INDEX OF
OBITUARIES
AND
MARRIAGES

IN
THE [BALTIMORE] SUN

1866-1870

WITH ADDENDUM
1861-1865

Francis P. O'Neill

HERITAGE BOOKS
2008

HERITAGE BOOKS
AN IMPRINT OF HERITAGE BOOKS, INC.

Books, CDs, and more—Worldwide

For our listing of thousands of titles see our website
at
www.HeritageBooks.com

Published 2008 by
HERITAGE BOOKS, INC.
Publishing Division
100 Railroad Ave. #104
Westminster, Maryland 21157

Copyright © 1996 Francis P. O'Neill

Other books by the author:

Index of Obituaries and Marriages in The [Baltimore] Sun, *1871-1875*
Index of Obituaries and Marriages in The [Baltimore] Sun, *1876-1880*

All rights reserved. No part of this book may be reproduced or transmitted in any form or by any means, electronic or mechanical, including photocopying, recording or by any information storage and retrieval system without written permission from the author, except for the inclusion of brief quotations in a review.

International Standard Book Numbers
Paperbound: 978-1-58549-341-8
Clothbound: 978-0-7884-7199-5

To Marla, who continues to bear up under the strain of being the wife of an antiquarian.

Contents

Acknowledgments **vi**

Forward **vii**

Statistics **ix**

Introduction **xi**

1866-1870 Index **1**

Acknowledgments

The secretary to the Library of the Maryland Historical Society, Miss Ann Grubb, did all the data entry for this index from cards which I compiled. Nobody -- least of all someone as nice as Ann -- deserves to have had to decipher my handwriting for as long as she did. My gratitude for her good humor and assiduity in the face of overwhelming odd squiggles is boundless and eternal.

Michael P. Shea, my friend, neighbor and Maryland Historical Society colleague, set up the database from which both this and the index to marriages and obituaries in *The Sun* for 1871-1875 were drawn, and bore up patiently (most of the time) before my invincible ignorance of exactly what that entailed. Every indexer needs someone as knowledgeable as Michael to rally to his or her aid, and anyone who had had such support in this case would probably have finished these volumes much sooner than I did.

Mr. Jack Grogaard volunteered to assist with the compilation of the 1861-1865 section of this volume, and did so to the obvious benefit of the work as a whole. He has my sincere thanks.

The Maryland Historical Society, under Head Library Penny Catzen, furnished me with logistical support, especially the microfilms of *The [Baltimore] Sun* from which I have compiled my information. The Maryland Historical Society holds film of these and other Maryland newspapers (as do other institutions like the Enoch Pratt Free Library in Baltimore and the Maryland State Archives in Annapolis) and researchers who have the opportunity to do so should refer to these microfilms for further information on the people list in this index and their families.

Francis P. O'Neill
December, 1995

A.M.D.G.

Foreword

The rapid growth of Baltimore's population in the period between 1850 and 1880 was mirrored by its marriage and death rates.[*] The city was expanding in all directions, while rapidly filling in the open spaces which had survived in its older neighborhoods, but its public services often were unable to keep pace with its private developers. The search for potable water, for example, was a race between supply and demand which was too often won by demand. It was publicly acknowledged that the increasing population had polluted downtown groundwater, and by the 1850s even the Jones Falls, whose waters were the source of most of the city's piped water, was recognized to be part of the problem rather than part of the solution. In 1854 the private Baltimore Water Company, convinced that the problem was too big to be overcome by private capital, sold out to the City of Baltimore. The city's answer, however -- a collection reservoir at Lake Roland, connected to a filtration reservoir in Hampden, connected to a distribution reservoir at Mount Royal and North Avenues -- came as too little, too late; by the mid-1860s, many neighborhoods already stood on ground higher than the Mount Royal reservoir and so could not be served by its gravity-powered pipelines, and the system often ran short of water, especially in hot weather.

The water department's response was to try to cut down on demand by raising the price of its service, which meant that many contractors, convinced that the poor would never be able to afford municipal rates, simply built their working-class tenements without connections to the city mains. This condemned the tenants of such houses and those of old houses in poor neighborhoods to their backyard or neighborhood pumps -- the same pumps that had been infecting them and their children all along. Not until the 1880s, when a reliable water supply at last was available to all Baltimoreans from the Loch Raven reservoir system, would the corner be turned on this problem, and even then it would still be many years before all Baltimore's homes could be tied into the system.

Private industry, although unwilling to commit itself to the problem of supplying the city with drinking water, was otherwise bullish on Baltimore, and enormous sums poured into the city even before the last echoes of the last guns of the Civil War had died away. Some of the investments, like the railroad tunnels that linked the city's three smaller carriers under the aegis of the Pennsylvania Railroad and broke the Baltimore & Ohio's traditional domination of land traffic, were breathtaking in their boldness; others were simply reckless, and helped pave the way for the approaching Panic of 1873 and the depression which followed it. Reckless capitalists expected workers to be reckless, too: the construction of the railroad tunnels cost dozens of lives through cave-ins which many times could have been

---

[*] J. Thomas Scharf's *1881 History of Baltimore City and County* gives the following figures for the city's successive U.S. census returns:

    1850 - 169,054   1870 - 267,599
    1860 - 212,418   1880 - 332,190

prevented by enforcement of the simplest of safety standards. Postwar Baltimore, however, was a city awash in cheap labor, as freed slaves competed with newly-arrived immigrants and newly-discharged soldiers for jobs, and a sense that human beings were worth less than the equipment they operated pervaded many workplaces.

All the same, families continued to be started, and there even were encouraging signs in the marriage notices as to the direction of society. Interracial continued to be unknown, but interfaith unions, while still uncommon, were at least occasionally reported,[**] and interethnic marriages appear with heartening regularity.[***] Germans no longer wed only other Germans, but Irish, Italians, and even Anglo-Saxons. The foundations of the city's future were being laid, and the announcements in its principle newspaper reflect that fact to us.

How faithfully they reflect it is another story. As I observed in the Foreword to my *Index to Obituaries and Marriages in The [Baltimore] Sun 1871-1875*, all sorts of mistakes could and did creep into a nineteenth-century newspaper by the time it came off the press, and all such must be passed on to modern researchers by the conscientious indexer. Furthermore, despite extensive checking, there are errors that may have entered in the course of the compilation of this index. For all such errors the compiler begs pardon; he hopes researchers still will be able to check *The Sun* itself (probably on microfilm) to confirm this information and possibly to get more than an index of this kind is designed to provide.

A closing word: I philosophized in the 1871-75 *Index* on the absence of very poor and non-English speaking Baltimoreans from the paid advertisements of *The Sun*, but use of my own tool has alerted me to one more group under-represented on the marriage and death announcement pages: the very rich. The Hoffmans, Wilsons, Carrolls, and Gilmors generally aren't in *The Sun* or in any other paper to which I've had access, and since they all spoke English and had plenty of money with which to pay for their notices, it took me some time to figure out why so few of them are present. Veblen must have snickered. It finally struck me that newspaper announcements are (or were) middle-class shorthand for the formal calls and engraved cards we read of in Edith Wharton. Wealthy Victorians felt such announcements to be beneath their dignity; having the money and the leisure to keep the transmission of good or bad news in their own hands, they did so, and felt only pity for those whose circumstances required them to do otherwise. The result? Nineteenth-century middle-class Baltimoreans are memorialized in this book and the newspapers it indexes; nineteenth-century upper-class Baltimoreans are memorialized, less accessibly, in the registers of then-fashionable churches and on the tombstones in Green Mount Cemetery. Somewhat ironic, that; but maybe it's the way they'd rather have it, even now.

[**] They can usually be identified by their occurrence in a pastor's study or the church parlor rather than in the sanctuary of the church.

[***] There were prejudices we've almost completely forgotten. Newly-arrived Irish immigrants often refused their children permission to marry the children of immigrants from Irish counties other than their own.

Statistics

Comparison of Civil Records and Index Statistics

Deaths Reported to the Baltimore
City Commissioner of Health

1866: N/A
1867: 5,225
1868: 6,178
1869: 6,497
1870: 7,262

Deaths Indexed in *Index of Obituaries and Marriages, 1866-1870*[*]

1866: 3,066
1867: 2,767
1868: 3,047
1869: 3,096
1870: 3,626

Marriage Licenses Granted by the Court of Common Pleas of Baltimore

1866: N/A
1867: 1,904
1868: 2,706
1869: 2,850
1870: 2,650

Marriages Indexed in *Index of Obituaries and Marriages, 1866-1870*[*]

1866: 1,278
1867: 1,299
1868: 1,368
1869: 1,402
1870: 1,262

Other Index Statisitcs

	Events	Entries	Citations
Female Deaths:	7,451	7,451	8,265
Male Deaths:	8,369	8,369	10,157
Unspec. Gender Deaths:	81	81	90
All Deaths:	15,901	15,901	18,512
Marriages:	6,714	13,428	13,770
Total for Index:	22,615	29,329	32,282

Statistics for Addition to 1861-1865 Index

	Events	Entries
Deaths:	1,772	1,772
Marriages:	9	18
Total:	1,781	1,790

---

[*] Note: Researchers should bear in mind that not every marriage or every death reported in *The Sun* took place in Baltimore. Many took place in other jurisdictions, and merely involved someone with some connection to Baltimore. Also, the total marriages or deaths for these five years do not exactly equal the totals for the entire index because events from years before this date range and for which no date was given are also contained in the index.

x *Statistics*

The 15 Most Frequent Causes of Death for Males and Females
from *Index to Obituaries and Marriages in The [Baltimore] Sun, 1866-1870**

Males

Cause	Deaths	avg. age
Drowning	313	27 yrs.
Consumption	176	36 yrs.
Railroad accident	95	34 yrs.
Heatstroke	94	40 yrs.
Heart disease	88	49 yrs.
Murder	74	32 yrs.
Suicide	69	43 yrs.
Paralysis	68	60 yrs.
Scarlet fever	58	5 yrs.
Pneumonia	53	36 yrs.
Typhoid	51	31 yrs.
Apoplexy	46	50 yrs.
Yellow fever	32	28 yrs.
Cholera	22	28 yrs.
Chronic croup	22	3 yrs.

Females

Cause	Deaths	avg. age
Consumption	159	37 yrs.
Scarlet fever	59	5 yrs.
Heart disease	42	49 yrs.
Pneumonia	27	38 yrs.
Typhoid	26	26 yrs.
Burned	23	17 yrs.
Brain congestion	21	23 yrs.
Drowned	18	35 yrs.
Paralysis	18	68 yrs.
Chronic croup	16	3 yrs.
Suicide	15	34 yrs.
Diptheria	14	4 yrs.
Heatstroke	12	49 yrs.
Lamp explosion	10	26 yrs.
Apoplexy	10	43 yrs.
Cholera infantum	10	1 yr.

* 15% of death entries in the index (2,378 of 15,901) give the cause of death. Broken down by gender, that is 21% for males (1,733 of 8,369), only 8% for females (617 of 7,451) and 35% for entries with unknown gender (28 of 81).

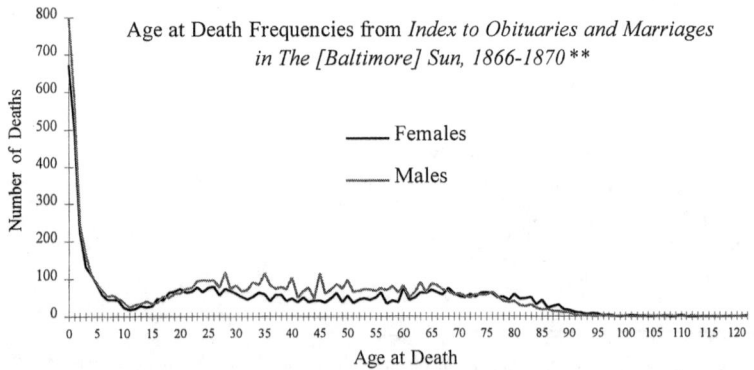

Age at Death Frequencies from *Index to Obituaries and Marriages in The [Baltimore] Sun, 1866-1870***

** 85% of death entries in the index (13,523 of 15,901) include age at death.

Introduction

Records

In general, records of marriages and deaths are of four types:

- **Personal records**, which are created and maintained by those most closely involved in the events they describe (*e.g.*, in family Bibles)
- **Religious records**, which are created by a clergyman and preserved among the records of his congregation or denomination
- **Civil records**, which are created by a government official and preserved by a public authority
- **Public records**, which are created by an organ of public communication and preserved as part of its product (*e.g.*, newspaper notices).

Before proceeding further with details on this particular index of public records, it may be as well to glance quickly at other types of records which may exist in Maryland. It would be natural to place the most confidence in civil records, but in Maryland such confidence is not always justified. While Marylanders repeatedly expressed a wish for full civil registration of vital records in the form of 19th-century laws requiring such, it was not until 1875 that their desire was realized, even in Baltimore. Prior to that time the records of marriages maintained by the Baltimore City Court of Common Pleas and of deaths maintained by the Baltimore City Commissioner of Health were usually deficient in detail and often incomplete in number. The Maryland State Archives has microfilm of the marriage license applications and marriage records kept by the Court of Common Pleas both before and after the enactment of the 1875 law, which makes clear how much more conscientiously the clergymen (who by law were the only Marylanders authorized to perform marriages in the 19th century) took their responsibilities to report their activities to the civil authorities after the passage of the 1875 law. The same was probably true of the physicians who were expected to return copies of death certificates to the Commissioner of Health.

Church records of marriages and deaths, while both universal in scope (at least in 19th-century Baltimore) and generally reliable, are only somewhat less diffused than private records, and therefore often difficult for researchers to track. This is especially true when churches have moved, merged, or simply disappeared. Newspaper notices often provide useful clues to an ancestor's religious affiliation when they name an officiating clergyman, even if they don't mention the congregation to which he was attached. Edna Kanely's 1991 guide to Maryland clergymen[1] can be the bridge between a clergyman's name and that of his congregation; beyond that, anyone in search of the congregation's records very often faces a long and arduous task.

---

[1] *Directory of Ministers and the Maryland Churches They Served, 1634-1990*, Edna Agatha Kanely (Westminster, MD: Family Line Publications, 1991).

xii *Introduction*

Finally, and most elusively, there are private records of marriages and deaths. They have the advantage of reliability, but the disadvantage of inaccessibility, since they traditionally have been diffused throughout the community, sometimes in the hands of those who treasured them, other times in the hands of those who discarded them. A movement is now underway by various libraries and historical societies to encourage those who have such private records which they no longer want to deposit either copies or the original document with such an institution where it can be cared for and made available to researchers. The Genealogical Council of Maryland has been leading an effort to publicize the location of all such institutionally-held private records in or related to Maryland, and the first fruits of their efforts became available in a 1989 volume entitled *Inventory of Maryland Bible Records*[2]. At the present time, however, and probably for the foreseeable future, private records are the most difficult of all the four classes of records of marriages and deaths for researchers who are not their legal owners to obtain.

The index you hold is an index of public records, specifically the 6,714 marriages and 15,901 deaths mentioned in one Baltimore newspaper -- *The Sun* -- between January 1st, 1866 and December 31st, 1870. Although there are similar indexes for other periods of *The Sun*'s existence, and for other Baltimore newspapers at other times, there is no other index to another Baltimore newspaper published during the same five-year period[3]. This is a pity, for while an informal survey has convinced me that there is not much difference between *The Sun*'s vital notices and those of its principal English-language competitor (the Baltimore *American*) during the last half of the 1860s, there are other Baltimore newspapers, especially German-language papers, indexes to which I feel sure would increase our stock of marriage and death information on mid-Victorian Baltimoreans to a great extent.

In my experience, many researchers cut themselves off from useful leads by an overly strict faith in the index with which they are working. It is well to remember the many points at which errors can creep into a work like this one: at the newspaper office, where a customer's unfamiliar accent, a clerk's bad handwriting or a compositor's hangover may very easily have converted your Great-Uncle Louis into your Great-Aunt Lois; at the microfilm reader, where I may unintentionally have done the same thing; or at the

---

[2] *Inventory of Maryland Bible Records* (Westminster, MD: Family Line Publications for the Genealogical Council of Maryland, 1989-).

[3] Other years of *The [Baltimore] Sun* are indexed in the following works:

Index to Marriages and Deaths in The [Baltimore] Sun, 1837-1850, compiled by Thomas L. Hollowak (Baltimore: Genealogical Publishing Company, 1978).

Departed This Life: Death Notices from The [Baltimore] Sun 1851-1860, compiled by Walter E. Arps, Jr. (Silver Spring, MD: Family Line Publications, 1985-1986).

Index to Marriages in The [Baltimore] Sun, 1851-1860, compiled by Thomas L. Hollowak (Baltimore: Genealogical Publishing Company, 1978).

Index to Obituaries and Marriages in The [Baltimore] Sun, 1861-1865, Joseph C. Maguire Jr. (Westminster, MD: Family Line Publications for The Maryland Historical Society, 1991).

Index to Obituaries and Marriages in The [Baltimore] Sun, 1871-1875, Francis P. O'Neill (Westminster, MD: Family Line Publications, 1995).

Introduction   xiii

computer, where my fingers may have flown a little faster than they ought to have done. It is a good idea to examine the microfilm of the original newspaper for anyone whose name even vaguely resembles the one for which you are searching, and to recall that even small children who don't actually figure in your family tree may lead you to their parents who do.

Sources

This index is based on microfilms of *The [Baltimore] Sun* produced and sold by University Microfilms International (UMI), 300 North Zeeb Road, Ann Arbor, Michigan. The main branch of Baltimore's Enoch Pratt Free Library has a complete collection (1837 to date) of *The [Baltimore] Sun* on UMI microfilm. The Maryland Historical Society's library currently contains the UMI films of the years 1860-1875, and hopes to obtain more of *The Sun* on microfilm in the future.

Researchers unable or unwilling to make use of microfilm, or those who find gaps in the run of papers filmed by UMI, may turn to the Albin O. Kuhn Library at the University of Maryland Baltimore County in Catonsville. Its Special Collections Department is the custodian of the Baltimore Sunpapers' archival collection of bound *Sun*s dating back to the first edition in 1837. The Department has limited hours, especially in the summer, and researchers planning to make use of its collections are urged to telephone in advance of any visit.

Indexing Methods

The Sun normally published four pages per issue in the 1860s and 1870s (there were, very rarely, supplemental pages), and the third page was almost always solid classified advertisements. The first page normally held the bulk of the news; the second page had editorials, marriage and obituary announcements and other kinds of paid notices, while the last page held the shipping news, business columns, and overflow from the other pages.

For most of the 1860s, *The Sun* printed in a seven-column format, which I have lettered A-G; at the very end of the decade, the format suddenly changed to eight columns and my designation becomes A-H. A story that appeared in the second column from the left on the first page would thus be designated 1B, and such a designation will be found after the date of the issue of the paper in which the story appeared, as

[67-Apr-13: 1B].

The dates outside the brackets refer to the date on which an event took place; unlike those within the brackets, they are generally of no use in terms of locating a story within *The Sun*, although they can be important for personal identification.

Many researchers may be put off by the fact that this is "only" an index and not an abstract of the marriages and deaths noted by *The Sun*s of its period. Unfortunately, such

xiv *Introduction*

*Sun*s contained so much information on each person that abstracts were not really feasible.*
An entry which reads only:

>Bayne, Lilly (66 yrs., 6 mos.) d. on 66-Jun-25 [66-Jun-27: 2C].

may actually lead one (as this does) to a notice on page 2, column C of June 27, 1866 which reads:

>BAYNE. - Fell asleep in Jesus, on the 25th instant, Mrs. LILLY BAYNE, consort of the late John N. Bayne, after a long and painful illness, which she bore with Christian fortitude, aged 66 years and 6 months. Her last words were, Thy will be done, O Lord. [Norfolk, Portsmouth and California papers please copy.]**
>>Weep not for me, my children dear,
>>I am not dead, but sleeping here:
>>I have gone to that world of eternal rest,
>>There, with Jesus, to be forever blest.

It is my intention to deposit the electronic database from which these indexes are drawn at the library of the Maryland Historical Society, where the information will be accessible in a variety of ways.

---

* See figure on page xv.

** In the days before wire services, journalists obtained most of their out-of-town news by exchanging copies of their newspapers for papers printed elsewhere. Notations like this were intended to tip off out-of-town colleagues -- in this case, the editors of the Norfolk and Portsmouth, VA papers and of papers in California -- that this person had connections in their readership areas who might be interested to learn that she had died. The editors in question would copy *The Sun*'s obituary notice into their papers, in exchange for which *The Sun*'s editor could lift information on Baltimoreans originally published in Norfolk, Portsmouth, or California.

MARRIED.

BROOKS—TAYMAN.—On June 2d, at the parsonage, by the Rev. Mr. Shrine, G. EDWIN BROOKS to Miss KATE C., adopted daughter of Mr. W. L. Tayman, both of this city.

BECKER—BROWN.—On the 30th ultimo, by the Rev. C. W. Ratke, FREDERICK BECKER to MARY LIZZIE BROWN, both of this city.

GILL—GRAY.—In St. Paul, Minnesota, on the 6th instant, by Rev. Dr. Patterson, WILLIAM H. GILL, of Baltimore, to Miss ANNA, daughter of George W. Gray, of Philadelphia. [Philadelphia papers please copy.]

HARDESTY—HUGHES.—July 9th, by Rev. Asbury R. Reiley, JOHN HARDESTY to HANNAH A. HUGHES, all of this city.

JAMISON—FERGUSON.—In the Twelfth Presbyterian Church, July 9th, by Rev. James M. Maxwell, CHARLES E. JAMISON and Miss ELLEN FERGUSON.

SNYDER—DE FORD.—On the 7th instant, by the Rev. J. S. Foulk, D. D., J. WILLIAM SNYDER, of Littlestown, Pa., to LAURA VIRGINIA DE FORD, of this city.

DIED.

ALLERS.—Yesterday morning, at seven o'clock, GEORGE W., infant son of John A. and Virginia Allers, aged 4 months and 19 days.

The friends of the family are respectfully requested to attend the funeral this (Saturday) morning, 11th instant, at ten o'clock, from No. 532 West Fayette street.

CURLETT.—Suddenly, on the 9th instant, E. M. CURLETT, eldest son of L. E. Curlett, in the 27th year of his age.

His friends and those of the family are respectfully invited to attend his funeral on to-morrow (Sunday) morning, 12th instant, at half-past seven o'clock, from the residence of his father, No. 120 Leestreet.

CLARK.—On the 6th instant, FLORA BELL, only daughter of John H. and Elizabeth Clark, aged 21 months and 9 days.

    Why should I weep, or why should I
      Be at her loss distressed;
    Why should I mourn, for her young heart
      Were ne'er by grief oppressed.
    No tears upon her grave be shed,
      But sweetest flowers be flung,
    The fittest offering thou cans't make
      To those who die so young.

The relatives and friends of the family are respectfully invited to attend the funeral to-morrow (Sunday) afternoon, 12th instant, at five o'clock, from the residence No. 129 South Bond street.

DORMAN.—Fell asleep in Jesus, on July 10th, at twenty minutes past one o'clock A. M., SARAH A., aged 38 years, second daughter of the late Thomas Dorman.

Her relatives and friends are respectfully invited to attend her funeral this (Saturday) morning, at ten o'clock, from her late residence, No. 75 South High street.

FUSSELBAUGH.—On Friday, 10th instant, at six o'clock P. M., HENRY BASCOM, son of Sarah R. and Wm. H. B. Fusselbaugh, aged 8 months and 2 days.

The relatives and friends of the family are respectfully ... the funeral this (Saturday) ... the residence of his

An actual size example of a section of column 2B
from *The Sun* (July 11, 1868)

Aaron, Charles F. m. Tarleton, Mary D. on 68-Sep-14 [68-Sep-17: 2B].
Aaron, Dorothea K. (79 yrs.) d. on 70-Jul-9 [70-Jul-11: 2C].
Aaron, Luvenia (26 yrs.) d. on 70-Jan-5 [70-Jan-7: 2F].
Aaron, Marcellus m. Hyer, Virginia D. on 70-Dec-18 [70-Dec-19: 2C].
Aaron, Samuel J. m. Russell, Mary Eliza on 66-Oct-30 [67-Jun-26: 2C].
Aaronson, Bertha d. Drowned [70-Feb-14: 1H].
Abbes, Jane Augusta m. Langford, Thomas on 69-Apr-29 [69-May-14: 2C].
Abbett, Samuel R. d. on 69-Mar-5 [69-Mar-6: 2B].
Abbett, Thomas M. (61 yrs.) d. on 66-Jul-17 [66-Jul-19: 1E].
Abbott, Elizabeth, Miss m. Ralph, James Murray on 66-Dec-27 [67-Feb-4: 2C].
Abbott, Elizabeth A. d. on 67-Mar-2 [67-Mar-4: 2D].
Abbott, Fanny Ella (2 yrs., 1 mo.) d. on 66-Aug-29 [66-Aug-30: 2B].
Abbott, George (66 yrs.) d. on 67-Jan-22 [67-Jan-24: 2C].
Abbott, Louisa (3 yrs.) d. on 68-Jan-10 in Street railway accident [68-Jan-11: 1G].
Abbott, M. Kate m. Bruce, Thomas Stockton on 67-Mar-12 [67-Apr-4: 2B].
Abbott, Maria K. d. on 68-Sep-7 [68-Sep-12: 2B].
Abbott, Mary Blanch (1 yr., 1 mo.) d. on 69-Jan-7 [69-Jan-9: 2C].
Abbott, Noah (50 yrs.) d. on 66-Dec-1 Murdered (Shooting) [66-Dec-3: 1G; 66-Dec-5: 1F].
Abbott, Serena W. m. Wonderly, Harry on 68-May-26 [68-May-28: 2B].
Abbott, Sophia (69 yrs.) d. on 69-Sep-27 [69-Sep-28: 2B; 69-Sep-30: 2B].
Abbott, Susan Adelaide (1 yr., 7 mos.) d. on 66-Jul-30 [66-Aug-6: 2C].
Abbott, Susan E. m. Dorr, Lawrence A. on 67-Nov-19 [67-Dec-27: 2D].
Abell, Edwin F. (1 yr., 8 mos.) d. on 70-Aug-4 [70-Aug-6: 2C].
Abell, Harry R. (3 yrs., 4 mos.) d. on 70-Nov-26 of Chronic croup [70-Nov-28: 2C].
Abell, Rosa m. Rogers, James P. on 68-Jun-2 [68-Jun-6: 2A].
Abell, William B. (66 yrs.) d. on 70-Apr-22 [70-Apr-23: 2B].
Abendschein, H. (26 yrs.) d. on 69-Nov-29 [69-Dec-6: 2C].
Abercrombie, Rebecca (21 yrs.) d. on 68-Feb-12 [68-Feb-13: 2C].
Abercrombie, William H. m. Quinn, Louisa J. on 69-Nov-28 [70-Jan-4: 2C].
Abey, Elizabeth (19 yrs., 2 mos.) d. on 67-Aug-13 [67-Aug-14: 2B].
Abey, Elizabeth (76 yrs.) d. on 70-Feb-13 [70-Feb-19: 2B].
Abey, Joseph W. m. Crandall, Thomas W. on 69-Mar-17 [69-Mar-18: 2C; 69-Mar-19: 1H].
Abey, Lizzie (1 yr., 11 mos.) d. on 68-Aug-27 [68-Aug-29: 2B].
Abey, Minnie m. Crandall, Thomas W. [69-Jan-13: 2D].
Able, A. E. m. La Barrer, Francis, Sr. on 69-Jan-19 [69-Mar-16: 2C].
Abraham, Annie Beatrice (2 yrs., 3 mos.) d. on 68-Dec-4 of Lung inflammation [68-Dec-5: 2C].
Abrahams, Cora W. m. Johnson, Albert A. on 68-Jul-7 [68-Jul-10: 2C].
Abrahams, Francis (37 yrs.) d. on 69-Jul-18 [69-Jul-19: 1G].
Abrahams, Georgie Littig (5 yrs.) d. on 69-Dec-28 [69-Dec-30: 2C].
Abrahams, H. Kate m. Stran, Thomas P. on 66-Nov-8 [66-Nov-12: 2C; 66-Nov-19: 2C].
Abrams, Washington (66 yrs.) d. on 69-Dec-3 [69-Dec-4: 2C; 69-Dec-6: 2C].
Abrams, Willie d. on 68-Sep-8 [68-Sep-10: 2B].
Abreo, Nicholas Lambdin (10 yrs., 4 mos.) d. on 67-Jul-23 [67-Jul-25: 2C].
Aburn, Susannah (74 yrs.) d. on 67-Sep-22 [67-Sep-24: 2A].
Achenbach, Carrie m. White, Joseph K. T. on 69-Nov-19 [69-Nov-22: 2C].
Achum, Hannah d. on 70-May-1 [70-May-3: 2C].
Ackerman, C. C. m. James, Anna L. on 68-May-25 [68-Jun-4: 2B].
Ackerman, David Romaine (10 yrs.) d. on 69-May-31 of Typhoid [69-Jun-8: 2B].
Ackerman, Ida M. m. Burnham, Charles on 67-Feb-5 [67-Jul-29: 2D].
Ackland, Mary C. m. Will, Andrew on 66-Sep-13 [66-Sep-15: 2B].
Ackler, William F. m. Hughes, Maggie A. on 67-Nov-5 [67-Nov-6: 2B].
Acomb, William (66 yrs.) d. on 67-Jan-23 [67-Jan-24: 2C; 67-Jan-25: 2C].
Acre, Myrta M. m. Starr, John, Jr. on 67-Oct-29 [67-Nov-1: 2B].
Acton, Clarence Edgar (3 yrs., 6 mos.) d. on 69-Feb-20 [69-Feb-22: 2C].
Acton, Hal Ely (1 yr., 4 mos.) d. on 70-Jan-19 [70-Jan-20: 2C].

1

Adair, John m. Reid, M. A. on 69-Jun-17 [69-Jun-28: 2C].
Adair, Josie (10 yrs.) d. on 69-Nov-18 [69-Nov-20: 2C].
Adair, Mary m. Gilliard, Nicholas on 68-May-21 [68-May-25: 2A].
Adams, Addie m. Winter, Harry S. on 69-Oct-20 [69-Oct-23: 2B].
Adams, Aloysius M. (36 yrs.) d. on 70-Apr-16 [70-Apr-19: 2B].
Adams, Alvin Quincy (4 mos.) d. on 70-Jul-29 [70-Aug-2: 2C].
Adams, Anne Mary m. Hoover, Edgar I. on 70-Nov-22 [70-Nov-26: 2B].
Adams, Benjamin F. m. Bond, Jane A. on 68-Dec-3 [69-Jan-18: 2C].
Adams, Blanche Lee (4 mos.) d. on 66-Jul-26 [66-Jul-28: 2C].
Adams, C. C. d. on 68-Mar-5 [68-Mar-7: 2B].
Adams, Charles A. (40 yrs.) d. on 69-May-25 [69-May-27: 2C].
Adams, Charles H. (20 yrs., 7 mos.) d. on 70-Sep-2 Drowned [70-Nov-11: 2B].
Adams, Charlotte (3 mos.) d. on 68-Jan-29 [68-Feb-1: 2C].
Adams, Cora Lee (3 mos.) d. on 67-Jun-18 [67-Jun-20: 2B].
Adams, Edward W. m. Henderson, Julia on 68-Oct-14 [68-Nov-7: 2B].
Adams, Elizabeth (72 yrs.) d. on 68-Oct-22 [68-Oct-23: 2B].
Adams, Elizabeth m. Wood, J. Alexander on 67-Nov-12 [67-Nov-16: 2B].
Adams, Elizabeth L. (60 yrs.) d. on 66-Nov-16 [66-Nov-17: 2B].
Adams, Ellie L. m. King, John C. on 66-Sep-6 [66-Sep-8: 2B].
Adams, Frank m. Cannon, Fannie B. on 67-Oct-23 [67-Oct-26: 2A].
Adams, George Howard d. on 67-Jun-20 [67-Jun-22: 2B].
Adams, J. B. (34 yrs.) d. on 70-Oct-18 [70-Oct-19: 2B; 70-Oct-20: 2B].
Adams, Jacob Hooper (37 yrs.) d. on 66-Feb-11 of Consumption [66-Feb-12: 2D].
Adams, James C. m. Eddy, Henrietta on 68-Jun-9 [68-Jun-12: 2B].
Adams, James H. (47 yrs.) d. on 66-Feb-22 [66-Feb-24: 2B].
Adams, James M. (8 mos.) d. on 69-Jun-19 [69-Jun-22: 2C].
Adams, James M. (46 yrs.) d. on 70-Mar-4 [70-Mar-8: 2C].
Adams, John m. Shaw, Mary Josephine on 66-May-3 [66-May-9: 2B].
Adams, John Carroll d. on 68-Aug-19 [68-Aug-22: 2A].
Adams, John W. m. Haslup, Ruth A. on 68-Nov-12 [68-Nov-17: 2C].
Adams, Joseph d. on 66-Jun-9 [66-Jun-12: 1G].
Adams, Joseph H. m. Livers, Caroline E. on 67-Nov-14 [67-Nov-18: 2B].
Adams, Joseph Searle (83 yrs.) d. on 67-Dec-12 [67-Dec-25: 2C].
Adams, Joseph Tarlton (11 yrs.) d. on 68-Oct-11 of Scarlet fever [68-Oct-13: 2C].
Adams, Josie R. m. Guy, Dixon on 68-Dec-31 [69-Feb-18: 2C].
Adams, Lillah m. Hayne, Theodore B. on 70-Apr-19 [70-Apr-30: 2A].
Adams, Lizzie V. m. Ahearn, John on 68-Nov-24 [68-Nov-28: 2C].
Adams, M. Washington m. Brady, Laura V. on 70-Jan-20 [70-Jan-29: 2B].
Adams, Mary A. (1 mo.) d. on 70-Jul-4 [70-Jul-6: 2C].
Adams, Mary E. m. Hall, N. Edwin on 68-Jan-21 [68-Jan-24: 2D].
Adams, Matilda m. Minor, George on 66-Nov-15 [66-Nov-17: 2C].
Adams, Sarah Adalene (23 yrs.) d. on 68-Aug-18 [69-Mar-27: 2B].
Adams, Sydney m. Slayman, Katie E. on 67-Jan-10 [67-Jan-19: 2C].
Adams, Thomas (45 yrs.) d. on 70-Jan-18 [70-Jan-19: 2C].
Adams, Thomas W. (44 yrs.) d. on 69-Aug-2 [69-Aug-3: 2C; 69-Aug-4: 1H, 2C].
Adams, William E. m. Lightner, Lizzie on 70-Dec-6 [70-Dec-10: 2B].
Adams, William H. m. McKenna, Annie J. on 67-Nov-6 [67-Nov-7: 2C].
Adams, William Kemp (15 yrs.) d. on 70-Aug-20 [70-Aug-24: 2C; 70-Aug-25: 2C].
Addington, J. C. m. Martin, Mary on 70-Sep-14 [70-Sep-23: 2C].
Addison, Anne (6 mos.) d. on 67-Jan-13 [67-Jan-14: 2C].
Addison, Annie M. (4 yrs., 2 mos.) d. on 68-Dec-13 of Croup [68-Dec-14: 2C].
Addison, Joseph T. m. Kinsley, Mary E. on 66-May-9 [66-May-16: 2C].
Addison, Priscilla (110 yrs.) d. on 66-Jul-17 [66-Jul-19: 2C].
Addison, Sallie d. on 66-Sep-5 [66-Sep-21: 2B].
Addison, Sallie L. m. Beck, Charles R. R. on 70-Oct-25 [70-Oct-27: 2B].

Addison, Samuel L. m. Chancellor, Ella H. on 69-Dec-22 [69-Dec-28: 2C].
Addison, Sue R. m. Sunderland, W. H. on 68-Sep-15 [68-Sep-17: 2B].
Addison, W. Edgar m. Postlethwaite, Sallie B. on 69-Nov-18 [69-Nov-20: 2B].
Addison, William MacKie (11 mos.) d. on 70-Oct-9 [70-Oct-10: 2B].
Adkinson, William (67 yrs.) d. on 69-Oct-25 [69-Oct-26: 2B].
Adkisson, Catherine A. (58 yrs.) d. on 67-Apr-15 [67-Apr-16: 2B].
Adkisson, W. H. m. Furlong, Irene E. on 68-Jan-22 [68-Jan-24: 2D].
Adler, Leon m. Wolf, Rebecca on 69-Aug-8 [69-Aug-17: 2C].
Adler, Sophia d. on 66-Nov-20 [66-Nov-21: 2C].
Adler, William Floss (4 mos.) d. on 68-Mar-13 [68-Mar-16: 2B].
Adley, William m. Wright, Frances on 67-Apr-30 [67-May-1: 2B].
Adolph, Henry m. Howard, Mary on 68-Sep-16 [68-Oct-8: 2B].
Adreon, George W. L. m. Uppercue, Maggie on 69-Dec-28 [70-Jan-8: 2B; 70-Jan-11: 2C].
Adreon, H. Clay (29 yrs.) d. on 69-Apr-29 [69-Apr-30: 2C].
Adreon, Harrison m. Guiteau, Jessie on 68-Jun-16 [68-Jun-19: 2B].
Adreon, Lina A. m. Maccubbin, Samuel J. on 66-May-17 [66-May-24: 2C].
Adreon, Minnie Grant (3 yrs., 2 mos.) d. on 69-Aug-7 [69-Aug-7: 2B].
Adrian, Emily C. m. Adrian, Stephen F. on 66-Apr-25 [66-Apr-27: 2C].
Adrian, Maryland M. d. on 70-Apr-1 [70-Apr-9: 2B].
Adrian, Stephen F. m. Adrian, Emily C. on 66-Apr-25 [66-Apr-27: 2C].
Aery, Elias m. Meeks, Mary Ann on 69-Apr-6 [69-Apr-10: 2B].
Agier, Catharine m. Turner, George C. on 67-Jul-29 [67-Oct-15: 2A].
Agnew, John D. m. Byrne, Lizzie C. on 67-Feb-19 [67-Feb-25: 2C].
Agnew, Rose Ellen d. on 69-Nov-24 [69-Nov-26: 2C].
Agnew, Thomas A. m. Martin, Mary A. on 66-Jun-28 [66-Jul-7: 2B].
Ahean, John d. on 69-Oct-7 of Dysentery [69-Oct-8: 2B].
Ahearn, John (32 yrs.) d. on 70-Aug-1 [70-Aug-6: 2C; 70-Aug-10: 2B].
Ahearn, John m. Adams, Lizzie V. on 68-Nov-24 [68-Nov-28: 2C].
Ahern, , Mrs. d. on 66-Jun-26 of Paralysis [66-Jun-28: 1G].
Ahern, Dennis (53 yrs.) d. on 67-Jan-27 [67-Jan-28: 2C].
Ahern, Francis I. m. Emory, Nannie M. on 68-Jun-16 [68-Jun-17: 2B; 68-Jun-18: 2B; 68-Jun-19: 2B].
Ahern, John d. on 69-Jul-24 [69-Jul-26: 2C].
Ahl, Barnerd D. (84 yrs.) d. on 66-Aug-27 [66-Aug-28: 2B].
Ahl, Romma m. McCafferty, Mary Ellen on 67-Oct-15 [67-Oct-21: 2B].
Ahrens, August d. on 66-Nov-9 in Machine accident [66-Nov-10: 4B; 66-Nov-12: 1F].
Aiken, George B. m. Wolvington, Mary T. on 70-Jun-9 [70-Jun-14: 2B].
Aiken, Matthew K. m. Jerome, Jennie on 67-Jan-8 [67-Jan-10: 2C].
Aires, Edward T. (1 yr., 5 mos.) d. on 68-Jul-30 [68-Aug-1: 2B].
Airey, , Miss (21 yrs.) d. on 67-Mar-1 [67-Mar-2: 2B].
Airey, Carroll B. (7 yrs.) d. on 68-May-14 Drowned [68-May-21: 1F].
Airey, George G. m. Patterson, Fannie B. on 70-Jun-21 [70-Jun-24: 2C].
Airey, George W. m. Davis, Lizzie J. on 69-Nov-16 [69-Nov-17: 2C].
Airey, James (51 yrs.) d. on 67-Apr-4 [67-Apr-5: 2B].
Airey, James m. Carrolle, Louisa A. on 66-May-3 [66-May-4: 2C].
Airey, James P. m. Werb, Mary A. on 70-Jan-29 [70-Feb-3: 2B].
Airey, Laura J. m. Ruley, Samuel H. on 67-Apr-25 [67-Apr-27: 2A].
Airey, Maggie C. m. Wood, Joseph E. on 67-Nov-19 [67-Nov-26: 2B].
Airey, Margaret Ann (81 yrs.) d. on 70-Nov-19 [70-Nov-21: 2C].
Airey, Mary C. m. Zepp, John H. on 67-Apr-11 [67-Apr-20: 2A].
Airey, Philip m. Mentzel, Sophia on 68-Oct-21 [68-Oct-30: 2C].
Airey, Robert W. (17 yrs.) d. on 70-Aug-24 in Railroad accident [70-Aug-25: 2B, 4D].
Aisquith, George m. Ireland, Mary on 68-Mar-31 [68-Apr-23: 2B].
Aitcheson, Mary m. Flister, Andrew F. on 69-May-27 [69-Jun-10: 2C].
Aitken, James Parker d. on 69-Dec-13 [69-Dec-14: 2C; 69-Dec-15: 2B].

Aken, Edwin C. m. Billingslea, Sallie on 68-Oct-6 [68-Oct-8: 2B].
Akers, Daniel, Jr. (24 yrs.) d. on 69-Feb-4 [69-Feb-6: 2C].
Akers, George W. (23 yrs.) d. on 69-Sep-28 [69-Sep-30: 2B; 69-Oct-1: 2B].
Akers, Laura Virginia d. on 70-Oct-6 [70-Oct-8: 2B].
Akers, Mary Grady (4 yrs.) d. on 67-Sep-27 [67-Sep-28: 2A].
Akers, Sarah A. m. Sturges, William J. on 66-Nov-20 [66-Nov-24: 2B; 66-Nov-27: 2B].
Akerst, John G. m. Girbrich, Eliza J. on 69-Sep-14 [69-Sep-24: 2B].
Albach, Mary m. Gengnagle, Henry on 68-Jul-7 [68-Aug-11: 2B].
Albaugh, E. Gover Cox d. on 69-Jun-19 [69-Jun-21: 2B].
Albaugh, Ira H. (25 yrs., 11 mos.) d. on 66-Jun-4 [66-Jun-14: 2B].
Albaugh, John Thomas (12 yrs., 1 mo.) d. on 66-Sep-22 [66-Sep-24: 2B].
Albaugh, Laura V. m. Tittle, George T. on 67-Oct-15 [68-Feb-7: 2C].
Albaugh, Mary F. m. Lewis, William S. on 67-Sep-11 [67-Sep-25: 2B].
Albaugh, Thomas m. Marsh, Emma J. on 70-Sep-15 [70-Sep-19: 2B].
Albaugh, William A. m. Snyder, Lillie E. on 67-Jan-2 [67-Jan-7: 2C].
Albaugh, William E. m. Thompson, Hannah J. on 70-Jun-8 [70-Jun-13: 2C].
Alberger, Adam (65 yrs.) d. on 68-May-31 [68-Jun-1: 2B; 68-Jun-2: 2B].
Albers, Charles F. m. Dunkell, Kate on 67-Dec-12 [67-Dec-17: 2B].
Albert, Andreas Conrad (3 yrs., 5 mos.) d. on 66-Mar-12 [66-Mar-13: 2B; 66-Mar-14: 2B].
Albert, Annie m. Keene, John T. on 69-May-17 [69-Jun-5: 2B].
Albert, Augustus J., Jr. m. Doughty, Julia on 67-Jul-3 [67-Jul-9: 2B].
Albert, Barbara (4 yrs., 11 mos.) d. on 66-Mar-4 [66-Mar-5: 2B; 66-Mar-6: 2B].
Albert, Henry C. m. Gunnison, Hannah G. on 69-Oct-21 [69-Oct-23: 2B; 69-Oct-25: 2B].
Albert, John (75 yrs.) d. on 66-Oct-6 [66-Oct-8: 2B; 66-Oct-9: 2A].
Albert, William Frederick (1 yr., 1 mo.) d. on 67-Dec-12 [67-Dec-14: 2B].
Albinson, Mary Anne (63 yrs.) d. on 67-Sep-19 [67-Sep-23: 2A].
Albrecht, August m. Logemann, Elenora on 66-May-8 [66-May-12: 2A].
Albrecht, F. W. (58 yrs.) d. on 70-Jan-16 [70-Jan-17: 2C].
Albrecht, Gustav (19 yrs.) d. on 70-Jul-25 [70-Jul-26: 2B].
Albrecht, Henriette (50 yrs., 3 mos.) d. on 68-Jun-28 [68-Jun-29: 2B].
Albrecht, Werner m. Meyer, Louisa on 66-Sep-18 [66-Sep-20: 2B].
Albrecht, William (57 yrs.) d. on 68-Oct-13 [68-Oct-15: 2C].
Albrecht, William J. (32 yrs., 3 mos.) d. on 69-Oct-20 [69-Oct-30: 2C].
Albright, Lavinia M. m. Langford, George W. on 70-Mar-10 [70-May-12: 2B].
Alcock, Clara Frances (20 yrs.) d. on 68-Dec-8 [68-Dec-9: 2C].
Alder, D. Slicker d. on 70-Nov-28 [70-Dec-6: 2C].
Alderson, Anna m. Weems, George W. on 67-Jun-18 [67-Jul-6: 2B].
Alderson, S. Fannie m. Cowles, James A. on 67-Jun-27 [67-Jun-29: 2B].
Alderson, Sarah A. (69 yrs.) d. on 69-Oct-7 [69-Oct-9: 2C].
Aldridge, , Mr. d. on 67-Mar-16 of Heart disease [67-Mar-19: 1F].
Aldridge, Eleonora m. Lamparter, E. on 69-Jul-8 [69-Jul-31: 2C].
Aler, Charles Howard (2 yrs., 10 mos.) d. [66-Feb-8: 2C].
Aler, Florence Olivia (16 yrs.) d. on 69-Sep-19 [69-Sep-20: 2B].
Aler, George E. (31 yrs.) d. [69-May-25: 2C].
Aler, Harry Clifton (1 yr., 4 mos.) d. on 66-Aug-7 [66-Aug-9: 2C].
Aler, Mary Elmira d. on 68-Aug-30 [68-Aug-31: 2B].
Aler, Reuben J. (24 yrs.) d. on 67-Dec-30 [67-Dec-31: 2C].
Aler, Reuben J. m. Paddington, Maggie on 66-Apr-12 [66-May-25: 2C].
Aler, Sylvanus R. (31 yrs.) d. on 67-Oct-15 [67-Oct-7: 2B].
Alexander, Charles Ambrose d. on 67-Oct-6 [67-Oct-8: 2B].
Alexander, Elizabeth C. m. Herbert, James R. on 68-Nov-10 [68-Nov-18: 2C].
Alexander, John Henry (54 yrs.) d. on 67-Mar-2 of Typhoid [67-Mar-4: 2D, 4E; 67-Mar-5: 1F].
Alexander, Meyer (46 yrs.) d. [70-Jan-27: 2C].
Alexander, Nathan m. Briggs, Clara V. on 69-Jul-4 [69-Jul-10: 2B].
Alexander, Priscilla d. on 67-Aug-5 [67-Aug-10: 2B].

Alexander, Robert (37 yrs.) d. [66-Dec-10: 2B; 66-Dec-11: 2B].
Alexander, Sadie R. m. Lockwood, George on 66-Jan-4 [66-Jan-16: 2C].
Alexander, Thomas (59 yrs.) d. on 69-May-20 [69-Aug-21: 2B].
Alexander, Thomas m. Lowry, Annie M. on 67-Jul-29 [67-Aug-14: 2B].
Alford, George C. m. Jacobs, Clara R. on 70-Dec-15 [70-Dec-19: 2C].
Alford, Mary (75 yrs.) d. on 69-Dec-29 [69-Dec-31: 2C].
Alger, Leila May (1 yr.) d. on 70-Sep-14 [70-Sep-16: 2B].
Alheit, Charlotte m. Hax, John on 68-Dec-26 [68-Dec-31: 2C].
Allan, Charles H. m. Jenkins, Lizzie W. on 68-Dec-17 [68-Dec-25: 2D].
Allan, Edmund Greenwood (2 yrs., 2 mos.) d. on 68-Sep-25 [68-Sep-26: 2B].
Allan, George S. (45 yrs.) d. on 68-Sep-20 [68-Sep-21: 2B].
Allan, William G., Mrs. (32 yrs.) d. [70-Jul-2: 2B].
Allan, William Galt d. on 68-Oct-15 [68-Oct-19: 2B].
Allard, Emma J. m. Higgins, Henry on 69-Feb-17 [69-Feb-24: 2C].
Allard, Emma P. (11 mos.) d. on 68-Jul-8 [68-Jul-10: 2C].
Allard, John (59 yrs.) d. on 68-Dec-9 [68-Dec-10: 2D].
Allard, John Edward (1 yr., 10 mos.) d. on 70-Jun-12 [70-Jun-13: 2C].
Allbright, Jessie P. (83 yrs.) d. on 69-Jun-30 [69-Jul-1: 1H, 2C].
Allbright, Mary M. (81 yrs.) d. on 69-Aug-16 [69-Aug-17: 2C].
Alldridge, Florence Alverta (10 mos.) d. on 69-Jan-24 [69-Jan-26: 2C].
Alldridge, W. T. m. Calvert, Kate C. on 66-Apr-29 [66-May-19: 2B].
Alldridge, William T. (25 yrs.) d. on 69-May-24 [69-May-25: 2C].
Allen, Alexander m. Wilson, Sarah A. on 70-Jul-8 [70-Sep-8: 2B].
Allen, Alice m. Bodine, William B. on 67-Apr-22 [67-Apr-23: 2B].
Allen, Barned (2 yrs., 9 mos.) d. on 70-Feb-7 [70-Feb-8: 2C].
Allen, Byron McCoubray (8 yrs.) d. on 68-Mar-2 [68-Mar-3: 2C; 68-Mar-4: 2C].
Allen, Carrie L. d. on 66-Mar-5 [66-Mar-8: 2B].
Allen, Elizabeth (66 yrs.) d. on 66-Jun-5 [66-Jun-6: 2B].
Allen, Elizabeth d. on 70-Aug-16 [70-Aug-18: 2C].
Allen, Emily (48 yrs., 9 mos.) d. on 67-Feb-23 [67-Feb-25: 2C].
Allen, Emma m. Dawes, Edward B., Jr. on 69-Aug-31 [69-Sep-8: 2B].
Allen, Emma m. Brannan, George A. on 69-Jan-6 [69-Jan-11: 2C].
Allen, George, Capt. (55 yrs.) d. on 67-Jun-1 of Liver Inflammation [67-Jun-3: 1F, 2B].
Allen, George W. (16 yrs.) d. on 66-Nov-6 Drowned [66-Nov-22: 1G; 66-Nov-23: 2C].
Allen, George W. m. Warner, Anna R. on 69-Sep-23 [69-Sep-25: 2B].
Allen, Henry D. m. Miller, Susan Ann on 70-Feb-3 [70-Feb-5: 2B].
Allen, Jane H. m. Taylor, William G. on 67-Aug-29 [67-Sep-5: 2B].
Allen, John C. (35 yrs.) d. on 67-Mar-7 Drowned [67-Mar-8: 1F; 67-Mar-12: 1F].
Allen, John E. (57 yrs.) d. on 70-Aug-19 [70-Aug-20: 2B, 4D].
Allen, John Wesley (4 mos.) d. on 67-Jun-16 [67-Jun-18: 2B].
Allen, Joseph (64 yrs.) d. on 69-Aug-14 [69-Aug-17: 2C].
Allen, Joseph H. m. McAllister, Kate on 70-Oct-19 [70-Oct-26: 2B].
Allen, L. m. Borton, Izetta on 69-Mar-18 [69-Apr-1: 2C].
Allen, Lennet (60 yrs.) d. on 69-Feb-7 of Pneumonia [69-Feb-8: 1G, 2C].
Allen, Lizzie B. (42 yrs.) d. on 70-Sep-4 [70-Sep-14: 2B].
Allen, Mamie E. (6 mos.) d. on 70-Sep-13 [70-Sep-17: 2B].
Allen, Margaret E. (59 yrs.) d. on 67-Oct-28 [67-Oct-29: 2B; 67-Oct-30: 2B].
Allen, Martha E. m. Emich, Nicholas on 68-Mar-24 [68-Apr-7: 2B].
Allen, Mary A. m. Horton, James M. on 67-Jan-24 [67-Jan-30: 2C].
Allen, Mary C. m. Grape, Joseph on 67-Apr-18 [67-Apr-22: 2A].
Allen, Mary E. m. Price, William T. on 69-Sep-7 [69-Sep-11: 2B].
Allen, Mary Hancock W. (7 mos.) d. on 69-Jun-4 [69-Jun-11: 2C].
Allen, Mary Jane (40 yrs.) d. on 67-Mar-10 [67-Mar-11: 2C; 67-Mar-12: 2C; 67-Mar-13: 2C].
Allen, Mary R. m. Campbell, James A. on 66-Nov-14 [66-Nov-19: 2B].
Allen, Peter R. (34 yrs.) d. on 70-May-28 [70-May-30: 2B].

Allen, Robert W. (55 yrs.) d. on 68-Jun-2 [68-Jun-3: 2B].
Allen, Robert W. m. Zimmerman, Dora E. on 70-Jun-1 [70-Jun-21: 2C].
Allen, William m. Evatt, Maggie E. on 66-Apr-23 [66-May-4: 2C].
Allen, William B. m. Barton, Susie V. on 66-Aug-7 [66-Aug-21: 2C].
Allen, William H. d. on 67-Aug-8 [67-Aug-9: 2C].
Allen, Willie M. (9 yrs.) d. on 70-Aug-9 [70-Aug-11: 2C].
Allenbaugh, John O. m. Daughaday, Mary E. on 67-Mar-21 [67-May-18: 2A].
Allender, J. Enlous m. Coard, Jennie S. on 70-Jan-20 [70-Jan-28: 2B].
Allender, Mary (88 yrs.) d. on 70-May-11 [70-May-12: 2B; 70-May-13: 2C].
Allerdice, John (38 yrs.) d. on 69-Oct-9 [69-Oct-11: 2C; 69-Oct-12: 2C].
Allers, George W. (5 mos.) d. on 68-Jul-10 [68-Jul-11: 2B].
Allers, Maggie m. Wenok, George J. on 67-Dec-12 [67-Dec-18: 2B].
Allison, Ann (86 yrs.) d. on 69-Nov-18 [69-Nov-22: 2C].
Allison, Catharine A. (25 yrs.) d. on 68-Dec-14 [68-Dec-16: 2C].
Allison, Jennie m. Jackson, E. M. on 67-May-16 [68-May-17: 2B].
Allison, Maggie E.S. (20 yrs.) d. on 68-Mar-4 [68-Mar-5: 2C; 68-Mar-6: 2C].
Allison, Mary Elizabeth (4 mos.) d. on 70-Jul-23 [70-Jul-28: 2C].
Allison, Rachel S. m. Bates, Franklin L. on 67-Jun-4 [67-Jun-8: 2B].
Allison, Robert H. m. Newman, E. Virginia on 66-Jun-7 [66-Oct-6: 2A].
Allison, Rose E. m. Lucchesi, David H. on 69-Feb-9 [69-Feb-17: 2C].
Allnutt, Benjamin m. White, Rachel on 66-Jan-16 [66-Feb-8: 2C].
Allnutt, Lertie C. m. Manning, George O. on 68-Nov-12 [68-Nov-16: 2C].
Allnutt, Sallie Smith (66 yrs.) d. on 66-Feb-17 [66-Feb-19: 2B].
Alloway, Martha (62 yrs.) d. on 68-Sep-28 [68-Sep-29: 2B; 68-Sep-30: 2B].
Alloway, Sallie m. Hamilton, Robert on 68-Jan-14 [68-Jan-21: 2C].
Allridge, John A. (1 yr., 3 mos.) d. on 68-May-12 [68-May-15: 2B].
Alls, Amanda V. (7 mos.) d. on 69-Aug-2 [69-Aug-3: 2C].
Allstan, Joseph S. m. Garner, Julia E. on 68-Apr-29 [68-Apr-30: 2B].
Allston, C. E. m. Coode, D. on 67-Jan-24 [67-Jan-26: 2C].
Allwell, Rebecca E. m. Couchman, William H. on 67-Nov-21 [68-Jan-1: 2C].
Allwell, Stephen S. m. Lee, Mary S. on 69-Aug-22 [69-Sep-2: 2B].
Allwell, William J. m. Rodley, Kate E. on 69-Mar-2 [69-Mar-3: 2B].
Almack, Mollie J. m. McJilton, J. N. on 67-Jan-10 [67-Jan-15: 2C].
Almaney, Henrietta m. Houston, Joel on 69-May-25 [69-Jun-5: 2B].
Alpenburg, E. J. M. m. Roeder, Emma on 70-Jun-4 [70-Jun-9: 2C].
Alsop, Mary J. m. Small, Charles W. on 68-Jun-4 [68-Jun-6: 2A].
Althier, Nancy A. (78 yrs.) d. on 66-Oct-9 [66-Oct-31: 2B; 66-Nov-3: 2B].
Altmeyer, Abraham m. Wiesenfeld, Rebecca on 68-Apr-22 [68-Apr-24: 2B].
Alton, James T. m. McJilton, Helen A. on 68-May-26 [68-May-28: 2B].
Altvater, Charles H. (11 yrs., 6 mos.) d. on 68-Jan-28 of Bowel inflammation [68-Jan-29: 2D; 68-Jan-30: 2C].
Altvater, Edward Williams m. Woodland, Cassie on 69-Nov-24 [69-Nov-26: 2B].
Altvater, John (40 yrs.) d. on 69-Feb-1 [69-Feb-2: 2C; 69-Feb-3: 2C].
Alwell, John M. (16 yrs., 10 mos.) d. on 68-Aug-16 [68-Aug-18: 2B].
Amboy, John (12 yrs.) d. on 68-May-31 Crushed by railing [67-Jun-1: 1E].
Ambrose, Elizabeth Dean (8 mos.) d. on 68-Aug-30 [68-Sep-1: 2B].
Ambrose, George W. (58 yrs.) d. on 69-Jul-18 [69-Aug-7: 2C].
Ambrose, Martha (40 yrs.) d. on 70-Nov-2 [70-Nov-4: 2C].
America, Jane E. m. Chandler, George F. on 67-Jun-2 [67-Jun-8: 2B].
Ames, Ann Jannette d. on 70-Aug-31 [70-Sep-2: 2C].
Ames, Annie m. Turner, Joshua on 66-Feb-12 [66-Feb-17: 2B].
Ames, George m. Doughty, Bettie B. on 66-Nov-19 [66-Dec-4: 2D].
Ames, George C., Esq. (69 yrs.) d. on 70-Feb-7 [70-Feb-15: 2C].
Ames, Mary F. d. on 70-Nov-20 [70-Nov-21: 2C].
Amey, Alonzo (2 yrs., 4 mos.) d. on 69-Nov-25 [69-Nov-27: 2C].

Amey, Laura V. m. Nicholson, Charles P. on 66-Jan-18 [66-Jan-22: 2C].
Amey, Sarah m. Amey, William on 65-Dec-18 [66-Apr-7: 2B].
Amey, William (11 mos.) d. on 69-Jul-5 [69-Jul-17: 2C].
Amey, William m. Amey, Sarah on 65-Dec-18 [66-Apr-7: 2B].
Amick, Mary E. m. Byrne, Joseph F. on 68-Nov-21 [68-Dec-1: 2C].
Ammidon, Frederick Brooks (6 mos.) d. on 70-Jun-29 of Brain congestion [70-Jun-30: 2C].
Ammidon, John Perry, Jr. (6 yrs.) d. on 70-Apr-18 of Brain fever [70-Apr-19: 2B; 70-Apr-20: 2B].
Amos, Anna A. m. Snyder, Henry on 68-Dec-1 [68-Dec-18: 2C].
Amos, B. F. m. Sylvester, Elizabeth on 66-Aug-12 [66-Aug-14: 2C].
Amos, Benjamin (96 yrs.) d. on 69-Oct-10 [69-Nov-3: 2C].
Amos, Charles E. m. Gontrom, Anna C. on 66-Mar-21 [66-May-4: 2C].
Amos, Corbin, Dr. (83 yrs.) d. on 66-Jul-21 [66-Jul-23: 1G, 2C].
Amos, George (50 yrs.) d. on 67-Aug-14 of Heatstroke [67-Aug-14: 1G; 67-Aug-15: 1F].
Amos, James T. m. Krebs, Louisa M. on 69-Jun-24 [69-Jun-28: 2C].
Amos, John H. (47 yrs.) d. on 69-Jul-25 [69-Jul-27: 2C].
Amos, John T. m. Arthur, Sarah J. on 67-Nov-14 [67-Nov-19: 2C].
Amos, Martha m. Slade, Washington M. on 67-Jan-29 [67-Feb-5: 2C].
Amos, Sarah (77 yrs.) d. on 69-Oct-7 [69-Oct-15: 2C].
Amoss, Alice J. m. Welty, F. H. on 68-Jul-18 [68-Oct-3: 2B].
Amoss, Annie E. m. Ford, Achilles on 67-Mar-27 [67-Apr-15: 2B].
Amoss, George Risteau d. on 67-Dec-9 [67-Dec-10: 2B].
Amoss, Jennie (11 mos.) d. on 68-Dec-8 [68-Dec-9: 2C].
Amoss, Mary C. m. Mallalieu, John B. on 68-Dec-23 [68-Dec-25: 2D].
Amoss, Theresa C. (28 yrs.) d. on 66-Sep-10 [66-Sep-11: 2B].
Amrain, George (59 yrs.) d. on 70-Apr-1 [70-Apr-2: 2A].
Amy, Charlotte E. m. Barnett, James A. on 68-Aug-11 [68-Aug-26: 2B].
Anderson, Alexander d. on 70-Jun-10 Drowned [70-Jun-13: 1G].
Anderson, Angela (10 mos.) d. on 70-Jul-17 [70-Jul-18: 2B].
Anderson, Bridget (28 yrs.) d. on 69-Dec-7 [69-Dec-8: 2C].
Anderson, Catherine m. Pagels, George H. Z. on 69-Sep-22 [69-Sep-24: 2B].
Anderson, Charles (2 yrs., 2 mos.) d. on 69-Feb-3 [69-Feb-4: 2C].
Anderson, E. m. Pagels, Edward on 66-Nov-12 [66-Nov-15: 2C].
Anderson, Edwin m. Krout, Annie on 66-Jan-18 [66-Feb-22: 2B].
Anderson, Elizabeth (70 yrs.) d. on 67-May-7 [67-May-9: 2A].
Anderson, Elizabeth (69 yrs.) d. on 66-Mar-12 [66-Mar-13: 2B].
Anderson, Elizabeth C. (76 yrs.) d. on 70-Aug-9 [70-Aug-11: 2C].
Anderson, Ellen (1 yr., 2 mos.) d. on 70-Dec-25 [70-Dec-26: 2C].
Anderson, Enoch m. Anderson, Mary E. on 68-Nov-5 [68-Nov-7: 2B].
Anderson, Fannie E. m. Henry, Robert J. on 68-Jun-30 [68-Jul-1: 2B].
Anderson, Franklin (75 yrs.) d. on 66-Apr-28 [66-May-1: 2A].
Anderson, George N. (24 yrs.) d. on 66-Jul-21 [66-Jul-23: 2C].
Anderson, Issac C. (61 yrs.) d. on 70-Sep-19 [70-Sep-20: 2B].
Anderson, James H. (18 yrs.) d. on 67-Jun-27 [67-Jun-28: 2B].
Anderson, Jane (5 yrs., 10 mos.) d. on 69-Jan-27 [69-Jan-28: 2C].
Anderson, John, Rev. d. on 67-Sep-22 of Heart disease [67-Sep-26: 1F].
Anderson, John H. m. Shipley, Charlotte on 66-Apr-12 [66-Apr-17: 2C].
Anderson, John H. m. Ensor, Amelia J. on 70-Jul-20 [70-Jul-25: 2C].
Anderson, Julia m. Tarter, Henry H. on 67-Aug-1 [67-Aug-6: 2C].
Anderson, Julius H. m. Thomas, Alice on 68-Jul-23 [68-Jul-25: 2B].
Anderson, Laura V. (22 yrs.) d. on 70-Nov-6 [70-Nov-7: 2B; 70-Nov-8: 2B].
Anderson, Lizzie m. Walsh, William L. on 68-Apr-15 [68-Apr-16: 2B].
Anderson, Lou E. m. Polk, William S. on 69-Jun-26 [69-Jul-1: 2C].
Anderson, Louisa m. Spriggs, William H. on 70-May-26 [70-Jun-10: 2B].
Anderson, Margaret (83 yrs.) d. on 70-Mar-23 [70-Mar-24: 2C].

Anderson, Maria (38 yrs.) d. on 69-Dec-13 [69-Dec-14: 2C].
Anderson, Mary (85 yrs.) d. on 67-Jan-9 [67-Jan-10: 2C; 67-Jan-11: 2C].
Anderson, Mary m. Farquharson, Francis L. on 67-Jun-10 [67-Jun-12: 2B].
Anderson, Mary D. (59 yrs.) d. on 69-Jan-26 [69-Jan-30: 2C].
Anderson, Mary E. m. Duvall, Franklin on 68-Nov-24 [68-Nov-28: 2C].
Anderson, Mary E. m. Anderson, Enoch on 68-Nov-5 [68-Nov-7: 2B].
Anderson, Mary Elizabeth (1 yr., 3 mos.) d. on 68-Apr-27 [68-Apr-28: 2B].
Anderson, Mary F. d. on 66-Oct-29 [66-Oct-31: 2B].
Anderson, Mary R. (75 yrs.) d. on 69-Feb-2 [69-Jan-6: 2C].
Anderson, Nannie F. m. Leishear, William B. on 70-Nov-23 [70-Nov-24: 2B].
Anderson, Oliver (5 yrs.) d. on 70-Sep-5 [70-Sep-7: 2B].
Anderson, Oliver H. m. Francis, Terella E. C. on 66-Jan-28 [66-Jan-30: 2B].
Anderson, Rebecca m. McDonald, Elias on 70-Jan-6 [70-Jan-8: 2B].
Anderson, Richard (78 yrs.) d. on 70-May-22 [70-May-24: 2C].
Anderson, Richard m. McLaughlin, Margaret on 69-Apr-1 [69-Apr-5: 2B].
Anderson, Richarda S. m. Mullikin, H. Clay [67-Jun-1: 2B].
Anderson, Rosanna (37 yrs.) d. on 70-Jan-29 [70-Jan-31: 2C].
Anderson, Samuel Eliot (1 yr., 6 mos.) d. on 67-Mar-17 [67-Mar-18: 2B].
Anderson, Theodora M. m. Norris, James B. on 68-Mar-23 [68-Apr-9: 2B].
Anderson, Thomas M. (33 yrs.) d. on 67-Jun-25 [67-Jun-26: 2C].
Anderson, Virginia m. Woodward, D. D. on 68-Jan-9 [68-Jan-16: 2C].
Anderson, Walter (23 yrs.) d. on 67-Sep-2 Drowned [67-Sep-3: 4C].
Anderson, William E. (52 yrs.) d. on 68-Jul-15 [68-Jul-16: 2C].
Anderson, William H. H. m. Brockett, Cornelia M. on 68-Feb-19 [68-Feb-22: 2B].
Anderson, Winfield D. S. m. Campbell, Mary M. Taney on 70-Oct-18 [70-Oct-19: 2B].
Anderton, Walter E. m. McCarthy, Victoria M. on 67-Jan-5 [67-Jan-11: 2C].
Andre, Alma M. (1 yr., 10 mos.) d. on 70-Jan-8 [70-Jan-10: 2C].
Andre, James Ridgway, Jr. (2 yrs., 6 mos.) d. [67-Jan-30: 2C; 67-Jan-31: 2C].
Andrew, , Mrs. d. on 69-Sep-2 [69-Sep-4: 2B].
Andrew, R. Franklin (17 yrs., 1 mo.) d. on 70-Feb-10 of Yellow fever [70-Mar-15: 2C].
Andrew, Sophia (82 yrs.) d. on 68-Feb-1 [68-Feb-7: 2C].
Andrew, Walter J. m. Fillinger, Mary J. on 67-Nov-19 [67-Nov-28: 2B].
Andrews, Annie P. m. Courtney, William T. on 66-Aug-23 [66-Sep-6: 2B].
Andrews, Benjamin m. Slater, Annie on 66-Jan-17 [66-Feb-2: 2C].
Andrews, Cornelia d. on 67-Jun-28 [].
Andrews, Elizabeth m. Tray, Samuel on 66-Aug-29 [66-Sep-1: 2B].
Andrews, Frances Delilah (7 mos.) d. on 68-May-27 [68-May-28: 2B].
Andrews, Henrietta S. (30 yrs.) d. on 69-Mar-31 [69-Apr-2: 2C].
Andrews, James (13 yrs.) d. on 66-Dec-14 [66-Dec-19: 2B].
Andrews, Margaret (55 yrs.) d. on 66-Dec-2 [66-Dec-7: 2B].
Andrews, Mary L. (24 yrs.) d. on 66-Apr-29 [66-Apr-30: 2B].
Andrews, Rebbie m. Moore, Joel on 70-Jan-1 [70-Jan-12: 2C].
Andrews, Thomas Edward m. Ryan, Mary Emma on 70-Jul-14 [70-Aug-6: 2C].
Andrews, Thomas H. m. Snyder, M. Virtu on 70-Mar-2 [70-Mar-3: 2C].
Anerson, Elizabeth (4 yrs., 7 mos.) d. on 69-Feb-2 [69-Feb-4: 2C].
Angelmier, Louise m. Webb, William W. on 67-Dec-20 [68-Mar-3: 2C].
Ankard, Joseph H. m. Mitchell, Maggie A. on 68-Jan-20 [68-Jan-22: 2C].
Annabel, Thurman C. m. Pearson, Annie E. on 68-May-26 [68-May-30: 2A].
Annan, Emily (24 yrs.) d. on 67-Jun-6 [67-Jun-7: 2B].
Annan, Samuel, Dr. d. on 68-Jan-19 [68-Jan-21: 2C; 68-Jan-20: 2C].
Annandale, William J. m. Mailhouse, Lizzie on 70-Feb-3 [70-Feb-10: 2C].
Annen, Jennie V. m. Wright, Richard on 70-Feb-11 [70-Mar-23: 2C].
Anshutz, Martha A. (48 yrs.) d. on 66-Feb-20 [66-Feb-22: 2B].
Anspach, Anna A. (3 yrs., 6 mos.) d. on 69-May-8 [69-May-18: 2C].
Anspach, Frederick R., Rev. (49 yrs.) d. on 67-Sep-17 [67-Sep-18: 2B; 67-Sep-19: 1G].

Anthony, Annie H. m. Dorsey, Clement H. on 70-May-28 [70-May-31: 2B].
Anthony, Emma C. m. Henricks, Arthur T. on 66-Apr-5 [66-Apr-11: 2B].
Anthony, Margaret m. Nicholson, Michael on 67-Oct-4 [67-Oct-5: 2B].
Anthony, Margaret Lee (10 mos.) d. on 66-Jan-15 [66-Jan-17: 2C].
Anthony, Mary R. m. Hammond, Richard E. on 69-Oct-7 [69-Oct-9: 2C].
Anthony, W. Fenwick m. Johnson, Henrietta L. M. on 66-Oct-23 [66-Oct-24: 2C].
Anzman, Joseph Anthony (7 mos.) d. on 66-Sep-27 [66-Sep-29: 2B].
Appel, Frederick (10 yrs.) d. on 67-May-18 Drowned [67-May-20: 1F].
Appell, Caroline C. m. Jackson, Charles McC. on 66-Apr-17 [66-Apr-18: 2B].
Apple, Margaret (50 yrs.) d. on 70-Mar-8 of Heart disease [70-Mar-10: 4G].
Appleby, Caroline (56 yrs.) d. on 67-Jun-15 [67-Jun-17: 2C].
Appleby, William (18 yrs.) d. on 70-Aug-10 [70-Aug-12: 2C].
Applegarth, Eleanor (7 yrs.) d. on 66-May-23 [66-May-24: 2C].
Applegarth, James A., Capt. d. on 66-Aug-31 of Remittent fever [66-Sep-13: 1G].
Applegarth, John A. m. Harrison, Josephine on 66-Oct-11 [66-Oct-18: 2B].
Applegarth, Kate m. Sanders, S. F. on 66-Nov-27 [66-Nov-28: 2B].
Applegarth, Maggie Cecilia m. Farnan, Thomas F. on 66-Apr-3 [66-Apr-11: 2B].
Applegarth, Mary Ann m. Henkel, Lewis on 68-Feb-3 [68-Feb-4: 2C].
Applegarth, Sarah E. m. Young, George H. on 68-Feb-6 [68-Feb-8: 2B].
Applegarth, Sarah Waddell (63 yrs.) d. on 70-Apr-25 [70-Apr-26: 2B].
Applegarth, Thomas J. (47 yrs.) d. on 69-Oct-20 [69-Oct-22: 2B].
Appler, Elizabeth m. Elliott, George on 69-Aug-8 [69-Oct-18: 2C].
Appleton, Eben m. Slade, Isabel on 68-Nov-24 [68-Dec-9: 2C].
Appold, James A. m. MacKenzie, Mollie on 66-Jul-25 [66-Aug-24: 2B].
Appold, Louvenia m. Stockman, George W. on 69-Nov-11 [69-Nov-13: 2B].
Archer, Ann (82 yrs.) d. on 67-Aug-20 [67-Aug-31: 2B].
Archer, Fanny Van Wick (18 yrs.) d. on 70-Nov-10 [70-Nov-12: 2B].
Archer, Mary E. G. m. Harlan, George S. on 70-Dec-14 [70-Dec-19: 2C].
Archer, Mary T. m. Shepard, Charles S. on 70-Sep-18 [70-Sep-23: 2C].
Archer, Nannie H. m. Thomas, Oliver H. on 68-Dec-1 [68-Dec-3: 2C].
Archer, Thomas (62 yrs.) d. on 70-Feb-17 [70-Feb-19: 2B].
Archer, William H. m. Goldsborough, Fannie V. W. on 69-Dec-28 [69-Dec-29: 2D].
Ardin, Mary Jane (62 yrs.) d. on 67-Mar-29 [67-Mar-29: 2C].
Ardleman, Andrew m. Harvey, Mary E. on 66-May-28 [66-Jun-2: 2B].
Armacost, Calvin A. m. Jackson, Mollie E. on 69-Sep-23 [69-Sep-25: 2B].
Armacost, Eliza (49 yrs.) d. [66-Dec-13: 2C].
Armacost, Frank Caldwell (2 yrs., 3 mos.) d. on 69-Nov-14 [69-Nov-15: 2C].
Armacost, Joseph m. Hartzell, Eliza on 66-Apr-30 [66-May-16: 2C].
Armacost, Maggie m. Kline, William on 68-Nov-17 [68-Nov-28: 2C].
Armacost, Priscilla (70 yrs.) d. on 70-Nov-18 [70-Nov-19: 2B].
Armager, Benjamin F. m. Harrison, Sallie E. on 68-Dec-17 [68-Dec-25: 2D].
Armager, Jesse S. d. on 69-Aug-17 [69-Aug-18: 2C; 69-Aug-19: 1H].
Armager, Juliet V. m. Staum, John W. on 69-Jun-22 [69-Jun-26: 2B].
Armat, John Hunter d. on 67-Dec-7 of Pneumonia [67-Dec-25: 2C].
Armendt, Frances Ann (30 yrs.) d. on 70-Jan-23 of Lamp explosion [70-Jan-24: 2C, 4F].
Armendt, William N. (1 yr., 4 mos.) d. on 70-Sep-6 [70-Sep-8: 2B].
Armiger, Alice (15 yrs.) d. on 66-Jan-14 [66-Jan-15: 2B].
Armiger, Benjamin (78 yrs.) d. on 67-Jan-9 [67-Jan-10: 2C].
Armiger, George Henry (9 mos.) d. on 67-May-22 [67-May-23: 2B].
Armiger, Henrietta (39 yrs.) d. on 66-Jan-6 [66-Jan-8: 2B].
Armiger, James Middleton (7 yrs., 9 mos.) d. on 70-Nov-30 of Scarlet fever [70-Dec-1: 2C; 70-Dec-2: 2C].
Armiger, Joseph H. m. Smith, Mary E. on 65-Feb-5 [66-Jun-8: 2B].
Armiger, Josiah C. m. Jubb, A. Rebecca on 70-Dec-8 [70-Dec-10: 2B].
Armiger, Mary (6 yrs.) d. on 66-May-5 [66-May-7: 2B].

Armiger, Mary Isabelle (4 mos.) d. on 66-Aug-22 [66-Aug-24: 2B].
Armiger, Richard m. Faringer, Carrie M. on 67-Mar-7 [67-Mar-9: 2B].
Armiger, Rosetta (51 yrs.) d. on 66-Apr-13 [66-Apr-14: 2B].
Armiger, Sarah (78 yrs.) d. on 69-Aug-4 [69-Aug-5: 2B].
Armiger, William (54 yrs.) d. on 70-Dec-3 [70-Dec-5: 2C].
Armistead, Sue Gordon m. Grady, C. Powell on 67-Nov-21 [67-Nov-23: 2B].
Armitage, Margaret (50 yrs.) d. on 68-Dec-22 [68-Dec-23: 2C].
Armor, Emily Ann Delia d. on 67-Oct-2 [67-Oct-4: 2B; 67-Oct-5: 2B].
Armor, Joseph G. (52 yrs.) d. on 69-Dec-17 of Brain congestion [70-Jan-3: 2C].
Armor, Minnie m. Holmes, Thomas on 66-Dec-18 [66-Dec-20: 2B].
Armor, Sedonia C. m. Dungan, H. G. on 68-Feb-12 [68-Feb-14: 2C].
Armstrong, Andrew (78 yrs.) d. on 69-Aug-19 [69-Aug-20: 1G, 2C; 69-Aug-21: 2B].
Armstrong, Belle H. m. Wessels, Littleton B. on 70-May-26 [70-Jun-2: 2B].
Armstrong, Catherine C. m. Eggleston, Edward J. on 69-Feb-9 [69-Feb-16: 2C].
Armstrong, Edward A. m. Hall, Regina B. on 68-Apr-19 [68-Jun-19: 2B].
Armstrong, Ethalinda d. [66-Jan-17: 2C].
Armstrong, Florence E. m. McCarty, William M. on 66-Jan-20 [66-Jan-23: 2C].
Armstrong, Hannah Ann d. on 66-Feb-20 [66-Feb-22: 2B].
Armstrong, Henry L. (34 yrs.) d. on 68-Feb-10 [68-Feb-12: 2B].
Armstrong, James (34 yrs.) d. on 67-Dec-17 of Want and exposure [67-Dec-18: 4D].
Armstrong, James (66 yrs.) d. on 66-Sep-4 [66-Sep-13: 3C].
Armstrong, James H. (38 yrs.) d. on 66-Apr-16 [66-Apr-18: 2B].
Armstrong, James S. (45 yrs.) d. on 67-Jun-16 [67-Jun-18: 2B].
Armstrong, John B. (40 yrs.) d. on 68-Jul-25 [68-Jul-27: 2B].
Armstrong, John H. m. Collins, Virginia on 66-Mar-7 [66-Mar-10: 2B].
Armstrong, John L. (34 yrs.) d. on 66-Jun-27 [66-Jun-28: 2C].
Armstrong, John M. m. Hughes, Clara L. on 70-Sep-15 [70-Oct-3: 2B].
Armstrong, Joseph Murphy (1 yr., 3 mos.) d. on 68-Apr-10 [68-Apr-11: 2A].
Armstrong, Juliett B. (69 yrs.) d. on 66-Jan-12 [66-Jan-13: 2C].
Armstrong, Lillie May (5 yrs.) d. on 68-Feb-20 [68-Feb-21: 2B].
Armstrong, Mary d. on 66-Apr-2 [66-Apr-5: 2B].
Armstrong, Mary (75 yrs.) d. on 66-Feb-6 [66-Feb-8: 2C].
Armstrong, Mary E. m. Levering, Eugene, Jr. on 68-Jan-23 [68-Jan-25: 2B].
Armstrong, Nettie J. m. Parramore, Thomas on 69-Jan-27 [69-Feb-4: 2C].
Armstrong, Rachel (56 yrs.) d. on 66-May-14 [66-May-16: 2C].
Armstrong, Richard (42 yrs.) d. on 67-Jul-23 [67-Jul-24: 2C].
Armstrong, S. Edward m. Murray, Kate Melvin on 69-Sep-21 [69-Sep-23: 2B].
Armstrong, Sallie V. m. Weiant, Wolsey T. on 69-Apr-15 [69-Apr-19: 2B].
Armstrong, Sarah R. m. Winter, Samuel on 69-Sep-30 [69-Oct-7: 2B].
Armstrong, Thomas (79 yrs.) d. on 68-Nov-14 of Paralysis [68-Nov-16: 1G, 2C; 68-Nov-17: 1H].
Armstrong, Thomas (26 yrs.) d. on 69-Sep-29 [69-Sep-30: 2B].
Armstrong, Victor D. m. Merryman, Rhettie on 68-Apr-16 [68-Apr-24: 2B].
Armstrong, William m. Weiant, Hannie M. on 69-Oct-27 [69-Nov-1: 2B].
Armstrong, William J. (36 yrs., 1 mo.) d. on 69-Jul-15 of Consumption [69-Aug-12: 2C].
Armstrong, William J. m. Clark, Fannie H. on 70-Nov-22 [70-Nov-26: 2B].
Arnol, Rebecca (62 yrs.) d. on 70-Mar-28 of Consumption [70-Mar-29: 2B].
Arnold, Alexander (5 yrs., 10 mos.) d. on 69-Feb-5 [69-Feb-6: 2C].
Arnold, Benjamin (65 yrs.) d. on 69-Sep-1 [69-Sep-2: 2B].
Arnold, D. W. m. Dulie, Mattie on 69-Jul-15 [69-Aug-3: 2C].
Arnold, George, Capt. (35 yrs.) d. on 68-Dec-17 [68-Jun-26: 2B].
Arnold, H. Tracy m. Ellicott, Sallie on 67-Sep-10 [67-Sep-11: 2B].
Arnold, John (33 yrs.) d. on 69-Mar-7 [69-Apr-13: 2B].
Arnold, John m. Wilbur, Mary A. P. on 67-Mar-5 [67-Mar-8: 2C].
Arnold, John m. McCauley, Arabella on 70-Apr-21 [70-Apr-26: 2B].

Arnold, John J. m. Thompson, Honnor A. on 70-Feb-3 [70-Mar-23: 2C].
Arnold, Kate m. Bayn, John M. on 66-Nov-7 [67-Feb-18: 2C].
Arnold, Laura V. m. Hooper, Thomas B. on 70-Aug-23 [70-Aug-25: 2B].
Arnold, Lilly May (2 yrs.) d. on 68-Aug-13 [68-Aug-14: 2C].
Arnold, Lizzie C. m. Hoag, James A. on 70-Mar-4 [70-May-4: 2C].
Arnold, Lizzie V. (32 yrs.) d. on 67-Feb-9 of Consumption [67-Feb-11: 2C].
Arnold, Mary E. m. Kepler, William P. on 66-Jun-25 [66-Oct-31: 2B].
Arnold, Thomas E. m. Mewbern, Eugenia on 68-Jun-11 [68-Jun-16: 2B].
Arnold, William (72 yrs.) d. on 67-Jul-4 [67-Jul-6: 2B].
Arnold, William S. m. Younger, Anna on 69-Jun-16 [69-Jun-26: 2B].
Arnott, Ellen (65 yrs.) d. on 67-Sep-8 [67-Sep-9: 2B].
Aro, Catherine (62 yrs.) d. on 67-Jan-5 [67-Jan-7: 2C].
Aro, Margaret A. m. Schienkle, Peter A. on 66-Jul-15 [66-Jul-23: 2C].
Aro, William Lewis (3 yrs.) d. on 69-Oct-27 [69-Oct-28: 2C].
Arscott, Richard m. Howell, Annie on 66-Mar-26 [66-Mar-28: 2C].
Arthur, Camilla E. m. McAlister, John A on 68-Feb-26 [68-Mar-12: 2B].
Arthur, Catherine (56 yrs.) d. on 70-Dec-28 [70-Dec-30: 2C].
Arthur, Delia m. Knipe, Oscar A. on 69-May-26 [69-Jun-10: 2C].
Arthur, Delia m. Benton, Charles S. on 70-Jun-30 [70-Jul-4: 2C].
Arthur, Emily J. (11 mos.) d. on 66-Jul-29 [66-Aug-4: 2C].
Arthur, Hattie (5 yrs.) d. on 68-Oct-25 [68-Oct-27: 2B].
Arthur, Hugh (90 yrs.) d. on 69-Jun-17 [69-Jun-18: 2C; 69-Jun-21: 1G].
Arthur, J. Fleming m. Harman, Lizzie K. on 66-Dec-20 [66-Dec-25: 2B].
Arthur, James D. O. m. Holton, Virginia on 67-Dec-26 [67-Dec-30: 2C].
Arthur, James H. m. Fontz, Mary Ellen on 70-Dec-20 [70-Dec-28: 2C].
Arthur, Maggie (9 mos.) d. on 68-Aug-30 [68-Aug-31: 2B].
Arthur, Maggie H. m. Boyd, J. W. on 67-Jun-18 [67-Jun-19: 2B].
Arthur, Margaret d. on 66-Mar-7 [66-Mar-8: 2B].
Arthur, Mary Elizabeth (23 yrs.) d. on 67-Jul-1 [67-Jul-6: 2B].
Arthur, Meriam (5 yrs., 2 mos.) d. on 69-Jul-2 [69-Jul-5: 2C].
Arthur, Rebecca m. Balls, Bartholomew on 68-Oct-15 [68-Oct-26: 2B].
Arthur, Rose (50 yrs.) d. on 67-Mar-2 [67-Mar-4: 2D].
Arthur, Sarah J. m. Amos, John T. on 67-Nov-14 [67-Nov-19: 2C].
Arthur, Susanna (1 yr., 8 mos.) d. on 68-Jul-11 [68-Jul-13: 2B].
Arthur, William d. on 66-Mar-28 Crushed by wall [66-Mar-29: 1G].
Arthurs, Robert (50 yrs.) d. on 66-Sep-9 [66-Sep-10: 2D].
Asendorf, C. H. m. Thiemeyer, Lizzie on 68-Dec-3 [68-Dec-7: 2C].
Asendorf, George H. m. Waltjen, Sophie A. on 69-Nov-23 [69-Dec-13: 2C].
Ash, Charles m. Wilson, M. Cornelia on 69-Oct-27 [69-Nov-2: 2B].
Ash, Elizabeth m. Spitz, Samuel on 66-Feb-6 [66-Feb-9: 2C].
Ash, George Thomas (4 mos.) d. on 69-Mar-20 [69-Mar-22: 2C].
Ash, Ida Jane (1 yr.) d. on 69-Jul-27 [69-Jul-28: 2D].
Ash, Isabella (64 yrs.) d. on 67-Sep-1 [67-Sep-2: 2B].
Ash, James (45 yrs.) d. on 70-Jul-17 of Heatstroke [70-Jul-18: 4D].
Ash, James F. (32 yrs.) d. on 66-Sep-14 [66-Sep-15: 2B].
Ash, Malvin (18 yrs.) d. on 67-Dec-30 [68-Jan-1: 2C; 68-Jan-6: 2C].
Ash, Martha (80 yrs.) d. on 67-Oct-22 [67-Oct-23: 2B].
Ash, Winson m. Brogdon, Henrietta on 67-May-2 [67-May-8: 2B].
Ash, Winston (63 yrs.) d. on 70-Feb-26 [70-Feb-28: 2C].
Ashbridge, Catherine S. m. Gorsuch, Edwin A. on 69-Dec-9 [69-Dec-11: 2B].
Ashburn, Judson A m. Dawson, Frances N. on 68-Dec-24 [68-Dec-25: 2D].
Ashburner, Charlotte (11 mos.) d. on 70-Jun-19 [70-Jun-20: 2B].
Ashbury, Joseph M. m. Elmer, Emma B. on 70-Oct-27 [70-Nov-12: 2B].
Ashcom, George W. m. Colton, Mary Ruth on 67-Dec-24 [67-Dec-25: 2C].
Ashdown, Mary Ann (66 yrs.) d. on 66-Jan-16 [66-Jan-18: 2C].

Asher, Mary C. m. Elliott, James J. on 67-Jan-3 [67-Jan-7: 2C].
Asher, William Francis (11 mos.) d. on 69-Apr-2 [69-Apr-5: 2B].
Ashley, William H. m. Hodges, Susie A. on 69-Dec-2 [69-Dec-7: 2C].
Ashman, Alfred (49 yrs.) d. on 69-Feb-21 [69-Feb-23: 2C].
Ashton, Charles E. (24 yrs.) d. on 69-Nov-8 of Consumption [69-Nov-9: 2C].
Ashton, John Mansfield (24 yrs.) d. on 67-Sep-4 of Consumption [67-Sep-5: 2B].
Ashton, May Susannah (4 mos.) d. on 67-Jul-2 [67-Jul-8: 2C].
Ashton, Washington R. (41 yrs.) d. on 68-Oct-26 [68-Nov-9: 2B].
Askew, Edward (28 yrs.) d. on 66-Nov-4 of Intemperance [66-Nov-5: 2B, 4A].
Askew, Mollie Cecilia (1 yr., 6 mos.) d. on 68-Jun-16 [68-Jun-17: 2B].
Askey, J. Robert m. Taylor, Lurannah M. on 67-Jan-10 [67-Jan-16: 2C; 67-Jan-19: 2C].
Askey, Susie F. m. Zimmerman, John C. on 67-Mar-3 [67-May-29: 2B].
Askins, William E., Capt. (40 yrs.) d. on 69-Mar-24 of Consumption [69-Mar-25: 2C].
Aspril, David S. m. Bruggmann, Anna M. M. on 66-Feb-19 [66-Feb-21: 2C].
Aspril, David Springer (9 mos.) d. on 70-Feb-18 [70-Feb-19: 2B].
Aspril, Emma Elizabeth (27 yrs., 10 mos.) d. on 70-May-20 of Consumption [70-May-21: 2B].
Aspril, George W. (25 yrs.) d. on 69-Sep-28 [69-Sep-29: 2B; 69-Sep-30: 1F, 2B].
Aspril, George W. m. Lightner, Fannie Jane on 67-Jun-4 [67-Jun-6: 2B].
Aspril, John (80 yrs.) d. on 67-Nov-7 [67-Nov-8: 2C].
Aspril, Mary Baker (6 mos.) d. on 69-Jun-10 [69-Jun-11: 2C].
Ast, Mollie Kimmell (2 yrs.) d. on 66-Mar-17 [66-Apr-28: 2A].
Ast, Rosalba Hoffman (3 yrs.) d. on 66-Jan-30 [66-Feb-26: 2B].
Ast, William Byron (7 yrs., 1 mo.) d. on 66-Apr-14 [66-May-3: 2C].
Athoe, Elizabeth (63 yrs.) d. on 67-Nov-10 [67-Nov-11: 2C].
Atkins, Benjamin (1 yr., 4 mos.) d. on 66-Aug-1 [66-Aug-7: 2C].
Atkins, Thomas m. Ward, Alice V. on 68-Aug-18 [68-Aug-25: 2B].
Atkinson, Ann P. (71 yrs.) d. on 70-Oct-28 [70-Oct-29: 2B].
Atkinson, Brodnay m. Purviance, Eliza on 69-Jan-28 [69-Jan-29: 2C].
Atkinson, George (63 yrs.) d. on 70-Jul-10 [70-Jul-11: 2C; 70-Jul-12: 2B].
Atkinson, Hannah P. (60 yrs.) d. on 68-Mar-27 [68-Mar-28: 2B].
Atkinson, Helen J. m. King, Bernard N. on 65-Sep-14 [66-Jan-31: 2C].
Atkinson, Israel (71 yrs.) d. on 66-Aug-12 [66-Aug-13: 2C].
Atkinson, J. E. m. Duvall, Virginia R. on 67-Oct-17 [67-Oct-18: 2C].
Atkinson, Joshua I (69 yrs.) d. on 69-May-1 of Congestive chill [69-May-3: 1H, 2C; 69-May-4: 1G].
Atkinson, Joshua I m. Conant, A. E. on 69-Apr-17 [69-Apr-20: 2B].
Atkinson, Mary E. m. Haslett, Samuel S. on 67-Jul-11 [67-Dec-27: 2D].
Atkinson, Nancy (71 yrs., 5 mos.) d. on 68-May-19 [68-May-28: 2B].
Atkinson, Orrie m. Popplein, George J. on 68-Jun-25 [68-Jun-27: 2B].
Atkinson, Samuel O. (30 yrs., 3 mos.) d. on 69-Mar-2 [69-Mar-5: 2C].
Atkinson, Thomas (78 yrs.) d. on 67-Jan-25 [67-Jan-26: 2C].
Atkinson, Thomas (51 yrs.) d. on 66-Oct-25 [66-Oct-27: 2B].
Atkinson, Thomas F. m. Kean, Mary A. on 69-Mar-11 [69-Mar-20: 2B].
Atkinson, William George m. Gogel, Kate W. on 67-Jun-13 [67-Jun-18: 2B].
Atkinson, William S. (40 yrs.) d. on 69-May-19 [69-May-20: 2C].
Atlee, Issac m. Kamerer, Louisa on 70-Nov-22 [70-Nov-28: 2C].
Atler, Lizzie S. m. Morgan, Randolph on 69-May-19 [69-May-21: 2C].
Atten, J. d. on 66-Dec-19 [66-Dec-24: 1G].
Atwell, Benjamin, Capt. (53 yrs.) d. on 66-Jan-23 [66-Jan-29: 1F; 66-Feb-10: 2C].
Atwell, Elizabeth (48 yrs.) d. on 69-Apr-11 [69-Apr-12: 2A].
Atwell, Emma m. Thierrauch, Lawson C. on 66-Jan-15 [66-Jan-17: 2C].
Atwell, Mollie E. m. Hopkins, Harrison on 68-Jun-4 [68-Jun-30: 2B].
Atwell, Susie C. m. Tucker, Alfred, Jr. on 66-Nov-20 [66-Dec-3: 2B].
Atwood, John (75 yrs., 2 mos.) d. on 69-Mar-26 [69-Mar-27: 2B].
Atwood, Robert m. Squirll, Jane on 68-Mar-5 [68-Mar-9: 2C].

Aubrey, Emma Virginia (1 mo.) d. on 66-Apr-28 [66-May-1: 2A].
Audibert, Harry (8 mos.) d. on 67-Nov-11 [67-Nov-15: 2B].
Audibert, John H (36 yrs.) d. on 68-Jun-6 [68-Jun-8: 2B].
Audibert, John William (5 mos.) d. on 66-Jul-11 [66-Jul-12: 2C].
Audoun, Emma Fuller m. McSherry, W. A. on 68-Nov-26 [68-Nov-28: 2C].
Audoun, Laura R. (19 yrs.) d. on 67-Jun-4 [67-Jun-5: 2B].
Augur, J. H. m. Barrett, Ella on 70-Jan-4 [70-Jan-5: 2C].
Augustus, Daniel (55 yrs.) d. on 70-Mar-15 [70-Mar-17: 2C].
Aulbach, John (51 yrs., 10 mos.) d. on 70-Jun-3 [70-Jun-4: 2B; 70-Jul-13: 2C].
Auld, Albert Ambrose (5 yrs.) d. on 66-Feb-10 [66-Feb-12: 2D].
Auld, Sarah E. d. on 67-Dec-18 [68-Jan-14: 2C].
Auld, Sarah Elizabeth m. Battie, George Elbert on 67-Jan-10 [67-Jan-16: 2C].
Aull, Jacob B. m. Collyer, Mary M. on 70-Dec-15 [70-Dec-26: 2C].
Ault, Mary Jane (51 yrs.) d. [69-Jan-20: 2C].
Ault, Samuel d. on 70-Jul-7 [70-Jul-9: 2B].
Ault, Samuel m. Clendemen, Kate R. on 68-Oct-29 [68-Nov-11: 2C].
Ault, William H. m. Smood, Elenore on 69-Oct-7 [69-Nov-2: 2B].
Aulthouse, Mary A. (30 yrs.) d. on 70-Mar-31 [70-Apr-1: 2B].
Austin, Elizabeth (48 yrs.) d. on 66-Feb-24 [66-Feb-26: 2B].
Austin, George Francis (9 yrs.) d. on 68-Oct-9 of Scarlet fever [68-Oct-13: 2C].
Austin, Georgianna M. D. m. Murphy, James D. on 66-Mar-6 [66-Mar-8: 2B].
Austin, James K. P. m. Chamberlaine, Martha A. on 66-Nov-1 [66-Dec-14: 2B].
Austin, Julia A. m. Smith, Abraham, Jr. on 69-Oct-21 [69-Oct-23: 2B].
Austin, Margaret m. Weyforth, George on 67-Nov-4 [67-Nov-30: 2C].
Austin, Sallie L. (24 yrs., 4 mos.) d. on 68-Oct-10 [68-Oct-12: 2B; 68-Oct-13: 2C].
Austin, Sophronia m. Nickerson, Charles W. on 69-Jun-23 [70-May-11: 2B].
Austin, Theodore G. m. Unduch, Mary E. on 66-May-31 [66-Jun-4: 2B].
Aveline, Jane E. m. Latchuem, John J. on 66-Feb-20 [66-Mar-22: 2B].
Avery, Ella L. m. Newnan, John T. on 68-Feb-18 [68-Mar-2: 2B].
Awbrey, Harry Ellmore (1 yr., 9 mos.) d. on 69-Jan-17 [69-Jan-18: 2C].
Awbrey, Mary E. m. Morrow, John F. on 67-Jan-29 [67-May-2: 2B].
Axe, David d. on 66-Dec-20 [67-Mar-30: 2C].
Ayers, Ruth (1 yr., 1 mo.) d. on 66-Sep-21 [66-Sep-29: 2B].
Ayler, Kate E. (15 yrs., 4 mos.) d. on 68-Sep-9 [68-Sep-12: 2B].
Aylsworth, Anna M. m. Longmore, Joseph S. on 70-Aug-2 [70-Aug-5: 2C].
Ayres, Charlotte m. Maddux, Alfred on 70-Jan-12 [70-Jan-17: 2C].
Ayres, Franklin C. d. on 69-Mar-14 [69-Mar-16: 2C].
Ayres, George W. m. Ensor, Sarah on 65-Dec-24 [66-Jan-15: 2B].
Ayres, Henrietta (67 yrs.) d. on 67-Jun-19 [67-Jun-20: 2B].
Ayres, Manie m. Cottingham, Harry M. on 70-Dec-13 [70-Dec-15: 2C].
Ayres, Robert H. (60 yrs.) d. on 68-Oct-9 [68-Dec-3: 2C].
Ayres, Sidonia (80 yrs.) d. on 69-Nov-20 [69-Nov-26: 2C].
Ayres, Sidonia m. Kemp, Morris J. on 70-Jun-2 [70-Jun-6: 2B].
Ayres, Thomas J. m. Norris, Alice A. on 66-Jan-25 [66-Feb-22: 2B].
Babb, John D., Jr. (38 yrs.) d. on 69-Aug-5 of Heart disease [69-Aug-7: 2B].
Babb, John D., Sr. (75 yrs.) d. on 69-Mar-31 [69-Apr-1: 2C; 69-Apr-2: 2C].
Babb, Wealthy H. (71 yrs.) d. on 67-Oct-1 [67-Oct-2: 2B; 67-Oct-3: 2B].
Babcock, Rowse, II m. Munger, Kate on 68-Apr-22 [68-Apr-23: 2B].
Baccigaluppo, Vincent (59 yrs.) d. on 69-Jul-25 of Heart disease [69-Jul-26: 1H, 2C].
Bach, Barbara E. A. m. McMaines, Charles J. on 69-Oct-11 [69-Oct-14: 2C].
Bachler, John M. (74 yrs.) d. on 67-Oct-26 [67-Oct-28: 2B].
Bachman, Mark m. Schaab, Kate on 67-Aug-6 [67-Aug-10: 2B].
Bachrach, Nathan m. Jacobi, Hannah on 67-Aug-5 [67-Aug-17: 2B; 67-Aug-21: 2B].
Bachrach, Simon d. on 69-Nov-6 [69-Nov-8: 1H].
Backus, Taylor d. [70-Jan-31: 1H].

Bacon, Aquilla (58 yrs.) d. on 70-Oct-20 of Heart disease [70-Oct-22: 4C].
Bacon, James C. (46 yrs.) d. on 68-Nov-23 [68-Nov-30: 2C].
Bacon, Pamela m. Green, William H. on 70-Sep-1 [70-Sep-2: 2C].
Bacon, Pamelia d. on 69-Apr-14 [69-Apr-15: 2B].
Badders, A. J. m. Ray, Clara A. on 70-Sep-12 [70-Sep-15: 2B].
Badders, Mary A. (78 yrs.) d. on 66-May-20 of Apoplexy [66-May-26: 1F; 66-May-28: 2B].
Badders, William (76 yrs.) d. on 66-Jul-27 [66-Jul-28: 2C].
Baden, Annie m. Grape, William Hamilton on 68-Jan-28 [68-Feb-4: 2C].
Baden, Louisa J. m. Ruff, John P. on 67-Sep-18 [67-Sep-26: 2B].
Baden, Richard W (19 yrs.) d. on 68-Feb-20 [68-Feb-22: 2B].
Baden, Thomas D. (29 yrs.) d. on 70-Jan-15 [70-Jan-17: 2C].
Bader, Anna Elizabeth (67 yrs.) d. on 68-May-14 [68-May-15: 2B].
Badger, Francis (25 yrs.) d. on 70-Oct-30 [70-Nov-2: 2C].
Badger, George Worfield (4 yrs., 7 mos.) d. on 69-Apr-2 [69-Apr-6: 2C].
Badger, Mary (22 yrs.) d. on 66-Feb-20 of Consumption [66-Feb-22: 2B].
Badger, Robert (29 yrs.) d. on 70-Dec-20 [70-Dec-21: 2C; 70-Dec-22: 2B].
Baer, Arthur Pue m. Price, Lizzie on 67-Feb-7 [67-Feb-16: 2D].
Baer, George H. m. Welling, Mary H. on 67-Nov-5 [67-Nov-12: 2C].
Baer, Jacob, Dr. (83 yrs.) d. on 66-Apr-10 [66-Apr-27: 2C].
Baer, James S. m. Fessler, Susan on 66-Nov-23 [66-Nov-27: 2B].
Baer, James Welling d. on 70-Mar-9 [70-Mar-10: 2C].
Baer, Mary E. m. Robelen, George F. on 68-Jul-27 [68-Jul-29: 2B].
Baer, Matilda Ridgely (10 mos.) d. on 68-May-28 [68-May-30: 2A; 68-Jun-1: 2B].
Baer, Nathan m. Lowenthal, Carrie on 70-Jan-2 [70-Feb-5: 2B].
Baer, Robert N. m. Corner, Mary on 70-Apr-14 [70-Apr-20: 2B].
Baer, Susannah (91 yrs.) d. on 66-Jan-12 [66-Jan-13: 2C].
Baer, William (79 yrs.) d. on 66-Jun-7 [66-Jun-14: 2A].
Baer, William H. m. Cherry, Lizzie A. on 67-Jun-20 [67-Jun-21: 2B].
Baer, Willie (1 yr., 2 mos.) d. on 69-Jul-4 [69-Jul-5: 2C].
Baetjer, Eliza L. m. Erich, Henry C. on 66-Feb-7 [66-Feb-9: 2C].
Baetjer, George m. Koppleman, Mary on 67-Sep-19 [67-Sep-23: 2A].
Baetjer, Henry (58 yrs.) d. on 69-Apr-13 [70-Apr-14: 2B; 70-Apr-15: 2B].
Baetjer, Henry m. Cronhardt, F. on 66-Aug-23 [66-Aug-27: 2B].
Bageley, Hannah Waters (53 yrs.) d. on 68-Nov-10 of Typhoid [68-Nov-14: 2B].
Baggett, John B. m. Foreman, Fannie V. on 69-Mar-18 [69-Mar-29: 2B].
Bagley, Clara A. m. Watkins, John B. on 69-Mar-25 [69-Mar-26: 2C; 69-Mar-27: 2B; 69-Mar-29: 2B].
Bagley, Horace m. Fairall, Henrietta S. on 70-May-19 [70-Jun-4: 2B].
Bagnall, Michael (55 yrs.) d. on 69-Sep-6 [69-Sep-8: 2B].
Bagwell, John m. Connelly, Mary Ann on 69-Apr-27 [69-May-4: 2B].
Bagwell, Nannie m. Handy, D. C. on 69-Nov-18 [69-Nov-20: 2B].
Bahn, Cassandra N m. Rinehart, Alexander on 68-Jan-9 [68-Jan-11: 2B].
Baier, Anna m. Weifforth, Jacob on 66-Sep-3 [66-Sep-5: 2B].
Baier, John (43 yrs.) d. on 66-Jun-26 [66-Jun-28: 2C].
Baile, Ginnie S. m. Getty, J. Frank on 70-Nov-1 [70-Nov-3: 2B].
Baile, Lewis N. m. Gorsuch, Jane on 66-Apr-10 [66-Apr-12: 2B].
Bailey, Alfred m. Going, J. C. on 69-Feb-19 [69-Feb-27: 2C].
Bailey, Amos V. m. Barnes, Hanora on 66-Mar-15 [66-Mar-16: 2B].
Bailey, Barbara (62 yrs.) d. [70-Aug-30: 2C].
Bailey, Caroline F. m. Newman, George L. on 68-Jan-2 [68-Jan-6: 2C].
Bailey, Charles W. m. Nash, Eliza J. on 66-May-2 [66-May-5: 2B].
Bailey, Charles W. m. Wilson, Martha L. on 69-May-24 [69-Jun-10: 2C].
Bailey, Charlotte m. Whitfield, Alexander on 69-Jan-14 [69-Jan-15: 2D].
Bailey, Cora Lee (1 yr., 4 mos.) d. on 69-May-10 [69-May-12: 2B].
Bailey, David G. (36 yrs.) d. on 66-Apr-20 [66-Apr-21: 2B].

Bailey, Edwin m. Caldwell, Lizzie on 68-Dec-24 [69-Feb-25: 2D].
Bailey, Edwin L. (43 yrs.) d. on 70-Apr-16 of Typhoid pneumonia [70-Apr-20: 2B].
Bailey, Eliza J. (22 yrs.) d. on 67-Sep-6 [67-Sep-9: 2B].
Bailey, Ephram (44 yrs.) d. on 69-Jul-17 of Heart disease [69-Jul-19: 2D].
Bailey, George W. (28 yrs.) d. on 69-Mar-20 of Consumption [69-Mar-22: 2C].
Bailey, Henry d. on 70-Jul-2 Drowned [70-Jul-4: 1H].
Bailey, Isabella M. m. Dobson, George H. on 70-Feb-16 [70-Feb-21: 2B; 70-Feb-22: 2C].
Bailey, John H. m. Cromwell, Lizzie S. on 67-Nov-12 [67-Nov-15: 2B].
Bailey, Julia A. m. Baker, Edwin F. on 70-Aug-11 [70-Aug-16: 2C].
Bailey, Kate m. Catrup, Samuel P. on 69-Dec-7 [69-Dec-13: 2C].
Bailey, Kate A. m. Thomas, A. C. on 67-Jul-21 [67-Jul-24: 2C].
Bailey, Marianne (4 yrs.) d. on 70-Aug-31 [70-Sep-1: 2B].
Bailey, Mary (58 yrs.) d. on 70-Mar-11 [70-Mar-12: 2C].
Bailey, Mary Ann (63 yrs.) d. on 68-Jun-13 [68-Jun-15: 2B].
Bailey, Susannah (44 yrs.) d. on 70-Feb-23 [70-Feb-24: 2C].
Bailey, William C. m. Webster, Sallie on 67-Jun-4 [67-Jun-10: 2B].
Bailey, William John (17 yrs., 7 mos.) d. on 66-Nov-13 [66-Nov-17: 2C].
Bailie, William L. m. Lambdin, Annie M. on 68-Feb-26 [68-Feb-28: 2D].
Baillie, Georgianna (19 yrs.) d. on 66-Jul-26 of Consumption [66-Jul-31: 2C].
Bailone, William B. (9 yrs.) d. on 66-Apr-8 [66-Apr-9: 2B; 66-Apr-10: 2C].
Baily, Joseph C. m. Marye, Ada on 69-Jul-13 [69-Jul-17: 2C].
Baily, M. Virginia m. Neidhammer, S. Lewis on 66-Oct-25 [66-Nov-6: 2B].
Baines, William F. m. Salmon, Sarah E. on 66-Dec-31 [67-Jan-8: 2B].
Baker, Annie m. Taverner, Edgar H. on 66-Feb-22 [66-Mar-5: 2B].
Baker, Catherine F. m. Ware, William on 66-Jul-24 [66-Jul-30: 2C].
Baker, Charles E. m. Whiteley, Mary E. on 67-Feb-5 [67-Feb-14: 2C].
Baker, Charles G. m. Strickler, Lydia on 67-Apr-4 [67-May-4: 2B].
Baker, Charles T. m. Kemp, Florence V. on 66-Oct-16 [66-Oct-23: 2B].
Baker, Christian (48 yrs.) d. on 70-Oct-16 [70-Oct-17: 2B].
Baker, Edward C. d. on 66-Dec-1 of Cholera morbus [66-Dec-15: 2B].
Baker, Edwin F. m. Bailey, Julia A. on 70-Aug-11 [70-Aug-16: 2C].
Baker, Elanora (74 yrs.) d. on 68-Oct-25 [68-Oct-26: 2B].
Baker, Elizabeth (73 yrs.) d. on 68-Jan-18 [68-Jan-21: 2C].
Baker, Fanny m. Carroll, Michael on 70-Feb-3 [70-Feb-14: 2C].
Baker, Francis A. (35 yrs.) d. on 66-Jan-12 [66-Jan-23: 2C].
Baker, Frederick Ashman (1 yr., 7 mos.) d. on 68-Sep-14 [68-Sep-16: 2B].
Baker, Henry m. Collyer, Ann E. on 70-Feb-2 [70-Feb-24: 2C].
Baker, Ida G. m. Simmonds, Herman on 70-Feb-17 [70-Feb-23: 2C].
Baker, Jane (84 yrs.) d. on 68-May-18 [68-May-20: 2A].
Baker, John F. d. on 66-Nov-26 of Bowel inflammation [66-Dec-15: 2B].
Baker, John G m. Crangle, Agnes on 68-Nov-24 [68-Nov-28: 2C].
Baker, Joseph (68 yrs.) d. on 70-Jul-12 [70-Jul-13: 2C; 70-Jul-14: 1H].
Baker, Joseph m. Douglass, Louisa on 67-May-23 [67-May-25: 2A].
Baker, Julia A. m. Carr, Wesley Cook on 70-Jul-7 [70-Dec-19: 2C].
Baker, Lewis (11 mos.) d. on 70-Oct-20 [70-Oct-25: 2B].
Baker, Lydia (73 yrs.) d. on 69-Oct-12 [69-Oct-14: 2C].
Baker, Mary A. (19 yrs.) d. on 66-Apr-14 of Consumption [66-Apr-16: 2B].
Baker, Mary Elizabeth (1 yr.) d. on 67-Sep-13 [67-Sep-14: 2A].
Baker, Mary R. m. Fales, E. Clark on 66-Jun-5 [66-Jun-27: 2C].
Baker, Merab (64 yrs.) d. on 70-Aug-18 [70-Aug-22: 2C].
Baker, Newton D. m. Dukehart, Mary on 68-Jun-11 [68-Jun-20: 2B].
Baker, Richard J. m. Browne, Mollie E. A. on 66-May-31 [66-Jun-11: 2B].
Baker, Risdon, Capt. d. on 66-Jul-17 [66-Jul-19: 1E].
Baker, Robert J. m. Dobson, Mary V. on 69-May-16 [69-Jun-8: 2B].
Baker, Robert Milton d. on 66-Jul-25 [66-Jul-27: 2C].

Baker, Sophia (31 yrs.) d. on 70-Oct-9 [70-Oct-10: 2B].
Baker, Susie m. Sutherland, George A. on 70-Dec-27 [70-Dec-30: 2C].
Baker, T. Otis m. Saunders, Olivia J. on 70-Mar-23 [70-Mar-30: 2B].
Baker, Theodore F. (27 yrs.) d. on 70-Jan-30 [70-Jan-31: 2C].
Baker, W. Henry m. Dingle, Louisa on 66-Jul-30 [66-Aug-10: 2C].
Baker, William (57 yrs.) d. on 67-Feb-4 [67-Feb-5: 2C; 67-Feb-6: 2C; 67-Feb-7: 1F].
Baker, William (86 yrs.) d. on 67-Mar-9 [67-Mar-11: 1F, 2C; 67-Mar-12: 2C].
Baker, William, Jr. m. Passano, Parthenia on 68-Jan-28 [68-Jan-31: 2C].
Baker, William M. m. O'Dell, Sallie E. on 70-Mar-2 [70-Mar-30: 2B].
Balderston, John P. m. Stokes, Ray V. on 70-Jun-1 [70-Jun-4: 2B].
Balderston, Margaret (95 yrs.) d. on 70-Jul-26 [70-Jul-27: 2C].
Balderston, Thomas C. m. Wethrald, Mary F. on 70-Nov-23 [70-Nov-28: 2C].
Balderston, William A. (24 yrs.) d. on 69-Apr-15 [69-Apr-16: 2B].
Baldwin, Albert Elsworth (4 mos.) d. on 70-Dec-4 [70-Dec-5: 2C].
Baldwin, Charles Gambrill (4 yrs., 4 mos.) d. on 70-Jul-21 [70-Jul-27: 2C].
Baldwin, Charles W. m. Hopkins, Annie C. on 68-Dec-1 [68-Dec-5: 2C].
Baldwin, Charley R. m. Hawkins, Mary on 67-Oct-8 [67-Oct-12: 2A].
Baldwin, Eliza Lee d. on 69-Oct-22 [69-Oct-23: 2B].
Baldwin, Emma M. m. Phelan, J. Wesley on 68-Oct-22 [68-Nov-3: 2B].
Baldwin, Emma V. Callow d. on 66-Aug-30 [66-Sep-1: 2B].
Baldwin, F. Annie C. m. Peregoy, Lewis A. on 69-Dec-20 [69-Dec-31: 2C].
Baldwin, Fannie d. on 67-Jul-21 [67-Jul-23: 2C].
Baldwin, George R. (58 yrs.) d. on 68-Jun-20 [68-Jun-22: 2B].
Baldwin, Gordon (2 yrs., 10 mos.) d. on 70-Apr-9 [70-Apr-11: 2B].
Baldwin, Hannah (84 yrs., 11 mos.) d. on 68-Mar-25 [68-Apr-9: 2B].
Baldwin, Jane Maria (68 yrs.) d. on 66-Mar-7 [66-Mar-9: 2B].
Baldwin, LeRoy E. m. Callow, Emma V. on 66-May-17 [66-May-18: 2C].
Baldwin, Leroy E. m. Hamilton, Virginia on 69-Dec-9 [69-Dec-13: 2C].
Baldwin, Lettitia L. (35 yrs.) d. on 69-May-28 of Consumption [69-Jun-4: 2C].
Baldwin, Levi J. (66 yrs.) d. on 69-Nov-10 [69-Nov-13: 2C].
Baldwin, Mary A. (53 yrs.) d. on 66-Oct-6 [66-Oct-8: 2B].
Baldwin, Nannie R. m. Passano, J. Ferdinand on 70-Apr-21 [70-Apr-22: 2C].
Baldwin, S. Emma m. Sloan, Frs. J. on 69-Dec-7 [69-Dec-13: 2C].
Baldwin, Sarah Catherine (7 yrs., 3 mos.) d. on 70-Nov-8 [70-Nov-8: 2B].
Baldwin, Silas m. Williar, Mary E. on 68-Apr-28 [68-Apr-30: 2B].
Baldwin, Sophia (85 yrs.) d. on 70-Jul-21 [70-Jul-22: 2C].
Baldwin, Summerfield m. Sewell, Juliet G. on 70-Jun-1 [70-Aug-2: 2B].
Ball, Annie m. Laughflin, Richard on 69-Sep-23 [69-Apr-22: 2B].
Ball, Annie P. m. Talbott, John T. on 69-Jun-1 [69-Jun-3: 2B].
Ball, Benjamin F. m. Hobbs, Alice on 70-Feb-16 [70-Feb-21: 2B].
Ball, David C. m. DeVere, Anna Clay on 67-Nov-7 [67-Nov-9: 2B].
Ball, David Emory d. on 70-Feb-22 [70-Feb-25: 2C].
Ball, Ella (1 yr., 1 mo.) d. on 66-Oct-18 [66-Oct-19: 2B].
Ball, Emily Howard (38 yrs.) d. on 69-Mar-4 [69-Mar-5: 2C].
Ball, Fayette (40 yrs.) d. [66-Aug-23: 2C].
Ball, Joann E. m. Boyle, John F. on 66-Jan-16 [66-Jan-20: 2C].
Ball, John Whitridge (3 mos.) d. on 66-Jul-22 [66-Jul-23: 2C].
Ball, Mary F. m. Perrine, Edward J. on 66-Mar-12 [66-Mar-14: 2B].
Ball, Maryland V. (20 yrs.) d. on 68-May-29 of Typhoid [68-Jun-13: 2B].
Ball, Robert d. on 66-Jun-14 Drowned [66-Jun-15: 1F; 66-Jun-18: 4C].
Ball, T. Sewall m. Haines, Esther L. on 67-May-7 [67-May-9: 2A].
Ball, William D. d. on 67-Aug-20 [67-Aug-21: 2B].
Ball, William O. (21 yrs.) d. on 66-Jan-12 [66-Jan-13: 2C].
Ball, William Whitridge (2 mos.) d. on 66-Jul-13 [66-Jul-14: 2B].
Balla, Henry (10 yrs.) d. on 69-Mar-16 in Railroad accident [69-Mar-17: 1G].

Balla, Mary A. (36 yrs.) d. on 70-Aug-17 [70-Aug-19: 2C].
Ballard, Clementine m. Jamison, C. C., Jr. on 66-Oct-1 [66-Oct-10: 2B].
Ballard, Edward J. (56 yrs.) d. on 67-Apr-13 [67-Apr-15: 2B].
Ballard, Fannie T. d. on 69-Oct-20 [69-Oct-21: 2B].
Ballard, Jacob Reed m. Connish, Henrietta E. on 70-Jan-18 [70-Jan-27: 2C].
Ballard, James T. m. Maihl, Eliza on 68-Jun-1 [68-Jun-15: 2B].
Ballard, Julia m. Ray, Charles H. on 68-Jan-6 [68-Jan-8: 2C].
Ballard, Mary A. m. Snyder, Benjamin B., Jr. on 66-Nov-15 [66-Nov-21: 2C].
Ballard, Norman (2 mos.) d. on 67-Jul-7 [67-Jul-8: 2C].
Ballard, Sarah (87 yrs.) d. on 69-Aug-16 [69-Aug-18: 2C].
Ballard, Sarah m. Watson, William, Jr. on 70-Sep-5 [70-Mar-14: 2C].
Ballard, Sarah Dennis (64 yrs.) d. on 66-Apr-13 of Consumption [66-Apr-18: 2C].
Ballauf, Charlotte A. (21 yrs.) d. on 68-Mar-9 [68-Mar-10: 2C].
Ballauf, William L. m. Switzer, Jennie C. on 67-Sep-13 [68-Jan-18: 2B].
Balloch, Lizzie M. d. on 66-Jan-9 [66-Jan-11: 2B].
Balls, Bartholomew m. Arthur, Rebecca on 68-Oct-15 [68-Oct-26: 2B].
Balmer, James (48 yrs.) d. on 66-Jul-29 of Heatstroke [66-Jul-30: 2C, 4D].
Baltzel, Mary (5 yrs.) d. on 69-Oct-18 [69-Oct-19: 2C].
Baltzell, Catharine (74 yrs.) d. on 68-Nov-17 [68-Nov-19: 2C].
Baltzell, Mollie m. Miller, J. Addison on 70-Nov-1 [70-Nov-7: 2A].
Baltzell, Ruth (68 yrs.) d. on 67-Jul-25 [67-Jul-30: 2C].
Bamberger, Edwin (2 yrs., 4 mos.) d. on 69-Jan-31 [69-Feb-2: 2C].
Bamberger, Edwin Francis (3 mos.) d. on 68-Jul-6 [68-Jul-9: 2B].
Bamberger, George Buckley (3 yrs., 2 mos.) d. on 68-Dec-31 [69-Jan-2: 2C].
Bamberger, Henry C. (35 yrs.) d. on 69-Jul-27 [69-Jul-28: 2D].
Bamberger, Moses m. Pels, Lizzie on 69-Feb-7 [69-Feb-9: 2C].
Bamberger, William A. m. Logan, Ellen on 66-May-1 [66-May-15: 2C].
Banan, William (7 yrs., 5 mos.) d. on 66-Oct-23 [66-Oct-25: 2C].
Bancroft, George S. (8 mos.) d. on 66-Jun-18 [66-Jun-19: 2B].
Bancroft, John (72 yrs.) d. on 70-Oct-6 [70-Oct-7: 2B].
Bancroft, John D. m. Willey, Mollie E. on 68-Jul-14 [68-Jul-16: 2C].
Bancroft, Lucy D. m. White, Edward T. on 67-May-27 [67-May-29: 2B].
Bandel, Anna Florence (5 mos.) d. on 66-May-22 [66-May-23: 2B].
Bandel, Charles S. (62 yrs.) d. on 69-Sep-2 [69-Sep-3: 2B].
Bandel, George E. m. Hammond, Elizabeth on 67-Feb-17 [67-Mar-4: 2D].
Bandel, J. Cook m. Bridge, Maggie A. on 69-Jun-24 [69-Jun-26: 2B].
Bandel, Julia C. m. Schwartz, William H. on 66-Dec-10 [66-Dec-12: 2B].
Bandel, Justina B. (75 yrs.) d. on 68-Apr-15 [68-Apr-16: 2B; 68-Apr-17: 2B].
Bandel, William Ruloff d. on 68-Jun-15 [68-Jun-16: 2B].
Bandell, Isabella A. m. Ferrandini, Francisco L. on 69-Jan-31 [69-Feb-4: 2C].
Bang, John (27 yrs.) d. on 67-May-31 of Consumption [67-Jun-3: 1G].
Bangert, Charles L. (22 yrs.) d. on 70-Nov-14 of Consumption [70-Nov-15: 2C].
Bangert, F. A. m. Humphries, Annie R. on 70-Apr-7 [70-Apr-27: 2B].
Bangs, Catherine (85 yrs.) d. on 66-Jun-24 [66-Jun-27: 2C].
Bangs, D. A. m. Elliott, Susan on 67-Aug-27 [67-Aug-30: 2B].
Bangs, Francis G. (64 yrs.) d. on 66-Feb-23 [66-Feb-28: 2C].
Bangs, John d. on 67-May-31 [67-Jun-3: 1G].
Bangs, John (53 yrs.) d. on 66-Oct-5 of Cholera [66-Oct-8: 2B; 66-Oct-6: 1F].
Bangs, John Thomas d. on 70-Apr-8 [70-Apr-9: 2B].
Bangs, M. Virginia m. Dodson, C. Marion on 69-Jan-27 [69-Jan-30: 2C].
Bangs, Marilla d. on 69-May-16 [69-May-20: 2C].
Bangs, Olivia m. Pearson, Summerfield on 70-Nov-8 [70-Nov-10: 2C].
Banister, Margaret (74 yrs.) d. on 66-Nov-5 [66-Nov-6: 2B; 66-Nov-7: 2C].
Bankard, Josephine J. m. Taylor, Milton N. on 68-Jun-25 [68-Jun-29: 2B].
Banks, Carrie m. Reynolds, Thomas W. on 69-Dec-18 [69-Dec-29: 2D].

Banks, Charlie William (10 mos.) d. on 68-Mar-16 [68-Mar-17: 2B].
Banks, David (48 yrs.) d. on 70-Sep-17 of Heart disease [70-Sep-19: 4C].
Banks, David (2 yrs.) d. on 70-Feb-6 [70-Feb-7: 2C].
Banks, Elisha (21 yrs.) d. on 69-Sep-16 Murdered (Stabbing) [69-Sep-17: 1G; 69-Sep-18: 1G].
Banks, Ellen m. Slingluff, J. Louis on 66-Nov-7 [66-Nov-10: 2B].
Banks, Emma J. m. Kahler, Charles P. on 69-May-11 [69-May-15: 2B].
Banks, Estella Mortina (8 mos.) d. on 69-Aug-25 [69-Aug-26: 2C].
Banks, Frank W. m. Gebhart, Amanda on 67-Dec-31 [68-Mar-9: 2C].
Banks, Henrietta m. Cole, John on 70-Oct-15 [70-Oct-17: 2B].
Banks, Isabella d. on 70-Jan-6 of Lamp explosion [70-Jan-8: 2B].
Banks, Lewis (27 yrs.) d. on 67-Apr-6 [67-Apr-8: 2B].
Banks, Margaret m. Hanson, James on 68-Dec-10 [68-Dec-12: 2C].
Banks, Mary Kate m. Casey, William E. on 70-Jul-4 [70-Jul-6: 2B].
Banks, Mollie B. m. Kimberly, Edward, Jr. on 67-Jun-10 [67-Jun-17: 2B].
Banks, R. G., Dr. (68 yrs.) d. on 69-Nov-5 [69-Nov-6: 2B].
Banks, Samuel m. Bull, Elizabeth Susanna Kelzer on 68-Aug-24 [68-Sep-12: 2B].
Bannan, Hugh C. (1 yr., 4 mos.) d. on 68-Dec-18 [68-Dec-19: 2B].
Bannan, Mary Catherine (3 yrs., 4 mos.) d. on 68-Nov-23 [68-Nov-25: 2B].
Bannan, Michael (42 yrs.) d. on 66-Sep-7 [66-Sep-8: 2B].
Bannas, Earrie Emma (1 yr., 5 mos.) d. on 69-Feb-18 [69-Feb-20: 2A].
Bannister, Emma Jane d. on 70-Oct-2 [70-Oct-7: 2B; 70-Oct-8: 2B].
Bannister, Georgetta m. Gore, Joseph on 70-Jan-20 [70-Jan-21: 2C].
Bannon, Agnes (4 yrs., 4 mos.) d. on 70-Nov-11 [70-Nov-14: 2B].
Bannon, John J. m. Clarke, Mary on 70-May-26 [70-May-31: 2B].
Bannon, John Joseph (10 mos.) d. on 70-Jul-25 [70-Jul-26: 2B].
Bansemer, Lillie d. on 67-Dec-23 [67-Dec-27: 2D].
Bansmith, Isabella Kenny d. on 66-Dec-15 [66-Dec-27: 2C].
Bantram, Richard (49 yrs.) d. on 67-Jul-4 of Heatstroke [67-Jul-6: 4D].
Bantz, Caroline (39 yrs.) d. on 70-Feb-28 [70-Mar-14: 2D].
Bantz, Eugene H. m. France, Lou M. on 67-Jun-4 [67-Jun-6: 2B].
Bantz, Harry H. m. Barnett, Annie E. on 70-Jan-25 [70-Feb-5: 2B; 70-Feb-8: 2C].
Bantz, Lou M. d. on 68-Mar-30 [68-Mar-31: 2B; 68-Apr-1: 2C].
Baragars, Elizabeth (58 yrs.) d. on 66-Apr-1 [66-Apr-2: 2B].
Barber, Belle (3 yrs., 6 mos.) d. on 67-Mar-7 [67-Mar-8: 2C; 67-Mar-18: 2C].
Barber, Charles H. (8 yrs., 6 mos.) d. on 68-Jul-7 Drowned [68-Jul-8: 2B].
Barber, Cordelia Jane (4 yrs., 3 mos.) d. on 66-Jan-6 of Chronic croup [66-Jan-8: 2B].
Barber, George A. m. Collinson, Belle C. on 69-Aug-5 [69-Aug-13: 2C].
Barber, Mary M. (88 yrs.) d. on 68-Apr-11 [68-Apr-15: 2B].
Barber, Philip J. m. Macauley, Mary E. on 66-Jun-14 [66-Jun-26: 2B].
Barbine, Elizabeth (75 yrs.) d. [66-Jan-26: 2B].
Barbine, Jacob F. m. Crawford, Isabella on 67-Dec-31 [68-Jan-4: 2C].
Barboe, Ida C. m. Robinson, Cornelius P. on 70-Feb-23 [70-Apr-2: 2A].
Barbour, Alfred (40 yrs.) d. on 68-Oct-1 of Suicide (Shooting) [68-Oct-2: 1F].
Barbour, Florence Virginia (7 mos.) d. on 70-Jan-8 [70-Jan-10: 2C].
Barbour, Thomas C. m. Edwards, Lizzie on 66-Aug-8 [66-Aug-13: 2C].
Barcher, Christopher W. m. Horney, Ellen M. on 66-Aug-8 [66-Aug-18: 2B].
Barcher, Emma m. Ilgenfritz, John on 69-Oct-5 [69-Nov-5: 2C].
Barchus, Alice P. (38 yrs.) d. on 66-May-5 [66-May-8: 2B].
Barclay, Mary Virginia (29 yrs.) d. on 66-Aug-17 [66-Aug-18: 2B; 66-Aug-28: 2B].
Barclay, Richard Read (4 yrs., 11 mos.) d. on 66-Nov-22 [66-Nov-23: 2C].
Bard, Jennie M. m. Dugdale, William on 66-Oct-18 [66-Oct-19: 2B].
Bardroff, John H. (5 mos.) d. on 69-Jan-18 [69-Jan-19: 2C].
Bardroff, Peter Henry (4 mos.) d. on 69-May-30 [69-May-31: 2C].
Bardwell, George S. m. Lynch, Mary E. [70-May-6: 2B].
Bargannini, D. L. m. Wingrove, Emma on 69-Jun-15 [69-Jun-16: 2C].

Bargar, Clara d. on 69-Oct-2 [69-Oct-5: 2B].
Bargar, Elizabeth (74 yrs.) d. on 67-Jul-10 of Brain congestion [67-Jul-11: 2C].
Bargar, Jacob T. m. Graham, Maggie J. on 70-Oct-12 [70-Oct-19: 2B].
Barickman, Kate m. Olwine, A. H., Jr. on 70-Dec-1 [70-Dec-12: 2C].
Barker, Annie Maria m. Wallace, J. on 68-Mar-31 [68-Apr-8: 2B].
Barker, C. W. m. Walsh, Annie on 69-Aug-23 [69-Sep-24: 2B].
Barker, Catherine (9 mos.) d. on 69-Apr-2 [69-Apr-5: 2B].
Barker, Daniel m. Holland, Mary E. on 68-Sep-8 [68-Sep-9: 2B].
Barker, George Y. m. Schaefer, Ellen B. on 68-Nov-24 [68-Nov-30: 2B].
Barker, Hattie E. m. Erdman, Charles H. on 70-Jan-19 [70-Jan-22: 2B].
Barker, Jesse m. Starr, Mary Rose on 67-Aug-5 [67-Aug-9: 2C].
Barker, John P. m. Cadwallader, Laura V. on 66-Oct-9 [66-Nov-8: 2C].
Barker, Joseph H. m. Chamberlaine, Fanny on 66-Dec-4 [66-Dec-6: 2B].
Barker, Mary d. on 69-Oct-27 [69-Oct-28: 2C].
Barker, Mary A. (48 yrs.) d. on 66-Jan-10 [66-Jan-12: 2C].
Barker, William F. m. Devall, Cordelia A. on 69-Aug-3 [69-Aug-4: 2B].
Barker, William R. (62 yrs.) d. on 66-Mar-10 [66-Mar-14: 2C].
Barklage, Henry A. m. McCarran, Maggie on 66-May-1 [66-May-4: 2C].
Barkman, Clara Virginia m. Donnelly, John M. on 69-Dec-23 [70-Jan-5: 2C].
Barkman, Jacob (18 yrs., 10 mos.) d. on 69-Apr-30 [69-May-1: 2B].
Barkman, Lewis Edwin (16 yrs.) d. on 66-Oct-13 [66-Oct-15: 2B].
Barkman, Mary Ann (82 yrs.) d. on 69-Jun-1 [69-Jun-2: 2B].
Barling, Annie Linton m. Tonge, Richard H. on 68-Apr-16 [68-Apr-25: 2B].
Barling, Sarah (79 yrs.) d. on 66-Aug-15 [66-Aug-17: 2C].
Barlow, Annie m. Maxwell, Thomas C. on 69-Feb-15 [69-Feb-17: 2C].
Barlow, Clinton m. Kirk, Laura L. on 70-Apr-8 [70-Apr-13: 2B].
Barlow, Emma m. Favour, Charles R. on 67-Jun-3 [67-Jun-7: 2B].
Barlow, Joseph M. m. Martin, Kate on 67-Feb-21 [67-Mar-7: 2C].
Barlow, Kate E. (2 yrs., 2 mos.) d. on 68-Jan-31 [68-Feb-3: 2C].
Barlow, Lizzie m. Kelly, William H. on 67-Jan-4 [67-Jan-10: 2C].
Barlow, Mary C. m. Stevenson, James H. on 67-May-28 [67-Jun-3: 2B].
Barnacle, Henry (10 yrs.) d. on 66-Apr-26 Drowned [66-Apr-27: 1G].
Barnard, James Louis (65 yrs.) d. on 69-Feb-23 [69-Feb-24: 2C].
Barnard, John D. m. Hopwood, Fannie on 69-May-6 [69-Jun-5: 2B].
Barnes, Agnes V. d. on 67-Jul-21 [67-Jul-23: 2C].
Barnes, Alexander Lincoln (4 yrs., 1 mo.) d. on 68-Dec-1 [68-Dec-2: 2C].
Barnes, Annie (82 yrs.) d. on 66-Mar-7 [66-Mar-8: 2B].
Barnes, Annie E. m. Davis, Joseph on 70-Nov-17 [70-Dec-5: 2C].
Barnes, Carrie E. m. Wigginton, W. Henry on 68-Oct-8 [68-Oct-13: 2C].
Barnes, Carrie Emma (1 yr., 5 mos.) d. on 69-Feb-18 [69-Feb-25: 2D].
Barnes, Charlotte m. Pierce, Joseph H. on 70-Jan-13 [70-Jan-15: 2C].
Barnes, Denton m. Taylor, Christie A. on 70-Feb-10 [70-Feb-25: 2C].
Barnes, Eddie (10 mos.) d. on 68-Jun-13 [68-Jun-15: 2B].
Barnes, Ellen J. m. Reddish, Lycurgus on 70-Nov-5 [70-Nov-19: 2B].
Barnes, Ellen R. (65 yrs.) d. on 69-Nov-5 [69-Nov-6: 2B].
Barnes, Emily F. m. Washington, Joseph on 67-Feb-11 [67-Feb-13: 2D].
Barnes, George E. m. Bartgis, Maggie E. on 69-Jan-21 [69-Jan-23: 2C].
Barnes, George W. m. Toole, Margaret Ann on 69-Oct-21 [69-Nov-4: 2B].
Barnes, Hannah A. m. Bright, Thomas on 66-Dec-27 [67-Jan-1: 2C].
Barnes, Hanora m. Bailey, Amos V. on 66-Mar-15 [66-Mar-16: 2B].
Barnes, Henry d. on 69-Sep-23 in Railroad accident [69-Sep-24: 1G].
Barnes, James Henry m. Peduzzi, Amelia on 67-Oct-26 [67-Nov-11: 2C].
Barnes, John H. (45 yrs.) d. on 67-Nov-13 [67-Dec-3: 2C].
Barnes, John R. (30 yrs.) d. on 68-May-22 of Consumption [68-May-23: 2A].
Barnes, Julia Ellen m. Hobbs, Edward Harman on 70-Feb-26 [70-Feb-28: 2C].

Barnes, Louisa E. m. Clayton, James H. on 67-Jan-3 [67-Jan-5: 2C].
Barnes, Maggie B. m. Riddle, George W. on 69-Feb-18 [69-Feb-23: 2C].
Barnes, Mary K. (81 yrs.) d. on 68-Apr-28 [68-Apr-29: 2B].
Barnes, Nannie Jamison (1 yr., 3 mos.) d. on 69-Aug-23 [69-Aug-24: 2B].
Barnes, Robert C., Jr. m. Leary, Emma on 70-Jan-6 [70-Jan-7: 2F].
Barnes, S. Annie m. Smith, Robert H. on 70-Sep-8 [70-Sep-10: 2B].
Barnes, Sallie A. m. Deaver, George T. on 66-Jul-19 [66-Jul-24: 2C].
Barnes, Susan (82 yrs.) d. on 67-Oct-9 [67-Oct-16: 2B].
Barnes, Thomas d. on 69-Sep-1 Drowned [69-Sep-4: 1H].
Barnes, Thomas B. (4 yrs., 5 mos.) d. on 69-May-4 [69-May-5: 2C].
Barnes, Thomas B. (34 yrs.) d. on 70-Nov-5 [70-Nov-7: 2B; 70-Nov-8: 2B].
Barnes, Walter S. m. Hudgins, Louisa M. on 66-Oct-3 [66-Oct-22: 2C].
Barnett, Andrew J. m. Shipley, P. Virginia on 67-Jan-9 [67-Feb-27: 2C].
Barnett, Annie E. m. Suell, James on 70-Aug-23 [70-Aug-25: 2B].
Barnett, Annie E. m. Bantz, Harry H. on 70-Jan-25 [70-Feb-5: 2B; 70-Feb-8: 2C].
Barnett, Charles F. m. Branson, Margaret L. on 67-Dec-17 [67-Dec-21: 2B].
Barnett, Henrietta V. m. Lerch, Harry A. on 70-Feb-3 [70-Apr-16: 2B].
Barnett, James A. m. Amy, Charlotte E. on 68-Aug-11 [68-Aug-26: 2B].
Barnett, Nicholas J. (60 yrs.) d. on 67-Oct-18 [67-Oct-21: 2B].
Barnett, Pierre Roszell (16 yrs., 6 mos.) d. on 66-Jun-16 Drowned [66-Jun-18: 2B, 4C].
Barnett, Violet Ross d. on 70-Jul-23 [70-Jul-26: 2C].
Barney, Annie m. Weston, Nathaniel on 67-Nov-28 [67-Dec-24: 2B].
Barney, Charles Ridgely (62 yrs.) d. on 67-Mar-10 [67-Mar-12: 2C; 67-Mar-14: 2C].
Barney, Charles S. m. Royce, Hattie E. on 69-Nov-6 [69-Dec-20: 2C].
Barney, Joshua (64 yrs.) d. on 67-Apr-2 [67-Apr-4: 2B].
Barney, Mary (25 yrs.) d. on 68-Aug-11 Drowned [68-Aug-13: 1F].
Barney, Thomas (35 yrs.) d. on 67-Mar-11 [67-Mar-12: 2C].
Barnfield, Henry (64 yrs.) d. on 68-Jan-17 [67-Jan-19: 2C].
Barnhill, Henry (4 mos.) d. on 66-Aug-21 [66-Aug-22: 2C].
Barnitz, Alexander H. (44 yrs.) d. on 67-Mar-25 [67-Mar-26: 2C].
Barns, John A. (35 yrs.) d. on 66-Sep-7 [66-Sep-8: 2B].
Barns, Mary A. m. Jacobs, John P. on 67-May-23 [67-Jun-5: 2B].
Barnsfield, Durethy Ann (55 yrs.) d. on 66-Dec-25 [66-Dec-27: 2C].
Barnsley, Isabel m. Kershaw, Henry on 70-Nov-1 [70-Nov-3: 2B].
Barnum, Annie m. Gordon, David C. [67-Feb-20: 2C].
Barnum, Fannie R. m. Warner, George on 68-Jan-30 [68-Apr-20: 2B].
Barnum, John R. d. on 70-Jan-30 [70-Feb-15: 2C].
Barnum, John R. m. Purnell, C. R. on 66-Dec-31 [67-Jan-2: 2C].
Barnum, Mary Ann Kirby (92 yrs.) d. on 66-Nov-14 [66-Nov-15: 1G, 2C].
Barnum, Richard, Dr. (61 yrs., 8 mos.) d. on 66-Oct-27 [66-Oct-29: 2B, 4C].
Barnwell, Michael (38 yrs.) d. on 66-Nov-26 [66-Nov-28: 2B].
Barr, James L. (26 yrs., 5 mos.) d. on 70-May-28 [70-May-30: 2B].
Barr, Maria G. (25 yrs.) d. on 67-Jan-21 of Consumption [67-Jan-22: 2C].
Barr, Mary A. Hopkins (17 yrs.) d. on 68-Aug-20 [68-Aug-22: 2A].
Barr, Samuel d. on 67-Dec-4 [67-Dec-5: 2C].
Barrack, Fannie E. m. Dame, Oliver M. on 70-Mar-18 [70-Apr-1: 2B].
Barranger, George W. m. Love, Almara Virginia on 66-Feb-12 [66-Feb-20: 2B].
Barranger, Harry C. m. Knell, Mami A. on 68-Jan-14 [68-Jan-20: 2B; 68-Jan-21: 2C].
Barranger, Isabella m. Smith, George S. on 66-May-1 [66-May-24: 2C].
Barranger, John A. m. Nicklas, Kate on 68-May-26 [68-Jun-26: 2B; 68-Jun-27: 2B].
Barranger, John Francis (89 yrs., 11 mos.) d. on 66-Apr-8 [66-Apr-9: 1G, 2B].
Barranger, Margaret (30 yrs.) d. on 66-Jul-15 [66-Jul-16: 2C].
Barranger, Mary Alice (1 yr.) d. on 70-Sep-11 [70-Sep-12: 2B].
Barrenger, Alice m. Cunningham, John D. on 68-Jan-1 [68-Jan-4: 2C].
Barrett, Ann Rebecca (13 yrs., 4 mos.) d. on 69-Mar-14 [69-Mar-15: 2C].

Barrett, Cicily Isabella (2 yrs., 6 mos.) d. on 68-Oct-27 [68-Oct-29: 2C].
Barrett, David Landers (5 yrs., 3 mos.) d. on 67-Jun-26 [67-Jun-28: 2B].
Barrett, Ella m. Augur, J. H. on 70-Jan-4 [70-Jan-5: 2C].
Barrett, Emily E. m. Brashears, Josephus Rous on 66-Dec-27 [66-Dec-31: 2C].
Barrett, Francis Reese (3 yrs.) d. on 70-Nov-11 [70-Nov-12: 2B].
Barrett, James Issac d. on 69-Jan-10 [69-Jan-12: 2C].
Barrett, Maggie F. m. Bell, Marion on 68-Sep-20 [68-Oct-6: 2B].
Barrett, Mary C. m. Cain, J. on 67-Mar-11 [67-Apr-25: 2B].
Barrett, McClellan (10 mos.) d. on 68-Jul-2 [68-Jul-9: 2B].
Barrett, Samuel m. Moore, Mary M. on 69-Aug-3 [69-Aug-28: 2B].
Barrett, Susan m. Grafton, Alexander on 66-May-10 [66-May-11: 2B].
Barrick, Samuel d. on 66-Jul-17 of Heatstroke [66-Jul-18: 1F].
Barringer, Elizabeth Wethered d. on 67-Jun-4 [67-Jun-5: 2B].
Barringer, Thomas m. Kohlhepp, Catharine on 67-Jul-9 [67-Jul-11: 2C].
Barrington, Catharine (72 yrs.) d. on 66-Mar-24 [66-Mar-26: 2B].
Barrington, Eveline M. m. Flack, Harry H. on 68-Nov-5 [68-Nov-10: 2C].
Barrington, Mina A. m. Chew, William S. on 68-Sep-29 [68-Oct-6: 2B].
Barroll, Mary Ann d. on 68-Jan-12 [68-Jan-13: 2C].
Barroll, Rebecca J. (65 yrs.) d. on 69-Aug-12 [69-Aug-13: 2C].
Barroll, Serena McLane m. Fisher, Harry on 66-May-10 [66-May-12: 2A].
Barron, John Francis (3 yrs.) d. on 70-Oct-4 [70-Oct-5: 2B].
Barron, Mary Ann m. McFlaherty, Daniel on 68-May-17 [68-May-22: 2C].
Barron, Mary K. (18 yrs.) d. on 68-Mar-11 [68-Mar-13: 2C].
Barron, William, Mrs. (73 yrs.) d. on 70-Jan-9 [70-Jan-10: 2C; 70-Jan-11: 2C].
Barrot, Odilon m. Forbes, Fanny on 68-Dec-14 [69-Jan-20: 2C].
Barrow, John D. (48 yrs.) d. on 67-Feb-9 [67-Feb-12: 2C].
Barrow, Thomas H. m. Holmes, Mollie A. on 66-Jun-14 [66-Jun-20: 2C].
Barry, Allen Howard (3 mos.) d. on 67-Jun-27 [67-Jun-28: 2B].
Barry, Amelia R. (9 mos.) d. on 68-Aug-5 [68-Aug-6: 2B].
Barry, Anna A. m. McDowell, Clarence on 70-Feb-2 [70-Feb-4: 2C].
Barry, Caroline F. d. on 70-Oct-22 [70-Oct-24: 2B].
Barry, Catherine (66 yrs.) d. on 68-Jun-4 [68-Jun-5: 2B; 68-Jun-6: 2A].
Barry, Daniel R. (30 yrs.) d. on 69-Sep-10 [69-Sep-11: 2B].
Barry, Edmund (34 yrs.) d. on 68-Apr-29 [68-May-1: 2B].
Barry, Edward m. Hamilton, Tillie on 69-Oct-5 [69-Oct-6: 2B].
Barry, Edward T. d. on 66-Sep-16 of Yellow fever [66-Sep-28: 2B].
Barry, Eliza d. on 69-Nov-18 [69-Nov-20: 2B].
Barry, H. V. d. on 67-May-5 [67-Jun-6: 2B].
Barry, James C. (74 yrs.) d. on 66-Apr-5 [66-Apr-7: 2B; 66-Apr-9: 1G].
Barry, John L. (73 yrs., 10 mos.) d. on 66-Oct-19 [66-Oct-20: 1G, 2B].
Barry, Joshua H. m. Morrison, Effie on 68-Oct-21 [68-Oct-23: 2B].
Barry, Josiah Bardwell (4 yrs., 4 mos.) d. on 69-May-22 [69-May-24: 2B].
Barry, Lizzie M. m. Shipley, C. Howard on 66-May-29 [66-Jun-1: 2B].
Barry, Louisa J. m. Dempsey, Jno. B. on 67-Jun-2 [67-Jun-11: 2B].
Barry, Maggie M. m. Milburne, Elijah S. on 68-Mar-3 [68-Mar-24: 2B].
Barry, Margaret (52 yrs.) d. on 66-May-30 [66-Jun-1: 2B].
Barry, Mary Eliza (2 yrs., 6 mos.) d. on 69-Apr-2 of Suffocation [69-Apr-3: 2B].
Barry, Mason Chesney (8 mos.) d. on 68-Aug-12 [68-Aug-14: 2C].
Barry, McClintock Y. m. McAlpine, Mary Ann on 66-Sep-4 [66-Sep-11: 2B].
Barry, Mollie Standish m. Bowman, Michael Edward on 66-Dec-6 [66-Dec-12: 2B].
Barry, Nora (62 yrs.) d. on 69-May-1 [69-May-3: 2C].
Barry, Richard A. m. Bull, Rebecca J. on 68-Oct-22 [68-Oct-31: 2B].
Barry, Samuel M. (77 yrs.) d. on 70-Aug-19 [70-Aug-20: 2B; 70-Aug-22: 2B].
Barry, William (35 yrs.) d. on 70-Nov-10 [70-Nov-2: 2C].
Bartel, Albert (25 yrs.) d. on 70-Jul-25 Drowned [70-Jul-26: 4C].

Bartgis, Maggie E. m. Barnes, George E. on 69-Jan-21 [69-Jan-23: 2C].
Barth, John H. (42 yrs.) d. on 67-Sep-19 of Yellow fever [67-Sep-21: 2A].
Barth, Joseph Chauncey (7 yrs.) d. on 66-Nov-30 [66-Dec-1: 2B].
Barth, Samuel m. Straus, Henrietta on 70-Nov-23 [70-Nov-29: 2C].
Barthold, Augustus (29 yrs.) d. on 66-Sep-27 [66-Sep-28: 2B; 66-Sep-29: 2B].
Bartholdt, Anna m. Nicoll, William J. on 69-Mar-1 [69-Mar-9: 2C].
Bartholomee, Eddie (3 yrs., 11 mos.) d. on 66-Nov-7 [66-Nov-9: 2C].
Bartholomee, Loulie A. (11 mos.) d. on 66-Oct-26 [66-Nov-9: 2C].
Bartholomee, Mary A. (58 yrs.) d. on 66-Mar-22 [66-Mar-23: 2C].
Bartholomew, Julia A. (64 yrs.) d. on 70-Jun-18 [70-Jun-20: 2C].
Bartholow, Lycurgus L. (33 yrs.) d. on 68-Nov-19 Drowned [68-Nov-20: 1H, 2C].
Bartler, Henrietta m. Jenkins, Ellis T. on 68-Jul-5 [68-Jul-8: 2B].
Bartleson, Alice (25 yrs.) d. on 70-Jan-20 [70-Jan-22: 2B].
Bartlett, Edward L. m. Farland, Julia A. on 66-Dec-6 [66-Dec-11: 2B].
Bartlett, Francis J. m. Shipley, Lettie C. on 70-Oct-12 [70-Oct-24: 2B].
Bartlett, George H. m. Seibert, Malvina A. E. on 66-Mar-20 [66-Mar-22: 2B].
Bartlett, Hannah d. on 67-Jan-15 [67-Jan-21: 2C].
Bartlett, Horace (3 yrs., 5 mos.) d. on 68-Sep-3 [68-Sep-4: 2A].
Bartlett, Jonathan m. Bartlett, Rebecca T. on 66-Dec-27 [67-Jan-11: 2C].
Bartlett, Mary m. Comegys, Benjamin on 66-Jan-25 [66-Jan-27: 2B].
Bartlett, Mary E. m. Strebeck, Peter on 69-Oct-21 [69-Oct-30: 2B].
Bartlett, Rebecca T. m. Bartlett, Jonathan on 66-Dec-27 [67-Jan-11: 2C].
Bartlett, Sarah A. d. on 66-Sep-18 [66-Sep-19: 2B].
Bartol, Nathaniel B. (58 yrs.) d. on 66-Feb-2 [66-Feb-8: 2C].
Barton, Ann Teresa (74 yrs.) d. on 68-Oct-14 [68-Oct-15: 2C; 68-Oct-16: 2B].
Barton, Clara C. (11 mos.) d. on 66-Jun-12 [66-Jun-16: 2B].
Barton, Holland Tecumseh (1 yr., 6 mos.) d. on 70-Jan-19 [70-Jan-21: 2C].
Barton, Jane (68 yrs.) d. on 67-Jul-4 [67-Jul-6: 2B; 67-Jul-8: 2C].
Barton, Jennie M. m. Gibson, William N. on 67-Feb-12 [67-Feb-20: 2C].
Barton, Laura J. m. McNeir, William J. on 66-Nov-5 [66-Nov-8: 2C].
Barton, Laura M. (20 yrs.) d. on 69-Aug-13 [69-Aug-24: 2C].
Barton, Laura S. m. Lewis, George W. on 67-Jun-13 [67-Jun-20: 2B].
Barton, Martha m. Kuhn, John on 66-Jun-25 [66-Jul-4: 2B].
Barton, Mary (84 yrs.) d. on 68-Jan-6 [68-Jan-7: 2B].
Barton, Mary J. m. Chisholm, Thomas H. on 70-Jun-27 [70-Jun-28: 2C].
Barton, Mary W. m. Craggs, John B. on 66-May-15 [66-May-19: 2B].
Barton, Mollie P. m. Seymour, William A. on 70-Feb-17 [70-Feb-19: 2B].
Barton, P. A. m. Finley, Sue on 70-Nov-24 [70-Dec-3: 2B].
Barton, Peter d. on 69-May-3 Drowned [69-May-7: 1G].
Barton, Susie V. m. Allen, William B. on 66-Aug-7 [66-Aug-21: 2C].
Barton, William J. (60 yrs.) d. on 70-Jun-20 [70-Jun-21: 2C; 70-Jun-22: 2C].
Barton, William N. (39 yrs.) d. on 68-Oct-12 [68-Oct-13: 2C].
Bartz, Wilhelmina m. Pfeiffer, Charles A. on 70-May-24 [70-May-28: 2B].
Bash, A. McCoomb m. Pearson, M. Caddie on 67-Nov-5 [67-Nov-9: 2B].
Bash, Edward H. m. Kerr, Mary on 70-Nov-3 [70-Nov-5: 2B].
Bassett, Kate C. (18 yrs., 2 mos.) d. on 66-Oct-4 [66-Oct-6: 2A].
Bassett, Mary m. Holt, Edwin A. on 68-Feb-4 [68-Feb-5: 2D].
Bassford, Albert E. (53 yrs.) d. on 66-Jan-23 [66-Jan-27: 2B].
Bastein, Francis Emil (40 yrs.) d. on 70-May-4 [70-May-5: 2B].
Batch, S. Ollie m. Tudor, Charles H. on 69-Nov-14 [69-Nov-20: 2B].
Batchelder, Laura Lincoln (5 yrs., 6 mos.) d. on 70-Aug-15 [70-Aug-17: 2C].
Batchelor, Eleanora m. Smith, Charles on 66-Oct-24 [66-Oct-30: 2B].
Batchelor, Eliza Jane m. Sadler, Joseph R. on 66-Jul-26 [66-Jul-28: 2C].
Batchelor, Harry Rollins (3 yrs., 4 mos.) d. on 70-Jul-27 [70-Jul-29: 2B].
Batchelor, Joseph (69 yrs.) d. on 68-Oct-31 [68-Nov-2: 2B].

Batchelor, Sarah J. (29 yrs.) d. on 69-Mar-25 [69-Mar-29: 2B].
Batchelor, Vinton Stewart (6 mos.) d. on 66-Mar-1 [66-Mar-2: 2B].
Batchelor, Wallace (38 yrs.) d. on 67-Jun-27 of Consumption [67-Jun-28: 2B; 67-Jun-29: 2A].
Bateman, Catherine (87 yrs.) d. on 70-Jul-27 of Dysentery [70-Jul-28: 2C].
Bateman, Eliza (66 yrs.) d. on 68-Feb-16 [68-Feb-17: 2B; 68-Feb-18: 2C].
Bateman, Lucina G. R. m. Stratton, Robert W. on 67-Dec-5 [67-Dec-12: 2B].
Bateman, Samuel D. m. Robinson, Lizzie G. on 66-Nov-14 [66-Nov-17: 2B].
Bateman, Susan (56 yrs.) d. on 70-Dec-23 [70-Dec-24: 2B].
Bates, Anna Cusic m. Wise, William W. on 68-Dec-22 [68-Dec-24: 2C].
Bates, Emma m. Blick, Thomas H. on 69-Feb-17 [69-Feb-23: 2C].
Bates, Franklin L. m. Allison, Rachel S. on 67-Jun-4 [67-Jun-8: 2D].
Bates, George C. m. Henderson, Susan J. on 66-Jun-28 [66-Jun-29: 2C].
Bates, Gertrude (4 yrs., 9 mos.) d. on 69-Mar-13 [69-Mar-15: 2C].
Bates, Henry d. on 70-Apr-3 [70-Apr-4: 2B].
Bates, John m. Griffith, Johanna on 70-Apr-19 [70-Apr-21: 2B].
Bates, Marcellena m. Webb, James Franklin on 68-Apr-14 [68-Apr-23: 2B].
Bates, Mary Ann (35 yrs.) d. on 66-Apr-11 [66-Apr-12: 2B].
Bates, Samuel d. on 69-Jan-30 [69-Feb-1: 2C].
Bates, Willis F. (20 yrs.) d. on 69-Feb-28 [69-Mar-2: 2C].
Batson, Sarah (44 yrs.) d. on 67-Mar-7 [67-Mar-8: 2C].
Battee, Ann (66 yrs.) d. on 66-Oct-10 [66-Oct-12: 2B].
Battee, Elizabeth (48 yrs.) d. on 70-Jul-17 [70-Jul-19: 2B].
Battee, George W. (53 yrs.) d. on 67-Oct-31 [67-Nov-1: 2B].
Battee, Julia Ann (68 yrs.) d. on 68-Dec-30 [68-Dec-31: 2D; 69-Jan-1: 2C].
Battee, Mary Elizabeth (11 mos.) d. on 66-Jul-19 [66-Jul-20: 2D].
Battee, Samuel (36 yrs.) d. on 69-Sep-14 Murdered (Assault) [69-Sep-16: 1F, 2B; 69-Sep-17: 1G].
Battee, Violetta B. (41 yrs.) d. on 68-Oct-2 [68-Oct-6: 2B].
Battenfeld, Philip Christion (69 yrs.) d. on 67-Jan-30 [67-Jan-31: 2C; 67-Feb-1: 2C].
Battenfield, Wilhelmina Maria (21 yrs., 1 mo.) d. on 68-Mar-11 [68-Mar-12: 2B].
Battie, George Elbert m. Auld, Sarah Elizabeth on 67-Jan-10 [67-Jan-16: 2C].
Bauer, Charles Bernhard (28 yrs.) d. on 68-Aug-6 [68-Aug-7: 2B].
Bauer, Josephine m. Edelman, Romwald [68-Apr-9: 2B].
Bauernschmidt, Elizabeth d. on 68-Sep-9 [68-Sep-9: 2B].
Bauers, Charles B. m. Hipsman, Mary on 67-Feb-26 [67-Mar-11: 2C].
Bauers, Sarah m. Muhly, Christian on 69-Feb-4 [69-Feb-8: 2C].
Baugher, Ella V. m. Nyman, William H. on 67-May-22 [67-Jun-1: 2B].
Baugher, J. Constantine d. on 70-Apr-22 of Consumption [70-Apr-25: 2B].
Baugher, Josiah L. (58 yrs.) d. on 66-Dec-2 of Carbuncle [66-Dec-3: 1G; 66-Dec-4: 2D; 66-Dec-5: 1F].
Baughman, Florence Louisa (3 yrs., 5 mos.) d. on 70-Mar-23 [70-Mar-25: 2C].
Baughman, George (66 yrs.) d. on 70-Sep-23 [70-Sep-24: 2B].
Baughman, Hettie M. (25 yrs.) d. on 70-Jul-2 [70-Jul-4: 2C].
Baughman, M. Annie m. Saumenig, John H. on 70-Apr-28 [70-Apr-30: 2A].
Baughman, Samuel W. m. Sanderson, Christiana A. V. on 68-Aug-10 [68-Aug-12: 2C].
Baumann, John Christian (35 yrs.) d. on 68-Nov-23 Drowned [68-Nov-25: 1G; 68-Nov-30: 1G].
Baumgardner, M. Olivia m. Overman, Jerome A. on 66-Nov-13 [66-Dec-1: 2B].
Baumgarten, Joseph (45 yrs.) d. on 70-Mar-14 [70-Mar-15: 2C].
Bausman, John P., Rev. (76 yrs.) d. on 69-May-18 [69-May-20: 1H, 2C].
Bausman, Kate m. Page, William on 70-Jul-5 [70-Jul-7: 2B].
Bausmith, Clarence Philip d. on 66-Jun-24 [66-Jun-25: 2B].
Bausmith, William Thomas (9 mos.) d. on 68-Jan-30 [68-Jan-31: 2C].
Bavington, James C m. Baxter, Mary Malinda on 68-Feb-2 [68-Feb-6: 2C].
Bawden, Elizabeth (43 yrs.) d. on 69-Sep-3 [69-Sep-4: 2B].
Bawden, Rachel C. (77 yrs.) d. on 67-Nov-1 [67-Nov-2: 2B].

Baxley, Claude m. Williams, Lena on 67-Sep-5 [67-Sep-11: 2B].
Baxley, George Williams (18 yrs.) d. on 69-Jan-18 [69-Jan-20: 2C].
Baxley, Gertie d. on 67-Jun-28 [67-Jul-1: 2B, 4C].
Baxter, Ann (35 yrs.) d. on 66-Apr-4 [66-Apr-6: 2B].
Baxter, Elijah T. (60 yrs.) d. on 69-May-23 [69-May-24: 2B].
Baxter, Emily Augusta (66 yrs.) d. on 68-Aug-29 of Consumption [68-Sep-3: 2B].
Baxter, Ida (4 yrs., 7 mos.) d. on 66-May-9 [66-May-10: 2B].
Baxter, James W. m. Sapp, Cidney S. on 67-May-2 [68-Feb-20: 2C].
Baxter, Mary Malinda m. Bavington, James C. on 68-Feb-2 [68-Feb-6: 2C].
Baxter, Rosena (34 yrs.) d. on 66-Oct-14 [66-Oct-16: 2B].
Baxter, Samuel m. Chambers, Agnes on 69-Mar-28 [69-Apr-6: 2C].
Bay, Fanny (73 yrs.) d. on 70-Aug-28 [70-Sep-2: 2C].
Bay, John W. m. Gallup, Emma W. on 68-Jan-16 [68-Jan-21: 2C].
Bay, Martha Elizabeth (4 yrs., 1 mo.) d. on 68-Apr-10 [68-Apr-11: 2A].
Bay, Nathan m. Bush, Margaret Emily on 67-Feb-21 [67-Feb-28: 2C].
Bayard, Richard H. (72 yrs.) d. on 68-Mar-4 [68-Mar-9: 2C].
Bayfield, James (90 yrs.) d. on 68-Feb-28 [68-Mar-14: 2B].
Bayfield, Mary d. on 70-Jun-7 [70-Jun-10: 2B].
Bayles, Elizabeth (86 yrs.) d. on 67-Aug-26 [67-Aug-27: 2B].
Bayles, William m. Carroll, Jane E. on 68-Jan-26 [68-Feb-1: 2B].
Bayless, Augusta J. m. Browne, Lewis R. on 66-Nov-8 [66-Nov-13: 2B].
Bayless, Elizabeth (63 yrs.) d. on 69-Jul-17 [69-Jul-19: 2C].
Bayless, George Rogers (1 yr.) d. on 69-Sep-5 [69-Sep-6: 2C].
Bayless, John T. m. Burke, Annie E. on 68-Mar-9 [68-Apr-27: 2B].
Bayless, Laura J. (30 yrs.) d. on 67-Mar-11 [67-Mar-13: 2C].
Bayless, Thomas (76 yrs.) d. on 70-Sep-16 [70-Sep-17: 2B, 4D].
Bayley, Clarence Elmer d. on 70-Nov-10 [70-Nov-12: 2B].
Bayley, Daniel S. m. Stanley, Sarah [66-Oct-26: 2B].
Bayley, Frederick A. m. Smith, Priscilla on 70-Sep-1 [70-Sep-10: 2B].
Bayley, John H. m. Lookingland, Mary C. on 68-Jul-12 [68-Jul-18: 2B].
Bayley, Louisa (42 yrs.) d. on 67-Jun-21 [67-Jun-22: 2B].
Bayley, Lucy Virginia (8 mos.) d. on 70-Apr-1 [70-Apr-2: 2A].
Bayley, Margaret (63 yrs.) d. on 66-May-22 [66-May-23: 2B].
Bayley, Mary Ann (69 yrs.) d. on 70-Sep-7 [70-Sep-8: 2B].
Bayley, Mary R. m. Diffenderffer, H. H. on 66-Nov-20 [66-Nov-23: 2C].
Bayley, Phyliss (84 yrs.) d. on 69-Mar-23 [69-Mar-25: 2C].
Baylies, Belle (4 yrs., 2 mos.) d. on 66-Jul-26 [66-Jul-27: 2C].
Baylies, Charles Edward d. on 66-Jun-9 [66-Jun-12: 2B].
Baylies, John H. m. Roach, Virginia A. on 69-Feb-18 [69-Feb-24: 2C].
Baylis, George H. (28 yrs.) d. on 68-Oct-14 [68-Nov-16: 2C].
Bayliss, Emma F. m. McPharson, John W. on 68-Nov-10 [68-Nov-16: 2C; 68-Nov-17: 2C].
Bayliss, Mary Emma m. Carvallo, Carlos on 67-Feb-28 [67-Mar-2: 2B].
Bayly, A. H. m. Craig, Margaret Armstrong on 67-Feb-12 [67-Feb-16: 2D].
Bayly, Abell W. (19 yrs.) d. on 67-Feb-23 [67-Mar-1: 2C; 67-Mar-2: 2B].
Bayly, Andrew T. (50 yrs.) d. on 70-Mar-1 [70-Mar-12: 2C].
Bayly, Charles B. m. Howard, Mary V. on 68-May-12 [68-May-14: 2B].
Bayly, Harry Zachary d. on 70-Nov-10 [70-Nov-12: 2B].
Bayly, Margaret (2 yrs.) d. on 67-Sep-19 [67-Sep-23: 2A].
Bayly, Mattie A. m. Shannon, John on 69-Jul-30 [69-Aug-10: 2C].
Bayly, Richard P. (56 yrs.) d. on 67-Jan-28 of Pneumonia [67-Jan-29: 2C; 67-Jan-30: 1G, 2C].
Bayly, Sue E. m. Hipkins, Fred S. on 69-May-3 [69-May-5: 2C].
Bayly, William (82 yrs.) d. on 66-Nov-3 [66-Nov-5: 2B].
Bayn, John M. m. Arnold, Kate on 66-Nov-7 [67-Feb-18: 2C].
Baynard, Louisa m. Chaney, Levi M. on 70-Apr-14 [70-Apr-20: 2B].
Bayne, Emily A. (26 yrs.) d. on 66-May-16 [66-May-19: 2B].

Bayne, John Carville (19 yrs.) d. on 70-Nov-24 Murdered (Shooting) [70-Nov-25: 4D; 70-Nov-26: 4C].
Bayne, John H. (66 yrs.) d. on 70-Aug-18 [70-Aug-27: 2A].
Bayne, Joseph (3 yrs., 10 mos.) d. on 68-Sep-26 [68-Oct-2: 2B].
Bayne, Lilly (66 yrs., 6 mos.) d. on 66-Jun-25 [66-Jun-27: 2C].
Bayne, Phebe A. m. Smith, Lynch T. on 67-Oct-16 [67-Oct-23: 2B].
Baynes, Charles D. d. on 70-Oct-4 of Diarrhea [70-Oct-17: 2B].
Baynes, Martha (68 yrs.) d. on 70-Oct-21 [70-Oct-22: 2B].
Baynes, William Seymour (1 yr., 2 mos.) d. on 67-Sep-28 [67-Oct-1: 2B].
Bazeman, Charlotte (52 yrs.) d. on 70-Jan-5 [70-Apr-29: 2B].
Beach, Annie S. m. Hands, Washington on 67-Oct-21 [67-Nov-14: 2B].
Beach, Carrie (32 yrs., 7 mos.) d. on 69-Apr-14 [69-Apr-16: 2B].
Beach, Frankie Blake (9 mos.) d. on 69-Apr-10 [69-Apr-16: 2B].
Beach, Maria (72 yrs.) d. on 69-Apr-12 [69-Apr-13: 2B].
Beach, Mary E. d. on 67-Jun-1 [67-Jun-3: 2B].
Beach, Mary E. m. Weisman, J. Frank on 70-Jun-9 [70-Jun-13: 2C].
Beach, William H. m. Flanagan, Mollie E. on 68-Apr-12 [68-Apr-21: 2B].
Beach, William J. m. Copper, Annie E. on 68-Jun-2 [68-Jun-5: 2B].
Beacham, Ellen S. (41 yrs.) d. on 69-Aug-20 [69-Aug-21: 2B].
Beacham, George H. m. Lambert, Josephine on 67-Nov-6 [67-Nov-9: 2B].
Beacham, Indiana C. m. Lewis, William F. on 69-Oct-20 [70-Apr-23: 2B].
Beacham, J. Summers m. Mason, Mary D. on 68-Oct-22 [68-Oct-24: 2B].
Beacham, James A. (47 yrs.) d. on 67-Dec-2 [67-Dec-3: 2C; 67-Dec-4: 2C].
Beacham, John S. m. Sanks, Henrietta on 67-Aug-20 [67-Aug-23: 2B].
Beacham, Liza (57 yrs.) d. on 67-Jun-4 [67-Jun-5: 2B; 67-Jun-6: 2B].
Beacham, Samuel T. m. Tilyard, Lizzie M. on 70-Nov-22 [70-Nov-30: 2C].
Beachamp, George R. m. Rae, Lidy on 69-May-30 [69-Jun-29: 2C].
Beachamp, John (58 yrs.) d. on 67-Aug-11 [67-Aug-12: 2C].
Beachamp, Lida R. (22 yrs.) d. on 70-Mar-10 [70-Mar-11: 2C].
Beachum, William S. m. Bidderson, Caroline on 66-Jul-30 [66-Jul-31: 2C].
Beal, Alexander m. Dunbar, Lucie A. on 70-May-26 [70-May-28: 2B].
Beal, Alexander L. (64 yrs.) d. on 67-Dec-3 [67-Feb-5: 2C].
Beal, Eliza H. (31 yrs.) d. on 70-Oct-14 [70-Nov-2: 2C].
Beal, Ellen E. (54 yrs.) d. on 67-Sep-12 [67-Sep-20: 2A].
Beal, Ignatious Langley (1 yr., 1 mo.) d. on 68-Dec-15 [68-Dec-24: 2C].
Beal, India Florence (1 yr., 9 mos.) d. on 67-Sep-4 [67-Sep-13: 2B].
Beale, C. M. m. Nottingham, William T. on 69-Jun-15 [69-Jun-17: 2C].
Beale, Henry E. (16 yrs.) d. on 68-May-22 of Gunshot wound [68-May-23: 1F; 68-May-25: 2A].
Beale, Joseph L. m. Thrift, M. R. on 69-Dec-9 [69-Dec-18: 2B].
Beale, William E. (55 yrs.) d. on 67-Feb-5 of Typhus [67-Feb-6: 1F; 67-Feb-7: 2C].
Beall, Alpheus B. (74 yrs.) d. on 68-Aug-19 [68-Aug-27: 1F].
Beall, Amanda M. d. on 68-Jul-22 [68-Jul-24: 2C].
Beall, Caroline M. (64 yrs.) d. on 67-Mar-21 [67-Mar-25: 2C].
Beall, Franklin Hopkins (7 mos.) d. on 69-Jul-17 [69-Jul-19: 2C].
Beall, James A. m. Smith, Ada on 69-Jul-7 [69-Jul-14: 2D].
Beall, Jennie Thompson (11 mos.) d. [66-Jul-6: 2B].
Beall, Laura E. m. Smith, Asa H. on 69-Dec-23 [69-Dec-30: 2C; 69-Dec-31: 2C].
Beall, Lucy M. (23 yrs.) d. on 68-Sep-25 [68-Sep-26: 2B].
Beall, Nathan F. m. Burton, Marcelene Burton on 67-Nov-7 [67-Nov-23: 2B].
Beall, Thomas B. m. Berry, Lucy M. on 67-Nov-7 [67-Nov-8: 2C].
Bealmear, Alice m. Evans, William on 70-Mar-17 [70-Mar-19: 2B].
Bealmear, Catherine (85 yrs.) d. on 66-Jul-27 [66-Jul-28: 2C].
Bealmear, Elizabeth A. m. Brewer, Philip M. on 69-Aug-31 [69-Sep-10: 2B].
Bealmear, James A. m. Robinson, Mamie on 69-Sep-28 [69-Oct-2: 2B].
Bealmear, Samuel m. Comegys, Mary E. on 69-Feb-25 [69-Mar-2: 2C].

Beam, George F. (36 yrs.) d. on 66-Jan-16 [66-Jan-17: 1G, 2C].
Beam, John H. (27 yrs.) d. on 69-Oct-14 [69-Oct-15: 2C; 69-Oct-16: 2B].
Beam, John H. m. Hartzell, Anna on 67-Apr-4 [67-Apr-11: 2B].
Beam, Lewis (33 yrs.) d. on 69-Jul-26 [69-Jul-28: 2D].
Beaman, Laura (4 mos.) d. on 66-Aug-13 [66-Aug-14: 2C].
Beamer, Henry (73 yrs.) d. on 67-Nov-22 [67-Nov-23: 2B].
Bean, Benjamin m. Scott, Rose on 70-Dec-6 [70-Dec-10: 2B].
Bean, Cezarina (4 yrs., 7 mos.) d. on 67-Jan-5 [67-Jan-8: 2B].
Bean, James B. (37 yrs.) d. Killed in avalanche [70-Oct-3: 4C].
Bean, Sarah F. (30 yrs.) d. on 68-Aug-20 [68-Aug-21: 2B].
Bean, Thomas A., Capt. (47 yrs.) d. on 67-Oct-31 [67-Nov-2: 2B; 67-Nov-4: 1G].
Beansby, Charles d. on 70-Jul-25 of Consumption [70-Jul-27: 4F].
Beard, Ann (76 yrs., 2 mos.) d. on 69-Oct-2 [69-Oct-4: 2C].
Beard, Barbara Ann d. on 66-Jun-5 [66-Jun-7: 2B].
Beard, Charles (17 yrs.) d. on 70-Feb-23 [70-Feb-24: 2C].
Beard, Fannie V. m. Lotz, J. Fred on 69-May-25 [69-Jun-2: 2B].
Beard, Issac B. m. Brewer, Mary E. on 68-Feb-27 [68-May-5: 2B].
Beard, James (89 yrs.) d. on 66-Aug-11 of Consumption [66-Aug-17: 2C].
Beard, Lucia Eulalia (1 yr., 3 mos.) d. on 69-Apr-19 [69-Apr-20: 2B].
Beard, Mary Ann d. on 68-Dec-11 [68-Dec-12: 2C].
Beard, Mary E. m. Caldwell, John S. on 70-Mar-22 [70-Apr-7: 2B].
Beard, Robert Edward (1 yr., 5 mos.) d. on 66-Jan-21 [66-Jan-26: 2B].
Beard, Sarah (52 yrs.) d. on 66-Oct-27 [66-Oct-29: 2B].
Beard, Thomas, Capt. (49 yrs.) d. on 67-Apr-24 [67-Apr-25: 2B].
Beasten, Susan M. (55 yrs.) d. on 70-Jan-6 [70-Jan-14: 2C].
Beatley, Isaiah (53 yrs.) d. on 67-Feb-13 [67-Feb-16: 2D].
Beatley, Mary Jane (46 yrs.) d. on 70-Apr-6 [70-Apr-8: 2C].
Beatty, George (74 yrs.) d. on 68-Aug-1 [68-Aug-3: 2B].
Beatty, John M. m. Olive, Mary on 69-Apr-14 [69-May-3: 2C].
Beatty, Joseph G. m. Cullen, Annie on 66-May-1 [66-May-3: 2C].
Beatty, Margaret d. on 70-Apr-18 [70-Apr-21: 2C].
Beatty, Michael (48 yrs.) d. on 69-Sep-16 [69-Sep-17: 2C].
Beatty, Thomas Lloyd (3 mos.) d. on 67-Aug-11 [67-Aug-13: 2B].
Beatty, William J. A. m. Neill, Jane A. on 69-Dec-28 [70-Jan-17: 2C].
Beaty, Josephine Isabella (2 mos.) d. on 68-Jul-20 [68-Jul-21: 2C].
Beauchamp, Annie m. Suding, Henry A. on 70-Aug-23 [70-Sep-29: 2B].
Beauchamp, John T. m. Hawkins, Kate on 70-Dec-1 [70-Dec-14: 2C].
Beauchamp, Sally Anne (60 yrs.) d. on 67-May-9 of Consumption [67-May-15: 2B].
Beauchamp, William N. (27 yrs.) d. on 67-Jun-25 of Consumption [67-Jun-26: 2C].
Beauchamp, William S. m. Dryden, Lue J. on 68-Jan-21 [68-Jan-23: 2C].
Beaumont, Alexander H. m. Schaeffer, Maggie on 67-Apr-18 [67-Apr-20: 2A].
Beaumont, Issac P. (49 yrs.) d. on 65-Oct-13 [66-Jan-5: 2C].
Beaumont, Mollie J. m. Davis, George W. on 70-Jan-26 [70-Jan-27: 2C].
Beaumont, Oliver T. m. Robey, L. Leota on 70-Mar-24 [70-Mar-29: 2B].
Beavens, William Robert (7 mos.) d. on 69-Jul-25 [69-Jul-26: 2C].
Beaver, Alice m. Browne, William Hardcastle on 69-Dec-16 [69-Dec-20: 2C].
Beck, August m. Scheib, Joanna L. on 66-Aug-30 [66-Sep-20: 2B].
Beck, Charles R. R. m. Addison, Sallie L. on 70-Oct-25 [70-Oct-27: 2B].
Beck, Ella H. (1 yr., 10 mos.) d. on 70-May-8 [70-May-10: 2B].
Beck, Ernest m. Kessler, Mary on 70-Jul-18 [70-Jul-19: 2B].
Beck, Frederick (69 yrs., 11 mos.) d. on 67-Jul-2 [67-Jul-3: 2B].
Beck, George A. m. Gemperling, Mary J. on 66-Apr-24 [66-Apr-25: 2B].
Beck, George W. (7 mos.) d. on 70-Jun-20 [70-Jun-21: 2C].
Beck, Jane S. (35 yrs.) d. on 69-Jul-17 [69-Jul-20: 2C; 69-Jul-21: 2C; 69-Jul-22: 2C].
Beck, John F. m. Shipley, Rebecca on 70-Oct-13 [70-Oct-18: 2B].

Beck, Margaret (32 yrs.) d. on 69-Jan-21 [69-Jan-22: 2D].
Beck, Margaret m. Hibline, George E. on 69-Aug-22 [69-Aug-25: 2C].
Beck, Maria (14 yrs.) d. on 68-Aug-6 [68-Aug-7: 2B; 68-Aug-8: 2B].
Beck, Michael d. on 68-Sep-19 in Railroad accident [68-Sep-21: 1F].
Beck, Thomas Henry Charles d. on 70-Dec-20 [70-Dec-22: 2B; 70-Dec-23: 2B].
Beck, Tobias (76 yrs.) d. on 66-Jun-26 [66-Jun-29: 1E].
Beck, William m. Smith, Anna C. on 66-Aug-14 [66-Aug-16: 2C].
Beck, William R. (1 yr.) d. [70-Aug-19: 2C].
Beckenbaugh, James J., Dr. (33 yrs.) d. on 69-May-13 [69-May-19: 2C].
Beckenbaugh, John M m. Douglas, Nannie C. on 68-Nov-19 [68-Nov-25: 2B].
Beckenmeyer, Mary m. Myers, Thomas on 68-Aug-13 [68-Aug-15: 2B].
Becker, Caroline m. Raabe, John F. on 68-Oct-6 [68-Oct-9: 2C].
Becker, Charles m. Tschudy, Theresa on 70-Aug-30 [70-Sep-13: 2B].
Becker, Frederick m. Brown, Mary Lizzie on 68-Jun-30 [68-Jul-11: 2B].
Becker, John (21 yrs.) d. on 70-Sep-8 [70-Sep-10: 2B].
Becker, John C. (1 yr., 6 mos.) d. on 66-Nov-19 [66-Nov-21: 2C].
Becker, John D. (79 yrs.) d. on 69-Jul-24 [69-Jul-26: 2C].
Becker, John George (25 yrs.) d. on 70-Aug-16 [70-Aug-17: 2C; 70-Aug-18: 2B].
Becker, Lina m. Matthei, Daniel on 68-Feb-2 [68-Feb-4: 2C].
Beckett, G. H. m. O'Grady, Eliza on 68-Jun-8 [68-Jul-25: 2B].
Beckett, Mary Hannah (1 yr., 7 mos.) d. on 68-Apr-20 [68-Apr-22: 2B].
Beckley, Constantine F. m. Koontz, Cornelia on 69-Feb-15 [69-Feb-19: 2C].
Beckley, Eliza A. (65 yrs.) d. on 66-Aug-24 [66-Aug-25: 2A].
Beckley, H. M. d. on 68-Sep-17 of Suicide (Poisoning) [68-Sep-18: 1F].
Beckley, John W. m. Colston, Florence on 70-Jan-26 [70-Jan-29: 2B].
Beckley, Kate (1 yr., 2 mos.) d. on 68-Feb-22 [68-Feb-28: 2D].
Beckley, Mary (7 mos.) d. on 67-Aug-6 [67-Aug-9: 2C].
Beckley, Rebecca (69 yrs.) d. on 67-Aug-15 [67-Aug-17: 2B].
Beckley, Sallie E. m. Gill, Heithe S. on 68-Nov-5 [68-Nov-6: 2C].
Beckmyer, Amelia, Miss m. Jones, William H. on 67-Aug-14 [67-Aug-17: 2B].
Beckmyre, Mary A m. Myers, Thomas R. D. on 68-Aug-13 [68-Aug-18: 2B].
Beckwith, Henry (50 yrs.) d. on 66-Apr-6 [66-Apr-10: 2C].
Beckwith, Jeremiah H., Rev. (33 yrs.) d. on 67-Jan-24 [67-Jan-25: 1E, 2C].
Becraft, George (34 yrs.) d. on 68-Apr-28 [68-Apr-29: 2B].
Bedell, Richard Gilmore (1 yr.) d. on 66-Jul-8 [66-Jul-19: 2C].
Bedell, Sarah Elizabeth (1 yr., 3 mos.) d. on 70-May-13 [70-May-14: 2A].
Bedencoff, Maggie m. Jackson, John L. on 70-Oct-30 [70-Nov-8: 2B].
Bedford, Jane D. (55 yrs.) d. on 66-Sep-17 [66-Sep-18: 2B].
Bedford, Janie d. on 70-Dec-27 [70-Dec-28: 2C].
Bedford, Rosalba J. (2 yrs., 3 mos.) d. on 68-Jul-15 [68-Jul-17: 2B].
Bedon, M. C. m. Wysong, R. on 69-Jan-27 [69-Feb-1: 2C].
Beebe, M. L. m. Magness, C. Wesley on 69-Aug-3 [69-Aug-5: 2B].
Beebe, Thaddeus (35 yrs.) d. on 70-Aug-25 [70-Aug-26: 2C].
Beecher, Maggie S. m. Sutor, Henry P. on 68-Oct-15 [68-Oct-27: 2B].
Beecher, Maria (59 yrs.) d. on 67-Jun-20 [67-Jun-22: 2B].
Beehler, Francis (64 yrs.) d. on 70-Nov-20 [70-Nov-21: 2C, 4D; 70-Nov-22: 2B].
Beehler, Mary E. m. Harvey, Robert M. on 70-Oct-13 [70-Oct-15: 2B].
Beeks, Willie (2 yrs., 8 mos.) d. on 70-Apr-10 [70-Apr-11: 2B].
Beeler, S. F. m. Short, Annie M. on 66-Mar-10 [66-Aug-20: 2C].
Beeler, Sarah Jane (32 yrs.) d. on 66-Nov-17 [66-Nov-19: 2B].
Beeman, James J. (43 yrs.) d. on 66-Jun-18 [66-Jun-30: 2B].
Beeman, Mary (65 yrs.) d. on 67-Dec-15 [67-Dec-19: 2B].
Beemer, Sarah Louise m. Noyes, Stephen D. on 67-Oct-16 [67-Oct-19: 2A].
Beers, George Henry (22 yrs.) d. on 66-Oct-27 [66-Oct-30: 2B].
Beers, Maggie A. m. Fuller, Robert H. on 66-Oct-4 [66-Oct-20: 2B].

Befelt, Clarence H. (4 mos.) d. on 70-Oct-1 [70-Oct-13: 2C].
Beggs, A. m. Thayer, N. J. on 66-Jul-23 [66-Jul-25: 2C].
Behr, Caroline Henrietta d. on 68-Aug-23 [68-Aug-24: 2B].
Behrend, Elon m. Leucht, Henrietta on 67-Jan-17 [67-Jan-19: 2C].
Behrends, C. (71 yrs., 6 mos.) d. on 70-Oct-11 [70-Oct-12: 2B; 70-Oct-13: 2C].
Behrends, Leopold m. Seliger, Rachel on 68-Mar-1 [68-Mar-12: 2B].
Beidle, Charles W. m. Musgrave, Josephine on 69-Mar-20 [69-Mar-29: 2B].
Beirne, Mary Howard m. Thomas, J. Hanson on 66-Oct-16 [66-Oct-19: 2B].
Beirne, Oliver m. Sprigg, Sallie C. on 68-Dec-29 [69-Jan-1: 2C].
Beissler, Nicholas E. m. Byrne, Mary A. on 69-Jul-8 [69-Jul-22: 2C].
Belbin, William (73 yrs.) d. on 67-Dec-17 [67-Dec-19: 2B].
Bell, Adelbert T. m. Hodges, Lou. M. on 68-Oct-15 [68-Oct-27: 2B].
Bell, Agnes m. Clarke, George B. on 67-Jun-24 [67-Jul-9: 2B].
Bell, Alice m. Nock, N. N. on 68-Jan-11 [68-Mar-20: 2B].
Bell, Andrew J. m. Watkins, Elizabeth on 66-Nov-29 [66-Dec-4: 2D].
Bell, C. H. m. White, L. B. on 70-Jan-4 [70-Jan-8: 2B].
Bell, Charles Brooke (3 mos.) d. on 70-Mar-19 [70-Mar-22: 2C].
Bell, Clara d. on 69-Sep-5 [69-Sep-10: 2B].
Bell, Clara E. m. Kelly, Dennis A. on 67-May-6 [67-May-8: 2B].
Bell, David m. Bersch, Mary A. on 69-Nov-17 [69-Nov-24: 2C].
Bell, Eliza J. (19 yrs.) d. on 67-Jul-7 [67-Jul-8: 2C].
Bell, Eliza W. m. Pryor, George W. on 68-Oct-20 [68-Nov-25: 2B].
Bell, Elizabeth (52 yrs.) d. on 66-Nov-26 [66-Nov-27: 2B].
Bell, Emma (5 mos.) d. on 70-Feb-2 [70-Feb-5: 2C].
Bell, Fannie S. m. Scott, Mittian F. on 67-Dec-19 [67-Dec-24: 2B].
Bell, James Alfred (5 yrs., 9 mos.) d. on 67-Jan-20 of Diptheria [67-Jan-22: 2C].
Bell, John E. (3 mos.) d. on 68-Apr-12 [68-Apr-13: 2B].
Bell, John E. m. Neigholf, Mary on 67-Apr-30 [67-May-2: 2B].
Bell, John R. m. Martin, Catherine on 66-Nov-1 [66-Nov-5: 2B].
Bell, John T. m. Rimby, Annie M. on 69-May-18 [69-May-20: 2C].
Bell, John W. m. Yearly, Eliza Jane on 66-Apr-24 [66-Apr-26: 2B].
Bell, John Winfield (15 yrs.) d. on 69-Nov-11 of Construction cave-in [69-Nov-12: 1G;
  69-Nov-13: 2C].
Bell, Joseph A. m. Hasson, Clara on 67-Apr-4 [67-Apr-6: 2B].
Bell, Keziah m. Courtney, James A. on 70-Jun-28 [70-Jun-30: 2C].
Bell, Lucy (1 yr., 4 mos.) d. on 66-Jul-31 [66-Aug-1: 2C].
Bell, Maggie Hudson m. Holland, George Poisal on 68-Jan-2 [68-Jan-4: 2C].
Bell, Maria S. (51 yrs.) d. on 70-Jul-3 [70-Jul-4: 2C].
Bell, Marion m. Barrett, Maggie F. on 68-Sep-20 [68-Oct-6: 2B].
Bell, Martha J. m. Brown, Enoch S. on 68-Jun-25 [68-Jun-30: 2B].
Bell, Mary Ann (48 yrs.) d. on 66-Jan-24 [66-Jan-25: 2C].
Bell, Mary Anne d. on 66-Aug-3 [66-Aug-4: 2C].
Bell, Mary Baldwin (1 yr., 2 mos.) d. on 67-Nov-5 [67-Nov-6: 2B].
Bell, Mary Leah (1 yr., 2 mos.) d. on 66-Jun-13 [66-Jun-18: 2B].
Bell, Mary Warren (1 yr., 1 mo.) d. on 66-Jul-20 [66-Jul-24: 2C].
Bell, Mollie A. m. Katzenberger, John H. on 67-Nov-27 [67-Nov-30: 2C].
Bell, Richard A. m. Evans, Lizzie G. on 68-Sep-24 [68-Dec-2: 2C].
Bell, Robert Lewis (9 mos.) d. on 68-Apr-6 [68-Apr-13: 2B; 68-Apr-28: 2B].
Bell, Sallie W. m. DeFord, Thomas on 69-May-20 [69-May-22: 2B].
Bell, Sarah (76 yrs.) d. on 66-Mar-25 [66-Mar-27: 2B].
Bell, Sarah (49 yrs.) d. on 66-Jun-2 [66-Jun-4: 2B].
Bell, Shadrach d. on 68-May-25 Murdered (Stabbing) [68-May-29: 1C].
Bell, Thomas B. m. Brown, Emma J. on 66-Feb-14 [66-Feb-16: 2B; 66-Feb-17: 2B].
Bell, William E. C. m. Smoot, Mary F. on 69-May-13 [69-May-18: 2C].
Bell, William H. m. Roberts, F. Augusta on 67-May-30 [67-Jun-4: 2A].

Bellash, Samuel G. W. (54 yrs.) d. on 70-Feb-11 [70-Feb-18: 2C].
Bellis, Elizabeth (20 yrs.) d. on 68-Apr-8 [68-Apr-10: 2B].
Bellis, John (54 yrs.) d. on 69-Dec-18 [69-Dec-20: 2C].
Bellis, William H. m. Tolson, Ella on 66-Aug-14 [66-Aug-31: 2B].
Bellmont, Thomas (45 yrs.) d. on 68-Jun-20 of Heatstroke [68-Jun-22: 1G].
Belmier, Charles d. on 69-May-28 Burned [69-May-31: 4B].
Belt, Fidelia R. d. on 66-Aug-7 [66-Aug-11: 2B; 66-Aug-13: 2C].
Belt, George Gordon (47 yrs.) d. on 69-Jun-3 Murdered (Shooting) [69-Jun-14: 1G; 69-Jun-15: 4B].
Belt, Hattie R. d. on 69-May-5 of Pneumonia [69-May-10: 2C].
Belt, James E. m. Hildebrandt, Maggie H. on 69-Feb-23 [69-Mar-3: 2B].
Belt, John S. m. Belt, Laura P. on 67-Dec-12 [67-Dec-30: 2C].
Belt, John W. m. Knox, Mahlah on 66-Dec-4 [66-Dec-8: 2B].
Belt, Laura E. d. on 69-Dec-10 [69-Dec-11: 2B].
Belt, Laura P. m. Belt, John S. on 67-Dec-12 [67-Dec-30: 2C].
Belt, Lucina m. Mitchell, William T. on 68-Nov-22 [68-Nov-28: 2C].
Belt, M. E. m. Haviland, Edgar P. on 69-Jan-6 [69-Jan-16: 2C].
Belt, Mary V. m. Reifsnider, John R. on 66-Apr-19 [66-May-10: 2B].
Belt, Robert V. m. Kirkwood, Josie W. on 69-Aug-10 [69-Aug-31: 2B].
Belt, Samuel J. m. Smith, S. Emma on 70-Jan-25 [70-Jan-28: 2B].
Belt, Sarah Eleanor Hardesty (1 yr., 8 mos.) d. on 66-Feb-10 [66-Oct-16: 2B].
Belt, T. H., Jr. m. Tyler, Maria on 69-Dec-8 [69-Dec-11: 2B].
Belt, Thomas W. m. Koch, Mary A. on 66-Jun-5 [66-Jun-18: 2C].
Belt, Walter S. m. Bernasco, Maria Virginia on 70-Mar-27 [70-Apr-25: 2B].
Belt, William Seton, Dr. (42 yrs.) d. on 70-Sep-6 [70-Sep-12: 2C].
Belvin, John A., Jr. m. Keesee, Mary O. on 67-Feb-21 [67-Feb-26: 2C].
Belvin, Naomi M. m. Lockhart, Andrew J. on 66-Sep-26 [66-Oct-5: 2B].
Bendan, Isadora (1 yr., 6 mos.) d. on 66-Jan-27 [66-Jan-29: 2C].
Bendann, Rosetta d. on 66-Aug-26 [66-Aug-27: 2B].
Bender, Emma d. on 67-Apr-8 [67-Apr-9: 2B].
Bender, George W. m. Faulkner, Maria L. on 65-Dec-27 [66-Jan-1: 2C].
Bender, John (64 yrs.) d. on 70-Mar-17 [70-Mar-18: 2C].
Bender, Mary Agnes m. Smith, James W. on 68-Jun-25 [68-Jun-26: 2B].
Bender, Mary K. R. m. Foulkes, Robert F. on 65-Dec-14 [66-Jan-1: 2C].
Bender, Walter G. (68 yrs.) d. on 70-May-12 [70-May-14: 2A].
Bendimire, Sophia (56 yrs.) d. on 69-Feb-22 [69-Mar-4: 2C].
Bendy, Eliza (74 yrs.) d. on 70-Nov-14 [70-Nov-15: 2C].
Benhoff, Alverda Zedora (9 mos.) d. on 70-Jun-16 [70-Jun-18: 2B].
Benhoff, William Oliver (2 yrs., 4 mos.) d. on 69-Oct-18 [69-Oct-23: 2B].
Benjamin, Alfred m. Carrol, Helen on 66-Nov-26 [66-Nov-29: 2B].
Benjamin, Joseph (18 yrs.) d. on 66-Jun-7 [66-Jun-9: 2B].
Benkuff, William m. Walker, Rebecca F. on 66-Jul-8 [66-Jul-14: 2B].
Bennamin, John m. Wilson, Mary J. on 68-Nov-22 [68-Nov-24: 2C].
Bennanzar, John (58 yrs.) d. on 70-Dec-8 [70-Dec-10: 2B].
Benner, Eliza (71 yrs.) d. on 68-Jan-31 [68-Feb-18: 2C].
Benner, H. H. m. Kleinle, Mary E. on 70-May-22 [70-Jun-10: 2B].
Benner, Lottie J. m. Brown, Thomas H. S. on 70-Sep-15 [70-Sep-20: 2B].
Benner, Louisa (54 yrs.) d. on 66-Jan-10 [66-Jan-15: 2C].
Benner, Samuel (7 yrs.) d. on 67-Jul-13 Drowned [67-Jul-15: 1F].
Benner, William H. (56 yrs.) d. on 69-Jul-8 [69-Jul-10: 2B].
Bennet, Harriet d. on 66-Nov-22 [66-Nov-23: 2C; 66-Nov-24: 2B].
Bennett, Annie C. m. Frush, Carroll V. on 66-Mar-19 [66-Mar-27: 2B].
Bennett, Edward W. m. Hoffman, Alexina on 68-Oct-29 [68-Oct-31: 2B].
Bennett, Eli m. Harden, Georgeana on 66-Feb-8 [66-Feb-22: 2B].
Bennett, Elizabeth C. (28 yrs.) d. on 67-May-8 Burned [67-May-9: 1F, 2A].

Bennett, Emma M. (2 yrs., 2 mos.) d. on 67-Dec-29 [67-Dec-31: 2C].
Bennett, Florence Amelia (4 yrs.) d. on 69-Apr-29 [69-May-1: 2B].
Bennett, George B. m. King, Georgie A. on 70-May-8 [70-May-12: 2B].
Bennett, George W. (44 yrs.) d. on 69-Apr-25 [69-Jun-10: 2C].
Bennett, Harry Rutledge (5 mos.) d. on 70-Jul-24 [70-Jul-27: 2C].
Bennett, James (1 yr., 3 mos.) d. on 68-Jul-22 [68-Jul-23: 2B].
Bennett, James A. (29 yrs., 4 mos.) d. on 70-Dec-10 [70-Dec-12: 2C].
Bennett, John Lewis (43 yrs., 10 mos.) d. on 70-Dec-19 [70-Dec-20: 2B].
Bennett, Larkin J. m. Conaway, Laura F. on 67-Dec-12 [68-Jan-1: 2C].
Bennett, Lillia (22 yrs.) d. on 69-Sep-26 [69-Sep-27: 2C].
Bennett, Lizzie S. m. Shipley, Edwin M. on 66-Dec-20 [66-Dec-25: 2B].
Bennett, Lucinda m. Burgess, Benjamin on 70-Nov-10 [70-Nov-26: 2B].
Bennett, Maggie m. Davidson, Robert J. on 68-Jul-28 [68-Aug-4: 2C].
Bennett, Martha W. m. Gillinder, James on 67-Apr-29 [67-May-2: 2B].
Bennett, Mary Ann (68 yrs.) d. on 69-Jun-23 [69-Jun-25: 2C].
Bennett, Mary Emma (1 yr., 10 mos.) d. on 66-Jul-12 [66-Jul-16: 2C].
Bennett, Mary J. (46 yrs.) d. on 70-Aug-4 [70-Aug-5: 2C; 70-Aug-6: 2C].
Bennett, Mary J. m. Prince, George E. on 66-Mar-28 [66-Apr-5: 2B].
Bennett, Pinkney J. m. Taylor, Irene C. on 68-Jun-9 [68-Jun-11: 2B].
Bennett, Samuel (56 yrs.) d. on 67-Dec-29 of Heart disease [67-Dec-30: 1E].
Bennett, Samuel H. m. Owings, Virginia F. on 66-Jan-28 [66-Feb-19: 2B].
Bennett, Susanna (65 yrs.) d. on 69-Jul-11 [69-Jul-12: 2C].
Bennett, Sylvanus (67 yrs.) d. on 67-Jul-8 [67-Jul-9: 2B].
Bennett, Thomas B. (35 yrs.) d. on 69-Dec-15 [69-Dec-16: 2C].
Bennett, Thomas J. m. Milburn, Mattie J. on 67-Dec-4 [67-Dec-27: 2D].
Bennett, William D. m. Mareen, Catherine E. on 68-Sep-17 [68-Oct-21: 2C].
Bennett, William F. (58 yrs.) d. on 69-Apr-2 [69-Apr-3: 2B].
Bennett, William H. d. on 68-Dec-22 [68-Dec-31: 2D].
Bennett, William Huntington m. Evans, Mary E. on 67-Nov-26 [67-Nov-30: 2C].
Bennett, William T. m. Mitchell, Emma E. on 69-Jul-19 [69-Aug-10: 2C].
Benney, David m. Johnson, Anninda on 67-Oct-26 [67-Dec-3: 2C].
Benney, Mary m. Squires, Alonzo on 67-Sep-23 [67-Dec-3: 2C].
Bennis, William d. on 68-Dec-8 [68-Dec-9: 2C].
Benny, Dasie Virginia (7 mos.) d. on 66-Aug-18 [66-Aug-23: 2C].
Benny, Emma G. (31 yrs.) d. on 69-Jun-29 of Pulmonary consumption [69-Jul-2: 2C].
Benny, James W. d. on 69-Oct-30 Drowned [69-Nov-1: 1G].
Benny, James W. m. Thompson, Emma G. on 68-Jan-7 [68-Jan-14: 2C].
Benny, Richard Oscar (8 yrs., 3 mos.) d. on 66-May-27 [66-May-28: 2B].
Benoit, C. Edwin (40 yrs.) d. on 70-Dec-26 of Liver disease [70-Dec-28: 4F; 70-Dec-29: 4B].
Benson, B. S. m. Marriott, Lucy on 67-Jan-3 [67-Jan-5: 2C].
Benson, Carrie (4 yrs., 5 mos.) d. on 68-Nov-28 [68-Dec-1: 2C].
Benson, Catherine m. Vermillion, George on 70-Jun-2 [70-Jun-4: 2B].
Benson, Ellen L (67 yrs.) d. on 68-Oct-28 [68-Oct-30: 2C].
Benson, Emma R. m. Holmes, John E. on 67-Apr-23 [67-Apr-26: 2B].
Benson, Everette E. (15 yrs., 8 mos.) d. on 70-Feb-18 [70-Feb-19: 2B].
Benson, Fannie (2 yrs., 7 mos.) d. on 69-Dec-27 [69-Dec-28: 2D].
Benson, Fanny Louise d. [69-Aug-24: 2C].
Benson, Florence Eugenia (8 mos.) d. on 68-Apr-21 [68-Apr-23: 2B].
Benson, Issac m. Berry, Louisa on 67-Oct-24 [67-Oct-26: 2A].
Benson, James W. m. Fisher, Laura on 69-Dec-21 [69-Dec-24: 2C].
Benson, Joseph m. McCoy, Jane E. on 68-Nov-12 [68-Nov-30: 2B].
Benson, Joseph K. m. Linthicum, Bettie V. on 69-Mar-9 [69-Mar-31: 2C].
Benson, Keturah (71 yrs.) d. on 67-Oct-13 [67-Oct-14: 2B; 67-Oct-15: 2A].
Benson, M. Virginia m. Englar, W. J. on 70-May-3 [70-May-4: 2C].
Benson, Mary m. Bokee, Morris H. on 70-Jun-13 [70-Jun-16: 2B].

Benson, Mary Emily (27 yrs.) d. on 66-Nov-8 of Childbirth [66-Nov-14: 2B].
Benson, Oregon R. m. Brian, Carvilla on 70-Oct-4 [70-Oct-10: 2B].
Benson, Peter Aulden (5 yrs., 2 mos.) d. on 70-Jun-28 [70-Jun-30: 2C].
Benson, Randolph S. m. Lauer, Catherine on 68-Jun-24 [68-Jun-26: 2B].
Benson, Walter Lee (1 yr., 2 mos.) d. on 67-Nov-17 [67-Nov-20: 2C].
Bent, Fred W. m. McLeod, Emma E. on 67-Sep-9 [67-Oct-9: 2B].
Benteen, Charles S. m. Gosewich, Annie C. on 67-Nov-19 [67-Nov-21: 2C].
Benteen, Edith (13 yrs.) d. on 68-Jan-9 [68-Jan-10: 2C; 68-Jan-11: 2B].
Benteen, Ella m. Robb, Duncan McC. on 68-Nov-12 [68-Nov-17: 2C].
Benthall, C. E. m. Kone, Franklin on 69-Nov-15 [69-Nov-18: 2C].
Benthall, Robert m. Cooksey, Mary Malloy on 70-Jun-9 [70-Jun-11: 2B].
Bentley, Eva Alexina (5 mos.) d. on 70-Jul-10 [70-Jul-12: 2B].
Bentley, Richard m. Jones, Roseta on 68-Jul-16 [68-Jul-18: 2B].
Bentley, Sarah Brooke m. Lea, William, Jr. on 67-Jun-20 [67-Jun-22: 2B].
Bentley, Sarah I. m. Mackey, S. Webster on 70-Oct-13 [70-Oct-18: 2B].
Bentley, William H. m. Mabee, Alexina on 68-Dec-16 [68-Dec-22: 2C].
Benton, Ann E. (44 yrs.) d. on 66-Dec-16 [66-Dec-20: 2B].
Benton, Charles S. m. Arthur, Delia on 70-Jun-30 [70-Jul-4: 2C].
Benton, Emily A. m. Nelson, T. R. on 70-Nov-25 [70-Dec-16: 2C].
Benton, George Washington (2 yrs., 1 mo.) d. on 66-Jul-16 [66-Aug-7: 2C].
Benton, J. Henry m. Bilson, Laura V. on 67-Dec-31 [68-Jan-4: 2C].
Benton, Levin (53 yrs.) d. on 68-Jul-4 [68-Jul-10: 2C].
Benton, Margretta R. m. Hyde, Joseph on 66-Feb-20 [66-Feb-26: 2B].
Benton, Rosaltha E. m. Swift, Nathan on 70-Mar-24 [70-Mar-30: 2B].
Benton, Thomas d. on 70-Jan-7 Drowned [70-Jan-8: 1G].
Benton, Thomas T. m. Blasser, Mollie E. on 66-Apr-17 [66-Apr-20: 2B].
Benton, William D. (56 yrs., 10 mos.) d. on 69-Jan-31 [69-Feb-3: 2C].
Bentz, Caroline Henderson (13 yrs.) d. on 66-Aug-19 [66-Sep-6: 2B].
Bentz, J. Henderson d. on 67-Feb-22 [67-Feb-28: 2C].
Bentz, Mary E. (7 mos.) d. on 70-Sep-21 [70-Sep-23: 2C].
Bentz, Mary Eugenia d. on 69-Oct-24 [69-Oct-27: 2B].
Bentzel, Henry m. Switzer, Mary E. on 68-Dec-23 [68-Dec-28: 2B].
Bentzel, Rebecca (30 yrs.) d. on 67-Mar-4 [67-Mar-6: 2C].
Benwire, Susannah (78 yrs.) d. on 69-Oct-22 [69-Oct-27: 2B].
Benz, Jesse W. m. Hahn, Katie on 68-Dec-23 [68-Dec-29: 2D].
Benzinger, Frederick J. d. on 66-Mar-10 [66-Mar-12: 2B].
Benzinger, John S (45 yrs.) d. on 69-Dec-13 [69-Dec-15: 2B].
Benzinger, Mary F. DeSales (39 yrs.) d. on 68-Oct-15 [68-Oct-17: 2B; 68-Oct-23: 1F].
Berg, Magdalene m. Steffens, Henry on 67-Jul-9 [67-Jul-10: 2B].
Bergen, Georgeanna m. Wonner, Michael on 67-Sep-15 [67-Oct-14: 2B].
Berger, Anastasia (64 yrs.) d. on 67-Sep-12 [67-Sep-14: 2A].
Berger, Clement (69 yrs.) d. on 68-May-8 [68-May-11: 2B].
Berger, Florence (1 yr., 4 mos.) d. on 70-Jul-22 [70-Jul-26: 2C].
Berger, Genevieve (69 yrs.) d. on 67-Oct-23 [70-Oct-26: 2B].
Berger, John (30 yrs.) d. on 70-Nov-23 [70-Nov-24: 2B].
Berger, John m. Senft, Wilhelmina on 68-Jun-17 [68-Jun-20: 2B].
Berger, Loretta C. F. (5 yrs.) d. on 70-Mar-26 [70-Mar-28: 2B].
Berger, Louisa H. m. McCaddin, James on 69-Mar-31 [69-Apr-2: 2C].
Berger, Marie (59 yrs.) d. on 69-Mar-5 [69-Mar-6: 2B].
Berger, Mary Eva (3 mos.) d. on 70-Mar-28 [70-Mar-29: 2C].
Berger, Willa m. Emory, Frederick B. on 69-Sep-6 [69-Oct-25: 2B].
Bergin, Arthur m. Duffy, Anna Maria on 69-Sep-19 [69-Sep-23: 2B].
Bergin, Mary (53 yrs.) d. on 70-Jul-4 [70-Jul-6: 2C].
Berkins, Mary A. m. Blucher, John M. on 66-Oct-21 [66-Oct-27: 2B].
Berkley, Emily W. d. on 67-Aug-7 [67-Aug-13: 2B].

Bernard, Arabella Wilson (17 yrs.) d. on 68-Jan-27 [68-Feb-5: 2D].
Bernard, Richard m. Duncan, F. Annie on 67-Jun-20 [67-Jun-27: 2B].
Bernasco, A. m. Kramer, C. H. on 68-Nov-8 [68-Nov-28: 2C].
Bernasco, Eleonora (4 yrs., 6 mos.) d. on 70-May-6 [70-May-9: 2B].
Bernasco, Maria Virginia m. Belt, Walter S. on 70-Mar-27 [70-Apr-25: 2B].
Bernhart, Emma Amelia (1 mo.) d. on 68-Jan-17 [68-Jan-21: 2C].
Bernheim, Emma L. m. Rueckert, J. F. on 67-Dec-19 [67-Dec-24: 2B].
Bernheimer, Henry m. Labe, Rebecca on 68-Oct-18 [68-Oct-20: 2B].
Bernoudy, Celanire m. McLain, William, Jr. on 67-Jan-15 [67-Jul-27: 2B].
Berrenger, Mary F. m. Lambdin, Thomas R. on 66-Nov-29 [67-Jan-5: 2C].
Berrett, Eugenia m. George, James, Jr. on 69-Oct-5 [69-Oct-8: 2B].
Berrey, Oscar d. on 68-Jun-30 in Railroad accident [68-Jul-2: 1G].
Berry, Alice E. m. Bourne, William L. on 68-Mar-5 [68-Mar-7: 2B].
Berry, Almira (42 yrs.) d. [69-Jan-4: 2C].
Berry, B. D. (48 yrs.) d. on 66-May-8 [66-May-9: 2B].
Berry, Charles A., Capt. (56 yrs.) d. on 66-Oct-4 [66-Oct-6: 1F, 2A].
Berry, Charles E. (20 yrs.) d. on 68-May-6 [68-May-7: 2B; 68-May-8: 2B].
Berry, Elizabeth m. Donigen, William on 67-Dec-19 [67-Dec-21: 2B].
Berry, Elizabeth A. m. Brian, George W. on 66-May-28 [66-Jun-14: 2B; 66-Jun-15: 2C].
Berry, Emory E. m. Kenny, Mollie A. B. on 70-Jul-28 [70-Sep-15: 2B].
Berry, Esther B. (78 yrs.) d. on 68-Oct-15 [68-Oct-30: 2C].
Berry, George W. (24 yrs.) d. on 69-Aug-11 [69-Aug-19: 2C].
Berry, George W. m. Wells, Eugenia M. on 67-Oct-22 [67-Nov-20: 2C].
Berry, George W. m. Delcher, Maggie J. on 69-Mar-8 [69-Mar-29: 2B].
Berry, Harry Mauduit (14 yrs.) d. on 70-Oct-31 [70-Nov-2: 2C].
Berry, Henry D. m. Meagher, Kate M. on 70-Sep-26 [70-Oct-1: 2B].
Berry, Jane (85 yrs.) d. on 68-Jul-2 [68-Jul-3: 2C].
Berry, John (58 yrs.) d. on 67-Jul-27 [67-Jul-30: 2C].
Berry, John B. (51 yrs.) d. on 69-Mar-8 [69-Mar-9: 2C].
Berry, Louisa m. Benson, Issac on 67-Oct-24 [67-Oct-26: 2A].
Berry, Lucy A. m. Hyson, Albert S. on 69-Feb-28 [69-Mar-3: 2B].
Berry, Lucy M. m. Beall, Thomas B. on 67-Nov-7 [67-Nov-8: 2C].
Berry, Maggie L. m. Weems, Theodore N. on 69-Sep-16 [69-Sep-17: 2C].
Berry, Mary E. m. Edmondson, Joseph A. on 67-Oct-22 [67-Oct-24: 2B].
Berry, Mary E. m. Donovan, M. W. on 66-Oct-17 [66-Oct-18: 2B].
Berry, May (6 mos.) d. on 67-Nov-28 [67-Dec-3: 2C].
Berry, Nimrod B. m. Wooden, Abbey on 69-Dec-29 [69-Dec-31: 2C].
Berry, R. R. m. Glass, Martha on 69-Jul-13 [69-Jul-15: 2C].
Berry, Robert D. (55 yrs.) d. on 70-Sep-10 [70-Sep-12: 2B].
Berry, Thomas W. (32 yrs.) d. on 69-Nov-5 of Suicide (Shooting) [69-Nov-6: 1H, 2C; 69-Nov-8: 1F].
Berryman, Fannie E. m. Edmonston, Charles on 68-Jan-14 [68-Jan-25: 2B].
Berryman, George G. m. Uhler, Julia on 68-Nov-19 [68-Nov-23: 2B].
Bersch, Henry, Sr. (80 yrs.) d. on 66-Nov-20 [66-Nov-21: 2C].
Bersch, Mary A. m. Bell, David on 69-Nov-17 [69-Nov-24: 2C].
Berteau, Emilie Beauzamy (76 yrs.) d. on 69-Aug-3 [69-Aug-5: 2B].
Berthey, Ann (85 yrs.) d. on 67-Jul-22 [67-Jul-23: 2C].
Bertier, Rachel (26 yrs.) d. on 67-Sep-26 of Consumption [67-Sep-27: 2B].
Bertram, Charles F. (29 yrs., 6 mos.) d. on 66-Nov-1 of Fall from roof [66-Nov-2: 2B, 4B; 66-Nov-3: 1G].
Bertrand, Eugene P., Lt. d. on 66-Sep-21 of Cholera [66-Oct-9: 2A; 66-Oct-12: 2B].
Bertrand, Henrietta E. d. on 67-Sep-22 [67-Oct-2: 2B].
Bervard, John m. Howard, Laura E. on 67-May-29 [67-Jun-1: 2B].
Bessee, Laura Virginia m. Moore, John Granville on 70-May-21 [70-Nov-3: 2B].
Besser, Jennia Amelia (4 yrs., 5 mos.) d. on 70-Apr-28 [70-Apr-30: 2A].

Bessinger, George (54 yrs.) d. on 66-Jan-6 [66-Jan-8: 1G].
Best, David (28 yrs.) d. on 69-Dec-28 [69-Dec-30: 2C].
Bestor, J. Rollin (54 yrs.) d. on 67-Sep-18 [67-Sep-24: 2A].
Bestor, Owen B. m. Cromwell, Hattie A. on 67-May-7 [67-May-14: 2B].
Bethune, J. D. m. Clark, Mary Agnes on 69-Jun-2 [69-Jun-4: 2C].
Betsmorth, James d. on 67-Jul-28 Drowned [67-Jul-29: 1E].
Betton, Jane (23 yrs., 4 mos.) d. on 66-May-1 [66-May-3: 2C].
Betton, Joseph Leonard (2 yrs., 1 mo.) d. on 68-Jul-6 [68-Jul-9: 2B].
Betton, Mary m. Jones, George on 68-May-26 [68-May-28: 2B].
Betton, Ophelia A. m. Keyser, Herman on 70-Mar-29 [70-Mar-31: 2C].
Betts, Albert A. m. Wood, Annie Eliza on 65-Oct-25 [66-Apr-17: 2C].
Betts, Hannah Virginia (8 yrs., 10 mos.) d. on 68-Mar-22 [68-Apr-3: 2C].
Betts, Henry T. (67 yrs.) d. on 67-Jun-19 [67-Jun-20: 2B].
Betts, John (74 yrs.) d. on 70-Jan-7 [70-Jan-8: 1H, 2B].
Betts, John Thomas (4 yrs., 10 mos.) d. on 69-Apr-28 [69-Apr-29: 2B].
Betts, Rosa Adelia (1 yr.) d. on 70-Mar-17 [70-Mar-22: 2C].
Betts, Roseanna d. on 66-Dec-29 [66-Dec-31: 2C].
Betts, Samuel C. m. Nelson, Emma F. on 66-Apr-4 [66-Apr-12: 2B].
Beuhler, Ellen m. Wirt, Calvin C. on 70-Dec-13 [70-Dec-16: 2C].
Beutelspacher, George m. Woolfenden, Sadie on 66-Aug-5 [67-Mar-27: 2C].
Bevan, Ann (46 yrs., 9 mos.) d. on 66-Mar-31 of Consumption [66-Apr-12: 2B].
Bevan, Charles m. Johnson, Agnes F. on 65-Oct-14 [66-Mar-19: 2C].
Bevan, Jeanettie (4 yrs.) d. on 67-Jan-17 of Scarlet fever [67-Jan-19: 2C].
Bevan, John W. m. Hopkins, Sallie S. on 70-Nov-1 [70-Nov-3: 2B].
Bevan, Kate Sergent d. on 66-Oct-28 [66-Oct-29: 2C].
Bevan, Miriam (3 yrs.) d. on 66-Dec-30 of Scarlet fever [67-Jan-3: 2C].
Bevans, James L. m. Peduzzi, Sarah F. on 70-Nov-3 [70-Nov-10: 2C].
Bevans, John m. Watts, Nancy on 66-Apr-19 [66-Apr-21: 2B].
Bevans, Joshua A. m. Hedeman, Sophia D. on 68-Oct-22 [68-Oct-24: 2B].
Bevans, Mary C. m. Rollins, Thomas on 69-Aug-12 [69-Aug-14: 2C].
Bevans, Mollie J. m. Murdock, Charles on 66-Dec-27 [67-Jan-1: 2C].
Bevans, Rachel J. m. Thomas, Van Beuren on 66-Feb-23 [66-Mar-2: 2B].
Bevans, Richard N. m. MacCubbin, Mary E. on 66-Dec-27 [67-Jan-2: 2C].
Bevans, Sarah A. d. on 68-Dec-1 [68-Dec-3: 2C].
Bevans, W. A. (2 mos.) d. on 67-Aug-16 [67-Aug-17: 2B].
Beveridge, Laura V. m. Eggleston, Bird on 67-Oct-15 [68-Jan-23: 2C].
Beveridge, Mary Jane (3 yrs., 10 mos.) d. on 69-Jul-11 of Scarlet fever [69-Jul-13: 2C].
Beveridge, Robert m. Williamson, Agnes on 70-Apr-5 [70-Apr-9: 2B].
Bevier, Katie E. m. Whiteside, A. S. on 66-Aug-22 [66-Sep-1: 2B].
Bew, Emma C. m. Stacey, Henry C. on 67-Apr-21 [67-Apr-23: 2B].
Bezeck, Margaret (66 yrs.) d. on 67-Mar-27 [67-Mar-29: 2B].
Beziat, Ellen F. m. Bollman, James H. on 67-Apr-19 [67-Apr-23: 2B].
Beziat, Jennie m. Watts, John W. on 69-Aug-24 [69-Sep-7: 2B].
Bians, William H. m. Salmon, Elizabeth Jane on 66-Dec-31 [67-Jan-9: 2B].
Bias, Charles (23 yrs., 4 mos.) d. on 66-Apr-5 [66-Apr-6: 2B].
Bias, John Henry (25 yrs.) d. on 68-Nov-1 [68-Nov-2: 2B].
Bias, Martha A. m. Williams, Asberry on 66-Jun-7 [66-Jun-20: 2C].
Bias, Mary Emma (14 yrs.) d. on 66-Nov-17 [66-Nov-19: 2B].
Bias, Richard m. Curtis, Mary Jane on 67-Feb-28 [67-Mar-4: 2D].
Bibb, Louisa Malvina (4 yrs., 3 mos.) d. on 66-Jan-25 of Diptheria [66-Jan-29: 2C].
Bickerton, Maggie A. m. Fay, Fordice on 66-May-23 [66-May-30: 2C].
Bickerton, Sarah (85 yrs.) d. on 70-Nov-30 [70-Dec-1: 2C; 70-Dec-2: 2C].
Bickley, Eliza A. (65 yrs.) d. on 66-Aug-24 [66-Aug-27: 2B].
Bidderson, Caroline m. Beachum, William Ss on 66-Jul-30 [66-Jul-31: 2C].
Bidderson, William (54 yrs.) d. on 66-Aug-28 [66-Aug-29: 2B].

Biddison, Alice L. m. Hoey, Henry on 68-Apr-14 [68-Apr-16: 2B].
Biddison, Benjamin (25 yrs.) d. on 66-Mar-18 [66-Mar-20: 2C].
Biddison, Elizabeth A. m. Edwards, John on 69-Aug-23 [69-Sep-25: 2B].
Biddison, Mary d. on 68-Jan-6 [68-Jan-7: 2B].
Biddison, Zachariah (73 yrs.) d. on 70-Dec-15 [70-Dec-17: 2B].
Biddle, George (1 yr.) d. on 68-Jul-3 [68-Jul-4: 2C].
Biddle, John T. m. Joice, Emily A. on 66-Jan-30 [66-Feb-6: 2D].
Biddle, Richard F. m. Kane, Susan on 67-Jan-1 [67-Jan-9: 2B].
Biddle, Samuel R. (69 yrs., 7 mos.) d. on 70-Jun-7 [70-Jun-9: 2C].
Biden, George d. on 68-Jul-24 Drowned [68-Jul-28: 1B].
Bidison, William T. m. German, Eliza on 69-Oct-24 [69-Oct-30: 2B].
Bidleman, Ferdinand (1 yr., 10 mos.) d. on 66-Jun-17 [66-Jun-19: 2B].
Bidleman, Ferdinand N. m. Ritter, Henrietta W. on 68-Oct-6 [68-Oct-7: 2C].
Biedenkopf, George m. Nevitt, Cordelia on 69-Jan-14 [69-Jan-21: 2C].
Bien, Annie E. m. McCann, William V. on 68-May-21 [68-May-26: 2B].
Bien, Susie m. Murray, James on 69-Jun-24 [69-Jul-22: 2C].
Bier, George H. m. Carter, Mary Randolph on 67-Dec-10 [67-Dec-18: 2B].
Bier, Josephine Virginia d. on 66-Apr-23 [66-Apr-24: 2B].
Bier, Oden Bowie (5 mos.) d. on 69-Mar-22 [69-Mar-23: 2C].
Bier, William Louis (8 yrs., 10 mos.) d. on 66-Oct-9 [66-Oct-11: 2C].
Bierbower, C. R. m. Blackiston, Kate on 70-Apr-28 [70-May-4: 2C].
Bierbower, Francis A. m. Fox, Mary A. on 69-Nov-18 [69-Nov-25: 2C].
Bierley, Mary (2 yrs.) d. on 69-Dec-4 of Chronic croup [69-Dec-4: 2C].
Bierley, William m. Mowbray, Ellen F. on 70-Oct-4 [70-Oct-15: 2B].
Biersock, George W. m. Kendig, Sallie C. on 67-Oct-31 [67-Nov-2: 2B].
Biggs, John T. (19 yrs.) d. on 66-Apr-12 [66-Apr-13: 2C].
Biggs, Julia Ann m. Keck, Samuel on 67-Nov-27 [67-Nov-30: 2C].
Biggs, Mary A. m. Ginnavan, J. T. on 69-Nov-7 [69-Nov-9: 2C].
Bigham, Ella Caldwell d. on 68-Jul-23 [68-Jul-31: 2C].
Bigham, John B. m. Brashears, Rachel Ann on 68-Oct-20 [68-Oct-23: 2B].
Bigham, John L. m. Passano, Rosa on 70-Nov-15 [70-Nov-16: 2C].
Bigham, Martha J. m. Prugh, Upton on 70-Nov-29 [70-Dec-10: 2B].
Bigley, M. Kate m. Nickle, Stephen E. on 69-Jun-9 [69-Aug-13: 2C].
Bihy, John, Jr. m. Corner, Kate on 69-Aug-22 [69-Aug-23: 2C].
Billings, Albert Q. m. Perry, Mary E. on 69-Mar-1 [69-Mar-2: 2C].
Billings, Felicia Louise (10 mos.) d. [68-May-27: 2B].
Billings, Leonora (3 yrs., 1 mo.) d. on 68-May-15 [68-May-16: 2A].
Billings, Winefred (11 mos.) d. on 70-May-22 [70-May-24: 2C].
Billingslea, A. m. Hopkins, Mollie J. on 66-Jan-2 [66-Jan-4: 2C].
Billingslea, Charlton W. m. McGonigal, Virginia on 69-Jul-14 [69-Jul-17: 2C].
Billingslea, Mary E. (24 yrs.) d. on 66-Apr-18 [66-Apr-20: 2B].
Billingslea, Sallie m. Aken, Edwin C. on 68-Oct-6 [68-Oct-8: 2B].
Billingsley, James m. Masson, Jennie on 70-Aug-16 [70-Aug-30: 2B].
Billingsley, S. W., Jr. m. Oler, Sarah A. on 66-Nov-29 [67-Jan-10: 2C].
Billingsley, Thomas A. m. Kent, Alice M. on 67-Dec-16 [67-Dec-23: 2B].
Billington, Elizabeth (93 yrs.) d. on 70-Jan-28 [70-Jan-29: 2B].
Billington, Lillie Ford (1 yr., 4 mos.) d. on 70-Apr-14 [70-Apr-16: 2B].
Billmeyer, Sarah m. Welsh, Edward on 70-Dec-27 [70-Dec-31: 2B].
Billmire, George A. m. Miller, Lizzie on 66-Mar-20 [66-Mar-26: 2B].
Billmire, W. Houry m. West, Lidie on 67-Jan-3 [67-Jan-7: 2C].
Billmyer, Emily J. m. Griggs, William O. on 69-Dec-15 [69-Dec-18: 2C].
Billmyer, Kate S. m. Sweetser, George W. on 67-Nov-2 [67-Nov-8: 2C].
Billmyer, Mattie m. Webster, John A. on 69-Aug-8 [69-Sep-20: 2C].
Billups, A. M. m. Maguire, Mary E. on 67-May-14 [67-May-23: 2B].
Billups, George M. (28 yrs.) d. on 66-Nov-11 [66-Nov-12: 2C].

Billups, Hattie (1 yr., 3 mos.) d. on 68-Mar-17 [68-Mar-19: 2B].
Bilmire, Mary m. Lafferty, Samuel on 69-Oct-16 [69-Oct-21: 2B].
Bilson, Andrew J. (49 yrs.) d. on 67-Jul-14 [67-Jul-16: 2C].
Bilson, Elizabeth (20 yrs., 3 mos.) d. on 68-Sep-7 [68-Sep-12: 2B].
Bilson, Elizabeth (91 yrs.) d. on 70-Nov-7 [70-Nov-9: 2C].
Bilson, Henry (55 yrs.) d. on 70-Dec-27 [70-Dec-28: 2C].
Bilson, Laura V. m. Benton, J. Henry on 67-Dec-31 [68-Jan-4: 2C].
Bilson, Margaret d. on 68-Apr-4 [68-Apr-7: 2B].
Bilson, Mary (50 yrs.) d. on 69-May-10 [69-May-11: 2B].
Bilson, Virginia M. m. Wilde, Augustin A. on 68-Dec-22 [69-Jan-11: 2C].
Bilson, William m. Pitts, Martha Hildred on 70-Dec-6 [70-Dec-15: 2C].
Bilson, Zachariah (46 yrs.) d. on 69-Oct-24 [69-Oct-26: 2B].
Bines, Josephine m. Wheeler, George on 66-Aug-12 [67-Feb-19: 2C].
Bines, Maggie m. Klug, Henry on 70-Oct-26 [70-Nov-9: 2C].
Bingham, Carrie J. m. Knodle, Charles S. on 68-Nov-24 [68-Dec-10: 2D].
Bingham, William W. (6 mos.) d. on 68-Dec-13 [68-Dec-14: 2C].
Binnex, John H. (31 yrs.) d. on 69-Dec-7 of Consumption [69-Dec-8: 1H, 2C; 69-Dec-9: 2C; 69-Dec-10: 1H].
Binnie, Agnes D. m. McClymont, Alexander G. on 70-Oct-6 [70-Oct-10: 2B].
Binnie, Jeanie m. Stevenson, William N. on 70-Jul-19 [70-Jul-26: 2B].
Binnie, Marion W. d. on 67-Jan-9 [67-Jan-11: 2C].
Binnix, John H. m. Hart, Elizabeth on 66-Feb-1 [66-Apr-20: 2B].
Binswanger, David m. Pragg, Lizzie on 70-Feb-6 [70-Feb-9: 2C].
Binswanger, Simon m. Pina, Sarah on 67-Jan-6 [67-Jan-9: 2B].
Binyon, Lillie m. Hellen, John F. on 67-Feb-7 [67-Feb-9: 2B].
Birch, Clinton S m. Emich, Julia A. on 68-May-25 [68-Jun-6: 2A].
Birch, Joseph H. m. Conner, Mollie E. on 69-Nov-1 [69-Nov-13: 2B].
Birckhead, Carrie M. d. on 67-Nov-12 [67-Nov-14: 2C].
Birckhead, Catherine Augusta M (73 yrs.) d. on 68-Feb-15 [68-Feb-17: 2B].
Birckhead, Grace Hannah (10 mos.) d. on 67-Aug-31 [67-Sep-3: 2B].
Birckhead, James (79 yrs.) d. on 70-Dec-1 [70-Dec-5: 2C].
Birckhead, John H. m. Hall, Caroline M. on 66-Sep-6 [66-Sep-10: 2D].
Birckhead, Lennox m. Harrison, Mary Wilson on 69-Jun-3 [69-Jun-9: 2C].
Birckhead, Mary C. d. on 69-Dec-11 [69-Dec-13: 2C].
Birckhead, Olivia m. Hanway, G. William on 66-Apr-24 [66-May-3: 2C].
Birckhead, Richard (48 yrs.) d. on 70-Nov-6 [70-Nov-9: 2C].
Birckhead, S. Lizzie m. Martin, H. T. on 68-Jun-4 [68-Jun-8: 2B].
Bird, Mary Adelaide m. Hyde, Arnold on 66-Dec-13 [66-Dec-15: 2B].
Bird, Mary Ann m. Owens, Edward on 69-Nov-21 [69-Nov-27: 2B].
Bird, Rebecca F (75 yrs.) d. on 66-Oct-9 [66-Oct-17: 2B].
Birkett, Georgiana (26 yrs.) d. on 68-Jul-8 [68-Jul-9: 2B].
Birkhead, Laura P. (4 yrs., 9 mos.) d. on 68-Dec-20 of Measles [68-Dec-22: 2C].
Birmingham, Thomas (45 yrs.) d. on 68-Apr-24 [68-Apr-28: 2B].
Birney, Laura J. (25 yrs.) d. on 68-Jun-18 [68-Jun-19: 2B].
Birnside, Henry (76 yrs.) d. on 66-Mar-22 [66-Mar-24: 2B].
Birnside, Virlinda d. on 67-May-27 [67-May-28: 2B].
Biscoe, Ellen S. d. on 70-Jan-9 [70-Jan-11: 2C].
Biscoe, Jenny Y. m. Glasscock, W. A. [69-Mar-6: 2B].
Biscoe, Susie V. m. Denton, Basil B. on 68-Mar-26 [68-Apr-1: 2C].
Bishop, Amanda M. m. Pierce, John C. on 70-Aug-25 [70-Oct-6: 2B].
Bishop, Anna (34 yrs.) d. on 70-Feb-25 [70-Feb-28: 2C].
Bishop, B. M. d. on 67-Sep-13 [67-Nov-30: 2C].
Bishop, Eliza Eugenia (23 yrs.) d. on 67-May-19 [67-May-24: 2B].
Bishop, Ella m. Hall, William H. on 68-Jun-11 [68-Jun-18: 2B].
Bishop, Elvira m. Wilderman, John on 69-Oct-4 [69-Oct-16: 2B].

Bishop, Ethelinda m. Pratt, William H. on 67-Feb-25 [67-Mar-1: 2C].
Bishop, Fanny (26 yrs.) d. on 70-Apr-19 [70-Apr-21: 2C].
Bishop, George (69 yrs.) d. on 67-Jan-5 of Paralysis [67-Jan-7: 2C].
Bishop, Hester M. m. Humes, Thomas J. on 67-Jan-3 [67-Jan-16: 2C].
Bishop, James (52 yrs.) d. on 67-Jul-1 of Fall from flagpole [67-Jul-2: 4C].
Bishop, James H. (36 yrs.) d. on 68-Oct-20 [68-Oct-22: 2C].
Bishop, John E. m. Cromwell, Fannie A. on 70-Jun-7 [70-Jun-14: 2B].
Bishop, Mary (68 yrs.) d. on 69-Oct-24 [69-Oct-25: 2B].
Bishop, Mollie Florence m. Causmelle, William J. on 70-Aug-11 [70-Sep-14: 2B].
Bishop, Nannie E. m. Percy, William R. on 67-Apr-23 [67-May-11: 2A].
Bishop, Reverdy m. Smith, Mary E. on 68-Jun-25 [68-Jun-27: 2B].
Bishop, Sarah Ann (42 yrs.) d. on 67-Oct-29 [67-Nov-2: 2B].
Bishop, Thomas Wilbur (7 yrs., 10 mos.) d. [70-Jul-19: 2B].
Bishop, William (62 yrs.) d. on 70-Mar-30 [70-Mar-31: 1H, 2C; 70-Apr-1: 1H].
Bishop, William Lewis (20 yrs.) d. on 67-Aug-25 Drowned [67-Aug-26: 2C; 67-Aug-28: 1F, 2B].
Bishop, William M. m. Warner, Harriette A. on 70-Oct-13 [70-Oct-20: 2B].
Bishop, William R. m. Holland, Maggie E. on 70-Sep-29 [70-Oct-3: 2B].
Bishope, F. A. m. Miller, John on 68-Oct-23 [68-Nov-30: 2B].
Biskett, Jennie R. (17 yrs.) d. on 70-Jun-13 [70-Jun-24: 2C; 70-Jun-25: 2C].
Bissett, Mary Ann (59 yrs.) d. on 67-Apr-13 [67-Apr-16: 2B].
Bisson, Mary Jane m. Boyd, Amos K. on 67-Jan-1 [67-Jan-3: 2B].
Bitner, Joseph m. Zimmerman, Elizabeth M. on 70-Jun-21 [70-Jun-23: 2C].
Bittejar, William (49 yrs.) d. on 70-Nov-25 [70-Nov-29: 2C].
Bitter, Maria (78 yrs.) d. on 68-Nov-8 Burned [68-Nov-9: 1F, 2B].
Bittijer, Lizzie M. m. Maguire, Hugh M. on 70-Nov-22 [70-Nov-25: 2D].
Bittinger, Elizabeth A. (75 yrs.) d. on 68-Jan-10 [68-Jan-11: 2B].
Bittinger, Lizzie A. m. Rodgers, Howard P. on 67-Apr-16 [67-Apr-19: 2B].
Bitzel, Sophia R. m. Cromwell, Andrew J. on 70-Feb-16 [70-Feb-22: 2C].
Bitzer, William m. Morrow, Frances on 68-Aug-18 [68-Aug-20: 2B].
Bixby, Daniel (31 yrs., 2 mos.) d. on 66-Jul-12 [66-Jul-16: 2C; 66-Jul-17: 2C].
Black, Adeline Virginia d. on 69-Feb-27 [69-Mar-1: 2C].
Black, Archibald (40 yrs.) d. on 70-Nov-12 [70-Nov-14: 2B].
Black, Duncan (20 yrs.) d. on 66-Jan-11 [66-Jan-13: 2C].
Black, Eleanora (1 yr., 6 mos.) d. on 69-Sep-29 [69-Sep-30: 2B].
Black, Elizabeth S. (46 yrs.) d. on 68-Nov-18 [68-Nov-19: 2C].
Black, Herrmann F. (51 yrs.) d. on 70-Mar-19 [70-Mar-21: 2C].
Black, John S. m. Woodland, Lucy C. on 70-Aug-10 [70-Aug-29: 2B].
Black, Mary m. Clayton, Henry on 69-Oct-10 [69-Oct-20: 2C].
Black, Nancy (62 yrs.) d. on 69-Aug-28 [69-Aug-30: 2B].
Black, William E. m. Harman, Kate P. on 69-Jan-21 [69-Jan-25: 2D].
Blackburn, Emma L. m. Lefebvre, Edward C. on 69-Feb-4 [69-Feb-13: 2C].
Blackburn, H. H. m. Clabaugh, Georgianna on 69-Oct-11 [69-Oct-12: 2C].
Blackburn, James A. m. Frizell, Marion on 70-Nov-28 [70-Dec-13: 2C].
Blackburn, Lucie m. Walter, Charles H. on 66-Apr-25 [66-Apr-27: 2C].
Blackburn, Martha Harriet (48 yrs.) d. on 66-Sep-26 [66-Sep-27: 2C; 66-Oct-1: 1F].
Blackburn, Nancy Jane (32 yrs.) d. on 70-Feb-2 [70-Feb-3: 2B].
Blackburn, Samuel (48 yrs.) d. on 66-Sep-29 of Cholera [66-Oct-1: 1F, 2B].
Blackburn, William C. m. Hipsley, Mollie J. on 66-Sep-12 [66-Sep-18: 2B].
Blackeby, Margaret Emeline (1 yr., 2 mos.) d. on 70-Jun-13 [70-Jun-14: 2B].
Blackford, Thomas d. on 66-Dec-20 in Machine accident [66-Dec-21: 1G].
Blackford, W. H. m. Potter, Alice B. on 69-Oct-5 [69-Oct-6: 2B].
Blackford, William E. m. Whaley, Maggie T. on 69-Jul-3 [69-Nov-18: 2C].
Blackinbridge, Samuel m. Davis, Henrietta on 66-Apr-15 [66-Apr-18: 2B].
Blackiston, Harvey C. (7 mos.) d. on 67-Jan-30 [67-Feb-1: 2C].
Blackiston, Helen M. m. Perry, Israel J. on 69-Nov-17 [69-Nov-23: 2C].

Blackiston, J. H. m. Davis, Annie on 70-Aug-29 [70-Sep-16: 2B].
Blackiston, J. Harry (16 yrs.) d. on 70-Oct-19 [70-Oct-20: 2B].
Blackiston, Kate m. Bierbower, C. R. on 70-Apr-28 [70-May-4: 2C].
Blacklar, Cassie G. m. Taylor, R. Emory on 68-Nov-12 [68-Nov-14: 2B].
Blacklar, Henry Slicer (4 yrs., 7 mos.) d. on 70-Aug-22 [70-Aug-24: 2C].
Blacklar, Mary Alice (29 yrs.) d. on 67-Apr-24 of Consumption [67-Apr-26: 2B].
Blacklar, William Bolton (7 mos.) d. on 68-Aug-23 [68-Aug-24: 2B].
Blacklock, David (77 yrs.) d. on 69-Nov-24 [69-Dec-4: 2C].
Blackson, Elizabeth (60 yrs.) d. on 66-Jan-8 [66-Jan-10: 2C].
Blackstone, Thomas (55 yrs.) d. on 66-Dec-20 [66-Dec-22: 2A].
Blades, Caroline E. (48 yrs.) d. on 69-Feb-2 of Stomach cancer [69-Feb-4: 2C].
Blades, Emma Magruder (9 mos.) d. on 66-Jul-1 [66-Jul-4: 2C].
Blades, George W. (16 yrs.) d. on 66-Jul-10 Drowned [66-Jul-13: 2C].
Blades, Louisa d. on 70-Mar-17 [70-Mar-19: 2B].
Blades, Mary F. m. Staylor, Vincent on 68-Aug-12 [68-Aug-15: 2B].
Blades, Thomas m. Kirby, Susan E. on 70-Dec-1 [70-Dec-23: 2B].
Blades, Willie B. (1 yr., 3 mos.) d. on 70-Jun-1 [70-Jun-2: 2B].
Blair, Anna Belle (45 yrs.) d. on 66-May-26 [66-May-28: 2B].
Blair, George Bond (56 yrs.) d. on 68-Sep-10 [68-Sep-14: 2B].
Blair, Grant Lincoln (1 yr., 1 mo.) d. on 67-Oct-1 [67-Oct-2: 2B].
Blair, J. A. m. Wilson, Mollie M. on 68-Jul-15 [68-Jul-18: 2B].
Blair, J. J. m. Wissel, Annie M. on 67-Aug-13 [67-Oct-1: 2B].
Blair, John (25 yrs.) d. on 70-Nov-12 [70-Nov-14: 2B].
Blair, Margaret (32 yrs., 1 mo.) d. on 67-Mar-20 [67-Mar-21: 2C].
Blair, Virginia E. m. Correll, S. D. on 66-Mar-19 [67-Mar-26: 2B].
Blake, Benson m. Kyle, Jennie T. on 69-Dec-16 [69-Dec-17: 2B].
Blake, Cato (90 yrs.) d. on 70-May-17 [70-May-19: 2C].
Blake, Clara (63 yrs.) d. on 66-May-30 [66-May-31: 2B; 66-Jun-1: 2B].
Blake, Edward V. (31 yrs.) d. on 69-Apr-17 of Consumption [69-Apr-19: 2B].
Blake, George D. (25 yrs., 5 mos.) d. on 68-Aug-4 [68-Aug-5: 2B].
Blake, George E. (23 yrs.) d. on 68-Aug-29 [68-Aug-31: 2B].
Blake, Jane T. (46 yrs.) d. on 66-Jan-23 [66-Jan-24: 2B].
Blake, Joel M. m. Livermore, Diantha on 66-Oct-10 [66-Oct-16: 2B].
Blake, John (76 yrs.) d. on 70-Jun-20 [70-Jun-21: 2C; 70-Jun-22: 2C].
Blake, John L. m. Johns, Susie on 70-Feb-10 [70-Feb-12: 2B; 70-Feb-14: 2C].
Blake, John R. m. McCartey, Mary Ann on 66-Nov-8 [66-Nov-12: 2C].
Blake, John W. (59 yrs.) d. on 68-Apr-3 of Apoplexy [68-Apr-4: 2B; 68-Apr-6: 1E].
Blake, Lavinia (26 yrs.) d. on 66-Jun-6 [66-Jun-23: 2B].
Blake, Mary J. m. Bowen, Josiah S. on 67-Jan-2 [67-Jan-9: 2B].
Blake, Matilda m. Jackson, John on 66-Aug-8 [66-Aug-11: 2B].
Blake, Mollie C. m. Tall, R. J. M. on 68-Apr-14 [68-Apr-28: 2B].
Blakemore, Clara A. d. on 70-Mar-21 [70-Mar-28: 2B].
Blakeney, Charles W. m. Karr, Lenni E. on 70-Dec-25 [70-Dec-30: 2C].
Blakeney, Jessie May (3 yrs., 3 mos.) d. on 67-Nov-10 [67-Nov-15: 2B].
Blakeney, Lydia Thomas (11 mos.) d. on 66-Jun-25 [66-Jun-26: 2B].
Blakeny, Elizabeth R. m. Disney, Nelson K. on 70-Oct-20 [70-Oct-22: 2B].
Blakeny, Mary J. m. Holston, John J. on 70-May-26 [70-May-31: 2B].
Blakey, Harriet d. on 66-Oct-30 [66-Nov-7: 2C].
Blanch, James M. (26 yrs.) d. on 66-Jan-30 [66-Feb-3: 2C].
Blanchard, Bennington G. m. Marsh, Mary Geneva on 70-Apr-19 [70-Apr-21: 2B].
Blanchard, Mary Ann m. Wyant, Joseph on 70-Dec-20 [70-Dec-31: 2B].
Blanchard, Thomas H. (76 yrs.) d. on 66-Feb-23 [66-Feb-27: 2B].
Bland, J. H. m. Burton, Columbia T. on 69-Jan-7 [69-Jan-9: 2C].
Bland, Theodore F. m. Kirk, Ida E. on 70-Oct-20 [70-Oct-25: 2B].
Blaney, Francilla m. Bond, Stephen J. on 67-Aug-14 [67-Aug-17: 2B].

Blaney, Harry C. m. Dorner, Kate E. on 69-Dec-9 [69-Dec-16: 2C].
Blaney, James (22 yrs.) d. on 68-Jun-20 Drowned [68-Jun-25: 1F].
Blaney, James J. m. Wagner, Caroline on 70-Apr-28 [70-Apr-30: 2A].
Blaney, John Shilling d. on 67-Jul-26 [67-Jul-27: 2B].
Blaney, Susie A. (28 yrs.) d. on 70-Mar-18 [70-Mar-19: 2B].
Blankenship, Thomas H. m. Crawford, Letta J. on 66-Oct-8 [66-Nov-10: 2B].
Blankford, Willie D. (10 mos.) d. on 68-Oct-6 [68-Oct-7: 2C].
Blasser, Mollie E. m. Benton, Thomas T. on 66-Apr-17 [66-Apr-20: 2B].
Bleakley, Laura V. A. m. Bremker, Frederick W. on 66-May-24 [66-Jun-1: 2B].
Bleakley, Samuel H. m. Brannon, Anna on 68-Jul-16 [68-Jul-18: 2B].
Bleakley, Sarah (53 yrs.) d. on 68-Jan-7 [68-Jan-8: 2C].
Bleakley, William H. m. Gravenstein, Laura J. on 68-Jun-18 [68-Jun-23: 2B].
Bleany, John (78 yrs.) d. on 66-Jul-2 of Erysipelas [66-Jul-3: 1G, 2C].
Bledsoe, John R. Lee (1 yr., 1 mo.) d. on 70-Jul-26 [70-Jul-28: 2C].
Bledsoe, Robert H. m. Walker, Virginia M. on 68-May-11 [68-May-15: 2B].
Blessing, Andrew m. Couskie, Amelia on 65-Dec-24 [66-Jan-2: 2C].
Blessing, Maggie E. d. on 70-Feb-22 [70-Feb-25: 2D].
Blew, Joel (37 yrs.) d. on 67-Jan-28 [67-Feb-4: 2C].
Blick, Thomas H. m. Bates, Emma on 69-Feb-17 [69-Feb-23: 2C].
Blight, Samuel m. Hines, Cynthia A. on 65-Sep-16 [66-Jan-6: 2B].
Blocher, Tillie M. m. Chiles, William S. on 67-Nov-27 [68-Jan-15: 2C].
Block, Augustus (31 yrs.) d. on 67-Sep-21 [67-Sep-23: 2A, 4C].
Block, Matilda m. Hazard, Henry on 69-Jan-11 [69-Jan-13: 2D].
Block, Rose Alphonsa (23 yrs.) d. on 66-Mar-4 [66-Mar-6: 2B].
Block, Simon J. (76 yrs.) d. on 70-Jan-5 [70-Jan-7: 2F, 4F].
Bloice, Susan E. (26 yrs.) d. on 67-Oct-23 [67-Oct-24: 2B].
Blome, Gottfried (2 yrs., 5 mos.) d. on 69-Jan-4 [69-Jan-6: 2C].
Blome, Henry George (5 yrs., 2 mos.) d. on 70-Mar-4 [70-Mar-5: 2B; 70-Mar-7: 2C].
Blondell, Elizabeth m. Smith, Andrew A. on 68-Nov-16 [68-Nov-18: 2C].
Bloomer, Charley (3 yrs.) d. on 68-Nov-30 of Diptheria [68-Nov-6: 2C].
Bloomer, John W. (72 yrs.) d. on 68-Apr-19 [68-Apr-20: 1G, 2B].
Bloomer, Mary J. m. Pumphrey, Walter J. on 66-Jun-28 [66-Jun-30: 2B].
Bloomer, Willie (4 yrs., 5 mos.) d. on 69-Feb-25 of Diptheria [69-Feb-26: 2D].
Bloomer, Willie Perry (6 yrs.) d. on 68-Oct-29 of Diptheria [68-Nov-6: 2C].
Bloss, Maggie m. Stewart, Ebeneezer C. on 68-Dec-3 [68-Dec-28: 2B].
Bloss, Mary m. Hedeman, Henry on 68-Oct-25 [68-Oct-27: 2B].
Blottenberger, Philip (49 yrs.) d. on 67-Nov-21 [67-Nov-23: 2B].
Blowas, Sarah L. m. Mitchell, Emory G. on 70-Feb-10 [70-Feb-14: 2C].
Bloxom, Euphemia B. m. Brown, Aaron A. on 69-Jun-18 [69-Jun-21: 2B].
Bloxom, George William (34 yrs.) d. on 66-Aug-9 [66-Aug-31: 2B].
Blucher, John M. m. Berkins, Mary A. on 66-Oct-21 [66-Oct-27: 2B].
Blum, Fredrica (38 yrs.) d. on 70-Feb-15 [70-Feb-17: 2C].
Blum, John G. (47 yrs.) d. on 70-May-6 [70-May-10: 2C].
Blum, John Herman (28 yrs.) d. on 67-Mar-5 [67-Mar-6: 2C; 67-Mar-7: 2C].
Blum, Joseph A. m. Reilly, Mary Ann on 68-Dec-15 [68-Dec-22: 2C].
Blumingdale, Victor (38 yrs.) d. on 67-Dec-23 [67-Dec-24: 4B].
Blundell, Anthony (62 yrs.) d. on 67-Oct-18 [67-Oct-19: 2A].
Blundell, Mary Jane (2 yrs., 4 mos.) d. on 68-Aug-31 [68-Sep-1: 2A].
Blunt, Amelia G. m. Salgee, John on 69-Sep-21 [69-Oct-5: 2B].
Blunt, Anna Maria m. Reightler, Joseph on 69-Mar-7 [69-Mar-15: 2C].
Blunt, Mary Ann (49 yrs.) d. on 70-Nov-23 [70-Nov-24: 2B].
Blunt, Peregrine (66 yrs.) d. on 66-Dec-4 [66-Dec-6: 2B].
Boardman, Francis E. m. Whalen, Mattie J. on 68-May-5 [68-Oct-9: 2C].
Boarman, Mary Agnes (54 yrs.) d. on 66-Feb-17 [66-Feb-19: 2B].
Boarman, Sarah Frances (15 yrs.) d. on 70-Jan-12 [70-Jan-13: 2D; 70-Jan-27: 2C].

Boarman, Thomas M. (46 yrs.) d. on 70-Jul-6 of Typhoid [70-Jul-9: 2B].
Boarman, William J. m. Garner, Annie on 68-Jul-2 [68-Jul-3: 2B].
Bobart, Charles (79 yrs., 7 mos.) d. on 69-Sep-17 of Typhoid [69-Sep-18: 1H; 69-Sep-20: 2C].
Bobart, Eliza A. m. Despeaux, Antony, Jr. on 66-Feb-1 [66-Feb-6: 2D].
Bobart, Sarah Amelia (1 yr., 11 mos.) d. on 68-Dec-15 [68-Dec-17: 2C].
Bobee, Mary Agnes (22 yrs.) d. on 69-Nov-1 of Consumption [69-Nov-2: 2B].
Bobst, Harman (30 yrs.) d. on 70-Jul-20 of Heatstroke [70-Jul-22: 4C].
Bock, Henry W. m. Granruth, Carrie on 68-Sep-10 [68-Sep-14: 2B].
Bode, William, Dr. (63 yrs.) d. on 66-Feb-15 [66-Feb-16: 2B].
Boden, Jane (86 yrs.) d. on 67-Mar-11 [67-Mar-13: 2C].
Bodensick, Francis Dawes (4 yrs., 3 mos.) d. on 68-Dec-17 [68-Dec-18: 2C].
Bodensick, Martha J. (5 yrs., 9 mos.) d. on 69-Dec-2 [69-Dec-3: 2C; 69-Dec-4: 2C].
Bodensick, Sophia (84 yrs.) d. on 70-Mar-13 [70-Mar-14: 2C].
Bodge, Daniel (42 yrs.) d. on 66-Jan-21 [66-Feb-7: 2C].
Bodge, William F. (24 yrs.) d. on 67-Sep-7 of Yellow fever [67-Sep-16: 2B].
Bodicker, Louis d. on 69-Jul-1 Drowned [69-Jul-5: 1G].
Bodine, William B. m. Allen, Alice on 67-Apr-22 [67-Apr-23: 2B].
Bodkin, Marie m. Kelly, Martin on 70-Jun-6 [70-Jun-8: 2C].
Boehm, Dorothea Eleonore (47 yrs.) d. on 70-Dec-5 [70-Dec-6: 2C; 70-Dec-7: 2C].
Boehm, Lewis C. (53 yrs.) d. on 68-Dec-2 [68-Dec-7: 2D].
Boehme, Augustus, Jr. m. Davis, Mary Josephine on 69-Mar-4 [69-Mar-11: 2C].
Boehme, Charles L. (23 yrs.) d. on 68-Jan-7 [68-Jan-9: 2C].
Boerner, Emma E. m. Emerson, Edwin A. on 66-Mar-13 [66-Apr-14: 2B].
Boerner, Isabella V. m. Scharf, William J. on 66-May-3 [66-May-17: 2C].
Boerum, Magdalen (81 yrs.) d. on 67-Mar-28 [67-Mar-29: 2B].
Boeschee, Elizabeth Matilda Cl (1 yr., 7 mos.) d. on 70-Oct-21 [70-Oct-22: 2B].
Boeshe, William H. m. Miller, Wilhelmine on 68-Nov-16 [68-Nov-18: 2C].
Boetler, Irene d. on 67-Aug-27 [67-Aug-30: 2B].
Boetler, Sophia C. m. Stier, Winfield S. on 70-Feb-11 [70-Feb-23: 2C].
Boewing, Charles F. d. on 69-Jun-23 of Accidental Drug Overdose [69-Jun-25: 1H].
Bogart, Hanna Ann (62 yrs.) d. on 66-May-27 [66-May-28: 2B].
Bogdan, Arthur m. Sutton, Nannie A. on 67-Sep-19 [67-Sep-20: 2A].
Boggs, James (48 yrs.) d. on 69-Jul-10 [69-Jul-12: 2D].
Boggs, Maggie Breckenridge (1 yr., 2 mos.) d. on 66-Apr-23 [66-Apr-24: 2B; 66-Apr-25: 2B].
Boggs, William A. (52 yrs.) d. on 68-May-1 [68-May-2: 2C].
Bohanan, James S. m. Pentz, Maggie E. on 66-Nov-1 [66-Nov-3: 2B].
Bohanon, Mollie R. m. Tucker, James on 66-Jun-5 [66-Jun-7: 2B].
Bohen, James A. J. d. on 67-May-27 [67-May-30: 2B].
Bohn, Maria W. m. Keck, Peter on 65-Dec-31 [66-Jan-6: 2B].
Bohn, Mary d. on 67-Nov-13 [67-Nov-18: 2B].
Bohrer, Christiana E. m. Hammel, Francis Owen on 69-Aug-31 [69-Sep-11: 2B].
Bohrer, Fannie (3 yrs., 10 mos.) d. on 67-Apr-2 [67-Apr-4: 2B].
Bohrer, Maria Forest m. Orendorf, J. T. M. on 68-Nov-17 [68-Nov-19: 2C].
Bohs, Margaret Ann (3 yrs.) d. on 68-Aug-31 [68-Sep-1: 2A].
Bokee, Charles Marston (3 yrs., 3 mos.) d. on 66-Mar-22 [66-Mar-24: 2B].
Bokee, Jessie Lee (2 yrs., 3 mos.) d. on 67-Jun-28 [67-Jun-29: 2A].
Bokee, Mary A. (64 yrs.) d. on 67-Nov-9 [67-Nov-11: 2C].
Bokee, Morris H. m. Benson, Mary on 70-Jun-13 [70-Jun-16: 2B].
Bokee, Virginia Lee (1 yr.) d. on 66-Oct-3 [66-Oct-4: 2B].
Bokel, Catherine (43 yrs.) d. on 69-Jun-15 [69-Jun-16: 2C].
Boker, J. Wesley (28 yrs.) d. on 67-Apr-2 [67-Apr-6: 2B].
Boland, Annie C. m. Russell, David G. on 67-May-23 [67-May-28: 2B].
Boland, Bridget (48 yrs.) d. on 68-Dec-1 [68-Dec-2: 2C].
Boland, Cassandra M. m. Musselman, John H. on 69-Dec-15 [69-Dec-16: 2C].
Boland, James (58 yrs.) d. on 70-May-19 [70-May-20: 2C].

Boland, James Thomas (25 yrs.) d. on 67-Mar-27 in Railroad accident [67-Apr-5: 2B; 67-Apr-6: 2B; 67-Apr-8: 2B].
Boland, Mary (46 yrs.) d. on 70-Apr-26 [70-Apr-27: 2B].
Boland, Mary Ann (20 yrs.) d. on 69-Nov-4 [69-Nov-5: 2C; 69-Nov-6: 2C].
Boland, Thomas (58 yrs.) d. on 67-Nov-19 [67-Nov-20: 2C].
Boland, William F. m. Poole, Emma G. on 68-Feb-19 [68-Dec-24: 2C].
Bolden, Amelia m. Ireland, Issac on 69-Oct-28 [69-Oct-29: 2B; 69-Oct-30: 2B].
Boler, Nelson (26 yrs.) d. on 68-Jul-3 Drowned [68-Jul-7: 4D].
Bolgiano, Bettie d. on 69-Dec-9 [69-Dec-11: 2B].
Bolgiano, Charles Lee (1 yr.) d. on 66-Feb-28 [66-Mar-1: 2B].
Bolgiano, Emma Grace (1 yr., 8 mos.) d. on 69-Aug-15 [69-Aug-16: 2B].
Bolgiano, Francis W. d. [67-Apr-27: 2A].
Bollman, Ann Barbara (80 yrs.) d. on 66-Jan-30 [66-Feb-1: 2C].
Bollman, Ann Catherine (54 yrs.) d. on 69-Jul-15 [69-Jul-16: 2C; 69-Jul-17: 2C; 69-Jul-19: 1F].
Bollman, Francis De Mangin (1 mo.) d. on 70-Aug-16 [70-Aug-18: 2C].
Bollman, J. Moellinger m. Brunt, Lutie on 69-Oct-19 [69-Oct-21: 2B].
Bollman, James H. m. Beziat, Ellen F. on 67-Apr-19 [67-Apr-23: 2B].
Bollman, Laura C. (19 yrs., 2 mos.) d. on 69-Jul-15 [69-Jul-16: 2C; 69-Jul-17: 2C; 69-Jul-19: 1F].
Bollman, Mary Ruby (5 mos.) d. on 67-Jul-1 [67-Jul-3: 2B].
Bolsom, B. F. m. White, Mattee E. on 69-Nov-30 [69-Dec-6: 2C].
Bolton, Alexander d. on 66-Sep-22 of Consumption [66-Oct-11: 1G].
Bolton, Edward Lee (11 mos.) d. on 70-Jul-24 [70-Jul-27: 2C].
Bolton, Florence (5 yrs.) d. on 70-Jan-21 [70-Jan-22: 2B].
Bolton, Louisa m. Nelson, James M. on 69-Sep-13 [69-Sep-16: 2B].
Bolton, Maria (71 yrs.) d. on 69-Jun-30 [69-Jul-1: 2C].
Bolton, Rachel A. m. Bosman, Thomas E. on 68-Jan-23 [68-Jan-25: 2B].
Bolton, Tymer (68 yrs.) d. on 66-Dec-5 [66-Dec-7: 2B].
Bomberger, Laura Virginia (2 yrs., 6 mos.) d. on 68-Jul-1 [68-Jul-7: 2B].
Bomberger, Lillie May (1 yr.) d. on 68-Jul-3 [68-Jul-7: 2B].
Bomberger, Robert (49 yrs.) d. on 68-Mar-29 [68-Apr-3: 2B].
Bonaparte, Jerome Napoleon (65 yrs.) d. on 70-Jun-17 [70-Jun-18: 2B; 70-Jun-20: 1G].
Bond, Almira m. Jackson, George W. on 67-Aug-31 [67-Sep-30: 2B].
Bond, Ann C. (83 yrs.) d. on 66-Jul-20 [66-Jul-24: 2C].
Bond, Anna d. on 66-Feb-15 [66-Feb-16: 2B].
Bond, Arthur W. m. Cecil, Josephine on 70-Dec-14 [70-Dec-15: 2C].
Bond, Bessie (1 yr.) d. on 69-Jul-25 [69-Jul-28: 2D].
Bond, Caroline E. (39 yrs.) d. on 69-Aug-22 [69-Aug-25: 2C].
Bond, Clara Howard m. Brown, P. B. on 69-Jun-8 [69-Jun-14: 2B].
Bond, Emma m. Cooke, Winfield on 69-May-19 [69-May-21: 2C].
Bond, Emma J. m. Kreis, Harry P. on 66-May-8 [66-May-9: 2B].
Bond, George (27 yrs.) d. on 68-Sep-12 [68-Sep-14: 2B].
Bond, George M. m. Coard, Annie E. on 68-Jan-2 [68-Jan-4: 2C].
Bond, James (76 yrs.) d. on 66-Dec-28 [66-Dec-29: 2C; 66-Dec-31: 1G].
Bond, James m. Lyon, Lizzie on 67-Apr-22 [67-Apr-24: 2B].
Bond, Jane A. m. Adams, Benjamin F. on 68-Dec-3 [69-Jan-18: 2C].
Bond, Janie m. Mecaslin, Adolph A. on 70-Nov-20 [70-Dec-7: 2C].
Bond, John (56 yrs.) d. on 70-Sep-1 [70-Sep-13: 2B].
Bond, John m. Suter, Sallie A. on 70-Jan-12 [70-Jan-15: 2C].
Bond, John, Jr. m. Wood, Hattie A. on 68-Oct-15 [68-Oct-19: 2B].
Bond, John Henry, Dr. (82 yrs.) d. on 67-Jan-14 [67-Mar-14: 2C].
Bond, Joseph H. (33 yrs.) d. on 67-Jun-29 of Explosion [67-Jun-27: 1E; 67-Jul-1: 2B, 4C].
Bond, Joshua B. m. Carson, Sarah Lizzie on 70-Nov-8 [70-Nov-12: 2B].
Bond, Julia A. (29 yrs.) d. on 70-Apr-21 [70-Apr-22: 2C; 70-Apr-23: 2B].

Bond, Julia Ann (72 yrs., 9 mos.) d. on 70-Feb-27 [70-Mar-7: 2C].
Bond, Laura E. d. on 69-Oct-20 [69-Oct-21: 2B].
Bond, Laura H. m. Corbaley, Robert C. on 67-Nov-5 [68-Nov-7: 2C].
Bond, Lizzie Lyon (3 mos.) d. on 70-Mar-9 of Scarlet fever [70-Mar-10: 2C; 70-Mar-11: 2C].
Bond, Mary Ann (89 yrs.) d. on 70-Aug-3 [70-Aug-13: 2C].
Bond, Mary C. m. Smith, George W. W. on 68-Jan-9 [68-Jan-14: 2C].
Bond, Mary Catherine m. Namuth, Edward F. on 66-Jan-1 [66-Jan-8: 2B; 66-Jan-11: 2B].
Bond, Michael d. on 70-Jul-11 [70-Jul-12: 2B].
Bond, Sophie C. m. Davison, George W. on 66-Oct-25 [66-Oct-29: 2B].
Bond, Stephen J. m. Blaney, Francilla on 67-Aug-14 [67-Aug-17: 2B].
Bond, Susan m. Kelly, Dandridge on 66-Aug-28 [66-Sep-22: 2B].
Bond, Susan E. H. m. Mallory, Charles F. on 70-Jan-27 [70-Jan-28: 2B].
Bond, Thomas (2 yrs., 1 mo.) d. on 70-Feb-28 of Scarlet fever [70-Mar-1: 2C; 70-Mar-2: 2C].
Bondarant, H. m. Welsh, S. Fannie on 69-Nov-3 [69-Nov-6: 2B].
Bonday, Laura Eugenia (6 mos.) d. on 69-Nov-3 [69-Nov-4: 2C].
Bone, Helen Lindsay (64 yrs.) d. on 68-Aug-21 [68-Aug-22: 2A].
Bone, Hugh, Sr. (68 yrs.) d. on 70-Jul-5 [70-Jul-6: 2C].
Bone, William Greenwood (1 mo.) d. on 67-Sep-13 [67-Sep-16: 2B].
Bone, William W. m. Wells, Catherine A. on 66-May-24 [66-Jul-13: 2C].
Boneau, De St. Marcel Elizabet (45 yrs.) d. on 67-May-24 [67-May-25: 2A].
Bonham, Emily Cora (25 yrs.) d. on 68-Aug-10 [68-Aug-14: 2C].
Bonham, Horace m. Lewis, Rebeckah F. on 70-Jan-27 [70-Jan-29: 2B].
Boninger, R. C. m. Garner, Bettie on 70-Oct-13 [70-Oct-15: 2B; 70-Oct-17: 2B].
Bonn, Anthony (72 yrs.) d. on 70-Oct-21 [70-Oct-22: 2B].
Bonn, Anthony S. m. Ewin, Martha A. on 66-Jun-19 [66-Jun-22: 2B].
Bonn, Emma V. m. Wilkinson, Thomas C. [70-Jun-4: 2B].
Bonn, Joseph m. Kemp, Fannie A. on 66-Apr-26 [66-May-2: 2B].
Bonn, Lewis V. m. Owens, Kate on 68-Nov-25 [68-Nov-28: 2C].
Bonn, Phinnie m. Silverthorn, Benjamin C. on 69-Feb-11 [69-Feb-13: 2C].
Bonn, Samuel G. m. Hayes, Sallie on 67-Jul-15 [67-Aug-1: 2C].
Bonney, James E. m. Phillips, Mollie E. on 67-Aug-26 [67-Sep-2: 2B].
Bonsal, Williamson (6 mos.) d. on 67-Jun-28 [67-Jul-19: 2C].
Boogher, D. R. m. Timanus, Emmie on 67-Nov-19 [67-Nov-22: 2C].
Booker, Henry C. m. Skinner, Mary R. on 66-Feb-8 [66-Feb-22: 2B].
Booker, James W. m. Knight, Eunice E. on 69-Mar-1 [69-Apr-28: 2B].
Booker, Thomas L. m. Hargrove, Sidney Virginia on 68-Feb-25 [68-Mar-3: 2C].
Boon, Charles (54 yrs.) d. on 70-Feb-18 [70-Feb-21: 2B].
Boon, Charles Edwin (2 mos.) d. on 69-Feb-1 [69-Feb-3: 2C].
Boon, Daniel Steven (3 yrs., 8 mos.) d. on 67-Jun-26 [67-Jun-27: 2B].
Boon, Gideon m. Ross, Sarah A. on 70-Aug-1 [70-Aug-3: 2C].
Boon, James (26 yrs.) d. on 69-Jun-22 Drowned [69-Jun-23: 1H].
Boon, Maria m. Dowing, Walter W. on 70-Jun-23 [70-Jul-2: 2B].
Boon, Martha d. on 66-Jun-12 of Consumption [66-Jun-13: 2B].
Boone, Ella E. (13 yrs.) d. on 68-Sep-4 of Bilious gastric fever [68-Sep-10: 2B].
Boone, Francis d. on 66-Jun-25 Drowned [66-Jun-26: 4C].
Boone, Frank Ward (2 yrs., 3 mos.) d. on 68-Sep-28 of Congestive chills [68-Oct-2: 2B].
Boone, Isaiah W. m. Stanford, Matilda on 70-Jan-18 [70-Jan-21: 2C].
Boone, James Henry (37 yrs.) d. on 69-Jul-10 [69-Jul-12: 2C].
Boone, Laura V. (6 mos.) d. on 68-Jul-29 [68-Jul-31: 2C].
Boone, Laura V. m. Turner, Beverly W. on 66-Feb-12 [66-Feb-13: 2C].
Boone, Mary A. (58 yrs.) d. on 66-Jan-22 [66-Jan-23: 2C].
Boone, Mary Elizabeth (1 yr., 1 mo.) d. on 67-Aug-28 [67-Aug-29: 2B].
Boone, Mary V. m. Moore, John H. on 70-May-5 [70-Jun-6: 2B].
Boone, Resin (56 yrs.) d. on 66-Jul-11 [66-Jul-12: 2C].
Boone, Samuel (43 yrs.) d. on 66-Apr-8 of Apoplexy [66-Apr-10: 2C, 4C].

Boone, William Henry (19 yrs.) d. on 66-Dec-6 [66-Dec-8: 2B].
Boone, William M. m. Kennedy, Sally P. on 66-Jan-31 [66-Feb-1: 2C].
Booth, Charles C. m. Gootee, Mary V. on 68-Oct-22 [68-Oct-26: 2B].
Booth, Eliza A. m. Yerkes, William H. on 67-Sep-3 [67-Sep-10: 2B].
Booth, Emma d. on 68-Jun-14 [68-Jun-16: 2B].
Booth, George W. m. Eubank, Sue M. on 66-Feb-13 [66-Feb-15: 2C].
Booth, Henry Addison (1 yr., 2 mos.) d. on 68-Jul-14 [68-Jul-16: 2C].
Booth, Izola Mills m. Stevenson, John W. on 69-Mar-2 [69-Oct-19: 2B].
Booth, John Washington (8 mos.) d. on 70-May-5 [70-May-6: 2B].
Booth, Josiah C. (26 yrs.) d. on 69-Oct-12 [69-Oct-14: 2C].
Booth, Mary R. (46 yrs.) d. on 66-May-15 [66-May-16: 2C].
Booth, Samuel James (16 yrs., 1 mo.) d. on 66-Apr-15 [66-Apr-16: 2B].
Booth, Walter, Gen. (79 yrs.) d. on 70-Apr-30 [70-May-5: 1G].
Booth, William H. (61 yrs.) d. on 69-Nov-12 of Suicide (Shooting) [69-Nov-13: 1H].
Bootman, Willie (14 yrs., 10 mos.) d. on 70-Oct-30 [70-Nov-3: 2C].
Booz, Anna Maria (1 yr., 4 mos.) d. on 70-Oct-8 [70-Oct-10: 2B].
Booz, Benjamin (79 yrs.) d. on 68-Nov-21 [68-Nov-23: 2B; 68-Nov-24: 2C].
Booz, Mary C. (52 yrs.) d. on 70-Dec-27 [70-Dec-28: 2C].
Booz, Rebecca A. (44 yrs.) d. on 68-Oct-8 [68-Oct-9: 2C; 68-Oct-10: 2B].
Booz, Regina (44 yrs.) d. on 70-Nov-7 [70-Nov-9: 2C].
Booz, Thomas F. (4 mos.) d. on 66-Aug-28 [66-Aug-29: 2B].
Booze, John W. (1 yr., 7 mos.) d. on 67-Mar-13 [67-Mar-14: 2C].
Booze, Marcellus J. (48 yrs.) d. on 68-Jun-2 [68-Jun-4: 2B].
Booze, Marcellus J. m. Hayes, Mary Lizzie on 67-Jan-2 [67-Jan-4: 2D].
Booze, Sarah F. (16 yrs., 11 mos.) d. on 69-Jul-21 [69-Jul-22: 2C].
Bopp, George m. Seibel, Lizzie on 66-Jul-3 [66-Jul-12: 2C].
Bopp, Lawrence (52 yrs.) d. on 68-Jan-25 [68-Jan-27: 2C; 68-Jan-28: 2D].
Boram, Thomas (18 yrs.) d. on 67-Jul-14 [67-Aug-9: 2C].
Boran, John Williamson (5 mos.) d. on 66-Feb-15 [66-Mar-13: 2C].
Borck, Agnes (19 yrs.) d. on 66-Jun-2 in Carriage accident [66-Jun-6: 1G].
Borck, John Rudolph (60 yrs.) d. on 66-Jul-17 of Heatstroke [66-Jul-18: 1F].
Bordley, Elizabeth C. m. Frampton, Nathaniel on 69-Nov-18 [69-Nov-20: 2B].
Bordley, Hannah M. m. Riggs, John W. on 69-Dec-23 [69-Dec-31: 2C].
Bordley, Harry Brice (17 yrs., 2 mos.) d. on 68-May-9 [68-May-11: 2B].
Bordley, Hiram J. (28 yrs.) d. on 69-Jan-2 [69-Jan-4: 2C; 69-Jan-5: 2C].
Bordley, James, Jr. m. Chamberlain, H. E. on 68-Oct-22 [68-Oct-27: 2B].
Bordley, John Barron (2 mos.) d. on 69-Feb-2 of Brain inflammation [69-Feb-4: 2C].
Bordley, Margaret (88 yrs.) d. on 68-Apr-9 [68-Apr-10: 2B].
Bordley, Mary A. m. Manly, Thomas E. on 68-Dec-10 [68-Dec-19: 2B].
Bordley, Thomas H. (28 yrs.) d. on 65-Dec-10 of Yellow fever [66-Feb-3: 2C].
Bordley, W. C., Jr. m. Fitzgerald, Laura on 67-Oct-31 [67-Nov-2: 2B].
Bordley, William Clayton (4 mos.) d. on 70-Jul-17 [70-Jul-18: 2C].
Bordley, William J. m. Ward, A. Blanche on 68-Oct-14 [68-Oct-20: 2B].
Bordley, William Ward (3 mos.) d. on 70-Jan-31 [70-Feb-11: 2C].
Borgelt, Sarah J. m. Boyer, William H. on 67-Apr-11 [67-Apr-12: 2C].
Borneman, Charles H. W. (1 yr., 4 mos.) d. on 68-Aug-30 [68-Sep-1: 2A].
Borneman, Henry Francis (1 yr., 8 mos.) d. on 70-Jul-27 [70-Jul-28: 2C].
Borneman, John H. William m. Gontrum, Mary A. Frances on 66-Mar-28 [66-May-8: 2B].
Borneman, William G. (39 yrs.) d. on 67-Dec-2 [68-Jan-17: 2C].
Bornemann, Elizabeth m. Nitze, Charles on 66-Jun-2 [66-Jun-14: 2B].
Borrouich, Thomas S. F. (17 yrs., 5 mos.) d. on 68-Jan-28 [68-Jan-30: 2C].
Borton, Izetta m. Allen, L. A. D. on 69-Mar-18 [69-Apr-1: 2C].
Bosee, Cathrine (62 yrs., 8 mos.) d. on 67-Aug-28 [67-Aug-31: 2B].
Bosee, Mary E. m. Nyce, J. Crawford on 67-Dec-3 [67-Dec-4: 2C].
Bosley, Amon m. Hanchett, Loretta C. on 68-May-7 [68-Jun-25: 2B].

Bosley, Carrie Emma (4 yrs.) d. on 70-Mar-15 [70-Mar-17: 2C].
Bosley, Clara Bell (2 yrs., 3 mos.) d. on 66-Jan-17 [66-Jan-19: 2C].
Bosley, Elijah (89 yrs.) d. on 69-Jul-13 [69-Jul-14: 2D].
Bosley, Infant (5 yrs.) d. Burned [66-Aug-6: 1G].
Bosley, Jane d. on 70-Mar-26 [70-Mar-28: 2B].
Bosley, John Of G. (49 yrs.) d. on 66-Nov-5 [66-Nov-7: 2C].
Bosley, Mary Virginia m. Parker, William R. on 66-Sep-29 [66-Oct-2: 2B].
Bosley, William T. (26 yrs.) d. on 68-Apr-10 [68-Apr-21: 2B; 68-Apr-22: 2B].
Bosman, Arianna m. Claridge, William H. on 69-Apr-5 [69-Apr-9: 2C].
Bosman, Elenderrean Virginia (11 yrs.) d. on 69-Jul-4 [69-Jul-7: 2C].
Bosman, Thomas E. m. Bolton, Rachel A. on 68-Jan-23 [68-Jan-25: 2B].
Boss, Abraham (40 yrs.) d. on 66-Jul-9 of Yellow fever [66-Jul-19: 2C].
Boss, Henrietta (35 yrs.) d. on 69-Dec-21 [69-Dec-22: 2B].
Boss, Mary E. m. McKenna, Frank L. on 66-Apr-12 [66-Apr-20: 2B].
Boss, Napoleon (38 yrs.) d. on 69-Jul-12 [69-Jul-14: 2D; 69-Jul-15: 2C].
Boss, Willie M. (2 yrs., 2 mos.) d. on 69-Mar-5 [69-Mar-6: 2B].
Bosselle, Louis m. Brown, Susie P. on 68-Feb-4 [68-Feb-5: 2D].
Bosson, Edward P. (48 yrs.) d. on 66-Jun-29 [66-Jul-2: 2B].
Boston, Charles (85 yrs.) d. on 70-Feb-7 [70-Feb-8: 2C, 4F; 70-Feb-9: 2C].
Boston, Edward A. d. on 68-Feb-26 [68-Feb-29: 2B].
Boston, Eleanora (1 yr., 4 mos.) d. on 68-Dec-11 [68-Dec-14: 2C].
Boston, J. William m. Leatherbury, Elizabeth K. on 68-Aug-27 [68-Aug-29: 2B].
Boston, Mary A. d. on 69-Apr-15 [69-Apr-16: 2B].
Boston, Sarah Ella (2 yrs., 6 mos.) d. on 69-Apr-28 [69-Apr-29: 2B].
Boston, Shoff m. Williams, Eliza on 70-Jun-28 [70-Jul-9: 2B].
Bostwick, Camilla G. m. Kirsch, Noah on 69-Nov-18 [69-Nov-30: 2C].
Boswell, Anna M. m. Cook, Joel M. on 68-Feb-4 [68-Sep-21: 2B].
Boswell, Annie E. m. Ryan, Robert S. on 66-Nov-20 [66-Nov-23: 2C].
Boswell, Arabella (79 yrs.) d. on 67-Oct-26 [67-Oct-29: 2B].
Boswell, Frederick A. m. Ferney, Mary E. on 70-Mar-31 [70-Apr-8: 2C].
Boswell, James E. (54 yrs.) d. on 70-Jul-19 [70-Jul-20: 2C].
Boswell, Maggie E. (26 yrs.) d. on 67-Dec-4 [67-Dec-6: 2C].
Boswell, Thomas M. Walter (11 mos.) d. on 68-Aug-11 [68-Sep-11: 2B].
Bosworth, Edward Apsey (1 yr., 3 mos.) d. on 70-Jun-7 [70-Jun-8: 2C].
Bosworth, George A. (20 yrs.) d. on 70-Jul-13 [70-Jul-14: 2B].
Bosworth, Julia A. (37 yrs.) d. on 70-Nov-28 [70-Dec-1: 2C].
Bosworth, Willie P. d. on 67-Aug-3 [67-Aug-6: 2C].
Boteler, Beverly Waugh (1 yr., 9 mos.) d. on 70-Jun-17 [70-Jun-20: 2C].
Boteler, Charles R. m. Mayher, Mary A. on 66-Feb-8 [66-Feb-12: 2D].
Boteler, Harry Ernest d. on 69-Oct-2 [70-Jun-20: 2C].
Boteler, Prudence m. Elgin, H. C. on 68-Dec-22 [68-Dec-24: 2C].
Boteler, Robert F. m. Gantt, Emily L. on 69-Sep-18 [69-Sep-20: 2C].
Boteler, Sarah (77 yrs.) d. on 66-Feb-8 [66-Feb-9: 2C].
Botterill, Bell m. Marshall, John on 68-Aug-20 [68-Aug-22: 2A].
Botterill, William (66 yrs.) d. on 70-Aug-7 [70-Aug-8: 2C].
Bottrell, Olivia A. m. Gray, Hezekiah L. on 70-Aug-23 [70-Aug-27: 2B].
Botts, Ishmael H. (33 yrs.) d. on 66-Dec-8 [66-Dec-13: 2B].
Bouchet, Michael Eugene (3 yrs., 1 mo.) d. on 69-Sep-18 [69-Sep-20: 2C].
Boughen, Ann (35 yrs.) d. on 69-Nov-17 [69-Nov-18: 2C].
Bouice, Stephen m. White, Achsah Griffith on 68-Dec-24 [68-Dec-31: 2C].
Bouis, Charlotte Virginia (40 yrs.) d. on 67-Apr-12 [67-Apr-13: 2B].
Bouis, Fannie A. (27 yrs.) d. on 66-Mar-1 [66-Mar-3: 2B].
Bouis, John H. m. Neville, Nannie on 69-Jan-19 [69-Jan-21: 2C].
Bouis, Laura Virginia d. on 66-Dec-25 [66-Dec-27: 2C].
Bouis, Stephen, Jr. m. White, Achsah G. on 68-Dec-24 [69-Jan-14: 2D].

Boulden, J. W. m. Miles, Bettie on 69-Oct-20 [69-Oct-21: 2B].
Boulden, Jane C. (67 yrs.) d. on 68-Apr-26 [68-Apr-27: 2B; 68-Apr-28: 2B].
Boulden, Lucinda d. on 69-May-3 [69-May-4: 2B].
Boulden, Richard R. D. m. Chester, Anna M. on 69-Oct-19 [69-Oct-21: 2B].
Boulden, William J. (35 yrs.) d. on 68-May-27 [68-May-29: 2B].
Bouldin, Harry Gough (6 mos.) d. on 68-Feb-20 [68-Feb-28: 2D].
Bouldin, Helen E. m. Long, William T. on 68-Dec-17 [68-Dec-21: 2B].
Bouldin, Jane A. (59 yrs.) d. on 67-Jan-6 [67-Jan-7: 2C; 67-Jan-8: 2B].
Bouldin, Laura Frances (11 mos.) d. [70-Aug-1: 2C].
Bouldin, Mollie m. Gilbert, A. Preston on 70-Oct-6 [70-Oct-7: 2B].
Bouldin, Richard F. (10 mos.) d. on 68-Apr-30 [68-May-1: 2B].
Boureoich, George (72 yrs.) d. on 69-Nov-21 [69-Nov-23: 2C].
Bourguet, Cecilia m. Hartung, Frederick on 70-Oct-20 [70-Oct-24: 2B].
Bourke, Johanna (53 yrs.) d. on 68-Oct-28 [68-Oct-29: 2B].
Bourman, Louisa m. Rutledge, John E. on 69-Apr-15 [69-Apr-17: 2A].
Bourne, James J. (44 yrs.) d. on 68-Nov-26 [68-Dec-3: 2C].
Bourne, William L. m. Berry, Alice E. on 68-Mar-5 [68-Mar-7: 2B].
Boursaud, A. (61 yrs.) d. on 69-Feb-6 [69-Feb-17: 2D].
Bouse, Sarah Adeline (31 yrs.) d. on 70-Apr-30 [70-May-2: 2B].
Bouse, William B. (1 yr., 8 mos.) d. on 66-Aug-28 [66-Aug-30: 2B].
Boushell, John S. m. Newnam, Fannie E. on 68-Aug-13 [68-Aug-17: 2B].
Bouton, A. G. m. Littig, Ella B. on 70-Jan-25 [70-Jan-29: 2B].
Bowen, Agnes C. m. McLaine, Samuel R. on 69-Oct-1 [69-Oct-9: 2C].
Bowen, Almira J. (50 yrs.) d. on 67-Oct-11 of Consumption [67-Oct-12: 2A].
Bowen, Benjamin (43 yrs.) d. on 66-Mar-28 [66-Apr-6: 2B].
Bowen, Benson O. m. Dempsey, Lida on 68-Dec-8 [68-Dec-14: 2C].
Bowen, Charles Foley (5 yrs., 3 mos.) d. on 69-Jun-13 [69-Jun-14: 2B].
Bowen, Charles T. m. Thomas, Martha on 69-Jun-17 [69-Jun-19: 2B].
Bowen, Clarence Clifton d. on 68-Jan-26 [68-Jan-29: 2D].
Bowen, Eleanora T. m. Haynes, George H. on 70-Jan-6 [70-Jan-8: 2B].
Bowen, Ellen Fitzhugh m. Pue, Ferdinand C. on 66-Jun-12 [66-Jun-14: 2B].
Bowen, Emma m. Tase, Andrew on 66-Jun-21 [66-Jun-25: 2B].
Bowen, Emmeline Z. (2 yrs., 1 mo.) d. on 69-Jan-1 [69-Jan-2: 2C].
Bowen, Fannie Belle (11 mos.) d. on 70-Jun-25 [70-Jun-27: 2C].
Bowen, George V. m. Gorsuch, Mary F. on 70-May-3 [70-May-9: 2B].
Bowen, Gerard m. Cable, Mary J. on 69-Dec-30 [70-Jan-12: 2C].
Bowen, Godfrey W. m. Heim, Annie E. on 67-Sep-10 [67-Sep-16: 2B].
Bowen, Harry Lewis (4 mos.) d. on 69-Feb-4 [69-Feb-5: 2C; 69-Feb-6: 2C].
Bowen, James Thomas Norval (2 mos.) d. on 68-Nov-28 [68-Dec-1: 2C].
Bowen, John E. m. Kemp, Sarah E. on 69-Nov-17 [69-Nov-20: 2B].
Bowen, John T. (50 yrs.) d. on 67-Sep-7 [67-Sep-12: 2B].
Bowen, Joseph (20 yrs.) d. on 66-Apr-11 in Railroad accident [66-Apr-12: 2B].
Bowen, Joseph L. m. Curvel, Albina A. on 66-Jan-13 [66-Jan-20: 2C].
Bowen, Joseph M. m. Hanway, Eliza L. on 66-Jan-17 [66-Jan-27: 2B].
Bowen, Josiah S. m. Blake, Mary J. on 67-Jan-2 [67-Jan-9: 2B].
Bowen, Laura Carroll (1 yr., 1 mo.) d. on 66-Aug-26 [66-Aug-27: 2B].
Bowen, Leah K. (27 yrs.) d. on 68-Sep-18 [68-Sep-19: 2B].
Bowen, Louisiana C. (47 yrs.) d. on 70-Jul-29 [70-Jul-30: 2B].
Bowen, Mary (44 yrs.) d. on 69-Dec-25 [70-Jan-10: 2C].
Bowen, Mary Ann (29 yrs.) d. on 69-Sep-19 [69-Sep-21: 2B].
Bowen, Minnie m. Bradley, James L. on 67-Dec-9 [67-Dec-13: 2C].
Bowen, Samuel W., Capt. (49 yrs.) d. on 67-Jun-9 [67-Jun-10: 2B, 1G; 67-Jun-11: 2B].
Bowen, Sarah E. m. Dixon, James U. on 69-Feb-18 [69-Feb-20: 2A].
Bowen, Steuart Lee (9 mos.) d. on 68-Jul-10 [68-Jul-15: 2B].
Bowen, Susan Virginia (29 yrs.) d. on 69-Nov-1 [69-Nov-3: 2C].

Bowen, T. Virginia m. Weller, Charles on 70-Mar-17 [70-Apr-5: 2B].
Bower, Emma C. m. Heath, George W. on 69-Nov-26 [69-Nov-29: 2C].
Bower, J. Jacob (51 yrs.) d. on 68-Apr-5 [68-Apr-6: 2B].
Bower, Mary m. Stembler, George on 66-Apr-24 [66-Apr-27: 2C].
Bower, William J. A. m. Freburger, Emma J. on 69-Dec-2 [69-Dec-11: 2B].
Bowerman, James Biays m. Hammond, H. A. on 67-Aug-7 [67-Aug-15: 2C].
Bowerman, Sallie S. m. Hayward, William B. on 66-Jun-5 [66-Jun-6: 2B].
Bowers, Annie Noble (9 yrs.) d. on 69-Feb-2 [69-Feb-3: 2C].
Bowers, Edward (49 yrs.) d. on 70-Jul-28 [70-Jul-30: 2B].
Bowers, Frederick J. (1 yr., 11 mos.) d. on 68-Jul-30 [68-Aug-1: 2B].
Bowers, John (50 yrs.) d. on 68-Jul-21 Drowned [68-Jul-22: 1G].
Bowers, John E. m. Brown, Elmira on 67-Oct-16 [67-Oct-19: 2A].
Bowers, Lavinia m. Leaming, Reuben H. on 69-Apr-20 [69-May-21: 2C].
Bowers, Mary E. m. Wallace, David W. on 68-Dec-9 [68-Dec-11: 2C].
Bowers, Nathan (50 yrs.) d. on 68-Aug-5 [68-Aug-6: 2B].
Bowers, William Henry (38 yrs.) d. on 68-Apr-3 [68-Apr-4: 2B].
Bowersock, Harry Fleming (1 yr., 11 mos.) d. on 67-Apr-30 [67-May-1: 2B].
Bowersock, William H. (22 yrs.) d. on 67-Dec-25 of Gunshot wound [67-Dec-27: 1F, 2D].
Bowersox, A. Maria m. Drakeley, Henry W. on 69-Jul-6 [69-Jul-7: 2C].
Bowersox, James W. m. Stall, Mary A. on 68-Dec-3 [68-Dec-11: 2C].
Bowersox, Laura V. m. Groves, William F. on 70-May-25 [70-Jul-29: 2B].
Bowes, Matilda M. m. Starr, John J. on 66-Nov-20 [66-Dec-8: 2B].
Bowes, Patrick (48 yrs.) d. on 70-Jan-11 [70-Jan-12: 2C; 70-Jan-13: 2D].
Bowhan, Ella J. m. Tilley, A. J. on 66-Aug-16 [66-Sep-4: 2B; 66-Sep-1: 2B].
Bowie, Arispah M. (7 mos.) d. on 70-Dec-17 [70-Dec-19: 2C].
Bowie, Benjamin A. J. (5 yrs.) d. on 70-Dec-13 of Scarlet fever [70-Dec-15: 2C].
Bowie, Catherine (71 yrs.) d. on 68-Apr-21 [68-Apr-23: 2B].
Bowie, Elizabeth (70 yrs.) d. on 66-Oct-1 [66-Oct-2: 2B].
Bowie, Ella J. m. Pendleton, John B. on 70-Apr-13 [70-Apr-16: 2B].
Bowie, Henry C. (26 yrs., 6 mos.) d. on 70-Jan-31 [70-Feb-2: 2B].
Bowie, Libby (33 yrs.) d. on 68-May-25 [68-May-28: 2B].
Bowie, Mary Isabella (11 mos.) d. on 68-Jul-31 [68-Aug-3: 2C].
Bowie, Oden H. (2 yrs., 2 mos.) d. on 70-Jun-23 [70-Jun-24: 2C].
Bowie, Reuben S. (80 yrs.) d. on 70-Jan-15 in Railroad accident [70-Jan-17: 1G, 2C].
Bowie, Washington m. Schley, Nettie on 68-Jun-23 [68-Jun-25: 2B].
Bowie, William F. G. (6 yrs.) d. on 70-Dec-5 [70-Dec-6: 2C].
Bowker, John W. (29 yrs.) d. on 67-Apr-2 [67-Apr-5: 2B].
Bowling, Alexander m. Turner, Lizzie J. on 68-Jun-2 [68-Jun-4: 2B].
Bowling, Annie Isabella m. Rimby, Jacob on 67-Oct-14 [67-Nov-21: 2C].
Bowling, Charles O. m. Claridge, Annie M. on 69-Jun-14 [69-Sep-6: 2C].
Bowling, George W. (18 yrs.) d. on 70-Aug-12 Drowned [70-Aug-15: 2C; 70-Aug-16: 4E; 70-Oct-3: 2B].
Bowling, Infant (1 mo.) d. on 70-Feb-10 [70-Feb-11: 2C].
Bowling, J. William (36 yrs.) d. on 67-Aug-30 [67-Sep-3: 2B].
Bowling, James Philip (42 yrs.) d. on 70-Oct-12 [70-Oct-14: 2B; 70-Oct-15: 2B].
Bowling, Joseph m. Vaughan, Mary E. on 67-Mar-12 [67-Apr-11: 2B].
Bowling, Rosa m. Dyer, T. Baker on 67-Oct-29 [67-Nov-1: 2B].
Bowling, William F. (65 yrs.) d. on 66-Jun-10 [66-Jun-18: 2B].
Bowman, Alonzo m. Sweeting, Bell S. on 70-Feb-10 [70-Feb-14: 2C].
Bowman, Emma G. m. Myers, O. A. on 69-Mar-18 [69-Mar-26: 2C].
Bowman, Laura M. m. Hart, Robert J. on 69-Jun-28 [69-Jul-16: 2C].
Bowman, Mollie Standish (23 yrs.) d. on 69-Mar-1 [69-Mar-2: 2C; 69-Mar-3: 2B].
Bowman, William Edward m. Barry, Mollie Standish on 66-Dec-6 [66-Dec-12: 2B].
Bowne, Joseph D. (30 yrs.) d. on 70-Apr-22 [70-Apr-23: 2B].
Bowser, Joseph P., Rev. d. on 70-Sep-15 [70-Sep-16: 1G].

Bowyer, Ann J. d. on 68-Jul-23 [68-Aug-12: 2C].
Box, Charlotte E. m. Girvin, James A. on 66-Dec-5 [67-Jan-4: 2D].
Boyce, Albert G. (59 yrs.) d. on 70-Nov-26 [70-Dec-6: 2C].
Boyce, George P. m. Pettengill, Hattie B. on 69-Dec-24 [70-Jan-25: 2C].
Boyce, John m. Feefel, Annie M. on 69-Feb-11 [69-Mar-9: 2C].
Boyce, Margaret Ann m. Schell, Richard J. on 69-Jan-14 [69-Jan-19: 2C].
Boyce, Mary F. (29 yrs., 5 mos.) d. on 67-May-21 [67-May-23: 2B].
Boyce, Mary Lavinia m. Slyers, James W. on 70-Feb-3 [70-Feb-5: 2B].
Boyce, Thomas (75 yrs.) d. on 68-Jun-5 [68-Jun-6: 2A].
Boyd, Albert H. (26 yrs., 1 mo.) d. on 69-May-28 in Railroad accident [69-May-29: 1H, 2B; 69-May-31: 2C].
Boyd, Aloysius (28 yrs.) d. on 69-Sep-2 [69-Sep-3: 2B].
Boyd, Amos K. m. Bisson, Mary Jane on 67-Jan-1 [67-Jan-3: 2B].
Boyd, Edgar Howard (11 mos.) d. on 70-Jul-4 [70-Jul-8: 2C].
Boyd, Eliza Lee (5 yrs., 3 mos.) d. on 68-Apr-1 [68-Apr-3: 2C].
Boyd, Elizabeth (40 yrs.) d. on 70-Jul-21 [70-Jul-22: 2C].
Boyd, Harvey (10 mos.) d. on 66-Jun-26 [66-Jun-29: 2C].
Boyd, Hugh (51 yrs.) d. on 66-May-5 [66-May-7: 2B].
Boyd, Imogene J. (1 yr., 4 mos.) d. on 70-Aug-23 [70-Aug-26: 2C].
Boyd, J. W. m. Arthur, Maggie H. on 67-Jun-18 [67-Jun-19: 2B].
Boyd, James (44 yrs.) d. on 70-Apr-14 of Consumption [70-Apr-15: 2B].
Boyd, James m. Saumerig, Amelia M. on 66-Jul-19 [66-Jul-25: 2C].
Boyd, James m. Hawkins, Mary L. on 69-Oct-31 [70-Jun-25: 2B].
Boyd, John, Jr. m. Hopkins, Emma V. on 68-Nov-10 [68-Nov-14: 2B].
Boyd, Joseph B. m. Dempsey, Mary Louisa on 66-Dec-18 [66-Dec-24: 2B].
Boyd, Joseph H. (48 yrs.) d. on 69-Jun-20 [69-Jun-22: 1G, 2C].
Boyd, Katie R. m. Herring, Howard McK. on 70-Apr-19 [70-Apr-21: 2B].
Boyd, Lillia Halston (1 yr.) d. on 69-Jun-3 [69-Jun-4: 2C].
Boyd, Maggie A. d. on 70-Aug-13 [70-Aug-15: 2B].
Boyd, Maggie F. m. Hoffman, Charles T. on 66-Jan-18 [66-Jan-20: 2C].
Boyd, Mary Gertrude (9 yrs., 3 mos.) d. on 70-Jan-14 [70-Jan-15: 2C; 70-Jan-17: 2C].
Boyd, Mary J. d. on 66-Dec-27 [66-Dec-28: 2C].
Boyd, R. E. m. Smith, Lizzie L. on 67-Sep-10 [67-Sep-17: 2A].
Boyd, Samuel Keyser d. on 67-Apr-20 [67-Apr-25: 2B].
Boyd, Sarah (56 yrs.) d. on 70-Jul-27 of Consumption [70-Jul-28: 2C].
Boyd, Sarah Cummings (2 mos.) d. on 70-Aug-9 [70-Aug-10: 2C].
Boyd, Temperance Ann (63 yrs.) d. on 67-Aug-28 [67-Aug-31: 2B].
Boyd, William Edward (7 mos.) d. on 68-Jul-27 [68-Aug-10: 2C].
Boyer, Edwin m. Spalding, M. Edwina on 69-Jul-14 [69-Jul-20: 2C].
Boyer, Perry (48 yrs., 2 mos.) d. on 67-Mar-23 [67-Mar-28: 2C].
Boyer, Thomas E m. Phillips, Anneta on 68-Jan-7 [68-Jan-8: 2C].
Boyer, William Dulin (10 mos.) d. on 69-Aug-6 [69-Aug-7: 2B].
Boyer, William H. m. Borgelt, Sarah J. on 67-Apr-11 [67-Apr-12: 2C].
Boyer, William W. m. Yellman, Mary J. on 68-Nov-17 [68-Nov-19: 2C].
Boylan, Ellen m. Martin, James on 67-Jan-1 [67-Jan-5: 2C; 67-Jan-4: 2D].
Boyle, A. H. m. Crawford, Annie E. on 69-Jan-13 [69-Jan-15: 2D].
Boyle, Agnes (82 yrs.) d. on 69-Aug-6 [69-Aug-7: 2B].
Boyle, Ann m. Cahill, Patrick on 67-Mar-4 [67-Mar-7: 2C].
Boyle, Bernard d. on 68-Apr-5 [68-Apr-6: 2B].
Boyle, Clarence Augustus (9 mos.) d. on 69-Aug-6 [69-Aug-7: 2C].
Boyle, Helen J. m. Irwin, P. H. on 66-Dec-4 [66-Dec-11: 2B].
Boyle, Helen L. m. Hooper, William B. on 70-Jun-29 [70-Jul-11: 2C].
Boyle, James W. m. Cottman, Maggie E. on 70-Mar-17 [70-Mar-18: 2C].
Boyle, James William (4 yrs., 2 mos.) d. on 70-Apr-30 [70-May-2: 2B].
Boyle, John (47 yrs.) d. on 70-Feb-16 [70-Feb-17: 2C].

Boyle, John F. m. Ball, Joann E. on 66-Jan-16 [66-Jan-20: 2C].
Boyle, John H. (52 yrs.) d. on 66-Feb-20 [66-Feb-24: 2B].
Boyle, Lawrence (54 yrs.) d. on 67-Jul-23 [67-Jul-24: 2C].
Boyle, Martin (4 mos.) d. on 67-Sep-20 [67-Sep-21: 2A].
Boyle, Mary d. on 69-Dec-4 [69-Dec-6: 2C].
Boyle, Michael (56 yrs.) d. on 70-Oct-26 [70-Oct-27: 2B].
Boyle, T. A. m. Coleman, Ellen A. on 69-Jun-15 [69-Jun-18: 2C].
Boyle, Theresa MacKenzie m. McConnor, Phineas S. on 69-Jan-28 [69-Feb-2: 2C].
Braby, Henry (59 yrs.) d. on 66-Oct-20 of Paralysis [66-Oct-22: 2C].
Braby, Mary J. m. Walker, John H. on 66-Oct-15 [66-Oct-16: 2B].
Brackenridge, Elizabeth (72 yrs.) d. on 69-Jun-11 [69-Jun-14: 2B, 4D].
Bracker, John H. m. Young, Margaret A. on 68-Jul-6 [68-Jul-7: 2B].
Brackett, John S. m. Gilmour, Mary D. on 69-Feb-18 [69-Feb-25: 2D].
Brackney, Francis I. (2 yrs., 9 mos.) d. on 70-Nov-17 [70-Nov-19: 2B].
Bradbury, Robert R. m. Love, Mary Emma on 69-Aug-9 [69-Dec-28: 2C].
Braddock, Roberta V. (41 yrs.) d. on 68-Jan-12 [68-Jan-13: 2C].
Braden, Robert A. m. Sprucebanks, Martha T. on 67-Jul-19 [67-Aug-1: 2C].
Braden, William (43 yrs.) d. on 66-Sep-21 [66-Sep-24: 4B; 66-Sep-25: 2B].
Bradenbaugh, William Thomas (24 yrs., 10 mos.) d. on 69-Oct-20 [69-Oct-23: 2B].
Bradford, Anna M. d. on 69-Jun-1 [69-Jun-8: 2B].
Bradford, Jefferson D. m. Sumner, Helen on 68-Jul-21 [68-Aug-12: 2C].
Bradford, John L. m. Wirt, Emma R. on 70-Apr-12 [70-Apr-16: 2B].
Bradford, Lemuel S. m. Ensley, Mary E. on 69-Oct-5 [69-Oct-7: 2B].
Bradford, Luther m. Ridgely, Lou E. on 70-Nov-30 [70-Dec-9: 2C].
Bradley, Amanda Alice (2 yrs., 5 mos.) d. on 67-Oct-22 [67-Oct-23: 2B].
Bradley, Edward (10 yrs.) d. on 69-Dec-15 [69-Dec-17: 2C].
Bradley, Edwin Gassaway (14 yrs.) d. on 70-Sep-8 [70-Sep-10: 2B].
Bradley, Ella Virginia (6 mos.) d. on 66-Jun-9 [66-Aug-8: 2C].
Bradley, Hooper (40 yrs.) d. on 66-May-22 Drowned [66-May-28: 1G].
Bradley, James m. Rowe, Mary L. on 70-May-29 [70-May-30: 2B].
Bradley, James L. m. Bowen, Minnie on 67-Dec-9 [67-Dec-13: 2C].
Bradley, John Sinclair (3 yrs., 3 mos.) d. on 70-Dec-19 [70-Dec-21: 2C].
Bradley, Margaret (27 yrs.) d. on 66-Jul-2 [66-Jul-4: 2B].
Bradley, Margaret (67 yrs.) d. on 66-Feb-15 [66-Feb-19: 2B].
Bradley, Mary Lou m. Miller, Theodore K. on 70-Jun-2 [70-Jun-6: 2B].
Bradley, Sallie E. m. McShane, James F. on 70-Feb-10 [70-Mar-11: 2C].
Bradley, Susan C. m. Meehan, Michael H. [66-Jul-21: 2C].
Bradley, William Mitchell (1 yr., 1 mo.) d. on 69-Mar-2 [69-Mar-3: 2B].
Bradley, Willie Hicks (1 yr., 11 mos.) d. on 66-Aug-3 [66-Aug-8: 2C].
Bradly, John H., Rev. (29 yrs.) d. on 68-Apr-21 [68-Apr-22: 2B].
Bradshaw, Joseph Augustus d. on 67-Dec-27 of Chronic croup [67-Dec-28: 2C].
Brady, Anna m. Geoghegan, Stewart A. on 67-Sep-17 [67-Dec-28: 2C].
Brady, Bridget Mary d. on 68-Sep-10 [68-Sep-11: 2B; 68-Sep-12: 2B].
Brady, Catherine (94 yrs.) d. on 70-May-25 [70-May-26: 2B].
Brady, Elisha (27 yrs.) d. on 67-Oct-22 Murdered (Shooting) [67-Oct-23: 1F, 2B].
Brady, Elisha C. m. Mackenhamer, Mary E. Macken on 66-Nov-20 [66-Nov-23: 2C].
Brady, Ella Granger (2 yrs., 8 mos.) d. on 69-Dec-16 [69-Dec-18: 2B].
Brady, Frederick (14 yrs.) d. on 66-Nov-27 in Railroad accident [66-Nov-29: 1G].
Brady, Georgia M. m. DeFord, Thomas G., Jr. on 70-Jan-25 [70-Jan-27: 2C].
Brady, Greenbury (59 yrs.) d. on 68-Feb-9 [68-Feb-10: 2C].
Brady, Hugh A. m. Cookes, Susannah on 68-Nov-26 [68-Nov-28: 2C].
Brady, James (60 yrs.) d. on 70-Dec-25 Drowned [70-Dec-28: 4E].
Brady, James m. Burke, Emma on 68-Jun-30 [68-Jul-2: 2C].
Brady, James m. Mocler, Kate on 67-Feb-13 [67-Feb-18: 2C].
Brady, James Henry (1 yr., 7 mos.) d. on 67-Jun-15 [67-Jun-21: 2B].

Brady, James W. (9 mos.) d. on 69-Dec-3 [69-Dec-4: 2C].
Brady, Joseph J. m. Countess, Annie B. V. on 70-Apr-27 [70-May-6: 2B].
Brady, Kate (30 yrs.) d. on 66-Sep-11 [66-Sep-15: 2B].
Brady, Laura V. m. Adams, M. Washington on 70-Jan-20 [70-Jan-29: 2B].
Brady, Lizzia m. Hutchinson, John W. on 69-Oct-17 [70-Jan-17: 2C].
Brady, Maggie m. Naylor, H. Louis on 69-Nov-25 [69-Dec-15: 2B].
Brady, Maggie V. m. Fossett, Henry C. on 70-Jul-12 [70-Jul-19: 2B].
Brady, Mary d. on 69-Oct-26 [69-Oct-28: 2C].
Brady, Mary A., Miss m. Streper, William on 66-Feb-11 [66-Feb-27: 2B].
Brady, Mary Catherine (40 yrs., 5 mos.) d. on 69-Aug-19 [69-Aug-21: 2B].
Brady, Mary Loretta (3 mos.) d. on 69-Mar-3 [69-Mar-6: 2C].
Brady, Rose (1 yr.) d. on 70-Jun-24 [70-Jun-25: 2B].
Brady, Sarah J. m. Klunk, Francis A. on 66-Nov-27 [67-Jan-10: 2C].
Brady, Thomas (70 yrs.) d. on 67-May-17 [67-May-31: 2B].
Brady, Thomas m. McCann, Elizabeth on 67-Sep-3 [67-Sep-7: 2A].
Brady, Thomas E. m. Lyons, Kate on 67-Oct-24 [67-Nov-6: 2B].
Brael, Maggie N. m. Jackson, Charles M. on 70-Jan-6 [70-Jan-7: 2F].
Braidwood, Maggie J. (31 yrs.) d. on 69-Mar-25 [69-Mar-27: 2B].
Bramble, Anna Catherine (34 yrs.) d. on 69-Jan-13 [69-Jan-14: 2D].
Bramble, Charles H. m. Sanders, Permelia on 70-Mar-8 [70-Mar-10: 2C].
Bramble, John T. Ford (17 yrs.) d. on 69-Jun-2 [69-Jun-3: 2B].
Bramble, Solomon W. (36 yrs.) d. on 70-Feb-18 of Consumption [70-Feb-19: 2B; 70-Feb-21: 2B].
Bramhall, George W. m. Jacques, Annie M. on 70-Nov-22 [70-Nov-24: 2B].
Bramwell, Henry V., Dr. (63 yrs.) d. on 68-Apr-27 [68-May-12: 2B].
Branan, George T. (23 yrs.) d. on 66-Sep-3 [66-Sep-4: 2B].
Branan, Margaret (18 yrs., 2 mos.) d. on 69-Apr-5 [69-Apr-7: 2C].
Branan, Mary A. d. on 70-Oct-3 [70-Oct-4: 2B].
Brand, Alexander J. m. Steuart, Fannie Glenn on 69-Oct-20 [69-Oct-22: 2B].
Brandau, George A. (21 yrs., 10 mos.) d. on 66-Aug-19 [66-Aug-20: 2C; 66-Aug-21: 2C].
Brandel, John M. (26 yrs., 9 mos.) d. on 67-Oct-14 [67-Oct-15: 2A].
Brandel, Lizzie A. m. Hennick, William F. on 70-Nov-22 [70-Dec-6: 2C].
Brandel, Susan Virginia (2 yrs., 7 mos.) d. on 66-Mar-30 [66-Apr-9: 2B].
Brandon, Amelia m. Schulter, John M. on 70-Dec-8 [70-Dec-14: 2C].
Brandt, , Mrs. (23 yrs.) d. on 70-Aug-26 of Apoplexy [70-Aug-27: 4D].
Brandt, Anthony m. Waidner, Amelia M. on 70-Sep-1 [70-Oct-4: 2B].
Brandt, Frederick H., Capt. (60 yrs.) d. on 68-Sep-28 of Paralysis [68-Sep-29: 1F].
Brandt, Hannah (80 yrs.) d. on 70-Dec-18 [70-Dec-21: 2C].
Brandt, Henry (50 yrs.) d. on 70-Oct-19 of Apoplexy [70-Oct-21: 4B].
Branen, Ann (44 yrs.) d. on 70-Jan-26 [70-Jan-28: 2B].
Brannaman, Jane (77 yrs.) d. on 68-Jun-5 [68-Jun-6: 2A].
Brannan, Annie D. (1 yr., 8 mos.) d. on 70-Sep-30 [70-Oct-1: 2B].
Brannan, Eliza J. m. Nelson, Franklin P. on 70-Mar-23 [70-Mar-26: 2B].
Brannan, Eliza Jane (53 yrs.) d. on 67-Nov-22 [67-Nov-23: 2B; 67-Nov-25: 2C].
Brannan, George A. m. Allen, Emma on 69-Jan-6 [69-Jan-11: 2C].
Brannan, John (72 yrs.) d. on 70-Jan-7 [70-Jan-8: 2B; 70-Jan-10: 2C; 70-Jan-11: 2C].
Brannan, Kate m. Smith, D. L. on 70-Jul-25 [70-Sep-12: 2B].
Brannan, Rica (13 yrs.) d. on 67-Jul-14 Drowned [67-Jul-15: 1F].
Brannan, Rosa Frances (1 yr., 11 mos.) d. on 70-Aug-8 [70-Aug-9: 2C].
Brannan, Thomas J. m. Schritz, Annie G. on 70-Aug-4 [70-Sep-9: 2B].
Brannen, Thomas H. m. North, Mary A. on 66-Oct-10 [66-Oct-18: 2B].
Brannon, Anna m. Bleakley, Samuel H. on 68-Jul-16 [68-Jul-18: 2B].
Brannon, Hannah m. Carle, Charles on 65-Nov-23 [66-Jan-4: 2C].
Bransby, Charles E. (35 yrs.) d. on 70-Jul-26 [70-Jul-28: 2C].
Branson, Margaret L. m. Barnett, Charles F. on 67-Dec-17 [67-Dec-21: 2B].

Branson, Sallie A. m. Courtney, William H. on 69-Apr-22 [69-Apr-24: 2B].
Branson, Willie J. d. on 68-Nov-5 [68-Nov-7: 2B].
Brant, Joseph E. m. Tucker, Jannett on 68-Apr-12 [68-Apr-18: 2A].
Brant, Mary Anne m. Brooks, J. Harris on 68-Oct-27 [68-Oct-30: 2C].
Brant, William M. m. Elsenroade, Maggie on 70-Dec-12 [70-Dec-15: 2C].
Brashears, Charles W. (7 yrs., 5 mos.) d. on 70-Jan-31 [70-Feb-2: 2B].
Brashears, Ellen m. Knighton, Joseph G. on 67-Sep-5 [67-Sep-10: 2B].
Brashears, Frank m. Duncan, Emma on 67-Sep-26 [67-Oct-21: 2B].
Brashears, John T. m. Long, Isabella G. on 67-Feb-25 [67-Mar-2: 2B].
Brashears, Josephus Rous m. Barrett, Emily E. on 66-Dec-27 [66-Dec-31: 2C].
Brashears, Laura R. m. Whiting, Stephen R. on 68-Jul-2 [68-Jul-7: 2B].
Brashears, Luther m. Gaither, Mattie A. on 68-Dec-17 [68-Dec-19: 2B].
Brashears, Mollie C., Miss m. Oler, Alexander M. on 66-Feb-20 [66-Feb-27: 2B].
Brashears, Rachel Ann m. Bigham, John B. on 68-Oct-20 [68-Oct-23: 2B].
Brashears, Samuel Thomas d. on 69-Jan-27 [69-Jan-30: 2C].
Brashears, Virginia m. McCubbin, John D. on 66-Jun-7 [66-Jun-8: 2B].
Brashears, William Henry d. on 70-Nov-19 [70-Nov-21: 4C].
Bratt, James E. m. Doll, Helen S. on 69-Jul-5 [69-Jul-13: 2C].
Bratt, Sarah (83 yrs.) d. on 68-Aug-24 [68-Aug-26: 2B].
Bratzel, John (37 yrs.) d. on 67-Apr-17 [67-Apr-18: 2B].
Bratzel, William Harry (1 yr., 2 mos.) d. on 68-Sep-16 [68-Sep-17: 2B].
Braul, George (37 yrs.) d. on 68-Jan-26 of Suicide (Hanging) [68-Jan-27: 1F].
Braun, Christian J. (56 yrs.) d. on 69-Dec-22 [69-Dec-23: 2B; 69-Dec-24: 2C; 69-Dec-25: 2C].
Brauns, Emma S. m. Keidel, Louis J. on 66-Jul-11 [66-Jul-13: 2C].
Brauns, F. W. m. Murdoch, Susan on 66-Dec-18 [66-Dec-19: 2B].
Brauns, Henry m. Stewart, Isabella on 69-Nov-11 [69-Nov-16: 2C].
Brautigam, John m. Thomas, Louisa on 70-Dec-13 [70-Dec-31: 2B].
Brawner, Andrew (66 yrs.) d. on 69-Dec-23 [69-Dec-24: 2C; 69-Dec-25: 2C].
Brawner, Andrew H. (38 yrs.) d. on 70-Jun-4 [70-Jun-6: 2B; 70-Jun-7: 1F].
Brawner, Charles A. (38 yrs., 3 mos.) d. on 69-Jun-17 [69-Jun-18: 2C; 69-Jun-19: 2B].
Brawner, Daniel Walter (28 yrs.) d. on 66-Jul-6 [66-Jul-7: 2B; 66-Jul-20: 2D].
Brawner, George A. (38 yrs., 7 mos.) d. on 68-Mar-20 [68-Mar-21: 2A].
Brawner, Howard Bennett (11 mos.) d. on 66-Jul-7 [66-Jul-9: 2C].
Brawner, Joseph M. (20 yrs.) d. on 69-Aug-20 [69-Aug-21: 2B].
Brawner, Robert G. m. Smith, Alice J. on 68-May-26 [68-May-28: 2B].
Brawner, William M. (26 yrs., 1 mo.) d. on 67-Jan-10 [67-Jan-12: 2C].
Bray, Charles D. m. Compton, Josephine on 70-Jul-27 [70-Jul-29: 2B].
Brayfield, Thomas Bernard (6 yrs., 10 mos.) d. on 68-Dec-16 [68-Dec-18: 2C].
Brayfield, William Arthur (2 yrs.) d. on 68-Aug-14 [68-Aug-18: 2B].
Brayshaw, John m. Zimmerman, Lizzie A on 68-Apr-28 [68-May-4: 2B].
Brazier, Laura J. m. Sumwalt, Samuel R. on 70-Jul-27 [70-Aug-2: 2C].
Brazier, Rebecca Jane m. Brown, Michael on 66-Apr-16 [66-Apr-19: 2B].
Breach, Mary Jane (42 yrs.) d. on 70-Mar-9 of Consumption [70-Mar-19: 2C; 70-Mar-21: 2C; 70-Mar-22: 2C].
Breaton, Rosa m. Dunn, Willie C. on 66-Sep-12 [66-Sep-13: 2C].
Breaton, Samuel R. (27 yrs.) d. on 69-Jun-15 [69-Jun-17: 2C].
Bredemeyer, Albert Ernest d. on 69-Jul-4 [69-Jul-5: 2C].
Bredemeyer, Charles H. m. Evans, Mame on 68-Jan-7 [68-Jan-9: 2C].
Bredemeyer, Louise J. d. on 67-May-8 [67-May-10: 2B].
Bredy, Elizabeth (23 yrs.) d. on 68-May-11 [68-May-12: 2B; 68-May-13: 2B].
Breed, W. K. Mercer (1 yr., 6 mos.) d. on 67-Dec-18 [67-Dec-19: 2B].
Breeden, Charles Andrew (8 yrs., 11 mos.) d. on 70-Sep-9 [70-Sep-17: 2B].
Breeden, Emma E. (1 yr., 4 mos.) d. on 69-Jul-10 [69-Jul-14: 2D].
Breeden, Henry Eugene (5 yrs., 10 mos.) d. on 70-Aug-20 [70-Aug-26: 2C].
Bregel, Henry m. Snyder, Louisa E. on 70-Apr-4 [70-Apr-9: 2B].

Brehme, Emil Hartenstein (11 mos.) d. on 70-Jul-19 [70-Jul-20: 2C].
Brehme, Wilhelm Traugott (8 mos.) d. on 66-Jun-23 of Scarlet fever [66-Jun-26: 2B].
Breidenstein, Martin (66 yrs.) d. on 68-Nov-9 Drowned [68-Nov-11: 1F; 68-Nov-12: 1H].
Breinig, Catherine (51 yrs.) d. on 69-Jan-2 [69-Jan-4: 2C].
Brelsford, H. W. m. Dell, Lizzie S. on 70-Jan-5 [70-Jan-8: 2B].
Bremker, Frederick W. m. Bleakley, Laura V. A. on 66-May-24 [66-Jun-1: 2B].
Brenan, Sarah Chew (39 yrs.) d. on 67-Aug-30 [67-Sep-2: 2B].
Brendel, Hannah E. d. on 69-Aug-13 [69-Sep-10: 2B].
Brener, Nathaniel H. m. Harryman, Sallie F. on 67-Aug-15 [67-Aug-21: 2B].
Brennan, James d. on 70-Feb-13 [70-Feb-14: 2C].
Brennan, John P. A. (65 yrs.) d. on 70-May-9 [70-May-10: 2B].
Brennan, Thomas (23 yrs.) d. on 68-Apr-23 [68-Apr-24: 2B; 68-Apr-25: 2B].
Brent, Ida (1 yr., 9 mos.) d. on 70-Aug-14 [70-Aug-16: 2C].
Brent, J. L. m. Kenner, Frances Rosella on 70-Apr-23 [70-May-12: 2B].
Brent, Leila L. m. Hunt, Dunbar on 67-Jun-4 [67-Jun-6: 2B].
Brent, Thomas Leigh (6 mos.) d. on 69-Jun-12 [69-Jun-14: 2C].
Brenton, Francis J. (41 yrs.) d. on 66-Mar-9 [66-Mar-15: 2C].
Brereton, Mollie (4 yrs., 1 mo.) d. on 66-Mar-4 [66-Mar-13: 2B].
Brerewood, Sarah N. m. Jackson, William R. on 70-Oct-18 [70-Oct-25: 2B].
Brevitt, Eliza R. (69 yrs., 11 mos.) d. on 67-Apr-10 [67-Apr-12: 2C].
Brevitt, Joseph P. m. Kirby, Annie S. on 70-Mar-19 [70-Mar-24: 2C].
Brewer, Charles (62 yrs.) d. on 69-Feb-9 [69-Feb-10: 2C].
Brewer, Charles m. High, Camille on 70-Dec-6 [70-Dec-8: 2B].
Brewer, Fannie T. m. Brewer, George on 68-Jul-1 [68-Jul-3: 2B].
Brewer, George m. Brewer, Fannie T. on 68-Jul-1 [68-Jul-3: 2B].
Brewer, James R. m. Dorsey, Annie Worthington on 68-Jun-11 [68-Jun-12: 2B].
Brewer, Mary E. m. Beard, Issac B. on 68-Feb-27 [68-May-5: 2B].
Brewer, Philip M. m. Bealmear, Elizabeth A. on 69-Aug-31 [69-Sep-10: 2B].
Brewer, Samuel (4 yrs., 3 mos.) d. on 69-Mar-26 [69-Mar-27: 2B].
Brewer, William R. m. Markland, Sarah on 66-May-17 [66-May-22: 2B].
Brewster, Hannah M. m. Milliken, Issac [66-May-28: 2B].
Brian, Carvilla m. Benson, Oregon R. on 70-Oct-4 [70-Oct-10: 2B].
Brian, Edward N. d. on 66-May-1 Murdered (Duelling) [66-Aug-31: 2B].
Brian, Emma V. m. Wheeler, Thomas J. on 69-Aug-17 [69-Sep-14: 2B].
Brian, George W. m. Berry, Elizabeth A. on 66-May-28 [66-Jun-11: 2B; 66-Jun-15: 2C].
Brian, Hannah Maria d. on 66-Nov-27 [66-Nov-28: 2B; 66-Nov-29: 2D].
Brian, Jeannette (1 yr., 3 mos.) d. on 67-Jun-26 [67-Jun-27: 2B].
Brian, John G. (66 yrs.) d. on 67-Feb-1 [67-Feb-2: 2C].
Brian, Joseph L. (27 yrs.) d. on 70-Nov-20 [70-Dec-2: 4E; 70-Dec-3: 2B].
Brian, M. A. m. Creamer, Emma A. on 70-May-26 [70-May-30: 2B].
Brian, Rebecca A. (42 yrs.) d. on 66-Sep-21 [66-Sep-22: 2B].
Brian, Robert Eugene (1 yr.) d. on 68-Dec-14 of Brain congestion [68-Dec-15: 2C].
Brian, William Arthur (1 yr., 11 mos.) d. on 69-Feb-22 [69-Feb-24: 2C].
Brice, Annie B. m. Childs, J. W. on 69-Sep-7 [69-Sep-28: 2B].
Brice, Charles C. m. Springer, Justina C. on 69-Mar-2 [69-Mar-4: 2C].
Brice, George H. d. on 68-Aug-11 [68-Aug-21: 2B].
Brice, Susan (47 yrs.) d. on 69-Apr-4 [69-Apr-5: 2B].
Brickman, Charles Louis (8 yrs., 10 mos.) d. on 70-Oct-13 [70-Oct-17: 2B].
Bride, Elizabeth d. on 66-Jul-17 [66-Jul-18: 2C].
Bride, Hannah E. m. Davidson, F. B. on 66-Dec-18 [66-Dec-19: 2B].
Bride, Mary J. m. Mathews, Wilbur F. on 67-Jun-19 [67-Jun-21: 2B].
Bride, Maude E. m. Scott, David J. on 68-Apr-22 [68-Apr-25: 2B].
Bridener, Mary Land-Street (6 yrs., 7 mos.) d. on 68-Nov-25 [68-Nov-26: 2B].
Bridener, Philip (44 yrs.) d. on 70-Feb-23 [70-Feb-25: 2C].
Bridge, Maggie A. m. Bandel, J. Cook on 69-Jun-24 [69-Jun-26: 2B].

Bridge, Richard Warren (7 mos.) d. on 69-Jan-10 [69-Jan-12: 2C].
Bridges, Allen Chapman (13 yrs.) d. on 66-May-30 [66-May-31: 2B].
Bridges, George H. (33 yrs.) d. on 70-Apr-24 [70-Apr-26: 2B].
Bridges, Grace (9 yrs.) d. on 68-Nov-22 [68-Nov-23: 2B; 68-Nov-24: 2C].
Bridges, Helen J. m. Schmucker, Samuel D. on 69-Nov-16 [69-Nov-18: 2C].
Bridges, Munroe m. Diggs, Eliza on 70-Jun-22 [70-Jun-28: 2C].
Briel, Anna Catherine (43 yrs., 8 mos.) d. on 69-Jan-8 [69-Jan-9: 2C].
Briel, G. W. m. Radecke, Maggie A. on 69-Oct-19 [69-Oct-28: 2C].
Brierly, Maggie J. m. Creighton, George W. on 70-May-5 [70-May-10: 2B].
Briggeman, C. A. m. Burk, Julia A. on 68-Oct-13 [68-Oct-15: 2C].
Briggs, , Mrs. (42 yrs.) d. on 70-Nov-29 [70-Dec-1: 2C].
Briggs, Ann (74 yrs.) d. on 70-Feb-3 [70-Feb-4: 2C].
Briggs, Clara V. m. Alexander, Nathan on 69-Jul-4 [69-Jul-10: 2B].
Bright, Elsie Read (3 yrs., 8 mos.) d. on 69-Nov-29 [69-Nov-30: 2C].
Bright, Emma m. Dunn, Benjamin F. on 68-Jun-2 [68-Jun-13: 2B].
Bright, Emma J. m. Colton, Theodore on 67-Oct-1 [67-Oct-3: 2B].
Bright, John F. m. Dixon, Georgia Helen on 66-Dec-20 [67-Jan-17: 2C].
Bright, Laura V. m. Sherler, William H. on 66-Feb-15 [66-Mar-19: 2C].
Bright, Mollie E. m. Down, Charles B. on 66-May-3 [66-May-4: 2C].
Bright, Sarah A. (55 yrs.) d. on 68-Jul-15 [68-Jul-18: 2B].
Bright, Thomas m. Barnes, Hannah A. on 66-Dec-27 [67-Jan-1: 2C].
Bright, William T. m. Coleman, Laura V. on 69-Feb-15 [69-Feb-22: 2C].
Brigman, Sarah (53 yrs.) d. on 66-Jan-17 [66-Jan-19: 2C; 66-Jan-20: 2C].
Brine, Thomas m. Clayton, Elizabeth on 67-Dec-29 [67-Dec-31: 2C].
Briney, John E. m. Evans, Mary A. on 68-Dec-22 [68-Dec-30: 2C].
Brink, Henry A. D. (36 yrs.) d. on 70-Nov-14 [70-Nov-15: 2C; 70-Nov-16: 2C; 70-Nov-18: 4C].
Brink, Hugo A. d. [70-Jul-20: 2C].
Brink, Isabella (44 yrs.) d. on 70-Jul-19 [70-Jul-20: 2C].
Brink, Louisa A. D. (27 yrs., 4 mos.) d. on 67-Aug-25 [67-Aug-26: 2D; 67-Aug-27: 2B; 67-Sep-7: 2B].
Brinker, Annie C. (17 yrs.) d. on 66-May-26 [66-May-28: 2B].
Brinkman, Frederick William (23 yrs.) d. on 66-Dec-6 of Consumption [66-Dec-7: 2B].
Brinkman, Henry N. (76 yrs.) d. on 67-Oct-22 [67-Oct-26: 2A].
Brinkman, Mary m. Stoll, Herman on 68-Jan-28 [68-Feb-3: 2C].
Brinkman, Sylvinia m. Ide, Ernst on 69-Feb-17 [69-Mar-15: 2C].
Brinsfield, William K. m. Jones, Annie R. on 66-May-20 [66-May-23: 2B].
Briscoe, Alexander M m. Toland, Alviare on 68-May-14 [68-Jun-16: 2B].
Briscoe, Charles E. (5 mos.) d. on 70-Dec-26 [70-Dec-28: 2C].
Briscoe, Eliza m. Jones, George W. on 69-Mar-16 [69-Mar-31: 2C].
Briscoe, Ellen T. M. m. Briscoe, Warner L. on 69-Mar-16 [69-Mar-19: 2C].
Briscoe, Emma m. Mather, Nathan C. on 70-Jun-2 [70-Jun-10: 2B].
Briscoe, Nicholas (14 yrs.) d. on 67-Sep-4 Drowned [67-Sep-5: 1F].
Briscoe, Sally R. G. (9 mos.) d. on 69-Aug-18 [69-Aug-20: 2C].
Briscoe, Samuel W. (31 yrs.) d. on 66-Oct-25 [66-Oct-27: 2B].
Briscoe, Thomas (1 mo.) d. on 66-Aug-6 [66-Aug-16: 2C].
Briscoe, Thomas d. on 66-May-14 [66-May-16: 2C].
Briscoe, Vincent d. on 67-Aug-19 [67-Aug-20: 2B].
Briscoe, Warner L. m. Briscoe, Ellen T. M. on 69-Mar-16 [69-Mar-19: 2C].
Britney, Alice d. on 69-Oct-22 [69-Oct-23: 2B].
Britt, Gaynor (74 yrs.) d. on 67-Aug-8 [67-Aug-9: 2C].
Britton, Alethia m. Hutchins, Clarence on 68-Nov-7 [68-Nov-19: 2C].
Britton, Bettie E. (21 yrs.) d. on 70-Aug-5 [70-Aug-6: 2C].
Britton, O. Parks m. Green, M. Bettie on 69-Dec-7 [69-Dec-10: 2C].
Broadbeck, William H. (22 yrs.) d. on 66-Feb-25 [66-Feb-27: 2B].
Broadbelt, Martha (60 yrs.) d. on 67-Jul-13 [67-Aug-14: 2C].

Broadbent, Eugene A. Ignatius d. on 70-May-9 [70-May-10: 2C].
Broadbent, J. C. (56 yrs.) d. on 70-Mar-25 [70-Mar-26: 2B].
Broadbent, Mary Eugenia m. Cleary, Douglas M. on 67-Apr-30 [67-May-2: 2B].
Broadbent, William, Jr. m. McCron, Jennie on 66-Sep-4 [66-Sep-5: 2B].
Broadbent, William, Sr. (71 yrs.) d. on 70-Jan-18 of Heart disease [70-Jan-20: 2C; 70-Jan-22: 1G].
Broadbent, William Walter d. on 70-Jan-26 [70-Jan-27: 2C].
Broadfoot, Ann L. Louisa (7 yrs., 1 mo.) d. on 70-May-26 [70-May-27: 2B; 70-May-28: 2B].
Broadfoot, Cassandra (86 yrs.) d. on 66-Feb-18 [66-Feb-20: 2B].
Brock, Henry C. m. Copes, Mattie R. on 70-Aug-29 [70-Sep-1: 2B].
Brockenbaugh, Letice F. m. Thomson, Meredith D. on 68-Jun-3 [68-Jun-6: 2A].
Brockenbough, Louisa C. m. Price, Elfred on 69-Apr-28 [69-May-1: 2B].
Brockett, Cornelia M. m. Anderson, William H. H. on 68-Feb-19 [68-Feb-22: 2B].
Brockner, Henry d. on 70-Jul-16 of Heatstroke [70-Jul-18: 4D].
Broderick, Alice E. (34 yrs.) d. on 67-May-19 [67-May-20: 2B; 67-May-21: 2B].
Broderick, Francis (45 yrs.) d. on 67-Nov-9 [67-Nov-12: 2C].
Broderick, Henry Edward (5 yrs., 1 mo.) d. on 69-Mar-4 [69-Mar-5: 2C; 69-Mar-6: 2B].
Broderick, John William (5 mos.) d. on 66-Nov-11 [66-Nov-13: 2B].
Broderick, Mary A. m. Rochford, John J. on 67-May-7 [67-May-10: 2B].
Brodie, John (62 yrs.) d. on 70-Sep-8 [70-Sep-10: 2B].
Brodrick, Timothy A. m. Wimpsett, Josephine Cicely on 69-Dec-30 [70-Jan-1: 2B].
Brogdon, Henrietta m. Ash, Winson on 67-May-2 [67-May-8: 2B].
Broglen, Daniel m. Buck, Isabella on 67-May-14 [67-May-16: 2B].
Brognard, Martha E. (41 yrs.) d. on 70-Jun-6 [70-Jun-10: 2B].
Brokaw, George A. (11 mos.) d. on 66-Jul-23 [66-Jul-24: 2C].
Brome, Astoria Belinda m. Maxwell, John T. on 69-Dec-7 [69-Dec-11: 2B].
Brome, Virginia L. m. Lenhart, George E. on 68-Jul-14 [68-Jul-20: 2B].
Bromley, Mary T. (33 yrs.) d. on 69-Aug-20 [69-Aug-21: 2B].
Bromwell, Gussie m. Bushey, Jacob M. on 70-Jan-19 [70-Jan-19: 2C].
Bromwell, John A. m. Linthicum, Rebecca on 66-Feb-18 [66-Feb-22: 2B].
Bromwell, Marian m. Whitley, Joseph on 67-Jul-17 [67-Jul-22: 2C].
Bronbaun, Christopher d. on 66-Feb-11 of Lung hemorrhage [66-Feb-12: 4C].
Brook, George E. m. White, Anna H. on 67-May-16 [67-May-18: 2A].
Brook, Olivia A. d. [66-Sep-15: 2B].
Brooke, Katie Lee m. Kern, Bentley on 70-Dec-29 [70-Dec-31: 2B].
Brooke, Nannie S. m. McLaughlin, J. Fairfax on 67-Dec-5 [67-Dec-9: 2B].
Brooke, Richard H. (65 yrs.) d. on 68-May-9 of Heart disease [68-May-11: 2B].
Brooke, Samuel L. (65 yrs.) d. on 69-May-28 [69-Jun-4: 2C].
Brookhart, Emma J. (23 yrs.) d. on 70-Feb-7 [70-Feb-10: 2C].
Brookhart, Roseann R. (25 yrs.) d. on 66-Jan-21 [66-Jan-22: 2C].
Brookhart, Sarah Deen MeCall (23 yrs.) d. on 68-Feb-12 [68-Feb-14: 2C].
Brookhart, Sarah Jane m. Townsend, Jesse M. on 67-Dec-8 [67-Dec-10: 2B].
Brookhart, Thomas (28 yrs.) d. on 68-Sep-4 [68-Sep-5: 2A].
Brookhart, Thomas J. m. Hanna, Bettie on 68-Apr-23 [68-May-15: 2B].
Brookholts, Rachel m. Huttenberger, Charles F. on 70-Aug-22 [70-Sep-5: 2C].
Brooking, H. G. m. Lambden, E. P. on 67-Dec-4 [67-Dec-6: 2C].
Brooks, Adaline Rebecca (4 mos.) d. on 66-Dec-26 [66-Dec-27: 2C].
Brooks, Almira m. Stansburg, C. on 70-Feb-27 [70-Mar-2: 2C].
Brooks, Annie E. m. Johnston, Alton R. on 69-Oct-29 [69-Nov-15: 2C].
Brooks, Benedict J. m. Sausser, Elizabeth A. on 68-Nov-30 [68-Dec-14: 2C].
Brooks, Bettie (30 yrs.) d. on 69-Oct-14 [69-Oct-15: 2C; 69-Oct-16: 2B].
Brooks, Catherine m. Dorsey, Caleb on 68-Dec-24 [68-Dec-29: 2D].
Brooks, Charles Oliver (2 yrs., 8 mos.) d. on 69-Aug-9 [69-Aug-13: 2C].
Brooks, Clement (8 yrs.) d. on 68-Aug-29 Drowned [68-Aug-31: 1G].
Brooks, Correll E. m. Netre, Sarah on 68-Nov-25 [68-Nov-26: 2B].

Brooks, Dennis Grant (8 yrs., 3 mos.) d. on 69-Jun-6 Drowned [69-Jun-7: 1H; 69-Jun-10: 2C].
Brooks, Edward W. m. Stuchfield, Josephine R. on 67-Sep-25 [67-Oct-15: 2A].
Brooks, Elizabeth d. on 70-Apr-7 [70-Apr-8: 2C].
Brooks, Emma L. m. Thomas, Daniel on 70-Feb-17 [70-Feb-22: 2C].
Brooks, G. Edwin m. Tayman, Kate C. on 68-Jun-2 [68-Jul-11: 2B].
Brooks, George W. m. Doyle, Mary on 67-Jun-27 [67-Jul-1: 2B].
Brooks, Hallie Fenton d. on 66-Nov-2 [66-Nov-9: 2C].
Brooks, Hester A. m. Conway, George W. on 67-Sep-26 [67-Sep-28: 2A].
Brooks, Hester A. m. Conaway, George W. on 66-Mar-20 [66-Mar-22: 2B].
Brooks, Isaiah C., Esq. m. Wheeler, Mariah C., Miss on 66-Feb-25 [66-Feb-27: 2B].
Brooks, Israel B. (24 yrs.) d. on 66-Dec-6 [66-Dec-8: 2B].
Brooks, J. Harris m. Brant, Mary Anne on 68-Oct-27 [68-Oct-30: 2C].
Brooks, J. Thomas m. Neighoff, Emma S. on 67-Dec-19 [67-Dec-31: 2C].
Brooks, Jacob (88 yrs.) d. on 67-Feb-21 [67-Feb-23: 2C].
Brooks, James M. m. Hutchinson, Virginia on 70-Jun-8 [70-Jun-28: 2C].
Brooks, Jane (1 yr., 4 mos.) d. on 69-Mar-8 [69-Mar-9: 2C].
Brooks, Jane (75 yrs.) d. on 70-May-30 [70-May-31: 2B; 70-Jun-1: 2B].
Brooks, Jemima (67 yrs.) d. on 69-Jan-31 [69-Feb-1: 2C].
Brooks, John d. on 68-Apr-30 of Snakebite [68-May-1: 1F].
Brooks, John (65 yrs.) d. on 66-Apr-3 [66-Apr-5: 2B].
Brooks, John (66 yrs.) d. on 66-Oct-2 [66-Oct-4: 1G].
Brooks, John H. m. Kennedy, Sarah R. on 67-Nov-26 [67-Dec-9: 2B].
Brooks, Joseph (74 yrs.) d. on 70-Jan-31 [70-Feb-1: 2B; 70-Feb-2: 2B].
Brooks, Joshua m. Yingling, Lummie on 66-Apr-12 [66-Apr-21: 2B].
Brooks, Josie m. Richardson, C. A. on 70-Jan-12 [70-Jan-14: 2C].
Brooks, Lucy A. m. Crisp, Edward T. on 68-Apr-8 [68-Apr-17: 2B].
Brooks, Margaret A. (27 yrs.) d. on 70-Apr-11 of Apoplexy [70-Apr-13: 1E, 2B].
Brooks, Martha m. Stizler, George W. on 67-Feb-3 [67-Mar-6: 2C].
Brooks, Mary m. McLernan, Matthew on 67-Dec-19 [67-Dec-24: 2B].
Brooks, Mary Augusta (9 yrs.) d. on 66-Jan-11 [66-Jan-12: 2C].
Brooks, Mary H. (61 yrs.) d. on 68-Dec-18 [68-Dec-21: 2B].
Brooks, N. C. (41 yrs.) d. on 69-Oct-17 [69-Oct-18: 2C].
Brooks, N. C. m. Crump, Christiana Octavia on 67-Jun-26 [67-Jun-27: 2B].
Brooks, Nathan C., Jr. (26 yrs.) d. on 69-Nov-16 of Typhoid pneumonia [69-Nov-17: 2C; 69-Nov-18: 2C].
Brooks, Richard H. m. Haines, Emma on 66-Aug-14 [66-Aug-17: 2C].
Brooks, Richard, Sr. (54 yrs.) d. on 70-Jul-4 [70-Jul-6: 2C].
Brooks, Robert Henry (11 mos.) d. on 67-Aug-4 [67-Aug-5: 2B].
Brooks, Robert S. m. Kurtze, Sarah L. on 69-Dec-29 [70-Jan-4: 2C].
Brooks, Samuel m. Hodges, Elizabeth on 66-Jun-7 [66-Jun-9: 2B].
Brooks, Sarah A. m. Smith, Joseph Merriken on 67-Oct-17 [67-Oct-19: 2A].
Brooks, Sarah Amanda (18 yrs., 6 mos.) d. on 66-Sep-2 [66-Sep-4: 2B].
Brooks, Sarah Jane m. Clazey, Albert on 68-Aug-12 [68-Aug-18: 2B].
Brooks, Thomas (40 yrs.) d. on 69-Oct-20 [69-Oct-21: 2B].
Brooks, Thomas D. m. Kelley, Mary O. on 68-Sep-15 [68-Sep-17: 2B].
Brooks, Thomas Pitman (9 mos.) d. on 69-Aug-23 [69-Aug-28: 2B].
Brooks, William m. Cole, Susie on 68-Nov-18 [68-Nov-21: 2C].
Brooks, William H. m. Pierce, Ella on 70-Dec-7 [70-Dec-12: 2C].
Brooks, William S. (56 yrs.) d. on 66-Apr-8 [66-Apr-10: 2C].
Brooks, William W. C. m. Weaver, Mary J. on 67-Apr-11 [67-Apr-24: 2B].
Brooks, Willie (2 yrs., 4 mos.) d. on 70-Feb-9 [70-Feb-10: 2C].
Broom, Laura Virginia d. on 67-Nov-29 [67-Nov-30: 2C].
Brophy, John P. m. Tyler, Bettie W. on 66-Sep-11 [66-Sep-13: 2C].
Brosanna, Eliza A. m. Stansfield, Benjamin L. on 70-Jan-26 [70-Jan-29: 2B].
Brosius, Sophie m. Sauer, Christian on 69-May-2 [69-May-4: 2B].

Brotzel, Jacob (68 yrs.) d. on 69-Nov-27 [69-Nov-29: 2C; 69-Nov-30: 2C].
Broud, Kate F. m. Williams, Francis on 66-Apr-5 [66-Apr-7: 2B].
Broughton, Henrietta (76 yrs.) d. on 69-Apr-24 [69-Apr-26: 2C].
Broughton, Samuel H., Capt. (38 yrs.) d. on 68-Feb-27 [68-Mar-7: 2C].
Broumel, Laura V. m. King, Andrew J. on 68-Apr-30 [68-May-2: 2C].
Broumel, Thomas O. (21 yrs.) d. on 66-Nov-28 [66-Nov-29: 2B; 66-Dec-3: 1F].
Brower, Wilbur G. m. Hopps, Sadie on 69-Dec-23 [70-Aug-9: 2C].
Brown, Aaron A. m. McCabe, Eliza J. on 67-Feb-21 [67-Feb-25: 2C].
Brown, Aaron A. m. Bloxom, Euphemia B. on 69-Jun-18 [69-Jun-21: 2B].
Brown, Abel, Jr. m. Henry, Charlotte Ann on 69-Aug-24 [69-Sep-6: 2C].
Brown, Alexander (9 mos.) d. on 66-Aug-14 [66-Aug-16: 2C].
Brown, Alice Leonora (5 mos.) d. on 68-Jul-9 [68-Jul-11: 2B].
Brown, Amelia T. m. Taylor, D. Wesley on 70-Nov-30 [70-Dec-7: 2C].
Brown, Ann (85 yrs.) d. on 70-Apr-26 [70-Apr-28: 2B].
Brown, Annie R. m. Hissey, John T. on 68-Jan-2 [68-Jan-4: 2C].
Brown, Arthur m. Horney, Mary R. on 70-Nov-7 [70-Dec-13: 2C].
Brown, B. Peyton m. Dickson, Harriet A. on 69-Apr-20 [69-Apr-21: 2A].
Brown, Benjamin (63 yrs.) d. on 66-Oct-5 [66-Oct-19: 2B; 66-Nov-15: 2C].
Brown, Benjamin B. m. Schultze, Lena on 70-Jan-1 [70-Jan-6: 2C].
Brown, Calvert m. Woodall, Priscilla E. on 69-Jul-6 [69-Jul-7: 2C].
Brown, Carrie S. m. O'Connell, William H. on 68-Apr-13 [68-Apr-22: 2B].
Brown, Cassandra V. (55 yrs.) d. on 69-Aug-30 [69-Aug-31: 2B; 69-Sep-2: 2B].
Brown, Charles m. Wheat, Julia A. on 67-Nov-12 [67-Nov-14: 2B].
Brown, Charles Henry d. on 67-Nov-12 Murdered (Shooting) [67-Nov-25: 1F].
Brown, Charles J., Col. (43 yrs.) d. on 68-Feb-3 of Pneumonia [68-Feb-4: 2C; 68-Feb-5: 2C, 1G; 68-Feb-6: 1G].
Brown, Charles O. (23 yrs.) d. on 67-May-31 [67-Jun-1: 2B].
Brown, Columbine A. m. Lang, Philip on 69-Jun-22 [69-Jun-26: 2B].
Brown, Costello C. (22 yrs.) d. on 69-Feb-1 of Typhoid [69-Feb-9: 2C].
Brown, Daniel (14 yrs.) d. on 68-Aug-10 of Heatstroke [68-Aug-11: 1G].
Brown, David (48 yrs.) d. on 67-Feb-18 [67-Feb-19: 2C].
Brown, David Martin (6 yrs., 7 mos.) d. on 67-Sep-29 [67-Oct-1: 2B].
Brown, David P. m. Jones, Mattie J. on 70-May-24 [70-May-27: 2B].
Brown, Diana d. on 66-Dec-19 [66-Dec-20: 2B].
Brown, Dollie A. m. Busey, William M. on 68-Oct-28 [68-Oct-31: 2B].
Brown, Edward (21 yrs.) d. on 70-Apr-5 [70-Apr-7: 2B].
Brown, Eleanor m. Burris, James H. on 66-Apr-18 [66-Apr-28: 2A].
Brown, Eliza J. (28 yrs.) d. on 68-Jun-17 [68-Jun-20: 2B].
Brown, Eliza J. m. Stull, Henry on 70-Feb-17 [70-Feb-21: 2B].
Brown, Elizabeth (73 yrs.) d. on 67-Apr-10 [67-Apr-11: 2B].
Brown, Elizabeth (47 yrs.) d. on 66-Oct-16 [66-Oct-17: 2B].
Brown, Elizabeth (80 yrs.) d. on 68-Nov-29 [69-Jan-18: 2D].
Brown, Elizabeth A. d. on 70-Sep-12 [70-Sep-14: 2B].
Brown, Elizabeth Ann (19 yrs., 4 mos.) d. on 68-Nov-21 [68-Nov-23: 2B].
Brown, Elizabeth Loretto (18 yrs.) d. on 66-Jul-3 [66-Jul-4: 2B].
Brown, Elizabeth Roberta (8 mos.) d. on 69-Jul-21 [69-Jul-22: 2C].
Brown, Ella May (16 yrs.) d. on 70-Apr-14 [70-Apr-15: 2B].
Brown, Ella Whedbee (9 yrs.) d. on 68-Mar-24 of Pneumonia [68-Mar-26: 2B].
Brown, Elmira m. Bowers, John E. on 67-Oct-16 [67-Oct-19: 2A].
Brown, Emily Jane (38 yrs.) d. on 70-May-1 [70-May-2: 2B; 70-May-3: 2B].
Brown, Emma T. m. Bell, Thomas B. on 66-Feb-14 [66-Feb-16: 2B; 66-Feb-17: 2B].
Brown, Enoch S. m. Bell, Martha J. on 68-Jun-25 [68-Jun-30: 2B].
Brown, Estelle d. on 70-Feb-9 [70-Feb-10: 2C].
Brown, Frances D. (20 yrs.) d. on 67-Sep-29 [67-Sep-30: 2B].
Brown, G. H. m. Hartsook, Rachel A. on 70-Jul-28 [70-Jul-30: 2B].

Brown, Garrett (77 yrs.) d. on 70-Jun-20 [70-Jun-21: 2C].
Brown, George (86 yrs.) d. on 67-Jan-21 of Paralysis [67-Jan-22: 2C; 67-Jan-23: 1G].
Brown, George m. Lanpher, Maggie on 67-Mar-18 [67-Mar-28: 2B].
Brown, George m. Lee, Jennie on 70-Jan-17 [70-Jun-18: 2B].
Brown, George A. (67 yrs.) d. on 70-May-11 [70-May-16: 2B].
Brown, George W. m. Holter, Mollie F. on 70-Jun-5 [70-Jun-22: 2C].
Brown, Helen Monona (3 yrs., 6 mos.) d. on 70-Jun-26 [70-Jun-27: 2C].
Brown, Henrietta H. (29 yrs.) d. on 67-Feb-4 [67-Feb-5: 2C].
Brown, Henry d. on 67-Jun-15 [67-Jun-20: 3C].
Brown, Henry (22 yrs.) d. Drowned [67-Jul-4: 1F].
Brown, Henry (65 yrs.) d. on 69-Aug-6 in Stevedore accident [69-Aug-7: 1H].
Brown, Henry m. Whittington, Virginia M. on 66-Jun-21 [66-Jun-22: 2B].
Brown, Henry G. m. Manro, Carrie T. on 67-Oct-3 [67-Oct-9: 2B; 67-Oct-10: 2B].
Brown, Henry Patterson (12 yrs., 4 mos.) d. on 69-Jun-30 [69-Jul-3: 2B].
Brown, Hezekiah m. Conaway, Jane on 70-Nov-20 [70-Nov-23: 2B].
Brown, Horatio W. m. Martin, Mary E. on 69-Nov-16 [69-Nov-20: 2B].
Brown, Infant (3 mos.) d. on 66-Jul-23 [66-Jul-24: 2C].
Brown, J. B. m. Parr, Katie on 69-Apr-21 [69-Apr-27: 2B].
Brown, J. Wilson m. Rothrock, R. Annie on 70-Nov-22 [70-Nov-25: 2D].
Brown, Jacob m. Ford, Mary Ann on 65-Dec-12 [66-Jan-1: 2C].
Brown, Jallie J. m. Cadwallader, Harrison C. on 67-May-18 [67-May-24: 2B].
Brown, James (55 yrs.) d. on 68-Jan-16 [68-Jan-18: 2B].
Brown, James m. Shalley, Mary on 70-May-19 [70-May-25: 2C].
Brown, James A. m. Hanna, Lizzie A. on 68-Nov-5 [68-Nov-7: 2B].
Brown, James Andrew m. Warner, Susan Miriam on 68-Dec-27 [69-Mar-2: 2C].
Brown, James E., Dr. d. on 66-Jan-12 [66-Jan-15: 1F].
Brown, James E. m. O'Rourke, Mary E. on 69-Jun-18 [69-Jul-15: 2C].
Brown, James F. m. Nicoll, Frances D. on 66-Jul-12 [66-Aug-11: 2B].
Brown, James M. (32 yrs.) d. on 66-Jul-17 of Heatstroke [66-Jul-19: 1F, 2C].
Brown, James R. m. Warrington, Palmyre on 69-Jan-28 [69-Feb-2: 2C].
Brown, Jane (76 yrs.) d. on 67-Jan-26 [67-Jan-28: 2C].
Brown, Jesse (22 yrs.) d. on 67-May-16 [67-May-17: 2B].
Brown, John (67 yrs.) d. on 66-Dec-30 [67-Jan-25: 2C].
Brown, John C. m. Buckingham, Lydia A. on 70-Aug-16 [70-Aug-23: 2B].
Brown, John Henry (17 yrs.) d. on 66-Jan-27 [66-Jan-29: 2B].
Brown, John T. (25 yrs.) d. on 67-Oct-13 [67-Oct-15: 2A].
Brown, John Thomas (6 yrs., 8 mos.) d. on 67-Aug-11 [67-Aug-12: 2C].
Brown, John W. m. Gray, Minnie V. on 67-May-22 [67-Jun-6: 2B].
Brown, John Wilson m. Howard, Laura Virginia on 66-Jan-25 [66-Feb-3: 2C].
Brown, Joseph (34 yrs.) d. on 67-Aug-26 in Street railway accident [67-Aug-27: 1G, 2B; 67-Aug-28: 1F].
Brown, Joseph m. Chalk, Elizabeth C. on 70-Jul-17 [70-Aug-8: 2C].
Brown, Josephine Augusta (30 yrs.) d. on 70-May-29 [70-May-31: 2B].
Brown, Joshua J. (51 yrs.) d. on 67-Jan-18 [67-Jan-19: 2C].
Brown, Julia A. (38 yrs.) d. on 66-Nov-9 [66-Nov-10: 2B].
Brown, Julia C. (11 mos.) d. on 68-Oct-19 [68-Oct-21: 2C].
Brown, Laura Gohen (7 mos.) d. on 66-May-7 [66-May-9: 2B].
Brown, Laura J. m. Reddish, William D. on 68-Oct-13 [68-Oct-20: 2B].
Brown, Laura V. (21 yrs.) d. on 67-Sep-10 of Typhoid [67-Sep-11: 2B; 67-Sep-12: 2B].
Brown, Lawrence H. (10 yrs.) d. on 67-Aug-1 [67-Aug-5: 2B].
Brown, Levi S. m. Orem, Elizabeth on 68-May-3 [68-May-5: 2B].
Brown, Lilian Isabel (3 mos.) d. on 70-Sep-26 [70-Sep-29: 2B].
Brown, Lizzie Mary A. m. McClean, John on 67-Apr-9 [67-May-7: 2B; 67-May-8: 2B].
Brown, M. Harold m. Paine, Martha J. on 68-Oct-7 [68-Oct-10: 2B].
Brown, M. Kate m. Camalier, George P. on 67-Mar-5 [67-Mar-8: 2C].

Brown, Maggie m. Madden, John J. on 67-Sep-23 [67-Oct-4: 2B].
Brown, Maggie m. Walters, John F. on 66-May-1 [66-Aug-20: 2C].
Brown, Maggie E. m. Doll, John W. on 69-Aug-3 [70-Mar-10: 2C].
Brown, Maggie M. m. Sank, Joseph H. on 70-Aug-2 [70-Aug-3: 2C].
Brown, Maggie Selester (1 yr., 5 mos.) d. on 66-Jan-1 of Whooping cough [66-Jan-2: 2C; 66-Jan-3: 2C].
Brown, Margaret Ann d. [68-Jul-22: 2C].
Brown, Margaret L. d. on 67-Jan-16 [67-Jan-18: 2C; 67-Jan-19: 2C].
Brown, Maria (72 yrs.) d. on 66-Aug-5 [66-Aug-7: 2C].
Brown, Maria A. Stanley d. on 68-Aug-5 [68-Aug-8: 2C].
Brown, Marion T. m. Osburn, Milton A. on 67-Feb-20 [67-Feb-22: 2D].
Brown, Martha Ann (20 yrs.) d. on 68-May-4 [68-May-6: 2B].
Brown, Mary (1 mo.) d. on 68-Jun-3 Smothered [68-Jun-4: 1G].
Brown, Mary d. on 67-Dec-13 [67-Dec-14: 2B].
Brown, Mary (71 yrs.) d. on 67-Mar-12 [67-Mar-14: 2C].
Brown, Mary (89 yrs.) d. on 67-Mar-25 [67-Mar-27: 2C].
Brown, Mary (78 yrs.) d. on 67-Jan-21 [67-Jan-22: 2C].
Brown, Mary d. on 67-Feb-2 [67-Feb-4: 2C].
Brown, Mary (81 yrs.) d. on 66-Nov-2 [66-Nov-3: 2B].
Brown, Mary d. on 70-Sep-29 [70-Oct-1: 2B].
Brown, Mary A. (48 yrs.) d. on 69-Mar-18 [69-Mar-19: 2C; 69-Mar-20: 2B].
Brown, Mary A. (32 yrs., 1 mo.) d. on 70-May-6 [70-May-9: 2C].
Brown, Mary A. m. Koffenberger, G. on 67-Jun-27 [67-Aug-3: 2B].
Brown, Mary Agnes (10 mos.) d. on 66-Mar-14 [66-Mar-16: 2B].
Brown, Mary Anna (4 yrs., 3 mos.) d. on 70-Apr-8 [70-Apr-12: 2B].
Brown, Mary D. d. on 67-Aug-28 of Paralysis [67-Aug-31: 2B].
Brown, Mary E. m. Johnson, Joseph P. on 67-May-30 [67-Jun-8: 2B].
Brown, Mary E. m. Taylor, William H. on 69-Feb-11 [69-Feb-12: 2C].
Brown, Mary E. W. m. Morton, G. Nash on 69-May-11 [69-May-15: 2B].
Brown, Mary Elizabeth (52 yrs.) d. on 67-Dec-21 [67-Dec-23: 2B].
Brown, Mary L. m. Merryman, Richard S. on 70-Feb-24 [70-Mar-19: 2B].
Brown, Mary Laura (19 yrs.) d. on 68-Aug-2 [68-Aug-3: 2B].
Brown, Mary Lizzie m. Becker, Frederick on 68-Jun-30 [68-Jul-11: 2B].
Brown, Mary V. m. Straney, Edward W. on 69-Jun-17 [69-Jul-5: 2C].
Brown, Mary Virginia (2 mos.) d. on 69-Jan-27 [69-Jan-28: 2C].
Brown, Matilda (72 yrs.) d. on 65-Dec-26 of Consumption [66-Jan-1: 2C].
Brown, Matilda R. m. Pue, Charles R., Jr. on 67-Dec-17 [67-Dec-21: 2B].
Brown, Mattie E. m. McCracken, Thomas C. on 68-Feb-13 [68-Feb-20: 2C].
Brown, Michael m. Brazier, Rebecca Jane on 66-Apr-16 [66-Apr-19: 2B].
Brown, Mollie E. m. Brown, William E. on 67-Apr-18 [67-May-22: 2B].
Brown, Nellie m. Lein, Harry B. on 69-Jul-8 [69-Jul-12: 2C; 69-Jul-10: 2B].
Brown, Nellie m. Leon, Harry B. on 69-Jul-8 [69-Jul-10: 2B].
Brown, Noah d. on 67-Oct-7 of Heart disease [67-Oct-8: 1G].
Brown, Norval Wilson (1 yr., 9 mos.) d. on 70-Dec-7 [70-Dec-8: 2C].
Brown, Oliver m. Doyle, Josephine on 69-Nov-16 [69-Nov-20: 2B].
Brown, Orphelia J. m. Halbert, Henry J. on 69-Dec-30 [70-Jan-21: 2C].
Brown, P. B. m. Bond, Clara Howard on 69-Jun-8 [69-Jun-14: 2C].
Brown, Pamelia (63 yrs.) d. on 69-Feb-24 [69-Feb-25: 2D].
Brown, Patrick (7 yrs.) d. on 68-Oct-27 [68-Oct-28: 1F].
Brown, Peter m. Hudson, Jennie on 70-May-12 [70-May-16: 2B].
Brown, Priscilla T. (44 yrs.) d. on 66-Feb-23 [66-Feb-27: 2B].
Brown, Randolph R. m. Depoe, Kate on 70-Jun-16 [70-Jun-25: 2B].
Brown, Rezin (65 yrs., 11 mos.) d. on 68-Nov-6 [68-Nov-9: 2B].
Brown, Richard W. (29 yrs., 1 mo.) d. on 69-Feb-21 [69-Feb-23: 2C].
Brown, Rinaldo (39 yrs.) d. on 66-Sep-7 [66-Sep-12: 2A; 66-Sep-13: 2C].

Brown, Robert (36 yrs.) d. on 68-Jan-6 [68-Jan-7: 2B].
Brown, Robert (14 yrs.) d. on 67-Jul-7 Drowned [67-Jul-8: 1G].
Brown, Robert P. (71 yrs.) d. on 69-Dec-17 [69-Dec-21: 2B].
Brown, Sallie A. m. Reynolds, William I. on 68-Sep-6 [68-Oct-10: 2B].
Brown, Sallie J. m. Cadwallader, Harrison C. on 67-May-18 [67-May-30: 2B].
Brown, Samuel (37 yrs.) d. on 66-Mar-31 of Suicide (Poisoning) [66-Apr-2: 1G, 2B; 66-Apr-3: 4C].
Brown, Samuel E. C. (18 yrs.) d. on 68-Mar-16 [68-Mar-20: 2B].
Brown, Sarah (2 yrs., 4 mos.) d. on 68-Nov-1 [68-Nov-3: 2B].
Brown, Sarah G. m. Harvey, C. T. on 70-Sep-27 [70-Oct-15: 2B].
Brown, Sarah J. (9 yrs., 9 mos.) d. on 67-Feb-11 [67-Feb-13: 2D].
Brown, Sebastian m. Clifton, Sue S. on 67-Sep-26 [67-Oct-1: 2B].
Brown, Stanley, Dr. (26 yrs.) d. on 67-Dec-16 [67-Dec-17: 2B].
Brown, Stephen Asbury (20 yrs.) d. on 66-Jul-28 [66-Jul-30: 2C].
Brown, Stewart (1 yr., 8 mos.) d. on 70-Jun-28 [70-Jun-30: 2C].
Brown, Susan C. m. Grape, George Sanders on 67-Dec-23 [67-Dec-24: 2B].
Brown, Susie B. (29 yrs.) d. on 69-Apr-8 [69-Apr-10: 2B].
Brown, Susie P. m. Bosselle, Louis on 68-Feb-4 [68-Feb-5: 2D].
Brown, T. R. m. Carrington, Hallie R. on 66-Dec-24 [66-Dec-27: 2C].
Brown, Thomas (49 yrs.) d. on 66-Oct-29 [66-Oct-30: 2B].
Brown, Thomas m. Forney, Susie B. on 68-Feb-17 [68-Apr-27: 2B].
Brown, Thomas m. Hollett, Ann Rebecca on 70-Jun-13 [70-Jul-2: 2B; 70-Jul-4: 2C].
Brown, Thomas H. S. m. Benner, Lottie J. on 70-Sep-15 [70-Sep-20: 2B].
Brown, Thomas M. m. Morris, Mary R. on 68-Feb-19 [68-Feb-20: 2C].
Brown, W. H. G., Rev. d. on 70-Nov-8 [70-Nov-10: 2C].
Brown, W. Judson m. Lawrence, Mary Louise on 70-Jun-9 [70-Jun-13: 2C].
Brown, Waldron P. m. Wright, Isabella M. on 70-Jan-13 [70-Jan-15: 2C].
Brown, Walter S. m. Oliver, Mary E. on 68-Oct-28 [68-Oct-30: 2C].
Brown, William (49 yrs.) d. on 69-Apr-25 [69-Apr-26: 2B].
Brown, William (48 yrs.) d. on 70-Dec-19 of Paralysis [70-Dec-20: 4C; 70-Dec-21: 2C; 70-Dec-22: 2B].
Brown, William B. (55 yrs.) d. on 70-Apr-15 [70-Apr-21: 2C].
Brown, William C. m. Disney, Mary A. on 68-Sep-19 [68-Sep-30: 2B].
Brown, William E. m. Brown, Mollie E. on 67-Apr-18 [67-May-22: 2B].
Brown, William F. m. Sakers, Maggie on 66-Oct-25 [66-Oct-27: 2B].
Brown, William Freeman (13 yrs.) d. on 67-Apr-2 [67-Apr-3: 2B; 67-Apr-4: 2B].
Brown, William H. d. on 67-Jul-25 [67-Aug-13: 2B].
Brown, William H., Lt. d. [69-Apr-27: 2C].
Brown, William H. m. Denny, Mary F. on 66-Oct-4 [66-Oct-12: 2B].
Brown, William H. m. Poteet, Annie on 70-Dec-20 [70-Dec-22: 2B].
Brown, William Henry (6 mos.) d. [69-Jul-3: 2B].
Brown, William O. m. Stockdale, Elizabeth A. on 68-Mar-8 [68-Mar-12: 2B].
Brown, William P. (76 yrs.) d. on 70-Aug-18 [70-Aug-20: 2B].
Brown, William T. m. Coombs, Mary E. on 67-Jun-3 [67-Jun-13: 2B].
Brown, William Thomas (14 yrs., 1 mo.) d. on 66-May-16 of Typhoid [66-May-18: 2C].
Brown, Willie (1 yr., 1 mo.) d. on 69-Apr-26 [69-Jun-8: 2B].
Brown, Willie (14 yrs.) d. on 69-May-20 of Gunshot wound [69-Mar-26: 1H].
Browne, David S. d. on 67-Jul-22 [67-Jul-23: 2C].
Browne, Etta K. d. on 69-Mar-17 [69-Mar-18: 2C].
Browne, Francis (31 yrs.) d. on 69-Jun-19 Drowned [69-Jun-23: 1H].
Browne, Lewis R. m. Bayless, Augusta J. on 66-Nov-8 [66-Nov-13: 2B].
Browne, Lizzie m. Clausen, C. F. on 67-Oct-22 [67-Oct-24: 2B].
Browne, Mollie E. A. m. Baker, RICHARD J. on 66-May-31 [66-Jun-11: 2B].
Browne, Stephen (23 yrs.) d. on 68-Jul-16 Drowned [68-Jul-17: 1G].
Browne, William Hardcastle m. Beaver, Alice on 69-Dec-16 [69-Dec-20: 2C].

Browning, Edward (66 yrs.) d. on 66-Jun-2 [66-Jun-5: 2B].
Browning, George G. m. Spangler, Lou T. on 69-Jun-6 [69-Aug-31: 2B].
Browning, Maggie (22 yrs., 6 mos.) d. on 68-Sep-21 [68-Sep-22: 2B].
Browning, Mary (89 yrs.) d. on 68-Jun-17 [68-Jun-18: 2B].
Browning, Nancy (60 yrs.) d. on 67-Jul-4 [67-Jul-10: 2B].
Browning, Olivia J. (48 yrs.) d. on 70-Feb-14 [70-Feb-15: 2C].
Browning, Samuel David m. Hanson, Ann Margaret on 70-Aug-24 [70-Aug-30: 2B].
Browning, Willie Patterson (1 yr., 6 mos.) d. on 69-Aug-4 [69-Aug-5: 2B; 69-Aug-6: 2C].
Brownlee, Ella J. m. Crosse, Elliot W. on 69-Nov-23 [69-Nov-25: 2C].
Brownley, Joseph (43 yrs.) d. on 68-Aug-18 [68-Aug-19: 2B].
Bruce, Edward m. Jordan, Laura V. on 68-Jan-6 [68-Jan-14: 2C].
Bruce, Georgia m. Mittler, Francis S. on 66-Mar-7 [66-Mar-13: 2B; 66-Mar-14: 2B].
Bruce, Robert (58 yrs.) d. on 67-Sep-26 of Chronic diarrhea [67-Sep-30: 2B].
Bruce, Sallie (14 yrs., 10 mos.) d. on 68-Mar-11 [68-Mar-14: 2B].
Bruce, Thomas Stockton m. Abbott, M. Kate on 67-Mar-12 [67-Apr-4: 2B].
Bruce, Virginia m. Lowecamp, John F. on 68-Oct-28 [68-Nov-10: 2C].
Bruchey, Annie M. m. Goolden, James on 67-Jun-12 [67-Jul-16: 2C].
Bruchey, Joseph (44 yrs., 5 mos.) d. on 66-Nov-24 of Paralysis [66-Nov-26: 2B].
Bruchey, Lydia Ann Rebecca (47 yrs.) d. on 69-Aug-17 [69-Aug-18: 2C].
Bruchey, William F. D. (1 yr.) d. on 69-Sep-3 [69-Sep-4: 2B].
Bruck, Henry M. m. Cook, Lizzie A. on 68-Sep-17 [68-Sep-22: 2B].
Bruckner, Catharine d. on 69-Oct-27 [69-Oct-28: 2C].
Bruehl, Clarence McDonald (3 yrs.) d. on 66-Nov-22 [66-Nov-23: 2C].
Bruehl, Eleanor Lizetta (60 yrs.) d. on 70-Oct-24 [70-Oct-25: 2B; 70-Oct-26: 2B].
Bruehl, George Edward (5 yrs., 2 mos.) d. on 66-Nov-20 [66-Nov-21: 2C].
Bruehl, Mary A. m. Kleibacker, C. B. on 69-Oct-14 [69-Oct-19: 2B].
Bruen, , Mrs. (75 yrs.) d. on 67-Aug-4 [67-Aug-5: 2B].
Bruff, Helen (21 yrs.) d. on 70-Jan-10 [70-Jan-11: 2C].
Bruff, Henry C. m. Dawson, Sallie B. on 69-Apr-14 [69-Apr-15: 2B].
Bruff, James M. (42 yrs.) d. on 66-Jul-23 [66-Jul-24: 1G, 2C].
Bruff, John K. m. Mitchell, Susan E. on 67-May-14 [67-Jun-21: 2B].
Bruff, John W. (50 yrs.) d. on 68-Mar-3 of Apoplexy [68-Mar-4: 2C; 68-Mar-5: 2C].
Bruff, Joseph E. m. Punderson, Helen on 69-Apr-29 [69-May-3: 2C].
Bruggman, Margaretta (52 yrs.) d. on 66-Oct-17 [66-Oct-18: 2B].
Bruggmann, Anna M. J. m. Aspril, David S. on 66-Feb-19 [66-Feb-21: 2C].
Brumble, Emma J. m. Landing, Benjamin J. on 69-Apr-3 [69-Apr-6: 2C].
Brummer, Anna Marie (34 yrs.) d. on 67-Apr-25 [67-Apr-26: 2B].
Brun, E. F. m. Merrill, V. G. on 70-Sep-22 [70-Sep-30: 2B].
Brundige, Hannah Gover (77 yrs.) d. on 70-May-27 [70-May-31: 2B].
Brundige, Hannah Stephenson d. on 70-Oct-28 [70-Oct-29: 2B].
Brundige, Kate H. m. Crowther, David W. on 70-Sep-7 [70-Sep-13: 2B; 70-Sep-14: 2B].
Brundige, Rosetta Wilson (5 mos.) d. [69-Aug-3: 2C].
Brundige, Susan H. d. [69-Jul-2: 2C].
Brundige, William, Sr. (80 yrs.) d. on 68-Jul-13 [68-Jul-14: 2B].
Brunker, James H. m. Farson, Inda T. on 69-Nov-11 [69-Nov-16: 2C].
Brunner, Christie L. d. on 67-Oct-21 [67-Oct-21: 2B; 67-Oct-22: 2A].
Brunt, Bella m. Scott, John E. on 66-May-23 [66-Jun-8: 2B].
Brunt, Eliza J. m. Dushane, James A. on 70-Jan-18 [70-Oct-20: 2C].
Brunt, Lutie C. m. Bollman, J. Moellinger on 69-Oct-19 [69-Oct-21: 2B].
Brunt, Mary Jacquelin (5 yrs., 5 mos.) d. on 66-Jun-10 [66-Jun-11: 2B; 66-Jun-13: 2B; 66-Jun-12: 2B].
Bruscup, Josephine C. m. Mobley, William H. on 70-Oct-19 [70-Oct-20: 2B].
Bruscup, William T. m. Delcher, Emma on 66-Jul-2 [66-Jul-10: 2C].
Brushwiller, Barbara (28 yrs.) d. on 70-Jun-5 [70-Jun-6: 2B].
Brushwiller, William (58 yrs.) d. on 70-Nov-11 [70-Nov-15: 2C; 70-Nov-16: 2C].

Brussel, Adolph m. Oppenheimer, Fannie on 67-May-5 [67-May-8: 2B].
Bruster, Caroline A. (34 yrs.) d. on 70-Aug-2 [70-Aug-3: 2C].
Bruster, James (45 yrs.) d. on 70-Jul-29 [70-Jul-30: 4E; 70-Aug-1: 4E].
Bruster, Mary Augusta (1 mo.) d. on 70-Aug-9 [70-Aug-13: 2C].
Brutche, Anna (24 yrs.) d. on 67-Mar-10 [67-Mar-12: 2C].
Bruxensten, Otto (29 yrs.) d. on 68-Jan-15 [68-Jan-17: 2C].
Bryan, Amanda m. Guyton, William T. on 67-Jul-14 [67-Jul-18: 2C].
Bryan, Andrew (46 yrs.) d. on 70-Jan-17 [70-Jan-18: 2C].
Bryan, Edward m. Clautice, Mary C. on 70-Apr-20 [70-Apr-23: 2B].
Bryan, Ellen (57 yrs.) d. on 67-Nov-17 [67-Nov-19: 2C].
Bryan, Ellenora (21 yrs.) d. on 66-Jan-30 [66-Feb-2: 2C].
Bryan, Emma F., Miss m. Parsons, D. E. on 69-Sep-18 [69-Sep-20: 2C].
Bryan, Emma V. (24 yrs.) d. on 69-Apr-14 [69-Apr-15: 2B].
Bryan, George Emory (29 yrs.) d. on 68-Jul-23 Drowned [68-Sep-24: 2B].
Bryan, Harriet (81 yrs.) d. on 66-May-19 [66-May-21: 2B].
Bryan, Harriet m. Scott, George S. on 70-Jan-6 [70-Jan-8: 2B].
Bryan, Issac R. m. Richardson, Mary V. on 69-Oct-14 [69-Oct-16: 2B; 69-Oct-18: 2C].
Bryan, James (73 yrs.) d. on 69-Jan-19 of Pleuro-pneumonia [69-Jan-20: 2C; 69-Jan-22: 2D].
Bryan, John H. (35 yrs.) d. on 70-Nov-12 of Epilepsy [70-Nov-14: 4C].
Bryan, William H. (38 yrs.) d. on 66-May-4 [66-May-5: 2B].
Bryant, William L. m. Franklin, Melissa N. on 69-Sep-2 [69-Sep-6: 2C].
Bryarly, Robert (60 yrs.) d. on 70-Jan-16 [70-Jan-17: 2C].
Bryarly, Wake, Dr. (49 yrs.) d. on 69-Mar-13 of Pneumonia [69-Mar-15: 2C; 69-Mar-16: 1G, 2C].
Bryden, Margaret (56 yrs.) d. on 69-Dec-11 [69-Dec-14: 2C].
Brydon, Edward M. m. Ferguson, Rhoda C. on 67-Jun-20 [67-Jun-22: 2B].
Bryne, Susan (80 yrs.) d. on 67-Jun-10 [67-Jul-6: 2B].
Bryson, Hugh (65 yrs.) d. on 66-Nov-27 [66-Nov-29: 2B].
Bryson, Margaret A. (47 yrs.) d. on 68-Oct-3 [68-Oct-5: 2B].
Bucannon, Andry d. on 66-Nov-8 [66-Nov-9: 2C].
Bucey, William H. m. Whittington, Laura Y. on 66-Mar-21 [66-Mar-22: 2B].
Buchanan, Ellen McMechen (2 mos.) d. on 69-Aug-7 [69-Aug-10: 2C].
Buchanan, James (79 yrs.) d. on 68-Aug-8 [68-Aug-10: 1G, 2B].
Buchanan, James M., Jr. m. Rogers, S. Teresa on 67-Mar-26 [67-Apr-8: 2B; 67-Apr-9: 2B].
Buchanan, Lizzie T. m. Sullivan, Felix R. on 68-Nov-17 [68-Nov-21: 2C].
Buchanan, Rebecca S. d. on 68-Feb-6 [68-Feb-7: 2C].
Buchanan, Robert S. d. on 70-Jun-13 [70-Jun-15: 2B].
Buchanan, Sallie Lloyd m. Screven, Thomas F. on 66-Oct-30 [66-Nov-7: 2C].
Buchen, George W. m. Petticord, Laura on 69-Nov-7 [69-Nov-15: 2C].
Bucher, Elenor m. Cross, John C. on 67-Sep-5 [67-Sep-18: 2B].
Bucher, George W. m. Byrne, Mary Alexina on 67-Oct-10 [67-Oct-16: 2B].
Buck, Aggie A. m. Randolph, John W., Jr. on 66-May-30 [66-Jun-2: 2B].
Buck, Cecilia (11 mos.) d. on 69-Aug-24 [69-Aug-25: 2C; 69-Aug-26: 2C].
Buck, Charles W. m. Jones, Fannie Currie on 68-Sep-1 [68-Sep-2: 2A].
Buck, Eliza Ann m. Welch, John on 68-Jun-2 [68-Jun-4: 2B].
Buck, Elizabeth (53 yrs.) d. on 66-Mar-20 [66-Mar-22: 2B].
Buck, Gabriella Clark d. on 67-May-21 [67-May-22: 2B].
Buck, Isabella m. Broglen, Daniel on 67-May-14 [67-May-16: 2B].
Buck, J. Eugene m. Hood, Josephine on 67-May-2 [67-May-7: 2B].
Buck, James (30 yrs.) d. on 66-Aug-11 [66-Aug-15: 2B].
Buck, James B. (62 yrs.) d. on 67-Dec-7 [67-Dec-9: 2B].
Buck, James F. m. Keller, Mary C. on 67-Sep-24 [67-Dec-11: 2B].
Buck, Laura Virginia E. (21 yrs., 4 mos.) d. on 68-Mar-7 [68-Mar-9: 2C].
Buck, Mary M. (85 yrs.) d. on 66-Feb-26 [66-Feb-27: 2B].
Buck, Sarah R. d. on 67-Jun-23 [67-Jun-24: 2B].

Buck, Susie E. m. Sheridan, Frank on 69-Oct-14 [69-Oct-19: 2B].
Buck, Theodore A. m. Miller, Grace on 68-Sep-16 [68-Nov-10: 2C].
Buck, Thomas C. m. Sharp, Lizzie G. on 69-Nov-2 [69-Nov-10: 2C].
Buck, William m. Huntemuller, Virginia on 69-Dec-8 [69-Dec-17: 2C].
Buck, William L. m. Starkey, Mary L. on 69-Aug-12 [69-Aug-18: 2C].
Buckingham, Alfred m. Yingling, Fannie on 70-Mar-17 [70-Apr-21: 2B].
Buckingham, Cora Mason (8 mos.) d. on 69-Apr-27 [69-Apr-29: 2C].
Buckingham, Ella V. m. Cochran, William F. on 67-Oct-9 [67-Oct-10: 2B].
Buckingham, F. M. (37 yrs.) d. on 66-Nov-17 [66-Nov-19: 2B; 66-Nov-20: 2B].
Buckingham, Fannie C. m. Hamilton, John A. on 68-Oct-15 [68-Oct-20: 2B].
Buckingham, George Clarence (6 mos.) d. on 68-Jan-20 [68-Jan-22: 2C].
Buckingham, George L. W. (37 yrs., 10 mos.) d. on 70-Mar-30 [70-Apr-19: 2B].
Buckingham, Georgianna A. m. Davis, William M. on 66-Jun-14 [66-Jun-15: 2C].
Buckingham, Greenbury m. Fallows, Harriet on 65-Dec-24 [66-Jan-6: 2B].
Buckingham, Lydia A. m. Brown, John C. on 70-Aug-16 [70-Aug-23: 2B].
Buckingham, M. Florence m. Webster, Thomas W. on 70-Feb-23 [70-Mar-3: 2C].
Buckingham, Mary D. (28 yrs.) d. on 68-Aug-1 [68-Aug-3: 2B].
Buckingham, Mary Emily m. Chase, George W. on 66-Dec-4 [66-Dec-13: 2B].
Buckingham, Olivia m. Esender, George T. [68-Dec-1: 2C].
Buckingham, Sidney E. m. Clymer, Francis D. on 67-Sep-5 [67-Sep-17: 2A].
Buckingham, Virginia m. Probest, George F. on 68-Jan-20 [68-Jan-21: 2C].
Buckle, Mary E. m. Connor, John A. on 67-Nov-27 [67-Nov-30: 2C].
Buckler, Isabel d. on 69-Jul-20 [69-Jul-22: 2C].
Buckler, John, Dr. (71 yrs.) d. on 66-Feb-24 of Heart disease [66-Feb-26: 1G, 2B; 66-Feb-28: 1E].
Buckler, William d. on 70-Apr-15 [70-Apr-18: 2B].
Buckley, Ann (64 yrs.) d. on 69-Nov-29 [69-Nov-30: 2C].
Buckley, Daniel (7 mos.) d. on 68-Mar-9 [68-Mar-11: 2B].
Buckley, Henry J. (50 yrs.) d. on 70-Nov-27 [70-Nov-29: 2C].
Buckley, James (27 yrs.) d. on 70-Aug-10 [70-Aug-11: 2C].
Buckley, Jane M. (75 yrs.) d. on 69-Nov-20 [69-Nov-22: 2C].
Buckley, Lydia m. Sillery, Charles on 69-Aug-12 [69-Aug-16: 2B].
Buckley, Robert L. (67 yrs.) d. on 67-Apr-3 [67-Apr-9: 2B].
Buckley, Willie (22 yrs.) d. on 66-Sep-24 of Consumption [66-Sep-25: 2B].
Buckman, George (40 yrs.) d. on 66-Apr-2 [66-Apr-3: 2B].
Buckmiller, Ollie M. m. Kime, James L. on 69-Sep-28 [69-Sep-30: 2B].
Buckner, Evelyn Carter (3 yrs., 3 mos.) d. on 70-Nov-27 [70-Nov-29: 2C].
Bucks, John m. Kennedy, Ellen on 67-Sep-23 [67-Sep-24: 2A].
Budd, Sarah Jane (6 yrs., 1 mo.) d. on 68-Feb-28 [68-Feb-29: 2B].
Budeke, Francis William (20 yrs.) d. on 69-Apr-7 [69-Apr-9: 2B].
Budeke, George H. m. Grothaus, Minnie on 69-Sep-14 [69-Sep-24: 2B].
Budeke, Wilhelmina (26 yrs.) d. on 70-Sep-18 [70-Sep-19: 2B; 70-Sep-20: 2B].
Buehler, Eliza d. on 67-May-31 [67-Jun-1: 2B].
Buehler, Thomas H. m. Schimp, Annie E. on 66-Aug-1 [66-Aug-7: 2C].
Buell, William P. m. Gary, S. Ellen on 69-Nov-1 [69-Nov-5: 2C].
Buhman, Lizzie d. on 70-Jul-27 of Heatstroke [70-Jul-28: 4E].
Bulack, Alice A. m. Martin, Josiah H. on 68-Jun-29 [68-Oct-5: 2B].
Bulack, Jacob (39 yrs.) d. on 70-Dec-15 [70-Dec-16: 2C; 70-Dec-17: 2B].
Bulack, Joseph m. McFarland, Mary Johnston on 70-Aug-31 [70-Sep-1: 2B].
Bulack, Maria d. on 68-Nov-18 [68-Nov-19: 2C; 68-Nov-20: 2C].
Bulack, Mary Jane m. Martin, John W. on 70-Jul-4 [70-Jul-22: 2C].
Bull, Caroline m. Kessler, Levi on 70-Oct-10 [70-Oct-17: 2C].
Bull, Elijah m. Mopps, Mary Eliza on 67-Jul-1 [67-Jul-6: 2B].
Bull, Eliza Ann (54 yrs.) d. on 69-May-24 [69-May-28: 2C].
Bull, Elizabeth Susanna Kelzer m. Banks, Samuel on 68-Aug-24 [68-Sep-12: 2B].

Bull, Emma H. m. Burton, Thomas W. on 70-Jan-19 [70-Jan-24: 2C].
Bull, Issac (78 yrs.) d. on 70-Sep-11 of Paralysis [70-Sep-15: 2B, 4D].
Bull, Katie Prentiss (2 yrs., 2 mos.) d. on 70-Jul-29 [70-Aug-1: 2C].
Bull, Lizzie M. d. on 68-Apr-5 [68-Apr-17: 2B].
Bull, Mary C. (1 yr., 10 mos.) d. on 70-May-19 [70-May-24: 2C].
Bull, Rachel d. on 66-Feb-11 [66-Feb-12: 2D].
Bull, Rebecca J. m. Barry, Richard A. on 68-Oct-22 [68-Oct-31: 2B].
Bull, Sarah E. m. Cooper, Thomas on 70-Oct-25 [70-Oct-28: 2C].
Bull, Shadrack (64 yrs.) d. on 67-Jun-13 [67-Jun-20: 2B].
Bullard, W. S. m. Kettlewell, Haddie on 67-Apr-25 [67-May-23: 2B].
Bullen, Clara May (6 mos.) d. on 66-Oct-5 [66-Oct-8: 2B].
Bullen, Henry m. Demuth, Hester A. on 66-Dec-27 [67-Jan-8: 2B].
Bullen, Jane (65 yrs.) d. on 67-Jul-1 [67-Jul-3: 2B].
Bullen, John DeMuth (11 mos.) d. on 70-Sep-14 [70-Sep-15: 2B].
Bullen, Prescott Dunnock (8 mos.) d. on 68-Jul-30 [68-Aug-1: 2B].
Bullock, Annie Bell (1 yr., 5 mos.) d. on 66-Jun-30 [66-Jul-2: 2B].
Bullock, Caroline Laurens (54 yrs.) d. on 67-Nov-4 [67-Nov-5: 2B; 67-Nov-6: 2B].
Bullock, Frank Everett (3 yrs., 5 mos.) d. on 68-May-10 [68-May-11: 2B].
Bullock, J. J. m. Lavendar, Lizzie [69-Feb-24: 2C].
Bullock, John S. m. Davis, Kate E. on 66-Jun-22 [66-Jun-26: 2B].
Bullock, Joseph J. (23 yrs.) d. on 66-Mar-19 [66-Mar-20: 2C].
Bullock, Kazwell J. (6 yrs.) d. on 68-Nov-2 [68-Nov-3: 2B].
Bullock, Mary Adie d. on 68-Nov-18 of Croup [68-Nov-19: 2C].
Bullock, Rhoda M. m. Sunstrom, Mark T. on 67-Apr-11 [67-Apr-12: 2C].
Bullock, Waller R. (36 yrs.) d. on 70-Nov-11 [70-Nov-12: 2B, 4C].
Bullock, Walter R. m. Canfield, Caroline on 70-Feb-3 [70-Feb-7: 2C; 70-Feb-8: 2C].
Bump, Jesse E. m. Hughes, Mary F. on 69-Jan-7 [69-Jan-15: 2D].
Bump, Orlando F. m. Weathers, Sarah E. on 70-Jul-27 [70-Jul-28: 2C].
Bunce, David m. Deal, Mary R. on 66-Mar-29 [66-Apr-7: 2B].
Bunce, George Burnett (2 mos.) d. on 66-Dec-11 [66-Dec-14: 2B].
Bunce, Mary m. Hubbel, Augustin on 66-Apr-5 [66-Apr-12: 2B].
Bunn, John S. m. Pitt, Eliza E. on 66-Jan-16 [66-Jan-19: 2C].
Bunn, Peter m. Shaab, Mary A. on 68-May-19 [68-Jun-4: 2B].
Bunster, Enrique S. m. McCrea, Katie on 69-Sep-21 [69-Dec-29: 2D].
Bunting, George W. (41 yrs.) d. on 68-Jan-28 [68-Jan-29: 2C].
Bunting, John (55 yrs.) d. on 69-Jul-17 [69-Jul-22: 2C; 69-Jul-23: 2C].
Bunting, John H. m. Noble, Emma J. on 69-Feb-11 [69-Feb-17: 2C].
Bunting, Maggie A. d. on 66-Jul-17 [66-Jul-18: 2C].
Bunting, Mary B. m. Nelson, Francis F. on 68-Feb-27 [68-Mar-2: 2B].
Bunting, May (1 yr., 6 mos.) d. on 70-Jul-19 [70-Aug-2: 2C].
Bunting, Virginia m. Maulsby, Augustus A. G. on 66-Apr-17 [66-Apr-30: 2B].
Bunting, W. A. m. Hart, Mary A. on 68-Jan-27 [68-Feb-7: 2C; 68-Feb-8: 2B].
Bunting, Zoe L. m. Rigby, Arthur on 69-Jun-9 [69-Jun-10: 2C].
Bunyan, Mary (57 yrs.) d. on 67-Jul-11 [67-Jul-13: 2B].
Burbage, John E. m. Warner, Annie S. on 68-Sep-17 [68-Sep-22: 2B].
Burbank, David Lyman (39 yrs.) d. on 68-Jul-13 [68-Aug-31: 2B].
Burbrier, Charles L. m. Ward, Mary E. E. on 67-Oct-8 [67-Oct-11: 2B].
Burch, David F. (67 yrs.) d. on 70-Apr-28 [70-Apr-30: 2A].
Burch, J. Alton m. Shepperson, Isabel Bird on 69-Nov-3 [69-Nov-13: 2B].
Burch, J. D. m. Hammett, J. E. on 68-Nov-10 [68-Nov-12: 2C].
Burchall, Jane (67 yrs.) d. on 70-Jul-22 [70-Jul-29: 2C].
Burchinal, Kate (21 yrs.) d. on 68-Aug-27 [68-Aug-29: 2B].
Burckhard, Willie (3 yrs., 4 mos.) d. on 69-Apr-6 [69-Apr-7: 2C].
Burdett, Aaron (69 yrs.) d. on 70-Feb-7 [70-Feb-8: 2C].
Burdett, Francis R. (48 yrs.) d. on 67-Sep-28 [67-Oct-1: 2B].

Burdette, Albert (25 yrs.) d. on 67-Apr-8 [67-Apr-9: 2B; 67-Apr-10: 2B].
Burer, John (12 yrs.) d. on 69-Nov-11 of Construction cave-in [69-Nov-12: 1G].
Burfoot, Mollie W. m. Waldman, George R. on 69-Apr-8 [69-Apr-17: 2A].
Burford, Willie E. d. on 69-Aug-27 [69-Aug-30: 2B].
Burgan, Elizabeth (80 yrs.) d. on 68-Mar-6 [68-Mar-7: 2B].
Burgen, Joshua (67 yrs.) d. on 70-Aug-16 [70-Aug-17: 2C].
Burger, Fannie A. m. Hall, Charles B. on 66-May-22 [66-May-23: 2B].
Burger, John N. m. Ramsay, Isabella D. on 69-Sep-14 [69-Sep-16: 2B].
Burger, Nicholas (66 yrs.) d. on 69-Aug-19 [69-Aug-20: 2C].
Burgess, Ann E. Hank d. on 68-May-28 [68-May-29: 2B].
Burgess, Benjamin m. Bennett, Lucinda on 70-Nov-10 [70-Nov-26: 2B].
Burgess, Caleb W. (67 yrs.) d. on 70-May-21 of Heart spasm [70-May-23: 1H, 2B].
Burgess, Elizabeth R. (54 yrs.) d. on 66-Nov-12 [66-Nov-13: 2B].
Burgess, Ellenora (4 yrs., 4 mos.) d. on 69-Jan-24 [69-Jan-25: 2D].
Burgess, Florence (2 yrs., 5 mos.) d. on 67-Jul-29 [67-Jul-30: 2C].
Burgess, George, Sr. d. on 67-Dec-30 [68-Jan-1: 2C].
Burgess, George R. m. Williamson, Emily J. on 70-Apr-28 [70-May-4: 2C].
Burgess, Henry Clayton (6 mos.) d. on 66-Jul-21 [66-Jul-25: 2C].
Burgess, Henry Howard (66 yrs.) d. on 66-Aug-1 [66-Aug-8: 2C].
Burgess, J. Albert (17 yrs.) d. on 69-Mar-3 [69-Mar-16: 2C].
Burgess, J. P. m. Richardson, Lizzie R. on 69-Jan-26 [69-Jan-28: 2C].
Burgess, Joshua (60 yrs.) d. on 67-Aug-26 [67-Sep-7: 2A].
Burgess, Mary E. m. Donsiff, Harry L. on 68-Sep-23 [68-Sep-26: 2B].
Burgess, Mary Maud (4 yrs., 7 mos.) d. on 69-Mar-24 [69-Mar-25: 2C].
Burgess, Mary Ozella (7 mos.) d. on 70-Jul-28 [70-Jul-29: 2C].
Burgess, Mollie A. W. m. Landing, George W., Jr. on 67-Apr-23 [67-Oct-3: 2B].
Burgess, Nelson (30 yrs.) d. on 69-Nov-12 Drowned [69-Nov-13: 1G].
Burgess, Sallie V. m. Jones, James G. on 67-May-21 [67-Jun-12: 2B].
Burgess, Samuel O. m. O'Laughlin, Mary B. on 67-May-22 [67-May-31: 2B].
Burgess, Sarah d. on 66-Jan-8 [66-Jan-13: 2C].
Burgess, Thomas D. (71 yrs.) d. on 70-Mar-22 of Pneumonia [70-Mar-28: 2B].
Burgess, W. G. m. Miller, Myra on 70-Feb-23 [70-Feb-28: 2C].
Burgess, William, Jr. m. Colladay, Emily F. on 68-Aug-18 [68-Aug-22: 2A].
Burgess, William T. m. Gibbons, Maggie E. on 70-Feb-28 [70-Mar-25: 2C].
Burgy, Emile H. (1 yr., 8 mos.) d. on 66-Nov-6 [66-Nov-9: 2C].
Burk, Charles H. (4 yrs.) d. on 69-Feb-7 [69-Feb-9: 2C].
Burk, Eliza (70 yrs.) d. on 68-Nov-11 [68-Nov-12: 2C].
Burk, John W. m. Gaither, Lizzie E. on 66-Dec-13 [66-Dec-17: 2B].
Burk, Julia A. m. Briggeman, C. A. on 68-Oct-13 [68-Oct-15: 2C].
Burk, Katie (1 yr., 7 mos.) d. on 70-Sep-4 [70-Sep-6: 2B].
Burk, Thomas (63 yrs.) d. on 69-May-21 [69-May-26: 2C].
Burke, A. J. m. Kroh, Georgia E. on 68-Aug-18 [69-Feb-24: 2C].
Burke, Annie E. m. Bayless, John T. on 68-Mar-9 [68-Apr-27: 2B].
Burke, Annie E. m. Catez, John B. on 67-Oct-22 [68-May-15: 2B].
Burke, Catherine (11 mos.) d. on 66-Oct-4 [66-Oct-5: 2B].
Burke, Eliza (72 yrs.) d. on 69-Feb-15 [69-Feb-17: 2C].
Burke, Eliza Julienne Willis (36 yrs.) d. on 70-Jan-3 [70-Jan-7: 2F].
Burke, Emily C. d. on 70-Mar-19 [70-Mar-24: 2C].
Burke, Emma m. Brady, James on 68-Jun-30 [68-Jul-2: 2C].
Burke, George R. d. on 70-May-2 [70-May-4: 2C].
Burke, George W. (71 yrs.) d. on 69-Apr-1 [69-Apr-2: 2C].
Burke, Honora (40 yrs.) d. on 69-Jun-25 [69-Jun-26: 2B].
Burke, J. M. m. Tatham, Rosa A. R. on 68-Nov-12 [68-Nov-26: 2B].
Burke, James (75 yrs.) d. on 66-Nov-30 [66-Dec-1: 2B].
Burke, John T. (4 yrs., 1 mo.) d. on 68-Dec-20 [68-Dec-21: 2B].

Burke, Joseph Vincent (2 yrs., 10 mos.) d. on 70-Nov-26 [70-Nov-29: 2C].
Burke, Kate E. m. Stokes, Thomas A. on 67-Nov-14 [67-Nov-18: 2B].
Burke, Lizzie A. m. McWilliams, Daniel on 68-Jul-2 [68-Jul-10: 2C].
Burke, M. Gertrude m. McLellan, John S. on 70-Sep-8 [70-Sep-13: 2B].
Burke, Martin (26 yrs.) d. on 68-Jul-16 of Heatstroke [68-Jul-17: 1D].
Burke, Martin H. (20 yrs., 5 mos.) d. on 69-Mar-29 [69-Mar-30: 2C].
Burke, Mary (25 yrs.) d. on 70-Mar-19 [70-Mar-22: 2C].
Burke, Mary Emma (24 yrs.) d. on 70-Oct-15 [70-Oct-17: 2B].
Burke, Michael d. on 69-Oct-1 [69-Oct-2: 2B].
Burke, Pamela A. m. Price, William S. on 69-Dec-14 [69-Dec-16: 2C].
Burke, Patrick (69 yrs.) d. on 67-Mar-10 [67-Mar-11: 2C].
Burke, Patrick R. (1 yr., 10 mos.) d. on 70-Nov-19 [70-Nov-21: 2C].
Burke, Sallie m. Taylor, George W. on 69-Aug-27 [69-Sep-11: 2B].
Burke, Sallie E. (18 yrs.) d. on 68-Feb-26 [68-Feb-27: 2C].
Burke, Walter Louis (6 mos.) d. on 69-Dec-10 [69-Dec-11: 2B].
Burke, William P. m. Pendergast, Bedelia on 69-Jun-9 [69-Jun-16: 2C].
Burkens, Mary Jane m. Metcalf, William H. on 66-Mar-25 [66-Apr-2: 2B].
Burkholder, Nettie m. Long, T. B. on 70-Jun-30 [70-Jul-1: 2B].
Burkman, Delila C. (37 yrs.) d. on 70-Feb-15 [70-Mar-9: 2C].
Burkmar, Dellila C. (37 yrs.) d. on 70-Feb-15 [70-Feb-23: 2C].
Burleigh, Anna McKim d. on 68-May-19 [68-May-21: 2B; 68-May-22: 2C].
Burleigh, Deborah M. m. Hartman, F. C. on 69-Oct-21 [69-Oct-29: 2B; 69-Oct-30: 2B].
Burley, Elizabeth m. Green, Joshua on 65-Dec-21 [66-Mar-6: 2B].
Burley, Issac (72 yrs., 8 mos.) d. on 66-Jul-7 [66-Jul-9: 2C].
Burley, Matilda m. Householder, William H. on 70-Feb-13 [70-Feb-28: 2C].
Burley, Osborn (52 yrs.) d. on 68-Sep-28 [68-Sep-29: 2B; 68-Sep-30: 1G, 2B].
Burlingame, W., Dr. (60 yrs.) d. on 68-Feb-11 [68-Feb-13: 2C].
Burlock, Joseph (77 yrs.) d. on 66-Apr-11 [66-Apr-12: 2B; 66-Apr-13: 2C].
Burman, Francis William Carl (3 yrs., 4 mos.) d. on 69-May-27 [69-May-28: 2C].
Burman, Harriett Amelia Randal (6 yrs., 3 mos.) d. on 69-May-7 of Croup [69-May-10: 2C].
Burman, Mary Agnes m. Dover, Jacob Z. on 68-Mar-5 [68-May-22: 2C].
Burman, Virginia P. m. Reed, John on 66-Sep-6 [66-Oct-9: 2A].
Burnes, Rachel (69 yrs.) d. on 66-May-15 [66-May-16: 2C].
Burneston, Mollie F. m. Wright, Benjamin F. on 69-Aug-4 [69-Aug-7: 2B].
Burnett, Alfred d. on 68-Mar-14 [68-Mar-16: 2B].
Burnett, Caroline P. (59 yrs.) d. on 66-Mar-14 [66-Mar-16: 2B].
Burnett, D. S. (59 yrs.) d. on 67-Jul-8 [67-Jul-9: 2B; 67-Jul-10: 2B; 67-Jul-11: 4E].
Burnett, George R. m. Dell, H. Virginia on 67-Sep-17 [67-Sep-21: 2A].
Burnett, Lulie m. Fifer, George F. on 70-May-11 [70-Sep-27: 2B].
Burnett, Mary Isabella (2 yrs., 4 mos.) d. on 69-Dec-1 [69-Dec-2: 2C].
Burnett, William Thomas (33 yrs.) d. on 68-Aug-6 [68-Aug-7: 2B; 68-Aug-8: 2B].
Burnett, Willienette m. Wood, Franklin on 70-Aug-29 [70-Sep-6: 2B].
Burnham, Charles m. Ackerman, Ida M. on 67-Feb-5 [67-Jul-20: 2D].
Burnham, Elizabeth m. Harrison, Josiah on 70-Oct-16 [70-Oct-22: 2B].
Burnham, Fanny d. on 66-Jan-5 [66-Jan-6: 2C].
Burnham, Henry d. on 66-Jun-4 in Swimming accident [66-Jun-8: 1F; 66-Jun-9: 2B].
Burnham, John T. (36 yrs., 6 mos.) d. on 70-Mar-27 [70-Mar-28: 2B; 70-Mar-29: 2B].
Burnham, Kate m. Stafford, Joseph B. on 69-Jan-12 [69-Jan-19: 2C].
Burnitt, William (56 yrs.) d. on 66-Jul-5 [66-Jul-7: 2B].
Burns, Agnes R. m. Kelly, Lawrence J. on 68-Jan-27 [68-Feb-19: 2C].
Burns, Annie M. m. Mulhall, James E. on 66-Jun-14 [66-Jun-20: 2C].
Burns, Arthur P., Dr. m. Stockett, Frank E. on 70-Jun-30 [70-Jul-11: 2C].
Burns, Ashton Claxton d. on 69-Jul-12 [69-Jul-14: 2D].
Burns, Catherine (65 yrs.) d. on 70-Dec-5 [70-Dec-6: 2C].
Burns, Charles S. m. Phair, Mollie on 68-Dec-20 [68-Dec-29: 2D].

Burns, Dennis (58 yrs.) d. on 70-Feb-8 [70-Feb-9: 2C].
Burns, Edward d. on 70-Jan-20 [70-Jan-22: 2C].
Burns, Elizabeth (70 yrs.) d. on 68-Apr-14 [68-Apr-15: 2B; 68-Apr-16: 2B].
Burns, Emmanuel (43 yrs., 4 mos.) d. on 70-Aug-17 [70-Aug-19: 2C].
Burns, George W. m. Pascault, Emily M. on 68-Oct-27 [68-Oct-29: 2B].
Burns, Harriet N. d. on 66-Feb-5 [66-Feb-7: 2C; 66-Feb-8: 2C].
Burns, James T. m. Ensor, Honour on 67-Dec-24 [67-Dec-25: 2C].
Burns, Jane (75 yrs.) d. on 66-Jan-13 [66-Jan-15: 2B].
Burns, John (2 yrs., 8 mos.) d. on 66-Apr-30 [66-May-2: 2B].
Burns, John d. on 66-Nov-24 in Railroad accident [66-Nov-28: 1G].
Burns, John (26 yrs.) d. on 70-Aug-26 [70-Aug-27: 2B].
Burns, John Edward (11 mos.) d. on 70-Mar-29 of Chronic croup [70-Mar-30: 2B].
Burns, John Samuel (1 yr., 2 mos.) d. on 70-Aug-3 [70-Aug-5: 2C].
Burns, John W. (41 yrs.) d. [68-Nov-6: 2C].
Burns, Joseph (58 yrs.) d. on 68-Oct-4 [68-Oct-5: 2C].
Burns, Julia (1 yr., 2 mos.) d. on 70-Aug-19 [70-Aug-20: 2B].
Burns, Kate (33 yrs.) d. on 67-Nov-26 [67-Nov-27: 2C].
Burns, Kate m. Young, James E. on 69-Oct-10 [69-Oct-12: 2C; 69-Oct-30: 2B].
Burns, Lena E. m. Johnson, Zachariah on 68-Oct-20 [68-Oct-21: 2B].
Burns, Lizzie (5 mos.) d. on 68-Jul-12 [68-Jul-14: 2B].
Burns, Louisa T. d. on 69-Nov-23 [69-Nov-24: 2C; 69-Nov-25: 2C].
Burns, Margaret (2 yrs.) d. on 69-Mar-12 [69-Mar-13: 2B].
Burns, Mary (8 yrs.) d. on 67-Feb-11 [67-Feb-12: 2C].
Burns, Mary Agnes (2 yrs., 4 mos.) d. on 70-Aug-4 [70-Aug-5: 2C].
Burns, Mary Ann (22 yrs.) d. on 70-Nov-23 [70-Dec-29: 2C].
Burns, Mary Ellen (36 yrs.) d. on 70-Nov-17 [70-Nov-18: 2C].
Burns, Mary M. m. O'Brien, James on 66-Nov-14 [66-Dec-13: 2B].
Burns, Owen (59 yrs.) d. on 69-Apr-8 [69-Apr-16: 2B].
Burns, R. K. (50 yrs., 9 mos.) d. on 66-Nov-3 [66-Nov-5: 2B].
Burns, Richard m. Wilson, S. Maria on 66-Jan-4 [66-Jan-6: 2B].
Burns, Robert L. (51 yrs.) d. on 68-Apr-27 of Pneumonia [68-Apr-28: 2B].
Burns, Robert McConnell (28 yrs.) d. on 67-Jul-8 [67-Oct-8: 2B].
Burns, Sarah (37 yrs.) d. on 67-Apr-12 [67-Apr-13: 2B].
Burns, Sarah J. m. Rixham, George B. on 69-Sep-20 [69-Sep-23: 2B].
Burns, Sarah J. m. Hubbel, Joseph A. on 69-Jul-1 [69-Jul-3: 2B].
Burns, Theodore (15 yrs.) d. on 70-Apr-12 [70-Apr-22: 2C].
Burns, William J. (27 yrs., 3 mos.) d. on 70-Aug-29 [70-Sep-3: 2B].
Burnside, James (60 yrs.) d. on 66-Aug-30 [66-Aug-31: 2B; 66-Sep-1: 2B].
Burnside, Jane m. Dickerson, George W. on 69-Jul-7 [69-Jul-8: 2C].
Burnup, Elizabeth (78 yrs.) d. on 66-Oct-6 [66-Oct-8: 2B].
Burrier, Angeline (46 yrs.) d. on 70-Sep-23 [70-Sep-24: 2B].
Burrier, Augustus m. Harper, Mary on 67-Jun-20 [67-Jun-22: 2B].
Burrier, Charles Tippett (11 mos.) d. on 69-Jan-30 [69-Feb-1: 2C].
Burrier, John R. m. Long, Mary Virginia on 70-Oct-31 [70-Nov-24: 2B].
Burrier, Sophia m. Smith, Joseph M. on 67-Nov-24 [67-Dec-3: 2C].
Burrier, Temperance (73 yrs.) d. on 66-Nov-8 [66-Nov-10: 2B].
Burris, Elizabeth Mason d. on 70-May-7 [70-May-9: 2B].
Burris, James H. m. Brown, Eleanor on 66-Apr-18 [66-Apr-28: 2A].
Burrough, Edward Emery (1 yr., 9 mos.) d. on 67-Dec-10 [67-Dec-11: 2B].
Burroughs, Elizabeth (63 yrs.) d. on 66-Jan-13 [66-Jan-17: 2C].
Burroughs, Joseph m. McLean, Georgie on 68-Apr-2 [68-Apr-4: 2B].
Burroughs, Mary E. d. on 67-Jan-5 [67-Jan-8: 2B].
Burrow, Clifton Paul (1 yr., 2 mos.) d. on 69-Jul-8 [69-Jul-13: 2C].
Burrows, Ann Maria m. Tender, James on 67-Aug-27 [67-Aug-28: 2B].
Burrows, Arthur Rhodes d. on 70-Oct-18 [70-Oct-22: 2B].

Burrows, Bettie L. m. Smith, G. Cookman on 66-Oct-23 [66-Oct-26: 2B].
Burrows, Daniel A. m. Rollins, Laura J. on 68-Dec-23 [68-Dec-29: 2D].
Burrows, Walter Rollins d. on 70-Jan-8 [70-Jan-10: 2C].
Burruss, William J. m. Moss, Ann Rebecca on 70-Apr-28 [70-May-2: 2B].
Burt, Amos S. m. Garrettson, Eleanora L. on 66-Mar-14 [66-Mar-17: 2B].
Burton, Annie Howard (3 yrs., 5 mos.) d. on 68-Dec-23 [68-Dec-24: 2C].
Burton, Columbia T. m. Bland, J. H. on 69-Jan-7 [69-Jan-9: 2C].
Burton, Elva R. m. Chase, Richard M. on 70-Apr-1 [70-Apr-16: 2B].
Burton, Harry W. m. Tappey, Mary V. on 66-Nov-27 [66-Dec-5: 2B].
Burton, Ida Virginia (4 mos.) d. on 67-May-3 [67-May-24: 2B].
Burton, Isabella d. on 68-Nov-23 [68-Nov-24: 2C].
Burton, Joseph (18 yrs.) d. on 66-Dec-19 [66-Dec-20: 2B].
Burton, Marcelene m. Beall, Nathan F. on 67-Nov-7 [67-Nov-23: 2B].
Burton, Nettie m. Chaney, James R. on 70-Nov-21 [70-Dec-8: 2B].
Burton, Richard A. m. Scaggs, Carrie V. on 68-Oct-1 [68-Oct-3: 2B].
Burton, Samuel (60 yrs.) d. on 69-Sep-24 Murdered (Stabbing) [69-Sep-27: 4C].
Burton, Sarah Jane (41 yrs.) d. on 70-Oct-3 of Consumption [70-Oct-4: 2B; 70-Oct-5: 2B].
Burton, Thomas W. m. Bull, Emma H. on 70-Jan-19 [70-Jan-24: 2C].
Burton, William m. Devlin, Mary Ann on 66-Aug-15 [66-Aug-23: 2C].
Burton, William N. m. Miles, Hattie B. on 67-Jul-9 [67-Aug-21: 2B].
Burwell, L. C. m. Cromwell, Benjamin M. on 66-Jan-16 [66-Jan-18: 2C].
Burwell, Laura Lee m. Davidson, Spencer on 69-Sep-9 [69-Sep-13: 2B].
Busby, Isaiah (9 yrs., 2 mos.) d. on 70-Jun-27 [70-Jun-28: 2C].
Busch, Abraham, Sr. (73 yrs.) d. on 69-Nov-18 [69-Nov-20: 2B].
Busch, Alice (4 yrs., 2 mos.) d. on 69-Sep-2 [69-Sep-15: 2B].
Busch, Caroline Virginia (19 yrs., 6 mos.) d. on 67-Feb-26 [67-Mar-1: 2C].
Busch, Emma m. Mills, Eugene on 70-Oct-31 [70-Dec-6: 2C].
Busch, George Edward (11 mos.) d. on 70-Jan-10 [70-Jan-11: 2C].
Busche, Nicholas (14 yrs.) d. on 67-Aug-14 Drowned [67-Aug-20: 1G; 67-Aug-21: 2B].
Buschman, Clement A. (53 yrs.) d. on 70-Apr-3 [70-Apr-4: 2B; 70-Apr-5: 2B; 70-Apr-6: 2B].
Buschman, Francis Albert (7 yrs., 1 mo.) d. on 69-May-28 [69-May-29: 2B].
Buschman, Katie m. Snyder, Thomas on 69-May-25 [69-Jun-1: 2B].
Buschman, Sallie (1 yr.) d. on 67-Sep-3 [67-Sep-5: 2B].
Buschmann, Kate m. Miller, C. W. on 67-May-5 [67-Jul-10: 2B].
Busey, Emma Virginia d. on 70-Aug-3 [70-Aug-4: 2C].
Busey, Kate O. m. Hall, Thomas T. on 68-Dec-21 [69-Mar-23: 2C].
Busey, L. m. Hogg, John on 66-Apr-4 [66-Apr-14: 2B].
Busey, William M. m. Brown, Dollie A. on 68-Oct-28 [68-Oct-31: 2B].
Bush, Anne Jones (24 yrs.) d. on 67-Jan-9 of Consumption [67-Jan-14: 2C].
Bush, James A. m. Hindman, Eliza B. on 67-Feb-14 [67-Feb-16: 2D].
Bush, Margaret Emily m. Bay, Nathan on 67-Feb-21 [67-Feb-28: 2C].
Bush, Peter m. McMillan, Martha on 68-Jan-2 [68-Jan-8: 2C].
Bush, Stella (2 yrs., 1 mo.) d. on 70-Jan-11 [70-Jan-19: 2C].
Bush, William (60 yrs.) d. on 69-Feb-4 [69-Feb-6: 2C].
Bushey, Jacob M. m. Bromwell, Gussie on 70-Jan-19 [70-Jan-19: 2C].
Bushman, Emma m. Kain, George on 70-Nov-15 [70-Nov-22: 2B].
Bushman, Frederick m. Sheldon, Sarah M. on 67-Apr-21 [67-May-14: 2B].
Bushman, Isabella C. (41 yrs.) d. on 68-Aug-1 [68-Aug-24: 2B].
Busic, Joshua (65 yrs.) d. on 66-May-24 [66-May-25: 2C].
Busick, Ella Virginia m. McKewen, Francis on 70-May-12 [70-Nov-18: 2C].
Bussard, Jane m. Mills, John A. on 66-Jun-12 [66-Jun-15: 2C].
Bussard, Matthew (68 yrs.) d. on 68-Feb-16 [68-Mar-13: 2C].
Bussey, J. Thomas m. Rowe, Julia P. on 67-Jan-16 [67-Jan-22: 2C].
Busus, Harriet (48 yrs.) d. on 69-Jan-13 [69-Jan-14: 2D].
Butcher, Willie E. (1 yr., 2 mos.) d. on 68-Sep-24 [68-Sep-26: 2B].

Butler, A. C., Dr. (76 yrs.) d. on 68-Aug-11 of Flatulant cholic [68-Aug-12: 1G, 2C].
Butler, Amanda H. m. Woolford, Thomas E. on 66-Nov-21 [66-Nov-24: 2B].
Butler, Anastasia (1 yr., 1 mo.) d. on 70-Feb-10 [70-Feb-11: 2C].
Butler, Ann M. m. Southern, Issac on 68-Oct-26 [68-Oct-30: 2C].
Butler, Annie Elizabeth (7 mos.) d. on 68-Nov-23 [68-Nov-24: 2C].
Butler, Bertha Cohen (11 mos.) d. on 67-Feb-24 [67-Feb-27: 2C].
Butler, Catherine (76 yrs.) d. on 69-Aug-4 [69-Aug-5: 2B].
Butler, Charles m. Dohm, Elizabeth J. on 68-Nov-24 [68-Dec-3: 2C].
Butler, Edward d. on 69-Jan-17 [69-Feb-9: 1G].
Butler, Edward F. (40 yrs.) d. on 69-Oct-1 [69-Oct-7: 2B].
Butler, Elizabeth (24 yrs.) d. on 69-Jun-1 [69-Jun-3: 2B].
Butler, Elizabeth (72 yrs.) d. on 70-Feb-17 [70-Feb-28: 2C].
Butler, Ellen m. Dorsey, James H. on 67-Nov-7 [67-Nov-18: 2B].
Butler, Evans m. Stanton, Susan Ann on 68-Oct-15 [68-Oct-17: 2B].
Butler, F. A. m. Stewart, H. H. on 70-Jun-21 [70-Jun-23: 2C].
Butler, Fanny H. (66 yrs.) d. on 70-Mar-17 [70-Mar-19: 2B].
Butler, George T. (9 yrs.) d. on 69-Mar-18 [69-Mar-19: 2C].
Butler, Henrietta (64 yrs.) d. on 69-Jul-27 [69-Jul-29: 2C].
Butler, Ida Sophia (1 yr., 5 mos.) d. on 66-Jun-7 [66-Jun-9: 2B].
Butler, James (82 yrs.) d. on 67-Jul-7 [67-Jul-8: 1G, 2C].
Butler, James (1 yr., 3 mos.) d. on 70-Aug-3 [70-Aug-4: 2C].
Butler, James J. m. Corcoran, Anastasia on 66-Dec-10 [66-Dec-20: 2B].
Butler, John, Sr. (62 yrs.) d. on 68-Feb-7 [68-Feb-8: 2B].
Butler, John H. m. Clark, Victorine P. on 67-Aug-20 [67-Sep-7: 2A].
Butler, John J., Dr. (34 yrs.) d. on 66-Feb-19 [66-Feb-20: 2B].
Butler, Lucy Welsh (2 yrs., 2 mos.) d. on 68-Feb-1 [68-Feb-3: 2C].
Butler, Maggie (9 mos.) d. on 70-Jul-12 [70-Jul-13: 2C].
Butler, Margaret (4 yrs.) d. on 69-Aug-15 [69-Aug-16: 2B].
Butler, Margaret (74 yrs.) d. on 69-Nov-6 [69-Nov-8: 2C].
Butler, Martha E. m. Oliver, Thomas J. on 68-Nov-26 [68-Nov-28: 2C].
Butler, Mary (40 yrs.) d. on 69-Sep-21 [69-Sep-23: 2B].
Butler, Mary d. on 70-May-3 Burned [70-May-5: 1G].
Butler, Mary C. m. Lawton, Robert B. on 66-May-30 [66-Jun-5: 2B].
Butler, Mary E. m. Phillips, William H. on 70-Aug-16 [70-Aug-24: 2C].
Butler, Mary F. (33 yrs.) d. on 70-Oct-7 of Heart disease [70-Oct-8: 4C].
Butler, Oliver N. m. Spence, Mary on 69-Oct-26 [69-Oct-30: 2B].
Butler, Rebecca (84 yrs.) d. on 67-Dec-20 [67-Dec-24: 2B].
Butler, Richard (97 yrs.) d. on 68-Dec-3 [68-Dec-4: 2D; 68-Dec-5: 2C].
Butler, Samuel, Jr. (17 yrs.) d. on 66-Jan-18 [66-Jan-19: 2C].
Butler, Sarah E. d. on 70-Jun-6 of Heart disease [70-Jun-7: 1H].
Butler, Susan (91 yrs.) d. on 69-Aug-26 [69-Sep-4: 2B].
Butler, Susie Blanch (1 yr., 4 mos.) d. on 66-Nov-18 [66-Nov-19: 2B].
Butler, Thomas d. on 66-Feb-4 of Heart disease [66-Apr-18: 1G].
Butler, Thomas H. m. Riggle, Laura on 67-Mar-25 [67-Apr-3: 2B].
Butler, Warren M. (1 yr., 3 mos.) d. on 67-Dec-24 of Consumption [67-Dec-25: 2C].
Butt, Henry (53 yrs.) d. on 67-Jun-6 [67-Jun-7: 2B].
Butterfield, Morris H. (56 yrs.) d. on 67-Feb-8 [67-Feb-13: 2D].
Butterworth, Mary Louisa (22 yrs.) d. on 66-Jul-11 [66-Jul-13: 2C].
Button, Charles Robert (2 yrs., 8 mos.) d. on 69-Mar-7 [69-Mar-8: 2C; 69-Mar-9: 2C].
Button, William Wallack (11 mos.) d. on 69-Feb-17 [69-Feb-19: 2C].
Butts, Alfred, Jr. (33 yrs.) d. on 67-Oct-18 [67-Oct-24: 2B].
Butts, William H. m. Gonce, Mary E. on 69-Oct-26 [69-Nov-17: 2C].
Buxensten, Franky King (1 yr., 7 mos.) d. on 68-Jul-22 [68-Jul-27: 2B].
Buxton, John H. m. Curtis, Jane E. on 66-Mar-27 [66-Mar-31: 2C].
Buzby, Frank Stockton (8 mos.) d. on 67-Jan-4 [67-Jan-5: 2C].

Buzby, Mary S. (14 yrs.) d. on 66-May-23 [66-May-24: 2C; 66-May-25: 2C].
Byard, Andrew J. m. Howard, Mary E. on 68-Nov-1 [68-Nov-6: 2C].
Byer, Catharine d. on 67-Jun-29 of Heart disease [67-Jul-10: 2B].
Byer, Louis m. Robinson, Susie E. on 66-Apr-8 [66-Apr-10: 2C].
Byer, Susie E. (23 yrs.) d. on 67-Dec-6 [67-Dec-7: 2B].
Byerly, Luther d. Drowned [68-Apr-8: 2A].
Byers, John Samuel (3 yrs., 3 mos.) d. on 67-Jan-8 [67-Jan-10: 2C].
Byers, John T. (31 yrs.) d. on 70-Jan-31 [70-Feb-1: 2B].
Byers, Kate E. m. Hayden, Horace Edwin on 68-Nov-30 [68-Dec-9: 2C].
Byers, Mary Ellen (9 mos.) d. on 67-Jun-10 [67-Jun-11: 2B].
Byers, Walter Byron (3 mos.) d. on 68-Feb-10 [68-Feb-11: 2C].
Byram, Margaret (88 yrs.) d. on 69-Dec-2 [69-Dec-20: 2C].
Byrd, Howard S. F. (6 mos.) d. on 70-Sep-29 [70-Sep-30: 2B].
Byrd, James E. m. Fletcher, Kate on 69-Dec-28 [70-Jan-4: 2C].
Byrd, Leila d. [69-Mar-20: 2B].
Byrd, Mary Shelden (49 yrs.) d. on 67-Jul-2 [67-Jul-6: 2B].
Byrne, Andrew J. d. on 68-Dec-18 [69-Jan-13: 2D].
Byrne, Anne (15 yrs., 4 mos.) d. on 66-Apr-1 [66-Apr-3: 2B].
Byrne, Bridget A. (41 yrs.) d. on 70-Jan-27 [70-Jan-28: 2B; 70-Jan-29: 2B].
Byrne, Daniel (33 yrs.) d. on 66-May-10 [66-May-12: 2A].
Byrne, Elizabeth M. d. on 66-Oct-12 [66-Nov-3: 2B].
Byrne, George Vincent (3 mos.) d. on 68-Sep-16 [68-Sep-18: 2B].
Byrne, John (46 yrs.) d. on 68-Dec-28 [68-Dec-29: 2D; 68-Dec-30: 2C].
Byrne, John H. d. on 67-Aug-25 [67-Aug-26: 2D].
Byrne, Joseph F. m. Amick, Mary E. on 68-Nov-21 [68-Dec-1: 2C].
Byrne, Lizzie C. m. Agnew, John D. on 67-Feb-19 [67-Feb-25: 2C].
Byrne, Mary A. m. Beissler, Nicholas E. on 69-Jul-8 [69-Jul-22: 2C].
Byrne, Mary Agnes (1 yr., 4 mos.) d. on 67-Mar-21 [67-Mar-22: 2C].
Byrne, Mary Alexina m. Bucher, George W. on 67-Oct-10 [67-Oct-16: 2B].
Byrne, Mary Ann d. on 70-Sep-20 [70-Sep-21: 2B].
Byrne, Mary E. d. on 68-Aug-20 [68-Aug-22: 2A; 68-Nov-14: 2B].
Byrne, Mary F. m. Reilly, William P. on 67-Nov-28 [67-Dec-3: 2C].
Byrne, Mary Halton (2 yrs., 11 mos.) d. on 70-Oct-18 [70-Oct-19: 2B; 70-Oct-20: 2B].
Byrne, Mary J. m. Lacy, Peter E. on 69-May-10 [69-May-12: 2B].
Byrne, Michael (60 yrs.) d. on 70-Oct-6 [70-Oct-8: 2B].
Byrne, Samuel E. m. Stuart, Laura V. on 67-Oct-29 [67-Nov-2: 2B].
Byrne, W. H. m. Halton, Mary J., Miss on 67-Jan-30 [67-Feb-12: 2C].
Byrne, Willie Vincent (2 yrs.) d. on 70-Nov-15 [70-Nov-16: 2C].
Byrnes, Catherine (27 yrs.) d. on 69-Dec-3 [69-Dec-4: 2C].
Byrnes, Edward d. on 70-Jan-28 [70-Jan-29: 2B; 70-Jan-31: 1H].
Byrnes, Hugh d. on 67-Nov-17 Drowned [67-Nov-30: 1G].
Byrnes, John Henry (2 yrs., 5 mos.) d. on 69-Jan-24 [69-Jan-26: 2C].
Byrnes, Martin (36 yrs.) d. on 70-Jan-30 [70-Jan-31: 2C].
Byrnes, Peter W. (48 yrs.) d. on 66-Oct-14 [66-Oct-15: 2B].
Byrnes, William (49 yrs.) d. on 70-Apr-8 [70-Apr-9: 1H, 2B].
Byron, Sarah J. m. Hopkins, Lewis Hopkins on 66-Apr-16 [66-Apr-10: 2B].
Cabell, N. F. m. Keller, Mary M. on 67-Aug-6 [67-Aug-7: 2C].
Cable, Mary J. m. Bowen, Gerard on 69-Dec-30 [70-Jan-12: 2C].
Cacy, Rosetta (64 yrs.) d. on 68-Feb-12 [68-Feb-14: 2C].
Cadden, John (25 yrs.) d. on 66-Sep-24 Murdered (Stabbing) [66-Sep-25: 1F, 2B].
Cadden, Margaret (82 yrs.) d. on 68-Feb-2 [68-Feb-4: 2D].
Cadden, Margaret Ann (10 mos.) d. on 70-Jan-20 [70-Jan-21: 2C].
Cade, Ella m. Robinson, George Millford on 70-Apr-28 [70-Apr-30: 2A].
Cademore, Susanna m. Dashiell, Charles E. on 69-Mar-17 [69-Mar-20: 2B].
Cadimore, Louisa (43 yrs.) d. on 68-Dec-17 [68-Dec-23: 2C].

Cadle, William (35 yrs.) d. on 67-Feb-9 Drowned [67-Feb-12: 4C].
Cadwallader, Harrison C m. Brown, Sallie J. on 67-May-18 [67-May-30: 2B].
Cadwallader, Harrison C. m. Brown, Jallie J. on 67-May-18 [67-May-24: 2B; 67-May-30: 2B].
Cadwallader, Laura V. m. Barker, John P. on 66-Oct-9 [66-Nov-8: 2C].
Caffrey, Ann (28 yrs.) d. on 69-Nov-13 [69-Nov-15: 2C].
Caffrey, Richard (3 yrs., 9 mos.) d. on 69-Jun-1 [69-Jun-3: 2B].
Cager, Jane (69 yrs.) d. on 67-Oct-27 [67-Oct-28: 2B].
Cahill, Ann (33 yrs.) d. on 66-May-30 [66-Jun-1: 2B].
Cahill, Frederick J. m. Reeder, Mary A. C. on 70-Oct-11 [70-Oct-17: 2B].
Cahill, John m. Wirtz, Kate on 67-Feb-14 [67-Feb-18: 2C].
Cahill, Joseph (2 yrs., 8 mos.) d. on 66-Nov-21 [66-Nov-22: 2C].
Cahill, Michael (43 yrs.) d. on 67-Apr-6 [67-Apr-8: 2B].
Cahill, Patrick m. Boyle, Ann on 67-Mar-4 [67-Mar-7: 2C].
Cail, Catharine (35 yrs.) d. on 68-Feb-14 [68-Feb-15: 1G].
Cain, Alice m. White, George D. on 70-Dec-6 [70-Dec-10: 2B].
Cain, Catherine (64 yrs.) d. on 69-Aug-9 [69-Aug-10: 2C].
Cain, Fannie m. Corrigan, James on 66-Jan-18 [66-Jan-19: 2C].
Cain, George m. Inkhouse, Mary A. on 69-Aug-30 [69-Nov-5: 2C].
Cain, J. m. Barrett, Mary C. on 67-Mar-11 [67-Apr-25: 2B].
Cain, John (66 yrs.) d. on 66-Jun-12 Crushed by wall [66-Jun-13: 1F, 2B].
Cain, Maggie C. m. Robinson, Spencer J. on 67-Jan-24 [67-Jan-28: 2C].
Cain, Margaret Louisa (24 yrs.) d. on 70-Sep-5 [70-Sep-7: 2B].
Cain, Mary E. m. Collins, Patrick [67-Aug-2: 2C].
Cain, Wilhelmina (1 yr., 3 mos.) d. on 67-Sep-23 [67-Sep-24: 2A].
Cain, Willie W. (2 yrs.) d. on 69-Oct-26 [69-Oct-27: 2B].
Cairns, Samuel d. on 70-May-11 [70-Jun-1: 1H].
Calahee, Margaret m. Mahany, John R. on 66-Jun-26 [66-Jun-28: 2C].
Calaman, Thomas (38 yrs.) d. on 68-Apr-25 [68-Apr-27: 2B].
Calder, William m. Norris, Sarah E. on 66-Apr-30 [66-May-3: 2C].
Caldwell, Charles Dunning (8 yrs.) d. on 67-Apr-21 of Scarlet fever [67-Apr-22: 2A].
Caldwell, Flora (96 yrs.) d. on 68-Feb-28 [68-Feb-29: 2B].
Caldwell, Frances m. Conaway, John S. on 68-Feb-20 [68-Feb-29: 2B].
Caldwell, George Earle (11 mos.) d. on 69-Feb-22 of Scarlet fever [69-Feb-23: 2D].
Caldwell, J. P. m. Koster, Carrie J. on 70-Aug-11 [70-Aug-15: 2B].
Caldwell, James Archer (11 mos.) d. on 69-Aug-5 [69-Aug-6: 2C].
Caldwell, John Carroll, Jr. (23 yrs.) d. on 69-Nov-18 [69-Nov-20: 2B].
Caldwell, John S. m. Beard, Mary E. on 70-Mar-22 [70-Apr-7: 2B].
Caldwell, Julia m. Walters, James C. on 69-Apr-13 [69-Apr-28: 2B].
Caldwell, Lizzie m. Bailey, Edwin on 68-Dec-24 [69-Feb-15: 2D].
Caldwell, Lizzie Jane m. Farrow, M. M. on 68-Apr-16 [68-May-4: 2B].
Caldwell, Mary J (39 yrs.) d. on 68-Mar-15 [68-Mar-17: 2C].
Caldwell, Samuel E. m. Kennedy, Sarah L. on 67-Jun-13 [67-Jun-28: 2B].
Caldwell, Sarah C. m. Parmer, Dennis on 67-Apr-27 [67-May-14: 2B].
Caldwell, Thomas (63 yrs.) d. on 68-Mar-28 [68-Mar-31: 2B].
Caldwell, William M. m. Clemment, Laura E. on 66-Aug-21 [66-Aug-24: 2B].
Caldwell, William Q. (62 yrs.) d. on 68-Apr-7 [68-Apr-8: 1G, 2B].
Call, Mary m. Gassaway, Samuel on 67-Feb-3 [67-Feb-7: 2C].
Callaghan, Charles (4 yrs.) d. on 66-Feb-19 [66-Feb-20: 2B].
Callahan, Caroline Percilla (6 mos.) d. on 70-Jul-31 [70-Aug-4: 2C].
Callahan, Dennis (36 yrs.) d. on 66-Jul-30 [66-Aug-1: 2C].
Callahan, Harriet Amanda (42 yrs., 7 mos.) d. on 69-May-18 [69-May-19: 2C].
Callahan, Margaret (45 yrs.) d. on 69-Feb-11 of Heart disease [69-Feb-12: 1G, 2C].
Callahan, Mary d. on 70-Feb-14 [70-Feb-16: 2C].
Callahan, Peter (24 yrs.) d. on 68-Mar-16 [68-Mar-27: 2C].
Callan, Bernard (60 yrs.) d. on 69-Sep-21 [69-Sep-22: 2C].

Callan, Francis, Sr. (68 yrs.) d. on 69-Mar-18 [69-Mar-20: 2B].
Callan, James J. (24 yrs.) d. on 69-May-11 Drowned [69-May-13: 1H].
Callan, Julia (50 yrs.) d. on 70-Mar-8 [70-Mar-9: 2C; 70-Mar-10: 2C].
Callan, Owen (33 yrs.) d. on 70-Nov-9 [70-Nov-10: 2C; 70-Nov-11: 2B].
Callander, Martha J. m. Miller, Jacob on 68-Aug-4 [68-Aug-5: 2B].
Callaway, Annie E. m. Iddins, Henry on 68-Nov-9 [68-Nov-16: 2C].
Callender, James Madison (2 yrs., 4 mos.) d. on 70-May-31 [70-Jun-2: 2B].
Calligan, Thomas (5 yrs.) d. on 68-Sep-27 [68-Sep-30: 1G, 2B].
Callinan, Thomas (1 yr., 11 mos.) d. on 69-Feb-28 [69-Mar-3: 2C].
Callinan, Winnifred (4 yrs., 11 mos.) d. on 68-Nov-11 [69-Mar-3: 2C].
Callis, Bella T. m. Moulton, William G. on 69-Dec-15 [69-Dec-18: 2B].
Callis, Fannie A. m. Clotworthy, Edward F. on 66-Oct-29 [66-Nov-5: 2B].
Callis, William (55 yrs.) d. on 66-Feb-9 [66-Feb-19: 2B].
Callow, Emma V. m. Baldwin, LeRoy E on 66-May-17 [66-May-18: 2C].
Calloway, Sallie Lavinia (6 yrs., 2 mos.) d. on 68-Jan-3 [68-Jan-4: 2C].
Caltrider, Elizabeth d. on 70-Oct-1 [70-Oct-13: 2C].
Caltrider, Frederick (83 yrs.) d. on 69-Apr-24 [69-May-1: 2B].
Calvert, Charles B. m. MacKubin, Eleanor on 66-Jun-14 [66-Jun-18: 2B].
Calvert, John A. (3 mos.) d. on 69-Sep-22 [69-Sep-23: 2B].
Calvert, Kate C. m. Alldridge, W. T. on 66-Apr-29 [66-May-19: 2B].
Calvert, Maggie A. (25 yrs.) d. on 69-Dec-23 [69-Dec-24: 2C; 69-Dec-25: 2C].
Calwel, Mary (58 yrs.) d. on 67-Jun-15 [67-Jun-19: 2B].
Calwell, James S. (48 yrs.) d. on 69-Jun-27 [69-Jun-28: 2C; 69-Jun-29: 2C].
Calwell, John, Jr. d. on 70-Jul-18 Drowned [70-Jul-20: 4E].
Calwell, John R. Kelso (9 mos.) d. on 66-Jul-22 [66-Jul-23: 2C].
Calwell, Rosanna M. m. Wherrett, James M. on 69-Oct-14 [69-Oct-19: 2C].
Calwell, Sophie N. (6 yrs., 2 mos.) d. on 69-Dec-5 [69-Dec-7: 2C].
Calwell, Thomas G. m. Jackson, Anne Eliza, Miss on 66-Feb-20 [66-Feb-27: 2B; 66-Feb-28: 2C].
Camalier, George P. m. Brown, M. Kate on 67-Mar-5 [67-Mar-8: 2C].
Camalier, George P. M. (24 yrs.) d. on 70-Nov-17 [70-Nov-18: 2C].
Camalier, George Van Howard (1 yr., 2 mos.) d. on 69-May-15 [69-May-17: 2B].
Cameron, Ann (68 yrs.) d. on 70-Jul-25 [70-Jul-28: 2C].
Cameron, Daniel W. (38 yrs.) d. on 69-Dec-8 [69-Dec-8: 2C].
Cameron, Elizabeth d. on 66-Dec-28 [67-Jan-2: 2C].
Cameron, John W. m. Williams, Mary C. on 68-Jun-25 [68-Jun-29: 2B].
Cameron, Margaret m. Walker, Edward M. on 66-Jan-4 [66-Jan-20: 2C].
Camichael, Jane (60 yrs., 7 mos.) d. on 70-May-6 [70-May-7: 2B].
Camp, Joseph (5 mos.) d. on 68-Sep-27 [68-Sep-29: 2B].
Camp, Joseph m. Weidler, Josephine on 67-Feb-27 [67-Mar-2: 2B].
Campbell, Alice Taney m. Etting, Frank M. on 68-Oct-27 [68-Oct-29: 2B].
Campbell, Annie C. m. Selke, David L. on 66-Apr-13 [66-Apr-17: 2C].
Campbell, Arthur (13 yrs.) d. on 68-Mar-16 of Suicide (Hanging) [68-Mar-18: 1G, 2B].
Campbell, Bridget (65 yrs.) d. on 66-Dec-21 [66-Dec-22: 2A].
Campbell, Caroline A. d. on 70-Aug-7 [70-Aug-29: 2C].
Campbell, Charles Bernard (5 yrs.) d. on 69-Mar-7 [69-Mar-8: 2C].
Campbell, Charles Hopkins (1 yr., 8 mos.) d. on 69-Sep-7 [69-Sep-8: 2B].
Campbell, Clara m. Colston, Frederick M. on 68-Oct-28 [68-Nov-4: 2C].
Campbell, Cora Lee (1 yr., 6 mos.) d. on 68-Aug-13 [68-Aug-15: 2B].
Campbell, Eliza d. on 70-Dec-12 [70-Dec-13: 2C; 70-Dec-14: 2C].
Campbell, Eliza Adeline (33 yrs.) d. on 66-Jun-1 of Suicide (Poisoning) [66-Jun-2: 2B; 66-Jun-4: 4C; 66-Jun-5: 1G].
Campbell, Ellen A. m. Connolly, Daniel A. on 68-Aug-6 [68-Aug-11: 2B].
Campbell, Harriet (78 yrs.) d. on 68-Nov-1 [68-Nov-2: 2B].
Campbell, Harry (2 yrs., 10 mos.) d. on 68-Jan-6 [68-Sep-29: 2B; 68-Sep-30: 1G, 2B].

Campbell, Hattie m. Perkins, J. Weston on 66-Jul-10 [66-Jul-19: 2C].
Campbell, Henry J. d. on 67-Mar-1 [67-Mar-2: 2B].
Campbell, Isabel R. m. Maguire, William West on 69-Nov-15 [69-Dec-30: 2C].
Campbell, James m. Eichelberger, Mary on 67-Feb-19 [67-Mar-5: 2C].
Campbell, James A. (50 yrs.) d. on 68-Oct-29 [68-Oct-30: 2C; 68-Oct-31: 2B; 68-Nov-2: 4C].
Campbell, James A. (2 yrs., 4 mos.) d. on 70-Dec-21 [70-Dec-23: 2B].
Campbell, James A. m. Allen, Mary R. on 66-Nov-14 [66-Nov-19: 2B].
Campbell, James E. (1 yr., 3 mos.) d. on 70-Mar-21 [70-Mar-23: 2C].
Campbell, James G. (55 yrs.) d. on 67-Dec-16 [67-Dec-17: 2B].
Campbell, James Ignatius d. on 69-Feb-7 [69-Feb-8: 2C].
Campbell, James Mason (60 yrs.) d. on 69-Jun-21 [69-Jun-23: 1E, 2C; 69-Jun-25: 1G].
Campbell, John, Col. (74 yrs.) d. on 67-Jun-8 in Carriage accident [67-Jun-12: 1F; 67-Jun-14: 2B].
Campbell, Johnnie (1 yr., 1 mo.) d. on 67-Sep-10 [67-Sep-13: 2B].
Campbell, Kate (34 yrs.) d. on 67-Jul-14 [67-Jul-16: 2C].
Campbell, Kate H. m. Ford, James R. on 66-Mar-6 [66-Mar-13: 2B].
Campbell, Maggie m. Hall, Franklin on 70-Jul-31 [70-Aug-18: 2B].
Campbell, Margaret Ann (54 yrs.) d. on 70-Nov-16 [70-Nov-17: 2C].
Campbell, Martha (9 yrs., 1 mo.) d. on 67-Mar-28 [67-Apr-1: 2C].
Campbell, Mary Agnes (2 yrs., 4 mos.) d. on 69-Mar-5 [69-Mar-6: 2B].
Campbell, Mary E. m. Williams, Levi on 67-Sep-12 [67-Sep-27: 2B].
Campbell, Mary M. Taney m. Anderson, Winfield D. S. on 70-Oct-18 [70-Oct-19: 2B].
Campbell, Michael (55 yrs.) d. [69-Dec-25: 2C].
Campbell, Michael J. (28 yrs.) d. on 67-Dec-29 [67-Dec-31: 2C].
Campbell, Mildred M. m. Evans, Inman H. on 67-Oct-23 [67-Oct-24: 2B].
Campbell, Peter (67 yrs.) d. on 68-Mar-24 [68-Mar-25: 2A; 68-Mar-26: 2B].
Campbell, R. B. Taney (28 yrs.) d. on 70-Jul-16 of Heatstroke [70-Jul-18: 4D; 70-Jul-19: 2B].
Campbell, Robert, Jr. m. Johnson, Laura on 66-Mar-13 [66-Mar-14: 2B].
Campbell, William (74 yrs.) d. on 68-May-4 [68-May-5: 2B].
Campbell, William (57 yrs.) d. on 66-Dec-10 [66-Dec-11: 2B].
Campbell, William (38 yrs.) d. on 70-Dec-26 [70-Dec-30: 2C].
Campbell, William H. m. Wright, Areminta on 68-Nov-5 [68-Nov-17: 2C].
Campbell, Willie J. (4 yrs., 1 mo.) d. on 70-Jul-26 [70-Jul-28: 2C].
Camper, Mary (74 yrs.) d. on 68-Mar-7 [68-Mar-9: 2C].
Camper, Thomas J. m. Davis, Georgie on 70-Apr-21 [70-Apr-23: 2B].
Campher, Stephen (84 yrs.) d. on 67-Aug-8 [67-Aug-10: 2B].
Campion, Jeremiah O. (21 yrs.) d. on 67-Jul-11 [67-Jul-12: 2C].
Cample, William (12 yrs.) d. on 67-Feb-14 in Railroad accident [67-Feb-15: 1F].
Canby, C. T. m. Fort, Zillah V. on 70-Jan-12 [70-Jan-21: 2C].
Canby, Edward L. (41 yrs.) d. on 69-Mar-18 [69-Mar-19: 2C].
Canby, Samuel (35 yrs.) d. on 70-Jul-26 [70-Jul-29: 2C].
Canfield, Caroline m. Bullock, Walter R. on 70-Feb-3 [70-Feb-7: 2C; 70-Feb-8: 2C].
Canfield, Charles m. White, Irene C. on 68-Jun-17 [68-Jun-22: 2B].
Canfield, James (40 yrs.) d. on 68-Jan-21 [68-Jan-22: 2C].
Canfield, Mary R. m. Jones, B. T. on 68-May-12 [68-May-14: 2B].
Canfield, Robert (71 yrs.) d. on 69-Dec-20 [69-Dec-21: 2B].
Canley, Mark (71 yrs.) d. on 70-Aug-15 [70-Aug-17: 2C].
Canlin, James (36 yrs.) d. on 67-Aug-29 [67-Aug-30: 2B].
Cann, B. B. m. Weems, Mollie S. on 68-May-14 [68-May-20: 2A].
Cann, Kate m. Thompson, William J. M. on 68-Sep-22 [68-Sep-24: 2B].
Cannally, Ellen m. Moffett, John on 66-Aug-9 [66-Aug-13: 2C].
Cannan, Arthur W. m. Gordshell, Louisa on 70-Oct-6 [70-Oct-8: 2B].
Cannoles, Elizabeth (75 yrs.) d. on 69-Dec-2 [69-Dec-3: 2C].
Cannoles, Harry Lee (6 yrs.) d. on 69-Sep-23 [69-Sep-24: 2B; 69-Sep-28: 2B].
Cannoles, John W. m. Weigel, Christine E. on 69-Sep-5 [69-Dec-20: 2C].

Cannoles, Mary (78 yrs.) d. on 66-Mar-9 [66-Mar-10: 2B].
Cannon, Annie R. m. Gardener, William H. on 66-Oct-29 [66-Nov-1: 2B].
Cannon, Charles K. (38 yrs.) d. on 69-Sep-12 [69-Sep-13: 2B; 69-Sep-14: 1H].
Cannon, Fannie B. m. Adams, Frank on 67-Oct-23 [67-Oct-26: 2A].
Cannon, Hutson (76 yrs.) d. on 70-Apr-28 [70-Apr-30: 2A].
Cannon, Maretta m. Smith, Samuel R. on 68-Nov-10 [68-Nov-14: 2B].
Cannon, Matilda J. Mitchel d. on 68-Oct-29 [68-Oct-31: 2B].
Canoles, John m. Dosh, Rebecca on 67-Oct-17 [67-Oct-26: 2A].
Canon, John A. m. Durham, Lizzie on 67-Nov-19 [67-Nov-23: 2B].
Canon, Levise (62 yrs.) d. on 70-Oct-4 [70-Oct-6: 2B].
Canter, Issac W. m. Hudson, Mary F. on 68-Nov-17 [68-Nov-19: 2C].
Canter, Issac W. m. Hall, Jennie on 70-Oct-25 [70-Oct-28: 2C].
Canter, James Milnor (1 yr.) d. on 68-Mar-18 [68-Mar-19: 2B].
Canter, Marie F. d. on 69-May-20 [69-May-22: 2B].
Canter, Rebecca B. d. on 69-Oct-11 [69-Oct-12: 2C].
Canter, Thomas Stephen (1 yr.) d. on 68-Mar-16 [68-Mar-8: 2B; 68-Mar-19: 2B].
Canty, Kate (21 yrs.) d. on 70-Feb-15 [70-Feb-17: 2C].
Capels, William m. Connolly, Sarah on 66-Aug-4 [66-Aug-20: 2C].
Caples, Anna M. m. Sherwood, Thomas N. on 66-Nov-15 [66-Nov-21: 2C].
Caples, Frederick m. Paul, Elizabeth on 70-Feb-17 [70-Feb-22: 2C].
Caples, Laura W. m. Ensor, Luke E. on 68-Oct-29 [68-Nov-7: 2B].
Caples, Mary m. Wells, Allen on 66-Nov-25 [66-Dec-7: 2B].
Caples, Robert F. m. Shipley, Elizabeth on 68-Feb-5 [68-Feb-7: 2C].
Caples, William M. (51 yrs.) d. on 69-Mar-21 [69-Mar-22: 2C].
Capp, Howard Parker (1 yr., 1 mo.) d. on 70-Sep-8 [70-Sep-27: 2B].
Capprise, Mary C. m. French, William L. on 67-Jun-19 [67-Jun-26: 2C].
Capron, Ann E. (63 yrs.) d. on 70-Dec-28 [70-Dec-30: 2C].
Capron, Julia V. m. Webb, Louis S. on 68-Aug-23 [68-Aug-25: 2B; 68-Aug-27: 2B].
Carano, Lewis Henry (7 yrs.) d. on 66-Sep-17 [66-Sep-18: 2B].
Carback, Margaret (67 yrs.) d. on 66-Mar-12 [66-Mar-14: 2B].
Carback, Sue m. Fowler, William on 70-Sep-15 [70-Sep-16: 2B].
Carback, William J. m. Sterling, Frances Rebecca on 70-Apr-7 [70-Apr-9: 2B].
Carberry, Michael (23 yrs.) d. on 69-Apr-16 [69-Apr-17: 2B].
Carcaud, Elizabeth Gray (5 yrs., 3 mos.) d. on 70-May-16 [70-May-17: 2B].
Card, Mary Cecil d. on 67-Apr-8 [67-Apr-9: 2B].
Card, William Edward d. on 67-Apr-7 [67-Apr-9: 2B].
Cardwell, Jackson m. Measell, Matta E. on 67-Dec-26 [68-Jan-15: 2C].
Cardwell, Matilda d. on 69-May-17 [69-May-19: 2C].
Carew, John W. m. Kelly, Maria P. on 68-Mar-12 [68-Mar-16: 2B].
Carey, Henry m. Gray, Isabella on 69-Dec-5 [69-Dec-10: 2C].
Carey, James (25 yrs.) d. on 68-May-12 [68-May-13: 2B].
Carey, Margaret (3 yrs., 4 mos.) d. on 70-May-2 [70-May-3: 2B].
Carey, Martin John (10 mos.) d. on 68-Aug-5 [68-Aug-6: 2B].
Carey, Mary Ann (36 yrs.) d. on 70-Nov-2 [70-Nov-3: 2B].
Carey, Mary Ellenora (9 mos.) d. on 70-Jun-29 [70-Jun-30: 2C].
Carey, Michael (28 yrs.) d. on 69-May-8 [69-May-10: 2B].
Carey, Robert (49 yrs.) d. on 69-Nov-3 [69-Nov-4: 2B].
Carey, Sarah (51 yrs.) d. on 67-Nov-11 Ruptured blood vessel [67-Nov-12: 1G, 2C].
Cariss, Samson (67 yrs.) d. on 70-Dec-22 of Paralysis [70-Dec-24: 2B; 70-Dec-28: 2C, 4D].
Carl, Joseph (77 yrs.) d. on 70-Jan-13 [70-Jan-15: 2C].
Carl, Lavina A. m. Ross, Warren B. on 69-Jun-15 [69-Jun-17: 2C].
Carle, Charles m. Brannon, Hannah on 65-Nov-23 [66-Jan-4: 2C].
Carle, Mary A. m. Hubert, George on 70-Apr-25 [70-Apr-28: 2B].
Carlin, Frances d. on 68-Apr-8 [68-Apr-9: 2B].
Carlin, John Lewis (5 yrs., 1 mo.) d. on 70-Jun-3 [70-Jun-6: 2B].

Carling, E. S. m. Hays, Eliza J. on 69-Aug-20 [69-Sep-6: 2C].
Carlisle, Burlington (53 yrs.) d. on 69-Feb-3 [69-Feb-4: 2C].
Carlisle, George Austin m. Jones, Sallie A. on 68-Aug-2 [68-Aug-5: 2B].
Carlisle, J. Howard, Maj. (45 yrs.) d. on 66-Dec-16 [66-Dec-18: 2B].
Carlisle, Mary M. m. Gent, Joshua G. on 70-Dec-14 [70-Dec-22: 2B].
Carlisle, Nicholas m. Wiker, Annie on 67-May-30 [67-May-31: 2B].
Carlos, Patrick (66 yrs.) d. on 69-Aug-18 [69-Aug-19: 2C].
Carloss, Mary d. on 70-Oct-31 [70-Nov-2: 2C].
Carlton, Arthur (6 mos.) d. on 67-Jul-24 [67-Jul-25: 2C].
Carlton, Hopewell Lynch m. Young, John C. on 67-Jan-10 [67-Jan-26: 2C].
Carmack, Emma M. m. Roberts, George S. on 68-May-28 [68-Jun-2: 2B].
Carman, Susan E. m. Maddux, Charles W. on 67-Mar-17 [67-Mar-26: 2C].
Carmichael, Anna J. m. Redmond, Robert A. on 67-May-12 [67-Jun-21: 2B].
Carmichael, Ellen R. m. Jordan, John R. on 67-Sep-17 [67-Oct-7: 2B].
Carmichael, William (34 yrs.) d. on 67-Jan-28 [67-Jan-29: 2C; 67-Jan-30: 2C].
Carmine, George W. m. Lainhart, Marietta on 68-Dec-22 [69-Nov-24: 2C].
Carmine, Mary A. S. (35 yrs.) d. on 68-Apr-2 [68-Apr-3: 2C].
Carmine, Rebecca (93 yrs.) d. on 68-Feb-11 [68-Feb-12: 2B].
Carmine, Susan m. Wright, Perry on 70-Nov-29 [70-Dec-16: 2C].
Carnar, John (28 yrs.) d. on 65-Oct-8 of Congestive chills [66-Feb-5: 2C].
Carnes, Patrick d. on 70-Feb-1 [70-Feb-2: 1F].
Carnes, Rebecca A. (47 yrs.) d. [67-Jan-1: 2C].
Carnes, Thomas (25 yrs.) d. on 66-Jan-19 Drowned [66-Jan-20: 1F].
Carnes, William (45 yrs.) d. on 69-Nov-20 [69-Nov-23: 2C].
Carney, James m. Hissey, Mary Ann on 69-Sep-27 [69-Oct-2: 2C].
Carney, John, Jr. m. Sweeny, Eliza on 67-Dec-8 [67-Dec-19: 2B].
Carney, Joseph m. Mills, Mollie R. on 69-Feb-23 [69-Mar-31: 2C].
Carney, Sarah E. (12 yrs., 3 mos.) d. on 66-Sep-14 of Typhoid [66-Sep-18: 2B].
Carnighan, Mary H. d. on 66-Dec-12 [66-Dec-14: 2B].
Carns, Emma (1 mo.) d. on 66-Oct-26 [66-Oct-27: 2B].
Carothers, Squire D. m. Levy, Sarah on 69-Nov-8 [69-Dec-9: 2C].
Carpenter, George W. m. Hauptman, Helen C. on 68-Nov-12 [68-Nov-18: 2C].
Carpenter, Rose Ann m. Walsh, B. B. on 65-Nov-5 [66-Feb-8: 2C].
Carpenter, Sophia (87 yrs.) d. on 70-Sep-14 [70-Sep-16: 2B].
Carpenter, Sophronia A. m. Tucker, James W. on 69-Sep-2 [69-Sep-6: 2C].
Carr, Alexander m. Wright, Sarah L. on 69-Jun-15 [69-Jun-18: 2C].
Carr, Andrew Johnson (3 yrs., 4 mos.) d. on 70-Jan-7 [70-Jan-11: 2C].
Carr, Annie m. Gowran, Michael on 66-Jan-30 [66-Feb-14: 2C].
Carr, Eliza d. on 70-Aug-8 [70-Aug-9: 2C].
Carr, Elizabeth (77 yrs.) d. on 70-Jan-6 [70-Jan-20: 2C].
Carr, Ella B. m. Fox, W. Tazewell on 69-Apr-22 [69-May-6: 2B].
Carr, Ellenora (77 yrs.) d. on 70-Sep-7 [70-Sep-9: 2B].
Carr, Homer S. m. Newman, Sarah E. on 70-Mar-23 [70-Mar-31: 2C].
Carr, John (1 yr.) d. on 66-Dec-23 [66-Dec-24: 2B].
Carr, John (30 yrs.) d. on 66-Oct-11 of Consumption [66-Oct-12: 2B].
Carr, John B. m. Waite, Annie on 66-Oct-9 [66-Oct-12: 2B].
Carr, John O. (54 yrs.) d. on 70-Apr-13 of Pneumonia [70-Apr-25: 2B].
Carr, Lizzie m. Dorsey, William C. on 67-Nov-13 [67-Nov-19: 2C].
Carr, M. Josephine (23 yrs.) d. on 70-May-12 [70-May-31: 2B].
Carr, Margaret S. m. Howard, Joseph A. on 67-May-9 [67-May-16: 2B].
Carr, Mary Elizabeth m. Horner, Charles Wesley on 68-Jun-1 [68-Jun-4: 2B].
Carr, Nicholas (52 yrs.) d. on 67-May-29 [67-May-30: 2B].
Carr, Sallie E. m. Lockard, Alfred F. on 70-Jan-20 [70-Jan-22: 2B].
Carr, Samuel m. Richardson, Charlotte on 70-Jul-4 [70-Jul-19: 2B].
Carr, Sarah (66 yrs.) d. on 67-Jan-3 of Heart disease [67-Jan-4: 2D].

Carr, Sarah Ann (37 yrs.) d. on 68-Nov-6 [68-Nov-7: 2B].
Carr, Susan d. on 67-Jul-23 [67-Jul-25: 2C].
Carr, W. Sanders m. Williamson, Bessie M. on 69-Nov-4 [69-Nov-9: 2C].
Carr, Wesley Cook m. Baker, Julia A. on 70-Jul-7 [70-Dec-19: 2C].
Carrall, William m. Thomas, Ann on 69-May-20 [69-May-22: 2B].
Carrick, H. m. Rienhart, A. A. on 70-Oct-4 [70-Oct-18: 2B].
Carrick, Lackey M. m. Carter, Virginia on 69-Dec-14 [69-Dec-25: 2C].
Carrington, Hallie R. m. Brown, T. R. on 66-Dec-24 [66-Dec-27: 2C].
Carrol, Helen m. Benjamin, Alfred on 66-Nov-26 [66-Nov-29: 2B].
Carroll, Albert H. m. Cockrill, Mollie P. on 68-Dec-1 [68-Dec-4: 2D].
Carroll, Andrew m. Sillery, Kate, Miss on 66-Feb-5 [66-Feb-27: 2B].
Carroll, Annie (51 yrs.) d. on 70-Jul-18 [70-Jul-19: 2B].
Carroll, Annie T. m. Taylor, Charles H. on 67-Nov-28 [67-Nov-30: 2C].
Carroll, Bridget m. Senate, Patrick on 67-Feb-26 [67-Feb-28: 2C].
Carroll, Caroline (60 yrs.) d. on 67-Feb-27 [67-Feb-28: 2C].
Carroll, Charles (62 yrs.) d. on 69-Nov-19 [69-Nov-20: 2B].
Carroll, Charles (10 mos.) d. on 70-Dec-30 [70-Dec-31: 2C].
Carroll, Charles R. (71 yrs.) d. on 70-Aug-12 [70-Aug-13: 2C, 4F].
Carroll, Drew P. (2 yrs.) d. on 68-Mar-6 [68-Mar-7: 2B].
Carroll, Elizabeth (85 yrs.) d. on 70-Sep-13 [70-Sep-14: 2B].
Carroll, Elizabeth Sedona (1 yr., 8 mos.) d. on 70-May-16 [70-May-17: 2B].
Carroll, Ella Louise (8 yrs.) d. on 69-Nov-8 of Scarlet fever [69-Nov-10: 2C].
Carroll, Emma E. m. Carson, William Thomas on 67-Dec-2 [67-Dec-14: 2B].
Carroll, George m. Lee, Sarah Jane on 67-Jul-21 [67-Jul-29: 2D].
Carroll, Henrietta M. (80 yrs.) d. on 70-Aug-29 [70-Sep-1: 2B].
Carroll, James J. m. Hamilton, Rachel A. on 68-Jun-14 [68-Jul-6: 2B].
Carroll, Jane E. m. Bayles, William on 68-Jan-26 [68-Feb-1: 2B].
Carroll, John (61 yrs.) d. on 69-May-29 [69-May-31: 2C].
Carroll, John Bennet (6 yrs.) d. on 70-Jan-15 [70-Jan-19: 2C].
Carroll, John Evans (2 yrs., 6 mos.) d. on 66-Feb-28 [66-Mar-1: 2B].
Carroll, John N. m. Thomas, Mary R. on 70-Apr-21 [70-Apr-23: 2B].
Carroll, John W. m. Harvey, Mary A. V. on 67-Oct-30 [67-Nov-2: 2B].
Carroll, Larkin m. Cowan, J. Elizabeth on 68-Dec-29 [69-Jan-4: 2C].
Carroll, Laura D. m. Shipley, E. E. on 70-Nov-10 [70-Nov-14: 2B].
Carroll, Lewis d. on 67-Sep-10 in Machine accident [67-Sep-14: 1F].
Carroll, Lilian Sabrina (1 yr., 2 mos.) d. on 66-Mar-8 [66-Mar-9: 2B].
Carroll, Margaret (55 yrs.) d. on 67-Sep-26 [67-Sep-28: 2A].
Carroll, Margaret (65 yrs.) d. on 66-Nov-15 [66-Nov-16: 2C].
Carroll, Margaret m. McCabe, Michael on 67-Feb-28 [67-Apr-15: 2B].
Carroll, Mary (16 yrs.) d. on 67-Apr-5 [67-Apr-6: 2C].
Carroll, Mary (70 yrs.) d. on 67-May-23 [67-May-25: 2A].
Carroll, Mary Anastasia (4 yrs., 5 mos.) d. on 67-Sep-19 [67-Sep-21: 2A].
Carroll, Mary Ann (2 yrs., 2 mos.) d. on 68-Dec-29 [69-Jan-6: 2C].
Carroll, Mary Jane m. Ogle, Atkin on 67-Sep-3 [67-Sep-5: 2B].
Carroll, Mary Magdalene (34 yrs.) d. on 66-Feb-13 [66-Feb-16: 2B].
Carroll, Michael m. Baker, Fanny on 70-Feb-3 [70-Feb-14: 2C].
Carroll, Minnie m. Unduch, H. H. on 70-Nov-20 [70-Nov-22: 2B].
Carroll, Nicholas C. (88 yrs.) d. on 68-Nov-11 [68-Nov-16: 2C; 68-Nov-19: 1H].
Carroll, Osborn m. Tyler, Hannah on 70-Dec-22 [70-Dec-23: 2B].
Carroll, P. H. (33 yrs.) d. on 67-Oct-21 [67-Oct-22: 2A].
Carroll, R. James m. Rawlins, Amelia B. on 67-Jun-27 [67-Jun-28: 2B; 67-Jun-29: 2B].
Carroll, Robert A. m. Cross, Sarah A. on 67-Apr-18 [67-Apr-20: 2A].
Carroll, St. John (44 yrs.) d. on 69-Dec-28 of Hemorrhage [69-Dec-29: 1G, 2D; 69-Dec-30: 2C; 69-Dec-31: 1G].
Carroll, Thomas Jefferson (1 yr.) d. on 67-Nov-20 [67-Nov-21: 2C].

Carroll, William (30 yrs.) d. on 66-Jan-11 in Railroad accident [66-Jan-12: 4C].
Carroll, William C. m. Gilpin, Mary M. on 68-Oct-19 [68-Oct-20: 2B].
Carroll, William F. m. Nolan, Harriet M. on 69-Oct-25 [69-Nov-3: 2C].
Carroll, William Henry (41 yrs.) d. on 68-Apr-3 [68-Apr-4: 2B].
Carroll, William J. (4 mos.) d. on 70-Feb-9 [70-Feb-10: 2C].
Carroll, William J. m. Millholland, Teresa on 67-Jan-15 [67-Jan-18: 2C].
Carrolle, Louisa A. m. Airey, James on 66-May-3 [66-May-4: 2C].
Carron, Patrick (64 yrs.) d. on 68-Jun-26 [68-Jun-27: 2B].
Carruthers, Angie Bell m. Evans, J. A. on 67-May-24 [67-Jun-4: 2A].
Carry, Nelson A. m. Jones, J. L. D. on 69-Jan-10 [69-Jan-12: 2C].
Carson, Catherine (51 yrs.) d. on 68-Oct-16 [68-Oct-21: 2C].
Carson, Charles L. m. Cornelius, Annie F. on 70-Dec-6 [70-Dec-10: 2B].
Carson, Emma L. m. Monroe, A. Warfield on 69-Dec-14 [69-Dec-16: 2C].
Carson, Emory (3 yrs., 2 mos.) d. on 70-Mar-17 [70-Mar-19: 2B].
Carson, John (74 yrs.) d. on 69-Mar-19 [69-Mar-20: 1H, 2B].
Carson, John B. d. on 66-Jul-22 [66-Jul-24: 2C].
Carson, John Emory (14 yrs., 10 mos.) d. on 66-Jan-4 [66-Jan-6: 2B].
Carson, Joseph (41 yrs.) d. on 67-Aug-12 [67-Aug-13: 1G; 67-Aug-14: 2B].
Carson, Lizzie A. m. Gregg, Thomas C. on 65-Dec-11 [66-Jan-11: 2B].
Carson, Maggie m. Chaillow, J. Frank on 66-Aug-30 [66-Sep-13: 2C].
Carson, Mary m. Lavender, James on 70-Dec-15 [70-Dec-17: 2B].
Carson, Mary E. (17 yrs.) d. on 66-Mar-20 [66-Mar-22: 2B].
Carson, Mary R. m. Howell, Darius M. on 67-Nov-7 [67-Nov-11: 2C].
Carson, Nannie V. m. Smith, J. Wesley on 69-Nov-24 [69-Nov-27: 2B].
Carson, Richard Keene (1 yr., 4 mos.) d. on 68-Feb-29 [68-Mar-3: 2C].
Carson, Sarah Lizzie m. Bond, Joshua B. on 70-Nov-8 [70-Nov-12: 2B].
Carson, Thomas J. (57 yrs.) d. on 69-May-11 [69-May-13: 1H, 2B; 69-May-14: 2C].
Carson, William Thomas m. Carroll, Emma E. on 67-Dec-2 [67-Dec-14: 2B].
Carstens, H. W. d. [69-Nov-29: 2C].
Carswell, Jonathan S. m. Jackson, Isabel R. on 67-Jan-8 [67-Jan-11: 2C].
Carswell, Walter Scott (20 yrs.) d. on 68-May-23 [68-May-25: 2A].
Carter, Alice C. m. Guerand, Eugene F. on 70-Feb-8 [70-Apr-2: 2A].
Carter, Alonzo Thomas (5 mos.) d. on 70-Jun-24 [70-Jun-25: 2C].
Carter, Amelia F. m. Devlin, Joseph on 66-Apr-25 [66-Apr-27: 2C].
Carter, C. Shirley m. Swann, Mary M. on 67-Oct-22 [67-Oct-24: 2B].
Carter, Carrie m. McGee, Michael J. on 69-Aug-11 [69-Aug-19: 2C].
Carter, Charles m. Robinson, Margaret on 66-Sep-25 [66-Oct-2: 2B].
Carter, Charles H. (31 yrs.) d. on 70-Aug-1 [70-Aug-2: 2C].
Carter, Charles L. m. Weaver, Venie J. on 68-May-20 [68-Jun-23: 2B].
Carter, Durus D. m. Wynkoop, Addie on 69-Oct-6 [69-Oct-11: 2C].
Carter, Eliza C. (77 yrs.) d. on 69-Nov-12 [69-Nov-13: 2C].
Carter, Elizabeth (71 yrs.) d. on 67-Jul-1 [67-Jul-3: 2B].
Carter, Emma J. d. on 67-Mar-13 [67-Mar-14: 2C].
Carter, Esther G. m. Hagner, William on 70-Feb-8 [70-Feb-18: 2C].
Carter, Francis R. m. Egan, Ella R. on 70-Jan-2 [70-Jan-26: 2C].
Carter, Frederick Wilson (3 mos.) d. on 69-Aug-17 [69-Aug-21: 2B].
Carter, Guy Norman (1 yr., 1 mo.) d. on 66-Jul-8 [66-Jul-9: 2C].
Carter, Helen E. m. Cook, Edward on 68-Feb-26 [68-Mar-7: 2B].
Carter, Henry (61 yrs.) d. on 67-Apr-14 [67-Apr-18: 2B].
Carter, Henry M. m. Llewellyn, M. Lulie on 70-Nov-24 [70-Nov-28: 2C].
Carter, Ida Eugenia (9 mos.) d. on 67-Apr-27 [67-Apr-29: 2B].
Carter, James m. Greer, Mary A. on 69-Jun-28 [69-Jul-2: 2C].
Carter, John m. Minnick, Sarah E. on 68-Jul-8 [68-Jul-10: 2C].
Carter, John Calvin, Dr. d. on 70-Dec-30 [70-Dec-31: 2B].
Carter, John M. m. Thomas, Florence S. on 67-Apr-25 [67-Apr-27: 2A].

Carter, John Sherman (1 yr., 1 mo.) d. on 67-Jun-20 [67-Jun-21: 2B; 67-Jun-22: 2B].
Carter, John W. (15 yrs.) d. on 70-Aug-9 Drowned [70-Aug-11: 4D].
Carter, John Willie (5 yrs., 7 mos.) d. on 67-Dec-12 [67-Dec-14: 2B].
Carter, Joseph F. m. Latchford, Mollie J. on 66-Jan-16 [66-Jan-18: 2C].
Carter, Laura L. V. m. Johnston, James, Jr. on 70-Sep-12 [70-Sep-28: 2B].
Carter, Lorenzo m. Johnson, Laura Virginia on 70-May-2 [70-May-4: 2C; 70-May-5: 2B].
Carter, Maria m. Renshaw, Robert H. on 69-Jun-8 [69-Jun-9: 2C].
Carter, Mary (24 yrs.) d. on 68-Dec-18 [68-Dec-19: 2B].
Carter, Mary Randolph m. Bier, George H. on 67-Dec-10 [67-Dec-18: 2B].
Carter, Mollie d. on 69-Apr-28 [69-Apr-30: 2C].
Carter, Rebecca B. (78 yrs.) d. on 66-Jan-6 of Paralysis [66-Jan-8: 2B; 66-Jan-9: 2B].
Carter, Robert C. m. Jones, Julia F. on 66-Jan-2 [66-Jan-3: 2C].
Carter, Rodney F. m. Zastrow, Amelia C. on 68-Apr-14 [68-Apr-18: 2A].
Carter, Ruth (83 yrs.) d. on 66-Nov-17 [66-Oct-19: 2B].
Carter, Samuel W. (48 yrs.) d. on 70-Oct-22 [70-Oct-24: 2B].
Carter, Sarah m. Cocks, Ambrose on 68-Apr-20 [68-Jun-6: 2A].
Carter, Sarah Virginia (1 yr.) d. on 68-Oct-18 [68-Oct-19: 2B].
Carter, Thomas H. m. Smith, G. A. on 67-Jul-18 [67-Jul-20: 2C].
Carter, Vincent Wylie (2 yrs., 8 mos.) d. on 68-Aug-22 [68-Aug-25: 2B].
Carter, Virginia m. Carrick, Lackey M. on 69-Dec-14 [69-Dec-25: 2C].
Carter, Walter S. m. Jones, Mollie A. on 67-Dec-18 [67-Dec-24: 2B].
Carter, William B. (28 yrs.) d. on 69-Jun-2 of Suicide (Poisoning) [69-Jun-4: 1G, 2C].
Carter, William M. (60 yrs.) d. on 66-Oct-19 [66-Oct-20: 2B].
Cartlich, George W. A. m. Wonderly, Sophia E. on 68-Jun-2 [68-Jun-4: 2B].
Carty, Edward (76 yrs.) d. on 67-Jul-5 [67-Jul-6: 2B].
Carvallo, Carlos m. Bayliss, Mary Emma on 67-Feb-28 [67-Mar-2: 2B].
Carvallo, Joseph Buckner Bayli (3 yrs.) d. on 69-Oct-10 of Dysentery [69-Oct-26: 2B].
Carver, Anna E. m. Daniels, David C. on 66-Jun-5 [66-Jun-6: 2B].
Carver, Emma V. m. White, John J. on 68-Jun-2 [68-Jun-9: 2B].
Carver, George W. m. Thorpe, Mary M. on 67-May-6 [67-May-11: 2A].
Carver, Mollie D. (4 yrs.) d. on 68-Oct-29 [68-Oct-30: 2C].
Carville, E. Kate m. Lowe, Wrightson L. on 70-Dec-8 [70-Dec-13: 2C].
Carville, Thomas B. m. Eareckson, Ann C. on 68-Nov-10 [68-Nov-12: 2C].
Carwithen, James C. (29 yrs.) d. on 69-Oct-26 [69-Oct-28: 2C].
Carwithen, Louis Lincoln (1 yr., 11 mos.) d. on 67-Mar-8 [67-Mar-9: 2B].
Carwithen, Philip (29 yrs.) d. on 66-Mar-13 [66-Mar-16: 2B].
Cary, Anna (19 yrs.) d. on 66-Jan-28 of Typhoid [66-Feb-13: 2C].
Cary, George (6 mos.) d. on 67-Oct-6 [67-Oct-8: 2B].
Cary, Tamar (75 yrs.) d. on 69-Nov-7 [69-Nov-10: 2C].
Cary, William F. (66 yrs.) d. on 68-Sep-23 [68-Sep-24: 2B; 68-Sep-25: 1G].
Case, Watson m. Daneker, Sadie V. on 69-Feb-2 [69-Feb-9: 2C].
Casey, Catherine (46 yrs., 3 mos.) d. on 66-May-12 [66-May-19: 2B].
Casey, Daniel P. (22 yrs.) d. on 70-Nov-28 [70-Nov-29: 2C; 70-Nov-30: 2C].
Casey, Elenora m. Woods, William H. on 70-Apr-27 [70-Apr-29: 2B].
Casey, Ellen (1 yr., 5 mos.) d. on 70-Jun-21 [70-Jun-22: 2C].
Casey, Michael d. on 67-Aug-12 Drowned [67-Aug-13: 1F].
Casey, William E. m. Banks, Mary Kate on 70-Jul-4 [70-Jul-6: 2B].
Cashmyer, Eleanora Theresa (1 yr., 2 mos.) d. on 70-Feb-28 [70-Mar-1: 2C].
Cashmyer, Philip James (1 yr., 11 mos.) d. on 68-Sep-18 [68-Sep-19: 2B].
Casilo, Marie m. Magruder, Haswell on 67-Apr-5 [67-Apr-10: 2B].
Caskey, Joseph m. Dumay, Louisa on 69-Jul-1 [69-Jul-7: 2C].
Caskey, Julia Ann (50 yrs.) d. on 67-Jul-5 [67-Jul-6: 2B].
Caskey, Mary E. (35 yrs.) d. on 66-Mar-16 [66-Mar-17: 2B].
Casley, Laura V. m. Sipple, George on 70-May-11 [70-Aug-18: 2B].
Caspari, Charles (58 yrs.) d. on 70-Oct-31 of Pneumonia [70-Nov-1: 2C; 70-Nov-2: 2B;

70-Nov-3: 2B].
Caspari, Martha A. d. on 68-Jun-24 [68-Jul-10: 2C].
Cassady, Fannie m. Shannon, Edward P. on 67-Oct-2 [67-Oct-9: 2B].
Cassady, Jane (77 yrs.) d. on 68-Apr-2 [68-Apr-3: 2C].
Cassard, J. D. m. Simms, Mary on 69-Dec-30 [69-Dec-31: 2C].
Cassard, Jesse L. m. Reese, Sophie R. on 67-Nov-5 [67-Nov-11: 2C].
Cassard, Louis R. m. Kensett, Eliza H. on 68-Nov-10 [68-Nov-13: 2C].
Cassard, M. Kate m. Drakeley, George E. on 67-Jun-4 [67-Jun-8: 2B].
Cassard, S. Kate m. Owens, Edward B. on 69-Nov-11 [69-Nov-16: 2C].
Cassard, Thomas Kensett (11 mos.) d. on 70-Jul-28 [70-Jul-29: 2B; 70-Jul-30: 2B].
Cassell, Abraham (57 yrs.) d. on 69-Mar-28 [69-Mar-30: 2C].
Cassell, Bell Chamberlain d. on 66-Dec-31 of Scarlet fever [67-Jan-1: 2C].
Cassell, Charles C. m. Lowery, Maggie A. on 67-Oct-31 [67-Nov-2: 2B].
Cassell, Joseph (86 yrs.) d. on 66-Dec-1 [66-Dec-3: 1G, 2B; 66-Dec-4: 4E].
Cassell, Thomas Mahlon (1 yr., 10 mos.) d. on 66-Jan-14 [66-Jan-15: 2C].
Casseres, Elizabeth d. on 68-Apr-25 [68-Apr-27: 2B].
Cassidy, C. Louisa d. on 70-Dec-23 [70-Dec-24: 2B].
Cassidy, Catherine (48 yrs.) d. on 66-Apr-11 [66-Apr-12: 2B].
Cassidy, Emma W. m. Fort, William F. on 66-Aug-29 [66-Sep-10: 2D].
Cassidy, Eugene (24 yrs.) d. on 67-Sep-22 [67-Sep-23: 2A].
Cassidy, Francis m. Eagan, Sarah on 67-Jun-10 [67-Jun-19: 2B].
Cassidy, Francis Patrick (5 yrs., 1 mo.) d. on 68-Aug-13 Drowned [68-Aug-14: 1G; 68-Aug-15: 2B].
Cassidy, Helen Emma (9 yrs.) d. on 66-May-6 [66-Mar-8: 2B].
Cassidy, Hugh (2 yrs., 9 mos.) d. on 70-Dec-12 [70-Dec-14: 2C].
Cassidy, Kate m. McFadden, Francis P. on 66-Nov-28 [66-Dec-1: 2B].
Cassidy, Maggie A. m. McShane, John on 69-Oct-19 [69-Oct-22: 2B].
Cassidy, Maria G. m. Travers, John M. on 69-Dec-29 [70-Jan-5: 2C].
Cassidy, Martin Louis (15 yrs.) d. on 70-Jan-23 [70-Jan-24: 2C].
Cassidy, Mary d. on 68-Feb-10 [68-Feb-12: 2B].
Cassidy, Sally (37 yrs.) d. on 70-Jul-19 [70-Jul-20: 2C].
Cassidy, Sarah (44 yrs.) d. [66-Jul-19: 2C].
Cassidy, Sarah Josephine (14 yrs.) d. on 69-Sep-13 [69-Sep-15: 2B].
Castillo, Patrick m. Lafferty, Agnes on 68-Jul-1 [68-Jul-3: 2B].
Castle, James Thomas (8 mos.) d. on 69-Aug-24 [69-Aug-26: 2C].
Castle, Thomas M. m. Tracy, Mollie E. on 65-Dec-28 [66-Jan-6: 2B].
Caswell, Robert B. m. Guiest, Georgeanna E. on 70-Dec-24 [70-Dec-29: 2C].
Cates, Susan m. Ellison, William Thomas on 66-Feb-9 [66-Feb-12: 2D].
Catez, John B. m. Burke, Annie E. on 67-Oct-22 [67-May-15: 2B].
Cathcart, Benjamin E. m. Lightner, Sallie A. on 69-Dec-14 [69-Dec-16: 2C].
Cathcart, Charles H. d. on 67-Jul-18 [67-Jul-19: 2C].
Cathcart, J. W. m. Marine, L. Emma on 68-Jun-22 [68-Jun-27: 2B].
Cathell, Emma m. Corbin, William S. on 67-Oct-15 [67-Oct-22: 2A].
Cathell, James R. m. Roberts, Mary E. on 65-Dec-26 [66-Jan-2: 2C].
Cathell, Mitchell K. (74 yrs.) d. on 69-Oct-5 [69-Oct-12: 2C].
Cathell, Priscilla (68 yrs.) d. on 67-Nov-28 [67-Nov-30: 2C].
Cathell, Rosie (24 yrs.) d. on 69-Jun-20 [69-Jun-22: 2C].
Cather, Hannah J. m. Dorsey, Charles H. on 70-Oct-20 [70-Oct-22: 2B].
Cather, Robert W. m. Jacobs, Sarah P. on 67-Jul-20 [67-Aug-23: 2B].
Cathers, Rachel A. m. Huritt, Joseph A. on 70-Oct-6 [70-Oct-15: 2B].
Catlett, Florence Lee (3 yrs., 3 mos.) d. on 67-Feb-13 [67-Feb-14: 2C].
Catlett, H. Bradley, Capt. (27 yrs.) d. on 70-Aug-21 [70-Aug-23: 2B].
Catlin, Charles M. m. Montague, Kate on 67-Jun-12 [67-Jun-13: 2C].
Catlin, Robert J. m. Merryman, Clara Augusta on 67-Apr-25 [67-Apr-29: 2B].
Caton, Bridget (62 yrs.) d. on 66-Mar-17 [66-Mar-19: 2C].

Caton, Isabella R. (35 yrs.) d. on 69-Dec-1 [69-Dec-2: 2C; 69-Dec-3: 2C].
Cator, Annie E. (25 yrs.) d. on 68-Mar-28 [68-Mar-30: 2B].
Cator, Grace Stuart   d. on 66-May-30 [66-May-31: 2B].
Cator, Mary E. m. Sanderson, W. Cook on 69-Dec-16 [69-Dec-21: 2B].
Cator, Mary J. m. Taylor, Benjamin F. on 69-Feb-23 [69-Feb-24: 2C].
Catrup, Samuel P. m. Bailey, Kate on 69-Dec-7 [69-Dec-13: 2C].
Catrup, William B. m. Jones, Eliza on 66-Jul-10 [66-Jul-13: 2C].
Catterton, William G. (39 yrs.) d. on 66-Nov-23 [66-Nov-24: 2B].
Caughy, Ann R. m. Herring, Clifford on 69-Oct-6 [69-Oct-9: 2C].
Caughy, Benjamin (61 yrs.) d. on 67-Jan-16 [67-Jan-17: 2C].
Caughy, Michael (77 yrs.) d. on 66-Jun-15 of Paralysis [66-Jun-16: 1F, 2B].
Caughy, Michael P. m. Pendergast, Mary R. on 67-Apr-25 [67-Apr-29: 2B; 67-Apr-30: 2B].
Cauley, Bridget (67 yrs.) d. on 69-Nov-4 [69-Nov-5: 2C].
Cauley, Roderick (65 yrs.) d. on 67-Oct-23 [67-Oct-24: 2B].
Caulfield, James (40 yrs.) d. on 68-Jan-21 [68-Jan-23: 2C].
Caulfield, Robert (71 yrs.) d. on 69-Dec-20 [69-Dec-22: 2B].
Caulfield, Valentine W. m. Howard, Anna A. on 67-Dec-11 [67-Dec-12: 2B].
Caulk, Annie M. (1 yr., 6 mos.) d. on 70-Sep-25 [70-Sep-26: 2B].
Caulk, Carrie L. (26 yrs.) d. on 70-Mar-29 [70-Apr-15: 2C].
Caulk, Cora (3 mos.) d. on 68-Nov-26 [68-Dec-1: 2C].
Caulk, Elizabeth A. m. Heath, Charles L. on 70-Aug-31 [70-Sep-2: 2C].
Caulk, Hester A. m. Winterbottom, James T. on 66-Dec-27 [66-Dec-29: 2C].
Caulk, Jacob (52 yrs.) d. on 66-Feb-16 [66-Feb-23: 2C].
Caulk, Joseph m. Weaver, Mary F. on 67-Feb-3 [67-Feb-18: 2C].
Caulk, William H. (25 yrs.) d. on 70-Aug-25 [70-Aug-27: 2B].
Causey, Mary J. m. Childs, William E. on 69-Dec-21 [69-Dec-28: 2C].
Causmelle, Mary A. m. Krumm, Louis P. on 70-Mar-8 [70-May-2: 2C].
Causmelle, William J. m. Bishop, Mollie Florence on 70-Aug-11 [70-Sep-14: 2B].
Cavana, Elizabeth m. Sterling, Christopher C. on 69-Sep-26 [69-Oct-5: 2B; 69-Oct-7: 2B].
Cavanagh, John (60 yrs.) d. on 68-Jul-30 [68-Jul-31: 2C; 68-Aug-1: 2B].
Cavanagh, Mary (47 yrs.) d. on 68-Oct-13 [68-Oct-14: 2B; 68-Oct-15: 2C].
Cavanaugh, Mary Cottle (35 yrs.) d. on 70-Jan-24 [70-Jan-25: 2C].
Caye, Margaret (63 yrs.) d. on 67-Aug-5 [67-Aug-6: 2C].
Cazier, Alice Marie (1 yr., 1 mo.) d. on 67-Jan-30 [67-Feb-1: 2C].
Cazier, Sadie E. (6 mos.) d. on 70-Aug-12 [70-Aug-13: 2C].
Cearey, Martin (40 yrs.) d. on 69-Jul-5 [69-Jul-12: 2D].
Cecil, George T. m. North, Lizzie J. on 68-Oct-19 [68-Oct-23: 2B].
Cecil, James m. Gosnell, Elizabeth Mary Cecil on 66-Apr-17 [66-Apr-19: 2B].
Cecil, Josephine m. Bond, Arthur W. on 70-Dec-14 [70-Dec-15: 2C].
Cecil, Nannie m. Holbrook, Francis X. on 70-Jul-14 [70-Jul-20: 2C].
Cephas, Elizabeth A. m. Smith, James C. on 67-Apr-25 [67-Apr-27: 2A].
Cesterle, Adam m. Wehn, Emma L. on 68-Jun-28 [68-Jun-30: 2B].
Chabot, Emilie m. Savage, William H. on 68-Apr-20 [68-May-7: 2B].
Chaffee, Matilda (81 yrs.) d. on 68-Feb-29 [68-Mar-2: 2B; 68-Mar-3: 2C].
Chaffinch, Anna Gertrude (1 yr., 2 mos.) d. on 69-Jan-17 [69-Jan-18: 2D].
Chaffinch, Robert E. (5 mos.) d. [69-Jul-24: 2C].
Chaillow, Barbara (52 yrs.) d. on 69-Nov-12 [69-Nov-13: 2C].
Chaillow, J. Frank m. Carson, Maggie on 66-Aug-30 [66-Sep-13: 2C].
Chaires, Samuel m. Whaland, Frances A. on 67-Dec-19 [67-Dec-21: 2B].
Chairs, Mary d. on 69-Aug-25 [69-Aug-27: 2B].
Chalfant, Christabel (2 yrs., 8 mos.) d. on 69-May-19 [69-May-20: 2C].
Chalk, Elizabeth C. m. Brown, Joseph on 70-Jul-17 [70-Aug-8: 2C].
Chalkley, Harrie Lacey (2 yrs., 4 mos.) d. on 70-Dec-18 [70-Dec-19: 2C].
Chalkley, Minnie Irene (6 yrs.) d. on 70-Sep-6 [70-Sep-7: 2B].
Challnor, Charles m. Powers, Margaret on 70-Feb-10 [70-Mar-8: 2C].

Chalmers, Susanna d. on 70-Apr-7 [70-Apr-8: 2C].
Chamberlain, Eliza V. m. Sisson, C. Roane on 69-Oct-5 [69-Oct-14: 2C].
Chamberlain, Farnando (51 yrs.) d. on 69-Dec-21 [69-Dec-24: 2C].
Chamberlain, H. E. m. Bordley, James on 68-Oct-22 [68-Oct-27: 2B].
Chamberlain, Mary Cordelia (1 yr., 3 mos.) d. on 66-May-5 [66-May-7: 2B].
Chamberlain, Mary R. m. Watkins, Nicholas N. on 68-Oct-29 [68-Nov-3: 2B].
Chamberlaine, Fanny m. Barker, Joseph H. on 66-Dec-4 [66-Dec-6: 2B].
Chamberlaine, Henry m. White, Henrietta Maria on 68-Nov-10 [68-Nov-11: 2C].
Chamberlaine, Martha A. m. Austin, James K.P. on 66-Nov-1 [66-Dec-14: 2B].
Chamberlaine, Mary A. d. on 66-Aug-7 [66-Aug-11: 2B].
Chamberlin, Thomas m. English, Fannie on 70-Oct-25 [70-Oct-27: 2B].
Chambers, Agnes m. Baxter, Samuel on 69-Mar-28 [69-Apr-6: 2C].
Chambers, Ann Elizabeth (46 yrs.) d. on 68-Apr-24 [68-May-13: 2B].
Chambers, Carrie M. m. Kenower, John A. on 70-Dec-22 [70-Dec-23: 2B].
Chambers, Ezekiel F. (79 yrs.) d. on 67-Jan-30 [67-Feb-2: 2A].
Chambers, George m. Crandell, H. A. Minerva on 68-Jul-15 [68-Jul-23: 2B].
Chambers, George Henry (12 yrs., 8 mos.) d. on 69-Jan-5 [69-Jan-6: 2C].
Chambers, George Maitland m. Dryden, Mary Rosealba on 66-Feb-12 [66-Feb-14: 2C].
Chambers, Grace (9 mos.) d. on 69-Nov-12 [69-Nov-20: 2C].
Chambers, H. Preston m. Harris, Isabella F. on 67-Dec-25 [68-Jan-15: 2C].
Chambers, Ida Estelle (1 yr., 1 mo.) d. on 68-Feb-1 [68-Feb-3: 2C].
Chambers, John Henry (38 yrs.) d. on 67-Jan-21 [67-Jan-23: 2C].
Chambers, John M. m. Gibson, Mary M. on 68-Apr-28 [68-Apr-30: 2B].
Chambers, John S. (25 yrs.) d. on 69-Aug-22 [69-Aug-24: 2B].
Chambers, Lee O'Neill (3 yrs., 3 mos.) d. on 68-Jan-13 [68-Jan-15: 2C].
Chambers, M. Fannie m. Pattison, Martin L. on 66-Jan-23 [66-Jan-30: 2B].
Chambers, Mary Virginia (16 yrs., 9 mos.) d. on 66-Apr-23 [66-Apr-25: 2B].
Champayne, Mary Leo (1 yr., 10 mos.) d. on 70-Mar-27 [70-Mar-28: 2B].
Champayne, Rachel Ann (75 yrs.) d. on 70-Nov-23 [70-Dec-13: 2C].
Champayre, David W. m. Wood, Annie M. on 66-Nov-8 [66-Nov-19: 2B].
Champney, Hiram J. m. Chaney, Victoria E. on 67-Dec-17 [68-Jan-18: 2B].
Champney, Rosa Eunice (1 yr., 2 mos.) d. on 70-Oct-25 [70-Oct-26: 2B].
Chance, Edward d. on 66-Feb-27 in Railroad accident [66-Feb-28: 1G].
Chance, F. E. (29 yrs.) d. on 68-Nov-7 [68-Nov-13: 2C].
Chance, James R. (53 yrs.) d. on 68-May-16 of Paralysis [68-May-18: 1G, 2B].
Chance, William A. A. (22 yrs.) d. on 68-Jul-29 [66-Jul-31: 2C].
Chanceaulme, Bella m. McCurdy, Richard J. on 66-Jan-1 [66-Jan-10: 2C].
Chancellor, Charles Chester d. on 70-Jul-4 [70-Jul-6: 2C].
Chancellor, Ella H. m. Addison, Samuel L. on 69-Dec-22 [69-Dec-28: 2C].
Chandlee, Cassandra (39 yrs.) d. on 68-Mar-2 [68-Mar-4: 2C].
Chandlee, Maggie (5 yrs.) d. on 70-Dec-9 [70-Dec-10: 2B].
Chandler, Clara Hamilton d. on 67-Aug-2 [67-Aug-3: 2B].
Chandler, George F. m. America, Jane E. on 67-Jun-2 [67-Jun-8: 2B].
Chandler, George W. (59 yrs.) d. on 70-Dec-11 [70-Dec-13: 2C].
Chandler, Jennie m. Hale, James A. on 68-Apr-16 [68-Apr-30: 2B].
Chandler, Kennard m. Glazier, Belle N. on 70-Nov-2 [70-Nov-14: 2B].
Chandler, Mary E. m. Wilhelm, George W.A. on 66-Mar-22 [66-Apr-27: 2B].
Chandler, Nancy A. (58 yrs.) d. on 70-Sep-4 [70-Sep-6: 2B].
Chandler, Sarah E. (47 yrs.) d. on 69-Feb-10 [69-Feb-12: 2C].
Chandler, William E. m. Windsor, Thibedeaux on 66-May-6 [66-May-8: 2B].
Chandler, Willie Augustus (1 yr., 7 mos.) d. on 68-Jun-30 [68-Jul-1: 2B].
Chandley, Annie E. m. Scarf, James H. on 66-Dec-25 [67-Jan-4: 2D].
Chaney, Almira m. Weir, Benjamin T. on 67-Jun-24 [67-Jun-26: 2C].
Chaney, Andrew m. Gardner, Sarah Maria on 70-Feb-24 [70-Mar-2: 2C].
Chaney, Andrew W. (38 yrs.) d. on 67-Feb-2 [67-Feb-6: 2C].

Chaney, Catherine (1 yr., 5 mos.) d. on 67-Dec-21 [67-Dec-23: 2B].
Chaney, Charles m. Gohlinghorst, Mary Elizabeth on 70-Jun-6 [70-Jun-9: 2C].
Chaney, Charles R. m. Meek, Mary E. on 66-Jan-21 [66-Jan-24: 2B].
Chaney, Eliza (39 yrs.) d. on 68-Jul-4 [68-Jul-6: 2B].
Chaney, Elizabeth m. Harrison, Edward on 69-May-2 [69-May-6: 2B].
Chaney, H. C. m. Griffith, Annie M. on 68-Nov-26 [68-Dec-19: 2B].
Chaney, H. C. m. Jordan, Kate G. on 66-Jul-26 [66-Aug-4: 2C].
Chaney, James R. m. Burton, Nettie on 70-Nov-21 [70-Dec-8: 2B].
Chaney, Julia A. m. Phelps, Richard D. on 69-Dec-16 [69-Dec-20: 2C].
Chaney, Levi M. m. Baynard, Louisa on 70-Apr-14 [70-Apr-20: 2B].
Chaney, Sarah m. Guteridge, William S. on 69-Dec-16 [69-Dec-22: 2B].
Chaney, Susan d. on 67-Oct-27 in Railroad accident [67-Oct-31: 1G].
Chaney, Victoria E. m. Champney, Hiram J. on 67-Dec-17 [68-Jan-18: 2B].
Chaney, William Edward m. Jones, Sarah Virginia on 66-Aug-8 [66-Aug-15: 2B].
Channel, Madeline (63 yrs.) d. on 67-Feb-28 [67-Mar-1: 2C].
Chany, Emma F. d. on 69-Jul-31 [69-Aug-2: 2C].
Chapin, Barbara (31 yrs.) d. on 70-Oct-12 [70-Oct-13: 2C].
Chapman, Carrie T. m. Reid, R. C. on 70-Nov-11 [70-Nov-12: 2B].
Chapman, Charles Louis (41 yrs.) d. on 66-Apr-14 [66-Apr-16: 2B].
Chapman, D. C. m. Harris, Anna M. on 69-Nov-23 [69-Nov-27: 2B].
Chapman, Elizabeth m. Stamp, Hendrick M. F. W. on 66-Dec-8 [66-Dec-10: 2B].
Chapman, Emma (44 yrs.) d. on 69-Apr-12 [69-Apr-13: 2B].
Chapman, Helen C. m. Montell, Edwin E. on 70-Jan-11 [70-Jan-18: 2C].
Chapman, J. J. m. Sauer, Catherine R. on 70-Dec-7 [70-Dec-9: 2C].
Chapman, James B. (54 yrs.) d. on 69-Sep-19 [69-Sep-21: 2B].
Chapman, John, Dr. (81 yrs.) d. on 69-Jun-13 [69-Jul-17: 2C].
Chapman, Mary (77 yrs.) d. on 67-Apr-24 [67-May-3: 2B].
Chapman, Mary E. (11 yrs.) d. on 69-Apr-8 [69-Apr-13: 2B].
Chapman, May m. Scofield, James on 69-Mar-22 [69-Mar-24: 2C].
Chappell, Alice (10 yrs.) d. on 67-May-6 [67-May-7: 2B; 67-May-8: 2B].
Chappell, Cornelius m. Millington, Florie E. on 68-Jun-24 [68-Jun-30: 2B].
Chappell, Edwin F. m. Whitehill, Julia on 68-Oct-1 [68-Oct-13: 2C].
Chappell, Florence Estelle (22 yrs.) d. on 69-Jul-25 [69-Jul-26: 2C; 69-Jul-27: 2C].
Chappell, Florence Estelle d. on 69-Aug-4 [69-Aug-5: 2C].
Chappell, Grace (2 yrs., 4 mos.) d. on 69-Apr-20 [69-Apr-21: 2B].
Chappell, Philip Walter d. on 68-Mar-3 [68-Mar-5: 2B].
Chappell, Thomas S. m. Hall, Agnes V. C. on 67-Jun-6 [67-Jun-15: 2B].
Charles, George C. m. Dickson, Kate on 67-May-25 [67-Jun-6: 2B].
Charles, John m. Morris, Annie [69-Dec-28: 2C; 69-Dec-29: 2D].
Charlet, Marcel (32 yrs.) d. on 70-Jul-18 [70-Jul-21: 2C].
Charlton, William Henry (11 mos.) d. on 69-Apr-26 [69-Apr-27: 2C].
Charron, Ellen M. m. Richard, Stephen on 66-Feb-21 [66-Feb-24: 2B].
Charron, Rebecca (46 yrs.) d. on 67-Sep-16 [67-Sep-17: 2A].
Chase, Catherine Elizabeth Jan (11 mos.) d. on 70-Jul-22 [70-Jul-23: 2B].
Chase, Cora Lee (1 yr., 3 mos.) d. on 69-Jun-7 [69-Jun-8: 2B].
Chase, David (43 yrs.) d. on 66-Jan-27 [66-Jan-30: 2B; 66-Jan-31: 1G].
Chase, Emily J. (79 yrs.) d. on 70-Feb-5 [70-Feb-7: 2C; 70-Feb-8: 2C].
Chase, Esther Elizabeth (27 yrs.) d. on 66-Jun-23 [66-Jul-6: 2B].
Chase, Francis Dawes (32 yrs.) d. on 67-Apr-18 [67-Apr-19: 2B].
Chase, George W. m. Buckingham, Mary Emily on 66-Dec-4 [66-Dec-13: 2B].
Chase, Georgie (3 yrs., 2 mos.) d. on 67-Oct-28 [67-Oct-29: 2B].
Chase, Henry m. Howard, Ella on 67-May-16 [67-May-20: 2B].
Chase, Hester S. d. on 69-Nov-3 [69-Nov-15: 2C].
Chase, James William (3 yrs., 6 mos.) d. on 70-Dec-13 [70-Dec-15: 2C].
Chase, Mary Ann (69 yrs.) d. on 68-Jul-27 [68-Jul-28: 2B].

Chase, Nellie m. Eastman, Edward on 68-Jun-18 [68-Jun-20: 2B].
Chase, Richard d. on 69-Sep-22 Drowned [69-Sep-23: 1G].
Chase, Richard M. m. Burton, Elva R. on 70-Apr-1 [70-Apr-16: 2B].
Chase, Samuel W., Rev. (67 yrs.) d. on 67-Mar-27 [67-Mar-29: 2B; 67-Mar-30: 1F; 67-Apr-1: 1F].
Chase, Wells (81 yrs.) d. on 69-Jul-24 [69-Jul-26: 1G, 2C; 69-Jul-27: 1G].
Chase, William S. (51 yrs.) d. on 69-Oct-26 [69-Jan-2: 2C].
Chassaing, J. H. m. Gratiot, Mary Louise on 66-Jul-5 [66-Jul-11: 2C].
Chatard, F. E., Jr. m. Miles, Josephine on 70-Jun-1 [70-Jun-4: 2B].
Chatard, Josephine M. m. Von Phul, Philip on 70-Oct-26 [70-Oct-28: 2C].
Chatard, Mary T. d. on 70-Jan-11 [70-Jan-12: 2C].
Chatelain, Julia d. on 66-Dec-10 of Consumption [66-Dec-28: 2C].
Cheeseborough, Susan Percy m. Sanders, Franklin on 69-Aug-12 [69-Aug-17: 2C].
Cheesebrough, R. C., Jr. m. Pagels, Sallie E. on 66-Jun-21 [66-Jun-25: 2B].
Chenoweth, Amy (87 yrs.) d. on 69-Sep-25 [69-Sep-29: 2B].
Chenoweth, Charles E. (27 yrs.) d. on 69-Apr-20 [69-Apr-21: 2B].
Chenoweth, Frank Gillmore (3 yrs.) d. on 67-Jan-8 of Scarlet fever [67-Jan-14: 2C].
Chenoweth, Lizzie A. (5 yrs.) d. on 67-Jan-11 of Scarlet fever [67-Jan-14: 2C].
Chenoweth, Oliver B. m. Morrison, Martha S. on 67-Sep-26 [67-Sep-27: 2B].
Chenoweth, Sarah Jane (34 yrs.) d. on 68-Oct-5 [68-Oct-6: 2B].
Chenowith, John (35 yrs.) d. on 66-Jun-9 of Consumption [66-Jun-16: 2B].
Chenowith, Richard, Lt. (39 yrs.) d. on 70-Aug-17 of Paralysis [70-Aug-18: 2B, 4E; 70-Aug-20: 4D].
Cherbonnier, Joseph H., Dr. (25 yrs.) d. on 70-Jul-12 [70-Jul-14: 2B].
Cherbonnier, Pierre (85 yrs.) d. on 66-Apr-5 [66-Apr-6: 2B].
Cherebonnier, Alida F. C. (12 yrs., 5 mos.) d. on 66-Nov-5 [66-Nov-7: 2C].
Cherry, Cornelia V. m. Saunders, J. Randolph on 69-Nov-25 [69-Dec-22: 2B].
Cherry, Joseph T. (16 yrs., 7 mos.) d. on 66-Oct-17 of Gunshot wound [66-Oct-18: 1G, 2B].
Cherry, Lizzie A. m. Baer, William H. on 67-Jun-20 [67-Jun-21: 2B].
Cheseborough, Emma F. d. on 67-Apr-2 [67-Apr-3: 2B; 67-Apr-4: 2B].
Cheshire, Eliza E. m. Colton, Charles on 70-Feb-17 [70-Feb-24: 2C].
Chesnay, Amanda m. Foster, Robert H. on 66-Jun-19 [66-Jul-28: 2C].
Chesney, Harriott m. Nelson, H. Clay on 70-Feb-17 [70-Mar-1: 2C].
Chesney, Robert (42 yrs.) d. on 70-Apr-9 [70-Apr-11: 2B].
Chesney, Samuel m. Walker, Alverda on 70-Aug-18 [70-Aug-20: 2B].
Chesnut, Mary E. m. McClay, George M. on 66-Nov-20 [66-Nov-23: 2C; 66-Nov-24: 2B].
Chester, Anna M. m. Dyer, Richard R. D. on 69-Oct-19 [69-Oct-21: 2B].
Chester, Anna M. m. Boulden, Richard R. D. on 69-Oct-19 [69-Oct-21: 2B].
Chester, George L. m. Norris, Eliza S. on 68-Jan-23 [68-Jan-28: 2D].
Chester, Isabel F. m. Hopps, William on 70-Jun-13 [70-Jun-14: 2B].
Chester, Martha V. m. Hardesty, George W. on 70-Jul-12 [70-Nov-26: 2B].
Chester, William H. m. Sprowl, Sarah E. on 67-May-15 [67-May-18: 2A].
Chetwood, R. E. m. McGowan, Kate A. on 67-Mar-5 [67-Mar-7: 2C].
Chew, Henry Banning (66 yrs.) d. on 66-Dec-12 [66-Dec-14: 2B; 66-Dec-15: 1G].
Chew, John Howser (6 mos.) d. on 70-Dec-8 [70-Dec-10: 2B].
Chew, Kate V. m. Knight, William on 69-Sep-16 [69-Sep-28: 2B].
Chew, Maria G. d. on 68-Apr-1 [68-Apr-3: 2C].
Chew, N. S. m. Peake, Sallie E. on 67-Feb-7 [67-Feb-13: 2D].
Chew, Perry m. Wilson, Vallow on 66-Sep-13 [66-Sep-14: 2B].
Chew, Robert B. m. Harris, Agnes on 69-Nov-3 [69-Nov-6: 2B].
Chew, Robert W. (51 yrs.) d. on 68-Apr-23 [68-Apr-25: 2B].
Chew, Samuel C. m. Gibson, Maria on 66-Apr-26 [66-Apr-30: 2B].
Chew, William S. m. Barrington, Mina A. on 68-Sep-29 [68-Oct-6: 2B].
Chickering, Jennie Estelle (2 yrs.) d. on 69-Jul-25 [69-Jul-28: 2D].
Chiffelle, Lillie d. on 67-Feb-20 [67-Feb-22: 2D].

Chiffelle, Thomas P. m. Goldsborough, Catharine W. on 68-Dec-22 [68-Dec-25: 2D].
Chilcoate, Elizabeth E. m. Ensor, John E. on 66-May-10 [66-May-12: 2A].
Child, Eliza J. G. d. on 66-Jan-10 [66-Jan-13: 2C].
Child, Ida M. d. on 69-Oct-21 [69-Oct-22: 2B].
Child, Joseph J., Capt. (42 yrs.) d. on 68-Jan-8 [68-Jan-17: 2C].
Child, Samuel (75 yrs.) d. on 66-Sep-19 [66-Sep-20: 2B].
Childerson, Margaret (65 yrs.) d. on 67-Nov-28 [67-Nov-30: 2C].
Childress, Alice Lei m. Lynham, E. N. on 68-Jul-8 [68-Jul-10: 2C].
Childs, Charles (41 yrs.) d. on 68-Mar-10 Murdered (Stabbing) [68-Mar-11: 2B, 4E; 68-Mar-12: 1G].
Childs, D. J. m. Davis, L. Jennie on 68-Nov-25 [68-Dec-21: 2B].
Childs, Frank Houston (2 mos.) d. on 69-Aug-2 [69-Aug-4: 2C].
Childs, George (61 yrs.) d. on 68-Feb-12 [68-Feb-20: 2C].
Childs, Harry Munroe (2 mos.) d. on 69-Apr-26 [69-Apr-28: 2B].
Childs, J. W. m. Brice, Annie B. on 69-Sep-7 [69-Sep-28: 2B].
Childs, Marcella m. Jones, Resin on 66-Jun-14 [66-Jun-15: 2C].
Childs, Marie E. m. Hobbs, C. Marion on 68-Apr-2 [68-Apr-9: 2B].
Childs, Martha A. m. Zangenberg, George C. J. on 66-Feb-22 [66-Feb-24: 2B].
Childs, Martha E. m. Way, W. R. on 70-Jul-19 [70-Aug-6: 2C].
Childs, Mary E. m. Orendorff, Adolphus J. on 67-Dec-24 [68-Feb-1: 2B].
Childs, Mathias S. m. Ruff, Mary E. on 68-Nov-3 [68-Nov-9: 2B].
Childs, Minnie S. (3 yrs., 5 mos.) d. on 69-Nov-21 [69-Nov-23: 2C].
Childs, N. S. m. Turnbull, Hattie on 67-May-29 [67-May-31: 2B].
Childs, Octavia (39 yrs.) d. on 70-Sep-5 [70-Sep-7: 2B].
Childs, Oliver Benjamin (3 yrs., 3 mos.) d. on 68-Jan-16 [68-Jan-20: 2C].
Childs, Rebecca B. m. Read, Elias A. on 66-Apr-9 [66-Apr-12: 2B].
Childs, Samuel m. Getty, Annie T. on 68-Nov-19 [68-Nov-21: 2C].
Childs, William E. m. Causey, Mary J. on 69-Dec-21 [69-Dec-28: 2C].
Chiles, William S. m. Blocher, Tillie M. on 67-Nov-27 [68-Jan-15: 2C].
Chilton, Laura Mason m. Wise, Peyton on 69-Nov-25 [69-Nov-27: 2B].
Chilton, Rachel (20 yrs.) d. on 67-Oct-19 in Railroad accident [67-Oct-21: 1F; 67-Oct-22: 1G].
Chilton, Susie m. Curlett, T. Spicer on 68-Nov-4 [68-Nov-7: 2B].
Chinn, Ann W. (66 yrs.) d. on 69-Jul-11 [69-Jul-12: 2C].
Chipmane, Mary A. m. Peddicord, Issac H. on 66-Jun-5 [66-Jun-6: 2B].
Chisholm, Charles H. m. Trust, Lizzie C. on 68-Sep-21 [68-Sep-24: 2B].
Chisholm, James W. H. m. Tracey, Matilda on 67-Oct-24 [67-Oct-28: 2B].
Chisholm, Mary Ellen (2 mos.) d. on 68-Oct-17 [68-Oct-20: 2B].
Chisholm, Thomas H. m. Barton, Mary J. on 70-Jun-27 [70-Jun-28: 2C].
Chisholm, Tilly (18 yrs., 8 mos.) d. on 70-Feb-3 [70-Feb-5: 2B].
Chism, Mary T. (9 yrs.) d. [67-Mar-9: 2B].
Chisney, , Mrs. d. on 66-Jul-8 of Heatstroke [66-Jul-9: 1G].
Chittenden, Catherine (66 yrs.) d. on 69-Mar-29 [69-Mar-31: 2C].
Chittenden, Charles H. m. Edwards, Mary on 66-Dec-28 [67-Jan-15: 2C].
Chivel, Maria (50 yrs.) d. on 67-Jan-20 [67-Feb-25: 2C].
Chiveral, Anna (80 yrs.) d. on 69-Oct-3 [69-Oct-5: 2B].
Chiveral, Emma J. m. Layton, James H. on 70-Nov-22 [70-Nov-24: 2B].
Chiveral, William D. m. Pearman, Sarah Jane on 69-Aug-12 [69-Aug-19: 2C].
Choate, Mary m. DeCaindry, William A. on 70-Sep-29 [70-Oct-1: 2B].
Choate, Mary J. m. Peddicord, Evan on 67-Jan-1 [67-Jan-12: 2C].
Choate, Susan A. m. Nolen, John on 67-Dec-17 [67-Dec-21: 2B].
Choupin, Agnes Eugenia (8 yrs., 10 mos.) d. on 67-Feb-7 [67-Feb-8: 2C].
Christ, George m. Davis, Julia A. on 70-Apr-27 [70-May-4: 2C].
Christhilf, George S. m. Odell, Laura F. on 67-Apr-24 [67-May-6: 2B].
Christhilf, Henry (80 yrs.) d. on 66-Nov-24 [66-Nov-26: 1G, 2B].
Christhilf, Henry B. m. Gill, Anna M. O. on 70-May-9 [70-May-23: 2B].

Christhilf, Sarah C. C. d. on 70-Apr-5 [70-Apr-6: 2B].
Christian, Richard (63 yrs., 1 mo.) d. on 68-Nov-26 [68-Nov-28: 2C].
Christie, Ann (54 yrs.) d. on 67-Sep-8 [67-Sep-9: 2B].
Christie, Joseph Rudolph (6 mos.) d. on 66-Aug-19 [66-Aug-21: 2C].
Christie, Lavinia d. on 66-Jun-21 [66-Jun-23: 2B].
Christie, Mannie m. Dorsey, Decatur on 66-Jan-4 [66-Jan-5: 2C].
Christofferson, Carl d. on 70-Jun-14 Drowned [70-Jun-15: 1H].
Christopher, Annie M. m. Mister, Issac S. on 66-May-1 [66-May-4: 2C].
Christopher, Christian W. (38 yrs.) d. on 67-Sep-17 [67-Sep-18: 2B].
Christopher, John Elmer (1 yr., 7 mos.) d. on 68-Nov-24 [68-Nov-26: 2B].
Christopher, Joseph M. (7 mos.) d. on 68-Mar-25 [68-Mar-30: 2B].
Christopher, Lola (7 mos.) d. on 66-Aug-2 [66-Aug-7: 2C].
Christopher, Mary R. m. Scott, William G. on 69-Nov-23 [69-Nov-26: 2B].
Christopher, Milton m. Cornelius, Louisa on 70-Nov-3 [70-Nov-7: 2A].
Christopher, Milton N. (1 yr., 4 mos.) d. on 66-Mar-10 [66-Mar-12: 2B; 66-Mar-13: 2B].
Christopher, Thomas J., Capt. (40 yrs.) d. on 70-Feb-4 Drowned [70-Mar-2: 2C].
Christopher, Thomas James m. Hammer, Lizzie on 67-May-8 [67-May-23: 2B].
Christy, Andrew d. on 68-Dec-27 of Exposure [69-Jan-2: 1H].
Christy, Henry (78 yrs.) d. on 67-Oct-14 [67-Oct-15: 2A; 67-Oct-16: 2B].
Chriswell, Leah (85 yrs.) d. on 68-Sep-24 [68-Sep-25: 2B].
Chunn, James T., Dr. (38 yrs.) d. on 67-Jan-24 [67-Jan-25: 2C].
Church, Amelia (56 yrs.) d. on 66-Jul-17 [66-Aug-1: 2C].
Church, Francis E. m. Randolph, Annie on 69-Feb-3 [69-Feb-5: 2C].
Church, Mary A. (29 yrs.) d. on 66-Mar-10 [66-Mar-13: 2B].
Church, Mary Blanch d. on 69-Aug-24 [69-Aug-25: 2C].
Church, Royal W. (32 yrs.) d. on 69-Nov-7 [69-Nov-8: 2C].
Church, Willie (13 yrs.) d. on 67-Mar-14 [67-Mar-15: 2C].
Cicirello, Antonio (32 yrs.) d. on 66-Oct-13 [66-Oct-15: 2B].
Cinnamond, George R. (52 yrs.) d. on 66-Feb-9 of Pneumonia [66-Feb-12: 2D, 4B; 66-Feb-14: 2C].
Cissel, Emma m. Galt, James V. on 66-Sep-25 [66-Sep-27: 2C].
Cissel, William L. m. Fletcher, Minnie on 65-Oct-5 [66-Jan-8: 2B].
Clabaugh, Georgianna m. Blackburn, H. H. on 69-Oct-11 [69-Oct-12: 2C].
Clabaugh, Janet m. Larrabee, Daniel on 69-Jun-10 [69-Jun-11: 2C].
Clabaugh, Mollie m. Rieman, Henry, Jr. on 70-Apr-26 [70-Apr-28: 2B].
Clagett, Fanny m. Young, R. A. on 69-Aug-3 [69-Aug-5: 2B].
Clagett, Harriet d. on 66-Nov-8 [66-Nov-9: 2C].
Clagett, Henry Brice (66 yrs.) d. on 67-Feb-13 [67-Feb-21: 2D].
Clagett, J. Thomas (25 yrs.) d. on 68-Sep-21 of Fall [68-Sep-22: 1G].
Clagett, Sarah d. on 66-Oct-24 [66-Oct-27: 2B].
Clagett, Thomas John d. on 66-Feb-26 [66-Feb-28: 2C].
Clagett, Walter Bowie (3 mos.) d. on 68-Nov-29 [68-Dec-1: 2C].
Clagett, Willie Tucker (1 mo.) d. on 66-Nov-25 [66-Dec-5: 2B].
Claggett, Ida May (1 yr., 9 mos.) d. on 68-Jan-15 [68-Jan-16: 2C].
Claggett, Lou m. Stauffer, S. Theodore on 69-Oct-12 [69-Oct-19: 2B].
Claggett, William d. on 68-Mar-19 [68-Mar-27: 2C; 68-Mar-30: 4E].
Claglett, Mary F. m. Knott, John E. on 67-Dec-26 [68-Jan-11: 2B].
Claiborne, Emily L. m. Suttle, C. F. on 66-Oct-2 [66-Oct-5: 2B; 66-Oct-6: 2A].
Clancey, Matthew (66 yrs.) d. on 70-Apr-2 [70-Apr-4: 2B].
Clancy, Annie E. d. on 69-Mar-26 of Consumption [69-Mar-27: 2B].
Clancy, John D. m. Orr, Agnes on 68-Feb-4 [68-Feb-11: 2C].
Clapp, Ann (87 yrs.) d. on 67-Oct-6 [67-Oct-7: 2B].
Clapp, Frank (33 yrs.) d. on 69-May-21 of Typhoid [69-May-24: 2B].
Clapp, Laura Elizabeth (7 mos.) d. on 66-Apr-25 [66-Apr-26: 2B].
Clare, Issac (82 yrs.) d. on 67-May-3 [67-May-4: 2B].

Claridge, Annie M. m. Bowling, Charles O. on 69-Jun-14 [69-Sep-6: 2C].
Claridge, Lloyd (65 yrs.) d. on 66-Apr-2 [66-Apr-4: 2B].
Claridge, William H. (4 mos.) d. on 70-Jul-4 [70-Jul-6: 2C].
Claridge, William H. (25 yrs., 7 mos.) d. on 70-Jul-29 [70-Jul-30: 2B].
Claridge, William H. m. Bosman, Arianna on 69-Apr-5 [69-Apr-9: 2C].
Claridge, William Z. d. on 69-Dec-20 Drowned [70-Jan-6: 1H; 70-Jan-8: 1G].
Clark, Ada E. m. Smith, William F. on 70-Feb-17 [70-Feb-24: 2C].
Clark, Albert (35 yrs.) d. on 69-Feb-27 in Machine accident [69-Mar-1: 1G, 2C].
Clark, Amanda m. Forsyth, Arthur P. on 70-Nov-24 [70-Dec-2: 2C].
Clark, Amanda J. m. Gordon, John H. on 69-Dec-14 [69-Dec-21: 2B].
Clark, Anna M. m. Haupt, George W. on 69-May-3 [69-May-10: 2B].
Clark, Anna R. m. Montague, Samuel H. A. on 70-May-3 [70-May-10: 2B].
Clark, Annie m. Gainer, Martin on 67-Nov-24 [67-Dec-13: 2C].
Clark, Annie M. m. Clark, William on 68-Jul-9 [68-Jul-14: 2B].
Clark, Annie M. m. Hall, James R. on 70-Mar-27 [70-Mar-29: 2B].
Clark, Annie Pentz (4 yrs., 9 mos.) d. on 69-May-8 [69-May-10: 2C].
Clark, Augustus B. m. Magaha, Mary M. on 69-Aug-15 [69-Sep-18: 2B].
Clark, Avis M. (51 yrs.) d. on 70-Nov-10 [70-Nov-16: 2C].
Clark, Benjamin, Jr. (27 yrs.) d. on 70-Sep-19 [70-Sep-23: 2C].
Clark, Benjamin J. (63 yrs.) d. on 70-Sep-7 [70-Sep-8: 2B; 70-Sep-9: 2B; 70-Sep-10: 4D].
Clark, Charles H. (24 yrs.) d. on 67-Jun-24 [67-Jun-25: 2B].
Clark, Cora Estelle (1 yr., 2 mos.) d. on 67-Sep-22 [67-Sep-23: 2A].
Clark, Daniel E. m. Schaum, Mary A. on 70-Jul-19 [70-Aug-1: 2C].
Clark, Daniel H. (63 yrs.) d. on 70-Jan-22 [70-Jan-25: 2C].
Clark, Edwin m. Manning, Laura V. on 70-Jan-13 [70-Jan-19: 2C].
Clark, Eleanor G. m. Jones, Talbot on 69-Jun-24 [69-Jun-28: 2C; 69-Jun-29: 2C].
Clark, Elizabeth P. m. Forsyth, Alexander D. on 69-Sep-15 [69-Sep-18: 2B].
Clark, Emma F. m. Roberts, John W. on 69-Feb-19 [69-Feb-24: 2C].
Clark, Emma L. m. Wilkinson, John W. B. on 67-Feb-18 [67-May-30: 2B].
Clark, Fannie H. m. Armstrong, William J. on 70-Nov-22 [70-Nov-26: 2B].
Clark, Flora Bell (1 yr., 9 mos.) d. on 68-Jul-9 [68-Jul-11: 2B].
Clark, Florence Virginia d. on 69-Jan-25 [69-Jan-26: 2C].
Clark, Francis P. m. Godfrey, Susanna A. on 68-Jun-28 [68-Jun-30: 2B].
Clark, Gabriel D., Jr. m. Edmonston, Emma on 69-Apr-13 [69-Apr-15: 2B].
Clark, George E. (10 mos.) d. on 67-Jul-28 [67-Aug-1: 2C].
Clark, Georgie m. Serpell, G. M. on 69-Sep-14 [69-Sep-15: 2B].
Clark, Harry Thomas (2 yrs., 7 mos.) d. on 68-Nov-4 [68-Nov-10: 2C].
Clark, Henry m. Galloway, Annie E. on 68-Oct-22 [68-Nov-6: 2B].
Clark, Henry m. Gross, Cordelia M. on 69-Dec-27 [69-Dec-28: 2C].
Clark, James R. (27 yrs.) d. on 67-Jan-20 [67-Jan-22: 2C].
Clark, James Thomas (2 yrs., 4 mos.) d. on 70-Oct-20 [70-Oct-21: 2C].
Clark, Jane (73 yrs.) d. on 70-Aug-30 [70-Aug-31: 2B].
Clark, Jane Ann Adeline m. Moore, Lemuel Mitchell on 68-Jun-20 [68-Jul-29: 2B].
Clark, John (80 yrs.) d. on 67-Jun-13 [67-Jun-14: 1F, 2B].
Clark, John (49 yrs.) d. on 70-Apr-24 [70-Apr-28: 2C].
Clark, John m. Manning, Margaret on 66-Apr-2 [66-Apr-26: 2B].
Clark, John H. (23 yrs.) d. on 66-Jan-23 [66-Jan-24: 2B].
Clark, John R. m. Owings, Susie D. on 70-Aug-21 [70-Sep-1: 2B].
Clark, Joseph (1 yr., 6 mos.) d. on 68-Jan-20 [68-Jan-22: 2C].
Clark, Joseph T., Capt. (40 yrs.) d. on 67-May-15 [67-May-25: 2B].
Clark, Julia E. m. Frey, Samuel W. on 66-Nov-22 [66-Nov-23: 2C].
Clark, Lemuel m. Middleton, Katie H. on 66-May-22 [66-May-29: 2B].
Clark, Lloyd (50 yrs.) d. on 66-Mar-17 [66-Mar-20: 2C].
Clark, Maggie m. Dawson, Edward L. on 66-Jul-5 [66-Jul-14: 2B].
Clark, Margaret (84 yrs.) d. on 70-May-19 [70-May-21: 2B].

Clark, Margaret Ann (45 yrs.) d. on 67-Sep-16 [67-Sep-18: 2B].
Clark, Margaret E. m. Hoffnagel, Robert D. on 69-May-19 [69-May-22: 2B].
Clark, Maria (63 yrs.) d. on 68-Dec-6 [68-Dec-11: 2C].
Clark, Maria D. m. Hamlin, James H. on 67-May-29 [67-Jun-22: 2B].
Clark, Mary (35 yrs.) d. on 67-Mar-20 [67-Mar-22: 2C; 67-Mar-23: 2C].
Clark, Mary (54 yrs.) d. on 66-Feb-3 [66-Feb-5: 2C].
Clark, Mary A. m. Magruder, George G. on 70-Dec-8 [70-Dec-10: 2B].
Clark, Mary Agnes m. Bethune, J. D. on 69-Jun-2 [69-Jun-4: 2C].
Clark, Mary Ann (3 yrs., 7 mos.) d. on 68-Dec-27 [68-Dec-28: 2B].
Clark, Mary Ann (75 yrs.) d. on 69-Feb-8 [69-Feb-9: 2C].
Clark, Mary E. m. Warfield, George T. on 68-Nov-25 [68-Dec-4: 2D].
Clark, Mary E. m. Polk, Lucius C. on 67-Nov-7 [67-Nov-13: 2C].
Clark, Mary Elizabeth (4 mos.) d. on 70-Nov-21 [70-Nov-23: 2B].
Clark, Mary Margaret (23 yrs.) d. on 69-Feb-11 [69-Feb-12: 2C; 69-Feb-13: 2C].
Clark, Mary R. m. Radley, Peter on 66-Jun-25 [66-Jun-27: 2C].
Clark, Mary S. (10 yrs., 1 mo.) d. on 67-Dec-10 [67-Dec-12: 2B].
Clark, Matthew (53 yrs.) d. on 67-Mar-8 [67-Mar-12: 1F, 2C].
Clark, Matthew Harry (6 yrs., 1 mo.) d. on 66-Jun-11 of Scarlet fever [66-Jul-4: 2B; 66-Jun-12: 2B].
Clark, Mollie A. m. Thurlow, William J. on 68-Feb-6 [68-Feb-10: 2C].
Clark, Nelson B. (55 yrs.) d. on 70-Jan-26 [70-Jan-29: 2B].
Clark, Peter (28 yrs.) d. on 66-Apr-16 of Consumption [66-Apr-17: 2C].
Clark, Pinkey (4 yrs., 8 mos.) d. on 66-Aug-13 [66-Aug-15: 2B].
Clark, Re Everett (77 yrs.) d. on 67-Mar-5 [67-Mar-7: 2C].
Clark, Rebecca J. (20 yrs.) d. on 70-Mar-14 [70-Mar-15: 2C].
Clark, Rebecca J. m. Heesh, John T. on 68-Mar-17 [68-Apr-13: 2B].
Clark, Robert G. (28 yrs.) d. on 70-Jan-3 in Railroad accident [70-Jan-4: 1H; 70-Jan-5: 2C].
Clark, Robert M. m. McCoy, Mattie on 69-Sep-1 [69-Sep-3: 2B].
Clark, Sarah (78 yrs.) d. on 69-Aug-7 [69-Aug-9: 2B].
Clark, Sarah A. m. Fales, Frank H. on 67-Jan-1 [67-Jan-5: 2C].
Clark, Sarah Elizabeth (29 yrs.) d. on 66-Mar-6 [66-Mar-7: 2B].
Clark, Sarah J. (26 yrs.) d. on 66-Mar-17 [66-Mar-20: 2C].
Clark, Sidney William (3 yrs., 1 mo.) d. on 66-Jun-29 of Scarlet fever [66-Jun-30: 2B; 66-Jul-4: 2B].
Clark, Susan S. (23 yrs.) d. on 66-Feb-9 of Poisoning [66-Feb-10: 1F].
Clark, Susanna R. m. Moog, G. W. on 68-Feb-4 [68-Feb-8: 2B].
Clark, Victorine P. m. Butler, John H. on 67-Aug-20 [67-Sep-7: 2A].
Clark, W. F. m. Frisch, Catharine on 70-Jun-6 [70-Jun-15: 2B].
Clark, Wheeler (74 yrs.) d. on 68-Feb-5 [68-Feb-6: 2C].
Clark, William (71 yrs.) d. on 67-Apr-6 [67-Apr-8: 1G, 2B].
Clark, William m. Clark, Annie M. on 68-Jul-9 [68-Jul-14: 2B].
Clark, William Of T. m. Dorsey, Jennie on 69-Dec-9 [69-Dec-13: 2C].
Clark, William Wilson (18 yrs.) d. on 66-Apr-17 [66-Apr-23: 2B].
Clarke, A. P. m. McLaughlin, Fannie on 70-Nov-22 [70-Nov-23: 2B].
Clarke, Addison m. Dunnington, Nancy on 69-Sep-15 [69-Sep-16: 2B].
Clarke, Annie M. (1 mo.) d. on 66-May-14 [66-May-15: 2C].
Clarke, Avis (63 yrs.) d. on 67-Jun-5 [67-Jun-6: 2B].
Clarke, Bridget (71 yrs.) d. on 69-Aug-30 [69-Aug-31: 2B].
Clarke, Charles H. (7 mos.) d. on 68-Jul-16 [68-Jul-17: 2B].
Clarke, Elizabeth D. (74 yrs.) d. on 70-Oct-24 [70-Oct-25: 2B].
Clarke, Emelia H. d. on 67-May-1 [67-May-7: 2B].
Clarke, George B. m. Bell, Agnes on 67-Jun-24 [67-Jul-9: 2B].
Clarke, George W. (46 yrs.) d. on 70-Jan-1 [70-Jan-3: 2C].
Clarke, George W. m. Stewart, Ella J. on 70-Sep-12 [70-Sep-14: 2B].
Clarke, John m. Wilson, Annie on 70-Mar-31 [70-May-12: 2B].

Clarke, Julianna Matthews d. on 70-Feb-24 [70-Feb-28: 2C].
Clarke, Katie Agatha d. on 68-Nov-24 [68-Nov-25: 2B].
Clarke, Laurence (49 yrs.) d. on 68-Dec-27 [68-Dec-28: 2B].
Clarke, Margaret (2 yrs., 10 mos.) d. on 66-Jun-27 [66-Jun-28: 2C].
Clarke, Maria Beverley (76 yrs.) d. on 68-Jan-9 [68-Jan-11: 2B].
Clarke, Mary d. on 69-Oct-27 [69-Oct-28: 2C].
Clarke, Mary m. Bannon, John J. on 70-May-26 [70-May-31: 2B].
Clarke, Phoebe A. d. on 68-Jan-5 [68-Jan-7: 2C].
Clarke, Ray S., Capt. (66 yrs.) d. on 70-Aug-23 of Apoplexy [70-Aug-24: 4D, 2C; 70-Aug-25: 2B].
Clarke, Sadie Duckett (18 yrs.) d. on 67-Mar-11 [67-Mar-12: 2C; 67-Mar-16: 2B].
Clarke, Samuel T. (37 yrs.) d. on 67-May-30 [67-Jun-5: 2B; 67-Jun-18: 2B].
Clarke, Susan (25 yrs.) d. on 67-Sep-28 [67-Sep-30: 2B].
Clarke, Sylvester (1 yr., 1 mo.) d. on 69-Dec-13 [69-Dec-14: 2C].
Clarke, Thomas m. Naughton, Kate on 66-Apr-4 [66-Apr-7: 2B].
Clarke, Walter T. (15 yrs.) d. on 67-Oct-7 of Heart disease [67-Oct-14: 2B].
Clarke, William F. m. Macon, Anna on 67-Nov-21 [67-Nov-23: 2B].
Clarke, William H. m. Owings, Carrie D. on 68-Jan-14 [68-Feb-5: 2D].
Clarke, William H. m. Pilkington, Serena D. on 70-May-9 [70-May-11: 2B].
Clarke, Willie E. (2 yrs.) d. on 66-Jun-23 [66-Jun-25: 2B].
Clarkson, Alfred (29 yrs., 4 mos.) d. on 69-Oct-5 [69-Oct-6: 2B].
Clarkson, Caroline Emily d. on 66-Jul-27 [66-Jul-28: 2C].
Clarkson, Emma E. (14 yrs., 6 mos.) d. on 66-Sep-17 [66-Sep-18: 2B].
Clarkson, Frank S. m. Hissey, Mary G. on 69-Jun-22 [69-Jun-24: 2C].
Clarkson, Nannie Reginald (7 mos.) d. on 70-Jul-8 [70-Jul-13: 2C].
Clarkston, E. M. m. Warwick, Sarah E. on 66-Dec-25 [66-Dec-28: 2C].
Clarvoe, C. W. m. Gill, Sallie J. on 67-Sep-24 [67-Sep-26: 2B].
Clary, John m. Murphy, Rose A. on 66-Jul-9 [66-Jul-11: 2C].
Clary, Rosa A. d. on 68-May-16 [68-May-18: 2B].
Clasey, Margaret (77 yrs.) d. on 69-May-21 [69-May-22: 2B].
Claspy, George W. m. Lane, Lizzie on 69-Mar-30 [69-Apr-12: 2A].
Claspy, Reese Helm (4 yrs., 1 mo.) d. on 69-Feb-22 [69-Feb-24: 2C].
Claude, Catharine A. m. Cortlan, Clinton on 70-Nov-30 [70-Dec-2: 2C].
Claude, Phoebe m. Kilburn, Willis on 70-Aug-25 [70-Aug-26: 2C].
Claude, Sue C. m. Morris, John on 66-May-31 [66-Jun-4: 2B].
Claus, Blanche Louisa (2 yrs., 8 mos.) d. on 70-Jul-22 [70-Jul-23: 2B].
Clausen, C. F. m. Browne, Lizzie on 67-Oct-22 [67-Oct-24: 2B].
Claussen, Catherina F. m. Lieb, Thomas on 67-Nov-24 [67-Nov-26: 2B].
Clautice, Agatha d. on 67-Aug-8 [67-Aug-9: 2C; 67-Aug-10: 2B].
Clautice, Frances Louisa d. on 70-Jun-17 [70-Jun-18: 2B].
Clautice, Francis (51 yrs.) d. [67-May-8: 2B; 67-May-9: 2A].
Clautice, Mary C. m. Bryan, Edward on 70-Apr-20 [70-Apr-23: 2B].
Clautice, William F. m. Sweeney, Alice J. on 70-Nov-17 [70-Nov-19: 2B].
Clautices, Charles Oliver (4 yrs., 6 mos.) d. on 69-Feb-4 of Brain inflammation [69-Feb-5: 2C; 69-Feb-6: 2C].
Clautices, William Henry (6 yrs., 5 mos.) d. on 69-Mar-2 of Dropsy [69-Mar-3: 2C; 69-Mar-4: 2C].
Claxton, Alexander d. on 67-Oct-29 [67-Oct-30: 2B].
Clay, William Henry (33 yrs.) d. on 70-Apr-14 [70-Apr-22: 2C].
Clay, William Oliver (1 yr., 3 mos.) d. on 69-May-12 [69-May-13: 2B].
Clayland, Mary E. d. on 68-Jan-5 of Pneumonia [68-Jan-9: 2C].
Clayland, Mary E. (67 yrs.) d. on 68-Oct-28 [68-Oct-29: 2B; 68-Oct-30: 2C].
Claypoole, Lucy m. Hughes, George N. on 68-Jul-30 [68-Aug-8: 2B].
Claypoole, Mary L. m. Merritt, James A. on 66-Jan-17 [66-Jan-19: 2C].
Clayton, Augustus L. m. Mumma, Josephine S. on 67-Nov-6 [67-Nov-11: 2C].

Clayton, Elizabeth m. Brine, Thomas on 67-Dec-29 [67-Dec-31: 2C].
Clayton, Henry m. Black, Mary on 69-Oct-10 [69-Oct-20: 2C].
Clayton, James H. m. Barnes, Louisa E. on 67-Jan-3 [67-Jan-5: 2C].
Clayton, Joseph S. m. Smith, Henrietta J. on 69-Dec-23 [69-Dec-30: 2C].
Clayton, Temperance R. m. Wisnom, Alexander H. on 69-Jan-11 [69-Mar-3: 2B].
Clayton, Theodore m. Keyser, Mary E. on 67-Dec-19 [67-Dec-20: 2B].
Clazey, Albert m. Brooks, Sarah Jane on 68-Aug-12 [68-Aug-18: 2B].
Clazey, George W. m. Seamont, Caroline on 69-Nov-28 [69-Nov-30: 2C].
Cleary, Douglas M. m. Broadbent, Mary Eugenia on 67-Apr-30 [67-May-2: 2B].
Cleary, Elizabeth B. m. Dinsmore, John on 66-Jun-24 [66-Jul-14: 2B].
Cleary, R. E. m. Fitzpatrick, Willie on 70-Jul-12 [70-Jul-19: 2B].
Cleaveland, Edwin R. m. Donaldson, Maggie H. on 68-Mar-4 [68-Mar-16: 2B].
Cleaveland, Thomas d. on 69-Jul-10 in Railroad accident [69-Jul-12: 1H].
Clefford, Austin m. McIntire, Jane E. on 66-Jun-12 [67-Apr-10: 2C].
Clefford, John H. m. McCoy, Jennie on 70-Aug-8 [70-Aug-10: 2B].
Clefford, Virginia Rose (1 yr., 9 mos.) d. on 69-Jan-2 [69-Jan-5: 2C].
Cleland, Margaret Theresa m. Kenna, Paul on 66-Jul-5 [66-Jul-10: 2C].
Clemants, Mary Elizabeth (34 yrs.) d. on 68-Sep-19 [68-Sep-21: 2B].
Clemency, Alexander (34 yrs.) d. on 68-Oct-24 [68-Oct-26: 2B].
Clemency, Sarah E. (26 yrs.) d. on 66-Mar-9 [66-Mar-14: 2C].
Clemens, George H. (4 yrs., 4 mos.) d. on 69-Mar-1 [69-Mar-3: 2C].
Clemens, Willie (1 yr., 1 mo.) d. on 68-Aug-10 [68-Aug-13: 2B].
Clement, Amanda d. on 66-Apr-10 [66-Apr-12: 2B].
Clement, Christopher d. on 68-Sep-26 of Fall from mast [68-Sep-28: 1G].
Clement, Jacob m. Hasson, Amanda on 66-Feb-7 [66-Feb-10: 2C].
Clements, Emma (40 yrs.) d. on 66-May-20 [66-May-23: 2B].
Clements, John (106 yrs.) d. on 70-Aug-18 [70-Aug-19: 2C, 4D].
Clements, John W. m. Moore, Mary E. on 66-Jul-27 [66-Nov-10: 2B].
Clements, Mary R. (34 yrs.) d. on 68-Mar-29 [68-Mar-30: 2B].
Clements, Robert m. Pierpont, Mary J. on 68-Sep-10 [68-Sep-24: 2B].
Clemm, Carrie R. m. Hyde, Edward I. on 68-Mar-25 [68-Mar-28: 2B].
Clemm, Margaret m. Parker, William H. on 66-May-14 [66-May-15: 2C].
Clemment, Laura E. m. Caldwell, William M. on 66-Aug-21 [66-Aug-24: 2B].
Clemmons, Emma (13 yrs., 3 mos.) d. on 66-Apr-18 [66-Apr-20: 2B].
Clemmont, Ann Eliza m. Ruckle, Edward H. on 68-Dec-15 [68-Dec-17: 2C].
Clemson, E. A. m. Norris, John B. on 66-Nov-13 [66-Nov-14: 2B].
Clendemen, Kate R. m. Ault, Samuel on 68-Oct-29 [68-Nov-11: 2C].
Cleveland, James B. m. Todhunter, Allison Douglas on 67-Mar-16 [67-Mar-18: 2B].
Cleveland, Joseph S. (52 yrs.) d. on 69-Nov-29 [69-Nov-30: 2C].
Cleveland, Josephine m. Wands, Alexander H. on 66-Oct-23 [66-Nov-6: 2B].
Clickner, John Reed d. on 67-May-19 [67-May-21: 2B].
Cliffe, Augusta m. Mahool, Thomas on 68-Dec-8 [68-Dec-10: 2D].
Cliffe, Hettie B. m. Jackson, James F. on 70-Oct-23 [70-Nov-3: 2B].
Cliffe, Jinnie Grace (9 mos.) d. on 70-Aug-6 [70-Aug-9: 2C].
Clifford, Ella (8 yrs.) d. on 67-Jun-19 of Diptheria [67-Jun-20: 2B].
Clifford, John S. (18 yrs.) d. on 67-Jun-14 [67-Jun-15: 2B].
Clifford, Mary (29 yrs.) d. on 67-Jul-30 [67-Jul-31: 2C].
Clifford, Thomas m. McGarigle, Anne M. on 70-Feb-14 [70-Feb-22: 2C].
Clift, Henry D. (47 yrs.) d. on 65-Nov-2 [66-Feb-22: 2B].
Clift, James H. (24 yrs.) d. on 69-Aug-20 [69-Aug-21: 2B].
Clifton, Louis Deluol d. on 67-Oct-5 of Yellow fever [67-Oct-21: 2B].
Clifton, Michael Edward d. on 66-Oct-22 [66-Oct-29: 2C].
Clifton, Sue S. m. Brown, Sebastian on 67-Sep-26 [67-Oct-1: 2B].
Clifton, Theodore Eccleston d. on 66-Mar-13 [66-Mar-15: 2C].
Clifton, Willy (4 yrs., 6 mos.) d. on 67-Aug-31 of Yellow fever [67-Sep-10: 2B].

Cline, Anna Alberta (5 yrs.) d. on 70-Oct-20 [70-Oct-22: 2B].
Cline, George Franklin (2 yrs., 1 mo.) d. on 70-Apr-26 of Typhoid [70-May-25: 2C].
Cline, Hugh H. m. Curtis, Leonora on 69-Jul-13 [69-Jul-21: 2C].
Cline, James P. (52 yrs.) d. on 66-Apr-27 of Consumption [67-Jan-24: 2C].
Cline, Mary E. m. Nagle, Henry A. on 67-Jul-16 [67-Jul-25: 2C].
Cline, Walter Stewart (3 mos.) d. on 66-Oct-7 [66-Oct-8: 2B].
Clingan, Anna E. m. Farrow, William H. on 68-Dec-15 [68-Dec-17: 2C].
Clipper, Stephen Randolph (1 yr., 2 mos.) d. on 70-Aug-16 [70-Aug-17: 2C].
Clisby, Louisa m. Dorsen, Lindsay T. on 69-Apr-22 [69-Apr-24: 2B].
Cloake, Patrick d. on 66-Nov-8 [66-Nov-9: 2C].
Clockley, William (63 yrs.) d. on 67-Jan-11 [67-Feb-4: 2C].
Cloman, Charlotte R. m. Noggle, Emmanuel on 65-Nov-30 [66-Feb-22: 2B].
Clonen, Michael P. (12 yrs., 2 mos.) d. on 67-Nov-4 [67-Nov-5: 2B].
Clopton, William S. m. Pitt, Fannie A. on 69-Jun-1 [69-Jun-2: 2B].
Close, Ella m. Little, William J. on 70-Oct-16 [70-Oct-24: 2B].
Close, Robert (53 yrs.) d. on 66-Jan-24 [66-Jan-25: 2C].
Clotworthy, Edward F. m. Callis, Fannie A. on 66-Oct-29 [66-Nov-5: 2B].
Clotworthy, Willie Steuart (11 yrs.) d. on 67-Dec-5 [67-Dec-7: 2B].
Clunan, Catherine d. on 69-Sep-19 [69-Sep-20: 2C].
Cluney, John (46 yrs.) d. on 69-Aug-5 [69-Aug-6: 2C].
Clunk, Mary E. (7 mos.) d. on 69-Sep-19 [69-Sep-20: 2C].
Cluskey, Joe E. m. Mullin, Michael A. on 70-Aug-9 [70-Aug-31: 2B].
Clymer, Francis D. m. Buckingham, Sidney E. on 67-Sep-5 [67-Sep-17: 2A].
Coad, George D. (56 yrs.) d. on 70-Dec-15 [70-Dec-16: 2C].
Coady, Thomas m. Walsh, Kate [68-Jul-17: 2B].
Coakley, P. H., Jr. (25 yrs.) d. on 67-Sep-11 [67-Sep-13: 2B].
Coakley, Sarah (69 yrs.) d. on 69-Apr-18 [69-Apr-19: 2B].
Coale, Alice Gertrude (5 yrs., 3 mos.) d. on 70-Sep-24 [70-Sep-26: 2B].
Coale, Harriet H. m. Hibberd, Job on 70-Nov-15 [70-Nov-22: 2B].
Coale, Issac, Jr. m. McDowell, Helen on 68-Oct-22 [68-Oct-27: 2B].
Coale, J. Olivia d. on 70-Jun-18 [70-Jun-20: 2B].
Coale, James Carey (9 yrs.) d. on 67-Aug-3 [67-Aug-6: 2C].
Coale, Lewis Chipmen (1 yr., 8 mos.) d. on 69-Jul-30 [69-Jul-31: 2C].
Coale, Mary Ann (74 yrs.) d. on 66-Apr-3 [66-Apr-4: 2C; 66-Apr-5: 2B].
Coale, Mary G. d. on 67-Jan-8 [67-Jan-10: 2C].
Coale, Rebecca S. m. Taylor, Joseph on 66-Nov-15 [66-Nov-16: 2C].
Coale, Skipwith Holland (1 yr., 3 mos.) d. on 70-Sep-19 [70-Sep-20: 2B].
Coale, William A. m. Freeman, Lizzie J. on 66-Jun-28 [66-Jul-4: 2B].
Coale, William F. (19 yrs.) d. [68-Feb-21: 2B].
Coan, Bridget (19 yrs.) d. on 70-Apr-14 [70-Apr-15: 2B].
Coard, Annie E. m. Bond, George M. on 68-Jan-2 [68-Jan-4: 2C].
Coard, Jennie S. m. Allender, J. Enlous on 70-Jan-20 [70-Jan-28: 2B].
Coarts, George W. m. Perry, Sallie E. on 68-Jun-12 [68-Jun-13: 2B].
Coates, George (43 yrs.) d. on 68-Jan-30 [68-Jan-31: 2C, 2B].
Coates, Kate Virginia (2 yrs., 8 mos.) d. on 69-May-18 of Scarlet fever [69-May-20: 2C; 69-Jul-5: 2C].
Coates, Maggie Lee (2 yrs., 6 mos.) d. on 69-Jun-15 of Scarlet fever [69-Jun-16: 2C; 69-Jun-17: 2C; 69-Jul-5: 2C].
Coates, Mary Jane m. Sellars, William on 66-Nov-13 [66-Nov-16: 2C].
Coates, Robert E. m. Williams, Hannah A. on 68-Mar-1 [68-Mar-7: 2B].
Coates, Thomas (1 yr., 2 mos.) d. on 69-Jul-3 of Scarlet fever [69-Jul-5: 2C].
Coath, Fannie S. m. Collett, Thomas E. on 66-Jun-8 [66-Sep-10: 2D].
Cobb, Annie M. m. Musgrove, Augustus on 70-Sep-8 [70-Oct-13: 2C].
Cobb, Ruth Ann d. on 66-May-22 [66-May-26: 2B].
Coblens, Julia m. Hamburger, Myer on 68-Feb-12 [68-Feb-22: 2B].

Coburn, John m. Moffett, Carrie A. on 69-Oct-5 [69-Oct-12: 2C].
Coburn, Sarah J. (15 yrs., 3 mos.) d. on 70-Feb-1 [70-Feb-2: 2B; 70-Feb-3: 2B].
Coburn, Susan Alice (26 yrs.) d. on 68-Oct-1 [68-Oct-2: 2B; 68-Oct-3: 2B].
Cochran, Annie L. m. Hynes, David S. on 70-Jul-4 [70-Aug-6: 2C; 70-Aug-8: 2C].
Cochran, Charles Buckingham d. on 68-Oct-8 [68-Oct-9: 2C].
Cochran, Florence A. m. George, J. on 66-Jan-11 [66-Jan-13: 2C].
Cochran, Mary E. m. Stitt, Joseph B. on 69-Dec-15 [69-Dec-17: 2C].
Cochran, Pleasant (73 yrs.) d. on 66-Jan-7 [66-Jan-23: 2C].
Cochran, Presley N. m. Hackett, Lizzie G. on 70-Aug-23 [70-Sep-7: 2B].
Cochran, Silas Morris d. on 66-Dec-16 [66-Dec-17: 1G; 66-Dec-18: 1E; 66-Dec-20: 1F].
Cochran, T. Ollie m. Kerr, Mary Dunbar on 67-Dec-10 [67-Dec-17: 2B].
Cochran, Thomas J. (59 yrs.) d. on 69-Apr-20 of Heart disease [69-Apr-21: 1G; 69-Apr-22: 1G, 2B; 69-Apr-23: 1G].
Cochran, William F. m. Buckingham, Ella V. on 67-Oct-9 [67-Oct-10: 2B].
Cochrane, John m. King, Mary E. on 66-Dec-6 [66-Dec-8: 2B].
Cochrane, Nellie M. m. Horn, Stephen on 67-Aug-21 [67-Aug-30: 2B].
Cochrane, William J. (9 yrs.) d. on 66-Jan-21 [66-Jan-22: 2C].
Cock, Sarah Carter d. on 70-Oct-15 [70-Oct-25: 2B].
Cockey, Annie S. m. McConky, Edward C. on 66-Oct-16 [66-Oct-20: 2B].
Cockey, Edward (63 yrs.) d. on 67-Aug-11 [67-Aug-13: 2B].
Cockey, Ellen Maria d. on 67-Oct-17 [67-Oct-21: 2B].
Cockey, George B. m. Emory, Maggie Wilmer on 67-Oct-8 [67-Oct-9: 2B; 67-Oct-14: 2B].
Cockey, John R. (61 yrs.) d. on 67-Nov-10 [67-Nov-11: 2C].
Cockey, Laura m. Talbott, J. Fred C. on 69-Feb-3 [69-Feb-22: 2C].
Cockey, Thomas B., Col. (81 yrs.) d. on 68-Apr-27 [68-Apr-29: 2B].
Cockey, W. H. m. Wantz, Lizzie on 67-Oct-8 [67-Oct-9: 2B].
Cockey, William H. (5 mos.) d. on 68-Nov-25 [68-Dec-9: 2C].
Cockrell, Irene L. m. Taylor, Robert B. on 69-Nov-25 [70-Jan-27: 2C].
Cockrill, Edward V. (58 yrs.) d. on 70-Feb-14 [70-Feb-15: 2C].
Cockrill, Mollie P. m. Carroll, Albert H on 68-Dec-1 [68-Dec-4: 2D].
Cocks, Ambrose m. Carter, Sarah on 68-Apr-20 [68-Jun-6: 2A].
Codd, Mary d. on 67-Mar-26 [67-Mar-27: 2C; 67-Mar-28: 2C].
Codd, William H. m. McCann, Maggie on 68-Oct-20 [68-Oct-23: 2B].
Codori, Sophia Charlotte (33 yrs.) d. on 70-Feb-12 [70-Feb-14: 2C].
Coe, Addie F. m. Douglass, Spencer on 69-Nov-12 [69-Nov-24: 2C].
Coe, Alexander Benson m. Scott, Mary M. on 66-Apr-24 [66-May-16: 2C].
Coe, Belle E. m. Palmer, Walter M. H. on 69-Sep-9 [69-Sep-10: 2B].
Coe, Charles (35 yrs.) d. on 70-Oct-20 of Intemperance and exposure [70-Oct-21: 4C].
Coe, Charles H. P. (31 yrs.) d. on 70-Oct-19 [70-Oct-24: 2B].
Coe, Charles R. (36 yrs.) d. on 70-Jun-15 [70-Jun-16: 2B].
Coe, Henrietta (28 yrs.) d. on 67-Dec-2 of Consumption [67-Dec-11: 2B].
Coe, Lee Andrew Jackson (1 mo.) d. on 67-Apr-25 [67-Apr-26: 2B].
Coe, Mary Pottee m. Ripley, E. H. on 67-Apr-24 [67-May-17: 2B].
Coe, Roderick D. m. Faithful, Maggie on 68-Jun-30 [68-Jul-1: 2B].
Coe, Theodore (26 yrs.) d. on 68-Dec-5 [68-Dec-7: 2C].
Coe, William H. (41 yrs.) d. on 70-Jul-19 [70-Aug-12: 2C].
Coe, William H. m. Taylor, Laura J. on 66-Oct-21 [66-Oct-30: 2B].
Coffey, Bridget d. on 70-Mar-19 [70-Mar-21: 2C].
Coffin, Charles G. m. Slasman, Emma J. on 66-Apr-25 [66-May-31: 2B].
Coffin, Lydia m. Thomas, George R. on 70-Oct-20 [70-Oct-24: 2B].
Coffin, Willie G. (12 yrs., 6 mos.) d. on 67-Aug-26 [67-Aug-27: 2B; 67-Aug-28: 2B].
Coffroth, Girtie V. m. Ross, John M. on 69-Feb-28 [69-Mar-4: 2C].
Cofran, Nettie m. Sipple, Charles O. on 66-Apr-2 [66-Apr-5: 2B; 66-Apr-6: 2B].
Coggins, Ann Maria (85 yrs.) d. on 67-Feb-4 [67-Feb-8: 2C].
Coggins, Annie Blanche (6 yrs., 10 mos.) d. on 68-Dec-5 [68-Dec-8: 2C].

Coggins, David A. m. Smick, Georgetta on 70-Jul-11 [70-Jul-26: 2B].
Coggins, Fannie Maria (10 mos.) d. on 69-Jul-25 of Brain inflammation [69-Jul-26: 2C].
Coggins, John m. Price, Martha J. on 68-Jun-3 [68-Jun-6: 2A].
Coggins, Lillie May (4 yrs., 8 mos.) d. on 69-Mar-13 [69-Mar-16: 2C].
Coghlan, Bridget (61 yrs.) d. on 66-Mar-5 [66-Mar-7: 2B].
Coghlan, Mary Ann (32 yrs.) d. on 70-Feb-18 [70-Feb-19: 2B].
Cogswell, Phoebe B. (68 yrs.) d. on 67-Jan-4 [67-Jan-9: 2C].
Cohee, Levin W. m. Daily, Mary A. on 70-Nov-22 [70-Nov-24: 2B].
Cohen, Annette, Capt. (27 yrs.) d. on 68-Apr-3 of Apoplexy [68-Apr-4: 2B; 68-Apr-14: 2A].
Cohen, Gerson (64 yrs.) d. on 70-Jul-4 [70-Jul-7: 2C].
Cohen, J. I. m. Mordecai, Ellen on 68-Oct-14 [68-Oct-16: 2B].
Cohen, Jacob I. (80 yrs.) d. on 69-Apr-6 [69-Apr-8: 1G, 2C; 69-Apr-9: 1H].
Cohen, Jacob L. m. May, Sarah on 69-May-2 [69-May-7: 2C].
Cohen, Joshua I., Dr. (70 yrs.) d. on 70-Nov-4 [70-Nov-5: 4D, 2B; 70-Nov-7: 2B; 70-Nov-8: 4D].
Cohn, M. G. m. Stoll, Emilie C. on 68-Jan-30 [68-Jan-31: 2C].
Colb, Jacob Elsworth (1 yr., 7 mos.) d. on 66-Oct-6 [66-Oct-12: 2B].
Colb, Sarah Elizabeth (5 yrs., 2 mos.) d. on 66-Oct-10 [66-Oct-12: 2B].
Colbeck, Ann C. (55 yrs.) d. on 70-Feb-19 [70-Feb-21: 2B].
Colbert, Amelia m. Wheatley, Thomas W. on 69-Jan-12 [69-Jan-15: 2D].
Colbert, Cornelius S. (8 yrs., 6 mos.) d. on 70-Jul-24 of Whooping cough [70-Jul-25: 2C].
Colbert, Matthias (66 yrs.) d. on 68-Nov-3 [68-Nov-4: 2C].
Colbert, Sallie E. m. Frank, Milton B. on 67-Jan-22 [67-Jan-24: 2C].
Colbert, Sarah (65 yrs.) d. on 70-Mar-15 [70-Mar-17: 2C].
Colbert, Sophia D. m. Tottle, John on 66-Apr-10 [66-Apr-14: 2B].
Colbert, Virginia m. Wellener, John T. on 69-May-18 [69-May-21: 2C].
Colborn, Lucy (37 yrs.) d. on 68-Jan-2 [68-Jan-18: 2B].
Colburn, Gilbert (17 yrs.) d. on 67-Aug-22 in Railroad accident [67-Aug-24: 1G].
Colburn, Milton d. on 67-Aug-22 in Railroad accident [67-Aug-24: 1G].
Colburn, Rollinson m. Lockwood, Helen M. on 67-Sep-5 [67-Sep-18: 2B].
Colburn, W. H. H. m. Whitenack, Carrie V. on 66-Feb-21 [66-Feb-26: 2B].
Colder, Mary Ellen m. Evert, Charles L. on 67-Oct-15 [67-Oct-17: 2B].
Cole, A. P. m. Dunn, Maria L. on 69-Jun-16 [69-Sep-21: 2B; 69-Sep-24: 2B].
Cole, Alexander (29 yrs.) d. on 68-Sep-20 [68-Sep-21: 2B].
Cole, Bennetta m. Knight, Upton on 70-Nov-21 [70-Nov-24: 2B].
Cole, Carrie Eugene (11 mos.) d. on 68-Aug-7 [68-Aug-10: 2C].
Cole, Carrie L. m. Kemp, Oscar T. on 70-Jun-15 [70-Jun-20: 2B].
Cole, Charles E. m. Young, Ella R. M. on 67-Jun-10 [67-Jun-22: 2B].
Cole, Eleanor d. on 66-Jun-26 [66-Jun-27: 2C].
Cole, Ellen (63 yrs.) d. on 68-Apr-26 [68-Apr-27: 2B].
Cole, Elmina (26 yrs.) d. on 68-Dec-27 [68-Dec-28: 2B].
Cole, Emily V. m. Green, William M. on 67-Mar-6 [67-Mar-15: 2C].
Cole, Emma C. (35 yrs.) d. on 69-Nov-16 [69-Nov-17: 2C; 69-Nov-18: 2C].
Cole, Emmeline Victoria d. on 68-Dec-8 [68-Dec-9: 2C; 68-Dec-10: 2D].
Cole, Florence A. (2 yrs., 4 mos.) d. on 70-Feb-25 [70-Feb-28: 2C].
Cole, Florence G. m. Fowble, Alfred on 67-Nov-28 [67-Dec-5: 2C].
Cole, George Henry (1 yr., 4 mos.) d. on 67-Sep-2 [67-Sep-3: 2B].
Cole, James m. Harris, Ida on 68-Nov-19 [68-Dec-8: 2C].
Cole, James m. Jones, Mary E. on 66-Jun-20 [66-Jun-30: 2B].
Cole, James H. m. Gorsuch, Bettie on 69-Jan-19 [69-Jan-27: 2C].
Cole, Jane Alverda m. Davis, Benjamin B. on 70-Apr-27 [70-May-11: 2B].
Cole, John (24 yrs., 1 mo.) d. on 66-Jul-19 [66-Jul-23: 2C].
Cole, John, Rev. d. on 68-Dec-30 [69-Jan-1: 2C].
Cole, John m. Middlekauff, Emma on 66-Jan-17 [66-Jan-20: 2C].
Cole, John m. Banks, Henrietta on 70-Oct-15 [70-Oct-17: 2B].

Cole, John M. (33 yrs.) d. on 66-Oct-18 [66-Mar-3: 2B].
Cole, John T. m. Leach, Lidia V. on 66-Sep-18 [66-Oct-1: 2B].
Cole, Josephine B. m. Kettlewell, R. C. on 68-Jan-20 [68-Feb-20: 2C].
Cole, Joshua (66 yrs.) d. on 69-Jul-18 [69-Jul-19: 2C].
Cole, Laura C. m. Logsdon, John T. on 66-Oct-9 [67-Jan-4: 2D].
Cole, Lizzie Roswell (10 yrs.) d. on 70-Aug-18 [70-Aug-20: 2B].
Cole, Mary Alice d. on 66-Jan-21 of Heart disease [66-Jan-23: 2C].
Cole, Mary Ann (66 yrs.) d. on 67-Apr-11 [67-Apr-12: 2C].
Cole, Mary Elizabeth (7 yrs., 8 mos.) d. on 66-May-7 [66-May-9: 2B].
Cole, Mary J. m. Gerhardt, Henry H. on 67-Feb-25 [67-Mar-2: 2B].
Cole, Michael (58 yrs.) d. on 68-Dec-5 [68-Dec-7: 2C].
Cole, Mollie E. m. Rodgers, Charles R. on 70-Dec-22 [70-Dec-30: 2C].
Cole, Moses M. m. Welsh, Allina on 68-Oct-14 [68-Oct-27: 2B].
Cole, Pennock I. m. East, Hattie on 67-Jan-30 [67-Feb-2: 2C].
Cole, Rachel Smith (1 yr., 10 mos.) d. on 70-Feb-14 [70-Feb-15: 2C].
Cole, Richard (56 yrs.) d. on 69-Feb-11 [69-Feb-12: 1G, 2C].
Cole, Rosa C. d. on 68-Aug-28 [68-Sep-5: 2A].
Cole, Sallie A. m. Kemp, Lewis on 68-May-26 [68-May-27: 2B].
Cole, Susan V. m. Welshons, John F. on 68-Dec-17 [68-Dec-22: 2C].
Cole, Susie m. Brooks, William on 68-Nov-18 [68-Nov-21: 2C].
Cole, Thomas (80 yrs.) d. on 70-Nov-17 [70-Nov-19: 2B].
Cole, William (77 yrs.) d. on 68-Mar-13 [68-Mar-14: 2B, 4E].
Cole, William d. on 68-May-30 of Apoplexy [68-Jun-1: 1F].
Cole, William B. m. Wolf, Sarah C. on 70-Mar-1 [70-Sep-1: 2B; 70-Sep-2: 2C].
Cole, William H. (44 yrs.) d. on 68-Nov-6 [68-Nov-7: 2B].
Cole, William H., Col. (51 yrs., 2 mos.) d. on 67-May-4 [67-May-6: 1G, 2B].
Cole, William W. m. Tanner, Eliza A. on 69-Nov-9 [69-Nov-11: 2C].
Cole, Willie H. (2 yrs., 3 mos.) d. on 67-Dec-18 [67-Dec-19: 2B; 67-Dec-20: 2B].
Colehouse, Randolph R. m. Dorsey, Margaret S. on 68-Oct-26 [68-Oct-27: 2B].
Colehouse, William T. (21 yrs., 2 mos.) d. on 66-Mar-23 [66-Mar-26: 2C].
Colein, Ida N. (4 mos.) d. on 68-Mar-12 [68-Mar-13: 2C].
Colein, T. R. m. Floyd, Alexina on 66-Jan-25 [66-Apr-11: 2B].
Coleman, Ann E. (44 yrs.) d. on 70-Jun-8 [70-Jun-10: 2B].
Coleman, Charles R. m. Guyton, Elenora on 68-May-31 [68-Jun-5: 2B].
Coleman, Charles R. m. Ferguson, Kate E. M. on 67-Dec-23 [68-Aug-3: 2B].
Coleman, Edith W. m. Oliver, William on 69-May-27 [69-May-29: 2B].
Coleman, Ella C. m. Forsyth, Alexander M. on 67-May-21 [67-May-22: 2B].
Coleman, Ella M. m. Pendergast, Jerome A. on 66-Oct-2 [66-Oct-3: 2B].
Coleman, Ellen A. m. Boyle, T. A. on 69-Jun-15 [69-Jun-18: 2C].
Coleman, Emily Jane (23 yrs., 4 mos.) d. on 70-Oct-5 [70-Oct-6: 2B; 70-Oct-7: 2B].
Coleman, Emma (9 mos.) d. on 67-Sep-16 [67-Sep-17: 2A].
Coleman, Erastus U. (27 yrs.) d. on 68-Apr-8 [68-Apr-9: 2B; 68-Apr-10: 2B].
Coleman, Fannie J. m. Forrest, E. Cole on 67-Jun-23 [67-Jun-27: 2B].
Coleman, George A. m. Smith, Carrie L. on 67-Nov-5 [67-Nov-12: 2C].
Coleman, Jackson (38 yrs.) d. on 69-Oct-29 [69-Oct-30: 2B].
Coleman, John (17 yrs., 11 mos.) d. on 70-Oct-2 [70-Oct-6: 2B].
Coleman, John Charles (1 yr., 3 mos.) d. on 70-May-29 [70-Jun-14: 2B].
Coleman, Joseph (56 yrs.) d. on 68-Feb-4 [68-Feb-19: 2C].
Coleman, Julia D. m. Howard, McHenry on 67-Jun-18 [67-Jun-22: 2B].
Coleman, Kate A. (42 yrs.) d. on 68-Nov-21 [68-Nov-23: 2B].
Coleman, Katie E. M. (20 yrs.) d. on 68-Jul-31 [68-Aug-3: 2B].
Coleman, Laura V. m. Bright, William T. on 69-Feb-15 [69-Feb-22: 2C].
Coleman, Lewis W. m. Smith, Kate on 69-Jan-29 [69-Feb-1: 2C].
Coleman, Lizzie B. m. Smith, Henry on 68-Dec-15 [68-Dec-16: 2C].
Coleman, Margaret (2 yrs., 8 mos.) d. on 70-Apr-7 [70-Apr-8: 2C].

Coleman, Martha R. m. Watson, James on 69-Apr-2 [69-Apr-17: 2A].
Coleman, Mary A. m. Gorsuch, John C. on 67-Dec-1 [68-Aug-13: 2B].
Coleman, Marzan m. Smallwood, Henry on 67-Aug-27 [67-Sep-21: 2A].
Coleman, Noah m. McGurk, Maggie on 70-Aug-1 [70-Sep-22: 2C].
Coleman, Royal B. m. Ryan, Anna Bell on 67-Jan-20 [67-Jan-24: 2C].
Coleman, Sarah Estelle (3 yrs., 8 mos.) d. on 69-Mar-4 [69-Mar-6: 2B].
Coleman, W. H. m. Tucker, Anna R. on 69-Dec-30 [70-Jan-4: 2C].
Coleman, William Henry (12 yrs., 3 mos.) d. on 67-Jul-3 of Typhoid [67-Jul-10: 2B].
Coles, Emma E. m. Powell, William H. on 69-Dec-21 [69-Dec-23: 2B].
Coles, William, Jr. m. Swan, Sophia C on 70-Feb-10 [70-Feb-12: 2B].
Coleson, Lou C. m. Watson, William H. on 70-Dec-26 [70-Dec-31: 2C].
Colfer, Cecilia (36 yrs.) d. on 70-Jan-20 [70-Jan-21: 2C; 70-Jan-22: 2B].
Colfer, John W. d. on 68-Aug-2 Poisoned [68-Aug-4: 1F; 68-Aug-5: 2B].
Colfor, Nicholas (52 yrs.) d. on 70-Aug-25 [70-Sep-10: 2B].
Colhoon, Jane d. on 66-Jul-14 [66-Jul-17: 2C].
Colin, George m. Foos, Mary C. on 66-Jan-26 [66-Mar-7: 2B].
Coll, Ellen (24 yrs.) d. on 67-Jun-23 [67-Jun-25: 2B].
Coll, John m. Walsh, Annie C. on 68-Jun-9 [68-Jun-18: 2B].
Colladay, Charles Henry (4 yrs.) d. on 67-Mar-26 [67-Mar-28: 2B].
Colladay, Emily F. m. Burgess, William, Jr. on 68-Aug-18 [68-Aug-22: 2A].
Colladay, Janie A. m. Stuart, George H. on 70-Oct-26 [70-Oct-29: 2B].
Colladay, Joseph Mason (30 yrs.) d. on 66-Apr-7 [66-Apr-10: 2C].
Collard, Mary J. m. Peregoy, John W. H. on 67-May-8 [67-May-25: 2A].
Collenberg, J. Henry (81 yrs.) d. on 70-Mar-8 [70-Mar-9: 2C].
Collett, Thomas E. m. Coath, Fannie S. on 66-Jun-8 [66-Sep-10: 2D].
Colley, Elizabeth Jane (3 yrs.) d. on 66-Mar-12 of Scarlet fever [66-Mar-14: 2B].
Colley, William H. (1 yr., 2 mos.) d. on 70-Mar-12 [70-Mar-14: 2C].
Collier, Ann M. (52 yrs.) d. on 70-Mar-23 [70-Mar-25: 2C].
Collier, Bessie (4 mos.) d. on 68-Jun-18 [68-Jun-25: 2B].
Collier, Charley (1 mo.) d. on 70-May-14 [70-May-16: 2B].
Collier, Eliza A. (37 yrs.) d. on 70-May-14 [70-May-16: 2B].
Collier, Elizabeth d. on 66-Jul-23 [66-Jul-27: 2C].
Collier, George K. m. Frazier, Lizzie on 69-Mar-4 [69-Mar-20: 2B].
Collier, J. C. m. Owens, Laura V. on 67-Dec-3 [67-Dec-24: 2B].
Collier, Mary (75 yrs.) d. on 67-Mar-13 [67-Mar-14: 2C].
Collier, Richard J. (57 yrs.) d. on 66-Sep-29 [66-Oct-2: 2B].
Collings, Mary Ann (24 yrs.) d. on 66-Jun-2 [66-Jun-4: 2B].
Collins, Anna Amanda m. Hollingshead, Robert K. on 67-Jun-3 [67-Jun-11: 2B].
Collins, Annie (79 yrs.) d. on 66-Jul-2 [66-Jul-3: 2C].
Collins, Annie (3 mos.) d. on 70-Jul-22 [70-Jul-26: 2C].
Collins, Bettie A. m. Flood, Samuel S. on 70-Nov-22 [70-Nov-24: 2B].
Collins, Bridget (35 yrs.) d. on 67-Jun-29 of Heart disease [67-Jul-1: 2B, 4C].
Collins, Cora Jane (1 yr., 11 mos.) d. on 68-Aug-14 [68-Aug-17: 2B].
Collins, Elizabeth A. (48 yrs.) d. on 66-Sep-11 [66-Sep-12: 2A].
Collins, Emma Beauregord (5 yrs.) d. on 67-Aug-2 [67-Aug-3: 2B].
Collins, Emma C. (46 yrs.) d. on 70-Apr-22 [70-Apr-23: 2B; 70-Apr-28: 2C].
Collins, Francis T. m. Roberts, Sarah on 67-Jan-20 [67-Jan-21: 2C].
Collins, George C. m. Cowley, Mary E. on 70-Dec-6 [70-Dec-28: 2C].
Collins, George W. (40 yrs.) d. on 69-Dec-4 [69-Dec-6: 2C].
Collins, George W. m. Fisher, Annie on 68-Aug-11 [68-Aug-25: 2B].
Collins, Georgiana (2 yrs., 8 mos.) d. on 68-Mar-28 [68-Mar-30: 2B].
Collins, Hanorah (76 yrs.) d. on 66-Jan-24 [66-Jan-25: 2C; 66-Jan-26: 2B].
Collins, Henry H. m. Fimple, Sallie E. S. on 68-Feb-20 [68-Mar-7: 2B].
Collins, Honor (61 yrs.) d. on 67-Sep-15 [67-Sep-16: 2B].
Collins, Issac, Rev. (81 yrs.) d. on 70-May-25 of Paralysis [70-May-26: 1H, 2C].

Collins, J. Eugene m. Garrot, Laura E. on 68-Feb-12 [68-Feb-13: 2C].
Collins, J. William m. Gerry, Lydia S. on 65-Dec-14 [66-Feb-7: 2C].
Collins, James (34 yrs.) d. on 68-Apr-28 [68-May-1: 2B].
Collins, James E. (29 yrs.) d. on 69-Aug-29 [69-Aug-31: 2B; 69-Sep-2: 2B; 69-Aug-30: 2B].
Collins, James Edward (8 mos.) d. on 68-Mar-22 [68-Mar-24: 2B].
Collins, John (52 yrs.) d. on 67-Jan-22 [67-Jan-24: 2C].
Collins, John (72 yrs., 10 mos.) d. on 66-Dec-11 [66-Dec-12: 1G, 2B; 66-Dec-13: 2B].
Collins, John m. Cunningham, Elizabeth S. on 67-Apr-25 [67-Apr-27: 2A].
Collins, John H. m. Ehrman, Mary A. on 67-Jul-2 [67-Jul-6: 2B].
Collins, John Michael (4 mos.) d. on 68-Aug-25 [68-Aug-26: 2B].
Collins, Joseph (40 yrs.) d. on 70-Feb-8 of Heart disease [70-Feb-9: 4F; 70-Feb-10: 2C].
Collins, Joseph m. Jeames, Catherine E. on 68-Apr-14 [68-Apr-22: 2B].
Collins, Julia m. Gorman, W. H. on 66-Apr-4 [66-Apr-4: 4B].
Collins, Katie (6 yrs., 5 mos.) d. on 66-Dec-2 [66-Dec-3: 2B].
Collins, Lizzie A. m. Swan, Samuel M. on 69-May-25 [69-May-28: 2C].
Collins, Maggie T. m. Monmonier, L. A. on 69-Apr-20 [69-Apr-26: 2B].
Collins, Maggie Webster (1 yr.) d. on 66-Jun-25 [66-Jun-29: 2C].
Collins, Margaret (48 yrs.) d. on 66-Apr-21 [66-Apr-23: 2B].
Collins, Margaret A. m. Conway, Robert T. on 68-Jun-1 [68-Jun-10: 2B].
Collins, Martha Alice (3 yrs., 2 mos.) d. on 68-Mar-17 [68-Mar-19: 2B].
Collins, Mary (78 yrs.) d. on 68-Nov-10 [68-Nov-11: 2C].
Collins, Mary (71 yrs.) d. on 66-Apr-1 [66-Apr-2: 2B].
Collins, Mary (1 yr., 2 mos.) d. on 70-Sep-2 [70-Sep-3: 2B].
Collins, Mary Agnes (3 yrs.) d. on 68-Jul-16 [68-Jul-18: 2B].
Collins, Mary Alice (6 yrs., 8 mos.) d. on 69-Mar-14 [69-Mar-15: 2C; 69-Mar-16: 2C].
Collins, Mary C. m. Quinn, William H. on 70-Jan-24 [70-Feb-22: 2C].
Collins, Mary J. m. McGary, William H. on 70-May-9 [70-May-14: 2A].
Collins, Michael (43 yrs.) d. on 68-Jul-15 of Heatstroke [68-Jul-17: 2B; 68-Jul-18: 1E].
Collins, Michael J. (20 yrs.) d. on 66-Apr-6 in Railroad accident [66-Apr-7: 2B].
Collins, Nellie A. m. Hoddinott, Elias C. on 68-Sep-15 [68-Oct-20: 2B].
Collins, Patrick m. Cain, Mary E. [67-Aug-2: 2C].
Collins, Patrick J. (30 yrs.) d. on 70-Sep-8 [70-Sep-12: 2B].
Collins, Rebecca m. Porter, William J. on 67-Nov-6 [67-Nov-13: 2C].
Collins, Spindelow m. Payne, Maria on 70-Jun-9 [70-Jun-23: 2C].
Collins, Susan Rebecca (9 yrs., 2 mos.) d. on 68-Dec-16 [68-Dec-19: 2B].
Collins, Susanna (68 yrs.) d. on 68-Dec-19 [68-Dec-21: 2B].
Collins, T. J. m. Patterson, Emma V. on 68-Dec-29 [69-Jan-9: 2C].
Collins, Thomas W. m. Green, M. Ada on 69-Dec-8 [69-Dec-11: 2B].
Collins, Virginia m. Armstrong, John H. on 66-Mar-7 [66-Mar-10: 2B].
Collins, W. E. m. Toomey, Mary C. on 68-Sep-8 [68-Sep-16: 2B].
Collinson, Belle C. m. Barber, George A. on 69-Aug-5 [69-Aug-13: 2C].
Collinson, Eliza J. m. Joyce, Cyrus N. on 69-Apr-22 [69-Apr-27: 2B].
Collison, Ann Emily (35 yrs.) d. on 68-May-9 [68-May-11: 2B].
Collison, Bettie W. (15 yrs., 7 mos.) d. on 69-Dec-18 [69-Jan-4: 2C].
Collison, George Washington (43 yrs.) d. [66-Jul-30: 4D].
Collyer, Ann E. m. Baker, Henry on 70-Feb-2 [70-Feb-24: 2C].
Collyer, Mary M. m. Aull, Jacob B. on 70-Dec-15 [70-Dec-26: 2C].
Colmary, Lidie J. m. Davis, John C. on 68-Nov-25 [68-Dec-2: 2C].
Colston, Florence m. Beckley, John W. on 70-Jan-26 [70-Jan-29: 2B].
Colston, Francis LaVancey (5 yrs., 1 mo.) d. on 70-Oct-12 [70-Oct-17: 2B].
Colston, Frederick M. m. Campbell, Clara on 68-Oct-28 [68-Nov-4: 2C].
Colston, Henriette Watson (3 yrs., 5 mos.) d. on 70-Sep-20 of Scarlet fever [70-Sep-23: 2C].
Colston, Josiah (76 yrs.) d. on 70-Jan-6 [70-Jan-10: 2C].
Colston, Pendleton (35 yrs.) d. on 67-Dec-8 [68-Jan-10: 2B; 67-Dec-12: 2B].
Colt, Amelia A. m. Knight, Jonathan W., Jr. on 68-May-26 [68-Jun-1: 2B].

Coltman, Mary E. (3 yrs., 4 mos.) d. on 69-May-6 [69-May-8: 2B].
Colton, Charles m. Cheshire, Eliza E. on 70-Feb-17 [70-Feb-24: 2C].
Colton, Edward C. m. Kauffman, Lavinia D. on 67-May-20 [67-May-23: 2B].
Colton, Georgie (6 mos.) d. on 66-Jun-13 [66-Jun-14: 2B].
Colton, Hannah Moore m. Wailes, C. A. on 69-Jan-12 [69-Jan-13: 2D].
Colton, Katie (9 mos.) d. on 69-Mar-26 [69-Mar-27: 2B].
Colton, Lodge m. Watts, Marian on 68-Apr-16 [68-Apr-18: 2A].
Colton, Mary Ruth m. Ashcom, George W. on 67-Dec-24 [67-Dec-25: 2C].
Colton, Theodore m. Bright, Emma J. on 67-Oct-1 [67-Oct-3: 2B].
Colton, W. H. m. Funkhauser, Sarah E. on 67-Sep-17 [67-Sep-20: 2A].
Colton, William H. (65 yrs.) d. on 66-Jan-6 [66-Jan-8: 2B].
Columber, Rebecca (72 yrs.) d. on 67-Mar-1 [67-Mar-12: 2C].
Colwell, William F. m. Johnson, Sarah Jane on 69-Nov-4 [69-Nov-30: 2C].
Combs, Charlotte C. m. McSherry, William Kilty on 70-Nov-30 [70-Dec-2: 2C].
Combs, William W. m. Slater, Isabel J. on 67-Dec-17 [67-Dec-20: 2B].
Comegys, Benjamin m. Bartlett, Mary on 66-Jan-25 [66-Jan-27: 2B].
Comegys, Harry F. (23 yrs.) d. on 68-Jan-17 of Consumption [68-Jan-18: 2B; 68-Jan-20: 2C].
Comegys, John Collier (2 yrs., 2 mos.) d. on 69-Nov-7 [69-Nov-16: 2C].
Comegys, Lilliam Emma (3 yrs., 9 mos.) d. on 66-Jan-21 [66-Jan-22: 2C].
Comegys, Mary E. m. Bealmear, Samuel on 69-Feb-25 [69-Mar-2: 2C].
Comegys, William m. Foreman, Rebecca E. on 67-Dec-31 [68-Jan-6: 2C].
Compton, John S. (18 yrs.) d. on 69-Aug-3 [69-Aug-18: 2C].
Compton, Josephine m. Bray, Charles D. on 70-Jul-27 [70-Jul-29: 2B].
Compton, Lemuel B. d. on 68-Jun-9 [68-Jun-10: 2B].
Compton, Thomas Jackson (24 yrs.) d. on 67-Feb-24 [67-Mar-12: 2C].
Comton, Worthington d. on 70-Sep-20 [70-Sep-27: 2B].
Conant, A. E. m. Atkinson, Joshua I. on 69-Apr-17 [69-Apr-20: 2B].
Conant, Samuel W. (81 yrs.) d. on 70-Jan-2 [70-Jan-4: 2C].
Conaway, Addison (51 yrs.) d. on 68-Jun-12 [68-Jun-20: 2B].
Conaway, Charles H. (10 mos.) d. on 68-Jun-12 [68-Jun-13: 2B].
Conaway, George W. m. Brooks, Hester A. on 66-Mar-20 [66-Mar-22: 2B].
Conaway, James M. m. Hodges, Emma on 69-Apr-10 [69-Apr-19: 2C].
Conaway, Jane m. Brown, Hezekiah on 70-Nov-20 [70-Nov-23: 2B].
Conaway, John S. m. Caldwell, Frances on 68-Feb-20 [68-Feb-29: 2B].
Conaway, Laura F. m. Bennett, Larkin J. on 67-Dec-12 [68-Jan-1: 2C].
Conaway, Louisa m. Sanders, William on 69-Jul-7 [69-Jul-12: 2C].
Conaway, Z. P. m. Wells, Elizabeth E. on 67-Feb-14 [67-Feb-21: 2D].
Concannon, Mary m. Mincher, Edward on 70-Nov-2 [70-Nov-5: 2B; 70-Nov-7: 2A].
Condiff, Littleton T. m. Condiff, Valentina on 66-Aug-3 [66-Aug-15: 2B].
Condiff, Valentina m. Condiff, Littleton T. on 66-Aug-3 [66-Aug-15: 2B].
Condon, Elizabeth A. (42 yrs.) d. on 70-Sep-28 [70-Sep-30: 2B].
Condon, Mary G. m. Graham, F. J. on 68-Apr-30 [68-Jun-5: 2B].
Condon, Rebecca d. on 70-Oct-2 [70-Oct-3: 2B].
Coner, Catherine (26 yrs.) d. on 66-Jun-29 [66-Jun-30: 2B].
Coneway, Georgeanna (37 yrs.) d. on 67-Aug-22 [67-Aug-23: 2B].
Congdon, Samuel H. m. Cromwell, Henrietta on 67-Nov-27 [67-Dec-2: 2C].
Conick, Edward W. (11 yrs., 7 mos.) d. on 66-Jan-25 [66-Jan-27: 2B].
Conine, Augusta m. Markley, Thaddeus W. on 66-Nov-29 [66-Dec-1: 2B].
Conine, Mary Lawrence Bull d. on 66-Jul-18 [66-Jul-19: 2C].
Conklin, William (19 yrs.) d. on 69-Mar-20 [69-Mar-22: 2C].
Conkling, William H., Capt. (79 yrs.) d. on 67-Dec-1 [67-Dec-2: 2C; 67-Dec-3: 1F, 2C].
Conley, Ella Maria (5 yrs.) d. on 69-Apr-20 [69-Apr-21: 2C].
Conley, Frances L. (25 yrs.) d. on 68-May-14 [68-May-16: 2A].
Conley, Mary Ann (22 yrs.) d. on 69-Sep-1 [69-Sep-4: 2B].
Conley, Mary Josephine m. Russell, William H. on 67-Jul-21 [67-Jul-24: 2C].

Conley, Sarah m. Gleason, Thomas on 67-Oct-2 [67-Oct-4: 2B].
Conlon, Edward D. (3 mos.) d. on 66-Jul-7 [66-Jul-10: 2C].
Conlon, Mary Agnes m. Rudden, John on 69-Nov-18 [69-Nov-25: 2C].
Conlon, Mary C. (8 mos.) d. on 68-Jun-13 [68-Jun-17: 2B].
Conn, Malcolm m. Pillsberry, Tillie S. on 70-Oct-28 [70-Nov-17: 2C].
Conn, Mary E. m. Hunt, Joseph on 68-Jan-14 [68-Jan-28: 2D].
Conn, Missouri (22 yrs.) d. on 66-Mar-12 [66-Mar-13: 2B].
Conn, Sarah S. m. Johnston, Frederick on 69-Mar-1 [69-Mar-10: 2C].
Connary, Kate B. m. McCabe, George W. E. on 67-Jul-2 [67-Jul-10: 2B].
Connel, Honora m. Murphy, Thomas A. on 68-Nov-8 [68-Nov-12: 2C].
Connell, Agnes (80 yrs.) d. on 70-Sep-24 [70-Sep-28: 2B].
Connell, James (1 yr., 5 mos.) d. on 70-Dec-17 of Chronic croup [70-Dec-19: 2C].
Connelly, Francis P. (1 yr., 5 mos.) d. on 66-Jun-21 [66-Jun-22: 2B].
Connelly, John (29 yrs.) d. on 66-Aug-2 [66-Aug-3: 2C].
Connelly, Mary (55 yrs.) d. on 67-Jun-26 [67-Jun-27: 2B].
Connelly, Mary Ann m. Bagwell, John on 69-Apr-27 [69-May-4: 2B].
Connelly, Mary Ellen d. on 69-Jul-21 [69-Jul-22: 2C].
Connelly, Michael (19 yrs.) d. on 70-Feb-23 [70-Mar-3: 2C].
Connelly, William J. m. McAleese, Martha A. on 68-Jan-28 [68-Feb-13: 2C].
Conner, Constantine Owen (37 yrs.) d. on 67-Sep-5 [67-Sep-6: 2B].
Conner, Elizabeth M. d. on 69-Oct-27 [69-Oct-29: 2B].
Conner, John (50 yrs.) d. on 69-Jan-25 Drowned [69-Jan-27: 1H].
Conner, John m. Shaw, Inez L. on 70-Jun-20 [70-Jun-24: 2C].
Conner, Laura Virginia m. Jones, Joseph T. on 68-Dec-1 [68-Dec-3: 2C].
Conner, Mary Jane m. Loudenslager, John Wesley on 70-Aug-23 [70-Sep-8: 2B].
Conner, Mollie E. m. Birch, Joseph H. on 69-Nov-1 [69-Nov-13: 2B].
Conner, Nannie Estelle (4 mos.) d. on 70-Sep-25 [70-Sep-26: 2B].
Conner, Richard J. K. (83 yrs.) d. on 67-Oct-7 [67-Oct-9: 2B].
Conner, Samuel H. (24 yrs.) d. on 67-Dec-6 in Railroad accident [67-Dec-7: 1F; 67-Dec-9: 2B].
Conner, Samuel H. m. Crouse, Caroline V. on 66-Feb-20 [66-Mar-6: 2B].
Conner, Thomas (50 yrs.) d. on 69-May-17 Drowned [69-May-18: 2C; 69-May-19: 1H].
Connery, Thomas d. on 68-Dec-15 Murdered (Assault) [68-Dec-18: 1H].
Connick, Carrie N. m. Slack, William H. on 69-Dec-1 [69-Dec-11: 2B].
Connish, Henrietta E. m. Ballard, Jacob Reed on 70-Jan-18 [70-Jan-27: 2C].
Connoll, Francis (35 yrs.) d. on 69-May-27 in Construction accident [69-May-29: 1H].
Connolly, Amelia m. Hook, Joseph A. on 67-Aug-13 [67-Aug-19: 2C].
Connolly, Anne (5 yrs.) d. on 68-Dec-9 [68-Dec-10: 2D].
Connolly, Catherine m. Quinn, William on 67-Apr-28 [67-May-22: 2B].
Connolly, Charles Ennis (4 yrs., 5 mos.) d. on 68-Dec-3 [68-Dec-4: 2D].
Connolly, Daniel A. m. Campbell, Ellen A. on 68-Aug-6 [68-Aug-11: 2B].
Connolly, Eliza (14 yrs.) d. on 70-Aug-20 [70-Aug-22: 2C].
Connolly, Emma d. on 70-Aug-11 [70-Aug-13: 2C].
Connolly, Honora (1 yr., 11 mos.) d. on 68-Oct-14 [68-Oct-15: 2B].
Connolly, Hugh (43 yrs.) d. on 70-Jul-4 [70-Jul-8: 2C].
Connolly, James (1 yr.) d. on 68-Sep-30 [68-Oct-1: 2B].
Connolly, John (1 yr.) d. on 70-Aug-3 [70-Aug-4: 2C].
Connolly, John (3 mos.) d. on 70-Oct-24 [70-Oct-25: 2B].
Connolly, John (40 yrs.) d. on 70-Aug-24 [70-Aug-25: 2C].
Connolly, John F. (59 yrs.) d. on 69-Jan-12 [69-Jan-13: 2D; 69-Jan-14: 1G].
Connolly, John T. m. Sherry, Mary A. on 69-Aug-9 [69-Aug-19: 2C].
Connolly, Louisa May (8 mos.) d. on 68-Feb-15 [68-Feb-19: 2C].
Connolly, Margaret Ann (4 mos.) d. on 69-Mar-31 [69-Apr-1: 2C].
Connolly, Mary m. Hammond, George on 70-Apr-6 [70-Apr-16: 2B].
Connolly, Mary Ann m. Daubrat, Frederick on 67-Apr-4 [67-Apr-10: 2B].
Connolly, Samuel F. (11 mos.) d. on 67-Aug-20 [67-Aug-27: 2B].

Connolly, Sarah m. Capels, William on 66-Aug-4 [66-Aug-20: 2C].
Connolly, Sarah Elizabeth m. Schaeffer, August on 69-Apr-2 [69-Jun-19: 2B].
Connolly, William Henry (14 yrs., 11 mos.) d. on 70-Jul-20 Drowned [70-Jul-22: 4C, 2C].
Connor, Cassandra d. on 70-May-3 [70-May-5: 2B].
Connor, John A. m. Buckle, Mary E. on 67-Nov-27 [67-Nov-30: 2C].
Connor, Mary Fane (2 yrs., 8 mos.) d. on 70-May-22 [70-May-25: 2C].
Connor, Richard (7 mos.) d. on 66-Sep-24 [66-Sep-25: 2B].
Connors, Mary A. O. m. McCormack, Joseph J. on 70-Sep-25 [70-Sep-28: 2B].
Conoley, Margaret E. (33 yrs.) d. on 67-Oct-27 [67-Oct-29: 2B].
Conoway, Laura (16 yrs., 9 mos.) d. on 70-Dec-30 [70-Dec-31: 2B].
Conoway, Mary M. m. Lauer, John [70-May-24: 2C].
Conrad, Calvin m. Corse, Annie C. on 69-Oct-12 [69-Oct-14: 2C].
Conrad, George D. W. (1 yr., 8 mos.) d. on 70-Nov-18 [70-Nov-19: 2B].
Conrad, Julia M. F. m. King, William G. H. on 69-Jan-14 [69-Jan-23: 2C].
Conrad, M. Kate d. on 69-Sep-13 [69-Sep-14: 2B].
Conrad, May L. m. Dodge, J. Heath on 70-Sep-28 [70-Oct-4: 2B].
Conrad, Sarah E. (71 yrs.) d. on 67-Feb-1 [67-Feb-2: 2C].
Conrad, Sarah Jane d. on 68-Sep-11 [68-Sep-12: 2B].
Conrad, T. M. m. Yingling, Kate V. on 67-Oct-17 [67-Nov-6: 2B].
Conrad, William D. m. Haney, Sarah Jane on 67-Mar-7 [67-Mar-8: 2B].
Conradt, Chris J. m. Suter, Geneva J. on 67-May-2 [67-May-8: 2B].
Conradt, Virginia m. Martien, William on 67-Jun-4 [67-Jun-12: 2B].
Conrey, J. F. m. Litsinger, Augusta on 67-Dec-24 [67-Dec-31: 2C].
Conroy, Catherine M. m. Kearney, William J. on 70-Nov-1 [70-Dec-16: 2C].
Conroy, Michael (36 yrs.) d. on 69-Nov-20 [69-Nov-22: 2C].
Conroy, Thomas (38 yrs.) d. on 68-Jul-19 [68-Jul-21: 2C].
Considine, Catherine (50 yrs.) d. on 70-Oct-1 [70-Oct-3: 2B].
Constable, Albert m. Groome, Lizzie B. on 66-Jun-13 [66-Jun-20: 2C].
Constable, Catherine d. on 70-Jul-11 [70-Jul-12: 2B].
Constable, Charles B. (35 yrs.) d. on 68-Jul-3 [68-Jul-4: 2C].
Constable, Isabel d. on 66-May-17 [66-May-18: 2C].
Constable, Sallie B. m. Hunt, Matthew W. on 70-Apr-28 [70-May-2: 2B].
Constance, Maggie L. (2 mos.) d. on 68-Jan-23 [68-Jan-25: 2B].
Constanstein, Mary m. Henderson, Samuel S. on 67-Jul-14 [67-Jul-26: 2C].
Constant, Franklin m. King, Matilda on 66-May-8 [66-May-10: 2B].
Constantine, Mary E. (25 yrs., 10 mos.) d. on 68-Oct-9 [68-Oct-13: 2C].
Constantine, Susannah m. Hitchcock, Edward G. on 66-Jun-27 [66-Jun-27: 2C].
Contee, Benjamin (46 yrs.) d. on 70-Feb-18 [70-Mar-26: 2C].
Converse, John H. m. Jones, Jane B. on 68-Oct-20 [68-Oct-21: 2C].
Conway, Alice d. on 70-Jun-27 [70-Jul-2: 2B].
Conway, Annie m. Robinson, W. Leslie on 67-May-23 [67-Apr-24: 2B].
Conway, Carrie Agnes (3 yrs., 3 mos.) d. on 67-Nov-15 [67-Nov-16: 2B].
Conway, Charles H. m. Jones, Alice on 68-Nov-12 [68-Nov-16: 2C].
Conway, Charles Joshua (4 yrs., 5 mos.) d. on 70-Dec-24 [70-Dec-26: 2C].
Conway, Edward Cooper (1 yr., 10 mos.) d. on 67-Aug-13 [67-Aug-14: 2B].
Conway, Elizabeth Ann (3 yrs., 4 mos.) d. on 66-Sep-26 [66-Sep-28: 2B].
Conway, George W. m. Brooks, Hester A. on 67-Sep-26 [67-Sep-28: 2A].
Conway, Grahame (8 mos.) d. on 66-Aug-27 [66-Aug-28: 2B].
Conway, Jesse B. (76 yrs.) d. on 66-Jan-5 of Pleurisy [66-Jan-13: 1G, 2C].
Conway, John R. (67 yrs.) d. on 69-Oct-29 [69-Oct-30: 2B].
Conway, M. Fannie m. Grahame, John H. on 68-Feb-20 [68-Feb-22: 2B].
Conway, Margaretta d. on 68-Sep-1 [68-Sep-3: 2B].
Conway, Minnie m. Sprague, James M. on 70-Sep-5 [70-Sep-14: 2B].
Conway, Noah (38 yrs.) d. on 67-Aug-2 Drowned [67-Aug-20: 2B; 67-Aug-21: 2B].
Conway, Owen (25 yrs.) d. on 68-Oct-24 in Boating accident [68-Oct-26: 4C, 2B].

Conway, Pamelia d. on 67-Oct-10 of Neuralgic rheumatism [67-Oct-18: 2C].
Conway, Robert J. (58 yrs.) d. on 68-Jun-1 [68-Jun-3: 2B].
Conway, Robert T. m. Collins, Margaret A. on 68-Jun-1 [68-Jun-10: 2B].
Conway, Thomas T. m. Lynch, Adelia on 69-Apr-29 [69-May-1: 2B].
Conway, William Henry (1 yr., 3 mos.) d. on 68-Nov-23 [68-Nov-24: 2C].
Conyers, Fannie (1 yr., 8 mos.) d. on 67-Dec-22 [67-Dec-23: 2B].
Coode, D. m. Allston, C. E. on 67-Jan-24 [67-Jan-26: 2C].
Coogan, Mary J. m. McKewen, James J. on 66-May-14 [66-May-19: 2B].
Cook, Adelea (86 yrs.) d. on 70-May-2 [70-May-3: 2B; 70-May-4: 2C].
Cook, Adelia B. m. Rice, John B. on 67-Jan-15 [67-Feb-5: 2C].
Cook, Adeline (79 yrs.) d. on 68-Jul-15 [68-Jul-17: 2B].
Cook, Alice Joseph (2 yrs., 6 mos.) d. on 69-Jan-13 [69-Jan-15: 2D].
Cook, Ann Laura (1 yr., 10 mos.) d. on 68-Nov-14 [68-Nov-24: 2C].
Cook, Anna G. m. Patterson, John H. on 67-Aug-27 [67-Aug-30: 2B].
Cook, Belle m. Lewis, A. B., Jr. on 69-Mar-4 [69-Mar-23: 2C].
Cook, Benjamin m. Pitcher, Martha C. on 66-Oct-24 [66-Nov-1: 2B].
Cook, C. O. m. Graves, Josephine H. on 69-Jan-21 [69-Jan-23: 2C].
Cook, Carrie A. d. on 67-Oct-11 [67-Oct-12: 2A].
Cook, Charles Morris (1 yr., 9 mos.) d. on 70-Nov-18 [70-Nov-19: 2B].
Cook, Charlotte (69 yrs.) d. on 69-Nov-18 [69-Nov-20: 2B].
Cook, Clifton Irving d. on 69-Jan-12 [69-Jan-14: 2D].
Cook, E. J., Dr. (49 yrs.) d. on 68-Mar-31 [68-Apr-16: 2B].
Cook, Edward m. Coster, Helen R. on 68-Feb-20 [68-Mar-6: 2C].
Cook, Edward m. Carter, Helen E. on 68-Feb-26 [68-Mar-7: 2B].
Cook, Elizabeth (88 yrs.) d. on 69-Jan-22 [69-Jan-23: 2C].
Cook, Elizabeth A. m. Michael, Francis W. on 66-Oct-15 [66-Oct-16: 2B].
Cook, Elizabeth B. m. Mercer, William J. on 69-Apr-22 [69-Apr-28: 2B].
Cook, Elizabeth S. (68 yrs.) d. on 70-Apr-21 [70-May-11: 2B].
Cook, Ellen (32 yrs.) d. on 66-Oct-14 [66-Oct-16: 2B].
Cook, Emeline (50 yrs.) d. on 69-Aug-13 [69-Aug-14: 2C].
Cook, Flora A. m. Garman, Warren C. on 70-Jun-18 [70-Nov-4: 2C].
Cook, Frederick, Jr. m. Griest, Emma F. on 67-Jun-18 [67-Jun-21: 2B].
Cook, George W. m. Thompson, Ella M. on 66-Jan-9 [66-Jan-13: 2C].
Cook, George W. M. (8 mos.) d. on 66-Jul-17 [66-Jul-21: 2C].
Cook, Helen R. m. Seebold, George W. on 68-Jul-27 [68-Aug-18: 2B].
Cook, Henry (71 yrs.) d. on 68-Jan-24 [68-Feb-6: 2C].
Cook, Henry (60 yrs.) d. on 66-Dec-14 [66-Oct-16: 1F].
Cook, Henry C. m. Sperry, Amelia C. on 69-Sep-21 [69-Oct-2: 2B].
Cook, Henry F. m. Jarboe, Eugenia on 67-Mar-28 [67-Mar-29: 2B].
Cook, J. Glenn m. Walter, Agnes B. on 70-Oct-20 [70-Oct-25: 2B].
Cook, James (52 yrs.) d. on 66-Aug-29 [66-Aug-31: 2B].
Cook, James H. (58 yrs.) d. on 69-Feb-22 [69-Feb-23: 2D].
Cook, James Harry (1 yr., 2 mos.) d. on 70-Nov-25 [70-Nov-26: 2C].
Cook, Joel M. m. Boswell, Anna M. on 68-Feb-4 [68-Sep-21: 2B].
Cook, John D. m. Stromenger, Lizzie on 68-Jan-7 [68-Jan-16: 2C].
Cook, John F. (85 yrs.) d. on 66-Mar-30 [66-Mar-31: 1F, 2C].
Cook, John T. m. Maihl, Leonora on 68-May-17 [68-May-19: 2B].
Cook, Joseph F. m. Glanville, Lucy A. on 68-Jan-22 [68-Jan-27: 2C].
Cook, Julia A. (32 yrs.) d. on 67-Jun-11 [67-Jun-12: 2B].
Cook, Julia A. m. Sweeney, Peter on 66-Jun-28 [66-Jun-30: 2B].
Cook, Lewis G. m. Eggleston, Lucretia V. on 69-Dec-2 [69-Dec-8: 2C].
Cook, Lizzie A. m. Bruck, Henry M. on 68-Sep-17 [68-Sep-22: 2B].
Cook, Lucy d. on 68-Jul-16 [68-Jul-20: 2B].
Cook, Margaret Ann (36 yrs.) d. on 66-Jan-27 [66-Jan-29: 2C].
Cook, Mary A. (66 yrs.) d. on 69-Apr-29 [69-May-1: 2B].

Cook, Mary Anna (2 yrs., 4 mos.) d. on 69-Feb-4 [69-Feb-5: 2C].
Cook, Mary C. m. Worden, William H. on 70-Sep-20 [70-Sep-30: 2B].
Cook, Matilda (30 yrs.) d. on 66-Jun-8 [66-Jun-9: 1F].
Cook, Philip Thomas (1 yr.) d. on 70-Mar-31 [70-Apr-1: 2B; 70-Apr-2: 2A].
Cook, Sallie E. L. d. on 68-Jan-9 [68-Jan-11: 2B].
Cook, Samuel G. B. m. Ludlow, Mary C. on 67-Jun-27 [67-Jul-9: 2B].
Cook, Sarah A. (48 yrs.) d. on 67-Aug-13 [67-Aug-14: 2B].
Cook, Silas, Capt. d. on 67-Sep-21 of Yellow fever [67-Oct-17: 1G].
Cook, Susan (76 yrs.) d. on 69-Nov-15 [69-Dec-14: 2C].
Cook, Thomas (60 yrs.) d. on 68-Jan-20 [68-Jan-23: 2C].
Cook, Walter T. m. Pollock, Sarah A. on 69-Jul-15 [69-Jul-27: 2C].
Cook, William (14 yrs.) d. on 70-Feb-18 of Accidental Hanging [70-Feb-19: 1F].
Cook, William Bell (52 yrs.) d. on 66-Mar-18 of Consumption [66-Mar-20: 2C].
Cook, William Henry (2 mos.) d. on 70-Apr-5 [70-Apr-6: 2C].
Cook, William J. (26 yrs.) d. Drowned [68-Aug-24: 1G].
Cooke, Eber F. (59 yrs.) d. on 68-Aug-13 of Consumption [68-Aug-14: 2C; 68-Aug-17: 1G].
Cooke, Etta (7 mos.) d. on 68-Jul-10 [68-Jul-11: 2B].
Cooke, George Addison (28 yrs.) d. on 69-Aug-20 [69-Aug-23: 2C; 69-Aug-25: 2C].
Cooke, Gilbert C. m. Timson, Sarah on 67-Jan-3 [67-Jan-4: 2D].
Cooke, Nellie (1 yr., 8 mos.) d. on 69-May-8 [69-May-10: 2C].
Cooke, Richard B. m. Kerfoot, Louisa L. on 66-Feb-15 [66-Feb-26: 2B].
Cooke, S. F. m. Lanpher, Annie E. on 66-Oct-25 [66-Oct-29: 2B; 66-Oct-30: 2B].
Cooke, T. m. Webster, Sophie Hodges on 67-Mar-20 [67-Apr-5: 2B].
Cooke, Warren (10 yrs.) d. on 69-Nov-3 [69-Nov-6: 2C].
Cooke, William A. m. Todd, Sarah E. on 66-Feb-8 [66-Feb-19: 2B].
Cooke, William H. m. James, M. Alice on 70-Jul-9 [70-Jul-19: 2B].
Cooke, William Logan (2 yrs.) d. on 70-Jul-17 [70-Jul-18: 2B].
Cooke, Winfield m. Bond, Emma on 69-May-19 [69-May-21: 2C].
Cookes, Mary (58 yrs.) d. on 69-Jul-12 [69-Jul-13: 2C].
Cookes, Susannah m. Brady, Hugh A. on 68-Nov-26 [68-Nov-28: 2C].
Cooksey, Annie Ramsay m. Etchberger, James S. on 69-Sep-7 [69-Sep-9: 2B].
Cooksey, Mary Ellis (5 mos.) d. on 66-Apr-8 [66-Apr-9: 2C].
Cooksey, Mary Malloy m. Benthall, Robert on 70-Jun-9 [70-Jun-11: 2B].
Cooksey, Rhoda E. m. Herbert, George M. on 67-Nov-4 [67-Nov-13: 2C].
Cooksey, Thomas Neilson, Capt. (33 yrs.) d. on 69-Feb-24 of Pneumonia [69-Feb-27: 1G, 2C; 69-Mar-1: 1G, 2C].
Coolahan, Catherine (45 yrs.) d. on 70-Mar-27 [70-Mar-28: 2B; 70-Mar-29: 2B].
Coolehan, Thomas Francis d. on 67-Mar-26 [67-Mar-28: 2B].
Cooley, John H. m. Elliott, Nellie B. on 66-Jan-2 [66-Jan-16: 2C].
Coombes, Richard J. m. McConkey, Eliza J. on 66-Nov-24 [66-Nov-26: 2B].
Coombs, Mary E. m. Brown, William T. on 67-Jun-3 [67-Jul-13: 2B].
Coonan, Charlie (1 yr., 1 mo.) d. on 69-Feb-20 [69-Feb-22: 2C].
Coonan, John (24 yrs., 11 mos.) d. on 70-Jul-5 of Fall from roof [70-Jul-6: 1H; 70-Jul-7: 1H, 2B].
Cooney, Charlie (3 mos.) d. on 68-Jul-26 [68-Aug-3: 2C].
Cooney, Ella S. Woodburn (7 mos.) d. on 66-Aug-15 [66-Aug-17: 2C].
Cooney, Laurence Holton (2 yrs., 6 mos.) d. on 70-Dec-5 [70-Dec-7: 2C].
Cooney, Margaret (68 yrs.) d. on 68-Jan-17 [68-Jan-18: 2B].
Cooney, Michael (30 yrs.) d. on 70-Jul-24 [70-Jul-25: 2C].
Cooney, William M. m. Henricks, Maggie Isabel on 67-Jul-16 [67-Jul-25: 2C].
Cooney, Willie H. (2 yrs., 4 mos.) d. on 67-Mar-7 [67-Mar-12: 2C].
Cooper, Ann C. (74 yrs.) d. on 69-Nov-28 [69-Nov-30: 2C].
Cooper, Ann M. m. Stites, William on 70-Nov-24 [70-Dec-19: 2C].
Cooper, Ann Sophia (25 yrs., 7 mos.) d. on 68-Apr-5 [68-Apr-7: 2B].
Cooper, Bernard G. m. Perine, Bessie Lee on 67-Aug-15 [67-Aug-17: 1G, 2B].

Cooper, Bishop (33 yrs.) d. [70-Sep-3: 2B].
Cooper, Charles Emmanuel (3 yrs.) d. on 69-Aug-5 [69-Aug-14: 2C].
Cooper, Edwin (65 yrs.) d. on 67-Jun-30 [67-Jul-13: 2B].
Cooper, Elizabeth (31 yrs.) d. on 66-May-21 [66-May-26: 2B].
Cooper, Ettie Eugenia (2 yrs., 6 mos.) d. on 70-Jul-8 [70-Jul-15: 2C].
Cooper, Fanny (31 yrs.) d. on 70-Sep-20 [70-Sep-21: 2B].
Cooper, Harriet m. Nicklos, John on 68-Mar-12 [68-Mar-17: 2C].
Cooper, Hester Ann m. Griffin, Eugene on 67-Dec-10 [67-Dec-19: 2B].
Cooper, Hugh A. (60 yrs.) d. on 70-Nov-11 [70-Nov-12: 2B; 70-Nov-14: 4C].
Cooper, Hugh A. m. Spedden, Maria L on 68-Mar-10 [68-Mar-12: 2B].
Cooper, Isabella (23 yrs.) d. on 69-Nov-20 [69-Nov-22: 2C].
Cooper, James d. on 67-Mar-4 [67-Mar-6: 2C].
Cooper, Janet H. m. Sylvester, William George on 67-Feb-21 [67-Feb-25: 2C].
Cooper, John H. m. Frisby, Josephine on 68-Feb-10 [68-Feb-11: 2C].
Cooper, Julia A. (67 yrs.) d. on 68-Nov-2 [68-Nov-5: 2C].
Cooper, Lizzie d. on 67-Jul-14 [67-Jul-15: 2C].
Cooper, Louisa (6 yrs.) d. on 67-Mar-16 Burned [67-Mar-18: 1E].
Cooper, Lucy Jane m. Logan, Benjamin on 68-Oct-6 [68-Oct-8: 2B].
Cooper, M. Ellie m. Miller, H. Best on 65-Dec-21 [66-Jan-10: 2C].
Cooper, Margaret Ann (18 yrs.) d. on 70-Feb-20 [70-Feb-21: 2C].
Cooper, Margaret E. m. Miller, Hezekiah B. on 65-Dec-21 [66-Jan-1: 2C].
Cooper, Maria d. on 70-May-27 [70-May-28: 2B].
Cooper, Martha A. m. McClelland, Theodore M. on 67-Jan-23 [67-Jan-28: 2C].
Cooper, Mary (69 yrs.) d. on 67-Apr-16 [67-Apr-17: 2B].
Cooper, Mary Agnes d. [68-Dec-23: 2C].
Cooper, Rebecca C. m. Sneed, John M. on 67-Jun-5 [67-Jun-15: 2B].
Cooper, Samuel m. Wait, Elizabeth A. on 66-May-21 [66-Jun-2: 2B].
Cooper, Thomas (69 yrs.) d. on 67-Sep-29 of Fall from bridge [67-Sep-30: 1F].
Cooper, Thomas (33 yrs.) d. on 69-Oct-1 of Consumption [69-Oct-5: 2B].
Cooper, Thomas m. Krauss, Sophie on 66-Jul-12 [66-Dec-15: 2B].
Cooper, Thomas m. Bull, Sarah E. on 70-Oct-25 [70-Oct-28: 2C].
Cooper, Virginia m. Latimer, Charles W. on 69-Apr-7 [69-Apr-8: 2C].
Cooper, Willie T. (11 mos.) d. on 68-Jul-16 [68-Jul-18: 2B].
Coote, Edward (30 yrs.) d. on 68-Feb-1 [68-Feb-7: 2C].
Coots, Margaret Catherine (4 mos.) d. on 67-Jun-27 [67-Jun-28: 2B].
Copenhaver, Sallie C. d. on 69-Jan-4 [69-Jan-5: 2C; 69-Jan-6: 2C].
Copenhaver, Susie m. Nichols, John E. on 70-Dec-20 [70-Dec-29: 2C].
Copes, Mattie R. m. Brock, Henry C. on 70-Aug-29 [70-Sep-1: 2B].
Copper, Annie E. m. Beach, William J. on 68-Jun-2 [68-Jun-5: 2B].
Copper, James D. m. Harding, Sarah A. on 67-Nov-5 [67-Nov-7: 2C].
Copper, Priscilla (84 yrs.) d. on 67-Nov-16 [67-Nov-23: 2B].
Coppinger, John (78 yrs.) d. on 69-Jan-29 [69-Jan-30: 2C].
Coram, R. Lee (7 mos.) d. on 70-Aug-29 [70-Aug-31: 2B].
Corame, William H. m. Leefe, Henrietta A. on 69-Apr-22 [69-May-4: 2B].
Corbaley, Robert C. m. Bond, Laura H. on 67-Nov-5 [67-Nov-7: 2C].
Corbell, William G. (43 yrs.) d. on 67-Oct-7 [67-Oct-9: 2B].
Corbett, Eddie d. on 70-Aug-22 [70-Aug-23: 4D].
Corbett, Mary Ann (7 mos.) d. on 66-Aug-6 [66-Aug-7: 2C].
Corbett, Thomas (25 yrs.) d. on 67-Oct-31 [67-Nov-6: 2B].
Corbin, Georgette m. Talbott, John F. on 70-Apr-10 [70-Apr-13: 2B].
Corbin, William S. m. Cathell, Emma on 67-Oct-15 [67-Oct-22: 2A].
Corcoran, Anastasia m. Butler, James J. on 66-Dec-10 [66-Dec-20: 2B].
Corcoran, Dennis (28 yrs.) d. on 70-Sep-8 [70-Sep-9: 2B; 70-Sep-10: 2B].
Corcoran, Joseph Patrick (18 yrs.) d. on 68-May-31 [68-Jun-3: 2B].
Corcoran, Kate T. (23 yrs., 5 mos.) d. on 69-Sep-13 [69-Sep-14: 2B].

Corcoran, Michael m. Spellman, Winifred on 70-May-11 [70-Jun-1: 2B].
Corcoran, Peter (28 yrs.) d. on 70-Apr-2 [70-Apr-4: 2B].
Cord, Maranda (31 yrs.) d. on 66-Jan-18 of Typhoid [66-Jan-29: 2C].
Cordell, L. C. (67 yrs.) d. on 70-Nov-14 [70-Nov-15: 2C].
Cordray, Ida Jones (2 mos.) d. on 67-Jan-17 [67-Jan-21: 2C].
Corey, Elizabeth (70 yrs.) d. on 67-Mar-12 [67-Mar-15: 2C].
Corey, Hannah d. on 68-Sep-7 [68-Oct-5: 2C].
Corey, Issac m. Keller, Margaret E. on 63-May-18 [67-Mar-28: 2B].
Coriell, Alvin m. Lawrence, Mary A. on 69-May-18 [69-Dec-4: 2C].
Coriell, Kate d. on 68-Apr-7 [68-Apr-8: 2B].
Corigan, Owen (27 yrs.) d. on 70-Jun-18 [70-Jun-20: 2B].
Cork, Albert m. Freeman, Emma on 68-Nov-11 [68-Nov-17: 2C].
Corkran, Amanda E. m. Tayman, Thomas on 68-Jan-28 [68-Jan-31: 2C].
Corkran, Edward Swain (2 yrs., 3 mos.) d. on 66-Jul-22 [66-Jul-27: 2C].
Corkran, Elizabeth (80 yrs.) d. on 66-Jul-7 [66-Jul-9: 2C; 66-Jul-10: 2C].
Corkran, Elizabeth Emily Withg (24 yrs.) d. on 66-Apr-10 [66-Apr-11: 2B; 66-Apr-12: 2B].
Corkran, James m. Corkran, Sarah A. on 69-May-27 [69-Jun-3: 2B].
Corkran, Kate T. m. Kelly, William J. on 68-Jun-2 [68-Jul-2: 2C].
Corkran, Sarah A. m. Corkran, James on 69-May-27 [69-Jun-3: 2B].
Corletto, Elizabeth (57 yrs.) d. on 66-Oct-28 [66-Oct-30: 2B].
Corletto, Emma F. m. Walker, Nathaniel C. on 69-May-11 [69-May-19: 2C].
Corletto, Georgiana (26 yrs.) d. on 70-Nov-23 [70-Nov-29: 2C].
Corliss, Kate J. d. on 69-Jul-2 [69-Jul-3: 2B].
Cornan, Theresia (84 yrs.) d. on 69-Dec-20 [69-Dec-21: 2B].
Cornelius, Annie F. m. Carson, Charles L. on 70-Dec-6 [70-Dec-10: 2B].
Cornelius, George W. m. Griffin, Emma C. on 67-Dec-18 [68-Feb-10: 2C].
Cornelius, George W. m. Ensor, Adaline V. on 69-Dec-26 [69-Dec-28: 2C].
Cornelius, Joshua T. (26 yrs.) d. on 67-Mar-3 of Typhus [67-Mar-5: 2C; 67-Mar-16: 2B].
Cornelius, Louisa m. Christopher, Milton on 70-Nov-3 [70-Nov-7: 2A].
Cornelius, Marietta Dungan (1 yr., 3 mos.) d. on 67-Apr-2 of Brain inflammation [67-Apr-3: 2B].
Cornelius, Samuel (73 yrs.) d. on 67-Apr-19 [67-Apr-20: 2A].
Cornell, Edwin m. Gallagher, Mattie A. on 69-Feb-22 [69-Mar-4: 2C].
Corner, Alice m. Ramsay, C. Gustaf on 68-Oct-22 [68-Oct-26: 2B].
Corner, Kate m. Bihy, John, Jr. on 69-Aug-22 [69-Aug-23: 2C].
Corner, Mary m. Baer, Robert N. on 70-Apr-14 [70-Apr-20: 2B].
Corner, Samuel m. Hulls, Mary Virginia on 69-Jun-16 [69-Jun-19: 2B].
Corner, Sarah (80 yrs.) d. on 66-Feb-1 [66-Feb-2: 2C].
Cornish, Susan N. (52 yrs.) d. on 68-Sep-27 [68-Sep-29: 2B].
Corns, Morris Richardson (6 mos.) d. on 68-Jul-29 [68-Jul-30: 2B].
Corns, Samuel T. (50 yrs.) d. on 70-Nov-29 [70-Dec-1: 2C].
Cornthwait, Alice Ann (84 yrs.) d. on 70-Jan-25 [70-Jan-26: 2C].
Cornthwait, Kate m. Drenner, Otho W. on 67-Sep-19 [67-Oct-14: 2B].
Cornwall, Benjamin B. (1 yr., 2 mos.) d. on 69-Mar-29 [69-Mar-30: 2C].
Cornwall, Sarah (3 mos.) d. on 69-Jul-2 [69-Jul-5: 2C].
Corr, Diodorus F. m. Crittenden, Sarah C. on 69-Nov-17 [69-Nov-18: 2C].
Correa, Sarah E. d. on 67-Jul-7 [67-Jul-8: 2C].
Correll, James M. m. Lawrenson, Olivia J. on 69-Dec-2 [69-Dec-7: 2C].
Correll, Mary R. m. Watts, Thomas on 67-May-21 [67-May-25: 2A].
Correll, Maude V. (3 mos.) d. on 68-Apr-4 [68-Apr-6: 2B].
Correll, Robert L. (34 yrs.) d. on 69-Dec-23 [69-Jan-13: 2D].
Correll, S. D. m. Blair, Virginia E. on 66-Mar-19 [66-Mar-26: 2B].
Corridon, Bryan m. Neely, Elizabeth on 67-Sep-15 [67-Sep-17: 2A].
Corrie, Samuel (45 yrs.) d. on 66-Nov-30 of Consumption [66-Dec-8: 2B].
Corrigan, Bartholomew (74 yrs.) d. on 66-Feb-24 [66-Mar-3: 2B].

Corrigan, Bessie (5 mos.) d. on 68-Jul-19 [68-Jul-24: 2C].
Corrigan, James m. Cain, Fannie on 66-Jan-18 [66-Jan-19: 2C].
Corrin, Isabella m. Stonebraker, Samuel on 69-May-25 [69-May-29: 2B].
Corse, Annie C. m. Conrad, Calvin on 69-Oct-12 [69-Oct-14: 2C].
Corse, George F. m. Sutton, Sarah on 66-Nov-13 [66-Nov-16: 2C].
Corse, William (65 yrs.) d. on 69-Mar-8 [69-Mar-10: 2C; 69-Mar-11: 2C].
Corsey, James B. (49 yrs.) d. on 69-Apr-9 [69-Apr-12: 2A].
Corsey, Robert m. Lemon, Rosanna Lemon on 69-Dec-23 [69-Dec-29: 2D].
Corson, A. C. (67 yrs.) d. on 70-Jun-15 [70-Jun-24: 2C].
Cortlan, Clinton m. Claude, Catharine A. on 70-Nov-30 [70-Dec-2: 2C].
Cortlan, Laura m. Norton, D. S. on 68-Jul-23 [68-Jul-27: 2B].
Cosby, Daniel W. (21 yrs.) d. on 69-May-10 [69-May-12: 2B].
Cosby, DeWitt m. Wooddy, Maggie C. on 68-Oct-1 [68-Oct-5: 2B].
Cosby, Sally King m. Webster, D. A. C. on 68-Nov-25 [68-Nov-30: 2B].
Cosgrove, Catherine (54 yrs.) d. on 69-Oct-17 [69-Oct-18: 2C].
Cosgrove, James (26 yrs.) d. on 68-May-24 of Fall from derrick [68-May-27: 2B; 68-May-28: 1F].
Coskerry, Carrie G. m. Tubman, F. Eugene on 67-Apr-11 [67-Apr-17: 2B].
Coskery, Eliza J. d. on 67-May-22 [67-May-24: 2B].
Coskery, F. S. m. Jackson, Rebecca A. on 69-Mar-17 [69-Mar-31: 2C].
Coskery, Oscar (1 yr., 1 mo.) d. on 69-Aug-17 [69-Aug-18: 2C].
Cost, Mary Catharine (25 yrs.) d. on 67-Oct-31 of Consumption [67-Nov-1: 2B].
Costello, Barbara (45 yrs.) d. on 67-Apr-26 [67-Apr-27: 2A].
Costello, John (50 yrs.) d. on 66-Jun-20 [66-Jun-21: 2B].
Costello, Margaret d. on 69-Dec-22 [69-Dec-23: 2B].
Costello, Thomas (70 yrs.) d. on 66-Dec-31 [67-Jan-1: 2C].
Coster, Etta Virginia (2 yrs., 2 mos.) d. on 66-Dec-29 [67-Jan-4: 2D].
Coster, Helen R. m. Cook, Edward on 68-Feb-20 [68-Mar-6: 2C].
Coster, James H. m. Kraft, Caroline C. on 66-Apr-9 [66-May-1: 2A].
Coster, Mary Ellen (1 yr., 1 mo.) d. on 69-Jun-29 [69-Jun-30: 2C].
Coster, Robert J. m. Wardenburg, Helena Marie on 66-Apr-3 [66-Apr-5: 2B].
Coster, S. L. m. Grover, B. A. on 69-Dec-26 [70-Feb-2: 2B].
Coster, William (72 yrs.) d. on 70-Feb-13 [70-Feb-25: 2D].
Coster, William E. (15 yrs., 4 mos.) d. on 68-Nov-29 [68-Nov-30: 2B].
Costlow, Michael m. Galloway, Gemima L. on 67-Sep-4 [67-Sep-18: 2B].
Costun, Mary T. (46 yrs.) d. on 70-Jul-28 Murdered (Stabbing) [70-Jul-29: 4D].
Cotrell, Rosanna m. Toughinbaugh, William on 68-Dec-24 [68-Dec-25: 2D].
Cotter, Mary Catherine (4 yrs., 2 mos.) d. on 68-Apr-22 [68-Apr-23: 2B; 68-Apr-24: 2B].
Cottingham, Harry M. m. Ayres, Manie on 70-Dec-13 [70-Dec-15: 2C].
Cottman, Herman Stuart m. Hullin, Corinne on 70-Jan-18 [70-Jan-28: 2B].
Cottman, Joseph B., Dr. (52 yrs.) d. on 68-Mar-29 [68-Apr-1: 2C].
Cottman, Maggie E. m. Boyle, James W. on 70-Mar-17 [70-Mar-18: 2C].
Cottrell, James W., Rev. (49 yrs.) d. on 66-Jun-12 [66-Jun-13: 2B].
Cottrell, Lizzie W. (25 yrs.) d. on 67-Dec-27 [67-Dec-28: 2C].
Cottrell, Sarah (81 yrs.) d. on 70-Apr-25 [70-Apr-26: 2B; 70-Apr-27: 2B].
Cottrell, Sarah Lemon (23 yrs.) d. on 69-Jan-26 [69-Jan-27: 2C; 69-Jan-28: 2C].
Cottrell, William Louis (6 mos.) d. on 68-Feb-20 [68-Feb-24: 2C].
Couch, Mary Agnes (1 yr., 3 mos.) d. on 66-Feb-15 [66-Feb-16: 2B].
Couch, Mary Agnes (25 yrs.) d. on 69-Jun-7 [69-Jun-9: 2C].
Couch, Rachel May m. Davis, William H. on 70-Dec-22 [70-Dec-26: 2C].
Couchman, Edwin D. m. Pfeltz, Kate on 66-Jan-5 [66-Jan-15: 2B].
Couchman, George Edgar (1 yr., 3 mos.) d. on 69-Dec-18 [69-Dec-21: 2B].
Couchman, Joseph m. Horn, Mary on 67-May-14 [67-May-25: 2A].
Couchman, Rebecca E. (22 yrs.) d. on 70-Dec-23 [70-Dec-24: 2B].
Couchman, William H. m. Allwell, Rebecca E., Miss on 67-Nov-21 [68-Jan-1: 2C].

Coughlan, Bridget (56 yrs.) d. on 69-Sep-12 [69-Sep-13: 2B; 69-Sep-14: 2B].
Coughlan, Cornelius (68 yrs.) d. on 70-Mar-16 [70-Mar-17: 2C; 70-Mar-18: 2C].
Coughlan, Elizabeth (73 yrs.) d. on 66-Nov-24 [66-Nov-27: 2B].
Coughlan, Jennie m. Morgan, George W. on 69-May-4 [69-May-7: 2C].
Coughlan, Margaret (55 yrs.) d. on 66-Aug-27 [66-Aug-29: 2B].
Coughlan, Marion Wallas d. on 69-Feb-17 [69-Feb-18: 2C].
Coughlan, Mary Agnes d. on 67-Aug-7 [67-Aug-8: 2B].
Coughlan, Mary E. m. Warnick, James B. on 66-Jun-24 [66-Jun-27: 2C].
Coughlan, Thomas F. m. Gillingham, Sarah V. on 66-Dec-27 [66-Dec-31: 2C].
Coughlan, William (1 mo.) d. on 69-Aug-12 [69-Aug-13: 2C].
Coughlin, John (68 yrs.) d. on 69-Dec-27 [69-Dec-28: 2C].
Coughlin, Kate J. m. Eliason, John A. on 66-Apr-10 [66-Apr-17: 2C].
Coulahan, Mary Ann (9 yrs.) d. on 66-Nov-28 [66-Nov-29: 2B].
Coulbourn, Angelline m. Gardner, John G. on 70-May-31 [70-Jun-2: 2B].
Coulbourn, J. Frank (22 yrs.) d. on 66-Oct-14 of Diptheria [66-Oct-19: 2B].
Coulbourn, Mary Corrilla (19 yrs.) d. on 66-Oct-14 [66-Oct-19: 2B].
Coulson, Elizabeth Ann (49 yrs.) d. on 66-Nov-22 [66-Nov-24: 2B].
Coulson, James (56 yrs.) d. on 66-Jun-13 [66-Jun-16: 2B].
Coulson, John B. (39 yrs.) d. on 69-Nov-8 [69-Nov-9: 2C].
Coulson, Nancy (67 yrs.) d. on 68-Jan-11 [68-Jan-13: 2C].
Coulson, Thomas H. (34 yrs.) d. on 66-Sep-2 [66-Sep-3: 2C].
Coulter, Deborah Morris (80 yrs.) d. on 68-May-27 [68-May-28: 2B; 68-May-29: 2B].
Coulter, George Beatty (4 yrs.) d. on 70-Oct-6 [70-Oct-8: 2B].
Coulter, Harry Alexander (2 yrs.) d. on 69-Nov-10 [69-Nov-11: 2C].
Coulter, Helen M. m. Woods, Charles F. on 66-Jun-28 [66-Jul-3: 2C].
Coulter, Isabella (57 yrs.) d. on 69-Mar-14 [69-Mar-16: 2C; 69-Mar-17: 2C].
Coulter, John Carson m. George, Jean on 70-Apr-5 [70-Apr-14: 2B].
Coulter, John J. m. Cox, Rebecca J. on 69-Jul-31 [69-Aug-3: 2C].
Coulter, Lizzie Jane (10 mos.) d. on 67-Aug-9 [67-Aug-10: 2B].
Coulter, Mary A. (60 yrs.) d. on 66-Aug-12 of Consumption [66-Aug-16: 2C].
Coulter, Noah B. m. Stoll, Laura J. on 66-Apr-12 [66-Apr-16: 2B].
Coulter, Sally (85 yrs.) d. on 68-May-22 [68-Jun-3: 2B].
Councell, William H. m. Harrison, Eugenia A. on 69-May-19 [69-May-22: 2B].
Councilman, Gertrude m. Owens, James R. on 68-Nov-25 [68-Dec-4: 2D].
Countee, Matilda (95 yrs.) d. on 67-Sep-27 [67-Oct-4: 2B].
Countess, Annie B. V. m. Brady, Joseph J. on 70-Apr-27 [70-May-6: 2B].
Countess, James C. m. McDonald, Alice on 67-Jan-17 [67-Feb-14: 2C].
Couper, Hannah (89 yrs.) d. on 67-Mar-22 [67-Mar-25: 2C].
Coupland, Ann (21 yrs.) d. on 68-Oct-3 [68-Oct-5: 2C].
Coupland, Dorothy Willing (79 yrs.) d. on 66-Feb-5 [66-Feb-6: 2D; 66-Feb-7: 2C].
Courcelle, Edouard (4 yrs., 9 mos.) d. on 68-Jan-21 [68-Jan-29: 2D].
Coursey, Charles N. m. Smith, Martha A. on 67-Jan-22 [67-Jan-28: 2C].
Coursey, E. R. m. Wilkins, James W. on 68-Mar-26 [68-Mar-30: 2B].
Coursey, Edward B. (67 yrs.) d. on 69-Sep-19 [69-Sep-20: 2C].
Coursey, Elizabeth (56 yrs.) d. on 68-Aug-31 [68-Sep-1: 2A].
Coursey, James A. m. Courthwait, Tilley W. on 68-Oct-15 [68-Oct-19: 2B].
Courtenay, Austin M. m. Valliant, M. Florence on 70-Aug-23 [70-Sep-26: 2B; 70-Sep-27: 2B].
Courthwait, Tilley W. m. Coursey, James A. on 68-Oct-15 [68-Oct-19: 2B].
Courtney, Clarence (8 mos.) d. on 68-Jul-31 [68-Aug-1: 2B].
Courtney, Edward (42 yrs.) d. on 68-Oct-6 [68-Oct-7: 2C].
Courtney, Ellen E. m. Donn, George W. on 69-Jan-7 [69-Jan-8: 2C].
Courtney, George A. m. Greble, Joe H. on 70-Feb-3 [70-Feb-7: 2C].
Courtney, George C. (7 mos.) d. on 70-Jul-28 [70-Jul-29: 2B].
Courtney, I. W. m. Unruh, Marietta on 67-May-13 [67-May-18: 2A].
Courtney, James (69 yrs.) d. on 70-May-6 [70-May-7: 2B].

Courtney, James A. m. Bell, Keziah on 70-Jun-28 [70-Jun-30: 2C].
Courtney, James P. (1 yr., 1 mo.) d. on 70-Nov-18 [70-Nov-19: 2B].
Courtney, John Bell m. Cunningham, Ellen T. on 69-Oct-11 [70-Feb-8: 4F].
Courtney, Lydia A. m. Mitchell, Thomas P. on 68-Dec-8 [68-Dec-9: 2C].
Courtney, Mary d. [70-Sep-28: 2B; 70-Sep-29: 2B].
Courtney, Mary B. (31 yrs.) d. on 70-Aug-22 [70-Aug-24: 2C].
Courtney, Sallie M. m. Mitchell, George V. on 66-Dec-6 [66-Dec-8: 2B].
Courtney, Susan (47 yrs.) d. on 67-Sep-24 [67-Sep-26: 2B].
Courtney, Susie (1 yr., 10 mos.) d. on 66-May-16 [66-May-17: 2C].
Courtney, William H. m. Branson, Sallie A. on 69-Apr-22 [69-Apr-24: 2B].
Courtney, William T. m. Andrews, Annie P. on 66-Aug-23 [66-Sep-6: 2B].
Courtney, Willie (6 yrs., 4 mos.) d. on 68-Mar-29 [68-Mar-30: 2B].
Courtois, Theodore A. (26 yrs.) d. on 68-Oct-29 [68-Oct-30: 2C].
Courts, Charles (46 yrs.) d. on 70-Apr-4 [70-Apr-6: 2C].
Courts, Emma m. Stall, William on 69-Jan-28 [69-Jan-29: 2C].
Courts, J. Edward m. Messersmith, Katie E. on 69-Oct-5 [69-Oct-9: 2C].
Cousins, Edward m. Draine, Maggie on 70-Mar-17 [70-Mar-19: 2B].
Cousins, Emma Davis (8 mos.) d. on 68-Aug-15 [68-Aug-17: 2B].
Cousins, John E. m. Merriken, Emma P. on 68-Jan-28 [68-Feb-12: 2B].
Couskie, Amelia m. Blessing, Andrew on 65-Dec-24 [66-Jan-2: 2C].
Covell, Joel E. m. Upperman, Emma on 66-May-15 [66-May-23: 2B].
Cover, Susan m. Klees, John on 69-Mar-30 [69-Apr-1: 2C].
Covington, Anna Beasley d. on 70-Mar-29 [70-Mar-30: 2B].
Covington, Charles Robinson (8 mos.) d. on 69-Jul-14 [69-Jul-17: 2C].
Covington, Emma V. (31 yrs.) d. on 70-May-19 [70-May-20: 2C].
Covington, Henrietta (66 yrs.) d. on 66-Jul-1 [66-Jul-2: 2B].
Covington, James H. m. Robinson, Emma V. on 67-Dec-16 [67-Dec-19: 2B].
Covington, Thomas S. m. Little, Sarah A. on 68-Dec-10 [68-Dec-16: 2C].
Cowan, J. Elizabeth m. Carroll, Larkin on 68-Dec-29 [69-Jan-4: 2C].
Cowan, James S. m. Wright, Nellie C. on 67-Jun-27 [67-Jul-4: 2B].
Cowan, John m. Himes, Kate on 69-Nov-25 [69-Dec-3: 2C].
Cowan, John J. (34 yrs.) d. on 67-Nov-15 [67-Nov-16: 2B].
Cowan, Lemuel C., Lt. d. [70-Mar-24: 1H].
Cowan, Mary d. on 66-Sep-23 of Fall [66-Sep-25: 1F].
Cowan, Thomas (50 yrs.) d. on 68-Dec-29 [68-Dec-30: 2C].
Cowan, William m. Denmead, Martha E. on 68-Nov-26 [68-Dec-30: 2C].
Coward, Estelle Mcdora (35 yrs.) d. on 66-Oct-15 of Apoplexy [66-Oct-17: 2B].
Cowardin, M. Alice m. Neale, E. Clarence on 66-Oct-25 [66-Oct-31: 2B].
Cowdery, Letitia N. m. Gissel, John on 67-Aug-27 [67-Sep-24: 2A].
Cowdon, Mary G. m. Graham, F. J. on 68-Apr-30 [68-Jun-4: 2B].
Cowen, Louisa m. Wherrett, Albert E. on 66-Oct-28 [66-Oct-30: 2B].
Cowles, E. Lela m. Hellen, Frank on 69-Sep-16 [69-Sep-17: 2C].
Cowles, James A. m. Alderson, S. Fannie on 67-Jun-27 [67-Jun-29: 2B].
Cowley, Annie R. m. Holland, Stokley on 69-Jan-7 [69-Jan-14: 2D].
Cowley, Mary E. m. Collins, George C. on 70-Dec-6 [70-Dec-28: 2D].
Cowley, Samuel T. m. McClellan, Eliza J. on 69-Mar-23 [69-Apr-6: 2C].
Cowman, Albert m. Phillips, Sallie E. on 70-Sep-15 [70-Sep-20: 2B].
Cowman, John G. m. Fisher, Laura Frances on 68-May-7 [68-May-15: 2B].
Cowman, Joseph, Jr. m. Fisher, Abbie L. on 70-Apr-28 [70-May-4: 2C].
Cowman, Mary A. (74 yrs.) d. on 69-Jan-29 [69-Jan-30: 2C].
Cowman, Mary Ann (54 yrs.) d. on 69-Oct-4 [69-Oct-5: 2B; 69-Oct-6: 2B].
Cowman, Richard (63 yrs.) d. on 70-Jan-6 of Paralysis [70-Jan-7: 2F; 70-Jan-8: 2B].
Cox, Abraham m. Williams, Mary E. on 70-Mar-22 [70-Mar-26: 2B].
Cox, Catherine (89 yrs., 6 mos.) d. on 70-Apr-18 [70-Apr-19: 2B; 70-Apr-20: 2B].
Cox, Eliza Jane Virginia (17 yrs., 10 mos.) d. on 67-Oct-16 [67-Oct-17: 2B].

Cox, Glennie Theresa (6 mos.) d. on 70-Mar-26 [70-Mar-28: 2B].
Cox, Issac (12 yrs.) d. on 67-Nov-6 [67-Nov-7: 2C; 67-Nov-8: 2C].
Cox, Issac m. Martin, Virginia A. on 67-Feb-11 [67-Feb-13: 2D].
Cox, Jack (110 yrs.) d. on 68-Nov-23 [68-Nov-28: 4D].
Cox, Jane d. on 70-Sep-20 [70-Sep-21: 2B; 70-Sep-22: 2C].
Cox, John R. m. Lamb, Mary M. on 69-Aug-5 [69-Aug-11: 2C].
Cox, Joseph H. (53 yrs., 3 mos.) d. on 68-Jun-8 [68-Jun-9: 2B].
Cox, Josephine m. Walker, John M. on 70-Oct-20 [70-Oct-22: 2B].
Cox, Lilly Elizabeth (3 yrs., 5 mos.) d. on 68-Dec-31 [69-Jan-2: 2C].
Cox, Luther J., Rev. (79 yrs.) d. on 70-Jul-26 [70-Jul-27: 4F, 2C].
Cox, Mary E. (95 yrs.) d. on 66-Apr-25 [66-Apr-27: 2C].
Cox, Mary R. m. Davis, James E. on 69-Sep-15 [69-Sep-22: 2C].
Cox, Meriam Louisa (1 yr., 2 mos.) d. on 68-Jul-13 [68-Jul-16: 2C; 68-Jul-17: 2C].
Cox, Rachel S. W. m. Gootee, Kelly on 69-Dec-30 [70-Jan-4: 2C; 70-Jan-5: 2C].
Cox, Rebecca J. m. Coulter, John J. on 69-Jul-31 [69-Aug-3: 2C].
Cox, Richard W. m. Norris, Fannie E. on 70-Jun-15 [70-Jun-18: 2B].
Cox, Shorlott (43 yrs., 7 mos.) d. on 67-Sep-18 [67-Sep-21: 2A].
Cox, Susan (65 yrs.) d. on 69-Feb-26 [69-Feb-27: 2C].
Cox, Susanna (84 yrs.) d. on 67-Mar-27 [67-Apr-2: 2B].
Cox, Willey (1 yr., 7 mos.) d. on 70-Jan-6 [70-Jan-7: 2F].
Cox, William (50 yrs.) d. on 69-Nov-18 [69-Nov-22: 2C].
Coxe, Katherine Cleveland m. Nash, Francis Philip on 67-Apr-25 [67-May-1: 2B].
Coxen, Florida (8 yrs.) d. on 70-Feb-8 [70-Feb-9: 2C].
Coxon, Emma (1 yr., 3 mos.) d. on 70-Aug-17 [70-Aug-19: 2C].
Coxon, Francis (1 mo.) d. on 68-Feb-16 [68-Feb-18: 2C].
Coxswain, Priscilla (40 yrs.) d. on 66-Jan-13 [66-Jan-15: 1G].
Coyle, Henry H. m. Thompson, Annie Isabella on 67-Mar-29 [67-May-14: 2B].
Coyle, Hugh J. (22 yrs.) d. on 67-Mar-22 [67-Mar-23: 2B].
Coyle, Mannie B. m. White, Thomas G. on 69-Jul-4 [69-Jul-7: 2C].
Coyle, Summerfield Supplee (8 mos.) d. on 67-Jul-16 [67-Jul-18: 2C].
Coyle, Wesley Walker (3 mos.) d. on 67-Jun-24 [67-Jul-18: 2C].
Coyne, Clara (1 yr., 10 mos.) d. on 68-Aug-5 [68-Aug-10: 2C].
Coyne, Florence (6 mos.) d. on 66-Sep-4 [66-Sep-5: 2B].
Coyne, Mary Catherine (35 yrs.) d. on 66-Sep-23 [66-Sep-24: 2B; 66-Sep-25: 2B].
Coyne, Mary E. m. Gieske, Charles on 67-Jun-11 [67-Jun-13: 2C].
Coyne, Patrick m. McKenna, Rose on 66-Nov-1 [66-Nov-9: 2C].
Crabbe, Gertie L. m. Lawder, Samuel M. on 66-Feb-1 [66-Feb-10: 2C].
Crabbs, Frederick Barron (2 yrs., 11 mos.) d. on 67-Apr-22 [67-Apr-24: 2B].
Crabson, Anna R. m. Wheeler, William A. on 67-Aug-28 [67-Sep-21: 2A].
Craeger, Mary Louisa m. Weaver, George H. on 67-Feb-18 [67-Feb-20: 2C].
Craft, George (79 yrs.) d. on 67-Jun-24 [67-Jun-29: 2A].
Craft, George B. (55 yrs.) d. on 69-Apr-25 [69-Apr-26: 2B; 69-Apr-27: 2C].
Craft, Jane Parker (13 yrs.) d. on 66-May-21 [66-May-22: 2B].
Craft, Mary Eleanor (19 yrs.) d. on 66-Jun-24 [66-Jun-25: 2B].
Crafton, J. A. m. Lutts, Hannah S. on 68-Jan-28 [68-Jan-31: 2C].
Crager, Josiah (16 yrs.) d. on 67-Apr-27 Drowned [67-Apr-29: 1F, 2B].
Crager, William Grason (25 yrs.) d. on 66-Jan-22 [66-Jan-23: 2C].
Cragg, Charles Griffin (1 yr., 8 mos.) d. on 69-Nov-23 [69-Nov-24: 2C].
Cragg, Hannah T. (83 yrs.) d. on 66-Jul-13 [66-Jul-17: 2C].
Cragg, John (70 yrs.) d. on 69-Oct-9 [69-Oct-11: 2C].
Cragg, Mary Alice (31 yrs.) d. on 70-Mar-9 [70-Mar-21: 2C].
Cragg, Robert m. Jones, Rachel A. on 67-Aug-13 [67-Aug-28: 2B].
Cragg, S. Wilkens m. Riggs, Mary Alice on 69-Sep-5 [69-Feb-8: 2C; 69-Feb-9: 2C].
Cragg, Samuel Edward (3 yrs.) d. on 69-Sep-5 [69-Sep-7: 2B].
Craggs, Elizabeth (65 yrs.) d. on 67-Jan-1 [67-Jan-3: 2B].

Craggs, John B. m. Barton, Mary W. on 66-May-15 [66-May-19: 2B].
Craggs, Susannah (47 yrs.) d. on 68-Jul-26 [68-Jul-28: 2B].
Craig, Alice M. (14 yrs., 4 mos.) d. on 66-Dec-24 [66-Jan-8: 2B].
Craig, Amelia T. m. Redgrave, William H. on 70-Jun-30 [70-Jul-8: 2C].
Craig, Annie E. m. Reese, William P. on 69-Feb-17 [69-Feb-19: 2C].
Craig, Bernard (3 yrs., 4 mos.) d. on 70-May-20 [70-May-21: 2B].
Craig, Elizabeth A. (79 yrs.) d. on 69-Jul-26 [69-Jul-27: 2C; 69-Jul-28: 2D].
Craig, Fannie m. Shamer, William on 66-Dec-30 [67-Jan-2: 2C].
Craig, Francis m. Quinn, Sarah on 68-Feb-4 [68-Feb-15: 2B].
Craig, Henry Robert Tucker (1 yr., 5 mos.) d. on 66-Apr-7 [66-Apr-9: 2B].
Craig, John A. m. Keene, Sallie Theobald on 68-Feb-4 [68-Feb-8: 2B].
Craig, John L. M. m. Patterson, Emily J. on 67-May-22 [67-Jun-3: 2B].
Craig, Margaret Armstrong m. Bayly, A. H. on 67-Feb-12 [67-Feb-16: 2D].
Craig, Oliver B. m. Franck, Kate on 66-Jan-25 [66-Jan-29: 2B].
Craig, Sarah (5 mos.) d. on 70-Jul-4 [70-Jul-7: 2C].
Craig, Thomas m. Crouch, Amanda E. on 67-May-21 [67-Aug-29: 2B].
Crain, Antoinette m. Linthicum, A. S. on 66-Jul-24 [66-Aug-3: 2C].
Cramblett, Emma V. m. Everitt, Francis A. on 66-Nov-18 [68-Jan-8: 2C].
Cramblitt, May F. d. on 70-Sep-21 [70-Sep-22: 2C].
Cramer, John A. d. on 70-Dec-28 [70-Dec-30: 2C].
Crammer, Mary E. m. Moyer, J. on 69-Dec-22 [70-Jan-5: 2C].
Crampton, Alice Savington (19 yrs.) d. on 69-Jul-5 [69-Jul-7: 2C].
Crampton, Johnson d. on 70-Sep-15 [70-Sep-19: 2B].
Crandall, F. M. m. Pyfer, Mary E. on 67-May-22 [67-May-24: 2B].
Crandall, Thomas W. m. Abey, Minnie [69-Jan-13: 2D].
Crandell, H. A. Minerva m. Chambers, George on 68-Jul-15 [68-Jul-23: 2B].
Crandell, Metamore (35 yrs.) d. on 68-Aug-2 [68-Aug-5: 2B].
Crane, Anne Moncure m. Seemuller, Augustus, Jr. on 69-Sep-23 [69-Sep-24: 2B].
Crane, Charles C. m. Zell, Virginia on 69-Jun-3 [69-Jun-5: 2B].
Crane, Charles T. m. Levering, Annie L. on 67-Sep-18 [67-Sep-19: 2B].
Crane, Clara D. (16 yrs., 8 mos.) d. on 69-Nov-1 of Dropsy [69-Nov-3: 2C].
Crane, Evaline C. m. Knapp, John T. on 68-May-24 [68-Nov-28: 2C].
Crane, George W. (41 yrs.) d. on 68-Nov-5 [68-Dec-5: 2C].
Crane, Mary m. Kidd, George on 68-Oct-5 [68-Oct-10: 2B].
Crane, S. E. F. m. Denig, E. C. on 70-Oct-4 [70-Oct-10: 2B].
Crane, Sarah M. d. on 69-Dec-31 [70-Jan-1: 2B].
Crane, William (77 yrs.) d. on 66-Sep-28 [66-Sep-29: 2B; 66-Oct-1: 1G].
Cranford, Ann E. (49 yrs.) d. on 69-Jun-16 [69-Jun-22: 2C].
Crangle, Agnes m. Baker, John G. on 68-Nov-24 [68-Nov-28: 2C].
Crangle, Mary A. m. Love, William H. on 70-Nov-17 [70-Nov-24: 2B].
Crangle, S. J. m. Stewart, Columbus J. on 67-Dec-24 [67-Dec-31: 2C].
Crapster, Milton H. m. Hunt, Susan M. on 66-Nov-15 [66-Nov-17: 2B].
Crate, Frederick m. Gossom, Fanny on 66-Nov-13 [66-Nov-20: 2B].
Crate, William Alexander (9 mos.) d. on 70-Jun-29 [70-Jul-1: 2B].
Craton, Kate m. Larkin, Thomas on 66-Sep-6 [66-Sep-8: 2B].
Craumer, Catherine (72 yrs.) d. on 69-May-24 [69-May-25: 2C].
Craumer, Francis M. m. Minnick, Louisa M. on 66-Jun-14 [66-Aug-4: 2C].
Craumer, James T. Thompson (2 yrs., 6 mos.) d. on 67-Aug-1 [67-Aug-2: 2C].
Craven, Anna d. on 69-Dec-22 [69-Dec-24: 2C].
Craven, William (77 yrs.) d. on 69-Nov-30 [69-Dec-6: 2C].
Craver, M. Monroe m. Outten, Mary F. on 66-Nov-6 [66-Nov-22: 2C].
Craver, Zachariah (68 yrs.) d. on 68-Sep-9 [68-Oct-14: 2B].
Crawford, Anna S. m. Ruth, Robert J. [66-Nov-3: 2B].
Crawford, Annie E. m. Gillingham, George O. on 68-Jul-23 [68-Jul-29: 2B].
Crawford, Annie E. m. Boyle, A. H. on 69-Jan-13 [69-Jan-15: 2D].

Crawford, Ellie B. m. Smith, James C. on 67-Jun-5 [67-Jun-15: 2B].
Crawford, George Heiner (21 yrs.) d. on 68-Oct-6 [68-Oct-17: 2B].
Crawford, George R. m. Giles, Lizzie F. on 69-Jul-22 [69-Jul-26: 2C].
Crawford, Isabella m. Barbine, Jacob F. on 67-Dec-31 [68-Jan-4: 2C].
Crawford, John m. Speck, Alice on 68-Dec-22 [69-Jan-1: 2C].
Crawford, John C. m. Nash, Eva A. on 66-May-2 [66-May-12: 2A].
Crawford, Letta J. m. Blankenship, Thomas H. on 66-Oct-8 [66-Nov-10: 2B].
Crawford, Martha A. m. Williams, Daniel on 67-Jun-6 [67-Jun-10: 2B].
Crawford, Mary (34 yrs.) d. on 67-Aug-26 [67-Aug-27: 2B].
Crawford, Mary F. m. Williams, John R. on 70-Nov-7 [70-Dec-16: 2C].
Crawford, Moses (26 yrs.) d. on 68-Dec-4 [68-Dec-5: 2C].
Crawford, Nancy (82 yrs.) d. on 69-Nov-21 [69-Nov-23: 2C].
Crawford, Rebecca A. (55 yrs.) d. on 68-Apr-2 [68-Apr-3: 2C].
Crawford, Rose Ann (29 yrs.) d. on 69-Aug-25 [69-Aug-26: 2C].
Crawford, Susie Florence (4 yrs., 9 mos.) d. on 66-Dec-15 [66-Dec-17: 2B].
Crawford, Thomas (17 yrs.) d. on 69-Jun-15 of Fall from roof [69-Jun-16: 2C, 4B].
Crawford, Thomas A. m. Waggner, Mary Olivia on 66-Aug-9 [66-Aug-20: 2C].
Crawley, Mary (25 yrs.) d. on 67-Jun-13 [67-Jun-14: 2B].
Creager, Elizabeth m. Otto, Henry on 66-Jul-29 [66-Aug-7: 2C].
Creager, George L. m. Kinsley, Virginia on 66-Jan-3 [66-Aug-25: 2A].
Creager, Laurie Virginia m. Knight, George on 68-Aug-11 [68-Sep-3: 2B].
Creagh, George W. (45 yrs.) d. on 70-Sep-22 [70-Sep-23: 2C].
Creagh, James (43 yrs.) d. on 68-Jul-8 [68-Jul-13: 2B; 68-Jul-21: 2C].
Creagh, James (3 yrs.) d. on 69-Apr-4 [69-Apr-6: 2C].
Creamer, Alexander F. m. McClaine, Mary C. on 68-Oct-1 [68-Nov-26: 2B; 68-Nov-28: 2C].
Creamer, Ann (65 yrs.) d. on 70-Aug-8 [70-Aug-10: 2B].
Creamer, Christina (64 yrs., 11 mos.) d. on 70-Jul-25 [70-Jul-26: 2B].
Creamer, David Cookman (11 mos.) d. on 68-Aug-8 [68-Aug-10: 2C].
Creamer, Emma m. Fuller, Charles F. on 66-Oct-18 [66-Oct-20: 2B].
Creamer, Emma A. m. Brian, M. A. on 70-May-26 [70-May-30: 2B].
Creamer, Jamima (49 yrs.) d. on 67-Nov-27 of Heart disease [67-Nov-28: 2C].
Creamer, Joshua S. (26 yrs.) d. on 70-May-20 Murdered (Stabbing) [70-May-21: 2B; 70-May-23: 1F].
Creamer, Marie Natalia (21 yrs.) d. on 68-Nov-5 [68-Nov-6: 2C].
Creamer, William (29 yrs.) d. on 69-Aug-8 [69-Aug-9: 2B].
Creegan, Joseph m. Cummings, Mary A. on 69-Jul-8 [69-Jul-23: 2C].
Creek, Thomas C. m. Folkes, Josephine R. on 68-May-28 [68-Jun-2: 2B].
Creem, Cornelius (30 yrs.) d. on 69-Aug-8 [69-Aug-10: 2C].
Creery, Joshua J. d. on 66-Dec-16 [67-Jan-28: 1F].
Creighton, Dora m. Parker, Charles R. on 68-Sep-14 [68-Sep-18: 2B].
Creighton, Dorothy d. on 70-Apr-11 [70-Apr-15: 2C].
Creighton, George W. m. Brierly, Maggie J. on 70-May-5 [70-May-10: 2B].
Creighton, Hattie A. m. Keen, John H on 67-Mar-12 [67-Mar-14: 2C].
Creighton, John H., Capt. d. on 67-Sep-22 [67-Sep-25: 2B].
Creighton, Mary Augusta m. Mitchell, William A. on 67-Jan-31 [67-Feb-5: 2C].
Creighton, Melissa C. m. Lewis, William H. on 67-Aug-14 [67-Aug-16: 2B].
Creighton, Patrick (62 yrs.) d. on 69-Oct-20 [69-Nov-1: 2B].
Creighton, Rosetta (34 yrs.) d. on 65-Dec-22 [66-Jan-3: 2C].
Creighton, Thomas (43 yrs.) d. on 66-Mar-15 of Pneumonia [66-Mar-16: 2B].
Creighton, William m. Traverse, Susie M. on 66-Dec-13 [66-Dec-15: 2B].
Cremin, Stephen A. m. Henkle, Amelia E. on 69-Jul-23 [69-Jul-24: 2B].
Creney, William R. (40 yrs.) d. on 68-Mar-5 [68-Mar-16: 2B].
Cressman, Mary Jane d. on 68-Nov-2 [68-Nov-3: 2B].
Cressy, Mary B. d. on 68-Apr-29 [68-Apr-30: 2B; 68-May-1: 2B].
Crew, Joseph E. d. on 66-Nov-29 Murdered (Stabbing) [66-Dec-1: 1G].

Crew, Martha S. m. Morris, James on 69-Apr-21 [69-Apr-29: 2B].
Crew, Mary Ann (40 yrs.) d. on 68-Jan-29 [68-Feb-4: 2D].
Crew, Victoria C. m. Smith, William H. on 69-Aug-3 [69-Aug-5: 2B].
Crey, Paula Domitilda (4 yrs., 6 mos.) d. on 70-Apr-11 [70-Apr-12: 2B; 70-Apr-13: 2B].
Crider, Mary R. (30 yrs.) d. on 69-Mar-5 of Consumption [69-Mar-8: 2C].
Cripps, Joseph (1 yr., 5 mos.) d. on 70-Aug-17 [70-Aug-18: 2B].
Crise, Almira m. Vaughan, Henry I. on 68-Feb-25 [68-Mar-2: 2B].
Crise, John m. Harris, Sallie on 67-Oct-7 [67-Nov-9: 2B; 67-Nov-11: 2C].
Crise, Josephine (45 yrs.) d. on 66-Feb-18 [66-Feb-19: 2B].
Crisp, Edward T. m. Brooks, Lucy A. on 68-Apr-8 [68-Apr-17: 2B].
Crisp, Martha J. (34 yrs., 8 mos.) d. on 67-Apr-20 [67-Apr-22: 2A].
Crisp, Sarah J. m. Shaw, Daniel E. on 67-Sep-2 [67-Sep-25: 2B].
Criss, Agnes m. Turnbull, Nesbit on 69-Oct-12 [69-Oct-21: 2B].
Criss, Mary (9 yrs.) d. on 67-Mar-3 of Scarlet fever [67-Mar-4: 2D; 67-Mar-6: 2C].
Crist, Charles H. m. Fisher, Emily E. on 67-Dec-26 [68-Jan-1: 2C].
Crist, Charlotta (71 yrs.) d. on 69-Mar-16 [69-Mar-23: 2C].
Crist, Henry m. Rousselot, Amelia on 68-Nov-5 [68-Nov-14: 2B].
Crist, Laura V. m. Parlett, Harry L. on 68-Mar-5 [68-Mar-19: 2B].
Crist, Philip m. Rouselot, Emma on 70-May-19 [70-Jun-18: 2B].
Crist, Sarah Ella m. Whiteside, Samuel on 67-Dec-17 [67-Dec-27: 2D].
Cristie, Nancy (52 yrs.) d. on 67-Sep-8 of Alcoholism [67-Sep-9: 4C].
Criswell, William (58 yrs., 4 mos.) d. on 69-Apr-21 [69-Apr-27: 2C].
Crittenden, Sarah C. m. Corr, Diodorus F. on 69-Nov-17 [69-Nov-18: 2C].
Crocken, George Beauregard (8 yrs., 9 mos.) d. on 68-May-15 [68-May-16: 2A].
Crocken, Nelson T. m. McKew, Ellen H. on 69-Jun-17 [69-Jul-20: 2C].
Crocker, Sarah (75 yrs.) d. on 68-Aug-30 [68-Sep-1: 2A].
Crocket, Rebecca (23 yrs.) d. on 67-Mar-25 [67-Mar-27: 2C].
Crockett, A. Jackson m. Jenkins, Samana on 70-Mar-28 [70-Apr-19: 2B].
Crockett, Martha (54 yrs.) d. on 69-Oct-1 [69-Oct-5: 2B].
Crockett, Walter C. m. Wilson, Marianna on 70-Feb-2 [70-Feb-5: 2B].
Crofoot, Mary A. m. Lee, William T. on 69-Sep-3 [69-Sep-7: 2B].
Crofoot, Mary Emma (4 yrs., 1 mo.) d. on 69-Feb-18 [69-Feb-20: 2A].
Croft, Mary Ann (67 yrs.) d. on 66-Aug-24 [66-Aug-25: 2A].
Croggan, R. C. m. Grafton, Katie on 70-Feb-22 [70-Feb-24: 2C; 70-Feb-25: 2C].
Croghan, Maggie m. Tylee, William C. on 69-Dec-21 [70-Jan-14: 2C].
Crombie, Clark (83 yrs.) d. on 67-Jul-15 [67-Jul-17: 2C].
Crombie, Lydia C. (22 yrs.) d. on 69-Feb-24 [69-Feb-25: 2D].
Crombie, Mary Greenwood (11 mos.) d. on 69-Aug-23 [69-Sep-7: 2B].
Cromwell, Alfred (8 mos.) d. on 69-Aug-8 [69-Aug-10: 2C].
Cromwell, Andrew J. m. Bitzel, Sophia R. on 70-Feb-16 [70-Feb-22: 2C].
Cromwell, Anna (23 yrs.) d. on 67-Aug-2 [67-Aug-3: 2B].
Cromwell, Annie M. (80 yrs.) d. on 67-Dec-6 [67-Dec-9: 2B].
Cromwell, Benjamin M. m. Burwell, L. C. on 66-Jan-16 [66-Jan-18: 2C].
Cromwell, Bettie B. (5 yrs.) d. on 70-Dec-12 [70-Dec-31: 2C].
Cromwell, Braxton B. (7 yrs., 1 mo.) d. on 70-Dec-24 [70-Dec-31: 2C].
Cromwell, Deborah (78 yrs.) d. on 69-Feb-1 [69-Feb-2: 2C; 69-Feb-3: 2C].
Cromwell, Dorcas (80 yrs.) d. on 68-Nov-2 [68-Nov-3: 2B].
Cromwell, Elizabeth m. Stevens, Leverin on 68-Mar-10 [68-Mar-12: 2B].
Cromwell, Ellen m. Turnbull, John T. on 66-May-30 [66-Jun-8: 2B].
Cromwell, Fannie A. m. Bishop, John E. on 70-Jun-7 [70-Jun-14: 2B].
Cromwell, Francis M. m. Woodall, Frances on 68-Jan-1 [68-Jan-4: 2C].
Cromwell, Grafton S. m. McPherson, Charlotte on 70-Feb-24 [70-Mar-2: 2C].
Cromwell, Hattie A. m. Bestor, Owen B. on 67-May-7 [67-May-14: 2B].
Cromwell, Henrietta m. Congdon, Samuel H. on 67-Nov-27 [67-Dec-2: 2C; 67-Dec-3: 2C].
Cromwell, Lambert m. Moore, Annie on 66-Sep-12 [66-Sep-24: 2B].

Cromwell, Levi (73 yrs.) d. on 68-Oct-7 [68-Oct-8: 2B; 68-Oct-10: 2B].
Cromwell, Lizzie S. m. Bailey, John H. on 67-Nov-12 [67-Nov-15: 2B].
Cromwell, Louisa m. Oliver, James F. on 70-Feb-10 [70-Mar-10: 2C].
Cromwell, Mary (32 yrs.) d. on 69-Apr-29 [69-May-1: 2B].
Cromwell, Mary A. (39 yrs., 3 mos.) d. on 69-Aug-24 [69-Aug-25: 2C].
Cromwell, Mary Slicer d. on 70-Sep-25 [70-Sep-30: 2B; 70-Oct-3: 2B].
Cromwell, Samuel O. (22 yrs., 8 mos.) d. on 68-Mar-5 [68-Mar-6: 2C; 68-Mar-7: 2B].
Cromwell, William Francis (34 yrs.) d. on 66-Jan-16 [66-Jan-17: 2C].
Cronan, N. Jeremiah (23 yrs.) d. on 68-Jul-16 of Heatstroke [68-Jul-17: 1D, 2B].
Croney, Charles W. G. m. Wonn, Minnie G. on 67-Jan-14 [67-Jan-16: 2C].
Croney, John W. (57 yrs.) d. on 67-Aug-11 [67-Aug-12: 2C; 67-Aug-13: 2B].
Cronhardt, F. m. Baetjer, Henry on 66-Aug-23 [66-Aug-27: 2B].
Cronhardt, Lina m. Unverzagt, George T. on 66-Jun-7 [66-Jun-11: 2B].
Cronin, Margaret (26 yrs.) d. on 67-Mar-9 [67-Mar-11: 2C].
Cronise, William H. V. m. Plume, Kate C. on 68-Apr-2 [68-Apr-29: 2B].
Cronmiller, Eliza J. d. on 66-Jun-13 [66-Jun-21: 2C].
Cronmiller, John m. Heath, Laura on 68-Nov-25 [68-Dec-3: 2C].
Cronsberry, Amelia O. m. Magness, Benjamin F. on 66-Jun-27 [66-Oct-9: 2A].
Crook, Augusta Isabella m. Madden, Joseph H. on 70-Feb-17 [70-Feb-18: 2C].
Crook, Catherine T. (68 yrs.) d. on 69-Jul-18 [69-Jul-19: 2C; 69-Jul-21: 2C].
Crook, Charles m. Laedrich, Angelique on 67-Jan-8 [67-Jan-31: 2C].
Crook, George W. d. on 69-Jan-25 [69-Jan-29: 2C].
Crook, George W. m. Kane, Catharine on 67-Jul-9 [67-Aug-6: 2C].
Crook, George W. M. (8 mos.) d. on 66-Jul-17 [66-Jul-28: 2C].
Crook, Henry m. McAllister, Agnes B. on 67-Apr-18 [67-Apr-20: 2A].
Crook, James (1 mo.) d. on 68-Apr-5 [68-Apr-10: 2B].
Crook, Jane A. m. Harper, John on 66-Nov-12 [66-Nov-13: 2B].
Crook, Thomas J. (4 yrs.) d. on 66-Oct-9 of Chronic croup [66-Oct-11: 2C].
Crook, Walter m. Funk, Lizzie on 70-Sep-19 [70-Oct-26: 2B].
Crook, Walter J. m. Heydenreich, Valene on 67-Aug-28 [67-Sep-5: 2B].
Crook, Willie (11 yrs.) d. on 66-Sep-11 [66-Sep-12: 2A].
Crooker, Clara m. Waterman, Thomas B. on 67-Jun-20 [67-Jun-22: 2B].
Crooks, Thomas B. m. McClure, Jane on 67-Apr-25 [67-May-10: 2B].
Crookshank, Jennie m. McKay, R. G. on 69-Nov-2 [69-Nov-4: 2B].
Crookshank, William F. (40 yrs.) d. on 69-Jan-10 [69-Jan-20: 2C].
Cropper, Z. H. H. d. on 69-Jan-16 [69-Feb-1: 2C].
Crosby, Charlie (4 yrs.) d. on 70-Oct-19 [70-Oct-20: 2B].
Crosby, Samuel (45 yrs.) d. on 70-Jul-15 Drowned [70-Jul-16: 1G].
Crosby, William S. m. Mincher, Kate on 67-Dec-2 [67-Dec-10: 2B].
Croshaw, Sue Ann m. Wilson, Robert on 70-Jul-11 [70-Jul-16: 2B].
Cross, Anna M. m. Sherwood, Benjamin on 70-Dec-1 [70-Dec-3: 2B].
Cross, Cordelia A. (31 yrs.) d. on 69-Apr-7 [69-Apr-9: 2B; 69-Apr-8: 2C].
Cross, David H. m. Hogner, Mary E. on 70-Jan-6 [70-Feb-28: 2C].
Cross, Frank W. m. Howell, Mollie A. on 68-Feb-27 [68-Mar-2: 2B].
Cross, Franklin T. m. Johnson, Mary J. on 69-Aug-17 [69-Aug-26: 2C].
Cross, Harriet (58 yrs.) d. on 70-Dec-17 [70-Dec-19: 2C].
Cross, Harriet R. m. Kelley, William H. on 70-Apr-19 [70-Apr-20: 2B].
Cross, Henry Wesley (6 mos.) d. on 67-Feb-20 [67-Feb-22: 2D].
Cross, J. H. M. m. Ewbanks, Mattie on 67-May-5 [67-Jul-16: 2C].
Cross, James R. m. Nicoll, Mary C. on 67-Mar-3 [67-Mar-14: 2C].
Cross, John C. m. Bucher, Elenor on 67-Sep-5 [67-Sep-18: 2B].
Cross, John Edwin (3 yrs., 6 mos.) d. on 67-Apr-3 [67-Apr-5: 2B].
Cross, John T. m. Weddegen, Mary on 70-Jun-20 [70-Nov-18: 2C].
Cross, Laura Alice d. on 68-Aug-27 [68-Aug-29: 2B].
Cross, Margaret (30 yrs.) d. on 68-May-27 [68-May-29: 2B].

Cross, Mary Margaret m. Mariner, William H. H. on 66-Dec-2 [66-Dec-5: 2B; 66-Dec-6: 2B].
Cross, Millard Fillmore m. Merrick, Emma Louise on 69-Dec-30 [70-Feb-2: 2B].
Cross, Samuel B. (6 yrs., 3 mos.) d. on 68-Nov-22 [68-Nov-23: 2B].
Cross, Sarah (65 yrs.) d. on 66-Jan-29 [66-Jan-29: 2B].
Cross, Sarah A. m. Carroll, Robert A. on 67-Apr-18 [67-Apr-20: 2A].
Cross, Thomas W. m. Fairbank, Laura A. on 66-Feb-27 [66-Mar-2: 2B].
Cross, Walter Bosley (70 yrs.) d. on 68-Feb-5 [68-Feb-7: 2C].
Cross, William Kemop (1 yr., 10 mos.) d. on 67-Oct-11 of Dipthoretic croup [67-Oct-15: 2A].
Crosse, Elliot W. m. Brownlee, Ella J. on 69-Nov-23 [69-Nov-25: 2C].
Crossman, George (45 yrs.) d. on 66-Nov-20 [66-Nov-21: 2C].
Crossmore, Alice (34 yrs.) d. on 69-Mar-26 [69-Mar-27: 2B].
Crosson, Eugene A. (26 yrs.) d. on 66-Aug-8 [66-Aug-14: 2C].
Crothers, Charles E. (24 yrs.) d. on 66-May-30 [66-Jun-1: 2B].
Crothers, David m. Knight, Hannah Marriner on 69-Feb-1 [69-Apr-27: 2B].
Crothers, Illinois (39 yrs.) d. on 70-Feb-24 [70-Feb-25: 2C].
Crothy, Daniel (1 yr., 5 mos.) d. on 66-Sep-30 [66-Oct-1: 2B].
Crotty, Mary (3 yrs.) d. on 66-Oct-9 [66-Oct-10: 2B].
Crouch, Amanda E. m. Craig, Thomas on 67-May-21 [67-Aug-29: 2B].
Crouch, Bertannia m. Roberts, John T. on 69-Apr-6 [69-Apr-9: 2B].
Crouch, Elizabeth (58 yrs.) d. on 67-Jan-31 [67-Feb-2: 2C].
Crouch, Margaret (70 yrs.) d. on 68-Feb-15 [68-Feb-17: 2B].
Crouch, Martha W. m. LaBarrer, Francis B., Jr. on 67-Mar-17 [67-Apr-11: 2B].
Crouch, Rebecca B. G. (51 yrs., 8 mos.) d. on 69-Jan-17 [69-Jan-20: 2C].
Crouch, S. Jennie m. Young, F. Garnett on 70-Jul-14 [70-Jul-19: 2B].
Crouse, Caroline V. m. Conner, Samuel H. on 66-Feb-20 [66-Mar-6: 2B].
Crouse, Florence Augusta (3 yrs., 8 mos.) d. on 69-Jan-1 [69-Jan-2: 2C].
Crouse, George, Sr. (67 yrs., 5 mos.) d. on 68-Jul-24 [68-Aug-7: 2B].
Crout, Mary F. m. McGinnes, John H. on 68-May-20 [68-May-25: 2A].
Crout, William F. m. Shilling, Mary R. on 68-May-28 [68-Jun-6: 2A].
Crow, Ann M. (74 yrs.) d. on 70-Apr-9 [70-Apr-11: 2B].
Crow, Ezekiel (59 yrs.) d. on 70-Aug-20 [70-Aug-22: 2B].
Crow, John (79 yrs.) d. on 70-Sep-29 [70-Oct-1: 2B].
Crow, Maggie Patterson d. on 70-Aug-14 [70-Aug-15: 2C].
Crowder, Robert Henry (6 mos.) d. on 66-Aug-9 [66-Aug-14: 2C].
Crowe, Ann (39 yrs.) d. on 66-Oct-9 of Consumption [66-Oct-12: 2B].
Crowell, Agnes P. m. Kisner, Henry C. on 69-Jan-12 [69-Jan-13: 2D].
Crowell, Frances m. Swain, Howard on 69-Jun-29 [69-Jun-30: 2C].
Crowfoot, Canfield (61 yrs.) d. on 68-Jun-3 of Lung hemorrhage [68-Jun-4: 2B].
Crowl, Henry (90 yrs.) d. on 66-Jan-10 [66-Jan-12: 2C, 4D].
Crowle, John m. Drury, Virginia on 66-Oct-23 [66-Oct-26: 2B].
Crowley, Charles Howard (1 yr., 4 mos.) d. on 70-Apr-30 [70-May-2: 2B].
Crowley, James A. m. Porter, Laura E. on 70-Sep-6 [70-Sep-10: 2B].
Crowley, Kate E. m. White, George R. on 65-Nov-20 [66-Jan-20: 2C].
Crowley, Patrick (20 yrs.) d. on 68-Mar-19 [68-Mar-26: 2B].
Crowley, Sally Cook d. on 69-Mar-5 [69-Mar-6: 2B].
Crown, Catherine H. (75 yrs.) d. on 70-Dec-25 of Paralysis [70-Dec-26: 2C].
Crown, Thomas (77 yrs.) d. on 67-Apr-12 [67-Apr-17: 2B].
Crowther, Charley (8 yrs., 2 mos.) d. on 67-Mar-5 of Scarlet fever [67-Mar-6: 2C].
Crowther, David W. m. Brundige, Kate H. on 70-Sep-7 [70-Sep-13: 2B; 70-Sep-14: 2B].
Crowther, Harry (2 yrs., 3 mos.) d. on 67-Mar-18 of Scarlet fever [67-Mar-19: 2C].
Crowther, Llewellyn m. Glass, Bessie on 70-Oct-13 [70-Oct-15: 2B].
Crowther, Matilda J. m. McKewin, Richard J. on 69-Jul-1 [69-Jul-14: 2D].
Croxall, Mary (77 yrs., 4 mos.) d. on 68-May-18 [68-May-20: 2A].
Croxall, Minnie E. m. Starr, John D. on 67-Jul-18 [67-Jul-25: 2C; 67-Aug-6: 2C].
Croyeau, Edward A. d. on 70-Jul-12 [70-Jul-14: 2B; 70-Jul-15: 2C].

Crozer, Emma m. Knowles, Gustavus W. on 70-Mar-29 [70-Apr-4: 2B].
Crozier, Annie M. m. Disney, William S. on 70-Jun-2 [70-Jun-17: 2B].
Crozier, Susan E. (10 yrs., 5 mos.) d. on 69-Jan-3 [69-Jan-4: 2C].
Crozier, Winona (12 yrs., 4 mos.) d. on 67-Nov-29 [67-Dec-2: 2C].
Crudden, Emma C. d. on 67-Feb-27 [67-Feb-28: 2C].
Crudden, Joseph m. McKean, Mary Jane on 66-Feb-22 [66-Nov-24: 2B].
Crudden, William m. King, Nancy on 69-Dec-23 [69-Dec-25: 2C].
Crumel, Rachel Ann (34 yrs.) d. on 68-May-26 [68-May-29: 2B].
Crumlish, Martha (23 yrs.) d. on 67-Sep-29 [67-Oct-1: 2B].
Crumm, Mary F. m. Miller, D. W. on 68-Apr-15 [68-Apr-17: 2B].
Crummer, Daniel d. on 68-Oct-6 [68-Oct-7: 1G; 68-Oct-8: 2B].
Crump, Christiana Octavia m. Brooks, N. C. on 67-Jun-26 [67-Jun-27: 2B].
Crump, Maria (75 yrs.) d. on 69-Jun-20 [69-Jul-20: 2C].
Crump, Robert A. m. Stewart, Alice L. on 67-Aug-6 [67-Sep-3: 2B].
Cruse, Edward (39 yrs.) d. on 69-Sep-16 [69-Sep-17: 2C].
Cruse, George W. (1 yr., 11 mos.) d. on 70-Jan-4 [70-Jan-5: 2C].
Cruse, Josephine (27 yrs.) d. on 66-Nov-6 [66-Nov-6: 2B].
Cruse, Mary Alice (4 yrs., 5 mos.) d. on 67-Jan-21 of Pneumonia [67-Jan-23: 2C].
Cruse, William T. (39 yrs.) d. on 67-Oct-5 Drowned [67-Oct-7: 1E; 67-Oct-12: 2B].
Cruser, C. M. m. Duncan, Mary E. on 66-Nov-7 [66-Nov-15: 2C].
Cruser, Harriet F. m. Meyers, Augustus on 67-Jun-6 [67-Aug-13: 2B].
Crutchly, Laura A. (29 yrs.) d. on 66-Sep-9 of Dysentery [66-Sep-10: 2D].
Cuddy, Louisa m. Everhard, W. J. on 69-Apr-14 [69-Apr-26: 2B].
Cuddy, Michael Joseph (6 mos.) d. on 70-Jul-27 [70-Jul-28: 2C].
Cuddy, Peter m. Monahan, Jane on 69-Jan-31 [69-Feb-6: 2C].
Cuddy, Rebecca m. Stabler, Edward on 69-Nov-17 [69-Nov-20: 2B].
Cuffy, James d. on 69-Apr-3 Murdered (Assault) [69-Apr-5: 1H].
Cugle, Edwin m. Zimmerman, Kate on 70-Oct-18 [70-Oct-20: 2B; 70-Oct-21: 2C].
Cugle, Miriam d. on 68-Oct-17 [68-Oct-19: 2B].
Culbbreth, Crawford m. Davis, Anna R. on 68-Feb-25 [68-Feb-27: 2C].
Culbertson, Sarah E. (30 yrs.) d. on 67-Sep-5 of Consumption [67-Sep-7: 2A].
Cull, Anna M. m. Maskell, Joseph H. on 66-Nov-20 [66-Nov-24: 2B].
Cullen, Ann (36 yrs.) d. on 66-Apr-13 [66-Apr-14: 2B].
Cullen, Annie m. Beatty, Joseph G. on 66-May-1 [66-May-3: 2C].
Cullen, John m. Loftus, Julia on 66-May-20 [66-May-23: 2B].
Cullen, Patrick (26 yrs.) d. on 70-May-9 Murdered (Shooting) [70-May-10: 1G, 2B; 70-May-11: 1F].
Cullen, Thomas J. (24 yrs.) d. on 70-Sep-19 [70-Sep-20: 2B].
Cullen, William T. m. Flishell, Elizabeth B. on 67-Jun-3 [67-Aug-31: 2B].
Culley, Mary Ann (66 yrs.) d. on 68-Nov-16 [68-Nov-18: 2C].
Cullimore, Flora d. [70-Jun-21: 2C].
Cullimore, James (60 yrs.) d. on 68-Feb-14 [68-Mar-5: 2C].
Cullimore, William H. m. Ward, Emily E. on 68-May-5 [68-May-18: 2B].
Cullings, James W. m. Truitt, Elenora H on 68-Jan-8 [68-Jan-16: 2C].
Cullison, Eli T. m. Faithful, Emma on 70-Oct-13 [70-Oct-29: 2B].
Cullison, George (21 yrs.) d. on 68-Dec-2 [68-Dec-4: 2D].
Cullison, George A. m. Fillmore, Jane on 67-Jun-9 [67-Jun-13: 2C].
Cullison, George E. (36 yrs.) d. on 66-Jan-30 [66-Jan-31: 2C].
Cullison, George W. (43 yrs.) d. on 66-Jul-24 [66-Jul-26: 2C].
Cullison, James Henry (4 mos.) d. on 70-Oct-26 [70-Oct-27: 2B].
Cullum, Harriet J. m. Larmour, John on 66-Feb-1 [66-Feb-5: 2C].
Cullum, John Wesley (10 mos.) d. on 66-Jul-30 [66-Aug-9: 2C].
Cullum, Margaret d. on 70-Oct-16 [70-Oct-18: 2C].
Cullum, Sarah Ellen Olevia (5 mos.) d. on 67-Dec-18 [67-Dec-20: 2B].
Culver, William Edward m. McClintock, Jennie on 68-Jan-9 [68-Jan-13: 2C].

Culverwell, Mary Ann (65 yrs.) d. on 70-Aug-8 [70-Aug-10: 2B].
Cumberland, Emma V. m. Emmart, Henry D. on 68-Dec-3 [68-Dec-21: 2B].
Cumming, Elizabeth Sexton d. on 68-Aug-1 [68-Aug-3: 2B].
Cumming, Margaret d. on 67-Apr-24 [67-May-6: 2B].
Cummings, Annie m. Rhoads, William R. on 70-Jul-7 [70-Jul-28: 2C].
Cummings, Ella Maben (6 yrs.) d. on 69-Dec-17 [69-Dec-18: 2B].
Cummings, Martha A. m. Wilkinson, James on 66-Mar-14 [66-Mar-20: 2C].
Cummings, Mary A. m. Creegan, Joseph on 69-Jul-8 [69-Jul-23: 2C].
Cummings, Sarah J. m. Wise, Nicholas J. on 67-Nov-21 [67-Nov-25: 2B].
Cummings, Thomas (74 yrs.) d. on 68-Jul-24 Drowned [68-Jul-30: 1G].
Cummins, Alexander (78 yrs.) d. on 67-Apr-20 [67-Apr-22: 1G, 2A].
Cummins, Jane P. (60 yrs.) d. on 68-Dec-6 [68-Dec-7: 2D].
Cummiskey, Eugene (45 yrs.) d. on 70-Nov-6 of Dropsy [70-Nov-7: 4C, 2B; 70-Nov-8: 2B; 70-Nov-10: 4C].
Cummiskey, Mary V. m. Hale, William D. on 67-Nov-26 [67-Dec-2: 2C].
Cumor, William (24 yrs.) d. on 70-Jan-1 [70-Jan-5: 2C].
Cundiff, Anne (68 yrs.) d. on 70-Jan-5 [70-Jan-7: 2F].
Cunigam, James d. on 66-Mar-2 [66-Mar-3: 2B].
Cunningham, Andrew J. (48 yrs.) d. on 67-May-17 [67-May-21: 2B].
Cunningham, Bridget A. (17 yrs.) d. on 67-Apr-22 [67-Apr-24: 2B].
Cunningham, Cecelia m. Mettee, Joseph S. on 66-Jun-6 [66-Oct-18: 2B].
Cunningham, Charles (45 yrs.) d. on 70-Feb-10 [70-Feb-14: 2C].
Cunningham, Charles S. (35 yrs.) d. on 69-Aug-13 [69-Aug-14: 2C].
Cunningham, Clara C. (8 mos.) d. on 69-Apr-13 [69-Apr-14: 2B].
Cunningham, Elizabeth S. m. Collins, John on 67-Apr-25 [67-Apr-27: 2A].
Cunningham, Ellen T. m. Courtney, John Bell on 69-Oct-11 [70-Feb-8: 4F].
Cunningham, Fannie m. Southall, G. B. on 68-Dec-8 [68-Dec-15: 2C].
Cunningham, James (53 yrs.) d. on 67-May-7 [67-May-8: 2B].
Cunningham, James (35 yrs.) d. on 66-Jun-7 [66-Jun-9: 2B].
Cunningham, James, Sr. (65 yrs.) d. on 70-Jul-21 of Heatstroke [70-Jul-22: 4D, 2C; 70-Jul-23: 2B].
Cunningham, John (47 yrs.) d. on 69-May-24 [69-Jun-14: 2C].
Cunningham, John A. H. (39 yrs.) d. on 70-Apr-20 [70-Apr-21: 2C].
Cunningham, John D. m. Barrenger, Alice on 68-Jan-1 [68-Jan-4: 2C].
Cunningham, John S. (1 yr., 9 mos.) d. on 70-Dec-6 [70-Dec-8: 2B].
Cunningham, John William d. on 66-Jan-29 of Consumption [66-Jan-30: 2B].
Cunningham, Joseph S. (36 yrs.) d. on 69-Nov-6 [69-Nov-8: 2C].
Cunningham, M. Augusta m. Diggs, Henry S. on 68-Jan-30 [68-Feb-3: 2C].
Cunningham, Maggie m. Foos, James K. on 66-Sep-20 [66-Sep-26: 2B].
Cunningham, Martha Elizabeth (60 yrs.) d. on 69-Feb-16 [69-Feb-18: 2C].
Cunningham, Mary (28 yrs.) d. on 68-Jun-3 [68-Jun-5: 2B].
Cunningham, Mary d. on 68-Jul-15 [68-Jul-16: 2C].
Cunningham, Mary (31 yrs.) d. on 66-Jun-17 [66-Jun-18: 2B].
Cunningham, Mary (44 yrs.) d. on 69-Nov-30 [69-Dec-1: 2C].
Cunningham, Merriken B. (58 yrs.) d. on 69-Apr-20 [69-Apr-21: 2B].
Cunningham, Michael (9 mos.) d. on 70-Sep-5 [70-Sep-6: 2B].
Cunningham, Sarah Ann (27 yrs.) d. on 67-Feb-2 [67-Feb-4: 2C].
Cunningham, Thomas (44 yrs.) d. on 66-Dec-14 [66-Dec-15: 2B].
Cunningham, Virginia D. C. (35 yrs.) d. on 66-Dec-17 [66-Dec-17: 2B].
Cunningham, Washington Eugene (18 yrs.) d. on 66-Sep-9 [66-Sep-10: 2D].
Cunningham, Wilbur Fisk m. Kramer, Rebecca E. on 68-Dec-29 [69-Jan-1: 2C].
Curkley, Lewis (50 yrs.) d. on 69-Jan-23 of Heart disease [69-Jan-25: 1H].
Curlett, Caroline E. (37 yrs.) d. on 67-Jul-19 [67-Jul-20: 2C].
Curlett, Elias Montague (27 yrs.) d. on 68-Jul-9 [68-Jul-11: 2B; 68-Jul-15: 2B].
Curlett, Ella (2 yrs., 4 mos.) d. on 69-Aug-28 [69-Sep-11: 2B].

Curlett, John m. Michael, Rebecca on 69-Jan-7 [69-Jan-8: 2C].
Curlett, Mollie S. M. m. Foster, Charles H. on 69-Nov-25 [69-Dec-10: 2C].
Curlett, T. Spicer m. Chilton, Susie on 68-Nov-4 [68-Nov-7: 2B].
Curlett, Thomas W. (49 yrs.) d. on 70-Apr-1 [70-Apr-2: 2A].
Curley, Barbara (82 yrs.) d. on 69-May-17 [69-May-18: 2C].
Curley, Barbara m. Tormy, John M. on 66-Apr-26 [66-Apr-27: 2C].
Curley, Clarence (13 yrs.) d. on 67-Jun-5 Drowned [67-Jun-6: 2B; 67-Jun-7: 1F].
Curley, Ella m. Middleton, William on 70-May-19 [70-May-23: 2B].
Curley, Ellenora (15 yrs., 10 mos.) d. on 66-Sep-28 [66-Oct-6: 2A].
Curley, Emma m. Morling, Frank L. on 66-Dec-6 [66-Dec-10: 2B].
Curley, George W. m. Walters, Marietta V. on 70-Jun-16 [70-Jun-21: 2C].
Curley, Ida m. Dyer, John J. on 69-Oct-11 [69-Apr-20: 2B].
Curley, James (83 yrs.) d. on 67-Aug-16 [67-Aug-17: 2B].
Curley, John D. m. Michael, Rebecca on 69-Jan-7 [69-Jan-9: 2C].
Curley, Kieran (29 yrs.) d. on 68-May-3 [68-May-4: 2B; 68-May-5: 2B].
Curley, Mary (4 yrs.) d. on 68-Jan-8 [68-Jan-9: 2C].
Curley, Mary Perrier (1 yr., 6 mos.) d. on 69-Feb-19 [69-Feb-22: 2C].
Curley, Michael (34 yrs.) d. on 70-May-2 [70-May-3: 2B].
Curran, Annie S. (16 yrs.) d. on 66-Nov-8 [66-Nov-9: 2C].
Curran, Cecilia J. m. Foley, David R. on 66-May-15 [66-May-24: 2C].
Curran, James (30 yrs.) d. on 66-Feb-12 [66-Feb-13: 2C].
Curran, Mary E. m. O'Brien, Daniel on 66-May-15 [66-May-24: 2C].
Curran, Patrick William (1 yr., 4 mos.) d. on 69-Jun-28 [69-Jun-29: 2C].
Curren, George (11 yrs., 2 mos.) d. on 66-Sep-16 [66-Sep-17: 2B].
Curren, Mary Catherine (10 mos.) d. on 70-Jul-20 [70-Jul-21: 2C].
Currey, A. Rebecca m. Denne, Charles H. on 68-Dec-24 [68-Dec-28: 2B].
Curry, Alfred W. m. Quigley, Mollie A. on 66-Oct-25 [66-Oct-27: 2B].
Curry, Daniel C. m. Lathe, Emma C. on 70-Apr-20 [70-Apr-22: 2C].
Curry, Edward J. m. Frisby, Sarah A. on 68-Feb-20 [68-Mar-7: 2B].
Curry, Hannah A. (59 yrs.) d. on 70-Aug-11 [70-Aug-15: 2C; 70-Aug-16: 2C].
Curry, James H. (34 yrs.) d. on 69-Jan-28 [69-Feb-1: 2C].
Curry, John (77 yrs.) d. on 68-Dec-5 [68-Dec-9: 2C].
Curry, Levi H. (64 yrs.) d. on 69-Apr-16 [69-Apr-17: 2A].
Curry, Lydia (74 yrs.) d. on 70-Nov-11 [70-Dec-12: 2C].
Curry, Sallie (10 yrs., 10 mos.) d. on 70-Sep-11 [70-Sep-24: 2B].
Curry, William (40 yrs.) d. on 68-Mar-8 [68-Mar-12: 2B].
Curtain, Francis Otley (2 yrs., 8 mos.) d. on 69-Feb-17 [69-Feb-19: 2C].
Curtain, Oliver P. m. Lamy, Marion O. on 66-May-13 [66-May-17: 2C; 66-May-18: 2C].
Curtin, Annie Margaret m. Moore, John W. on 70-Aug-1 [70-Aug-3: 2C].
Curtin, Robert R. (32 yrs.) d. on 70-Mar-1 [70-Mar-2: 2C; 70-Mar-3: 2C].
Curtin, Robert R. m. Hutton, Rosalind on 69-Apr-8 [69-Apr-9: 2B].
Curtis, Ella m. Fort, Leander D. on 68-Nov-5 [68-Nov-12: 2C].
Curtis, F. A. m. Gill, John on 66-Feb-15 [66-Feb-24: 2B].
Curtis, George C. (31 yrs., 2 mos.) d. on 66-Jul-25 [66-Jul-26: 2C].
Curtis, Ida Frances (1 yr., 6 mos.) d. on 69-Jul-16 [69-Jul-28: 2D].
Curtis, Jane E. m. Buxton, John H. on 66-Mar-27 [66-Mar-31: 2C].
Curtis, John D. (69 yrs.) d. on 68-Sep-23 [68-Sep-25: 2B].
Curtis, Kate E. Nedals (1 yr., 7 mos.) d. on 66-Mar-2 of Typhoid [66-Mar-3: 2B].
Curtis, Leonora m. Cline, Hugh H. on 69-Jul-13 [69-Jul-21: 2C].
Curtis, Mary Jane m. Bias, Richard on 67-Feb-28 [67-Mar-4: 2D].
Curvel, Albina A. m. Bowen, Joseph L. on 66-Jan-13 [66-Jan-20: 2C].
Curvell, Annie Florence (10 mos.) d. on 66-Jun-20 [66-Jun-21: 2B].
Curvil, David (50 yrs.) d. on 66-Mar-10 [66-Mar-12: 2B].
Curvil, Frances (85 yrs.) d. on 66-Nov-21 [66-Nov-24: 2B].
Cusack, Catharine (75 yrs.) d. on 68-Jan-1 [68-Jan-2: 2C].

Cushell, H. B. m. Jones, Hattie A. on 70-Feb-17 [70-Mar-3: 2C].
Cushing, Henry M. m. Tolson, Margaret E. on 68-Feb-13 [68-Feb-15: 2B].
Cushing, James P. D. m. Summers, Sallie F. on 70-Aug-16 [70-Aug-19: 2C].
Cushing, John, Jr. m. Whelan, Etta on 70-Apr-26 [70-Apr-28: 2B].
Cushley, Ellen m. Scally, John on 65-Nov-5 [66-Feb-8: 2C].
Cushley, Janie D. m. Terhune, John M. on 67-Jun-4 [67-Jun-7: 2B].
Cutalar, Harry (8 mos.) d. on 67-Jun-25 [67-Jun-26: 2C].
Cuthbert, Agnes d. on 68-Jul-15 [68-Jul-16: 2C].
Cutino, Joseph (50 yrs.) d. on 67-Apr-5 [67-Apr-6: 2B].
Cutler, Malinda m. Waltemeyer, William H. on 68-Sep-18 [68-Sep-21: 2B].
Cuttle, Ann d. on 69-Dec-17 [69-Dec-20: 2C].
D'Elpeux, Aline Ravin d. on 70-Jan-10 [70-Jan-19: 2D].
D'Espeaux, Mollie F. W. m. Eccleston, G. W. on 68-May-31 [68-Jul-21: 2C].
D'ouville, E. D'Aigneaux m. Prevost, Tullie J. on 66-May-29 [66-Jun-4: 2B].
D'Ouville, Eddie (10 mos.) d. on 68-Jan-9 [68-Jan-11: 2B].
Dabney, C. m. Nicol, Mary on 70-Feb-10 [70-Feb-19: 2B].
Dabour, John m. Leach, Kate on 68-Nov-26 [68-Dec-2: 2C].
DaCosta, Alena Rosa m. Dowling, John J. on 70-May-24 [70-May-26: 2C].
Dadds, Annie M. m. Ryan, James E. on 70-Jun-9 [70-Jun-15: 2B].
Dade, Bettie m. Fuggitt, N. B. on 67-Oct-15 [67-Oct-16: 2B].
Dade, Mary C. m. Wall, William E. on 70-Jan-25 [70-Jan-28: 2B].
Daffin, Charles Joseph d. on 70-Jul-17 [70-Jul-18: 2B].
Daffin, Florence (1 mo.) d. on 70-Oct-10 [70-Oct-11: 2C].
Daffin, Francis D. m. Moulton, M. Ida on 67-May-16 [67-May-20: 2B].
Daffin, Mary Emma d. on 69-Dec-6 [69-Dec-7: 2C].
Daffin, Robert S. d. on 67-Jul-30 [67-Jul-31: 2C; 67-Aug-1: 2C].
Dahme, Joseph Percy (10 mos.) d. on 69-Sep-8 [69-Sep-9: 2B].
Dahoney, John E. m. Gisriel, Mary Olivia on 68-Nov-3 [68-Nov-11: 2C].
Daicker, Elizabeth (54 yrs.) d. on 68-Feb-4 [68-Feb-6: 2C].
Daicker, Louisa m. Towner, James L. on 68-Feb-20 [68-Feb-22: 2B].
Daicker, Robert T. m. DeGaw, Annie E. on 69-Jul-13 [69-Jul-27: 2C].
Daiger, Charles Henry (3 mos.) d. on 68-Feb-28 [68-Mar-2: 2C].
Daiger, Letitia (1 yr., 1 mo.) d. on 70-Jul-15 [70-Jul-16: 2B].
Daiger, Peter Vin. McDermott (5 mos.) d. on 68-Jul-7 [68-Jul-11: 2B].
Daiger, Willie Vincent (1 yr., 1 mo.) d. on 67-Oct-15 [67-Oct-16: 2B].
Dail, Alice V. m. Hebb, John L. on 68-Dec-13 [66-Dec-15: 2B; 66-Dec-17: 2B].
Dail, Vernon R. (1 yr., 7 mos.) d. on 66-Jul-8 [66-Jul-10: 2C].
Dailey, Catherine (45 yrs.) d. on 67-Apr-21 [67-Apr-22: 2A; 67-Apr-23: 2B].
Dailey, James (60 yrs.) d. on 68-Feb-22 [68-Feb-24: 2C].
Dailey, John (35 yrs.) d. on 69-Aug-3 [69-Aug-5: 2B; 69-Aug-6: 2C].
Dailey, William F. (34 yrs.) d. on 69-Mar-1 [69-Mar-23: 2C].
Daily, Daniel Eugene (1 yr., 6 mos.) d. on 67-Sep-18 [67-Sep-19: 2B].
Daily, Elijah (56 yrs.) d. on 68-Oct-19 [68-Oct-20: 1G, 2B].
Daily, Ellen (30 yrs.) d. on 67-Nov-23 [67-Nov-25: 2C; 67-Nov-26: 2B].
Daily, John m. Ryan, Honora on 66-Oct-16 [66-Oct-18: 2B].
Daily, Margaret (2 yrs., 10 mos.) d. on 69-Sep-13 [69-Sep-14: 2B].
Daily, Mary A. m. Cohee, Levin W. on 70-Nov-22 [70-Nov-24: 2B].
Daily, Mary Ellen (7 yrs., 5 mos.) d. on 68-Jan-29 [68-Jan-30: 2C].
Daily, Samuel Vansant (10 yrs.) d. on 66-Dec-25 [66-Dec-27: 2C].
Daily, Susan m. Green, Israel J. on 70-Oct-23 [70-Nov-24: 2B].
Daimond, James m. Gambrell, Sarah E. on 68-Jan-14 [68-Jan-17: 2C].
Dalby, Jane M. (33 yrs.) d. on 68-Jul-16 [68-Jul-20: 2B].
Daley, Annie (76 yrs.) d. on 70-Nov-12 [70-Nov-22: 2C].
Daley, Catherine m. Loane, James R. on 68-Nov-1 [68-Nov-9: 2B].
Daley, Emma d. on 68-Dec-10 [68-Dec-11: 2C; 68-Dec-12: 2C].

Daley, Helen E. m. Sweaney, Randolph B. on 66-Oct-23 [66-Oct-25: 2C].
Daley, Margaret (40 yrs.) d. on 69-Oct-12 [69-Oct-14: 2C].
Daley, Nannie d. on 66-Apr-21 [66-Apr-25: 2B].
Daley, Rose L. m. Hayden, Hal. G. on 68-Jun-25 [68-Jul-24: 2C].
Daley, Sallie m. Van Tromp, John on 66-Jul-12 [66-Jul-16: 2C].
Daley, William Martin (23 yrs.) d. on 66-Jul-2 [66-Jul-3: 2C].
Dall, Joseph Edward (3 yrs., 4 mos.) d. on 69-Apr-18 [69-Apr-19: 2B].
Dall, Thomas Atkinson (8 yrs.) d. on 69-Jan-24 [69-Jan-25: 2D].
Dallam, B. Bush (46 yrs.) d. on 66-Nov-7 [66-Nov-13: 2B].
Dallam, Charles F. m. Yates, Emily S. on 68-Jan-23 [68-Jan-27: 2C].
Dallam, Josephine d. on 69-Jul-28 [69-Aug-3: 2C].
Dallam, Josias W. (59 yrs.) d. on 70-Oct-20 [70-Oct-24: 2B].
Dallwig, E. A. m. Kraft, Sallie L. on 70-Apr-3 [70-Apr-6: 2B].
Dalrymple, Kate Marsh (23 yrs.) d. on 66-Aug-20 [66-Aug-21: 2C].
Dalrymple, Margaret R. m. Harrison, Charles S. on 66-Dec-6 [66-Dec-8: 2B; 66-Dec-10: 2B].
Dalrymple, Mollie E. m. Phillips, John R. on 69-Jun-15 [69-Jun-17: 2C].
Dalrymple, William D., Dr. (49 yrs.) d. on 67-Apr-13 of Typhoid [67-Apr-15: 1F, 2C; 67-May-11: 2A].
Dalrymple, William F. (68 yrs.) d. on 66-Aug-2 [66-Aug-3: 1G, 2C].
Dalsheimer, Eugenie m. Friedenwald, Issac on 66-Dec-25 [66-Dec-29: 2C].
Dalton, Charles F., Dr. (51 yrs.) d. on 66-Jan-1 of Consumption [66-Feb-14: 2C].
Dalton, Elizabeth A. (54 yrs.) d. on 69-Jan-29 [69-Jan-30: 2C].
Dalton, James (8 yrs., 10 mos.) d. on 69-Oct-5 [69-Oct-12: 2C].
Daly, Eliza m. Maguire, Patrick on 68-Feb-5 [68-Jun-26: 2B].
Daly, James m. Hudner, Margaret on 66-May-24 [66-May-31: 2B].
Daly, Samuel P. Ducket (2 yrs.) d. on 69-Jan-13 [69-Jan-14: 2D].
Dambmann, Gustav F. P. m. Rettler, Louisa A. on 68-Jan-6 [68-Jan-7: 2B].
Dame, Oliver M. m. Barrack, Fannie E. on 70-Mar-18 [70-Apr-1: 2B].
Dameron, Charles B. (23 yrs.) d. on 68-Oct-29 [68-Nov-2: 2B].
Dameron, Mary (98 yrs.) d. on 66-Jul-8 [66-Jul-9: 2C].
Dames, John H. m. Giesendaffer, Hannah E. on 67-May-29 [67-May-31: 2B].
Damman, Ann M. d. on 68-Jul-7 [68-Jul-8: 2B].
Dammann, A. E. m. McDonald, Emma on 70-Nov-26 [70-Nov-30: 2C].
Dammann, Annie Elizabeth (50 yrs.) d. on 69-May-20 [69-May-21: 2C].
Dammann, Mary E. d. on 66-Oct-8 [66-Oct-10: 2B].
Dammann, Mary Virginia (21 yrs.) d. on 70-Jan-18 [70-Jan-19: 2C].
Dance, E. Scott m. Jenkins, Sue R. on 70-Nov-24 [70-Nov-29: 2C].
Dandelet, Lucille (40 yrs.) d. on 66-Oct-1 [66-Oct-2: 2B; 66-Oct-3: 2B].
Dandelet, Susie C. m. King, George W. on 67-Nov-27 [67-Dec-5: 2C].
Dane, Margaret (84 yrs.) d. on 69-Mar-10 [69-Mar-11: 2C].
Danehey, Edward (68 yrs.) d. on 69-Mar-29 [69-Mar-30: 2C].
Daneker, Clar Keener (1 yr., 3 mos.) d. on 70-Jul-17 [70-Jul-19: 2C].
Daneker, Jennie m. Kirkwood, S. A. on 67-May-25 [67-Jun-4: 2A].
Daneker, Sadie V. m. Case, Watson on 69-Feb-2 [69-Feb-9: 2C].
Daneker, William H. m. Kerner, Carrie E. on 67-Oct-29 [67-Nov-5: 2B].
Danforth, Francis Lippitt (57 yrs.) d. on 67-Apr-30 [67-May-13: 2B].
Daniel, A. R. m. Eastham, Anna on 66-Dec-11 [66-Dec-18: 2B].
Daniel, Alice Isabella m. Lyon, M. Johnson on 68-Apr-28 [68-May-1: 2B].
Daniel, John Warwick m. Murrell, Julia E. on 69-Nov-24 [69-Nov-30: 2C].
Daniel, Myra (39 yrs.) d. on 68-Nov-22 [68-Nov-30: 2C].
Daniels, David C. m. Carver, Anna E. on 66-Jun-5 [66-Jun-6: 2B].
Danskin, Washington A., Jr. (28 yrs.) d. on 67-Apr-3 [67-Apr-4: 2B].
Darby, James m. Lumberson, Kate on 66-May-16 [66-Jun-5: 2B].
Darby, Lewis (5 mos.) d. on 68-Jan-6 [68-Jan-7: 2C].
Darby, Margaret (28 yrs.) d. on 67-Sep-13 [67-Sep-14: 2A].

Darby, Philip m. Furlong, Hattie A. on 69-Jan-14 [69-Jan-18: 2C].
Darby, Rose M. m. Jones, John A. on 66-Jan-9 [66-Jan-11: 2B].
Dare, Elizabeth (92 yrs.) d. on 68-Nov-3 [68-Nov-5: 2C].
Dare, Ephram E. m. Edwards, Martha J. on 66-Sep-9 [67-May-28: 2B].
Dare, Margaret (84 yrs.) d. on 67-Oct-25 [67-Oct-26: 2A].
Dare, Nannie m. Peterson, George P. on 70-Jan-13 [70-Jan-19: 2C].
Dare, Sophie S. m. Morgan, Samuel Ross on 70-Jul-19 [70-Jul-21: 2C].
Dargen, Elizabeth m. Sullivan, James on 68-Jan-27 [68-Jan-30: 2C].
Darling, James H. m. Shaw, Mary A. on 69-Dec-31 [70-Jan-5: 2C].
Darling, Laura J. m. Ford, John D. on 66-Apr-30 [66-May-3: 2C].
Darling, Lawrence Molineaux d. on 68-Jul-19 [68-Jul-20: 2B].
Darragh, Ann Jane d. on 69-Dec-27 [69-Dec-28: 2C; 69-Dec-29: 2D].
Darraugh, Daniel (60 yrs.) d. on 67-May-5 [67-May-6: 2B].
Darraugh, Robert J. (28 yrs.) d. on 66-Dec-27 of Consumption [66-Dec-29: 2C].
Darrell, Augustus (28 yrs.) d. on 68-Dec-22 [68-Dec-24: 2C].
Darrington, Mary m. Dunlap, C. Lewis on 68-Jul-16 [68-Jul-17: 2B].
Dary, William H. (54 yrs.) d. on 66-Oct-23 [66-Oct-24: 2C].
Dasch, John P. (49 yrs.) d. on 68-Oct-27 [68-Oct-28: 2B].
Dasch, Mary E. m. Powers, Warren T. on 68-Apr-16 [68-Apr-18: 2A].
Dashields, Susanna (31 yrs., 1 mo.) d. on 69-Aug-5 [69-Aug-9: 2C].
Dashields, Thomas m. Waugh, Jennie on 69-Feb-4 [69-Feb-12: 2C].
Dashiell, Charles E. m. Cademore, Susanna on 69-Mar-17 [69-Mar-20: 2B].
Dashiell, Daniel (40 yrs.) d. on 68-Nov-24 of Fall from roof [68-Nov-25: 1H].
Dashiell, Ellen Maria (2 yrs., 5 mos.) d. on 68-Apr-2 of Whooping cough [68-Apr-10: 2B].
Dashiell, Emily W. (45 yrs.) d. on 66-Nov-25 [66-Nov-26: 2B].
Dashiell, Maggie Louisa (6 mos.) d. on 68-Mar-9 [68-Mar-10: 2C].
Dashiell, Mary (90 yrs.) d. on 69-May-8 [69-May-10: 2B; 69-May-11: 2B; 69-May-12: 2B].
Dashiell, Robert (70 yrs.) d. on 70-Jan-15 [70-Jan-17: 2C].
Dashiell, William O. m. Holbrook, Jane on 68-Nov-25 [68-Nov-28: 2C].
Daub, Christian m. Guemann, Dina on 66-Feb-11 [66-Feb-13: 2C].
Daubrat, Frederick m. Connolly, Mary Ann on 67-Apr-4 [67-Apr-10: 2B].
Daughaday, Emma Florence (1 yr., 6 mos.) d. on 67-Mar-2 [67-Mar-4: 2D].
Daughaday, Henrietta (30 yrs.) d. on 67-Jan-21 [67-Jan-22: 2C].
Daughaday, Joseph (32 yrs.) d. on 67-Nov-22 [67-Nov-30: 2C].
Daughaday, Mary E. m. Allenbaugh, John O. on 67-Mar-21 [67-May-18: 2A].
Daughaday, Richard (62 yrs.) d. on 68-Nov-10 [68-Nov-12: 2C; 68-Nov-13: 2C].
Daughaday, William, Rev. (69 yrs.) d. on 66-May-20 [66-May-22: 2B].
Daughert, August (22 yrs.) d. on 69-May-20 of Suicide (Shooting) [69-May-21: 1H].
Daugherty, Catherine (89 yrs.) d. on 70-Jan-22 [70-Jan-24: 2C].
Daugherty, Elizabeth (77 yrs.) d. on 67-Dec-14 [67-Dec-16: 2B].
Daugherty, Lilley May (2 mos.) d. on 67-Sep-16 [67-Sep-18: 2B].
Daugherty, Sarah (43 yrs.) d. on 68-Dec-3 [68-Dec-4: 2D].
Daugherty, Thomas (68 yrs.) d. on 67-May-13 [67-May-14: 2B].
Daugherty, William C. (25 yrs.) d. on 69-Jan-9 [69-Jan-14: 2D].
Daugherty, William Henry (7 yrs., 11 mos.) d. on 66-Oct-30 [66-Oct-31: 2B].
Davault, John Jacob (63 yrs.) d. on 70-Jul-20 [70-Jul-21: 2C].
Davenport, Joseph (77 yrs.) d. on 68-Feb-26 [68-Feb-28: 2D].
Davenport, Laura V. (22 yrs.) d. on 67-Feb-14 [67-Feb-15: 2C].
David, Patrick (13 yrs.) d. on 67-Jun-15 Drowned [67-Jun-17: 1F].
Davids, Josiah J. (54 yrs.) d. on 66-Sep-19 of Apoplexy [66-Sep-21: 1G, 2B].
Davidson, Charles d. on 70-Jul-4 [70-Jul-6: 2C].
Davidson, Charles N. d. on 66-Jun-3 [66-Jun-8: 2B].
Davidson, F. B. m. Bride, Hannah E. on 66-Dec-18 [66-Dec-19: 2B].
Davidson, Henrietta (29 yrs.) d. on 70-Apr-2 [70-Apr-4: 2C].
Davidson, Howard Lee (1 yr., 1 mo.) d. on 68-Jan-27 [68-Jan-28: 2D].

Davidson, James H. (32 yrs.) d. on 70-Jan-9 of Consumption [70-Jan-10: 2C; 70-Jan-11: 2C].
Davidson, John Gardner (63 yrs.) d. on 70-Oct-26 [70-Oct-27: 2B].
Davidson, Joseph H. m. Davis, Lotte on 70-Nov-2 [70-Nov-11: 2B].
Davidson, Louisa m. Hyde, John on 69-Apr-6 [69-Apr-20: 2B].
Davidson, Maria M. d. on 69-Feb-20 of Consumption [69-Feb-22: 2C].
Davidson, Robert J. m. Bennett, Maggie on 68-Jul-28 [68-Aug-4: 2C].
Davidson, Samuel A., Dr. (47 yrs.) d. on 66-Jul-2 [66-Jul-3: 1G, 2C; 66-Jul-4: 2B].
Davidson, Sarah E. A. (2 yrs., 3 mos.) d. on 70-Apr-7 [70-Apr-8: 2C].
Davidson, Spencer m. Burwell, Laura Lee on 69-Sep-9 [69-Sep-13: 2B].
Davidson, Susannah (59 yrs.) d. on 70-Oct-27 [70-Oct-28: 2C; 70-Oct-29: 2B].
Davidson, T. W. (27 yrs.) d. on 68-Aug-10 [68-Aug-13: 2B].
Davidson, William B. (27 yrs., 6 mos.) d. on 67-Jul-3 [67-Jul-4: 2B].
Davies, William d. on 70-Mar-1 [70-Mar-8: 2C].
Davis, Alexander T. m. Ellis, Elizabeth A. on 70-May-9 [70-Oct-11: 2B].
Davis, Allace J. m. McGinniss, William L. on 69-Nov-8 [69-Nov-12: 2C].
Davis, Amelia (42 yrs.) d. on 67-Mar-23 [67-Mar-25: 2C].
Davis, Angeline d. on 68-Feb-2 of Heart disease [68-Feb-3: 1F].
Davis, Ann (56 yrs.) d. on 68-Dec-11 [68-Dec-12: 2C].
Davis, Ann (94 yrs.) d. [68-May-9: 2B].
Davis, Anna Louisa (2 yrs., 1 mo.) d. on 68-Sep-19 [68-Sep-21: 2B].
Davis, Anna R. m. Culbbreth, Crawford on 68-Feb-25 [68-Feb-27: 2C].
Davis, Annie m. Blackiston, J. H. on 70-Aug-29 [70-Sep-16: 2B].
Davis, Annie E. (16 yrs.) d. on 66-Aug-8 [66-Aug-10: 2C].
Davis, Avonia Hoffman (2 yrs., 4 mos.) d. on 69-Jan-15 [69-Jan-20: 2C].
Davis, Benjamin B. m. Cole, Jane Alverda on 70-Apr-27 [70-May-11: 2B].
Davis, Benjamin D. (36 yrs.) d. on 66-Mar-12 [66-Mar-13: 2B; 66-Mar-14: 2B].
Davis, Bettie A. (30 yrs., 1 mo.) d. [69-May-6: 2B].
Davis, Blanche Estelle (9 mos.) d. on 70-Jul-25 [70-Jul-26: 2B].
Davis, Caroline m. Kessler, Henry on 70-Jan-20 [70-Feb-1: 2B].
Davis, Carrie V. (20 yrs.) d. on 66-Jun-23 [66-Jul-9: 2C].
Davis, Catherine (88 yrs.) d. on 66-Jan-7 [66-Jan-9: 2B].
Davis, Catherine M. (21 yrs.) d. on 66-Oct-17 of Congestive chills [66-Oct-18: 2B].
Davis, Charles (72 yrs.) d. on 67-Aug-6 of Dropsy [67-Aug-7: 1F].
Davis, Charles G. (9 mos.) d. on 70-Apr-30 of Whooping cough [70-May-2: 2B].
Davis, Charles W. m. Henthorn, Eliza J. on 70-Sep-28 [70-Oct-3: 2B].
Davis, Clinton H. m. Gravenstine, Jennie on 70-Jul-7 [70-Jul-11: 2C].
Davis, Daniel (53 yrs.) d. on 66-Feb-2 [66-Feb-3: 2C].
Davis, David (30 yrs.) d. on 70-Nov-11 [70-Nov-12: 2B].
Davis, Edward A. m. Madden, Christina Kate on 66-May-15 [66-May-22: 2B].
Davis, Elizabeth d. on 67-Oct-2 [67-Oct-4: 2B].
Davis, Elizabeth (61 yrs.) d. on 66-Nov-22 [66-Nov-24: 2B].
Davis, Elizabeth (35 yrs.) d. on 66-Sep-3 [66-Sep-5: 2B].
Davis, Elizabeth A. m. Eaton, Joseph S. on 66-Aug-18 [66-Aug-25: 2A].
Davis, Emily Sarah m. Franklin, Lewis A. on 66-Dec-12 [67-Jan-8: 2B].
Davis, Emma E. (1 yr.) d. on 70-Sep-13 [70-Sep-14: 2B; 70-Sep-15: 2B].
Davis, Emmaline d. on 67-Jul-1 [67-Jul-4: 2B].
Davis, Fannie E. m. Freburger, Charles E. on 69-Jun-8 [69-Jun-10: 2C].
Davis, Findlay H. Burns (6 mos.) d. on 66-Dec-21 [66-Dec-24: 2B].
Davis, Florence May (5 mos.) d. on 67-Jul-4 [67-Jul-6: 2B].
Davis, Frances H. (20 yrs., 4 mos.) d. on 68-Oct-12 [68-Oct-17: 2B].
Davis, Frank E. m. Small, Emma E. on 67-May-25 [67-May-28: 2B].
Davis, Freddy (2 yrs.) d. on 69-Oct-14 [69-Oct-15: 2C].
Davis, Frederick (74 yrs.) d. on 69-Jun-3 [69-Jun-4: 2C; 69-Jun-5: 1G].
Davis, Frederick A. (23 yrs.) d. on 66-Sep-26 of Cholera [66-Oct-12: 2B].
Davis, George m. Howard, Margaret Ann on 70-Apr-14 [70-Apr-20: 2B].

Davis, George A. (1 yr., 3 mos.) d. on 66-Jan-21 [66-Jan-24: 2B].
Davis, George A. m. Josenhans, Henrietta C. on 68-Jul-16 [69-Mar-16: 2C].
Davis, George C. m. Petty, Sallie Maud on 70-Feb-24 [70-Mar-1: 2C].
Davis, George E. d. on 68-May-8 [68-May-12: 2B].
Davis, George Eugene (2 yrs., 3 mos.) d. on 68-Jan-20 [68-Jan-21: 2C].
Davis, George H. (38 yrs.) d. on 68-Jan-27 of Consumption [68-Feb-3: 2C].
Davis, George Lynn Lachlan (57 yrs.) d. on 69-Dec-24 [69-Dec-25: 1G, 2C; 70-Jan-11: 1F].
Davis, George M. (26 yrs.) d. on 69-Sep-13 [69-Sep-16: 2B].
Davis, George W. (30 yrs.) d. on 69-Dec-21 [69-Dec-22: 2B].
Davis, George W. m. Beaumont, Mollie J. on 70-Jan-26 [70-Jan-27: 2C].
Davis, Georgianna m. Westerman, Francis H. on 66-Jan-17 [66-Jan-19: 2C].
Davis, Georgie m. Camper, Thomas J. on 70-Apr-21 [70-Apr-23: 2B].
Davis, Hannah C. m. Keyser, John P. on 69-Jan-17 [69-Jan-23: 2C].
Davis, Hannah Jessie d. on 67-Aug-5 [67-Aug-6: 2C; 67-Aug-7: 2C; 67-Aug-8: 2B].
Davis, Harriet (61 yrs.) d. on 68-Apr-16 of Typhoid pneumonia [68-Apr-17: 2B; 68-Apr-18: 2A].
Davis, Harry Vincent (3 mos.) d. on 67-Feb-15 [67-Feb-18: 2C].
Davis, Henrietta m. Blackinbridge, Samuel on 66-Apr-15 [66-Apr-18: 2B].
Davis, Henry Clay (3 yrs.) d. on 67-Apr-10 of Pneumonia [67-Apr-12: 2C].
Davis, Hester A. m. Haney, McHenry on 68-May-24 [68-May-26: 2B].
Davis, Howard (43 yrs.) d. on 70-Jul-4 [70-Jul-6: 2C].
Davis, Ida (8 yrs., 9 mos.) d. on 66-Feb-18 [66-Feb-20: 2B].
Davis, J. Mattie m. Simon, August on 66-Sep-12 [66-Sep-18: 2B].
Davis, Jackson m. Slye, Marion G. on 69-Nov-4 [69-Nov-6: 2B; 69-Nov-10: 2C].
Davis, James E. m. Cox, Mary R. on 69-Sep-15 [69-Sep-22: 2C].
Davis, John (66 yrs.) d. on 66-Mar-23 [66-Mar-24: 2B].
Davis, John, Jr. m. Wood, Mary A. on 67-Dec-30 [68-Mar-3: 2C].
Davis, John C. m. Colmary, Lidie J. on 68-Nov-25 [68-Dec-2: 2C].
Davis, John F. (29 yrs.) d. on 70-Sep-11 [70-Sep-12: 2B].
Davis, John H. m. Pierpoint, Elizabeth on 68-Jan-12 [68-Jan-25: 2B].
Davis, John H. m. Small, L. on 70-Sep-22 [70-Sep-27: 2B].
Davis, Joseph m. Barnes, Annie E. on 70-Nov-17 [70-Dec-5: 2C].
Davis, Joseph L. m. Downs, Florence A. on 70-Mar-9 [70-Mar-19: 2B].
Davis, Joseph P. m. Harbaugh, Nellie on 66-Aug-9 [66-Aug-17: 2C].
Davis, Joshua (28 yrs.) d. on 67-Feb-9 Drowned [67-Feb-12: 4C].
Davis, Julia A. m. Christ, George on 70-Apr-27 [70-May-4: 2C].
Davis, Kate m. Lanahan, Michael on 67-Oct-14 [67-Nov-13: 2C].
Davis, Kate m. Keller, Peter F. on 67-Oct-3 [67-Oct-7: 2B].
Davis, Kate m. George, Samuel E. on 70-Apr-26 [70-Apr-29: 2B].
Davis, Kate E. m. Bullock, John S. on 66-Jun-22 [66-Jun-26: 2B].
Davis, L. H. m. McDuffy, Eliza Melvina on 70-May-1 [70-May-3: 2B].
Davis, L. Jennie m. Childs, D. J. on 68-Nov-25 [68-Dec-21: 2B].
Davis, Laura Jane (1 yr., 7 mos.) d. on 70-Dec-6 [70-Dec-7: 2C].
Davis, Laurence C. m. Griffith, Mary E. on 66-Mar-29 [66-Apr-30: 2B].
Davis, Letta E. m. Maddox, Edward on 68-Oct-6 [68-Nov-3: 2B].
Davis, Lizzie H. m. Ickler, John on 68-Mar-17 [68-Mar-18: 2B].
Davis, Lizzie J. m. Airey, George W. on 69-Nov-16 [69-Nov-17: 2C].
Davis, Lotte m. Davidson, Joseph H. on 70-Nov-2 [70-Nov-11: 2B].
Davis, Luliona Augusta (2 yrs., 4 mos.) d. on 68-Oct-31 [68-Nov-4: 2C].
Davis, Margaret (65 yrs.) d. on 66-Nov-22 [66-Nov-26: 2C].
Davis, Margaret Ann (45 yrs.) d. on 68-Mar-22 [68-Mar-23: 2B].
Davis, Maria V. d. on 66-May-5 [66-May-10: 2B].
Davis, Mary (67 yrs.) d. on 70-Jul-26 [70-Aug-4: 2C].
Davis, Mary (77 yrs.) d. on 70-Jan-21 [70-Jan-25: 2C].
Davis, Mary A. J. (24 yrs.) d. on 68-Apr-6 [68-Apr-8: 2B].

Davis, Mary Ann (47 yrs.) d. on 69-Dec-4 [69-Dec-8: 2C].
Davis, Mary E. (34 yrs.) d. on 66-Aug-20 [66-Aug-22: 2C].
Davis, Mary E. m. Huff, Charles A. O. on 69-Dec-16 [69-Dec-17: 2C].
Davis, Mary Jane d. on 66-Dec-29 [67-Jan-1: 2C].
Davis, Mary Josephine m. Boehme, Augustus, Jr. on 69-Mar-4 [69-Mar-11: 2C].
Davis, Mary Rebecca (1 yr.) d. on 69-Jul-23 [69-Jul-24: 2C].
Davis, Mary V. m. Greacen, John on 67-Feb-26 [67-Feb-28: 2C].
Davis, Mary W. m. Hutton, Samuel on 69-Feb-23 [69-Mar-22: 2C].
Davis, Minnie Ellsworth (5 yrs., 7 mos.) d. on 67-Apr-18 [67-Apr-19: 2B].
Davis, Noah (63 yrs.) d. on 67-Apr-7 [67-Apr-9: 2B].
Davis, Prestley Thomas (50 yrs.) d. on 67-Aug-27 Drowned [67-Aug-30: 1G; 67-Aug-31: 2B].
Davis, R. A., Sr. (64 yrs.) d. on 68-Mar-11 [68-Mar-13: 2C].
Davis, Rebecca (67 yrs.) d. on 66-May-28 [66-May-30: 2C].
Davis, Richard m. Hinton, Manie on 70-Oct-10 [70-Oct-26: 2B].
Davis, Robert (37 yrs.) d. on 68-Mar-12 [68-Mar-13: 2C].
Davis, Sallie E. m. Stewart, John T. B. on 69-Sep-3 [69-Nov-23: 2C].
Davis, Sarah A. m. Reiter, Albert H. on 70-Oct-18 [70-Oct-22: 2B].
Davis, Sarah E. Turner (8 mos.) d. on 67-Sep-18 [67-Sep-20: 2A].
Davis, Sarah J. (64 yrs.) d. on 69-Mar-31 [69-Apr-2: 2C].
Davis, Silas W. m. Hobbs, Alverda V. on 66-Feb-6 [66-Feb-8: 2C].
Davis, Thomas H. J. (58 yrs.) d. on 70-Nov-1 [70-Nov-2: 2C].
Davis, Thomas V. d. on 68-Jan-10 [68-Jan-11: 2B].
Davis, W. R. m. Shackelford, Shirley on 69-Dec-15 [69-Dec-17: 2C].
Davis, Wallis (1 mo.) d. on 69-Aug-1 [69-Aug-3: 2C].
Davis, William (27 yrs.) d. on 67-Jul-5 of Consumption [67-Jul-6: 2B].
Davis, William m. Hopkins, Amelia on 68-Sep-24 [68-Sep-29: 2B].
Davis, William m. Fowler, Rachel on 67-Jul-21 [67-Jul-24: 2C].
Davis, William Albert (7 mos.) d. on 67-Jul-23 [67-Jul-27: 2B].
Davis, William E. m. McKay, Albenia on 70-Sep-7 [70-Sep-15: 2B].
Davis, William H. (35 yrs.) d. on 66-Jul-24 [66-Jul-27: 2C].
Davis, William H. m. Tyte, Annie E. on 67-Feb-5 [67-Feb-20: 2C].
Davis, William H. m. Ford, Hannah Jessie on 66-Apr-26 [66-Apr-30: 2B].
Davis, William H. m. Couch, Rachel May on 70-Dec-22 [70-Dec-26: 2C].
Davis, William M. m. Buckingham, Georgianna A. on 66-Jun-14 [66-Jun-15: 2C].
Davis, William Wilkins (24 yrs.) d. on 66-Mar-2 [66-Mar-5: 2B].
Davis, William Winn (26 yrs.) d. on 66-Oct-12 [66-Oct-16: 2B].
Davis, Willie Langdale (1 yr., 6 mos.) d. on 69-Dec-11 [69-Dec-15: 2B].
Davison, George W. m. Bond, Sophie C. on 66-Oct-25 [66-Oct-29: 2B].
Davison, Henry J. m. Howard, Ella C. on 66-Jun-21 [66-Jun-25: 2B].
Davisson, Andrew J. m. Levey, Sarah E. on 68-Apr-1 [68-Apr-3: 2C].
Davisson, Anne Elizabeth m. Jackson, William on 66-Jan-4 [66-Jan-12: 2C].
Davny, Henry m. Mumma, Elizabeth on 69-Sep-6 [69-Sep-8: 2B].
Davy, Peter (6 yrs.) d. on 68-Sep-4 [68-Sep-5: 2A].
Daw, Nannie J., Miss m. Stone, L. P., Dr. on 70-Sep-8 [70-Sep-24: 2B].
Dawes, Edward B., Jr. m. Allen, Emma on 69-Aug-31 [69-Sep-3: 2B].
Dawes, Ella E. m. Keen, Jesse W. on 70-Aug-4 [70-Sep-3: 2B].
Dawes, John S., Capt. (42 yrs.) d. on 68-Feb-20 [68-Feb-21: 2B; 68-Mar-14: 2B].
Dawley, Tonnie m. Warfield, J. D. on 68-Apr-15 [68-Apr-17: 2B].
Dawson, Cassandra (80 yrs.) d. on 70-Mar-18 [70-Mar-23: 2C].
Dawson, Catherine (84 yrs.) d. on 69-Mar-29 [69-Mar-29: 2B; 69-Mar-30: 2C].
Dawson, Charles (39 yrs.) d. on 66-Jul-17 of Heatstroke [66-Jul-18: 1F; 66-Jul-21: 2C].
Dawson, Edward L. m. Clark, Maggie on 66-Jul-5 [66-Jul-14: 2B].
Dawson, Elizabeth E. (25 yrs., 6 mos.) d. on 67-Nov-13 [67-Nov-14: 2B].
Dawson, Ella G. m. Kennard, Philemon T. on 69-Apr-20 [69-May-5: 2C].
Dawson, Frances N. m. Ashburn, Judson A on 68-Dec-24 [68-Dec-25: 2D].

Dawson, James (32 yrs.) d. on 67-Mar-3 [67-Mar-4: 2D].
Dawson, Kate M. m. Lockwood, George C. on 69-Jan-5 [69-Jan-6: 2C].
Dawson, Manie m. Morrow, John H. on 68-Oct-22 [68-Oct-23: 2B].
Dawson, Sallie B. m. Bruff, Henry C. on 69-Apr-14 [69-Apr-15: 2B].
Dawson, William, Jr. (71 yrs.) d. on 70-Feb-11 [70-Feb-12: 2C].
Dawson, William H. H. m. King, Sue S. on 68-Jul-4 [68-Jul-23: 2B].
Day, Albert m. Stirling, Susan B. on 69-May-27 [69-Jun-3: 2B].
Day, Ann E. (61 yrs.) d. on 68-Dec-6 [68-Dec-7: 2C].
Day, Charlotte Mary Orso d. on 70-Nov-19 [70-Nov-22: 2C].
Day, Elvira m. Morris, John W. on 70-Oct-20 [70-Oct-22: 2B].
Day, H. R. d. on 66-Jan-22 [66-Feb-1: 1G].
Day, Henry d. [67-Apr-20: 1F].
Day, Kate C. m. Houston, James on 70-Aug-7 [70-Aug-9: 2C].
Day, Laura V. m. Warfield, Nathan O. on 69-Dec-7 [69-Dec-7: 2C].
Day, Levi (69 yrs.) d. [69-Nov-16: 2C].
Day, Robert m. Proctor, Effie on 70-Oct-25 [70-Nov-2: 2C].
Day, Sarah (90 yrs.) d. on 70-Dec-26 [70-Dec-28: 2C].
Day, William T. m. Hobbs, Almira Virginia on 67-Jun-4 [67-Jun-8: 2B].
Dayton, Annie m. Otto, Simon on 69-Nov-21 [69-Dec-15: 2B].
De Baufre, Mary V. m. Van Rossum, John H. on 67-Feb-28 [67-Mar-2: 2B].
De Baugh, Lizzie (20 yrs.) d. on 66-Aug-10 [66-Aug-18: 2B].
De Beaufre, Sarah A. (5 mos.) d. on 67-Jul-6 [67-Jul-8: 2C].
De Bow, John (73 yrs.) d. on 70-Apr-18 [70-Apr-20: 2B].
De Bow, Martha Virginia (34 yrs.) d. on 70-Sep-11 [70-Sep-14: 2B].
De Courcey, Jane m. Phillips, George on 68-Sep-20 [68-Sep-29: 2B].
De Frantice, Levin d. on 66-Aug-22 of Fall [66-Aug-23: 1G].
De La Faille, Marie Planat m. Evans, Theodore W. on 68-Sep-8 [68-Sep-9: 2B].
De Ronceray, Louis m. Vander Weyde, Jennie on 67-Oct-9 [67-Oct-24: 2B].
De Valin, Charles E. m. Levins, Mary S. on 68-Jul-6 [68-Jul-7: 2B].
De Valin, John H. m. Seymour, Lizzie F. on 68-May-19 [68-Jun-2: 2B].
De Vere, Sallie M. m. Wiggins, Lester T. on 68-Nov-19 [68-Nov-23: 2B].
De Walt, Louisa (53 yrs.) d. on 68-Dec-28 [68-Dec-29: 2D].
De Ward, Mary A. m. Jones, George W. on 67-Sep-5 [67-Sep-10: 2B].
Deady, Ellie T. m. Downs, William on 67-Dec-24 [67-Dec-27: 2D].
Deal, Addie m. Hales, S. on 70-Dec-16 [70-Dec-17: 2B].
Deal, Anne M. m. Roycroft, John A. on 69-Jul-8 [69-Aug-28: 2B].
Deal, Henry (48 yrs.) d. on 67-Sep-4 [67-Sep-5: 2B; 67-Sep-6: 2B].
Deal, Mary A. m. Scott, Charles A. on 67-Mar-4 [67-Mar-14: 2C].
Deal, Mary R. m. Bunce, David on 66-Mar-29 [66-Apr-7: 2B].
Deale, Alice J. m. Higgins, Joseph W. on 67-Aug-6 [67-Aug-9: 2C].
Deale, James N., Dr. (25 yrs.) d. on 67-Mar-9 [67-Mar-19: 2C].
Deale, Mary F. m. Owens, Charles W. on 69-Apr-27 [69-May-6: 2B].
Deale, W. Edward m. Earicsson, Julia S. on 69-Dec-4 [69-Dec-8: 2C].
Deale, Walter Gault (10 mos.) d. on 68-Jul-6 [68-Jul-7: 2B].
Deale, William G. (67 yrs.) d. on 68-Apr-10 [68-Apr-11: 2A; 68-Apr-13: 2B].
Dean, Harriet m. Enlows, John on 70-Dec-10 [70-Dec-13: 2C].
Dean, James m. Gorsuch, Hannah A. on 67-Feb-28 [67-Mar-16: 2B].
Dean, Margaret (43 yrs.) d. on 70-Mar-5 [70-Mar-9: 2C].
Dean, Margaret N. d. on 70-Jun-11 [70-Jun-13: 2C; 70-Jun-14: 2B].
Dean, Mary (81 yrs.) d. on 66-Nov-14 [66-Nov-19: 2B].
Dean, Samuel Albert (9 mos.) d. on 68-Jun-10 [68-Jun-11: 2B].
Dean, Seneca m. Reed, Mary D. on 69-Oct-22 [69-Nov-6: 2B].
Dearing, Anna Warren d. on 70-Aug-30 [70-Aug-31: 2B].
Dearing, Bettie m. Franklin, Benjamin on 69-Mar-24 [69-Mar-31: 2C].
Dearring, Sarah A. (60 yrs.) d. on 68-Feb-21 of Consumption [68-Feb-22: 2B].

Deaver, Alice H. m. McCabe, Jefferson on 68-Jul-30 [68-Aug-1: 2B].
Deaver, Ann Victoria d. on 66-Sep-11 [66-Sep-12: 2A].
Deaver, Clarence Edward (4 mos.) d. on 70-Feb-8 [70-Feb-11: 2C].
Deaver, Ford (63 yrs.) d. on 69-Jun-14 [69-Jun-17: 2C].
Deaver, George (45 yrs.) d. on 69-Jan-15 in Railroad accident [69-Jan-16: 1H].
Deaver, George T. m. Barnes, Sallie A. on 66-Jul-19 [66-Jul-24: 2C].
Deaver, George Washington (4 yrs.) d. on 68-Dec-27 [68-Dec-29: 2D].
Deaver, H. T. m. Horsey, Keenie on 68-Jun-24 [68-Jun-27: 2B].
Deaver, Mary Ann (65 yrs.) d. on 70-Nov-20 [70-Nov-22: 2B].
Deaver, Mary C. m. DeHoff, George P. on 66-Jun-28 [66-Jul-31: 2C; 66-Aug-1: 2C].
Deaver, Stephen F. m. Singleton, Mary E. on 68-Apr-12 [68-Apr-28: 2B].
Deaver, William John H. (27 yrs., 10 mos.) d. on 67-Jan-13 [67-Jan-15: 2C; 67-Jan-16: 2C].
DeBegna, M. Cecelia d. on 66-Oct-16 [66-Oct-27: 4A].
DeBis, Mary (66 yrs.) d. on 69-Oct-3 of Heart disease [69-Oct-5: 1H].
DeBow, Barbara A. m. Holtz, Edwin D. on 66-Feb-20 [66-Feb-23: 2C].
Debow, Barbara Ann (47 yrs.) d. on 66-Sep-24 [66-Sep-25: 2B].
DeBow, Lemuel (58 yrs.) d. on 69-Mar-31 [69-Apr-1: 2C; 69-Apr-2: 2C].
Debring, Mary A. m. Schanberger, Henry A. on 67-Feb-26 [67-Mar-1: 2C].
DeCaindry, William A. m. Choate, Mary on 70-Sep-29 [70-Oct-1: 2B].
DeCamp, Cora V. m. Drury, Charles B. on 66-Aug-28 [66-Sep-3: 2C].
Decker, Frances E. m. Oehrl, John G. on 70-Nov-20 [70-Nov-25: 2D].
Decker, John m. Henrickle, E. P. on 70-Mar-6 [70-Mar-15: 2C].
Decker, Lewis m. Dixon, Sarah A. on 69-Apr-19 [69-Apr-23: 2B].
DeComrick, Amelia W. d. on 68-Apr-26 [68-Apr-27: 2B].
DeCormas, Nina m. Oliver, James R. on 67-Sep-26 [67-Sep-27: 2B].
Decorsey, Thomas Leonard (38 yrs.) d. on 69-Aug-2 [69-Aug-10: 2C].
Dee, Edward Francis (1 yr., 6 mos.) d. on 66-Sep-27 [66-Sep-28: 2B].
Dee, Thomas (56 yrs.) d. on 69-Oct-9 [69-Oct-13: 2C].
Deeds, Virginia m. Uhler, J. H. on 69-Aug-3 [69-Aug-4: 2C].
Deegan, Mary Regina (9 mos.) d. on 66-Jun-26 [66-Jul-4: 2C].
Deegs, Sophia A. m. Mitchell, John on 70-Dec-18 [70-Dec-22: 2B].
Deemeg, Julia m. Flach, Bernhard on 70-Jul-26 [70-Aug-10: 2B].
Deems, Anna Lucille (8 mos.) d. on 68-Dec-8 [68-Dec-10: 2D].
Deems, Annie May (2 yrs., 5 mos.) d. on 68-Dec-27 [68-Dec-29: 2D].
Deems, Ella Columbia d. on 66-Jul-27 [66-Jul-28: 2C].
Deems, George W. (21 yrs.) d. on 69-Mar-21 [69-Mar-23: 2C].
Deems, George W., Rev. (84 yrs.) d. on 70-Jul-3 [70-Jul-4: 2C; 70-Jul-6: 1H].
Deems, Scotia Anna m. White, John J. on 67-Jan-1 [67-Jan-3: 2B].
Deems, Susanna (84 yrs.) d. on 69-Jan-31 [69-Feb-1: 2C; 69-Feb-2: 2C].
Deets, Elizabeth (75 yrs.) d. on 66-Nov-26 [66-Nov-27: 2B].
Deets, George m. Miers, Barbara on 66-Mar-1 [66-Mar-14: 2B].
Deets, Hannah (68 yrs., 11 mos.) d. on 66-Nov-3 [66-Nov-6: 2B].
DeFord, Anna m. Wright, James B. on 67-Feb-28 [67-Mar-5: 2C].
Deford, Benjamin (71 yrs.) d. on 70-Apr-17 of Paralysis [70-Apr-18: 1G; 70-Apr-19: 2B].
DeFord, India K. (3 yrs., 6 mos.) d. on 67-Jun-21 [67-Jul-29: 2D].
DeFord, Issac d. on 68-Feb-18 [68-Feb-20: 2C].
DeFord, Laura Virginia m. Snyder, J. William on 68-Jul-7 [68-Jul-11: 2B].
DeFord, Thomas m. Bell, Sallie W. on 69-May-20 [69-May-22: 2B].
DeFord, Thomas G., Jr. m. Brady, Georgia M. on 70-Jan-25 [70-Jan-27: 2C].
DeGarmendia, Anita Teresa (7 yrs.) d. on 68-Jul-8 [68-Jul-9: 2B].
DeGaw, Annie E. m. Daicker, Robert T. on 69-Jul-13 [69-Jul-27: 2C].
Degaw, Lovedy (1 yr., 8 mos.) d. on 70-Jul-28 [70-Jul-29: 2B].
Degaw, Tabitha (80 yrs.) d. on 66-Mar-2 [66-Mar-5: 2B].
DeGraw, George L. m. Leonard, Virginia on 68-Jan-1 [68-May-4: 2B].
Dehms, Samuel (36 yrs.) d. on 70-Mar-16 of Heart disease [70-Mar-17: 1H].

Dehn, Louis m. Trumbo, Jane H. on 68-Feb-9 [68-Feb-13: 2C].
DeHoff, George P. m. Deaver, Mary C. on 66-Jun-28 [66-Jul-31: 2C; 66-Aug-1: 2C].
DeHoff, Harry A. (5 mos.) d. on 67-Jul-12 [67-Jul-13: 2B].
DeHoff, J. m. Naill, Bell on 70-Apr-21 [70-Apr-26: 2B].
Deibel, Louis (17 yrs., 11 mos.) d. on 66-Feb-7 [66-Feb-8: 2C; 66-Feb-9: 2C].
Deibel, Maggie m. Megenhardt, Frederick on 66-Oct-9 [66-Oct-16: 2B].
Deibel, Wilhelmine m. Moog, James R. on 68-Dec-22 [68-Dec-25: 2D].
Deichelborer, Michael (32 yrs.) d. on 66-Mar-20 [66-Mar-22: 2B].
Deichmann, Augustus m. Taylor, Amanda P. on 67-May-7 [67-May-11: 2A].
Deigel, Daniel m. Getman, Mary A. on 68-Feb-18 [68-Feb-25: 2C].
Deitch, William m. Green, Jennie on 66-Aug-5 [66-Aug-13: 2C].
Deiter, Caroline (80 yrs.) d. on 70-Oct-30 [70-Oct-31: 2B].
Deitz, Mary Louisa (78 yrs.) d. on 68-Jan-5 [68-Jan-7: 2B].
DeKubber, Jacob m. Newton, Susanna on 66-May-22 [66-May-30: 2C].
Delahay, James C. (55 yrs.) d. on 70-Jul-14 of Suicide (Shooting) [70-Jul-15: 1G; 70-Jul-16: 1F].
Delahaye, Ferdinand (32 yrs.) d. on 70-Apr-23 [70-Apr-25: 2B].
Delaney, Catherine m. Ryder, William on 66-Apr-25 [66-Apr-26: 2B].
Delaney, Charles (1 yr., 7 mos.) d. on 66-May-10 [66-May-11: 2B].
Delaney, Daniel A. (15 yrs.) d. on 66-Jan-5 [66-Jan-10: 2C].
Delaney, James G. (34 yrs.) d. on 69-Jan-4 [69-Jan-30: 2C].
Delaney, Louise m. McGlone, Bernard F. on 69-Nov-25 [69-Dec-18: 2B].
Delaney, Mary Grace (2 yrs., 4 mos.) d. on 66-Apr-15 [66-Apr-17: 2C].
Delaney, Willie Nelson (5 yrs., 2 mos.) d. on 66-Jan-27 [66-Jan-30: 2B].
Delano, Mary A. (69 yrs.) d. on 68-Nov-5 [68-Nov-6: 2C].
Delano, Mary Ann (68 yrs.) d. on 67-Oct-11 [67-Oct-24: 2B].
Delany, Eliza (56 yrs.) d. on 68-Feb-25 [68-Feb-27: 2C].
Delany, James H. m. Delavie, Julia on 68-Sep-1 [68-Sep-3: 2B].
Delaplane, Edmund Hiteshue (6 mos.) d. on 70-Jun-18 [70-Jun-20: 2C].
Delaplane, John (75 yrs.) d. on 68-Feb-10 [68-Feb-15: 2B].
Delavie, Julia m. Delany, James H. on 68-Sep-1 [68-Sep-3: 2B].
Delcher, Anna E. m. Morgan, George M. on 67-Sep-11 [67-Sep-18: 2B].
Delcher, Emma m. Bruscup, William T. on 66-Jul-2 [66-Jul-10: 2C].
Delcher, Maggie J. m. Berry, George W. on 69-Mar-8 [69-Mar-29: 2B].
Delcher, S. C. m. Lainhart, R. D. on 67-Sep-5 [67-Dec-2: 2C].
Delcher, Thomas B. m. Namuth, Mary A. on 66-Sep-11 [66-Sep-15: 2B].
Delcher, William G. (50 yrs.) d. on 69-Feb-6 [69-Feb-8: 2C].
Delevie, Hannah d. on 69-Mar-23 [69-Mar-24: 2C].
Delius, , Mrs. (64 yrs.) d. on 70-Jul-18 of Heart disease [70-Jul-20: 4D].
Dell, H. Virginia m. Burnett, George R. on 67-Sep-17 [67-Sep-21: 2A].
Dell, J. Everett m. Shekell, Margie on 68-Jul-21 [68-Jul-30: 2B].
Dell, L. Gobright m. Phelan, Jennie on 66-Jun-19 [66-Jun-22: 2B].
Dell, Lizzie S. m. Brelsford, H. W. on 70-Jan-5 [70-Jan-8: 2B].
Dell, Mary Corina (11 mos.) d. on 70-Aug-2 [70-Aug-3: 2C].
Dell, Mary Jane d. on 70-Jul-26 [70-Jul-27: 2C; 70-Jul-28: 2C].
Dell, Samuel Lamborn (3 yrs.) d. on 66-Dec-16 [66-Dec-17: 2B].
Dellaplane, Ella m. Nelson, John M. on 68-Oct-20 [68-Oct-21: 2C].
Delphey, Laura V. m. Walter, William H. on 70-May-4 [70-May-10: 2B].
DeMass, Fannie A. m. Smith, Joseph A. on 68-May-28 [68-May-29: 2B].
Demelman, Lina m. Hutzler, Charles on 67-Dec-8 [67-Dec-10: 2B].
Demitz, Rebecca M. m. Sank, James W. on 69-Apr-13 [69-May-10: 2B].
Demmitt, Florence R. m. Tormey, Frank A. on 66-Sep-14 [66-Sep-24: 2B].
DeMoss, David m. Holloway, Jennie on 66-Jun-7 [66-Jun-8: 2B].
Dempsey, Jno. B. m. Barry, Louisa J. on 67-Jun-2 [67-Jun-11: 2B].
Dempsey, Lida m. Bowen, Benson O. on 68-Dec-8 [68-Dec-14: 2C].

Dempsey, Mary (77 yrs.) d. on 67-Dec-26 [67-Dec-27: 2D].
Dempsey, Mary Louise m. Boyd, Joseph B. on 66-Dec-18 [66-Dec-24: 2B].
Dempsey, Sarah Jane (47 yrs.) d. on 67-Feb-7 [67-Feb-9: 2B; 67-Feb-11: 2C].
Dempsey, Warren Sherman (6 yrs.) d. on 70-Aug-24 [70-Aug-29: 2C].
Demuth, G. O. m. Willis, Elizabeth H. on 67-Nov-21 [67-Nov-23: 2B].
DeMuth, George M. D. (22 yrs.) d. on 67-Dec-2 [67-Dec-6: 2C].
DeMuth, Hester A. m. Bullen, Henry on 66-Dec-27 [67-Jan-8: 2B].
Denbow, Annie E. m. Tuder, Joseph H. on 70-Aug-29 [70-Aug-31: 2B].
Denby, Rebecca J. m. Dorsey, Evan L. on 66-Nov-27 [66-Dec-1: 2B].
Denby, William L. m. McKewen, Ella on 67-Sep-8 [67-Dec-27: 2D].
Denehey, Jennie (52 yrs.) d. on 66-Apr-26 [66-Apr-28: 2A].
Denig, E. C. m. Crane, S. E. F. on 70-Oct-4 [70-Oct-10: 2B].
Deninger, J. B. m. Taylor, Mollie on 67-Jun-11 [67-Jun-21: 2B].
Denison, Ann Eliza (54 yrs.) d. on 68-Sep-7 [68-Sep-8: 2B].
Denison, Eliza J. m. Ortlip, Malon on 66-Mar-18 [66-Mar-20: 2C].
Denison, Henry C. (36 yrs.) d. on 70-Aug-18 of Typhoid [70-Aug-19: 2C, 4D].
Denison, Mary Carroll (28 yrs.) d. on 68-Apr-22 [68-Apr-23: 2B; 68-Apr-24: 2B].
Denison, Matilda J. m. Griffin, W. Hunter on 68-Feb-6 [68-Feb-10: 2C].
Denkel, Valentine (65 yrs.) d. on 66-May-6 [66-May-7: 2B].
Denkin, Mary Ann (30 yrs.) d. on 68-Aug-16 [68-Aug-18: 2B].
Denkin, William (14 yrs.) d. on 70-Jul-6 [70-Jul-7: 2B].
Denman, Henry, Capt. (28 yrs.) d. on 69-Jun-21 [69-Jun-28: 2C].
Denmead, Clara m. Miller, William A. on 69-Jul-20 [69-Jul-22: 2C].
Denmead, Henry, Jr. (69 yrs.) d. on 68-Dec-14 [68-Dec-16: 2C; 68-Dec-17: 2C].
Denmead, Howard Johnson (2 yrs., 2 mos.) d. on 68-May-29 [68-Jun-2: 2B].
Denmead, Lizzie A. m. Groff, Benjamin F. on 70-Apr-19 [70-Apr-26: 2B].
Denmead, Martha E. m. Cowan, William on 68-Nov-26 [68-Dec-30: 2C].
Denmead, Olivia (81 yrs., 3 mos.) d. on 68-Jul-11 [68-Jul-13: 2B].
Denne, Charles H. m. Currey, A. Rebecca on 68-Dec-24 [68-Dec-28: 2B].
Denney, Peter (57 yrs.) d. on 67-Aug-20 [67-Aug-22: 2B].
Dennie, Thomas d. on 68-Jan-24 [68-Feb-26: 2C].
Denning, Charles m. Robinson, Georgiana on 68-Feb-19 [68-Feb-20: 2C].
Dennis, Andrew T. m. McKey, Eliza on 67-Oct-17 [67-Oct-19: 2A].
Dennis, Benjamin Lamane (2 mos.) d. on 67-Sep-2 [67-Sep-3: 2B].
Dennis, Cora Grace (2 yrs., 4 mos.) d. on 67-May-15 [67-May-16: 2B].
Dennis, Elenor m. Leaf, George on 68-Oct-29 [68-Nov-3: 2B].
Dennis, Emma T. (1 yr., 5 mos.) d. on 66-Jan-23 [66-Jan-24: 2B].
Dennis, Emory (59 yrs.) d. on 67-Jan-7 [67-Jan-8: 2B].
Dennis, Frederick Columbus (85 yrs.) d. on 67-Dec-3 [67-Dec-4: 2C; 67-Dec-5: 1G, 2C].
Dennis, John m. Meyers, Kate on 66-Dec-17 [66-Dec-19: 2B].
Dennis, John L. m. Hammond, Henrietta on 70-Sep-22 [70-Sep-24: 2B].
Dennis, Joseph Robb (5 yrs.) d. on 69-May-10 of Scarlet fever [69-May-11: 2B].
Dennis, Kate J. m. Loane, William T. Valiant on 66-Oct-25 [66-Nov-29: 2B].
Dennis, L. Q. m. Martin, S. E. on 68-Jan-29 [68-Feb-1: 2B].
Dennis, Mary E. (41 yrs.) d. on 66-Nov-30 of Consumption [66-Dec-11: 2B].
Dennis, Mary E. m. Weekes, Charles on 67-Nov-19 [67-Nov-20: 2C].
Dennis, Mary J. m. Wirth, Andrew on 69-May-18 [69-May-15: 2C].
Dennis, Naomi S. m. Smith, A. A. on 67-Jul-30 [67-Aug-1: 2C].
Dennis, Rebecca J. Bonn (3 mos.) d. on 68-Oct-28 [68-Oct-29: 2C].
Dennis, William (5 mos.) d. on 66-May-6 [66-May-8: 2B].
Dennison, Ann (48 yrs.) d. on 67-Jul-7 [67-Jul-8: 2C].
Denny, Charles F. m. Griffin, Sarah H. on 67-Oct-10 [67-Oct-15: 2A].
Denny, Frank Shaw (6 mos.) d. [67-Feb-9: 2B].
Denny, James W. m. Wiggins, Mary E. on 70-Dec-14 [70-Dec-23: 2B].
Denny, Mary F. m. Brown, William H. on 66-Oct-4 [66-Oct-12: 2B].

Denny, Richard W. m. Spencer, Eliza C. on 69-Dec-21 [69-Dec-23: 2B].
Denoe, Washington B. (29 yrs.) d. on 69-Aug-8 of Bilious fever [69-Aug-31: 2B].
Denson, Elizabeth (55 yrs.) d. on 67-May-5 [67-May-6: 2B].
Denson, James H. (56 yrs.) d. on 61-Nov-27 [66-Jul-9: 2C].
Denson, Lizzie m. Herron, George S. on 70-Oct-13 [70-Oct-27: 2B].
Denson, Maria E. (75 yrs.) d. on 69-Feb-26 [69-Mar-1: 2C].
Denton, Basil B. m. Biscoe, Susie V. on 68-Mar-26 [68-Apr-1: 2C].
Denton, Wilson m. Mitchel, Margaret G. on 68-Mar-24 [68-Mar-27: 2C].
Dentz, Simon m. Winkler, Catharine on 68-Oct-12 [68-Oct-13: 2C].
Dentzel, Henry H. d. on 69-Aug-4 [69-Aug-5: 2B].
Dentzell, Imogene A. d. on 69-May-23 [69-May-25: 2C].
Denvir, Mary (47 yrs.) d. on 67-Jan-3 [67-Jan-4: 2D; 67-Jan-5: 2C].
DePaepe, C. m. Lohmuller, D. on 68-Nov-3 [68-Nov-6: 2C].
DePaepe, Matilda C. (16 yrs., 11 mos.) d. on 67-Jul-7 [67-Jul-11: 2C; 67-Dec-25: 2C].
DePass, John (57 yrs.) d. on 70-Aug-26 [70-Aug-29: 2C].
Depkin, Elizabeth M. (2 yrs., 4 mos.) d. on 70-Jan-11 [70-Jan-13: 2D].
Depoe, Kate m. Brown, Randolph R. on 70-Jun-16 [70-Jun-25: 2D].
Deppish, Francis m. Quigley, Mary on 68-Dec-6 [69-Feb-22: 2C].
Derenberger, Henry m. Finnigan, Alice on 68-Apr-21 [68-Jun-6: 2A].
DeRinzie, E. Horton m. Spencer, M. A. on 70-May-19 [70-May-20: 2C].
Derks, Benjamin d. on 70-May-4 Drowned [70-May-7: 1H].
DeRonceray, Jennie d. on 69-Jan-25 [69-Jan-27: 2C].
Derr, Ann Elizabeth (43 yrs.) d. on 69-Jan-31 [69-Feb-1: 2C].
Derr, Samuel B. m. Ruckle, Jennie on 66-Apr-1 [66-Apr-3: 2B].
Derr, William Henry (24 yrs., 6 mos.) d. on 70-Jun-21 [70-Jun-22: 2C].
Derrenberger, George d. on 69-Feb-1 [69-Feb-8: 2C].
Derricks, Harriet R. m. Stevens, James E. on 69-May-19 [69-May-20: 2C].
Derry, William (9 yrs.) d. on 66-Apr-2 in Wagon accident [66-Apr-4: 1G, 2B].
Desch, Peter (40 yrs.) d. on 66-Mar-11 [66-Mar-12: 2B].
DeShields, George H. (17 yrs.) d. on 66-Jul-9 [66-Jul-10: 2C].
Deshields, Olivia F. m. Hoffman, J. L. on 68-Jun-9 [68-Oct-16: 2B].
Deshon, Estelle Mailland m. King, John on 67-Oct-17 [67-Oct-21: 2B].
Despeaux, Anthony (71 yrs.) d. on 68-Feb-9 [68-Feb-11: 1G, 2C].
Despeaux, Antony, Jr. m. Bobart, Eliza Ann on 66-Feb-1 [66-Feb-6: 2D].
Despeaux, Charles H. m. Joseph, Annie on 68-Aug-27 [68-Sep-3: 2B].
Despeaux, Henry J. (45 yrs.) d. on 66-Oct-13 [66-Oct-15: 2B].
Destimonia, Amy m. Gent, Richard C. on 69-Aug-9 [69-Sep-16: 2B].
Deter, Charles Oscor (14 yrs., 2 mos.) d. on 69-Mar-4 [69-Mar-6: 2C].
Dettmer, H. m. Wimmer, Anna M. on 67-Oct-8 [67-Oct-12: 2A].
Deubler, O. K. m. McCusker, L. C. on 67-Dec-18 [67-Dec-25: 2C].
Devall, Cordelia A. m. Barker, William F. on 69-Aug-3 [69-Sep-4: 2B].
Dever, Annie m. Kimble, Alfred W. on 69-Jan-12 [69-Jan-21: 2C].
DeVere, Anna Clay m. Ball, David C. on 67-Nov-7 [67-Nov-9: 2B].
Devese, Charles M. (8 yrs.) d. on 70-Dec-21 [70-Dec-23: 2B].
Devinney, William (1 yr., 3 mos.) d. on 67-Nov-1 [67-Nov-2: 2B].
Deviter, Jane F. (81 yrs.) d. on 70-Sep-16 [70-Sep-17: 2B].
Devitt, Elizabeth d. on 69-May-10 [69-May-18: 2C].
Devitt, P. H. (1 mo.) d. on 68-Dec-28 [69-Jan-4: 2C].
Devlain, James m. Meagher, Sarah on 70-Jun-9 [70-Jun-10: 2B].
Devlin, Felix P. (50 yrs.) d. on 66-Jul-3 [66-Jul-4: 2B].
Devlin, Joanna Kelly (23 yrs.) d. on 69-Jan-10 [69-Jan-12: 2C].
Devlin, Joseph m. Carter, Amelia F. on 66-Apr-25 [66-Apr-27: 2C].
Devlin, Mary Ann m. Burton, William on 66-Aug-15 [66-Aug-23: 2C].
Devouges, Alphonse m. O'Farrell, Teresa on 69-Dec-30 [70-Jan-14: 2C].
Devouges, Eugenie E. m. O'Farrell, Charles on 68-Dec-29 [69-Jan-4: 2C].

Devries, Cornelia d. [66-Jul-28: 2C].
Dew, John Walter (2 yrs., 3 mos.) d. on 70-Jun-9 [70-Jun-10: 2B].
Dew, Joshua S. m. Hall, Lucretia on 70-Jan-1 [70-Jan-3: 2C].
Dew, Walter John (23 yrs.) d. on 70-May-2 [70-May-3: 2B].
Dewalt, J. Christopher (54 yrs.) d. on 66-Sep-27 of Dysentery [66-Oct-1: 2B; 66-Oct-8: 2B].
DeWalt, John C. m. Remmey, Isabel A. on 66-Jun-14 [66-Jun-23: 2B].
DeWitt, Juliana d. on 66-Jun-6 [66-Jun-8: 2B].
Dewlin, Andrew Jackson (50 yrs.) d. on 70-Jul-22 [70-Jul-29: 2C].
Dewling, Christina (50 yrs., 4 mos.) d. on 69-Feb-1 [69-Feb-3: 2C].
Dews, Zack, Jr. m. Shackelford, Mollie E. on 70-Dec-22 [70-Dec-28: 2C].
Diamond, George H. m. Ford, Mollie E. on 66-Sep-6 [66-Sep-12: 2A].
Diamond, Jane B. (67 yrs.) d. on 66-Jul-8 [66-Jul-10: 2C].
Diamond, Rebecca Jane (7 mos.) d. on 70-Jun-21 [70-Jun-22: 2C].
Diblee, Robert m. Egerton, Clara S. on 69-Jan-27 [69-Jan-29: 2C].
Dice, Ella Roszell d. on 66-May-31 [66-Jun-7: 2B].
Dickens, Mary C. m. Jones, Thomas F. on 66-Nov-11 [66-Nov-22: 2C].
Dickerson, George W. m. Burnside, Jane on 69-Jul-7 [69-Jul-8: 2C].
Dickerson, Henry S. (45 yrs.) d. on 69-Sep-2 [69-Sep-4: 1H].
Dickerson, Juliet M. (52 yrs.) d. on 67-Feb-10 [67-Feb-13: 2D; 67-Feb-12: 2C].
Dickerson, Lillie Heath (1 yr.) d. on 67-Nov-28 [67-Nov-30: 2C].
Dickerson, Rebecca E. (47 yrs.) d. on 68-Jul-23 [68-Jul-24: 2C; 68-Jul-25: 2B].
Dickey, Emma Estella Opie (2 mos.) d. on 66-Mar-21 [66-Mar-22: 2B].
Dickey, George S. (71 yrs.) d. on 69-May-28 [69-May-29: 2B].
Dickey, W. W. m. Jackson, Sarah E. on 66-Oct-23 [66-Oct-25: 2C].
Dickey, William Henry Richard (1 mo.) d. on 67-Jun-22 [67-Jun-24: 2B].
Dickinson, E. Harvey (33 yrs.) d. on 70-Feb-8 Drowned [70-Mar-30: 2B].
Dickinson, Nellie Worthington (8 mos.) d. on 67-May-27 [67-May-29: 2B].
Dickinson, Susie m. Hiss, Benjamin S. on 69-May-2 [69-May-7: 2C].
Dickson, Harriet A. m. Brown, B. Peyton on 69-Apr-20 [69-Apr-21: 2B].
Dickson, Issac N., Jr. (10 mos.) d. on 69-Jul-12 [69-Aug-3: 2C].
Dickson, James (75 yrs.) d. on 67-Nov-4 [67-Nov-5: 2B].
Dickson, James Howard (8 mos.) d. on 68-Jul-7 [68-Jul-10: 2C].
Dickson, John (59 yrs.) d. on 68-Mar-30 [68-Apr-2: 2C].
Dickson, Kate m. Charles, George C. on 67-May-25 [67-Jun-6: 2B].
Dickson, Martha (60 yrs.) d. on 70-Feb-8 [70-Feb-10: 2C].
Dickson, William (87 yrs.) d. on 69-Nov-25 [69-Nov-27: 2C].
Dickson, William m. Watchman, Fanny on 66-Dec-24 [67-Mar-28: 2B].
Dicus, James A. m. McDaniel, Kate G. on 69-Apr-20 [69-May-8: 2B].
Didenhover, Mary A. m. Poulton, Robert A. on 67-Dec-31 [68-Jan-11: 2B].
Dieckman, Lizzie m. Tietgen, Charles on 67-Oct-29 [67-Nov-12: 2C].
Diehl, John m. Fremin, M. L. on 66-Sep-11 [66-Sep-14: 2B].
Diehl, John m. Stoner, Mary J. on 70-Dec-1 [70-Dec-3: 2B].
Diehl, Theodore m. Usilton, Esther A. on 70-Dec-9 [70-Dec-28: 2C].
Diering, John Henry (1 yr., 6 mos.) d. on 70-Aug-25 [70-Aug-29: 2C].
Dieterly, Emma (10 mos.) d. on 68-Jul-25 [68-Jul-27: 2B].
Dietrich, Christiane d. on 66-Nov-15 [66-Nov-16: 2C].
Dietrick, John B. (31 yrs., 3 mos.) d. on 67-Feb-12 of Heart disease [67-Feb-13: 1F; 67-Feb-14: 2C].
Dietz, G. Jacob (43 yrs.) d. on 70-May-25 [70-May-26: 2C; 70-May-27: 2B].
Dietz, George P. (39 yrs.) d. on 69-May-23 [69-May-24: 2B].
Dietz, John M. (37 yrs.) d. on 69-Nov-28 [69-Nov-29: 2C].
Diffenbach, W. H. H. m. Swenk, Annie on 66-Jul-19 [66-Jul-26: 2C].
Diffenbaugh, John m. Eggleston, Annie on 66-Mar-5 [66-Mar-7: 2B].
Diffenderfer, Mary m. Tipton, J. Emory on 69-Nov-3 [69-Nov-6: 2C].
Diffenderfer, Michael D. m. Talbot, Rebecca A. on 69-Jun-2 [69-Jun-11: 2C].

Diffenderffer, Anna Mary (9 mos.) d. on 66-Jun-24 [66-Jun-25: 2B; 66-Jun-26: 2B].
Diffenderffer, Elizabeth (80 yrs.) d. on 66-Nov-10 [66-Nov-12: 2C].
Diffenderffer, Ellen Rich (6 yrs., 5 mos.) d. on 66-Feb-27 of Typhoid [66-Mar-19: 2C].
Diffenderffer, H. H. m. Bayley, Mary R. on 66-Nov-20 [66-Nov-23: 2C].
Diffenderffer, Harry Lee (4 yrs.) d. on 66-Dec-14 [66-Dec-18: 2B].
Diffenderffer, Harvey B. Nash (1 yr., 8 mos.) d. on 70-Jan-11 [70-Jan-12: 2C].
Diffenderffer, James T. m. Murphy, Mary on 66-Jun-13 [66-Jun-15: 2C].
Diffenderffer, M. Natalie (2 yrs., 8 mos.) d. on 70-Jan-3 of Scarlet fever [70-Jan-4: 2C; 70-Jan-12: 2C].
Diffenderffer, Michael, Dr. (81 yrs.) d. on 70-Sep-17 [70-Sep-19: 2B].
Diffenderffer, Salome Decker (5 yrs., 6 mos.) d. on 66-Sep-23 [66-Sep-26: 2B].
Diffey, Alexander (94 yrs.) d. on 69-Apr-24 [69-Apr-29: 2C].
Diffey, Susie V. m. Walters, James E. on 70-Dec-8 [70-Dec-14: 2C].
Diffily, Michael (42 yrs.) d. on 67-Aug-13 [67-Aug-14: 2B].
Diffley, John Thomas (10 mos.) d. on 67-Sep-6 [67-Sep-7: 2A].
Diggs, Annie Virginia (6 mos.) d. on 70-Jun-23 [70-Jun-24: 2C].
Diggs, Charles F. m. Hall, Camilla F. on 70-Oct-25 [70-Oct-27: 2B].
Diggs, Eliza m. Bridges, Munroe on 70-Jun-22 [70-Jun-28: 2C].
Diggs, Henry S. m. Cunningham, M. Augusta on 68-Jan-30 [68-Feb-3: 2C].
Diggs, Josephine B. (37 yrs.) d. on 67-Mar-10 [67-Mar-11: 2C; 67-Mar-12: 2C].
Diggs, Julia F. (12 yrs., 8 mos.) d. on 69-Nov-19 [69-Nov-20: 2B].
Diggs, Kate B. m. Harrison, Samuel on 69-Jan-14 [69-Jan-20: 2C].
Diggs, Louisa (45 yrs.) d. on 70-Feb-9 of Lockjaw [70-Feb-11: 4E].
Dignan, James L. (1 yr., 11 mos.) d. on 69-Mar-9 [69-Mar-10: 2C].
Dignan, Lawrence (2 yrs., 1 mo.) d. on 66-Sep-26 [66-Sep-27: 2C].
Dignan, Sallie m. Nixon, John on 66-Apr-5 [66-Apr-30: 2B].
Dignan, Thomas (9 mos.) d. on 70-Feb-13 [70-Feb-14: 2C].
Dignen, Lawrence V. (23 yrs.) d. on 68-Jan-17 [68-Jan-18: 2B].
Dignen, Mary Elizabeth d. on 69-Jun-23 [69-Jun-24: 2C].
Dike, Edward G. m. Thomas, Kate on 66-Dec-24 [66-Dec-27: 2C].
Dikes, William H. m. Riggs, Fanny on 68-Aug-11 [68-Aug-12: 2C].
Dill, Catharine J. m. Sachs, Mell on 67-Sep-24 [67-Sep-25: 2B].
Dill, M. Catherine m. Small, Frank R. on 67-Oct-23 [67-Oct-25: 2B].
Dillaway, Genevieve m. Watts, George O. on 69-Oct-28 [69-Nov-4: 2B].
Dillenger, John (28 yrs.) d. on 70-Jun-12 Drowned [70-Jun-13: 1H; 70-Jun-15: 1G].
Dillerhide, Frances (72 yrs.) d. on 69-Jun-22 of Apoplexy [69-Jun-23: 1G, 2C].
Dillow, Ellen Virginia (6 mos.) d. on 67-Aug-5 [67-Aug-7: 2C].
Dils, Charles B. m. Duwees, Lizzie S. on 69-Jun-24 [69-Nov-9: 2C].
Dilts, George S. (1 mo.) d. on 70-Aug-3 [70-Aug-6: 2C].
Dilworth, Jeremiah m. Murray, Sarah on 68-Jan-19 [68-Jan-29: 2C].
Diment, James C. m. Hanberry, Eliza on 69-Dec-13 [69-Dec-14: 2C].
Diment, Susan M. m. Pomroy, Charles H. on 70-Dec-5 [70-Dec-7: 2C].
Dimmitt, Nellie (8 yrs.) d. on 66-Nov-24 [66-Nov-26: 2B].
Dimmock, Charles W. m. Webb, Emma D. on 70-Feb-10 [70-Feb-12: 2B].
Dimond, Ann E. (89 yrs.) d. on 67-Feb-5 [67-Feb-7: 2C].
Dingle, Louisa m. Baker, W. Henry on 66-Jul-30 [66-Aug-10: 2C].
Dinmore, Christopher (29 yrs.) d. on 69-Sep-20 [69-Sep-22: 2C].
Dinsmore, George (24 yrs.) d. on 67-Sep-9 of Cholera [68-Apr-4: 2B].
Dinsmore, James J. (47 yrs.) d. on 70-Dec-23 [70-Dec-26: 2C].
Dinsmore, John m. Cleary, Elizabeth B. on 66-Jun-24 [66-Jul-14: 2B].
Dishler, Antone (47 yrs.) d. on 70-Jul-24 of Heatstroke [70-Jul-25: 4D].
Disney, Andrew J. m. Miles, Harriet V. on 66-Feb-22 [66-Mar-5: 2B].
Disney, Anna Theresa (11 yrs., 4 mos.) d. on 70-Aug-30 [70-Aug-31: 2B; 70-Sep-1: 2B].
Disney, Benjamin m. Gibbons, Martha on 66-Mar-20 [66-Mar-22: 2B].
Disney, Benjamin F. m. Downs, Sarah E. on 67-Jan-31 [67-Feb-18: 2C].

Disney, Deborah (72 yrs.) d. on 66-Mar-25 [66-Mar-27: 2B].
Disney, Ellen R. (28 yrs.) d. on 68-Apr-29 [68-Apr-30: 2B; 68-May-1: 2B].
Disney, Hannah A. m. Rennolds, Lindsay H on 70-May-17 [70-May-19: 2C].
Disney, John W. (47 yrs.) d. on 67-Feb-6 [67-Feb-8: 2C].
Disney, John W. m. Rumney, Alice on 66-Feb-20 [66-Feb-23: 2C].
Disney, Joseph A. m. Goodrick, Laura on 69-Mar-30 [69-Apr-2: 2C].
Disney, Lizzie A. m. Zimmerman, George R. on 69-Nov-25 [69-Nov-27: 2B].
Disney, Luther Widerman (1 yr., 2 mos.) d. on 68-Jul-28 [68-Jul-29: 2B].
Disney, Maria E. m. Lowman, Nicholas on 67-Mar-7 [67-Mar-8: 2C].
Disney, Mary A. m. Brown, William C. on 68-Sep-19 [68-Sep-30: 2B].
Disney, Mary Elizabeth (17 yrs.) d. on 67-Sep-25 [67-Sep-26: 2B].
Disney, Mary R. (13 yrs., 4 mos.) d. on 69-Sep-7 [69-Sep-8: 2B].
Disney, Nelson K. m. Blakeny, Elizabeth R. on 70-Oct-20 [70-Oct-22: 2B].
Disney, Rachel m. Stephens, David N. on 70-Oct-6 [70-Oct-7: 2B].
Disney, Samuel m. Peddicord, Amelia on 69-Mar-4 [69-Mar-8: 2C].
Disney, Stirling T. (24 yrs.) d. on 70-Nov-28 [70-Nov-30: 2C].
Disney, Stirling T. m. McMillen, Sarah A. on 66-Nov-29 [67-Oct-2: 2B].
Disney, Wesley (75 yrs.) d. on 68-May-10 [68-May-11: 1F, 2B].
Disney, William S. m. Crozier, Annie M. on 70-Jun-2 [70-Jun-17: 2B].
Disus, James (50 yrs.) d. on 66-Aug-7 [66-Aug-9: 2C].
Dittman, Edward F. (30 yrs.) d. on 68-Feb-27 [68-Feb-29: 2B; 68-Mar-2: 2B].
Dittman, George W. (19 yrs.) d. on 70-Jul-24 Drowned [70-Jul-25: 4E, 2C; 70-Jul-27: 4D].
Dittman, John H., Sr. (61 yrs.) d. on 68-Jun-6 [68-Jun-8: 2B].
Dittman, Susan R. (36 yrs.) d. on 70-Apr-5 [70-Apr-7: 2B; 70-Apr-8: 2C].
Dittus, Thomas F. m. Keller, Hester L. on 68-Oct-29 [68-Nov-4: 2C].
Ditty, C. Irving m. Schwartz, Sophia L. on 68-Oct-1 [68-Oct-5: 2B].
Ditzell, Maggie m. Woollen, Thomas on 67-Mar-11 [67-Apr-15: 2B].
Diven, Katie A. (15 yrs.) d. on 68-Apr-3 [68-Apr-4: 2B].
Diven, Laura V. m. Thompson, Owen on 68-Dec-29 [69-Jan-1: 2C].
Diviny, Catherine (2 yrs.) d. on 69-Oct-27 [69-Oct-28: 2C].
Diviny, Ellen (37 yrs.) d. on 70-Mar-28 [70-Mar-30: 2B].
Dix, Edward H. (51 yrs.) d. on 69-Apr-11 [69-Apr-13: 2B].
Dix, Thomas H. (34 yrs.) d. on 69-May-30 [69-May-31: 2C].
Dix, William W. (62 yrs.) d. on 66-Jun-14 [66-Jun-15: 2C].
Dixon, Amanda m. Montgomery, Joseph Charles on 66-Jul-10 [66-Jul-12: 2C].
Dixon, Annie E. m. Wilson, George H. on 70-Oct-18 [70-Dec-6: 2C].
Dixon, Bridget (63 yrs.) d. on 68-Sep-19 [68-Sep-21: 2B].
Dixon, Clara Idella (8 yrs.) d. on 68-Nov-14 [68-Nov-16: 2C].
Dixon, George R. (35 yrs.) d. on 67-May-20 [67-May-27: 2B].
Dixon, Georgia Helen m. Bright, John F. on 66-Dec-20 [67-Jan-17: 2C].
Dixon, Issac F., Jr. (26 yrs.) d. on 70-May-30 of Typhoid [70-May-31: 2B; 70-Jun-1: 2B].
Dixon, James, Jr. (28 yrs.) d. on 67-Feb-11 [67-Feb-13: 2D].
Dixon, James U. m. Bowen, Sarah E. on 69-Feb-18 [69-Feb-20: 2A].
Dixon, John H. m. Green, Jennie on 68-Dec-15 [68-Dec-17: 2C].
Dixon, John N. d. on 69-Apr-12 [69-Apr-13: 2B].
Dixon, Joseph C. (2 yrs., 10 mos.) d. on 68-Sep-27 [68-Sep-29: 2B].
Dixon, Lizzie A. m. Hopkins, Issac F. on 69-Dec-21 [69-Dec-30: 2C].
Dixon, Lizzie Richards (44 yrs., 10 mos.) d. on 67-May-27 [67-Jun-5: 2B].
Dixon, Mary E. (2 yrs., 6 mos.) d. on 67-Sep-5 of Gunshot wound [67-Sep-6: 4C].
Dixon, Mary T. (24 yrs.) d. on 67-Sep-10 [67-Sep-11: 2B].
Dixon, Matthew (24 yrs.) d. on 66-Sep-11 [66-Sep-12: 2A].
Dixon, Nicholas Edward (10 mos.) d. on 66-Aug-2 [66-Aug-4: 2C].
Dixon, Patrick (30 yrs.) d. on 67-Dec-2 [67-Dec-3: 2C].
Dixon, Sarah A. m. Decker, Lewis on 69-Apr-19 [69-Apr-23: 2B].
Dixon, Sarah E. (36 yrs.) d. on 69-Aug-20 [69-Aug-26: 2C].

Dixon, Sydney d. on 68-Jul-19 Drowned [68-Jul-21: 4E].
Dixon, Thomas m. Freeman, Rebecca H. on 68-Nov-5 [68-Nov-7: 2B].
Dixon, W. A. m. Henderson, Caroline E. [68-Jul-9: 2B].
Dixon, William m. Gilpin, Arabella on 70-Oct-14 [70-Oct-17: 2B].
Dixon, William T. m. Oudesluys, Mary W. on 69-Nov-4 [69-Nov-8: 2C].
Dixson, David m. O'Donnell, S. A. on 69-Feb-4 [69-May-11: 2B].
Dobaker, Adam (86 yrs.) d. on 70-Dec-26 [70-Dec-28: 2C, 4D].
Dobbin, George Leonard (26 yrs.) d. on 67-Sep-5 [67-Sep-6: 2B, 4B].
Dobbin, Mary A. (48 yrs.) d. on 70-Jul-11 [70-Jul-12: 2B; 70-Jul-13: 2C].
Dobbin, Robert Lee (2 yrs., 7 mos.) d. [68-Jul-16: 2C].
Dobbs, Mary V. m. Fricker, John A. on 70-Jun-21 [70-Jun-23: 2C].
Doberer, Gottlieb m. Schaible, Amelia W. on 66-May-24 [66-May-28: 2B].
Doberer, John (58 yrs., 2 mos.) d. on 66-Mar-1 [66-Mar-2: 2B; 66-Mar-3: 2B].
Dobins, Mary Anne m. Orme, Thomas P. on 68-Jan-30 [68-Feb-3: 2C].
Dobler, Barbara (53 yrs.) d. on 66-Jul-30 [66-Jul-31: 2C].
Dobler, Daniel, Mrs. (65 yrs.) d. on 67-Jun-17 [67-Jun-18: 2B].
Dobler, David, Jr. m. Folkes, Elizabeth C. on 70-Dec-1 [70-Dec-3: 2B].
Dobler, Maria J. m. Schumacher, James R. on 66-Feb-13 [66-Feb-28: 2C].
Dobler, Mary Ann (48 yrs.) d. [70-Jul-2: 2B].
Dobson, Daniel H. (24 yrs., 3 mos.) d. on 68-Jun-5 [68-Jun-22: 2B].
Dobson, Daniel H. m. Krause, Mary Virginia on 68-Mar-9 [68-Mar-11: 2B].
Dobson, George H. m. Bailey, Isabella M. on 70-Feb-16 [70-Feb-21: 2B; 70-Feb-22: 2C].
Dobson, George W. (20 yrs.) d. on 70-Apr-26 [70-Apr-27: 2B].
Dobson, John m. Floyd, Matilda C. on 67-Jan-17 [67-Jan-19: 2C].
Dobson, Lebby (80 yrs.) d. on 67-Jan-15 [67-Jan-17: 2C].
Dobson, Martha L. (27 yrs.) d. on 66-Jun-13 [66-Jun-15: 2C; 66-Jun-16: 2B].
Dobson, Mary V. m. Baker, Robert J. on 69-May-16 [69-Jun-8: 2B].
Dobson, Sallie J. m. Ould, Perry on 68-Jul-22 [68-Jul-24: 2C].
Dockerty, Mary E. m. Sheckles, Cephas H. on 68-Jul-9 [68-Jul-14: 2B].
Dockstader, Sanford I. m. Love, Florence L. on 67-Sep-5 [67-Sep-7: 2A].
Dodd, Catharine (68 yrs.) d. on 70-Mar-23 of Pneumonia [70-Mar-24: 2C].
Dodd, Martha Ann (16 yrs.) d. on 70-Nov-27 [70-Nov-29: 2C].
Dodd, Mary E. (36 yrs.) d. on 70-Feb-15 of Pneumonia [70-Feb-17: 2C].
Dodd, Orson Gore (7 mos.) d. on 70-Jun-16 of Cholera infantum [70-Jun-18: 2B].
Dodd, Thomas S. (30 yrs.) d. on 66-Feb-10 [66-Feb-12: 2D].
Dode, Eulena (88 yrs.) d. on 68-Mar-4 [68-Mar-5: 2C].
Dode, Josephine d. on 70-May-19 [70-May-21: 2B].
Dode, Peter (86 yrs.) d. on 66-May-23 [66-May-24: 2C].
Dodge, George R. (58 yrs.) d. on 66-Aug-9 [66-Aug-10: 1G, 2C; 66-Aug-11: 2B; 66-Aug-13: 1G].
Dodge, J. Heath m. Conrad, May L. on 70-Sep-28 [70-Oct-4: 2B].
Dodge, Lois Adela m. Ely, Jesse F. on 70-Jun-16 [70-Jun-24: 2C].
Dodge, Mollie m. M'Cauley, W. S. on 66-Jun-21 [66-Jun-23: 2B].
Dodge, Orestes Lettel (2 yrs., 4 mos.) d. on 69-Feb-7 [69-Feb-9: 2C].
Dods, Elizabeth (81 yrs.) d. on 66-Dec-11 [66-Dec-12: 2B].
Dodson, Amelia J. m. Ridgway, D. C. on 67-Jul-11 [67-Jul-15: 2C].
Dodson, C. Marion m. Bangs, M. Virginia on 69-Jan-27 [69-Jan-30: 2C].
Dodson, C. R. m. Kavanaugh, Berrie on 70-Mar-1 [70-Mar-11: 2C].
Dodson, Peter m. Humphries, Mary Ann on 69-Nov-10 [69-Nov-12: 2C].
Dodville, Caroline (78 yrs.) d. on 70-Sep-16 [70-Sep-20: 2B].
Doe, Sammy W. (6 yrs., 5 mos.) d. on 70-Jun-27 [70-Jul-18: 2B].
Doenges, Elizabeth (7 mos.) d. on 66-Jul-16 [66-Jul-17: 2C].
Doenges, Fred J. m. Miller, Mary E. on 70-Jun-14 [70-Jun-24: 2C].
Doerr, Louisa (28 yrs.) d. on 68-Mar-17 [68-Mar-20: 2B].
Doft, Mary I. (38 yrs.) d. on 67-Dec-9 [67-Dec-11: 2B].

Doged, Almira G. m. Smith, Cyrus A. on 70-Mar-24 [70-Mar-29: 2C].
Doged, Eliza d. on 69-Feb-16 [69-Feb-17: 2C].
Doged, James S. (17 yrs., 6 mos.) d. on 70-Apr-3 [70-Apr-4: 2B; 70-Apr-5: 2B].
Doged, M. Harrison (26 yrs.) d. on 66-Feb-26 [66-Feb-28: 2C].
Doged, Sallie E. m. McGrath, H. J. on 69-Mar-11 [69-Mar-12: 2C].
Dohm, Elizabeth J. m. Butler, Charles on 68-Nov-24 [68-Dec-3: 2C].
Dohme, Charles E. m. Schulz, Ida on 66-Apr-5 [66-Apr-6: 2B].
Doize, Celina (24 yrs.) d. on 67-Oct-1 of Yellow fever [67-Oct-8: 2B].
Doize, Henriette Marie d. on 67-Sep-22 of Yellow fever [67-Sep-28: 2A].
Dolan, James, Rev. (56 yrs.) d. on 70-Jan-12 [70-Jan-13: 2B, 2D; 70-Jan-14: 1G, 2C].
Dolan, John m. Malone, Mary V. on 69-Mar-18 [69-Jul-8: 2C].
Dolan, Mary Virginia m. Murphy, Owen J. on 70-Sep-8 [70-Oct-15: 2B].
Dolan, Patrick (40 yrs.) d. on 68-Jan-15 [68-Jan-17: 2C].
Dolan, Thomas (15 yrs.) d. on 70-Jun-19 Drowned [70-Jun-20: 1H, 2B].
Dolan, Valentine (54 yrs.) d. on 70-Jul-4 [70-Jul-6: 2C].
Doland, John (33 yrs.) d. on 67-Apr-3 [67-Apr-4: 2B].
Dolbow, Reuben N. m. Taylor, Anna E. on 67-Jan-18 [67-Jan-19: 2C].
Doleman, George H. (25 yrs.) d. on 67-Sep-4 [67-Sep-5: 2B].
Dolen, James (53 yrs.) d. on 69-Jul-9 [69-Jul-15: 2C].
Doll, Helen S. m. Bratt, James E. on 69-Jul-5 [69-Jul-13: 2C].
Doll, Jane E. d. on 68-Feb-26 [68-Feb-28: 2D].
Doll, John W. m. Brown, Maggie E. on 69-Aug-3 [70-Mar-10: 2C].
Dollan, Michael (23 yrs.) d. on 70-Mar-11 [70-Mar-12: 2C].
Dollard, Elizabeth (67 yrs.) d. on 70-Jun-11 [70-Jun-13: 2C].
Dollard, James (22 yrs.) d. on 69-Apr-19 [69-Apr-21: 2B].
Dolliver, Mollie (3 yrs.) d. on 69-Nov-5 [69-Nov-6: 2C].
Dolphin, Emma m. Edwards, John R. on 66-Mar-24 [66-Mar-31: 2C].
Dolphin, Jennie m. Dorsey, B. C. on 69-Dec-7 [69-Dec-13: 2C].
Donaghoe, Hannah (34 yrs.) d. on 67-Nov-9 [67-Nov-11: 2C].
Donahue, George d. on 69-May-3 Drowned [69-May-7: 1G].
Donahue, Timothy (31 yrs.) d. on 66-Nov-2 [66-Nov-3: 2B].
Donald, James m. Rice, Maggie on 69-Sep-1 [69-Sep-21: 2B].
Donaldson, Arthur M. m. Rutter, Almire C. on 66-Oct-7 [66-Oct-24: 2C].
Donaldson, Camilla d. on 67-Jun-16 [67-Jun-18: 2B].
Donaldson, Catherine (85 yrs.) d. on 66-Mar-29 [66-Mar-30: 2C].
Donaldson, Elexener m. Hall, James P. on 69-Oct-28 [69-Oct-30: 2B].
Donaldson, Eliza Cook (5 yrs., 4 mos.) d. on 67-Jul-28 [67-Aug-1: 2C].
Donaldson, J. J. m. Youngman, M. M. on 65-Nov-16 [66-Jan-4: 2C].
Donaldson, John m. Donaldson, Margaret on 66-Sep-11 [66-Sep-12: 2A].
Donaldson, John Johnston (78 yrs.) d. on 66-Sep-18 [66-Sep-19: 2B].
Donaldson, Maggie H. m. Cleaveland, Edwin R. on 68-Mar-4 [68-Mar-16: 2B].
Donaldson, Margaret Harrison (1 yr., 5 mos.) d. on 66-Oct-21 [66-Oct-22: 2C].
Donaldson, Margaret Harrisson m. Donaldson, John on 66-Sep-11 [66-Oct-22: 2C].
Donaldson, Mary A. m. James, John R. on 69-Nov-3 [69-Nov-5: 2C].
Donaldson, Samuel C. m. Hazard, Camilla on 65-Dec-27 [66-Jan-10: 2C].
Donaldson, Sue m. Evans, Samuel M. on 66-Sep-8 [66-Sep-21: 2B].
Donaldson, Thomas W. m. Thompson, Ella H. on 67-May-20 [67-May-21: 2B].
Donaldson, Ward H. m. Gosnel, Cassandra on 67-May-28 [67-Jun-5: 2B].
Donallen, Elizabeth m. Roberts, W. H. on 68-Oct-27 [68-Nov-12: 2C].
Donallen, Erwin Louis (21 yrs.) d. on 70-Oct-30 [70-Oct-31: 2B; 70-Nov-1: 2C].
Donelan, Bridget (24 yrs.) d. [70-Oct-13: 2C].
Donelson, Harriet Isabella (7 mos.) d. on 70-Jul-24 [70-Jul-25: 2C].
Donigan, Annie E. m. Hampson, William A. on 67-Nov-25 [68-Jan-4: 2C].
Donigen, William m. Berry, Elizabeth on 67-Dec-19 [67-Dec-21: 2B].
Donley, Mary E. (23 yrs.) d. on 69-Jul-5 Drowned [69-Jul-7: 4C].

Donn, George W. m. Courtney, Ellen E. on 69-Jan-7 [69-Jan-9: 2C].
Donnegan, Kate m. Kelley, James on 69-Sep-5 [69-Sep-10: 2B].
Donnellan, Martin m. Macnamara, Maggie A. on 69-Jan-18 [69-Jan-27: 2C].
Donnelly, Ambrose (1 yr., 3 mos.) d. on 69-Apr-6 [69-Apr-27: 2C].
Donnelly, Catherine S. (48 yrs.) d. on 66-Sep-29 [66-Oct-8: 2B].
Donnelly, Charles (71 yrs., 2 mos.) d. on 68-Dec-23 [69-Jan-6: 2C].
Donnelly, Charles H. (7 yrs.) d. on 70-Jun-24 [70-Jun-28: 2C].
Donnelly, Charles J. m. Muir, Emma on 69-Jan-24 [69-Feb-3: 2C].
Donnelly, Charles J. P. (5 yrs., 6 mos.) d. on 66-Jun-21 [66-Jun-22: 2B].
Donnelly, E., Mrs. (73 yrs.) d. on 67-Nov-20 [67-Nov-21: 2C].
Donnelly, Ellen (18 yrs.) d. on 66-Aug-19 Drowned [66-Aug-20: 1F, 2C].
Donnelly, Emma m. Rice, C. E. on 68-Nov-15 [68-Nov-30: 2B].
Donnelly, Frank (6 mos.) d. on 70-Apr-1 [70-Apr-2: 2A].
Donnelly, Hugh (1 yr., 1 mo.) d. on 66-Jan-24 [66-Jan-25: 2C].
Donnelly, John (16 yrs.) d. on 68-Feb-7 [68-Feb-8: 2B].
Donnelly, John m. Morison, Annie M. T. on 69-Dec-8 [69-Dec-14: 2C].
Donnelly, John M. m. Barkman, Clara Virginia on 69-Dec-23 [70-Jan-5: 2C].
Donnelly, Maggie F. d. on 66-Jan-14 [66-Jan-16: 2C].
Donnelly, Maggie Teresa (1 yr., 6 mos.) d. on 66-Jun-28 [66-Jun-29: 2C].
Donnelly, Sara (60 yrs.) d. on 68-Jul-20 [68-Jul-21: 2C].
Donnelly, Thomas m. Murphy, Bridget on 69-Jun-27 [69-Jul-3: 2B].
Donnelly, Thomas James (11 mos.) d. on 70-Aug-24 [70-Aug-26: 2C].
Donohue, Bernard Joseph (7 mos.) d. on 67-Jul-25 [67-Jul-26: 2C].
Donohue, Bridget (13 yrs.) d. on 67-Feb-1 of Brain congestion [67-Feb-2: 2C].
Donohue, Daniel O. (76 yrs.) d. on 70-Jul-18 [70-Jul-19: 2B].
Donohue, Edward (5 mos.) d. on 70-Aug-9 [70-Aug-10: 2B].
Donohue, Elizabeth (29 yrs.) d. on 68-Jul-2 [68-Jul-4: 2C].
Donohue, Fannie E. m. Wellener, Bazil S. on 69-Dec-28 [70-Jan-6: 2C].
Donohue, Ida Virginia (7 mos.) d. on 68-Aug-15 [68-Aug-17: 2B].
Donohue, James H. m. Doyle, Susie V. on 69-Jan-12 [69-Jan-20: 2C].
Donohue, John Francis (3 yrs., 10 mos.) d. on 69-Aug-17 [69-Aug-18: 2C].
Donoker, John (32 yrs.) d. on 66-Sep-20 [66-Sep-21: 2B].
Donolon, James (1 yr., 7 mos.) d. on 66-Jun-1 [66-Jun-2: 2B].
Donovan, Edward (23 yrs.) d. on 70-Nov-12 of Gunshot wound [70-Nov-14: 2B; 70-Nov-15: 2C; 70-Nov-14: 4D].
Donovan, M. W. m. Berry, Mary E. on 66-Oct-17 [66-Oct-18: 2B].
Donovan, Michael m. Stansbury, Mary Elizabeth on 66-Apr-25 [66-Apr-28: 2A].
Donovan, William d. on 67-Jul-5 of Heatstroke [67-Jul-6: 4D].
Donsiff, Harry L. m. Burgess, Mary E. on 68-Sep-23 [68-Sep-26: 2B].
Dooley, James d. on 66-Oct-10 Drowned [66-Oct-13: 1F].
Dooley, Mary Jane d. on 66-Oct-10 Drowned [66-Oct-13: 1F].
Dooley, Thomas d. on 66-Oct-10 Drowned [66-Oct-13: 1F].
Doolittle, Jane m. Toner, John on 69-Apr-10 [69-Apr-13: 2B].
Doolittle, William W. (35 yrs.) d. on 68-May-27 of Suicide (Drowning) [68-May-29: 1E; 68-Jun-2: 2B].
Dooner, Hugh (78 yrs.) d. on 67-Nov-25 [67-Nov-26: 2B].
Dooris, Mary (40 yrs.) d. on 68-Aug-29 [68-Sep-1: 2B].
Dooris, Mary m. Faith, Andrew on 70-May-20 [70-Jul-16: 2B].
Doran, Ann d. on 69-Dec-25 of Consumption [69-Dec-28: 2D].
Doran, Kate m. Ryan, Thomas on 67-Nov-26 [67-Dec-3: 2C].
Dorm, Lizzie m. Sherer, John on 69-Nov-2 [69-Nov-4: 2B].
Dorm, Maggie (21 yrs., 5 mos.) d. on 67-Dec-26 [67-Dec-27: 2D; 67-Dec-28: 2C].
Dorman, Charles Francis (1 yr., 5 mos.) d. on 66-May-3 [66-May-5: 2B; 66-May-7: 2B].
Dorman, Samuel (36 yrs.) d. on 68-Jan-6 of Consumption [68-Jan-7: 2B].
Dorman, Sarah A. (38 yrs.) d. on 68-Jul-10 [68-Jul-11: 2B].

Dorman, Stephen L. (71 yrs.) d. on 67-Jan-16 [67-Jan-17: 2C].
Dorming, Rachel R. m. Hopkins, Philip T. on 69-Feb-18 [69-Feb-24: 2C].
Dorn, Philip m. Franck, Nettie T. on 67-Dec-31 [68-Jan-6: 2C].
Dorner, Kate E. m. Blaney, Harry C. on 69-Dec-9 [69-Dec-16: 2C].
Dorney, William W. (63 yrs.) d. on 66-Jan-10 [66-Jan-17: 2C].
Dorr, Lawrence A. m. Abbott, Susan E. on 67-Nov-19 [67-Dec-27: 2D].
Dorrett, Susan E. m. Wilkinson, William J. G. on 68-May-27 [68-May-29: 2B].
Dorrett, William W. m. Jones, Laura B. on 69-May-18 [69-May-20: 2C].
Dorritee, Harriet (36 yrs.) d. on 68-Oct-28 [68-Oct-29: 2B; 68-Oct-30: 2C].
Dorritee, Lorenzo m. Hanly, Mary on 67-Nov-30 [67-Dec-6: 2C].
Dorritee, Robert E. (54 yrs.) d. on 69-Jan-26 [69-Jan-27: 2C; 69-Jan-28: 2C].
Dorrittee, Robert E. (54 yrs.) d. on 69-Jan-26 [69-Jan-27: 2C; 69-Jan-28: 2C].
Dorry, Edward G. (53 yrs.) d. on 66-Oct-10 [66-Oct-11: 2C; 66-Oct-12: 2B].
Dorschel, Agnes Louisa (6 mos.) d. on 69-Jul-4 [69-Jul-7: 2C].
Dorschel, Emma Josephine (1 yr., 6 mos.) d. on 68-Dec-10 [68-Dec-12: 2C].
Dorsen, Lindsay T. m. Clisby, Louisa on 69-Apr-22 [69-Apr-24: 2B].
Dorsett, Herbert (1 yr., 2 mos.) d. [68-Jun-29: 2B].
Dorsey, Alexander (55 yrs.) d. on 70-Jun-26 [70-Jun-27: 2C].
Dorsey, Andrew m. Key, Fannie on 70-Oct-13 [70-Oct-15: 2B].
Dorsey, Anna M. m. Nelson, Tenant on 70-Jun-9 [70-Jun-24: 2C].
Dorsey, Annie Worthington m. Brewer, James R. on 68-Jun-11 [68-Jun-12: 2B].
Dorsey, Asbury (31 yrs.) d. on 66-Apr-7 [66-Apr-23: 2C].
Dorsey, Augusta A. d. on 70-May-30 [70-Jun-1: 2B; 70-Jun-3: 2B].
Dorsey, Augustus E. (61 yrs.) d. on 69-Dec-9 [69-Dec-10: 2C].
Dorsey, B. m. Thompson, Hattie S. on 66-Dec-20 [66-Dec-22: 2A].
Dorsey, B. C. m. Dolphin, Jennie on 69-Dec-7 [69-Dec-13: 2C].
Dorsey, Bell (17 yrs., 10 mos.) d. [66-May-31: 2B].
Dorsey, Bessie d. on 69-Sep-22 [69-Sep-23: 2B].
Dorsey, Caleb (68 yrs.) d. on 67-Apr-6 [67-Apr-9: 2B].
Dorsey, Caleb (89 yrs.) d. on 69-Sep-6 [69-Sep-7: 2B].
Dorsey, Caleb m. Brooks, Catherine on 68-Dec-24 [68-Dec-29: 2D].
Dorsey, Charles H. m. Cather, Hannah J. on 70-Oct-20 [70-Oct-22: 2B].
Dorsey, Charles S. W. d. on 66-Mar-6 [66-Mar-7: 2B].
Dorsey, Chloe m. Wilhelm, H. on 68-Mar-12 [68-Mar-14: 2B].
Dorsey, Clara m. Hooper, John on 67-May-30 [67-Jun-1: 2B].
Dorsey, Clement H. m. Anthony, Annie H on 70-May-28 [70-May-31: 2B].
Dorsey, David A. (48 yrs.) d. on 68-Mar-5 [68-Mar-12: 2B].
Dorsey, Decatur m. Christie, Mannie on 66-Jan-4 [66-Jan-5: 2C].
Dorsey, Eliza A. (52 yrs.) d. on 69-Oct-14 [69-Oct-15: 2C].
Dorsey, Elizabeth M. (5 mos.) d. on 67-Jun-18 [67-Jun-20: 2B].
Dorsey, Ella M. m. Nichlas, John on 70-Oct-4 [70-Oct-7: 2B; 70-Oct-8: 2B].
Dorsey, Emma m. Ellis, John E. on 67-Nov-21 [67-Nov-26: 2B].
Dorsey, Evan L. m. Denby, Rebecca J. on 66-Nov-27 [66-Dec-1: 2B].
Dorsey, George W. (5 yrs., 2 mos.) d. on 70-Mar-22 [70-Mar-24: 2C].
Dorsey, James H. m. Butler, Ellen on 67-Nov-7 [67-Nov-18: 2B].
Dorsey, James Henry (11 mos.) d. on 68-Jan-21 [68-Jan-23: 2C].
Dorsey, James P. m. Hall, Emma on 66-Oct-18 [66-Oct-29: 2C].
Dorsey, James R. (45 yrs.) d. on 69-Aug-24 [69-Aug-26: 2C].
Dorsey, Jemima (106 yrs.) d. on 66-Jul-18 [66-Jul-19: 2C].
Dorsey, Jemimma d. on 66-Jul-18 [66-Jan-19: 2C].
Dorsey, Jennie m. Clark, William Of T. on 69-Dec-9 [69-Dec-13: 2C].
Dorsey, John C. m. Owings, Alverdo S. on 69-Jun-24 [69-Jul-8: 2C].
Dorsey, John Patrick (2 yrs., 5 mos.) d. on 68-Jan-10 [68-Jan-11: 2B].
Dorsey, John Thomas (61 yrs.) d. on 68-Jul-10 [68-Jul-14: 2C].
Dorsey, Joseph S. (53 yrs.) d. on 70-Dec-5 [70-Dec-6: 2C].

Dorsey, Joseph Thomas (1 yr., 4 mos.) d. on 69-May-4 [69-May-5: 2C].
Dorsey, Josephine A. m. Fowler, James F. on 67-Sep-26 [67-Oct-17: 2B].
Dorsey, Julia m. Wilhelm, James T. on 69-Nov-25 [69-Nov-29: 2C].
Dorsey, Kate (22 yrs.) d. on 68-Jul-13 [68-Jul-14: 2B].
Dorsey, Kate H. m. Winder, Richard B. on 69-Apr-15 [69-Apr-16: 2B].
Dorsey, Katharine Mason (1 yr.) d. on 67-Aug-21 [67-Aug-29: 2B].
Dorsey, Lloyd E. m. Worthington, Laura on 69-Oct-26 [69-Oct-30: 2B].
Dorsey, Luther d. on 66-Dec-17 in Carriage accident [66-Dec-22: 4C].
Dorsey, Maggie L. (5 mos.) d. on 67-Jun-12 [67-Jun-20: 2B].
Dorsey, Margaret m. Simpson, Joseph on 69-Mar-11 [69-Mar-22: 2C].
Dorsey, Margaret S. m. Colehouse, Randolph R. on 68-Oct-26 [68-Oct-27: 2B].
Dorsey, Martha E. m. Moltin, Samuel on 69-Sep-12 [69-Sep-21: 2B].
Dorsey, Mary (83 yrs., 1 mo.) d. on 70-Aug-29 [70-Aug-30: 2B].
Dorsey, Mary m. Mack, James on 70-Sep-13 [70-Sep-15: 2B].
Dorsey, Mary A. (60 yrs.) d. on 67-Sep-15 [67-Sep-17: 2A].
Dorsey, Mary Catherine m. Guy, Edwin K. on 69-Oct-21 [69-Oct-22: 2B].
Dorsey, Mary Elenor m. Lynn, A. Luther on 66-Oct-18 [66-Oct-22: 2C].
Dorsey, Matilda (74 yrs.) d. on 69-Mar-13 [69-Mar-24: 2C].
Dorsey, Matilda Heath d. on 67-Feb-13 [67-Feb-14: 2C].
Dorsey, Mattie B. m. Riggs, Joshua W. on 67-Oct-2 [67-Oct-5: 2B].
Dorsey, Michael (96 yrs.) d. on 68-May-24 [68-May-25: 2A].
Dorsey, Michael (68 yrs.) d. on 67-Jul-11 [67-Jul-12: 2C].
Dorsey, Nannie Poultney m. Fisher, Charles on 68-Apr-15 [68-Apr-16: 2B].
Dorsey, Nicholas (85 yrs.) d. on 67-Feb-23 [67-Feb-28: 1G, 2C].
Dorsey, Patrick (29 yrs.) d. on 70-Aug-13 in Street railway accident [70-Aug-15: 4D].
Dorsey, Rachel d. on 67-Jul-3 [67-Jul-4: 2B].
Dorsey, Rebecca (78 yrs.) d. on 70-Nov-30 [70-Dec-3: 2B].
Dorsey, Richard H. m. Hammond, Mary M. on 69-Sep-1 [69-Sep-2: 2B].
Dorsey, Richard J., Dr. d. on 69-Mar-2 [69-Mar-4: 2C].
Dorsey, Robert d. on 68-Feb-4 [68-Feb-5: 2D].
Dorsey, Samuel Y. (79 yrs.) d. on 67-Mar-12 [67-Apr-2: 2B].
Dorsey, Sarah F. m. Rasin, A. R. on 67-Oct-17 [67-Oct-21: 2B].
Dorsey, Sarah R. d. on 67-Oct-31 [67-Nov-1: 2B].
Dorsey, Selman (34 yrs.) d. on 69-Jul-30 of Consumption [69-Jul-31: 2C; 69-Sep-4: 2B].
Dorsey, Susan E. A. (77 yrs.) d. on 66-Jul-25 [66-Jul-26: 2C].
Dorsey, Susan F. (18 yrs.) d. on 69-Jan-9 [69-Jan-13: 2D].
Dorsey, Theodore C. m. Whitman, H. Victorine on 68-Apr-15 [68-Apr-17: 2B].
Dorsey, W. H. B. m. Ebert, Fannie V. on 67-Nov-20 [67-Nov-27: 2B].
Dorsey, W. T., Dr. (22 yrs.) d. on 70-Apr-15 [70-Apr-16: 2B].
Dorsey, William (40 yrs.) d. on 68-Jul-27 [68-Jul-28: 2B].
Dorsey, William A. m. Leatherwood, Mary A. on 67-Nov-26 [67-Dec-3: 2C].
Dorsey, William C. m. Carr, Lizzie on 67-Nov-13 [67-Nov-19: 2C].
Dorsey, William H. m. Sprenkle, Sarah E. on 66-Mar-18 [66-Apr-4: 2B].
Dorsey, William Patrick (2 yrs., 9 mos.) d. on 70-Dec-15 [70-Dec-17: 2B].
Dorsey, Willie W. (17 yrs.) d. on 66-Feb-4 [66-Feb-5: 2C].
Dory, Benjamin m. Shaffer, Sarah Jane on 66-Sep-17 [66-Oct-2: 2B].
Dos Santos, James Murray d. on 67-Jan-9 [67-Jan-30: 2C].
Dosh, Maggie m. Krichten, John H. on 67-Aug-4 [67-Aug-7: 2C].
Dosh, Rebecca m. Canoles, John on 67-Oct-17 [67-Oct-17: 2A].
Doubleday, Lottie M. m. O'Dell, Walter on 69-Dec-2 [69-Dec-4: 2C].
Douch, William m. McCauley, Cornelia A. on 67-Apr-23 [67-May-14: 2B].
Doud, Bartholomew (55 yrs.) d. on 69-Sep-25 [69-Sep-27: 2C].
Doud, James William (30 yrs.) d. on 70-Oct-2 [70-Oct-29: 2B].
Dougherty, Allen (75 yrs.) d. on 70-Oct-19 [70-Oct-21: 2C].
Dougherty, Ann (37 yrs.) d. on 70-Nov-6 in Carriage accident [70-Nov-7: 2B; 70-Nov-8: 4D].

Dougherty, Bernard J. d. on 69-May-2 [69-May-4: 2B].
Dougherty, Charles J. d. on 69-Jan-1 [69-Jan-2: 2C].
Dougherty, Edward John (19 yrs.) d. on 69-Apr-26 [69-May-7: 2C].
Dougherty, Edward L. d. on 69-Jun-24 [69-Jun-25: 2C].
Dougherty, Elizabeth m. Martin, Patrick H. on 69-Jan-26 [69-Feb-8: 2C].
Dougherty, Ellen E. d. on 66-Mar-8 [66-Mar-9: 2B].
Dougherty, Emma (1 yr., 3 mos.) d. on 67-Jun-4 [67-Jun-6: 2B].
Dougherty, George W. m. Woods, Mary J. on 66-Jan-7 [66-Oct-20: 2B].
Dougherty, Hannah (58 yrs.) d. on 68-Nov-5 [68-Nov-7: 2B].
Dougherty, Hugh Garthwait (8 mos.) d. on 69-Jan-15 [69-Jan-18: 2D].
Dougherty, James (37 yrs.) d. on 68-Oct-20 [68-Oct-22: 2C].
Dougherty, James (75 yrs.) d. on 66-Apr-1 [66-Apr-2: 2B].
Dougherty, John J. (23 yrs.) d. on 69-Mar-22 [69-Mar-23: 2C].
Dougherty, John J. m. Garthwait, Mary A. on 67-May-21 [67-Jun-1: 2B].
Dougherty, Margaret Ann (74 yrs.) d. on 68-Jan-6 [68-Jan-14: 2C].
Dougherty, Mary (80 yrs.) d. on 68-Apr-11 [68-Apr-13: 2B].
Dougherty, Mary d. on 69-Feb-14 [69-Feb-16: 2C].
Dougherty, Patrick (78 yrs.) d. on 67-Aug-23 [67-Aug-24: 2B].
Dougherty, Samuel Sewel (2 yrs., 3 mos.) d. on 67-Dec-29 [67-Dec-31: 2C].
Dougherty, Thomas E. m. Maddox, Margaret J. on 70-Jun-30 [70-Jul-2: 2B].
Doughty, Bettie B. m. Ames, George T. on 66-Nov-19 [66-Dec-4: 2D].
Doughty, James, Sr. (76 yrs.) d. on 70-Dec-26 [70-Jan-4: 2C].
Doughty, Julia m. Albert, Augustus J., Jr. on 67-Jul-3 [67-Jul-9: 2B].
Doughty, Mary Ann (71 yrs.) d. on 70-Aug-3 [70-Aug-5: 2C].
Doughty, Thomas P. m. Waters, Maggie M. on 70-Feb-24 [70-Feb-28: 2C].
Douglas, George (1 yr., 1 mo.) d. on 69-Jul-17 [69-Jul-19: 2C].
Douglas, George (79 yrs.) d. [69-Apr-8: 1H].
Douglas, Nannie C. m. Beckenbaugh, John M. on 68-Nov-19 [68-Nov-25: 2B].
Douglass, Catherine C. m. Lehman, Henry on 69-Aug-2 [69-Oct-14: 2C].
Douglass, Clara E. m. Rother, Rod M. on 70-Jul-3 [70-Jul-6: 2B].
Douglass, Frank H. (24 yrs.) d. [70-Aug-12: 2C].
Douglass, James B. (62 yrs., 1 mo.) d. on 67-Jul-27 [67-Jul-31: 2C].
Douglass, John (66 yrs.) d. on 67-Jan-17 [67-Jan-19: 2C].
Douglass, Joseph H. H. (4 mos.) d. on 68-Jul-17 [68-Jul-21: 2C].
Douglass, Louisa m. Baker, Joseph on 67-May-23 [67-May-25: 2A].
Douglass, Robert A. (39 yrs.) d. on 70-Sep-21 [70-Sep-22: 2C].
Douglass, Sarah Talitha (50 yrs., 5 mos.) d. on 67-Jun-11 [67-Jun-12: 2B].
Douglass, Spencer m. Coe, Addie F. on 69-Nov-12 [69-Nov-24: 2C].
Douglass, Walter C. m. Johnson, Ellen on 69-Dec-9 [69-Dec-17: 2C].
Douley, Alice A. m. Payne, Richard on 67-May-14 [67-May-15: 2B].
Douthat, William H. m. Walton, Mary A. on 68-May-28 [68-Jun-4: 2B].
Dove, Marmaduke (44 yrs.) d. on 66-Sep-2 [66-Sep-7: 2B].
Dove, William C. (49 yrs.) d. on 67-Aug-21 [67-Aug-22: 2B].
Dove, Willie Case (2 mos.) d. on 68-Jul-8 [68-Jul-10: 2C].
Dover, Jacob Z. m. Burman, Mary Agnes on 68-Mar-5 [68-May-22: 2C].
Dowd, Mary E. d. on 66-Oct-27 [66-Oct-30: 4C].
Dowd, Mary Isabella (3 yrs., 2 mos.) d. on 68-May-5 [68-May-7: 2B].
Dowell, Jefferson Davis (8 yrs., 5 mos.) d. on 69-Jun-28 [69-Jul-5: 2C].
Dowell, John T. (7 mos.) d. on 68-Jul-16 [68-Jul-17: 2B].
Dowell, Marie Nathalie m. Pollard, Edward A. [67-Apr-6: 2B].
Dowing, Walter W. m. Boon, Maria on 70-Jun-23 [70-Jul-2: 2B].
Dowley, John d. on 66-Aug-25 Drowned [66-Oct-10: 1F].
Dowling, Frances M. m. Hale, Charles W. on 70-May-23 [70-May-24: 2C].
Dowling, John J. m. DaCosta, Alena Rose on 70-May-24 [70-May-26: 2C].
Dowling, Mary E. m. Small, John F. on 69-Apr-27 [69-Apr-30: 2C].

Down, Charles B. m. Bright, Mollie E. on 66-May-3 [66-May-4: 2C].
Downes, Mary (25 yrs.) d. on 67-Aug-16 of Heart disease [67-Aug-17: 1G].
Downey, Benjamin F. m. West, Alice A. on 67-Mar-25 [67-Mar-27: 2C].
Downey, Catherine m. Paul, Samuel B. on 70-Jun-15 [70-Jun-17: 2B].
Downey, Fanny (27 yrs.) d. on 67-Dec-15 [67-Dec-17: 2B].
Downey, Henrietta m. Vanockey, Lewis on 68-Nov-26 [68-Dec-23: 2C].
Downey, Laura E. m. Mitchell, Augustus on 68-Oct-8 [68-Oct-9: 2C].
Downey, Laura V. m. Roszel, John H. on 66-May-17 [66-May-24: 2C].
Downey, Margaret M. m. Hopkins, Howard W. on 69-Sep-1 [69-Sep-2: 2B; 69-Sep-3: 2B].
Downing, Eliza (58 yrs.) d. on 66-May-8 [66-May-9: 2B; 66-May-10: 2B].
Downing, Nathaniel F. (70 yrs., 1 mo.) d. on 70-Nov-4 [70-Nov-5: 2B].
Downs, Anna Cornelius (4 yrs., 10 mos.) d. on 70-Nov-15 [70-Nov-16: 2C].
Downs, Annie Sophia (9 mos.) d. on 69-Jun-27 [69-Jun-28: 2C].
Downs, Florence A. m. Davis, Joseph L. on 70-Mar-9 [70-Mar-19: 2B].
Downs, Frank Albert (1 yr., 10 mos.) d. on 70-Jan-25 [70-Jan-27: 2C].
Downs, J. B. m. Ryley, George on 66-Jan-10 [66-Jan-17: 2C].
Downs, James H. m. Gordshell, Mary F. on 66-Jul-3 [66-Nov-27: 2B].
Downs, John G. m. Poulton, Mary Alverda on 67-Jan-31 [67-Feb-18: 2C].
Downs, John J. m. Ziegler, Emma A. on 67-Apr-25 [67-Apr-29: 2B].
Downs, Margaret (71 yrs.) d. on 67-Dec-3 [67-Dec-4: 2C; 67-Dec-5: 2C].
Downs, Sarah E. m. Disney, Benjamin F. on 67-Jan-31 [67-Feb-18: 2C].
Downs, William L. m. Deady, Ellie T. on 67-Dec-24 [67-Dec-27: 2D].
Doxen, Kinsey J. m. Harvey, Elizabeth A. on 66-May-15 [66-Jun-5: 2B].
Doyer, Emma m. Tarr, Wesley B. on 69-Mar-2 [69-Mar-22: 2C].
Doyle, Adele (9 mos.) d. on 70-Jul-14 [70-Jul-16: 2B].
Doyle, Catherine (16 yrs., 6 mos.) d. on 70-Feb-8 [70-Feb-9: 2C].
Doyle, Charley (5 mos.) d. on 70-Jan-3 [70-Jan-6: 2C].
Doyle, Elizabeth (22 yrs.) d. on 70-Aug-23 [70-Aug-25: 2C].
Doyle, James (76 yrs.) d. on 67-Jan-9 [67-Jan-11: 2C].
Doyle, James M. m. Timmons, Maggie E. on 68-Nov-3 [68-Nov-9: 2B].
Doyle, John (2 mos.) d. on 70-Jul-27 [70-Jul-29: 2C].
Doyle, Josephine m. Brown, Oliver on 69-Nov-16 [69-Nov-20: 2B].
Doyle, Kate (12 yrs.) d. on 69-Dec-21 [69-Dec-22: 2B; 69-Dec-23: 2B].
Doyle, Maggie J. m. Griffin, Thomas J. on 69-Aug-5 [69-Aug-9: 2B].
Doyle, Mary m. Brooks, George W. on 67-Jun-27 [67-Jul-1: 2B].
Doyle, Mary Ann (84 yrs.) d. on 69-May-5 [69-May-6: 2B].
Doyle, Michael (55 yrs.) d. on 68-Aug-22 Murdered (Shooting) [68-Aug-25: 1F; 68-Aug-26: 4B].
Doyle, Patrick d. on 67-Dec-25 [67-Dec-27: 2D].
Doyle, Patrick (51 yrs.) d. on 66-Feb-13 [66-Feb-14: 2C; 66-Feb-15: 2C].
Doyle, Susie V. m. Donohue, James H. on 69-Jan-12 [69-Jan-20: 2C].
Doyle, Thomas J. (30 yrs.) d. on 66-May-23 [66-May-30: 2C].
Doyle, William (77 yrs.) d. on 66-Nov-13 [66-Nov-14: 2B; 66-Nov-15: 2C].
Doyle, William J. m. Gallagher, Jennie on 67-Oct-3 [67-Oct-8: 2B].
Drachman, Philip m. Katzenstein, Rosa on 68-Apr-21 [68-Apr-24: 2B].
Drage, Charles (21 yrs.) d. on 67-Apr-27 Drowned [67-May-2: 1G].
Draine, Maggie m. Cousins, Edward on 70-Mar-17 [70-Mar-19: 2B].
Drake, John O. m. Finley, Anna H. on 67-Oct-16 [67-Oct-18: 2C].
Drake, Katie (15 yrs.) d. on 68-Feb-22 [69-Feb-24: 2C].
Drakeley, George E. m. Cassard, M. Kate on 67-Jun-4 [67-Jun-8: 2B].
Drakeley, Harry Cassard (1 yr., 9 mos.) d. on 70-May-8 [70-May-9: 2B].
Drakeley, Henry W. m. Bowersox, A. Maria on 69-Jul-6 [69-Jul-7: 2C].
Drakeley, Herbert (8 mos.) d. on 70-Apr-22 [70-Apr-23: 2B].
Drakely, Mary E. (42 yrs.) d. on 67-Feb-26 [67-Feb-27: 2C].
Drame, Annie E. d. on 68-Oct-5 [68-Oct-8: 2B].
Drame, James E. (1 yr., 3 mos.) d. on 69-Sep-22 [69-Sep-23: 2B].

Drane, Catherine (56 yrs.) d. on 69-Apr-26 [69-Apr-29: 2C].
Drechsler, Annie Rosanna (11 mos.) d. on 67-Feb-18 [67-Feb-23: 2C].
Drege, Jacob R. (68 yrs.) d. on 66-Jul-5 [66-Jul-7: 2B].
Dreibing, Marion E. m. Leech, Thomas on 69-May-23 [69-Oct-13: 2C].
Drenner, Otho W. m. Cornthwait, Kate on 67-Sep-19 [67-Oct-14: 2B].
Drew, Eliza Ramsay d. on 70-Oct-19 [70-Oct-21: 2C].
Drew, Mary d. on 68-Jul-24 [68-Jul-25: 2B].
Drexel, Francis F. m. Steudler, Laura V. on 68-Mar-11 [68-Mar-14: 2B].
Drexler, Emily S. m. Greenfield, Thomas S. on 70-Feb-23 [70-Mar-1: 2C].
Dreyer, Henry A. m. Mason, Mary E. on 66-Jan-1 [66-Jan-15: 2B].
Drill, Mary E. d. on 70-Oct-25 [70-Oct-27: 2B].
Drill, Sallie B. (1 yr., 1 mo.) d. on 66-Aug-19 [66-Aug-20: 2C].
Driscol, John (37 yrs.) d. on 67-Dec-13 Drowned [67-Dec-16: 1G].
Driscoll, Ellen (40 yrs.) d. on 69-May-8 [69-May-10: 2B].
Driscoll, Mary J. (28 yrs.) d. on 70-Oct-5 [70-Oct-22: 2B].
Driver, Robert E. Lee (3 mos.) d. on 68-Jul-18 [68-Jul-23: 2B].
Driver, Silas m. Williams, Catherine on 69-Sep-30 [69-Oct-2: 2B].
Drohan, Clara J. (1 yr., 8 mos.) d. on 69-Sep-13 of Catarrh [69-Sep-15: 2B].
Drohan, Elizabeth Graham (2 yrs., 3 mos.) d. on 70-Dec-27 [70-Dec-28: 2C].
Drohan, Thomas m. Hall, Kate E. [67-Oct-2: 2B].
Drohan, Thomas Graham (4 yrs., 4 mos.) d. on 69-Dec-31 [70-Jan-3: 2C].
Droney, Dennis (79 yrs.) d. on 68-Oct-4 [68-Oct-5: 2C].
Drost, Laura (34 yrs.) d. on 69-Aug-5 [69-Aug-7: 2B; 69-Aug-10: 2C].
Drost, Lydia (68 yrs.) d. on 67-Mar-23 [67-Mar-25: 2C].
Droste, John H. (73 yrs.) d. on 67-Oct-31 [67-Nov-1: 2B; 67-Nov-2: 2B].
Droste, William H. m. Start, Maria C. on 67-May-16 [67-May-18: 2A].
Droste, William Malvin (1 yr.) d. on 70-Jul-11 [70-Jul-12: 2C].
Drought, Ida Bell (1 yr., 6 mos.) d. on 70-Mar-14 [70-Mar-16: 2C].
Drugan, Mary C. m. Eney, Joseph R. on 68-Jan-7 [68-Jan-10: 2C].
Drummond, Evan (70 yrs.) d. on 70-Feb-17 of Consumption [70-Feb-19: 2B].
Drummond, Levin J. (47 yrs.) d. on 66-Jan-10 [66-Jan-11: 2B; 66-Jan-12: 2C; 66-Jan-13: 1G].
Drummond, Robert (60 yrs., 5 mos.) d. on 66-Aug-19 [66-Sep-7: 2B].
Drurry, Catherine (50 yrs.) d. on 69-Aug-5 [69-Aug-6: 2C].
Drury, Charles B. m. DeCamp, Cora V. on 66-Aug-28 [66-Sep-3: 2C].
Drury, Helen E. m. Ricketts, John on 69-Aug-4 [69-Aug-6: 2C].
Drury, Virginia m. Crowle, John on 66-Oct-23 [66-Oct-26: 2B].
Dryden, Annie M. m. Kensett, John R. on 67-Nov-12 [67-Nov-15: 2B].
Dryden, Catherine d. on 70-Sep-23 [70-Sep-24: 2B].
Dryden, Charles H. (50 yrs.) d. on 68-Jan-1 Murdered (Shooting) [68-Jan-2: 1F, 2C].
Dryden, E. Julia m. Klockgether, D., Jr. on 65-Dec-21 [66-Jan-1: 2C].
Dryden, Ella Mae (5 yrs., 3 mos.) d. on 67-Aug-6 of Scarlet fever [67-Aug-7: 2C].
Dryden, John H. (66 yrs.) d. on 68-Feb-25 of Liver inflammation [68-May-9: 2B].
Dryden, Joseph H. m. Taylor, Mary E. on 67-Nov-12 [67-Dec-18: 2B].
Dryden, Lue J. m. Beauchamp, William S. on 68-Jan-21 [68-Jan-23: 2C].
Dryden, Mary Rosealba m. Chambers, George Maitland on 66-Feb-12 [66-Feb-14: 2C].
Dryden, Robert W. (2 yrs., 4 mos.) d. on 66-May-29 [66-May-30: 2C].
Dryden, Sarah C. m. Watkins, Leonard G. on 66-Nov-12 [66-Nov-15: 2C].
Dryden, Virginia A. m. Mansfield, Benjamin F. on 67-May-28 [67-May-30: 2B].
Dryden, W. Sidney m. Walters, Mary A. on 67-Jan-23 [67-Feb-1: 2C].
Dryer, Amelia (80 yrs.) d. on 68-Aug-31 [68-Sep-1: 1G].
Du Barry, Edmund m. Williams, Laura on 68-Nov-12 [68-Nov-14: 2B].
Du Barry, Edmund Louis (1 mo.) d. on 69-Sep-30 [69-Oct-4: 2C].
Du Flocq, Louis H. m. Megraw, Carrie M. on 66-Feb-6 [66-Feb-13: 2C].
Du Hamel, James (76 yrs.) d. on 69-Sep-30 [69-Oct-1: 2B].
Duane, John m. Garvey, Kate on 66-Feb-7 [66-Feb-13: 2C].

Duane, John Thomas (9 mos.) d. on 70-May-3 [70-May-4: 2C].
DuBarry, William Duane m. Inloes, Ella on 66-Oct-9 [66-Oct-11: 2C].
DuBois, Edward S. m. Robinson, Theodora on 70-Mar-1 [70-Mar-29: 2B].
Dubois, John m. Spencer, Jane on 66-Sep-4 [66-Sep-12: 2A].
Dubois, Sarah E. (3 yrs.) d. on 70-Feb-7 [70-Feb-18: 2C].
Dubois, Sarah E. m. Milligan, Robert W. on 70-Feb-17 [70-Feb-18: 2C].
Dubosq, Henry (69 yrs.) d. on 67-Jul-10 [67-Jul-13: 2B; 67-Jul-15: 2C].
Dubree, George W. m. Labraque, Louise J. on 68-Jan-12 [68-Jan-14: 2C].
Dubree, Rebecca (70 yrs.) d. on 66-Nov-14 [66-Nov-16: 2C].
DuBreuil, Aristide (54 yrs.) d. on 66-Mar-22 [66-Mar-29: 2B].
DuBuisson, Anna Elizabeth (3 mos.) d. on 67-Mar-22 [67-Mar-23: 2B].
Ducatel, Hyppolitte G. (60 yrs.) d. on 70-Jun-20 [70-Jun-28: 2C].
Ducatel, Josephine d. on 67-Apr-13 [67-Apr-15: 2B].
Duck, Charles Edward m. Forbes, Martha Bush on 69-Nov-23 [69-Nov-24: 2C].
Ducker, Henry H. (47 yrs.) d. on 69-Nov-27 [69-Dec-2: 2C].
Ducket, Mary m. Hammond, Peter on 66-Sep-27 [66-Sep-27: 2C].
Duckett, Katie (1 yr.) d. on 70-Jan-21 [70-Jan-22: 2B].
Duckett, Sophia m. Hall, Alexander on 69-Dec-8 [69-Dec-9: 2C].
Duckett, William (3 yrs., 3 mos.) d. on 69-Feb-8 [69-Feb-10: 2C].
Duckstein, Jeanette A. m. Feuss, Andrew C. on 66-Apr-5 [66-Apr-19: 2B].
Dudalez, Alonzo G. m. McCabe, Nety C. on 66-Dec-31 [67-Jan-1: 2C].
Dudderow, John W., Dr. (25 yrs.) d. on 67-Mar-1 of Typhoid [67-Mar-2: 2B; 67-Mar-4: 4F].
Dudley, Charles G. B. (10 mos.) d. on 70-Aug-20 [70-Aug-23: 2B].
Dudley, Charles G. B. m. Peters, Clara J. on 69-Jan-12 [69-Jan-19: 2C].
Dudley, Charlotte d. on 68-Jan-9 [68-Jan-16: 2C].
Dudley, Frederick M. m. Whitlock, Mary E. on 67-May-14 [67-May-18: 2A].
Dudley, Johannah Rebecca (1 yr., 9 mos.) d. on 67-Aug-8 [67-Aug-10: 2B].
Dudley, John C. (20 yrs.) d. on 66-Jan-17 [66-Jan-18: 2C].
Dudrow, Martha m. Finch, William W. on 65-Dec-31 [67-Jan-3: 2C].
Duen, Mary Alice (57 yrs.) d. on 68-May-27 [68-Jun-5: 2B].
Duer, Mary J. m. Gnosspelius, G. A. on 68-Aug-25 [68-Sep-2: 2A].
Duer, Sarah (88 yrs.) d. on 67-Sep-30 [67-Oct-1: 2B].
Duering, John S. (70 yrs.) d. on 66-Feb-25 [66-Feb-26: 2B].
Duff, Celestine d. on 70-Apr-23 [70-Apr-25: 2B].
Duff, Eliza Jane d. on 66-Dec-4 [66-Dec-5: 2B].
Duff, Elizabeth (80 yrs.) d. on 69-Sep-16 [69-Sep-22: 2C].
Duff, Fannie H. m. Painter, Joel F. on 67-May-30 [67-Jun-21: 2B].
Duff, Henry, Capt. (67 yrs.) d. on 69-Mar-16 [69-Mar-17: 2C; 69-Mar-18: 1H].
Duff, Ida Isabel m. Hunt, William M. on 70-Jan-20 [70-Jan-27: 2C].
Duff, J. Luther m. Jessop, Hattie E. on 69-Aug-23 [69-Aug-25: 2C].
Duff, Luther Jessop (3 mos.) d. on 70-Sep-14 [70-Sep-15: 2B].
Duff, Mary J. m. Heisel, R. F. on 70-Jan-25 [70-Jan-29: 2B].
Duffey, Thomas (34 yrs.) d. on 66-Feb-8 [66-Feb-9: 2C; 66-Feb-10: 2C].
Duffey, Thomas Vincent (8 mos.) d. on 70-Mar-15 [70-Mar-16: 2C].
Duffy, Anna Belle (3 yrs., 6 mos.) d. on 67-Jul-23 [67-Jul-25: 2C].
Duffy, Anna Maria m. Bergin, Arthur on 69-Sep-19 [69-Sep-23: 2B].
Duffy, John (8 yrs.) d. on 66-Jul-20 [66-Jul-21: 2C].
Duffy, John (63 yrs.) d. on 66-Oct-17 [66-Oct-18: 2B; 66-Oct-19: 2B].
Duffy, John (40 yrs.) d. on 69-Apr-27 [69-Apr-29: 2B].
Duffy, Katey (8 yrs., 4 mos.) d. on 66-Nov-9 [66-Nov-10: 2B].
Duffy, Mary (38 yrs.) d. on 69-Jul-19 [69-Jul-20: 2C; 69-Jul-21: 2C].
Duffy, Patrick (28 yrs.) d. on 70-Jul-13 of Heatstroke [70-Jul-14: 1H].
Duffy, Thomas B. (1 yr., 8 mos.) d. on 70-Nov-8 [70-Nov-12: 2B].
Dufie, Mary A. m. Fosbenner, Alexander on 66-May-22 [66-Jun-4: 2B].
Dugan, Alexander (36 yrs.) d. on 70-Jul-20 [70-Jul-21: 2C].

Dugan, Charles D. (70 yrs.) d. on 70-Mar-16 in Street railway accident [70-Mar-18: 2C, 4E].
Dugan, Frederick J. (5 mos.) d. on 69-Aug-11 [69-Aug-13: 2C].
Dugan, James (35 yrs.) d. on 69-Oct-11 [69-Oct-12: 2C].
Dugan, James (31 yrs.) d. on 70-Mar-17 [70-Mar-19: 2B].
Dugan, John T. d. on 68-Jan-24 [68-Jan-25: 2B].
Dugan, Josephine (1 yr., 9 mos.) d. [69-Jul-12: 2D].
Dugan, Leila C. (20 yrs.) d. on 67-Dec-26 [67-Dec-30: 2C].
Dugan, Mary Agnes (2 yrs., 2 mos.) d. on 70-Dec-10 [70-Dec-12: 2C].
Dugdale, William m. Bard, Jennie M. on 66-Oct-18 [66-Oct-19: 2B].
Duggan, Francis James d. on 70-Sep-3 [70-Sep-5: 2C].
DuHamel, Martha (76 yrs.) d. on 67-Aug-1 [67-Aug-2: 2C].
DuHamel, William (70 yrs.) d. on 67-Mar-28 [67-Apr-4: 2B].
Duhurst, Anna S. m. Latta, Samuel M. on 68-May-14 [68-May-16: 2A].
Duhurst, Elizabeth m. Gallion, Charles Green on 70-Aug-4 [70-Aug-15: 2C].
Duhurst, Francis G. m. Merriken, Mary M. on 68-Oct-12 [68-Oct-23: 2B].
Duhurst, Francis Merriken d. on 68-Jun-27 [68-Jun-29: 2B].
Duhurst, Hannah (58 yrs.) d. on 68-Dec-1 [68-Dec-4: 2D].
Duhurst, Mary (88 yrs.) d. on 69-Nov-27 [69-Nov-29: 2C].
Duke, Josephine (2 yrs., 1 mo.) d. on 69-Oct-7 of Diptheria [69-Oct-8: 2B].
Duke, Margaret (4 yrs., 3 mos.) d. on 68-Jan-19 [68-Jan-20: 2C].
Duke, Susanna (49 yrs.) d. on 69-Dec-18 [69-Dec-20: 2C; 69-Dec-21: 2B].
Dukehart, Harry Franklin (3 mos.) d. on 70-Jul-18 [70-Jul-21: 2C].
Dukehart, Henry (73 yrs.) d. on 66-Dec-8 of Paralysis [66-Dec-10: 1G; 66-Dec-11: 2B].
Dukehart, John M. m. Mantz, Rebecca on 66-Jul-29 [66-Sep-3: 2C].
Dukehart, Lydia A. (26 yrs.) d. on 68-Dec-21 [68-Dec-23: 2C].
Dukehart, Mary m. Baker, Newton D. on 68-Jun-11 [68-Jun-20: 2B].
Dukehart, Mary Kate (1 mo.) d. on 67-Mar-14 [67-Mar-21: 2C].
Dukehart, Mollie Elizabeth (4 mos.) d. on 69-Aug-5 [69-Aug-21: 2B].
Dukehart, Parthenia B. m. Webb, Thomas W. on 68-Nov-17 [68-Nov-19: 2C; 68-Nov-20: 2C].
Dukehart, Parthenia E. m. Wickliffe, Andrew J. on 69-Oct-21 [69-Oct-23: 2B; 69-Oct-25: 2B].
Dukehart, Sarah Jane m. Potter, Charles on 69-Jan-6 [69-Jan-12: 2C].
Dukehart, Valerius (83 yrs.) d. on 66-Sep-3 [66-Sep-5: 2B, 4B].
Duker, Henry N. (46 yrs.) d. on 70-Dec-24 [70-Dec-26: 2C].
Dukes, Helen d. on 68-Nov-2 [68-Nov-3: 2B].
Dukes, James (83 yrs.) d. on 70-Jul-5 [70-Jul-7: 2B].
Dukson, John m. Gorsuch, Annie on 66-Apr-17 [66-Apr-28: 2A].
Dulaney, Emma J. m. Eader, J. R. on 70-Nov-23 [70-Dec-1: 2C].
Dulaney, James H. m. Shipley, Sarah Virginia on 66-Mar-15 [66-Mar-17: 2B].
Dulaney, William (53 yrs.) d. on 66-Oct-9 [66-Oct-10: 2B].
Dulany, Julia L. m. Peabody, Jose K. on 70-Dec-3 [70-Dec-7: 2C].
Dulany, William J. C., Jr. (2 mos.) d. on 70-Jun-3 [70-Jun-4: 2B].
Duley, Nicey Neal (16 yrs.) d. on 70-Dec-5 [70-Dec-6: 2C].
Dulie, Mattie m. Arnold, D. W. on 69-Jul-15 [69-Aug-3: 2C].
Dull, Catherine (40 yrs.) d. on 70-Dec-16 [70-Dec-17: 2B].
Dull, James (72 yrs.) d. on 68-Mar-5 [68-Mar-6: 2C].
Dull, John C. m. Kelly, Margaret Ann [67-Oct-11: 2B].
Dull, Marie A. m. Valentine, Thomas B. on 68-Feb-20 [68-Feb-22: 2B].
Duly, Mary Frances Mills (32 yrs.) d. on 66-Nov-3 [66-Nov-9: 2C].
Duly, Thomas F. m. Naylor, Belle on 69-May-25 [69-May-28: 2C].
Dumay, Louisa m. Caskey, Joseph on 69-Jul-1 [69-Jul-7: 2C].
Dumbolton, George (32 yrs.) d. on 68-Oct-24 [68-Oct-26: 2B].
Dumont, Frank m. Williams, Ellen Elizabeth on 66-Feb-15 [66-Feb-24: 2B].
Dumont, John F. (28 yrs.) d. on 67-Jan-23 [67-Mar-1: 2C].
Dunbar, Caroline E. d. on 69-Mar-21 of Pneumonia [69-Mar-29: 2B].

Dunbar, Lucie A. m. Beal, Alexander on 70-May-26 [70-May-28: 2B].
Dunbar, Rachel m. Walker, John H. on 68-Dec-24 [68-Dec-29: 2D].
Dunbracco, Evelyn (9 yrs.) d. on 66-Dec-18 [66-Dec-19: 2B].
Dunbracco, Margaretta (2 mos.) d. on 66-Dec-31 [67-Jan-7: 2C].
Duncan, Cassandra (88 yrs.) d. on 70-Jul-24 [70-Jul-25: 2C].
Duncan, Cassandra m. Partridge, L. W. on 70-Jan-6 [70-Jan-10: 2C].
Duncan, Cornelia (1 yr., 6 mos.) d. on 70-Apr-19 [70-Apr-20: 2B].
Duncan, Emma m. Brashears, Frank on 67-Sep-26 [67-Oct-21: 2B].
Duncan, F. Annie m. Bernard, Richard on 67-Jun-20 [67-Jun-27: 2B].
Duncan, J. J. m. Phelan, Susie A. on 68-Jan-2 [68-Jan-4: 2C].
Duncan, Joseph (39 yrs.) d. on 66-Mar-27 [66-Mar-28: 2C; 66-Mar-29: 2B].
Duncan, Margaret S. d. on 69-Feb-28 [69-Mar-1: 2C; 69-Mar-2: 2C].
Duncan, Mary E. m. Cruser, C. M. on 66-Nov-7 [66-Nov-15: 2C].
Duncan, N. J. H. m. Hiss, Mary Jane on 69-Nov-16 [69-Nov-18: 2C].
Duncan, Thomas (65 yrs.) d. on 70-Jan-29 of Epilepsy [70-Jan-31: 1H].
Duncan, William Y. m. Tweedale, Amelia on 69-Jun-8 [69-Jun-10: 2C; 69-Jun-12: 2B].
Dungan, Elizabeth d. on 68-Aug-14 [68-Aug-17: 2B].
Dungan, Francis D. (70 yrs.) d. on 70-Apr-24 [70-Apr-28: 2C].
Dungan, H. G. m. Armor, Sedonia C. on 68-Feb-12 [68-Feb-14: 2C].
Dungan, Louis (10 mos.) d. on 69-Jul-3 [69-Jul-5: 2C].
Dungan, Mina S. (4 yrs., 6 mos.) d. on 66-Jun-9 [66-Jun-11: 2B].
Dungan, Sallie Ann m. Pitzer, John Bernard on 66-Jan-3 [66-Jan-11: 2B].
Dungan, William H. (5 mos.) d. on 66-May-24 [66-Jun-11: 2B].
Dunger, Wilhelmina m. Maydwell, Theodore F. on 70-Oct-11 [70-Oct-21: 2C].
Dunham, Alverda S. m. Stokes, John H. on 68-Sep-11 [66-Sep-25: 2B].
Dunichan, Bridget (74 yrs.) d. on 67-Jun-7 [67-Jun-8: 2B].
Dunigan, Ann (33 yrs.) d. on 67-May-22 [67-May-25: 2A].
Dunigan, Patrick (72 yrs.) d. on 70-Mar-23 [70-Mar-25: 2C].
Dunigan, Sarah E. m. Justice, John W. on 68-Dec-21 [68-Dec-28: 2B].
Dunkell, Kate m. Albers, Charles F. on 67-Dec-12 [67-Dec-17: 2B].
Dunkerly, George W. m. Harvey, Rebecca Jane on 69-Sep-9 [69-Sep-15: 2B].
Dunkerly, Minerva (36 yrs.) d. on 68-Aug-25 [68-Dec-2: 2B].
Dunkerly, William Matthew d. on 66-Nov-4 [66-Nov-8: 2C].
Dunlap, C. Lewis m. Darrington, Mary on 68-Jul-16 [68-Jul-17: 2B].
Dunlap, Henry (18 yrs.) d. on 67-Jul-24 Drowned [67-Jul-25: 1F; 67-Jul-26: 2C; 67-Jul-27: 1G, 2B].
Dunlap, Mary (1 yr., 4 mos.) d. on 67-Jul-26 [67-Jul-27: 2B].
Dunlap, Melville S. m. Jacobs, Laura V. on 70-Mar-31 [70-Apr-6: 2B].
Dunlap, W. D. m. Fahnestock, Sue on 66-Sep-20 [66-Sep-21: 2B].
Dunn, Amelia S. m. Urbach, William J. on 70-Jun-7 [70-Jun-9: 2C].
Dunn, Andrew (1 yr., 3 mos.) d. on 68-Aug-20 [68-Aug-21: 2B].
Dunn, Benjamin F. m. Bright, Emma on 68-Jun-2 [68-Jun-13: 2B].
Dunn, Bridget m. Gibson, John Henry on 68-Jan-6 [68-Jan-11: 2B].
Dunn, Charles Howard (1 yr., 7 mos.) d. on 68-Dec-10 [68-Dec-12: 2C].
Dunn, Christopher J. m. Nelligan, Mary on 70-Oct-10 [70-Nov-7: 2A].
Dunn, Cornelia Adelaide (8 yrs., 9 mos.) d. on 67-Jan-30 [67-Jan-31: 2C].
Dunn, Daniel (1 yr., 5 mos.) d. on 69-Sep-29 [69-Sep-30: 2B].
Dunn, Edward (49 yrs.) d. on 66-Aug-30 [66-Aug-31: 2B].
Dunn, Edward m. Ward, Mary on 67-Sep-14 [67-Nov-28: 2C].
Dunn, Edward H. m. Thorpe, Mary Louisa on 66-Jul-26 [66-Jul-28: 2C].
Dunn, Eliza m. McEntee, James J. on 70-Oct-20 [70-Oct-24: 2B].
Dunn, Hannah (70 yrs.) d. on 66-Jul-17 [66-Jul-19: 2C].
Dunn, Hetty (83 yrs.) d. on 70-Sep-15 [70-Sep-17: 2B].
Dunn, Issac B m. Tatham, George F. [68-Oct-12: 2B].
Dunn, Jacob m. Weaver, Mary L. on 70-Jan-12 [70-Feb-5: 2B].

Dunn, Jessie Webster (6 mos.) d. on 70-Feb-26 [70-Mar-2: 2C].
Dunn, John m. Price, Josephine A. on 66-Feb-13 [66-Feb-24: 2B].
Dunn, John, Jr. (18 yrs.) d. on 69-Jul-16 [69-Jul-17: 2C; 69-Jul-27: 2C].
Dunn, John Cummings (7 mos.) d. on 69-Oct-4 [69-Oct-5: 2B].
Dunn, Joseph m. O'Connor, Sarah on 67-Nov-4 [67-Nov-9: 2B].
Dunn, Katie P. m. Whittelsey, E. J. on 70-Nov-22 [70-Dec-6: 2C].
Dunn, Louisa Klein d. on 69-Oct-20 [69-Oct-21: 2B].
Dunn, Margaret (27 yrs.) d. on 66-Jan-7 [66-Jan-9: 2B].
Dunn, Margaret Donaldson (6 yrs., 4 mos.) d. on 67-Jan-18 [67-Jan-19: 2C].
Dunn, Maria L. m. Cole, A. P. on 69-Jun-16 [69-Sep-21: 2B; 69-Sep-24: 2B].
Dunn, Mary (36 yrs.) d. on 69-Oct-7 [69-Oct-8: 2C].
Dunn, Mary E. m. Myers, John J. on 69-May-11 [69-May-13: 2B].
Dunn, Michael (36 yrs.) d. on 67-Dec-1 [67-Dec-2: 1G, 2C; 67-Dec-3: 2C; 67-Dec-4: 2C].
Dunn, Rose A. d. on 66-Aug-2 [66-Aug-3: 2C].
Dunn, Susan Anna (90 yrs.) d. on 68-Nov-25 [68-Nov-26: 2B].
Dunn, Thomas (60 yrs.) d. on 69-Mar-28 [69-Mar-29: 2B].
Dunn, William (65 yrs.) d. on 70-Apr-27 Crushed in cave-in [70-May-2: 2B].
Dunn, William Henry (10 yrs., 11 mos.) d. on 67-Jan-30 [67-Jan-31: 2C].
Dunn, Willie C. m. Breaton, Rosa on 66-Sep-12 [66-Sep-13: 2C].
Dunn, Winter M. d. on 70-Jul-19 [70-Jul-23: 3D].
Dunning, Halsey, Rev. d. on 69-Jan-11 [69-Jan-12: 2C; 69-Jan-13: 1G, 2D; 69-Jan-14: 1G].
Dunning, James H. (27 yrs.) d. on 66-Jul-16 [66-Jul-18: 2C].
Dunning, Mary (66 yrs.) d. on 66-Mar-23 [66-Apr-24: 2C].
Dunnington, Nancy m. Clarke, Addison on 69-Sep-15 [69-Sep-16: 2B].
Dunock, Samuel Ross (41 yrs.) d. on 66-Feb-15 [66-Mar-13: 2C].
Duns, Margaret (59 yrs.) d. on 67-Oct-19 of Typhoid [67-Nov-20: 2C].
Dunsmore, Mary T. m. Welsh, James on 70-Nov-22 [70-Dec-15: 2C].
Duoning, James (47 yrs.) d. on 66-Jul-24 [66-Aug-8: 2C].
Dupuy, Charles H. d. on 69-Feb-4 of Accidental Poisoning [69-Feb-5: 1F; 69-Feb-6: 1H; 69-Feb-8: 1H].
Durborow, Alverta d. on 70-Oct-24 [70-Oct-27: 2B].
Durborow, Eliza Woods (34 yrs.) d. on 69-Jan-9 [69-Jan-15: 2D].
Durgan, William (53 yrs.) d. on 70-Jun-30 [70-Jul-2: 2B].
Durham, Amelia m. Fowler, Randolph on 70-Dec-15 [70-Dec-19: 2C].
Durham, Catharine m. Miller, Jacob C. on 69-Jun-16 [69-Jun-17: 2C].
Durham, Clara Virginia (1 yr., 8 mos.) d. on 70-Sep-14 [70-Sep-16: 2B].
Durham, Edward (21 yrs.) d. on 66-Sep-5 in Railroad accident [66-Sep-7: 4B].
Durham, Eliza m. Walter, William H. on 70-Apr-20 [70-Apr-29: 2B].
Durham, Emma C. (2 yrs., 10 mos.) d. on 70-Dec-6 [70-Dec-8: 2C].
Durham, Lizzie m. Canon, John A. on 67-Nov-19 [67-Nov-23: 2B].
Durham, Martha P. m. Sohl, Henry S. on 67-Mar-21 [67-Apr-2: 2B].
Durham, Mary A. m. Rogers, Frederick on 67-Aug-15 [67-Aug-24: 2B].
Durham, Mary Ann Rogers (9 yrs., 8 mos.) d. on 67-Sep-11 [67-Sep-12: 2B].
Durity, Rebecca Minerva (38 yrs.) d. on 69-Nov-1 [69-Nov-4: 2C].
Durkee, Elizabeth C. (69 yrs.) d. on 67-Jun-25 [67-Jul-1: 2B].
Durkee, John A. (66 yrs.) d. on 66-Jan-24 [66-Jan-30: 1F].
Durkee, John L. m. Durkee, Mary on 68-Sep-10 [68-Sep-11: 2B].
Durkee, Joseph H. m. Eaverson, Cora L. on 69-Nov-2 [69-Nov-4: 2B].
Durkee, Mary m. Durkee, John L. on 68-Sep-10 [68-Sep-11: 2B].
Durkin, Thomas d. [67-Oct-8: 2B].
Durkins, Mary m. Smith, James H. on 66-Feb-1 [66-Feb-2: 2C].
Durning, Martha d. on 66-Jul-18 [66-Jul-19: 2C].
Durocher, Maria L. (69 yrs.) d. on 68-Mar-11 [68-Mar-12: 2B].
Durr, Amelia T. m. Urbach, William J. on 70-Jun-7 [70-Jun-14: 2B].
Durst, Catherine Y. (53 yrs.) d. on 68-Jun-18 of Consumption [68-Jun-19: 2B; 68-Jun-20: 2B].

Durst, Cordelia F. (36 yrs.) d. on 70-May-17 [70-May-18: 2B].
Durst, Sarah E. m. Kines, John W. on 66-May-22 [66-May-30: 2C].
Duschane, John (50 yrs.) d. on 67-Dec-31 [68-Jan-2: 2C; 68-Sep-9: 1G].
Dushane, Harriet R. m. Root, C. S. on 68-Jul-22 [68-Jul-24: 2C].
Dushane, James A. m. Brunt, Eliza J. on 70-Jan-18 [70-Jan-20: 2C].
Dutrow, Jonathan Manro m. Snyder, Rebecca Catherine on 66-Apr-19 [66-Apr-23: 2B].
Dutrow, Margaret (62 yrs.) d. on 70-Jul-4 [70-Jul-6: 2C].
Dutrow, Mary (22 yrs.) d. on 67-Mar-23 [67-Mar-25: 2C].
Dutton, John W. m. Lewis, Emma V. on 69-Jun-1 [69-Jun-3: 2B].
Dutton, Kate m. Pitt, William T. on 68-Nov-11 [68-Nov-17: 2C].
Dutton, Libby (1 yr., 10 mos.) d. on 70-Aug-26 [70-Aug-30: 2C].
Dutton, Lydia G. m. Norris, William H. on 67-Dec-26 [68-Jan-8: 2C].
Dutzell, Franklin (50 yrs.) d. on 70-Aug-26 in Stevedore accident [70-Aug-27: 4D].
Duval, M. Emily d. on 67-Apr-30 [67-May-16: 2B].
Duvall, A. Leslie m. Watkins, Emily on 70-Nov-26 [70-Nov-30: 2C].
Duvall, Antoinette d. on 69-Sep-13 of Yellow fever [69-Dec-9: 2C].
Duvall, Benjamin F. m. Smith, Mary C. on 68-May-14 [68-Oct-20: 2B].
Duvall, Charles M. m. Hollingsworth, Mollie on 66-Dec-29 [66-Dec-31: 2C].
Duvall, Charles W. (26 yrs.) d. on 67-Aug-27 in Railroad accident [67-Aug-29: 1G, 2B].
Duvall, D. (63 yrs.) d. on 69-Jan-30 [69-Feb-5: 2C].
Duvall, Edwin W. m. Nichols, Caroline on 69-Sep-23 [69-Oct-8: 2B].
Duvall, Eliza R. m. Price, Benjamin on 68-Oct-29 [68-Nov-2: 2B].
Duvall, Elizabeth (52 yrs.) d. on 68-Nov-26 of Cancer [68-Nov-30: 2C].
Duvall, Ellen Lavinia m. Steuart, James H. on 69-Apr-18 [69-Apr-20: 2B].
Duvall, Eugene Post (2 mos.) d. on 67-Aug-17 [67-Aug-19: 2C].
Duvall, Evans m. Green, Josie on 70-Nov-22 [70-Nov-24: 2B].
Duvall, Ferdinand m. Linthicum, Annie E. on 66-Nov-20 [66-Nov-27: 2B].
Duvall, Frances F. m. Kyle, George H. on 67-Jan-1 [67-Jan-3: 2B].
Duvall, Franklin m. Anderson, Mary E. on 68-Nov-24 [68-Nov-28: 2C].
Duvall, Fred (2 yrs., 8 mos.) d. on 67-Feb-16 [67-Feb-19: 2C].
Duvall, G. C. m. Gant, Mollie on 66-Feb-13 [66-Feb-21: 2C].
Duvall, George W. m. Phillips, Mary B. on 66-Oct-18 [66-Nov-3: 2B].
Duvall, Grayson W. m. Rauterberg, Mary on 70-May-10 [70-May-16: 2B].
Duvall, Hannah Elizabeth (2 yrs., 7 mos.) d. on 67-Mar-24 [67-Mar-25: 2C].
Duvall, Harry C. m. Mettee, Maggie C. on 67-Jan-1 [67-Jan-3: 2B].
Duvall, Kate m. Ellicott, George, Jr. on 67-Dec-24 [67-Dec-25: 2C].
Duvall, Lizzie M. m. Miller, Hamilton J. on 67-Mar-20 [67-Apr-1: 2C].
Duvall, Louisa m. Silver, Frank on 68-Nov-16 [68-Nov-19: 2C].
Duvall, Lydia A. d. on 68-Aug-19 [68-Aug-21: 2B].
Duvall, Mareen M., Dr. (63 yrs.) d. on 68-Sep-3 [68-Sep-4: 2A].
Duvall, Maria d. of Pneumonia [68-Apr-23: 2B].
Duvall, Maria Blanche (7 mos.) d. on 68-Apr-9 [68-May-1: 2B].
Duvall, Marshall m. Fort, Susie R. on 68-Jun-4 [68-Jun-22: 2B].
Duvall, Mary (87 yrs.) d. on 66-Feb-5 [66-Feb-7: 2C; 66-Feb-9: 2C].
Duvall, Mary E. m. Shaffer, Ira W. on 66-Jun-10 [66-Jun-26: 2B].
Duvall, Mary Jane m. Gray, H. Otis on 66-Apr-26 [66-Apr-27: 2C; 66-Apr-28: 2A].
Duvall, S. Turner m. Lawrence, Kate M. on 68-Sep-22 [68-Sep-25: 2B].
Duvall, Sallie D. d. on 67-Sep-10 [67-Sep-11: 2B; 67-Sep-12: 2B].
Duvall, Susie R. m. Kennard, A. A. on 66-Jun-14 [66-Jun-15: 2C].
Duvall, Vinton W. m. Smith, Augusta J. on 68-Oct-13 [68-Oct-15: 2C].
Duvall, Virginia R. m. Atkinson, J. E. on 67-Oct-17 [67-Oct-18: 2C].
Duvall, William B. (55 yrs.) d. on 69-Feb-2 [69-Feb-3: 2C; 69-Feb-6: 2C].
Duvall, William J. (26 yrs., 2 mos.) d. on 66-Aug-20 of Consumption [66-Aug-22: 2C].
Duvall, William T. (20 yrs.) d. on 70-Aug-31 [70-Sep-1: 2B].
Duve, Emma (1 yr., 1 mo.) d. on 69-Jun-27 [69-Jun-28: 2C].

Duwees, J. C. (52 yrs.) d. on 68-May-27 [68-May-29: 2B].
Duwees, Lizzie S. m. Dils, Charles B. on 69-Jun-24 [69-Nov-9: 2C].
Duwees, Mary M. (19 yrs.) d. on 67-Mar-10 [67-Mar-12: 2C].
Dwen, Lawrence (61 yrs.) d. on 67-Jun-19 [67-Jun-20: 2B].
Dwen, Maria L. m. Hartmier, Richard J. on 65-Dec-26 [66-Jan-2: 2C].
Dwen, Mary Alice (67 yrs.) d. on 68-May-27 [68-Jun-6: 2A].
Dwen, Peter S. (34 yrs.) d. on 67-Sep-19 of Yellow fever [67-Sep-20: 2A].
Dwinelle, Mary E. d. on 70-Apr-13 [70-Apr-14: 2B; 70-Apr-15: 2B].
Dwyer, Anna Eliza (2 yrs.) d. on 66-Feb-12 [66-Feb-13: 2C; 66-Nov-28: 2B].
Dwyer, George W. (36 yrs.) d. on 70-Feb-22 [70-Feb-24: 2C].
Dwyer, John Frederick d. on 66-Jul-13 [66-Jul-18: 2C].
Dwyer, Kate m. Hook, Joseph on 67-Apr-23 [67-Apr-26: 2B].
Dwyer, Mary Elizabeth (89 yrs.) d. on 68-Jun-23 [68-Jun-26: 2B].
Dwyer, Michael (40 yrs.) d. on 69-Oct-22 of Suicide (Jumped from window) [69-Oct-23: 4E; 69-Oct-25: 4C].
Dwyer, Walter Macgill (1 mo.) d. on 66-Nov-17 [66-Nov-28: 2B].
Dyer, C. W. m. Johnson, Emma C. on 67-Nov-5 [67-Nov-12: 2C].
Dyer, Carrie I. d. on 70-Jan-10 [70-Jan-11: 2C; 70-Jan-12: 2C; 70-Jan-13: 2D].
Dyer, Horatio P. m. Morton, M. Jennie [70-Apr-13: 2B].
Dyer, J. F. m. Gormley, Mary E. on 69-Oct-6 [69-Oct-14: 2C].
Dyer, Jane m. Hartlove, Asbury on 69-Apr-13 [69-Apr-28: 2B].
Dyer, John J. m. Curley, Ida on 69-Oct-11 [69-Apr-20: 2B].
Dyer, Laura V. m. Sargent, George W. on 69-Aug-26 [69-Aug-31: 2B].
Dyer, Major (32 yrs.) d. on 69-Jul-11 [69-Jul-14: 2D].
Dyer, Margaret (50 yrs.) d. on 67-Oct-19 of Heart disease [67-Oct-21: 1E].
Dyer, Richard R. D. m. Chester, Anna M. on 69-Oct-19 [69-Oct-21: 2B].
Dyer, Stephen (28 yrs.) d. on 66-Oct-19 of Construction cave-in [66-Oct-20: 1G].
Dyer, T. Baker m. Bowling, Rosa on 67-Oct-29 [67-Nov-1: 2B].
Dyer, Walter J. L. m. Taylor, Carrie J. on 66-Oct-10 [66-Oct-16: 2B].
Dykers, John m. Haynes, Sarah E. on 67-Nov-7 [67-Nov-16: 2B].
Dyott, Sarah A. m. Legg, John on 69-Dec-22 [69-Dec-23: 2B].
Dysart, Moses A. (78 yrs.) d. on 70-Dec-16 [70-Dec-19: 2C].
Dyson, Mary (49 yrs.) d. on 66-Mar-6 [66-Mar-10: 2B].
Eachus, Florence Louisa (5 yrs.) d. on 68-Jan-7 [68-Jan-8: 2C].
Eader, J. R. m. Dulaney, Emma J. on 70-Nov-23 [70-Dec-1: 2C].
Eagan, Catherine (67 yrs.) d. on 66-Sep-26 [66-Sep-27: 2C].
Eagan, Eliza C. m. Wilson, James H. on 67-May-26 [67-Jun-4: 2A].
Eagan, Mary C. m. Hibline, John J. on 70-Dec-1 [70-Dec-8: 2B].
Eagan, Mary Ellen (6 yrs.) d. on 70-Oct-14 [70-Oct-15: 2B].
Eagan, Mary Ellen (2 yrs., 10 mos.) d. on 70-Dec-10 [70-Dec-12: 2C].
Eagan, Owen (53 yrs.) d. on 66-Apr-28 [66-Apr-30: 2B].
Eagan, Sarah m. Cassidy, Francis on 67-Jun-10 [67-Jun-19: 2B].
Eagan, William (1 yr., 2 mos.) d. on 69-Aug-16 [69-Aug-17: 2C].
Eager, Elizabeth (60 yrs.) d. on 68-May-21 [68-May-25: 2A].
Eager, Joseph m. Tatum, Maggie on 66-Mar-20 [66-Apr-12: 2B].
Eagleston, Charles m. Wolf, Mary on 70-Jan-18 [70-Jan-20: 2C].
Eagleston, Mary (23 yrs.) d. on 70-Sep-13 [70-Sep-14: 2B].
Eagleston, Mary E. m. Newkirk, Joseph V., Jr. on 67-Jun-10 [67-Jun-17: 2B].
Eagleston, William H. m. Wittler, Mary on 69-Dec-12 [69-Dec-24: 2C].
Eansey, Julia A. (81 yrs.) d. on 66-Aug-27 [66-Aug-29: 2B].
Eardley, Solomon m. Henderson, Louisa on 69-May-20 [69-Jun-2: 2B].
Eareckson, Albert (1 yr., 8 mos.) d. on 66-Mar-24 [66-Mar-26: 2B].
Eareckson, Alexander Thompson (1 yr., 3 mos.) d. on 70-Oct-23 [70-Oct-26: 2B].
Eareckson, Ann C. m. Carville, Thomas B. on 68-Nov-10 [68-Nov-12: 2C].
Eareckson, Frederick G. m. Thompson, S. M. on 67-Feb-28 [67-Mar-21: 2C].

Eareckson, Kate (2 yrs., 5 mos.) d. on 67-Jan-17 [67-Jan-26: 2C].
Eareckson, Rose (4 yrs., 3 mos.) d. on 67-Jan-9 [67-Jan-16: 2C].
Earhart, Laura T. m. Welch, Edward R. on 67-Oct-21 [67-Oct-23: 2B; 67-Oct-25: 2B].
Earhart, Virginia L. m. Tolson, Thomas H. on 68-Jun-25 [68-Jun-26: 2B].
Earicsson, Julia S. m. Deale, W. Edward on 69-Dec-4 [69-Dec-8: 2C].
Earl, Eliza Ann (42 yrs.) d. on 70-Sep-19 [70-Sep-20: 2B].
Earl, Florence Abbrilla (1 yr.) d. on 70-Aug-28 [70-Aug-29: 2C].
Earle, Sarah m. Marshall, Edward on 69-Nov-3 [69-Nov-5: 2C].
Earles, James H. (33 yrs., 11 mos.) d. on 66-Jul-18 of Consumption [66-Jul-23: 2C].
Early, Bernard J. m. Murphy, Agnes A. on 67-Oct-29 [67-Oct-30: 2B].
Earnish, E. (76 yrs.) d. on 68-Apr-7 [68-Apr-9: 2B].
Earp, Amanda Ellen (12 yrs., 5 mos.) d. on 69-Mar-16 [69-Mar-18: 2C].
Earp, Amos m. Shaw, Marian E. on 69-Jan-12 [69-Jan-14: 2D].
Earp, John W. m. Shipley, C. Elizabeth on 67-Apr-2 [67-Apr-5: 2B].
Earreckson, Thomas B. (42 yrs.) d. on 70-Aug-4 [70-Aug-5: 2C; 70-Aug-6: 2C].
Eary, Ella V. m. Fletcher, James A. on 68-Oct-19 [68-Oct-26: 2B].
East, Hattie m. Cole, Pennock I. on 67-Jan-30 [67-Feb-2: 2C].
East, Hattie A. m. Monmonier, Louis on 66-Mar-13 [66-Mar-26: 2B].
East, Henry, Capt. d. on 66-Jun-1 Drowned [66-Jun-5: 1F].
East, Henry, Sr. (57 yrs.) d. on 66-Jun-21 [66-Jun-23: 2B].
East, Henry T. m. King, Elizabeth A. on 68-Aug-20 [68-Aug-28: 2B].
East, Robert P. m. Gibson, Anna on 69-Nov-14 [69-Dec-3: 2C].
Easten, James W. d. on 67-Sep-20 [67-Sep-21: 2A].
Easter, Anna H. (39 yrs.) d. on 68-May-18 [68-May-20: 2A; 68-May-21: 2B].
Easter, John, Jr. (46 yrs.) d. on 69-Jul-1 [69-Jul-2: 2C; 69-Jul-3: 2B].
Easter, John, Jr. m. Quarles, Mollie E. C. on 66-Dec-20 [66-Dec-25: 2B].
Easter, Peter (62 yrs., 2 mos.) d. on 69-Mar-31 [69-Apr-2: 2C].
Eastham, Anna m. Daniel, A. R. on 66-Dec-11 [66-Dec-18: 2B].
Eastly, John d. on 68-May-2 [68-May-4: 2B].
Eastman, Catherine (93 yrs.) d. on 70-Jan-9 [70-Jan-10: 2C].
Eastman, Edward m. Chase, Nellie on 68-Jun-18 [68-Jun-20: 2B].
Easton, Allie A. m. Trout, John A. on 67-Sep-5 [67-Nov-23: 2B].
Easton, Stanley (25 yrs.) d. on 70-Dec-11 [70-Dec-14: 2C].
Eaton, Elizabeth (35 yrs.) d. on 68-Dec-6 [68-Dec-8: 2C].
Eaton, Janie m. Taylor, Sidney B on 69-Jan-7 [69-Jan-15: 2D].
Eaton, Joseph S. m. Davis, Elizabeth A. on 66-Aug-18 [66-Aug-25: 2A].
Eaton, Mary S. m. Sederberg, Charles A. on 70-May-17 [70-May-21: 2B].
Eaverson, Cora L. m. Durkee, Joseph H. on 69-Nov-2 [69-Nov-4: 2B].
Ebaugh, Andrew C. m. Tucker, Ida H. on 70-Apr-21 [70-Jun-2: 2B].
Ebaugh, Carrie m. Krafft, Daniel J. on 68-Sep-1 [68-Sep-8: 2B].
Ebaugh, Eliza J. m. Gillingham, C. Raborg on 70-Jun-4 [70-Jun-6: 2B].
Ebbert, George (85 yrs.) d. on 66-Jan-22 [66-Jan-23: 1F, 2C].
Ebberts, George W. m. Milis, Charlotte on 67-Apr-11 [67-Apr-30: 2A].
Ebberts, Josephine A. (31 yrs.) d. on 68-Feb-2 [68-Feb-5: 2D].
Eberhart, Catharine m. Vogelsang, Jacob on 66-Apr-1 [66-Apr-3: 2B].
Eberhart, George Lewis (1 yr., 4 mos.) d. on 68-Dec-19 [68-Dec-23: 2C].
Eberhart, Henry (54 yrs.) d. on 69-Jul-25 [69-Jul-27: 2C].
Eberhart, Henry m. Wallace, Isabella E. on 67-Sep-29 [67-Oct-1: 2B].
Ebert, Fannie V. m. Dorsey, W. H. B. on 67-Nov-20 [67-Nov-27: 2B].
Eberwein, August (27 yrs.) d. on 68-Jul-31 Drowned [68-Aug-5: 1G].
Eborn, Mary C. m. Morris, Abraham on 68-Mar-8 [68-Mar-14: 2B].
Ebsworth, Annie (1 yr., 8 mos.) d. on 68-Jan-27 [68-Jan-29: 2C].
Ebsworth, Annie (1 yr.) d. on 68-Nov-19 [68-Nov-20: 2C].
Ebsworth, Puella Dolores (6 mos.) d. on 70-Aug-24 [70-Aug-25: 2C].
Ebsworth, Thomas J. (66 yrs.) d. on 67-Jul-1 [67-Jul-2: 2B].

Eccleston, G. W. m. D'Espeaux, Mollie F. W. on 68-May-31 [68-Jun-21: 2C].
Eccleston, James J. Grant (4 yrs., 10 mos.) d. on 70-Feb-13 [70-Feb-15: 2C].
Eck, John L. m. Hilderbrand, Priscilla on 67-Mar-26 [67-Apr-4: 2B].
Eck, William F. m. Hildebrand, Annie on 67-Feb-5 [67-Feb-7: 2C].
Eckert, George W. m. Kraft, Abby S. on 66-Apr-26 [66-Apr-28: 2A].
Eckert, Jerome (15 yrs., 8 mos.) d. on 68-Feb-4 [68-Feb-6: 2C].
Eckert, Linda Tippett d. on 68-Sep-1 [68-Sep-2: 2B].
Eckhardt, Charles m. Riggins, Fannie on 69-Oct-18 [69-Oct-19: 2B].
Eckloff, Joseph E. m. Smith, Kate V. on 68-Sep-8 [68-Sep-14: 2B].
Eckloff, Mary A. m. Leese, Martin W. on 70-Sep-15 [70-Sep-23: 2C].
Eddins, Richard W. m. Furlong, Virginia A. on 66-Dec-13 [66-Dec-17: 2B].
Eddins, Susan E. m. Grinnell, John B. on 67-May-26 [67-May-30: 2B].
Eddy, Augustus, Rev. (71 yrs.) d. on 70-Feb-9 [70-Feb-12: 2C].
Eddy, Gardner W. m. Parson, Lucinda C. on 69-Mar-25 [69-Mar-29: 2B].
Eddy, Henrietta m. Adams, James C. on 68-Jun-9 [68-Jun-12: 2B].
Eddy, Olive M. m. Hasselman, Otto H. on 70-Apr-21 [70-Apr-23: 2B].
Edelen, Amos d. on 69-Mar-24 of Suicide (Hanging) [69-Mar-29: 1G].
Edelen, L. C. m. Lewis, Annie E. on 67-Apr-23 [67-Apr-27: 2A].
Edelen, Sarah E. m. Frazier, William W. on 66-Mar-20 [66-Mar-22: 2B].
Edeler, Charles H. m. McCauley, Mary W. on 69-Jun-3 [69-Jun-19: 2B].
Edelman, Romwald m. Bauer, Josephine [68-Apr-9: 2B].
Edelman, Sabina (89 yrs.) d. on 70-Feb-1 [70-Feb-2: 2B; 70-Feb-3: 2B].
Eden, Annie Elizabeth (12 yrs., 11 mos.) d. on 66-Feb-7 [66-Feb-8: 2C].
Eden, Elizabeth (61 yrs.) d. on 70-Dec-2 [70-Dec-3: 2B].
Eden, Mary Arrabella (3 yrs., 5 mos.) d. on 68-Mar-10 [68-Mar-12: 2B].
Eden, Richard Ellis (4 mos.) d. on 68-Jan-27 [68-Mar-12: 2B].
Edgar, Charles W. m. Waters, Mary on 70-Sep-27 [70-Sep-29: 2B].
Edgar, George H. m. Slater, Helen on 68-Jun-16 [68-Jun-19: 2B].
Edgar, Mary E. m. Linton, John on 68-Nov-26 [68-Nov-28: 2C].
Edgerton, Anna (65 yrs.) d. on 70-May-16 [70-May-17: 2B].
Edgerton, Thomas m. Watson, Mary E. on 66-Aug-21 [66-Aug-23: 2C].
Edkins, Joseph W. m. Leach, Allie on 66-Feb-20 [66-Apr-18: 2B].
Edkins, Sarah A. m. Lofgren, P. G. on 68-May-7 [68-May-16: 2A].
Edmeades, Elizabeth E. m. Pilsch, Jacob on 67-Dec-2 [67-Dec-3: 2C].
Edmonds, Hannah B. m. Griffith, George A. on 66-Nov-7 [66-Nov-10: 2B].
Edmonds, James Pouder d. on 69-Jan-30 [69-Feb-1: 2C].
Edmonds, Jane d. on 69-Nov-30 [69-Dec-2: 2C].
Edmonds, Mary J. m. Shorey, Miles Chase on 70-Jan-6 [70-Jan-10: 2C].
Edmonds, William Emory (3 mos.) d. on 70-Nov-18 [70-Nov-19: 2B].
Edmondson, Arthur T. (19 yrs.) d. on 69-May-20 [69-May-24: 2B].
Edmondson, Eleanor (73 yrs.) d. on 70-May-19 [70-May-21: 2B].
Edmondson, Joseph A. m. Berry, Mary E. on 67-Oct-22 [67-Oct-24: 2B].
Edmondson, W. Winder m. Hooper, Maggie L. on 67-Nov-28 [67-Nov-30: 2C].
Edmondson, William Leeds (20 yrs.) d. on 68-Feb-29 of Typhoid [68-Mar-3: 2C].
Edmonston, Charles m. Berryman, Fannie E. on 68-Jan-14 [68-Jan-25: 2B].
Edmonston, Emma m. Clark, Gabriel D., Jr. on 69-Apr-13 [69-Apr-15: 2B].
Edmonston, Francis O. m. Streets, Mary Emma on 69-Jun-7 [69-Jun-8: 2B].
Edmonston, Tilghman (45 yrs.) d. on 68-May-17 [68-May-19: 2B].
Edwards, Agnes Virginia (1 yr., 8 mos.) d. on 68-Aug-2 [68-Aug-6: 2B].
Edwards, Charles G. m. Frey, Mary L. on 68-Dec-3 [68-Dec-24: 2C].
Edwards, Emma T. m. Graff, James H. on 66-Nov-8 [66-Nov-10: 2B].
Edwards, Eveline (32 yrs.) d. on 69-Feb-26 [69-Feb-27: 2C].
Edwards, Fannie Bird (9 mos.) d. on 66-Jun-25 [66-Jun-27: 2C].
Edwards, Frank Slattery (7 mos.) d. on 67-Jul-1 [67-Jul-8: 2C].
Edwards, George Ross d. on 68-May-2 [68-May-4: 2B].

Edwards, Ida Rosalie (5 mos.) d. on 69-Sep-28 [69-Sep-30: 2B].
Edwards, James (71 yrs.) d. on 70-May-1 [70-May-3: 2B].
Edwards, James B. (43 yrs.) d. on 70-Dec-16 of Typhoid [70-Dec-17: 2B, 4C].
Edwards, James Lewis (8 yrs.) d. on 67-Aug-16 [67-Aug-19: 2C].
Edwards, James Ponley (6 yrs., 11 mos.) d. on 66-Jan-1 of Typhoid [66-Jan-6: 2C].
Edwards, John m. Biddison, Elizabeth A. on 69-Aug-23 [69-Sep-25: 2B].
Edwards, John R. m. Dolphin, Emma on 66-Mar-24 [66-Mar-31: 2C].
Edwards, Joseph H., Sr. (86 yrs.) d. on 70-Nov-18 [70-Nov-19: 2B].
Edwards, Joshua Colfax (3 mos.) d. on 70-Jan-11 [70-Jan-12: 2C].
Edwards, Julia E. m. Jenkins, John on 66-Nov-13 [66-Nov-17: 2C].
Edwards, Laura V. (27 yrs.) d. on 69-Oct-15 [69-Oct-19: 2C].
Edwards, Lizzie S. m. Barbour, Thomas C. on 66-Aug-8 [66-Aug-13: 2C].
Edwards, Louisa E. m. Snell, J. Marvin on 68-Jun-16 [68-Jun-23: 2B].
Edwards, Margaret (56 yrs.) d. on 67-Oct-24 [67-Oct-25: 2B].
Edwards, Margaret Victoria (37 yrs., 9 mos.) d. on 69-Apr-28 [69-Apr-29: 2B].
Edwards, Martha J. m. Dare, Ephram E. on 66-Sep-9 [67-May-28: 2B].
Edwards, Mary m. Chittenden, Charles H. on 66-Dec-28 [67-Jan-15: 2C].
Edwards, Mary Ross d. on 66-Jul-12 [66-Aug-13: 2C].
Edwards, Nannie E. m. Green, William H. on 69-Feb-16 [69-Feb-20: 2A].
Edwards, Susan (77 yrs.) d. on 70-Jun-6 [70-Jun-7: 2C].
Edwards, Thomas D. (1 yr.) d. on 67-Nov-24 [67-Nov-27: 2C].
Effing, Bernard (42 yrs.) d. on 66-Feb-9 of Hanging [66-Feb-10: 1F].
Effort, Catherine M. d. on 67-Mar-13 [67-Mar-15: 2C].
Egan, Annie M. (6 mos.) d. on 70-Jun-25 [70-Jun-27: 2C].
Egan, Ella R. m. Carter, Francis R. on 70-Jan-2 [70-Jan-26: 2C].
Egbert, James E. d. on 68-Dec-31 [69-Dec-15: 2D].
Egbert, James H. (51 yrs.) d. on 68-Dec-31 [69-Jan-15: 2D].
Egerton, Ann Rebecca (1 yr.) d. on 68-Jun-25 [68-Jul-1: 2B].
Egerton, Clara S. m. Diblee, Robert on 69-Jan-27 [69-Jan-29: 2C].
Egerton, J. Chesley m. Leffler, Virginia on 69-Nov-17 [69-Nov-22: 2C].
Egerton, Samuel E. (7 mos.) d. on 68-Jul-13 [68-Jul-14: 2B].
Egerton, Samuel E. m. Wilson, Elizabeth D. on 66-Nov-20 [66-Nov-22: 2C].
Eggleston, Abram (36 yrs.) d. on 69-Apr-10 [69-Apr-12: 2A].
Eggleston, Anna m. Jones, William A. M. on 68-Aug-5 [68-Aug-6: 2B].
Eggleston, Annie m. Diffenbaugh, John on 66-Mar-5 [66-Mar-7: 2B].
Eggleston, Bird m. Beveridge, Laura V. on 67-Oct-15 [68-Jan-23: 2C].
Eggleston, Carrie m. Waidner, Jacob B. on 66-Mar-22 [66-Mar-27: 2B].
Eggleston, Edward J. m. Armstrong, Catherine C. on 69-Feb-9 [69-Feb-16: 2C].
Eggleston, Emily m. Tracey, James on 67-Sep-15 [67-Sep-17: 2A].
Eggleston, John T. m. Miller, Elizabeth A. on 67-Jan-23 [67-Mar-5: 2C].
Eggleston, Lucretia V. m. Cook, Lewis G. on 69-Dec-2 [69-Dec-8: 2C].
Eggling, Charles P. (8 mos.) d. on 68-May-22 [68-May-23: 2A].
Eggling, Mary E. (4 yrs.) d. on 70-Feb-10 [70-Feb-12: 2C].
Egner, Caroline (14 yrs., 10 mos.) d. on 66-Dec-19 [66-Dec-20: 2B; 66-Dec-21: 2B].
Ehlen, Annie M. m. Parker, Llewellyn L. on 68-Apr-14 [68-Apr-17: 2B].
Ehlen, Charlie E. (2 yrs.) d. on 70-Apr-24 of Chronic croup [70-Apr-26: 2B].
Ehlen, Ellen (48 yrs.) d. on 66-Nov-6 [66-Nov-7: 2C].
Ehlen, Thomas A. m. Schelle, Kate R. on 67-Jul-2 [67-Jul-10: 2B].
Ehlers, Bernard H. m. Littleton, Mary G. on 66-Sep-5 [66-Sep-25: 2B].
Ehlers, Eudora (2 yrs., 5 mos.) d. on 69-Mar-13 [69-Mar-15: 2C].
Ehlers, Frank Bernard (2 mos.) d. on 69-Jul-28 [69-Aug-2: 2C].
Ehlers, Lewis (66 yrs.) d. on 66-Aug-27 [66-Sep-8: 2B].
Ehlers, Louisa (59 yrs.) d. on 70-Sep-13 [70-Sep-14: 2B].
Ehlers, Sophie (1 yr., 4 mos.) d. on 69-Apr-12 [69-Apr-14: 2B].
Ehlies, Ellen d. on 67-Aug-1 [67-Aug-2: 2C].

Ehrhart, Ann (66 yrs.) d. on 69-Mar-12 [69-Mar-13: 2B].
Ehrman, Anna Margaret (31 yrs.) d. on 68-Oct-3 [68-Oct-5: 2C].
Ehrman, Annie m. Hartenstein, Alvin on 69-Nov-16 [69-Nov-18: 2C].
Ehrman, B. (47 yrs.) d. on 67-Sep-11 of Heart disease [67-Sep-12: 1F].
Ehrman, Florence d. on 70-Aug-4 [70-Aug-5: 2C].
Ehrman, George M. m. Eichler, Sallie A. on 66-May-14 [66-May-18: 2C].
Ehrman, Henrietta M. (40 yrs.) d. on 68-Oct-5 [68-Oct-7: 2C].
Ehrman, John (69 yrs.) d. on 66-Jan-1 [66-Jan-2: 2C].
Ehrman, Louis m. Gronau, Virginia on 69-Oct-28 [69-Oct-30: 2B].
Ehrman, M. m. Rider, Freddie on 67-Jun-12 [67-Jun-14: 2B].
Ehrman, Mary A. m. Collins, John H. on 67-Jul-2 [67-Jul-6: 2B].
Eichelberger, Charles E. m. Horpel, Louisa on 68-Jun-22 [68-Jun-24: 2B].
Eichelberger, Charles H. m. Gramblitt, Keturah B. on 65-Sep-18 [66-Apr-17: 2C].
Eichelberger, Fannie (2 yrs., 1 mo.) d. on 66-Jan-12 of Chronic croup [66-Jan-13: 2C].
Eichelberger, George Howard (3 mos.) d. on 67-Sep-22 [67-Sep-23: 2A].
Eichelberger, George N. m. Levett, Annie M. on 66-Jun-25 [66-Jul-3: 1C].
Eichelberger, Henrietta M. (66 yrs.) d. on 67-May-6 [67-May-13: 2B].
Eichelberger, J. Franklin (71 yrs.) d. on 70-Nov-22 [70-Nov-24: 4C].
Eichelberger, L. S., Dr. (44 yrs.) d. on 68-Sep-2 [68-Sep-7: 2A].
Eichelberger, L. S. m. Richstein, Lizzie on 66-Apr-24 [66-May-24: 2C].
Eichelberger, Laura (1 mo.) d. on 66-Dec-11 [66-Dec-12: 2B].
Eichelberger, Lucille Jane (1 mo.) d. on 69-Jun-3 [69-Jun-5: 2B].
Eichelberger, Mary m. Campbell, James on 67-Feb-19 [67-Mar-5: 2C].
Eichhorn, Mary E. (82 yrs.) d. on 70-Jan-6 [70-Jan-8: 2B; 70-Jan-10: 2C].
Eichlberger, Ferdinand Chatard (1 yr., 2 mos.) d. on 68-Dec-28 [68-Dec-30: 2D].
Eichler, Sallie A. m. Ehrman, George M. on 66-May-14 [66-May-18: 2C].
Eichman, George Marden (3 yrs.) d. on 66-Nov-19 Murdered (Stabbing) [66-Nov-20: 4B; 66-Nov-21: 2C].
Eickel, Henry W. (2 yrs., 6 mos.) d. on 68-Jan-20 of Diptherial croup [68-Jan-21: 2C; 68-Jan-22: 2C].
Eickel, Mary Elveta (7 mos.) d. on 67-Dec-6 [67-Dec-7: 2B].
Eigenbrodt, Christian, Jr. m. Stetzenbach, Amelia on 69-Jul-28 [69-Aug-30: 2B].
Eilert, Mary (71 yrs., 7 mos.) d. on 68-Oct-26 [68-Nov-3: 2B].
Eilsa, Maggie m. Leitz, Charles F. on 70-Jan-5 [70-Jan-25: 2C].
Eisla, Jacob F (49 yrs.) d. on 69-Jul-10 [69-Jul-12: 2C].
Eisler, John (63 yrs.) d. on 66-Feb-26 [66-Feb-28: 2C; 66-Mar-1: 2B].
Eitel, Philip d. on 67-Jul-24 of Heatstroke [67-Jul-26: 1G].
Elcliff, Frederick d. on 70-Oct-10 of Suicide (Shooting) [70-Oct-12: 4D].
Elder, Allen (67 yrs.) d. on 67-Aug-29 [67-Aug-30: 1G, 2B].
Elder, Basil S. (96 yrs.) d. on 69-Oct-13 [69-Oct-14: 1H, 2C; 69-Oct-15: 2C].
Elder, C. Maurice m. Van Valzah, Lucy G. on 67-Nov-19 [67-Nov-23: 2B].
Elder, Catherine (69 yrs.) d. on 70-Feb-28 [70-Mar-2: 2C].
Elder, Charlotte H. m. Hardesty, B. McLean on 70-Apr-26 [70-Apr-30: 2A].
Elder, George H. d. on 66-Jul-18 [66-Jul-19: 2C].
Elder, Ida Estella (2 yrs.) d. on 66-Jan-31 [66-Feb-8: 2C].
Elder, Laura A. m. Ellicott, Joseph T. on 66-Sep-4 [66-Sep-21: 2B].
Elder, P. Laurensson m. Williams, Octavia on 69-Jan-28 [69-Feb-2: 2C].
Elder, Samuel (71 yrs.) d. on 66-Mar-8 of Apoplexy [66-Mar-9: 1F, 2B; 66-Mar-10: 2B].
Elderdice, Mary (76 yrs.) d. on 67-Dec-3 [67-Dec-7: 2B].
Elderkin, James K. (43 yrs.) d. on 68-Jan-1 [68-Jun-22: 2B].
Eldridge, Charlotte d. on 69-Jun-24 [69-Jun-25: 2C].
Eldridge, Harry (5 yrs.) d. on 66-Jun-13 [66-Jun-14: 2B].
Eldridge, Robert m. Oliver, Hannah on 70-Apr-14 [70-Apr-16: 2B].
Elfrey, Philip J. m. King, Sarah E. on 67-Aug-6 [67-Aug-22: 2B].
Elgin, H. C. m. Boteler, Prudence on 68-Dec-22 [68-Dec-24: 2C].

Elias, Samuel m. Elias, Sara F. on 68-Apr-27 [68-Apr-29: 2B].
Elias, Sara F. m. Elias, Samuel on 68-Apr-27 [70-Apr-29: 2B].
Eliason, John A. m. Coughlin, Kate J. on 66-Apr-10 [66-Apr-17: 2C].
Eliason, Mattie J. m. Green, John on 66-Apr-10 [66-Apr-17: 2A].
Eliason, Samuel S. H. m. Woods, Mary A. on 70-Dec-20 [70-Dec-31: 2B].
Elkhardt, Carrie m. Herrmann, John on 70-Jul-10 [70-Jul-15: 2C].
Elkins, Joseph D. (47 yrs.) d. on 68-Nov-15 [68-Nov-18: 2C].
Ellender, Martha H. m. Fitzer, Edward F. on 69-Dec-27 [69-Dec-31: 2C].
Ellender, Sarah E. m. Moore, Randolph L. on 67-Jun-11 [67-Jun-19: 2B].
Ellermeyer, Charles A. (18 yrs.) d. on 67-Oct-17 Murdered (Shooting) [67-Oct-18: 1E; 67-Oct-19: 4A; 67-Oct-21: 1F].
Ellett, F. M. m. Hewlett, Rebecca on 66-Jun-21 [66-Jun-23: 2B].
Elliott, Agnes Barbara (57 yrs.) d. on 66-Jan-21 [66-Jan-22: 2C].
Ellicott, Andrew (65 yrs.) d. on 66-Jul-6 [66-Jul-7: 2B].
Ellicott, Benjamin (71 yrs.) d. on 67-Feb-1 [67-Feb-2: 2C].
Ellicott, Carroll W. m. Pierce, Belle on 68-Jun-29 [68-Jul-7: 2B].
Ellicott, Emily d. on 66-Dec-23 [66-Dec-25: 2B].
Ellicott, Evam T., Jr. d. on 67-Apr-5 [67-Apr-6: 2B].
Ellicott, Evan T. (74 yrs.) d. on 66-Dec-21 [66-Dec-24: 1F, 2B].
Ellicott, George (71 yrs.) d. on 69-Dec-16 [69-Dec-17: 1H, 2C].
Ellicott, George, Jr. m. Duvall, Kate on 67-Dec-24 [67-Dec-25: 2C].
Ellicott, Joseph T. m. Elder, Laura A. on 66-Sep-4 [66-Sep-21: 2B].
Ellicott, Margaret m. Woodhull, Alfred A. on 68-Dec-15 [68-Dec-16: 2C].
Ellicott, Pattie Tyson m. Haines, Ephraim on 66-Apr-3 [66-Apr-6: 2B].
Ellicott, Sallie m. Arnold, H. Tracy on 67-Sep-10 [67-Sep-11: 2B].
Ellicott, Sarah E. d. on 66-Dec-22 [66-Dec-24: 2B].
Ellicott, William H. (29 yrs.) d. on 70-Aug-8 [70-Aug-11: 2C].
Ellinger, Elenora m. Rose, William P. on 67-Oct-23 [67-Oct-24: 2B].
Elliot, Elizabeth D. m. Murphy, James D. on 70-Feb-22 [70-Feb-24: 2C; 70-Feb-26: 2C].
Elliot, George D. m. Jenkins, Sarah E. on 69-Oct-28 [69-Dec-6: 2C].
Elliot, John Thomas Clayton d. on 68-Aug-4 [68-Aug-6: 2B].
Elliot, Kate E. d. on 65-Aug-11 [66-Aug-10: 2C].
Elliot, William H. (19 yrs.) d. on 66-Jan-10 [66-Jan-12: 2C].
Elliott, Edward (54 yrs.) d. on 66-Mar-25 [66-Mar-27: 2B].
Elliott, Eleanor (67 yrs.) d. on 69-Aug-22 [69-Aug-24: 2B].
Elliott, Ellen Eliza (29 yrs.) d. on 69-Oct-10 [69-Oct-11: 2C].
Elliott, Fannie m. Leef, Albert F. on 70-Aug-1 [70-Aug-3: 2C].
Elliott, George m. Appler, Elizabeth on 69-Aug-8 [69-Oct-18: 2C].
Elliott, George m. Jenkins, Sarah on 69-May-18 [69-May-20: 2C].
Elliott, George G. m. McComas, Elizabeth S. on 66-Aug-2 [66-Aug-7: 2C].
Elliott, James J. m. Asher, Mary C. on 67-Jan-3 [67-Jan-7: 2C].
Elliott, John (53 yrs.) d. on 68-Nov-24 in Railroad accident [68-Nov-26: 1H].
Elliott, John (65 yrs.) d. on 66-May-14 [66-May-15: 2C; 66-May-16: 2C].
Elliott, John B., Dr. d. on 69-Jun-4 [69-Jun-10: 2C].
Elliott, John W. (1 yr., 4 mos.) d. on 70-Aug-29 [70-Aug-31: 2B].
Elliott, Joseph P. m. Janney, Margaret H. on 70-Feb-23 [70-Feb-25: 2C].
Elliott, Julia A. m. Williams, Thomas B. on 66-Mar-6 [66-Mar-10: 2B].
Elliott, Lewis A. m. Krebs, Mary C. on 69-Dec-21 [70-Jan-11: 2C].
Elliott, Margaret d. on 69-Mar-12 [69-Mar-15: 2C].
Elliott, Mary Ellen (13 yrs.) d. on 70-Aug-7 [70-Aug-8: 2C].
Elliott, Mary J. m. Etchison, John H. on 69-Jan-5 [69-Jan-18: 2C].
Elliott, Nellie B. m. Cooley, John H. on 66-Jan-2 [66-Jan-16: 2C].
Elliott, Rebecca d. on 70-Dec-28 [70-Dec-29: 2C].
Elliott, Rebecca m. Huster, William G. on 67-Apr-21 [67-Apr-24: 2B].
Elliott, Robert (44 yrs.) d. on 68-Sep-11 [68-Sep-15: 2B].

Elliott, Susan m. Bangs, D. A. on 67-Aug-27 [67-Aug-30: 2B].
Elliott, Susan Bangs d. on 70-Apr-5 [70-Apr-6: 2C].
Elliott, Thomas J. R. m. Johnson, Amelia on 66-Nov-14 [66-Nov-21: 2C; 66-Nov-22: 2C].
Elliott, Thomas J. R. m. Johnston, Amelia on 66-Nov-14 [66-Nov-22: 2C].
Elliott, W. Wallace m. Issacs, Emma E. on 70-Mar-2 [70-Mar-7: 2C].
Elliott, Walter Foxhall (5 yrs.) d. on 70-Jul-28 [70-Jul-25: 2C].
Elliott, William H. m. Layfield, Ella Virginia on 66-Oct-23 [66-Oct-26: 2B].
Elliotte, Ellen m. Jenkins, T. Christopher on 69-Jan-27 [69-Jan-30: 2C].
Ellis, Agnes (7 yrs.) d. on 70-Sep-30 [70-Oct-1: 2B].
Ellis, Alice Barranger (16 yrs.) d. on 66-Nov-7 [66-Nov-9: 2C].
Ellis, Edward d. on 67-Jan-3 [67-Jan-5: 2C].
Ellis, Elizabeth A. m. Davis, Alexander T. on 70-May-9 [70-Oct-11: 2B].
Ellis, John C. H., Capt. (73 yrs.) d. on 66-Sep-8 in Carriage accident [66-Sep-11: 2B, 4B; 66-Sep-12: 2A].
Ellis, John E. m. Dorsey, Emma on 67-Nov-21 [67-Nov-26: 2B].
Ellis, Sallie m. Harvey, J. W., Jr. on 68-Feb-6 [68-Sep-1: 2A].
Ellis, Samuel H. (56 yrs.) d. on 69-May-18 [69-May-19: 2C; 69-May-20: 2C].
Ellison, William Thomas m. Cates, Susan on 66-Feb-9 [66-Feb-12: 2D].
Elmer, Emma B. m. Ashbury, Joseph M. on 70-Oct-27 [70-Nov-12: 2B].
Elmer, Mary Estelle (10 mos.) d. on 70-Nov-6 [70-Nov-7: 2B].
Elmore, Charles Dawson (4 mos.) d. on 66-Aug-2 [66-Aug-3: 2C].
Elmore, Hannah (79 yrs.) d. on 70-Sep-18 [70-Sep-19: 2B; 70-Sep-20: 2B].
Elsenroade, Maggie m. Brant, William M. on 70-Dec-12 [70-Dec-13: 2C].
Elseroad, Lewis N. m. Hoburg, Carrie on 68-Jan-1 [68-Jan-17: 2C].
Elsroad, Frankie (1 yr., 7 mos.) d. on 70-Aug-3 [70-Aug-6: 2C].
Elsroad, R. m. Hammen, M. Z. on 70-Nov-10 [70-Nov-15: 2C].
Eltonhead, Molley E. T. m. Grace, Charles H. on 68-Oct-7 [68-Oct-12: 2B].
Eltonhead, William T. m. Johns, Aggie on 67-Jan-23 [67-Feb-1: 2C].
Ely, Arabella (17 yrs.) d. on 70-Jun-19 [70-Jun-21: 2C].
Ely, Charles Francis (2 yrs., 5 mos.) d. on 70-Sep-7 [70-Sep-8: 2B].
Ely, Charles W. m. Hagerty, Amelia on 68-Jun-16 [68-Jun-20: 2B].
Ely, Ellen N. m. Tapper, William H. on 70-Jan-2 [70-Jan-4: 2C].
Ely, Eunice Noyes (79 yrs.) d. on 70-Jul-25 [70-Jul-26: 2B].
Ely, Jesse F. m. Dodge, Lois Adela on 70-Jun-16 [70-Jun-24: 2C].
Ely, Joseph F. m. Kraus, Elmira on 67-May-26 [67-May-29: 2B].
Ely, Minnie N. (10 mos.) d. on 70-Jul-25 [70-Jul-27: 2C].
Ely, Samuel McComas (9 mos.) d. on 68-Jun-13 [68-Jun-15: 2B].
Ely, Samuel S. m. Stocksdale, Hannah E. on 68-Nov-18 [68-Nov-21: 2C].
Elzey, Sue B. d. on 66-Apr-7 [66-Apr-9: 2B].
Elzey, Willie m. Lynde, F. M. on 68-Apr-29 [68-Apr-30: 2B].
Emerick, Annie Elizabeth (11 mos.) d. on 67-Apr-3 of Brain congestion [67-Apr-6: 2B].
Emerick, Thomas K. (28 yrs.) d. on 69-Jan-1 [69-Jan-2: 2C].
Emerick, William H. (43 yrs.) d. on 70-Jan-30 [70-Jan-31: 2C; 70-Feb-2: 1G].
Emerson, Charles H. m. Slaughter, Fannie Rose on 68-Jul-9 [68-Jul-13: 2B].
Emerson, Edwin A. m. Boerner, Emma E. on 66-Mar-13 [66-Apr-14: 2B].
Emerson, Jennie m. Morgan, H. Suter on 66-May-10 [66-May-16: 2C].
Emery, Mary Ann d. on 70-Nov-6 [70-Nov-7: 2B; 70-Nov-8: 2B].
Emery, Mary Jane d. on 67-Jul-28 [67-Jul-30: 2C].
Emery, Sabine, Col. (34 yrs.) d. on 68-Mar-24 [68-Mar-25: 1G; 68-Mar-26: 2B].
Emich, Julia A. m. Birch, Clinton S. on 68-May-25 [68-Jun-6: 2A].
Emich, Marcella m. Lannan, William on 70-Dec-27 [70-Dec-28: 2C].
Emich, Nellie m. Fee, Jacob on 69-Sep-27 [69-Oct-5: 2B].
Emich, Nicholas (29 yrs.) d. on 68-Aug-20 [68-Aug-26: 2B].
Emich, Nicholas m. Allen, Martha E. on 68-Mar-24 [68-Apr-7: 2B].
Emich, Sarah L m. Huffington, William O. on 68-Sep-21 [68-Oct-1: 2B].

Emlen, Charles m. Roff, Lavinia on 69-Jan-7 [69-Jan-9: 2C].
Emmart, Catherine (72 yrs., 11 mos.) d. on 70-Apr-12 [70-Apr-13: 2B].
Emmart, Emily Jane (19 yrs.) d. on 66-Jul-25 [66-Jul-27: 2C].
Emmart, Henry D. m. Cumberland, Emma V. on 68-Dec-3 [68-Dec-21: 2B].
Emmart, Martha A. m. Reed, Hiram F. on 67-Apr-11 [67-Apr-18: 2B].
Emmart, Michael, Sr. (60 yrs.) d. on 66-Nov-17 [66-Nov-19: 2B].
Emmart, Michael A. (23 yrs.) d. on 66-Aug-16 of Cholera [66-Aug-18: 1G, 2B].
Emmart, Sallie E. m. Iglehart, Emery E. on 68-Nov-12 [68-Nov-14: 2B].
Emmart, Thomas m. Wardell, Emma on 70-Sep-19 [70-Dec-29: 2C].
Emmart, Vernon S. m. Hindes, Minnie on 68-Jun-4 [68-Jun-15: 2B].
Emmet, Jacob m. Williams, Sarah on 67-Jan-28 [67-Feb-8: 2C].
Emmitt, Joseph d. on 68-Jun-30 [68-Jul-1: 1G].
Emmons, Antonia Thornton m. White, Edmond on 70-Sep-20 [70-Sep-24: 2B].
Emmons, H. E. (39 yrs.) d. on 67-Jan-1 [67-Jan-8: 2B].
Emmons, Lizzie (23 yrs.) d. on 66-May-21 [66-May-24: 2C].
Emory, Ann (67 yrs.) d. on 68-Oct-28 [68-Oct-31: 2B].
Emory, D. Hopper m. Sadtler, Mary C. on 66-Nov-22 [66-Nov-28: 2B].
Emory, Ellen Barry m. Quinlan, Joseph E. on 66-Apr-24 [66-Apr-28: 2A].
Emory, Frederick B. m. Berger, Willa on 69-Sep-6 [69-Oct-25: 2B].
Emory, Hester Clark (9 mos.) d. on 69-Aug-2 [69-Aug-10: 2C].
Emory, Joe m. Rhodes, Joseph on 69-Mar-30 [69-Jul-13: 2C].
Emory, M. Lizzie m. Lucy, Thomas on 67-Aug-1 [67-Aug-3: 2B].
Emory, Maggie Wilmer m. Cockey, George B. on 67-Oct-8 [67-Oct-9: 2B; 67-Oct-14: 2B].
Emory, Maria (63 yrs.) d. on 69-Sep-23 [69-Sep-24: 2C; 69-Sep-25: 2B].
Emory, Maria Louisa (2 yrs., 1 mo.) d. on 66-Jan-21 of Lung congestion [66-Jan-24: 2B].
Emory, Mary C. (24 yrs., 2 mos.) d. on 70-Jan-20 [70-Jan-21: 2C; 70-Jan-22: 2B].
Emory, Mary E. d. on 70-Mar-9 [70-Mar-11: 2C].
Emory, Nannie M. m. Ahern, Francis I. on 68-Jun-16 [68-Jun-17: 2B; 68-Jun-18: 2B; 68-Jun-19: 2B].
Emory, Richard m. Hall, Agnes S. on 70-Jan-4 [70-Jan-12: 2B].
Emory, Sue m. Nichols, N. K. on 69-Jun-1 [69-Jun-12: 2B].
Emory, Thomas H. m. Evans, Albertine F. on 66-Oct-16 [66-Oct-18: 2B].
Emrich, Amelia M. (1 yr., 1 mo.) d. on 68-Dec-23 [68-Dec-24: 2C].
Emrick, Mary C. m. Saunders, William W. on 68-Mar-4 [68-Nov-26: 2B].
Eney, John E. m. Freeburger, Amanda on 67-Jun-12 [67-Jun-20: 2B].
Eney, Joseph R. m. Drugan, Mary C. on 68-Jan-7 [68-Jan-10: 2C].
Engel, C. H. m. Sand, Mary E. on 69-Jan-19 [69-Feb-1: 2C].
Engel, John O. (47 yrs., 7 mos.) d. on 69-Mar-30 [69-Mar-31: 2C; 69-Apr-1: 2C].
Engel, Julius L. m. Stine, Matilda on 66-Jun-7 [66-Jan-9: 2B].
Engelmyer, August (13 yrs.) d. on 67-Apr-1 in Railroad accident [67-Apr-2: 4B].
Engers, Mary (12 yrs.) d. on 67-Jan-6 Burned [67-Jan-8: 1G].
England, Carrie A. m. Winters, James on 68-Oct-1 [68-Oct-17: 2B].
England, John H. m. Lewis, Mary on 66-Oct-18 [66-Nov-10: 2B].
England, Mary d. on 67-Mar-10 [67-Mar-14: 2C; 67-Mar-15: 2C].
Englar, W. J. m. Benson, M. Virginia on 70-May-3 [70-May-4: 2C].
Engle, Matilda (43 yrs.) d. on 66-Jul-15 [66-Jul-17: 2C].
Engle, William A. (1 yr., 6 mos.) d. on 70-Feb-4 [70-Feb-5: 2C].
Engle, William J. m. McLane, Sarah B. on 67-Oct-6 [67-Oct-8: 2B].
Englebrecht, Carrie Florence (16 yrs.) d. on 70-Nov-15 [70-Nov-26: 2C].
Englehart, Mary (60 yrs.) d. on 66-Apr-19 [66-Apr-20: 2B].
Engler, Elizabeth (30 yrs.) d. on 70-Jan-6 of Consumption [70-Jan-8: 2B].
Engler, Emma L. m. Gibbons, James E. on 70-Nov-17 [70-Nov-19: 2B].
Engles, Elizabeth F. (64 yrs.) d. on 66-Aug-4 of Consumption [66-Aug-7: 2C].
English, Alice (17 yrs.) d. on 67-Oct-31 [67-Nov-2: 2B].
English, Fannie m. Chamberlin, Thomas on 70-Oct-25 [70-Oct-27: 2B].

English, Marshall d. on 70-Aug-10 [70-Aug-15: 2B].
Enlows, John m. Dean, Harriet on 70-Dec-10 [70-Dec-13: 2C].
Ennalls, Henrett Ann m. Ross, Perry on 67-Jul-18 [67-Jul-20: 2C].
Ennis, Elizabeth V. (4 yrs.) d. on 69-Jun-24 [69-Jun-25: 2C].
Ennis, Harriet A. d. on 67-Aug-18 [67-Aug-19: 2C].
Ennis, John (65 yrs.) d. on 68-Sep-2 [68-Sep-3: 2B].
Ennis, Moses (30 yrs.) d. on 68-Sep-14 Drowned [68-Oct-13: 2C].
Ennis, Sarah Catherine (23 yrs., 11 mos.) d. on 66-Aug-22 [66-Aug-25: 2A].
Ennis, Thomas H. m. Nevitt, Virginia on 68-Dec-17 [68-Dec-23: 2C].
Enos, H. K. m. Tyson, Olive O. B. on 66-Aug-1 [66-Aug-2: 2C].
Ensey, Grace E. m. Ward, Asa, Jr. on 66-Dec-17 [66-Dec-19: 2B].
Ensley, Mary E. m. Bradford, Lemuel S. on 69-Oct-5 [69-Oct-7: 2B].
Ensminger, Ophelia L. m. Gies, John, Jr. on 70-Dec-1 [70-Dec-6: 2C].
Ensor, Adaline V. m. Cornelius, George W. on 69-Dec-26 [69-Dec-28: 2C].
Ensor, Amelia J. m. Anderson, John H. on 70-Jul-20 [70-Jul-25: 2C].
Ensor, Benjamin F. m. Joyce, Emma P. on 66-Sep-2 [67-Jan-14: 2C].
Ensor, Columbus A. (38 yrs.) d. on 66-Mar-23 [66-Mar-26: 2B].
Ensor, George Washington (6 yrs., 7 mos.) d. on 69-Oct-25 [69-Oct-27: 2B].
Ensor, Honour m. Burns, James T. on 67-Dec-24 [67-Dec-25: 2C].
Ensor, John E. m. Chilcoate, Elizabeth E. on 66-May-10 [66-May-12: 2A].
Ensor, Luke E. m. Caples, Laura W. on 68-Oct-29 [68-Nov-7: 2B].
Ensor, Maggie A. m. Ross, G. Howard on 69-Oct-1 [69-Oct-5: 2B].
Ensor, Sarah (69 yrs.) d. on 70-Jun-24 [70-Jun-25: 2B].
Ensor, Sarah Rebecca m. Ayres, George W. on 65-Dec-24 [66-Jan-15: 2B].
Entler, Amelia m. Rodenmayer, John on 66-Oct-17 [66-Oct-18: 2B].
Entz, Andrew (1 yr., 3 mos.) d. on 68-Aug-17 [68-Aug-18: 2B].
Entz, Harry Lyttleton (8 mos.) d. on 70-Aug-3 [70-Aug-4: 2C; 70-Aug-5: 2C].
Eplinger, Edward m. Schiller, Caroline on 70-May-26 [70-May-30: 2B].
Epple, Rosa m. Reeger, John C., Jr. on 69-May-2 [69-May-11: 2B].
Eppley, Mary L. (24 yrs.) d. on 67-Jan-1 [67-Jan-2: 2C].
Epron, Peter (73 yrs.) d. on 66-Nov-27 [66-Nov-29: 2B].
Erb, Howard m. McCabe, Georgene on 69-Aug-26 [69-Aug-27: 2B].
Erdman, Amanda L. m. Wise, Silas L. on 69-Aug-5 [69-Aug-7: 2B].
Erdman, Barbara E. m. Lamley, Jacob F. on 69-Mar-30 [69-Apr-7: 2C].
Erdman, Charles H. m. Barker, Hattie E. on 70-Jan-19 [70-Jan-22: 2B].
Erdman, Frank S. m. Graves, Mollie on 69-Sep-29 [69-Oct-1: 2B].
Erdman, Kate W. (2 yrs., 1 mo.) d. on 68-Mar-15 [68-Mar-16: 2B].
Erdman, William H., Jr. m. McGlone, Mary E. on 66-Nov-22 [66-Dec-13: 2B].
Erek, Jennie B. d. on 70-Jul-20 [70-Jul-21: 2C].
Erek, William H. (45 yrs.) d. on 68-Feb-12 [68-Feb-14: 2C].
Erich, Christiana (57 yrs.) d. on 69-May-5 [69-May-6: 2B].
Erich, Florence Nightengale (3 yrs., 10 mos.) d. on 70-Apr-29 [70-Apr-30: 2A].
Erich, Henrietta m. Hook, J. G. on 69-Aug-14 [69-Sep-18: 2B].
Erich, Henry C. m. Baetjer, Eliza L. on 66-Feb-7 [66-Feb-9: 2C].
Ermeling, Margaret (55 yrs., 1 mo.) d. on 68-Aug-6 [68-Aug-7: 2B; 68-Aug-8: 2C].
Ermer, Henry m. Kaiser, Amelia M. on 68-Jun-1 [68-Jun-10: 2B].
Ermey, William H. (28 yrs.) d. on 68-Feb-12 [68-Feb-13: 2C; 68-Feb-14: 2C].
Erskine, George m. Henthorn, Ann Jane on 69-Sep-1 [69-Sep-11: 2B].
Ervin, Ann m. Lednum, William Dallas on 68-Dec-28 [69-Mar-16: 2C].
Ervin, Anna (34 yrs.) d. on 67-Feb-8 [67-Feb-9: 2B].
Ervin, John (53 yrs.) d. on 66-Mar-7 [66-Mar-15: 2C].
Eschbach, Elizabeth C. d. on 70-Jan-5 [70-Jan-7: 2F].
Eschbach, Leo m. Lucchesi, Maggie T. on 69-Mar-30 [69-Apr-3: 2B].
Eschbach, Margaret (64 yrs.) d. on 67-Sep-29 [67-Sep-30: 2B; 67-Oct-1: 2B].
Esender, George T. m. Buckingham, Olivia [68-Dec-1: 2C].

Esenger, Emma L. d. on 66-Jul-11 [66-Aug-8: 2C].
Esgate, Thomas D. (33 yrs.) d. on 68-Jan-22 [68-Feb-5: 2B, 2D].
Esham, F. W. m. Watkins, John W. on 68-Sep-29 [68-Oct-2: 2B].
Eshelman, Emma m. Richards, T. S. on 67-Feb-20 [67-Feb-23: 2C].
Eshrick, Sarah W. (50 yrs.) d. on 69-Feb-3 [69-Feb-4: 2C; 69-Feb-5: 2C].
Esler, Edward d. on 67-Nov-16 [67-Nov-18: 2B].
Eslin, Louisa S. (23 yrs.) d. on 68-May-21 [68-May-22: 2C].
Espey, Charles Lawson (4 mos.) d. on 70-Jul-24 [70-Jul-26: 2C].
Espey, William S. (65 yrs.) d. on 67-Oct-19 [67-Oct-21: 2B].
Espy, Emma Matilda (18 yrs.) d. on 66-Aug-13 of Consumption [66-Aug-15: 2B].
Essert, George (50 yrs.) d. on 67-Apr-9 Drowned [67-Apr-10: 1G].
Essig, Bertha (12 yrs., 5 mos.) d. on 70-Jun-24 [70-Jun-25: 2B].
Estabrooke, Mary (37 yrs.) d. on 70-May-16 of Childbirth [70-May-19: 2C].
Esteley, Frederick (48 yrs.) d. on 70-Jul-11 [70-Jul-16: 2B].
Estep, Mary M. m. Williams, J. J. on 70-Aug-18 [70-Aug-23: 2B].
Etchberger, James S. m. Cooksey, Annie Ramsay on 69-Sep-7 [69-Sep-9: 2B].
Etchison, John H. m. Elliott, Mary J. on 69-Jan-5 [69-Jan-18: 2C].
Etchison, Maggie A. m. Silance, John H. on 70-Feb-2 [70-Feb-8: 2C].
Etchison, Virginia W. m. Jackson, James G. on 67-May-30 [67-Jun-4: 2A].
Etherington, Sarah (78 yrs.) d. on 67-Aug-13 [67-Aug-14: 2B].
Etherington, Virginia E. m. Jones, David A. on 70-Jun-7 [70-Jul-9: 2C].
Etris, Agnes (20 yrs., 8 mos.) d. on 69-Sep-15 [69-Sep-16: 2B].
Etter, Philip L. (43 yrs.) d. on 66-Jul-10 [66-Jul-13: 2C].
Etting, Frank M. m. Campbell, Alice Taney on 68-Oct-27 [68-Oct-29: 2B].
Ettle, Annie B. m. Roberts, Thomas on 68-Feb-4 [68-Feb-8: 2B].
Eubank, Sue M. m. Booth, George W. on 66-Feb-13 [66-Feb-15: 2C].
Euler, George W. m. Moore, Laura J. on 67-Dec-4 [67-Dec-7: 2B].
Eunick, Edward H. m. Toner, Rebecca A. on 68-Jan-1 [68-Jan-22: 2C].
Eustace, Catherine (24 yrs.) d. on 70-Feb-5 [70-Feb-7: 2C].
Eustis, George, Mrs. d. on 67-Dec-4 [67-Dec-10: 2B].
Evans, Albertine F. m. Emory, Thomas H. on 66-Oct-16 [66-Oct-18: 2B].
Evans, Andrew J. m. Moore, Sarah A. on 68-Dec-3 [69-Jan-7: 2C].
Evans, Annie Augusta (7 mos.) d. on 68-Mar-18 [68-Mar-19: 2B; 68-Mar-20: 2B].
Evans, Arthur Olander (6 mos.) d. on 70-Feb-26 [70-Mar-1: 2C].
Evans, Catherine Josephine d. on 68-Apr-26 of Lung congestion [68-Apr-28: 2B].
Evans, Charles W. m. Jenkins, Elma on 70-Nov-22 [70-Nov-26: 2B].
Evans, Charles William (2 yrs., 6 mos.) d. on 69-Dec-3 [69-Dec-6: 2C].
Evans, D'Oyley m. McDonald, Annie C. on 68-Sep-8 [68-Sep-9: 2B].
Evans, Daniel (1 yr., 2 mos.) d. on 67-Jul-11 [67-Jul-13: 2B].
Evans, Edward (28 yrs.) d. on 67-Feb-12 [67-Feb-14: 2C].
Evans, Eliza A. d. on 69-Sep-18 [69-Sep-20: 2C].
Evans, Elizabeth (73 yrs.) d. on 66-Jan-28 [66-Jan-30: 2B].
Evans, Elizabeth J. d. on 66-Dec-11 [66-Dec-18: 2B; 66-Dec-19: 2B; 66-Dec-28: 2C].
Evans, Ella Varden (5 yrs., 5 mos.) d. on 67-Jan-4 [67-Jan-7: 2C].
Evans, Ellen (9 mos.) d. on 67-Sep-28 of Bowel inflammation [67-Sep-30: 2B].
Evans, Esther (88 yrs.) d. on 68-Feb-7 [68-Feb-8: 2B].
Evans, Fannie A. (29 yrs.) d. on 66-Nov-19 [66-Nov-21: 2C].
Evans, G. W., Jr. m. Stigers, Ambrosia on 68-Jul-15 [68-Jul-18: 2B].
Evans, George m. Willis, Wellie on 66-Jan-25 [66-Jan-26: 2B].
Evans, Hugh Davey (77 yrs.) d. on 68-Jul-16 of Heatstroke [68-Jul-17: 1G, 2B; 68-Jul-18: 1G].
Evans, Inman H. m. Campbell, Mildred M. on 67-Oct-23 [67-Oct-24: 2B].
Evans, Issac, Sr. (81 yrs.) d. on 66-Sep-22 [66-Sep-24: 2B].
Evans, J. A. m. Carruthers, Angie Bell on 67-May-24 [67-Jun-4: 2A].
Evans, Joseph (8 yrs., 11 mos.) d. on 67-Mar-13 of Scarlet fever [67-Mar-14: 2C].
Evans, Joseph (69 yrs.) d. on 70-Sep-17 [70-Sep-19: 2B].

Evans, Joseph (54 yrs.) d. on 70-Nov-2 [70-Nov-3: 2C].
Evans, Julia A. m. Young, William H. on 66-Oct-17 [66-Oct-23: 2B].
Evans, Laura (19 yrs.) d. on 70-Nov-24 [70-Nov-25: 2D; 70-Nov-26: 2B].
Evans, Laura E. (42 yrs.) d. on 66-Dec-31 of Consumption [67-Jan-4: 2D].
Evans, Lizzie G. m. Bell, Richard A. on 68-Sep-24 [68-Dec-2: 2C].
Evans, Louis P. (26 yrs.) d. on 66-Apr-4 of Consumption [66-Apr-23: 2B].
Evans, Mame m. Bredemeyer, Charles H. on 68-Jan-7 [68-Jan-9: 2C].
Evans, Martha (22 yrs.) d. on 69-Dec-12 [69-Dec-13: 2C].
Evans, Mary (54 yrs.) d. on 69-Dec-24 [69-Dec-25: 2C].
Evans, Mary m. Lewis, Wilson on 66-May-28 [66-Jun-1: 2B].
Evans, Mary m. Williams, Hugh Huntington on 67-Nov-26 [67-Nov-30: 2C].
Evans, Mary A. m. Briney, John E. on 68-Dec-22 [68-Dec-30: 2C].
Evans, Mary E. m. Hood, Joshua on 68-Feb-6 [68-Feb-19: 2C].
Evans, Mary E. m. Bennett, William Huntington on 67-Nov-26 [67-Nov-30: 2C].
Evans, Mary Wareham (13 yrs., 1 mo.) d. on 69-Apr-16 [69-Apr-22: 2B].
Evans, Matilda (39 yrs.) d. on 69-Aug-21 [69-Aug-23: 2C].
Evans, Robert (56 yrs.) d. on 67-Jan-4 [67-Jan-8: 2B].
Evans, Ruth (76 yrs.) d. on 67-Jul-4 [67-Jul-6: 2B].
Evans, Samuel M. m. Donaldson, Sue on 66-Sep-8 [66-Sep-21: 2B].
Evans, Stanley (5 yrs.) d. on 68-Feb-9 [68-Feb-10: 2C; 68-Feb-11: 2C].
Evans, Theodore W. m. De La Faille, Marie Planat on 68-Sep-8 [68-Sep-9: 2B].
Evans, Thomas (80 yrs.) d. on 66-Mar-16 [66-Mar-17: 1G, 2B].
Evans, Thomas (90 yrs.) d. on 70-Jul-20 [70-Jul-21: 2C].
Evans, Thomas Layton (9 mos.) d. on 67-Jan-12 [67-Jan-14: 2C].
Evans, Virginia d. on 70-Jan-6 [70-Jan-19: 2D].
Evans, W. W. m. Wiltberger, Edith M. on 68-Aug-12 [68-Sep-9: 2B].
Evans, William (63 yrs.) d. on 69-May-16 [69-May-17: 2B].
Evans, William m. Morrisett, Helena A. on 69-Mar-17 [69-Mar-26: 2C].
Evans, William m. Bealmear, Alice on 70-Mar-17 [70-Mar-19: 2B].
Evans, William Henry (24 yrs.) d. on 67-Oct-10 [67-Nov-15: 2B].
Evans, William R. m. Linton, Marie Perkins on 70-Feb-10 [70-Feb-14: 2C].
Evans, Willie Ann m. Peterson, John on 70-Aug-12 [70-Aug-23: 2B].
Evanson, Charles Gilbert d. on 70-Mar-6 [70-Mar-8: 2C].
Evatt, Edward (62 yrs.) d. on 69-Jul-14 [69-Jul-15: 2C].
Evatt, George K. m. McCarthy, Lizzie on 66-Apr-10 [66-May-15: 2C].
Evatt, Maggie E. m. Allen, William on 66-Apr-23 [66-May-4: 2C].
Everest, Phebe A. (64 yrs.) d. on 69-Feb-4 [69-Feb-6: 2C].
Everett, James T. (36 yrs.) d. on 66-Jan-29 [66-Jan-30: 2B].
Everett, Maggie m. Perry, Alexander on 66-Feb-4 [66-Feb-6: 2D].
Everett, Thomas H. m. Lehr, Sophia on 68-Aug-2 [68-Aug-3: 2B].
Everhard, W. J. m. Cuddy, Louisa on 69-Apr-14 [69-Apr-26: 2B].
Everhart, David (60 yrs.) d. on 67-Jun-15 [67-Jun-17: 2B].
Everhart, George P. m. Hauer, Mary E. on 66-Jun-5 [66-Jun-11: 2B].
Everhart, Jacob (81 yrs.) d. on 70-Jun-26 [70-Jun-27: 2C; 70-Jun-28: 1G].
Everhart, Martin (63 yrs., 7 mos.) d. on 69-Jul-23 [69-Jul-26: 2C].
Everhart, William H. m. Howser, Emma S. on 69-Aug-15 [69-Aug-23: 2C].
Everhart, William J. (23 yrs.) d. on 70-Jul-4 [70-Jul-6: 2C].
Everist, Elizabeth (76 yrs.) d. on 70-Jul-9 [70-Jul-11: 2C].
Everist, Elizabeth (68 yrs.) d. on 70-Nov-17 [70-Nov-18: 2C].
Everist, Ruth (79 yrs.) d. on 69-Apr-2 [69-Apr-3: 2B].
Everitt, Francis A. m. Cramblett, Emma V. on 66-Nov-18 [68-Jan-6: 2B].
Everitt, Francis Thomas (10 mos.) d. on 70-Jun-19 [70-Jun-21: 2C].
Everitt, Mary A. m. Stoddard, Thomas J. on 69-Aug-18 [69-Aug-31: 2B].
Everson, George H. (1 yr., 6 mos.) d. on 69-Aug-11 [69-Aug-13: 2C].
Everson, Lizzie P. (3 yrs., 2 mos.) d. on 69-Aug-11 [69-Aug-13: 2C].

Evert, Charles L. m. Colder, Mary Ellen on 67-Oct-15 [67-Oct-17: 2B].
Ewall, Mary m. Stone, John L. on 69-Nov-17 [69-Nov-18: 2C].
Ewalt, George m. Smith, Mary J. on 70-Jun-30 [70-Jul-7: 2B].
Ewalt, Henry m. McElwee, Mary E. on 70-Mar-10 [70-Mar-23: 2C].
Ewalt, Philip (68 yrs.) d. on 67-Aug-30 [67-Sep-2: 2B].
Ewart, Clara Virginia (5 yrs.) d. on 68-Nov-18 of Scarlet fever [68-Nov-19: 2C].
Ewbanks, Mattie m. Cross, J. H. M. on 67-May-5 [67-Jul-16: 2C].
Ewen, Jeremiah E. (36 yrs.) d. on 68-Mar-8 [68-Mar-9: 2C].
Ewen, Sarah Catherine m. Keene, Charles E. on 70-Jul-19 [70-Jul-21: 2C].
Ewin, Martha A. m. Bonn, Anthony S. on 66-Jun-19 [66-Jun-22: 2B].
Ewing, Edith d. on 70-Sep-7 [70-Sep-8: 2B].
Ewing, Rebert Lee (9 mos.) d. on 66-Jul-1 of Cholera infantum [66-Jul-2: 2B].
Eyler, Henry S. m. France, Ann Louisa on 68-Apr-26 [68-May-1: 2B].
Eyster, M. Larue m. Nones, Harry S. on 68-Oct-12 [68-Oct-24: 2B].
Eytinge, Simon (82 yrs.) d. on 69-Aug-25 [69-Aug-26: 2C; 69-Aug-27: 1H, 2B].
Facey, Henry J. m. Leibin, Amelia on 66-Sep-20 [66-Sep-25: 2B].
Fadeley, Rebecca (30 yrs.) d. on 68-Mar-8 [68-Mar-10: 2C].
Fagan, Mary (22 yrs.) d. on 69-Oct-17 [69-Oct-18: 2C].
Fagan, Mary M. (21 yrs.) d. on 66-Aug-20 [66-Aug-22: 2C].
Fagan, Matthew J. (21 yrs.) d. on 66-Sep-16 of Consumption [66-Sep-17: 2B].
Fagen, Hugh E. m. Hanson, Emma on 68-Jul-5 [68-Jul-7: 2B].
Fager, Cornelius (78 yrs.) d. on 67-Aug-4 [67-Aug-6: 2C].
Fager, Fredericka (50 yrs.) d. on 66-Nov-21 [66-Nov-22: 2C].
Faherty, Bartholomew (40 yrs.) d. on 69-Sep-3 [69-Sep-4: 2B].
Faherty, Mary A. Appolonia (1 yr., 7 mos.) d. on 70-Aug-25 of Cholera infantum [70-Aug-29: 2C].
Faherty, Thomas (65 yrs.) d. on 70-May-23 [70-May-24: 2C].
Fahey, John (77 yrs.) d. on 68-Dec-14 [68-Dec-16: 2C].
Fahey, John (34 yrs.) d. on 66-Feb-25 [66-Feb-26: 2B; 66-Feb-27: 2B].
Fahey, Mary (38 yrs.) d. on 69-Mar-28 [69-Mar-30: 2C].
Fahey, Michael (28 yrs.) d. on 67-Mar-14 [67-Mar-15: 2B].
Fahey, Sarah (1 yr., 2 mos.) d. on 68-Dec-2 [68-Dec-3: 2C; 68-Dec-4: 2D].
Fahey, Sarah (1 yr., 2 mos.) d. on 70-Jun-28 [70-Jun-30: 2C].
Fahnestock, Elizabeth d. on 69-Dec-3 [69-Dec-6: 2C].
Fahnestock, Grace S. d. on 67-Jul-25 [67-Aug-8: 2B].
Fahnestock, Mary (88 yrs.) d. on 66-Jul-23 [66-Jul-26: 2C].
Fahnestock, Sue m. Dunlap, W. D. on 66-Sep-20 [66-Sep-21: 2B].
Fahs, Mary Amelia (86 yrs.) d. on 69-Jun-26 [69-Jun-28: 2C].
Faid, Mary m. Glue, Ignatius on 69-Jan-2 [69-Jan-5: 2C; 69-Jan-6: 2C].
Fails, Anna M. m. Nelson, Alexander on 69-Apr-27 [69-May-21: 2C].
Fairall, Henrietta S. m. Bagley, Horace on 70-May-19 [70-Jun-4: 2B].
Fairbank, Andrew J., Jr. (4 mos.) d. on 70-Jul-1 [70-Jul-16: 2B].
Fairbank, Anna E. (44 yrs.) d. on 70-Feb-27 [70-Feb-28: 2C].
Fairbank, Florence (10 mos.) d. on 70-Dec-24 [70-Dec-26: 2C].
Fairbank, Frank M. m. Perrigo, Sophia L. on 70-Oct-27 [70-Oct-29: 2B].
Fairbank, Josiah, Jr. m. Pumphrey, Rachel A. on 65-Nov-30 [66-Feb-14: 2C].
Fairbank, Laura A. m. Cross, Thomas W. on 66-Feb-27 [66-Mar-2: 2B].
Fairbank, Nellie d. on 70-Nov-7 [70-Nov-8: 2B].
Fairbank, Sadie Estella (8 mos.) d. on 70-Mar-10 [70-Mar-12: 2C].
Fairbank, Samuel, Dr. (29 yrs.) d. on 68-May-5 [68-May-6: 2B].
Fairbank, Thomas J. m. Martin, Libbie E. on 70-Sep-7 [70-Sep-10: 2B].
Fairbanks, Annie T. m. Jones, Henry C. on 70-Jan-2 [70-Jan-4: 2C].
Fairbanks, Christopher C. (60 yrs.) d. on 69-Jul-29 [69-Jul-30: 2C].
Fairbanks, Ida Eudora d. on 66-Apr-18 [66-Apr-20: 2B].
Fairbanks, James D. m. Hudgins, Alice on 66-Oct-16 [66-Oct-22: 2C].

Fairbanks, Kate m. Watts, J. W. on 69-Nov-9 [69-Dec-15: 2B].
Fairbanks, Kate Randall (5 mos.) d. on 69-Jul-20 [69-Jul-23: 2C].
Fairchild, Alexina m. Glanville, J. Offley on 66-Nov-5 [66-Nov-10: 2B].
Fairchild, Charles H. (42 yrs.) d. on 66-Jan-12 [66-Jan-15: 2C].
Fairchild, Frances E. m. Nicoll, Benjamin G. on 68-May-27 [68-Jun-4: 2B].
Fairchild, Kate m. Kirk, F. Dev. on 69-Sep-1 [69-Sep-3: 2B; 69-Sep-4: 2B].
Fairfax, Charles Snowden (40 yrs.) d. on 69-Apr-4 [69-Apr-5: 1G, 2B; 69-Apr-7: 1G].
Faith, Andrew m. Dooris, Mary on 70-May-20 [70-Jul-16: 2B].
Faithful, Emma m. Cullison, Eli T. on 70-Oct-13 [70-Oct-29: 2B].
Faithful, Maggie m. Coe, Roderick D. on 68-Jun-30 [68-Jul-1: 2B].
Faithful, Margaret (80 yrs.) d. on 67-Feb-9 [67-Feb-12: 2C].
Faithful, William Edgar (5 mos.) d. on 69-Feb-9 [69-Feb-11: 2C].
Falck, Emma Blanchard (6 mos.) d. on 69-Feb-23 [69-Feb-25: 2D; 69-Feb-26: 2D].
Falck, Frederick m. Reed, Amanda on 67-Dec-1 [68-Jun-8: 2B].
Falck, George M. m. Miller, Jessie A. on 70-May-10 [70-May-12: 2B].
Falck, John B. m. Stinson, Kate C. on 67-May-23 [67-May-28: 2B].
Falconar, Caroline E. d. on 67-Jun-30 [67-Jul-1: 2B].
Falconer, Robert B. (19 yrs.) d. on 68-Sep-5 [68-Sep-11: 2B].
Fales, E. Clark m. Baker, Mary R. on 66-Jun-5 [66-Jun-27: 2C].
Fales, Eleanora F. (57 yrs.) d. on 70-Aug-11 [70-Aug-12: 2C; 70-Aug-13: 2C].
Fales, Frank H. m. Clark, Sarah A. on 67-Jan-1 [67-Jan-5: 2C].
Fales, Laura V. m. Peterson, William N. on 70-Jul-31 [70-Aug-6: 2C].
Fales, Mary R. (23 yrs.) d. on 67-Oct-15 [67-Oct-17: 2B; 67-Oct-18: 2C].
Fales, Squire M. (74 yrs.) d. on 70-Aug-17 [70-Sep-17: 2B].
Falk, Louisa J. M. m. Richter, Gustave on 69-Apr-4 [69-Apr-6: 2C].
Falkner, Caroline G. W. m. Nichols, James W. on 66-Nov-29 [66-Dec-1: 2B].
Fall, , Mrs. (46 yrs.) d. on 68-Oct-23 of Epilepsy [68-Oct-24: 4B].
Fallen, James (3 yrs., 9 mos.) d. on 68-Oct-10 [68-Oct-12: 2B].
Fallen, Willy Joseph (11 mos.) d. on 69-Sep-15 [69-Sep-16: 2B; 69-Sep-17: 2C].
Fallin, Isabella Frances m. Ringrose, John A. on 67-Jun-23 [67-Jul-10: 2B].
Fallon, Battie (18 yrs.) d. [68-Oct-27: 2B].
Fallon, Edward Francis (1 yr.) d. on 69-Aug-22 [69-Aug-23: 2C].
Fallon, Thomas (20 yrs.) d. on 67-May-29 [67-May-30: 2B; 67-May-31: 2B].
Falloom, James (41 yrs.) d. on 67-Oct-23 of Intemperance [67-Oct-24: 1G, 2B].
Fallows, Harriet m. Buckingham, Greenbury on 65-Dec-24 [66-Jan-6: 2B].
Falls, Henrietta Jane d. on 70-Mar-10 [70-Mar-17: 2C].
Falls, Marie L. d. on 66-Aug-6 [66-Aug-7: 2C].
Falls, Matilda R. d. on 70-Jul-16 [70-Jul-18: 2B].
Fanchen, Jno. d. on 68-Mar-13 of Suicide (Hanging) [68-Mar-16: 1G].
Fanliken, Joseph (45 yrs.) d. on 68-Jul-16 of Heatstroke [68-Jul-17: 1D].
Fant, Edward S. d. on 66-May-21 [66-Jun-9: 2B].
Fantom, Elenora (56 yrs.) d. on 67-Dec-30 [68-Jan-1: 2C].
Farber, John M. (71 yrs.) d. on 69-Aug-11 [69-Aug-12: 2C].
Farber, M. H. m. Stalfort, Amelia on 68-Jun-11 [68-Jun-13: 2B].
Fardwell, Issac, Capt. (67 yrs.) d. on 67-May-18 [67-May-20: 2B].
Fardwell, Issac (37 yrs.) d. on 66-Sep-20 [66-Sep-21: 2B].
Fardy, John T. (48 yrs.) d. on 67-Jul-22 of Consumption [67-Jul-24: 1G, 2C].
Faringer, Carrie M. m. Armiger, Richard on 67-Mar-7 [67-Mar-9: 2B].
Farland, Alice (8 mos.) d. on 70-Jul-28 [70-Jul-29: 2C].
Farland, Ida May (11 mos.) d. on 69-Sep-13 of Teething [69-Sep-14: 2B].
Farland, Julia A. m. Bartlett, Edward L. on 66-Dec-6 [66-Dec-11: 2B].
Farley, A. R. m. Pollard, W. A. on 69-Dec-23 [70-Jan-4: 2C].
Farley, Ida m. Sweikert, William on 69-Jan-13 [69-Jan-18: 2C].
Farlow, Ida V. m. Gill, Thomas on 68-Aug-8 [69-Apr-27: 2B; 69-Apr-28: 2B].
Farmer, James A. m. Jones, Mary J. on 68-Feb-27 [68-Feb-29: 2B].

Farmer, Philip (85 yrs.) d. on 70-Mar-17 [70-Mar-21: 2C].
Farnan, Ellen (63 yrs.) d. on 69-Feb-9 [69-Feb-10: 2C].
Farnan, James J. m. Jenkins, Sarah E. on 68-Dec-29 [69-Jan-1: 2C].
Farnan, John (35 yrs.) d. on 69-Sep-11 [69-Sep-13: 2B].
Farnan, Thomas F. m. Applegarth, Maggie Cecilia on 66-Apr-3 [66-Apr-11: 2B].
Farquarson, Francis Alexander (1 yr., 11 mos.) d. on 70-Nov-27 [70-Nov-29: 2C].
Farquarson, Hannah d. on 70-Aug-9 [70-Aug-10: 2B; 70-Aug-11: 2C].
Farquhar, Annie Poultney (13 yrs., 6 mos.) d. on 68-May-10 [68-May-11: 2B].
Farquharson, Francis L. m. Anderson, Mary on 67-Jun-10 [67-Jun-12: 2B].
Farquharson, W. E. m. Sanner, Marian on 68-Oct-6 [68-Oct-7: 2C].
Farran, J. Frank m. Martin, Pauline V. on 66-Jun-28 [66-Jul-7: 2B].
Farrar, A. E. m. Laurence, Jennie Webb on 70-Aug-7 [70-Aug-16: 2C].
Farrel, Bartholomew (48 yrs.) d. on 69-Aug-31 [69-Sep-1: 2B].
Farrel, Thomas (75 yrs.) d. on 68-Feb-22 [68-Feb-24: 2C].
Farrell, Annie (24 yrs.) d. on 66-Feb-5 of Consumption [66-Feb-6: 2D].
Farrell, Cora Virginia (1 yr.) d. on 67-Sep-15 [67-Sep-16: 2B].
Farrell, James Higgins (1 yr., 8 mos.) d. on 69-May-25 [69-May-26: 2C].
Farrell, John (36 yrs.) d. on 70-Dec-28 of Apoplexy [70-Dec-29: 2C, 4B; 70-Dec-30: 2C].
Farrell, John m. Fitzpatrick, Elizabeth on 70-Jan-19 [70-Jan-28: 2B].
Farrell, John C. m. Stapleton, Ella on 70-May-16 [70-May-18: 2B].
Farrell, Margaret (76 yrs.) d. on 69-Feb-12 [69-Feb-13: 2C].
Farrell, Mary E. (3 yrs.) d. on 70-Sep-4 [70-Sep-5: 2C].
Farrell, Mary Lizzie (4 yrs.) d. on 66-Aug-2 [66-Aug-4: 2C].
Farrell, Mattie Ann (1 yr., 9 mos.) d. on 66-Jul-16 of Brain inflammation [66-Jul-17: 2C].
Farrell, Michael (64 yrs.) d. on 70-Jan-20 [70-Jan-21: 2C].
Farrell, Robert Lee (1 yr., 1 mo.) d. on 66-Mar-28 [66-Mar-29: 2B].
Farrelly, John d. on 66-Jan-16 [66-Jan-17: 2C].
Farringer, Benjamin F. (33 yrs.) d. on 68-Mar-8 [68-Mar-9: 2C; 68-Mar-10: 2C].
Farrow, Eugenia m. Pearson, James F. on 66-Oct-25 [66-Oct-26: 2B].
Farrow, M. M. m. Caldwell, Lizzie Jane on 68-Apr-16 [68-May-4: 2B].
Farrow, Maria L. m. Tudor, Henry C. on 69-Dec-7 [69-Dec-9: 2C].
Farrow, William H. m. Clingan, Anna E. on 68-Dec-15 [68-Dec-17: 2C].
Farson, Inda T. m. Brunker, James H. on 69-Nov-11 [69-Nov-16: 2C].
Farson, Mary E. m. Harr, Charles E. on 66-Sep-18 [66-Sep-24: 2B].
Fastie, John F. (30 yrs.) d. on 69-Jan-28 [69-Jan-30: 2C].
Faton, William Henry (20 yrs.) d. on 70-Oct-29 Murdered (Stabbing) [70-Nov-1: 4C; 70-Nov-2: 4D].
Faucett, Annie E. m. Moore, Archibald D. on 66-Jan-24 [66-Jan-27: 2B].
Faulkner, A. B. m. Robinson, Louisa A. on 67-Nov-19 [67-Nov-23: 2B].
Faulkner, Cornelia m. Walton, Joseph F. on 66-Feb-11 [66-Feb-15: 2C].
Faulkner, Maria L. m. Bender, George W. on 65-Dec-27 [66-Jan-11: 2C].
Faulkner, Thomas m. Law, Susanna on 66-May-1 [66-May-3: 2C].
Faulkner, William (54 yrs.) d. on 67-Mar-29 [67-Mar-30: 2C].
Faust, Emma (4 yrs.) d. on 70-Sep-5 [70-Sep-6: 2B; 70-Sep-7: 2B].
Fauth, Edward E. (10 yrs.) d. on 70-Feb-5 [70-Feb-7: 2C].
Favier, Camille (3 yrs., 4 mos.) d. on 69-Mar-27 [69-Mar-30: 2B].
Favier, Mary V. m. Foos, John C. on 69-Mar-14 [69-Mar-18: 2C].
Favour, Charles R. m. Barlow, Emma on 67-Jun-3 [67-Jun-7: 2B].
Fawcett, Annie M. m. Shaw, William E. on 66-Jan-18 [66-Jan-22: 2C].
Fawkes, Maria L. m. Mansfield, James A. on 68-Jun-25 [68-Jul-2: 2C].
Faxon, Eben (43 yrs.) d. on 68-Mar-8 [68-Mar-9: 2C, 4E; 68-Mar-10: 2C].
Fay, Bridget (60 yrs.) d. on 68-Mar-31 [68-Apr-1: 2C].
Fay, Fordice m. Bickerton, Maggie A., Mrs. on 66-May-23 [66-May-30: 2C].
Fay, Lawrence (65 yrs.) d. on 70-Aug-16 [70-Aug-17: 2C].
Fay, Patrick (45 yrs.) d. on 67-Feb-6 Crushed by wall [67-Feb-7: 1E].

Fay, Thomas Laurence (3 mos.) d. on 70-Feb-25 [70-Feb-26: 2C].
Fearing, George R. m. Travers, Harriet on 69-Sep-1 [69-Sep-16: 2B].
Fearson, Mary Ann (63 yrs.) d. on 67-Apr-21 [67-May-6: 2B].
Feast, John N. (80 yrs.) d. on 68-Oct-1 [68-Oct-3: 4C].
Feast, Mary Ann (47 yrs.) d. on 70-Jul-18 [70-Jul-19: 2C].
Feast, Samuel, Sr. (72 yrs.) d. on 68-Feb-27 of Fall [68-Feb-28: 1G, 2D; 68-Feb-29: 2B].
Fechtig, Isabella (69 yrs.) d. on 69-Aug-20 [69-Aug-30: 2B].
Fee, Jacob m. Emich, Nellie on 69-Sep-27 [69-Oct-5: 2B].
Fee, Mary (63 yrs.) d. on 66-Nov-13 [66-Nov-15: 2C].
Feefel, Annie M. m. Boyce, John on 69-Feb-11 [69-Mar-9: 2C].
Feelay, Anny (14 yrs.) d. on 70-Feb-18 [70-Feb-19: 2B].
Feelemyer, Isadora m. Fox, Frank S. on 66-Feb-22 [66-Feb-23: 2C].
Feeney, Ellen (11 mos.) d. on 69-Apr-16 [69-Apr-17: 2B].
Feeney, Patrick (63 yrs.) d. on 66-Oct-17 [66-Oct-19: 2B].
Feeny, Anne Catherine (5 mos.) d. on 66-Jul-5 [66-Jul-7: 2C].
Feetsch, Kate m. Sturbits, John on 69-May-25 [69-Jun-15: 2C].
Fefel, Carrie C. d. on 69-May-24 [69-May-28: 2C].
Fefel, George W. m. Zell, Barbara A. on 70-Jul-7 [70-Jul-14: 2B].
Fefel, Joseph, Jr. (42 yrs.) d. on 67-Jan-8 of Typhoid [67-Jan-10: 2C].
Fegan, Isabella (38 yrs.) d. on 69-Jul-16 [69-Jul-23: 2C].
Fehely, William (80 yrs.) d. on 67-Dec-4 [67-Dec-6: 2C].
Fehleisen, Bertha M. m. Wild, Frederick W. on 69-Nov-25 [69-Nov-29: 2C; 69-Dec-1: 2C].
Fehleisen, Magdalena d. on 70-Jan-4 [70-Jan-5: 2C].
Feil, Lizzie M. (16 yrs.) d. on 70-Mar-26 [70-Mar-28: 2B].
Feinour, Elizabeth C. m. Hearn, Charles E. on 67-Apr-18 [67-Jun-18: 2B].
Feinour, Thomas E. W. (29 yrs.) d. on 70-Jan-28 [70-Jan-31: 1H; 70-Feb-2: 2B].
Feldhaus, A. J. m. Whitlock, Barbara S. on 68-Apr-9 [68-Apr-11: 2A].
Feldhaus, Joseph C. m. Weaver, Sue on 69-Nov-18 [69-Nov-24: 2C].
Feldhaus, Mary Jane d. on 66-Sep-26 of Consumption [66-Sep-27: 2C; 66-Sep-28: 2B].
Felgner, J. W. (29 yrs.) d. on 67-Oct-11 of Yellow fever [67-Oct-23: 2B].
Felker, Ruth E. (19 yrs., 11 mos.) d. on 68-Feb-17 [68-Feb-18: 2C].
Fell, J. Sands m. Simpson, Fannie on 67-Dec-23 [68-Feb-17: 2B].
Fell, Margaret d. on 68-Feb-14 Burned [68-Feb-15: 1F].
Felthousen, William H. (38 yrs.) d. on 70-Mar-17 of Consumption [70-Mar-21: 2C; 70-Mar-31: 2C].
Fenby, Theodosia (83 yrs.) d. on 66-Dec-16 [66-Dec-17: 2B; 66-Dec-18: 2B].
Fendall, Joshua F., Dr. (46 yrs.) d. on 69-Oct-30 [69-Nov-17: 2C].
Fenemore, Martha A. m. Wood, James W. on 69-Sep-15 [69-Sep-20: 2C].
Fenemore, William S. (73 yrs., 3 mos.) d. on 69-Oct-27 [69-Oct-28: 2C].
Fenhagen, Thomas A., Capt. (52 yrs.) d. on 70-Nov-14 in Machine accident [70-Nov-15: 2C, 4C].
Feninada, Thomas d. on 68-Oct-14 [68-Oct-15: 1F].
Fennel, Katie (5 yrs.) d. on 70-Aug-16 [70-Aug-17: 2C].
Fennell, Mattie F. m. Mundorff, David on 67-Oct-14 [67-Oct-17: 2B].
Fenneman, John T. m. Warfield, Helen on 69-May-20 [69-Jun-26: 2B].
Fennemore, James T. m. Wood, Catherine J. on 69-Dec-2 [69-Dec-4: 2C].
Fennessy, Julia Anne (3 yrs., 6 mos.) d. on 69-Mar-1 [69-Mar-2: 2C; 69-Mar-5: 2C].
Fennessy, Michael Joseph (1 yr., 10 mos.) d. on 70-Nov-30 [70-Dec-1: 2C].
Fennessy, Thomas (1 yr., 1 mo.) d. on 68-Aug-17 [68-Aug-18: 2B].
Fensley, William, Sr. (100 yrs.) d. on 66-Oct-25 [66-Oct-26: 2B].
Fenton, D. A. m. McClellan, Eliza D. on 66-Feb-25 [66-Mar-29: 2B].
Fenton, Laura m. Welsh, William E. on 70-Mar-31 [70-Apr-2: 2A].
Fentress, Anna Maria (35 yrs.) d. on 68-Feb-13 [68-Feb-15: 2B].
Fenwick, Helen C. S. d. on 70-Sep-8 [70-Sep-9: 2B].
Fenwick, Martin, Dr. (80 yrs.) d. on 66-Sep-2 [66-Sep-4: 2B].

Ferbee, Napoleon H. (49 yrs.) d. on 70-Aug-31 of Dysentery [70-Sep-2: 2C; 70-Sep-3: 4C].
Ferciot, Charles N. m. McGuire, Mary A. on 69-Dec-28 [70-Jan-3: 2C].
Ferciot, Sophie d. on 68-Oct-24 of Brain congestion [68-Oct-26: 2B].
Ferguson, Charles m. King, Ellen on 69-Mar-25 [69-Apr-1: 2C].
Ferguson, Eliza (83 yrs.) d. [70-Sep-29: 2B].
Ferguson, Elizabeth (68 yrs.) d. on 66-Oct-1 [66-Oct-6: 2A].
Ferguson, Ellen m. Jamison, Charles E. on 68-Jul-9 [68-Jul-11: 2B].
Ferguson, James DuGue m. Simons, Henrietta Wragg on 68-Oct-22 [68-Nov-10: 2C].
Ferguson, Kate M. m. Coleman, Charles R. on 67-Dec-23 [68-Aug-3: 2B].
Ferguson, Louis Elbridge (2 yrs., 4 mos.) d. on 68-Dec-18 of Measles [68-Dec-21: 2C].
Ferguson, Margaret (69 yrs.) d. on 67-Feb-7 [67-Feb-8: 2C].
Ferguson, Margaret m. McCormick, John on 69-Nov-17 [69-Nov-26: 2B].
Ferguson, Margaret S. (8 yrs., 4 mos.) d. on 66-Oct-11 [66-Oct-12: 2B].
Ferguson, Mary H. m. Wallis, Robert V. on 69-Sep-23 [69-Sep-24: 2B].
Ferguson, Mary V. m. Hutchinson, Joshua S. on 66-Aug-23 [66-Aug-27: 2B].
Ferguson, Rhoda C. m. Brydon, Edward M. on 67-Jun-20 [67-Jun-22: 2B].
Ferguson, Thomas (61 yrs., 7 mos.) d. on 68-Sep-11 [68-Sep-14: 2B].
Ferguson, Thomas B. m. Swann, Jeanie B. on 67-Apr-23 [67-Apr-25: 2B].
Ferguson, William (79 yrs.) d. on 67-Mar-18 [67-Mar-19: 2C].
Ferguson, William m. Taylor, Anna on 67-Dec-17 [67-Dec-25: 2C].
Ferguson, William James (1 yr.) d. on 66-Aug-7 [66-Aug-8: 2C].
Ferguson, Willie Oscar d. on 70-Apr-16 [70-Apr-19: 2B].
Fergusson, Catherine (77 yrs.) d. on 70-Nov-18 [70-Nov-19: 2B].
Ferguston, James (35 yrs.) d. on 70-Jan-18 Drowned [70-Jan-24: 4F].
Fernan, Richard d. on 67-Sep-15 [67-Sep-17: 1G].
Fernau, Charles Richard (19 yrs.) d. [67-Sep-16: 2B].
Ferney, Mary E. m. Boswell, Frederick A. on 70-Mar-31 [70-Apr-8: 2C].
Ferrandini, , Mrs. d. on 70-Dec-23 Burned [70-Dec-24: 4C].
Ferrandini, Annie Elizabeth (1 yr.) d. on 66-Apr-23 [66-Apr-25: 2B].
Ferrandini, Francisco L. m. Bandell, Isabella A. on 69-Jan-31 [69-Feb-4: 2C].
Ferrandini, Harrietta A. M. m. Murphy, Joseph F. on 69-Mar-30 [69-Apr-1: 2C].
Ferrandini, Josephine A. m. Smyder, William Louis on 70-Jun-30 [70-Jul-12: 2B].
Ferree, Alexander Grant (1 yr., 7 mos.) d. on 66-Oct-3 [66-Oct-4: 2B].
Ferrell, Annie (19 yrs.) d. on 66-Jul-24 [66-Jul-25: 2C; 66-Jul-26: 2C].
Ferrell, Christiana W. d. on 67-Jan-15 [67-Jan-17: 2C].
Ferrell, Elizabeth Jane (9 mos.) d. on 70-Dec-25 [70-Dec-26: 2C].
Ferrell, Mary (67 yrs.) d. on 70-Sep-5 [70-Sep-6: 2B].
Ferrell, Thomas m. Smith, Laura V. on 67-May-4 [67-May-8: 2B].
Ferris, A. S. m. Metzger, Sophia A. on 67-Apr-30 [67-Jun-5: 2B].
Ferris, William H. m. Simms, Annie M. on 69-Mar-11 [69-Mar-15: 2C].
Ferry, Ella V. m. Woodworth, William R. on 67-Jun-13 [67-Jun-18: 2B].
Ferry, Maggie J. m. Goodhand, George W. on 69-Jan-12 [69-Jan-19: 2C].
Fessler, Susan m. Baer, James S. on 66-Nov-23 [66-Nov-27: 2B].
Festionel, Ann d. on 69-Jun-20 Burned [69-Jun-21: 1G].
Fetterman, L. B. m. Gloninger, Augusta on 69-Jun-23 [69-Jun-29: 2C].
Fetting, W. G. (19 yrs.) d. on 70-Sep-2 [70-Sep-5: 2C].
Feuss, Andrew C. m. Duckstein, Jeanette A. on 66-Apr-5 [66-Apr-19: 2B].
Feuss, Henry O. m. Winkelman, Henrietta on 68-Nov-18 [68-Nov-21: 2C].
Fick, Barbara m. Shorey, Samuel F. on 69-Jul-19 [69-Jul-23: 2C].
Fick, Ferdinand (60 yrs.) d. on 66-Apr-21 of Apoplexy [66-Apr-23: 1F].
Fiddis, Clinton A. (6 yrs., 6 mos.) d. on 69-May-5 [69-May-12: 2B].
Field, A. W. (40 yrs.) d. on 67-Mar-9 [67-Mar-11: 2C; 67-Mar-12: 2C].
Field, J. T. m. Minifie, Mary E. on 68-Oct-28 [68-Oct-29: 2B].
Field, John A. m. Goforth, Kate on 66-Dec-15 [66-Dec-20: 2B].
Field, Mary (5 mos.) d. on 67-Jul-8 [67-Jul-9: 2B].

Field, Mary (78 yrs.) d. on 70-Aug-28 [70-Aug-30: 2B].
Field, Penelope J. d. on 70-Dec-5 [70-Dec-7: 2C].
Fielding, Kate L. m. Hinder, Frederick on 68-Oct-20 [68-Oct-27: 2B].
Fields, Charles Leroy (36 yrs.) d. on 70-Nov-13 [70-Nov-14: 2B].
Fields, Eliza (73 yrs.) d. on 69-Dec-14 [69-Dec-15: 2B].
Fields, Harry B. m. Kelly, Albina V. on 70-Sep-8 [70-Nov-17: 2C].
Fields, Hester d. on 66-Dec-4 [66-Dec-5: 2B].
Fields, James (64 yrs.) d. on 67-Sep-26 [67-Sep-27: 2B].
Fields, James (76 yrs.) d. on 67-May-25 [67-May-27: 1F, 2B].
Fields, James m. Mayberry, Laura E. V. on 67-Jan-1 [67-Jan-5: 2C].
Fields, Martha (39 yrs.) d. on 66-Sep-23 [66-Sep-25: 2B].
Fields, Martha (33 yrs.) d. on 70-Jun-9 [70-Jun-10: 2B].
Fields, Mary (90 yrs.) d. on 69-Aug-16 [69-Aug-18: 2C].
Fields, Susan A. m. Williams, Robert A. on 70-Jul-14 [70-Jul-19: 2B].
Fields, Susan A. V. m. Jones, Robert L. on 68-Apr-28 [68-May-2: 2C].
Fifer, Francis A. (27 yrs.) d. on 66-Apr-14 [66-Apr-17: 2C].
Fifer, George E. m. Burnett, Lulie on 70-May-11 [70-Sep-27: 2B].
Fifer, Martha m. White, Hiram F. on 66-Apr-4 [66-Apr-5: 2B].
Fifer, Mary Eliza (7 mos.) d. on 68-Oct-11 [68-Oct-12: 2B].
Fifer, Robert S. m. Grant, Anna E. on 66-Mar-15 [66-Mar-17: 2B].
Fifer, Sallie Jane d. on 68-Jul-30 [68-Jul-31: 2C].
Filben, Michael (19 yrs., 6 mos.) d. on 70-May-6 [70-May-7: 2B].
Filchner, Kate m. Hayward, R. R. on 67-Mar-5 [67-Apr-10: 2B].
Files, Anna Frances (2 yrs., 1 mo.) d. on 68-Jan-13 [68-Jan-14: 2C].
Fillinger, Elexiner m. Poole, James E. on 69-May-12 [69-Jun-8: 2B].
Fillinger, James L. m. Gise, Sallie J. on 70-Dec-1 [70-Dec-5: 2C].
Fillinger, Mary J. m. Walter, Andrew J. on 67-Nov-19 [67-Nov-28: 2C].
Fillinger, Mary J. m. Andrew, Walter J. on 67-Nov-19 [67-Nov-28: 2C].
Fillmore, Jane m. Cullison, George A. on 67-Jun-9 [67-Jun-13: 2C].
Fimple, Mary (69 yrs.) d. on 68-Sep-19 [68-Sep-21: 2B].
Fimple, Sallie E. S. m. Collins, Henry H. on 68-Feb-20 [68-Mar-7: 2B].
Finch, Elizabeth S. m. Messer, Lewis W. [69-Jan-14: 2D].
Finch, George J. m. Wills, Elizabeth J. on 66-Jun-26 [66-Jun-29: 2C].
Finch, William W. m. Dudrow, Martha J. on 65-Dec-31 [66-Jan-3: 2C].
Finck, Bernard m. Warnick, Sallie R. on 68-May-12 [68-May-27: 2B].
Finck, Sallie R. d. on 70-Nov-16 [70-Nov-17: 2C].
Fincknauer, William F. (23 yrs.) d. on 70-May-1 [70-May-4: 2C].
Fincknaur, Harry (18 yrs.) d. on 69-Jul-18 [69-Jul-20: 2C].
Findlay, Archibald Irwin (7 mos.) d. on 66-Jul-17 [66-Jul-30: 2C].
Findlay, Mary C. d. on 68-Mar-28 [68-Mar-30: 2B; 68-Mar-31: 2B].
Findlay, Mary Therese (2 yrs., 9 mos.) d. on 70-Aug-19 [70-Aug-20: 2B].
Findly, Owen (66 yrs.) d. on 66-Jul-6 [66-Jul-7: 2B].
Finegan, Rebecca (60 yrs.) d. on 70-Aug-1 [70-Aug-2: 2C].
Fink, Henry d. on 68-Aug-5 of Fall from roof [68-Aug-7: 1G].
Fink, Herman d. on 70-Mar-21 of Suicide (Poisoning) [70-Mar-22: 4D].
Finlay, Ellen d. on 69-Nov-18 [69-Nov-23: 2C].
Finlayson, L. A. m. Houston, S. T. on 69-Jan-23 [69-Feb-6: 2C].
Finley, Agnes (2 yrs., 1 mo.) d. on 67-Feb-11 [67-Feb-14: 2C].
Finley, Anna H. m. Drake, John O. on 67-Oct-16 [67-Oct-18: 2C].
Finley, Jane (83 yrs.) d. on 70-Nov-7 [70-Nov-8: 2B].
Finley, Lizzie M. m. Guyton, Benjamin F. on 68-Jan-15 [68-Jan-23: 2C].
Finley, Louis Thomas Camillus (17 yrs.) d. on 68-Sep-22 [68-Sep-24: 2B].
Finley, Mary E. m. McNamee, John F. on 69-May-30 [69-Jun-3: 2B].
Finley, Robert Smith m. Keenan, Emma on 69-Nov-23 [69-Nov-24: 2C].
Finley, Sue m. Barton, P. A. on 70-Nov-24 [70-Dec-3: 2B].

Finn, Infant (8 mos.) d. on 70-Sep-12 [70-Sep-13: 2B].
Finnegan, Annie d. on 70-Sep-19 [70-Sep-21: 2B].
Finnegan, Clara (2 yrs., 6 mos.) d. on 66-Jan-27 [66-Jan-29: 2B].
Finnegan, Mary d. on 69-Dec-20 [69-Dec-21: 2B].
Finnegan, Michael m. Rafferty, Sarah on 67-Nov-1 [67-Nov-21: 2C].
Finnegan, Sarah (1 yr., 1 mo.) d. on 70-Nov-9 [70-Nov-11: 2B].
Finnegan, William (3 yrs., 10 mos.) d. on 68-Feb-2 [68-Feb-3: 2C].
Finnegan, Winnifred m. McKenna, Peter on 68-Jan-17 [68-Oct-2: 2B].
Finneran, John Joseph (4 yrs., 4 mos.) d. on 70-Dec-19 [70-Dec-20: 2B].
Finnerau, Thomas (5 mos.) d. on 66-Oct-29 [66-Oct-30: 2B].
Finney, David B. (38 yrs.) d. on 70-Apr-12 [70-Apr-14: 2B].
Finney, Eliza U. d. on 67-Apr-19 of Consumption [67-Apr-24: 2B].
Finney, John (45 yrs.) d. Drowned [67-Mar-23: 1F].
Finney, Lewis H. (73 yrs.) d. on 69-May-23 [69-May-31: 4B].
Finnigan, Alice m. Derenberger, Henry on 68-Apr-21 [68-Jun-6: 2A].
Fint, Maggie m. Griffith, Barzillar on 69-Jun-15 [69-Jun-23: 2C].
Fiquet, Dominick (90 yrs.) d. on 66-Feb-28 [66-Mar-1: 2B].
Firn, Cornelius m. O'Connor, Mary A. on 68-Oct-26 [69-May-29: 2B].
Firoved, Charles Anderson (8 mos.) d. on 66-Dec-19 [66-Dec-22: 2B].
Firoved, George Marion (1 yr., 10 mos.) d. on 66-Sep-21 [66-Sep-22: 2B].
Firth, Jonas (53 yrs.) d. on 66-Oct-1 of Suicide (Drowning) [66-Oct-2: 1E, 2B].
Fischer, Charles Henry Martin (4 mos.) d. on 68-Jul-2 [68-Jul-7: 2B].
Fischer, Ernst (54 yrs.) d. on 69-Mar-1 [69-Mar-9: 2C].
Fischer, George J. (56 yrs.) d. on 66-Feb-21 [66-Feb-23: 2C].
Fischer, John Charles m. Joeckel, Elizabeth on 66-Dec-11 [66-Dec-31: 2C].
Fischer, Louis C. m. Gill, Annie on 66-Nov-22 [66-Nov-24: 2B].
Fischer, Otto m. Hellwig, Katie on 66-May-13 [66-Jul-9: 2C].
Fish, Charlie Herbert (10 mos.) d. on 69-Aug-1 of Brain fever [69-Aug-5: 2C].
Fish, Marion (2 yrs., 6 mos.) d. on 69-Aug-4 [69-Aug-5: 2C; 69-Aug-6: 2C].
Fish, Ross Calcott (1 yr., 5 mos.) d. on 67-Oct-17 [67-Oct-18: 2C].
Fish, Sarah A. (1 yr., 4 mos.) d. on 68-Aug-25 [68-Aug-26: 2B].
Fish, Willie J. (3 yrs., 7 mos.) d. on 69-May-26 [69-Jun-2: 2B].
Fishback, Mary (3 yrs.) d. on 67-Mar-20 Burned [67-Mar-21: 1F].
Fisher, Abbie L. m. Cowman, Joseph, Jr. on 70-Apr-28 [70-May-4: 2C].
Fisher, Agnes (55 yrs.) d. on 68-Jul-15 [68-Jul-17: 2B].
Fisher, Aminta Elizabeth m. Green, Charles on 69-May-20 [69-May-26: 2C].
Fisher, Annie m. Collins, George W. on 68-Aug-11 [68-Aug-25: 2B].
Fisher, B. F. m. Zimmerman, S. A. on 70-Feb-22 [70-Mar-5: 2B].
Fisher, Benny F. (1 yr., 1 mo.) d. on 70-Dec-27 of Chronic croup [70-Dec-28: 2C].
Fisher, Charles D. m. Dorsey, Nannie Poultney on 68-Apr-15 [68-Apr-16: 2B].
Fisher, Charles G. m. Lloyd, Phillie C. on 69-Dec-15 [69-Dec-22: 2B].
Fisher, Charles Rush (2 mos.) d. on 66-Apr-24 [66-Apr-28: 2A].
Fisher, Charles V. (8 yrs.) d. on 68-Apr-29 [68-Apr-30: 2B].
Fisher, Elizabeth (61 yrs.) d. on 69-Jan-8 of Consumption [69-Jan-9: 2C].
Fisher, Emily E. m. Crist, Charles H. on 67-Dec-26 [68-Jan-1: 2C].
Fisher, Emma A. m. Nugent, Charles F. on 70-Mar-1 [70-Apr-9: 2B].
Fisher, George A. m. Webster, Maggie on 70-Apr-12 [70-Apr-16: 2B].
Fisher, George W. (43 yrs.) d. on 67-Dec-30 [68-Jan-7: 2C].
Fisher, Georgie m. Holtz, George W. on 69-Jun-8 [69-Jun-15: 2C].
Fisher, Harry m. Barroll, Serena Mc Lane on 66-May-10 [66-May-12: 2A].
Fisher, Harry Bramwell (3 mos.) d. on 66-Jan-24 [66-Jan-26: 2B].
Fisher, Harry Gilmor (7 mos.) d. on 67-Apr-13 [67-Apr-19: 2B].
Fisher, Ida Almira (1 yr., 8 mos.) d. on 69-Jul-3 [69-Jul-12: 2D].
Fisher, Issac (22 yrs., 9 mos.) d. on 70-Sep-22 [70-Sep-26: 2B].
Fisher, Issac (49 yrs., 6 mos.) d. on 70-Dec-7 [70-Dec-8: 2C].

Fisher, J. Harmanus m. McCulloh, Josephine L. on 69-Jan-13 [69-Jan-14: 2D].
Fisher, John (52 yrs.) d. on 68-Aug-26 [68-Aug-27: 2B].
Fisher, John A. (65 yrs.) d. on 70-Nov-20 [70-Nov-22: 2B].
Fisher, Laura m. Benson, James W. on 69-Dec-21 [69-Dec-24: 2C].
Fisher, Laura E. m. Gilroy, John on 69-Apr-1 [69-Apr-10: 2B].
Fisher, Laura Frances m. Cowman, John G. on 68-May-7 [68-May-15: 2B].
Fisher, Lillie May (5 mos.) d. on 68-Mar-30 [68-Mar-31: 2B].
Fisher, Lucy (32 yrs.) d. on 67-Jun-30 of Typhoid [67-Jul-2: 2B].
Fisher, M. A. m. Maris, W. D. on 70-Feb-2 [70-Feb-10: 2C].
Fisher, Margaret Ann (62 yrs.) d. on 66-Oct-1 [66-Oct-3: 2B].
Fisher, Mary Jane M. d. on 67-Feb-8 [67-Feb-9: 2B; 67-Feb-11: 2C].
Fisher, Nattie Crawford (2 yrs., 1 mo.) d. on 68-Mar-22 [68-Mar-26: 2B].
Fisher, Sarah (34 yrs.) d. on 67-Aug-7 [67-Aug-13: 2B].
Fisher, Sarah (69 yrs.) d. on 70-Dec-10 [70-Dec-12: 2C].
Fisher, Virginia (26 yrs.) d. on 69-Nov-12 [69-Nov-13: 2C; 69-Nov-20: 2C].
Fisher, William (59 yrs.) d. on 67-Jan-18 [67-Jan-19: 2C; 67-Jan-21: 1F].
Fisher, William H. m. Reitz, Sophia C. on 67-May-9 [67-May-13: 2B].
Fisher, Willie Wilkens (9 mos.) d. on 69-Dec-23 of Scarlet fever [69-Dec-25: 2C].
Fishpaugh, Margaret A. m. Litsinger, Augustus M. on 67-Aug-6 [67-Aug-9: 2C].
Fishpaw, Marion C. m. Printz, Artemas S. on 67-Apr-18 [67-May-1: 2B].
Fisk, Phebe A. (52 yrs., 7 mos.) d. on 67-Aug-10 [67-Aug-13: 2B].
Fister, John (66 yrs.) d. on 68-Feb-3 [68-Feb-4: 2C].
Fitch, A. P. (55 yrs.) d. on 66-Feb-6 [66-Feb-7: 2C].
Fitch, Edward M. m. Wiggins, Nannie M. on 66-Oct-15 [66-Oct-18: 2B].
Fitch, John E. (41 yrs.) d. on 69-Jan-3 [69-Jan-4: 2C].
Fitch, Joshua (77 yrs.) d. on 70-May-31 [70-Jun-1: 2B].
Fitch, Thomas (40 yrs.) d. on 66-Jul-18 of Heatstroke [66-Jul-19: 1F, 2C; 66-Aug-3: 2C].
Fitchett, Dickson m. Stevens, Sarah A. on 66-Jun-25 [66-Jun-30: 2B].
Fite, Mary O. (83 yrs.) d. on 69-Jul-25 [69-Jul-31: 2C].
Fithian, Ephraim (77 yrs.) d. on 68-Jan-3 [68-Jan-4: 2C].
Fitzer, Edward F. m. Ellender, Martha H. on 69-Dec-27 [69-Dec-31: 2C].
Fitzgerald, , Mr. d. on 68-Feb-14 in Railroad accident [68-Feb-15: 1F].
Fitzgerald, Catherine d. on 67-Aug-24 [67-Apr-26: 2D].
Fitzgerald, David d. on 68-Dec-17 Murdered (Shooting) [68-Dec-19: 4C; 68-Dec-21: 4C].
Fitzgerald, James H. m. Robinson, Annie E. on 70-May-19 [70-May-21: 2B].
Fitzgerald, Kate (18 yrs.) d. on 67-May-21 [67-May-22: 2B; 67-May-23: 2B; 67-May-24: 2B].
Fitzgerald, Laura m. Bordley, W. C., Jr. on 67-Oct-31 [67-Nov-2: 2B].
Fitzgerald, Mary Margaret m. Smith, Charles Fisher on 67-Dec-10 [67-Dec-13: 2C].
Fitzgerald, Richard B., Capt. (62 yrs.) d. on 69-Mar-14 [69-Mar-16: 1F, 2C; 69-Mar-19: 1H].
Fitzgerald, Virginia (6 yrs.) d. on 68-Aug-3 [68-Aug-5: 2B].
Fitzgerald, William H. m. Morrison, Mary R. on 69-Nov-16 [69-Nov-25: 2C].
Fitzgibbon, John (21 yrs.) d. on 68-Nov-6 [68-Nov-6: 2C].
Fitzhugh, Ann d. on 67-Aug-6 [67-Aug-15: 2C].
Fitzhugh, F. M. m. Fort, Olivia on 67-Jul-13 [67-Aug-2: 2C].
Fitzhugh, Sarah Wharton d. on 69-Nov-13 [69-Nov-16: 2C].
Fitzmaurice, Anne d. on 66-Apr-7 [66-Apr-26: 2B].
Fitzpatrick, Catherine (45 yrs.) d. on 66-Nov-1 [66-Nov-2: 2B; 66-Nov-3: 2B].
Fitzpatrick, Charles William (6 mos.) d. on 70-Aug-18 of Cholera infantum [70-Jul-19: 2C].
Fitzpatrick, Elizabeth m. Farrell, John on 70-Jan-19 [70-Jan-28: 2B].
Fitzpatrick, Ellen (15 yrs.) d. on 70-Aug-26 [70-Aug-27: 2B].
Fitzpatrick, Francis A. (21 yrs.) d. on 69-Jun-8 [69-Jun-9: 2C].
Fitzpatrick, Francis Patrick (2 yrs., 6 mos.) d. on 69-Aug-4 [69-Aug-5: 2B].
Fitzpatrick, George (25 yrs.) d. on 68-Jul-15 [68-Jul-25: 2B].
Fitzpatrick, Hannah (61 yrs.) d. on 69-Apr-6 [69-Apr-7: 2C; 69-Apr-8: 2C].
Fitzpatrick, J. C. S. (33 yrs.) d. on 70-Sep-11 [70-Sep-12: 2B].

Fitzpatrick, J. C. S. m. Griffin, Bessie on 68-Oct-1 [68-Oct-2: 2B].
Fitzpatrick, James m. Tagney, Joe V. on 69-Jan-28 [69-Feb-6: 2C].
Fitzpatrick, Katy (5 yrs., 3 mos.) d. on 69-May-1 [69-May-3: 2C].
Fitzpatrick, Michael (65 yrs.) d. on 66-Dec-30 [66-Dec-31: 2C].
Fitzpatrick, Patrick (77 yrs.) d. on 66-Dec-3 [66-Dec-4: 2D].
Fitzpatrick, William m. Wareham, Annie on 68-Dec-13 [68-Dec-15: 2C].
Fitzpatrick, Willie m. Cleary, R. E. on 70-Jul-12 [70-Jul-19: 2B].
Fitzpatrick, Willie Bingham d. on 70-May-12 [70-May-14: 2A].
Fitzsimmons, Daniel G. d. on 66-Feb-10 [66-Feb-24: 2B].
Fitzsimmons, John (45 yrs.) d. on 68-Nov-4 of Intemperance [68-Nov-5: 1G].
Fitzsimons, John (66 yrs.) d. on 69-Jul-7 [69-Aug-26: 2C].
Fizell, Rebecca m. Jones, James A. on 68-Nov-5 [68-Nov-7: 2B].
Fizone, Jacob m. Murty, Annie R. on 70-Apr-19 [70-Oct-25: 2B].
Flach, Bernhard m. Deemeg, Julia on 70-Jul-26 [70-Aug-10: 2B].
Flack, Harry H. m. Barrington, Eveline M. on 68-Nov-5 [68-Nov-10: 2C].
Flack, J. Simms O. d. on 68-Jul-31 [68-Aug-1: 2B].
Flagherty, Lewis R. D. m. Swift, Caroline on 66-Mar-14 [66-Mar-28: 2C].
Flaharty, John Summerfield d. on 67-Apr-1 [67-Apr-4: 2B].
Flaherty, Anna Cecilia (2 mos.) d. on 70-Sep-4 [70-Sep-6: 2B].
Flaherty, Barbara m. Hartley, Charles H. on 70-Jun-2 [70-Jun-9: 2C].
Flaherty, Bridget Burns (37 yrs.) d. on 67-Nov-8 [67-Nov-9: 2B].
Flaherty, Catherine (19 yrs., 6 mos.) d. on 67-Apr-17 [67-Apr-18: 2B].
Flaherty, Clara (5 yrs., 6 mos.) d. on 66-Apr-16 [66-Apr-18: 2B].
Flaherty, Edward (76 yrs.) d. on 70-May-20 [70-May-21: 2B].
Flaherty, James (23 yrs.) d. on 70-Aug-11 [70-Aug-12: 2C].
Flaherty, Maggie E. m. Garrett, Richard S. on 69-Jan-12 [69-Feb-4: 2C].
Flaherty, Michael (34 yrs.) d. on 69-May-24 in Railroad accident [69-Dec-27: 1F, 2D].
Flaherty, Thomas (37 yrs.) d. on 69-Oct-28 of Suffocation [69-Oct-30: 2B, 4B].
Flaherty, Uriah J. (1 yr., 4 mos.) d. on 68-Dec-14 of Pneumonia [68-Dec-15: 2C; 68-Dec-16: 2C].
Flahn, Lewis m. Sheiry, Margaret J. on 68-Jul-20 [68-Sep-14: 2B].
Flamm, Elizabeth m. Knorr, Friedrich F. on 65-Oct-24 [66-Apr-18: 2B].
Flanagan, Mollie E. m. Beach, William H. on 68-Apr-12 [68-Apr-21: 2B].
Flanagan, Thomas (34 yrs.) d. on 69-Jan-3 [69-Jan-4: 2C].
Flanigan, Elizabeth (6 yrs., 10 mos.) d. on 69-Jan-10 [69-Jan-11: 2C].
Flanigan, Michael (7 yrs.) d. on 67-May-6 [67-May-7: 2B].
Flannegan, Andrew McE m. Schuelor, J. Nannie C. on 66-Apr-5 [66-Apr-19: 2B; 66-Apr-20: 2B].
Flannigan, Andrew, Sr. (71 yrs.) d. on 70-Jun-21 [70-Jun-23: 1H, 2C].
Flannigan, Andrew McElderry (41 yrs., 1 mo.) d. on 70-Sep-12 [70-Sep-22: 2C].
Flannigan, James (2 yrs.) d. on 68-Aug-25 [68-Aug-26: 2B].
Flarity, Philip (44 yrs.) d. on 66-Jan-9 [66-Jan-11: 2B].
Flashell, William H. m. Freeman, Mary E. on 66-Nov-18 [67-Jan-8: 2C].
Flather, Edwin (27 yrs., 1 mo.) d. on 67-Feb-19 [67-Feb-22: 2D].
Flatley, Mary (29 yrs., 2 mos.) d. on 69-Oct-27 [69-Oct-29: 2C].
Flautt, Joseph T. m. Foos, Susie W. on 66-Feb-13 [66-Mar-9: 2B].
Flautt, Mary Ida (4 mos.) d. on 67-Jun-29 [67-Jul-2: 2B].
Flaxcomb, Margaret (48 yrs.) d. on 70-Jun-23 [70-Jun-24: 2C].
Flayhart, Joshua Albert Ellswo (1 yr., 11 mos.) d. on 67-Oct-25 [67-Oct-26: 2A].
Flayhart, Sophie (15 yrs., 4 mos.) d. on 66-Feb-19 [66-Feb-23: 2C].
Fledderman, G. Eugene (5 mos.) d. on 70-Jun-17 [70-Jun-18: 2B].
Fledderman, Minnie m. Hammer, John A. on 66-Feb-6 [66-Feb-12: 2D].
Fleeharty, John T. m. Rigby, Milcah on 69-Aug-3 [69-Aug-4: 2C].
Fleeharty, Walter Anderson (1 yr., 7 mos.) d. on 69-Jul-18 [69-Jul-20: 2C].
Fleetwood, Christian A. m. Iredell, Sara L. on 69-Nov-18 [69-Nov-22: 2C].

Fleischer, Simon m. Joseph, Betty on 70-Dec-18 [70-Dec-24: 2B].
Fleischman, Hannah m. Manley, James, Jr. on 70-Sep-13 [70-Sep-20: 2B].
Fleischman, John (41 yrs.) d. on 66-Jul-24 [66-Jul-25: 2C].
Fleishall, Fannie A. m. Taylor, James on 70-Sep-1 [70-Sep-13: 2B].
Fleishell, Andrew J. (2 yrs., 6 mos.) d. on 66-Jul-5 [66-Jul-7: 2B].
Fleming, Bridget (50 yrs.) d. on 66-Sep-28 [66-Sep-29: 2B].
Fleming, Douglas m. Marriet, Lizzie on 69-Feb-16 [69-Feb-23: 2C].
Fleming, Ellen (29 yrs.) d. on 67-Apr-12 [67-May-9: 2A].
Fleming, John Perkins, Dr. (40 yrs.) d. on 68-Aug-13 [68-Aug-14: 1G, 2C; 68-Aug-15: 2B; 68-Aug-17: 1F].
Fleming, Patrick (63 yrs.) d. [68-Feb-3: 2C].
Flemming, Ann (88 yrs.) d. on 66-Aug-27 [66-Aug-28: 2B].
Flemming, Bridget (66 yrs.) d. on 67-Jan-16 [67-Jan-18: 2C].
Flemming, Henry D. (52 yrs.) d. on 66-Jun-17 [66-Jun-18: 2B].
Flemming, James B. (41 yrs.) d. on 66-Mar-11 [66-Mar-13: 2B].
Flemming, Margaret (65 yrs.) d. on 69-May-17 [69-May-18: 2C].
Flemming, Mary (7 yrs.) d. on 69-May-12 [69-May-14: 2C].
Fletcher, James A. m. Eary, Ella V. on 68-Oct-19 [68-Oct-26: 2B].
Fletcher, James Edward Leach (2 yrs., 10 mos.) d. on 69-Feb-15 [69-Feb-17: 2C].
Fletcher, James S. m. Taylor, Henrietta P. on 69-Sep-20 [69-Mar-29: 2B].
Fletcher, Kate m. Byrd, James E. on 69-Dec-28 [70-Jan-4: 2C].
Fletcher, Maria L. (30 yrs.) d. on 67-Sep-4 [67-Sep-5: 2B].
Fletcher, Minnie m. Cissel, William L. on 65-Oct-5 [66-Jan-8: 2B].
Fletcher, Stephen G. (19 yrs.) d. on 67-Mar-4 Murdered (Shooting) [67-Mar-5: 1G, 2C].
Fletcher, William (57 yrs.) d. on 69-Apr-2 [69-Apr-3: 2B].
Fleury, Harriet (65 yrs.) d. on 65-Nov-24 [66-Jan-9: 2B].
Fleury, Michael (70 yrs.) d. on 70-Jul-25 of Heatstroke [70-Jul-27: 4E].
Flint, Ann (86 yrs.) d. on 70-Jan-31 [70-Feb-1: 2B; 70-Feb-2: 2B].
Flint, Richard d. on 70-Sep-5 [70-Sep-13: 2B].
Flint, William A. (10 yrs.) d. on 70-Jul-16 [70-Jul-19: 2C].
Flishell, Elizabeth B. m. Cullen, William T. on 67-Jun-3 [67-Aug-31: 2B].
Flister, Andrew F. m. Aitcheson, Mary on 69-May-27 [69-Jun-10: 2C].
Flohr, Henry (26 yrs.) d. on 68-Apr-7 of Apoplexy [68-Apr-8: 1G].
Flood, Bessie (22 yrs.) d. on 67-Oct-18 [67-Oct-21: 2B].
Flood, Ida M. (7 yrs., 5 mos.) d. on 69-Jan-28 of Pneumonia and typhoid [69-Feb-6: 2C].
Flood, Samuel S. m. Collins, Bettie A. on 70-Nov-22 [70-Nov-24: 2B].
Florence, Belle m. Simpson, C. Owen on 67-Nov-21 [67-Nov-30: 2C].
Florer, William H. m. McCreary, Cornelia L. on 67-Jul-11 [67-Jul-13: 2B].
Flory, Alice A. m. Marriott, Samuel N. on 67-Aug-18 [67-Aug-20: 2B].
Flory, Thomas E. m. Lockard, Mollie W. on 67-Sep-25 [67-Sep-26: 2B].
Floss, Sarah A. (49 yrs.) d. on 67-Mar-1 [67-Mar-5: 2C].
Floyd, Alexina m. Colein, T. R. on 66-Jan-25 [66-Apr-11: 2B].
Floyd, Elizabeth (69 yrs.) d. on 69-Jan-10 [69-Jan-12: 2C].
Floyd, Joseph (66 yrs.) d. on 67-Nov-30 [67-Dec-2: 2C].
Floyd, Matilda C. m. Dobson, John on 67-Jan-17 [67-Jan-19: 2C].
Floyd, William m. Kenny, Kate A. on 69-Jan-12 [69-Jan-15: 2D].
Floyd, William H. (23 yrs.) d. on 67-Jul-17 [67-Jul-19: 2C].
Fluharty, Hester A. m. Hubbard, Jesse H. T. on 68-Apr-7 [68-Apr-15: 2B].
Fluharty, Mary Ramsey (9 mos.) d. on 66-Jul-1 [66-Jul-3: 2C].
Flyn, Johana d. on 66-Oct-25 [66-Oct-26: 2B].
Flynn, Johanna d. on 66-Oct-25 [66-Oct-16: 2B].
Flynn, Johanna J. m. Hughes, John on 66-May-1 [66-May-7: 2B; 66-May-8: 2B].
Flynn, Kate A. m. Kitson, Samuel on 67-Jul-23 [67-Aug-7: 2C].
Flynn, Matthew (60 yrs.) d. on 66-Apr-5 [66-Apr-6: 2B].
Flynn, Maurice (48 yrs.) d. on 67-May-3 of Consumption [67-May-4: 2B].

Flynn, Roger (68 yrs.) d. on 66-Jul-15 [66-Jul-16: 2C].
Flynn, Simon (47 yrs.) d. on 67-Jun-4 [67-Jun-5: 2B].
Flynn, William d. on 69-Dec-23 [69-Dec-24: 2C].
Foans, A. B. (51 yrs.) d. on 67-Mar-21 [67-Mar-25: 2C].
Foard, A. J., Dr. d. on 68-Mar-18 [68-Apr-1: 1G].
Foard, Benjamin m. Wilson, Elizabeth Ann on 70-Aug-2 [70-Aug-4: 2C; 70-Aug-10: 2B].
Foard, Charles Dexter (32 yrs.) d. on 66-Nov-12 [66-Nov-15: 2C].
Foard, Harriet E. d. on 68-Mar-2 [68-Mar-5: 2C].
Foard, Josiah (68 yrs.) d. on 66-Oct-17 [66-Oct-18: 2B].
Foard, Mary (74 yrs.) d. on 69-Apr-9 [69-Apr-10: 2B].
Foard, Mary Parker d. on 67-Nov-25 [67-Nov-26: 2B; 67-Nov-27: 2C].
Foard, Susanna A. (72 yrs.) d. on 67-Dec-4 [67-Dec-6: 2C].
Foard, William (1 yr., 5 mos.) d. on 66-Sep-7 [66-Sep-8: 2B].
Foble, J. James m. Shepherd, Ella on 68-Oct-8 [68-Oct-9: 2C].
Focke, Charles W., Capt. (65 yrs.) d. on 69-Jul-25 [69-Jul-26: 2C].
Focke, Frederick K. m. Skeels, Marion A. [69-Jul-15: 2C].
Focke, Mary Anne d. on 67-Mar-21 [67-Mar-22: 2C].
Fogle, Ida Estelle (4 mos.) d. on 66-Jun-28 of Brain congestion [66-Jun-30: 2B].
Fogle, Lillie May d. on 69-Aug-25 of Gastric fever [69-Aug-27: 2B].
Fogt, Theodore d. on 70-Sep-3 of Heart disease [70-Sep-5: 4E].
Foley, Ann (50 yrs.) d. on 67-Nov-10 [67-Nov-11: 2C].
Foley, Ann (43 yrs.) d. on 69-Nov-25 [69-Nov-26: 2C].
Foley, David R. m. Curran, Cecilia J. on 66-May-15 [66-May-24: 2C].
Foley, Ella J. (12 yrs., 11 mos.) d. on 67-Apr-26 [67-Apr-27: 2A].
Foley, Jane (24 yrs.) d. on 66-Sep-26 [66-Sep-28: 2B].
Foley, John (35 yrs.) d. on 68-Jul-16 of Heatstroke [68-Jul-21: 4D].
Foley, John B., Rev. (49 yrs.) d. on 67-Dec-31 [68-Jan-2: 1F, 2C].
Foley, John W. (28 yrs.) d. on 66-Jan-2 [66-Jan-3: 2C].
Foley, Margaret (75 yrs.) d. on 70-Dec-7 [70-Dec-9: 2C].
Foley, Martha V. m. Syer, Robert on 69-May-24 [69-May-25: 2C].
Foley, Mary (7 yrs., 2 mos.) d. on 69-Apr-13 [69-Apr-14: 2B].
Foley, Matthew (81 yrs.) d. on 66-Oct-5 in Street railway accident [66-Oct-6: 1F, 2A; 66-Oct-9: 4B].
Foley, Michael d. on 66-Oct-5 [66-Oct-6: 2A].
Folk, Edwin C. m. Mylins, Annie on 70-Oct-23 [70-Oct-26: 2B].
Folkes, Elizabeth C. m. Dobler, David, Jr. on 70-Dec-1 [70-Dec-3: 2B].
Folkes, Josephine R. m. Creek, Thomas C. on 68-May-28 [68-Jun-2: 2B].
Follett, F. C., Capt. d. on 69-Apr-9 of Suicide (Shooting) [69-Apr-12: 1G].
Follmer, Henry m. Heiser, Louisa on 68-Sep-23 [68-Sep-25: 2B].
Foltz, George (47 yrs., 4 mos.) d. of Brain congestion [69-Mar-22: 2C].
Foltz, Henry C. m. Miller, Annie on 69-Dec-23 [69-Dec-25: 2C].
Fonce, Sarah (41 yrs.) d. on 66-Oct-26 [66-Oct-27: 2B].
Fonerden, Clarence A. m. Sherwood, Emma V. on 70-Oct-31 [70-Nov-1: 2C].
Fonerden, Eliza d. on 66-Jun-21 [66-Jun-23: 2B].
Fonerden, John, Dr. d. on 69-May-6 [69-May-7: 1H; 69-May-8: 1H, 2B].
Fontaine, A. Wilson (7 mos.) d. on 67-Dec-23 [67-Dec-24: 2B].
Fontaine, Minnie Belle (1 yr., 7 mos.) d. on 70-Jun-8 [70-Jun-9: 2C].
Fontz, Jacob H. m. Johnson, Henrietta H. on 70-May-19 [70-May-24: 2C].
Fontz, Mary Ann (66 yrs.) d. on 69-Oct-10 [69-Oct-12: 2C].
Fontz, Mary Ellen m. Arthur, James H. on 70-Dec-20 [70-Dec-28: 2C].
Fooks, Henrietta E. m. Palmer, William C. on 68-Dec-15 [68-Dec-24: 2C].
Fooks, J. J. m. Parsons, M. E. on 70-Sep-26 [70-Oct-22: 2B].
Fooler, Mary M. Florence (10 mos.) d. on 69-Apr-12 [69-Apr-14: 2B].
Foos, Annie E. (19 yrs.) d. on 66-Nov-21 [66-Nov-23: 2C].
Foos, Ida E. (1 yr., 10 mos.) d. on 69-Apr-11 [69-Apr-12: 2A].

Foos, James K. m. Cunningham, Maggie on 66-Sep-20 [66-Sep-26: 2B].
Foos, John C. (3 yrs.) d. on 70-Feb-24 [70-Feb-26: 2C].
Foos, John C. m. Knihoff, Annie C. on 66-May-10 [66-May-17: 2C].
Foos, John C. m. Favier, Mary V. on 69-Mar-14 [69-Apr-18: 2C].
Foos, John S. m. Spafford, Mary O. on 69-Sep-9 [69-Sep-13: 2B].
Foos, John W. (5 yrs., 5 mos.) d. on 70-May-30 [70-Jun-1: 2B].
Foos, Mary C. m. Colin, George on 66-Jan-26 [66-Mar-7: 2B].
Foos, Susie W. m. Flautt, Joseph T. on 66-Feb-13 [66-Mar-9: 2B].
Foose, Catherine E. m. Schepler, Francis on 69-Sep-8 [69-Sep-18: 2B].
Foot, Matilda (73 yrs.) d. on 69-Mar-14 [69-Jun-9: 2C].
Foran, Ann T. (45 yrs.) d. on 66-Apr-19 [66-Apr-20: 2B; 66-Apr-21: 2B].
Foran, Esther Elizabeth (11 mos.) d. on 67-Aug-11 [67-Aug-12: 2C].
Forbes, Fanny m. Barrot, Odilon on 68-Dec-14 [69-Jan-20: 2C].
Forbes, Harry (2 yrs., 9 mos.) d. on 70-Oct-10 [70-Oct-12: 2B].
Forbes, Lewis m. Lippincott, Emma H. on 69-Nov-18 [69-Nov-20: 2B].
Forbes, Martha Bush m. Duck, Charles Edward on 69-Nov-23 [69-Nov-24: 2C].
Forbes, Susan Gordon d. on 68-Dec-25 [68-Dec-29: 2D].
Force, Lottie C. m. Hoffman, George W. on 66-Dec-12 [67-Jan-3: 2B].
Force, William C. (27 yrs.) d. on 67-Jan-26 [67-Feb-7: 2C].
Forckus, John W. m. Spears, Martha A. on 66-Jun-10 [66-Jun-22: 2B].
Ford, Achilles m. Amoss, Annie E. on 67-Mar-27 [67-Apr-15: 2B].
Ford, Alice C. (2 yrs., 4 mos.) d. on 69-Mar-15 of Measles [69-Mar-16: 2C; 69-Mar-24: 2C].
Ford, Alverda A. m. Suter, Frank T. on 70-Oct-25 [70-Oct-27: 2B].
Ford, Annie L. m. Palmer, John M. on 68-Oct-15 [68-Oct-16: 2B].
Ford, Bettie E. (24 yrs., 2 mos.) d. of Consumption [70-Apr-15: 2B].
Ford, Charles E. m. Nunnally, Maria on 68-Oct-4 [68-Oct-6: 2B].
Ford, David (68 yrs.) d. on 68-Oct-9 [68-Oct-10: 2B].
Ford, Eddy (8 yrs.) d. on 69-Feb-17 [69-Feb-20: 2B].
Ford, Elizabeth Ann (35 yrs.) d. on 70-Jun-24 [70-Jun-28: 2C].
Ford, Emily d. on 70-Mar-23 of Consumption [70-Jul-16: 2B].
Ford, Florence Lee (6 yrs.) d. on 69-Mar-29 [69-Mar-30: 2C].
Ford, Hannah (52 yrs.) d. on 68-Apr-19 [68-Apr-20: 2B].
Ford, Hannah Jessie m. Davis, William H. on 66-Apr-26 [66-Apr-30: 2B].
Ford, Hiram J., Capt. (32 yrs.) d. on 68-Oct-27 of Gunshot wound [68-Oct-29: 1G, 2B].
Ford, Issac m. Taylor, Sarah E. on 67-Oct-24 [67-Oct-30: 2B].
Ford, James B. (1 yr., 4 mos.) d. on 68-Aug-25 [68-Aug-27: 2B].
Ford, James R. m. Campbell, Kate H. on 66-Mar-6 [66-Mar-13: 2B].
Ford, Jane E. m. Lowe, John W. on 69-Jan-17 [69-Feb-6: 2C].
Ford, Jerry (72 yrs.) d. on 69-Jul-24 [69-Jul-27: 2C].
Ford, John D. m. Darling, Laura J. on 66-Apr-30 [66-May-3: 2C].
Ford, John L. (13 yrs.) d. on 70-Oct-4 [70-Oct-6: 2B].
Ford, John S. (38 yrs.) d. on 66-Aug-13 [66-Sep-13: 2C].
Ford, John T. (17 yrs.) d. on 69-Jun-2 in Railroad accident [69-Jun-3: 1F; 69-Jun-7: 1H].
Ford, John Thomas m. Ningardt, Mary Virginia on 69-Dec-28 [70-Jan-1: 2B].
Ford, Kate E. m. Lee, B. Frank on 67-Mar-14 [67-Mar-16: 2B].
Ford, Lambert (13 yrs.) d. on 70-Oct-4 [70-Oct-17: 2B].
Ford, Louisa m. Price, James M. on 67-Sep-12 [67-Sep-21: 2A].
Ford, Martha A. d. on 67-Jun-30 [67-Jul-1: 2B].
Ford, Martha W. (34 yrs.) d. on 69-Jul-10 [69-Jul-17: 2C].
Ford, Mary A. (4 mos.) d. on 69-May-25 [69-May-26: 2C].
Ford, Mary A. m. Richards, James George on 66-Mar-18 [66-Apr-7: 2B].
Ford, Mary Ann m. Brown, Jacob on 65-Dec-12 [66-Jan-1: 2C].
Ford, Mary Frances d. on 70-Jan-20 [70-Jan-21: 2C; 70-Jan-22: 2B].
Ford, Michael d. Drowned [70-Dec-3: 2B].
Ford, Mollie (7 yrs., 10 mos.) d. on 69-Sep-18 of Diptheria [69-Sep-20: 2C].

Ford, Mollie E. m. Diamond, George H. on 66-Sep-6 [66-Sep-12: 2A].
Ford, Patrick (45 yrs.) d. on 69-Jan-17 [69-Jan-18: 2C].
Ford, R. Wesley m. Wright, Sallie E. on 70-Jan-27 [70-Jan-29: 2B; 70-Feb-3: 2B].
Ford, Reuben (6 yrs., 9 mos.) d. on 70-Oct-14 [70-Oct-17: 2B].
Ford, Robert R. (1 yr., 2 mos.) d. on 69-Mar-21 of Measles [69-Mar-24: 2C].
Ford, William H. (46 yrs.) d. on 67-Oct-30 [67-Oct-31: 2B].
Ford, William H. m. Harris, Margaret J. on 68-Jul-5 [68-Aug-15: 2B].
Foreman, Catherine (56 yrs.) d. on 67-Jul-13 of Typhoid [67-Jul-16: 2C].
Foreman, Fannie V. m. Baggett, John B. on 69-Mar-18 [69-Mar-29: 2B].
Foreman, Lea m. Ingram, Belle on 67-Feb-5 [67-Feb-7: 2C].
Foreman, Leonard W. (57 yrs.) d. on 69-Dec-20 [69-Dec-22: 2B].
Foreman, Lizzie A. m. German, George J. on 68-Apr-27 [68-Apr-30: 2B].
Foreman, Rebecca E. m. Comegys, William on 67-Dec-31 [68-Jan-6: 2C].
Forester, James d. on 68-Feb-9 [68-Feb-10: 2C].
Forman, Amelia m. Johnson, Thomas C. on 68-Sep-22 [68-Sep-26: 2B].
Forman, Arthur J. (61 yrs.) d. [67-Dec-10: 2B].
Forman, Issac, Rev. (84 yrs.) d. on 70-Apr-16 of Paralysis [70-Apr-18: 2B; 70-Apr-19: 1H].
Forman, Philip J. (26 yrs., 3 mos.) d. on 67-Jan-18 [67-Jan-19: 2C].
Forman, Virginia m. Willis, Z. L. C. on 69-Nov-25 [69-Nov-29: 2C].
Forney, Bayley (1 yr.) d. on 69-Apr-28 [69-Apr-29: 2C].
Forney, Charlotte R. m. Furlong, William H. on 68-Sep-10 [68-Sep-19: 2B].
Forney, Elizabeth (48 yrs., 9 mos.) d. on 70-Nov-22 [70-Nov-24: 2B].
Forney, Georgie (5 yrs.) d. on 69-Apr-27 [69-Apr-28: 2B].
Forney, Issac C. (67 yrs.) d. on 69-Jun-11 [69-Jun-12: 2B].
Forney, Jemima (76 yrs.) d. on 69-Feb-10 [69-Feb-12: 2C].
Forney, John Snoden (42 yrs.) d. on 66-Jun-1 [66-Jun-5: 2B].
Forney, Lizzie Brett (2 yrs., 8 mos.) d. on 67-Jul-26 [67-Jul-27: 2B].
Forney, Martha A. m. Hanson, Homer H. on 68-Feb-13 [68-Feb-15: 2B].
Forney, Millie m. Young, William S. on 70-Jun-29 [70-Jul-4: 2C].
Forney, Mollie G. m. Holmes, William, Jr. on 70-Nov-20 [70-Nov-28: 2C].
Forney, Susie B. m. Brown, Thomas on 68-Feb-17 [68-Apr-27: 2B].
Fornshill, Columbus C. (39 yrs.) d. on 67-Jun-25 Murdered (Shooting) [67-Jun-26: 1F, 2C].
Forrest, Charles (20 yrs.) d. on 68-May-8 [68-May-9: 2B].
Forrest, E. Cole m. Coleman, Fannie J. on 67-Jun-23 [67-Jun-27: 2B].
Forrest, Emma L. m. Ward, Issac L. on 67-Jul-16 [67-Jul-18: 2C].
Forrest, Leonard d. on 66-Nov-16 [66-Nov-17: 1G, 2B].
Forrest, Mary (94 yrs.) d. on 69-Jul-13 [69-Jul-14: 2D].
Forrest, Mary E. m. Watts, Charles A. on 69-Feb-18 [69-Apr-19: 2B].
Forrest, Monroe (24 yrs.) d. on 66-Jun-22 of Brain concussion [66-Jun-23: 2B].
Forrest, Moreau d. on 66-Nov-24 of Yellow fever [66-Dec-22: 2B].
Forrester, Benjamin F. (63 yrs., 5 mos.) d. on 67-Jan-25 [67-Jan-26: 2C].
Forrester, George m. Hurtt, Frances A. on 67-Dec-18 [68-Jul-31: 2C].
Forrester, Jessie m. McLean, John on 67-Jul-12 [67-Jul-23: 2C].
Forrester, John R. m. Joyce, Lavenia on 69-Jul-4 [69-Jul-9: 2C].
Forrester, Josephine m. Gatch, Thomas B. on 68-Sep-9 [68-Oct-8: 2B].
Forrester, Julia Ann (33 yrs., 8 mos.) d. on 66-Dec-30 [67-Jan-1: 2C].
Forrester, Mary Cookman (1 yr., 8 mos.) d. on 67-Dec-2 [67-Dec-4: 2C].
Forrester, Mary Elizabeth (9 yrs.) d. on 70-Dec-9 of Scarlet fever [70-Dec-12: 2C].
Forrester, Rosalia (6 yrs.) d. on 70-Dec-1 [70-Dec-3: 2B].
Forrester, William E. m. Marrow, Laura B. on 70-Apr-21 [70-Apr-28: 2B].
Forrester, William H. m. Isenberg, Jennie on 68-Sep-8 [68-Sep-12: 2B].
Forster, Barbara Ann (71 yrs.) d. on 66-Jul-8 [66-Jul-9: 2C].
Forster, G. H. m. Simon, Rose R. on 67-Oct-3 [67-Oct-5: 2B].
Forster, Mary H. (80 yrs.) d. on 67-Dec-5 [67-Dec-6: 2C].
Forsyth, Alexander D. m. Clark, Elizabeth P. on 69-Sep-15 [69-Sep-18: 2B].

Forsyth, Alexander M. m. Coleman, Ella C. on 67-May-21 [67-May-22: 2B].
Forsyth, Arthur P. m. Clark, Amanda on 70-Nov-24 [70-Dec-2: 2C].
Forsyth, Henry (63 yrs.) d. on 66-Aug-16 [66-Aug-25: 2A].
Forsyth, Jarrett M. (45 yrs.) d. on 70-Jun-19 Drowned [70-Jun-20: 1G; 70-Jun-21: 2C].
Forsyth, Joseph F. m. Spidle, Mary J. on 68-Aug-23 [69-Aug-23: 2C].
Forsyth, Richard Henry (13 yrs.) d. on 70-Jun-11 Drowned [70-Jun-13: 1G, 2C].
Forsyth, William H. m. Welling, Belle C. on 68-Jan-21 [68-Jan-23: 2C].
Forsythe, Elizabeth F. (28 yrs.) d. on 67-May-3 of Heart disease [67-May-4: 2B; 67-May-24: 2B].
Forsythe, Elizabeth J. (36 yrs.) d. on 70-Mar-13 [70-Mar-14: 2C].
Forsythe, Florence Virginia (5 yrs., 3 mos.) d. on 70-Nov-24 [70-Nov-25: 2D].
Forsythe, L. E. m. Hunt, Emma V. on 68-Dec-17 [68-Dec-31: 2C].
Fort, Alfie V. m. Jordan, J. W. on 66-Oct-11 [66-Oct-16: 2B].
Fort, Ella Virginia (4 yrs.) d. on 70-Nov-14 [70-Nov-15: 2C].
Fort, Harriet d. on 69-Mar-13 [69-Mar-16: 2C].
Fort, Ida C. (17 yrs.) d. on 69-Sep-6 [69-Sep-7: 2B].
Fort, Leander D. m. Curtis, Ella on 68-Nov-5 [68-Nov-12: 2C].
Fort, Mary Anna (6 yrs., 4 mos.) d. on 70-Oct-24 [70-Oct-25: 2B].
Fort, Olivia m. Fitzhugh, F. M. on 67-Jul-13 [67-Aug-2: 2C].
Fort, Otis S. (18 yrs.) d. on 67-Jun-2 of Consumption [67-Jun-5: 2B].
Fort, Susie R. m. Duvall, Marshall on 68-Jun-4 [68-Jun-22: 2B].
Fort, Thomas m. Latchford, Alice on 69-Jun-20 [69-Jun-24: 2C].
Fort, William Bernard (1 yr., 6 mos.) d. on 70-Nov-9 [70-Nov-10: 2C].
Fort, William F. (27 yrs.) d. on 69-Jan-16 [69-Jan-18: 2D].
Fort, William F. m. Cassidy, Emma W. on 66-Aug-29 [66-Sep-10: 2D].
Fort, Zillah V. m. Canby, C. T. on 70-Jan-12 [70-Jan-21: 2C].
Fortenbaugh, Charles m. Raab, Lizzie B. on 70-Jun-16 [70-Jul-23: 2B].
Fortling, Elizabeth (69 yrs.) d. on 69-Aug-29 [69-Aug-30: 2B].
Fortling, Leonard (37 yrs.) d. on 67-Mar-26 [67-Mar-27: 2C].
Fortman, Stephen Adolphus (1 yr., 6 mos.) d. on 69-Aug-5 [69-Aug-10: 2C].
Fortune, Julia (49 yrs.) d. on 66-Apr-2 [66-Apr-4: 2B].
Forwood, Christine m. Mitchell, James H. on 66-Aug-23 [66-Aug-29: 2B].
Forwood, Samuel E. m. White, Mary E. on 69-Dec-16 [69-Dec-18: 2C].
Fosbenner, Alexander m. Dufie, Mary A. on 66-May-22 [66-Jun-4: 2B].
Fosbenner, Ella m. Ward, Joseph W. on 70-Oct-20 [70-Oct-24: 2B].
Fosler, Almira F. m. Johnson, Richard on 68-Apr-30 [68-May-6: 2B].
Foss, Emma A. (1 yr., 5 mos.) d. on 70-Jan-31 [70-Feb-1: 2B].
Foss, Florria m. High, William T. J. on 66-Nov-22 [66-Dec-7: 2B].
Foss, Laura A. m. Holtzman, Thomas R. on 66-Sep-27 [66-Sep-29: 2B].
Fossebenner, William G. (45 yrs.) d. on 69-Aug-13 Drowned [69-Aug-16: 1G; 69-Aug-19: 2C].
Fossett, Arabella m. Gordon, Charles M. on 67-Nov-26 [67-Nov-28: 2C].
Fossett, Henry C. m. Brady, Maggie V. on 70-Jul-12 [70-Jul-19: 2B].
Fossett, John (84 yrs.) d. on 70-Jul-14 [70-Jul-16: 2B].
Foster, Annie A. m. Smith, Louis J. on 68-May-26 [68-May-28: 2B].
Foster, Annie D. (22 yrs.) d. on 66-Nov-28 [66-Nov-29: 2B].
Foster, Benjamin Howard (3 yrs.) d. on 68-May-20 [68-May-21: 2B].
Foster, Caroline F. (35 yrs.) d. on 70-Aug-6 [70-Aug-8: 2C].
Foster, Catherine J. (69 yrs.) d. on 67-Jun-11 [67-Jun-13: 2C].
Foster, Charles H. m. Curlett, Mollie S. M. on 69-Nov-25 [69-Dec-10: 2C].
Foster, Elizabeth (61 yrs., 3 mos.) d. on 67-Jul-13 [67-Jul-15: 2C].
Foster, Ella C. (6 mos.) d. on 68-Aug-29 [68-Sep-1: 2B].
Foster, Ella E. (5 yrs., 10 mos.) d. on 67-Nov-14 [67-Nov-15: 2B].
Foster, Emma m. Leach, C. M. on 68-Dec-3 [68-Dec-5: 2C].
Foster, H. D. m. Williams, Mary A. on 68-Sep-20 [68-Oct-17: 2B].
Foster, Isabel Marshall (2 mos.) d. on 68-May-27 [68-May-28: 2B].

Foster, James, Sr. (79 yrs.) d. on 70-Jun-5 [70-Jun-6: 2B].
Foster, James Thomas (9 yrs., 5 mos.) d. on 70-Jun-7 [70-Jun-9: 2C].
Foster, Jessie Florence (4 yrs.) d. on 66-Oct-18 [66-Oct-19: 2B].
Foster, John Alvey (2 yrs., 6 mos.) d. on 70-Mar-22 of Bronchitis and whooping cough [70-Mar-24: 2C].
Foster, Kate m. Gehring, Charles J. on 67-Nov-27 [67-Nov-28: 2C].
Foster, Lucretia D. m. McGinley, Durban on 67-Nov-25 [68-Mar-2: 2B].
Foster, Mary (56 yrs.) d. on 66-Aug-31 of Suicide (Poisoning) [66-Sep-3: 4C; 66-Sep-4: 4C].
Foster, Mary (69 yrs.) d. on 69-Feb-22 [69-Feb-24: 2C].
Foster, Rachel m. Lare, Lewis G. on 66-Nov-15 [66-Nov-20: 2B].
Foster, Robert m. Woods, Susan on 69-Sep-2 [69-Sep-20: 2C].
Foster, Robert H. m. Chesnay, Amanda on 66-Jun-19 [66-Jul-28: 2C].
Foster, Samuel (54 yrs.) d. on 68-Feb-12 [68-Feb-24: 2C].
Foster, Solina P. (63 yrs.) d. on 70-Jun-30 [70-Jul-1: 2B].
Foudriat, Celine m. Muth, John P. on 70-Oct-18 [70-Nov-1: 2C].
Foulk, Eliza (68 yrs.) d. on 68-Oct-9 [68-Oct-12: 2B].
Foulkes, Mary K. R. d. on 69-Jul-14 [69-Jul-16: 2C].
Foulkes, Robert F. m. Bender, Mary K. R. on 65-Dec-14 [66-Jan-1: 2C].
Fountain, Amanda J. m. Spurrier, John E. on 69-Oct-11 [69-Oct-13: 2C].
Fountain, Ella (8 mos.) d. on 66-Jul-16 [66-Jul-20: 2D].
Fountain, George A. Thawley (4 mos.) d. on 66-Mar-29 [66-Mar-31: 2C].
Fountain, Helen Eugenia (2 mos.) d. on 70-Jan-22 [70-Jan-24: 2C].
Fountain, Hennie m. Meeds, Thomas E. on 68-Jan-7 [68-Jan-9: 2C].
Fountain, Julia M. m. Jump, Robert H. on 66-Jul-31 [66-Aug-11: 2B].
Fountain, Maggie J. m. Hitchens, John H. on 67-Feb-13 [67-Feb-16: 2D].
Fountain, Manie Baxter (9 yrs.) d. on 68-Dec-3 [68-Dec-4: 2D; 68-Dec-5: 2C].
Fountain, Martha Virginia (2 yrs.) d. on 70-May-5 [70-May-6: 2B].
Fountain, Mary A. (38 yrs.) d. on 69-Jul-11 [69-Jul-12: 2C].
Fountain, William d. on 68-Jul-24 Drowned [68-Jul-28: 1B].
Fout, Mary C. m. Lyeth, John T. on 69-Nov-9 [69-Nov-15: 2C].
Foutz, J. Lyle (10 mos.) d. on 70-Mar-1 [70-Mar-2: 2C].
Foutz, Margaret m. Kelso, John on 66-Jul-9 [66-Jul-14: 2B].
Fowble, Alfred m. Cole, Florence G. on 67-Nov-28 [67-Dec-5: 2C].
Fowble, George m. Kemp, Missouri on 70-Nov-15 [70-Nov-26: 2B].
Fowble, Rosa May (9 mos.) d. on 66-Feb-25 of Whooping cough [66-Feb-27: 2B].
Fowble, William A. m. Plummer, S. A. on 70-Jan-16 [70-Feb-16: 2C].
Fowler, Alfred d. on 67-Dec-12 in Railroad accident [67-Dec-13: 1G].
Fowler, Amelia Sophia (46 yrs.) d. on 69-Feb-2 [69-Feb-3: 2C; 69-Feb-4: 2C].
Fowler, Clara Lee (17 yrs.) d. on 69-Mar-3 [69-Mar-5: 2C].
Fowler, Ella m. Linthicum, William H. on 69-Jan-21 [69-Feb-10: 2C].
Fowler, Emily R. m. Richardson, William H. on 69-Jun-17 [69-Jun-23: 2C].
Fowler, Emma (8 mos.) d. on 70-Jul-13 [70-Jul-15: 2C].
Fowler, Ettie Almer (1 yr., 6 mos.) d. on 69-Jul-30 [69-Aug-2: 2C].
Fowler, Fannie E. m. Remore, George E. on 67-Jun-27 [67-Aug-6: 2C].
Fowler, George W. (36 yrs.) d. on 67-Jul-26 [67-Jul-27: 2B].
Fowler, James F. m. Dorsey, Josephine A. on 67-Sep-26 [67-Oct-17: 2B].
Fowler, John, Capt. (47 yrs.) d. on 68-May-27 Drowned [68-May-30: 2A].
Fowler, John (65 yrs.) d. on 68-Mar-6 [68-Mar-7: 2B].
Fowler, John W. m. Houston, Mary on 69-Aug-3 [69-Aug-10: 2C].
Fowler, Margaret E. m. Harris, William H. on 68-Oct-27 [68-Nov-5: 2C].
Fowler, Margery A. W. m. Marshall, John on 70-May-19 [70-May-21: 2B].
Fowler, Mary (83 yrs.) d. on 70-Sep-1 [70-Sep-3: 2B].
Fowler, Mary Ann (77 yrs.) d. on 69-Jun-7 [69-Jul-8: 2C].
Fowler, Mary Anne (83 yrs.) d. on 68-Aug-19 [68-Aug-20: 2B].
Fowler, Mary T. m. Heydorn, M. on 68-Apr-22 [68-May-28: 2B].

Fowler, Monroe m. Ritter, Annie E. on 68-May-7 [68-May-11: 2B].
Fowler, Philip W. (48 yrs.) d. on 66-Dec-7 [66-Dec-8: 2B].
Fowler, Rachel m. Davis, William on 67-Jul-21 [67-Jul-24: 2C].
Fowler, Randolph m. Durham, Amelia on 70-Dec-15 [70-Dec-17: 2C].
Fowler, Rasin m. Moore, Maggie on 68-Dec-31 [69-Jan-5: 2C].
Fowler, Sallie A. d. on 67-Jul-5 [67-Jul-6: 2B].
Fowler, Sarah Alice (24 yrs.) d. on 66-Jul-16 [66-Jul-25: 2C].
Fowler, Susan (79 yrs.) d. on 68-Mar-13 [68-Mar-14: 2B].
Fowler, Susan R. m. Litzinger, William R. on 68-Mar-18 [68-Apr-3: 2C].
Fowler, William m. Carback, Sue on 70-Sep-15 [70-Sep-16: 2B].
Fowler, William T. (42 yrs.) d. on 70-Aug-28 [70-Aug-30: 2C; 70-Aug-29: 2B].
Fowner, Emma V. (2 yrs., 2 mos.) d. on 67-Oct-3 [67-Oct-4: 2B].
Fowner, Louisa R. (3 yrs., 8 mos.) d. on 67-Oct-2 [67-Oct-4: 2B].
Fox, Andrew (30 yrs.) d. on 68-Jun-30 [68-Jul-4: 2C].
Fox, Ann (56 yrs.) d. on 70-Sep-21 [70-Sep-23: 2C].
Fox, Christopher d. on 67-Sep-28 [67-Sep-30: 1F].
Fox, Edward W. m. Rex, Sybill on 66-Mar-22 [66-Mar-23: 2C].
Fox, Elizabeth (95 yrs.) d. on 69-Aug-20 [69-Aug-27: 2B].
Fox, Frank S. m. Feelemyer, Isadora on 66-Feb-22 [66-Feb-23: 2C].
Fox, James J. m. Quinn, Kate on 66-Dec-23 [66-Dec-25: 2B].
Fox, Joseph (1 yr., 9 mos.) d. on 69-Dec-20 [69-Dec-22: 2B].
Fox, Lewis C. m. Kraft, Anna E. on 68-Apr-30 [68-May-5: 2B].
Fox, Luther A. m. Glossbrenner, Henrietta C. on 69-Sep-9 [69-Sep-15: 2B].
Fox, Martha Adeline (31 yrs.) d. on 68-Jan-20 [68-Jan-23: 2C].
Fox, Mary (66 yrs.) d. on 68-Nov-27 [68-Nov-28: 2C].
Fox, Mary A. m. Bierbower, Francis A. on 69-Nov-18 [69-Nov-25: 2C].
Fox, Nina Carr (4 mos.) d. on 70-Jul-24 [70-Jul-26: 2B].
Fox, Susan d. on 66-Jun-22 [66-Jun-23: 2B].
Fox, Thomas J. E. (82 yrs.) d. on 66-Jul-10 [66-Jul-12: 2C].
Fox, W. Tazewell m. Carr, Ella B. on 69-Apr-22 [69-May-6: 2B].
Foxcroft, William (74 yrs.) d. on 66-Aug-7 [66-Aug-8: 2C].
Foxwell, Annie E. m. Merchant, John R. on 67-Aug-5 [67-Aug-10: 2B].
Foxwell, Benjamin m. Paul, Anna M. on 67-Oct-8 [67-Oct-9: 2B].
Foxwell, Benjamin F. m. Vansant, Sarah J. on 66-Apr-22 [66-Apr-26: 2B].
Foxwell, Mary Ann (47 yrs.) d. on 70-Feb-13 [70-Feb-19: 2B].
Foy, Charlie (1 yr., 10 mos.) d. on 70-Jul-26 [70-Jul-27: 2C].
Foy, Lina d. on 70-Apr-25 [70-Apr-26: 2B; 70-Apr-27: 2B].
Foy, Philip Charles d. on 70-Apr-3 [70-Apr-9: 2B].
Frailey, Alice m. McMahan, John B. on 69-Dec-30 [70-Jan-1: 2B].
Frailey, Elizabeth (82 yrs.) d. on 68-Oct-8 [68-Oct-9: 2C].
Frailey, Mary E. m. McGreevy, A. R. on 66-Dec-11 [66-Dec-12: 2B].
Fraley, Amanda (38 yrs.) d. on 67-Jan-9 [67-Jan-14: 2C].
Frame, Alice m. Starr, Edward V. on 69-Jun-24 [69-Jul-1: 2C].
Frame, George m. Stewart, Mary M. on 69-Apr-29 [69-May-5: 2C].
Frame, James m. Mathiot, Clara L. on 70-Apr-28 [70-May-3: 2B].
Frames, John Minett d. on 70-Jul-18 [70-Jul-19: 2C].
Framiller, Adolphus d. on 70-Aug-25 Drowned [70-Aug-27: 4E; 70-Aug-29: 4D].
Frampton, Nathaniel m. Bordley, Elizabeth C. on 69-Nov-18 [69-Nov-20: 2B].
Frampton, Susan (39 yrs.) d. on 68-Sep-29 [68-Oct-2: 2B].
France, Ann Louisa m. Eyler, Henry S. on 68-Apr-26 [68-May-1: 2B].
France, Bettie m. Nailor, W. T. on 70-Sep-15 [70-Sep-16: 2B].
France, Henry m. Whitten, Lizzie F. on 68-Sep-6 [68-Oct-10: 2B].
France, John d. on 66-Sep-14 of Fall [66-Sep-15: 1G].
France, John m. King, Lucy on 66-Sep-20 [66-Sep-21: 2B].
France, Lou M. m. Bantz, Eugene H. on 67-Jun-4 [67-Jun-6: 2B].

France, Sarah Elenore (3 yrs., 11 mos.) d. on 68-Dec-17 [68-Dec-18: 2C; 68-Dec-19: 2B].
Francis, Charles m. Willingham, Martha A. on 68-Dec-17 [68-Dec-18: 2C].
Francis, Estelle (1 yr., 9 mos.) d. on 69-Sep-29 [69-Sep-30: 2B].
Francis, John William (17 yrs.) d. on 67-Apr-25 [67-Apr-26: 2B].
Francis, Mary Jane m. Irons, John T. on 67-Mar-12 [67-Mar-21: 2C].
Francis, Robert d. on 66-Jul-18 [66-Jul-19: 2C].
Francis, Robert m. Woods, Mary E. on 68-Oct-26 [68-Nov-10: 2C].
Francis, Terella E. C. m. Anderson, Oliver H. on 66-Jan-28 [66-Jan-30: 2B].
Francis, Thomas (70 yrs.) d. on 66-Jan-7 [66-Jan-8: 2B; 66-Jan-9: 2B].
Franck, Kate m. Craig, Oliver B. on 66-Jan-25 [66-Jan-29: 2B].
Franck, Nettie T. m. Dorn, Philip on 67-Dec-31 [68-Jan-6: 2C].
Franckhouser, Mary (55 yrs.) d. on 67-Feb-18 [67-Feb-20: 2C].
Frank, Carrie m. Hecht, Jacob H. on 67-Jan-23 [67-Jan-26: 2C].
Frank, Hannah m. Woolf, H. E. on 69-Apr-11 [69-Apr-20: 2B].
Frank, John A. m. Hopps, Mary J. on 68-Sep-18 [68-Oct-13: 2C].
Frank, John Custis Lee (2 mos.) d. on 66-Apr-3 [66-Apr-4: 2B].
Frank, John G. (59 yrs.) d. on 68-Jun-26 [68-Jun-27: 2B].
Frank, Lena m. Gardner, Frederick on 69-Jun-28 [69-Jun-30: 2C].
Frank, Mary E. d. on 66-Feb-25 [66-Feb-26: 2B].
Frank, Mary V. H. (1 yr.) d. on 69-Sep-10 [69-Sep-11: 2B].
Frank, Milton B. m. Colbert, Sallie E. on 67-Jan-22 [67-Jan-24: 2C].
Frank, Oscar W., Capt. (28 yrs.) d. on 67-Aug-29 Drowned [67-Aug-31: 2B, 4B; 67-Sep-5: 1G].
Frank, S. L. m. Rayner, Bertha on 69-Dec-16 [69-Dec-18: 2B].
Frank, Simon (62 yrs.) d. on 69-Jul-28 [69-Jul-30: 2C].
Franke, Henrietta (50 yrs., 4 mos.) d. on 70-Aug-18 [70-Aug-19: 2C].
Frankfottier, Sarah d. on 67-Dec-9 [67-Dec-11: 2B].
Frankland, Matilda m. Heiss, Alexander on 68-Dec-10 [68-Dec-23: 2C].
Frankland, W. E. m. Williams, Alice V. on 66-Dec-20 [66-Dec-24: 2B].
Franklin, Annie m. Maitland, James F. on 66-May-17 [66-May-18: 2C].
Franklin, Annie m. Treadway, Nelson R. on 70-Apr-7 [70-Apr-9: 2B].
Franklin, Benjamin m. Dearing, Bettie on 69-Mar-24 [69-Mar-31: 2C].
Franklin, Ellen (53 yrs.) d. on 66-Feb-11 [66-Feb-12: 2D].
Franklin, Garrett (66 yrs.) d. on 70-Jul-12 [70-Jul-13: 2C].
Franklin, Jarrett (74 yrs.) d. on 67-Apr-13 [67-Apr-19: 2B].
Franklin, John, Jr. m. Thorburn, Maggie McC on 67-Apr-14 [67-Apr-17: 2B].
Franklin, John, Sr. (60 yrs.) d. on 67-May-3 [67-May-4: 2B].
Franklin, John E. m. Skinner, Marietta on 67-Jan-1 [67-Jan-5: 2E].
Franklin, John R. m. Martin, Kate on 68-Dec-9 [68-Dec-11: 2C].
Franklin, Joseph F. (44 yrs.) d. on 68-Jul-15 of Heatstroke [68-Jul-16: 2C; 68-Jul-20: 1E].
Franklin, Lewis A. m. Davis, Emily Sarah on 66-Dec-12 [67-Jan-8: 2B].
Franklin, Melissa N. m. Bryant, William L. on 69-Sep-2 [69-Sep-6: 2C].
Franklin, Phillis d. on 67-May-13 [67-May-16: 2B].
Franz, John A. m. Thompsen, Mary A. on 66-Jan-16 [66-Feb-2: 2C].
Fraser, Ellen J. m. Steuart, Alexander S. on 70-Aug-11 [70-Aug-15: 2B].
Fraser, William m. Meiser, Kate on 70-Dec-20 [70-Dec-26: 2C].
Fray, Mary Elizabeth (68 yrs.) d. on 69-Jul-28 [69-Jul-29: 2C].
Frayser, Mary T. m. Wilkinson, Stephen A. on 66-Dec-12 [67-Jan-1: 2C].
Frazer, Anne G. m. Wilson, John W. on 68-Apr-21 [68-Apr-23: 2B].
Frazer, Elizabeth d. on 67-Nov-10 [67-Nov-11: 2C; 67-Nov-12: 2C].
Frazer, Ellen L. m. Gough, Arthur on 67-Jun-27 [67-Jun-29: 2B].
Frazier, Charles E. m. Hines, Mary E. on 67-Feb-28 [67-Mar-4: 2D].
Frazier, Elizabeth (37 yrs.) d. on 66-Oct-7 [66-Oct-8: 2B].
Frazier, Frances A. (37 yrs.) d. on 67-Nov-28 [67-Dec-2: 2C].
Frazier, Isabella B. m. Sensner, George W. on 68-Mar-26 [68-Apr-3: 2C].
Frazier, James, Capt. (85 yrs.) d. on 66-Jul-18 [66-Jul-19: 1E, 2C; 66-Jul-20: 2D].

Frazier, James, Jr. (57 yrs.) d. on 70-Dec-21 [70-Dec-28: 2C].
Frazier, John (59 yrs.) d. on 66-Nov-8 [66-Nov-9: 2C].
Frazier, John M. (42 yrs.) d. on 70-Feb-27 [70-Mar-2: 1H; 70-Mar-4: 2C; 70-Mar-5: 1H, 2B; 70-Mar-7: 2C].
Frazier, Lizzie m. Collier, George K. on 69-Mar-4 [69-Mar-20: 2B].
Frazier, Lydia Ann d. on 67-Apr-6 [67-Apr-8: 2B].
Frazier, Margaret d. on 70-Jul-2 [70-Jul-6: 2C].
Frazier, Martina A. m. Newton, Henry C. on 69-Oct-25 [69-Oct-27: 2B].
Frazier, Rosanna m. Strickling, Jesse on 69-Mar-9 [69-Nov-1: 2B].
Frazier, Sarah Ann m. Redmond, John B. on 67-Apr-21 [67-May-2: 2B].
Frazier, Sarah Jane d. on 67-Sep-18 [67-Sep-19: 2B].
Frazier, Virginia C. m. Quinan, John A. on 69-Jul-13 [69-Jul-15: 2C].
Frazier, William W. m. Edelen, Sarah E. on 66-Mar-20 [66-Mar-22: 2B].
Freberger, Mary E. m. Stowman, Edward D. on 70-Jan-27 [70-Jan-29: 2B].
Freburger, Charles E. m. Davis, Fannie E. on 69-Jun-8 [69-Jun-10: 2C].
Freburger, Emeline (32 yrs., 3 mos.) d. on 66-Sep-1 [66-Sep-3: 2C; 66-Sep-4: 2B].
Freburger, Emma J. m. Bower, William J. A. on 69-Dec-2 [69-Dec-11: 2B].
Freburger, Henry G. (79 yrs.) d. on 66-Dec-12 [66-Dec-14: 2B].
Freburger, James M. m. Short, Kate A. on 68-Oct-19 [68-Oct-27: 2B].
Freburger, John W. m. Meeks, Josephine E. on 68-Jun-9 [68-Jun-25: 2B].
Freburger, Sarah Ann (26 yrs.) d. on 66-Jul-17 [66-Jul-18: 2C].
Frederick, Ada m. Koonce, H. A. on 69-Apr-13 [69-Apr-29: 2B].
Frederick, Ann (31 yrs.) d. on 68-Jan-17 of Lamp explosion [68-Jan-20: 1F, 2C].
Frederick, Ann Rebetha (11 mos.) d. on 68-Jul-18 [68-Jul-20: 2B].
Frederick, Annie m. Stockdale, John on 66-Sep-18 [66-Sep-20: 2B].
Frederick, Benjamin F. m. Jackson, Martha A. on 68-Sep-9 [68-Sep-14: 2B].
Frederick, Georgeanna m. Harford, Charles Dallas on 68-Sep-28 [68-Oct-1: 2B].
Frederick, Henrietta (34 yrs.) d. on 69-May-21 [69-May-22: 2B].
Frederick, John (59 yrs.) d. on 68-Jan-8 [68-Jan-9: 2C].
Frederick, Julia A. Virginia m. Welsh, David C. on 70-Nov-29 [70-Dec-7: 2C].
Frederick, Laura V. m. Hutson, Thomas A. D. on 69-Nov-16 [69-Nov-25: 2C].
Frederick, Lydia A. m. Harrison, Robert R. on 67-Dec-23 [68-Sep-14: 2B].
Frederick, Mary Ann (21 yrs.) d. on 69-Jun-10 [69-Jun-11: 2C].
Frederick, Mary Jane m. Keller, John H. on 66-Oct-2 [66-Oct-25: 2C].
Frederick, Sarah Elizabeth (4 mos.) d. on 69-Jun-29 [69-Jun-30: 2C].
Frederick, Theodore Mottu (2 yrs., 10 mos.) d. on 69-Dec-14 [69-Dec-15: 2B].
Frederick, William T. m. Weaver, A. Cornelia on 68-Oct-12 [68-Oct-16: 2B].
Fredericks, Lewis m. Weston, Ellen on 68-Feb-27 [68-Feb-29: 2B].
Fredericks, Mary E. m. Wolf, George W. on 67-Oct-14 [67-Oct-22: 2A].
Frederickson, Victor d. on 66-Mar-31 of Apoplexy [66-Apr-2: 1F].
Free, Mary (64 yrs.) d. on 70-Jun-15 [70-Jun-17: 2B].
Freeberger, James H. (2 yrs.) d. on 70-May-22 of Cholera infantum [70-May-24: 2C].
Freeburger, Amanda m. Eney, John E. on 67-Jun-12 [67-Jun-20: 2B].
Freeburger, Morris Gilbert (5 mos.) d. on 69-Mar-6 [69-Mar-9: 2C].
Freeburger, Peter (76 yrs.) d. on 67-May-20 [67-May-23: 2B].
Freedy, Dietrich m. Zoellers, Kate on 70-Mar-1 [70-Mar-3: 2C].
Freeland, Elenora d. on 67-Sep-25 [67-Sep-28: 2A].
Freeland, Eliza (59 yrs.) d. on 68-Jun-15 [68-Jun-17: 2B].
Freeland, Elizabeth m. Mason, Julian J. on 70-Oct-4 [70-Oct-6: 2B].
Freeland, Jarrett King (5 mos.) d. on 70-Jun-30 [70-Jul-2: 2B].
Freeland, John H. d. on 67-Feb-5 [67-Jul-19: 2C].
Freeland, John T. m. King, Annie E. on 68-Oct-6 [68-Oct-10: 2B].
Freeland, Lemuel Duvall (2 yrs., 2 mos.) d. on 66-Mar-15 [66-Mar-21: 2C].
Freeland, Mary m. Smith, J. Addison on 70-Feb-17 [70-Feb-19: 2B].
Freeland, Mary J. m. Weller, Jacob on 66-Mar-21 [66-Mar-22: 2B].

Freeland, William S. m. Mules, Annie R. on 69-Oct-26 [69-Oct-30: 2B].
Freeland, Zachary T. m. Meekins, Georgianna on 69-Nov-17 [69-Nov-20: 2B].
Freeman, Amanda m. Robinson, William H. on 69-Nov-4 [69-Nov-11: 2C].
Freeman, Charles m. Pitt, Maria W. on 67-Mar-6 [67-Mar-8: 2C].
Freeman, Charles G. (62 yrs.) d. on 67-Mar-16 [67-Mar-18: 2B].
Freeman, Charles L. d. on 70-Feb-15 [70-Feb-16: 2C].
Freeman, Edward D. m. Johnson, Georgianna on 68-May-28 [68-May-29: 2B].
Freeman, Edward Wilhelm (5 yrs.) d. on 70-Jan-5 of Scarlet fever [70-Jan-13: 2D].
Freeman, Emma m. Cork, Albert on 68-Nov-11 [68-Nov-17: 2C].
Freeman, H. Vann m. Leedy, W. Franklin on 69-Apr-1 [69-Apr-6: 2C].
Freeman, James A. m. Van Vick, Mary E. on 66-Mar-28 [66-Apr-10: 2C].
Freeman, Lizzie J. m. Coale, William A. on 66-Jun-28 [66-Jul-4: 2B].
Freeman, Mary E. m. Flashell, William H. on 66-Nov-18 [67-Jan-8: 2B].
Freeman, Mary Irene Bishop (3 yrs., 2 mos.) d. on 70-Jan-9 of Scarlet fever [70-Jan-13: 2D].
Freeman, Rebecca H. m. Dixon, Thomas on 68-Nov-5 [68-Nov-17: 2B].
Freer, Richard Shaw (5 yrs., 3 mos.) d. on 68-Nov-27 of Chronic croup [68-Dec-2: 2C].
Freibey, Labella m. Snyder, Augustus on 69-Apr-5 [69-Apr-6: 2C].
Freidenrich, Hennie m. Gold, Louis on 70-Jan-5 [70-Jan-8: 2B].
Freill, James (27 yrs.) d. on 67-Nov-29 [67-Nov-30: 2C].
Freise, Mary H. (39 yrs.) d. on 66-May-10 [66-May-11: 2B].
Fremin, M. L. m. Diehl, John on 66-Sep-11 [66-Sep-14: 2B].
French, Alpheus R. m. Ross, Annie M. on 68-Jan-15 [68-Jan-16: 2C].
French, Andrew m. Swope, Maggie on 70-May-10 [70-May-13: 2C].
French, Charles Dorsey (3 yrs., 1 mo.) d. on 69-Oct-8 [69-Oct-9: 2C].
French, Charles Oliver (4 mos.) d. on 70-Feb-25 [70-Feb-28: 2C].
French, Cornelius (34 yrs.) d. on 67-May-21 [67-May-22: 2B].
French, Ella K. m. Hunter, William K. on 67-Dec-19 [68-Jan-4: 2C; 68-Jan-6: 2C].
French, Ellen Estelle d. on 69-Oct-14 [69-Oct-15: 2C].
French, Harry H. (12 yrs.) d. on 68-Jul-13 [68-Jul-14: 2C].
French, John H. (36 yrs.) d. on 68-Jan-9 [68-Jan-13: 2C; 68-Jan-14: 2C; 68-Jan-15: 2C].
French, Lizzie A. m. Morgan, Edward T. on 66-Nov-15 [66-Nov-17: 2B].
French, Thomas (37 yrs.) d. on 70-Dec-8 [70-Dec-12: 2C].
French, William L. m. Capprise, Mary C. on 67-Jun-19 [67-Jun-26: 2C].
Freshour, Mary C. m. Williamson, John B. on 67-May-14 [67-May-27: 2B].
Freund, Charlotte Louise d. on 70-Oct-21 of Croup and diptheria [70-Oct-22: 2B].
Frew, Ellen M. McGowan, George on 67-Nov-7 [67-Nov-12: 2C].
Frew, Sarah J. m. Waidner, Charles W. on 67-May-23 [67-May-29: 2B].
Frey, Amelia d. on 67-May-31 [67-Jun-3: 2B].
Frey, Edwin B. m. Jones, Mary E. on 67-Jun-20 [67-Jun-22: 2B].
Frey, Harry Melvin (8 mos.) d. on 68-Jul-10 [68-Jul-11: 2B].
Frey, Hippolitz d. on 70-Apr-7 in Railroad accident [70-Apr-8: 1G].
Frey, James H. m. Sample, Lavinia E. on 67-Mar-27 [67-Mar-29: 2B].
Frey, Lizzie C. M. m. Sherwood, Issac N. on 68-Sep-9 [68-Sep-11: 2B].
Frey, Mary Ann (49 yrs.) d. on 66-Feb-9 [66-Feb-12: 2D].
Frey, Mary L. m. Edwards, Charles G. on 68-Dec-3 [68-Dec-24: 2C].
Frey, Robert Miltenberger (6 mos.) d. on 69-Jan-10 [69-Jan-11: 2C; 69-Jan-12: 2C].
Frey, Samuel (1 yr., 7 mos.) d. on 67-Oct-12 [67-Oct-14: 2B].
Frey, Samuel W. m. Clark, Julia E. on 66-Nov-22 [66-Nov-23: 2C].
Frey, Solomon K. m. Jones, Mary H. on 68-May-4 [68-May-8: 2B].
Freyer, John m. Harp, Emma C. on 70-Jun-23 [70-Jul-4: 2C].
Frick, George (10 yrs.) d. on 68-Jan-8 [68-Jan-9: 2C].
Frick, George, Dr. (77 yrs.) d. on 70-Mar-26 [70-Apr-11: 2B; 70-Apr-29: 4C].
Frick, John J. m. Myers, Mary L. on 69-Sep-7 [69-Sep-9: 2B].
Frick, Mary (72 yrs.) d. on 66-Oct-13 [66-Oct-15: 2B].
Fricker, John A. m. Dobbs, Mary V. on 70-Jun-21 [70-Jun-23: 2C].

Fricker, Mary Jane (36 yrs.) d. on 67-Feb-20 [67-Feb-21: 2C].
Fricks, Amelia m. Hyson, William H. on 66-Dec-23 [66-Dec-29: 2C].
Friedenwald, Issac m. Dalsheimer, Eugenie on 66-Dec-25 [66-Dec-29: 2C].
Friedhofer, William m. Moore, Martha on 66-Dec-23 [67-Jan-8: 2B].
Friedhoffer, Mary J. m. Miller, Stephen M. on 66-Dec-26 [66-Dec-29: 2C; 66-Dec-31: 2C].
Frisbie, Mary C. d. on 70-May-8 [70-May-10: 2B].
Frisby, Ann (82 yrs.) d. on 70-Dec-17 [70-Dec-19: 2C].
Frisby, Josephine m. Cooper, John H. on 68-Feb-10 [68-Feb-11: 2C].
Frisby, Sarah A. m. Curry, Edward J. on 68-Feb-20 [68-Mar-7: 2B].
Frisch, Caroline L. (43 yrs.) d. on 66-Mar-23 [66-Mar-24: 2B].
Frisch, Catharine m. Clark, W. F. on 70-Jun-6 [70-Jun-15: 2B].
Frisch, John W. (58 yrs.) d. on 70-Jun-30 [70-Jul-2: 2B].
Frist, Lizzie Harrison m. Hanks, J. Edwin on 66-Jul-19 [66-Jul-21: 2C].
Fritz, Elanor d. on 70-Jul-22 [70-Jul-23: 2B].
Frizell, Marion m. Blackburn, James A. on 70-Nov-28 [70-Dec-13: 2C].
Frizzell, Sarah J. m. Lednum, James F. on 68-Nov-19 [68-Nov-24: 2C].
Frizzle, A. Henning m. Poole, Anna on 66-Nov-29 [66-Dec-1: 2B].
Frock, Joseph M. (22 yrs., 6 mos.) d. on 68-Oct-18 [68-Oct-20: 2B].
Froelich, John C. m. Wilmot, Rebecca E. on 66-Sep-20 [66-Sep-28: 2B].
Froelich, Wilmot Henry (7 mos.) d. on 68-Jul-26 [68-Jul-28: 2B].
Frohrlich, John (27 yrs.) d. on 68-Nov-24 of Epilepsy [68-Nov-25: 1H].
Frost, George (17 yrs.) d. on 66-Feb-8 in Machine accident [66-Feb-9: 1F].
Frost, Harriet (57 yrs.) d. on 66-Dec-15 [66-Dec-19: 2B].
Frost, Mary L. (63 yrs.) d. on 66-Nov-19 [66-Nov-22: 2C].
Frost, Thomas m. Hooper, Agnes on 70-Jul-19 [70-Aug-4: 2C].
Frost, William (61 yrs.) d. on 68-Jan-12 [68-Jan-13: 2C].
Frush, Carroll V. m. Bennett, Annie C. on 66-Mar-19 [66-Mar-27: 2B].
Frush, Charles F. (35 yrs.) d. [69-Sep-10: 2B].
Frush, Jacob (76 yrs.) d. on 69-Jun-18 [69-Jun-19: 2B].
Fry, Edward E. m. Joines, Fannie on 69-May-11 [69-Jun-17: 2C].
Fry, John E. m. Hellen, Helen Mar on 69-Mar-10 [69-May-3: 2C].
Fry, John H., Capt. (55 yrs.) d. on 67-May-25 Drowned [67-Jun-5: 1F; 67-Jun-10: 2B].
Fry, Joseph (76 yrs.) d. on 68-Nov-6 [68-Nov-7: 2C].
Fry, Robert J. m. Wall, Amelia on 66-Mar-1 [66-Mar-5: 2B].
Fry, T. W. G., Maj. d. on 69-May-17 [69-Jun-10: 2C].
Frye, Eliza J. m. Slattery, John J. on 69-Dec-30 [70-Jan-14: 2C].
Fryer, Elijah S. d. [70-Sep-12: 2C].
Fryfogle, George (59 yrs.) d. on 67-Dec-29 [68-Feb-15: 2B].
Fuchs, Guido m. Verdier, Marie Therese Blanche on 67-Jan-21 [67-Feb-5: 2C].
Fuerth, W. G. m. Lauer, Lilly on 69-Aug-11 [69-Aug-12: 2C; 69-Aug-13: 2C].
Fuggitt, N. B. m. Dade, Bettie on 67-Oct-15 [67-Oct-16: 2B].
Fugle, James m. Walter, Laura J. on 70-Feb-15 [70-Feb-19: 2B].
Fulenkamp, Mary C. m. Hogg, Solomon S. on 67-Nov-20 [67-Nov-23: 2B].
Fulford, Ida V. m. Proudfoot, George W. on 70-Jan-27 [70-Feb-1: 2B; 70-Feb-3: 2B].
Fuller, A. Octavia m. Leber, W. Frank on 69-Oct-19 [69-Oct-22: 2B].
Fuller, Alexander m. Middlemis, Jane E. on 68-Dec-29 [68-Dec-31: 2C].
Fuller, Alvan B. m. Treadway, Sarah E. on 66-Dec-13 [66-Dec-17: 2B].
Fuller, Carrie Howe d. on 68-Sep-22 [68-Sep-24: 2B; 68-Sep-25: 2B].
Fuller, Charles F. m. Creamer, Emma on 66-Oct-18 [66-Oct-20: 2B].
Fuller, Edwin T. (28 yrs.) d. on 66-Dec-13 [66-Dec-15: 2B].
Fuller, Emma m. Spear, Edwin W. on 69-Jun-8 [69-Jun-10: 2C].
Fuller, Frances M. (59 yrs.) d. on 66-Nov-9 [66-Nov-10: 2B].
Fuller, Jane (79 yrs.) d. on 69-Dec-7 [69-Dec-9: 2C].
Fuller, Jennie m. Mask, Charles M. on 70-Jan-13 [70-Jan-18: 2C].
Fuller, John M. (33 yrs.) d. on 65-Dec-30 [66-Jan-1: 2C].

Fuller, Maggie A. d. on 70-Jun-23 [70-Jun-25: 2B].
Fuller, Margaret A. m. Kilpatrick, Thomas on 68-Jun-9 [68-Jun-23: 2B].
Fuller, Mary N. m. Lewin, John C. on 68-May-7 [68-May-21: 2B].
Fuller, Patrick (12 yrs.) d. on 68-Oct-9 [68-Oct-10: 2B].
Fuller, Philip C. d. on 70-Jul-18 [70-Aug-3: 2C].
Fuller, Robert H. m. Beers, Maggie A. on 66-Oct-4 [66-Oct-20: 2B].
Fuller, Sadie R. d. on 70-Jun-13 [70-Jun-14: 2B; 70-Jun-15: 2B].
Fuller, Sarah Ellen (19 yrs.) d. on 67-Jan-27 [67-Jan-29: 2C].
Fuller, Thomas J. m. Williams, Savilla A. on 66-Dec-13 [66-Dec-17: 2B].
Fuller, William S. m. Gordon, Laura on 69-Dec-19 [69-Dec-21: 2B].
Fullerton, Charles H. B. (8 yrs.) d. on 66-Mar-18 [66-Mar-19: 2C; 66-Mar-20: 2C].
Fullerton, Irene m. Gallagher, Frank J. on 68-Nov-19 [68-Dec-15: 2C].
Fullum, Joseph J. m. Mager, Mary on 66-Jun-5 [66-Jun-9: 2B].
Fullum, Martin Eugene (4 mos.) d. on 69-Sep-17 [69-Sep-18: 2B].
Fullwood, Margaret J. (26 yrs.) d. on 69-Dec-7 of Lamp explosion [69-Dec-8: 1H, 2C].
Fulman, George W. (26 yrs., 3 mos.) d. on 66-Nov-15 [66-Nov-16: 2C].
Fulton, Emily Jane d. on 69-Jul-20 [69-Jul-21: 1G, 2C; 69-Jul-22: 2C; 69-Jul-23: 1H].
Fulton, Nannie (6 mos.) d. on 68-Aug-26 [68-Sep-3: 2B].
Fulton, Susan (44 yrs.) d. on 70-May-31 [70-Jun-1: 2B].
Funck, Henry (49 yrs.) d. on 67-Aug-14 of Apoplexy [67-Aug-15: 2C].
Funk, Civie C. m. Gorsuch, D. A. on 68-Dec-22 [68-Dec-25: 2D].
Funk, John W. (38 yrs., 6 mos.) d. on 68-May-18 [68-May-20: 2A].
Funk, John W. m. Jarvis, Virginia F. on 70-Mar-24 [70-Mar-28: 2B].
Funk, Lizzie m. Crook, Walter on 70-Sep-19 [70-Oct-26: 2B].
Funk, Mary Virginia (4 yrs.) d. on 68-Nov-7 of Chronic croup [68-Nov-9: 2B].
Funk, Rudolph (34 yrs.) d. on 68-Sep-6 [68-Sep-7: 2A].
Funk, Sarah (74 yrs.) d. on 67-Feb-18 [67-Feb-27: 2C].
Funkhauser, Sarah E. m. Colton, W. H. on 67-Sep-17 [67-Sep-20: 2A].
Funkhouse, Elijah R. m. Leitch, Lizzie R. on 68-Jan-13 [68-Jan-16: 2C].
Furguson, Celia m. Stein, C. E. on 69-Sep-27 [69-Oct-27: 2B].
Furguson, Julia m. Litchfield, John on 66-Dec-25 [67-Jan-15: 2C].
Furlong, Hattie A. m. Darby, Philip on 69-Jan-14 [69-Jan-18: 2C].
Furlong, Irene E. P. m. Adkisson, W. H. H. on 68-Jan-22 [68-Jan-24: 2D].
Furlong, Sarah (97 yrs.) d. on 70-Dec-30 [70-Dec-31: 2C].
Furlong, Virginia A. m. Eddins, Richard W. on 66-Dec-13 [66-Dec-17: 2C].
Furlong, William G. (47 yrs.) d. on 70-Dec-2 [70-Dec-3: 2B].
Furlong, William H. m. Forney, Charlotte R. on 68-Sep-10 [68-Sep-10: 2B].
Furr, Jennie M. m. Priest, John H. on 67-Oct-9 [67-Oct-14: 2B].
Fusselbaugh, Henry Bascom (8 mos.) d. on 68-Jul-10 [68-Jul-11: 2B].
Fussell, Louis N. (13 yrs., 7 mos.) d. on 70-Jan-23 [70-Jan-25: 2C].
Fusting, Clara m. McDonnell, James on 70-Apr-27 [70-May-3: 2B].
Fusting, Sarah A. m. Latsch, John B. on 68-Apr-16 [68-Apr-30: 2B].
Gable, Appellius m. Thumser, Louisa F. on 68-Dec-31 [69-Jan-9: 2C].
Gable, Henry (87 yrs.) d. on 69-Dec-11 [69-Dec-13: 2C].
Gable, John A. m. Stembler, C. E. on 69-Aug-4 [69-Sep-4: 2B].
Gabrio, William F. m. Heck, Mary on 67-May-29 [67-May-30: 2B].
Gadd, Luther M. m. Penn, Nancy A. on 67-Oct-17 [67-Nov-4: 2B].
Gaddess, Lizzie m. Kefauver, Charles M. on 66-Dec-13 [66-Dec-22: 2A].
Gaebler, Charles (63 yrs.) d. on 70-Jan-14 of Mania a potu [70-Jan-17: 1H].
Gaehle, Henry F. (30 yrs., 3 mos.) d. on 66-May-31 [66-Jun-1: 2B].
Gaehle, Henry Louis (1 yr., 7 mos.) d. on 66-Jul-3 [66-Jul-12: 2C].
Gaerber, Johana (73 yrs., 6 mos.) d. on 68-Aug-16 [68-Aug-19: 2B].
Gahagan, Bridget d. on 67-Nov-27 [67-Nov-28: 2C].
Gahagan, William (37 yrs.) d. on 68-Sep-18 [68-Sep-19: 2B].
Gahan, James (38 yrs.) d. on 68-Mar-13 [68-Mar-14: 2B].

Gahan, Mary Frances (9 mos.) d. on 67-Aug-2 [67-Aug-3: 2B].
Gahegan, Thomas (52 yrs.) d. on 69-Nov-24 [69-Nov-25: 2C].
Gain, Mary (72 yrs.) d. on 70-Sep-20 [70-Sep-22: 2C].
Gainer, Martin m. Clark, Annie on 67-Nov-24 [67-Dec-13: 2C].
Gaither, Catharine d. on 70-Mar-25 [70-Mar-28: 2B].
Gaither, E. m. Ross, Lou on 70-Oct-20 [70-Jan-22: 2B].
Gaither, Edwin Francis (3 mos.) d. on 69-Apr-22 [69-Apr-30: 2C].
Gaither, Ernest Mordant (11 mos.) d. on 70-Jul-21 [70-Jul-26: 2C].
Gaither, Henrietta d. on 68-Feb-17 [68-Apr-3: 2C].
Gaither, Henry Vernon (3 mos.) d. on 69-Apr-27 [69-Apr-30: 2C].
Gaither, Lizzie E. m. Burk, John W. on 66-Dec-13 [66-Dec-17: 2B].
Gaither, Mary Agnes m. Lilly, David on 70-Jan-3 [70-Jan-7: 2F].
Gaither, Mattie A. m. Brashears, Luther on 68-Dec-17 [68-Dec-19: 2B].
Gaither, Rezin (28 yrs.) d. on 68-May-26 [68-Jun-12: 2B].
Gaither, Thomas (53 yrs.) d. on 67-Aug-8 [67-Aug-15: 2C].
Gaither, Washington (81 yrs.) d. [66-Feb-7: 2C].
Gaither, William d. on 68-Sep-6 [68-Sep-8: 2B].
Gaitley, Mary Ann (1 yr.) d. on 68-Nov-5 [68-Nov-6: 2C].
Gaitley, Mary J. m. Walsh, Thomas on 70-Apr-26 [70-Apr-27: 2B].
Galbraith, Lillie Toner (1 mo.) d. on 69-Feb-28 [69-Mar-2: 2C; 69-Mar-3: 2C].
Gale, Charlotte E. d. on 69-Dec-11 [69-Dec-13: 2C].
Gale, Hattie m. Grape, Thomas E. on 66-Jan-1 [66-Jan-4: 2C].
Gale, James Harper m. Harris, Laura [69-Nov-17: 2C].
Gale, Mary (74 yrs.) d. on 68-Sep-23 [68-Sep-25: 2B].
Gale, Mary Elizabeth (34 yrs.) d. on 67-Oct-13 [67-Oct-15: 2A].
Gale, Thomas (79 yrs.) d. on 70-Apr-30 [70-May-2: 2B].
Gallagher, Agnes Afenia (1 yr., 4 mos.) d. on 66-Nov-17 [66-Nov-19: 2B].
Gallagher, Alexander Foreman (11 mos.) d. on 69-Mar-17 of Pneumonia [69-Mar-18: 2C].
Gallagher, Bridget (31 yrs.) d. on 66-Feb-25 [66-Feb-26: 2B].
Gallagher, Francis (2 yrs., 5 mos.) d. on 66-Jan-21 [66-Jan-22: 2C].
Gallagher, Francis, Capt. (51 yrs.) d. on 66-Dec-10 of Consumption [66-Dec-11: 1F, 2B; 66-Dec-12: 2B; 66-Dec-13: 4C].
Gallagher, Frank J. m. Fullerton, Irene on 68-Nov-19 [68-Dec-15: 2C].
Gallagher, Howard L. m. Price, Anna E. on 68-Oct-1 [69-Feb-10: 2C].
Gallagher, Isabel Griffith (10 mos.) d. on 69-Sep-23 [69-Sep-24: 2B].
Gallagher, James (58 yrs.) d. on 70-Aug-30 [70-Aug-31: 2B].
Gallagher, Jane (76 yrs.) d. on 66-Jul-17 [66-Jul-18: 2C].
Gallagher, Jennie m. Doyle, William J. on 67-Oct-3 [67-Oct-8: 2B].
Gallagher, Kate m. Rochfort, John E. on 68-Jan-16 [68-Feb-4: 2C].
Gallagher, Margaret (35 yrs.) d. on 70-Jan-9 [70-Jan-10: 2C].
Gallagher, Margaret A. (2 yrs.) d. on 68-Aug-21 [68-Aug-22: 2A].
Gallagher, Martin (16 yrs., 7 mos.) d. on 70-Jun-2 [70-Jun-3: 2B].
Gallagher, Mattie A. m. Cornell, Edwin on 69-Feb-22 [69-Mar-4: 2C].
Gallaher, Eliza Arris (34 yrs., 3 mos.) d. on 67-Dec-22 [68-Jan-4: 2C].
Gallaher, Horatio Eugene (9 mos.) d. on 70-Jun-12 [70-Jun-14: 2B].
Gallaway, James L. m. Green, Mary E. on 66-Jun-5 [66-Jun-26: 2B].
Gallaway, Mary D. (73 yrs.) d. on 68-Aug-25 [68-Aug-26: 2B; 68-Aug-27: 2B].
Gallaway, Pamela J. m. Reddish, Louis on 70-Feb-28 [70-Mar-11: 2C].
Galligher, Alice Anne (10 mos.) d. on 68-Aug-22 [68-Aug-24: 2B].
Gallion, Charles Green m. Duhurst, Elizabeth on 70-Aug-4 [70-Aug-15: 2C].
Gallion, Jacob H. d. on 69-Oct-13 of Typhoid [69-Oct-15: 2C].
Galloway, Absalom m. Whittaker, Avrilla B. on 66-Sep-20 [66-Oct-21: 2B].
Galloway, Anna M. (11 mos.) d. on 66-Apr-17 of Chronic croup [66-Apr-19: 2B].
Galloway, Annie E. m. Clark, Henry on 68-Oct-22 [68-Nov-7: 2B].
Galloway, Charles B. m. Smith, Susan Jane on 68-Feb-4 [68-Feb-10: 2C].

Galloway, Fred George Calvert (1 yr., 3 mos.) d. on 65-Dec-30 [66-Jan-2: 2C; 66-Jan-3: 2C].
Galloway, Gemima L. m. Costlow, Michael on 67-Sep-4 [67-Sep-18: 2B].
Galloway, Henrietta m. Kemp, J. F. on 66-Jan-11 [66-Jan-25: 2C].
Galloway, John m. Magraw, Rebecca on 70-Mar-8 [70-Mar-11: 2C].
Galloway, Mary m. Smith, Philip on 68-Oct-11 [69-Apr-7: 2C].
Galloway, Mary A. m. Smithson, William H. on 68-Oct-4 [68-Oct-6: 2B].
Galloway, May Ella m. Marston, R. Jarrett on 66-Jan-22 [66-Feb-13: 2C].
Gallup, Emma W. m. Bay, John W. on 68-Jan-16 [68-Jan-21: 2C].
Gallup, Kate M. m. Holloway, Charles E. on 67-Feb-28 [67-Mar-11: 2C].
Gallup, Thomas F. d. on 68-Jun-1 [68-Jun-20: 2B].
Galt, J. Murray m. Wands, Ella W. on 68-Jul-28 [68-Nov-20: 2C].
Galt, James V. m. Cissel, Emma on 66-Sep-25 [66-Sep-25: 2C].
Galvin, Emma M. m. Martin, John G. on 66-Mar-28 [66-Mar-30: 2C].
Galvin, John (67 yrs.) d. on 67-Nov-1 [67-Nov-2: 2B].
Galvin, William (8 mos.) d. on 69-Apr-22 [69-Aug-24: 2B].
Gambel, Emma (1 yr., 6 mos.) d. on 66-Jan-17 [66-Jan-18: 2C].
Gambel, Maggie A. m. Rowland, Edward on 66-Aug-29 [66-Sep-1: 2B].
Gambell, Mary V. m. Holmes, John on 68-Aug-10 [68-Sep-16: 2B].
Gamber, John d. on 67-Mar-25 [67-Mar-26: 2C; 67-Mar-27: 2C].
Gamble, Ann d. on 66-Feb-25 [66-Mar-1: 2B].
Gamble, Julia Ann (52 yrs.) d. on 68-Jul-9 [68-Jul-10: 2C; 68-Jul-11: 2B].
Gamble, Robert, Col. (87 yrs.) d. on 67-May-23 [67-May-24: 2B].
Gambrall, Mary B. d. on 70-Feb-7 [70-Feb-18: 2C].
Gambrell, James H. m. Sapp, Martha J. on 68-Jun-25 [68-Jul-27: 2B].
Gambrell, Jesse B. (8 yrs.) d. on 69-Jul-29 [69-Jul-31: 2C].
Gambrell, Sarah E. m. Daimond, James on 68-Jan-14 [68-Jan-17: 2C].
Gambrill, Albert m. Webb, Laura V. on 70-Oct-27 [70-Nov-1: 2C].
Gambrill, Baby (1 mo.) d. on 70-Jul-25 [70-Jul-26: 2C].
Gambrill, Charles A. (63 yrs.) d. on 69-Feb-20 of Dropsy [69-Feb-22: 1G, 2C].
Gambrill, George T. m. Owings, Rebecca on 69-Jun-8 [69-Jun-11: 2C].
Gambrill, Henry W. (34 yrs.) d. on 67-Sep-19 [67-Sep-20: 2A; 67-Sep-21: 4B].
Gambrill, Howard W. m. McDonald, Mary on 69-Apr-28 [69-May-11: 2B].
Gambrill, Mary d. on 68-Jul-16 [68-Jul-18: 2B].
Gambrill, Mary m. Jones, I. Thomas on 69-Jun-3 [69-Jun-4: 2C].
Gambrill, Rebecca (22 yrs.) d. on 69-Dec-13 [69-Dec-14: 2C; 69-Dec-15: 2B].
Gambrill, Sallie A. m. Potter, D. E. on 69-Apr-29 [69-May-8: 2B].
Gambrill, Stephen m. Gorman, Kate on 69-Dec-22 [69-Dec-28: 2C].
Gammie, George m. Nash, Nellie on 67-May-21 [67-May-29: 2B].
Ganbin, Eliza M. (33 yrs.) d. on 69-Jun-28 [69-Jun-29: 2C].
Ganbin, Nelly Elizabeth d. on 69-Jun-24 [69-Jun-25: 2C].
Ganby, John (25 yrs.) d. on 70-Jul-25 Drowned [70-Jul-26: 4C].
Ganish, Rachel V. m. Knight, William J. on 68-Mar-18 [68-Mar-20: 2B].
Ganley, John F. (47 yrs.) d. on 66-Jan-27 [66-Jan-30: 2B].
Gannon, Delia M. S. d. on 68-Dec-12 [68-Dec-14: 2C].
Gannon, James d. on 67-Feb-9 Drowned [67-Feb-12: 4C].
Gannon, Thomas (40 yrs.) d. on 69-Jun-14 in Railroad accident [69-Jun-15: 4B].
Gansey, Cora N. (14 yrs., 10 mos.) d. on 69-Apr-8 [69-Apr-10: 2B].
Gant, Mollie m. Duvall, G. C. on 66-Feb-13 [66-Feb-21: 2C].
Gantt, Ava L. m. Pirie, William on 70-May-26 [70-Jun-8: 2C].
Gantt, Emily L. m. Boteler, Robert F on 69-Sep-18 [69-Sep-20: 2C].
Gantt, Harriet (46 yrs.) d. on 69-Jul-2 [69-Jul-9: 2C].
Gantt, William T., Dr. (66 yrs.) d. on 68-Jun-29 [68-Jul-1: 2B].
Garaghty, Charles M. m. Hamlin, Louisa on 66-Sep-6 [66-Sep-11: 2B].
Garber, Harry S. (8 mos.) d. on 70-Sep-30 [70-Oct-3: 2B].
Garber, Henry S. m. Mallon, Sibbie F. on 66-Jun-19 [66-Jun-22: 2B].

Gardener, Ann m. McGregor, Robert on 67-Nov-7 [68-May-13: 2B].
Gardener, Elizabeth A. m. Hanson, John N. on 66-Nov-26 [67-Feb-4: 2C].
Gardener, Joseph (23 yrs.) d. on 66-Oct-9 [66-Oct-11: 2C].
Gardener, William H. m. Cannon, Annie R. on 66-Oct-29 [66-Nov-1: 2B].
Gardiner, Annie M. (70 yrs.) d. on 70-Jul-26 [70-Jul-28: 2C].
Gardiner, F. A. m. Turner, Prissie on 68-Nov-24 [68-Nov-26: 2B].
Gardiner, Hannah E. m. Miller, Jacob on 68-Dec-24 [69-Jan-20: 2C].
Gardiner, Helen E. m. Mettee, Mezick C. on 70-Apr-7 [70-Apr-12: 2B].
Gardiner, Joseph (53 yrs.) d. on 69-Apr-5 [69-Apr-10: 2B].
Gardiner, Mary m. Hanna, George on 69-Dec-14 [69-Dec-20: 2C].
Gardiner, Nancy Ann Buchanan (65 yrs.) d. on 68-Feb-11 [68-Feb-13: 2C].
Gardiner, William J. m. Hook, Sarah Kate on 69-Dec-2 [69-Dec-18: 2B].
Gardmer, Mary Amm (61 yrs.) d. on 67-Sep-6 [67-Sep-7: 2A].
Gardner, Almore Marion (11 mos.) d. on 66-Aug-7 of Cholera infantum [66-Aug-8: 2C].
Gardner, Amanda C. m. Hall, Charles C. E. on 68-May-5 [68-May-11: 2B].
Gardner, Araminta J. m. Smith, Eb on 70-Oct-3 [70-Oct-12: 2B].
Gardner, Elizabeth (68 yrs.) d. on 70-Jun-2 [70-Jun-3: 2B].
Gardner, Elizabeth m. Steele, John T. on 66-Dec-21 [67-Jan-5: 2C].
Gardner, Elizabeth m. Pearse, Charles C. on 66-Jun-5 [66-Jun-22: 2B].
Gardner, Emma S. m. Walsh, Jeff J. on 69-Mar-30 [69-Apr-1: 2C].
Gardner, Ephraim (81 yrs.) d. on 69-Jul-1 [69-Jul-2: 2C; 69-Jul-3: 2B].
Gardner, Frederick m. Frank, Lena on 69-Jun-28 [69-Jun-30: 2C].
Gardner, George W. m. Lieman, Josephine C. on 67-Jan-6 [67-Jan-8: 2B].
Gardner, George Washington (1 yr., 8 mos.) d. on 70-Aug-5 [70-Aug-6: 2C].
Gardner, J. B. (70 yrs., 6 mos.) d. on 70-Sep-6 [70-Sep-9: 2B].
Gardner, James Wesley m. Jackson, Mary Ellen on 67-Jan-15 [67-Jan-23: 2C].
Gardner, John (52 yrs.) d. on 66-Nov-9 [66-Nov-10: 2B].
Gardner, John G. m. Coulbourn, Angelline on 70-May-31 [70-Jun-2: 2B].
Gardner, John R. m. Randall, Sarah on 69-May-29 [69-Jun-5: 2B].
Gardner, John S. P. m. Hardesty, Lavinia on 70-Feb-11 [70-Feb-12: 2B].
Gardner, Johns m. Moran, Mary Jane on 69-Nov-10 [69-Nov-24: 2C].
Gardner, L. N. m. Hall, Delia M. on 66-Nov-29 [66-Dec-3: 2B].
Gardner, Louisa M. m. Quinn, Hugh on 69-Aug-15 [69-Oct-6: 2B].
Gardner, Maria (78 yrs.) d. on 70-Oct-30 [70-Oct-31: 2B; 70-Nov-1: 2C; 70-Nov-2: 2C].
Gardner, Mary (63 yrs.) d. on 68-Apr-12 [68-Apr-13: 2B].
Gardner, Mary (76 yrs.) d. on 67-Dec-19 [67-Dec-21: 2B].
Gardner, Mary Alice (30 yrs.) d. on 68-Dec-26 [68-Dec-28: 2B].
Gardner, Maurinda (47 yrs.) d. on 68-May-5 [68-May-6: 2B].
Gardner, Patience d. on 67-Jun-26 [67-Jun-28: 2B].
Gardner, Rebecca A. m. Tudor, Issac F. on 68-Nov-7 [68-Nov-24: 2C].
Gardner, Sarah Maria m. Chaney, Andrew on 70-Feb-24 [70-Mar-2: 2C].
Gardner, Virginia m. Norris, John B. on 70-Apr-26 [70-May-2: 2B].
Gardner, William C. m. Hardy, Susan on 69-Dec-22 [69-Dec-24: 2C].
Gardner, William F. m. Vondersmith, Willie H. on 67-Sep-19 [67-Sep-24: 2A].
Gardner, William H. m. Irving, Kate on 70-Oct-11 [70-Oct-19: 2B].
Gardner, Winter Davis (1 yr., 2 mos.) d. on 68-Sep-21 [68-Sep-22: 2B].
Garhart, Jacob (57 yrs.) d. on 70-Sep-13 [70-Sep-14: 2B].
Garity, Annie d. on 66-Apr-28 [66-Apr-30: 2B].
Garland, Daniel d. on 68-Mar-9 of Consumption [68-Mar-11: 2B].
Garland, L. F. m. Montgomery, A. J. on 66-Aug-8 [66-Aug-15: 2B].
Garland, Margaret Ann d. on 69-Oct-20 [69-Oct-21: 2B; 69-Oct-29: 2C].
Garman, Warren C. m. Cook, Flora A. on 70-Jun-18 [70-Nov-4: 2C].
Garmendia, Prospero Tomas (11 mos.) d. on 68-Jul-15 [68-Jul-17: 2B].
Garmendia, Thomas Meredith (1 mo.) d. on 70-Jul-25 [70-Jul-26: 2C].
Garner, Alice F. m. Welsh, Charles D. on 70-May-17 [70-Jun-10: 2B].

Garner, Annie m. Boarman, William J. on 68-Jul-2 [68-Jul-3: 2B].
Garner, Bettie m. Boninger, R. C. on 70-Oct-13 [70-Oct-15: 2B; 70-Oct-17: 2B].
Garner, Ellen C. m. Lindsey, John Y. on 67-Jun-17 [67-Jun-18: 2B].
Garner, Julia E. m. Allstan, Joseph S. on 68-Apr-29 [68-Apr-30: 2B].
Garner, Susannah (79 yrs.) d. on 67-Sep-22 [67-Oct-7: 2B].
Garner, T. H. R., Dr. (1 mo.) d. on 67-Jan-7 [67-Jan-8: 2B].
Garnett, Benjamin M. d. on 66-Feb-10 [66-Feb-13: 2C; 66-Feb-14: 2C].
Garnett, Mary A. m. Rasin, William J. on 67-Nov-19 [67-Nov-26: 2B].
Garrell, James C., Capt. (77 yrs.) d. on 67-Nov-27 [67-Dec-4: 2C].
Garrett, Ann Elizabeth m. Hunter, Alexander on 68-Jan-9 [68-Jan-16: 2C].
Garrett, Henry S. (50 yrs.) d. on 67-Oct-10 [67-Oct-11: 1G, 2B; 67-Oct-14: 1F; 67-Oct-12: 2B].
Garrett, James H. m. Realy, Annie R. on 67-Feb-21 [67-Jul-26: 2B].
Garrett, John H. (35 yrs.) d. on 66-Jul-18 of Heatstroke [66-Jul-20: 1F, 2D].
Garrett, Margaret (45 yrs.) d. on 70-Dec-16 [70-Dec-17: 2B].
Garrett, Margaret m. Watson, John W. on 66-Apr-15 [66-Apr-18: 2B].
Garrett, Mary E. m. Pettinger, Richard V. on 69-May-11 [69-May-19: 2C].
Garrett, Mary R. (1 yr., 3 mos.) d. on 68-Aug-18 [68-Aug-20: 2B].
Garrett, Richard S. m. Flaherty, Maggie e. on 69-Jan-12 [69-Feb-4: 2C].
Garrett, Sarah A. (56 yrs.) d. on 69-Sep-20 [69-Dec-15: 2B].
Garrett, T. Harrison m. Whitridge, Alice D. on 70-Feb-15 [70-Feb-18: 2C].
Garrett, William d. on 66-Jan-7 [66-Jan-15: 2C].
Garrett, William A. (41 yrs.) d. on 68-Feb-17 [68-Feb-20: 2C].
Garrett, William H. m. Hoffman, Anna on 67-Nov-18 [67-Nov-22: 2C].
Garrettson, Bennett (78 yrs.) d. on 68-Oct-26 [68-Dec-18: 2C].
Garrettson, Caroline (57 yrs., 7 mos.) d. on 67-Sep-22 [67-Dec-4: 2C].
Garrettson, Eleanora L. m. Burt, Amos S. on 66-Mar-14 [66-Mar-17: 2B].
Garrettson, Florence m. Spooner, Henry T. on 68-Dec-24 [68-Dec-30: 2C].
Garrigan, Philip (57 yrs.) d. on 67-Nov-18 [67-Nov-19: 2C].
Garrish, John J. (8 mos.) d. on 68-Jul-20 [68-Jul-30: 2B].
Garrison, Ann (71 yrs.) d. on 70-Nov-16 [70-Nov-18: 2C].
Garrison, George Lincoln (6 yrs., 6 mos.) d. on 66-Jul-23 [66-Jul-24: 2C].
Garrison, Laura m. Sprigle, George on 66-May-13 [66-May-30: 2C].
Garrison, Mary Margaret (23 yrs.) d. on 66-Jun-21 [66-Jun-22: 2B].
Garrot, Laura E. m. Collins, J. Eugene on 68-Feb-12 [68-Feb-13: 2C].
Garrott, Ann d. on 67-Jun-13 [67-Jun-14: 2B].
Garrott, Sallie m. McDuell, William H. on 67-Apr-24 [67-Apr-29: 2B].
Garrott, William (63 yrs.) d. on 66-Jan-7 [66-Jan-12: 2C].
Garthwait, John A. m. Johnson, Sarah Jane on 66-Nov-18 [66-Nov-24: 2B].
Garthwait, Mary A. m. Dougherty, John J. on 67-May-21 [67-Jun-1: 2B].
Gartland, Daniel (28 yrs.) d. on 68-Mar-27 [68-Mar-28: 2B].
Gartside, Ruth (76 yrs.) d. on 66-Dec-19 [67-Mar-14: 2C].
Garvey, James (56 yrs.) d. on 67-Jul-4 [67-Jul-6: 2B].
Garvey, Kate m. Duane, John on 66-Feb-7 [66-Feb-13: 2C].
Garvey, Katie (6 mos.) d. on 70-Aug-28 [70-Aug-29: 2B].
Garvey, Patrick (32 yrs.) d. on 69-Feb-17 [69-Feb-18: 2C].
Garvey, Peter James (1 yr.) d. on 69-Jul-13 [69-Jul-14: 2D].
Gary, James S. (62 yrs.) d. on 70-Mar-7 [70-Mar-8: 2C; 70-Mar-9: 2C].
Gary, James S., Jr. (9 yrs., 1 mo.) d. on 69-Dec-27 [69-Dec-28: 2D; 69-Dec-29: 2D].
Gary, S. Ellen m. Buell, William P. on 69-Nov-1 [69-Nov-5: 2C].
Gaskins, Doretta Priscilla (6 mos.) d. on 66-Jan-20 [66-Jan-22: 2C].
Gaskins, Priscilla (62 yrs.) d. on 67-May-11 [67-May-13: 2B].
Gassaway, Elizabeth A. (69 yrs.) d. on 69-Nov-23 [69-Nov-24: 2C].
Gassaway, Henry (5 mos.) d. on 69-Jun-26 [69-Jun-29: 2C].
Gassaway, Henry d. on 69-Jul-10 [69-Jul-12: 2C].

Gassaway, Samuel m. Call, Mary on 67-Feb-3 [67-Feb-7: 2C].
Gassaway, Samuel B. d. on 67-Jan-1 [67-Jan-2: 2C].
Gassaway, Theodore m. Meyer, Paulina on 67-Jan-4 [67-Jan-14: 2C].
Gaston, Robert m. Wright, Annie on 67-Feb-28 [67-Mar-2: 2B].
Gatch, Thomas B. m. Forrester, Josephine on 68-Sep-9 [68-Oct-8: 2B].
Gatch, Willie H. (9 mos.) d. on 70-Jun-29 of Cholera infantum [70-Jul-2: 2B].
Gatchell, Hugh McElderry m. Tyler, Mary Addison on 68-Jan-30 [68-Feb-1: 2B].
Gatchell, John G. m. Martin, Jane Gatchell on 68-Nov-26 [68-Nov-28: 2C].
Gatechair, Mary d. on 69-Jan-23 [69-Jan-25: 2D].
Gately, John d. on 68-Jul-6 [68-Jul-7: 2B].
Gately, John (22 yrs., 8 mos.) d. on 67-Feb-6 [67-Feb-7: 2C].
Gately, John, Sr. (71 yrs.) d. on 69-Oct-27 [69-Oct-28: 2C; 69-Oct-29: 2C].
Gates, Thomas Baker (66 yrs.) d. on 68-Feb-10 [68-Feb-12: 2B].
Gaubatz, Elise (92 yrs.) d. on 68-Mar-23 [68-Mar-24: 2B].
Gaubatz, Maria Elizabeth (21 yrs.) d. on 67-Apr-21 [67-Apr-23: 2B].
Gaule, Catherine (70 yrs.) d. on 68-Apr-27 [68-Apr-28: 2B; 68-Apr-29: 2B].
Gaule, Thomas (75 yrs.) d. on 69-Dec-3 [69-Dec-4: 2C].
Gauline, John B. (61 yrs.) d. on 67-Dec-1 [67-Dec-6: 2C].
Gauline, Joseph C. (59 yrs.) d. on 67-Jan-22 [67-Jan-26: 2C].
Gault, Annie D. m. Polk, Nathaniel W. on 70-Nov-15 [70-Nov-16: 2C].
Gault, John Summerfield (5 mos.) d. on 66-Apr-18 [66-Apr-19: 2B].
Gault, William A. m. Paine, Sallie J. on 70-Nov-15 [70-Nov-16: 2C].
Gaunt, John (73 yrs.) d. on 67-Feb-9 [67-Feb-11: 2C].
Gaunt, Kate T. m. Pearce, John E. on 70-Apr-26 [70-May-10: 2B].
Gaunt, Leonora S. m. Shealey, William J. on 67-May-14 [67-May-16: 2B].
Gaunt, Samuel B. m. Love, Mary Ann on 69-Jun-2 [69-Sep-7: 2B].
Gaus, Louisa m. Klockgether, Albert A. on 69-Sep-9 [69-Oct-28: 2C].
Gaus, Louisa m. Klockgether, Albert A. on 70-Sep-9 [70-Oct-4: 2B].
Gavet, Isabel m. Reinicker, Edward S. on 70-Nov-16 [70-Nov-23: 2B].
Gavier, George F. d. on 67-Dec-12 in Railroad accident [67-Dec-13: 1G].
Gavin, Carrie A. (19 yrs.) d. on 70-Jun-11 [70-Jun-13: 2C].
Gawthorp, George (9 yrs.) d. on 67-Feb-7 [67-Feb-8: 2C].
Gay, James (66 yrs.) d. on 67-Aug-3 [67-Aug-6: 2C].
Gaynor, B. E. m. Nolan, T. on 70-Sep-15 [70-Oct-4: 2B].
Gaynor, Bertha Genevive (4 mos.) d. on 69-Jun-24 [69-Jun-25: 2C].
Gazan, Nathan m. Kean, Sophia on 67-Mar-24 [67-Mar-26: 2C].
Geagan, John Fran. Jefferson (5 yrs.) d. on 66-Mar-11 [66-Mar-13: 2B].
Geakle, Wilbeth (20 yrs.) d. on 66-Jul-17 [66-Jul-19: 1F].
Geartling, Mary Elizabeth d. on 66-Nov-21 [66-Nov-22: 2C].
Geary, Charles A. (32 yrs.) d. on 70-Aug-22 of Consumption [70-Aug-23: 2B, 4E; 70-Aug-24: 2C].
Geary, Ellen (45 yrs.) d. on 69-Jan-19 [69-Jan-21: 2C].
Geary, J. Alford (38 yrs.) d. on 69-Mar-24 [69-Mar-26: 2C].
Gebhart, Amanda m. Banks, Frank W. on 67-Dec-31 [68-Mar-9: 2C].
Geddes, Charles Edward (11 mos.) d. on 69-Aug-5 [69-Aug-6: 2C; 69-Aug-7: 2B].
Gee, Sally B. m. Hamilton, M. A. on 68-Jul-8 [68-Jul-18: 2B].
Geekie, Grace (6 mos.) d. on 70-Jan-27 [70-Jan-28: 2B].
Geekie, Jesse (5 yrs.) d. on 70-Dec-18 [70-Dec-19: 2C].
Gees, Benjamin F. (39 yrs.) d. on 68-Mar-18 [68-Mar-19: 2B; 68-Mar-20: 1F, 2B].
Gees, Frances C. m. Keckler, Jacob J. on 67-Nov-13 [67-Nov-21: 2C].
Gees, Frank Owen (16 yrs., 9 mos.) d. on 70-Jun-16 [70-Jun-17: 2B; 70-Jun-18: 2B].
Gees, Lewis Selby d. on 69-Apr-16 [69-Apr-17: 2B].
Gees, Olivia L. m. Whitehouse, George A. on 67-May-28 [67-Aug-28: 2B].
Gegner, Eva M. d. on 69-Mar-2 [69-Mar-4: 2C].
Gehring, Charles J. m. Foster, Kate on 67-Nov-27 [67-Nov-28: 2C].

Gehring, Lottie m. Huzza, Luther D. on 67-Nov-28 [67-Dec-2: 2C].
Gehring, Maddie (3 mos.) d. on 69-Jan-11 [69-Jan-13: 2D].
Gehrman, Julia A. m. Lovejoy, Henry A. L. on 68-Mar-18 [68-Aug-20: 2B].
Gehrmann, Adelaide V. m. Lovejoy, Charles Amos on 70-Aug-25 [70-Aug-30: 2B].
Gehrmann, August (40 yrs.) d. on 68-Nov-2 [68-Nov-3: 2B].
Gehrmann, J. A. J., Dr. (24 yrs., 3 mos.) d. on 70-Nov-17 [70-Nov-18: 2C; 70-Nov-19: 2B].
Geigan, Harry S. d. on 69-Nov-11 [69-Nov-13: 2C].
Geiger, E. L.H. m. Gress, Kate E. on 70-Apr-12 [70-Apr-23: 2B].
Geiger, Mary m. Scherer, Henry on 67-Sep-5 [67-Sep-6: 2B].
Geiglein, John m. Myers, Mary on 69-Sep-12 [69-Sep-29: 2B].
Geigler, Carrie m. Stewart, William M. on 70-Aug-16 [70-Aug-27: 2B].
Geiglin, Barbara E. m. Wright, John W. on 67-Jan-21 [67-Jan-30: 2C].
Geis, John d. on 70-Jul-13 [70-Jul-14: 1H].
Geis, Rosa m. Stevenson, Edward on 69-Oct-5 [69-Oct-12: 2C].
Geis, Teresa m. Gorsuch, Lewis C. on 68-Nov-26 [68-Dec-1: 2C].
Geisendaffer, Richard Fuller (18 yrs., 6 mos.) d. on 67-Oct-7 [67-Oct-8: 2B].
Geisendaffer, W. J. m. Townsend, Georgie A. on 67-Nov-12 [68-Feb-4: 2C].
Geiser, John Adam (33 yrs.) d. on 68-Apr-20 [68-Apr-21: 2B].
Geiss, Margaret d. on 69-Sep-13 [69-Sep-17: 2C].
Geist, Martin D. m. Joice, Rosa E. on 69-Dec-21 [70-Jan-24: 2C].
Gekler, Mary (73 yrs.) d. on 70-Nov-3 [70-Nov-4: 2C; 70-Nov-5: 2B].
Gelbach, Charles A. (4 mos.) d. on 70-Mar-16 [70-Mar-17: 2C].
Gelbach, William H. m. Harvey, Lottie B. on 67-Feb-5 [67-Feb-8: 2C].
Gelston, H. D. (88 yrs.) d. on 67-Oct-27 [67-Oct-30: 2B].
Gelston, Robert Bruce (28 yrs.) d. on 66-Jan-3 [66-Jan-5: 2C].
Gemeny, Lillie May (1 yr., 1 mo.) d. on 67-Jun-7 [67-Jun-10: 2B].
Gemmill, Rebecca (47 yrs.) d. on 68-Mar-18 [68-Mar-20: 2B].
Gemmill, Walter m. Musgrove, Sarah on 69-Jun-1 [69-Jun-3: 2B].
Gemmill, William Porter (27 yrs., 4 mos.) d. on 66-Jan-21 [66-Feb-6: 2D].
Gemperling, Mary J. m. Beck, George A. on 66-Apr-24 [66-Apr-25: 2B].
Gemundt, Charles (45 yrs., 1 mo.) d. on 69-Jul-3 [69-Jul-5: 2C].
Gengnagle, Henry (27 yrs., 10 mos.) d. on 70-May-28 Drowned [70-May-30: 1F, 2B].
Gengnagle, Henry m. Albach, Mary on 68-Jul-7 [68-Aug-11: 2B].
Gengnagle, Julia m. Kolby, William Frederick on 67-May-7 [67-May-23: 2B].
Gent, Hannah E. (51 yrs.) d. on 69-Mar-6 [69-Mar-8: 2C].
Gent, Joshua G. m. Carlisle, Mary M. on 70-Dec-14 [70-Dec-22: 2B].
Gent, Maggie J. m. Kirwan, James O. on 66-Feb-20 [66-Feb-28: 2C].
Gent, Richard C. m. Destimonia, Amy on 69-Aug-9 [69-Sep-16: 2B].
Gentern, Charles A. (25 yrs.) d. on 69-Jul-20 of Suicide (Poisoning) [69-Jul-22: 1H].
Gentry, John H. (48 yrs.) d. on 67-Sep-9 [67-Sep-18: 2B].
Geoghegan, Charles Travers (5 mos.) d. on 69-Feb-28 [69-Mar-2: 2C].
Geoghegan, Clara Celoane (7 mos.) d. on 70-Jun-27 [70-Jun-28: 2C].
Geoghegan, Emma D. m. Henry, Solomon on 68-Sep-10 [68-Nov-16: 2C].
Geoghegan, Henrietta m. Williamson, Edward on 67-Oct-16 [67-Oct-19: 2A].
Geoghegan, Isadora m. Hamett, Elmire on 66-Feb-19 [66-Mar-19: 2C].
Geoghegan, Kate A. m. Hubbard, George W. on 69-Dec-14 [70-Feb-7: 2C].
Geoghegan, Laura Virginia (4 yrs.) d. on 70-Sep-7 [70-Sep-8: 2B; 70-Sep-9: 2B].
Geoghegan, Louisa m. Perry, W. H. on 66-May-10 [66-May-18: 2C].
Geoghegan, Stewart A. m. Brady, Anna on 67-Sep-17 [67-Dec-28: 2C].
Geoghegan, Virginia (1 yr., 2 mos.) d. on 66-Jul-11 [66-Jul-13: 2C].
Geoghegan, William Albert (11 mos.) d. on 70-Jul-20 [70-Jul-21: 2C].
Geoghgan, Elizabeth J. m. Lambdin, Daniel B. on 68-Jun-23 [68-Jul-14: 2B].
George, Alfred (41 yrs.) d. on 67-Jun-3 [67-Jun-4: 2A].
George, Ann Sanders (10 mos.) d. on 68-Aug-23 [68-Aug-24: 2B].
George, Anna (10 yrs.) d. on 68-Oct-17 [68-Oct-19: 2B].

George, Annie Fitzhugh (5 mos.) d. on 69-Jul-6 [69-Jul-8: 2C].
George, Archibald Lord (1 yr.) d. on 70-Jul-13 [70-Jul-15: 2C].
George, Clarence O. m. Mooer, Laura on 66-Feb-15 [66-Feb-20: 2B].
George, Florence A. d. on 67-Jul-23 of Typhoid [67-Jul-25: 2C].
George, J. Brown m. Cochran, Florence A. on 66-Jan-11 [66-Jan-13: 2C].
George, James (7 mos.) d. on 67-Sep-30 [67-Oct-10: 2B].
George, James, Jr. m. Berrett, Eugenia on 69-Oct-5 [69-Oct-8: 2B].
George, James B. (75 yrs.) d. on 69-Feb-1 of Erysipelas [69-Feb-3: 1G, 2C].
George, James B., Jr. (43 yrs.) d. on 69-Mar-22 [69-Mar-24: 2C].
George, Jean m. Coulter, John Carson on 70-Apr-5 [70-Apr-14: 2B].
George, John B. (41 yrs.) d. on 68-Dec-4 [68-Dec-5: 2C; 68-Dec-7: 1H].
George, John T. m. Selby, Maggie E. on 67-Oct-9 [67-Oct-11: 2B].
George, Mary Cope (12 yrs.) d. on 69-Apr-14 [69-Apr-15: 2B; 69-Apr-16: 2B].
George, Mary E. (69 yrs.) d. on 69-Feb-15 [69-Feb-16: 2C].
George, Mary E. m. Maulsby, D. L., Jr. on 69-Jun-3 [69-Jun-7: 2B].
George, Octavius (42 yrs.) d. on 68-May-20 [68-May-21: 2B].
George, Samuel E. m. Davis, Kate on 70-Apr-26 [70-Apr-29: 2B].
George, Sophia H. d. on 70-Feb-22 [70-Feb-24: 2C; 70-Feb-25: 2C].
George, Thomas d. on 70-Jun-3 [70-Jun-4: 2B].
George, Thomas J. m. Sanders, Sophie M. on 66-Dec-13 [66-Dec-18: 2B].
George, Victor Francis d. on 67-Aug-11 of Bilious fever [67-Sep-6: 2B].
Geppritch, Tresa m. Merriken, Jacob D. on 69-Jun-27 [69-Jul-3: 2B].
Gerard, Mary C. d. on 68-Jan-11 [68-Jan-13: 2C].
Gerding, Louis Henry (4 yrs., 4 mos.) d. on 70-Jul-10 [70-Jul-11: 2C].
Gere, Hattie A. m. Jayne, S. C. on 69-Nov-18 [69-Dec-4: 2C].
Gere, Verdie M. m. Thompson, George B. on 70-Dec-22 [70-Dec-26: 2C].
Gerhardt, Henry H. m. Cole, Mary J. on 67-Feb-25 [67-Mar-2: 2B].
Gerhardt, Mary E. (74 yrs.) d. on 66-Mar-13 [66-Mar-14: 2C].
Gerhart, Gottlieb d. on 68-Feb-1 in Wagon accident [68-Feb-4: 1E].
Gerhegan, Lizzie M. m. Maguire, William D. on 67-Apr-25 [67-Apr-29: 2B].
German, Andrew J. m. Holland, Ann R. on 66-May-8 [66-May-10: 2B].
German, Benjamin C. m. Welch, Mary G. on 66-Mar-4 [66-Mar-6: 2B].
German, Catharine A. m. Grubb, Richard B., Jr. on 66-Jun-18 [67-Feb-26: 2C].
German, Charles Carroll (1 yr., 5 mos.) d. on 70-Jan-2 [70-Jan-4: 2C].
German, Dorcas d. on 66-Oct-16 [66-Oct-17: 2B].
German, Eliza m. Bidison, William T. on 69-Oct-24 [69-Oct-30: 2B].
German, Frederick (28 yrs.) d. on 69-Jul-4 Drowned [69-Jul-5: 1F, 2C].
German, George J. m. Foreman, Lizzie A. on 68-Apr-27 [68-Apr-30: 2B].
German, Issac (67 yrs.) d. on 67-Sep-2 [67-Sep-4: 2B].
German, Jerome B. m. Mattingly, Kate on 67-Sep-24 [67-Sep-26: 2B].
German, Job (72 yrs.) d. on 68-Nov-27 [68-Nov-28: 2C].
German, John W. m. Poisal, Maggie E. on 68-Aug-11 [68-Aug-15: 2B].
German, Joseph m. Hunt, Mary J. on 67-Oct-1 [67-Oct-7: 2B].
German, Lemuel m. Pierce, Eunice on 69-Feb-25 [69-Mar-1: 2C].
German, Levin Clarke (2 yrs., 5 mos.) d. on 68-Aug-27 [68-Aug-28: 2B; 68-Aug-29: 2B].
German, Mary (72 yrs.) d. [69-Jul-23: 2C].
German, Mary A. m. Roden, George on 66-Feb-1 [66-Feb-3: 2C].
German, Thomas E. J. m. Sultzer, Susan A. on 67-Sep-4 [67-Sep-11: 2B].
German, Thomas S. m. LeMerchant, Josina E. on 68-Jan-28 [68-Feb-4: 2C].
German, Willie (10 mos.) d. on 69-Mar-23 [69-Mar-24: 2C].
Gerry, E. H. m. Scarborough, Annie on 68-Sep-22 [68-Sep-23: 2B].
Gerry, Lydia S. m. Collins, J. William on 65-Dec-14 [66-Feb-7: 2C].
Gerstmeyer, Barney (42 yrs., 3 mos.) d. on 69-Oct-26 of Fall from horse [69-Oct-27: 4C; 69-Oct-28: 2C].
Getman, Mary A. m. Deigel, Daniel on 68-Feb-18 [68-Feb-25: 2C].

Gettert, Jacob (46 yrs.) d. on 70-Sep-23 [70-Sep-24: 2B].
Gettier, Anna Catherine (75 yrs.) d. on 66-Feb-17 [66-Feb-19: 2B].
Gettier, Edward S. (34 yrs.) d. on 68-Mar-14 [68-Mar-20: 2B].
Gettier, Ira Lee (9 mos.) d. on 69-Feb-21 [69-Feb-22: 2C].
Gettier, M. Kate m. Stuart, James A. on 70-Nov-24 [70-Nov-26: 2B].
Gettier, Thomas H. (2 mos.) d. on 69-Feb-28 [69-Mar-1: 2C].
Gettier, Willie A. (1 yr., 6 mos.) d. on 68-May-16 [68-May-19: 2B].
Getty, Annie T. m. Childs, Samuel on 68-Nov-19 [68-Nov-21: 2C].
Getty, Francis, Capt. (91 yrs.) d. on 67-Sep-28 [67-Sep-30: 2B].
Getty, J. Frank m. Baile, Ginnie S. on 70-Nov-1 [70-Nov-3: 2B].
Getty, T. M., Col. (50 yrs.) d. on 67-Oct-30 [67-Oct-31: 1G; 67-Nov-1: 2B].
Gettys, Mary C. m. Spamer, George W. on 66-May-2 [66-May-16: 2C].
Getz, Mary A. m. Vansant, Augustus L. on 66-May-1 [66-May-8: 2B].
Getzendanner, Mary A. (49 yrs.) d. on 67-May-16 [67-May-22: 2B].
Ghee, James Nicholas (10 mos.) d. on 66-Feb-20 [66-Feb-21: 2C].
Ghee, Kate (10 mos.) d. on 70-May-27 [70-May-31: 2B].
Ghee, William Thomas (4 yrs., 5 mos.) d. on 66-Oct-3 [66-Oct-5: 2B].
Ghequiers, Cecilia d. on 66-Apr-5 [66-Apr-11: 2B].
Gibbins, Oliver m. Taunea, Keziah on 67-Dec-26 [68-Jan-3: 2C].
Gibbon, J. H. (74 yrs.) d. on 68-Dec-16 of Erysipelas and pneumonia [68-Dec-17: 1G].
Gibbon, Mary d. on 66-Jun-4 [66-Jun-5: 2B].
Gibbons, Annie (25 yrs.) d. on 70-Aug-31 of Consumption [70-Sep-23: 2C].
Gibbons, Fannie Lyon d. on 70-Jan-27 [70-Jan-29: 2B].
Gibbons, James (5 mos.) d. on 68-Jun-15 [68-Jun-16: 2B].
Gibbons, James E. m. Engler, Emma L. on 70-Nov-17 [70-Nov-19: 2B].
Gibbons, Maggie E. m. Burgess, William T. on 70-Feb-28 [70-Mar-25: 2C].
Gibbons, Martha m. Disney, Benjamin on 66-Mar-20 [66-Mar-22: 2B].
Gibbons, Sarah F. m. Laib, Edward W. on 69-Feb-9 [69-Feb-11: 2C].
Gibbons, Stephen m. Logsdon, Fannie, Miss on 66-Nov-27 [66-Nov-28: 2B].
Gibbons, William (79 yrs.) d. on 70-Jul-30 [70-Aug-1: 2C].
Gibbons, William J. (40 yrs.) d. on 67-Jul-3 [67-Jul-8: 2C; 67-Jul-11: 2C].
Gibbs, Elizabeth m. Miller, Elisha H. on 70-Oct-20 [70-Oct-29: 2B].
Gibbs, Sue m. Hoffman, William on 67-Nov-21 [68-Jan-9: 2C].
Gibbs, Theodore d. on 67-May-23 Drowned [67-May-24: 1F].
Gibbs, William H. (24 yrs.) d. on 66-Jan-23 of Consumption [66-Jan-24: 2B].
Gibbs, William Joseph (1 yr., 6 mos.) d. on 69-Feb-14 [69-Feb-16: 2C].
Giblan, Elizabeth (64 yrs.) d. on 70-Sep-3 [70-Sep-5: 2C].
Giblin, Annie Teresa m. Leonard, Michael on 67-Aug-4 [67-Aug-17: 2B].
Gibling, Mary Ann (28 yrs.) d. on 68-Aug-14 [68-Aug-15: 2B].
Gibney, Ellen (40 yrs.) d. on 70-Apr-12 [70-Apr-13: 2B].
Gibney, George J. (40 yrs.) d. on 66-Jun-7 [66-Jun-8: 2B; 66-Jun-9: 2B].
Gibney, Mary Louise A. (19 yrs.) d. on 68-Oct-12 [68-Oct-13: 2C].
Gibson, A. F. m. Kerr, Fanny A. on 69-Oct-13 [69-Oct-14: 2C].
Gibson, Ann d. on 68-Jul-8 [68-Jul-9: 2B].
Gibson, Anna m. East, Robert P. on 69-Nov-14 [69-Dec-3: 2C].
Gibson, Annie E. m. Hoffman, Emory B. on 69-Sep-7 [69-Sep-16: 2B].
Gibson, Arnold m. Reaves, Maria on 70-May-1 [70-May-21: 2B].
Gibson, Charles Rawlings (9 mos.) d. on 67-Mar-24 [67-Mar-25: 2C].
Gibson, Charles W. (20 yrs.) d. on 66-Oct-30 [66-Nov-1: 2B].
Gibson, David (30 yrs.) d. on 69-Apr-3 of Apoplexy [69-Apr-5: 1H].
Gibson, Elizabeth Jane d. on 66-Oct-10 [66-Oct-13: 2B].
Gibson, Ella m. Richardson, B. O. on 70-Oct-26 [70-Nov-9: 2C].
Gibson, Emily A. (73 yrs.) d. on 68-Nov-6 [68-Nov-7: 2B].
Gibson, Fanny A. d. on 70-Jul-17 [70-Jul-18: 2B].
Gibson, George McIlrath (45 yrs.) d. on 68-Feb-20 of Fall on ice [68-Feb-22: 1G, 2B].

Gibson, George W. m. Gilbert, Agnes B. on 70-Sep-21 [70-Sep-27: 2B].
Gibson, J. Henry (34 yrs.) d. on 68-Dec-21 [68-Dec-22: 2C].
Gibson, James Francis (3 mos.) d. on 70-Oct-31 [70-Nov-1: 2C].
Gibson, Jane Viney (7 mos.) d. on 69-Mar-3 [69-Mar-4: 2C].
Gibson, John (1 yr., 8 mos.) d. on 69-Jun-30 [69-Jul-1: 2C].
Gibson, John m. Weems, Cornelia on 69-Sep-2 [69-Sep-6: 2C].
Gibson, John F. (21 yrs.) d. on 68-Nov-28 [68-Nov-30: 2B].
Gibson, John Henry m. Dunn, Bridget on 68-Jan-6 [68-Jan-21: 2C].
Gibson, John W. m. McElroy, Mary on 68-Jul-7 [68-Jul-14: 2B].
Gibson, Joseph (37 yrs.) d. on 70-Oct-15 of Consumption [70-Oct-17: 2B, 4D].
Gibson, Laura C. m. Weaver, John C. on 70-Mar-19 [70-Mar-26: 2B].
Gibson, Maggie Allen (2 yrs., 2 mos.) d. on 69-Jan-10 of Chronic croup [69-Jan-15: 2D].
Gibson, Malachi (51 yrs.) d. on 70-Jul-12 [70-Jul-13: 2C].
Gibson, Margaret Ann (32 yrs.) d. on 70-Apr-26 [70-Apr-27: 2B; 70-Apr-28: 2B].
Gibson, Maria m. Chew, Samuel C. on 66-Apr-26 [66-Apr-30: 2B].
Gibson, Mary A. (47 yrs.) d. on 67-Jun-29 [67-Jul-1: 2B].
Gibson, Mary A. (27 yrs.) d. on 70-Jul-22 [70-Jul-25: 2C].
Gibson, Mary Cecilia (2 mos.) d. on 70-Jun-21 [70-Jun-23: 2C].
Gibson, Mary Ella (8 yrs., 3 mos.) d. on 66-Aug-14 [66-Aug-15: 2B].
Gibson, Mary M. m. Chambers, John M. on 68-Apr-28 [68-Apr-30: 2B].
Gibson, Patrick (59 yrs.) d. on 68-Feb-4 [68-Feb-6: 2C; 68-Feb-7: 1G, 2C].
Gibson, Robert (33 yrs.) d. on 68-May-30 [68-Jun-3: 1F, 2B].
Gibson, Rowland G. m. Stapleton, Mary A. on 69-Jun-7 [69-Jun-11: 2C].
Gibson, Thomas A. m. Rohrbough, Esta E. on 68-Nov-24 [68-Dec-29: 2D].
Gibson, William N. m. Barton, Jennie M. on 67-Feb-12 [67-Feb-20: 2C].
Gibson, Woolman m. Richardson, Addie on 68-Feb-28 [68-May-12: 2B].
Gidding, Richard (1 yr., 1 mo.) d. on 70-Dec-3 [70-Dec-5: 2C].
Giddings, Luther m. Wells, Mary Wallace on 69-Jul-15 [69-Jul-17: 2C].
Gidings, Marshal F. (43 yrs.) d. on 68-Sep-2 [68-Sep-3: 2B].
Gienger, George (46 yrs.) d. on 69-Oct-30 of Suicide (Hanging) [69-Nov-1: 2C, 1G].
Gies, John, Jr. m. Ensminger, Ophelia L. on 70-Dec-1 [70-Dec-6: 2C].
Giese, L W. H. (80 yrs.) d. on 66-Nov-9 [66-Nov-10: 2B; 66-Nov-12: 2C].
Giese, Lillian m. LeMassena, Theodore F. on 70-Jun-22 [70-Jun-23: 2C].
Giesendaffer, Charles P. m. Green, Fannie M. on 67-Mar-28 [67-Jun-25: 2B].
Giesendaffer, Hannah E. m. Dames, John H. on 67-May-29 [67-May-31: 2B].
Giesendaffer, Luther (27 yrs.) d. on 70-Aug-18 [70-Aug-20: 2B].
Gieske, Charles m. Coyne, Mary E. on 67-Jun-11 [67-Jun-13: 2C].
Gieske, Louis m. Schwing, Mary on 67-Oct-3 [67-Oct-4: 2B].
Giesriel, Frederick (43 yrs.) d. on 67-Sep-23 [67-Sep-24: 2A; 67-Sep-25: 2B].
Giessendaffer, Hannah (67 yrs.) d. on 70-Aug-31 [70-Sep-1: 2B].
Gifford, William m. McCoubray, Alice C. on 68-Jul-12 [68-Sep-9: 2B].
Gilback, John D. m. Hunt, Susan R. on 67-Oct-1 [67-Oct-7: 2B].
Gilbert, A. Preston m. Bouldin, Mollie on 70-Oct-6 [70-Oct-7: 2B].
Gilbert, Agnes B. m. Gibson, George W. on 70-Sep-21 [70-Sep-27: 2B].
Gilbert, Calvin m. Griffin, Sarah F. on 70-Dec-20 [70-Dec-30: 2C].
Gilbert, Irenus Asbury (21 yrs.) d. on 70-May-19 [70-Jun-4: 2B].
Gilbert, John Emory (6 mos.) d. on 69-Jul-28 [69-Jul-30: 2C].
Gilbert, Sarah d. on 70-Jan-23 [70-Jan-27: 2C].
Gildea, Julia Ann (66 yrs.) d. on 69-Jan-1 [69-Jan-4: 2C].
Gildea, Kate m. Tierney, Patrick E. on 69-Oct-7 [70-Jan-19: 2C].
Gildea, Laura Paulina (1 yr., 8 mos.) d. on 67-Jan-2 [67-Jan-3: 2B].
Gildersleeve, William Reynolds d. on 69-Jan-3 [69-Jan-4: 2C].
Gile, Aquilla, Jr. (35 yrs.) d. on 68-Nov-10 [68-Nov-18: 2C].
Giles, Cassie W. (23 yrs.) d. on 70-Mar-3 [70-Mar-5: 2B].
Giles, Eliza (35 yrs.) d. on 66-Jul-31 of Boiler explosion [66-Aug-1: 1F].

Giles, George W. (47 yrs.) d. on 69-Aug-30 [69-Sep-2: 2B].
Giles, Henry M. (36 yrs.) d. on 68-Nov-25 in Wagon accident [68-Nov-26: 1H; 68-Nov-28: 2C].
Giles, Jarreta (24 yrs., 5 mos.) d. on 68-Jan-18 of Consumption [68-Jan-20: 2C].
Giles, Laura V. m. Purnell, Washington J. on 67-Nov-30 [67-Dec-2: 2C].
Giles, Lizzie F. m. Crawford, George R. on 69-Jul-22 [69-Jul-26: 2C].
Giles, Mariam (56 yrs.) d. on 69-Dec-17 [69-Dec-18: 2B].
Giles, Robert Vinton (24 yrs., 6 mos.) d. on 67-Sep-5 Drowned [67-Sep-11: 2B].
Giles, Steuart (17 yrs., 5 mos.) d. on 70-Nov-8 [70-Nov-11: 2B; 70-Nov-12: 4C].
Giles, Thomas Patterson (2 yrs., 4 mos.) d. on 66-Mar-16 of Brain congestion [66-Mar-20: 2C].
Giles, William Fell m. Kealhofer, Lutie on 66-Apr-11 [66-Apr-17: 2C].
Gill, A. E. m. Harris, S. R. on 68-Nov-17 [69-Feb-24: 2C].
Gill, Adaline (1 mo.) d. on 69-Jul-11 [69-Jul-12: 2D].
Gill, Ann E. d. on 69-Feb-18 [69-Feb-20: 2B].
Gill, Anna M. O. m. Christhilf, Henry B. on 70-May-9 [70-May-23: 2B].
Gill, Annie m. Fischer, Louis C. on 66-Nov-22 [66-Nov-24: 2B].
Gill, Annie R. (20 yrs.) d. on 69-May-28 [69-May-29: 2B].
Gill, Cardella Frost (10 mos.) d. on 70-Nov-15 [70-Nov-19: 2B].
Gill, Charles Albert (13 yrs., 3 mos.) d. on 70-Nov-17 [70-Nov-19: 2B].
Gill, Christie H. m. Rutter, Joseph H. J. on 67-Jun-10 [67-Jun-10: 2B].
Gill, Edward (80 yrs.) d. on 67-Dec-6 [67-Dec-9: 2B].
Gill, Elisha P. (57 yrs.) d. on 68-Feb-11 [68-Feb-13: 2C].
Gill, Elizabeth McDonald (46 yrs.) d. on 70-Jan-12 [70-Jan-15: 2C].
Gill, Flora (82 yrs.) d. on 69-Oct-17 [69-Oct-18: 2C; 69-Oct-19: 2C].
Gill, George W. (22 yrs.) d. on 70-Sep-20 [70-Sep-22: 2C].
Gill, Harry T. (12 yrs.) d. on 67-Mar-15 [67-Mar-19: 2C].
Gill, Heithe S. m. Beckley, Sallie E. on 68-Nov-5 [68-Nov-6: 2C].
Gill, John m. Spence, Louisa W. on 66-Nov-27 [66-Nov-29: 2B].
Gill, John m. Curtis, F. A. on 66-Feb-15 [66-Feb-24: 2B].
Gill, John C. (11 mos.) d. on 67-Jul-17 [67-Jul-23: 2C].
Gill, John R. m. McComas, Martha A. E. on 68-Feb-20 [68-Feb-27: 2C].
Gill, John W. m. Tipton, Julia A. on 70-Mar-24 [70-Mar-25: 2C].
Gill, Joseph m. Hutchins, Florence E. on 70-Jan-19 [70-Jan-22: 2B; 70-Feb-1: 2B].
Gill, Margaret F. (40 yrs.) d. on 70-Jul-1 [70-Jul-7: 2C].
Gill, Mary Ann (35 yrs.) d. on 67-Jan-29 [67-Jan-31: 2C].
Gill, Mary E. m. Putts, Charles J. on 66-Sep-9 [66-Sep-14: 2B].
Gill, Sallie J. m. Clarvoe, C. W. on 67-Sep-24 [67-Sep-26: 2B].
Gill, Thaddeus Schuyler (3 mos.) d. on 68-Oct-25 [68-Oct-26: 2B].
Gill, Theophilus P. m. Starr, Mary Elizabeth on 69-Jun-24 [69-Jun-26: 2B].
Gill, Thomas B. m. Farlow, Ida V. on 68-Aug-8 [69-Apr-27: 2B; 69-Apr-28: 2B].
Gill, William H. m. Gray, Anna on 68-Jul-6 [68-Jul-11: 2B].
Gill, William H. m. Kennerly, Martha on 69-Jul-4 [69-Jul-7: 2C].
Gill, William James m. Whitaker, Matilda E. on 66-Jun-26 [66-Nov-1: 2B].
Gill, William R. m. Manson, Mary M. on 67-Jan-15 [67-Jan-19: 2C].
Gillaspy, Druscilla (43 yrs.) d. on 69-May-2 [69-May-3: 2C].
Gillen, Daniel (42 yrs.) d. on 68-May-7 [68-May-9: 2B].
Gillen, Robert (33 yrs.) d. on 68-May-9 [68-May-12: 2B].
Gillenham, William James m. Harvey, Alice L. on 69-Dec-23 [70-Jan-20: 2C].
Gilleran, James (57 yrs.) d. on 70-Jan-7 [70-Jan-8: 2B].
Gillespie, Joseph J. m. Guyton, Lizzie F. on 68-Sep-24 [68-Sep-26: 2B].
Gillespie, Martha (80 yrs.) d. on 69-Jul-22 [69-Jul-23: 2C].
Gillespie, Mary d. on 67-Oct-21 [67-Oct-22: 2A].
Gillespie, Nannie L. m. May, E. Ferdinand on 67-Jun-27 [67-Jul-1: 2B].
Gillespie, Sadie E. m. McCallum, A. C. on 67-Feb-14 [67-Feb-18: 2C].
Gillespie, Stephen (73 yrs.) d. on 68-Feb-7 [68-Feb-8: 2B].
Gillet, Annie S. m. Parker, James H. on 69-Oct-28 [69-Oct-30: 2B].

Gillette, Charles, Rev. (52 yrs.) d. on 69-Mar-6 [69-Mar-8: 1G; 69-Mar-9: 4D].
Gilley, Charles W. m. Lyon, Mary A. on 68-Jun-4 [68-Jun-5: 2B].
Gilliard, Edward (57 yrs.) d. on 67-Jul-29 [67-Jul-30: 2C].
Gilliard, Nicholas m. Adair, Mary on 68-May-21 [68-May-25: 2A].
Gilligan, Catherine Elizabeth (5 mos.) d. on 70-Jun-13 [70-Jun-14: 2B].
Gilligan, Harry Clay d. on 68-Aug-9 [68-Aug-13: 2B].
Gilligan, John J. (20 yrs.) d. on 70-Jan-18 [70-Jan-19: 2C; 70-Jan-20: 2C].
Gilligan, Michael (36 yrs.) d. on 68-Dec-2 [68-Dec-3: 2C].
Gillin, Mary (80 yrs.) d. on 67-May-8 [67-May-10: 2B].
Gillinder, James m. Bennett, Martha W. on 67-Apr-29 [67-May-2: 2B].
Gillingham, Annie R. m. Shuster, William H. on 68-Nov-24 [68-Dec-4: 2D].
Gillingham, C. Raborg m. Ebaugh, Eliza J. on 70-Jun-4 [70-Jun-6: 2B].
Gillingham, Charles Brooks (3 mos.) d. on 69-Jul-3 [69-Jul-5: 2C].
Gillingham, Edward (55 yrs.) d. on 70-Aug-12 [70-Aug-15: 2C].
Gillingham, Ella Howard (5 mos.) d. on 70-Dec-18 [70-Dec-19: 2C].
Gillingham, George O. m. Crawford, Annie E. on 68-Jul-23 [68-Jul-29: 2D].
Gillingham, Mary Ann (23 yrs.) d. on 68-Aug-14 [68-Aug-17: 2B].
Gillingham, Sarah V. m. Coughlan, Thomas on 66-Dec-27 [66-Dec-31: 2C].
Gilliss, Joseph A. m. Hardesty, Georgie on 70-Dec-20 [70-Dec-23: 2B].
Gillum, 'Doc' (45 yrs.) d. on 70-Aug-4 Drowned [70-Aug-5: 1H].
Gilman, Ellen m. Porter, William Henry on 70-Oct-13 [70-Oct-14: 2B].
Gilmer, Charles S. (49 yrs.) d. on 66-Sep-21 [66-Sep-22: 2B; 66-Sep-24: 4C].
Gilmor, Sarah R. L. d. on 66-Mar-18 [66-Mar-20: 2C].
Gilmor, William (56 yrs.) d. on 70-Jul-21 [70-Jul-23: 2B].
Gilmore, Emma m. Harrison, William on 68-Apr-15 [68-Apr-18: 2A].
Gilmore, Michael (25 yrs.) d. on 70-May-26 [70-May-27: 2B].
Gilmore, Robert (50 yrs.) d. on 70-Jan-1 of Pneumonia [70-Jan-3: 1G; 70-Jan-6: 2C].
Gilmour, H. C. m. Rutter, Julia on 69-Jun-10 [69-Jun-15: 2C].
Gilmour, Mary D. m. Brackett, John S. on 69-Feb-18 [69-Feb-25: 2D].
Gilpin, Anna (66 yrs.) d. on 69-Oct-18 [69-Nov-17: 2C].
Gilpin, Arabella m. Dixon, William on 70-Oct-14 [70-Oct-17: 2B].
Gilpin, Mary M. m. Carroll, William C. on 68-Oct-19 [68-Oct-20: 2B].
Gilpin, Sarah Ann (48 yrs.) d. on 68-Jan-3 [68-Jan-4: 2C].
Gilroy, John m. Fisher, Laura E. on 69-Apr-1 [69-Apr-10: 2B].
Gimmill, Rose Ann (30 yrs.) d. on 69-Aug-23 [69-Sep-18: 2B].
Ginn, Achsah (82 yrs.) d. on 67-Dec-21 [67-Dec-23: 2B].
Ginn, Irene (10 mos.) d. on 68-Nov-30 [68-Dec-3: 2C].
Ginnaman, Eliza Malvina (5 mos.) d. on 66-Jun-27 [66-Jul-10: 2C].
Ginnavan, George W. (2 mos.) d. on 68-Sep-3 [68-Sep-29: 2B].
Ginnavan, J. T. m. Biggs, Mary A. on 69-Nov-7 [69-Nov-9: 2C].
Ginnavan, Susan m. Hinton, Zachariah on 70-Jun-5 [70-Jun-10: 2B].
Ginnavan, William Westley (3 mos.) d. on 70-Jul-25 [70-Oct-25: 2B].
Girard, Kate m. Hall, George H. on 70-May-26 [70-Jun-3: 2B].
Giraud, Orilla d. on 68-Dec-26 [68-Dec-30: 2C].
Girbrich, Eliza J. m. Akerst, John G. on 69-Sep-14 [69-Sep-24: 2B].
Girding, George (65 yrs.) d. on 69-Sep-23 Drowned [69-Sep-25: 1H].
Girvin, Florence Little (2 yrs., 5 mos.) d. on 70-Jul-22 [70-Jul-23: 2B; 70-Aug-30: 2C].
Girvin, James (72 yrs.) d. on 69-Mar-3 [69-Mar-4: 1H, 2C; 69-Mar-5: 2C].
Girvin, James A. m. Box, Charlotte E. on 66-Dec-5 [67-Jan-4: 2D].
Girvin, John (33 yrs.) d. on 68-Jun-8 Drowned [68-Jun-30: 2C].
Girvin, Mary E. m. Peters, Winfield on 69-Nov-10 [69-Nov-15: 2C].
Gischel, John Henry (3 yrs., 9 mos.) d. on 69-Jan-25 [69-Jan-26: 2C].
Gise, Sallie J. m. Fillinger, James L. on 70-Dec-1 [70-Dec-5: 2C].
Gisriel, Mary Olivia m. Dahoney, John E. on 68-Nov-3 [68-Nov-11: 2C].
Gissel, John m. Cowdery, Letitia N. on 67-Aug-27 [67-Sep-24: 2A].

Gist, Joseph (57 yrs.) d. on 70-Dec-27 [70-Dec-28: 2C; 70-Dec-29: 2C].
Gist, W. Irving m. Moore, Mary on 67-Feb-25 [67-Mar-12: 2C].
Gittenger, Ella (20 yrs.) d. on 70-Jun-11 [70-Jun-14: 2B].
Gittings, Ann Emory m. Yellott, George Washington, Jr. [69-Feb-6: 2C].
Gittings, Caroline Carter (43 yrs.) d. on 66-Apr-14 [66-Apr-16: 2B].
Gittings, D. T. m. King, Laura A. on 68-Sep-15 [68-Sep-17: 2B].
Gittings, Julia Evans m. Morris, J. Champlin on 69-Nov-25 [69-Nov-26: 2B].
Gittings, Martin V. (26 yrs.) d. on 66-Aug-23 [66-Aug-24: 2B].
Givan, J. L. m. Reed, M. A. on 69-Apr-13 [69-Apr-17: 2A].
Givins, Joseph H. (28 yrs.) d. on 68-Dec-29 [68-Dec-30: 2C].
Gladding, Edward (25 yrs.) d. on 66-Sep-1 Drowned [66-Sep-3: 4C].
Gladfelter, Rebecca (54 yrs.) d. on 68-Jan-17 of Intermittant fever [68-Jan-18: 2B].
Gladfelter, Walter Thomas (5 mos.) d. on 70-Jun-22 [70-Jun-23: 2C].
Glading, Charles F. m. Ward, Sallie J. on 67-Dec-26 [68-Jan-1: 2C].
Gladson, Rebecca (76 yrs.) d. on 70-Mar-14 [70-Mar-15: 2C].
Glady, William (10 yrs.) d. on 70-Jul-10 Drowned [70-Jul-12: 1G].
Glaeser, Margaret K. d. on 70-Feb-3 [70-Feb-5: 2B].
Glancy, Margaret m. Woods, John on 66-May-8 [66-Sep-17: 2B].
Glanding, Laura V. m. Hissey, William, Jr. on 69-Oct-14 [69-Oct-21: 2B].
Glanding, Sarah (88 yrs.) d. on 68-Jan-2 [68-Jan-3: 2C].
Glanding, Sarah E. m. Jennings, John M. on 69-Jul-13 [69-Jul-15: 2C].
Glann, Elizabeth (84 yrs.) d. on 68-Jan-25 [68-Jan-27: 2C].
Glanville, Alma d. on 69-Jul-24 [69-Jul-26: 2C].
Glanville, Ida M. m. Whiting, A. Lawrence on 66-May-24 [66-Jun-6: 2B].
Glanville, J. Offley m. Fairchild, Alexina on 66-Nov-5 [66-Nov-10: 2B].
Glanville, James W. (63 yrs.) d. on 66-Jan-9 of Consumption [66-Jan-10: 2C; 66-Jan-11: 2B].
Glanville, Lucy A. m. Cook, Joseph F. on 68-Jan-22 [68-Jan-27: 2C].
Glanville, Robert B. m. Joyce, Josephine H. on 66-Apr-30 [66-May-3: 2C].
Glasco, Catherine (67 yrs.) d. on 66-Mar-4 [66-Mar-6: 2B].
Glaser, Edward m. Popp, Barbara on 68-Jun-4 [68-Jun-6: 2A].
Glass, Bessie Digges m. Crowther, Llewellyn on 70-Oct-13 [70-Oct-15: 2B].
Glass, Issac (34 yrs.) d. on 66-May-8 of Consumption [66-May-9: 2B; 66-May-10: 2B].
Glass, John (40 yrs.) d. on 66-Dec-5 Drowned [66-Dec-8: 2B].
Glass, Martha m. Berry, R. R. on 69-Jul-13 [69-Jul-15: 2C].
Glass, Rachel Ann m. Saunders, Joseph A. on 66-Jan-7 [66-Jan-16: 2C].
Glass, William m. Gough, Mary E. on 68-Feb-13 [68-Feb-14: 2C].
Glass, William D. (54 yrs.) d. on 69-Aug-23 of Heart disease [69-Aug-24: 1H, 2C].
Glasscock, W. A. m. Biscoe, Jenny Y. [69-Mar-6: 2B].
Glasscocke, Mary A. d. on 67-Nov-13 [67-Nov-14: 2B; 67-Nov-15: 2B].
Glassgow, John L. m. Smith, Emmeline on 67-Feb-11 [67-Feb-13: 2D].
Glavines, Charles Albert (1 yr.) d. on 68-Dec-26 [68-Dec-28: 2B].
Glazier, Belle N m. Chandler, Kennard on 70-Nov-2 [70-Nov-14: 2B].
Gleason, Thomas m. Conley, Sarah on 67-Oct-2 [67-Oct-4: 2B].
Gleeson, Bridget (30 yrs.) d. on 70-Mar-22 [70-Mar-24: 2C].
Gleeson, T. James m. Thompson, Frances on 68-May-6 [68-May-25: 2A].
Gleghorn, Robert (17 yrs., 9 mos.) d. on 67-Feb-25 [67-Feb-26: 2C].
Glenn, Charles W. (21 yrs.) d. on 69-May-12 in Railroad accident [69-May-13: 1H, 2B].
Glenn, Elias (29 yrs.) d. on 68-Mar-5 [68-Mar-10: 2C].
Glenn, Emily Amelia (2 yrs., 4 mos.) d. on 66-Nov-22 [66-Nov-23: 2C].
Glenn, James, Sr. (46 yrs.) d. on 68-Nov-12 in Machine accident [68-Nov-13: 1H, 2C].
Glenn, John m. Jordan, Mary A. on 69-Oct-17 [69-Oct-26: 2B].
Glenn, John H. m. Williams, Elizabeth F. on 70-Jul-14 [70-Jul-23: 2B].
Glenn, Lewis W. (67 yrs.) d. on 68-Jun-7 of Apoplexy [68-Jun-12: 1B].
Glenn, M. E. m. Smith, H. M. on 66-Jun-28 [66-Aug-3: 2C].
Glenn, William Enoch P. (1 yr., 6 mos.) d. on 66-Mar-17 [66-Mar-19: 2C].

Glennan, Thomas, Jr. (26 yrs.) d. on 68-Dec-5 [68-Dec-15: 2C].
Glines, Olivia (2 yrs., 9 mos.) d. on 66-Mar-1 [66-Mar-2: 2B].
Glocker, A. Campbell m. Paine, Juliet A. on 70-Dec-20 [70-Dec-22: 2B].
Glocker, Theodore W. m. Kirby, Mollie on 69-Dec-9 [69-Dec-10: 2C].
Gloninger, Augusta m. Fetterman, L. B. on 69-Jun-23 [69-Jun-29: 2C].
Gloss, Lizzie m. Rowe, E. H. on 69-Sep-28 [69-Oct-1: 2B].
Glossbrenner, Henrietta C. m. Fox, Luther A. on 69-Sep-9 [69-Sep-15: 2B].
Glossner, Ernest (48 yrs.) d. on 67-Nov-24 [67-Nov-25: 2C].
Glossner, John Paulus (24 yrs., 8 mos.) d. on 70-Sep-29 of Consumption [70-Oct-1: 2B].
Glover, William H. m. Thumlert, Maggie A. on 69-Jan-21 [69-Jan-23: 2C].
Glowman, Clara Isabella (53 yrs.) d. on 69-Nov-29 [69-Dec-1: 2C].
Gluck, Mary Louisa Catharine (8 yrs., 5 mos.) d. on 70-Jan-18 [70-Jan-20: 2C].
Glue, Ignatius m. Faid, Mary on 69-Jan-2 [69-Jan-5: 2C; 69-Jan-6: 2C].
Glue, William Ignatius (2 mos.) d. on 70-Jan-6 [70-Jan-7: 2F].
Glynn, Mattie Seabright (1 yr., 6 mos.) d. on 69-Apr-8 of Brain fever [69-Apr-9: 2B].
Gnosspelius, G. A. m. Duer, Mary J. on 68-Aug-25 [68-Sep-2: 2A].
Gobright, Louisa R. (78 yrs.) d. on 66-Jul-12 [66-Jul-13: 2C].
Gobright, William H. m. Hart, Matilda on 67-Nov-6 [67-Nov-7: 2C].
Godey, Charlotte m. Warner, William Henry on 67-Oct-2 [67-Oct-5: 2B].
Godfrey, Benjamin Edward (3 yrs., 9 mos.) d. on 67-Jul-20 [67-Jul-22: 2C].
Godfrey, Charles (28 yrs.) d. on 68-Oct-9 of Yellow fever [68-Dec-3: 2C].
Godfrey, James H. (42 yrs.) d. on 70-Oct-24 in Railroad accident [70-Oct-27: 2B].
Godfrey, Maria (57 yrs.) d. on 69-Jul-4 [69-Jul-7: 2C].
Godfrey, Sarah (79 yrs.) d. on 69-Feb-15 [69-Feb-16: 2C; 69-Feb-17: 2C].
Godfrey, Susanna A. m. Clark, Francis P. on 68-Jun-28 [68-Jun-30: 2B].
Godman, Brutus (90 yrs.) d. on 67-Mar-24 [67-Mar-25: 2C].
Godman, Charles (10 mos.) d. on 69-Jul-16 [69-Jul-17: 2C].
Godman, Emma Louisa (22 yrs.) d. on 67-May-27 of Dropsy and scarlet fever [67-May-28: 2B].
Godman, G. Robert m. Muir, Emma on 66-Apr-2 [66-Apr-19: 2B].
Godman, John T. (44 yrs., 7 mos.) d. on 66-Dec-15 [66-Dec-21: 2B].
Godman, Laura V. m. Rodgers, James W. on 68-Jun-11 [68-Jun-16: 2B].
Godman, Laura V. m. Peppler, Charles on 68-Dec-22 [68-Dec-30: 2C].
Godman, William J. m. Jackson, Anna V. on 68-Apr-23 [68-Apr-25: 2B].
Godwin, Almira (34 yrs.) d. on 68-Feb-15 [68-Feb-17: 2C].
Godwin, Ann (67 yrs.) d. on 69-May-25 [69-May-26: 2C].
Godwin, Emma E. m. Roseberry, Samuel J. on 69-May-20 [69-May-27: 2C; 69-May-28: 2C].
Godwin, Julia A. (48 yrs.) d. on 68-Jun-3 [68-Jun-16: 2B].
Godwin, Martha d. on 68-Aug-19 [68-Aug-21: 2B].
Godwin, R. L. m. Taliaferro, G. C. on 69-Apr-30 [69-Sep-1: 2B].
Godwin, Thomas W. m. Whiting, Indiana on 67-Dec-11 [67-Dec-14: 2B].
Godwin, William (61 yrs.) d. on 68-Oct-31 of Paralysis [68-Nov-2: 2B].
Goertz, Henry (14 yrs., 6 mos.) d. on 69-Jun-3 Drowned [69-Jun-4: 1G; 69-Jun-5: 2B].
Goforth, George W. (54 yrs.) d. [67-Nov-14: 2B].
Goforth, Kate m. Field, John A. on 66-Dec-15 [66-Dec-20: 2B].
Gogel, Anna E. m. Hughes, Robert on 66-Jun-6 [66-Jun-11: 2B].
Gogel, Jacob F. (87 yrs.) d. on 66-Oct-14 [66-Oct-16: 2B; 66-Oct-17: 2B].
Gogel, Kate W. m. Atkinson, William George on 67-Jun-13 [67-Jun-18: 2B].
Goghean, Margaret A. m. Lambert, Elijah on 68-May-18 [68-May-20: 2A].
Goghegan, Philemon (35 yrs.) d. on 68-Feb-15 [68-Feb-20: 2B].
Gogings, Mary A. (47 yrs.) d. on 68-Sep-1 [68-Sep-4: 2A].
Gohlinghorst, Mary Elizabeth m. Chaney, Charles on 70-Jun-6 [70-Jun-9: 2C].
Going, J. C. m. Bailey, Alfred on 69-Feb-19 [69-Feb-27: 2C].
Gold, Charles W., Capt. d. on 67-Aug-20 Drowned [67-Sep-18: 2B].
Gold, Louis m. Freidenrich, Hennie on 70-Jan-5 [70-Jan-8: 2B].

Golden, Mary C. m. Harrington, Patrick A. on 70-Jan-23 [70-Jan-29: 2B].
Goldman, Lucinda (122 yrs., 8 mos.) d. on 70-Dec-27 [70-Dec-29: 4B].
Goldsborough, Catharine W. m. Chiffelle, Thomas P. on 68-Dec-22 [68-Dec-25: 2D].
Goldsborough, Eddie Roberts (1 yr., 11 mos.) d. on 69-Sep-10 [69-Sep-14: 2B].
Goldsborough, Emma F. d. on 70-Jul-25 of Consumption [70-Jul-29: 2C].
Goldsborough, Fannie V. W. m. Archer, William H. on 69-Dec-28 [69-Dec-29: 2D].
Goldsborough, John (83 yrs.) d. on 69-Feb-11 [69-Feb-13: 2C].
Goldsborough, Maggie D. m. Owen, William H. [68-Oct-8: 2B].
Goldsborough, Richard H. m. Martin, Henrietta M. F. on 70-May-31 [70-Jun-6: 2B].
Goldsborough, W. Ewell m. Laird, Mattie P. on 69-Jan-7 [69-Jan-16: 2C; 69-Jan-18: 2C].
Goldsmith, Egbert S. m. Miller, Virginia S. on 70-Nov-22 [70-Nov-30: 2C].
Goldsmith, Esther m. Sackerman, Henry on 70-Jan-2 [70-Jan-5: 2C].
Goldsmith, George W. (25 yrs.) d. on 66-Oct-12 of Cholera [66-Oct-15: 2B].
Goldsmith, Harry (2 yrs., 3 mos.) d. on 67-Jul-3 [67-Jul-6: 2B].
Goldsmith, Isabella m. Shomberg, Israel on 67-Apr-28 [67-Apr-29: 1G].
Goldsmith, John T. (68 yrs.) d. on 66-Jan-27 [66-Jan-31: 2C].
Goldsmith, M. M. m. White, James McKenny on 68-Apr-30 [68-May-1: 2B].
Goldsmith, Rachel A. m. Kirkley, Charles P. on 66-Aug-27 [66-Oct-11: 2C].
Goldsmith, Sarah H. (84 yrs.) d. [69-Mar-9: 2C].
Goldsmith, Sophia m. Hirshberg, Moses H. on 69-Dec-19 [70-Jan-3: 2C].
Goldstein, Aaron (75 yrs.) d. on 70-Nov-2 [70-Nov-3: 2C].
Golibart, Mary d. on 68-Mar-21 [68-Mar-23: 2B; 68-Mar-24: 2B].
Golibart, Simon R. (45 yrs.) d. on 70-Jan-7 [70-Jan-10: 2C].
Golibart, Simon R. m. Meakin, Maria on 69-Sep-30 [69-Oct-9: 2C].
Gonce, Mary E. m. Butts, William H. on 69-Oct-26 [69-Nov-17: 2C].
Gontrom, Anna C. m. Amos, Charles E. on 66-Mar-21 [66-May-4: 2C].
Gontrum, Florence E. (2 yrs., 1 mo.) d. on 69-Feb-11 [69-Feb-24: 2C].
Gontrum, Mary A. Frances m. Borneman, John H. William on 66-Mar-28 [66-May-8: 2B].
Good, Josephine M. m. Herbst, Arthur C. on 69-Nov-3 [69-Nov-15: 2C].
Good, M. Howard m. Leypold, Mary S. on 66-Feb-6 [66-Feb-10: 2C].
Good, Patrick d. on 67-Sep-19 [67-Sep-27: 2C].
Goodacre, Daniel (71 yrs.) d. on 69-Apr-5 [69-Apr-5: 2B; 69-Apr-6: 2C].
Goodacre, Mary (67 yrs.) d. on 70-Mar-2 [70-Mar-3: 2C].
Goodall, Margaret (86 yrs.) d. on 69-Dec-26 [69-Dec-21: 2B].
Goodhand, George W. m. Ferry, Maggie J. on 69-Jan-12 [69-Jan-19: 2C].
Goodhand, John (56 yrs.) d. on 66-Apr-5 [66-Apr-7: 2B].
Goodloe, Richard Fuller d. [69-Jan-1: 2C].
Goodman, John W. m. Pollard, Maggie on 67-Oct-31 [67-Dec-6: 2C].
Goodman, Maggie (23 yrs.) d. on 69-Nov-14 [69-Nov-15: 2C; 69-Nov-16: 2C].
Goodmanson, George Franklin d. on 67-Jul-8 [67-Jul-10: 2B].
Goodrick, Laura m. Disney, Joseph A. on 69-Mar-30 [69-Apr-2: 2C].
Goodrick, Mary Ann (36 yrs.) d. on 66-Nov-4 [66-Nov-5: 2B].
Goodrick, Virginia (16 yrs.) d. on 66-Nov-4 [66-Nov-5: 2B].
Goodwin, Charles m. Lawrence, Lulia A. on 69-Oct-27 [69-Oct-28: 2C].
Goodwin, Elizabeth H. m. Price, Thomas B. on 66-Apr-5 [67-Apr-7: 2B].
Goodwin, Ellen E. m. Ward, Abraham on 69-Jun-11 [69-Jun-22: 2C].
Goolden, James m. Bruchey, Annie M. on 67-Jun-12 [67-Jul-16: 2C].
Goolrick, Charles Deane d. on 70-Jul-23 [70-Jul-29: 2C].
Gootee, Kelly m. Cox, Rachel S. on 69-Dec-30 [70-Jan-4: 2C; 70-Jan-5: 2C].
Gootee, Mary V. m. Booth, Charles C. on 68-Oct-22 [68-Oct-26: 2B].
Gootee, Sarah A. (64 yrs.) d. on 70-Oct-17 [70-Oct-18: 2B].
Gordon, A. M. E., Lt. (26 yrs.) d. on 67-Sep-28 of Yellow fever [67-Oct-23: 2B].
Gordon, A. M. E. m. Quincy, Sue W. on 67-Jul-25 [67-Jul-30: 2C].
Gordon, Allen B. (22 yrs.) d. on 64-May-21 [66-Jan-23: 2C].
Gordon, Anna C. (83 yrs.) d. on 67-Oct-8 [67-Oct-9: 2B].

Gordon, Bazil F. (25 yrs.) d. on 66-Mar-9 [66-Mar-14: 2C].
Gordon, Bernard (1 yr., 11 mos.) d. on 66-Dec-17 [66-Dec-21: 2B].
Gordon, Bridget (80 yrs.) d. on 70-Aug-10 [70-Aug-11: 2C].
Gordon, Charles M. m. Fossett, Arabella on 67-Nov-26 [67-Nov-28: 2C].
Gordon, David C. m. Barnum, Annie [67-Feb-20: 2C].
Gordon, F. Skipwith m. Wheeler, Mary T. on 66-Jan-9 [66-Jan-11: 2B].
Gordon, Florence D. m. Tebbs, William F. on 68-Nov-3 [68-Nov-6: 2C].
Gordon, Harry (2 yrs., 1 mo.) d. on 68-Aug-23 [68-Aug-29: 2B].
Gordon, J. Frisby, Jr. (6 yrs.) d. on 69-Dec-17 [69-Dec-18: 2B].
Gordon, James (60 yrs.) d. on 70-Feb-26 of Heart disease [70-Feb-28: 1H].
Gordon, John H. m. Clark, Amanda J. on 69-Dec-14 [69-Dec-21: 2B].
Gordon, Josiah (39 yrs.) d. on 68-Nov-11 Murdered (Shooting) [68-Nov-13: 1G; 68-Nov-14: 2B].
Gordon, Laura m. Fuller, William S. on 69-Dec-19 [69-Dec-21: 2B].
Gordon, Maggie Amelia (8 mos.) d. on 70-May-3 [70-May-4: 2C].
Gordon, Mahala (84 yrs., 11 mos.) d. on 67-Jun-14 [67-Jun-17: 2C].
Gordon, Mary (59 yrs.) d. on 67-Oct-13 [67-Oct-15: 2A].
Gordon, Robert L. (3 mos.) d. on 68-Jan-10 [68-Jan-11: 2B].
Gordon, Samuel m. Lane, Annie on 66-Apr-26 [66-May-28: 2B].
Gordon, Sarah Maria (63 yrs.) d. on 69-Jun-10 [69-Jun-11: 2C].
Gordridge, George K. m. Murphy, Ella S. on 67-Nov-27 [67-Dec-2: 2C].
Gordshell, Louisa m. Cannan, Arthur W. on 70-Oct-6 [70-Oct-8: 2B].
Gordshell, Mary F. m. Downs, James H. on 66-Jul-3 [66-Nov-27: 2B].
Gore, Alfred F. m. Haughey, Sallie E. on 67-Jul-23 [68-Jan-10: 2C].
Gore, Amos (73 yrs.) d. on 69-Nov-18 [69-Dec-15: 2B].
Gore, Joseph m. Bannister, Georgetta on 70-Jan-20 [70-Jan-21: 2C].
Gore, Sarah E. (33 yrs.) d. on 70-Sep-10 [70-Sep-17: 2B].
Gorge, Thomas J. m. Grason, Elizabeth Ridgely on 68-Dec-9 [68-Dec-11: 2C].
Gorges, Minnie (5 yrs., 1 mo.) d. on 68-Dec-26 [68-Dec-28: 2C].
Gorman, Albert Ignatius (11 mos.) d. on 69-Oct-29 [69-Oct-30: 2B].
Gorman, Ellen m. McMann, Michael on 70-May-30 [70-Jun-9: 2C].
Gorman, Francis De Sales (3 yrs., 2 mos.) d. on 70-May-18 [70-May-20: 2C].
Gorman, Henry (40 yrs.) d. on 69-Sep-7 of Consumption [69-Sep-8: 2B].
Gorman, James (72 yrs.) d. on 70-Nov-10 [70-Nov-11: 2B].
Gorman, Kate m. Gambrill, Stephen on 69-Dec-22 [69-Dec-28: 2C].
Gorman, Mary Ann (71 yrs.) d. on 69-Jun-15 [69-Jun-17: 2C].
Gorman, Mary E. m. Marriott, Thomas on 66-Jan-26 [66-Jan-27: 2B].
Gorman, Mary O. m. Tierney, Thomas on 67-Feb-13 [67-Feb-26: 2C].
Gorman, W. H. m. Collins, Julia on 66-Apr-4 [66-Apr-16: 2B].
Gorman, William M. d. [70-Apr-9: 2B].
Gorman, William M. (20 yrs.) d. on 66-Dec-1 [66-Dec-3: 2B].
Gormley, Jennie m. Sutherland, J. B. on 69-Sep-15 [69-Sep-18: 2B].
Gormley, John (65 yrs.) d. on 68-Apr-15 of Pneumonia [68-Apr-16: 2B].
Gormley, Mary E. m. Dyer, J. F. on 69-Oct-6 [69-Oct-14: 2C].
Gorrell, Cassie m. Harkins, William A. on 68-Dec-15 [68-Dec-18: 2C].
Gorsuch, Amanda m. Watson, Henry F. on 69-Nov-4 [69-Nov-6: 2B].
Gorsuch, Amanda M. P. m. Hartzell, John on 67-Jun-18 [67-Jun-24: 2B].
Gorsuch, Annie m. Dukson, John on 66-Apr-17 [66-Apr-28: 2A].
Gorsuch, Bettie m. Cole, James H. on 69-Jan-19 [69-Jan-27: 2C].
Gorsuch, D. A. m. Funk, Civie C. on 68-Dec-22 [68-Dec-25: 2D].
Gorsuch, Daniel H. m. Greenwood, Susie C. on 67-Apr-25 [67-Apr-30: 2A].
Gorsuch, Edwin A. m. Ashbridge, Catherine S. on 69-Dec-9 [69-Dec-11: 2B].
Gorsuch, Elizabeth (89 yrs.) d. on 67-Jul-23 [67-Jul-25: 2C].
Gorsuch, Florence Chatard (8 mos.) d. on 68-Jul-2 [68-Jul-4: 2C].
Gorsuch, Hannah A. m. Dean, James on 67-Feb-28 [67-Mar-16: 2B].

Gorsuch, James K. P. m. Little, Susannah on 69-Feb-25 [69-Oct-14: 2C].
Gorsuch, Jane m. Baile, Lewis N. on 66-Apr-10 [66-Apr-12: 2B].
Gorsuch, John C. m. Coleman, Mary A. on 67-Dec-1 [68-Aug-13: 2B].
Gorsuch, John H. m. Whiting, Kate L. on 68-Sep-10 [68-Sep-15: 2B].
Gorsuch, John Thomas Levi (11 mos.) d. on 67-Jun-29 [67-Jul-2: 2B].
Gorsuch, Laura V. m. Hampy, F. W. [66-Feb-27: 2B].
Gorsuch, Leonard Miles (1 yr., 7 mos.) d. on 68-Aug-4 [68-Aug-5: 2B].
Gorsuch, Lewis C. m. Geis, Teresa on 68-Nov-26 [68-Dec-1: 2C].
Gorsuch, Liza (58 yrs.) d. on 70-Apr-24 of Brain inflammation [70-Apr-26: 2B].
Gorsuch, Lizzie A. m. Rainsford, Theodore A. on 67-Jul-31 [67-Aug-17: 2B].
Gorsuch, Mary F. m. Bowen, George V. on 70-May-3 [70-May-9: 2B].
Gorsuch, Mary L. m. Hogg, George C. on 68-Apr-14 [68-Apr-15: 2B].
Gorsuch, Noah F. m. Lester, Ellen A. on 68-Jan-14 [68-Jan-17: 2C].
Gorsuch, Priscilla (91 yrs.) d. on 68-Nov-28 [68-Nov-30: 2B].
Gorsuch, Robert Fayette (4 mos.) d. on 70-Jun-16 [70-Jun-23: 2C].
Gorsuch, Silas W. m. McMahon, Lizzie on 66-Oct-9 [66-Dec-29: 2C].
Gorsuch, Theodore m. Sherwood, Margaret G. on 67-Dec-5 [67-Dec-7: 2B].
Gorsuch, Thomas T., Jr. m. Mayes, S. Temple on 66-Feb-20 [66-Mar-2: 2B].
Gorsuch, William (59 yrs.) d. on 70-Nov-25 [70-Dec-3: 2B].
Gorsuch, William Peregrine (7 mos.) d. on 70-Mar-2 [70-Mar-5: 2B].
Gorsuch, William S. m. Messersmith, Louisa A. on 68-Jun-23 [68-Jun-25: 2B].
Gorsuch, William S. m. Sutton, Martha A. on 66-May-3 [66-May-14: 2B].
Gorton, Mary Emma (10 yrs., 6 mos.) d. on 67-Mar-10 [67-Mar-11: 2C].
Gosden, John T. (63 yrs.) d. on 70-Mar-25 [70-Mar-29: 2C].
Gosewich, Annie C. m. Benteen, Charles S. on 67-Nov-19 [67-Nov-21: 2C].
Goshell, Eugenia D. (45 yrs.) d. on 70-Dec-28 [70-Dec-29: 2C].
Goslin, Ellis m. Hall, Mary M. C. on 70-Dec-27 [70-Dec-31: 2B].
Goslin, Martha W. m. Willis, James on 69-Feb-25 [69-Feb-27: 2C].
Gosman, Anna Maria (74 yrs.) d. on 67-Jul-19 [67-Jul-20: 2C].
Gosman, Maria Theresa m. Rouse, R. on 66-Jun-28 [66-Jul-31: 2C].
Gosneider, Sarah J. m. Halliday, James on 67-Jun-16 [67-Jul-31: 2C].
Gosnel, Cassandra m. Donaldson, Ward H. on 67-May-28 [67-Jun-5: 2B].
Gosnell, , Capt. d. on 66-Oct-8 of Cholera [66-Oct-9: 4B].
Gosnell, Annie May (1 yr., 3 mos.) d. on 66-Aug-11 [66-Aug-16: 2C].
Gosnell, Elizabeth J. (19 yrs.) d. on 66-Nov-13 [66-Nov-17: 2C].
Gosnell, Elizabeth Mary Cecil m. Cecil, James on 66-Apr-17 [66-Apr-19: 2B].
Gosnell, Ella Lionne (1 yr., 6 mos.) d. on 69-Apr-16 [69-Apr-20: 2B].
Gosnell, Esther J. M. (45 yrs.) d. on 69-May-2 [69-May-3: 2C].
Gosnell, George T. (49 yrs.) d. on 70-Jun-24 of Erysipelas [70-Jun-25: 1G, 2B].
Gosnell, Grace Lee m. Parlett, Thomas E. on 68-Nov-17 [68-Nov-21: 2C].
Gosnell, James Wray (18 yrs.) d. on 68-Oct-6 [68-Oct-8: 2B].
Gosnell, Maggie A. m. Moore, William R. W. on 69-Apr-20 [69-Apr-28: 2B].
Gosnell, Rachel A. m. Meyers, Jacob W. on 67-Sep-11 [67-Sep-18: 2B].
Gosnell, Thomas (72 yrs.) d. on 69-Sep-24 [69-Sep-25: 2B].
Gosnell, Walter E. m. Trainer, Mary M. on 69-Jul-20 [69-Aug-16: 2B].
Goss, Emma Virginia (24 yrs.) d. on 67-Oct-21 [67-Oct-22: 2A].
Goss, Francis Marion (1 yr., 2 mos.) d. on 67-Nov-11 [67-Nov-13: 2C].
Goss, Maggie E. m. Henry, George W. on 69-Sep-22 [69-Oct-12: 2C].
Gossman, Florence K. m. Harrison, James R. on 70-May-17 [70-Jun-3: 2B].
Gossom, Fanny E. m. Crate, Frederick on 66-Nov-13 [66-Nov-20: 2B].
Gott, Alice (59 yrs.) d. on 68-Jul-20 [68-Jul-21: 2C].
Gott, Amelia (80 yrs., 11 mos.) d. [69-Apr-8: 2C].
Gottlieb, Philip (53 yrs.) d. on 69-Apr-26 [69-Apr-27: 2C].
Gottlob, Adolph d. on 70-Sep-14 Drowned [70-Sep-17: 4D].
Gottman, Fredericka (51 yrs.) d. on 67-Jan-18 [67-Jan-21: 2C].

Goudy, Elizabeth J. m. Gunther, Hammond on 70-Nov-24 [70-Nov-28: 2C].
Goudy, John (58 yrs.) d. on 68-Apr-23 [68-Apr-24: 2B; 68-Apr-25: 2B].
Goudy, Susan (27 yrs.) d. on 66-Jun-13 of Heart disease [66-Jun-14: 2B].
Gough, Alice (56 yrs.) d. on 68-Sep-29 [68-Sep-30: 2B; 68-Oct-1: 2B].
Gough, Arthur m. Frazer, Ellen L. on 67-Jun-27 [67-Jun-29: 2B].
Gough, Benedict d. on 70-Jan-20 [70-Jan-21: 2C; 70-Jan-22: 2B].
Gough, Charles E. m. Webb, Mary on 70-Nov-21 [70-Nov-22: 2B].
Gough, Fanny m. Wilson, Benjamin on 67-Oct-17 [67-Oct-21: 2B].
Gough, Harry D. d. on 67-Dec-2 [67-Dec-6: 2B].
Gough, Harry O. d. on 70-May-28 of Paralysis [70-Jun-11: 2B].
Gough, James (33 yrs.) d. on 70-Sep-24 [70-Sep-26: 2B].
Gough, Mary E. m. Glass, William on 68-Feb-13 [68-Feb-14: 2C].
Gough, Thomas W. m. Maguire, Mary G. on 66-Oct-24 [66-Oct-27: 2B].
Gould, Emma G. d. on 69-Dec-3 [69-Dec-4: 2C; 69-Dec-6: 2C].
Gould, Jane W. d. on 66-Oct-1 [66-Oct-29: 2C].
Gould, Maggie A. m. Wright, William H. on 66-Sep-13 [66-Sep-14: 2B].
Gould, T. P. (45 yrs.) d. on 70-Jul-28 [70-Jul-29: 2C].
Gould, Thomas N. (13 yrs., 7 mos.) d. on 66-Nov-16 [66-Nov-17: 2B].
Goulden, Patrick Henry (1 yr., 7 mos.) d. on 66-May-19 [66-May-21: 2B].
Gouley, Addie L. m. Hartman, Henry C. on 70-Oct-5 [70-Oct-12: 2B].
Gouley, Louis E. N. (28 yrs.) d. on 70-Mar-23 of Convulsions [70-Mar-15: 2C, 4E].
Gourley, George (61 yrs.) d. on 70-Aug-7 [70-Aug-9: 2C].
Gourley, James (36 yrs.) d. on 68-Dec-20 [68-Dec-21: 2B].
Gover, Emma Eudora (9 mos.) d. on 66-Jul-6 [66-Jul-7: 2B].
Gover, Robert m. Griffin, S. E. on 69-Apr-26 [69-Sep-1: 2B].
Gover, Samuel A. m. Matthews, Temperance on 69-May-4 [69-May-12: 2B].
Govett, Lewis Washington m. Richardson, Rebecca E. on 68-Dec-28 [68-Dec-29: 2D].
Gowens, Catherine (70 yrs.) d. on 69-Jun-9 [69-Jun-10: 2C].
Gowran, Michael m. Carr, Annie on 66-Jan-30 [66-Feb-14: 2C].
Grace, Charles H. m. Eltonhead, Molley E. T. on 68-Oct-7 [68-Oct-12: 2B].
Grace, Jacob A. (74 yrs.) d. on 67-May-22 [67-May-23: 2C].
Grace, James (60 yrs.) d. on 69-Jul-17 Drowned [69-Jul-19: 1F].
Grace, Mary R. d. on 69-Dec-17 [69-Dec-20: 2C].
Grace, Meta m. Mueller, Louis H. on 70-Apr-19 [70-Apr-23: 2B].
Grace, Rose De Clare d. on 66-Aug-19 [66-Aug-21: 2C].
Gracey, Annie M. (24 yrs.) d. on 67-Nov-15 [67-Nov-18: 2B].
Gracey, Henry, Sr. (81 yrs.) d. on 69-Sep-13 [69-Sep-14: 2B].
Gracey, Robert (69 yrs.) d. on 69-Apr-21 [69-Apr-22: 2B].
Gracey, Robert Morris (1 yr., 3 mos.) d. on 68-Mar-28 [68-Mar-30: 2B].
Gracey, William A. m. Smith, Annie R. on 70-May-22 [70-Oct-17: 2B].
Gracon, John (36 yrs.) d. on 67-May-19 of Hydrophobia [67-May-20: 1F].
Gradville, Mary Elizabeth (20 yrs.) d. on 70-Feb-9 [70-Feb-23: 2C].
Gradwohl, F. W. m. Pfister, Mary E. on 67-Jun-26 [67-Jul-1: 2B].
Grady, C. Powell m. Armistead, Sue Gordon on 67-Nov-21 [67-Nov-23: 2B].
Grady, Frank T. m. Louthan, Helen M. on 70-Jan-11 [70-Jan-13: 2D].
Grady, James (57 yrs.) d. on 68-Oct-20 [68-Oct-23: 2B].
Grady, Jane Powell m. Norris, George W. on 67-Feb-20 [67-Feb-23: 2C].
Grady, John d. on 65-Dec-31 of Assault [66-Jan-1: 1G, 2C].
Grady, Maggie m. Lepper, Charles V. on 67-Jun-13 [67-Jun-19: 2B].
Graf, Frederick B. (54 yrs.) d. on 66-Jan-12 of Pneumonia [66-Jan-13: 1G, 2C].
Graff, August (20 yrs.) d. on 70-Jul-20 Drowned [70-Jul-22: 4C].
Graff, Harriet Theodora d. on 70-Feb-7 [70-Feb-9: 2C].
Graff, James H. m. Edwards, Emma T. on 66-Nov-8 [66-Nov-10: 2B].
Graff, John D. (65 yrs.) d. on 68-Sep-9 [68-Sep-11: 2B].
Grafflin, Amanda P. m. Waters, T. Sollers on 68-Nov-26 [68-Nov-30: 2B].

Grafflin, George W. m. Wright, Mary P. on 67-Jan-4 [67-Jan-8: 2B].
Grafflin, Lewis F. m. Lyon, Mary E. B. on 68-Aug-18 [68-Nov-28: 2C].
Grafflin, Margaret P. m. Lyon, Augustus I. on 67-Oct-17 [67-Oct-19: 2A].
Grafflin, Marie Stansbury (16 yrs.) d. on 68-May-18 [68-May-19: 2B].
Grafflin, William Stewart (1 yr., 5 mos.) d. on 70-Jan-29 [70-Jan-31: 2C].
Graft, Thomas D. m. Kurtz, Ella on 66-Oct-8 [66-Nov-2: 2B].
Grafton, Alexander m. Barrett, Susan on 66-May-10 [66-May-11: 2B].
Grafton, Hettie David (1 yr.) d. on 70-Jul-23 [70-Jul-28: 2C].
Grafton, Katie m. Croggan, R. C. on 70-Feb-22 [70-Feb-24: 2C; 70-Feb-25: 2C].
Grafton, McHenry (37 yrs.) d. on 67-Mar-28 [67-Mar-29: 1F, 2B].
Graham, Amanda (30 yrs.) d. on 68-Jul-9 [68-Jul-10: 2C].
Graham, Ann (71 yrs., 1 mo.) d. on 70-Oct-15 of Paralysis [70-Oct-28: 2C].
Graham, Ann Elizabeth (51 yrs.) d. on 70-Jan-12 of Consumption [70-Jun-13: 2C].
Graham, Ann M. (78 yrs.) d. on 67-May-23 [67-May-24: 2B; 67-May-25: 2A].
Graham, Annie V. m. Sanner, A. A. on 69-Nov-30 [69-Dec-1: 2C].
Graham, Campbell (67 yrs.) d. on 66-Nov-8 [66-Nov-9: 2C; 66-Nov-10: 4B, 2B].
Graham, F. J. m. Cowdon, Mary G. on 68-Apr-30 [68-Jun-4: 2B; 68-Jun-5: 2B].
Graham, F. J. m. Condon, Mary G. on 68-Apr-30 [68-Jun-5: 2B].
Graham, George Washington (16 yrs.) d. on 67-Sep-5 [67-Sep-6: 2B].
Graham, Henry G. m. Kirkland, Amelia on 66-Aug-3 [66-Sep-3: 2C].
Graham, James D., Lt. d. on 68-Jun-18 [68-Jun-24: 1F].
Graham, Jane R. m. Schi, Ferdinand J. on 68-Mar-5 [68-Mar-13: 2C].
Graham, John (56 yrs.) d. on 68-Nov-19 [68-Nov-20: 2C].
Graham, John W. m. Sham, Lizzie on 70-Jul-12 [70-Jul-30: 2B].
Graham, Joseph A. m. Keen, Amelia R. on 67-Sep-19 [67-Sep-21: 2A].
Graham, Lizzie A. m. Houck, John T. on 69-Oct-19 [69-Oct-21: 2B].
Graham, Maggie J. m. Bargar, Jacob T. on 70-Oct-12 [70-Oct-19: 2B].
Graham, Mero S. (38 yrs.) d. on 67-Jul-18 of Consumption [67-Jul-19: 2C].
Graham, Michael (49 yrs.) d. on 68-Jul-2 [68-Jul-4: 2C].
Graham, Samuel m. Hilton, Mary E. on 70-Nov-7 [70-Nov-16: 2C].
Grahame, John M. m. Conway, M. Fannie on 68-Feb-20 [68-Feb-22: 2B].
Grain, John M. (47 yrs.) d. on 69-Feb-6 [69-Feb-8: 2C].
Grain, Lilly Isabel d. on 68-Aug-11 [68-Aug-13: 2B].
Gramblitt, Keturah B. m. Eichelberger, Charles H. on 65-Sep-18 [66-Apr-17: 2C].
Grammer, Alice W. m. Wherry, William M. on 68-Jun-10 [68-Jun-12: 2B].
Granberry, Annie M. m. Whitehurst, L. H. on 69-Oct-28 [69-Oct-30: 2B].
Granbery, Lizzie Lee (3 yrs.) d. on 69-Jan-17 [69-Jan-18: 2D].
Graner, Margaret C. m. Smith, Jerome M. on 70-Jan-18 [70-Jan-22: 2B].
Granger, Emma Ellsworth (5 yrs., 10 mos.) d. on 67-Dec-10 [67-Dec-11: 2B].
Granger, Florence May d. on 68-Jan-12 [68-Jan-13: 2C].
Granger, Frances Marion (5 yrs.) d. on 68-Jan-9 of Scarlet fever [68-Jan-11: 2C; 68-Jan-13: 2C].
Granger, Harriet (36 yrs.) d. on 69-Dec-3 [69-Dec-4: 2C].
Granger, Henry (77 yrs.) d. on 69-Jan-10 [69-Jan-11: 2C; 69-Jan-12: 2C].
Granger, James E. (34 yrs.) d. on 68-Jun-8 Murdered (Shooting) [68-Jun-9: 1F; 68-Jun-10: 2B].
Granger, John Cannadine m. Henkle, Laura Virginia on 69-Apr-22 [69-Apr-23: 2B].
Granger, Levin, Capt. (45 yrs.) d. on 70-Oct-31 [70-Nov-2: 2C; 70-Nov-3: 2B].
Granger, Maggie E. (1 yr., 9 mos.) d. on 66-May-15 [66-May-31: 2B].
Granger, Nathan (77 yrs.) d. on 66-Feb-27 [66-Feb-28: 2C].
Granger, Pere C. d. on 66-Feb-13 [66-Feb-27: 2B].
Granger, Sarah M. m. Taylor, William Harding on 68-Feb-11 [68-Feb-15: 2B].
Granger, Walter (3 mos.) d. on 67-Jun-26 [67-Jun-27: 2B].
Granger, William H. m. Hinman, Virginia E. on 70-May-25 [70-Jun-6: 2B].
Grannan, John B. (6 yrs.) d. on 66-Nov-30 [66-Dec-1: 2B].

Grannan, Mary Ann (28 yrs.) d. on 67-Dec-18 [67-Dec-20: 2B].
Grannis, Mary A. (36 yrs.) d. on 70-Jul-1 [70-Jul-2: 2B].
Grannus, John (34 yrs.) d. on 70-Jun-23 Drowned [70-Jun-25: 1G].
Granruth, Carrie m. Bock, Henry W. on 68-Sep-10 [68-Sep-14: 2B].
Granruth, William G. m. Hartlove, Maggie on 67-Jun-11 [67-Jun-24: 2B].
Grant, Alice (93 yrs.) d. on 67-Mar-11 [67-Mar-12: 2C].
Grant, Anna E. m. Fifer, Robert S. on 66-Mar-15 [66-Mar-17: 2B].
Grant, Catherine (50 yrs.) d. on 70-Sep-3 [70-Sep-5: 2C].
Grant, Ellen (33 yrs.) d. on 68-Jul-9 [68-Jul-10: 2C].
Grant, James (1 mo.) d. on 66-Jan-9 [66-Jan-11: 2B].
Grant, Jane A. (51 yrs.) d. on 70-Apr-5 [70-Apr-6: 2C; 70-Apr-7: 2C].
Grant, John m. Russell, Amanda P. on 66-Nov-6 [66-Nov-12: 2C].
Grant, Maggie J. m. Gwynne, William A. on 67-Feb-24 [67-Mar-1: 2C].
Grant, Malcolm m. Russell, Euphemia on 66-Jul-2 [66-Jul-4: 2B].
Grant, Margaret (67 yrs.) d. on 67-Jun-13 [67-Jun-14: 2B].
Grant, Mark (43 yrs.) d. on 67-May-9 [67-May-10: 2B].
Grant, Mary d. on 68-Jul-15 of Heatstroke [68-Jul-17: 1D].
Grant, Nancy (81 yrs.) d. on 69-Aug-7 [69-Aug-7: 2B].
Grant, Richard Hamilton (10 mos.) d. on 68-Sep-17 [68-Sep-26: 2B].
Grape, Andrew (50 yrs.) d. on 67-May-20 Drowned [67-May-27: 1F].
Grape, Elizabeth d. on 70-Oct-20 [70-Oct-21: 2C].
Grape, George Sanders m. Brown, Susan C. on 67-Dec-23 [67-Dec-24: 2B].
Grape, Georgia m. Rennolds, H. T. on 70-May-12 [70-May-19: 2C].
Grape, Henry Allen (8 mos.) d. on 69-Mar-31 [69-Apr-1: 2C; 69-Apr-2: 2C].
Grape, Joseph m. Allen, Mary C. on 67-Apr-18 [67-Apr-22: 2A].
Grape, Samuel m. Malone, Emma Jane on 68-Jan-15 [68-Jan-22: 2C].
Grape, Sarah Jane d. on 70-Jul-7 [70-Jul-8: 2C].
Grape, Thomas E. m. Gale, Hattie on 66-Jan-1 [66-Jan-4: 2C].
Grape, W. S. m. Richardson, Ella M. on 69-Sep-7 [69-Sep-28: 2B].
Grape, William Hamilton m. Baden, Annie on 68-Jan-28 [68-Feb-4: 2C].
Grasbinder, E. m. Numsen, William N. on 70-Oct-4 [70-Oct-24: 2B].
Grason, Elizabeth Ridgely m. Gorge, Thomas J. on 68-Dec-9 [68-Dec-11: 2C].
Grason, William (81 yrs.) d. on 68-Jul-2 [68-Jul-4: 2C].
Gratiot, Mary Louise m. Chassaing, J. H. on 66-Jul-5 [66-Jul-11: 2C].
Gravenstein, Laura J. m. Bleakley, William H. on 68-Jun-18 [68-Jun-23: 2B].
Gravenstine, Emer Jane (46 yrs.) d. on 69-Feb-8 [69-Feb-11: 2C].
Gravenstine, Jennie m. Davis, Clinton H. on 70-Jul-7 [70-Jul-11: 2C].
Graves, Anna m. Morris, James on 67-Jun-27 [67-Jun-29: 2B].
Graves, C. Lynn m. Smith, Lavinia E. on 68-Jun-11 [68-Jun-12: 2B].
Graves, Jinny (6 mos.) d. on 66-Feb-28 [66-Mar-3: 2B].
Graves, Josephine H. m. Cook, C. O. on 69-Jan-21 [69-Jan-23: 2C].
Graves, Mollie m. Erdman, Frank S. on 69-Sep-29 [69-Oct-1: 2B].
Graves, Sarah Isabella m. Way, Lewis E. on 67-Aug-7 [67-Aug-14: 2B].
Graw, Maggie M. (2 yrs., 6 mos.) d. [66-May-25: 2C].
Gray, Alberta V. m. Rosier, Jacob on 68-Dec-1 [68-Dec-5: 2C].
Gray, Alexander P. (57 yrs.) d. on 66-Jul-9 [66-Jul-10: 2C].
Gray, Alexius (69 yrs.) d. on 69-Dec-1 [69-Dec-6: 2C].
Gray, Alice M. m. Hillegeist, Arnold E. on 66-Feb-7 [66-Feb-22: 2B].
Gray, Anna m. Gill, William H. on 68-Jul-6 [68-Jul-11: 2B].
Gray, Annie (54 yrs.) d. on 70-Aug-4 [70-Aug-6: 2C].
Gray, Benjamin F. m. O'Brine, Agnes on 70-Sep-1 [70-Nov-18: 2C].
Gray, Ellenora d. on 68-Jan-31 [68-Feb-1: 2B].
Gray, Elmer (3 yrs., 5 mos.) d. on 70-Dec-28 [70-Dec-30: 2C].
Gray, Fannie m. Richardson, John R. on 69-Dec-2 [69-Dec-20: 2C].
Gray, George B. (3 mos.) d. on 70-Jul-3 [70-Jul-7: 2C].

Gray, H. Otis m. Duvall, Mary Jane on 66-Apr-26 [66-Apr-27: 2C; 66-Apr-28: 2B].
Gray, Hezekiah L. m. Bottrell, Olivia A. on 70-Aug-23 [70-Aug-27: 2B].
Gray, Howard P. m. Skinner, Imogen on 69-Oct-5 [69-Oct-12: 2C].
Gray, Irene Sands (1 yr., 5 mos.) d. on 68-Oct-13 [68-Oct-14: 2B].
Gray, Isabella m. Carey, Henry on 69-Dec-5 [69-Dec-10: 2C].
Gray, Jacob E. m. Meredith, Louisa C. on 67-Mar-19 [67-Mar-25: 2C].
Gray, James (38 yrs.) d. on 68-Jul-4 [68-Jul-7: 2B].
Gray, James m. Wheeler, Christianetta on 67-Jun-17 [67-Jun-20: 2B].
Gray, James L. (37 yrs.) d. on 67-Feb-2 [67-Feb-4: 2C].
Gray, James Thomas (4 yrs., 8 mos.) d. on 68-Jul-20 [68-Jul-21: 2C].
Gray, John (54 yrs.) d. on 70-Jun-16 of Heart disease [70-Jun-18: 2B].
Gray, Laura (3 mos.) d. on 70-Nov-13 [70-Nov-14: 2B].
Gray, Maggie m. Swain, Edward on 66-Nov-11 [66-Nov-13: 2B].
Gray, Martha Ann (66 yrs.) d. on 66-Jan-15 [66-Jan-17: 2C].
Gray, Mary (68 yrs.) d. on 69-Apr-28 [69-Apr-30: 2C].
Gray, Mary A. (63 yrs.) d. on 70-Mar-2 [70-Mar-5: 2B].
Gray, Minnie V. m. Brown, John W. on 67-May-22 [67-Jun-6: 2B].
Gray, Patrick (45 yrs.) d. on 68-May-6 [68-May-7: 2B].
Gray, Roberta F. m. Taylor, Henry on 66-Jul-30 [66-Aug-3: 2C].
Gray, Sadie T. m. Woodall, William T. on 70-Apr-14 [70-Apr-16: 2B].
Gray, Sammy (1 yr., 6 mos.) d. on 70-Aug-25 [70-Aug-26: 2C].
Gray, Susan A. (27 yrs.) d. on 68-Feb-12 [68-Feb-13: 2C; 68-Feb-14: 2C].
Gray, Thomas W. (3 yrs.) d. on 68-Jun-26 [68-Jun-27: 2B].
Gray, William Leonard Whalen (4 yrs., 8 mos.) d. on 68-Dec-2 [68-Dec-3: 2C].
Gray, Willie Leon (9 yrs., 1 mo.) d. on 68-Jul-27 [68-Jul-28: 2B; 68-Jul-29: 2B].
Graydon, James m. Tracey, Eliza on 69-Jan-4 [69-Jan-16: 2C].
Greacen, John m. Davis, Mary V. on 67-Feb-26 [67-Feb-28: 2C].
Greaner, William d. on 68-Dec-29 [69-Jan-1: 1H].
Greasley, Jacob H. m. Messersmith, Mary F. on 70-Nov-8 [70-Nov-11: 2B].
Greasley, Louisa H. m. Nelker, A. H. on 69-Jul-6 [69-Jul-17: 2C].
Greason, John (1 yr.) d. on 67-Jan-31 [67-Feb-4: 2C].
Greason, Joseph H. m. Zeigler, Elizabeth M. on 67-Jun-10 [67-Sep-9: 2B].
Greason, Margaret Ann (33 yrs.) d. on 68-Jan-27 [68-Jan-28: 2D].
Greason, Thomas, Jr. m. Spence, Mary E. on 67-Sep-17 [67-Sep-24: 2A].
Greatfield, Julia d. on 70-Jul-30 [70-Aug-15: 2C].
Grebe, Conrad d. on 68-Oct-14 in Machine accident [68-Oct-14: 1G; 68-Oct-15: 1F].
Greble, Benjamin (74 yrs.) d. on 70-Jun-7 in Railroad accident [70-Jun-8: 1G, 2C].
Greble, Joe H. m. Courtney, George A. on 70-Feb-3 [70-Feb-7: 2C].
Greely, Anna Mary Josephine (17 yrs., 6 mos.) d. on 69-May-12 [69-May-13: 2B].
Greeme, Elizabeth (33 yrs.) d. on 70-Apr-4 [70-Apr-5: 2B].
Green, Adelaide V. m. Tennant, Robert R. on 69-Dec-14 [69-Dec-16: 2C; 69-Dec-18: 2B].
Green, Agnes Virginia (28 yrs.) d. on 70-Sep-29 [70-Oct-1: 2B].
Green, Amon (57 yrs.) d. on 69-Apr-9 [69-Apr-10: 2B; 69-Apr-12: 1H].
Green, Ann G. d. on 69-Mar-19 [69-Mar-20: 2B].
Green, Catherine d. on 66-Feb-8 [66-Feb-10: 2C].
Green, Catherine Ann d. on 68-Sep-25 [68-Oct-14: 2B].
Green, Charles m. Fisher, Aminta Elizabeth on 69-May-20 [69-May-26: 2C].
Green, Charles E. (7 yrs.) d. on 68-Nov-20 of Scarlet fever [68-Dec-3: 2C].
Green, Charles Herbert (1 yr., 4 mos.) d. on 68-Aug-22 [68-Aug-26: 2B].
Green, Clara E. m. Hellman, J. A. on 69-Jan-26 [69-Jan-30: 2C].
Green, David S. (3 yrs.) d. on 68-Nov-29 of Scarlet fever [68-Dec-3: 2C].
Green, Edward d. on 67-Mar-23 [67-Apr-15: 2C].
Green, Eliza (75 yrs.) d. on 67-Mar-15 [67-Mar-16: 2B].
Green, Elizabeth (79 yrs.) d. on 69-Apr-2 [69-Apr-3: 2B].
Green, Ella P. m. Smith, Joseph F. on 69-Sep-29 [69-Oct-2: 2B].

Green, Fannie M. m. Giesendaffer, Charles P. on 67-Mar-28 [67-Jun-25: 2B].
Green, George (27 yrs.) d. on 66-Mar-29 of Suicide (Stabbing) [66-Mar-30: 1G].
Green, Israel J. m. DAILY, SUSAN on 70-Oct-23 [70-Nov-24: 2B].
Green, James H. (37 yrs.) d. on 68-Feb-17 [68-Feb-18: 2C].
Green, James Henry (11 mos.) d. on 68-Dec-24 [68-Dec-30: 2D].
Green, Jennie m. Dixon, John H. on 68-Dec-15 [68-Dec-17: 2C].
Green, Jennie m. Deitch, William on 66-Aug-5 [66-Aug-13: 2C].
Green, John F. m. Eliason, Mattie J. on 66-Apr-10 [66-Aug-17: 2C].
Green, John M., Capt. (63 yrs.) d. on 70-Apr-15 [70-Apr-16: 2B; 70-Apr-18: 2B].
Green, John N. (1 yr., 6 mos.) d. on 66-Jul-28 [66-Jul-30: 2C].
Green, John W. m. Owens, Agnes on 67-Sep-19 [67-Nov-20: 2C].
Green, Josephine m. Hampton, William A. on 66-Sep-9 [66-Sep-11: 2B].
Green, Joshua m. Burley, Elizabeth on 65-Dec-21 [66-Mar-6: 2B].
Green, Josie m. Duvall, Evans on 70-Nov-22 [70-Nov-24: 2B].
Green, Laura J. m. Morse, George W. on 67-Apr-25 [67-May-24: 2B].
Green, Louisa m. Roff, John N. on 66-Jan-1 [66-Jan-15: 2B].
Green, Lucy A. (60 yrs.) d. on 68-Jun-14 [68-Jun-20: 2B].
Green, M. Ada m. Collins, Thomas W. on 69-Dec-8 [69-Dec-11: 2B].
Green, M. Bettie m. Britton, O. Parks on 69-Dec-7 [69-Dec-10: 2C].
Green, M. Louisa m. Runge, Emil E. on 69-Sep-14 [69-Oct-5: 2B].
Green, Mary E. m. Gallaway, James L. on 66-Jun-5 [66-Jun-26: 2B].
Green, Mary Elizabeth m. Murphy, Richard D. on 70-Dec-20 [70-Dec-28: 2C].
Green, Mary Louisa (1 yr., 3 mos.) d. on 67-May-12 [67-May-13: 2B].
Green, Mary M. m. Harrison, Robert E. on 66-May-1 [66-Jul-4: 2B].
Green, Milton W. m. Robinson, Sophia E. on 66-Oct-1 [66-Nov-6: 2B].
Green, Mollie E. (1 yr., 9 mos.) d. on 67-Jan-20 [67-Jan-21: 2C; 67-Jan-22: 2C; 67-Jan-23: 2C].
Green, Nancy (57 yrs., 7 mos.) d. on 67-Apr-15 of Consumption [67-Apr-16: 2B].
Green, Nancy (81 yrs.) d. on 69-Nov-26 [69-Nov-27: 2B].
Green, O. C. m. Price, Sallie H. on 67-Nov-27 [67-Nov-28: 2C].
Green, Pemberton W. m. Morrison, Emma on 69-Jan-13 [69-Jan-18: 2C].
Green, Samuel (30 yrs.) d. on 67-Mar-24 [67-Mar-25: 2C; 67-Mar-26: 2C].
Green, Samuel (75 yrs.) d. on 69-Jan-31 [69-Feb-2: 2C].
Green, Samuel m. Williams, Georgeanna on 70-Jan-16 [70-Jan-20: 2C].
Green, Sarah A. m. Washbourn, John T. on 67-Nov-18 [67-Dec-30: 2C].
Green, Sarah H. d. on 69-Jan-24 [69-Jan-25: 2D].
Green, Selena Grace (8 mos.) d. on 69-Jul-6 [69-Jul-8: 2C].
Green, Thomas (53 yrs.) d. on 68-Nov-20 [68-Nov-21: 2C].
Green, Thomas m. Redman, Annie E. on 69-Dec-15 [69-Dec-21: 2B].
Green, Thomas J. (25 yrs.) d. on 68-Dec-27 [68-Dec-28: 2B].
Green, Vincent (42 yrs.) d. Drowned [70-Jul-4: 1H].
Green, William (65 yrs.) d. on 67-Feb-16 [67-Feb-19: 2C].
Green, William H. m. Edwards, Nannie E. on 69-Feb-16 [69-Feb-20: 2A].
Green, William H. m. Bacon, Pamela on 70-Sep-1 [70-Sep-2: 2C].
Green, William M. m. Cole, Emily V. on 67-Mar-6 [67-Mar-15: 2C].
Green, William Morris (4 mos.) d. on 70-Jun-11 [70-Jun-13: 2C].
Greenbaum, Emmanuel m. Seliger, Lina on 68-Oct-18 [68-Oct-24: 2B].
Greene, Benson M. m. Lester, Emma J. on 68-May-7 [68-May-11: 2B].
Greene, Bernard (38 yrs.) d. on 69-Mar-7 [69-Mar-8: 2C; 69-Mar-9: 2C].
Greene, Charles Piper d. on 66-Jun-2 [66-Jun-6: 2B].
Greene, Lawrence C. (10 mos.) d. on 68-Jul-13 of Brain congestion [68-Jul-18: 2B].
Greener, Mary Amanda (28 yrs.) d. on 68-Sep-4 [68-Sep-7: 2A].
Greenfield, Annie Isabella (18 yrs., 5 mos.) d. on 68-Feb-5 [68-Feb-6: 2C].
Greenfield, Aquilla H. (2 yrs., 6 mos.) d. on 68-Jul-30 [68-Jul-31: 2C; 68-Aug-1: 2B].
Greenfield, George Orem (1 yr., 6 mos.) d. on 70-Aug-5 [70-Aug-6: 2C].

Greenfield, Harriet (18 yrs., 1 mo.) d. on 66-Sep-8 of Consumption [66-Sep-10: 2D].
Greenfield, Margaret W. (46 yrs.) d. on 66-Jun-14 [66-Jun-15: 2C].
Greenfield, Thomas H. m. Maccubbin, Amelia N. on 67-Dec-5 [67-Dec-7: 2B].
Greenfield, Thomas S. m. Drexler, Emily S. on 70-Feb-23 [70-Mar-1: 2C].
Greenley, Mary E. m. Thawley, W. E. on 67-Nov-26 [67-Nov-28: 2C].
Greensfelder, Bernard (56 yrs.) d. on 68-May-21 [68-May-22: 2C; 68-May-23: 2A].
Greensfelder, Rebecca m. Hirshberg, Nathan on 69-May-23 [69-May-29: 2B].
Greensfelder, Samuel B. (21 yrs.) d. on 68-Aug-20 [68-Aug-22: 2A].
Greentree, Mervin Z (6 mos.) d. on 67-Mar-31 of Scarlet fever [67-Apr-2: 2B].
Greentree, Willie H. (9 yrs., 2 mos.) d. on 67-Apr-28 of Scarlet fever [67-Apr-29: 2B].
Greenwell, Jane E. (19 yrs., 6 mos.) d. on 66-Sep-29 [66-Oct-1: 2B].
Greenwood, Abraham (39 yrs.) d. on 68-Feb-8 [68-Feb-10: 2C].
Greenwood, James Nelson d. on 65-Sep-25 [66-Jun-20: 2C; 66-Jun-21: 2C].
Greenwood, James W. m. Hopkins, Susie R. on 67-Jan-31 [67-Feb-6: 2C].
Greenwood, Perrygan (62 yrs.) d. on 69-Apr-11 [69-Apr-12: 2A].
Greenwood, Susie C. m. Gorsuch, Daniel H. on 67-Apr-25 [67-Apr-30: 2A].
Greenwood, Walter m. Lee, Maggie on 67-Jun-27 [67-Jul-3: 2B].
Greer, Alexander d. of Heart disease [67-Oct-16: 1G].
Greer, Benjamin A. m. McCoy, Anne M. on 70-Nov-9 [70-Nov-11: 2B].
Greer, Issac (76 yrs.) d. on 67-Jul-12 of Heart disease [67-Jul-13: 2B; 67-Jul-15: 1G].
Greer, J. Allen m. Pope, Jennie E. on 69-Nov-10 [69-Nov-26: 2B].
Greer, James Richard (2 mos.) d. on 68-Jul-12 [68-Jul-14: 2C].
Greer, Margaret m. Harris, James on 66-Dec-20 [66-Dec-22: 2A].
Greer, Mary A. m. Carter, James on 69-Jun-28 [69-Jul-2: 2C].
Greer, William (54 yrs.) d. on 70-Mar-10 of Pneumonia [70-Mar-11: 2C].
Gregg, Celina C. m. Smith, Jesse on 65-Dec-12 [66-Jan-11: 2B].
Gregg, Letitia d. on 70-Jan-2 [70-Jan-8: 2B].
Gregg, Mary (26 yrs.) d. on 66-Nov-15 [66-Nov-16: 2C].
Gregg, Mary E. (16 yrs.) d. on 66-Jan-29 [66-Mar-6: 2B].
Gregg, Nancy (84 yrs.) d. on 67-Apr-28 [67-May-1: 2B].
Gregg, Robert A. d. on 68-Nov-2 [68-Nov-9: 2B].
Gregg, Susan (50 yrs.) d. on 69-May-2 [69-May-3: 2C].
Gregg, Thomas C. m. Carson, Lizzie A. on 65-Dec-11 [66-Jan-11: 2B].
Gregg, Tillie m. Mitchell, A. Godfrey on 69-Feb-23 [69-Mar-18: 2C].
Gregg, Z. T. m. Swain, Harriet V. on 70-Jun-15 [70-Jun-20: 2B].
Gregory, James C. m. Layton, Georgianna B. on 65-Mar-5 [66-Mar-5: 2B].
Gregory, Lavinia R. (69 yrs.) d. on 67-Apr-8 [67-Apr-11: 2B].
Grepp, John d. on 66-Feb-17 Murdered (Stabbing) [66-Feb-19: 1F].
Gress, Kate E. m. Geiger, E. L. H. on 70-Apr-12 [70-Apr-23: 2B].
Greves, Katie M. m. Joyce, J. A. on 67-Nov-12 [67-Nov-22: 2C].
Grew, John S. (49 yrs., 6 mos.) d. on 70-Oct-23 [70-Oct-24: 2B].
Grewe, Mary (71 yrs.) d. on 67-Mar-21 [67-Mar-25: 2C].
Grey, Agnes Stella (7 yrs.) d. on 66-May-27 [66-Jun-4: 2B].
Grey, James (64 yrs.) d. on 69-Jun-2 [69-Jun-5: 2B].
Greyson, John m. Grome, Nicolina Louisa on 66-Dec-31 [67-Jan-4: 2D].
Grice, Elizabeth (55 yrs.) d. on 67-Apr-7 [67-Apr-9: 2B].
Griefe, August (10 yrs.) d. on 68-Sep-6 of Fall from roof [68-Sep-7: 1F].
Grier, Sultina H. m. Harkins, John T. on 68-Jan-2 [68-Jan-16: 2C].
Griest, Emma F. m. Cook, Frederick, Jr. on 67-Jun-18 [67-Jun-21: 2B].
Griest, Joseph D. m. Seabrook, Mary Virginia on 66-Jul-12 [66-Jul-24: 2C].
Grieves, Adele m. Moorehead, C. Curtis on 70-Nov-16 [70-Nov-18: 2C].
Griffin, Adeline Rebecca (1 yr., 8 mos.) d. on 68-Sep-23 [68-Oct-7: 2C].
Griffin, Annie L. m. Vincent, William H. on 68-Sep-21 [68-Oct-5: 2B].
Griffin, Bessie m. Fitzpatrick, J. C. S. on 68-Oct-1 [68-Oct-2: 2B].
Griffin, Charles H. (18 yrs., 2 mos.) d. on 69-Apr-17 [69-Apr-19: 2B].

Griffin, Clara C. (57 yrs.) d. on 70-Nov-7 of Consumption [70-Nov-11: 2B].
Griffin, Dorothea m. Smith, John on 65-Dec-26 [66-Jan-1: 2C].
Griffin, Eliza (45 yrs.) d. on 70-Jun-12 of Heart disease [70-Jun-13: 1H].
Griffin, Emma C. m. Cornelius, George W. on 67-Dec-18 [68-Feb-10: 2C].
Griffin, Eugene m. Cooper, Hester Ann on 67-Dec-10 [67-Dec-19: 2B].
Griffin, Henrietta M. (55 yrs.) d. on 70-Feb-25 [70-Feb-26: 2C].
Griffin, James (17 yrs.) d. on 67-Jun-15 [67-Jun-17: 1F].
Griffin, James m. McDonald, Amelia on 68-Dec-17 [68-Dec-18: 2C].
Griffin, James E. m. O'Neale, A. Adelaide on 67-Apr-18 [67-Apr-25: 2B].
Griffin, James Ogle (1 yr., 9 mos.) d. on 68-Nov-2 [68-Nov-4: 2C].
Griffin, John (43 yrs.) d. on 66-May-6 [66-May-7: 2B].
Griffin, John Thomas m. Johnson, Laura Virginia on 69-Jul-1 [69-Jul-5: 2C].
Griffin, Julianna S. (60 yrs.) d. on 70-Feb-18 [70-Feb-26: 2C].
Griffin, Levi m. Swanberry, Mary A. on 68-Apr-30 [68-Jun-26: 2B].
Griffin, Mary Jane m. Hayes, Daniel on 68-May-28 [68-Jun-9: 2B].
Griffin, Paul (86 yrs.) d. on 69-Oct-30 [69-Nov-1: 2B].
Griffin, Robert J. (7 mos.) d. on 68-Dec-26 of Pneumonia [68-Dec-28: 2B].
Griffin, S. E. m. Gover, Robert on 69-Apr-26 [69-Sep-1: 2B].
Griffin, Samuel Franklin (11 yrs., 7 mos.) d. on 66-Nov-25 [66-Nov-26: 2B].
Griffin, Samuel J. (41 yrs.) d. on 68-Nov-2 [68-Nov-3: 2B].
Griffin, Sarah F. m. Gilbert, Calvin on 70-Dec-20 [70-Dec-30: 2C].
Griffin, Sarah H. m. Denny, Charles F. on 67-Oct-10 [67-Oct-15: 2A].
Griffin, Thomas J. m. Doyle, Maggie J. on 69-Aug-5 [69-Aug-9: 2B].
Griffin, W. Hunter m. Denison, Matilda J. on 68-Feb-6 [68-Feb-10: 2C].
Griffing, Daniel S. (50 yrs.) d. on 67-Feb-2 [67-Feb-4: 2C; 67-Feb-5: 2C].
Griffiss, Eliza W. (83 yrs.) d. on 69-Aug-25 [69-Aug-26: 2C; 69-Aug-27: 2B].
Griffiss, Elizabeth Ann Jerome (29 yrs.) d. on 68-Jan-30 [68-Feb-1: 2B].
Griffiss, Florence (8 yrs.) d. on 69-Jan-25 [69-Jan-26: 2C].
Griffiss, Kate (6 yrs.) d. on 70-Apr-26 [70-Apr-27: 2B].
Griffith, A. J. m. White, A. V. on 68-Nov-10 [68-Nov-11: 2C].
Griffith, Annie M. m. Chaney, H. C. on 68-Nov-26 [68-Dec-19: 2B].
Griffith, Barbara (74 yrs.) d. on 69-Mar-24 [69-Mar-25: 2C; 69-Mar-26: 2C].
Griffith, Barzillar m. Fint, Maggie on 69-Jun-15 [69-Jun-23: 2C].
Griffith, Daniel G. (67 yrs.) d. on 70-Nov-29 [70-Dec-1: 2C].
Griffith, David I m. Thorpe, Gertrude on 67-Jan-22 [67-Jan-24: 2C].
Griffith, Edward (86 yrs.) d. on 67-Jul-4 [67-Jul-6: 2B].
Griffith, Elizabeth (81 yrs.) d. on 67-Dec-25 [67-Dec-28: 2C].
Griffith, Elizabeth (59 yrs.) d. on 66-Jan-3 [66-Jan-4: 2C; 66-Jan-5: 2C].
Griffith, Elizabeth C. (52 yrs.) d. on 67-Apr-27 [67-Apr-30: 2A].
Griffith, G. Mason m. Startzman, Emma on 70-Apr-14 [70-Apr-19: 2B].
Griffith, George A. m. Edmonds, Hannah B. on 66-Nov-7 [66-Nov-10: 2B].
Griffith, Ginnie L. (30 yrs.) d. on 70-Mar-10 [70-Mar-17: 2C].
Griffith, Hiram Elmer (1 yr., 4 mos.) d. on 69-Jan-18 [69-Jan-19: 2C].
Griffith, Howard (73 yrs.) d. on 66-Oct-10 [66-Oct-11: 1G, 2C].
Griffith, Issac (53 yrs., 2 mos.) d. on 66-Oct-21 of Paralysis [66-Oct-22: 2C].
Griffith, Johanna m. Bates, John on 70-Apr-19 [70-Apr-21: 2B].
Griffith, Joseph (16 yrs.) d. on 68-Sep-18 Struck by pole [68-Sep-19: 1G].
Griffith, Josephine m. Smith, Milton E. on 67-Feb-19 [67-Mar-2: 2B].
Griffith, Laura m. Smith, Samuel D. on 66-Apr-24 [66-Apr-27: 2C].
Griffith, Levi P. (57 yrs.) d. on 66-Oct-3 [66-Oct-5: 2B].
Griffith, Lizzie m. Riffle, Thomas on 68-Sep-15 [68-Sep-28: 2B].
Griffith, Lucy P. m. Holmes, Alexander T. on 67-Apr-30 [67-May-9: 2A].
Griffith, Maggie A. (25 yrs., 2 mos.) d. on 68-Jul-16 [68-Jul-17: 2C].
Griffith, Margaret (64 yrs.) d. on 69-Jan-30 [69-Feb-1: 2C].
Griffith, Margaret m. Hulse, Henry on 68-Dec-15 [68-Dec-22: 2C].

Griffith, Maria (78 yrs.) d. on 68-Oct-27 [68-Oct-28: 2B].
Griffith, Maria C. d. on 69-Apr-21 [69-Apr-23: 2B].
Griffith, Maria J. m. Snowden, J. C. on 67-Oct-24 [67-Oct-28: 2B].
Griffith, Martha Rebecca (3 yrs., 3 mos.) d. on 70-Jun-28 of Whooping cough [70-Jun-30: 2C].
Griffith, Mary E. m. Davis, Laurence C. on 66-Mar-29 [66-Apr-30: 2B].
Griffith, Mary J. (2 yrs.) d. on 69-Apr-19 [69-Apr-20: 2B].
Griffith, Rebecca Jane (30 yrs.) d. on 69-Nov-3 [69-Nov-5: 2C].
Griffith, Ruth (78 yrs.) d. on 69-Feb-20 [69-Feb-23: 2D].
Griffith, Spencer Vinton (14 yrs., 8 mos.) d. on 68-Jan-3 [68-Jan-4: 2C].
Griffith, Teresa m. Taylor, Milton N. on 70-Oct-6 [70-Dec-14: 2C].
Griffith, Thomas (67 yrs.) d. on 70-Jan-28 [70-Feb-2: 2C].
Griffith, Ulysses (58 yrs.) d. on 69-Jan-17 [69-Jan-13: 2D].
Griffith, Vermadela m. McIntire, George H. on 68-Dec-22 [68-Dec-24: 2C].
Griffith, Virginia Ervin (3 mos.) d. on 69-Feb-28 [69-Mar-3: 2C].
Griffith, W. Curtis m. Royston, Fredericka M. on 68-Dec-3 [68-Dec-5: 2C].
Griffith, William (76 yrs.) d. on 70-May-21 [70-May-23: 2B].
Griffith, William Henry (6 mos.) d. on 66-Mar-8 [66-Mar-9: 2B].
Griffiths, James E. m. Keese, Minnie on 70-Oct-19 [70-Oct-22: 2B].
Griggs, Mary V. (24 yrs.) d. on 69-Nov-19 [69-Nov-20: 2B].
Griggs, William O. m. Billmyer, Emily J. on 69-Dec-15 [69-Dec-18: 2B].
Grim, Edward J. m. Meredith, Laura V. on 68-Mar-3 [68-Mar-17: 2C].
Grimes, Ann (80 yrs.) d. on 67-Sep-21 [67-Sep-27: 2B].
Grimes, Carrie V. m. Swann, James on 67-Apr-9 [67-Apr-13: 2B].
Grimes, Charles W. m. Oler, Rovenia R. on 66-Dec-20 [66-Dec-25: 2B].
Grimes, Edward (80 yrs.) d. on 67-May-29 [67-May-30: 1F, 2B].
Grimes, Elizabeth C. (30 yrs.) d. on 68-Aug-19 [68-Aug-21: 2B].
Grimes, Elnor (77 yrs.) d. on 69-May-19 [69-May-24: 2B].
Grimes, George W. (29 yrs.) d. on 70-May-10 of Consumption [70-May-11: 2B].
Grimes, James H. m. Mathews, Margaret B. on 66-Aug-16 [66-Sep-6: 2B].
Grimes, Laura F. (2 yrs., 4 mos.) d. on 70-Dec-26 of Dropsy [70-Dec-28: 2C].
Grimes, Maggie A. m. Russell, Charles F. on 70-May-10 [70-May-13: 2C].
Grimes, Marcella R. m. Ritter, Thomas H. on 68-Apr-2 [68-Apr-7: 2B].
Grimes, Martha E. (17 yrs.) d. on 68-Oct-6 [68-Oct-9: 2C].
Grimes, Sarah E. m. Scott, Henry C. on 69-Jun-20 [69-Jun-26: 2B].
Grimes, William K. m. Johnson, E. Pauline on 69-Nov-23 [69-Dec-11: 2B].
Grimes, William S. (6 yrs.) d. on 68-Sep-3 [68-Sep-5: 2A].
Grimshaw, M. Louisa d. on 68-Apr-23 [68-Apr-25: 2B].
Grimshaw, Solomon d. on 66-Feb-5 [66-Feb-10: 2C].
Grinder, Mary (19 yrs.) d. on 70-Aug-18 [70-Aug-19: 4E].
Grine, Paul (57 yrs.) d. on 70-Nov-10 [70-Nov-12: 2B].
Grinnell, John B. m. Eddins, Susan E. on 67-May-26 [67-May-30: 2B].
Griscom, Powel (50 yrs.) d. on 67-May-16 in Wagon accident [67-May-18: 1G].
Griswold, Bessie m. Thelin, William T. on 68-Sep-24 [68-Sep-25: 2B].
Griswold, Chester (85 yrs.) d. on 67-Nov-27 [67-Nov-30: 2C].
Griswold, J. F. (84 yrs.) d. on 70-Feb-20 [70-Feb-22: 2C].
Griswold, Mary Ann (69 yrs.) d. on 67-Jan-1 [67-Jan-3: 2B].
Grobe, Elizabeth (5 yrs.) d. on 66-Sep-14 [66-Sep-15: 2B].
Groff, Benjamin F. m. Denmead, Lizzie A. on 70-Apr-19 [70-Apr-26: 2B].
Groff, J. Humphreys m. King, Ollie J. on 68-Apr-30 [68-May-4: 2B].
Groff, Mary C. m. Tyson, Joshua J. H. on 69-May-19 [69-May-26: 2C].
Grogan, Thomas (19 yrs.) d. on 70-Oct-21 [70-Oct-22: 2B].
Grome, Nicolina Louisa m. Greyson, John on 66-Dec-31 [67-Jan-4: 2D].
Gronau, Virginia m. Ehrman, Louis on 69-Oct-28 [69-Oct-30: 2B].
Groome, John C. (67 yrs.) d. on 66-Nov-30 [66-Dec-3: 2B].
Groome, Lizzie B. m. Constable, Albert on 66-Jun-13 [66-Jun-20: 2C].

Grooms, Jane A. (45 yrs.) d. on 70-Apr-2 [70-Apr-4: 2B].
Grooms, Nelson T. (5 yrs.) d. on 66-Feb-22 [66-Feb-23: 2C].
Grooms, Virginia (1 yr., 9 mos.) d. on 66-Apr-21 [66-Apr-23: 2B].
Grooms, William M. m. Reddish, Joanna on 70-Nov-3 [70-Nov-30: 2C].
Grooscors, Agnes Mary (2 yrs., 9 mos.) d. on 70-Jul-2 [70-Jul-4: 2C; 70-Jul-7: 2C].
Grooscors, Herman H. d. on 70-Jul-16 [70-Jul-19: 2C].
Grosbernd, Henry m. Newton, Mary J. on 69-Mar-9 [69-Mar-27: 2C].
Groscup, Alverta m. Scarborough, William on 70-Oct-13 [70-Oct-22: 2B].
Groscup, Alverta Holliday (1 yr., 4 mos.) d. on 67-Sep-25 [67-Oct-1: 2B].
Groscup, Charles H. m. Kirk, Rachel H. on 70-Apr-28 [70-May-7: 2B].
Groscup, Frederick J. m. Nelson, Mollie T. on 67-Oct-31 [67-Nov-2: 2B].
Grosh, May (2 yrs., 5 mos.) d. on 69-Oct-7 [69-Oct-9: 2C].
Gross, Adam (70 yrs.) d. on 69-Dec-28 [69-Dec-30: 2C].
Gross, Benjamin m. Smith, Mary A. on 67-Jan-31 [67-Feb-2: 2C].
Gross, Cordelia M. m. Clark, Henry on 69-Dec-27 [69-Dec-28: 2C].
Gross, Harry T. m. Timanus, Cilla J. on 70-Oct-27 [70-Oct-29: 2B].
Gross, J. I., Jr. m. Morrison, Maggie E. on 66-Dec-26 [67-Jan-3: 2B].
Gross, John I. (72 yrs.) d. on 69-Mar-22 [69-Mar-23: 1G, 2C].
Gross, Lena m. Walter, Henry on 68-May-3 [68-May-12: 2B].
Gross, Louis E. (26 yrs.) d. on 70-Jul-5 [70-Jul-16: 2B].
Gross, Philip T. m. Watts, Josephine on 68-Aug-20 [68-Aug-21: 2B].
Gross, Rosena C. m. JOHNSON, ISSAC J. on 66-Feb-5 [66-Feb-9: 2C].
Gross, William S. (54 yrs.) d. on 68-May-8 [68-May-11: 2B].
Grote, Frederick m. Kramer, Elizabeth on 68-Nov-17 [68-Nov-24: 2C].
Grote, John (64 yrs.) d. on 69-Apr-23 [69-Apr-24: 2B].
Grothaus, Annie E. m. MacDonald, J. H. on 70-Feb-22 [70-Mar-7: 2C].
Grothaus, David m. Peduzzi, Mary R. on 69-Sep-21 [69-Sep-24: 2B].
Grothaus, Minnie m. Budeke, George H. on 69-Sep-14 [69-Sep-24: 2B].
Grothouse, Mary C. m. Larmour, Robert B. on 67-Oct-3 [67-Oct-4: 2B].
Ground, Annie H. m. Zellers, John on 68-Jul-1 [68-Jul-7: 2B].
Ground, Emma (29 yrs.) d. on 68-Jul-23 [68-Jul-24: 2C].
Grove, Ella N. m. Schultz, William A. on 68-Jan-9 [68-Jan-10: 2C].
Grove, Henrietta Randall (6 yrs., 10 mos.) d. on 66-Oct-7 [66-Oct-9: 2A].
Grove, Mary (64 yrs.) d. on 70-Apr-8 [70-Apr-9: 2B].
Grove, Salome F. m. Howell, Murdock on 68-Apr-16 [68-Apr-18: 2A].
Grove, Samuel E. m. Todd, Ruth on 67-Jun-7 [67-Jun-12: 2B].
Grove, Seth S. (27 yrs.) d. on 68-Dec-10 [68-Dec-14: 2C; 68-Dec-15: 2C; 68-Dec-16: 2C].
Grover, B. A. m. Coster, S. L. on 69-Dec-26 [70-Feb-2: 2B].
Grover, Charles d. on 66-Jun-23 [66-Jun-25: 2B].
Groverman, Richard H. m. Selden, Fannie S. on 69-Jan-27 [69-Feb-11: 2C].
Groves, William F. m. Bowersox, Laura V. on 70-May-25 [70-Jul-29: 2B].
Grubb, George (79 yrs.) d. on 69-Oct-3 [69-Oct-4: 2C].
Grubb, Martha L. d. on 70-Sep-4 [70-Sep-5: 2C; 70-Sep-6: 2B].
Grubb, Matilda (44 yrs.) d. on 70-May-7 [70-May-9: 2B].
Grubb, Richard B., Jr. m. German, Catharine A. on 66-Jun-18 [67-Feb-26: 2C].
Grubb, William A. J. (43 yrs.) d. on 68-May-15 of Consumption [68-May-16: 2B].
Grubb, Z. Taylor m. Lyons, Emma J. on 70-Aug-11 [70-Sep-15: 2B].
Gruber, Ann (71 yrs., 1 mo.) d. on 69-Feb-16 of Pneumonia [69-Mar-24: 2C].
Gruber, William H. (27 yrs., 4 mos.) d. on 70-Apr-26 [70-Apr-27: 2B; 70-Apr-28: 2B].
Grueber, Sophie (47 yrs.) d. on 70-Mar-21 [70-Mar-23: 2C].
Gruetter, Annie C. m. Waidner, Louis A., Jr. on 69-Nov-25 [69-Nov-30: 2C].
Gruinbeck, Margaret A. m. Mariner, Charles W. on 69-Feb-9 [69-Feb-12: 2C].
Grumbine, Irene d. on 70-Aug-12 [70-Aug-24: 2C].
Grumble, John C. m. Williams, Lydia C. on 67-Jun-20 [67-Jul-4: 2B].
Grupy, Jacob m. Kesler, Ellen C. on 70-Jan-6 [70-Jan-14: 2C].

Gruver, Carrie C. m. Lancaster, Martin V. B. on 67-Aug-1 [67-Sep-20: 2A].
Gruver, George W. (65 yrs.) d. on 70-Nov-8 of Apoplexy [70-Nov-9: 4C, 2C].
Gude, Anna m. Sickel, William H. on 70-Jun-29 [70-Jul-6: 2B].
Gude, Charles William (1 mo.) d. on 66-Feb-21 [66-Feb-24: 2B].
Gude, Henry Herman (10 mos.) d. on 67-Nov-6 [67-Nov-9: 2B].
Gude, Mary Elizabeth (4 yrs., 9 mos.) d. on 67-Oct-28 of Diptheria [67-Oct-31: 2B].
Guemann, Dina m. Daub, Christian on 66-Feb-11 [66-Feb-13: 2C].
Guerand, Eugene F. m. Carter, Alice C. on 70-Feb-8 [70-Apr-2: 2A].
Guerand, Francis (68 yrs.) d. on 70-Oct-26 [70-Oct-27: 2C].
Guest, Charlotte (78 yrs.) d. on 66-Jun-7 [66-Jun-8: 2B].
Guest, Elizabeth (81 yrs.) d. on 69-Sep-2 [69-Sep-3: 2B].
Guest, Florence Estelle (1 yr., 6 mos.) d. on 68-Dec-30 [68-Dec-31: 2D].
Guiest, Georgeanna E. m. Caswell, Robert B. on 70-Dec-24 [70-Dec-29: 2C].
Guild, Reese Holmes d. on 67-Sep-25 [67-Sep-27: 2C].
Guildener, Eliza d. on 68-Apr-14 of Heart disease [68-Apr-15: 2B; 68-Apr-16: 2B].
Guise, Mary C. (59 yrs.) d. on 69-Oct-26 [69-Oct-27: 2B; 69-Oct-28: 2C].
Guiteau, Jessie m. Adreon, Harrison on 68-Jun-16 [68-Jun-19: 2B].
Gulding, E. Lookingland (48 yrs.) d. on 67-Aug-24 [67-Apr-25: 2B].
Gulicek, Adelbert d. on 70-Aug-3 of Suicide (Stabbing) [70-Aug-5: 1H].
Gunby, Elizabeth A. (78 yrs.) d. on 66-Nov-26 [66-Nov-27: 2B].
Gunby, John S. d. on 70-Apr-10 Drowned [70-Apr-22: 2C; 70-Apr-23: 2B].
Gunby, Julia F. m. Malone, Lemuel on 66-Jan-10 [66-Jan-15: 2B].
Gunby, Mary S. (77 yrs.) d. on 67-Mar-10 [67-Mar-12: 2C].
Gunnel, Josephine E. (39 yrs.) d. on 68-Jan-7 [68-Jan-9: 2C].
Gunning, Annie (1 yr., 7 mos.) d. on 70-Feb-1 [70-Feb-2: 2B].
Gunnison, Hannah G. m. Albert, Henry C. on 69-Oct-21 [69-Oct-23: 2B; 69-Oct-25: 2B].
Gunther, Adolph m. Wise, Rosalie on 68-Sep-28 [68-Oct-6: 2B].
Gunther, Charles m. Radecke, Maggie on 66-Oct-17 [66-Oct-25: 2C].
Gunther, Hammond m. Goudy, Elizabeth J. on 70-Nov-24 [70-Nov-28: 2C].
Gunz, Frances M. m. Hoffman, John W. on 70-Feb-27 [70-Apr-7: 2B].
Gupton, John H. (53 yrs.) d. on 70-Aug-6 [70-Aug-12: 2C].
Guptul, John (53 yrs.) d. on 70-Aug-6 [70-Aug-15: 2C].
Gurney, Henry Paul (1 mo.) d. on 68-Mar-15 [68-Apr-14: 2A].
Gurney, Mary Lavinia m. Lange, Jacob P. on 70-Feb-23 [70-Feb-24: 2C].
Gurney, Rosedelle (1 yr., 4 mos.) d. on 66-Sep-4 [66-Sep-5: 2B].
Gustus, Israel m. Wise, Elizabeth on 68-Feb-18 [68-Feb-19: 2C].
Guteridge, William S. m. Chaney, Sarah on 69-Dec-16 [69-Dec-22: 2B].
Gutmann, John B. (46 yrs.) d. on 69-Dec-2 of Heart disease [69-Dec-4: 2C].
Guy, Alice R. m. Williams, David E. on 67-Jan-29 [67-Feb-11: 2C].
Guy, Caroline C. m. Webster, George on 66-Jun-12 [66-Jul-7: 2B].
Guy, Charles H. m. Smith, Minty on 66-Mar-29 [66-Mar-31: 2C].
Guy, Dixon m. Adams, Josie R. on 68-Dec-31 [69-Feb-18: 2C].
Guy, Edwin K. m. Dorsey, Mary Catherine on 69-Oct-21 [69-Oct-22: 2B].
Guy, Elizabeth (67 yrs.) d. on 68-Nov-1 [68-Nov-3: 2B].
Guy, Frank A. m. Sanner, Mary V. on 69-Nov-4 [69-Nov-6: 2B].
Guy, Moses (37 yrs.) d. on 69-Oct-29 [69-Oct-30: 2C].
Guy, Rutha (85 yrs.) d. on 67-Aug-13 [67-Aug-14: 2B].
Guy, Samuel, Capt. (59 yrs., 3 mos.) d. on 66-Mar-5 [66-Mar-26: 2C].
Guyer, John, Rev. d. on 67-Dec-13 of Bowel dropsy [67-Dec-21: 1G].
Guyton, Addie D. m. Spicer, Simeon on 68-May-21 [68-May-30: 2A].
Guyton, Benjamin F. m. Finley, Lizzie M. on 68-Jan-15 [68-Jan-23: 2C].
Guyton, Charles T. (37 yrs.) d. on 70-Mar-22 [70-Mar-23: 2C].
Guyton, Elenora m. Coleman, Charles R. on 68-May-31 [68-Jun-5: 2B].
Guyton, James (73 yrs.) d. on 68-Aug-12 [68-Sep-1: 2B].
Guyton, James (13 yrs.) d. on 66-Sep-27 [66-Sep-28: 2B].

Guyton, Lizzie F. m. Gillespie, Joseph J. on 68-Sep-24 [68-Sep-26: 2B].
Guyton, Marion (21 yrs.) d. on 66-Sep-3 [66-Sep-4: 2B; 66-Sep-5: 2B].
Guyton, Orville (21 yrs.) d. on 67-Sep-11 [67-Sep-12: 2B].
Guyton, William T. m. Bryan, Amanda on 67-Jul-14 [67-Jul-18: 2C].
Gwinn, Ellen m. Johnson, Samuel on 67-Dec-15 [67-Dec-17: 2B].
Gwinn, George m. Shure, Charles A. on 69-Jun-24 [69-Jun-26: 2B].
Gwinn, John H. m. Hopkins, Louisa on 70-Aug-16 [70-Aug-24: 2C].
Gwinn, Laura C. m. Hoffman, John R. on 69-Oct-14 [69-Oct-19: 2B].
Gwinn, Nancy A. (90 yrs.) d. on 70-Jul-8 [70-Jul-12: 2C].
Gwinn, Sarah (64 yrs.) d. on 68-Dec-25 [68-Dec-30: 2D].
Gwinn, William Edward (18 yrs.) d. on 70-Sep-26 [70-Sep-27: 2B].
Gwinn, William R. m. McKay, Sarah M. on 68-Jan-28 [68-Jan-29: 2C].
Gwinnell, Randolph m. Wilson, Susan on 69-Feb-4 [69-Feb-8: 2C].
Gwyn, Charles L. m. Taliaferro, Maggie B. on 68-Apr-28 [68-May-5: 2B].
Gwyn, Hugh Barrett (2 yrs., 10 mos.) d. on 69-Dec-30 [69-Jan-1: 2C].
Gwynn, A. J. m. Keene, Louise on 68-Jan-8 [68-Jan-9: 2C].
Gwynn, J. P., Capt. d. on 67-Oct-9 [67-Nov-12: 1G].
Gwynne, William A. m. Grant, Maggie J. on 67-Feb-24 [67-Mar-1: 2C].
Gylard, Charlotte (79 yrs.) d. on 70-Mar-15 [70-Mar-16: 2C].
Haas, Conrad m. Schoop, Louisa Margaret on 69-Aug-15 [69-Aug-21: 2B].
Haas, Rosa m. Krug, Thomas on 70-Aug-21 [70-Sep-27: 2B].
Haase, Herman m. Plaggemeyer, Anna on 69-Jan-17 [69-Jan-23: 2C].
Habersett, William (87 yrs.) d. on 66-Jul-2 [66-Jul-4: 2B].
Habighorst, Frederick d. on 66-Aug-4 [66-Aug-6: 2C].
Hable, Herman (60 yrs.) d. on 70-Dec-23 of Heart disease [70-Dec-24: 4D].
Habliston, Arunah A. (9 yrs., 10 mos.) d. on 66-Aug-10 Trampled by horse [66-Aug-11: 2B].
Habliston, Arunah S. (10 yrs.) d. on 66-Aug-7 [66-Aug-11: 1F].
Habliston, Henry N. G., Rev. (76 yrs.) d. on 70-Apr-2 [70-Apr-4: 1G, 2B; 70-Apr-5: 4D].
Hack, Augusta C. m. Mann, Arthur H. on 68-Aug-4 [68-Aug-8: 2B].
Hack, Cavey (2 yrs., 6 mos.) d. on 69-Sep-25 [69-Sep-30: 2B].
Hack, Charles d. on 68-Jul-16 of Brain congestion [68-Jul-17: 1F].
Hack, Emma V. m. Peters, Clarence on 67-Jan-10 [67-Jan-30: 2C].
Hack, John B. d. on 66-Jul-17 of Heatstroke [66-Jul-19: 1F].
Hack, Sallie R. d. on 69-Oct-28 [69-Nov-2: 2B].
Hack, William A. (54 yrs.) d. on 66-Dec-8 of Paralysis [66-Dec-10: 1G, 2B].
Hack, Willis A., Jr. (3 yrs., 9 mos.) d. on 69-Mar-9 [69-Mar-10: 2C].
Hacker, Louise m. Townsend, Calvin D. on 69-Oct-14 [69-Oct-18: 2C].
Hacket, George A., Capt. (64 yrs.) d. on 70-Apr-21 [70-Apr-23: 2B; 70-Apr-25: 1H].
Hackett, Charles d. on 69-Mar-25 Burned [69-Mar-26: 1H].
Hackett, Lizzie G. m. Cochran, Presley N. on 70-Aug-23 [70-Sep-7: 2B].
Hackett, Love R. m. Turpin, F. T. on 70-Dec-15 [70-Dec-31: 2B].
Hackett, Mary E. (61 yrs.) d. on 70-Mar-1 [70-Mar-2: 2C].
Hackett, R. G. d. on 68-Feb-15 of Heart disease [68-Feb-17: 1G].
Hackett, Rebecca (62 yrs.) d. on 67-Apr-2 of Dropsy [67-Apr-8: 2B].
Hackett, Robert Wesley (9 mos.) d. on 66-Aug-18 [66-Aug-22: 2C].
Hackett, S. Holland m. Sollers, Amelia on 67-Dec-12 [67-Dec-23: 2B].
Hackett, Sophia (48 yrs.) d. on 66-Nov-3 [66-Nov-5: 2B].
Hackett, Wesley Grant (2 mos.) d. on 67-Jan-13 [67-Jan-16: 2C].
Hackett, William H. (1 yr., 3 mos.) d. on 67-Sep-1 [67-Sep-2: 2B].
Hackney, Mary E. m. Johnson, William T. on 66-Nov-6 [66-Nov-10: 2B].
Hadaway, James H. (47 yrs.) d. on 70-Apr-15 [70-Apr-16: 2B].
Haddaway, Eleanora m. Wood, Isaiah E. on 66-Feb-7 [66-Feb-13: 2C].
Haddaway, Jasper McCauley (1 yr., 1 mo.) d. on 70-Jun-27 [70-Jun-28: 2C].
Haddaway, Oakley M. (45 yrs.) d. on 70-May-17 [70-May-18: 2B].
Hadel, Charles A. m. Kemp, Ella on 70-Feb-3 [70-Feb-9: 2C].

Haden, Florence E. m. Hood, J. M. on 67-Jul-17 [67-Jul-26: 2C].
Haehnlen, Maggie d. on 67-Sep-30 [67-Oct-1: 2B].
Hagan, Charles H. (1 yr., 2 mos.) d. on 66-Oct-10 [66-Oct-12: 2B].
Hagan, Daniel (63 yrs.) d. on 67-Jul-9 [67-Jul-11: 2C].
Hagan, Hugh (73 yrs.) d. on 68-Sep-9 [68-Sep-10: 2B].
Hagan, Mollie A. m. Scanlon, Michael A. on 69-Aug-18 [70-Feb-8: 2C].
Hagan, Peter m. McKenna, Mary C. on 69-May-27 [69-Jun-3: 2B].
Hagan, Petie (2 yrs., 3 mos.) d. on 66-Jul-16 [66-Jul-17: 2C].
Hagany, Sarah d. on 70-Jun-10 [70-Jun-16: 2B].
Hagelin, Charles M. (21 yrs., 8 mos.) d. on 70-Sep-8 [70-Sep-9: 2B].
Hagelin, Mary (60 yrs.) d. on 68-Sep-29 [68-Oct-3: 2B].
Hager, Emma m. Saunders, Joseph L. on 69-Jul-6 [69-Dec-23: 2B].
Hager, Margaret m. Rose, Robert C. on 69-Oct-11 [69-Oct-29: 2B].
Hagerty, Amelia m. Ely, Charles W. on 68-Jun-16 [68-Jun-20: 2B].
Hagerty, Ellen (35 yrs.) d. on 70-Nov-15 of Intemperance and exposure [70-Nov-16: 4D; 70-Nov-17: 2C].
Hagerty, Emily L. (7 yrs.) d. on 66-May-8 [66-May-9: 2B; 66-May-10: 2B].
Hagerty, Fannie m. Magarrell, J. F. on 67-Dec-12 [67-Dec-16: 2B].
Hagerty, Kate d. on 66-Jul-8 [66-Jul-9: 2C].
Hagerty, Kate m. Krager, George W. on 70-Oct-13 [70-Nov-4: 2C].
Hagerty, Margaret m. Ward, Thomas on 67-Apr-22 [68-Feb-11: 2C].
Hagerty, Mary (25 yrs.) d. on 70-Sep-16 [70-Sep-17: 2B].
Hagerty, Patrick (38 yrs.) d. on 69-Mar-23 Crushed by stone [69-Mar-24: 1H; 69-Mar-25: 2C].
Haggaman, George d. on 68-May-26 of Epilepsy [68-May-27: 1F].
Hagger, John W. (10 yrs.) d. on 69-Jul-7 Drowned [69-Jul-9: 4C; 69-Jul-12: 2D].
Haggerty, Elizabeth A. (28 yrs.) d. on 67-May-30 [67-May-31: 2B].
Haggerty, James W., Jr. m. Miller, Margaret W. on 70-Oct-6 [70-Oct-15: 2B].
Hagner, Adam (44 yrs.) d. on 69-Oct-15 [69-Oct-19: 2C].
Hagner, Cora Virginia (1 yr., 2 mos.) d. on 68-Aug-7 [68-Aug-8: 2C].
Hagner, Florence (9 yrs.) d. on 68-May-14 [68-May-15: 2B].
Hagner, William m. Carter, Esther G. on 70-Feb-8 [70-Feb-18: 2C].
Hahn, Charles Oliver (7 mos.) d. on 70-Dec-21 [70-Dec-22: 2B; 70-Dec-23: 2B].
Hahn, Daniel H. m. Towner, Melissa J. on 66-Nov-13 [66-Nov-15: 2C].
Hahn, Harry Francis (1 yr., 9 mos.) d. on 70-Dec-27 [70-Dec-29: 2C].
Hahn, Henry m. Shipley, Annie E. on 67-Dec-5 [67-Dec-7: 2B].
Hahn, John m. O'Neal, Kate A. on 67-Nov-6 [67-Nov-9: 2B].
Hahn, John, Sr. d. on 70-Jul-1 [70-Jul-2: 2B].
Hahn, John Ferdinand (8 mos.) d. on 70-Mar-31 [70-Apr-1: 2B].
Hahn, Katie m. Benz, Jesse W. on 68-Dec-23 [68-Dec-29: 2D].
Hahn, Margaret d. on 69-Jul-11 [69-Jul-14: 2D].
Hahn, Mary m. Hays, James H on 67-Jan-24 [67-Jan-28: 2C].
Hahn, Minnie m. Mansdorper, John George on 69-Dec-26 [70-Jan-4: 2C].
Hahn, Susan (67 yrs.) d. on 66-Aug-7 [66-Aug-8: 2C].
Haies, Aida Ellsworth (4 yrs., 5 mos.) d. on 67-Sep-8 [67-Sep-10: 2B].
Haight, Elizabeth Ann (23 yrs.) d. on 66-Dec-9 [66-Dec-10: 2B].
Haigley, Henry m. Weigel, Mary on 67-Apr-29 [67-Jun-20: 2B].
Haile, Amanda T. m. Jessop, George W. on 69-Dec-23 [70-Feb-21: 2B].
Haile, Minerva m. Moore, Samuel on 68-Dec-10 [69-Jan-8: 2C].
Haines, Christianna (41 yrs.) d. on 67-Jan-21 [67-Jan-22: 2C].
Haines, Emma m. Brooks, Richard on 66-Aug-14 [66-Aug-17: 2C].
Haines, Ephraim m. Ellicott, Pattie Tyson on 66-Apr-3 [66-Apr-6: 2B; 66-Apr-7: 2B].
Haines, Esther L. m. Ball, T. Sewell on 67-May-7 [67-May-9: 2A].
Haines, Frederick d. on 66-Jan-4 Drowned [66-Jan-8: 1F].
Haines, Mary (61 yrs.) d. on 66-Mar-27 [66-Apr-24: 2B].
Haines, Oakley P. m. Hopkins, Annie E. on 66-Oct-24 [66-Oct-29: 2B].

Haines, Rachel (85 yrs.) d. on 68-Apr-16 [68-Apr-21: 2B].
Haire, Michael (25 yrs.) d. on 69-Oct-5 [69-Oct-7: 2B].
Hakesley, Edward M. m. McComas, Alverta F. on 68-Dec-29 [68-Dec-31: 2C].
Hakesley, George Edward (6 mos.) d. on 70-Dec-19 [70-Dec-20: 2B].
Halbach, Charles (65 yrs.) d. on 70-Jun-6 [70-Jun-7: 2C; 70-Jun-8: 2C].
Halben, George d. on 70-Jul-1 of Heatstroke [70-Jul-2: 1G].
Halbert, Edward D. m. Hall, Georgia S. on 69-Oct-2 [69-May-12: 2B].
Halbert, Henry U. m. Brown, Orphelia J. on 69-Dec-30 [70-Jan-21: 2C].
Halbert, Mary A. m. Price, John L. on 68-Oct-21 [68-Oct-24: 2B; 68-Oct-26: 2B].
Halbert, Samuel (32 yrs.) d. on 69-Apr-15 of Consumption [69-Apr-27: 2C].
Halbig, Eva (60 yrs.) d. on 68-May-20 [68-May-22: 2C].
Hale, B. E. m. Proctor, Peter on 66-Oct-18 [66-Oct-20: 2B].
Hale, Charles W. m. Dowling, Frances M. on 70-May-23 [70-May-24: 2C].
Hale, Cornelia W. m. Ridgaway, J. Lee on 67-Jul-24 [67-Oct-21: 2B].
Hale, George E. m. Smith, Georgie H. on 69-Feb-3 [69-Feb-25: 2D].
Hale, James A. m. Chandler, Jennie on 68-Apr-16 [68-Apr-30: 2B].
Hale, Maria (83 yrs.) d. on 69-Mar-12 [69-Mar-13: 2B].
Hale, Sarah A. (67 yrs.) d. on 67-Aug-7 [67-Aug-8: 2B].
Hale, Sarah A. R. m. Mercer, Cyrus T. on 66-Feb-22 [66-Mar-2: 2B].
Hale, William D. m. Cummiskey, Mary V. on 67-Nov-26 [67-Dec-2: 2C].
Hales, S. m. Deal, Addie on 70-Dec-16 [70-Dec-17: 2B].
Haley, Ann (70 yrs.) d. on 70-Feb-17 [70-Feb-19: 2B].
Haley, John (26 yrs.) d. on 66-Jun-26 of Heatstroke [66-Jun-27: 1G].
Haley, Nellie S. m. Stirling, Yates on 67-Aug-29 [67-Sep-24: 2A].
Haley, Nicholas (52 yrs.) d. on 66-Jul-25 [66-Jul-31: 2C].
Halfpenny, Sarah Jane m. Lutz, Otto on 69-Nov-30 [69-Dec-2: 2C].
Hall, A. A. m. Hooper, Mary M. on 69-Jun-10 [69-Jun-11: 2C].
Hall, Agnes S. m. Emory, Richard on 70-Jan-4 [70-Jan-12: 2C].
Hall, Agnes V. C. m. Chappell, Thomas S. on 67-Jun-6 [67-Jun-15: 2B].
Hall, Alexander (39 yrs.) d. on 69-Aug-16 Drowned [69-Aug-17: 1H, 2C].
Hall, Alexander m. Duckett, Sophia on 69-Dec-8 [69-Dec-9: 2C].
Hall, Annie E. (40 yrs.) d. on 69-Apr-18 [69-Apr-20: 2B].
Hall, Annie Maria m. Shaw, George W. on 66-Jul-1 [66-Jul-3: 2C].
Hall, Aquilla (80 yrs.) d. on 70-Sep-9 [70-Sep-13: 1H, 2B].
Hall, Camilla F. m. Diggs, Charles F. on 70-Oct-25 [70-Oct-27: 2B].
Hall, Caroline M. m. Birckhead, John H. on 66-Sep-6 [66-Sep-10: 2D].
Hall, Charles B. m. Burger, Fannie A. on 66-May-22 [66-May-23: 2B].
Hall, Charles C. E. m. Gardner, Amanda C. on 68-May-5 [68-May-11: 2B].
Hall, Deborah (63 yrs.) d. on 67-May-15 [67-May-20: 2B].
Hall, Delia M. m. Gardner, L. N. on 66-Nov-29 [66-Dec-3: 2B].
Hall, Delilah (74 yrs.) d. on 67-Aug-3 [67-Aug-5: 2B].
Hall, Edward (1 yr.) d. on 67-Mar-28 of Dropsy [67-Mar-30: 2B].
Hall, Edward H. m. Haynes, Lydia B. on 70-Feb-10 [70-Mar-7: 2C].
Hall, Elenora Ruth Carroll (31 yrs.) d. on 69-Jan-8 [69-Jan-11: 2C].
Hall, Eliza (54 yrs.) d. on 66-Apr-16 [66-Apr-17: 2C].
Hall, Eliza (69 yrs.) d. on 69-Apr-10 [69-Apr-13: 2B].
Hall, Eliza Kitora (10 mos.) d. on 66-Jul-20 [66-Jul-21: 2C].
Hall, Elizabeth Ann (77 yrs.) d. on 70-Apr-24 [70-Apr-25: 2B; 70-Apr-26: 2B].
Hall, Emma m. Dorsey, James P. on 66-Oct-18 [66-Oct-29: 2B].
Hall, Emma C. m. Yearley, William H. on 67-Jun-27 [67-Jul-6: 2B].
Hall, F. Walters m. Robinson, Kate G. on 67-Apr-23 [67-Apr-25: 2B].
Hall, Fannie King (2 yrs.) d. on 70-Aug-8 [70-Aug-9: 2C].
Hall, Fanny m. Richards, Frisby on 68-Jun-18 [68-Jun-23: 2B].
Hall, Franklin m. Campbell, Maggie on 70-Jul-31 [70-Aug-18: 2B].
Hall, Frederick D. m. Johnson, Mary R. on 66-Mar-1 [66-Mar-5: 2B].

Hall, Freeborn G. (43 yrs.) d. on 69-Oct-17 [69-Oct-18: 2C; 69-Oct-19: 1H].
Hall, George (38 yrs.) d. on 67-Aug-20 [67-Aug-21: 2B; 67-Aug-22: 2B].
Hall, George m. Van Horn, Rebecca on 70-May-25 [70-May-27: 2B].
Hall, George H. m. Girard, Kate on 70-May-26 [70-Jun-3: 2B].
Hall, George William d. on 66-Jul-26 [66-Jul-27: 2C].
Hall, Georgia S. m. Halbert, Edward D. on 69-Oct-2 [69-May-12: 2B].
Hall, Henrietta (94 yrs.) d. on 68-Apr-30 [68-May-1: 2B].
Hall, Ibbie (5 yrs.) d. on 70-Nov-17 [70-Nov-18: 2C].
Hall, James (67 yrs.) d. on 70-Nov-17 [70-Nov-18: 2C].
Hall, James (3 yrs., 7 mos.) d. on 70-Jun-25 of Diptheria [70-Jun-28: 2C].
Hall, James P. m. Donaldson, Elexener on 69-Oct-28 [69-Oct-30: 2B].
Hall, James R. m. Hopkins, Alice C. on 67-Nov-27 [67-Nov-30: 2C].
Hall, James R. m. Clark, Annie M. on 70-Mar-27 [70-Mar-29: 2B].
Hall, James William (20 yrs.) d. on 69-Oct-23 of Heart disease [69-Oct-25: 2C].
Hall, Jane T. m. Kuhn, John on 66-Sep-27 [66-Oct-2: 2B].
Hall, Jennie m. Canter, Issac on 70-Oct-25 [70-Oct-28: 2C].
Hall, John (58 yrs.) d. on 68-Dec-14 [68-Dec-16: 2C].
Hall, John (23 yrs.) d. on 68-Jun-27 [68-Jul-1: 2B].
Hall, John d. on 70-Aug-2 of Construction cave-in [70-Aug-3: 2C, 4E].
Hall, John J. m. Richardson, Juliet P. on 67-Oct-3 [67-Nov-8: 2C].
Hall, Joshua M. (47 yrs.) d. on 66-Jun-20 [66-Jun-21: 1F, 2B].
Hall, Kate m. Young, Thomas H. on 69-Nov-30 [69-Dec-2: 2C].
Hall, Kate E. m. Drohan, Thomas [67-Oct-2: 2B].
Hall, Laura m. Kennedy, Walter S. on 69-Dec-7 [69-Dec-9: 2C].
Hall, Lenora (8 mos.) d. on 70-Mar-4 [70-Mar-5: 2B].
Hall, Liffie m. Oliver, James on 67-Jun-19 [67-Jun-22: 2B].
Hall, Lucretia m. Dew, Joshua S. on 70-Jan-1 [70-Jan-3: 2C].
Hall, Maggie A. (31 yrs.) d. on 70-Apr-6 of Consumption [70-Apr-7: 2B].
Hall, Margaret Lenora (10 mos.) d. on 69-Feb-27 [69-Mar-1: 2C].
Hall, Mary (68 yrs.) d. on 70-Apr-27 [70-May-3: 2B].
Hall, Mary m. McCann, Daniel on 67-Nov-7 [67-Nov-11: 2C].
Hall, Mary A. (32 yrs.) d. on 66-Apr-8 [66-Apr-10: 2C].
Hall, Mary A. d. on 69-Dec-16 [69-Dec-18: 2B].
Hall, Mary Alice (1 yr., 4 mos.) d. on 68-Sep-2 [68-Sep-3: 2B].
Hall, Mary Carr d. on 68-Feb-7 [68-Mar-9: 2C; 68-Mar-10: 2C].
Hall, Mary J. C. m. Goslin, Ellis on 70-Dec-27 [70-Dec-31: 2B].
Hall, Mary Jane (3 yrs., 6 mos.) d. on 68-Apr-17 [68-Apr-18: 2A].
Hall, Mary Jane (25 yrs.) d. on 67-Feb-21 [67-Feb-22: 2D].
Hall, Mary V. m. Watkins, Leonard G. on 70-Jul-22 [70-Sep-9: 2B].
Hall, Mary Washington (6 mos.) d. on 70-Aug-4 [70-Aug-5: 2C].
Hall, Millie A. m. Wright, Isaiah M. on 66-Nov-8 [66-Nov-15: 2C].
Hall, N. Edwin m. Adams, Mary E. on 68-Jan-21 [68-Jan-24: 2D].
Hall, Owen D. m. Wise, Sarah C. on 70-Mar-13 [70-Apr-5: 2B].
Hall, Regina B. m. Armstrong, Edward A. on 68-Apr-19 [68-Jun-19: 2B].
Hall, Reuben B. (11 yrs., 8 mos.) d. on 69-Sep-26 of Typhoid [69-Oct-9: 2C].
Hall, Richard Drason d. on 66-Mar-2 [66-Mar-5: 2B].
Hall, Rosina (60 yrs.) d. on 69-Apr-14 [69-Apr-19: 2B].
Hall, S. D. m. Iglehart, P. V. on 66-Dec-27 [67-Jan-24: 2C].
Hall, Sallie L. m. Hipkins, David C. on 70-Aug-24 [70-Sep-8: 2B].
Hall, Sarah Ann (75 yrs.) d. on 69-Jun-3 [69-Jun-4: 2C; 69-Jun-5: 2B].
Hall, Sarah B. (66 yrs.) d. on 66-Mar-19 [66-Mar-25: 2C].
Hall, Sarah E. m. Sears, James on 70-Apr-26 [70-May-3: 2B].
Hall, Sarah R. d. on 70-Feb-15 [70-Feb-16: 2C].
Hall, Sophia C. m. Plaskitt, Joshua on 67-Oct-8 [67-Oct-12: 2A].
Hall, Sophie m. Read, Robert F. on 70-Jul-5 [70-Jul-6: 2B].

Hall, Susan (76 yrs.) d. on 70-Jun-8 [70-Jun-9: 2C].
Hall, Theodorick L. S. (4 mos.) d. [67-Dec-10: 2B].
Hall, Thomas T. m. Busey, Kate O. on 68-Dec-21 [69-Mar-23: 2C].
Hall, William d. on 66-Dec-13 of Cholera [66-Oct-15: 4B].
Hall, William A. (32 yrs.) d. on 67-Jul-3 [67-Jul-10: 2B].
Hall, William H. m. Bishop, Ella on 68-Jun-11 [68-Jun-18: 2B].
Hall, William Henry (17 yrs.) d. on 70-Oct-25 [70-Oct-28: 2C].
Hall, William Melvin (3 yrs.) d. on 70-Jan-19 of Pneumonia [70-Jan-20: 2C].
Hall, Willie A. (11 mos.) d. on 70-Aug-12 [70-Aug-13: 2C].
Hall, Willie E. (1 yr., 9 mos.) d. on 69-Aug-17 [69-Aug-19: 2C].
Hallear, Mary A. (33 yrs.) d. on 68-May-10 [68-May-12: 2B].
Haller, Abner (37 yrs.) d. on 69-Jul-4 Drowned [69-Jul-7: 4C; 69-Jul-8: 1H; 69-Jul-12: 2D].
Hallet, Ida d. on 70-Dec-1 [70-Dec-3: 2B, 4E].
Halley, Catharine Jane (27 yrs.) d. on 67-Mar-8 [67-Mar-11: 2C].
Halliday, Christina (31 yrs.) d. on 70-May-19 [70-May-20: 2C; 70-May-21: 2B].
Halliday, James m. Gosneider, Sarah J. on 67-Jun-16 [67-Jul-31: 2C].
Halligan, Ann (68 yrs.) d. on 69-Nov-1 [69-Nov-2: 2B; 69-Nov-3: 2C].
Hallisy, E. m. Sorgler, Theodore T. on 67-Aug-8 [67-Aug-15: 2C].
Hallnay, George F. m. Shook, Elenora V. on 69-Dec-12 [70-Jan-13: 2D].
Halloran, Dennis (26 yrs.) d. on 66-Dec-3 [66-Dec-4: 2D].
Hallowell, Mary J. d. on 70-Mar-13 [70-Mar-16: 2C; 70-Mar-17: 2C].
Hallworth, Hannah (44 yrs.) d. on 67-Mar-7 [67-Mar-8: 2C].
Halpine, Winnie A. m. Schultz, Frederick on 67-Jan-30 [67-Feb-2: 2C].
Halsey, Stephen P. m. Holmes, Rebecca E. on 70-Jan-19 [70-Jan-21: 2C].
Halstead, Alfred T. m. Hergesheimer, Hannah on 68-May-28 [68-Jun-6: 2A].
Halton, Mary J., Miss m. Byrne, W. H. on 67-Jan-30 [67-Feb-12: 2C].
Halverson, Oswald R. (20 yrs.) d. on 69-Dec-20 of Fall from mast [70-Feb-24: 4E].
Hambleton, Clara m. Noel, Henry R. on 69-Dec-2 [69-Dec-4: 2C].
Hamblett, Ann (46 yrs.) d. on 69-Apr-19 [69-Apr-21: 2B].
Hamburger, Myer m. Coblens, Julia on 68-Feb-12 [68-Feb-22: 2B].
Hamel, Annie J. (2 yrs., 3 mos.) d. on 66-Mar-22 [66-Mar-24: 2B].
Hamel, Annie Maria (28 yrs.) d. on 69-Jan-13 [69-Jan-15: 2D].
Hamer, George Robert (2 yrs., 11 mos.) d. on 70-Jul-21 [70-Jul-22: 2C].
Hamer, Ida m. Tyler, James E. on 70-Nov-10 [70-Nov-15: 2C].
Hamett, Elmire m. Geoghegan, Isadora on 66-Feb-19 [66-Mar-19: 2C].
Hamil, Patrick (40 yrs.) d. on 70-Jun-17 [70-Jun-18: 2B].
Hamill, Ann (1 yr., 4 mos.) d. on 68-Sep-11 [68-Sep-12: 2B].
Hamill, Margaret J. m. Penny, Edward G. on 69-Jan-7 [69-Jan-8: 2C].
Hamill, Mary m. Redman, James E. on 68-Jan-25 [68-Feb-3: 2C].
Hamill, Robert H. m. Nickum, Margaret V. on 66-Sep-3 [66-Sep-5: 2B; 66-Sep-6: 2B].
Hamill, Samuel m. Jones, Virginia on 68-Oct-15 [68-Oct-16: 2B].
Hamilton, Alexander D. m. Shepard, Emma on 68-Feb-11 [68-Feb-14: 2C].
Hamilton, Annie Virginia (3 yrs.) d. on 69-Aug-10 [69-Aug-26: 2C].
Hamilton, Bella Maria (11 mos.) d. on 68-Jul-19 [68-Jul-20: 2B].
Hamilton, Bettie A. m. Spragins, Stith B. on 66-May-29 [66-Jun-2: 2B].
Hamilton, Caleb B., Jr. m. Hogg, Clara E. on 66-Sep-27 [66-Oct-20: 2B].
Hamilton, Catherine (31 yrs.) d. on 66-Oct-15 [66-Oct-16: 2B; 66-Oct-17: 2B].
Hamilton, Charles E. (13 yrs.) d. on 69-Sep-20 [69-Sep-27: 2C].
Hamilton, Dessie M. m. Hellen, C. W. on 67-Aug-16 [67-Aug-22: 2B].
Hamilton, Eliza (70 yrs.) d. on 70-Jul-9 [70-Jul-13: 2C].
Hamilton, Elizabeth d. on 68-Feb-21 of Consumption [68-Feb-22: 2B].
Hamilton, Estelle Mayer m. Van Kleeck, F. B. on 69-Jun-10 [69-Jun-11: 2C].
Hamilton, Eva Laselle (18 yrs., 1 mo.) d. on 66-Oct-15 [66-Oct-19: 2B].
Hamilton, Francis m. James, Susie Emily on 67-Mar-31 [67-Apr-3: 2B].
Hamilton, George D. m. Stansbury, Sarah E. on 70-Oct-24 [70-Nov-7: 2A].

Hamilton, Grace Agnes m. O'Brien, John on 68-Dec-21 [68-Dec-29: 2D].
Hamilton, Helen (41 yrs.) d. on 68-May-6 [68-May-7: 2B].
Hamilton, Helen d. on 66-Jun-18 [66-Jun-20: 2C].
Hamilton, Isabella m. Henderson, Thomas R. on 66-Aug-1 [66-Aug-6: 2C].
Hamilton, J. Frank m. Stansbury, Joanna on 69-May-26 [69-Jun-2: 2B].
Hamilton, Jacob m. Stevens, Laura A. on 66-Nov-22 [66-Dec-10: 2B].
Hamilton, James (77 yrs.) d. on 69-Oct-29 [69-Nov-1: 2C].
Hamilton, James K. P. m. Harrison, Sarah J. on 69-Feb-9 [69-Feb-19: 2C].
Hamilton, John m. Linton, Ann on 68-Nov-9 [68-Nov-17: 2C].
Hamilton, John A. m. Buckingham, Fannie C. on 68-Oct-15 [68-Oct-20: 2B].
Hamilton, John H. (29 yrs.) d. on 69-Oct-5 [69-Oct-13: 2C].
Hamilton, John Henry (11 mos.) d. on 70-Jul-15 [70-Jul-16: 2B].
Hamilton, John T. m. Hudson, Mary A. on 70-Nov-24 [70-Nov-29: 2C].
Hamilton, Joseph E. (37 yrs.) d. on 66-Oct-29 [66-Oct-30: 2B].
Hamilton, Kate (8 mos.) d. on 68-Jul-29 [68-Jul-30: 2B].
Hamilton, M. A. m. Gee, Sally B. on 68-Jul-8 [68-Jul-18: 2B].
Hamilton, Margaret (60 yrs.) d. on 68-Mar-13 [68-Mar-14: 2B].
Hamilton, Mary d. on 70-Jul-4 [70-Jul-12: 2C].
Hamilton, Mary A. m. Search, Newton C. on 68-Nov-17 [68-Nov-24: 2C].
Hamilton, Mary Bruce d. on 70-Feb-5 [70-Feb-14: 2C].
Hamilton, Mary Isabel (1 yr., 1 mo.) d. on 67-Jun-25 [67-Jun-27: 2B].
Hamilton, Rachel A. m. Carroll, James J. on 68-Jun-14 [68-Jul-6: 2B].
Hamilton, Rebecca m. Thomas, Joseph L. on 67-Sep-17 [67-Sep-21: 2A].
Hamilton, Robert m. Alloway, Sallie on 68-Jan-14 [68-Jan-21: 2C].
Hamilton, Sally m. Rhoads, James E. on 67-Jan-8 [67-Feb-5: 2C].
Hamilton, Sarah (74 yrs.) d. on 70-Aug-4 [70-Aug-6: 2C].
Hamilton, Stewart m. Miller, Joanna on 68-Aug-6 [68-Aug-11: 2B].
Hamilton, Stewart m. Martin, Mary on 67-Feb-28 [67-Mar-6: 2C].
Hamilton, Thomas Henry (14 yrs., 6 mos.) d. on 70-Dec-27 [70-Dec-28: 2C].
Hamilton, Tillie m. Barry, Edward on 69-Oct-5 [69-Oct-6: 2B].
Hamilton, Virginia m. Baldwin, Leroy E. on 69-Dec-9 [69-Dec-13: 2C].
Hamilton, William (38 yrs.) d. on 70-Jun-22 [70-Jun-23: 2C].
Hamilton, Willie Edgar (3 yrs.) d. on 70-Jul-9 [70-Jul-16: 2B].
Hamlen, William C., Capt. (61 yrs.) d. on 67-Jun-26 [67-Jun-27: 2B].
Hamlin, Frances (87 yrs.) d. on 70-Jul-29 [70-Jul-30: 2C].
Hamlin, James H. m. Clark, Maria D. on 67-May-29 [67-Jun-22: 2B].
Hamlin, Josephine d. on 70-Mar-29 [70-Apr-4: 2C].
Hamlin, Louisa m. Garaghty, Charles M. on 66-Sep-6 [66-Sep-11: 2B].
Hammack, George M. (46 yrs.) d. on 69-Jan-28 [69-Feb-2: 2C].
Hamman, Annie Mary (1 yr., 10 mos.) d. on 66-Dec-23 [66-Dec-24: 2B].
Hamman, Dorothy m. Steer, William F., Jr. on 70-Mar-30 [70-Apr-5: 2B].
Hammann, Elizabeth m. Langley, Dallas on 66-May-10 [66-Jun-21: 2B].
Hammann, Mary m. Lindeman, John on 68-Nov-15 [68-Nov-21: 2C].
Hammel, Francis Owen m. Bohrer, Christiana E. on 69-Aug-31 [69-Sep-11: 2B].
Hammel, Jacob (65 yrs.) d. on 66-Apr-18 [66-Apr-19: 2B; 66-Apr-20: 2B].
Hammel, Maggie m. Koehler, Ferdinand on 69-Jul-14 [69-Jul-19: 2C].
Hammen, Louis Lawrence (1 yr., 10 mos.) d. on 70-Oct-31 [70-Nov-1: 2C].
Hammen, M. Z. m. Elsroad, R. on 70-Nov-10 [70-Nov-15: 2C].
Hammer, John A. m. Fledderman, Minnie on 66-Feb-6 [66-Feb-12: 2D].
Hammer, Josephine m. Mayatte, Alfons on 66-Aug-5 [66-Aug-14: 2C].
Hammer, Julia F. m. Sanders, James W. on 69-Jun-13 [69-Jun-15: 2C].
Hammer, Lizzie m. Christopher, Thomas James on 67-May-8 [67-May-23: 2B].
Hammer, Peter C. (35 yrs.) d. on 66-Jul-17 [66-Aug-1: 2C].
Hammersley, Mary D. m. Horner, Albert N. on 69-Feb-9 [69-Feb-17: 2C].
Hammerslough, Lewis (66 yrs.) d. on 70-Sep-19 [70-Sep-21: 2B].

Hammersly, William N. m. Magers, Hessie V. on 67-Jan-17 [67-Jan-24: 2C].
Hammett, George R. (16 yrs.) d. on 68-Jun-28 [68-Jul-3: 2C].
Hammett, J. E. m. Burch, J. D. on 68-Nov-10 [68-Nov-12: 2C].
Hammill, Patrick (65 yrs.) d. on 70-Apr-19 [70-Apr-20: 2B; 70-Apr-21: 2C].
Hammond, Arthur Warfield (1 yr., 4 mos.) d. [69-Jul-8: 2C].
Hammond, Catherine C. (70 yrs.) d. on 68-Dec-19 [68-Dec-21: 2B, 4D].
Hammond, Elizabeth m. Bandel, George E. on 67-Feb-17 [67-Mar-4: 2D].
Hammond, Ella J. m. Merryman, Charles D. on 70-Mar-10 [70-Mar-22: 2C].
Hammond, Ellen A. d. on 69-Nov-21 [69-Nov-24: 2C].
Hammond, George m. Connolly, Mary on 70-Apr-6 [70-Apr-16: 2B].
Hammond, H. Jane A. m. Bowerman, James Biays on 67-Aug-7 [67-Aug-15: 2C].
Hammond, Henrietta m. Dennis, John L. on 70-Sep-22 [70-Sep-24: 2B].
Hammond, John m. Stockman, Sophia on 68-May-29 [68-Jun-2: 2B].
Hammond, John A. (45 yrs.) d. on 68-Sep-30 of Consumption [68-Oct-3: 2B].
Hammond, John L. (81 yrs.) d. on 68-May-12 [68-May-13: 2B].
Hammond, Joshua m. Ledley, Augusta on 69-Jun-29 [69-Jun-30: 2C].
Hammond, Mary M. m. Dorsey, Richard H. on 69-Sep-1 [69-Sep-2: 2B].
Hammond, Matilda A. d. on 67-Oct-21 [67-Oct-26: 2A].
Hammond, Nannie m. Tubman, Samuel A. on 66-Apr-17 [66-Apr-28: 2A].
Hammond, Nellie E. m. Wann, James H. on 68-Dec-3 [68-Dec-28: 2B].
Hammond, Peter m. Ducket, Mary on 66-Sep-27 [66-Sep-27: 2C].
Hammond, Richard E. m. Anthony, Mary R. on 69-Oct-7 [69-Oct-9: 2C].
Hammond, Susan M. (36 yrs.) d. on 66-Apr-22 [66-Apr-23: 2B].
Hammond, William S. m. Thomas, Lizzie A. on 66-Mar-6 [66-Mar-8: 2B].
Hammontree, Mary m. Watson, James E. on 66-Jul-2 [66-Jul-4: 2B].
Hamner, Jane m. Vickers, Albert on 67-Oct-15 [67-Oct-19: 2A].
Hampson, A. J. m. O'Leary, Annie on 70-Mar-24 [70-Mar-25: 2C; 70-Mar-26: 2B].
Hampson, William A. m. Donigan, Annie E. on 67-Nov-25 [68-Jan-4: 2C].
Hampton, Josephine (26 yrs.) d. on 70-Jun-28 [70-Jun-29: 2C].
Hampton, William A. m. Green, Josephine on 66-Sep-9 [66-Sep-11: 2B].
Hampy, F. W. m. Gorsuch, Laura V. [66-Feb-27: 2B].
Hamtramck, Florence m. Shepherd, James H. on 67-Mar-5 [67-Mar-8: 2C].
Han, John N. m. Hancock, Kate on 70-Nov-30 [70-Dec-8: 2B].
Hanan, Anna Jane (10 yrs.) d. on 70-Jan-13 [70-Jan-15: 2C].
Hanan, William Pinkney (7 mos.) d. on 66-Jul-26 [66-Jul-27: 2C].
Hanberry, Eliza m. Diment, James C. on 69-Dec-13 [69-Dec-14: 2C].
Hance, Ella Chesley m. McCaw, W. R. on 70-Nov-8 [70-Nov-29: 2C].
Hance, Julia m. Lebrun, Henry on 66-Apr-25 [68-Jan-31: 2C].
Hanchett, Loretta C. m. Bosley, Amon on 68-May-7 [68-Jun-25: 2B].
Hancock, Elizabeth (59 yrs.) d. on 66-Feb-28 [66-Mar-2: 2B].
Hancock, Francis M. d. on 70-Jun-4 [70-Jun-6: 2B].
Hancock, Francis M. m. Patterson, Mary Isabel on 70-May-23 [70-Jun-6: 2B].
Hancock, Kate m. Han, John N. on 70-Nov-30 [70-Dec-8: 2B].
Hancock, Mamie Lizzie (10 mos.) d. on 70-Jul-15 [70-Jul-19: 2C].
Hancock, Mary Ann (26 yrs.) d. on 67-Feb-3 [67-Feb-5: 2C].
Hancock, Maud (1 yr., 11 mos.) d. on 68-Jan-24 [68-Jan-29: 2D].
Hancock, Orlando m. Johnson, Martha A. on 66-Oct-4 [66-Oct-11: 2C].
Hancock, Sarah A. (41 yrs.) d. on 65-Nov-26 [66-Jun-12: 2B].
Hand, Alexander (78 yrs.) d. on 68-Nov-11 [68-Nov-12: 2C].
Hand, Alice Jane (2 yrs., 2 mos.) d. on 68-Nov-22 [68-Nov-23: 2B].
Hand, Margaret A. d. on 70-Oct-31 [70-Nov-1: 2C; 70-Nov-2: 2C].
Hand, Mary J. m. Phelps, J. B. T. on 66-May-31 [66-Jun-6: 2B].
Hand, Willie (1 mo.) d. on 69-Dec-27 [69-Dec-28: 2D].
Handley, Mollie A. m. Turpin, Albert S. on 67-Jun-6 [67-Jun-8: 2B].
Hands, Mary (23 yrs.) d. on 68-Nov-12 [68-Nov-14: 2B].

Hands, Washington m. Beach, Annie S. on 67-Oct-21 [67-Nov-14: 2B].
Handy, A. Ward m. Nicholson, Hattie E. on 70-Apr-28 [70-May-10: 2B].
Handy, Arianna m. Sutro, Otto on 69-Oct-28 [69-Oct-29: 2B].
Handy, D. C. m. Bagwell, Nannie on 69-Nov-18 [69-Nov-20: 2B].
Handy, James A. m. Trives, Rachel S. on 69-Jun-2 [69-Jun-3: 2B].
Handy, John Francis (3 yrs., 4 mos.) d. on 67-Oct-20 [67-Oct-21: 2B].
Handy, Lindsay Talliaferro (9 mos.) d. on 67-Jul-3 [67-Jul-6: 2B].
Hanes, George B. (9 mos.) d. on 67-Jun-30 of Cholera infantum [67-Jul-1: 2B].
Haney, Charles M. (48 yrs.) d. on 69-Jun-16 of Apoplexy [69-Jun-17: 2C, 4C; 69-Jun-19: 1G, 2B].
Haney, Frances Edith (1 yr., 1 mo.) d. on 67-Aug-20 [67-Sep-11: 2B].
Haney, McHenry m. Davis, Hester A. on 68-May-24 [68-May-26: 2B].
Haney, Sarah Jane m. Conrad, William D. on 67-Mar-7 [67-Mar-9: 2B].
Hanitramck, Eliza m. Williamson, L. on 69-Jan-20 [69-Jan-25: 2D].
Hank, August d. on 69-Jun-17 of Cholera morbus [69-Jun-18: 1G].
Hank, Serena Peale (68 yrs.) d. on 70-Jul-9 [70-Jul-13: 2C].
Hank, William, Rev. (73 yrs.) d. on 69-Mar-31 [69-Apr-5: 2B].
Hanks, Emma Virginia (20 yrs.) d. on 68-Feb-16 [68-Feb-18: 2C].
Hanks, Euell O. (20 yrs., 3 mos.) d. on 70-Dec-13 of Consumption [70-Dec-15: 2C].
Hanks, J. Edwin m. Frist, Lizzie Harrison on 66-Jul-19 [66-Jul-21: 2C].
Hanlen, John (63 yrs.) d. on 67-Jul-8 of Consumption [67-Jul-9: 2B; 67-Jul-10: 2B].
Hanlen, Mary Ann d. on 67-May-19 [67-May-20: 2B; 67-May-21: 2B].
Hanlin, James (45 yrs.) d. on 68-Jan-27 [68-Jan-28: 2D].
Hanlon, Agnes C. d. on 69-Apr-20 [69-Apr-21: 2B; 69-Apr-22: 2B; 69-Oct-7: 2B].
Hanlon, Edward (49 yrs.) d. on 70-Jun-16 [70-Jun-17: 2B].
Hanlon, Francis T. (6 mos.) d. on 66-Aug-3 [66-Aug-4: 2C].
Hanly, Andrew (30 yrs.) d. on 67-May-22 [67-May-23: 2C].
Hanly, George Edward (9 yrs.) d. on 68-Jun-14 [68-Jun-15: 2B].
Hanly, Martin C. d. on 69-Dec-4 [69-Dec-6: 2C].
Hanly, Mary m. Dorritee, Lorenzo on 67-Nov-30 [67-Dec-6: 2C].
Hanly, Patrick J. (22 yrs.) d. on 69-Jan-13 [69-Jan-14: 2D].
Hann, Charles m. Macher, Susie P. on 70-Jun-9 [70-Jun-14: 2B].
Hann, H. Clay m. Yeagel, Sarah on 68-Oct-29 [68-Nov-9: 2B].
Hanna, Alexander B. m. Myers, Amelia on 66-Apr-23 [66-Apr-25: 2B].
Hanna, Amelia (29 yrs.) d. [69-Jul-21: 2C; 69-Jul-22: 2C].
Hanna, Annie d. on 70-Dec-14 [70-Dec-16: 2C].
Hanna, Araminta Morrison (2 mos.) d. on 68-Nov-13 [68-Nov-14: 2B].
Hanna, Bettie m. Brookhart, Thomas J. on 68-Apr-23 [68-May-15: 2B].
Hanna, George m. Gardiner, Mary on 69-Dec-14 [69-Dec-20: 2C].
Hanna, Henry, Jr. d. on 66-Feb-25 Burned [66-Feb-26: 1F].
Hanna, Kate Chase (4 mos.) d. on 67-Jul-2 [67-Jul-6: 2B].
Hanna, Lizzie A. m. Brown, James A. on 68-Nov-5 [68-Nov-7: 2B].
Hanna, Louise (1 yr., 6 mos.) d. on 69-Sep-16 [69-Sep-18: 2B].
Hanna, Mary S. (72 yrs.) d. on 70-Oct-26 [70-Oct-27: 2B].
Hanna, William Eagin (32 yrs.) d. on 70-Oct-9 [70-Oct-11: 2B].
Hannagan, Margaret (71 yrs.) d. on 68-May-21 [68-May-22: 2C; 68-May-23: 2A].
Hannagan, Peter (17 yrs.) d. on 66-Jan-11 Drowned [66-Mar-6: 1F, 2B].
Hannah, Lillie (1 yr., 7 mos.) d. on 69-Jan-1 [69-Jan-2: 2C].
Hannah, Madam d. on 68-Jan-22 [68-Jan-23: 2C].
Hannah, Thomas L. (18 yrs.) d. on 66-Oct-14 [66-Oct-15: 2B].
Hannan, George (35 yrs.) d. on 67-Jul-30 of Suicide (Stabbing) [67-Jul-31: 1E].
Hannan, Patrick (40 yrs.) d. on 67-Sep-7 of Consumption [67-Sep-9: 2B].
Hanney, Mary A. (68 yrs.) d. on 69-Jan-6 [69-Jan-7: 2C].
Hannon, Bernard (52 yrs.) d. on 68-Sep-24 Murdered (Assault) [68-Sep-25: 1G, 2B; 68-Sep-26: 2B, 4C].

Hanrahan, Agnes (2 yrs., 4 mos.) d. on 70-Aug-22 [70-Aug-23: 2B].
Hanratta, James (26 yrs.) d. on 69-Oct-28 [69-Oct-29: 2C].
Hanratty, Patrick (27 yrs.) d. on 66-Apr-18 [66-Apr-19: 2B].
Hanson, Ann Margaret m. Browning, Samuel David on 70-Aug-24 [70-Aug-30: 2B].
Hanson, Annie (8 mos.) d. on 70-Aug-26 [70-Aug-27: 2B].
Hanson, Casaner (56 yrs.) d. on 66-Nov-25 [66-Nov-27: 2B].
Hanson, Eli (66 yrs.) d. on 67-Oct-6 [67-Oct-11: 2B].
Hanson, Elias (32 yrs.) d. on 67-Apr-24 of Consumption [67-Apr-26: 2B].
Hanson, Ella W. (5 mos.) d. on 70-Jul-26 [70-Jul-27: 2C].
Hanson, Ellie (2 yrs.) d. on 67-Feb-2 [67-Feb-7: 2C].
Hanson, Emma m. Fagen, Hugh E. on 68-Jul-5 [68-Jul-7: 2B].
Hanson, F. B. m. Wakeland, M. C. on 67-Jan-10 [67-Jan-18: 2C].
Hanson, Homer H. m. Forney, Martha A. on 68-Feb-13 [68-Feb-15: 2B].
Hanson, Ida Elizabeth (5 mos.) d. on 66-Jun-4 [66-Jun-8: 2B].
Hanson, Isabel m. Keagle, Henry on 70-Aug-9 [70-Sep-21: 2B].
Hanson, James m. Banks, Margaret on 68-Dec-10 [68-Dec-12: 2C].
Hanson, James Henry (1 yr.) d. on 69-Aug-8 [69-Aug-10: 2C].
Hanson, John N. m. Gardener, Elizabeth A. on 66-Nov-26 [67-Feb-4: 2C].
Hanson, Laura Davis (9 mos.) d. on 68-Nov-2 [68-Nov-4: 2C].
Hanson, Martha Ann (20 yrs.) d. on 69-Mar-28 [69-Apr-8: 2C].
Hanson, Mary B. (59 yrs.) d. on 70-Nov-27 [70-Nov-29: 2C].
Hanson, Mary E. d. on 68-Jun-27 [68-Jun-29: 2B].
Hanson, Mary T. (22 yrs.) d. on 70-Dec-12 [70-Dec-14: 4E].
Hanson, Washington R. m. Williams, Elenora Teresa on 70-May-10 [70-May-25: 2C].
Hanson, William E. (49 yrs.) d. on 68-Feb-29 [68-Mar-2: 2B].
Hanson, Willie (1 yr., 1 mo.) d. on 67-Apr-1 [67-Apr-2: 2B].
Hanway, Eleanor (71 yrs.) d. on 70-Dec-22 [70-Dec-23: 2B].
Hanway, Eliza L. m. Bowen, Joseph M. on 66-Jan-17 [66-Jan-27: 2B].
Hanway, G. William m. Birckhead, Olivia on 66-Apr-24 [66-May-3: 2C].
Hanway, Hattie B. m. Rouse, John G. on 66-Apr-25 [66-May-7: 2B].
Hanway, Sarah V. m. Kenly, James F. on 70-Nov-30 [70-Dec-20: 2B].
Hanzsche, Lizzie d. on 70-Oct-13 [70-Oct-14: 2B].
Hanzsche, Mary Elizabeth (10 mos.) d. on 69-Jun-17 [69-Jun-19: 2B].
Hanzsche, Robert (8 mos.) d. on 67-Jun-25 [67-Jun-27: 2B].
Hapner, Cordelia (38 yrs.) d. on 67-Mar-7 [67-Mar-9: 2B].
Happoldt, Eugenia A. m. Lombard, Henry C. on 66-Oct-18 [66-Oct-29: 2B].
Happoldt, Eveleen T. m. Wright, Joseph T. on 70-Dec-8 [70-Dec-20: 2B].
Happoldt, Jane (58 yrs.) d. on 69-Jun-4 [69-Jun-5: 2B].
Happoldt, Marian L. m. Kirk, William W. on 69-Mar-22 [69-Mar-26: 2C].
Harback, Charles m. Warren, Mary J. on 68-Aug-18 [68-Dec-4: 2D].
Harback, Emily Verona (2 yrs., 2 mos.) d. on 70-Dec-9 [70-Dec-12: 2C].
Harban, Katie d. on 69-Jan-30 of Typhoid [69-Feb-2: 2C].
Harbaugh, Benjamin (76 yrs.) d. on 69-Sep-30 [69-Oct-2: 2B].
Harbaugh, Ella Virginia (8 mos.) d. on 66-Jul-1 [66-Jul-3: 2C].
Harbaugh, Nellie m. Davis, Joseph P. on 66-Aug-9 [66-Aug-17: 2C].
Harbaugh, T. F. (34 yrs., 8 mos.) d. on 70-Aug-29 [70-Aug-31: 2B].
Harbaugh, T. J. m. Shuler, Julia on 70-Sep-28 [70-Oct-1: 2B].
Harbert, George (22 yrs.) d. on 67-Aug-10 [67-Aug-13: 2B].
Harbert, W. H. H. m. Nicholson, Millie J. on 68-May-13 [68-May-15: 2B].
Harburger, A. m. Oberndorf, Fannie on 69-Feb-8 [69-Feb-22: 2C; 69-Feb-23: 2C; 69-Feb-24: 2C].
Harburger, Issac (30 yrs.) d. on 68-Feb-19 [68-Feb-20: 2C; 68-Feb-21: 2B].
Harcourt, Francis Howard (2 yrs., 10 mos.) d. on 70-Feb-8 of Scarlet fever [70-Feb-9: 2C].
Harcourt, Lottie (4 yrs., 3 mos.) d. on 70-Jan-18 of Scarlet fever [70-Jan-20: 2C].
Harden, Catherine m. Ringgold, Samuel on 66-Nov-29 [66-Dec-6: 2B].

Harden, Edwin Summerfield (8 mos.) d. on 66-Jul-8 [66-Jul-13: 2C].
Harden, Emma (5 yrs., 1 mo.) d. on 67-Mar-9 [67-Mar-13: 2C].
Harden, Georgeana m. Bennett, Eli on 66-Feb-8 [66-Feb-22: 2B].
Harden, John, Jr. (21 yrs.) d. on 70-Aug-28 [70-Aug-29: 2C].
Harden, Penelope (74 yrs.) d. on 66-May-24 [66-May-26: 2B].
Hardenbrook, Walter Rooke (7 mos.) d. on 68-Apr-16 [68-Apr-18: 2C].
Hardester, Charles m. Pickering, Sarah E. on 67-Jan-7 [67-Jan-27: 2C].
Hardester, George E. m. Mayo, Josephine E. A. on 66-Aug-30 [66-Sep-11: 2B].
Hardester, Maria (1 yr., 7 mos.) d. on 66-Aug-15 [66-Aug-16: 2C].
Hardesty, Annie (24 yrs.) d. on 67-Jan-16 [67-Jan-17: 2C].
Hardesty, B. McLean m. Elder, Charlotte H. on 70-Apr-26 [70-Apr-30: 2A].
Hardesty, Belle m. Robb, John on 68-Nov-5 [68-Nov-9: 2B].
Hardesty, Charles R. (46 yrs.) d. on 67-Oct-7 [67-Oct-8: 2B].
Hardesty, Eliza Mclean d. on 66-Jan-12 of Apoplexy [66-Jan-15: 1G, 2C].
Hardesty, George W. m. Chester, Martha V. on 70-Jul-12 [70-Nov-26: 2B].
Hardesty, Georgie m. Gilliss, Joseph A. on 70-Dec-20 [70-Dec-23: 2B].
Hardesty, John m. Hughes, Hannah A. on 68-Jul-9 [68-Jul-11: 2B].
Hardesty, John J. (57 yrs.) d. on 68-Oct-8 of Paralysis [68-Oct-9: 1F, 2C].
Hardesty, Lavinia m. Gardner, John S. P. on 70-Feb-11 [70-Feb-12: 2B].
Hardesty, Lizzie D. m. Owens, Alexander, Jr. on 67-Nov-21 [67-Nov-23: 2B].
Hardesty, Mary Cromwell (52 yrs.) d. on 66-Feb-12 [66-Feb-14: 2C].
Hardesty, Mary Custis d. on 69-May-12 [69-May-13: 2B; 69-May-14: 2C].
Hardesty, Mary Custis (5 mos.) d. on 69-Mar-30 [69-Apr-1: 2C].
Hardesty, Mary E. m. Wilson, Edwin C. on 67-Jul-22 [67-Jul-23: 2C].
Hardesty, Matilda m. Siebert, David on 68-Jun-10 [68-Jun-12: 2B].
Hardesty, Richard C. (64 yrs.) d. on 67-Oct-7 [67-Oct-12: 2B].
Hardesty, Sarah (92 yrs.) d. on 68-Feb-9 [68-Feb-12: 2C].
Hardesty, Thomas J. (62 yrs.) d. on 67-Jun-10 [67-Jun-14: 2B].
Hardesty, Thomas J. m. Miller, Frances V. on 69-Dec-14 [70-Aug-23: 2C].
Hardesty, William T. (45 yrs.) d. on 70-Mar-4 [70-Mar-14: 2D].
Harding, , Capt. d. on 66-May-14 [66-May-16: 2C; 66-May-15: 2C].
Harding, Albert (5 mos.) d. on 66-Oct-27 [66-Oct-23: 2B].
Harding, Caroline T. d. on 68-Sep-29 [68-Oct-1: 2B].
Harding, George d. on 66-Oct-13 of Cholera [66-Oct-15: 4B].
Harding, James E. m. Lyons, Ellen on 69-Nov-9 [69-Nov-22: 2C].
Harding, M. B. m. Tubman, Willie A. on 70-Apr-5 [70-Apr-21: 2B].
Harding, M. Virginia m. Iglehart, J. H. on 69-Mar-9 [69-Mar-10: 2C].
Harding, Mary d. on 66-Oct-13 of Cholera [66-Oct-15: 4B].
Harding, Priscilla (81 yrs.) d. on 66-Sep-12 [66-Sep-27: 2C].
Harding, Sarah A. m. Copper, James D. on 67-Nov-5 [67-Nov-7: 2C].
Harding, William H. (35 yrs.) d. on 70-Jun-19 [70-Jun-21: 2B].
Hardisty, Alice Eugenia m. Small, William on 67-Apr-25 [67-Apr-27: 2A].
Hardman, Asa S. m. Watts, Mary E. H. on 67-Jun-7 [67-Jun-8: 2B].
Hardy, Andrew J. (10 mos.) d. on 67-Nov-30 [67-Dec-2: 2C].
Hardy, Anna F. (25 yrs.) d. on 66-Mar-4 [66-Mar-7: 2B].
Hardy, Caroline F. A. (17 yrs.) d. on 68-May-6 [68-May-8: 2B].
Hardy, Dennis (35 yrs.) d. on 70-Apr-26 in Railroad accident [70-Apr-27: 1H].
Hardy, Emma E. (1 yr.) d. on 70-Jun-19 [70-Jun-20: 2B].
Hardy, Emma Rose (9 mos.) d. on 68-Dec-19 [68-Dec-21: 2B].
Hardy, George E. W. m. Regester, Eliza J. on 68-Oct-6 [68-Oct-8: 2B].
Hardy, Hugh M. (55 yrs.) d. on 67-Oct-18 [67-Oct-19: 2A].
Hardy, James (35 yrs.) d. on 66-Jul-16 of Heatstroke [66-Jul-17: 1F].
Hardy, Susan m. Gardner, William C. on 69-Dec-22 [69-Dec-24: 2C].
Hare, E. m. West, Charles on 69-May-13 [69-Jun-2: 2B].
Hare, Henry m. Stinhagen, Sarah on 66-Oct-6 [66-Oct-18: 2B].

Hare, John R. m. McConniken, Minnie E. on 67-Oct-15 [67-Oct-16: 2B].
Harford, Charles Dallas m. Frederick, Georgeanna on 68-Sep-28 [68-Oct-1: 2B].
Harford, Helen (63 yrs.) d. on 68-Mar-5 [68-Mar-7: 2B].
Harford, Henrietta Emma Helen (6 mos.) d. on 67-Oct-7 [67-Oct-8: 2B].
Harford, Marion (7 mos.) d. on 70-Jun-27 [70-Jun-28: 2C].
Hargrave, Frances m. Tate, James E. on 68-Oct-28 [68-Nov-5: 2C].
Hargrove, Sidney Virginia m. Booker, Thomas L. on 68-Feb-25 [68-Mar-3: 2C].
Harig, John Bernard (83 yrs.) d. on 69-May-1 [69-May-3: 1H, 2C].
Harig, John Joseph m. Spies, Julia A. on 68-Sep-8 [68-Sep-10: 2B].
Harig, Mary A. d. on 67-May-14 [67-May-15: 2B].
Haring, Frederick M. (20 yrs.) d. on 66-Feb-20 [66-Feb-21: 2D].
Hariss, Charles O. (40 yrs.) d. on 67-Jan-5 [67-Jan-7: 2C].
Harker, Andrew J. (53 yrs.) d. on 67-Jun-19 [67-Jun-21: 2B].
Harker, Henrietta (44 yrs.) d. on 70-Oct-29 [70-Oct-31: 2B].
Harker, Ida May d. on 68-Oct-3 [68-Oct-5: 2C].
Harker, James H. W., Jr. (1 yr., 6 mos.) d. on 70-Jun-9 [70-Jun-10: 2B].
Harker, Mary Rebecca (6 yrs.) d. on 66-Dec-22 [67-Jan-3: 2C].
Harker, Samuel (30 yrs.) d. on 68-Oct-10 of Heart disease [68-Oct-12: 1F].
Harkins, John H. m. Toy, Sallie E. on 68-Nov-11 [68-Nov-12: 2C].
Harkins, John T. m. Grier, Sultina H. on 68-Jan-2 [68-Jan-16: 2C].
Harkins, William A. m. Gorrell, Cassie on 68-Dec-15 [68-Dec-18: 2C].
Harkness, Margaret (1 yr.) d. on 68-Aug-19 [68-Aug-20: 2B].
Harkness, Margaret A. d. on 68-Jun-5 [68-Jun-6: 2A].
Harkness, Margaret J. (56 yrs.) d. on 69-May-9 [69-May-11: 2B].
Harkness, Mary Elizabeth (21 yrs., 4 mos.) d. on 69-Dec-23 [69-Dec-24: 2C; 69-Dec-25: 2C].
Harkness, Mutary (74 yrs.) d. on 67-Dec-9 [67-Dec-10: 2B].
Harkness, Robert Patterson (1 yr., 10 mos.) d. on 67-Aug-12 [67-Aug-14: 2B].
Harlan, Esther m. Hawkins, William L. on 66-Jul-31 [66-Aug-3: 2C].
Harlan, George S. m. Archer, Mary E. G. on 70-Dec-14 [70-Dec-19: 2C].
Harley, Huldah (59 yrs.) d. on 67-Jul-21 [67-Jul-22: 2C].
Harley, Joseph W. (21 yrs.) d. on 67-Sep-1 [67-Sep-2: 2B].
Harlon, John (25 yrs.) d. on 67-Jun-14 [67-Jun-15: 1G, 2B].
Harlow, Issac (66 yrs.) d. on 69-Oct-23 [69-Oct-27: 2B; 69-Oct-28: 2C].
Harman, Edward L. m. Wagner, Rosa C. on 69-Nov-18 [69-Nov-20: 2B].
Harman, Elizabeth d. on 66-Aug-19 of Lung hemorrhage [66-Aug-21: 2C].
Harman, Gussie d. on 69-Jul-9 [69-Jan-12: 2C].
Harman, Jacob T. (51 yrs.) d. on 68-Feb-8 [68-Feb-10: 2B].
Harman, John Of Andrew d. on 66-Jan-1 [66-Jan-3: 2C; 66-Jan-5: 2C].
Harman, Kate P. m. Black, William E. on 69-Jan-21 [69-Jan-25: 2D].
Harman, Lizzie K. m. Arthur, J. Fleming on 66-Dec-20 [66-Dec-25: 2B].
Harman, Samuel (59 yrs.) d. on 70-Feb-28 [70-Mar-1: 2C].
Harman, William H. (50 yrs.) d. on 68-Aug-14 [68-Aug-18: 2B].
Harman, William H., Jr. m. Travis, Zenophine on 68-Oct-15 [68-Oct-19: 2B].
Harney, James (60 yrs.) d. on 69-Aug-9 of Epilepsy [69-Aug-11: 1H].
Harney, Luke (50 yrs.) d. on 69-May-3 [69-May-4: 2B].
Harney, St. George d. [69-Feb-25: 1H].
Harnickel, Wilhelmine m. O'Donnell, George W. on 68-Nov-24 [68-Dec-5: 2C].
Harp, Emma C. m. Freyer, John on 70-Jun-23 [70-Jul-4: 2C].
Harp, John Hezekiah (51 yrs.) d. on 68-Aug-24 [68-Aug-25: 2B].
Harp, Laurence d. on 69-Jul-12 in Railroad accident [69-Jul-13: 4C].
Harp, Nicholas d. on 70-Nov-17 Drowned [70-Nov-22: 4D].
Harper, Ann (60 yrs.) d. on 68-May-6 [68-May-8: 2B].
Harper, Ann m. Westcott, James on 66-May-15 [66-May-18: 2C].
Harper, Harriet T. m. Phillips, Wesley on 66-Sep-11 [66-Sep-12: 2A].
Harper, Helen J. D. m. Shipley, H. C. on 68-Dec-3 [68-Dec-4: 2D].

Harper, J. H. d. on 66-Aug-13 of Cholera morbus [66-Aug-15: 4C].
Harper, J. S., Dr. (41 yrs.) d. on 70-Jul-29 [70-Jul-30: 2B].
Harper, James Emory m. Prince, Catherine Amelia on 68-Mar-31 [68-Apr-3: 2C].
Harper, James H., Rev. (78 yrs.) d. on 68-Mar-10 [68-Mar-11: 2B].
Harper, John (50 yrs.) d. on 67-Feb-15 of Construction cave-in [67-Feb-20: 2C; 67-Feb-23: 1G].
Harper, John m. Crook, Jane A. on 66-Nov-12 [66-Nov-14: 2B].
Harper, John Wesley (9 mos.) d. on 69-Jul-21 [69-Jul-24: 2C].
Harper, Mary m. Burrier, Augustus on 67-Jun-20 [67-Jun-22: 2B].
Harper, Mary A. (68 yrs.) d. on 69-Feb-19 [69-Feb-20: 2A].
Harper, Prestbury (68 yrs.) d. on 67-Mar-30 [67-Apr-1: 2C].
Harper, Samuel m. Houston, Maggie J. on 67-Jan-1 [67-Jan-4: 2D].
Harper, Samuel W. (24 yrs.) d. on 67-Nov-3 [67-Nov-5: 2B].
Harr, Charles E. m. Farson, Mary E. on 66-Sep-18 [66-Sep-24: 2B].
Harr, John N. d. on 69-Feb-5 [69-Feb-8: 2C].
Harr, Peter (79 yrs.) d. on 70-Jul-26 [70-Jul-27: 2C; 70-Jul-28: 2C].
Harrell, Carmia (23 yrs.) d. on 68-Apr-16 [68-Apr-17: 2B].
Harriday, Virginia m. Stevens, Thomas on 68-Dec-22 [68-Dec-23: 2C].
Harries, Mary m. Hatton, George C. on 69-Aug-19 [69-Sep-17: 2C].
Harrigan, Andrew (66 yrs.) d. on 67-May-12 [67-May-15: 2B].
Harrigan, Ellen m. Hughes, Henry on 66-Feb-5 [66-Feb-23: 2C].
Harrigan, Mary d. on 66-Jul-18 [66-Jul-19: 2C].
Harriman, Sophia Simmons (28 yrs.) d. on 70-Mar-18 [70-Mar-19: 2B].
Harrington, Daniel (26 yrs., 7 mos.) d. on 69-Feb-27 Murdered (Shooting) [69-Mar-1: 1G; 69-Mar-2: 1H, 2C].
Harrington, Edmund (11 mos.) d. on 68-Jul-17 [68-Jul-24: 2C].
Harrington, John (76 yrs.) d. on 67-Aug-9 [67-Aug-12: 2C].
Harrington, Mary E. (41 yrs.) d. on 69-Jul-8 [69-Jul-10: 2B].
Harrington, Patrick A. m. Golden, Mary C. on 70-Jan-23 [70-Jan-29: 2B].
Harrington, Samuel (66 yrs.) d. on 67-Aug-17 [67-Aug-19: 2C].
Harris, Agnes m. Chew, Robert B. on 69-Nov-3 [69-Nov-6: 2B].
Harris, Ann Ennels (86 yrs.) d. on 68-Jan-24 [68-Jan-28: 2D; 68-Jan-29: 2D].
Harris, Anna Amelia m. Wallace, George A. on 70-Nov-29 [70-Dec-2: 2C].
Harris, Anna M. m. Chapman, D. C. on 69-Nov-23 [69-Nov-27: 2B].
Harris, Anna R. m. Mathews, Henry on 68-Nov-5 [68-Nov-7: 2B].
Harris, Annie C. m. Jamison, Robert on 68-Sep-29 [68-Oct-1: 2B].
Harris, Annie C. m. Owens, Benjamin B. on 69-Nov-18 [69-Nov-20: 2B].
Harris, Annie J. (1 yr., 11 mos.) d. on 67-Oct-13 [67-Oct-14: 2B].
Harris, Augusta F. m. Rockwell, Alfred H. on 68-Sep-28 [68-Sep-30: 2B].
Harris, David (26 yrs.) d. on 68-Mar-20 [68-Mar-21: 2A].
Harris, E. G. m. Zeigler, Mollie F. on 67-Nov-12 [67-Nov-14: 2B; 67-Nov-15: 2B].
Harris, Edna m. Ockamay, James H. on 66-Oct-9 [66-Oct-10: 2B].
Harris, Elizabeth (82 yrs., 11 mos.) d. on 69-Jan-5 [69-Feb-6: 2C].
Harris, Ellen (42 yrs.) d. on 70-Feb-22 [70-Feb-24: 2C].
Harris, George C. (15 yrs., 4 mos.) d. on 66-Nov-4 [66-Nov-6: 2B].
Harris, Gulielma d. on 70-Aug-5 [70-Aug-6: 2C].
Harris, Henry Wilson (54 yrs.) d. on 69-Apr-29 [69-Apr-30: 2C].
Harris, Hicks (65 yrs.) d. on 66-Apr-25 [66-Apr-28: 2A].
Harris, Ida m. Cole, James on 68-Nov-19 [68-Dec-8: 2C].
Harris, Imogene d. on 66-Mar-23 [66-Mar-28: 2C].
Harris, Isabella F. m. Chambers, H. Preston on 67-Dec-25 [68-Jan-15: 2C].
Harris, James m. Greer, Margaret on 66-Dec-20 [66-Dec-22: 2A].
Harris, James C. d. on 66-Aug-30 [66-Sep-1: 2B].
Harris, John Henry d. on 67-Jun-20 Drowned [67-Jun-22: 1G].
Harris, John L. m. Nizer, Sarah E. on 69-Mar-31 [69-May-20: 2C].

Harris, John P. m. McNeir, Anna R. on 67-May-28 [67-Jun-1: 2B].
Harris, Joseph (72 yrs.) d. on 68-May-18 [68-May-22: 2C].
Harris, Joseph (17 yrs.) d. on 66-Feb-19 [66-Feb-21: 2C].
Harris, Laura m. Gale, James Harper [69-Nov-17: 2C].
Harris, Lethe Ann (55 yrs.) d. on 69-Apr-22 [69-Apr-23: 2B; 69-Apr-24: 2B].
Harris, Louisa (33 yrs.) d. on 69-Aug-13 [69-Aug-14: 2C].
Harris, Margaret J. m. Ford, William H. on 68-Jul-5 [68-Aug-15: 2B].
Harris, Maria L. m. Jessop, George A. on 65-Dec-14 [66-Jan-1: 2C].
Harris, Mary H. m. Keefer, Albert W. on 70-Nov-23 [70-Nov-29: 2C].
Harris, Mary Jane (47 yrs.) d. on 70-Dec-21 [70-Dec-22: 2B].
Harris, Nancy M. m. Steigerwald, John W. on 66-Jan-11 [66-Jan-25: 2C].
Harris, Richard (68 yrs.) d. on 66-Nov-15 [66-Nov-20: 2B].
Harris, S. R. m. Gill, A. E. on 68-Nov-17 [69-Feb-14: 2C].
Harris, Sallie m. Crise, John on 67-Oct-7 [67-Nov-9: 2B; 67-Nov-11: 2C].
Harris, Samuel, Jr. (59 yrs.) d. on 70-Jun-12 [70-Jun-14: 1G, 2B; 70-Jun-15: 1H].
Harris, Samuel K. m. Hayward, Clara M. on 70-Feb-3 [70-Feb-5: 2B].
Harris, Samuel Y. m. Jones, Minnie on 70-Apr-28 [70-May-3: 2B].
Harris, Sarah Ann (33 yrs.) d. on 70-Aug-21 [70-Aug-22: 2B].
Harris, Sarah G. d. on 69-Jan-3 [69-Jan-4: 2C; 69-Jan-5: 2C].
Harris, Susan C. (18 yrs.) d. on 70-May-7 [70-May-9: 2C].
Harris, Susan T. (71 yrs.) d. on 66-May-29 [66-May-31: 2B].
Harris, Thomas (11 yrs.) d. on 67-Jul-28 Drowned [67-Jul-29: 1F].
Harris, Thomas Furlong (19 yrs.) d. on 66-Apr-19 [66-Apr-21: 2B].
Harris, Thomas G. d. on 68-Jan-16 [68-Jan-29: 2D].
Harris, William H. m. Fowler, Margaret E. on 68-Oct-27 [68-Nov-5: 2C].
Harrisk, Mary Dornin (3 yrs., 7 mos.) d. on 67-May-9 of Scarlet fever [67-May-14: 2B].
Harrison, Ann Louisa (24 yrs., 9 mos.) d. on 70-Sep-15 [70-Sep-17: 2B].
Harrison, Anna d. on 67-Dec-24 [67-Dec-25: 2C].
Harrison, Anne Jennetta Grant (10 mos.) d. on 67-Apr-26 [67-Apr-29: 2B].
Harrison, Annie (1 yr.) d. on 66-Jul-8 [66-Jul-9: 2C].
Harrison, Araminta C. (78 yrs.) d. on 66-Feb-9 [66-Feb-10: 2C].
Harrison, Bridget Annie (23 yrs., 11 mos.) d. on 70-Jun-6 [70-Jun-27: 2C].
Harrison, Champion J. m. Stier, Annie M. on 69-Jan-18 [69-Jan-25: 2D].
Harrison, Charles A. (1 yr., 7 mos.) d. on 67-Jun-1 [67-Jun-6: 2B].
Harrison, Charles O. m. Rankin, Agnes on 69-Oct-27 [69-Oct-30: 2B].
Harrison, Charles S. m. Dalrymple, Margaret R. on 66-Dec-6 [66-Dec-8: 2B; 66-Dec-10: 2B].
Harrison, Edward m. Chaney, Elizabeth on 69-May-2 [69-May-6: 2B].
Harrison, Edwin A. Dalrymple (10 mos.) d. on 68-Aug-3 [68-Aug-4: 2C].
Harrison, Elizabeth d. on 66-Mar-12 [66-Mar-16: 2B].
Harrison, Emily E. m. Lyon, Samuel H. on 69-Jul-8 [69-Jul-9: 2C].
Harrison, Eugenia A. m. Councell, William H. on 69-May-19 [69-May-22: 2B].
Harrison, James (82 yrs., 1 mo.) d. on 70-Oct-20 [70-Oct-21: 2C].
Harrison, James M. (55 yrs.) d. on 69-Feb-8 [69-Feb-9: 2C].
Harrison, James P. m. Hosmer, Hattie A. on 70-Dec-8 [70-Dec-22: 2B].
Harrison, James R. m. Gossman, Florence K. on 70-May-17 [70-Jun-3: 2B].
Harrison, Jesse (97 yrs.) d. on 66-Nov-6 [66-Nov-8: 2C].
Harrison, John m. Sheckels, Bernettie on 70-Oct-4 [70-Oct-5: 2B].
Harrison, John O. (2 yrs., 5 mos.) d. on 68-Nov-28 [68-Nov-30: 2C].
Harrison, John W. m. Maccubbin, Mollie F. on 66-Dec-20 [66-Dec-24: 2B].
Harrison, Joseph Marion (6 yrs., 6 mos.) d. on 70-Jul-17 [70-Jul-22: 2C].
Harrison, Josephine m. Applegarth, John A. on 66-Oct-11 [66-Oct-18: 2B].
Harrison, Josiah m. Burnham, Elizabeth on 70-Oct-16 [70-Oct-22: 2B].
Harrison, Louisa Emma (8 mos.) d. on 66-Jul-30 [66-Jul-31: 2C].
Harrison, M. A. d. on 66-Nov-1 [66-Nov-2: 2B].
Harrison, Maria (71 yrs.) d. on 66-Jan-25 [66-Jan-26: 2B].

Harrison, Martha m. Turner, H. T. on 68-Jun-11 [68-Jun-23: 2B].
Harrison, Mary A. (57 yrs.) d. on 70-May-8 [70-May-9: 2B; 70-May-10: 2B].
Harrison, Mary Jane (47 yrs.) d. on 70-Dec-21 [70-Dec-23: 2B].
Harrison, Mary Spencer m. Noble, Horace on 68-Oct-20 [68-Nov-2: 2B].
Harrison, Mary Wilson m. Birckhead, Lennox on 69-Jun-3 [69-Jun-9: 2C].
Harrison, Phil. L. m. Willson, Mary L. on 66-Jun-26 [66-Jun-28: 2C].
Harrison, Richard H. (4 yrs., 7 mos.) d. on 69-Aug-10 [69-Aug-11: 2C].
Harrison, Robert E. m. Green, Mary M. on 66-May-1 [66-Jul-4: 2B].
Harrison, Robert O. (22 yrs.) d. on 67-Dec-11 [67-Dec-13: 2C].
Harrison, Robert R. m. Frederick, Lydia A. on 67-Dec-23 [68-Sep-14: 2B].
Harrison, Sallie E. m. Armager, Benjamin F. on 68-Dec-17 [68-Dec-25: 2D].
Harrison, Samuel m. Diggs, Kate B. on 69-Jan-14 [69-Jan-20: 2C].
Harrison, Sarah A. (63 yrs.) d. on 69-Feb-17 [69-Feb-20: 2A].
Harrison, Sarah J. m. Young, John W. on 66-Mar-26 [66-Apr-7: 2B].
Harrison, Sarah J. m. Hamilton, James K. P. on 69-Feb-9 [69-Feb-19: 2C].
Harrison, Sidney (48 yrs.) d. on 66-Oct-26 [66-Oct-29: 2C].
Harrison, Susanna Spencer (11 mos.) d. on 68-Jul-5 [68-Jul-8: 2B].
Harrison, Susannah (85 yrs.) d. on 66-Oct-6 [66-Oct-8: 2B].
Harrison, Susie m. Ross, George L. on 68-May-17 [68-May-21: 2B; 68-May-22: 2C].
Harrison, Susie V. (20 yrs.) d. on 69-May-2 [69-May-8: 2B].
Harrison, Thomas Beauchamp (6 mos.) d. on 68-Mar-12 [68-Mar-24: 2B].
Harrison, Thomas Francis (10 mos.) d. on 68-Dec-16 [68-Dec-18: 2C].
Harrison, William (72 yrs.) d. on 70-Jan-25 [70-Jan-26: 1G, 2C].
Harrison, William m. Howard, Emma J. on 68-May-7 [68-May-9: 2B].
Harrison, William m. Gilmore, Emma on 68-Apr-15 [68-Apr-18: 2A].
Harrison, William Edward (11 yrs.) d. on 69-May-17 [69-May-18: 2C; 69-May-19: 2C].
Harrison, William Evans (1 yr., 10 mos.) d. on 70-Mar-19 [70-Mar-21: 2C].
Harrison, William Henry (2 yrs., 8 mos.) d. on 66-Oct-29 [66-Oct-30: 2B].
Harrison, William J. (75 yrs.) d. on 66-Jun-11 [66-Jun-27: 2C].
Harrison, William N. (62 yrs.) d. on 68-Jul-16 [68-Jul-17: 1F, 2B].
Harrison, William S. (93 yrs.) d. on 69-Aug-8 [69-Aug-18: 2C].
Harrisse, Nanine (69 yrs.) d. on 70-Mar-14 [70-Mar-15: 2C].
Harryman, Charles C. m. Poteet, Elizabeth H. on 69-May-24 [69-Jun-1: 2B].
Harryman, David S. (52 yrs.) d. on 68-Apr-7 [68-Apr-9: 2B].
Harryman, Sallie F. m. Brener, Nathaniel H. on 67-Aug-15 [67-Aug-21: 2B].
Harsh, Moses (33 yrs.) d. on 68-Feb-28 [68-Mar-2: 2C; 68-Mar-3: 2C; 68-Mar-6: 2C].
Hart, Ann Rachel (72 yrs.) d. on 68-May-2 [68-May-5: 2B].
Hart, Annie d. on 70-Nov-11 [70-Nov-12: 2B].
Hart, Charles S. (1 yr., 3 mos.) d. on 70-Aug-3 [70-Aug-4: 2C].
Hart, Elizabeth m. Binnix, John H. on 66-Feb-1 [66-Apr-20: 2B].
Hart, Frank m. Scott, John T. on 68-Jan-1 [68-Jan-11: 2B].
Hart, Frank Gilbert (2 yrs., 4 mos.) d. on 68-Apr-6 [68-Jun-3: 2B].
Hart, George A. m. Schaefer, Mary E. on 67-Dec-26 [68-Jan-2: 2C].
Hart, Harriet (76 yrs.) d. on 68-Aug-4 [68-Aug-5: 2B].
Hart, Harry S. d. on 67-Jun-21 [67-Jun-22: 2B].
Hart, Henrietta V. m. Parvis, John H. on 70-Mar-16 [70-Mar-21: 2C].
Hart, Hettie Jane m. Mordecai, David on 66-Nov-13 [66-Nov-15: 2C].
Hart, James (9 yrs.) d. on 66-May-1 [66-May-2: 2B].
Hart, Josephine m. Meldick, John on 70-Nov-13 [70-Nov-17: 2C].
Hart, Lizzie May (10 yrs.) d. on 66-Oct-2 [66-Oct-4: 2B].
Hart, Malcolm m. Shaw, Katie E. on 70-Jun-30 [70-Jul-4: 2C].
Hart, Mary A. m. Bunting, W. A. on 68-Jan-27 [68-Feb-7: 2C; 68-Feb-8: 2B].
Hart, Matilda m. Gobright, William H. on 67-Nov-6 [67-Nov-7: 2C].
Hart, Nettie m. Humrichouse, W. H. on 70-Dec-15 [70-Dec-17: 2B].
Hart, Rebecca P. (72 yrs.) d. on 67-Mar-2 [67-Mar-20: 2C].

Hart, Robert J. m. Bowman, Laura M. on 69-Jun-28 [69-Jul-16: 2C].
Hart, Sarah E. d. on 67-Jan-2 [67-Jan-3: 2B].
Hart, Victoria A. m. Wagner, George on 66-Feb-6 [66-Feb-8: 2C].
Hart, William James (17 yrs.) d. on 70-Feb-12 of Yellow fever [70-Apr-2: 2B].
Harten, Francis Simpson (1 yr., 8 mos.) d. on 67-Sep-18 [67-Sep-19: 2B].
Hartenstein, Alvin m. Ehrman, Annie on 69-Nov-16 [69-Nov-18: 2C].
Hartigan, John T. m. Keelan, Mary Teresa on 70-Feb-16 [70-Feb-26: 2C].
Harting, Charles m. McMillan, Margaret A. on 66-Sep-11 [66-Sep-15: 2B].
Hartke, Joseph E. m. Shick, Annie K. on 70-Feb-24 [70-Feb-26: 2C].
Hartley, Charles H. m. Flaherty, Barbara on 70-Jun-2 [70-Jun-9: 2C].
Hartley, Elizabeth A. m. Shinnick, Ormsby W. on 67-Jan-31 [67-Feb-2: 2C].
Hartley, George (7 mos.) d. on 70-Jul-12 [70-Jul-14: 2B].
Hartley, Georgeanna (5 mos.) d. on 69-Jun-29 [69-Jul-1: 2C].
Hartley, Henry (21 yrs.) d. on 69-Nov-3 [69-Nov-5: 2C; 69-Nov-4: 2C].
Hartley, Howard m. Wardenburg, Sallie E. on 70-Apr-28 [70-May-2: 2B].
Hartley, Susannah (83 yrs.) d. on 67-Feb-17 [67-Feb-19: 2C].
Hartline, Henry (64 yrs.) d. of Erysipelas [67-Jul-24: 1G].
Hartlove, Asbury m. Dyer, Jane on 69-Apr-13 [69-Apr-28: 2B].
Hartlove, Elinzeena m. Linthicum, Thomas S. on 69-Feb-25 [69-Feb-26: 2D].
Hartlove, Joseph M. m. Rider, Elizabeth H. on 66-Apr-11 [66-Apr-21: 2B].
Hartlove, Maggie m. Granruth, William G. on 67-Jun-11 [67-Jun-24: 2B].
Hartlove, Mary C. (3 yrs., 11 mos.) d. on 68-Oct-10 [68-Oct-13: 2C].
Hartlove, Thomas P. m. Sherwood, Laura J. on 69-Jun-29 [69-Jul-2: 2C].
Hartlove, Westley (57 yrs.) d. on 70-Jul-11 [70-Jul-12: 2C].
Hartlove, William W. m. Wessels, Annie E. on 69-Nov-18 [69-Nov-20: 2B].
Hartmaier, Henry m. Volz, Mary Lizzie on 67-Jan-8 [67-Jan-10: 2C].
Hartmaier, Mary Elizabeth (10 mos.) d. on 70-Sep-20 [70-Sep-22: 2C].
Hartman, F. C. m. Burleigh, Deborah M. on 69-Oct-21 [69-Oct-29: 2B; 69-Oct-30: 2B].
Hartman, Fannie m. Hartman, Henry on 70-Feb-9 [70-Feb-17: 2C].
Hartman, Gottfried Herman (37 yrs.) d. on 69-Jul-17 of Apoplexy [69-Jul-19: 1G].
Hartman, Henry m. Hartman, Fannie on 70-Feb-9 [70-Feb-17: 2C].
Hartman, Henry C. m. Gouley, Addie L. on 70-Oct-5 [70-Oct-12: 2B].
Hartman, John d. on 70-Jul-1 of Suicide (Drowning) [70-Jul-2: 1G].
Hartman, John d. on 68-Jul-16 of Heatstroke [68-Jul-18: 1E].
Hartman, John m. Williams, Mary on 66-Feb-19 [66-Feb-20: 2B].
Hartman, John Henry (9 mos.) d. on 67-Jul-31 [67-Aug-20: 2B].
Hartman, Julia Ann (20 yrs., 8 mos.) d. on 68-Jul-30 [68-Jul-31: 2C].
Hartman, Lewis (35 yrs.) d. on 70-Aug-1 Drowned [70-Aug-2: 4D].
Hartman, Martha Irene (8 mos.) d. on 69-Feb-13 [69-Feb-15: 2C].
Hartman, Mary (78 yrs.) d. on 70-Nov-13 [70-Nov-15: 2C].
Hartman, Mary Catherine (27 yrs.) d. on 69-Nov-28 [69-Nov-30: 2C].
Hartman, Milton F. m. Norfolk, Louise S. on 66-May-9 [66-May-14: 2B].
Hartman, Philip m. Thomas, Julia A. on 67-Feb-14 [67-Apr-23: 2B].
Hartman, Philip m. Thomas, Mary Ellen on 70-Nov-23 [70-Dec-3: 2B].
Hartman, Samuel (73 yrs.) d. on 67-Mar-6 [67-Mar-7: 2C; 67-Mar-8: 2C].
Hartman, William m. Miller, Eliza on 69-Apr-18 [69-May-15: 2B].
Hartmann, Maggie Elizabeth (9 mos.) d. on 68-Aug-19 [68-Aug-21: 2B].
Hartmier, Richard Dwen d. on 68-Aug-20 [68-Aug-22: 2A].
Hartmier, Richard J. m. Dwen, Maria L. on 65-Dec-26 [66-Jan-2: 2C].
Hartsock, S. M. m. Lewis, Mary E. on 69-Jan-13 [69-Jan-16: 2C].
Hartsook, Rachel A. m. Brown, G. H. on 70-Jul-28 [70-Jul-30: 2B].
Hartung, Frederick m. Bourguet, Cecilia on 70-Oct-20 [70-Oct-24: 2B].
Hartung, John F. (68 yrs., 4 mos.) d. on 68-Sep-9 [68-Sep-10: 2B].
Hartz, Stima (26 yrs.) d. on 68-Jul-29 [68-Aug-20: 2B].
Hartze, Charlotte m. Wood, Robert on 66-Sep-13 [66-Sep-18: 2B].

Hartzell, Amenia Belle (7 yrs.) d. on 69-May-9 [69-May-10: 2C, 2B; 69-May-11: 2B].
Hartzell, Ann Maria (58 yrs.) d. on 67-Jan-3 [67-Jan-5: 2C].
Hartzell, Anna m. Beam, John H. on 67-Apr-4 [67-Apr-11: 2B].
Hartzell, Cora Lavenia (3 mos.) d. on 69-Jul-19 [69-Jul-27: 2C].
Hartzell, Cornelius (44 yrs.) d. on 66-Nov-30 [66-Dec-3: 2B].
Hartzell, David m. Hough, M. A. on 68-May-25 [68-May-28: 2B].
Hartzell, Eliza m. Armacost, Joseph on 66-Apr-30 [66-May-16: 2C].
Hartzell, Frederick m. Henry, Mary on 69-Dec-14 [69-Dec-16: 2C].
Hartzell, John m. Gorsuch, Amanda M. P. on 67-Jun-18 [67-Jun-24: 2B].
Hartzell, John C. m. Pfisterer, Mary P. on 67-Sep-17 [67-Sep-27: 2B].
Hartzell, Lavinia m. Hoffman, John on 66-Jul-1 [67-May-24: 2B].
Hartzell, Mary Ella m. Henneman, John H. on 67-Aug-29 [67-Sep-24: 2A].
Hartzell, Sarah Agnes (17 yrs.) d. on 69-Nov-9 [69-Nov-11: 2C].
Hartzell, William (36 yrs.) d. on 67-Feb-28 [67-Mar-2: 2B].
Hartzell, William Henry (3 mos.) d. on 69-Jul-25 [69-Jul-27: 2C].
Harvey, Alfred A. (25 yrs.) d. on 68-Nov-8 [68-Nov-9: 2B; 68-Nov-10: 2C].
Harvey, Alfred Henry (2 yrs.) d. on 66-Jan-1 [66-Jan-3: 2C].
Harvey, Alice L. m. Gillenham, William James on 69-Dec-23 [70-Jan-20: 2C].
Harvey, C. T. m. Brown, Sarah G. on 70-Sep-27 [70-Oct-15: 2B].
Harvey, Cassandra Jane d. on 69-May-21 [69-May-22: 2B].
Harvey, Charles T. m. Kinsley, Ellenora on 69-Nov-23 [69-Nov-26: 2B].
Harvey, Elizabeth A. m. Doxen, Kinsey J. on 66-May-15 [66-Jun-5: 2B].
Harvey, Ellen m. Trull, George on 66-Nov-6 [66-Nov-9: 2C].
Harvey, Genila m. Jones, Arthur W. on 67-Jul-14 [67-Jul-17: 2C].
Harvey, J. W., Jr. m. Ellis, Sallie on 68-Feb-6 [68-Sep-1: 2A].
Harvey, James E. m. Ward, Laura V. on 67-Feb-12 [67-Feb-13: 2D].
Harvey, Kate m. Roberts, Harry on 69-Oct-28 [69-Nov-2: 2B].
Harvey, Lilly (2 yrs., 6 mos.) d. on 66-Jun-5 [66-Jun-6: 2B].
Harvey, Lottie B. m. Gelbach, William H. on 67-Feb-5 [67-Feb-8: 2C].
Harvey, Mary (78 yrs.) d. on 68-Apr-28 [68-May-4: 2B].
Harvey, Mary (64 yrs.) d. on 69-Sep-6 [69-Sep-8: 2B].
Harvey, Mary A. m. Carroll, John W. on 67-Oct-30 [67-Nov-2: 2B].
Harvey, Mary E. m. Ardleman, Andrew on 66-May-28 [66-Jun-2: 2B].
Harvey, Mary Onderdonk d. on 69-Apr-5 [69-Apr-7: 2C; 69-Apr-8: 2C].
Harvey, Rebecca Jane m. Dunkerly, George W. on 69-Sep-9 [69-Sep-15: 2B].
Harvey, Robert M. m. Beehler, Mary E. on 70-Oct-13 [70-Oct-15: 2B].
Harvey, Sallie A. m. Tydings, Thomas J. on 67-Dec-22 [67-Dec-31: 2C].
Harvey, Susie m. Lowe, John H. on 68-Jul-9 [68-Jul-23: 2B].
Harvey, William d. on 67-Dec-28 in Railroad accident [67-Dec-30: 1E].
Harvey, William Charles (53 yrs.) d. on 68-Jul-26 [68-Jul-28: 2B; 68-Jul-29: 1G, 2B].
Harvey, William P. m. Jordan, Jennie on 66-Jun-28 [66-Jul-12: 2C].
Harvey, Willie H. (11 mos.) d. on 68-Dec-18 [68-Dec-19: 2B].
Harward, Mary E. m. Hellen, William H. on 67-Nov-21 [67-Nov-28: 2C; 67-Dec-3: 2C].
Harward, William C. m. Zimmerman, E. Dora on 70-Apr-9 [70-Apr-12: 2B].
Harwood, Eliza W. d. on 69-Jul-17 [69-Jul-19: 2D].
Harwood, Sarah E. (49 yrs.) d. on 68-Jul-12 [68-Jul-13: 2B].
Haskell, Alice M. m. Keyes, James on 70-Aug-9 [70-Sep-2: 2C].
Haslett, Samuel S. m. Atkinson, Mary E. on 67-Jul-11 [67-Dec-27: 2D].
Haslup, Laura A. m. Toy, Thomas B. on 69-Feb-25 [69-Feb-27: 2C].
Haslup, Ruth A. m. Adams, John W. on 68-Nov-12 [68-Nov-17: 2C].
Hasselberger, Mary C. (24 yrs.) d. on 69-Dec-8 [69-Dec-11: 2B].
Hasselman, Otto H. m. Eddy, Olive M. on 70-Apr-21 [70-Apr-23: 2B].
Hassett, John F. m. Matthews, Lizzie A. on 69-May-5 [69-May-8: 2B].
Hasson, Amanda m. Clement, Jacob on 66-Feb-7 [66-Feb-10: 2C].
Hasson, Clara m. Bell, Joseph A. on 67-Apr-4 [67-Apr-6: 2B].

Hasson, Elijah (7 yrs., 6 mos.) d. on 68-Jul-28 [68-Jul-30: 2B].
Hasson, J. A. m. Millar, Sarah E. on 66-May-10 [66-May-16: 2C].
Hasson, John A. (24 yrs.) d. on 67-Jun-3 [67-Jun-4: 2A; 67-Jun-5: 2B].
Hasson, Mary (40 yrs.) d. on 68-Feb-17 [68-Feb-18: 2C].
Hasson, Rebecca B. (65 yrs.) d. on 66-Jun-25 [66-Jun-27: 2C].
Hatch, Frank J. (14 yrs., 6 mos.) d. on 70-Nov-17 [70-Nov-18: 2C].
Hattcher, Leno (4 yrs.) d. on 70-Jun-24 of Accidental Blow [70-Jun-27: 1G].
Hatter, Martin Henry (2 yrs., 10 mos.) d. on 67-Dec-21 [67-Dec-23: 2B].
Hatton, Ellen (83 yrs.) d. on 66-Mar-2 [66-Mar-3: 2B].
Hatton, George C. m. Harries, Mary on 69-Aug-19 [69-Sep-17: 2C].
Hatton, Joseph C. m. Steed, Addie L. on 67-Dec-4 [67-Dec-9: 2B].
Haueisen, Lydia Augusta d. on 66-Aug-28 [66-Aug-30: 2B].
Hauer, Mary E. m. Everhart, George P. on 66-Jun-5 [66-Jun-11: 2B].
Haughey, Sallie E. m. Gore, Alfred F. on 67-Jul-23 [68-Jan-10: 2C].
Haulley, Franklin (18 yrs.) d. on 68-Oct-14 [68-Oct-15: 2C].
Haun, Sallie E. m. Matthews, John P. on 69-Dec-28 [69-Dec-29: 2D].
Haupt, George W. m. Clark, Anna M. on 69-May-3 [69-May-10: 2B].
Haupt, Mary Ann (28 yrs.) d. on 70-Jul-7 [70-Aug-2: 2C].
Haupt, Mary Catherine Louisa (1 yr.) d. on 70-Aug-7 [70-Sep-9: 2B].
Haupt, Matthias (72 yrs.) d. on 67-Feb-26 [67-Feb-28: 1G, 2C; 67-Mar-1: 2C].
Hauptman, Emily Jane (43 yrs.) d. on 66-Mar-31 [66-Apr-2: 2B].
Hauptman, Helen C. m. Carpenter, George W. on 68-Nov-12 [68-Nov-18: 2C].
Hausdaffer, Florence Lee (1 yr., 7 mos.) d. on 70-Nov-9 [70-Nov-11: 2B].
Hause, Alexander P. m. Musselman, Lizzie on 66-Apr-24 [66-Apr-26: 2B].
Hause, Jennie (8 yrs.) d. on 66-Nov-15 [66-Nov-17: 2B].
Hause, Rebecca d. on 68-Feb-22 [68-Feb-24: 2C].
Hauselt, William F. d. on 70-Aug-2 [70-Aug-3: 2C].
Haush, Charles (8 yrs.) d. on 67-Sep-12 in Wagon accident [67-Sep-13: 1F].
Hautz, Nicholas (55 yrs.) d. on 70-Apr-5 of Fall from window [70-Apr-6: 1H].
Havenner, Thomas (20 yrs., 5 mos.) d. on 69-May-24 [69-May-26: 2C].
Havenner, Thomas H. (54 yrs.) d. on 70-Jan-12 [70-Jan-13: 2D].
Havez, Alice Clara (3 yrs.) d. on 70-Sep-6 [70-Sep-7: 2B; 70-Sep-8: 2B].
Haviland, Edgar P. m. Belt, M. E. on 69-Jan-6 [69-Jan-16: 2C].
Haviland, Isabella (62 yrs.) d. on 68-May-16 [68-May-18: 2B].
Hawk, Peter d. on 68-Jul-24 Drowned [68-Jul-28: 1B].
Hawkins, Aaron (75 yrs.) d. on 67-Jun-23 [67-Jun-24: 2B].
Hawkins, Abbey m. Owens, Stephen B. on 68-Feb-7 [68-Aug-11: 2B].
Hawkins, Addie E. m. McLaughlin, J. T. W. on 69-Sep-16 [69-Sep-22: 2C].
Hawkins, Amelia C. m. Litsinger, William D. on 69-Mar-16 [69-Mar-19: 2C].
Hawkins, Andrew Edgar (4 yrs.) d. on 70-Oct-11 [70-Oct-12: 2B; 70-Oct-13: 2C].
Hawkins, Eddy (1 mo.) d. on 68-Apr-7 [68-Apr-16: 2B].
Hawkins, George P. (41 yrs.) d. on 66-May-28 [66-May-29: 2B].
Hawkins, James W. (27 yrs.) d. on 70-Mar-1 [70-Mar-2: 2C].
Hawkins, Kate m. Beauchamp, John T. on 70-Dec-1 [70-Dec-14: 2C].
Hawkins, Keziah (60 yrs.) d. on 67-Jun-17 [67-Jun-18: 2B].
Hawkins, Lola Z. (10 mos.) d. on 69-Oct-9 [69-Oct-11: 2C].
Hawkins, Mary m. Baldwin, Charley R. on 67-Oct-8 [67-Oct-12: 2A].
Hawkins, Mary Ellen m. Kimberly, Augustus G. on 66-Jun-28 [66-Jun-29: 2C].
Hawkins, Mary L. m. Boyd, James on 69-Oct-31 [70-Jun-25: 2B].
Hawkins, William L. m. Harlan, Esther on 66-Jul-31 [66-Aug-3: 2C].
Hawley, Florence (1 yr.) d. on 70-Dec-27 [70-Dec-29: 2C].
Hawley, Ravana K., Jr. d. on 68-Jun-29 [68-Jul-4: 2C].
Hawn, Cordelia (9 mos.) d. on 70-Jul-10 [70-Jul-22: 2C].
Hawn, William H. H. m. Snyder, Belinda A. on 66-Aug-14 [66-Aug-17: 2C].
Hax, John m. Alheit, Charlotte on 68-Dec-26 [68-Dec-31: 2C].

Hay, Carrie d. on 68-Sep-8 [68-Sep-12: 2B].
Hay, John, Dr. (42 yrs.) d. on 68-Aug-26 [68-Sep-3: 2B].
Hay, John Carroll (1 yr., 8 mos.) d. on 70-Mar-10 [70-Mar-11: 2C].
Hay, M. Ann d. on 67-Jan-10 [67-Jan-11: 2C].
Hay, William M. m. Mitchell, Carrie J. on 67-Mar-27 [67-Apr-3: 2B].
Hayden, Bernard (59 yrs.) d. on 67-Oct-17 [67-Oct-19: 2B].
Hayden, George J. (57 yrs.) d. on 67-Apr-14 [67-Apr-15: 2B].
Hayden, Hal. G. m. Daley, Rose L. on 68-Jun-25 [68-Jul-24: 2C].
Hayden, Horace Edwin m. Byers, Kate E. on 68-Nov-30 [68-Dec-9: 2C].
Hayden, Mary Eliza (2 mos.) d. on 66-Jun-16 [66-Jun-22: 2B].
Hayden, Mary Elizabeth d. [68-Dec-23: 2C].
Hayden, Wilmer Gillet (1 yr., 2 mos.) d. on 70-Aug-23 [70-Aug-25: 2C].
Hayes, Achasiah m. Snookes, George on 69-Oct-25 [69-Oct-27: 2B].
Hayes, Daniel m. Griffin, Mary Jane on 68-May-28 [68-Jun-9: 2B].
Hayes, Edward m. Ryan, Bridget on 68-Feb-4 [68-Feb-18: 2C].
Hayes, Johanna (2 mos.) d. on 70-Feb-28 [70-Mar-1: 2C].
Hayes, Mary Lizzie m. Booze, Marcellus J. on 67-Jan-2 [67-Jan-4: 2D].
Hayes, Robert H. (7 yrs.) d. on 66-Sep-28 [66-Sep-29: 2B].
Hayes, Sallie m. Bonn, Samuel G. on 67-Jul-15 [67-Aug-1: 2C].
Hayes, Virginia (45 yrs.) d. on 69-Oct-17 [69-Oct-19: 2C].
Hayes, William B. (3 yrs., 2 mos.) d. on 70-Apr-8 [70-Apr-9: 2B].
Hayghe, James S. (21 yrs.) d. on 70-Oct-20 [70-Oct-22: 2B].
Hayne, Mary Anne (67 yrs.) d. on 68-Jul-14 [68-Jul-17: 2C].
Hayne, Theodore B. m. Adams, Lillah on 70-Apr-19 [70-Apr-30: 2A].
Haynes, Antie Brown (36 yrs.) d. on 70-Feb-20 of Pleuro-pneumonia [70-Feb-24: 2C].
Haynes, Arabella Lavinia m. Robinson, William Smith on 69-Nov-9 [69-Dec-28: 2C].
Haynes, Charles d. on 70-Oct-14 of Brain congestion [70-Oct-15: 2B].
Haynes, George H. m. Bowen, Eleanora T. on 70-Jan-6 [70-Jan-8: 2B].
Haynes, Lydia B. m. Hall, Edward H. on 70-Feb-10 [70-Mar-7: 2C].
Haynes, Micha Ann (72 yrs.) d. on 70-Oct-23 [70-Oct-24: 2B].
Haynes, Sarah E. m. Dykers, John on 67-Nov-7 [67-Nov-16: 2B].
Haynes, William H. (49 yrs.) d. on 67-Aug-1 [67-Aug-3: 2B].
Haynie, Emma E. d. on 69-Nov-3 [69-Dec-8: 2C].
Haynie, Marian Albina (19 yrs.) d. on 67-Aug-6 [67-Aug-7: 2C].
Haynie, Willard S. (45 yrs.) d. on 66-Jul-23 [66-Jul-24: 2C].
Hays, Alejandro Albizu d. on 70-Aug-2 [70-Aug-4: 2C].
Hays, Charles Edward (10 mos.) d. on 70-Aug-18 [70-Aug-19: 2C].
Hays, David (75 yrs.) d. on 70-Aug-7 [70-Aug-8: 2C; 70-Aug-9: 2C].
Hays, Edward P. m. Selvage, Mary E. on 66-Nov-5 [66-Nov-12: 2C].
Hays, Eliza J. m. Carling, E. S. on 69-Aug-20 [69-Sep-6: 2C].
Hays, Helen Marr (5 yrs., 6 mos.) d. on 68-Oct-4 [68-Oct-7: 2C].
Hays, Infant d. on 66-Nov-16 [66-Nov-17: 2B].
Hays, James (48 yrs.) d. on 67-Mar-26 of Consumption [67-Mar-27: 2C].
Hays, James H. m. Hahn, Mary on 67-Jan-24 [67-Jan-28: 2C].
Hays, John B. (55 yrs., 3 mos.) d. on 70-Nov-20 Crushed by wall [70-Nov-21: 4B; 70-Nov-22: 2B; 70-Nov-23: 2B, 4B, 4C].
Hays, Nicholas (25 yrs.) d. on 70-Nov-17 Drowned [70-Nov-19: 4D].
Hays, Priscilla Stansbury d. on 66-Apr-9 of Consumption [66-Apr-10: 2C].
Hays, Simon Scott (5 yrs., 6 mos.) d. on 67-Feb-16 [67-Feb-18: 2C].
Hays, Walter C. (68 yrs., 4 mos.) d. on 66-Aug-13 [66-Aug-17: 2C].
Hays, William H. m. McAllister, Laura V. on 70-Feb-14 [70-Feb-24: 2C].
Hays, Willie S. (1 yr., 10 mos.) d. on 68-Aug-12 [68-Aug-13: 2B].
Hayszelton, Robert Collins (19 yrs., 3 mos.) d. on 67-Feb-28 [67-Mar-1: 2C].
Hayward, Augusta d. on 69-Mar-9 [69-Mar-10: 2C].
Hayward, Clara M. m. Harris, Samuel K. on 70-Feb-3 [70-Feb-5: 2B].

Hayward, Gertrude (6 mos.) d. on 69-Mar-7 [69-Mar-8: 2C; 69-Mar-10: 2C].
Hayward, Harry P. (28 yrs.) d. on 67-Nov-5 in Carriage accident [67-Nov-6: 1F; 67-Nov-7: 2C].
Hayward, Jonas H. (51 yrs.) d. on 66-May-25 [66-May-26: 1F, 2B; 66-May-28: 1E].
Hayward, R. R. m. Filchner, Kate on 67-Mar-5 [67-Apr-10: 2B].
Hayward, Samuel J. m. Wehn, Annie Louise on 70-Mar-6 [70-Mar-9: 2C].
Hayward, Thomas J. m. Roberts, Blanche A. on 69-Jun-15 [69-Jun-18: 2C].
Hayward, William B. m. Bowerman, Sallie S. on 66-Jun-5 [66-Jun-6: 2B].
Hayward, William W. m. Weller, Kate on 66-Oct-4 [66-Oct-5: 2B].
Haywood, Lewis (21 yrs.) d. on 69-Dec-25 [69-Dec-28: 2D].
Haywood, Victoria m. Wheeler, Charles H. on 67-Nov-25 [67-Nov-30: 2C].
Hazard, Camilla m. Donaldson, Samuel C. on 65-Dec-27 [66-Jan-10: 2C].
Hazard, Henry m. Block, Matilda on 69-Jan-11 [69-Jan-13: 2D].
Hazelip, Estella Jane (12 yrs.) d. on 69-Nov-27 [69-Dec-1: 2C; 69-Dec-3: 2C].
Hazeltine, Sarah Hart d. on 70-Oct-2 [70-Oct-7: 2B].
Hazlett, C. C. m. McKnew, Sallie J. on 68-Jun-1 [68-Jun-6: 2A].
Hazlett, Mary A. m. Hunter, Thomas A. on 70-Jun-14 [70-Jun-16: 2B].
Hazlewood, N. H. m. Marriott, Mollie E. on 66-Nov-22 [66-Nov-27: 2B].
Hazlitt, Boston (35 yrs.) d. on 67-Mar-8 [67-Mar-9: 2B].
Hazzard, Mary L. m. Tignor, W. J. on 70-Nov-24 [70-Nov-28: 2C].
Heacock, Florence Amelia (7 yrs.) d. on 70-Sep-28 [70-Sep-30: 2B].
Head, Henry H. m. Oler, Bricie on 69-Feb-4 [69-Feb-17: 2C].
Head, Maggie, Miss m. Pedrick, George G. on 67-Dec-26 [68-Jan-2: 2C; 68-Jan-3: 2C].
Headley, Edward (3 yrs., 1 mo.) d. on 69-Nov-4 [69-Nov-5: 2C].
Heagerty, Mary (27 yrs.) d. on 70-Apr-14 [70-Apr-15: 2B].
Heagy, Mary E. (37 yrs., 1 mo.) d. on 68-Dec-15 [69-Jan-6: 2C].
Heagy, Mary E. m. King, William A. on 69-Jun-27 [69-Jun-29: 2C].
Heald, Callie F. m. Price, Richard W. on 70-Nov-3 [70-Nov-7: 2A].
Heald, William (81 yrs.) d. on 68-Nov-10 [68-Nov-11: 2C; 68-Nov-12: 1G; 68-Nov-16: 1G; 68-Nov-12: 2C].
Healy, E. Alice (7 mos.) d. on 68-Apr-30 [68-May-1: 2B].
Healy, James (1 yr., 5 mos.) d. on 68-Sep-11 [68-Sep-12: 2B].
Healy, James E., Dr. (44 yrs.) d. on 67-Jul-18 [67-Jul-20: 2C].
Healy, John (9 mos.) d. on 69-Dec-23 [69-Dec-25: 2C].
Healy, John J. m. Jennings, Maggie A. on 67-Aug-8 [67-Aug-16: 2B].
Healy, Margaret Catherine (1 yr.) d. on 66-Jul-10 [66-Jul-14: 2B].
Healy, Mary (10 yrs., 3 mos.) d. on 69-Oct-10 [69-Oct-11: 2C].
Healy, Richard (23 yrs.) d. on 67-Sep-8 [67-Sep-10: 2B].
Healy, Thomas J. m. Steever, Nellie B. on 69-Oct-25 [69-Nov-3: 2C].
Heaphy, Margaret (56 yrs.) d. on 70-Nov-14 [70-Nov-15: 2C].
Heaphy, Richard (19 yrs.) d. on 70-Sep-19 [70-Sep-20: 2B].
Heaps, William H. m. Swartz, Ellenora on 69-Nov-16 [69-Nov-29: 2C].
Heapy, Kate m. Murray, John on 68-Oct-6 [68-Oct-20: 2B].
Heard, John, Sr. (90 yrs.) d. on 66-Oct-7 [66-Oct-9: 2A, 4C].
Hearn, Charles E. m. Feinour, Elizabeth C. on 67-Apr-18 [67-Jun-21: 2B].
Hearn, Ellen Virginia (7 mos.) d. on 68-Jan-10 [68-Jan-14: 2C].
Hearn, Enoch Miller (3 mos.) d. on 66-Jul-26 [66-Aug-1: 2C].
Heartlaner, William Wallace (1 yr., 6 mos.) d. on 68-Jul-5 [68-Jul-16: 2C].
Heath, Alice A. Virginia (1 yr., 7 mos.) d. on 67-Apr-5 [67-Apr-6: 2B].
Heath, Charles L. m. Caulk, Elizabeth A. on 70-Aug-31 [70-Aug-31: 2C].
Heath, Clarence Barnes (6 mos.) d. on 67-Jun-30 [67-Jul-3: 2B].
Heath, George W. m. Bower, Emma C. on 69-Nov-26 [69-Nov-29: 2C].
Heath, J. B. m. Williams, Fannie E. on 69-May-28 [69-May-29: 2B].
Heath, Laura m. Cronmiller, John on 68-Nov-25 [68-Dec-3: 2C].

Heath, Mary d. on 68-Oct-12 [68-Oct-14: 2B].
Heath, Patrick (40 yrs.) d. on 67-Oct-25 Drowned [67-Oct-31: 1F; 67-Nov-4: 1F].
Heath, William F. m. Waller, Hannah M. on 68-Nov-15 [68-Nov-26: 2B].
Heath, William George (9 mos.) d. on 66-Sep-6 [66-Sep-10: 2D].
Heaton, Eliza (72 yrs.) d. on 68-Nov-20 [68-Nov-21: 2C].
Heaton, Gideon d. on 70-Jan-29 [70-Jan-31: 2C].
Heavel, Frederick (82 yrs.) d. on 66-Oct-18 [66-Oct-19: 2B; 66-Oct-20: 2B].
Heavell, George H. (18 yrs.) d. on 70-Aug-4 [70-Aug-5: 2C].
Heaverley, Caroline (34 yrs., 9 mos.) d. on 68-Jan-9 [68-Jan-11: 2B].
Heavy, Bridget (6 mos.) d. on 70-Feb-4 [70-Feb-5: 2B].
Hebb, John L. m. Dail, Alice V. on 66-Dec-13 [66-Dec-15: 2B; 66-Dec-17: 2B].
Hebden, Margaret (85 yrs.) d. on 70-Mar-21 [70-Mar-22: 2C].
Heber, Elizabeth (53 yrs.) d. on 70-Jul-15 [70-Jul-30: 2C].
Hechinger, Ferdinand m. Winternitz, Virginia on 70-Jan-20 [70-Jan-25: 2C].
Hecht, Jacob H. m. Frank, Carrie on 67-Jan-23 [67-Jan-26: 2C].
Heck, Adalhaidt m. Wolf, Henry on 67-Aug-15 [67-Aug-19: 2C].
Heck, C. J. m. Johnston, Minnie on 69-Aug-1 [69-Aug-3: 2C].
Heck, Mary (77 yrs.) d. on 66-Jun-22 [66-Jun-23: 2B].
Heck, Mary m. Gabrio, William F. on 67-May-29 [67-May-30: 2B].
Heck, Nathaniel m. Stouffer, Elizabeth on 68-Mar-25 [68-Mar-27: 2C; 68-Mar-28: 2B].
Heckman, John W. m. Lambden, Carrie A. on 70-Jan-6 [70-Jan-14: 2C; 70-Jan-15: 2C].
Heddinger, Theodore George (1 yr., 4 mos.) d. on 68-Dec-4 [68-Dec-7: 2D].
Heddrick, E. Lucinda m. Kennell, Samuel G. on 66-Aug-25 [66-Sep-1: 2B].
Hedeman, Henry m. Bloss, Mary on 68-Oct-25 [68-Oct-27: 2B].
Hedeman, Sophia D. m. Bevans, Joshua A. on 68-Oct-22 [68-Oct-24: 2B].
Hedley, Harry Eugene (6 mos.) d. on 67-Jul-15 [67-Jul-16: 2C].
Hedley, John H. (1 yr., 11 mos.) d. on 66-Jul-16 [66-Jul-17: 2C].
Hedrick, Richard Jackson (3 yrs., 5 mos.) d. on 66-May-16 [66-May-18: 2C].
Heesh, Catherine (101 yrs.) d. on 67-Jan-23 [67-Jan-24: 2C].
Heesh, John T. m. Clark, Rebecca J. on 68-Mar-17 [68-Apr-13: 2B].
Heffenor, Katy m. Magaha, Charles D. on 70-Aug-18 [70-Sep-15: 2B].
Hefferman, Celeste W. m. Ruhl, John C. on 69-Jun-9 [69-Jun-19: 2B].
Heffler, George (11 yrs.) d. on 67-Aug-20 [67-Aug-21: 1F].
Heffner, Anna M. C. m. Scott, Lewis on 69-Dec-5 [69-Dec-10: 2C].
Heffner, John d. on 67-Jan-18 of Suicide (Poisoning) [67-Jan-19: 1G; 67-Jan-21: 1F].
Heffner, Patrick (68 yrs.) d. on 68-Jun-30 [68-Jul-2: 2C].
Heginbotham, Charles (61 yrs.) d. on 70-Nov-10 [70-Nov-19: 2B].
Heide, George d. on 70-Aug-2 [70-Aug-5: 2C].
Heider, Christian (50 yrs., 11 mos.) d. on 70-Sep-2 [70-Sep-3: 2B].
Heighe, John M. m. Ross, Sallie on 70-Jan-12 [70-Jan-17: 2C].
Heilig, Charles E. d. on 70-May-30 [70-Aug-9: 2C].
Heiliger, Lewis A. (21 yrs.) d. on 70-May-9 [70-May-10: 2C; 70-May-11: 1G].
Heilner, Meier m. Seliger, Hannah on 66-Mar-25 [66-Mar-27: 2B].
Heim, Annie E. m. Bowen, Godfrey W. on 67-Sep-10 [67-Sep-16: 2B].
Heim, Charles A. (25 yrs.) d. on 69-Feb-23 [69-Feb-24: 2C].
Heim, Charles G. m. Nicodemus, Bessie on 70-Nov-23 [70-Nov-29: 2C].
Heim, Jacob B. (51 yrs.) d. on 70-Jan-26 [70-Jan-27: 2C].
Heim, Martha A. m. McCann, George on 68-Apr-2 [68-Apr-7: 2B].
Heim, William H. m. Weiner, Annie V. on 68-Oct-20 [68-Oct-24: 2B].
Heimiller, Henry F. m. Kane, Louisa on 68-May-17 [68-Jul-31: 2C].
Heimiller, Mary Elizabeth (9 mos.) d. on 70-Jul-16 [70-Jul-18: 2B].
Heims, F. m. Smith, Bergeda on 69-Jan-11 [69-Jan-13: 2D].
Hein, Henry d. on 67-Mar-23 Drowned [67-Apr-1: 1G].
Heindel, Harriet m. Schultz, Samuel on 67-Dec-26 [67-Dec-28: 2C].
Heine, Fannie E. m. Pertner, Augustus on 68-Jun-21 [68-Jul-8: 2B].

Heinecke, Annie E. (53 yrs.) d. on 69-Jun-12 [69-Jun-15: 2C].
Heinecke, Thomas August m. Pfaff, Elizabeth on 69-Sep-19 [69-Sep-21: 2B].
Heinekamp, Mary E. m. Walter, William on 69-May-25 [69-May-27: 2C].
Heiner, Eugene Boyd (2 mos.) d. on 70-Mar-28 [70-Mar-29: 2C].
Heiner, G. Payson (24 yrs.) d. on 69-Nov-17 of Consumption [69-Nov-30: 1G, 2C].
Heiner, Mary (53 yrs.) d. on 66-Sep-18 [66-Sep-19: 2B; 66-Sep-20: 2B].
Heintz, Henry d. on 68-Jul-16 of Heatstroke [68-Jul-17: 1D].
Heinz, Catie (13 yrs., 6 mos.) d. on 66-Mar-3 [66-Mar-5: 2B].
Heinz, Frederick (26 yrs.) d. on 68-Feb-21 [68-Mar-7: 2C].
Heinzman, Kate m. Schwinn, George on 66-Oct-28 [66-Nov-3: 2B].
Heinzman, Lou H. m. LaPorte, Will H. on 70-Jun-20 [70-Jun-28: 2C].
Heird, Henry James (2 yrs., 10 mos.) d. on 70-Oct-10 [70-Oct-11: 2B].
Heird, Nancy (72 yrs.) d. on 70-Sep-30 [70-Oct-1: 2B].
Heird, Nannie J. m. Mellor, Eli J. on 67-Nov-26 [67-Nov-30: 2C].
Heironimus, H. W. m. Wood, Mary J. on 68-Apr-15 [68-Apr-18: 2A].
Heisel, R. F. m. Duff, Mary J. on 70-Jan-25 [70-Jan-29: 2B].
Heiser, Louisa m. Follmer, Henry on 68-Sep-23 [68-Sep-25: 2B].
Heiss, Alexander m. Frankland, Matilda on 68-Dec-10 [68-Dec-23: 2C].
Heldmann, Henry J. m. Scheib, Adeline on 70-Sep-13 [70-Sep-26: 2B].
Helfrich, Charles M. (34 yrs.) d. on 69-Jun-28 [69-Jun-29: 2C].
Helfrich, George W. S. (4 yrs.) d. on 69-Sep-16 [69-Sep-17: 2C].
Helfrich, Rudolph m. Konig, Lizzie on 67-Apr-11 [67-Apr-17: 2B].
Helfrich, Willie Amos (8 mos.) d. on 70-Apr-28 [70-Apr-30: 2B].
Hellen, C. W. m. Hamilton, Dessie M. on 67-Aug-16 [67-Aug-22: 2B].
Hellen, Frank m. Cowles, E. Lela on 69-Sep-16 [69-Sep-17: 2C].
Hellen, Helen Mar m. Fry, John F. on 69-Mar-10 [69-May-3: 2C].
Hellen, John F. m. Binyon, Lillie on 67-Feb-7 [67-Feb-9: 2B].
Hellen, Thomas H. m. Small, M. Lettie [67-Nov-28: 2C].
Hellen, William H. m. Harward, Mary E. on 67-Nov-21 [67-Nov-28: 2C; 67-Dec-3: 2C].
Heller, M. H. m. Shakman, Annie on 70-Sep-28 [70-Oct-20: 2B].
Hellman, J. A. m. Green, Clara E. on 69-Jan-26 [69-Jan-30: 2C].
Hellman, Mary E. m. Vernetson, W. E. on 67-May-9 [67-May-11: 2A].
Hellwig, Caroline (53 yrs.) d. on 66-Nov-6 [66-Nov-7: 2C].
Hellwig, Henry m. Stang, Elizabeth on 67-Sep-22 [67-Sep-24: 2A].
Hellwig, Katie m. Fischer, Otto on 66-May-13 [66-Jul-9: 2C].
Helm, Agnes P. m. Kloman, Edward F. on 66-Nov-6 [66-Nov-9: 2C].
Helm, George (8 yrs.) d. on 68-Sep-10 Drowned [68-Sep-11: 1G].
Helm, Henrietta m. Vansant, James E. on 69-Jan-7 [69-Jan-8: 2C].
Helmkin, Mary E. (47 yrs.) d. on 66-Nov-10 [66-Nov-12: 2C].
Helmling, Annie Estelle (9 mos.) d. on 68-Oct-16 [68-Oct-28: 2B].
Helmling, Henry (53 yrs.) d. on 66-Mar-29 [66-Mar-31: 2C].
Helsby, Sue m. Wiley, Edward P. on 69-Oct-21 [69-Oct-28: 2C].
Hemmell, John C. m. Leak, Virginia on 66-Apr-3 [66-Apr-26: 2B].
Hemmell, John D. (62 yrs.) d. on 68-Dec-8 of Apoplexy [68-Dec-9: 2C].
Hemmick, Ann C. d. on 67-Jul-18 [67-Jul-20: 2C].
Hemmick, Wheatley N. m. Jones, Margaret E. on 70-Mar-6 [70-Jul-4: 2C].
Hempel, Frederick (41 yrs.) d. on 67-Aug-4 [67-Aug-5: 2B].
Hemphill, James (33 yrs.) d. on 68-Oct-14 of Heart disease [68-Oct-15: 2C].
Hemsley, Mary m. Sterrett, Samuel on 66-Oct-29 [66-Oct-31: 2B].
Henaman, William Henry (1 yr., 4 mos.) d. on 67-Oct-18 of Brain fever [67-Oct-19: 2B].
Henbeck, Mary Amelia (5 yrs.) d. on 69-Apr-11 [69-Apr-13: 2B].
Henck, Carrie d. on 66-Jun-14 [66-Jun-16: 2B].
Henderson, d. on 68-Sep-28 of Apoplexy [68-Sep-30: 1G].
Henderson, Anna m. Lambson, William B. on 66-Dec-27 [67-Jan-1: 2C].
Henderson, Anna Keene (4 mos.) d. on 70-Feb-3 [70-Feb-4: 2C].

Henderson, Anthony (63 yrs.) d. on 66-Oct-18 [66-Oct-19: 2B].
Henderson, Caroline E. m. Dixon, W. A. [68-Jul-9: 2B].
Henderson, Carrie E. m. Wadhams, A. V. on 70-Feb-28 [70-Mar-4: 2C].
Henderson, Clorinda T. (24 yrs.) d. on 67-Dec-20 [67-Dec-21: 2B].
Henderson, George Washington (1 yr., 1 mo.) d. on 66-Jul-14 [66-Jul-16: 2C].
Henderson, Hannah Amanda m. Watts, William, Jr. on 66-Feb-13 [66-Feb-17: 2B].
Henderson, Isabella S. m. Kierstead, Andrew J. on 66-Jan-25 [66-Jan-29: 2B; 66-Jan-30: 2B].
Henderson, J. Augustine m. Meyer, Clorinda on 66-Feb-13 [66-Feb-20: 2B].
Henderson, James m. House, Louise H. on 68-Feb-4 [68-Feb-5: 2D].
Henderson, James A., Jr. (26 yrs.) d. on 68-Oct-3 of Accidental Suffocation [68-Oct-5: 1F, 2C].
Henderson, John (26 yrs.) d. on 67-Aug-4 [67-Aug-5: 2B].
Henderson, John N. (37 yrs.) d. on 67-Jan-18 [67-Jan-19: 2C].
Henderson, Josephine d. on 67-Mar-13 [67-Mar-15: 2C].
Henderson, Julia m. Adams, Edward W. on 68-Oct-14 [68-Nov-7: 2B].
Henderson, Julia Ann (28 yrs.) d. on 68-Mar-11 [68-Mar-13: 2C].
Henderson, Landonia E. (10 mos.) d. on 66-Jun-25 [66-Jun-27: 2C].
Henderson, Laura Virginia (17 yrs.) d. on 67-Aug-6 [67-Aug-8: 2B].
Henderson, Louisa m. Eardley, Solomon on 69-May-20 [69-Jun-2: 2B].
Henderson, Mary (72 yrs.) d. on 66-Sep-11 [66-Sep-13: 2C].
Henderson, Rebecca (71 yrs.) d. on 69-Aug-16 [69-Aug-21: 2B].
Henderson, Samuel S. m. Constanstein, Mary on 67-Jul-14 [67-Jul-26: 2C].
Henderson, Seth W. (6 mos.) d. on 67-Aug-17 [67-Aug-21: 2B].
Henderson, Susan J. m. Bates, George C. on 66-Jun-28 [66-Jun-29: 2C].
Henderson, Thomas R. m. Hamilton, Isabella on 66-Aug-1 [66-Aug-6: 2C].
Henderson, William (67 yrs.) d. on 67-Mar-28 [67-Mar-29: 2B].
Henderson, William H. m. Townsend, Mary E. on 69-Dec-21 [70-Jan-11: 2C].
Henderson, William T. m. Watts, Julia A. on 68-Nov-17 [68-Nov-18: 2C].
Henderson, William T. m. Martin, Ella on 68-Aug-31 [68-Sep-1: 2A].
Henery, John Edward (1 yr., 8 mos.) d. on 68-Sep-13 [68-Sep-14: 2B].
Henkel, Charles m. Shuemacker, Mary on 70-Sep-29 [70-Oct-3: 2B].
Henkel, Lewis m. Applegarth, Mary Ann on 68-Feb-3 [68-Feb-4: 2C].
Henkel, Louisa m. Walker, Thaddeus on 67-Sep-28 [67-Oct-1: 2B].
Henkle, Amelia E. m. Cremin, Stephen A. on 69-Jul-23 [69-Jul-24: 2C].
Henkle, Annie Gertrude (19 yrs.) d. on 67-Nov-19 [67-Nov-20: 2C].
Henkle, Eli, Rev. (80 yrs.) d. on 67-Aug-24 [67-Sep-2: 2B, 4C].
Henkle, J. M., Rev. (48 yrs.) d. on 69-May-7 [69-May-15: 2B].
Henkle, Katie (6 yrs.) d. on 69-Aug-28 [69-Aug-31: 2B].
Henkle, Laura Virginia m. Granger, John Cannadine on 69-Apr-22 [69-Apr-23: 2B].
Henly, David m. Joyce, Sarah E. on 68-Jun-30 [68-Jul-7: 2B].
Henneberger, Rachel Wilson d. on 70-Feb-20 [70-Feb-22: 2C].
Henneberry, John (10 yrs., 3 mos.) d. on 67-May-19 [67-May-21: 2B].
Henneman, Ann L. (46 yrs.) d. on 69-Oct-1 [69-Oct-2: 2B].
Henneman, Clara Mary (7 mos.) d. on 69-Jun-4 [69-Jun-7: 2B].
Henneman, John H. m. Hartzell, Mary Ella on 67-Aug-29 [67-Sep-24: 2A].
Hennick, Annie E. m. Watkins, Thomas C. on 68-Dec-6 [69-Jun-2: 2B].
Hennick, Charles Lee (1 yr., 1 mo.) d. on 69-Aug-15 [69-Aug-18: 2C].
Hennick, Josias G. (33 yrs.) d. on 70-Mar-11 of Consumption [70-Mar-14: 2C].
Hennick, William F. m. Brandel, Lizzie A. on 70-Nov-22 [70-Dec-6: 2C].
Hennicks, Mattie V. m. Rutter, Wilbur on 68-Jan-23 [68-Jan-31: 2C].
Henning, Elizabeth (87 yrs.) d. on 70-Mar-30 [70-Mar-31: 2C; 70-Apr-1: 2B].
Henning, George C. m. Parker, Sue A. on 68-Oct-16 [68-Oct-27: 2B].
Henning, Jacob (30 yrs.) d. on 70-Oct-16 in Railroad accident [70-Oct-18: 4D].
Henning, Mary R. m. Renwick, R., Jr. on 66-Jan-24 [66-Jan-27: 2B].
Henning, Susie m. Pisani, Egisto on 70-Jan-9 [70-Jan-15: 2C].

Henning, William S. m. Taylor, Mary A. on 70-Oct-11 [70-Oct-20: 2B].
Hennings, Jeremiah B. (64 yrs.) d. on 68-Oct-6 [68-Oct-7: 2C; 68-Oct-8: 2B].
Henrice, John (60 yrs.) d. on 66-Jul-17 of Heatstroke [66-Jul-19: 1F].
Henrickle, E. P. m. Decker, John on 70-Mar-6 [70-Mar-15: 2C].
Henricks, Arthur T. m. Anthony, Emma C. on 66-Apr-5 [66-Apr-11: 2B].
Henricks, Maggie Isabel m. Cooney, William M. on 67-Jul-16 [67-Jul-25: 2C].
Henrix, Rosamond Ridgaway (3 yrs., 8 mos.) d. on 67-Apr-19 of Scarlet fever [67-Apr-24: 2B].
Henry, Ann Maria (48 yrs.) d. on 66-May-8 [66-May-9: 2B].
Henry, Arthur (55 yrs.) d. on 66-Nov-18 [66-Nov-20: 2B].
Henry, Augustine d. on 70-Feb-6 of Heart disease [70-Feb-8: 4G].
Henry, Caleb F. m. Sank, Mary Eliza on 66-Jan-15 [66-Jan-19: 2C].
Henry, Charles Livingston (7 yrs.) d. on 67-Jul-10 [67-Jul-11: 2C].
Henry, Charles S. (19 yrs.) d. on 67-Jul-31 [67-Aug-1: 2C].
Henry, Charlotte Ann m. Brown, Abel, Jr. on 69-Aug-24 [69-Sep-6: 2C].
Henry, David d. on 69-May-9 Drowned [69-May-11: 1H].
Henry, Elizabeth (33 yrs.) d. on 68-Jan-29 of Lamp explosion [68-Jan-30: 2C; 68-Jan-31: 1E].
Henry, George B. (23 yrs.) d. on 67-Sep-3 [67-Sep-4: 2B].
Henry, George W. m. Goss, Maggie E. on 69-Sep-22 [69-Oct-12: 2C].
Henry, Hugh W., Dr. (79 yrs.) d. on 70-Feb-12 [70-Feb-15: 2C].
Henry, James d. on 70-Jul-20 of Heatstroke [70-Jul-21: 1F; 70-Jul-22: 2C].
Henry, Jemima (64 yrs.) d. on 69-Apr-23 [69-Apr-24: 2B].
Henry, John (18 yrs.) d. on 66-Jun-26 Drowned [66-Jun-28: 1F].
Henry, John (21 yrs.) d. on 66-Apr-23 Drowned [66-Apr-26: 1G].
Henry, John B., Rev. d. on 68-Jan-30 [68-Feb-1: 2B].
Henry, John E. m. Kelley, Annie C. on 67-Mar-5 [67-Mar-16: 2B].
Henry, John W. (1 yr., 1 mo.) d. on 69-Aug-5 [69-Aug-6: 2C].
Henry, Joseph (27 yrs.) d. on 66-Sep-16 [66-Sep-17: 2B].
Henry, Joseph D. m. Stewart, Rebecca F. on 69-Jan-6 [69-Jan-25: 2D].
Henry, Margaret (21 yrs.) d. on 70-Dec-6 [70-Dec-7: 2C].
Henry, Martha m. Satterfield, John F. on 67-Nov-6 [68-Apr-30: 2B].
Henry, Martha A. (35 yrs.) d. on 68-Jun-22 [68-Jun-23: 2B].
Henry, Mary m. Hartzell, Frederick on 69-Dec-14 [69-Dec-16: 2C].
Henry, Mary Ann (16 yrs., 4 mos.) d. on 66-Mar-6 [66-Mar-8: 2B].
Henry, Mary Virginia (20 yrs., 9 mos.) d. on 67-Dec-6 [67-Dec-7: 2B].
Henry, Mattie m. Robinson, G. Oscar on 70-Dec-6 [70-Dec-13: 2C].
Henry, Mitilda Irene (18 yrs.) d. [70-May-26: 2C; 70-May-27: 2B].
Henry, Robert J. m. Anderson, Fannie E. on 68-Jun-30 [68-Jul-1: 2B].
Henry, Robert John (8 mos.) d. on 69-Jul-8 [69-Jul-9: 2C].
Henry, Samuel T. (40 yrs.) d. on 70-Apr-2 of Accidental blow [70-Apr-4: 1F, 2B].
Henry, Solomon m. Geoghegan, Emma D. on 68-Sep-10 [68-Nov-16: 2C].
Henry, Thomas (28 yrs.) d. on 66-Jul-5 of Heart disease [66-Jul-6: 1G, 2B].
Henry, Thomas W. (42 yrs.) d. on 69-Oct-19 [69-Oct-21: 2B].
Henry, William T. m. Mabee, Matilda Irene on 69-Sep-19 [69-Sep-27: 2C].
Henshall, James (61 yrs.) d. on 67-Sep-7 [67-Oct-1: 2B].
Henthorn, Ann Jane m. Erskine, George on 69-Sep-1 [69-Sep-11: 2B].
Henthorn, Eliza J. m. Davis, Charles W. on 70-Sep-28 [70-Oct-3: 2B].
Hentz, Lawrence (8 mos.) d. on 69-Sep-21 [69-Sep-22: 2C].
Henze, Orilla m. Hulse, George T. on 66-Nov-27 [66-Nov-29: 2B].
Herbanm, Adam (4 yrs.) d. on 66-Sep-23 Burned [66-Sep-25: 1G].
Herbert, Amanda Virginia (10 yrs., 1 mo.) d. on 66-Jul-28 [66-Jul-31: 2C].
Herbert, Fannie m. Lee, Alfred G. on 66-Oct-18 [66-Oct-23: 2B].
Herbert, Francis (79 yrs., 11 mos.) d. on 70-Oct-17 [70-Oct-18: 2B].
Herbert, Gabriel (45 yrs.) d. on 68-May-21 [68-May-22: 2C].
Herbert, George M. m. Cooksey, Rhoda E. on 67-Nov-4 [67-Nov-13: 2C].
Herbert, George N. m. Sullivan, Annie on 68-Jun-17 [68-Jun-19: 2B].

Herbert, George W. m. Moore, Mary on 69-May-13 [69-Jun-9: 2C].
Herbert, James R. m. Alexander, Elizabeth C. on 68-Nov-10 [68-Nov-18: 2C].
Herbert, Joseph B. m. Nulton, Kate M. on 68-Jun-3 [68-Jun-25: 2B].
Herbert, Margaret Ann d. on 68-Oct-14 [68-Oct-15: 2C].
Herbert, Sallie E. m. Hook, George W. on 69-Oct-5 [69-Oct-8: 2B].
Herbst, Arthur C. m. Good, Josephine M. on 69-Nov-3 [69-Nov-15: 2C].
Herck, David (60 yrs.) d. on 70-Jan-31 of Heart disease [70-Feb-1: 1H].
Herford, Meyer Spawger (66 yrs.) d. on 70-May-16 [70-May-17: 2B; 70-May-18: 2B].
Hergesheimer, Anna m. Oakes, Samuel H. on 69-Jan-28 [69-Feb-3: 2C].
Hergesheimer, Hannah m. Halstead, Alfred T. on 68-May-28 [68-Jun-6: 2A].
Hergesheimer, Sarah (59 yrs.) d. on 68-Apr-3 [68-Apr-29: 2B].
Hergesheimer, Sarah m. Lambdin, George W., Sr. on 66-Feb-14 [66-Feb-21: 2C].
Herget, George E. m. Miskimon, Lizzie J. on 68-Dec-17 [69-Jan-1: 2C].
Herget, Robert F. V. (13 yrs.) d. on 69-Mar-24 [69-Mar-27: 2B].
Herkenhine, George Henry m. Sebastian, Augusta on 68-Jul-2 [68-Aug-3: 2B].
Herkenhine, Henry Ernst (54 yrs.) d. on 66-Oct-26 [66-Oct-27: 2B].
Herkert, Conrad d. on 67-Nov-2 Drowned [67-Nov-4: 1G].
Herling, George L. (76 yrs.) d. on 66-Jun-24 [66-Jun-26: 2B].
Herman, John m. Rhinehart, Emelia on 68-Jul-2 [68-Jul-4: 2C].
Hermann, Henry W. m. Oehal, Rose D. on 68-Jun-4 [68-Jun-6: 2A].
Herold, Amelia F. m. Zange, August on 68-Nov-26 [68-Nov-28: 2C].
Herold, Charles F. m. Schillinger, Ettie M. on 69-Feb-9 [69-Feb-11: 2C].
Herold, Mary Ann Bly (10 mos.) d. on 67-Oct-21 [67-Oct-22: 2A].
Herold, Mary M. m. Snyder, Charles M. on 69-Apr-20 [69-Apr-26: 2B].
Herold, Nellie A. (6 mos.) d. on 70-Jul-1 [70-Jul-2: 2B].
Herold, William Marion (9 mos.) d. on 68-Aug-23 [68-Aug-25: 2B].
Heron, Caroline (49 yrs.) d. on 68-Jan-6 [68-Jan-7: 2C].
Herpel, John H. m. Unger, Margarethe on 70-Jul-5 [70-Jul-5: 2B].
Herpel, Mary Frances (27 yrs., 1 mo.) d. on 69-Sep-13 [69-Sep-15: 2B].
Herring, Annie E. m. Tongue, Johnzie on 69-Mar-9 [69-Sep-12: 2C].
Herring, Carrie E. m. Williar, Harry D. on 69-Oct-19 [69-Oct-21: 2B].
Herring, Charles Lewis (10 mos.) d. on 66-Jan-31 [66-Feb-2: 2C].
Herring, Clifford (26 yrs.) d. on 70-May-7 [70-May-9: 2B; 70-May-10: 2B; 70-May-13: 2C].
Herring, Clifford m. Caughy, Ann R. on 69-Oct-6 [69-Oct-9: 2C].
Herring, Elizabeth M. m. Hughson, Charles J. on 69-Nov-25 [69-Nov-30: 2C].
Herring, Georgie G. (7 yrs., 1 mo.) d. on 70-Feb-9 [70-Feb-10: 2C; 70-Feb-11: 2C].
Herring, Henry (77 yrs.) d. on 68-Mar-7 [68-Mar-9: 2C, 4E].
Herring, Henry (6 mos.) d. on 66-Apr-13 [66-Apr-14: 2B].
Herring, Howard McK. m. Boyd, Katie R. on 70-Apr-19 [70-Apr-21: 2B].
Herring, Imogene E. m. Sykes, James on 70-Mar-15 [70-Mar-19: 2B].
Herring, Julia m. Marshall, Charles on 70-Nov-24 [70-Nov-26: 2B].
Herring, Lewis E. m. Turner, Emma J. on 69-Jan-13 [69-Jan-27: 2C].
Herring, Louisa (60 yrs.) d. on 67-Jan-20 [67-Jan-21: 2C; 67-Jan-22: 2C].
Herring, Malcolm Lowry d. on 69-Mar-30 of Apoplexy [69-Mar-31: 2C; 69-Apr-1: 2C].
Herring, Sarah E. m. Wild, Henry C. on 67-Mar-14 [67-Mar-15: 2C].
Herrlich, Charles (3 yrs., 3 mos.) d. on 69-Nov-9 [69-Nov-10: 2C].
Herrmann, John M. m. Elkhardt, Carrie on 70-Jul-10 [70-Jul-15: 2C].
Herron, George S. m. Denson, Lizzie on 70-Oct-13 [70-Oct-27: 2B].
Herron, James, Rev. (98 yrs.) d. on 66-Jan-14 [66-Jan-19: 2C].
Herron, James L. d. [67-Aug-3: 1F].
Herron, William A. m. Titlow, Effie J. on 70-Feb-22 [70-Feb-28: 2C].
Hersch, Margaretta C. (41 yrs.) d. [67-Mar-14: 2C].
Hersch, Martin (82 yrs.) d. on 69-Nov-16 [69-Nov-17: 2C].
Hersh, Charles S. m. Leach, Anna R. on 69-Aug-11 [69-Aug-25: 2C].
Herzberg, Mayer (79 yrs.) d. on 70-Oct-5 [70-Oct-6: 2B; 70-Oct-7: 2B].

Herzog, John, Sr. (73 yrs.) d. on 70-Jan-28 [70-Jan-29: 2B].
Heslip, Susan P. (79 yrs.) d. on 68-Mar-5 [68-Mar-6: 2C].
Hess, Elias d. on 67-Aug-14 Drowned [67-Aug-16: 1G].
Hess, Ida Mary d. on 66-Sep-23 [66-Oct-3: 2B].
Hess, John Reynolds (32 yrs.) d. on 66-Aug-30 [66-Aug-31: 2B].
Hess, Kate m. Trail, William H. [69-Jan-27: 2C].
Hess, Killon m. Kircher, Virginia on 69-Nov-9 [69-Nov-13: 2B; 69-Dec-11: 2B].
Hess, Louis F. (23 yrs., 3 mos.) d. on 66-Apr-29 [66-May-1: 2A].
Hess, Tillie m. Reuther, Carl on 66-May-8 [66-May-15: 2C].
Hess, William U. m. Wall, Helen A. on 67-Feb-12 [67-Feb-18: 2C].
Hesse, Pilkey Montraville (1 yr., 6 mos.) d. on 69-Jul-25 [69-Jul-27: 2C].
Hessemer, Edwin I. m. Stesch, Eugenia F. C. on 70-Oct-2 [70-Oct-5: 2B].
Hessey, D. Stewart m. Smith, L. Addie on 68-Jan-22 [68-Jan-23: 2C].
Heter, George Lewis m. Wimpsett, Mary Paleaner on 69-Oct-18 [69-Oct-22: 2B].
Hetzell, John Alfred (15 yrs.) d. on 67-Mar-1 [67-Mar-2: 2B].
Heubeck, Franklin (3 yrs.) d. on 69-May-15 [69-May-17: 2B].
Heuisler, Ann E. m. McCurdy, James R. on 67-Feb-12 [67-Apr-2: 2B].
Heuisler, Katie (11 mos.) d. on 68-Jul-14 [68-Jul-16: 2C].
Hevel, William Henry m. Kirby, Deborah on 69-May-11 [69-May-15: 2B].
Heveren, H. A. m. Way, Scott on 68-Jan-9 [68-Jan-15: 2C].
Heveren, William (52 yrs.) d. on 66-Dec-16 [66-Dec-17: 2B].
Hevy, David m. Macean, Mary on 66-Dec-25 [67-Jan-5: 2C].
Hewell, Lewis, Capt. (68 yrs.) d. on 66-Sep-24 [66-Sep-25: 2B; 66-Sep-26: 2B].
Hewes, Eli M. (31 yrs.) d. on 68-Nov-14 [68-Nov-16: 2C].
Hewes, James m. Perkins, Lucy Madeline on 69-Oct-5 [69-Oct-18: 2C].
Hewes, M. Warner m. Worthington, Anna Lee on 67-Jul-23 [67-Jul-25: 2C].
Hewing, Maria (77 yrs.) d. on 69-Dec-24 [69-Dec-25: 2C].
Hewitt, Eli (64 yrs.) d. on 68-Apr-10 of Suicide (Stabbing) [68-Apr-11: 1F; 68-Apr-20: 2B].
Hewitt, John m. Pearson, Margaret J. on 66-Oct-25 [66-Oct-30: 2B].
Hewitt, Mary E. m. Shipley, William H. on 67-Nov-7 [67-Nov-14: 2B].
Hewitt, Mary Elizabeth (9 yrs., 2 mos.) d. on 69-Feb-13 [69-Feb-15: 2C].
Hewlett, Rebecca m. Ellett, F. M. on 66-Jun-21 [66-Jun-23: 2B].
Hexter, Heineman (81 yrs.) d. on 67-Aug-4 [67-Aug-6: 2C].
Heydenreich, Valene m. Crook, Walter J. on 67-Aug-28 [67-Sep-5: 2B].
Heydorn, M. m. Fowler, Mary T. on 68-Apr-22 [68-May-28: 2B].
Heyn, Catherine F. d. on 67-Jul-5 [67-Jul-6: 2B].
Heyser, Clara m. Webb, Levi on 68-Feb-20 [68-Feb-26: 2C].
Hibberd, Job m. Coale, Harriet H. on 70-Nov-15 [70-Nov-22: 2B].
Hibberd, Joseph (88 yrs.) d. on 66-Nov-22 [66-Nov-27: 2B].
Hibbitt, George A. m. Murphy, Rose A. on 66-Oct-16 [66-Oct-17: 2B].
Hibbitts, Anne Augusta (1 yr., 4 mos.) d. on 69-Jan-3 [69-Jan-4: 2C].
Hibler, Henry B. m. Moore, Louisa E. on 68-Dec-16 [68-Dec-29: 2D].
Hibline, Barbara Matilda (10 mos.) d. on 70-Dec-2 [70-Dec-3: 2B].
Hibline, George E. m. Beck, Margaret on 69-Aug-22 [69-Aug-25: 2C].
Hibline, John J. m. Eagan, Mary C. on 70-Dec-1 [70-Dec-8: 2B].
Hickenbotham, William m. Sizns, Elizabeth on 66-Jun-25 [66-Jun-30: 2B].
Hickey, Edward B. J. m. Posey, Mary V. on 66-Jun-24 [66-Jun-29: 2C].
Hickey, John F., Rev. (77 yrs.) d. on 69-Feb-15 [69-Feb-16: 1F; 69-Feb-17: 2C; 69-Feb-18: 1G; 69-Feb-17: 1G].
Hickey, Mary J. m. McJilton, William G. on 66-Mar-19 [66-Jul-24: 2C].
Hickey, William Edward (15 yrs., 6 mos.) d. on 66-Feb-16 of Consumption [66-Feb-17: 2B].
Hickley, James (40 yrs.) d. on 68-Apr-10 [68-Apr-11: 2A; 68-Apr-13: 1G].
Hickley, Kate R. m. Reynolds, Charles A. on 68-Apr-30 [68-May-4: 2B].
Hickley, Robert (40 yrs.) d. on 66-Apr-23 [66-Apr-25: 2B].
Hickley, Thomas (83 yrs.) d. on 68-May-22 [68-May-25: 2A].

Hickman, Frank T. m. Larkin, Sarah V. on 66-Jun-28 [66-Jun-30: 2B].
Hickman, John (84 yrs.) d. on 70-Mar-4 [70-Mar-5: 1H, 2B].
Hickman, Nathaniel, Gen. (72 yrs.) d. on 68-Mar-12 [68-Mar-13: 2C; 68-Mar-14: 2B; 68-Mar-16: 1E].
Hicks, Ann E. m. Thomas, Cornelius A. on 67-Jul-2 [67-Jul-4: 2B].
Hicks, Emily A. m. Van Ruth, Florus M. on 66-May-16 [66-May-19: 2B].
Hicks, Franklin S. m. Phillips, Lucretia A. on 69-Apr-21 [69-Apr-27: 2B].
Hicks, George (65 yrs.) d. on 68-Jun-17 [68-Jun-18: 2B].
Hicks, George A. (31 yrs.) d. on 66-Oct-6 of Cholera [66-Oct-8: 1G, 2B].
Hicks, George L. m. Hicks, Nannie on 67-Mar-8 [67-Mar-18: 2B].
Hicks, Georgianna McCord (3 yrs., 6 mos.) d. on 66-Sep-2 [66-Sep-3: 2C].
Hicks, John G. m. Rigby, Mary O. on 69-Nov-17 [69-Nov-20: 2B].
Hicks, John W. m. Turnbaugh, Eliza Jane on 69-Dec-19 [69-Dec-23: 2B].
Hicks, Joseph m. Williar, Mary J. on 69-Apr-13 [69-Apr-16: 2B].
Hicks, Mary E. m. Kraft, Charles V. on 66-Nov-1 [66-Nov-2: 2B].
Hicks, Nannie m. Hicks, George L. on 67-Mar-8 [67-Mar-18: 2B].
Hicks, William H. (41 yrs.) d. on 70-Feb-4 [70-Feb-19: 2B].
Hickson, John S. (66 yrs.) d. on 70-Nov-22 [70-Nov-23: 2B].
Hieller, Line Fredericka (4 yrs., 9 mos.) d. on 69-Jan-1 [69-Jan-4: 2C].
Hieller, Louis C. (3 mos.) d. on 66-Jul-4 [66-Jul-6: 2B].
Hiem, Bartholomew (32 yrs., 9 mos.) d. on 70-Apr-12 [70-Apr-14: 2B].
Higby, George H. C. (1 yr., 4 mos.) d. on 70-Aug-31 [70-Sep-1: 2B].
Higby, Joseph H. m. Thomas, Martha E. on 69-Jun-28 [69-Jul-8: 2C].
Higdon, Elizabeth (55 yrs.) d. on 66-Sep-22 [66-Sep-24: 2B].
Higdon, Harry Herbert (1 yr., 3 mos.) d. on 67-Aug-20 [67-Aug-21: 2B].
Higdon, Leah m. Hilton, John T. on 68-Jul-13 [68-Jul-17: 2B].
Higdon, Mary E. m. Lee, Charles T. on 67-Feb-28 [67-Mar-5: 2C].
Higdon, Mary E. m. Simmons, Richard L. on 69-Nov-18 [69-Nov-22: 2C].
Higdon, Mary Isabella (25 yrs.) d. on 69-Dec-11 [69-Dec-13: 2C].
Higgins, Alice Blanche m. Martin, Henry B. on 67-Apr-25 [67-Apr-26: 2B].
Higgins, Catharine m. Schaub, John on 67-Nov-19 [67-Nov-22: 2C].
Higgins, E. m. Hindes, W. H. on 70-Feb-3 [70-Apr-2: 2A].
Higgins, Edwin m. Ould, Rebecca S. on 66-Nov-1 [66-Nov-7: 2C].
Higgins, Eliza d. on 67-Feb-1 [67-Feb-2: 2C].
Higgins, Elizabeth d. on 68-Mar-5 [68-Mar-6: 2C].
Higgins, Emma Jane (23 yrs.) d. on 70-Aug-2 [70-Aug-4: 2C].
Higgins, Henry m. Allard, Emma J. on 69-Feb-17 [69-Feb-24: 2C].
Higgins, J. Richard m. White, Jennie A. on 69-Feb-1 [69-Feb-11: 2C].
Higgins, James, Dr. (50 yrs.) d. on 70-Mar-25 of Pneumonia [70-Mar-26: 1H, 2B].
Higgins, James H. m. Whitten, Laura J. on 66-Apr-19 [66-Apr-26: 2B].
Higgins, James Lee (33 yrs.) d. on 68-Jan-23 [68-Jan-28: 2D].
Higgins, Joanna W. (26 yrs.) d. on 70-Mar-13 [70-Mar-14: 2D].
Higgins, John (83 yrs., 2 mos.) d. on 66-Jun-4 [66-Jun-6: 2B].
Higgins, Joseph W. m. Deale, Alice J. on 67-Aug-6 [67-Aug-9: 2C].
Higgins, Josephine Robinson (51 yrs.) d. on 70-Jun-25 [70-Jun-27: 2C].
Higgins, Joshua (59 yrs.) d. on 66-Nov-21 [66-Nov-24: 2C].
Higgins, Maria m. Jeanneret, Louis P. on 66-Feb-13 [66-Feb-21: 2C].
Higgins, Mary (35 yrs.) d. on 69-Nov-21 [69-Nov-23: 2C].
Higgins, Mary (50 yrs.) d. on 70-Oct-12 [70-Oct-13: 2C; 70-Oct-14: 2B].
Higgins, Mary J. m. Smyth, William on 69-Jan-28 [69-Feb-4: 2C].
Higgins, Philip A. d. on 67-Jun-14 of Suicide (Poisoning) [67-Jun-17: 1F].
Higgins, Rose (1 yr., 1 mo.) d. on 69-Mar-8 [69-Mar-10: 2C; 69-Mar-11: 2C].
Higgins, W. George m. Mewburn, Susie on 70-May-26 [70-May-30: 2B].
Higgins, William M. m. Taylor, Margaret on 69-Jul-15 [69-Aug-21: 2B].
Higgins, William T. m. Seward, Margaret A. on 66-Aug-5 [66-Aug-18: 2B].

High, Anna Belle (1 yr., 1 mo.) d. on 67-Sep-9 [67-Sep-11: 2B].
High, Annie M. m. Israel, S. G. on 69-Feb-15 [69-Feb-19: 2C].
High, Camille m. Brewer, Charles on 70-Dec-6 [70-Dec-8: 2B].
High, David (66 yrs.) d. on 66-Mar-15 [66-Mar-17: 2B].
High, Florence Foss (19 yrs.) d. on 68-Apr-24 [68-Apr-27: 2B].
High, John W. m. Konze, Amelia on 70-Nov-8 [70-Nov-12: 2B].
High, Mary A. (27 yrs.) d. on 66-Jan-1 [66-Jan-2: 2C].
High, Mary Ella (1 yr., 10 mos.) d. on 66-Aug-11 [66-Aug-14: 2C].
High, Samuel E. m. Ray, Marietta on 69-Dec-2 [69-Dec-4: 2C].
High, William T. (30 yrs.) d. on 67-Feb-14 [67-Feb-16: 2D; 67-Feb-18: 2C].
High, William T. J. m. Foss, Florria on 66-Nov-22 [66-Dec-7: 2B].
High, William W. m. Jones, Amanda M. on 70-Jun-21 [70-Jul-25: 2C].
High, Willie (1 yr.) d. on 66-Oct-17 [66-Oct-18: 2B].
Highland, Anna d. on 66-Feb-25 Burned [66-Feb-26: 1F].
Highland, Lina d. on 66-Feb-25 Burned [66-Feb-26: 1F].
Highnat, Caroline (86 yrs.) d. on 68-Apr-4 [68-Apr-6: 2B].
Hilberg, Anna Margoretta (83 yrs.) d. on 66-Aug-17 [66-Aug-18: 2B].
Hilberg, Frank (8 mos.) d. on 66-Jun-23 [66-Jun-25: 2B].
Hilberg, S. Kate m. Rodenmayer, Frank T. on 69-Nov-11 [69-Nov-18: 2C].
Hilbert, Barbara m. Tempel, Thomas on 70-Aug-21 [70-Aug-25: 2B].
Hilbert, Maria L. (18 yrs.) d. on 66-Jul-2 [66-Jul-3: 2C].
Hild, Anthony m. McGarigle, Margaret F. on 68-Jan-16 [68-Jan-17: 2C].
Hild, Jane E. (42 yrs.) d. on 67-Jul-4 of Consumption [67-Jul-6: 2B].
Hild, Juliet M. (20 yrs.) d. on 67-Apr-8 [67-Apr-8: 2D].
Hild, Mary J. (5 mos.) d. on 67-Jul-26 [67-Aug-5: 2B].
Hildebrand, , Mr. d. on 70-Sep-1 [70-Sep-2: 4D].
Hildebrand, Annie d. on 69-Sep-27 Burned [69-Sep-29: 1H].
Hildebrand, Annie m. Eck, William F. on 67-Feb-5 [67-Feb-7: 2C].
Hildebrand, Harry F. m. McMechen, Emma V. on 68-Jul-23 [68-Aug-6: 2B].
Hildebrand, Susan J. m. Keckler, John G. on 70-Jun-2 [70-Jun-28: 2C].
Hildebrandt, Achsa E. m. Litchfield, George J. on 69-Dec-14 [69-Dec-16: 2C].
Hildebrandt, Achsah A. (47 yrs.) d. on 66-Jun-12 [66-Jun-13: 2B].
Hildebrandt, George W. (10 yrs., 6 mos.) d. on 70-Jan-1 [70-Jan-5: 2C].
Hildebrandt, Maggie H. m. Belt, James E. on 69-Feb-23 [69-Mar-3: 2B].
Hilderbrand, Priscilla m. Eck, John L. on 67-Mar-26 [67-Apr-4: 2B].
Hildt, E. Kate m. Shepherd, Owens on 70-Dec-14 [70-Dec-17: 2B].
Hilgenberg, Emilie d. on 69-May-30 [69-May-31: 2C].
Hill, A. P. m. Johnson, M. V. on 70-Oct-6 [70-Oct-7: 2B].
Hill, Amanda M. d. on 70-Jun-8 [70-Jun-22: 2C].
Hill, Anna Virginia (10 mos.) d. on 69-Jun-27 [69-Jun-28: 2C].
Hill, Edward m. Wood, Susan E. on 66-Sep-24 [66-Sep-29: 2B].
Hill, Eliza (54 yrs.) d. on 68-Aug-7 [68-Aug-8: 2C].
Hill, Florence Hank. d. on 68-Jul-20 [68-Jul-22: 2C].
Hill, Francis Turner (8 yrs.) d. on 67-May-8 [67-May-9: 2A].
Hill, George M. (2 mos.) d. on 69-Nov-17 [69-Nov-26: 2D].
Hill, Georgeanna (1 yr., 6 mos.) d. on 68-Jul-27 [68-Jul-28: 2B].
Hill, John (20 yrs.) d. on 68-Jun-28 Drowned [68-Jun-29: 1G].
Hill, John E. m. Miller, Elizabeth A. on 69-Apr-21 [69-Aug-24: 2B].
Hill, John T. m. Weaver, Maggie on 68-Nov-26 [68-Nov-28: 2C].
Hill, Joseph H. (31 yrs.) d. on 67-Jan-29 [67-Jan-31: 2C].
Hill, Joshua (67 yrs., 7 mos.) d. on 70-Aug-21 [70-Aug-22: 2B].
Hill, Laura Augusta (1 yr., 5 mos.) d. on 68-Aug-7 [68-Aug-8: 2C].
Hill, Lawrence P. m. Stickney, Amanda M. on 68-Nov-5 [68-Nov-17: 2C].
Hill, Maggie Ellen (3 yrs., 6 mos.) d. on 68-May-13 [68-May-14: 2B].
Hill, Marianne Hynson (1 yr., 1 mo.) d. on 67-Jul-10 [67-Jul-11: 2C].

Hill, Martha A. (67 yrs.) d. on 67-Jan-17 [67-Jan-19: 2C].
Hill, Mary A. (25 yrs.) d. on 67-Feb-10 [67-Feb-12: 2C].
Hill, Norman F. m. Roberts, Carrie E. on 69-Oct-6 [69-Oct-8: 2B].
Hill, Richard (64 yrs.) d. on 69-Oct-29 [69-Oct-30: 2B].
Hill, Richard m. Morton, Mary on 68-Apr-20 [68-Apr-25: 2B].
Hill, Rosalie m. Holtzman, John on 69-May-13 [69-May-14: 2C].
Hill, Thomas (63 yrs.) d. on 68-Oct-25 [68-Oct-27: 2B].
Hill, William (91 yrs.) d. on 68-Dec-17 [68-Dec-19: 2B].
Hill, William (28 yrs.) d. on 66-Dec-20 [66-Dec-21: 2B].
Hill, William (40 yrs.) d. on 70-Oct-19 Drowned [70-Oct-25: 4C].
Hillander, Bernard (53 yrs.) d. on 70-Jul-11 of Suicide (Hanging) [70-Jul-12: 1H].
Hilleary, William T. m. Kennard, Margaret J. B. on 66-Nov-29 [67-Jun-26: 2C].
Hilleary, William Tilghman d. on 67-Dec-2 [67-Dec-3: 2C].
Hillegeist, Arnold E. m. Gray, Alice M. on 66-Feb-7 [66-Feb-22: 2B].
Hillen, Charles (44 yrs.) d. on 69-Oct-14 [69-Oct-15: 2C].
Hilliard, Ann M. (66 yrs.) d. on 66-May-28 [66-May-30: 2C].
Hillman, Charles Brook Boyle (6 mos.) d. on 70-Apr-30 [70-May-2: 2B].
Hillman, Stanislaus A. m. Smith, Mary E. on 69-Feb-28 [69-May-17: 2B].
Hillock, Mary (77 yrs.) d. on 67-Mar-25 of Heart disease [67-Mar-26: 2C; 67-Mar-27: 2C].
Hillyard, John W. (36 yrs.) d. on 66-Oct-1 [66-Oct-2: 2B].
Hilton, Amanda V. m. Mills, Job on 68-May-14 [68-May-21: 2B].
Hilton, Andrew J. (7 yrs.) d. on 70-Mar-9 [70-Mar-14: 2D].
Hilton, John T. m. Higdon, Leah on 68-Jul-13 [68-Jul-17: 2B].
Hilton, Marion (31 yrs.) d. on 67-Jun-15 [67-Jun-25: 2B].
Hilton, Mary E. m. Graham, Samuel on 70-Nov-7 [70-Nov-16: 2C].
Hilton, Mary Emma (9 mos.) d. on 66-Aug-21 [66-Aug-23: 2C].
Hilton, William H. (41 yrs.) d. on 67-Feb-12 [67-Feb-13: 2D].
Hilts, Ida (8 mos.) d. on 68-Aug-8 [68-Aug-10: 2C].
Himes, Kate m. Cowan, John on 69-Nov-25 [69-Dec-3: 2C].
Hinchliffe, Erath (81 yrs.) d. on 67-Jun-2 [67-Jul-26: 2C].
Hinder, Frederick m. Fielding, Kate L. on 68-Oct-20 [68-Oct-27: 2B].
Hindes, Kate Frost (2 mos.) d. on 69-Aug-10 [69-Aug-11: 2C].
Hindes, Mary (81 yrs.) d. on 68-Jan-10 [68-Jan-11: 2B].
Hindes, Mary A. (47 yrs.) d. on 67-Dec-29 [67-Dec-30: 2C; 67-Dec-31: 2C].
Hindes, Minnie m. Emmart, Vernon S. on 68-Jun-4 [68-Jun-15: 2B].
Hindes, Samuel (62 yrs.) d. on 70-Jun-7 [70-Jun-8: 1H, 2C; 70-Jun-9: 2C].
Hindes, Samuel m. Stokes, Adeline M. on 70-Jul-10 [70-Jul-25: 2C].
Hindes, Susie m. Hooper, Henry on 67-Apr-25 [67-Apr-29: 2B].
Hindes, W. H. m. Higgins, E. on 70-Feb-3 [70-Apr-2: 2A].
Hindman, Eliza B. m. Bush, James A. on 67-Feb-14 [67-Feb-16: 2D].
Hinds, Charles H. m. Sumwalt, Rachel on 70-Aug-28 [70-Oct-17: 2B].
Hinds, Edward J. m. Lightner, Margaret A. on 67-Oct-13 [67-Oct-14: 2B].
Hinds, Thomas, Capt. (78 yrs.) d. on 68-Oct-29 [68-Nov-4: 2C].
Hinds, William R. (18 yrs.) d. on 69-Aug-3 [69-Aug-4: 2C].
Hineker, Frederick (39 yrs.) d. on 66-Jun-18 [66-Jun-26: 2B; 66-Jun-27: 2C].
Hineker, Lavinia (74 yrs.) d. on 69-Oct-1 [69-Oct-8: 2B].
Hiner, George W. (50 yrs., 2 mos.) d. on 67-Mar-6 of Consumption [67-Mar-8: 2B].
Hiner, Sarah J. (55 yrs.) d. on 70-Mar-17 [70-Mar-18: 2C; 70-Mar-19: 2B].
Hines, Caleb B. m. Miller, Annie M. on 66-Dec-26 [66-Dec-27: 2C].
Hines, Catherine E. (48 yrs.) d. on 69-Aug-29 [69-Aug-30: 2B].
Hines, Cynthia A. m. Blight, Samuel on 65-Sep-16 [66-Jan-6: 2B].
Hines, Elizabeth (78 yrs.) d. on 67-May-3 [67-May-17: 2B].
Hines, George M. (50 yrs.) d. on 68-Mar-4 [68-Apr-2: 2C].
Hines, Henry (2 yrs., 3 mos.) d. on 66-Oct-29 [66-Oct-31: 2B].
Hines, James (3 yrs., 7 mos.) d. on 66-Jun-13 [66-Jun-15: 2C].

Hines, Maggie m. Hume, William on 70-Aug-25 [70-Sep-7: 2B].
Hines, Mary E. m. Frazier, Charles E. on 67-Feb-28 [67-Mar-4: 2D].
Hines, Michael (52 yrs.) d. on 70-Jan-6 [70-Jan-7: 2F].
Hines, Sarah (13 yrs., 10 mos.) d. on 70-Apr-30 [70-May-2: 2B].
Hines, Susie E. m. Phillips, A. A., Jr. on 66-Jun-21 [66-Aug-18: 2B].
Hinesman, Margaret d. on 70-Feb-17 [70-Feb-25: 2D].
Hinkel, James Perves (6 yrs.) d. on 66-Dec-27 [66-Dec-29: 2C; 66-Dec-31: 2C].
Hinkle, Harry Ridgaway (4 yrs., 9 mos.) d. on 67-Feb-3 [67-Feb-4: 2C].
Hinkley, Edward (2 yrs., 10 mos.) d. on 70-Feb-24 [70-Feb-28: 2C].
Hinkley, George (40 yrs.) d. on 66-Mar-4 [66-Mar-6: 2B].
Hinkley, Hargrove, Dr. (45 yrs.) d. on 66-Nov-14 [66-Nov-29: 2C].
Hinman, Anna Maria (40 yrs.) d. on 70-May-10 [70-May-11: 2B; 70-May-12: 2B].
Hinman, Edward H. C. (23 yrs.) d. on 70-Apr-15 [70-Apr-20: 2B].
Hinman, Hiram Lincoln (2 yrs., 2 mos.) d. on 67-Jul-12 [67-Jul-24: 2C].
Hinman, Virginia E. m. Granger, William H. on 70-May-25 [70-Jun-6: 2B].
Hinman, W. C. m. Long, M. Josie on 69-Dec-27 [69-Dec-28: 2C].
Hinsley, John (53 yrs.) d. on 68-Feb-13 [68-Feb-15: 2B].
Hinton, Anne E. m. Lafferty, Robert on 66-Apr-3 [66-Jun-11: 2B].
Hinton, Harry W. (9 mos.) d. on 66-Dec-26 [66-Dec-28: 2C].
Hinton, Manie m. Davis, Richard on 70-Oct-10 [70-Oct-26: 2B].
Hinton, Sarah (62 yrs.) d. on 70-Jan-27 [70-Jan-31: 2C].
Hinton, Thomas (75 yrs.) d. on 66-Mar-13 Drowned [66-Mar-15: 1G; 66-Mar-16: 2B].
Hinton, William (43 yrs.) d. on 66-Feb-3 Drowned [66-Feb-23: 2C].
Hinton, Zachariah m. Ginnavan, Susan on 70-Jun-5 [70-Jun-10: 2B].
Hipkins, David C. m. Hall, Sallie L. on 70-Aug-24 [70-Sep-8: 2B].
Hipkins, Fred S. m. Bayly, Sue E. on 69-May-3 [69-May-5: 2C].
Hipkins, Richard m. Kerr, Lilla B. on 67-Mar-25 [67-Mar-26: 2C].
Hipkins, Sarah J. m. Kirwan, John R. on 70-Apr-7 [70-May-31: 2B].
Hipsley, Ann (60 yrs.) d. on 69-Feb-6 [69-Feb-8: 2C].
Hipsley, Margaretta A. m. Jorden, Henry F. on 66-Jun-28 [66-Jun-30: 2B].
Hipsley, Mollie J. m. Blackburn, William C. on 66-Sep-12 [66-Sep-18: 2B].
Hipsman, Mary m. Bauers, Charles B. on 67-Feb-26 [67-Mar-11: 2C].
Hirsch, Fanny (14 yrs.) d. on 66-Mar-1 [66-Mar-3: 2B].
Hirsch, Florence Lizzie (1 yr., 6 mos.) d. on 68-Jun-18 [68-Jun-29: 2B].
Hirsch, Lazarus (65 yrs.) d. on 69-Mar-23 of Suicide (Hanging) [69-Mar-24: 1G].
Hirsh, William (32 yrs.) d. on 66-Jan-15 of Gunshot wound [66-Jan-16: 1G, 2C; 66-Jan-17: 2C].
Hirshback, Mary E. m. Williams, Levi on 68-Aug-24 [68-Sep-7: 2A].
Hirshberg, Moses H. m. Goldsmith, Sophia on 69-Dec-19 [70-Jan-3: 2C].
Hirshberg, Nathan m. Greensfelder, Rebecca on 69-May-23 [69-May-29: 2B].
Hirst, Elizabeth m. Meek, William H. [67-Mar-16: 2B].
Hiser, Elizabeth (62 yrs.) d. on 68-Jul-28 [68-Jul-31: 2C].
Hiser, R. Virginia (27 yrs.) d. on 68-Jul-18 [68-Jul-20: 2B].
Hiss, Benjamin S. m. Dickinson, Susie on 69-May-2 [69-May-7: 2C].
Hiss, Bettie S. (17 yrs.) d. on 70-Apr-22 [70-Apr-25: 2B].
Hiss, Ellen E. (37 yrs.) d. on 69-Mar-1 [69-Mar-4: 2C].
Hiss, Jacob C. (34 yrs.) d. on 67-May-3 [67-May-4: 2B].
Hiss, Mary F. (4 yrs., 5 mos.) d. on 70-Nov-25 [70-Nov-26: 2B].
Hiss, Mary Jane m. Duncan, N. J. H. on 69-Nov-16 [69-Nov-18: 2C].
Hiss, Sarah E. (34 yrs., 3 mos.) d. on 68-Jul-29 [68-Aug-1: 2B].
Hiss, Walter Tolley Altener (11 mos.) d. on 70-Aug-27 [70-Aug-29: 2B; 70-Aug-30: 2B].
Hissey, John T. m. Brown, Annie R. on 68-Jan-2 [68-Jan-4: 2C].
Hissey, Lida m. Lare, Francis D. on 69-Dec-16 [69-Dec-18: 2B].
Hissey, Mary Ann m. Carney, James on 69-Sep-27 [69-Oct-2: 2B].
Hissey, Mary G. m. Clarkson, Frank S. on 69-Jun-22 [69-Jun-24: 2C].

Hissey, Vincent G. d. on 67-Aug-8 [67-Aug-10: 2B].
Hissey, William (59 yrs.) d. on 69-Mar-6 [69-Mar-8: 2C].
Hissey, William, Jr. m. Glanding, Laura V. on 69-Oct-14 [69-Oct-21: 2B].
Hitafer, Margaret Hank (36 yrs., 10 mos.) d. on 68-Jul-21 [68-Jul-22: 2B].
Hitch, Elizabeth (80 yrs.) d. [67-Dec-2: 2C].
Hitchcock, Catharine (84 yrs.) d. on 69-Dec-3 [69-Dec-8: 2C].
Hitchcock, Edward G. m. Constantine, Susannah on 66-Jun-27 [66-Jun-28: 2C].
Hitchens, John H. m. Fountain, Maggie J. on 67-Feb-13 [67-Feb-16: 2D].
Hitchins, Anna m. Jenkins, Alexander on 66-Jan-30 [66-Feb-7: 2C].
Hites, Thomas E. m. Murphy, Ella C on 66-Mar-19 [66-Apr-23: 2B].
Hiteshew, Catherine d. on 68-Jul-5 [68-Jul-8: 2B].
Hiteshue, W. Albert m. Scott, Ettie on 68-Jan-2 [68-Jan-7: 2B].
Hitselberger, Anne E. d. on 66-Nov-8 [66-Nov-9: 2C].
Hitselberger, Frances A. (28 yrs.) d. on 70-Jul-25 [70-Jul-26: 2B].
Hitzel, S. Emma m. Hogg, Edwin A. on 70-May-13 [70-May-25: 2C].
Hitzelberger, Charles W. (31 yrs.) d. on 70-Jan-12 [70-Jan-14: 2C].
Hitzelberger, Hannah Ann (68 yrs.) d. on 66-Aug-19 [66-Aug-20: 2C].
Hitzelberger, Helen C. m. Jones, William D. on 70-May-24 [70-May-25: 2C].
Hoadley, Frances A. m. White, C. B. on 69-Dec-21 [70-Jan-3: 2C].
Hoag, James A. m. Arnold, Lizzie C. on 70-Mar-4 [70-May-4: 2C].
Hoban, David (62 yrs.) d. on 69-Feb-4 [69-Feb-5: 2C].
Hoban, John Francis (1 yr.) d. on 70-Aug-14 [70-Aug-15: 2B].
Hobbs, Alice m. Ball, Benjamin F. on 70-Feb-16 [70-Feb-21: 2B].
Hobbs, Almira Virginia m. Day, William T. on 67-Jun-4 [67-Jun-8: 2B].
Hobbs, Alverda V. m. Davis, Silas W. on 66-Feb-6 [66-Feb-8: 2C].
Hobbs, Ann Rebecca d. on 66-Nov-16 [66-Nov-17: 2B].
Hobbs, Annie C. m. Peaster, Henry [66-Sep-21: 2B].
Hobbs, B. E. (25 yrs.) d. on 69-Aug-13 [69-Aug-24: 2C].
Hobbs, Brice (60 yrs.) d. on 68-Dec-27 [68-Dec-28: 2B].
Hobbs, C. Marion m. Childs, Marie E. on 68-Apr-2 [68-Apr-9: 2B].
Hobbs, Charles R. m. Meyers, Frances on 67-Sep-22 [67-Oct-22: 2A].
Hobbs, Denard (54 yrs.) d. on 70-Oct-27 of Consumption [70-Oct-29: 2B].
Hobbs, Edward Harman m. Barnes, Julia Ellen on 70-Feb-26 [70-Feb-28: 2C].
Hobbs, Elizabeth (24 yrs.) d. on 66-Jan-4 [66-Jan-22: 2C].
Hobbs, Emma E. (1 yr., 1 mo.) d. on 69-Nov-1 [69-Nov-2: 2B].
Hobbs, Frank Trevelyan (1 yr., 3 mos.) d. on 70-Dec-7 [70-Dec-9: 2C].
Hobbs, George B. (3 yrs., 5 mos.) d. on 67-Mar-12 [67-Mar-13: 2C].
Hobbs, George F. m. Kessler, Cammie S. on 68-Oct-22 [69-Apr-27: 2B].
Hobbs, Hannah d. on 67-May-9 [67-May-10: 2B].
Hobbs, Joseph R., Jr. (9 mos.) d. on 70-Jan-9 of Dropsy [70-Jan-10: 2C].
Hobbs, Laura A. (25 yrs.) d. on 66-Nov-19 [66-Nov-21: 2C; 66-Nov-27: 2B].
Hobbs, Mary (89 yrs.) d. on 69-Nov-27 [69-Nov-30: 2C].
Hobbs, Nancy (49 yrs.) d. on 69-Feb-4 [69-Feb-5: 2C].
Hobbs, Napoleon B. d. on 70-Aug-26 [70-Sep-3: 2B].
Hobbs, Rachel (75 yrs.) d. on 66-Jan-19 [66-Jan-22: 2C].
Hobbs, Ruth Elizabeth m. McLean, Arthur on 66-Dec-11 [66-Dec-15: 2B].
Hobbs, Samuel A. m. Lemmon, Emma Warfield on 66-Dec-8 [66-Dec-12: 2B].
Hobbs, Sarah (34 yrs.) d. on 69-Nov-30 [69-Dec-2: 2C].
Hobbs, Wesley (42 yrs.) d. on 69-Nov-13 [69-Nov-16: 2C].
Hobbs, Yelverton T. m. Wright, Amanda J on 69-May-20 [69-May-26: 2C].
Hobday, Alma Elizabeth (1 yr., 8 mos.) d. on 67-Apr-2 of Catarrh fever [67-Apr-3: 2B].
Hobday, Erastus Lord Edward d. on 67-Sep-21 [67-Sep-23: 2A].
Hoben, Bridget (45 yrs.) d. on 66-Aug-19 Drowned [66-Aug-20: 1F, 2C].
Hobhal, Hester R. m. Michael, Jacob C. on 69-Nov-18 [69-Nov-20: 2B].
Hobin, Mary (81 yrs.) d. on 70-Jan-12 [70-Jan-14: 2C].

Hobleman, Johana m. Wehr, Frederick on 67-Aug-1 [67-Aug-3: 2B].
Hoblitzel, James Woodside (112 yrs.) d. on 68-Mar-17 [68-Mar-18: 2B].
Hoblitzell, P. W. m. Hollingshead, Mary C. on 67-May-30 [67-May-31: 2B].
Hoblitzell, Sue G. m. Zimmerman, J. C. on 67-Nov-7 [67-Nov-11: 2C].
Hoburg, Carrie m. Elseroad, Lewis N. on 68-Jan-1 [68-Jan-17: 2C].
Hoch, John G. m. Schwartz, Josephine C. on 66-Sep-9 [66-Sep-27: 2C].
Hochadel, James S. m. Lauster, Anna E. on 66-Dec-16 [66-Dec-17: 2B].
Hocker, Margaret d. on 69-Nov-5 Drowned [69-Nov-6: 1H].
Hockritt, Salome m. Shaw, Richard on 70-May-24 [70-May-26: 2C].
Hoddinott, Elias C. m. Collins, Nellie A. on 68-Sep-15 [68-Oct-20: 2B].
Hodge, William E. m. Moffatt, Mary on 68-Sep-10 [68-Sep-12: 2B].
Hodgekinson, Annie R. d. [66-Nov-10: 2B].
Hodges, Benjamin M. (93 yrs.) d. on 67-Jul-27 [67-Jul-29: 1F, 2D].
Hodges, Elizabeth m. Brooks, Samuel on 66-Jun-7 [66-Jun-9: 2B].
Hodges, Emma m. Conaway, James M. on 69-Apr-10 [69-Aug-19: 2C].
Hodges, Estelle Caroline (5 mos.) d. on 66-Oct-29 [66-Oct-30: 2B].
Hodges, Galena (7 mos.) d. on 67-Jul-21 [67-Jul-23: 2C].
Hodges, Harry (2 yrs., 3 mos.) d. on 68-Dec-10 [68-Dec-15: 2C].
Hodges, Jennings (8 mos.) d. on 67-Sep-1 [67-Sep-3: 2B].
Hodges, John Henry (12 yrs.) d. on 67-Jan-13 [67-Jan-14: 2C; 67-Jan-23: 2C].
Hodges, Joseph d. on 69-Jan-15 [69-Jan-16: 2C].
Hodges, Julia A. m. Reaymond, Moses B. on 66-Oct-21 [66-Oct-24: 2C].
Hodges, Lou. M. m. Bell, Adelbert T. on 68-Oct-15 [68-Oct-27: 2B].
Hodges, Margaret (3 yrs., 3 mos.) d. on 68-Apr-19 [68-Apr-20: 2B].
Hodges, Mary Worthington (7 mos.) d. on 68-Aug-9 [68-Aug-11: 2B].
Hodges, Robert (64 yrs.) d. on 68-Jan-7 [68-Jan-9: 2C].
Hodges, Sarah (78 yrs.) d. on 70-Apr-8 [70-Apr-9: 2B].
Hodges, Susie A. m. Ashley, William H. on 69-Dec-2 [69-Dec-7: 2C].
Hodgkiss, Ann (88 yrs.) d. on 66-Oct-4 [66-Oct-5: 2B].
Hodnett, Emily Adde (17 yrs.) d. on 68-Nov-8 [68-Nov-9: 2B].
Hodnett, Jason T. m. Rathell, Emily Adele on 68-Aug-26 [68-Sep-8: 2B].
Hodnett, John H. m. Pettit, Ozella Lucinda on 68-Oct-19 [68-Oct-22: 2C].
Hodson, T. S. m. Mauck, Alice on 66-Feb-7 [66-Feb-10: 2C].
Hoey, Henry m. Biddison, Alice L. on 68-Apr-14 [68-Apr-16: 2B].
Hoey, William Thomas (39 yrs.) d. on 66-Oct-26 [66-Nov-6: 2B].
Hoff, Addie S. m. Shirley, Henry C. on 67-Nov-14 [67-Nov-16: 2B].
Hoff, Augusta F. m. Large, Charles A. on 67-Aug-1 [67-Aug-5: 2B].
Hoff, Dannie C. (8 yrs.) d. on 68-Jan-25 of Diptheric croup [68-Jan-27: 2C; 68-Jan-28: 2D].
Hoff, J. Wilbur m. Scharf, Teresa on 70-Dec-13 [70-Dec-15: 2C].
Hoff, John F. (24 yrs.) d. on 66-Dec-11 [66-Dec-13: 2B].
Hoffernan, Hugh (48 yrs.) d. on 67-Sep-30 [67-Oct-1: 2B].
Hoffman, Ada Cecilia d. on 66-May-29 [66-May-31: 2B].
Hoffman, Alexina m. Bennett, Edward W. on 68-Oct-29 [68-Oct-31: 2B].
Hoffman, Amelia m. Schiminger, Rudolph on 65-Dec-11 [66-Mar-1: 2B].
Hoffman, Anna m. Garrett, William H. on 67-Nov-18 [67-Nov-22: 2C].
Hoffman, Anna Barbara (1 yr.) d. on 68-Feb-18 of Diptheria [68-Feb-20: 2C].
Hoffman, Caroline Rogers d. on 67-Mar-27 [67-Mar-28: 2B].
Hoffman, Charles Force (4 mos.) d. on 70-Jul-23 [70-Jul-25: 2C].
Hoffman, Charles H. (25 yrs., 11 mos.) d. on 69-Sep-28 [69-Sep-30: 2B].
Hoffman, Charles T. m. Boyd, Maggie F. on 66-Jan-18 [66-Jan-20: 2C].
Hoffman, Charles Thomas (3 mos.) d. on 69-Jan-29 [69-Feb-1: 2C].
Hoffman, Christopher (25 yrs.) d. on 67-Feb-22 of Consumption [67-Feb-23: 2C].
Hoffman, E. Joeline (24 yrs.) d. on 68-Jul-15 [68-Jul-16: 2C].
Hoffman, Elizabeth (40 yrs.) d. on 68-Jan-2 [68-Jan-4: 4F].
Hoffman, Ellen (28 yrs.) d. on 70-Apr-14 [70-Apr-16: 2B].

Hoffman, Emory B. m. Gibson, Annie E. on 69-Sep-7 [69-Sep-16: 2B].
Hoffman, Frederick B. m. Stine, Emma C. on 70-Jul-5 [70-Jul-9: 2B].
Hoffman, George W. m. Force, Lottie C. on 66-Dec-12 [67-Jan-3: 2B].
Hoffman, Henry (36 yrs.) d. on 68-Apr-19 [68-Apr-20: 4C].
Hoffman, Isabella m. Zeitler, Edward on 66-May-3 [66-May-5: 2B].
Hoffman, J. Adam m. Schneider, Louisa on 68-Jan-2 [68-Jan-4: 2C].
Hoffman, J. L. m. Deshields, Olivia F. on 68-Jun-9 [68-Oct-16: 2B].
Hoffman, Jacob (63 yrs.) d. on 67-Nov-5 of Heart disease [67-Nov-6: 1G; 67-Nov-7: 1G].
Hoffman, John d. on 67-Aug-14 of Heatstroke [67-Aug-15: 1F].
Hoffman, John m. Hartzell, Lavinia on 66-Jul-1 [67-May-24: 2B].
Hoffman, John L. (56 yrs.) d. on 70-May-10 [70-May-16: 2B].
Hoffman, John R. m. Wright, E. Joeline on 67-Jul-16 [67-Jul-19: 2C].
Hoffman, John R. m. Gwinn, Laura C. on 69-Oct-14 [69-Oct-19: 2B].
Hoffman, John W. m. Gunz, Frances M. on 70-Feb-27 [70-Apr-7: 2B].
Hoffman, Josiah M. Kuhn, Albenia on 68-Sep-1 [68-Sep-3: 2B].
Hoffman, Kate Wright d. on 68-Jun-8 [68-Jun-9: 2B].
Hoffman, Levi B. (28 yrs.) d. [66-Aug-17: 2C].
Hoffman, Lewis (53 yrs.) d. on 69-Apr-24 [69-Apr-26: 2B].
Hoffman, Lizzie d. on 66-Apr-15 [66-Apr-16: 2B].
Hoffman, Louisa m. Riach, Alexander F. on 68-Nov-11 [68-Nov-17: 2C].
Hoffman, Lucie Belle (9 mos.) d. on 70-Jun-1 [70-Jun-2: 2B].
Hoffman, Margaret (56 yrs.) d. on 68-Jan-28 [68-Feb-1: 2C].
Hoffman, Martha L. (39 yrs.) d. on 68-Mar-9 [68-Mar-11: 2B].
Hoffman, Mary E. m. Jones, R. Emmett on 70-Jan-3 [70-Jan-31: 2C].
Hoffman, Mary Frances (2 yrs., 1 mo.) d. on 67-Apr-28 [67-Apr-29: 2B].
Hoffman, Mary Jane m. Rouse, Edwin W. on 69-Sep-14 [69-Sep-16: 2B].
Hoffman, Philip m. Krener, Mary on 67-Nov-5 [67-Nov-19: 2C].
Hoffman, Rachel d. on 66-Aug-18 [66-Aug-20: 2C].
Hoffman, Valentine (71 yrs.) d. on 67-May-15 [67-May-21: 2B].
Hoffman, William m. Gibbs, Sue on 67-Nov-21 [68-Jan-9: 2C].
Hoffman, William E. m. Rizer, Mollie E. F. on 67-Feb-21 [67-Mar-11: 2C].
Hoffmeister, Emma (7 mos.) d. on 68-Sep-28 [68-Sep-30: 2B].
Hoffnagel, Robert D. m. Clark, Margaret E. on 69-May-19 [69-May-22: 2B].
Hoffsnider, John m. Jones, Harriet on 68-May-7 [68-May-9: 2B].
Hofmeister, William (23 yrs.) d. on 69-Oct-17 [69-Oct-19: 2C].
Hogan, Agnes Delia (1 yr., 6 mos.) d. on 68-Dec-8 [68-Dec-9: 2C].
Hogan, Katie (2 yrs., 3 mos.) d. on 69-Nov-4 [69-Nov-6: 2C].
Hogan, Louis (2 yrs., 6 mos.) d. on 69-Feb-5 [69-Feb-6: 2C].
Hogan, Mary (79 yrs.) d. on 67-Dec-31 [68-Jan-1: 2C].
Hogan, Mary Ann (6 yrs.) d. on 70-Dec-14 Burned [70-Dec-16: 4E].
Hoge, Lydia A. m. Shaw, Moses on 68-Apr-9 [68-Apr-23: 2B].
Hogg, Clara E. m. Hamilton, Caleb B., Jr. on 66-Sep-27 [66-Oct-20: 2B].
Hogg, Edward Mateer (3 yrs., 11 mos.) d. on 69-Feb-11 [69-Feb-12: 2C].
Hogg, Edwin A. m. Hitzel, S. Emma on 70-May-13 [70-May-25: 2C].
Hogg, Eliza Ann d. on 69-Mar-4 [69-Mar-5: 2C].
Hogg, George C. m. Gorsuch, Mary L. on 68-Apr-14 [68-Apr-15: 2B].
Hogg, James (19 yrs.) d. on 68-Dec-26 [68-Dec-28: 2B].
Hogg, John m. Busey, L. on 66-Apr-4 [66-Apr-14: 2B].
Hogg, Julia d. on 70-Jul-10 [70-Jul-11: 2C].
Hogg, Sallie M. m. Watts, Thomas B. on 70-Jan-27 [70-Jan-31: 2C].
Hogg, Samuel R. (2 yrs., 6 mos.) d. on 69-Jan-11 [69-Jan-12: 2C].
Hogg, Solomon S. m. Fulenkamp, Mary C. on 67-Nov-20 [67-Nov-23: 2B].
Hogg, Thomas H. m. Stallings, Lizzie on 69-Apr-20 [69-Apr-22: 2B].
Hogg, William A. m. Litz, Mary Jane on 69-May-20 [69-Jun-15: 2C].
Hogg, William H. (21 yrs.) d. on 69-Oct-9 of Construction cave-in [69-Oct-11: 1G, 2C].

Hogg, Willima (65 yrs.) d. on 67-Dec-3 [67-Dec-4: 2C; 67-Dec-5: 2C].
Hogner, Mary E. m. Cross, David H. on 70-Jan-6 [70-Feb-28: 2C].
Hohn, John Thomas (7 mos.) d. on 69-Aug-7 [69-Aug-9: 2B].
Hohn, Theophilus m. Pritchard, Annie M. on 69-Jan-19 [69-Jan-26: 2C].
Hohne, Mary d. on 70-Apr-22 [70-Apr-25: 2B].
Hokamp, Mary Ann m. Meyer, A. B. H. on 66-Oct-16 [66-Oct-24: 2C].
Holan, Lewis m. Sewell, Libbie V. on 65-Dec-25 [66-Jan-2: 2C].
Holbrook, Eliza (65 yrs.) d. on 67-Jan-24 [67-Jan-25: 2C; 67-Jan-26: 2C].
Holbrook, Francis X. m. Cecil, Nannie on 70-Jul-14 [70-Jul-20: 2C].
Holbrook, George Atkinson d. [66-May-9: 2B].
Holbrook, Jane m. Dashiell, William O. on 68-Nov-25 [68-Nov-28: 2C].
Holbrook, S. E. m. O'Dell, J. Dixon on 69-Jun-30 [69-Jul-10: 2B].
Holbrook, W. G. m. Kidd, Louisa C. on 66-Aug-6 [66-Aug-16: 2C].
Holbrook, William G. d. on 68-Oct-19 of Congestive fever [68-Oct-23: 1F; 68-Oct-24: 2B; 68-Oct-26: 4E].
Holdefer, Josephine m. Sanner, Thomas W. on 70-Apr-7 [70-Apr-11: 2B].
Holden, Catherine (50 yrs.) d. on 66-Jan-5 [66-Jan-6: 2B].
Holden, Elizabeth (23 yrs.) d. on 66-Nov-7 [66-Nov-8: 2C].
Holden, Fritz d. on 70-Jul-9 Drowned [70-Jul-12: 1G].
Holden, G. W. m. Willis, Lizzie on 66-Jun-7 [66-Jun-19: 2B].
Holden, Henry J. (74 yrs.) d. on 67-Oct-22 [67-Nov-7: 2C].
Holden, Margaret (7 mos.) d. on 69-Jun-13 [69-Jun-14: 2B].
Holden, Mary C. m. McCauley, Jasper G. on 69-Oct-20 [69-Oct-22: 2B].
Holden, Mary Elizabeth (27 yrs.) d. on 69-May-8 [69-May-10: 2C].
Holdsworth, George H. m. Lee, Lizzie T. on 67-Nov-28 [67-Dec-5: 2C].
Holland, Amanda d. on 67-Jul-6 [67-Jul-8: 2C].
Holland, Amanda Steuart (3 yrs., 7 mos.) d. on 67-Mar-21 of Chronic croup [67-Mar-28: 2C].
Holland, Amos T. m. Welsh, Mollie A. on 70-Nov-3 [70-Nov-8: 2B].
Holland, Ann R. m. German, Andrew J. on 66-May-8 [66-May-10: 2B].
Holland, Annie m. Yoe, George P. on 70-May-11 [70-May-11: 2B; 70-May-14: 2A].
Holland, Archibald (81 yrs.) d. on 66-Jan-9 [66-Jan-13: 2C, 1G].
Holland, Cassandra (58 yrs.) d. on 67-Aug-28 of Heart disease [67-Aug-29: 1G, 2B].
Holland, George Poisal m. Bell, Maggie Hudson on 68-Jan-2 [68-Jan-4: 2C].
Holland, Hattie (1 yr.) d. on 66-Feb-3 [66-Feb-5: 2C].
Holland, John M. m. Knell, Laura J. on 70-Mar-3 [70-Mar-16: 2C].
Holland, Johnston m. Nelson, Mary Jane on 70-Dec-8 [70-Dec-10: 2B].
Holland, Laura J. (27 yrs.) d. on 70-Oct-25 [70-Oct-26: 2B].
Holland, Madge (9 mos.) d. on 67-Apr-7 [67-Apr-8: 2B].
Holland, Maggie E. m. Bishop, William R. on 70-Sep-29 [70-Oct-3: 2B].
Holland, Margaret (37 yrs.) d. on 68-Jul-16 of Brain congestion [68-Jul-17: 1G].
Holland, Marion M. d. on 66-Dec-10 [66-Dec-11: 2B].
Holland, Mary m. Shipley, Alfred A. on 67-Feb-12 [67-Feb-14: 2C].
Holland, Mary E. m. Barker, Daniel on 68-Sep-8 [68-Sep-9: 2B].
Holland, Mattie V. m. Richardson, William W. on 70-Oct-27 [70-Nov-3: 2B].
Holland, Stokley m. Cowley, Annie R. on 69-Jan-7 [69-Jan-14: 2D].
Holland, William H. m. Hubbard, Mary E. on 67-Dec-16 [67-Dec-18: 2B].
Hollands, Emily m. Hooper, Thomas W. on 68-Jan-14 [68-Jan-25: 2B].
Holle, Henry (32 yrs., 4 mos.) d. on 66-Nov-26 [66-Nov-27: 2B].
Hollen, Sarah m. Roberson, William H. on 68-Aug-12 [68-Aug-15: 2B].
Holler, John d. on 70-Jul-15 of Heart disease [70-Jul-16: 2B].
Holler, Mary m. Wiesman, William V. on 68-May-12 [68-May-21: 2B].
Hollett, Ann Rebecca m. Brown, Thomas on 70-Jun-13 [70-Jul-2: 2B; 70-Jul-4: 2C].
Holliday, Caroline m. Mitchel, Theodorick on 65-Dec-26 [66-Aug-31: 2B].
Holliday, Eliza V. m. Meekins, John D. on 69-Apr-27 [69-Apr-30: 2C].
Holliday, Jesse L. (56 yrs.) d. on 66-Apr-30 [66-May-1: 1G, 2A].

Hollifield, William (60 yrs.) d. on 70-Apr-6 [70-Apr-7: 2B].
Hollinberger, John J. m. Toft, Sarah E. on 67-Oct-1 [67-Oct-4: 2B].
Hollingshead, Carrie R. m. Needham, Asa, Jr. on 66-Jun-7 [66-Jun-8: 2B].
Hollingshead, Mary C. m. Hoblitzell, P. W. on 67-May-30 [67-May-31: 2B].
Hollingshead, Robert K. m. Collins, Anna Amanda on 67-Jun-3 [67-Jun-11: 2B].
Hollingshead, Samuel, Capt. (60 yrs.) d. on 70-Aug-9 [70-Aug-18: 2C].
Hollingsworth, Anna B. d. on 70-Apr-10 [70-Apr-11: 2B; 70-Apr-12: 2B].
Hollingsworth, Jarrett (57 yrs.) d. on 66-Jan-7 [66-Feb-12: 2D].
Hollingsworth, John H. m. Oden, Ellen on 68-Nov-5 [68-Nov-7: 2B].
Hollingsworth, Luther m. Holt, Mary E. A. on 69-Feb-23 [69-Feb-25: 2D].
Hollingsworth, Mollie m. Duvall, Charles M. on 66-Dec-29 [66-Dec-31: 2C].
Hollingsworth, R. E. (74 yrs.) d. on 68-Oct-30 [68-Oct-31: 2B].
Hollins, Frederick W. (30 yrs.) d. on 67-Oct-23 of Consumption [67-Dec-24: 2B; 67-Dec-27: 1G].
Hollins, George (62 yrs.) d. on 68-Nov-7 [68-Nov-9: 2B].
Hollins, Jesse (79 yrs.) d. on 69-Apr-8 [69-Apr-10: 2B; 69-Apr-13: 1F].
Hollins, Maria Sterrett (19 yrs.) d. on 66-Feb-13 [66-Feb-15: 2C; 66-Feb-16: 2B].
Hollins, Rebecca (81 yrs.) d. on 69-May-27 [69-May-28: 2C].
Hollis, Eli d. on 70-Sep-21 Drowned [70-Sep-22: 4B].
Hollis, William B. m. Townsend, Hannah E. on 69-May-11 [69-May-13: 2B].
Holloway, Charles E. m. Gallup, Kate M. on 67-Feb-28 [67-Mar-11: 2C].
Holloway, Charles Howard (3 mos.) d. on 70-Feb-17 [70-Feb-25: 2D].
Holloway, Edward (46 yrs.) d. on 66-Apr-20 [66-Apr-21: 2B; 66-Apr-23: 1E].
Holloway, George (60 yrs.) d. on 68-Feb-5 [68-Feb-6: 2C].
Holloway, George E. m. Shook, Elenora V. on 70-Jan-12 [70-Jan-14: 2C].
Holloway, Jennie m. DeMoss, David on 66-Jun-7 [66-Jun-8: 2B].
Holloway, M. Annie (22 yrs.) d. on 70-May-16 [70-May-17: 2B].
Hollyday, David (62 yrs.) d. on 67-Dec-14 [67-Dec-19: 2B].
Hollyday, George S. (71 yrs.) d. on 70-Mar-11 [70-Mar-15: 2C].
Hollyday, William (64 yrs.) d. on 68-Jul-16 [68-Jul-20: 2B].
Holmes, A. Reese (22 yrs.) d. on 66-Sep-26 [66-Sep-27: 2C].
Holmes, Alexander (5 mos.) d. on 70-Jul-19 [70-Jul-20: 2C].
Holmes, Alexander T. m. Griffith, Lucy P. on 67-Apr-30 [67-May-9: 2A].
Holmes, Alfred (1 yr., 8 mos.) d. on 67-Nov-5 [67-Nov-8: 2C].
Holmes, Byron H. m. Wallace, Sallie E. on 68-Oct-27 [68-Nov-9: 2B].
Holmes, Charles E. H. m. Steiner, Valietta on 67-Nov-4 [67-Nov-7: 2C].
Holmes, Henry, Capt. d. on 67-Apr-13 [67-Apr-15: 2B].
Holmes, Janey m. Parlett, Harry on 69-Apr-15 [69-Apr-20: 2B].
Holmes, John m. Johnston, Carrie on 68-Jul-14 [68-Jul-31: 2C].
Holmes, John m. Gambell, Mary V. on 68-Aug-10 [68-Sep-16: 2B].
Holmes, John E. m. Benson, Emma R. on 67-Apr-23 [67-Apr-26: 2B].
Holmes, John T. m. Inscoe, Elizabeth J. on 68-Nov-12 [68-Nov-16: 2C].
Holmes, Josephine d. on 69-Nov-14 Burned [69-Nov-15: 1H].
Holmes, Mary Ann (53 yrs.) d. on 66-Apr-4 [66-Apr-5: 2B; 66-Apr-6: 2B].
Holmes, Milton W. m. Rhodes, Virginia E. on 70-May-5 [70-May-10: 2B].
Holmes, Mollie A. m. Barrow, Thomas H. on 66-Jun-14 [66-Jun-20: 2C].
Holmes, Rebecca E. m. Halsey, Stephen P. on 70-Jan-19 [70-Jan-21: 2C].
Holmes, Reuben A. m. Woolsey, Mary Virginia on 66-Dec-6 [66-Dec-11: 2B].
Holmes, Somerville (31 yrs.) d. on 68-May-12 [68-May-14: 2B].
Holmes, Susan E. m. Robbins, John M. on 66-Dec-4 [67-Mar-26: 2C].
Holmes, Thomas m. Armor, Minnie on 66-Dec-18 [66-Dec-20: 2B].
Holmes, Thomas H. (66 yrs.) d. on 70-Oct-9 [70-Oct-12: 2B].
Holmes, William, Jr. m. Forney, Mollie G. on 70-Nov-20 [70-Nov-28: 2C].
Holmes, William G., Jr. m. Tucker, Mollie E. on 67-Aug-22 [67-Aug-28: 2B].
Holmes, William Scarlett (8 mos.) d. on 70-Jun-20 [70-Jun-21: 2C].

Holmes, William T. m. Taylor, Annie B. on 66-Aug-20 [66-Oct-3: 2B].
Holston, John J. (52 yrs.) d. on 69-Apr-29 [69-May-1: 2B].
Holston, John J. m. Blakeny, Mary J. on 70-May-26 [70-May-31: 2B].
Holston, Mary Elizabeth (18 yrs.) d. on 67-Oct-28 [67-Oct-29: 2B].
Holt, Edwin A. m. Bassett, Mary on 68-Feb-4 [68-Feb-5: 2D].
Holt, Harry Brittell (8 mos.) d. on 70-Jul-17 [70-Jul-19: 2C].
Holt, Harry C. m. Wrightson, Amelia R. on 70-Jan-12 [70-Jan-14: 2C; 70-Jan-15: 2C].
Holt, John (61 yrs.) d. on 70-Oct-18 [70-Oct-25: 2B].
Holt, Mary E. A. m. Hollingsworth, Luther on 69-Feb-23 [69-Feb-25: 2D].
Holt, Thomas d. on 67-Feb-9 Drowned [67-Feb-12: 4C].
Holt, William (28 yrs.) d. on 66-Dec-10 [66-Dec-14: 2B].
Holt, William m. McKenny, Mary A. on 65-Dec-14 [66-Jan-9: 2B].
Holter, Mollie F. m. Brown, George W. on 70-Jun-5 [70-Jun-22: 2C].
Holthaus, Fannie m. Homer, Charles C. on 69-Mar-4 [69-Mar-8: 2C].
Holthaus, Harry C. m. Riefle, Hetty V. on 68-Nov-5 [68-Nov-10: 2C; 68-Nov-11: 2C].
Holton, George Thomas (1 yr., 4 mos.) d. on 70-Dec-28 [70-Dec-29: 2C; 70-Dec-30: 2C].
Holton, Isaiah (33 yrs.) d. on 69-Aug-5 [69-Aug-6: 2C].
Holton, John m. Travers, Mary Emma on 68-Nov-17 [68-Nov-19: 2C].
Holton, Thomas (13 yrs.) d. on 70-Oct-12 [70-Oct-13: 2C].
Holton, Virginia m. Arthur, James D. O. on 67-Dec-26 [67-Dec-30: 2C].
Holtz, Annie W. m. Johnson, A. E. on 70-Dec-20 [70-Dec-24: 2B].
Holtz, Edwin D. m. DeBow, Barbara A. on 66-Feb-20 [66-Feb-23: 2C].
Holtz, Emmanuel m. Mayben, Mary on 67-Oct-23 [67-Nov-4: 2B].
Holtz, George m. LaPorte, Clara on 68-May-1 [68-May-6: 2B].
Holtz, George W. m. Fisher, Georgie on 69-Jun-8 [69-Jun-15: 2C].
Holtz, Mollie E. m. Tottle, William A. on 69-Jun-15 [69-Jun-16: 2C].
Holtz, Nellie H. (8 yrs.) d. on 69-Jan-23 [69-Jan-26: 2C].
Holtzman, John m. Hill, Rosalie on 69-May-13 [69-May-14: 2C].
Holtzman, Margaret Cooper (4 mos.) d. on 66-Jul-29 [66-Jul-31: 2C].
Holtzman, Thomas R. m. Foss, Laura A. on 66-Sep-27 [66-Sep-29: 2B].
Homer, Charles C. m. Holthaus, Fannie on 69-Mar-4 [69-Mar-8: 2C].
Honeywell, Marion Grant (2 yrs.) d. on 66-May-12 [66-May-14: 2B].
Hood, A. J. m. Rimby, F. Virginia on 69-Dec-26 [69-Dec-27: 2D].
Hood, J. M. m. Haden, Florence E. on 67-Jul-17 [67-Jul-26: 2C].
Hood, James H. m. Owings, Anna E. on 69-Dec-21 [69-Dec-23: 2B].
Hood, John m. Smith, Mamie F. on 66-Nov-22 [66-Dec-4: 2D].
Hood, Josephine m. Buck, J. Eugene on 67-May-2 [67-May-7: 2B].
Hood, Joshua m. Evans, Mary E. on 68-Feb-6 [68-Feb-19: 2C].
Hood, Matilda Ann (59 yrs.) d. on 66-Jul-22 [66-Jul-23: 2C].
Hood, Steven G. m. Turner, Emma A. on 66-Oct-25 [66-Oct-27: 2B].
Hooenberger, Franz (34 yrs.) d. on 69-Jun-26 of Apoplexy [69-Jun-28: 1G].
Hoofer, Charles A. d. on 67-Apr-18 Drowned [67-Apr-20: 1F].
Hooff, J. Johnston m. Loney, Fannie on 68-Jul-16 [68-Jul-18: 2B].
Hoofnagle, Eleanora (53 yrs.) d. on 69-Feb-25 [69-Feb-26: 2D].
Hoofnagle, Sarah A. (47 yrs.) d. on 70-Nov-28 [70-Nov-29: 2C; 70-Nov-30: 2C].
Hoofnagle, Sarah A. m. Virtue, John on 68-Sep-29 [68-Oct-1: 2B].
Hoofnagle, William m. Twing, Agnes Carr on 68-Mar-1 [68-Mar-5: 2C].
Hoofnagle, William D. m. Owings, Agnes C. on 68-Mar-1 [68-Mar-7: 2B].
Hoogewerff, Harry d. on 66-Dec-3 [66-Dec-7: 2B].
Hook, Eleanor A. (23 yrs.) d. on 67-Dec-29 [68-Jan-3: 2C].
Hook, Elizabeth (21 yrs., 10 mos.) d. on 69-Apr-1 [69-Apr-3: 2B].
Hook, Elizabeth Ann (45 yrs.) d. on 69-Sep-25 [69-Sep-27: 2C].
Hook, Enoch F., Sr. (55 yrs.) d. on 67-Dec-14 [67-Dec-16: 2B].
Hook, George E. (16 yrs.) d. on 68-Dec-27 [68-Dec-28: 2B].
Hook, George F. (23 yrs.) d. on 67-Jul-25 [67-Jul-27: 2B].

Hook, George W. m. Herbert, Sallie E. on 69-Oct-5 [69-Oct-8: 2B].
Hook, George W. m. Ritinger, Rosania on 70-Apr-28 [70-Jun-17: 2B].
Hook, Hannah (77 yrs.) d. on 69-Jun-15 [69-Jun-17: 2C].
Hook, J. G. m. Erich, Henrietta on 69-Aug-14 [69-Sep-18: 2B].
Hook, John (89 yrs.) d. on 67-Feb-3 [67-Feb-5: 2C].
Hook, John A. m. Wilderman, Ellie A. on 65-Dec-14 [66-Jan-24: 2B].
Hook, Joseph m. Dwyer, Kate on 67-Apr-23 [67-Apr-26: 2B].
Hook, Joseph A. m. Connolly, Amelia on 67-Aug-13 [67-Aug-19: 2C].
Hook, Lalla Kenly (1 yr.) d. on 66-Aug-8 [66-Aug-21: 2C].
Hook, M. C. m. Rasin, A. R. on 66-May-8 [66-Aug-17: 2C].
Hook, M. R. m. Lay, Annie M. on 66-Mar-17 [66-Mar-20: 2C].
Hook, Margaret (21 yrs.) d. on 67-Mar-5 [67-Mar-7: 2C].
Hook, Mary Ann d. on 67-Nov-24 [67-Dec-6: 2C].
Hook, Mary E. (1 yr., 1 mo.) d. on 69-Apr-29 [69-Apr-30: 2C].
Hook, Rebekah (83 yrs.) d. on 67-Nov-13 [67-Nov-14: 2B; 67-Nov-15: 2B].
Hook, Samuel E. (26 yrs.) d. on 66-Nov-1 [66-Nov-3: 2B].
Hook, Samuel R. m. Kennedy, Mary J. on 67-Dec-1 [67-Dec-10: 2B].
Hook, Sarah Jane (35 yrs.) d. on 66-Dec-15 [66-Dec-17: 2B].
Hook, Sarah Kate m. Gardiner, William J. on 69-Dec-2 [69-Dec-18: 2B].
Hook, Thomas, Col. (77 yrs.) d. on 69-May-12 [69-May-13: 1H, 2B].
Hook, Warren Glenn (1 yr., 7 mos.) d. on 68-Aug-10 [68-Aug-11: 2B].
Hooper, Agnes m. Frost, Thomas on 70-Jul-19 [70-Aug-4: 2C].
Hooper, Charles Leander (1 yr., 11 mos.) d. on 70-Nov-15 [70-Nov-16: 2C; 70-Nov-17: 2C].
Hooper, Edward (1 yr., 11 mos.) d. on 66-Sep-5 of Water on the brain [66-Sep-6: 2B].
Hooper, Elizabeth (71 yrs.) d. on 68-Sep-15 [68-Sep-16: 2B].
Hooper, Ella Gladding d. on 67-Jul-26 [67-Jul-27: 2B].
Hooper, Eugene H. (26 yrs.) d. on 68-Dec-7 [68-Jan-24: 1G, 2D; 68-Apr-20: 2B].
Hooper, Florence T. m. Simon, Frederic W. on 69-Nov-16 [69-Nov-17: 2C; 69-Nov-23: 2C].
Hooper, Henry m. Hindes, Susie on 67-Apr-25 [67-Apr-29: 2B].
Hooper, Isadora Helena (11 mos.) d. on 67-Aug-3 [67-Aug-5: 2B].
Hooper, James B. (57 yrs.) d. on 66-Apr-1 [66-Apr-3: 2B].
Hooper, James H. H. (1 yr., 9 mos.) d. on 66-May-2 [66-May-3: 2C].
Hooper, James I. (72 yrs.) d. on 70-Jul-26 [70-Jul-27: 2C].
Hooper, John m. Dorsey, Clara on 67-May-30 [67-Jun-1: 2B].
Hooper, John H., Capt. (59 yrs.) d. on 67-Jan-10 [67-Jan-12: 2C].
Hooper, John J. (22 yrs.) d. on 70-Apr-10 [70-Apr-12: 2B].
Hooper, Joseph J. m. Lightner, Mary V. on 66-Jun-10 [66-Jun-19: 2B].
Hooper, Kate J. m. Roop, Josiah L. on 68-May-28 [68-May-30: 2A].
Hooper, L. E. m. Wheeler, Maria L. on 67-Jan-6 [67-Jan-12: 2C].
Hooper, Lillie Josephine d. on 67-Jul-14 [67-Jul-15: 2C].
Hooper, Maggie L. m. Edmondson, W. Winder on 67-Nov-28 [67-Nov-30: 2C].
Hooper, Maria L. m. Stewart, John W. on 68-Jun-9 [68-Jun-16: 2B].
Hooper, Marietta Greenwell (29 yrs.) d. on 67-Apr-10 [67-Apr-11: 2B].
Hooper, Mary E. (6 mos.) d. on 68-Jun-14 [68-Jun-16: 2B].
Hooper, Mary M. m. Hall, A. A. on 69-Jun-10 [69-Jun-11: 2C].
Hooper, Mary Virginia (28 yrs.) d. on 70-Apr-26 [70-Apr-27: 2B; 70-Apr-28: 2B].
Hooper, Pauline J. d. on 67-Jun-30 [67-Jul-1: 2B].
Hooper, Sallie M. m. Reese, William D. on 68-Jan-16 [68-Jan-17: 2C].
Hooper, Samuel (82 yrs.) d. on 66-Feb-9 [66-Feb-13: 2C].
Hooper, Samuel N. m. Kennard, Addie S. on 68-Mar-19 [68-Mar-21: 2A].
Hooper, Thomas B. m. Arnold, Laura V. on 70-Aug-23 [70-Aug-25: 2B].
Hooper, Thomas H. (26 yrs.) d. on 66-Aug-13 [66-Aug-14: 2C; 66-Aug-15: 2C].
Hooper, Thomas T., Capt. (62 yrs.) d. on 68-Jan-8 [68-Jan-10: 2C].
Hooper, Thomas W. m. Hollands, Emily on 68-Jan-14 [68-Jan-25: 2B].
Hooper, William B. m. Boyle, Helen L. on 70-Jun-29 [70-Jul-11: 2C].

Hooper, William Ijams d. on 70-Jan-11 [70-Jan-12: 2C].
Hoopes, Charles (45 yrs.) d. on 70-Dec-5 [70-Dec-6: 2C; 70-Dec-7: 2C].
Hoopes, Sarah R. (62 yrs.) d. on 68-Aug-29 [68-Aug-31: 2B].
Hoopman, Rachel m. Osborn, Amos on 70-Dec-14 [70-Dec-21: 2C].
Hoopper, Mary Rebecca (8 yrs.) d. on 67-Sep-30 of Scarlet fever [67-Oct-2: 2B].
Hoover, Ann Dora (5 yrs., 10 mos.) d. on 69-Nov-19 [69-Nov-20: 2B].
Hoover, Edgar I. m. Adams, Anne Mary on 70-Nov-22 [70-Nov-26: 2B].
Hoover, Francis, Col. (66 yrs.) d. on 70-May-15 [70-May-16: 2B; 70-May-17: 2B, 4B; 70-May-18: 1F].
Hoover, Francis Edgar (3 yrs., 8 mos.) d. on 70-Jan-17 [70-Jan-18: 2C].
Hoover, Francis W. (35 yrs.) d. on 70-Apr-4 of Lung congestion [70-Apr-5: 4D, 2B; 70-Apr-6: 2C; 70-Apr-8: 1H].
Hoover, George m. Wagner, Annie E. on 65-Jul-20 [66-Jan-6: 2B].
Hoover, Harrison T. m. Putts, Julia C. on 68-May-28 [68-May-29: 2B].
Hoover, John P. d. on 66-Jul-18 [66-Jul-19: 1F].
Hoover, Jonah D. (49 yrs.) d. on 70-Jun-5 [70-Jun-7: 2C].
Hoover, Mary (21 yrs.) d. on 69-Aug-29 [69-Aug-30: 2B; 69-Aug-31: 2B; 69-Sep-1: 2B].
Hoover, Mary Francis De Sale, (26 yrs.) d. on 68-Dec-5 of Heart disease [68-Dec-11: 1G].
Hoover, Willie A. (6 mos.) d. on 70-Aug-11 [70-Aug-12: 2C].
Hope, Robert J. m. Wardenburg, Ra on 69-Jan-12 [69-Jan-14: 2D].
Hopkins, Alice B. (9 yrs.) d. on 66-Jun-24 [66-Jun-25: 2B; 66-Jul-10: 2C].
Hopkins, Alice C. m. Hall, James R. on 67-Nov-27 [67-Nov-30: 2C].
Hopkins, Amelia m. Davis, William on 68-Sep-24 [68-Sep-29: 2B].
Hopkins, Anna P. McCord (2 mos.) d. on 66-Mar-2 [66-Mar-6: 2B].
Hopkins, Annie C. (10 mos.) d. on 68-Aug-25 [68-Aug-26: 2B].
Hopkins, Annie C. m. Baldwin, Charles W. on 68-Dec-1 [68-Dec-5: 2C].
Hopkins, Annie E. m. Haines, Oakley P. on 66-Oct-24 [66-Oct-29: 2B].
Hopkins, B. L. m. Reasin, A. V. on 68-Sep-10 [68-Sep-11: 2B].
Hopkins, Emma V. m. Boyd, John, Jr. on 68-Nov-10 [68-Nov-14: 2B].
Hopkins, George G. (28 yrs.) d. on 69-Jul-6 [69-Jul-8: 2C].
Hopkins, H. Harrison m. Richards, Annie Custis on 67-Jun-5 [67-Jun-12: 2B].
Hopkins, Hannah (67 yrs.) d. on 68-Mar-24 [68-Mar-26: 2B].
Hopkins, Hannah Ann d. on 69-Jul-28 [69-Aug-23: 2C].
Hopkins, Harrison m. Atwell, Mollie E. on 68-Jun-4 [68-Jun-30: 2B].
Hopkins, Harry L. (1 yr., 8 mos.) d. on 66-Jul-26 [66-Jul-30: 2C].
Hopkins, Hester (25 yrs.) d. on 69-Sep-7 [69-Sep-8: 2B; 69-Sep-9: 2B].
Hopkins, Howard Bowen (2 mos.) d. on 68-Aug-22 [68-Aug-25: 2B].
Hopkins, Howard W. m. Downey, Margaret M. on 69-Sep-1 [69-Sep-2: 2B; 69-Sep-3: 2B].
Hopkins, Howell (63 yrs.) d. on 69-Mar-20 [69-Mar-26: 2C].
Hopkins, Ida Rebecca (13 yrs., 10 mos.) d. on 68-Jul-4 [68-Jul-8: 2B].
Hopkins, Issac F. m. Dixon, Lizzie A. on 69-Dec-21 [69-Dec-30: 2C].
Hopkins, J. Reynolds m. Winsett, Mollie L. on 69-Mar-11 [69-Mar-18: 2C].
Hopkins, J. Seth m. Ludlow, Charlotte Sellman on 69-Nov-3 [69-Nov-5: 2C].
Hopkins, Jacob H. (42 yrs.) d. on 70-Jul-24 [70-Aug-5: 2C].
Hopkins, James (67 yrs.) d. on 67-Feb-22 [67-Feb-23: 2C].
Hopkins, Jamiel L. (52 yrs.) d. on 69-Apr-19 [69-Apr-21: 2B].
Hopkins, Jennie m. Joynes, Willie F. on 70-May-19 [70-May-23: 2B; 70-May-24: 2C].
Hopkins, Jennie S. (2 yrs., 6 mos.) d. on 68-Oct-25 [68-Oct-27: 2B].
Hopkins, Joel, Dr. (85 yrs.) d. on 68-Feb-23 [68-Feb-24: 2C; 68-Feb-25: 2C].
Hopkins, John H., Jr. m. Worthington, Mary G. on 70-Jun-16 [70-Jun-22: 2C].
Hopkins, John T. (42 yrs.) d. on 68-Feb-20 [68-Feb-22: 2B; 68-Feb-24: 1G].
Hopkins, Joseph (33 yrs.) d. on 68-Jan-1 [68-Jan-2: 2C].
Hopkins, Josephine H. (29 yrs.) d. on 69-Oct-14 [69-Oct-15: 2C].
Hopkins, Laura B. m. Sellers, Jacob C. on 69-Feb-18 [69-Feb-22: 2C].
Hopkins, Lavinia (24 yrs.) d. on 69-Feb-4 [69-Feb-18: 2C].

Hopkins, Lewis S. m. Byron, Sarah J. on 66-Apr-16 [66-Apr-19: 2B].
Hopkins, Louisa m. Gwinn, John H. on 70-Aug-16 [70-Aug-24: 2C].
Hopkins, Margaret A. (56 yrs.) d. on 70-Mar-5 [70-Mar-7: 2C].
Hopkins, Mary Anne (71 yrs.) d. on 68-Sep-4 [68-Sep-17: 2B].
Hopkins, Mary Johnson m. Woodward, William, Jr. on 68-Dec-10 [68-Dec-31: 2C].
Hopkins, Mary L. m. Wilcox, E. B. on 69-Sep-7 [69-Sep-9: 2B].
Hopkins, Mollie J. m. Billingslea, A. on 66-Jan-2 [66-Jan-4: 2C].
Hopkins, Philip T. m. Dorming, Rachel B. on 69-Feb-18 [69-Feb-24: 2C].
Hopkins, Robert D. m. Powder, Fannie E. on 69-Feb-4 [69-Feb-9: 2C].
Hopkins, Sallie S. m. Bevan, John W. on 70-Nov-1 [70-Nov-3: 2B].
Hopkins, Samuel (64 yrs.) d. on 67-Sep-4 [67-Sep-5: 2B; 67-Sep-6: 4B].
Hopkins, Samuel (66 yrs., 4 mos.) d. on 66-Jul-17 [66-Jul-25: 2C].
Hopkins, Samuel m. Schley, Rachel on 66-Sep-23 [66-Sep-25: 2B].
Hopkins, Samuel E. m. Stoddert, Mary E. S. on 66-Apr-24 [66-Apr-25: 2B].
Hopkins, Sophia D. d. on 67-Oct-22 [67-Oct-23: 2B].
Hopkins, Susan B. (62 yrs.) d. on 66-Mar-9 [66-Mar-20: 2C].
Hopkins, Susie R. m. Greenwood, James W. on 67-Jan-31 [67-Feb-6: 2C].
Hopkins, Thomas (64 yrs.) d. on 70-Aug-31 [70-Sep-1: 2B].
Hopkins, William (64 yrs., 6 mos.) d. on 66-Apr-21 [66-Apr-23: 2B].
Hopkins, William C. d. on 66-Oct-9 [66-Oct-16: 2B].
Hopkins, William F. m. Shock, Minnie O. on 68-Apr-6 [68-Apr-8: 2B].
Hopkins, William F. m. Welsh, Lizzie on 68-Dec-29 [69-Jan-2: 2C].
Hopkins, William M. (65 yrs.) d. on 67-Oct-12 [67-Oct-15: 2A].
Hopkins, William Of Levin (51 yrs.) d. on 70-May-10 [70-May-11: 2B; 70-May-12: 2B].
Hopkins, William S. (54 yrs.) d. on 69-Feb-16 [69-Feb-17: 1H, 2C].
Hoppell, George W. m. Torrington, Eleanora on 67-Aug-1 [67-Aug-7: 2C].
Hopper, Annie E. m. Morgan, George A. on 70-Mar-6 [70-May-3: 2B].
Hopper, Emmeline V. d. on 67-Dec-13 [67-Dec-14: 2B].
Hopper, John Wesley (13 yrs., 11 mos.) d. on 67-Mar-21 [67-Mar-23: 2B].
Hopper, M. Fannie (33 yrs., 2 mos.) d. on 66-May-23 [66-May-30: 2C].
Hopper, Nellie (87 yrs.) d. on 68-Aug-16 [68-Aug-26: 2B].
Hopper, S. W. T. m. Webb, Mary C. on 70-May-12 [70-May-14: 2A].
Hopper, William H. m. Russell, Annie E. on 70-Nov-15 [70-Nov-16: 2C; 70-Nov-17: 2C].
Hopper, Willie Griffin (3 yrs., 4 mos.) d. on 69-Sep-23 [69-Oct-1: 2B].
Hopps, Annie E. m. Wooden, John T. on 67-Nov-21 [68-Apr-21: 2B].
Hopps, Annie R. m. Smith, John on 65-Sep-21 [66-Mar-5: 2B].
Hopps, John, Sr. (65 yrs.) d. on 70-Jan-21 [70-Jan-22: 2C].
Hopps, Mary J. m. Frank, John A. on 68-Sep-18 [68-Oct-13: 2C].
Hopps, Sadie m. Brower, Wilbur G. on 69-Dec-23 [70-Aug-9: 2C].
Hopps, Thomas Henry (14 yrs.) d. on 70-Apr-23 of Suicide (Hanging) [70-Apr-25: 1G].
Hopps, William m. Chester, Isabel F. on 70-Jun-13 [70-Jun-14: 2B].
Hopwood, Fannie m. Barnard, John D. on 69-May-6 [69-Jun-5: 2B].
Horan, Sophia E. (35 yrs.) d. on 67-Nov-4 [67-Nov-5: 2B].
Horgan, Mary (77 yrs.) d. on 69-Dec-4 [69-Dec-6: 2C].
Hormes, Amelia (60 yrs., 11 mos.) d. on 67-Mar-20 [67-Mar-21: 2C].
Horn, Catherine (88 yrs.) d. on 69-Jun-18 [69-Jun-19: 2B; 69-Jun-21: 2B].
Horn, Clara V. (26 yrs.) d. on 69-Nov-18 [69-Nov-20: 2B].
Horn, Emma (27 yrs.) d. on 69-Dec-5 [69-Dec-6: 2C; 69-Dec-7: 2C].
Horn, Ferdinand (51 yrs.) d. on 70-Apr-13 [70-Apr-14: 2B; 70-Apr-15: 2B].
Horn, Florence Louisa (5 yrs., 2 mos.) d. on 69-Oct-4 [69-Oct-5: 2B].
Horn, George M. m. Kelley, Carrie M. on 69-Jan-19 [69-Jan-25: 2D].
Horn, Henry (77 yrs.) d. on 70-Mar-8 [70-Mar-9: 2C].
Horn, J. V., Jr. m. Miller, Hannie on 68-Nov-10 [68-Nov-12: 2C].
Horn, John S. (24 yrs.) d. on 66-Nov-28 [66-Nov-29: 2B].
Horn, Lillian May (1 yr., 1 mo.) d. on 69-Oct-11 [69-Oct-13: 2C].

Horn, Martha A. m. Moore, James T. on 66-May-8 [66-May-9: 2B].
Horn, Mary m. Couchman, Joseph on 67-May-14 [67-May-25: 2A].
Horn, Mary A. m. Rice, Frederick on 66-Jan-25 [66-Jan-27: 2B].
Horn, Michael (28 yrs.) d. on 69-Jan-4 [69-Jan-5: 2C].
Horn, Philip Reppert (10 mos.) d. on 69-Dec-16 of Scarlet fever [69-Dec-18: 2B].
Horn, Stephen m. Cochrane, Nellie M. on 67-Aug-21 [67-Aug-30: 2B].
Horn, Susie C. m. Shane, Harry C. on 67-May-7 [67-May-10: 2B].
Hornbrook, Sarah m. Ziegler, Frederick on 70-Nov-17 [70-Nov-28: 2C].
Horner, Albert N. m. Hammersley, Mary D. on 69-Feb-9 [69-Feb-17: 2C].
Horner, Charles Wasley m. Carr, Mary Elizabeth on 68-Jun-1 [68-Jun-6: 2B].
Horner, George D. m. Spilman, Estelle on 68-Sep-16 [68-Sep-29: 2B].
Horner, John A. (10 mos.) d. on 70-Jun-24 [70-Jun-27: 2C].
Horner, Kate m. Lyeth, Samuel H., Jr. on 67-Nov-12 [67-Nov-14: 2B].
Horner, Laura E. m. Smallwood, John on 69-Sep-7 [69-Sep-23: 2B].
Horner, Sarah J. (36 yrs.) d. on 66-Nov-13 of Brain congestion [66-Nov-16: 2C].
Horner, Sarah S. (24 yrs.) d. on 68-Mar-8 [68-Mar-9: 2C].
Horney, B. Franklin (8 yrs.) d. on 66-Apr-14 of Brain inflammation [66-Apr-16: 2B].
Horney, Ellen M. m. Barcher, Christopher W. on 66-Aug-8 [66-Aug-18: 2B].
Horney, Mary (68 yrs.) d. on 69-May-4 [69-May-6: 2B].
Horney, Mary R. m. Brown, Arthur on 70-Nov-7 [70-Dec-13: 2C].
Horney, Sallie F. m. Neily, R. Augustus on 66-Dec-4 [66-Dec-6: 2B].
Horney, Sammy (1 yr., 6 mos.) d. on 70-Jul-16 [70-Jul-19: 2C].
Horney, Sarah m. Kirby, Thomas H. on 67-Oct-29 [68-Jan-21: 2C].
Horney, William H. m. Sands, Eugenie F. on 66-Dec-26 [67-Jan-3: 2B].
Horney, William N. (45 yrs.) d. on 69-Dec-7 [69-Dec-9: 2C].
Horpel, Louisa m. Eichelberger, Charles on 68-Jun-22 [68-Jun-24: 2B].
Horrigan, Cornelius (53 yrs.) d. on 68-May-30 [68-Jun-1: 2B].
Horrigan, David (84 yrs.) d. on 66-Sep-16 [66-Sep-18: 2B].
Horsey, Edith (4 yrs., 2 mos.) d. on 70-Apr-2 [70-Apr-4: 2B].
Horsey, Keenie m. Deaver, H. T. on 68-Jun-24 [68-Feb-27: 2B].
Horsey, Mary Grammer (7 mos.) d. on 68-Jun-15 [68-Jul-16: 2C].
Horst, Henry (3 yrs., 3 mos.) d. on 69-Aug-11 [69-Aug-13: 2C].
Hort, William Francis m. Supplee, Hattie L. on 69-Apr-20 [69-Apr-26: 2B].
Horton, James M. m. Allen, Mary A. on 67-Jan-24 [67-Jan-30: 2C].
Horton, Rebecca E. m. Leary, Cornelius L. L. on 66-Jan-16 [66-Jan-18: 2C].
Horton, William (44 yrs.) d. on 70-Jul-9 [70-Aug-22: 2C].
Horwell, Edward C. (69 yrs.) d. on 68-Jan-26 [68-Jan-28: 2D].
Hosey, Kate M. m. McGregor, James H. on 66-Nov-22 [67-Mar-26: 2C].
Hoshour, John (53 yrs.) d. on 70-Oct-20 [70-Oct-27: 2B].
Hosking, Ann (97 yrs.) d. on 70-Dec-1 [70-Dec-5: 2C].
Hoskins, Martha Corrinne (5 mos.) d. on 70-Mar-22 [70-Mar-23: 2C].
Hosmer, Amos H. (81 yrs., 1 mo.) d. on 70-Feb-27 of Pneumonia [70-Mar-2: 2C].
Hosmer, Charley (2 yrs., 8 mos.) d. on 70-Apr-5 of Scarlet fever [70-Apr-22: 2C].
Hosmer, Harriet (76 yrs.) d. on 66-Aug-14 [66-Aug-18: 2B].
Hosmer, Hattie A. m. Harrison, James P. on 70-Dec-8 [70-Dec-22: 2B].
Hosmer, Jeanie d. on 67-Jan-3 [67-Jan-4: 2D].
Hosner, Ada C. d. on 66-Feb-28 [66-Mar-16: 2B].
Hosner, S. A. d. on 65-Dec-10 [66-Mar-16: 2B].
Hossbach, Philip (46 yrs.) d. on 69-Oct-21 [69-Oct-22: 2B].
Houck, Alfred E. (25 yrs.) d. on 70-Sep-12 [70-Sep-13: 2B; 70-Sep-14: 4C].
Houck, Anthony V. (51 yrs.) d. on 70-Dec-5 [70-Dec-7: 2C].
Houck, Carrie Sommerville (2 yrs., 5 mos.) d. on 70-Apr-30 [70-May-2: 2B].
Houck, Charles W. (1 mo.) d. on 67-Jun-11 [67-Jun-12: 2B].
Houck, Chloe M. (80 yrs.) d. on 66-Jul-17 [66-Jul-21: 2C].
Houck, Frank Clark (9 mos.) d. on 68-Sep-6 [68-Sep-7: 2A].

Houck, Henry J. m. Stone, Eugenia M. on 66-Dec-4 [66-Dec-7: 2B].
Houck, Jennie (9 yrs.) d. on 69-May-8 of Scarlet fever [69-May-10: 2C].
Houck, John T. m. Graham, Lizzie A. on 69-Oct-19 [69-Oct-21: 2B].
Houck, Laura (10 mos.) d. on 67-Jan-15 [67-Jan-16: 2C].
Houck, Lydia A. m. Ingle, William P. on 68-Apr-14 [68-Apr-24: 2B].
Houck, M. Tillie m. Simmons, Charles E. on 68-Dec-3 [68-Dec-7: 2C].
Houck, Margaret (42 yrs.) d. on 66-Jan-3 [66-Jan-5: 2C].
Houck, William James (1 mo.) d. on 68-Aug-27 [68-Aug-28: 2B].
Hough, Charles Miller (1 yr., 2 mos.) d. on 68-Sep-21 [68-Oct-1: 2B].
Hough, Harry Lee (4 mos.) d. on 66-Aug-28 [66-Aug-30: 2B].
Hough, M. A. m. Hartzell, David on 68-May-25 [68-May-28: 2B].
Hough, Mary d. on 70-Feb-11 [70-Feb-24: 2C].
Hough, Robert (57 yrs.) d. on 68-Jan-8 [68-Jan-9: 2C; 68-Jan-10: 1G, 2C].
Hough, William D. m. Norris, Mary R. on 70-Feb-8 [70-Feb-10: 2C].
Houghton, Louisa M. (35 yrs.) d. on 70-Mar-24 [70-Mar-25: 2C].
Houlton, George J. (52 yrs.) d. on 66-Sep-30 [66-Oct-2: 2B].
House, Emma F. (28 yrs.) d. on 70-Mar-17 [70-Mar-19: 2B].
House, Louise H. m. Henderson, James on 68-Feb-4 [68-Feb-5: 2D].
Householder, William H. m. Burley, Matilda on 70-Feb-13 [70-Feb-28: 2C].
Houseman, Anna Druscilla (2 yrs.) d. on 70-Jun-19 [70-Jun-20: 2C].
Houseman, George W. m. Shaw, Welthy Ann on 66-Dec-3 [66-Dec-5: 2B].
Houston, Ann (67 yrs.) d. on 66-Aug-13 of Food poisoning [66-Aug-15: 4C].
Houston, Emily m. Stanton, James on 66-Jun-14 [66-Jun-18: 2B].
Houston, James m. Day, Kate C. on 70-Aug-7 [70-Aug-9: 2C].
Houston, Joel m. Almaney, Henrietta on 69-May-25 [69-Jun-5: 2B].
Houston, Maggie J. m. Harper, Samuel on 67-Jan-1 [67-Jan-4: 2D].
Houston, Mary m. Fowler, John W. on 69-Aug-3 [69-Aug-10: 2C].
Houston, Mary Ann (28 yrs.) d. on 70-Sep-22 [70-Sep-23: 2C].
Houston, Mary Levinia m. Scharf, Elisha T. on 67-Jan-2 [67-Jan-23: 2C].
Houston, S. T. m. Finlayson, L. A. on 69-Jan-23 [69-Feb-6: 2C].
Houston, Samuel T. d. on 68-Jul-15 [68-Jul-16: 1G].
Hover, James O. (33 yrs.) d. on 66-Nov-22 [66-Nov-23: 2C].
Hover, Matilda J. (59 yrs.) d. on 66-Nov-8 [66-Nov-13: 2B].
Hovington, Richard d. on 66-Oct-12 of Cholera [66-Oct-15: 4B].
Howard, , Mrs. (70 yrs.) d. on 69-Sep-9 [69-Sep-11: 2B].
Howard, Anna A. m. Caulfield, Valentine W. on 67-Dec-11 [67-Dec-12: 2B].
Howard, Annie (4 mos.) d. on 66-Oct-8 [66-Oct-9: 2A].
Howard, Bertha Florence (4 yrs., 1 mo.) d. on 68-Aug-1 [68-Aug-3: 2B].
Howard, Bridget d. on 68-Dec-9 of Dropsy [68-Dec-10: 2D].
Howard, Charles (37 yrs.) d. on 68-Apr-24 [68-Apr-25: 2B].
Howard, Charles (68 yrs.) d. on 69-Jun-18 [69-Jun-21: 1G, 2B].
Howard, Deborah Ridgely d. on 66-Feb-16 [66-Feb-17: 2B].
Howard, Elizabeth (77 yrs.) d. on 68-Jun-10 [68-Jun-11: 2B].
Howard, Elizabeth Graham (2 yrs., 6 mos.) d. on 68-Apr-8 of Diptheria [68-Apr-9: 2B].
Howard, Ella m. Chase, Henry on 67-May-16 [67-May-20: 2B].
Howard, Ella C. m. Davison, Henry J. on 66-Jun-21 [66-Jun-25: 2B].
Howard, Emma J. m. Harrison, William on 68-May-7 [68-May-9: 2B].
Howard, Fannie m. Saltzer, James E. on 68-Dec-17 [68-Dec-18: 2C].
Howard, Harry E. (6 mos.) d. on 70-Jul-21 [70-Jul-23: 2B].
Howard, James (73 yrs.) d. on 70-Mar-19 of Typhoid [70-Mar-21: 1G, 2C].
Howard, Jane G. m. King, Joseph on 69-Jun-1 [69-Jun-4: 2C].
Howard, Joseph A. m. Carr, Margaret S. on 67-May-9 [67-May-16: 2B].
Howard, Joshua (72 yrs.) d. on 68-Sep-1 [68-Sep-2: 2A].
Howard, Laura E. m. Bervard, John on 67-May-29 [67-Jun-1: 2B].
Howard, Laura Virginia m. Brown, John Wilson on 66-Jan-25 [66-Feb-3: 2C].

Howard, Louisa M. (74 yrs.) d. on 69-Nov-9 [69-Nov-10: 2C].
Howard, Mabel m. Picard, William T. on 69-Dec-14 [69-Dec-17: 2C].
Howard, Maggie R. (7 mos.) d. on 68-Apr-22 [68-Apr-27: 2B].
Howard, Margaret Ann m. Davis, George on 70-Apr-14 [70-Apr-20: 2B].
Howard, Mary m. Adolph, Henry on 68-Sep-16 [68-Oct-8: 2B].
Howard, Mary Ann (64 yrs.) d. on 67-Aug-11 [67-Aug-12: 2C].
Howard, Mary Ann (32 yrs.) d. on 66-Feb-7 [66-Feb-9: 2C].
Howard, Mary E. m. Byard, Andrew J. on 68-Nov-1 [68-Nov-6: 2C].
Howard, Mary V. m. Bayly, Charles B. on 68-May-12 [68-May-14: 2B].
Howard, McHenry m. Coleman, Julia D. on 67-Jun-18 [67-Jun-22: 2B].
Howard, Parthenia (60 yrs.) d. on 70-Mar-21 of Paralysis [70-Mar-24: 2C].
Howard, Parthenia (9 mos.) d. on 67-Mar-16 [67-Mar-18: 2B].
Howard, Richard M. m. Perdue, Ella S. on 66-Oct-30 [66-Nov-8: 2C].
Howard, Sally (33 yrs.) d. on 70-Jun-21 of Brain congestion [70-Jun-28: 2C].
Howard, William (40 yrs.) d. on 70-Dec-2 [70-Dec-3: 2B].
Howard, William m. Smith, Rachel on 66-Jun-7 [66-Jun-21: 2B].
Howard, William Gilmor (9 mos.) d. on 69-Jul-7 [69-Jul-8: 2C].
Howard, William L. White (39 yrs., 8 mos.) d. on 70-Nov-30 of Bowel inflammation [70-Dec-1: 2C].
Howe, Eddie (6 mos.) d. on 69-Jun-20 [69-Jun-22: 2C].
Howe, Fannie C. d. on 70-Mar-30 [70-Apr-12: 2B].
Howe, Martin (6 mos.) d. on 69-Jun-20 [69-Jun-22: 2C].
Howe, Patrick (55 yrs.) d. [69-Dec-21: 2B].
Howe, Sarah (72 yrs., 10 mos.) d. on 66-Feb-1 [66-Feb-9: 2C].
Howe, Thomas T. d. on 70-Nov-4 of Consumption [70-Nov-22: 2C].
Howell, Annie m. Arscott, Richard on 66-Mar-26 [66-Mar-28: 2C].
Howell, Darius C. (21 yrs.) d. on 70-May-7 [70-May-9: 2B; 70-May-10: 2C].
Howell, Darius M. m. Carson, Mary R. on 67-Nov-7 [67-Nov-11: 2C].
Howell, George E. (9 yrs., 10 mos.) d. on 67-Jul-14 of Fall from tree [67-Jul-15: 1G, 2C].
Howell, Isabel m. Ronsaville, David W. on 66-Jan-1 [66-Jan-8: 2B].
Howell, Mary B. m. Seemuller, William on 67-Nov-14 [67-Nov-18: 2B].
Howell, Mary Carson (7 mos.) d. on 70-Jun-29 [70-Jun-30: 2C].
Howell, Mollie A. m. Cross, Frank W. on 68-Feb-27 [68-Mar-2: 2B].
Howell, Murdock m. Grove, Salome F. on 68-Apr-16 [68-Apr-18: 2A].
Howell, Permelia B. m. Nalls, Benjamin F. on 67-Aug-15 [67-Aug-20: 2B].
Howell, Rebecca L. d. on 70-Jul-20 [70-Jul-23: 2B].
Howes, E. L. m. Wilson, Mary E. on 66-Mar-7 [66-Mar-10: 2B].
Howland, Lothrop (26 yrs.) d. on 66-Apr-28 [66-Apr-30: 2B].
Howland, Russell (23 yrs.) d. on 69-Jan-30 of Consumption [69-Feb-1: 2C; 69-Feb-2: 2C; 69-Feb-3: 2C; 69-Mar-6: 2C].
Howser, Emma S. m. Everhart, William H. on 69-Aug-15 [69-Aug-23: 2C].
Howser, Jacob (73 yrs.) d. on 66-Oct-2 [66-Oct-20: 2C].
Howser, Martha (52 yrs.) d. on 66-Jan-9 [66-Jan-11: 2B].
Hoxter, Mary A. (34 yrs.) d. on 69-Dec-18 [69-Dec-20: 2C].
Hoye, James A. (34 yrs.) d. on 70-Mar-20 [70-Mar-23: 2C].
Hoye, Thomas (70 yrs.) d. on 69-Aug-28 [69-Sep-3: 2B].
Hoyer, Annie B. m. Steibel, Francis P. on 66-Nov-29 [66-Dec-8: 2B; 66-Dec-10: 2B].
Hoyer, William H. m. Jenkins, Julia A. on 67-Nov-26 [67-Dec-5: 2C].
Hubbard, Alva m. Noble, Ella on 70-Dec-8 [70-Dec-10: 2B].
Hubbard, Andrew J. m. White, Sarah A. on 68-Oct-13 [68-Oct-17: 2B].
Hubbard, Annie Virginia (1 yr., 4 mos.) d. on 68-Apr-22 [68-Apr-25: 2B].
Hubbard, B. (39 yrs.) d. on 70-Jan-23 [70-Feb-15: 2C].
Hubbard, George W. m. Geoghegan, Kate A. on 69-Dec-14 [70-Feb-7: 2C].
Hubbard, Jeanette (20 yrs.) d. on 68-Jan-23 [68-Jan-24: 2D].
Hubbard, Jesse H. T. m. Fluharty, Hester A. on 68-Apr-7 [68-Apr-15: 2B].

Hubbard, John Wesley d. on 70-Jul-25 of Consumption [70-Jul-26: 2C; 70-Jul-27: 2C].
Hubbard, Josephine F. m. Siddons, George H. on 69-Mar-4 [69-Mar-6: 2B].
Hubbard, Lavinia (37 yrs.) d. on 68-Apr-12 [68-Apr-14: 2A].
Hubbard, Lewis (25 yrs.) d. on 66-Oct-9 [66-Oct-11: 2C].
Hubbard, Mary E. m. Michell, Joseph C. on 68-Apr-9 [68-Apr-11: 2A].
Hubbard, Mary E. m. Holland, William H. on 67-Dec-16 [67-Dec-18: 2B].
Hubbard, Mary Elizabeth m. Sturgeon, Lindsey on 66-Apr-2 [66-Apr-6: 2B].
Hubbard, Matilda d. on 68-Mar-11 [68-Mar-31: 2B].
Hubbard, Nannie m. Sturgis, Zadoc on 67-May-6 [67-May-8: 2B].
Hubbard, Rebecca (54 yrs.) d. on 66-Jan-1 [66-Jan-4: 2C].
Hubbard, Sarah C. (16 yrs.) d. on 67-Mar-24 [67-Mar-25: 2C; 67-Mar-26: 2C].
Hubbard, V. R. G. m. Piercy, J. H. on 68-Nov-5 [68-Nov-17: 2C].
Hubbard, Wallace (16 yrs.) d. on 66-Sep-4 Drowned [66-Sep-5: 2B, 4B].
Hubbard, William m. Koons, Rosa on 68-Oct-29 [68-Nov-6: 2C; 68-Nov-7: 2B].
Hubbel, Augustin m. Bunce, Mary on 66-Apr-5 [66-Apr-12: 2B].
Hubbel, Benedict (73 yrs.) d. on 69-Nov-25 [69-Nov-27: 2B].
Hubbel, Joseph A. m. Burns, Sarah J. on 69-Jul-1 [69-Jul-3: 2B].
Hubbell, Bernard m. Stone, Mary E. on 68-Oct-7 [68-Nov-10: 2C].
Hubbell, Carrie V. m. Musselman, H. D. on 68-Oct-8 [68-Oct-10: 2B].
Hubbell, Clark (37 yrs.) d. on 69-Mar-11 [69-Mar-15: 2C].
Hubbell, Henry (9 mos.) d. on 70-Mar-27 [70-Mar-28: 2B; 70-Mar-29: 2C].
Hubel, Benedict (21 yrs.) d. on 65-Dec-31 [66-Jan-4: 2C].
Hubel, Rosa (59 yrs.) d. on 67-Jul-17 [67-Jul-18: 2C].
Huber, John A. m. King, Kate on 69-Mar-11 [69-Mar-16: 2C].
Huber, Maria L. m. Rothrock, Joseph on 68-Feb-24 [68-Mar-21: 2A].
Hubers, Lizzie (25 yrs., 7 mos.) d. on 70-May-16 [70-May-17: 2B].
Hubert, George m. Carle, Mary A. on 70-Apr-25 [70-Apr-28: 2B].
Hubert, Jeremiah (53 yrs.) d. on 68-Dec-26 [68-Dec-29: 2D].
Huck, Catharina (46 yrs.) d. on 66-Jan-15 [66-Jan-19: 2C].
Huck, Kate M. (20 yrs.) d. on 68-Jul-8 [68-Jul-11: 2B].
Hudgins, Alice m. Fairbanks, James D. on 66-Oct-16 [66-Oct-22: 2C].
Hudgins, Angeline m. Powell, Alexander W. on 66-Jul-19 [66-Jul-21: 2C].
Hudgins, Hezekiah (3 yrs.) d. on 66-Sep-26 of Croup [66-Oct-20: 2B].
Hudgins, James C. m. Robinson, Anna J. on 69-Feb-25 [69-Mar-9: 2C].
Hudgins, Lewis, Sr., Capt. (69 yrs.) d. on 66-Dec-26 [67-Feb-12: 2C].
Hudgins, Lilly Bell (2 mos.) d. on 69-Feb-24 [69-Feb-27: 2C].
Hudgins, Louisa M. m. Barnes, Walter S. on 66-Oct-3 [66-Oct-22: 2C].
Hudgins, Lucretia m. Van Newkirk, Francis M. on 68-Nov-29 [68-Dec-2: 2C].
Hudner, Margaret m. Daly, James on 66-May-24 [66-May-31: 2B].
Hudson, David W. (76 yrs.) d. on 66-Oct-30 [66-Nov-1: 2B, 4B].
Hudson, E. J., Dr. (28 yrs.) d. on 69-Aug-30 of Suicide (Poisoning) [69-Aug-31: 1G].
Hudson, Harriet A. d. on 69-Oct-29 [69-Oct-30: 2B; 69-Nov-1: 2B].
Hudson, Jennie m. Brown, Peter on 70-May-12 [70-May-16: 2B].
Hudson, John M. m. Townsend, Sarah C. on 67-Oct-31 [67-Nov-5: 2B].
Hudson, Mary A. m. Hamilton, John T. on 70-Nov-24 [70-Nov-29: 2C].
Hudson, Mary F. m. Canter, Issac W. on 68-Nov-17 [68-Nov-19: 2C].
Hudson, Paul Lee (9 mos.) d. on 67-Feb-9 of Croup [67-Feb-13: 2D].
Hudson, Robert (10 mos.) d. on 70-Jul-20 [70-Jul-22: 2C].
Hudwalker, Henry m. Knapp, Emma E. on 70-Sep-13 [70-Sep-15: 2B].
Hues, Hester A. (78 yrs.) d. on 66-Dec-27 [66-Dec-29: 2C].
Huett, Emille (30 yrs.) d. on 68-Mar-28 [68-Mar-30: 2B].
Huff, Charles A. O. m. Davis, Mary E. on 69-Dec-16 [69-Dec-17: 2C].
Huff, William J. (24 yrs.) d. on 70-Feb-27 [70-Feb-28: 2C].
Huffington, H. C. m. Pratt, Lizzie on 69-Jan-4 [69-Jan-5: 2C].
Huffington, William O. m. Emich, Sarah L. on 68-Sep-21 [68-Oct-1: 2B].

Huger, Benjamin, Jr., Capt. d. on 67-Sep-27 [67-Sep-28: 2A].
Huger, Eliza Celestine d. on 67-Oct-3 [67-Oct-4: 2B].
Hugg, Elizabeth A. (37 yrs.) d. on 67-Nov-15 [67-Nov-19: 2C].
Hugg, Emory m. Yeager, Ella on 69-Jun-16 [69-Jun-22: 2C].
Hugg, George W. m. Webb, Emma P. on 70-May-17 [70-Aug-24: 2C].
Hugg, Jacob W., Sr., Capt. (69 yrs., 7 mos.) d. on 70-Feb-26 [70-Feb-28: 1G, 2C; 70-Mar-1: 2C].
Hugg, William H. m. Nice, Mary J. on 70-Aug-26 [70-Aug-27: 2B; 70-Aug-29: 2B].
Huggins, Ida (9 yrs.) d. on 68-Oct-17 [68-Oct-19: 2B].
Huggins, Jane Cochran (2 mos.) d. on 69-Jun-29 [69-Jul-2: 2C].
Huggins, Sarah E. m. Patterson, George C. on 67-Aug-7 [67-Aug-12: 2C].
Hugh, Martin (1 yr., 2 mos.) d. on 67-Jul-7 [67-Jul-8: 2C].
Hughes, Alexander m. Willson, Margaret on 66-May-3 [66-May-30: 2C].
Hughes, Alfred W. m. Miller, Martha V. on 66-Apr-30 [66-May-17: 2C].
Hughes, Alice (69 yrs.) d. on 69-Jan-28 [69-Jan-29: 2C].
Hughes, Ann (1 yr., 4 mos.) d. on 68-Jul-19 [68-Jul-20: 2B].
Hughes, Ann d. on 69-Jun-26 [69-Jun-26: 2B].
Hughes, Carrie Inloe (1 yr., 2 mos.) d. on 68-Sep-25 [68-Sep-26: 2B].
Hughes, Clara L. m. Armstrong, John M. on 70-Sep-15 [70-Oct-3: 2B].
Hughes, Emily m. Wells, George on 67-Sep-5 [67-Sep-7: 2A].
Hughes, George N. m. Claypoole, Lucy on 68-Jul-30 [68-Aug-8: 2B].
Hughes, Hannah A. m. Hardesty, John on 68-Jul-9 [68-Jul-11: 2B].
Hughes, Hannah E. (1 mo.) d. of Inanition [68-Aug-28: 2B].
Hughes, Henrietta (52 yrs.) d. on 66-Oct-15 [66-Oct-18: 2B].
Hughes, Henry m. Harrigan, Ellen on 66-Feb-5 [66-Feb-23: 2C].
Hughes, Hugh (55 yrs.) d. on 66-Dec-29 [66-Dec-31: 2C; 67-Jan-1: 2C].
Hughes, James (52 yrs.) d. on 66-Mar-28 [66-Mar-30: 2C].
Hughes, James E., Rev. d. on 67-Sep-23 [67-Oct-3: 2B].
Hughes, John m. Flynn, Johanna J. on 66-May-1 [66-May-7: 2B; 66-May-8: 2B].
Hughes, Laura S. m. Sanner, Basil P. on 67-Feb-11 [67-Feb-19: 2C].
Hughes, Lizzie m. Rees, William S. on 68-Dec-15 [69-Jan-16: 2C].
Hughes, Louisa (44 yrs.) d. on 70-Jun-29 [70-Jun-30: 2C; 70-Jul-1: 2B].
Hughes, Maggie A. m. Ackler, William F. on 67-Nov-5 [67-Nov-6: 2B].
Hughes, Margaret (100 yrs.) d. on 67-Mar-19 [67-Mar-20: 2C].
Hughes, Maria Lavinia (28 yrs.) d. on 68-Dec-27 [68-Dec-29: 2D].
Hughes, Mary d. on 68-Dec-12 [68-Dec-14: 2C].
Hughes, Mary m. Unwin, Edward on 70-Jun-14 [70-Jun-15: 2B].
Hughes, Mary C. m. Kent, William A. on 69-Aug-11 [69-Aug-18: 2C].
Hughes, Mary Ellen (19 yrs.) d. on 66-Jan-19 [66-Jan-20: 2C; 66-Jan-21: 1G].
Hughes, Mary F. m. Bump, Jesse E. on 69-Jan-7 [69-Jan-15: 2D].
Hughes, Mary J. m. Moncure, W. P. on 69-Apr-8 [69-Apr-10: 2B].
Hughes, Mary Jane (80 yrs.) d. on 69-May-11 [69-May-13: 2B].
Hughes, Mary Roberta (1 yr., 2 mos.) d. on 68-Dec-8 [68-Dec-9: 2C].
Hughes, Minnie P. d. on 67-Sep-29 [67-Oct-10: 2B].
Hughes, Patrick (75 yrs.) d. on 70-Aug-22 [70-Aug-23: 2B].
Hughes, Patrick (55 yrs.) d. on 70-Jan-23 [70-Jan-28: 2C].
Hughes, Patrick H. (39 yrs.) d. on 68-Jun-27 [68-Jul-2: 2C].
Hughes, Peter d. on 67-Aug-13 [67-Aug-15: 2C].
Hughes, Peter (22 yrs.) d. on 70-Jul-18 [70-Jul-19: 2C].
Hughes, Robert m. Gogel, Anna E. on 66-Jun-6 [66-Jun-11: 2B].
Hughes, Rosa (19 yrs.) d. on 66-Apr-22 [66-Apr-24: 2B].
Hughes, Sarah d. on 66-Apr-17 [66-Apr-19: 2B; 66-Apr-20: 2B].
Hughes, Teresa (72 yrs.) d. on 67-May-22 [67-Jun-1: 2B].
Hughes, Virginia E. m. Mitchen, E. Madison on 70-Dec-22 [70-Dec-26: 2C].
Hughes, William (58 yrs.) d. on 67-Mar-1 [67-Mar-4: 2D].

Hughes, William Henry (3 mos.) d. on 68-Jul-5 [68-Jul-9: 2B].
Hughes, William Henry (22 yrs.) d. on 67-May-26 [67-May-27: 2B].
Hughes, William S. m. Weaver, Ellen G. on 66-Nov-19 [66-Nov-27: 2B].
Hughes, William T. (57 yrs.) d. on 70-Jan-27 of Consumption [70-Jan-29: 2B].
Hughes, William Whitfield (28 yrs., 5 mos.) d. on 67-Apr-7 [67-Apr-9: 2B].
Hughlett, Caroline m. Lindsay, Richard A. on 69-Sep-30 [69-Oct-4: 2C].
Hughson, Charles J. m. Herring, Elizabeth M. on 69-Nov-25 [69-Nov-30: 2C].
Hull, Agnes d. on 70-Aug-14 [70-Aug-16: 2C].
Hull, Elizabeth (70 yrs.) d. on 67-Apr-26 [67-Apr-27: 2A].
Hull, Josiah L. J. (7 yrs.) d. on 66-Dec-25 [66-Dec-27: 2C].
Hull, Julia m. Newport, John E. on 67-Apr-10 [67-Apr-12: 2C].
Hull, Mary C. d. on 69-Jul-14 [69-Jul-17: 2C].
Hull, Rebecca d. on 69-Jun-24 [69-Jun-26: 2B].
Hull, Rose d. on 66-Sep-13 [66-Sep-14: 2B].
Hullin, Corinne m. Cottman, Herman Stuart on 70-Jan-18 [70-Jan-28: 2B].
Hulls, Mary Virginia m. Corner, Samuel on 69-Jun-16 [69-Jun-19: 2B].
Hulse, Elizabeth Ann (72 yrs.) d. [68-Aug-22: 2A].
Hulse, George T. m. Henze, Orilla on 66-Nov-27 [66-Nov-29: 2B].
Hulse, Henry m. Griffith, Margaret on 68-Dec-15 [68-Dec-22: 2C].
Hulse, James H. m. Sleat, Mary J. on 70-Nov-22 [70-Dec-31: 2B].
Hulse, John I., Dr. d. on 69-Mar-10 [69-Mar-23: 2C].
Hults, William H. m. Mass, E. V. on 66-May-21 [66-May-24: 2C].
Hultz, Catherine C. (77 yrs.) d. on 70-May-23 [70-May-25: 2C].
Hume, Maggie J. m. Wolff, C. C. on 67-Mar-14 [67-Mar-18: 2B].
Hume, Margaret A. (64 yrs.) d. on 68-Jan-23 [68-Jan-24: 2D].
Hume, William m. Hines, Maggie on 70-Aug-25 [70-Sep-7: 2B].
Humes, Emma V. m. Kolb, William W. on 70-Mar-22 [70-Apr-9: 2B].
Humes, Susanna (73 yrs.) d. on 67-Aug-8 [67-Aug-9: 2C; 67-Aug-10: 2B].
Humes, Thomas J. m. Bishop, Hester M. on 67-Jan-3 [67-Jan-16: 2C].
Hummel, Conrad (6 yrs.) d. on 70-Mar-11 in Railroad accident [70-Mar-12: 1H].
Hummer, Maggie (25 yrs.) d. on 70-Mar-3 [70-Mar-4: 2C].
Humphreys, Elizabeth Jane (75 yrs.) d. on 67-May-6 [67-May-7: 2B; 67-May-8: 2B].
Humphreys, Ellen Eliza (2 yrs., 2 mos.) d. on 66-Dec-24 of Scarlet fever [66-Dec-27: 2C].
Humphreys, May Underwood (11 mos.) d. on 66-Dec-17 of Scarlet fever [66-Dec-19: 2B].
Humphreys, Thomas W. m. Waltjen, Catherine J. on 67-Nov-20 [68-Jul-17: 2B; 68-Jul-18: 2B].
Humphries, Annie R. m. Bangert, F. A. on 70-Apr-7 [70-Apr-27: 2B].
Humphries, Mary Ann m. Dodson, Peter on 69-Nov-10 [69-Nov-12: 2C].
Humrichouse, W. H. m. Hart, Nettie on 70-Dec-15 [70-Dec-17: 2B].
Humrickhouse, Mary Elizabeth (36 yrs.) d. on 70-Jul-16 of Apoplexy [70-Jul-18: 4E].
Hunckel, Philip m. Nesbit, Lizzie on 66-Jun-14 [66-Jun-18: 2B].
Hungerford, Sophia W. d. on 66-May-13 [66-May-16: 2C].
Hunichenn, Henry (34 yrs.) d. on 66-Aug-30 [66-Sep-1: 2B].
Hunt, Alice (36 yrs., 3 mos.) d. on 66-Mar-7 [66-Mar-9: 2B].
Hunt, Chloe Ann (63 yrs.) d. on 66-Nov-23 [66-Nov-24: 2B].
Hunt, Dunbar m. Brent, Leila L. on 67-Jun-4 [67-Jun-6: 2B].
Hunt, Emma V. m. Forsythe, L. E. on 68-Dec-17 [68-Dec-31: 2C].
Hunt, John A. (19 yrs.) d. on 68-Dec-12 [68-Dec-14: 2C].
Hunt, John A. (35 yrs.) d. on 67-Jul-2 [67-Jul-3: 2B; 67-Jul-11: 2C].
Hunt, Joseph m. Conn, Mary E. on 68-Jan-14 [68-Jan-28: 2D].
Hunt, Mary A. m. Reider, David J. on 67-Dec-8 [67-Dec-17: 2B].
Hunt, Mary J. (23 yrs.) d. on 70-Apr-1 [70-Apr-2: 2A].
Hunt, Mary J. m. German, Joseph on 67-Oct-1 [67-Oct-7: 2B].
Hunt, Matthew W. m. Constable, Sallie B. on 70-Apr-28 [70-May-2: 2B].
Hunt, Prudence (77 yrs.) d. on 67-Aug-2 [67-Aug-3: 2B].

Hunt, Ridie m. Marshall, George W. on 69-Nov-18 [69-Nov-20: 2C].
Hunt, S. V. m. Pistel, George H. on 68-Oct-22 [68-Oct-23: 2B].
Hunt, Susan M. m. Crapster, Milton H. on 66-Nov-15 [66-Nov-17: 2B].
Hunt, Susan R. m. Gilback, John D. on 67-Oct-1 [67-Oct-7: 2B].
Hunt, Thomas J. (36 yrs.) d. on 65-Dec-15 [66-Jan-29: 2C].
Hunt, Virginia A. (41 yrs., 5 mos.) d. on 69-Jun-5 [69-Jun-8: 2B].
Hunt, W. Hopkins m. Pearce, Sallie A. on 66-Oct-23 [66-Oct-25: 2C].
Hunt, William M. m. Duff, Ida Isabel on 70-Jan-20 [70-Jan-27: 2C].
Huntemuller, Alice (8 mos.) d. on 68-Jul-5 [68-Jul-6: 2B].
Huntemuller, Alice F. m. Mitchell, Robert M. on 66-Jan-2 [66-Jan-15: 2B].
Huntemuller, Herman (5 yrs., 6 mos.) d. on 68-Dec-19 of Scarlet fever [68-Dec-21: 2C; 68-Dec-28: 2C].
Huntemuller, Mamie (3 yrs., 4 mos.) d. on 68-Dec-27 of Scarlet fever [68-Dec-28: 2C].
Huntemuller, Matilda Sophia (66 yrs.) d. on 69-May-2 [69-May-3: 2C].
Huntemuller, Virginia m. Buck, William on 69-Dec-8 [69-Dec-17: 2C].
Hunter, Adeline (37 yrs.) d. on 67-Jul-25 [67-Jul-26: 2C].
Hunter, Alexander m. Garrett, Ann Elizabeth on 68-Jan-9 [68-Jan-16: 2C].
Hunter, Ann Louisa (6 mos.) d. on 66-Aug-2 [66-Aug-3: 2C].
Hunter, David Alexander (1 yr.) d. on 69-Feb-17 [69-Feb-19: 2C].
Hunter, Elizabeth m. Montgomery, Samuel on 68-Mar-19 [68-Mar-24: 2B].
Hunter, Emily m. Porter, Zeley W. on 70-Aug-11 [70-Sep-23: 2C].
Hunter, George Hoover d. on 67-Aug-8 [67-Aug-9: 2C].
Hunter, Grace Carroll (8 mos.) d. on 70-Mar-7 [70-Mar-8: 2C].
Hunter, H. Lawson W. (11 mos.) d. on 66-Sep-3 [66-Sep-10: 2D].
Hunter, James, Rev. d. on 68-May-1 [68-Jun-13: 2B].
Hunter, James Donaldson d. on 68-Jan-22 of Spasmodic croup [68-Jan-24: 2D].
Hunter, Louisa Jane (2 yrs., 2 mos.) d. on 70-Nov-27 [70-Nov-29: 2C].
Hunter, Marion (30 yrs.) d. on 70-Sep-21 [70-Sep-22: 2C].
Hunter, Mary E. (2 yrs., 2 mos.) d. on 66-May-30 [66-Jun-1: 2B].
Hunter, Nellie Blanche (7 yrs., 2 mos.) d. on 69-May-14 [69-May-15: 2B].
Hunter, Peter S. m. Norris, Clarinda on 67-Nov-19 [67-Nov-20: 2C].
Hunter, Rachel (67 yrs.) d. on 66-Feb-11 of Paralysis [66-Feb-13: 2C; 66-Feb-14: 2C].
Hunter, Samuel (29 yrs.) d. on 69-Mar-6 [69-Mar-8: 2C].
Hunter, Samuel m. Mister, Annie Maria on 68-Feb-13 [68-Feb-14: 2C].
Hunter, Thomas A. m. Hazlett, Mary A. on 70-Jun-14 [70-Jun-16: 2B].
Hunter, William G. m. Roszelle, Nannie D. on 70-Jun-16 [70-Jun-21: 2C].
Hunter, William K. m. French, Ella K. on 67-Dec-19 [68-Jan-4: 2C; 68-Jan-6: 2C].
Huppman, Annie d. on 69-Aug-30 [69-Aug-31: 2B; 69-Sep-1: 2B].
Huritt, Joseph A. m. Cathers, Rachel A. on 70-Oct-6 [70-Oct-15: 2B].
Hurkamp, J. Henry (47 yrs.) d. on 68-Aug-31 [68-Sep-1: 2A].
Hurley, Annie R. (7 yrs., 6 mos.) d. on 68-Apr-16 [68-Apr-18: 2A; 68-Apr-20: 2B].
Hurley, Fannie H. m. Whitemore, J. F. on 69-Aug-23 [69-Nov-4: 2B].
Hurley, George W. (1 yr., 9 mos.) d. on 68-Aug-29 [68-Sep-1: 2B].
Hurley, Ida Jane (6 yrs.) d. on 69-Apr-9 [69-Apr-10: 2B].
Hurley, Janava (16 yrs.) d. on 70-Nov-30 [70-Dec-2: 2C].
Hurley, R. A. m. Littleton, F. Drucie on 70-Aug-23 [70-Aug-24: 2C; 70-Aug-25: 2B].
Hurley, S. Mortimer m. Parke, M. Letitia [68-Jul-8: 2B].
Hurly, Timothy (6 yrs., 9 mos.) d. on 66-Nov-25 [66-Nov-27: 2B].
Hursh, William Alexander (3 yrs., 1 mo.) d. on 70-Jan-1 [70-Jan-5: 2C].
Hurst, Annetta (9 mos.) d. on 66-Mar-8 [66-Mar-9: 2B].
Hurst, Bridget (62 yrs.) d. on 70-Sep-19 [70-Sep-19: 2B].
Hurst, Jacob B. m. Stansbury, Mary E. on 66-Jun-14 [66-Jun-30: 2B].
Hurst, M. J. m. Johnes, T. S. on 69-Oct-28 [69-Oct-29: 2B].
Hurst, Martina Augusta (9 mos.) d. on 70-May-4 [70-May-5: 2B].
Hurst, Mary (30 yrs.) d. on 68-Jun-18 of Consumption [68-Jun-19: 2B].

Hurst, Samuel Webster d. on 66-Jul-14 [66-Jul-19: 2C].
Hurst, William R. (36 yrs.) d. on 68-Jun-14 of Paralysis [68-Jun-15: 1G, 2B; 68-Jun-16: 2B; 68-Jun-17: 2B].
Hurt, George A. m. Schaeffer, Mary A. on 67-Dec-26 [67-Dec-31: 2C].
Hurtt, Florence (1 yr., 9 mos.) d. on 68-Aug-11 [68-Aug-12: 2C].
Hurtt, Frances A. m. Forrester, George on 67-Dec-18 [68-Jul-31: 2C].
Hurtt, James T. (34 yrs.) d. on 67-Nov-22 of Yellow fever [67-Dec-14: 2B].
Hurtt, Martha V. (21 yrs.) d. on 69-Feb-22 [69-Feb-24: 2C; 69-Mar-6: 2C].
Hurtt, Provie A. m. Thompson, George W. on 70-Apr-6 [70-Apr-15: 2B].
Hurty, Dennis (45 yrs.) d. on 68-Mar-18 [68-Mar-19: 2B].
Hurxthal, Lewis (48 yrs.) d. on 68-Aug-1 [68-Aug-5: 2C].
Husgen, James (50 yrs.) d. on 68-Nov-16 [68-Nov-18: 2C].
Hush, Annie Primrose (1 yr.) d. on 66-Mar-6 [66-Mar-7: 2B].
Hush, Ida M. m. Williams, Denard S. on 69-Apr-29 [69-May-3: 2C].
Hush, Samuel C. (4 mos.) d. on 70-Jun-23 [70-Jun-28: 2C].
Hush, Samuel C. m. Wharry, Mary J. on 69-Apr-27 [69-May-4: 2B].
Hush, Samuel J. m. McCabe, Alice on 69-Sep-24 [69-Oct-13: 2C].
Hushbeck, Mary Ann (80 yrs.) d. on 68-May-11 [68-May-12: 2B].
Husing, Mary Elizabeth (15 yrs., 4 mos.) d. on 69-Apr-3 [69-Apr-5: 2B].
Husing, Mildred Veronica (6 yrs., 4 mos.) d. on 69-Mar-21 [69-Mar-22: 2C].
Hussey, Eddie (1 yr., 6 mos.) d. on 66-Oct-17 [66-Oct-20: 2B].
Hussey, Jacob A. d. on 66-May-4 [66-May-25: 2C].
Hussey, James (59 yrs.) d. on 68-Jan-9 [68-Jan-11: 2B].
Hussey, James R. m. Randell, Columbia J. on 66-Mar-29 [66-Apr-5: 2B].
Hussing, John D., Sr. (57 yrs.) d. on 70-Jan-7 [70-Jan-8: 2B; 70-Jan-11: 2C].
Hussman, Charles F. W. m. Wernsing, Mary A. on 66-Apr-19 [66-Apr-23: 2B].
Hussmeyer, Elizabeth Dora m. Pittroff, John P. on 68-Apr-16 [68-Apr-20: 2B].
Husten, Henrietta m. Pierce, Henry on 67-Dec-15 [67-Dec-19: 2B].
Huster, Anne E. (9 mos.) d. on 67-Jun-4 [67-Jun-7: 2B].
Huster, Emma F. m. Mullan, Charles X. on 66-Jul-2 [66-Jul-17: 2C].
Huster, Gottlieb (92 yrs., 9 mos.) d. on 68-Aug-29 [68-Sep-2: 1F].
Huster, Lizzie A. m. May, Philip M. on 70-Feb-22 [70-Mar-15: 2C].
Huster, Maria m. Rupley, Charles P. on 67-May-7 [67-May-8: 2B].
Huster, William G. m. Elliott, Rebecca on 67-Apr-21 [67-Apr-24: 2B].
Hutchens, Sarah m. Libren, Christopher on 67-Apr-2 [67-Apr-4: 2B].
Hutchings, Isabella (6 mos.) d. on 70-Feb-13 of Pneumonia [70-Feb-15: 2C].
Hutchins, Anna Amelia (8 mos.) d. on 70-Oct-17 [70-Oct-24: 2B].
Hutchins, Anna R. (28 yrs.) d. on 69-Oct-23 of Consumption [69-Oct-25: 2C].
Hutchins, Clara V. m. Turner, Samuel R. on 68-Feb-4 [68-Feb-13: 2C].
Hutchins, Clarence m. Britton, Alethia on 68-Nov-7 [68-Nov-19: 2C].
Hutchins, Eliza (60 yrs.) d. on 70-Apr-30 [70-May-2: 2B].
Hutchins, Florence E. m. Gill, Joseph on 70-Jan-19 [70-Jan-22: 2B; 70-Feb-1: 2B].
Hutchins, Helen Jane (1 yr., 2 mos.) d. on 66-Mar-29 [66-Apr-4: 2C].
Hutchins, Henry C. m. Ross, Clara on 70-Jan-27 [70-Jan-29: 2B; 70-Feb-3: 2B].
Hutchins, Joseph J. (36 yrs.) d. on 69-Nov-4 [69-Nov-5: 2C].
Hutchins, Lizzie m. Topham, John P. on 67-Sep-3 [67-Oct-1: 2B].
Hutchins, Matilda (1 yr., 1 mo.) d. on 70-Feb-20 [70-Feb-28: 2C].
Hutchins, Nicholas (67 yrs.) d. on 67-Nov-28 [67-Dec-20: 2B].
Hutchins, Richard Britton (4 mos.) d. on 70-May-23 [70-May-26: 2C].
Hutchins, Samuel (16 yrs.) d. on 67-Mar-17 [67-Mar-20: 2C].
Hutchins, William H. (20 yrs.) d. on 67-Mar-24 [67-Mar-25: 2C].
Hutchinson, Charlotte L. (20 yrs.) d. on 70-Apr-16 [70-Apr-18: 2B].
Hutchinson, George F. m. McClelland, Charlotte L. on 68-Nov-10 [68-Nov-12: 2C].
Hutchinson, George J. m. Phillips, Etta on 67-Nov-13 [67-Dec-5: 2C].
Hutchinson, James m. Reisinger, Annie M. on 66-Aug-5 [66-Nov-17: 2B].

Hutchinson, John W. m. Brady, Lizzia on 69-Oct-17 [70-Jan-17: 2C].
Hutchinson, Joshua S. m. Ferguson, Mary V. on 66-Aug-23 [66-Aug-27: 2B].
Hutchinson, Lizzie Wilder (33 yrs.) d. on 69-Mar-8 of Typhoid [69-Mar-9: 2C; 69-Mar-10: 2C].
Hutchinson, Mary T. m. Thompson, William on 69-Oct-19 [69-Nov-11: 2C].
Hutchinson, Virginia m. Brooks, James M. on 70-Jun-8 [70-Jun-28: 2C].
Hutchison, Charles E. m. Sargent, Mary A. E. on 70-Nov-17 [70-Nov-29: 2C].
Hutson, Catherine (52 yrs.) d. on 68-Apr-16 of Pneumonia [68-Apr-17: 2B].
Hutson, Deborah (77 yrs.) d. on 69-Mar-27 [69-Mar-29: 2B].
Hutson, George H (52 yrs.) d. on 69-Oct-11 [69-Oct-13: 2C].
Hutson, John (25 yrs.) d. on 67-Nov-20 [67-Nov-21: 2C; 67-Nov-22: 2C].
Hutson, Thomas A. D. m. Frederick, Laura V. on 69-Nov-16 [69-Nov-25: 2C].
Huttenberger, Charles F. m. Brookholts, Rachel on 70-Aug-22 [70-Sep-5: 2C].
Huttenberger, Charles F. m. Saville, Eliza A. on 70-Apr-7 [70-Apr-26: 2B].
Hutton, Ann d. on 69-Mar-6 [69-Mar-10: 2C].
Hutton, G. M. (62 yrs.) d. on 70-Apr-28 [70-May-21: 2B].
Hutton, James D. d. on 68-Aug-15 [68-Oct-7: 2C].
Hutton, Job (74 yrs.) d. on 70-Mar-30 [70-Mar-31: 2C].
Hutton, Rosalind m. Curtin, Robert R. on 69-Apr-8 [69-Apr-9: 2B].
Hutton, Samuel m. Davis, Mary W. on 69-Feb-23 [69-Mar-22: 2C].
Hutzler, Charles m. Demelman, Lina on 67-Dec-8 [67-Dec-10: 2B].
Hutzler, Charles G. m. Sonneborn, Hennie on 70-Jun-14 [70-Jun-16: 2B].
Huzza, Charity (76 yrs.) d. on 66-Aug-13 [66-Aug-14: 2C].
Huzza, Luther D. m. Gehring, Lottie on 67-Nov-28 [67-Dec-2: 2C].
Hyam, Abraham (77 yrs.) d. on 69-Jun-5 [69-Jun-7: 1H, 2B].
Hyatt, Roberta Underwood (10 mos.) d. on 66-Apr-26 [66-Apr-28: 2A].
Hyde, Arnold m. Bird, Mary Adelaide on 66-Dec-13 [66-Dec-15: 2B].
Hyde, Catherine (65 yrs.) d. on 69-May-25 [69-May-26: 2C].
Hyde, Charlotte m. Smith, Nicholas on 66-Dec-24 [66-Dec-27: 2C].
Hyde, Clemence T. m. Keith, William H. on 66-Oct-23 [66-Oct-26: 2B].
Hyde, David d. on 67-Apr-25 [67-Apr-27: 2A].
Hyde, Edward I. m. Clemm, Carrie R. on 68-Mar-25 [68-Mar-28: 2B].
Hyde, Ida Pratt m. Janes, Henry on 67-Aug-1 [67-Aug-7: 2C].
Hyde, Jacob W. d. on 66-Sep-18 of Cholera [66-Oct-17: 2B].
Hyde, James H. (72 yrs.) d. on 70-Aug-19 [70-Aug-22: 2C].
Hyde, John m. Davidson, Louisa on 69-Apr-6 [69-Apr-20: 2B].
Hyde, Joseph m. Benton, Margretta R. on 66-Feb-20 [66-Feb-26: 2B].
Hyde, Josephine (33 yrs.) d. on 69-Aug-29 [69-Sep-1: 2B].
Hyde, Mary (58 yrs.) d. on 70-Feb-24 [70-Feb-25: 2C].
Hyde, Mary A. d. on 69-May-27 [69-May-29: 2B].
Hyde, Mary Adelaide (7 yrs., 10 mos.) d. on 66-Jun-14 [66-Jun-15: 2C].
Hyde, Melinda (76 yrs.) d. on 68-Jun-29 [68-Jun-30: 2B].
Hyde, Oliver (83 yrs.) d. on 67-Jun-8 [67-Jun-10: 2B].
Hyde, Prudence G. d. on 68-May-7 [68-May-8: 2B].
Hyde, Richard Ridgely (14 yrs.) d. on 68-Jul-2 [68-Jul-13: 2B].
Hyde, Susan E. d. on 67-Jul-13 [67-Jul-15: 2C].
Hyde, Warren G. m. Martins, Anna S. on 68-May-14 [68-May-16: 2A].
Hyde, William H. m. Kime, Elizabeth on 69-Sep-28 [69-Sep-30: 2B].
Hyer, Virginia D. m. Aaron, Marcellus on 70-Dec-18 [70-Dec-19: 2C].
Hyland, John G. d. on 68-Oct-8 [68-Oct-9: 2C].
Hyman, John d. on 67-Jun-13 [67-Jun-15: 2B].
Hymos, Hughey d. on 66-Oct-5 of Cholera [66-Oct-6: 1F].
Hynds, Maria Louisa (27 yrs.) d. on 70-Apr-6 [70-Apr-14: 2C].
Hynes, David S. m. Cochran, Annie L. on 70-Jul-4 [70-Aug-6: 2C; 70-Aug-8: 2C].
Hynes, James (21 yrs.) d. on 66-Feb-21 of Lung inflammation [66-Feb-23: 2C].
Hynson, Ann Rebecca (48 yrs.) d. on 67-Mar-4 [67-Mar-5: 2C; 67-Mar-6: 2C].

Hynson, Benjamin T. m. Kenly, Anna M. on 68-May-5 [68-May-6: 2B].
Hynson, Charles E. m. Sanders, Virginia B. on 70-Mar-29 [70-Apr-1: 2B].
Hynson, Charles L. m. Stewart, Annie E. on 66-Oct-17 [66-Oct-19: 2B].
Hynson, Mary Lizzie (9 mos.) d. on 67-Feb-9 [67-Feb-11: 2C].
Hynson, Mary W. m. Sollers, Andrew Jackson on 69-Apr-7 [69-Apr-12: 2A].
Hysan, Mary Esther (1 yr., 4 mos.) d. on 70-Dec-1 [70-Dec-3: 2B].
Hyson, Albert S. m. Berry, Lucy A. on 69-Feb-28 [69-Mar-3: 2B].
Hyson, James W. (24 yrs.) d. on 70-Jul-13 [70-Jul-30: 2C].
Hyson, James W. m. Meyers, Mary F. on 69-Mar-25 [69-Mar-31: 2C].
Hyson, Sarah E. m. Newkirk, James on 69-Mar-18 [69-Mar-20: 2B].
Hyson, William (22 yrs.) d. on 70-Jul-13 of Fall [70-Jul-15: 1G].
Hyson, William H. m. Fricks, Amelia on 66-Dec-23 [66-Dec-29: 2C].
Hythe, William (14 yrs.) d. on 67-Jun-5 Drowned [67-Jun-7: 1F].
Ickler, John m. Davis, Lizzie H. on 68-Mar-17 [68-Mar-18: 2B].
Idding, Emily S. W. (23 yrs.) d. on 66-Jun-20 [66-Jun-21: 2B].
Iddins, Henry m. Callaway, Annie E. on 68-Nov-9 [68-Nov-16: 2C].
Ide, Ernst m. Brinkman, Sylvinia on 69-Feb-17 [69-Mar-15: 2C].
Iglehart, Ann (87 yrs.) d. on 69-Mar-27 [69-Apr-6: 2C].
Iglehart, Ann Eliza d. on 67-May-13 [67-May-14: 2B].
Iglehart, Anna Louisa m. Richardson, Henry W. on 70-Apr-26 [70-May-2: 2B].
Iglehart, Emery E. m. Emmart, Sallie E. on 68-Nov-12 [68-Nov-14: 2B].
Iglehart, Harwood m. Kent, A. Owen on 66-Aug-16 [66-Aug-21: 2C].
Iglehart, Issac m. Stansfield, Josephine on 69-Feb-2 [69-Feb-6: 2C].
Iglehart, J. H. m. Harding, M. Virginia on 69-Mar-9 [69-Mar-10: 2C].
Iglehart, John (82 yrs.) d. on 69-Apr-30 [69-May-6: 2B].
Iglehart, John H. d. on 67-Dec-27 [67-Dec-28: 2C].
Iglehart, John R. d. on 67-Sep-17 [67-Sep-18: 2B].
Iglehart, P. V. m. Hall, S. D. on 66-Dec-27 [67-Jan-24: 2C].
Igo, John Henry (7 mos.) d. on 67-Jun-17 [67-Jun-18: 2B].
Igo, Leonard Francis d. on 70-Sep-2 [70-Sep-3: 2B].
Igo, Willie Edward d. on 68-Jul-8 [68-Jul-9: 2B].
Ijams, Harriet (69 yrs.) d. on 67-Sep-29 [67-Sep-30: 2B].
Ijams, Hattie m. Smith, George W. on 66-Nov-22 [66-Dec-31: 2C].
Ijams, Joseph A. m. Waters, Violetta A. on 65-Nov-24 [66-Jul-7: 2B].
Ijams, Rosetta C. (21 yrs.) d. on 66-Oct-25 [66-Oct-27: 2B].
Ijams, William H. (48 yrs.) d. on 66-Apr-19 [66-Apr-21: 2B].
Iler, William B. (41 yrs.) d. on 70-Jan-17 of Heart disease [70-Feb-5: 2C; 70-Feb-7: 2C].
Ilgenfritz, John m. Barcher, Emma on 69-Oct-5 [69-Nov-5: 2C].
Ilgenfritz, Sarah E. (30 yrs.) d. on 68-Apr-8 [68-Apr-9: 2B].
Ilgenfritz, Walter Dunning (3 yrs., 8 mos.) d. on 69-Jan-11 of Scarlet fever [69-Jan-15: 2D].
Imler, Charles Christian m. Readasell, Margaret on 67-Aug-6 [67-Aug-12: 2C].
Ing, John Hadley (4 yrs.) d. on 69-Feb-27 [69-Mar-1: 2C].
Ingalls, Dimond m. Peters, Anna M. on 67-Sep-26 [67-Oct-3: 2B].
Ingalls, John D. m. Johnson, Alverdia on 69-Apr-5 [69-Apr-9: 2C].
Ingle, James Allen (25 yrs.) d. on 69-Mar-5 [69-Mar-13: 2C].
Ingle, William P. m. Houck, Lydia A. on 68-Apr-14 [68-Apr-24: 2B].
Inglesby, Mary (60 yrs.) d. on 70-Nov-21 [70-Nov-22: 2B; 70-Nov-23: 2B].
Ingleson, Judith (66 yrs.) d. on 67-Mar-17 [67-Mar-18: 2B; 67-Mar-19: 2C].
Inglis, Anna Maria (82 yrs.) d. on 66-Dec-21 [66-Dec-22: 2B].
Ingraham, J. Geiger m. Kosure, Clara Virginia on 68-Jun-2 [68-Jun-3: 2B].
Ingram, Belle m. Foreman, Lea on 67-Feb-5 [67-Feb-7: 2C].
Inkhouse, Mary A. m. Cain, George on 69-Aug-30 [69-Nov-5: 2C].
Inloes, Charles E. m. Thompson, Mary Carroll on 68-Feb-18 [68-Feb-19: 2C].
Inloes, Ella m. DuBarry, William Duane on 66-Oct-9 [66-Oct-11: 2C].
Inloes, Emma Ellen (2 mos.) d. on 68-Nov-7 [68-Nov-9: 2B].

Inloes, H. A., Jr. m. Uhthoff, Carrie H. on 67-Apr-25 [67-Apr-27: 2A].
Inloes, Henry A., Jr., Dr. (27 yrs.) d. on 70-Jun-16 [70-Jun-17: 2B; 70-Jun-18: 2B].
Inloes, Martha A. (50 yrs.) d. on 66-Jul-11 [66-Jul-17: 2C].
Inloes, Mary (74 yrs.) d. on 67-Mar-25 [67-Mar-26: 2C; 67-Mar-27: 2C; 67-Mar-28: 2B].
Inloes, S. Emma (20 yrs.) d. on 66-Apr-11 [66-Apr-12: 2B].
Innes, Cora (8 mos.) d. on 69-Apr-28 [69-Apr-29: 2B].
Inscoe, Elizabeth J. m. Holmes, John T. on 68-Nov-12 [68-Nov-16: 2C].
Insley, Corbin W. m. Mister, Annie on 70-May-17 [70-May-19: 2C].
Insley, Richard H. m. Mister, Maria F. on 70-Nov-20 [70-Nov-23: 2B].
Insley, Zebedee m. Pritchet, Amanda on 67-Nov-14 [67-Nov-16: 2B].
Iredell, Sara L. m. Fleetwood, Christian A. on 69-Nov-18 [69-Nov-22: 2C].
Ireland, George Bourne (1 yr., 3 mos.) d. on 69-Oct-9 of Whooping cough and congestive chill [69-Oct-23: 2B].
Ireland, George Gideon (9 yrs., 8 mos.) d. on 69-Jul-27 [69-Jul-30: 2C].
Ireland, Issac m. Bolden, Amelia on 69-Oct-28 [69-Oct-29: 2B; 69-Oct-30: 2B].
Ireland, Mary m. Aisquith, George on 68-Mar-31 [68-Apr-23: 2B].
Ireland, Samuel R. (23 yrs.) d. on 68-Sep-4 [68-Sep-5: 2A; 68-Sep-7: 2A].
Ironmonger, Charles S. m. Nace, Henrietta on 69-Dec-30 [70-Jan-4: 2C].
Irons, Ann (75 yrs.) d. on 68-Dec-26 [68-Dec-28: 2B; 68-Dec-29: 2D].
Irons, John T. m. Francis, Mary Jane on 67-Mar-12 [67-Mar-21: 2C].
Irons, Sarah H. (31 yrs.) d. on 68-Sep-19 [68-Sep-22: 2B].
Irons, William m. Lewis, Mary C. on 69-Aug-3 [69-Aug-7: 2B].
Irvin, George W. (50 yrs.) d. on 68-Apr-16 [68-Apr-18: 2A; 68-Apr-20: 1G].
Irvine, Carter P. m. Rennolds, Mary T. on 69-May-11 [69-May-18: 2C].
Irving, Elizabeth E. (64 yrs.) d. on 68-Oct-25 [68-Oct-26: 2B; 68-Oct-27: 2B].
Irving, Julia A. M. d. on 70-Feb-1 [70-Feb-3: 2B].
Irving, Kate m. Gardner, William H. on 70-Oct-11 [70-Oct-19: 2B].
Irving, Mary E. m. Steiger, John Carroll on 68-Feb-19 [68-Mar-13: 2C].
Irwin, Belle m. Neff, Charles W. on 65-Dec-20 [66-Jan-20: 2C].
Irwin, Cornelia Griggins d. on 69-Mar-9 [69-Mar-13: 2C].
Irwin, Deborah L. (68 yrs.) d. on 70-Mar-19 [70-Apr-21: 2C].
Irwin, Henrietta J. m. Woodrow, J. Frank on 68-Aug-25 [68-Aug-28: 2B].
Irwin, Henry, Capt. d. [68-Jul-13: 2A].
Irwin, James (5 yrs., 4 mos.) d. on 69-Jan-31 [69-Feb-1: 2C].
Irwin, Margaret d. on 68-Sep-13 [68-Sep-14: 2B].
Irwin, Mary Agnes (1 mo.) d. on 68-Jun-25 [68-Jun-26: 2B].
Irwin, P. H. m. Boyle, Helen J. on 66-Dec-4 [66-Dec-11: 2B].
Irwin, William m. Polmyer, Pamela on 70-Jan-27 [70-Jan-28: 2B].
Isenberg, Jennie m. Forrester, William H. on 68-Sep-8 [68-Sep-12: 2B].
Isett, John (62 yrs.) d. on 66-Aug-5 of Consumption [66-Aug-7: 2C].
Isett, Robert W. R. (20 yrs.) d. on 66-Sep-18 of Consumption [66-Sep-14: 2B].
Israel, DeWitt C. d. on 68-Dec-3 [69-Jan-1: 2C].
Israel, Edward d. on 69-Aug-6 [69-Aug-11: 2C; 69-Aug-12: 2C].
Israel, Kate (2 yrs., 1 mo.) d. on 69-Aug-14 [69-Apr-24: 2B].
Israel, Richard (73 yrs.) d. on 68-Feb-13 [68-Feb-26: 2C].
Israel, S. G. m. High, Annie M. on 69-Feb-15 [69-Feb-19: 2C].
Israel, T. Woodward (23 yrs.) d. on 66-Dec-3 [66-Dec-7: 2B].
Issacs, Charlotte m. Issacs, Tobias on 69-Jul-29 [69-Jul-31: 2C].
Issacs, Emma E. m. Elliott, W. Wallace on 70-Mar-2 [70-Mar-7: 2C].
Issacs, Rebecca J. d. on 66-May-28 of Consumption [66-May-29: 2B].
Issacs, Tobias m. Issacs, Charlotte on 69-Jul-29 [69-Jul-31: 2C].
Ives, Elizabeth m. Todd, James H. on 67-Sep-3 [67-Sep-7: 2A].
Ives, James H. m. Medinger, Emma R. on 70-Dec-15 [70-Dec-19: 2C].
Jackens, Taylor d. on 67-Dec-24 of Gunshot wound [67-Dec-27: 1G].
Jackson, Alfred S. (60 yrs.) d. on 66-Dec-26 Drowned [67-Jun-24: 1F, 2B].

Jackson, Anna V. m. Godman, William J. on 68-Apr-23 [68-Apr-25: 2B].
Jackson, Anne Eliza m. Calwell, Thomas G. on 66-Feb-20 [66-Feb-27: 2B; 66-Feb-28: 2C].
Jackson, Annie M. d. on 70-Sep-28 [70-Sep-29: 2B; 70-Sep-30: 2B].
Jackson, Arthur N. m. Rayner, Mary J. on 68-May-20 [68-May-22: 2C].
Jackson, Arthur Rayner (4 mos.) d. on 70-Mar-31 [70-Apr-1: 2B].
Jackson, Bethiah (76 yrs.) d. on 69-Jan-9 [69-Jan-11: 2C].
Jackson, Caroline C. (34 yrs.) d. on 69-Jan-3 [69-Jan-5: 2C].
Jackson, Charles Edwin (8 mos.) d. on 66-May-6 [66-May-7: 2B].
Jackson, Charles M. m. Brael, Maggie N. on 70-Jan-6 [70-Jan-7: 2F].
Jackson, Charles McC. m. Appell, Caroline C. on 66-Apr-17 [66-Apr-18: 2B].
Jackson, E. M. m. Allison, Jennie on 67-May-16 [67-May-17: 2B].
Jackson, Edward T. m. Long, Helen M. on 69-Oct-20 [69-Oct-21: 2B].
Jackson, Elizabeth (69 yrs.) d. on 70-Feb-27 [70-Mar-2: 2D].
Jackson, Elizabeth A. m. Koller, Issac A. on 67-Jul-15 [67-Jul-31: 2C].
Jackson, Emma A. m. Wheeler, G. F. on 67-Jun-13 [67-Jun-17: 2B].
Jackson, Frank C. m. Kuhn, Theresa S. on 70-Oct-13 [70-Oct-19: 2B].
Jackson, Frederick Skipwith (15 yrs.) d. on 68-Jul-24 [68-Jul-28: 2B].
Jackson, George H. m. Markland, Bettie M. on 68-Jun-16 [68-Jun-20: 2B].
Jackson, George W. m. Bond, Almira on 67-Aug-31 [67-Sep-30: 2B].
Jackson, Harold m. Wilmore, Hester on 68-Oct-1 [68-Oct-3: 2B].
Jackson, Hattie Florence (1 yr.) d. on 70-Oct-12 [70-Oct-13: 2C].
Jackson, Henry (40 yrs.) d. on 69-Dec-12 [69-Dec-14: 2C].
Jackson, Henry (60 yrs.) d. on 70-Mar-17 in Machine accident [70-Mar-19: 2B; 70-Mar-21: 1H].
Jackson, Isabel R. m. Carswell, Jonathan on 67-Jan-8 [67-Jan-11: 2C].
Jackson, Issac H. (49 yrs.) d. on 67-Aug-21 of Kidney disease [67-Aug-30: 2B].
Jackson, James D. (15 yrs.) d. on 66-Apr-8 [66-Apr-9: 2B].
Jackson, James F. m. Cliffe, Hettie B. on 70-Oct-23 [70-Nov-3: 2B].
Jackson, James G. m. Etchison, Virginia W. on 67-May-30 [67-Jun-4: 2A].
Jackson, Jane m. Scott, Joseph on 69-Oct-19 [69-Oct-26: 2B].
Jackson, John m. Blake, Matilda on 66-Aug-8 [66-Aug-11: 2B].
Jackson, John H. (53 yrs.) d. on 70-Feb-27 [70-Mar-2: 2C].
Jackson, John L. m. Bedencoff, Maggie on 70-Oct-30 [70-Nov-8: 2B].
Jackson, Josephine C. m. Morgan, Joseph A. on 68-Aug-25 [68-Sep-1: 2A].
Jackson, Lilly Maud (2 yrs.) d. on 68-Aug-20 [68-Aug-21: 2B].
Jackson, Louisa Canter (60 yrs.) d. on 69-Nov-3 [69-Nov-5: 2C].
Jackson, Lucy S. m. Trotter, William on 68-Oct-21 [68-Nov-2: 2B].
Jackson, M. Helen m. Mackall, John B. on 66-Dec-5 [66-Dec-8: 2B].
Jackson, Maggie A. (21 yrs.) d. on 70-Apr-1 [70-Apr-2: 2A].
Jackson, Martha A. m. Frederick, Benjamin F. on 68-Sep-9 [68-Sep-14: 2B].
Jackson, Mary (67 yrs.) d. on 66-Jul-24 [66-Jul-25: 2C].
Jackson, Mary m. Miller, William G. on 67-Apr-23 [67-Apr-27: 2A].
Jackson, Mary E. m. McClelland, David P. on 68-Dec-25 [68-Dec-29: 2D].
Jackson, Mary E. m. Tubman, John T. on 66-Aug-8 [66-Aug-10: 2C].
Jackson, Mary Ellen m. Gardner, James Wesley on 67-Jan-15 [67-Jan-23: 2C].
Jackson, Mary F. m. King, John, Jr. on 67-Aug-20 [67-Aug-21: 2B].
Jackson, Mollie E. m. Armacost, Calvin A. on 69-Sep-23 [69-Sep-25: 2B].
Jackson, Nason (13 yrs.) d. on 66-Jul-13 Drowned [66-Jul-14: 1F].
Jackson, Rebecca A. m. Coskery, F. S. on 69-Mar-17 [69-Mar-31: 2C].
Jackson, Ruth Ann Rebecca (1 yr., 5 mos.) d. on 70-Dec-13 [70-Dec-14: 2C].
Jackson, Sarah E. m. Dickey, W. W. on 66-Oct-23 [66-Oct-25: 2C].
Jackson, Stephen M. (70 yrs.) d. on 68-Nov-3 [68-Nov-4: 2C].
Jackson, Tatlow m. Ludlow, Sally W. on 66-Jun-13 [66-Jun-15: 2C].
Jackson, William m. Davisson, Anne Elizabeth on 66-Jan-4 [66-Jan-12: 2C].
Jackson, William Hutchinson (28 yrs.) d. on 70-Nov-20 [70-Nov-22: 2B].

Jackson, William R. (58 yrs.) d. on 66-Feb-1 of Pneumonia [66-Feb-2: 1G, 2C; 66-Feb-3: 2C].
Jackson, William R. m. Brerewood, Sarah N. on 70-Oct-18 [70-Oct-25: 2B].
Jacob, James Albert (41 yrs.) d. on 67-Dec-20 [68-Jan-4: 2C].
Jacob, Sarah (82 yrs.) d. on 69-May-10 [69-May-12: 2B].
Jacobi, Hannah m. Bachrach, Nathan on 67-Aug-5 [67-Aug-17: 2B; 67-Aug-21: 2B].
Jacobs, Clara R. m. Alford, George C. on 70-Dec-15 [70-Dec-19: 2C].
Jacobs, Collis F. m. Underwood, Sarah J. on 68-Apr-2 [68-Apr-8: 2B].
Jacobs, Georgeann (22 yrs., 6 mos.) d. on 66-Dec-11 [66-Dec-27: 2C].
Jacobs, Hannah m. Levy, Louis on 68-Jun-21 [68-Jun-23: 2B].
Jacobs, Isabella m. Rothschild, Theodore on 70-Jun-19 [70-Jun-25: 2B].
Jacobs, John D. (36 yrs.) d. on 68-Jan-3 [68-Jan-17: 2C].
Jacobs, John P. m. Barns, Mary A. on 67-May-23 [67-Jun-5: 2B].
Jacobs, Laura V. m. Dunlap, Melville S. on 70-Mar-31 [70-Apr-6: 2B].
Jacobs, Sarah m. Kerngood, A. on 69-Dec-19 [69-Dec-28: 2C].
Jacobs, Sarah P. m. Cather, Robert W. on 67-Jul-20 [67-Aug-23: 2B].
Jacobs, Thomas E. m. Leddon, Susanna R. on 68-Feb-27 [68-Mar-2: 2B].
Jacobs, Zachariah S. (5 mos.) d. on 70-Aug-6 [70-Aug-8: 2C].
Jacobsen, Carl C. m. Roberts, Frances M. on 67-Nov-21 [67-Nov-22: 2B].
Jacobsen, Charles (38 yrs.) d. on 68-Oct-19 [68-Oct-23: 2B].
Jacobsen, Emma m. Williams, Dalrymple on 68-Apr-28 [68-Apr-30: 2B].
Jacobsen, Gill (4 yrs., 7 mos.) d. on 66-Mar-1 [66-Mar-2: 2B].
Jacobsen, Maria E. (69 yrs.) d. on 68-Feb-29 [68-Mar-2: 2B].
Jacobson, Alfred d. on 66-Feb-6 [66-Feb-7: 2C].
Jacobson, Kate V. m. Jefferson, Joseph A. on 70-Dec-14 [70-Dec-17: 2B].
Jacques, Annie M. m. Bramhall, George W. on 70-Nov-22 [70-Nov-24: 2B].
Jakes, Charlotte (65 yrs.) d. on 70-Dec-2 [70-Dec-15: 2C].
Jamart, Kate A. (36 yrs.) d. on 68-May-11 [68-May-12: 2B].
James, Anna L. m. Ackerman, C. C. on 68-May-25 [68-Jun-4: 2B].
James, Annie m. Sanderson, George H. on 67-Nov-21 [67-Nov-25: 2C].
James, Arthur (1 yr.) d. on 66-May-26 [66-May-28: 2B].
James, DeWitt Clinton (26 yrs.) d. on 66-May-9 Murdered (Shooting) [66-May-10: 1F; 66-May-11: 1E, 2B; 66-May-12: 1F].
James, Eliza R. (23 yrs.) d. on 69-Mar-23 [69-Mar-24: 2C; 69-Mar-25: 2C].
James, Gilbert C. (50 yrs.) d. on 70-Aug-6 [70-Aug-8: 2C].
James, Janie (22 yrs.) d. on 69-Jan-22 [69-Feb-6: 2C].
James, John R. (35 yrs.) d. on 70-Feb-16 [70-Feb-18: 2C].
James, John R. m. Donaldson, Mary A. on 69-Nov-3 [69-Nov-5: 2C].
James, Lizzie A. m. Philips, Thomas N. S. on 67-Nov-17 [68-Apr-10: 2B].
James, M. Alice m. Cooke, William H. on 70-Jul-9 [70-Jul-19: 2B].
James, Richard D. (49 yrs.) d. on 66-Apr-5 [66-Apr-6: 2B].
James, Sarah Jane (27 yrs.) d. on 69-Mar-1 of Consumption [69-Mar-3: 2C].
James, Stephen P. m. Lynch, Martha E. on 66-Jul-12 [66-Jul-26: 2C].
James, Susannah (65 yrs.) d. on 70-Jul-29 [70-Jul-30: 2B].
James, Susie Emily m. Hamilton, Francis on 67-Mar-31 [67-Apr-3: 2B].
James, William S. (39 yrs.) d. on 69-Jul-16 [69-Jul-19: 2D].
James, William W. m. Laurence, Bettie on 66-Dec-15 [66-Dec-18: 2B].
Jameson, Harriet Maria d. on 67-Jun-27 [67-Jun-28: 2B].
Jameson, Louisa J. (23 yrs.) d. on 67-Jul-7 [67-Jul-8: 2C].
Jameson, William, Capt. (90 yrs.) d. on 68-Oct-28 [68-Oct-29: 2B].
Jameson, William S. (39 yrs.) d. on 69-Jul-16 [69-Jul-17: 2C].
Jamison, C. C., Jr. m. Ballard, Clementine on 66-Oct-1 [66-Oct-10: 2B].
Jamison, Charles E. m. Ferguson, Ellen on 68-Jul-9 [68-Jul-11: 2B].
Jamison, Henrietta (46 yrs.) d. on 66-Jul-13 of Consumption [66-Jul-17: 2C].
Jamison, Margaret (41 yrs.) d. on 69-Aug-14 [69-Apr-16: 2B].
Jamison, Mollie B. m. Norton, W. J. on 70-Oct-11 [70-Oct-13: 2C].

Jamison, Robert m. Harris, Annie C. on 68-Sep-29 [68-Oct-1: 2B].
Jamison, W. D., Dr. (47 yrs.) d. on 68-Feb-17 [68-Feb-19: 2C; 68-Feb-20: 2C].
Jamison, William Douglas (1 yr., 3 mos.) d. on 68-Apr-23 [68-Apr-25: 2B].
Janes, Henry m. Hyde, Ida Pratt on 67-Aug-1 [67-Aug-7: 2C].
Janney, Margaret H. m. Elliott, Joseph P. on 70-Feb-23 [70-Feb-25: 2C].
Janowitz, Daniel m. Meyer, Mary A. on 67-Jan-28 [67-Mar-14: 2C].
January, Carrie m. Klausman, Lawrence on 67-Sep-17 [67-Sep-21: 2A].
January, Selenia C. (25 yrs., 4 mos.) d. on 66-Jun-30 [66-Jul-3: 2C].
Janvier, Edmund De H m. Minor, Juliet Gilmer on 68-Nov-10 [68-Nov-12: 2C].
Janvier, Margaret N. (33 yrs.) d. on 66-Oct-18 [66-Oct-20: 2B].
Jarboe, Eugenia m. Cook, Henry F. on 67-Mar-28 [67-Mar-29: 2B].
Jarboe, Walter S. m. Warner, Agnes A. on 68-Jan-9 [68-Jan-11: 2B].
Jarrett, Archer d. on 69-Jul-6 of Fall from window [69-Jul-9: 4C].
Jarrett, Lefevre (46 yrs.) d. on 70-Feb-25 of Paralysis [70-Feb-26: 1H; 70-Feb-28: 1G, 2C; 70-Mar-1: 1E].
Jarrett, Lizzie Quigley (1 yr., 2 mos.) d. on 67-Dec-8 [67-Dec-9: 2B].
Jarvis, Catherine m. Skinner, Thomas W. on 66-Dec-18 [66-Dec-20: 2B].
Jarvis, Robert B. (47 yrs.) d. on 69-Sep-13 of Bilious dysentery [69-Sep-17: 2C; 69-Sep-29: 2B].
Jarvis, Virginia F. m. Funk, John W. on 70-Mar-24 [70-Mar-28: 2B].
Jatho, Eliza J. d. on 66-Jun-26 [66-Jun-28: 2C].
Jay, Albert (3 yrs., 4 mos.) d. on 70-Oct-22 of Spine disease [70-Oct-24: 2B].
Jay, Alice M. d. on 70-Oct-15 [70-Oct-17: 2B].
Jay, Charles E. (40 yrs.) d. on 67-Sep-1 of Consumption [67-Sep-3: 2B].
Jay, Harry Lee (4 mos.) d. on 66-Aug-31 [66-Sep-1: 2B].
Jay, James Edward (3 mos.) d. on 68-Aug-6 [68-Aug-8: 2C].
Jay, Thomas Wilson (69 yrs.) d. on 70-Sep-28 [70-Sep-30: 2B].
Jay, William Henry d. on 67-Feb-3 [67-Feb-5: 2C].
Jay, William Johnston (4 mos.) d. on 67-Aug-15 [67-Aug-17: 2B].
Jayne, B. G. m. Palmer, Florence E. M. on 66-Oct-23 [66-Dec-28: 2C].
Jayne, S. C. m. Gere, Hattie A. on 69-Nov-18 [69-Dec-4: 2C].
Jeames, Catherine E. m. Collins, Joseph on 68-Apr-14 [68-Apr-22: 2B].
Jean, George B. m. Selby, Emily W. on 67-Dec-26 [67-Dec-28: 2C].
Jean, Jennie Phelps (4 mos.) d. on 70-Aug-8 [70-Aug-11: 2C].
Jean, Marie Rose Valillee (11 mos.) d. on 67-Jul-20 [67-Jul-22: 2C].
Jean, Nellie m. Watkins, Gassaway on 69-Mar-29 [69-Apr-2: 2C].
Jean, Sue E. d. on 66-Sep-19 [66-Sep-21: 2B].
Jeanneret, Louis P. m. Higgins, Maria on 66-Feb-13 [66-Feb-21: 2C].
Jeffers, George W. m. Pumphrey, Ann C. on 68-Mar-10 [68-Mar-14: 2B].
Jeffers, Joseph M. m. Woodall, Jennie on 69-Jan-28 [69-Feb-5: 2C].
Jeffers, Mary Kate (2 yrs., 2 mos.) d. on 66-Aug-19 [66-Aug-20: 2C].
Jeffers, Myrtie (8 mos.) d. on 70-Sep-12 [70-Sep-14: 2B].
Jefferson, Amanda E. m. Tracy, Edward F. on 66-Jun-13 [66-Jun-15: 2C].
Jefferson, Elizabeth m. Pinkett, Job on 66-Jan-11 [66-Jan-13: 2C].
Jefferson, Joseph A. m. Jacobson, Kate V. on 70-Dec-14 [70-Dec-17: 2B].
Jefferson, Mary E. m. Murphy, Charles on 68-May-3 [68-May-5: 2B].
Jefferson, Mary E. m. Montgomery, William T. on 67-May-14 [67-May-29: 2B; 67-May-30: 2B].
Jefferson, Sarah H. m. Lowry, John E. on 67-Jul-2 [67-Jul-4: 2B].
Jefferson, Thomas (22 yrs.) d. [66-Jan-31: 1G].
Jeffrey, Matilda Wethered (82 yrs.) d. on 68-May-8 [68-May-12: 2B].
Jeffreys, Thomas R. (46 yrs.) d. on 66-Jan-2 [66-Jan-4: 2C].
Jeffries, Benjamin m. Litzinger, Rebecca E. on 68-Jul-28 [68-Jul-31: 2C].
Jeffries, Harry C. (8 yrs., 4 mos.) d. on 70-Mar-5 [70-Mar-7: 2C].
Jelks, Cincinatus m. Server, Marietta on 66-Dec-20 [66-Dec-23: 2B].

Jelley, Hugh (36 yrs.) d. on 66-Dec-28 [66-Dec-29: 2C].
Jelley, John (29 yrs.) d. on 68-Nov-29 of Apoplexy [68-Nov-30: 1H; 68-Dec-1: 2C].
Jelly, Elizabeth (71 yrs.) d. on 66-Jul-17 [66-Jul-18: 2C].
Jenifer, Emily Barton (2 yrs., 5 mos.) d. on 67-Jan-31 [67-Feb-2: 2C].
Jenifer, Lillie T. C. m. Mitchell, John H. on 70-Oct-11 [70-Oct-12: 2B].
Jenifer, Nannie Courtenay (18 yrs.) d. on 67-Jan-7 of Typhoid pneumonia [67-Jan-9: 2B].
Jenkins, Alexander m. Hitchins, Anna on 66-Jan-30 [66-Feb-7: 2C].
Jenkins, Alfred (10 mos.) d. on 70-Aug-3 [70-Aug-4: 2C].
Jenkins, Alfred, Jr. m. Roper, Nettie H. on 68-Oct-22 [68-Oct-28: 2B].
Jenkins, Alice B. (26 yrs.) d. on 70-Oct-14 [70-Oct-15: 2B].
Jenkins, Ann (76 yrs.) d. on 67-Jun-7 [67-Jun-12: 2B].
Jenkins, Anna m. Shriver, Albert on 66-Apr-26 [66-May-2: 2B].
Jenkins, Annie E. m. Linn, Daniel H. on 68-Dec-22 [69-Jan-1: 2C].
Jenkins, Annie M. m. Schleigh, William H. on 70-Jul-25 [70-Aug-13: 2C].
Jenkins, Annie S. m. Scott, Isaiah M. on 70-Dec-7 [70-Dec-14: 2C].
Jenkins, Clara Vandervoort (2 yrs., 6 mos.) d. on 69-Feb-16 [69-Feb-17: 2D; 69-Feb-18: 2C].
Jenkins, Claude Alouisius (9 yrs.) d. on 69-Nov-17 [69-Nov-18: 2C; 69-Nov-20: 2C].
Jenkins, Conway M. m. Taft, Lottie on 70-Nov-24 [70-Nov-30: 2C].
Jenkins, Eliza (70 yrs.) d. on 70-Mar-22 [70-Mar-24: 2C].
Jenkins, Eliza O. m. Scott, John T. on 70-Dec-21 [70-Dec-23: 2B].
Jenkins, Elizabeth Gwynn d. on 66-May-8 [66-May-10: 2B].
Jenkins, Ellis T. m. Bartler, Henrietta on 68-Jul-5 [68-Jul-8: 2B].
Jenkins, Elma m. Evans, Charles W. on 70-Nov-22 [70-Nov-26: 2B].
Jenkins, George C. m. Key, Kate on 68-Nov-19 [68-Nov-24: 2C].
Jenkins, George Taylor d. on 67-Feb-13 [67-Feb-16: 2D].
Jenkins, Gonzaga, Sr. (24 yrs.) d. on 69-Sep-15 of Consumption [69-Sep-16: 1H].
Jenkins, Henry (89 yrs.) d. on 69-Dec-31 [70-Jan-1: 2B].
Jenkins, Henry m. Warfield, Manelia E. S. on 69-Oct-27 [69-Oct-30: 2B].
Jenkins, Henry Worthington (1 yr., 6 mos.) d. on 69-Mar-5 [69-Mar-10: 2C].
Jenkins, Isabella m. Jenkins, Michael on 66-Oct-2 [66-Oct-6: 2A].
Jenkins, J. Rebecca m. Smyser, Henry C. on 67-Sep-5 [67-Sep-11: 2B].
Jenkins, James m. Nash, Anne Louisa on 68-Jun-8 [68-Jun-10: 2B].
Jenkins, James T. (44 yrs.) d. on 66-Aug-9 of Consumption [66-Aug-11: 1G; 66-Aug-15: 2C].
Jenkins, Job (33 yrs.) d. on 67-Sep-24 [67-Sep-26: 2B].
Jenkins, John m. Edwards, Julia E. on 66-Nov-13 [66-Nov-17: 2C].
Jenkins, Joseph W., Jr. m. Rogers, M. Ellen on 67-Oct-9 [67-Oct-14: 2B].
Jenkins, Julia A. m. Hoyer, William H. on 67-Nov-26 [67-Dec-5: 2C].
Jenkins, Lizzie W. m. Allan, Charles H. on 68-Dec-17 [68-Dec-25: 2D].
Jenkins, M. V. m. Wall, Patrick on 69-Dec-27 [70-Jan-1: 2B].
Jenkins, Mary Ann (60 yrs.) d. on 68-Dec-2 [68-Dec-3: 2C].
Jenkins, Mary Armour m. Saxton, William H. on 67-Oct-8 [67-Oct-11: 2B].
Jenkins, Mary Rosalia (1 yr., 4 mos.) d. on 70-Aug-8 [70-Aug-10: 2C].
Jenkins, Matilda Dale m. Lee, Charles O'Donnell on 69-Nov-11 [69-Nov-18: 2C].
Jenkins, Michael m. Jenkins, Isabella on 66-Oct-2 [66-Oct-6: 2A].
Jenkins, Oliver L., Rev. (56 yrs.) d. on 69-Jul-11 [69-Jul-12: 1H, 2D].
Jenkins, Oliver L. m. Procter, Agnes on 69-Sep-3 [70-Jan-24: 2C].
Jenkins, Samana m. Crockett, A. Jackson on 70-Mar-28 [70-Apr-19: 2B].
Jenkins, Sarah m. Elliott, George on 69-May-18 [69-May-20: 2C].
Jenkins, Sarah E. m. Elliot, George D. on 69-Oct-28 [69-Dec-6: 2C].
Jenkins, Sarah E. m. Farnan, James J. on 68-Dec-29 [69-Jan-1: 2C].
Jenkins, Sue R. m. Dance, E. Scott on 70-Nov-24 [70-Nov-29: 2C].
Jenkins, T. Christopher m. Elliotte, Ellen on 69-Jan-27 [69-Jan-30: 2C].
Jenkins, Theodore (57 yrs.) d. on 66-Dec-15 [66-Dec-19: 2B].
Jenkins, William (80 yrs.) d. on 66-Aug-15 [66-Aug-23: 2C].
Jenks, Hattie Clemm d. on 68-Mar-28 [68-Apr-3: 2C].

Jenness, Sade J. m. Leitch, B. Frank on 67-Oct-10 [67-Oct-17: 2B].
Jennings, Edith d. on 69-Apr-28 [69-Apr-30: 2C].
Jennings, George (33 yrs.) d. on 70-Jul-13 [70-Jul-15: 2C].
Jennings, John M. m. Glanding, Sarah E. on 69-Jul-13 [69-Jul-15: 2C].
Jennings, Katie (7 mos.) d. on 67-Jul-10 of Lung congestion [67-Jul-12: 2C].
Jennings, Maggie A. m. Healy, John J. on 67-Aug-8 [67-Aug-16: 2B].
Jennings, Patrick (60 yrs.) d. on 67-Feb-6 Crushed by wall [67-Feb-7: 1E, 2C].
Jennings, Samuel T. (34 yrs.) d. on 66-Jun-8 [66-Jun-9: 2B].
Jennings, Thomas (70 yrs.) d. on 66-Aug-29 of Heart disease [66-Aug-30: 1G].
Jerome, Elizabeth Ann (29 yrs.) d. on 68-Jan-30 [68-Feb-18: 2C].
Jerome, Jennie m. Aiken, Matthew K. on 67-Jan-8 [67-Jan-10: 2C].
Jerome, John H. T. m. Kimberly, Olivia on 69-Jun-11 [69-Jun-15: 2C].
Jerome, Sarah A. m. Shipley, E. A. on 66-Mar-15 [66-Mar-17: 2B].
Jerone, Mary R. d. on 66-Apr-4 [66-Apr-5: 2B].
Jervis, George William (3 yrs., 5 mos.) d. on 67-Aug-29 [67-Aug-30: 2B].
Jervis, John Augustin T. (6 yrs., 4 mos.) d. on 66-Jan-5 [66-Jan-6: 2C].
Jervis, Sallie A. m. Ridgely, John T. on 68-Apr-2 [68-Apr-9: 2B].
Jess, Sarah J. m. Warfield, J. A. on 70-Jun-30 [70-Jul-12: 2B].
Jessop, Annie Lauinia (2 yrs., 11 mos.) d. on 66-Aug-16 [66-Aug-17: 2C].
Jessop, George A. m. Harris, Maria L. on 65-Dec-14 [66-Jan-1: 2C].
Jessop, George Lee (4 yrs., 8 mos.) d. on 68-Feb-26 of Pneumonia [68-Mar-4: 2C].
Jessop, George W. m. Haile, Amanda T. on 69-Dec-19 [70-Feb-21: 2B].
Jessop, Georgianna m. Waltham, C. S. on 66-Jul-5 [66-Jul-16: 2C].
Jessop, Hattie E. m. Duff, J. Luther on 69-Aug-23 [69-Aug-25: 2C].
Jessop, Joshua (63 yrs., 2 mos.) d. on 69-Aug-25 [69-Aug-31: 2B].
Jessop, William (66 yrs.) d. on 66-Jan-23 [66-Jan-25: 2C].
Jessop, William Clinton (5 mos.) d. on 68-Feb-24 of Brain inflammation [68-Mar-4: 2C].
Jessup, George m. Startzman, Sally A. on 67-Mar-5 [67-Mar-6: 2C].
Jewell, Tryon J. m. Leary, Kate on 66-Mar-8 [66-Mar-9: 2B].
Jewens, William m. Lyon, Margaret on 69-Feb-4 [69-Feb-11: 2C].
Jillard, John (89 yrs.) d. on 66-Nov-1 [66-Nov-2: 2B].
Jinkens, John (63 yrs.) d. on 66-Mar-26 of Consumption [66-Mar-28: 2C].
Jockel, Mary Anna Elizabeth (37 yrs.) d. on 69-Jan-25 [69-Jan-26: 2C].
Jocobs, Drewry Otley (6 mos.) d. on 68-Jul-30 [68-Aug-4: 2C].
Joeckel, Elizabeth (52 yrs.) d. on 70-Dec-6 [70-Dec-7: 2C].
Joeckel, Elizabeth m. Fischer, John Charles on 66-Dec-11 [66-Dec-31: 2C].
Johannes, C. Maria (69 yrs.) d. on 68-Oct-3 [68-Oct-5: 2C].
Johannes, Eddie (1 yr., 2 mos.) d. on 69-Oct-2 [69-Oct-5: 2B].
Johannes, Mirian Irene (5 mos.) d. on 69-Jun-13 [69-Jun-15: 2C].
Johenning, John Frederick (71 yrs.) d. on 69-Nov-12 [69-Nov-13: 2C].
Johnes, T. S. m. Hurst, M. J. on 69-Oct-28 [69-Oct-29: 2B].
Johns, Aggie m. Eltonhead, William T. on 67-Jan-23 [67-Feb-1: 2C].
Johns, E. J. m. Riley, W. H. on 65-Dec-15 [66-Jul-28: 2C].
Johns, Eleanor d. on 68-Dec-5 [68-Dec-9: 2C].
Johns, Eleanor (9 mos.) d. on 69-Jul-29 [69-Aug-2: 2C].
Johns, Jason Stockbridge (2 yrs., 7 mos.) d. on 69-May-25 [69-May-28: 2C].
Johns, Laura L. (37 yrs.) d. on 68-Oct-7 [68-Oct-13: 2C].
Johns, Leonard m. Lee, Frances on 66-Apr-17 [66-Apr-27: 2C].
Johns, Maggie m. Long, Henry J. on 67-Sep-25 [67-Oct-1: 2B].
Johns, Mary Ardean (8 yrs.) d. on 69-Mar-17 [69-Mar-18: 2C].
Johns, Richard (48 yrs.) d. on 69-Jun-22 of Suicide (Shooting) [69-Jun-24: 1G; 69-Jul-24: 1H].
Johns, Sarah Elizabeth (10 mos.) d. on 67-Jun-23 [67-Jun-24: 2B].
Johns, Susie m. Blake, John L. on 70-Feb-10 [70-Feb-12: 2B; 70-Feb-14: 2C].
Johns, Virginia m. Snyder, John on 69-Jan-14 [69-Feb-15: 2C].
Johns, William Jesse (23 yrs.) d. on 69-Feb-1 [69-Feb-5: 2C].

Johnson, A. E. m. Holtz, Annie W. on 70-Dec-20 [70-Dec-24: 2B].
Johnson, Agnes A. m. Martin, William H. on 66-May-24 [66-May-29: 2B].
Johnson, Agnes F. m. Bevan, Charles on 65-Oct-14 [66-Mar-19: 2C].
Johnson, Aimee E. m. Stanley, Alfred on 67-Aug-6 [67-Aug-14: 2B].
Johnson, Albert A. m. Abrahams, Cora W. on 68-Jul-7 [68-Jul-10: 2C].
Johnson, Albert C. (1 yr., 11 mos.) d. on 68-May-9 [68-May-11: 2B].
Johnson, Alexander W., Jr. (28 yrs.) d. on 67-Oct-10 [67-Oct-12: 2B].
Johnson, Alverdia m. Ingalls, John D. on 69-Apr-5 [69-Apr-9: 2C].
Johnson, Amelia m. Elliott, Thomas J. R. on 66-Nov-14 [66-Nov-21: 2C].
Johnson, Annie d. on 68-Aug-26 [68-Aug-27: 2B; 68-Aug-28: 2B].
Johnson, Annie S. m. West, Thomas M. on 70-Nov-22 [70-Nov-24: 2B].
Johnson, Anninda m. Benney, David on 67-Oct-26 [67-Dec-3: 2C].
Johnson, Aquilla (90 yrs.) d. on 69-Apr-19 [69-Apr-20: 1G, 2B].
Johnson, Arthur Eugene (3 yrs., 5 mos.) d. on 67-Jul-4 [67-Jul-6: 2B].
Johnson, C. D. m. Tree, Annie F. on 65-Oct-2 [66-Mar-24: 2B].
Johnson, Charles W. m. Smith, Lucretia C. on 69-Mar-11 [69-Mar-18: 2C; 69-Mar-20: 2B].
Johnson, Charlotte Elizabeth (9 yrs., 4 mos.) d. on 70-Jan-16 [70-Jan-17: 2C].
Johnson, Christopher (68 yrs.) d. on 68-Feb-14 [68-Feb-15: 2B].
Johnson, Clara L. m. Johnson, William J. on 69-Dec-2 [69-Dec-4: 2C].
Johnson, Crawford H. m. Roberts, Lizzie W. on 66-Nov-20 [66-Dec-4: 2D].
Johnson, Douglas Clark (10 yrs.) d. [69-Sep-30: 2B].
Johnson, E. Dorsey (29 yrs.) d. on 69-Aug-9 [69-Aug-10: 2C; 69-Aug-11: 2C].
Johnson, E. Pauline m. Grimes, William K. on 69-Nov-23 [69-Dec-11: 2B].
Johnson, Edward (52 yrs.) d. on 68-Aug-21 [68-Aug-22: 2A].
Johnson, Edward M. m. Lewis, Caroline J. on 66-Jul-30 [66-Aug-1: 2C].
Johnson, Edwin Austin (1 yr., 2 mos.) d. on 67-Mar-11 [67-Mar-13: 2C].
Johnson, Elisha S. (76 yrs., 10 mos.) d. on 66-Dec-9 [66-Dec-11: 2B].
Johnson, Eliza (56 yrs.) d. on 67-Oct-6 of Paralysis [67-Oct-8: 1G].
Johnson, Eliza A. (46 yrs.) d. on 70-Jun-12 [70-Jun-13: 2C].
Johnson, Eliza J. m. Keller, John on 66-Jul-26 [66-Aug-1: 2C].
Johnson, Elizabeth m. Johnson, James on 66-Sep-20 [66-Sep-22: 2B].
Johnson, Ella (1 yr., 4 mos.) d. on 70-Mar-1 [70-Mar-2: 2C].
Johnson, Ella m. Kerr, Charles Kerr on 67-Apr-25 [67-Apr-26: 2B].
Johnson, Ella V. m. McGahan, John C. on 68-Apr-12 [68-Apr-15: 2B].
Johnson, Ellen m. Douglass, Walter C. on 69-Dec-9 [69-Dec-17: 2C].
Johnson, Emma C. m. Dyer, C. W. on 67-Nov-5 [67-Nov-12: 2C].
Johnson, Enoch V. (37 yrs.) d. on 66-Jan-3 [66-Jan-6: 2C].
Johnson, George T. (26 yrs.) d. on 67-Jan-25 [67-Jan-26: 2C].
Johnson, George W. d. on 66-Dec-22 of Fall [66-Dec-24: 1F].
Johnson, George W. m. Tatum, Mollie on 70-Jun-23 [70-Jul-12: 2B].
Johnson, Georgianna m. Freeman, Edward D. on 68-May-28 [68-May-29: 2B].
Johnson, Hannah (23 yrs.) d. on 69-Mar-6 [69-Mar-8: 2C].
Johnson, Hannah A. m. Nelson, Peter on 67-Feb-14 [67-Feb-18: 2C].
Johnson, Harriet (38 yrs.) d. on 66-Sep-30 [66-Oct-2: 2B].
Johnson, Harriet (67 yrs.) d. on 69-Mar-21 [69-Mar-23: 2C].
Johnson, Henrietta H. m. Fontz, Jacob H. on 70-May-19 [70-May-24: 2C].
Johnson, Henrietta L. M. m. Anthony, W. Fenwick on 66-Oct-23 [66-Oct-24: 2C].
Johnson, Hester Ann d. on 70-Dec-17 Murdered (Assault) [70-Dec-19: 4D].
Johnson, Howard (60 yrs.) d. on 69-Oct-28 [69-Oct-29: 2C].
Johnson, Hugh (43 yrs.) d. on 66-Dec-16 [66-Dec-18: 2B].
Johnson, Ida d. on 67-Jul-4 Drowned [67-Jul-6: 4C, 4D].
Johnson, Ida Levinia (4 mos.) d. on 66-Jan-24 [66-Jan-25: 2C].
Johnson, Issac J. m. Gross, Rosena C. on 66-Feb-5 [66-Feb-9: 2C].
Johnson, James m. Johnson, Elizabeth on 66-Sep-20 [66-Sep-22: 2B].
Johnson, James Edward m. Wakeman, Elizabeth R. B. on 68-Sep-8 [68-Sep-19: 2B].

Johnson, James M. (47 yrs.) d. on 67-Feb-7 [67-Feb-8: 2C].
Johnson, James M. (30 yrs.) d. on 69-Dec-31 [70-Jan-1: 2B].
Johnson, James M. (2 yrs., 6 mos.) d. on 70-May-11 [70-May-12: 2B].
Johnson, James Milburn m. McElroy, Jennie on 66-Oct-30 [67-Jan-3: 2B].
Johnson, James R. (36 yrs.) d. on 67-Mar-18 [67-Mar-20: 2C].
Johnson, Jane d. on 67-Nov-12 [67-Nov-14: 2B].
Johnson, Jesse m. Yeager, Carrie M. on 68-Oct-6 [68-Oct-15: 2C].
Johnson, Joanna m. Plater, John on 66-Aug-30 [66-Sep-5: 2B].
Johnson, John (86 yrs.) d. on 66-Nov-29 [66-Dec-1: 2B].
Johnson, John D. m. White, Lizzie V. on 70-Nov-23 [70-Nov-24: 2B].
Johnson, Joseph d. on 68-Aug-27 Drowned [68-Aug-29: 1G].
Johnson, Joseph (57 yrs.) d. on 66-Oct-3 of Consumption [66-Oct-4: 2B].
Johnson, Joseph Gess (29 yrs., 3 mos.) d. on 70-Oct-5 [70-Oct-15: 2B].
Johnson, Joseph P. m. Brown, Mary E. on 67-May-30 [67-Jun-8: 2B].
Johnson, Josephine A. (8 yrs., 8 mos.) d. on 69-May-12 [69-May-14: 2C].
Johnson, Joshua (39 yrs.) d. on 70-Aug-29 in Railroad accident [70-Aug-30: 2C, 4D].
Johnson, Laura m. Martin, Joseph on 67-Jan-15 [67-Jan-17: 2C].
Johnson, Laura m. Campbell, Robert, Jr. on 66-Mar-13 [66-Mar-14: 2B].
Johnson, Laura C. m. Jones, C. W. on 68-Feb-19 [68-Feb-22: 2B].
Johnson, Laura Virginia m. Griffin, John Thomas on 69-Jul-1 [69-Jul-5: 2C].
Johnson, Laura Virginia m. Carter, Lorenzo on 70-May-2 [70-May-4: 2C; 70-May-5: 2B].
Johnson, Laurence McCauley (2 yrs., 4 mos.) d. on 70-Dec-14 [70-Dec-15: 2C].
Johnson, Lizzie A. m. Sadler, John R. on 70-Sep-8 [70-Oct-1: 2B].
Johnson, Louisa F. (25 yrs., 6 mos.) d. on 69-Nov-20 [69-Nov-22: 2C].
Johnson, Lucinda (102 yrs.) d. on 67-Oct-15 [67-Oct-17: 2B].
Johnson, M. A. m. Tudor, J. C. on 70-Feb-10 [70-Feb-18: 2C].
Johnson, M. Tyler d. on 68-Oct-15 [68-Oct-17: 1G, 2B].
Johnson, M. V. m. Hill, A. P. on 70-Oct-6 [70-Oct-7: 2B].
Johnson, Maggie M. m. Smart, Benjamin G. on 67-Jul-22 [67-Jul-29: 2D].
Johnson, Margaret H. (32 yrs.) d. on 69-Jun-21 [69-Jun-25: 2C].
Johnson, Maria d. on 67-Oct-20 [67-Nov-14: 2C].
Johnson, Martha A. m. Hancock, Orlando on 66-Oct-4 [66-Oct-11: 2C].
Johnson, Mary (54 yrs.) d. on 68-May-14 [68-May-15: 2B].
Johnson, Mary d. on 69-Jul-19 of Scarlet fever [69-Jul-22: 2C].
Johnson, Mary Ann (61 yrs.) d. on 67-Jan-8 [67-Jan-9: 2C].
Johnson, Mary C. m. Knight, Augustine on 67-Jul-18 [68-Jan-13: 2C].
Johnson, Mary E. (70 yrs., 7 mos.) d. on 68-Sep-24 [68-Sep-26: 2B].
Johnson, Mary E. m. Randall, George C. on 68-Jan-28 [68-Feb-10: 2C].
Johnson, Mary Elizabeth (16 yrs.) d. on 70-Dec-4 [70-Dec-5: 2C].
Johnson, Mary F. (87 yrs.) d. on 69-Dec-11 [69-Dec-24: 2C].
Johnson, Mary J. m. Cross, Franklin T. on 69-Aug-17 [69-Aug-26: 2C].
Johnson, Mary R. m. Hall, Frederick D. on 66-Mar-1 [66-Mar-5: 2B].
Johnson, Mary Tyler (7 mos.) d. on 67-Aug-6 [67-Aug-8: 2B].
Johnson, Moses (67 yrs.) d. on 67-Feb-28 [67-Mar-2: 2B].
Johnson, Oliver Taylor (2 yrs., 2 mos.) d. on 70-Jan-10 [70-Jan-11: 2C].
Johnson, Olivia Gertrude (7 yrs.) d. on 70-Jan-26 [70-Jan-28: 2B].
Johnson, Owen (57 yrs., 1 mo.) d. on 68-Jan-8 [68-Jan-10: 2C; 68-Jan-29: 2D].
Johnson, Peter C. (36 yrs.) d. on 68-Jul-20 [68-Jul-22: 2B].
Johnson, Philip d. on 66-Oct-29 of Gunshot wound [66-Oct-31: 4B].
Johnson, Rebecca d. on 67-Nov-12 [67-Nov-13: 2C].
Johnson, Richard m. Fosler, Almira F. on 68-Apr-30 [68-May-6: 2B].
Johnson, Richard W. (61 yrs., 9 mos.) d. on 70-Feb-15 [70-Feb-22: 2C].
Johnson, Robert d. on 69-Mar-9 of Heart disease [69-Mar-11: 1H].
Johnson, Robert B. d. on 68-Jun-21 in Railroad accident [68-Jun-22: 1F].
Johnson, Robert Melville (4 yrs., 11 mos.) d. on 66-May-22 [66-May-24: 2C].

Johnson, Samuel m. Gwinn, Ellen on 67-Dec-15 [67-Dec-17: 2B].
Johnson, Samuel m. Prescoe, Sarah L. on 70-Apr-4 [70-Apr-6: 2B].
Johnson, Sarah (83 yrs.) d. on 70-Jun-1 [70-Jun-3: 2B].
Johnson, Sarah (84 yrs.) d. on 70-Nov-24 [70-Nov-29: 2C].
Johnson, Sarah A. (34 yrs.) d. on 66-Mar-26 [66-Mar-26: 2C].
Johnson, Sarah Jane m. Garthwait, John A. on 66-Nov-18 [66-Nov-24: 2B].
Johnson, Sarah Jane m. Colwell, William F. on 69-Nov-4 [69-Nov-30: 2C].
Johnson, Sarah Lizzie (1 mo.) d. on 68-Jan-19 [68-Jan-22: 2C].
Johnson, Susan (90 yrs.) d. on 66-Nov-27 [66-Dec-1: 2B].
Johnson, Susan Bray m. Martin, William Hammet on 70-Oct-27 [70-Nov-1: 2C].
Johnson, Susan C. m. McKinley, William on 66-Oct-18 [66-Oct-20: 2B].
Johnson, Thomas (75 yrs.) d. on 65-Dec-31 [66-Jan-2: 1G, 2B].
Johnson, Thomas C. m. Forman, Amelia on 68-Sep-22 [68-Sep-26: 2B].
Johnson, Thomas F. m. Tilghman, Fanny A. on 70-Feb-1 [70-Feb-3: 2B].
Johnson, Washington (3 yrs.) d. on 67-Mar-10 Burned [67-Mar-11: 1F].
Johnson, Washington Packie d. on 70-Sep-25 of Typhoid [70-Sep-29: 2B].
Johnson, Wilhelmina (88 yrs.) d. on 70-Dec-4 [70-Dec-6: 2C; 70-Dec-7: 2C].
Johnson, William d. on 68-Jun-13 Murdered (Shooting) [68-Jun-26: 1G].
Johnson, William d. on 66-Oct-24 Murdered (Shooting) [66-Oct-25: 1G].
Johnson, William Edward m. Waters, Julia on 70-Aug-8 [70-Aug-13: 2C].
Johnson, William H. (19 yrs.) d. on 69-Sep-7 [69-Sep-8: 2B].
Johnson, William J. m. Johnson, Clara L. on 69-Dec-2 [69-Dec-4: 2C].
Johnson, William J. m. Ross, Jessie on 70-Dec-8 [70-Dec-10: 2B].
Johnson, William Reynolds (14 yrs.) d. on 66-Dec-18 [66-Dec-19: 2B].
Johnson, William S. (34 yrs.) d. on 70-Feb-1 [70-Feb-2: 2B; 70-Feb-3: 2B].
Johnson, William S. m. Pere, Ann Maria on 67-May-9 [67-May-16: 2B].
Johnson, William T. (24 yrs.) d. on 68-May-12 [68-May-13: 2B].
Johnson, William T. m. Hackney, Mary E. on 66-Nov-6 [66-Nov-10: 2B].
Johnson, Zachariah m. Burns, Lena E. on 68-Oct-20 [68-Oct-21: 2B].
Johnston, Agnes m. Prior, Samuel C. on 68-Sep-14 [68-Sep-17: 2B].
Johnston, Alton R. m. Brooks, Annie E. on 69-Oct-29 [69-Nov-15: 2C].
Johnston, Amelia m. Elliott, Thomas J. R. on 66-Nov-14 [66-Nov-22: 2C].
Johnston, Ann M. d. on 70-Oct-15 [70-Nov-11: 2B].
Johnston, Carrie m. Holmes, John on 68-Jul-14 [68-Jul-31: 2C].
Johnston, Edward E. m. Reiter, Ann Leonora on 66-Dec-13 [66-Dec-13: 2B].
Johnston, Eleanora Tilghman (5 mos.) d. on 66-Aug-4 [66-Aug-6: 2C].
Johnston, Eliza Gates (8 yrs.) d. on 67-Oct-13 [67-Oct-14: 2B; 67-Oct-15: 2A].
Johnston, Elizabeth Frances (28 yrs., 2 mos.) d. on 68-May-6 [68-May-7: 2B].
Johnston, Fayette m. Keys, Leonore on 69-Jan-12 [69-Jan-19: 2C].
Johnston, Fergus (86 yrs.) d. on 69-Jul-4 [69-Jul-5: 2C].
Johnston, Frederick m. Conn, Sarah S. on 69-Mar-1 [69-Mar-10: 2C].
Johnston, James m. Richardson, Martha A. on 70-Oct-19 [70-Oct-29: 2B].
Johnston, James, Jr. m. Carter, Laura L.V. on 70-Sep-12 [70-Sep-28: 2B].
Johnston, Mary (51 yrs.) d. on 70-Dec-30 [70-Dec-31: 2C].
Johnston, Mary M. m. Scrivner, James on 69-May-11 [69-May-18: 2C].
Johnston, Minnie m. Heck, C. J. on 69-Aug-1 [69-Aug-3: 2C].
Johnston, William (68 yrs.) d. on 68-Jul-7 [68-Jul-8: 2B; 68-Jul-10: 1G].
Johnston, William d. on 70-Mar-24 [70-Mar-26: 2B].
Johnston, Willie E. m. Perkin, Frank A. on 69-Jan-19 [69-Jan-21: 2C].
Joice, Daniel (84 yrs.) d. on 67-May-21 of Paralysis [67-May-22: 1G].
Joice, Emily A. m. Biddle, John T. on 66-Jan-30 [66-Feb-6: 2D].
Joice, George H. (51 yrs., 2 mos.) d. on 67-Dec-21 [67-Dec-23: 2B].
Joice, Rosa E. m. Geist, Martin D. on 69-Dec-21 [70-Jan-24: 2C].
Joice, Thomas m. Schwatka, Sophia on 70-Jun-23 [70-Jun-24: 2C].
Joiner, Ellen Veronica (10 mos.) d. on 67-Jul-26 [67-Aug-17: 2B].

Joines, Fannie m. Fry, Edward E. on 69-May-11 [69-Jun-17: 2C].
Jolliffe, Charles C. m. Merryman, Sadie R. on 70-Aug-18 [70-Aug-29: 2B].
Jolliffe, W. H. m. Matthews, Lucy on 69-Dec-8 [69-Dec-9: 2C].
Jolly, John C. (62 yrs.) d. on 67-Nov-21 [67-Nov-23: 2B].
Jonas, Charles E. (23 yrs.) d. on 67-May-23 [67-May-24: 2B; 67-May-25: 2B].
Jones, Alice m. Conway, Charles H. on 68-Nov-12 [68-Nov-16: 2C].
Jones, Alonzo F. m. Schenckel, Louisa on 66-Jun-8 [66-Nov-5: 2B].
Jones, Amanda M. m. High, William W. on 70-Jun-21 [70-Jul-25: 2C].
Jones, Amelia (82 yrs.) d. on 66-Dec-31 [67-Jan-4: 2D].
Jones, Andrew D. (78 yrs.) d. on 70-Aug-10 [70-Aug-11: 2C].
Jones, Ann (61 yrs.) d. on 69-Nov-24 of Pneumonia [69-Dec-1: 2C].
Jones, Ann (76 yrs.) d. on 70-Mar-14 [70-Mar-16: 2C].
Jones, Ann C. (49 yrs.) d. on 69-May-29 [69-Jun-7: 2B].
Jones, Ann Louisa (2 yrs., 1 mo.) d. on 67-Jul-15 [67-Jul-16: 2C].
Jones, Anna S. m. Reese, J. Fisher on 67-Oct-8 [67-Oct-10: 2B].
Jones, Annie (28 yrs.) d. on 69-Jul-3 [69-Jul-8: 2C].
Jones, Annie m. Waterworth, Alexander on 67-May-21 [67-Jun-7: 2B].
Jones, Annie E. m. Storey, Norman H. on 70-Mar-24 [70-Apr-4: 2B].
Jones, Annie J. m. Thomas, James B. on 68-Jun-4 [68-Jun-20: 2B].
Jones, Annie R. m. Brinsfield, William K. on 66-May-20 [66-May-23: 2B].
Jones, Arthur W. m. Harvey, Genila on 67-Jul-14 [67-Jul-17: 2C].
Jones, Asariah m. Price, Martha A. on 68-Aug-27 [68-Sep-15: 2B].
Jones, B. T. m. Canfield, Mary R. on 68-May-12 [68-May-14: 2B].
Jones, Basil d. on 69-Nov-2 in Railroad accident [69-Nov-5: 1H].
Jones, Beaswell d. on 67-Mar-23 Drowned [67-Apr-1: 1G].
Jones, Benjamin d. Drowned [67-Apr-22: 1F].
Jones, Benjamin d. on 66-Oct-6 Murdered (Shooting) [66-Oct-8: 1F; 66-Oct-9: 4C].
Jones, Bennett B. (59 yrs., 8 mos.) d. on 69-Jan-14 [69-Jan-16: 2C].
Jones, C. W. m. Johnson, Laura C. on 68-Feb-19 [68-Feb-22: 2B].
Jones, Caroline Alfonses (7 mos.) d. on 67-Jul-2 [67-Jul-3: 2B].
Jones, Catherine (80 yrs.) d. on 66-Apr-6 [66-Apr-17: 2C].
Jones, Charles (28 yrs.) d. on 66-Dec-17 [66-Dec-18: 2B].
Jones, Charles F. (1 yr., 7 mos.) d. on 70-Aug-16 [70-Aug-17: 2C].
Jones, Charles Henry (1 yr., 8 mos.) d. on 68-Sep-11 [68-Sep-12: 2B].
Jones, Charles W. m. Woolford, A. Augusta on 69-May-4 [69-May-15: 2B].
Jones, Clinton Henderson (1 yr., 7 mos.) d. on 70-Jan-7 of Chronic croup [70-Jan-11: 2C].
Jones, Colin Q. C. (35 yrs.) d. on 66-Aug-24 [66-Aug-25: 2A].
Jones, David A. m. Etherington, Virginia E. on 70-Jun-7 [70-Jun-9: 2C].
Jones, Dorothy (77 yrs.) d. on 67-Apr-19 [67-Apr-20: 2A].
Jones, Edward (12 yrs.) d. on 68-Oct-6 Drowned [68-Oct-8: 1F].
Jones, Edward (32 yrs.) d. on 67-Nov-10 of Consumption [67-Nov-11: 2C; 67-Nov-12: 2C].
Jones, Edward C. m. Walker, Mary F. on 66-Apr-29 [66-May-15: 2C].
Jones, Edward J. m. Knight, Lavinia on 70-Sep-18 [70-Oct-11: 2B].
Jones, Eliza d. on 67-Apr-29 [67-Apr-30: 2A].
Jones, Eliza m. Catrup, William B. on 66-Jul-10 [66-Jul-13: 2C].
Jones, Eliza A. (62 yrs.) d. on 68-Jan-22 [68-Jan-23: 2C].
Jones, Elizabeth R. m. Jones, William T. on 67-Dec-11 [67-Dec-21: 2B].
Jones, Elvary Jane (15 yrs., 4 mos.) d. on 66-Mar-20 [66-Mar-22: 2B].
Jones, Emma m. Webster, Joseph J. G. on 69-Jul-14 [69-Jul-16: 2C].
Jones, Emma Maude d. on 67-Mar-2 [67-Mar-4: 2D; 67-Mar-5: 2C].
Jones, Emma Maude M. (6 mos.) d. on 67-Aug-4 [67-Aug-5: 2B].
Jones, Ernest W. R. (7 yrs.) d. on 68-Oct-7 [68-Oct-9: 2C].
Jones, Eugene W. m. Walsh, Emilie Hughes on 70-Jun-22 [70-Jun-25: 2B].
Jones, Evan m. Turner, Ellen Amanda on 69-Nov-25 [69-Nov-29: 2C].
Jones, F. D. m. Jones, Sarah Geneva on 69-May-8 [69-May-10: 2B].

Jones, Fannie B. (16 yrs.) d. on 68-Apr-19 [68-Apr-20: 2B].
Jones, Fannie Currie m. Buck, Charles W. on 68-Sep-1 [68-Sep-2: 2A].
Jones, Florence Allifair (5 yrs.) d. on 66-Nov-12 [66-Nov-14: 2B].
Jones, Florence Allipha d. on 69-Sep-6 [69-Sep-7: 2B].
Jones, Francis W. m. Vieweg, Emma on 68-Nov-17 [68-Dec-21: 2B].
Jones, George (1 yr., 6 mos.) d. on 69-Apr-20 [69-Apr-22: 2B; 69-May-5: 2C].
Jones, George m. Betton, Mary on 68-May-26 [68-May-28: 2B].
Jones, George W. (35 yrs.) d. on 67-Jul-13 Drowned [67-Jul-15: 1F].
Jones, George W. (34 yrs.) d. of Yellow fever [67-Sep-25: 2B].
Jones, George W. m. De Ward, Mary A. on 67-Sep-5 [67-Sep-10: 2B].
Jones, George W. m. Proctor, Mary A. on 66-May-3 [66-May-4: 2C].
Jones, George W. m. Briscoe, Eliza on 69-Mar-16 [69-Mar-31: 2C].
Jones, Georgie d. on 69-Aug-12 [69-Aug-13: 2C].
Jones, Gilbert (57 yrs.) d. on 67-Apr-4 [67-Apr-6: 2B].
Jones, Harriet d. on 69-Nov-29 [69-Nov-30: 2C; 69-Dec-1: 2C].
Jones, Harriet m. Hoffsnider, John on 68-May-7 [68-May-9: 2B].
Jones, Harry McComas (2 yrs., 4 mos.) d. on 66-Jun-2 [66-Jun-4: 2B].
Jones, Harry W. (19 yrs., 10 mos.) d. [66-Aug-4: 2C].
Jones, Hattie A. m. Cushell, H. B. on 70-Feb-17 [70-Mar-3: 2C].
Jones, Henry C. m. Simms, Elizabeth on 67-Nov-12 [67-Nov-14: 2B].
Jones, Henry C. m. Fairbanks, Annie T. on 70-Jan-2 [70-Jan-4: 2C].
Jones, Hettie G. m. Roche, P. J. on 66-Oct-11 [66-Oct-13: 2B].
Jones, Hugh (93 yrs.) d. [70-Oct-11: 2C].
Jones, I. Thomas m. Gambrill, Mary on 69-Jun-3 [69-Jun-4: 2C].
Jones, Isaiah m. Salter, Eliza on 66-Mar-17 [66-Mar-29: 2B].
Jones, Israel B. m. Woods, Lotta on 69-Jun-1 [69-Jun-8: 2B].
Jones, J. Crawford d. on 70-Jul-1 [70-Jul-2: 2B].
Jones, J. Guest m. Prigg, Olivia R. on 68-Oct-1 [68-Oct-12: 2B].
Jones, J. L. D. m. Carry, Nelson A. on 69-Jan-10 [69-Jan-12: 2C].
Jones, J. P., Dr. (31 yrs., 10 mos.) d. on 69-May-3 [69-May-15: 2B].
Jones, J. Preston m. Wartman, Dorrie on 68-Dec-13 [69-Mar-15: 2C].
Jones, Jacob (1 mo.) d. on 69-May-3 [69-May-5: 2C].
Jones, James d. on 66-Oct-7 Drowned [66-Oct-8: 1G].
Jones, James d. on 66-Feb-14 of Pneumonia [66-Mar-2: 1G].
Jones, James, Sr. (58 yrs.) d. on 69-Jan-8 [69-Jan-11: 2C].
Jones, James A. m. Fizell, Rebecca on 68-Nov-5 [68-Nov-7: 2B].
Jones, James G. m. Burgess, Sallie V. on 67-May-21 [67-Jun-12: 2B].
Jones, Jane (61 yrs.) d. on 67-Jan-19 [67-Jan-21: 2C].
Jones, Jane (63 yrs.) d. on 70-Dec-10 [70-Dec-28: 2C].
Jones, Jane B. m. Converse, John H. on 68-Oct-20 [68-Oct-21: 2C].
Jones, Jennie m. Rodrigue, A. [70-Oct-18: 2B].
Jones, John A. m. Darby, Rose M. on 66-Jan-9 [66-Jan-11: 2B].
Jones, John L. m. Rimmey, Martha on 68-Jul-23 [68-Jul-30: 2B].
Jones, John M. m. Paynter, Mary J. on 66-Aug-6 [66-Aug-15: 2B].
Jones, John T. (19 yrs.) d. on 68-Sep-9 [68-Sep-17: 2B].
Jones, John Walton (38 yrs.) d. on 68-Dec-5 of Suicide (Poisoning) [68-Dec-7: 1H; 68-Dec-8: 1G].
Jones, Joseph Ellison (4 yrs., 10 mos.) d. on 67-Jan-30 of Scarlet fever [67-Jan-31: 2C].
Jones, Joseph T. m. Conner, Laura Virginia on 68-Dec-1 [68-Dec-3: 2C].
Jones, Josephine (24 yrs.) d. on 68-Jan-5 of Consumption [68-Jan-20: 2C].
Jones, Julia A. d. on 70-Jun-19 [70-Jun-20: 2B; 70-Jun-21: 2C].
Jones, Julia F. m. Carter, Robert on 66-Jan-2 [66-Jan-3: 2C].
Jones, Kate Emmart (1 yr., 3 mos.) d. on 66-Mar-6 [66-Mar-8: 2B].
Jones, Laura m. Lawrence, Richard H. on 70-Dec-15 [70-Dec-24: 2B].
Jones, Laura B. m. Dorrett, William W. on 69-May-18 [69-May-20: 2C].

Jones, Leah (83 yrs.) d. on 69-Oct-7 [69-Oct-18: 2C; 69-Oct-19: 2C].
Jones, Leonard J. (4 yrs., 7 mos.) d. on 66-Sep-8 [66-Sep-10: 2D; 66-Sep-11: 2B].
Jones, Leonard S. Healy (3 mos.) d. on 66-Jul-19 [66-Jul-20: 2D].
Jones, Levin (56 yrs.) d. on 66-Feb-9 [66-Feb-16: 2B].
Jones, Levin T. m. Phillips, Margaret H. on 68-Jul-6 [68-Sep-10: 2B].
Jones, Lewis (15 yrs.) d. on 70-Sep-10 [70-Sep-12: 2C].
Jones, Lillie W. m. Willis, John H. on 70-Apr-5 [70-Oct-11: 2B].
Jones, Lina m. Scholl, John .. on 68-Dec-2 [69-Jan-11: 2C].
Jones, Lizzie J. (18 yrs.) d. on 67-Mar-28 [67-Mar-30: 2B; 67-Apr-4: 2B].
Jones, Lizzie P. m. Swinney, Epaphroditus on 66-Oct-17 [66-Oct-18: 2B].
Jones, Louise A. m. Schusler, John on 68-Nov-26 [68-Dec-18: 2C].
Jones, Maggie S. m. Kolb, William Augustus on 66-May-24 [66-Jun-4: 2B].
Jones, Mahala Ann (27 yrs.) d. on 66-Oct-15 [66-Oct-17: 2B].
Jones, Margaret (29 yrs.) d. on 67-Nov-1 [67-Nov-2: 2B].
Jones, Margaret D. (17 yrs.) d. on 70-Mar-6 [70-Mar-7: 2C].
Jones, Margaret E. m. Hemmick, Wheatley N. on 70-Mar-6 [70-Jul-4: 2C].
Jones, Mary (57 yrs., 1 mo.) d. on 67-Nov-16 [67-Nov-21: 2C].
Jones, Mary (60 yrs.) d. on 67-Jan-27 [67-Jan-29: 2C].
Jones, Mary (46 yrs.) d. on 70-Oct-10 [70-Oct-12: 2C].
Jones, Mary Ann m. Kolb, William A. on 69-Jan-2 [69-Jan-13: 2D].
Jones, Mary Ann E. (64 yrs.) d. on 68-Jul-4 [68-Jul-6: 2B].
Jones, Mary Catherine (20 yrs.) d. on 70-Aug-27 [70-Aug-29: 2B].
Jones, Mary Claire F. m. Montgomery, James M. on 70-Aug-14 [70-Aug-18: 2B].
Jones, Mary E. d. on 66-May-24 [66-May-25: 2C].
Jones, Mary E. (44 yrs.) d. on 69-Jul-8 [69-Jul-9: 2C].
Jones, Mary E. m. Kahler, J. A. Charles on 68-Dec-9 [68-Dec-11: 2C].
Jones, Mary E. m. Frey, Edwin B. on 67-Jun-20 [67-Jun-22: 2B].
Jones, Mary E. m. Cole, James on 66-Jun-20 [66-Jun-30: 2B].
Jones, Mary E. m. Keirle, Nathaniel G. on 70-Jan-5 [70-Jan-7: 2F].
Jones, Mary Franklin (5 mos.) d. on 67-Aug-4 [67-Aug-5: 2B].
Jones, Mary G. m. Wyatt, Thomas J. on 67-Dec-3 [67-Dec-5: 2C].
Jones, Mary H. m. Frey, Solomon K. on 68-May-4 [68-May-8: 2B].
Jones, Mary Irene Bell (5 mos.) d. on 70-Jul-31 [70-Aug-2: 2C].
Jones, Mary J. m. Farmer, James A. on 68-Feb-27 [68-Feb-29: 2B].
Jones, Mary Rutter (15 yrs., 8 mos.) d. on 70-Aug-25 [70-Aug-26: 2C].
Jones, Mary T. m. Wivel, Francis P. on 66-May-22 [66-May-26: 2B].
Jones, Mary V. d. on 67-Mar-24 [67-Mar-25: 2C].
Jones, Mattie J. m. Brown, David P. on 70-May-24 [70-May-27: 2B].
Jones, Minnie m. Harris, Samuel Y. on 70-Apr-28 [70-May-3: 2B].
Jones, Minnie Lyeth d. on 70-Feb-2 [70-Feb-3: 2B].
Jones, Mollie A. m. Rees, A. J. on 67-Jun-20 [67-Jun-22: 2B].
Jones, Mollie A. m. Carter, Walter S. on 67-Dec-18 [67-Dec-24: 2B].
Jones, Nelson m. Tilmon, Mary E. on 69-Nov-11 [69-Nov-13: 2B].
Jones, Olivia (29 yrs.) d. on 69-Nov-20 of Consumption [69-Nov-23: 2C].
Jones, Planner (45 yrs.) d. on 66-Oct-12 [66-Oct-13: 2B].
Jones, R. Emmett m. Hoffman, Mary E. on 70-Jan-3 [70-Jan-31: 2C].
Jones, Rachel A. m. Cragg, Robert on 67-Aug-13 [67-Aug-28: 2B].
Jones, Rebecca (66 yrs.) d. on 66-Feb-1 [66-Feb-3: 2C].
Jones, Rebecca J. (48 yrs.) d. on 69-Nov-21 [69-Nov-23: 2C].
Jones, Resin m. Childs, Marcella on 66-Jun-14 [66-Jun-15: 2C].
Jones, Richard D. (49 yrs.) d. on 66-Apr-5 [66-Apr-7: 2B].
Jones, Robert m. Miller, Elizabeth on 66-Apr-5 [66-Apr-14: 2B].
Jones, Robert H. m. Marshall, Maggie on 69-Sep-9 [69-Sep-22: 2C].
Jones, Robert L. m. Fields, Susan A. V. on 68-Apr-28 [68-May-2: 2C].
Jones, Robert M. m. Straney, Mary A. on 69-Apr-6 [69-May-1: 2B].

Jones, Roseta m. Bentley, Richard on 68-Jul-16 [68-Jul-18: 2B].
Jones, S. Oleita (1 yr., 4 mos.) d. [70-Jul-29: 2C].
Jones, Sallie A. m. Carlisle, George Austin on 68-Aug-2 [68-Aug-5: 2B].
Jones, Sallie K. m. Morris, Thomas H. on 66-Nov-1 [66-Nov-7: 2C].
Jones, Sarah (65 yrs.) d. on 66-Nov-5 [66-Nov-7: 2C].
Jones, Sarah A. (63 yrs.) d. on 70-Nov-19 [70-Nov-21: 2C].
Jones, Sarah Ann (82 yrs.) d. on 68-Apr-20 [68-Apr-22: 2B].
Jones, Sarah Eliza (7 mos.) d. on 69-Jan-5 of Lung congestion [69-Jan-9: 2C].
Jones, Sarah Geneva m. Jones, F. D. on 69-May-8 [69-May-10: 2B].
Jones, Sarah Jane (27 yrs.) d. on 69-Mar-1 [69-Mar-6: 2C].
Jones, Sarah Virginia m. Chaney, William Edward on 66-Aug-8 [66-Aug-15: 2B].
Jones, Sibelah (83 yrs.) d. on 66-Jun-18 [66-Jun-20: 2C].
Jones, Sophia d. on 68-Jan-26 [68-Jan-30: 2C].
Jones, Susan d. on 67-Sep-19 [67-Sep-21: 2A].
Jones, Susan H. (60 yrs.) d. on 66-Jun-5 [66-Jun-9: 2B].
Jones, Susannah (56 yrs.) d. on 67-Feb-5 of Cancer [67-Feb-7: 2C].
Jones, Susie T. m. Martin, J. H. on 67-Aug-28 [67-Sep-10: 2B].
Jones, T. P. m. Mace, S. Virginia on 70-Dec-22 [70-Dec-28: 2C].
Jones, Talbot m. Clark, Eleanor G. on 69-Jun-24 [69-Jun-28: 2C; 69-Jun-29: 2C].
Jones, Thomas, Capt. (56 yrs.) d. on 66-Oct-24 [66-Oct-31: 2B].
Jones, Thomas m. Richards, Sadoria on 66-Dec-29 [66-Dec-31: 2C].
Jones, Thomas C. (62 yrs.) d. on 66-Oct-7 [66-Oct-9: 2A].
Jones, Thomas F. m. Dickens, Mary C. on 66-Nov-11 [66-Nov-22: 2C].
Jones, Turbot (59 yrs., 6 mos.) d. on 70-Jun-25 [70-Jun-27: 2C].
Jones, Virginia m. Hamill, Samuel on 68-Oct-15 [68-Oct-16: 2B].
Jones, W. W., Capt. (32 yrs.) d. on 66-Oct-3 Drowned [66-Oct-24: 2C].
Jones, Waitman, Dr. (50 yrs.) d. on 68-Jan-29 [68-Jan-31: 2C; 68-Feb-1: 2B].
Jones, Walter C., Capt. (40 yrs.) d. on 70-Jun-19 [70-Jun-20: 2B; 70-Jun-21: 2C; 70-Jun-22: 2C].
Jones, Walter Miller (3 yrs., 4 mos.) d. on 66-Apr-19 [66-Apr-20: 2B].
Jones, William, Capt. (66 yrs.) d. on 68-Oct-28 [68-Oct-29: 2B; 68-Oct-30: 2C].
Jones, William (58 yrs.) d. on 70-Sep-8 Burned [70-Sep-10: 2B, 4C].
Jones, William A. H. m. Eggleston, Anna on 68-Aug-5 [68-Aug-6: 2B].
Jones, William C., Capt. (31 yrs.) d. on 70-Apr-10 [70-Apr-22: 2C; 70-Apr-25: 1H].
Jones, William C. (6 mos.) d. on 70-Oct-8 [70-Oct-10: 2B].
Jones, William C. m. Nichols, Isabel on 66-Apr-5 [66-Apr-13: 2C].
Jones, William C., Jr. m. Pearson, Elizabeth J. on 67-Feb-18 [67-Jun-17: 2B].
Jones, William D. m. Hitzelberger, Helen C. on 70-May-24 [70-May-25: 2C].
Jones, William H. (41 yrs.) d. on 70-Dec-29 of Erysipelas [70-Dec-30: 2C, 4D; 70-Dec-31: 2C].
Jones, William H. d. on 67-Aug-14 [67-Aug-17: 2B].
Jones, William H. d. on 66-Apr-6 [66-Apr-7: 2B].
Jones, William H. m. Taylor, Kate A. on 67-Sep-13 [67-Nov-23: 2B].
Jones, William H. m. Matthews, Emma Maud on 66-Apr-25 [66-Apr-30: 2B].
Jones, William H. m. Beckmyer, Amelia, Miss on 67-Aug-14 [67-Aug-17: 2B].
Jones, William M. m. Paca, Eliza E. on 67-Sep-1 [67-Sep-9: 2B].
Jones, William T. m. Simms, Maria on 68-May-5 [68-May-8: 2B].
Jones, William T. m. Jones, Elizabeth R. on 67-Dec-11 [67-Dec-21: 2B].
Jones, William Thomas (4 mos.) d. on 68-Jul-4 [68-Jul-6: 2B].
Jones, Willie (6 mos.) d. on 70-Aug-3 [70-Aug-5: 2C].
Jordan, Charles E. m. Magil, Annie on 70-Jul-19 [70-Jul-30: 2B].
Jordan, Eliza J. (44 yrs.) d. on 70-Aug-14 [70-Aug-15: 2B].
Jordan, Elizabeth m. Keister, William on 66-Mar-17 [66-Mar-19: 2B].
Jordan, Ellen (22 yrs.) d. on 69-May-20 [69-May-22: 2B].
Jordan, Emma (2 yrs., 10 mos.) d. on 66-Jun-25 [66-Jun-27: 2C].
Jordan, German (76 yrs.) d. on 66-Feb-25 [66-Mar-1: 2B].

Jordan, Henry d. on 70-Aug-15 [70-Aug-20: 4E].
Jordan, J. W. m. Fort, Alfie V. on 66-Oct-11 [66-Oct-16: 2B].
Jordan, Jennie m. Harvey, William P. on 66-Jun-28 [66-Jul-12: 2C].
Jordan, John R. m. Carmichael, Ellen R. on 67-Sep-17 [67-Oct-7: 2B].
Jordan, Kate G. m. Chaney, H. C. on 66-Jul-26 [66-Aug-4: 2C].
Jordan, Laura V. m. Bruce, Edward on 68-Jan-6 [68-Jan-14: 2C].
Jordan, Margaret m. Zeller, John W. on 68-Nov-19 [68-Nov-21: 2C].
Jordan, Mary A. m. Glenn, John on 69-Oct-17 [69-Oct-26: 2B].
Jordan, Pauline m. Walter, Abram on 69-Jan-27 [69-Feb-13: 2C].
Jordan, Rosa (6 yrs., 1 mo.) d. on 67-Jul-16 [67-Jul-17: 2C].
Jordan, Rosa Emma (10 mos.) d. on 68-Aug-25 [68-Aug-26: 2B].
Jordan, Rufus E. m. Woolford, Lillie G. on 69-Jun-22 [69-Jun-28: 2C].
Jordan, William G. m. Preston, Mary A. on 69-Sep-7 [69-Oct-20: 2C].
Jorden, Henry F. m. Hipsley, Margaretta A. on 66-Jun-28 [66-Jun-30: 2B].
Jordon, Annetta Estelle (4 yrs., 8 mos.) d. on 66-Mar-11 [66-Mar-13: 2B].
Jordon, Fanny, Sr. (85 yrs.) d. on 67-Jun-13 [67-Jul-12: 1F].
Jordon, Isom (74 yrs., 1 mo.) d. on 70-Jan-29 [70-Jan-31: 2C].
Jordon, James H. (28 yrs., 1 mo.) d. on 67-Nov-12 [67-Nov-13: 2C].
Jory, Jennette m. Klockgether, Albert A. on 66-Aug-22 [66-Aug-25: 2A].
Jory, John G. m. Wagner, Maggie on 69-Nov-16 [69-Nov-20: 2B].
Josenhans, Caroline (47 yrs., 3 mos.) d. on 66-Oct-20 [66-Oct-22: 2C].
Josenhans, Charles H. m. Snyder, Elenor F on 69-Oct-19 [69-Oct-26: 2B].
Josenhans, Henrietta C. m. Davis, George A. on 68-Jul-16 [69-Mar-16: 2C].
Joseph, Annie m. Despeaux, Charles H. on 68-Aug-27 [68-Sep-3: 2B].
Joseph, Babette m. Westheimer, David on 70-Sep-20 [70-Sep-22: 2C].
Joseph, Betty m. Fleischer, Simon on 70-Dec-18 [70-Dec-24: 2B].
Joseph, George (53 yrs.) d. on 68-Jul-19 [68-Jul-21: 2C].
Joseph, Jessel (63 yrs.) d. on 68-Apr-1 [68-Apr-2: 2C; 68-Apr-3: 2C].
Joseph, John (35 yrs.) d. on 66-Sep-30 [66-Oct-1: 2B].
Joseph, Margaret E. m. Myers, George W. on 67-Aug-22 [67-Aug-24: 2B].
Joseph, Sophie (1 yr., 6 mos.) d. on 68-May-23 [68-May-26: 2B].
Jourdan, Elenora d. on 67-Dec-29 [67-Dec-31: 2C].
Jourley, Andrew (32 yrs.) d. on 70-Feb-20 [70-Feb-22: 2C].
Joy, G. W. m. Woodford, Marion on 68-Dec-31 [68-Jan-1: 2C].
Joyce, Charles m. Lee, Ellen on 70-Mar-31 [70-Apr-2: 2A].
Joyce, Cyrus N. m. Collinson, Eliza J. on 69-Apr-22 [69-Apr-27: 2B].
Joyce, Emma P. m. Ensor, Benjamin F. on 66-Sep-2 [67-Jan-14: 2C].
Joyce, Florence (3 yrs.) d. on 65-Dec-29 [66-Jan-5: 2C].
Joyce, George A. (17 yrs., 4 mos.) d. on 67-May-10 of Consumption [67-May-11: 2A].
Joyce, J. A. m. Greves, Katie M. on 67-Nov-12 [67-Nov-22: 2C].
Joyce, Josephine H. m. Glanville, Robert B . on 66-Apr-30 [66-May-3: 2C].
Joyce, Kate A. m. Moke, James E. on 67-Apr-25 [67-Apr-30: 2A].
Joyce, Katie m. Lowry, Irving on 69-Oct-5 [69-Oct-7: 2B].
Joyce, Lavenia m. Forrester, John R. on 69-Jul-4 [69-Jul-9: 2C].
Joyce, Sarah E. m. Henly, David on 68-Jun-30 [68-Jul-7: 2B].
Joyce, Sarah Elizabeth (8 mos.) d. on 67-Jul-5 [67-Jul-9: 2B].
Joyce, William (53 yrs.) d. on 68-Nov-1 of Paralysis [68-Nov-2: 4C; 68-Nov-3: 2B; 68-Nov-13: 2C].
Joyes, Jesse (75 yrs.) d. on 70-Jun-2 [70-Jun-7: 2C].
Joynes, David J. m. Livingston, Mary S. on 69-Aug-10 [69-Sep-24: 2B].
Joynes, Elisha (21 yrs.) d. on 67-Dec-17 of War wounds [67-Dec-19: 2B].
Joynes, Johnny (9 mos.) d. on 70-Aug-15 [70-Aug-16: 2C].
Joynes, Willie F. m. Hopkins, Jennie on 70-May-19 [70-May-23: 2B; 70-May-24: 2C].
Jubb, A. Rebecca m. Armiger, Josiah C. on 70-Dec-8 [70-Dec-10: 2B].
Jubb, Dabora m. Munroe, Joseph G on 67-Sep-26 [67-Nov-5: 2B].

Jubb, William J., Capt. (40 yrs.) d. on 67-Sep-6 [67-Sep-26: 2B].
Judah, David (77 yrs.) d. on 66-May-28 [66-May-29: 2B].
Judah, E. Douglas m. Rider, Rosie on 68-Aug-6 [68-Aug-7: 2B].
Judd, John m. Walter, Laura J. on 68-Nov-24 [68-Dec-18: 2C].
Judge, Ann (48 yrs.) d. on 66-Jan-16 [66-Jan-18: 2C].
Judge, Francis A. m. Logue, Mary A. on 70-Oct-13 [70-Oct-14: 2B].
Judkins, Eugenia F. (17 yrs.) d. on 67-Aug-18 [67-Aug-20: 2B].
Julien, Anne (75 yrs.) d. on 69-Mar-4 [69-Mar-5: 2C].
Jump, Robert H. m. Fountain, Julia M. on 66-Jul-31 [66-Aug-11: 2B].
Jump, Sarah D. (26 yrs.) d. on 68-Sep-16 [68-Sep-17: 2B].
Jungling, Friedrich m. Kraft, Catharine J. on 70-Feb-22 [70-Mar-3: 2C].
Junkins, George F. m. Waldron, Georgia M. on 69-Jun-8 [69-Jun-12: 2B].
Jurdan, Francis m. Stapleton, Mary Ann [70-Oct-8: 2B].
Jurgens, J. H. m. Kimble, C. E. on 65-Dec-24 [66-Jan-27: 2B].
Jurgens, Maggie m. Wieman, Leopold on 70-Apr-26 [70-Apr-28: 2B].
Justi, William Bassett (1 yr.) d. on 69-Dec-7 [69-Dec-9: 2C].
Justice, Ann (51 yrs.) d. on 68-Apr-9 [68-Apr-13: 2B].
Justice, Franklin Sommerfield (4 yrs., 2 mos.) d. on 68-Jul-28 of Dysentery [68-Jul-31: 2C].
Justice, John W. m. Dunigan, Sarah E. on 68-Dec-21 [68-Dec-28: 2B].
Justice, Mahlon (45 yrs.) d. on 66-Nov-8 of Typhoid [66-Nov-13: 2B].
Justis, Charles E. (27 yrs.) d. on 68-Jan-23 [68-Jan-24: 2D; 68-Jan-25: 2B].
Justis, J. Chris m. Leans, Lou M. on 68-Nov-12 [68-Nov-19: 2C].
Justus, John d. on 70-Apr-1 Drowned [70-Apr-4: 1H].
Kabernagel, Mary Elise (38 yrs.) d. on 67-May-10 [67-May-11: 2A].
Kabernagle, Amelia D. m. Schaub, Frederick on 69-Nov-18 [69-Nov-30: 2C].
Kabernagle, Mary E. m. Wehr, Herman on 67-Apr-16 [67-Apr-20: 2A].
Kaghn, Michael d. on 67-Nov-15 in Railroad accident [67-Nov-18: 1F].
Kahler, Charles P. m. Banks, Emma J. on 69-May-11 [69-May-15: 2B].
Kahler, Emma J. (21 yrs.) d. on 69-Jun-18 [69-Jun-19: 2B].
Kahler, J. A. Charles m. Jones, Mary E. on 68-Dec-9 [68-Dec-11: 2C].
Kain, George m. Bushman, Emma on 70-Nov-15 [70-Nov-22: 2B].
Kain, Virginia (33 yrs.) d. on 67-Aug-27 [67-Aug-31: 2B].
Kaiser, Amelia M. m. Ermer, Henry on 68-Jun-1 [68-Jun-10: 2B].
Kaiser, John H. m. Miller, Catharine M. on 68-Dec-16 [68-Dec-24: 2C].
Kalbfus, Lewis (74 yrs.) d. on 68-Apr-22 [68-Apr-23: 2B; 68-Apr-24: 2B].
Kalkman, Charles W. m. Polk, Carrie on 69-Oct-26 [69-Nov-4: 2B; 69-Nov-5: 2C].
Kalkman, Henry F. (58 yrs.) d. on 69-Apr-6 [69-Apr-16: 2B].
Kalling, Annie Elizabeth m. Unverzagt, William on 68-Jul-2 [68-Jul-28: 2B].
Kamerer, Louisa m. Atlee, Issac on 70-Nov-22 [70-Nov-28: 2C].
Kammerer, William A. m. Streiwig, Emma L. on 70-Oct-27 [70-Nov-2: 2C].
Kamps, Mary (27 yrs.) d. on 66-Jul-10 [66-Jul-11: 2B].
Kane, Bernard (70 yrs.) d. on 69-Jun-13 [69-Jun-14: 2B].
Kane, Catharine m. Crook, George W. on 67-Jul-9 [67-Aug-6: 2C].
Kane, Eugene T. (5 mos.) d. on 66-Jul-15 of Brain inflammation [66-Jul-28: 2C].
Kane, G. K., Rev. (81 yrs.) d. on 69-Sep-27 [69-Sep-28: 2B; 69-Sep-29: 1G].
Kane, James (42 yrs.) d. on 66-Jul-17 of Heatstroke [66-Jul-18: 1F, 2C].
Kane, John (76 yrs.) d. on 68-Jul-30 [68-Aug-1: 2B].
Kane, John P. m. Kirwan, Mary C. on 66-Sep-12 [67-Feb-4: 2C].
Kane, Louisa m. Heimiller, Henry F. on 68-May-17 [68-Jul-31: 2C].
Kane, Mary E. (8 yrs., 9 mos.) d. on 69-Mar-23 [69-Mar-29: 2B].
Kane, O. P. (56 yrs.) d. on 66-Sep-4 of Consumption [66-Sep-6: 2B].
Kane, P. (35 yrs.) d. on 70-Nov-30 [70-Dec-1: 2C; 70-Dec-2: 2C].
Kane, Susan m. Biddle, Richard F. on 67-Jan-1 [67-Jan-9: 2B].
Kann, Mena (69 yrs.) d. on 67-May-26 [67-May-27: 2B].
Kann, Nathan (12 yrs.) d. on 67-Jun-12 [67-Jun-14: 2B].

Kanne, William H. m. Ohlendorff, Johanna F. E. on 69-Jan-7 [69-Jan-8: 2C].
Kaprziewa, Dominic (7 yrs.) d. on 67-Jun-15 Drowned [67-Jun-17: 1F].
Karmrodt, Lewis (1 yr., 10 mos.) d. on 69-May-6 [69-May-8: 2B].
Karr, Cora Ellis (3 yrs.) d. on 70-May-22 [70-May-23: 2B].
Karr, Lenni E. m. Blakeney, Charles W. on 70-Dec-25 [70-Dec-30: 2C].
Kasten, C. A., Jr. m. Meyers, Emma on 70-May-12 [70-May-24: 2C].
Kating, Katie m. Russell, William H. on 69-Oct-14 [69-Oct-20: 2C].
Katzenberger, John H. m. Bell, Mollie A. on 67-Nov-27 [67-Nov-30: 2C].
Katzenberger, Louis Edward (10 mos.) d. on 67-Jun-21 [67-Jun-22: 2B].
Katzenstein, Rosa m. Drachman, Philip on 68-Apr-21 [68-Apr-24: 2B].
Kauder, George A. J. (2 yrs., 1 mo.) d. on 66-Jul-29 [66-Jul-30: 2C].
Kauderer, Willie Wallace (1 yr., 6 mos.) d. on 68-Jul-6 [68-Jul-7: 2B].
Kauffman, Blanche Matilda (7 mos.) d. on 69-Jul-15 [69-Jul-20: 2C].
Kauffman, Cleantha M. m. Miller, Thomas G. on 69-Jun-23 [69-Jun-29: 2C].
Kauffman, George (67 yrs.) d. on 66-Nov-6 [66-Nov-22: 2C].
Kauffman, Helen S. m. Wilmer, William B. on 70-May-5 [70-May-9: 2B].
Kauffman, Lavinia D. m. Colton, Edward C. on 67-May-20 [67-May-23: 2B].
Kauffman, Marion Meeds (1 yr., 11 mos.) d. on 67-Sep-3 [67-Sep-5: 2B].
Kauffman, William H. (28 yrs.) d. on 66-Nov-24 [66-Nov-29: 2C].
Kaufman, Bessie Curtis d. on 69-Jan-27 [69-Jan-28: 2C].
Kaufman, Elizabeth (30 yrs.) d. on 69-Apr-11 [69-Apr-13: 2B].
Kaufmann, Louis Joseph (26 yrs.) d. on 68-Aug-23 [68-Aug-25: 2B].
Kaufmann, William m. Ray, Mary E. on 68-Dec-15 [69-Jan-12: 2C].
Kavanagh, James Martin (2 mos.) d. on 70-Oct-19 [70-Oct-20: 2B].
Kavanagh, Patrick, Capt. (63 yrs.) d. on 70-Jul-7 of Cholera morbus [70-Jul-8: 1H, 2C; 70-Jul-9: 2B].
Kavanagh, Steven F. (3 yrs., 6 mos.) d. on 70-Jul-10 [70-Jul-11: 2C].
Kavanaugh, Allan T. (1 yr., 7 mos.) d. on 70-Mar-20 [70-Mar-22: 2C].
Kavanaugh, Berrie m. Dodson, C. R. on 70-Mar-1 [70-Mar-11: 2C].
Kavanaugh, Edward (65 yrs.) d. on 70-Aug-25 [70-Aug-26: 2C].
Kavanaugh, John (24 yrs.) d. on 68-Jul-24 Drowned [68-Jul-28: 1B].
Kavanaugh, Maggie L. (24 yrs.) d. on 70-Sep-11 [70-Sep-12: 2B].
Kavenaugh, Mary (55 yrs.) d. on 69-Oct-7 [69-Oct-8: 2B].
Kaylor, Elizabeth J. (51 yrs.) d. on 68-Jul-3 [68-Jul-4: 2C].
Kayser, Albert (6 yrs., 6 mos.) d. on 69-May-3 [69-May-4: 2B].
Keach, Cyril W. (53 yrs.) d. on 66-Aug-11 [66-Aug-13: 2C].
Keach, Mary E. (12 yrs.) d. on 67-Feb-19 [67-Feb-21: 2C].
Keach, S. Amelia m. Russell, Alex. H. on 69-Feb-2 [69-Feb-17: 2C].
Keagle, Henry m. Hanson, Isabel on 70-Aug-9 [70-Sep-21: 2B].
Keagle, James K. (1 yr.) d. on 68-Jul-2 [68-Jul-3: 2B].
Keagle, William m. Meek, Mabel F. on 69-Dec-28 [70-Jan-11: 2C].
Kealhofer, Lutie m. Giles, William Fell on 66-Apr-11 [66-Apr-17: 2C].
Kean, James m. Levering, Sallie C. on 67-Sep-10 [67-Sep-14: 2A].
Kean, John (24 yrs.) d. on 70-Aug-20 [70-Sep-2: 2C].
Kean, Mary A. m. Atkinson, Thomas F. on 69-Mar-11 [69-Mar-20: 2B].
Kean, Priscilla d. on 67-Feb-15 [67-Feb-25: 2C].
Kean, Sophia m. Gazan, Nathan on 67-Mar-24 [67-Mar-26: 2C].
Keane, Fanny d. on 68-Aug-28 [68-Aug-29: 2B].
Kearney, Mary (1 yr., 3 mos.) d. on 70-Jul-18 [70-Jul-19: 2C].
Kearney, Susan (28 yrs.) d. on 69-Apr-6 [69-Apr-7: 2C].
Kearney, Thomas J. m. Whelan, Agnes Olivia on 67-Dec-25 [68-Jan-6: 2C].
Kearney, William J. m. Conroy, Catherine M. on 70-Nov-1 [70-Dec-16: 2C].
Kearns, Henry m. Seth, Margaret A. on 66-Jun-25 [66-Aug-2: 2C].
Keaton, Fannie L. d. on 68-Aug-23 [68-Aug-26: 2B].
Keaton, James P. m. Small, Frances L. on 66-Dec-25 [67-Jan-4: 2D].

Kechling, Theodore (23 yrs.) d. on 68-Jul-16 of Heatstroke [68-Jul-17: 1D].
Keck, Julia A. (31 yrs.) d. on 70-Jul-10 [70-Jul-11: 2C].
Keck, Peter m. Bohn, Maria W. on 65-Dec-31 [66-Jan-6: 2B].
Keck, Samuel (58 yrs.) d. on 70-Oct-24 in Railroad accident [70-Oct-25: 4D; 70-Oct-26: 2B].
Keck, Samuel m. Biggs, Julia Ann on 67-Nov-27 [67-Nov-30: 2C].
Keck, Samuel Gilbert m. Slingman, Mary Anna on 66-Jan-7 [66-Feb-13: 2C].
Keckler, Catharine E. (20 yrs., 11 mos.) d. on 70-Mar-13 [70-Mar-14: 2C; 70-Mar-15: 2C].
Keckler, Jacob J. m. Gees, Frances C. on 67-Nov-13 [67-Nov-21: 2C].
Keckler, John G. m. Hildebrand, Susan J. on 70-Jun-2 [70-Jun-28: 2C].
Keech, Sallie M. m. Ramsburg, Newton A. on 67-Oct-22 [67-Oct-26: 2A].
Keefe, John F. m. Trumbo, Susan M. on 66-Apr-17 [66-Apr-20: 2B].
Keefe, Kate m. Kilfoyle, Thomas on 66-May-16 [66-May-30: 2C].
Keefe, Patrick d. on 68-Jul-17 [68-Jul-18: 2B].
Keefer, Albert W. m. Harris, Mary H. on 70-Nov-23 [70-Nov-29: 2C].
Keefer, John (52 yrs.) d. on 70-Feb-21 [70-Feb-22: 2C].
Keefer, Sarah Jane (47 yrs.) d. on 68-Jan-23 [68-Jan-24: 2D].
Keegan, John T. (27 yrs.) d. on 68-Sep-6 of Consumption [68-Sep-8: 1G].
Keegan, Mary Ellen (2 yrs., 3 mos.) d. on 67-Sep-2 [67-Sep-3: 2B].
Keelan, Mary Teresa m. Hartigan, John T. on 70-Feb-16 [70-Feb-26: 2C].
Keeling, Joseph W. m. Salgee, Oriana on 70-Oct-13 [70-Oct-21: 2C].
Keen, Amelia R. m. Graham, Joseph A. on 67-Sep-19 [67-Sep-21: 2A].
Keen, Charles Oliver (4 mos.) d. on 69-Jul-8 [69-Jul-9: 2C].
Keen, Edward (80 yrs.) d. on 70-Nov-13 [70-Nov-14: 2B].
Keen, Elizabeth H. (3 yrs., 10 mos.) d. on 69-Jul-21 of Brain fever [69-Jul-22: 2C].
Keen, Jesse W. m. Dawes, Ella E. on 70-Aug-4 [70-Sep-3: 2B].
Keen, John M. Creighton, Hattie A. on 67-Mar-12 [67-Mar-14: 2C].
Keen, Lottie m. Preece, R. W. on 67-Nov-14 [67-Dec-10: 2B].
Keen, Rosalie Elvira (20 yrs.) d. on 66-Aug-17 [66-Aug-18: 2B].
Keen, Sallie Gaskins (1 yr., 4 mos.) d. on 67-Jul-2 [67-Jul-6: 2B].
Keenan, Alma (2 yrs., 3 mos.) d. on 70-Mar-31 [70-Apr-1: 2B; 70-Apr-2: 2B].
Keenan, Blanche Elmina d. on 70-Jul-26 [70-Jul-28: 2C].
Keenan, Catherine (26 yrs.) d. on 66-Aug-5 [66-Aug-7: 2C].
Keenan, Charles d. on 67-Apr-24 [67-Apr-25: 2B].
Keenan, Dennis (84 yrs.) d. on 67-Jul-21 [67-Jul-22: 2C].
Keenan, Elizabeth (83 yrs.) d. on 69-May-29 of Pneumonia [69-Jun-1: 2B].
Keenan, Emma m. Finley, Robert Smith on 69-Nov-23 [69-Nov-24: 2C].
Keenan, Emma Josephine d. on 67-Mar-21 [67-Mar-22: 2C; 67-Mar-23: 2B].
Keenan, James (45 yrs.) d. on 70-Oct-5 [70-Oct-6: 2B].
Keenan, James E. m. Miles, Adie on 67-Mar-5 [67-Mar-9: 2B].
Keenan, John Watson m. Morris, Sarah E. on 67-May-6 [67-May-11: 2A].
Keenan, Lizzie A. m. McClure, William G. [66-Dec-11: 2B].
Keenan, Mary A. (76 yrs.) d. on 68-Jan-12 [68-Jan-14: 2C].
Keene, Charles E. m. Ewen, Sarah Catherine on 70-Jul-19 [70-Jul-21: 2C].
Keene, John (54 yrs.) d. on 69-Jan-24 [69-Feb-15: 2C].
Keene, John R. m. Kraft, Jennette on 67-Oct-3 [67-Oct-8: 2B].
Keene, John T. m. Albert, Annie on 69-May-17 [69-Jun-5: 2B].
Keene, Joseph Herbert (8 mos.) d. on 70-Mar-8 [70-Mar-9: 2C].
Keene, Joseph R. m. Nugent, Annie A. on 66-Jan-18 [66-Jan-29: 2B].
Keene, Lena d. on 70-Mar-7 [70-Mar-15: 2C].
Keene, Louise m. Gwynn, A. J. on 68-Jan-8 [68-Jan-9: 2C].
Keene, Mary F. (19 yrs.) d. on 70-Oct-10 [70-Oct-12: 2C].
Keene, Sallie Theobald m. Craig, John A. on 68-Feb-4 [68-Feb-8: 2B].
Keener, Mary Clare (70 yrs.) d. on 67-Oct-31 [67-Nov-1: 2B].
Keese, Minnie m. Griffiths, James E. on 70-Oct-19 [70-Oct-22: 2B].
Keesee, Mary O. m. Belvin, John A., Jr. on 67-Feb-21 [67-Feb-26: 2C].

Kefauver, Charles M. m. Gaddess, Lizzie on 66-Dec-13 [66-Dec-22: 2A].
Kegan, Elizabeth (10 mos.) d. on 70-Aug-8 [70-Aug-9: 2C].
Kehoe, Edward (1 yr.) d. on 70-Nov-7 [70-Nov-8: 2B].
Kehoe, Jessie d. on 68-Sep-27 of Consumption [68-Oct-1: 2B].
Kehoe, Mathew (86 yrs.) d. on 70-Nov-20 [70-Nov-21: 2C].
Kehoe, Richard Thomas (7 yrs., 9 mos.) d. on 69-Sep-14 [69-Sep-15: 2B].
Keibard, Ellen S. (47 yrs.) d. on 70-Dec-13 [70-Dec-14: 2C].
Keidel, Charlotte Emma (3 yrs., 1 mo.) d. on 68-Dec-20 [68-Dec-21: 2B].
Keidel, Fredericka Karthaus d. on 67-Oct-30 [67-Nov-1: 2B; 67-Nov-2: 2B].
Keidel, Henry m. Lawrence, Adela on 69-Jun-17 [69-Jun-19: 2B].
Keidel, Louis J. m. Brauns, Emma S. on 66-Jul-11 [66-Jul-13: 2C].
Keighler, Alice L. (27 yrs.) d. on 69-Apr-20 [69-Apr-21: 2C].
Keighler, Frank Ames (23 yrs.) d. on 69-Apr-19 [69-Apr-22: 2B].
Keighler, John H. (67 yrs.) d. on 66-Sep-24 [66-Sep-26: 2B].
Keil, Catharine M. m. Keil, Philip on 67-Aug-25 [67-Apr-27: 2B].
Keil, George, Sr. (67 yrs.) d. on 66-Mar-13 of Dropsy [66-Mar-16: 2B].
Keil, Philip m. Keil, Catharine M. on 67-Aug-25 [67-Aug-27: 2B].
Keil, Sarah (26 yrs., 1 mo.) d. of Chronic diarrhea [70-Jan-29: 2B].
Keiler, Rosanna m. Slemaker, Jacob H. on 66-May-22 [66-Jul-16: 2C].
Keilholtz, Sophia (33 yrs., 1 mo.) d. on 67-Jan-30 [67-Feb-1: 2C].
Keily, Richard W. (60 yrs.) d. on 68-May-4 [68-May-6: 2B].
Keirle, Henry C. (35 yrs.) d. on 70-Jul-20 [70-Jul-29: 2C].
Keirle, Nathaniel G. m. Jones, Mary E. on 70-Jan-5 [70-Jan-7: 2F].
Keiser, Nicholas (74 yrs.) d. on 67-Apr-23 [67-Apr-27: 2A].
Keisling, Richard (18 yrs.) d. on 70-Jun-24 Drowned [70-Jun-25: 1G].
Keister, Fredericka (61 yrs.) d. on 70-Mar-20 [70-Mar-21: 2C].
Keister, William m. Jordan, Elizabeth on 66-Mar-17 [66-Mar-19: 2C].
Keith, William H. m. Hyde, Clemence T. on 66-Oct-23 [66-Oct-26: 2B].
Keithley, Isabel m. Thomas, Joseph H. on 66-Dec-25 [66-Dec-29: 2C].
Keithley, Thomas H. d. [67-Apr-15: 2B].
Keithly, Jane d. [66-Mar-29: 2B].
Keizer, Mary d. on 70-Aug-23 of Cholera infantum [70-Aug-24: 2C].
Kelbaugh, George M. (1 yr.) d. on 69-Sep-21 [69-Sep-23: 2B].
Kelchner, Maggie R. m. Spencer, J. N. on 69-May-25 [69-Jun-22: 2C].
Keleher, Dennis (22 yrs.) d. on 66-Nov-10 [66-Nov-12: 2C].
Keleher, John (11 mos.) d. on 69-Sep-13 [69-Sep-14: 2B].
Keleher, John (26 yrs.) d. on 70-Jan-7 [70-Jan-8: 2B].
Keleher, Margaret (66 yrs.) d. on 66-Oct-3 [66-Oct-4: 2B].
Kelhart, Louis (45 yrs.) d. on 67-Sep-10 in Railroad accident [67-Sep-11: 1G].
Kell, Charles Philip (5 mos.) d. on 69-Jun-21 [69-Jun-22: 2C].
Kell, Honoria (1 yr., 1 mo.) d. on 68-Jul-26 [68-Jul-27: 2B; 68-Jul-28: 2B].
Keller, Andrew J. (1 yr., 10 mos.) d. on 66-May-11 of Chronic croup [66-May-12: 2A].
Keller, Hester L. m. Dittus, Thomas F. on 68-Oct-29 [68-Nov-4: 2C].
Keller, John m. Johnson, Eliza J. on 66-Jul-26 [66-Aug-1: 2C].
Keller, John C. (42 yrs.) d. on 67-Sep-17 [67-Sep-19: 2B].
Keller, John H. m. Frederick, Mary Jane on 66-Oct-2 [66-Oct-25: 2C].
Keller, John William d. on 69-May-24 [69-May-25: 2C].
Keller, Josiah G. m. Yingling, Mollie M. on 66-Jun-12 [66-Jun-19: 2B].
Keller, Laura M. (3 yrs., 4 mos.) d. on 68-Aug-14 in Wagon accident [68-Aug-15: 1G, 2B].
Keller, Margaret E. m. Corey, Issac on 63-May-18 [67-Mar-28: 2B].
Keller, Mary Anne (9 mos.) d. on 68-Jul-12 [68-Jul-13: 2B].
Keller, Mary C. m. Buck, James F. on 67-Sep-24 [67-Dec-11: 2B].
Keller, Mary M. m. Cabell, N. F. on 67-Aug-6 [67-Aug-7: 2C].
Keller, Peter F. m. Davis, Kate on 67-Oct-3 [67-Oct-7: 2B].
Keller, Samuel (3 yrs.) d. on 69-Apr-5 of Water on the brain [69-Apr-6: 2C].

Keller, Samuel P. m. Swartz, Mary E. on 68-Nov-17 [68-Dec-8: 2C].
Keller, Virginia A. m. Romoser, Edward M. on 68-Oct-13 [68-Oct-20: 2B].
Keller, William L. (43 yrs.) d. on 69-Mar-2 [69-Mar-4: 2C].
Keller, William L. (23 yrs.) d. on 70-Dec-28 [70-Dec-29: 2C; 70-Dec-30: 2C].
Kelley, A. H. d. on 68-Sep-22 [68-Oct-2: 2B].
Kelley, Annie d. on 68-Sep-22 [68-Oct-2: 2B].
Kelley, Annie C. m. Henry, John E. on 67-Mar-5 [67-Mar-16: 2B].
Kelley, Carrie M. m. Horn, George M. on 69-Jan-19 [69-Jan-25: 2D].
Kelley, Clara d. on 68-Sep-22 [68-Oct-2: 2B].
Kelley, Dandridge, Jr. (19 yrs., 3 mos.) d. on 70-Oct-20 [70-Oct-22: 2B].
Kelley, Daniel M. (73 yrs.) d. on 70-Jan-7 [70-Jan-8: 2B].
Kelley, Emmanuel m. North, Violet on 67-Dec-3 [67-Dec-5: 2C].
Kelley, James m. Donnegan, Kate on 69-Sep-5 [69-Sep-10: 2B].
Kelley, Jane m. Phillips, William A. on 67-Jan-6 [67-Jan-16: 2C].
Kelley, John m. Schaeffer, Margaret on 66-Nov-5 [66-Nov-22: 2C].
Kelley, John A. m. Pearce, Sarah E. on 69-May-6 [69-May-11: 2B; 69-May-12: 2B].
Kelley, Julia (52 yrs.) d. on 70-Apr-12 [70-Apr-14: 2B].
Kelley, Julia (62 yrs.) d. on 70-Jun-5 [70-Jun-6: 2B].
Kelley, Martin (42 yrs.) d. on 67-Nov-29 [67-Nov-30: 2C].
Kelley, Mary (33 yrs.) d. on 68-Mar-4 [68-Mar-5: 2C].
Kelley, Mary E. m. Parks, Edwin D. on 68-Feb-6 [68-Feb-12: 2B].
Kelley, Mary O. m. Brooks, Thomas D. on 68-Sep-15 [68-Sep-17: 2B].
Kelley, Phillip (54 yrs.) d. on 70-Oct-16 [70-Oct-17: 2B].
Kelley, Rachel M. m. Shipley, John on 70-Jun-5 [70-Jun-8: 2C].
Kelley, S. C. m. Markland, Charles H. on 69-Oct-26 [69-Oct-27: 2B].
Kelley, William (46 yrs.) d. on 66-Apr-29 [66-May-1: 2A].
Kelley, William H. m. Cross, Harriet R. on 70-Apr-19 [70-Apr-20: 2B].
Kelliher, Mary (16 yrs., 2 mos.) d. on 67-Sep-18 [67-Sep-20: 2A].
Kellog, Orson (76 yrs.) d. on 68-Nov-18 [68-Nov-19: 2C; 68-Nov-20: 1H].
Kellogg, W. L. H. m. Lauderman, Adeline on 63-Nov-12 [66-Oct-23: 2B].
Kellum, Annie E. m. Livingston, James H. on 68-May-12 [68-May-14: 2B].
Kelly, Albina V. m. Fields, Harry B. on 70-Sep-8 [70-Nov-17: 2C].
Kelly, Amanda m. Rose, Levi L. on 66-Jul-10 [66-Jul-20: 2D].
Kelly, Ann (32 yrs.) d. on 68-Aug-28 [68-Aug-29: 2B].
Kelly, Ann (33 yrs.) d. on 68-May-30 [68-Jun-1: 2B].
Kelly, Basil (36 yrs.) d. on 66-Mar-5 [66-Mar-7: 2B].
Kelly, Bridget (44 yrs.) d. on 67-Mar-26 [67-Mar-28: 2B; 67-Mar-29: 2B].
Kelly, Bridget (44 yrs.) d. on 66-Apr-22 [66-Apr-23: 2B].
Kelly, Bridget (47 yrs.) d. on 70-Feb-14 [70-Feb-15: 2C; 70-Feb-16: 2C].
Kelly, Catharine (9 yrs.) d. on 66-Dec-22 in Wagon accident [66-Dec-24: 1G].
Kelly, Catherine S. (53 yrs.) d. on 69-Jun-13 [69-Jun-15: 2C].
Kelly, Cornelia m. Reynolds, Francis S. on 68-May-4 [68-May-11: 2B].
Kelly, Dandridge m. Bond, Susan on 66-Aug-28 [66-Sep-22: 2B].
Kelly, Dennis A. m. Bell, Clara E. on 67-May-6 [67-May-8: 2B].
Kelly, Dennis Henry (22 yrs.) d. of Consumption [67-Feb-18: 2C].
Kelly, Edward (55 yrs.) d. on 67-Oct-25 [67-Oct-26: 2A].
Kelly, Edward (2 mos.) d. on 67-Jul-3 [67-Jul-4: 2B].
Kelly, Edward d. on 70-Jun-17 [70-Jun-18: 2B].
Kelly, Eliza (62 yrs.) d. on 70-May-4 [70-May-6: 2B].
Kelly, Elizabeth (75 yrs.) d. on 67-Oct-19 [67-Oct-21: 2B].
Kelly, Ellen (3 yrs., 1 mo.) d. [68-Jan-3: 2C].
Kelly, Ellen (49 yrs.) d. on 70-Aug-12 [70-Aug-13: 2C].
Kelly, Emma Malissa (9 mos.) d. on 67-Jan-9 of Consumption [67-Jan-15: 2C].
Kelly, Evelyn (4 yrs., 4 mos.) d. on 70-Dec-15 of Scarlet fever [70-Dec-20: 2B].
Kelly, Frank G. (7 yrs.) d. on 68-Sep-18 [68-Oct-9: 2C].

Kelly, George d. on 66-Nov-6 Drowned [66-Dec-1: 1G].
Kelly, Georgeanna m. Krebs, John J. on 68-Aug-17 [68-Sep-2: 2A].
Kelly, Ina d. on 70-Dec-26 [70-Dec-28: 2C].
Kelly, James (53 yrs.) d. on 66-Aug-25 [66-Aug-27: 2B].
Kelly, James (47 yrs.) d. on 66-Jun-8 of Consumption [66-Jun-9: 2B; 66-Jun-11: 1F].
Kelly, James m. Parish, Sarah E. on 70-Mar-21 [70-Apr-7: 2B].
Kelly, James m. McCarthy, Annie on 70-Nov-1 [70-Nov-8: 2B].
Kelly, James F. (1 yr., 9 mos.) d. on 68-Aug-3 [68-Aug-4: 2C].
Kelly, James M. m. Magness, Rebecca on 69-Aug-3 [69-Aug-10: 2C].
Kelly, James T. m. Kraft, Mary E. on 68-May-5 [68-May-8: 2B].
Kelly, John (58 yrs.) d. on 66-Aug-25 [66-Aug-27: 2B].
Kelly, John F. (8 mos.) d. on 70-Jul-30 [70-Aug-1: 2C].
Kelly, John J. (1 yr., 7 mos.) d. on 68-Oct-8 [68-Oct-9: 2C].
Kelly, Josephine M. m. Roberts, James E. on 68-Jun-16 [68-Jun-18: 2B].
Kelly, Julia (33 yrs.) d. on 66-Jul-28 [66-Jul-31: 2C].
Kelly, Kate (32 yrs.) d. on 67-Nov-20 [67-Nov-21: 2C; 67-Nov-22: 2C].
Kelly, Lawrence J. m. Burns, Agnes R. on 68-Jan-27 [68-Feb-19: 2C].
Kelly, Margaret d. on 68-Aug-20 [68-Aug-21: 2B].
Kelly, Margaret Ann m. Dull, John C. [67-Oct-11: 2B].
Kelly, Maria P. m. Carew, John W. on 68-Mar-12 [68-Mar-16: 2B].
Kelly, Martin m. Bodkin, Marie on 70-Jun-6 [70-Jun-8: 2C].
Kelly, Mary (28 yrs.) d. on 68-Oct-4 [68-Oct-5: 2C].
Kelly, Mary (53 yrs.) d. on 67-Jun-14 [67-Jun-15: 2B].
Kelly, Mary (75 yrs.) d. on 66-Dec-29 [66-Dec-31: 2C].
Kelly, Mary Ann (27 yrs.) d. on 66-Aug-9 [66-Aug-10: 2C].
Kelly, Mary E. (10 mos.) d. on 68-Feb-19 [68-Feb-20: 2C].
Kelly, Michael (49 yrs.) d. on 69-Aug-13 [69-Aug-14: 2C].
Kelly, N. E. m. Sloan, L. J. on 69-Nov-23 [69-Nov-30: 2C].
Kelly, Nancy (80 yrs.) d. on 69-Nov-17 [69-Nov-18: 2C].
Kelly, Patrick (32 yrs.) d. on 69-Mar-22 [69-Mar-24: 2C].
Kelly, Solomon (11 yrs.) d. on 69-Mar-11 [69-Mar-19: 2C].
Kelly, Susan (46 yrs.) d. on 67-Mar-15 [67-Mar-19: 2C].
Kelly, Susie m. Maynes, Andrew R. on 67-Jul-7 [67-Jul-17: 2C].
Kelly, Thomas B. (2 yrs., 9 mos.) d. on 67-Mar-6 [67-Mar-7: 2C].
Kelly, Timothy (86 yrs.) d. on 67-Apr-13 [67-Apr-15: 1F, 2B].
Kelly, William C. (1 yr., 1 mo.) d. on 70-Jul-7 [70-Jul-8: 2C].
Kelly, William H. m. Barlow, Lizzie on 67-Jan-4 [67-Jan-10: 2C].
Kelly, William J. m. Corkran, Kate T. on 68-Jun-2 [68-Jul-2: 2C].
Kelly, William Thomas (5 mos.) d. on 70-May-2 [70-May-3: 2B].
Kelman, Henry d. on 66-Mar-2 of Fall [66-Mar-3: 1F].
Kelsey, Mida m. Miller, Robert J. on 68-Oct-29 [68-Nov-5: 2C].
Kelso, Alexander K. (20 yrs.) d. on 69-May-7 [69-May-10: 2C].
Kelso, John m. Foutz, Margaret on 66-Jul-9 [66-Jul-14: 2B].
Kemp, Ann m. Russell, Charles on 69-Mar-3 [69-Mar-16: 2C].
Kemp, Cecilia J. m. Kraft, George W. on 70-Feb-9 [70-Feb-21: 2B].
Kemp, Charles M. m. O'Keefe, Matilda on 69-Jun-7 [69-Jun-9: 2C].
Kemp, Edward Donald d. on 68-Feb-12 of Stomach cramps [68-Feb-13: 1F, 2C].
Kemp, Edwin Clyde (5 mos.) d. on 70-Aug-13 [70-Aug-15: 2C].
Kemp, Elizabeth (78 yrs.) d. on 70-Jul-17 [70-Jul-20: 2C].
Kemp, Ella m. Hadel, Charles A. on 70-Feb-3 [70-Feb-9: 2C].
Kemp, Fannie A. m. Bonn, Joseph on 66-Apr-26 [66-May-2: 2B].
Kemp, Florence V. m. Baker, Charles T. on 66-Oct-16 [66-Oct-23: 2B].
Kemp, J. F. m. Galloway, Henrietta on 66-Jan-11 [66-Jan-25: 2C].
Kemp, John m. Storms, Rachel Jane, Miss on 66-Feb-22 [66-Feb-27: 2B].
Kemp, John T. d. on 66-Aug-11 [66-Aug-13: 2C].

Kemp, Joseph F. (51 yrs.) d. on 66-Oct-5 [66-Oct-6: 2A].
Kemp, Lewis m. Cole, Sallie A. on 68-May-26 [68-May-27: 2B].
Kemp, Mary E. m. Zeigler, David on 69-Jan-26 [69-Jan-30: 2C].
Kemp, Missouri m. Fowble, George on 70-Nov-15 [70-Nov-26: 2B].
Kemp, Morris J. m. Ayres, Sidonia on 70-Jun-2 [70-Jun-6: 2B].
Kemp, Oscar T. m. Cole, Carrie L. on 70-Jun-15 [70-Jun-20: 2B].
Kemp, Rebecca d. on 66-Dec-19 [66-Dec-21: 2B; 66-Dec-22: 2B].
Kemp, Richard m. Mitchell, J. M. on 67-Aug-24 [67-Aug-28: 2B].
Kemp, Sarah E. m. Bowen, John E. on 69-Nov-17 [69-Nov-20: 2B].
Kemp, Susie E. m. Stevens, Charles on 70-Dec-1 [70-Dec-3: 2B].
Kemp, William Henry d. on 70-Jul-14 [70-Jul-15: 2C].
Kendall, Amanda m. Sparks, William H. H. on 66-Dec-18 [66-Dec-31: 2C].
Kendall, George (6 mos.) d. on 66-May-1 [66-May-2: 2B].
Kendall, Henry Andrew d. on 66-Jan-14 [66-Jan-18: 2C].
Kendall, Henry M. (59 yrs.) d. on 68-Nov-2 [68-Nov-3: 2B].
Kendall, Joseph V. m. Stees, Mary C. on 67-Jul-16 [67-Jul-30: 2C].
Kendig, Frank (72 yrs.) d. [68-Jul-6: 2B].
Kendig, Sallie C. m. Biersock, George W. on 67-Oct-31 [67-Nov-2: 2B].
Kendrick, Eliza Jane (29 yrs.) d. on 70-Sep-27 [70-Sep-28: 2B].
Kenehan, James (11 yrs., 3 mos.) d. on 70-Sep-5 [70-Sep-6: 2B].
Kenly, Anna M. m. Hynson, Benjamin T. on 68-May-5 [68-May-6: 2B].
Kenly, James F. m. Hanway, Sarah V. on 70-Nov-30 [70-Dec-20: 2B].
Kenly, Margaret m. Thomas, James on 66-Aug-29 [66-Nov-12: 2C].
Kenly, Oliver G. m. Stewart, Lou L. on 67-Oct-1 [67-Oct-8: 2B].
Kenna, Paul m. Cleland, Margaret Theresa on 66-Jul-5 [66-Jul-10: 2C].
Kennady, Emma Elizabeth (2 yrs., 7 mos.) d. on 66-Jan-22 [66-Jan-24: 2B].
Kennard, A. A. m. Duvall, Susie R. on 66-Jun-14 [66-Jun-15: 2C].
Kennard, Addie S. m. Hooper, Samuel N. on 68-Mar-19 [68-Mar-21: 2A].
Kennard, B. F. m. Magruder, Kate C. on 66-Jun-19 [66-Jun-21: 2B].
Kennard, Emma D. d. on 69-Jul-8 [69-Jul-9: 2C].
Kennard, Frank Lesner (17 yrs.) d. on 68-Feb-2 [68-Feb-3: 2C].
Kennard, Laura J. m. Owens, Richard H. on 68-Nov-17 [68-Nov-19: 2C].
Kennard, Margaret J. B. m. Hilleary, William T. on 66-Nov-29 [67-Jun-26: 2C].
Kennard, Philemon T. m. Dawson, Ella G. on 69-Apr-20 [69-May-5: 2C].
Kennard, Priscilla A. (55 yrs.) d. on 67-Sep-14 [67-Sep-16: 2B].
Kennard, Virginia C. (33 yrs.) d. on 70-Nov-21 [70-Nov-23: 2B].
Kennedy, , Mrs. (55 yrs.) d. on 69-Dec-15 [69-Dec-17: 2C].
Kennedy, Alexander d. on 70-Jan-28 [70-Jan-29: 2B].
Kennedy, Amanda M. d. on 70-Nov-20 [70-Nov-21: 2C].
Kennedy, Anna E. (2 yrs., 7 mos.) d. on 70-Aug-8 [70-Aug-9: 2C].
Kennedy, Calvin (8 mos.) d. on 69-Jul-5 [69-Jul-7: 2C].
Kennedy, Catherine P. d. on 66-Feb-25 [66-Feb-28: 2C].
Kennedy, Elizabeth (64 yrs.) d. on 68-Mar-22 [68-Mar-24: 2B].
Kennedy, Elizabeth m. Nicholson, Thomas G. on 67-Jul-16 [67-Aug-31: 2B].
Kennedy, Ellen (26 yrs.) d. on 70-Feb-24 [70-Feb-26: 2C].
Kennedy, Ellen m. Bucks, John on 67-Sep-23 [67-Sep-24: 2A].
Kennedy, Emma L. m. Rasch, Gustav A. on 66-Apr-26 [66-May-1: 2A].
Kennedy, Hamill H. (39 yrs.) d. on 69-Mar-12 [69-Mar-17: 2C].
Kennedy, James (50 yrs.) d. on 66-Jul-9 [66-Jul-10: 2C].
Kennedy, John (28 yrs.) d. on 70-Jul-17 of Heatstroke [70-Jul-18: 2B].
Kennedy, John C. (22 yrs.) d. on 67-Nov-9 [67-Dec-7: 2B].
Kennedy, John P. d. on 67-Aug-29 of Suicide (Drowning) [67-Sep-2: 4C].
Kennedy, John P. d. on 70-Aug-18 [70-Aug-22: 4D].
Kennedy, Lizzie T. d. on 70-May-24 [70-May-25: 2C].
Kennedy, Margaret (11 mos.) d. on 69-Dec-4 [69-Dec-6: 2C].

Kennedy, Mary (54 yrs.) d. on 69-Mar-8 [69-Mar-9: 2C].
Kennedy, Mary Agnes (20 yrs., 2 mos.) d. on 70-Jul-26 of Lung hemorrhage [70-Jul-29: 2C].
Kennedy, Mary J. m. Hook, Samuel R. on 67-Dec-1 [67-Dec-10: 2B].
Kennedy, Mary Jane m. Robb, Joseph A. on 66-May-15 [66-May-26: 2B].
Kennedy, Molly (18 yrs., 4 mos.) d. on 68-Jan-18 [68-Jan-30: 2C].
Kennedy, Nicholas Lambert (8 yrs.) d. on 67-Feb-13 [67-Feb-20: 2C].
Kennedy, S. D. m. Selden, Mary on 69-Jun-22 [69-Jun-24: 2C].
Kennedy, Sally P. m. Boone, William M. on 66-Jan-31 [66-Feb-1: 2C].
Kennedy, Samuel Willie d. on 68-Dec-8 of Dropsy [68-Dec-11: 2C].
Kennedy, Sarah A. m. McMahon, John on 70-Jan-17 [70-Feb-2: 2B].
Kennedy, Sarah L. m. Caldwell, Samuel E. on 67-Jun-13 [67-Jun-28: 2B].
Kennedy, Sarah R. m. Brooks, John H. on 67-Nov-26 [67-Dec-9: 2B].
Kennedy, Timothy P. (49 yrs.) d. on 70-Dec-28 [70-Dec-29: 2C; 70-Dec-30: 2C].
Kennedy, Virginia m. Pendleton, Edmund on 69-Jun-23 [69-Jun-29: 2C].
Kennedy, Walter S. m. Hall, Laura on 69-Dec-7 [69-Dec-9: 2C].
Kennedy, William J. m. Lalor, Margaret on 67-Aug-15 [67-Aug-17: 2B].
Kennell, Samuel G. m. Heddrick, E. Lucinda on 66-Aug-25 [66-Sep-1: 2B].
Kenner, Frances Rosella m. Brent, J. L. on 70-Apr-23 [70-May-12: 2B].
Kennerly, Martha m. Gill, William H. on 69-Jul-4 [69-Jul-7: 2C].
Kenney, Edward (77 yrs.) d. on 66-May-11 [66-May-12: 2A].
Kenney, Ellen (38 yrs.) d. on 67-Dec-7 Burned [67-Dec-10: 1F].
Kenney, J. J., Jr. m. Myers, Sallie E. on 67-Jul-7 [67-Jul-11: 2C].
Kenney, Patrick W. (47 yrs.) d. on 69-Aug-19 [69-Aug-21: 2B].
Kenney, Sophia m. Wolf, Charles P. on 66-Dec-6 [66-Dec-21: 2B].
Kenney, Thomas (59 yrs., 6 mos.) d. on 69-Mar-28 [69-Mar-29: 2B; 69-Mar-30: 2C].
Kenney, William (10 mos.) d. on 69-Oct-4 [69-Oct-5: 2B].
Kenny, A. m. Parlet, Zachariah on 66-Apr-15 [66-Apr-20: 2B].
Kenny, Ann Curly d. on 67-Dec-8 [67-Dec-10: 2B].
Kenny, Annie E. d. on 70-Oct-3 [70-Oct-4: 2B].
Kenny, Bridget d. on 70-Oct-6 [70-Oct-8: 2B].
Kenny, Frankie (2 yrs., 2 mos.) d. on 67-Sep-11 [67-Sep-13: 2B].
Kenny, Isabella (65 yrs.) d. on 67-Dec-22 [67-Dec-23: 2B].
Kenny, James (11 mos.) d. on 67-Aug-11 [67-Aug-12: 2C].
Kenny, John (23 yrs., 9 mos.) d. on 68-Jun-16 Murdered (Stabbing) [68-Jun-17: 1E, 2B].
Kenny, Kate A. m. Floyd, William on 69-Jan-12 [69-Jan-15: 2D].
Kenny, Lewis (53 yrs.) d. on 68-Apr-21 of Suicide (Hanging) [68-Apr-23: 1G].
Kenny, Mary Anne (4 yrs.) d. on 69-Dec-3 [69-Dec-4: 2C].
Kenny, Mollie A. B. m. Berry, Emory E. on 70-Jul-28 [70-Sep-15: 2B].
Kenny, Robert (3 yrs., 2 mos.) d. on 66-Jun-7 [66-Jun-8: 2B].
Kenower, John A. m. Chambers, Carrie M. on 70-Dec-22 [70-Dec-23: 2B].
Kensella, James m. Moffett, Hannah on 67-May-22 [67-May-29: 2B].
Kensett, Eliza H. m. Cassard, Louis R. on 68-Nov-10 [68-Nov-13: 2C].
Kensett, John R. m. Dryden, Annie M. on 67-Nov-12 [67-Nov-15: 2B].
Kensett, Mary Amelia Rogers (2 yrs., 5 mos.) d. on 69-Feb-22 [69-Feb-23: 2D].
Kensett, Thomas (8 mos.) d. on 69-Nov-1 [69-Nov-2: 2B; 69-Nov-3: 2C].
Kent, A. Owen m. Iglehart, Harwood on 66-Aug-16 [66-Aug-21: 2C].
Kent, Alice Lee (76 yrs.) d. on 68-Aug-24 [68-Aug-25: 2B].
Kent, Alice M. m. Billingsley, Thomas A. on 67-Dec-16 [67-Dec-23: 2B].
Kent, Daniel (25 yrs.) d. on 68-Nov-22 [68-Nov-24: 2C].
Kent, Kate Virginia (1 yr., 5 mos.) d. on 68-Aug-12 [68-Aug-14: 2C].
Kent, William A. m. Hughes, Mary C. on 69-Aug-11 [69-Aug-18: 2C].
Kent, William Thomas (2 mos.) d. on 70-Oct-17 [70-Oct-18: 2B].
Kepler, Annie Augusta d. on 69-Jan-8 [69-Jan-12: 2C].
Kepler, Clara Evelyn (3 mos.) d. on 68-Jun-21 [68-Jun-22: 2B].
Kepler, Mollie m. Lee, John L. on 68-Nov-18 [68-Nov-21: 2C].

Kepler, William P. m. Arnold, Mary E. on 66-Jun-25 [66-Oct-31: 2B].
Keplinger, William Oscar (1 yr., 8 mos.) d. on 66-Jul-20 [66-Jul-21: 2C].
Kerchman, Bernard (24 yrs.) d. on 70-Jun-26 of Heatstroke [70-Jun-27: 1F].
Kerchner, Anna Maria (65 yrs.) d. on 70-May-5 [70-May-6: 2B; 70-May-7: 2B].
Kerchner, Francis A. B. (8 yrs., 8 mos.) d. on 67-May-29 [67-May-30: 2B].
Kerchner, William Joseph (4 mos.) d. on 69-Mar-19 [69-Mar-20: 2B].
Kerfoot, Louisa L. m. Cooke, Richard B. on 66-Feb-15 [66-Feb-26: 2B].
Kerlinger, George A. (39 yrs., 11 mos.) d. on 69-Sep-10 of Consumption [69-Sep-21: 2B].
Kermode, Emily Isabella (11 mos.) d. on 68-Nov-17 [68-Nov-18: 2C].
Kermode, John (43 yrs.) d. on 70-Apr-3 of Heart neuralgia [70-Apr-4: 1G, 2C; 70-Apr-6: 2C].
Kern, Bentley m. Brooke, Katie Lee on 70-Dec-29 [70-Dec-31: 2B].
Kern, Peter (15 yrs.) d. on 66-Aug-19 of Fall from wagon [66-Aug-20: 1F].
Kernan, Amanda d. on 67-Aug-26 [67-Aug-29: 2B].
Kernan, James (76 yrs.) d. on 67-Apr-12 [67-Apr-13: 2B; 67-Apr-15: 1F].
Kernan, James H. (54 yrs.) d. on 70-Aug-26 [70-Aug-27: 4E, 2B].
Kernan, Lawrence Eugene (5 yrs., 3 mos.) d. on 70-Jul-18 [70-Jul-19: 2C].
Kernan, Patrick L. (69 yrs.) d. on 67-Jun-5 [67-Jun-6: 1G, 2B].
Kernan, Peter (61 yrs.) d. on 69-Mar-12 [69-Mar-13: 2C; 69-Mar-15: 2C].
Kernan, Thomas P. m. O'Donnell, C. A.M. on 69-Jan-31 [69-Feb-22: 2C].
Kernan, William P. m. Morgan, Hester Ann on 69-Aug-26 [69-Aug-28: 2B].
Kerner, Carrie E. m. Daneker, William H. on 67-Oct-29 [67-Nov-5: 2B].
Kerney, Mary J. m. Kirby, Thomas J. on 70-Jun-16 [70-Jun-21: 2C].
Kerney, P. Murray (20 yrs.) d. on 70-Dec-22 [70-Dec-23: 2B; 70-Dec-24: 2B].
Kerngood, A. m. Jacobs, Sarah on 69-Dec-19 [69-Dec-28: 2C].
Kerngood, Morris (9 mos.) d. on 69-Aug-12 [69-Aug-13: 2C].
Kerngood, William m. Mandelbaum, Carrie on 68-Jan-8 [68-Jan-10: 2C].
Kerns, Gertrude M. (9 mos.) d. on 70-Aug-18 [70-Aug-19: 2C].
Kerr, Charles Goldsborough m. Johnson, Ella on 67-Apr-25 [67-Apr-27: 2B].
Kerr, Edward (68 yrs.) d. on 66-Jan-5 [66-Jan-6: 2B].
Kerr, Edward m. Sinsz, Sophia on 67-Nov-28 [67-Dec-10: 2B].
Kerr, Eliza Goldsborough (77 yrs.) d. on 70-Dec-14 [70-Dec-15: 2C; 70-Dec-16: 2C; 70-Dec-17: 2B].
Kerr, Fanny d. on 66-Jul-11 [66-Jul-13: 2C].
Kerr, Fanny A. m. Gibson, A. F. on 69-Oct-13 [69-Oct-14: 2C].
Kerr, George (35 yrs.) d. on 67-Aug-27 [67-Aug-30: 2B].
Kerr, James (57 yrs.) d. on 66-Jun-19 [66-Jun-20: 2C].
Kerr, James, Sr. (72 yrs.) d. on 67-Feb-25 of Typhoid pneumonia [67-Feb-28: 2C].
Kerr, John W. m. Keys, Ada P. on 67-Feb-14 [67-Feb-19: 2C].
Kerr, Lilla B. m. Hipkins, Richard on 67-Mar-25 [67-Mar-26: 2C].
Kerr, Margaret (53 yrs.) d. on 66-Apr-10 of Suicide (Poisoning) [66-Apr-12: 4C].
Kerr, Mary m. Bash, Edward H. on 70-Nov-3 [70-Nov-5: 2B].
Kerr, Mary Dunbar m. Cochran, T. Ollie on 67-Dec-10 [67-Dec-17: 2B].
Kerr, Thomas m. McDonald, Hannah on 69-Jun-22 [69-Jul-3: 2B].
Kerr, William m. Silver, Virginia on 68-Dec-15 [68-Dec-17: 2C].
Kershaw, Henry m. Barnsley, Isabel on 70-Nov-1 [70-Nov-3: 2B].
Kershner, Edward d. on 70-Jan-27 [70-Jan-28: 2B; 70-Jan-29: 2B].
Keser, Robert J. m. Stanley, Margaret Ann on 68-May-21 [68-May-23: 2A].
Kesler, Ellen C. m. Grupy, Jacob on 70-Jan-6 [70-Jan-14: 2C].
Kesling, Julia (35 yrs.) d. on 67-Oct-17 [67-Oct-19: 2B].
Kesmodel, Gustav m. McJilton, Sallie E. on 69-Nov-29 [70-Mar-3: 2C].
Kessler, Cammie S. m. Hobbs, George F. on 68-Oct-22 [69-Apr-27: 2B].
Kessler, Charles S. (23 yrs.) d. on 70-Dec-2 [70-May-20: 2C].
Kessler, Elizabeth A. m. Underwood, George A. on 68-Aug-18 [68-Aug-24: 2B].
Kessler, Harry d. on 70-Jun-23 of Brain fever [70-Jun-24: 1H].
Kessler, Henry m. Davis, Caroline on 70-Jan-20 [70-Feb-1: 2B].

Kessler, Henry C. m. McClintock, Bell on 67-Jan-8 [67-Jan-9: 2B].
Kessler, Levi m. Bull, Caroline on 70-Oct-10 [70-Nov-17: 2C].
Kessler, Mary m. Beck, Ernest on 70-Jul-18 [70-Jul-19: 2B].
Kessler, Samuel m. Nathans, Helena V. on 66-Nov-7 [66-Nov-26: 2B; 66-Nov-27: 2B].
Kessler, Sophie R. (1 yr., 7 mos.) d. on 70-Feb-2 of Chronic croup [70-Feb-3: 2B].
Kestel, Mary Ignatia, Sr. (26 yrs.) d. on 68-Nov-14 [68-Nov-16: 2C; 68-Nov-17: 1H].
Ketchum, Frederick M. (40 yrs.) d. on 70-Oct-3 of Consumption [70-Oct-4: 2B].
Kettering, Adam C. (36 yrs., 3 mos.) d. on 70-Oct-11 [70-Oct-13: 2C].
Kettering, Henry m. Rabe, Elizabeth on 70-Jul-26 [70-Aug-20: 2B].
Kettlewell, Emily Marian m. Lough, George F. on 70-Apr-28 [70-May-7: 2B].
Kettlewell, Haddie m. Bullard, W. S. on 67-Apr-25 [67-May-23: 2B].
Kettlewell, R. C. m. Cole, Josephine on 68-Jan-20 [68-Feb-20: 2C].
Key, A. W. Blackburn (10 yrs., 8 mos.) d. on 70-Apr-21 [70-Apr-22: 2C].
Key, Alice m. Smith, James on 69-Oct-26 [69-Oct-28: 2C].
Key, Anna m. McClean, William on 70-Mar-24 [70-Apr-4: 2C].
Key, Charles H. d. on 69-Jun-29 [69-Jul-3: 2B].
Key, Fannie m. Dorsey, Andrew on 70-Oct-13 [70-Oct-15: 2B].
Key, Francis (59 yrs.) d. on 66-Apr-4 [66-Apr-6: 1G, 2B].
Key, George W. (13 yrs.) d. on 66-Oct-21 [66-Oct-22: 2C].
Key, Kate m. Jenkins, George C on 68-Nov-19 [68-Nov-19: 2C].
Key, Margaret A. m. Pitcher, James M. on 69-Apr-7 [69-May-21: 2C].
Key, Murray m. Troup, Clelia on 69-Nov-16 [69-Nov-18: 2C].
Keyes, E. L. m. Loughborough, Sallie M. on 70-Apr-26 [70-Apr-28: 2B].
Keyes, James m. Haskell, Alice M. on 70-Aug-9 [70-Sep-2: 2C].
Keyes, Jane (69 yrs.) d. on 66-Jun-5 [66-Jun-6: 2B].
Keyhan, Mary Ann m. Streckfus, Leonard on 70-Apr-26 [70-Apr-28: 2A].
Keys, Ada P. m. Kerr, John W. on 67-Feb-14 [67-Feb-19: 2C].
Keys, Alexander S. (4 yrs., 4 mos.) d. on 67-Feb-26 [67-Feb-27: 2C].
Keys, Bayly d. on 68-Jul-3 [68-Jul-4: 2C].
Keys, James Hanson (3 yrs., 11 mos.) d. on 68-Dec-6 [68-Dec-7: 2C].
Keys, John m. Tasker, Kate on 69-May-6 [69-May-8: 2B].
Keys, Leonore m. Johnston, Fayette on 69-Jan-12 [69-Jan-19: 2C].
Keys, Mary B. d. on 70-Jan-19 [70-Jan-21: 2C].
Keys, Ruth M. d. on 70-Jul-1 [70-Jul-2: 2B].
Keyser, Charles C., Dr. (46 yrs.) d. on 67-May-17 of Typhoid [67-May-18: 1G, 2A; 67-May-20: 1G].
Keyser, David M. (17 yrs.) d. on 68-Nov-13 [68-Nov-16: 2C].
Keyser, Ellenora (9 mos.) d. on 70-Aug-3 [70-Aug-4: 2C].
Keyser, George (35 yrs.) d. on 66-Jul-17 [66-Jul-18: 2C].
Keyser, Herman m. Betton, Ophelia A. on 70-Mar-29 [70-Mar-31: 2C].
Keyser, John P. m. Davis, Hannah C. on 69-Jan-17 [69-Jan-23: 2C].
Keyser, Mabel Wyman (6 mos.) d. on 68-Jun-16 [68-Jun-18: 2B].
Keyser, Martha W. m. Levering, Joshua on 70-Nov-24 [70-Nov-28: 2C].
Keyser, Mary E. m. Clayton, Theodore on 67-Dec-19 [67-Dec-20: 2B].
Keyser, Samuel m. Thompson, Julia Therese on 68-Apr-14 [68-Apr-17: 2B].
Keyser, William L. m. Phelps, Margaret A. on 66-Jul-5 [66-Jul-11: 2C].
Keyton, Thomas m. Tolloway, Cleary on 67-Jan-20 [67-Jan-31: 2C].
Keyworth, Elizabeth (68 yrs., 4 mos.) d. on 70-Jul-22 [70-Jul-23: 2B].
Kibler, Catherine (75 yrs., 1 mo.) d. on 70-Dec-29 [70-Dec-30: 2C; 70-Dec-31: 2C].
Kidd, Andrew F. m. Norton, Sarah on 69-Feb-15 [69-Mar-24: 2C].
Kidd, Emma (25 yrs., 3 mos.) d. on 70-Jan-15 [70-Jan-24: 2C].
Kidd, George m. Crane, Mary on 68-Oct-5 [68-Oct-10: 2B].
Kidd, John H. m. O'Brien, Maggie on 68-Feb-19 [68-Mar-4: 2C].
Kidd, Louisa C. m. Holbrook, W. G. on 66-Aug-6 [66-Aug-16: 2C].
Kidd, Nelson m. Whitehouse, Mary Emma on 66-Jan-2 [66-Jan-15: 2B].

Kidd, Thomas J. m. Nunan, Annie M. on 68-Jun-22 [68-Jul-14: 2B].
Kieffer, Charles d. on 66-Feb-1 of Consumption [66-Feb-2: 2C].
Kieley, Ann E. (54 yrs.) d. on 70-Jul-26 of Congestive chills [70-Aug-18: 2C].
Kiely, David (68 yrs.) d. on 68-Aug-22 [68-Aug-25: 2B].
Kierchner, Edward m. Schmidt, Catherine on 69-Sep-12 [69-Sep-20: 2C].
Kiernan, Patrick (56 yrs.) d. on 70-Jul-19 [70-Jul-20: 2C].
Kierstead, Andrew J. m. Henderson, Isabella S. on 66-Jan-25 [66-Jan-29: 2B; 66-Jan-30: 2B].
Kiggins, James (53 yrs.) d. on 66-Sep-4 [66-Sep-5: 2B].
Kilbourn, D. T. d. on 69-Nov-23 [69-Nov-30: 2C].
Kilburn, Willis m. Claude, Phoebe on 70-Aug-25 [70-Aug-26: 2C].
Kilduff, Anna Lizzie (3 yrs., 3 mos.) d. on 67-Sep-12 [67-Sep-13: 2B].
Kilelea, Catherine (58 yrs.) d. on 70-Jul-13 [70-Jul-15: 2C].
Kiley, Maggie (6 yrs., 5 mos.) d. on 69-Sep-17 [69-Sep-18: 2B].
Kilfoyle, Thomas m. Keefe, Kate on 66-May-16 [66-May-30: 2C].
Kilgore, John S. m. Miller, M. on 69-Dec-14 [69-Dec-16: 2C].
Kilgour, Anna L. (29 yrs., 1 mo.) d. on 68-Apr-8 [68-Apr-9: 2B; 68-Apr-10: 2B].
Killalea, John (23 yrs.) d. on 70-Jul-17 [70-Jul-18: 2B].
Killalea, M. Patrick d. on 67-Nov-23 [67-Nov-25: 2C].
Killalea, Mary (28 yrs.) d. [67-Nov-28: 2C].
Killer, Caspar (64 yrs.) d. on 70-May-4 [70-May-6: 2B].
Killman, Harriet J. m. Ward, Thomas on 67-Jun-30 [67-Jul-31: 2C].
Killmond, Elizabeth (65 yrs.) d. on 66-Dec-10 [66-Dec-11: 2B].
Kilpatrick, Mary A. m. Wain, Daniel on 69-Apr-8 [69-Apr-10: 2B].
Kilpatrick, Robert W. m. Sowle, Aggie A. on 69-Sep-29 [69-Oct-12: 2C].
Kilpatrick, Thomas m. Fuller, Margaret A. on 68-Jun-9 [68-Jun-23: 2B].
Kilty, Mary E. d. [70-Aug-6: 2C].
Kimball, George S. (26 yrs.) d. on 69-Feb-11 of Consumption [69-Feb-12: 2C].
Kimberly, Augustus G. m. Hawkins, Mary Ellen on 66-Jun-28 [66-Jun-29: 2C].
Kimberly, Charles Homer (21 yrs.) d. on 70-Aug-20 of Typhoid [70-Aug-22: 2B, 4E; 70-Aug-23: 4E].
Kimberly, Charles Wesley (45 yrs.) d. on 70-Jun-1 of Dropsy [70-Jun-2: 1H, 2B; 70-Jun-3: 1G].
Kimberly, Edward, Jr. m. Banks, Mollie B. on 67-Jun-10 [67-Jun-17: 2B].
Kimberly, Elizabeth (84 yrs.) d. on 66-Mar-22 [66-Mar-23: 2C; 66-Mar-24: 2B; 66-Mar-27: 1F].
Kimberly, Harry, Sr. (62 yrs.) d. on 70-May-16 [70-May-17: 2B; 70-May-18: 2B; 70-May-19: 2C].
Kimberly, Olivia m. Jerome, John on 69-Jun-11 [69-Jun-15: 2C].
Kimble, Alfred W. m. Dever, Annie on 69-Jan-12 [69-Jan-21: 2C].
Kimble, C. E. m. Jurgens, J. H. on 65-Dec-24 [66-Jan-27: 2B].
Kimble, Ida May (1 yr., 10 mos.) d. on 68-Dec-22 [68-Dec-23: 2C].
Kimble, Leonard (34 yrs.) d. on 70-Aug-2 [70-Aug-3: 2C].
Kime, Elizabeth m. Hyde, William H. on 69-Sep-28 [69-Sep-30: 2B].
Kime, James L. m. Buckmiller, Ollie M. on 69-Sep-28 [69-Sep-30: 2B].
Kimmel, Mary E. m. Ochs, John T. on 68-Sep-22 [68-Sep-30: 2B].
Kimmell, Herbert Stanley (1 yr., 3 mos.) d. on 69-Jan-23 [69-Feb-10: 2C].
Kimmell, John D. (37 yrs.) d. on 70-Jun-20 of Heart disease [70-Jun-22: 1H].
Kimmet, G. A. m. Stouffer, Maggie A. on 68-Jun-25 [68-Jul-2: 2C].
Kincade, Catherine (73 yrs.) d. on 68-Jul-13 [68-Jul-14: 2C].
Kincaid, Annie Amelia (5 yrs., 8 mos.) d. on 67-Mar-11 [67-Mar-12: 2C].
Kincaid, William J. (38 yrs.) d. on 68-Dec-27 [68-Dec-28: 2B].
Kindig, Henry W. m. Leonard, Margaret A. on 66-May-20 [66-May-22: 2B].
Kindleberger, D. m. Poor, Mattie on 68-Oct-8 [68-Oct-9: 2C].
Kines, Albert C. (3 yrs., 9 mos.) d. on 70-Dec-25 [70-Dec-26: 2C].

Kines, Charles Ehrman (9 mos.) d. on 67-Nov-9 [67-Nov-11: 2C].
Kines, John W. m. Durst, Sarah E. on 66-May-22 [66-May-30: 2C].
Kines, Susan M. (28 yrs.) d. on 68-Apr-11 [68-Apr-13: 2B].
King, Amos (54 yrs.) d. on 66-Jun-11 [66-Jun-12: 2B].
King, Andrew J. m. Broumel, Laura V. on 68-Apr-30 [68-May-2: 2C].
King, Ann (94 yrs.) d. on 66-Dec-6 [66-Dec-7: 2B].
King, Anna Wilhelmine (1 yr., 1 mo.) d. of Teething [70-Dec-26: 2C].
King, Annie E. m. Freeland, John T. on 68-Oct-6 [68-Oct-10: 2B].
King, Bernard N. m. Atkinson, Helen J. on 65-Sep-14 [66-Jan-31: 2C].
King, C. Pauline m. Rathford, Gilbert B. on 70-Jan-25 [70-Jan-29: 2B; 70-Feb-1: 2B].
King, Catherine R. (37 yrs.) d. on 68-May-14 [68-May-19: 2B].
King, Charles Edwards (19 yrs.) d. on 66-Dec-8 [66-Dec-10: 2B].
King, Charles F., Rev. (52 yrs.) d. on 70-Mar-20 [70-Mar-22: 2C].
King, Cisela (43 yrs.) d. on 69-Sep-12 [69-Sep-13: 2B].
King, David d. on 68-Jul-8 of Gunshot wound [68-Jul-10: 1F].
King, Eliza (68 yrs.) d. on 70-Nov-11 [70-Nov-12: 2B].
King, Eliza Ann (41 yrs.) d. on 69-Mar-6 [69-Mar-8: 2C].
King, Eliza Jane (17 yrs., 8 mos.) d. on 66-May-27 [66-May-28: 2B].
King, Elizabeth (45 yrs.) d. on 70-Sep-12 [70-Sep-13: 2B; 70-Sep-14: 2B].
King, Elizabeth A. m. East, Henry T. on 68-Aug-20 [68-Aug-28: 2B].
King, Ellen m. Ferguson, Charles on 69-Mar-25 [69-Apr-1: 2C].
King, Frances Caroline (19 yrs.) d. on 67-Sep-1 [67-Sep-5: 2B].
King, Francis (31 yrs.) d. on 70-Oct-14 in Railroad accident [70-Oct-17: 4D].
King, Francis Albert (5 mos.) d. on 66-Feb-19 [66-Feb-20: 2B].
King, George (16 yrs.) d. on 68-Jun-13 Drowned [68-Jun-15: 1F].
King, George W., Capt. (71 yrs.) d. on 69-Apr-21 [69-Apr-23: 1H, 2B; 69-Apr-24: 1G].
King, George W. m. Dandelet, Susie C. on 67-Nov-27 [67-Dec-5: 2C].
King, George Washington (15 yrs., 11 mos.) d. on 66-Oct-29 [66-Oct-31: 2B].
King, Georgie A. m. Bennett, George B. on 70-May-8 [70-May-12: 2B].
King, Hester B. (70 yrs.) d. on 68-Nov-22 [68-Nov-23: 2B; 68-Nov-24: 2C].
King, J. Merryman (1 yr.) d. on 70-Aug-13 [70-Aug-15: 2B].
King, Jacob (84 yrs., 7 mos.) d. on 69-Jul-14 [69-Jul-15: 2C].
King, Jacob (59 yrs., 1 mo.) d. on 70-Jan-23 [70-Jan-24: 2C; 70-Jan-25: 2C].
King, James (63 yrs.) d. on 67-Jun-9 [67-Jun-11: 2B].
King, James A. (13 yrs., 2 mos.) d. on 68-May-28 of Lockjaw [68-May-30: 2A].
King, John m. Deshon, Estelle Mailland on 67-Oct-17 [67-Oct-21: 2B].
King, John, Jr. m. Jackson, Mary F. on 67-Aug-20 [67-Aug-21: 2B].
King, John Albert H. (33 yrs., 3 mos.) d. on 66-Jan-22 of Typhoid [66-Aug-24: 2B].
King, John C. m. Adams, Ellie L. on 66-Sep-6 [66-Sep-8: 2B].
King, Joseph m. Howard, Jane G. on 69-Jun-1 [69-Jun-4: 2C].
King, Joshua T. (63 yrs.) d. on 69-Mar-7 [69-Mar-8: 2C].
King, Kate m. Huber, John A. on 69-Mar-11 [69-Mar-16: 2C].
King, Laura A. m. Gittings, D. T. on 68-Sep-15 [68-Sep-17: 2B].
King, Lloyd W. m. Scaggs, Mollie R. on 68-Nov-11 [68-Nov-13: 2C].
King, Lottie d. on 68-Aug-18 [68-Aug-20: 2B].
King, Louis Barnes (2 yrs., 2 mos.) d. on 69-Nov-11 [69-Nov-13: 2C].
King, Lucy m. France, John on 66-Sep-20 [66-Sep-21: 2B].
King, M. Frances (31 yrs.) d. on 70-Oct-14 in Railroad accident [70-Oct-15: 2B].
King, Maria m. Owings, Israel on 67-Sep-9 [67-Sep-11: 2B].
King, Mary m. Somers, William E. on 69-Nov-28 [69-Nov-30: 2C].
King, Mary m. Lee, Emory G. on 70-Feb-17 [70-Feb-25: 2C].
King, Mary A. d. on 68-Dec-12 [68-Dec-14: 2C].
King, Mary A. m. McManus, Edward P. on 68-Oct-8 [68-Oct-10: 2B].
King, Mary E. m. Cochrane, John on 66-Dec-6 [66-Dec-8: 2B].
King, Mary E. m. Wilson, S. Hauen on 69-Sep-1 [69-Sep-3: 2B].

King, Mary Helen (6 mos.) d. on 67-Apr-13 [67-Apr-15: 2B].
King, Mary J. (28 yrs.) d. on 66-Jun-24 [66-Jun-26: 2B].
King, Matilda m. Constant, Franklin on 66-May-8 [66-May-10: 2B].
King, Michael, Mrs. (79 yrs.) d. on 70-Mar-7 [70-Mar-8: 2C].
King, Mollie E. m. Williams, H. B. on 70-Dec-15 [70-Dec-20: 2B].
King, Nancy m. Crudden, William on 69-Dec-23 [69-Dec-25: 2C].
King, Nellie Harman (9 mos.) d. on 66-May-14 [66-May-16: 2C].
King, Ollie J. m. Groff, J. Humphreys on 68-Apr-30 [68-May-4: 2B].
King, Patrick J. m. Tootell, Leila G. on 66-Apr-12 [66-Apr-20: 2B].
King, Rebecca A. (33 yrs.) d. on 68-Jan-3 [68-Jan-4: 2C].
King, Rebecca A. m. Reeves, I. Cooper on 69-Sep-1 [69-Sep-3: 2B].
King, Robert (1 yr.) d. on 70-Oct-13 [70-Oct-14: 2B].
King, Robert Armstrong (6 yrs.) d. on 68-Jan-2 [68-Jan-3: 2C; 68-Jan-4: 2C].
King, Rosalina F. m. Mullikin, Frank on 68-Oct-29 [68-Nov-2: 2B].
King, Rose E. L. (16 yrs.) d. on 69-Aug-25 [69-Aug-26: 2C].
King, Rosie M. (20 yrs.) d. on 68-Jun-27 [68-Jul-4: 2C].
King, Rufus m. Warner, Susie M. on 67-Dec-17 [67-Dec-18: 2B].
King, Samuel (47 yrs.) d. on 70-Aug-5 Drowned [70-Aug-6: 4E].
King, Sarah C. m. Marston, Henry W. on 68-Jan-23 [68-Jan-27: 2C].
King, Sarah E. m. Elfrey, Philip J. on 67-Aug-6 [67-Aug-22: 2B].
King, Sue S. m. Dawson, William H. H. on 68-Jul-4 [68-Jul-23: 2B].
King, Susan Caroline (3 yrs.) d. on 68-Aug-19 [68-Aug-20: 2B; 68-Aug-21: 2B].
King, William A. m. Heagy, Mary E. on 69-Jun-27 [69-Jun-29: 2C].
King, William G. H. m. Conrad, Julia M. F. on 69-Jan-14 [69-Jan-23: 2C].
Kinge, Martin m. Roose, Sarah A. on 67-Jun-9 [67-Jun-14: 2B; 67-Jun-24: 2B].
Kingsland, M. S. m. Popplein, Susie M. on 68-Jan-16 [68-Jan-20: 2C].
Kinnaird, Clintonia W. (18 yrs., 2 mos.) d. on 68-Jun-9 of Spinal congestion [68-Jun-10: 1G, 2B; 68-Jun-11: 1E].
Kinnear, John W. m. Wildy, Agnes on 68-Apr-22 [68-Apr-25: 2B].
Kinnear, Mary K. (50 yrs.) d. on 69-Apr-30 [69-May-1: 2B].
Kinnersley, Martha Gertrude (3 yrs., 10 mos.) d. on 69-Nov-7 [69-Nov-10: 2C].
Kinnersley, Sammy Brunner (1 yr., 11 mos.) d. on 69-Oct-28 [69-Oct-30: 2B].
Kinnier, George, Jr. m. McLean, Sarah A. on 67-Aug-8 [67-Aug-15: 2C; 67-Aug-16: 2B].
Kinnier, William (26 yrs.) d. on 70-Jun-15 [70-Jun-16: 2B; 70-Jun-17: 2B].
Kinningham, Mary B. m. Kreis, John on 66-Oct-23 [67-May-20: 2B].
Kinsey, Charles Fleming (1 yr., 3 mos.) d. on 68-Dec-18 [68-Dec-22: 2C].
Kinsey, Thomas Sumwall (3 yrs., 1 mo.) d. on 66-Nov-27 [66-Nov-28: 2B].
Kinsley, Ellenora m. Harvey, Charles T. on 69-Nov-23 [69-Nov-26: 2B].
Kinsley, Mary E. m. Addison, Joseph T. on 66-May-9 [66-May-16: 2C].
Kinsley, Samuel G. (1 mo.) d. on 68-Dec-5 [68-Dec-7: 2D].
Kinsley, Virginia m. Creager, George L. on 66-Jan-3 [66-Aug-25: 2A].
Kinsley, William (57 yrs.) d. on 70-Dec-6 [70-Dec-8: 2C].
Kinslow, Annie (1 yr., 1 mo.) d. on 69-Sep-3 [69-Sep-4: 2B].
Kipp, John G. m. LeFevre, Sarah R. on 70-Jan-19 [70-Apr-25: 2B].
Kirby, Anna R. m. McLean, John Of William on 69-Aug-31 [69-Sep-7: 2B].
Kirby, Annie Rebecca (7 yrs., 8 mos.) d. on 70-Sep-19 [70-Sep-19: 2B].
Kirby, Annie S. m. Brevitt, Joseph P. on 70-Mar-19 [70-Mar-24: 2C].
Kirby, Benjamin Alfred (3 yrs.) d. on 69-Mar-5 [69-Mar-6: 2C].
Kirby, Clara Anna (3 yrs., 4 mos.) d. on 69-Feb-19 [69-Feb-20: 2A].
Kirby, Deborah m. Hevel, William Henry on 69-May-11 [69-May-15: 2B].
Kirby, Edith (52 yrs.) d. on 67-Apr-6 [67-Apr-8: 2B].
Kirby, Edward (57 yrs.) d. on 69-Feb-17 [69-Feb-18: 2C].
Kirby, Elizabeth (82 yrs.) d. on 67-Dec-2 [67-Dec-4: 2C; 67-Dec-5: 2C].
Kirby, Ellen B. (26 yrs.) d. on 69-Feb-7 [69-Feb-8: 2C].
Kirby, George Marion (11 mos.) d. on 68-Aug-18 [68-Aug-19: 2B].

Kirby, James Ellenslie (2 yrs., 5 mos.) d. on 66-Feb-12 [66-Feb-14: 2C].
Kirby, Jane (81 yrs.) d. on 66-Mar-20 [66-Mar-21: 2C].
Kirby, Laura E. B. Lloyd (20 yrs., 9 mos.) d. on 66-Sep-13 [66-Sep-14: 2B].
Kirby, Lizzie (28 yrs.) d. on 69-Oct-30 [69-Nov-1: 2C].
Kirby, Lizzie m. Little, John Henry on 70-Dec-1 [70-Dec-10: 2B].
Kirby, Maggie Florence (9 mos.) d. on 70-Nov-3 [70-Nov-5: 2B].
Kirby, Mollie m. Glocker, Theodore W. on 69-Dec-9 [69-Dec-10: 2C].
Kirby, Patrick (28 yrs.) d. on 70-Apr-3 [70-Apr-4: 2C].
Kirby, Phillis m. Maxwell, Charles E. on 67-Sep-19 [67-Sep-21: 2A].
Kirby, Sarah J. (54 yrs.) d. on 70-Mar-1 [70-Mar-26: 2B].
Kirby, Sarah J. (51 yrs.) d. on 70-Jul-2 [70-Jul-4: 2C].
Kirby, Susan E. m. Blades, Thomas on 70-Dec-1 [70-Dec-23: 2B].
Kirby, Theodore T. m. Oram, Parcella F. on 68-Oct-22 [68-Oct-27: 2B].
Kirby, Thomas H. m. Horney, Sarah on 67-Oct-29 [68-Jan-21: 2C].
Kirby, Thomas J. m. Kerney, Mary J. on 70-Jun-16 [70-Jun-21: 2C].
Kirby, Virginia m. Terres, J. B. on 68-Jun-11 [68-Jul-4: 2C].
Kirby, William m. Starr, Sarah on 69-Dec-12 [69-Dec-14: 2C].
Kirby, William George (1 yr., 1 mo.) d. on 69-Mar-1 [69-Mar-3: 2C].
Kirch, John H., Capt. d. on 67-Sep-4 [67-Sep-5: 2B].
Kircher, Sidnea R. d. on 67-Apr-19 [67-Apr-27: 2A].
Kircher, Virginia m. Hess, Killon on 69-Nov-9 [69-Nov-13: 2B; 69-Dec-11: 2B].
Kirchmeir, Franziska m. Volk, Kayatan on 67-Aug-20 [67-Aug-22: 2B].
Kirk, Elenor Ann (50 yrs.) d. on 70-Jun-9 [70-Jun-11: 2B].
Kirk, Eliza d. on 69-Jan-10 [69-Jan-12: 2C].
Kirk, Elizabeth (43 yrs.) d. on 66-Jan-22 [66-Jan-23: 2C].
Kirk, F. DeV. m. Fairchild, Kate on 69-Sep-1 [69-Sep-3: 2B; 69-Sep-4: 2B].
Kirk, Fanny Augusta (1 yr., 1 mo.) d. on 67-Feb-27 [67-Feb-28: 2C].
Kirk, Ida E. m. Bland, Theodore F. on 70-Oct-20 [70-Oct-25: 2B].
Kirk, John A. (61 yrs.) d. on 69-Apr-11 [69-Apr-12: 2A; 69-Apr-13: 2B].
Kirk, Laura L. m. Barlow, Clinton on 70-Apr-8 [70-Apr-13: 2B].
Kirk, Lizzie Hopkins (3 yrs., 11 mos.) d. on 67-Jul-14 [67-Jul-15: 2C].
Kirk, Martha M. (20 yrs., 4 mos.) d. on 70-Feb-8 [70-Feb-15: 2C].
Kirk, Mary Elizabeth (15 yrs., 8 mos.) d. on 69-Dec-6 [69-Dec-14: 2C].
Kirk, Rachel H. m. Groscup, Charles H. on 70-Apr-28 [70-May-7: 2B].
Kirk, Samuel, Jr. (29 yrs.) d. on 70-Mar-13 [70-Mar-14: 1H, 2C].
Kirk, Sarah E. m. Marsh, John H. on 68-Feb-26 [68-Feb-27: 2C].
Kirk, William W m. Happoldt, Marian L. on 69-Mar-22 [69-Mar-26: 2C].
Kirkby, Mary Leonia (1 yr., 2 mos.) d. on 70-Feb-12 [70-Feb-14: 2C].
Kirkland, Amelia m. Graham, Henry G. on 66-Aug-3 [66-Sep-3: 2C].
Kirkland, Anna Elizabeth (18 yrs.) d. on 69-Oct-23 [69-Oct-25: 2C].
Kirkland, Edward M. m. Towson, Estelle M. on 68-Oct-20 [68-Oct-22: 2C].
Kirkland, John W. d. on 70-Mar-22 [70-Mar-25: 2C].
Kirkley, Charles P. m. Goldsmith, Rachel A. on 66-Aug-27 [66-Oct-11: 2C].
Kirkley, John Crum (11 mos.) d. on 68-Aug-25 [68-Aug-27: 2B].
Kirkpatrick, Mary A. (60 yrs.) d. on 69-Aug-15 [69-Aug-16: 2B].
Kirkwood, Ann (68 yrs.) d. on 68-May-2 [68-May-4: 2B].
Kirkwood, Annie Holliday (1 yr.) d. on 68-Sep-15 [68-Sep-16: 2B].
Kirkwood, Cora (1 yr.) d. on 66-Mar-29 [66-Mar-31: 2C].
Kirkwood, Josie W. m. Belt, Robert V. on 69-Aug-10 [69-Aug-31: 2B].
Kirkwood, Mollie J. m. Van Trump, Volney on 66-Oct-25 [66-Oct-27: 2B].
Kirkwood, S. A. m. Daneker, Jennie on 67-May-25 [67-Jun-4: 2A].
Kirsch, Frederick (67 yrs., 7 mos.) d. on 69-Feb-28 [69-Mar-1: 2C].
Kirsch, Noah m. Bostwick, Camilla G. on 69-Nov-18 [69-Nov-30: 2C].
Kirwan, Emily (56 yrs.) d. on 70-Aug-31 [70-Sep-1: 2B].
Kirwan, Georgeanna K. m. Weston, John A. on 70-Apr-20 [70-Apr-22: 2C].

Kirwan, James O. m. Gent, Maggie J. on 66-Feb-20 [66-Feb-28: 2C].
Kirwan, John R. m. Hipkins, Sarah J. on 70-Apr-7 [70-May-31: 2B].
Kirwan, Louisa C. m. Storm, J. on 66-Jan-23 [66-Feb-8: 2C].
Kirwan, Mary C. m. Kane, John P. on 66-Sep-12 [67-Feb-4: 2C].
Kirwan, William Travers, Capt. (49 yrs.) d. on 67-Aug-31 of Bilious fever [67-Sep-2: 2B; 67-Sep-7: 2A].
Kirwin, Mary H. m. Potter, Thomas on 68-Apr-20 [68-Apr-23: 2B].
Kiser, Elizabeth (35 yrs.) d. on 68-Nov-15 [68-Nov-16: 2C].
Kisner, Henry C. m. Crowell, Agnes P. on 69-Jan-12 [69-Jan-13: 2D].
Kitchin, William A. (27 yrs.) d. on 67-Nov-23 [67-Nov-25: 2C].
Kitson, Emma Virginia (2 yrs., 11 mos.) d. on 67-Jun-8 [67-Jun-10: 2B].
Kitson, Samuel m. Flynn, Kate A. on 67-Jul-23 [67-Aug-7: 2C].
Kitts, John (108 yrs.) d. on 70-Sep-18 [70-Sep-19: 4B; 70-Sep-20: 2B; 70-Sep-21: 4B].
Kizer, Nicholas (45 yrs.) d. on 67-Apr-23 Drowned [67-May-1: 1F].
Klassen, Charles (83 yrs.) d. on 66-Nov-16 [66-Nov-17: 1G, 2B; 66-Nov-19: 2B].
Klassen, Cordelia S. d. on 66-Jan-15 of Consumption [66-Jan-16: 2C].
Klatte, Charles (32 yrs.) d. on 67-Nov-22 [67-Nov-23: 2B].
Klausman, Lawrence m. January, Carrie on 67-Sep-17 [67-Sep-21: 2A].
Klees, Daniel B. (12 yrs., 10 mos.) d. on 66-Nov-30 [66-Dec-1: 2B].
Klees, John m. Cover, Susan on 69-Mar-30 [69-Apr-1: 2C].
Kleff, Francis (1 yr., 7 mos.) d. on 70-Oct-5 [70-Oct-7: 2B].
Kleibacker, C. B. m. Bruehl, Mary E. on 69-Oct-14 [69-Oct-19: 2B].
Klein, H. W. m. Schaible, L. D. on 68-Sep-15 [68-Sep-19: 2B].
Kleinjohn, Charles H. m. Waitz, Lauretta A. C. on 69-Jul-17 [69-Jul-27: 2C].
Kleinle, Louisa m. Simpson, Charles W. on 70-Apr-13 [70-May-27: 2B].
Kleinle, Mary E. m. Benner, H. H. on 70-May-22 [70-Jun-10: 2B].
Kleinle, Michael (57 yrs.) d. on 68-Dec-25 [68-Dec-28: 2C].
Kleinle, William m. Ogier, Mary on 69-Sep-14 [69-Sep-16: 2B].
Klessne, Harriet (28 yrs.) d. on 66-Nov-22 [66-Nov-23: 2C].
Klett, R. A. m. Williams, Mary A. on 66-Jul-3 [66-Jul-18: 2C].
Kline, Jacob R. m. Shue, Rebecca on 67-Feb-12 [67-Mar-7: 2C].
Kline, Kate R. m. McAfee, Job W. on 69-Jun-24 [69-Jun-29: 2C].
Kline, Morris P. m. Murgatroyd, Alice S. on 70-Nov-2 [70-Nov-5: 2B].
Kline, William m. Armacost, Maggie on 68-Nov-17 [68-Nov-28: 2C].
Klinefelter, G. W. (49 yrs.) d. on 70-Jun-1 [70-Jun-17: 2B].
Klinefelter, Overton H. d. on 70-Sep-24 [70-Sep-26: 2B].
Klinefelter, Thomas C. (10 yrs.) d. on 68-Dec-21 [68-Dec-23: 2C].
Klockgether, Albert A. m. Jory, Jennette on 66-Aug-22 [66-Aug-25: 2A].
Klockgether, Albert A. m. Gaus, Louisa on 69-Sep-9 [69-Oct-28: 2C].
Klockgether, Albert A. m. Gaus, Louisa on 70-Sep-9 [70-Oct-4: 2B].
Klockgether, Charlotte (69 yrs.) d. on 68-Jan-22 [68-Jan-23: 2C].
Klockgether, D., Jr. m. Dryden, E. on 65-Dec-21 [66-Jan-1: 2C].
Klockgether, E. Julia d. on 66-Jul-27 [66-Aug-1: 2C].
Kloman, Edward F. m. Helm, Agnes P. on 66-Nov-6 [66-Nov-9: 2C].
Kloman, Felix (75 yrs.) d. on 66-Apr-9 [66-Apr-11: 2B].
Klueber, Oscar Julius (2 yrs., 8 mos.) d. on 70-Nov-8 [70-Nov-7: 2B].
Klug, Henry m. Bines, Maggie on 70-Oct-26 [70-Nov-9: 2C].
Klunk, Elizabeth (79 yrs.) d. on 69-Apr-6 [69-Apr-15: 2B].
Klunk, Francis A. m. Brady, Sarah J. on 66-Nov-27 [67-Jan-10: 2C].
Klunk, Maurice William (4 mos.) d. on 70-Oct-25 [70-Oct-26: 2B].
Klyensteber, Frederick (45 yrs.) d. on 66-Jul-18 of Heatstroke [66-Jul-20: 1F, 2D].
Knap, Rebecca (70 yrs.) d. on 66-Sep-9 [66-Sep-10: 2D].
Knapp, Emma E. m. Hudwalker, Henry on 70-Sep-13 [70-Sep-15: 2B].
Knapp, Harry C. N. (4 yrs., 4 mos.) d. on 69-Sep-17 [69-Sep-18: 2B].
Knapp, John m. Swinney, Victoria Virginia on 69-Dec-19 [69-Dec-25: 2C].

273

Knapp, John T. m. Crane, Evaline C. on 68-May-24 [68-Nov-28: 2C].
Knauf, Catherine (51 yrs., 5 mos.) d. [68-Sep-21: 2B].
Knauf, Philip H. m. McCall, Maggie A. on 69-Apr-18 [69-Apr-19: 2B].
Knell, Amelie m. Shipley, Benjamin F. on 70-Oct-13 [70-Oct-15: 2B].
Knell, Laura J. m. Holland, John M. on 70-Mar-3 [70-Mar-16: 2C].
Knell, Mami A. m. Barranger, Harry C. on 68-Jan-14 [68-Jan-20: 2B; 68-Jan-21: 2C].
Knickman, Elizabeth m. Wolf, August on 68-Sep-20 [68-Sep-22: 2B].
Knickman, Jacob (2 yrs., 1 mo.) d. on 68-Oct-24 [68-Oct-27: 2B].
Knickman, John (60 yrs.) d. on 66-Oct-17 [66-Oct-18: 2B].
Knierem, Emma Wilhelmina (1 yr.) d. on 67-Jul-17 [67-Mar-2: 2B].
Knierem, Virginia Estelle (4 yrs., 2 mos.) d. on 67-Feb-28 [67-Mar-2: 2B].
Knight, A. E. (49 yrs.) d. on 66-Jan-26 [66-Jan-27: 2B].
Knight, Anne M. d. on 68-Oct-11 [68-Oct-15: 2C].
Knight, Augustine m. Johnson, Mary C. on 67-Jul-18 [68-Jan-13: 2C].
Knight, Bell Hooper W. d. on 68-Jan-24 [68-Jan-25: 2B].
Knight, Elizabeth Cecile (17 yrs., 6 mos.) d. on 69-May-4 [69-May-5: 2C].
Knight, Ellen S. (28 yrs.) d. on 70-Jan-26 [70-Jan-27: 2C].
Knight, Emma A. m. Slyder, Izadore A. on 67-Mar-12 [67-Mar-14: 2C].
Knight, Eunice E. m. Booker, James W. on 69-Mar-1 [69-Apr-28: 2B].
Knight, Francis Reilly (2 yrs.) d. on 66-Jul-1 [66-Jul-2: 2B].
Knight, George m. Creager, Laurie Virginia on 68-Aug-11 [68-Sep-3: 2B].
Knight, Hannah (59 yrs.) d. on 68-Oct-12 [68-Oct-13: 2C].
Knight, Hannah Marriner m. Crothers, David on 69-Feb-1 [69-Apr-27: 2B].
Knight, James Henry (6 mos.) d. on 67-Jun-24 [67-Jun-26: 2C].
Knight, James Joseph d. on 68-Sep-29 [68-Sep-30: 2B].
Knight, John J. m. Waskey, Mary F. on 68-Dec-23 [68-Dec-24: 2C].
Knight, John T. m. Sands, Laura V. on 66-Jul-3 [66-Jul-6: 2B].
Knight, Jonathan W., Jr. m. Colt, Amelia A. on 68-May-26 [68-Jun-1: 2B].
Knight, Julianna M. (74 yrs.) d. on 68-Feb-20 [68-Feb-24: 2C].
Knight, Lavinia m. Jones, Edward J. on 70-Sep-18 [70-Oct-11: 2B].
Knight, Lewis m. Roche, L. W. on 70-Feb-15 [70-Feb-24: 2C].
Knight, Mary Amelia m. Sanks, John W. on 68-Oct-1 [68-Oct-5: 2B].
Knight, Mary Eliza (30 yrs.) d. on 68-May-10 [68-May-12: 2B].
Knight, Michael (76 yrs.) d. on 68-Jul-19 [68-Jul-20: 2B].
Knight, Rachel m. Trezise, Thomas on 69-Dec-23 [70-Jan-21: 2C].
Knight, Samuel T., Jr., Dr. (20 yrs.) d. on 70-Feb-12 [70-Feb-14: 2C; 70-Feb-15: 2C].
Knight, Theodore B. (56 yrs.) d. on 70-Nov-19 [70-Dec-1: 2C; 70-Dec-2: 2C].
Knight, Upton m. Cole, Bennetta on 70-Nov-21 [70-Nov-24: 2B].
Knight, William m. Chew, Kate V. on 69-Sep-16 [69-Sep-28: 2B].
Knight, William H m. McCleary, Laura V on 66-Jun-5 [66-Jun-7: 2B].
Knight, William H. m. Morris, Amanda M. C. A. on 70-Jan-18 [70-Jan-24: 2C].
Knight, William J. m. Ganish, Rachel V. on 68-Mar-18 [68-Mar-20: 2B].
Knight, William Thomas (3 mos.) d. on 67-Nov-11 [67-Nov-22: 2C].
Knighton, Harriet P. (72 yrs.) d. on 68-Aug-9 [68-Aug-11: 2B].
Knighton, Harry H. m. Price, Harrietta A. M. on 66-Nov-15 [66-Nov-29: 2B].
Knighton, Henry H. (20 yrs.) d. on 69-Dec-19 [69-Dec-20: 2C; 69-Dec-21: 2B].
Knighton, Joseph G. m. Brashears, Ellen on 67-Sep-5 [67-Sep-10: 2B].
Knihoff, Annie C. m. Foos, John C. on 66-May-10 [66-May-17: 2C].
Knipe, Oscar A. m. Arthur, Delia on 69-May-26 [69-Jun-10: 2C].
Knipe, Robert R. (17 yrs.) d. on 70-Aug-7 [70-Aug-8: 2C].
Knipe, Rosie M. m. Rote, John T. on 69-Jun-21 [69-Jun-25: 2C].
Knipe, Sarah (73 yrs.) d. on 69-Oct-21 [69-Oct-23: 2B].
Knipp, Mary m. Smith, Walter W. on 68-Nov-12 [68-Nov-17: 2C].
Knode, Israel (60 yrs.) d. on 68-Jan-7 [68-Jan-8: 2C].
Knode, John G. (33 yrs.) d. on 66-Dec-29 of Brain congestion [66-Dec-31: 2C].

Knodle, Charles S. m. Bingham, Carrie J. on 68-Nov-24 [68-Dec-10: 2D].
Knoepp, Sophia m. Rissau, Herman H. on 67-Jul-18 [67-Jul-22: 2C].
Knorr, Elizabeth Emily (1 yr., 9 mos.) d. on 67-Jun-3 [67-Jun-4: 2A].
Knorr, Friedrich F. m. Flamm, Elizabeth on 65-Oct-24 [66-Apr-18: 2B].
Knott, Adam (70 yrs.) d. on 69-Mar-18 of Intemperance and exposure [69-Mar-19: 1H].
Knott, Edward (81 yrs.) d. on 66-Aug-5 [66-Aug-8: 2C].
Knott, Elenora (59 yrs.) d. on 69-May-13 [69-May-14: 2C; 69-May-15: 2B].
Knott, J. Wesley m. Martin, Mary E. on 68-Aug-11 [68-Aug-19: 2B].
Knott, Jane M. (69 yrs.) d. on 69-Nov-26 [69-Nov-27: 2B].
Knott, John E. m. Claglett, Mary F. on 67-Dec-26 [68-Jan-11: 2B].
Knott, Maggie E. (1 yr., 3 mos.) d. on 66-Oct-31 [66-Nov-16: 2C].
Knotts, Joseph W. m. Reel, Fanny on 69-Nov-3 [69-Nov-10: 2C].
Knowles, Gustavus W. m. Crozer, Emma on 70-Mar-29 [70-Apr-4: 2B].
Knowles, Mary (70 yrs.) d. on 66-Mar-9 of Heart disease [66-Mar-10: 1F].
Knox, Ernestine (65 yrs.) d. on 70-Nov-21 [70-Nov-23: 2B].
Knox, Joseph d. on 68-Jul-30 [68-Dec-29: 2D].
Knox, Lottie d. on 66-Jul-19 [66-Jul-20: 2D].
Knox, Mahlah m. Belt, John W. on 66-Dec-4 [66-Dec-8: 2B].
Koa, Patrick Henry (1 yr., 4 mos.) d. on 66-Jun-1 [66-Jun-2: 2B].
Koch, Carl d. on 70-Apr-16 [70-Apr-19: 2B].
Koch, Mary A. m. Belt, Thomas W. on 66-Jun-5 [66-Jun-18: 2C].
Koch, Nancy (71 yrs.) d. on 69-Jun-11 [69-Jun-14: 2C].
Koch, William m. Stalfort, Kate on 69-May-18 [69-May-19: 2C].
Koechling, C. W., Dr. d. on 68-Sep-26 [68-Oct-17: 2B].
Koechling, Wilhelmine (28 yrs.) d. on 69-Mar-31 [69-Apr-2: 2C].
Koehler, Ferdinand m. Hammel, Maggie on 69-Jul-14 [69-Jul-19: 2C].
Koehler, George (49 yrs.) d. on 66-Dec-25 Drowned [66-Dec-27: 1F].
Koffenberger, Anne Barbara (50 yrs.) d. on 69-Jun-27 [69-Jun-28: 2C].
Koffenberger, G. m. Brown, Mary A. on 67-Jun-27 [67-Aug-3: 2B].
Koffenberger, Henry J. (1 yr., 6 mos.) d. on 70-Feb-2 [70-Feb-4: 2C].
Koffenberger, Maggie Agnes (1 yr., 3 mos.) d. on 68-Jul-15 [68-Jul-18: 2B].
Kohler, Adolph (48 yrs.) d. on 67-Apr-30 of Heart disease [67-May-2: 1G].
Kohler, Emil d. on 66-Sep-5 [66-Sep-8: 2B].
Kohlhepp, Catharine m. Barringer, Thomas on 67-Jul-9 [67-Jul-11: 2C].
Kohlhepp, Hartman (45 yrs., 3 mos.) d. on 69-Nov-25 [69-Nov-26: 2D].
Koke, John Frederick (1 yr., 9 mos.) d. on 68-May-15 [68-May-16: 2B].
Kolb, Jacob (27 yrs.) d. on 66-Oct-5 [66-Oct-6: 2A].
Kolb, Maggie S. (25 yrs.) d. on 68-Jan-9 [68-Jan-13: 2C].
Kolb, William A. m. Jones, Mary Ann on 69-Jan-2 [69-Jan-3: 2D].
Kolb, William Augustus m. Jones, Maggie S. on 66-May-24 [66-Jun-4: 2B].
Kolb, William W. m. Humes, Emma V. on 70-Mar-22 [70-Apr-9: 2B].
Kolb, Wilson W. (62 yrs.) d. on 69-Jan-14 [69-Jan-15: 2D].
Kolberstadt, John (55 yrs.) d. on 69-May-1 of Spasms [69-May-3: 1G].
Kolby, William Frederick m. Gengnagle, Julia on 67-May-7 [67-May-23: 2B].
Koller, Charles E. m. Pierce, Mary M. on 69-Nov-4 [70-Jan-4: 2C].
Koller, Issac A. m. Jackson, Elizabeth A. on 67-Jul-15 [67-Jul-31: 2C].
Koller, James B. m. Sheffer, Josephine on 70-Jan-4 [70-Jan-7: 2F].
Koller, John W. m. Loucks, Bell L. on 68-Nov-17 [68-Nov-19: 2C].
Kone, Franklin m. Benthall, C. E. on 69-Nov-15 [69-Nov-18: 2C].
Kone, Jane (42 yrs.) d. on 67-Sep-15 [67-Sep-17: 2A].
Konig, Lizzie m. Helfrich, Rudolph on 67-Apr-11 [67-Apr-17: 2B].
Konze, Amelia m. High, John W. on 70-Nov-8 [70-Nov-12: 2B].
Koockogey, Mary Lizzie (34 yrs.) d. on 70-Feb-20 [70-Feb-21: 2B].
Koonce, H. A. m. Frederick, Ada on 69-Apr-13 [69-Apr-29: 2B].
Koons, Anna m. Mettee, Michael on 68-Dec-20 [68-Dec-30: 2C].

Koons, Daniel L. (33 yrs.) d. on 68-Mar-19 [68-Mar-21: 2A].
Koons, J. E. m. Null, Lydia E. on 67-Mar-12 [67-Mar-20: 2C].
Koons, John (52 yrs.) d. on 69-Mar-6 [69-Mar-15: 2C].
Koons, Margaret m. Nurbaum, Harvey on 67-Nov-26 [67-Nov-27: 2B].
Koons, Rosa m. Hubbard, William on 68-Oct-29 [68-Nov-6: 2C; 68-Nov-7: 2B].
Koons, T. H. m. Rooney, Alice M. on 65-Sep-27 [66-Sep-27: 2C].
Koontz, Charles F. (32 yrs.) d. on 67-Feb-3 [67-Feb-4: 2C].
Koontz, Cornelia m. Beckley, Constantine F. on 69-Feb-15 [69-Feb-19: 2C].
Koontze, John (50 yrs.) d. on 69-Mar-6 of Fall from roof [69-Mar-8: 1H].
Koors, Emma (7 yrs., 9 mos.) d. on 67-Aug-2 [67-Aug-3: 2B].
Koper, Rudolph (43 yrs.) d. on 67-Apr-30 [67-May-1: 2B].
Koppelman, Catharine M. (56 yrs.) d. on 68-Feb-5 [68-Feb-6: 2C; 68-Feb-7: 2C].
Koppelman, Charles Albert (2 yrs., 5 mos.) d. on 69-May-6 [69-May-7: 2C].
Koppelman, George Edward d. on 66-Feb-4 [66-Feb-5: 2C].
Koppelman, John Henry (57 yrs.) d. on 69-May-13 [69-May-15: 2B].
Koppelman, Lizzie C. m. Weaver, Charles on 66-Jan-16 [66-Jan-19: 2C].
Koppleman, Mary m. Baetjer, George on 67-Sep-19 [67-Sep-23: 2A].
Koran, Barre m. Shepler, Christopher on 69-Nov-25 [69-Dec-10: 2C].
Korb, Henry d. on 68-Jul-19 Murdered (Stabbing) [68-Jul-20: 1F].
Kornman, Henry (64 yrs.) d. on 68-Aug-18 [68-Aug-19: 2B].
Koster, Carrie J. m. Caldwell, J. on 70-Aug-11 [70-Aug-15: 2C].
Koster, Kate d. on 66-Nov-21 [66-Nov-22: 2C].
Kosure, Clara Virginia m. Ingraham, J. on 68-Jun-2 [68-Jun-3: 2B].
Koth, Maggie m. Miller, Thomas H. on 70-Oct-10 [70-Oct-21: 2C].
Krafft, Daniel J. m. Ebaugh, Carrie on 68-Sep-1 [68-Sep-8: 2B].
Kraft, Abby S. m. Eckert, George W. on 66-Apr-26 [66-Apr-28: 2A].
Kraft, Anna E. m. Fox, Lewis C. on 68-Apr-30 [68-May-5: 2B].
Kraft, Caroline C. m. Coster, James H. on 66-Apr-9 [66-May-1: 2A].
Kraft, Catharine J. m. Jungling, Friedrich on 70-Feb-22 [70-Mar-3: 2C].
Kraft, Catherine (47 yrs.) d. on 70-Oct-12 [70-Oct-13: 2C].
Kraft, Charles m. Snyder, Mary Regine on 67-Oct-8 [67-Oct-14: 2B].
Kraft, Charles L. (40 yrs.) d. on 66-Jul-28 of Stomach gout [66-Aug-2: 1G; 66-Aug-4: 2C].
Kraft, Charles V. m. Hicks, Mary E. on 66-Nov-1 [66-Nov-2: 2B].
Kraft, Christina m. Muhlhofer, William on 69-Feb-25 [69-Feb-27: 2C].
Kraft, Edward Thomas (2 mos.) d. on 67-Dec-29 [67-Dec-31: 2C].
Kraft, Elizabeth (25 yrs.) d. on 68-Nov-1 [68-Nov-2: 2C].
Kraft, Elizabeth (80 yrs.) d. on 69-Nov-2 [69-Nov-4: 2C; 69-Nov-5: 2C].
Kraft, George W. m. Kemp, Cecilia J. on 70-Feb-9 [70-Feb-21: 2B].
Kraft, Hester F. (61 yrs.) d. on 66-Oct-17 [66-Oct-18: 2B].
Kraft, Jacob (65 yrs.) d. on 70-Jun-30 [70-Jul-2: 2B].
Kraft, Jennette m. Keene, John R. on 67-Oct-3 [67-Oct-8: 2B].
Kraft, Joseph Paul (2 mos.) d. on 70-May-10 [70-May-11: 2B].
Kraft, Lewis (37 yrs.) d. on 65-Dec-9 [66-Apr-11: 2B].
Kraft, Lewis m. Omer, Virginia on 68-Sep-28 [68-Oct-1: 2B].
Kraft, Louisa P. m. Young, J. Christopher on 68-Oct-27 [69-Jan-12: 2C].
Kraft, Marion M. C. (17 yrs.) d. on 68-Sep-18 [68-Sep-19: 2B].
Kraft, Mary A. m. Roy, Robert on 67-Feb-5 [67-Mar-26: 2C].
Kraft, Mary E. m. Kelly, James T. on 68-May-5 [68-May-8: 2B].
Kraft, Sallie L. m. Dallwig, E. A. on 70-Apr-3 [70-Apr-6: 2B; 70-Apr-2: 2C].
Kraft, Sophie S. m. Smith, Eugene R. on 68-Feb-4 [68-Feb-11: 2C; 68-Feb-12: 2B].
Krager, Ellen Georgiana (1 yr., 2 mos.) d. on 66-Aug-2 [66-Aug-3: 2C].
Krager, Frederick (11 mos.) d. on 68-Aug-17 [68-Aug-18: 2B].
Krager, George W. m. McKenna, Mollie on 66-Sep-17 [66-Sep-19: 2B].
Krager, George W. m. Hagerty, Kate on 70-Oct-13 [70-Nov-4: 2C].
Krager, John L. (42 yrs.) d. on 70-Aug-28 [70-Aug-29: 2C, 4D].

Krager, John Phillips (6 yrs.) d. on 67-Feb-27 [67-Feb-28: 2C].
Krager, Mollie (21 yrs.) d. on 67-Jun-10 [67-Jun-11: 2B].
Kramer, C. H. m. Bernasco, A. on 68-Nov-8 [68-Nov-28: 2C].
Kramer, Elizabeth m. Grote, Frederick on 68-Nov-17 [68-Nov-24: 2C].
Kramer, Emanuel (55 yrs.) d. on 66-Jun-4 of Suicide (Hanging) [66-Jun-6: 1G].
Kramer, Florence (3 yrs.) d. on 70-Dec-1 of Scarlet fever [70-Dec-5: 2C].
Kramer, Jacob (83 yrs.) d. [68-Mar-30: 2B].
Kramer, Mary (52 yrs.) d. on 69-May-1 [69-May-3: 2C].
Kramer, Oscar d. on 70-Jun-16 [70-Jun-17: 2B].
Kramer, Rebecca E. m. Cunningham, Wilbur Fisk on 68-Dec-29 [69-Jan-1: 2C].
Kramer, Samuel m. Shane, Matilda on 70-Feb-21 [70-Feb-22: 2C].
Kramm, Willie G. m. Stover, Robert W. on 67-Sep-20 [68-May-30: 2A].
Kramme, Frederick (56 yrs.) d. on 69-Nov-23 [69-Nov-25: 2C].
Krantz, George (30 yrs., 7 mos.) d. on 70-Oct-10 [70-Oct-11: 2C; 70-Oct-12: 2C].
Krantz, John C. (44 yrs., 11 mos.) d. on 70-Aug-31 [70-Sep-1: 2B; 70-Sep-2: 2C].
Krantz, Sarah E. m. Roberts, James L. on 69-Jul-13 [69-Jul-20: 2C].
Krastel, John m. Mulvey, Mary on 70-May-19 [70-Jun-10: 2B].
Kratzer, John (14 yrs.) d. on 69-Jul-8 in Wagon accident [69-Jul-9: 4C].
Kraus, Elmira m. Ely, Joseph F. on 67-May-26 [67-May-29: 2B].
Krause, Emile W. (1 yr., 6 mos.) d. on 68-Aug-3 [68-Aug-4: 2C].
Krause, Jane C. (68 yrs.) d. on 66-May-2 [66-May-4: 2C].
Krause, Mary Virginia m. Dobson, Daniel H. on 68-Mar-9 [68-Mar-11: 2B].
Krauss, Sophie m. Cooper, Thomas on 66-Jul-12 [66-Dec-15: 2B].
Krauss, William H. (1 yr., 10 mos.) d. on 68-Jul-15 [68-Jul-16: 2C].
Krausse, Henry (29 yrs.) d. on 70-Oct-10 Murdered (Shooting) [70-Oct-11: 4D; 70-Oct-12: 4C].
Krebs, Adeline (36 yrs.) d. on 67-Sep-25 [67-Sep-26: 2B].
Krebs, David N. m. McCabe, Sarah O. on 69-Apr-26 [69-May-17: 2B].
Krebs, Eliza Jane d. on 70-May-3 of Consumption [70-May-4: 2C, 2B].
Krebs, George L. m. Shaw, Imogene on 66-Jan-30 [66-Feb-5: 2C].
Krebs, George W. C. m. Paine, Mary G. on 70-Sep-27 [70-Sep-30: 2B].
Krebs, Harry Warner (2 mos.) d. on 67-Jul-4 [67-Jul-6: 2B].
Krebs, Henry B. (33 yrs.) d. on 67-Jun-7 [67-Jun-8: 2B].
Krebs, Jacob (93 yrs.) d. on 67-Oct-9 [67-Oct-10: 2B; 67-Oct-11: 1G, 2B].
Krebs, John J. m. Kelly, Georgeanna on 68-Aug-17 [68-Sep-2: 2A].
Krebs, Louisa M. m. Amos, James T. on 69-Jun-24 [69-Jun-28: 2C].
Krebs, Margaret (88 yrs.) d. on 66-Aug-31 [66-Sep-1: 2B].
Krebs, Maria d. on 68-Jan-15 [68-Jan-17: 2C].
Krebs, Mary C. m. Elliott, Lewis A. on 69-Dec-21 [70-Jan-11: 2C].
Krebs, Mary E. (60 yrs.) d. on 66-Jul-16 [66-Jul-17: 2C].
Krebs, Mary Elizabeth (2 yrs.) d. on 67-Oct-27 [67-Oct-28: 2B].
Krebs, William, Rev. (52 yrs.) d. on 70-Sep-26 [70-Sep-27: 2B; 70-Sep-28: 2B; 70-Sep-29: 4B].
Krebs, William George (64 yrs.) d. on 66-Apr-24 of Pulmonary disease [66-Apr-25: 1F; 66-Aug-25: 2B].
Kregar, Fanny R. (20 yrs.) d. on 66-Feb-11 [66-Feb-12: 2D].
Kregel, Otto (37 yrs.) d. on 68-Jun-10 [68-Jun-11: 2B; 68-Jun-12: 2B].
Kreideweis, William m. McNulty, Margaret on 68-Dec-31 [69-Feb-5: 2C].
Kreil, Andrew (86 yrs.) d. on 69-Aug-22 [69-Aug-23: 2C].
Kreis, Harry P. m. Bond, Emma J. on 66-May-8 [66-May-9: 2B].
Kreis, John m. Kinningham, Mary B. on 66-Oct-23 [67-May-20: 2B].
Kreis, Joseph William (6 mos.) d. on 69-Aug-27 [69-Aug-30: 2B].
Kreitman, Emma Lillie (4 yrs.) d. on 66-Jan-12 [66-Jan-13: 2C].
Kreitman, John (26 yrs.) d. on 69-Jan-1 [69-Jan-4: 2C].
Kremelberg, Joseph William (2 yrs., 2 mos.) d. on 69-Jul-16 [69-Jul-20: 2C].
Kremer, Anna Margaret (61 yrs.) d. on 66-Mar-14 [66-Mar-16: 2B].
Kremer, Nelly (1 yr., 2 mos.) d. on 69-Jan-4 [69-Jan-5: 2C].

Krener, Mary m. Hoffman, Philip on 67-Nov-5 [67-Nov-19: 2C].
Kretchmer, Carrie Belle (12 yrs.) d. on 66-Mar-13 [66-Mar-14: 2C].
Kreutzer, Emma m. Muesse, Henry on 69-Oct-17 [69-Oct-21: 2B].
Kreutzer, George (46 yrs.) d. on 67-May-28 [67-May-29: 2B].
Krews, Sydney Alberta (3 yrs., 4 mos.) d. on 66-Jun-5 [66-Jun-6: 2B].
Krichten, John H. m. Dosh, Maggie on 67-Aug-4 [67-Aug-7: 2C].
Krichton, Mary R. m. Miner, J. P. on 67-Dec-3 [68-Jan-22: 2C].
Kridel, William (23 yrs.) d. [66-Dec-28: 2C].
Kries, John A. (63 yrs., 3 mos.) d. on 66-Jan-29 [66-Jan-30: 2B].
Krise, Elizabeth m. Mercer, William H. on 67-Nov-7 [67-Nov-16: 2B].
Krise, William Henry (1 yr., 8 mos.) d. on 68-Sep-20 [68-Sep-21: 2B].
Kriteman, Sarah Rebecca (5 yrs., 4 mos.) d. on 66-Jan-2 [66-Jan-4: 2C].
Kritte, Charles (8 yrs.) d. on 70-Jul-30 [70-Aug-1: 4G].
Kritzer, Christian d. on 67-Oct-12 [67-Oct-16: 2B].
Kroder, John (62 yrs.) d. on 67-Oct-31 [67-Nov-1: 2B].
Kroeger, Ernest August (1 yr., 4 mos.) d. on 69-Aug-8 [69-Aug-9: 2C; 69-Aug-10: 2C].
Kroh, Georgia E. m. Burke, A. J. on 68-Aug-18 [69-Feb-24: 2C].
Kroh, Philip A. m. Sterling, Mary Ellen on 66-Dec-13 [66-Dec-14: 2B].
Krone, J. B. C. m. McDonald, Maria on 66-Feb-28 [66-Mar-2: 2B].
Krousse, Charles F. (1 yr., 5 mos.) d. on 70-Aug-7 [70-Aug-9: 2C].
Krousse, John C. (2 yrs., 11 mos.) d. on 68-Feb-11 [68-Feb-13: 2C].
Krout, Annie m. Anderson, Edwin on 66-Jan-18 [66-Feb-22: 2B].
Krout, Emma Ellen (9 mos.) d. on 68-Sep-14 [68-Sep-15: 2B].
Krug, Thomas m. Haas, Rosa on 70-Aug-21 [70-Sep-27: 2B].
Krumm, Caroline E. m. Spamer, William on 68-Nov-15 [68-Nov-26: 2B].
Krumm, Emma A. m. Stratten, Julius Thor on 69-Oct-10 [69-Oct-18: 2C; 69-Oct-19: 2B].
Krumm, Louis P. m. Causmelle, Mary A. on 70-Mar-8 [70-May-2: 2B].
Krummer, Aaron (33 yrs.) d. on 66-Jul-14 of Heatstroke [66-Jul-16: 1G].
Kubel, W. A. (28 yrs.) d. on 67-Oct-7 [67-Oct-9: 2B].
Kugler, George W., Capt. d. on 68-Feb-15 of Pneumonia [68-Feb-26: 2C].
Kugler, John Coates (1 mo.) d. on 69-Aug-11 [69-Aug-12: 2C].
Kugler, Octavia A. m. Williams, Augustus A. on 67-Apr-13 [67-Apr-15: 2B].
Kugler, Thomas H. m. Thompson, Sarah M. on 68-Jul-7 [68-Jul-15: 2B].
Kuhan, Cornelius m. Morwood, Mary Lucy on 69-Aug-13 [69-Aug-16: 2B].
Kuhleman, Charles F. m. Schultheis, Mary on 70-Jun-22 [70-Jun-25: 2B].
Kuhn, Agnes Elizabeth d. on 70-May-14 [70-May-16: 2B].
Kuhn, Albenia m. Hoffman, Josiah on 68-Sep-1 [68-Sep-3: 2B].
Kuhn, Alphonsus (19 yrs.) d. on 66-Jan-8 [66-Jan-11: 2B].
Kuhn, Anna (19 yrs.) d. on 69-Jan-12 [69-Jan-15: 2D].
Kuhn, Annie (23 yrs.) d. on 68-Oct-12 of Epilepsy [68-Oct-13: 1F].
Kuhn, Augustus (20 yrs.) d. on 68-Dec-1 [68-Dec-2: 2C].
Kuhn, John m. Hall, Jane T. on 66-Sep-27 [66-Oct-2: 2B].
Kuhn, John m. Barton, Martha on 66-Jun-25 [66-Jul-4: 2B].
Kuhn, Joshua M. (57 yrs.) d. on 67-May-21 [67-May-22: 2B].
Kuhn, Matilda (31 yrs.) d. on 69-Oct-7 [69-Oct-8: 2B; 69-Oct-9: 2C].
Kuhn, Minnie (1 yr., 2 mos.) d. on 66-Aug-2 [66-Aug-3: 2B].
Kuhn, Theresa S. m. Jackson, Frank C. on 70-Oct-13 [70-Oct-19: 2B].
Kunkel, Charles H. m. Redsecker, Hallie S. on 70-May-31 [70-Jun-4: 2B].
Kunsman, Edward Slaughter (9 mos.) d. on 66-Sep-8 [66-Sep-10: 2D].
Kunsman, George R. (43 yrs.) d. on 70-Sep-24 [70-Sep-26: 2B, 4D].
Kunsman, Harriet D. (34 yrs.) d. on 67-Oct-22 [67-Oct-23: 2B].
Kunsman, Sarah E. (78 yrs.) d. on 70-Jul-17 [70-Jul-19: 2C].
Kunsman, William H. (43 yrs.) d. on 69-Sep-25 [69-Sep-27: 2C].
Kunsman, William H. m. Tolson, Georganna on 69-Sep-24 [69-Sep-25: 2B].
Kurtz, Alice m. Thomas, Edward F. on 69-May-20 [69-May-22: 2B].

Kurtz, Anna M. (44 yrs.) d. on 69-Apr-28 [69-May-1: 2B].
Kurtz, Benjamin, Rev. (71 yrs.) d. on 65-Dec-29 [66-Jan-1: 2C; 66-Jan-2: 1G].
Kurtz, Elizabeth F. d. on 69-May-13 [69-May-14: 2C].
Kurtz, Ella m. Graft, Thomas D. on 66-Oct-8 [66-Nov-2: 2B].
Kurtz, Freddie d. on 66-Jul-6 [66-Jul-13: 2C].
Kurtz, Harry (7 yrs., 1 mo.) d. on 68-Dec-20 [68-Dec-30: 2C].
Kurtz, Louise DePue m. Virnon, George R. on 68-Oct-8 [68-Oct-13: 2C].
Kurtz, Maggie T. m. Stanfield, Caleb F. on 67-Oct-2 [67-Oct-10: 2B].
Kurtz, Minnie Florence (1 mo.) d. on 70-Apr-20 [70-Apr-22: 2C].
Kurtz, Pheba (72 yrs.) d. on 70-Apr-29 [70-Apr-30: 2B].
Kurtz, Samuel (70 yrs.) d. on 66-Nov-10 [66-Nov-12: 2C].
Kurtz, Willie d. on 66-Feb-13 [66-Feb-14: 2C].
Kurtze, Sarah L. m. Brooks, Robert S. on 69-Dec-29 [70-Jan-4: 2C].
Kurzman, B. (18 yrs.) d. on 67-Mar-12 of Suicide (Drowning) [67-Mar-13: 1F].
Kuster, Henry d. on 66-Jul-1 Drowned [66-Jul-3: 1F; 66-Jul-4: 1G].
Kuszmaul, Emily A. T. (22 yrs.) d. on 68-Sep-23 [68-Sep-25: 2B].
Kuszmaul, John m. Scott, Emily A. T. on 66-Jan-1 [66-Jan-19: 2C].
Kutfreen, John d. on 70-May-30 of Fall [70-May-31: 1H].
Kyle, Adam B. (86 yrs.) d. on 69-Apr-12 [69-Apr-15: 1F, 2B].
Kyle, George H. m. Duvall, Frances F. on 67-Jan-1 [67-Jan-3: 2B].
Kyle, H. T. d. on 70-Jan-23 of Pneumonia [70-Jan-25: 2C].
Kyle, Jennie T. m. Blake, Benson on 69-Dec-16 [69-Dec-17: 2C].
Kyle, Sarah (74 yrs.) d. on 69-Feb-24 [69-Feb-26: 2D].
Kyle, Thomas (65 yrs.) d. on 66-Oct-29 [66-Oct-30: 2B].
Kyne, Anna m. Sullivan, Cornelius on 67-Nov-7 [67-Nov-11: 2C].
La Barrer, Francis, Sr. m. Able, A. E. on 69-Jan-19 [69-Mar-16: 2C].
La Porte, Clara E. m. Williams, Thomas W. on 69-Apr-1 [69-Apr-2: 2C; 69-Apr-3: 2B].
La Porte, Eliza (54 yrs., 4 mos.) d. on 69-Jun-4 [69-Jun-5: 2B].
Labar, Michael (56 yrs.) d. on 68-Apr-6 [68-Apr-7: 2B].
LaBarrer, Francis B., Jr. m. Crouch, Martha W. on 67-Mar-17 [67-Apr-11: 2B].
LaBarrer, Lavinia (42 yrs.) d. on 66-Dec-3 [66-Dec-4: 2D].
LaBarrer, Martha W. (23 yrs.) d. on 68-Dec-20 [68-Dec-22: 2C].
Labby, Frances A. m. Zink, Louis on 70-Jun-30 [70-Jul-8: 2C].
Labby, Lewis (49 yrs.) d. on 69-May-28 [69-May-29: 2B].
Labe, Rebecca m. Bernheimer, Henry on 68-Oct-18 [68-Oct-20: 2B].
Labenstein, William d. on 68-Aug-24 of Apoplexy [68-Aug-25: 1F].
Labenvein, Louis (6 yrs.) d. on 67-Jul-1 Drowned [67-Jul-2: 4D].
Labraque, Louise J. m. Dubree, George W. on 68-Jan-12 [68-Jan-14: 2C].
Labroquere, Bernard T. (89 yrs.) d. on 69-Jan-5 [69-Jan-7: 2C].
Lacey, Ellen Elizabeth (5 yrs., 2 mos.) d. on 68-May-27 [68-May-28: 2B].
Lacey, Lizzie C. m. Wherrett, Robert M. on 66-Sep-23 [66-Sep-27: 2C].
Lackey, M. F. m. Laurenson, Margaretta on 69-Oct-26 [69-Nov-6: 2B].
Lackey, Mary Levina (1 yr., 1 mo.) d. on 68-Dec-7 [68-Dec-9: 2C].
Lacy, Elizabeth Emily (9 yrs., 5 mos.) d. on 70-Apr-9 [70-Apr-11: 2B].
Lacy, John Francis (1 mo.) d. on 67-Jul-23 [67-Jul-25: 2C].
Lacy, Lizzie m. McHenry, Patrick on 67-Feb-27 [67-Mar-6: 2C].
Lacy, Maurice Fitzgerald d. on 70-Mar-15 [70-Mar-16: 2C; 70-Mar-17: 2C].
Lacy, Peter E. m. Byrne, Mary J. on 69-May-10 [69-May-12: 2B].
Laedrich, Angelique m. Crook, Charles on 67-Jan-8 [67-Jan-31: 2C].
Laessig, August (1 yr., 3 mos.) d. on 66-Jan-26 [66-Jan-27: 2C].
Laessig, John G. d. on 66-Sep-4 [66-Sep-5: 2B].
Lafevre, Maggie (26 yrs.) d. on 70-May-31 [70-Jun-2: 2B].
Lafferty, Agnes m. Castillo, Patrick on 68-Jul-1 [68-Jul-3: 2B].
Lafferty, Ellen (37 yrs.) d. on 67-Apr-19 [67-Apr-20: 2A].
Lafferty, Ellen A. (12 yrs.) d. on 69-Apr-2 [69-Apr-3: 2B].

Lafferty, John C. B. (6 yrs., 8 mos.) d. on 69-Feb-20 [69-Feb-23: 2D].
Lafferty, Murdock Hugh (1 yr., 7 mos.) d. on 66-Jul-31 [66-Aug-1: 2C].
Lafferty, Robert m. Hinton, Anne E. on 66-Apr-3 [66-Jun-11: 2B].
Lafferty, Samuel m. Bilmire, Mary on 69-Oct-16 [69-Oct-21: 2B].
Lafferty, William (1 yr., 5 mos.) d. on 70-Jul-18 [70-Jul-19: 2C].
LaFore, James L. (26 yrs.) d. on 68-Aug-22 [68-Aug-26: 2B].
Laib, Edward W. m. Gibbons, Sarah F. on 69-Feb-9 [69-Feb-11: 2C].
Laib, Harry (2 mos.) d. on 70-Aug-4 [70-Aug-5: 2C].
Laib, Jacob (65 yrs.) d. on 70-Jan-1 [70-Jan-3: 2C].
Laib, John C. (63 yrs.) d. on 69-Sep-29 [69-Sep-30: 2B; 69-Oct-1: 2B].
Laib, Sarah F. (21 yrs.) d. on 70-Nov-25 [70-Nov-26: 2B].
Lainhart, Juliet F. m. Weaver, Edmund E. J. on 69-Oct-26 [69-Oct-30: 2B].
Lainhart, Marietta m. Carmine, George on 68-Dec-22 [69-Nov-24: 2C].
Lainhart, R. D. m. Delcher, S. C. on 67-Sep-5 [67-Dec-2: 2C].
Laird, Mattie P. m. Goldsborough, W. Ewell on 69-Jan-7 [69-Jan-16: 2C; 69-Jan-18: 2C].
Lake, Amelia m. Vanock, William H. on 66-Sep-26 [66-Dec-15: 2B].
Lake, Effie (60 yrs.) d. on 69-Nov-20 [69-Dec-4: 2C].
Lake, Herman B., Jr. m. Steindle, Barbara on 70-Jun-6 [70-Jun-7: 2C].
Lake, James B., Jr. m. Thayer, Mary R. on 70-Sep-6 [70-Oct-5: 2B].
Lake, John m. Tompson, Mary Rebecca on 68-Jan-28 [68-Feb-4: 2C].
Lake, Mary A. d. on 69-Dec-1 of Consumption [69-Dec-4: 2C].
Laley, Laura M. m. Storm, E. M. on 69-Apr-5 [69-Apr-7: 2C].
Laley, T. K. m. Spencer, R. L. on 66-Dec-4 [66-Dec-6: 2B].
Lally, J. Augustine (1 yr., 9 mos.) d. on 70-Dec-22 [70-Dec-23: 2B].
Lalor, Lawrence Patrick (2 yrs., 4 mos.) d. on 69-Feb-5 [69-Feb-6: 2C].
Lalor, Margaret m. Kennedy, William J. on 67-Aug-15 [67-Aug-17: 2B].
Lamb, Charles W., Dr. (29 yrs.) d. on 67-Jan-6 [67-Jan-7: 2C; 67-Jan-8: 2B].
Lamb, Emily Ward m. Stansbury, L. Frank on 67-Oct-30 [67-Nov-2: 2B].
Lamb, George M. (53 yrs.) d. on 68-Apr-16 [68-Apr-17: 2B].
Lamb, James (21 yrs.) d. on 70-Apr-8 Drowned [70-Apr-20: 1H; 70-Apr-22: 2C].
Lamb, Joseph m. Schiermer, Elizabeth Rosetta on 67-Jan-17 [67-Jan-21: 2C].
Lamb, Mary M. m. Cox, John R. on 69-Aug-5 [69-Aug-11: 2C].
Lamb, Robert m. Schepler, Margaret A. on 66-Oct-16 [66-Oct-20: 2B].
Lamb, Thomas P. (48 yrs.) d. on 67-Aug-26 [67-Aug-30: 2B].
Lambden, Carrie A. m. Heckman, John W. on 70-Jan-6 [70-Jan-14: 2C; 70-Jan-15: 2C].
Lambden, E. P. m. Brooking, H. G. on 67-Dec-4 [67-Dec-6: 2C].
Lambden, Maggie Eloise (1 yr., 7 mos.) d. on 66-Mar-16 [66-Mar-19: 2C].
Lambdin, Annie M. m. Bailie, William L. on 68-Feb-26 [68-Feb-28: 2D].
Lambdin, Daniel B. m. Geoghgan, Elizabeth J. on 68-Jun-23 [68-Jul-14: 2B].
Lambdin, Emily B. (65 yrs.) d. on 69-Jul-26 [69-Jul-27: 2C].
Lambdin, George W. m. Hergesheimer, Sarah on 66-Feb-14 [66-Feb-21: 2C].
Lambdin, Margaret A. m. Spencer, George W. on 66-Sep-20 [66-Sep-25: 2B].
Lambdin, Martha E. m. Volans, William C. on 68-Apr-7 [68-Apr-10: 2B].
Lambdin, Mary E. m. Sears, John K. on 70-Apr-28 [70-Apr-30: 2A].
Lambdin, Mary Elizabeth (1 yr., 4 mos.) d. on 67-Sep-2 [67-Sep-3: 2B].
Lambdin, N. B. m. Webb, Emma W. on 70-May-5 [70-May-25: 2C].
Lambdin, Olivia G. (9 yrs.) d. on 69-Jan-30 [69-Feb-1: 2C].
Lambdin, Thomas A. J. m. Taylor, Helen C. on 68-Dec-20 [68-Dec-22: 2C].
Lambdin, Thomas H. (39 yrs.) d. on 67-Feb-26 [67-Feb-28: 2C].
Lambdin, Thomas R. m. Berrenger, Mary F. on 66-Nov-29 [67-Jan-5: 2C].
Lambdin, Willie S. (1 yr.) d. on 70-Nov-2 [70-Nov-4: 2C].
Lambert, Annie Isabel (1 yr., 7 mos.) d. on 70-Jul-27 [70-Jul-28: 2C].
Lambert, Charlotte (47 yrs.) d. on 66-May-14 [66-May-15: 2C].
Lambert, Elijah m. Goghean, Margaret A. on 68-May-18 [68-May-20: 2C].
Lambert, John (31 yrs.) d. on 69-Jun-14 [69-Jun-19: 2B].

Lambert, John P. (9 mos.) d. on 66-Apr-20 [66-Apr-21: 2B].
Lambert, Joseph (64 yrs.) d. on 69-Apr-9 [69-Apr-10: 2B].
Lambert, Josephine m. Beacham, George H. on 67-Nov-6 [67-Nov-9: 2B].
Lambert, Philip (39 yrs.) d. on 66-Aug-10 of Consumption [66-Aug-11: 2B].
Lambrecht, George H. (58 yrs.) d. on 69-Feb-26 [69-Feb-27: 2C; 69-Mar-1: 2C].
Lambson, William B. m. Henderson, Anna on 66-Dec-27 [67-Jan-1: 2C].
Lame, James William (2 yrs., 11 mos.) d. on 68-Oct-29 [68-Nov-2: 2B].
Lamkin, S. Lewis m. Middleton, Matilda W. on 68-Jan-23 [68-Jan-28: 2D].
Lamley, Charles G. m. Trott, Margaret A. on 69-Dec-14 [69-Dec-23: 2B].
Lamley, Jacob F. m. Erdman, Barbara E. on 69-Mar-30 [69-Apr-7: 2C].
Lamley, Thomas P. (67 yrs.) d. on 66-Apr-5 [66-Apr-6: 2B].
Lammot, Moses (82 yrs.) d. [68-Jun-6: 1G].
Lampanius, Annie L. (7 yrs.) d. on 68-Dec-10 [68-Dec-12: 2C].
Lamparter, E. m. Aldridge, Eleonora on 69-Jul-8 [69-Jul-31: 2C].
Lampertsteoffer, Margaret (23 yrs.) d. on 66-Jul-17 [66-Jul-19: 1F].
Lamping, F. Emma m. Wells, William H. on 67-Oct-16 [67-Oct-18: 2C].
Lamy, Marion O. m. Curtain, Oliver P. on 66-May-13 [66-May-17: 2C; 66-May-18: 2C].
Lanahan, Mary d. on 67-Sep-24 [67-Sep-26: 2B; 67-Sep-27: 2B].
Lanahan, Mary A. m. Reilly, Charles E. on 70-Jul-26 [70-Aug-3: 2C].
Lanahan, Mary C. m. Reeder, Oliver on 68-Nov-13 [68-Nov-25: 2B].
Lanahan, Michael m. Davis, Kate on 67-Oct-14 [67-Nov-13: 2C].
Lanahan, William (56 yrs.) d. on 68-Aug-8 [68-Aug-10: 2B].
Lancaster, Columbus L. (57 yrs.) d. on 66-Jun-9 [66-Jun-13: 2B].
Lancaster, Issac T., Capt. (30 yrs.) d. on 68-Apr-4 of Apoplexy [68-Apr-6: 1E, 2B].
Lancaster, John W. m. Vanhorn, Lydia V. on 66-Sep-25 [66-Oct-3: 2B].
Lancaster, Louis J. m. Wootten, Mary E. on 68-Feb-20 [68-Mar-20: 2C].
Lancaster, Martha M. m. Miller, John W. on 66-Aug-19 [66-Aug-27: 2B].
Lancaster, Martin V. B. m. Gruver, Carrie C. on 67-Aug-1 [67-Sep-20: 2A].
Lancaster, Mary (66 yrs.) d. on 66-Nov-1 [66-Nov-2: 2B].
Lancaster, Sallie D. m. Marshall, James W. on 69-Nov-16 [69-Nov-20: 2B].
Landers, Bernard (40 yrs.) d. on 70-Oct-9 [70-Oct-11: 2C].
Landin, Issac James m. Pritchard, Laura U. on 70-Jun-22 [70-Aug-20: 2B].
Landing, Benjamin J. m. Brumble, Emma J. on 69-Apr-3 [69-Apr-6: 2C].
Landing, George W., Jr. m. Burgess, Mollie A. W. on 67-Apr-23 [67-Oct-3: 2B].
Landis, David (21 yrs.) d. on 67-Nov-3 [67-Nov-4: 2B].
Landis, Emma M. m. Root, George H. on 67-Oct-8 [67-Oct-12: 2A].
Landon, Elizabeth P. (66 yrs.) d. on 67-Dec-24 [67-Dec-25: 2C].
Landon, George (2 mos.) d. on 68-Apr-11 [68-Apr-14: 2A].
Landrigan, Sarah (80 yrs.) d. on 68-Jul-16 of Heatstroke [68-Jul-17: 2B, 1D].
Landry, Eliza M. C. (78 yrs.) d. on 70-Feb-25 [70-Feb-26: 2C].
Landstreet, Margaret Gray (2 yrs., 7 mos.) d. on 68-Oct-21 [68-Oct-23: 2B].
Landy, John Augustus (1 yr.) d. on 66-Aug-22 [66-Aug-23: 2C].
Lane, Ann M. (66 yrs.) d. on 67-Oct-20 [67-Oct-24: 2B].
Lane, Annie m. Gordon, Samuel on 66-Apr-26 [66-May-28: 2B].
Lane, Caroline L. m. Renoff, Frederick J. on 69-Aug-23 [69-Aug-30: 2B].
Lane, Charles (39 yrs.) d. on 66-Feb-14 of Consumption [66-Feb-15: 2C].
Lane, Christopher m. Pease, Anne on 68-Mar-4 [68-Mar-30: 2B].
Lane, Elizabeth Jane (56 yrs.) d. on 66-Nov-8 [66-Nov-10: 2B].
Lane, Jane A. (41 yrs.) d. on 69-Apr-18 [69-May-3: 2C].
Lane, Lizzie m. Claspy, George W. on 69-Mar-30 [69-Apr-12: 2A].
Lane, Mary A. H. (62 yrs.) d. on 70-Nov-25 [70-Dec-3: 2B].
Lane, Mary Rebecca (29 yrs., 2 mos.) d. on 66-May-21 [66-May-23: 2B].
Lang, Elizabeth m. Sluter, Jeremiah H. on 69-Feb-25 [69-Mar-17: 2C].
Lang, Philip m. Brown, Columbine A. on 69-Jun-22 [69-Jun-26: 2B].
Langan, Thomas m. Morgan, Mary M. on 68-Jul-21 [68-Aug-27: 2B].

Langdon, Ann Maria m. Ramsey, Robert J. on 66-Jan-1 [66-Jan-9: 2B].
Langdon, Eliza M. (67 yrs.) d. on 67-Feb-28 [67-Mar-2: 2B].
Langdon, Nannie Lisle (21 yrs.) d. on 68-Sep-19 [68-Sep-21: 2B].
Langdon, Thomas P. m. White, Nannie Lisle on 68-Jan-29 [68-Jan-31: 2C].
Langdorf, Frederica (22 yrs.) d. on 69-Jun-17 [69-Jun-18: 2C; 69-Jun-19: 2B].
Lange, Jacob P. m. Gurney, Mary Lavinia on 70-Feb-23 [70-Feb-24: 2C].
Lange, Louise d. on 68-Aug-30 [68-Sep-1: 2B].
Lange, Nettie (24 yrs.) d. on 69-Aug-9 [69-Aug-10: 2C; 69-Aug-11: 2C].
Lange, William m. Weiss, Caroline on 69-Oct-26 [69-Nov-23: 2C].
Langford, George W. m. Albright, Lavinia M. on 70-Mar-10 [70-May-12: 2B].
Langford, Mary E. m. Page, Charles I on 67-Dec-25 [67-Dec-28: 2C].
Langford, Thomas m. Abbes, Jane Augusta on 69-Apr-29 [69-May-14: 2C].
Langley, Charles E. (28 yrs.) d. on 67-Mar-1 [67-Mar-4: 2D].
Langley, Dallas m. Hammann, Elizabeth on 66-May-10 [66-Jun-21: 2B].
Langley, Hezekiah m. White, Susan P. on 66-Feb-8 [66-Feb-10: 2C].
Langley, M. Josephine m. Ross, J. T. on 68-Jun-24 [68-Jun-25: 2B].
Langmaid, James Nelson d. on 67-Jul-11 [67-Jul-17: 2C].
Langsdale, Margaret (29 yrs.) d. on 70-Dec-25 [70-Dec-26: 2C].
Langville, Mary Ella (3 yrs.) d. on 68-Jan-24 [68-Jan-27: 2C].
Langville, Sarah Elizabeth (56 yrs.) d. on 66-Jun-22 [66-Jun-23: 2B].
Langville, Willie F. (2 yrs., 1 mo.) d. on 66-Jan-18 of Diptheria [66-Jan-20: 2C].
Lanier, Margaret S. d. on 70-Nov-5 [70-Nov-7: 2B].
Lanigan, John m. Worden, Annie on 68-Nov-25 [68-Dec-7: 2C].
Lanigan, Mary (35 yrs., 10 mos.) d. on 66-Dec-13 [66-Dec-18: 2B].
Lankford, Harriet (68 yrs.) d. on 70-Feb-4 [70-Feb-5: 2C].
Lankford, Martha A. (70 yrs.) d. on 69-Apr-19 [69-Apr-21: 2C].
Lankford, Ruth (19 yrs.) d. on 67-Jul-4 Murdered (Shooting) [67-Jul-6: 4C].
Lankford, Thomas (2 yrs., 11 mos.) d. on 68-Oct-27 [68-Oct-28: 2B].
Lankfort, Elizabeth (16 yrs., 11 mos.) d. on 66-Apr-18 [66-Apr-19: 2B].
Lannan, Annie m. Shea, Thomas F. on 66-May-13 [66-May-19: 2B].
Lannan, William m. Emich, Marcella on 70-Dec-27 [70-Dec-28: 2C].
Lanpher, Annie E. m. Cooke, S. F. on 66-Oct-25 [66-Oct-29: 2B; 66-Oct-30: 2B].
Lanpher, John (19 yrs.) d. on 70-Feb-18 [70-Feb-19: 2B].
Lanpher, John W. (45 yrs.) d. on 68-Nov-8 [68-Nov-9: 2B].
Lanpher, Maggie m. Brown, George on 67-Mar-18 [67-Mar-28: 2B].
Lanpher, Margaret (40 yrs.) d. on 69-Apr-12 [69-Apr-24: 2B].
Lansdale, Frank Scott (5 yrs.) d. on 68-Nov-25 [68-Nov-26: 2B].
Lansdowne, G. E. S. m. Parks, Leanora B. on 66-Dec-5 [66-Dec-8: 2B].
Lant, Martha m. Robinson, John E. on 70-Nov-16 [70-Nov-29: 2C].
Lantz, Charles m. Young, Kate on 69-Nov-9 [69-Nov-14: 2B].
Lantz, Elizabeth (70 yrs.) d. on 67-Jan-16 [67-Jan-28: 2C].
Lantz, J. Max m. Murndorff, Kate on 66-Mar-15 [66-Mar-17: 2B].
Lantz, Joseph (57 yrs.) d. on 66-Mar-20 [66-Mar-21: 2C].
Lantz, Mary Catherine (9 yrs.) d. on 69-Jun-6 [69-Jun-8: 2B].
Lapeyre, Jacques (39 yrs.) d. on 68-May-11 [68-May-12: 2B].
Laporte, Clara m. Holtz, George on 68-May-1 [68-May-6: 2B].
LaPorte, Emma L. m. Taylor, James J. W. on 70-Oct-4 [70-Oct-11: 2B].
LaPorte, Henry, Jr. m. Meseke, Mollie L. on 67-Aug-22 [67-Aug-30: 2B].
LaPorte, Will H. m. Heinzman, Lou H. on 70-Jun-20 [70-Jun-28: 2C].
Laragy, John T. (2 mos.) d. on 68-Oct-18 [68-Oct-19: 2B].
Lare, Francis D. m. Hissey, Lida on 69-Dec-16 [69-Dec-18: 2B].
Lare, Lewis G. m. Foster, Rachel on 66-Nov-15 [66-Nov-20: 2B].
Large, Charles A. m. Hoff, Augusta F. on 67-Aug-1 [67-Aug-5: 2B].
Larkin, Bernard Thomas (1 yr., 3 mos.) d. on 69-Jan-14 [69-Jan-16: 2C].
Larkin, Eugenie Beauregard (7 yrs., 2 mos.) d. on 68-Jul-24 of Heart hypertrophy [68-Jul-25:

2B].
Larkin, J. Milton Asbury (35 yrs.) d. on 65-Jun-27 of Consumption [66-Apr-4: 2C].
Larkin, John Jacob (11 yrs.) d. on 68-Jan-13 of Whooping cough [68-Jan-15: 2C].
Larkin, Michael (49 yrs.) d. on 68-Dec-13 [68-Dec-14: 2C].
Larkin, Sarah V. m. Hickman, Frank J. on 66-Jun-28 [66-Jun-30: 2B].
Larkin, Thomas (53 yrs.) d. on 69-Jan-1 [69-Jan-2: 2C].
Larkin, Thomas m. Craton, Kate on 66-Sep-6 [66-Sep-8: 2B].
Larkin, William D. F. (17 yrs.) d. on 68-Feb-9 [68-Feb-11: 2C].
Larmour, J. Warrell m. Miller, Lou K. on 67-Jul-2 [67-Jul-6: 2B; 67-Jul-8: 2C].
Larmour, John m. Cullum, Harriet J. on 66-Feb-1 [66-Feb-3: 2C].
Larmour, Joseph (14 yrs.) d. on 70-Jul-6 Drowned [70-Jul-7: 1H].
Larmour, Lou Miller d. on 67-Aug-20 [67-Aug-21: 2B].
Larmour, Margaret m. Williams, William on 69-Nov-30 [69-Dec-14: 2C].
Larmour, Robert B. m. Grothouse, Mary C. on 67-Oct-3 [67-Oct-4: 2B].
Larmour, W. B. m. Moffitt, Jennie on 68-Feb-25 [68-Feb-27: 2C].
Laroque, Edward (18 yrs.) d. on 68-Sep-18 [68-Sep-19: 2B].
Laroque, Eugenie d. on 69-Mar-11 [69-Mar-12: 2C].
Laroque, Mathilde Marie (15 yrs.) d. on 70-Apr-27 [70-Apr-28: 2B].
Larrabee, Daniel m. Clabaugh, Janet on 69-Jun-10 [69-Jun-11: 2C].
Larrabee, Harrison C. m. Turley, Louise B. on 68-Sep-30 [68-Oct-2: 2B].
Larsh, Silas, Dr. (62 yrs.) d. on 66-Apr-26 [66-Apr-28: 2A].
Last, Mary d. on 67-Jul-6 [67-Jul-8: 1G].
Latch, Sarah d. on 70-Mar-14 [70-Mar-22: 2C].
Latchford, Alice m. Fort, Thomas on 69-Jun-20 [69-Jun-24: 2C].
Latchford, Jane (49 yrs.) d. on 68-Oct-22 [68-Oct-24: 2B].
Latchford, John (17 yrs.) d. on 70-Dec-22 [70-Dec-22: 2B].
Latchford, Lewis m. Snyder, Maggie E. on 69-May-16 [69-May-29: 2B].
Latchford, Margaret (37 yrs.) d. on 67-Feb-4 [67-Feb-5: 2C].
Latchford, Mary (75 yrs.) d. on 70-Apr-9 of Pheumonia [70-Apr-11: 2B].
Latchford, Mary A. (41 yrs.) d. on 68-Aug-27 [68-Aug-29: 2B].
Latchford, Mollie J. m. Carter, Joseph F. on 66-Jan-16 [66-Jan-18: 2C].
Latchuem, John J. m. Aveline, Jane E. on 66-Feb-20 [66-Mar-22: 2B].
Latham, George T. (1 yr., 11 mos.) d. on 68-Jun-23 [68-Jun-24: 2B].
Latham, Sarah R. m. White, Charles E. on 68-Oct-13 [68-Oct-17: 2B].
Lathe, Emma C. m. Curry, Daniel C. on 70-Apr-20 [70-Apr-22: 2C].
Latimer, Charles W. m. Cooper, Virginia on 69-Apr-7 [69-Apr-8: 2C].
Latimer, Fanny (1 yr., 4 mos.) d. on 68-Aug-31 [68-Sep-2: 2A].
Latimer, James B., Col. (77 yrs.) d. on 69-Jul-12 [69-Jul-14: 1H, 2D].
Latimer, Priscilla d. on 68-Mar-3 [68-Mar-4: 2C].
Latrobe, Charles H. m. Robinson, Rosa Wirt on 69-Dec-14 [69-Dec-23: 2B].
Latrobe, Henry, Jr. m. Meseke, Mollie E. on 67-Aug-22 [67-Aug-29: 2B].
Latrobe, Kate m. Weston, Cornelius on 67-Jul-8 [67-Jul-11: 2C].
Latrobe, Lettie G. d. [67-May-23: 2C].
Latrobe, Mary E. m. Onderdonk, Henry on 68-Dec-17 [68-Dec-22: 2C].
LaTrobe, Rosa Wirt d. on 70-Jul-12 [70-Jul-13: 2C; 70-Jul-14: 2B].
Latsch, John B. m. Fusting, Sarah A. on 68-Apr-16 [68-Apr-30: 2B].
Latta, Eliza Jane (42 yrs.) d. on 67-Sep-24 [67-Sep-26: 2B].
Latta, John (54 yrs., 9 mos.) d. on 70-May-10 [70-May-12: 2B].
Latta, Samuel M. m. Duhurst, Anna S. on 68-May-14 [68-May-16: 2A].
Lattimore, Mary F. (23 yrs.) d. on 69-Jan-1 [69-Jan-4: 2C].
Laub, John d. on 69-Feb-28 of Suicide (Poisoning) [69-Feb-10: 1F; 69-Mar-30: 1G].
Laudenslager, Eliza (34 yrs., 5 mos.) d. on 70-Apr-23 [70-Apr-26: 2B].
Lauder, Sophia M. (61 yrs.) d. on 70-Jun-18 [70-Jun-20: 2B].
Lauderman, Adeline m. Kellogg, W. L. H. on 63-Nov-12 [66-Oct-23: 2B].
Lauer, Catherine m. Benson, Randolph S. on 68-Jun-24 [68-Jun-26: 2B].

Lauer, Ella (3 yrs., 3 mos.) d. on 70-Apr-12 [70-Apr-19: 2B].
Lauer, John m. Conoway, Mary M. [70-May-24: 2C].
Lauer, Lewis (53 yrs.) d. on 69-Feb-12 [69-Feb-13: 2C].
Lauer, Lilly m. Fuerth, W. G. on 69-Aug-11 [69-Aug-12: 2C; 69-Aug-13: 2C].
Lauer, Martha Ann (44 yrs.) d. on 69-Jul-3 [69-Jul-7: 2C].
Lauer, Mary Eliza d. on 70-Oct-24 [70-Oct-25: 2B].
Laughflin, Richard m. Ball, Annie on 69-Sep-23 [69-Apr-22: 2B].
Laughlin, Clara (3 yrs., 7 mos.) d. on 66-Jun-28 [66-Jun-29: 2C].
Laughlin, Jennie Miller (1 yr., 7 mos.) d. on 66-May-23 of Scarlet fever [66-May-26: 2B].
Laughlin, Nettie m. Simpson, D. T. on 69-Nov-15 [69-Nov-27: 2B].
Laureen, Ella B. m. Rutledge, William H. M. on 70-Dec-13 [70-Dec-14: 2C].
Laurence, Bettie m. James, William W. on 66-Dec-15 [66-Dec-18: 2B].
Laurence, Jennie Webb m. Farrar, A. E. on 70-Aug-7 [70-Aug-16: 2C].
Laurenson, Margaretta m. Lackey, M. F. on 69-Oct-26 [69-Nov-6: 2B].
Laurenson, Sallie R. m. Monmonier, J. Carroll on 69-Jan-14 [69-Jan-21: 2C].
Lauster, Anna E. m. Hochadel, James on 66-Dec-16 [66-Dec-19: 2B].
Lautenbach, Robert m. Nason, Eudora on 68-Jan-7 [68-Jan-13: 2C].
Lauver, Milton A. m. Stansfield, Helen C on 66-Nov-29 [66-Dec-4: 2D].
Lavendar, Lizzie m. Bullock, J. J. [69-Feb-24: 2C].
Lavender, James m. Carson, Mary on 70-Dec-15 [70-Dec-17: 2B].
Law, Annie J. m. Welsh, D. H. on 70-Feb-7 [70-Mar-1: 2C].
Law, Elizabeth D. m. Spear, James O. on 68-Jun-10 [68-Jun-12: 2B].
Law, James S. (62 yrs.) d. on 69-Oct-22 [69-Oct-23: 2B].
Law, Mary Howard m. Murdoch, John on 69-Nov-10 [69-Nov-13: 2B].
Law, Susanna m. Faulkner, Thomas on 66-May-1 [66-May-3: 2C].
Lawder, Carrie A. m. Seneca, Robert on 67-Dec-26 [68-Jan-1: 2C].
Lawder, Samuel M. m. Crabbe, Gertie L. on 66-Feb-1 [66-Feb-10: 2C].
Lawder, Walter Barkman (2 mos.) d. on 67-Feb-9 [67-Feb-11: 2C].
Lawkins, T. Lewis m. Middleton, Matilda W. on 68-Jan-23 [68-Jan-27: 2C].
Lawless, R. J. m. Smith, Mary A. on 69-Oct-12 [69-Oct-23: 2B].
Lawn, Catherine d. [70-Jun-25: 2B].
Lawn, Edward (40 yrs.) d. on 69-Nov-9 [69-Nov-10: 2C].
Lawrason, Annie Elizabeth m. Taylor, Thomas on 66-Aug-30 [66-Sep-3: 2C].
Lawrason, William W. (56 yrs.) d. on 70-Jan-7 [70-Jan-11: 2C].
Lawrence, Adela m. Keidel, Henry on 69-Jun-17 [69-Jun-19: 2B].
Lawrence, Ann L. (72 yrs.) d. on 68-Apr-13 [68-Apr-15: 2B].
Lawrence, Daniel H., Jr., Dr. (22 yrs.) d. on 70-May-23 Drowned [70-May-25: 1G; 70-May-30: 2B].
Lawrence, Edward Reno Hurst (8 mos.) d. on 68-Aug-8 [68-Aug-11: 2B].
Lawrence, Francis Edward d. on 67-Aug-13 [67-Aug-15: 2C].
Lawrence, George W. (6 yrs.) d. [66-Aug-17: 2C].
Lawrence, Kate M. m. Duvall, S. Turner on 68-Sep-22 [68-Sep-25: 2B].
Lawrence, Lulia A. m. Goodwin, Charles on 69-Oct-27 [69-Oct-28: 2C].
Lawrence, M. S. m. Morton, S. R. on 68-Nov-30 [68-Dec-15: 2C].
Lawrence, Margaret m. Spence, Joseph on 70-Dec-1 [70-Dec-12: 2C].
Lawrence, Mary A. m. Coriell, Alvin on 69-May-18 [69-Dec-4: 2C].
Lawrence, Mary Clare (16 yrs., 3 mos.) d. on 69-Jan-18 of Consumption [69-Jan-20: 2C].
Lawrence, Mary Louise m. Brown, W. Judson on 70-Jun-9 [70-Jun-13: 2C].
Lawrence, Richard D. (46 yrs.) d. on 66-Dec-29 [67-Feb-5: 2C].
Lawrence, Richard H. m. Jones, Laura on 70-Dec-15 [70-Dec-24: 2B].
Lawrence, Sarah A. (60 yrs.) d. on 70-Jul-9 [70-Jul-16: 2B].
Lawrenson, Olivia J. m. Correll, James M. on 69-Dec-2 [69-Dec-7: 2C].
Laws, Ada A. m. Lee, R. C. on 66-Feb-7 [66-Feb-28: 2C].
Laws, Joseph Quinton d. on 67-Sep-23 [67-Sep-27: 2C].
Lawson, Sarah (90 yrs.) d. on 68-Oct-18 [68-Oct-29: 2C].

Lawton, Ellie m. Norwood, Thomas on 70-May-26 [70-May-30: 2B].
Lawton, Robert B. m. Butler, Mary C. on 66-May-30 [66-Jun-5: 2B].
Lawton, Sarah (40 yrs.) d. on 67-Sep-27 [67-Sep-28: 2A].
Lawton, Walter E. m. Reed, Adele Louise on 70-Jan-1 [70-Jan-4: 2C].
Lay, Annie M. m. Hook, M. R. on 66-Mar-17 [66-Mar-20: 2C].
Layer, Louisa F. m. Woolf, Daniel F. on 68-Mar-5 [68-Mar-12: 2B].
Layfield, Ella Virginia m. Elliott, William H. on 66-Oct-23 [66-Oct-26: 2B].
Layfield, Lillie E. (19 yrs.) d. on 69-Jun-24 [69-Jun-29: 2C].
Layfield, William W. (58 yrs., 1 mo.) d. on 66-Oct-27 [66-Nov-2: 2B].
Layre, Wilhelmina m. Wagner, Casper on 66-Oct-9 [66-Oct-26: 2B].
Layton, Georgianna B. m. Gregory, James C. on 65-Mar-5 [66-Mar-5: 2B].
Layton, James H. m. Chiveral, Emma J. on 70-Nov-22 [70-Nov-24: 2B].
Lazear, Frances B. d. on 67-Jan-24 [67-Jan-31: 2C].
Le Grand, Sarah d. on 69-Oct-23 [69-Oct-27: 2B].
Lea, William, Jr. m. Bentley, Sarah Brooke on 67-Jun-20 [67-Jun-22: 2B].
Leach, Allie m. Edkins, Joseph W. on 66-Feb-20 [66-Apr-18: 2B].
Leach, Anna R. m. Hersh, Charles S. on 69-Aug-11 [69-Aug-25: 2C].
Leach, C. M. m. Foster, Emma on 68-Dec-3 [68-Dec-5: 2C].
Leach, Catherine (62 yrs.) d. on 70-Sep-26 [70-Sep-28: 2B].
Leach, Edward (1 yr.) d. on 69-Oct-31 [69-Nov-2: 2B].
Leach, Granville Rusk (5 mos.) d. on 70-Aug-3 [70-Aug-4: 2C].
Leach, James, Jr. (30 yrs.) d. on 66-Dec-1 [66-Dec-3: 2B].
Leach, James Henry (1 yr., 4 mos.) d. on 68-Aug-16 [68-Aug-17: 2B].
Leach, Kate m. Dabour, John on 68-Nov-26 [68-Dec-2: 2C].
Leach, Lidia V. m. Cole, John T. on 66-Sep-18 [66-Oct-1: 2B].
Leach, Mary A. m. Scholl, William R. on 70-Aug-23 [70-Sep-13: 2B].
Leach, Mary Ann (54 yrs.) d. on 66-Mar-26 of Consumption [66-Mar-27: 2B].
Leaf, Emma J. m. Spies, Edward on 70-Mar-24 [70-Mar-29: 2B].
Leaf, George m. Dennis, Elenor on 68-Oct-29 [68-Nov-3: 2B].
League, Angeline A. d. on 70-Sep-2 [70-Sep-3: 2B].
League, Columbus (59 yrs.) d. on 66-Jul-1 [66-Jul-2: 2B].
League, Elizabeth (64 yrs., 3 mos.) d. on 66-Dec-30 of Heart disease [67-Jan-1: 2C; 67-Jan-2: 2C].
League, Ella m. Williams, John on 70-Jul-5 [70-Jul-7: 2B].
League, Georgette m. Paynter, John C. on 67-Jun-13 [67-Jun-19: 2B].
League, Sarah Ann (54 yrs.) d. on 70-Jul-6 [70-Jul-7: 2C].
Leahy, Mary d. on 68-Oct-10 [68-Oct-12: 2B].
Leak, Virginia m. Hemmell, John C. on 66-Apr-3 [66-Apr-26: 2B].
Leaken, John d. [67-Nov-18: 2B].
Leakin, Margaret (80 yrs.) d. on 68-Jan-23 [68-Jan-24: 2D; 68-Jan-25: 2B].
Leakin, Sheppard C., Gen. (78 yrs.) d. on 67-Nov-20 [67-Nov-21: 2C; 67-Nov-22: 1F, 2C].
Leaming, James R. m. Strobel, Kate Lawton on 68-Nov-5 [68-Nov-9: 2B].
Leaming, Reuben H. m. Bowers, Lavinia on 69-Apr-20 [69-May-21: 2C].
Leamy, Jennings d. on 66-May-7 [66-May-11: 2B].
Leanard, Anna Frances m. Monro, Samuel on 68-Dec-21 [68-Dec-28: 2B].
Leans, Lou M. m. Justis, J. Chris. on 68-Nov-12 [68-Nov-19: 2C].
Leary, Alice (34 yrs.) d. on 68-Feb-25 [68-Feb-27: 2C].
Leary, Andrew Wells (1 yr., 10 mos.) d. on 68-Mar-25 [68-Mar-26: 2B; 68-Mar-27: 2C; 69-Apr-21: 2C; 69-Apr-22: 2B].
Leary, Cornelius L. L. m. Horton, Rebecca E. on 66-Jan-16 [66-Jan-18: 2C].
Leary, Daniel d. on 67-Oct-2 [67-Oct-3: 2B].
Leary, Ellen Louise m. Robie, James on 68-Oct-14 [69-Jan-9: 2C].
Leary, Emma m. Barnes, Robert C., Jr. on 70-Jan-6 [70-Jan-7: 2F].
Leary, George Sims (2 yrs., 11 mos.) d. on 69-Apr-20 [69-Apr-21: 2C; 69-Apr-22: 2B].
Leary, Jennie m. Mallster, William T. on 70-Feb-1 [70-Feb-8: 2C; 70-Feb-15: 2C].

Leary, John (2 yrs., 9 mos.) d. on 69-May-24 [69-May-26: 2C].
Leary, Kate m. Jewell, Tryon J. M. on 66-Mar-8 [66-Mar-9: 2B].
Leary, Martha A. (61 yrs.) d. on 69-Apr-11 [69-Apr-12: 2A; 69-Apr-13: 2B].
Leary, Norah (6 yrs.) d. on 68-Jul-9 [68-Jul-10: 2C].
Leatherbury, Elizabeth K. m. Boston, J. William on 68-Aug-27 [68-Aug-29: 2B].
Leatherwood, Mary A. m. Dorsey, William A. on 67-Nov-26 [67-Dec-3: 2C].
Leatrick, [son] (8 yrs.) d. on 70-Dec-22 of Lamp explosion [70-Dec-23: 4E].
Leavett, Florence V. m. Stevenson, Samuel E. on 70-Dec-6 [70-Dec-14: 2C].
Leavitt, Victoria C. m. Wilkins, William A. on 66-Mar-21 [66-Mar-28: 2C].
Lebark, Maria H. (70 yrs.) d. on 66-Sep-21 [66-Sep-22: 2B].
Leber, W. Frank m. Fuller, A. Octavia on 69-Oct-19 [69-Oct-22: 2B].
LeBron, Mary Elizabeth (37 yrs.) d. on 68-Nov-12 [68-Nov-13: 2C].
LeBrou, Joseph A., Capt. (57 yrs.) d. on 67-Aug-25 [67-Aug-27: 2B; 67-Aug-28: 1G, 2B].
LeBrun, Henry m. Hance, Julia on 66-Apr-25 [68-Jan-31: 2C].
Lecates, Hester P. m. Sclote, Augustus on 69-Dec-29 [70-Jan-14: 2C].
Leche, William Augustus (16 yrs.) d. on 70-Aug-26 of Gunshot wound [70-Sep-1: 2B].
Leckie, Robert (56 yrs.) d. on 66-Jul-3 [66-Jul-6: 2B].
LeCompte, Lake Durst (4 yrs., 3 mos.) d. on 70-Aug-21 [70-Aug-22: 2C].
LeCompte, Margaret Ann d. on 68-Aug-1 [68-Aug-7: 2B].
Leddon, Fannie A. (25 yrs.) d. on 68-Dec-15 of Consumption [68-Dec-16: 2C].
Leddon, Mary J. m. Morrow, William H. on 70-Feb-6 [70-Feb-12: 2B; 70-Feb-14: 2C].
Leddon, Susanna R. m. Jacobs, Thomas E. on 68-Feb-27 [68-Mar-2: 2B].
Leddy, Mary Catherine (28 yrs.) d. on 66-Jul-16 [66-Jul-21: 2C].
Ledley, Alexander D. m. Mansfield, Marceline on 66-Aug-23 [66-Aug-27: 2B].
Ledley, Arthur Stuart (6 mos.) d. on 68-Nov-3 [68-Nov-9: 2B].
Ledley, Augusta m. Hammond, Joshua on 69-Jun-29 [69-Jun-30: 2C].
Ledley, Benjamin P. m. Wilson, Mary A. on 66-Aug-16 [66-Sep-28: 2B].
Ledley, Daniel A. (3 yrs., 4 mos.) d. on 68-Jan-3 [68-Jan-7: 2C].
Ledley, Elizabeth (75 yrs.) d. on 67-Nov-12 [67-Nov-14: 2C].
Ledley, John C. m. Wiggins, Amanda C. on 69-Aug-30 [69-Sep-1: 2B].
Lednum, Ary May (7 mos.) d. on 70-Mar-26 [70-Mar-29: 2C].
Lednum, James F. m. Frizzell, Sarah J. on 68-Nov-19 [68-Nov-24: 2C].
Lednum, William Dallas m. Ervin, Ann on 68-Dec-28 [69-Mar-16: 2C].
Ledsinger, John H. (34 yrs., 5 mos.) d. on 70-Aug-19 [70-Aug-22: 2C].
Ledwith, Mary (92 yrs.) d. on 68-Feb-17 [68-Feb-18: 2C].
Lee, Abraham B. (10 mos.) d. on 68-Jul-5 [68-Jul-7: 2B].
Lee, Alfred G. m. Herbert, Fannie on 66-Oct-18 [66-Oct-23: 2B].
Lee, Alice May (3 yrs., 9 mos.) d. on 70-May-22 [70-May-23: 2B].
Lee, Amanda Hulse (4 mos.) d. on 69-Jun-23 [69-Jun-26: 2B].
Lee, B. Frank m. Ford, Kate E. on 67-Mar-14 [67-Mar-16: 2B].
Lee, Belinda m. Townsend, Joseph C. on 69-Jun-3 [69-Jun-4: 2C].
Lee, Bessie m. Sherman, H. Gibson on 69-Dec-14 [69-Dec-20: 2C].
Lee, Bettie d. on 70-Nov-4 [70-Nov-7: 2B].
Lee, Caroline Elizabeth (1 mo.) d. on 69-Jun-13 of Sore throat [69-Jun-18: 2C].
Lee, Caroline Virginia (4 mos.) d. on 68-Jul-16 [68-Jul-21: 2C].
Lee, Catey (2 yrs., 3 mos.) d. on 70-Mar-9 of Scarlet fever [70-Mar-10: 2C].
Lee, Charles O'Donnell m. Jenkins, Matilda Dale on 69-Nov-11 [69-Nov-18: 2C].
Lee, Charles T. m. Higdon, Mary E. on 67-Feb-28 [67-Mar-5: 2C].
Lee, Edward (66 yrs.) d. on 67-Nov-7 [67-Nov-8: 2C].
Lee, Edward (8 mos.) d. on 66-Apr-28 [66-May-1: 2A].
Lee, Edward D. m. Lloyd, Anna Elizabeth on 68-Jun-2 [68-Jun-10: 2B].
Lee, Eleanor (75 yrs.) d. on 69-Apr-16 [69-Apr-27: 2C].
Lee, Elijah B. (32 yrs.) d. on 67-Aug-27 [67-Aug-29: 2B].
Lee, Elijah W. m. Wilson, Jennie on 70-Nov-9 [70-Dec-10: 2B].
Lee, Ella Maria (3 yrs., 8 mos.) d. on 66-Sep-10 [66-Sep-12: 2A].

Lee, Ellen m. Joyce, Charles on 70-Mar-31 [70-Apr-2: 2A].
Lee, Elmira F. (4 yrs., 9 mos.) d. on 70-Oct-28 [70-Nov-10: 2C].
Lee, Emory G. m. King, Mary on 70-Feb-17 [70-Feb-25: 2C].
Lee, Fannie (29 yrs.) d. on 68-Mar-24 [69-Mar-27: 2B].
Lee, Florence (5 mos.) d. on 66-Oct-5 [66-Oct-6: 2A].
Lee, Frances m. Johns, Leonard on 66-Apr-17 [66-Apr-27: 2C].
Lee, Frances Anna m. Wilson, William G. on 67-Apr-15 [67-Apr-18: 2B].
Lee, Frank Waters (13 yrs.) d. on 70-Jan-19 of Pneumonia [70-Jan-20: 2C; 70-Jan-21: 2C; 70-Jan-22: 2C].
Lee, Freddie W. (2 yrs., 3 mos.) d. on 70-Oct-12 [70-Nov-10: 2C].
Lee, George A. m. Weaver, Elizabeth A. on 68-Feb-18 [68-Mar-5: 2C].
Lee, Hannah (64 yrs.) d. on 69-Jun-11 [69-Jun-12: 2B].
Lee, Harry (22 yrs.) d. on 69-Aug-5 Drowned [69-Aug-6: 1G; 69-Aug-9: 1G; 69-Aug-10: 1G].
Lee, Henry A. m. Whittington, Eveline W. on 68-Oct-6 [68-Oct-28: 2B].
Lee, Ida Amelia (4 yrs., 10 mos.) d. on 66-Jul-5 [66-Jul-7: 2C].
Lee, James H. (30 yrs.) d. Drowned [68-Dec-23: 4D].
Lee, James Leonard (5 mos.) d. on 67-Sep-23 [67-Sep-24: 2A].
Lee, Jennie m. Brown, George on 70-Jan-17 [70-Jun-18: 2B].
Lee, Jesse W. m. White, Emeline on 66-Jan-25 [66-Jan-29: 2B].
Lee, John (22 yrs.) d. on 66-Jul-17 [66-Jul-20: 2D].
Lee, John m. Noble, Eliza A. on 66-Apr-17 [66-Apr-28: 2A].
Lee, John L. m. Kepler, Mollie on 68-Nov-18 [68-Nov-21: 2C].
Lee, John T. (24 yrs.) d. on 69-Apr-29 [69-May-1: 2B].
Lee, John W. m. Sinclair, Mary A. on 66-Sep-4 [66-Sep-17: 2B].
Lee, Joseph E. (40 yrs.) d. on 70-Jul-21 of Heatstroke [70-Jul-22: 2C; 70-Jul-23: 4E].
Lee, Josephine (6 mos.) d. on 69-Dec-22 [69-Dec-23: 2B].
Lee, Josephine m. Price, Bruce on 70-Apr-20 [70-Apr-26: 2B].
Lee, Laura V. m. Van Order, David G. on 67-Jul-11 [67-Sep-15: 2B].
Lee, Lillian May (1 yr., 8 mos.) d. on 70-Dec-5 [70-Dec-6: 2C].
Lee, Lizzie T. d. on 70-Feb-26 [70-Feb-28: 2C].
Lee, Lizzie T. m. Holdsworth, George H. on 67-Nov-28 [67-Dec-5: 2C].
Lee, Maggie m. Greenwood, Walter on 67-Jun-27 [67-Jul-3: 2B].
Lee, Maggie J. m. Reed, Michael H. on 69-Aug-18 [69-Aug-23: 2C].
Lee, Mary E. (50 yrs.) d. on 70-Feb-3 [70-Feb-5: 2B].
Lee, Mary S. m. Allwell, Stephen S. on 69-Aug-22 [69-Sep-2: 2B].
Lee, R. C. m. Laws, Ada A. on 66-Feb-7 [66-Feb-28: 2C].
Lee, Ralph (79 yrs.) d. on 70-Dec-1 [70-Dec-3: 2B].
Lee, Richard B. (27 yrs.) d. on 69-Mar-1 [69-Mar-2: 2C].
Lee, Richard Henry m. Wilson, Isabella George on 68-Oct-27 [68-Oct-29: 2B].
Lee, Sarah (82 yrs.) d. on 70-Sep-27 [70-Sep-28: 2B].
Lee, Sarah Ann (2 yrs., 2 mos.) d. on 67-Sep-9 [67-Sep-10: 2B].
Lee, Sarah Jane m. Carroll, George on 67-Jul-21 [67-Jul-29: 2D].
Lee, Stephen L. (65 yrs.) d. on 70-Dec-6 of Consumption [70-Dec-10: 2C].
Lee, Susannah (83 yrs.) d. on 69-Nov-21 [69-Dec-11: 2B].
Lee, Susie A. m. Stephens, Charles L. on 70-Feb-1 [70-Feb-8: 2C].
Lee, William (66 yrs.) d. on 69-Sep-3 [69-Sep-4: 2B].
Lee, William T. m. Crofoot, Mary A. on 69-Sep-3 [69-Sep-7: 2B].
Leech, David (28 yrs.) d. on 67-Nov-24 [67-Nov-26: 2B].
Leech, David (5 yrs., 8 mos.) d. on 69-Nov-25 [69-Nov-26: 2D].
Leech, Emily (26 yrs.) d. on 68-Jun-20 of Brain congestion [68-Jun-23: 2B].
Leech, George T. m. Stevens, Susan S. on 69-Apr-13 [69-Apr-21: 2B].
Leech, Margaret Ann (7 mos.) d. on 69-Apr-25 [69-Apr-26: 2B].
Leech, Margaret Ann (4 mos.) d. on 70-Aug-17 [70-Aug-18: 2B].
Leech, Mary C. (65 yrs.) d. on 68-Jul-5 [68-Jul-7: 2B].
Leech, Ruth (85 yrs.) d. on 67-Dec-10 [67-Dec-12: 2B].

Leech, Thomas m. Dreibing, Marion E. on 69-May-23 [69-Oct-13: 2C].
Leech, William Henry (5 mos.) d. on 66-Mar-9 [66-Mar-10: 2B].
Leecount, Ella (48 yrs.) d. on 70-Aug-17 [70-Aug-26: 2C].
Leeden, Alice Jane m. McCaffrey, Thomas on 69-Apr-27 [69-May-11: 2B].
Leeds, Alexander m. Sheckels, Maria E. on 69-May-20 [69-May-26: 2C].
Leedy, W. Franklin m. Freeman, H. Vann on 69-Apr-1 [69-Apr-6: 2C].
Leef, Albert F. m. Elliott, Fannie on 70-Aug-1 [70-Aug-3: 2C].
Leef, Charles G. m. Otter, Mary H. on 66-Apr-24 [66-May-1: 2A].
Leef, Harry Milton (1 yr., 1 mo.) d. on 70-Sep-5 [70-Sep-7: 2B].
Leef, Henry G. m. Miller, Amelia M. on 66-Mar-20 [66-Mar-28: 2C].
Leefe, Henrietta A. m. Corame, William H. on 69-Apr-22 [69-May-4: 2B].
Leeke, Henry (73 yrs.) d. on 66-Aug-16 [66-Aug-18: 2B].
Leeke, J. Aldgate m. Weaver, Elizabeth Thirkel on 66-May-29 [66-Jun-6: 2B].
Leeke, Lizzie (1 yr.) d. on 67-Jul-31 [67-Aug-2: 2C].
Leeke, Willie H. (7 yrs., 3 mos.) d. on 68-Jul-15 [68-Jul-16: 2C].
Lees, William (63 yrs.) d. on 70-Mar-26 [70-Mar-28: 2B; 70-Mar-29: 2C].
Leese, Martin W. m. Eckloff, Mary A. on 70-Sep-15 [70-Sep-23: 2C].
Leeson, Bertha (9 mos.) d. on 67-Nov-30 of Brain fever [67-Dec-2: 2C].
LeFaivre, Ferdinand (29 yrs.) d. on 67-Apr-2 [67-Apr-3: 2B].
LeFaivre, Gustave J. m. Phelan, Mary A. on 70-Oct-20 [70-Oct-24: 2B].
Lefebvre, Edward C. m. Blackburn, Emma L. on 69-Feb-4 [69-Feb-13: 2C].
LeFevre, Charles (65 yrs.) d. on 67-Nov-17 [67-Nov-18: 2B; 67-Nov-19: 2C].
LeFevre, Laura Virginia (10 mos.) d. on 67-Apr-22 [67-Aug-23: 2B].
LeFevre, Mary E. (26 yrs., 2 mos.) d. on 67-Dec-9 [67-Dec-10: 2B; 67-Dec-11: 2B].
LeFevre, Sarah R. m. Kipp, John G. on 70-Jan-19 [70-Apr-25: 2B].
LeFevre, Willie (1 yr., 4 mos.) d. on 66-Jul-9 [66-Jul-10: 2C].
Leffler, Charles H. (31 yrs.) d. on 70-Jul-18 of Heatstroke [70-Jul-20: 4C, 2C].
Leffler, Virginia m. Egerton, J. Chesley on 69-Nov-17 [69-Nov-22: 2C].
Legg, John m. Dyott, Sarah A. on 69-Dec-22 [69-Dec-23: 2B].
Legg, Joseph m. Parker, Elizabeth on 68-Oct-29 [68-Oct-31: 2B].
Legg, Mary Ann (81 yrs.) d. on 69-Oct-30 [69-Nov-1: 2C].
Legg, Matilda E. (1 yr., 4 mos.) d. on 70-Oct-12 [70-Oct-14: 2B].
Legg, Thomas M. m. Wright, E. Lou on 68-May-25 [68-Jun-9: 2B].
Leggett, Carrie H. m. Whitmarsh, Henry C. on 66-Apr-16 [66-Apr-18: 2B].
Lehman, George A. m. Rhodes, Sarah J. on 70-May-12 [70-May-14: 2A].
Lehman, Henry m. Douglass, Catherine C. on 69-Aug-2 [69-Oct-14: 2C].
Lehman, Josephine E. m. Phillips, Albert on 66-Oct-4 [66-Oct-22: 2C].
Lehman, Robert m. Ridgely, Hettie T. on 66-Mar-29 [66-Mar-31: 2C].
Lehmen, Jacob S. m. Orndorff, Rachel S. on 70-Feb-17 [70-Mar-14: 2C].
Lehmen, Mary E. (48 yrs., 4 mos.) d. on 69-Oct-6 [69-Oct-7: 2B; 69-Oct-8: 2B].
Lehnert, Ernest m. Mullmyer, Minnie on 70-Nov-10 [70-Nov-11: 2B].
Lehr, Sophia m. Everett, Thomas H. on 68-Aug-2 [68-Aug-3: 2B].
Lehr, William d. on 70-Jan-8 Murdered (Shooting) [70-Jan-10: 1G].
Lehrs, Mary Ann (70 yrs.) d. on 70-Jul-5 [70-Jul-6: 2C].
Lehrs, Olga Alexandrina (5 yrs.) d. on 68-Jul-3 [68-Aug-12: 2C; 68-Aug-13: 2B].
Leib, E. Trego (36 yrs.) d. on 68-Apr-25 [68-Apr-28: 2B].
Leibin, Amelia m. Facey, Henry J. on 66-Sep-20 [66-Sep-25: 2B].
Leiman, Emily J. m. Welch, John W. on 66-Mar-12 [66-Mar-14: 2B].
Leimann, Conrad (50 yrs., 1 mo.) d. [68-May-22: 2C].
Lein, Harry B. m. Brown, Nellie on 69-Jul-8 [69-Jul-12: 2C].
Leinss, Annie E. (8 mos.) d. on 67-Jun-2 [67-Jun-4: 2A].
Leinsz, Mary (38 yrs.) d. on 70-Aug-9 [70-Aug-10: 2B; 70-Aug-11: 2C].
Leisen, Julian Alphonsus (3 yrs., 9 mos.) d. on 70-Aug-13 [70-Aug-15: 2C].
Leisenring, John G. Morris d. on 67-Jan-24 [67-Jan-25: 2C].
Leisenring, William M. Kemp d. on 68-Feb-24 [68-Feb-25: 2C].

Leishear, Adolphus m. Thurston, Elizabeth on 70-Mar-30 [70-Apr-16: 2B].
Leishear, Elijah (74 yrs.) d. on 65-Dec-31 [66-Jan-2: 2C].
Leishear, Elijah, Jr. (37 yrs.) d. on 67-Jan-15 [67-Jan-16: 2C; 67-Jan-17: 2C].
Leishear, Maria Eliza (52 yrs., 10 mos.) d. on 67-Oct-4 [67-Oct-8: 2B].
Leishear, Mary (45 yrs.) d. on 67-Mar-2 [67-Mar-11: 2C].
Leishear, Richard H. (58 yrs.) d. on 68-Jan-21 [68-Jan-22: 2C].
Leishear, William B. m. Anderson, Nannie F. on 70-Nov-23 [70-Nov-24: 2B].
Leister, Andrew J. (4 yrs., 10 mos.) d. on 70-Mar-30 [70-Apr-1: 2B].
Leister, Israel (57 yrs.) d. on 66-Jan-26 [66-Jan-29: 2C].
Leitch, B. Frank m. Jenness, Sade J. on 67-Oct-10 [67-Oct-17: 2B].
Leitch, Edward G. (56 yrs.) d. on 68-Jun-7 [68-Jun-8: 2B].
Leitch, Edward G., Jr. m. Skinner, Laura V. on 67-Dec-31 [68-Jan-3: 2C].
Leitch, Lizzie R. m. Funkhouse, Elijah R. on 68-Jan-13 [68-Jan-16: 2C].
Leitch, Zorah m. Wells, Oliver McKee on 69-Jun-17 [69-Jun-30: 2C].
Leitz, Charles F. m. Eilsa, Maggie on 70-Jan-5 [70-Jan-25: 2C].
Leitz, Mary Catherine m. Wolf, George Louis on 70-Mar-1 [70-Mar-9: 2C].
Leland, Priscilla F. m. Purucker, J. W. on 70-Feb-27 [70-Mar-12: 2C].
LeMassena, Theodore F. m. Giese, Lillian on 70-Jun-22 [70-Jun-23: 2C].
Lemate, Henrietta W. D. m. Rodhe, Andrew on 70-May-22 [70-May-25: 2C].
Lemates, William (2 yrs., 1 mo.) d. on 68-Oct-5 [68-Oct-6: 4C, 2B].
Lemcke, Alexander R. m. Wells, Sarah J. on 68-May-6 [68-May-16: 2A].
Lemcke, Edgar Wells d. on 69-Sep-16 [69-Sep-20: 2C].
Lemcke, Mary J. m. Logemann, Henry on 66-Mar-29 [66-Apr-4: 2B].
Lemel, Sidney L. m. Shaw, John W. on 69-Nov-18 [69-Nov-20: 2B].
LeMerchant, Josina E. m. German, Thomas S. on 68-Jan-28 [68-Feb-4: 2C].
Lemmon, Andrew H., Dr. (75 yrs.) d. on 66-Jul-12 [66-Jul-16: 2C].
Lemmon, Benny Frank (2 yrs., 1 mo.) d. on 68-Oct-31 [68-Nov-4: 2C].
Lemmon, Emma Warfield m. Hobbs, Samuel A. on 66-Dec-8 [66-Dec-8: 2B].
Lemmon, Estella May (1 yr., 1 mo.) d. on 66-Dec-1 [66-Dec-3: 2B].
Lemmon, James (60 yrs.) d. on 67-Mar-7 [67-Mar-9: 2B].
Lemmon, John Edward d. on 69-Jul-29 [69-Jul-30: 2C].
Lemmon, Joseph Cromwell (1 yr., 11 mos.) d. on 66-Sep-17 [66-Sep-20: 2B].
Lemmon, Joshuine d. on 66-Oct-27 [66-Oct-30: 2B].
Lemmon, Mary G. D. (61 yrs.) d. [68-Dec-2: 2C; 68-Dec-3: 2C].
Lemmon, Mattie J. m. Stansbury, James E. on 68-Jul-23 [68-Aug-5: 2B].
Lemmon, Robert G. (37 yrs.) d. on 70-Oct-20 of Apoplexy [70-Oct-22: 2B].
Lemmon, Sarah d. on 66-Nov-7 [66-Nov-9: 2C].
Lemmon, William (67 yrs.) d. on 69-Jul-17 Kicked by horse [69-Jul-19: 1G; 69-Jul-20: 2C].
Lemmon, William A. m. Lewis, Elizabeth J. on 67-Dec-10 [68-Jan-11: 2B].
Lemmons, James J. (49 yrs.) d. on 68-Feb-10 [68-Feb-12: 2B].
Lemon, Annie m. McClaskey, Charles E. on 69-Oct-14 [69-Oct-26: 2B].
Lemon, Rosanna m. Corsey, Robert on 69-Dec-23 [69-Dec-29: 2D].
Lenard, Michael m. Tully, Ann on 67-Mar-4 [67-Mar-23: 2B].
Lenhart, George E. m. Brome, Virginia L. on 68-Jul-14 [68-Jul-20: 2B].
Lennex, Charles T. m. Southers, Mary on 69-Jun-29 [69-Jul-1: 2C].
Lennord, Ann (34 yrs.) d. on 70-Oct-31 [70-Nov-1: 2C].
Lennox, George Washington (14 yrs., 1 mo.) d. on 66-Apr-13 [66-Apr-14: 2B].
Lentz, Carrie m. Russell, F. D. on 66-Dec-20 [66-Dec-24: 2B].
Lentz, Mary (65 yrs.) d. on 67-Nov-2 [67-Nov-4: 2B].
Lentz, Peter (38 yrs.) d. on 66-May-2 [66-May-3: 2C].
Leon, Harry B. m. Brown, Nellie on 69-Jul-8 [69-Jul-10: 2B].
Leonard, Alex B. F. (28 yrs.) d. on 70-Apr-1 [70-Apr-5: 2B].
Leonard, George W. m. Weaver, Anna Carrie on 70-Jun-28 [70-Sep-12: 2B].
Leonard, John T. m. Parker, Virginia on 69-May-25 [69-May-27: 2C].
Leonard, Jonathan m. Wright, Mary F. on 69-Jan-14 [69-Feb-1: 2C].

Leonard, M. E. m. Lloyd, Edward H. on 66-May-17 [66-May-22: 2B].
Leonard, Margaret A. m. Kindig, Henry W. on 66-May-20 [66-May-22: 2B].
Leonard, Maria m. Moran, John on 68-Nov-29 [68-Dec-1: 2C].
Leonard, Michael m. Giblin, Annie Teresa on 67-Aug-4 [67-Aug-17: 2B].
Leonard, Virginia m. DeGraw, George L. on 68-Jan-1 [68-May-4: 2B].
Leonard, William T. (23 yrs.) d. on 67-Sep-12 [67-Sep-13: 2B].
Leonhardt, Henry (29 yrs., 2 mos.) d. on 67-Jul-26 [67-Jul-27: 2B].
Leport, Lucy m. Scarf, William T. on 66-Nov-12 [66-Nov-21: 2C].
Lepper, Charles V. m. Grady, Maggie on 67-Jun-13 [67-Jun-19: 2B].
Leprew, Augustus m. Pasters, Alice on 67-Mar-13 [67-Jun-11: 2B].
Lepson, Amelia D. m. Shipley, Washington on 68-Jan-14 [68-Jan-18: 2B].
Lepson, George W. m. Ricktor, Adelia S. on 67-May-14 [67-Sep-2: 2B].
Lepson, Linnie S. m. McFrederick, James on 67-Dec-19 [67-Dec-23: 2B].
Lepson, Peter (52 yrs.) d. on 70-Apr-20 [70-Apr-21: 2C; 70-Apr-22: 2C].
Lerch, Harry A. m. Barnett, Henrietta V. on 70-Feb-3 [70-Apr-16: 2B].
Lerch, Vernon Watkins (3 yrs.) d. on 66-Nov-24 [66-Nov-27: 2B].
Lertz, Theodor (10 yrs., 5 mos.) d. on 66-Oct-29 [66-Oct-30: 2B].
Leshea, Anna S. (76 yrs.) d. on 70-Apr-20 [70-Apr-23: 2B].
Leslie, James (64 yrs.) d. on 69-Jun-5 [69-Jun-7: 2B].
Leslie, John (69 yrs.) d. on 66-Oct-2 [66-Oct-3: 2B].
Lessner, Thomas Wildy (2 yrs.) d. on 68-May-11 [68-May-12: 2B].
Lester, Anna Netta (45 yrs., 2 mos.) d. on 67-Jan-1 [67-Jan-2: 2C].
Lester, Charles H. m. Shackelford, Elizabeth H. on 69-May-12 [69-May-17: 2B].
Lester, Ellen A. m. Gorsuch, Noah F. on 68-Jan-14 [68-Jan-17: 2C].
Lester, Emma J. m. Greene, Benson M. on 68-May-7 [68-May-11: 2B].
Lester, Joseph R. m. Markey, Lucy E. on 68-May-5 [68-May-11: 2B].
Lethco, William (31 yrs.) d. on 66-Jul-17 of Heatstroke [66-Jul-18: 1F].
LeTourneau, F. W. W. d. on 70-Aug-31 [70-Sep-2: 2C].
Letterer, Anne (54 yrs.) d. on 67-Feb-5 [67-Feb-6: 2C].
Letterman, Annie R. d. on 70-Dec-27 [70-Dec-29: 2C; 70-Dec-30: 2C].
Letterman, Mary D. d. on 67-Oct-30 [67-Nov-8: 2C].
Leucht, Henrietta m. Behrend, Elon on 67-Jan-17 [67-Jan-19: 2C].
Leveaux, Mathilde Felice m. Winans, Clinton on 69-Sep-16 [69-Oct-11: 2C].
Levering, Aaron (46 yrs.) d. on 67-Jan-2 [67-Jan-4: 2D].
Levering, Annie L. m. Crane, Charles T. on 67-Sep-18 [67-Sep-19: 2B].
Levering, Clinton (58 yrs.) d. on 69-Aug-23 [69-Aug-25: 2C].
Levering, Elizabeth (61 yrs.) d. on 69-Sep-16 [69-Sep-18: 2B].
Levering, Eugene (52 yrs.) d. on 70-Jun-19 [70-Jun-20: 1H, 2C; 70-Jun-21: 2C].
Levering, Eugene, Jr. m. Armstrong, Mary E. on 68-Jan-23 [68-Jan-25: 2B].
Levering, Frederick A. (54 yrs.) d. on 66-Jul-3 [66-Jul-4: 1G, 2B].
Levering, Joshua m. Keyser, Martha W. on 70-Nov-24 [70-Nov-28: 2C].
Levering, Laura (26 yrs.) d. on 68-Sep-9 [68-Sep-10: 2B].
Levering, Louisa Ferguson d. on 67-Jan-5 [67-Jan-8: 2B].
Levering, Mary E. (21 yrs.) d. on 68-Mar-3 [68-Mar-5: 2C; 68-Mar-6: 2C].
Levering, Peter J. (36 yrs.) d. on 70-Mar-25 [70-Mar-26: 2B].
Levering, Sallie C. m. Kean, James on 67-Sep-10 [67-Sep-14: 2A].
Levering, Samuel S. (40 yrs.) d. on 70-Apr-27 [70-Apr-28: 2B].
Levering, Stuart Ely (7 mos.) d. on 69-Oct-6 [69-Oct-7: 2B].
Levering, Susan (63 yrs.) d. on 70-Aug-14 [70-Aug-15: 2B; 70-Aug-16: 2C].
Levering, T. H. m. Singer, Susie L. on 69-Oct-7 [69-Oct-9: 2C].
Leverton, Annie M. m. Wheeler, William H. on 66-May-31 [66-Jun-9: 2B].
Leverton, William W. (8 yrs., 9 mos.) d. on 69-May-10 [69-Mar-11: 2C].
Levett, Annie M. m. Eichelberger, George N. on 66-Jun-25 [66-Jul-3: 1C].
Levey, Sarah E. m. Davisson, Andrew J. on 68-Apr-1 [68-Apr-3: 2C].
Levins, Mary S. m. De Valin, Charles E. on 68-Jul-6 [68-Jul-7: 2B].

Levoy, Christopher d. on 66-Oct-10 Drowned [66-Oct-13: 1F].
Levoy, Ellen d. on 66-Oct-11 Drowned [66-Oct-19: 1F].
Levy, Amelia P. m. Rupp, R. F. on 66-Aug-16 [66-Aug-30: 2B].
Levy, Charles W. (35 yrs.) d. on 66-Nov-17 Crushed by stone [66-Nov-19: 1G].
Levy, Joseph M. (71 yrs.) d. on 66-Oct-26 [66-Oct-27: 2B].
Levy, L. G. m. Miller, Maggie L. on 70-Jul-30 [70-Aug-9: 2C].
Levy, Laura O. m. Phipps, William E. on 69-Feb-18 [69-Dec-24: 2C].
Levy, Lewis d. on 66-Apr-29 Drowned [66-Apr-30: 1F].
Levy, Louis m. Jacobs, Hannah on 68-Jun-21 [68-Jun-23: 2B].
Levy, Robert (3 mos.) d. on 70-Apr-1 [70-Apr-2: 2B].
Levy, Sarah m. Carothers, Squire D. on 69-Nov-8 [69-Dec-9: 2C].
Levy, Thomas P. (73 yrs.) d. on 66-Sep-2 [66-Sep-10: 2D].
Lewin, Ann (74 yrs.) d. on 66-Oct-23 [66-Oct-24: 2C].
Lewin, Ida Bell (2 yrs., 10 mos.) d. on 68-Jun-18 of Chronic croup [68-Jun-20: 2B].
Lewin, John C. m. Fuller, Mary N. on 68-May-7 [68-May-21: 2B].
Lewin, John H. (36 yrs.) d. on 70-Nov-27 [70-Nov-29: 2C].
Lewin, Mary C. (25 yrs., 8 mos.) d. on 67-Jul-1 [67-Jul-2: 2B].
Lewin, Sarah L. m. Thompson, Thomas H. on 66-Dec-24 [66-Dec-31: 2C].
Lewin, William (53 yrs., 3 mos.) d. on 70-Jun-15 [70-Jun-16: 2B].
Lewin, Willie J. A. (1 yr., 5 mos.) d. on 68-Aug-5 [68-Aug-6: 2B].
Lewis, A. B., Jr. m. Cook, Belle on 69-Mar-4 [69-Mar-23: 2C].
Lewis, Albert Ellsworth (1 yr., 6 mos.) d. on 66-May-17 [66-May-19: 2B].
Lewis, Alfred E. m. Ware, Sarah on 67-Dec-18 [67-Dec-23: 2B].
Lewis, Allen T. (48 yrs.) d. on 68-Oct-10 [68-Oct-12: 2B, 1F].
Lewis, Alonzo B. m. Scarburgh, Mary A. on 67-Dec-17 [67-Dec-19: 2B].
Lewis, Amelia T. m. Mercer, Robert T. on 67-Jun-4 [67-Jun-10: 2B].
Lewis, Ann d. on 70-Jan-30 [70-Feb-1: 2B].
Lewis, Annie E. m. Edelen, L. C. on 67-Apr-23 [67-Apr-27: 2A].
Lewis, Caroline J. m. Johnson, Edward M. on 66-Jul-30 [66-Aug-1: 2C].
Lewis, Charles H. m. Wethers, Virginia J. on 66-Jul-19 [66-Jul-27: 2C; 66-Aug-15: 2B].
Lewis, Charles M. m. Weathers, Virginia A. on 66-Jul-19 [66-Aug-15: 2B].
Lewis, Delia R. m. Renshaw, James H. on 70-Oct-23 [70-Dec-28: 2C].
Lewis, Edmund H. (68 yrs.) d. on 66-Oct-20 [66-Oct-22: 2C; 66-Oct-23: 2B].
Lewis, Edwin (6 mos.) d. on 68-Jul-25 [68-Jul-27: 2B].
Lewis, Elizabeth (70 yrs.) d. [66-Jan-16: 2C].
Lewis, Elizabeth (80 yrs.) d. on 66-Dec-11 [66-Dec-12: 2B].
Lewis, Elizabeth m. Russel, Edward J. on 69-May-4 [69-May-6: 2B].
Lewis, Elizabeth J. m. Lemmon, William A. on 67-Dec-10 [68-Jan-11: 2B].
Lewis, Emma V. m. Dutton, John W. on 69-Jun-1 [69-Jun-3: 2B].
Lewis, Frances A. m. Wilson, William H. on 68-Dec-31 [69-Jan-9: 2C].
Lewis, Francis (51 yrs.) d. on 66-Dec-3 [66-Dec-4: 2D; 66-Dec-5: 2B].
Lewis, Frank m. Wheeler, Fannie M. on 69-Nov-4 [69-Nov-6: 2B].
Lewis, George C. m. Pearson, Henrietta J. on 66-Oct-30 [67-May-1: 2B].
Lewis, George H. m. Morse, Mollie J. on 69-Apr-7 [69-Apr-9: 2B].
Lewis, George T. m. Taylor, Sarah J. on 67-Dec-12 [67-Dec-17: 2B].
Lewis, George W. m. Barton, Laura S. on 67-Jun-13 [67-Jun-20: 2B].
Lewis, Harriet J. (25 yrs.) d. on 68-Jul-12 [68-Jul-14: 2C].
Lewis, Henry m. Moran, Mary Bridget on 70-Sep-4 [70-Oct-22: 2B].
Lewis, Henry Caspar (1 mo.) d. on 69-Jan-2 [69-Jan-4: 2C].
Lewis, Henry W. Webster (11 mos.) d. on 68-Nov-16 [68-Nov-18: 2C].
Lewis, Hettie (24 yrs.) d. on 70-Dec-8 [70-Dec-10: 2B].
Lewis, James (22 yrs.) d. on 70-Jun-18 Murdered (Stabbing) [70-Jun-20: 1G].
Lewis, Jane (28 yrs.) d. on 67-Jan-25 [67-Jan-29: 2C].
Lewis, John (54 yrs.) d. on 68-Nov-22 [68-Nov-24: 2C; 68-Nov-25: 2B].
Lewis, John G. (23 yrs.) d. on 67-Jan-27 [67-Jan-29: 2C].

Lewis, John T. (61 yrs.) d. on 66-May-13 of Heart disease [66-May-15: 2C; 66-May-16: 2C; 66-May-17: 1F].
Lewis, John William m. Paublitz, Sarah J. on 67-Apr-14 [67-Apr-20: 2A].
Lewis, Joseph F. (19 yrs., 10 mos.) d. on 68-Dec-15 [68-Dec-16: 2C].
Lewis, Josephine Paschal (42 yrs.) d. on 66-Nov-13 [66-Nov-17: 2C].
Lewis, Lennox B. B. d. on 70-Oct-4 of Cholera infantum [70-Oct-6: 2B].
Lewis, Mary (74 yrs.) d. on 69-Apr-5 [69-Apr-6: 2C].
Lewis, Mary m. England, John H. on 66-Oct-18 [66-Nov-10: 2B].
Lewis, Mary Agnes (4 yrs., 5 mos.) d. on 69-May-17 [69-May-19: 2C].
Lewis, Mary C. (35 yrs.) d. on 70-May-7 [70-May-9: 2B].
Lewis, Mary C. m. Irons, William on 69-Aug-3 [69-Aug-7: 2B].
Lewis, Mary E. m. Hartsock, S. M. on 69-Jan-13 [69-Jan-16: 2C].
Lewis, Mary E. T. m. Sellens, John on 66-May-6 [66-Jul-9: 2C].
Lewis, Mary F. m. McKinnell, John C. on 67-Dec-19 [67-Dec-23: 2B].
Lewis, Mary J. m. Oliver, Thomas A. J. on 67-Jun-11 [67-Jun-13: 2C].
Lewis, Permelia Jane (1 yr., 11 mos.) d. on 68-Jan-9 [68-Jan-14: 2C].
Lewis, Rebecca Sophia d. on 68-Apr-14 [68-Apr-15: 2B; 68-Apr-16: 2B].
Lewis, Rebeckah F. m. Bonham, Horace on 70-Jan-27 [70-Jan-29: 2B].
Lewis, Richard T. (17 yrs.) d. on 69-Jun-16 [69-Jun-18: 2C].
Lewis, Stella Morse d. on 70-Jan-29 [70-Jan-31: 2C].
Lewis, Thomas B. (39 yrs.) d. on 68-Oct-11 [68-Oct-15: 2C; 68-Oct-16: 2B; 68-Oct-17: 2B].
Lewis, William F. m. Beacham, Indiana C. on 69-Oct-20 [70-Apr-23: 2B].
Lewis, William H. m. Creighton, Melissa C. on 67-Aug-14 [67-Aug-16: 2B].
Lewis, William K. m. Lutman, Mary A. on 66-Feb-19 [66-Feb-24: 2B].
Lewis, William S. m. Albaugh, Mary F. on 67-Sep-11 [67-Sep-25: 2B].
Lewis, William T. m. Personette, Elizabeth C. on 70-Jul-7 [70-Jul-9: 2B].
Lewis, Wilson m. Evans, Mary on 66-May-28 [66-Jun-1: 2B].
Leypold, Mary S. m. Good, M. Howard on 66-Feb-6 [66-Feb-10: 2C].
Liberty, Ann (33 yrs.) d. on 69-Aug-26 [69-Aug-27: 2B].
Libren, Christopher m. Hutchens, Sarah on 67-Apr-2 [67-Apr-4: 2B].
Lichtenthaeler, Samuel (60 yrs.) d. on 67-Oct-2 [67-Oct-5: 2B; 67-Oct-7: 2B].
Lichty, Strickler Groom (5 yrs., 9 mos.) d. on 67-Jul-2 [67-Jul-4: 2B].
Lidard, Harry (4 yrs., 6 mos.) d. on 69-Aug-12 [69-Aug-13: 2C].
Lidard, John P. (37 yrs.) d. on 67-Oct-24 [67-Oct-25: 2B].
Lieb, Thomas m. Claussen, Catherina F. on 67-Nov-24 [67-Nov-26: 2B].
Lieman, Josephine C. m. Gardner, George W. on 67-Jan-6 [67-Jan-8: 2B].
Lightner, Fannie Jane m. Aspril, George W. on 67-Jun-4 [67-Jun-6: 2B].
Lightner, Lizzie m. Adams, William E. on 70-Dec-6 [70-Dec-10: 2B].
Lightner, Margaret A. m. Hinds, Edward J. on 67-Oct-13 [67-Oct-14: 2B].
Lightner, Mary V. m. Hooper, Joseph J. on 66-Jun-10 [66-Jun-19: 2B].
Lightner, Sallie A. m. Cathcart, Benjamin E. on 69-Dec-14 [69-Dec-16: 2C].
Lightner, William P. (47 yrs.) d. on 67-Sep-27 [67-Sep-28: 1F, 2A; 67-Sep-30: 1F].
Liley, Washington (53 yrs.) d. on 68-Mar-23 of Consumption [68-Mar-25: 2A].
Lillard, Virginia Amelia (26 yrs.) d. on 66-Dec-16 [66-Dec-25: 2C].
Lillobrise, Isabella (26 yrs., 11 mos.) d. of Consumption [70-Sep-5: 2C].
Lilly, Alonzo, Jr. m. Ludlow, Kate W. on 70-Nov-15 [70-Nov-17: 2C].
Lilly, Clarissa m. Shipley, Robert on 67-Apr-17 [67-Apr-20: 2A].
Lilly, David m. Gaither, Mary Agnes on 70-Jan-3 [70-Jan-7: 2F].
Lilly, Dorcas d. on 66-Oct-20 in Railroad accident [66-Oct-22: 1E].
Lilly, Florence Keys (4 mos.) d. on 67-Apr-14 [67-Apr-16: 2B].
Lilly, John m. Sable, Mary Jane on 66-Dec-24 [67-Jan-5: 2C].
Lilly, John H. (21 yrs., 4 mos.) d. on 68-Feb-25 [68-Mar-4: 2C].
Lilly, Lucinda R. (64 yrs.) d. on 70-Jul-25 [70-Jul-26: 2B; 70-Jul-27: 2C].
Lilly, Mary E. (20 yrs., 4 mos.) d. on 69-May-26 [69-May-28: 2C].
Lilly, Solomon H. (24 yrs.) d. on 66-Feb-11 [66-Feb-13: 4C].

Lillybridge, Octavius C. m. White, Helen V. on 70-Jan-13 [70-Jan-18: 2C].
Limberg, William m. Snyder, Mary on 67-Oct-24 [67-Nov-1: 2B].
Linaweaver, Josephine McKay (15 yrs.) d. on 68-Sep-28 [68-Sep-29: 2B].
Lincoln, Joseph (60 yrs.) d. on 66-May-28 [66-Jun-5: 2B].
Lincoln, N. L. m. Moale, Nannie M. Smith on 66-Oct-30 [66-Nov-15: 2C].
Lincoln, Nannie W. Moale d. on 69-Jun-5 [69-Jun-7: 2B].
Lindeman, Elizabeth (6 mos.) d. on 70-Jun-14 [70-Jun-17: 2B].
Lindeman, Henry m. Rudiger, Alvina on 68-Aug-25 [68-Aug-29: 2B].
Lindeman, John m. Hammann, Mary on 68-Nov-15 [68-Nov-21: 2C].
Lindeman, Louisa Amelia d. on 67-Mar-29 [67-Mar-30: 2B].
Linden, Annie Hamilton (3 mos.) d. on 67-Jun-27 [67-Jun-29: 2A].
Linden, Catharine d. on 66-May-31 in Railroad accident [66-Jun-2: 1F].
Linden, John Thomas (4 mos.) d. on 69-Jul-31 [69-Aug-2: 2C].
Lindenman, Conrad (89 yrs.) d. on 66-Aug-4 [66-Aug-6: 2C].
Linder, Louis F. m. Piquette, Nora M. on 69-Jun-21 [69-Jul-20: 2C].
Lindner, Henry d. on 66-Jul-17 of Heatstroke [66-Jul-20: 1F].
Lindsay, Dora Julia (2 yrs., 11 mos.) d. on 69-May-10 [69-May-11: 2B].
Lindsay, Granville m. Whitehead, Agnes L. on 70-Sep-8 [70-Sep-12: 2B].
Lindsay, Harry Lee (3 yrs., 1 mo.) d. on 69-Mar-11 [69-Mar-12: 2C; 69-Mar-13: 2C].
Lindsay, Helen (11 mos.) d. on 69-Apr-29 [69-May-1: 2B].
Lindsay, Richard A. m. Hughlett, Caroline on 69-Sep-30 [69-Oct-4: 2C].
Lindsay, William G. m. Meakin, Dollie J. on 70-Nov-24 [70-Nov-28: 2C].
Lindsey, John J. (50 yrs.) d. on 68-Nov-9 [68-Nov-11: 2C].
Lindsey, John Y. m. Garner, Ellen C. on 67-Jun-17 [67-Jun-18: 2B].
Lindsley, Benjamin F. (32 yrs.) d. on 69-Sep-24 [69-Sep-27: 2C].
Lindstrom, Oscar m. Ross, Mary on 70-Oct-8 [70-Nov-28: 2C].
Linehan, Ann (85 yrs.) d. on 67-Oct-21 [67-Oct-28: 2B].
Lineweaver, George L. (1 yr., 3 mos.) d. on 66-May-13 [66-May-15: 2C].
Lingenfelder, Henry m. Parks, Emma V. on 69-Oct-28 [69-Nov-2: 2B].
Linhard, Annie Cora (1 yr., 2 mos.) d. on 66-Jul-12 [66-Jul-13: 2C].
Linhard, Annie M. (37 yrs.) d. on 66-Aug-2 of Consumption [66-Aug-3: 2C].
Linhard, Charlie William (5 mos.) d. on 68-Jul-22 [68-Jul-27: 2B].
Linhard, Margaret H. (76 yrs.) d. on 67-Apr-6 [67-Apr-8: 2B].
Linhard, Thomas (68 yrs.) d. on 67-Feb-18 of Heart disease [67-Feb-20: 2C; 67-Feb-21: 1F].
Lininburger, Jacob A. (4 yrs., 8 mos.) d. on 70-Nov-5 [70-Nov-7: 2B].
Link, Frederick C., Jr. (2 yrs.) d. on 68-Sep-22 [68-Sep-24: 2B].
Link, John (9 yrs.) d. Drowned [67-Apr-13: 1G].
Linn, Daniel H. m. Jenkins, Annie E. on 68-Dec-22 [69-Jan-1: 2C].
Linn, Margaret Ann d. on 67-Jul-28 [67-Jul-30: 2C].
Linn, Mary Joseph (1 yr., 2 mos.) d. on 70-Jul-22 [70-Jul-23: 2B].
Linn, Peter (75 yrs.) d. on 68-Jul-2 [68-Jul-3: 2B].
Linnehan, John (46 yrs.) d. on 70-Aug-7 [70-Aug-8: 2C].
Linnenkemper, Herman (33 yrs.) d. on 70-Feb-2 [70-Feb-3: 2B; 70-Feb-4: 2C].
Linnenkemper, Herman m. Walter, Elizabeth on 67-Jan-22 [67-Jan-26: 2C].
Linsey, Jennie m. Richmond, George W. on 68-Aug-12 [68-Aug-20: 2B].
Linthicum, A. S. m. Crain, Antoinette on 66-Jul-24 [66-Aug-3: 2C].
Linthicum, Anna d. on 69-Nov-25 [69-Dec-1: 2C].
Linthicum, Annette (25 yrs.) d. on 68-Sep-14 [68-Sep-15: 2B; 68-Sep-16: 2B].
Linthicum, Annie E. m. Duvall, Ferdinand on 66-Nov-20 [66-Nov-27: 2B].
Linthicum, Bettie V. m. Benson, Joseph K. on 69-Mar-9 [69-Mar-31: 2C].
Linthicum, Charles Ellsworth (8 yrs., 8 mos.) d. on 67-Sep-5 [67-Sep-6: 2B].
Linthicum, Clarence Robinson (7 mos.) d. on 67-Dec-2 [67-Dec-3: 2C].
Linthicum, David Thomas (1 yr., 4 mos.) d. on 66-Dec-29 [67-Jan-8: 2B].
Linthicum, Frank H. (1 yr., 9 mos.) d. on 69-Jan-1 [69-Jan-7: 2C].
Linthicum, Henrietta m. Newbury, D. W. on 68-Nov-12 [68-Dec-3: 2C].

Linthicum, James A. m. Slagg, Mary J. on 70-Aug-25 [70-Aug-27: 2B].
Linthicum, Leah Frances (33 yrs., 7 mos.) d. on 69-Nov-24 [69-Nov-27: 2C].
Linthicum, Leonidas (19 yrs., 6 mos.) d. on 66-Sep-24 [66-Sep-25: 2B].
Linthicum, Matilda D. m. Williams, William G. on 69-Sep-21 [69-Oct-15: 2C].
Linthicum, Rebecca m. Bromwell, John A. on 66-Feb-18 [66-Feb-22: 2B].
Linthicum, Samuel Philander (5 mos.) d. on 67-Sep-15 of Cholera infantum [67-Sep-19: 2B].
Linthicum, Thomas F. (67 yrs.) d. on 70-Dec-13 [70-Dec-14: 2C].
Linthicum, Thomas S. m. Hartlove, Elinzeena on 69-Feb-25 [69-Feb-26: 2D].
Linthicum, Victoria (2 yrs.) d. on 67-Apr-6 [67-Apr-11: 2B].
Linthicum, William (68 yrs., 5 mos.) d. on 66-Aug-27 [66-Aug-28: 2B; 66-Sep-15: 2B].
Linthicum, William H. m. Fowler, Ella on 69-Jan-21 [69-Feb-10: 2C].
Linton, Ann m. Hamilton, John on 68-Nov-9 [68-Nov-17: 2C].
Linton, John m. Edgar, Mary E. on 68-Nov-26 [68-Nov-28: 2C].
Linton, Joseph m. Rider, Annie on 67-Oct-23 [67-Oct-24: 2A].
Linton, Louisa C. m. Oldham, Joseph D. on 69-Aug-26 [69-Sep-1: 2B].
Linton, Marie Perkins m. Evans, William R. on 70-Feb-10 [70-Feb-14: 2C].
Linton, Samuel (45 yrs.) d. on 70-Jan-23 of Consumption [70-Jan-24: 2C, 4F].
Linton, William K. (48 yrs.) d. on 69-Oct-20 [69-Nov-12: 2C].
Linzey, John H. m. Watson, Margaret A. on 68-Mar-12 [68-Mar-17: 2C].
Lipp, Agnes Virginia (2 yrs., 11 mos.) d. on 70-Aug-9 of Diptheria [70-Aug-10: 2C].
Lipp, George d. on 66-Apr-7 of Construction cave-in [66-Apr-9: 1G].
Lippard, James William (6 mos.) d. on 66-May-4 [66-May-9: 2B].
Lippey, George (73 yrs.) d. on 68-Jan-14 [68-Jan-16: 2C].
Lippey, Willie (1 yr., 1 mo.) d. on 68-Sep-9 [68-Sep-12: 2B].
Lippincott, Emma H. m. Forbes, Lewis on 69-Nov-18 [69-Nov-20: 2B].
Lips, Ida A. F. (1 yr., 1 mo.) d. on 69-Jul-6 [69-Jul-7: 2C].
Lipscomb, J. D. m. Ricketts, Sallie on 70-Nov-16 [70-Nov-22: 2B].
Lipscomb, Philip D., Rev. (72 yrs.) d. on 70-Jan-4 [70-Jan-6: 2C; 70-Jan-7: 4F].
Lisle, Mary E. (29 yrs.) d. on 70-Nov-22 [70-Nov-30: 2C].
Lisle, Nettie m. Rivers, J. L. on 67-Apr-24 [67-Dec-27: 2D].
Lisner, Cecilia m. Sommerfeld, Adolph on 67-Feb-24 [67-Mar-1: 2C].
List, Ella Elizabeth (1 yr., 6 mos.) d. on 69-Jun-28 [69-Jun-30: 2C].
Litchfield, George J. m. Hildebrandt, Achsa E. on 69-Dec-14 [69-Dec-16: 2C].
Litchfield, John C. m. Furguson, Julia on 66-Dec-25 [67-Jan-15: 2C].
Litsinger, Augusta m. Conrey, J. F. on 67-Dec-24 [67-Dec-31: 2C].
Litsinger, Augustus M. m. Fishpaugh, Margaret A. on 67-Aug-6 [67-Aug-9: 2C].
Litsinger, William D. m. Hawkins, Amelia C. on 69-Mar-16 [69-Mar-19: 2C].
Littell, William W. (53 yrs.) d. on 69-Apr-18 [69-Apr-26: 2C].
Littig, Ella B. m. Bouton, A. G. on 70-Jan-25 [70-Jan-29: 2B].
Littig, Jane R. (64 yrs.) d. on 70-Feb-6 of Heart disease [70-Feb-7: 2C; 70-Feb-8: 2C].
Littig, John M. m. Sterett, Sallie E. on 69-Nov-17 [69-Nov-29: 2C].
Littig, Luther (63 yrs.) d. on 67-Sep-10 [67-Sep-13: 2B].
Little, Amelia A. m. Woods, Alex. P. on 67-Jun-12 [67-Jun-18: 2B].
Little, Ann (71 yrs.) d. on 69-Mar-15 [69-Mar-16: 2C; 69-Mar-17: 2C].
Little, Catherine (49 yrs.) d. on 68-Sep-19 [68-Sep-21: 2B].
Little, Catherine (79 yrs.) d. on 67-Jul-18 [67-Jul-19: 2C].
Little, Charles m. Pryor, Amanda on 70-Nov-27 [70-Dec-9: 2C].
Little, Charles G. (25 yrs.) d. on 67-Jul-26 [67-Jul-27: 2B].
Little, George d. on 66-Sep-12 of Cholera [66-Oct-13: 2B].
Little, Henry d. on 62-Sep-19 [66-Jul-13: 1G].
Little, Irene Morrison (9 yrs., 9 mos.) d. on 68-May-3 [68-May-4: 2B].
Little, J. Q. (37 yrs.) d. on 70-Apr-7 of Heart disease [70-Apr-8: 2C; 70-Apr-9: 2B].
Little, Jane (65 yrs.) d. on 67-Jan-3 [67-Jan-4: 2D; 67-Jan-5: 2C].
Little, John (38 yrs.) d. on 69-May-16 [69-May-17: 2B; 69-May-18: 2C].
Little, John Henry m. Kirby, Lizzie on 70-Dec-1 [70-Dec-10: 2B].

Little, Lewis P. m. Rhinehart, Sallie V. on 69-Aug-23 [69-Aug-30: 2B].
Little, Louisa V. m. Matthews, John on 68-Nov-10 [68-Nov-12: 2C].
Little, Robert Wilson (1 yr., 5 mos.) d. on 70-Jun-24 [70-Jun-25: 2B].
Little, Sarah A. m. Covington, Thomas S. on 68-Dec-10 [68-Dec-16: 2C].
Little, Susannah m. Gorsuch, James K. P. on 69-Feb-25 [69-Oct-14: 2C].
Little, William Edward (2 yrs., 2 mos.) d. on 70-Jan-15 [70-Jan-17: 2D].
Little, William J. m. Close, Ella on 70-Oct-16 [70-Oct-24: 2B].
Littlefield, Sallie C. S. (32 yrs.) d. on 68-Jul-24 [68-Jul-25: 2B].
Littleton, F. Drucie m. Hurley, R. A. on 70-Aug-23 [70-Aug-24: 2C; 70-Aug-25: 2B].
Littleton, Mary G. m. Ehlers, Bernard H. on 66-Sep-5 [66-Sep-25: 2B].
Litz, Mary Jane m. Hogg, William A. on 69-May-20 [69-Jun-15: 2C].
Litzinger, Rebecca E. m. Jeffries, Benjamin on 68-Jul-28 [68-Jul-31: 2C].
Litzinger, William R. m. Fowler, Susan R. on 68-Mar-18 [68-Apr-3: 2C].
Livermore, Diantha m. Blake, Joel N. on 66-Oct-10 [66-Oct-16: 2B].
Livermore, Margie B. d. on 68-Jan-12 [68-Jan-15: 2C].
Livers, Caroline E. m. Adams, Joseph H. on 67-Nov-14 [67-Nov-18: 2B].
Livesey, Albert (23 yrs.) d. on 67-Apr-16 Crushed by stone [67-Apr-17: 1G, 2B].
Livesey, Susan Caroline d. on 67-Jul-7 [67-Jul-8: 2C].
Livesey, Victoria m. Somerville, Thomas J. [70-Nov-12: 2B].
Livingston, Agnes Eugenie (1 mo.) d. on 70-Apr-4 [70-Apr-5: 2B].
Livingston, George A. (34 yrs.) d. on 66-Jul-6 [66-Jul-7: 2B].
Livingston, George W. m. Peregoy, Alice V. on 68-Aug-11 [68-Sep-5: 2A].
Livingston, James H. m. Kellum, Annie E. on 68-May-12 [68-May-14: 2B].
Livingston, John P. (47 yrs.) d. on 69-Apr-28 [69-Apr-30: 2C].
Livingston, Livingus m. Young, Eliza on 68-Apr-28 [68-Apr-30: 2B].
Livingston, Mary Jennett (6 mos.) d. on 69-Jul-2 of Brain fever [69-Jul-9: 2C].
Livingston, Mary S. m. Joynes, David J. on 69-Aug-10 [69-Sep-24: 2B].
Livingston, Willie (1 yr., 8 mos.) d. on 69-Sep-16 [69-Sep-17: 2C].
Livsey, Alice Jane (2 mos.) d. on 67-Jun-25 [67-Jun-26: 2C].
Livsey, Sophia J. (35 yrs.) d. on 67-May-26 [67-Mar-28: 2B].
Llewellyn, M. Lulie m. Carter, Henry M. on 70-Nov-24 [70-Nov-28: 2C].
Llewellyn, Mary Louisa (4 yrs.) d. on 66-Oct-24 of Croup [66-Oct-25: 2C].
Lloyd, Anna Elizabeth m. Lee, Edward D. on 68-Jun-2 [68-Jun-10: 2B].
Lloyd, Edward H. (1 mo.) d. on 70-Oct-18 [70-Oct-19: 2B].
Lloyd, Edward H. m. Leonard, M. E. on 66-May-17 [66-May-22: 2B].
Lloyd, Eliza A. m. Weaver, Jacob B on 69-Nov-29 [69-Dec-1: 2C].
Lloyd, George W. (15 yrs.) d. on 66-Jun-5 [66-Jun-7: 2B].
Lloyd, Jennie (20 yrs.) d. on 70-Sep-16 [70-Sep-17: 2B].
Lloyd, Laura E. (20 yrs., 9 mos.) d. on 66-Sep-13 [66-Sep-15: 2B].
Lloyd, M. Lutie m. Walmsley, Robert H. on 67-Jan-15 [67-Jan-31: 2C].
Lloyd, Mary (45 yrs.) d. on 69-Jun-23 [69-Jun-24: 2C].
Lloyd, Mary Ann (52 yrs.) d. on 66-Jul-22 [66-Jul-24: 2C].
Lloyd, Mary R. (14 yrs.) d. on 67-Mar-5 [67-Mar-6: 2C].
Lloyd, Phillie C. m. Fisher, Charles G. on 69-Dec-15 [69-Dec-22: 2B].
Lloyd, William m. Stincendaffer, Anna on 66-Aug-12 [66-Aug-18: 2B].
Lloyd, William B. (53 yrs.) d. on 66-Jul-2 [66-Jul-3: 2C].
Loan, Daniel (50 yrs.) d. on 67-May-22 [67-May-23: 2C].
Loane, Charles (1 yr., 2 mos.) d. on 69-Aug-26 [69-Aug-27: 2B].
Loane, Emma F. m. Shields, Richard B. on 70-Jul-6 [70-Jul-12: 2B].
Loane, James R. m. Daley, Catherine on 68-Nov-1 [68-Nov-9: 2B].
Loane, Jane E. (32 yrs.) d. on 66-May-28 [66-May-28: 2B].
Loane, John (46 yrs.) d. on 70-Nov-18 of Paralysis [70-Nov-19: 2B, 4D].
Loane, John R. (19 yrs.) d. on 68-Aug-8 [68-Aug-10: 2C].
Loane, Joseph (11 mos.) d. on 70-Jul-16 [70-Jul-18: 2C].
Loane, Joseph G. (1 yr., 10 mos.) d. on 66-Apr-8 [66-Apr-9: 2B; 66-Apr-10: 2C].

Loane, Joseph Michael (6 yrs., 6 mos.) d. on 67-May-11 [67-May-14: 2B].
Loane, Martha Jane (20 yrs.) d. on 70-Aug-19 [70-Aug-20: 2B].
Loane, Mary E. m. Whittlesey, William E. on 68-Nov-3 [68-Nov-10: 2C].
Loane, Mollie D. M. m. Snow, William B. on 66-Dec-20 [66-Dec-22: 2A].
Loane, Rebecca d. on 69-Nov-29 [69-Nov-30: 2C; 69-Dec-1: 2C].
Loane, William T. Valiant m. Dennis, Kate J. on 66-Oct-25 [66-Nov-29: 2B].
Loane, Willie (4 mos.) d. on 69-Jul-16 [69-Jul-20: 2C].
Lobe, Annette m. Straus, William H. on 69-May-19 [69-May-22: 2B].
Lobenstein, Jonas M. (73 yrs.) d. on 68-Mar-5 [68-Mar-6: 2C].
Lockard, Alfred F. m. Carr, Sallie E. on 70-Jan-20 [70-Jan-22: 2B].
Lockard, Mollie W. m. Flory, Thomas E. on 67-Sep-25 [67-Sep-26: 2B].
Locke, Laura Virginia d. on 66-Jan-12 [66-Jan-13: 2C].
Lockhart, Andrew J. m. Belvin, Naomi M. on 66-Sep-26 [66-Oct-5: 2B].
Lockhart, William Edward (1 yr., 6 mos.) d. on 68-Aug-26 [68-Aug-27: 2B].
Lockington, Lucy m. Meagher, Lewis J. on 69-Apr-4 [69-Apr-9: 2B].
Locks, Benjamin d. on 69-Sep-7 in Construction accident [69-Sep-8: 4E].
Locks, Stephen m. Ward, Josephine on 67-Dec-12 [67-Dec-14: 2B].
Lockwood, Aquilla (82 yrs.) d. on 69-Oct-23 [69-Oct-25: 2C, 4C].
Lockwood, George m. Alexander, Sadie R. on 66-Jan-4 [66-Jan-16: 2C].
Lockwood, George C. m. Dawson, Kate M. on 69-Jan-5 [69-Jan-6: 2C].
Lockwood, Harold Weed (1 yr.) d. on 69-Dec-2 [69-Dec-3: 2C].
Lockwood, Hattie (9 yrs.) d. on 67-Jun-24 [67-Jun-25: 2B].
Lockwood, Helen M. m. Colburn, Rollinson on 67-Sep-5 [67-Sep-18: 2B].
Lockwood, John, Sr. d. on 66-Nov-23 [66-Dec-1: 2B].
Lockwood, Rodney Clarence (13 yrs., 3 mos.) d. on 69-Jun-22 [69-Jun-23: 2C].
Lodge, John H. m. Wayman, Harriet D. on 70-May-12 [70-Jun-1: 2B].
Loebenstein, Martha (73 yrs.) d. on 70-Jul-17 [70-Jul-19: 2C].
Loewrer, Peter (33 yrs.) d. on 68-Jul-17 of Heatstroke [68-Jul-18: 1E].
Lofgren, P. G. m. Edkins, Sarah A. on 68-May-7 [68-May-16: 2A].
Loftis, Margaret m. McGreevy, James on 69-Mar-4 [69-Mar-13: 2B].
Loftus, Hannah J. m. Zimmerman, Joseph A. H. on 69-Jan-1 [69-Jan-4: 2C].
Loftus, Julia m. Cullen, John on 66-May-20 [66-May-23: 2B].
Logan, Alexander (28 yrs.) d. on 68-Jan-28 [68-Jan-29: 2C].
Logan, Anne Rebecca d. on 70-Mar-11 [70-Mar-12: 2C].
Logan, Benjamin m. Cooper, Lucy Jane on 68-Oct-6 [68-Oct-8: 2B].
Logan, Ellen m. Bamberger, William A. on 66-May-1 [66-May-15: 2C].
Logan, John m. O'Neill, Mary A. on 69-Aug-26 [69-Sep-10: 2B].
Logan, Joseph Thomas (46 yrs.) d. on 66-Apr-12 [66-Apr-13: 2C].
Logan, Josephine (39 yrs.) d. on 70-Jan-14 [70-Jan-19: 2D].
Logan, Margaret (75 yrs.) d. on 67-Jan-19 [67-Feb-1: 2C].
Logan, Mary (73 yrs.) d. on 70-Nov-1 [70-Nov-2: 2C; 70-Nov-3: 2B].
Logan, Mary M. d. on 70-Nov-1 of Consumption [70-Nov-2: 2C; 70-Nov-3: 2B].
Logan, Willie James (6 yrs.) d. on 70-Aug-1 Burned [70-Aug-2: 2C, 4E].
Logemann, Elenora m. Albrecht, August on 66-May-8 [66-May-12: 2A].
Logemann, Henry m. Lemcke, Mary J. on 66-Mar-29 [66-Apr-4: 2B].
Logsdon, Fannie, Miss m. Gibbons, Stephen on 66-Nov-27 [66-Nov-28: 2B].
Logsdon, Imogene m. Watts, Nathaniel on 66-Oct-18 [66-Oct-19: 2B].
Logsdon, John T. m. Cole, Laura C. on 66-Oct-9 [67-Jan-4: 2D].
Logsdon, Mary Kate (1 yr., 4 mos.) d. on 69-Jan-9 [69-Jan-11: 2C].
Logsdon, Nimrod C. m. Morrow, Martha on 66-Sep-11 [66-Sep-12: 2A].
Logsdon, William (53 yrs.) d. on 66-Apr-29 [66-May-1: 2A].
Logue, George E. d. on 67-Oct-4 [67-Oct-12: 2B].
Logue, James A. m. Lucas, Cecilia on 70-Jul-21 [70-Jul-25: 2C].
Logue, Kate m. Tyler, John T. on 66-Feb-15 [66-Feb-17: 2B].
Logue, M. Josephine m. Mustin, A., Jr. on 67-Mar-27 [67-Mar-29: 2B].

Logue, Mary A. m. Twist, Henry B. on 68-Apr-16 [69-May-5: 2B].
Logue, Mary A. m. Judge, Francis A. on 70-Oct-13 [70-Oct-14: 2B].
Logue, William H. m. Monmonier, Pamela J. on 70-Nov-24 [70-Nov-29: 2C].
Lohman, Charles Theodore (2 yrs., 1 mo.) d. on 70-Nov-1 of Chronic croup [70-Nov-3: 2C].
Lohmuller, D. m. DePaepe, C. on 68-Nov-3 [68-Nov-6: 2C].
Lohmuller, William C. (22 yrs., 4 mos.) d. on 69-Jan-5 [69-Jan-6: 2C].
Lohrmann, John Henry (63 yrs.) d. on 69-Mar-6 [69-Mar-9: 2C].
Loker, Emma Florence (9 mos.) d. on 67-Jul-1 [67-Jul-2: 2B].
Lomax, James (88 yrs.) d. on 66-Jan-20 [66-Jan-22: 1G, 2C].
Lombard, Harry Hamilton (1 yr.) d. on 68-Jul-4 [68-Jul-6: 2B].
Lombard, Henry C. m. Happoldt, Eugenia A. on 66-Oct-18 [66-Oct-29: 2B].
Loney, Ellen L. S. m. Wirts, William T. on 69-Aug-31 [69-Sep-20: 2C].
Loney, Fannie m. Hooff, J. Johnston on 68-Jul-16 [68-Jul-18: 2B].
Loney, Lewis H. m. McLoughlin, Rosa on 66-Dec-19 [66-Dec-22: 2A].
Loney, Mary Ann (75 yrs.) d. on 70-Jan-27 [70-Jan-29: 2B].
Loney, William (70 yrs.) d. on 66-Aug-12 [66-Aug-14: 2C].
Long, Annie m. Toulson, J. H. on 70-Sep-19 [70-Dec-16: 2C].
Long, Carrie m. Sackerman, Louis on 70-May-22 [70-Jun-11: 2B].
Long, Cornelius B. m. Love, Ellen A. on 67-Jun-27 [67-Jun-29: 2B].
Long, Daniel (45 yrs.) d. on 70-May-2 Drowned [70-May-4: 1G, 2C].
Long, Edgar (16 yrs.) d. on 70-Jan-8 [70-Jan-17: 2C].
Long, Ellen Malinda (7 mos.) d. [68-Nov-21: 2C].
Long, George E. (28 yrs.) d. on 67-Mar-14 [67-Mar-16: 2B].
Long, Hannah (76 yrs.) d. on 67-Feb-10 [67-Feb-12: 2C].
Long, Harriet M. d. on 66-Jan-16 [66-Jan-18: 2C].
Long, Helen M. m. Jackson, Edward T. on 69-Oct-20 [69-Oct-21: 2B].
Long, Henry (4 yrs.) d. on 67-Mar-19 Burned [67-Mar-20: 1F].
Long, Henry J. m. Johns, Maggie on 67-Sep-25 [67-Oct-1: 2B].
Long, Henry K., Col. (80 yrs.) d. on 67-Nov-20 [67-Nov-21: 2C; 67-Nov-22: 1F].
Long, Isabella G. m. Brashears, John T. on 67-Feb-25 [67-Mar-2: 2B].
Long, Janey F. (24 yrs.) d. on 70-Sep-12 [70-Sep-19: 2B].
Long, John (60 yrs.) d. on 68-Dec-23 Drowned [68-Dec-24: 1H].
Long, John T. (47 yrs.) d. on 69-Dec-11 [69-Dec-13: 2C].
Long, John W. (1 yr., 4 mos.) d. on 66-Apr-28 [66-May-1: 2A].
Long, Joseph L. (47 yrs.) d. on 66-Oct-17 [66-Oct-18: 2B].
Long, L. J. (39 yrs.) d. on 69-Dec-18 [69-Dec-20: 2C].
Long, Laura m. Wood, John H. on 67-Mar-31 [67-Apr-18: 2B].
Long, Laura H. m. Wheeler, Benjamin F. on 67-Jun-26 [67-Jun-29: 2B].
Long, M. Josie m. Hinman, W. C. on 69-Dec-27 [69-Dec-28: 2C].
Long, Maria (79 yrs.) d. on 67-Nov-21 [67-Nov-23: 2B].
Long, Marion L. d. on 70-Jan-10 [70-Jan-17: 2D].
Long, Mary Virginia m. Burrier, John R. on 70-Oct-31 [70-Nov-24: 2B].
Long, Philip (11 yrs.) d. on 68-Jul-16 Drowned [68-Jul-18: 1F].
Long, Robert Joseph (17 yrs.) d. on 66-Apr-7 [66-Apr-9: 2C].
Long, Samuel (61 yrs.) d. on 68-Apr-9 of Consumption [68-Apr-10: 2B; 68-Apr-11: 2A].
Long, Samuel B. (40 yrs.) d. on 67-Apr-4 of Brain congestion [67-Apr-5: 1F].
Long, Sarah d. on 69-Dec-7 [69-Dec-9: 2C].
Long, T. B. m. Burkholder, Nettie on 70-Jun-30 [70-Jul-1: 2B].
Long, William d. on 68-Nov-21 [68-Nov-24: 2C].
Long, William H. m. North, Jane F. on 66-Nov-22 [66-Nov-27: 2B].
Long, William T. m. Bouldin, Helen on 68-Dec-17 [68-Dec-21: 2B].
Longley, Caroline Emma (2 yrs., 4 mos.) d. on 67-Nov-10 [67-Nov-12: 2C].
Longley, Elizabeth d. on 68-Jan-20 [68-Jan-21: 2C].
Longley, Ellenora d. on 69-Jul-2 [69-Jul-3: 2B].
Longley, George W. (28 yrs.) d. on 67-Jun-30 of Consumption [67-Jul-1: 2B].

Longley, Mary d. on 66-Jul-21 [66-Jul-21: 2C].
Longmore, Joseph S. m. Aylsworth, Anna M. on 70-Aug-2 [70-Aug-5: 2C].
Longnecker, David (76 yrs.) d. on 66-May-8 [66-May-9: 2B].
Longnecker, John H. (53 yrs.) d. on 70-Nov-11 [70-Nov-12: 4C, 2B].
Lookingland, Margaret m. Youse, William on 68-Dec-28 [68-Dec-30: 2C].
Lookingland, Mary C. m. Bayley, John H. on 68-Jul-12 [68-Jul-18: 2B].
Lord, George Boardman (4 yrs.) d. on 66-Oct-1 of Croup [66-Oct-2: 2B].
Lorentz, Bernhard A. m. Steeger, Elizabeth on 68-Apr-6 [68-Apr-7: 2B].
Lorenz, Henry (48 yrs.) d. on 70-Dec-26 [70-Dec-28: 2C].
Lorge, Mary E. (26 yrs.) d. on 66-Feb-2 of Consumption [66-Feb-3: 2C].
Lorman, Helen V. (19 yrs.) d. on 69-Nov-19 [69-Dec-3: 2C; 69-Nov-20: 2C].
Lorman, Howell S. m. Trippe, Helen on 68-Dec-10 [68-Dec-19: 2B].
Lorman, Margaret (73 yrs.) d. on 66-Jul-10 [66-Jul-12: 2C].
Lorz, Caroline (28 yrs.) d. on 66-Mar-16 [66-Mar-17: 2B].
Loscom, James Edward (1 mo.) d. on 70-Sep-12 [70-Sep-14: 2B].
Lott, William (24 yrs.) d. on 69-Sep-11 in Railroad accident [69-Sep-13: 1H, 2B].
Lotz, Dora m. Streib, Jacob on 68-Sep-15 [68-Sep-30: 2B].
Lotz, J. Fred m. Beard, Fannie V. on 69-May-25 [69-Jun-2: 2B].
Loucks, Bell L. m. Koller, John W. on 68-Nov-17 [68-Nov-19: 2C].
Loud, Clarence Allen (1 yr., 11 mos.) d. [67-Sep-3: 2B; 67-Sep-4: 2B].
Loud, Conrad d. on 70-Mar-30 of Hemorrhage [70-Mar-31: 1H].
Louden, Issac (28 yrs.) d. on 66-Aug-24 [66-Nov-20: 2B].
Loudenslager, Alice Elizabeth (6 mos.) d. on 68-Dec-13 [68-Dec-14: 2C].
Loudenslager, John Wesley m. Conner, Mary Jane on 70-Aug-23 [70-Sep-8: 2B].
Loudenslager, Sylvanus (48 yrs.) d. on 66-Nov-18 [66-Nov-20: 2B].
Louderman, James C. (60 yrs.) d. on 67-May-11 [67-May-14: 2B].
Louge, Bell m. Martin, F. on 68-Dec-25 [69-Jan-4: 2C].
Lough, George F. m. Kettlewell, Emily Marian on 70-Apr-28 [70-May-7: 2B].
Loughborough, Maria Louisa m. Zane, Edmund P. on 67-Apr-23 [67-Apr-26: 2B].
Loughborough, Sallie M. m. Keyes, E. L. on 70-Apr-26 [70-Apr-28: 2B].
Lougherty, Elizabeth d. on 66-May-24 [66-May-25: 2C].
Loughran, Anny (5 yrs., 8 mos.) d. on 70-Apr-11 [70-Apr-12: 2B].
Lounsberry, Charles W. m. Torrington, Jane on 68-Jan-24 [68-Jan-28: 2D].
Louthan, Helen M. m. Grady, Frank T. on 70-Jan-11 [70-Jan-12: 2D].
Love, Almara Virginia m. Barranger, George W. on 66-Feb-12 [66-Feb-20: 2B].
Love, Ellen A. m. Long, Cornelius B. on 67-Jun-27 [67-Jun-29: 2B].
Love, Florence L. m. Dockstader, Sanford I. on 67-Sep-5 [67-Sep-7: 2A].
Love, Mary Ann m. Gaunt, Samuel B. on 69-Jun-2 [69-Sep-7: 2B].
Love, Mary Emma m. Bradbury, Robert R. on 69-Aug-9 [69-Dec-28: 2C].
Love, Serena A. (29 yrs.) d. on 70-Jul-30 [70-Aug-1: 2C].
Love, Susan m. Williamson, George D. on 66-Apr-10 [66-Apr-14: 2B].
Love, William H. m. Crangle, Mary A. on 70-Nov-17 [70-Nov-24: 2B].
Love, William J. (3 yrs., 1 mo.) d. on 70-Aug-15 [70-Aug-16: 2C].
Loveday, Ida m. Sargent, H. G. C. on 67-Nov-7 [67-Nov-22: 2C].
Lovejoy, Charles Amos m. Gehrmann, Adelaide V. on 70-Aug-25 [70-Aug-30: 2B].
Lovejoy, Elizabeth d. on 67-Mar-11 [67-Mar-16: 2B].
Lovejoy, Henry A. L. m. Gehrman, Julia A. on 68-Mar-18 [68-Aug-20: 2B].
Lovejoy, Willard R. m. Schley, Louisa A. on 69-Dec-8 [69-Dec-13: 2C].
Lovejoy, William H. d. on 67-Nov-21 [68-Jan-13: 2C].
Lovell, Lydia A. m. Phillips, Nathan on 67-Oct-1 [67-Oct-8: 2B].
Lovering, Francis J. (30 yrs., 7 mos.) d. on 67-Jan-25 [67-Jan-26: 2C].
Lovering, Lottie m. Rider, William E. on 67-Oct-8 [67-Oct-14: 2B].
Lovering, Susan E. M. d. on 68-Apr-11 [68-Apr-16: 2B].
Low, A. m. Low, A. Mann on 66-Oct-11 [66-Oct-16: 2B].
Low, A. Mann m. Low, A. on 66-Oct-11 [66-Oct-16: 2B].

Low, Catherine (62 yrs.) d. on 66-Oct-22 [66-Oct-24: 2C].
Lowdenslager, George (63 yrs.) d. on 66-Aug-26 [66-Aug-27: 2B].
Lowe, John H. m. Harvey, Susie on 68-Jul-9 [68-Jul-23: 2B].
Lowe, John W. m. Ford, Jane E. on 69-Jan-17 [69-Feb-6: 2C].
Lowe, Margaret A. E. d. on 67-Nov-10 [67-Nov-23: 2B].
Lowe, Owen Cleveland (3 mos.) d. on 66-Jun-21 [66-Jun-22: 2B].
Lowe, Rebecca (68 yrs.) d. on 68-Jan-27 [68-Jan-28: 2D].
Lowe, Walter (10 mos.) d. on 70-May-1 [70-May-2: 2B].
Lowe, Wrightson L. m. Carville, E. Kate on 70-Dec-8 [70-Dec-13: 2C].
Lowecamp, John F. m. Bruce, Virginia on 68-Oct-28 [68-Nov-10: 2C].
Lowekamp, Charles B. m. Tumbleson, Mary Ellen on 68-Oct-8 [68-Oct-19: 2B].
Lowell, John B. m. Welch, Annie E. on 66-Nov-18 [66-Nov-27: 2B].
Lowenstein, Walter H. m. Wolf, Emma on 68-May-4 [68-May-7: 2B].
Lowenthal, Abraham (37 yrs.) d. on 68-Jul-24 Drowned [68-Jul-27: 1D].
Lowenthal, Carrie m. Baer, Nathan on 70-Jan-2 [70-Feb-5: 2B].
Lowery, George E. m. Regester, Maggie A. on 68-Jun-9 [68-Jun-10: 2B].
Lowery, Issac L. m. Sterret, Rachel M. on 67-May-9 [67-May-10: 2B].
Lowery, Johannah (23 yrs.) d. on 68-Feb-15 [68-Feb-24: 2C].
Lowery, Maggie A. m. Cassell, Charles C. on 67-Oct-31 [67-Nov-2: 2B].
Lowery, Mary (76 yrs.) d. on 70-Jun-26 [70-Jun-27: 2C].
Lowman, Mary M. m. Redmiles, Richard F. on 67-Feb-17 [67-Feb-27: 2C].
Lowman, Nicholas m. Disney, Maria E. on 67-Mar-7 [67-Mar-8: 2C].
Lowman, Sarah M. m. Pocock, George W. on 67-Feb-7 [67-Feb-27: 2C].
Lowndes, E. S. d. on 70-Jan-25 [70-Jan-31: 2C].
Lowrey, Annie Jane (1 yr., 1 mo.) d. on 68-Jul-30 [68-Jul-31: 2C].
Lowry, Alfred m. Snyder, Margaret on 68-Apr-3 [68-Apr-7: 2B].
Lowry, Annie E. m. Whitney, Daniel on 66-Sep-13 [66-Sep-14: 2B].
Lowry, Annie M. m. Alexander, Thomas on 67-Jul-29 [67-Aug-14: 2B].
Lowry, Benjamin F. (2 yrs., 9 mos.) d. on 69-Mar-14 [69-Mar-16: 2C].
Lowry, Irving m. Joyce, Katie on 69-Oct-5 [69-Oct-7: 2B].
Lowry, James Amon (10 mos.) d. on 70-Apr-24 [70-Apr-28: 2C].
Lowry, John E. m. Jefferson, Sarah H. on 67-Jul-2 [67-Jul-4: 2B].
Lowry, Maria d. on 66-May-17 [66-Jun-1: 2B].
Lowry, Matilda (56 yrs.) d. on 69-Jan-1 [69-Jan-2: 2C].
Lowry, Sarah d. on 68-Sep-9 [68-Sep-11: 2B].
Lowther, Adah Z. m. Ward, George W. on 70-Dec-15 [70-Dec-28: 2C].
Lucas, Amanda E. (27 yrs.) d. on 70-Mar-19 [70-Mar-21: 2C].
Lucas, Cecilia m. Logue, James A. on 70-Jul-21 [70-Jul-25: 2C].
Lucas, Gertrude (2 yrs., 2 mos.) d. on 70-Jun-14 [70-Jun-15: 2B].
Lucas, James B. m. Lucas, Nellie B. on 68-Apr-6 [68-Apr-9: 2B].
Lucas, Joshua J. (33 yrs.) d. on 67-Oct-3 [67-Oct-5: 2B].
Lucas, Nellie B. m. Lucas, James B. on 68-Apr-6 [68-Apr-9: 2B].
Lucas, R. Henry m. Rider, H. Isabel on 70-Sep-26 [70-Oct-5: 2B; 70-Oct-7: 2B].
Lucas, Sallie Sophia (7 yrs., 4 mos.) d. on 69-May-12 [69-May-14: 2C].
Lucas, Sarah R. m. Owens, Hugh A. on 69-Jan-13 [69-Jan-19: 2C].
Lucas, Thomas Trotton (1 yr., 4 mos.) d. on 68-Mar-15 [68-Mar-16: 2B].
Lucchesi, David H. m. Allison, Rose E. on 69-Feb-9 [69-Feb-17: 2C].
Lucchesi, F. A. m. Mason, Ida I. on 68-Apr-16 [68-May-4: 2B].
Lucchesi, Frederick (58 yrs.) d. on 69-Sep-3 [69-Sep-4: 2B].
Lucchesi, Maggie T. m. Eschbach, Leo on 69-Mar-30 [69-Apr-3: 2B].
Lucchesi, Mark (24 yrs., 1 mo.) d. on 70-Mar-1 [70-Mar-2: 2C; 70-Mar-3: 2C].
Lucius, Philip B. (24 yrs.) d. on 66-Jul-2 of Consumption [66-Jul-23: 2C].
Luckett, James H. (54 yrs.) d. on 66-Jul-17 of Heatstroke [66-Jul-18: 1F; 66-Jul-20: 2D].
Luckett, Mollie C. m. Stewart, F. A. on 68-Nov-30 [68-Dec-7: 2C].
Luckett, Ralph d. Drowned [68-Apr-8: 2A].

Lucy, Lizzie B. m. Whiteford, M. Crook on 69-Jul-27 [69-Aug-4: 2C].
Lucy, Thomas m. Emory, M. on 67-Aug-1 [67-Aug-3: 2B].
Ludeking, J. P. (59 yrs.) d. on 68-Apr-21 [68-Apr-23: 2B].
Ludeking, Margaret (70 yrs.) d. on 68-Aug-14 [68-Aug-17: 2B].
Ludlow, Charlotte Sellman m. Hopkins, J. Seth on 69-Nov-3 [69-Nov-5: 2C].
Ludlow, Kate W. m. Lilly, Alonzo, Jr. on 70-Nov-15 [70-Nov-17: 2C].
Ludlow, Mary C. m. Cook, Samuel G. B. on 67-Jun-27 [67-Jul-9: 2B].
Ludlow, Sally W. m. Jackson, Tatlow on 66-Jun-13 [66-Jun-15: 2C].
Ludowieg, A. m. Timanus, Fannie on 70-Oct-6 [70-Oct-31: 2B].
Ludwig, Andrew (51 yrs., 8 mos.) d. on 66-Apr-17 [66-Apr-19: 2B].
Ludwig, Augustus (8 yrs., 4 mos.) d. on 70-Aug-14 Drowned [70-Aug-15: 2B, 4E].
Ludwig, John (48 yrs.) d. on 67-Mar-3 [67-Mar-4: 2D].
Ludwig, John A. m. Small, M. Augusta on 68-Jun-4 [68-Jun-8: 2B].
Lum, Isabella m. Waldren, George Edward on 67-Apr-28 [67-May-7: 2B].
Lumberson, Erixon L. m. Reese, Naomi S. on 69-Dec-9 [69-Dec-13: 2C].
Lumberson, Kate m. Darby, James on 66-May-16 [66-Jun-5: 2B].
Lumsdon, Martha M. m. Magruder, J. F. D. on 70-Nov-5 [70-Nov-18: 2C].
Lumsdon, William O., Rev. (63 yrs.) d. on 68-May-14 [68-May-18: 2B].
Lundy, John Patrick (1 yr., 5 mos.) d. on 70-Nov-7 [70-Nov-8: 2B].
Lunean, Elise m. Wolf, Isidore on 67-Jul-9 [67-Jul-10: 2B].
Lupton, Charles S. m. Magruder, Veale M. on 67-Nov-12 [67-Nov-26: 2B].
Lupton, Martha (89 yrs.) d. on 69-Mar-23 [69-Mar-25: 2C].
Lurman, Gustave W. (58 yrs.) d. on 66-Jul-8 of Paralysis [66-Jul-9: 1G, 2C].
Lurty, Sallie A. m. Skinner, A. S. on 67-Feb-14 [67-Feb-19: 2C].
Lusby, Henry (85 yrs.) d. on 67-Mar-22 [67-Mar-23: 2B].
Lusby, Lawrence Winfield (4 mos.) d. on 70-Mar-12 [70-Mar-14: 2C].
Lusby, Mary A. m. Vickers, Horace R. on 69-Sep-12 [69-Oct-13: 2C].
Lusby, Nevit Latrobe (10 yrs.) d. on 69-Sep-8 [69-Sep-9: 2B].
Lusby, Nicholas (76 yrs.) d. on 67-Mar-19 [67-Mar-21: 2C].
Lushbaugh, Martin L. (47 yrs.) d. on 70-Sep-28 [70-Sep-29: 2B].
Luthold, Carrie m. Meisner, Henry on 66-Nov-28 [66-Dec-6: 2B].
Lutman, Mary A. m. Lewis, William K. on 66-Feb-19 [66-Feb-24: 2B].
Luttman, Alfred m. Saunders, Louisa on 67-Jan-15 [67-Jan-17: 2C].
Lutts, Elizabeth A. (56 yrs.) d. on 70-Mar-16 [70-Mar-19: 2B].
Lutts, Georgie m. Norris, Thomas E. on 66-Nov-22 [66-Dec-1: 2B].
Lutts, Hannah S. m. Crafton, J. A. on 68-Jan-28 [68-Jan-31: 2C].
Lutts, Mary A. (61 yrs.) d. [70-Nov-12: 2B].
Lutz, Charles F. E. d. on 70-Jun-9 of Suicide (Stabbing) [70-Nov-14: 4D].
Lutz, John m. Saunders, Sarah R. on 68-Apr-2 [68-Apr-6: 2B].
Lutz, John P. d. on 68-Apr-5 [68-Apr-6: 2B; 68-Apr-7: 2B].
Lutz, Maggie V. m. Morgan, Charles L. on 66-May-17 [66-May-24: 2C].
Lutz, Mary E. m. Starr, George W., Jr. on 68-May-5 [68-May-16: 2A].
Lutz, Otto m. Halfpenny, Sarah Jane on 69-Nov-30 [69-Dec-2: 2C].
Lutz, Valentine (92 yrs.) d. on 66-Aug-9 [66-Aug-11: 2B; 66-Aug-16: 2C].
Lycett, Edward (77 yrs.) d. [69-Apr-2: 2C; 69-Apr-3: 2B].
Lycett, Michael T. m. McNeal, Ann Rebecca A. on 68-Nov-30 [68-Dec-8: 2C].
Lydy, Henry (78 yrs.) d. on 67-Aug-13 [67-Aug-21: 2B].
Lyebrand, Joseph E. (20 yrs.) d. on 66-Sep-22 [66-Sep-24: 2B].
Lyell, William L. (46 yrs.) d. on 70-Aug-6 [70-Aug-10: 2C].
Lyeth, John T. m. Fout, Mary C. on 69-Nov-9 [69-Nov-15: 2C].
Lyeth, Kate (24 yrs.) d. on 70-Dec-4 [70-Dec-5: 2C].
Lyeth, Martha (90 yrs.) d. on 70-Mar-21 [70-Mar-22: 2C; 70-Mar-23: 2C].
Lyeth, Samuel H., Jr. m. Horner, Kate on 67-Nov-12 [67-Nov-14: 2B].
Lyles, Margaret m. Paddy, Thomas E. on 69-Jan-7 [69-Jan-9: 2C].
Lyles, Mary Eliza (18 yrs.) d. on 66-Jan-9 [66-Jan-13: 2C].

Lyles, Nancy G. m. Smith, Horace E. on 68-Jun-9 [68-Jun-11: 2B].
Lyles, William Thomas (8 mos.) d. on 68-Oct-20 [68-Oct-21: 2C].
Lynch, Adelia m. Conway, Thomas T. on 69-Apr-29 [69-May-1: 2B].
Lynch, Alexander d. on 68-Mar-10 of Apoplexy [68-Mar-11: 4E; 68-Mar-12: 1G].
Lynch, Celia (55 yrs.) d. on 68-Dec-7 [68-Dec-8: 2C; 68-Dec-9: 2C].
Lynch, Cinderella m. Walter, Joseph L. on 69-Jul-22 [69-Jul-29: 2C; 69-Jul-30: 2C].
Lynch, Emily (29 yrs.) d. on 66-Apr-26 [66-Apr-30: 2B].
Lynch, George (34 yrs.) d. on 66-Mar-6 of Consumption [66-Mar-8: 2B].
Lynch, James m. Oldson, Mollie G. on 69-Jun-22 [69-Jul-27: 2C].
Lynch, James Thomas (1 yr., 6 mos.) d. on 70-Jul-27 [70-Jul-28: 2C].
Lynch, Joshua (40 yrs.) d. on 66-Jun-23 [66-Jun-25: 2B].
Lynch, Lizzie m. Williams, William H. on 70-Jul-28 [70-Dec-16: 2C].
Lynch, Martha E. m. James, Stephen P. on 66-Jul-12 [66-Jul-26: 2C].
Lynch, Martha M. m. Warnick, William B. on 68-Nov-25 [68-Dec-28: 2B].
Lynch, Mary (30 yrs.) d. on 66-Jul-20 [66-Jul-21: 2C].
Lynch, Mary E. m. Bardwell, George S [70-May-6: 2B].
Lynch, Mary M. (25 yrs.) d. on 70-Jul-7 of Consumption [70-Jul-14: 2B].
Lynch, Mathew (76 yrs.) d. on 69-Jul-9 [69-Jul-10: 2B].
Lynch, Matthew (10 mos.) d. on 67-Feb-18 [67-Feb-19: 2C].
Lynch, Matthew (50 yrs.) d. on 66-Jul-27 [66-Jul-28: 2C].
Lynch, Patrick (64 yrs.) d. on 68-Jun-10 [68-Jun-11: 2B].
Lynch, Patrick (75 yrs.) d. on 69-Feb-15 [69-Feb-17: 1H, 2C].
Lynch, Percy Pelham (4 yrs.) d. on 70-Jul-19 [70-Aug-27: 2B].
Lynch, Ralph (31 yrs., 2 mos.) d. on 69-Nov-8 [69-Nov-10: 2C; 69-Nov-9: 2C].
Lynch, Ruth C. (73 yrs.) d. on 70-Oct-18 [70-Oct-19: 2B; 69-Oct-20: 2B].
Lynch, Sarah m. Mitchell, Edward on 66-Oct-25 [66-Oct-27: 2B].
Lynch, William (40 yrs.) d. on 66-Jun-4 of Construction cave-in [66-Jun-5: 1F].
Lynch, Zoe d. on 66-Sep-3 of Typhoid [66-Sep-4: 2B].
Lynd, Mary A. m. McKenna, Arthur on 68-Nov-16 [68-Nov-20: 2C].
Lynde, F. M. m. Elzey, Willie on 68-Apr-29 [68-Apr-30: 2B].
Lynde, R. D., Dr. d. on 66-Feb-2 [66-Mar-23: 2C; 66-Mar-24: 2B; 66-Jun-2: 2B].
Lynham, E. N. m. Childress, Alice Lei on 68-Jul-8 [68-Jul-10: 2C].
Lynn, A. Luther m. Dorsey, Mary Elenor on 66-Oct-18 [66-Oct-22: 2C].
Lyon, Augusta P. D. m. Watkins, Frank D. on 68-Oct-16 [68-Oct-19: 2B].
Lyon, Augustus I. m. Grafflin, Margaret P. on 67-Oct-17 [67-Oct-19: 2A].
Lyon, Charles G. (80 yrs.) d. on 67-Jun-21 in Carriage accident [67-Jun-22: 2B; 67-Jun-24: 1E].
Lyon, Emily Kuhn (21 yrs.) d. on 70-Jun-26 [70-Jun-27: 2C].
Lyon, Estalia (3 mos.) d. on 69-Jun-26 [69-Jun-28: 2C].
Lyon, John (34 yrs.) d. Drowned [68-Nov-5: 1G].
Lyon, John C., Rev. (67 yrs.) d. on 68-May-21 [68-May-22: 2C; 68-May-23: 1G].
Lyon, Lizzie m. Bond, James on 67-Apr-22 [67-Apr-24: 2B].
Lyon, M. Johnson m. Daniel, Alice Isabella on 68-Apr-28 [68-May-1: 2B].
Lyon, Margaret m. Jewens, William on 69-Feb-4 [69-Feb-11: 2C].
Lyon, Mary A. m. Gilley, Charles W. on 68-Jun-4 [68-Jun-5: 2B].
Lyon, Mary E. B. m. Grafflin, Lewis F. on 68-Aug-18 [68-Nov-28: 2C].
Lyon, Mollie J. m. Schaeffer, William G. on 70-Jan-18 [70-Jan-20: 2C].
Lyon, Richard H. (65 yrs.) d. on 68-Nov-11 [68-Nov-12: 2C].
Lyon, Robert d. on 69-Mar-11 of Pneumonia [69-Apr-23: 2B].
Lyon, Samuel H. m. Harrison, Emily E. on 69-Jul-8 [69-Jul-9: 2C].
Lyon, Walter M. m. Thorburn, Jessie D. on 67-Apr-14 [67-Apr-17: 2B].
Lyons, Bridget (85 yrs.) d. on 68-Oct-25 [68-Oct-26: 2B].
Lyons, Catherine (30 yrs.) d. on 70-Sep-9 [70-Sep-12: 2B].
Lyons, Ellen m. Harding, James E. on 69-Nov-9 [69-Nov-22: 2C].
Lyons, Emma J. m. Grubb, Z. Taylor on 70-Aug-11 [70-Sep-15: 2B].

Lyons, James (38 yrs.) d. on 70-Nov-18 of Suicide (Poisoning) [70-Nov-19: 4D].
Lyons, James (1 yr., 7 mos.) d. on 70-Aug-18 [70-Aug-19: 2C].
Lyons, Jeremiah (24 yrs.) d. on 67-Jun-30 [67-Jul-1: 2B].
Lyons, John H. (32 yrs.) d. on 67-Oct-13 [67-Oct-15: 2A].
Lyons, Joseph E. (3 yrs., 4 mos.) d. on 67-May-19 Drowned [67-May-20: 1E, 2B].
Lyons, Kate m. Brady, Thomas E. on 67-Oct-24 [67-Nov-6: 2B].
Lyons, Mary Alverdia (1 yr., 4 mos.) d. on 68-May-19 [68-Jul-20: 2B; 68-Jul-21: 2C].
Lyons, Ruhamah (57 yrs., 1 mo.) d. on 70-Nov-14 [70-Nov-19: 2B].
Lyons, Thomas (50 yrs.) d. on 66-Jul-17 [66-Jul-18: 1F, 2C].
Lyshear, William H. m. Watts, Emma on 66-Feb-4 [66-Feb-9: 2C].
Lyster, Catherine C. d. on 67-Feb-19 [67-Feb-20: 2C].
Lytle, John H. m. Taylor, Sallie M. on 69-Jun-15 [69-Jun-23: 2C].
Lytle, Sadie (1 mo.) d. on 70-Feb-14 [70-Feb-21: 2C].
M'Cauley, W. S. m. Dodge, Mollie E. on 66-Jun-21 [66-Jun-23: 2B].
Mabbott, Carrie S. m. Smoot, Albert on 66-Mar-22 [66-Mar-26: 2B].
Mabee, Alexina m. Bentley, William H. on 68-Dec-16 [68-Dec-22: 2C].
Mabee, Matilda Irene m. Henry, William T. on 69-Sep-19 [69-Sep-27: 2C].
Maben, James A. m. Taylor, Carrie A. on 66-Jan-24 [66-Jan-27: 2B].
Macalister, Hiram L. m. Ross, Laura S. on 68-Jul-23 [68-Jul-24: 2C].
Macaulay, James H. (2 mos.) d. on 66-Dec-1 of Diptheria [66-Dec-3: 2B].
Macauley, Mary E. m. Barber, Philip J. on 66-Jun-14 [66-Jun-26: 2B].
Maccubbin, Amelia N m. Greenfield, Thomas H. on 67-Dec-5 [67-Dec-7: 2B].
Maccubbin, James S. (41 yrs.) d. on 69-Feb-28 [69-Mar-1: 2C].
Maccubbin, John T. m. Watkins, Ellen on 67-Jun-18 [67-Jun-27: 2B].
MacCubbin, Joshua L. m. McAllister, Mary C. on 67-Jul-10 [67-Jul-12: 2C].
Maccubbin, Mary E. m. Bevans, Richard N. on 66-Dec-27 [67-Jan-2: 2C].
Maccubbin, Mollie F. m. Harrison, John W. on 66-Dec-20 [66-Dec-24: 2B].
Maccubbin, R. W., Jr. m. Owings, Kate on 69-Nov-25 [69-Nov-29: 2C].
MacCubbin, Samuel (8 mos.) d. on 68-Jul-16 [68-Jul-17: 2C].
Maccubbin, Samuel Hamilton (5 yrs., 8 mos.) d. on 69-Nov-21 [69-Nov-3: 2C].
Maccubbin, Samuel J. m. Adreon, Lina A. on 66-May-17 [66-May-24: 2C].
MacDermott, Thomas (19 yrs.) d. on 70-Jul-19 [70-Jul-20: 2C; 70-Jul-21: 2C].
Macdonald, Flora (6 yrs., 4 mos.) d. on 66-Jan-22 [66-Jan-23: 2C].
MacDonald, J. H. m. Grothaus, Annie E. on 70-Feb-22 [70-Mar-7: 2C].
Macdougal, Mary Frances (8 mos.) d. on 67-Jul-25 [67-Jul-26: 2C].
Mace, Ann d. on 70-Feb-10 [70-Feb-12: 2C].
Mace, Ellen (28 yrs.) d. on 66-Dec-7 of Consumption [66-Dec-8: 2B].
Mace, John H. (30 yrs.) d. on 69-Feb-7 [69-Feb-9: 2C].
Mace, Oscar A. (1 yr., 1 mo.) d. on 69-Apr-25 [69-Apr-26: 2B].
Mace, S. Virginia m. Jones, T. P. on 70-Dec-22 [70-Dec-28: 2C].
Mace, William m. Tyler, Kate E. on 68-Apr-29 [68-May-5: 2B].
Macean, Mary m. Hevy, David on 66-Dec-25 [67-Jan-5: 2C].
Macgill, Elizabeth (72 yrs.) d. on 69-Sep-7 [69-Sep-8: 2B].
MacGregor, Kate d. on 67-Oct-29 [67-Nov-1: 2B].
Machen, Charles (8 yrs., 9 mos.) d. on 67-Jan-3 [67-Jan-3: 2B].
Machen, Thomas (70 yrs.) d. on 69-Dec-4 [69-Dec-6: 2C].
Macher, Elbert Kinnett (10 mos.) d. on 69-Jul-22 [69-Jul-23: 2C].
Macher, Fannie E. m. Meeks, Samuel J. on 68-Jun-4 [68-Jun-6: 2B].
Macher, Katie Elberta (8 mos.) d. on 70-Jul-14 [70-Jul-15: 2C].
Macher, Susie P. m. Hann, Charles on 70-Jun-9 [70-Jun-14: 2B].
MacIntosh, William T. m. Walter, Hannah on 67-May-22 [67-Sep-11: 2B].
Mack, James m. Dorsey, Mary on 70-Sep-13 [70-Sep-15: 2B].
Mackall, Elizabeth Louisa (9 yrs.) d. on 66-Jun-18 [66-Jun-20: 2C].
Mackall, Harriet m. Remington, W. Williams on 70-Sep-22 [70-Sep-26: 2B].
Mackall, Henry Covington (4 yrs., 4 mos.) d. on 66-Nov-30 [66-Dec-10: 2C].

Mackall, John B. m. Jackson, M. Helen on 66-Dec-5 [66-Dec-8: 2B].
Mackall, Levin C. m. Walker, Martha J. on 69-Dec-14 [69-Dec-22: 2B].
Mackall, Virginia m. McCabe, John Collins on 68-Sep-15 [68-Sep-18: 2B].
Macken, Bridget (59 yrs.) d. on 68-Sep-27 [68-Sep-29: 2B].
Macken, Ida May (1 yr., 7 mos.) d. on 69-Jun-23 [69-Jun-28: 2C].
Mackenhamer, George N. m. Wolf, Belle on 67-Sep-11 [67-Sep-17: 2A].
Mackenhamer, Mary E. m. Brady, Elisha C. on 66-Nov-20 [66-Nov-23: 2C].
Mackenna, Mary Cecilia d. on 66-Sep-27 [66-Sep-29: 2B].
Mackenzie, Ida Cora (3 mos.) d. on 70-Nov-30 [70-Dec-2: 2C].
Mackenzie, Ida Lavinia (4 yrs., 7 mos.) d. on 69-Mar-4 [69-Mar-5: 2C].
Mackenzie, Jennie L. (18 yrs.) d. on 70-Oct-1 [70-Oct-3: 2B].
MacKenzie, John C., Dr. (42 yrs.) d. on 66-Apr-4 [66-Apr-5: 2B; 66-Apr-7: 2C].
Mackenzie, Mollie m. Appold, James A. on 66-Jul-25 [66-Aug-24: 2B].
Mackenzie, Ruey d. on 66-Nov-4 [66-Nov-5: 2B].
Mackenzie, Thomas (73 yrs.) d. on 66-Jun-3 [66-Jun-4: 2B; 66-Jun-5: 2B].
Mackenzie, Thomas G. (26 yrs.) d. on 67-Jan-1 [67-Jan-3: 2B].
Mackenzie, William Henry (11 yrs.) d. on 68-Sep-12 [68-Sep-14: 2B].
Mackey, S. Webster m. Bentley, Sarah I. on 70-Oct-13 [70-Oct-18: 2B].
Mackey, Sallie E. m. Standiford, A. M. on 69-Feb-12 [69-Feb-22: 2C].
Mackey, William A. d. on 68-Nov-23 in Railroad accident [68-Nov-28: 4D].
Mackey, Zulike D. m. Schley, Arthur on 68-Jul-22 [68-Jul-27: 2B].
Mackie, Charles B., Rev. (75 yrs.) d. on 66-Jun-5 of Paralysis [66-Jun-12: 2B].
Mackin, Georgeanna m. Shiole, Charles F. on 68-May-7 [68-May-9: 2B].
Mackin, Harry G. (7 yrs.) d. on 66-Jul-16 [66-Jul-19: 2C; 66-Aug-16: 2C].
Mackin, Katie Irene (3 yrs.) d. on 66-Aug-8 [66-Aug-16: 2C].
Mackinheimer, Laura J. m. Wheeler, Andrew T. on 69-Aug-12 [69-Aug-14: 2C].
Mackinheimer, William (64 yrs.) d. on 67-Oct-12 [67-Oct-14: 2B].
Macklin, John A. m. Tidy, Mary M. on 68-Oct-29 [68-Nov-7: 2B].
Macklin, Mary N. d. on 69-May-23 [69-May-24: 2B; 69-May-25: 2C].
Mackrill, William R. (36 yrs.) d. on 69-Aug-25 of Consumption [69-Sep-14: 2B].
Mackubin, Clarence H. m. Mackubin, Kate M. on 68-Jul-19 [68-Jul-29: 2B].
Mackubin, Eleanor m. Calvert, Charles B. on 66-Jun-14 [66-Jun-18: 2B].
Mackubin, James m. Peter, Gabriella on 68-Nov-5 [68-Nov-9: 2B].
MacKubin, Kate M. m. Mackubin, Clarence H. on 68-Jul-19 [68-Jul-29: 2B].
Maclenan, John (35 yrs.) d. on 69-Oct-26 [69-Oct-27: 2B].
Maclenan, Margaret (27 yrs.) d. on 67-Apr-15 [67-Apr-17: 2B; 67-Apr-18: 2B].
MacNally, Mary E. d. on 68-Jun-10 [68-Jun-11: 2B].
Macnamara, Maggie A. m. Donnellan, Martin on 69-Jan-18 [69-Jan-27: 2C].
MacNeal, Charles L. m. Smick, Sarah E. on 67-Nov-27 [67-Nov-28: 2C].
MacNeal, Ida H. m. Robbins, Russel, Jr. on 70-Nov-10 [70-Nov-14: 2B].
MacNeal, Monica Ann (56 yrs.) d. on 66-Feb-2 [66-Feb-3: 2C].
MacNeal, P. Douglas m. Wilkins, Mary A. on 70-Oct-20 [70-Oct-24: 2B].
Macomber, Mary C. (32 yrs.) d. on 70-Jul-21 [70-Jul-25: 2C].
Macon, Anna m. Clarke, William F. on 67-Nov-21 [67-Nov-23: 2B].
Mactavish, Charles Carroll (50 yrs.) d. on 68-Mar-12 of Paralysis [68-Mar-14: 2B; 68-Mar-16: 1F, 2B].
Mactavish, Emily (74 yrs.) d. on 67-Jan-26 [67-Jan-29: 2C; 67-Jan-30: 1F].
Mactier, Emily Tennant d. on 68-Oct-22 [68-Oct-24: 2B].
Madden, Catherine (41 yrs.) d. on 69-Oct-25 [69-Oct-26: 2B].
Madden, Christina Kate m. Davis, Edward A. on 66-May-15 [66-May-22: 2B].
Madden, Dennis (3 yrs., 2 mos.) d. on 70-Dec-28 [70-Dec-30: 2C].
Madden, Emma m. Rayner, Henry on 69-Dec-28 [69-Dec-29: 2D].
Madden, Janie H. m. Pumphrey, Lloyd D on 68-Apr-26 [68-Apr-29: 2B].
Madden, John J. m. Brown, Maggie on 67-Sep-23 [67-Oct-4: 2B].
Madden, Joseph H. m. Crook, Augusta Isabella on 70-Feb-17 [70-Feb-18: 2C].

Madden, Mary Augusta (1 yr., 6 mos.) d. on 70-Aug-3 [70-Aug-5: 2C].
Madden, Mary Jane Stimax d. on 66-Jun-10 [66-Jun-11: 2B].
Madden, Thomas (33 yrs.) d. on 69-Apr-9 [69-Apr-10: 1G, 2B].
Madden, Thomas C. m. Merklen, Caroline V. on 69-Sep-13 [69-Sep-16: 2B].
Maddex, William T. (3 yrs., 10 mos.) d. on 68-May-26 [68-May-28: 2B].
Maddox, Anna Maria (69 yrs.) d. on 69-Apr-9 [69-Apr-10: 2B].
Maddox, Charlotte Ann (13 yrs., 1 mo.) d. on 66-Aug-19 [66-Aug-21: 2C].
Maddox, Edward m. Davis, Letta E. on 68-Oct-6 [68-Nov-3: 2B].
Maddox, Elizabeth L. (6 yrs., 8 mos.) d. on 66-Oct-23 [66-Oct-24: 2C].
Maddox, George A. (43 yrs., 1 mo.) d. on 70-Oct-25 [70-Oct-26: 2B].
Maddox, James (38 yrs.) d. on 68-Feb-19 [68-Feb-20: 2C].
Maddox, Jennie D. m. Milton, Charles H. on 69-Nov-18 [69-Nov-23: 2C].
Maddox, Margaret J. m. Dougherty, Thomas E. on 70-Jun-30 [70-Jul-2: 2B].
Maddox, William J. (41 yrs.) d. on 67-Nov-6 [67-Nov-7: 2C; 67-Nov-8: 2C].
Maddox, William Theobald (80 yrs.) d. on 70-Feb-6 [70-Feb-7: 2C; 70-Feb-8: 4G].
Maddux, Alfred m. Ayres, Charlotte on 70-Jan-12 [70-Jan-17: 2C].
Maddux, Charles W. m. Carman, Susan E. on 67-Mar-17 [67-Mar-26: 2C].
Maddux, James Thomas (18 yrs., 11 mos.) d. on 68-Jul-15 [68-Jul-16: 2C].
Madigan, Anna Chinn (9 mos.) d. on 68-Jul-8 [68-Jul-9: 2B].
Madigan, Elleanora d. on 68-Jun-12 [68-Jun-13: 2B].
Madigan, Patrick (60 yrs.) d. on 66-Jul-11 [66-Jul-12: 2C].
Maestar, Charles (14 yrs.) d. on 67-Aug-5 in Railroad accident [67-Aug-6: 1G].
Maffitt, William Ryan (8 mos.) d. on 69-Apr-14 [69-Apr-15: 2B].
Magaha, Agnes Celia (8 yrs., 8 mos.) d. on 66-Jul-17 [66-Jul-19: 2C].
Magaha, Charles D. m. Heffenor, Katy on 70-Aug-18 [70-Sep-15: 2B].
Magaha, Mary M. m. Clark, Augustus on 69-Aug-15 [69-Sep-18: 2B].
Magaha, Sarah C. m. Nally, George W. on 67-Jul-18 [67-Jul-20: 2C].
Magan, Sophie W. (82 yrs.) d. on 67-May-6 [67-May-7: 2B].
Magarity, Edith I. (2 yrs., 5 mos.) d. on 68-Aug-26 [68-Aug-27: 2B].
Magarrell, J. F. m. Hagerty, Fannie on 67-Dec-12 [67-Dec-16: 2B].
Magaw, John L. (1 yr., 5 mos.) d. on 66-Aug-19 [66-Aug-20: 2C].
Magee, John (53 yrs.) d. on 68-Jul-15 [68-Jul-16: 2C].
Magee, Margaret Cooper d. on 70-Jul-12 [70-Jul-13: 2C].
Magee, Mary Cole (2 yrs., 6 mos.) d. on 68-Jun-6 [68-Jun-6: 2A].
Magee, Mary S. (21 yrs.) d. on 70-Aug-2 [70-Aug-3: 2C; 70-Aug-4: 2C].
Magee, Samuel C. m. Williams, Mary S. on 67-Jul-8 [67-Jul-10: 2B].
Mager, Mary m. Fullum, Joseph J. on 66-Jun-5 [66-Jun-9: 2B].
Magers, Elias S. (1 yr., 6 mos.) d. on 70-Aug-9 [70-Aug-10: 2C].
Magers, Hessie V. m. Hammersly, William N. on 67-Jan-17 [67-Jan-24: 2C].
Magers, John M. m. White, Hannah R. on 68-Feb-25 [68-Feb-28: 2D].
Magers, Thomas A. (17 yrs.) d. on 70-May-25 [70-May-26: 2C; 70-May-27: 2B].
Magher, Mary (57 yrs.) d. on 68-Oct-28 [68-Oct-29: 2C].
Magil, Annie m. Jordan, Charles E. on 70-Jul-19 [70-Jul-30: 2B].
Magill, John A. d. on 66-Jul-25 of Heatstroke [66-Aug-8: 2C].
Magill, Mary A. (11 mos.) d. on 66-Jul-5 [66-Jul-6: 2B].
Maginnis, C. J. d. on 67-Aug-23 [67-Aug-24: 2B].
Magischrift, Herman (40 yrs.) d. on 70-Oct-11 in Railroad accident [70-Oct-12: 4C; 70-Oct-13: 4D].
Magness, Benjamin F. m. Cronsberry, Amelia O. on 66-Jun-27 [66-Oct-9: 2A].
Magness, C. Wesley m. Meekins, Sarah A. on 67-May-9 [67-May-13: 2B].
Magness, C. Wesley m. Beebe, M. L. on 69-Aug-3 [69-Aug-5: 2C].
Magness, Julia Ann (31 yrs.) d. on 68-Apr-5 [68-Apr-9: 2B].
Magness, Rebecca m. Kelly, James M. on 69-Aug-3 [69-Aug-10: 2C].
Magness, Sarah Ann (22 yrs.) d. on 68-Jan-6 [68-Jan-8: 2C].
Magness, Susan Ida (8 yrs.) d. on 67-May-13 Struck by lightning [67-May-16: 1G, 2B].

Magrath, Mary Julia (12 yrs.) d. on 67-Mar-28 of Brain congestion [67-Mar-29: 2B].
Magraw, David (10 yrs.) d. on 68-Oct-3 Drowned [68-Oct-5: 1G].
Magraw, Elizabeth m. Maguire, Philip on 69-Jan-17 [69-Jan-23: 2C].
Magraw, Emily W. (52 yrs.) d. on 70-Mar-25 [70-Mar-28: 2B].
Magraw, Henry S. (52 yrs.) d. on 67-Feb-4 of Apoplexy [67-Feb-4: 1F, 2C].
Magraw, James C. (64 yrs.) d. on 68-Jul-3 [68-Jul-4: 2C].
Magraw, Katey Agnes (1 yr.) d. on 70-Jul-13 [70-Jul-14: 2B].
Magraw, Rebecca m. Galloway, John on 70-Mar-8 [70-Mar-11: 2C].
Magraw, Robert M. d. on 66-Jun-13 of Paralysis [66-Jun-14: 2A].
Magraw, Robert N. m. Nussear, Mary M. on 69-Aug-11 [69-Aug-16: 2B].
Magraw, Stephen C. m. Webster, Jennie S. on 69-Feb-22 [69-Feb-24: 2C].
Magruder, Bettie Mills m. Slothower, Morris B. on 68-Oct-13 [68-Oct-14: 2B].
Magruder, Daniel Randall m. Sollers, Mary on 67-Dec-12 [67-Dec-23: 2B].
Magruder, Edwin (1 mo.) d. on 67-Mar-25 [67-Mar-26: 2C].
Magruder, F. G. m. Watts, Annie S. on 67-Jul-2 [67-Jul-24: 2C].
Magruder, George G. m. Clark, Mary A. on 70-Dec-8 [70-Dec-10: 2B].
Magruder, Hamline m. Sisson, Hallie C. on 69-Apr-22 [69-Apr-24: 2B].
Magruder, Haswell m. Casilo, Marie on 67-Apr-5 [67-Apr-10: 2B].
Magruder, J. F. D. m. Lumsdon, Martha M. on 70-Nov-5 [70-Nov-18: 2C].
Magruder, Kate C. m. Kennard, B. F. on 66-Jun-19 [66-Jun-21: 2B].
Magruder, Van m. Owen, Thomas J. on 69-Nov-18 [69-Nov-25: 2C].
Magruder, Veale M. m. Lupton, Charles S. on 67-Nov-12 [67-Nov-26: 2B].
Maguire, Alexander (4 yrs.) d. on 68-Jan-13 [68-Jan-14: 2C].
Maguire, Annie (26 yrs.) d. on 70-Jun-24 [70-Jun-25: 2B].
Maguire, Eliza J. m. Stewart, John T. on 67-May-18 [67-May-22: 2B].
Maguire, Hugh M. m. Bittijer, Lizzie M. on 70-Nov-22 [70-Nov-25: 2D].
Maguire, James (73 yrs.) d. on 69-Oct-22 [69-Oct-26: 2B].
Maguire, James Alexandria (34 yrs.) d. on 67-Apr-29 [67-May-1: 2B].
Maguire, James B. m. McConnell, Alice on 67-Jun-26 [67-Jul-3: 2B].
Maguire, John (2 yrs., 9 mos.) d. on 67-Mar-7 [67-Mar-8: 2C].
Maguire, Joseph Mitchell (22 yrs.) d. on 66-Jan-6 of Chronic diarrhea [66-Jan-8: 2B; 66-Jan-9: 2B].
Maguire, Julia (53 yrs.) d. on 67-Nov-16 [67-Nov-18: 2B].
Maguire, M. m. Ortlip, Eliza J. on 69-Apr-18 [69-Apr-28: 2B].
Maguire, Mary E. m. Billups, A. M. on 67-May-14 [67-May-23: 2B].
Maguire, Mary G. m. Gough, Thomas W. on 66-Oct-24 [66-Oct-27: 2B].
Maguire, Patrick m. Daly, Eliza on 68-Feb-5 [68-Jun-26: 2B].
Maguire, Philip m. Magraw, Elizabeth on 69-Jan-17 [69-Jan-23: 2C].
Maguire, Robert (27 yrs.) d. on 66-Feb-9 [66-Feb-23: 2C].
Maguire, Susan (30 yrs.) d. on 66-Jul-31 [66-Aug-2: 2C].
Maguire, William D. (28 yrs.) d. on 67-Dec-27 [67-Dec-28: 2C].
Maguire, William D. m. Gerhegan, Lizzie M. on 67-Apr-25 [67-Apr-29: 2B].
Maguire, William West m. Campbell, Isabel R. on 69-Nov-15 [69-Dec-30: 2C].
Mahan, Milo, Rev. (52 yrs.) d. on 70-Sep-3 [70-Sep-5: 2C; 70-Sep-6: 4C; 70-Sep-7: 4C].
Mahaney, Mary m. Thompson, John W. on 70-Dec-2 [70-Dec-10: 2B].
Mahaney, Susan (62 yrs.) d. on 68-Oct-31 [68-Nov-2: 2B].
Mahany, John R. m. Calahee, Margaret on 66-Jun-26 [66-Jun-28: 2C].
Mahany, Nathan d. on 66-Jun-9 [66-Jun-15: 2C].
Maharg, Sadie (3 mos.) d. on 68-Jul-1 [68-Jul-2: 2C].
Maher, Norah (33 yrs.) d. on 69-Dec-24 of Consumption [69-Dec-25: 2C].
Mahon, Annie Agnes (4 mos.) d. on 70-Apr-29 [70-Apr-30: 2B].
Mahon, John J. m. Ward, Mary E. on 70-May-6 [70-May-11: 2B].
Mahon, Kate (28 yrs.) d. on 67-Oct-31 [67-Nov-1: 2B; 67-Nov-2: 2B].
Mahon, Margaret Ann (9 mos.) d. on 68-Jul-9 [68-Jul-10: 2C].
Mahon, Mary E. (4 yrs.) d. on 69-Feb-25 [69-Feb-26: 2D].

Mahool, George W. d. on 70-Apr-17 [70-May-23: 2C].
Mahool, Thomas m. Cliffe, Augusta on 68-Dec-8 [68-Dec-10: 2D].
Mahorner, Sarah Ann (66 yrs., 9 mos.) d. on 70-Nov-4 [70-Nov-8: 2B].
Maier, Mary A. m. Mann, John C. on 69-Sep-12 [69-Sep-18: 2B].
Maihl, Eliza m. Ballard, James T. on 68-Jun-1 [68-Jun-15: 2B].
Maihl, Leonora m. Cook, John T. on 68-May-17 [68-May-19: 2B].
Mailhouse, Betty (80 yrs.) d. on 70-Jun-26 [70-Jun-27: 2C; 70-Jun-28: 2C].
Mailhouse, Lizzie m. Annandale, William on 70-Feb-3 [70-Feb-10: 2C].
Main, Kate S. m. Routzahn, William H. on 67-Jan-10 [67-Jan-12: 2C].
Mainley, Sarah J. m. Mears, John W. on 68-Sep-11 [69-Mar-29: 2B].
Mainster, Samuel (37 yrs.) d. on 70-Sep-2 [70-Sep-3: 2B].
Mainster, Theodora S. (7 mos.) d. [68-Aug-10: 2C].
Maischein, Peter (72 yrs.) d. on 69-Dec-23 of Suicide (Stabbing) [69-Dec-24: 1H].
Maith, Mary C. m. North, Thomas L. on 67-Oct-8 [67-Oct-10: 2B].
Maith, Sarah E. (10 yrs., 7 mos.) d. on 68-Aug-2 [68-Aug-4: 2C].
Maitland, James F. m. Franklin, Annie on 66-May-17 [66-May-18: 2C].
Maitland, Mary (3 yrs., 4 mos.) d. on 68-Aug-13 [68-Aug-14: 2C].
Maize, Carrie M. m. Schwatka, William F. on 69-Oct-5 [69-Oct-6: 2B].
Major, B. C. (34 yrs.) d. on 69-Aug-23 of Suicide (Poisoning) [69-Aug-24: 1H].
Maken, John H. m. Tucker, Maria L. on 67-Dec-15 [67-Dec-23: 2B].
Makinson, Dorothy (60 yrs., 2 mos.) d. on 66-Mar-30 [66-Mar-31: 2C].
Malambre, James M. m. Woods, Emma V. on 68-Jan-31 [68-Jan-17: 2C].
Malcolm, Harry m. Pearson, Marian on 68-Apr-2 [68-Apr-7: 2B].
Males, Gulie Elma d. on 70-Jun-22 [70-Jun-24: 2C].
Mallalieu, Flora d. on 68-Aug-1 [68-Aug-8: 2C].
Mallalieu, J. Edwin d. on 69-Nov-22 [69-Nov-24: 2C].
Mallalieu, John B. m. Amoss, Mary C. on 68-Dec-23 [68-Dec-25: 2D].
Mallalieu, Louise Hinkle (2 yrs., 3 mos.) d. on 68-Jan-6 [68-Jan-8: 2C].
Mallen, James (65 yrs.) d. on 66-Sep-26 [66-Sep-27: 2C; 66-Sep-28: 2B].
Mallen, Margaret (51 yrs.) d. on 69-Apr-16 [69-Apr-17: 2B].
Mallen, Margaret A. m. Shunk, Benjamin on 66-May-29 [66-Jun-2: 2B; 66-Jun-4: 2B].
Mallen, Mary A. m. McGraw, John on 68-Apr-16 [68-Apr-22: 2B].
Mallette, James Augustus d. on 66-Oct-25 [66-Oct-26: 2B; 66-Oct-27: 2B].
Mallinckrodt, Charles W. (22 yrs.) d. on 68-Sep-9 [68-Sep-10: 2B].
Mallinckrodt, William Warner (25 yrs.) d. on 66-Dec-25 [66-Dec-27: 2C].
Mallon, Charles (31 yrs.) d. on 70-Nov-8 [70-Nov-9: 2C; 70-Nov-10: 2C].
Mallon, Francis (73 yrs.) d. on 67-Mar-6 [67-Mar-8: 2C; 67-Mar-9: 2B].
Mallon, Sibbie F. m. Garber, Henry S. on 66-Jun-19 [66-Jun-22: 2B].
Mallonee, Comilla Elizabeth (1 mo.) d. on 67-Jul-10 [67-Jul-12: 2C].
Mallonee, Mary Sue (35 yrs., 2 mos.) d. on 66-Oct-5 of Brain congestion [66-Oct-23: 2B].
Mallonee, Rachel m. McLane, Asbury on 70-Sep-12 [70-Sep-21: 2B].
Mallonee, William Alfred (5 yrs., 1 mo.) d. on 66-Oct-20 [66-Oct-24: 2C].
Mallory, Charles F. m. Bond, Susan E. H. on 70-Jan-27 [70-Jan-28: 2B].
Malloy, Eugene (27 yrs.) d. on 70-Nov-17 [70-Nov-19: 2B].
Malloy, Martha (7 yrs.) d. on 70-Nov-29 of Scarlet fever [70-Nov-30: 2C].
Malloy, Mary Ann Davidson d. on 67-Aug-3 [67-Aug-6: 2C].
Mallster, William T. m. Leary, Jennie on 70-Feb-1 [70-Feb-8: 2C; 70-Feb-15: 2C].
Malo, James d. on 70-Jul-27 of Heatstroke [70-Jul-28: 4E].
Malone, Daniel m. Sullivan, Christina T. on 66-Oct-1 [66-Nov-13: 2B].
Malone, Emma Jane m. Grape, Samuel on 68-Jan-15 [68-Jan-22: 2C].
Malone, Lemuel m. Gunby, Julia F. on 66-Jan-10 [66-Jan-15: 2B].
Malone, Marianne d. on 68-Aug-8 [68-Aug-10: 2C].
Malone, Mary d. on 70-Sep-15 [70-Sep-16: 2B].
Malone, Mary Ellen (11 mos.) d. on 70-Aug-29 [70-Aug-30: 2B].
Malone, Mary V. m. Dolan, John on 69-Mar-18 [69-Jul-8: 2C].

Maloney, James A. m. Murry, Lizzie Ogden on 68-Jan-27 [68-Feb-21: 2C].
Maloney, James Marian (3 yrs.) d. on 69-Mar-2 [69-Mar-4: 2C].
Maloney, John (45 yrs.) d. on 68-Dec-2 of Fall from trestle [68-Dec-4: 1G, 2D].
Maloney, Julia m. Worden, R. on 68-Sep-1 [68-Sep-4: 2A].
Maloney, Mary (47 yrs.) d. on 69-Nov-21 [69-Nov-22: 2C].
Maloney, Mathon (60 yrs.) d. on 68-May-19 [68-May-20: 2A].
Maloney, Michael (26 yrs.) d. on 68-Jul-17 of Heatstroke [68-Jul-20: 1E].
Maloney, Patrick (26 yrs.) d. on 68-Jul-19 [68-Jul-20: 2B].
Malony, William H. (2 yrs., 5 mos.) d. on 66-Dec-22 [66-Dec-24: 2B].
Malooley, Catherine (6 yrs., 5 mos.) d. on 67-May-31 [67-Jun-1: 2B].
Malooly, Katie (9 mos.) d. on 68-Aug-28 [68-Aug-29: 2B].
Maltby, Jane (68 yrs.) d. on 68-Aug-11 [68-Aug-12: 2C].
Manahan, Adele (11 yrs.) d. on 69-May-30 [69-May-31: 2C].
Mandelbaum, Carrie m. Kerngood, William on 68-Jan-8 [68-Jan-10: 2C].
Manders, A. E. (22 yrs.) d. on 68-Mar-4 [68-Mar-5: 2C].
Manger, Frederick Forrest (2 yrs., 1 mo.) d. on 67-Jan-22 [67-Jan-23: 2C].
Mangum, Richie d. on 69-Mar-30 [69-Apr-1: 2C].
Manion, James (24 yrs.) d. on 68-Apr-5 [68-Apr-6: 2B].
Manion, Matthew (24 yrs.) d. on 69-Aug-23 of Brain congestion [69-Aug-24: 1H].
Manion, Patrick (52 yrs.) d. on 68-Jul-2 [68-Jul-4: 2C].
Mankin, Mary J. L. m. Wherrett, George Z. on 67-Dec-3 [67-Dec-6: 2C].
Manley, James, Jr. m. Fleischman, Hannah on 70-Sep-13 [70-Sep-20: 2B].
Manly, Thomas E. m. Bordley, Mary A. on 68-Dec-10 [68-Dec-19: 2B].
Manly, William G. m. Moffitt, Rebecca on 67-Apr-4 [67-Apr-9: 2B].
Manly, William H. (32 yrs.) d. on 70-Mar-12 [70-Mar-14: 2C].
Manly, William R., Jr. (1 yr., 6 mos.) d. on 67-Aug-28 [67-Aug-29: 2B].
Mann, Ann Louisa (30 yrs.) d. on 66-Jul-28 [66-Jul-30: 2C].
Mann, Anne Louisa (1 yr., 11 mos.) d. on 70-Aug-31 [70-Sep-1: 2B].
Mann, Arthur H. m. Hack, Augusta C. on 68-Aug-4 [68-Aug-8: 2B].
Mann, Helen (4 mos.) d. on 69-Jun-14 [69-Jun-15: 2C].
Mann, John (78 yrs.) d. on 70-Dec-21 [70-Dec-22: 2B; 70-Dec-23: 2B].
Mann, John C. m. Maier, Mary A. on 69-Sep-12 [69-Sep-18: 2B].
Mann, Josephine m. Weems, Tennyson on 68-Jun-2 [68-Jun-24: 2B].
Mann, Maria E. H. m. Shryock, Thomas J. on 69-Oct-21 [69-Oct-23: 2B].
Mann, Mary (53 yrs.) d. on 66-Jul-2 [66-Jul-3: 2C].
Mann, Mary Jennie (1 yr., 5 mos.) d. on 68-Sep-15 [68-Sep-17: 2B].
Mann, Susan A. m. Plunkett, Edward J. on 68-Jul-21 [68-Oct-13: 2C].
Mann, Walter G. (1 yr., 9 mos.) d. on 66-Jul-12 [66-Jul-13: 2C].
Mann, William Howard (44 yrs.) d. on 66-Jun-17 [66-Jun-18: 2B].
Mannar, James B. (2 yrs., 9 mos.) d. of Panama fever [66-Jul-26: 2C].
Mannar, Martha A. H. (69 yrs.) d. on 69-May-10 [69-May-12: 2B; 69-May-19: 2C].
Mannar, Mary C. m. Richardson, John on 66-Apr-5 [66-Apr-7: 2B].
Manner, Annie m. Simms, Thomas on 70-Feb-1 [70-Feb-10: 2C].
Manning, Fannie T. (1 yr., 6 mos.) d. on 68-Aug-13 [68-Aug-14: 2C].
Manning, George O. m. Allnutt, Lertie C. on 68-Nov-12 [68-Nov-16: 2C].
Manning, Grace (6 mos.) d. on 70-Aug-1 [70-Aug-3: 2C].
Manning, Henry (48 yrs.) d. on 66-Sep-19 [66-Sep-20: 1G, 2B].
Manning, John (40 yrs.) d. on 66-Mar-16 Drowned [66-Mar-19: 1G].
Manning, Laura V. m. Clark, Edwin on 70-Jan-13 [70-Jan-19: 2C].
Manning, Malachi (44 yrs.) d. on 69-Nov-15 [69-Nov-17: 2C].
Manning, Margaret m. Clark, John on 66-Apr-2 [66-Apr-26: 2B].
Manning, Thomas (41 yrs.) d. on 67-Oct-7 [67-Oct-8: 2B].
Manning, Thomas S. d. on 67-Nov-19 [67-Nov-26: 4E].
Mannion, Patrick (55 yrs.) d. on 66-Dec-6 [66-Dec-7: 2B].
Manns, Emma (4 mos.) d. on 67-Sep-12 [67-Sep-14: 2A].

Manns, Frederick A. m. Remmy, Emma A. on 67-Aug-1 [67-Aug-10: 2B].
Manns, Margaret (1 mo.) d. on 70-Sep-12 [70-Sep-13: 2B].
Manro, Carrie T. m. Brown, Henry G. on 67-Oct-3 [67-Oct-9: 2B; 67-Oct-10: 2B].
Mansdorfer, John G. (32 yrs.) d. on 70-Sep-25 [70-Sep-26: 2B].
Mansdorper, John George m. Hahn, Minnie on 69-Dec-26 [70-Jan-4: 2C].
Mansfield, Benjamin W. m. Dryden, Virginia A. on 67-May-28 [67-May-30: 2B].
Mansfield, James A. m. Fawkes, Maria L. on 68-Jun-25 [68-Jul-2: 2C].
Mansfield, James D. (3 yrs., 11 mos.) d. on 69-Dec-31 of Measles [69-Jan-7: 2C].
Mansfield, Marceline m. Ledley, Alexander D on 66-Aug-23 [66-Aug-27: 2B].
Mansfield, Mary m. Pugh, Ananias on 68-May-25 [68-May-27: 2B].
Mansfield, Richard Henry (11 mos.) d. on 67-Aug-14 [67-Aug-16: 2B].
Mansfield, Samuel m. Plack, Lucetta F. on 70-Jun-9 [70-Jun-20: 2B].
Mansfield, William m. Phillips, Mary E. on 69-Jul-11 [69-Jul-14: 2D].
Manson, Indiana F. (32 yrs.) d. on 70-Jul-21 [70-Jul-22: 2C; 70-Jul-23: 2B].
Manson, James Guy (2 yrs., 5 mos.) d. on 66-Jun-2 [66-Jun-4: 2B; 66-Jun-8: 2B].
Manson, Mary M. m. Gill, William R. on 67-Jan-15 [67-Jan-19: 2C].
Mansur, Ellen A. d. on 69-Mar-22 [69-Mar-23: 2C].
Mantle, George W. (25 yrs.) d. on 66-Jun-21 [66-Jun-23: 2B].
Mantler, John L. m. Sauerwein, Virginia R. on 69-Sep-1 [69-Sep-16: 2B].
Mantz, David Allen (37 yrs.) d. on 66-Dec-27 [66-Dec-29: 2C].
Mantz, Eliza (69 yrs.) d. on 69-Apr-9 [69-Apr-20: 2B].
Mantz, Rebecca m. Dukehart, John M. on 66-Jul-29 [66-Sep-3: 2C].
Mantz, Sophia (67 yrs.) d. on 70-Jun-3 [70-Jun-4: 2B].
Manuel, Sarah (19 yrs.) d. on 65-Jul-29 of Typhoid [66-Jun-20: 2C].
Maple, H. L. (26 yrs.) d. on 70-Jan-8 of Consumption [70-Jan-11: 2C].
Marcelas, Charles M. W. d. on 67-Feb-3 [67-Feb-28: 2C].
Marcellett, Mary Josephine m. Webber, John Philip on 68-Sep-29 [68-Oct-1: 2B].
March, James (2 yrs., 1 mo.) d. on 70-Oct-18 [70-Oct-20: 2B].
Marchant, Ella Nora (11 mos.) d. on 68-Jun-17 [68-Jun-23: 2B].
Marchildon, Julia m. Reily, James E. on 69-Jun-15 [69-Jun-25: 2C].
Marchonnetti, Sebastian (65 yrs.) d. on 66-May-19 [66-May-21: 2B].
Marck, John L. (51 yrs.) d. on 67-Jan-8 [67-Jan-9: 2C].
Marcuse, Jacob (38 yrs.) d. on 70-Sep-8 [70-Sep-14: 2B].
Marden, Sallie S. m. Thompson, A. D. on 67-Mar-5 [67-Mar-6: 2C].
Marean, Thomas (84 yrs.) d. on 68-Jul-16 [68-Jul-17: 2C].
Mareen, Catherine E. m. Bennett, William D. on 68-Sep-17 [68-Oct-21: 2C].
Mareks, George H. m. Martin, Claudia E. on 67-Nov-10 [67-Nov-16: 2B].
Marhencke, H. H. (39 yrs.) d. on 66-Aug-25 [66-Aug-27: 2B].
Marine, Anna T. m. Wallace, George W. on 67-Dec-24 [68-Jan-21: 2C].
Marine, L. Emma m. Cathcart, J. W. on 68-Jun-22 [68-Jun-27: 2B].
Marine, Winfield Franklin d. on 69-Aug-26 [69-Aug-28: 2B].
Mariner, Charles W. m. Gruinbeck, Margaret A. on 69-Feb-9 [69-Feb-12: 2C].
Mariner, William H. H. m. Cross, Mary Margaret on 66-Dec-2 [66-Dec-5: 2B; 66-Dec-6: 2B].
Maris, W. D. m. Fisher, M. A. on 70-Feb-2 [70-Feb-10: 2C].
Mark, Calvin B. (28 yrs., 3 mos.) d. on 68-Jul-13 [68-Jul-14: 2C; 68-Jul-22: 2C].
Mark, Emma J. m. Saums, Christian C. on 67-Dec-3 [67-Dec-18: 2B].
Mark, George W. m. Stevens, Ann J. on 70-Nov-1 [70-Nov-2: 2C].
Mark, Nicholas (56 yrs.) d. on 70-May-22 of Paralysis [70-May-23: 2B; 70-May-24: 2C].
Marker, Elizabeth (84 yrs.) d. on 70-Jan-10 [70-Jan-11: 2C].
Markey, Lucy E. m. Lester, Joseph R. on 68-May-5 [68-May-11: 2B].
Markland, Allie m. Wiles, James A. on 66-Dec-11 [67-Jan-3: 2B].
Markland, Bettie M. m. Jackson, George H. on 68-Jun-16 [68-Jun-20: 2B].
Markland, Charles H. m. Kelley, S. C. on 69-Oct-26 [69-Oct-27: 2B].
Markland, Charles Henry (18 yrs., 6 mos.) d. on 68-Nov-5 [68-Nov-6: 2C].
Markland, Sarah m. Brewer, William R. on 66-May-17 [66-May-22: 2B].

Markley, Thaddeus W. m. Conine, Augusta on 66-Nov-29 [66-Dec-1: 2B].
Markoe, Maria Kerr (1 yr., 2 mos.) d. on 70-Aug-24 [70-Aug-25: 2C].
Marlaey, Harry (5 mos.) d. on 70-Jul-29 [70-Jul-30: 2C].
Marley, James (80 yrs.) d. on 69-Dec-26 [69-Dec-27: 2D; 69-Dec-28: 2D].
Marley, John Y. (1 yr., 2 mos.) d. on 66-Aug-24 [66-Aug-25: 2A].
Marley, Mary Ann (10 mos.) d. [68-Sep-29: 2B].
Marley, Richard (77 yrs., 8 mos.) d. on 69-May-7 [69-May-8: 1G; 69-May-10: 1H; 69-May-8: 2B].
Marlin, Eveline m. Ryer, John D. on 66-Jun-5 [66-Jun-13: 2B].
Maroney, Eliza (32 yrs.) d. [69-Jan-4: 2C].
Marquett, Mary (70 yrs.) d. on 67-Dec-13 [67-Dec-14: 2B].
Marr, George (58 yrs.) d. on 69-Nov-3 [69-Nov-4: 2C].
Marr, William (77 yrs.) d. on 69-Mar-13 [69-Mar-15: 2C].
Marren, Terrance d. on 70-Apr-14 Drowned [70-Apr-19: 2B].
Marren, Terrence (72 yrs.) d. on 70-Jan-14 [70-Jan-15: 1H, 2C].
Marrian, James A. m. Miles, Sallie A. [69-Apr-10: 2B].
Marriet, Lizzie m. Fleming, Douglas on 69-Feb-16 [69-Feb-23: 2C].
Marriott, Barzillai (63 yrs.) d. on 70-Mar-12 [70-Mar-14: 1H, 2C].
Marriott, Byron m. Rogers, Kate on 70-Aug-25 [70-Sep-3: 2B].
Marriott, Elisha James (53 yrs.) d. on 66-Dec-5 [66-Dec-10: 2C].
Marriott, Ellen d. on 68-Aug-25 [68-Jul-26: 2B].
Marriott, Eugene E. m. Trott, Mary Louisa on 70-Jul-7 [70-Jul-8: 2C].
Marriott, Jane McKim d. on 68-Apr-30 [68-May-2: 2C; 68-May-4: 2B].
Marriott, Kate d. on 69-Feb-22 [69-Feb-24: 2C].
Marriott, Kate (1 yr., 2 mos.) d. on 69-Feb-6 [69-Feb-8: 2C].
Marriott, Lucy (26 yrs.) d. on 67-Sep-13 [67-Sep-14: 2A].
Marriott, Lucy m. Benson, B. S. on 67-Jan-3 [67-Jan-5: 2C].
Marriott, Mollie E. m. Hazlewood, N. H. on 66-Nov-22 [66-Nov-27: 2B].
Marriott, Richard Waters (71 yrs.) d. on 70-May-12 [70-May-14: 2B].
Marriott, Samuel N. m. Flory, Alice A. on 67-Aug-18 [67-Aug-20: 2B].
Marriott, Telfair Wilson (10 yrs.) d. on 66-Jul-5 [66-Jul-6: 2B; 66-Jul-7: 2B].
Marriott, Thomas m. Gorman, Mary E. on 66-Jan-26 [66-Jan-27: 2B].
Marrison, John M. (21 yrs.) d. on 67-Oct-31 [67-Nov-2: 2B].
Marron, Thomas m. Walbach, Eliza L. on 66-Apr-26 [66-May-2: 2B].
Marron, William L. m. Walbach, Mary on 68-Jan-29 [68-Feb-1: 2B].
Marrow, Laura B. m. Forrester, William E. on 70-Apr-21 [70-Apr-28: 2B].
Marsden, Alice Williams (1 yr., 5 mos.) d. on 70-May-16 [70-May-17: 2B].
Marsden, Helen Haste (3 mos.) d. on 67-Feb-19 [67-Feb-26: 2C].
Marsh, Charles H. (28 yrs.) d. on 67-Jan-25 [67-Jan-29: 2C].
Marsh, Charles Howard (2 yrs., 2 mos.) d. on 70-Feb-26 [70-Feb-28: 2C].
Marsh, Chester S. d. on 70-Dec-13 [70-Dec-28: 2C].
Marsh, Eleanora B. (77 yrs.) d. on 70-May-3 [70-May-4: 2C].
Marsh, Eliza (40 yrs.) d. on 67-Aug-4 of Consumption [67-Aug-5: 2B].
Marsh, Emma J. m. Albaugh, Thomas on 70-Sep-15 [70-Sep-19: 2B].
Marsh, George d. on 70-Apr-21 [70-Apr-22: 2C].
Marsh, Hugh W. (53 yrs.) d. on 70-Nov-26 [70-Nov-28: 2C].
Marsh, James William d. on 70-Apr-21 [70-Apr-22: 2C].
Marsh, John H. m. Kirk, Sarah E. on 68-Feb-26 [68-Feb-27: 2C].
Marsh, Johnnie (3 yrs., 8 mos.) d. on 70-Feb-20 [70-Feb-21: 2B].
Marsh, Mary Geneva m. Blanchard, Bennington G. on 70-Apr-19 [70-Apr-21: 2B].
Marsh, Mary Jane d. on 70-Apr-21 [70-Apr-22: 2C].
Marshall, Alexander H. m. Miller, Maggie on 67-Jun-4 [67-Jun-17: 2B].
Marshall, Belle (30 yrs.) d. on 69-May-16 [69-May-17: 2B].
Marshall, Catherine A. (38 yrs.) d. on 70-Nov-7 [70-Nov-8: 2B].
Marshall, Charles (1 yr., 1 mo.) d. on 69-Jul-6 [69-Jul-8: 2C].

Marshall, Charles m. Herring, Julia on 70-Nov-24 [70-Nov-26: 2B].
Marshall, Edward m. Earle, Sarah on 69-Nov-3 [69-Nov-5: 2C].
Marshall, Elizabeth (56 yrs.) d. on 67-Jan-12 [67-Jan-14: 2C].
Marshall, Frank (22 yrs.) d. on 70-Apr-2 [70-Apr-5: 2B].
Marshall, George W. m. Hunt, Ridie on 69-Nov-18 [69-Nov-20: 2B].
Marshall, Harry Grant (6 yrs.) d. on 69-Apr-8 of Chronic croup [69-Apr-9: 2B].
Marshall, James W. m. Lancaster, Sallie D. on 69-Nov-16 [69-Nov-20: 2B].
Marshall, Jane (30 yrs.) d. on 70-Nov-3 of Intemperance and exposure [70-Nov-4: 4C].
Marshall, Jane P. (41 yrs., 10 mos.) d. on 69-Dec-23 [69-Dec-24: 2C].
Marshall, John (24 yrs.) d. on 68-Aug-19 [68-Aug-22: 2A].
Marshall, John m. Botterill, Bell on 68-Aug-20 [68-Aug-22: 2A].
Marshall, John m. Fowler, Margery A. W. on 70-May-19 [70-May-21: 2B].
Marshall, Laura V. m. Price, Frank S. on 66-Jul-30 [66-Aug-6: 2C].
Marshall, Lorama m. Wilson, James on 68-Dec-16 [69-Jan-6: 2C].
Marshall, Maggie m. Jones, Robert H. on 69-Sep-9 [69-Sep-22: 2C].
Marshall, Margaret (39 yrs.) d. on 67-Jun-8 [67-Jun-10: 2B].
Marshall, Margaret Cora (1 yr., 7 mos.) d. on 69-Oct-17 [69-Oct-19: 2C].
Marshall, Margaret R. (35 yrs.) d. on 68-Jun-26 [68-Jul-1: 2B].
Marshall, Mary Ann (18 yrs., 2 mos.) d. on 67-Dec-4 [67-Dec-5: 2C].
Marshall, Mary Ann (48 yrs.) d. on 67-Feb-18 [67-Feb-19: 2C].
Marshall, Samuel V. (33 yrs.) d. on 70-Dec-19 [70-Dec-20: 2B].
Marshall, Sarah (1 yr., 1 mo.) d. on 69-Aug-23 [69-Aug-24: 2B].
Marshall, Sarah (64 yrs.) d. on 70-Aug-31 [70-Sep-1: 2B].
Marshall, Theodore W. (23 yrs.) d. on 70-Nov-4 [70-Nov-5: 2B].
Marshall, Thomas W. (23 yrs.) d. on 70-Nov-4 [70-Nov-7: 2B].
Marshall, Urath d. on 67-Jan-29 [67-Jan-30: 2C].
Marston, Henry W. m. King, Sarah C. on 68-Jan-23 [68-Jan-27: 2C].
Marston, Mary E. m. Wood, George M. D. on 66-Sep-11 [66-Sep-17: 2B].
Marston, R. Jarrett m. Galloway, May Ella on 66-Jan-22 [66-Feb-13: 2C].
Martenet, Charles Joseph (2 yrs., 6 mos.) d. on 69-Jan-17 [69-Jan-19: 2C].
Martenet, George Dorsey (3 yrs., 3 mos.) d. on 67-May-18 [67-May-22: 2B].
Martenet, John Gilbert (1 yr., 4 mos.) d. on 69-Jun-30 [69-Jul-1: 2C].
Martenet, Mary Edwardina (5 yrs., 3 mos.) d. on 66-Dec-16 [66-Dec-18: 2B].
Martien, Florence I. (6 mos.) d. on 66-Dec-25 [66-Dec-27: 2C].
Martien, William m. Conradt, Virginia on 67-Jun-4 [67-Jun-12: 2B].
Martin, A. S. m. Morris, Tillie L. on 68-Mar-1 [68-Mar-3: 2C].
Martin, Abbie m. Rinehardt, A. on 68-Dec-22 [69-Jan-4: 2C].
Martin, Agnes Gertrude (2 yrs., 8 mos.) d. on 68-Oct-24 [68-Oct-26: 2B].
Martin, Ann Elizabeth (66 yrs.) d. on 69-Sep-29 [69-Sep-30: 2B].
Martin, Arthur Lawrence (9 mos.) d. on 70-Aug-5 [70-Aug-17: 2C].
Martin, Basil N. m. McCuen, Clara on 66-Apr-24 [66-May-1: 2A].
Martin, Bessie A. (3 yrs., 3 mos.) d. on 70-Feb-5 [70-Feb-7: 2C].
Martin, Catharine M. (37 yrs., 8 mos.) d. on 70-Mar-9 [70-Mar-11: 2C; 70-Mar-12: 2C].
Martin, Catherine m. Bell, John R. on 66-Nov-1 [66-Nov-5: 2B].
Martin, Claudia E. m. Mareks, George H. on 67-Nov-10 [67-Nov-16: 2B].
Martin, D. W. m. Sewell, Martha E. on 69-Dec-27 [69-Feb-2: 2C].
Martin, Daniel (63 yrs.) d. on 67-Dec-3 [67-Dec-6: 2C].
Martin, Edna Ann (85 yrs.) d. on 68-Nov-29 [68-Dec-1: 2C].
Martin, Eli m. Stifler, Eliza J. on 68-Dec-27 [69-Jan-2: 2C].
Martin, Eliza (66 yrs.) d. on 67-Oct-15 [67-Oct-17: 2B].
Martin, Elizabeth (81 yrs.) d. on 67-Jul-6 [67-Jul-11: 2C].
Martin, Elizabeth m. Rinecker, John W. on 67-Feb-9 [67-Mar-6: 2C].
Martin, Elizabeth P. (40 yrs.) d. on 70-Apr-18 of Suicide (Stabbing) [70-Apr-19: 1H, 2B].
Martin, Ella m. Henderson, William T. on 68-Aug-31 [68-Sep-1: 2A].
Martin, Ella m. Stine, C. Edwin on 70-Nov-17 [70-Nov-29: 2C].

Martin, Emma (3 yrs., 7 mos.) d. on 69-Oct-31 [69-Nov-1: 2C].
Martin, Eugene Camillus d. on 68-Dec-19 [68-Dec-23: 2C].
Martin, Eva R. m. Miller, James A. on 66-Dec-24 [66-Dec-27: 2C].
Martin, F. m. Louge, Bell on 68-Dec-25 [69-Jan-4: 2C].
Martin, Fanny (11 mos.) d. on 69-Jul-18 [69-Jul-21: 2C].
Martin, George, Capt. (43 yrs.) d. on 67-Dec-4 [67-Dec-5: 1G; 67-Dec-6: 2C].
Martin, George B. m. Richardson, Virginia S. on 70-Mar-6 [70-Apr-16: 2B].
Martin, George E. (9 mos.) d. on 69-Jul-3 [69-Jul-5: 2C].
Martin, George W. m. Pierce, Emma on 68-Jan-21 [68-Jan-22: 2C].
Martin, H. T. m. Birckhead, S. Lizzie on 68-Jun-4 [68-Jun-8: 2B].
Martin, Henrietta M. F. m. Goldsborough, Richard H. on 70-May-31 [70-Jun-6: 2B].
Martin, Henry B. m. Higgins, Alice Blanche on 67-Apr-25 [67-Apr-26: 2B].
Martin, Henry Stevens (7 mos.) d. on 70-Jul-19 [70-Jul-22: 2C].
Martin, Howard (1 yr.) d. on 69-Feb-2 [69-Feb-9: 2C].
Martin, Hugh, Capt. (69 yrs.) d. on 67-Jun-17 [67-Jun-22: 2B; 67-Jun-24: 1F].
Martin, J. H. m. Jones, Susie T. on 67-Aug-28 [67-Sep-10: 2B].
Martin, James m. Boylan, Ellen on 67-Jan-1 [67-Jan-4: 2D; 67-Jan-5: 2C].
Martin, Jane Gatchell m. Gatchell, John G. on 68-Nov-26 [68-Nov-28: 2C].
Martin, John (66 yrs.) d. on 66-May-25 [66-May-26: 2B].
Martin, John d. on 69-May-20 [69-May-21: 2C].
Martin, John A. (8 mos.) d. on 70-Aug-1 [70-Aug-9: 2C].
Martin, John B. m. Wilson, Anna A. on 66-Nov-1 [66-Nov-3: 2B].
Martin, John G. (5 yrs., 1 mo.) d. on 69-Feb-22 [69-Feb-23: 2C].
Martin, John G. m. Galvin, Emma M. on 66-Mar-28 [66-Mar-30: 2C].
Martin, John W. m. Bulack, Mary Jane on 70-Jul-4 [70-Jul-22: 2C].
Martin, Joseph m. Johnson, Laura on 67-Jan-15 [67-Jan-17: 2C].
Martin, Joseph K. (32 yrs.) d. on 66-Feb-16 of Consumption [66-Feb-27: 2B].
Martin, Josiah H. m. Bulack, Alice A. on 68-Jun-29 [68-Oct-5: 2B].
Martin, Julius (50 yrs., 2 mos.) d. on 70-Apr-11 [70-Apr-13: 2B].
Martin, Kate m. Franklin, John R. on 68-Dec-9 [68-Dec-11: 2C].
Martin, Kate m. Barlow, Joseph M. on 67-Feb-21 [67-Mar-7: 2C].
Martin, Leila M. m. Yates, Charles A. on 67-Dec-17 [67-Dec-23: 2B].
Martin, Lewis d. on 70-Dec-14 Drowned [70-Dec-16: 4E].
Martin, Lewis G. m. Montgomery, Virginia on 66-Mar-8 [66-Apr-4: 2B].
Martin, Libbie E. m. Fairbank, Thomas J. on 70-Sep-7 [70-Sep-10: 2B].
Martin, Lorano D. d. on 69-Jul-17 of Paralysis [69-Jul-19: 2D].
Martin, Maria M. d. [67-Jan-10: 2C].
Martin, Mary (70 yrs.) d. on 69-Nov-13 [69-Nov-15: 2C].
Martin, Mary (39 yrs.) d. on 69-Dec-30 [69-Jan-1: 2C].
Martin, Mary m. Hamilton, Stewart on 67-Feb-28 [67-Mar-6: 2C].
Martin, Mary m. Addington, J. C. on 70-Sep-14 [70-Sep-23: 2C].
Martin, Mary A. m. Agnew, Thomas A. on 66-Jun-28 [66-Jul-7: 2B].
Martin, Mary E. m. Knott, J. Wesley on 68-Aug-11 [68-Aug-19: 2B].
Martin, Mary E. m. Brown, Horatio W. on 69-Nov-16 [69-Nov-20: 2B].
Martin, Mary Elizabeth (86 yrs.) d. on 69-Mar-23 [69-Mar-25: 2C].
Martin, Mary Ella (1 yr., 3 mos.) d. on 70-Apr-9 of Diptheria [70-Apr-11: 2B].
Martin, Mary Emma (10 mos.) d. on 70-Dec-27 [70-Dec-30: 2C].
Martin, Michael (6 yrs., 1 mo.) d. on 70-Sep-6 [70-Sep-7: 2B].
Martin, Patrick H. m. Dougherty, Elizabeth on 69-Jan-26 [69-Feb-8: 2C].
Martin, Pauline V. m. Farran, J. Frank on 66-Jun-28 [66-Jul-7: 2B].
Martin, Percy Darrington (9 mos.) d. on 67-Oct-11 [67-Oct-14: 2B].
Martin, Robert Harry (1 yr., 11 mos.) d. on 68-Oct-10 of Lung congestion [68-Oct-14: 2B].
Martin, Robert N. (70 yrs.) d. on 70-Jul-20 [70-Jul-21: 1F].
Martin, S. E. m. Dennis, L. Q. on 68-Jan-29 [68-Feb-1: 2B].
Martin, Sarah E. (1 yr., 3 mos.) d. on 69-Feb-5 [69-Feb-6: 2C].

Martin, Sarah Jane m. Sorrell, James H. on 70-Apr-28 [70-May-3: 2B].
Martin, Susan E. m. Miller, Thomas on 69-Apr-11 [69-Apr-13: 2B].
Martin, Thomas d. on 68-Aug-31 Crushed by tree [68-Sep-1: 1G].
Martin, Thomas (11 yrs., 2 mos.) d. on 69-Nov-7 [69-Nov-8: 2C].
Martin, Thomas E. (43 yrs.) d. on 70-Jul-28 [70-Jul-29: 2C, 4D; 70-Jul-30: 4D].
Martin, Thomas R. (28 yrs.) d. on 70-Jul-3 [70-Jul-12: 2C].
Martin, Virginia A. m. Cox, Issac on 67-Feb-11 [67-Feb-13: 2D].
Martin, W. D. m. Shaddoc, Jennie on 67-Jan-31 [67-Feb-16: 2D].
Martin, Walter (1 yr., 4 mos.) d. on 66-Oct-19 [66-Oct-20: 2B].
Martin, William (8 yrs., 9 mos.) d. on 69-Apr-17 [69-Apr-26: 2C].
Martin, William (77 yrs.) d. on 69-Jan-9 [69-Jan-11: 1H, 2C].
Martin, William E. (42 yrs.) d. on 67-Jul-24 [67-Jul-25: 2C].
Martin, William E., Gen. (55 yrs.) d. on 69-Nov-11 [69-Nov-12: 1G, 2C; 69-Nov-13: 1H].
Martin, William H. m. Johnson, Agnes A. on 66-May-24 [66-May-29: 2B].
Martin, William Hammet m. Johnson, Susan Bray on 70-Oct-27 [70-Nov-1: 2C].
Martin, William S. (24 yrs.) d. on 68-Oct-25 [68-Oct-27: 2B].
Martin, William Thomas (31 yrs.) d. on 70-Oct-12 [70-Oct-14: 2B].
Martine, Catherine S. m. Morgan, John F. on 66-Jan-10 [66-Jan-12: 2C].
Martini, John (11 mos.) d. on 68-Jul-31 [68-Aug-1: 2B].
Martins, Anna S. m. Hyde, Warren G. on 68-May-14 [68-May-16: 2A].
Martz, Joseph (42 yrs.) d. of Paralysis [67-Jul-16: 2C].
Marye, Ada m. Baily, Joseph C. on 69-Jul-13 [69-Jul-17: 2C].
Mask, Charles Edward (5 mos.) d. on 68-Feb-16 [68-Feb-17: 2C].
Mask, Charles M. m. Fuller, Jennie on 70-Jan-13 [70-Jan-18: 2C].
Mask, John Q. A. (27 yrs.) d. on 68-Jul-8 of Gunshot wound [68-Jul-10: 1G, 2C; 68-Jul-11: 1G].
Maskell, Joseph H. m. Cull, Anna M. on 66-Nov-20 [66-Nov-24: 2B].
Maskell, Walter Howard (10 mos.) d. on 68-Sep-10 [68-Sep-11: 1G, 2B].
Maslin, Philip Walter (3 mos.) d. on 69-Jul-23 [69-Jul-26: 2C].
Mason, Anna (74 yrs.) d. on 68-Nov-29 [68-Nov-30: 2B].
Mason, Charles (72 yrs.) d. on 67-Aug-11 [67-Aug-13: 2B].
Mason, David (40 yrs.) d. on 68-Jun-30 [68-Jul-2: 2C].
Mason, E. Wellford m. Simpson, Mary Belle on 68-Nov-25 [68-Nov-26: 2B].
Mason, George A. m. Thomas, Alice E. on 69-Dec-14 [69-Dec-18: 2B].
Mason, George A. m. Rankle, Ruth Matilda on 70-Aug-8 [70-Dec-2: 2C].
Mason, George W. (34 yrs.) d. on 66-Jun-8 [66-Jun-9: 2B].
Mason, Georgeanna Macgill (25 yrs.) d. on 66-Apr-7 [66-Apr-9: 2B].
Mason, Ida I. m. Lucchesi, F. A. on 68-Apr-16 [68-May-4: 2B].
Mason, James (41 yrs.) d. on 66-Mar-18 [66-Mar-19: 2C].
Mason, James A. m. Millington, Maggie on 66-Jun-5 [66-Jun-7: 2B].
Mason, John (75 yrs.) d. on 70-Jul-25 [70-Jul-26: 2C; 70-Jul-27: 2C].
Mason, Julian J. m. Freeland, Elizabeth on 70-Oct-4 [70-Oct-6: 2B].
Mason, Maggie E. (11 mos.) d. on 66-Aug-8 [66-Aug-9: 2C].
Mason, Margaret (52 yrs.) d. on 67-Mar-27 [67-Mar-30: 2C].
Mason, Mary (74 yrs.) d. on 69-May-15 [69-May-17: 2B].
Mason, Mary D. m. Beacham, J. Summers on 68-Oct-22 [68-Oct-24: 2B].
Mason, Mary E. m. Nice, William A. on 65-Nov-6 [66-Jan-31: 2C].
Mason, Mary E. m. Dreyer, Henry A. on 66-Jan-1 [66-Jan-15: 2B].
Mason, Mary Ellen d. on 70-May-15 [70-May-16: 2B].
Mason, Mary Simpson (8 mos.) d. on 70-Jul-21 [70-Aug-2: 2C].
Mason, N. Carroll m. Stayman, Kate E. on 67-Nov-21 [67-Dec-2: 2C].
Mason, Samuel, Jr. d. on 67-Aug-12 of Cholera [67-Apr-3: 2B].
Mason, Thomas Aloysius (6 yrs.) d. on 66-Feb-2 [66-Feb-5: 2C].
Mason, William, Capt. (68 yrs.) d. on 68-Feb-21 [68-May-4: 2B].
Mason, William A. (34 yrs.) d. on 68-Jul-5 [68-Jul-7: 2B].

Mass, E. V. m. Hults, William H. on 66-May-21 [66-May-24: 2C].
Mass, Franklin (43 yrs.) d. on 70-Oct-1 of Suicide (Shooting) [70-Oct-3: 4B].
Mass, Samuel (73 yrs.) d. on 67-Jun-2 [67-Jun-17: 2C; 67-Jun-21: 2B, 4C].
Massey, James (30 yrs.) d. on 66-Nov-15 [66-Nov-16: 2C].
Massey, L. M. m. Turner, John, Jr. on 67-Apr-9 [67-Apr-13: 2B; 67-Apr-15: 2B].
Massey, Mary Ann m. Shrifogle, W. H. on 66-Nov-18 [66-Nov-24: 2B].
Masson, Jennie m. Billingsley, James on 70-Aug-16 [70-Aug-30: 2B].
Masson, Susannah F. m. Smith, Wesley on 69-May-5 [69-May-11: 2B].
Mastbaum, Sarah m. Reinhart, Harry E. on 70-Jun-15 [70-Jul-19: 2B].
Masten, Mary (23 yrs., 3 mos.) d. on 69-Oct-11 [69-Oct-13: 2C].
Masterman, Mary E. m. Pattison, R. E. on 68-Jan-30 [68-Feb-3: 2C].
Mater, William (35 yrs.) d. on 69-Aug-18 of Paralysis [69-Aug-19: 2B].
Mates, Eliza Ann m. Redmond, Robert on 69-Oct-14 [69-Oct-27: 2B].
Mates, William (35 yrs.) d. on 69-Aug-18 of Paralysis [69-Aug-27: 2B].
Mathany, John Morris (5 mos.) d. on 69-Dec-20 [69-Dec-22: 2B].
Mather, Nathan C. m. Briscoe, Emma on 70-Jun-2 [70-Jun-10: 2B].
Mather, Thomas (72 yrs.) d. on 67-Feb-1 [67-Feb-2: 2C].
Mathes, Elizabeth Caroline (5 mos.) d. on 70-Jun-20 [70-Jun-21: 2C].
Mathews, Charles (58 yrs.) d. on 69-Jun-23 of Heart disease [69-Jun-24: 1G].
Mathews, Ellen A. (63 yrs.) d. on 70-Mar-30 [70-Mar-31: 2C].
Mathews, Henry m. Harris, Anna R. on 68-Nov-5 [68-Nov-7: 2B].
Mathews, Lemuel E. m. Mitchell, Ella A. on 70-Feb-23 [70-Feb-24: 2C].
Mathews, Margaret (56 yrs.) d. on 66-Apr-21 [66-Apr-24: 2B].
Mathews, Margaret B. m. Grimes, James H. on 66-Aug-16 [66-Sep-6: 2B].
Mathews, Nora L. m. Mittnacht, Henry on 69-Mar-3 [69-Mar-8: 2C].
Mathews, Patrick d. on 70-Jun-26 [70-Jun-27: 2C].
Mathews, Wilbur F. m. Bride, Mary J. on 67-Jun-19 [67-Jun-21: 2B].
Mathias, John A. m. Montgomery, Ida C. on 68-May-7 [68-May-9: 2B].
Mathias, Tunnier d. on 66-Sep-1 of Suicide (Hanging) [66-Sep-4: 4C].
Mathias, William A. (19 yrs.) d. on 70-Jan-2 [70-Jan-3: 2C; 70-Jan-4: 2C].
Mathiot, Annie M. d. on 69-Jun-10 [69-Jun-12: 2B].
Mathiot, Charles (47 yrs.) d. on 68-Jun-29 of Heart disease [68-Jun-30: 1G, 2B; 68-Jul-1: 2B].
Mathiot, Charles Albert (8 yrs., 6 mos.) d. on 69-Oct-14 of Typhoid [69-Oct-16: 2B].
Mathiot, Clara L. m. Frame, James on 70-Apr-28 [70-May-3: 2B].
Mathison, Alexander, Jr. (5 mos.) d. on 68-Jul-28 [68-Jul-29: 2B].
Mathison, Emma (64 yrs.) d. on 68-Mar-11 [68-Mar-12: 2B].
Mathison, John (67 yrs., 9 mos.) d. on 67-Apr-21 [67-Apr-22: 2A].
Matson, Minnie J. m. Prichard, George W. on 67-Nov-7 [68-Mar-2: 2B].
Matson, Mollie E. m. Neely, James M. on 69-Nov-4 [69-Nov-9: 2C].
Mattfeldt, Charles W. m. Wernex, Mary A. on 66-May-6 [66-Jun-16: 2B].
Matthai, C. E. m. Spielman, Margaret Elizabeth on 68-Nov-17 [68-Dec-3: 2C].
Matthai, John N. (16 yrs.) d. on 68-Aug-1 Drowned [68-Aug-3: 1F, 2B].
Matthei, Daniel m. Becker, Lina on 68-Feb-2 [68-Feb-4: 2C].
Matthews, Ann M. d. on 67-Jan-4 [67-Jan-8: 2B].
Matthews, Ann Maria (59 yrs.) d. on 68-Feb-4 [68-Feb-6: 2C].
Matthews, Anna J. m. Travis, L. Alonzo on 68-May-20 [68-May-26: 2B].
Matthews, Charles (54 yrs.) d. on 69-Jun-23 [69-Jun-30: 2C].
Matthews, Charles S. m. Rochester, Jane on 70-Sep-5 [70-Sep-7: 2B].
Matthews, Edward (55 yrs.) d. on 69-May-4 of Suicide (Shooting) [69-May-8: 1G; 69-May-5: 1G].
Matthews, Eli m. Price, Sallie E. on 68-Nov-10 [68-Nov-18: 2C].
Matthews, Eli Scott (10 mos.) d. on 66-Jul-15 [66-Jul-17: 2C].
Matthews, Elizabeth (79 yrs.) d. on 69-Mar-10 of Paralysis [69-Mar-12: 2C].
Matthews, Elizabeth H. (52 yrs.) d. on 67-Oct-18 [67-Oct-22: 2A].
Matthews, Emma Maud m. Jones, William H. on 66-Apr-25 [66-Apr-30: 2B].

Matthews, George W. m. Mules, Mary J. on 66-Apr-26 [66-May-11: 2B].
Matthews, Harry (5 mos.) d. on 67-Jul-13 [67-Jul-13: 2B].
Matthews, Howard James (6 mos.) d. on 66-Aug-18 [66-Aug-23: 2C].
Matthews, James (48 yrs.) d. on 67-Aug-17 [67-Aug-19: 2C].
Matthews, John d. on 70-Oct-17 of Cholera [70-Nov-11: 4D].
Matthews, John m. Little, Louisa V. on 68-Nov-10 [68-Nov-12: 2C].
Matthews, John P. m. Haun, Sallie E. on 69-Dec-28 [69-Dec-29: 2D].
Matthews, Joseph D. (58 yrs.) d. on 67-Jan-7 [67-Jan-8: 2B; 67-Jan-9: 2C].
Matthews, Joshua m. Waugh, Jennie on 70-Jun-1 [70-Jun-2: 2B].
Matthews, Lizzie A. m. Hassett, John F. on 69-May-5 [69-May-8: 2B].
Matthews, Lucy m. Jolliffe, W. H. on 69-Dec-8 [69-Dec-9: 2C].
Matthews, Mary V. m. Spedden, M. L. on 67-Oct-17 [67-Oct-19: 2A; 67-Oct-21: 2B].
Matthews, Mordecai H., Jr. (22 yrs.) d. on 67-May-7 [67-May-8: 2B].
Matthews, Rachel (81 yrs.) d. on 69-Apr-19 [69-Apr-20: 2B; 69-Apr-21: 2C].
Matthews, Randolph m. Scharf, Martha A. on 68-Nov-10 [68-Nov-18: 2C].
Matthews, Sarah (88 yrs.) d. on 67-May-19 [67-May-20: 2B].
Matthews, Temperance m. Gover, Samuel A. on 69-May-4 [69-May-12: 2B].
Matthews, Thomas R., Jr. m. Roberts, Susan A. on 66-Dec-19 [66-Dec-22: 2A].
Matthews, William (96 yrs., 8 mos.) d. on 70-Sep-12 [70-Sep-16: 2B].
Matthews, William Dorsett (5 yrs., 8 mos.) d. on 68-Oct-5 of Diptheria [68-Oct-10: 2B].
Matthews, Willie Riley (1 yr., 1 mo.) d. on 68-Jul-3 [68-Jul-7: 2B].
Matthews, Wilson m. Waugh, Maggie C. on 68-Mar-5 [68-Mar-12: 2B].
Mattingly, Jennie d. on 69-Oct-17 [69-Oct-19: 2C].
Mattingly, Kate m. German, Jerome B. on 67-Sep-24 [67-Sep-26: 2B].
Mattingly, Sophia (32 yrs.) d. on 70-Dec-23 [70-Dec-24: 2B].
Mattson, John (50 yrs.) d. on 69-Jan-27 [69-Jan-29: 2C].
Mattson, Lizzie H. m. Nyce, Hugh J. on 68-Nov-18 [68-Nov-24: 2C].
Mauck, Alice m. Hodson, T. S. on 66-Feb-7 [66-Feb-10: 2C].
Maughlin, Hugh A. m. Sherwood, Mary E. on 69-Feb-11 [69-Feb-23: 2C].
Maughlin, James (31 yrs., 4 mos.) d. on 69-Apr-23 [69-Apr-24: 2B].
Maul, Eleanor (54 yrs.) d. on 68-Nov-13 [68-Nov-16: 2C].
Maull, Edward A. m. Shane, Lizzie R. on 70-May-17 [70-May-18: 2B].
Maulsby, Augustus A. G. m. Bunting, Virginia on 66-Apr-17 [66-Apr-30: 2B].
Maulsby, D. L., Jr. m. George, Mary E. on 69-Jun-3 [69-Jun-7: 2B].
Maulsby, Sarah d. on 70-Aug-31 [70-Sep-2: 2C].
Maulsby, Virginia E. (21 yrs.) d. on 66-May-21 [66-May-25: 2C].
Maunder, Louisa (39 yrs.) d. on 70-Mar-27 [70-Mar-28: 2B].
Maureau, Marie Louise Fortunie d. on 66-Apr-23 [66-Apr-25: 2B].
Mause, John Henry (23 yrs., 10 mos.) d. on 70-Feb-3 [70-Feb-4: 2C; 70-Feb-5: 2B].
Maxfield, J. Harry (4 yrs., 9 mos.) d. on 70-Dec-24 [70-Dec-28: 2C].
Maxwell, Agnes Mowbray (1 yr., 2 mos.) d. on 67-Dec-10 [67-Dec-11: 2B; 67-Dec-12: 2B].
Maxwell, Ann (88 yrs.) d. on 66-Jan-2 [66-Jan-3: 2C].
Maxwell, Charles E. m. Kirby, Phillis on 67-Sep-19 [67-Sep-21: 2A].
Maxwell, David m. Rathvon, Emma E. on 70-Mar-15 [70-Mar-17: 2C].
Maxwell, George W. m. Wardenburg, Mary A. on 66-Oct-16 [66-Oct-18: 2B].
Maxwell, Griffith d. on 70-Jul-30 [70-Aug-1: 2C].
Maxwell, Issac P. m. Snyder, Annie M. on 69-Mar-18 [69-Mar-19: 2C].
Maxwell, James (33 yrs.) d. on 69-Jun-2 [69-Jun-3: 2B].
Maxwell, James Davidson (13 yrs.) d. on 66-Jul-18 [66-Jul-24: 2C].
Maxwell, John T. m. Brome, Astoria Belinda on 69-Dec-7 [69-Dec-11: 2B].
Maxwell, John W., Jr. m. Wright, Sarah E. on 68-Jan-21 [68-Jan-22: 2C].
Maxwell, Margaret A., Mrs. m. Woolfendon, James on 67-Mar-28 [67-Mar-30: 2B].
Maxwell, Thomas C. m. Barlow, Annie on 69-Feb-15 [69-Feb-17: 2C].
Maxwell, William S. m. Yearley, Elizabeth M. on 68-Apr-21 [68-Apr-25: 2B].
Maxwell, Willie Shipley (1 yr., 2 mos.) d. on 70-Jun-21 [70-Jun-23: 2C].

May, E. Ferdinand (37 yrs.) d. on 69-Oct-8 [69-Oct-9: 2C].
May, E. Ferdinand m. Gillespie, Nannie L. on 67-Jun-27 [67-Jul-1: 2B].
May, Frederick L. (55 yrs.) d. on 69-Jan-15 [69-Jan-19: 2C].
May, Henrietta m. Newman, Louis on 68-Feb-27 [68-Feb-29: 2B].
May, Henry (50 yrs.) d. on 66-Sep-25 [66-Sep-26: 2B; 66-Sep-28: 4A].
May, Henry MacKall (1 yr., 4 mos.) d. on 70-Jul-23 [70-Jul-29: 2C].
May, Joseph T. m. Palmer, Sallie M. on 68-Jan-5 [68-Jan-14: 2C].
May, M. Amanda (32 yrs.) d. on 70-Apr-14 [70-Apr-15: 2B].
May, Maud Egerton (9 mos.) d. on 69-Jun-16 [69-Jun-19: 2B].
May, Philip M. m. Huster, Lizzie A. on 70-Feb-22 [70-Mar-15: 2C].
May, Sarah m. Cohen, Jacob L. on 69-May-2 [69-May-7: 2C].
May, Sue K. m. Stuart, William R. on 68-Nov-30 [69-Jan-14: 2D].
May, W. m. Watchman, Sarah A. on 69-Mar-24 [69-Mar-27: 2B].
Mayatte, Alfons m. Hammer, Josephine on 66-Aug-5 [66-Aug-14: 2C].
Mayben, Mary m. Holtz, Emmanuel on 67-Oct-23 [67-Nov-4: 2B].
Mayberry, James K. Polk (22 yrs.) d. on 66-Oct-16 [66-Oct-17: 2B].
Mayberry, Laura m. Fields, James on 67-Jan-1 [67-Jan-5: 2C].
Maybury, Sarah Rebecca (24 yrs.) d. on 66-Sep-7 [66-Sep-10: 2D].
Maydwell, Hezekiah (53 yrs.) d. on 68-Aug-17 [68-Oct-9: 2C].
Maydwell, John C. (58 yrs.) d. on 67-Jun-10 in Street railway accident [68-Jan-30: 2C; 67-Jun-11: 1F, 2B].
Maydwell, Theodore F. m. Dunger, Wilhelmina on 70-Oct-11 [70-Oct-21: 2C].
Mayent, Mary d. on 66-Jan-31 Burned [66-Feb-2: 1G].
Mayer, Alfred M. m. Snowden, Maria L. on 69-Jun-30 [69-Jul-9: 2C].
Mayer, Kitty Duckett d. on 68-May-2 [68-May-6: 2B].
Mayes, Charles E. (19 yrs.) d. on 68-Aug-23 [68-Aug-27: 2B].
Mayes, Mattie J. m. Thompson, William J. on 67-Mar-14 [67-Jul-9: 2B].
Mayes, S. Tempie m. Gorsuch, Thomas T., Jr. on 66-Feb-20 [66-Mar-2: 2B].
Mayfield, Sarah (25 yrs., 8 mos.) d. on 70-Apr-19 [70-Apr-30: 2B].
Mayger, Richard Randolph d. on 70-Feb-4 of Suicide (Shooting) [70-Feb-5: 2C; 70-Feb-7: 1G].
Mayher, Mary A. m. Boteler, Charles R. on 66-Feb-8 [66-Feb-12: 2D].
Mayhew, Abby E. (73 yrs.) d. on 66-Apr-12 [66-Apr-13: 2C].
Maykranz, Willie H. (1 yr., 5 mos.) d. on 66-Aug-24 [66-Aug-25: 2A].
Maynard, John Wesley (65 yrs.) d. on 69-Sep-23 [69-Sep-25: 2B].
Maynard, Rachel E. d. on 67-Apr-23 [67-Apr-24: 2B].
Maynard, William Pyfer (6 mos.) d. on 66-Jun-15 [66-Jun-19: 2B].
Maynard, Willie H. (1 yr., 5 mos.) d. on 68-Sep-1 [68-Sep-3: 2B].
Maynes, Andrew R. m. Kelly, Susie on 67-Jul-7 [67-Jul-17: 2C].
Mayo, Josephine Orphelia m. Hardester, George E. on 66-Aug-30 [66-Sep-11: 2B].
Mayo, Thomas (42 yrs.) d. on 66-Oct-24 [66-Oct-26: 2B].
Mayron, Christian (68 yrs.) d. on 70-Jan-26 [70-Jan-27: 2C; 70-Jan-28: 2B].
Mays, J. Emory m. McClintock, Martha on 69-Apr-11 [69-Apr-21: 2B].
Mays, Lizzie A. m. Michael, David E. on 70-Jan-25 [70-Feb-1: 2B].
McAbee, Charles (35 yrs.) d. on 66-Nov-29 [66-Dec-1: 2B].
McAbee, John W. (38 yrs.) d. on 70-Jan-25 [70-Feb-2: 2C].
McAdam, , Mrs. (75 yrs.) d. on 68-Oct-6 [68-Oct-7: 2C].
McAdams, Rose (24 yrs.) d. on 67-Feb-28 of Consumption [67-Mar-1: 2C].
McAfee, Job W. m. Kline, Kate R. on 69-Jun-24 [69-Jun-29: 2C].
McAleer, Clara L. m. McSherry, James, Jr. on 67-Jan-21 [67-Jan-26: 2C].
McAleese, James P., Capt. (30 yrs.) d. on 68-Oct-20 Drowned [68-Nov-5: 2C; 68-Nov-6: 2C].
McAleese, Martha A. m. Connelly, William J. on 68-Jan-28 [68-Feb-13: 2C].
McAlister, John A. m. Arthur, Camilla E. on 68-Feb-26 [68-Mar-12: 2B].
McAlister, Mary Wallace (1 yr., 11 mos.) d. on 66-May-5 [66-Jun-6: 2B].
McAllister, Adelaide Emma m. Parkhill, Charles on 70-Jul-14 [70-Jul-22: 2C].
McAllister, Agnes B. m. Crook, Henry on 67-Apr-18 [67-Apr-20: 2A].

McAllister, Elizabeth (80 yrs.) d. on 68-Dec-8 [68-Dec-9: 2C].
McAllister, Florence d. on 67-May-12 [67-May-13: 2B].
McAllister, John (61 yrs.) d. on 70-Jun-4 [70-Jun-7: 2C].
McAllister, Kate m. Allen, Joseph H. on 70-Oct-19 [70-Oct-26: 2B].
McAllister, Laura V. m. Hays, William H. on 70-Feb-14 [70-Feb-24: 2C].
McAllister, Lizzie m. McCarty, Chandler on 67-Aug-27 [67-Aug-28: 2B].
McAllister, Marietta (51 yrs.) d. on 70-Apr-9 [70-Apr-11: 2B].
McAllister, Mary (10 mos.) d. on 70-Sep-8 [70-Sep-9: 2B].
McAllister, Mary C. m. Maccubbin, Joshua L. on 67-Jun-2 [67-Jul-12: 2C].
McAllister, Pamelia (18 yrs.) d. on 66-Oct-17 [66-Oct-18: 2B].
McAllister, Robert J. (5 yrs., 2 mos.) d. on 69-Jan-3 [69-Jan-5: 2C].
McAllister, Sarah E. d. on 70-Apr-16 [70-Apr-18: 2B].
McAllister, William (5 mos.) d. on 67-Jan-14 [67-Jan-15: 2C].
McAlpine, Mary Ann m. Barry, McClintock Y. on 66-Sep-4 [66-Sep-11: 2B].
McAneny, Joseph (45 yrs.) d. on 68-Mar-9 [68-Mar-10: 2C].
McAtee, John Street (2 yrs., 7 mos.) d. on 66-Mar-3 of Diptheria [66-Mar-5: 2B].
McAuley, Mary Vincent (30 yrs.) d. on 68-Mar-13 [68-Mar-20: 1F].
McAvoy, Emma (14 yrs.) d. on 66-Mar-20 [66-Mar-21: 2C].
McAvoy, Francis (68 yrs.) d. on 70-Jul-4 [70-Jul-6: 2C].
McAvoy, Mary Jane m. Shreck, William M. on 66-Jun-3 [66-Jul-10: 2C].
McAvoy, Rose Emma (10 mos.) d. on 67-Jun-30 [67-Jul-2: 2B].
McBee, Charles B. m. Miller, Maggie A. on 67-Jul-12 [67-Jul-30: 2C].
McBee, Wilson, Sr. (63 yrs.) d. on 66-Jul-25 [66-Jul-26: 2C].
McBerryman, Standish m. Warner, Elizabeth A. on 68-Oct-15 [68-Oct-16: 2B].
McBride, Catherine (43 yrs.) d. on 70-Jun-2 [70-Jun-4: 2B].
McBride, Harriet Louisa d. on 67-Apr-3 [67-Apr-12: 2C].
McBride, Harry m. Servenais, Emily on 67-Sep-9 [67-Sep-10: 2B].
McBride, John (41 yrs.) d. on 69-Apr-17 Killed by falling timber [69-Apr-19: 1F, 2B; 69-Apr-20: 1F].
McBride, Rosa (2 yrs., 2 mos.) d. on 69-Sep-9 [69-Sep-10: 2B].
McBriety, William m. Plunkett, Ellen on 68-Nov-19 [68-Dec-2: 2C].
McCabe, Alice m. Hush, Samuel J. on 69-Sep-24 [69-Oct-13: 2C].
McCabe, Eliza J. m. Brown, Aaron A. on 67-Feb-21 [67-Feb-25: 2C].
McCabe, George W. E. m. Connary, Kate B. on 67-Jul-2 [67-Jul-10: 2B].
McCabe, Georgene m. Erb, Howard on 69-Aug-26 [69-Aug-27: 2B].
McCabe, Jefferson m. Deaver, Alice H. on 68-Jul-30 [68-Aug-1: 2B].
McCabe, John Collins m. Mackall, Virginia on 68-Sep-15 [68-Sep-18: 2B].
McCabe, M., Mrs. (65 yrs.) d. on 68-Jul-15 of Heatstroke [68-Jul-17: 1D].
McCabe, Maria V. (43 yrs.) d. on 67-Jul-17 [67-Jul-22: 2C].
McCabe, Martha (61 yrs.) d. on 68-Jun-27 [68-Jul-1: 2B].
McCabe, Mary d. on 66-Jul-28 [66-Aug-2: 2C].
McCabe, Mary (16 yrs.) d. on 70-Sep-6 [70-Sep-7: 2B].
McCabe, Michael m. Carroll, Margaret on 67-Feb-28 [67-Apr-18: 2B].
McCabe, Nety C. m. Dudalez, Alonzo G. on 66-Dec-31 [67-Jan-1: 2C].
McCabe, Owen m. McCann, Mary on 66-Jan-28 [66-Feb-5: 2C].
McCabe, Patrick (70 yrs.) d. on 67-Nov-26 [67-Nov-27: 2C].
McCabe, Rose Ann (56 yrs.) d. on 69-Sep-13 [69-Sep-22: 2C].
McCabe, Sarah O. m. Krebs, David N. on 69-Apr-26 [69-May-17: 2B].
McCabe, Solomon, Jr. (8 yrs., 10 mos.) d. on 70-Mar-2 [70-Mar-3: 2C].
McCabe, W. Gordon m. Osborne, Jennie on 67-Apr-9 [67-Apr-15: 2B].
McCabe, William H. m. Walker, Virginia P. on 70-Feb-18 [70-Feb-25: 2C].
McCaddin, Francis George (1 yr., 6 mos.) d. on 68-Nov-19 [68-Nov-20: 2C].
McCaddin, James m. Berger, Louisa H. on 69-Mar-31 [69-Apr-2: 2C].
McCaddin, Margaret (70 yrs.) d. on 70-Jan-5 [70-Jan-6: 2C; 70-Jan-8: 2B].
McCaddin, Richard m. Pennington, Lizzie A. on 60-Sep-10 [70-Jun-8: 2C].

McCaferty, Susan (76 yrs.) d. on 69-Dec-24 [69-Dec-25: 2C].
McCafferty, Elizabeth (82 yrs.) d. on 66-Aug-18 [66-Aug-20: 2C; 66-Aug-22: 2C].
McCafferty, John (52 yrs., 1 mo.) d. on 69-Aug-17 [69-Aug-18: 2C].
McCafferty, Mary Ellen m. Ahl, Romma on 67-Oct-15 [67-Oct-21: 2B].
McCaffray, Alice Carmichael (1 yr., 5 mos.) d. on 70-Aug-26 [70-Aug-27: 2B].
McCaffray, James m. McNelly, Maggie A. on 69-Oct-31 [69-Nov-1: 2B].
McCaffrey, Andrew J. (24 yrs.) d. on 67-Aug-11 [67-Aug-12: 2C].
McCaffrey, Francis J. (36 yrs.) d. on 66-Jan-15 [66-Jan-19: 2C; 66-Jan-27: 2B].
McCaffrey, Susan A. (68 yrs.) d. on 69-Mar-13 [69-Mar-15: 2C].
McCaffrey, Thomas m. Leeden, Alice Jane on 69-Apr-27 [69-May-11: 2B].
McCaghey, John A. (10 mos.) d. on 68-Aug-21 [68-Aug-24: 2B].
McCahan, Harry (33 yrs.) d. on 69-Feb-13 [69-Feb-18: 2C].
McCahan, Mary Malloy (7 yrs., 4 mos.) d. on 66-Jun-26 [66-Jun-27: 2C].
McCahan, William James (3 mos.) d. on 69-Jan-9 [69-Jan-11: 2C].
McCaigney, Peter d. on 66-Jun-13 in Railroad accident [66-Jun-16: 1F].
McCall, Bridget (60 yrs.) d. on 69-Oct-4 [69-Oct-6: 2B].
McCall, Maggie A. m. Knauf, Philip H. on 69-Apr-18 [69-Apr-19: 2B].
McCall, Mary Jane m. Murphy, John W. on 66-Sep-6 [66-Sep-15: 2B].
McCall, Michael (93 yrs.) d. on 66-Feb-1 [66-Feb-2: 2C].
McCall, Michael (60 yrs.) d. on 69-Nov-12 [69-Nov-13: 2C].
McCall, Patrick (34 yrs.) d. on 67-Apr-9 [67-Apr-11: 2B].
McCall, William Arthur (22 yrs.) d. on 68-Nov-14 [68-Nov-17: 2C, 1H].
McCallum, A. C. m. Gillespie, Sadie E. on 67-Feb-14 [67-Feb-18: 2C].
McCamley, Sarah m. McCloskey, William on 68-Nov-22 [68-Nov-28: 2C].
McCaniel, George W. (50 yrs.) d. on 68-Aug-6 [68-Aug-8: 2C].
McCann, Daniel m. Hall, Mary on 67-Nov-7 [67-Nov-11: 2C].
McCann, Edward (2 yrs., 8 mos.) d. on 70-Aug-26 [70-Aug-27: 2B].
McCann, Elizabeth (69 yrs.) d. on 70-Dec-3 [70-Dec-10: 2C; 70-Dec-12: 2C].
McCann, Elizabeth m. Brady, Thomas on 67-Sep-3 [67-Sep-7: 2A].
McCann, George (30 yrs.) d. on 68-Jul-16 [68-Jul-17: 2C].
McCann, George m. Heim, Martha A. on 68-Apr-2 [68-Apr-7: 2B].
McCann, Ida Virginia Glaspy (11 yrs.) d. on 68-Apr-26 [68-Apr-27: 2B].
McCann, J. B. m. Shea, Mary on 69-Dec-21 [70-Jan-26: 2C].
McCann, James m. Paul, Sarah A. on 69-Apr-6 [69-Apr-7: 2C].
McCann, Laura m. Yardley, Charles on 67-Jan-24 [67-Jan-25: 2C].
McCann, Lloyd (67 yrs.) d. on 68-Mar-29 [68-Mar-31: 2B].
McCann, Maggie m. Codd, William H. on 68-Oct-20 [68-Oct-23: 2B].
McCann, Mary m. McCabe, Owen on 66-Jan-28 [66-Feb-5: 2C].
McCann, Mary Ann (42 yrs.) d. on 66-Apr-28 [66-Apr-30: 2B].
McCann, Mary Della (1 yr., 8 mos.) d. on 68-Dec-8 [68-Dec-10: 2D].
McCann, Michael (38 yrs.) d. on 68-Jun-13 [68-Jun-15: 2B].
McCann, Michael (56 yrs.) d. on 69-Dec-10 Murdered (Shooting) [69-Dec-11: 1G, 2B].
McCann, Peter d. on 70-Apr-14 [70-Apr-14: 2B].
McCann, Sarah (77 yrs.) d. on 69-Jan-31 [69-Feb-1: 2C; 69-Feb-2: 2C].
McCann, Sarah m. Muldoon, James on 69-Nov-28 [69-Dec-16: 2C].
McCann, William V. m. Bien, Annie E. on 68-May-21 [68-May-26: 2B].
McCanna, Michael (35 yrs.) d. on 69-Jan-22 [69-Jan-23: 2C].
McCannon, James (72 yrs., 5 mos.) d. on 70-Jun-13 [70-Jun-14: 2B].
McCaraher, Daniel (44 yrs.) d. on 67-Jan-24 [67-Jan-25: 2C].
McCardell, Ann Mariner (59 yrs.) d. on 68-Nov-21 [68-Nov-23: 2B].
McCardell, John (66 yrs.) d. on 70-Apr-13 [70-Apr-15: 2B].
McCardell, John Thomas (1 yr., 1 mo.) d. on 69-Jan-10 [69-Jan-12: 2C].
McCarran, Maggie m. Barklage, Henry A. on 66-May-1 [66-May-4: 2C].
McCarron, John Francis (1 yr., 2 mos.) d. on 66-Jun-20 [66-Jun-21: 2C].
McCarron, Mary d. on 70-Aug-11 [70-Aug-13: 2C].

McCartey, Mary Ann m. Blake, John R. on 66-Nov-8 [66-Nov-12: 2C].
McCarthy, Ann (50 yrs.) d. on 66-May-11 [66-May-12: 2A].
McCarthy, Annie m. Kelly, James on 70-Nov-1 [70-Nov-8: 2B].
McCarthy, Daniel A. (24 yrs.) d. on 66-Dec-19 [66-Dec-20: 2B].
McCarthy, Daniel J. d. on 70-Jul-28 [70-Jul-30: 2C].
McCarthy, James (16 yrs.) d. on 67-Aug-17 of Boiler explosion [67-Aug-19: 1F; 67-Aug-21: 1F].
McCarthy, Joseph Bernard (4 yrs., 2 mos.) d. on 70-Aug-2 [70-Aug-4: 2C].
McCarthy, Lizzie m. Evatt, George K. on 66-Apr-10 [66-May-15: 2C].
McCarthy, Michael (31 yrs.) d. Drowned [68-Apr-2: 2C; 68-Apr-3: 4C].
McCarthy, Victoria M. m. Anderton, Walter E. on 67-Jan-5 [67-Jan-11: 2C].
McCartney, Mary (?? yrs.) d. on 70-Apr-13 [70-Apr-14: 2B; 70-Apr-15: 2B].
McCartney, Mary A. m. Norris, Michael A. on 68-Jun-11 [68-Jul-13: 2B].
McCartney, Patrick (51 yrs.) d. on 66-Oct-27 of Consumption [66-Oct-30: 2B].
McCartney, Peter (39 yrs.) d. on 66-Oct-10 [66-Oct-11: 2C].
McCarty, Agnes A. (3 mos.) d. on 66-Nov-27 [66-Dec-3: 2B].
McCarty, Annie m. Smith, Robert Z. on 69-Jul-6 [69-Dec-29: 2D].
McCarty, Chandler m. McAllister, Lizzie on 67-Aug-27 [67-Aug-28: 2B].
McCarty, James m. Simmons, Bertha on 66-Jul-3 [66-Jul-7: 2B].
McCarty, William (25 yrs.) d. on 66-Mar-16 Drowned [66-Mar-17: 1G].
McCarty, William M. m. Armstrong, Florence E. on 66-Jan-20 [66-Jan-23: 2C].
McCauley, Arabella m. Arnold, John on 70-Apr-21 [70-Apr-26: 2B].
McCauley, Cornelia A. m. Douch, William on 67-Apr-23 [67-May-14: 2B].
McCauley, Edward H. d. on 66-Aug-15 [66-Aug-16: 2C].
McCauley, Jasper G. m. Holden, Mary C. on 69-Oct-20 [69-Oct-22: 2B].
McCauley, John (63 yrs.) d. on 67-Apr-27 [67-Apr-29: 2B].
McCauley, John A. (2 yrs., 2 mos.) d. on 69-Feb-20 [69-Feb-22: 2C].
McCauley, Joseph O. m. Parlett, Matilda Rebecca on 66-Mar-8 [66-Mar-12: 2B].
McCauley, Laurence, Rev. (30 yrs.) d. on 66-Apr-20 of Consumption [66-Apr-21: 2B; 66-Apr-23: 1F, 2B; 66-Apr-24: 1F].
McCauley, Mary W. m. Edeler, Charles H. on 69-Jun-3 [69-Jun-19: 2B].
McCauley, Ruth A. m. Sweeting, Edward on 67-Apr-9 [67-Apr-11: 2B].
McCauley, William E. m. McLaughlin, Sallie I. on 70-Nov-17 [70-Nov-22: 2B].
McCaulley, Elizabeth (63 yrs.) d. on 68-Nov-21 [68-Nov-23: 2B].
McCaw, W. R. m. Hance, Ella Chesley on 70-Nov-8 [70-Nov-29: 2C].
McCay, Annie (28 yrs.) d. on 68-Aug-16 [68-Aug-22: 2A].
McCay, Sarah Jane (9 yrs., 2 mos.) d. on 66-Mar-2 of Diptheria [66-Mar-3: 2B].
McCeney, George d. on 66-Apr-8 [66-Apr-16: 2B].
McCeney, Sallie m. McCeney, Thomas on 70-Apr-20 [70-Apr-22: 2C].
McCeney, Thomas m. McCeney, Sallie on 70-Apr-20 [70-Apr-22: 2C].
McClain, Sarah Ann (34 yrs.) d. on 69-Jul-27 [69-Jul-28: 2D].
McClaine, Mary C. m. Creamer, Alexander F. on 68-Oct-1 [68-Nov-26: 2B; 68-Nov-28: 2C].
McClary, John William (10 mos.) d. on 68-Oct-26 [68-Oct-27: 2B].
McClaskey, Charles E. m. Lemon, Annie on 69-Oct-14 [69-Oct-26: 2B].
McClatchie, Margarette (82 yrs.) d. on 70-Apr-8 [70-Apr-11: 2B].
McClay, George M. m. Chesnut, Mary E. on 66-Nov-20 [66-Nov-23: 2C; 66-Nov-24: 2B].
McClean, John m. Brown, Lizzie Mary A. on 67-Apr-9 [67-May-7: 2B; 67-May-8: 2B].
McClean, Mary (2 mos.) d. on 70-Oct-24 [70-Oct-26: 2B].
McClean, William m. Key, Anna on 70-Mar-24 [70-Apr-4: 2C].
McCleary, Isabella (20 yrs.) d. [69-May-5: 2C].
McCleary, John W. m. Snyder, Ella on 69-Feb-11 [69-Feb-13: 2C].
McCleary, Laura V. m. Knight, William H. on 66-Jun-5 [66-Jun-7: 2B].
McCleary, Mary T. (77 yrs.) d. on 67-Mar-18 [67-Mar-19: 2C; 67-Mar-20: 2C].
McCleary, Moses Wesley m. Williams, Minerva on 69-Feb-25 [69-Mar-3: 2B].
McClellan, Charles Albert (9 mos.) d. on 69-Jun-30 [69-Jul-1: 2C].

McClellan, Eliza D. m. Fenton, D. A. on 66-Feb-25 [66-Mar-29: 2B].
McClellan, Eliza J. m. Cowley, Samuel T. on 69-Mar-23 [69-Apr-6: 2C].
McClellan, George F. (24 yrs.) d. on 67-Nov-15 of Consumption [67-Nov-18: 2C].
McClellan, John Thomas (3 yrs., 4 mos.) d. on 70-Feb-25 [70-Feb-28: 2C].
McClellan, Kate (27 yrs.) d. on 69-Aug-5 [69-Aug-10: 2C].
McClellan, Raymond Duvall (6 mos.) d. on 70-Dec-6 [70-Dec-8: 2C].
McClellan, Walter d. on 69-Jul-22 [69-Jul-31: 2C].
McClelland, Charlotte L. m. Hutchinson, George F. on 68-Nov-10 [68-Nov-12: 2C].
McClelland, David P. m. Jackson, Mary E. on 68-Dec-25 [68-Dec-29: 2D].
McClelland, Elizabeth (18 yrs.) d. on 70-Aug-30 [70-Aug-31: 2B].
McClelland, Hannah N. (9 mos.) d. on 67-Jul-24 [67-Jul-25: 2C].
McClelland, Margaret Eugenie (1 yr.) d. on 70-Aug-31 [70-Sep-1: 2B].
McClelland, Robert (74 yrs.) d. on 70-Jul-24 [70-Jul-25: 2C].
McClelland, Theodore M. m. Cooper, Martha A. on 67-Jan-23 [67-Jan-28: 2C].
McClenaghan, Daniel (37 yrs.) d. on 69-Feb-18 of Pneumonia [69-Feb-19: 2C].
McClenan, James (1 yr., 6 mos.) d. on 69-Nov-14 [69-Nov-15: 2C].
McClernan, Patrick (35 yrs.) d. on 70-Feb-15 Murdered (Stabbing) [70-Feb-16: 1H; 70-Feb-17: 1G; 70-Jun-14: 1F].
McClintock, Bell m. Kessler, Henry C. on 67-Jan-8 [67-Jan-9: 2B].
McClintock, Curtis W. (29 yrs.) d. on 67-Jan-30 [67-Jan-31: 2C].
McClintock, Jennie m. Culver, William Edward on 68-Jan-9 [68-Jan-13: 2C].
McClintock, Martha m. Mays, J. Emory on 69-Apr-11 [69-Apr-21: 2B].
McClintock, Mary Winfield (1 yr., 4 mos.) d. on 68-Nov-28 of Chronic croup [68-Nov-30: 2C].
McCloskey, William m. McCamley, Sarah on 68-Nov-22 [68-Nov-28: 2C].
McCluney, Thomas, Sr. (59 yrs.) d. on 69-Jul-27 [69-Jul-28: 2D].
McClure, James F. m. Richardson, Amanda on 69-Mar-4 [69-Apr-5: 2B].
McClure, Jane m. Crooks, Thomas B. on 67-Apr-25 [67-May-10: 2B].
McClure, Minnie (1 mo.) d. on 66-Jul-4 [66-Jul-7: 2C].
McClure, William G. m. Keenan, Lizzie A. [66-Dec-11: 2B].
McClusky, Kate m. Minniegue, Albert M. on 70-Jul-27 [70-Nov-16: 2C].
McClymont, Alexander G. m. Binnie, Agnes D. on 70-Oct-6 [70-Oct-10: 2B].
McColgan, , Mr. (50 yrs.) d. on 66-Jul-17 of Heatstroke [66-Jul-19: 1F].
McColgan, John (77 yrs.) d. on 67-May-4 of Pneumonia [67-May-6: 1G, 2B].
McColl, John (82 yrs.) d. on 66-Oct-10 [66-Oct-11: 2C].
McColloff, Thomas (11 mos.) d. on 68-Dec-28 [68-Dec-29: 2D].
McComas, Alverta m. Hakesley, Edward on 68-Dec-29 [68-Dec-31: 2C].
McComas, Charlotte Ann (43 yrs.) d. on 67-Nov-11 [67-Nov-20: 2C].
McComas, Cora Bell (1 yr., 1 mo.) d. on 69-Feb-7 [69-Feb-9: 2C].
McComas, Elizabeth S. m. Elliott, George G. on 66-Aug-2 [66-Aug-7: 2C].
McComas, Florence Lee (1 yr., 4 mos.) d. on 67-Dec-25 [67-Dec-27: 2C].
McComas, Georgeanna (11 mos.) d. on 68-Jun-8 [68-Jun-10: 2B].
McComas, H. Clay m. Parker, Mary on 70-Dec-1 [70-Dec-5: 2C].
McComas, Holcombe R. (3 yrs., 4 mos.) d. on 70-Apr-13 [70-Apr-15: 2C].
McComas, John W. (25 yrs.) d. on 66-Feb-9 of Pneumonia [66-Feb-12: 2D; 66-Feb-15: 2C, 4E].
McComas, Martha Ann E. m. Gill, John R. on 68-Feb-20 [68-Feb-27: 2C; 68-Feb-29: 2B].
McComas, Mary Ann (79 yrs.) d. on 68-Feb-28 [68-Feb-29: 2B].
McComas, Mary M. (11 mos.) d. on 70-Aug-28 [70-Aug-29: 2C].
McComas, Mary T. J. (27 yrs.) d. on 69-Mar-18 [69-Mar-20: 2B].
McComas, Nicholas (37 yrs.) d. on 69-Apr-10 Murdered (Shooting) [69-Apr-13: 1F].
McComas, Parker (3 yrs., 1 mo.) d. on 70-Mar-10 [70-Mar-11: 2C; 70-Mar-12: 2C].
McComas, Robert (49 yrs., 6 mos.) d. on 67-Jun-22 [67-Jun-24: 2B].
McComas, Robert A. (19 yrs., 3 mos.) d. on 67-Jan-12 of Lung disease [67-Jan-14: 2C].
McComas, Sidney A. (58 yrs.) d. on 67-Mar-3 [67-Mar-4: 2D].
McComas, Sophie m. Slade, Alfred H. on 67-May-21 [67-Jun-21: 2B].
McComb, William Owen d. on 69-Jun-20 [69-Jun-21: 2B].

McConica, Charles C. (25 yrs., 8 mos.) d. on 67-Nov-6 [67-Nov-7: 2C; 67-Nov-8: 2C].
McConkey, Eliza J. m. Coombes, Richard J. on 66-Nov-24 [66-Nov-26: 2B].
McConkey, James (62 yrs.) d. on 70-Jul-29 in Wagon accident [70-Jul-30: 4E].
McConkey, Tabitha d. on 68-Nov-16 [68-Nov-17: 2C; 68-Nov-18: 2C].
McConky, Edward D. m. Cockey, Annie S. on 66-Oct-16 [66-Oct-20: 2B].
McConky, James (63 yrs.) d. on 70-Jul-29 [70-Jul-30: 2C].
McConky, Mary D. d. on 70-May-12 [70-May-14: 2B].
McConn, Richard (71 yrs.) d. on 70-Sep-7 [70-Sep-8: 2B; 70-Sep-9: 2B].
McConnell, Alice m. Maguire, James B. on 67-Jun-26 [67-Jul-3: 2B].
McConnell, Elizabeth (80 yrs.) d. on 66-Aug-5 [66-Aug-6: 1G].
McConnell, Mary Elizabeth (8 yrs., 3 mos.) d. on 66-May-1 [66-May-3: 2C].
McConnell, Thomas (61 yrs.) d. on 66-Jan-29 [66-Jan-31: 2C].
McConnell, Thomas (65 yrs.) d. on 70-May-28 [70-May-30: 2B].
McConniken, Cecilia (26 yrs.) d. on 69-Aug-28 [69-Aug-30: 2B].
McConniken, Minnie E. m. Hare, John R. on 67-Oct-15 [67-Oct-16: 2B].
McConnor, Phineas S. m. Boyle, Theresa on 69-Jan-28 [69-Feb-2: 2C].
McCord, Felix (45 yrs.) d. Drowned [70-Feb-10: 4E].
McCormack, Joseph J. m. Connors, Mary A. O. on 70-Sep-25 [70-Sep-28: 2B].
McCormack, Moira (22 yrs.) d. on 66-Dec-10 [66-Dec-12: 2B].
McCormic, Eddy F. (4 yrs., 3 mos.) d. on 67-May-7 of Typhoid [67-May-10: 2B].
McCormic, George W. (5 yrs., 6 mos.) d. on 66-Oct-13 of Diptheria [66-Oct-16: 2C].
McCormick, Alice d. on 70-Dec-24 of Scarlet fever [70-Dec-26: 2C].
McCormick, Belle (1 yr., 4 mos.) d. on 68-Jan-27 [68-Jan-31: 2C].
McCormick, Clara S. m. Owens, Zachary T. on 69-Jan-25 [69-Jan-26: 2C].
McCormick, Elizabeth A. S. d. on 66-Dec-24 [66-Dec-25: 2B].
McCormick, Francis Thomas (10 mos.) d. on 66-Mar-16 [66-Mar-17: 2B].
McCormick, Fred (25 yrs.) d. on 68-Jul-25 [68-Aug-25: 2B].
McCormick, John m. Ferguson, Margaret on 69-Nov-17 [69-Nov-26: 2B].
McCormick, John T. m. Mullen, Lizzie on 70-Mar-27 [70-Apr-13: 2B].
McCormick, Julia (1 yr., 5 mos.) d. on 70-Mar-13 [70-Mar-14: 2C].
McCormick, Margaret S. (39 yrs.) d. on 68-Apr-26 [68-Apr-27: 2B].
McCormick, Mary A. (23 yrs.) d. on 68-Jul-21 [68-Jul-22: 2B; 68-Aug-5: 2C].
McCormick, Patrick (43 yrs.) d. on 66-Sep-2 [66-Sep-4: 2B].
McCormick, Rebecca m. Ragsdale, J. K. P. on 69-Nov-18 [69-Nov-22: 2C].
McCormick, Richard (3 yrs., 8 mos.) d. on 68-Feb-24 [68-Feb-25: 2C; 68-Feb-26: 2B].
McCormick, Samuel (1 yr., 2 mos.) d. on 68-Sep-13 [68-Sep-14: 2B].
McCormick, Samuel G. (23 yrs.) d. on 66-Feb-26 [66-Feb-27: 2B].
McCormick, William m. Power, Mary Ellen on 70-Feb-24 [70-Mar-11: 2C].
McCormick, William N. m. Toulson, Laura on 65-Dec-25 [66-Jan-1: 2C].
McCormick, William Peregrine (8 mos.) d. on 66-Jul-21 [66-Jul-24: 2C].
McCoubray, Alice C. m. Gifford, William on 68-Jul-12 [68-Sep-9: 2B].
McCoubray, Georgeanna W. d. on 67-Jul-31 [67-Aug-1: 2C].
McCoull, George C. (68 yrs.) d. on 70-Dec-16 [70-Dec-17: 2B].
McCourt, Dennis (35 yrs.) d. on 67-Nov-24 of Suicide (Shooting) [67-Nov-25: 1G].
McCourt, Felix m. Murry, Sarah E. on 67-Oct-8 [67-Oct-11: 2B].
McCourt, James (75 yrs.) d. on 68-Jul-30 [68-Aug-1: 2B].
McCourt, Mary d. on 66-Apr-22 [66-Apr-24: 2B].
McCoy, Anne M. m. Greer, Benjamin A. on 70-Nov-9 [70-Nov-11: 2B].
McCoy, Bettie Mana d. on 70-Jul-15 [70-Jul-16: 2B].
McCoy, Edwin F. m. Smith, Cornelia Rowland on 70-Oct-12 [70-Oct-20: 2B].
McCoy, Elizabeth (61 yrs.) d. on 70-Jul-6 [70-Jul-7: 2B].
McCoy, Henry B., Capt. (40 yrs.) d. on 66-Dec-28 [66-Dec-29: 2C].
McCoy, J. Findley m. Shotts, Venie R. on 68-Sep-17 [68-Oct-9: 2C].
McCoy, James (5 mos.) d. on 66-Apr-19 [66-Apr-27: 2C].
McCoy, Jane E. m. Benson, Joseph on 68-Nov-12 [68-Nov-30: 2C].

McCoy, Jennie m. Clefford, John H. on 70-Aug-8 [70-Aug-10: 2B].
McCoy, Lucretia V. d. on 70-Aug-7 [70-Aug-8: 2C; 70-Aug-9: 2C; 70-Aug-10: 2C; 70-Aug-18: 2C].
McCoy, Magdalene (89 yrs.) d. on 70-Sep-25 [70-Sep-26: 2B].
McCoy, Margaretta d. on 69-Sep-11 [69-Sep-11: 2B].
McCoy, Mattie m. Clark, Robert M. on 69-Sep-1 [69-Sep-3: 2B].
McCoy, Washington R. m. Odend'hal, Magdalen M. on 66-Apr-4 [66-Apr-7: 2B].
McCoy, William D. d. on 68-Aug-13 Drowned [68-Aug-17: 1F].
McCoy, William Francis (6 yrs., 8 mos.) d. on 66-May-15 [66-May-16: 2C].
McCrackan, Hannah E. (34 yrs.) d. on 70-Apr-18 [70-Apr-19: 2B].
McCrackan, James (77 yrs.) d. on 70-Sep-9 [70-Sep-10: 2B].
McCracken, Alex. Andrew (99 yrs.) d. on 69-Jan-23 [69-Jan-25: 2D].
McCracken, Alexander d. on 69-Jan-23 [69-Jan-25: 2D].
McCracken, Thomas C. m. Brown, Mattie E. on 68-Feb-13 [68-Feb-20: 2C].
McCracken, William (11 mos.) d. on 68-Aug-8 [68-Aug-13: 2B].
McCrae, Gavin (63 yrs.) d. on 67-May-2 of Pneumonia [67-May-29: 2B].
McCraight, Jane m. Wood, Edward K. on 70-Jul-26 [70-Jul-28: 2C].
McCrea, Katie m. Bunster, Enrique S. on 69-Sep-21 [69-Dec-29: 2D].
McCready, Annie Lewis (3 yrs., 4 mos.) d. on 69-Nov-22 [69-Dec-20: 2C].
McCreary, Cornelia L. m. Florer, William H. on 67-Jul-11 [67-Jul-13: 2B].
McCreary, Sarah Elizabeth (38 yrs.) d. on 70-Oct-11 [70-Oct-15: 2B].
McCreary, Willard D. (1 yr., 5 mos.) d. on 69-Aug-16 [69-Aug-21: 2B].
McCristal, John (1 yr., 10 mos.) d. on 70-Apr-25 [70-Apr-28: 2C].
McCron, Jennie m. Broadbent, William, Jr. on 66-Sep-4 [66-Sep-5: 2B].
McCrone, Helen H. (39 yrs.) d. on 67-Jun-3 [67-Jun-5: 2B].
McCrone, Sarah (61 yrs.) d. on 66-Dec-31 [67-Jan-2: 2C].
McCrory, Catherine (26 yrs.) d. on 70-Jul-18 of Heart disease [70-Jul-19: 2C].
McCubbin, Aaron H. (61 yrs.) d. on 68-Jul-30 [68-Jul-31: 2C].
McCubbin, Amanda (24 yrs.) d. on 68-Jul-26 [68-Jul-31: 2C].
McCubbin, John D. m. Brashears, Virginia on 66-Jun-7 [66-Jun-8: 2B].
McCubbin, M. Nellie (3 yrs., 5 mos.) d. on 67-Feb-24 [67-Feb-26: 2C].
McCubbin, Margaret Elizabeth d. on 66-Apr-4 [66-Apr-6: 2B].
McCubbin, Nicholas (70 yrs.) d. on 70-Mar-31 [70-Apr-1: 2B].
McCubbin, Rhoda (66 yrs.) d. on 69-Mar-30 [69-Mar-31: 2C].
McCubbin, Sarah Ann m. Treadwell, John on 70-Nov-24 [70-Nov-28: 2C].
McCubbin, Sarah R. m. Rice, Duane on 68-Dec-27 [68-Dec-30: 2C].
McCubbins, Peter B. m. Standiford, Rachel A. on 66-Feb-20 [66-Feb-22: 2B].
McCue, John (65 yrs.) d. on 67-Aug-18 [67-Aug-19: 2C].
McCuen, Clara m. Martin, Basil N. on 66-Apr-24 [66-May-1: 2A].
McCulloh, Chauncey m. Ward, Alice R. on 70-Aug-6 [70-Aug-25: 2B].
McCulloh, Ella d. on 69-Dec-10 [69-Dec-13: 2C].
McCulloh, Ellen (33 yrs.) d. on 70-Sep-4 [70-Sep-5: 2C; 70-Sep-6: 2B].
McCulloh, James H., Dr. (78 yrs.) d. on 69-Dec-21 of Paralysis [69-Dec-25: 2C; 69-Dec-28: 1G].
McCulloh, Josephine L. m. Fisher, J. Harmanus on 69-Jan-13 [69-Jan-14: 2D].
McCullough, Annie E. m. Phillips, William A. on 69-Aug-22 [69-Aug-24: 2B].
McCullough, Benjamin (75 yrs.) d. on 67-Jan-23 [67-Feb-2: 1F].
McCullough, Harry (1 yr., 5 mos.) d. on 67-Sep-27 [67-Sep-28: 2A].
McCullough, Samuel (79 yrs.) d. on 68-Jun-27 [68-Jul-3: 2C].
McCullough, Sarah (75 yrs.) d. on 67-Apr-13 [67-Apr-15: 2B].
McCunn, George d. on 68-Jul-16 of Heatstroke [68-Jul-17: 1D].
McCurdy, James R. m. Heuisler, Ann E. on 67-Feb-12 [67-Apr-2: 2B].
McCurdy, Mary Jane (1 yr., 1 mo.) d. on 66-Jan-28 [66-Jan-30: 2B].
McCurdy, Mary Jane d. on 66-Apr-8 [66-Apr-9: 2B; 66-Apr-10: 2C].
McCurdy, Nannie Pearl (1 yr., 8 mos.) d. on 70-Jun-7 [70-Jun-9: 2C].

McCurdy, Richard J. m. Chanceaulme, Bella on 66-Jan-1 [66-Jan-10: 2C].
McCurley, Elizabeth (54 yrs.) d. on 66-Sep-17 [66-Sep-19: 2B].
McCurley, Fannie m. Walter, Edward H. on 70-Jan-18 [70-Jan-22: 2B].
McCurley, Issac m. Stran, H. Annie on 70-Jan-13 [70-Jan-17: 2C].
McCurley, Issac McKim, Dr. (31 yrs.) d. on 68-Dec-25 [68-Dec-28: 2C; 68-Dec-29: 2D].
McCurley, James m. Stauter, Susannah Sandford on 67-Apr-1 [67-Apr-4: 2B; 67-Apr-5: 2B].
McCurley, John M., Jr. (38 yrs.) d. on 70-Jul-20 Drowned [70-Jul-21: 1G, 2C].
McCurly, William (26 yrs.) d. on 68-Nov-20 [68-Nov-21: 2C].
McCusker, Annie d. on 68-Jul-7 [68-Jul-8: 2B].
McCusker, Bridget d. on 69-May-9 [69-May-11: 2C].
McCusker, L. C. m. Deubler, O. K. on 67-Dec-18 [67-Dec-25: 2C].
McCusker, Thomas (58 yrs.) d. on 68-Oct-20 of Consumption [68-Oct-22: 2C].
McCutchan, Elizabeth (81 yrs.) d. on 70-Dec-18 [70-Dec-19: 2C].
McCutchan, George, Capt. (85 yrs.) d. on 70-Dec-22 [70-Dec-23: 2B; 70-Dec-24: 2B; 70-Dec-31: 4C].
McCutchan, George Henry (25 yrs.) d. on 70-Nov-19 [70-Nov-19: 2B].
McCutchan, Sarah Jane (14 yrs.) d. on 68-Oct-20 [68-Oct-22: 2C].
McCutchins, Ann (83 yrs.) d. on 68-Jul-1 [68-Jul-2: 2C].
McDaniel, Kate G. m. Dicus, James A. on 69-Apr-20 [69-May-8: 2B].
McDaniel, Leanna (20 yrs.) d. on 67-May-14 [67-May-16: 2B].
McDermot, James H. m. Neveils, Anna on 69-Jul-18 [69-Jul-21: 2C].
McDermott, Ann Agnes (38 yrs.) d. on 67-Feb-7 [67-Feb-9: 2B].
McDermott, Charles T. d. on 69-Apr-14 [69-Apr-16: 2B].
McDermott, James (75 yrs.) d. on 69-Jun-4 [69-Jun-5: 2B].
McDermott, Margaret (35 yrs.) d. on 68-Sep-28 [68-Sep-29: 2B].
McDermott, Mary d. on 69-Aug-3 [69-Aug-5: 2C].
McDermott, Mary (73 yrs.) d. on 69-Apr-13 of Heart disease [69-Apr-15: 2B; 69-Apr-14: 2B].
McDermott, Michael (13 yrs.) d. on 67-Sep-4 Murdered (Stabbing) [67-Sep-11: 1G].
McDermott, Thomas (61 yrs.) d. on 66-Oct-25 [66-Oct-27: 2B].
McDermott, Timothy (49 yrs.) d. on 66-Jan-30 of Pneumonia [66-Jan-31: 2C; 66-Feb-11: 2C].
McDevitt, Anna (56 yrs.) d. on 70-Sep-20 [70-Sep-21: 2B].
McDevitt, Bernard (44 yrs.) d. on 68-Oct-7 [68-Oct-8: 2B; 68-Oct-9: 2C].
McDevitt, Edward d. on 66-Jul-18 [66-Jul-19: 1F].
McDevitt, John (75 yrs.) d. on 66-Sep-30 [66-Oct-1: 1G, 2B].
McDonald, Alice m. Countess, James C. on 67-Jan-17 [67-Feb-14: 2C].
McDonald, Amelia m. Griffin, James on 68-Dec-17 [68-Dec-18: 2C].
McDonald, Annie C. m. Evans, D'Oyley on 68-Sep-8 [68-Sep-9: 2B].
McDonald, Daniel (7 yrs.) d. on 66-Jan-28 [66-Feb-1: 2C].
McDonald, Elias m. Anderson, Rebecca on 70-Jan-6 [70-Jan-8: 2B].
McDonald, Emma m. Dammann, A. E. on 70-Nov-26 [70-Nov-30: 2C].
McDonald, Hannah m. Kerr, Thomas on 69-Jun-22 [69-Jul-3: 2B].
McDonald, Maria (71 yrs.) d. on 70-Jul-20 [70-Jul-21: 2C].
McDonald, Maria m. Krone, J. B. C. on 66-Feb-28 [66-Mar-2: 2B].
McDonald, Mary (28 yrs.) d. on 68-Dec-20 [68-Dec-21: 2B; 68-Dec-22: 2C].
McDonald, Mary (81 yrs.) d. on 67-Aug-9 [67-Sep-25: 2B].
McDonald, Mary (90 yrs.) d. on 70-Oct-30 [70-Oct-31: 2B].
Mcdonald, Mary m. Thomas, Raleigh C. on 68-Nov-25 [68-Nov-30: 2B].
McDonald, Mary m. Gambrill, Howard W. on 69-Apr-28 [69-May-11: 2B].
McDonald, Mary Margaret (2 yrs., 5 mos.) d. on 69-Feb-17 of Pneumonia [69-Feb-18: 2C].
McDonald, Michael d. on 66-Jan-20 Drowned [66-Feb-12: 4C; 66-Feb-14: 2C].
McDonald, Samuel (40 yrs.) d. on 70-Jul-20 of Apoplexy [70-Jul-21: 1F, 2C].
McDonald, Sarah d. on 66-Feb-27 [66-Feb-28: 2C; 66-Mar-1: 2B].
McDonald, Thomas (45 yrs.) d. on 67-Feb-5 [67-Feb-7: 2C].
McDonald, Willie (1 mo.) d. on 66-May-13 [66-May-17: 2C].
McDonnall, Charles (24 yrs.) d. on 69-Sep-20 [69-Sep-11: 2B; 69-Oct-23: 2B].

McDonnel, Martin m. Thompson, Emma Belle on 67-Apr-3 [67-Apr-15: 2B].
McDonnell, , Mr. (94 yrs.) d. on 66-Oct-10 [66-Oct-26: 1G].
McDonnell, Elijah m. North, Caroline V. on 69-Sep-29 [69-Oct-7: 2B].
McDonnell, Honora (44 yrs.) d. on 70-Jun-9 [70-Jun-10: 2B].
McDonnell, James (45 yrs.) d. on 66-Dec-24 [66-Dec-25: 2B].
McDonnell, James m. Fusting, Clara on 70-Apr-27 [70-May-3: 2B].
McDonnell, John (48 yrs.) d. on 69-Mar-22 [69-Mar-24: 2C].
McDonnell, Lizzie (2 yrs., 3 mos.) d. [70-Sep-24: 2B].
McDonnell, Lizzie m. Price, Winfield S. on 69-Aug-5 [69-Aug-6: 2C].
McDonnell, Patrick (51 yrs.) d. on 69-Jun-13 [69-Jun-15: 2C].
McDonough, Felix (21 yrs.) d. on 68-Jul-16 Drowned [68-Jul-17: 1G].
McDonough, James (65 yrs.) d. on 66-Oct-9 of Consumption [66-Oct-10: 2B].
McDonough, John A. m. Walton, Mollie L. on 69-Jan-26 [69-Feb-22: 2C].
McDonough, Martin d. on 68-Dec-4 in Railroad accident [68-Dec-5: 1H].
McDonough, Michael m. Ryan, Ellen on 69-Jun-23 [69-Jul-19: 2C].
McDougal, Mary m. Scharf, John Thomas on 69-Dec-2 [69-Dec-3: 2C].
McDowell, Allace Elizabeth (2 yrs.) d. on 66-Dec-13 [66-Dec-15: 2B].
McDowell, Charles Clinton (9 yrs., 2 mos.) d. on 70-Apr-3 of Scarlet fever [70-Apr-5: 2B].
McDowell, Clarence m. Barry, Anna A. on 70-Feb-2 [70-Feb-4: 2C].
McDowell, Elizabeth d. on 67-Aug-8 [67-Aug-9: 2C].
McDowell, Helen m. Coale, Issac, Jr. on 68-Oct-22 [68-Oct-27: 2B].
McDowell, James (41 yrs.) d. on 67-Nov-6 of Consumption [67-Nov-14: 2C].
McDowell, John B., Dr. (64 yrs.) d. on 68-Jul-8 [68-Jul-17: 2C].
McDowell, W. G. m. Stone, Marion L. on 66-Jan-18 [66-Jan-20: 2C].
McDuell, William H. m. Garrott, Sallie on 67-Apr-24 [67-Apr-29: 2B].
McDuffy, Eliza Melvina m. Davis, L. H. on 70-May-1 [70-May-3: 2B].
McEldon, William B. m. Omelea, Mary on 70-May-5 [70-May-16: 2B].
McEldowney, Mary m. Moore, John on 68-Oct-20 [68-Oct-27: 2B].
McElhaney, Charles (33 yrs.) d. on 69-Mar-30 [69-Mar-31: 2C].
McElhiney, William J. m. Watkins, Mary on 67-Jun-4 [67-Jun-5: 2B].
McElray, Mary (30 yrs.) d. on 67-Oct-25 [67-Oct-31: 2B].
McElray, Mary (32 yrs.) d. on 69-Nov-4 [69-Nov-6: 2C].
McElroy, Daniel m. Patterson, Eliza A. on 68-Nov-3 [68-Nov-12: 2C].
McElroy, George W. (49 yrs.) d. on 66-Nov-1 [66-Nov-7: 2C].
McElroy, James (35 yrs.) d. on 66-Mar-2 [66-Mar-3: 2B].
McElroy, Jennie m. Johnson, James Milburn on 66-Oct-30 [67-Jan-3: 2B].
McElroy, John (17 yrs.) d. on 67-Aug-13 [67-Aug-15: 2C].
McElroy, Martha m. Reissinger, William H. on 70-Jul-7 [70-Jul-15: 2C].
McElroy, Mary d. on 69-Jun-1 [69-Jun-2: 2B].
McElroy, Mary m. Gibson, John W. on 68-Jul-7 [68-Jul-14: 2B].
McElroy, Mary E. (1 yr., 8 mos.) d. on 68-Aug-23 [68-Aug-24: 2B].
McElroy, Sarah (84 yrs.) d. on 68-May-17 [68-May-18: 2B].
McElroy, William m. Robinson, Lizzie on 65-Dec-28 [66-Jan-2: 2C].
McElroy, Willie R. (1 yr., 6 mos.) d. on 70-Jul-31 [70-Aug-1: 2C].
McElvey, Georgeanna Clay (14 yrs.) d. on 66-Apr-2 [66-Apr-4: 2C].
McElwee, Mary A. (40 yrs.) d. on 67-Sep-21 of Consumption [67-Oct-9: 2B].
McElwee, Mary E. m. Ewalt, Henry on 70-Mar-10 [70-Mar-23: 2C].
McElwee, William (44 yrs.) d. on 69-Aug-12 [69-Aug-13: 2C].
McEnany, Peter m. Monahan, Sarah on 70-Feb-14 [70-Feb-17: 2C].
McEnnis, James J. m. Swann, Carrie V. on 70-Sep-22 [70-Sep-26: 2B].
McEntee, James J. m. Dunn, Eliza on 70-Oct-20 [70-Oct-24: 2B].
McEvoy, Thomas (12 yrs.) d. on 69-Apr-28 [69-Apr-29: 2B].
McEwen, Hugh J. (30 yrs.) d. on 66-Oct-19 [66-Oct-23: 2B].
McFadden, Francis P. m. Cassidy, Kate on 66-Nov-28 [66-Dec-1: 2B].
McFadden, Johnny Willis (9 mos.) d. on 70-Sep-16 [70-Sep-17: 2B].

McFadden, Michael H. (23 yrs.) d. on 69-Jan-7 [69-Jan-8: 2C].
McFadden, Rose (27 yrs.) d. on 70-Sep-20 of Consumption [70-Sep-22: 2C].
McFadden, Willie H. C. (5 mos.) d. on 69-Mar-1 [69-Mar-3: 2C].
McFaddin, Francis m. Smith, Sarah F. on 68-Jan-20 [68-Feb-5: 2D].
McFalls, Gertrude R. m. Middlekoff, John C. on 70-Dec-6 [70-Dec-31: 2B].
McFarland, James Henry (2 yrs., 5 mos.) d. on 66-Jul-2 [66-Jul-3: 2C].
McFarland, James Keyser d. on 68-May-28 [68-May-29: 2B].
McFarland, Mary Johnston m. Bulack, Joseph on 70-Aug-31 [70-Sep-1: 2B].
McFaul, Eneas (80 yrs.) d. on 69-Jun-5 [69-Jun-12: 2B].
McFaul, Mary d. on 66-Jan-6 [66-Jan-26: 2B].
McFern, Edward (31 yrs.) d. on 70-Aug-2 [70-Aug-3: 2C].
McFlaherty, Daniel m. Barron, Mary Ann on 68-May-17 [68-May-22: 2C].
McFrederick, A. J. m. Strubie, Mary J. on 69-Oct-26 [69-Oct-29: 2B].
McFrederick, James m. Lepson, Linnie S. on 67-Dec-19 [67-Dec-23: 2B].
McGahan, John C. m. Johnson, Ella V. on 68-Apr-12 [68-Apr-15: 2B].
McGall, Christena (66 yrs.) d. on 70-Jan-22 [70-Jan-24: 2C].
McGall, Elizabeth (47 yrs.) d. on 70-Mar-13 [70-Mar-14: 2C].
McGann, Anne (83 yrs.) d. on 68-Dec-30 [68-Dec-31: 2D].
McGann, Catharine (36 yrs.) d. on 67-Feb-6 [67-Feb-8: 2C].
McGarigle, Anne M. m. Clifford, Thomas on 70-Feb-14 [70-Feb-22: 2C].
McGarigle, Margaret F. m. Hild, Anthony on 68-Jan-16 [68-Jan-17: 2C].
McGarigle, Mary Theresa (2 yrs.) d. on 70-Jul-29 [70-Jul-30: 2C].
McGarity, James Francis (4 yrs., 9 mos.) d. on 69-Jan-11 [69-Jan-12: 2C; 69-Jan-13: 2D].
McGarity, Mary Gertrude (2 yrs., 10 mos.) d. on 70-Nov-10 [70-Nov-11: 2B].
McGarrell, John (62 yrs.) d. on 66-Oct-13 [66-Oct-16: 2B].
McGarrigale, Mary (4 yrs., 10 mos.) d. on 66-Nov-28 [66-Nov-29: 2C].
McGarrity, James (37 yrs.) d. on 69-Jun-1 [69-Jun-2: 2B; 69-Jun-3: 2B].
McGarry, Henrietta (6 mos.) d. on 67-Jul-10 [67-Jul-11: 2C].
McGarvey, William C. m. Uhl, Mary on 66-Nov-29 [66-Dec-1: 2B].
McGary, William H. m. Collins, Mary J. on 70-May-9 [70-May-14: 2A].
McGaw, Albert B. (23 yrs.) d. on 68-Aug-11 [68-Aug-15: 2B].
McGaw, Sally A. (62 yrs.) d. on 66-Jun-25 [66-Jun-26: 2B].
McGeary, Thomas (28 yrs.) d. on 70-Jul-16 Drowned [70-Jul-18: 4E].
McGee, Agnes Loretta d. on 68-Apr-20 [68-Apr-21: 2B].
McGee, Bernard (62 yrs.) d. on 70-Jul-29 [70-Jul-30: 2C].
McGee, Bridget (30 yrs.) d. on 68-Jun-7 [68-Jun-9: 2B].
McGee, John O. (43 yrs.) d. on 69-Feb-26 [69-Feb-27: 2C].
McGee, Kate A. m. McMillen, William H. on 69-Oct-18 [69-Mar-3: 2B].
McGee, Mary Virginia (2 yrs., 5 mos.) d. on 70-Mar-23 [70-Mar-25: 2C].
McGee, Michael (37 yrs.) d. on 67-Jul-5 [67-Jul-6: 2B].
McGee, Michael J. m. Carter, Carrie on 69-Aug-11 [69-Aug-19: 2C].
McGee, Rose (88 yrs.) d. on 70-Jun-22 [70-Jun-23: 2C].
McGee, Thomas m. Pollard, Annie A. on 70-Sep-12 [70-Sep-23: 2C].
McGee, Thomas J. m. Thomas, Annie M. on 67-Apr-28 [67-May-7: 2B].
McGeehan, Emma (1 yr., 11 mos.) d. on 67-Dec-25 [67-Dec-28: 2C].
McGeeney, Ellen (50 yrs.) d. on 68-Feb-29 of Consumption [68-Mar-2: 2B].
McGeeney, Margaret (5 yrs., 8 mos.) d. on 70-Aug-5 [70-Aug-6: 2C].
McGeeney, Patrick (84 yrs.) d. on 66-May-26 [66-May-28: 2B].
McGervy, M. Theodosia, Sr. (60 yrs.) d. on 69-Nov-1 [69-Nov-10: 1H].
McGill, William (28 yrs.) d. on 68-Jan-22 [68-Jan-24: 1G].
McGinley, Durban m. Foster, Lucretia D. on 67-Nov-25 [68-Mar-2: 2B].
McGinley, Durbin (23 yrs.) d. on 69-Apr-9 [69-Apr-10: 2B].
McGinley, George W. (19 yrs.) d. on 67-Oct-10 [67-Oct-11: 2B; 67-Oct-15: 2A].
McGinn, Anastasia E. (21 yrs.) d. on 67-Sep-5 [67-Sep-6: 2B].
McGinn, Anne (65 yrs.) d. [67-Feb-16: 2D].

McGinnes, John H. m. Crout, Mary F. on 68-May-20 [68-May-25: 2A].
McGinnis, Anna d. on 68-Nov-22 [68-Nov-23: 2B].
McGinnis, Annie M. m. Parry, Marion W. on 70-Apr-9 [70-Nov-30: 2C].
McGinnis, John Ulysses Grant d. on 68-Oct-16 [68-Nov-2: 2B].
McGinnis, Mary F. O. d. on 70-Nov-4 [70-Nov-8: 2B].
McGinnis, Susan d. on 69-Jun-30 [69-Jul-5: 2C].
McGinniss, Maria (70 yrs.) d. on 68-Feb-24 [68-Feb-27: 2C].
McGinniss, William L. m. Davis, Allace J. on 69-Nov-8 [69-Nov-12: 2C].
McGinty, Henry, Jr. m. Schellenberger, Kate on 69-Jun-20 [69-Jun-29: 2C].
McGivney, Ann (54 yrs.) d. on 69-Feb-10 [69-Feb-12: 2C].
McGlannan, Thomas Philip (27 yrs.) d. on 68-Nov-24 [68-Nov-25: 2B].
McGlennon, Eliza V. m. Mumma, John on 69-Nov-10 [69-Nov-16: 2C].
McGlennon, Rose Catherine (10 mos.) d. on 68-Sep-29 [68-Oct-10: 2B].
McGlone, Bernard F. m. Delaney, Louise on 69-Nov-25 [69-Dec-18: 2B].
McGlone, Mary E. m. Erdman, William H., Jr. on 66-Nov-22 [66-Dec-13: 2B].
McGlue, Henry S. m. Thomas, Ann R. on 66-Apr-18 [66-Apr-19: 2B].
McGnive, Mary (31 yrs.) d. on 69-Nov-26 [69-Nov-27: 2B].
McGonigal, Virginia m. Billingslea, Charlton W. on 69-Jul-14 [69-Jul-17: 2C].
McGonigle, Catherine Golden (8 yrs., 11 mos.) d. on 70-Oct-10 [70-Oct-12: 2C].
McGookin, John (26 yrs.) d. on 68-Aug-15 [68-Aug-20: 2B].
McGowan, Bernard m. Thrush, Martha V. on 66-Sep-20 [66-Oct-3: 2B].
McGowan, Eliza (68 yrs.) d. on 67-Dec-27 [68-Jan-1: 2C].
McGowan, Eliza Barton (34 yrs.) d. on 66-Apr-29 [66-Aug-30: 2B].
McGowan, George m. Frew, Ellen on 67-Nov-7 [67-Nov-12: 2C].
McGowan, Hugh (69 yrs.) d. on 67-Aug-26 [67-Aug-27: 2B].
McGowan, John C. d. on 66-Dec-4 [66-Dec-5: 2B].
McGowan, John William Price (20 yrs.) d. on 68-Aug-15 [68-Aug-17: 2B].
McGowan, Kate A. m. Chetwood, R. E. on 67-Mar-5 [67-Mar-7: 2C].
McGowan, Martha V. (26 yrs.) d. on 69-Jan-22 [69-Jan-23: 2C].
McGowan, Mary (30 yrs.) d. on 66-Jul-26 [66-Jul-27: 2C].
McGowan, Mary A. (20 yrs.) d. on 68-Sep-19 [68-Sep-21: 2B].
McGowan, Owen (74 yrs.) d. on 70-Oct-26 [70-Oct-27: 2B].
McGowan, Thomas (28 yrs.) d. on 66-Aug-23 [66-Aug-25: 2A].
McGowan, Thomas (1 yr., 2 mos.) d. on 66-May-21 [66-May-23: 2B].
McGowan, Thomas Oliver (3 mos.) d. on 66-Dec-18 [66-Dec-21: 2B].
McGowan, Thomson m. Roland, S. E on 67-Jul-17 [67-Jul-30: 2C].
McGowan, William (42 yrs.) d. on 66-Oct-9 [66-Oct-10: 2B].
McGrane, Patrick (43 yrs.) d. on 68-May-17 [68-May-18: 2B; 68-May-20: 2A].
McGrath, Ellinore (75 yrs.) d. on 66-Mar-27 [66-Apr-4: 2C].
McGrath, H. J. m. Doged, Sallie E. on 69-Mar-11 [69-Mar-12: 2C].
McGrath, J. D. m. McIntire, Lucy E. on 70-Sep-20 [70-Sep-22: 2C].
McGrath, James (3 mos.) d. on 70-Dec-5 [70-Dec-6: 2C].
McGrath, Julia d. on 70-Jul-30 [70-Aug-1: 2C].
McGrath, Mary Elizabeth (1 yr.) d. on 70-Jul-22 [70-Jul-23: 2B].
McGrath, Mary Julia (11 yrs., 9 mos.) d. on 67-Mar-28 of Brain congestion [67-Mar-30: 2C].
McGraw, John (30 yrs.) d. on 70-Nov-4 [70-Nov-5: 2B].
McGraw, John m. Mallen, Mary A. on 68-Apr-16 [68-Apr-22: 2B].
McGraw, Leonora (18 yrs., 8 mos.) d. on 69-Sep-22 [69-Sep-23: 2B].
McGraw, Mary (11 yrs., 3 mos.) d. on 67-Feb-22 [67-Feb-23: 2C].
McGreevy, A. Hamilton R. m. Frailey, Mary E. on 66-Dec-11 [66-Dec-12: 2B].
McGreevy, James m. Loftis, Margaret on 69-Mar-4 [69-Mar-13: 2B].
McGreevy, James Edward (2 yrs., 5 mos.) d. on 66-Oct-5 [66-Oct-6: 2A].
McGreevy, John (48 yrs.) d. on 70-Oct-24 [70-Oct-25: 4E; 70-Oct-26: 2B].
McGreevy, Rebecca (83 yrs.) d. on 70-Dec-21 [70-Dec-22: 2B].
McGregor, James H. m. Hosey, Kate M. on 66-Nov-22 [67-Mar-26: 2C].

McGregor, Robert m. Gardener, Ann on 67-Nov-7 [68-May-13: 2B].
McGregor, William (25 yrs.) d. on 68-Sep-1 [68-Sep-2: 2B].
McGreivy, Mary Ann O'Connor (88 yrs.) d. on 66-Nov-24 [66-Nov-26: 2C].
McGuigan, Bernard d. on 66-Mar-17 Murdered (Stabbing) [66-Mar-20: 1F].
McGuilgan, John Ignatius (1 yr., 4 mos.) d. on 69-Nov-14 [69-Nov-15: 2C].
McGuinas, Sarah (85 yrs.) d. on 70-Nov-25 [70-Nov-26: 2C].
McGuire, Alford C. (5 yrs., 9 mos.) d. on 70-Jun-29 of Scarlet fever [70-Jul-4: 2C].
McGuire, Frances Ann (48 yrs.) d. on 67-Jun-6 [67-Jun-8: 2B].
McGuire, George W. (9 yrs., 2 mos.) d. on 70-Jun-29 of Scarlet fever [70-Jul-4: 2C].
McGuire, Herbert (8 mos.) d. on 70-Jan-11 [70-Jan-13: 2D].
McGuire, James (42 yrs.) d. on 66-Jan-3 [66-Jan-4: 2C].
McGuire, Lizzie (3 yrs., 6 mos.) d. on 68-Nov-23 Burned [68-Nov-25: 1H].
McGuire, Mary A. m. Ferciot, Charles N. on 69-Dec-28 [70-Jan-3: 2C].
McGurk, Catherine d. on 70-May-8 [70-May-9: 2B].
McGurk, Maggie m. Coleman, Noah on 70-Aug-1 [70-Sep-22: 2C].
McHenry, Charlie (1 yr., 1 mo.) d. on 69-Aug-27 [69-Aug-28: 2B].
McHenry, James (4 yrs.) d. on 69-Sep-7 of Diptheria [69-Sep-9: 2B].
McHenry, Patrick m. Lacy, Lizzie L. on 67-Feb-27 [67-Mar-6: 2C].
McHenry, William F. (37 yrs.) d. on 68-Aug-25 Murdered (Shooting) [68-Aug-26: 4C, 2B; 68-Aug-28: 1F].
McHugh, Thomas (48 yrs.) d. on 69-May-24 [69-May-25: 2C; 69-May-26: 2C].
McIlhaney, John (2 yrs., 4 mos.) d. on 68-Apr-16 [68-Apr-17: 2B].
McIlhany, Willie Lee (7 mos.) d. on 69-Mar-1 [69-Mar-3: 2C].
McIlvain, Henry C. m. Nicholson, Fanny on 70-Oct-11 [70-Oct-13: 2C].
McIlvaine, Robert (28 yrs., 8 mos.) d. on 66-Dec-13 of Explosion [66-Dec-14: 1F, 2B].
McIlvaine, Willie G. (6 yrs., 5 mos.) d. on 68-Sep-27 [68-Sep-28: 2B].
McIlwein, John (6 yrs., 11 mos.) d. on 69-May-2 [69-May-3: 2C].
McInnes, T. W. m. Orchiese, Mary A. on 70-Jan-5 [70-Jan-18: 2C].
McIntire, Ann d. on 67-Jul-17 [67-Jul-26: 2C].
McIntire, Barney (35 yrs.) d. on 68-Sep-7 [68-Sep-11: 2B].
McIntire, George H. m. Griffith, Vermadela on 68-Dec-22 [68-Dec-24: 2C].
McIntire, Jane E. m. Clefford, Austin on 66-Jun-12 [67-Apr-10: 2B].
McIntire, Lucy E. m. McGrath, J. D. on 70-Sep-20 [70-Sep-22: 2C].
McIntire, Patrick (76 yrs.) d. on 66-Mar-31 [66-Apr-2: 2B].
McIntire, Sallie J. m. Sloan, J. Theodore on 70-Jan-5 [70-Jan-8: 2B].
McIntosh, John d. on 70-Jun-8 of Lung hemorrhage [70-Jun-13: 1H].
McIntyre, Gilbert (20 yrs.) d. on 67-Dec-15 [67-Dec-18: 2B].
McIntyre, James (1 yr., 3 mos.) d. on 67-Jul-19 of Bowel inflammation [67-Jul-20: 2C].
McIntyre, James (39 yrs.) d. on 69-Apr-15 [69-Apr-17: 2B].
McIntyre, Mary (38 yrs.) d. on 66-Jan-18 [66-Jan-20: 2C].
McIntyre, Mary (48 yrs.) d. on 70-Oct-25 [70-Oct-26: 2B].
McIntyre, Mary m. Miller, F. W. on 70-Jan-27 [70-Jan-29: 2B].
McIntyre, Sarah (38 yrs.) d. on 67-Sep-29 [67-Sep-30: 2B].
McJilton, D. A., Rev. d. on 70-May-9 [70-May-12: 2B].
McJilton, Helen A. m. Alton, James T. on 68-May-26 [68-May-28: 2B].
McJilton, J. N. m. Almack, Mollie J. on 67-Jan-10 [67-Jan-15: 2C].
McJilton, John N., Jr. (14 yrs.) d. on 69-Apr-15 [69-Apr-19: 2B].
McJilton, Sallie E. m. Kesmodel, Gustav on 69-Nov-29 [70-Mar-3: 2C].
McJilton, W. W. d. on 69-Oct-3 [69-Oct-7: 2B].
McJilton, William G. m. Hickey, Mary J. on 66-Mar-19 [66-Jul-24: 2C].
McKail, Anthony (98 yrs.) d. on 67-Oct-10 [67-Oct-12: 2A].
McKay, Albenia m. Davis, William E. on 70-Sep-7 [70-Sep-15: 2B].
McKay, Annie J. m. White, Edmund on 70-Apr-12 [70-Apr-15: 2B].
McKay, Charles J. (3 mos.) d. on 69-Jul-27 [69-Jul-28: 2D].
McKay, Donald m. Triplett, Eliza J. on 70-Feb-1 [70-Feb-2: 2B].

McKay, Harry C. (22 yrs.) d. on 66-Nov-23 [66-Nov-24: 2C].
McKay, Mary (32 yrs.) d. on 66-May-3 [66-May-5: 2B].
McKay, R. G. m. Crookshank, Jennie on 69-Nov-2 [69-Nov-4: 2B].
McKay, Sarah M. m. Gwinn, William R. on 68-Jan-28 [68-Jan-29: 2C].
McKean, Anna Frances (5 yrs.) d. on 70-Dec-3 [70-Dec-5: 2C].
McKean, Annie M. (19 yrs.) d. on 67-May-20 of Bilious Pneumonia [67-May-28: 2B].
McKean, Mary Jane m. Crudden, Joseph on 66-Feb-22 [66-Feb-24: 2B].
McKean, William H. d. on 66-Jun-21 [66-Jun-23: 2B].
McKee, Alice (1 yr., 1 mo.) d. on 69-Sep-3 [69-Sep-4: 2B].
McKee, Andrew E. (43 yrs.) d. on 68-May-5 [68-May-7: 2B].
McKee, Caroline (22 yrs.) d. on 69-Dec-10 [69-Dec-11: 2B].
McKee, James W. (4 yrs.) d. on 69-Dec-5 of Scarlet fever [69-Dec-10: 2C].
McKee, Mary Theresa m. Waggaman, Samuel J. on 70-Sep-21 [70-Sep-22: 2C].
Mckeel, Arthur D d. on 69-Mar-2 [69-Mar-4: 2C].
McKeever, John (47 yrs.) d. on 70-Mar-23 of Consumption [70-Mar-24: 2C; 70-Mar-25: 2C].
McKeever, Julia (6 mos.) d. on 68-Feb-10 [68-Feb-11: 2C].
McKeever, Julia (1 yr., 3 mos.) d. on 70-Jun-3 [70-Jun-4: 2B].
McKeldin, David W. (40 yrs.) d. on 66-Sep-17 of Consumption [66-Sep-21: 2B].
McKeldin, Maria Louisa (20 yrs.) d. on 66-Jul-20 [66-Jul-23: 2C].
McKeldin, Sarah (18 yrs., 7 mos.) d. on 67-Jan-11 of Consumption [67-Jan-14: 2C].
McKeldin, Sarah Virginia (11 mos.) d. on 70-Dec-16 [70-Dec-20: 2B].
McKelvy, Henrietta (4 yrs.) d. on 69-Nov-16 of Diptheria [69-Nov-17: 2C].
McKenna, Ann d. on 68-Jul-21 [68-Jul-22: 2B; 68-Jul-23: 2B].
McKenna, Ann (61 yrs.) d. on 68-Oct-17 [68-Oct-19: 2B].
McKenna, Annie J. m. Adams, William H. on 67-Nov-6 [67-Apr-29: 2B].
McKenna, Arthur m. Lynd, Mary A. on 68-Nov-16 [68-Nov-20: 2C].
McKenna, Bernard T. d. on 68-Nov-13 [68-Nov-14: 2B].
McKenna, Catherine (28 yrs.) d. on 66-Oct-14 [66-Oct-13: 2B].
McKenna, Catherine m. McShane, Edward on 67-Apr-21 [67-Apr-29: 2B].
McKenna, Ella (6 mos.) d. on 70-Feb-16 [70-Feb-17: 2C].
McKenna, Felix (30 yrs.) d. on 66-Jul-17 [66-Jul-18: 2C].
McKenna, Francis (58 yrs.) d. on 68-Oct-31 [68-Nov-2: 2B].
McKenna, Francis (31 yrs.) d. on 66-Oct-24 of Consumption [66-Oct-26: 2B].
McKenna, Frank L. m. Boss, Mary E. on 66-Apr-12 [66-Apr-20: 2B].
McKenna, James (31 yrs.) d. on 70-Apr-2 of Pneumonia [70-Apr-4: 2C].
McKenna, James (3 yrs., 9 mos.) d. on 70-May-9 [70-May-10: 2C].
McKenna, John P. (6 mos.) d. on 69-Feb-6 [69-Feb-8: 2C].
McKenna, Mary C. m. Hagan, Peter on 69-May-27 [69-Jun-3: 2B].
McKenna, Michael (65 yrs.) d. on 66-Jul-18 [66-Jul-19: 2C].
McKenna, Mollie m. Krager, George W. on 66-Sep-17 [66-Sep-19: 2B].
McKenna, Peter m. Finnegan, Winnifred on 68-Jan-17 [68-Oct-2: 2B].
McKenna, Rose m. Coyne, Patrick on 66-Nov-1 [66-Nov-9: 2C].
McKenna, Sarah (74 yrs.) d. on 69-Jun-11 [69-Jun-12: 2B].
McKenney, Caroline S. (55 yrs.) d. on 67-Jan-26 [67-Jan-28: 2C].
McKenney, Samuel J. (26 yrs.) d. on 66-Dec-16 [66-Dec-19: 2B].
McKenny, Mary A. m. Holt, William on 65-Dec-14 [66-Jan-9: 2B].
McKenzie, Agnes (84 yrs.) d. on 70-Feb-3 [70-Feb-5: 2B].
McKenzie, Ann Jane (34 yrs.) d. on 68-Dec-21 [68-Dec-22: 2C].
McKenzie, George W. (39 yrs.) d. on 66-Aug-22 [66-Aug-24: 2B; 66-Aug-25: 2A].
McKeown, John T. m. Thompson, Mary Ann on 66-Aug-22 [66-Aug-30: 2B].
McKeown, Sarah Ann m. Woods, James C. on 66-Dec-5 [66-Dec-11: 2B].
McKernan, Catharine (22 yrs.) d. on 68-Jan-26 of Consumption [68-Jan-27: 2C].
McKew, Elizabeth (63 yrs.) d. on 68-Jan-25 [68-Jan-27: 2C].
McKew, Ellen H. m. Crocken, Nelson T. on 69-Jun-17 [69-Jun-20: 2C].
McKewan, Hugh (70 yrs.) d. on 70-Sep-5 [70-Sep-7: 2B].

McKewen, Ella m. Denby, William L. on 67-Sep-8 [67-Dec-27: 2D].
McKewen, Francis m. Busick, Ella Virginia on 70-May-12 [70-Nov-18: 2C].
McKewen, Freddie J. d. on 66-Dec-31 of Scarlet fever [67-Jan-2: 2C].
McKewen, James J. m. Coogan, Mary J. on 66-May-14 [66-May-19: 2B].
McKewen, Nicholas J. (2 yrs., 7 mos.) d. on 70-Mar-18 [70-Mar-19: 2B].
McKewin, Richard J. m. Crowther, Matilda J. on 69-Jul-1 [69-Jul-14: 2D].
McKewin, William (61 yrs.) d. on 68-Oct-1 [68-Oct-2: 2B].
McKey, Eliza m. Dennis, Andrew T. on 67-Oct-17 [67-Oct-19: 2A].
McKey, John d. on 69-Oct-19 [69-Oct-20: 2C].
McKim, Augustus (19 yrs.) d. on 68-Aug-18 [68-Aug-26: 2B].
McKim, Duncan (5 yrs.) d. on 69-Jan-3 [69-Jan-4: 2C].
McKim, Haslett m. Winthrop, Harriet R. on 70-Sep-15 [70-Sep-19: 2B].
McKim, Hollins (3 yrs., 1 mo.) d. on 68-Dec-27 of Diptheria [68-Dec-28: 2C].
McKim, Susan Anne (54 yrs.) d. on 66-Feb-7 [66-Feb-8: 2C].
McKim, William (8 yrs.) d. on 69-Jan-20 of Diptheria [69-Jan-21: 2C].
McKinley, Eliza R. m. Mitchell, Philip E. on 66-Dec-23 [66-Dec-28: 2C].
McKinley, Margaret (51 yrs.) d. on 66-Nov-4 of Consumption [66-Nov-5: 2B].
McKinley, Mary A. d. on 67-Feb-3 [67-Feb-5: 2C].
McKinley, Susannah Cecilia m. Steen, Samuel Isaiah on 68-Oct-28 [70-Mar-24: 2C; 70-Mar-26: 2B].
McKinley, William (57 yrs.) d. on 68-Jun-16 of Paralysis [68-Jun-17: 1F, 2B].
McKinley, William m. Johnson, Susan C. on 66-Oct-18 [66-Oct-20: 2B].
McKinnell, Emma Virginia (8 mos.) d. on 69-Jun-29 [69-Jul-3: 2B].
McKinnell, John C. m. Lewis, Mary F. on 67-Dec-19 [67-Dec-23: 2B].
McKinney, Augustus Myers (6 mos.) d. on 67-Mar-14 [67-Mar-15: 2C].
McKinney, Maria m. Stewart, James on 67-Jul-10 [67-Jul-24: 2C].
McKinney, William (43 yrs.) d. on 70-Apr-9 of Boiler explosion [70-Apr-11: 2B].
McKinny, Bernard (41 yrs.) d. on 69-Mar-20 of Consumption [69-Mar-24: 2C].
McKinny, Margery C. (1 yr., 3 mos.) d. on 68-Jun-28 [68-Oct-9: 2C].
McKitrich, Laura T. (3 mos.) d. on 69-Sep-27 [69-Sep-28: 2B].
McKitrick, Harry (1 yr.) d. on 70-Jul-1 [70-Jul-2: 2B].
McKittrick, Robert A. d. on 68-Jul-2 [68-Jul-4: 2C].
McKnew, Emma H. m. Turner, J. W. on 68-Jun-2 [68-Jun-5: 2B].
McKnew, N. C. (38 yrs.) d. on 69-Mar-22 of Consumption [69-Mar-24: 2C; 69-Mar-25: 2C].
McKnew, Sallie J. m. Hazlett, C. C. on 68-Jun-1 [68-Jun-6: 2A].
McLain, Mary m. Sheehan, Daniel F. on 68-Dec-27 [68-Dec-31: 2C].
McLain, Patrick d. on 68-Jul-15 of Brain congestion [68-Jul-17: 1D; 68-Jul-18: 1E].
McLain, Richard Thomas (9 yrs.) d. on 66-Feb-23 in Wagon accident [66-Feb-24: 2B].
McLain, William, Jr. m. Bernoudy, Celanire on 67-Jan-15 [67-Jul-27: 2B].
McLaine, Samuel R. m. Bowen, Agnes C. on 69-Oct-1 [69-Oct-9: 2C].
McLanahan, James B. m. Yager, Kate on 69-Nov-9 [69-Nov-30: 2C].
McLane, Asbury m. Mallonee, Rachel on 70-Sep-12 [70-Sep-21: 2B].
McLane, Edward E. (50 yrs.) d. on 69-Oct-12 [69-Oct-15: 2C].
McLane, James Goreking (4 yrs., 10 mos.) d. on 67-Dec-21 of Scarlet fever [67-Dec-23: 2B].
McLane, Sarah B. m. Engle, William J. on 67-Oct-6 [67-Oct-8: 2B].
McLarney, Patrick (62 yrs.) d. on 66-Dec-7 [66-Dec-8: 2B].
McLaughlin, Alice (4 yrs., 7 mos.) d. on 70-Dec-27 [70-Dec-28: 2C].
McLaughlin, Alice Gertrude (4 mos.) d. on 68-Jun-20 [68-Jun-22: 2B].
McLaughlin, Andrew Thomas (3 yrs., 4 mos.) d. on 66-Aug-25 [66-Aug-27: 2B].
McLaughlin, Ann J. (68 yrs.) d. on 69-Mar-12 [69-Mar-15: 2C].
McLaughlin, Charles (53 yrs.) d. on 68-May-31 [68-Jun-2: 2B].
McLaughlin, Fannie m. Clarke, A. P. on 70-Nov-22 [70-Nov-23: 2B].
McLaughlin, Francis, Mrs. (25 yrs.) d. on 67-Apr-13 [67-Apr-15: 2B].
McLaughlin, Francis W. (25 yrs.) d. on 69-Jul-8 [69-Jul-10: 2B].
McLaughlin, George (30 yrs.) d. on 67-Jan-1 [67-Jan-3: 2C].

McLaughlin, George Reuben (1 yr.) d. on 66-Sep-9 [66-Sep-10: 2D].
McLaughlin, J. Fairfax m. Brooke, Nannie S. on 67-Dec-5 [67-Dec-9: 2B].
McLaughlin, J. G. m. Whiteford, Jennie on 70-Jun-27 [70-Jun-28: 2C].
McLaughlin, J. George d. on 69-Nov-2 [69-Nov-5: 2C].
McLaughlin, J. T. W. m. Hawkins, Addie E. on 69-Sep-16 [69-Sep-22: 2C].
McLaughlin, James (48 yrs.) d. on 66-Oct-8 [66-Oct-9: 2A].
McLaughlin, John Edwin (4 yrs., 2 mos.) d. on 66-Dec-25 [66-Dec-27: 2C].
McLaughlin, John Patrick (4 yrs., 11 mos.) d. on 70-May-31 [70-Jun-1: 2B].
McLaughlin, Joseph J. (43 yrs.) d. on 70-Dec-15 [70-Dec-16: 2C].
McLaughlin, Margaret m. Anderson, Richard on 69-Apr-1 [69-Apr-5: 2B].
McLaughlin, Marie L. m. Salomon, Oscar E. on 70-Jan-9 [70-Jan-11: 2C].
McLaughlin, Mary (37 yrs.) d. on 67-Dec-15 [67-Dec-16: 2B].
McLaughlin, Mary m. Ryan, William on 66-Dec-10 [66-Dec-13: 2B].
McLaughlin, Robert H. (2 yrs., 7 mos.) d. on 69-Jan-22 of Pneumonia [69-Jan-23: 2C].
McLaughlin, Sallie I. m. McCauley, William E. on 70-Nov-17 [70-Nov-22: 2B].
McLaughlin, Sarah d. on 67-Dec-22 [67-Dec-23: 2B].
McLaughlin, Therese (6 mos.) d. [67-Mar-15: 2C].
McLea, William H. (38 yrs.) d. on 69-Jul-5 [69-Jul-7: 2C].
McLean, Alexander Maria Corner (10 mos.) d. on 69-Jan-20 [69-Jan-22: 2D].
McLean, Arthur m. Hobbs, Ruth Elizabeth on 66-Dec-11 [66-Dec-15: 2B].
McLean, Dixon Crawford (7 yrs., 11 mos.) d. on 67-Feb-26 [67-Feb-27: 2C].
McLean, Eliza (87 yrs.) d. on 67-May-21 [67-May-23: 2C].
McLean, Fannie Riggin d. on 67-Sep-22 [67-Oct-2: 2B].
McLean, Georgie m. Burroughs, Joseph on 68-Apr-2 [68-Apr-4: 2B].
McLean, Ida m. Pyatt, Charles E. on 66-Dec-20 [67-Feb-19: 2C].
McLean, John m. Forrester, Jessie on 67-Jul-12 [67-Jul-23: 2C].
McLean, John William m. Kirby, Anna R. on 69-Aug-31 [69-Sep-7: 2B].
McLean, Maggie m. Roulston, Robert on 70-Oct-6 [70-Oct-14: 2B].
McLean, Margaret Eugenia m. Yost, Richard D. on 68-Jun-25 [68-Jun-29: 2B].
McLean, Mary G. m. Rogers, Daniel on 66-Jan-30 [66-Feb-2: 2C].
McLean, Rose Anna (19 yrs.) d. on 70-May-21 [70-May-23: 2C].
McLean, Samuel Adams (1 yr.) d. on 68-Dec-13 [68-Dec-14: 2C].
McLean, Sarah A. m. Kinnier, George on 67-Aug-8 [67-Aug-15: 2C; 67-Aug-16: 2B].
McLean, William H. m. Seabert, Mary on 69-Oct-3 [69-Oct-5: 2B].
McLean, William J. m. Netre, Olivia on 70-Feb-7 [70-Feb-10: 2C].
McLean, William West (48 yrs.) d. on 69-Nov-8 [69-Nov-11: 1G; 69-Nov-12: 2C].
McLeary, Elizabeth Jane (30 yrs.) d. on 66-Feb-25 [66-Feb-26: 2B].
McLellan, John S. m. Burke, M. Gertrude on 70-Sep-8 [70-Sep-13: 2B].
McLeod, Alexander m. Rathbun, Maggie Allison on 68-Jul-16 [68-Jul-17: 2B].
McLeod, Emma E. m. Bent, Fred W. on 67-Sep-9 [67-Oct-9: 2B].
McLernan, Matthew m. Brooks, Mary on 67-Dec-19 [67-Dec-24: 2B].
McLetchie, Andrew, Dr. (30 yrs.) d. on 67-Oct-13 [67-Nov-8: 2C].
McLevy, James d. on 67-Sep-28 [67-Sep-30: 2B].
McLoud, Francis (42 yrs.) d. on 66-May-6 [66-May-7: 2B].
McLoughlin, Rosa m. Loney, Lewis H. on 66-Dec-19 [66-Dec-22: 2A].
McMagh, Bernard (55 yrs.) d. on 70-Feb-15 [70-Feb-17: 2C].
McMahan, John B. m. Frailey, Alice on 69-Dec-30 [70-Jan-1: 2B].
McMahan, Terrence m. McShane, Annie on 67-Nov-25 [67-Dec-12: 2B].
McMahon, Elizabeth (65 yrs.) d. on 70-Dec-2 [70-Dec-3: 2B].
McMahon, Francis Michael (11 mos.) d. on 69-Aug-19 [69-Aug-20: 2C].
McMahon, James T. (33 yrs.) d. on 68-Apr-2 of Consumption [68-Apr-3: 2C].
McMahon, John (14 yrs.) d. on 67-May-1 of Hydrophobia [67-May-4: 1F].
McMahon, John m. Kennedy, Sarah A. on 70-Jan-17 [70-Feb-2: 2B].
McMahon, Lizzie m. Gorsuch, Silas W. on 66-Oct-9 [66-Dec-29: 2C].
McMahon, Maggie Loretto (6 mos.) d. on 69-Nov-26 [69-Nov-27: 2C].

McMahon, Mary Alice (1 yr., 2 mos.) d. on 68-Feb-7 [68-Feb-8: 2B].
McMahon, Mary F. (77 yrs.) d. on 66-Aug-9 [66-Aug-13: 2C].
McMahon, Michael (64 yrs.) d. on 67-Dec-20 [67-Dec-20: 2B].
McMahon, Michael (54 yrs.) d. on 66-Jul-18 of Intemperance and exposure [66-Jul-19: 1F, 2C].
McMahon, Patrick (85 yrs.) d. on 70-Mar-25 [70-Mar-26: 2B].
McMaines, Charles J. m. Bach, Barbara E. A. on 69-Oct-11 [69-Oct-14: 2C].
McMaines, Elizabeth m. Naff, Albert on 67-Oct-15 [68-Mar-16: 2B].
McMaines, John (53 yrs.) d. on 70-Aug-24 [70-Aug-26: 2C].
McMaines, William m. Pumphrey, Isabella W. on 66-Sep-19 [66-Sep-21: 2B].
McMains, A. E. (76 yrs.) d. on 68-Jul-1 [68-Aug-18: 2B].
McMann, Mary Ann d. on 66-Dec-25 of Typhoid [66-Dec-27: 2C].
McMann, Michael m. Gorman, Ellen on 70-May-30 [70-Jun-9: 2C].
McManus, Alexander (74 yrs.) d. on 70-May-6 of Lung hemorrhage [70-May-10: 2C].
McManus, Catharine (27 yrs.) d. on 68-Nov-10 [68-Nov-21: 2C].
McManus, Edward P. m. King, Mary A. on 68-Oct-8 [68-Oct-10: 2B].
McManus, Eliza Ann (45 yrs., 10 mos.) d. on 69-Jun-16 [69-Jun-17: 2C].
McManus, Florence d. on 70-Apr-7 [70-Apr-8: 2C; 70-Apr-9: 2B].
McManus, Frederick A. m. Wier, Florence on 68-Oct-1 [68-Oct-3: 2B].
McManus, John (2 yrs., 5 mos.) d. on 66-Sep-4 [66-Sep-5: 2B].
McManus, Joseph H. d. on 70-Mar-3 [70-Mar-4: 2C].
McManus, Kate (21 yrs.) d. on 68-Sep-30 [68-Oct-2: 2B].
McManus, Samuel Lyeth (7 yrs.) d. on 69-Nov-25 of Chronic croup [69-Nov-27: 2B].
McManus, Thomas (50 yrs.) d. on 68-Jul-27 [68-Jul-28: 2B].
McMechen, Emma V. m. Hildebrand, Harry F. on 68-Jul-23 [68-Aug-6: 2B].
McMechen, Sarah A. (62 yrs.) d. on 67-Mar-18 [67-Mar-19: 2C].
McMechin, James d. on 66-Mar-2 Drowned [66-Mar-3: 1G].
McMillan, John G. (42 yrs.) d. on 70-Nov-15 [70-Nov-16: 2C].
McMillan, Margaret A. m. Harting, Charles on 66-Sep-11 [66-Sep-15: 2B].
McMillan, Martha m. Bush, Peter on 68-Jan-2 [68-Jan-8: 2C].
McMillan, Mary Jane d. on 68-Jun-22 [68-Jun-24: 2B].
McMillard, Mary A. m. Rust, Thomas on 66-Sep-20 [66-Oct-4: 2B].
McMillen, Sarah A. m. Disney, Stirling T on 66-Nov-29 [67-Nov-29: 2B].
McMillen, William H. m. McGee, Kate A. on 69-Oct-18 [69-Mar-3: 2B].
McMullan, Anna M. d. on 68-Jan-25 [68-Jan-30: 2C].
McMullen, Ellen m. Simpson, Alexander on 67-Nov-11 [67-Nov-22: 2C].
McMullen, John (80 yrs.) d. on 70-Sep-18 [70-Sep-19: 2B; 70-Sep-20: 2B; 70-Sep-21: 2B].
McMullen, Maggie m. Wilmer, Gideon L. on 69-Oct-7 [69-Oct-15: 2C].
McMullen, Margaret (76 yrs.) d. on 70-Mar-20 [70-Mar-21: 2C].
McMullen, Mary J. d. on 66-May-14 [66-May-15: 2C; 66-May-16: 2C].
McMullin, Lambert (24 yrs.) d. on 67-Nov-14 of Consumption [67-Nov-18: 2C].
McMurray, Ann (82 yrs.) d. on 68-Nov-25 [68-Nov-28: 2C].
McMurray, John (42 yrs.) d. on 67-Jan-22 [67-Jan-28: 2C].
McMurray, Sally (75 yrs.) d. on 69-Oct-7 [69-Oct-8: 2B].
McNabb, Anna E. m. Preston, Herbert A. on 69-Oct-19 [69-Oct-20: 2C].
McNabb, Mary E. m. Sanford, Edward H. on 68-Mar-24 [68-Mar-26: 2B].
McNally, Bridget d. on 66-Nov-16 [66-Nov-17: 2B].
McNally, Elizabeth (38 yrs.) d. on 69-Apr-21 [69-Apr-22: 2B].
McNally, Francis (26 yrs.) d. on 68-Jul-13 [68-Jul-14: 2C].
McNally, Hugh (56 yrs.) d. on 66-Oct-28 [66-Oct-30: 2B].
McNally, James (72 yrs.) d. on 70-Feb-20 of Congestive chills [70-Feb-21: 2B; 70-Feb-22: 2C].
McNally, John (39 yrs.) d. on 68-Mar-27 in Railroad accident [68-Mar-28: 1F, 2B].
McNally, John m. Switzer, Elizabeth on 68-Oct-4 [68-Oct-6: 2B].
McNally, Louisa D. d. on 69-Mar-1 [69-Mar-2: 2C; 69-Mar-3: 2C].
McNally, Sarah (1 yr., 3 mos.) d. on 69-Apr-25 [69-Apr-26: 2B].

McNamara, Ann d. on 67-Dec-25 Murdered (Shooting) [67-Dec-27: 1F; 67-Dec-28: 1G].
McNamara, Caleb (77 yrs.) d. on 67-Oct-11 [67-Oct-12: 2A].
McNamara, Daniel (4 yrs., 1 mo.) d. on 69-Dec-8 [69-Dec-9: 2C].
McNamara, Leander (10 mos.) d. on 68-Sep-10 [68-Sep-11: 2B].
McNamara, Mary Ellen (40 yrs.) d. on 68-Mar-4 [68-Mar-6: 2C].
McNamee, James (55 yrs.) d. on 70-Mar-31 of Typhoid pneumonia [70-Apr-1: 1H; 70-Apr-2: 2B; 70-Apr-4: 1G].
McNamee, John F. m. Finley, Mary E. on 69-May-30 [69-Jun-3: 2B].
McNamee, Rose (36 yrs.) d. on 69-Dec-30 [70-Jan-1: 2B; 69-Dec-31: 2C].
McNamee, Virginia W. m. Vaughan, Walter W. on 70-Dec-15 [70-Dec-21: 2C].
McNaney, Charles G. (4 yrs., 6 mos.) d. on 70-Nov-25 [70-Nov-26: 2C].
McNaugh, John (35 yrs.) d. on 67-Jun-20 in Machine accident [67-Jun-21: 4C].
McNaughton, Michael (55 yrs.) d. on 67-Sep-5 [67-Sep-6: 2B].
McNeal, Ann Rebecca A. m. Lycett, Michael T. on 68-Nov-30 [68-Dec-8: 2C].
McNeal, George d. on 70-Jun-9 of Asthma and heart disease [70-Jun-10: 1H].
McNeal, Mary E. m. Preston, Thomas H. on 70-May-19 [70-May-24: 2C].
McNeal, Sarah (81 yrs.) d. on 69-Jun-30 [69-Jul-1: 2C].
McNeal, William (69 yrs.) d. on 66-Nov-13 [66-Nov-15: 2C].
McNear, Hannah E. (1 yr., 5 mos.) d. on 69-Feb-28 [69-Mar-3: 2C].
McNeil, John G. (69 yrs.) d. on 70-Jun-9 [70-Jun-11: 2B].
McNeil, Susan (63 yrs.) d. on 68-Nov-25 [68-Nov-26: 2B].
McNeill, Ahmica Alice (19 yrs.) d. on 68-May-25 [68-May-27: 2B].
McNeir, Anna R. m. Harris, John P. on 67-May-28 [67-Jun-1: 2B].
McNeir, Elizabeth (29 yrs.) d. on 67-Feb-6 [67-Feb-8: 2C].
McNeir, William J. m. Barton, Laura J. on 66-Nov-5 [66-Nov-8: 2C].
McNelly, James Barton (29 yrs.) d. on 67-Jun-18 of Consumption [67-Jun-20: 2B].
McNelly, Maggie A. m. McCaffray, James on 69-Oct-31 [69-Nov-1: 2B].
McNemar, Harrison m. Ogg, Lue on 66-Feb-8 [66-Feb-9: 2C].
McNerhany, Margaret (35 yrs.) d. on 67-May-15 [67-May-17: 2B].
McNevin, John P. (74 yrs.) d. on 66-Nov-15 [66-Nov-16: 2C; 66-Nov-17: 2B].
McNew, Thomas Wilbert (1 yr., 5 mos.) d. on 70-Mar-26 [70-Mar-30: 2C].
McNight, Thomas (30 yrs., 6 mos.) d. on 69-Sep-8 [69-Sep-13: 2B].
McNinch, Ella S. (7 yrs.) d. on 68-Oct-2 [68-Oct-3: 2B].
McNinch, William (36 yrs.) d. on 66-Jan-21 in Street railway accident [66-Jan-22: 1F, 2C; 66-Jan-23: 2C].
McNulty, Margaret m. Kreideweis, William on 68-Dec-31 [69-Feb-5: 2C].
McNulty, Mary Ellen (6 yrs.) d. on 66-Jan-9 [66-Jan-10: 2C].
McNulty, Thomas (1 yr., 10 mos.) d. on 69-Jan-1 [69-Jan-2: 2C].
McPhail, Leonard Casse, Dr. (59 yrs.) d. on 67-Mar-23 [67-Mar-26: 1G, 2C].
McPharson, John W. m. Bayliss, Emma F. on 68-Nov-10 [68-Nov-16: 2C; 68-Nov-17: 2C].
McPherson, Charlotte m. Cromwell, Grafton S. on 70-Feb-24 [70-Mar-2: 2C].
McPherson, Jefferson Davis (9 yrs., 6 mos.) d. on 70-Nov-11 [70-Nov-12: 2B].
McPherson, John (51 yrs.) d. on 67-Jul-9 [67-Jul-17: 2C].
McPherson, John H. T. (45 yrs., 11 mos.) d. on 66-Aug-26 [66-Aug-27: 2B].
McPherson, John W. m. Parker, Annie P. on 70-May-12 [70-May-14: 2A].
McPherson, Margaret E. (47 yrs.) d. on 66-Jun-10 of Consumption [66-Jun-12: 2B].
McPherson, Samuel J. (35 yrs.) d. on 70-Feb-8 [70-Feb-24: 2C].
McQuaid, Elizabeth (51 yrs.) d. on 68-Jul-3 [68-Jul-4: 2C].
McQuaid, Frank (4 mos.) d. on 70-Jul-22 [70-Aug-10: 2C].
McQuaid, Mary (5 mos.) d. on 70-Aug-8 [70-Aug-10: 2C].
McQuewen, Mary (87 yrs.) d. on 67-Jan-26 [67-Jan-28: 2C].
McQuillan, James (70 yrs.) d. on 66-Dec-16 [66-Dec-17: 2B].
McQuillan, Mary Ann (23 yrs.) d. on 69-Oct-20 of Phthistia pulmonalis [69-Oct-22: 2B].
McReady, Josephine Virginia (10 yrs., 10 mos.) d. on 68-Aug-25 [68-Aug-29: 2B].
McShane, Annie m. McMahan, Terrence on 67-Nov-25 [67-Dec-12: 2B].

McShane, Edward m. McKenna, Catherine on 67-Apr-21 [67-Apr-24: 2B].
McShane, Helen Rosalia (2 yrs., 5 mos.) d. [68-Mar-18: 2B].
McShane, James F. m. Bradley, Sallie E. on 70-Feb-10 [70-Mar-11: 2C].
McShane, John m. Cassidy, Maggie A. on 69-Oct-19 [69-Oct-22: 2B].
McShane, Winifred d. on 69-May-19 [69-May-20: 2C].
McSherry, Clementine (46 yrs.) d. on 70-Jan-14 [70-Jan-15: 2C].
McSherry, Edward Norris (10 yrs.) d. on 70-Nov-25 of Scarlet fever [70-Nov-26: 2C].
McSherry, Eliza T. (42 yrs.) d. on 68-Mar-25 [68-Mar-27: 2C].
McSherry, Henry F., Dr. (30 yrs.) d. on 67-Oct-1 [67-Nov-30: 2C].
McSherry, James, Jr. m. McAleer, Clara L. on 67-Jan-21 [67-Jan-26: 2C].
McSherry, W. A. m. Audoun, Emma Fuller on 68-Nov-26 [68-Nov-28: 2C].
McSherry, William Kilty m. Combs, Charlotte C. on 70-Nov-30 [70-Dec-2: 2C].
McSoarley, Anna d. on 68-Apr-28 [68-Apr-30: 2B].
McSorley, John (42 yrs.) d. on 69-Aug-4 [69-Aug-5: 2C].
McSweeney, John Patrick (3 yrs., 4 mos.) d. on 69-Feb-6 [69-Feb-15: 2C].
McSweeny, Catherine (65 yrs.) d. on 67-Feb-21 [67-Feb-23: 2C].
McSweeny, Sarah m. Welsh, John W. on 70-Sep-15 [70-Sep-24: 2B].
McSwiney, Annie (17 yrs.) d. on 67-Sep-17 [67-Sep-18: 2B].
McSwiney, Edmond (2 mos.) d. on 69-Jun-15 [69-Jun-16: 2C].
McSwinney, Hanora (1 yr., 9 mos.) d. on 69-Oct-5 [69-Oct-6: 2B].
McTague, Patrick (29 yrs.) d. on 68-Jan-10 [68-Jan-11: 2B].
McVay, Hannah (83 yrs.) d. on 70-Aug-28 [70-Aug-29: 2C].
McVay, Patrick (33 yrs.) d. on 66-Jul-18 [66-Jul-19: 2C].
McVeigh, James H., Jr. m. Ratcliffe, Mary F. on 70-Jan-18 [70-Jan-19: 2C].
McVille, Elenora m. Sullivan, Daniel on 69-Nov-17 [69-Nov-24: 2C].
McWhinney, Lizzie d. on 68-Aug-17 [68-Aug-18: 2B].
McWilliam, Mary (65 yrs.) d. on 67-Sep-6 [67-Sep-7: 2A].
McWilliams, Catherine J. (55 yrs.) d. on 68-Mar-15 [68-Mar-17: 2C].
McWilliams, Daniel m. Burke, Lizzie A. on 68-Jul-2 [68-Jul-10: 2C].
McWilliams, Ellen d. on 70-Dec-21 of Heart disease [70-Dec-22: 4E].
McWilliams, Hugh m. Opitz, Elizabeth on 69-Sep-15 [69-Sep-18: 2B].
Mead, Annie m. Moore, John T. on 68-Nov-12 [68-Nov-14: 2B].
Mead, Benneta Star (6 mos.) d. on 70-Apr-20 of Whooping cough [70-Apr-22: 2C].
Mead, Samuel L. (48 yrs.) d. on 69-Mar-17 [69-Mar-19: 2C].
Mead, Sarah E. m. Smith, Walter D. on 70-Aug-18 [70-Aug-20: 2B].
Meade, W. C. m. Waring, Carrie F. on 68-Apr-7 [68-Apr-10: 2B].
Meads, Ellie m. Nicoll, William T. on 68-Mar-1 [68-Mar-3: 2C].
Meads, George E. (20 yrs.) d. on 66-Jan-20 [66-Jan-22: 2C].
Meads, Harry (6 yrs.) d. on 70-Jan-12 [70-Jan-14: 2C].
Meads, Maggie E. m. Raffle, Joseph S. on 70-Jun-8 [70-Jun-9: 2B].
Meagher, Kate M. m. Berry, Henry D. on 70-Sep-26 [70-Oct-1: 2B].
Meagher, Lewis J. m. Lockington, Lucy on 69-Apr-4 [69-Apr-9: 2B].
Meagher, Sarah m. Devlain, James on 70-Jun-9 [70-Jun-10: 2B].
Meakin, Alice A. m. Perkins, Edward K. on 67-Mar-28 [67-Mar-30: 2B].
Meakin, Dollie J. m. Lindsay, William G. on 70-Nov-24 [70-Nov-28: 2C].
Meakin, Emma A. (8 yrs.) d. on 68-Mar-31 [68-Apr-2: 2C].
Meakin, Maria m. Golibart, Simon R. on 69-Sep-30 [69-Oct-9: 2C].
Meakin, Mary A. m. Smith, Walter G. on 67-Oct-3 [67-Oct-9: 2B].
Meakin, Sarah J. m. Taft, Alfred H. on 70-Nov-24 [70-Nov-28: 2C].
Mealy, Otho (58 yrs.) d. on 68-Jan-30 [68-Feb-1: 2C].
Meara, Hannah (40 yrs.) d. on 66-Jul-31 [66-Aug-6: 2C].
Meares, Catherine (72 yrs.) d. on 70-Mar-2 [70-Mar-4: 2C].
Meares, Catherine G. d. on 70-Mar-29 [70-Mar-31: 2C].
Mearh, Elenora (15 yrs.) d. on 68-Jan-13 [68-Jan-15: 2C].
Mears, Ida (1 mo.) d. on 69-Jul-11 [69-Jul-15: 2C].

Mears, John W. m. Mainley, Sarah J. on 68-Sep-11 [69-Mar-29: 2B].
Mears, Joseph Washington (3 yrs., 3 mos.) d. on 69-Apr-19 [69-Apr-22: 2B].
Measell, Matta E. m. Cardwell, Jackson on 67-Dec-26 [68-Jan-15: 2C].
Mecaslin, Adolph A. m. Bond, Janie on 70-Nov-20 [70-Dec-7: 2C].
Medairy, Edwin d. on 69-May-22 [69-May-24: 2B].
Medairy, Frank Welsh (9 mos.) d. on 68-Sep-10 [68-Sep-11: 2B].
Medairy, Summerfield (42 yrs.) d. on 70-Jun-11 [70-Jun-13: 2C].
Medcalf, Elijah (68 yrs.) d. on 66-Jul-9 [66-Jul-10: 2C].
Medcalf, Sarah (60 yrs., 1 mo.) d. on 70-Jul-8 [70-Jul-9: 2B].
Medcalfe, Daniel Allen (25 yrs.) d. on 70-Jan-16 of Consumption [70-Jan-18: 2C].
Medcalfe, Sarah A. m. Platt, George W. on 70-Feb-14 [70-Feb-24: 2C].
Medinger, Charles Chase (7 mos.) d. on 68-May-7 of Pneumonia [68-May-9: 2B].
Medinger, Charles G. (11 mos.) d. on 66-Mar-25 [66-Mar-27: 2B].
Medinger, Elizabeth Pfaff (1 yr., 3 mos.) d. on 67-May-22 of Scarlet fever [67-May-24: 2B].
Medinger, Emma R. m. Ives, James H. on 70-Dec-15 [70-Dec-19: 2C].
Medtart, Ann Mary (72 yrs.) d. on 67-Feb-27 [67-Mar-2: 2B].
Meeds, Mary C. d. on 69-Jan-3 [69-Jan-6: 2C].
Meeds, Samuel (61 yrs.) d. on 67-Feb-18 [67-Feb-19: 2C].
Meeds, Thomas E. m. Fountain, Hennie on 68-Jan-7 [68-Jan-9: 2C].
Meegan, Mary A. (86 yrs.) d. on 68-Jul-15 [68-Jul-16: 2C].
Meehan, Bartholomew d. on 68-Sep-24 [68-Sep-26: 2B].
Meehan, John (9 mos.) d. on 66-May-12 [66-May-14: 2B].
Meehan, John Joseph (5 mos.) d. on 67-Aug-5 [67-Aug-6: 2C].
Meehan, Michael H. m. Bradley, Susan C. [66-Jul-21: 2C].
Meek, Mabel F. m. Keagle, William on 69-Dec-28 [70-Jan-11: 2C].
Meek, Mary E. m. Chaney, Charles R. on 66-Jan-21 [66-Jan-24: 2B].
Meek, William H. m. Hirst, Elizabeth [67-Mar-16: 2B].
Meeker, C. Irwin m. Smith, Kate C. on 66-Dec-6 [66-Dec-8: 2B].
Meekings, Samuel d. on 66-Oct-28 [66-Oct-31: 2B; 66-Nov-2: 2B].
Meekins, Eliza V. d. on 70-Oct-26 [70-Oct-27: 2B].
Meekins, Georgianna m. Freeland, Zachary T. on 69-Nov-17 [69-Nov-20: 2B].
Meekins, Isabella Dorathea (1 yr., 9 mos.) d. on 67-Sep-1 [67-Sep-5: 2B].
Meekins, John D. m. Holliday, Eliza V. on 69-Apr-27 [69-Apr-30: 2C].
Meekins, Maria M. m. Russel, Henry P. on 70-Jan-31 [70-Feb-16: 2C].
Meekins, Mary A. m. Shields, John L. on 70-Jul-21 [70-Jul-26: 2B].
Meekins, Samuel m. Smith, Sarah E. on 66-Jun-14 [66-Jun-18: 2B].
Meekins, Sarah A. m. Magness, C. Wesley on 67-May-9 [67-May-13: 2B].
Meeks, Ann Rebecca (26 yrs.) d. on 66-Mar-2 [66-Mar-3: 2B].
Meeks, Josephine E. m. Freburger, John W. on 68-Jun-9 [68-Jun-25: 2B].
Meeks, Mary Ann m. Aery, Elias on 69-Apr-6 [69-Apr-10: 2B].
Meeks, Mary Jane (53 yrs.) d. on 67-Feb-19 [67-Feb-20: 2C; 67-Feb-21: 2C].
Meeks, Samuel J. m. Macher, Fannie E. on 68-Jun-4 [68-Jun-16: 2B].
Meeks, William H. (25 yrs.) d. on 70-May-14 [70-May-17: 2B].
Meers, Terrance A. (5 yrs., 6 mos.) d. on 69-Jul-18 [69-Jul-19: 2C].
Meeter, John F. m. Zwanzger, Mary B. on 67-Feb-12 [67-Feb-16: 2D].
Meeth, Anna (6 mos.) d. on 69-Sep-14 [69-Sep-15: 2B].
Megarry, Lizzie Ann (4 yrs.) d. on 67-Oct-22 [67-Oct-23: 2B].
Megary, Joseph Austin d. on 70-Jun-14 [70-Jun-15: 2B].
Megee, Joseph Howard (3 mos.) d. on 67-Jul-24 [67-Jul-26: 2C].
Megenhardt, Frederick m. Deibel, Maggie on 66-Oct-9 [66-Oct-16: 2B].
Megenhardt, Louis Deibel (1 yr., 11 mos.) d. on 69-May-25 [69-May-26: 2C].
Meginnis, John (95 yrs.) d. on 69-Mar-3 [69-Mar-5: 2C].
Meginniss, Willie Osborn (1 yr., 1 mo.) d. on 67-Sep-3 [67-Sep-5: 2B].
Megraw, Carrie M. m. Du Flocq, Louis H. on 66-Feb-6 [66-Feb-13: 2C].
Mehlgarten, August (56 yrs.) d. on 69-Jan-29 of Hemorrhage [69-Jan-30: 1H, 2C].

Mehlgarten, Charles m. Vogell, Alvina F. on 70-Feb-22 [70-Mar-3: 2C].
Mehr, Annie C. A. (1 yr., 2 mos.) d. on 69-Sep-5 [69-Sep-8: 2B].
Mehrens, John (60 yrs.) d. on 67-Feb-13 of Suicide (Poisoning) [67-Mar-15: 2C; 67-Mar-16: 1F, 2B].
Mehrs, Harry m. Ulrich, Mary C. on 67-Sep-10 [67-Sep-12: 2B].
Meisel, George d. on 68-Jul-15 [68-Jul-16: 1F].
Meisel, Louis J. m. Steel, Sarah J. on 67-Jun-11 [67-Jun-29: 2B].
Meiser, Kate m. Fraser, William on 70-Dec-20 [70-Dec-26: 2C].
Meisner, Henry m. Luthold, Carrie on 66-Nov-28 [66-Dec-6: 2B].
Meisner, John d. on 66-Dec-21 [66-Dec-22: 2B; 66-Dec-24: 2B].
Meisz, Christina (88 yrs.) d. on 69-Dec-6 [69-Dec-7: 2C; 69-Dec-8: 2C].
Meixsel, Elizabeth (76 yrs.) d. on 68-Apr-6 [68-Apr-8: 2B].
Meixsell, Howard F. (37 yrs.) d. on 67-Jul-5 [67-Jul-6: 2B].
Melcher, Annie Lawrence (1 yr., 9 mos.) d. on 68-Dec-28 [68-Dec-30: 2C].
Melchior, Annie Regina (1 yr., 2 mos.) d. on 68-Jul-23 [68-Jul-25: 2B].
Melchior, Edward m. Smalzel, Mary E. on 66-Sep-20 [66-Sep-26: 2B].
Melchior, Johanna M. C. (78 yrs.) d. on 69-Sep-19 [69-Sep-23: 2C].
Melchior, John Charles (75 yrs.) d. on 66-May-25 [66-May-26: 2B].
Melchior, Katy R. F. (1 yr., 1 mo.) d. on 70-Feb-4 [70-Feb-5: 2C].
Melchior, Willie (10 mos.) d. on 68-Aug-23 [68-Aug-25: 2B].
Meldick, John m. Hart, Josephine on 70-Nov-13 [70-Nov-17: 2C].
Melia, Mary (1 yr., 6 mos.) d. on 70-Mar-17 [70-Mar-18: 2C].
Melius, Louis m. Vaughan, Lottie Amelia on 69-Jun-1 [69-Jun-9: 2C].
Meller, Alexander E. (3 yrs., 7 mos.) d. on 67-Aug-1 [67-Aug-5: 2B].
Mellin, Susanna (78 yrs.) d. on 68-Jan-29 [68-Jan-30: 2C].
Mellon, Catherine (79 yrs.) d. on 70-Sep-18 [70-Sep-20: 2B].
Mellor, Clara d. on 66-Oct-13 [66-Oct-22: 2C].
Mellor, Eli J. m. Heird, Nannie J. on 67-Nov-26 [67-Nov-30: 2C].
Melville, Eliza Jane (39 yrs., 10 mos.) d. on 69-Oct-31 [69-Nov-1: 2C].
Melville, Elizabeth (79 yrs.) d. on 66-Oct-20 [66-Oct-26: 2B].
Melvin, Mary E. d. on 66-Mar-8 of Pneumonia [66-Mar-10: 2B].
Melzick, Mary H. m. Stoops, William T. on 68-Jul-16 [68-Jul-18: 2B].
Mench, Mary A. m. Pollock, James A. on 69-Nov-17 [69-Dec-4: 2C].
Menslage, Kate m. Smith, Charles E. on 66-Jul-12 [66-Jul-19: 2C].
Mentzel, Sophia m. Airey, Philip on 68-Oct-21 [68-Oct-30: 2C].
Menzies, Adeline Louise (8 mos.) d. on 66-Nov-10 [66-Nov-12: 2C].
Menzies, Carrie L. m. Staylor, William A. on 70-Oct-6 [70-Oct-10: 2B].
Menzies, F. B. (44 yrs.) d. on 70-Dec-21 [70-Dec-22: 2B; 70-Dec-23: 2B].
Mercer, Cyrus T. m. Hale, Sarah A. R. on 66-Feb-22 [66-Mar-2: 2B].
Mercer, Elisha T. (38 yrs.) d. [67-Jul-27: 2B].
Mercer, Emily m. Mercer, William E. on 66-Apr-24 [66-Apr-27: 2C].
Mercer, George W. (55 yrs.) d. on 67-May-27 [67-May-28: 2B].
Mercer, Raymond Reich (1 yr., 6 mos.) d. on 68-Jan-30 [68-Feb-4: 2D].
Mercer, Robert T. m. Lewis, Amelia T. on 67-Jun-4 [67-Jun-10: 2B].
Mercer, Ruth E. m. Warfield, Thomas J. on 66-Mar-6 [66-Mar-13: 2B].
Mercer, William E. m. Mercer, Emily on 66-Apr-24 [66-Apr-27: 2C].
Mercer, William J. m. Cook, Elizabeth B. on 69-Apr-22 [69-Apr-28: 2B].
Mercer, William M. m. Krise, Elizabeth on 67-Nov-7 [67-Nov-16: 2B].
Merchant, B. m. Slemmer, S. Fannie on 68-May-28 [68-Jun-2: 2B].
Merchant, John R. m. Foxwell, Annie E. on 67-Aug-5 [67-Aug-10: 2B].
Merchant, Willie P. d. on 67-Aug-25 [67-Aug-28: 2B].
Merecraft, George m. White, Letitia V. [69-Sep-15: 2B].
Meredeth, Willie Casper (1 yr., 7 mos.) d. on 70-Feb-3 [70-Feb-5: 2C].
Meredith, Abby A. (22 yrs., 3 mos.) d. on 69-Jan-6 [69-Jan-11: 2C].
Meredith, Aureola Beatrice d. on 66-Jul-20 [66-Jul-21: 2C].

Meredith, Benjamin F. (20 yrs., 6 mos.) d. on 70-Jan-4 [70-Jan-6: 2C].
Meredith, Daniel R. m. Sherwood, Annie R. on 70-Feb-10 [70-Mar-1: 2C].
Meredith, Elizabeth m. Wolff, Alexander on 68-Oct-1 [68-Oct-2: 2B].
Meredith, John A. (21 yrs., 3 mos.) d. on 67-Apr-29 of Typhoid [67-May-18: 2A].
Meredith, Laura V. m. Grim, Edward J. on 68-Mar-3 [68-Mar-17: 2C].
Meredith, Louisa C. m. Gray, Jacob E. on 67-Mar-19 [67-Mar-25: 2C].
Meredith, Mary E. m. Schlinkman, Herman H. on 65-Nov-12 [66-Jan-15: 2B].
Meredith, Sarah E. m. Shields, John J. on 67-Aug-29 [67-Sep-3: 2B].
Merk, C. F. August (44 yrs., 2 mos.) d. on 66-Nov-1 of Dropsy [66-Nov-3: 2B].
Merker, Fidie Ledley (8 yrs.) d. on 68-Nov-28 [68-Nov-30: 2C].
Merker, Sallie m. Saville, W. Oliver on 66-Oct-9 [66-Oct-11: 2C].
Merklen, Caroline V. m. Madden, Thomas C. on 69-Sep-13 [69-Sep-16: 2B].
Merrett, Frances J. m. Woolford, Napoleon B. on 68-Aug-27 [68-Sep-19: 2B].
Merrett, Mary A. m. Wilkins, E. M. on 66-May-8 [66-May-11: 2B].
Merriam, Rosalind m. Strini, S. on 67-Apr-30 [67-May-9: 2A].
Merrick, Emma Louise m. Cross, Millard Fillmore on 69-Dec-30 [70-Feb-2: 2B].
Merriken, Arthur (8 mos.) d. on 67-May-8 [67-May-13: 2B].
Merriken, Cora May (2 yrs., 9 mos.) d. on 69-Feb-22 [69-Feb-23: 2D].
Merriken, Emma P. m. Cousins, John E. on 68-Jan-28 [68-Feb-12: 2B].
Merriken, Jacob D. m. Geppritch, Tresa on 69-Jun-27 [69-Jul-3: 2B].
Merriken, John D. (32 yrs.) d. on 69-Nov-27 [69-Nov-30: 2C].
Merriken, Mary M. m. Duhurst, Francis G. on 68-Oct-12 [68-Oct-23: 2B].
Merriken, Willmor (1 yr., 2 mos.) d. on 69-Aug-16 [69-Aug-17: 2C].
Merrill, Adele m. Orendorf, Joseph C. on 70-May-23 [70-Jun-1: 2B].
Merrill, Catherine M. m. Rice, William D. on 67-Dec-12 [67-Dec-16: 2B].
Merrill, V. G. m. Brun, E. F. on 70-Sep-22 [70-Sep-30: 2B].
Merritt, Amelia (19 yrs.) d. on 68-Oct-22 [68-Oct-23: 2B; 68-Oct-24: 2B].
Merritt, Anna Elizabeth d. on 70-Apr-27 [70-Apr-28: 2B].
Merritt, Annie E. m. Vincent, Richard on 67-Dec-26 [67-Dec-27: 2D].
Merritt, Eliza (64 yrs.) d. on 68-Oct-11 [68-Oct-12: 2B].
Merritt, Eliza C. (1 yr., 7 mos.) d. on 69-Mar-4 [69-Mar-5: 2C].
Merritt, James H. m. Claypoole, Mary L. on 66-Jan-17 [66-Jan-19: 2C].
Merritt, Mary A. m. Springs, John on 66-Sep-4 [66-Sep-25: 2B].
Merritt, Mary L. (24 yrs.) d. on 67-Oct-7 [67-Oct-8: 2B; 67-Oct-9: 2B].
Merritt, Mary Louisa d. [68-Feb-14: 2C].
Merritt, Thomas A. m. Todd, Sallie E. on 69-Dec-8 [69-Dec-11: 2B].
Merryman, Araminta d. on 70-Apr-6 [70-Apr-7: 2C].
Merryman, Barnett K. (44 yrs., 5 mos.) d. on 68-Jul-12 [68-Aug-13: 2B].
Merryman, Charles D. m. Hammond, Ella J. on 70-Mar-10 [70-Mar-22: 2C].
Merryman, Charles H. m. Taylor, Mollie R. on 69-Oct-20 [69-Oct-23: 2B].
Merryman, Charles Powell (3 mos.) d. on 67-Jul-20 [67-Jul-26: 2C].
Merryman, Clara Augusta m. Catlin, Robert J. on 67-Apr-25 [67-Apr-29: 2B].
Merryman, Dorcas (72 yrs.) d. on 66-Jul-20 [66-Jul-24: 2C].
Merryman, Elenora d. on 70-Sep-9 [70-Sep-10: 2B].
Merryman, Joseph R. d. on 66-Jan-15 [66-Jan-16: 2C].
Merryman, Laura Virginia d. on 70-Oct-3 [70-Oct-5: 2B].
Merryman, Levi (73 yrs.) d. on 69-Apr-6 of Typhoid pneumonia [69-Apr-8: 2C; 69-Apr-9: 2B].
Merryman, Rhettie m. Armstrong, Victor D. on 68-Apr-16 [68-Apr-24: 2B].
Merryman, Richard S. m. Brown, Mary L. on 70-Feb-24 [70-Mar-19: 2B].
Merryman, Sadie R. m. Jolliffe, Charles C. on 70-Aug-18 [70-Aug-29: 2B].
Mertz, Mary Jane (35 yrs.) d. on 70-Mar-23 of Typhoid pneumonia [70-Mar-24: 2C].
Meseke, Mollie E. m. Latrobe, Henry, Jr. on 67-Aug-22 [67-Aug-29: 2B].
Meseke, Mollie L. m. LaPorte, Henry, Jr. on 67-Aug-22 [67-Aug-30: 2B].
Mesner, Jacob G. (18 yrs.) d. on 70-Nov-24 [70-Nov-26: 2C].
Messer, Gustus E. m. Thomas, Lavinia V. on 69-May-13 [69-Jun-19: 2B].

Messer, John H. (29 yrs., 11 mos.) d. on 68-Dec-27 of Typhoid [69-Jan-5: 2C].
Messer, Lewis W. m. Finch, Elizabeth S. [69-Jan-14: 2D].
Messersmith, Edward P. (7 mos.) d. on 68-Feb-11 [68-Feb-12: 2C].
Messersmith, George Henry (14 yrs., 10 mos.) d. on 70-Feb-10 [70-Feb-11: 2C].
Messersmith, Katie E. m. Courts, J. Edward on 69-Oct-5 [69-Oct-9: 2C].
Messersmith, Louisa A. m. Gorsuch, William S. on 68-Jun-23 [68-Jun-25: 2B].
Messersmith, Mary H. m. Greasley, Jacob H. on 70-Nov-8 [70-Nov-11: 2B].
Messing, Susanna (70 yrs.) d. on 66-Dec-12 of Fall [66-Dec-14: 1F, 2B].
Messinger, Levin A. m. Morgan, Sophie Louise on 68-Aug-6 [68-Sep-1: 2A].
Metcalf, William H. m. Burkens, Mary Jane on 66-Mar-25 [66-Apr-2: 2B].
Metcalfe, Thomas P. (50 yrs., 11 mos.) d. on 67-Oct-30 [67-Nov-7: 2C].
Mett, Jacob d. on 69-Sep-7 of Heatstroke [69-Sep-8: 4F].
Mettam, Kate L. m. Watts, Philip on 68-May-28 [68-May-29: 2B].
Mettee, Anna M. C. d. on 70-May-21 [70-May-23: 2B].
Mettee, Annie (4 yrs., 8 mos.) d. on 68-Aug-18 [68-Aug-19: 2B].
Mettee, Annie V. (1 yr., 2 mos.) d. on 69-Aug-9 [69-Aug-10: 2C].
Mettee, Charles Leonard (42 yrs.) d. on 70-Jul-20 [70-Jul-21: 2C].
Mettee, Joseph S. m. Cunningham, Cecelia on 66-Jun-6 [66-Oct-18: 2B].
Mettee, Maggie C. m. Duvall, Harry C. on 67-Jan-1 [67-Jan-3: 2B].
Mettee, Mary (58 yrs.) d. on 70-Dec-14 [70-Dec-16: 2C].
Mettee, Mary Catherine d. on 67-Jun-14 [67-Jun-15: 2B].
Mettee, Mezick C. m. Gardiner, Helen E. on 70-Apr-7 [70-Apr-12: 2B].
Mettee, Michael m. Koons, Anna on 68-Dec-20 [68-Dec-30: 2C].
Mettee, Milford Morris (15 yrs., 1 mo.) d. on 66-Feb-9 [66-Feb-10: 2C].
Metz, Anna Elizabeth (6 yrs., 6 mos.) d. on 67-Jan-6 [67-Jan-7: 2C].
Metz, Emma Craig (2 yrs., 8 mos.) d. on 66-Nov-8 [66-Nov-10: 2B].
Metz, Louisa (41 yrs.) d. on 67-Feb-14 [67-Feb-16: 2D].
Metzger, Rebecca A. d. on 69-Dec-20 [69-Dec-21: 2B].
Metzger, Sophia A. m. Ferris, A. S. on 67-Apr-30 [67-Jun-5: 2B].
Metzler, Philip (69 yrs.) d. on 70-Apr-29 [70-May-6: 2B].
Meushaw, Franklin m. Smith, Annie Eliza on 70-Feb-23 [70-Feb-25: 2C].
Mewbern, Eugenia m. Arnold, Thomas E. on 68-Jun-11 [68-Jun-16: 2B].
Mewburn, Carrie V. (3 yrs.) d. on 67-Nov-5 [67-Nov-6: 2B].
Mewburn, N. J. m. Murphy, Katurah on 67-Aug-28 [67-Dec-10: 2B].
Mewburn, Susie m. Higgins, W. George on 70-May-26 [70-May-26: 2B].
Mewshaw, Dennis (49 yrs.) d. on 68-Jul-28 [68-Aug-1: 2B].
Meyenberg, W. M. (39 yrs.) d. on 68-Sep-11 [68-Sep-14: 2B].
Meyer, A. B. H. m. Hokamp, Mary Ann on 66-Oct-16 [66-Oct-24: 2C].
Meyer, Charles (8 yrs., 2 mos.) d. on 68-Aug-11 Burned [68-Aug-13: 1G, 2B].
Meyer, Clorinda m. Henderson, J. Augustine on 66-Feb-13 [66-Feb-20: 2B].
Meyer, Eliza Sophia (19 yrs., 7 mos.) d. on 70-Jan-30 of Consumption [70-Jan-31: 2C; 70-Feb-1: 2B].
Meyer, Harman H. (50 yrs.) d. on 67-May-5 [67-May-17: 2B].
Meyer, Henry (28 yrs.) d. on 69-Feb-2 [69-Feb-4: 2C].
Meyer, Jacob m. Wagner, Mary E. on 69-Dec-26 [70-Jan-4: 2C].
Meyer, Louisa m. Albrecht, Werner on 66-Sep-18 [66-Sep-20: 2B].
Meyer, Mary A. m. Janowitz, Daniel on 67-Jan-28 [67-Mar-14: 2C].
Meyer, Paulina m. Gassaway, Theodore on 67-Jan-4 [67-Jan-14: 2C].
Meyer, Sarah Jane (20 yrs.) d. on 66-Jul-21 [66-Jul-25: 2C].
Meyers, A. B. H. (28 yrs.) d. on 70-Jul-21 of Heatstroke [70-Jul-22: 2C; 70-Jul-23: 4E].
Meyers, Augustus m. Cruser, Harriet F. on 67-Jun-6 [67-Aug-13: 2B].
Meyers, Charles Bernhard (62 yrs., 6 mos.) d. on 68-Jan-7 [68-Jan-9: 2C].
Meyers, Emma m. Kasten, C. A. on 70-May-12 [70-May-24: 2C].
Meyers, Frances m. Hobbs, Charles R. on 67-Sep-22 [67-Oct-22: 2A].
Meyers, Henrietta (31 yrs., 11 mos.) d. on 67-Nov-10 of Typhoid gastritis [67-Nov-11: 2C].

Meyers, Jacob W. m. Gosnell, Rachel A. on 67-Sep-11 [67-Sep-18: 2B].
Meyers, John R. (59 yrs.) d. on 66-May-19 [66-May-21: 2B].
Meyers, John V. (48 yrs.) d. on 67-Jan-4 [67-Jan-7: 2C].
Meyers, Joshua (48 yrs.) d. on 70-Oct-1 [70-Oct-8: 2B].
Meyers, Kate m. Dennis, John on 66-Dec-17 [66-Dec-19: 2B].
Meyers, Louisa A. m. Rochester, Henry on 68-Nov-9 [68-Nov-23: 2B].
Meyers, Mary F. m. Hyson, James W. on 69-Mar-25 [69-Mar-31: 2C].
Meyler, James F. (46 yrs.) d. on 70-Mar-17 [70-Mar-18: 2C].
Mezick, Thomas J. (62 yrs.) d. on 68-May-10 [68-May-11: 2B; 68-May-12: 2B].
Michael, David E. m. Mays, Lizzie A. on 70-Jan-25 [70-Feb-1: 2B].
Michael, Ethan (69 yrs.) d. on 68-Sep-10 [68-Sep-14: 2B].
Michael, Eugene Bush (1 yr., 4 mos.) d. on 69-Mar-30 [69-Apr-3: 2B].
Michael, Francis W. m. Cook, Elizabeth A. on 66-Oct-15 [66-Oct-16: 2B].
Michael, George William (1 yr., 8 mos.) d. on 69-Oct-21 [69-Oct-23: 2B].
Michael, Henry (75 yrs., 1 mo.) d. on 66-Feb-3 [66-Feb-5: 1G, 2C].
Michael, Jacob C. m. Hobhal, Hester R. on 69-Nov-18 [69-Nov-20: 2B].
Michael, James (62 yrs.) d. on 70-Apr-9 [70-Apr-11: 2B].
Michael, Lizzie m. Smith, Judson H. on 70-Aug-17 [70-Aug-18: 2B; 70-Aug-31: 2B].
Michael, Louis D. (33 yrs.) d. on 66-Dec-24 [66-Dec-27: 2C].
Michael, Rebecca m. Curlett, John on 69-Jan-7 [69-Jan-8: 2C].
Michael, Rebecca m. Curley, John D. on 69-Jan-7 [69-Jan-9: 2C].
Michael, Sarah J. (49 yrs.) d. on 69-Nov-3 [69-Nov-4: 2C].
Michael, William Wallace d. on 66-Nov-27 [66-Nov-29: 2C].
Michael, Zoe T. (25 yrs.) d. on 68-Feb-28 [68-Feb-29: 2B].
Michel, William (55 yrs.) d. on 66-Oct-16 of Gunshot wound [66-Oct-17: 1G, 2B].
Michell, Joseph C. m. Hubbard, Mary E. on 68-Apr-9 [68-Apr-11: 2A].
Mickin, Mary Jane m. Owens, James T. on 67-Nov-28 [67-Nov-30: 2C].
Micklethwait, Walter m. Ramsey, Mary on 67-Jul-16 [67-Jul-20: 2C].
Micon, Thomas H. (39 yrs.) d. on 68-Mar-25 [68-Mar-31: 2B; 68-Apr-1: 2C].
Middlekauff, Emma m. Cole, John on 66-Jan-17 [66-Jan-20: 2C].
Middlekoff, John C. m. McFalls, Gertrude R. on 70-Dec-6 [70-Dec-31: 2B].
Middlemis, Jane E. m. Fuller, Alexander on 68-Dec-29 [68-Dec-31: 3C].
Middleton, Alice S. m. Whiting, James A. on 68-Feb-6 [68-Feb-10: 2C].
Middleton, Annie Gwynn (5 yrs.) d. on 69-Oct-31 [69-Nov-1: 2C].
Middleton, Charles F. (54 yrs.) d. on 68-May-6 of Paralysis [68-May-7: 1G, 2B; 68-May-8: 2B].
Middleton, Charles K. m. Smoot, Edith E. on 69-Sep-1 [69-Sep-6: 2C].
Middleton, John D., Dr. (45 yrs.) d. on 70-Apr-26 of Heart disease [70-Apr-27: 2B].
Middleton, Katie H. m. Clark, Lemuel on 66-May-22 [66-May-29: 2B].
Middleton, Lidie Berry (10 yrs.) d. on 69-Nov-10 [69-Nov-11: 2C].
Middleton, Mary Ellen (43 yrs.) d. on 67-May-25 [67-May-27: 2B].
Middleton, Mary Julia m. Yeatman, W. Wallace on 67-Mar-14 [67-Mar-23: 2B].
Middleton, Mary P. m. Winslow, Benjamin F. on 67-Dec-31 [68-Jan-6: 2C].
Middleton, Matilda W. m. Lawkins, T. Lewis on 68-Jan-23 [68-Jan-27: 2C].
Middleton, Matilda W. m. Lamkin, S. Lewis on 68-Jan-23 [68-Jan-28: 2D].
Middleton, Richard (83 yrs.) d. on 69-Oct-6 [69-Oct-7: 2B].
Middleton, Robert Stevens d. on 67-Mar-5 of Consumption [67-Mar-11: 2C].
Middleton, William m. Curley, Ella on 70-May-19 [70-May-23: 2B].
Miers, Barbara m. Deets, George on 66-Mar-1 [66-Mar-14: 2B].
Miete, Amelie m. Theiss, Charles F. on 67-May-23 [67-May-27: 2B].
Mifflin, Lou V. m. Stegall, M. S. on 70-Sep-27 [70-Nov-17: 2C].
Mifflin, Lydia D. (2 yrs., 8 mos.) d. on 67-Jul-18 [67-Jul-20: 2C].
Milan, David L. (31 yrs.) d. on 68-Jul-31 [68-Aug-7: 2B].
Milbourne, Clara J. m. Reister, John E. on 68-Jan-2 [68-Jan-4: 2C].
Milbourne, Florence Edith (10 mos.) d. on 66-Nov-21 [66-Nov-22: 2C].
Milburn, Alfred H. m. Peddicord, Emma J. on 69-Jun-27 [69-Jul-12: 2C].

Milburn, Ann S. (58 yrs.) d. on 67-Mar-11 [67-Mar-19: 2C].
Milburn, Mary Emma (2 mos.) d. on 68-Apr-16 [68-Apr-18: 2A].
Milburn, Mattie J. m. Bennett, Thomas J. on 67-Dec-4 [67-Dec-27: 2D].
Milburne, Elijah S. m. Barry, Maggie M. on 68-Mar-3 [68-Mar-24: 2B].
Mildeck, Augustus d. on 69-May-2 [69-May-3: 1H].
Miles, Abram S. m. Williams, Emma R. on 69-Apr-22 [69-Apr-26: 2B].
Miles, Adie m. Keenan, James E. on 67-Mar-5 [67-Mar-9: 2B].
Miles, Bettie m. Boulden, J. W. on 69-Oct-20 [69-Oct-21: 2B].
Miles, Charles M. (33 yrs.) d. on 70-Nov-28 [70-Nov-29: 2C].
Miles, Elizabeth d. on 69-Jan-7 [69-Jan-9: 2C].
Miles, Harriet V. m. Disney, Andrew J. on 66-Feb-22 [66-Mar-5: 2B].
Miles, Hattie B. m. Burton, William N. on 67-Jul-9 [67-Aug-21: 2B].
Miles, Henry (55 yrs.) d. on 69-Nov-15 [69-Nov-16: 2C].
Miles, Imogene T. m. Mudd, John F. on 69-Jun-3 [69-Jun-16: 2C].
Miles, Josephine m. Chatard, F. E., Jr. on 70-Jun-1 [70-Jun-4: 2B].
Miles, Mary A. (49 yrs., 10 mos.) d. on 66-Dec-31 [67-Jan-3: 2B].
Miles, Robert (57 yrs.) d. on 68-Jun-17 [68-Jun-24: 2B].
Miles, Robert (48 yrs.) d. on 66-Feb-16 [66-Feb-20: 2B; 66-Feb-23: 1A].
Miles, Robert Filmore (2 yrs.) d. on 68-Oct-1 [68-Oct-3: 2B].
Miles, Sallie A. m. Marrian, James A. [69-Apr-10: 2B].
Milholland, Arthur V. m. Reilly, Maggie A. on 68-May-14 [68-May-28: 2B].
Milholland, Bridget (73 yrs.) d. on 67-Nov-25 [67-Nov-26: 2B].
Milholland, Catherine (38 yrs.) d. on 68-May-18 [68-May-20: 2A].
Milis, Charlotte m. Ebberts, George W. on 67-Apr-11 [67-Apr-30: 2A].
Millan, George S. m. Pierce, Elizabeth S. on 66-Oct-16 [66-Oct-25: 2C].
Millar, Alexander m. Millar, Matilda on 67-Mar-14 [67-Mar-27: 2C].
Millar, John Marshall (3 yrs., 2 mos.) d. on 67-Dec-27 of Membraneous croup [67-Dec-30: 2C].
Millar, Matilda m. Millar, Alexander on 67-Mar-14 [67-Mar-27: 2C].
Millar, Sarah E. m. Hasson, J. A. on 66-May-10 [66-May-16: 2C].
Millard, Rachel d. on 68-Apr-20 [68-Apr-22: 2B].
Miller, Adolph (35 yrs.) d. on 66-Apr-17 [66-Apr-18: 1G].
Miller, Adolphus H. m. Newton, Laura A. on 69-Dec-16 [69-Dec-20: 2C].
Miller, Alfred B. m. Saunders, Hannah R. on 69-Jun-17 [69-Jun-21: 2B].
Miller, Amelia J. (34 yrs.) d. on 69-Nov-9 [69-Nov-16: 2C].
Miller, Amelia M. m. Leef, Henry G. on 66-Mar-20 [66-Mar-28: 2C].
Miller, Andrew Lewis (3 yrs., 4 mos.) d. on 66-Nov-14 [66-Nov-16: 2C].
Miller, Anna m. Rixse, George A. on 66-Jun-20 [66-Jun-22: 2B].
Miller, Anna Sherlock d. on 68-Sep-20 [68-Sep-22: 2B].
Miller, Anna T. m. Murray, Stirling on 66-Nov-6 [66-Nov-9: 2C].
Miller, Annie m. Hines, Caleb B. on 66-Dec-26 [66-Dec-27: 2C].
Miller, Annie m. Foltz, Henry C. on 69-Dec-23 [69-Dec-25: 2C].
Miller, Annie Isabelle (9 yrs., 2 mos.) d. on 69-Apr-18 of Scarlet fever [69-Apr-19: 2B].
Miller, Anthony (66 yrs.) d. on 68-Mar-31 [68-Apr-2: 2C].
Miller, Augustine (73 yrs.) d. on 67-May-30 [67-May-31: 2B].
Miller, B. H. d. on 66-Jul-16 of Heatstroke [66-Jul-18: 1F].
Miller, C. W. m. Buschmann, Kate on 67-May-5 [67-Jul-10: 2B].
Miller, Catharine M. m. Kaiser, John H. on 68-Dec-16 [68-Dec-24: 2C].
Miller, Catherine d. on 70-Aug-24 [70-Aug-25: 2C].
Miller, Charles (35 yrs.) d. on 68-Dec-18 [68-Dec-19: 2B].
Miller, Charles Edward (1 yr., 1 mo.) d. on 70-Oct-6 [70-Oct-7: 2B].
Miller, Charles Tilman Grommee (22 yrs.) d. on 69-Mar-9 of Pneumonia [69-Mar-11: 2C].
Miller, Charlotte H. (34 yrs.) d. on 70-Aug-28 [70-Aug-29: 2C].
Miller, Clara Eugenia m. Mills, Daniel on 67-Sep-4 [67-Sep-30: 2B].
Miller, D. W. m. Crumm, Mary F. on 68-Apr-15 [68-Apr-17: 2B].
Miller, Daisy Rebecca (2 mos.) d. on 68-Oct-11 [68-Oct-16: 2B].

Miller, Daniel (58 yrs.) d. on 70-Jul-25 of Heart disease [70-Jul-26: 2C, 4C; 70-Jul-27: 2C; 70-Jul-28: 4D].
Miller, David S. (44 yrs.) d. on 66-Sep-21 [66-Nov-21: 2C].
Miller, Edward (25 yrs.) d. on 68-Mar-25 Drowned [68-Mar-26: 1F].
Miller, Edward (36 yrs.) d. on 69-Jun-28 [69-Jun-29: 2C].
Miller, Edward A., Dr. (64 yrs.) d. on 67-Jan-9 [67-Jan-10: 2C].
Miller, Edward Blackburn (6 mos.) d. on 68-Aug-16 [68-Aug-21: 2B].
Miller, Edward Shriver (21 yrs.) d. [70-Jun-22: 2C; 70-Jun-23: 2C].
Miller, Edwin G. (5 mos.) d. on 69-Jun-26 [69-Jun-28: 2C].
Miller, Elisha H. m. Gibbs, Elizabeth on 70-Oct-20 [70-Oct-29: 2B].
Miller, Eliza m. Hartman, William on 69-Apr-18 [69-May-15: 2B].
Miller, Elizabeth (71 yrs.) d. on 70-Nov-16 [70-Nov-18: 2C].
Miller, Elizabeth m. Jones, Robert on 66-Apr-5 [66-Apr-14: 2B].
Miller, Elizabeth A. m. Eggleston, John T. on 67-Jan-23 [67-Mar-5: 2C].
Miller, Elizabeth A. m. Hill, John E. on 69-Apr-21 [69-Apr-24: 2B].
Miller, Ella m. Snyder, Henry Lee on 70-Dec-22 [70-Dec-28: 2C].
Miller, Emily m. Potter, Charles C. on 68-Mar-10 [68-Mar-11: 2B].
Miller, Enoch (63 yrs.) d. on 70-Nov-2 [70-Nov-3: 2C].
Miller, F. W. m. McIntyre, Mary on 70-Jan-27 [70-Jan-29: 2B].
Miller, Fannie m. Patterson, William L. on 66-Apr-17 [66-May-4: 2C].
Miller, Fannie A. m. Weiner, Henry M. on 68-May-6 [68-May-8: 2B].
Miller, Frances V. m. Hardesty, Thomas J. on 69-Dec-14 [70-Aug-23: 2B].
Miller, Frank Carroll (1 yr., 11 mos.) d. on 69-Sep-4 [69-Sep-6: 2C].
Miller, George (35 yrs.) d. Drowned [66-May-14: 1F].
Miller, George W. m. Watts, Maggie J. on 69-Dec-8 [69-Dec-9: 2C].
Miller, Grace m. Buck, Theodore A. on 68-Sep-16 [68-Nov-10: 2C].
Miller, H. Best m. Cooper, M. Ellie on 65-Dec-21 [66-Jan-10: 2C].
Miller, Hamilton J. m. Duvall, Lizzie M. on 67-Mar-20 [67-Apr-1: 2C].
Miller, Hannie m. Horn, J. V., Jr. on 68-Nov-10 [68-Nov-12: 2C].
Miller, Harman H. (32 yrs.) d. on 68-Jan-13 in Railroad accident [68-Jan-14: 1F; 68-Jan-16: 1F].
Miller, Harriet J. d. on 68-Sep-30 [68-Oct-2: 2B].
Miller, Henrietta m. Wyvill, Samuel W. on 67-Feb-13 [67-Feb-18: 2C].
Miller, Henry (25 yrs.) d. on 67-Oct-28 [67-Oct-30: 2B].
Miller, Henry W. d. on 67-Jan-27 [67-Feb-11: 2C].
Miller, Hezekiah (78 yrs.) d. on 69-Apr-1 [69-Apr-3: 2B].
Miller, Hezekiah B. m. Cooper, Margaret E. on 65-Dec-21 [66-Jan-1: 2C].
Miller, Isabella m. Sherwood, J. R. on 67-May-6 [67-May-15: 2B].
Miller, Isabella m. Phillips, William H. on 66-Jun-19 [66-Jun-22: 2B].
Miller, J. Addison m. Baltzell, Mollie on 70-Nov-1 [70-Nov-7: 2A].
Miller, J. Howard (2 yrs., 4 mos.) d. on 66-Jan-27 [66-Jan-29: 2B].
Miller, J. W. m. Overbeck, Lizzie on 68-Apr-30 [68-May-2: 2C].
Miller, Jacob m. Callander, Martha J. on 68-Aug-4 [68-Aug-5: 2B].
Miller, Jacob m. Gardiner, Hannah E. on 68-Dec-24 [69-Jan-20: 2C].
Miller, Jacob C. m. Durham, Catharine on 69-Jun-16 [69-Jun-17: 2C].
Miller, Jacob P. (72 yrs., 4 mos.) d. on 66-Oct-4 [66-Oct-9: 2A].
Miller, James A. m. Martin, Eva R. on 66-Dec-24 [66-Dec-24: 2C].
Miller, James Dodson (4 mos.) d. on 68-Mar-19 [68-Mar-23: 2B].
Miller, James Edward (1 yr., 8 mos.) d. on 67-Apr-16 [67-Apr-17: 2B].
Miller, Jane (11 mos.) d. on 67-Feb-17 [67-Feb-18: 2C].
Miller, Jeffersonia Davis (5 yrs., 6 mos.) d. on 70-Feb-5 [70-Feb-7: 2C].
Miller, Jessie A. m. Falck, George M. on 70-May-10 [70-May-12: 2B].
Miller, Joanna m. Hamilton, Stewart on 68-Aug-6 [68-Aug-11: 2B].
Miller, John (45 yrs.) d. on 70-Dec-4 [70-Dec-5: 2C; 70-Dec-6: 2C].
Miller, John m. Bishope, F. A. on 68-Oct-23 [68-Nov-30: 2B].

Miller, John D. (49 yrs.) d. on 68-Jul-21 [68-Jul-22: 2B].
Miller, John S. m. Sands, Hattie on 68-Jan-30 [68-Feb-3: 2C].
Miller, John W. m. Lancaster, Martha M. on 66-Aug-19 [66-Aug-27: 2B].
Miller, John W. m. Mitchell, Beulah O. on 70-Nov-17 [70-Nov-19: 2B].
Miller, Lewis Shackleford (4 yrs., 4 mos.) d. on 70-Mar-13 of Scarlet fever [70-Mar-15: 2C].
Miller, Lizzie m. Billmire, George A. on 66-Mar-20 [66-Mar-26: 2B].
Miller, Lizzie S. d. on 68-Jun-25 [68-Jun-26: 2B].
Miller, Llewellyn m. Osburn, Mary Anna on 68-Oct-29 [68-Oct-21: 2B].
Miller, Lou K. m. Larmour, J. Warrell on 67-Jul-2 [67-Jul-6: 2B; 67-Jul-8: 2C].
Miller, M. m. Kilgore, John S. on 69-Dec-14 [69-Dec-16: 2C].
Miller, Maggie m. Marshall, Alexander H. on 67-Jun-4 [67-Jun-17: 2B].
Miller, Maggie A. m. McBee, Charles B. on 67-Jul-12 [67-Jul-30: 2C].
Miller, Maggie E. m. Schott, Henry on 68-May-19 [68-Sep-28: 2B].
Miller, Maggie L. m. Levy, L. G. on 70-Jul-30 [70-Aug-9: 2C].
Miller, Margaret (72 yrs.) d. on 66-Jun-7 [66-Jun-8: 2B].
Miller, Margaret A. (1 yr.) d. on 66-Dec-28 [66-Dec-29: 2C].
Miller, Margaret Ann (24 yrs.) d. on 68-Jan-26 [68-Jan-28: 2D].
Miller, Margaret W. m. Haggerty, James W., Jr. on 70-Oct-6 [70-Oct-15: 2B].
Miller, Martha J. m. Winn, Frederick S. on 67-Nov-14 [67-Nov-18: 2B].
Miller, Martha V. m. Hughes, Alfred W. on 66-Apr-30 [66-May-17: 2C].
Miller, Martin L. m. Sisselburger, Elizabeth A. on 69-Oct-5 [69-Oct-11: 2C].
Miller, Mary (1 yr., 8 mos.) d. on 70-Jan-30 [70-Jan-31: 2C].
Miller, Mary E. m. Doenges, Fred J. on 70-Jun-14 [70-Jun-24: 2C].
Miller, Mary Elizabeth m. Zepp, Leonard on 68-Jun-9 [68-Jun-10: 2B].
Miller, Mary Ellen (29 yrs., 6 mos.) d. on 66-Nov-16 [66-Nov-17: 2B].
Miller, Mary L. m. Segerman, Thomas on 66-Jan-4 [66-Jan-6: 2B].
Miller, Mary Shaw (60 yrs.) d. on 68-Aug-2 [68-Aug-3: 2B].
Miller, Michael (64 yrs.) d. on 66-Nov-24 [66-Nov-29: 2C].
Miller, Mollie F. m. Nash, William Wadsworth on 69-Oct-18 [69-Oct-23: 2B].
Miller, Myra m. Burgess, W. G. on 70-Feb-23 [70-Feb-28: 2C].
Miller, Nellie Blanch (1 yr., 7 mos.) d. on 69-Jun-26 of Diptheria and croup [69-Jun-28: 2C].
Miller, Peter (67 yrs.) d. on 69-Oct-9 [69-Oct-13: 2C].
Miller, Richard (56 yrs.) d. on 68-May-14 [68-May-16: 2B].
Miller, Richard (22 yrs.) d. on 67-Sep-15 [67-Sep-16: 2B].
Miller, Richard A. m. Waller, Sophie on 67-Jan-18 [67-Jan-19: 2C].
Miller, Robert J. m. Kelsey, Mida on 68-Oct-29 [68-Nov-5: 2C].
Miller, Sallie m. Sherwood, Charles on 66-May-17 [67-Feb-16: 2D].
Miller, Sarah d. on 68-Nov-20 [68-Nov-21: 2C].
Miller, Sarah (86 yrs.) d. on 66-Mar-19 [66-Mar-20: 2C; 66-Mar-21: 2C].
Miller, Stephen J. (4 mos.) d. on 68-Mar-15 [68-Mar-16: 2B].
Miller, Stephen Maxwell m. Friedhoffer, Mary J. on 66-Dec-26 [66-Dec-29: 2C; 66-Dec-31: 2C].
Miller, Susan Ann m. Allen, Henry D. on 70-Feb-3 [70-Feb-5: 2B].
Miller, Theodore K. m. Bradley, Mary Lou on 70-Jun-2 [70-Jun-6: 2B].
Miller, Thomas m. Martin, Susan E. on 69-Apr-11 [69-Apr-13: 2B].
Miller, Thomas G. m. Kauffman, Cleantha M. on 69-Jun-23 [69-Jun-29: 2C].
Miller, Thomas H. m. Koth, Maggie on 70-Oct-10 [70-Oct-21: 2C].
Miller, Thomas Randolph (1 yr.) d. on 67-Mar-10 [67-Mar-12: 2C].
Miller, Virginia m. Rich, Edward R. on 66-May-29 [66-May-31: 2B].
Miller, Virginia S. m. Goldsmith, Egbert S. on 70-Nov-22 [70-Nov-30: 2C].
Miller, Walter Campbell (1 yr., 1 mo.) d. on 68-Sep-8 [68-Sep-9: 2B; 68-Sep-10: 2B].
Miller, Walter T. H. (54 yrs.) d. on 68-Oct-10 [68-Oct-15: 2B].
Miller, Wilhelmine m. Boeshe, William H. on 68-Nov-16 [68-Nov-18: 2C].
Miller, William A. m. Denmead, Clara on 69-Jul-20 [69-Jul-22: 2C].
Miller, William Edward (3 mos.) d. on 66-Nov-27 [66-Nov-28: 2B].

Miller, William G. m. Jackson, Mary on 67-Apr-23 [67-Apr-27: 2A].
Miller, William T. (25 yrs.) d. on 68-Nov-29 [68-Nov-30: 2B].
Millholland, Teresa m. Carroll, William J. on 67-Jan-15 [67-Jan-18: 2C].
Millichop, Lydia P. (76 yrs.) d. on 70-Nov-24 [70-Nov-26: 2C].
Milligan, Robert W. m. Dubois, Sarah E. on 70-Feb-17 [70-Feb-18: 2C].
Milliken, Issac m. Brewster, Hannah M. [66-May-28: 2B].
Millikin, Sadie V. (8 yrs.) d. on 69-May-1 [69-May-3: 2C].
Milliman, Mary A. (82 yrs.) d. on 67-Jan-2 [67-Jan-4: 2D].
Millington, Florie E. m. Chappell, Cornelius on 68-Jun-24 [68-Jun-30: 2B].
Millington, John N. (65 yrs.) d. on 68-Feb-11 [68-Jan-12: 4D].
Millington, Maggie m. Mason, James A. on 66-Jun-5 [66-Jun-7: 2B].
Milliron, Elizabeth d. on 67-Sep-1 [67-Sep-4: 2B].
Millis, Carrie Belle (1 yr., 7 mos.) d. on 67-Sep-7 [67-Sep-9: 2B].
Mills, Almira Phelps m. Peace, Charles F. on 70-Nov-2 [70-Nov-3: 2B].
Mills, Ann Elizabeth (69 yrs.) d. on 69-Nov-4 [69-Nov-5: 2C].
Mills, Anne Buchanan (75 yrs.) d. on 67-Dec-17 [67-Dec-18: 2B].
Mills, Catherine (87 yrs.) d. on 67-Jan-23 [67-Jan-24: 2C].
Mills, Charles M. d. on 69-Jul-15 [69-Jul-17: 2C].
Mills, Charlotte A. m. Stone, Charles Wesley on 68-Jun-24 [68-Jun-27: 2B].
Mills, Cora Bell (7 mos.) d. on 66-Jul-15 [66-Aug-2: 2C].
Mills, Cornelia (1 yr., 8 mos.) d. on 66-Jun-13 of Dysentery [66-Jun-15: 2C].
Mills, Daniel m. Miller, Clara Eugenia on 67-Sep-4 [67-Sep-30: 2B].
Mills, Emily Slonaker d. on 70-Nov-2 Drowned [70-Nov-17: 2C].
Mills, Eugene m. Busch, Emma on 70-Oct-31 [70-Dec-6: 2C].
Mills, Ezekiel m. Porter, Virginia on 70-Nov-15 [70-Nov-16: 2C].
Mills, Florence d. on 67-Jul-30 [67-Jul-31: 2C].
Mills, Florence Virginia (2 mos.) d. on 69-Jul-10 [69-Jul-16: 2C].
Mills, Job m. Hilton, Amanda V. on 68-May-14 [68-May-21: 2B].
Mills, John A. m. Bussard, Jane on 66-Jun-12 [66-Jun-15: 2C].
Mills, John H. D. m. Simmons, Maggie E. on 66-Feb-28 [66-Mar-6: 2B].
Mills, Kate (28 yrs.) d. on 69-Apr-6 [69-Apr-9: 2C].
Mills, Mary E. (24 yrs., 7 mos.) d. on 66-Mar-4 [66-Mar-6: 2B].
Mills, Mollie R. m. Carney, Joseph on 69-Feb-23 [69-Mar-31: 2C].
Mills, Oaks (19 yrs.) d. on 66-Oct-4 [66-Oct-27: 2B].
Mills, Penelope (86 yrs.) d. on 70-Mar-4 [70-Mar-5: 2B].
Mills, Priscilla E. (9 yrs.) d. on 69-Jan-31 [69-Feb-2: 2C].
Mills, Robert (67 yrs.) d. on 67-Dec-15 [67-Dec-18: 2B].
Mills, Robert d. on 66-Feb-10 [66-Jan-12: 2D].
Mills, Sallie P. m. Sutton, Otho on 68-Jul-21 [68-Aug-10: 2B].
Mills, Thomas H. m. White, Denney on 68-May-28 [68-May-30: 2A].
Mills, William R., Rev. d. on 69-Dec-19 [69-Dec-23: 4F].
Mills, William V. m. Ward, Helen L. on 66-May-1 [66-May-4: 2C].
Milnes, Vic m. Reay, Henry S. on 66-Nov-6 [66-Nov-17: 2C].
Milnor, Bessie Stephens (9 mos.) d. on 67-Jul-22 [67-Jul-23: 2C; 67-Jul-24: 2C].
Milnor, John P. (74 yrs.) d. on 67-Jun-20 [67-Jun-22: 2B].
Milnor, Lily Pancoast d. on 67-Mar-11 [67-Mar-12: 2C].
Milroy, Grace (67 yrs.) d. on 66-Jul-30 [66-Jul-30: 2C].
Milstead, Georgie m. Moriarty, P. M. on 69-Sep-15 [69-Oct-1: 2B].
Milstead, Ignatius (76 yrs., 4 mos.) d. on 69-Mar-11 [69-May-12: 2B].
Milstead, John H. m. Rhoads, E. M. on 68-Dec-31 [69-Jan-23: 2C].
Miltenberger, Anthony F. W., G (80 yrs.) d. on 69-Oct-21 [69-Oct-22: 2B; 69-Oct-23: 2B, 4D].
Milton, Charles H. m. Maddox, Jennie D. on 69-Nov-18 [69-Nov-23: 2C].
Mince, Daniel (45 yrs.) d. on 67-Mar-8 [67-Mar-9: 2B].
Mince, Thomas S. d. [68-Aug-17: 1G].
Mincher, Edward m. Concannon, Mary on 70-Nov-2 [70-Nov-5: 2B; 70-Nov-7: 2A].

Mincher, Kate m. Crosby, William S. on 67-Dec-2 [67-Dec-10: 2B].
Minck, Jonnie (4 yrs., 7 mos.) d. on 70-Dec-25 [70-Dec-28: 2D].
Minck, Tommie (7 mos.) d. on 70-Dec-24 [70-Dec-28: 2D].
Miner, Annie (5 yrs.) d. [70-May-23: 2B].
Miner, J. P. m. Krichton, Mary R. on 67-Dec-3 [68-Jan-22: 2C].
Mines, Annie L. m. Moale, J. Gorham on 66-Feb-8 [66-Feb-13: 2C].
Mingo, Catherine (20 yrs.) d. on 66-Aug-14 [66-Aug-18: 2B].
Minifie, Mary E. m. Field, J. T. on 68-Oct-28 [68-Oct-29: 2B].
Minis, Leila m. Poultney, S. Eugene on 69-Nov-4 [69-Nov-9: 2C].
Minnick, Francis (37 yrs.) d. on 68-Nov-30 [68-Dec-2: 2C].
Minnick, Francis H. Gruppy (1 yr., 6 mos.) d. on 68-Aug-6 [68-Aug-8: 2C].
Minnick, Louisa M. m. Craumer, Francis M. on 66-Jun-14 [66-Aug-4: 2C].
Minnick, Mary Ann (73 yrs.) d. on 68-Nov-3 [68-Nov-4: 2C].
Minnick, Mary J. E. m. Nutwell, John B. on 69-Dec-30 [70-Jan-4: 2C].
Minnick, Sarah E. m. Carter, John on 68-Jul-8 [68-Jul-10: 2C].
Minniegue, Albert M. m. McClusky, Kate on 70-Jul-27 [70-Nov-16: 2C].
Minnoge, John (35 yrs.) d. on 67-Jun-20 [67-Jun-21: 2B].
Minor, George m. Adams, Matilda on 66-Nov-15 [66-Nov-17: 2C].
Minor, Juliet Gilmer m. Janvier, Edmund De H on 68-Nov-10 [68-Nov-12: 2C].
Minor, Michael Thomas (7 yrs.) d. [70-Jul-27: 2C].
Minton, Charles (36 yrs.) d. on 67-Jun-4 [67-Jun-8: 2B].
Minwegan, Joseph (70 yrs.) d. on 67-Oct-11 [67-Oct-12: 2A].
Misel, Mary Selina (20 yrs.) d. on 66-Oct-12 [66-Oct-13: 2B].
Miskel, Patrick (39 yrs.) d. on 66-Aug-6 [66-Aug-8: 2C].
Miskelly, Joseph (51 yrs.) d. on 70-Feb-14 [70-Mar-3: 2C].
Miskelly, Mary (94 yrs.) d. on 70-Feb-17 [70-Feb-18: 2C].
Miskelly, Mary Lizzie d. on 67-Nov-2 [67-Nov-4: 2B].
Miskimon, Elizabeth (53 yrs.) d. on 69-Dec-18 [69-Dec-20: 2C].
Miskimon, Lizzie J. m. Herget, George E. on 68-Dec-17 [69-Jan-1: 2C].
Miskimon, Mary (70 yrs.) d. on 66-Dec-18 [66-Dec-19: 2B].
Misnering, Henry (23 yrs.) d. on 66-May-7 Murdered (Stabbing) [66-May-8: 1F].
Missildine, Henrietta (13 yrs.) d. on 68-Jul-18 [68-Jul-20: 2B].
Missing, Catharine M. (34 yrs.) d. on 68-Sep-15 [68-Sep-17: 2B].
Missing, Ernest m. Roger, Catherine on 69-Apr-22 [69-Apr-26: 2B].
Mister, Annie m. Insley, Corbin W. on 70-May-17 [70-May-19: 2C].
Mister, Annie Maria m. Hunter, Samuel on 68-Feb-13 [68-Feb-14: 2C].
Mister, Issac S. m. Christopher, Annie M. on 66-May-1 [66-May-4: 2C].
Mister, Levin R. (68 yrs.) d. on 66-Oct-13 [66-Oct-17: 2B].
Mister, Maria F. m. Insley, Richard H. on 70-Nov-20 [70-Nov-23: 2B].
Mitchel, Margaret G. m. Denton, Wilson on 68-Mar-24 [68-Mar-27: 2C].
Mitchel, Rebecca (73 yrs.) d. on 67-Apr-27 [67-Apr-29: 2B].
Mitchel, Theodorick m. Holliday, Caroline on 65-Dec-26 [66-Aug-31: 2B].
Mitchell, A. Godfrey m. Gregg, Tillie on 69-Feb-23 [69-Mar-18: 2C].
Mitchell, Agnes Virginia (4 yrs., 2 mos.) d. on 66-Dec-13 Burned [66-Dec-15: 1G, 2B].
Mitchell, Amanda m. Williams, John L. on 68-Jan-21 [68-Jan-25: 2B].
Mitchell, Amelia (16 yrs.) d. on 68-Jan-1 [68-Jan-4: 2C].
Mitchell, Ann d. on 66-Aug-12 [66-Aug-13: 2C].
Mitchell, Annie Druscilla (1 mo.) d. on 67-Aug-9 [67-Aug-10: 2B].
Mitchell, Augustus m. Downey, Laura E. on 68-Oct-8 [68-Oct-9: 2C].
Mitchell, Beulah O. m. Miller, John W. on 70-Nov-17 [70-Nov-19: 2B].
Mitchell, Carrie J. m. Hay, William M. on 67-Mar-27 [67-Apr-3: 2B].
Mitchell, Catharine Susan (36 yrs.) d. on 69-Oct-23 of Consumption [69-Oct-29: 2C].
Mitchell, David J. m. Naugle, Mary C. on 67-Dec-10 [67-Dec-16: 2B].
Mitchell, Edgar W. (14 yrs., 3 mos.) d. on 68-Sep-23 [68-Sep-24: 2B].
Mitchell, Edmund Morgan (3 mos.) d. on 68-Jul-18 [68-Jul-20: 2B].

Mitchell, Edward (58 yrs.) d. on 70-Nov-23 [70-Nov-24: 2C; 70-Nov-25: 2D].
Mitchell, Edward m. Lynch, Sarah on 66-Oct-25 [66-Oct-27: 2B].
Mitchell, Elisha (61 yrs.) d. on 69-Jan-26 [69-Jan-27: 2C].
Mitchell, Eliza Rebecca (19 yrs.) d. on 68-Jan-7 [68-Jan-21: 2C].
Mitchell, Elizabeth (89 yrs.) d. on 70-Feb-8 [70-May-24: 2C].
Mitchell, Elizabeth A. m. Stockdale, Joshua N. on 69-Apr-13 [69-Apr-15: 2B].
Mitchell, Elizabeth Ann (20 yrs.) d. on 69-Jan-10 [69-Jan-12: 2C].
Mitchell, Ella A. m. Mathews, Lemuel E. on 70-Feb-23 [70-Feb-24: 2C].
Mitchell, Ella May (1 yr., 2 mos.) d. on 70-Nov-5 [70-Nov-8: 2B].
Mitchell, Emma E. m. Bennett, William T. on 69-Jul-19 [69-Aug-10: 2C].
Mitchell, Emory G. m. Blowas, Sarah L. on 70-Feb-10 [70-Feb-14: 2C].
Mitchell, Ernest Linwood (2 yrs., 5 mos.) d. on 68-May-21 [68-May-22: 2C].
Mitchell, Ezekiel, Sr. (63 yrs.) d. on 66-Oct-16 [66-Oct-19: 2B].
Mitchell, George R. m. Strayler, Mary C. on 66-May-3 [66-May-5: 2B].
Mitchell, George V. m. Courtney, Sallie M. on 66-Dec-6 [66-Dec-8: 2B].
Mitchell, George W. (33 yrs.) d. on 70-Aug-19 [70-Aug-20: 2B].
Mitchell, George W. m. Ruckle, Mollie L. on 67-Jan-1 [67-Jan-3: 2B].
Mitchell, Harry Clay (10 yrs.) d. on 70-Feb-7 [70-Feb-9: 2C].
Mitchell, Henrietta M. (49 yrs.) d. on 67-Jul-16 of Heart paralysis [67-Jul-17: 1F; 67-Jul-18: 2C].
Mitchell, Henry Judson (9 mos.) d. on 68-Aug-1 [68-Aug-5: 2C].
Mitchell, Hettie May (1 yr.) d. on 68-Jul-2 [68-Jul-3: 2B].
Mitchell, Isabel (9 mos.) d. on 66-Dec-8 [66-Dec-10: 2B].
Mitchell, J. M. m. Kemp, Richard on 67-Aug-24 [67-Aug-28: 2B].
Mitchell, Jacob C. (19 yrs.) d. on 69-Jan-31 [69-Feb-3: 2C].
Mitchell, James H. m. Forwood, Christine on 66-Aug-23 [66-Aug-29: 2B].
Mitchell, Joanna m. Satterfield, Andrew on 70-Nov-24 [70-Nov-28: 2C].
Mitchell, John (51 yrs.) d. on 66-Oct-29 [66-Oct-31: 2B].
Mitchell, John m. Deegs, Sophia A. on 70-Dec-18 [70-Dec-22: 2B].
Mitchell, John H. (29 yrs.) d. on 66-Apr-20 of Consumption [66-Apr-21: 1G, 2B].
Mitchell, John H. m. Jenifer, Lillie T. C. on 70-Oct-11 [70-Oct-12: 2B].
Mitchell, John R. m. Shaffer, Lizzie A. on 68-Nov-26 [68-Dec-4: 2D].
Mitchell, John Wesley m. Pusey, Mary E. on 67-Jan-24 [67-Jan-26: 2C].
Mitchell, Joseph, Dr. d. on 70-Apr-25 [70-May-24: 2C].
Mitchell, Joshua Slicer (9 yrs., 10 mos.) d. on 68-Jan-5 [68-Jan-7: 2C].
Mitchell, Julia Ann (51 yrs.) d. on 69-Mar-18 [69-Mar-19: 2C].
Mitchell, Maggie A. m. Ankard, Joseph H. on 68-Jan-20 [68-Jan-22: 2C].
Mitchell, Margaret (67 yrs.) d. on 66-Jun-13 [66-Jun-15: 2C].
Mitchell, Mary Ann (52 yrs.) d. on 68-Sep-22 [68-Sep-23: 2B].
Mitchell, Mary J. m. Shaw, Charles H. on 69-Oct-14 [69-Oct-19: 2B].
Mitchell, Olive d. [70-Jul-19: 2C].
Mitchell, Philip E. m. McKinley, Eliza R. on 66-Dec-23 [66-Dec-28: 2C].
Mitchell, R. H. B., Rev. d. on 69-May-18 [69-May-19: 2C].
Mitchell, Robert (66 yrs.) d. on 68-Jan-14 [68-Jan-15: 2C; 68-Jan-16: 2C].
Mitchell, Robert M. m. Huntemuller, Alice F. on 66-Jan-2 [66-Jan-15: 2B].
Mitchell, Sadie E. (7 mos.) d. on 69-Aug-11 [69-Aug-12: 2C].
Mitchell, Samuel Jefferson (12 yrs., 3 mos.) d. on 68-Jan-11 Drowned [68-Jan-13: 1F; 68-Jan-14: 2C].
Mitchell, Sue (25 yrs.) d. on 69-Nov-9 [69-Nov-10: 2C].
Mitchell, Susan E. m. Bruff, John K. on 67-May-14 [67-Jun-21: 2B].
Mitchell, T. E. m. Ramsburgh, Charlotte on 69-Oct-5 [69-Oct-8: 2B].
Mitchell, Thomas P. m. Courtney, Lydia A. on 68-Dec-8 [68-Dec-9: 2C].
Mitchell, Walter, Gen. (69 yrs.) d. [70-Apr-2: 2B].
Mitchell, William m. Spedden, Mary E. on 70-Dec-20 [70-Dec-29: 2C].
Mitchell, William A. m. Creighton, Mary Augusta on 67-Jan-31 [67-Feb-5: 2C].

Mitchell, William H., Capt. (42 yrs.) d. on 67-Oct-29 Drowned [67-Dec-3: 2C].
Mitchell, William T. m. Belt, Lucina on 68-Nov-22 [68-Nov-28: 2C].
Mitchen, E. Madison m. Hughes, Virginia E. on 70-Dec-22 [70-Dec-26: 2C].
Mittan, Theodore E. (22 yrs.) d. on 66-Dec-29 [66-Dec-31: 2C].
Mittendorf, Mary Jane m. Reinhart, George P. on 70-May-19 [70-May-21: 2B].
Mittler, Fanny d. on 69-Jan-16 [69-Jan-18: 2D].
Mittler, Francis S. m. Bruce, Georgia on 66-Mar-7 [66-Mar-13: 2B; 66-Mar-14: 2B].
Mittnacht, Henry m. Mathews, Nora L. on 69-Mar-3 [69-Mar-8: 2C].
Mitzell, John (62 yrs., 7 mos.) d. on 69-Feb-10 [69-Feb-13: 2C].
Moale, Augusta m. Nicholas, Wilson C. on 66-Oct-16 [66-Oct-19: 2B].
Moale, J. Gorham m. Mines, Annie L. on 66-Feb-8 [66-Feb-13: 2C].
Moale, Maria Konig d. on 70-Mar-4 [70-Mar-5: 2B].
Moale, Nannie M. Smith m. Lincoln, N. L. on 66-Oct-30 [66-Nov-15: 2C].
Moale, Richard H. d. on 69-Feb-18 of Brain congestion [69-Feb-19: 1H, 2C; 69-Feb-20: 2A; 69-Feb-23: 2D].
Moan, Mary (29 yrs.) d. on 69-Jan-7 of Consumption [69-Jan-8: 2C].
Moan, Michael O. (66 yrs.) d. on 69-Feb-7 of Asthma [69-Feb-8: 2C; 69-Feb-9: 2C].
Mobley, William H. m. Bruscup, Josephine C. on 70-Oct-19 [70-Oct-20: 2B].
Mocler, Kate m. Brady, James on 67-Feb-13 [67-Feb-18: 2C].
Moetz, Louisa (41 yrs.) d. [67-Feb-15: 2C].
Moffatt, Mary m. Hodge, William E. on 68-Sep-10 [68-Sep-12: 2B].
Moffet, Margaret Ann m. Taylor, William on 68-May-14 [68-May-21: 2B].
Moffett, Anna (85 yrs.) d. on 69-Jun-6 [69-Jun-7: 2B].
Moffett, Carrie A. m. Coburn, John on 69-Oct-5 [69-Oct-12: 2C].
Moffett, Hannah m. Kensella, James on 67-May-22 [67-May-29: 2B].
Moffett, Jacob L. (20 yrs.) d. on 70-Mar-16 [70-Mar-17: 2C; 70-Mar-18: 2C].
Moffett, John m. Cannally, Ellen on 66-Aug-9 [66-Aug-13: 2C].
Moffitt, Jennie m. Larmour, W. B. on 68-Feb-25 [68-Feb-27: 2C].
Moffitt, Rebecca m. Manly, William G. on 67-Apr-4 [67-Apr-9: 2B].
Mohler, Jacob T. (67 yrs.) d. on 69-Mar-4 [69-Mar-5: 2C].
Mohler, Marian Elizabeth d. on 68-Apr-20 [68-Apr-28: 2B].
Mohler, Marion Elizabeth d. on 68-Apr-20 [].
Mohrman, Lizzie (28 yrs.) d. on 66-Nov-2 [66-Nov-8: 2C].
Moke, James E. m. Joyce, Kate A. on 67-Apr-25 [67-Apr-30: 2A].
Molinard, Julian Robinson (1 yr., 3 mos.) d. on 67-Jan-23 [67-Jan-26: 2C].
Molloy, James (23 yrs.) d. on 66-Sep-27 [66-Sep-28: 2B; 66-Sep-29: 2C].
Molloy, Kate C. m. Neer, N. Franklin on 67-Jun-6 [67-Jun-8: 2B; 67-Jun-11: 2B].
Molloy, Michael (21 yrs.) d. on 66-Aug-14 [66-Aug-16: 2C].
Molloy, Thomas F. (20 yrs.) d. on 70-Mar-16 [70-Mar-18: 2C].
Moloy, Mary Anne (48 yrs.) d. on 66-Jul-16 [66-Jul-17: 2C].
Molseed, William, Capt. d. on 68-Sep-4 Drowned [68-Oct-15: 1F].
Moltin, Samuel m. Dorsey, Martha E. on 69-Sep-12 [69-Sep-21: 2B].
Moltz, Eliza d. on 70-Jul-29 [70-Aug-1: 2C].
Monaghan, Margaret (18 yrs.) d. on 67-May-13 [67-May-14: 2B].
Monaghan, Mary (73 yrs.) d. on 68-Feb-6 [68-Feb-7: 2C].
Monaghan, Peter (10 mos.) d. on 70-May-19 [70-May-20: 2C].
Monaghan, Roseanna (37 yrs.) d. on 67-Dec-17 [67-Dec-18: 2B; 67-Dec-19: 2B].
Monahan, George d. on 67-Aug-20 [67-Aug-21: 2B].
Monahan, Jane m. Cuddy, Peter on 69-Jan-31 [69-Feb-6: 2C].
Monahan, Sarah m. McEnany, Peter on 70-Feb-14 [70-Feb-17: 2C].
Moncure, W. P. m. Hughes, Mary J. on 69-Apr-8 [69-Apr-10: 2B].
Monday, Lottie A. m. Vincente, J. on 70-Jun-2 [70-Jun-9: 2C].
Mondowney, Anna Maria d. on 66-Jun-14 [66-Jun-18: 2B].
Money, Margaret J. m. Willson, James J. on 69-May-12 [69-May-15: 2B].
Monk, Mary (18 yrs.) d. on 68-Oct-26 [68-Oct-27: 2B].

Monk, William Aabury d. on 70-Feb-24 [70-Feb-26: 2C].
Monkur, J. C. S., Dr. (67 yrs.) d. on 67-Jan-2 of Pneumonia [67-Jan-3: 2C; 67-Jan-4: 2D; 67-Jan-5: 2C].
Monmonier, Charles G. (60 yrs.) d. on 69-Sep-29 [69-Sep-30: 2B; 69-Oct-1: 2B].
Monmonier, Charles L. (31 yrs.) d. on 70-Dec-25 [70-Dec-28: 2C].
Monmonier, J. Carroll m. Laurenson, Sallie R. on 69-Jan-14 [69-Jan-21: 2C].
Monmonier, L. A. m. Collins, Maggie T. on 69-Apr-20 [69-Apr-26: 2B].
Monmonier, Louis m. East, Hattie A. on 66-Mar-13 [66-Mar-26: 2B].
Monmonier, Mary F. m. Taylor, William H. on 70-Feb-7 [70-Feb-9: 2C].
Monmonier, Pamela J. m. Logue, William H. on 70-Nov-24 [70-Nov-29: 2C].
Monro, Samuel m. Leanard, Anna Frances on 68-Dec-21 [68-Dec-28: 2B].
Monroe, A. Warfield m. Carson, Emma L. on 69-Dec-14 [69-Dec-16: 2C].
Monroe, David M. m. Wright, Emma N. on 67-Feb-16 [67-Feb-20: 2C].
Monroe, Georgianna (67 yrs.) d. on 70-Jan-2 [70-Jan-4: 2C].
Monroe, Mary (60 yrs.) d. on 69-Oct-19 [69-Oct-21: 2B].
Monsarrat, George, Col. d. on 69-Dec-11 [69-Dec-22: 2B].
Monsarrat, Nicholas (79 yrs.) d. on 68-Nov-6 of Paralysis [68-Nov-7: 1F, 2B].
Montague, James Douglas d. on 66-Jan-2 [66-Jan-4: 2C].
Montague, Kate m. Catlin, Charles M. on 67-Jun-12 [67-Jun-13: 2C].
Montague, Mary A. (44 yrs.) d. on 70-Jul-22 [70-Jul-23: 2B].
Montague, Samuel H. A. m. Clark, Anna R. on 70-May-3 [70-May-10: 2B].
Montague, W. Powhatan m. Sinclair, Lelia on 70-Jul-19 [70-Jul-23: 2B].
Montague, William W. (19 yrs.) d. on 66-Dec-23 [66-Dec-27: 2C].
Montell, Edwin E. m. Chapman, Helen C. on 70-Jan-11 [70-Jan-18: 2C].
Montgomery, A. J. m. Garland, L. F. on 66-Aug-8 [66-Aug-15: 2B].
Montgomery, Agnes B. m. Russell, Charles B. on 67-Apr-9 [67-Apr-17: 2B].
Montgomery, Alice (21 yrs.) d. on 67-Apr-3 [67-Apr-4: 2B].
Montgomery, Alvoerda d. [67-Jun-17: 2B].
Montgomery, Catharine Velleria (1 yr., 3 mos.) d. on 68-Sep-24 [68-Oct-1: 2B].
Montgomery, Ellen J. (4 mos.) d. on 68-Jun-21 [68-Jun-22: 2B].
Montgomery, Henry (8 yrs., 7 mos.) d. on 68-May-30 Drowned [68-Jun-1: 1F, 2B].
Montgomery, Ida C. m. Mathias, John A. on 68-May-7 [68-May-9: 2B].
Montgomery, James M. m. Jones, Mary Claire F. on 70-Aug-14 [70-Aug-18: 2C].
Montgomery, Johanna (2 mos.) d. on 66-Dec-22 [66-Dec-25: 2C].
Montgomery, John d. on 69-Jul-28 of Fall [69-Jul-29: 4E; 69-Jul-30: 1H].
Montgomery, Joseph Charles m. Dixon, Amanda on 66-Jul-10 [66-Jul-12: 2C].
Montgomery, Mary Margaret (19 yrs.) d. on 69-Sep-15 [69-Sep-16: 2B].
Montgomery, Samuel m. Hunter, Elizabeth on 68-Mar-19 [68-Mar-24: 2B].
Montgomery, Virginia m. Martin, Lewis G. on 66-Mar-8 [66-Apr-4: 2B].
Montgomery, William (22 yrs.) d. on 67-Jan-27 [67-Jan-28: 2C].
Montgomery, William S. (67 yrs.) d. on 69-Sep-3 [69-Sep-4: 2B].
Montgomery, William T. m. Jefferson, Mary E. on 67-May-14 [67-May-29: 2B; 67-May-30: 2B].
Moody, Louise E. (9 mos.) d. on 68-Aug-16 [68-Aug-17: 2B].
Moody, Sarah Devenia (3 yrs., 4 mos.) d. on 69-Nov-11 [69-Nov-12: 2C].
Mooer, Laura m. George, Clarence O. on 66-Feb-15 [66-Feb-20: 2B].
Moog, G. W. m. Clark, Susanna R. on 68-Feb-4 [68-Feb-8: 2B].
Moog, James R. m. Deibel, Wilhelmine on 68-Dec-22 [68-Dec-25: 2D].
Moon, Catherine (47 yrs.) d. on 67-Mar-9 of Paralytic apoplexy [67-Mar-11: 2C].
Moon, Edward B. (11 mos.) d. on 70-Sep-3 [70-Sep-6: 2B].
Moon, Ellen (40 yrs.) d. on 69-Apr-5 [69-Apr-7: 2C].
Moon, Lucinda m. Wittington, Charles A. on 69-Sep-22 [69-Sep-24: 2B].
Moon, Mary L. Carr m. Thomas, Augustus M. on 66-Oct-16 [66-Oct-18: 2B].
Moon, Thomas O. m. Shaffer, Ellen A. on 68-Jun-8 [68-Jun-17: 2B].
Moon, William (56 yrs.) d. on 67-Jun-17 [67-Jul-6: 2B].

Mooney, Catherine (1 yr., 1 mo.) d. [70-Jul-7: 2B].
Mooney, James Richard (2 yrs., 8 mos.) d. on 68-Jan-1 [68-Jan-2: 2C].
Mooney, N., Mrs. (48 yrs.) d. on 70-Jul-18 [70-Jul-19: 2C].
Mooney, Oliver (18 yrs.) d. on 67-May-8 of Boiler explosion [67-May-9: 1F, 2A].
Mooney, William H. (28 yrs.) d. on 68-Jul-14 [68-Jul-15: 2B; 68-Jul-16: 2C].
Moor, John (58 yrs.) d. on 67-Apr-1 [67-Apr-3: 2B].
Moor, Lister D m. Snowden, Ella D on 67-Feb-7 [67-Feb-15: 2C].
Moore, Ann C. d. on 70-Sep-3 [70-Sep-5: 2C].
Moore, Annie m. Cromwell, Lambert on 66-Sep-12 [66-Sep-24: 2B].
Moore, Annie M. m. Pryor, James V. on 69-Jul-19 [69-Jul-21: 2C].
Moore, Anthony (72 yrs.) d. on 66-Jun-20 [66-Jun-21: 2B].
Moore, Archibald D. m. Faucett, Annie E. on 66-Jan-24 [66-Jan-27: 2B].
Moore, Benseles m. Robinson, Elizabeth on 70-Apr-14 [70-Apr-16: 2B].
Moore, Camilla Collins (62 yrs.) d. on 66-Feb-21 [66-Feb-22: 2B].
Moore, Catherine (91 yrs.) d. on 67-May-16 [67-May-17: 2B].
Moore, Charles (46 yrs.) d. on 70-Nov-4 [70-Nov-5: 2B; 70-Nov-7: 4D].
Moore, Charles H. m. Tapman, Martha S. on 68-Aug-30 [68-Sep-1: 2A].
Moore, Chessie C. m. Morse, Charles N. on 66-Aug-23 [66-Sep-6: 2B].
Moore, Clara Catherine (9 mos.) d. on 70-Sep-1 [70-Sep-2: 2C].
Moore, Cora Lee (3 mos.) d. on 67-Apr-2 [67-Apr-6: 2B].
Moore, Eleanor m. Taylor, Caleb S. on 69-Jun-10 [69-Jun-23: 2C].
Moore, Ella (4 mos.) d. on 66-Jun-18 [66-Jun-20: 2C].
Moore, Ezekiel (16 yrs.) d. [66-Aug-15: 2B].
Moore, Frances (85 yrs.) d. on 66-Apr-11 [66-Apr-12: 2B].
Moore, Francina m. Taylor, George M. on 70-Jun-21 [70-Jul-4: 2C; 70-Jul-6: 2C].
Moore, H. F. m. Walsh, Emma A. on 69-Feb-2 [69-Feb-5: 2C].
Moore, James Ross (19 yrs.) d. on 68-Apr-15 [68-Apr-17: 2B].
Moore, James T. m. Horn, Martha A. on 66-May-8 [66-May-9: 2B].
Moore, Joel m. Andrews, Rebbie on 70-Jan-1 [70-Jan-12: 2C].
Moore, John m. McEldowney, Mary on 68-Oct-20 [68-Oct-27: 2B].
Moore, John Granville m. Bessee, Laura Virginia on 70-May-21 [70-Nov-3: 2B].
Moore, John H. m. Boone, Mary V. on 70-May-5 [70-Jun-6: 2B].
Moore, John T. m. Mead, Annie on 68-Nov-12 [68-Nov-14: 2B].
Moore, John W. m. Curtin, Annie Margaret on 70-Aug-1 [70-Aug-3: 2C].
Moore, Julia A. (46 yrs.) d. on 66-Mar-20 [66-Mar-21: 2C].
Moore, Laura J m. Euler, George W. on 67-Dec-4 [67-Dec-7: 2B].
Moore, Laura V. m. Pole, William, Jr. on 66-Aug-9 [66-Aug-13: 2C].
Moore, Lemuel Mitchell m. Clark, Jane Ann Adeline on 68-Jun-20 [68-Jul-29: 2B].
Moore, Louisa E. m. Hibler, Henry B. on 68-Dec-16 [68-Dec-29: 2D].
Moore, Maggie m. Fowler, Rasin on 68-Dec-31 [69-Jan-5: 2C].
Moore, Maggie E. m. Smith, S. B. on 66-Jan-31 [66-Mar-14: 2B].
Moore, Margaret K. m. Waidner, William F. on 69-Feb-9 [69-Feb-25: 2D].
Moore, Maria Louisa m. Murdoch, J. Campbell on 67-Nov-26 [67-Nov-28: 2C].
Moore, Martha m. Friedhofer, William on 66-Dec-23 [67-Jan-8: 2B].
Moore, Martha M. d. on 69-Jul-3 [69-Jul-9: 2C].
Moore, Mary m. Gist, W. Irving on 67-Feb-25 [67-Mar-12: 2C].
Moore, Mary m. Herbert, George W. on 69-May-13 [69-Jun-9: 2C].
Moore, Mary E. (36 yrs.) d. on 66-Jun-22 [66-Jun-23: 2B; 66-Jun-25: 2B].
Moore, Mary E. m. Clements, John W. on 66-Jul-27 [66-Nov-10: 2B].
Moore, Mary Florence (1 yr., 2 mos.) d. on 66-Sep-13 [66-Sep-14: 2B].
Moore, Mary Lizzie (1 yr., 11 mos.) d. on 67-Mar-11 [67-Mar-13: 2C].
Moore, Mary M. m. Barrett, Samuel on 69-Aug-3 [69-Aug-28: 2B].
Moore, Mary Sarah (1 yr., 1 mo.) d. on 70-Mar-14 [70-Mar-15: 2C].
Moore, Mollie (23 yrs., 5 mos.) d. on 69-Oct-5 [69-Oct-7: 2B].
Moore, Mollie A. m. Norris, Daniel A. on 68-Sep-28 [68-Sep-30: 2B].

Moore, Rachel Anne m. Rank, William D. on 66-Apr-26 [66-Apr-27: 2C].
Moore, Randolph L. m. Ellender, Sarah E. on 67-Jun-11 [67-Jun-19: 2B].
Moore, Robert George (30 yrs.) d. [68-Jan-29: 2C; 68-Jan-30: 2C].
Moore, Robert V. m. O'Brion, Susan M. on 68-May-12 [68-May-20: 2A].
Moore, Samuel m. Saunders, Harriet P. on 66-Sep-3 [66-Sep-6: 2B].
Moore, Samuel m. Haile, Minerva on 68-Dec-10 [69-Jan-8: 2C].
Moore, Sarah A. m. Evans, Andrew J. on 68-Dec-3 [69-Jan-7: 2C].
Moore, Thomas m. Rosenberger, Annie M. on 68-Oct-27 [68-Nov-23: 2B].
Moore, Thomas J. (67 yrs.) d. on 69-Aug-2 [69-Aug-4: 2C].
Moore, William Allison (24 yrs.) d. on 67-Sep-25 [67-Oct-10: 2B].
Moore, William H. (22 yrs.) d. on 70-Jun-12 Murdered (Assault) [70-Jun-13: 1F, 2C; 70-Jun-14: 1F].
Moore, William P. (2 yrs., 5 mos.) d. on 68-Mar-24 [68-Mar-25: 2A].
Moore, William R. W. m. Gosnell, Maggie A. on 69-Apr-20 [69-Apr-28: 2B].
Moore, Willie W. (8 yrs.) d. on 69-Jan-12 [69-Jan-13: 2D].
Moorehead, C. Curtis m. Grieves, Adele on 70-Nov-16 [70-Nov-18: 2C].
Moorehead, Mary (70 yrs.) d. on 67-Jan-28 [67-Jan-28: 2C; 67-Jan-29: 2C].
Moores, Henry C. (29 yrs.) d. on 70-Jul-9 [70-Jul-11: 2C].
Moorhead, James (30 yrs.) d. on 66-Jul-18 of Heatstroke [66-Jul-19: 1E, 1F].
Mopps, Mary Eliza m. Bull, Elijah on 67-Jul-1 [67-Jul-6: 2B].
Moran, Catherine (32 yrs.) d. on 69-Jan-5 [69-Jan-7: 2C].
Moran, Ellie (1 yr., 8 mos.) d. on 69-Jan-15 [69-Jan-16: 2C].
Moran, Isabell d. on 69-Feb-28 [69-Mar-1: 2C].
Moran, James d. on 68-Aug-19 [68-Aug-21: 2B].
Moran, James (25 yrs.) d. on 70-Mar-20 [70-Mar-21: 2C; 70-Mar-22: 2C].
Moran, Jennie F. (20 yrs.) d. on 70-Feb-20 [70-Feb-21: 2B].
Moran, John m. Leonard, Maria on 68-Nov-29 [68-Dec-1: 2C].
Moran, Joseph A. (30 yrs.) d. on 67-Aug-14 [68-Mar-26: 2B].
Moran, Laura E. m. Woodhouse, E. N. on 70-Jan-6 [70-Jan-20: 2C].
Moran, Lydia Ellen (18 yrs.) d. on 66-Mar-17 [66-Mar-19: 2C].
Moran, Mary Bridget m. Lewis, Henry on 70-Sep-4 [70-Oct-22: 2B].
Moran, Mary Jane m. Gardner, Johns on 69-Nov-10 [69-Nov-24: 2C].
Moran, Patrick (35 yrs.) d. on 66-Dec-14 [66-Dec-15: 2B].
Morand, James B. d. [68-Mar-5: 2C].
Mordecai, David m. Hart, Hettie Jane on 66-Nov-13 [66-Nov-15: 2C].
Mordecai, Ellen m. Cohen, J. I. on 68-Oct-14 [68-Oct-16: 2B].
Morehead, Martha E. m. Wilkes, J. on 67-Aug-1 [67-Aug-31: 2B].
Moreland, Daniel Selby (1 yr., 6 mos.) d. on 66-Sep-6 [66-Sep-8: 2B].
Moreland, John H (29 yrs.) d. on 67-Mar-1 of Brain fever [67-Mar-2: 2B].
Moreland, M. E. m. Parson, John T. on 67-Sep-3 [67-Sep-4: 2B].
Moreton, Samuel (70 yrs.) d. on 70-Dec-3 [70-Dec-7: 2C].
Morgan, Ann B. (67 yrs.) d. on 69-Oct-9 [69-Oct-16: 2B].
Morgan, Charity (63 yrs.) d. on 67-Mar-8 [67-Mar-9: 2C].
Morgan, Charles (2 mos.) d. on 67-Sep-1 [67-Sep-2: 2B].
Morgan, Charles L. m. Lutz, Maggie V. on 66-May-17 [66-May-24: 2C].
Morgan, Edward T. m. French, Lizzie A. on 66-Nov-15 [66-Nov-17: 2B].
Morgan, Elizabeth (78 yrs.) d. on 66-Oct-21 [66-Oct-24: 2C].
Morgan, Esther A d. on 67-Dec-25 [67-Dec-27: 2D].
Morgan, George m. Schley, Mary M. on 69-Jun-22 [69-Jun-23: 2C].
Morgan, George A. m. Hopper, Annie E. on 70-Mar-6 [70-May-3: 2B].
Morgan, George M. m. Delcher, Anna E. on 67-Sep-11 [67-Sep-18: 2B].
Morgan, George W. m. Coughlan, Jennie on 69-May-4 [69-May-7: 2C].
Morgan, H. Suter m. Emerson, Jennie on 66-May-10 [66-May-16: 2C].
Morgan, Hester Ann m. Kernan, William P. on 69-Aug-26 [69-Aug-28: 2B].
Morgan, John F. m. Martine, Catherine S. on 66-Jan-10 [66-Jan-12: 2C].

Morgan, Joseph A. m. Jackson, Josephine C. on 68-Aug-25 [68-Sep-1: 2A].
Morgan, Katie (14 yrs., 7 mos.) d. on 69-Jul-16 [69-Jul-20: 2C].
Morgan, Maggie A. d. on 69-Dec-23 of Croup [69-Dec-28: 2D].
Morgan, Maggie J. m. Pope, Thomas L. on 70-Feb-8 [70-Feb-11: 2C].
Morgan, Mary (53 yrs.) d. on 69-Oct-17 [69-Oct-18: 2C].
Morgan, Mary M. m. Langan, Thomas on 68-Jul-21 [68-Aug-27: 2B].
Morgan, Molly (20 yrs.) d. on 68-Feb-18 of Consumption [68-Feb-19: 2C].
Morgan, R. Adelaide m. Osborne, F. M. W. on 69-Dec-7 [69-Dec-11: 2B].
Morgan, Randolph m. Atler, Lizzie S. on 69-May-19 [69-May-21: 2C].
Morgan, Samuel (58 yrs.) d. on 69-Oct-13 [69-Oct-15: 2C].
Morgan, Samuel Ross m. Dare, Sophie S. on 70-Jul-19 [70-Jul-21: 2C].
Morgan, Sarah Susannah (7 yrs., 5 mos.) d. on 67-Mar-24 [67-Mar-26: 2C].
Morgan, Sophie Louise m. Messinger, Levin A. on 68-Aug-6 [68-Sep-1: 2A].
Morgan, Susan (24 yrs.) d. on 68-Sep-5 [68-Sep-8: 2B].
Morgan, Thomas E. m. Tarleton, Sarah H. on 68-Mar-15 [68-Mar-17: 2C].
Morgan, Thomas E. m. Osborn, L. Jennie on 70-Feb-17 [70-Feb-22: 2C].
Morgan, William James (25 yrs.) d. on 70-Jan-27 [70-Jan-27: 2C].
Morgan, William Thomas (27 yrs.) d. on 68-Feb-20 [68-Feb-21: 2B].
Morhiser, Richard Swann d. on 69-Aug-3 [69-Aug-6: 2C].
Moriarty, Margaret (21 yrs.) d. on 68-Dec-20 [68-Dec-21: 2B; 68-Dec-22: 2C].
Moriarty, P. M. m. Milstead, Georgie on 69-Sep-15 [69-Oct-1: 2B].
Morison, Annie M. T. m. Donnelly, John on 69-Dec-8 [69-Dec-14: 2C].
Morison, George F. (48 yrs.) d. on 70-Sep-4 [70-Sep-5: 2C; 70-Sep-6: 4C].
Morison, Horace (59 yrs.) d. on 70-Aug-5 [70-Aug-10: 2C].
Morison, Lucy Fiske d. on 66-May-25 [66-Jun-9: 2B].
Morison, William George (16 yrs., 5 mos.) d. on 69-Oct-30 [69-Nov-2: 2B].
Moritz, J. D. m. Steuart, Lizzie on 68-Apr-16 [68-Apr-20: 2B].
Morkin, Margaret (62 yrs.) d. on 70-Mar-26 [70-Mar-28: 2B].
Morkin, Michael (63 yrs.) d. on 70-Mar-20 [70-Mar-21: 2C].
Morling, Frank L. m. Curley, Emma on 66-Dec-6 [66-Dec-10: 2B].
Morningstar, Charles d. on 68-Aug-14 in Railroad accident [68-Aug-17: 1G].
Morran, Charles Thomas (9 mos.) d. on 66-Sep-20 [66-Sep-21: 2B].
Morran, Thomas m. Stansbury, Mollie A. on 69-Feb-18 [69-Feb-19: 2C].
Morris, Abraham m. Eborn, Mary C. on 68-Mar-8 [68-Mar-14: 2B].
Morris, Amanda M. C. A. m. Knight, William H. on 70-Jan-18 [70-Jan-24: 2C].
Morris, Ann M. m. Prince, John O. on 67-Apr-23 [67-Apr-25: 2B].
Morris, Annie m. Charles, John [69-Dec-28: 2C; 69-Dec-29: 2C].
Morris, Annie m. Orem, Francis on 69-Dec-28 [70-Jan-1: 2B].
Morris, Annie m. Richards, Thomas on 70-Jan-15 [70-Jan-19: 2C].
Morris, Augustus Theodore (5 mos.) d. on 70-Aug-20 [70-Sep-14: 2B].
Morris, Eddie (3 yrs., 7 mos.) d. on 70-Jun-30 [70-Jul-2: 2B].
Morris, Elijah J. m. Taylor, Telucker J. on 69-Apr-22 [69-Apr-24: 2B].
Morris, J. Champlin m. Gittings, Julia Evans on 69-Nov-25 [69-Nov-26: 2B].
Morris, James m. Graves, Anna on 67-Jun-27 [67-Jun-29: 2B].
Morris, James m. Crew, Martha S. on 69-Apr-21 [69-Apr-29: 2B].
Morris, James A. (75 yrs.) d. on 69-Sep-6 [69-Sep-8: 2B; 69-Sep-7: 2B].
Morris, John m. Claude, Sue C. on 66-May-31 [66-Jun-4: 2B].
Morris, John W. m. Day, Elvira on 70-Oct-20 [70-Oct-22: 2B].
Morris, Kate (36 yrs.) d. on 70-Jan-26 of Consumption [70-Jan-28: 2B].
Morris, Levin G. (25 yrs., 3 mos.) d. on 70-Nov-29 [70-Nov-30: 2C].
Morris, Mary Ann (71 yrs.) d. on 68-Jan-31 [68-Feb-1: 2C].
Morris, Mary R. m. Brown, Thomas M. on 68-Feb-19 [68-Feb-20: 2C].
Morris, Owen m. Porter, Temperance K. on 68-May-6 [68-Jun-6: 2A].
Morris, Sarah E. m. Keenan, John Watson on 67-May-6 [67-May-11: 2A].
Morris, Temperance K. (30 yrs.) d. on 69-May-1 [69-May-3: 2C].

Morris, Thomas H. m. Jones, Sallie K. on 66-Nov-1 [66-Nov-7: 2C].
Morris, Tillie L. m. Martin, A. S. on 68-Mar-1 [68-Mar-3: 2C].
Morris, William W. (4 mos.) d. on 67-Mar-30 [67-Apr-1: 2C].
Morrisett, Helena A. m. Evans, William on 69-Mar-17 [69-Mar-26: 2C].
Morrison, Alice A. (23 yrs.) d. on 67-Oct-9 [67-Oct-10: 2B; 67-Oct-11: 2B].
Morrison, Arthur (59 yrs.) d. on 67-Aug-8 [67-Aug-9: 2C].
Morrison, Carrie (3 yrs.) d. on 69-Mar-30 of Diptheria [69-Apr-5: 2B].
Morrison, Effie m. Barry, Joshua H. on 68-Oct-21 [68-Oct-23: 2B].
Morrison, Elizabeth (37 yrs.) d. on 68-Aug-16 [68-Aug-21: 2B].
Morrison, Emma m. Green, Pemberton W. on 69-Jan-13 [69-Jan-18: 2C].
Morrison, Frances W. m. Russell, Eugene J. on 66-Aug-2 [66-Aug-4: 2C].
Morrison, George C. (28 yrs.) d. on 67-Sep-14 of Yellow fever [67-Sep-30: 2B].
Morrison, Harriet (68 yrs.) d. on 70-Jul-24 [70-Jul-27: 2C].
Morrison, Henry W. (37 yrs., 9 mos.) d. on 70-Nov-7 [70-May-17: 2B].
Morrison, James S. m. Taylor, Almira C. on 70-Dec-7 [70-Dec-15: 2C].
Morrison, John (22 yrs.) d. on 67-Oct-31 in Construction accident [67-Nov-1: 1F].
Morrison, Joseph L. m. Shorey, Alice A. on 66-May-17 [66-May-19: 2B].
Morrison, Maggie m. Reid, B. G. W. on 67-Feb-20 [67-Feb-21: 2C].
Morrison, Maggie E. m. Gross, J. I., Jr. on 66-Dec-26 [67-Jan-3: 2B].
Morrison, Martha S. m. Chenoweth, Oliver B. on 67-Sep-26 [67-Sep-27: 2B].
Morrison, Mary m. Myers, George G. on 70-Jul-12 [70-Jul-19: 2B].
Morrison, Mary Anne (62 yrs.) d. on 68-Sep-24 [68-Sep-25: 2B].
Morrison, Mary Frances d. on 70-Jul-8 [70-Jul-11: 2C].
Morrison, Mary H. (85 yrs.) d. on 70-Feb-21 [70-Feb-28: 2C].
Morrison, Mary R. m. Fitzgerald, William H. on 69-Nov-16 [69-Nov-25: 2C].
Morrison, Mollie Mills (1 yr., 3 mos.) d. on 68-May-10 [68-May-12: 2B].
Morrison, Rosa (12 yrs.) d. on 70-Feb-3 of Consumption [70-Feb-5: 2B].
Morrison, Roseanna (84 yrs.) d. on 66-Mar-17 [66-Mar-30: 2C].
Morrison, Susan (42 yrs.) d. on 69-Sep-20 [69-Sep-21: 2B].
Morrison, William D. m. Tharp, Pauline Ve on 68-Mar-3 [68-Mar-25: 2A].
Morrow, A. C. m. Sherwood, Mary A. on 66-Jul-26 [66-Jul-28: 2C].
Morrow, Ann Jane d. on 67-Sep-29 of Consumption [67-Sep-30: 2B; 67-Oct-1: 2B].
Morrow, Elenora B. (6 yrs.) d. on 70-Jan-17 of Croup [70-Jan-18: 2C].
Morrow, Fannie Eliza (2 mos.) d. on 67-Jul-6 [67-Jul-9: 2B].
Morrow, Frances m. Bitzer, William on 68-Aug-18 [68-Aug-20: 2B].
Morrow, George G. m. Skinner, Roberta J. on 66-Oct-18 [66-Oct-20: 2B].
Morrow, James S. m. Sanks, Lida A. on 68-Oct-1 [68-Oct-5: 2B].
Morrow, John F. m. Awbrey, Mary E. on 67-Jan-29 [67-May-2: 2B].
Morrow, John H. m. Dawson, Manie on 68-Oct-22 [68-Oct-23: 2B].
Morrow, Maggie Lizzie (2 mos.) d. on 67-Jul-5 [67-Jul-6: 2B; 67-Jul-9: 2B].
Morrow, Martha m. Logsdon, Nimrod C. on 66-Sep-11 [66-Sep-12: 2A].
Morrow, Mary E. m. York, William on 70-Feb-11 [70-Mar-9: 2C].
Morrow, Mary G. m. Reip, Thomas H. on 68-Sep-29 [68-Oct-28: 2B].
Morrow, Phebe m. Sturgis, John I. on 67-Dec-26 [67-Dec-30: 2C].
Morrow, William H. m. Leddon, Mary J. on 70-Feb-6 [70-Feb-12: 2B; 70-Feb-14: 2C].
Morry, Elizabeth (89 yrs.) d. on 66-Nov-20 [66-Nov-21: 2C; 66-Nov-22: 2C].
Morse, Charles (51 yrs.) d. on 70-Jul-30 [70-Aug-1: 2C].
Morse, Charles N. m. Moore, Chessie C. on 66-Aug-23 [66-Sep-6: 2B].
Morse, George W. m. Green, Laura J. on 67-Apr-25 [67-May-24: 2B].
Morse, Mollie J. m. Lewis, George H. on 69-Apr-7 [69-Apr-9: 2B].
Morsell, Ann Cornwall d. on 69-Oct-30 [69-Nov-3: 2C].
Mortimer, Amelia C. (18 yrs.) d. on 66-Aug-31 [66-Sep-1: 2B].
Mortimer, Leonal C. (7 mos.) d. on 69-Jun-16 [69-Jun-18: 2C].
Mortimer, Willie Stevenson (5 mos.) d. on 70-Apr-23 [70-Apr-26: 2B].
Morton, Alexander (54 yrs.) d. on 66-Jul-17 of Imprudence and exposure [66-Jul-19: 1F].

Morton, Ann (43 yrs.) d. on 69-Oct-11 [69-Oct-12: 2C].
Morton, Dixon (68 yrs.) d. on 67-Jan-5 [67-Jan-10: 2C].
Morton, G. Nash m. Brown, Mary E. W. on 69-May-11 [69-May-15: 2B].
Morton, George C. (66 yrs.) d. on 68-Nov-1 [68-Nov-3: 2B].
Morton, George W. d. on 70-Aug-11 [70-Aug-12: 4C].
Morton, James (43 yrs.) d. on 69-Oct-9 [69-Oct-12: 2C].
Morton, Kate (13 yrs.) d. on 69-Oct-10 [69-Oct-12: 2C].
Morton, M. Jennie m. Dyer, Horatio P. [70-Apr-13: 2B].
Morton, Margaret (73 yrs.) d. on 68-Dec-25 [68-Dec-30: 2D].
Morton, Mary m. Hill, Richard on 68-Apr-20 [68-Apr-25: 2B].
Morton, S. R. m. Lawrence, M. S. on 68-Nov-30 [68-Dec-15: 2C].
Morwood, Mary Lucy m. Kuhan, Cornelius on 69-Aug-13 [69-Aug-16: 2B].
Mory, Frederick W. m. Waidner, Dollie E. on 67-Oct-13 [67-Dec-17: 2B].
Moses, Henry (61 yrs.) d. on 68-Dec-20 [68-Dec-22: 2C].
Mosher, Annie E. (22 yrs.) d. on 70-Apr-26 [70-Apr-27: 2B].
Mosher, Elizabeth (87 yrs.) d. on 66-May-12 [66-May-14: 2B].
Mosher, Laura V. m. Murphy, J. James on 70-Oct-20 [70-Nov-24: 2B].
Mosher, Martin (56 yrs.) d. on 69-Dec-22 [69-Dec-24: 2C].
Mosher, Mary (87 yrs.) d. on 70-Dec-9 [70-Dec-12: 2C].
Mosher, William, Dr. (72 yrs.) d. on 69-Jul-12 [69-Jul-13: 2C].
Moss, Ann Rebecca m. Burruss, William J. on 70-Apr-28 [70-May-2: 2B].
Most, Henry H. (88 yrs.) d. on 66-Oct-28 [66-Oct-29: 2C].
Most, Willie Becham (4 mos.) d. on 69-Jul-18 [69-Jul-19: 2D].
Mott, William, Capt. d. on 67-Jan-5 Drowned [67-Jan-16: 1F].
Motter, Rebecca A. d. on 69-May-2 of Consumption [69-May-5: 2C].
Mottu, Herbert Newton (7 mos.) d. on 68-Jul-26 [68-Jul-27: 2B].
Moulton, M. Ida m. Daffin, Francis D. on 67-May-16 [67-May-20: 2B].
Moulton, William G. m. Callis, Bella T. on 69-Dec-15 [69-Dec-18: 2B].
Mount, George W. m. Tucker, Imogene on 67-Nov-26 [67-Nov-28: 2C].
Mowatt, Sue E. d. on 66-Dec-9 [66-Dec-10: 2B; 66-Dec-11: 2B].
Mowbray, Agnes E. (28 yrs.) d. on 68-May-23 [68-May-25: 2A].
Mowbray, Ellen F. m. Bierley, William on 70-Oct-4 [70-Oct-15: 2B].
Mowbray, Francis Stewart (2 yrs., 6 mos.) d. on 68-Jul-29 of Diptheria [68-Aug-8: 2C].
Mowbray, Mary A. m. Palmer, A. W. on 67-Nov-26 [67-Dec-5: 2C].
Mowbray, William C. (23 yrs.) d. on 68-Jul-7 [68-Jul-8: 2B].
Mowell, Peter (64 yrs.) d. on 69-Nov-7 [69-Nov-9: 1H, 2C].
Mowton, George (49 yrs.) d. on 68-Mar-9 of Heart disease [68-Mar-11: 2B].
Mowton, Rebecca (75 yrs.) d. on 69-Sep-11 [69-Sep-13: 2B; 69-Sep-14: 2B].
Moxley, C. Henry (24 yrs.) d. on 67-Jan-1 [67-Jan-2: 2C; 67-Jan-3: 2B].
Moxley, Ida Amelia (6 yrs., 5 mos.) d. on 70-Oct-6 [70-Oct-7: 2B].
Moxley, Reuben Kennedy (9 yrs., 8 mos.) d. on 70-Jul-16 [70-Jul-20: 2C].
Moxley, William (60 yrs.) d. on 70-Jan-16 [70-Feb-17: 2C].
Moyer, J. m. Crammer, Mary E. on 69-Dec-22 [70-Jan-5: 2C].
Moylan, Harry (9 mos.) d. on 68-Oct-18 [68-Oct-19: 2B].
Moylan, Joseph (4 yrs., 3 mos.) d. on 66-Jul-1 [66-Jul-2: 2B].
Moylan, Joseph (5 mos.) d. on 70-May-26 [70-May-28: 2B].
Moylan, Michael (42 yrs.) d. on 68-May-17 [68-May-18: 2B].
Muckelroy, Elizabeth (69 yrs.) d. on 70-Jun-30 [70-Jul-2: 2B].
Mudd, John F. m. Miles, Imogene T. on 69-Jun-3 [69-Jun-16: 2C].
Mudge, William R. m. Zeigler, Gotlibin M. on 67-Sep-23 [67-Sep-25: 2B].
Mueller, Elizabeth (68 yrs., 2 mos.) d. on 68-Aug-19 [68-Aug-21: 2B].
Mueller, John m. Vogel, Mary on 69-Nov-7 [69-Nov-8: 2C].
Mueller, John G. d. on 70-Jun-19 [70-Jul-12: 2C; 70-Jul-16: 2B].
Mueller, Louis H. m. Grace, Meta on 70-Apr-19 [70-Apr-23: 2B].
Muesse, Henry m. Kreutzer, Emma on 69-Oct-17 [69-Oct-21: 2B].

Mugan, Bridget d. on 69-Jul-1 [69-Jul-2: 2C].
Muhl, August Charles (15 yrs., 11 mos.) d. on 70-Nov-16 [70-Nov-18: 2C].
Muhlhofer, Mary E. S. (28 yrs.) d. on 67-Nov-13 [67-Nov-14: 2C].
Muhlhofer, William m. Kraft, Christina on 69-Feb-25 [69-Feb-27: 2C].
Muhly, Christian m. Bauers, Sarah on 69-Feb-4 [69-Feb-8: 2C].
Muir, Emma m. Godman, G. Robert on 66-Apr-2 [66-Apr-19: 2B].
Muir, Emma m. Donnelly, Charles J. on 69-Jan-24 [69-Feb-3: 2C].
Muir, Jennet (54 yrs.) d. on 66-Feb-11 [66-Feb-13: 2C].
Muir, Laura A. m. Weitzel, John C. on 66-May-7 [66-May-9: 2B].
Muir, Robert D. d. on 67-Sep-11 of Heart congestion [67-Sep-25: 2B].
Muirhead, John W. m. Offutt, Zorah Ann on 66-Sep-4 [66-Sep-10: 2D].
Mulcahy, Patrick (33 yrs.) d. on 67-Nov-20 [67-Nov-22: 2C].
Muldoon, James m. McCann, Sarah on 69-Nov-28 [69-Dec-16: 2C].
Mules, Alfred H. m. Watts, Mary C. on 70-Apr-7 [70-Apr-14: 2B].
Mules, Annie R. m. Freeland, William S. on 69-Oct-26 [69-Oct-30: 2B].
Mules, Margaret A. m. Reed, Jacob on 68-Nov-12 [68-Nov-19: 2C].
Mules, Margaret J. (30 yrs.) d. on 68-Jun-6 [68-Jun-8: 2B].
Mules, Mary J. m. Matthews, George W. on 66-Apr-26 [66-May-11: 2B].
Mulhair, Thomas (65 yrs.) d. on 70-Feb-7 [70-Feb-8: 2C].
Mulhall, James E. m. Burns, Annie M. on 66-Jun-14 [66-Jun-20: 2C].
Mulkern, Mary (4 mos.) d. on 68-Nov-30 [68-Dec-1: 2C].
Mull, Maria (65 yrs.) d. on 68-Nov-1 [68-Nov-2: 2B, 4B].
Mullan, Bridget (48 yrs.) d. on 68-Jun-19 [68-Jun-20: 2B].
Mullan, Charles X. m. Huster, Emma F. on 66-Jul-2 [66-Jul-17: 2C].
Mullan, Eugene Lieutaud (4 mos.) d. on 70-Jul-26 [70-Jul-28: 2C].
Mullan, John (77 yrs.) d. on 66-Jul-22 [66-Jul-23: 2C].
Mullan, Jonathan (73 yrs.) d. on 69-Jan-20 [69-Jan-21: 2C; 69-Jan-22: 2D; 69-Jan-23: 1H].
Mullan, Peter (79 yrs.) d. on 69-Aug-8 [69-Aug-9: 2C].
Mullan, Sarah (65 yrs.) d. on 68-Jun-7 of Lung congestion [68-Jun-8: 2B; 68-Jun-9: 2B].
Mullen, Charles E. (1 yr., 10 mos.) d. on 70-Jun-21 [70-Jun-23: 2C].
Mullen, Eliza (75 yrs.) d. on 70-Dec-19 [70-Dec-20: 2B; 70-Dec-21: 2C].
Mullen, Jane (65 yrs.) d. on 69-Jul-7 [69-Jul-8: 2C].
Mullen, John m. Wallace, Mary J. on 69-Nov-18 [69-Dec-28: 2C].
Mullen, Jonathan (74 yrs.) d. on 69-Jan-19 [69-Jan-23: 1H; 69-Jan-22: 2D].
Mullen, Lizzie m. McCormick, John T. on 70-Mar-27 [70-Apr-13: 2B].
Mullen, Martha m. Wolf, John B. on 69-Jan-11 [69-Jan-13: 2D].
Mullen, Martin J. (4 mos.) d. on 69-Jan-8 [69-Jan-9: 2C].
Mullen, Rachel Ann d. on 66-May-9 [66-May-11: 2B].
Mullen, Sarah Jane (19 yrs., 3 mos.) d. on 68-Sep-3 [68-Sep-4: 2A; 68-Sep-5: 2A].
Mullen, Sarah V. m. Smith, William S. on 69-Jun-28 [69-Jul-13: 2C].
Mullen, Thomas (40 yrs.) d. on 66-Mar-13 [66-Mar-14: 2C].
Muller, Ellen (72 yrs.) d. on 68-Mar-30 [68-Apr-2: 2C].
Muller, John R., Dr. (39 yrs.) d. on 67-Mar-21 [67-Mar-22: 2C; 67-Mar-23: 2B].
Muller, John Randolph d. on 68-Dec-28 [68-Dec-29: 2D; 68-Dec-30: 2C; 68-Dec-31: 2D].
Muller, Narcissa A. m. Stabler, John on 68-Sep-24 [68-Oct-1: 2B].
Mullerkin, Margaret (44 yrs.) d. on 68-Dec-21 [68-Dec-22: 2C].
Mullet, Eugenia C. m. Rice, John W. on 70-Jun-22 [70-Jun-25: 2B; 70-Jun-27: 2C].
Mullett, Carrie A. m. Richardson, Joshua N. on 69-Dec-30 [70-Jan-4: 2C].
Mullett, Thomas, Sr. (79 yrs.) d. on 66-Aug-13 [66-Aug-14: 2C].
Mulligan, Bridget (31 yrs.) d. on 66-Aug-21 [66-Aug-22: 2C].
Mulligan, Catharine (30 yrs.) d. on 70-Dec-21 [70-Dec-22: 2B].
Mulligan, Cynthia A. (45 yrs.) d. on 66-Feb-24 [66-Feb-26: 2B].
Mulligan, Henry (50 yrs.) d. on 70-Jul-7 [70-Jul-8: 2C].
Mulligan, John J. d. on 66-Oct-21 [66-Oct-30: 4C].
Mulligan, Sarah (10 mos.) d. on 70-Jun-28 [70-Jun-30: 2C].

Mulligan, Sarah Jane (25 yrs.) d. on 70-Dec-28 [70-Dec-29: 2C].
Mullikin, Frank m. King, Rosalina F. on 68-Oct-29 [68-Nov-2: 2B].
Mullikin, H. Clay m. Anderson, Richarda S. [67-Jun-1: 2B].
Mullikin, Joseph H. m. Sherwood, Rebecca E. on 68-Oct-21 [68-Oct-24: 2B].
Mullikin, Minnie Search (6 mos.) d. on 70-Apr-29 [70-May-3: 2B].
Mullikin, Samuel H. H. (1 yr., 3 mos.) d. on 69-Aug-31 [69-Sep-10: 2B].
Mullin, Catherine (64 yrs.) d. on 66-Jul-28 [66-Jul-31: 2C].
Mullin, Margaret (1 yr., 8 mos.) d. on 66-Jun-11 [66-Jun-12: 2B].
Mullin, Michael A. m. Cluskey, Joe E. on 70-Aug-9 [70-Aug-31: 2B].
Mullin, Owen (53 yrs.) d. on 68-Nov-6 [68-Nov-7: 2B].
Mullin, Timothy (32 yrs.) d. on 66-Apr-14 [66-Apr-16: 2B].
Mulliner, E. E., Capt. d. on 67-Jan-20 of Iceboat collision [67-Jan-25: 1F].
Mullmyer, Minnie m. Lehnert, Ernest on 70-Nov-10 [70-Nov-11: 2B].
Mulvey, Mary m. Krastel, John on 70-May-19 [70-Jun-10: 2B].
Mulvey, William E. m. Stevens, Martha V. on 67-Jun-20 [67-Jun-25: 2B].
Mulville, Mary (62 yrs.) d. on 66-Nov-10 [66-Nov-12: 2C].
Mumford, Virginia A. m. Turner, Joseph on 67-Nov-12 [67-Nov-19: 2C].
Mumma, Ann (74 yrs., 9 mos.) d. on 67-May-23 [67-May-24: 2B].
Mumma, Elizabeth m. Davny, Henry on 69-Sep-6 [69-Sep-8: 2B].
Mumma, Jacob J. (44 yrs.) d. on 66-Jul-8 [66-Jul-9: 2C].
Mumma, John m. McGlennon, Eliza V. on 69-Nov-10 [69-Nov-16: 2C].
Mumma, Josephine S m. Clayton, Augustus L. on 67-Nov-6 [67-Nov-11: 2C].
Mumma, Julia m. Nourse, William H. on 69-Sep-20 [69-Dec-16: 2C].
Mumma, Mary Ann m. Smith, Eli B. on 67-May-21 [67-May-24: 2B].
Mundee, William Gilbert (78 yrs.) d. on 70-Jan-15 [70-Jan-17: 2C].
Munder, Charles F. (43 yrs.) d. on 68-Apr-26 [68-Apr-28: 2B].
Munder, Frank (2 yrs., 4 mos.) d. on 70-May-6 [70-May-7: 2B].
Munder, John Gottlieb (70 yrs.) d. on 70-Nov-8 [70-Nov-10: 2C].
Mundorff, David m. Fennell, Mattie F. on 67-Oct-14 [67-Oct-17: 2B].
Mundorff, Mary (52 yrs.) d. on 67-Jul-2 [67-Jul-3: 2B].
Munger, Kate m. Babcock, Rowse on 68-Apr-22 [68-Apr-23: 2B].
Munos, Mary Agnes (3 mos.) d. on 70-Oct-10 [70-Oct-11: 2C].
Munoz, Manuel m. Ross, Harriet on 67-Jan-22 [67-Jan-29: 2C].
Munroe, E. A. (70 yrs.) d. on 66-Oct-18 [66-Nov-5: 2B].
Munroe, Joseph G. m. Jubb, Dabora on 67-Sep-26 [67-Nov-5: 2B].
Munroe, Richmond (78 yrs.) d. on 66-Aug-25 [66-Aug-28: 1G, 2B].
Munson, Margaret d. on 66-Jul-25 of Consumption [66-Jul-26: 2C].
Munson, William Albert (23 yrs.) d. on 68-Nov-10 [68-Nov-12: 2C].
Murdoch, Almira E. m. Wright, George W. on 66-Apr-9 [66-Apr-11: 2B].
Murdoch, Ann d. on 69-Aug-22 [69-Aug-23: 2C; 69-Aug-24: 2B].
Murdoch, J. Campbell m. Moore, Maria Louisa on 67-Nov-26 [67-Nov-28: 2C].
Murdoch, John m. Law, Mary Howard on 69-Nov-10 [69-Nov-13: 2B].
Murdoch, Martha J. m. Norwood, Franklin on 70-Oct-6 [70-Oct-13: 2C].
Murdoch, Susan m. Brauns, F. W. on 66-Dec-18 [66-Dec-19: 2B].
Murdock, Albert T. m. Todd, Mary J. on 68-May-14 [68-May-15: 2B].
Murdock, Ann Sophia (53 yrs., 8 mos.) d. on 67-Oct-6 [67-Oct-7: 2B].
Murdock, Charles m. Bevans, Mollie J. on 66-Dec-27 [67-Jan-1: 2C].
Murdock, Minnie Allen d. on 69-Jun-26 [69-Jun-28: 2C].
Murdock, Thomas (70 yrs.) d. on 68-Dec-3 [68-Dec-4: 2D].
Murdock, Thomas d. on 66-Oct-29 Drowned [66-Nov-1: 4B].
Murdock, William B. (16 yrs.) d. on 68-Aug-6 [68-Aug-18: 2B].
Murgatroyd, Alice S. m. Kline, Morris P. on 70-Nov-2 [70-Nov-5: 2B].
Murguiondo, Lammot d. on 68-Aug-12 [68-Aug-13: 2B; 68-Aug-14: 2C].
Murker, John (88 yrs.) d. on 68-Aug-25 [68-Aug-26: 2B; 68-Aug-27: 2B].
Murndorff, Kate m. Lantz, J. Max on 66-Mar-15 [66-Mar-17: 2B].

Murphy, A. J. (25 yrs.) d. on 67-Apr-1 of Lung disease [67-Apr-2: 4C].
Murphy, A. Margaret (35 yrs.) d. on 70-Mar-30 of Consumption [70-Mar-31: 2C; 70-Apr-1: 2B].
Murphy, Agnes A. m. Early, Bernard J. on 67-Oct-29 [67-Oct-30: 2B].
Murphy, Alice (1 yr., 4 mos.) d. on 69-Jun-28 [69-Jun-29: 2C].
Murphy, Annie (10 mos.) d. on 69-Oct-27 [69-Oct-28: 2C].
Murphy, Bridget m. Donnelly, Thomas on 69-Jun-27 [69-Jul-3: 2B].
Murphy, Catharine (1 yr., 8 mos.) d. on 67-Oct-19 [67-Oct-21: 2B].
Murphy, Charles m. Jefferson, Mary E. on 68-May-3 [68-May-5: 2B].
Murphy, Dennis (24 yrs., 9 mos.) d. on 68-Sep-22 [68-Sep-23: 2B].
Murphy, Dennis (28 yrs.) d. on 70-Jul-17 of Heatstroke [70-Jul-18: 2B, 4D].
Murphy, Elizabeth d. on 70-Dec-10 [70-Dec-12: 2C].
Murphy, Ella C. m. Hites, Thomas E. on 66-Mar-19 [66-Apr-23: 2B].
Murphy, Ella S. m. Gordridge, George K. on 67-Nov-27 [67-Dec-2: 2C].
Murphy, Florence (6 mos.) d. on 69-Jun-20 [69-Jun-21: 2B].
Murphy, George Sheffield (7 mos.) d. on 67-Oct-15 [67-Oct-16: 2D].
Murphy, Georgie (22 yrs.) d. on 66-Dec-22 [66-Dec-25: 2B].
Murphy, Hannah d. on 70-May-22 of Lamp explosion [70-May-23: 1H].
Murphy, Hannah Bond (38 yrs.) d. on 67-Nov-1 [67-Nov-8: 2C].
Murphy, Henry (64 yrs.) d. on 68-Feb-2 [68-Feb-3: 2C].
Murphy, J. James m. Mosher, Laura V. on 70-Oct-20 [70-Nov-24: 2B].
Murphy, James (31 yrs.) d. on 68-May-14 [68-May-15: 2B].
Murphy, James d. on 69-Apr-21 of Fall from window [69-Apr-23: 1H].
Murphy, James (24 yrs.) d. on 70-Jul-5 Murdered (Assault) [70-Jul-6: 1G; 70-Jul-7: 2B; 70-Jul-8: 1F].
Murphy, James D. m. Austin, Georgianna M. D. on 66-Mar-6 [66-Mar-8: 2B].
Murphy, James D. m. Elliot, Elizabeth on 70-Feb-22 [70-Feb-24: 2C; 70-Feb-26: 2C].
Murphy, James J. (66 yrs.) d. on 66-Sep-7 [66-Sep-13: 2C].
Murphy, Jane (24 yrs., 4 mos.) d. on 70-Jul-27 [70-Jul-28: 2C; 70-Jul-29: 2C].
Murphy, Jesse D. (45 yrs.) d. on 66-Dec-25 Murdered (Shooting) [66-Dec-27: 1G].
Murphy, John (35 yrs.) d. on 68-Jul-2 [68-Jul-4: 2C].
Murphy, John (60 yrs.) d. on 68-Jan-9 [68-Jan-11: 2B].
Murphy, John (60 yrs.) d. on 68-Jun-9 [68-Jun-10: 2B].
Murphy, John Joseph (1 yr., 5 mos.) d. on 66-Feb-24 [66-Feb-26: 2B].
Murphy, John Robb (38 yrs.) d. on 68-Feb-6 [68-Feb-28: 2D].
Murphy, John W. m. McCall, Mary Jane on 66-Sep-6 [66-Sep-15: 2B].
Murphy, Joseph (20 yrs., 4 mos.) d. on 69-Dec-18 [69-Dec-20: 2C].
Murphy, Joseph F. m. Ferrandini, Harrietta A. M. on 69-Mar-30 [69-Apr-1: 2C].
Murphy, Katurah m. Mewburn, N. J. on 67-Aug-28 [67-Dec-10: 2B].
Murphy, Maggie A. (20 yrs., 5 mos.) d. on 67-Aug-27 [67-Aug-30: 2B; 67-Sep-6: 2B].
Murphy, Maggie Ann (1 yr., 8 mos.) d. on 68-Nov-2 [68-Nov-3: 2B].
Murphy, Margaret Elizabeth (41 yrs.) d. on 69-Oct-27 [69-Oct-28: 2C; 69-Oct-29: 2C; 69-Nov-1: 2C].
Murphy, Mary (36 yrs.) d. on 67-Aug-21 [67-Aug-22: 2B].
Murphy, Mary (55 yrs.) d. on 69-Jul-6 [69-Jul-8: 2C].
Murphy, Mary m. Diffenderffer, James T. D. on 66-Jun-13 [66-Jun-15: 2C].
Murphy, Mary A. d. on 68-Jul-24 Drowned [68-Aug-6: 1G].
Murphy, Mary C. m. Sadler, John on 69-Jun-28 [69-Jul-5: 2C].
Murphy, Mary Frances (4 mos.) d. on 67-Sep-1 [67-Sep-2: 2B].
Murphy, Michael (1 yr., 1 mo.) d. on 66-Oct-21 [66-Oct-22: 2C].
Murphy, Michael d. on 69-May-23 of Construction cave-in [69-May-25: 1H].
Murphy, Michael d. on 70-Nov-5 [70-Nov-8: 2B].
Murphy, Owen J. m. Dolan, Mary Virginia on 70-Sep-8 [70-Oct-15: 2B].
Murphy, Patrick d. on 68-Sep-29 [68-Oct-1: 2B].
Murphy, Patrick (60 yrs.) d. on 68-Apr-23 [68-Apr-24: 2B; 68-Apr-25: 2B].

Murphy, Placette Caze d. on 69-Dec-27 [70-Jan-18: 2C].
Murphy, Richard D. m. Green, Mary Elizabeth on 70-Dec-20 [70-Dec-28: 2C].
Murphy, Rose A. m. Clary, John on 66-Jul-9 [66-Jul-11: 2C].
Murphy, Rose A. m. Hibbitt, George A. on 66-Oct-16 [66-Oct-17: 2B].
Murphy, Sallie M. m. Sanderson, L. W. on 69-Jul-4 [69-Jul-7: 2C].
Murphy, Sarah (82 yrs.) d. on 66-Oct-8 [66-Oct-9: 2A].
Murphy, Sarah (57 yrs.) d. on 70-Jul-14 [70-Jul-15: 2C].
Murphy, Sarah A. m. Sands, Thomas E. on 67-Nov-7 [67-Nov-14: 2B].
Murphy, Sarah B. (70 yrs.) d. on 67-Feb-19 [67-Feb-23: 2C].
Murphy, Thomas (39 yrs.) d. on 68-Nov-16 [68-Nov-17: 2C].
Murphy, Thomas (45 yrs., 9 mos.) d. on 67-Nov-19 in Machine accident [67-Nov-21: 2C; 67-Nov-22: 1G; 67-Nov-23: 1F; 67-Dec-12: 2B].
Murphy, Thomas A. m. Connel, Honora on 68-Nov-8 [68-Nov-12: 2C].
Murphy, William (2 yrs., 4 mos.) d. on 66-Nov-27 [66-Nov-29: 2B].
Murphy, William (8 mos.) d. on 70-Jan-31 [70-Feb-1: 2B].
Murphy, William m. Oliver, Cassandra Lee on 69-Feb-7 [69-Feb-25: 2D].
Murphy, William T. J. (32 yrs.) d. on 67-Aug-10 [67-Aug-15: 2C].
Murphy, William Tecumseh (5 mos.) d. on 67-Jul-7 [67-Jul-9: 2B].
Murphy, Willie (1 yr., 9 mos.) d. on 70-Jul-15 [70-Jul-16: 2B].
Murrall, Hannah (42 yrs.) d. on 70-May-24 [70-May-25: 2C].
Murray, Bridget (38 yrs.) d. on 68-Jul-30 [68-Jul-31: 2C].
Murray, Charles Albert d. on 69-Jun-29 [69-Jun-30: 2C].
Murray, Edward (35 yrs.) d. on 70-Jun-26 [70-Jun-28: 2C].
Murray, Eliza Ann (49 yrs.) d. on 68-Nov-20 [68-Nov-21: 2C].
Murray, Elizabeth (28 yrs.) d. on 67-Sep-21 Murdered (Shooting) [67-Sep-23: 4B; 67-Sep-24: 1F].
Murray, Francis Key, Capt. (48 yrs.) d. on 68-Jul-11 [68-Jul-14: 2C].
Murray, Gertey (1 yr., 1 mo.) d. on 67-Dec-10 [67-Dec-12: 2B].
Murray, Henrietta M. d. on 70-Oct-18 [70-Oct-19: 2B].
Murray, Herron C. m. Williams, Cordelia Carey on 68-Oct-26 [68-Nov-24: 2C].
Murray, Hugh (55 yrs.) d. on 67-Oct-6 of Intemperance and exposure [67-Oct-7: 1F].
Murray, James (31 yrs.) d. on 66-Apr-20 [66-Apr-24: 2B].
Murray, James d. on 70-Nov-16 [70-Nov-17: 2C].
Murray, James m. Ross, Mattie J. on 66-May-17 [66-May-19: 2B].
Murray, James m. Bien, Susie on 69-Jun-24 [69-Jul-22: 2C].
Murray, Jesse m. Virley, Catherine on 67-Jun-11 [67-Jun-18: 2C].
Murray, Johanna (28 yrs.) d. [68-Oct-19: 2B].
Murray, John (55 yrs.) d. on 67-Feb-16 [67-Feb-18: 2C].
Murray, John m. Heapy, Kate on 68-Oct-6 [68-Oct-20: 1F].
Murray, John J. (24 yrs.) d. on 66-Feb-25 [66-Feb-27: 2B].
Murray, John Lincoln (2 yrs., 4 mos.) d. on 69-Mar-18 [69-Mar-19: 2C].
Murray, Kate d. on 70-Mar-13 [70-Mar-15: 2C].
Murray, Kate Melvin m. Armstrong, S. Edward on 69-Sep-21 [69-Sep-23: 2B].
Murray, Lucy (13 yrs., 7 mos.) d. on 70-Jan-23 [70-Jan-24: 2C].
Murray, Maggie (15 yrs.) d. on 66-Aug-19 Drowned [66-Aug-20: 1F; 66-Aug-21: 1G, 2C].
Murray, Margaret (70 yrs.) d. on 67-Mar-8 [67-Mar-9: 2B].
Murray, Margaret (45 yrs.) d. on 70-Jul-17 [70-Jul-19: 2C].
Murray, Martha E d. on 70-Apr-30 [70-May-2: 2B].
Murray, Mary Anne (3 yrs.) d. on 68-Nov-13 [68-Nov-14: 2B].
Murray, Mary C. d. on 66-Jun-29 [66-Jun-30: 2B].
Murray, Mary Elizabeth (58 yrs., 10 mos.) d. on 67-Sep-11 [67-Sep-12: 2B].
Murray, Mary Jane d. on 67-Feb-23 [67-Feb-25: 2C].
Murray, Mary Virginia d. on 70-May-19 [70-May-20: 2C; 70-May-21: 2B].
Murray, Richard C. (66 yrs.) d. on 68-Oct-9 of Paralysis [68-Oct-10: 2B; 68-Oct-12: 1G].
Murray, Sallie (36 yrs.) d. on 69-May-1 [69-May-4: 2B].

Murray, Samuel (70 yrs.) d. on 68-Feb-14 [68-Feb-15: 2B].
Murray, Sarah m. Dilworth, Jeremiah on 68-Jan-19 [68-Jan-29: 2C].
Murray, Stirling m. Miller, Anna T. on 66-Nov-6 [66-Nov-9: 2C].
Murray, William (74 yrs.) d. on 66-Jul-17 [66-Jul-18: 2C].
Murray, William H., Dr. (37 yrs.) d. on 68-Mar-14 [68-Mar-16: 2B; 68-Mar-17: 1G].
Murray, William H. (35 yrs.) d. on 69-Oct-23 [69-Oct-25: 2C; 69-Oct-26: 2B].
Murrell, Julia E. m. Daniel, John Warwick on 69-Nov-24 [69-Nov-30: 2C].
Murry, Annie m. Smith, Robert on 69-Apr-18 [69-May-21: 2C].
Murry, Jemmy (3 yrs., 9 mos.) d. on 69-Sep-17 [69-Sep-18: 2B].
Murry, Laura V m. White, Robert H on 70-Nov-28 [70-Dec-2: 2C].
Murry, Lizzie Ogden m. Maloney, James A. on 68-Jan-27 [68-Feb-21: 2B].
Murry, Patrick (43 yrs.) d. on 66-Aug-30 [66-Aug-31: 2B].
Murry, Sarah E. m. McCourt, Felix on 67-Oct-8 [67-Oct-11: 2B].
Murry, William (47 yrs.) d. on 69-Jul-15 [69-Jul-17: 2C].
Murteugh, Mary (40 yrs.) d. on 70-Aug-9 [70-Aug-10: 2C].
Murty, Annie R m. Fizone, Jacob on 70-Apr-19 [70-Oct-25: 2B].
Murty, Mary (52 yrs.) d. on 67-Oct-13 [67-Oct-14: 2B].
Muse, Addie B. m. Reid, Edward on 67-May-19 [67-May-21: 2B].
Muse, Lawrence W. m. Smith, Rana on 69-Feb-26 [69-Mar-3: 2B].
Musgrave, Charles Edward d. on 66-Jul-20 [66-Jul-23: 2C].
Musgrave, Ellen d. on 70-Oct-10 [70-Oct-11: 2C; 70-Oct-12: 2C].
Musgrave, Josephine m. Beidle, Charles W. on 69-Mar-20 [69-Mar-29: 2B].
Musgrove, Augustus W. m. Cobb, Annie M. on 70-Sep-8 [70-Oct-13: 2C].
Musgrove, Margaret Y. m. Penn, Richard on 69-May-2 [69-May-6: 2B].
Musgrove, Sarah m. Gemmill, Walter on 69-Jun-1 [69-Jun-3: 2B].
Musselman, Emily F. m. Skinner, W. Hammond on 69-May-12 [69-May-14: 2C].
Musselman, H. D. m. Hubbell, Carrie V. on 68-Oct-8 [68-Oct-10: 2B].
Musselman, John H. m. Boland, Cassandra M. on 69-Dec-15 [69-Dec-16: 2C].
Musselman, Lizzie d. on 67-Aug-9 [67-Aug-10: 2B].
Musselman, Lizzie m. Hause, Alexander P. on 66-Apr-24 [66-Apr-26: 2B].
Musser, Alexander M m. Reid, Mary A on 70-Oct-24 [70-Oct-29: 2B].
Musseter, Harriet J. m. Willis, W. M. on 70-Oct-11 [70-Dec-2: 2C].
Mussetter, Mary J. m. Owens, Samuel on 68-Nov-18 [68-Nov-28: 2C].
Musterman, Anna Catharine (80 yrs., 11 mos.) d. on 68-Oct-13 [68-Oct-15: 2C].
Mustin, A., Jr. m. Logue, M. Josephine on 67-Mar-27 [67-Mar-29: 2B].
Muth, Edith (1 yr., 6 mos.) d. on 69-Oct-3 [69-Oct-12: 2C].
Muth, Francis X. (4 yrs., 4 mos.) d. on 70-Mar-31 [70-Apr-1: 2B].
Muth, George L. m. Shaab, Mary Lizzie on 69-May-18 [69-May-22: 2B].
Muth, Ida May (3 yrs., 9 mos.) d. on 69-Oct-3 [69-Oct-12: 2C].
Muth, John P m. Foudriat, Celine on 70-Oct-18 [70-Nov-1: 2C].
Muth, Lizzie V. m. Repp, Charles W. on 69-Sep-28 [69-Oct-19: 2B].
Muth, Mary Innocent d. on 68-Aug-26 [68-Aug-27: 2B; 68-Aug-28: 2B].
Muzzy, Helen Lydia d. on 70-Oct-13 of Heart disease [70-Oct-14: 4D].
Myatt, Joseph (44 yrs.) d. on 69-Dec-8 [69-Dec-10: 2C].
Myer, Charles Marshall (1 yr., 5 mos.) d. on 66-Jun-24 [66-Jun-25: 2B].
Myer, Elizabeth (9 yrs.) d. on 67-Jun-7 in Wagon accident [67-Jun-8: 1G].
Myer, John (9 yrs.) d. on 66-Jul-5 Drowned [66-Jul-7: 1G].
Myers, Alice C. d. on 66-Apr-16 [66-Apr-17: 2C; 66-Apr-18: 2B; 66-Apr-24: 2B].
Myers, Amelia m. Hanna, Alexander B. on 66-Apr-23 [66-Apr-25: 2B].
Myers, Charles (67 yrs.) d. on 66-Sep-2 [66-Sep-3: 2C].
Myers, Charles N. (5 yrs., 7 mos.) d. on 69-May-16 [69-May-18: 2C].
Myers, Charles Tancred (14 yrs.) d. Drowned [66-Sep-20: 2B].
Myers, Daniel F. (58 yrs.) d. on 70-Aug-16 of Typhoid [70-Aug-17: 2C, 4E; 70-Aug-18: 2B; 70-Aug-20: 4D].
Myers, Eddie (1 mo.) d. on 70-Oct-9 [70-Oct-10: 2B].

Myers, Edward (46 yrs.) d. on 69-Dec-8 [69-Dec-10: 2C].
Myers, Emma Maria (5 mos.) d. [70-Jul-19: 2C].
Myers, Euphemia A. m. Taylor, Henry S. on 66-Mar-20 [66-Mar-27: 2B].
Myers, Fannie Victoria (2 yrs., 1 mo.) d. on 69-Sep-28 of Brain congestion [69-Oct-11: 2C].
Myers, George G m. Morrison, Mary on 70-Jul-12 [70-Jul-19: 2B].
Myers, George W. (25 yrs.) d. on 70-Jul-27 [70-Jul-28: 2C; 70-Jul-29: 2C; 70-Aug-20: 2B].
Myers, George W. m. Joseph, Margaret E. on 67-Aug-22 [67-Aug-24: 2B].
Myers, Henry, Col. (75 yrs.) d. on 70-Jul-7 [70-Jul-9: 2B].
Myers, Herman d. on 70-Feb-25 of Construction cave-in [70-Feb-28: 1H].
Myers, Hester A. m. Norris, John on 66-Nov-22 [66-Nov-24: 2B].
Myers, Humphrey m. Pettit, Sarah Jane on 68-Nov-12 [68-Nov-23: 2B].
Myers, Ida Gertrude (1 yr., 1 mo.) d. on 70-Jan-28 [70-Jan-29: 2B].
Myers, Jacob (63 yrs.) d. on 68-Jun-26 [68-Jun-27: 2B].
Myers, Jacob (1 yr.) d. on 66-Dec-19 [66-Dec-21: 2B].
Myers, James E. m. Sangston, Lillie C. on 68-Oct-7 [68-Oct-9: 2C].
Myers, James W. (7 yrs., 8 mos.) d. on 68-Nov-20 [68-Nov-21: 2C].
Myers, John Edwards (6 mos.) d. on 67-Feb-22 [67-Feb-23: 2C].
Myers, John J. m. Dunn, Mary E. on 69-May-11 [69-May-13: 2B].
Myers, Joseph (68 yrs.) d. on 70-Nov-25 of Consumption [70-Nov-28: 2C].
Myers, Kate E. (31 yrs., 4 mos.) d. on 70-Apr-20 [70-Apr-21: 2C].
Myers, Louis (42 yrs., 11 mos.) d. on 70-Jan-26 [70-Jan-27: 2B].
Myers, Mary (76 yrs.) d. on 68-Jun-6 [68-Jun-8: 2B].
Myers, Mary m. Geiglein, John on 69-Sep-12 [69-Sep-29: 2B].
Myers, Mary A. m. Rupp, William on 67-Oct-17 [67-Oct-30: 2B].
Myers, Mary L. m. Frick, John J. on 69-Sep-7 [69-Sep-9: 2B].
Myers, Mary R. (39 yrs.) d. on 66-May-15 [66-May-16: 2C].
Myers, Milcah Amelia (1 yr., 1 mo.) d. on 66-Aug-2 [66-Aug-4: 2C].
Myers, O. A. m. Bowman, Emma G. on 69-Mar-18 [69-Mar-26: 2C].
Myers, Rebecca d. on 66-Oct-29 [66-Oct-30: 2B].
Myers, Robert (24 yrs.) d. on 66-Jan-30 [66-Feb-6: 2D].
Myers, Sallie E. m. Kenney, J. J., Jr. on 67-Jul-7 [67-Jul-11: 2C].
Myers, Thomas m. Beckenmeyer, Mary on 68-Aug-13 [68-Aug-15: 2B].
Myers, Thomas R. D. m. Beckmyre, Mary A. on 68-Aug-13 [68-Aug-18: 2B].
Myers, William (5 yrs.) d. on 70-Sep-8 Drowned [70-Sep-9: 4D].
Myers, Willie (4 mos.) d. on 70-Oct-18 [70-Oct-19: 2B].
Mylins, Annie m. Folk, Edwin C on 70-Oct-23 [70-Oct-26: 2B].
Myrsinger, Annie E. (6 yrs., 7 mos.) d. on 68-Dec-7 [68-Dec-8: 2C].
Myrsinger, Willie (2 yrs., 2 mos.) d. on 68-Aug-13 [68-Aug-14: 2C].
Myrta, Mary d. on 70-Aug-9 of Lamp explosion [70-Aug-10: 4E].
Mytinger, C. H. m. Richardson, Mary Weems on 67-Feb-28 [67-Mar-7: 2C].
Nabb, George W. (75 yrs.) d. on 70-Oct-12 [70-Oct-14: 2B].
Nace, Elizabeth Murray (87 yrs.) d. on 66-May-8 [66-May-10: 2B].
Nace, Eugene Gilyard (2 yrs., 4 mos.) d. on 68-Feb-24 [68-Feb-25: 2C].
Nace, Henrietta m. Ironmonger, Charles S on 69-Dec-30 [70-Jan-4: 2C].
Nace, Sarah Ann (11 mos.) d. on 68-Sep-12 [68-Sep-15: 2B].
Nachman, Jacob (1 yr., 6 mos.) d. on 66-Jul-11 [66-Jul-12: 2C].
Naff, Albert m. McMaines, Elizabeth on 67-Oct-15 [68-Mar-16: 2B].
Naff, John Augustus (5 yrs., 4 mos.) d. on 68-Nov-12 [68-Nov-17: 2C].
Naff, William Henry (2 yrs., 6 mos.) d. on 68-Nov-14 [68-Nov-17: 2C].
Nagle, Charles (35 yrs.) d. on 68-Jul-16 of Heatstroke [68-Jul-17: 1D].
Nagle, Emma (12 yrs., 8 mos.) d. on 69-Jul-24 [69-Jul-26: 2C].
Nagle, George O m. Winters, Martha H on 70-Nov-18 [70-Dec-14: 2C].
Nagle, Henry A. m. Cline, Mary C. on 67-Jul-16 [67-Jul-25: 2C].
Nagle, John P. (29 yrs.) d. on 69-Jul-24 of Bowel inflammation [69-Jul-26: 1G; 69-Jul-27: 1H].
Nagle, Lizzie (20 yrs., 6 mos.) d. on 69-Aug-6 [69-Aug-7: 2B].

Nagle, Lucretia (53 yrs.) d. on 68-Feb-17 [68-Feb-19: 2C].
Nagle, Margaret (56 yrs.) d. on 69-Oct-16 [69-Oct-18: 1G].
Nagle, William F. (28 yrs.) d. on 66-Jun-26 of Consumption [66-Jun-27: 2C; 66-Jun-28: 1G; 66-Jul-7: 2C].
Naill, Bell B m. DeHoff, J. B. on 70-Apr-21 [70-Apr-26: 2B].
Nailor, W. T. m. France, Bettie on 70-Sep-15 [70-Sep-16: 2B].
Nalhardt, Aaron (88 yrs.) d. on 69-Oct-31 of Suicide (Hanging) [69-Nov-1: 1H].
Nalle, Phillip m. Zimmerman, Mary A. on 69-Feb-24 [69-Feb-26: 2D; 69-Feb-27: 2C].
Nalls, Benjamin F m. Howell, Permelia B. on 67-Aug-15 [67-Aug-20: 2B].
Nally, Christa C. m. Wood, Adam L. on 68-Sep-21 [68-Sep-29: 2B].
Nally, George W. m. Magaha, Sarah C. on 67-Jul-18 [67-Jul-20: 2C].
Namuth, Edward F. m. Bond, Mary Catherine on 66-Jan-1 [66-Jan-8: 2B; 66-Jan-11: 2B].
Namuth, Mary A. m. Delcher, Thomas B. on 66-Sep-11 [66-Sep-15: 2B].
Nants, Margaretta Boyer (76 yrs.) d. on 66-Nov-8 [66-Nov-9: 2C].
Nants, Olivia m. Wilson, Joseph Kent on 69-Jun-15 [69-Jun-17: 2C].
Napier, Mary A. (65 yrs.) d. on 69-Feb-20 [69-Feb-22: 2C].
Nash, Anne Louisa m. Jenkins, James on 68-Jun-8 [68-Jun-10: 2B].
Nash, Eliza J. m. Bailey, Charles W. on 66-May-2 [66-May-5: 2B].
Nash, Elizabeth E. (6 yrs., 9 mos.) d. on 66-Jan-4 [66-Jan-5: 2C].
Nash, Eva A. m. Crawford, John C. on 66-May-2 [66-May-12: 2A].
Nash, Francis Philip m. Coxe, Katherine Cleveland on 67-Apr-25 [67-May-1: 2B].
Nash, James (24 yrs.) d. on 70-Oct-23 [70-Oct-25: 2B].
Nash, John W. (26 yrs.) d. on 69-Aug-22 of Apoplexy [69-Aug-23: 1G, 2C; 69-Aug-24: 2B].
Nash, John W. m. Talbott, Emma on 68-Oct-13 [68-Oct-15: 2C].
Nash, Nellie m. Gammie, George on 67-May-21 [67-May-29: 2B].
Nash, William H. (37 yrs., 6 mos.) d. on 70-Mar-24 [70-Mar-26: 2B].
Nash, William Wadsworth m. Miller, Mollie F. on 69-Oct-18 [69-Oct-23: 2B].
Nason, Eudora m. Lautenbach, Robert on 68-Jan-7 [68-Jan-13: 2C].
Nathans, Helena V. m. Kessler, Samuel on 66-Nov-7 [66-Nov-26: 2B; 66-Nov-27: 2B].
Natherwood, Charles A. d. [69-Apr-3: 2B].
Nattall, Mary J. d. on 70-Dec-13 [70-Dec-14: 2C].
Naughlin, John Workman (17 yrs.) d. on 67-Mar-19 [67-Mar-20: 2C].
Naughton, Eddy (9 mos.) d. on 68-Aug-17 [68-Aug-18: 2B].
Naughton, John (35 yrs.) d. on 68-Nov-4 [68-Nov-5: 2C].
Naughton, Kate m. Clarke, Thomas on 66-Apr-4 [66-Apr-7: 2B].
Naugle, Mary C. m. Mitchell, David J on 67-Dec-10 [67-Dec-16: 2B].
Naylor, Belle m. Duly, Thomas F. on 69-May-25 [69-May-28: 2C].
Naylor, H. Louis m. Brady, Maggie on 69-Nov-25 [69-Dec-15: 2B].
Naylor, Henry m. Templeman, Charlotte on 70-Feb-2 [70-Feb-7: 2C].
Naylor, Susanna m. Wilson, James R. on 67-Jun-10 [67-Jul-1: 2B].
Neal, Harriet E. m. Oram, Vincent H. on 69-Apr-29 [69-May-11: 2B].
Neal, Henry C. m. Sermon, Laura V. on 67-Oct-31 [67-Nov-8: 2C].
Neal, James G. d. on 69-Sep-27 [69-Oct-2: 2B].
Neal, Mary W. m. Parke, George M. on 70-Jan-25 [70-Jan-27: 2C].
Neale, Adeline R. m. Vanderford, William H. on 69-Nov-25 [69-Nov-27: 2B].
Neale, E. Clarence m. Cowardin, M. Alice on 66-Oct-25 [66-Oct-31: 2B].
Neale, Ellen d. on 67-Sep-7 [67-Sep-9: 2B].
Neale, Ferdinand De Barthe (8 mos.) d. on 70-Aug-7 [70-Aug-8: 2C].
Neale, J. Harry m. Short, Nina F. on 66-Jan-10 [66-Jan-15: 2B].
Neale, Louisa (74 yrs.) d. on 70-Mar-4 [70-Mar-8: 2C].
Nearing, Adam m. Rossler, Margaret R. on 68-Aug-6 [68-Aug-14: 2C].
Nedwell, M. J. m. Wamsley, J. S. on 69-Feb-23 [69-Mar-16: 2C].
Neeb, John (73 yrs.) d. on 69-Apr-16 [69-Apr-17: 2B].
Needham, Asa, Jr. m. Hollingshead, Carrie R. on 66-Jun-7 [66-Jun-8: 2B].
Needhamer, Mary Clara (5 mos.) d. on 69-Apr-14 [69-Apr-16: 2B].

Needles, Elizabeth (81 yrs.) d. on 70-Aug-30 [70-Sep-1: 2B].
Needles, Walter M. d. on 69-Jan-21 [69-Jan-22: 2D].
Neel, Bell m. Sellman, Alonzo on 70-Jul-13 [70-Jul-14: 2B].
Neely, Annie (60 yrs.) d. on 68-May-21 [68-May-22: 2C].
Neely, Caroline H. (28 yrs.) d. on 69-Jul-1 [69-Jul-2: 2C].
Neely, Elizabeth m. Corridon, Bryan on 67-Sep-15 [67-Sep-17: 2A].
Neely, James M. m. Matson, Mollie E. on 69-Nov-4 [69-Nov-9: 2C].
Neely, Mattie d. on 70-Jul-4 [70-Jul-12: 2C].
Neenan, Michael (1 yr., 10 mos.) d. on 67-Dec-19 Burned [67-Dec-21: 1G, 2B].
Neer, N. Franklin m. Molloy, Kate C. on 67-Jun-6 [67-Jun-8: 2B; 67-Jun-11: 2B].
Neff, Charles W. m. Irwin, Belle on 65-Dec-20 [66-Jan-20: 2C].
Neiderman, George, Sr. d. on 66-Jul-6 [66-Jul-7: 2B].
Neidhamer, George Lewis (4 yrs., 4 mos.) d. on 67-Jan-27 of Scarlet fever [67-Jan-29: 2C].
Neidhamer, John George (36 yrs.) d. on 69-Jan-13 of Consumption [69-Jan-14: 1H, 2D].
Neidhammer, Mary Clara (8 yrs., 6 mos.) d. on 66-Dec-20 of Scarlet fever [66-Dec-22: 2B].
Neidhammer, S. Lewis m. Baily, M. Virginia on 66-Oct-25 [66-Nov-6: 2B].
Neidhammer, Willie d. on 68-Jan-21 [].
Neighoff, Emma S. m. Brooks, J. Thomas on 67-Dec-19 [67-Dec-31: 2C].
Neigholf, Mary m. Bell, John E. on 67-Apr-30 [67-May-1: 2B].
Neihoff, Joseph I. (34 yrs.) d. on 70-Feb-5 [70-Feb-9: 2C].
Neill, James (21 yrs., 1 mo.) d. on 69-Sep-6 of Consumption [69-Sep-8: 2B].
Neill, Jane A m. Beatty, William J. A. on 69-Dec-28 [70-Jan-17: 2C].
Neill, Rebecca T. (72 yrs.) d. on 69-Nov-20 [69-Nov-25: 2C].
Neill, Thomas B. m. Smith, Sarah J. on 68-Apr-9 [68-Apr-11: 2A].
Neilson, Joseph Walter (3 yrs., 1 mo.) d. on 69-Nov-25 Burned [69-Nov-27: 2C, 4D].
Nelson, Mary Ann (76 yrs.) d. on 70-Oct-25 [70-Oct-27: 2B].
Neily, Janie (2 yrs.) d. on 70-Jun-26 [70-Jun-28: 2C].
Neily, R. Augustus m. Horney, Sallie F. on 66-Dec-4 [66-Dec-6: 2B].
Neligan, Maggie d. on 68-Jul-12 [68-Jul-13: 2B].
Neligan, Maurice (34 yrs.) d. on 69-Apr-19 [69-Apr-20: 2B].
Nelker, A. H. m. Greasley, Louisa H. on 69-Jul-6 [69-Jul-17: 2C].
Nelker, John Freddy (10 mos.) d. on 66-Jun-9 [66-Jun-11: 2B].
Nelligan, Mary m. Dunn, Christopher J. on 70-Oct-10 [70-Nov-7: 2A].
Nelms, Mary A. (82 yrs.) d. on 66-Jan-28 [66-Feb-19: 1B, 2B].
Nelson, Alexander m. Fails, Anna M. on 69-Apr-27 [69-May-21: 2C].
Nelson, Alexander Hagner (7 yrs.) d. on 69-Apr-7 [69-Apr-10: 2B].
Nelson, Annie L. (8 yrs., 11 mos.) d. on 66-Feb-5 [66-Feb-8: 2C].
Nelson, Edward T. (21 yrs., 8 mos.) d. on 66-Oct-21 [66-Oct-22: 2C].
Nelson, Emma F. m. Betts, Samuel C. on 66-Apr-4 [66-Apr-12: 2B].
Nelson, Fannie B. m. Taylor, Charles J. on 68-Mar-12 [68-Mar-24: 2B].
Nelson, Fannie P. d. on 68-May-11 [68-May-18: 2B].
Nelson, Francis F. m. Bunting, Mary B. on 68-Feb-27 [68-Mar-2: 2B].
Nelson, Frank T. (26 yrs.) d. [68-Jul-8: 2B].
Nelson, Franklin P. m. Brannan, Eliza J. on 70-Mar-23 [70-Mar-26: 2B].
Nelson, Garrett H. m. Nelson, Georgia on 69-Feb-25 [69-Mar-10: 2C].
Nelson, Georgia m. Nelson, Garrett H. on 69-Feb-25 [69-Mar-10: 2C].
Nelson, H. Clay m. Chesney, Harriott on 70-Feb-17 [70-Mar-1: 2C].
Nelson, Henry (69 yrs.) d. on 67-Jan-3 [67-Jan-9: 2C].
Nelson, James M. m. Bolton, Louisa on 69-Sep-13 [69-Sep-16: 2B].
Nelson, John (23 yrs.) d. on 66-Nov-13 Murdered (Shooting) [66-Nov-14: 2B, 4B].
Nelson, John d. on 66-Aug-2 Drowned [66-Aug-3: 1G].
Nelson, John m. Reese, Mary C. on 66-Sep-6 [66-Sep-18: 2B].
Nelson, John Emerson (2 mos.) d. on 67-Jan-9 [67-Jan-11: 2C].
Nelson, John M. m. Dellaplane, Ella on 68-Oct-20 [68-Oct-21: 2C].
Nelson, Louisa G. d. on 69-Sep-21 [69-Oct-7: 2B].

Nelson, Martin m. West, Virginia on 69-Mar-24 [69-Apr-2: 2C].
Nelson, Mary B. (63 yrs.) d. on 66-Jul-18 [66-Jul-19: 2C].
Nelson, Mary C. m. Offley, H. E. on 68-May-27 [68-Jun-4: 2B].
Nelson, Mary Jane m. Holland, Johnston on 70-Dec-8 [70-Dec-10: 2B].
Nelson, Mollie M. m. Stromenger, Charles H. on 66-Oct-11 [66-Oct-16: 2B].
Nelson, Mollie T. m. Groscup, Frederick J. on 67-Oct-31 [67-Nov-2: 2B].
Nelson, Nathan (75 yrs.) d. on 66-Oct-17 [66-Oct-22: 2C].
Nelson, Peter m. Johnson, Hannah A. on 67-Feb-14 [67-Feb-18: 2C].
Nelson, Sarah Ann d. on 68-Mar-13 [68-Mar-14: 2B].
Nelson, Sophia G. (18 yrs., 2 mos.) d. on 67-Oct-17 [67-Oct-19: 2B].
Nelson, T. R. m. Benton, Emily A. on 70-Nov-25 [70-Dec-16: 2C].
Nelson, Tenant m. Dorsey, Anna M. on 70-Jun-9 [70-Jun-24: 2C].
Nenninger, Annie Louisa F. (80 yrs.) d. on 68-May-6 [68-May-11: 2B; 68-May-12: 2B].
Nermann, Junita Pinwell (34 yrs.) d. on 67-Feb-15 [67-Feb-16: 2D].
Nesbit, Lizzie m. Hunckel, Philip on 66-Jun-14 [66-Jun-18: 2B].
Ness, Alfred S. (50 yrs.) d. on 69-May-16 [69-May-18: 2C].
Ness, George W. (41 yrs.) d. on 70-Apr-11 [70-Apr-12: 2B].
Netre, Ferdinand (27 yrs.) d. on 67-Jun-18 [67-Jun-19: 2B; 67-Jun-20: 2B].
Netre, John G. m. Waldmann, Emeline M. on 67-Oct-29 [67-Nov-2: 2B].
Netre, Maggie E. (9 mos.) d. on 69-Jun-18 [69-Jun-19: 2B].
Netre, Olivia m. McLean, William J. on 70-Feb-7 [70-Feb-10: 2C].
Netre, Sarah m. Brooks, Correll E. on 68-Nov-25 [68-Nov-26: 2B].
Neuschafert, Louisa m. Petignat, Peter on 66-Jul-31 [66-Aug-6: 2C].
Nevaker, Edward Benjamin (1 yr., 5 mos.) d. on 69-Aug-27 [69-Sep-1: 2B].
Nevaker, Ida Virginia (13 yrs.) d. on 66-Aug-30 [66-Aug-31: 2B].
Neveils, Anna m. McDermot, James H. on 69-Jul-18 [69-Jul-21: 2C].
Neviker, Mary C. m. Yewell, John W. on 66-Aug-16 [66-Aug-25: 2A].
Neville, Nannie m. Bouis, John H. on 69-Jan-19 [69-Jan-21: 2C].
Nevin, John (35 yrs.) d. on 69-Jan-19 [69-Jan-22: 2D].
Nevins, John (46 yrs.) d. on 69-May-25 of Heart disease and dropsy [69-May-31: 2C].
Nevitt, Cordelia m. Biedenkopf, George on 69-Jan-14 [69-Jan-21: 2C].
Nevitt, Virginia m. Ennis, Thomas H. on 68-Dec-17 [68-Dec-23: 2C].
Nevius, Reuben S. m. Tuomey, Minnie on 67-Aug-1 [67-Aug-3: 2B].
Nevker, Catherine Jane (34 yrs.) d. on 66-Dec-18 of Consumption [67-Jan-4: 2D].
Newbell, Julia A. m. Werner, Gustave on 68-Oct-4 [69-Apr-3: 2B].
Newberry, Albert S. m. Wall, Prudie E. on 68-Jan-1 [68-Jan-4: 2C].
Newbold, Lila B. (3 mos.) d. on 67-Jul-19 of Cholera infantum [67-Jul-22: 2C].
Newbury, D. W. m. Linthicum, Henrietta on 68-Nov-12 [68-Dec-3: 2C].
Newby, Georgeanna (43 yrs.) d. on 68-Aug-28 [68-Sep-30: 2B; 68-Oct-1: 2B].
Newcome, Mary (64 yrs.) d. on 69-Mar-14 [69-Mar-16: 2C].
Newcomer, Frank (9 yrs.) d. on 66-Dec-1 [66-Dec-3: 2B].
Newcomer, William P. m. Winter, Scandra R. on 70-Aug-30 [70-Sep-6: 2B].
Newell, Sarah A. (48 yrs.) d. on 70-Mar-1 [70-Mar-2: 2C].
Newkirk, James m. Hyson, Sarah E. on 69-Mar-18 [69-Mar-20: 2B].
Newkirk, Joseph V., Jr. m. Eagleston, Mary E. on 67-Jun-10 [67-Jun-27: 2B].
Newkirk, Josephine (33 yrs.) d. on 70-Aug-5 [70-Aug-15: 2C].
Newman, E. Virginia m. Allison, Robert H. on 66-Jun-7 [66-Oct-6: 2A].
Newman, Edwin (5 mos.) d. on 68-Jun-19 of Measles [68-Jun-23: 2B].
Newman, George L. m. Bailey, Caroline F. on 68-Jan-2 [68-Jan-6: 2C].
Newman, Henry N. (74 yrs.) d. on 70-Aug-4 [70-Aug-6: 2C].
Newman, Jacob Emory (37 yrs., 2 mos.) d. on 67-Sep-5 [67-Sep-7: 2A].
Newman, Louis m. May, Henrietta on 68-Feb-27 [68-Feb-29: 2B].
Newman, Margaret m. Thompson, Alexander on 68-Apr-19 [68-Apr-29: 2B].
Newman, Margaretta (38 yrs.) d. on 67-Jul-1 [67-Jul-17: 2C].
Newman, Moses (45 yrs.) d. on 67-Jan-10 [67-Jan-12: 2C].

Newman, Olivia A. (38 yrs.) d. on 70-Dec-24 of Pneumonia [70-Dec-26: 2C].
Newman, Sarah E m. Carr, Homer S on 70-Mar-23 [70-Mar-31: 2C].
Newman, Thomas Francis (2 mos.) d. on 68-Apr-5 [68-Apr-6: 2B].
Newman, William H. m. Rogers, Ellen Stewart on 66-Oct-18 [66-Oct-20: 2B].
Newman, William S. (6 yrs.) d. on 70-Sep-12 Drowned [70-Sep-14: 4B].
Newnam, Fannie E. m. Boushell, John S. on 68-Aug-13 [68-Aug-17: 2B].
Newnan, John T. m. Avery, Ella L. on 68-Feb-18 [68-Mar-2: 2B].
Newnan, Timothy (52 yrs.) d. on 69-May-8 [69-May-11: 2C].
Newport, John E. m. Hull, Julia on 67-Apr-10 [67-Apr-12: 2C].
Newton, Amelia d. on 67-Jul-29 [67-Jul-30: 2C].
Newton, Annie M. (38 yrs.) d. on 67-Jul-6 [67-Jul-11: 2C].
Newton, Emma Ezelia (3 yrs., 3 mos.) d. on 69-Feb-25 [69-Feb-26: 2D].
Newton, Henry C. m. Frazier, Martina A. on 69-Oct-25 [69-Oct-27: 2B].
Newton, Issac m. Slaughter, Emma M. on 66-May-30 [66-Jun-18: 2B].
Newton, John B. m. Stanley, Laura V. on 66-Jun-7 [66-Jun-16: 2B].
Newton, John Wesley (2 yrs.) d. [68-Aug-15: 2B].
Newton, Laura A. m. Miller, Adolphus H. on 69-Dec-16 [69-Dec-20: 2C].
Newton, Mary J. m. Grosbernd, Henry on 69-Mar-9 [69-Mar-27: 2C].
Newton, Mary V. (2 yrs., 1 mo.) d. on 67-Jul-9 [67-Jul-11: 2C].
Newton, Susanna m. DeKubber, Jacob on 66-May-22 [66-May-30: 2C].
Newton, Thomas Moore (1 yr., 5 mos.) d. on 70-Dec-10 [70-Dec-13: 2C].
Niblet, Joshua S. (54 yrs.) d. on 66-Jun-23 [66-Jun-25: 2B].
Nice, Mary Ann (81 yrs.) d. on 67-Mar-15 [67-Mar-18: 2C].
Nice, Mary J., Miss m. Hugg, William H. on 70-Aug-26 [70-Aug-27: 2B; 70-Aug-29: 2B].
Nice, William A. m. Mason, Mary E. on 65-Nov-6 [66-Jan-31: 2C].
Nichlas, John m. Dorsey, Ella M. on 70-Oct-4 [70-Oct-7: 2B; 70-Oct-8: 2B].
Nicholas, Henry Moale d. on 69-Sep-7 [69-Sep-9: 2B].
Nicholas, Jacob (38 yrs.) d. on 68-Oct-6 of Heart disease [68-Oct-7: 1G].
Nicholas, Mary Jane m. Riley, Luther C. on 66-Jan-2 [66-Feb-13: 2C].
Nicholas, Wilson C. m. Moale, Augusta on 66-Oct-16 [66-Oct-19: 2B].
Nicholas, Winney (32 yrs.) d. on 70-Aug-1 [70-Sep-2: 2C].
Nicholes, Henrietta (110 yrs.) d. on 69-Aug-1 [69-Aug-2: 1H, 2C].
Nicholls, E. m. Whittington, A. E. on 66-Aug-18 [66-Aug-21: 2C].
Nichols, Blanche m. Worthington, Joshua F. C. on 68-Oct-6 [68-Oct-9: 2C].
Nichols, Caroline m. Duvall, Edwin F. on 69-Sep-23 [69-Oct-8: 2B].
Nichols, Eliza m. Squires, Alfred A. on 67-Jul-22 [67-Jul-24: 2C].
Nichols, Fanny M. m. Sakers, John T. on 66-Feb-6 [66-Feb-9: 2B].
Nichols, George M. (24 yrs., 3 mos.) d. on 70-Apr-1 [70-Apr-6: 2C].
Nichols, Isabel m. Jones, William C. on 66-Apr-5 [66-Apr-13: 2C].
Nichols, James W. m. Falkner, Caroline G. W on 66-Nov-29 [66-Dec-1: 2B].
Nichols, Jane M. (65 yrs.) d. on 70-Nov-8 [70-Nov-9: 2C; 70-Dec-3: 2B].
Nichols, John E m. Copenhaver, Susie on 70-Dec-20 [70-Dec-29: 2C].
Nichols, Joseph B. (30 yrs.) d. on 66-Mar-29 [66-Apr-2: 2B].
Nichols, Josephine m. Stowell, Joseph W. on 66-Dec-24 [67-Jan-5: 2C].
Nichols, Kate d. on 70-Jun-13 of Lamp explosion [70-Jun-14: 1G; 70-Jun-15: 1E].
Nichols, M. Cornelia m. Stabler, Philip T. on 70-Nov-10 [70-Nov-16: 2C].
Nichols, N. K. m. Emory, Sue on 69-Jun-1 [69-Jun-12: 2B].
Nichols, Thomas (23 yrs.) d. on 66-Oct-22 in Machine accident [66-Oct-23: 4C].
Nicholson, Albert (12 yrs.) d. on 70-Dec-8 [70-Dec-9: 2C].
Nicholson, Alexander (63 yrs.) d. on 69-Aug-1 [69-Aug-2: 2C].
Nicholson, Ann Jane d. on 69-Jul-3 [69-Jul-7: 2C].
Nicholson, Caroline (56 yrs.) d. on 67-Aug-4 [67-Aug-7: 2C].
Nicholson, Caroline J. (51 yrs.) d. on 68-Sep-29 [68-Oct-1: 2B].
Nicholson, Carrie d. on 67-May-15 [67-May-16: 2B].
Nicholson, Charles P. m. Amey, Laura V. on 66-Jan-18 [66-Jan-23: 2C].

Nicholson, Doratha A. (51 yrs.) d. on 67-Dec-6 [67-Dec-7: 2B].
Nicholson, Edward J. (2 yrs.) d. on 70-Nov-6 [70-Nov-8: 2B].
Nicholson, Fanny m. McIlvain, Henry C. on 70-Oct-11 [70-Oct-13: 2C].
Nicholson, George W. (1 yr., 2 mos.) d. on 66-May-5 [66-May-7: 2B].
Nicholson, Georgeanna (26 yrs.) d. on 66-Feb-11 [66-Feb-14: 2C].
Nicholson, H. R. m. Pitts, Martha on 69-Apr-29 [69-May-10: 2B].
Nicholson, Hattie E. m. Handy, A. Word on 70-Apr-28 [70-May-10: 2B].
Nicholson, Jacob C. (65 yrs.) d. on 68-Dec-20 [68-Dec-21: 2B; 68-Dec-22: 2C; 68-Dec-23: 4D].
Nicholson, James E. m. Reed, Mary Victoria on 66-Feb-1 [66-Feb-10: 2C].
Nicholson, Michael m. Anthony, Margaret on 67-Oct-4 [67-Oct-5: 2B].
Nicholson, Millie J. m. Harbert, W. H. H. on 68-May-13 [68-May-15: 2B].
Nicholson, Thomas G. m. Kennedy, Elizabeth on 67-Jul-16 [67-Aug-31: 2B].
Nicholson, William (15 yrs., 5 mos.) d. on 66-Jul-18 [66-Jul-20: 2D].
Nickerson, Charles W. m. Austin, Sophronia on 69-Jun-23 [70-May-11: 2B].
Nicklas, Florence E. P. (1 yr., 10 mos.) d. on 67-Dec-18 [67-Dec-20: 2B].
Nicklas, Kate m. Barranger, John A. on 68-May-26 [68-Jun-26: 2B; 68-Jun-27: 2B].
Nicklas, William m. Zimmerman, Anna Olivia on 69-Nov-18 [69-Dec-30: 2C].
Nickle, Stephen E. m. Bigley, M. Kate on 69-Jun-9 [69-Aug-13: 2C].
Nickles, Mary C m. Rankle, William on 70-Oct-23 [70-Nov-16: 2C].
Nicklos, John m. Cooper, Harriet on 68-Mar-12 [68-Mar-17: 2C].
Nickman, Carolina m. Swab, F. on 66-Aug-12 [66-Aug-28: 2B; 66-Aug-29: 2B].
Nickolson, Joseph (40 yrs.) d. on 70-Jul-22 of Cholera morbus [70-Jul-23: 4F, 2B].
Nickolson, Sarah E. (20 yrs., 4 mos.) d. [69-Jul-27: 2C].
Nickum, Margaret V. m. Hamill, Robert H. on 66-Sep-3 [66-Sep-5: 2B; 66-Sep-6: 2B].
Nicodemus, Bessie m. Heim, Charles G. on 70-Nov-23 [70-Nov-29: 2C].
Nicodemus, M. Angela m. Shriver, Calvin S. on 70-Jan-4 [70-Jan-10: 2C].
Nicodemus, Mary Isabel (1 yr., 6 mos.) d. on 69-Mar-31 [69-Apr-5: 2B].
Nicol, Mary m. Dabney, C. on 70-Feb-10 [70-Feb-19: 2B].
Nicolai, Antoinette Beatrice m. Waggner, George E. on 70-Nov-29 [70-Dec-8: 2B].
Nicolai, J. Marbury Turner (10 mos.) d. on 69-Jul-29 [69-Jul-30: 2C; 69-Jul-31: 2C].
Nicolai, Marian Augusta (33 yrs., 5 mos.) d. on 70-Aug-7 [70-Aug-8: 2C; 70-Aug-9: 2C].
Nicolai, William Frederick (1 yr., 11 mos.) d. on 68-Nov-6 [68-Nov-7: 2B].
Nicoll, Benjamin Brevard (1 yr., 4 mos.) d. on 70-Jun-29 [70-Jun-30: 2C].
Nicoll, Benjamin G. m. Fairchild, Frances E. on 68-May-27 [68-Jun-4: 2B].
Nicoll, Frances D. m. Brown, James F. on 66-Jul-12 [66-Aug-11: 2B].
Nicoll, Mary C. m. Cross, James R. on 67-Mar-3 [67-Mar-14: 2C].
Nicoll, Rebecca B. (19 yrs.) d. on 69-Oct-10 [69-Oct-11: 2C; 69-Oct-12: 2C].
Nicoll, William J. m. Bartholdt, Anna on 69-Mar-1 [69-Mar-9: 2C].
Nicoll, William T. m. Meads, Ellie on 68-Mar-1 [68-Mar-3: 2C].
Nicolson, Elizabeth J. (22 yrs.) d. on 68-Mar-2 [68-Mar-4: 2C].
Niedhammer, Willie (1 yr., 5 mos.) d. on 68-Jan-21 [68-Jan-22: 2C].
Niernsee, John R. m. Shelton, Annie on 69-Oct-6 [69-Oct-11: 2C].
Night, Willie Grant (1 yr., 5 mos.) d. on 70-Nov-6 [70-Nov-8: 2B].
Nihoff, Susan (28 yrs.) d. on 67-Nov-30 [67-Dec-2: 2C].
Nimmo, Jane m. Price, Jared M. on 70-Dec-8 [70-Dec-23: 2B].
Nimmo, John E. (45 yrs.) d. on 67-Jul-2 [67-Jul-3: 2B].
Nimmo, John Elliott d. on 68-Aug-4 [68-Aug-6: 2B].
Ninde, Amanda B. (48 yrs.) d. on 68-Sep-23 [68-Sep-25: 2B].
Ningardt, Mary Virginia m. Ford, John Thomas on 69-Dec-28 [70-Jan-1: 2B].
Nitze, Charles m. Bornemann, Elizabeth on 66-Jun-2 [66-Jun-14: 2B].
Nixon, J. B. d. on 67-Oct-26 of Pneumonia [67-Oct-28: 1F].
Nixon, John m. Dignan, Sallie on 66-Apr-5 [66-Apr-30: 2B].
Nizer, Sarah Alice d. [67-Dec-28: 2C].
Nizer, Sarah E. m. Harris, John L. on 69-Mar-31 [69-May-20: 2C].
Noble, Eliza A. m. Lee, John on 66-Apr-17 [66-Apr-28: 2A].

Noble, Ella m. Hubbard, Alva on 70-Dec-8 [70-Dec-10: 2B].
Noble, Emma J. m. Bunting, John H. on 69-Feb-11 [69-Feb-17: 2C].
Noble, Harrison Winship (8 mos.) d. on 70-Jul-18 [70-Jul-21: 2C].
Noble, Horace m. Harrison, Mary Spencer on 68-Oct-20 [68-Nov-2: 2B].
Noble, James (55 yrs.) d. on 66-Jan-15 [66-Jan-17: 2C].
Nock, N. N. m. Bell, Alice on 68-Jan-11 [68-Mar-20: 2B].
Nockton, Bridget (70 yrs.) d. on 68-Oct-12 [68-Oct-14: 2B].
Noel, Ella Sherman (2 yrs., 3 mos.) d. on 67-Mar-19 [67-Mar-21: 2C].
Noel, Henry R. m. Hambleton, Clara on 69-Dec-2 [69-Dec-4: 2C].
Noggle, Emmanuel m. Cloman, Charlotte R. on 65-Nov-30 [66-Feb-22: 2B].
Nolan, Harriet M. m. Carroll, William F. on 69-Oct-25 [69-Nov-3: 2C].
Nolan, Mary (86 yrs.) d. on 66-Feb-23 [66-Feb-24: 2B].
Nolan, Mary Catherine (2 yrs., 7 mos.) d. on 69-Dec-20 [69-Dec-21: 2B].
Nolan, Matthew (66 yrs.) d. on 67-Oct-7 [67-Oct-9: 2B].
Nolan, Mollie A. m. Shepperd, James A. on 66-Jan-16 [66-Jan-19: 2C].
Nolan, Patrick (36 yrs.) d. on 66-Jun-17 [66-Jun-18: 2B; 66-Jun-19: 2B].
Nolan, Patrick (42 yrs.) d. on 69-Dec-12 [69-Dec-13: 2C; 69-Dec-14: 2C].
Nolan, T. m. Gaynor, B. E on 70-Sep-15 [70-Oct-4: 2B].
Noland, Wineford (38 yrs.) d. on 67-Mar-14 [67-Mar-15: 2C].
Nold, John (30 yrs.) d. on 70-Jul-17 Drowned [70-Jul-18: 4E].
Nolen, Annie m. Southcomb, Joseph on 67-Sep-27 [67-Sep-27: 2B].
Nolen, John m. Choate, Susan A. on 67-Dec-17 [67-Dec-21: 2B].
Noll, Jacob (40 yrs.) d. on 70-Jul-17 Drowned [70-Jul-18: 4D].
Nolley, Marcellus J. m. Sturman, Edmonia J. on 69-Feb-23 [69-Mar-1: 2C].
Nolting, Robert (15 yrs., 8 mos.) d. on 70-Feb-13 [70-Feb-15: 2C].
Nones, Harry S. m. Eyster, M. LaRue on 68-Oct-12 [68-Oct-24: 2B].
Nones, Mary D. (21 yrs.) d. on 66-May-13 [66-May-15: 2C].
Noonan, Annie (18 yrs.) d. on 67-Sep-25 [67-Sep-27: 2B].
Noonan, Catherine (50 yrs.) d. on 68-Feb-8 [68-Feb-10: 2C].
Noonan, Ellie d. on 69-Oct-13 [69-Oct-16: 2B].
Noonan, F. H. m. Thomas, Fanny on 69-Nov-9 [69-Nov-11: 2C].
Norback, Virginia m. Rynerson, John on 68-Apr-6 [68-Apr-7: 2B; 68-Apr-8: 2B].
Norfolk, Louise S. m. Hartman, Milton F. on 66-May-9 [66-May-14: 2B].
Norman, Ella (11 mos.) d. on 67-Jun-23 [67-Jun-26: 2C].
Norman, George (41 yrs.) d. on 69-Apr-5 [69-Apr-7: 2C].
Norman, Montezuma M. (25 yrs., 6 mos.) d. on 69-Jul-14 [69-Jul-20: 2C].
Norris, Adam (83 yrs.) d. on 69-Feb-24 [69-Feb-25: 2D].
Norris, Alice A. m. Ayres, Thomas J. on 66-Jan-25 [66-Feb-22: 2B].
Norris, Ann (73 yrs.) d. on 67-Nov-24 [67-Dec-5: 2C].
Norris, Ann Simeon (49 yrs.) d. on 66-Jan-16 [66-Jan-17: 2C].
Norris, B. B. (84 yrs.) d. on 66-Nov-17 [66-Nov-19: 1G, 2B].
Norris, B. F. (59 yrs.) d. on 67-Nov-7 [67-Nov-9: 2B].
Norris, Benjamin F. (21 yrs., 3 mos.) d. on 66-Jul-3 [66-Jul-19: 2C].
Norris, Clarinda m. Hunter, Peter S. on 67-Nov-19 [67-Nov-20: 2C].
Norris, Daniel A. m. Moore, Mollie A. on 68-Sep-28 [68-Sep-30: 2B].
Norris, Eliza S. (1 yr., 1 mo.) d. on 70-Aug-14 [70-Aug-15: 2C].
Norris, Eliza S. m. Chester, George L. on 68-Jan-23 [68-Jan-28: 2D].
Norris, Fannie E. m. Cox, Richard W. on 70-Jun-15 [70-Jun-18: 2B].
Norris, Francis m. Stevens, Lizzie C. on 70-Aug-30 [70-Nov-29: 2C].
Norris, George Dufur (6 yrs., 1 mo.) d. on 70-Sep-12 [70-Sep-17: 2B].
Norris, George W. m. Grady, Jane Powell on 67-Feb-20 [67-Feb-23: 2C].
Norris, Georgie O. m. Warns, Francis G. on 68-Nov-8 [68-Nov-13: 2B].
Norris, J. Rivan (32 yrs.) d. on 70-Sep-8 [70-Sep-12: 2C].
Norris, James B. m. Anderson, Theodora M. on 68-Mar-23 [68-Apr-9: 2B].
Norris, John m. Myers, Hester A. on 66-Nov-22 [66-Nov-24: 2B].

Norris, John B. m. Clemson, E. A. on 66-Nov-13 [66-Nov-14: 2B].
Norris, John B. m. Gardner, Virginia on 70-Apr-26 [70-May-2: 2B].
Norris, John Chowning (1 yr., 5 mos.) d. on 68-Dec-15 [68-Dec-17: 2C].
Norris, John D. (68 yrs.) d. on 70-Aug-30 [70-Aug-31: 2B; 70-Sep-1: 2B].
Norris, John Jay (58 yrs.) d. on 68-Jul-30 [68-Jul-31: 2C].
Norris, Mary (84 yrs.) d. on 68-Jul-8 [68-Jul-10: 2C].
Norris, Mary m. Perry, George L. on 68-Nov-26 [68-Nov-28: 2C].
Norris, Mary Ann (77 yrs.) d. on 70-Aug-14 [70-Aug-18: 2C].
Norris, Mary R. m. Hough, William D. on 70-Feb-8 [70-Feb-10: 2C].
Norris, Matilda d. on 69-Jun-26 of Apoplexy [69-Jun-28: 1G].
Norris, Michael A. m. McCartney, Mary A. on 68-Jun-11 [68-Jul-13: 2B].
Norris, Nimrod (64 yrs.) d. on 67-Jan-16 of Consumption [67-Jan-18: 2C].
Norris, R. W., Jr. m. Oster, Emma S. on 68-May-12 [68-May-16: 2A].
Norris, Rachel (83 yrs.) d. on 67-Sep-24 [67-Sep-25: 2B].
Norris, Samuel (62 yrs.) d. on 68-Feb-7 [68-Feb-8: 2B].
Norris, Sarah E. m. Calder, William on 66-Apr-30 [66-May-3: 2C].
Norris, Sarah Verena (4 yrs.) d. on 66-Oct-15 [66-Oct-18: 2B].
Norris, Sophia C. m. Webster, Richard E. on 67-Jun-6 [67-Jun-8: 2B].
Norris, Susie R. m. Sellman, Benjamin F. on 68-Jun-16 [68-Jun-23: 2B].
Norris, Thomas A. d. on 67-Nov-28 [67-Nov-30: 2C].
Norris, Thomas C. (28 yrs.) d. on 67-Jan-19 [67-Jan-21: 2C].
Norris, Thomas E. m. Lutts, Georgie on 66-Nov-22 [66-Dec-1: 2B].
Norris, William G. (88 yrs.) d. on 70-Jun-30 [70-Jul-1: 1H, 2B; 70-Jul-2: 2B].
Norris, William H. (70 yrs.) d. on 70-Nov-6 [70-Nov-8: 2B].
Norris, William H. m. Dutton, Lydia G. on 67-Dec-26 [68-Jan-8: 2C].
Norriss, Samuel Howard d. on 70-Jun-4 [70-Jun-8: 2C].
North, Alverda F m. Price, Thomas L. on 70-Jun-2 [70-Jun-4: 2B].
North, Caroline V. m. McDonnell, Elijah on 69-Sep-29 [69-Oct-7: 2B].
North, James (46 yrs.) d. on 67-Apr-12 [67-Apr-13: 2B].
North, Jane F. m. Long, William H. on 66-Nov-22 [66-Nov-27: 2B].
North, Jennie C. (15 yrs.) d. on 70-Mar-26 [70-Mar-29: 2C].
North, Lizzie J. m. Cecil, George T. on 68-Oct-19 [68-Oct-23: 2B].
North, Mary A m. Willey, Marcellus on 70-Dec-27 [70-Dec-29: 2B].
North, Mary A. m. Brannen, Thomas H. on 66-Oct-10 [66-Oct-18: 2B].
North, Susan A. (66 yrs.) d. on 70-Feb-20 [70-Feb-26: 2C].
North, Thomas L. m. Maith, Mary C. on 67-Oct-8 [67-Oct-10: 2B].
North, Violet m. Kelley, Emmanuel on 67-Dec-3 [67-Dec-5: 2C].
Norton, D. S. m. Cortlan, Laura on 68-Jul-23 [68-Jul-27: 2B].
Norton, Sarah m. Kidd, Andrew F. on 69-Feb-15 [69-Mar-24: 2C].
Norton, W. J. m. Jamison, Mollie B. on 70-Oct-11 [70-Oct-13: 2C].
Norwood, Charles C. (41 yrs.) d. on 68-Oct-29 [68-Oct-30: 2C; 68-Oct-31: 2B].
Norwood, Frank H. (3 yrs.) d. on 68-Oct-24 [68-Oct-27: 2B].
Norwood, Franklin m. Murdoch, Martha J. on 70-Oct-6 [70-Oct-13: 2C].
Norwood, George W. (24 yrs., 7 mos.) d. on 70-May-21 [70-May-26: 2C; 70-May-27: 2B].
Norwood, Isabella (36 yrs.) d. on 68-Aug-31 [68-Sep-1: 2B].
Norwood, Ralph (42 yrs.) d. on 66-Nov-2 [66-Nov-9: 2C].
Norwood, Thomas m. Lawton, Ellie M. on 70-May-26 [70-May-30: 2B].
Norwood, Thomas S. m. Schroeder, Mollie A. on 70-May-30 [70-May-31: 2B].
Nottingham, William T. m. Beale, C. M. on 69-Jun-15 [69-Jun-17: 2C].
Noughton, Patrick (65 yrs.) d. on 68-Jun-17 [68-Jun-18: 2B].
Nourse, William H. m. Mumma, Julia on 69-Sep-20 [69-Dec-16: 2C].
Noyes, Charlotte C. d. on 70-May-17 [70-May-19: 2C; 70-May-20: 2C].
Noyes, Edward Abbott (1 yr., 3 mos.) d. on 67-Jul-26 [67-Jul-22: 2C].
Noyes, Stephen D. m. Beemer, Sarah Louise on 67-Oct-16 [67-Oct-19: 2A].
Noyes, William Galsber d. on 70-Nov-22 [70-Nov-23: 2B].

Nugent, Annie A. m. Keene, Joseph R. on 66-Jan-18 [66-Jan-29: 2B].
Nugent, Catherine Ann (25 yrs.) d. on 69-Jul-20 [69-Jul-21: 2C].
Nugent, Cecilia M. m. Turner, William B. on 68-Oct-7 [68-Oct-29: 2B].
Nugent, Charles F. m. Fisher, Emma A. on 70-Mar-1 [70-Apr-9: 2B].
Nugent, Elizabeth (4 yrs., 3 mos.) d. on 70-Aug-22 [70-Aug-23: 2B].
Nugent, Hannah (85 yrs.) d. on 69-Jul-12 [69-Jul-13: 2C].
Nugent, Mary (50 yrs.) d. on 68-Jul-4 [68-Jul-6: 2B].
Nugent, Sarah E. (26 yrs.) d. on 66-Sep-23 of Typhoid [66-Sep-24: 2B; 66-Sep-26: 2B].
Nugent, William (30 yrs.) d. on 67-Jul-31 of Lung hemorrhage [67-Aug-13: 2B].
Null, Lydia E m. Koons, J. E. on 67-Mar-12 [67-Mar-20: 2C].
Nulton, Kate M. m. Herbert, Joseph B. on 68-Jun-3 [68-Jun-25: 2B].
Numbers, Avarilla m. Osborne, George A. on 70-Apr-26 [70-May-2: 2B].
Numbers, Mary (71 yrs.) d. on 68-Sep-23 [68-Oct-3: 2B].
Numsen, Mary Catherine (30 yrs.) d. on 68-Mar-16 [68-Mar-17: 2C; 68-Mar-18: 2B].
Numsen, Matilda Gideona (3 yrs., 7 mos.) d. on 68-Apr-10 [68-Apr-15: 2B].
Numsen, William N. m. Grasbinder, E. on 70-Oct-4 [70-Oct-24: 2B].
Nunan, Annie M. m. Kidd, Thomas J. on 68-Jun-22 [68-Jul-14: 2B].
Nunnally, Maria m. Ford, Charles E. on 68-Oct-4 [68-Oct-6: 2B].
Nunnamaker, Sallie (59 yrs.) d. on 69-Jul-8 [69-Jul-9: 2C].
Nurbaum, Harvey m. Koons, Margaret on 67-Nov-26 [67-Nov-27: 2B].
Nussear, Mary M. m. Magraw, Robert H. on 69-Aug-11 [69-Aug-16: 2B].
Nusz, Mary Elizabeth (2 yrs., 7 mos.) d. on 69-Mar-25 [69-Mar-26: 2C].
Nuthall, George Sprague (4 yrs., 10 mos.) d. on 69-Dec-9 [69-Dec-11: 2B; 69-Dec-14: 2C].
Nutwell, Emma J. m. Nutwell, Wesley L. on 67-Mar-30 [67-Apr-12: 2C].
Nutwell, James E. (28 yrs.) d. on 70-Jun-14 [70-Jun-18: 2B].
Nutwell, John B. m. Minnick, Mary J. E. on 69-Dec-30 [70-Jan-4: 2C].
Nutwell, John S. E. (65 yrs.) d. on 69-Sep-21 [69-Sep-22: 2C].
Nutwell, Wesley L. m. Nutwell, Emma J. on 67-Mar-30 [67-Apr-12: 2C].
Nyburg, J. S. (24 yrs.) d. on 68-Oct-9 [68-Oct-10: 2B].
Nyce, B. Brook (38 yrs.) d. on 67-Jun-16 of Suicide (Shooting) [67-Jun-15: 1E; 67-Jun-17: 1G, 2B; 67-Jun-22: 1F].
Nyce, Emma m. Schaefer, Louis G. on 68-Dec-26 [68-Jan-11: 2B].
Nyce, Hugh J. (25 yrs., 4 mos.) d. on 70-Mar-16 [70-Mar-18: 2C; 70-Mar-19: 2B; 70-Mar-21: 2C].
Nyce, Hugh J. m. Mattson, Lizzie H. on 68-Nov-18 [68-Nov-24: 2C].
Nyce, J. Crawford m. Bosee, Mary E. on 67-Dec-3 [67-Dec-4: 2C].
Nyman, William H. m. Baugher, Ella V. on 67-May-22 [67-Jun-1: 2B].
O'Boyle, Martin (60 yrs.) d. on 68-Jan-8 [68-Jan-10: 2C].
O'Brien, Charles Edward (3 yrs.) d. on 69-Feb-13 [69-Feb-15: 2C].
O'Brien, Daniel m. Curran, Mary E. on 66-May-15 [66-May-24: 2C].
O'Brien, James (43 yrs.) d. on 67-Jan-9 of Heart congestion [67-Jan-10: 1G; 67-Jan-11: 2C].
O'Brien, James m. Burns, Mary M. on 66-Nov-14 [66-Dec-13: 2B].
O'Brien, John m. Hamilton, Grace Agnes on 68-Dec-21 [68-Dec-29: 2D].
O'Brien, John m. Studman, Mary Jane on 68-Nov-7 [68-Dec-5: 2C].
O'Brien, Laurence (53 yrs.) d. on 69-Sep-10 of Mania a potu [69-Sep-11: 2B; 69-Sep-13: 1H].
O'Brien, Maggie m. Kidd, John H. on 68-Feb-19 [68-Mar-4: 2C].
O'Brien, Maggie m. Schley, Edward on 67-Sep-26 [67-Nov-4: 2B].
O'Brien, Mary H. (29 yrs., 10 mos.) d. on 69-Oct-2 [69-Oct-5: 2B].
O'Brien, Patrick (25 yrs.) d. on 68-Dec-9 of Construction cave-in [68-Dec-10: 4F; 68-Dec-11: 2C].
O'Brien, Patrick (60 yrs.) d. on 67-Dec-9 of Heart disease [67-Dec-10: 1E; 67-Dec-11: 2B].
O'Brien, Sarah (50 yrs.) d. on 66-Feb-26 [66-Feb-28: 2C].
O'Brine, Agnes m. Gray, Benjamin F. on 70-Sep-1 [70-Nov-18: 2C].
O'Brion, Susan M. m. Moore, Robert V. on 68-May-12 [68-May-20: 2A].
O'Byron, Rosa S. m. Rathbun, Davis L. on 67-May-30 [67-Jun-3: 2B].

O'Callaghan, Joseph, Rev. (45 yrs.) d. Crushed by table [69-Feb-18: 1H; 69-Jan-30: 1G; 69-Feb-13: 1H].
O'Connell, Elizabeth (48 yrs.) d. on 67-May-31 [67-Jun-1: 1G, 2B].
O'Connell, Ellen (65 yrs.) d. on 69-Dec-16 [69-Dec-17: 2C].
O'Connell, Honoria d. on 68-Jul-5 [68-Jul-6: 2B].
O'Connell, Mary Ellen (10 mos.) d. on 69-Oct-27 [69-Oct-28: 2C].
O'Connell, Michael (2 yrs.) d. on 70-Apr-11 [70-Apr-12: 2B; 70-Apr-13: 2B].
O'Connell, Philip d. on 68-Jul-16 [68-Jul-17: 2C].
O'Connell, Philip (5 yrs., 6 mos.) d. on 66-Jun-15 [66-Jun-16: 2B].
O'Connell, Thomas d. on 67-Nov-15 Drowned [67-Nov-16: 1F].
O'Connell, William H. m. Brown, Carrie S. on 68-Apr-13 [68-Apr-22: 2B].
O'Connor, , Mrs. (38 yrs.) d. on 69-Aug-29 of Lamp explosion [69-Aug-31: 1G].
O'Connor, Bridget d. on 68-Apr-8 [68-Apr-11: 2A].
O'Connor, Daniel (78 yrs.) d. on 68-Dec-8 [68-Dec-9: 2C; 68-Dec-10: 2D].
O'Connor, Eliza C. (57 yrs.) d. on 69-Feb-6 [69-Feb-8: 2C].
O'Connor, Ellen (53 yrs.) d. on 68-Jan-28 [68-Jan-29: 2C].
O'Connor, Francis P. H. (29 yrs.) d. on 70-May-13 [70-May-14: 2B; 70-May-16: 2B].
O'Connor, Hercules (43 yrs.) d. on 68-Jan-12 [68-Jan-21: 2C].
O'Connor, Honora (60 yrs.) d. on 67-Apr-19 [67-Apr-20: 2A].
O'Connor, James (31 yrs.) d. on 68-Aug-3 [68-Aug-5: 2B].
O'Connor, James d. on 66-Apr-12 Murdered (Stabbing) [66-Apr-17: 4D].
O'Connor, Johanna (1 yr., 6 mos.) d. on 68-Jul-22 [68-Jul-23: 2B].
O'Connor, Mary d. on 69-Jan-30 [69-Feb-1: 2C].
O'Connor, Mary A. m. Firn, Cornelius on 68-Oct-26 [69-May-29: 2B].
O'Connor, Mary Ellen (1 yr., 4 mos.) d. on 66-Jan-22 [66-Jan-23: 2C].
O'Connor, Michael (34 yrs.) d. on 69-Dec-27 [69-Dec-28: 2D].
O'Connor, Peter d. on 66-Jul-17 of Heatstroke [66-Jul-19: 1F].
O'Connor, Sarah m. Dunn, Joseph on 67-Nov-4 [67-Nov-9: 2B].
O'Connor, Thomas d. on 69-Sep-17 of Lamp explosion [69-Sep-21: 1H].
O'Connor, William J., Jr. m. Scheick, Josephine on 70-Feb-10 [70-Mar-28: 2B].
O'Dell, Elizabeth H. (29 yrs.) d. on 67-Feb-6 [67-Feb-7: 2C].
O'Dell, J. Dixon m. Holbrook, S. E. on 69-Jun-30 [69-Jul-10: 2B].
O'Dell, Sallie E. m. Baker, William M. on 70-Mar-2 [70-Mar-30: 2B].
O'Dell, Walter m. Doubleday, Lottie M. on 69-Dec-2 [69-Dec-4: 2C].
O'Donald, Edward B. (3 mos.) d. on 66-Nov-12 [66-Nov-13: 2B].
O'Donald, George D. (1 yr., 5 mos.) d. on 65-Dec-30 [66-Jan-1: 2C].
O'Donnell, Ada m. Wootton, Henry E. on 68-Oct-13 [68-Oct-14: 2B].
O'Donnell, C. A. M. m. Kernan, Thomas P. on 69-Jan-31 [69-Feb-22: 2C].
O'Donnell, Charles Roatledge, (76 yrs.) d. on 70-Nov-18 [70-Dec-14: 2C].
O'Donnell, David (21 yrs.) d. on 70-Nov-4 of Consumption [70-Nov-5: 2B].
O'Donnell, Eleanora Pascault (72 yrs.) d. on 70-Jul-26 [70-Jul-28: 2C].
O'Donnell, Eveline Cameron d. on 66-Sep-29 [66-Oct-9: 2B].
O'Donnell, George W. m. Harnickel, Wilhelmine on 68-Nov-24 [68-Dec-5: 2C].
O'Donnell, Hannah (4 yrs., 10 mos.) d. on 70-Aug-20 [70-Aug-24: 2C].
O'Donnell, John (74 yrs.) d. on 70-May-18 [70-May-20: 2C].
O'Donnell, Mary (48 yrs.) d. on 67-Mar-3 [67-Mar-5: 2C].
O'Donnell, Patrick H. (27 yrs., 1 mo.) d. on 70-Apr-25 Drowned [70-Apr-26: 1H; 70-Apr-27: 1H, 2B].
O'Donnell, S. A. m. Dixson, David on 69-Feb-4 [69-May-11: 2B].
O'Donohue, Mary Ann (37 yrs.) d. on 69-Sep-15 [69-Sep-16: 2B].
O'Donovan, Frank Grant (1 mo.) d. on 69-Mar-18 [69-Mar-23: 2C; 69-Mar-22: 2C].
O'Donovan, John H., Dr. d. on 69-Jun-18 of Apoplexy [69-Jun-19: 2B; 69-Jun-21: 1F].
O'Donovan, Mary Louisa (2 yrs., 11 mos.) d. on 67-Jan-4 [67-Jan-8: 2B].
O'Doud, Hannah (46 yrs.) d. on 67-Jul-2 [67-Jul-3: 2B].
O'Dowd, Thomas Patrick (5 mos.) d. on 69-Mar-26 [69-Mar-27: 2B].

O'Farrell, Charles m. Devouges, Eugenie E. on 68-Dec-29 [69-Jan-4: 2C].
O'Farrell, Teresa m. Devouges, Alphonse on 69-Dec-30 [70-Jan-14: 2C].
O'Ferrall, Michael (23 yrs.) d. on 68-Feb-25 [68-Feb-26: 2C].
O'Grady, Eliza m. Beckett, G. H. on 68-Jun-8 [68-Jul-25: 2B].
O'Grady, Emma Jane (1 yr., 5 mos.) d. on 70-Sep-22 [70-Sep-23: 2C].
O'Grady, Mary Jane (20 yrs.) d. on 70-Jan-20 [70-Jan-21: 2C; 70-Jan-22: 2C].
O'Halloran, Ada Kathleen m. Tucker, Thomas W. on 67-Jul-10 [67-Jul-17: 2C].
O'Hanlon, Bridget (35 yrs.) d. on 70-Jan-22 [70-Jan-24: 2C].
O'Hara, Bridget (9 yrs.) d. on 66-Oct-12 [66-Oct-13: 2B].
O'Hara, James (7 yrs., 8 mos.) d. on 66-May-1 [66-May-2: 2B].
O'Hara, James, Sr. (64 yrs.) d. on 66-Mar-5 of Heart disease [66-Mar-6: 1F, 2B; 66-Mar-7: 2B].
O'Hara, Jane (49 yrs.) d. on 67-Jun-24 [67-Jun-27: 2B].
O'Hara, Matilda Jane (50 yrs.) d. on 66-Apr-10 of Pneumonia [66-Apr-11: 2B; 66-Apr-12: 2B].
O'Hara, Nancy d. on 66-Dec-31 [67-Jan-30: 2C].
O'Hara, Patrick (82 yrs.) d. on 70-Nov-1 [70-Nov-3: 2C].
O'Hara, Sarah Ann (62 yrs.) d. on 70-Feb-22 [70-Feb-23: 2C].
O'Keefe, Arthur Joseph (28 yrs.) d. on 70-Apr-29 [70-Apr-30: 2B].
O'Keefe, Catherine (37 yrs.) d. on 69-Apr-2 [69-Apr-3: 2B].
O'Keefe, David, Dr. (45 yrs.) d. on 70-Mar-2 of Typhoid [70-Mar-4: 1H, 2C; 70-Mar-5: 1G, 2B; 70-Mar-7: 1G].
O'Keefe, Joseph (60 yrs.) d. on 68-Feb-6 Drowned [68-Feb-7: 1G, 2C].
O'Keefe, Joseph (21 yrs.) d. on 67-Dec-8 [67-Dec-9: 2B].
O'Keefe, Lizzie (2 yrs., 6 mos.) d. on 68-Jul-19 [68-Jul-21: 2C].
O'Keefe, Matilda m. Kemp, Charles M. on 69-Jun-7 [69-Jun-9: 2C].
O'Laughlen, Margaret (3 mos.) d. on 68-Jan-19 [68-Jan-21: 2C].
O'Laughlin, J. S. m. Osborne, Mollie S. on 67-Jul-25 [67-Jul-27: 2B].
O'Laughlin, Mary B. m. Burgess, Samuel O. on 67-May-22 [67-May-31: 2B].
O'Leary, Annie m. Hampson, A. J. on 70-Mar-24 [70-Mar-25: 2C; 70-Mar-26: 2B].
O'Leary, Hattie A. m. Shutt, August L. on 66-Oct-25 [66-Oct-26: 2B; 66-Oct-27: 2B].
O'Leary, John (11 mos.) d. on 66-Mar-22 [66-Mar-23: 2C].
O'Leary, Laura Virginia (9 mos.) d. on 68-Dec-15 [68-Dec-16: 2C].
O'Leary, Martin (32 yrs.) d. on 69-Nov-8 [69-Nov-9: 2C].
O'Leary, Mary Agnes (28 yrs., 4 mos.) d. on 70-Dec-10 [70-Dec-12: 2C].
O'Leary, William Edward (1 yr., 8 mos.) d. on 70-Sep-11 [70-Sep-12: 2C].
O'Leary, William F., Capt. (29 yrs.) d. on 68-Jun-22 of Yellow fever [68-Jun-24: 1F; 68-Jul-8: 2B].
O'Loughlin, Clara Elizabeth (4 mos.) d. on 67-Jun-28 [67-Jun-29: 2A].
O'Loughlin, Francis J. m. Smith, Isabella on 68-May-24 [68-May-29: 2B].
O'Loughlin, Michael (28 yrs.) d. on 67-Sep-23 of Yellow fever [67-Sep-26: 1F].
O'Loughlin, Michael (48 yrs.) d. on 69-Feb-5 [69-Feb-8: 2C].
O'Loughlin, William (1 yr., 8 mos.) d. on 70-Jan-21 [70-Jan-22: 2C].
O'Mealey, Thomas (47 yrs.) d. on 68-Jan-12 [68-Jan-13: 2C].
O'Mealy, Bridget (35 yrs.) d. on 66-Sep-13 [66-Sep-15: 2B].
O'Meara, John J. d. on 70-Mar-11 [70-Mar-18: 2C].
O'Neal, Ann d. on 68-Mar-11 [68-Mar-13: 2C].
O'Neal, Charles C. (6 mos.) d. on 69-Jul-14 [69-Mar-29: 2B].
O'Neal, Edward H. (1 yr., 2 mos.) d. on 69-Mar-28 [69-Mar-29: 2B].
O'Neal, Kate A. m. Hahn, John on 67-Nov-6 [67-Nov-9: 2B].
O'Neal, Mary H. d. on 69-Dec-22 [69-Dec-23: 2B].
O'Neale, A. Adelaide m. Griffin, James E. on 67-Apr-18 [67-Apr-25: 2B].
O'Neale, Anna (61 yrs.) d. on 67-Dec-20 [67-Dec-23: 2B].
O'Neale, Jane S. d. on 66-May-24 [66-May-25: 2C].
O'Neil, Ann (75 yrs.) d. on 70-May-19 [70-May-21: 2B].
O'Neil, Jeremiah F., Jr., Rev. (42 yrs.) d. on 68-Nov-6 [68-Nov-9: 1G, 2B].

O'Neil, Michael (50 yrs.) d. on 70-Jun-24 [70-Jun-25: 2B].
O'Neile, Stephen (1 yr.) d. on 66-Aug-30 [66-Aug-31: 2B].
O'Neill, d. [66-Jan-18: 1G].
O'Neill, Alice M. d. on 66-Aug-25 [66-Sep-5: 2B].
O'Neill, Daniel (45 yrs.) d. on 70-May-2 [70-May-4: 2C].
O'Neill, Elizabeth (6 yrs., 5 mos.) d. on 67-May-30 [67-May-31: 2B].
O'Neill, J. Irene (4 yrs., 2 mos.) d. on 70-Jul-3 [70-Jul-4: 2C].
O'Neill, James (1 yr., 5 mos.) d. on 69-Jul-4 [69-Jul-5: 2C].
O'Neill, John (70 yrs.) d. on 68-Feb-24 [68-Feb-25: 2C; 68-Feb-26: 2C].
O'Neill, John (63 yrs.) d. on 70-Jul-1 [70-Jul-2: 2B].
O'Neill, John m. Whitney, Georgie on 66-Nov-29 [66-Dec-1: 2B].
O'Neill, Louisa (40 yrs.) d. on 69-Aug-26 [69-Aug-27: 2B].
O'Neill, Margaret Ann (11 mos.) d. on 66-Jul-5 [66-Jul-6: 2B].
O'Neill, Mary A. m. Logan, John on 69-Aug-26 [69-Sep-10: 2B].
O'Neill, Patrick (77 yrs.) d. on 70-Aug-20 [70-Aug-22: 2B].
O'Neill, Robert (5 mos.) d. [69-Aug-16: 2C].
O'Neill, Thomas (7 mos.) d. on 67-Sep-4 [67-Sep-5: 2B].
O'Neill, William Edmond d. on 68-Jul-8 [68-Jul-9: 2B].
O'Reilly, Alexander (46 yrs.) d. on 70-Feb-25 [70-Mar-3: 2C].
O'Rorke, Patrick d. on 66-Jul-17 [66-Jul-18: 2C].
O'Rourke, Harry (1 yr., 8 mos.) d. on 66-Jun-13 [66-Jun-14: 2B].
O'Rourke, Mary E. m. Brown, James E. on 69-Jun-18 [69-Jul-15: 2C].
O'Rourke, Mollie (3 yrs., 2 mos.) d. on 70-Jan-12 [70-Jan-13: 2D; 70-Jan-14: 2C].
O'Toole, Frances (37 yrs.) d. on 70-Jan-3 [70-Jan-3: 2C].
Oakes, Samuel H. m. Hergesheimer, Anna on 69-Jan-28 [69-Feb-3: 2C].
Oakey, James (22 yrs.) d. on 66-Mar-19 Drowned [66-Mar-21: 1F].
Oakford, Charles B. (7 yrs.) d. on 67-Nov-23 [67-Nov-25: 2C].
Oakford, Grace (4 yrs.) d. on 68-Jan-21 [68-Jan-22: 2C].
Oakford, Hall Baldwin (9 mos.) d. on 68-Jan-18 [68-Jan-20: 2C].
Oates, Ann d. on 66-May-2 [66-May-9: 2B; 66-May-10: 2B].
Oates, Charles T. m. Smith, Catherine on 70-May-18 [70-May-21: 2B].
Ober, Catherine (86 yrs.) d. on 67-Feb-2 [67-Feb-4: 2C].
Ober, Charles W. H. (1 yr., 11 mos.) d. on 68-Feb-29 [68-Mar-2: 2B].
Ober, Elinor Sophia d. on 69-Feb-19 [69-Feb-20: 2B].
Ober, John Henry (2 mos.) d. on 70-May-9 [70-May-10: 2C].
Oberndorf, Emilie d. on 69-Feb-25 [69-Feb-27: 2C].
Oberndorf, Fannie m. Harburger, A. on 69-Feb-8 [69-Feb-22: 2C; 69-Feb-23: 2C; 69-Feb-24: 2C].
Oberndorf, Georgia Ann (29 yrs.) d. on 68-Apr-18 [68-Apr-20: 2B].
Ochs, George m. Thomas, Barbara on 67-Oct-20 [67-Nov-1: 2B].
Ochs, John T. m. Kimmel, Mary E. on 68-Sep-22 [68-Sep-30: 2B].
Ockamay, James H. m. Harris, Edna on 66-Oct-9 [66-Oct-10: 2B].
Ockerme, Moses (63 yrs.) d. on 70-Mar-1 [70-Mar-2: 2C].
Ockes, Margaret (57 yrs.) d. on 69-Mar-11 [69-Mar-13: 2C].
Odell, Laura F. m. Christhilf, George S. on 67-Apr-24 [67-May-6: 2B].
Oden, Ellen m. Hollingsworth, John H. on 68-Nov-5 [68-Nov-7: 2B].
Odend'hal, Magdalen M. m. McCoy, Washington R. on 66-Apr-4 [66-Apr-7: 2B].
Odenhal, John (47 yrs.) d. on 70-Jul-27 Drowned [70-Jul-29: 4E; 70-Jul-30: 2C].
Odendonk, Elizabeth (81 yrs.) d. on 68-Dec-8 [68-Dec-12: 2C].
Oehal, Rose D. m. Hermann, Henry W. on 68-Jun-4 [68-Jun-6: 2A].
Oehrl, John G. m. Decker, Frances E. on 70-Nov-20 [70-Nov-25: 2D].
Oelmann, Dorothea (39 yrs.) d. on 68-Mar-29 [68-Mar-30: 2B; 68-Mar-31: 2B].
Offley, H. E. m. Nelson, Mary C. on 68-May-27 [68-Jun-4: 2B].
Offley, Michael (51 yrs.) d. on 70-Feb-18 [70-Feb-19: 2B].
Offner, Emma B. (5 yrs.) d. on 66-Jul-16 of Bilious dysentery [66-Jul-17: 2C].

Offutt, Agnes S.   d. on 70-Jan-18 [70-Jan-20: 2C].
Offutt, Livia (10 yrs., 10 mos.) d. on 68-Dec-15 [68-Dec-22: 2C].
Offutt, Zorah Ann   m. Muirhead, John W. on 66-Sep-4 [66-Sep-10: 2D].
Ogden, John Wesley (39 yrs.) d. on 70-Feb-27 [70-Feb-28: 2C].
Ogden, Josephine   m. Yunker, John George on 67-Feb-17 [67-Feb-20: 2C].
Ogden, Mary Alice (5 mos.) d. on 69-Apr-29 [69-May-7: 2C].
Ogg, Lue   m. McNemar, Harrison on 66-Feb-8 [66-Feb-9: 2C].
Ogier, Anna Elizabeth (16 yrs., 11 mos.) d. on 66-Jan-14 of Consumption [66-Jan-15: 2C; 66-Jan-16: 2C].
Ogier, Henry Clinton (1 yr., 4 mos.) d. on 66-Jul-4 [66-Jul-14: 2B].
Ogier, Mary Elizabeth (15 yrs., 11 mos.) d. on 69-Jul-23 [69-Jul-24: 2C].
Ogier, Mary Emma   m. Kleinle, William on 69-Sep-14 [69-Sep-16: 2B].
Ogle, Adkin (51 yrs.) d. on 69-Dec-10 in Railroad accident [69-Dec-11: 1G, 2B].
Ogle, Atkin   m. Carroll, Mary Jane on 67-Sep-3 [67-Sep-5: 2B].
Ogle, Elizabeth C. (42 yrs.) d. on 66-May-22 [66-May-23: 2B].
Ogle, Joseph (76 yrs.) d. on 69-Aug-26 of Fall from roof [69-Aug-27: 1H, 2B].
Ogle, Maud (4 mos.) d. on 70-Nov-17 [70-Nov-18: 2C].
Ogle, Theodosia   m. Rust, J. Franklin on 68-Nov-4 [68-Nov-6: 2C].
Ogle, Virginia G. (1 yr., 3 mos.) d. on 68-Sep-4 [68-Sep-5: 2A].
Ohers, Catherine (56 yrs.) d. on 70-Sep-27 Drowned [70-Oct-1: 4B].
Ohlendorff, Johanna F. E.   m. Kanne, William H. on 69-Jan-7 [69-Jan-8: 2C].
Ohrenschall, Christina   m. Winkelman, John H. on 69-Mar-23 [69-Mar-29: 2B].
Ohrenschall, F. A.   m. Schwartz, Augusta E. on 70-Feb-22 [70-Mar-1: 2C].
Olcott, Joel White (79 yrs.) d. on 66-Jul-4 [66-Jul-6: 2B].
Oldershaw, Thomas (29 yrs.) d. on 67-Aug-9 [67-Aug-12: 2C].
Oldham, Joseph D.   m. Linton, Louisa C. on 69-Aug-26 [69-Sep-1: 2B].
Oldham, Sallie I.   m. Wright, George F. on 65-Aug-17 [66-Jan-30: 2B].
Oldham, William H. (45 yrs.) d. on 70-Apr-11 [70-Apr-12: 2B].
Oldham, Willie Anna   d. on 70-Jul-14 [70-Jul-18: 2C].
Oldson, Mollie G.   m. Lynch, James on 69-Jun-22 [69-Jul-27: 2C].
Oler, Alexander M.   m. Brashears, Mollie C., Miss on 66-Feb-20 [66-Feb-27: 2B].
Oler, Bricie   m. Head, Henry H. on 69-Feb-4 [69-Feb-17: 2C].
Oler, Fanny Philipi   d. on 68-Mar-23 [68-Mar-30: 2C].
Oler, Jacob   d. on 68-Jun-2 [68-Jun-3: 2B].
Oler, Rovenia R.   m. Grimes, Charles W. on 66-Dec-20 [66-Dec-25: 2B].
Oler, Sarah A.   m. Billingsley, S. W., Jr. on 66-Nov-29 [67-Jan-10: 2C].
Oler, William Edwin (9 mos.) d. on 68-Aug-2 [68-Aug-4: 2C].
Oler, William Howard   d. on 68-Mar-21 [68-Apr-2: 2C].
Olive, Charles H.   m. Thomas, Cora on 69-Mar-2 [69-Mar-4: 2C].
Olive, Elitha (75 yrs.) d. on 67-Jan-12 [67-Jan-25: 2C].
Olive, Lizzie   m. Reed, N. G. on 69-Oct-5 [69-Oct-7: 2B].
Olive, Mary   m. Beatty, John M. on 69-Apr-14 [69-May-3: 2C].
Oliver, Angelina (31 yrs.) d. on 70-Apr-7 Drowned [70-Apr-8: 1H].
Oliver, Cassandra Lee   m. Murphy, William on 69-Feb-7 [69-Feb-25: 2D].
Oliver, George (40 yrs.) d. on 69-Mar-2 [69-Mar-3: 2C].
Oliver, George Allen (5 yrs.) d. on 66-Jan-15 [66-Jan-27: 2B].
Oliver, Hannah (87 yrs.) d. on 69-Nov-5 [69-Nov-6: 2C].
Oliver, Hannah   m. Eldridge, Robert on 70-Apr-14 [70-Apr-16: 2B].
Oliver, James   m. Hall, Liffie on 67-Jun-19 [67-Jun-22: 2B].
Oliver, James F.   m. Cromwell, Louisa on 70-Feb-10 [70-Mar-10: 2C].
Oliver, James R.   m. DeCormas, Nina on 67-Sep-26 [67-Sep-27: 2B].
Oliver, John (1 yr., 10 mos.) d. on 70-Nov-21 [70-Nov-24: 2C].
Oliver, John A. (66 yrs.) d. on 69-Mar-8 [69-Mar-10: 2C].
Oliver, Lewis (28 yrs.) d. on 66-Sep-7 Drowned [66-Sep-10: 1G].
Oliver, Margaret (56 yrs.) d. on 66-Dec-12 [66-Dec-13: 2B; 66-Dec-14: 4B].

Oliver, Maria (68 yrs.) d. on 70-May-20 [70-May-21: 2B].
Oliver, Mary Ann (43 yrs.) d. on 70-Oct-26 [70-Oct-27: 2B].
Oliver, Mary E. m. Brown, Walter S. on 68-Oct-28 [68-Oct-30: 2C].
Oliver, Thomas A. J. m. Lewis, Mary J. on 67-Jun-11 [67-Jun-13: 2C].
Oliver, Thomas J. m. Butler, Martha E. on 68-Nov-26 [68-Nov-28: 2C].
Oliver, William m. Coleman, Edith W. on 69-May-27 [69-May-29: 2B].
Olvis, Margaret (63 yrs.) d. on 68-Dec-8 [68-Dec-10: 2D].
Olwine, A. H., Jr. m. Barickman, Kate on 70-Dec-1 [70-Dec-12: 2C].
Omelea, Mary m. McEldon, William B. on 70-May-5 [70-May-16: 2B].
Omer, Virginia m. Kraft, Lewis on 68-Sep-28 [68-Oct-1: 2B].
Onderdonk, Henry m. Latrobe, Mary E. on 68-Dec-17 [68-Dec-22: 2C].
Onion, Edward D. m. Rawlings, Julia A. on 68-Jun-25 [68-Jul-8: 2B].
Onion, Elizabeth Ann (38 yrs.) d. on 66-Mar-1 [66-Mar-2: 2B].
Onion, Howard m. Payne, Lizzie on 68-Jun-15 [68-Jun-19: 2B].
Onion, John R. m. Smyser, Sallie C. on 66-Dec-27 [66-Dec-28: 2C].
Onion, Lizzie R. d. on 70-Nov-14 [70-Dec-6: 2C].
Onion, Mary Elizabeth (5 mos.) d. on 66-Jul-25 [66-Jul-26: 2C].
Onion, Mary G. m. White, Francis on 70-Nov-23 [70-Nov-24: 2B].
Onion, Thomas A. m. Rock, Elizabeth M. on 70-Aug-14 [70-Sep-13: 2B].
Onion, Thomas Bond (73 yrs.) d. on 69-May-27 [69-May-28: 2C; 69-May-29: 1H].
Opie, Nannie (2 yrs., 1 mo.) d. on 70-Nov-28 [70-Nov-29: 2C].
Opitz, Charles W. (1 mo.) d. on 66-Jan-15 [66-Jan-17: 2C].
Opitz, Elizabeth m. McWilliams, Hugh on 69-Sep-15 [69-Sep-18: 2B].
Opitz, Elizabeth M. Rentz (26 yrs.) d. on 66-Jan-7 [66-Jan-12: 2C].
Opitz, John m. Phiffer, Clara J. on 67-Oct-24 [67-Nov-5: 2B].
Oppenheim, Betsy (26 yrs.) d. on 68-Apr-22 [68-Apr-24: 2B].
Oppenheimer, Fannie m. Brussel, Adolph on 67-May-5 [67-May-8: 2B].
Oram, Kate m. Starr, David J. on 69-Sep-2 [69-Sep-7: 2B].
Oram, Parcella F. m. Kirby, Theodore T. on 68-Oct-22 [68-Oct-27: 2B].
Oram, Vincent H. m. Neal, Harriet E. on 69-Apr-29 [69-May-11: 2B].
Orchiese, Mary A. m. McInnes, T. W. on 70-Jan-5 [70-Jan-18: 2C].
Orem, Ann Elizabeth (38 yrs.) d. on 66-Mar-19 [66-Mar-20: 2C; 66-Mar-21: 2C].
Orem, Eleanor d. on 69-Jan-8 [69-Jan-9: 2C; 69-Jan-11: 2C].
Orem, Elizabeth m. Brown, Levi S. on 68-May-3 [68-May-5: 2B].
Orem, Francis m. Morris, Annie on 69-Dec-28 [70-Jan-1: 2B].
Orem, George E. (24 yrs.) d. on 66-Mar-9 [66-May-11: 2B].
Orem, J. Chase (34 yrs.) d. on 70-May-28 [70-May-30: 2B].
Orem, John M. m. Rose, Sophia G. on 66-Sep-20 [66-Sep-25: 2B].
Orem, Mollie L. m. Worick, John H. on 70-Sep-13 [70-Sep-15: 2B].
Orem, Sophie B. m. West, William H. on 70-Oct-27 [70-Nov-1: 2C].
Orem, Sydney M. m. Seth, James on 70-Mar-29 [70-Apr-11: 2B; 70-Apr-12: 2B].
Orem, William G. (53 yrs.) d. on 66-Jan-13 of Dysentery and hip disease [66-Jun-4: 2B].
Orem, William Westley (56 yrs.) d. on 70-Sep-16 [70-Sep-17: 2B, 4D].
Orendorf, J. T. M. m. Bohrer, Maria Forrest on 68-Nov-17 [68-Nov-19: 2C].
Orendorf, Joseph C. m. Merrill, Adele on 70-May-23 [70-Jun-1: 2B].
Orendorf, Maria Louise (10 mos.) d. on 70-Jul-17 [70-Jul-18: 2B].
Orendorff, Adolphus J. m. Childs, Mary E. on 67-Dec-24 [68-Feb-1: 2B].
Orme, D. G. (65 yrs.) d. on 66-Jan-8 [66-Jan-16: 2C].
Orme, Thomas P. m. Dobins, Mary Anne on 68-Jan-30 [68-Feb-3: 2C].
Orndorff, Ellen E. d. on 66-May-14 [66-May-15: 2C].
Orndorff, Harriet (26 yrs.) d. on 69-Jun-10 [69-Jun-12: 2B].
Orndorff, John T. (28 yrs.) d. on 68-Mar-4 in Railroad accident [68-Mar-6: 2C].
Orndorff, Rachel S. m. Lehmen, Jacob S. on 70-Feb-17 [70-Mar-14: 2C].
Orne, Jane E. (66 yrs.) d. on 70-Mar-3 [70-Mar-5: 2B].
Orr, Agnes m. Clancy, John D. on 68-Feb-4 [68-Feb-11: 2C].

Orr, Edward Creighton (4 yrs., 3 mos.) d. on 66-Nov-1 [66-Nov-3: 2B].
Orrell, Edward Francis (1 yr., 5 mos.) d. on 66-Jun-16 [66-Jun-29: 2C].
Orrell, Walter Vickers d. on 66-Sep-10 [66-Sep-13: 2C].
Orrick, Edward Gerhart (12 yrs., 4 mos.) d. on 70-Mar-16 [70-Mar-17: 2C].
Orrick, Ella m. Slothower, J. A. on 66-Mar-24 [66-May-8: 2B].
Orrick, William K. (61 yrs.) d. on 69-Jan-17 [69-Jan-18: 2D].
Orrison, Lanie F. m. Shaw, Marshall G. on 68-Aug-25 [68-Sep-2: 2A].
Orrit, Frank (36 yrs.) d. on 70-Jul-26 of Heatstroke [70-Jul-28: 4E].
Orth, Louis m. Roth, Ella, Miss on 67-Feb-10 [67-Feb-12: 2C].
Orth, Mary E. m. Sickel, L. D. on 67-Oct-6 [67-Oct-11: 2B].
Ortlip, Eliza J. m. Maguire, M. on 69-Apr-18 [69-Apr-28: 2B].
Ortlip, George W. (22 yrs.) d. on 68-Feb-8 in Railroad accident [68-Feb-10: 1F, 2C].
Ortlip, Mahlon (47 yrs.) d. on 66-Oct-5 [66-Oct-6: 2A].
Ortlip, Malon m. Denison, Eliza J. on 66-Mar-18 [66-Mar-20: 2C].
Ortlip, Willie (5 yrs., 6 mos.) d. on 66-Sep-20 [66-Sep-21: 2B].
Ortman, Ann m. Riepe, Lothar on 66-Apr-24 [66-Apr-25: 2B].
Ortwine, Adelaide m. Robinson, Eugene D. on 69-Aug-24 [69-Sep-6: 2C].
Ortwine, Annie Elizabeth (72 yrs.) d. on 67-Aug-26 [67-Aug-29: 2B].
Orvier, Marie Gabriella m. Sauerwein, Charles D. on 67-Aug-23 [67-Sep-12: 2B].
Osborn, Amos m. Hoopman, Rachel on 70-Dec-14 [70-Dec-21: 2C].
Osborn, Elmer Ellsworth (1 yr., 7 mos.) d. on 67-Jun-19 [67-Jul-9: 2B].
Osborn, L. Jennie m. Morgan, Thomas E. on 70-Feb-17 [70-Feb-22: 2C].
Osborn, Phebe (57 yrs.) d. on 66-Sep-18 [66-Sep-22: 2B].
Osborn, Rebecca (76 yrs.) d. on 69-Dec-22 [69-Dec-24: 2C].
Osborn, Susannah (90 yrs.) d. on 70-Aug-28 [70-Aug-29: 2C; 70-Aug-30: 2B].
Osborne, A. E. (64 yrs.) d. on 70-Sep-22 [70-Sep-23: 2C].
Osborne, F. M. W. m. Morgan, R. Adelaide on 69-Dec-7 [69-Dec-11: 2B].
Osborne, George A. m. Numbers, Avarilla on 70-Apr-26 [70-May-2: 2B].
Osborne, Jennie m. McCabe, W. Gordon on 67-Apr-9 [67-Apr-15: 2B].
Osborne, Mollie S. m. O'Laughlin, J. S. on 67-Jul-25 [67-Jul-27: 2B].
Osbourn, Anna A. E. McLay m. Street, Charles O. on 66-Apr-24 [66-Apr-27: 2C].
Osbourn, Howard (18 yrs.) d. on 67-Jun-29 [67-Jul-1: 2B].
Osbourn, James G., Jr. m. Paul, Mary E. on 68-Jan-14 [68-Jan-16: 2C].
Osbourn, Joshua m. Robinson, Sarah A. M. on 67-Jul-30 [67-Aug-1: 2C].
Osbourn, Joshua m. Robinson, Rebecca on 70-Feb-24 [70-Mar-21: 2C].
Osbourn, Sarah A. M. (24 yrs.) d. on 68-Aug-11 [68-Aug-13: 2B].
Osbourn, Thomas B. (18 yrs.) d. on 69-Apr-11 [69-Apr-12: 2A].
Osburn, Mary Anna m. Miller, Llewellyn on 68-Oct-29 [68-Oct-31: 2B].
Osburn, Mary Jane (39 yrs.) d. on 70-Dec-9 [70-Dec-10: 2B].
Osburn, Milton A. m. Brown, Marion T. on 67-Feb-20 [67-Feb-22: 2D].
Osing, Ida Catherine (11 mos.) d. on 68-Sep-1 [68-Sep-3: 2B].
Ostendorf, Alexander (20 yrs., 9 mos.) d. on 66-Feb-16 [66-Feb-17: 2B; 66-Feb-19: 2B].
Ostendorf, Anton (51 yrs.) d. on 69-May-27 [69-May-28: 2C; 69-May-29: 2B].
Ostendorf, Edward Anthony (5 yrs., 7 mos.) d. on 69-May-20 [69-May-21: 2C].
Ostendorf, Henry (30 yrs.) d. on 69-Dec-5 [69-Dec-6: 2C].
Ostendorf, Mary Margaret (3 yrs., 10 mos.) d. on 69-May-13 [69-May-14: 2C].
Oster, Emma S. m. Norris, R. W., Jr. on 68-May-12 [68-May-16: 2A].
Oster, Fannie A. m. Thomas, B. D. on 69-Feb-24 [69-Mar-1: 2C].
Osterhus, Rudolph H. (81 yrs.) d. on 67-Jun-4 [67-Jun-5: 2B].
Osterman, Joseph A. (39 yrs.) d. on 69-Jan-19 of Consumption [69-Jan-20: 2C].
Ott, Otto m. Smith, Jennie W. on 69-Dec-13 [69-Dec-18: 2B].
Otten, Sarah Jane m. Walsh, John J. on 69-Feb-8 [69-Feb-18: 2C].
Otter, Joseph E. (28 yrs.) d. on 67-Jan-22 [67-Jan-23: 2C].
Otter, Mary H. m. Leef, Charles G. on 66-Apr-24 [66-May-1: 2A].
Ottmiller, , Mrs. (53 yrs.) d. on 67-May-14 [67-May-16: 1G].

Otto, David Ross (10 mos.) d. on 69-May-11 of Pneumonia [69-May-13: 2B].
Otto, Frederick A. m. Ross, Himena on 66-Jun-14 [66-Jun-28: 2C; 66-Jun-30: 2B].
Otto, Henry m. Creager, Elizabeth on 66-Jul-29 [66-Aug-7: 2C].
Otto, Simon m. Dayton, Annie on 69-Nov-21 [69-Jan-15: 2B].
Oudesluys, Harriet d. on 66-Apr-11 [66-Apr-12: 2B; 66-Apr-13: 2C].
Oudesluys, Mary W. m. Dixon, William T. on 69-Nov-4 [69-Nov-8: 2C].
Ould, Perry m. Dobson, Sallie J. on 68-Jul-22 [68-Jul-24: 2C].
Ould, Rebecca S. m. Higgins, Edwin on 66-Nov-1 [66-Nov-7: 2C].
Oursler, Amanda M. (68 yrs.) d. on 67-Dec-4 [68-Jan-14: 2C].
Outten, Mary F. m. Craver, M. Monroe on 66-Nov-6 [66-Nov-22: 2C].
Overbeck, Lizzie m. Miller, J. W. on 68-Apr-30 [68-May-2: 2C].
Overman, Jerome A. m. Baumgardner, M. Olivia on 66-Nov-13 [66-Dec-1: 2B].
Owen, John, Rev. d. on 67-Oct-16 of Yellow fever [67-Oct-29: 2B].
Owen, Marcus (45 yrs.) d. on 69-Oct-15 [69-Oct-16: 2B].
Owen, Mary d. on 67-Sep-5 [67-Sep-9: 2B].
Owen, Thomas J. m. Magruder, Van on 69-Nov-18 [69-Nov-25: 2C].
Owen, William C. d. on 69-Jun-25 [69-Jul-3: 2B].
Owen, William H. m. Goldsborough, Maggie D. [68-Oct-8: 2B].
Owens, Agnes m. Green, John W. on 67-Sep-19 [67-Nov-20: 2C].
Owens, Alexander, Jr. m. Hardesty, Lizzie D. on 67-Nov-21 [67-Nov-23: 2B].
Owens, Alice (23 yrs.) d. on 70-Mar-6 [70-Mar-18: 2C].
Owens, Benjamin B. m. Harris, Annie C. on 69-Nov-18 [69-Nov-20: 2B].
Owens, Charles Stevens (12 yrs.) d. on 67-Mar-23 [67-Mar-25: 2C].
Owens, Charles W. m. Deale, Mary F. on 69-Apr-27 [69-May-6: 2B].
Owens, Edward (31 yrs.) d. on 68-Feb-3 in Railroad accident [68-Feb-4: 1F; 68-Feb-5: 2D].
Owens, Edward m. Bird, Mary Ann on 69-Nov-21 [69-Nov-27: 2B].
Owens, Edward B. m. Cassard, S. Kate on 69-Nov-11 [69-Nov-16: 2C].
Owens, Elizabeth (66 yrs.) d. on 66-Mar-3 of Consumption [66-Mar-16: 2B].
Owens, Elizabeth Estelle (6 mos.) d. on 67-Aug-13 [67-Aug-15: 2C].
Owens, Francis (34 yrs.) d. on 66-Dec-31 [67-Jan-2: 2C].
Owens, Hugh A. m. Lucas, Sarah R. on 69-Jan-13 [69-Jan-19: 2C].
Owens, Ida Laura (1 yr., 10 mos.) d. on 66-Dec-22 [67-Jan-10: 2C].
Owens, James R. m. Councilman, Gertrude on 68-Nov-25 [68-Dec-4: 2D].
Owens, James S., Dr. (63 yrs.) d. on 66-Mar-5 [66-Mar-6: 1E, 2B].
Owens, James T. m. Mickin, Mary Jane on 67-Nov-28 [67-Nov-30: 2C].
Owens, James W. m. Ratcliffe, Bettie H. on 68-Jan-16 [68-Jan-18: 2B].
Owens, Joanna (34 yrs.) d. on 66-Oct-5 [66-Oct-6: 2A].
Owens, John (39 yrs.) d. on 67-May-30 [67-Jun-1: 2B].
Owens, John A. (23 yrs.) d. on 70-Apr-10 [70-Apr-27: 2B].
Owens, John T. d. on 70-Aug-15 in Railroad accident [70-Aug-16: 4D; 70-Aug-18: 4D].
Owens, Kate m. Bonn, Lewis V. on 68-Nov-25 [68-Nov-28: 2C].
Owens, Laura V. m. Collier, J. C. on 67-Dec-3 [67-Dec-24: 2B].
Owens, Maria H. m. Richardson, Henry on 68-Oct-13 [68-Oct-14: 2B].
Owens, Michael (70 yrs.) d. on 68-Mar-22 [68-Mar-23: 2B].
Owens, Owen Griffith (68 yrs.) d. on 68-Jan-12 [68-Jan-16: 1F].
Owens, Priscilla m. Waidner, John J. on 69-Feb-1 [69-Feb-9: 2C].
Owens, Richard H. m. Kennard, Laura J. on 68-Nov-17 [68-Nov-19: 2C].
Owens, Robert W. m. Randall, Ida on 70-Sep-29 [70-Oct-3: 2B].
Owens, Samuel m. Mussetter, Mary J. on 68-Nov-18 [68-Nov-28: 2C].
Owens, Sarah Ann (35 yrs.) d. on 67-Mar-3 [67-Mar-5: 2C].
Owens, Stephen B. m. Hawkins, Abbey on 68-Feb-7 [68-Aug-11: 2B].
Owens, William Benjamin (6 mos.) d. on 69-Dec-10 [69-Dec-11: 2B].
Owens, Zachary T. m. McCormick, Clara S. on 69-Jan-25 [69-Jan-26: 2C].
Owings, Agnes Carr m. Hoofnagle, William D. on 68-Mar-1 [68-Mar-7: 2B].
Owings, Alverdo S. m. Dorsey, John C. on 69-Jun-24 [69-Jul-7: 2C].

Owings, Anna E. m. Hood, James H. on 69-Dec-21 [69-Dec-23: 2B].
Owings, Basil (71 yrs.) d. on 69-Feb-7 [69-Feb-9: 2C].
Owings, Carrie D. m. Clarke, William H. on 68-Jan-14 [68-Feb-5: 2D].
Owings, Eliza A. (41 yrs., 6 mos.) d. on 68-Mar-23 [68-Mar-25: 2A].
Owings, Ellen d. on 67-Nov-27 [67-Nov-28: 2C].
Owings, Ellen B. d. on 68-Mar-6 [68-Mar-7: 2C].
Owings, Eunice C. m. Taylor, W. M. on 69-Dec-23 [70-Jan-4: 2C].
Owings, George W. (10 yrs., 1 mo.) d. on 68-Dec-5 [68-Dec-7: 2D].
Owings, George Washington (38 yrs.) d. on 70-Jun-28 of Heatstroke [70-Jun-29: 1G, 2C].
Owings, Henry H., Maj. (70 yrs.) d. on 69-Oct-26 [69-Oct-27: 2B].
Owings, Israel m. King, Maria on 67-Sep-9 [67-Sep-11: 2B].
Owings, John A. (57 yrs.) d. on 70-Aug-9 [70-Aug-11: 2C].
Owings, Kate m. Maccubbin, R. W., Jr. on 69-Nov-25 [69-Nov-29: 2C].
Owings, Mary (72 yrs.) d. on 68-Apr-26 [68-Apr-27: 2B].
Owings, Mollie V. (25 yrs.) d. on 70-Apr-24 of Consumption [70-Apr-26: 2B].
Owings, Nannie (2 yrs., 4 mos.) d. on 66-Nov-20 [66-Nov-23: 2C].
Owings, Nannie T. (3 yrs.) d. on 70-Apr-27 [70-Apr-29: 2B].
Owings, Perry T. m. Watson, Maggie S. on 70-Apr-28 [70-May-12: 2B].
Owings, Rebecca m. Gambrill, George T. on 69-Jun-8 [69-Jun-11: 2C].
Owings, Samuel A. d. on 69-Jan-16 Drowned [69-Jan-18: 1G].
Owings, Samuel Beall (52 yrs.) d. on 69-Dec-27 of Neuralgia [69-Dec-29: 1G, 2D].
Owings, Sarah R. (61 yrs.) d. on 68-Jul-17 [68-Aug-14: 2C].
Owings, Susie D. m. Clark, John R. on 70-Aug-21 [70-Sep-1: 2B].
Owings, Thomas, Dr. (64 yrs.) d. on 66-Dec-18 [66-Dec-19: 2B, 4E; 66-Dec-20: 2B].
Owings, Virginia (58 yrs.) d. on 68-Jul-24 Drowned [68-Jul-28: 1B].
Owings, Virginia F. m. Bennett, Samuel H. on 66-Jan-28 [66-Feb-19: 2B].
Owings, William G. m. Ward, Miranda on 66-Sep-13 [66-Sep-15: 2B].
Owins, Mary Idora (2 yrs., 11 mos.) d. on 66-May-5 [66-May-7: 2B].
Pabst, Mary Magdelena (2 yrs., 2 mos.) d. on 66-Mar-18 [66-Mar-19: 2C; 66-Mar-20: 2C].
Pabst, Victor (11 yrs.) d. on 69-May-31 Drowned [69-Jun-5: 1G].
Paca, Eliza E. m. Jones, William M. on 67-Sep-1 [67-Sep-9: 2B].
Pacetti, Thomas A. m. Richardson, Emma S. on 68-May-12 [68-May-16: 2A].
Paddington, Carrie m. Startzman, J. H. on 69-Oct-14 [69-Oct-16: 2B; 69-Oct-18: 2C].
Paddington, Edward (19 yrs.) d. on 70-Nov-6 [70-Nov-8: 2B].
Paddington, Maggie m. Aler, Reuben J. on 66-Apr-12 [66-May-25: 2C].
Paddon, Sarah C. m. Wilkins, James D. on 66-Oct-25 [66-Oct-29: 2B].
Paddy, Thomas E. m. Lyles, Margaret on 69-Jan-7 [69-Jan-9: 2B].
Padgett, Esther (38 yrs.) d. on 67-Jan-19 [66-Jan-21: 2C].
Page, Addie S. m. Snethen, Worthington N. on 67-Jul-17 [67-Aug-1: 2C].
Page, Albert (49 yrs.) d. on 70-May-3 [70-May-4: 2C].
Page, Anne d. on 70-Feb-7 [70-Feb-12: 2C].
Page, Charles I. m. Langford, Mary E. on 67-Dec-25 [67-Dec-28: 2C].
Page, William m. Bausman, Kate on 70-Jul-5 [70-Jul-7: 2B].
Pagels, Edward m. Anderson, E. on 66-Nov-12 [66-Nov-15: 2C].
Pagels, George H. Z. m. Anderson, Catherine on 69-Sep-22 [69-Sep-24: 2B].
Pagels, Sallie E. m. Cheesebrough, R. C. on 66-Jun-21 [66-Jun-25: 2B].
Pagon, William H. m. Pattison, Carrie H. on 70-Dec-8 [70-Dec-13: 2C].
Paine, Caroline R. (5 yrs., 10 mos.) d. on 66-Jun-21 [66-Jun-22: 2B].
Paine, Charles T. (42 yrs.) d. on 67-Aug-12 [67-Aug-14: 2B].
Paine, Eugene J. R. (2 yrs., 3 mos.) d. on 69-May-30 [69-Mar-31: 2C; 69-Apr-1: 2C].
Paine, Ida Belle (1 yr.) d. on 66-Aug-19 [66-Aug-21: 2C].
Paine, Joseph H. m. Stevenson, Mary A. on 70-Nov-23 [70-Nov-24: 2B; 70-Nov-25: 2D].
Paine, Juliet A. m. Glocker, A. Campbell on 70-Dec-20 [70-Dec-22: 2B].
Paine, Martha J. m. Brown, M. Harold on 68-Oct-7 [68-Oct-10: 2B].
Paine, Mary G. m. Krebs, George W. C. on 70-Sep-27 [70-Sep-30: 2B].

Paine, Sallie J. m. Gault, William A. on 70-Nov-15 [70-Nov-16: 2C].
Painter, Edith Eyre (7 mos.) d. on 68-Jul-9 [68-Jul-11: 2B].
Painter, Joel F. m. Duff, Fannie H. on 67-May-30 [67-Jun-21: 2B].
Painter, Virginia E. (50 yrs.) d. on 67-May-5 [67-May-7: 2B].
Palagano, Camillo Charles (4 yrs., 5 mos.) d. on 69-Feb-19 [69-Feb-22: 2C].
Palmenton, J. R. (65 yrs.) d. on 68-Jul-16 of Heatstroke [68-Jul-17: 1D].
Palmer, A. W. m. Mowbray, Mary A. on 67-Nov-26 [67-Dec-5: 2C].
Palmer, Anna Elizabeth (7 mos.) d. on 67-Jul-5 [67-Jul-6: 2B].
Palmer, Florence E. M. m. Jayne, B. G. on 66-Oct-23 [66-Dec-28: 2C].
Palmer, Ichobad Bartlett (43 yrs.) d. on 67-Aug-10 [67-Aug-12: 2C].
Palmer, John M. m. Ford, Annie L. on 68-Oct-15 [68-Oct-16: 2B].
Palmer, John W. d. on 70-Oct-29 [70-Nov-7: 2B].
Palmer, Margaret A. (35 yrs.) d. on 66-Jan-21 [66-Jan-23: 2C].
Palmer, Rebecca N. (63 yrs.) d. on 67-Aug-6 [67-Aug-9: 2C].
Palmer, Sallie M. m. May, Joseph T. on 68-Jan-5 [68-Jan-14: 2C].
Palmer, Thomas J. (48 yrs.) d. on 68-Jun-19 [68-Jun-20: 2B].
Palmer, Walter M. H. m. Coe, Belle E. on 69-Sep-9 [69-Sep-10: 2B].
Palmer, William C. m. Fooks, Henrietta E. on 68-Dec-15 [68-Dec-24: 2C].
Pancoast, Arthur D. m. Wingate, Sarah J. on 70-Jun-2 [70-Jun-4: 2B].
Pancoast, John Howard d. on 69-Nov-26 [69-Nov-27: 2C].
Pancoast, Rachel d. on 70-Feb-10 of Consumption [70-Feb-12: 2C].
Pannill, William d. on 70-Nov-16 [70-Nov-17: 4D].
Pape, Bertha m. Prior, Edward A. on 68-Apr-4 [68-Apr-7: 2B].
Pardoe, Archibald Reid (6 mos.) d. on 68-Sep-24 [68-Sep-26: 2B].
Pardoe, Ginnie (9 mos.) d. on 66-Aug-10 [66-Aug-13: 2C].
Parish, Emma R. (22 yrs.) d. on 70-Jun-4 [70-Jun-7: 2C].
Parish, Lou Ella (6 mos.) d. on 67-Jul-10 [67-Jul-11: 2C].
Parish, Milton Taylor (10 mos.) d. [70-Mar-10: 2C].
Parish, Sarah E. m. Kelly, James on 70-Mar-21 [70-Apr-7: 2B].
Parke, George M. m. Neal, Mary W. on 70-Jan-25 [70-Jan-27: 2C].
Parke, M. Letitia m. Hurley, S. Mortimer [68-Jul-8: 2B].
Parker, Akfred d. on 67-Apr-23 of Fall [67-Apr-24: 1F].
Parker, Annie P. m. McPherson, John W. on 70-May-12 [70-May-14: 2A].
Parker, Betty Merryman (5 mos.) d. on 66-Aug-9 [66-Aug-10: 2C].
Parker, Cecilia V. m. Schultz, Frederick W. on 68-Nov-11 [68-Nov-13: 2C].
Parker, Charles R. m. Creighton, Dora on 68-Sep-14 [68-Sep-18: 2B].
Parker, Daniel M. m. Smith, H. J. on 67-Nov-28 [67-Nov-30: 2C].
Parker, Edwin L. (58 yrs.) d. on 68-Sep-5 [68-Sep-7: 1G, 2A].
Parker, Elias (27 yrs.) d. on 66-Feb-4 [66-Feb-5: 2C].
Parker, Elizabeth m. Legg, Joseph on 68-Oct-29 [68-Oct-31: 2B].
Parker, Ellen E. d. on 69-Mar-5 [69-Mar-8: 2C].
Parker, Emily Mason (4 mos.) d. on 66-Jul-24 [66-Aug-1: 2C].
Parker, James d. on 70-Feb-8 [70-Feb-9: 2C].
Parker, James H. m. Gillet, Annie S. on 69-Oct-28 [69-Oct-30: 2B].
Parker, Julia d. on 69-Oct-17 of Paralysis [69-Oct-19: 1H].
Parker, Julia A. m. Polk, Josiah B. on 68-Sep-28 [68-Sep-29: 2B].
Parker, Laura A. m. Whippey, C. F. on 67-Nov-27 [67-Dec-2: 2C].
Parker, Lilly Irena (1 yr., 5 mos.) d. on 69-Jul-27 [69-Aug-24: 2C].
Parker, Llewellyn L. m. Ehlen, Annie M. on 68-Apr-14 [68-Apr-17: 2B].
Parker, Mary m. McComas, H. Clay on 70-Dec-1 [70-Dec-5: 2C].
Parker, Mary E. (18 yrs.) d. on 68-Aug-22 [68-Aug-25: 2B].
Parker, Mary E. (57 yrs.) d. on 68-Nov-11 [68-Nov-12: 2C].
Parker, Sue A. m. Henning, George C. on 68-Oct-16 [68-Oct-27: 2B].
Parker, Virginia m. Leonard, John T. on 69-May-25 [69-May-27: 2C].
Parker, William (43 yrs.) d. on 68-Mar-25 [68-Mar-27: 2C].

Parker, William H. m. Phillips, Emily L. on 68-Nov-5 [68-Nov-7: 2B].
Parker, William H. m. Clemm, Margaret on 66-May-14 [66-May-15: 2C].
Parker, William R. m. Bosley, Mary Virginia on 66-Sep-29 [66-Oct-2: 2B].
Parkerson, Christopher, Rev. (70 yrs.) d. on 67-Apr-30 [67-May-2: 1G, 2B].
Parkhill, Charles m. McAllister, Adelaide Emma on 70-Jul-14 [70-Jul-22: 2C].
Parkhill, John H. d. on 69-May-3 [69-May-4: 2B].
Parkhurst, George Cushins (1 yr.) d. on 66-Jul-29 [66-Jul-30: 2C].
Parkins, Alfred, Jr. m. Walter, Maggie on 67-Jan-2 [67-Jan-31: 2B].
Parkinson, James R. (70 yrs.) d. on 66-Jul-5 [66-Jul-6: 2B; 66-Jul-7: 2B].
Parks, Charles A. m. Patterson, Annie E. on 67-Apr-30 [67-Sep-4: 2B].
Parks, Edwin D. m. Kelley, Mary E. on 68-Feb-6 [68-Feb-12: 2B].
Parks, Ellen Mariah (30 yrs.) d. on 66-Apr-21 [66-Apr-23: 2B].
Parks, Emma V. m. Lingenfelder, Henry on 69-Oct-28 [69-Nov-2: 2B].
Parks, Emmeline (42 yrs.) d. on 67-Sep-25 Murdered (Stabbing) [67-Sep-26: 1E].
Parks, Fannie m. Parsons, George W. on 70-Jul-25 [70-Aug-5: 2C].
Parks, James Franklin (4 yrs.) d. on 67-May-11 [67-May-17: 2B].
Parks, James Harry d. on 66-Jul-1 [66-Jul-6: 2B].
Parks, Joseph B. (46 yrs., 2 mos.) d. on 70-Jul-2 [70-Jul-4: 2C].
Parks, Joshua (80 yrs.) d. on 70-Jan-28 [70-Feb-10: 2C].
Parks, Julia A. m. Parks, Levin D. on 69-Apr-14 [69-Apr-16: 2B].
Parks, Leanora B. m. Lansdowne, G. E. S. on 66-Dec-5 [66-Dec-8: 2B].
Parks, Levin D. m. Parks, Julia A. on 69-Apr-14 [69-Apr-16: 2B].
Parks, Levin T. B. (28 yrs.) d. on 69-Oct-14 [69-Oct-16: 2B].
Parks, Mary Ellen (18 yrs.) d. on 66-Sep-11 [66-Sep-18: 2B].
Parks, Robert Franklin (30 yrs.) d. on 66-Aug-3 [66-Aug-6: 2C].
Parks, Samuel Henry (4 mos.) d. on 68-Feb-20 [68-Feb-22: 2B].
Parks, Sarah A. (65 yrs.) d. on 70-May-19 [70-May-21: 2B].
Parlet, Zachariah m. Kenny, A. on 66-Apr-15 [66-Apr-20: 2B].
Parlett, Achsah S. m. Parlett, William D. on 66-Apr-3 [66-Apr-5: 2B].
Parlett, Emma J. (24 yrs.) d. on 67-May-29 [67-May-31: 2B].
Parlett, Emma Virginia m. Smith, Henry Peters on 67-Sep-19 [67-Sep-23: 2A].
Parlett, Harry m. Holmes, Janey on 69-Apr-15 [69-Apr-20: 2B].
Parlett, Harry L. m. Crist, Laura V. on 68-Mar-5 [68-Mar-19: 2B].
Parlett, Hezekiah m. Talbott, Mary Jane on 65-Dec-25 [66-Jan-1: 2C].
Parlett, Lizzie V. m. Warren, William B. on 68-Sep-10 [68-Oct-24: 2B].
Parlett, Matilda R. d. on 66-Nov-10 [66-Nov-12: 2C].
Parlett, Matilda Rebecca m. McCauley, Joseph O. on 66-Mar-8 [66-Mar-12: 2B].
Parlett, Molly May (1 yr., 8 mos.) d. on 66-Jan-5 [66-Jan-6: 2B].
Parlett, Moses Lee (39 yrs., 11 mos.) d. on 70-Aug-12 [70-Aug-13: 2C].
Parlett, Temperance (62 yrs.) d. on 70-Apr-23 [70-Apr-25: 2B].
Parlett, Thomas E. m. Gosnell, Grace Lee on 68-Nov-17 [68-Nov-21: 2C].
Parlett, William D. m. Parlett, Achsah S. on 66-Apr-3 [66-Apr-5: 2B].
Parlett, William O. m. Slaughter, Harriet L. on 67-Jul-16 [67-Jul-18: 2C].
Parmer, Dennis m. Caldwell, Sarah C. on 67-Apr-27 [67-May-14: 2B].
Parnell, Mary A. m. Quinn, Patrick on 69-Nov-29 [69-Dec-7: 2C].
Parr, Emily W. m. Simpson, Louis, Jr. on 69-Oct-21 [69-Oct-23: 2B].
Parr, Frances C. (26 yrs.) d. on 69-Jun-16 of Consumption [69-Jun-21: 2B].
Parr, James L. (49 yrs.) d. on 68-Nov-9 [68-Nov-10: 2C].
Parr, Katie m. Brown, J. B. on 69-Apr-21 [69-Apr-27: 2B].
Parr, Mary Preston (9 mos.) d. on 68-Jul-11 [68-Jul-13: 2B].
Parramore, Thomas m. Armstrong, Nettie J. on 69-Jan-27 [69-Feb-4: 2C].
Parran, Samuel (43 yrs., 8 mos.) d. on 69-Apr-6 [69-Apr-8: 2C].
Parrish, Elizabeth d. on 68-May-17 [68-May-18: 2B].
Parrish, James H. m. Sanderson, Emily M. on 68-May-12 [68-May-15: 2B].
Parrish, Thomas (79 yrs.) d. on 68-Jun-26 [68-Jul-2: 2C].

Parrott, George W. (20 yrs.) d. on 66-Oct-22 [66-Oct-30: 4C; 66-Oct-31: 2B].
Parrott, John David d. on 67-Aug-8 [67-Aug-9: 2C].
Parrott, Rebecca J. (71 yrs.) d. on 66-May-24 [66-May-26: 2B].
Parry, Charley D. (4 yrs.) d. on 69-Dec-12 of Scarletina [69-Dec-16: 2C].
Parry, James D. (1 yr., 3 mos.) d. on 70-Apr-27 of Whooping cough [70-Apr-30: 2B].
Parry, Kate A. m. Warren, Lawrence J. on 67-Jun-6 [67-Jun-8: 2B].
Parry, Katey D. (2 yrs., 9 mos.) d. on 69-Dec-14 of Scarletina [69-Dec-16: 2C].
Parry, Marion W. m. McGinnis, Annie M. on 70-Apr-9 [70-Nov-30: 2C].
Parson, John T. m. Moreland, M. E. on 67-Sep-3 [67-Sep-4: 2B].
Parson, Lucinda C. m. Eddy, Gardner W. on 69-Mar-25 [69-Mar-29: 2B].
Parsons, D. E. m. Bryan, Emma F., Miss on 69-Sep-18 [69-Sep-20: 2C].
Parsons, Ezeliea Medora (10 mos.) d. on 70-Feb-15 [70-Feb-17: 2C].
Parsons, George W. m. Parks, Fannie on 70-Jul-25 [70-Aug-5: 2C].
Parsons, Lizzie Blanche (1 yr., 11 mos.) d. on 68-Jan-10 [68-Jan-11: 2B].
Parsons, Lorenzo (48 yrs.) d. on 67-Mar-5 [67-Mar-6: 2C].
Parsons, M. E. m. Fooks, J. J. on 70-Sep-26 [70-Oct-22: 2B].
Parsons, Mary Ann (51 yrs.) d. on 70-Nov-28 [70-Nov-29: 2C].
Parsons, Mary Elizabeth (56 yrs.) d. on 69-Jul-8 [69-Jul-30: 2C].
Parsons, Rufus M. m. Patrick, Laura E. on 68-Nov-18 [68-Dec-22: 2C].
Parsons, William Augustus (3 mos.) d. on 70-Nov-30 [70-Dec-1: 2C].
Partridge, Fanny d. on 70-Jan-8 of Typhoid [70-Jan-24: 2C, 4G].
Partridge, John L. (38 yrs.) d. on 68-Oct-13 [68-Oct-16: 2B].
Partridge, L. W. m. Duncan, Cassandra on 70-Jan-6 [70-Jan-10: 2C].
Partridge, Marie A. (35 yrs.) d. on 70-Apr-26 [70-Apr-27: 2B].
Partridge, Rossberry (28 yrs.) d. on 69-Nov-25 [69-Nov-29: 2C].
Partridge, William d. on 68-Jul-24 Drowned [68-Jul-28: 1B].
Partridge, William, Jr. (40 yrs.) d. on 70-Mar-24 [70-Apr-27: 2B].
Parvis, John H. m. Hart, Henrietta V. on 70-Mar-16 [70-Mar-21: 2C].
Pascal, Elizabeth (83 yrs.) d. on 70-Jun-19 [70-Jun-20: 2B].
Pascal, John N. d. on 70-Oct-7 [70-Oct-8: 2B].
Pascault, Emily d. on 68-Oct-4 [68-Oct-6: 2B].
Pascault, Emily M. m. Burns, George W. on 68-Oct-27 [68-Oct-29: 2B].
Passano, J. Ferdinand m. Baldwin, Nannie R. on 70-Apr-21 [70-Apr-22: 2C].
Passano, Joseph, Jr. (44 yrs.) d. on 69-Sep-15 [69-Sep-16: 2B].
Passano, Louis (52 yrs.) d. on 70-Apr-26 of Liver disease [70-Apr-27: 1H, 2B].
Passano, Maria Merrill (1 mo.) d. on 69-Feb-8 [69-Feb-11: 2C].
Passano, Parthenia m. Baker, William, Jr. on 68-Jan-28 [68-Oct-28: 2C].
Passano, Rosa m. Bigham, John L. on 70-Nov-15 [70-Nov-16: 2C].
Passeay, James Albert (32 yrs.) d. on 66-Nov-30 of Typhus [66-Dec-1: 2B; 66-Dec-3: 1G].
Pasterfield, George G. (24 yrs.) d. on 66-Apr-19 [66-Apr-20: 2B].
Pasterfield, Margaret (48 yrs.) d. on 67-Feb-8 [67-Feb-9: 2B].
Pasters, Alice m. LePrew, Augustus on 67-Mar-13 [67-Jun-11: 2B].
Pasters, Elizabeth m. Stevens, William H. on 67-Aug-15 [67-Aug-20: 2B].
Pasters, John James (2 yrs., 4 mos.) d. on 68-Jul-20 [68-Jul-21: 2C].
Patrick, Elizabeth (53 yrs.) d. on 68-Nov-10 [68-Nov-11: 2C].
Patrick, John Henry d. on 66-Mar-1 Drowned [66-Mar-21: 2C].
Patrick, Laura E. m. Parsons, Rufus M. on 68-Nov-18 [68-Dec-22: 2C].
Patrick, Maria (63 yrs.) d. on 67-Jun-20 [67-Jun-21: 2B; 67-Jun-24: 1G; 67-Jun-25: 2B].
Patten, Benjamin R. m. Porter, Frances A. on 68-Aug-12 [68-Aug-27: 2B].
Patten, Gertrude Harrison (10 mos.) d. on 69-Jun-12 [69-Jun-14: 2C].
Patterson, Abraham d. on 67-Jun-18 of Fall from window [67-Jun-19: 1F].
Patterson, Agnes m. Spencer, A. D. R. on 69-Jun-10 [69-Jun-29: 2C].
Patterson, Annie E. m. Parks, Charles A. on 67-Apr-30 [67-Sep-4: 2B].
Patterson, Anny (2 yrs., 4 mos.) d. on 69-Sep-23 [69-Sep-24: 2B].
Patterson, Corrie d. on 68-Aug-28 [68-Aug-29: 2B].

Patterson, Daniel (54 yrs.) d. on 70-May-25 [70-May-26: 2C].
Patterson, Eliza A. m. McElroy, Daniel on 68-Nov-3 [68-Nov-12: 2C].
Patterson, Elizabeth (63 yrs.) d. on 70-Apr-19 [70-Apr-21: 2C].
Patterson, Emeline (41 yrs.) d. [67-Dec-3: 2C].
Patterson, Emily J. m. Craig, John L. M. on 67-May-22 [67-Jun-3: 2B].
Patterson, Emma V. m. Collins, T. J. on 68-Dec-29 [69-Jan-9: 2C].
Patterson, Fannie B. m. Airey, George G. on 70-Jun-21 [70-Jun-24: 2C].
Patterson, Fitzhugh Coyle (9 yrs., 1 mo.) d. on 70-Mar-17 [70-Mar-21: 2C; 70-Mar-22: 2C].
Patterson, Frederick E. m. Powell, Lillie on 70-Dec-7 [70-Dec-13: 2C].
Patterson, George (74 yrs.) d. on 69-Nov-19 [69-Nov-22: 2C, 4B].
Patterson, George C. m. Huggins, Sarah E. on 67-Aug-7 [67-Aug-12: 2C].
Patterson, Hannah (83 yrs.) d. on 66-Mar-9 [66-Mar-10: 2B].
Patterson, Harriet E. (72 yrs.) d. on 69-Feb-13 [69-Feb-18: 2C].
Patterson, Helen Bredemeyer (5 mos.) d. on 68-Aug-9 [68-Aug-11: 2B].
Patterson, J. J. d. on 69-Aug-19 Drowned [69-Aug-20: 1G; 69-Aug-21: 4E].
Patterson, Jennie M. m. Suter, William H. on 68-Mar-25 [68-Dec-28: 2B].
Patterson, John H. m. Cook, Anna G on 67-Aug-27 [67-Aug-30: 2B].
Patterson, John T. (17 yrs.) d. of Yellow fever [68-Mar-14: 2B].
Patterson, Joseph B. m. Walker, Florence K on 66-Jun-5 [67-Feb-9: 2B].
Patterson, Joseph W. (80 yrs.) d. on 66-Oct-13 [66-Oct-15: 2B, 4C].
Patterson, Mary (74 yrs.) d. on 70-Nov-9 [70-Nov-10: 2C].
Patterson, Mary A. (60 yrs.) d. on 68-Feb-14 [68-Feb-19: 2C].
Patterson, Mary A. (42 yrs.) d. on 69-Feb-20 [69-Feb-23: 2D].
Patterson, Mary A. (50 yrs.) d. on 69-Apr-19 [69-Apr-20: 2B].
Patterson, Mary B. (85 yrs.) d. on 68-Dec-27 [68-Dec-31: 2C].
Patterson, Mary Emma d. on 70-Jun-18 of Consumption [70-Jun-20: 2B].
Patterson, Mary Isabel m. Hancock, Francis M. on 70-May-23 [70-Jun-6: 2B].
Patterson, Mary Jane d. on 69-Aug-31 [69-Sep-1: 2B; 69-Sep-2: 2B].
Patterson, Mary R. (38 yrs.) d. on 68-Jun-27 [68-Jun-29: 2B].
Patterson, Mary R. (21 yrs.) d. on 67-Mar-30 of Suicide (Poisoning) [67-Apr-1: 2C; 67-Apr-2: 4D].
Patterson, Mary V. (2 yrs., 6 mos.) d. on 70-Nov-13 [70-Nov-14: 2B].
Patterson, Michael (58 yrs.) d. on 67-Apr-13 [67-Apr-15: 2B].
Patterson, Oliver C. m. Shipley, M. E. on 68-Apr-9 [68-May-1: 2B].
Patterson, Robert (36 yrs.) d. on 66-Jun-14 [66-Jun-18: 2B].
Patterson, Sarah E. (85 yrs.) d. on 69-Oct-29 [69-Nov-4: 2C].
Patterson, Sarah Rebecca (3 yrs., 7 mos.) d. on 70-Dec-22 [70-Dec-23: 2B].
Patterson, William (80 yrs.) d. on 66-Jul-10 [66-Jul-13: 1G].
Patterson, William L. m. Miller, Fannie on 66-Apr-17 [66-May-4: 2C].
Pattison, Carrie H. m. Pagon, William H. on 70-Dec-8 [70-Dec-13: 2C].
Pattison, Martin L. m. Chambers, M. Fannie on 66-Jan-23 [66-Jan-30: 2B].
Pattison, Mary Sherwood (39 yrs.) d. on 68-Jul-23 [68-Sep-24: 2B].
Pattison, R. E. m. Masterman, Mary E. on 68-Jan-30 [68-Feb-3: 2C].
Pattison, Susan H. (26 yrs.) d. on 66-Jun-1 [66-Jun-2: 2B].
Patton, David H. m. Roe, Emily on 66-Jun-26 [66-Jun-29: 2C].
Paublitz, Sarah J. m. Lewis, John William on 67-Apr-14 [67-Apr-20: 2A].
Paul, Amelia A. m. Schnibe, George C. on 70-Jan-19 [70-Jan-22: 2B].
Paul, Anna M. m. Foxwell, Benjamin on 67-Oct-8 [67-Oct-9: 2B].
Paul, Augustus (8 yrs.) d. on 66-Jan-27 of Gunshot wound [66-Jan-29: 1F].
Paul, Elizabeth m. Caples, Frederick on 70-Feb-17 [70-Feb-22: 2C].
Paul, Gwinnett J. (3 yrs., 10 mos.) d. on 66-Feb-23 [66-Feb-24: 2B].
Paul, Henry Key (17 yrs., 2 mos.) d. on 67-May-19 Drowned [67-May-21: 2B].
Paul, Mary E. m. Osbourn, James G., Jr. on 68-Jan-14 [68-Jan-16: 2C].
Paul, Samuel B. m. Downey, Catherine on 70-Jun-15 [70-Jun-17: 2B].
Paul, Sarah A. m. McCann, James on 69-Apr-6 [69-Apr-7: 2C].

Paulin, John E. m. Reed, Augusta A. on 67-Jun-4 [67-Jun-11: 2B].
Paulus, George (59 yrs.) d. on 65-Nov-28 [66-Jan-17: 2C].
Pawley, Ruth A. (53 yrs.) d. on 66-Aug-29 [66-Aug-31: 2B].
Pawley, Sarah A. (61 yrs.) d. on 69-Nov-1 [69-Nov-2: 2B; 69-Nov-3: 2C].
Pawley, William R. (10 mos.) d. on 67-Aug-15 [67-Aug-20: 2B].
Pawson, Sarah U. d. on 67-Oct-30 [67-Nov-1: 2B].
Paxton, Jane M. (74 yrs.) d. on 70-Apr-29 [70-Apr-30: 2B].
Paxton, Mattie B. m. Pollard, Walter F. on 66-Apr-17 [66-Apr-27: 2C].
Payant, Edward m. Phillips, Albina C. on 66-Oct-16 [66-Oct-22: 2C].
Payant, Mollie E. C. (10 mos.) d. on 70-Jan-8 [70-Jan-10: 2C].
Payne, Benjamin E. (73 yrs.) d. on 70-Jul-29 [70-Aug-3: 2C].
Payne, Benjamin N. (63 yrs., 2 mos.) d. on 70-Feb-26 [70-Feb-28: 1G, 2C].
Payne, George C. (4 mos.) d. on 66-Jul-17 [66-Jul-18: 2C].
Payne, George C. m. Ridgaway, Emma A. on 68-Nov-17 [68-Nov-21: 2C].
Payne, J. Thomas m. Ross, Emma on 68-Apr-23 [68-Apr-27: 2B].
Payne, Julia H. m. Thornley, John on 66-Sep-25 [66-Oct-5: 2B].
Payne, Laura P. (21 yrs., 2 mos.) d. on 66-May-29 [66-May-30: 2C].
Payne, Lizzie R. m. Onion, Howard on 68-Jun-15 [68-Jun-19: 2B].
Payne, Maria m. Collins, Spindelow on 70-Jun-9 [70-Jun-23: 2C].
Payne, Richard m. Douley, Alice A. on 67-May-14 [67-May-15: 2B].
Paynter, John C. m. League, Georgette on 67-Jun-13 [67-Jun-14: 2B].
Paynter, Mary J. m. Jones, John M. on 66-Aug-6 [66-Aug-15: 2B].
Peabody, George d. on 69-Nov-4 [69-Nov-8: 1F; 69-Nov-9: 1G].
Peabody, Jose K. m. Dulany, Julia L. on 70-Dec-3 [70-Dec-7: 2C].
Peace, Charles F. m. Mills, Almira Phelps on 70-Nov-2 [70-Nov-3: 2B].
Peace, George (51 yrs.) d. on 70-Aug-30 [70-Sep-3: 2B].
Peacock, George N. (5 yrs., 9 mos.) d. on 70-Nov-9 of Consumption [70-Nov-10: 2C].
Peacock, Ingram E. (79 yrs.) d. on 66-Dec-27 [66-Dec-28: 2C].
Peacock, Richard (68 yrs., 7 mos.) d. on 66-Sep-1 of Apoplexy [66-Sep-3: 2C].
Peacock, Samuel, Sr. (74 yrs.) d. on 66-Mar-23 [66-Mar-24: 1G, 2B].
Peake, Hattie Baylor (10 mos.) d. on 66-Jul-24 [66-Aug-9: 2C].
Peake, Sallie E. m. Chew, N. S. on 67-Feb-7 [67-Feb-13: 2D].
Peake, William m. Smith, Mollie on 68-Aug-25 [68-Aug-28: 2B].
Pearce, Emily C. (11 yrs.) d. on 70-Feb-1 [70-Feb-3: 2B].
Pearce, Franklin F. m. White, Mary F. on 66-Jul-15 [66-Jul-17: 2C].
Pearce, John E. m. Gaunt, Kate T. on 70-Apr-26 [70-May-10: 2B].
Pearce, Joseph (67 yrs.) d. on 68-Feb-4 [68-Feb-7: 2C].
Pearce, Kate Russell m. Prentiss, John H. on 66-Oct-2 [66-Oct-3: 2B].
Pearce, Lizzie Wells (1 yr., 11 mos.) d. on 69-Dec-28 [69-Dec-29: 2D].
Pearce, Sallie A. m. Hunt, W. Hopkins on 66-Oct-23 [66-Oct-25: 2C].
Pearce, Sarah Ann (74 yrs., 9 mos.) d. on 66-Jul-19 [66-Jul-20: 2D].
Pearce, Sarah E. m. Kelley, John A. on 69-May-6 [69-May-11: 2B; 69-May-12: 2B].
Pearman, Sarah Jane m. Chiveral, William D. on 69-Aug-12 [69-Aug-19: 2C].
Pearsall, John m. Woodward, Susannah on 66-Jun-3 [67-May-31: 2B].
Pearse, Charles C. m. Gardner, Elizabeth on 66-Jun-5 [66-Jun-22: 2B].
Pearson, Andrew C. m. Soper, Hester on 67-May-3 [67-May-7: 2B].
Pearson, Annie E. m. Annabel, Thurman C. on 68-May-26 [68-May-30: 2A].
Pearson, Elizabeth J. m. Jones, William C. on 67-Feb-18 [67-Jun-17: 2B].
Pearson, Henrietta J. m. Lewis, George C. on 66-Oct-30 [67-May-11: 2B].
Pearson, James F. m. Farrow, Eugenia on 66-Oct-25 [66-Oct-26: 2B].
Pearson, James Solomon (12 yrs., 10 mos.) d. on 68-May-23 [68-May-26: 2B].
Pearson, M. Caddie m. Bash, A. McCoomb on 67-Nov-5 [67-Nov-9: 2B].
Pearson, Margaret J. m. Hewitt, John on 66-Oct-25 [66-Oct-30: 2B].
Pearson, Marian m. Malcolm, Harry on 68-Apr-2 [68-Apr-7: 2B].
Pearson, Robert Fergusson (21 yrs.) d. on 66-Oct-21 [66-Oct-31: 2B].

Pearson, Summerfield m. Bangs, Olivia on 70-Nov-8 [70-Nov-10: 2C].
Pease, Anne m. Lane, Christopher on 68-Mar-4 [68-Mar-30: 2B].
Pease, Francis N. m. Rodenmyer, Elizabeth on 69-Dec-23 [70-Mar-14: 2C].
Pease, Isabelle m. Shipley, James W. on 68-Feb-20 [68-Mar-30: 2B].
Peasley, James (25 yrs.) d. on 70-Jun-21 of Typhus [70-Jun-22: 2C].
Peaster, Henry m. Hobbs, Annie C. [66-Sep-21: 2B].
Peck, Caroline (37 yrs.) d. on 70-Aug-9 [70-Aug-10: 2C].
Peck, Harriet (71 yrs.) d. on 70-Jun-19 [70-Jun-20: 2B].
Peck, James (74 yrs.) d. on 70-Jul-24 [70-Jul-26: 2C].
Peck, Stephen (63 yrs.) d. on 66-Feb-26 [66-Feb-28: 2C; 66-Mar-1: 1F].
Pecor, Charlotte (76 yrs.) d. on 67-Apr-25 [67-Apr-26: 2B].
Peddicord, Amelia m. Disney, Samuel on 69-Mar-4 [69-Mar-8: 2C].
Peddicord, Charles A. L. m. Ruff, Christiana on 70-Nov-15 [70-Nov-29: 2C].
Peddicord, Emma J. m. Milburn, Alfred H. on 69-Jun-27 [69-Jul-12: 2C].
Peddicord, Evan m. Choate, Mary J. on 67-Jan-1 [67-Jan-12: 2C].
Peddicord, Issac H. m. Chipmane, Mary A. on 66-Jun-5 [66-Jun-6: 2B].
Peddicord, Sallie E. m. Sauter, William on 66-May-8 [66-May-16: 2C].
Peddicord, Van Dorn (8 mos.) d. on 67-Mar-9 [67-Mar-16: 2B].
Pedrick, Ann Orelia (9 mos.) d. on 69-Jun-3 [69-Jun-5: 2B].
Pedrick, Charles (24 yrs.) d. on 68-Nov-22 in Railroad accident [68-Nov-23: 1H; 68-Nov-24: 2C; 68-Nov-25: 1H].
Pedrick, E. Franklin m. Spedden, Martha V. on 68-Sep-23 [68-Oct-3: 2B].
Pedrick, George G. m. Head, Maggie on 67-Dec-26 [68-Jan-2: 2C; 68-Jan-3: 2C].
Pedrick, Joshua V. (59 yrs.) d. on 68-Feb-22 [68-Feb-25: 2C].
Peduzzi, Amelia m. Barnes, James Henry on 67-Oct-26 [67-Nov-11: 2C].
Peduzzi, Mary R. m. Grothaus, David on 69-Sep-21 [69-Sep-24: 2B].
Peduzzi, Sarah F. m. Bevans, James L. on 70-Nov-3 [70-Nov-10: 2C].
Peet, Susan d. on 69-May-26 [69-May-27: 2C].
Peinart, Charles d. on 66-Jul-18 of Heatstroke [66-Jul-20: 1F].
Peirson, Emil Carter (7 mos.) d. on 69-Jun-22 [69-Jun-24: 2C].
Peirson, Thomas G. m. Russell, Mary E. on 70-Oct-6 [70-Oct-13: 2C].
Pels, Lizzie m. Bamberger, Moses on 69-Feb-7 [69-Feb-9: 2C].
Pembrook, Josie M. C. (21 yrs.) d. on 69-Jan-30 [69-Feb-17: 2D].
Pendergast, Bedelia m. Burke, William P. on 69-Jun-9 [69-Jun-16: 2C].
Pendergast, Charles, Capt. (76 yrs.) d. on 67-Oct-7 of Pneumonia [67-Oct-8: 2B; 67-Oct-9: 1F, 2B].
Pendergast, Jerome A. m. Coleman, Ella M. on 66-Oct-2 [66-Oct-3: 2B].
Pendergast, John (36 yrs.) d. on 66-May-31 [66-Jun-1: 2B].
Pendergast, Mary E. d. on 67-Apr-9 [67-Apr-10: 2B].
Pendergast, Mary R. m. Caughy, Michael P. on 67-Apr-25 [67-Apr-29: 2B; 67-Apr-30: 2B].
Pendergast, William (80 yrs.) d. on 67-Sep-11 [67-Sep-12: 2B].
Penders, John d. on 69-May-3 Drowned [69-May-7: 1G].
Pendexter, Henry d. on 69-Aug-11 [69-Aug-12: 2C].
Pendexter, William d. on 70-Jul-19 of Heatstroke [70-Jul-20: 4C].
Pendleton, Edmund m. Kennedy, Virginia on 69-Jun-23 [69-Jun-29: 2C].
Pendleton, Edmund m. Yost, Virginia on 69-Jun-23 [69-Jun-28: 2C].
Pendleton, John B. m. Bowie, Ella J. on 70-Apr-13 [70-Apr-16: 2B].
Penington, Ann Ellis (43 yrs.) d. on 67-Oct-1 of Consumption [67-Oct-3: 2B].
Penington, Ingram E. (16 yrs., 6 mos.) d. on 68-Nov-25 [68-Nov-28: 2C].
Penington, William Cooper m. Woodall, Rebecca on 67-Dec-4 [67-Dec-5: 2C].
Penn, Charlotte A (38 yrs.) d. on 67-May-28 [67-May-30: 2B].
Penn, Jacob, Jr. d. on 68-Feb-27 [68-Feb-29: 2B].
Penn, Josie Pettit (2 yrs., 1 mo.) d. on 67-Apr-15 [67-Apr-16: 2B].
Penn, Matthew J. A. m. Shipley, Margaret Ann on 67-Sep-16 [67-Sep-21: 2A].
Penn, Nancy A. m. Gadd, Luther M. on 67-Oct-17 [67-Nov-4: 2B].

Penn, Richard m. Musgrove, Margaret Y. on 69-May-2 [69-May-6: 2B].
Penn, Sophia (48 yrs.) d. on 67-Jun-19 of Consumption [67-Jun-20: 2B].
Penn, Thomas P. m. Sheid, Hattie A. on 70-Aug-29 [70-Sep-8: 2B].
Penn, Willie S. (3 yrs., 8 mos.) d. on 70-Jun-24 [70-Jun-25: 2B].
Pennington, Daniel H. m. Taylor, Adaline on 66-Jun-7 [66-Jun-9: 2B].
Pennington, E. Burke m. Tucker, Mary A. on 70-Dec-8 [70-Dec-10: 2B].
Pennington, Lizzie A. m. McCaddin, Richard on 60-Sep-10 [70-Jun-8: 2C].
Pennington, William James (49 yrs.) d. on 67-May-20 [67-May-22: 2B].
Penny, Edward G. m. Hamill, Margaret J. on 69-Jan-7 [69-Jan-8: 2C].
Penrice, Marion Louisa m. Reed, Emit W. on 69-Aug-3 [69-Aug-7: 2B].
Penrose, Lizzie d. on 66-Mar-25 of Diptheria [66-Mar-27: 2B].
Pensel, Henry J. m. Reigel, Eva on 70-Jan-18 [70-Jan-31: 2C].
Pentland, Charles Jennings (4 yrs., 8 mos.) d. on 69-Jul-16 [69-Jul-17: 2C].
Pentland, Ella Margaret (17 yrs., 2 mos.) d. on 67-Oct-10 [67-Oct-12: 2A].
Pentland, John P. A. (24 yrs.) d. on 69-Aug-8 [69-Aug-9: 2C; 69-Aug-10: 2C].
Pentz, Annie E. m. Reaney, Charles on 67-Jul-4 [67-Jul-8: 2C].
Pentz, Henry B., Jr. m. Perry, Georgie A. on 69-Feb-1 [69-Feb-19: 2C].
Pentz, Henry S. (59 yrs.) d. on 67-Apr-4 [67-Apr-5: 2B].
Pentz, Jessie May (1 yr., 5 mos.) d. on 68-Jul-22 [68-Jul-23: 2B].
Pentz, John J. m. Rose, Ella Teresa on 69-Sep-21 [69-Sep-24: 2B].
Pentz, Maggie E. (18 yrs.) d. on 69-Jan-28 [69-Jan-29: 2C].
Pentz, Maggie E. m. Bohanan, James S. on 66-Nov-1 [66-Nov-3: 2B].
Pentz, Margaret L. (46 yrs.) d. on 67-May-22 of Heart disease [67-May-24: 1F, 2B; 67-May-25: 2B].
Pentz, William F. m. Taylor, Rebecca on 70-May-26 [70-Jun-18: 2B].
Peppercorn, Francis F. m. Williams, Sarah A. on 67-Nov-1 [67-Nov-4: 2B].
Peppler, Alexander George m. Schmidt, Anna Maria on 66-Feb-20 [66-Feb-22: 2B].
Peppler, Charles m. Godman, Laura V. on 68-Dec-22 [68-Dec-30: 2C].
Peppler, Mary Lizzie (8 mos.) d. on 69-Jul-2 [69-Jul-3: 2B].
Percell, Johannah (50 yrs.) d. on 66-Mar-2 [66-Mar-5: 2B].
Percy, William R. m. Bishop, Nannie E. on 67-Apr-23 [67-May-11: 2A].
Perdue, Ella S. m. Howard, Richard M. on 66-Oct-30 [66-Nov-8: 2C].
Pere, Ann Maria m. Johnson, William S. on 67-May-9 [67-May-16: 2B].
Peregoy, Adaline S. (49 yrs.) d. on 69-Nov-2 [69-Nov-3: 2C].
Peregoy, Alice V. m. Livingston, George W. on 68-Aug-11 [68-Sep-5: 2A].
Peregoy, Catherine Elizabeth d. on 67-Mar-20 [67-Mar-25: 2C].
Peregoy, Catherine M. (64 yrs.) d. on 70-May-15 of Heart disease [70-May-16: 2B].
Peregoy, Charles F. m. Turner, Mary E. on 67-Jun-27 [67-Jun-29: 2B].
Peregoy, George W. m. Vincent, Margaret J. on 68-Mar-3 [68-Mar-24: 2B].
Peregoy, George W. m. Phelps, Laura V. on 70-Dec-7 [70-Dec-19: 2C].
Peregoy, James C. (81 yrs.) d. on 70-Dec-20 [70-Dec-21: 2C].
Peregoy, John W. H. m. Collard, Mary J. on 67-May-8 [67-May-25: 2A].
Peregoy, Joshua (45 yrs.) d. on 69-Aug-23 [69-Aug-24: 2B].
Peregoy, Lewis A. m. Baldwin, F. Annie C. on 69-Dec-20 [69-Dec-31: 2C].
Peregoy, Margaret J. McC. (32 yrs., 7 mos.) d. on 69-Jan-29 [69-Jan-30: 2C].
Peregoy, Nicholas (79 yrs.) d. on 69-Aug-4 [69-Aug-6: 2C].
Peregoy, Rose Agnes (1 yr., 2 mos.) d. on 67-Mar-15 [67-Mar-18: 2C; 67-Mar-25: 2C].
Peregoy, Ruth (94 yrs.) d. on 69-Dec-13 [69-Dec-14: 2C].
Peregoy, Sarah (83 yrs.) d. on 70-Jul-11 [70-Jul-13: 2C].
Peregoy, Sarah Elizabeth (4 mos.) d. on 67-Sep-30 [67-Oct-1: 2B].
Peregoy, Sarah Lizzie m. Tucker, Jacob R. on 66-Sep-6 [66-Sep-19: 2B].
Peregoy, William Henry (31 yrs.) d. on 66-Sep-17 Murdered (Shooting) [66-Sep-18: 2B, 4B; 66-Sep-22: 2B].
Perger, Maria (36 yrs.) d. on 70-Aug-20 [70-Aug-22: 4D].
Perine, Bessie Lee m. Cooper, Bernard G. on 67-Aug-15 [67-Aug-17: 1G, 2B].

Perine, Edward Burns (5 mos.) d. on 70-Jun-11 [70-Jun-13: 2C].
Perine, William A. d. on 70-Apr-8 of Heart disease [70-May-3: 2B].
Perkin, Frank A. m. Johnston, Willie E. on 69-Jan-19 [69-Jan-21: 2C].
Perkins, Ann J., Mrs. (55 yrs.) d. on 70-Jul-22 of Heatstroke [70-Jul-23: 4E; 70-Jul-30: 2C].
Perkins, Debbie d. on 67-Mar-18 [67-Mar-21: 2C].
Perkins, Edward (69 yrs.) d. on 68-Feb-18 of Paralysis [68-Feb-19: 2C].
Perkins, Edward K. m. Meakin, Alice A. on 67-Mar-28 [67-Mar-30: 2B].
Perkins, Emma Deett (1 yr., 5 mos.) d. on 70-Aug-20 [70-Aug-22: 2C].
Perkins, Francis (21 yrs.) d. on 69-May-19 of Brain congestion [69-May-22: 2B].
Perkins, George H. T. m. Spencer, Nannie on 70-Jan-27 [70-Feb-1: 2B].
Perkins, Harriet E. d. on 68-Jul-2 [68-Jul-6: 2B].
Perkins, Henry (50 yrs.) d. on 67-Jan-3 [67-Jan-9: 2C].
Perkins, J. Weston m. Campbell, Hattie on 66-Jul-10 [66-Jul-19: 2C].
Perkins, Leonard B. (7 mos.) d. on 68-Feb-6 [68-Feb-7: 2C].
Perkins, Lucretia D. (69 yrs.) d. on 68-Mar-14 [68-Mar-16: 2B].
Perkins, Lucy (2 yrs.) d. on 70-Oct-22 [70-Oct-24: 2B].
Perkins, Lucy Madeline m. Hewes, James on 69-Oct-5 [69-Oct-18: 2C].
Perkins, Richard K. m. Pierce, Amanda on 66-Nov-8 [66-Nov-10: 2B].
Perkins, Washington Doane (26 yrs.) d. on 69-Jan-26 [69-Jan-27: 2C].
Perkins, William (30 yrs.) d. on 70-Oct-15 [70-Oct-17: 2B].
Perkinson, D. F. m. Speights, Laura V. on 69-Mar-23 [69-May-4: 2B].
Perkinson, Ida Virginia (16 yrs., 1 mo.) d. on 70-Jul-8 [70-Jul-12: 2C].
Perl, George William (2 mos.) d. on 70-Jun-27 [70-Jun-30: 2C].
Perrigo, Daniel (87 yrs.) d. on 68-Jan-14 [68-Jan-15: 2C; 68-Jan-16: 2C; 68-Jan-17: 1G, 2C].
Perrigo, Sophia L. m. Fairbank, Frank M. on 70-Oct-27 [70-Oct-29: 2B].
Perrine, Ann (79 yrs.) d. on 70-Dec-2 [70-Dec-3: 2B].
Perrine, Edward J. m. Ball, Mary F. on 66-Mar-12 [66-Mar-14: 2B].
Perrine, Richard J. m. Stansbury, S. Lizzie on 68-May-19 [68-May-20: 2A].
Perry, Alexander m. Everett, Maggie on 66-Feb-4 [66-Feb-6: 2D].
Perry, Ancell C. (9 mos.) d. on 66-Jul-15 [66-Jul-16: 2C].
Perry, Augustus (1 mo.) d. on 70-Mar-31 [70-Apr-6: 2C].
Perry, George L. m. Norris, Mary on 68-Nov-26 [68-Nov-28: 2C].
Perry, Georgie A. m. Pentz, Henry B., Jr. on 69-Feb-1 [69-Feb-19: 2C].
Perry, Israel J. m. Blackiston, Helen M. on 69-Nov-17 [69-Nov-23: 2C].
Perry, John Hicks Travers (8 yrs., 2 mos.) d. on 69-May-29 [69-Jun-3: 2B].
Perry, Maria G. (3 yrs., 4 mos.) d. on 67-Feb-3 [67-Feb-5: 2C].
Perry, Marion E. m. Tress, Washington on 70-Aug-2 [70-Aug-5: 2C].
Perry, Mary Ann (60 yrs.) d. on 69-Sep-20 [69-Sep-21: 2B].
Perry, Mary E. m. Billings, Albert Q. on 69-Mar-1 [69-Mar-2: 2C].
Perry, R. Ross m. Thaw, Mary Callie on 70-Nov-15 [70-Nov-17: 2C].
Perry, Robert Andrew (2 yrs., 9 mos.) d. on 68-Nov-28 [68-Nov-30: 2C].
Perry, Sallie E. m. Coarts, George W. on 68-Jun-12 [68-Jun-13: 2B].
Perry, Sarah E. m. White, John F. on 67-Jan-6 [67-Jan-18: 2C].
Perry, W. H. m. Geoghegan, Louisa on 66-May-10 [66-May-18: 2C].
Person, Mary (70 yrs.) d. on 68-Nov-8 [68-Nov-10: 2C].
Personette, Elizabeth C. m. Lewis, William T. on 70-Jul-7 [70-Jul-9: 2B].
Personette, George (52 yrs.) d. on 69-Jun-4 [69-Jun-12: 2B].
Pertenia, Mary Ann (26 yrs.) d. on 66-Apr-15 [66-Apr-17: 2C].
Pertner, Augustus m. Heine, Fannie E. on 68-Jun-21 [68-Jul-8: 2B].
Pescud, S. B. m. Schacht, S. on 66-Mar-9 [66-Sep-1: 2B].
Pest, Philip (33 yrs.) d. on 66-Jul-17 of Heatstroke [66-Jul-18: 1F].
Peter, Albert (4 yrs., 7 mos.) d. on 69-Mar-16 of Scarlet fever [69-Mar-18: 2C].
Peter, Catherine (34 yrs.) d. [70-Oct-8: 2B].
Peter, Charles Louis (7 yrs., 6 mos.) d. on 69-Mar-14 of Scarlet fever [69-Mar-18: 2C].
Peter, Gabriella m. Mackubin, James on 68-Nov-5 [68-Nov-9: 2B].

Peter, Jacob (1 yr., 7 mos.) d. on 69-Mar-13 of Scarlet fever [69-Mar-18: 2C].
Peterkin, George W., Jr. d. on 70-Jul-13 [70-Jul-16: 2B].
Peterman, Elizabeth (66 yrs.) d. [69-Apr-22: 1G].
Peters, Anna M. m. Ingalls, Dimond on 67-Sep-26 [67-Oct-3: 2B].
Peters, Clara J. m. Dudley, Charles G. B. on 69-Jan-12 [69-Jan-19: 2C].
Peters, Clarence m. Hack, Emma V. on 67-Jan-10 [67-Jan-30: 2C].
Peters, George Albert (41 yrs.) d. on 67-Dec-5 [67-Dec-6: 2C; 67-Dec-7: 2B].
Peters, Jesse T. (68 yrs.) d. on 67-Jul-7 [67-Jul-8: 2C].
Peters, Kate m. Trasey, Samuel S. on 70-Jan-5 [70-Jan-8: 2B].
Peters, Maria (80 yrs.) d. on 70-Jul-28 [70-Jul-29: 2C, 4E; 70-Aug-1: 2C].
Peters, Mary C. m. Ullrich, Henry C. on 67-Jun-5 [67-Jun-7: 2B].
Peters, Mary Estelle (1 yr.) d. on 68-Aug-18 [68-Aug-19: 2B].
Peters, Sally (75 yrs.) d. on 70-Jul-27 [70-Jul-29: 4E, 2C; 70-Aug-1: 2C].
Peters, Winfield m. Girvin, Mary E. on 69-Nov-10 [69-Nov-15: 2C].
Peterson, Eleanor J. (34 yrs.) d. on 66-Dec-28 [67-Jan-2: 2C].
Peterson, George P. m. Dare, Nannie on 70-Jan-13 [70-Jan-19: 2C].
Peterson, John m. Evans, Willie Ann on 70-Aug-12 [70-Aug-23: 2B].
Peterson, Joseph d. on 67-Jul-27 [67-Jul-29: 2D].
Peterson, Peter Stanislaus (34 yrs.) d. on 69-Aug-22 [69-Aug-23: 2C].
Peterson, William N. m. Fales, Laura V. on 70-Jul-31 [70-Aug-6: 2C].
Petignat, Peter m. Neuschafert, Louisa on 66-Jul-31 [66-Aug-6: 2C].
Pettebone, Evan Miller (1 yr., 10 mos.) d. on 70-Oct-20 [70-Oct-26: 2B].
Pettebone, Philip (68 yrs.) d. on 70-Sep-30 [70-Oct-4: 2B].
Pettengill, Hattie B. m. Boyce, George P. on 69-Dec-24 [70-Jan-25: 2C].
Petticord, Laura m. Buchen, George W. on 69-Nov-7 [69-Nov-15: 2C].
Petticord, Martha A. (23 yrs.) d. on 66-Nov-10 [66-Nov-12: 2C].
Petticord, Sarah Francis m. White, Joseph on 68-Feb-2 [68-Feb-4: 2C].
Pettinger, Richard V. m. Garrett, Mary E. on 69-May-11 [69-May-19: 2C].
Pettit, Alfred T., Dr. (36 yrs.) d. on 65-Mar-31 [65-Apr-7: 2B].
Pettit, Elizabeth E. d. on 69-Nov-5 of Lung inflammation [69-Nov-11: 2C].
Pettit, Ozella Lucinda m. Hodnett, John H. on 68-Oct-19 [68-Oct-22: 2C].
Pettit, Sarah Jane m. Myers, Humphrey on 69-Nov-12 [69-Nov-23: 2B].
Pettit, Sylvester m. Zimmerman, Annie on 66-Feb-8 [66-Feb-10: 2C; 66-Feb-13: 2C].
Petty, Sallie Maud m. Davis, George C. on 70-Feb-24 [70-Mar-1: 2C].
Peyser, Abraham d. on 68-Jul-24 Drowned [68-Jul-25: 1D; 68-Jul-27: 1D].
Peyser, Albert m. Shieldesheim, Johanna on 68-Feb-16 [68-Feb-18: 2C].
Pfaff, Ann Barbara (1 yr., 4 mos.) d. on 66-Feb-15 [66-Feb-16: 2B].
Pfaff, Conrad d. on 66-Jul-17 [66-Jul-18: 1F].
Pfaff, Elizabeth m. Heinecke, Thomas August on 69-Sep-19 [69-Sep-21: 2B].
Pfaff, Jacob (44 yrs.) d. on 66-Jan-9 of Battle wounds [66-Jan-11: 2B].
Pfalzgraf, Christina (66 yrs.) d. on 66-Nov-5 [66-Nov-6: 2B].
Pfeifer, John F. (35 yrs.) d. on 68-Oct-3 [68-Oct-5: 2C].
Pfeiffer, Charles A. m. Bartz, Wilhelmina on 70-May-24 [70-May-28: 2B].
Pfeiffer, Charles Frederick (5 yrs., 11 mos.) d. [69-Apr-3: 2B].
Pfeiffer, John G. (62 yrs., 10 mos.) d. on 69-Feb-5 [69-Feb-6: 2C].
Pfeil, John (66 yrs.) d. [67-Jan-8: 2B].
Pfelty, Martha (20 yrs.) d. on 69-May-7 [69-May-8: 2B].
Pfeltz, Albertina (25 yrs.) d. on 69-Oct-28 [69-Oct-30: 2B].
Pfeltz, Ann Maria (82 yrs.) d. on 70-Dec-7 [70-Dec-9: 2C].
Pfeltz, Kate m. Couchman, Edwin D. on 66-Jan-5 [66-Jan-15: 2B].
Pfeltz, Mary m. Touchton, William H. on 69-Aug-3 [69-Sep-14: 2B].
Pfenge, Henry P. (7 yrs.) d. on 67-Apr-5 Drowned [67-Aug-6: 1G].
Pfister, Margaret (89 yrs.) d. on 66-Sep-1 [66-Sep-3: 2C].
Pfister, Mary E. m. Gradwohl, F. W. on 67-Jun-26 [67-Jul-1: 2B].
Pfisterer, Mary P. m. Hartzell, John C. on 67-Sep-17 [67-Sep-27: 2B].

Pfisterer, William m. Schwartz, M. Josephine on 70-Apr-17 [70-Apr-19: 2B].
Pfisterer, William J. (2 yrs., 7 mos.) d. on 69-Dec-30 [69-Dec-31: 2C].
Pflaunlacher, Samuel m. Wornitz, Emma on 66-Feb-18 [66-Feb-20: 2B].
Phair, Mollie m. Burns, Charles S. on 68-Dec-20 [68-Dec-29: 2D].
Phalin, Frankey J. (3 yrs., 10 mos.) d. on 70-Mar-28 [70-Mar-30: 2B].
Pheabus, William B. (1 yr., 1 mo.) d. on 68-Mar-28 [68-Mar-30: 2C].
Phebus, Sarah Catherine (14 yrs., 5 mos.) d. on 66-Aug-6 [66-Aug-15: 2C].
Phebus, Temperance A. (5 yrs.) d. on 68-Nov-16 [68-Nov-19: 2C].
Pheister, Joseph d. on 68-Jul-17 of Heatstroke [68-Jul-18: 1E].
Phelan, Elizabeth (72 yrs.) d. on 68-Sep-26 [68-Sep-28: 2B].
Phelan, J. Wesley m. Baldwin, Emma M. on 68-Oct-22 [68-Nov-3: 2B].
Phelan, Jennie m. Dell, L. Gobright on 66-Jun-19 [66-Jun-12: 2B].
Phelan, Mary A. m. LeFaivre, Gustave J. on 70-Oct-20 [70-Oct-24: 2B].
Phelan, Susie A. m. Duncan, J. James on 68-Jan-2 [68-Jan-4: 2C].
Phelps, Charles E. m. Woodward, Martha E. on 68-Dec-29 [68-Dec-31: 2C].
Phelps, J. B. T. m. Hand, Mary J. on 66-May-31 [66-Jun-6: 2B].
Phelps, James G. m. Thompson, Regina M. on 67-Oct-15 [67-Oct-21: 2B].
Phelps, Jane M. (17 yrs.) d. on 68-May-26 of Consumption [68-May-28: 2B].
Phelps, Joseph T. (51 yrs., 9 mos.) d. on 70-Apr-23 [70-Jun-18: 2B].
Phelps, Joshua T. (23 yrs.) d. on 70-Oct-5 of Typhoid dysentery [70-Oct-10: 2B].
Phelps, Laura V. m. Peregoy, George V. on 70-Dec-7 [70-Dec-19: 2C].
Phelps, Margaret A. m. Keyser, William L. on 66-Jul-5 [66-Jul-11: 2C].
Phelps, Myraanna (10 yrs., 6 mos.) d. on 66-Aug-24 [66-Aug-28: 2B].
Phelps, Nelson (72 yrs.) d. [68-Mar-4: 2C; 68-Mar-5: 2C].
Phelps, Rachel d. on 68-Mar-11 [68-Mar-13: 2C].
Phelps, Richard D. m. Chaney, Julia A. on 69-Dec-16 [69-Dec-20: 2C].
Phelps, Silas Robert (6 yrs., 2 mos.) d. on 66-Jun-25 of Brain congestion [66-Jun-26: 2B].
Phiffer, Clara J. m. Opitz, John on 67-Oct-24 [67-Nov-5: 2B].
Philan, Josephine A. m. Wilson, William R. on 67-May-21 [67-Feb-9: 2B].
Philipp, Christine (22 yrs., 2 mos.) d. on 69-Feb-12 [69-Feb-15: 2C].
Philips, Harriet (54 yrs.) d. on 68-Jan-31 [68-Feb-1: 2C].
Philips, Thomas N. S. m. James, Lizzie A. on 67-Nov-17 [68-Apr-10: 2B].
Phillip, Joseph (73 yrs.) d. on 66-Oct-4 [66-Oct-6: 2A].
Phillippe, Judas (65 yrs.) d. on 69-Jun-11 of Suicide (Hanging) [69-Jun-14: 4C].
Phillips, A. A., Jr. m. Hines, Susie E. on 66-Jun-21 [66-Aug-18: 2B].
Phillips, Albert m. Lehman, Josephine E. on 66-Oct-4 [66-Oct-22: 2B].
Phillips, Albina C. m. Payant, Edward on 66-Oct-16 [66-Oct-22: 2C].
Phillips, Anneta m. Boyer, Thomas E. on 68-Jan-7 [68-Jan-8: 2C].
Phillips, Annie Salome (60 yrs., 7 mos.) d. on 68-Oct-8 [68-Oct-10: 2B].
Phillips, Arania Jane (28 yrs.) d. on 68-Feb-20 [68-Feb-27: 2C].
Phillips, Carrie R. d. on 69-Oct-31 [69-Nov-1: 2C; 69-Nov-2: 2B].
Phillips, Charity A. B. d. on 70-Jul-29 [70-Jul-30: 2C].
Phillips, Clara Virginia (4 mos.) d. on 66-Jul-30 [66-Jul-31: 2C].
Phillips, Cora Elizabeth (3 mos.) d. on 68-Nov-15 [68-Nov-17: 2C].
Phillips, Eliza Jane m. Wilson, W. W. on 67-May-19 [67-Oct-11: 2B].
Phillips, Elizabeth I. (5 mos.) d. on 67-Aug-28 [67-Aug-29: 2B].
Phillips, Emily L. m. Parker, William M on 68-Nov-5 [68-Nov-7: 2B].
Phillips, Etta E. m. Hutchinson, George J. on 67-Nov-13 [67-Dec-5: 2C].
Phillips, Frances J. (41 yrs.) d. on 66-Dec-9 [66-Dec-10: 1G, 2B].
Phillips, George m. De Courcey, Jane on 68-Sep-20 [68-Sep-29: 2B].
Phillips, Hester P. (78 yrs.) d. on 66-Mar-6 [66-Mar-8: 2B].
Phillips, Ida Virginia (4 yrs., 10 mos.) d. on 69-Oct-12 [69-Oct-13: 2C].
Phillips, John (48 yrs.) d. on 66-May-24 [66-May-25: 2C; 66-May-26: 2B].
Phillips, John (54 yrs.) d. on 70-Feb-2 of Suicide (Shooting) [70-Feb-3: 1G].
Phillips, John E. W. (1 yr., 8 mos.) d. on 67-Feb-28 [67-Mar-2: 2B].

Phillips, John R. m. Dalrymple, Mollie E. on 69-Jun-15 [69-Jun-17: 2C].
Phillips, John T. (53 yrs.) d. on 70-Jun-28 [70-Jun-30: 2C].
Phillips, John Wilson (9 yrs., 2 mos.) d. on 70-Aug-15 [70-Aug-17: 2C].
Phillips, Joshua (54 yrs.) d. on 68-May-25 [68-May-27: 2B].
Phillips, Lewis Dwinelle (1 yr., 11 mos.) d. on 68-Jul-19 [68-Jul-20: 2B].
Phillips, Lucretia A. m. Hicks, Franklin S. on 69-Apr-21 [69-Apr-27: 2B].
Phillips, Lucy (1 yr.) d. on 68-Jul-20 [68-Jul-31: 2C].
Phillips, Margaret H. m. Jones, Levin T. on 68-Jul-6 [68-Sep-10: 2B].
Phillips, Mary B. K. m. Duvall, George on 66-Oct-18 [66-Nov-3: 2B].
Phillips, Mary E. m. Mansfield, William on 69-Jul-11 [69-Jul-14: 2D].
Phillips, Mollie E. m. Bonney, James E. on 67-Aug-26 [67-Sep-2: 2B].
Phillips, Nathan m. Lovell, Lydia A. on 67-Oct-1 [67-Oct-8: 2B].
Phillips, Paul Herbert d. on 68-Nov-2 [68-Nov-4: 2C].
Phillips, Sallie E. m. Cowman, Albert on 70-Sep-15 [70-Sep-20: 2B].
Phillips, Samuel, Capt. (42 yrs.) d. on 66-Dec-8 [66-Dec-10: 1G, 2B].
Phillips, Wesley m. Harper, Harriet T. on 66-Sep-11 [66-Sep-12: 2A].
Phillips, William A. m. Kelley, Jane on 67-Jan-6 [67-Jan-16: 2C].
Phillips, William A. m. McCullough, Annie E. on 69-Aug-22 [69-Aug-24: 2B].
Phillips, William B. (63 yrs.) d. on 69-Oct-11 [69-Oct-12: 2C; 69-Oct-13: 2C].
Phillips, William B. m. Veeder, Carrie E. on 69-Feb-22 [69-Feb-25: 2D].
Phillips, William H. m. Miller, Isabella on 66-Jun-19 [66-Jun-22: 2B].
Phillips, William H. m. Butler, Mary E. on 70-Aug-16 [70-Aug-24: 2C].
Phillips, William J., Capt. (49 yrs.) d. on 66-Aug-27 [66-Aug-28: 2B; 66-Sep-18: 2B].
Philpotts, Willie C. (15 yrs.) d. on 66-Jan-21 [66-Feb-28: 2C].
Phipps, Ann (91 yrs., 6 mos.) d. on 67-Apr-3 [67-Apr-5: 2B].
Phipps, James A. (1 yr., 3 mos.) d. on 69-Jul-26 [69-Jul-27: 2C].
Phipps, William E. m. Levy, Laura O. on 69-Feb-18 [69-Feb-24: 2C].
Phipps, William H. (74 yrs.) d. on 67-Jul-17 [67-Jul-19: 2C].
Phoebus, Nelly (7 mos.) d. on 66-Feb-27 [66-Mar-1: 2B].
Picard, William T. m. Howard, Mabel on 69-Dec-14 [69-Dec-17: 2C].
Picker, John C. (46 yrs.) d. on 67-Mar-8 [67-Mar-9: 2B].
Pickering, Samuel (44 yrs.) d. on 68-Aug-31 [68-Sep-1: 2B].
Pickering, Sarah E. m. Hardester, Charles on 67-Jan-7 [67-Jan-21: 2C].
Picket, Jerome, Capt. d. [66-Dec-15: 2B].
Pickett, Jerome, Capt. (54 yrs.) d. on 65-Oct-22 [66-Mar-27: 2B; 66-Jan-20: 1F].
Pickrell, Violetta d. on 70-Mar-13 [70-Mar-18: 2C].
Pieper, Henry J. (3 yrs., 3 mos.) d. on 69-Jan-30 [69-Feb-1: 2C].
Pierce, Amanda m. Perkins, Richard K. on 66-Nov-8 [66-Nov-10: 2B].
Pierce, Belle m. Ellicott, Carroll W. on 68-Jun-29 [68-Jul-7: 2B].
Pierce, Catherine (67 yrs.) d. [67-Feb-5: 2C].
Pierce, Elizabeth S. m. Millan, George S. on 66-Oct-16 [66-Oct-25: 2C].
Pierce, Ella m. Brooks, William H. on 70-Dec-7 [70-Dec-12: 2C].
Pierce, Emma m. Martin, George W. on 68-Jan-21 [68-Jan-22: 2C].
Pierce, Eunice m. German, Lemuel on 69-Feb-25 [69-Mar-1: 2C].
Pierce, George (16 yrs.) d. on 67-Sep-10 Drowned [67-Sep-16: 1G].
Pierce, Henry m. Husten, Henrietta on 67-Dec-15 [67-Dec-19: 2B].
Pierce, John C. m. Bishop, Amanda M. on 70-Aug-25 [70-Oct-6: 2B].
Pierce, Joseph (76 yrs.) d. on 70-Aug-22 [70-Aug-24: 2C].
Pierce, Joseph H. m. Barnes, Charlotte on 70-Jan-13 [70-Jan-15: 2C].
Pierce, Josephine m. Rowles, William Henry on 66-Jan-28 [66-Jan-30: 2B].
Pierce, Mary M. m. Koller, Charles E. on 69-Nov-4 [70-Jan-4: 2C].
Pierce, Stephen A. d. on 69-Dec-30 [69-Feb-4: 2C].
Pierce, William M. m. Williams, Mollie on 68-Jan-15 [68-Jan-16: 2C].
Piercy, J. H. m. Hubbard, V. R. G. on 68-Nov-5 [68-Nov-17: 2B].
Piercy, Norris Eugene (1 mo.) d. on 70-Jan-10 [70-Jan-12: 2C].

Piercy, Virginia May (2 mos.) d. on 68-Jul-2 [68-Jul-11: 2B].
Pierpoint, Elizabeth (90 yrs.) d. on 68-Nov-25 [68-Dec-1: 2C].
Pierpoint, Elizabeth m. Davis, John H. on 68-Jan-12 [68-Jan-25: 2B].
Pierpont, Mary J. m. Clements, Robert on 68-Sep-10 [68-Sep-27: 2B].
Pierpont, Samuel A. Lincoln d. on 68-Oct-20 [68-Oct-22: 2C].
Pierpont, Sarah Ann (44 yrs.) d. on 66-May-29 [66-Jun-5: 2B].
Pierpont, William T. m. Yealdhall, Elizabeth J. on 67-Aug-8 [67-Aug-20: 2B].
Piet, Mary Samuel, Sr. (40 yrs.) d. on 68-Dec-6 [68-Dec-11: 1G].
Piet, Susan (73 yrs.) d. on 69-May-26 [69-May-28: 2C].
Pietsch, C. Francis m. Wells, Florence A. on 66-Jun-14 [66-Jun-26: 2B].
Piggot, Louis DeLaigle (6 yrs.) d. on 66-Aug-29 Drowned [66-Aug-31: 1F].
Piggot, Thomas (39 yrs.) d. on 68-Mar-15 [68-Mar-17: 1G].
Piggott, A. Snowden, Dr. (47 yrs.) d. on 69-Feb-13 of Paralysis [69-Feb-15: 1E; 69-Feb-17: 1H, 2D].
Pike, Ignatius d. on 66-Mar-24 [66-Mar-26: 2B].
Pilchard, Ann (53 yrs.) d. on 68-Jul-27 [68-Jul-28: 2B].
Pilkington, Serena D. m. Clarke, William H. on 70-May-9 [70-May-11: 2B].
Pillsberry, Tillie S. m. Conn, Malcolm on 70-Oct-28 [70-Nov-17: 2C].
Pilsch, Elizabeth G. (76 yrs., 5 mos.) d. on 69-Feb-25 [69-Feb-26: 2D; 69-Feb-27: 2C].
Pilsch, Jacob m. Edmeades, Elizabeth E. on 67-Dec-2 [67-Dec-3: 2C].
Pilson, Martha (64 yrs.) d. on 69-Sep-7 [69-Sep-14: 2B].
Pilson, Mary J. m. Seymour, Joseph L. on 68-Apr-28 [68-Apr-29: 2B].
Pina, Sarah m. Binswanger, Simon on 67-Jan-6 [67-Jan-9: 2B].
Pindel, , Mrs. d. on 67-Mar-21 [67-Mar-25: 2C].
Pindell, Adolphus T. m. Yellott, Jane H. on 68-Nov-5 [68-Nov-12: 2C].
Pindell, Thomas, Col. (70 yrs.) d. on 70-Jul-26 [70-Jul-27: 2C; 70-Jul-28: 2C].
Pindle, Edward (5 yrs.) d. on 70-Jul-28 Drowned [70-Jul-29: 4F].
Pindle, Rebecca (62 yrs.) d. on 67-Mar-21 [67-Mar-28: 2C].
Pine, Mary H. (74 yrs.) d. on 68-Oct-14 [68-Oct-17: 2B].
Pink, Nicholas (76 yrs.) d. on 67-Sep-30 [67-Oct-2: 2B].
Pinkett, Job m. Jefferson, Elizabeth on 66-Jan-11 [66-Jan-13: 2C].
Pinkney, James W. (17 yrs.) d. on 66-Oct-3 [66-Oct-4: 2B].
Pinkney, Jane d. on 70-Feb-23 [70-Feb-25: 2C].
Piper, Frank A. d. [70-May-19: 2C].
Piper, Horace H. (39 yrs.) d. on 66-Nov-2 [66-Nov-9: 2C].
Piper, Susan (83 yrs.) d. on 70-Feb-28 [70-Mar-2: 2C].
Piper, William B. (51 yrs.) d. on 68-Jul-16 of Heatstroke [68-Jul-18: 1E].
Piper, William Ulysses, Jr. (10 mos.) d. on 70-Jun-27 [70-Jul-6: 2C].
Piper, William Ulysses S. (1 yr.) d. on 68-Oct-8 [68-Oct-9: 2C].
Piquett, David C. (44 yrs.) d. on 68-Jan-1 [68-Jan-18: 2B].
Piquette, Nora M. m. Linder, Louis F. on 69-Jun-21 [69-Jul-20: 2C].
Pirie, George, Dr. (45 yrs.) d. on 67-Nov-1 [67-Nov-2: 2B].
Pirie, William m. Gantt, Ava L. on 70-May-26 [70-Jun-8: 2C].
Pisani, Egisto m. Henning, Susie on 70-Jan-9 [70-Jan-15: 2C].
Pistel, George H. m. Hunt, S. V. on 68-Oct-22 [68-Oct-23: 2B].
Pitcher, Columbus O. (33 yrs.) d. on 70-Oct-7 [70-Oct-8: 2B].
Pitcher, J. Porus m. Pumphrey, Mary A. on 68-Jan-13 [68-Jan-18: 2B].
Pitcher, James (9 yrs.) d. on 70-Aug-27 [70-Sep-19: 2B].
Pitcher, James M. m. Key, Margaret A. on 69-Apr-7 [69-May-21: 2C].
Pitcher, Martha C. m. Cook, Benjamin on 66-Oct-24 [66-Nov-1: 2B].
Pitcher, Mattie Cook (1 yr., 8 mos.) d. on 70-Sep-18 [70-Sep-19: 2B].
Pitroff, Elanora Louisa (8 yrs., 3 mos.) d. on 70-Jul-14 [70-Jul-15: 2C].
Pitt, Eliza E. m. Bunn, John S. on 66-Jan-16 [66-Jan-19: 2C].
Pitt, Fannie A. m. Clopton, William S. on 69-Jun-1 [69-Jun-2: 2B].
Pitt, Henry Clay (25 yrs.) d. on 70-Oct-10 [70-Oct-11: 2C; 70-Oct-12: 2C].

Pitt, Maria W. m. Freeman, Charles on 67-Mar-6 [67-Mar-8: 2C].
Pitt, William T. m. Dutton, Kate on 68-Nov-11 [68-Nov-17: 2C].
Pittroff, Anna Barbara (26 yrs., 11 mos.) d. [67-Apr-15: 2B; 67-Apr-16: 2B].
Pittroff, John P. m. Hussmeyer, Elizabeth Dora on 68-Apr-16 [68-Apr-20: 2B].
Pitts, Elizabeth B. d. on 66-Jun-12 [66-Jun-14: 2B].
Pitts, John W. (29 yrs.) d. on 69-Nov-8 [69-Nov-10: 2C; 69-Nov-11: 2C; 69-Nov-12: 2C].
Pitts, Martha m. Nicholson, H. R. on 69-Apr-29 [69-May-10: 2B].
Pitts, Martha Hildred m. Bilson, William on 70-Dec-6 [70-Dec-15: 2C].
Pitzer, John Bernard m. Dungan, Sallie Ann on 66-Jan-3 [66-Jan-11: 2B].
Placide, Emma C. (32 yrs.) d. on 66-Sep-9 [66-Sep-10: 2D].
Placide, Henry B. (39 yrs.) d. on 70-Oct-11 [70-Oct-12: 2C; 70-Oct-13: 2C].
Placide, Henry S. (69 yrs.) d. on 68-Nov-24 [68-Nov-25: 2B; 68-Nov-26: 2B; 68-Dec-22: 2C].
Placide, Louisa d. on 70-Jan-9 [70-Jan-11: 2C].
Placide, W. Harrison (30 yrs.) d. on 67-Jun-9 [67-Jun-10: 2B; 67-Jun-11: 2B].
Plack, Lucetta F. m. Mansfield, Samuel on 70-Jun-9 [70-Jun-20: 2B].
Plaggemeyer, Anna m. Haase, Herman on 69-Jan-17 [69-Jan-23: 2C].
Plaskitt, John (71 yrs.) d. on 67-Jul-3 [67-Jul-4: 1F, 2B].
Plaskitt, Joshua m. Hall, Sophia C. on 67-Oct-8 [67-Oct-12: 2A].
Plater, John m. Johnson, Joanna on 66-Aug-30 [66-Sep-5: 2B].
Platt, Emma m. Schotta, John on 69-Feb-2 [69-Feb-8: 2C].
Platt, George W. m. Medcalfe, Sarah A. on 70-Feb-14 [70-Feb-24: 2C].
Pleasants, Basil Brooke (70 yrs.) d. on 68-Sep-24 [68-Oct-5: 2C].
Pledge, Ida V. m. Stubbs, Wilbur on 70-Jan-4 [70-Jan-10: 2C].
Plitt, Amelia m. Plitt, George on 67-Nov-19 [67-Nov-23: 2B].
Plitt, Annie S. m. Sadtler, George T. on 66-Jul-10 [66-Jul-19: 2C].
Plitt, George m. Plitt, Amelia on 67-Nov-19 [67-Nov-23: 2B].
Plowman, Elizabeth (74 yrs.) d. on 67-Mar-5 [67-Mar-6: 2C].
Plume, Kate C. m. Cronise, William H. V. on 68-Apr-2 [68-Apr-29: 2B].
Plummer, Hattie Fay (4 yrs., 8 mos.) d. on 70-Dec-21 [70-Dec-23: 2B].
Plummer, J. W. m. Youce, Clara V. on 66-Apr-5 [66-Apr-9: 2B].
Plummer, John B. (46 yrs.) d. on 68-Dec-16 of Fall from roof [68-Dec-17: 1G; 68-Dec-18: 2C].
Plummer, John Contee (7 mos.) d. on 69-Jul-2 [69-Jul-14: 2D].
Plummer, Kate m. Van Rossum, William E. on 70-Feb-21 [70-Mar-10: 2C].
Plummer, Mary (36 yrs.) d. on 67-Oct-9 [67-Oct-12: 2B].
Plummer, Mary A. m. Simpson, A. J. on 67-Jul-3 [67-Jul-4: 2B].
Plummer, Mary E. m. Smart, William T. on 69-Mar-22 [69-Mar-27: 2B].
Plummer, Mordecai, Jr. m. Pratt, Adeline on 67-Feb-11 [67-Feb-12: 2C].
Plummer, Richard (90 yrs.) d. on 69-Sep-14 [69-Sep-30: 2B].
Plummer, Richard (66 yrs.) d. on 70-Aug-12 [70-Aug-13: 2C].
Plummer, S. A. m. Fowble, William A. on 70-Jan-16 [70-Feb-16: 2C].
Plummer, Samuel (66 yrs.) d. on 68-May-12 [68-May-13: 2B].
Plummer, Samuel (66 yrs.) d. on 69-Jan-8 of Dropsy [69-Jan-21: 2C].
Plunkett, Edward J. m. Mann, Susan A. on 68-Jul-21 [68-Jul-23: 2C].
Plunkett, Ellen m. McBriety, William on 68-Nov-19 [68-Dec-2: 2C].
Pochon, Charles M. L. d. on 66-Nov-26 [66-Nov-27: 2B; 66-Nov-28: 2B].
Pochon, Sophie m. Willcox, Edward J. on 68-Aug-18 [68-Aug-19: 2B].
Pocock, George W. m. Lowman, Sarah M. on 67-Feb-7 [67-Feb-27: 2C].
Pocock, John (75 yrs.) d. on 67-Jun-29 [67-Jul-1: 2B].
Poe, George, Jr. m. Wallace, Maggie A. on 69-Mar-17 [69-Mar-20: 2B].
Poe, Toulmin A. (35 yrs., 6 mos.) d. on 70-Nov-15 [70-Nov-18: 2C].
Poe, William C. m. Robertson, Eleanora H. on 68-Oct-13 [68-Oct-20: 2B].
Pohlan, Augusta m. Wilson, William T. on 69-Sep-23 [69-Oct-2: 2B].
Poisal, Maggie E. m. German, John W. on 68-Aug-11 [68-Aug-15: 2B].
Poist, James E. (57 yrs., 4 mos.) d. on 69-Jul-15 [69-Aug-10: 2C].
Poits, Sarah A. (38 yrs.) d. on 69-Dec-16 [69-Dec-17: 2C].

Pole, William, Jr. m. Moore, Laura V. on 66-Aug-9 [66-Aug-13: 2C].
Polk, Carrie m. Kalkman, Charles W. on 69-Oct-26 [69-Nov-4: 2B; 69-Nov-5: 2C].
Polk, Gillis W. (65 yrs.) d. on 66-Feb-17 [66-Feb-21: 2D].
Polk, Grace (16 yrs.) d. on 68-Dec-14 of Brain congestion [68-Dec-15: 2C; 68-Jan-20: 2C].
Polk, James, Col. (76 yrs.) d. on 68-Dec-6 of Stomach cancer [68-Dec-7: 1G, 2D].
Polk, Josiah B. m. Parker, Julia A. on 68-Sep-28 [68-Sep-29: 2B].
Polk, Letitia J. (70 yrs.) d. on 69-Apr-26 [69-Apr-27: 2C].
Polk, Lizzie C. m. Warfield, Joshua D. on 68-Oct-20 [68-Oct-26: 2B].
Polk, Lucius C m. Clark, Mary E. on 67-Nov-7 [67-Nov-13: 2C].
Polk, Mary K. (7 yrs.) d. on 68-Aug-6 [68-Aug-8: 2C].
Polk, Nathaniel W. m. Gault, Annie D. on 70-Nov-15 [70-Nov-16: 2C].
Polk, William S. m. Anderson, Lou E. on 69-Jun-26 [69-Jul-1: 2C].
Pollard, Annie A. m. McGee, Thomas on 70-Sep-12 [70-Sep-23: 2C].
Pollard, Edward A. m. Dowell, Marie Nathalie [67-Apr-6: 2B].
Pollard, James m. Tyler, Susie on 70-Dec-15 [70-Dec-17: 2B].
Pollard, John (69 yrs.) d. on 67-Feb-1 [67-Feb-2: 2C].
Pollard, Maggie m. Goodman, John W. on 67-Oct-31 [67-Dec-6: 2C].
Pollard, Patrick (52 yrs.) d. on 67-Mar-19 [67-Mar-20: 2C; 67-Mar-21: 2C].
Pollard, Sarah Jane (2 yrs., 10 mos.) d. on 66-Mar-15 [66-Mar-16: 2B].
Pollard, Seth (78 yrs.) d. on 68-Jun-22 [68-Jun-23: 2B].
Pollard, W. A. m. Farley, A. R. on 69-Dec-23 [70-Jan-4: 2C].
Pollard, Walter F. m. Paxton, Mattie B. on 66-Apr-17 [66-Apr-27: 2C].
Pollitt, Carrie (11 yrs., 4 mos.) d. on 70-Jun-22 [70-Jun-23: 2C].
Pollitt, J. Francis (38 yrs.) d. on 68-Jan-27 [68-Jan-30: 2C].
Pollock, Eliza G. (57 yrs.) d. on 70-Aug-25 [70-Aug-26: 2C].
Pollock, Elizabeth (37 yrs.) d. on 67-Sep-25 [67-Sep-26: 2B].
Pollock, James A. m. Mench, Mary A. on 69-Nov-17 [69-Dec-4: 2C].
Pollock, Sarah A. m. Cook, Walter T. on 69-Jul-15 [69-Jul-27: 2C].
Polmyer, Pamela m. Irwin, William on 70-Jan-27 [70-Jan-28: 2B].
Polmyer, William (49 yrs.) d. on 69-Jun-11 of Apoplexy [69-Jun-12: 1H, 2B; 69-Jun-14: 4C].
Pomeroy, Alice d. on 67-Oct-12 [67-Oct-25: 2B].
Pomeroy, William H. d. on 67-Oct-6 [67-Oct-25: 2B].
Pomroy, Charles H. m. Diment, Susan M. on 70-Dec-5 [70-Dec-7: 2C].
Ponice, Henry (54 yrs.) d. on 67-Aug-9 Drowned [67-Aug-10: 1G].
Pool, Ann R. (58 yrs.) d. on 68-Sep-26 [68-Sep-28: 2B].
Pool, Jane m. Rutledge, Charles William on 69-Sep-20 [69-Sep-28: 2B].
Poole, Anna m. Frizzle, A. Henning on 66-Nov-29 [66-Dec-1: 2B].
Poole, Debbie m. Thompson, George W. on 69-Oct-6 [69-Oct-21: 2B].
Poole, Elizabeth (57 yrs.) d. on 68-Dec-7 [68-Dec-8: 2C].
Poole, Emma G. m. Boland, William F. on 68-Feb-19 [68-Feb-24: 2C].
Poole, James E. m. Fillinger, Elexiner on 69-May-12 [69-Jun-8: 2B].
Poole, John H. m. Upperman, Lydia A. on 70-Jun-5 [70-Jun-11: 2B].
Poor, Frank Mayhew (3 yrs.) d. on 68-Oct-2 of Lung congestion [68-Oct-7: 2C].
Poor, Kenny (9 yrs.) d. on 66-Dec-8 [66-Dec-10: 2C].
Poor, Mattie m. Kindleberger, D. on 68-Oct-8 [68-Oct-9: 2C].
Pope, Ann (84 yrs.) d. on 70-Aug-15 [70-Aug-16: 2C; 70-Aug-17: 2C].
Pope, Daniel (82 yrs.) d. on 68-Dec-9 [68-Dec-14: 2C].
Pope, Hannah L. d. on 68-Sep-10 [68-Sep-11: 2B].
Pope, Jennie E. m. Greer, J. Allen on 69-Nov-10 [69-Nov-26: 2B].
Pope, Thomas E. m. Rice, Mattie M. on 66-Jan-23 [66-Jan-26: 2B].
Pope, Thomas L. m. Morgan, Maggie J. on 70-Feb-8 [70-Feb-11: 2C].
Popp, Barbara m. Glaser, Edward on 68-Jun-4 [68-Jun-6: 2A].
Popplein, George J. m. Atkinson, Orrie on 68-Jun-25 [68-Jun-27: 2B].
Popplein, Susie M. m. Kingsland, M. S. on 68-Jan-16 [68-Jan-20: 2C].
Porter, Alexander d. on 66-Oct-10 Drowned [66-Oct-13: 1F].

Porter, Annette M. d. on 68-Aug-8 [68-Aug-14: 2C].
Porter, Charles Hugh (10 mos.) d. on 70-Sep-1 [70-Sep-3: 2B].
Porter, David m. Sego, Rebecca E. on 66-Mar-13 [66-May-18: 2C].
Porter, Edwin J. (1 yr., 1 mo.) d. on 67-Jul-2 [67-Jul-3: 2B].
Porter, Elizabeth (70 yrs.) d. on 67-Feb-26 [67-Feb-27: 2C; 67-Feb-28: 2C].
Porter, Elizabeth (60 yrs.) d. on 66-May-3 [66-May-8: 2B].
Porter, Frances A. m. Patten, Benjamin R. on 68-Aug-12 [68-Aug-27: 2B].
Porter, George Henry (2 mos.) d. on 68-Jul-3 [68-Jul-20: 2B].
Porter, J. Mercer m. Ruskell, Abbie on 70-Nov-15 [70-Nov-23: 2B].
Porter, James F. (34 yrs.) d. on 66-Jul-11 [66-Jul-14: 2B].
Porter, John O. m. Porter, Malvina on 70-Mar-9 [70-Mar-12: 2C].
Porter, Laura E. m. Crowley, James A. on 70-Sep-6 [70-Sep-10: 2B].
Porter, Lillie (1 yr., 3 mos.) d. on 66-Feb-4 [66-Feb-5: 2C].
Porter, Malvina m. Porter, John O. on 70-Mar-9 [70-Mar-12: 2C].
Porter, S. Julia m. Rollins, Thornton on 66-Oct-25 [66-Oct-27: 2B].
Porter, Temperance K. m. Morris, Owen on 68-May-6 [68-Jun-6: 2A].
Porter, Virginia (1 yr.) d. on 70-Feb-14 [70-Feb-15: 2C].
Porter, Virginia m. Mills, Ezekiel on 70-Nov-15 [70-Nov-16: 2C].
Porter, W. D. m. Pugh, Elizabeth on 70-Oct-19 [70-Feb-24: 2C].
Porter, William E. m. Tanner, Annie S. on 66-Oct-17 [66-Oct-19: 2B].
Porter, William F., Capt. (56 yrs.) d. on 66-Nov-15 of Consumption [66-Nov-17: 2B; 66-Nov-20: 4C].
Porter, William Henry m. Gilman, Ellen on 70-Oct-13 [70-Oct-14: 2B].
Porter, William J. m. Collins, Rebecca on 67-Nov-6 [67-Nov-13: 2C].
Porter, Zeley W. m. Hunter, Emily on 70-Aug-11 [70-Sep-23: 2C].
Ports, Catherine Ann (41 yrs.) d. on 70-Oct-11 [70-Oct-13: 2C].
Ports, T. Frank (28 yrs.) d. on 66-Nov-3 [66-Nov-6: 2B].
Posey, John (23 yrs.) d. on 68-Jun-16 Drowned [68-Jun-20: 2B].
Posey, Mary V. m. Hickey, Edward B. J. on 66-Jun-24 [66-Jun-29: 2C].
Post, John Eager Howard d. on 69-Jun-29 [69-Jul-2: 2C].
Post, Margaret Elizabeth d. on 69-Apr-17 [69-Apr-19: 2B].
Post, William M., Dr. (43 yrs.) d. on 70-Nov-3 [70-Nov-8: 2B].
Postlethwaite, Sallie B. m. Addison, W. Edgar on 69-Nov-18 [69-Nov-20: 2B].
Potee, Mary (85 yrs.) d. on 70-Oct-13 [70-Oct-14: 2B].
Potee, Mary A. (46 yrs.) d. on 68-Mar-4 [68-Mar-6: 2B].
Potee, William F. m. Schwer, Catherine on 66-Mar-19 [66-Mar-21: 2C].
Potee, William Jackson (2 yrs., 3 mos.) d. on 69-Jan-7 [69-Jan-8: 2C].
Poteet, Annie m. Brown, William H. on 70-Dec-20 [70-Dec-22: 2B].
Poteet, Elizabeth H. m. Harryman, Charles C. on 69-May-24 [69-Jun-1: 2B].
Poteet, Sarah C. (26 yrs.) d. on 66-Oct-21 [66-Nov-2: 2B].
Potter, Alice B. m. Blackford, W. H. on 69-Oct-5 [69-Oct-6: 2B].
Potter, Charles m. Dukehart, Sarah Jane on 69-Jan-6 [69-Jan-12: 2C].
Potter, Charles C. m. Miller, Emily on 68-Mar-10 [68-Mar-11: 2B].
Potter, Charlie Fuller (1 yr., 7 mos.) d. on 68-May-7 [68-May-8: 2B].
Potter, D. E. m. Gambrill, Sallie A. on 69-Apr-29 [69-May-8: 2B].
Potter, James William (6 yrs., 5 mos.) d. on 69-Oct-9 [69-Oct-11: 2C].
Potter, Mary Catherine (19 yrs.) d. on 66-Sep-25 [66-Sep-26: 2B].
Potter, Mary E. (42 yrs.) d. on 67-Mar-1 [67-Mar-2: 2B].
Potter, Oscar F. d. on 70-Dec-23 [70-Dec-24: 2B].
Potter, Sarah T. d. on 68-Nov-4 [68-Nov-7: 2B].
Potter, Thomas m. Kirwin, Mary H. on 68-Apr-20 [68-Apr-23: 2B].
Pouder, Leonard (67 yrs.) d. on 68-Nov-7 [68-Nov-9: 2B].
Poultney, Philip (71 yrs.) d. on 69-Aug-10 [69-Aug-11: 2C; 69-Aug-12: 1H, 2C].
Poultney, S. Eugene m. Minis, Leila on 69-Nov-4 [69-Nov-9: 2C].
Poultney, T., Jr. m. Ward, Queen on 67-Jan-3 [67-Jan-14: 2C].

Poulton, Charles A. m. Runkles, Mary F. on 70-Nov-10 [70-Nov-14: 2B].
Poulton, Henry Mulliken (7 mos.) d. on 70-Mar-29 [70-Mar-30: 2B].
Poulton, John (69 yrs.) d. on 68-Jul-8 [68-Jul-14: 2C].
Poulton, Mary Alverda m. Downs, John G. on 67-Jan-31 [67-Feb-18: 2C].
Poulton, Robert A. m. Didenhover, Mary A. on 67-Dec-31 [68-Jan-11: 2B].
Powder, Fannie E. m. Hopkins, Robert D. on 69-Feb-4 [69-Feb-9: 2C].
Powel, Elizabeth E. (50 yrs.) d. on 69-Feb-23 [69-Feb-25: 2D].
Powell, Alexander W. m. Hudgins, Angeline on 66-Jul-19 [66-Jul-21: 2C].
Powell, Hiram S. (2 yrs., 8 mos.) d. on 70-Sep-28 [70-Sep-30: 2B].
Powell, James (54 yrs.) d. on 70-Aug-31 [70-Sep-1: 2B].
Powell, Lillie m. Patterson, Frederick E. on 70-Dec-7 [70-Dec-13: 2C].
Powell, Louisa d. on 70-Jan-8 [70-Jan-10: 2C].
Powell, Michael (50 yrs.) d. on 69-Aug-21 of Heatstroke [69-Aug-23: 1G].
Powell, Robert (39 yrs.) d. on 69-Dec-25 [69-Dec-29: 2D].
Powell, William H. m. Coles, Emma E. on 69-Dec-21 [69-Dec-23: 2B].
Power, James, Rev. (68 yrs.) d. on 66-Feb-28 [66-Mar-2: 2B].
Power, John (38 yrs.) d. on 67-Jan-3 [67-Jan-4: 2D].
Power, Kate (4 yrs.) d. on 67-Dec-5 [67-Dec-6: 2C].
Power, Mary Ellen m. McCormick, William on 70-Feb-24 [70-Mar-11: 2C].
Powers, Benjamin S. (22 yrs.) d. on 68-Nov-25 [68-Dec-15: 2C].
Powers, John (11 mos.) d. on 70-Sep-12 [70-Sep-21: 2B].
Powers, Margaret m. Challnor, Charles on 70-Feb-10 [70-Mar-8: 2C].
Powers, Richard (45 yrs.) d. on 69-Oct-30 [69-Nov-1: 2C].
Powers, Warren T. m. Dasch, Mary E. on 68-Apr-16 [68-Apr-18: 2A].
Pragg, Lizzie m. Binswanger, David on 70-Feb-6 [70-Feb-9: 2C].
Pralle, Dietrich (61 yrs.) d. on 69-Nov-7 of Heart disease [69-Nov-8: 1G; 69-Nov-9: 2C; 69-Nov-10: 1G].
Prather, Fanny E. d. on 67-Mar-15 of Pneumonia [67-Mar-23: 2C].
Pratt, Adeline m. Plummer, Mordecai, Jr. on 67-Feb-11 [67-Feb-12: 2C].
Pratt, Albert Dean d. on 66-Dec-30 [67-Jan-1: 2C; 66-Dec-31: 2C].
Pratt, Janie m. Stevenson, Emory H. on 70-Nov-20 [70-Dec-16: 2C].
Pratt, John d. on 69-Aug-30 Murdered (Shooting) [69-Sep-1: 1G].
Pratt, John d. on 70-May-10 [70-May-12: 1G].
Pratt, Lizzie m. Huffington, H. C. on 69-Jan-4 [69-Jan-5: 2C].
Pratt, Mary V. m. Shipley, Benjamin W. on 68-May-14 [68-May-21: 2B].
Pratt, Thomas G. (66 yrs.) d. on 69-Nov-9 [69-Nov-10: 2C; 69-Nov-11: 1F].
Pratt, William H. m. Bishop, Ethelinda on 67-Feb-25 [67-Mar-1: 2C].
Prechtel, George F. m. Schillinger, Mary M. on 70-Aug-25 [70-Sep-8: 2B].
Preece, R. W. m. Keen, Lottie on 67-Nov-14 [67-Dec-10: 2B].
Prendergast, Mary (42 yrs.) d. on 67-Sep-7 [67-Sep-9: 2B].
Prendergast, Thomas d. on 69-May-27 [69-May-29: 2B].
Prentice, Harry Wood (5 yrs., 3 mos.) d. on 70-Dec-8 [70-Dec-9: 2C].
Prentiss, John H. m. Pearce, Kate Russell on 66-Oct-2 [66-Oct-3: 2B].
Prentiss, T. Melville (9 mos.) d. on 69-Sep-23 [69-Sep-24: 2C].
Prescoe, Sarah L. m. Johnson, Samuel on 70-Apr-4 [70-Apr-6: 2B].
Presstman, Adolph W. (9 yrs.) d. on 68-May-3 [68-May-4: 2B].
Presstman, Anna Frances d. on 69-Mar-10 [69-Mar-11: 2C; 69-Mar-12: 2C].
Presstman, Robert Francis (6 yrs.) d. on 68-Sep-22 [68-Sep-24: 2B].
Preston, Benjamin Huger (1 yr., 1 mo.) d. on 66-Oct-25 [66-Oct-26: 2B].
Preston, Caroline m. Simonds, John on 69-Apr-1 [69-Apr-6: 2C].
Preston, Herbert A. m. McNabb, Anna E. on 69-Oct-19 [69-Oct-20: 2C].
Preston, Ida V. (2 yrs., 11 mos.) d. on 69-Oct-24 [69-Oct-26: 2B].
Preston, Jacob A. (72 yrs.) d. on 68-Aug-2 [68-Aug-4: 2C; 68-Aug-5: 2C].
Preston, Jane (68 yrs.) d. on 70-Nov-10 [70-Nov-11: 2B].
Preston, John F. m. Thomas, Eliza P. on 69-Jan-5 [69-Jan-13: 2D].

Preston, M. Laura m. Shannon, James on 67-Dec-4 [67-Dec-5: 2C].
Preston, Mary A. m. Jordan, William G. on 69-Sep-7 [69-Oct-20: 2C].
Preston, Mary Ann (44 yrs.) d. on 67-Dec-1 [67-Dec-2: 2C].
Preston, Sarah Virginia (17 yrs., 5 mos.) d. on 68-Aug-5 [68-Aug-7: 2B].
Preston, Thomas H. m. McNeal, Mary E. on 70-May-19 [70-May-24: 2C].
Preston, William Thomas (1 yr., 4 mos.) d. on 69-Aug-25 [69-Aug-26: 2C].
Pretzman, William W. m. Whitman, Malinda F. on 68-Nov-11 [68-Nov-25: 2B].
Preusch, John d. on 68-May-7 Drowned [68-May-15: 1F].
Prevost, Adeline (11 yrs.) d. on 68-Mar-11 [68-Mar-14: 2B].
Prevost, F. L. (41 yrs.) d. [67-Jun-28: 1G].
Prevost, Tullie J. m. D'Ouville, E. D'Aigneaux on 66-May-29 [66-Jun-4: 2B].
Price, Alverda (6 yrs., 3 mos.) d. on 69-Oct-17 of Scarlet fever [69-Oct-27: 2B].
Price, Amelia m. Thompson, Wallace on 68-Jan-7 [68-Jan-29: 2C].
Price, Ann S. (85 yrs.) d. on 69-Oct-18 [69-Oct-22: 2B].
Price, Anna E. m. Gallagher, Howard L. on 68-Oct-1 [69-Feb-10: 2C].
Price, Annie Lavinia (22 yrs.) d. on 66-Jan-12 [66-Feb-26: 2B].
Price, Antonia Frances (1 yr., 5 mos.) d. on 66-Dec-6 [66-Dec-7: 2B].
Price, Augustus M. (68 yrs.) d. on 70-Jul-20 [70-Jul-21: 1G, 2C].
Price, Beale m. Worthington, Lavinia on 69-Jun-3 [69-Jun-8: 2B].
Price, Benjamin m. Duvall, Eliza R. on 68-Oct-29 [68-Nov-2: 2B].
Price, Benjamin R. (59 yrs.) d. on 66-Sep-23 [66-Sep-26: 2B].
Price, Bessie d. on 69-Jan-3 [69-Jan-5: 2C].
Price, Bruce m. Lee, Josephine on 70-Apr-20 [70-Apr-26: 2B].
Price, Carrie Cecilia (2 yrs., 2 mos.) d. on 70-Apr-10 [70-Apr-11: 2B].
Price, Charles M. d. on 70-Apr-20 [70-Apr-25: 2B].
Price, Charley T. (14 yrs., 6 mos.) d. on 69-Feb-18 [69-Feb-25: 2D].
Price, Charlie R. (5 yrs., 8 mos.) d. on 69-May-10 of Scarlet fever [69-May-11: 2C; 69-May-12: 2B].
Price, Charlotte (75 yrs.) d. on 67-Dec-9 [67-Dec-10: 2B].
Price, David Thomas d. on 67-Aug-11 [67-Aug-12: 2C; 67-Aug-13: 2B].
Price, Denwood C. (44 yrs.) d. on 69-Jul-12 [69-Jul-13: 2C].
Price, Eleanor (97 yrs.) d. on 70-Oct-20 [70-Oct-21: 2C].
Price, Elfred m. Brockenbough, Louisa C. on 69-Apr-28 [69-May-1: 2B].
Price, Elizabeth (70 yrs.) d. on 70-Feb-14 [70-Feb-23: 2C].
Price, Ellen (73 yrs.) d. on 68-Aug-19 [68-Aug-21: 2B].
Price, Emeline m. Simms, Joseph on 66-Jun-13 [66-Jun-23: 2B].
Price, Emily H. d. on 66-Jul-17 of Heatstroke [66-Jul-19: 1E, 2C].
Price, Emma McClellan (4 yrs., 6 mos.) d. on 67-Jan-1 [67-Jan-8: 2B].
Price, Frank (1 yr., 5 mos.) d. on 68-Dec-8 of Pneumonia [68-Dec-9: 2C].
Price, Frank S. m. Marshall, Laura V. on 66-Jul-30 [66-Aug-6: 2C].
Price, George T. m. Roberts, Elizabeth J. on 65-Dec-28 [66-Mar-10: 2B].
Price, George T. m. Wallet, Sarah on 66-May-20 [66-Oct-9: 2A].
Price, Hager d. [66-Mar-17: 2B].
Price, Harriet B. d. on 69-Dec-13 [69-Dec-17: 2C].
Price, Harrietta A. M. m. Knighton, Harry H. on 66-Nov-15 [66-Nov-29: 2B].
Price, Harry Woodward (6 yrs.) d. on 66-Jun-13 [66-Jun-15: 2C].
Price, James (56 yrs.) d. on 70-Feb-19 [70-Feb-22: 2C].
Price, James M. m. Ford, Louisa on 67-Sep-12 [67-Sep-21: 2A].
Price, James T. m. Young, Laura H. on 70-Jan-14 [70-Jan-18: 2C].
Price, Jared M. m. Nimmo, Jane on 70-Dec-8 [70-Dec-23: 2B].
Price, John (84 yrs.) d. on 70-Aug-12 [70-Feb-23: 2C].
Price, John Allen (1 yr., 4 mos.) d. on 69-Apr-6 [69-Apr-9: 2C].
Price, John L. m. Halbert, Mary A. on 68-Oct-21 [68-Oct-24: 2B; 68-Oct-26: 2B].
Price, John Sanderson d. on 68-Jul-17 [68-Jul-21: 2C; 68-Jul-22: 2C].
Price, Joseph d. on 68-Jun-28 [68-Jul-1: 2B].

Price, Josephine A. m. Dunn, John on 66-Feb-13 [66-Feb-24: 2B].
Price, Laura K. (1 yr., 7 mos.) d. on 69-Jan-13 [69-Jan-14: 2D; 69-Jan-15: 2D].
Price, Lizzie m. Baer, Arthur Pue on 67-Feb-7 [67-Feb-16: 2D].
Price, Lizzie Ellen d. on 67-Jul-27 [67-Aug-2: 2C].
Price, Martha A. m. Jones, Asariah Jones on 68-Aug-27 [68-Sep-15: 2B].
Price, Martha J. m. Coggins, John on 68-Jun-3 [68-Jun-6: 2A].
Price, Mary A. m. Sterling, B. F. on 68-Dec-27 [68-Dec-29: 2D].
Price, Mary L. (19 yrs.) d. on 66-May-14 [66-Mar-15: 2C].
Price, Mary S. (50 yrs.) d. on 68-Jan-17 [68-Jan-18: 2B].
Price, Mattie E. m. Zimmerman, George E. on 66-Jan-30 [66-Feb-6: 2D].
Price, Michael Edward (39 yrs.) d. on 67-Sep-7 of Yellow fever [67-Sep-23: 2A].
Price, Mollie A. m. Warren, P. T. on 68-Feb-20 [68-Feb-22: 2B].
Price, Oliver m. Royston, Ella on 67-Nov-28 [67-Nov-30: 2C].
Price, Penelope H. (61 yrs.) d. [69-Jan-7: 2C].
Price, Peter, Sr. (88 yrs.) d. on 69-Mar-13 [69-Mar-15: 2C].
Price, Richard W. m. Heald, Callie F. on 70-Nov-3 [70-Nov-7: 2A].
Price, Robert F. d. on 66-May-26 in Railroad accident [66-May-28: 1F; 66-May-29: 1F].
Price, Romeo (81 yrs.) d. on 67-Apr-2 [67-Apr-4: 1G, 2B].
Price, Sallie E. m. Matthews, Eli on 68-Nov-10 [68-Nov-18: 2C].
Price, Sallie H. m. Green, O. C. on 67-Nov-27 [67-Nov-28: 2C].
Price, Samuel (9 yrs.) d. on 69-Jun-28 Drowned [69-Jun-30: 1H; 69-Jul-2: 2C].
Price, Samuel W., Rev. (32 yrs.) d. on 66-Jan-8 of Typhoid pneumonia [66-Jan-20: 1F].
Price, Sarah Ann m. Van Newkirk, Joseph on 70-Dec-7 [70-Dec-9: 2C].
Price, Sarah E. m. Trimble, Charles T. on 70-Aug-30 [70-Sep-3: 2B].
Price, Stephen (65 yrs.) d. on 68-Jun-20 [68-Jun-22: 2B].
Price, Thomas B. m. Goodwin, Elizabeth H. on 66-Apr-5 [66-Apr-7: 2B].
Price, Thomas L. m. North, Alverda F. on 70-Jun-2 [70-Jun-4: 2B].
Price, Violetta (54 yrs.) d. on 70-Mar-17 [70-Mar-19: 2B].
Price, William (75 yrs.) d. on 68-Nov-25 [68-Nov-28: 2C, 4C].
Price, William S. m. Burke, Pamela A. on 69-Dec-14 [69-Dec-16: 2C].
Price, William T. m. Allen, Mary E. on 69-Sep-7 [69-Sep-11: 2B].
Price, Winfield S. m. McDonnell, Lizzie on 69-Aug-5 [69-Aug-6: 2C].
Prichard, George W. m. Matson, Minnie J. on 67-Nov-7 [68-Mar-2: 2B].
Prichard, William d. on 70-Sep-11 of Heart disease [70-Sep-13: 1H].
Priddy, Lulie M. (23 yrs.) d. on 70-Apr-26 [70-Apr-28: 2C].
Pridgeon, Ella May (5 yrs., 1 mo.) d. on 70-Mar-23 [70-Mar-24: 2C].
Pridgeon, Hester (20 yrs., 9 mos.) d. on 69-Sep-17 [69-Sep-20: 2C].
Pridham, W. F., Capt. (45 yrs.) d. on 66-Jul-17 of Heatstroke [66-Jul-19: 2C; 66-Jul-20: 1F].
Priest, John H. m. Furr, Jennie M. on 67-Oct-9 [67-Oct-14: 2B].
Prigg, Julius A. m. Winters, Lizzie B. on 70-Apr-19 [70-May-5: 2B].
Prigg, Olivia R. m. Jones, J. Guest on 68-Oct-1 [68-Oct-12: 2B].
Prime, Carrie (2 yrs., 7 mos.) d. on 68-Feb-8 [68-Feb-10: 2C].
Prime, Eddie (4 yrs., 9 mos.) d. on 69-Feb-25 [69-Feb-26: 2D].
Prime, Frank Hersey (10 mos.) d. on 67-Jul-24 [67-Jul-27: 2B].
Primrose, Josephine H. (5 yrs.) d. on 68-Mar-11 [68-Mar-12: 2B].
Prince, Ada Sidney (3 yrs., 3 mos.) d. on 67-Oct-12 [67-Oct-14: 2B].
Prince, Catherine Amelia m. Harper, James Emory on 68-Mar-31 [68-Apr-3: 2C].
Prince, George E. m. Bennett, Mary J. on 66-Mar-28 [66-Apr-5: 2B].
Prince, John O. m. Morris, Ann M. on 67-Apr-23 [67-Apr-25: 2B].
Prince, Mary F. d. on 70-Dec-3 [70-Dec-5: 2C].
Printy, Bernard (51 yrs.) d. on 70-Sep-22 [70-Sep-24: 2B].
Printy, Bernard A. (20 yrs., 9 mos.) d. on 69-Oct-22 [69-Oct-25: 2C].
Printz, Artemas S. m. Fishpaw, Marion C. on 67-Apr-18 [67-May-1: 2B].
Prinz, Matilda m. Schlarb, Philip F. on 69-Sep-2 [69-Sep-6: 2C].
Prior, Edward A. m. Pape, Bertha on 68-Apr-4 [68-Apr-7: 2B].

Prior, Frederick C. (37 yrs.) d. on 66-Jul-22 [66-Jul-23: 2C].
Prior, Samuel C. m. Johnston, Agnes on 68-Sep-14 [68-Sep-17: 2B].
Pritchard, Annie M. m. Hohn, Theophilus on 69-Jan-19 [69-Jan-26: 2C].
Pritchard, Arthur (18 yrs., 2 mos.) d. on 69-Dec-1 [69-Dec-10: 2C].
Pritchard, Laura U. m. Landin, Issac James on 70-Jun-22 [70-Aug-20: 2B].
Pritchard, Levin (67 yrs.) d. on 66-Feb-13 of Heart disease [66-Feb-15: 2C, 4D].
Pritchard, M. William d. on 67-Nov-10 [67-Nov-11: 2C].
Pritchard, Maria d. on 68-Dec-5 [68-Dec-8: 2C].
Pritchard, William (45 yrs.) d. on 68-Sep-4 [68-Sep-11: 2B].
Pritchet, Amanda m. Insley, Zebedee on 67-Nov-14 [67-Nov-16: 2B].
Pritchett, Edward J. (28 yrs.) d. on 66-Jun-28 [66-Jul-11: 2C].
Pritchett, George W. (34 yrs.) d. on 66-Jun-28 Drowned [66-Jul-11: 2C].
Pritchett, James (26 yrs.) d. on 67-Sep-17 [67-Sep-19: 2B].
Pritchett, James T. d. Murdered (Stabbing) [66-May-23: 1G].
Pritchett, Mary Frances (31 yrs.) d. on 69-Jul-30 [69-Jul-31: 2C].
Probest, George E. m. Buckingham, Virginia on 68-Jan-20 [68-Jan-21: 2C].
Procter, Agnes m. Jenkins, Oliver L. on 69-Sep-3 [70-Jan-24: 2C].
Proctor, Effie m. Day, Robert on 70-Oct-25 [70-Nov-2: 2C].
Proctor, Henry D. (65 yrs.) d. [68-Jul-28: 2B].
Proctor, Joseph Edwin (3 yrs., 11 mos.) d. on 67-Apr-21 [67-Apr-30: 2A].
Proctor, Josephine (20 yrs.) d. on 70-Jun-25 [70-Jul-25: 2C].
Proctor, Mary A. m. Jones, George W. on 66-May-3 [66-May-4: 2C].
Proctor, Peter m. Hale, B. E. on 66-Oct-18 [66-Oct-20: 2B].
Proudfoot, George W. m. Fulford, Ida V. on 70-Jan-27 [70-Feb-1: 2B; 70-Feb-3: 2B].
Provost, Sarah Catherine (26 yrs.) d. on 66-Aug-21 [66-Aug-23: 2C].
Pruett, Willia James (1 mo.) d. on 69-Nov-18 [69-Nov-20: 2C].
Prugh, Upton m. Bigham, Martha J. on 70-Nov-29 [70-Dec-10: 2B].
Prunty, Francis Patrick (5 yrs., 3 mos.) d. on 66-Feb-17 [66-Feb-22: 2B].
Pryor, Amanda m. Little, Charles on 70-Nov-27 [70-Dec-9: 2C].
Pryor, Delasmatyr (1 yr., 9 mos.) d. on 66-Aug-6 [66-Aug-7: 2C].
Pryor, Elizabeth (55 yrs.) d. on 70-Jan-14 [70-Mar-15: 2C].
Pryor, George W. m. Bell, Eliza W. on 68-Oct-20 [68-Nov-25: 2B].
Pryor, James V. m. Moore, Annie M. on 69-Jul-19 [69-Jul-21: 2C].
Pryor, John A. m. Reese, Mary M. on 67-Jul-31 [67-Aug-3: 2B].
Pryor, Lizzie m. Tarman, William W. on 69-Dec-23 [70-Jan-23: 2B].
Pryor, Thomas Moran (3 yrs., 2 mos.) d. on 69-Apr-1 [69-Apr-3: 2B].
Pue, Charles R., Jr. m. Brown, Matilda R. on 67-Dec-17 [67-Dec-21: 2B].
Pue, Ferdinand C. m. Bowen, Ellen Fitzhugh on 66-Jun-12 [66-Jun-14: 2B].
Pue, Michael m. Schell, Margaret J. on 67-Jun-18 [67-Jul-4: 2B].
Pue, Peggy (95 yrs.) d. on 70-Apr-1 [70-Apr-4: 2C].
Pugh, Ananias m. Mansfield, Mary on 68-May-25 [68-May-27: 2B].
Pugh, Elizabeth m. Porter, W. D. on 70-Oct-19 [70-Feb-24: 2C].
Pugh, William G. m. Stevenson, Mary on 70-May-26 [70-May-31: 2B].
Pugsley, John H. m. Williamson, Lavinia, Mrs. on 67-Mar-28 [67-Mar-30: 2B].
Pugsley, Sarah Adelaide d. on 70-Oct-31 of Typhoid [70-Nov-2: 2C].
Pullen, John (63 yrs.) d. on 67-Dec-29 [68-Jan-4: 2C; 68-Jan-3: 2C].
Pullen, William (51 yrs.) d. on 68-Jul-12 [68-Jul-14: 2C].
Pullett, Mary Elenora (2 yrs.) d. on 68-Sep-6 [68-Sep-7: 2A].
Pumphrey, Alice Virginia (1 yr., 3 mos.) d. on 69-Oct-23 [69-Oct-28: 2C].
Pumphrey, Ann C. m. Jeffers, George W. on 68-Mar-10 [68-Mar-14: 2B].
Pumphrey, Anna Rebecca (4 mos.) d. on 68-May-6 [68-Jul-1: 2B].
Pumphrey, Ebeneezer, Jr. m. Tickner, Amelia R. on 67-May-28 [67-Jun-14: 2A].
Pumphrey, Isabella W. m. McMaines, William on 66-Sep-19 [66-Sep-21: 2B].
Pumphrey, Lloyd m. Madden, Janie H. on 68-Apr-26 [68-Apr-29: 2B].
Pumphrey, Mary A. m. Pitcher, J. Porus on 68-Jan-13 [68-Jan-18: 2B].

Pumphrey, Rachel A. m. Fairbank, Josiah, Jr. on 65-Nov-30 [66-Feb-14: 2C].
Pumphrey, Walter J. m. Bloomer, Mary J. on 66-Jun-28 [66-Jun-30: 2B].
Punderson, Helen m. Bruff, Joseph E. on 69-Apr-29 [69-May-3: 2C].
Purcell, George K. m. White, Mary E. on 66-Dec-13 [66-Dec-15: 2B].
Purcell, John J. (26 yrs.) d. on 70-Apr-8 [70-Apr-12: 2B].
Purcell, William A. (19 yrs.) d. on 70-Jan-7 [70-Jan-8: 2B].
Purden, Mary A. (64 yrs.) d. on 69-Dec-22 [70-Jan-1: 2B; 69-Dec-23: 2B].
Purden, Mary Ann (80 yrs.) d. on 66-Aug-19 [66-Aug-22: 2C].
Purdy, Samuel Radcliffe (6 yrs.) d. on 66-Sep-9 of Scarlet fever [66-Sep-10: 2D].
Purnell, C. R. m. Barnum, John R. on 66-Dec-31 [67-Jan-2: 2C].
Purnell, Charles B. (64 yrs.) d. on 66-Apr-20 [66-Apr-21: 2B; 66-Apr-23: 1E].
Purnell, Cornelia Eugenia (5 mos.) d. on 68-Mar-28 [68-Mar-30: 2C].
Purnell, Hurst (10 mos.) d. on 67-Oct-7 [67-Oct-9: 2B].
Purnell, Laura Kate (4 mos.) d. on 70-Dec-10 [70-Dec-12: 2C].
Purnell, Washington J. m. Giles, Laura V. on 67-Nov-30 [67-Dec-2: 2C].
Purucker, J. W. m. Leland, Priscilla F. on 70-Feb-27 [70-Mar-12: 2C].
Purviance, Eliza m. Atkinson, Brodnay on 69-Jan-28 [69-Jan-29: 2C].
Purviance, Robert, Jr. (65 yrs.) d. on 66-Aug-28 [66-Aug-30: 1G, 2B; 66-Aug-31: 2B].
Purvis, Ella M. m. Rutter, Fred G. on 68-Nov-18 [68-Nov-23: 2B].
Pusey, Mary E. m. Mitchell, John Wesley on 67-Jan-24 [67-Jan-26: 2C].
Putsche, Mary Carlina (1 yr.) d. on 68-Aug-9 [68-Aug-10: 2B].
Putts, Charles J. m. Gill, Mary E. on 66-Sep-9 [66-Sep-14: 2B].
Putts, John W. (68 yrs.) d. on 70-Jan-2 [70-Jan-3: 2C].
Putts, Julia C. m. Hoover, Harrison T. on 68-May-28 [68-May-29: 2B].
Pyatt, Charles E. m. McLean, Ida R. on 66-Dec-20 [67-Feb-19: 2C].
Pyfer, Mary E. m. Crandall, F. M. on 67-May-22 [67-May-24: 2B].
Pyfer, Philip M. (51 yrs.) d. on 68-Nov-7 [68-Nov-9: 2B; 68-Nov-10: 2C].
Pyle, Sarah Elizabeth m. Snyder, William Henry on 67-Feb-28 [67-Mar-6: 2C].
Pyle, Stephen Girard (2 yrs., 6 mos.) d. on 70-Apr-27 [70-Apr-29: 2B].
Quaid, Honora (52 yrs.) d. on 66-Jul-20 [66-Jul-21: 2C].
Quaid, James (7 yrs., 7 mos.) d. on 68-Dec-17 [68-Dec-18: 2C].
Quaid, Kate (5 yrs., 5 mos.) d. on 68-Dec-16 [68-Dec-17: 2C].
Quaid, Mary (9 yrs., 11 mos.) d. on 68-Dec-14 [68-Dec-15: 2C].
Quail, Charles E. m. Weishampel, Emma C. on 67-Jun-4 [67-Jun-6: 2B].
Quail, Elizabeth C. (33 yrs.) d. on 67-Jun-6 [67-Jun-7: 2B].
Quail, Robert Lee (1 yr., 4 mos.) d. on 67-Sep-21 [67-Sep-24: 2A].
Quandt, Otto d. on 69-Jun-2 Drowned [69-Jun-3: 1G].
Quarles, Belinda A. m. Strovel, George R. on 67-Sep-30 [67-Oct-2: 2B].
Quarles, Mollie E. C. m. Easter, John, Jr. on 66-Dec-20 [66-Dec-25: 2B].
Quaty, Christopher m. Severin, Maggie A. on 69-Oct-19 [69-Oct-23: 2B].
Quay, Mary Ann (64 yrs.) d. on 68-Aug-15 [68-Aug-17: 2B].
Quebeck, George Washington d. on 66-Jul-4 [66-Jul-10: 2C].
Queen, Elizabeth d. on 68-Dec-20 of Heart disease [68-Dec-21: 4D].
Queen, John (23 yrs.) d. on 69-Sep-5 [69-Sep-6: 2C].
Queen, Moses (45 yrs.) d. on 67-Jun-3 of Heart disease [67-Jun-4: 1G].
Queen, William (64 yrs.) d. on 66-Oct-11 [66-Oct-12: 2B].
Quell, Amy E. (1 yr., 8 mos.) d. on 70-Mar-3 of Brain congestion [70-Mar-4: 2C; 70-Mar-5: 2B].
Quell, Eva d. on 70-Aug-1 [70-Oct-22: 2B].
Quell, Grace d. on 70-Aug-1 [70-Oct-22: 2B].
Quell, Magdalen Getty (6 mos.) d. on 67-Jun-23 [67-Oct-1: 2B].
Quick, Annie Rebecca (1 yr.) d. on 70-Aug-9 [70-Aug-10: 2C].
Quick, James m. Ray, Mary S. on 70-Mar-30 [70-Apr-1: 2B].
Quigg, William F. d. on 66-Dec-11 of Consumption [66-Dec-24: 2C].
Quigley, Fannie Cooper (5 yrs.) d. on 66-Feb-2 [66-Feb-3: 2C].

Quigley, John (65 yrs.) d. on 66-Sep-22 [66-Sep-24: 2B].
Quigley, Kate m. Turner, James on 68-Feb-20 [68-Feb-29: 2B].
Quigley, Mary m. Deppish, Francis on 68-Dec-6 [69-Feb-22: 2C].
Quigley, Mollie A. m. Curry, Alfred W. on 66-Oct-25 [66-Oct-27: 2B].
Quin, Mary Elon (8 mos.) d. on 70-Aug-14 [70-Aug-15: 2C].
Quinan, John A. m. Frazier, Virginia C. on 69-Jul-13 [69-Jul-15: 2C].
Quincy, Rachel Denison (1 mo.) d. on 68-Aug-20 [68-Aug-22: 2A].
Quincy, Sue W. m. Gordon, A. M. E. on 67-Jul-25 [67-Jul-30: 2C].
Quinlan, Agnes E. m. Stevenson, Wesley G. on 66-Oct-15 [66-Oct-17: 2B].
Quinlan, Anna Elizabeth d. on 68-Nov-16 [68-Nov-17: 2C].
Quinlan, Joseph E. m. Emory, Ellen Barry on 66-Apr-24 [66-Apr-28: 2A].
Quinlan, M. L. m. Swift, J. H. on 69-Feb-2 [69-Feb-9: 2C].
Quinlan, Susannah (101 yrs.) d. on 67-Oct-13 [67-Oct-19: 2B].
Quinlin, James M. (34 yrs.) d. on 67-Sep-11 of Yellow fever [67-Sep-26: 2B].
Quinn, Catherine (37 yrs.) d. on 66-Sep-15 [66-Sep-17: 2B].
Quinn, Charles Eugene (3 mos.) d. on 69-Jan-14 [69-Jan-15: 2D].
Quinn, Francis B. (9 yrs., 10 mos.) d. on 68-Dec-29 [68-Dec-31: 2D].
Quinn, Hugh m. Gardner, Louisa M. on 69-Aug-15 [69-Oct-6: 2B].
Quinn, John (24 yrs.) d. on 70-Aug-29 [70-Aug-30: 2B].
Quinn, Kate m. Fox, James J. on 66-Dec-23 [66-Dec-25: 2B].
Quinn, Louisa J. m. Abercrombie, William H. on 69-Nov-28 [70-Jan-4: 2C].
Quinn, Mary (65 yrs.) d. on 70-Nov-1 [70-Nov-2: 2C].
Quinn, Mary A. (58 yrs.) d. on 70-Mar-13 [70-Mar-14: 2C].
Quinn, Mary C. (10 mos.) d. on 69-Feb-8 [69-Feb-9: 2C].
Quinn, Patrick m. Parnell, Mary A. on 69-Nov-29 [69-Dec-7: 2C].
Quinn, Rosanna (55 yrs.) d. on 70-May-4 [70-May-6: 2B].
Quinn, Sarah m. Craig, Francis on 68-Feb-4 [68-Feb-15: 2B].
Quinn, Thomas F. (27 yrs.) d. on 66-Jul-15 Drowned [66-Jul-16: 1F; 66-Jul-21: 2C].
Quinn, William (26 yrs.) d. on 66-Jul-17 of Heatstroke [66-Jul-19: 1F, 2C].
Quinn, William m. Connolly, Catherine on 67-Apr-28 [67-May-22: 2B].
Quinn, William H. m. Collins, Mary C. on 70-Jan-24 [70-Feb-22: 2C].
Quynn, Edward Irons d. on 69-Jun-3 [69-Jun-8: 2D].
Quynn, J. H. S. m. Sewell, Ruth Anna, Miss on 66-Feb-22 [66-Feb-27: 2B].
Raab, Lizzie B. m. Fortenbaugh, Charles on 70-Jun-16 [70-Jul-23: 2B].
Raabe, John F. m. Becker, Caroline on 68-Oct-6 [68-Oct-9: 2C].
Rabe, Elizabeth m. Kettering, Henry on 70-Jul-26 [70-Aug-20: 2B].
Rabe, Henry m. Steinmier, Mary on 70-Feb-24 [70-Mar-16: 2C].
Rabe, John F. (32 yrs.) d. on 68-Jul-3 [68-Jul-4: 2C].
Raborg, C. H., Dr. (51 yrs.) d. on 69-Jun-29 [69-Jun-30: 2C; 69-Jul-1: 2C].
Raborg, Carrie M. m. Rhodes, S. T. on 68-Nov-24 [68-Nov-25: 2B].
Raborg, George Goddard d. on 70-Mar-22 [70-Mar-24: 2C].
Raborg, Joseph S. m. Weigel, Rose on 68-Oct-19 [68-Oct-26: 2B].
Racktun, August d. Drowned [66-Feb-24: 1F].
Radcliffe, John, Mrs. d. on 67-Feb-13 of Suicide (Jumped from window) [67-Feb-16: 1G].
Radecke, Louisa m. Schriner, Albert on 68-Jan-28 [68-Jan-31: 2C; 68-Feb-1: 2B].
Radecke, Maggie m. Gunther, Charles on 66-Oct-17 [66-Oct-25: 2C].
Radecke, Maggie A. m. Briel, G. W. on 69-Oct-19 [69-Oct-28: 2C].
Radecke, Margarata S. m. Schultheis, George E. on 66-Jan-24 [66-Jan-26: 2B].
Radley, Peter m. Clark, Mary R. on 66-Jun-25 [66-Jun-27: 2C].
Rae, Elizabeth A. m. Shaw, Joshua B. on 70-Oct-4 [70-Oct-8: 2B].
Rae, Lidy m. Beachamp, George R. on 69-May-30 [69-Jun-29: 2C].
Rae, Mary Ann (82 yrs.) d. on 69-Feb-12 [69-Feb-16: 2C].
Rae, Mary Ann (46 yrs.) d. on 70-Feb-6 of Consumption [70-Feb-7: 2C; 70-Feb-8: 2C].
Rae, Robert William (2 yrs., 1 mo.) d. on 67-Apr-10 [67-Apr-11: 2B].
Raferty, Margaret Ann (18 yrs., 7 mos.) d. on 70-Jan-16 [70-Jan-17: 2C].

Rafferty, Annie m. Sexton, Thomas on 67-Feb-21 [67-Feb-25: 2C].
Rafferty, Bernard (39 yrs.) d. on 68-Jan-29 [68-Jan-31: 2C].
Rafferty, John (34 yrs.) d. on 69-Jun-18 of Consumption [69-Jun-19: 2B].
Rafferty, Sarah m. Finnegan, Michael on 67-Nov-1 [67-Nov-21: 2C].
Raffle, Joseph S. m. Meads, Maggie E. on 70-Jun-8 [70-Jul-9: 2B].
Ragan, Louisa (21 yrs.) d. on 66-Jan-3 [66-Jan-12: 2C].
Ragan, Mary d. on 67-Feb-25 [67-Feb-26: 2C].
Ragan, Michael (48 yrs.) d. on 66-Jul-19 [66-Jul-20: 1F].
Ragsdale, J. K. P. m. McCormick, Rebecca on 69-Nov-18 [69-Nov-22: 2C].
Ragsdale, Rebecca (22 yrs.) d. on 70-Aug-26 [70-Aug-27: 2B].
Rahe, Johannh (26 yrs., 2 mos.) d. on 68-Mar-9 [68-Mar-11: 2B; 68-Mar-12: 2B].
Rahner, George d. on 69-May-29 of Suicide (Drowning) [69-Jun-1: 1H].
Rainehart, John (55 yrs.) d. on 66-Oct-11 [66-Oct-12: 1G].
Rainey, Lucy B. d. on 70-Aug-26 [70-Aug-31: 2B].
Rains, Lewis, Capt. (78 yrs.) d. on 68-Oct-18 of Apoplexy [68-Oct-26: 4C, 2B].
Rains, Reuben Hill (8 mos.) d. on 69-Jul-1 [69-Jul-3: 2B].
Rainsford, Theodore A. m. Gorsuch, Lizzie on 67-Jul-31 [67-Aug-17: 2B].
Raitt, Charles H. (69 yrs.) d. on 67-Aug-28 [67-Sep-10: 2B].
Ralph, James Murray m. Abbott, Elizabeth, Miss on 66-Dec-27 [67-Feb-4: 2C].
Ralston, Mary E. J. (11 mos.) d. on 70-Jun-11 [70-Jun-13: 2C].
Ralston, Sarah A. (2 mos.) d. on 68-Mar-13 [68-Mar-14: 2B].
Ramsay, C. Gustaf m. Corner, Alice on 68-Oct-22 [68-Oct-26: 2B].
Ramsay, Charles S. d. on 68-Jul-18 [68-Jul-22: 2C].
Ramsay, Granville Knight d. on 69-May-16 [69-May-18: 2C].
Ramsay, Helen Mary (70 yrs.) d. on 70-Jan-20 [70-Jan-27: 2C].
Ramsay, Isabella D. m. Burger, John N. on 69-Sep-14 [69-Sep-16: 2B].
Ramsay, Joseph B. (21 yrs., 3 mos.) d. on 67-Sep-20 [67-Sep-21: 2A].
Ramsburg, Eleanor Keech d. on 69-Jul-10 [69-Jul-14: 2D].
Ramsburg, Newton A. m. Keech, Sallie M. on 67-Oct-22 [67-Oct-26: 2A].
Ramsburgh, Charlotte m. Mitchell, T. E. on 69-Oct-5 [69-Oct-8: 2B].
Ramsey, Arabella (77 yrs.) d. on 66-May-24 [66-May-25: 2C].
Ramsey, Caroline C. m. Wheeler, A. Carroll on 68-Nov-5 [68-Nov-7: 2B].
Ramsey, Eliza (49 yrs.) d. on 69-Aug-21 [69-Aug-23: 2C].
Ramsey, Eliza J. m. White, James H. on 70-Dec-28 [70-Dec-31: 2B].
Ramsey, Mary m. Micklethwait, Walter on 67-Jul-16 [67-Jul-20: 2C].
Ramsey, Mortimer m. Williams, Charlotte on 70-Jan-11 [70-Apr-1: 2B].
Ramsey, Nellie m. Smith, James R. on 69-Sep-22 [69-Sep-25: 2B].
Ramsey, Robert J. m. Langdon, Ann Maria on 66-Jan-1 [66-Jan-9: 2B].
Randall, George C. m. Johnson, Mary E. on 68-Jan-28 [68-Feb-10: 2C].
Randall, Hannah (80 yrs., 5 mos.) d. on 70-Feb-28 [70-Mar-1: 2C].
Randall, Henrietta (83 yrs., 1 mo.) d. on 66-Jun-26 [66-Jun-27: 2C].
Randall, Ida m. Owens, Robert W. on 70-Sep-29 [70-Oct-3: 2B].
Randall, Johanna (33 yrs.) d. on 66-Oct-20 of Fall [66-Oct-22: 1F, 2C].
Randall, Kate Brady d. on 70-Nov-14 [70-Nov-19: 2B].
Randall, Laura Virginia d. on 68-Dec-22 [68-Dec-23: 2C; 68-Dec-24: 2C].
Randall, Mary (29 yrs.) d. on 70-Jan-30 [70-Feb-1: 2B].
Randall, Robert (52 yrs.) d. on 69-Dec-29 [69-Dec-31: 2C].
Randall, Robert John d. on 69-Dec-6 [69-Dec-7: 2C].
Randall, Sarah (83 yrs.) d. on 66-Aug-18 [66-Aug-20: 2C].
Randall, Sarah m. Gardner, John R. on 69-May-29 [69-Jun-5: 2B].
Randall, William A. m. Standfield, Rachel E. on 69-Dec-23 [69-Dec-31: 2C].
Randell, Columbia J. m. Hussey, James R. on 66-Mar-29 [66-Apr-5: 2B].
Randle, Charles Q. (3 yrs.) d. on 68-Aug-23 [68-Aug-25: 2B].
Randle, Ella V. (1 yr.) d. on 69-Mar-3 [69-Mar-4: 2C].
Randle, Horatio Nelson (1 yr., 9 mos.) d. on 70-Aug-6 [70-Aug-8: 2C].

Randolph, Agnes Ann (6 mos.) d. on 68-Aug-31 [68-Sep-1: 2B; 68-Sep-2: 2A].
Randolph, Annie m. Church, Francis E. on 69-Feb-3 [69-Feb-5: 2C].
Randolph, Eliza (78 yrs.) d. on 68-Jul-11 [68-Jul-14: 2C].
Randolph, John W., Jr. (25 yrs.) d. on 69-Nov-20 [69-Nov-22: 2C].
Randolph, John W., Jr. m. Buck, Aggie A. on 66-May-30 [66-Jun-2: 2B].
Randolph, Robert L. m. Taylor, Martha A. on 68-Sep-17 [68-Oct-7: 2C].
Rank, William D. m. Moore, Rachel Annie on 66-Apr-26 [66-Apr-27: 2C].
Rankin, Agnes m. Harrison, Charles O. on 69-Oct-27 [69-Oct-30: 2B].
Rankin, Sarah (68 yrs.) d. on 67-Jan-4 [67-Jan-5: 2C].
Rankin, Susanna m. Watson, George W. on 69-Apr-22 [69-Apr-23: 2B].
Rankle, Ruth Matilda m. Mason, George A. on 70-Aug-8 [70-Dec-2: 2C].
Rankle, William m. Nickles, Mary C. on 70-Oct-23 [70-Nov-16: 2C].
Rapier, Mary (29 yrs.) d. on 66-Nov-3 [66-Nov-16: 1G].
Rapin, Gerhardt A. (52 yrs.) d. on 70-Sep-24 [70-Sep-26: 2B].
Rapley, Hannah (63 yrs.) d. on 68-Mar-12 [68-Mar-14: 2B].
Rappold, Ruth d. on 70-Jun-20 [70-Jun-23: 2C].
Rasch, Gustav A. m. Kennedy, Emma L. on 66-Apr-26 [66-May-1: 2A].
Rasin, A. R. m. Dorsey, Sarah F. on 67-Oct-17 [67-Oct-21: 2B].
Rasin, A. R. m. Hook, M. C. on 66-May-8 [66-Aug-17: 2C].
Rasin, Alfred Ringgold (29 yrs., 7 mos.) d. on 69-Sep-20 [69-Sep-21: 2B].
Rasin, Howard Claypoole (2 yrs., 4 mos.) d. on 68-Nov-12 [68-Nov-13: 2C].
Rasin, Mary C. (23 yrs.) d. on 67-Mar-10 [67-Mar-11: 2C].
Rasin, Mary Clare (6 mos.) d. on 67-Aug-14 [67-Aug-15: 2C].
Rasin, William J. m. Garnett, Mary A. on 67-Nov-19 [67-Nov-26: 2B].
Ratcliffe, Bettie H. m. Owens, James W. on 68-Jan-16 [68-Jan-18: 2B].
Ratcliffe, Mary F. m. McVeigh, James H., Jr. on 70-Jan-18 [70-Jan-19: 2C].
Rathbun, Davis L. m. O'Byron, Rosa S. on 67-May-30 [67-Jun-3: 2B].
Rathbun, Maggie Allison m. McLeod, Alexander on 68-Jul-16 [68-Jul-17: 2B].
Rathell, Emily Adele m. Hodnett, Jason T. on 68-Aug-26 [68-Sep-8: 2B].
Rathell, Mary (72 yrs.) d. on 70-Jul-15 [70-Jul-30: 2C].
Rathford, Gilbert B. m. King, C. Pauline on 70-Jan-25 [70-Jan-29: 2B; 70-Feb-1: 2B].
Rathie, Lizzie m. Woodall, James on 66-Jan-30 [66-Feb-7: 2C].
Rathvon, Emma E. m. Maxwell, David on 70-Mar-15 [70-Mar-17: 2C].
Rauck, Ann Gibson (37 yrs.) d. on 70-Jun-25 [70-Jun-27: 2C].
Rausch, Amelia Louisa d. on 68-Sep-3 [68-Sep-5: 2A].
Rausch, J. H. Philip (2 yrs., 11 mos.) d. on 68-Aug-17 [68-Aug-18: 2B].
Rausch, John H. (27 yrs.) d. on 68-Oct-22 [68-Oct-24: 2B; 68-Oct-26: 4C].
Rausch, Maggie M. m. Strodtman, William H. on 68-Oct-27 [68-Nov-10: 2C].
Rausche, James (40 yrs.) d. on 67-Aug-20 of Brain concussion [67-Aug-21: 1F].
Rausher, Louis (31 yrs.) d. on 68-Sep-24 [68-Sep-25: 2B].
Rauterberg, Mary m. Duvall, Grayson W. on 70-May-10 [70-May-16: 2B].
Rawlings, Benjamin (91 yrs.) d. on 68-Mar-24 [68-Mar-28: 2B; 68-Mar-30: 2C].
Rawlings, George A., Capt. (51 yrs.) d. on 69-Aug-20 of Stomach inflammation [69-Aug-21: 2B, 4D; 69-Aug-23: 1G].
Rawlings, James Ellsworth (3 yrs., 1 mo.) d. on 69-Sep-24 of Brain fever [69-Sep-25: 2B].
Rawlings, Julia A. m. Onion, Edward D. on 68-Jun-25 [68-Jul-8: 2B].
Rawlings, Tabitha (88 yrs.) d. on 67-Mar-2 [67-Apr-1: 2C].
Rawlins, Amelia B. m. Carroll, R. James on 67-Jun-27 [67-Jun-28: 2B; 67-Jun-29: 2B].
Ray, Annie (4 yrs., 2 mos.) d. [69-Oct-30: 2C].
Ray, Charles H. m. Ballard, Julia on 68-Jan-6 [68-Jan-8: 2C].
Ray, Clara A. m. Badders, A. J. on 70-Sep-12 [70-Sep-15: 2B].
Ray, Fannie Virginia (2 yrs., 1 mo.) d. on 68-Mar-3 [68-Mar-4: 2C].
Ray, Honora (52 yrs.) d. on 67-Nov-4 [67-Nov-5: 2B].
Ray, Marietta m. High, Samuel E. on 69-Dec-2 [69-Dec-4: 2C].
Ray, Mary (25 yrs.) d. on 70-Jun-18 of Suicide (Jumped from balcony) [70-Jun-20: 1H].

Ray, Mary E. m. Kaufmann, William on 68-Dec-15 [69-Jan-12: 2C].
Ray, Mary S. m. Quick, James on 70-Mar-30 [70-Apr-1: 2B].
Ray, Thomas (13 yrs., 8 mos.) d. on 66-Feb-14 of Consumption [66-Feb-17: 2B].
Raymo, Willie F. (6 mos.) d. on 69-Sep-6 [69-Sep-7: 2B].
Raymond, Calvin Colton d. on 69-Oct-1 of Typhoid [69-Oct-18: 2C].
Raymond, Charles W. m. Stump, Mary E. on 66-Sep-14 [66-Dec-6: 2B].
Raymond, Lucy E. E. m. Wilkins, William J. on 67-Dec-24 [67-Dec-27: 2D].
Raymond, Lucy H. d. on 68-Sep-5 [68-Sep-7: 2A].
Raymond, William E. (45 yrs.) d. on 68-Apr-5 [68-Apr-7: 2B].
Rayner, Bertha m. Frank, S. L. on 69-Dec-16 [69-Dec-18: 2B].
Rayner, Henry m. Madden, Emma on 69-Dec-28 [69-Dec-29: 2D].
Rayner, Mary J. m. Jackson, Arthur N. on 68-May-20 [68-May-22: 2C].
Raynor, Samuel (55 yrs.) d. on 69-Apr-6 [69-Apr-13: 2B].
Rea, Ann E. d. on 68-Feb-28 [68-Feb-29: 2B].
Rea, Annie m. Trine, William H. on 68-Nov-26 [68-Nov-28: 2C].
Rea, Charles H. (40 yrs.) d. on 69-Sep-30 [69-Oct-1: 2B].
Rea, Emma G. m. Shaw, William A. on 67-Apr-16 [67-Apr-20: 2A].
Read, Charles W. m. Shriver, Sarah A. on 66-Apr-10 [66-Apr-12: 2B].
Read, E. William m. Stromenger, Mary on 69-Jun-29 [69-Jun-30: 2C].
Read, Elias A. m. Childs, Rebecca B. on 66-Apr-9 [66-Apr-12: 2B].
Read, Elizabeth May (7 mos.) d. on 69-Aug-7 of Cholera infantum [69-Aug-10: 2C].
Read, Fannie m. Smith, George on 68-Oct-13 [68-Oct-19: 2B].
Read, George S. m. Scarborough, Emma on 70-Apr-26 [70-Apr-30: 2A].
Read, Grace (79 yrs.) d. on 69-Apr-18 [69-Apr-21: 2C; 69-Apr-27: 2C].
Read, Henry C. Larrabee (10 mos.) d. on 68-Jun-22 [68-Jun-23: 2B].
Read, James L. m. Schaum, Sophie on 67-Dec-10 [68-Jan-11: 2B].
Read, John G. (60 yrs.) d. on 70-Jul-11 [70-Jul-12: 2C].
Read, Joseph Bernard (1 yr., 9 mos.) d. on 66-Apr-29 [66-May-4: 2C].
Read, Josephine (9 mos.) d. on 67-Jan-10 [67-Jan-17: 2C].
Read, Julia (9 mos.) d. on 67-Sep-6 [67-Sep-7: 2A].
Read, Lydia M. (72 yrs.) d. on 70-Apr-15 [70-Apr-16: 2B].
Read, Maria Estella (3 mos.) d. on 70-Sep-5 [70-Sep-9: 2B].
Read, Mary m. Talbot, Joshua F. C. Talbot on 68-Jun-16 [67-Jul-3: 2B].
Read, Robert F. m. Hall, Sophie on 70-Jul-5 [70-Jul-6: 2B].
Read, William E. m. Steele, Lydia on 67-Jan-11 [67-Jan-13: 2C].
Read, William M. (1 yr., 2 mos.) d. on 68-Feb-10 [68-Feb-15: 2B].
Readasell, Margaret m. Imler, Charles Christian on 67-Aug-6 [67-Aug-12: 2C].
Ready, Mary D. (34 yrs.) d. on 70-Feb-17 [70-Feb-19: 2B].
Reagan, Maria L. m. Rock, James P. on 68-Oct-8 [68-Nov-9: 2B].
Reaisin, William H. (51 yrs.) d. on 67-Mar-4 [67-Mar-5: 1G, 2C].
Real, Charles d. on 69-May-31 Drowned [69-Jun-4: 1G].
Realy, Annie R. m. Garrett, James H. on 67-Feb-21 [67-Jul-27: 2B].
Reamy, Albert V. (41 yrs.) d. on 69-Nov-8 [69-Nov-10: 2C].
Reaney, Charles H. m. Pentz, Annie E. on 67-Jul-4 [67-Jul-8: 2C].
Reaney, Joseph (2 mos.) d. on 66-Feb-20 [66-Feb-22: 2B].
Reaney, Lucien Duteil (5 yrs., 9 mos.) d. on 67-Nov-10 [67-Nov-11: 2C].
Reardon, E. B. d. on 69-Mar-26 [69-Mar-27: 2B].
Reardon, John d. on 69-Jun-21 [69-Jun-24: 1G].
Reasin, A. V. m. Hopkins, B. L. on 68-Sep-10 [68-Sep-11: 2B].
Reather, Daisy May (2 mos.) d. on 70-Aug-4 [70-Aug-5: 2C].
Reaves, Maria m. Gibson, Arnold on 70-May-1 [70-May-2: 2B].
Reay, Henry S. m. Milnes, Vic on 66-Nov-6 [66-Nov-17: 2C].
Reay, Martha S. (6 mos.) d. on 70-Aug-27 [70-Aug-29: 2C].
Reay, Sarah (76 yrs.) d. on 68-Nov-20 [68-Nov-21: 2C].
Reaymond, Moses B. m. Hodges, Julia A. on 66-Oct-21 [66-Oct-24: 2C].

Rechenberg, Adolph A. E. F. m. Schneider, Mary on 69-Feb-4 [69-Feb-6: 2C].
Reckert, Ann Matilda d. on 69-Aug-8 [69-Aug-10: 2C].
Reckert, Elizabeth Sarah d. on 69-Aug-6 [69-Aug-10: 2C].
Reckert, Harriet Emily (17 yrs.) d. on 67-Feb-2 [67-Feb-4: 2C].
Reckert, Louis (40 yrs.) d. on 68-Nov-6 of Heart disease [68-Nov-9: 1F].
Reckert, Matilda Elizabeth (25 yrs.) d. on 67-Feb-5 [67-Feb-7: 2C].
Reckett, William G. (27 yrs.) d. on 69-Jan-11 [69-Jan-16: 2C].
Reckit, Anna Jenkins (2 yrs., 5 mos.) d. on 68-Feb-2 [68-Feb-4: 2D].
Reckitt, Mary Evaline (2 yrs., 6 mos.) d. on 68-Feb-14 [68-Feb-15: 2B].
Redden, George S. (66 yrs.) d. on 69-Jul-6 [69-Jul-8: 2C].
Redden, Katie (3 yrs., 7 mos.) d. on 70-Nov-12 [70-Nov-14: 2B].
Redden, Rosa E. m. Vivarttas, Aloha on 66-May-1 [66-May-5: 2B].
Reddesh, Louisa (51 yrs.) d. on 67-Dec-1 [67-Dec-3: 2C].
Redding, Catherine (65 yrs.) d. on 68-Oct-13 [68-Oct-14: 2B].
Reddish, Elizabeth (46 yrs.) d. on 68-Oct-20 [68-Oct-21: 2C].
Reddish, Joanna m. Grooms, William M. on 70-Nov-3 [70-Nov-30: 2C].
Reddish, Louis m. Gallaway, Pamela J. on 70-Feb-28 [70-Mar-11: 2C].
Reddish, Lycurgus m. Barnes, Ellen J. on 70-Nov-5 [70-Nov-19: 2B].
Reddish, Martha Jane (25 yrs., 2 mos.) d. on 66-May-1 [66-May-4: 2C].
Reddish, William D. m. Brown, Laura J. on 68-Oct-13 [68-Oct-20: 2B].
Reddy, Thomas J. (25 yrs.) d. on 67-Feb-28 [67-Mar-1: 2C].
Redgrave, Harriet (78 yrs.) d. on 66-Jun-5 [66-Jun-12: 2B].
Redgrave, Helen Raborg d. on 70-Feb-28 of Scarlet fever [70-Mar-2: 2D].
Redgrave, I. Frank (29 yrs.) d. on 68-Feb-19 of Typhoid pneumonia [68-Feb-21: 2B].
Redgrave, J. Ford (2 yrs., 1 mo.) d. on 67-Jun-1 [67-Jun-6: 2B].
Redgrave, J. Frank m. Stewart, Fannie A. on 67-Nov-21 [67-Nov-25: 2C].
Redgrave, J. W. Hammond (3 yrs., 1 mo.) d. of Pneumonia [68-Apr-24: 2B].
Redgrave, Janie Nolen (4 mos.) d. on 68-Aug-5 of Cholera infantum [68-Aug-7: 2B].
Redgrave, William H. m. Craig, Amelia T. on 70-Jun-30 [70-Jul-8: 2C].
Redgraves, Anna (86 yrs.) d. on 68-Jun-14 [68-Jun-16: 2B].
Redifer, Emma J. m. Woods, Hudson A. on 66-Dec-27 [67-Jan-3: 2B].
Redman, Ann (76 yrs.) d. on 67-Jul-31 [67-Aug-3: 2B].
Redman, Annie E. m. Green, Thomas on 69-Dec-15 [69-Dec-21: 2B].
Redman, James E. m. Hamill, Mary on 68-Jan-25 [68-Feb-3: 2C].
Redman, John d. on 66-May-11 of Construction cave-in [66-May-12: 1F].
Redmiles, Richard F. m. Lowman, Mary M. on 67-Feb-17 [67-Feb-27: 2C].
Redmond, Ann (58 yrs.) d. on 70-Oct-8 [70-Oct-10: 2B].
Redmond, B. C. m. Ryall, P. H. on 68-Dec-22 [68-Dec-28: 2B].
Redmond, John B. m. Frazier, Sarah Ann on 67-Apr-21 [67-May-2: 2B].
Redmond, John Byrne (18 yrs.) d. on 69-Feb-25 [69-Feb-26: 2D].
Redmond, Robert m. Mates, Eliza Ann on 69-Oct-14 [69-Oct-27: 2B].
Redmond, Robert A. m. Carmichael, Anna J. on 67-May-12 [67-Jun-21: 2B].
Redsecker, Hallie S. m. Kunkel, Charles H. on 70-May-31 [70-Jun-4: 2B].
Redsecker, Jacob (68 yrs.) d. on 68-Oct-14 [68-Oct-16: 2B].
Reece, Jacob (58 yrs.) d. on 70-Nov-30 [70-Dec-1: 2C].
Reed, Abner M. m. Stembler, Maggie on 70-Dec-6 [70-Dec-24: 2B].
Reed, Adele Louise m. Lawton, Walter E. on 70-Jan-1 [70-Jan-4: 2C].
Reed, Amanda m. Falck, Frederick on 67-Dec-1 [68-Jun-8: 2B].
Reed, Andrew J. (46 yrs.) d. on 68-Sep-11 [68-Oct-28: 2B].
Reed, Ann Rebecca (9 mos.) d. on 69-Mar-19 [69-Mar-20: 2C].
Reed, Augusta A. m. Paulin, John E. on 67-Jun-4 [67-Jun-11: 2B].
Reed, Benjamin F. m. Wilkens, Elizabeth O. on 70-Apr-19 [70-Apr-21: 2B].
Reed, Bessie Hutchinson (5 yrs., 7 mos.) d. on 67-Feb-16 [67-Feb-18: 2C].
Reed, Brucie T. (26 yrs.) d. on 68-Jul-9 of Consumption [68-Jun-16: 2C].
Reed, Charles Arthur (1 yr., 3 mos.) d. on 68-Jul-16 [68-Jul-20: 2B].

Reed, Charlotte (10 mos.) d. on 68-Dec-2 [68-Dec-3: 2C].
Reed, David m. Sollers, Maggie A. on 68-Oct-22 [69-Feb-19: 2C].
Reed, Delila A. (69 yrs.) d. on 66-Mar-24 [66-Mar-30: 2C].
Reed, Ella May (1 yr., 1 mo.) d. on 70-Oct-12 [70-Oct-14: 2B].
Reed, Emit W. m. Penrice, Marion Louisa on 69-Aug-3 [69-Aug-7: 2B].
Reed, Francis A. (22 yrs.) d. on 66-Apr-1 of Typhus [66-Jun-29: 2C].
Reed, Hiram F. m. Emmart, Martha A. on 67-Apr-11 [67-Apr-18: 2B].
Reed, J. Seymour (1 yr., 2 mos.) d. on 70-Oct-13 [70-Oct-14: 2B].
Reed, Jacob m. Mules, Margaret A. on 68-Nov-12 [68-Nov-19: 2C].
Reed, James A., Dr. d. Drowned [70-Apr-14: 1F, 2B].
Reed, John d. on 68-May-2 Drowned [68-Aug-17: 1G].
Reed, John m. Burman, Virginia P. on 66-Sep-6 [66-Oct-9: 2A].
Reed, Julia V. m. Stewart, William J. on 70-Aug-17 [70-Sep-10: 2B].
Reed, Leonard Kirby (2 mos.) d. on 66-Jul-16 [66-Jul-17: 2C].
Reed, M. A. m. Givan, J. L. on 69-Apr-13 [69-Apr-17: 2A].
Reed, Margaret J. Lee d. on 70-Oct-30 [70-Oct-31: 2C].
Reed, Mary (19 yrs., 7 mos.) d. on 67-Oct-4 [67-Oct-5: 2B].
Reed, Mary D. m. Dean, Seneca on 69-Oct-22 [69-Nov-6: 2B].
Reed, Mary Ellen (29 yrs.) d. on 66-May-8 [66-May-9: 2B].
Reed, Mary Rebecca (1 yr., 5 mos.) d. on 66-Dec-29 [66-Dec-31: 2C].
Reed, Mary Victoria m. Nicholson, James E. on 66-Feb-1 [66-Feb-10: 2C].
Reed, Michael H. m. Lee, Maggie J. on 69-Aug-18 [69-Aug-23: 2C].
Reed, N. G. m. Olive, Lizzie on 69-Oct-5 [69-Oct-7: 2B].
Reed, Oliver H., Sr. (63 yrs.) d. on 66-Mar-5 [66-Mar-7: 2B].
Reed, P. R. m. West, A. C. on 66-Feb-28 [66-Mar-2: 2B].
Reed, Rachel (74 yrs.) d. on 67-Jan-21 [67-Jan-26: 2C].
Reed, Randolph (34 yrs.) d. on 69-Mar-31 [69-Apr-1: 2C].
Reed, Susannah R. (61 yrs.) d. on 67-Mar-22 [67-Mar-23: 2B].
Reed, Thomas H. C. m. Worthington, Drucie on 66-Dec-20 [67-Jan-4: 2D].
Reed, William R. (1 yr., 8 mos.) d. on 69-Jan-16 [69-Jan-19: 2C].
Reeder, Mary A. C. m. Cahill, Frederick J. on 70-Oct-11 [70-Oct-17: 2B].
Reeder, Oliver m. Lanahan, Mary C. on 68-Nov-13 [68-Nov-25: 2B].
Reeger, John C., Jr. m. Epple, Rosa on 69-May-2 [69-May-11: 2B].
Reel, Fanny m. Knotts, Joseph W. on 69-Nov-3 [69-Nov-10: 2C].
Rees, A. J. m. Jones, Mollie A. on 67-Jun-20 [67-Jun-22: 2B].
Rees, William S. m. Hughes, Lizzie on 68-Dec-15 [69-Jan-16: 2C].
Reese, Alexina d. on 66-Feb-23 [66-Apr-25: 2B].
Reese, Alice Maud (6 yrs., 11 mos.) d. on 69-Jan-16 of Scarlet fever [69-Jan-19: 2C].
Reese, Ann Hallowell (17 yrs., 4 mos.) d. on 70-Aug-7 [70-Aug-9: 2C].
Reese, Edward Samuel (3 yrs., 4 mos.) d. on 66-Mar-4 [66-Mar-5: 2B].
Reese, Ellen Anna d. on 69-Jul-8 [69-Jul-9: 2C].
Reese, Ellen R. d. on 67-Jun-14 [67-Jun-15: 2B].
Reese, Emma (11 yrs., 10 mos.) d. on 69-Jan-12 of Heart disease [69-Jan-14: 2D].
Reese, Estelle Evangeline (13 yrs.) d. on 69-Jan-3 [69-Jan-4: 2C].
Reese, Esther (76 yrs.) d. on 70-Nov-7 [70-Nov-8: 2B].
Reese, Gideon D. d. on 68-Dec-31 [69-Jan-2: 2C].
Reese, Henry Lawton (2 yrs., 3 mos.) d. on 66-Nov-23 [66-Nov-24: 2B].
Reese, Henry O. m. Watkins, Emma V. on 67-Oct-8 [67-Oct-9: 2B].
Reese, Herman Frederick (2 yrs., 1 mo.) d. on 69-Jan-8 of Scarlet fever [69-Jan-9: 2C].
Reese, Ida Wilson (1 yr., 3 mos.) d. on 66-Dec-3 [66-Dec-6: 2B].
Reese, J. Fisher m. Jones, Anna S. on 67-Oct-8 [67-Oct-10: 2B].
Reese, John Marshall (2 yrs., 2 mos.) d. on 66-Sep-2 [66-Sep-4: 2B].
Reese, John W. (65 yrs.) d. on 67-Apr-28 [67-May-1: 2B].
Reese, Margaret K. (64 yrs.) d. on 66-Mar-18 [66-Mar-19: 2C; 66-Mar-20: 2C].
Reese, Mary C. m. Nelson, John on 66-Sep-6 [66-Sep-18: 2B].

Reese, Mary Elizabeth (48 yrs.) d. on 68-Apr-3 of Consumption [68-Apr-15: 2B].
Reese, Mary M. m. Pryor, John A. on 67-Jul-31 [67-Aug-3: 2B].
Reese, Minnie Ann (1 yr., 7 mos.) d. on 67-Mar-2 [67-Mar-4: 2D].
Reese, Naomi S. m. Lumberson, Erixon L. on 69-Dec-9 [69-Dec-13: 2C].
Reese, Priscilla (40 yrs.) d. on 66-Apr-10 [66-Apr-12: 2B].
Reese, Sarah T. m. Turner, Rodwell on 70-Jun-8 [70-Jun-11: 2B].
Reese, Sophie C. m. Stewart, William C. on 69-Nov-18 [69-Nov-20: 2B].
Reese, Sophie R. m. Cassard, Jesse L. on 67-Nov-5 [67-Nov-11: 2C].
Reese, Thomas (3 yrs.) d. on 67-May-29 in Railroad accident [67-May-31: 1F; 67-Jun-1: 1F].
Reese, Warren Lacey (10 yrs., 7 mos.) d. on 69-Jan-9 of Scarlet fever [69-Jan-19: 2C].
Reese, William D. m. Hooper, Sallie M. on 68-Jan-16 [68-Jan-17: 2C].
Reese, William M. (78 yrs.) d. on 70-Nov-24 [70-Nov-25: 2D; 70-Nov-26: 2C].
Reese, William P. m. Craig, Annie E. on 69-Feb-17 [69-Feb-19: 2C].
Reese, William Pitcher (1 yr., 2 mos.) d. on 69-Nov-21 [69-Nov-22: 2C; 69-Nov-23: 2C].
Reeside, H. H. m. Shearer, Maggie G. on 69-Dec-21 [69-Dec-22: 2B].
Reeves, I. Cooper m. King, Rebecca A. on 69-Sep-1 [69-Sep-3: 2B].
Reeves, John Wesley (1 yr., 4 mos.) d. on 68-Jun-28 Drowned [68-Jun-29: 1G, 2B].
Reeves, William Derr (1 yr., 8 mos.) d. on 69-May-15 [69-May-18: 2C].
Regan, Margaret m. Wagner, Alexander on 69-Nov-17 [70-Feb-3: 2B].
Regester, Eliza J. m. Hardy, George E. W. on 68-Oct-6 [68-Oct-8: 2B].
Regester, Maggie A. m. Lowery, George E. on 68-Jun-9 [68-Jun-10: 2B].
Rehbine, William H. H. m. Shaw, Mary E. on 67-Jun-12 [67-Jun-29: 2B].
Rehn, Johnnie B. d. on 66-Jan-18 of Pneumonia [66-Jan-20: 2C].
Reichert, Charles William G. m. Wells, Ruth A. on 69-Jul-13 [69-Jul-27: 2C].
Reid, B. G. W. m. Morrison, Maggie on 67-Feb-20 [67-Feb-21: 2C].
Reid, Edward m. Muse, Addie B. on 67-May-19 [67-May-21: 2B].
Reid, Ellen (86 yrs.) d. on 66-Feb-18 [66-Feb-20: 2B].
Reid, James (25 yrs.) d. on 68-Jan-9 [68-Jan-10: 2C].
Reid, James H. (64 yrs.) d. on 69-May-19 of Paralysis [69-May-20: 1H; 69-May-21: 1H].
Reid, Jane A. m. Russell, William W. on 66-Jun-14 [66-Jun-23: 2B].
Reid, Jessie Isabella (6 yrs.) d. on 69-May-9 [69-Jun-4: 2C].
Reid, John O. (45 yrs.) d. on 68-Mar-13 in Railroad accident [68-Mar-16: 1F].
Reid, M. A. m. Adair, John on 69-Jun-17 [69-Jun-28: 2C].
Reid, Mary d. on 66-Apr-15 [66-Apr-16: 2B].
Reid, Mary A. m. Musser, Alexander M. on 70-Oct-24 [70-Oct-29: 2B].
Reid, R. C. m. Chapman, Carrie T. on 70-Nov-11 [70-Nov-12: 2B].
Reider, David J. m. Hunt, Mary A. on 67-Dec-8 [67-Dec-17: 2B].
Reifsnider, John R. m. Belt, Mary V. on 66-Apr-19 [66-May-10: 2B].
Reigart, Catherine (77 yrs.) d. on 68-May-30 [68-Jun-1: 2B].
Reigel, Eva m. Pensel, Henry J. on 70-Jan-18 [70-Jan-31: 2C].
Reigenhart, Emma V. (25 yrs.) d. on 70-Jul-17 [70-Aug-1: 2C].
Reigher, James M. m. Wyatt, Emma on 69-Oct-22 [69-Oct-29: 2B].
Reightler, Joseph m. Blunt, Anna Maria on 69-Mar-7 [69-Mar-15: 2C].
Reign, Sarah d. on 70-Sep-15 [70-Sep-17: 2B].
Reihl, Harry (1 yr., 7 mos.) d. on 69-Jun-3 [69-Jun-5: 2B].
Reiley, Asbury Lincoln (1 yr., 6 mos.) d. on 66-Jul-23 [66-Jul-25: 2C].
Reilley, Mary (70 yrs.) d. on 68-Apr-12 [68-Apr-14: 2A].
Reilley, Mary Ann d. on 67-Dec-3 [67-Dec-4: 2C; 67-Dec-5: 2C].
Reilly, Charles E. m. Lanahan, Mary A. on 70-Jul-26 [70-Aug-3: 2C].
Reilly, Edwin d. on 69-Sep-30 [69-Oct-1: 2B].
Reilly, Elizabeth (42 yrs.) d. on 68-Aug-2 [68-Aug-3: 2B; 68-Aug-4: 2C].
Reilly, Francis (57 yrs.) d. on 68-Dec-19 [68-Dec-21: 2C].
Reilly, James F. (29 yrs.) d. on 68-Jul-15 [68-Jul-18: 2B].
Reilly, Julia A. m. Snyder, Harry S. on 68-Jan-21 [69-Aug-17: 2C].
Reilly, Julia Ann (5 yrs., 4 mos.) d. on 70-Feb-16 [70-Feb-17: 2C].

Reilly, Maggie (1 yr., 7 mos.) d. on 69-Feb-7 [69-Feb-8: 2C].
Reilly, Maggie A. m. Milholland, Arthur V. on 68-May-14 [68-May-28: 2B].
Reilly, Mary Ann m. Blum, Joseph A. on 68-Dec-15 [68-Dec-22: 2C].
Reilly, Mary Catherine (1 yr., 5 mos.) d. on 70-May-28 [70-May-30: 2B].
Reilly, Peter J. J. m. White, Jane E. on 70-Jan-19 [70-Feb-12: 2C].
Reilly, Philip (65 yrs.) d. on 69-Jul-2 of Apoplexy [69-Jul-3: 2B].
Reilly, Rose (2 yrs.) d. on 69-Jul-24 [69-Jul-26: 2C].
Reilly, Rose d. on 70-Oct-20 [70-Oct-22: 2B].
Reilly, Thomas Francis (14 yrs., 3 mos.) d. on 67-Jan-2 [67-Jan-3: 2B].
Reilly, William P. m. Byrne, Mary F. on 67-Nov-28 [67-Dec-3: 2C].
Reily, Alpheus L. d. on 68-Sep-16 [68-Sep-18: 2B].
Reily, James E. m. Marchildon, Julia on 69-Jun-15 [69-Jun-25: 2C].
Reinhardt, Blanche Amanda (2 yrs., 6 mos.) d. on 69-Feb-20 [69-Feb-22: 2C].
Reinhardt, Charles Henry (2 yrs., 2 mos.) d. on 69-Dec-2 [69-Dec-3: 2C].
Reinhardt, Emma V. (25 yrs.) d. on 70-Jul-17 [70-Jul-18: 2B].
Reinhardt, George M. m. Sunderland, Isabella E. on 66-Mar-22 [66-Mar-28: 2C].
Reinhardt, Henry Mull (19 yrs.) d. on 70-Sep-19 [70-Sep-20: 2B].
Reinhardt, John C. (87 yrs., 2 mos.) d. on 70-Mar-1 [70-Mar-2: 2C].
Reinhardt, Margaret Ann (1 mo.) d. on 67-Nov-28 [67-Nov-30: 2C].
Reinhardt, Matilda d. on 69-Apr-16 [69-Apr-17: 2B].
Reinhart, Albert Reginald (4 mos.) d. on 68-Jul-20 [68-Jul-21: 2C].
Reinhart, George P. m. Mittendorf, Mary Jane on 70-May-19 [70-May-21: 2B].
Reinhart, Harry E. m. Mastbaum, Sarah on 70-Jun-15 [70-Jul-19: 2B].
Reinhart, Mary Ann E. (24 yrs.) d. on 68-Apr-6 [68-Apr-7: 2B; 68-Apr-8: 2B].
Reinicker, Edward S. m. Gavet, Isabel on 70-Nov-16 [70-Nov-23: 2B].
Reip, Thomas H. m. Morrow, Mary G. on 68-Sep-29 [68-Oct-28: 2B].
Reisinger, Annie M. m. Hutchinson, James on 66-Aug-5 [66-Nov-17: 2B].
Reisinger, Bertha J. m. Richardson, John S. on 67-Nov-28 [67-Dec-17: 2B].
Reisinger, Fannie E. m. Sleeger, George A. on 70-Nov-6 [70-Nov-15: 2C].
Reisinger, Hannah (48 yrs., 11 mos.) d. on 69-Sep-6 of Consumption [69-Sep-8: 2B].
Reissinger, William H. m. McElroy, Martha on 70-Jul-7 [70-Jul-15: 2C].
Reister, John E. m. Milbourne, Clara J. on 68-Jan-2 [68-Jan-4: 2C].
Reister, Maggie E. m. Schaefer, Henry on 68-Jun-4 [68-Jul-14: 2B].
Reiter, Albert H. m. Davis, Sarah A. on 70-Oct-18 [70-Oct-22: 2B].
Reiter, Ann Leonora m. Johnston, Edward E. on 66-Dec-13 [66-Dec-15: 2B].
Reiter, Emma Cheseborough (2 yrs., 5 mos.) d. on 68-Oct-15 [68-Oct-16: 2B; 68-Oct-17: 2B].
Reitz, John (46 yrs.) d. on 70-Jun-24 of Heart paralysis [70-Jun-25: 1G, 2B].
Reitz, Lavinia A. (21 yrs.) d. on 66-Feb-25 [66-Feb-26: 2B; 66-Feb-27: 2B].
Reitz, Sophia C. m. Fisher, William H. on 67-May-9 [67-May-13: 2B].
Remick, Freddie Albert (9 yrs., 11 mos.) d. on 69-Dec-26 [69-Dec-27: 2D].
Remington, W. Williams m. Mackall, Harriet on 70-Sep-22 [70-Sep-26: 2B].
Remmey, Isabel A. m. DeWalt, John C. on 66-Jun-14 [66-Jun-23: 2C].
Remmy, Emma A. m. Manns, Frederick A. on 67-Aug-1 [67-Aug-10: 2B].
Remmy, Joseph Edward (1 yr., 1 mo.) d. on 67-Oct-10 [67-Oct-12: 2A].
Remmy, William Winfield (21 yrs.) d. on 69-Apr-14 of Typhoid [69-Apr-15: 2B].
Remore, George E. m. Fowler, Fannie E. on 67-Jun-27 [67-Aug-6: 2C].
Renehan, John Foley (3 yrs., 4 mos.) d. on 67-Jan-27 [67-Jan-28: 2C].
Renehan, Josephine Cecilia (10 mos.) d. on 69-Apr-6 [69-Apr-7: 2C].
Renner, George, Jr. m. Swing, Mollie P. on 68-Sep-29 [68-Oct-8: 2B].
Rennolds, H. T. m. Grape, Georgia on 70-May-12 [70-May-19: 2C].
Rennolds, Helen A. m. Rennolds, William Lindsay on 67-Dec-23 [67-Dec-28: 2C].
Rennolds, Henry S. (64 yrs.) d. on 69-Sep-27 [69-Sep-28: 2B].
Rennolds, Lindsay H. m. Disney, Hannah A. on 70-May-17 [70-May-19: 2C].
Rennolds, Mary (62 yrs.) d. on 67-Jul-29 [67-Jul-30: 2C].
Rennolds, Mary T. m. Irvine, Carter R. on 69-May-11 [69-May-18: 2C].

Rennolds, William D. m. Tubman, Julia L. on 66-Nov-15 [66-Nov-19: 2B].
Rennolds, William Lindsay m. Rennolds, Helen A. on 67-Dec-23 [67-Dec-28: 2C].
Rennous, Susie d. on 70-Oct-21 [70-Oct-22: 2B; 70-Oct-27: 2B].
Renoff, Frederick J. m. Lane, Caroline L. on 69-Aug-23 [69-Aug-30: 2B].
Renshaw, Harriet d. on 70-Aug-22 [70-Aug-25: 2C].
Renshaw, James (55 yrs.) d. on 66-Apr-19 [66-Apr-26: 2B].
Renshaw, James H. m. Lewis, Delia R. on 70-Oct-23 [70-Dec-28: 2C].
Renshaw, Robert H. m. Carter, Maria on 69-Jun-8 [69-Jun-9: 2C].
Rentz, George F. (33 yrs., 4 mos.) d. on 70-Dec-17 [70-Dec-19: 2C].
Rentz, Jacob F. (68 yrs.) d. on 67-Aug-23 [67-Aug-24: 2B].
Renwick, John F. (27 yrs.) d. on 69-Jun-23 [69-Jun-24: 2C].
Renwick, R., Jr. m. Henning, Mary R. on 66-Jan-24 [66-Jan-27: 2B].
Renwick, Thomas Oliver (19 yrs.) d. on 69-Oct-8 [69-Oct-9: 2C].
Renwick, William Selter Hennin (2 mos.) d. on 69-Jan-9 [69-Jan-11: 2C].
Renwick, William Telfer (20 yrs.) d. on 68-Jul-12 [68-Jul-14: 2C].
Repp, Charles W. m. Muth, Lizzie V. on 69-Sep-28 [69-Oct-19: 2B].
Requardt, Harriet E. (1 yr., 6 mos.) d. on 67-Jan-1 [67-Jan-3: 2C].
Requardt, Julia J. d. on 67-Jan-14 [67-Jan-15: 2C].
Rettler, Louisa A. m. Dambmann, Gustav F. P. on 68-Jan-6 [68-Jan-7: 2B].
Reuter, Lisette (2 yrs., 3 mos.) d. on 68-Jun-5 [68-Jun-6: 2A].
Reuther, Carl m. Hess, Tillie on 66-May-8 [66-May-15: 2C].
Rex, Sybill m. Fox, Edward W. on 66-Mar-22 [66-Mar-23: 2C].
Rexs, Charles m. Smith, Emily on 67-Sep-24 [67-Sep-26: 2B].
Reynolds, Anthony d. on 67-May-28 Drowned [67-May-29: 1F, 2B].
Reynolds, Caroline (26 yrs.) d. on 68-Feb-14 [68-Feb-15: 2B].
Reynolds, Caroline M. d. on 70-Mar-24 [70-Mar-25: 2C].
Reynolds, Charles A. m. Hickley, Kate R. on 68-Apr-30 [68-May-4: 2B].
Reynolds, Charles E. (25 yrs.) d. on 69-May-25 of Pneumonia [69-May-26: 2C].
Reynolds, Eliza d. on 66-Jul-18 [66-Jul-19: 2C].
Reynolds, Eliza Ann (6 yrs., 7 mos.) d. on 70-Mar-18 [70-Mar-19: 2C].
Reynolds, Ellen (66 yrs.) d. on 70-Jul-2 [70-Jul-6: 2C].
Reynolds, Francis S. m. Kelly, Cornelia E. on 68-May-4 [68-May-11: 2B].
Reynolds, H. R. (39 yrs.) d. on 67-Jan-23 of Pneumonia [67-Jan-24: 2C; 67-Jan-25: 2C].
Reynolds, Henry R. (59 yrs.) d. on 68-Dec-28 of Heart disease [68-Dec-29: 2D, 4C; 68-Dec-30: 2D; 68-Dec-31: 1G].
Reynolds, Josiah (59 yrs., 6 mos.) d. on 67-May-29 of Brain congestion [67-May-30: 1F, 2B; 67-May-31: 2B].
Reynolds, Kate (1 yr.) d. on 67-Jul-5 [67-Jul-6: 2B].
Reynolds, Kate (1 yr., 6 mos.) d. on 70-Jul-18 [70-Jul-19: 2C].
Reynolds, Lucy A. H. d. on 68-Dec-16 [68-Dec-18: 2C].
Reynolds, Luther M. m. Willis, Mary L. on 67-Oct-26 [67-Oct-30: 2B].
Reynolds, Mary Ann (8 yrs.) d. on 70-Feb-3 [70-Feb-5: 2C].
Reynolds, Mary E. m. Tracy, Samuel W. on 69-Feb-8 [69-Feb-23: 2C].
Reynolds, Patrick m. Turner, Maria on 67-May-19 [67-May-23: 2B].
Reynolds, Perry (47 yrs.) d. on 69-Dec-4 [69-Dec-6: 2C].
Reynolds, Thomas m. Singleton, Mary Virginia on 66-Nov-4 [66-Nov-24: 2B].
Reynolds, Thomas W. m. Banks, Carrie on 69-Dec-18 [69-Dec-29: 2D].
Reynolds, William (40 yrs.) d. on 68-Oct-26 [68-Oct-27: 2B].
Reynolds, William (29 yrs.) d. on 68-May-3 [68-May-4: 2B; 68-May-5: 2B].
Reynolds, William Allen (1 yr., 5 mos.) d. on 69-Aug-22 [69-Aug-24: 2C].
Reynolds, William Francis (1 yr., 4 mos.) d. on 69-Feb-23 [69-Feb-24: 2C].
Reynolds, William I. m. Brown, Sallie A. on 68-Sep-6 [68-Oct-10: 2B].
Reynolds, William John (1 yr., 9 mos.) d. on 68-Nov-2 [68-Nov-4: 2C].
Rhames, William m. Sherwood, Abbie M. on 69-Mar-15 [69-Mar-17: 2C].
Rhea, George W. m. Wingate, Louisa on 66-Jun-12 [66-Jun-15: 2C].

Rhinehart, Charles (69 yrs.) d. on 66-Mar-14 [66-Mar-15: 2C; 66-Mar-16: 2B].
Rhinehart, Elizabeth (33 yrs.) d. on 66-Aug-27 [66-Aug-28: 2B].
Rhinehart, Emelia m. Herman, John on 68-Jul-2 [68-Jul-4: 2C].
Rhinehart, Sallie U. m. Little, Lewis P. on 69-Aug-23 [69-Aug-30: 2B].
Rhinender, Adam (8 yrs.) d. on 69-Oct-24 Drowned [69-Nov-8: 1G].
Rhoades, Isabella (45 yrs.) d. on 66-Jan-28 [66-Jan-29: 2C].
Rhoads, E. M. m. Milstead, John H. on 68-Dec-31 [69-Jan-23: 2C].
Rhoads, Eliza A. d. on 70-Jul-25 [70-Jul-27: 2C].
Rhoads, James E. m. Hamilton, Sally on 67-Jan-8 [67-Feb-5: 2C].
Rhoads, William R. m. Cummings, Annie on 70-Jul-7 [70-Jul-28: 2C].
Rhodes, Emma J. (74 yrs.) d. on 68-Aug-24 [68-Aug-25: 2B].
Rhodes, F. W. m. Smith, Mary E. on 69-Nov-21 [69-Nov-27: 2B].
Rhodes, Gilbert Welty (1 mo.) d. on 67-Jul-7 [67-Jul-8: 2C].
Rhodes, Joseph m. Emory, Joe on 69-Mar-30 [69-Jul-13: 2C].
Rhodes, Lucy Churchill (79 yrs.) d. on 70-Jan-7 [70-Jan-18: 2C].
Rhodes, Mary A. (38 yrs.) d. on 70-Aug-18 [70-Aug-20: 2B].
Rhodes, S. T. m. Raborg, Carrie M. on 68-Nov-24 [68-Nov-25: 2B].
Rhodes, Sarah J. m. Lehman, George A. on 70-May-12 [70-May-14: 2A].
Rhodes, Virginia E. m. Holmes, Milton W. on 70-May-5 [70-May-10: 2B].
Rhodes, William Edwin d. on 69-Feb-5 [69-Feb-8: 2C].
Rhodes, Zachariah Blowers (78 yrs.) d. on 70-Jan-1 [70-Jan-7: 2F, 4F].
Rhor, John d. on 67-Jul-4 in Railroad accident [67-Jul-6: 4C].
Riach, Alexander F. m. Hoffman, Louisa on 68-Nov-11 [68-Nov-17: 2C].
Riach, Margaret (1 yr., 10 mos.) d. on 69-Jul-24 [69-Jul-28: 2D].
Rial, Michael K. m. Sitzler, Emma D. on 67-Jul-3 [67-Sep-26: 2B].
Ricards, John R., Sr. d. on 70-Dec-28 of Paralysis [70-Dec-29: 2C; 70-Dec-31: 4B].
Ricaud, Sarah E. d. on 69-Oct-24 [69-Oct-26: 2B].
Rice, Bell (1 yr., 3 mos.) d. on 70-Aug-16 [70-Aug-17: 2C].
Rice, C. E. m. Donnelly, Emma on 68-Nov-15 [68-Nov-30: 2B].
Rice, Duane H. m. McCubbin, Sarah R. on 68-Dec-27 [68-Dec-30: 2C].
Rice, Edith Mantz d. on 66-Mar-11 [66-Mar-13: 2B].
Rice, Elizabeth Jane (43 yrs.) d. on 67-Sep-29 [67-Oct-1: 2B].
Rice, Frederick m. Horn, Mary A. on 66-Jan-25 [66-Jan-27: 2B].
Rice, John (31 yrs.) d. on 66-Feb-23 of Gunshot wound [66-Feb-24: 1F].
Rice, John B. m. Cook, Adelia B. on 67-Jan-15 [67-Feb-5: 2C].
Rice, John W. m. Mullet, Eugenia C. on 70-Jun-22 [70-Jun-25: 2B; 70-Jun-27: 2C].
Rice, Judah, Sr. (54 yrs.) d. on 70-Aug-30 [70-Sep-1: 2B].
Rice, Maggie m. Donald, James on 69-Sep-1 [69-Sep-21: 2B].
Rice, Maggie Lee (6 yrs., 7 mos.) d. on 69-Nov-9 [69-Nov-10: 2C].
Rice, Mary (93 yrs., 9 mos.) d. on 67-Jan-25 [67-Jan-30: 2C].
Rice, Mary (50 yrs.) d. on 67-Feb-20 [67-Feb-21: 2C].
Rice, Mary M. d. on 66-Sep-8 [66-Sep-13: 2C].
Rice, Mattie M. m. Pope, Thomas E. on 66-Jan-23 [66-Jan-26: 2B].
Rice, Peter (73 yrs.) d. on 66-Sep-21 [66-Sep-22: 2B].
Rice, Sallie E. d. on 67-Jun-27 [67-Jun-28: 2B; 67-Jul-2: 2B].
Rice, William (31 yrs.) d. on 70-Jul-8 of Heart disease [70-Jul-9: 1H, 2B].
Rice, William D. m. Merrill, Catherine M. on 67-Dec-12 [67-Dec-16: 2B].
Rich, Edward R. m. Miller, Virginia on 66-May-29 [66-May-31: 2B].
Rich, George Augustus (21 yrs.) d. on 67-Jan-20 [67-Jan-26: 2C].
Rich, Lizzie d. on 67-Nov-4 [67-Nov-5: 2B].
Rich, Mary Elizabeth (16 yrs.) d. on 69-Jun-18 [69-Jun-19: 2B].
Rich, Mary W. d. on 69-Nov-3 [69-Nov-4: 2C].
Rich, Nannie Owings d. on 66-Jun-25 [66-Jun-27: 2C].
Richard, Stephen m. Charron, Ellen M. on 66-Feb-21 [66-Feb-24: 2B].
Richards, Annie Custis m. Hopkins, H. Harrison on 67-Jun-5 [67-Jun-12: 2B].

Richards, Charles Lewis (1 yr., 9 mos.) d. on 68-Feb-20 of Chronic croup [68-Feb-22: 2B].
Richards, Frisby m. Hall, Fanny on 68-Jun-18 [68-Jun-23: 2B].
Richards, Georgeanna (20 yrs.) d. on 70-Jan-5 [70-Jan-6: 2C].
Richards, Henry d. on 70-Aug-12 of Execution (Hanging) [70-Aug-13: 1C].
Richards, James (24 yrs.) d. on 68-Jul-26 [68-Jul-27: 2B; 68-Jul-28: 2B].
Richards, James George m. Ford, Mary A. on 66-Mar-18 [66-Apr-7: 2B].
Richards, James P. m. Swann, Emma S. on 70-Apr-12 [70-Apr-16: 2B].
Richards, Lillie May (1 yr., 3 mos.) d. on 66-Apr-17 [66-Apr-18: 2C].
Richards, Mary R. m. Thomas, Richard C. on 69-Jan-12 [69-Jan-29: 2C].
Richards, Sadoria m. Jones, Thomas on 66-Dec-29 [66-Dec-31: 2C].
Richards, T. S. m. Eshelman, Emma on 67-Feb-20 [67-Feb-23: 2C].
Richards, T. T. S., Rev. d. on 69-Dec-26 [69-Dec-27: 2D].
Richards, Theodore (1 yr., 7 mos.) d. on 70-Jul-5 [70-Jul-6: 2C].
Richards, Thomas m. Morris, Annie on 70-Jan-15 [70-Jan-19: 2C].
Richardson, Addie m. Gibson, Woolman on 68-Feb-28 [68-May-12: 2B].
Richardson, Amanda m. McClure, James F. on 69-Mar-4 [69-Apr-5: 2B].
Richardson, Andrew Lipscomb (28 yrs.) d. on 69-May-11 [69-May-12: 2B].
Richardson, B. O. m. Gibson, Ella on 70-Oct-26 [70-Nov-9: 2C].
Richardson, C. A. m. Brooks, Josie on 70-Jan-12 [70-Jan-14: 2C].
Richardson, Catharine Martenet (75 yrs.) d. on 70-Oct-4 of Heart disease [70-Oct-17: 2B; 70-Oct-18: 2C].
Richardson, Charlotte m. Carr, Samuel on 70-Jul-4 [70-Jul-19: 2B].
Richardson, Claudia Henkle (1 yr.) d. on 69-Jul-30 [69-Aug-5: 2C].
Richardson, Edward J. (66 yrs.) d. on 68-Aug-29 [68-Aug-31: 1G, 2B].
Richardson, Eliza N. (74 yrs., 7 mos.) d. on 70-Sep-9 [70-Sep-15: 2B].
Richardson, Elizabeth (93 yrs.) d. on 67-Mar-4 [67-Mar-14: 2C].
Richardson, Ella M. m. Grape, W. S. on 69-Sep-7 [69-Sep-28: 2B].
Richardson, Emma S. m. Pacetti, Thomas A. on 68-May-12 [68-May-16: 2A].
Richardson, Henry m. Owens, Maria H. on 68-Oct-13 [68-Oct-14: 2B].
Richardson, Henry B. (43 yrs.) d. on 68-Jun-19 [68-Jul-4: 2C].
Richardson, Henry W. m. Iglehart, Anna Louisa on 70-Apr-26 [70-May-2: 2B].
Richardson, Ida R. (2 yrs., 4 mos.) d. on 67-Mar-8 [67-Mar-12: 2C].
Richardson, James O. m. Young, Felicite E. on 67-Feb-21 [67-Feb-23: 2C].
Richardson, James W. (50 yrs.) d. on 66-Jul-17 of Heatstroke [66-Jul-18: 1F, 2C].
Richardson, Johanna Frances (50 yrs.) d. on 66-Jan-5 [66-Jan-17: 2C].
Richardson, John m. Mannar, Mary C. on 66-Apr-5 [66-Apr-7: 2B].
Richardson, John R. m. Gray, Fannie on 69-Dec-2 [69-Dec-20: 2C].
Richardson, John S. m. Reisinger, Bertha J. on 67-Nov-28 [67-Dec-17: 2B].
Richardson, John W. (60 yrs.) d. on 66-Sep-27 [66-Oct-1: 2B].
Richardson, John W. (65 yrs.) d. on 70-Apr-3 of Paralysis [70-Apr-4: 1G, 2C; 70-Apr-5: 2B].
Richardson, Joshua N. m. Mullett, Carrie A. on 69-Dec-30 [70-Jan-4: 2C].
Richardson, Juliet P. m. Hall, John J. on 67-Oct-3 [67-Nov-8: 2C].
Richardson, Julius Garey d. on 67-Sep-10 [67-Sep-11: 2B].
Richardson, Linneaus Washingto (25 yrs.) d. on 69-Aug-22 of Heart disease [69-Aug-27: 2B].
Richardson, Lizzie Dorsey (18 yrs., 3 mos.) d. on 68-Mar-14 [68-May-21: 2B].
Richardson, Lizzie R. m. Burgess, J. P. on 69-Jan-26 [69-Jan-28: 2C].
Richardson, Llewellyn Poulton (1 yr., 9 mos.) d. on 69-Sep-2 [69-Sep-14: 2B].
Richardson, Martha A. m. Johnston, James on 70-Oct-19 [70-Oct-29: 2B].
Richardson, Mary (62 yrs.) d. on 67-Mar-30 [67-Apr-1: 2C].
Richardson, Mary Martha (33 yrs.) d. on 67-Nov-6 [67-Nov-7: 2C].
Richardson, Mary Robinson (7 mos.) d. on 67-Nov-14 [67-Nov-15: 2B].
Richardson, Mary V. m. Bryan, Issac R. on 69-Oct-14 [69-Oct-16: 2B; 69-Oct-18: 2C].
Richardson, Mary Weems m. Mytinger, C. H. on 67-Feb-28 [67-Mar-7: 2C].
Richardson, Nancy Pauline (4 yrs., 1 mo.) d. on 69-Mar-21 [69-Mar-22: 2C].
Richardson, Rebecca E. m. Govett, Lewis Washington on 68-Dec-28 [68-Dec-29: 2D].

Richardson, S. Barry (22 yrs.) d. on 69-Oct-16 [69-Oct-18: 2C].
Richardson, Sarah Reese d. on 70-Nov-20 [70-Nov-22: 2C].
Richardson, Thomas B. (67 yrs.) d. on 68-May-15 of Paralysis [68-May-18: 1G, 2B].
Richardson, Thomas Oliver Lock (13 yrs., 6 mos.) d. on 66-Nov-28 of Fall from roof [66-Nov-29: 1G; 66-Dec-1: 2B].
Richardson, Virginia S. m. Martin, George B. on 70-Mar-6 [70-Apr-16: 2B].
Richardson, Wallace P. m. Strong, Elizabeth A. on 69-Dec-12 [69-Dec-15: 2B].
Richardson, Wilbur James (4 mos.) d. on 67-Jul-30 [67-Aug-1: 2C].
Richardson, William H. m. Fowler, Emily R. on 69-Jun-17 [69-Jun-23: 2C].
Richardson, William W. m. Holland, Mattie V. on 70-Oct-27 [70-Nov-3: 2B].
Richars, Frances d. on 67-Feb-4 [67-Feb-5: 2C].
Richerson, Mary (60 yrs.) d. on 68-Dec-6 of Hemorrhage [68-Dec-12: 2C].
Richey, James I. (25 yrs.) d. on 67-Apr-20 of Consumption [67-Apr-30: 2A].
Richey, Maggie S. m. Yeager, M. B. on 67-May-21 [67-Jun-27: 2B].
Richey, Robert Miles (1 yr., 3 mos.) d. on 68-Apr-11 [68-Apr-15: 2B].
Richfield, Ann Louisa m. Thomas, John H. on 67-Jan-30 [67-Feb-4: 2C].
Richman, Clayton S. m. Tolson, Lilian M. on 70-Jun-13 [70-Jun-18: 2B].
Richmond, George W. m. Linsey, Jennie on 68-Aug-12 [68-Aug-20: 2B].
Richmond, Jemima d. on 67-Oct-19 of Consumption [67-Oct-22: 2A].
Richstein, Lizzie m. Eichelberger, L. S. on 66-Apr-24 [66-May-24: 2C].
Richter, Elizabeth J. (38 yrs.) d. on 68-Aug-15 [68-Aug-18: 2B].
Richter, Gustave m. Falk, Louisa J. M. on 69-Apr-4 [69-Apr-6: 2C].
Richtor, Ann Mariah (1 yr., 10 mos.) d. on 67-Aug-4 [67-Aug-7: 2C].
Richtor, Florence Annetta d. on 67-Aug-4 [67-Aug-7: 2C].
Rickard, John m. Thompson, Rebecca on 67-Sep-26 [67-Oct-22: 2A].
Rickert, Lena m. Wisner, H. on 67-Jun-16 [67-Jun-21: 2B].
Rickett, William G. (27 yrs.) d. on 69-Jan-11 [69-Jan-12: 2C].
Ricketts, David F. (33 yrs.) d. on 66-Jan-8 [66-Jan-10: 2C].
Ricketts, James Poole d. on 66-Oct-11 [66-Oct-17: 2B].
Ricketts, John m. Drury, Helen E. on 69-Aug-4 [69-Aug-6: 2D].
Ricketts, Mary (75 yrs.) d. on 69-Feb-15 [69-Feb-16: 2C; 69-Feb-17: 2D].
Ricketts, Sallie m. Lipscomb, J. D. on 70-Nov-16 [70-Nov-22: 2B].
Ricktor, Adelia S. m. Lepson, George W. on 67-May-14 [67-Sep-2: 2B].
Ricktor, Ida Virginia (5 mos.) d. on 70-Jun-1 [70-Jun-3: 2B].
Ricktor, Thomas (50 yrs.) d. on 70-Jul-25 [70-Jul-26: 2C].
Riddle, Charles Edward (26 yrs.) d. on 66-Apr-7 [66-Apr-10: 2C; 66-Apr-11: 2B].
Riddle, George W. m. Barnes, Maggie B. on 69-Feb-18 [69-Feb-23: 2C].
Riddle, John (75 yrs.) d. on 66-Oct-31 of Paralysis [66-Nov-7: 1F].
Riddle, Sophia (76 yrs.) d. on 70-May-30 [70-Jun-2: 2B].
Riddlemoser, Robert Lee (2 yrs., 2 mos.) d. on 66-Jun-22 [66-Jun-23: 2B; 66-Jun-27: 2C].
Ridenour, Catherine R. (66 yrs.) d. on 70-Mar-12 [70-Mar-18: 2C].
Ridenour, Charles Cavalier (7 yrs., 9 mos.) d. on 68-Dec-25 [68-Dec-29: 2D].
Ridenour, Harry (5 yrs., 1 mo.) d. on 68-Dec-23 [68-Dec-29: 2D].
Ridenour, M. A. m. Roadcap, Macey A. on 70-Jun-26 [70-Jul-15: 2C].
Ridenour, Willie Rider (3 yrs.) d. on 69-Jan-6 [69-Jan-8: 2C].
Rider, Aaron (69 yrs.) d. on 69-Mar-8 of Heart disease [69-Mar-12: 4D].
Rider, Annie m. Linton, Joseph on 67-Oct-23 [67-Oct-26: 2A].
Rider, Edward, Sr. (77 yrs.) d. on 66-Nov-25 [66-Nov-27: 2B, 4B].
Rider, Elizabeth H. m. Hartlove, Joseph M. on 66-Apr-11 [66-Apr-21: 2B].
Rider, Freddie m. Ehrman, M. on 67-Jun-12 [67-Jun-14: 2B].
Rider, Georgette (10 mos.) d. on 68-Mar-17 [68-Mar-19: 2B].
Rider, Ginette (53 yrs., 8 mos.) d. on 66-Nov-1 [66-Nov-3: 2B; 66-Nov-10: 2B].
Rider, H. Isabel m. Lucas, R. Henry on 70-Sep-26 [70-Oct-5: 2B; 70-Oct-7: 2B].
Rider, Leopold m. Stern, R. on 67-Nov-24 [67-Nov-25: 2C].
Rider, Lizzie m. Stevenson, John M. on 67-Apr-18 [67-Apr-20: 2A].

Rider, Margaret Elizabeth (5 mos.) d. on 69-Jan-27 [69-Jan-29: 2C].
Rider, Nettie (9 mos.) d. on 69-Jul-21 [69-Jul-22: 2C].
Rider, Rosie m. Judah, E. Douglas on 68-Aug-6 [68-Aug-7: 2B].
Rider, Washington (64 yrs.) d. on 66-Mar-26 [66-Mar-28: 2C].
Rider, William E. m. Lovering, Lottie on 67-Oct-8 [67-Oct-14: 2B].
Ridgaway, Emma A. m. Payne, George C. on 68-Nov-17 [68-Nov-21: 2C].
Ridgaway, George Thomas (2 yrs., 1 mo.) d. on 67-Sep-2 [67-Sep-3: 2B].
Ridgaway, J. Lee m. Hale, Cornelia W. on 67-Jul-24 [67-Oct-21: 2B].
Ridgaway, James R. (21 yrs.) d. on 68-Feb-28 [68-Feb-29: 2B].
Ridgaway, Julia E. m. Rose, Charles H. on 68-May-7 [68-May-20: 2B].
Ridgeley, Caroline (62 yrs.) d. on 69-Jul-4 [69-Jul-5: 2C].
Ridgely, Catherine M. d. on 70-Sep-29 [70-Sep-30: 2B; 70-Oct-1: 2B].
Ridgely, Daniel Bowley (55 yrs.) d. on 68-May-5 of Heart disease [68-May-7: 1B, 2B].
Ridgely, Eliza E. (65 yrs.) d. on 67-Dec-20 [67-Dec-21: 2B].
Ridgely, Hettie T. m. Lehman, Robert on 66-Mar-29 [66-Mar-31: 2C].
Ridgely, Isaiah (76 yrs.) d. on 68-Apr-12 of Paralysis [68-Apr-21: 2B].
Ridgely, John [of Hampton] (78 yrs.) d. on 67-Jul-16 [67-Jul-17: 1G, 2C].
Ridgely, John T. m. Jervis, Sallie A. on 68-Apr-2 [68-Apr-9: 2B].
Ridgely, Lloyd G. (45 yrs.) d. on 68-Nov-3 of Suicide (Jumped from roof) [68-Nov-4: 1G, 2C].
Ridgely, Lou E. m. Bradford, Luther on 70-Nov-30 [70-Dec-9: 2C].
Ridgely, Mary (86 yrs.) d. on 68-Jan-1 [68-Jan-2: 2C].
Ridgely, Mary Bell Cowden (1 yr., 3 mos.) d. on 66-Aug-24 [66-Aug-29: 2B].
Ridgely, Richard D. m. Turner, Lottie M. on 68-Mar-25 [68-Mar-30: 2B].
Ridgely, Sarah Ann (15 yrs.) d. on 68-May-18 [68-May-20: 2A].
Ridgely, Sarah Talbott (48 yrs.) d. on 67-May-10 of Consumption [67-May-15: 2B].
Ridgely, Shelly Baer (17 yrs.) d. on 69-Apr-7 [69-Apr-9: 2C; 69-Apr-10: 2B].
Ridgely, William A. (8 yrs., 2 mos.) d. on 67-May-12 [67-May-16: 2B].
Ridgely, William H. d. on 68-Mar-7 [68-Mar-9: 2C].
Ridgley, Nicholas Herbert (10 mos.) d. on 69-Jul-22 [69-Jul-23: 2C].
Ridgway, D. C. m. Dodson, Amelia J. on 67-Jul-11 [67-Jul-15: 2C].
Ridout, Ann (79 yrs.) d. on 68-Jul-29 [68-Jul-30: 2B].
Ridout, John (76 yrs.) d. on 68-Oct-15 [68-Oct-27: 2C].
Ridout, Margaret A. d. on 70-Oct-13 [70-Oct-18: 2C].
Riedinger, Caroline (21 yrs., 6 mos.) d. on 68-Jan-6 [68-Jan-8: 2C].
Riefle, Hetty V. m. Holthaus, Harry C. on 68-Nov-5 [68-Nov-10: 2C; 68-Nov-11: 2C].
Riegel, Theodore Grant (6 mos.) d. on 68-Aug-10 of Lung congestion [68-Aug-13: 2B].
Rieger, Francis m. Thompson, Mary J. on 68-Dec-25 [68-Dec-29: 2D].
Riehl, Edward Friederick (5 mos.) d. on 68-Jul-25 [68-Jul-27: 2B].
Rieman, Henry, Jr. m. Clabaugh, Mollie on 70-Apr-26 [70-Apr-28: 2B].
Rieman, Robert G. (39 yrs.) d. on 70-Dec-26 [70-Dec-28: 2C, 4D; 70-Dec-29: 2C; 70-Dec-30: 4D].
Rienhart, A. A. m. Carrick, H. on 70-Oct-4 [70-Oct-18: 2B].
Riepe, Lothar m. Ortman, Ann on 66-Apr-24 [66-Apr-25: 2B].
Rierdon, Edward (45 yrs.) d. on 66-Nov-14 [66-Nov-16: 2C].
Rierdon, Margaret (39 yrs.) d. on 68-Nov-25 [68-Nov-26: 2B].
Ries, Benjamin (1 yr., 1 mo.) d. on 66-Feb-20 [66-Feb-22: 2B].
Riesinger, Charles Ellsworth (6 yrs., 10 mos.) d. on 69-Mar-2 [69-Mar-5: 2C].
Riffle, Ava M. V. d. on 66-May-15 of Consumption [66-May-19: 2B].
Riffle, Thomas m. Griffith, Lizzie on 68-Sep-15 [68-Sep-28: 2B].
Rigby, Annie J. m. Smith, E. T. on 68-Dec-2 [68-Dec-5: 2C].
Rigby, Arthur m. Bunting, Zoe L. on 69-Jun-9 [69-Jun-10: 2C].
Rigby, Deborah (58 yrs.) d. on 70-Jul-26 [70-Jul-27: 2C; 70-Jul-28: 2C].
Rigby, Florence Washington d. on 67-Apr-20 [67-Apr-22: 2A].
Rigby, Mary H. (63 yrs.) d. on 69-Aug-29 [69-Aug-30: 2B; 69-Aug-31: 2B].
Rigby, Mary O. m. Hicks, John G. on 69-Nov-17 [69-Nov-20: 2B].

Rigby, Milcah m. Fleeharty, John T. on 69-Aug-3 [69-Aug-4: 2C].
Rigger, Mary Clementine m. Wells, Thomas on 69-Sep-28 [69-Nov-2: 2B].
Riggin, E. A. W. d. on 69-Aug-1 [69-Aug-2: 2C].
Riggin, James Francis (10 mos.) d. on 70-Dec-31 [70-Jan-1: 2B].
Riggin, Napoleon B. (33 yrs., 9 mos.) d. on 69-Sep-14 [69-Sep-15: 2B; 69-Sep-16: 2B].
Riggin, William L. P. m. Throop, Mary C. on 70-Sep-15 [70-Sep-17: 2B].
Riggins, Fannie m. Eckhardt, Charles on 69-Oct-18 [69-Oct-19: 2B].
Riggle, Emily m. Whitlock, George on 68-Aug-16 [68-Aug-19: 2B].
Riggle, Laura m. Butler, Thomas H. on 67-Mar-25 [67-Apr-3: 2B].
Riggs, Fanny m. Dikes, William H. on 68-Aug-11 [68-Aug-12: 2C].
Riggs, George R. d. on 70-Jan-23 [70-Jan-24: 4F].
Riggs, John W. m. Bordley, Hannah M. on 69-Dec-23 [69-Dec-31: 2C].
Riggs, Joshua W. m. Dorsey, Mattie B. on 67-Oct-2 [67-Oct-5: 2B].
Riggs, Mary Alice m. Cragg, S. Wilkins on 69-Sep-5 [69-Feb-8: 2C; 69-Sep-9: 2C].
Riggs, Mary Ann (73 yrs.) d. on 70-Feb-26 [70-Mar-21: 2C].
Riggs, Rebecca (83 yrs.) d. on 68-Dec-19 [68-Dec-21: 2C].
Riggs, Remus (78 yrs.) d. on 67-Dec-18 [67-Dec-20: 2B].
Rigney, Mary E. (1 yr., 10 mos.) d. on 68-Sep-18 [68-Sep-19: 2B].
Riley, Alice (78 yrs.) d. on 66-Jul-8 [66-Jul-9: 2C].
Riley, Ann Eliza (1 yr., 1 mo.) d. on 66-Jan-4 [66-Jan-6: 2B].
Riley, Benjamin Nalls (9 mos.) d. on 70-Jul-29 [70-Aug-1: 2C].
Riley, Dennis (55 yrs.) d. on 70-Nov-17 of Heart disease [70-Nov-18: 2C, 4C].
Riley, Ella Carson (12 yrs., 6 mos.) d. on 69-Aug-21 [69-Aug-23: 2C].
Riley, Emily d. on 67-Jan-15 [67-Jan-17: 2C; 67-Jan-18: 2C].
Riley, John T. (10 yrs.) d. on 70-Apr-9 [70-Apr-11: 2B].
Riley, John W. W. d. on 68-Aug-27 [68-Sep-1: 2B].
Riley, Luther C. m. Nicholas, Mary Jane on 66-Jan-2 [66-Feb-13: 2C].
Riley, Margaret Ann m. Solon, Thomas on 69-Sep-6 [69-Sep-21: 2B].
Riley, Mary A. m. Winkel, Henry A. on 67-Sep-8 [67-Sep-25: 2B].
Riley, Mary Ellen (22 yrs.) d. on 69-Jun-9 [69-Jun-10: 2C].
Riley, Theodore B. m. Tindall, Miriam E. on 69-Aug-3 [69-Aug-9: 2B].
Riley, Theodore B. m. Sindall, Miriam E. on 69-Aug-3 [69-Aug-7: 2B].
Riley, Valerious (76 yrs.) d. on 66-Jul-18 [66-Jul-20: 1G, 2D].
Riley, W. H. m. Johns, E. J. on 65-Dec-15 [66-Jul-28: 2C].
Riley, William Thomas (20 yrs.) d. on 64-Dec-19 [69-May-29: 2B].
Rimby, Annie M. m. Bell, John T. on 69-May-18 [69-May-20: 2C].
Rimby, F. Virginia m. Hood, A. J. on 69-Dec-26 [69-Dec-27: 2D].
Rimby, Jacob m. Bowling, Annie Isabella on 67-Oct-14 [67-Nov-21: 2C].
Rimby, Rachel (57 yrs.) d. on 67-May-3 [67-May-4: 2B].
Rimmey, Martha m. Jones, John L. on 68-Jul-23 [68-Jul-30: 2B].
Rinck, George (77 yrs.) d. on 68-Mar-25 [68-Mar-26: 2B].
Rind, William A. (33 yrs.) d. on 69-Mar-28 [69-Apr-7: 2C].
Rine, William d. on 67-Apr-13 in Machine accident [67-Apr-19: 1G].
Rineck, Mary A. (56 yrs., 3 mos.) d. on 70-Oct-11 [70-Oct-13: 2C].
Rinecker, John W. m. Martin, Elizabeth on 67-Feb-9 [67-Mar-6: 2C].
Rinehardt, A. m. Martin, Abbie on 68-Dec-22 [69-Jan-4: 2C].
Rinehart, Alexander m. Bahn, Cassandra N. on 68-Jan-9 [68-Jan-11: 2B].
Rinehart, Maggie A. (28 yrs.) d. on 67-Apr-14 [67-Apr-15: 2C].
Ring, Richard (37 yrs.) d. on 70-Nov-7 [70-Nov-8: 2B].
Ring, Washington d. on 66-Mar-13 Drowned [66-Mar-14: 1F].
Ringgold, Alex H. d. on 67-Dec-12 [67-Dec-24: 2B].
Ringgold, C. F. m. Wickes, Sarah V. on 68-Jan-22 [68-Jan-29: 2C].
Ringgold, Eliza W. (79 yrs.) d. on 69-May-15 [69-May-17: 2B].
Ringgold, Ettie C. m. Tolson, J. Carrow on 67-Jul-18 [67-Jul-22: 2C].
Ringgold, Florence DeCoursey (10 yrs., 6 mos.) d. on 69-Apr-5 [69-Apr-7: 2C].

Ringgold, Frances Ann d. on 67-Jul-5 [67-Jul-6: 2B].
Ringgold, James B. (60 yrs.) d. on 66-Feb-8 [66-Feb-10: 2C].
Ringgold, Mary (85 yrs.) d. on 70-Jan-12 [70-Jan-14: 2C].
Ringgold, Mary C. (62 yrs.) d. on 66-Feb-11 [66-Feb-13: 2C].
Ringgold, Mary Emma (1 yr., 8 mos.) d. on 67-Mar-15 [67-Mar-16: 2B].
Ringgold, Samuel m. Harden, Catherine on 66-Nov-29 [66-Dec-6: 2B].
Ringold, Martha A. (40 yrs.) d. on 69-Apr-27 [69-Apr-28: 2B].
Ringrose, Elizabeth m. Slemaker, John H. on 67-Apr-2 [67-Apr-4: 2B].
Ringrose, John A. m. Fallin, Isabella Frances on 67-Jun-23 [67-Jul-10: 2B].
Ringrose, John W. d. on 69-Dec-2 [69-Dec-3: 2C; 69-Dec-4: 2C].
Rink, Elizabeth (79 yrs.) d. on 68-Sep-4 of Paralysis [68-Sep-5: 1G, 2A].
Riordan, Baptista, Sr. (32 yrs.) d. on 68-Oct-29 [68-Nov-6: 1G].
Riordan, Ella Virginia (1 yr., 11 mos.) d. on 70-May-23 [70-May-24: 2C].
Riordan, John B. m. Tindle, Sarah E. on 67-Nov-14 [67-Nov-27: 2B].
Riordan, John J. m. Storck, Annie M. on 67-Jun-4 [67-Jun-7: 2B].
Riordan, Mary Ellen d. on 70-Feb-14 [70-Feb-16: 2C].
Ripley, E. H. m. Coe, Mary Pottee on 67-Apr-24 [67-May-17: 2B].
Ripley, Joseph Edward (2 yrs., 4 mos.) d. on 67-Mar-19 of Scarlet fever [67-Mar-21: 2C].
Ripple, Catherine A. (1 yr., 5 mos.) d. on 67-Dec-23 [68-Jan-7: 2C].
Ripple, Emily W. m. Wright, George E. on 69-Mar-18 [69-Mar-23: 2C].
Ripple, Francis M. (32 yrs.) d. on 67-Feb-4 [67-Feb-12: 2C].
Ripple, George Martin (2 yrs., 3 mos.) d. on 69-May-30 [69-May-31: 2C].
Ripple, Lewis m. Smith, Laura A. on 66-Jan-4 [66-Jan-5: 2C].
Rissau, Herman H. m. Knoepp, Sophia on 67-Jul-18 [67-Jul-22: 2C].
Risteau, Annie W. m. Wilson, J. Oliver on 68-Aug-4 [68-Aug-5: 2C].
Risteau, Thomas C., Dr. (71 yrs.) d. on 66-Feb-3 [66-Feb-5: 1G, 2C].
Riston, Margaret d. on 69-Feb-22 [69-Mar-1: 2C; 69-Mar-2: 2C].
Riston, Virginia Clarence (8 yrs.) d. on 69-Oct-17 [69-Nov-20: 2C].
Ritchie, Elspie (68 yrs.) d. on 68-Sep-26 [68-Sep-28: 2B].
Ritchie, Frank (10 mos.) d. on 70-Apr-15 [70-Apr-16: 2B].
Ritchie, George Harrison d. on 68-Oct-5 [68-Oct-8: 2B].
Ritchie, William (63 yrs.) d. on 66-Aug-24 [66-Aug-25: 2A].
Ritinger, Rosania m. Hook, George W. on 70-Apr-28 [70-Jun-17: 2B].
Rittberg, Elizabeth (37 yrs.) d. on 70-May-8 [70-May-9: 2B; 70-May-10: 2C].
Ritter, Alfred G. (24 yrs.) d. on 67-Aug-5 of Typhoid [67-Aug-6: 2C].
Ritter, Annie E. m. Fowler, Monroe on 68-May-7 [68-May-11: 2B].
Ritter, Henrietta W. m. Bidleman, Ferdinand N. on 68-Oct-6 [68-Oct-7: 2C].
Ritter, James A. (33 yrs.) d. on 67-Aug-31 [67-Sep-25: 2B].
Ritter, John Thomas (44 yrs., 5 mos.) d. on 70-Dec-20 [70-Dec-21: 2C].
Ritter, John W. m. Tilghman, Martha A. on 67-Dec-29 [68-Jan-7: 2B].
Ritter, Johnzie (47 yrs.) d. on 68-Aug-17 [68-Aug-19: 2B].
Ritter, Mary E. (53 yrs., 8 mos.) d. on 68-Jul-30 [68-Aug-3: 2C].
Ritter, Sidney E. d. on 66-Mar-2 [66-Mar-3: 2B].
Ritter, Sidney M. (66 yrs.) d. on 68-Mar-7 [68-Mar-9: 2C].
Ritter, Thomas (71 yrs.) d. on 68-Mar-14 [68-Mar-16: 2B].
Ritter, Thomas H. m. Grimes, Marcella R. on 68-Apr-2 [68-Apr-7: 2B].
Ritter, William L. m. Rowan, Sarah H. on 67-Nov-26 [67-Nov-30: 2C].
Ritterpush, Terese (29 yrs.) d. on 67-Jan-9 [67-Jan-11: 2C].
Rivera, Mary A. (65 yrs.) d. on 70-Oct-20 [70-Oct-25: 2B].
Rivers, J. L. m. Lisle, Nettie on 67-Apr-24 [67-Dec-27: 2D].
Rivers, Maria (29 yrs.) d. on 66-Mar-31 [66-Apr-2: 2B].
Rixham, George B. m. Burns, Sarah J. on 69-Sep-20 [69-Sep-23: 2B].
Rixham, Isabella Marjorie (9 mos.) d. on 69-Jul-5 [69-Jul-8: 2C].
Rixse, George A. m. Miller, Anna on 66-Jun-20 [66-Jun-22: 2B].
Rizer, Mollie E. F. m. Hoffman, William E. on 67-Feb-21 [67-Mar-11: 2C].

Roach, Annie (85 yrs.) d. on 69-Jul-29 [69-Jul-30: 2C].
Roach, James J. (55 yrs.) d. on 69-Jan-24 [69-Jan-25: 2D; 69-Jan-26: 2C].
Roach, John Edward (8 mos.) d. on 68-Mar-5 [68-Mar-6: 2C].
Roach, Kate m. Smith, William B. on 69-Apr-29 [69-May-25: 2C].
Roach, Michael d. on 69-Sep-15 Murdered (Stabbing) [69-Sep-16: 1G].
Roach, Virginia A. m. Baylies, John H. on 69-Feb-18 [69-Feb-24: 2C].
Roadcap, Macey A. m. Ridenour, M. A. on 70-Jun-26 [70-Jul-15: 2C].
Roan, Mary (21 yrs.) d. on 67-Feb-14 [67-Feb-15: 2C].
Robb, Duncan McC. m. Benteen, Ella on 68-Nov-12 [68-Nov-17: 2C].
Robb, John (88 yrs.) d. on 68-Nov-1 [68-Nov-2: 2B].
Robb, John, Rev. (87 yrs.) d. on 69-Feb-26 [69-Feb-26: 1G; 69-Mar-1: 1H].
Robb, John m. Hardesty, Belle on 68-Nov-5 [68-Nov-9: 2B].
Robb, John A., Capt. (75 yrs.) d. on 67-Jan-28 of Paralysis [67-Jan-29: 1F; 67-Jan-30: 2C; 67-Jan-31: 2C; 67-Feb-1: 1F].
Robb, Joseph A. m. Kennedy, Mary Jane on 66-May-15 [66-May-26: 2B].
Robbins, Addie L. (22 yrs.) d. on 66-Jul-20 [66-Jul-21: 2C].
Robbins, Alice B. (31 yrs.) d. on 70-Nov-27 [70-Dec-13: 2C].
Robbins, Charles E. (22 yrs.) d. on 66-Nov-1 [66-Nov-3: 2B].
Robbins, Ellen m. Wright, Henry on 66-Jan-17 [66-Jan-22: 2C].
Robbins, John H. (41 yrs.) d. on 70-Aug-8 [70-Aug-10: 2C].
Robbins, John M. m. Holmes, Susan E. on 66-Dec-4 [67-Mar-26: 2C].
Robbins, Mary F. (40 yrs.) d. on 69-Jun-16 [69-Jun-18: 2C].
Robbins, Moses S. (67 yrs.) d. on 67-Sep-13 [67-Sep-14: 2A].
Robbins, Russel, Jr. m. MacNeal, Ida H. on 70-Nov-10 [70-Nov-14: 2B].
Robelen, George F. m. Baer, Mary E. on 68-Jul-27 [68-Jul-29: 2B].
Roberson, William H. m. Hollen, Sarah on 68-Aug-12 [68-Aug-15: 2B].
Roberts, Alice Glenn (1 yr., 6 mos.) d. on 68-Dec-7 [68-Dec-8: 2C].
Roberts, Annie M. m. Winter, George on 69-Jan-12 [69-Jan-18: 2C].
Roberts, Antone (35 yrs.) d. on 69-Sep-1 of Hemorrhage [69-Sep-2: 1H].
Roberts, Bertania C. (20 yrs.) d. on 70-May-20 [70-May-24: 2C].
Roberts, Blanche A. m. Hayward, Thomas J. on 69-Jun-15 [69-Jun-18: 2C].
Roberts, Carrie E. m. Hill, Norman F. on 69-Oct-6 [69-Oct-8: 2B].
Roberts, Charity (75 yrs.) d. on 67-Apr-30 [67-May-3: 2B].
Roberts, Charles (47 yrs.) d. on 67-May-28 [67-May-29: 2B].
Roberts, Charles M. m. Swann, Fannie A. on 67-Jun-11 [67-Jun-19: 2B].
Roberts, Elizabeth d. on 70-Oct-26 [70-Oct-29: 2B].
Roberts, Elizabeth J. m. Price, George T. on 65-Dec-28 [66-Mar-10: 2B].
Roberts, Emma C. (3 yrs., 9 mos.) d. on 69-May-26 of Brain congestion [69-May-28: 2C].
Roberts, Emma V. m. Temple, William G. on 68-Jan-21 [68-Jan-31: 2C].
Roberts, F. Augusta m. Bell, William H. on 67-May-30 [67-Jun-4: 2A].
Roberts, Frances M. m. Jacobsen, Carl C. on 67-Nov-21 [67-Nov-22: 2B].
Roberts, George C. M., Dr. (64 yrs.) d. on 70-Jan-15 [70-Jan-17: 1G, 2D].
Roberts, George S. m. Carmack, Emma M on 68-May-28 [68-Jun-2: 2B].
Roberts, George Washington (11 mos.) d. on 69-Aug-13 [69-Aug-14: 2C].
Roberts, Gracie (11 mos.) d. on 70-Feb-18 [70-Feb-21: 2C].
Roberts, Harry m. Harvey, Kate on 69-Oct-28 [69-Nov-2: 2B].
Roberts, Helen V. d. on 70-Apr-2 [70-Apr-6: 2C].
Roberts, Hugh, Sr. (70 yrs.) d. on 67-Jul-17 [67-Jul-18: 1G, 2C; 67-Jul-19: 2C].
Roberts, Jacob d. on 68-Sep-12 Drowned [68-Sep-16: 1G].
Roberts, James E. m. Kelly, Josephine M. on 68-Jun-16 [68-Jun-18: 2B].
Roberts, James L. m. Krantz, Sarah E. on 69-Jul-13 [69-Jul-20: 2C].
Roberts, Jane S. (87 yrs.) d. on 69-Jun-16 [69-Jun-17: 2C; 69-Jun-18: 2C].
Roberts, Jefferson D. (9 yrs., 1 mo.) d. on 70-Jul-25 Drowned [70-Jul-27: 4F, 2C].
Roberts, John H. L. m. Whitney, Sarah R. on 69-Oct-19 [70-Jan-10: 2C].
Roberts, John T. m. Crouch, Bertannia on 69-Apr-6 [69-Apr-9: 2B].

Roberts, John W. m. Clark, Emma F. on 69-Feb-19 [69-Feb-24: 2C].
Roberts, Joseph (29 yrs.) d. on 68-Sep-19 in Railroad accident [68-Sep-21: 1G, 2B].
Roberts, Lemuel, Jr. (19 yrs., 6 mos.) d. on 66-Oct-29 of Typhoid [66-Nov-6: 2B].
Roberts, Lewis James (2 yrs., 7 mos.) d. on 69-Feb-24 [69-Feb-27: 2C].
Roberts, Lizzie W. m. Johnson, Crawford H. on 66-Nov-20 [66-Dec-4: 2D].
Roberts, Malaska (5 yrs.) d. on 66-Nov-17 [66-Nov-19: 2B; 66-Nov-20: 2B].
Roberts, Margaret Jane m. Winn, Joshua on 68-Apr-21 [68-Apr-23: 2B].
Roberts, Maria Lamina (2 yrs.) d. on 66-Aug-16 [66-Aug-17: 2C].
Roberts, Mary E. m. Cathell, James R. on 65-Dec-26 [66-Jan-2: 2C].
Roberts, Sarah m. Collins, Francis T. on 67-Jan-20 [67-Jan-22: 2C].
Roberts, Susan A. m. Matthews, Thomas R. on 66-Dec-19 [66-Dec-19: 2A].
Roberts, Susannah Morrel (89 yrs.) d. on 69-Nov-19 [69-Nov-23: 2C].
Roberts, Thomas m. Ettle, Annie B. on 68-Feb-4 [68-Feb-8: 2B].
Roberts, Virginia m. Tower, Alonzo on 70-Nov-10 [70-Nov-19: 2B].
Roberts, W. H. m. Donallen, Elizabeth on 68-Oct-27 [68-Nov-12: 2C].
Roberts, Wilhelmina (82 yrs.) d. [67-Feb-20: 2C; 67-Feb-21: 2C].
Roberts, William (22 yrs., 7 mos.) d. on 67-Sep-12 Murdered (Stabbing) [67-Sep-13: 1F; 67-Sep-14: 1F, 2A].
Roberts, Willie (1 yr., 8 mos.) d. on 67-Sep-18 [67-Sep-19: 2B].
Robertson, D. A. (45 yrs.) d. on 68-Oct-1 [68-Oct-3: 2B].
Robertson, Eleanora H. m. Poe, William C. on 68-Oct-13 [68-Oct-20: 2B].
Robertson, Elizabeth M. (73 yrs.) d. on 68-Aug-10 [68-Aug-12: 2C].
Robertson, Elizabeth V. d. on 67-Jan-24 of Pneumonia [67-Jan-25: 2C].
Robertson, Emma W. (27 yrs.) d. on 70-Apr-9 of Typhoid [70-Apr-11: 2B].
Robertson, Frank S. m. Wheeler, Ella on 68-Jan-30 [68-Feb-1: 2B].
Robertson, Henrietta (69 yrs.) d. on 67-Apr-16 [67-Apr-17: 2B; 67-Apr-18: 2B].
Robertson, Margaret (87 yrs.) d. on 66-May-1 [66-May-2: 2B; 66-May-3: 2C].
Robertson, Mary m. Watkins, Thomas on 69-Oct-7 [69-Oct-12: 2C].
Robertson, Mary A. d. on 69-Nov-12 [69-Nov-15: 2C].
Robertson, Nathaniel C., Sr. (76 yrs.) d. on 67-Feb-9 [67-Feb-11: 2C].
Robertson, William m. Valiant, Mary Sue on 70-May-11 [70-May-13: 2C].
Robey, L. Leota m. Beaumont, Oliver T. on 70-Mar-24 [70-Mar-29: 2B].
Robey, William H. m. Smith, Mary V. on 69-Jul-5 [69-Jul-9: 2C].
Robie, James m. Leary, Ellen Louise on 68-Oct-14 [69-Jan-9: 2C].
Robier, Clarence Eugene (1 yr., 2 mos.) d. on 70-Sep-6 [70-Sep-7: 2B].
Robinson, Alcinda (1 yr., 4 mos.) d. on 70-Jul-8 [70-Jul-11: 2C].
Robinson, Alexander (27 yrs.) d. on 67-Apr-24 [67-Apr-26: 2B].
Robinson, Amelia J. (1 yr., 1 mo.) d. on 67-May-5 [67-May-7: 2B].
Robinson, Ann d. on 70-Dec-4 [70-Dec-5: 2C].
Robinson, Anna J. m. Hudgins, James C. on 69-Feb-25 [69-Mar-9: 2C].
Robinson, Anna M. d. on 69-Dec-2 [69-Dec-4: 2C].
Robinson, Annie E. m. Fitzgerald, James H. on 70-May-19 [70-May-21: 2B].
Robinson, Charles (74 yrs.) d. on 68-Jan-24 [68-Feb-5: 2B].
Robinson, Charles (57 yrs.) d. on 69-May-13 [69-May-20: 2C].
Robinson, Cornelius P. m. Barboe, Ida C. on 70-Feb-23 [70-Apr-2: 2A].
Robinson, D. Otley (29 yrs.) d. on 68-Mar-13 [68-Mar-14: 2B].
Robinson, Deborah d. on 66-Nov-29 [66-Dec-1: 2B].
Robinson, Edmund m. Walker, Emma L. on 66-May-16 [66-Jul-16: 2C].
Robinson, Edward Cornelius (3 mos.) d. on 66-Dec-13 [66-Dec-15: 2B].
Robinson, Edward W. (58 yrs.) d. on 68-Jan-30 [68-Feb-4: 2D].
Robinson, Eliza d. on 70-Sep-27 of Suicide (Self-immolation) [70-Sep-29: 4C].
Robinson, Elizabeth d. on 69-Jan-28 [69-Jan-29: 2C].
Robinson, Elizabeth (1 yr., 6 mos.) d. on 69-Feb-18 [69-Feb-20: 2B].
Robinson, Elizabeth m. Moore, Benseles on 70-Apr-14 [70-Apr-16: 2B].
Robinson, Elizabeth M. (74 yrs.) d. on 68-Aug-9 of Fall on stairs [68-Aug-11: 1G].

Robinson, Emma m. Weaver, Jacob on 66-Dec-11 [67-Jan-5: 2C].
Robinson, Emma V. m. Covington, James H. on 67-Dec-16 [67-Dec-19: 2B].
Robinson, Eugene D. m. Ortwine, Adelaide on 69-Aug-24 [69-Sep-6: 2C].
Robinson, G. Oscar m. Henry, Mattie on 70-Dec-6 [70-Dec-13: 2C].
Robinson, George Law m. Williams, Margaret Gordon on 69-Nov-16 [69-Nov-17: 2C].
Robinson, George Millford m. Cade, Ella on 70-Apr-28 [70-Apr-30: 2A].
Robinson, George Walter (6 mos.) d. on 68-Aug-2 [68-Aug-24: 2B].
Robinson, Georgiana m. Denning, Charles on 68-Feb-19 [68-Feb-20: 2C].
Robinson, Ida May (2 yrs., 3 mos.) d. on 66-Feb-27 [66-Feb-28: 2C].
Robinson, James Williams (1 yr., 11 mos.) d. on 70-May-7 [70-May-9: 2B].
Robinson, John (77 yrs.) d. on 68-Mar-31 [68-Apr-1: 4C; 68-Apr-3: 2C].
Robinson, John d. on 67-May-27 of Paralysis [67-Jun-13: 2C].
Robinson, John (17 yrs., 8 mos.) d. on 69-Sep-22 [69-Sep-23: 2B; 69-Sep-24: 2C].
Robinson, John E. m. Lant, Martha on 70-Nov-16 [70-Nov-29: 2C].
Robinson, Joseph m. Robinson, Maggie L. on 69-May-18 [69-Jun-3: 2B].
Robinson, Joseph Allen Otley (5 mos.) d. on 68-Apr-11 of Pneumonia [68-Apr-13: 2B].
Robinson, Joseph D. Atley (29 yrs., 1 mo.) d. on 68-Mar-13 of Consumption [68-Mar-20: 2B].
Robinson, Julia Ann d. on 66-Oct-29 [66-Oct-31: 2B].
Robinson, Kate G. m. Hall, F. Walters on 67-Apr-23 [67-Apr-25: 2B].
Robinson, Laura (35 yrs.) d. on 67-Dec-2 [67-Dec-4: 2C].
Robinson, Laura Ann (10 mos.) d. on 68-Sep-26 [68-Sep-26: 2B].
Robinson, Laura C. m. Tydings, John L. on 70-Feb-14 [70-Feb-15: 2C].
Robinson, Lizzie m. McElroy, William on 65-Dec-28 [66-Jan-2: 2C].
Robinson, Lizzie G. m. Bateman, Samuel D. on 66-Nov-14 [66-Nov-17: 2B].
Robinson, Louisa A. m. Faulkner, A. B. on 67-Nov-19 [67-Nov-23: 2B].
Robinson, Maggie L. m. Robinson, Joseph on 69-May-18 [69-Jun-3: 2B].
Robinson, Mamie m. Bealmear, James A. on 69-Sep-28 [69-Oct-2: 2B].
Robinson, Margaret m. Carter, Charles on 66-Sep-25 [66-Oct-2: 2B].
Robinson, Mary E. (37 yrs.) d. on 70-Jun-22 [70-Jun-22: 2B].
Robinson, Peter (76 yrs.) d. on 70-Jul-27 of Dropsy [70-Jul-30: 2C].
Robinson, Rebecca m. Osbourn, Joshua on 70-Feb-24 [70-Mar-21: 2C].
Robinson, Rhodie M. m. Thrift, Fleet W. on 67-Oct-19 [67-Oct-22: 2A].
Robinson, Robert Stewart (21 yrs.) d. on 70-Feb-1 [70-Feb-2: 2B; 70-Feb-3: 2B].
Robinson, Rosa Wirt m. Latrobe, Charles H. on 69-Dec-14 [69-Dec-23: 2B].
Robinson, Rowland Edwin (22 yrs.) d. on 66-Aug-9 [66-Aug-10: 2C].
Robinson, Samuel, Sr. (75 yrs.) d. on 67-Feb-10 [67-Feb-11: 1G, 2C].
Robinson, Sarah (76 yrs.) d. on 66-Nov-6 [66-Nov-7: 2C; 66-Nov-8: 2C].
Robinson, Sarah A. M. m. Osbourn, Joshua on 67-Jul-30 [67-Aug-1: 2C].
Robinson, Sophia E. m. Green, Milton W. on 66-Oct-1 [66-Nov-6: 2B].
Robinson, Spencer J. m. Cain, Maggie C. on 67-Jan-24 [67-Jan-28: 2C].
Robinson, Stephen (63 yrs.) d. on 68-Mar-29 [68-Mar-30: 2B, 4E; 68-Mar-31: 2B].
Robinson, Susie E. m. Byer, Louis on 66-Apr-8 [66-Apr-10: 2C].
Robinson, Sylvester Smith (22 yrs.) d. on 70-Feb-19 [70-Feb-21: 2B].
Robinson, Theodora m. DuBois, Edward S. on 70-Mar-1 [70-Mar-29: 2B].
Robinson, Thomas H. (75 yrs.) d. on 70-Sep-21 [70-Sep-23: 2C].
Robinson, W. Leslie m. Conway, Annie on 67-May-23 [67-May-24: 2B].
Robinson, W. T. m. Wilkins, Mathew Jane on 68-Apr-16 [68-Apr-24: 2B].
Robinson, William m. Wilson, Isabella G. on 66-Sep-13 [66-Sep-18: 2B].
Robinson, William B. m. Walter, Annie V. on 67-Jan-2 [67-Jan-3: 2B].
Robinson, William H. m. Freeman, Amanda on 69-Nov-4 [69-Nov-11: 2C].
Robinson, William L. d. on 68-Jul-23 [68-Aug-4: 2C].
Robinson, William Smith m. Haynes, Arabella Lavinia on 69-Nov-9 [69-Dec-28: 2C].
Roby, Charles J. m. Tumblinson, Lizzie J. on 66-Nov-20 [66-Nov-24: 2B].
Roby, H. N. (52 yrs.) d. on 68-Mar-23 [68-Mar-24: 1G, 2B; 68-Mar-25: 2A].
Roche, Charles Francis (3 yrs., 3 mos.) d. on 68-Jul-28 [68-Jul-30: 2B].

Roche, Emily T. (1 yr., 10 mos.) d. on 67-Sep-24 [67-Sep-26: 2B].
Roche, L. W. m. Knight, Lewis on 70-Feb-15 [70-Feb-24: 2C].
Roche, Margaret (50 yrs.) d. on 66-Sep-26 [66-Sep-27: 2C].
Roche, Mary (80 yrs.) d. on 69-May-28 [69-May-29: 2B].
Roche, Matthew R. (41 yrs.) d. on 68-Nov-29 [68-Dec-1: 2C].
Roche, P. J. m. Jones, Hettie G. on 66-Oct-11 [66-Oct-13: 2B].
Roche, Thomas H. (32 yrs.) d. on 68-May-7 [68-Jun-5: 2B].
Roche, William (76 yrs.) d. on 69-Sep-26 [69-Sep-27: 2C].
Rochefort, Edward (57 yrs.) d. on 67-Sep-14 in Wagon accident [67-Sep-16: 1G].
Rochester, Henry m. Meyers, Louisa A. on 68-Nov-9 [68-Nov-23: 2B].
Rochester, Jane m. Matthews, Charles S. on 70-Sep-5 [70-Sep-7: 2B].
Rochester, Matthew Newkirk (33 yrs.) d. on 68-Oct-29 in Wagon accident [68-Oct-30: 1F; 68-Oct-31: 1G; 68-Nov-2: 2B].
Rochester, William (68 yrs.) d. on 67-Dec-20 [67-Dec-24: 2B, 4B].
Rochford, John J. m. Broderick, Mary A. on 67-May-7 [67-May-10: 2B].
Rochfort, Edward (31 yrs.) d. on 70-Jan-3 [70-Jan-4: 1H, 2C; 70-Jan-5: 2C].
Rochfort, John E. m. Gallagher, Kate on 68-Jan-16 [68-Feb-4: 2C].
Rochfort, Winnifred (28 yrs.) d. on 67-Jun-9 [67-Jun-10: 2B].
Rock, Cecilia (2 yrs.) d. on 66-Oct-16 [66-Oct-17: 2B].
Rock, Elizabeth M. m. Onion, Thomas A. on 70-Aug-14 [70-Sep-13: 2B].
Rock, George Moroland (1 yr., 1 mo.) d. on 68-Aug-20 [68-Aug-21: 2B].
Rock, James P. m. Reagan, Maria L. on 68-Oct-8 [68-Nov-9: 2B].
Rock, John d. on 69-Oct-14 of Fall from mast [70-Jan-24: 4G].
Rock, Thomas (1 yr., 3 mos.) d. on 67-Oct-20 [67-Oct-21: 2B].
Rock, Timothy (13 yrs.) d. on 66-Apr-27 [66-Apr-28: 2A].
Rock, Warren T. m. Trimble, Hallie N. on 70-Oct-28 [70-Oct-31: 2B].
Rockhold, George Thomas (4 yrs., 5 mos.) d. on 66-May-5 of Measles [66-May-7: 2B].
Rockhold, William Lewis (11 mos.) d. on 68-Mar-5 [68-Mar-6: 2C].
Rockwell, Alfred H. m. Harris, Augusta F. on 68-Sep-28 [68-Sep-30: 2B].
Rockwell, William S. d. on 70-Jan-23 [70-Jan-24: 4F; 70-Jan-28: 1G].
Rodberg, Rosa (6 yrs., 5 mos.) d. on 70-Mar-20 Burned [70-Mar-21: 2C, 1G].
Roden, George m. German, Mary A. on 66-Feb-1 [66-Feb-3: 2C].
Rodenmayer, Frank T. m. Hilberg, S. Kate on 69-Nov-11 [69-Nov-18: 2C].
Rodenmayer, John m. Entler, Amelia on 66-Oct-17 [66-Oct-18: 2B].
Rodenmayer, Mary (78 yrs.) d. on 66-Jan-5 [66-Jan-6: 2B].
Rodenmyer, Elizabeth m. Pease, Francis N. on 69-Dec-23 [70-Mar-14: 2C].
Roder, Adolphe m. Somers, Mary Jane on 67-Mar-12 [67-Apr-23: 2B].
Rodgers, Charles R. m. Cole, Mollie E. on 70-Dec-22 [70-Dec-30: 2C].
Rodgers, Daniel B. (71 yrs.) d. on 70-Jan-17 [70-Jan-18: 2C].
Rodgers, Elizabeth A. m. Wroten, Augustus on 68-Mar-9 [68-Mar-18: 2B].
Rodgers, Elizabeth Jane (1 yr., 2 mos.) d. on 68-Jul-13 [68-Jul-14: 2C].
Rodgers, Howard P. m. Bittinger, Lizzie A. on 67-Apr-16 [67-Apr-19: 2B].
Rodgers, James Edward (6 yrs., 5 mos.) d. on 69-May-7 [69-May-8: 2B].
Rodgers, James W. m. Godman, Laura V. on 68-Jun-11 [68-Jun-16: 2B].
Rodgers, Oliver (1 yr., 3 mos.) d. on 68-Dec-15 [68-Dec-16: 2C].
Rodgers, Sarah Frances m. Topham, Joseph L. on 69-Jun-1 [69-Jun-4: 2C].
Rodhe, Andrew m. Lemate, Henrietta W. D. on 70-May-22 [70-May-25: 2C].
Rodley, Kate E. m. Allwell, William J. on 69-Mar-2 [69-Mar-3: 2B].
Rodney, George (11 yrs.) d. on 66-Jun-12 in Railroad accident [66-Jun-13: 1G, 2B].
Rodrigue, A. m. Jones, Jennie [70-Oct-18: 2B].
Roe, Annie F. (22 yrs.) d. on 67-Feb-3 [67-Feb-4: 2C].
Roe, Annie Laura (1 yr., 2 mos.) d. on 68-Nov-16 [68-Nov-18: 2C].
Roe, Emily m. Patton, David H. on 66-Jun-26 [66-Jun-29: 2C].
Roe, John (35 yrs.) d. on 68-Aug-14 Murdered (Stabbing) [68-Aug-15: 1F].
Roe, Robert (3 mos.) d. on 68-Aug-7 [68-Aug-8: 2C].

Roe, Thomas B. m. Youngs, Mary Ellen on 66-Apr-19 [66-Apr-26: 2B].
Roeder, Emma m. Alpenburg, E. J. M. on 70-Jun-4 [70-Jun-9: 2C].
Roelkey, George A. d. on 70-Feb-16 in Railroad accident [70-Feb-17: 1H; 70-Feb-18: 1H].
Roese, Mary E. m. Trust, George on 68-Jun-30 [68-Jul-7: 2B].
Roesler, Catharine Barbara (55 yrs.) d. [70-Jan-27: 2C; 70-Jan-28: 2C].
Roff, John N. m. Green, Louisa on 66-Jan-1 [66-Jan-15: 2B].
Roff, Lavinia m. Emlen, Charles on 69-Jan-7 [69-Jan-9: 2C].
Roger, Catherine m. Missing, Ernest on 69-Apr-22 [69-Apr-26: 2B].
Rogers, Alice A. (68 yrs.) d. on 68-Jan-27 [68-Jan-29: 2C].
Rogers, Andrew J. m. Stewart, Anna E. on 66-Feb-21 [66-Feb-26: 2B].
Rogers, Anthony d. on 68-Jan-16 of Construction cave-in [68-Jan-18: 1F].
Rogers, C. Howard (55 yrs.) d. on 70-Nov-18 [70-Nov-19: 2B].
Rogers, Carrie B. m. Williams, John Q. on 66-Sep-20 [66-Sep-22: 2B].
Rogers, Charles McG. (14 yrs.) d. on 68-Nov-7 [68-Nov-11: 2C].
Rogers, Christiana d. on 70-Oct-13 [70-Oct-14: 2B].
Rogers, Daniel m. McLean, Mary G. on 66-Jan-30 [66-Feb-2: 2C].
Rogers, Elizabeth (87 yrs.) d. on 67-Oct-10 [67-Oct-11: 2B].
Rogers, Elizabeth J. (10 mos.) d. on 70-Mar-24 [70-Mar-25: 2C].
Rogers, Ellen m. Watkins, Samuel on 67-Jan-24 [67-Jan-29: 2C].
Rogers, Ellen Stewart m. Newman, William H. on 66-Oct-18 [66-Oct-20: 2B].
Rogers, Eugenia (2 yrs., 7 mos.) d. on 66-Apr-27 [66-May-5: 2B].
Rogers, Frank, Dr. (48 yrs.) d. on 70-Jan-20 [70-Jan-27: 2C].
Rogers, Frederick m. Durham, Mary A. on 67-Aug-15 [67-Aug-24: 2B].
Rogers, Henry C. m. Woodward, Mary B. on 68-Aug-25 [68-Aug-29: 2B].
Rogers, Issac S. d. on 68-Apr-12 [68-Apr-14: 2A].
Rogers, James Lloyd d. on 70-Mar-18 [70-Mar-21: 2C].
Rogers, James P. m. Abell, Rosa on 68-Jun-2 [68-Jun-6: 2A].
Rogers, James R. m. Stephen, Bettie on 69-Mar-10 [69-Mar-13: 2B].
Rogers, Jonathan (18 yrs.) d. on 69-Feb-3 [69-Feb-4: 2C].
Rogers, Kate m. Marriott, Byron on 70-Aug-25 [70-Sep-3: 2B].
Rogers, M. Ellen m. Jenkins, Joseph W., Jr. on 67-Oct-9 [67-Oct-14: 2B].
Rogers, Martha Ann (64 yrs.) d. on 66-Apr-5 [66-Apr-7: 2B].
Rogers, Mary (46 yrs.) d. on 70-Mar-12 [70-Mar-14: 2D].
Rogers, Mary Grafton (11 yrs.) d. on 66-Jul-22 [66-Jul-23: 2C].
Rogers, Mary Rebecca (4 mos.) d. on 67-Jul-25 [67-Jul-26: 2C].
Rogers, Mary Woodward (7 mos.) d. on 70-Feb-18 [70-Feb-23: 2C].
Rogers, Michael W. d. on 70-Jan-30 [70-Feb-2: 2C].
Rogers, Narcise (50 yrs.) d. on 67-Aug-18 [67-Aug-19: 2C].
Rogers, Nicholas S. (33 yrs.) d. on 68-Apr-7 [68-Apr-8: 2B; 68-Apr-9: 2B].
Rogers, Patrick (49 yrs.) d. on 70-Mar-20 [70-Mar-21: 2C].
Rogers, Philip m. Smith, E. Kate on 66-Apr-11 [66-Apr-16: 2B].
Rogers, Phillip (49 yrs.) d. on 68-Mar-21 [68-Mar-23: 2B].
Rogers, Rebecca Owen d. [68-Aug-15: 2B].
Rogers, Robert Lyon d. on 69-Aug-2 [69-Aug-6: 2C].
Rogers, Rowland (83 yrs.) d. on 66-Mar-11 [66-Mar-13: 2B].
Rogers, S. Teresa m. Buchanan, James M., Jr. on 67-Mar-26 [67-Apr-8: 2B; 67-Apr-9: 2B].
Rogers, Sarah Jane m. Waters, John F on 66-May-24 [66-May-26: 2B].
Rogers, Sauah (22 yrs.) d. on 66-Apr-1 [66-Apr-3: 2B].
Rogers, Susan m. Sears, Dewitt C. on 68-Oct-11 [68-Oct-21: 2C].
Rogers, Terrence (35 yrs.) d. on 70-Aug-6 [70-Aug-8: 2C].
Rohleder, Joseph A. m. Wehage, Maggie on 69-Sep-7 [69-Sep-13: 2B].
Rohr, Joseph Stanislaus d. on 69-Mar-11 [69-Mar-13: 2C].
Rohrbaugh, Daniel (55 yrs.) d. on 68-Jun-1 in Railroad accident [68-Jun-6: 1F].
Rohrbough, Esta E. m. Gibson, Thomas A. on 68-Nov-24 [68-Dec-29: 2D].
Rokers, Maria Ann (31 yrs.) d. on 66-Oct-9 [66-Oct-10: 2B].

Roland, S. E. m. McGowan, Thomson on 67-Jul-17 [67-Jul-30: 2C].
Rolando, Henry (49 yrs.) d. on 69-Mar-20 of Paralysis [69-Mar-22: 4C].
Rolando, John Buckler (12 yrs.) d. on 68-Mar-14 [68-Mar-16: 2B].
Roles, Mary F. (44 yrs.) d. on 67-Feb-25 of Consumption [67-Apr-4: 2B].
Roll, Henry (8 yrs.) d. on 67-Jun-14 Drowned [67-Jun-17: 1F].
Rolla, Albert (50 yrs.) d. on 69-Mar-16 of Suicide (Drowning) [69-Mar-17: 1G].
Rollins, Clara Roselle (5 yrs., 11 mos.) d. on 66-Jun-22 [66-Jun-26: 2B].
Rollins, Harriet E. m. Wilson, John W. on 67-Aug-26 [67-Sep-9: 2B].
Rollins, Jesse (63 yrs.) d. on 67-May-20 of Bowel inflammation [67-May-21: 1F].
Rollins, Laura J. m. Burrows, Daniel A. on 68-Dec-23 [68-Dec-29: 2D].
Rollins, Mary Frances (9 mos.) d. on 66-Sep-11 [66-Sep-13: 2C].
Rollins, Thomas m. Bevans, Mary C. on 69-Aug-12 [69-Aug-14: 2C].
Rollins, Thornton m. Porter, S. Julia on 66-Oct-25 [66-Oct-27: 2B].
Rollins, William d. on 69-Dec-5 [69-Dec-10: 2C].
Rollison, Thomas m. Townsend, Josephine on 68-Jan-16 [68-Feb-12: 2B].
Roloson, Delia Teresa (5 yrs., 6 mos.) d. on 68-Jul-3 [68-Jul-6: 2B].
Roloson, Henry Lewis (1 yr., 8 mos.) d. on 68-Apr-26 [68-Apr-30: 2B].
Roloson, Lucy Rosella m. Smith, Edmund Morton on 66-Dec-12 [66-Dec-17: 2B].
Roloson, William H. (22 yrs.) d. on 67-Nov-10 [67-Nov-20: 2C].
Rolph, James d. on 66-Dec-22 of congestive chills [66-Dec-24: 2B].
Rome, Arthur Thompson (3 yrs., 7 mos.) d. on 67-Nov-20 of Hydrophobia [67-Nov-22: 1G; 67-Nov-23: 2B].
Romey, Francis G. m. Wambach, Emma L. on 70-Jul-12 [70-Aug-30: 2B].
Romoser, Alfred Andrew (1 yr., 2 mos.) d. on 70-Feb-23 [70-Feb-25: 2C].
Romoser, Edward G. (1 yr., 5 mos.) d. on 70-Jul-16 [70-Jul-18: 2B].
Romoser, Edward M. m. Keller, Virginia A. on 68-Oct-13 [68-Oct-20: 2B].
Romroser, John G. m. Wolfangel, Mary E. on 68-Mar-12 [68-Mar-16: 2B].
Ronemous, Burton Leonard (3 mos.) d. on 70-Jul-25 [70-Jul-27: 2C].
Roney, , Mr. (72 yrs.) d. on 70-Feb-20 [70-Feb-22: 2C].
Roney, Ann (50 yrs.) d. on 70-Mar-17 [70-Mar-19: 2C].
Roney, Eddie Warden (2 yrs., 1 mo.) d. on 68-Aug-24 of Cholera infantum [68-Sep-11: 2B].
Roney, Mary (74 yrs.) d. on 70-Apr-27 [70-Apr-28: 2C].
Roney, William (21 yrs.) d. on 68-Jun-22 Drowned [68-Jun-23: 1G; 68-Jul-1: 1G].
Ronsaville, David W. m. Howell, Isabel on 66-Jan-1 [66-Jan-8: 2B].
Roof, James N. m. Stansbury, Nannie M. on 70-Jan-11 [70-Jan-12: 2C].
Rook, William E. d. on 68-May-26 of Suicide (Hanging) [68-May-29: 1C].
Rooney, Agnes (16 yrs.) d. on 68-Apr-14 [68-Apr-15: 2B].
Rooney, Alice M. m. Koons, T. H. on 65-Sep-27 [66-Sep-27: 2C].
Rooney, Catherine (1 yr., 6 mos.) d. on 67-Jul-15 [67-Jul-16: 2C].
Rooney, James F. d. on 66-May-29 [66-May-30: 2C].
Rooney, Mary (38 yrs.) d. on 68-Sep-1 [68-Sep-2: 2A].
Rooney, Mary m. Warren, James on 70-May-6 [70-May-11: 2B].
Rooney, Mary Bell (8 yrs.) d. on 70-Oct-15 [70-Oct-15: 2B].
Rooney, Rose (43 yrs.) d. on 69-Jun-20 [69-Jun-21: 2B].
Rooney, William (27 yrs.) d. on 67-Dec-5 [67-Dec-6: 2C].
Roop, Devinia (33 yrs.) d. on 67-Oct-27 [67-Oct-29: 2B].
Roop, Josiah L. m. Hooper, Kate J. on 68-May-28 [68-May-30: 2A].
Rooper, Benjamin A. (11 mos.) d. on 70-Nov-1 [70-Nov-2: 2C].
Roose, George (6 yrs., 5 mos.) d. on 69-Feb-25 [69-Feb-26: 2D].
Roose, Sarah A. m. Kinge, Martin on 67-Jun-9 [67-Jun-14: 2B; 67-Jun-24: 2B].
Root, C. S. m. Dushane, Harriet R. on 68-Jul-22 [68-Jul-24: 2C].
Root, Emma M. (26 yrs.) d. on 69-Jul-12 [69-Jul-13: 2C].
Root, George H. m. Landis, Emma M. on 67-Oct-8 [67-Oct-12: 2A].
Root, Henry R. (50 yrs.) d. on 70-Jan-11 [70-Jan-12: 2C].
Root, John D. (45 yrs.) d. on 66-Nov-8 Murdered (Shooting) [66-Nov-9: 2C, 4A].

Root, Sarah (72 yrs.) d. on 69-Jul-9 [69-Jul-10: 2B].
Root, William Denison (1 yr., 4 mos.) d. on 66-Jul-27 [66-Jul-28: 2C].
Roper, Martha A. d. on 68-Apr-9 [68-Apr-13: 2B].
Roper, Nettie H. m. Jenkins, Alfred, Jr. on 68-Oct-22 [68-Oct-28: 2B].
Ropplett, Joseph Henry (7 mos.) d. on 67-Aug-10 [67-Aug-12: 2C].
Roque, Ella (11 yrs., 6 mos.) d. on 69-Dec-27 of Lamp explosion [69-Dec-28: 2C; 69-Dec-29: 1G].
Roque, Harriet (65 yrs.) d. on 68-Feb-11 [68-Feb-12: 2C].
Rose, Charles H. m. Ridgaway, Julia E. on 68-May-7 [68-May-21: 2B].
Rose, Clara Elizabeth (10 mos.) d. on 68-Aug-8 [68-Aug-10: 2B].
Rose, Ella Teresa m. Pentz, John J. on 69-Sep-21 [69-Sep-24: 2B].
Rose, Howard Bennett (2 mos.) d. on 68-Jul-29 [68-Jul-30: 2B].
Rose, John Henry (38 yrs.) d. on 69-Jun-24 [69-Jun-25: 2C].
Rose, John W. C. (39 yrs.) d. on 68-Jun-29 of Consumption [68-Jun-30: 2B].
Rose, Levi L. m. Kelly, Amanda on 66-Jul-10 [66-Jul-20: 2D].
Rose, Mary Elizabeth (6 mos.) d. on 70-Jul-25 [70-Jul-26: 2C].
Rose, Robert C. m. Hager, Margaret on 69-Oct-11 [69-Oct-29: 2B].
Rose, S. Francis m. Seward, Mary L. on 69-Apr-1 [69-May-4: 2B].
Rose, Sophia G. m. Orem, John M. on 66-Sep-20 [66-Sep-25: 2B].
Rose, Teresa (74 yrs.) d. on 70-Mar-7 [70-Mar-8: 2C; 70-Mar-9: 2C].
Rose, William H. (62 yrs.) d. on 69-Jul-11 of Apoplexy [69-Jul-12: 1H; 69-Jul-13: 2C].
Rose, William P. m. Ellinger, Elenora on 67-Oct-23 [67-Oct-24: 2B].
Roseberry, Samuel J. m. Godwin, Emma E. on 69-May-20 [69-May-27: 2C; 69-May-28: 2C].
Roseman, Charles Edward (12 yrs.) d. on 66-Jun-4 [66-Jun-6: 2B].
Rosenbaum, Charles m. Whitmarsh, Ella on 69-Jan-17 [69-Jan-22: 2D].
Rosenberger, Annie M. m. Moore, Thomas on 68-Oct-27 [68-Nov-23: 2B].
Rosene, Charles Bond (9 mos.) d. [66-Sep-13: 2C].
Rosensteel, Ambrose A. m. Wiedfeld, Rebecca E. on 66-Jun-7 [66-Jun-14: 2B].
Rosensteel, Elizabeth (80 yrs.) d. on 70-Nov-18 [70-Nov-21: 2C].
Rosensteel, Mary F. m. Stuart, Charles G. on 68-Feb-11 [68-Feb-14: 2C].
Rosenstock, Abraham (21 yrs.) d. on 69-Apr-21 [69-Apr-24: 2B; 69-Apr-28: 2B].
Rosenstock, Willie (3 mos.) d. on 69-Jun-30 [69-Jul-10: 2B].
Rosenswig, Emmie L. m. Schultz, Harry R. on 68-Nov-24 [68-Dec-3: 2C].
Rosier, Jacob m. Gray, Alberta V. on 68-Dec-1 [68-Dec-5: 2C].
Rosier, Joseph Grant (9 mos.) d. on 69-Aug-14 [69-Aug-17: 2C].
Ross, Alexander m. Winks, Annie E. on 68-Jun-30 [68-Jul-18: 2B; 68-Jul-21: 2C].
Ross, Annie M. m. French, Alpheus R. on 68-Jan-15 [68-Jan-16: 2C].
Ross, Bridget Ann (19 yrs.) d. on 70-May-9 [70-May-13: 2C].
Ross, Charles C. (47 yrs.) d. on 69-Jan-18 [69-Jan-19: 2C].
Ross, Clara m. Hutchins, Henry C. on 70-Jan-27 [70-Jan-29: 2B; 70-Feb-3: 2B].
Ross, David J. (46 yrs.) d. on 66-Apr-20 [66-Apr-21: 2B; 66-Apr-23: 1E].
Ross, Eliza m. Williamson, James A. on 66-Jun-19 [66-Jun-20: 2C].
Ross, Emma m. Payne, J. Thomas on 68-Apr-23 [68-Apr-27: 2B].
Ross, Frances R. (62 yrs.) d. on 69-Mar-2 [69-Mar-3: 2C].
Ross, G. Howard m. Ensor, Maggie A. on 69-Oct-1 [69-Oct-5: 2B].
Ross, George L. m. Harrison, Susie on 68-May-17 [68-May-21: 2B; 68-May-22: 2C].
Ross, Harriet m. Munoz, Manuel on 67-Jan-22 [67-Jan-29: 2C].
Ross, Himena m. Otto, Frederick A. on 66-Jun-14 [66-Jun-28: 2C; 66-Jun-30: 2B].
Ross, J. T. m. Langley, M. Josephine on 68-Jun-24 [68-Jun-25: 2B].
Ross, James D. m. Wren, Ann on 65-Dec-28 [66-Jan-3: 2C].
Ross, James Ellmore d. on 69-Jun-25 [69-Jun-28: 2C; 69-Jul-5: 2C].
Ross, Jessie m. Johnson, William J. on 70-Dec-8 [70-Dec-10: 2B].
Ross, Jessie m. Thomson, William J. on 70-Dec-8 [70-Dec-12: 2C].
Ross, John M. m. Coffroth, Girtie C. on 69-Feb-28 [69-Mar-4: 2C].
Ross, Laura S. m. MacAlister, Hiram L. on 68-Jul-23 [68-Jul-24: 2C].

Ross, Laura V. m. Wright, George S. on 67-Sep-17 [67-Sep-24: 2A].
Ross, Lou m. Gaither, E. on 70-Oct-20 [70-Oct-22: 2B].
Ross, Mary m. Lindstrom, Oscar on 70-Oct-8 [70-Nov-28: 2C].
Ross, Mary Jane (27 yrs.) d. on 66-Jun-7 [66-Jun-8: 2B].
Ross, Mattie J. m. Murray, James on 66-May-17 [66-May-19: 2B].
Ross, Perry m. Ennalls, Henrett Ann on 67-Jul-18 [67-Jul-20: 2C].
Ross, Robert J. (48 yrs.) d. on 70-Feb-27 [70-Mar-7: 2C].
Ross, Robert T. (50 yrs.) d. on 69-May-23 [69-Jun-5: 2B].
Ross, Sallie m. Heighe, John M. on 70-Jan-12 [70-Jan-17: 2C].
Ross, Sarah A. m. Boon, Gideon on 70-Aug-1 [70-Aug-3: 2C].
Ross, Sarah E. (57 yrs.) d. on 70-Jul-24 [70-Jul-25: 2C].
Ross, Teresa (66 yrs.) d. on 70-Mar-7 [70-Mar-9: 2C; 70-Mar-10: 2C; 70-Jun-29: 2C].
Ross, Thomas, Sr. (71 yrs.) d. on 70-Jul-6 [70-Jul-8: 2C].
Ross, Warren B. m. Carl, Lavina A. on 69-Jun-15 [69-Jun-17: 2C].
Ross, William C. (50 yrs.) d. on 69-May-4 Crushed by wall [69-May-5: 2C; 69-May-6: 1H].
Rossler, Margaret R. m. Nearing, Adam on 68-Aug-6 [68-Aug-14: 2C].
Rost, Augustus m. Zirkler, Lizzie on 67-Mar-27 [67-Apr-12: 2C].
Rost, John A. d. on 68-Jun-29 of Suicide (Shooting) [68-Jul-1: 1G].
Rost, Mary B. m. Schueler, John on 67-Oct-20 [67-Oct-23: 2B].
Rost, Theodore (48 yrs.) d. on 67-Sep-7 in Construction accident [67-Sep-9: 4B].
Roszel, John H. m. Downey, Laura V. on 66-May-17 [66-May-24: 2C].
Roszel, Laura Virginia (20 yrs., 5 mos.) d. on 68-Sep-23 [68-Sep-24: 2B; 68-Oct-10: 2B].
Roszel, Mary Sophie (3 yrs.) d. on 68-Dec-20 [68-Dec-21: 2C].
Roszell, Ennalls (73 yrs.) d. on 67-Feb-22 [67-Feb-26: 2C].
Roszelle, Nannie D. m. Hunter, William G. on 70-Jun-16 [70-Jun-21: 2C].
Rote, Jacob (68 yrs.) d. on 68-Apr-15 [68-Apr-17: 2B].
Rote, John T. m. Knipe, Rosie M. on 69-Jun-21 [69-Jun-25: 2C].
Roten, Alice (2 yrs., 7 mos.) d. on 70-Oct-19 [70-Oct-24: 2B].
Roth, Ella, Miss m. Orth, Louis on 67-Feb-10 [67-Feb-12: 2C].
Rothel, Ann (57 yrs.) d. on 66-Sep-6 [66-Sep-7: 2B].
Rother, Rod M. m. Douglass, Clara E. on 70-Jul-3 [70-Jul-6: 2B].
Rothert, John Herman (13 yrs., 10 mos.) d. on 69-Aug-29 [69-Aug-30: 2B].
Rothert, John William (41 yrs., 3 mos.) d. on 66-Jun-25 [66-Jun-26: 2B].
Rothrock, Andrew J. (24 yrs.) d. on 68-Apr-5 [68-Apr-6: 2B; 68-Apr-7: 2B].
Rothrock, Joseph m. Huber, Maria L. on 68-Feb-24 [68-Mar-21: 2A].
Rothrock, R. Annie m. Brown, J. Wilson on 70-Nov-22 [70-Nov-25: 2D].
Rothschild, Theodore m. Jacobs, Isabella on 70-Jun-19 [70-Jun-25: 2B].
Roulet, Arthur (42 yrs.) d. on 66-Dec-27 [66-Dec-28: 2C; 66-Dec-29: 2C].
Roulston, Margaret Ann d. on 68-May-28 [68-May-29: 2B].
Roulston, Robert m. McLean, Maggie on 70-Oct-6 [70-Oct-14: 2B].
Rountree, Catherine (80 yrs.) d. on 69-Feb-20 of Paralysis [69-Feb-22: 1H, 2C].
Rountree, William H. H. m. White, Frances on 67-Mar-14 [67-May-1: 2B; 67-May-2: 2B].
Rourk, Daniel d. on 69-Jul-1 Drowned [69-Jul-2: 4D; 69-Jul-3: 1H].
Rourke, Ella (10 yrs., 9 mos.) d. on 69-Jun-20 [69-Jun-21: 2B].
Rourke, Mary Rebecca (33 yrs.) d. on 70-Jan-7 of Consumption [70-Jan-10: 2C].
Rous, John G. (61 yrs.) d. on 67-Dec-19 [67-Dec-20: 2B; 67-Dec-21: 2B].
Rouse, Edwin W. m. Hoffman, Mary Jane on 69-Sep-14 [69-Sep-16: 2B].
Rouse, John G. m. Hanway, Hattie B. on 66-Apr-25 [66-May-7: 2B].
Rouse, R. m. Gosman, Maria Theresa on 66-Jun-28 [66-Jul-31: 2C].
Rouse, Virginia F. m. Willis, Columbus C. on 67-Apr-16 [67-Apr-20: 2A].
Rouselot, Emma m. Crist, Philip on 70-May-19 [70-Jun-18: 2B].
Roussell, Anton Ferdinand (39 yrs.) d. on 68-Mar-18 [68-Mar-20: 2B].
Rousselot, Amelia m. Crist, Henry on 68-Nov-5 [68-Nov-14: 2B].
Rousselot, Augustus H. (29 yrs., 3 mos.) d. on 66-May-24 [66-May-25: 2C].
Routzahn, William H. m. Main, Kate S. on 67-Jan-10 [67-Jan-12: 2C].

Roux, Edwin S. m. Timanus, Mary E. on 68-Jun-18 [68-Jun-24: 2B].
Rowan, Sarah H. m. Ritter, William L. on 67-Nov-26 [67-Nov-30: 2C].
Rowan, Stephen m. Shields, Annie on 70-Mar-1 [70-Mar-8: 2C].
Rowe, Charles Edward (1 yr., 8 mos.) d. on 66-Mar-1 [66-Mar-2: 2B].
Rowe, E. H. m. Gloss, Lizzie on 69-Sep-28 [69-Oct-1: 2B].
Rowe, Harry Albert (1 yr., 10 mos.) d. on 68-Sep-14 [68-Sep-18: 2B].
Rowe, John (67 yrs.) d. on 66-Dec-31 [67-Jan-2: 2C].
Rowe, Julia P. m. Bussey, J. Thomas on 67-Jan-16 [67-Jan-22: 2C].
Rowe, Levi (52 yrs.) d. on 70-Nov-26 [70-Nov-28: 2C].
Rowe, Margaret C. (65 yrs.) d. on 66-Sep-19 [66-Sep-20: 2B].
Rowe, Mary L. m. Bradley, James on 70-May-29 [70-May-30: 2B].
Rowe, Nettie A. m. Zimmerman, George H. on 66-Oct-8 [66-Oct-9: 2A].
Rowland, Edward m. Gambel, Maggie A. on 66-Aug-29 [66-Sep-1: 2B].
Rowland, J. Melville (1 yr., 11 mos.) d. on 69-Jul-22 of Brain fever [69-Jul-27: 2C].
Rowland, Maude H. (1 yr., 2 mos.) d. on 66-Jun-25 [66-Jun-28: 2C].
Rowland, William Lee d. on 70-Jul-8 of Cholera infantum [70-Jul-9: 2B].
Rowles, Catherine (30 yrs.) d. on 68-Jun-17 [68-Jun-22: 2B].
Rowles, William Henry m. Pierce, Josephine on 66-Jan-28 [66-Jan-30: 2B].
Roxbury, Edward m. Smart, Martha W. on 68-Nov-3 [68-Nov-7: 2B].
Roy, Robert m. Kraft, Mary A. on 67-Feb-5 [67-Mar-26: 2C].
Roy, Sarah Elizabeth (29 yrs., 1 mo.) d. on 67-Nov-28 [67-Nov-30: 2C].
Royce, Hattie E. m. Barney, Charles S. on 69-Nov-6 [69-Dec-20: 2C].
Roycroft, George (70 yrs.) d. on 68-Feb-5 [68-Feb-7: 2C].
Roycroft, John A. m. Deal, Anne M. on 69-Jul-8 [69-Aug-28: 2B].
Royston, Eleanor Roberta (4 mos.) d. on 67-Jun-25 [67-Jun-26: 2C].
Royston, Elizabeth (69 yrs.) d. on 70-Feb-26 [70-Feb-28: 2C].
Royston, Ella m. Price, Oliver on 67-Nov-28 [67-Nov-30: 2C].
Royston, Fredericka M. m. Griffith, W. Curtis on 68-Dec-3 [68-Dec-5: 2C].
Royston, Hattie Lila (1 yr., 6 mos.) d. on 69-Aug-14 [69-Aug-17: 2C].
Royston, John W. (51 yrs.) d. on 66-Dec-14 [66-Dec-15: 2B].
Royston, Sylvanus M. (31 yrs.) d. on 66-Jul-24 [66-Jul-30: 2C].
Ruark, Alexander, Capt. d. [66-Apr-18: 2C].
Ruark, Anna C. (32 yrs.) d. on 66-Jun-10 [66-Jun-11: 2B].
Ruark, Edwin R. m. Travers, Helen M. on 68-Feb-19 [68-Jun-18: 2B].
Ruark, Mary E. m. Supple, Thomas A. on 66-May-3 [66-May-11: 2B].
Rubrick, , Mr. d. on 66-Jul-17 of Cholera morbus [66-Jul-19: 1E].
Ruby, Fannie (11 mos.) d. on 69-Feb-17 of Lung congestion [69-Feb-18: 2C; 69-Feb-19: 2C].
Ruby, William (3 yrs., 8 mos.) d. on 70-Nov-24 of Chronic croup [70-Nov-25: 2D].
Ruckle, Charles Tolley (1 yr., 4 mos.) d. on 66-Aug-6 [66-Aug-7: 2C].
Ruckle, Edward H. m. Clemmont, Ann Eliza on 68-Dec-15 [68-Dec-17: 2C].
Ruckle, Harry Lee (2 yrs.) d. on 68-Dec-13 [68-Dec-15: 2C].
Ruckle, Jennie m. Derr, Samuel B. on 66-Apr-1 [66-Apr-3: 2B].
Ruckle, Mollie L. m. Mitchell, George W. on 67-Jan-1 [67-Jan-3: 2B].
Ruckle, Oscar m. Steevers, Susie on 66-Dec-4 [66-Dec-8: 2B].
Ruckle, William T. m. Sisselberger, Mary A. on 67-Dec-30 [68-Jan-2: 2C].
Ruddach, Washington d. on 67-Feb-19 [67-Feb-21: 2C].
Rudden, John m. Conlon, Mary Agnes on 69-Nov-18 [69-Nov-25: 2C].
Rudenstein, John, Dr. (45 yrs.) d. on 69-Dec-9 [69-Dec-29: 2D].
Rudiger, Alvina m. Lindeman, Henry on 68-Aug-25 [68-Aug-29: 2B].
Rudolf, John A. m. Wyble, Kate on 70-May-31 [70-Jun-4: 2B].
Rudolph, Clara (3 yrs., 2 mos.) d. on 70-Jul-26 [70-Jul-28: 2C].
Rueckert, J. F. m. Bernheim, Emma L. on 67-Dec-19 [67-Dec-24: 2B].
Rufenacht, Frederick d. on 70-May-4 Murdered (Stabbing) [70-May-5: 1G; 70-May-6: 1G; 70-Oct-18: 4C].
Ruff, Christiana m. Peddicord, Charles A. L. on 70-Nov-15 [70-Nov-29: 2C].

Ruff, Jacob (38 yrs.) d. on 70-Dec-10 [70-Dec-12: 2C].
Ruff, John P. m. Baden, Louisa J. on 67-Sep-18 [67-Sep-26: 2B].
Ruff, Louisa J. (33 yrs.) d. on 70-Sep-13 [70-Sep-14: 2B].
Ruff, Mary C. m. Seager, Thomas, Jr. on 66-May-2 [66-May-4: 2C].
Ruff, Mary E. m. Childs, Mathias S. on 68-Nov-3 [68-Nov-9: 2B].
Ruff, Winfield (11 mos.) d. on 70-May-14 [70-May-17: 2B].
Ruhl, John C. m. Hefferman, Celeste W. on 69-Jun-9 [69-Jun-19: 2B].
Ruley, Samuel H. m. Airey, Laura J. on 67-Apr-25 [67-Apr-27: 2A].
Rullman, , Mr. d. on 69-Feb-11 of Consumption [69-Feb-12: 1G].
Rullmann, Elizabeth (47 yrs.) d. on 70-Sep-30 [70-Oct-3: 2B].
Rummell, Charles B. (29 yrs.) d. on 69-Jul-25 of Consumption [69-Jul-26: 2C].
Rummell, Charles J. (4 mos.) d. on 68-Dec-18 [68-Dec-22: 2C].
Rummell, Charles V. (29 yrs.) d. on 69-Jul-25 [69-Jul-27: 2C].
Rummels, William d. on 67-Apr-26 in Railroad accident [67-Apr-27: 1G].
Rumney, Alice m. Disney, John W. on 66-Feb-20 [66-Feb-23: 2C].
Rumney, Charles W. m. Wimpsett, Emma F. M. on 68-Mar-3 [68-Aug-25: 2B].
Rumney, Lucinda (87 yrs.) d. on 66-Mar-15 [66-Mar-19: 2C].
Rundle, J. Dallas (24 yrs.) d. on 68-Oct-7 of Consumption [68-Oct-8: 2B; 68-Nov-7: 2B].
Rundle, John S. m. Shaffer, Mary E. on 66-Jul-12 [66-Jul-25: 2C].
Runge, Emil E. m. Green, M. Louisa on 69-Sep-14 [69-Oct-5: 2B].
Runkles, Mary F. m. Poulton, Charles A. on 70-Nov-10 [70-Nov-14: 2B].
Rupley, Charles P. m. Huster, Maria on 67-May-7 [67-May-8: 2B].
Rupley, Maggie V. d. on 66-Jan-19 [66-Jan-20: 2C; 66-Jan-22: 2C].
Rupp, Franklin Eugene (1 yr., 6 mos.) d. on 70-Mar-17 [70-Mar-19: 2C].
Rupp, R. F. m. Levy, Amelia P. on 66-Aug-16 [66-Aug-30: 2B].
Rupp, Sarah Catherine (9 mos.) d. on 68-May-13 [68-May-16: 2B].
Rupp, William m. Myers, Mary A. on 67-Oct-17 [67-Oct-30: 2B].
Ruppert, Catharine (52 yrs., 1 mo.) d. on 68-Nov-24 [68-Nov-25: 2B; 68-Nov-26: 2B].
Ruppert, Jacob (26 yrs., 4 mos.) d. on 66-Dec-13 [66-Dec-14: 2B].
Ruppert, Mary M. (37 yrs., 9 mos.) d. on 70-Apr-27 [70-Apr-30: 2B].
Rush, Catharine P. m. Schelle, Peter S. on 68-Sep-8 [68-Oct-16: 2B].
Rush, Edward (1 yr., 3 mos.) d. on 67-Aug-11 [67-Aug-12: 2C].
Rush, May W. (79 yrs.) d. on 69-Jul-20 [69-Jul-21: 2C].
Rusk, William R. (4 mos.) d. on 69-Dec-23 [69-Dec-29: 2D].
Ruskell, Abbie m. Porter, J. Mercer on 70-Nov-15 [70-Nov-23: 2B].
Ruskell, William m. Todd, S. Fannie on 70-Jan-12 [70-Jan-18: 2C].
Russe, Caspar (28 yrs.) d. on 68-Jan-13 of Building collapse [68-Jan-18: 1G].
Russel, Edward J. m. Lewis, Elizabeth on 69-May-4 [69-May-6: 2B].
Russel, Henry P. m. Meekins, Maria M. on 70-Jan-31 [70-Feb-16: 2C].
Russell, Alex. H. m. Keach, S. Amelia on 69-Feb-2 [69-Feb-17: 2C].
Russell, Amanda P. m. Grant, John on 66-Nov-6 [66-Nov-12: 2C].
Russell, Ann (79 yrs.) d. on 69-Jan-31 [69-Feb-2: 2C].
Russell, Ann (67 yrs.) d. on 69-Jun-11 [69-Jun-12: 2B].
Russell, Ann (58 yrs.) d. on 70-Oct-19 [70-Oct-20: 2B; 70-Oct-21: 2C].
Russell, Annie E. m. Hopper, William H. on 70-Nov-15 [70-Nov-16: 2C; 70-Nov-17: 2C].
Russell, Benjamin F. m. Wood, Mary A. on 68-Mar-9 [68-Jun-16: 2B].
Russell, Charles m. Kemp, Ann on 69-Mar-3 [69-Mar-16: 2C].
Russell, Charles B. m. Montgomery, Agnes B. on 67-Apr-9 [67-Apr-17: 2B].
Russell, Charles F. m. Grimes, Maggie A. on 70-May-10 [70-May-13: 2C].
Russell, Charles G. (35 yrs.) d. on 69-Jul-4 of Mania a potu [69-Jul-5: 1G].
Russell, Charles R. m. Tonge, Ella R. on 69-Sep-16 [69-Sep-18: 2B].
Russell, Charles W. d. on 67-Nov-22 [67-Nov-23: 2B; 67-Nov-25: 1E].
Russell, Christian, Mrs. (82 yrs.) d. on 69-Mar-18 [69-Mar-19: 2C; 69-Mar-20: 2B].
Russell, David G. m. Boland, Annie C. on 67-May-23 [67-May-28: 2B].
Russell, Elizabeth (33 yrs.) d. on 69-Jun-13 [69-Jun-14: 2B; 69-Jun-15: 2C].

Russell, Ellen C. (23 yrs.) d. on 66-Aug-5 [66-Aug-6: 2C; 66-Aug-7: 2C].
Russell, Eugene J. m. Morrison, Frances W. on 66-Aug-2 [66-Aug-4: 2C].
Russell, Euphemia m. Grant, Malcolm on 66-Jul-2 [66-Jul-4: 2B].
Russell, Eva (1 yr.) d. on 68-Aug-11 [68-Aug-13: 2B].
Russell, F. D. m. Lentz, Carrie on 66-Dec-20 [66-Dec-24: 2B].
Russell, George (60 yrs.) d. on 66-Oct-16 of Paralysis [66-Oct-18: 2B].
Russell, George W., Capt. (58 yrs.) d. on 69-Mar-16 of Cancer [69-Mar-17: 1F, 2C; 69-Mar-18: 1H].
Russell, Henry (2 yrs., 9 mos.) d. on 66-Sep-9 [66-Sep-13: 2C].
Russell, Henry O. m. Rutledge, Mary J. on 69-Oct-6 [69-Oct-9: 2C].
Russell, James (1 yr., 10 mos.) d. on 69-Oct-14 [69-Oct-16: 2B].
Russell, John Shearer (2 yrs., 5 mos.) d. on 68-Nov-29 [68-Nov-30: 2C].
Russell, Louisa S. d. on 69-Oct-27 [69-Oct-29: 2C].
Russell, Mary A. (11 mos.) d. on 70-Mar-19 [70-Mar-22: 2C].
Russell, Mary Ann (4 yrs., 1 mo.) d. on 66-Mar-25 of Scarlet fever [66-Mar-26: 2B].
Russell, Mary E. m. Peirson, Thomas G. on 70-Oct-6 [70-Oct-13: 2C].
Russell, Mary Eliza m. Aaron, Samuel J. on 66-Oct-30 [66-Jun-26: 2C].
Russell, Mary Rebecca (3 mos.) d. on 67-Mar-18 [67-Mar-19: 2C].
Russell, Nancy (51 yrs.) d. on 70-Dec-28 [70-Dec-30: 2C].
Russell, Nicholas (25 yrs.) d. on 66-Aug-30 [66-Aug-31: 2B].
Russell, Richard B. (72 yrs., 6 mos.) d. on 69-Apr-6 [69-Apr-7: 2C].
Russell, Ruth (73 yrs.) d. on 69-Feb-15 [69-Feb-17: 2D].
Russell, S. Emma m. Vandersloot, F. Edward on 69-Sep-27 [69-Sep-29: 2B].
Russell, Sallie D. m. Watters, W. J. H. on 67-Nov-19 [67-Nov-27: 2B].
Russell, Sarah (68 yrs.) d. on 66-Aug-8 [66-Aug-11: 2B].
Russell, Sarah Louisa (1 mo.) d. on 68-Aug-24 [68-Aug-26: 2B].
Russell, Susan (68 yrs.) d. on 70-Jul-28 [70-Jul-30: 2C].
Russell, W. A. m. Thomas, Abbie A. on 69-Sep-7 [69-Oct-1: 2B].
Russell, William (54 yrs.) d. on 66-Oct-27 [66-Oct-29: 2C].
Russell, William H. m. Conley, Mary Josephine on 67-Jul-21 [67-Jul-24: 2C].
Russell, William H. m. Kating, Katie on 69-Oct-14 [69-Oct-20: 2C].
Russell, William W. m. Reid, Jane A. on 66-Jun-14 [66-Jun-23: 2B].
Russell, Willie Asbury (9 mos.) d. on 70-Dec-14 [70-Dec-16: 2C].
Russell, Willie Joseph (2 mos.) d. on 66-Aug-10 [66-Aug-16: 2C].
Russell, Willis Clarence d. on 66-Mar-15 [66-Mar-16: 2B].
Russell, Wilson Lemon (2 yrs.) d. on 69-Dec-1 of Chronic croup [69-Dec-3: 2C].
Russelle, Anna E. m. Walker, George on 70-Jun-1 [70-Jun-11: 2B].
Russom, Jane E. (53 yrs.) d. on 68-Feb-3 [68-Feb-4: 2C].
Rust, J. Franklin m. Ogle, Theodosia on 68-Nov-4 [68-Nov-6: 2C].
Rust, John (48 yrs.) d. on 68-Dec-9 Drowned [68-Dec-10: 4F].
Rust, Thomas m. McMillard, Mary A. on 66-Sep-20 [66-Oct-4: 2B].
Ruth, Josiah Henry (10 mos.) d. on 70-Feb-9 [70-Feb-10: 2C].
Ruth, Mary Elizabeth (1 yr., 8 mos.) d. on 69-Jan-17 [69-Jan-19: 2C].
Ruth, Robert J. m. Crawford, Anna S. [66-Nov-23: 2B].
Rutherdale, George G. (14 yrs.) d. on 68-Jan-16 [68-Jan-17: 2C].
Ruthrauff, Annie Florence (12 yrs.) d. on 67-May-4 [67-May-6: 2B; 67-May-7: 2B; 67-Aug-27: 2B].
Rutledge, Charles J. (4 yrs., 11 mos.) d. on 67-Jul-19 [67-Jul-20: 2C].
Rutledge, Charles William m. Pool, Jane on 69-Sep-20 [69-Sep-28: 2B].
Rutledge, John E. m. Bourman, Louisa on 69-Apr-15 [69-Apr-17: 2A].
Rutledge, Maltby Cochran (2 yrs., 4 mos.) d. on 66-Nov-25 [66-Nov-26: 2C].
Rutledge, Mary (68 yrs.) d. on 69-Oct-31 [69-Nov-1: 2C].
Rutledge, Mary J. m. Russell, Henry O. on 69-Oct-6 [69-Oct-9: 2C].
Rutledge, William H. M. m. Laureen, Ella B. on 70-Dec-13 [70-Dec-14: 2C].
Rutter, Almire C. m. Donaldson, Arthur M. on 66-Oct-7 [66-Oct-24: 2C].

Rutter, Elila McLure (71 yrs.) d. on 67-Jul-27 [67-Jul-29: 2D].
Rutter, Evelina d. on 66-Apr-11 of Consumption [66-Apr-12: 2B].
Rutter, Fred G. m. Purvis, Ella M. on 68-Nov-18 [68-Nov-23: 2B].
Rutter, Ida F. d. on 67-Sep-9 [67-Sep-10: 2B].
Rutter, Joseph H. J. m. Gill, Christie H. on 67-Jun-6 [67-Jun-10: 2B].
Rutter, Julia m. Gilmour, H. C. on 69-Jun-10 [69-Jun-15: 2C].
Rutter, Thomas B. (78 yrs.) d. on 67-Nov-3 [67-Nov-5: 1G, 2B].
Rutter, W. H. m. Thackery, Sallie D. on 68-Jan-15 [68-Jan-30: 2C].
Rutter, Wilbur m. Hennicks, Mattie V. on 68-Jan-23 [68-Jan-31: 2C].
Rutter, William Thomas (17 yrs., 10 mos.) d. on 66-Nov-19 [66-Nov-20: 2B].
Ryall, P. H. m. Redmond, B. C. on 68-Dec-22 [68-Dec-28: 2B].
Ryan, Alice M. (16 yrs., 9 mos.) d. on 70-Jan-17 [70-Jan-18: 2C].
Ryan, Anna (1 yr., 5 mos.) d. on 70-Oct-9 [70-Oct-10: 2B].
Ryan, Anna Bell m. Coleman, Royal B. on 67-Jan-20 [67-Jan-24: 2C].
Ryan, Bridget m. Hayes, Edward on 68-Feb-4 [68-Feb-18: 2C].
Ryan, Edward (36 yrs.) d. on 66-May-30 of Consumption [66-Jun-1: 2B].
Ryan, Elenora m. Smith, Charles F. on 67-Dec-17 [67-Dec-30: 2C].
Ryan, Ellen m. McDonough, Michael on 69-Jun-23 [69-Jul-19: 2C].
Ryan, Hanorah (43 yrs.) d. on 69-Jan-26 [69-Jan-28: 2C].
Ryan, Honora m. Daily, John on 66-Oct-16 [66-Oct-18: 2B].
Ryan, James (42 yrs.) d. on 69-May-9 [69-May-10: 2C].
Ryan, James E. m. Dadds, Annie M. on 70-Jun-9 [70-Jun-15: 2B].
Ryan, Jeremiah (45 yrs.) d. on 67-Jun-18 [67-Jun-19: 2B; 67-Jun-20: 2B].
Ryan, Johanna (4 yrs., 4 mos.) d. on 66-Mar-6 [66-Mar-8: 2B].
Ryan, John (7 yrs., 9 mos.) d. on 68-Nov-28 [68-Nov-30: 2C].
Ryan, John (55 yrs.) d. on 68-Sep-25 [68-Sep-26: 2B].
Ryan, John (1 yr., 8 mos.) d. on 66-May-8 [66-May-9: 2B].
Ryan, John J. d. on 70-Nov-18 [70-Nov-19: 2B].
Ryan, Julia (3 yrs., 8 mos.) d. on 66-May-3 [66-May-5: 2B].
Ryan, Mary E. (19 yrs.) d. on 69-Aug-27 [69-Aug-28: 2B].
Ryan, Mary Ellen (6 mos.) d. on 66-Aug-28 [66-Aug-29: 2B].
Ryan, Mary Emma m. Andrews, Thomas Edward on 70-Jul-14 [70-Aug-6: 2C].
Ryan, Michael d. on 66-Jul-6 Drowned [66-Jul-7: 1G; 66-Jul-9: 1G].
Ryan, Olita Chatard (6 mos.) d. on 70-Jul-12 [70-Jul-14: 2B].
Ryan, Robert S. m. Boswell, Annie E. on 66-Nov-20 [66-Nov-23: 2C].
Ryan, Thomas m. Doran, Kate on 67-Nov-26 [67-Dec-3: 2C].
Ryan, William m. McLaughlin, Mary on 66-Dec-10 [66-Dec-13: 2B].
Ryans, Thomas (46 yrs.) d. on 66-Nov-13 [66-Nov-15: 2C].
Ryder, William m. Delaney, Catherine on 66-Apr-25 [66-Apr-26: 2B].
Ryer, John D. m. Marlin, Eveline on 66-Jun-5 [66-Jun-13: 2B].
Ryland, Josephine m. Scott, Abram V. on 67-Nov-26 [67-Nov-30: 2C].
Ryley, George m. Downs, J. B. on 66-Jan-10 [66-Jan-17: 2C].
Rynehart, Samuel, Jr. m. Young, Mary A. on 66-Aug-26 [66-Aug-27: 2B; 66-Aug-28: 2B].
Rynerson, John m. Norback, Virginia on 68-Apr-6 [68-Apr-7: 2B; 68-Apr-8: 2B].
Ryninger, Margaret (79 yrs.) d. on 70-Mar-22 [70-Mar-28: 2B].
Sable, Mary Jane m. Lilly, John on 66-Dec-24 [67-Jan-5: 2C].
Sachs, Mell m. Dill, Catharine J. on 67-Sep-24 [67-Sep-25: 2B].
Sackerman, Henry m. Goldsmith, Esther on 70-Jan-2 [70-Jan-5: 2C].
Sackerman, Louis (80 yrs.) d. on 68-Sep-8 [68-Sep-9: 2B].
Sackerman, Louis m. Long, Carrie on 70-May-22 [70-Jun-11: 2B].
Sackman, Henry (44 yrs.) d. on 66-Feb-18 [66-Jun-26: 2B].
Saddler, William H. d. on 68-May-9 of Heart disease [68-May-11: 1F].
Sadler, Eliza (56 yrs.) d. on 70-Dec-25 [70-Dec-28: 2C].
Sadler, George E. m. Weems, Kate C. on 69-Dec-23 [69-Dec-25: 2C].
Sadler, Helen F. (3 yrs., 4 mos.) d. on 69-Feb-23 [69-Feb-24: 2C].

Sadler, John m. Murphy, Mary C. on 69-Jun-28 [69-Jul-5: 2C].
Sadler, John R. m. Johnson, Lizzie A. on 70-Sep-8 [70-Oct-1: 2B].
Sadler, Joseph R. m. Batchelor, Eliza Jane on 66-Jul-26 [66-Jul-28: 2C].
Sadtler, Charles Stanley (8 yrs.) d. on 69-Oct-10 [69-Oct-13: 2C].
Sadtler, George T. m. Plitt, Annie S. on 66-Jul-10 [66-Jul-19: 2C].
Sadtler, Mary C. m. Emory, D. Hopper on 66-Nov-22 [66-Nov-28: 2B].
Sahm, Henry (7 mos.) d. on 69-Apr-17 [69-Apr-19: 2B].
Sakers, John T. m. Nichols, Fanny M. on 66-Feb-6 [66-Feb-9: 2B].
Sakers, Maggie m. Brown, William F. on 66-Oct-25 [66-Oct-27: 2B].
Saladin, Mary Caroline d. on 69-Aug-3 [69-Aug-4: 2C].
Sale, Henrietta F. (27 yrs.) d. on 66-Jul-7 [66-Jul-10: 2C].
Salgee, John m. Blunt, Amelia G. on 69-Sep-21 [69-Oct-5: 2B].
Salgee, Oriana m. Keeling, Joseph W. on 70-Oct-13 [70-Oct-21: 2C].
Salisbury, Laura J. (40 yrs.) d. on 67-Nov-5 [67-Dec-18: 2B].
Salisbury, Sallie S. (83 yrs.) d. on 70-Oct-13 [70-Oct-14: 2B].
Salley, Ellen (56 yrs.) d. on 66-Jan-19 [66-Jan-22: 2C].
Salmon, Elizabeth Jane m. Bians, William H. on 66-Dec-31 [67-Jan-9: 2B].
Salmon, P. Adolphus (43 yrs.) d. on 69-Dec-29 [69-Dec-31: 2C].
Salmon, Sarah E. m. Baines, William F. on 66-Dec-31 [67-Jan-8: 2B].
Salom, Mary E. m. Van Reuth, A. P. on 67-Feb-21 [67-Feb-23: 2C].
Salomon, Oscar E. M. m. McLaughlin, Marie L. on 70-Jan-9 [70-Jan-11: 2C].
Salter, Eliza m. Jones, Isaiah on 66-Mar-17 [66-Mar-29: 2B].
Saltzer, James E. m. Howard, Fannie on 68-Dec-17 [68-Dec-18: 2C].
Salzkorn, Dorothea (71 yrs.) d. on 70-Oct-28 [70-Oct-29: 2B].
Sample, Lavinia E. m. Frey, James H. on 67-Mar-27 [67-Mar-29: 2B].
Sampson, Amanda V. m. Washam, Issac on 67-May-6 [67-May-8: 2B].
Sampson, Selicour (54 yrs.) d. on 67-Feb-6 of Heart disease [67-Feb-7: 2C].
Samson, Harriet Louisa (2 yrs., 9 mos.) d. on 67-Jul-11 [67-Jul-12: 2C].
Samuel, Euphemia M. (1 yr., 3 mos.) d. on 68-Jul-14 [68-Jul-15: 2B].
Sand, Mary E. m. Engel, C. H. on 69-Jan-19 [69-Feb-1: 2C].
Sand, Peter (22 yrs.) d. on 68-Jul-3 [68-Jul-4: 2C].
Sanders, Ann (76 yrs.) d. on 69-Oct-6 [69-Oct-8: 2B].
Sanders, Charles L. (35 yrs.) d. on 67-May-9 [67-May-10: 2B; 67-May-11: 2A].
Sanders, Eugene A. (24 yrs.) d. on 66-Aug-14 [66-Aug-29: 2B; 66-Sep-1: 2B].
Sanders, Franklin m. Cheeseborough, Susan Percy on 69-Aug-12 [69-Aug-17: 2C].
Sanders, George P. (35 yrs., 6 mos.) d. on 67-Mar-2 [67-May-4: 2C; 67-May-7: 2B].
Sanders, James W. m. Hammer, Julia F. on 69-Jun-13 [69-Jun-15: 2C].
Sanders, Joseph F. (77 yrs.) d. on 66-Oct-22 [66-Oct-24: 1G, 2C].
Sanders, Katie Margery (1 yr., 11 mos.) d. on 68-Dec-18 [68-Dec-21: 2C].
Sanders, Levin (40 yrs.) d. on 66-Aug-16 Drowned [66-Aug-17: 4C].
Sanders, Mary Ann m. Slater, Thomas W. on 67-Feb-27 [67-Mar-7: 2C].
Sanders, Matilda A. (44 yrs.) d. on 66-Nov-5 [66-Nov-10: 2B].
Sanders, Permelia m. Bramble, Charles H. on 70-Mar-8 [70-Mar-10: 2B].
Sanders, S. F. m. Applegarth, Kate on 66-Nov-27 [66-Nov-28: 2B].
Sanders, Samuel Herbert (3 mos.) d. on 70-Jul-15 [70-Jul-18: 2C].
Sanders, Solomon S. (36 yrs.) d. on 70-Oct-6 [70-Oct-8: 2B].
Sanders, Sophie M. m. George, Thomas J. on 66-Dec-13 [66-Dec-18: 2B].
Sanders, Virginia B. m. Hynson, Charles E. on 70-Mar-29 [70-Apr-1: 2B].
Sanders, William m. Conaway, Louisa on 69-Jul-7 [69-Jul-12: 2C].
Sanderson, Catherine (70 yrs.) d. on 66-Jan-19 [66-Jan-20: 2C].
Sanderson, Charles (17 yrs., 9 mos.) d. on 66-Aug-15 [66-Aug-16: 2C].
Sanderson, Christiana A. V. m. Baughman, Samuel W. on 68-Aug-10 [68-Aug-12: 2C].
Sanderson, Emily Jane (54 yrs.) d. on 66-May-29 [66-May-30: 2C].
Sanderson, Emily M. m. Parrish, James H. on 68-May-12 [68-May-15: 2B].
Sanderson, George H. m. James, Annie on 67-Nov-21 [67-Nov-25: 2C].

Sanderson, L. W. m. Murphy, Sallie M. on 69-Jul-4 [69-Jul-7: 2C].
Sanderson, Nannie B. (1 yr., 8 mos.) d. on 67-Aug-6 [67-Aug-7: 2C].
Sanderson, W. Cook m. Cator, Mary E. on 69-Dec-16 [69-Dec-21: 2B].
Sandman, Joseph H. (38 yrs.) d. on 70-Jan-24 [70-Jan-27: 2C].
Sands, Ella May d. on 70-Aug-11 [70-Aug-13: 2C].
Sands, Eugenie F. m. Horney, William H. on 66-Dec-26 [67-Jan-3: 2B].
Sands, Hattie m. Wilson, John F. on 68-Jan-30 [68-Feb-1: 2B; 68-Feb-3: 2C].
Sands, Hattie m. Miller, John S. on 68-Jan-30 [68-Feb-3: 2C].
Sands, Henry R. (35 yrs.) d. on 67-Apr-23 [67-Apr-24: 2B; 67-Apr-25: 2B].
Sands, Jane W. (59 yrs.) d. on 70-Mar-3 [70-Mar-5: 2B].
Sands, Laura V. m. Knight, John T. on 66-Jul-3 [66-Jul-6: 2B].
Sands, Phealix (67 yrs.) d. on 68-Jun-13 [68-Jun-15: 2B].
Sands, Polly (68 yrs.) d. on 70-Oct-20 [70-Oct-21: 2C].
Sands, Richard m. Woodward, Helen on 68-Aug-1 [68-Sep-30: 2B].
Sands, Thomas E. m. Murphy, Sarah A. on 67-Nov-7 [67-Nov-14: 2B].
Sanford, Edward H. m. McNabb, Mary E. on 68-Mar-24 [68-Mar-26: 2B].
Sangster, Mary Ann (75 yrs.) d. on 68-Jun-1 [68-Jun-2: 2B].
Sangston, Anne M. (2 mos.) d. on 70-Jun-25 [70-Jun-28: 2C].
Sangston, Benjamin W. (31 yrs.) d. on 68-Jun-30 [68-Jul-1: 2B; 68-Jul-2: 2C].
Sangston, Florence (16 yrs.) d. on 66-Jun-23 [66-Jun-25: 2B].
Sangston, John (23 yrs.) d. on 70-Oct-8 [70-Oct-10: 2B].
Sangston, Lillie C. m. Myers, James E. on 68-Oct-7 [68-Oct-9: 2C].
Sangston, Lillie Lee (2 yrs., 2 mos.) d. on 67-Sep-12 [67-Sep-13: 2B].
Sangston, Mary Emma (5 yrs., 4 mos.) d. on 69-May-28 [69-Jun-5: 2B].
Sangston, Sallie Stevens d. on 69-Dec-31 [70-Jan-1: 2B].
Sangston, Sue Wright d. on 69-Nov-24 [69-Nov-25: 2C; 69-Nov-26: 2D].
Sangston, William Stevens (30 yrs.) d. on 66-Aug-13 [66-Jun-15: 2C].
Sangston, William Stevens (4 mos.) d. on 66-Aug-13 [66-Aug-14: 2C].
Sanguinetti, Erina m. Stornone, Gregory on 68-Nov-11 [68-Nov-21: 2C].
Sank, Corben A. m. Welch, Julie J. on 66-Apr-4 [66-Apr-7: 2B].
Sank, Elizabeth (40 yrs.) d. on 68-Jan-10 [68-Jan-13: 2C].
Sank, James W. m. Demitz, Rebecca M. on 69-Apr-13 [69-May-10: 2B].
Sank, Joseph H. m. Brown, Maggie M. on 70-Aug-2 [70-Aug-3: 2C].
Sank, Mary Eliza m. Henry, Caleb F. on 66-Jan-15 [66-Jan-19: 2C].
Sank, Nicholas (90 yrs., 1 mo.) d. on 66-Sep-6 [66-Sep-7: 2B].
Sanks, Henrietta m. Beacham, John S. on 67-Aug-20 [67-Aug-23: 2B].
Sanks, Jane (55 yrs.) d. on 69-Apr-30 [69-May-3: 2C].
Sanks, John M. (7 yrs., 2 mos.) d. on 68-Oct-21 [68-Oct-22: 2C].
Sanks, John W. m. Knight, Mary Amelia on 68-Oct-1 [68-Oct-5: 2B].
Sanks, Lida m. Shorey, William F. on 69-Sep-30 [69-Oct-4: 2C].
Sanks, Lida A. m. Morrow, James S. on 68-Oct-1 [68-Oct-5: 2B].
Sanks, Mary Eliza (1 yr.) d. on 69-Sep-25 of Chronic croup [69-Sep-27: 2C].
Sanner, A. A. m. Graham, Annie V. on 69-Nov-30 [69-Dec-1: 2C].
Sanner, Basil P. m. Hughes, Laura S. on 67-Feb-11 [67-Feb-19: 2C].
Sanner, Eddie (3 yrs.) d. on 66-Nov-20 [66-Nov-23: 2C].
Sanner, Ernest Lee (1 yr., 6 mos.) d. on 68-Sep-18 [68-Sep-19: 2B].
Sanner, Harry Lee (9 mos.) d. on 67-Apr-11 [67-Apr-12: 2C].
Sanner, James Andrew (9 mos.) d. on 66-Aug-13 [66-Aug-15: 2C].
Sanner, John F. (40 yrs.) d. on 68-Jul-16 of Heatstroke [68-Jul-17: 1D; 68-Jul-18: 2B].
Sanner, Jonathan B. (3 mos.) d. on 67-Dec-1 [67-Dec-5: 2C].
Sanner, Marian m. Farquharson, W. E. on 68-Oct-6 [68-Oct-7: 2C].
Sanner, Martha Washington (13 yrs.) d. on 66-Dec-23 [66-Dec-25: 2B].
Sanner, Mary V. m. Guy, Frank A. on 69-Nov-4 [69-Nov-6: 2B].
Sanner, Thomas W. m. Holdefer, Josephine on 70-Apr-7 [70-Apr-11: 2B].
Sansbury, Alice A. (8 yrs., 7 mos.) d. on 66-Aug-20 [66-Aug-21: 2C].

Sansbury, Edward (82 yrs.) d. on 70-Aug-28 [70-Aug-30: 2C].
Sapp, Catherine H. (14 yrs., 10 mos.) d. on 69-Mar-29 [69-Mar-31: 2C].
Sapp, Cidney S. m. Baxter, James W. on 67-May-2 [68-Feb-20: 2C].
Sapp, Daniel, Sr. (75 yrs.) d. on 70-Jan-28 [70-Jan-28: 2B].
Sapp, Elizabeth Rosalia (28 yrs.) d. on 67-Oct-21 [67-Oct-22: 2A].
Sapp, Jacob Edward (4 yrs., 4 mos.) d. on 69-Jun-20 [69-Jun-22: 2C].
Sapp, Joseph F. m. Wright, Louisa on 70-Feb-8 [70-Feb-15: 2C].
Sapp, Justina (74 yrs.) d. on 69-Jul-16 [69-Jul-17: 2C].
Sapp, Laura Virginia (2 yrs., 1 mo.) d. on 69-Jun-20 [69-Jun-21: 2B].
Sapp, Martha J. m. Gambrell, James H. on 68-Jun-25 [68-Jun-27: 2B].
Sapp, Sarah m. Viney, Douglas on 69-Oct-17 [69-Oct-20: 2C].
Sapp, William H. (20 yrs., 3 mos.) d. on 67-Feb-3 of Consumption [67-Feb-11: 2C].
Sappington, John, Dr. (68 yrs.) d. on 69-Nov-18 [69-Nov-25: 2C].
Sappington, John K., Dr. (78 yrs.) d. on 68-Aug-8 [68-Aug-10: 2C; 68-Aug-11: 2B].
Sappington, R. Dorsey (22 yrs.) d. on 70-Jul-6 [70-Jul-19: 2C].
Sappington, Richard Lee (1 yr., 2 mos.) d. on 67-May-10 [67-May-11: 2A].
Sargent, George W. m. Dyer, Laura V. on 69-Aug-26 [69-Aug-31: 2B].
Sargent, H. G. C. m. Loveday, Ida on 67-Nov-7 [67-Nov-22: 2C].
Sargent, Mary A. E. m. Hutchison, Charles E. on 70-Nov-17 [70-Nov-29: 2C].
Sarmon, Sophia (7 yrs., 3 mos.) d. on 67-Aug-18 [67-Sep-10: 2B].
Satterfield, Andrew m. Mitchell, Joanna on 70-Nov-24 [70-Nov-28: 2C].
Satterfield, Eleanor E. m. Staylor, Louis P. on 66-Aug-9 [66-Aug-14: 2C].
Satterfield, John F. m. Henry, Martha on 67-Nov-6 [68-Apr-30: 2B].
Satterfield, Rachel A. A. (22 yrs., 11 mos.) d. on 67-Feb-12 [67-Feb-22: 2D].
Satterfield, Samuel S. (66 yrs.) d. [66-Apr-3: 2B].
Sauer, Catherine R. m. Chapman, J. on 70-Dec-7 [70-Dec-9: 2C].
Sauer, Christian m. Brosius, Sophie on 69-May-2 [69-May-4: 2B].
Sauer, Margaretta (67 yrs.) d. on 68-Feb-23 [68-Feb-24: 2C].
Sauerhoff, George T. (35 yrs.) d. on 68-Aug-27 [68-Aug-28: 2B; 68-Aug-29: 2B].
Sauerhoff, Mary Elizabeth m. Taylor, James W. W. on 66-Mar-22 [66-Mar-27: 2B].
Sauerhoff, Oscar F. m. Wetter, Emma L. on 69-Sep-14 [69-Sep-28: 2B].
Sauerwald, Margaretha d. on 69-Dec-23 [69-Dec-24: 2C].
Sauerwald, Mary Genevive d. on 68-Mar-18 [68-Apr-14: 2A].
Sauerwein, Charles D. m. Orvier, Marie Gabriella on 67-Aug-23 [67-Sep-12: 2B].
Sauerwein, Edwin m. Taylor, Annie on 69-May-13 [69-May-15: 2B].
Sauerwein, Emma m. West, George P. on 68-Dec-8 [68-Dec-12: 2C].
Sauerwein, Margaret F. (43 yrs.) d. on 70-Oct-31 [70-Nov-1: 2C].
Sauerwein, Mary M. (68 yrs.) d. on 67-Nov-5 [67-Nov-6: 2B].
Sauerwein, Virginia R. m. Mantler, John L. on 69-Sep-1 [69-Sep-16: 2B].
Saul, Ann E. (55 yrs.) d. on 68-Jun-24 [68-Jun-26: 2B].
Saul, James F. m. Shrudes, Sallie on 69-Mar-8 [69-Mar-30: 2C].
Saumenig, A. C. (53 yrs.) d. on 69-Oct-6 [69-Oct-7: 2B; 69-Oct-8: 2B].
Saumenig, John H. m. Baughman, M. Annie on 70-Apr-28 [70-Apr-30: 2A].
Saumenig, William R. m. Stauffer, Mary E. on 69-Apr-8 [69-Apr-13: 2B].
Saumerig, Amelia M. m. Boyd, James on 66-Jul-19 [66-Jul-25: 2C].
Saums, Christian C. m. Mark, Emma J. on 67-Dec-3 [67-Dec-18: 2B].
Saums, John J. d. on 69-Jun-25 [69-Jun-26: 2B].
Saums, Mary Ellen Helfenstein (36 yrs., 7 mos.) d. on 69-Apr-2 [69-Apr-3: 2B].
Saunders, Barbara (60 yrs., 8 mos.) d. on 68-Sep-27 [68-Sep-29: 2B].
Saunders, Hannah R. m. Miller, Alfred B. on 69-Jun-17 [69-Jun-21: 2B].
Saunders, Harriet P. m. Moore, Samuel on 66-Sep-3 [66-Sep-6: 2B].
Saunders, Issac M. D. (22 yrs.) d. on 66-Sep-4 [66-Sep-5: 2B].
Saunders, J. Randolph m. Cherry, Cornelia V. on 69-Nov-25 [69-Dec-22: 2B].
Saunders, John Joseph m. Vaughan, Sarah C. on 66-Feb-13 [66-Feb-20: 2B].
Saunders, Joseph A. m. Glass, Rachel Ann on 66-Jan-7 [66-Jan-16: 2C].

Saunders, Joseph L. m. Hager, Emma on 69-Jul-6 [69-Dec-23: 2B].
Saunders, Kate M. m. Waring, Robert K. on 70-May-3 [70-May-6: 2B].
Saunders, Louisa m. Luttman, Alfred on 67-Jan-15 [67-Jan-17: 2C].
Saunders, Marie m. Sinclair, Matthew on 66-Aug-2 [66-Aug-30: 2B].
Saunders, Olivia J. m. Baker, T. on 70-Mar-23 [70-Mar-30: 2B].
Saunders, Sarah (17 yrs.) d. on 69-Sep-3 [69-Sep-7: 2B].
Saunders, Sarah R. m. Lutz, John on 68-Apr-2 [68-Apr-6: 2B].
Saunders, Solomon (23 yrs.) d. on 70-May-14 [70-May-17: 2B].
Saunders, Theodore P. m. Stevens, Sarah Louisa on 70-Dec-20 [70-Dec-22: 2B].
Saunders, William W. m. Emrick, Mary C. on 68-Mar-4 [68-Nov-26: 2B].
Sauner, Andrew Jackson (41 yrs.) d. on 66-May-28 [66-May-29: 2B].
Sauner, Laura (1 yr.) d. on 70-Jan-16 [70-Jan-18: 2C].
Sauner, William F. (1 yr., 10 mos.) d. on 67-Sep-7 [67-Sep-9: 2B].
Sauntry, Michael (1 yr., 9 mos.) d. on 66-Jul-27 [66-Jul-28: 2C].
Sausser, Elizabeth A. m. Brooks, Benedict J. on 68-Nov-30 [68-Dec-14: 2C].
Sauter, Christian (36 yrs.) d. on 68-Feb-21 [68-Feb-22: 2B].
Sauter, Christian (9 mos.) d. on 69-Feb-10 [69-Feb-11: 2C; 69-Feb-13: 2C].
Sauter, Frederick Augustus (2 yrs., 6 mos.) d. on 69-Feb-12 [69-Feb-13: 2C].
Sauter, Mary Elizabeth (13 yrs.) d. on 68-Apr-7 [68-Apr-8: 2B].
Sauter, William m. Peddicord, Sallie E. on 66-May-8 [66-May-16: 2C].
Savage, Clara I. (1 yr., 10 mos.) d. on 70-Aug-24 [70-Aug-25: 2C].
Savage, Samuel F. (32 yrs.) d. on 68-Nov-2 [68-Nov-4: 2C].
Savage, William H. m. Chabot, Emilie on 68-Apr-20 [68-May-7: 2B].
Saville, Daisy Caroline d. on 67-Nov-23 [67-Nov-28: 2C].
Saville, Eliza A. m. Huttenberger, Charles F. on 70-Apr-7 [70-Apr-26: 2B].
Saville, W. Oliver m. Merker, Sallie on 66-Oct-9 [66-Oct-11: 2C].
Savin, Mary A. m. Walbach, Jno. B. on 67-Jun-6 [67-Jun-10: 2B].
Savoy, Alfred (41 yrs.) d. on 66-Dec-12 [66-Dec-13: 2B].
Saxton, Louisa (19 yrs.) d. on 70-May-19 [70-May-20: 2C; 70-May-21: 2B].
Saxton, William G. (77 yrs.) d. on 68-May-9 of Dropsy [68-May-11: 2B].
Saxton, William H. m. Jenkins, Mary Armour on 67-Oct-8 [67-Oct-11: 2B].
Saylor, John W. m. Thompson, Isabella on 66-Feb-1 [66-Feb-6: 2D].
Sayre, Caroline F. (63 yrs.) d. on 66-Jan-9 [66-Jan-12: 2C].
Sayre, George W. (22 yrs.) d. on 66-Apr-7 [66-Apr-10: 2C].
Sayre, John (74 yrs.) d. on 70-Aug-23 [70-Sep-13: 2B].
Scaggs, Carrie V. m. Burton, Richard A. on 68-Oct-1 [68-Oct-3: 2B].
Scaggs, Mollie R. m. King, Lloyd W. on 68-Nov-11 [68-Nov-13: 2C].
Scales, Carrie m. Wood, John F. on 68-Dec-25 [69-Jan-6: 2C].
Scally, Ellen (1 yr., 4 mos.) d. on 69-Oct-14 [69-Oct-15: 2C].
Scally, Hugh d. on 70-Apr-30 in Wagon accident [70-Jul-21: 2C].
Scally, John m. Cushley, Ellen on 65-Nov-5 [66-Feb-8: 2C].
Scally, Luke (65 yrs.) d. on 69-Feb-11 [69-Feb-12: 2C].
Scanlon, Ellen (45 yrs.) d. on 70-Sep-19 [70-Sep-20: 2B].
Scanlon, Michael A. m. Hagan, Mollie A. on 69-Aug-18 [70-Feb-8: 2C].
Scannal, John (5 yrs., 6 mos.) d. on 66-Apr-13 [66-Apr-14: 2B].
Scarborough, Annie m. Gerry, E. H. on 68-Sep-22 [68-Sep-23: 2B].
Scarborough, Emma m. Read, George S. on 70-Apr-26 [70-Apr-30: 2A].
Scarborough, George B. (14 yrs., 11 mos.) d. on 67-Sep-8 [67-Sep-10: 2B].
Scarborough, James m. Wills, Mary C. on 69-Oct-18 [69-Dec-28: 2C].
Scarborough, Kate (4 yrs., 5 mos.) d. on 68-Dec-6 [68-Dec-8: 2C].
Scarborough, Pauline M. (42 yrs.) d. on 70-Mar-9 [70-Feb-10: 2C].
Scarborough, Robert m. Thompson, Mattie J. on 66-Feb-1 [66-Feb-21: 2C].
Scarborough, William m. Groscup, Alverta on 70-Oct-13 [70-Oct-22: 2B].
Scarborough, William A. (31 yrs.) d. on 70-Oct-8 [70-Oct-10: 2B].
Scarburgh, Mary A. m. Lewis, Alonzo B. on 67-Dec-17 [67-Dec-19: 2B].

Scarf, James H. m. Chandley, Annie E. on 66-Dec-25 [67-Jan-4: 2D].
Scarf, Lucy (18 yrs.) d. on 68-Nov-30 [68-Dec-1: 2C].
Scarf, William T. m. Leport, Lucy on 66-Nov-12 [66-Nov-21: 2C].
Scarff, Elizabeth (88 yrs.) d. on 68-Aug-6 [68-Aug-7: 2B].
Scarff, Henry J. d. on 70-Sep-10 [70-Sep-19: 2B].
Schaab, Kate m. Bachman, Mark on 67-Aug-6 [67-Aug-10: 2B].
Schaaf, Catherine m. Wittig, George H. on 68-May-10 [68-May-13: 2B].
Schacht, S. m. Pescud, S. B. on 66-Mar-9 [66-Sep-1: 2B].
Schaefer, Caroline (31 yrs.) d. on 68-May-31 [68-Jun-1: 2B].
Schaefer, Ellen B. m. Barker, George Y. on 68-Nov-24 [68-Nov-30: 2B].
Schaefer, Emma Jane (1 yr., 11 mos.) d. on 68-Oct-7 of Diptheria [68-Oct-8: 2B; 68-Oct-10: 2B].
Schaefer, George A. (33 yrs.) d. on 66-Mar-7 [66-Mar-10: 2B].
Schaefer, Henry m. Reister, Maggie E. on 68-Jun-4 [68-Jul-14: 2B].
Schaefer, Louis G. m. Nyce, Emma on 68-Dec-26 [68-Jan-11: 2B].
Schaefer, Maria Margrethe (74 yrs.) d. on 67-Jul-15 [67-Jul-16: 2C; 67-Jul-17: 2C].
Schaefer, Mary E. m. Hart, George A. on 67-Dec-26 [68-Jan-2: 2C].
Schaefer, Sarah Anna (57 yrs.) d. on 69-Nov-23 [69-Nov-24: 2C].
Schaeffer, August m. Connolly, Sarah Elizabeth on 69-Apr-2 [69-Jun-19: 2B].
Schaeffer, Caroline m. Tweeddale, Jacob on 67-Dec-23 [67-Dec-30: 2C].
Schaeffer, Charity V. (31 yrs.) d. on 68-Nov-17 [68-Nov-23: 2B].
Schaeffer, John C. (17 yrs.) d. on 67-Aug-18 Drowned [67-Aug-19: 1G; 67-Aug-20: 1G].
Schaeffer, Maggie m. Beaumont, Alexander H. on 67-Apr-18 [67-Apr-20: 2A].
Schaeffer, Margaret m. Kelley, John on 66-Nov-5 [66-Nov-22: 2C].
Schaeffer, Mary A. m. Hurt, George A. on 67-Dec-26 [67-Dec-31: 2C].
Schaeffer, William A. (74 yrs.) d. on 66-Jan-11 [66-Jan-12: 2C; 66-Jan-13: 1G].
Schaeffer, William G. m. Lyon, Mollie J. on 70-Jan-18 [70-Jan-20: 2C].
Schafer, Christian M. S. m. Winter, Tillie on 66-Feb-21 [66-Feb-23: 2C].
Schafer, Mary Roseanna (1 yr.) d. on 66-Aug-21 [66-Aug-22: 2C].
Schaff, John Edwin (9 yrs., 1 mo.) d. on 70-Aug-20 of Fall [70-Aug-25: 2C].
Schaible, Amelia W. m. Doberer, Gottlieb on 66-May-24 [66-May-28: 2B].
Schaible, Charles F. (56 yrs.) d. on 70-Sep-8 [70-Sep-9: 2B; 70-Sep-10: 2B].
Schaible, John Frederick R. (17 yrs., 3 mos.) d. on 70-Jul-22 of Heatstroke [70-Jul-25: 2C; 70-Jul-26: 2C].
Schaible, L. D. m. Klein, H. W. on 68-Sep-15 [68-Sep-19: 2B].
Schanberger, Henry A. m. Debring, Mary A. on 67-Feb-26 [67-Mar-1: 2C].
Scharf, Clara (4 mos.) d. on 66-Aug-14 [66-Aug-15: 2C].
Scharf, Elisha T. m. Houston, Mary Levina on 67-Jan-2 [67-Jan-23: 2C].
Scharf, Francis (1 yr., 7 mos.) d. on 66-Jul-5 [66-Jul-6: 2B].
Scharf, Hannah (46 yrs.) d. on 66-Aug-28 [66-Aug-29: 2B].
Scharf, John Thomas m. McDougal, Mary on 69-Dec-2 [69-Dec-3: 2C].
Scharf, Margreth (27 yrs.) d. on 67-May-2 [67-May-4: 2B].
Scharf, Martha m. Matthews, Randolph on 68-Nov-10 [68-Nov-18: 2C].
Scharf, Mary Matilda (1 mo.) d. on 70-Mar-31 [70-Apr-2: 2B].
Scharf, Teresa m. Hoff, J. Wilbur on 70-Dec-13 [70-Dec-15: 2C].
Scharf, Thomas G. Lee (6 yrs., 7 mos.) d. on 69-Nov-21 [69-Nov-22: 2C].
Scharf, William m. Woodward, Alice on 67-Jun-3 [67-Jun-5: 2B].
Scharf, William J. m. Boerner, Isabella V. on 66-May-3 [66-May-17: 2C].
Scharff, Issac Newton m. Woodward, Maggie A. on 66-Sep-12 [66-Nov-9: 2C].
Scharp, Mary E. m. Unglaub, Philip on 69-Sep-12 [69-Sep-14: 2B].
Schaub, Frederick m. Kabernagle, Amelia D. on 69-Nov-18 [69-Nov-30: 2C].
Schaub, John d. on 66-Jul-16 of Heatstroke [66-Jul-18: 1F].
Schaub, John m. Higgins, Catharine on 67-Nov-19 [67-Nov-22: 2C].
Schaufelberger, Louis P. (22 yrs.) d. [70-Dec-30: 2C].
Schaum, Christopher J. m. Schillinger, Amelia S. on 69-Mar-2 [69-Mar-23: 2C].

Schaum, Mary A. m. Clark, Daniel E. on 70-Jul-19 [70-Aug-1: 2C].
Schaum, Sophie m. Read, James L. on 67-Dec-10 [68-Jan-11: 2B].
Schaun, Mary E. (29 yrs.) d. on 66-Dec-4 [66-Dec-5: 2B].
Scheckells, Mary F. (42 yrs.) d. on 67-Jan-28 [67-Jan-30: 2C].
Scheerer, Ellennora David (1 yr., 2 mos.) d. on 66-Sep-19 [66-Sep-20: 2B].
Scheib, Adeline m. Heldmann, Henry J. on 70-Sep-13 [70-Sep-26: 2B].
Scheib, Joanna L. m. Beck, August on 66-Aug-30 [66-Sep-20: 2B].
Scheick, Josephine m. O'Connor, William J., Jr. on 70-Feb-10 [70-Mar-28: 2B].
Scheldt, Otho F., Dr. (29 yrs.) d. on 66-Jan-24 of Typhoid [66-Jan-29: 2C].
Schell, Albin (34 yrs.) d. on 69-Aug-13 [69-Aug-14: 1G, 2C].
Schell, Margaret d. on 66-Jan-7 of Pneumonia [66-Jan-13: 2C].
Schell, Margaret J. m. Pue, Michael on 67-Jun-18 [67-Jul-4: 2B].
Schell, Richard J. m. Boyce, Margaret Ann on 69-Jan-14 [69-Jan-19: 2C].
Schelle, Kate R. m. Ehlen, Thomas A. on 67-Jul-2 [67-Jul-10: 2B].
Schelle, Peter S. m. Rush, Catharine P. on 68-Sep-8 [68-Oct-16: 2B].
Schellenberger, Kate m. McGinty, Henry, Jr. on 69-Jun-20 [69-Jun-29: 2C].
Schem, John Leonard (23 yrs.) d. on 68-Jun-15 Kicked by horse [68-Jun-16: 1G, 2B].
Schenck, Alexander D. m. Turner, Maggie R. on 69-May-4 [69-May-6: 2B].
Schenckel, Florence E. (3 mos.) d. on 70-Jan-2 [70-Jan-4: 2C].
Schenckel, Louisa m. Jones, Alonzo F. on 66-Jun-8 [66-Nov-5: 2B].
Schenthal, Menna (59 yrs.) d. on 66-Jan-25 [66-Jan-26: 2B].
Schepler, Edward (14 yrs., 10 mos.) d. on 69-Jan-30 [69-Feb-1: 2C].
Schepler, Francis William m. Foose, Catherine E. on 69-Sep-8 [69-Sep-18: 2B].
Schepler, Louisa m. Smith, Alfred Lee on 69-Oct-28 [69-Nov-16: 2C].
Schepler, Margaret A. m. Lamb, Robert on 66-Oct-16 [66-Oct-20: 2B].
Scherbenzueler, John d. on 70-Feb-26 of Construction cave-in [70-Feb-28: 1H].
Scherer, Henry m. Geiger, Mary on 67-Sep-5 [67-Sep-6: 2B].
Scheuler, Edna E. m. Travers, Samuel H. on 66-May-15 [66-May-16: 2C].
Scheurman, Herman (35 yrs.) d. on 66-Jul-14 [66-Jul-16: 2C].
Schi, Ferdinand J. m. Graham, Jane R. on 68-Mar-5 [68-Mar-13: 2C].
Schienkle, Peter A. m. Aro, Margaret A. on 66-Jul-15 [66-Jul-23: 2C].
Schierbaum, August, Jr. (16 yrs.) d. on 69-Sep-3 of Heart disease [69-Sep-4: 1H, 2B].
Schiermer, Elizabeth Rosetta m. Lamb, Joseph on 67-Jan-17 [67-Jan-17: 2C].
Schiller, Caroline m. Eplinger, Edward on 70-May-26 [70-May-30: 2B].
Schillinger, Amelia S. m. Schaum, Christopher J. on 69-Mar-2 [69-Mar-23: 2C].
Schillinger, Emma (14 yrs., 1 mo.) d. on 70-Feb-25 [70-Feb-26: 2C].
Schillinger, Ettie M. m. Herold, Charles F. on 69-Feb-9 [69-Feb-11: 2C].
Schillinger, Mary M. m. Prechtel, George F. on 70-Aug-25 [70-Sep-8: 2B].
Schiminger, Rudolph m. Hoffman, Amelia on 65-Dec-11 [66-Mar-1: 2B].
Schimp, Annie E. m. Buehler, Thomas H. on 66-Aug-1 [66-Aug-7: 2C].
Schimp, Edwin d. on 70-Jul-18 [70-Jul-21: 2C].
Schimp, Harry (2 yrs., 9 mos.) d. on 68-Dec-25 [68-Dec-30: 2D].
Schimp, John A. (70 yrs.) d. on 66-Jun-27 [66-Jun-28: 2C].
Schirmyer, John Henry (10 mos.) d. on 70-Mar-7 [70-Mar-9: 2C].
Schlankman, Joseph Mensey (9 mos.) d. on 70-Aug-29 [70-Aug-30: 2B].
Schlarb, Baby d. on 70-Aug-5 [70-Aug-6: 2C].
Schlarb, Philip F. m. Prinz, Matilda on 69-Sep-2 [69-Sep-6: 2C].
Schleigh, William H. m. Jenkins, Annie M. on 70-Jul-25 [70-Aug-13: 2C].
Schlens, Katie (1 yr.) d. on 66-Jun-25 [66-Jun-26: 2B].
Schley, Ann Cadwallader d. on 70-Jun-10 [70-Jun-11: 2B].
Schley, Arthur m. Mackey, Zulike D. on 68-Jul-22 [68-Jul-27: 2B].
Schley, Edward m. O'Brien, Maggie on 67-Sep-26 [67-Nov-4: 2B].
Schley, Francis Hoopes (5 yrs., 5 mos.) d. on 68-Aug-29 [68-Aug-31: 2B].
Schley, Georgeanna M. (56 yrs.) d. on 67-Apr-13 [67-Apr-16: 2B].
Schley, Louisa A. m. Lovejoy, Willard on 69-Dec-8 [69-Dec-13: 2C].

Schley, Mary M. m. Morgan, George on 69-Jun-22 [69-Jun-23: 2C].
Schley, Nettie m. Bowie, Washington on 68-Jun-23 [68-Jun-25: 2B].
Schley, Rachel m. Hopkins, Samuel on 66-Sep-23 [66-Sep-25: 2B].
Schley, William C. m. Teackle, Ellen S. on 68-Dec-17 [68-Dec-22: 2C].
Schley, William H. (49 yrs., 8 mos.) d. on 70-Mar-26 [70-Mar-28: 2B].
Schlinkman, Herman H. m. Meredith, Mary E. on 65-Nov-12 [66-Jan-15: 2B].
Schlogel, Emmanuel (16 yrs.) d. on 70-Aug-23 Drowned [70-Aug-25: 4E].
Schlosser, Catherine (59 yrs.) d. on 69-Aug-4 of Consumption [69-Aug-10: 2C].
Schlotfeld, Laura Virginia (19 yrs.) d. on 70-Feb-4 [70-Feb-7: 2C].
Schlott, Conrad (56 yrs., 8 mos.) d. on 68-Jul-17 [68-Jul-18: 2B].
Schmenner, Daniel (1 mo.) d. on 66-Apr-11 [66-Apr-12: 2B; 66-Apr-14: 2B].
Schmick, Anna Catherine m. Schwartz, Jacob on 66-Sep-20 [66-Sep-24: 2B].
Schmick, Philip m. Weymouth, Fannie on 66-Mar-1 [66-Mar-20: 2C].
Schmidt, Ann d. on 70-Jan-21 of Intemperance [70-Jan-24: 4F].
Schmidt, Anna Maria m. Peppler, Alexander George on 66-Feb-20 [66-Feb-22: 2B].
Schmidt, Catherine m. Kierchner, Edward on 69-Sep-12 [69-Sep-20: 2C].
Schmidt, George W. d. on 70-Aug-27 Drowned [70-Aug-29: 4D].
Schmidt, Henry (42 yrs.) d. on 70-Oct-29 [70-Oct-31: 2C].
Schmidt, Henry D. (3 yrs., 5 mos.) d. on 68-Apr-28 [68-Apr-29: 2B].
Schmidt, Martin d. on 69-Aug-21 Drowned [69-Aug-23: 1H].
Schmidt, Mary A. d. on 69-Mar-14 [69-Mar-16: 2C].
Schmidt, Rosa m. Veith, John on 69-Dec-30 [70-Jan-6: 2C].
Schmitt, Mary Catherine (3 yrs., 1 mo.) d. on 67-Jul-5 [67-Jul-6: 2B].
Schmitz, Eliza (37 yrs., 3 mos.) d. on 66-Apr-3 of Brain congestion [66-Apr-4: 2C; 66-Apr-5: 2B].
Schmitz, Henry (37 yrs., 5 mos.) d. on 67-Jul-31 [67-Aug-1: 2C].
Schmitz, Theodore (47 yrs.) d. on 68-Jun-7 [68-Jun-8: 2B].
Schmucker, Samuel D. m. Bridges, Helen J. on 69-Nov-16 [69-Nov-18: 2C].
Schnauder, Mary m. Soter, George F. on 70-Feb-27 [70-Mar-2: 2C].
Schnauffer, Wilhelmina (5 yrs.) d. on 69-Oct-22 [69-Oct-26: 2B].
Schnavely, Issac (73 yrs.) d. on 70-Mar-11 [70-Mar-29: 2C].
Schneider, Frederick (66 yrs.) d. on 69-May-3 [69-May-8: 2B].
Schneider, George Henry (10 mos.) d. on 68-Nov-2 [68-Nov-4: 2C].
Schneider, Louisa m. Hoffman, J. Adam on 68-Jan-2 [68-Jan-4: 2C].
Schneider, Mary m. Rechenberg, Adolph A. E. F. on 69-Feb-4 [69-Feb-6: 2C].
Schnibbe, M. Elizabeth (26 yrs., 3 mos.) d. on 66-Mar-5 [66-Mar-7: 2B].
Schnibe, George C. m. Paul, Amelia A. on 70-Jan-19 [70-Jan-22: 2B].
Schnuck, John Henry (39 yrs.) d. on 66-Jun-13 of Typhoid [66-Jun-14: 2B].
Schofield, Benjamin (58 yrs.) d. on 70-Jul-22 [70-Jul-23: 2B].
Schofield, Ellen Catherine (1 yr., 6 mos.) d. on 70-Jul-18 [70-Jul-19: 2C].
Schofield, George Washington (6 yrs.) d. on 66-Oct-7 [66-Oct-8: 2B].
Schofield, William Henry (2 mos.) d. on 66-Jul-27 [66-Jul-28: 2C].
Scholl, John L. m. Jones, Lina on 68-Dec-2 [69-Jan-11: 2C].
Scholl, Rosina (81 yrs.) d. on 70-Dec-18 [70-Dec-19: 2C].
Scholl, William R. m. Leach, Mary A. on 70-Aug-23 [70-Sep-13: 2B].
Schoolfield, L. Harrison m. Tillson, Lizzie M. on 69-Aug-30 [69-Sep-4: 2B].
Schoop, Louisa Margaret m. Haas, Conrad on 69-Aug-15 [69-Aug-21: 2B].
Schott, Charles C. (26 yrs., 4 mos.) d. on 68-Dec-8 [68-Dec-10: 2D].
Schott, Henry m. Miller, Maggie E. on 68-May-19 [68-Sep-28: 2B].
Schott, Willie (4 yrs., 5 mos.) d. on 66-Apr-8 [66-Apr-9: 2C].
Schotta, John m. Platt, Emma on 69-Feb-2 [69-Feb-8: 2C].
Schreiber, Mary m. Trager, John Christian on 70-Jul-31 [70-Aug-2: 2C].
Schreiner, Albert (5 mos.) d. on 69-Mar-28 [69-Mar-30: 2C].
Schriner, Albert m. Radecke, Louisa on 68-Jan-28 [68-Jan-31: 2C; 68-Feb-1: 2B].
Schriner, Charles Harman (1 mo.) d. on 70-Jan-8 [70-Jan-14: 2C].

Schriner, Ella Sophia (1 mo.) d. on 70-Jan-11 [70-Jan-14: 2C].
Schriner, Mary Catherine (19 yrs., 2 mos.) d. on 66-Feb-22 [66-Feb-23: 2C].
Schritz, Annie G. m. Brannan, Thomas J. on 70-Aug-4 [70-Sep-9: 2B].
Schroeder, Amelia (10 yrs.) d. on 69-Nov-12 in Railroad accident [69-Nov-13: 1G].
Schroeder, Henry (83 yrs.) d. on 70-Jan-10 [70-Jan-17: 2D].
Schroeder, Joseph Frederick (4 mos.) d. on 70-Jul-26 [70-Jul-27: 2C].
Schroeder, Mollie A. m. Norwood, Thomas S. on 70-May-30 [70-May-31: 2B].
Schubert, Emily m. Walter, J. E. on 69-May-24 [69-May-26: 2C; 69-May-27: 2C].
Schuchts, Harry B. (1 yr., 3 mos.) d. on 68-Dec-30 [69-Jan-1: 2C].
Schuchts, James H. m. Wilson, Urith on 69-Mar-31 [69-Apr-3: 2B].
Schucking, Constantin m. Sutro, Elise on 66-May-8 [66-May-9: 2B].
Schuckle, Charles F. (39 yrs.) d. [70-Nov-3: 2C].
Schuckle, William (18 yrs., 6 mos.) d. on 70-Sep-5 [70-Sep-6: 2B].
Schueler, John m. Rost, Mary B. on 67-Oct-20 [67-Oct-23: 2B].
Schuelor, J. Nannie C. m. Flannegan, Andrew McE. on 66-Apr-5 [66-Apr-19: 2B; 66-Apr-20: 2B].
Schul, Louisa Malvina (2 yrs., 10 mos.) d. on 69-Jan-1 [69-Jan-4: 2C].
Schul, Malvina (1 yr.) d. on 69-Jan-1 [69-Jan-4: 2C].
Schulenberg, Henry m. Spangler, Williamanna on 67-Sep-10 [67-Sep-17: 2B].
Schuler, Frederick A. (42 yrs.) d. on 66-Apr-16 [66-Apr-18: 2C].
Schull, John Albert (13 yrs.) d. on 69-Sep-12 [69-Sep-13: 2B].
Schulter, John M. m. Brandon, Amelia on 70-Dec-8 [70-Dec-14: 2C].
Schultheis, George E. m. Radecke, Margarata S. on 66-Jan-24 [66-Jan-26: 2B].
Schultheis, Mary m. Kuhleman, Charles F., Jr. on 70-Jun-22 [70-Jun-25: 2B].
Schulthus, Frederick d. on 70-Jul-27 of Heatstroke [70-Jul-28: 4E].
Schultz, Albert d. on 67-Aug-6 [67-Aug-8: 2B].
Schultz, Charles d. on 68-Aug-9 Drowned [68-Aug-10: 1G].
Schultz, Elizabeth d. on 66-Oct-5 [66-Oct-6: 1F].
Schultz, Frederick m. Halpine, Winnie A. on 67-Jan-30 [67-Feb-2: 2C].
Schultz, Frederick W. m. Parker, Cecilia V. on 68-Nov-11 [68-Nov-13: 2C].
Schultz, Harry R. m. Rosenswig, Emmie L. on 68-Nov-24 [68-Dec-3: 2C].
Schultz, Samuel m. Heindel, Harriet on 67-Dec-26 [67-Dec-28: 2C].
Schultz, William A. m. Grove, Ella N. on 68-Jan-9 [68-Jan-10: 2C].
Schultz, William A. m. Tweedall, Martha A. on 70-Sep-11 [70-Sep-20: 2B].
Schultze, Charles d. [70-Jul-23: 2B].
Schultze, J. L. d. [69-Mar-22: 2C].
Schultze, Lena m. Brown, Benjamin B. on 70-Jan-1 [70-Jan-6: 2C].
Schulz, Ida m. Dohme, Charles E. on 66-Apr-5 [66-Apr-6: 2B].
Schulze, John L. (24 yrs.) d. on 69-Jan-19 Drowned [69-Jan-20: 4F; 69-Jan-21: 2C].
Schulze, John W. J. G. L. (6 mos.) d. on 68-Sep-11 [68-Sep-12: 2B].
Schumacher, C. H. (63 yrs.) d. on 67-Nov-12 [67-Nov-15: 2B].
Schumacher, H. A. m. Warwick, Mary on 66-Dec-25 [66-Dec-28: 2C].
Schumacher, James R. m. Dobler, Maria J. on 66-Feb-13 [66-Feb-28: 2C].
Schuman, Burwell E. m. Whiting, William H. on 68-Nov-5 [68-Nov-9: 2B].
Schunck, Charles Henry (5 yrs., 8 mos.) d. on 66-Nov-8 [66-Nov-14: 2B].
Schunck, Jacob Henry (11 mos.) d. on 69-Jan-13 [69-Jan-14: 2D].
Schunstrong, James (45 yrs.) d. on 67-Jun-16 [67-Jun-17: 2B].
Schusler, John m. Jones, Louise A. on 68-Nov-26 [68-Dec-18: 2C].
Schutz, Elizabeth V. (83 yrs.) d. on 70-Jun-21 [70-Jun-22: 2C].
Schutz, Lawrence m. Turnbull, Annie E. on 67-Jun-9 [67-Jun-12: 2B].
Schutz, Louisa (32 yrs.) d. on 67-Jun-11 [67-Jun-14: 2B].
Schutze, John C. (86 yrs.) d. on 69-Oct-30 [69-Nov-2: 2B; 69-Nov-3: 2C].
Schutze, Sophia Hannah (10 yrs.) d. on 70-Jun-24 [70-Jun-28: 2C].
Schwab, Clara (10 yrs.) d. on 69-Jul-6 [69-Jul-7: 2C].
Schwab, Hannah (20 yrs.) d. on 67-Feb-25 [67-Feb-26: 2C].

Schwartz, Augusta E. m. Ohrenschall, F. A. on 70-Feb-22 [70-Mar-1: 2C].
Schwartz, Harry Andrew (1 yr., 1 mo.) d. on 70-Sep-23 [70-Sep-26: 2B].
Schwartz, Jacob m. Schmick, Anna Catherine on 66-Sep-20 [66-Sep-24: 2B].
Schwartz, Josephine C. m. Hoch, John G. on 66-Sep-9 [66-Sep-27: 2C].
Schwartz, M. Josephine m. Pfisterer, William on 70-Apr-17 [70-Apr-19: 2B].
Schwartz, Philip Henry (1 yr., 8 mos.) d. on 69-Mar-1 of Chronic croup [69-Mar-3: 2C].
Schwartz, Sophia L. m. Ditty, C. Irving on 68-Oct-1 [68-Oct-5: 2B].
Schwartz, William Andrew (5 mos.) d. on 68-Mar-28 [68-Mar-30: 2B].
Schwartz, William H. m. Bandel, Julia C. on 66-Dec-10 [66-Dec-12: 2B].
Schwartze, Ellen W. (7 mos.) d. [69-Jun-30: 2C].
Schwartzhaupt, Elizabeth Louis (2 yrs., 2 mos.) d. on 66-Sep-4 [66-Sep-5: 2B].
Schwartzhaupt, Margarett (60 yrs.) d. on 69-Mar-13 [69-Mar-15: 2C].
Schwarz, John, Sr. (51 yrs.) d. on 68-Jun-30 [68-Jul-2: 2C].
Schwarz, John V. m. Wieghorst, Elizabeth on 66-Jul-10 [66-Jul-13: 2C].
Schwarzenberg, Edward (45 yrs.) d. on 66-Jul-21 [66-Jul-24: 2C].
Schwatka, Sophia m. Joice, Thomas on 70-Jun-23 [70-Jun-24: 2C].
Schwatka, William F. m. Maize, Carrie M. on 69-Oct-5 [69-Oct-6: 2B].
Schweikert, Mary (41 yrs.) d. on 69-Sep-23 of Consumption [69-Sep-24: 2B].
Schweitzer, Joseph (76 yrs.) d. on 68-May-13 [68-May-14: 2B].
Schwer, Catherine m. Potee, William F. on 66-Mar-19 [66-Mar-21: 2C].
Schwind, Philip d. on 67-Mar-28 [67-Mar-30: 2B].
Schwing, Mary m. Gieske, Louis on 67-Oct-3 [67-Oct-4: 2B].
Schwinn, George m. Heinzman, Kate on 66-Oct-28 [66-Nov-3: 2B].
Sclote, Augustus m. Lecates, Hester P. on 69-Dec-29 [70-Jan-14: 2C].
Scofield, James m. Chapman, May on 69-Mar-22 [69-Mar-24: 2C].
Scoggins, Robert Columbus (1 yr., 1 mo.) d. on 70-Jul-5 [70-Jul-7: 2B].
Scott, Abram V. m. Ryland, Josephine on 67-Nov-26 [67-Nov-30: 2C].
Scott, Amy E. m. Wallis, J. William on 70-Nov-30 [70-Dec-2: 2C].
Scott, Bertha (8 yrs., 10 mos.) d. on 69-May-24 [69-May-25: 2C].
Scott, Charles (19 yrs., 8 mos.) d. on 66-Dec-21 [66-Dec-22: 2B].
Scott, Charles A. m. Deal, Mary A. on 67-Mar-4 [67-Mar-14: 2C].
Scott, Charles M. (31 yrs.) d. on 68-Jul-8 [68-Jul-9: 2B].
Scott, Charles Willis (30 yrs.) d. on 69-Dec-22 [69-Dec-23: 2B].
Scott, David J. m. Bride, Maude E. on 68-Apr-22 [68-Apr-25: 2B].
Scott, Elizabeth (58 yrs.) d. on 66-Oct-14 [66-Oct-16: 2C].
Scott, Elizabeth (34 yrs.) d. on 70-Jan-13 [70-Feb-3: 2B].
Scott, Ella d. on 66-Aug-9 [66-Aug-11: 2B].
Scott, Ella F. d. on 69-Oct-7 of Pneumonia [69-Oct-8: 2B].
Scott, Emily A. T. m. Kuszmaul, John on 66-Jan-1 [66-Jan-19: 2C].
Scott, Ettie m. Hiteshue, W. Albert on 68-Jan-2 [68-Jan-7: 2B].
Scott, Eva Kate (5 mos.) d. on 69-Dec-19 [69-Dec-20: 2C].
Scott, Evan (71 yrs.) d. on 66-Aug-8 [66-Aug-25: 2A].
Scott, George Oliver (14 yrs.) d. on 67-May-23 [67-May-24: 2B].
Scott, George S. m. Bryan, Harriet on 70-Jan-6 [70-Jan-8: 2B].
Scott, H. Levering (12 yrs.) d. on 70-Sep-2 of Typhoid [70-Sep-6: 2B].
Scott, Henry C. m. Grimes, Sarah E. on 69-Jun-20 [69-Jun-26: 2B].
Scott, Isaiah M. m. Jenkins, Annie S. on 70-Dec-7 [70-Dec-14: 2C].
Scott, James d. on 67-Mar-5 in Railroad accident [67-Mar-7: 1F].
Scott, James (69 yrs.) d. on 69-Feb-5 [69-Feb-6: 2C].
Scott, James J. (35 yrs.) d. on 69-Sep-28 [69-Sep-29: 2B].
Scott, James Jewett (11 mos.) d. on 66-Aug-20 [66-Aug-21: 2C].
Scott, James W. (71 yrs.) d. on 69-Feb-1 [69-Feb-2: 2C].
Scott, John C. m. Wylie, Mary Frances on 68-May-28 [68-Aug-17: 2B].
Scott, John E. m. Brunt, Bella on 66-May-23 [66-Jun-8: 2B].
Scott, John O. m. Stigers, Anna A. E. on 69-Feb-25 [69-Mar-1: 2C].

Scott, John T. (36 yrs.) d. on 66-Dec-1 [66-Dec-3: 2B].
Scott, John T. m. Hart, Frank on 68-Jan-1 [68-Jan-11: 2B].
Scott, John T. m. Jenkins, Eliza O. on 70-Dec-21 [70-Dec-23: 2B].
Scott, Joseph d. on 68-Jan-23 of Intemperance [68-Jan-24: 1G].
Scott, Joseph m. Jackson, Jane on 69-Oct-19 [69-Oct-26: 2B].
Scott, Juliet R. (60 yrs.) d. on 66-Mar-20 [66-Mar-24: 2B].
Scott, Leander James (1 yr., 1 mo.) d. on 70-Feb-8 [70-Feb-9: 2C].
Scott, Lewis m. Heffner, Anna M. C. on 69-Dec-5 [69-Dec-10: 2C].
Scott, Maggie E. (4 mos.) d. on 68-Oct-2 [68-Oct-3: 2B].
Scott, Margaret (92 yrs.) d. on 66-Aug-22 [66-Sep-20: 2B].
Scott, Mary (81 yrs.) d. on 67-Jan-14 [67-Jan-16: 2C].
Scott, Mary (75 yrs.) d. on 69-Feb-5 [69-Feb-6: 2C].
Scott, Mary (88 yrs.) d. on 70-Oct-17 [70-Oct-18: 2C].
Scott, Mary A. (43 yrs.) d. on 69-Mar-5 [69-Mar-6: 2C].
Scott, Mary Ann (67 yrs.) d. on 69-May-18 [69-May-19: 2C].
Scott, Mary E. (45 yrs.) d. on 68-Nov-17 [68-Nov-25: 2B].
Scott, Mary M. m. Coe, Alexander Benson on 66-Apr-24 [66-May-16: 2C].
Scott, Mittian T. m. Bell, Fannie S. on 67-Dec-19 [67-Dec-24: 2B].
Scott, Oscar W. (11 yrs., 1 mo.) d. on 68-Oct-3 [68-Oct-5: 2C].
Scott, Robert Lewis (4 mos.) d. on 68-Feb-10 [68-Feb-14: 2C].
Scott, Rose m. Bean, Benjamin on 70-Dec-6 [70-Dec-10: 2B].
Scott, Sue m. Winchester, A. P. on 67-Nov-6 [67-Nov-9: 2B].
Scott, Walter Leon (2 yrs., 1 mo.) d. on 70-Apr-3 [70-Apr-4: 2C].
Scott, William (84 yrs.) d. on 67-Jul-24 [67-Jul-25: 2C].
Scott, William D. (53 yrs.) d. on 69-Dec-21 [69-Dec-22: 2B; 69-Dec-23: 2B].
Scott, William G. m. Christopher, Mary R. on 69-Nov-23 [69-Nov-26: 2B].
Scotti, Laura J. m. Thomas, James E. on 68-Mar-17 [68-Mar-21: 2A].
Scotti, William Wesley (2 yrs.) d. on 66-Jun-19 [66-Jun-20: 2C].
Screven, Mary (5 yrs.) d. on 69-Mar-9 [69-Mar-10: 2C].
Screven, Thomas F. m. Buchanan, Sallie Lloyd on 66-Oct-30 [66-Nov-7: 2C].
Scrimger, Clarence D. (15 yrs.) d. on 69-May-30 [69-Jun-1: 2B].
Scrivener, Kate (31 yrs.) d. on 70-Jan-18 [70-Jan-22: 2C; 70-Feb-21: 2C].
Scrivner, James m. Johnston, Mary M. on 69-May-11 [69-May-18: 2C].
Scully, Charles Richard (3 yrs., 8 mos.) d. on 70-Nov-1 [70-Nov-2: 2C].
Seabert, Mary m. McLean, William H. on 69-Oct-3 [69-Oct-5: 2B].
Seabrook, Mary Virginia m. Griest, Joseph D. on 66-Jul-12 [66-Jul-24: 2C].
Seager, Henry (23 yrs., 2 mos.) d. on 70-Dec-8 [70-Dec-9: 2C].
Seager, Jesse Colien d. on 67-Jul-14 [67-Aug-5: 2B].
Seager, Lillian Gertrude (1 yr., 4 mos.) d. on 70-Mar-20 [70-Mar-22: 2C].
Seager, Thomas, Jr. m. Ruff, Mary C. on 66-May-2 [66-May-4: 2C].
Seamont, Caroline m. Clazey, George W. on 69-Nov-28 [69-Nov-30: 2C].
Search, Magdalene (54 yrs.) d. on 67-Aug-11 [67-Oct-7: 2B].
Search, Margaret d. on 66-Nov-4 [66-Nov-5: 2B; 66-Nov-6: 2B].
Search, Newton C. m. Hamilton, Mary A. on 68-Nov-17 [68-Nov-24: 2C].
Searley, Ellen M. (26 yrs.) d. on 68-Jun-8 of Typhoid [68-Jun-9: 2B; 68-Jun-10: 2B].
Searley, Mollie E. (11 yrs., 3 mos.) d. on 69-Apr-8 [69-Apr-10: 2B].
Sears, Dewitt C. m. Rogers, Susan on 68-Oct-11 [68-Oct-21: 2C].
Sears, George W. (37 yrs.) d. on 68-May-24 [68-May-27: 2B].
Sears, James m. Hall, Sarah E. on 70-Apr-26 [70-May-3: 2B].
Sears, John K. m. Lambdin, Mary E. on 70-Apr-28 [70-Apr-30: 2A].
Sears, Julia Ann (60 yrs.) d. on 67-Aug-8 [67-Aug-13: 2B].
Sears, Melvina (26 yrs.) d. on 66-Dec-27 of Suicide (Stabbing) [66-Dec-28: 1F; 66-Dec-29: 2C].
Sears, Samuel Thomas (6 yrs., 6 mos.) d. on 70-May-12 [70-May-14: 2B].
Sears, Sarah E. m. Trazzare, Thomas E. on 66-Sep-11 [66-Sep-18: 2B].
Seaver, Catherine (30 yrs.) d. on 66-Jul-17 of Heatstroke [66-Jul-19: 1F].

Seaver, Martha d. on 68-Sep-17 [68-Sep-18: 2B].
Seay, Thomas H. (28 yrs.) d. on 69-Jun-7 [69-Jun-8: 2B].
Sebastian, Augusta m. Herkenhine, George Henry on 68-Jul-2 [68-Aug-3: 2B].
Seche, Joseph (88 yrs.) d. on 70-Jul-24 [70-Jul-28: 2C].
Seche, Mary E. (81 yrs.) d. on 70-Jul-22 [70-Jul-28: 2C].
Sederberg, Charles A. m. Eaton, Mary S. on 70-May-17 [70-May-21: 2B].
Sedwick, W. A. m. Somervell, Emma on 66-Nov-15 [66-Nov-17: 2B].
Seebold, George W. m. Cook, Helen R. on 68-Jul-27 [68-Aug-18: 2B].
Seed, Easter (85 yrs.) d. on 68-Sep-16 [68-Sep-17: 2B; 68-Sep-18: 2B].
Seemuller, Augustus, Jr. m. Crane, Anne Moncure on 69-Sep-23 [69-Sep-24: 2B].
Seemuller, Henrietta d. on 69-Mar-10 [69-Mar-12: 2C; 69-Mar-13: 2C].
Seemuller, William m. Howell, Mary B. on 67-Nov-14 [67-Nov-18: 2B].
Seesnop, Catherine (78 yrs.) d. on 68-Mar-24 [68-Mar-26: 2B].
Segerman, Bessie (1 yr., 5 mos.) d. on 68-Aug-22 [68-Aug-24: 2B].
Segerman, Henry H. m. Stall, Jennie on 70-Oct-20 [70-Oct-24: 2B].
Segerman, Mary Eliza (1 yr., 10 mos.) d. on 67-Feb-4 [67-Feb-6: 2C].
Segerman, Thomas m. Miller, Mary L. on 66-Jan-4 [66-Jan-6: 2C].
Sego, Rebecca E. m. Porter, David on 66-Mar-13 [66-May-18: 2C].
Seibel, Lizzie m. Bopp, George on 66-Jul-3 [66-Jul-12: 2C].
Seibert, Annie L. (1 yr., 9 mos.) d. on 70-Apr-30 [70-May-2: 2B; 70-May-3: 2B].
Seibert, Frederick d. on 67-Aug-20 Murdered (Assault) [67-Aug-21: 1F].
Seibert, Henry (46 yrs.) d. on 67-Aug-4 Drowned [67-Aug-5: 1G].
Seibert, Maggie Bell (1 yr., 9 mos.) d. on 66-Jun-10 [66-Jun-12: 2B].
Seibert, Malvina A. E. m. Bartlett, George H. on 66-Mar-20 [66-Mar-22: 2B].
Seibold, Emma Rosina (1 yr., 5 mos.) d. on 70-Jul-28 [70-Jul-29: 2C].
Seidenstricker, Edward C. (7 yrs.) d. on 67-Mar-19 [67-Mar-20: 2C].
Seidenstricker, May (6 mos.) d. on 67-Jun-29 [67-Jul-2: 2B].
Seim, Henry (15 yrs.) d. on 67-Mar-3 of Suicide (Poisoning) [67-Mar-4: 4F].
Seim, Henry, Jr. m. Wright, Annie E. on 66-Oct-22 [66-Oct-25: 2C].
Seip, Maggie Amanda (2 yrs., 5 mos.) d. on 66-Aug-23 [66-Aug-27: 2B].
Seip, Mary Rose (8 mos.) d. on 66-Jun-26 [66-Jun-29: 2C].
Seipp, Henry F. m. Tarlton, Mary Louise on 68-Dec-29 [69-Jan-11: 2C].
Seipp, Louis (58 yrs.) d. on 69-Apr-24 of Suicide (Drowning) [69-Apr-26: 1G].
Seipp, Mary E. (30 yrs.) d. on 69-Jan-16 [69-Jan-18: 2D].
Seis, Elizabeth J. (21 yrs.) d. on 68-Feb-3 [68-Feb-4: 2D].
Seitz, Adam (84 yrs.) d. on 70-Nov-11 [70-Nov-18: 2C].
Seitz, Charles (56 yrs.) d. on 70-Oct-9 [70-Oct-10: 2B].
Seitz, Henry m. Smith, E. Mary on 66-Jun-28 [66-Jun-30: 2B].
Selby, Blanche Marie (6 mos.) d. on 70-Aug-9 [70-Aug-11: 2C].
Selby, C. W. m. Selby, Sophia E. on 70-Jun-30 [70-Jul-9: 2B].
Selby, Emily W. m. Jean, George B. on 67-Dec-26 [67-Dec-28: 2C].
Selby, Joseph m. White, E. Blanche on 68-Feb-19 [68-Feb-21: 2B].
Selby, Maggie E. m. George, John T. on 67-Oct-9 [67-Oct-11: 2B].
Selby, Maud d. on 66-Oct-27 [66-Oct-29: 2C].
Selby, Nicholas Richard (35 yrs.) d. on 70-Sep-20 [70-Sep-21: 2B; 70-Sep-22: 2C, 4B].
Selby, Richard M. (58 yrs.) d. on 67-May-8 [67-May-10: 2B].
Selby, Sophia E. m. Selby, C. W. on 70-Jun-30 [70-Jul-9: 2B].
Selby, Susannah (81 yrs., 2 mos.) d. on 68-Apr-17 [68-Apr-18: 2A].
Selby, Susannah (68 yrs.) d. on 69-Nov-6 [69-Nov-12: 2C].
Selby, Thomas Sellman (25 yrs.) d. on 68-Mar-2 [68-Mar-4: 2C].
Selden, Fannie S. m. Groverman, Richard H. on 69-Jan-27 [69-Feb-11: 2C].
Selden, Mary m. Kennedy, S. D. on 69-Jun-22 [69-Jun-24: 2C].
Seliger, Edel (63 yrs.) d. on 68-Jul-7 [68-Jul-8: 2B; 68-Jul-9: 2B].
Seliger, Hannah m. Heilner, Meier on 66-Mar-25 [66-Mar-27: 2B].
Seliger, Lina m. Greenbaum, Emmanuel on 68-Oct-18 [68-Oct-24: 2B].

Seliger, Rachel m. Behrends, Leopold on 68-Mar-1 [68-Mar-12: 2B].
Seling, A. Catharine m. Shaffer, Joseph R. on 68-Dec-20 [68-Dec-25: 2D].
Selke, David L. m. Campbell, Annie C. on 66-Apr-13 [66-Apr-17: 2C].
Sellars, William m. Coates, Mary Jane on 66-Nov-13 [66-Nov-16: 2C].
Sellens, John m. Lewis, Mary E. T. on 66-May-6 [66-Jul-9: 2C].
Sellers, Jacob C. m. Hopkins, Laura B. on 69-Feb-18 [69-Feb-22: 2C].
Sellers, Mary Catherine (81 yrs.) d. on 68-Feb-24 [68-Feb-25: 2C; 68-Feb-26: 2C].
Sellick, James (26 yrs.) d. on 67-Nov-18 in Railroad accident [67-Nov-19: 1G].
Sellinger, Julius (40 yrs.) d. on 70-Jun-29 of Suicide (Poisoning) [70-Jun-30: 1F].
Sellman, Alonzo m. Neel, Bell on 70-Jul-13 [70-Jul-14: 2B].
Sellman, Benjamin F. m. Norris, Susie R. on 68-Jun-16 [68-Jun-23: 2B].
Sellman, Ella Mary (3 mos.) d. on 69-Jul-4 [69-Jul-20: 2C].
Sellman, John F. d. on 66-Jun-17 of Paralysis [66-Jun-19: 2B; 66-Jun-20: 2C].
Sellman, John S. (64 yrs.) d. on 69-Jan-27 [69-Feb-6: 2C].
Sellman, Sallie S. (59 yrs.) d. on 70-May-25 [70-May-28: 2B].
Seltzer, Mary Ann (56 yrs.) d. on 69-Mar-9 [69-Mar-11: 2C; 69-Mar-12: 2C].
Selvage, Mary E. m. Hays, Edward P. on 66-Nov-5 [66-Nov-12: 2C].
Selway, Robert (66 yrs.) d. on 69-Oct-22 [69-Oct-23: 2B].
Semmes, Robert Doyne (36 yrs.) d. on 70-Dec-17 [70-Dec-19: 2C].
Semone, Conrad H. (62 yrs.) d. on 68-Jul-1 [68-Jul-4: 2C].
Semper, George d. on 68-Sep-11 in Railroad accident [68-Sep-12: 1G].
Senate, Patrick m. Carroll, Bridget on 67-Feb-26 [67-Feb-28: 2C].
Senderling, Anna May d. on 67-Dec-24 of Pleuritic pneumonia [67-Dec-25: 2C].
Seneca, Robert m. Lawder, Carrie A. on 67-Dec-26 [68-Jan-1: 2C].
Seney, Sophia d. on 66-Apr-11 [66-Apr-12: 2B].
Senft, Wilhelmina m. Berger, John on 68-Jun-17 [68-Jun-20: 2B].
Senner, Lillie May (4 yrs.) d. on 69-Mar-26 [69-Mar-27: 2B].
Senseney, Catherine d. on 68-Feb-27 [68-Feb-29: 2B].
Sensner, George W. m. Frazier, Isabella B. on 68-Mar-26 [68-Apr-3: 2C].
Sent, Mary (71 yrs.) d. [69-Jan-2: 2C].
Sermon, Laura V. m. Neal, Henry C. on 67-Oct-31 [67-Nov-8: 2C].
Sermons, Robert (38 yrs.) d. on 70-Jan-5 [70-Jan-7: 2F; 70-Jan-8: 1H].
Serpell, G. M. m. Clark, Georgie on 69-Sep-14 [69-Sep-15: 2B].
Servenais, Emily m. McBride, Harry on 67-Sep-9 [67-Sep-10: 2B].
Server, Elizabeth (45 yrs.) d. on 66-Feb-14 [66-Feb-16: 2B].
Server, Laura V. m. Staley, Cornelius on 68-Apr-28 [68-Apr-30: 2B].
Server, Marietta m. Jelks, Cincinatus on 66-Dec-20 [66-Dec-23: 2B].
Sessions, Ida Virginia (2 yrs., 6 mos.) d. on 68-Jun-27 [68-Jun-29: 2B].
Sessions, Joseph A. D. m. Voyce, Ellenora on 69-Dec-21 [69-Dec-29: 2D].
Sessions, W. P. D. m. White, M. E. on 68-Jan-1 [68-Jan-6: 2C].
Seth, Elizabeth T. (72 yrs.) d. on 67-Oct-16 [67-Oct-24: 2B].
Seth, James m. Orem, Sydney M. on 70-Mar-29 [70-Apr-11: 2B; 70-Apr-12: 2B].
Seth, Margaret A. m. Kearns, Henry on 66-Jun-25 [66-Aug-2: 2C].
Seufert, Charles (45 yrs.) d. on 70-Dec-11 [70-Dec-12: 2C].
Seveir, Susanna (81 yrs.) d. on 67-Apr-13 [67-Apr-15: 2B].
Severin, Maggie A. m. Quaty, Christopher on 69-Oct-19 [69-Oct-23: 2C].
Sevier, George Calvin (1 yr., 7 mos.) d. on 66-Aug-3 [66-Aug-4: 2C].
Sewall, Thomas, Rev. (50 yrs.) d. on 70-Aug-11 [70-Aug-12: 2C, 4C; 70-Aug-15: 4D].
Seward, George Albert (5 mos.) d. on 70-Feb-27 [70-Mar-1: 2C].
Seward, James, Sr. (43 yrs.) d. on 68-Jul-16 [68-Jul-17: 2C].
Seward, Louisa (45 yrs.) d. on 70-Feb-2 [70-Feb-4: 2C].
Seward, Margaret A. m. Higgins, William T. on 66-Aug-5 [66-Aug-18: 2B].
Seward, Mary L. m. Rose, S. Francis on 69-Apr-1 [69-May-4: 2B].
Sewell, Amelia A. (36 yrs.) d. on 67-Mar-27 [67-Mar-28: 2B].
Sewell, Ella m. Slingluff, Fielder C. on 66-Oct-3 [66-Oct-6: 2A].

Sewell, Emma Isabella (5 mos.) d. on 70-Jun-22 of Cholera infantum [70-Jun-23: 2C].
Sewell, Fielder Bowie (1 yr., 11 mos.) d. on 68-Jan-29 [68-Feb-7: 2C].
Sewell, James, Rev. (76 yrs.) d. on 66-Nov-27 [66-Nov-29: 1G; 66-Dec-1: 1F].
Sewell, James B. T. (27 yrs.) d. on 67-Apr-4 of Consumption [67-Apr-6: 2B].
Sewell, James M. d. on 69-Aug-5 Drowned [69-Aug-6: 1G; 69-Aug-9: 1G; 69-Aug-10: 1G].
Sewell, John (6 yrs.) d. on 67-Aug-30 [67-Aug-31: 2B].
Sewell, John T. m. Wellener, Mary J. on 69-Apr-8 [69-Apr-21: 2B].
Sewell, Juliet G. m. Baldwin, Summerfield on 70-Jun-1 [70-Jun-2: 2B].
Sewell, Lewis (30 yrs.) d. on 67-Aug-22 in Railroad accident [67-Aug-24: 1G].
Sewell, Libbie V. m. Holan, Lewis on 65-Dec-25 [66-Jan-2: 2C].
Sewell, Martha E. m. Martin, D. W. on 69-Dec-27 [69-Feb-2: 2C].
Sewell, Mary Alice (7 mos.) d. on 68-Jul-16 [68-Jul-20: 2B].
Sewell, Ruth Anna, Miss m. Quynn, J. H. S. on 66-Feb-22 [66-Feb-27: 2B].
Sewell, Sallie A. (4 yrs., 10 mos.) d. on 66-Aug-6 [66-Aug-8: 2C].
Sewell, Septimus d. on 69-Aug-5 Drowned [69-Aug-6: 1G; 69-Aug-9: 1G; 69-Aug-10: 1G].
Sewell, Thomas S. (64 yrs.) d. on 67-Sep-8 [67-Sep-18: 2B].
Sexton, Thomas m. Rafferty, Annie on 67-Feb-21 [67-Feb-25: 2C].
Sexton, William James (14 yrs.) d. on 70-Nov-18 in Wagon accident [70-Nov-19: 2B, 4D].
Seymore, John (18 yrs.) d. on 67-Nov-30 of Consumption [67-Dec-2: 2C].
Seymore, John (50 yrs.) d. on 67-May-5 [67-May-6: 1F; 67-May-7: 1G].
Seymour, Charlotte (41 yrs.) d. on 67-Mar-12 [67-Mar-13: 2C].
Seymour, Daniel (40 yrs.) d. on 69-Jul-28 in Elevator accident [69-Jul-29: 4D].
Seymour, Dora m. Zepp, Charles on 69-Aug-15 [69-Aug-20: 2C].
Seymour, Joseph L. m. Pilson, Mary J. on 68-Apr-28 [68-Apr-29: 2B].
Seymour, Julia Lindred (4 yrs., 3 mos.) d. on 70-Aug-22 [70-Aug-23: 2B].
Seymour, Lizzie F. m. De Valin, John H. on 68-May-19 [68-Jun-2: 2B].
Seymour, Nora V. m. Willen, Samuel J. on 66-Nov-5 [66-Nov-6: 2B].
Seymour, William A. m. Barton, Mollie P. on 70-Feb-17 [70-Feb-19: 2B].
Seymour, William Andrew J. (6 mos.) d. on 67-Jun-25 [67-Jun-26: 2C].
Shaab, Mary A. m. Bunn, Peter on 68-May-19 [68-Jun-4: 2B].
Shaab, Mary Lizzie m. Muth, George L. on 69-May-18 [69-May-22: 2B].
Shackelford, Elizabeth H. m. Lester, Charles H. on 69-May-12 [69-May-17: 2B].
Shackelford, Frances T. d. on 69-Sep-26 of Typhoid pneumonia [69-Oct-8: 2B].
Shackelford, Mary (82 yrs.) d. on 70-Jun-20 [70-Jun-21: 2C; 70-Jun-22: 2C].
Shackelford, Mollie E. m. Dews, Zack, Jr. on 70-Dec-22 [70-Dec-28: 2D].
Shackelford, Shirley m. Davis, W. R. on 69-Dec-15 [69-Dec-17: 2C].
Shaddoc, Jennie m. Martin, W. D. on 67-Jan-31 [67-Feb-16: 2D].
Shade, John d. on 68-Sep-2 [68-Sep-30: 1C].
Shadrick, Joshua A. (26 yrs., 3 mos.) d. on 68-Nov-23 [68-Nov-25: 2B; 68-Nov-26: 2B].
Shaeffer, Ada E. (9 yrs., 6 mos.) d. on 69-Feb-24 [69-Feb-25: 2D].
Shaeffer, Charles (65 yrs.) d. on 67-Aug-21 Drowned [67-Aug-23: 1F, 2B].
Shafer, George W. m. Waltjen, Mary D. on 66-Aug-29 [66-Sep-5: 2B].
Shaffer, Caroline Christopher (1 yr., 1 mo.) d. on 67-Mar-9 of Scarlet fever [67-Mar-12: 2C].
Shaffer, Charles Henry (3 yrs., 6 mos.) d. on 67-Feb-28 [67-Mar-1: 2C].
Shaffer, Ellen A. m. Moon, Thomas O. on 68-Jun-8 [68-Jun-17: 2B].
Shaffer, George William (2 yrs., 1 mo.) d. on 69-Dec-9 [69-Dec-10: 2C].
Shaffer, Ira W. m. Duvall, Mary E. on 66-Jun-10 [66-Jun-26: 2B].
Shaffer, James (2 mos.) d. on 69-Jul-15 [69-Jul-16: 2C].
Shaffer, Joseph R. m. Seling, A. Catharine on 68-Dec-20 [68-Dec-25: 2D].
Shaffer, Lizzie A. m. Mitchell, John R. on 68-Nov-26 [68-Dec-4: 2B].
Shaffer, Mary Ann (60 yrs.) d. on 67-Jan-20 [67-Jan-22: 2C].
Shaffer, Mary C. (68 yrs., 3 mos.) d. on 67-Oct-16 [67-Oct-18: 2C].
Shaffer, Mary E. m. Rundle, John S. on 66-Jul-12 [66-Jul-25: 2C].
Shaffer, Sarah Jane m. Dory, Benjamin on 66-Sep-17 [66-Oct-2: 2B].
Shaffner, Samuel (63 yrs.) d. on 68-Aug-17 [68-Aug-18: 2B].

Shakespear, Virginia S. (1 yr., 7 mos.) d. on 66-Jun-8 [66-Jul-11: 2C].
Shakman, Annie m. Heller, M. H. on 70-Sep-28 [70-Oct-20: 2B].
Shalley, Mary m. Brown, James on 70-May-19 [70-May-25: 2C].
Shallus, Samuel William (4 mos.) d. on 69-May-6 [69-May-8: 2B].
Sham, Lizzie m. Graham, John W. on 70-Jul-12 [70-Jul-30: 2B].
Shamburg, William D. (58 yrs.) d. on 69-Jun-1 [69-Jun-2: 2B].
Shamer, James Theodore (11 mos.) d. on 68-Aug-19 [68-Aug-20: 2B].
Shamer, William m. Craig, Fannie on 66-Dec-30 [67-Jan-2: 2C].
Shamey, John (35 yrs.) d. on 67-Aug-20 Drowned [67-Sep-16: 2B].
Shamhan, Martin (47 yrs.) d. on 67-Jun-30 [67-Jul-1: 2B].
Shamleffer, John m. Short, Maggie Annie on 67-Feb-11 [67-Feb-13: 2D; 67-Feb-14: 2C].
Shanahan, Maggie B. (23 yrs.) d. on 67-Sep-30 [67-Oct-30: 2B].
Shanahan, Margaret (3 mos.) d. [69-Jul-14: 2D].
Shanaman, John (42 yrs.) d. on 66-Nov-10 of Fall from roof [66-Nov-12: 1F, 2C; 66-Dec-6: 2B].
Shane, Harry C. m. Horn, Susie C. on 67-May-7 [67-May-10: 2B].
Shane, Helen Rosenia (2 yrs., 5 mos.) d. [68-Mar-17: 2C].
Shane, Lizzie R. m. Maull, Edward A. on 70-May-17 [70-May-18: 2B].
Shane, Matilda m. Kramer, Samuel on 70-Feb-21 [70-Feb-22: 2C].
Shane, Virginia Roxanna (23 yrs.) d. on 69-Jan-14 [69-Jan-16: 2C].
Shaney, Margaret (49 yrs.) d. on 67-Feb-21 [67-Feb-23: 2C].
Shanks, Mary (62 yrs.) d. on 69-Nov-9 [69-Nov-10: 2C].
Shanks, R. C., Capt. d. on 70-Apr-13 [70-Apr-14: 2C].
Shannessy, John (28 yrs.) d. on 70-Sep-22 [70-Sep-24: 2B].
Shannon, Bridget (64 yrs.) d. on 69-Oct-6 [69-Oct-7: 2B; 69-Oct-8: 2B].
Shannon, Edward P. m. Cassady, Fannie on 67-Oct-2 [67-Oct-9: 2B].
Shannon, James m. Preston, M. Laura on 67-Dec-4 [67-Dec-5: 2C].
Shannon, John m. Bayly, Mattie A. on 69-Jul-30 [69-Aug-10: 2C].
Shannon, John A. m. Sloan, Ida A. on 68-Sep-14 [68-Sep-22: 2B].
Shannon, Lizzie A. (9 yrs.) d. on 69-Dec-1 [69-Dec-2: 2C; 69-Dec-3: 2C].
Shannon, Maggie J. m. Wallace, Robert B. on 70-May-10 [70-May-16: 2B].
Shannon, Nathaniel (66 yrs., 3 mos.) d. on 70-May-4 [70-May-5: 2B; 70-May-6: 2B].
Shannon, W. R. (44 yrs.) d. on 68-Jan-4 [68-Jan-6: 2C].
Share, Charles T. (26 yrs.) d. on 67-Jul-12 [67-Jul-13: 2B].
Share, Eliza d. on 66-Oct-18 [66-Oct-19: 2B].
Sharkey, Mary (68 yrs.) d. on 70-Dec-13 [70-Dec-14: 2C; 70-Dec-15: 2C].
Sharp, Adam d. on 68-May-30 of Suicide (Struck by train) [68-Jun-6: 1F].
Sharp, Lizzie G. m. Buck, Thomas C. on 69-Nov-2 [69-Nov-10: 2C].
Sharp, Peter (19 yrs.) d. on 70-Nov-4 in Railroad accident [70-Nov-5: 4D].
Sharp, Solacie m. Wilson, Alfred A. on 69-Feb-7 [69-Feb-10: 2C].
Sharrets, Samuel F. m. Watkins, Amanda F. on 69-Jun-2 [69-Jun-10: 2C].
Sharretts, Edward Everett (7 yrs., 2 mos.) d. on 66-Dec-8 [66-Dec-10: 2C].
Shart, Issac (68 yrs.) d. on 70-Mar-5 [70-Mar-7: 2C].
Shattuck, Warrell (42 yrs.) d. on 67-Dec-19 [67-Dec-27: 2D].
Shaw, Benjamin m. Whiting, Mary on 69-Oct-26 [69-Oct-28: 2C].
Shaw, Carrie Louisa (5 mos.) d. on 66-Jul-13 [66-Jul-14: 2B].
Shaw, Charles H. m. Mitchell, Mary J. on 69-Oct-14 [69-Oct-19: 2B].
Shaw, Daniel E. m. Crisp, Sarah J. on 67-Sep-2 [67-Sep-25: 2B].
Shaw, Elizabeth B. (41 yrs.) d. on 68-Jul-1 [68-Jul-6: 2B].
Shaw, Ernest (2 mos.) d. on 67-Jul-11 [67-Jul-23: 2C].
Shaw, Florence V. m. Toner, J. C. on 66-Mar-19 [66-Mar-20: 2C].
Shaw, George W. m. Hall, Annie Maria on 66-Jul-1 [66-Jul-3: 2C].
Shaw, Imogene m. Krebs, George L. on 66-Jan-30 [66-Feb-5: 2C].
Shaw, Inez L. m. Conner, John on 70-Jun-20 [70-Jun-24: 2C].
Shaw, James V. B. (33 yrs.) d. on 70-Apr-15 [70-Apr-19: 2B].

Shaw, James W. (87 yrs.) d. on 66-Jul-17 [66-Jul-20: 2D].
Shaw, John W. m. Lemel, Sidney L. on 69-Nov-18 [69-Nov-20: 2B].
Shaw, Jonathan (50 yrs.) d. on 70-Feb-17 of Suicide (Shooting) [70-Jan-18: 1G].
Shaw, Joseph d. on 66-Oct-9 [66-Dec-13: 2B].
Shaw, Joseph (60 yrs.) d. on 69-Jan-13 [69-Jan-15: 2D].
Shaw, Joseph K. (13 yrs.) d. on 70-Aug-27 [70-Aug-29: 2C].
Shaw, Joshua B. m. Rae, Elizabeth A. on 70-Oct-4 [70-Oct-8: 2B].
Shaw, Katie E. m. Hart, Malcolm on 70-Jun-30 [70-Jul-4: 2C].
Shaw, Marian E. m. Earp, Amos on 69-Jan-12 [69-Jan-14: 2D].
Shaw, Marshall G. m. Orrison, Lanie F. on 68-Aug-25 [68-Sep-1: 2A].
Shaw, Mary A. m. Darling, James H. on 69-Dec-31 [70-Jan-5: 2C].
Shaw, Mary E. m. Rehbine, William H. on 67-Jun-12 [67-Jun-29: 2B].
Shaw, Mary Josephine m. Adams, John on 66-May-3 [66-May-9: 2B].
Shaw, Moses m. Hoge, Lydia A. on 68-Apr-9 [68-Apr-23: 2B].
Shaw, Richard m. Hockritt, Salome on 70-May-24 [70-May-26: 2C].
Shaw, Robert (54 yrs.) d. on 69-Apr-22 [69-Apr-26: 2C].
Shaw, Sophia (55 yrs.) d. on 67-Sep-3 [67-Sep-7: 2B].
Shaw, Susan m. Slaughter, John T. on 66-Apr-18 [66-Jun-18: 2B].
Shaw, Susan Ann (43 yrs.) d. on 69-Aug-5 [69-Aug-6: 2C; 69-Aug-7: 2C].
Shaw, Susan Cora (9 mos.) d. on 70-Apr-6 [70-Apr-7: 2C].
Shaw, Sylvanus T. (33 yrs.) d. on 68-Jul-28 of Consumption [68-Jul-29: 2B].
Shaw, Thomas (38 yrs.) d. on 67-Oct-16 of Intemperance and exposure [67-Oct-17: 1G].
Shaw, Welthy Ann m. Houseman, George W. on 66-Dec-3 [66-Dec-5: 2B].
Shaw, William A. m. Rea, Emma G. on 67-Apr-16 [67-Apr-20: 2A].
Shaw, William E. m. Fawcett, Annie M. on 66-Jan-18 [66-Jan-22: 2C].
Shea, Mary m. McCann, J. B. on 69-Dec-21 [70-Jan-26: 2C].
Shea, Rose (34 yrs.) d. on 70-Sep-4 [70-Sep-5: 2C].
Shea, Thomas (32 yrs.) d. on 67-Nov-2 [67-Nov-5: 2B].
Shea, Thomas F. (36 yrs.) d. on 69-Jun-1 of Apoplexy [69-Jun-2: 2B; 69-Jun-3: 1G].
Shea, Thomas F. m. Lannan, Annie on 66-May-13 [66-May-19: 2B].
Shealey, William J. m. Gaunt, Leonora S. on 67-May-14 [67-May-16: 2B].
Shearer, John (81 yrs.) d. on 66-Jan-27 [66-Jan-29: 2C].
Shearer, Maggie G. m. Reeside, H. H. on 69-Dec-21 [69-Dec-22: 2B].
Shearlock, John (55 yrs.) d. on 66-Aug-17 [66-Aug-18: 2B].
Sheckells, Anna Church d. on 69-May-14 [69-May-18: 2C].
Sheckells, Margaret R. (32 yrs.) d. on 67-Oct-11 [67-Oct-12: 2A].
Sheckels, Augustus Striker d. on 68-Dec-10 of Lung congestion [68-Dec-12: 2C].
Sheckels, Bernettie m. Harrison, John on 70-Oct-4 [70-Oct-5: 2B].
Sheckels, Lillie Clemens (2 mos.) d. on 70-Sep-10 [70-Sep-13: 2B].
Sheckels, Maria E. m. Leeds, Alexander on 69-May-20 [69-May-26: 2C].
Sheckels, W. Pinkney m. Stirling, Mary Elizabeth on 68-Aug-11 [68-Aug-12: 2C].
Sheckels, William H. (51 yrs.) d. on 68-Apr-12 [68-Apr-13: 2B].
Sheckles, Cephas H. m. Dockerty, Mary E. on 68-Jul-9 [68-Jul-14: 2B].
Sheedy, John (64 yrs.) d. on 69-Sep-4 [69-Sep-6: 2C].
Sheehan, Daniel F. m. MCIAIN, MARY on 68-Dec-27 [68-Dec-31: 2C].
Sheehan, George A. d. on 68-Apr-19 Murdered (Poisoning) [68-Jul-7: 4C; 68-Sep-9: 1G].
Sheehan, Helen Regine d. on 67-Aug-9 [67-Aug-10: 2B].
Sheehan, John F. (27 yrs.) d. on 69-Aug-7 [69-Aug-9: 2C].
Sheehan, Timothy (62 yrs.) d. on 67-Jul-4 of Pleurisy [67-Jul-6: 2B].
Sheehey, Teresa (1 yr., 2 mos.) d. on 68-Apr-16 [68-Apr-17: 2B; 68-Apr-18: 2A].
Sheeler, George W. m. Williams, Ellanora on 67-Oct-15 [67-Oct-17: 2B].
Sheets, Bessie (10 mos.) d. on 69-Jun-23 [69-Jun-28: 2C].
Sheets, Elizabeth (64 yrs., 3 mos.) d. on 69-Oct-26 [69-Oct-27: 2B].
Sheets, Jacob (40 yrs.) d. on 70-Jun-29 [70-Jun-30: 2C].
Sheffer, Josephine m. Koller, James B. on 70-Jan-4 [70-Jan-7: 2F].

Sheffer, Lillian Estelle (2 yrs., 1 mo.) d. [66-Nov-22: 2C].
Sheffer, Matilda (38 yrs.) d. on 67-Jun-24 [67-Jun-26: 2C].
Sheffer, Willie (1 yr.) d. on 67-Mar-17 [67-Mar-18: 2C].
Sheffield, John (38 yrs.) d. on 66-Jun-22 [66-Jun-23: 2B].
Sheffield, William Robinson (76 yrs.) d. on 70-May-21 [70-May-23: 2B; 70-May-24: 2C].
Shehan, Catherine (19 yrs.) d. on 69-Sep-27 [69-Sep-30: 2B].
Shehan, Edward (8 yrs., 7 mos.) d. on 68-Aug-9 Drowned [68-Aug-11: 1G, 2B].
Sheid, Hattie A m. Penn, Thomas P. on 70-Aug-29 [70-Sep-8: 2B].
Sheiry, Catherine (47 yrs.) d. on 69-Dec-22 [69-Dec-24: 2C].
Sheiry, Margaret J. m. Flahn, Lewis on 68-Jul-20 [68-Sep-14: 2B].
Shekell, Margie m. Dell, J. Everett on 68-Jul-21 [68-Jul-30: 2B].
Sheldon, John (81 yrs.) d. on 70-Jan-21 [70-Jan-22: 2C].
Sheldon, Margaret Elizabeth (1 yr., 11 mos.) d. on 66-Jan-27 [66-Jan-29: 2C].
Sheldon, Sarah M. m. Bushman, Frederick on 67-Apr-21 [67-May-14: 2B].
Shelley, Emily M. (48 yrs.) d. on 69-Jun-6 [69-Jun-9: 2C].
Shellhouse, William (29 yrs.) d. on 69-Jun-12 Drowned [69-Jun-17: 4C].
Shelton, Annie m. Niernsee, John R. on 69-Oct-6 [69-Dec-11: 2C].
Shenhart, Theodore (16 yrs.) d. on 68-Apr-8 Drowned [68-Apr-10: 1G].
Shepard, Charles S. m. Archer, Mary T. on 70-Sep-18 [70-Sep-23: 2C].
Shepard, Emma m. Hamilton, Alexander D. on 68-Feb-11 [68-Feb-14: 2C].
Shepherd, Anna H. (27 yrs.) d. on 68-Jan-14 [68-Jan-23: 2C].
Shepherd, E. C. m. Shock, Amelia E. on 70-Aug-17 [70-Aug-18: 2B].
Shepherd, Ella m. Foble, J. James on 68-Oct-8 [68-Oct-9: 2C].
Shepherd, George (69 yrs.) d. on 69-May-5 [69-Jul-31: 2C].
Shepherd, H. S. m. Snyder, Katie R. on 68-Dec-20 [68-Dec-31: 2C].
Shepherd, James H. m. Hamtramck, Florence on 67-Mar-5 [67-Mar-8: 2C].
Shepherd, Owens m. Hildt, E. Kate on 70-Dec-14 [70-Dec-17: 2B].
Shepler, Christopher m. Koran, Barre on 69-Nov-25 [69-Dec-10: 2C].
Sheppard, Amelia (2 mos.) d. on 68-Jan-29 [68-Jan-30: 2C].
Sheppard, E. Laura d. on 70-Oct-9 [70-Oct-11: 2C].
Sheppard, Ella F. (25 yrs., 3 mos.) d. on 70-Nov-22 [70-Nov-24: 2C].
Sheppard, Franklin Averill (2 mos.) d. on 70-May-26 [70-Jun-1: 2B].
Sheppard, George Thomas (33 yrs.) d. on 70-Oct-28 [70-Oct-29: 2B].
Sheppard, Harry Morgan d. [68-Jul-2: 2C].
Sheppard, Isabella G. d. on 70-Jul-5 of Consumption [70-Jul-6: 2C].
Sheppard, N. A. (72 yrs.) d. on 69-Jun-12 [69-Jun-15: 2C].
Shepperd, James A. m. Nolan, Mollie A. on 66-Jan-16 [66-Jan-19: 2C].
Shepperd, Mary Addell (7 mos.) d. on 70-Jul-25 [70-Jul-30: 2C].
Shepperson, Isabel Bird m. Burch, J. Alton on 69-Nov-3 [69-Nov-13: 2B].
Sherer, John m. Dorm, Lizzie on 69-Nov-2 [69-Nov-4: 2B].
Sheridan, Annie L. d. on 68-May-19 of Consumption [68-May-26: 2B].
Sheridan, Frank m. Buck, Susie E. on 69-Oct-14 [69-Oct-19: 2B].
Sheridan, Jane L. (62 yrs.) d. on 66-Jun-22 [66-Jun-23: 2B].
Sheridan, Samuel d. on 68-Apr-25 [68-May-6: 2B].
Sherler, William H. m. Bright, Laura V. on 66-Feb-15 [66-Mar-19: 2C].
Sherman, H. Gibson m. Lee, Bessie on 69-Dec-14 [69-Dec-20: 2C].
Shermer, Charles (56 yrs.) d. on 68-Apr-8 [68-Apr-9: 2B].
Sherry, Mary A. m. Connolly, John T. on 69-Aug-9 [69-Aug-19: 2C].
Sherwood, Abbie M. m. Rhames, William on 69-Mar-15 [69-Mar-17: 2C].
Sherwood, Annie R. m. Meredith, Daniel R. on 70-Feb-10 [70-Mar-1: 2C].
Sherwood, Benjamin m. Cross, Anna M. on 70-Dec-1 [70-Dec-3: 2B].
Sherwood, Charles K. m. Miller, Sallie on 66-May-17 [67-Feb-16: 2D].
Sherwood, Clara m. Waters, John H. on 70-Apr-28 [70-Apr-30: 2A].
Sherwood, Eliza d. on 68-Nov-20 [68-Nov-21: 2C].
Sherwood, Emma V. m. Fonerden, Clarence A. on 70-Oct-31 [70-Nov-11: 2C].

Sherwood, F. Frank m. Wood, Lizzie E. on 68-Oct-29 [68-Nov-3: 2B].
Sherwood, Florence Louise (7 mos.) d. on 68-Mar-28 [68-Mar-31: 2B].
Sherwood, George H. Hamilton (2 yrs., 5 mos.) d. on 67-Dec-28 of Chronic croup [67-Dec-31: 2C].
Sherwood, Giles Edward (10 yrs.) d. on 66-Jul-27 Drowned [66-Jul-28: 1F, 2C].
Sherwood, Howell P. (63 yrs.) d. on 69-Feb-15 [69-Feb-17: 2D].
Sherwood, Issac N. m. Trey, Lizzie C. M. on 68-Sep-9 [68-Sep-15: 2B].
Sherwood, Issac N. m. Frey, Lizzie C. M. on 68-Sep-9 [68-Sep-11: 2B].
Sherwood, J. R. m. Miller, Isabella on 67-May-6 [67-May-15: 2B].
Sherwood, Jesse Asbury (62 yrs.) d. on 66-Jul-17 of Heatstroke [66-Jul-24: 2C].
Sherwood, Laura J. m. Hartlove, Thomas P. on 69-Jun-29 [69-Jul-2: 2C].
Sherwood, Maggie A. m. Wells, William A. on 66-Oct-25 [66-Oct-27: 2B].
Sherwood, Margaret G. m. Gorsuch, Theodore on 67-Dec-5 [67-Dec-7: 2B].
Sherwood, Mary A. (42 yrs.) d. on 68-May-7 [68-May-9: 2B].
Sherwood, Mary A. m. Morrow, A. C. on 66-Jul-26 [66-Jul-28: 2C].
Sherwood, Mary E. m. Maughlin, Hugh A. on 69-Feb-11 [69-Feb-23: 2C].
Sherwood, Matilda (64 yrs.) d. on 68-Jul-25 [68-Jul-30: 2B].
Sherwood, Rebecca m. Mullikin, Joseph H. on 68-Oct-21 [68-Oct-24: 2B].
Sherwood, Richard P. (58 yrs.) d. on 66-Nov-14 [66-Nov-15: 1G, 2C; 66-Nov-16: 2C].
Sherwood, Thomas J. (70 yrs.) d. on 70-Dec-1 [70-Dec-8: 2C].
Sherwood, Thomas N. m. Caples, Anna M. on 66-Nov-15 [66-Nov-21: 2C].
Sherwood, William S. (52 yrs.) d. on 66-Jun-7 [66-Jun-8: 1F, 2B; 66-Jun-9: 2B; 66-Jun-11: 1F].
Sheubrook, Annie (9 yrs., 9 mos.) d. on 67-Jan-16 of Lamp explosion [67-Jan-17: 2C; 67-Jan-23: 2C; 67-Jan-17: 1F].
Shevelin, Mary Elizabeth (23 yrs.) d. on 69-Sep-2 [69-Sep-3: 2B].
Shible, Peter (67 yrs.) d. on 67-Jun-20 [67-Jul-12: 2C].
Shick, Annie K. m. Hartke, Joseph E. on 70-Feb-24 [70-Feb-26: 2C].
Shieldesheim, Johanna m. Peyser, Albert on 68-Feb-16 [68-Feb-18: 2C].
Shields, Annie m. Rowan, Stephen on 70-Mar-1 [70-Mar-8: 2C].
Shields, Ellen (2 yrs., 8 mos.) d. on 69-Apr-14 [69-Apr-15: 2B].
Shields, James J. (38 yrs.) d. on 67-Jan-28 in Railroad accident [67-Jan-29: 1F; 67-Jan-30: 2C; 67-Feb-4: 2C].
Shields, Jane (29 yrs.) d. on 67-Nov-23 [67-Nov-25: 2C].
Shields, John J. m. Meredith, Sarah E. on 67-Aug-29 [67-Sep-3: 2B].
Shields, John L. m. Meekins, Mary A. on 70-Jul-21 [70-Jul-26: 2B].
Shields, John Patrick (1 yr., 3 mos.) d. on 69-Apr-2 [69-Apr-3: 2B].
Shields, Mary M. (62 yrs.) d. on 66-Jun-13 [66-Jun-14: 2B].
Shields, Richard B. m. Loane, Emma F. on 70-Jul-6 [70-Jul-12: 2B].
Shilling, Kate Frances (1 yr., 9 mos.) d. on 68-Oct-29 [68-Oct-30: 2C; 68-Oct-31: 2B].
Shilling, Mary R. m. Crout, William F. on 68-May-28 [68-Jun-6: 2A].
Shillingberger, Elizabeth (83 yrs.) d. on 68-Jan-13 [68-Jan-14: 2C].
Shinnick, Charles Carroll (3 mos.) d. on 67-Sep-14 [67-Sep-16: 2B].
Shinnick, Charles Martin (1 yr., 2 mos.) d. on 66-Oct-26 [66-Oct-27: 2B].
Shinnick, Elizabeth A. (21 yrs., 6 mos.) d. on 70-Oct-5 [70-Oct-6: 2B; 70-Oct-7: 2B].
Shinnick, Margaret (56 yrs.) d. on 70-Apr-3 [70-Apr-4: 2C; 70-Apr-5: 2B].
Shinnick, Ormsby W. m. Hartley, Elizabeth A. on 67-Jan-31 [67-Feb-2: 2C].
Shiole, Charles F. m. Mackin, Georgeanna on 68-May-7 [68-May-9: 2B].
Shipley, Alfred A. m. Holland, Mary on 67-Feb-12 [67-Feb-14: 2C].
Shipley, Alverta L. m. Stunz, William P. on 67-Apr-18 [67-Apr-25: 2C].
Shipley, Ann (86 yrs.) d. on 67-Sep-3 [67-Sep-6: 2B].
Shipley, Annie E. m. Hahn, Henry on 67-Dec-5 [67-Dec-7: 2B].
Shipley, Archimedes (65 yrs.) d. on 67-Jan-24 in Railroad accident [67-Jan-25: 1F; 67-Jan-26: 2C].
Shipley, Benjamin F. m. Knell, Amelie on 70-Oct-13 [70-Oct-15: 2B].

Shipley, Benjamin W. m. Pratt, Mary M. on 68-May-14 [68-May-21: 2B].
Shipley, C. Elizabeth m. Earp, John W. on 67-Apr-2 [67-Apr-5: 2B].
Shipley, C. Howard m. Barry, Lizzie M. on 66-May-29 [66-Jun-1: 2B].
Shipley, Charles W. m. Tracy, Mary on 66-Nov-8 [66-Nov-9: 2C].
Shipley, Charlotte m. Anderson, John H. on 66-Apr-12 [66-Apr-17: 2C].
Shipley, Columbus m. White, Elizabeth A. on 68-Jan-2 [68-Jan-17: 2C].
Shipley, E. A. m. Jerome, Sarah A. on 66-Mar-15 [66-Mar-17: 2B].
Shipley, E. E. m. Carroll, Laura D. on 70-Nov-10 [70-Nov-14: 2B].
Shipley, Edwin C. (5 yrs., 4 mos.) d. on 66-Oct-17 of Typhoid [66-Oct-18: 2B].
Shipley, Edwin M. m. Bennett, Lizzie S. on 66-Dec-20 [66-Dec-25: 2B].
Shipley, Elizabeth m. Caples, Robert F. on 68-Feb-5 [68-Feb-7: 2C].
Shipley, Emma (21 yrs., 3 mos.) d. on 66-Aug-8 [66-Aug-9: 2C].
Shipley, Emma Rebecca (6 mos.) d. on 67-Jan-11 [67-Jan-15: 2C].
Shipley, George m. Taneyhill, Mary on 68-Jul-1 [69-Apr-9: 2B].
Shipley, George Ambrose (4 mos.) d. on 68-Aug-24 [68-Aug-25: 2B].
Shipley, George W. (5 yrs.) d. on 67-Feb-24 [67-Mar-2: 2B].
Shipley, Gustavus W. d. on 68-Feb-24 [68-Feb-26: 2C].
Shipley, H. C. m. Harper, Helen J. D. on 68-Dec-3 [68-Dec-4: 2D].
Shipley, J. Wesley (1 yr., 3 mos.) d. on 67-Sep-10 of Scarlet fever [67-Sep-11: 2B].
Shipley, James W. m. Pease, Isabelle on 68-Feb-20 [68-Mar-30: 2B].
Shipley, John m. Kelley, Rachel M. on 70-Jun-5 [70-Jun-8: 2C].
Shipley, Joseph Ennis (1 yr., 10 mos.) d. on 69-Mar-1 of Measles [69-Mar-2: 2C; 69-Mar-12: 2C].
Shipley, Katie Virginia I. (7 mos.) d. on 68-Aug-19 [68-Aug-20: 2B].
Shipley, L. G. d. on 70-Apr-2 [70-Apr-8: 2C; 70-Apr-9: 2B].
Shipley, Leonard Marshall (1 yr., 6 mos.) d. on 70-Aug-29 [70-Aug-30: 2C].
Shipley, Lettie C. m. Bartlett, Francis J. on 70-Oct-12 [70-Oct-24: 2B].
Shipley, Lizzie (23 yrs.) d. on 66-May-24 [66-May-25: 2C].
Shipley, Lloyd G. (57 yrs.) d. on 70-Oct-10 [70-Oct-11: 2C].
Shipley, M. E. m. Patterson, Oliver C. on 68-Apr-9 [68-May-1: 2B].
Shipley, Margaret Ann m. Penn, Matthew J. A. on 67-Sep-16 [67-Sep-21: 2A].
Shipley, Marian (2 mos.) d. on 69-Jan-8 [69-Jan-11: 2C].
Shipley, Mary (82 yrs.) d. on 70-Aug-22 [70-Aug-23: 2B].
Shipley, Mary V. m. Suits, Robert L. on 66-Sep-6 [66-Sep-10: 2D].
Shipley, Mary Virginia (18 yrs., 3 mos.) d. on 67-Feb-20 [67-Feb-27: 2C].
Shipley, Naomi m. Thomas, George on 68-Dec-29 [69-Jan-9: 2C].
Shipley, P. Virginia m. Barnett, Andrew J. on 67-Jan-9 [67-Feb-27: 2C].
Shipley, Rebecca m. Beck, John F. on 70-Oct-13 [70-Oct-18: 2B].
Shipley, Rebecca A. (45 yrs.) d. on 68-Oct-18 [68-Oct-19: 2B].
Shipley, Robert m. Lilly, Clarissa on 67-Apr-17 [67-Apr-20: 2A].
Shipley, Samuel d. on 67-Jun-19 of Suicide (Hanging) [67-Jun-20: 1F].
Shipley, Samuel H. d. on 70-Sep-15 in Railroad accident [70-Sep-20: 2B].
Shipley, Samuel Lewis (59 yrs., 7 mos.) d. on 67-May-10 [67-May-15: 2B].
Shipley, Samuel Oliver (1 yr., 5 mos.) d. on 70-Oct-10 [70-Oct-11: 2C].
Shipley, Sarah Virginia m. Dulaney, James H. on 66-Mar-15 [66-Mar-17: 2B].
Shipley, Washington m. Lepson, Amelia D. on 68-Jan-14 [68-Jan-18: 2B].
Shipley, William (72 yrs.) d. on 69-Sep-17 [69-Sep-18: 2B].
Shipley, William H. m. Hewitt, Mary E. on 67-Nov-7 [67-Nov-14: 2B].
Shipley, William S. (28 yrs.) d. on 70-Jun-28 [70-Jul-2: 2B].
Shipley, William T. m. Wesley, L. R. on 69-Nov-25 [69-Nov-26: 2B].
Shirland, T. J., Dr. (35 yrs.) d. on 66-Dec-7 of Suicide (Stabbing) [66-Dec-8: 1G].
Shirley, Henry C. m. Hoff, Addie S. on 67-Nov-14 [67-Nov-16: 2B].
Shirley, Nancy (55 yrs.) d. on 67-Jan-21 [67-Jan-25: 2C].
Shock, Amelia E. m. Shepherd, E. C. on 70-Aug-17 [70-Aug-18: 2B].
Shock, Clara Freedly (6 mos.) d. on 68-Jul-5 [68-Jul-7: 2B].

Shock, Evelyn (3 mos.) d. on 66-Jun-22 [66-Jun-25: 2B].
Shock, George H. (69 yrs.) d. on 68-Aug-7 [68-Aug-8: 2C].
Shock, Minnie O. m. Hopkins, William F. on 68-Apr-6 [68-Apr-8: 2B].
Shock, Virginia (29 yrs.) d. on 67-Jun-17 [67-Jun-18: 2B].
Shoemaker, Alfred d. on 66-Mar-12 [66-Mar-14: 2C].
Shoemaker, Ann M. (74 yrs.) d. on 68-Sep-21 [68-Sep-22: 2B].
Shoemaker, George W. (43 yrs.) d. on 66-Dec-28 [66-Dec-29: 2C].
Shoemaker, Jonathan d. on 67-Dec-7 [67-Dec-9: 2B].
Shoemaker, Rachel (72 yrs.) d. on 67-Jan-17 [67-Jan-18: 2C].
Shomberg, Israel m. Goldsmith, Isabella on 67-Apr-28 [67-Apr-29: 1G].
Shook, Catherine (97 yrs.) d. on 67-Sep-16 [67-Sep-18: 2B, 4D].
Shook, Elenora V. m. Hallnay, George F. on 69-Dec-12 [70-Jan-13: 2D].
Shook, Elenora V. m. Holloway, George E. on 70-Jan-12 [70-Jan-14: 2C].
Shorb, D. McNeal (28 yrs.) d. on 66-Jul-10 [66-Jul-12: 2C].
Shorb, James A., Dr. d. on 67-Oct-31 [67-Nov-14: 2C].
Shorey, Alice A. m. Morrison, Joseph L. on 66-May-17 [66-May-19: 2B].
Shorey, Miles Chase m. Edmonds, Mary J. on 70-Jan-6 [70-Jan-10: 2C].
Shorey, N. B. m. Tyler, Mattie E. on 66-May-17 [66-May-19: 2B].
Shorey, Samuel F. m. Fick, Barbara on 69-Jul-19 [69-Jul-23: 2C].
Shorey, William F. m. Sanks, Lida on 69-Sep-30 [69-Oct-4: 2C].
Short, Annie M. m. Beeler, S. F. on 66-Mar-10 [66-Aug-20: 2C].
Short, Kate A. m. Freburger, James M. on 68-Oct-19 [68-Oct-27: 2B].
Short, Maggie Annie m. Shamleffer, John Sham on 67-Feb-11 [67-Feb-13: 2D; 67-Feb-14: 2C].
Short, Mary Ann (55 yrs., 3 mos.) d. on 69-Mar-24 [69-Mar-25: 2C].
Short, Nina F. m. Neale, J. Harry on 66-Jan-10 [66-Jan-15: 2B].
Short, Perry (33 yrs.) d. on 67-Sep-27 Drowned [67-Oct-4: 1F; 67-Oct-10: 2B].
Shorter, Eliza Ann (60 yrs.) d. on 68-Jan-25 [68-Jan-27: 2C].
Shorter, P. W. m. Travers, Medora on 66-Jan-4 [66-Jan-6: 2B].
Shorter, William m. Smith, Harriet Emma on 66-May-13 [66-May-22: 2B].
Shortt, Mary M. (77 yrs.) d. on 68-Jan-25 [68-Jan-27: 2C].
Shott, Anna E. (7 yrs., 5 mos.) d. on 67-Dec-19 [67-Dec-21: 2B].
Shott, Charles H. (47 yrs.) d. on 70-Apr-20 [70-Apr-22: 2C].
Shott, Eliza (43 yrs.) d. on 69-Dec-26 of Consumption [70-Jan-8: 2B].
Shotts, Venie R. m. McCoy, J. Findlay on 68-Sep-17 [68-Oct-9: 2C].
Showacre, John Benjamin (1 yr., 5 mos.) d. on 68-Oct-6 [68-Oct-7: 2C].
Showacre, Lucretia C. (1 yr., 6 mos.) d. on 66-Jul-13 [66-Jul-17: 2C].
Shreck, Jacob N. (63 yrs.) d. on 69-Apr-4 of Consumption [69-Apr-6: 2C].
Shreck, William M. m. McAvoy, Mary Jane on 66-Jun-3 [66-Jul-10: 2C].
Shreek, Hester Elizabeth (59 yrs.) d. on 66-Jan-21 [66-Feb-1: 2C; 66-Feb-2: 2C].
Shreenes, Martha A. W. m. Solomon, Joseph Stan on 66-Dec-9 [67-Jan-1: 2C].
Shreve, J. Jefferson m. Tilghman, Rosalie on 66-Jan-26 [66-Jan-29: 2B].
Shrifogle, W. H. m. Massey, Mary Ann on 66-Nov-18 [66-Nov-24: 2B].
Shriner, Albert E. (17 yrs.) d. on 67-Mar-24 [67-Mar-27: 2C].
Shriver, Albert m. Jenkins, Anna on 66-Apr-26 [66-May-2: 2B].
Shriver, Ann Eva (79 yrs.) d. on 66-Jun-26 [66-Jun-27: 2C].
Shriver, Anne m. Tompkins, John A. on 67-Feb-26 [67-Feb-27: 2C].
Shriver, Calvin S. m. Nicodemus, M. Angela on 70-Jan-4 [70-Jan-10: 2C].
Shriver, E. Eme m. Tyler, R. Bradley on 69-Mar-11 [69-Mar-13: 2B].
Shriver, Edith (4 yrs., 2 mos.) d. on 70-Dec-2 [70-Dec-3: 2B].
Shriver, Frederick d. on 68-Feb-4 of Fall on shipboard [68-Feb-5: 1F].
Shriver, Henry Hooper (2 yrs., 9 mos.) d. on 69-Apr-28 [69-Apr-29: 2C].
Shriver, Rebecca (63 yrs.) d. on 69-Sep-17 [69-Sep-21: 2B].
Shriver, Sarah A. m. Read, Charles W. on 66-Apr-10 [66-Apr-12: 2B].
Shriver, Susan Wilson d. on 68-Apr-20 [68-Apr-21: 2B].

Shrudes, Sallie m. Saul, James F. on 69-Mar-8 [69-Mar-30: 2C].
Shryack, James Frederick (27 yrs.) d. on 69-Jun-2 [69-Jun-3: 2B; 69-Jun-18: 2C].
Shryock, Thomas J. m. Mann, Maria E. H. on 69-Oct-21 [69-Oct-23: 2B].
Shue, Elize (65 yrs.) d. on 68-Nov-28 [68-Nov-30: 2C].
Shue, Rebecca m. Kline, Jacob R. on 67-Feb-12 [67-Mar-7: 2C].
Shuemacker, Mary m. Henkel, Charles on 70-Sep-29 [70-Oct-3: 2B].
Shuler, Julia m. Harbaugh, T. J. on 70-Sep-28 [70-Oct-1: 2B].
Shultheis, Alberta (2 yrs., 9 mos.) d. on 69-Sep-27 [69-Sep-28: 2B; 69-Sep-29: 2B].
Shultz, Caroline Matilda (27 yrs.) d. on 67-Jun-29 [67-Jul-1: 2B].
Shultz, Charles H. m. Sumsh, Froney on 68-Dec-1 [68-Dec-7: 2C].
Shunk, Benjamin m. Mallen, Margaret A. on 66-May-29 [66-Jun-2: 2B; 66-Jun-4: 2B].
Shure, Charles A. m. Gwinn, George on 69-Jun-24 [69-Jun-26: 2B].
Shure, Harry W. m. Wahl, Georgie on 67-Oct-30 [67-Oct-31: 2B].
Shuster, William H. m. Gillingham, Annie R. on 68-Nov-24 [68-Dec-4: 2D].
Shuter, James m. Stratton, Sallie W. on 67-Jun-18 [67-Jun-26: 2C].
Shutt, August L. m. O'Leary, Hattie A. on 66-Oct-25 [66-Oct-26: 2B; 66-Oct-27: 2B].
Shutt, Barbara (88 yrs.) d. on 70-Apr-18 [70-Apr-22: 2C].
Shutt, William S. (5 yrs., 4 mos.) d. on 69-Sep-2 [69-Sep-3: 2B].
Shutz, John (52 yrs.) d. on 69-Jun-4 [69-Jun-5: 2B].
Shyme, John A. (50 yrs.) d. of Consumption [67-Mar-19: 2C].
Sickel, Edward m. Trust, Alice M. on 68-Sep-10 [68-Sep-12: 2B].
Sickel, Gertrude (65 yrs.) d. on 67-Dec-3 [67-Dec-4: 2C; 67-Dec-5: 2C].
Sickel, L. D. m. Orth, Mary E. on 67-Oct-6 [67-Oct-11: 2B].
Sickel, Mary R. d. on 70-Aug-19 [70-Aug-20: 2B].
Sickel, William H m. Gude, Anna on 70-Jun-29 [70-Jul-6: 2B].
Siddons, George H. m. Hubbard, Josephine F. on 69-Mar-4 [69-Mar-6: 2B].
Siebert, Charles (40 yrs.) d. on 68-Aug-21 of Fall from horse [68-Aug-28: 1G].
Siebert, David m. Hardesty, Matilda on 68-Jun-10 [68-Jun-12: 2B].
Siebert, Julius (14 yrs.) d. on 69-Mar-25 Crushed by lumber [69-Mar-26: 1H].
Siegmann, John G. (49 yrs.) d. on 70-Dec-7 [70-Dec-8: 2C; 70-Dec-9: 2C].
Siegmann, Louisa d. on 68-Oct-8 [68-Oct-10: 2B].
Siemers, Herrman (65 yrs.) d. [70-Sep-12: 2B; 70-Sep-13: 2B].
Siemers, Maria (63 yrs.) d. on 68-Oct-11 [68-Oct-2: 2B; 68-Oct-3: 2B].
Silance, John H. m. Etchison, Maggie A. on 70-Feb-2 [70-Feb-8: 2C].
Silbereisen, Louisa (97 yrs., 9 mos.) d. on 70-Nov-11 [70-Nov-16: 2C].
Silence, Adanegah (4 yrs., 4 mos.) d. on 67-Feb-19 [67-Feb-19: 2C].
Silk, Thomas R. (61 yrs.) d. on 70-Nov-3 [70-Nov-5: 2B].
Sillery, Charles m. Buckley, Lydia on 69-Aug-12 [69-Aug-16: 2B].
Sillery, Kate, Miss m. Carroll, Andrew, Miss on 66-Feb-5 [66-Feb-27: 2B].
Silver, Alice H. (62 yrs.) d. on 68-Jan-28 [68-Feb-10: 2C].
Silver, Frank m. Duvall, Louisa on 68-Nov-16 [68-Nov-19: 2C].
Silver, Virginia A. m. Kerr, William on 68-Dec-15 [68-Dec-17: 2C].
Silverthorn, Benjamin C. m. Bonn, Phinnie on 69-Feb-11 [69-Feb-13: 2C].
Simering, William (47 yrs., 8 mos.) d. on 69-Dec-16 of Consumption [69-Dec-17: 2C].
Simes, Edgar C. (56 yrs.) d. on 67-Feb-19 [67-Feb-23: 2C].
Simmonds, Emma D. (22 yrs.) d. on 69-Jan-1 [69-Jan-4: 2C].
Simmonds, Herman m. Baker, Ida G. on 70-Feb-17 [70-Feb-23: 2C].
Simmons, Alice m. Worthington, Nicholas J. on 67-Oct-17 [67-Oct-19: 2A].
Simmons, Annie R. (16 yrs.) d. on 70-Mar-6 [70-Mar-8: 2C].
Simmons, Bertha m. McCarty, James on 66-Jul-3 [66-Jul-7: 2B].
Simmons, Catherine (64 yrs.) d. on 69-Nov-30 [69-Dec-1: 2C].
Simmons, Charles E. m. Houck, M. Tillie on 68-Dec-3 [68-Dec-7: 2C].
Simmons, Frank G. m. Snyder, Maggie F. on 69-Apr-20 [69-Apr-26: 2B].
Simmons, John Wesley (11 mos.) d. on 67-Feb-17 of Scarlet fever [67-Feb-18: 2C].
Simmons, Maggie E. m. Mills, John H. D. on 66-Feb-28 [66-Mar-6: 2B].

Simmons, Mamie C. (8 mos.) d. on 70-Aug-22 [70-Aug-23: 2B].
Simmons, Marion Virginia d. [70-Dec-24: 2B].
Simmons, Mary Ann d. on 68-Jul-3 [68-Jul-4: 2C].
Simmons, Mary E. d. on 69-Jun-29 [69-Jul-1: 2C].
Simmons, Richard L. m. Higdon, Mary E. on 69-Nov-18 [69-Nov-22: 2C].
Simmons, Robert H. m. Stallings, Sarah E. on 66-Dec-11 [67-Feb-7: 2C].
Simmons, Samuel B. (4 yrs.) d. on 67-Feb-7 of Scarlet fever [67-Feb-9: 2B].
Simmons, William m. Smallwood, Jane on 66-Aug-2 [66-Aug-7: 2C].
Simms, Annie M. m. Ferris, William H. on 69-Mar-11 [69-Mar-15: 2C].
Simms, Elizabeth m. Jones, Henry C. on 67-Nov-12 [67-Nov-14: 2B].
Simms, Eva A. m. Wells, William M. on 70-Jun-30 [70-Jul-9: 2B].
Simms, George m. Straup, Elizabeth on 66-Feb-1 [66-Feb-19: 2B].
Simms, Joseph (71 yrs.) d. on 68-Jan-26 [68-Jan-27: 2C; 68-Jan-28: 2D, 4E].
Simms, Joseph m. Price, Emeline on 66-Jun-13 [66-Jun-23: 2B].
Simms, Maria m. Jones, William T. on 68-May-5 [68-May-8: 2B].
Simms, Mary m. Cassard, J. D. on 69-Dec-30 [69-Dec-31: 2C].
Simms, Sarah (55 yrs.) d. on 67-Jan-21 of Pneumonia [67-Jan-23: 2C].
Simms, Thomas m. Manner, Annie on 70-Feb-1 [70-Feb-10: 2C].
Simon, August m. Davis, J. Mattie on 66-Sep-12 [66-Sep-18: 2B].
Simon, Edmund m. Ware, Virginia on 68-Dec-29 [68-Dec-30: 2C].
Simon, Frederic W. m. Hooper, Florence T. on 69-Nov-16 [69-Nov-17: 2C; 69-Nov-23: 2C].
Simon, Mathias (47 yrs.) d. on 68-Oct-19 [68-Oct-20: 2B; 68-Oct-21: 2C; 68-Oct-22: 1G].
Simon, Rose R. m. Forster, G. H. on 67-Oct-3 [67-Oct-5: 2B].
Simonds, John m. Preston, Caroline on 69-Apr-1 [69-Apr-6: 2C].
Simonds, John W. m. Weir, Isabella on 66-Apr-8 [66-May-1: 2A].
Simons, Henrietta Wragg m. Ferguson, James DuGue on 68-Oct-22 [68-Nov-10: 2C].
Simons, Mary T. G. d. on 68-Feb-2 [68-Feb-11: 2C; 68-Feb-12: 2C].
Simpson, A. J. m. Plummer, Mary A. on 67-Jul-3 [67-Jul-9: 2B].
Simpson, Alexander m. McMullen, Ellen on 67-Nov-11 [67-Nov-22: 2C].
Simpson, Andrew J. (24 yrs.) d. on 67-Feb-24 [67-Feb-25: 2C].
Simpson, Anne Shields (48 yrs.) d. on 67-Apr-27 [67-Apr-29: 2B].
Simpson, Blanche (10 mos.) d. on 68-Jul-15 [68-Jul-17: 2C].
Simpson, C. Owen m. Florence, Belle on 67-Nov-21 [67-Nov-30: 2C].
Simpson, Charles C. m. White, Martha A. on 67-Nov-11 [67-Nov-12: 2C].
Simpson, Charles W. m. Kleinle, Louisa on 70-Apr-13 [70-May-27: 2B].
Simpson, D. T. m. Laughlin, Nettie on 69-Nov-15 [69-Nov-27: 2B].
Simpson, Dennis (61 yrs.) d. on 66-Jan-23 [66-Jan-27: 2B].
Simpson, Elizabeth (61 yrs.) d. on 70-Apr-9 [70-Apr-11: 2B; 70-Apr-12: 2B].
Simpson, Fannie m. Fell, J. Sands on 67-Dec-23 [68-Feb-17: 2B].
Simpson, Florence (27 yrs.) d. on 69-Sep-23 [69-Oct-4: 2C].
Simpson, George B. (35 yrs.) d. on 66-Oct-7 [66-Oct-19: 2B].
Simpson, Harriet (60 yrs.) d. on 69-Aug-15 [69-Aug-16: 2C].
Simpson, Ida May (2 mos.) d. on 69-Jun-29 [69-Jun-30: 2C].
Simpson, J. H. d. on 70-Feb-23 of Paralysis [70-Mar-2: 2D].
Simpson, Jane A. (58 yrs., 4 mos.) d. [69-Apr-3: 2B].
Simpson, John Wesley (1 yr., 6 mos.) d. on 69-Apr-5 [69-Apr-6: 2C].
Simpson, Joseph m. Dorsey, Margaret on 69-Mar-11 [69-Mar-22: 2C].
Simpson, Louis, Jr. m. Parr, Emily W. on 69-Oct-21 [69-Oct-23: 2B].
Simpson, Margaret (71 yrs.) d. on 67-May-10 [67-May-11: 2A].
Simpson, Mary Belle m. Mason, E. Mason on 68-Nov-25 [68-Nov-26: 2B].
Simpson, Mary L. (23 yrs.) d. on 68-Jun-10 of Consumption [68-Jun-11: 2B].
Simpson, Sallie m. Townsend, John T. on 69-Aug-8 [69-Aug-28: 2B].
Simpson, William S. (16 yrs.) d. on 66-Mar-27 [66-Mar-29: 2B; 66-Mar-31: 2C].
Simpson, William S. (45 yrs.) d. on 70-Jul-30 [70-Aug-2: 2C].
Simpson, William Thomas (4 yrs., 5 mos.) d. on 69-Mar-8 of Croup [69-Mar-9: 2C].

Simpson, Willie Edward (10 mos.) d. on 69-Aug-1 [69-Aug-2: 2C].
Sinclair, Arthur m. Willett, Drusilla on 67-Sep-3 [67-Sep-5: 2B].
Sinclair, Charles M. (1 yr., 3 mos.) d. on 70-Oct-25 [70-Oct-26: 2B].
Sinclair, Charles S. McKain (37 yrs.) d. on 70-Jul-5 [70-Jul-6: 2C].
Sinclair, Cyrus (3 yrs., 5 mos.) d. on 69-May-28 [69-May-29: 2B].
Sinclair, George M. (3 mos.) d. on 70-Jun-22 [70-Jun-24: 2C].
Sinclair, Lelia m. Montague, W. Powhatan on 70-Jul-19 [70-Jul-23: 2B].
Sinclair, Margaret (107 yrs.) d. on 69-Jul-10 [69-Jul-13: 2C].
Sinclair, Mary A. m. Lee, John W. on 66-Sep-4 [66-Sep-17: 2B].
Sinclair, Mary Ann (95 yrs.) d. on 68-Oct-7 [68-Oct-9: 2C].
Sinclair, Matthew m. Saunders, Marie on 66-Aug-2 [66-Aug-30: 2B].
Sinclair, Regina (48 yrs.) d. on 70-Nov-7 [70-Nov-17: 2C].
Sinclair, William R. (56 yrs.) d. on 69-Sep-12 [69-Sep-18: 2B].
Sindall, Alice Roberta (9 yrs.) d. on 66-Jun-28 [66-Jun-30: 2B].
Sindall, Charles A. (4 mos.) d. on 68-Jul-17 [68-Jul-18: 2B].
Sindall, Eleanor Anna (21 yrs., 10 mos.) d. on 69-Nov-26 [69-Nov-27: 2C].
Sindall, Jane d. on 67-Sep-13 [67-Sep-14: 2A].
Sindall, Miriam E. m. Riley, Theodore B. on 69-Aug-3 [69-Aug-7: 2B].
Sindall, Philip d. on 66-Jul-29 [66-Jul-30: 2C].
Singer, Susie L. m. Levering, T. H. on 69-Oct-7 [69-Oct-9: 2C].
Singewald, Henry (7 mos.) d. on 69-Jul-28 [69-Jul-31: 2C].
Singewald, Henry C. (21 yrs.) d. on 68-Aug-30 [68-Sep-1: 2B].
Singleton, John (45 yrs.) d. on 70-May-27 [70-May-28: 2B].
Singleton, Mary E. m. Deaver, Stephen F. on 68-Apr-12 [68-Apr-28: 2B].
Singleton, Mary Margaret (4 yrs., 1 mo.) d. on 67-Feb-3 [67-Feb-4: 2C].
Singleton, Mary Virginia m. Reynolds, Thomas on 66-Nov-4 [66-Nov-24: 2B].
Singleton, William H. H. m. Snyder, Mary Anna on 70-Jun-15 [70-Jun-22: 2C].
Sinner, David m. Tuttle, Mary on 70-Jan-7 [70-Jan-11: 2C; 70-Jan-18: 2C].
Sinnott, Michael d. on 68-Sep-6 [68-Sep-8: 2B].
Sinskey, Ellen (1 yr.) d. on 68-Oct-10 [68-Oct-12: 2B].
Sinskey, Henry d. on 66-Jan-17 [66-Jan-19: 2C].
Sinsz, Sophia m. Kerr, Edward on 67-Nov-28 [67-Dec-10: 2B].
Sipple, Charles O. m. Cofran, Nettie on 66-Apr-2 [66-Apr-5: 2B; 66-Apr-6: 2B].
Sipple, George m. Casley, Laura V. on 70-May-11 [70-Aug-18: 2B].
Sipple, M. R. C. (66 yrs.) d. on 66-Jan-29 [66-Jan-30: 2B].
Sipple, Nettie (26 yrs.) d. on 67-Mar-2 [67-Mar-5: 2C].
Sipple, Sarah Emma (3 yrs., 4 mos.) d. on 70-Nov-3 [70-Nov-4: 2C].
Sipple, Thomas E. (15 yrs., 5 mos.) d. on 69-Sep-3 [69-Sep-6: 2B].
Sipple, William Francis (7 yrs., 5 mos.) d. on 70-Oct-26 [70-Oct-27: 2B].
Sirich, John H. (46 yrs.) d. on 66-Oct-15 [66-Oct-19: 2B].
Sisco, Isabella A. m. Taylor, George W. on 66-Jan-25 [66-Jan-27: 2B].
Sisselberger, Mary ANEY, Miss m. Ruckle, William T. on 67-Dec-30 [68-Jan-2: 2B].
Sisselburger, Elizabeth A. m. Miller, Martin L. on 69-Oct-5 [69-Oct-11: 2C].
Sisson, C. Roane m. Chamberlain, Eliza V. on 69-Oct-5 [69-Oct-14: 2C].
Sisson, Hallie C. m. Magruder, Hamline on 69-Apr-22 [69-Apr-24: 2B].
Sisson, Nettie (8 yrs.) d. on 66-May-15 [66-May-16: 2C].
Sitler, Morris (59 yrs.) d. on 66-Aug-2 [66-Aug-4: 2C].
Sitters, Issac d. on 68-Jul-15 of Heatstroke [68-Jul-17: 1D].
Sitzler, Emma D. m. Rial, Michael K. on 67-Jul-3 [67-Sep-26: 2B].
Sitzler, Leonard F. m. Thompson, Medora H. on 70-Jul-14 [70-Jul-27: 2C].
Six, George W. (21 yrs.) d. on 70-Dec-21 [70-Dec-24: 2B].
Sizns, Elizabeth m. Hickenbotham, William on 66-Jun-25 [66-Jun-30: 2B].
Skeels, Marion A. m. Focke, Frederick K. [69-Jul-15: 2C].
Skillman, Catherine Ann (64 yrs.) d. on 66-Jan-11 [66-Jan-15: 2C].
Skinner, A. S. m. Lurty, Sallie A. on 67-Feb-14 [67-Feb-19: 2C].

Skinner, Emma V. m. Woolford, Benjamin W. on 70-May-12 [70-May-18: 2B].
Skinner, G. B. m. Wingate, M. Kate on 69-Jan-3 [69-Mar-18: 2C].
Skinner, Imogen m. Gray, Howard P. on 69-Oct-5 [69-Oct-12: 2C].
Skinner, Laura V., Miss m. Leitch, Edward G., Jr. on 67-Dec-31 [68-Jan-3: 2C].
Skinner, Marianna m. West, H. Montgomery on 70-Jan-20 [70-Jan-28: 2B].
Skinner, Marietta m. Franklin, John E. on 67-Jan-1 [67-Jan-5: 2C].
Skinner, Mary J. d. on 70-Aug-25 [70-Aug-27: 2B].
Skinner, Mary R. m. Booker, Henry C. on 66-Feb-8 [66-Feb-22: 2B].
Skinner, Precilla M. (38 yrs.) d. on 67-Feb-7 [67-Feb-9: 2B].
Skinner, Roberta J. m. Morrow, George G. on 66-Oct-18 [66-Oct-20: 2B].
Skinner, Ruth (92 yrs.) d. on 70-Mar-21 [70-Apr-19: 2B].
Skinner, Sarah Jane d. on 66-Sep-30 [66-Oct-9: 2B].
Skinner, Thomas m. Stansbury, Mary F. on 67-Sep-15 [67-Sep-19: 2B].
Skinner, Thomas m. Tubman, Sarah A. on 69-Feb-18 [69-Feb-20: 2A].
Skinner, Thomas W. m. Jarvis, Catherine on 66-Dec-18 [66-Dec-20: 2B].
Skinner, W. Hammond m. Musselman, Emily F. on 69-May-12 [69-May-14: 2C].
Skipper, Catherine (42 yrs., 2 mos.) d. on 68-Nov-15 [68-Nov-17: 2C].
Skipper, Dorsey (68 yrs.) d. on 69-Feb-9 [69-Feb-10: 2C].
Skivington, Catherine (48 yrs.) d. on 67-May-8 [67-May-9: 2A].
Skuer, Otto B. m. Thomas, Sarah J. E. on 70-Jan-1 [70-Jan-4: 2C].
Slack, Amos William (39 yrs.) d. on 70-Aug-31 [70-Sep-23: 2C].
Slack, Belinda d. on 67-Apr-26 [67-Apr-27: 2A].
Slack, Jasper N. (28 yrs.) d. on 69-Apr-5 [69-Apr-6: 2C; 69-Apr-7: 2C].
Slack, Minnie m. Thomson, Alexander on 66-May-10 [66-May-11: 2B].
Slack, William H. m. Connick, Carrie N. on 69-Dec-1 [69-Dec-11: 2B].
Slacum, Ida May (1 mo.) d. on 67-Aug-16 [67-Aug-20: 2B].
Slade, Alcinda Wilhelm d. on 69-Nov-23 [69-Nov-27: 2C].
Slade, Alfred H. m. McComas, Sophie on 67-May-21 [67-Jun-21: 2B].
Slade, Ella (16 yrs.) d. on 68-Aug-1 [68-Aug-15: 2B].
Slade, Isabel m. Appleton, Eben on 68-Nov-24 [68-Dec-9: 2C].
Slade, Meriken (15 yrs.) d. on 66-Aug-11 in Riding accident [66-Aug-18: 1F].
Slade, Washington M. m. Amos, Martha on 67-Jan-29 [67-Feb-5: 2C].
Slade, William H. (59 yrs.) d. on 66-Aug-4 [66-Aug-6: 2C; 66-Aug-11: 1G].
Slagg, Mary J. m. Linthicum, James A. on 70-Aug-25 [70-Aug-27: 2B].
Slagle, David (69 yrs.) d. on 70-Jul-6 [70-Jul-9: 2B].
Slagle, Hannah (66 yrs., 9 mos.) d. on 67-Jun-7 [67-Jun-12: 2B].
Slagle, John W. d. on 70-Mar-25 of Typhoid pneumonia [70-Apr-7: 2C; 70-Apr-8: 2C].
Slagle, Ross (1 yr., 4 mos.) d. on 68-Aug-6 [68-Aug-8: 2C].
Slasman, Emma J. m. Coffin, Charles G. on 66-Apr-25 [66-May-31: 2B].
Slater, Abraham (74 yrs.) d. on 68-Mar-12 [68-Mar-14: 2B].
Slater, Annie m. Andrews, Benjamin on 66-Jan-17 [66-Feb-2: 2C].
Slater, Eliza (64 yrs.) d. on 66-Nov-26 [66-Nov-27: 2B; 66-Nov-28: 2B].
Slater, Helen m. Edgar, George H. on 68-Jun-16 [68-Jun-19: 2B].
Slater, Isabel J. m. Combs, William W. on 67-Dec-17 [67-Dec-20: 2B].
Slater, Mary Dunichan (31 yrs.) d. on 68-Jan-16 [68-Jan-17: 2C].
Slater, Mary J. m. Snyder, Daniel on 68-Apr-9 [68-Apr-11: 2A].
Slater, Mary S. (62 yrs.) d. on 69-Apr-9 [69-Apr-10: 2B].
Slater, Thomas W. m. Sanders, Mary Ann on 67-Feb-27 [67-Mar-7: 2C].
Slater, Willie T. (1 yr.) d. on 69-Oct-28 [69-Oct-29: 2C; 69-Oct-30: 2C].
Slattery, John J. m. Frye, Eliza J. on 69-Dec-30 [70-Jan-14: 2C].
Slattery, Michael, Rev. (58 yrs.) d. on 66-Oct-3 of Paralysis [66-Oct-4: 1F, 2B; 66-Oct-5: 2B].
Slaughter, Edmonia (23 yrs.) d. on 70-Oct-8 [70-Oct-12: 2C].
Slaughter, Emily G. m. Stewart, William A. on 69-Mar-16 [69-Mar-17: 2C].
Slaughter, Emma M. m. Newton, Issac on 66-May-30 [66-Jun-18: 2B].
Slaughter, Fannie Rose m. Emerson, Charles H. on 68-Jul-9 [68-Jul-13: 2B].

Slaughter, Harriet L. m. Parlett, William O. on 67-Jul-16 [67-Jul-18: 2C].
Slaughter, John T. m. Shaw, Susan on 66-Apr-18 [66-Jun-18: 2B].
Slaughter, William H. (1 yr., 7 mos.) d. on 68-May-20 [68-May-21: 2B].
Slavin, Bridget (25 yrs.) d. on 70-Nov-5 [70-Nov-7: 2B].
Slavin, Margaret (1 yr., 8 mos.) d. on 69-Feb-26 [69-Feb-27: 2C].
Slavin, Mary (66 yrs.) d. on 66-Jun-9 [66-Jun-11: 2B].
Slawson, Charles Henry (1 yr., 7 mos.) d. on 69-Apr-1 [69-Apr-6: 2C].
Slayman, Katie E. m. Adams, Sydney on 67-Jan-10 [67-Jan-19: 2C].
Slaysman, Alexander (72 yrs.) d. on 69-Feb-27 [69-Mar-1: 2C].
Sleat, Mary J. m. Hulse, James H. on 70-Nov-22 [70-Dec-31: 2B].
Slee, George W. (47 yrs.) d. on 66-Apr-22 [66-Sep-5: 2B].
Slee, John N. (35 yrs.) d. on 66-Apr-15 of Brain congestion [66-Apr-16: 2B].
Slee, William (56 yrs.) d. on 68-Jul-22 [68-Aug-3: 2C].
Sleeger, Daniel F. S. (9 mos.) d. on 69-Mar-2 [69-Mar-4: 2C].
Sleeger, George A. m. Reisinger, Fannie E. on 70-Nov-6 [70-Nov-15: 2C].
Sleepack, Hanna m. Wegner, Charles J. on 68-Jun-9 [68-Jun-13: 2B].
Slemaker, Eliza (52 yrs.) d. on 66-Feb-4 [66-Feb-6: 2D].
Slemaker, Jacob H. m. Keiler, Rosanna on 66-May-22 [66-Jul-16: 2C].
Slemaker, John H. m. Ringrose, Elizabeth on 67-Apr-2 [67-Apr-4: 2B].
Slemmer, Jesse Levering (74 yrs.) d. on 70-Jul-23 [70-Jul-30: 2C; 70-Aug-1: 4G].
Slemmer, S. Fannie m. Merchant, B. on 68-May-28 [68-Jun-2: 2B].
Slicer, Elizabeth (62 yrs.) d. on 69-Jun-14 [69-Jun-15: 2C; 69-Jun-16: 2C].
Slicer, Hattee E. (8 yrs., 7 mos.) d. on 66-Jun-26 [66-Jun-28: 2C].
Slicer, Henry W. (36 yrs.) d. on 67-Oct-20 of Typhoid [67-Oct-22: 1F, 2A].
Sliner, Mary A. d. on 67-Apr-8 [67-Apr-9: 2B].
Slingluff, Carrie Orme (1 yr.) d. on 68-Jul-29 [68-Jul-31: 2C].
Slingluff, Ella Sewell d. on 69-Jan-5 [69-Jan-6: 2C; 69-Jan-7: 2C].
Slingluff, Ellen (25 yrs.) d. on 69-Jun-20 [69-Jun-21: 2B].
Slingluff, Fielder C. m. Sewell, Ella on 66-Oct-3 [66-Oct-6: 2A].
Slingluff, J. Louis m. Banks, Ellen on 66-Nov-7 [66-Nov-10: 2B].
Slingluff, Reuben H., Dr. (42 yrs.) d. on 68-Mar-26 [68-Apr-3: 2C].
Slingluff, Trueman C. m. Tilghman, Anna R. on 68-Oct-22 [68-Oct-24: 2B].
Slingman, Mary Anna m. Keck, Samuel Gilbert on 66-Jan-7 [66-Feb-13: 2C].
Slinkman, Lillian May (1 yr., 3 mos.) d. on 69-Aug-23 [69-Aug-24: 2B].
Sloan, Frs. J. m. Baldwin, S. Emma on 69-Dec-7 [69-Dec-13: 2C].
Sloan, George E. (47 yrs.) d. on 66-Mar-30 of Paralysis [66-Mar-31: 1F, 2C; 66-Apr-2: 2B].
Sloan, Ida M. m. Shannon, John A. on 68-Sep-14 [68-Sep-22: 2B].
Sloan, J. Theodore m. McIntire, Sallie J. on 70-Jan-5 [70-Jan-8: 2B].
Sloan, James (55 yrs.) d. on 70-Oct-12 [70-Oct-13: 2C].
Sloan, John, Capt. (80 yrs.) d. on 70-Nov-20 [70-Nov-22: 2C].
Sloan, L. J. m. Kelly, N. E. on 69-Nov-23 [69-Nov-30: 2C].
Sloan, Leila Estelle (3 yrs., 9 mos.) d. on 69-Jul-15 [69-Jul-17: 2C].
Sloan, Pemberton (39 yrs.) d. on 68-Sep-2 [68-Sep-3: 2B].
Sloan, Rosalie m. Snead, A. B. on 68-Nov-10 [68-Dec-10: 2D].
Sloan, William Frederick (40 yrs.) d. on 70-Oct-3 [70-Oct-4: 2B].
Slothour, Ella Orrick d. on 67-May-10 [67-May-25: 2B].
Slothower, George (1 yr., 2 mos.) d. on 67-Mar-31 [67-Apr-1: 1C].
Slothower, J. A. m. Orrick, Ella on 66-Mar-24 [66-May-8: 2B].
Slothower, Morris B. m. Magruder, Bettie Mills on 68-Oct-13 [68-Oct-14: 2B].
Slouey, Mary (77 yrs.) d. on 69-Nov-16 [69-Nov-17: 2C; 69-Nov-18: 2C].
Sluter, Jeremiah H. m. Lang, Elizabeth on 69-Feb-25 [69-Mar-17: 2C].
Slyder, Izadore A. m. Knight, Emma A. on 67-Mar-12 [67-Mar-14: 2C].
Slye, Marion G. m. Davis, Jackson on 69-Nov-4 [69-Nov-6: 2B; 69-Nov-10: 2C].
Slyers, James W. m. Boyce, Mary Lavinia on 70-Feb-3 [70-Feb-5: 2B].
Small, Charles W. m. Alsop, Mary J. on 68-Jun-4 [68-Jun-6: 2A].

Small, Charles Wesley (7 mos.) d. on 68-Feb-17 [68-Feb-21: 2B].
Small, Edward A. m. Thacker, Mollie E. on 70-Jan-19 [70-Jan-29: 2B].
Small, Emma E. m. Davis, Frank E. on 67-May-25 [67-May-28: 2B].
Small, Frances L. m. Keaton, James P. on 66-Dec-25 [67-Jan-4: 2D].
Small, Frank R. m. Dill, M. Catherine on 67-Oct-23 [67-Oct-25: 2B].
Small, John F. m. Dowling, Mary E. on 69-Apr-27 [69-Apr-30: 2C].
Small, Joseph m. Upton, Susie R. on 69-Nov-16 [69-Nov-18: 2C].
Small, L. m. Davis, John H. on 70-Sep-22 [70-Sep-27: 2B].
Small, M. Augusta m. Ludwig, John A. on 68-Jun-4 [68-Jun-8: 2B].
Small, M. Lettie m. Hellen, Thomas J. [67-Nov-28: 2C].
Small, Mabel Hepburn (10 mos.) d. on 67-Jul-11 [67-Jul-12: 2C].
Small, Maggie A. m. Toft, L. L. on 68-Nov-25 [68-Nov-30: 2C].
Small, Vinton B. (20 yrs., 8 mos.) d. on 68-Aug-23 [68-Aug-26: 2B].
Small, William (19 yrs.) d. on 69-Dec-11 of Lung congestion [69-Dec-11: 2B].
Small, William m. Hardisty, Alice Eugenia on 67-Apr-25 [67-Apr-27: 2A].
Small, William D. (37 yrs.) d. on 68-Apr-11 [68-Apr-17: 2B].
Smalley, Reuben Henry (2 yrs., 6 mos.) d. on 67-Dec-10 [67-Dec-12: 2B].
Smallwood, Henry (27 yrs.) d. on 69-Jun-1 Crushed by stone [69-Jun-2: 1H].
Smallwood, Henry m. Coleman, Marzan on 67-Aug-27 [67-Sep-21: 2A].
Smallwood, Jane m. Simmons, William on 66-Aug-2 [66-Aug-7: 2C].
Smallwood, John m. Horner, Laura E. on 69-Sep-7 [69-Sep-23: 2B].
Smalzel, Mary E. m. Melchior, Edward on 66-Sep-20 [66-Sep-26: 2B].
Smardon, Charlotte (68 yrs.) d. on 66-Dec-21 [66-Dec-22: 2B].
Smardon, Elias (73 yrs.) d. on 66-Aug-19 [66-Aug-20: 2C].
Smart, Benjamin G. m. Johnson, Maggie M. on 67-Jul-22 [67-Jul-29: 2D].
Smart, Martha W. m. Roxbury, Edward on 68-Nov-3 [68-Nov-7: 2B].
Smart, William T. m. Plummer, Mary E. on 69-Mar-22 [69-Mar-27: 2B].
Smead, James E. (4 yrs., 6 mos.) d. on 69-Feb-13 [69-Feb-17: 2D].
Smick, Georgetta m. Coggins, David A. on 70-Jul-11 [70-Jul-26: 2B].
Smick, Sarah E. m. MacNeal, Charles L. on 67-Nov-27 [67-Nov-28: 2C].
Smith, A. A. m. Dennis, Naomi S. on 67-Jul-30 [67-Jul-1: 2C].
Smith, Abraham, Jr. m. Austin, Julia A. on 69-Oct-21 [69-Oct-23: 2B].
Smith, Ada m. Beall, James A. on 69-Jul-7 [69-Jul-14: 2D].
Smith, Alexander M. (27 yrs.) d. on 69-Sep-18 [69-Sep-20: 2C].
Smith, Alfred m. Wentz, Cecilia on 68-Feb-18 [68-Mar-7: 2B].
Smith, Alfred Archibald (26 yrs.) d. on 69-Oct-29 [69-Nov-20: 2C].
Smith, Alfred Downs (1 yr., 6 mos.) d. on 66-Sep-30 [66-Oct-18: 2B].
Smith, Alfred Lee m. Schepler, Louisa on 69-Oct-28 [69-Nov-16: 2C].
Smith, Alice J. m. Brawner, Robert G. on 68-May-26 [68-May-28: 2B].
Smith, Alice M. (25 yrs.) d. on 70-Jun-10 [70-Jun-11: 2B].
Smith, Amzi m. Van Patten, Hannah M. on 69-Dec-21 [69-Dec-23: 2B].
Smith, Anastasia m. White, Peter L. on 67-Aug-5 [67-Aug-7: 2C].
Smith, Andrew (75 yrs.) d. on 66-Mar-1 [66-Mar-2: 1G, 2B].
Smith, Andrew A. m. Blondell, Elizabeth on 68-Nov-16 [68-Nov-18: 2C].
Smith, Andrew M. (61 yrs.) d. on 68-Nov-7 [68-Dec-30: 2D].
Smith, Ann Rebecca m. Stallings, John W. on 68-Feb-3 [68-Feb-5: 2D].
Smith, Ann Teackle (2 yrs., 8 mos.) d. on 69-Oct-9 [69-Oct-11: 2C].
Smith, Anna C. m. Beck, William on 66-Aug-14 [66-Aug-16: 2C].
Smith, Anna J. C. m. Welsh, Warner M. on 70-Dec-22 [70-Dec-23: 2B].
Smith, Anna M. m. Taylor, Thomas O. on 68-Dec-17 [68-Dec-18: 2C].
Smith, Anna M. m. White, William G. on 66-Oct-17 [66-Oct-25: 2C; 66-Oct-26: 2B].
Smith, Anna Margaret (7 yrs., 2 mos.) d. on 67-Jan-5 [67-Jan-7: 2C].
Smith, Anna Maria d. on 67-Sep-28 Burned [67-Oct-1: 1F].
Smith, Anne E. (2 yrs., 7 mos.) d. on 68-Jul-15 [68-Jul-17: 2C].
Smith, Annie Eliza m. Meushaw, Franklin on 70-Feb-23 [70-Feb-25: 2C].

Smith, Annie R. m. Wilkinson, W. H. B. on 66-Dec-18 [66-Dec-28: 2C].
Smith, Annie R. m. Gracey, William A. on 70-May-22 [70-Oct-17: 2B].
Smith, Arthur W. (36 yrs.) d. on 66-Apr-22 [66-May-5: 2B].
Smith, Asa (83 yrs.) d. on 69-Nov-11 [69-Nov-15: 2C].
Smith, Asa H. m. Beall, Laura E. on 69-Dec-23 [69-Dec-30: 2C; 69-Dec-31: 2C].
Smith, Augusta J. m. Duvall, Vinton W. on 68-Oct-13 [68-Oct-15: 2C].
Smith, Augustus Webster d. on 68-Jul-2 [68-Jul-4: 2C].
Smith, Bell Howard (4 mos.) d. on 69-Mar-17 [69-Mar-20: 2B].
Smith, Bergeda m. Heims, F. on 69-Jan-11 [69-Jan-13: 2D].
Smith, Bernard (29 yrs.) d. on 67-May-15 in Railroad accident [67-May-16: 1G].
Smith, Bridget (51 yrs.) d. on 66-Jul-15 [66-Jul-16: 2C].
Smith, Caroline (90 yrs.) d. on 66-Dec-30 [66-Dec-31: 2C].
Smith, Caroline (14 yrs.) d. on 70-Oct-19 [70-Oct-31: 2C].
Smith, Caroline H. (41 yrs., 11 mos.) d. on 69-Mar-10 [69-Mar-11: 2C; 69-Mar-12: 2C].
Smith, Carrie L. m. Coleman, George A. on 67-Nov-5 [67-Nov-12: 2C].
Smith, Carrie W. (10 mos.) d. on 67-Aug-12 [67-Aug-13: 2B; 67-Aug-14: 2C].
Smith, Catherine (72 yrs.) d. on 69-Jul-15 [69-Jul-16: 2C].
Smith, Catherine m. Oates, Charles T. on 70-May-18 [70-May-21: 2B].
Smith, Catherine Grace (2 yrs., 3 mos.) d. on 67-May-20 [67-May-22: 2B].
Smith, Catherine M. (81 yrs.) d. on 70-Sep-23 [70-Sep-24: 2B].
Smith, Charity d. on 69-Nov-14 [69-Nov-16: 2C].
Smith, Charles (51 yrs.) d. on 68-Dec-6 of Consumption [68-Dec-7: 2D].
Smith, Charles d. on 67-Apr-21 [67-Apr-23: 2B].
Smith, Charles d. on 69-May-20 Drowned [69-May-26: 1H].
Smith, Charles m. Batchelor, Eleanora on 66-Oct-24 [66-Oct-30: 2B].
Smith, Charles E. m. Menslage, Kate on 66-Jul-12 [66-Jul-19: 2C].
Smith, Charles F. m. Ryan, Elenora on 67-Dec-17 [67-Dec-30: 2C].
Smith, Charles Fisher m. Fitzgerald, Mary Margaret on 67-Dec-10 [67-Dec-13: 2C].
Smith, Charles T., Jr. (6 yrs., 2 mos.) d. on 68-Dec-4 [68-Dec-5: 2C].
Smith, Clara Isabel (1 yr.) d. on 68-Sep-11 [68-Sep-12: 2B].
Smith, Cornelia Rowland m. McCoy, Edwin F. on 70-Oct-12 [70-Oct-20: 2B].
Smith, Cyrus A. m. Doged, Almira G. on 70-Mar-24 [70-Mar-29: 2B].
Smith, D. L. m. Brannan, Kate on 70-Jul-25 [70-Sep-12: 2B].
Smith, David (4 mos.) d. on 67-Feb-9 [67-Feb-12: 2C].
Smith, Delia H. m. Smith, Oliver T. on 68-Oct-29 [68-Oct-31: 2B].
Smith, Dennis (1 yr., 1 mo.) d. on 68-Nov-23 [68-Nov-24: 2C].
Smith, Dora d. on 66-Aug-30 of Measles [66-Aug-31: 2B].
Smith, E. Kate m. Rogers, Philip on 66-Apr-11 [66-Apr-16: 2B].
Smith, E. Mary m. Seitz, Henry on 66-Jun-28 [66-Jun-30: 2B].
Smith, E. T. m. Rigby, Annie J. on 68-Dec-2 [68-Dec-5: 2C].
Smith, Eb m. Gardner, Araminta J. on 70-Oct-3 [70-Oct-12: 2B].
Smith, Ebeneezer d. on 66-Oct-15 of Cholera [66-Oct-16: 1F].
Smith, Edmund Morton m. Roloson, Lucy Rosella on 66-Dec-12 [66-Dec-17: 2B].
Smith, Edward G. m. Ullrich, Mary E. on 66-Oct-31 [66-Nov-1: 2B].
Smith, Edward Worrell, Capt. (38 yrs.) d. on 68-Sep-19 [68-Oct-26: 2B].
Smith, Elenor (78 yrs.) d. on 66-Feb-1 [66-Feb-2: 2C].
Smith, Eli B. m. Mumma, Mary Ann on 67-May-21 [67-May-24: 2B].
Smith, Elihu (9 mos.) d. on 69-Jul-16 [69-Jul-17: 2C].
Smith, Eliza (78 yrs.) d. on 69-Jun-3 [69-Jun-4: 2C].
Smith, Eliza A. (50 yrs.) d. on 66-Jan-10 [66-Jan-13: 2C].
Smith, Eliza G. (69 yrs.) d. on 68-Sep-30 [68-Oct-1: 2B].
Smith, Eliza J. (53 yrs.) d. on 68-Sep-6 [68-Sep-11: 2B].
Smith, Eliza Louisa D. (9 mos.) d. on 70-Jul-12 [70-Jul-15: 2C].
Smith, Elizabeth (34 yrs.) d. on 68-Mar-1 [68-Mar-3: 2C].
Smith, Elizabeth (52 yrs.) d. on 68-Dec-15 [68-Dec-30: 2D].

Smith, Elizabeth (80 yrs.) d. on 68-Mar-10 [68-Mar-11: 2B].
Smith, Elizabeth (67 yrs.) d. on 66-Oct-12 [66-Oct-16: 2C].
Smith, Elizabeth (88 yrs.) d. on 66-Jul-26 [66-Jul-27: 2C].
Smith, Elizabeth m. Zahnmesser, Sebastian on 65-Oct-29 [66-Jan-2: 2C].
Smith, Elizabeth J. (18 yrs.) d. on 69-Mar-4 [69-Mar-6: 2C].
Smith, Emil m. Wolff, Johanna M. on 69-Sep-2 [69-Sep-4: 2B].
Smith, Emil J. (3 yrs., 10 mos.) d. on 70-Oct-30 [70-Nov-1: 2C].
Smith, Emily m. Rexs, Charles on 67-Sep-24 [67-Sep-26: 2B].
Smith, Emily S. d. on 68-Sep-18 [68-Sep-19: 2B].
Smith, Emily Virginia Ann d. on 69-Jun-28 [69-Jul-2: 2C].
Smith, Emma E. (32 yrs.) d. on 67-Jul-2 [67-Jul-3: 2B].
Smith, Emmeline m. Glassgow, John L. on 67-Feb-11 [67-Feb-13: 2D].
Smith, Eugene R. m. Kraft, Sophie S. on 68-Feb-4 [68-Feb-11: 2C; 68-Feb-12: 2B].
Smith, Evaline B. (18 yrs.) d. on 67-Jan-3 [67-Jan-5: 2C].
Smith, Fannie C. d. on 70-Jul-27 [70-Jul-28: 2C; 70-Jul-30: 2C].
Smith, Frances A. m. Warner, Jonathan on 68-Aug-18 [68-Aug-27: 2B; 68-Aug-28: 2B].
Smith, Frederick d. on 66-Oct-5 Burned [66-Oct-6: 1F].
Smith, Frederick m. Waddell, Louisa A. on 70-May-31 [70-Jun-9: 2C].
Smith, Frederick Duvall (1 yr., 10 mos.) d. on 69-Oct-25 [69-Nov-11: 2C].
Smith, G. A. m. Carter, Thomas H. on 67-Jul-18 [67-Jul-20: 2C].
Smith, G. Cookman m. Burrows, Bettie L. on 66-Oct-23 [66-Oct-26: 2B].
Smith, George (31 yrs.) d. on 66-Sep-26 [66-Sep-27: 2C].
Smith, George m. Read, Fannie on 68-Oct-13 [68-Oct-19: 2B].
Smith, George A. (3 yrs., 7 mos.) d. on 70-Dec-13 of Scarlet fever [70-Dec-14: 2C].
Smith, George A. Z. (85 yrs.) d. on 66-Mar-7 [66-Mar-7: 2B; 66-Mar-8: 2B].
Smith, George M. m. Zollicoffer, Sallie on 69-Dec-22 [69-Dec-24: 2C].
Smith, George S. m. Barranger, Isabella M. on 66-May-1 [66-May-24: 2C].
Smith, George Thomas (2 yrs., 10 mos.) d. on 66-Sep-24 [66-Sep-25: 2B].
Smith, George W. d. [70-Aug-30: 2B].
Smith, George W. m. Ijams, Hattie on 66-Nov-22 [66-Dec-31: 2C].
Smith, George W. W. m. Bond, Mary C. on 68-Jan-9 [68-Jan-14: 2C].
Smith, George William (6 mos.) d. on 68-Jul-26 [68-Jul-27: 2B].
Smith, Georgie H. m. Hale, George E. on 69-Feb-3 [69-Feb-25: 2D].
Smith, Gideon B., Dr. (74 yrs.) d. on 67-Mar-24 [67-Mar-25: 2C; 67-Mar-26: 1F, 2C].
Smith, Grace Galena (1 yr., 1 mo.) d. on 68-Aug-25 [68-Aug-27: 2B].
Smith, Griffin (69 yrs.) d. on 67-Nov-28 [67-Nov-30: 2C].
Smith, H. J. m. Parker, Daniel M. on 67-Nov-28 [67-Nov-30: 2C].
Smith, H. M. m. Glenn, M. E. on 66-Jun-28 [66-Aug-3: 2C].
Smith, Hannah Ann (76 yrs.) d. on 70-Mar-17 [70-Mar-18: 2C].
Smith, Harrie Austin (1 yr.) d. on 66-Jun-7 [66-Jun-8: 2B].
Smith, Harriet Emma m. Shorter, William on 66-May-13 [66-May-22: 2B].
Smith, Harriet T. m. Sprigg, James F. on 66-Oct-8 [66-Oct-12: 2B].
Smith, Harry A. d. on 66-Jul-18 [66-Jul-19: 2C].
Smith, Harry Brooks (1 yr., 11 mos.) d. on 70-Aug-1 of Whooping cough [70-Aug-2: 2C; 70-Aug-3: 2C].
Smith, Harry Chapman (5 yrs., 7 mos.) d. on 68-Aug-7 [68-Aug-8: 2C].
Smith, Harry Clay (3 yrs.) d. on 66-Dec-6 of Croup [66-Jan-16: 2C].
Smith, Helen Kate (16 yrs.) d. on 69-Nov-19 [69-Nov-20: 2C].
Smith, Henrietta d. on 67-Aug-2 [67-Aug-8: 2B].
Smith, Henrietta J. m. Clayton, Joseph S. on 69-Dec-23 [69-Dec-30: 2C].
Smith, Henry (23 yrs.) d. on 66-May-16 Drowned [66-May-17: 1G].
Smith, Henry m. Coleman, Lizzie B. on 68-Dec-15 [68-Dec-16: 2C].
Smith, Henry D. (32 yrs., 7 mos.) d. on 66-Jul-13 [66-Jul-14: 2B].
Smith, Henry Peters m. Parlett, Emma Virginia on 67-Sep-19 [67-Sep-23: 2A].
Smith, Henry Price (4 yrs.) d. on 67-Sep-18 [67-Sep-25: 2B].

Smith, Henry Washington (1 yr., 3 mos.) d. on 68-Aug-6 [68-Aug-8: 2C].
Smith, Horace (43 yrs.) d. on 67-Apr-3 [67-Apr-5: 2B; 67-Apr-6: 1G, 2C].
Smith, Horace E. m. Lyles, Nancy G. on 68-Jun-9 [68-Jun-11: 2B].
Smith, Howard (1 yr., 8 mos.) d. on 68-Aug-20 [68-Aug-22: 2A].
Smith, Howard (9 yrs., 6 mos.) d. on 66-Aug-4 [66-Aug-6: 2C].
Smith, Howard Montgomery (5 mos.) d. on 66-Jul-3 [66-Jul-4: 2B].
Smith, Hugh M. (66 yrs., 10 mos.) d. on 69-Mar-9 of Consumption [69-Mar-16: 2C].
Smith, Isabel m. Taylor, William H. on 69-Dec-21 [69-Dec-22: 2B].
Smith, Isabella m. O'Loughlin, Francis J. on 68-May-24 [68-May-29: 2B].
Smith, Isma (62 yrs.) d. on 69-Oct-3 [69-Oct-4: 2C].
Smith, J. Addison m. Freeland, Mary on 70-Feb-17 [70-Feb-19: 2B].
Smith, J. B. d. on 69-Oct-25 [69-Oct-29: 2C].
Smith, J. Hopkinson (40 yrs.) d. on 66-Jan-15 [66-Jan-17: 2C; 66-Jan-18: 2C].
Smith, J. Wesley m. Carson, Nannie on 69-Nov-24 [69-Nov-27: 2B].
Smith, James (82 yrs.) d. on 66-Sep-15 [66-Sep-17: 2B].
Smith, James (35 yrs.) d. on 66-Oct-9 of Hemorrhage [66-Oct-10: 1G].
Smith, James m. Key, Alice on 69-Oct-26 [69-Oct-28: 2C].
Smith, James C. m. Cephas, Elizabeth A. on 67-Apr-25 [67-Apr-27: 2A].
Smith, James C. m. Crawford, Ellie B. on 67-Jun-5 [67-Jun-15: 2B].
Smith, James H. m. Durkins, Mary on 66-Feb-1 [66-Feb-2: 2C].
Smith, James Henry (45 yrs.) d. on 68-Apr-24 [68-Apr-25: 2B].
Smith, James P. (54 yrs.) d. on 69-Jun-4 [69-Jun-8: 2B].
Smith, James R. (28 yrs.) d. on 69-Oct-27 [69-Oct-28: 2C].
Smith, James R. m. Ramsey, Nellie on 69-Sep-22 [69-Sep-25: 2B].
Smith, James W. m. Bender, Mary Agnes on 68-Jun-25 [68-Jun-26: 2B].
Smith, Jamima (55 yrs.) d. on 70-Aug-20 [70-Aug-22: 2C].
Smith, Jane d. on 67-Nov-3 [67-Nov-4: 2B].
Smith, Jane (77 yrs.) d. on 70-Sep-25 [70-Sep-26: 2B; 70-Sep-27: 2B].
Smith, Jane (72 yrs.) d. on 70-Aug-3 [70-Aug-4: 2C].
Smith, Jennie (8 yrs.) d. on 70-Nov-12 [70-Nov-14: 2B].
Smith, Jennie m. Sprague, George H. on 69-Jan-10 [69-Jan-28: 2C].
Smith, Jennie W. m. Ott, Otto on 69-Dec-13 [69-Dec-18: 2B].
Smith, Jerome M. m. Graner, Margaret C. on 70-Jan-18 [70-Jan-22: 2B].
Smith, Jesse m. Gregg, Celina C. on 65-Dec-12 [66-Jan-11: 2B].
Smith, Jessie d. on 70-Jul-16 [70-Jul-18: 2B].
Smith, Johannah L. m. Swope, Charles C. on 70-Jun-23 [70-Jun-30: 2C].
Smith, John (67 yrs.) d. on 68-Jan-31 [68-Feb-1: 2C; 68-Feb-3: 2C].
Smith, John d. on 68-Jan-6 of Consumption [68-Jan-7: 1F].
Smith, John (66 yrs.) d. on 66-Nov-21 [66-Nov-23: 2C].
Smith, John (37 yrs.) d. on 66-Jul-16 of Heatstroke [66-Jul-17: 1F].
Smith, John m. Hopps, Annie R. on 65-Sep-21 [66-Mar-5: 2B].
Smith, John m. Griffin, Dorothea on 65-Dec-26 [66-Jan-1: 2C].
Smith, John m. Smith, Marcelina on 69-Sep-19 [69-Sep-21: 2B].
Smith, John A. (44 yrs.) d. on 69-Apr-9 [69-Apr-12: 2A].
Smith, John C. (58 yrs.) d. on 68-Dec-10 of Pneumonia [68-Dec-11: 1G, 2C; 68-Dec-14: 1H, 2C].
Smith, John C. (45 yrs., 10 mos.) d. on 67-May-2 of Consumption [67-May-3: 2B].
Smith, John F. m. Whorton, Amanda M. on 66-Feb-19 [66-Feb-24: 2B].
Smith, John I. (4 mos.) d. on 68-Mar-2 [68-Mar-3: 2C].
Smith, John Lee (11 mos.) d. on 67-Dec-28 of Chronic croup [67-Dec-30: 2C].
Smith, John P. (60 yrs.) d. on 69-Dec-29 [69-Dec-30: 2C; 69-Dec-31: 2C].
Smith, John S. m. Thomas, Mary S. on 69-Sep-2 [69-Nov-9: 2C].
Smith, John Spear, Gen. (80 yrs.) d. on 66-Nov-17 [66-Nov-22: 2C; 66-Nov-23: 1G].
Smith, John Thomas (7 mos.) d. on 70-Jun-18 [70-Jun-20: 2B].
Smith, John Wesley (33 yrs.) d. on 67-Nov-13 [67-Nov-27: 2C].

Smith, Joseph (50 yrs.) d. on 70-Sep-9 of Consumption [70-Sep-10: 4D].
Smith, Joseph A. m. DeMass, Fannie A. on 68-May-28 [68-May-29: 2B].
Smith, Joseph F. m. Green, Ella P. on 69-Sep-29 [69-Oct-2: 2B].
Smith, Joseph Grant (2 yrs., 5 mos.) d. on 66-Aug-6 [66-Aug-7: 2C].
Smith, Joseph L. (33 yrs., 7 mos.) d. on 66-Feb-27 [66-Mar-3: 2B].
Smith, Joseph L. (26 yrs.) d. on 70-Jun-7 [70-Jun-8: 2C].
Smith, Joseph M. m. Burrier, Sophia on 67-Nov-24 [67-Dec-3: 2C].
Smith, Joseph Merriken m. Brooks, Sarah A. on 67-Oct-17 [67-Oct-19: 2A].
Smith, Joseph Sim, Maj. (29 yrs.) d. on 67-Sep-8 of Yellow fever [67-Sep-25: 2B].
Smith, Josephus (29 yrs.) d. on 67-Feb-2 [67-Feb-13: 2D].
Smith, Joshua (66 yrs.) d. on 68-Jun-24 Drowned [68-Jun-27: 1G; 68-Aug-1: 2B].
Smith, Judson H. m. Michael, Lizzie on 70-Aug-17 [70-Aug-18: 2B; 70-Aug-31: 2B].
Smith, Julia (60 yrs.) d. on 67-Apr-22 [67-Apr-23: 2B].
Smith, Julia (24 yrs.) d. on 67-Jul-15 [67-Jul-16: 2C].
Smith, Kate d. on 69-May-21 [69-May-22: 2B].
Smith, Kate m. Coleman, Lewis W. on 69-Jan-29 [69-Feb-1: 2C].
Smith, Kate Ann d. on 68-Aug-24 [68-Aug-28: 2B].
Smith, Kate C. m. Meeker, C. Irvin on 66-Dec-6 [66-Dec-8: 2B].
Smith, Kate V. m. Eckloff, Joseph E. on 68-Sep-8 [68-Sep-14: 2B].
Smith, L. Addie m. Hessey, D. Stewart on 68-Jan-22 [68-Jan-23: 2C].
Smith, Laura A. m. Stone, Benjamin F. on 67-Oct-29 [67-Nov-4: 2B].
Smith, Laura A. m. Ripple, Lewis on 66-Jan-4 [66-Jan-5: 2C].
Smith, Laura V. m. Ferrell, Thomas on 67-May-4 [67-May-8: 2B].
Smith, Lavinia E. m. Graves, C. Lynn on 68-Jun-11 [68-Jun-12: 2B].
Smith, Lawrence B. (2 yrs., 6 mos.) d. on 68-Aug-27 [68-Aug-28: 2B].
Smith, Letitia (10 mos.) d. on 68-Jul-29 [68-Aug-1: 2B].
Smith, Lillie Ann (8 yrs., 4 mos.) d. on 67-Nov-12 [67-Nov-13: 2C].
Smith, Lilly (33 yrs.) d. on 67-Nov-26 [67-Nov-27: 2C].
Smith, Lizzie Ellen d. on 66-Aug-9 [66-Aug-10: 2C].
Smith, Lizzie L. m. Boyd, R. E. on 67-Sep-10 [67-Sep-17: 2A].
Smith, Louis J. m. Foster, Annie A. on 68-May-26 [68-May-28: 2B].
Smith, Louisa C. m. Stritehoof, Frank on 66-May-31 [66-Jun-23: 2B].
Smith, Louisa T. (70 yrs.) d. on 70-Aug-13 [70-Aug-17: 2C].
Smith, Lucretia C. m. Johnson, Charles W. on 69-Mar-11 [69-Mar-18: 2C; 69-Mar-20: 2B].
Smith, Lydia (66 yrs.) d. on 68-Aug-4 [68-Aug-5: 2B].
Smith, Lynch T. m. Bayne, Phebe A. on 67-Oct-16 [67-Oct-23: 2B].
Smith, Maggie Grace Stevenson d. on 67-Mar-26 [67-Mar-27: 2C].
Smith, Maggie L. (1 yr., 4 mos.) d. on 68-Oct-24 [68-Oct-27: 2B].
Smith, Maggie May (5 mos.) d. on 69-Jun-21 [69-Jun-22: 2C].
Smith, Mahala m. Taylor, Angelo on 66-Jan-18 [66-Jan-23: 2C].
Smith, Mamie F. m. Hood, John on 66-Nov-22 [66-Dec-4: 2D].
Smith, Marcelina m. Smith, John on 69-Sep-19 [69-Sep-21: 2B].
Smith, Margaret (60 yrs.) d. on 67-Oct-1 [67-Oct-3: 2B].
Smith, Margaret (3 yrs., 2 mos.) d. on 65-Dec-31 [66-Jan-1: 2C].
Smith, Margaret Ann (53 yrs.) d. on 68-Apr-27 [68-Apr-29: 2B].
Smith, Margaret E. (4 yrs., 8 mos.) d. on 67-Nov-11 [67-Nov-13: 2C].
Smith, Margaret E. (38 yrs., 6 mos.) d. on 69-Oct-20 [69-Oct-22: 2B].
Smith, Margaret S. (43 yrs.) d. on 69-Mar-27 [69-Mar-29: 2B].
Smith, Marian R. m. Strong, Richard P. on 68-Feb-6 [68-Feb-14: 2C].
Smith, Martha A. m. Coursey, Charles M. on 67-Jan-22 [67-Jan-28: 2C].
Smith, Martha J. m. Townshend, James H. on 69-Jun-29 [69-Jul-1: 2C].
Smith, Martha Jane (25 yrs.) d. on 69-Feb-1 [69-Feb-3: 2C].
Smith, Mary (68 yrs.) d. on 68-Dec-31 [69-Jan-5: 2C].
Smith, Mary (81 yrs.) d. on 66-Feb-23 [66-Feb-27: 2B].
Smith, Mary A. m. Gross, Benjamin on 67-Jan-31 [67-Feb-2: 2C].

Smith, Mary A. m. Lawless, R. J. on 69-Oct-12 [69-Oct-23: 2B].
Smith, Mary Ann (69 yrs.) d. on 69-May-1 [69-May-4: 2B].
Smith, Mary C. m. Duvall, Benjamin F. on 68-May-14 [68-Oct-20: 2B].
Smith, Mary E. d. on 69-Oct-5 [69-Oct-7: 2B].
Smith, Mary E. m. Bishop, Reverdy on 68-Jun-25 [68-Jun-27: 2B].
Smith, Mary E. m. Armiger, Joseph H. on 65-Feb-5 [66-Jun-8: 2B].
Smith, Mary E. m. Rhodes, F. W. on 69-Nov-21 [69-Nov-27: 2B].
Smith, Mary E. m. Hillman, Stanislaus A. on 69-Feb-28 [69-May-17: 2B].
Smith, Mary Elizabeth (2 yrs., 4 mos.) d. on 70-Mar-21 [70-Mar-23: 2C].
Smith, Mary Emma (6 mos.) d. on 69-Jan-28 [69-Jan-29: 2C].
Smith, Mary J. m. Ewalt, George on 70-Jun-30 [70-Jul-7: 2B].
Smith, Mary Jane (30 yrs.) d. on 66-Jan-23 of Consumption [66-Jan-24: 2B].
Smith, Mary L. (25 yrs.) d. on 68-Feb-24 [68-Mar-6: 2C].
Smith, Mary M. d. on 67-Dec-3 of Consumption [67-Dec-5: 2C].
Smith, Mary V. d. on 67-May-4 [67-May-10: 2B].
Smith, Mary V. m. Robey, William H. on 69-Jul-5 [69-Jul-9: 2C].
Smith, Mary Virginia (7 yrs., 4 mos.) d. on 66-Mar-1 of Brain fever [66-Mar-2: 2B].
Smith, Mary Virginia d. on 69-Mar-21 [69-Mar-22: 2C; 69-Mar-23: 2C].
Smith, Mary W. E. d. on 67-Jul-20 [67-Jul-22: 2C].
Smith, Matthias (85 yrs.) d. on 66-Feb-28 [66-Mar-1: 2B].
Smith, Michael d. on 68-Jul-16 of Heatstroke [68-Jul-17: 1D].
Smith, Milton E. m. Griffith, Josephine on 67-Feb-19 [67-Mar-2: 2B].
Smith, Minty m. Guy, Charles H. on 66-Mar-29 [66-Mar-31: 2C].
Smith, Mollie m. Peake, William on 68-Aug-25 [68-Aug-28: 2B].
Smith, Mollie A. m. Warner, J. Philip on 66-Jan-17 [66-Feb-16: 2B].
Smith, Mollie E. (24 yrs.) d. on 66-Mar-29 [66-Mar-30: 2C; 66-Mar-31: 2C].
Smith, Mordecai K. m. Thomas, Eleanor on 68-Apr-15 [68-Apr-17: 2B].
Smith, Moses (104 yrs.) d. on 67-Jul-5 [67-Jul-13: 2B].
Smith, Nancy (83 yrs.) d. on 70-May-28 [70-May-30: 2B].
Smith, Nicholas m. Hyde, Charlotte on 66-Dec-24 [66-Dec-27: 2C].
Smith, Oliver T. m. Smith, Delia H. on 68-Oct-29 [68-Oct-31: 2B].
Smith, Owen K. m. Walker, Laura V. on 67-Oct-16 [67-Oct-17: 2B].
Smith, Patrick (78 yrs.) d. on 70-Aug-16 [70-Aug-17: 2C].
Smith, Patsy (110 yrs.) d. on 66-Mar-28 [66-Mar-31: 1G].
Smith, Philip m. Galloway, Mary on 68-Oct-11 [69-Apr-7: 2C].
Smith, Philip H. m. Wells, Hallie A. on 70-Jun-16 [70-Jun-21: 2C].
Smith, Priscilla m. Bayley, Frederick A. on 70-Sep-1 [70-Sep-10: 2B].
Smith, Rachel m. Howard, William on 66-Jun-7 [66-Jun-21: 2B].
Smith, Rana m. Muse, Lawrence W. on 69-Feb-26 [69-Mar-3: 2B].
Smith, Rebecca (91 yrs.) d. on 68-Mar-11 [68-Mar-12: 2B; 68-Mar-13: 2C].
Smith, Rebecca (78 yrs.) d. on 66-Apr-11 [66-Apr-12: 2B; 66-Apr-13: 2C].
Smith, Richard m. Temes, Harriet A. on 67-Sep-16 [67-Sep-17: 2A].
Smith, Robert (74 yrs.) d. on 68-Mar-25 [68-Mar-27: 2B].
Smith, Robert m. Murry, Annie on 69-Apr-18 [69-May-21: 2C].
Smith, Robert Emmett (6 mos.) d. on 70-Jun-22 [70-Jun-23: 2C].
Smith, Robert H. m. Barnes, S. Annie on 70-Sep-8 [70-Sep-10: 2B].
Smith, Robert Z. m. McCarty, Annie on 69-Jul-6 [69-Dec-29: 2D].
Smith, Rose Philemena (21 yrs.) d. on 66-Apr-23 [66-Apr-24: 2B].
Smith, S. B. m. Moore, Maggie E. on 66-Jan-31 [66-Mar-14: 2B].
Smith, S. Emma m. Belt, Samuel J. on 70-Jan-25 [70-Jan-28: 2B].
Smith, Sallie R. m. Tyson, Robert on 69-Nov-25 [69-Nov-29: 2C].
Smith, Samuel (58 yrs.) d. on 68-Oct-17 of Paralysis [68-Oct-19: 2B].
Smith, Samuel D. m. Griffith, Laura on 66-Apr-24 [66-Apr-27: 2C].
Smith, Samuel E. (1 yr., 11 mos.) d. on 68-Apr-26 [68-Apr-27: 2B].
Smith, Samuel H. (56 yrs.) d. on 70-Jul-18 [70-Jul-19: 2C].

Smith, Samuel R. m. Cannon, Maretta on 68-Nov-10 [68-Nov-14: 2B].
Smith, Sarah A. m. Vogt, John G. on 66-Feb-27 [66-Mar-8: 2B; 66-Mar-9: 2B].
Smith, Sarah Adams (17 yrs.) d. on 66-Sep-3 [66-Sep-4: 2B].
Smith, Sarah E. (6 yrs., 8 mos.) d. on 67-Oct-17 [67-Oct-19: 2B].
Smith, Sarah E. m. Meekins, Samuel on 66-Jun-14 [66-Jun-18: 2B].
Smith, Sarah F. m. McFaddin, Francis on 68-Jan-20 [68-Feb-5: 2D].
Smith, Sarah F. m. Trexler, Charles T. on 70-May-26 [70-Jun-7: 2C].
Smith, Sarah J. m. Neill, Thomas B. on 68-Apr-9 [68-Apr-11: 2A].
Smith, Sarah Joan d. on 69-Mar-25 [69-Apr-15: 2B].
Smith, Sarah R. Goodwin (13 yrs., 11 mos.) d. on 67-Sep-28 [67-Oct-1: 2B].
Smith, Sidney (35 yrs.) d. on 69-Oct-20 [69-Oct-27: 2B].
Smith, Stephen (38 yrs.) d. on 68-Nov-24 [68-Nov-28: 2C].
Smith, Susan Jane m. Galloway, Charles B. on 68-Feb-4 [68-Feb-10: 2C].
Smith, Susanna (27 yrs.) d. on 70-Feb-24 [70-Feb-25: 2C; 70-Feb-26: 2C].
Smith, Susannah d. on 67-May-2 [67-May-4: 2B; 67-May-9: 2A].
Smith, Thomas (86 yrs.) d. on 68-Aug-13 [68-Aug-15: 2B].
Smith, Thomas, Mrs. (42 yrs.) d. on 69-Feb-9 [69-Feb-16: 2C].
Smith, Thomas F., Rev. d. [67-Dec-7: 2B].
Smith, Thomas Irving d. on 69-Mar-5 [69-Mar-8: 2C].
Smith, Victorine D. m. White, George W. on 69-Jul-25 [70-Mar-14: 2C].
Smith, Virginia (28 yrs.) d. on 67-Nov-13 [67-Nov-14: 2C; 67-Nov-15: 2B; 67-Dec-6: 2C].
Smith, Walter D. m. Mead, Sarah E. on 70-Aug-18 [70-Aug-20: 2B].
Smith, Walter G. m. Meakin, Mary A. on 67-Oct-3 [67-Oct-9: 2B].
Smith, Walter W. m. Knipp, Mary on 68-Nov-12 [68-Nov-17: 2C].
Smith, Wesley m. Masson, Susannah F. on 69-May-5 [69-May-11: 2B].
Smith, William d. on 68-Sep-7 Drowned [68-Sep-8: 1G].
Smith, William (54 yrs.) d. on 68-Apr-5 [68-Apr-7: 2B].
Smith, William (80 yrs., 3 mos.) d. on 67-Nov-7 [67-Nov-14: 2C].
Smith, William (63 yrs.) d. on 67-Jul-3 of Heart disease [67-Jul-9: 2B].
Smith, William d. on 66-Feb-17 of Heart disease [66-Feb-19: 1G].
Smith, William (41 yrs.) d. on 69-Mar-1 [69-Mar-4: 2C].
Smith, William (77 yrs.) d. on 70-Nov-22 [70-Nov-24: 2C].
Smith, William m. Wooden, Elizabeth on 68-Mar-18 [68-Apr-7: 2B].
Smith, William B. (43 yrs.) d. on 67-Oct-15 [67-Oct-17: 2B].
Smith, William B. m. Roach, Kate on 69-Apr-29 [69-May-25: 2C].
Smith, William F m. Clark, Ada E. on 70-Feb-17 [70-Feb-24: 2C].
Smith, William H. d. on 68-Nov-21 [68-Nov-23: 2B].
Smith, William H. m. Woodland, Mariah C. on 69-Sep-21 [69-Sep-24: 2B].
Smith, William H. m. Crew, Victoria C. on 69-Aug-3 [69-Aug-5: 2B].
Smith, William Henry (30 yrs.) d. on 70-Jan-22 [70-Jan-24: 2C].
Smith, William J.Jr m. Springer, Anna C. on 70-Jun-30 [70-Jul-7: 2B].
Smith, William S. m. Young, Alexena C. on 67-Nov-19 [67-Dec-5: 2C].
Smith, William S. m. Mullen, Sarah V. on 69-Jun-28 [69-Jul-13: 2C].
Smith, Willie (4 yrs.) d. on 70-Nov-2 in Wagon accident [70-Nov-3: 4C].
Smith, Willie (5 yrs., 9 mos.) d. on 70-Dec-1 [70-Dec-2: 2C].
Smith, Willie Ahl (1 yr.) d. on 70-Oct-19 [70-Oct-20: 2B].
Smithson, Laura A. m. Williams, George W. on 68-Nov-11 [68-Nov-28: 2C].
Smithson, William H. m. Galloway, Mary A. on 68-Oct-4 [68-Oct-6: 2B].
Smood, Elenore m. Ault, William H. on 69-Oct-7 [69-Nov-2: 2B].
Smoot, Albert m. Mabbott, Carrie S. on 66-Mar-22 [66-Mar-26: 2B].
Smoot, Edith E. m. Middleton, Charles K. on 69-Sep-1 [69-Sep-6: 2C].
Smoot, Ella d. on 70-Jul-3 [70-Jul-6: 2C].
Smoot, Mary F. m. Bell, William E. C. on 69-May-13 [69-May-18: 2C].
Smoot, Richard m. Witten, Elea W. on 66-Oct-4 [66-Oct-16: 2B].
Smoot, Sarah E. (44 yrs.) d. on 69-May-21 [69-May-22: 2B].

Smoot, William H. (25 yrs.) d. on 69-Dec-8 of Consumption [69-Dec-10: 2C].
Smothers, Anthony d. on 68-Sep-15 Drowned [68-Sep-16: 1G].
Smothers, Jesse d. on 66-Oct-2 [66-Oct-3: 2B].
Smull, William G., Dr. d. on 69-Nov-23 of Typhoid [69-Nov-26: 2C].
Smyder, William m. Ferrandini, Josephine A. on 70-Jun-30 [70-Jul-12: 2B].
Smyser, Henry C. m. Jenkins, J. Rebecca on 67-Sep-5 [67-Sep-11: 2B].
Smyser, Kate (34 yrs.) d. on 69-Feb-16 [69-Feb-17: 2D].
Smyser, Sallie C. m. Onion, John R. on 66-Dec-27 [66-Dec-28: 2C].
Smyth, William m. Higgins, Mary J. on 69-Jan-28 [69-Feb-4: 2C].
Snack, Sarah (47 yrs.) d. on 69-May-7 of Consumption [69-May-8: 2B].
Snack, William Edward (16 yrs.) d. [66-Nov-2: 2B].
Snavely, Elizabeth (77 yrs.) d. on 70-Jul-5 [70-Jul-6: 2C].
Snavely, Elizabeth Ann (30 yrs.) d. on 67-Jan-14 [67-Jan-15: 2C].
Snavely, Emma Virginia (15 yrs.) d. on 66-Mar-14 [66-Mar-15: 2C].
Snavely, Joseph F. m. Williams, Maria on 68-Nov-12 [68-Nov-14: 2B].
Snavely, Mary Elizabeth (39 yrs.) d. on 67-Oct-15 [67-Oct-16: 2B].
Snead, A. B. m. Sloan, Rosalie on 68-Nov-10 [68-Dec-10: 2D].
Snead, Charles W. m. Snead, Sue U. on 67-Dec-19 [67-Dec-24: 2B].
Snead, Sarah A. S. (45 yrs.) d. on 69-Jan-13 [69-Jan-14: 2D; 69-Jan-15: 2D].
Snead, Sue U. m. Snead, Charles W. on 67-Dec-19 [67-Dec-19: 2B].
Sneath, Charlie Spicer (5 yrs.) d. on 68-May-26 [68-May-28: 2B].
Sneed, John M. m. Cooper, Rebecca C. on 67-Jun-5 [67-Jun-15: 2B].
Sneeringer, William J. m. Uniack, Mary on 68-Jun-1 [68-Jun-3: 2B].
Snell, Charles d. on 70-Apr-27 of Epilepsy [70-Apr-28: 1G].
Snell, J. Marvin m. Edwards, Louisa E. on 68-Jun-16 [68-Jun-23: 2B].
Snell, Lorestin m. Wells, Clara S. on 69-Oct-6 [69-Oct-12: 2C].
Snell, Munroe m. Stirrat, Nettie M. on 70-Jan-13 [70-Jan-17: 2C].
Snethen, Worthington N. m. Page, Addie S. on 67-Jul-17 [67-Aug-1: 2C].
Snookes, George m. Hayes, Achasiah on 69-Oct-25 [69-Oct-27: 2B].
Snow, Annie W. (44 yrs.) d. on 68-May-18 [68-May-22: 2C].
Snow, William B. m. Loane, Mollie D. M. on 66-Dec-20 [66-Dec-22: 2A].
Snowden, Achsah Frick d. on 69-May-31 [69-Apr-2: 2C].
Snowden, Arthur, Dr. d. on 69-Jul-28 Drowned [69-Aug-4: 1G; 69-Aug-5: 2C; 69-Aug-19: 1H].
Snowden, Ella D. m. Moor, Lister D. on 67-Feb-7 [67-Feb-15: 2C].
Snowden, Gustavus W. (9 yrs.) d. on 70-May-23 [70-May-31: 2B].
Snowden, Henry, Col. (81 yrs.) d. on 68-Dec-4 [68-Dec-16: 2C].
Snowden, J. C. m. Griffith, Maria J. on 67-Oct-24 [67-Oct-28: 2B].
Snowden, Lawrence (2 mos.) d. on 67-Oct-25 [67-Nov-5: 2B].
Snowden, Maria L. m. Mayer, Alfred on 69-Jun-30 [69-Jul-9: 2C].
Snowden, Mary E. d. on 69-Mar-31 [69-Apr-1: 2C].
Snowden, Rezin H. (70 yrs.) d. on 66-Jul-23 [66-Jul-24: 2C].
Snowden, William (4 mos.) d. on 66-Aug-3 [66-Aug-4: 2C].
Snyder, Aleana (37 yrs.) d. on 67-Nov-4 [67-Nov-5: 2B].
Snyder, Ann E. (28 yrs.) d. on 70-Nov-22 [70-Nov-23: 2C].
Snyder, Annie M. m. Maxwell, Issac P. on 69-Mar-18 [69-Mar-19: 2C].
Snyder, Augustus m. Freibey, Labella on 69-Apr-5 [69-Apr-6: 2C].
Snyder, Azariah H. m. Williams, Mary A. on 70-Feb-8 [70-Feb-12: 2C].
Snyder, Belinda A. m. Hawn, William H. H. on 66-Aug-14 [66-Aug-17: 2C].
Snyder, Benjamin B., Jr. m. Ballard, Mary A. on 66-Nov-15 [66-Nov-21: 2C].
Snyder, Catherine L. d. on 67-Mar-3 [67-Mar-5: 2C].
Snyder, Charles M. m. Herold, Mary M. on 69-Apr-20 [69-Apr-26: 2B].
Snyder, Daniel m. Slater, Mary J. on 68-Apr-9 [68-Apr-11: 2A].
Snyder, Elenor F. m. Josenhans, Charles H. on 69-Oct-19 [69-Oct-26: 2B].
Snyder, Eliza Jane (5 yrs.) d. on 70-Dec-24 [70-Dec-26: 2C].
Snyder, Elizabeth (24 yrs., 10 mos.) d. on 66-Oct-13 of Scarlet fever [66-Oct-18: 2B].

Snyder, Ella m. McCleary, John W. on 69-Feb-11 [69-Feb-13: 2C].
Snyder, Emma C. (9 yrs., 2 mos.) d. on 66-Oct-5 of Scarlet fever [66-Oct-8: 2B; 66-Oct-18: 2B].
Snyder, George Cookman (25 yrs.) d. on 68-Dec-19 [68-Dec-21: 2C].
Snyder, Harry S. m. Reilly, Julia A. on 68-Jan-21 [69-Aug-17: 2C].
Snyder, Henry m. Amos, Anna A. on 68-Dec-1 [68-Dec-18: 2C].
Snyder, Henry Lee m. Miller, Ella on 70-Dec-22 [70-Dec-28: 2C].
Snyder, J. William m. DeFord, Laura Virginia on 68-Jul-7 [68-Jul-11: 2B].
Snyder, John m. Johns, Virginia on 69-Jan-14 [69-Feb-15: 2C].
Snyder, John Henry (41 yrs.) d. on 67-Jul-3 of Yellow fever [67-Oct-31: 2B].
Snyder, Julia d. on 67-Feb-7 [67-Feb-8: 2C].
Snyder, Kate Gertrude (3 yrs., 3 mos.) d. on 69-Oct-8 [69-Oct-14: 2C].
Snyder, Katie R. m. Shepherd, H. S. on 68-Dec-20 [68-Dec-31: 2C].
Snyder, Lillie E. m. Albaugh, William A. on 67-Jan-2 [67-Jan-7: 2C].
Snyder, Louisa C. m. Whitehouse, James on 66-Nov-13 [66-Nov-15: 2C].
Snyder, Louisa E. m. Bregel, Henry on 70-Apr-4 [70-Apr-9: 2B].
Snyder, M. Virtu m. Andrews, Thomas H. on 70-Mar-2 [70-Mar-3: 2C].
Snyder, Maggie E. m. Latchford, Lewis on 69-May-16 [69-May-29: 2B].
Snyder, Maggie F. m. Simmons, Frank G. on 69-Apr-20 [69-Apr-26: 2B].
Snyder, Margaret m. Lowry, Alfred on 68-Apr-3 [68-Apr-7: 2B].
Snyder, Martyn (33 yrs.) d. on 66-Sep-13 Drowned [66-Sep-15: 1F].
Snyder, Mary (26 yrs., 4 mos.) d. on 66-Oct-14 of Scarlet fever [66-Oct-18: 2C].
Snyder, Mary (63 yrs.) d. on 70-May-10 [70-May-11: 2B; 70-May-12: 2B].
Snyder, Mary m. Limberg, William on 67-Oct-24 [67-Nov-1: 2B].
Snyder, Mary Anna m. Singleton, William H. H. on 70-Jun-15 [70-Jun-22: 2C].
Snyder, Mary E. m. Stevenson, George Espy on 69-May-25 [69-May-27: 2C].
Snyder, Mary J. d. on 68-Oct-21 of Brain congestion [68-Oct-22: 2C].
Snyder, Mary Regine m. Kraft, Charles on 67-Oct-8 [67-Oct-14: 2B].
Snyder, Mazie V. m. Sullivan, George R. on 69-May-18 [69-May-19: 2C].
Snyder, Rebecca Catharine m. Dutrow, Jonathan Manro on 66-Apr-19 [66-Apr-23: 2B].
Snyder, Sallie Gertrude d. on 69-Feb-5 [69-Feb-8: 2C].
Snyder, Sophia (23 yrs., 1 mo.) d. on 69-Mar-15 [69-Mar-17: 2C].
Snyder, Susan S. (42 yrs.) d. on 67-Aug-5 [67-Aug-6: 2C].
Snyder, Thomas m. Buschman, Katie on 69-May-25 [69-Jun-1: 2B].
Snyder, Walter Davis d. on 70-Aug-7 [70-Aug-9: 2C].
Snyder, William Henry m. Pyle, Sarah Elizabeth on 67-Feb-28 [67-Mar-6: 2C].
Sohl, Harry Hammond (5 mos.) d. on 70-Oct-3 [70-Oct-4: 2B].
Sohl, Henry S. m. Durham, Martha P. on 67-Mar-21 [67-Apr-2: 2B].
Sohn, Mary E. (18 yrs.) d. on 69-Nov-12 of Hydrophobia [69-Nov-15: 1H].
Solback, Clara (63 yrs., 6 mos.) d. on 67-Mar-31 [67-Apr-2: 2B].
Sollers, Amelia m. Hackett, S. Holland on 67-Dec-12 [67-Dec-23: 2B].
Sollers, Andrew Jackson m. Hynson, Mary W. on 69-Apr-7 [69-Apr-12: 2A].
Sollers, Annie Elizabeth (3 yrs., 11 mos.) d. on 69-Feb-7 of Chronic croup [69-Feb-10: 2C].
Sollers, Maggie A. m. Reed, David on 68-Oct-22 [69-Feb-19: 2C].
Sollers, Mary m. Magruder, Daniel Randall on 67-Dec-12 [67-Dec-23: 2B].
Solomon, Carrie m. Stewart, Septimus H. on 66-Feb-12 [66-Feb-17: 2B].
Solomon, Joseph Stan m. Shreenes, Martha A. W. on 66-Dec-9 [67-Jan-1: 2C].
Solomon, Thomas W. m. Speake, Emma J. on 70-Jan-18 [70-Jan-25: 2C].
Solon, Thomas m. Riley, Margaret Ann on 69-Sep-6 [69-Sep-21: 2B].
Solter, Ella Virginia (2 yrs., 2 mos.) d. on 67-May-28 [67-May-29: 2B].
Solter, George Wasington (2 yrs., 7 mos.) d. on 70-Nov-11 [70-Nov-15: 2C].
Somer, Carrie (1 yr., 2 mos.) d. on 70-Sep-9 [70-Sep-16: 2B].
Somer, Ida (1 yr., 2 mos.) d. on 70-Sep-8 [70-Sep-16: 2B].
Somerlott, Frederick (32 yrs.) d. on 70-Jul-15 [70-Jul-16: 2B; 70-Jul-26: 2C].
Somers, Mary Jane m. Roder, Adolphe on 67-Mar-12 [67-Apr-23: 2B].

Somers, William E. m. King, Mary on 69-Nov-28 [69-Nov-30: 2C].
Somervell, Emma m. Sedwick, W. A. on 66-Nov-15 [66-Nov-17: 2B].
Somervill, Elizabeth (25 yrs.) d. on 69-Sep-19 [69-Sep-21: 2B].
Somerville, Thomas J. m. Livesey, Victoria [70-Nov-12: 2B].
Sommerfeld, Adolph m. Lisner, Cecilia A. on 67-Feb-24 [67-Mar-1: 2C].
Sommerkamp, Charles F. (36 yrs.) d. on 69-Dec-29 [70-Jan-13: 2D; 70-Jan-15: 2C].
Sommerlock, Anna (33 yrs.) d. on 68-Nov-14 [68-Nov-16: 2C].
Sommers, James M. (33 yrs.) d. on 69-Apr-22 Crushed by wall [69-Apr-23: 1G, 2B; 69-Apr-26: 1F].
Sommers, Mary G. (22 yrs.) d. on 66-Sep-14 [66-Sep-15: 2B].
Sonneborn, Hennie m. Hutzler, Charles G. on 70-Jun-14 [70-Jun-16: 2B].
Sonnemon, Robert (40 yrs.) d. on 67-Jan-26 [67-Feb-9: 2B].
Sonnenburg, William Richard (7 mos.) d. on 70-Feb-3 [70-Feb-4: 2C].
Sonnermon, Matilda (49 yrs.) d. on 67-Jan-24 [67-Jan-26: 2C].
Soper, Grace d. on 67-Jan-6 [67-Jan-7: 2C].
Soper, Hester m. Pearson, Andrew C. on 67-May-3 [67-May-7: 2B].
Soran, Eugene Olliver (3 mos.) d. on 67-Nov-27 [67-Nov-28: 2C].
Sorgler, Theodore T. m. Hallisy, E. on 67-Aug-8 [67-Aug-15: 2C].
Sorrel, Francis (78 yrs.) d. on 70-May-5 [70-May-11: 2B].
Sorrell, James H. m. Martin, Sarah Jane on 70-Apr-28 [70-May-3: 2B].
Soter, George F. m. Schnauder, Mary on 70-Feb-27 [70-Mar-2: 2C].
Soubiron, Catharine (82 yrs.) d. on 70-Mar-9 [70-Mar-11: 2C].
Souder, Mary Elizabeth d. on 69-Mar-1 [69-Mar-3: 2C].
Soulter, Margaret (88 yrs.) d. on 68-Nov-10 [68-Nov-12: 2C].
Southall, G. B. m. Cunningham, Fannie on 68-Dec-8 [68-Dec-15: 2C].
Southard, Sallie C. (13 yrs.) d. on 70-Mar-1 [70-Mar-2: 2C].
Southcomb, Joseph m. Nolen, Annie on 67-Sep-27 [67-Sep-27: 2B].
Southern, Issac m. Butler, Ann M. on 68-Oct-26 [68-Oct-30: 2C].
Southers, Mary m. Lennex, Charles T. on 69-Jun-29 [69-Jul-1: 2C].
Sowle, Aggie A. m. Kilpatrick, Robert W. on 69-Sep-29 [69-Oct-12: 2C].
Spackman, Elizabeth (32 yrs.) d. on 67-Jun-18 [67-Oct-7: 2B].
Spafford, Mary O. m. Foos, John S. on 69-Sep-9 [69-Sep-13: 2B].
Spalding, M. Edwina m. Boyer, Edwin on 69-Jul-14 [69-Jul-20: 2C].
Spamer, George W. d. on 66-Sep-5 [66-Sep-6: 2B].
Spamer, George W. m. Gettys, Mary C. on 66-May-2 [66-May-16: 2C].
Spamer, Willard Andrew (11 mos.) d. on 70-Jul-18 [70-Jul-19: 2C].
Spamer, William m. Krumm, Caroline E. on 68-Nov-15 [68-Nov-26: 2B].
Spangler, Alfred Morris (23 yrs.) d. on 69-May-9 [69-May-10: 2C].
Spangler, Lou T. m. Browning, George G. on 69-Jun-6 [69-Aug-31: 2B].
Spangler, Mary M. (20 yrs.) d. on 67-Aug-9 [67-Aug-10: 2B].
Spangler, Williamanna m. Schulenberg, Henry on 67-Sep-10 [67-Sep-17: 2A].
Sparklin, Hester A. (26 yrs.) d. on 67-Apr-16 [67-Apr-17: 2B].
Sparklin, James W. m. Thomas, Alice on 67-Apr-7 [67-Apr-17: 2B].
Sparklin, Mary Rebecca (2 mos.) d. on 68-May-19 [68-May-27: 2B].
Sparklin, William F. m. Wilkins, Frances M. on 69-Apr-1 [69-Apr-13: 2B].
Sparks, Freddie Mason (2 yrs., 11 mos.) d. on 69-Apr-20 [69-Apr-22: 2B].
Sparks, John Howard d. on 70-Nov-25 [70-Dec-5: 2C].
Sparks, Rachel Jane (18 yrs., 4 mos.) d. on 68-Sep-29 [68-Oct-6: 2B].
Sparks, William H. H. m. Kendall, Amanda on 66-Dec-18 [66-Dec-31: 2C].
Sparrow, Anthony (45 yrs.) d. on 67-May-22 [67-May-23: 2C].
Spavin, Belinda d. on 69-Sep-20 [69-Sep-24: 2C].
Spavin, Robert, Capt. (63 yrs.) d. on 68-Sep-22 [68-Sep-24: 2B].
Spavin, William (58 yrs.) d. on 68-Aug-28 [68-Sep-1: 2B].
Speake, Emma J. m. Solomon, Thomas W. on 70-Jan-18 [70-Jan-25: 2C].
Speake, Grace Amelia (8 mos.) d. on 70-Jun-19 [70-Jun-20: 2C].

Spear, E. P. (35 yrs.) d. on 70-Jul-21 of Heatstroke [70-Jul-22: 4D; 70-Jul-23: 4E].
Spear, Edwin W. m. Fuller, Emma on 69-Jun-8 [69-Jun-10: 2C].
Spear, Florence D. (10 yrs., 7 mos.) d. on 66-Jul-21 [66-Jul-23: 2C].
Spear, James O. m. Law, Elizabeth D. on 68-Jun-10 [68-Jun-12: 2B].
Spear, John W. (54 yrs.) d. on 70-Nov-18 [70-Nov-19: 2B].
Spear, William (65 yrs.) d. on 66-Jul-18 [66-Jul-19: 1E, 2C; 66-Jul-20: 2D].
Spearman, Kate (11 mos.) d. on 70-Oct-23 [70-Oct-24: 2B].
Spearman, Mary d. on 68-Mar-11 [68-Mar-13: 2C].
Spears, Martha A. m. Forckus, John W. on 66-Jun-10 [66-Jun-22: 2B].
Speck, Alice m. Crawford, John on 68-Dec-22 [69-Jan-1: 2C].
Speck, Mary (61 yrs.) d. on 68-Aug-13 of Paralysis [68-Aug-15: 1G, 2B].
Spedden, Alfred (39 yrs.) d. on 68-Mar-9 [68-Mar-10: 2C].
Spedden, Ann Rebecca (50 yrs.) d. on 69-Oct-19 [69-Oct-21: 2B].
Spedden, M. L. m. Matthews, Mary V. on 67-Oct-17 [67-Oct-19: 2A; 67-Oct-21: 2B].
Spedden, Maria L. m. Cooper, Hugh A. on 68-Mar-10 [68-Mar-12: 2B].
Spedden, Martha V. m. Pedrick, E. Franklin on 68-Sep-23 [68-Oct-3: 2B].
Spedden, Mary E. m. Mitchell, William on 70-Dec-20 [70-Dec-29: 2C].
Spedden, Mary Grace (3 yrs., 4 mos.) d. on 69-Mar-14 [69-Mar-16: 2C].
Spedden, Rebecca (53 yrs.) d. on 70-Jan-6 [70-Jan-7: 2F].
Spedden, S. Kate m. Woodrow, William E. on 66-Jan-22 [66-Jan-25: 2C].
Spedden, Thomas (53 yrs.) d. on 66-Jul-9 [66-Jul-11: 2C].
Spedden, Thomas H. (25 yrs., 2 mos.) d. on 70-Sep-28 [70-Sep-30: 2B].
Spedden, Virginia m. White, C. B. on 70-Nov-3 [70-Nov-8: 2B].
Speeres, Elenora Elmira (1 yr., 1 mo.) d. on 69-Apr-5 [69-Apr-6: 2C].
Speiden, Maria (56 yrs., 7 mos.) d. on 66-Oct-28 [66-Oct-30: 2C].
Speights, Laura V. m. Perkinson, D. F. on 69-Mar-23 [69-May-4: 2B].
Speights, Thomas J. m. Walter, Clara on 69-Nov-8 [70-Jan-7: 2F].
Spellissy, Hannora (37 yrs.) d. on 66-Oct-30 [66-Oct-31: 2B].
Spellman, Winifred m. Corcoran, Michael on 70-May-11 [70-Jun-1: 2B].
Spelman, John d. on 68-Apr-8 [68-Apr-10: 2B].
Spelman, Matthew (55 yrs.) d. on 70-Feb-17 of Intemperance and exposure [70-Feb-18: 1H].
Spence, Cornelia (48 yrs.) d. on 66-Jun-28 [66-Jun-29: 2C].
Spence, George (46 yrs.) d. on 69-Jun-12 [69-Jun-12: 2B].
Spence, Gioeme Keith (79 yrs.) d. on 69-Jan-24 [69-Feb-13: 2C].
Spence, Joseph m. Lawrence, Margaret on 70-Dec-1 [70-Dec-12: 2C].
Spence, Louisa W. m. Gill, John on 66-Nov-27 [66-Nov-29: 2B].
Spence, Mary m. Butler, Oliver N. on 69-Oct-26 [69-Oct-30: 2B].
Spence, Mary E. m. Greason, Thomas, Jr. on 67-Sep-17 [67-Sep-24: 2A].
Spence, Minnie F. (9 mos.) d. on 69-Jun-29 [69-Jun-30: 2C].
Spence, R. T. m. Waldron, Virginia on 68-Oct-1 [68-Oct-3: 2B].
Spence, Samuel (40 yrs., 1 mo.) d. on 66-Mar-4 in Railroad accident [66-Mar-5: 1G, 2B].
Spencer, A. D. R. m. Patterson, Agnes on 69-Jun-10 [69-Jun-29: 2C].
Spencer, Benjamin Franklin (3 yrs., 7 mos.) d. on 66-Apr-13 [66-Apr-16: 2B].
Spencer, Caleb M. (35 yrs.) d. on 66-May-13 of Consumption [66-May-16: 1G, 2C].
Spencer, Clara Virginia (2 yrs., 1 mo.) d. on 70-Dec-26 [70-Dec-29: 2C].
Spencer, Daniel M. (29 yrs.) d. on 67-Oct-25 [67-Oct-26: 2A].
Spencer, Eliza C. m. Denny, Richard W. on 69-Dec-21 [69-Dec-23: 2B].
Spencer, Frances E. d. on 68-May-5 [68-May-7: 2B].
Spencer, George W. m. Lambdin, Margaret A. on 66-Sep-20 [66-Sep-25: 2B].
Spencer, J. N. m. Kelchner, Maggie R. on 69-May-25 [69-Jun-22: 2C].
Spencer, Jane m. Dubois, John on 66-Sep-4 [66-Sep-12: 2A].
Spencer, John Ashcom (3 mos.) d. on 67-Apr-28 [67-Apr-29: 2B].
Spencer, Kate Florence (10 mos.) d. on 67-Aug-21 [67-Aug-22: 2B].
Spencer, M. A. m. DeRinzie, E. Horton on 70-May-19 [70-May-20: 2C].
Spencer, Nannie m. Perkins, George H. T. on 70-Jan-27 [70-Feb-1: 2B].

Spencer, R. L. m. Laley, T. K. on 66-Dec-4 [66-Dec-6: 2B].
Spencer, Samuel H. m. Tittle, Virginia E. on 67-Dec-10 [68-Jul-28: 2B].
Spencer, Sarah (92 yrs.) d. on 70-Mar-3 [70-Mar-8: 2C].
Spencer, Susan (55 yrs.) d. on 70-Nov-29 [70-Nov-30: 2C].
Spencer, Susan (72 yrs.) d. on 70-Mar-29 [70-Apr-4: 2C].
Spencer, William H. (38 yrs.) d. on 68-Mar-10 [68-Mar-12: 2B].
Sperry, Amelia C. m. Cook, Henry on 69-Sep-21 [69-Oct-2: 2B].
Spicer, Ferdinand Sewell (1 yr.) d. on 66-Oct-25 [66-Oct-27: 2B].
Spicer, Henrietta J. d. on 67-Dec-21 [67-Dec-25: 2C].
Spicer, John Durham (11 mos.) d. on 70-Jul-25 [70-Jul-26: 2C].
Spicer, Joseph T. (36 yrs., 10 mos.) d. on 66-May-6 [66-May-8: 2B].
Spicer, Simeon m. Guyton, Addie D. on 68-May-21 [68-May-30: 2A].
Spicer, Virginia C. d. on 70-Oct-12 [70-Oct-13: 2C].
Spidle, Mary J. m. Forsyth, Joseph F. on 68-Aug-23 [69-Feb-23: 2C].
Spielman, Margaret Elizabeth m. Matthai, C. E. on 68-Nov-17 [68-Dec-3: 2C].
Spies, Catherine (54 yrs.) d. on 70-Jan-23 [70-Jan-24: 2C].
Spies, Edward m. Leaf, Emma J. on 70-Mar-24 [70-Mar-29: 2B].
Spies, Eliza (63 yrs.) d. on 67-Mar-25 [67-Mar-26: 2C].
Spies, Julia A. m. Harig, John Joseph on 68-Sep-8 [68-Sep-10: 2B].
Spies, Margaret (82 yrs.) d. on 69-Aug-25 [69-Aug-26: 2C].
Spiess, Clara Virginia d. on 68-Dec-23 [68-Dec-24: 2C].
Spilker, Charles, Sr. (59 yrs.) d. on 68-Mar-3 of Paralysis [68-Mar-4: 2C; 68-Mar-5: 1G].
Spiller, Ann Augusta d. on 70-Jan-21 [70-Feb-3: 2B].
Spillman, F. Willie (3 yrs., 1 mo.) d. on 70-Aug-31 [70-Sep-2: 2C].
Spillman, George E. (1 yr., 4 mos.) d. on 70-Aug-31 [70-Sep-2: 2C].
Spillman, J. Henry (6 yrs., 4 mos.) d. on 70-Sep-1 [70-Sep-2: 2C].
Spilman, Estelle m. Horner, George D. on 68-Sep-16 [68-Sep-29: 2B].
Spilman, William J. m. Steuart, Virginia on 70-Sep-15 [70-Sep-19: 2B].
Spink, Sarah Anne d. on 66-Oct-29 [66-Nov-2: 2B].
Spitz, Samuel m. Ash, Elizabeth on 66-Feb-6 [66-Feb-9: 2C].
Spoechrl, Fritz d. on 69-Jun-12 Burned [69-Jun-15: 4C].
Spooner, Henry T. m. Garrettson, Florence on 68-Dec-24 [68-Dec-30: 2C].
Spradling, Thomas J. (20 yrs.) d. on 66-Aug-5 Drowned [66-Aug-7: 1G].
Spragins, Stith B. m. Hamilton, Bettie A. on 66-May-29 [66-Jun-2: 2B].
Sprague, Elisha R. (50 yrs.) d. on 67-Jul-23 [67-Aug-15: 1F; 67-Aug-23: 2B].
Sprague, George H. m. Smith, Jennie on 69-Jan-10 [69-Jan-28: 2C].
Sprague, Helen M. m. Wherrett, Andrew J. on 66-Jun-18 [66-Jun-21: 2B].
Sprague, James M. m. Conway, Minnie on 70-Sep-5 [70-Sep-14: 2B].
Sprenkle, Arthur Gill (11 mos.) d. on 69-Jan-26 [69-Jan-27: 2C].
Sprenkle, Charles (3 yrs.) d. on 69-Jan-24 [69-Jan-27: 2C].
Sprenkle, Sarah E. m. Dorsey, William H. on 66-Mar-18 [66-Apr-4: 2B].
Sprigg, Elizabeth d. on 70-Apr-19 [70-Apr-25: 2B].
Sprigg, James F. m. Smith, Harriet T. on 66-Oct-8 [66-Oct-12: 2B].
Sprigg, Sallie C. m. Beirne, Oliver on 68-Dec-29 [69-Jan-1: 2C].
Spriggs, William H. m. Anderson, Louisa on 70-May-26 [70-Jun-10: 2B].
Sprigle, George m. Garrison, Laura on 66-May-13 [66-May-30: 2C].
Springer, Anna C. m. Smith, William J., Jr. on 70-Jun-30 [70-Jul-7: 2B].
Springer, Charles d. on 66-Jun-2 of Suicide (Shooting) [66-Jun-4: 4B; 66-Jun-5: 1F; 66-Jun-6: 1G].
Springer, Charles Frederick d. on 66-Nov-15 [66-Nov-16: 2C; 66-Nov-17: 2B].
Springer, Justina C. m. Brice, Charles C. on 69-Mar-2 [69-Mar-4: 2C].
Springs, John m. Merritt, Mary A. on 66-Sep-4 [66-Sep-25: 2B].
Springs, Johnny (1 yr., 11 mos.) d. on 69-Oct-25 [69-Oct-26: 2B].
Sprowl, Mary A. m. Warnick, John F. on 66-Oct-7 [66-Oct-12: 2B].
Sprowl, Paul (1 yr., 7 mos.) d. on 68-Mar-6 [68-Mar-7: 2C].

Sprowl, Sarah E. m. Chester, William H. on 67-May-15 [67-May-18: 2A].
Sprucebanks, Martha T. m. Braden, Robert A. on 67-Jul-19 [67-Aug-1: 2C].
Spurrer, Thomas d. on 68-Jul-1 in Railroad accident [68-Jul-2: 1G].
Spurrier, Elizabeth Kortwright (43 yrs.) d. on 68-Apr-2 [68-Apr-6: 2B].
Spurrier, Greenbury (83 yrs.) d. on 66-Dec-29 [67-Jan-8: 1G, 2C].
Spurrier, John E. m. Fountain, Amanda J. on 69-Oct-11 [69-Oct-13: 2C].
Spurrier, Mary G. d. on 69-Jun-16 [69-Jun-26: 2B].
Spurrier, William (61 yrs.) d. on 70-Feb-23 in Railroad accident [70-Feb-24: 4E; 70-Feb-25: 2C].
Squires, Alfred A. m. Nichols, Eliza on 67-Jul-22 [67-Jul-24: 2C].
Squires, Alonzo m. Benney, Mary on 67-Sep-23 [67-Dec-3: 2C].
Squires, George Washington d. on 69-Sep-3 [69-Sep-4: 2B].
Squirll, Jane m. Atwood, Robert on 68-Mar-5 [68-Mar-9: 2C].
St. John, Albert Hopkins (1 yr., 8 mos.) d. on 70-Oct-1 [70-Oct-3: 2B].
St. John, Frederick (27 yrs.) d. on 67-Apr-28 [67-Apr-30: 2A].
Staab, John m. Weaver, Hannah on 69-Oct-11 [69-Dec-1: 2C].
Stablein, J. Harry (3 mos.) d. on 68-Jul-21 [68-Jul-22: 2C].
Stabler, Edward m. Cuddy, Rebecca on 69-Nov-17 [69-Nov-20: 2B].
Stabler, George J. B. m. Thomas, Henrietta on 68-May-12 [68-May-20: 2A].
Stabler, John m. Muller, Narcissa A. on 68-Sep-24 [68-Oct-1: 2B].
Stabler, Philip T. m. Nichols, M. Cornelia on 70-Nov-10 [70-Nov-16: 2C].
Stabler, William (35 yrs.) d. on 67-Feb-9 [67-Feb-13: 2B].
Stacey, Henry C. m. Bew, Emma C. on 67-Apr-21 [67-Apr-23: 2B].
Stack, Catherine d. on 68-Aug-15 [68-Aug-17: 2B].
Stack, John G. (23 yrs.) d. on 68-Dec-22 [68-Dec-28: 2B; 68-Dec-29: 2D].
Stack, Mary A. (26 yrs.) d. on 70-Dec-24 [70-Dec-28: 2D].
Stacker, Caroline (51 yrs.) d. on 69-Dec-12 [69-Dec-13: 2C].
Staeblein, Charles Theodore (1 yr., 1 mo.) d. on 66-Oct-30 [66-Nov-1: 2B].
Stafford, Joseph B. m. Burnham, Kate on 69-Jan-12 [69-Jan-19: 2C].
Stafford, Nicholas (70 yrs.) d. on 66-Jul-11 [66-Jul-13: 2C].
Stafford, William J. (35 yrs.) d. Drowned [69-Apr-22: 1F].
Stagmyer, Margaret Hughes (26 yrs.) d. on 69-Jan-13 [69-Jan-15: 2D].
Stair, Henry W. (37 yrs., 7 mos.) d. on 70-Dec-9 [70-Dec-13: 2C].
Staley, , Mr. d. on 67-Jan-21 in Railroad accident [67-Jan-23: 1G].
Staley, Cornelius m. Server, Laura V. on 68-Apr-28 [68-Apr-30: 2B].
Stalfort, Amelia m. Farber, M. H. on 68-Jun-11 [68-Jun-13: 2B].
Stalfort, Frederick (62 yrs.) d. on 70-Aug-8 [70-Aug-10: 2C; 70-Aug-11: 2C].
Stalfort, Kate m. Koch, William on 69-May-18 [69-May-19: 2C].
Stall, Jennie m. Segerman, Henry H. on 70-Oct-20 [70-Oct-24: 2B].
Stall, Mary A. m. Bowersox, James W. on 68-Dec-3 [68-Dec-11: 2C].
Stall, Sarah Jane (44 yrs.) d. on 66-Nov-3 [66-Nov-5: 2B].
Stall, William m. Courts, Emma on 69-Jan-28 [69-Jan-29: 2C].
Stallings, Fanny (38 yrs.) d. on 67-Nov-18 [67-Nov-19: 2C].
Stallings, John W. m. Smith, Ann Rebecca on 68-Feb-3 [68-Feb-5: 2D].
Stallings, Lizzie m. Hogg, Thomas H. on 69-Apr-20 [69-Apr-22: 2B].
Stallings, Martha (78 yrs., 1 mo.) d. on 70-Apr-8 [70-Apr-9: 2B].
Stallings, Sarah E. (41 yrs.) d. on 69-Oct-24 [69-Oct-25: 2C; 69-Oct-26: 2B].
Stallings, Sarah E. m. Simmons, Robert H. on 66-Dec-11 [67-Feb-7: 2C].
Stallings, Ulysses Grant (1 yr., 1 mo.) d. on 70-Mar-9 [70-Mar-10: 2C].
Stambaugh, Lillian Elsie (5 mos.) d. on 67-Jul-5 [67-Jul-6: 2B].
Stamp, Elizabeth (40 yrs.) d. on 69-Aug-5 [69-Aug-6: 2C].
Stamp, Elizabeth d. on 69-Jun-26 [69-Jun-28: 2C; 69-Jun-29: 2C].
Stamp, Hendrick M. F. W. m. Chapman, Elizabeth on 66-Dec-8 [66-Dec-10: 2B].
Standbury, Mary Anne (61 yrs.) d. on 69-Mar-4 [69-Mar-5: 2C].
Standfield, Rachel E. m. Randall, William A. on 69-Dec-23 [69-Dec-31: 2C].

Standford, Henry (60 yrs.) d. on 67-May-4 [67-May-6: 1G, 2B; 67-May-7: 1F].
Standiford, A. M. m. Mackey, Sallie E. on 69-Feb-12 [69-Feb-22: 2C].
Standiford, Issac C. m. Zimmer, Henrietta on 69-Jan-4 [69-Mar-8: 2C].
Standiford, Rachel A. m. McCubbins, Peter B. on 66-Feb-20 [66-Feb-22: 2B].
Stanfield, Caleb m. Kurtz, Maggie T. on 67-Oct-2 [67-Oct-5: 2B; 67-Oct-10: 2B].
Stanfield, William d. on 68-Jun-29 [68-Jul-2: 2C].
Stanford, Matilda m. Boone, Isaiah W. on 70-Jan-18 [70-Jan-21: 2C].
Stang, Elizabeth m. Hellwig, Henry on 67-Sep-22 [67-Sep-24: 2A].
Stanley, Alfred m. Johnson, Aimee E. on 67-Aug-6 [67-Aug-14: 2B].
Stanley, Eben E., Rev. (52 yrs.) d. on 66-Oct-3 [66-Oct-4: 2B].
Stanley, Eliza (43 yrs.) d. on 66-Aug-15 [66-Aug-21: 2C].
Stanley, John P. E. d. on 69-Mar-14 [69-Mar-15: 2C].
Stanley, Laura V. m. Newton, John B. on 66-Jun-7 [66-Jun-16: 2B].
Stanley, Margaret Ann m. Keser, Robert J. on 68-May-21 [68-May-23: 2A].
Stanley, Sarah (40 yrs.) d. on 68-Nov-8 of Consumption [68-Nov-9: 1F].
Stanley, Sarah m. Bayley, Daniel S. [66-Oct-26: 2B].
Stanly, Rebecca d. on 70-Dec-22 of Consumption and heart disease [70-Dec-23: 4D].
Stansburg, C. m. Brooks, Almira on 70-Feb-27 [70-Mar-2: 2C].
Stansbury, Adam D. (12 yrs.) d. on 69-Nov-12 [69-Nov-13: 2C].
Stansbury, Amelia M. d. on 66-Nov-22 [66-Nov-23: 2C].
Stansbury, Andrew J. (24 yrs.) d. on 69-Mar-25 [69-Mar-26: 2C].
Stansbury, Ann (68 yrs.) d. on 68-Jul-24 Drowned [68-Jul-28: 2B, 1B].
Stansbury, Calvin m. Wickert, Margaret J. on 68-Apr-30 [68-May-2: 2C].
Stansbury, Charity (76 yrs.) d. on 68-Jan-7 [68-Jan-8: 2C].
Stansbury, Elizabeth (52 yrs.) d. on 69-Feb-2 [69-Feb-3: 2C].
Stansbury, George M. Lamb (1 yr., 5 mos.) d. on 70-Mar-2 [70-Mar-3: 2C].
Stansbury, Harry Lee (9 mos.) d. on 70-Jul-13 [70-Jul-14: 2B].
Stansbury, James E. m. Lemmon, Mattie J. on 68-Jul-23 [68-Aug-5: 2B].
Stansbury, Joanna m. Hamilton, J. Frank on 69-May-26 [69-Jun-2: 2B].
Stansbury, Joseph S. (47 yrs.) d. on 70-Apr-15 of Paralysis [70-Apr-19: 2B].
Stansbury, L. Frank m. Lamb, Emily Ward on 67-Oct-30 [67-Nov-2: 2B].
Stansbury, Margaret E. d. on 67-May-22 [67-May-23: 2C].
Stansbury, Mary m. Skinner, Thomas on 67-Sep-15 [67-Sep-19: 2B].
Stansbury, Mary A. (54 yrs.) d. on 66-Mar-20 [66-Mar-21: 2C].
Stansbury, Mary Ann (67 yrs.) d. on 68-May-16 [68-May-18: 2B].
Stansbury, Mary E. m. Hurst, Jacob B. on 66-Jun-14 [66-Jun-30: 2B].
Stansbury, Mary Elizabeth m. Donovan, Michael on 66-Apr-25 [66-Apr-28: 2A].
Stansbury, Mollie A. m. Morran, Thomas on 69-Feb-18 [69-Feb-19: 2C].
Stansbury, Nannie M. m. Roof, James N. on 70-Jan-11 [70-Jan-12: 2C].
Stansbury, R. Peters d. on 67-Nov-30 [67-Dec-2: 2C].
Stansbury, S. Lizzie m. Perrine, Richard J. on 68-May-19 [68-May-20: 2A].
Stansbury, Sarah E. m. Hamilton, George D. on 70-Oct-24 [70-Nov-7: 2A].
Stansbury, Tabitha (83 yrs.) d. on 66-Dec-17 [66-Dec-18: 2B].
Stansbury, William H. m. Yeatman, Sue A. on 69-Jun-24 [69-Jun-30: 2C].
Stansbury, William Hammond (57 yrs.) d. on 66-Mar-15 [66-Mar-17: 2B].
Stansfield, Benjamin L. m. Brosanna, Eliza A. on 70-Jan-26 [70-Jan-29: 2B].
Stansfield, Helen C. m. Lauver, Milton A. on 66-Nov-29 [66-Nov-4: 2D].
Stansfield, Josephine m. Iglehart, Issac on 69-Feb-2 [69-Feb-6: 2C].
Stanton, Elizabeth (27 yrs.) d. on 70-Nov-13 [70-Nov-15: 2C].
Stanton, Fannie Thomas (3 yrs.) d. on 68-Nov-8 [68-Nov-9: 2B].
Stanton, James m. Houston, Emily on 66-Jun-14 [66-Jun-18: 2B].
Stanton, John (43 yrs.) d. on 67-Jun-19 [67-Jun-22: 2B].
Stanton, Maggie (2 yrs., 6 mos.) d. on 68-Aug-7 [68-Aug-8: 2C].
Stanton, Margarite Frances (23 yrs.) d. on 69-Jan-12 [69-Jan-13: 2D; 69-Jan-14: 2D].
Stanton, Rachel (17 yrs.) d. on 66-Mar-16 [66-Mar-17: 2B].

Stanton, Susan Ann m. Butler, Evans on 68-Oct-15 [68-Oct-17: 2B].
Staph, Andrew m. Tucker, Ann Maria on 66-Oct-29 [66-Nov-1: 2B].
Stapleford, Charles Winlock (8 mos.) d. on 70-Jul-11 [70-Jul-12: 2C].
Stapleford, George Winlock (11 mos.) d. on 69-Nov-22 [69-Nov-23: 2C].
Stapleford, Sarah Ann (23 yrs.) d. on 70-Mar-15 of Consumption [70-Mar-15: 2C].
Stapleford, Willie (6 mos.) d. on 68-Mar-15 [68-Mar-17: 2C].
Staples, Clarence E. (8 mos.) d. on 70-Jul-17 [70-Jul-18: 2B].
Stapleton, Ella m. Farrell, John C. on 70-May-16 [70-May-18: 2B].
Stapleton, Isabella (34 yrs.) d. on 67-Aug-13 [67-Aug-14: 2C].
Stapleton, Mary A. m. Gibson, Rowland G. on 69-Jun-7 [69-Jun-11: 2C].
Stapleton, Mary Ann m. Jurdan, Francis [70-Oct-8: 2B].
Stapleton, Maximillian E. (38 yrs.) d. on 68-Dec-18 [68-Dec-21: 2C].
Stapleton, Reginald E. (63 yrs.) d. on 68-Jul-26 [68-Jul-27: 2B].
Stapleton, Timothy, Jr. (23 yrs.) d. on 69-Aug-18 [69-Aug-19: 2C].
Stark, James (21 yrs.) d. on 66-Nov-19 [66-Nov-20: 2B].
Stark, John (26 yrs.) d. on 67-Aug-7 of Consumption [67-Aug-8: 2B].
Stark, John d. on 70-Mar-12 of Construction cave-in [70-Mar-15: 4E].
Stark, Simon (76 yrs.) d. on 69-May-20 [69-May-21: 1G, 2C].
Starke, Powhatan B., Dr. (47 yrs.) d. on 70-Sep-10 [70-Sep-12: 2B; 70-Sep-13: 1H].
Starkey, Charlotte m. Vain, Scott on 70-May-31 [70-Jun-24: 2C].
Starkey, Ida Estelle (6 yrs., 5 mos.) d. on 70-Dec-24 of Brain fever [70-Dec-26: 2C].
Starkey, Mary L. m. Buck, William L. on 69-Aug-12 [69-Aug-18: 2C].
Starkey, William H. m. Vain, Elizabeth J. on 70-Jul-31 [70-Aug-10: 2B].
Starkweather, , Mrs. (61 yrs.) d. on 68-Nov-16 in Railroad accident [68-Nov-18: 1G].
Starlings, Margaret (50 yrs.) d. on 66-Jul-16 [66-Jul-17: 2C].
Starr, Ann (82 yrs.) d. [69-Jul-7: 2C; 69-Jul-8: 2C].
Starr, Charles Howard (4 yrs., 5 mos.) d. on 69-Oct-28 [69-Oct-29: 2C].
Starr, David Issac (25 yrs.) d. on 70-Mar-23 of Consumption [70-Mar-25: 2C].
Starr, David J. m. Oram, Kate on 69-Sep-2 [69-Sep-7: 2B].
Starr, Edward V. m. Frame, Alice on 69-Jun-24 [69-Jul-1: 2C].
Starr, George L. S. (10 mos.) d. on 66-Sep-2 [66-Sep-5: 2B].
Starr, George W., Jr. m. Lutz, Mary E. on 68-May-5 [68-May-16: 2A].
Starr, Henry (8 yrs.) d. on 69-Oct-18 of Diptheria [69-Oct-19: 2C].
Starr, John, Jr. m. Acre, Myrta M. on 67-Oct-29 [67-Nov-1: 2B].
Starr, John D. m. Croxall, Minnie E. on 67-Jul-18 [67-Jul-25: 2C; 67-Aug-6: 2C].
Starr, John J. m. Bowes, Matilda M. on 66-Nov-20 [66-Dec-8: 2B].
Starr, John Thomas (2 yrs., 6 mos.) d. on 70-Jan-24 [70-Feb-5: 2C].
Starr, Mary Elizabeth m. Gill, Theophilus P. on 69-Jun-24 [69-Jun-26: 2B].
Starr, Mary Rose m. Barker, Jesse on 67-Aug-5 [67-Aug-9: 2C].
Starr, Myrta A. (28 yrs.) d. on 69-Mar-4 [69-Mar-10: 2C].
Starr, Sarah m. Kirby, William on 69-Dec-12 [69-Dec-14: 2C].
Starr, Wesley (77 yrs.) d. on 66-May-9 [66-May-10: 1F, 2B; 66-May-11: 2B; 66-May-12: 1F].
Starr, William Penn (4 yrs., 1 mo.) d. on 66-Apr-22 [66-Apr-23: 2B].
Starr, William T. (33 yrs., 8 mos.) d. on 69-Mar-20 [69-Mar-22: 2C].
Start, Maria C. m. Droste, William H. on 67-May-16 [67-May-18: 2A].
Startzman, David d. on 66-May-27 [66-May-28: 2B; 66-May-29: 2B].
Startzman, Emma m. Griffith, G. Mason on 70-Apr-14 [70-Apr-19: 2B].
Startzman, J. H. m. Paddington, Carrie on 69-Oct-14 [69-Oct-16: 2B; 69-Oct-18: 2C].
Startzman, Sally A. m. Jessup, George on 67-Mar-5 [67-Mar-6: 2C].
Stauf, Henry (44 yrs.) d. on 69-Dec-26 [69-Dec-28: 2D; 69-Dec-27: 2D].
Stauffer, George W. (60 yrs.) d. on 70-Feb-21 [70-Feb-23: 2C].
Stauffer, Henry d. on 66-Nov-8 [66-Nov-29: 2C].
Stauffer, Mary E. m. Saumenig, William R. on 69-Apr-8 [69-Apr-13: 2B].
Stauffer, S. Theodore m. Claggett, Lou on 69-Oct-12 [69-Oct-19: 2B].
Staum, John W. m. Armager, Juliet V. on 69-Jun-22 [69-Jun-26: 2B].

Stauter, Susannah Sandford m. McCurley, James on 67-Apr-1 [67-Apr-4: 2B; 67-Apr-5: 2B].
Staylor, Frederick George (3 mos.) d. on 70-Feb-18 [70-Feb-19: 2B].
Staylor, Harry (2 yrs.) d. on 66-Aug-3 [66-Aug-4: 2C].
Staylor, Isabella Frances (3 mos.) d. on 66-Jul-10 [66-Jul-11: 2C].
Staylor, Louis P. m. Satterfield, Eleanor E. on 66-Aug-9 [66-Aug-14: 2C].
Staylor, Mark J. (30 yrs.) d. on 70-Mar-27 [70-Mar-28: 2B; 70-Mar-29: 2C].
Staylor, Susan Rose (1 yr., 1 mo.) d. on 66-Jul-11 [66-Jul-12: 2C].
Staylor, Vincent m. Blades, Mary F. on 68-Aug-12 [68-Aug-15: 2B].
Staylor, William A. m. Menzies, Carrie L. on 70-Oct-6 [70-Oct-10: 2B].
Stayman, Kate E. m. Mason, N. Carroll on 67-Nov-21 [67-Dec-2: 2C].
Stayton, Elizabeth (79 yrs.) d. on 68-Apr-29 [68-May-1: 2B].
Steadman, Adeline S. (58 yrs.) d. on 68-Jan-6 [68-Jan-7: 2C].
Steadman, Harry (7 yrs., 4 mos.) d. on 70-May-13 [70-May-16: 2B].
Steadman, James Hooper (3 yrs., 8 mos.) d. on 70-Jan-31 [70-Feb-1: 2C].
Steadman, Margaret (88 yrs., 11 mos.) d. on 70-Dec-20 [70-Dec-22: 2B].
Steadman, Mary M. (22 yrs.) d. on 70-Nov-13 [70-Nov-14: 2B; 70-Nov-15: 2C; 70-Nov-16: 4C].
Steangler, Mary (20 yrs.) d. on 70-Jan-7 of Suicide (Hanging) [70-Jan-8: 1H].
Stearn, John d. on 70-Jul-19 of Heatstroke [70-Jul-21: 1F].
Stearns, John L. (69 yrs.) d. on 67-May-1 of Heart disease [67-May-20: 2B].
Stearns, Louisa H. (58 yrs.) d. on 67-Aug-13 [67-Aug-15: 2C].
Steb, Conrad (45 yrs.) d. on 66-Sep-3 in Wagon accident [66-Sep-5: 4B].
Steck, Mary C. d. on 70-Oct-18 [70-Oct-20: 2B].
Steed, Addie L. m. Hatton, Joseph C. on 67-Dec-4 [67-Dec-9: 2B].
Steed, Augustin O'Donnell (7 mos.) d. on 68-Nov-17 [68-Nov-18: 2C].
Steed, Elmina d. on 70-Feb-11 [70-Feb-12: 2C].
Steed, Richard Arthur (1 yr., 6 mos.) d. on 66-Aug-31 [66-Sep-1: 2B].
Steeger, Elizabeth m. Lorentz, Bernhard A. on 68-Apr-6 [68-Apr-7: 2B].
Steel, Sarah J. m. Meisel, Louis J. on 67-Jun-11 [67-Jun-29: 2B].
Steele, Arthur Gale (23 yrs.) d. on 67-Oct-9 of Yellow fever [67-Oct-31: 2B; 67-Nov-1: 1F].
Steele, Charles H. (1 yr., 6 mos.) d. on 69-Mar-6 [69-Mar-9: 2C].
Steele, Henry M. d. on 69-Mar-10 [69-Mar-12: 2C].
Steele, James (16 yrs.) d. on 66-Dec-25 [67-Jan-4: 2D].
Steele, James (30 yrs.) d. on 70-Oct-24 of Fall from pier [70-Oct-26: 4B].
Steele, John (63 yrs.) d. on 67-Jul-28 [67-Jul-29: 2D; 67-Jul-30: 2C].
Steele, John T. m. Gardner, Elizabeth on 66-Dec-21 [67-Jan-5: 2C].
Steele, Lydia m. Read, William E. on 67-Jan-11 [67-Jan-13: 2C].
Steele, Martha J. m. Zimmerman, William E. on 68-Nov-19 [68-Nov-23: 2B].
Steele, Mary Ann (60 yrs.) d. on 66-Jan-2 [66-Jan-4: 2C].
Steele, William A. (32 yrs.) d. on 68-Jul-24 Drowned [68-Aug-6: 1G, 2B].
Steen, Clara (1 yr., 1 mo.) d. on 67-Aug-31 [67-Sep-11: 2B].
Steen, John m. Steen, Lizzie on 70-Sep-19 [70-Sep-20: 2B].
Steen, Lizzie m. Steen, John on 70-Sep-19 [70-Sep-20: 2B].
Steen, Mary A. d. on 68-Nov-5 [68-Nov-7: 2B].
Steen, Samuel Isaiah m. McKinley, Susannah Cecilia on 68-Oct-28 [70-Mar-24: 2C; 70-Mar-26: 2B].
Steen, Ulysses S. Grant (5 mos.) d. on 70-Sep-24 [70-Sep-27: 2B].
Steer, Charles Edward d. on 68-Sep-6 [68-Sep-7: 2A].
Steer, William F., Jr. m. Hamman, Dorothy on 70-Mar-30 [70-Apr-5: 2B].
Steer, William Henry (2 yrs., 3 mos.) d. on 68-Oct-5 [68-Oct-7: 2C].
Stees, Mary C. m. Kendall, Joseph V. on 67-Jul-16 [67-Jul-30: 2C].
Steever, Nellie B. m. Healy, Thomas J. on 69-Oct-25 [69-Nov-3: 2C].
Steevers, Susie m. Ruckle, Oscar on 66-Dec-4 [66-Dec-8: 2B].
Steffe, Harry (7 yrs., 7 mos.) d. on 68-May-22 of Scarlet fever [68-May-26: 2B].
Steffe, John Franklin (3 mos.) d. on 70-Jul-17 [70-Jul-18: 2B].

Steffens, Henry m. Berg, Magdalene on 67-Jul-9 [67-Jul-10: 2B].
Stegall, M. S. m. Mifflin, Lou V. on 70-Sep-27 [70-Nov-17: 2C].
Steger, William m. Vollandt, Johanna C. on 67-Jun-2 [67-Jun-4: 2A].
Stehl, Justus V. m. Wilson, Eliza A. on 69-Oct-27 [69-Nov-1: 2B].
Steibel, Francis P. m. Hoyer, Annie B. on 66-Nov-29 [66-Dec-8: 2B; 66-Dec-10: 2B].
Steibel, Jeanette m. Weck, John W. on 69-Jul-24 [69-Jul-30: 2C].
Steigelman, Abraham (74 yrs.) d. on 70-Sep-25 [70-Sep-26: 2B].
Steigelman, Eliza (1 yr.) d. on 69-Jun-26 [69-Jun-29: 2C].
Steiger, John Carroll m. Irving, Mary E. on 68-Feb-19 [68-Mar-13: 2C].
Steigers, Ellen d. on 67-Mar-11 [67-Mar-13: 2C].
Steigerwald, John W. m. Harris, Nancy M. on 66-Jan-11 [66-Jan-25: 2C].
Stein, A. T. m. Troxell, Martha I. on 67-Dec-24 [67-Dec-28: 2C].
Stein, C. E. m. Furguson, Celia on 69-Sep-27 [69-Oct-27: 2B].
Stein, Catherine (56 yrs.) d. on 69-May-18 [69-May-20: 2C].
Stein, Frances Rosina (47 yrs.) d. on 69-Jun-28 [69-Jun-29: 2C].
Stein, Julia (21 yrs.) d. on 66-Dec-10 [66-Dec-15: 2B].
Steinacker, Godfried (70 yrs.) d. on 70-Feb-4 [70-Feb-5: 2C].
Steindle, Barbara m. Lake, Herman B., Jr. on 70-Jun-6 [70-Jun-7: 2C].
Steiner, Edwin Thomas d. on 66-Jun-22 [66-Jun-23: 2B].
Steiner, Elizabeth (78 yrs.) d. on 66-Jun-11 [66-Jun-13: 2B].
Steiner, Ferdinand (18 yrs.) d. on 66-Aug-24 of Gunshot wound [66-Aug-25: 1G].
Steiner, John Michael (65 yrs., 4 mos.) d. on 67-Nov-15 of Heart disease [67-Nov-16: 1G, 2B].
Steiner, John Michael (4 mos.) d. on 70-Mar-16 [70-Mar-18: 2C; 70-Mar-19: 2D].
Steiner, Sophia (60 yrs.) d. on 68-May-9 [68-May-11: 2B].
Steiner, Valietta m. Holmes, Charles E. H. on 67-Nov-4 [67-Nov-7: 2C].
Steinmier, Mary m. Rabe, Henry on 70-Feb-24 [70-Mar-16: 2C].
Stellman, Louisa (10 mos.) d. on 66-Jul-2 [66-Jul-4: 2C].
Stembler, C. E. m. Gable, John A. on 69-Aug-4 [69-Sep-4: 2B].
Stembler, George m. Bower, Mary on 66-Apr-24 [66-Apr-27: 2C].
Stembler, Maggie m. Reed, Abner M. on 70-Dec-6 [70-Dec-24: 2B].
Stembler, Nicholas (1 yr., 5 mos.) d. on 66-Aug-25 [66-Aug-27: 2B].
Stembler, Willy A. (56 yrs.) d. on 68-Nov-14 [68-Nov-16: 2C].
Stengel, John George Frederick (72 yrs.) d. on 68-Jan-20 [68-Jan-31: 2C].
Stenson, C. R. d. on 68-Jan-5 [68-Jan-7: 2C].
Stephen, Bettie m. Rogers, James R. on 69-Mar-10 [69-Mar-13: 2B].
Stephen, Joseph H. (65 yrs.) d. on 68-Nov-2 in Railroad accident [68-Nov-3: 1G].
Stephen, Julia (73 yrs.) d. on 66-Dec-28 [67-Jan-3: 2C].
Stephens, Anna K. m. Watkins, George R. on 67-Oct-3 [67-Oct-4: 2B].
Stephens, Charles L. m. Lee, Susie A. on 70-Feb-1 [70-Feb-8: 2C].
Stephens, David N. m. Disney, Rachel on 70-Oct-6 [70-Oct-7: 2B].
Stephens, J. J. m. Vincell, Mollie E. on 67-Dec-17 [67-Dec-19: 2B].
Stephens, James H., Sr. (63 yrs., 9 mos.) d. on 68-Nov-2 in Railroad accident [68-Nov-3: 2B].
Stephens, John T. (50 yrs.) d. on 68-Apr-6 [68-Apr-9: 2B].
Stephens, Louis Elliott (5 mos.) d. on 70-May-6 [70-May-9: 2C].
Stephens, Thomas A. (45 yrs.) d. on 69-May-8 [69-May-11: 2C].
Stephenson, Henry, Jr. d. on 69-Apr-26 Murdered (Assault) [69-May-13: 1G].
Stephenson, Matthew Burnell (2 yrs.) d. on 69-Nov-21 [69-Nov-22: 2C].
Sterett, Sallie E. m. Littig, John M. on 69-Nov-17 [69-Nov-29: 2C].
Sterling, B. F. m. Price, Mary A. on 68-Dec-27 [68-Dec-29: 2D].
Sterling, Christopher C. m. Cavana, Elizabeth on 69-Sep-26 [69-Oct-5: 2B; 69-Oct-7: 2B].
Sterling, Frances Rebecca m. Carback, William J. on 70-Apr-7 [70-Apr-9: 2B].
Sterling, Mary Ellen m. Kroh, Philip A. on 66-Dec-13 [66-Dec-14: 2B].
Stern, , Mr. d. on 70-Dec-18 of Heart disease [70-Dec-20: 4C].
Stern, Mary m. Strauss, Bernard on 69-Sep-16 [69-Sep-18: 2B].
Stern, R. m. Rider, Leopold on 67-Nov-24 [67-Nov-25: 2C].

Stern, Sallie m. Strassburger, Victor C. on 66-Mar-18 [66-Mar-20: 2C].
Sterner, Mary Magdalene, Sr. (50 yrs.) d. on 67-Nov-5 [67-Nov-6: 2B].
Sterret, Rachel M. m. Lowery, Issac L. on 67-May-9 [67-May-10: 2B].
Sterrett, Cecilia J. d. on 70-Jul-18 [70-Jul-20: 2C].
Sterrett, Jesse (70 yrs.) d. on 69-Jul-2 in Railroad accident [69-Jul-5: 1G].
Sterrett, Joeanna d. on 70-Jun-25 of Consumption [70-Jun-27: 2C].
Sterrett, Samuel m. Hemsley, Mary on 66-Oct-29 [66-Oct-31: 2B].
Stesch, Eugenia F. C. m. Hessemer, Edwin I. on 70-Oct-2 [70-Oct-5: 2B].
Stetson, William S. (43 yrs.) d. on 66-May-16 [66-May-29: 2B].
Stetzenbach, Amelia m. Eigenbrodt, Christian, Jr. on 69-Jul-28 [69-Aug-30: 2B].
Steuart, Alexander S. m. Fraser, Ellen J. on 70-Aug-11 [70-Aug-15: 2B].
Steuart, Ann E. (68 yrs.) d. on 67-Jun-10 of Heart disease [67-Jun-12: 2B; 67-Jun-13: 1F].
Steuart, David, Jr. d. on 69-Jan-3 [69-Jan-8: 2C].
Steuart, Fannie Glenn m. Brand, Alexander J. on 69-Oct-20 [69-Oct-22: 2B].
Steuart, George H., Gen. (77 yrs.) d. on 67-Oct-22 [67-Oct-23: 1G, 2B].
Steuart, Grace (8 mos.) d. on 70-Jul-19 [70-Jul-21: 2C].
Steuart, James E. d. on 67-Oct-1 [67-Oct-4: 1F; 67-Oct-7: 2B].
Steuart, James H. m. Duvall, Ellen Lavinia on 69-Apr-18 [69-Apr-20: 2B].
Steuart, Lizzie m. Moritz, J. D. on 68-Apr-16 [68-Apr-20: 2B].
Steuart, Lizzie Jane (5 yrs., 8 mos.) d. on 66-Mar-28 [66-Mar-31: 2C].
Steuart, Virginia m. Spilman, William J. on 70-Sep-15 [70-Sep-19: 2B].
Steudler, Laura V. m. Drexel, Francis F. on 68-Mar-11 [68-Mar-14: 2B].
Stevens, Albert d. on 66-Mar-21 [66-Mar-22: 2C].
Stevens, Ann J. m. Mark, George W. on 70-Nov-1 [70-Nov-2: 2C].
Stevens, Ann Jane (2 yrs., 1 mo.) d. on 67-Sep-28 [67-Sep-30: 2B].
Stevens, C. S. C. (35 yrs.) d. on 68-Sep-15 [68-Oct-15: 2C].
Stevens, Camilla (9 mos.) d. on 69-Aug-6 [69-Aug-7: 2C].
Stevens, Charles (67 yrs.) d. on 67-Sep-10 [67-Sep-16: 2B].
Stevens, Charles m. Kemp, Susie E. on 70-Dec-1 [70-Dec-3: 2B].
Stevens, Elizabeth A. (23 yrs.) d. on 69-Oct-1 [69-Oct-2: 2B].
Stevens, Elizabeth Ann (16 yrs.) d. on 69-Sep-7 [69-Sep-8: 2B].
Stevens, Elizabeth Kate (6 yrs.) d. on 67-Feb-6 [67-Feb-7: 2C; 67-Feb-8: 2C].
Stevens, George O. (5 yrs., 1 mo.) d. on 70-Jul-30 of Dysentery [70-Aug-1: 2C].
Stevens, James (59 yrs.) d. on 70-Sep-2 [70-Sep-3: 2B].
Stevens, James E. m. Derricks, Harriet R. on 69-May-19 [69-May-20: 2C].
Stevens, John R. m. Wright, Grace A. on 67-Jun-6 [67-Jul-9: 2B].
Stevens, John T. (48 yrs., 5 mos.) d. on 66-Aug-27 [66-Aug-28: 2B].
Stevens, Laura A. m. Hamilton, Jacob on 66-Nov-22 [66-Dec-10: 2B].
Stevens, Leverin m. Cromwell, Elizabeth on 68-Mar-10 [68-Mar-12: 2B].
Stevens, Lizzie C. m. Norris, Francis on 70-Aug-30 [70-Nov-29: 2C].
Stevens, Louisa (43 yrs.) d. on 67-Feb-13 [67-Feb-16: 2D].
Stevens, Martha E. (15 yrs.) d. on 67-Dec-9 [67-Dec-10: 2B].
Stevens, Martha V. m. Mulvey, William E. on 67-Jun-20 [67-Jun-25: 2B].
Stevens, Mary (92 yrs.) d. on 66-Feb-19 [66-Feb-23: 2C].
Stevens, Nellie (8 mos.) d. on 70-Jul-16 [70-Jul-18: 2C].
Stevens, Sarah A. m. Fitchett, Dickson on 66-Jun-25 [66-Jun-30: 2B].
Stevens, Sarah L. m. Wilson, Samuel G. on 68-Jun-18 [68-Jun-20: 2B].
Stevens, Sarah Louisa m. Saunders, Theodore P. on 70-Dec-20 [70-Dec-22: 2B].
Stevens, Susan S. m. Leech, George T. on 69-Apr-13 [69-Apr-21: 2B].
Stevens, Thomas m. Harriday, Virginia on 68-Dec-22 [68-Dec-23: 2C].
Stevens, Viola (1 yr.) d. on 70-Aug-2 [70-Aug-3: 2C].
Stevens, Walter Husted, Gen. (40 yrs.) d. on 67-Nov-12 [67-Nov-30: 2C].
Stevens, William H. m. Pasters, Elizabeth on 67-Aug-15 [67-Aug-20: 2B].
Stevenson, Bessie (1 yr., 7 mos.) d. on 68-Aug-9 [68-Aug-10: 2B].
Stevenson, Cator (75 yrs.) d. on 69-Mar-14 [69-Mar-22: 2C].

Stevenson, Charlie Lee (2 yrs., 1 mo.) d. on 70-Feb-16 [70-Feb-18: 2C].
Stevenson, Edmund (39 yrs.) d. on 70-Jan-31 [70-Feb-2: 2B; 70-Feb-3: 2B].
Stevenson, Edward m. Geis, Rosa on 69-Oct-5 [69-Oct-12: 2C].
Stevenson, Emory H. m. Pratt, Janie on 70-Nov-20 [70-Dec-16: 2C].
Stevenson, George Espy m. Snyder, Mary E. on 69-May-25 [69-May-27: 2C].
Stevenson, Harry (29 yrs.) d. on 69-May-6 Murdered (Assault) [69-May-7: 1G, 2C].
Stevenson, Harry Clinton (5 mos.) d. on 66-May-27 [66-May-29: 2B].
Stevenson, Henry (72 yrs.) d. on 68-Jun-6 [68-Jun-9: 2B].
Stevenson, James H. m. Barlow, Mary C. on 67-May-28 [67-Jun-3: 2B].
Stevenson, John M. (83 yrs.) d. on 70-Jun-8 [70-Jun-9: 2C].
Stevenson, John M. m. Rider, Lizzie on 67-Apr-18 [67-Apr-20: 2A].
Stevenson, John W. m. Booth, Izola Mills on 69-Mar-2 [69-Oct-19: 2B].
Stevenson, John Willis (6 mos.) d. on 70-Sep-7 [70-Sep-8: 2B].
Stevenson, Maggie m. Vincente, Edward P. on 68-Nov-10 [68-Nov-14: 2B].
Stevenson, Mary m. Pugh, William G. on 70-May-26 [70-May-31: 2B].
Stevenson, Mary A. m. Paine, Joseph H. on 70-Nov-23 [70-Nov-24: 2B; 70-Nov-25: 2D].
Stevenson, Mary Catherine (1 yr.) d. on 69-Mar-11 [69-Mar-13: 2C].
Stevenson, Samuel E. m. Leavett, Florence V. on 70-Dec-6 [70-Dec-14: 2C].
Stevenson, Wesley, Rev. (69 yrs., 1 mo.) d. on 70-Mar-14 [70-Mar-15: 2C; 70-Mar-16: 1H].
Stevenson, Wesley G. m. Quinlan, Agnes E. on 66-Oct-15 [66-Oct-17: 2B].
Stevenson, William N. m. Binnie, Jeanie on 70-Jul-19 [70-Jul-26: 2B].
Steward, Margaret (75 yrs.) d. on 69-Feb-28 [69-Mar-1: 2C].
Stewart, Albin D. (18 yrs.) d. on 68-Mar-22 [68-Mar-24: 2B].
Stewart, Alice L. m. Crump, Robert A. on 67-Aug-6 [67-Sep-3: 2B].
Stewart, Ann (48 yrs.) d. on 69-Sep-3 [69-Sep-17: 2C].
Stewart, Ann C. (61 yrs.) d. on 66-Dec-20 [66-Dec-22: 2B].
Stewart, Anna E. m. Rogers, Andrew J. on 66-Feb-21 [66-Feb-26: 2B].
Stewart, Annie E. m. Hynson, Charles L. on 66-Oct-17 [66-Oct-19: 2B].
Stewart, Barbara m. Wooden, Wilbur F. on 68-Jul-12 [68-Jul-14: 2B].
Stewart, Bessie d. on 68-Jul-20 [68-Jul-22: 2C].
Stewart, Charles (28 yrs.) d. on 68-Aug-16 Drowned [68-Aug-17: 1G].
Stewart, Charles Glen (4 yrs.) d. on 70-Dec-27 [70-Dec-28: 2D].
Stewart, Charles Lewis (6 yrs., 1 mo.) d. on 66-Jan-13 [66-Jan-15: 2C].
Stewart, Charles Wesley (32 yrs.) d. on 69-Aug-14 in Railroad accident [69-Aug-16: 2C; 69-Aug-17: 1H].
Stewart, Columbus J. m. Crangle, S. J. on 67-Dec-24 [67-Dec-31: 2C].
Stewart, Ebeneezer C. m. Bloss, Maggie on 68-Dec-3 [68-Dec-28: 2B].
Stewart, Eliza (71 yrs.) d. on 70-Feb-18 [70-Feb-19: 2B].
Stewart, Elizabeth d. on 67-Feb-10 [67-Feb-11: 2C].
Stewart, Ella J. m. Clarke, George W. on 70-Sep-12 [70-Sep-14: 2B].
Stewart, Ellen F. d. on 66-Sep-20 of Cholera [66-Oct-17: 2B].
Stewart, Emma Jane (11 yrs., 9 mos.) d. on 69-May-22 [69-May-25: 2C].
Stewart, Emma Ogier (2 yrs., 5 mos.) d. on 70-Aug-23 [70-Aug-24: 2C].
Stewart, F. A. m. Luckett, Mollie C. on 68-Nov-30 [68-Dec-7: 2C].
Stewart, Fannie A. m. Redgrave, J. Frank on 67-Nov-21 [67-Nov-25: 2C].
Stewart, Flora May (7 mos.) d. on 69-Oct-13 [69-Oct-15: 2C].
Stewart, Frederick August (1 mo.) d. on 66-Apr-6 [66-Apr-7: 2B].
Stewart, H. H. m. Butler, F. A. on 70-Jun-21 [70-Jun-23: 2C].
Stewart, Harry (3 yrs., 8 mos.) d. on 69-May-6 [69-May-13: 2B].
Stewart, Henry D. d. on 66-Jul-17 [66-Jul-19: 1E].
Stewart, Howard (6 yrs.) d. on 67-Mar-22 [67-Mar-23: 2C].
Stewart, Irene (1 yr., 10 mos.) d. on 70-Jul-28 [70-Jul-29: 2C].
Stewart, Isabella (78 yrs.) d. on 67-Aug-13 [67-Aug-14: 2C].
Stewart, Isabella m. Brauns, Henry on 69-Nov-11 [69-Nov-16: 2C].
Stewart, James (79 yrs.) d. on 67-May-19 [67-May-21: 2B].

Stewart, James (23 yrs., 11 mos.) d. on 70-Oct-18 [70-Oct-21: 2C].
Stewart, James m. McKinney, Maria on 67-Jul-10 [67-Jul-24: 2C].
Stewart, James B. (2 yrs., 10 mos.) d. on 69-Feb-12 [69-Feb-13: 2C].
Stewart, James Edgar, Capt. (59 yrs.) d. on 70-Sep-6 of Apoplexy [70-Sep-8: 4E; 70-Sep-9: 4C; 70-Sep-10: 2B].
Stewart, John (68 yrs.) d. on 68-Aug-20 [68-Aug-21: 2B].
Stewart, John (80 yrs.) d. on 67-Apr-12 [67-Apr-13: 2B].
Stewart, John (53 yrs.) d. on 66-Aug-20 [66-Aug-21: 2C].
Stewart, John H. (36 yrs.) d. on 70-Mar-23 [70-Mar-25: 2C; 70-Mar-26: 2B].
Stewart, John R. (1 yr., 1 mo.) d. on 68-Sep-13 [68-Sep-15: 2B].
Stewart, John T. m. Maguire, Eliza J. on 67-May-18 [67-May-22: 2B].
Stewart, John T. B. m. Davis, Sallie E. on 69-Sep-3 [69-Nov-23: 2C].
Stewart, John W. m. Hooper, Maria L. on 68-Jun-9 [68-Jun-16: 2B].
Stewart, Joseph F. (34 yrs.) d. on 66-Dec-3 [66-Dec-5: 2B].
Stewart, Joseph W. (71 yrs.) d. on 68-Jan-13 [68-Jan-14: 2C; 68-Jan-15: 2C].
Stewart, Lou E. m. Kenly, Oliver G. on 67-Oct-1 [67-Oct-8: 2B].
Stewart, Margaret (69 yrs.) d. on 67-Dec-31 [68-Jan-1: 2C].
Stewart, Marian (7 mos.) d. on 66-Nov-3 [66-Nov-5: 2B].
Stewart, Marry Morton d. on 69-Jun-30 [69-Jul-1: 2C].
Stewart, Martha (69 yrs.) d. on 70-Jul-11 [70-Jul-12: 2C; 70-Jul-13: 2C].
Stewart, Mary (7 yrs., 7 mos.) d. on 70-Oct-1 [70-Oct-3: 2B].
Stewart, Mary A. d. on 66-Jun-17 [66-Jun-19: 2B].
Stewart, Mary M. m. Frame, George on 69-Apr-29 [69-May-5: 2C].
Stewart, Mary Ogier (69 yrs.) d. on 67-Dec-29 [68-Jan-2: 2C].
Stewart, May (10 yrs.) d. on 68-Jul-8 [68-Jul-9: 2B].
Stewart, Rebecca F. m. Henry, Joseph D. on 69-Jan-6 [69-Jan-25: 2D].
Stewart, Rosanne (1 mo.) d. on 70-May-8 [70-May-9: 2B].
Stewart, Sallie E. m. Tucker, David L. on 70-Nov-15 [70-Nov-26: 2B].
Stewart, Septimus H. m. Solomon, Carrie on 66-Feb-12 [66-Feb-17: 2B].
Stewart, William (55 yrs.) d. on 66-Jan-2 [66-Jan-3: 2C].
Stewart, William A. m. Slaughter, Emily G. on 69-Mar-16 [69-Mar-17: 2C].
Stewart, William C. (73 yrs.) d. on 70-Sep-24 [70-Sep-26: 2B].
Stewart, William C. m. Reese, Sophie C. on 69-Nov-18 [69-Nov-20: 2B].
Stewart, William H. (35 yrs.) d. on 68-May-11 [68-May-12: 2B].
Stewart, William J. m. Reed, Julia V. on 70-Aug-17 [70-Sep-10: 2B].
Stewart, William M. m. Geigler, Carrie on 70-Aug-16 [70-Aug-27: 2B].
Stewart, William Wesley (1 yr., 4 mos.) d. on 67-Oct-31 [67-Nov-1: 2B].
Stickney, Amanda M. m. Hill, Lawrence P. on 68-Nov-5 [68-Nov-17: 2C].
Stickney, Mary M. (81 yrs.) d. on 70-Nov-6 [70-Nov-7: 2B].
Stidham, P. Alonzo (26 yrs., 6 mos.) d. on 67-Aug-6 of Consumption [67-Aug-7: 2C].
Stidman, Elizabeth Kate d. on 67-Jun-22 [67-Jun-24: 2B].
Stidman, Robert (1 yr.) d. on 70-Jul-1 [70-Jul-2: 2B].
Stier, Annie M. m. Harrison, Champion J. on 69-Jan-18 [69-Jan-25: 2D].
Stier, George (28 yrs.) d. on 66-Jun-30 [66-Jul-4: 2C; 66-Jul-6: 2B].
Stier, Hannah (64 yrs.) d. on 70-Jul-14 [70-Jul-18: 2C].
Stier, Winfield S. m. Boetler, Sophia C. on 70-Feb-11 [70-Feb-23: 2C].
Stiffler, Mary E. (25 yrs.) d. on 69-Feb-17 [69-Feb-22: 2C].
Stifler, Eliza J. m. Martin, Eli on 68-Dec-27 [69-Jan-2: 2C].
Stigers, Ambrosia m. Evans, G. W., Jr. on 68-Jul-15 [68-Jul-18: 2B].
Stigers, Anna A. E. m. Scott, John O. on 69-Feb-25 [69-Mar-1: 2C].
Stigers, Mary Philomela d. on 70-Jul-31 [70-Aug-5: 2C].
Stimpson, James H. d. on 67-Aug-20 Murdered (Killed by Indians) [67-Sep-10: 1E; 68-Jun-16: 2B].
Stincendaffer, Anna m. Lloyd, William on 66-Aug-12 [66-Aug-18: 2B].
Stinchacomb, Anna (85 yrs.) d. on 70-Apr-20 [70-Apr-22: 2C].

Stinchcomb, Hannah (71 yrs.) d. on 70-Oct-30 [70-Nov-1: 2C].
Stinchcomb, Laura Virginia (25 yrs.) d. on 68-May-27 [68-May-29: 2B].
Stinchcomb, Nelson Perry (6 yrs.) d. on 69-Dec-23 [69-Dec-25: 2C].
Stinchcomb, Victor B d. on 67-Aug-16 [67-Aug-26: 2D].
Stine, C. Edwin m. Martin, Ella on 70-Nov-17 [70-Nov-29: 2C].
Stine, Emma C. m. Hoffman, Frederick B. on 70-Jul-5 [70-Jul-9: 2B].
Stine, George D. (48 yrs.) d. on 68-Mar-31 [68-Apr-1: 2C; 68-Apr-2: 2C].
Stine, Jacob (6 mos.) d. on 66-Mar-11 [66-Mar-13: 2B].
Stine, Joseph C. (26 yrs.) d. on 70-Mar-17 [70-Mar-18: 2C].
Stine, Matilda m. Engel, Julius L. on 66-Jan-7 [66-Jan-9: 2B].
Stine, Richard Henry Smith (8 yrs.) d. on 70-Dec-12 of Scarlet fever [70-Dec-13: 2C].
Stinhagen, Sarah m. Hare, Henry on 66-Oct-6 [66-Oct-18: 2B].
Stinnicke, Maria C. (70 yrs.) d. on 69-Jan-28 [69-Jan-30: 2C; 69-Feb-8: 1F; 69-Feb-9: 1H].
Stinson, Kate L. m. Falck, John B. on 67-May-23 [67-May-28: 2B].
Stinson, R. James m. Talbott, Maggie on 67-Dec-5 [67-Dec-9: 2B].
Stire, Carson m. Williams, Ellie on 70-Jan-10 [70-Jan-14: 2C].
Stirley, Charles Henry (27 yrs.) d. on 66-Jan-15 of Dropsy [66-Jan-16: 2C].
Stirling, Christopher C. (26 yrs.) d. on 70-Sep-16 in Railroad accident [70-Sep-17: 2B, 4D].
Stirling, Mary Elizabeth m. Sheckels, W. Pinkney on 68-Aug-11 [68-Aug-12: 2C].
Stirling, Susan B. m. Day, Albert on 69-May-27 [69-Jun-3: 2B].
Stirling, William G. (2 mos.) d. on 67-Jul-14 [67-Jul-16: 2C].
Stirling, Yates m. Haley, Nellie S. on 67-Aug-29 [67-Sep-24: 2A].
Stirrat, Nancy W. d. on 70-Jul-29 [70-Jul-30: 2C].
Stirrat, Nettie M. m. Snell, Munroe on 70-Jan-13 [70-Jan-17: 2C].
Stitcher, Agnes (1 mo.) d. on 67-Sep-8 [67-Sep-10: 2B].
Stitcher, Ellen (65 yrs.) d. on 66-Nov-13 [66-Nov-14: 2B; 66-Nov-15: 2C].
Stitcher, John Wesley (2 yrs., 10 mos.) d. on 66-Mar-24 [66-Mar-26: 2B].
Stitcher, Mary Elizabeth d. on 67-Sep-1 [67-Sep-3: 2B].
Stites, M. Alice m. Wightman, George A. on 70-Dec-22 [70-Dec-29: 2C].
Stites, William m. Cooper, Ann M. on 70-Nov-24 [70-Dec-19: 2C].
Stitt, Joseph B. m. Cochran, Mary E. on 69-Dec-15 [69-Dec-17: 2C].
Stiver, Charles Henry (1 yr., 4 mos.) d. on 67-Nov-21 [67-Nov-23: 2B].
Stizler, George W. m. Brooks, Martha on 67-Feb-3 [67-Mar-6: 2C].
Stober, Jacob (66 yrs.) d. on 67-Aug-28 of Apoplexy [67-Aug-29: 2B].
Stockdale, Adline (55 yrs.) d. on 69-Jan-20 [69-Jan-21: 2C; 69-Jan-22: 2D].
Stockdale, Elizabeth A. m. Brown, William O. on 68-Mar-8 [68-Mar-12: 2B].
Stockdale, John m. Frederick, Annie on 66-Sep-18 [66-Sep-20: 2B].
Stockdale, Joshua N. m. Mitchell, Elizabeth A. on 69-Apr-13 [69-Apr-15: 2B].
Stockett, Charles Ellsworth (1 yr., 5 mos.) d. on 69-Jul-2 [69-Jul-7: 2C].
Stockett, Christiana W. (3 yrs., 6 mos.) d. on 69-Jul-15 [69-Jul-21: 2C].
Stockett, Frank E. m. Burns, Arthur P., Dr. on 70-Jun-30 [70-Jul-11: 2C].
Stockett, Lillie May (1 yr., 5 mos.) d. on 67-Mar-11 [67-Mar-13: 2C].
Stockett, William H. (11 yrs.) d. on 68-Apr-5 [68-Apr-8: 2B].
Stockman, George W. m. Appold, Louvenia on 69-Nov-11 [69-Nov-13: 2B].
Stockman, J. Garrison m. Taylor, Mary E. on 69-Dec-15 [69-Dec-30: 2C].
Stockman, Sophia m. Hammond, John on 68-May-29 [68-Jun-2: 2B].
Stocksdale, Edmund H. (68 yrs.) d. on 69-May-20 [69-May-22: 2B].
Stocksdale, Hannah E. m. Ely, Samuel S. on 68-Nov-18 [68-Nov-21: 2C].
Stocksdale, Jessie N. (10 mos.) d. on 69-Jul-19 [69-Jul-20: 2C].
Stocksdale, Providence (72 yrs.) d. on 68-Apr-25 [68-May-1: 2B].
Stocksdale, Susanna (18 yrs., 6 mos.) d. on 68-Mar-12 [68-Mar-21: 2A].
Stockton, Edward (2 yrs.) d. on 66-May-8 [66-May-10: 2B].
Stoddard, Fred Sinclair (1 yr., 9 mos.) d. on 67-May-28 [67-May-29: 2B].
Stoddard, John W. (52 yrs.) d. on 69-Apr-21 in Railroad accident [69-Apr-23: 1H; 69-Apr-24: 2B].

Stoddard, Kate K. m. Wheatley, William F. on 69-Oct-7 [69-Oct-9: 2C].
Stoddard, Mary A. H. (56 yrs.) d. on 69-Aug-8 [69-Aug-9: 2C].
Stoddard, Thomas J. m. Everitt, Mary A. on 69-Aug-18 [69-Aug-31: 2B].
Stoddert, John T. (80 yrs.) d. on 70-Jul-19 [70-Jul-21: 1F].
Stoddert, Mary E. S. m. Hopkins, Samuel E. on 66-Apr-24 [66-Apr-25: 2B].
Stoebe, Herman m. Vollandt, Maggie on 67-Feb-12 [67-Feb-15: 2C].
Stokes, Adeline M. m. Hindes, Samuel on 70-Jul-10 [70-Jul-25: 2C].
Stokes, Bradley T. m. Whitney, Maria Louisa on 69-Oct-21 [69-Oct-25: 2B].
Stokes, Jane (58 yrs.) d. on 68-Jul-31 of Consumption [68-Aug-7: 2B].
Stokes, John H. m. Dunham, Alverda S. on 66-Sep-11 [66-Sep-25: 2B].
Stokes, Joseph Cornelius (23 yrs.) d. on 67-May-23 [67-May-25: 2B].
Stokes, Ray V. m. Balderston, John P. on 70-Jun-1 [70-Jun-4: 2B].
Stokes, Thomas A. m. Burke, Kate E. on 67-Nov-14 [67-Nov-18: 2B].
Stokes, William B. (84 yrs.) d. on 66-Oct-7 [66-Oct-8: 2B].
Stoll, Emilie C. m. Cohn, M. G. on 68-Jan-30 [68-Jan-31: 2C].
Stoll, Herman m. Brinkman, Mary on 68-Jan-28 [68-Feb-3: 2C].
Stoll, Laura J. m. Coulter, Noah B. on 66-Apr-12 [66-Apr-16: 2B].
Stoll, Mary A. (37 yrs.) d. on 69-Aug-18 [69-Aug-20: 2C].
Stolpp, Carrie L. m. Thomas, Nelson C. on 70-Feb-24 [70-Mar-3: 2C; 70-Mar-4: 2C].
Stolpp, Lewis (59 yrs.) d. on 66-Aug-19 [66-Aug-20: 2C].
Stone, Benjamin F. m. Smith, Laura A. on 67-Oct-29 [67-Nov-4: 2B].
Stone, Charles Wesley m. Mills, Charlotte A. on 68-Jun-24 [68-Jun-27: 2B].
Stone, Eugenia M. m. Houck, Henry J. on 66-Dec-4 [66-Dec-7: 2B].
Stone, George S. (20 yrs.) d. on 70-Jul-24 [70-Jul-26: 2C].
Stone, Helen A. d. on 67-Feb-26 of Paralysis [67-Feb-28: 2C].
Stone, John L. m. Ewall, Mary on 69-Nov-17 [69-Nov-18: 2C].
Stone, John T. (23 yrs.) d. on 68-Sep-13 [68-Sep-14: 2B].
Stone, L. P., Dr. m. Daw, Nannie J., Miss on 70-Sep-8 [70-Sep-24: 2B].
Stone, Marion L. m. McDowell, W. G. on 66-Jan-18 [66-Jan-20: 2C].
Stone, Mary E. m. Hubbell, Bernard on 68-Oct-7 [68-Nov-10: 2C].
Stone, Mary Eliza (90 yrs.) d. on 67-Jan-5 [67-Jan-10: 2C].
Stone, Mary Virginia (1 yr., 2 mos.) d. on 67-May-2 [67-May-4: 2B].
Stone, Theodore L. d. on 66-Aug-20 of Cholera [66-Sep-18: 2B].
Stone, Yelverton P. m. Tarr, Leida J. on 67-Sep-24 [67-Sep-30: 2B].
Stonebraker, Jacob (77 yrs.) d. on 67-Feb-26 [67-Mar-7: 1G].
Stonebraker, Samuel m. Corrin, Isabella on 69-May-25 [69-May-29: 2B].
Stoner, Mary J. m. Diehl, John on 70-Dec-1 [70-Dec-3: 2B].
Stonestreet, Mary Philomela (49 yrs., 5 mos.) d. on 67-Jun-21 [67-Jun-28: 1G].
Stoops, William T. m. Melzick, Mary H. on 68-Jul-16 [68-Jul-18: 2B].
Storck, Annie M. m. Riordan, John J. on 67-Jun-4 [67-Jun-7: 2B].
Storer, Mary E. (26 yrs.) d. on 68-Jul-15 [68-Jul-17: 2C].
Stores, Alice Maryland (1 yr., 1 mo.) d. [66-Jan-18: 2C].
Storey, Norman H. m. Jones, Annie E. on 70-Mar-24 [70-Apr-4: 2B].
Storke, Richard (25 yrs.) d. on 67-Jan-29 [67-Jan-30: 2C].
Storm, E. L. (34 yrs.) d. on 67-Apr-17 [67-Apr-18: 2B].
Storm, E. M. m. Laley, Laura M. on 69-Apr-5 [69-Apr-7: 2C].
Storm, J. P. L. m. Kirwan, Louisa C. on 66-Jan-23 [66-Feb-8: 2C].
Storms, Rachel Jane, Miss m. Kemp, John on 66-Feb-22 [66-Feb-27: 2B].
Stornone, Gregory m. Sanguinetti, Erina on 68-Nov-11 [68-Nov-21: 2C].
Story, Carrie (4 yrs., 10 mos.) d. on 67-Mar-10 [67-Mar-11: 2C].
Story, Harry Lee (11 mos.) d. on 67-Mar-8 [67-Mar-11: 2C].
Story, John T. (3 yrs., 6 mos.) d. on 67-Mar-9 [67-Mar-11: 2C].
Stouffer, Elizabeth m. Heck, Nathaniel on 68-Mar-25 [68-Mar-27: 2C; 68-Mar-28: 2B].
Stouffer, John (83 yrs.) d. on 66-Aug-22 [66-Aug-23: 2C; 66-Aug-24: 1G, 2B].
Stouffer, Maggie A. m. Kimmet, G. A. on 68-Jun-25 [68-Jul-2: 2C].

Stout, Ann B. (72 yrs., 10 mos.) d. on 68-Jul-22 [68-Aug-21: 2B].
Stover, Jacob (71 yrs.) d. on 68-Oct-25 [68-Oct-29: 2C].
Stover, Robert W. m. Kramm, Willie G. on 67-Sep-20 [68-May-30: 2A].
Stowe, Daniel m. Walker, Bettie on 70-Aug-10 [70-Aug-17: 2C].
Stowe, Mary A. (31 yrs.) d. on 68-Jul-22 [68-Jul-24: 2C].
Stowell, Joseph W. m. Nichols, Josephine on 66-Dec-24 [67-Jan-5: 2C].
Stowman, Edward D. m. Freberger, Mary E. on 70-Jan-27 [70-Jan-29: 2B].
Straith, Nannie Alexander (2 yrs., 6 mos.) d. on 68-Apr-21 [68-Apr-24: 2B].
Straler, Sarah A. (39 yrs., 4 mos.) d. on 68-Apr-19 [68-Apr-21: 2B].
Stran, H. Annie m. McCurley, Issac on 70-Jan-13 [70-Jan-17: 2C].
Stran, Thomas P. m. Abrahams, H. Kate on 66-Nov-8 [66-Nov-12: 2C; 66-Nov-19: 2B].
Strandberg, Daniel (48 yrs.) d. on 67-Oct-7 [67-Oct-17: 2B].
Strandberg, Henry J. d. on 67-May-10 [67-May-16: 1G].
Straney, Ann M. (64 yrs.) d. on 69-Nov-29 [69-Dec-1: 2C].
Straney, Charles (35 yrs.) d. on 66-Jul-23 of Drowning [66-Jul-25: 1F; 66-Jul-27: 2C].
Straney, Edward W. m. Brown, Mary V. on 69-Jun-17 [69-Jul-5: 2C].
Straney, John (70 yrs.) d. on 69-May-9 [69-May-10: 2C].
Straney, Mary A. m. Jones, Robert M. on 69-Apr-6 [69-May-1: 2B].
Stranley, Robert Rose (19 yrs.) d. on 67-Aug-22 [67-Sep-5: 2B; 67-Sep-10: 2B].
Stranley, William Francis (21 yrs.) d. on 67-Aug-24 [67-Sep-5: 2B; 67-Sep-10: 2B].
Strassburger, Victor C. m. Stern, Sallie on 66-Mar-18 [66-Mar-20: 2C].
Stratmyer, Anna Mary (4 yrs., 1 mo.) d. on 68-Nov-17 [68-Nov-19: 2C].
Stratner, Lewis (34 yrs.) d. on 70-Oct-27 [70-Oct-28: 2C].
Stratten, Julius Thor m. Krumm, Emma A. on 69-Oct-10 [69-Oct-18: 2C; 69-Oct-19: 2B].
Stratton, Ellen (85 yrs.) d. on 67-Nov-9 [67-Nov-11: 2C].
Stratton, Robert W. m. Bateman, Lucina G. R. on 67-Dec-5 [67-Dec-12: 2B].
Stratton, Sallie W. m. Shuter, James on 67-Jun-18 [67-Jun-26: 2C].
Straup, Elizabeth m. Simms, George on 66-Feb-1 [66-Feb-19: 2B].
Straus, Henrietta m. Barth, Samuel on 70-Nov-23 [70-Nov-29: 2C].
Straus, Solomon m. Ullman, Mina on 69-Dec-22 [69-Dec-25: 2C].
Straus, William H. m. Lobe, Annette on 69-May-19 [69-May-22: 2B].
Strauss, Bernard m. Stern, Mary on 69-Sep-16 [69-Sep-18: 2B].
Strayler, Amelia (31 yrs.) d. on 70-Feb-24 [70-Feb-26: 2C].
Strayler, Mary C. m. Mitchell, George R. on 66-May-3 [66-May-5: 2B].
Strebeck, Peter m. Bartlett, Mary E. on 69-Oct-21 [69-Oct-30: 2B].
Streckfus, Leonard m. Keyhan, Mary Ann on 70-Apr-26 [70-Apr-28: 2A].
Street, Charles Dalrymple (2 mos.) d. on 66-Apr-29 [66-May-12: 2A].
Street, Charles O. m. Osbourn, Anna A. E. McLay on 66-Apr-24 [66-Apr-27: 2C].
Street, Joseph (40 yrs.) d. on 69-Jul-18 of Apoplexy [69-Jul-19: 1G].
Street, Nellie Curtis d. on 70-Dec-1 [70-Dec-2: 2C].
Street, Robert Dalrymple (9 mos.) d. on 67-Dec-13 [67-Dec-21: 2B].
Streets, John, Capt. (70 yrs.) d. on 69-Sep-5 [69-Sep-6: 1H, 2C].
Streets, Mary Emma m. Edmonston, Francis O. on 69-Jun-7 [69-Jun-8: 2B].
Streets, Sarah (72 yrs.) d. on 69-Aug-10 [69-Aug-11: 2C; 69-Aug-12: 2B].
Streett, A. J., Dr. (69 yrs.) d. on 67-Nov-9 [67-Nov-15: 2B].
Streett, Jacob Rutledge (5 mos.) d. on 69-Dec-18 [69-Dec-23: 2B].
Streett, Lawrence A. (6 mos.) d. on 69-Sep-22 [69-Sep-23: 2B].
Streett, Marion d. on 70-May-17 [70-May-18: 2B].
Streever, LaFayette (36 yrs.) d. on 69-Sep-2 [69-Sep-3: 2B].
Streib, Jacob m. Lotz, Dora on 68-Sep-15 [68-Sep-30: 2B].
Streiwig, Emma L. m. Kammerer, William A. on 70-Oct-27 [70-Nov-2: 2C].
Streng, Amelia (1 yr., 4 mos.) d. on 66-Jun-29 [66-Jun-30: 2B].
Streng, Charles Henry (1 yr., 6 mos.) d. on 68-Nov-3 [68-Nov-5: 2C].
Streper, Mary A. (25 yrs.) d. on 69-Nov-4 [69-Nov-5: 2C; 69-Nov-6: 2C].
Streper, William m. Brady, Mary A., Miss on 66-Feb-11 [66-Feb-27: 2B].

Strickler, Lydia m. Baker, Charles G. on 67-Apr-4 [67-May-4: 2B].
Strickling, Jesse m. Frazier, Rosanna on 69-Mar-9 [69-Nov-1: 2B].
Strider, John d. on 68-Sep-2 [].
Strider, Maria V. d. on 68-Jul-15 [68-Jul-17: 2C].
Strini, S. m. Merriam, Rosalind on 67-Apr-30 [67-May-9: 2A].
Stritehoof, Frank m. Smith, Louisa C. on 66-May-31 [66-Jun-23: 2B].
Strobel, Amanda F. (28 yrs., 8 mos.) d. on 67-Jun-27 [67-Jul-2: 2B].
Strobel, Kate Lawton m. Leaming, James R. on 68-Nov-5 [68-Nov-9: 2B].
Strodtman, William H. (22 yrs., 4 mos.) d. on 69-Apr-5 [69-Apr-7: 2C].
Strodtman, William H. m. Rausch, Maggie M. on 68-Oct-27 [68-Nov-10: 2C].
Stromberg, Wilhelmina Magarett d. on 66-Dec-7 [66-Dec-8: 2B].
Stromenger, Charles H. m. Nelson, Mollie M. on 66-Oct-11 [66-Oct-16: 2B].
Stromenger, Lizzie m. Cook, John D. on 68-Jan-7 [68-Jan-16: 2C].
Stromenger, Mary m. Read, E. William on 69-Jun-29 [69-Jun-30: 2C].
Strong, Elizabeth A. m. Richardson, Wallace P. on 69-Dec-12 [69-Dec-15: 2B].
Strong, George W. m. Towson, Emma K. on 66-Jul-1 [66-Jul-6: 2B; 66-Jul-17: 2C].
Strong, Molly (3 yrs., 1 mo.) d. on 67-Apr-2 [67-Apr-3: 2B].
Strong, Richard P. m. Smith, Marian R. on 68-Feb-6 [68-Feb-14: 2C].
Strong, Roberta May (1 yr., 10 mos.) d. on 68-Sep-19 [69-Jan-19: 2C].
Strong, Samuel J. D. (1 yr., 6 mos.) d. on 66-Jun-30 [66-Jul-2: 2B].
Strovel, George S. m. Quarles, Belinda A. on 67-Sep-30 [67-Oct-2: 2B].
Strow, Mary C. (59 yrs.) d. on 66-Sep-20 [66-Oct-3: 2B].
Strubie, Mary J. m. McFrederick, A. on 69-Oct-26 [69-Oct-29: 2B].
Stuart, Agnes E. m. Townsend, Alpheus A. on 67-Oct-24 [67-Oct-25: 2B].
Stuart, Catharine Ann (21 yrs.) d. on 67-Jul-2 [67-Jul-3: 2B].
Stuart, Charles G. m. Rosensteel, Mary F. on 68-Feb-11 [68-Feb-14: 2C].
Stuart, David, Jr. d. on 69-Nov-25 [69-Nov-27: 2C].
Stuart, Edgar d. on 69-Aug-13 [69-Aug-17: 2C].
Stuart, Elizabeth C. (31 yrs.) d. on 66-Mar-7 [66-Mar-8: 2B].
Stuart, George H. m. Colladay, Janie A. on 70-Oct-26 [70-Oct-29: 2B].
Stuart, Harriet (77 yrs.) d. on 67-Aug-16 [67-Aug-17: 2B].
Stuart, James A. m. Gettier, M. Kate on 70-Nov-24 [70-Nov-26: 2B].
Stuart, John B. m. Wilson, Annie M. on 66-Jan-4 [66-Jan-11: 2B].
Stuart, Laura V. m. Byrne, Samuel E. on 67-Oct-29 [67-Nov-2: 2B].
Stuart, Mary d. on 70-Dec-24 [70-Dec-28: 2D].
Stuart, Mary Ann (50 yrs.) d. on 69-Jun-29 [69-Jun-29: 2C].
Stuart, Rose Lee (1 yr., 8 mos.) d. on 70-Aug-4 [70-Aug-5: 2C].
Stuart, William R. m. May, Sue K. on 68-Nov-30 [69-Jan-14: 2D].
Stubbs, Hervey Shriver (1 yr., 4 mos.) d. on 66-Aug-28 [66-Aug-30: 2B].
Stubbs, Wilbur m. Pledge, Ida V. on 70-Jan-4 [70-Jan-10: 2C].
Stuchfield, Josephine R. m. Brooks, Edward W. on 67-Sep-25 [67-Oct-15: 2A].
Studman, Mary Jane m. O'Brien, John on 68-Nov-7 [68-Dec-5: 2C].
Stull, Henry m. Brown, Eliza J. on 70-Feb-17 [70-Feb-21: 2B].
Stump, Elizabeth m. Volz, Peter T. on 67-May-7 [67-May-9: 2A].
Stump, Emmeline (38 yrs.) d. on 70-Sep-4 of Heart disease [70-Sep-5: 2C, 4D].
Stump, J. Henry m. White, Maggie on 67-May-16 [67-May-28: 2B].
Stump, Mary d. on 70-Jul-4 [70-Jul-6: 2C].
Stump, Mary E. m. Raymond, Charles on 66-Sep-14 [66-Dec-6: 2B].
Stunz, Charles Shipley d. on 68-Jun-29 [68-Jun-30: 2B].
Stunz, G. William P. (1 mo.) d. on 69-Aug-26 [69-Aug-27: 2B].
Stunz, William P. m. Shipley, Alverta L. on 67-Apr-18 [67-Apr-25: 2B].
Sturbits, John m. Feetsch, Kate on 69-May-25 [69-Jun-15: 2C].
Sturgeon, Caroline F. (22 yrs.) d. on 68-Jun-28 Burned [68-Jun-29: 1F].
Sturgeon, Lindsey m. Hubbard, Mary Elizabeth on 66-Apr-2 [66-Apr-6: 2B].
Sturgeon, Margaret (80 yrs.) d. on 67-Apr-29 [67-Apr-30: 2A].

Sturges, William J. m. Akers, Sarah A. on 66-Nov-20 [66-Nov-24: 2B; 66-Nov-27: 2B].
Sturgis, John I. m. Morrow, Phebe on 67-Dec-26 [67-Dec-30: 2C].
Sturgis, Nannie d. on 67-May-6 [67-May-8: 2B].
Sturgis, Zadoc m. Hubbard, Nannie on 67-May-6 [67-May-8: 2B].
Sturling, Amanda M. m. Thornton, Beniah on 70-Jun-26 [70-Aug-1: 2C].
Sturman, Edmonia J. m. Nolley, Marcellus J. on 69-Feb-23 [69-Mar-1: 2C].
Suding, Henry A. m. Beauchamp, Annie on 70-Aug-23 [70-Sep-29: 2B].
Suell, James m. Barnett, Annie E. on 70-Aug-23 [70-Aug-25: 2B].
Sugden, George (58 yrs.) d. on 67-Apr-23 [67-Apr-25: 2B].
Suits, Robert L. m. Shipley, Mary V. on 66-Sep-6 [66-Sep-10: 2D].
Sullans, David H. d. on 67-Mar-23 Drowned [67-Mar-27: 1G].
Sullivan, Amelia (75 yrs.) d. on 70-Jan-3 [70-Jan-4: 2C].
Sullivan, Ann (57 yrs.) d. on 67-Jun-20 [67-Jun-26: 2C].
Sullivan, Annie m. Herbert, George N. on 68-Jun-17 [68-Jun-19: 2B].
Sullivan, Bessie m. Weaver, William E. on 69-Dec-16 [70-Mar-2: 2C].
Sullivan, Catherine (37 yrs.) d. on 70-Feb-6 [70-Feb-7: 2C].
Sullivan, Christina T. m. Malone, Daniel on 66-Oct-1 [66-Nov-13: 2B].
Sullivan, Cornelius m. Kyne, Anna on 67-Nov-7 [67-Nov-11: 2C].
Sullivan, Daniel m. McVille, Elenora on 69-Nov-17 [69-Nov-24: 2C].
Sullivan, Daniel Steffe (2 mos.) d. on 67-Feb-26 [67-Mar-2: 2B].
Sullivan, Elizabeth d. on 70-Feb-3 [70-Feb-8: 2C].
Sullivan, Felix R. m. Buchanan, Lizzie T. on 68-Nov-17 [68-Nov-21: 2C].
Sullivan, George R. m. Snyder, Mazie V. on 69-May-18 [69-May-19: 2C].
Sullivan, Henry C. m. Van Bokern, Mary on 66-Jul-17 [66-Jul-21: 2C].
Sullivan, James (45 yrs.) d. on 66-Mar-5 [66-Mar-6: 2B].
Sullivan, James m. Dargen, Elizabeth on 68-Jan-27 [68-Jan-30: 2C].
Sullivan, James W. (46 yrs.) d. on 68-Nov-1 [68-Nov-2: 4B, 2B].
Sullivan, Jeremiah (76 yrs.) d. on 67-Apr-22 [67-Apr-23: 2B].
Sullivan, John d. on 68-Jul-24 Drowned [68-Jul-28: 1B].
Sullivan, John William (7 yrs., 4 mos.) d. on 67-Jan-4 [67-Jan-5: 2C].
Sullivan, Leanna B. (20 yrs.) d. on 69-Apr-20 [69-Apr-22: 2B].
Sullivan, Mahala (60 yrs.) d. on 67-Nov-15 [67-Nov-16: 2B].
Sullivan, Mary A. d. on 66-Nov-1 [66-Nov-2: 2B; 66-Nov-3: 2B].
Sullivan, Mary Ellen (5 mos.) d. on 67-Aug-19 [67-Aug-20: 2B].
Sullivan, Mary Irene (1 yr., 2 mos.) d. on 66-Dec-1 [66-Dec-3: 2B].
Sullivan, Michael (60 yrs.) d. on 66-Oct-19 [66-Oct-20: 2B].
Sullivan, Mollie J. m. Tolley, Thomas E. on 68-Jul-16 [68-Jul-20: 2B].
Sullivan, Nicholas (31 yrs.) d. on 69-Oct-7 [69-Oct-16: 2B].
Sullivan, Robert (56 yrs.) d. on 67-Sep-24 [67-Sep-25: 2B, 1G].
Sullivan, Robert P. R. (9 yrs.) d. on 68-Apr-12 [68-Apr-13: 2B].
Sullivan, Ruth (53 yrs.) d. on 67-Jul-23 [67-Jul-24: 2C].
Sullivan, Ruth A. (21 yrs.) d. on 69-Sep-3 [69-Sep-4: 2B].
Sullivan, Ruth Lennox (11 mos.) d. on 68-Sep-1 [68-Sep-5: 2A].
Sullivan, Sarah (22 yrs.) d. on 66-Jun-3 [66-Jun-7: 2B].
Sullivan, Sarah A. (24 yrs.) d. on 67-Aug-7 [67-Aug-9: 2C].
Sullivan, Thomas (35 yrs.) d. on 68-Aug-16 Murdered (Stabbing) [68-Aug-17: 1G].
Sultzer, Susan (83 yrs.) d. on 69-Mar-19 [69-Mar-20: 2B].
Sultzer, Susan A. m. German, Thomas E. on 67-Sep-4 [67-Sep-11: 2B].
Summers, Charles G. m. Thomas, Mary Rogers on 69-Oct-5 [69-Oct-9: 2C].
Summers, George D. (45 yrs.) d. on 70-Dec-9 [70-Dec-10: 2B].
Summers, George Dawson (5 mos.) d. on 68-Jul-5 [68-Jul-6: 2B].
Summers, James N. (18 yrs.) d. on 68-Jul-24 Drowned [68-Aug-3: 2C; 68-Jul-28: 1B].
Summers, M. Bettie m. Wright, J. L. on 70-May-11 [70-May-19: 2C].
Summers, Sallie F. m. Cushing, James P. D. on 70-Aug-16 [70-Aug-19: 2C].
Summers, Thomas B. d. on 70-Oct-8 [70-Oct-10: 2B, 4C].

Summers, Willie Warren (8 mos.) d. on 66-Jun-28 [66-Jun-30: 2B].
Sumner, Helen m. Bradford, Jefferson D. on 68-Jul-21 [68-Aug-12: 2C].
Sumsh, Froney m. Shultz, Charles H. on 68-Dec-1 [68-Dec-7: 2C].
Sumwalt, Alexander (62 yrs.) d. on 69-Dec-13 of Pneumonia [69-Dec-15: 2B].
Sumwalt, Frederick G. (36 yrs.) d. [67-Feb-6: 2C].
Sumwalt, George M. (1 yr., 1 mo.) d. on 70-Aug-16 [70-Aug-18: 2C].
Sumwalt, Jesse (62 yrs.) d. on 66-Apr-18 [66-Apr-19: 2B; 66-Apr-20: 1G].
Sumwalt, John T. (78 yrs.) d. on 68-Aug-20 [68-Aug-21: 1G, 2B].
Sumwalt, Louisa (65 yrs.) d. on 70-Sep-27 [70-Sep-30: 2B].
Sumwalt, Martha J. d. on 68-Sep-13 [68-Sep-15: 2B].
Sumwalt, Rachel (68 yrs.) d. on 68-Aug-30 [68-Aug-31: 2B].
Sumwalt, Rachel m. Hinds, Charles H. on 70-Aug-28 [70-Oct-17: 2B].
Sumwalt, Rose May Anna d. on 68-Feb-12 of Consumption [68-Feb-13: 2C].
Sumwalt, Samuel R. m. Brazier, Laura J. on 70-Jul-27 [70-Aug-2: 2C].
Sumwalt, Sarah A. (14 yrs., 1 mo.) d. on 70-Aug-9 [70-Aug-18: 2C].
Sunderland, Isabella E. m. Reinhardt, George M. on 66-Mar-22 [66-Mar-28: 2C].
Sunderland, W. H. m. Addison, Sue R. on 68-Sep-15 [68-Sep-17: 2B].
Sunery, Henry d. on 70-Mar-3 [70-Mar-4: 1H].
Sunstrom, Calvin m. Wilson, Isabella V. on 69-May-9 [69-May-11: 2B].
Sunstrom, Mark T. m. Bullock, Rhoda M. on 67-Apr-11 [67-Apr-12: 2C].
Sunstrom, Rachel m. Trueman, Josiah C. on 69-Jul-28 [69-Jul-31: 2C].
Supple, Sophia C. m. Wellen, Amos F. on 67-May-7 [67-May-14: 2B].
Supple, Thomas A. m. Ruark, Mary E. on 66-May-3 [66-May-11: 2B].
Supplee, Harriet (61 yrs.) d. on 70-Apr-11 of Consumption [70-Apr-12: 2B; 70-Apr-13: 2B].
Supplee, Hattie L. m. Hort, William Francis on 69-Apr-20 [69-Apr-26: 2B].
Suter, Frank T. m. Ford, Alverda A. on 70-Oct-25 [70-Oct-27: 2B].
Suter, Geneva J. m. Conradt, Chris J. on 67-May-2 [67-May-8: 2B].
Suter, Kate A. d. on 66-Nov-8 [66-Nov-9: 2C].
Suter, Sallie A. m. Bond, John on 70-Jan-12 [70-Jan-15: 2C].
Suter, William H. m. Patterson, Jennie E. on 68-Mar-25 [68-Dec-28: 2B].
Sutherland, George A. m. Baker, Susie on 70-Dec-27 [70-Dec-30: 2C].
Sutherland, J. B. m. Gormley, Jennie on 69-Sep-15 [69-Sep-18: 2B].
Sutherland, James (36 yrs.) d. on 66-Dec-31 [67-Jan-3: 2C].
Sutherland, John S. m. Taylor, Sarah Emma on 70-Sep-8 [70-Sep-17: 2B].
Sutherland, Sidney E. (14 yrs.) d. on 66-Jan-5 [66-Jan-6: 2B].
Sutor, Henry P. m. Beecher, Maggie S. on 68-Oct-15 [68-Oct-27: 2B].
Sutro, Elise m. Schucking, Constantin on 66-May-8 [66-May-9: 2B].
Sutro, Otto m. Handy, Arianna on 69-Oct-28 [69-Oct-29: 2B].
Suttle, C. F. m. Claiborne, Emily L. on 66-Oct-2 [66-Oct-5: 2B; 66-Oct-6: 2A].
Suttle, Frances (76 yrs.) d. on 69-Oct-17 [69-Oct-18: 2C].
Sutton, Charles (27 yrs.) d. on 66-Jan-20 [66-Jan-22: 2C].
Sutton, James R. (42 yrs.) d. on 68-Feb-11 of Hydrophobia [68-Feb-12: 2C; 68-Feb-13: 2C].
Sutton, Jonathon P. S. (21 yrs.) d. on 68-Aug-20 [68-Aug-21: 2B].
Sutton, Martha A. m. Gorsuch, William S. on 66-May-3 [66-May-14: 2B].
Sutton, Mary A. (41 yrs.) d. on 68-May-6 [68-May-7: 2B; 68-May-8: 2B].
Sutton, Mary C. (18 yrs.) d. on 68-Mar-14 [68-Mar-16: 2B].
Sutton, Mollie E. m. Torsch, John W. on 66-Mar-29 [66-Apr-6: 2B].
Sutton, Mollie Guona (17 yrs.) d. on 68-Jan-19 of Brain congestion [68-Jan-20: 1F, 2C; 68-Jan-21: 2C].
Sutton, Nannie A. m. Bogdan, Arthur on 67-Sep-19 [67-Sep-20: 2A].
Sutton, Otho m. Mills, Sallie P. on 68-Jul-21 [68-Aug-10: 2B].
Sutton, Samuel V. (29 yrs.) d. on 68-Jul-4 of Lung hemorrhage [68-Jul-9: 2B].
Sutton, Sarah m. Corse, George F. on 66-Nov-13 [66-Nov-16: 2C].
Swab, F. m. Nickman, Carolina on 66-Aug-12 [66-Aug-28: 2B; 66-Aug-29: 2B].
Swain, Abraham R., Capt. (54 yrs.) d. on 70-Nov-22 [70-Dec-13: 2C].

Swain, Charlotte H. (47 yrs.) d. on 67-May-27 [67-May-28: 2B; 67-May-29: 2B].
Swain, Eddie (2 yrs., 8 mos.) d. on 70-Apr-8 [70-Apr-9: 2B].
Swain, Edward (10 yrs., 9 mos.) d. on 66-Jan-12 of Scarlet fever [66-Jan-15: 2C].
Swain, Edward m. Gray, Maggie on 66-Nov-11 [66-Nov-13: 2B].
Swain, Eliza (4 yrs., 6 mos.) d. on 65-Dec-30 [66-Jan-1: 2C].
Swain, Harriet V. m. Gregg, Z. T. on 70-Jun-15 [70-Jun-20: 2B].
Swain, Howard m. Crowell, Frances on 69-Jun-29 [69-Jun-30: 2C].
Swain, John (84 yrs.) d. on 70-Apr-6 [70-Apr-7: 2C].
Swain, Laura Virginia d. on 70-Jul-21 [70-Jul-22: 2C].
Swain, Mary A. (20 yrs.) d. on 69-Nov-8 [69-Nov-9: 2C].
Swain, Mollie d. on 70-May-17 [70-May-17: 2B].
Swain, Tamer M. d. on 66-May-24 [66-May-26: 2B].
Swain, William Emmet (3 yrs.) d. on 66-Aug-2 [66-Aug-3: 2C].
Swain, William M. (58 yrs., 9 mos.) d. on 68-Feb-16 [68-Feb-17: 2A; 68-Feb-19: 2C; 68-Feb-20: 2C].
Swan, Alice A. m. Woodward, George W. on 68-Jul-21 [68-Aug-19: 2B].
Swan, Eliza James (3 yrs.) d. on 69-Aug-22 [69-Aug-23: 2C].
Swan, Horace D. (62 yrs.) d. on 67-Nov-24 [67-Nov-27: 2C; 67-Nov-28: 2C].
Swan, Samuel M. m. Collins, Lizzie A. on 69-May-25 [69-May-28: 2C].
Swan, Sophia C. m. Coles, William, Jr. on 70-Feb-10 [70-Feb-12: 2B].
Swan, William (80 yrs.) d. on 67-Apr-15 [67-Apr-16: 1G, 2B].
Swanberry, Mary A. m. Griffin, Levi on 68-Apr-30 [68-Jun-26: 2B].
Swanger, J. P., Rev. (32 yrs.) d. on 67-Jun-29 [67-Jul-1: 2B].
Swann, Carrie V. m. McEnnis, James J. on 70-Sep-22 [70-Sep-26: 2B].
Swann, Emma S. m. Richards, James P. on 70-Apr-12 [70-Apr-16: 2B].
Swann, Fannie A. m. Roberts, Charles M. on 67-Jun-11 [67-Jun-19: 2B].
Swann, James m. Grimes, Carrie V. on 67-Apr-9 [67-Apr-13: 2B].
Swann, James H. (26 yrs.) d. on 68-Sep-13 [68-Sep-14: 2B].
Swann, Jeanie B. m. Ferguson, Thomas on 67-Apr-23 [67-Apr-25: 2B].
Swann, Mary M. m. Carter, C. Shirley on 67-Oct-22 [67-Oct-24: 2B].
Swann, Thomas, Jr. (31 yrs.) d. on 66-Aug-7 [66-Aug-8: 1G, 2C; 66-Aug-9: 2C].
Swann, Thomas Warren (8 mos.) d. on 67-Feb-28 [67-Mar-2: 2B].
Swann, William Albert (4 mos.) d. on 66-Oct-31 [66-Nov-1: 2B].
Swartz, Ellenora m. Heaps, William H. on 69-Nov-16 [69-Nov-29: 2C].
Swartz, Mary E. m. Keller, Samuel P. on 68-Nov-17 [68-Dec-8: 2C].
Sweaney, Charles Henry (5 yrs., 2 mos.) d. on 66-May-22 [66-May-23: 2B].
Sweaney, Randolph B. m. Daley, Helen E. on 66-Oct-23 [66-Oct-25: 2C].
Sweany, Clara E. (38 yrs.) d. on 68-Jun-14 [68-Jun-15: 2B; 68-Jun-16: 2B].
Swearer, Benjamin m. Williams, Kate C. on 68-Jun-2 [68-Jun-3: 2B].
Swearer, Charles (7 yrs.) d. on 67-Oct-13 of Chronic croup [67-Oct-15: 2A].
Swearer, Charles Corney (1 yr., 3 mos.) d. on 70-Jul-23 [70-Jul-25: 2C].
Swearer, Francis (4 yrs., 9 mos.) d. on 70-Jun-27 [70-Jun-28: 2C].
Sweeney, Alice J. m. Clautice, William F. on 70-Nov-17 [70-Nov-19: 2B].
Sweeney, Bridget C. (26 yrs.) d. on 68-Jun-13 [68-Jun-15: 2B].
Sweeney, Daniel (34 yrs.) d. on 68-Sep-5 [68-Sep-5: 2A].
Sweeney, James Henry (11 yrs.) d. on 67-Mar-6 [67-Mar-7: 2C].
Sweeney, Owen d. on 67-Aug-5 [67-Aug-7: 2C].
Sweeney, Peter d. on 69-Oct-9 of Paralysis [69-Oct-11: 1G, 1H].
Sweeney, Peter m. Cook, Julia A. on 66-Jun-28 [66-Jun-30: 2B].
Sweeney, Priscilla d. on 69-Jul-17 [69-Jul-19: 2D].
Sweeny, Eliza m. Carney, John, Jr. on 67-Dec-8 [67-Dec-19: 2B].
Sweeny, Martha W. d. on 69-Nov-4 [69-Nov-5: 2C].
Sweet, A. C. m. Taylor, Lydia A. on 66-Jan-9 [66-Jan-23: 2C].
Sweeting, Bell S. m. Bowman, Alonzo on 70-Feb-10 [70-Feb-14: 2C].
Sweeting, Benjamin F. (2 yrs., 7 mos.) d. on 66-Jun-18 [66-Jun-19: 2B; 66-Jun-20: 2C].

Sweeting, Edward m. McCauley, Ruth A. on 67-Apr-9 [67-Apr-11: 2B].
Sweetser, George W. m. Billmyer, Kate S. on 67-Nov-2 [67-Nov-8: 2C].
Sweglar, Robert E. Lee (1 yr., 3 mos.) d. on 67-Dec-6 [67-Dec-7: 2B].
Sweikert, William m. Farley, Ida on 69-Jan-13 [69-Jan-18: 2C].
Swenk, Annie m. Diffenbach, W. H. H. on 66-Jul-19 [66-Jul-26: 2C].
Swertzer, Charles (43 yrs.) d. on 70-Dec-10 of Apoplexy [70-Dec-16: 2C].
Swett, Carrie (4 yrs.) d. on 66-Jan-9 [66-Jan-10: 2C].
Swick, Alphonsus Lee (3 yrs., 9 mos.) d. on 68-Aug-13 [68-Aug-15: 2B].
Swick, Elizabeth (13 yrs., 4 mos.) d. on 69-Mar-31 [69-Apr-2: 2C].
Swick, Joseph F. (16 yrs.) d. on 66-Aug-24 [66-Aug-27: 1G; 66-Oct-20: 2C].
Swift, Alice A. m. Thompson, James F. on 66-Nov-22 [66-Nov-24: 2B].
Swift, Caroline m. Flagherty, Lewis R. D. on 66-Mar-14 [66-Mar-28: 2C].
Swift, J. H. m. Quinlan, M. L. on 69-Feb-2 [69-Feb-9: 2C].
Swift, Lizzie E. m. Unkle, George on 70-Mar-29 [70-Mar-30: 2B].
Swift, Loretta Frances (2 mos.) d. on 70-Feb-12 [70-Feb-14: 2C].
Swift, Mary D. (83 yrs.) d. on 70-Apr-30 [70-May-10: 2C].
Swift, Nathan m. Benton, Rosaltha E. on 70-Mar-24 [70-Mar-30: 2B].
Swift, Thirza May (1 yr., 2 mos.) d. on 68-Jul-3 [68-Jul-10: 2C].
Swigert, Christian (55 yrs.) d. on 70-Nov-28 of Suicide (Shooting) [70-Nov-29: 4C].
Swindell, George E. m. Wiegel, Julia E. on 70-Jan-13 [70-Jan-17: 2C].
Swing, Mollie P. m. Renner, George, Jr. on 68-Sep-29 [68-Oct-8: 2B].
Swinney, Epaphroditus m. Jones, Lizzie P. on 66-Oct-17 [66-Oct-18: 2B].
Swinney, Victoria Virginia m. Knapp, John on 69-Dec-19 [69-Dec-25: 2C].
Swinney, Willis (11 mos.) d. on 68-Jul-24 [68-Jul-25: 2B].
Switzer, Elizabeth m. McNally, John on 68-Oct-4 [68-Oct-6: 2B].
Switzer, Ella F. m. Uppercu, Thomas S. on 68-Jun-1 [68-Jun-23: 2B].
Switzer, Isabella (24 yrs.) d. on 66-Jan-11 [66-Jan-13: 2C].
Switzer, Jennie C. m. Ballauf, William L. on 67-Sep-13 [68-Jan-18: 2B].
Switzer, Mary E. m. Bentzel, Henry on 68-Dec-23 [68-Dec-28: 2B].
Switzer, Mary Isabella (2 mos.) d. on 69-Mar-25 [69-Mar-30: 2C].
Swope, Charles C. m. Smith, Johannah L. on 70-Jun-23 [70-Jun-30: 2C].
Swope, Maggie m. French, Andrew on 70-May-10 [70-May-13: 2C].
Sword, John W. (64 yrs.) d. on 70-Apr-21 [70-Apr-22: 2C; 70-Apr-23: 2B].
Sword, Matilda Ann d. on 69-Dec-15 [70-Feb-18: 2C].
Swormstedt, Henrietta d. on 68-Sep-6 [68-Sep-7: 2A].
Syer, Robert m. Foley, Martha V. on 69-May-24 [69-May-25: 2C].
Sykes, Atwell (10 yrs.) d. on 66-Jun-5 Drowned [66-Jun-6: 1G].
Sykes, Cecilia (60 yrs.) d. on 67-Feb-4 [67-Feb-6: 2C].
Sykes, James m. Herring, Imogene E. on 70-Mar-15 [70-Mar-19: 2B].
Sykes, Martha d. on 69-Feb-14 [69-Feb-15: 2C; 69-Feb-16: 2C].
Sykes, Mary Virginia (20 yrs.) d. on 67-Mar-12 [67-Mar-14: 2C].
Sykes, Sallie Edith (16 yrs., 1 mo.) d. on 67-Jan-4 [67-Jan-7: 2C].
Sykes, Sarah V. (18 yrs.) d. on 70-May-25 [70-May-31: 2B].
Sylvester, Elizabeth m. Amos, B. F. on 66-Aug-12 [66-Aug-14: 2C].
Sylvester, Lydia (70 yrs.) d. on 66-Dec-19 [66-Dec-21: 2B].
Sylvester, William George m. Cooper, Janet H. on 67-Feb-21 [67-Feb-25: 2C].
Symington, Andrew Johnston d. on 69-Dec-26 [69-Dec-28: 2D].
Symington, John F. (23 yrs.) d. on 67-Jan-26 [67-Jan-28: 2C].
Symonds, Charles A. (3 yrs., 11 mos.) d. on 70-Sep-15 [70-Sep-17: 2B].
Symonds, Willie H. (1 yr., 11 mos.) d. on 70-Sep-22 [70-Sep-23: 2C].
Szemelenyi, Fritz d. on 67-Jun-14 [67-Jun-15: 2B].
Tabler, John L. (30 yrs.) d. on 70-Apr-25 of Epilepsy [70-Apr-30: 2B].
Tableton, John (64 yrs.) d. on 70-Mar-15 [70-Mar-17: 2C].
Taft, Alfred H. m. Meakin, Sarah J. on 70-Nov-24 [70-Nov-28: 2C].
Taft, Lottie m. Jenkins, Conway M. on 70-Nov-24 [70-Nov-30: 2C].

Tagart, Elizabeth L. d. on 70-Nov-2 [70-Nov-4: 2C].
Tagart, Helen (1 yr.) d. on 69-Jan-1 [69-Jan-6: 2C].
Tagart, William d. on 66-May-22 [66-May-24: 2C].
Taggert, William (18 yrs.) d. on 67-Nov-11 of Consumption [67-Nov-12: 2C].
Tagney, Joe V. m. Fitzpatrick, James on 69-Jan-28 [69-Feb-6: 2C].
Talbot, Caleb Allen (8 mos.) d. [66-Aug-28: 2B].
Talbot, James A. C. m. Wise, Linnie S. on 66-Mar-27 [66-Apr-12: 2B].
Talbot, Joshua F. C. m. Read, Mary on 68-Jun-16 [68-Jul-3: 2B].
Talbot, Margaret m. Tipton, W. on 67-Jun-24 [67-Jun-26: 2C].
Talbot, Mary Ann d. on 69-Jan-31 [69-Feb-2: 2C].
Talbot, Mary Jane (47 yrs.) d. on 70-Feb-17 [70-Feb-18: 2C].
Talbot, Rebecca A. m. Diffenderfer, Michael D. on 69-Jun-2 [69-Jun-11: 2C].
Talbott, Charles Hutchinson (6 yrs., 10 mos.) d. on 66-Mar-25 [66-Mar-26: 2C].
Talbott, Emma m. Nash, John W. on 68-Oct-13 [68-Oct-25: 2C].
Talbott, George H. m. Wiley, Eliza Jane on 69-Oct-6 [69-Nov-1: 2B].
Talbott, Hamilton M. (30 yrs.) d. on 70-Mar-4 [70-Mar-5: 2B].
Talbott, J. Fred C. m. Cockey, Laura on 69-Feb-3 [69-Feb-22: 2C].
Talbott, John (63 yrs.) d. on 66-Nov-28 [66-Nov-29: 2C].
Talbott, John F. m. Corbin, Georgette on 70-Apr-10 [70-Apr-13: 2B].
Talbott, John T. m. Ball, Annie P. on 69-Jun-1 [69-Jun-3: 2B].
Talbott, Joshua F. C. (73 yrs.) d. on 69-Mar-24 [69-Mar-26: 2C].
Talbott, Louisa (63 yrs.) d. on 66-Feb-26 [66-Feb-28: 2C].
Talbott, Maggie m. Stinson, R. James on 67-Dec-5 [67-Dec-9: 2B].
Talbott, Mariam (42 yrs.) d. on 69-Feb-17 [69-Feb-25: 2D].
Talbott, Mary Jane m. Parlett, Hezekiah on 65-Dec-25 [66-Jan-1: 2C].
Talbott, Sarah (77 yrs.) d. on 68-Jun-15 [68-Jun-16: 2B].
Talbott, Thomas E. (48 yrs.) d. on 70-Mar-10 [70-Mar-11: 2C].
Talbott, Thomas J. (65 yrs.) d. on 69-Mar-5 [69-Mar-6: 2C].
Talbott, Thomas J., Jr. m. Waters, Mattie M. on 67-Nov-21 [67-Nov-27: 2B].
Talbott, William C. (27 yrs., 4 mos.) d. on 66-May-5 [66-May-8: 2B].
Taliaferro, Emma (30 yrs.) d. on 68-May-11 [68-Mar-12: 2B].
Taliaferro, G. C. m. Godwin, R. L. on 69-Apr-30 [69-Sep-1: 2B].
Taliaferro, Maggie B. m. Gwyn, Charles L. on 68-Apr-28 [68-May-5: 2B].
Tall, R. J. H. m. Blake, Mollie C. on 68-Apr-14 [68-Apr-28: 2B].
Tall, S. Columbus, Esq. m. Wheeler, Maggie T., Miss on 66-Feb-21 [66-Feb-27: 2B].
Tall, Sarah d. on 66-Oct-13 [66-Oct-19: 2B].
Tall, Sarah J. (30 yrs.) d. on 68-Jan-30 [68-Jan-31: 2C].
Tall, William (43 yrs., 1 mo.) d. on 68-Jul-10 of Cholera morbus [68-Jul-14: 2C].
Talley, William A. (27 yrs.) d. on 69-Dec-12 of Consumption [69-Dec-13: 2C; 69-Dec-14: 2C].
Tanderlin, Hendrik d. on 70-Jul-29 [70-Jul-30: 4D].
Tanera, Mary G. d. on 68-Mar-5 [68-Mar-7: 2C].
Taney, Harriet (79 yrs.) d. on 66-Jul-2 [66-Jul-4: 2C].
Taneyhill, Mary m. Shipley, George on 68-Jul-1 [69-Apr-9: 2B].
Tanner, Annie S. m. Porter, William E. on 66-Oct-17 [66-Oct-19: 2B].
Tanner, Eliza A. m. Cole, William W. on 69-Nov-9 [69-Nov-11: 2C].
Tanner, John Harvey (10 mos.) d. on 70-Aug-24 [70-Aug-25: 2C].
Tanner, Mary Darby (16 yrs.) d. on 67-Aug-14 of Typhoid [67-Aug-17: 2B].
Tanneyhill, Samuel (52 yrs.) d. on 68-Jun-29 [68-Jun-30: 2B].
Tapman, Harry T. m. Waldman, Aggie E. on 67-Jan-1 [67-Jan-5: 2C].
Tapman, John M. (58 yrs., 10 mos.) d. on 70-Apr-15 [70-Apr-16: 2B].
Tapman, Martha S. m. Moore, Charles H. on 68-Aug-30 [68-Sep-1: 2A].
Tapper, William H. m. Ely, Ellen N. on 70-Jan-2 [70-Jan-4: 2C].
Tappey, Mary V. m. Burton, Harry W. on 66-Nov-27 [66-Dec-5: 2B].
Tarleton, James R. m. Wright, Maggie J. on 68-Oct-29 [68-Nov-11: 2C].
Tarleton, Mary D. m. Aaron, Charles F. on 68-Sep-14 [68-Sep-17: 2B].

Tarleton, Sarah H. m. Morgan, Thomas E. on 68-Mar-15 [68-Mar-17: 2C].
Tarlton, Mary Louise m. Seipp, Henry F. on 68-Dec-29 [69-Jan-11: 2C].
Tarman, William W. m. Pryor, Lizzie on 69-Dec-23 [70-Jan-22: 2B].
Tarr, John T. (48 yrs., 3 mos.) d. on 69-Apr-20 [69-Apr-21: 2C].
Tarr, Leida J. m. Stone, Yelverton P. on 67-Sep-24 [67-Sep-30: 2B].
Tarr, Margaret DuPlessis (25 yrs.) d. on 67-Sep-17 [67-Sep-18: 2B].
Tarr, Wesley B. m. Doyer, Emma on 69-Mar-2 [69-Mar-22: 2C].
Tarr, William H., Rev. (72 yrs., 11 mos.) d. on 70-Jul-19 [70-Jul-20: 2C].
Tarring, George W. (40 yrs.) d. on 69-Nov-26 [69-Nov-27: 2C].
Tarter, Hagar (87 yrs.) d. on 66-Jul-28 [66-Jul-28: 2C].
Tarter, Henry H. m. Anderson, Julia on 67-Aug-1 [67-Aug-6: 2C].
Tase, Andrew m. Bowen, Emma on 66-Jun-21 [66-Jun-25: 2B].
Tasker, Kate m. Keys, John on 69-May-6 [69-May-8: 2B].
Tate, James E. m. Hargrave, Frances on 68-Oct-28 [68-Nov-5: 2C].
Tate, James Thomas (36 yrs.) d. on 67-Jan-2 [68-Jan-3: 2C].
Tate, Susan A. S. (1 yr., 6 mos.) d. on 66-Aug-2 [66-Aug-3: 2C].
Tates, Samuel d. on 66-Dec-26 [66-Dec-27: 1G].
Tatham, George F. m. Dunn, Issac B. [68-Oct-12: 2B].
Tatham, Rosa A. R. m. Burke, J. M. on 68-Nov-12 [68-Nov-26: 2B].
Tatham, Sue E. m. Williams, Zeddie F. on 66-Apr-11 [66-Apr-17: 2C].
Tatum, Maggie m. Eager, Joseph on 66-Mar-20 [66-Apr-12: 2B].
Tatum, Missouri (18 yrs.) d. on 67-Aug-5 [67-Aug-8: 2B].
Tatum, Mollie m. Johnson, George W. on 70-Jun-23 [70-Jul-12: 2B].
Taunea, Keziah m. Gibbins, Oliver on 67-Dec-26 [68-Jan-3: 2C].
Taverner, Edgar H. m. Baker, Annie on 66-Feb-22 [66-Mar-5: 2B].
Taylor, Adaline m. Pennington, Daniel H. on 66-Jun-7 [66-Jun-9: 2B].
Taylor, Almira C. m. Morrison, James S. on 70-Dec-7 [70-Dec-15: 2C].
Taylor, Amanda P. m. Deichmann, Augustus on 67-May-7 [67-May-11: 2A].
Taylor, Angelo m. Smith, Mahala on 66-Jan-18 [66-Jan-23: 2C].
Taylor, Anna m. Ferguson, William on 67-Dec-17 [67-Dec-25: 2C].
Taylor, Anna E. m. Dolbow, Reuben N. on 67-Jan-18 [67-Jan-19: 2C].
Taylor, Anne Maria (7 yrs., 9 mos.) d. on 70-Dec-8 of Scarlet fever [70-Dec-9: 2C].
Taylor, Annie m. Sauerwein, Edwin on 69-May-13 [69-May-15: 2B].
Taylor, Annie B. m. Holmes, William T. on 66-Aug-20 [66-Oct-3: 2B].
Taylor, Annie Sidney (1 yr.) d. on 67-Sep-19 [67-Sep-27: 2C].
Taylor, Bell Madera (15 yrs.) d. on 66-Jan-15 [66-Jan-16: 2C; 66-Jan-17: 2C].
Taylor, Benjamin F. m. Cator, Mary J. on 69-Feb-23 [69-Feb-24: 2C].
Taylor, Benjamin S. (24 yrs.) d. on 67-May-7 [67-May-8: 2B].
Taylor, Caleb S. m. Moore, Eleanor on 69-Jun-10 [69-Jun-23: 2C].
Taylor, Carrie A. m. Maben, James A. on 66-Jan-24 [66-Jan-27: 2B].
Taylor, Carrie J. m. Dyer, Walter J. L. on 66-Oct-10 [66-Oct-16: 2B].
Taylor, Catherine (69 yrs.) d. on 68-Mar-11 [68-Mar-12: 2B; 68-Mar-13: 2C].
Taylor, Catherine (73 yrs.) d. on 67-Dec-20 [67-Dec-23: 2B].
Taylor, Celinda (65 yrs.) d. on 66-Jul-20 [66-Jul-21: 2C].
Taylor, Charles Edgar (1 yr.) d. on 67-Jan-31 [67-Feb-2: 2C].
Taylor, Charles H. (8 mos.) d. on 67-Sep-1 [67-Sep-2: 2B].
Taylor, Charles H. m. Carroll, Annie T. on 67-Nov-28 [67-Nov-30: 2C].
Taylor, Charles J. m. Nelson, Fannie B. on 68-Mar-12 [68-Mar-24: 2B].
Taylor, Christie A. m. Barnes, Denton on 70-Feb-10 [70-Feb-25: 2C].
Taylor, D. Wesley m. Brown, Amelia T. on 70-Nov-30 [70-Dec-7: 2C].
Taylor, David Cornelius (6 yrs., 7 mos.) d. on 67-Sep-5 [67-Sep-12: 2B].
Taylor, Edgar G. d. on 67-Apr-9 [67-Apr-11: 2B].
Taylor, Edward (58 yrs.) d. on 70-Jan-1 [70-Jan-15: 2C].
Taylor, Edward Everett (7 yrs., 3 mos.) d. on 68-Feb-17 [68-Feb-18: 2C].
Taylor, Elijah (82 yrs.) d. on 67-Nov-21 [67-Nov-22: 2C; 67-Nov-23: 1E, 2B].

Taylor, Eliza Ann d. on 66-Dec-29 Murdered (Assault) [66-Dec-31: 1F].
Taylor, Elizabeth (33 yrs.) d. on 68-Aug-8 [68-Aug-18: 2B].
Taylor, Elizabeth (29 yrs.) d. on 66-Oct-9 [66-Oct-9: 2A].
Taylor, Elizabeth A. (40 yrs., 6 mos.) d. on 70-Jul-9 [70-Jul-11: 2C].
Taylor, Elizabeth Ester (10 mos.) d. on 67-Mar-14 of Scarlet fever [67-Mar-15: 2C].
Taylor, Elizabeth J. (23 yrs., 9 mos.) d. on 66-Feb-12 [66-Feb-13: 2C].
Taylor, Ella Moseana (3 yrs.) d. on 66-Mar-6 [66-Mar-7: 2B].
Taylor, Ellen (38 yrs.) d. on 69-Dec-17 [69-Dec-20: 2C].
Taylor, Ellen (66 yrs.) d. on 69-Nov-27 [69-Dec-9: 2C].
Taylor, Ellen V. (61 yrs.) d. on 70-Jul-7 [70-Jul-8: 2C; 70-Jul-14: 2B].
Taylor, Emily (55 yrs.) d. on 68-May-31 [68-Jun-2: 1G].
Taylor, Emma H. m. Ward, George H. on 69-Aug-12 [69-Aug-13: 2C].
Taylor, Evelyn Juliett m. Wright, Thomas Clayton on 68-Nov-18 [68-Nov-21: 2C].
Taylor, Frances C. (18 yrs.) d. on 69-May-8 [69-May-10: 2C].
Taylor, Frances T. D. d. on 70-Jun-23 [70-Jun-24: 2C; 70-Jun-25: 2C].
Taylor, George, Dr. (36 yrs., 5 mos.) d. on 67-Aug-5 of Yellow fever [67-Aug-8: 1G, 2B].
Taylor, George (82 yrs.) d. on 70-Sep-21 [70-Sep-23: 2C].
Taylor, George M. m. Moore, Francina on 70-Jun-21 [70-Jul-4: 2C; 70-Jul-6: 2C].
Taylor, George W. m. Sisco, Isabella A on 66-Jan-25 [66-Jan-27: 2B].
Taylor, George W. m. Burke, Sallie on 69-Aug-27 [69-Sep-11: 2B].
Taylor, Helen C. m. Lambdin, Thomas A. J. on 68-Dec-20 [68-Dec-22: 2C].
Taylor, Henrietta P. m. Fletcher, James S. on 69-Sep-20 [69-Mar-29: 2B].
Taylor, Henry m. Gray, Roberta F. on 66-Jul-30 [66-Aug-3: 2C].
Taylor, Henry McKeson d. on 70-May-9 [70-May-10: 2C].
Taylor, Henry S. m. Myers, Euphemia A. on 66-Mar-20 [66-Mar-27: 2B].
Taylor, Horace Vincent (1 yr., 2 mos.) d. on 70-Jan-27 [70-Jan-28: 2C].
Taylor, Ida (27 yrs.) d. on 67-May-18 [67-May-20: 2B].
Taylor, Irene C. m. Bennett, Pinkney J. on 68-Jun-9 [68-Jun-11: 2B].
Taylor, Isabella (75 yrs.) d. on 70-Mar-14 [70-Mar-15: 2C; 70-Mar-16: 2C].
Taylor, Isabella F. (4 mos.) d. on 69-May-8 [69-May-11: 2C].
Taylor, Issac (67 yrs.) d. on 67-May-19 [67-May-21: 2B].
Taylor, James, Capt. (50 yrs.) d. on 67-May-20 [67-May-23: 1E].
Taylor, James (34 yrs.) d. on 67-Jan-14 [67-Jan-16: 2C].
Taylor, James m. Fleishall, Fannie on 70-Sep-1 [70-Sep-3: 2B].
Taylor, James B. m. Tipton, Hannah E. on 67-Jul-18 [67-Jul-20: 2C].
Taylor, James H. C. (36 yrs.) d. on 67-Jan-23 of Typhoid [67-Jan-24: 2C].
Taylor, James J. W. m. LaPorte, Emma L. on 70-Oct-4 [70-Oct-11: 2B].
Taylor, James W. W. m. Sauerhoff, Mary Elizabeth on 66-Mar-22 [66-Mar-27: 2B].
Taylor, Jane (53 yrs.) d. on 68-Dec-15 [68-Dec-17: 2C].
Taylor, Jane (48 yrs.) d. on 67-Oct-15 of Consumption [67-Oct-23: 2B].
Taylor, John W. m. Welch, Sallie E. on 67-Jan-15 [67-Jan-19: 2C].
Taylor, Joseph (72 yrs.) d. on 68-Feb-27 [68-Mar-2: 2C].
Taylor, Joseph d. on 67-Feb-11 [67-Feb-13: 2D; 67-Feb-12: 2C].
Taylor, Joseph (75 yrs.) d. on 70-Dec-14 [70-Dec-15: 2C].
Taylor, Joseph (29 yrs.) d. on 70-May-28 [70-Jun-2: 2B].
Taylor, Joseph m. Coale, Rebecca S. on 66-Nov-15 [66-Nov-16: 2C].
Taylor, Josephine (41 yrs.) d. on 70-Apr-25 [70-Apr-27: 1H].
Taylor, Josephine I. (24 yrs.) d. on 69-Mar-10 of Consumption [69-Mar-16: 2C].
Taylor, Joshua, Gen. (88 yrs.) d. on 66-Nov-12 [66-Nov-14: 2B].
Taylor, Joshua (58 yrs.) d. on 69-Mar-28 [69-Apr-3: 2B].
Taylor, Kate A. d. on 67-Feb-11 [67-Feb-13: 2D].
Taylor, Kate A. m. Jones, William H. on 67-Sep-13 [67-Nov-23: 2B].
Taylor, Laura E. m. Tonge, William G. D. on 70-Jun-15 [70-Jun-16: 2B].
Taylor, Laura J. m. Coe, William H. on 66-Oct-21 [66-Oct-30: 2B].
Taylor, Lemuel K. (43 yrs.) d. on 69-Mar-20 [69-Mar-22: 2C].

Taylor, Lewis Thomas (16 yrs., 1 mo.) d. on 70-Sep-9 [70-Sep-13: 2B].
Taylor, Littleton (65 yrs.) d. on 67-Apr-11 [67-Apr-13: 2B].
Taylor, Lurannah m. Askey, J. Robert on 67-Jan-10 [67-Jan-16: 2C; 67-Jan-19: 2C].
Taylor, Lydia A. m. Sweet, A. C. on 66-Jan-9 [66-Jan-23: 2C].
Taylor, Mager J. (67 yrs.) d. on 66-Apr-19 of Apoplexy [66-Apr-20: 2B].
Taylor, Mager W. (31 yrs.) d. on 67-Jul-31 [67-Aug-1: 2C].
Taylor, Maggie (17 yrs., 2 mos.) d. on 67-Feb-19 of Typhoid [67-Feb-21: 2C; 67-Feb-23: 2C].
Taylor, Margaret E. m. Higgins, William M. on 69-Jul-15 [69-Aug-21: 2B].
Taylor, Margaret J. (42 yrs.) d. on 68-Feb-13 [68-Feb-14: 2C; 68-Feb-15: 2B].
Taylor, Margaret Powell (61 yrs.) d. on 67-Jun-23 [67-Jun-24: 2B].
Taylor, Maria d. on 68-Feb-13 [68-Feb-14: 2C; 68-Feb-15: 2B].
Taylor, Martha A. m. Randolph, Robert L. on 68-Sep-17 [68-Oct-7: 2C].
Taylor, Martha E. (11 yrs., 3 mos.) d. on 70-Aug-22 [70-Aug-24: 2C].
Taylor, Mary (85 yrs.) d. on 68-Nov-10 [68-Nov-12: 2C].
Taylor, Mary (72 yrs.) d. on 68-Sep-18 [68-Sep-21: 2B].
Taylor, Mary A. m. Henning, William S. on 70-Oct-11 [70-Oct-20: 2B].
Taylor, Mary A. C. (64 yrs.) d. on 69-May-26 [69-May-28: 2C].
Taylor, Mary Alice (7 mos.) d. on 68-Mar-28 [68-May-2: 2C].
Taylor, Mary Ann (59 yrs.) d. on 66-May-28 [66-May-29: 2B].
Taylor, Mary E. (62 yrs.) d. on 66-Mar-16 [66-Mar-17: 2B].
Taylor, Mary E. m. Dryden, Joseph H. on 67-Nov-12 [67-Dec-18: 2B].
Taylor, Mary E. m. Stockman, J. Garrison on 69-Dec-15 [69-Dec-30: 2C].
Taylor, Mary Jane (58 yrs.) d. on 68-Jan-5 [68-Jan-6: 2C].
Taylor, Mary Jane (29 yrs., 8 mos.) d. on 68-Nov-5 [68-Nov-6: 2C].
Taylor, Mary V. m. Winter, Samuel G. on 67-May-15 [67-Jun-6: 2B].
Taylor, Milton N. m. Bankard, Josephine J. on 68-Jun-25 [68-Jun-29: 2B].
Taylor, Milton N. m. Griffith, Teresa on 70-Oct-6 [70-Dec-14: 2C].
Taylor, Mollie m. Deninger, J. B. on 67-Jun-11 [67-Jun-21: 2B].
Taylor, Mollie R. m. Merryman, Charles H. on 69-Oct-20 [69-Oct-23: 2B].
Taylor, R. Emory m. Blacklar, Cassie G. on 68-Nov-12 [68-Nov-14: 2B].
Taylor, Rachel Ann (3 yrs., 9 mos.) d. on 67-Aug-6 [67-Aug-8: 2B; 67-Aug-10: 2B].
Taylor, Rebecca m. Pentz, William F. on 70-May-26 [70-Jun-18: 2B].
Taylor, Richard (50 yrs.) d. on 69-Mar-16 in Machine accident [69-Mar-17: 1G, 2C].
Taylor, Robert (88 yrs.) d. on 69-Sep-16 [69-Sep-17: 2C; 69-Sep-18: 1H, 2B].
Taylor, Robert B. m. Cockrell, Irene L. on 69-Nov-25 [70-Jan-27: 2C].
Taylor, Sallie M. m. Lytle, John H. on 69-Jun-15 [69-Jun-23: 2C].
Taylor, Samuel B. (12 yrs.) d. on 66-Mar-6 in Riding accident [66-Mar-10: 2B].
Taylor, Sarah A. (54 yrs., 10 mos.) d. on 68-Jan-26 [68-Feb-5: 2D].
Taylor, Sarah E. m. Ford, Issac on 67-Oct-24 [67-Oct-30: 2B].
Taylor, Sarah Emma m. Sutherland, John S. on 70-Sep-8 [70-Sep-17: 2B].
Taylor, Sarah J. m. Lewis, George T. on 67-Dec-12 [67-Dec-17: 2B].
Taylor, Sharlotte (4 yrs., 6 mos.) d. on 70-Dec-8 of Scarlet fever [70-Dec-9: 2C].
Taylor, Sidney B. m. Eaton, Janie on 69-Jan-7 [69-Jan-15: 2D].
Taylor, Telucker J. m. Morris, Elijah J. on 69-Apr-22 [69-Apr-24: 2B].
Taylor, Thomas (73 yrs.) d. on 69-Sep-26 [69-Sep-27: 2C; 69-Sep-28: 2B].
Taylor, Thomas m. Lawrason, Annie Elizabeth on 66-Aug-30 [66-Sep-3: 2C].
Taylor, Thomas O. m. Smith, Anna M. on 68-Dec-17 [68-Dec-18: 2C].
Taylor, W. M. m. Owings, Eunice C. on 69-Dec-23 [70-Jan-4: 2C].
Taylor, William m. Moffet, Margaret Ann on 68-May-14 [68-May-21: 2B].
Taylor, William m. Tithin, Mary on 68-Sep-18 [68-Sep-22: 2B].
Taylor, William A. (36 yrs.) d. on 66-Nov-27 of Boiler explosion [66-Nov-28: 2B; 66-Nov-29: 2C].
Taylor, William G. m. Allen, Jane H. on 67-Aug-29 [67-Sep-5: 2B].
Taylor, William H. m. Smith, Isabel on 69-Dec-21 [69-Dec-22: 2B].
Taylor, William H. m. Brown, Mary E. on 69-Feb-11 [69-Feb-12: 2C].

Taylor, William H. m. Monmonier, Mary F. on 70-Feb-7 [70-Feb-9: 2C].
Taylor, William H. R. m. Tisdale, Elizabeth W. on 68-Oct-13 [68-Oct-20: 2B].
Taylor, William Harding m. Granger, Sarah M. on 68-Feb-11 [68-Feb-15: 2B].
Taylor, William Tyer (1 yr.) d. on 69-Nov-6 of Scarlet fever [69-Nov-10: 2C].
Taylor, William W., Capt. (56 yrs.) d. on 67-Jan-3 of Typhoid pneumonia [67-Jan-4: 2D; 67-Jan-5: 2C; 67-Jan-7: 2C].
Taylor, William Washington (7 mos.) d. on 66-Mar-9 [66-Mar-10: 2B].
Taylor, Willie W. (4 yrs., 1 mo.) d. on 69-Oct-22 [69-Oct-26: 2B].
Tayman, Kate C. m. Brooks, G. Edwin on 68-Jun-2 [68-Jul-11: 2B].
Tayman, Thomas m. Corkran, Amanda E. on 68-Jan-28 [68-Jan-31: 2C].
Teackle, Ellen S. m. Schley, William C. on 68-Dec-17 [68-Dec-22: 2C].
Teal, Ann Marie (68 yrs.) d. on 68-Jun-19 [68-Jun-20: 2B].
Teasdale, Thomas, Capt. d. on 69-May-9 of Chronic diarrhea [69-May-11: 1H].
Tebbs, William F. m. Gordon, Florence D. on 68-Nov-3 [68-Nov-6: 2C].
Teepe, Emma Louisa (2 mos.) d. on 66-Jul-15 [66-Jul-18: 2C].
Teepe, William H. (41 yrs., 7 mos.) d. on 66-Jul-21 [66-Jul-23: 2C].
Tegeler, George (3 yrs., 5 mos.) d. on 70-Oct-15 [70-Oct-17: 2B].
Temes, Harriet A. m. Smith, Richard on 67-Sep-16 [67-Sep-17: 2A].
Tempel, Thomas m. Hilbert, Barbara on 70-Aug-21 [70-Aug-25: 2B].
Temple, Amanda C. d. on 67-Feb-12 [67-Feb-16: 2D].
Temple, Anna Maria (64 yrs.) d. on 70-Mar-17 [70-Mar-19: 2C].
Temple, Margery (89 yrs.) d. on 70-Dec-14 [70-Dec-19: 2C].
Temple, William G. m. Roberts, Emma V. on 68-Jan-21 [68-Jan-31: 2C].
Temple, William J. m. Whittaker, Avarilla P. on 68-Dec-1 [68-Dec-16: 2C].
Templeman, Charlotte m. Naylor, Henry on 70-Feb-2 [70-Feb-7: 2C].
Tender, James m. Burrows, Ann Maria on 67-Aug-27 [67-Aug-28: 2B].
Tennant, Robert Lee (7 mos.) d. on 70-Jun-28 [70-Jun-29: 2C].
Tennant, Robert R. m. Green, Adelaide V. on 69-Dec-14 [69-Dec-16: 2C; 69-Dec-18: 2B].
Tennis, John M. m. Ward, Maggie on 67-Dec-30 [68-Jan-8: 2C].
Tennison, Catherine (42 yrs.) d. on 69-Dec-16 [69-Dec-17: 2C].
Terhune, John M. m. Cushley, Janie D. on 67-Jun-4 [67-Jun-7: 2B].
Terhune, John W. (1 yr., 1 mo.) d. on 69-Nov-29 [69-Nov-30: 2C; 69-Dec-1: 2C].
Terrell, Hattie Scott (2 yrs., 4 mos.) d. on 70-Jan-22 of Pneumonia [70-Jan-24: 2C].
Terres, Charles E. m. Tuslin, Marian W. on 70-Jun-15 [70-Jun-17: 2B].
Terres, J. B. m. Kirby, Virginia on 68-Jun-11 [68-Jul-4: 2C].
Tesdorpf, J. H. (34 yrs.) d. on 66-Dec-13 [66-Jan-3: 2C; 66-Jan-4: 2C].
Tessier, J. Andrew (52 yrs.) d. on 67-Aug-20 [67-Aug-23: 2B].
Test, Abraham (48 yrs.) d. on 68-Jan-6 [68-Jan-7: 1F].
Thacker, Mollie E. m. Small, Edward A. on 70-Jan-19 [70-Jan-29: 2B].
Thackery, Sallie D. m. Rutter, W. H. on 68-Jan-15 [68-Jan-30: 2C].
Thadel, John (56 yrs.) d. on 70-Jul-26 of Heatstroke [70-Jul-28: 4E].
Thamart, Augusta (20 yrs.) d. on 69-Feb-4 [69-Feb-5: 2C].
Tharp, Jonathan, Dr. (51 yrs.) d. on 68-Aug-1 [68-Aug-3: 2B].
Tharp, Pauline Ve m. Morrison, William D. on 68-Mar-3 [68-Mar-25: 2A].
Thater, Catherine Amelia (16 yrs., 8 mos.) d. on 66-Aug-14 [66-Aug-15: 2B].
Thater, Charles (54 yrs.) d. on 68-Aug-8 [68-Aug-10: 2B].
Thater, Elizabeth (74 yrs.) d. on 70-Nov-13 [70-Nov-15: 2C].
Thater, William Henry (9 yrs.) d. on 69-May-30 [69-May-31: 2C].
Thaw, Mary Callie m. Perry, R. Ross on 70-Nov-15 [70-Nov-17: 2C].
Thawley, W. E. m. Greenley, Mary E. on 67-Nov-26 [67-Nov-28: 2C].
Thayer, Henrietta (43 yrs.) d. on 66-May-28 [66-May-29: 2B].
Thayer, Mary R. m. Lake, James B., Jr. on 70-Sep-6 [70-Oct-5: 2B].
Thayer, N. J. m. Beggs, A. on 66-Jul-23 [66-Jul-25: 2C].
Thays, Catherine (65 yrs.) d. on 69-Sep-19 [69-Sep-21: 2B].
Theiss, Charles F. m. Miete, Amelie on 67-May-23 [67-May-27: 2B].

Thelin, William (74 yrs.) d. on 70-Apr-24 [70-Apr-26: 2B].
Thelin, William T. m. Griswold, Bessie on 68-Sep-24 [68-Sep-25: 2B].
Thesing, John H. (22 yrs.) d. on 70-Aug-21 of Suicide (Drowning) [70-Aug-24: 4D].
Thiede, Florence Augusta (1 yr., 1 mo.) d. on 69-Jan-5 [69-Jan-7: 2C].
Thiemeyer, Charles d. on 69-Sep-20 [69-Sep-21: 2B].
Thiemeyer, Lizzie m. Asendorf, C. H. on 68-Dec-3 [68-Dec-7: 2C].
Thierrauch, Angeline m. Wagner, Frederick on 67-Mar-24 [67-Mar-25: 2C].
Thierrauch, Lawson C. m. Atwell, Emma on 66-Jan-15 [66-Jan-17: 2C].
Thirkeld, L. May (1 yr., 6 mos.) d. on 66-Jul-18 [66-Jul-23: 2C].
Thole, George H. (13 yrs., 3 mos.) d. on 69-Feb-19 [69-Feb-27: 2C].
Thomas, A. d. on 67-Feb-7 [67-Feb-9: 2B].
Thomas, A. C. m. Bailey, Kate A. on 67-Jul-21 [67-Jul-24: 2C].
Thomas, Abbie A. m. Russell, W. A. on 69-Sep-7 [69-Oct-1: 2B].
Thomas, Ada m. Wilbur, Joseph T. on 68-Dec-1 [68-Dec-5: 2C].
Thomas, Alice m. Anderson, Julius H. on 68-Jul-23 [68-Jul-25: 2B].
Thomas, Alice m. Sparklin, James W. on 67-Apr-7 [67-Apr-17: 2B].
Thomas, Alice E. m. Mason, George A. on 69-Dec-14 [69-Dec-18: 2B].
Thomas, Ann m. Carrall, William on 69-May-20 [69-May-22: 2B].
Thomas, Ann R. m. McGlue, Henry S. on 66-Apr-18 [66-Apr-19: 2B].
Thomas, Annie M. m. McGee, Thomas J. on 67-Apr-28 [67-May-7: 2B].
Thomas, Augustus M. (11 mos.) d. on 68-Jul-12 [68-Jul-13: 2B].
Thomas, Augustus M. m. Moon, Mary L. Carr on 66-Oct-16 [66-Oct-18: 2B].
Thomas, B. D. m. Oster, Fannie A. on 69-Feb-24 [69-Mar-1: 2C].
Thomas, Barbara m. Ochs, George on 67-Oct-20 [67-Nov-1: 2B].
Thomas, Barbara A. (35 yrs.) d. on 67-Nov-20 [67-Nov-21: 2C; 67-Nov-22: 2C].
Thomas, Catherine Stewart d. on 66-Sep-29 [66-Oct-2: 2B].
Thomas, Charles Fenby d. on 69-May-14 [69-May-15: 2B].
Thomas, Charles H. (20 yrs.) d. on 67-Mar-1 of Heart disease [67-Mar-4: 4F].
Thomas, Charles Henry (45 yrs.) d. on 67-Jan-20 [67-Jan-22: 2C].
Thomas, Christina (18 yrs., 10 mos.) d. on 68-Mar-25 [68-Mar-27: 2C].
Thomas, Clarence Williams d. on 70-Jun-21 [70-Jun-23: 2C].
Thomas, Cora m. Olive, Charles H. on 69-Mar-2 [69-Mar-4: 2C].
Thomas, Cornelius A. m. Hicks, Ann E. on 67-Jul-2 [67-Jul-4: 2B].
Thomas, Daniel m. Brooks, Emma L. on 70-Feb-17 [70-Feb-22: 2C].
Thomas, Douglas H. m. Whitridge, Alice Lee on 70-Jan-25 [70-Jan-27: 2C; 70-Jan-29: 2B].
Thomas, Edward B. (67 yrs.) d. on 66-Jan-27 of Pneumonia [66-Feb-9: 2C].
Thomas, Edward B. (55 yrs.) d. on 66-Sep-26 [66-Oct-13: 2B; 66-Oct-15: 2B].
Thomas, Edward F. m. Kurtz, Alice on 69-May-20 [69-May-22: 2B].
Thomas, Edward Murphy (8 mos.) d. on 66-Sep-18 [66-Sep-19: 2B].
Thomas, Eleanor m. Smith, Mordecai K. on 68-Apr-15 [68-Apr-17: 2B].
Thomas, Eliza (63 yrs.) d. on 67-Jun-24 [67-Jun-27: 2B].
Thomas, Eliza P. m. Preston, John F. on 69-Jan-5 [69-Jan-13: 2D].
Thomas, Elizabeth (66 yrs.) d. on 66-Jul-31 [66-Aug-2: 2C].
Thomas, Elizabeth D. d. on 66-Oct-15 [66-Oct-16: 2B].
Thomas, Ellen Howard d. on 67-Oct-7 [67-Oct-8: 2B].
Thomas, Ephraim (69 yrs.) d. on 66-Jan-11 [66-Jan-12: 2C].
Thomas, Evan Philip (69 yrs.) d. on 66-Jun-4 [66-Jun-27: 2C].
Thomas, Fanny m. Noonan, F. H. on 69-Nov-9 [69-Nov-11: 2C].
Thomas, Florence S. m. Carter, John M. on 67-Apr-25 [67-Apr-27: 2A].
Thomas, Frank (9 yrs., 6 mos.) d. on 68-Oct-14 [68-Oct-21: 2C].
Thomas, Frank m. Woods, Mary on 67-Oct-1 [67-Oct-3: 2B].
Thomas, Franklin (38 yrs.) d. on 67-Nov-25 [67-Nov-26: 2B].
Thomas, Frederick (80 yrs.) d. on 68-Dec-21 [68-Dec-30: 2D].
Thomas, George (50 yrs.) d. on 67-Oct-27 [67-Oct-28: 2B].
Thomas, George m. Shipley, Naomi on 68-Dec-29 [69-Jan-9: 2C].

Thomas, George R. m. Coffin, Lydia on 70-Oct-20 [70-Oct-24: 2B].
Thomas, Harriet d. on 66-Jun-19 [66-Jun-22: 2B].
Thomas, Henrietta m. Stabler, George J. B. on 68-May-12 [68-May-20: 2A].
Thomas, Herbert Alexander d. on 69-Feb-24 [69-Feb-25: 2D].
Thomas, Hester M. (29 yrs.) d. on 67-Oct-27 [67-Oct-30: 2B].
Thomas, J. Hanson m. Beirne, Mary Howard on 66-Oct-16 [66-Oct-19: 2B].
Thomas, James (42 yrs.) d. on 69-May-23 [69-May-24: 2B].
Thomas, James m. Kenly, Margaret on 66-Aug-29 [66-Nov-12: 2C].
Thomas, James B. m. Jones, Annie J. on 68-Jun-4 [68-Jun-20: 2B].
Thomas, James E. m. Scotti, Laura J. on 68-Mar-17 [68-Mar-21: 2A].
Thomas, John (67 yrs.) d. on 67-May-22 [67-May-23: 2C].
Thomas, John (40 yrs.) d. on 66-Mar-7 of Stabbing [66-Mar-9: 1F].
Thomas, John d. on 66-Dec-17 Burned [66-Dec-19: 4E].
Thomas, John (48 yrs.) d. on 70-Dec-14 of Lung congestion [70-Dec-15: 2C, 4E; 70-Dec-16: 2C].
Thomas, John H., Capt. (56 yrs.) d. on 70-Sep-23 [70-Sep-24: 2B].
Thomas, John H. m. Richfield, Ann Louisa on 67-Jan-30 [67-Feb-4: 2C].
Thomas, John Wesley (2 yrs., 2 mos.) d. on 70-Aug-22 [70-Aug-25: 2C].
Thomas, Joseph H. m. Keithley, Isabel on 66-Dec-25 [66-Dec-29: 2C].
Thomas, Joseph L. m. Hamilton, Rebecca on 67-Sep-17 [67-Sep-21: 2A].
Thomas, Julia A. m. Hartman, Philip on 67-Feb-14 [67-Apr-23: 2B].
Thomas, Kate m. Dike, Edward G. on 66-Dec-24 [66-Dec-27: 2C].
Thomas, Laura W. m. Warfield, Cecilius E. on 70-Jan-18 [70-Jan-27: 2C].
Thomas, Lavinia V. m. Messer, Gustus E. on 69-May-13 [69-Jun-19: 2B].
Thomas, Lavinia William H. m. Williams, John H. on 70-May-10 [70-May-14: 2A].
Thomas, Lewis C. (30 yrs.) d. on 69-Feb-11 [69-Feb-18: 2C].
Thomas, Lilly (5 yrs., 1 mo.) d. on 67-Jan-20 [67-Jan-21: 2C].
Thomas, Lizzie A. m. Hammond, William S. on 66-Mar-6 [66-Mar-8: 2B].
Thomas, Louisa m. Brautigam, John on 70-Dec-13 [70-Dec-31: 2B].
Thomas, Luther m. Williams, Annie L. on 69-Sep-2 [69-Sep-4: 2B].
Thomas, Lydia (35 yrs.) d. on 66-May-31 of Heart disease [66-Jun-2: 1G].
Thomas, Martha m. Bowen, Charles T. on 69-Jun-17 [69-Jun-19: 2B].
Thomas, Martha Downs (6 mos.) d. on 69-Jul-4 [69-Jul-5: 2C].
Thomas, Martha E. m. Higby, Joseph H. on 69-Jun-28 [69-Jul-8: 2C].
Thomas, Mary Ann (55 yrs.) d. on 67-Jun-7 [67-Jun-8: 2B].
Thomas, Mary C. m. Waidner, Frederick A. on 69-Sep-9 [69-Nov-30: 2C].
Thomas, Mary Elizabeth (35 yrs.) d. on 67-Nov-3 [67-Nov-4: 2B; 67-Nov-5: 2B].
Thomas, Mary Ellen m. Hartman, Philip on 70-Nov-23 [70-Dec-3: 2B].
Thomas, Mary L. d. on 69-Jun-5 [69-Jun-7: 2B].
Thomas, Mary Margarette m. Weiss, William on 70-Mar-31 [70-Apr-19: 2B].
Thomas, Mary R. m. Carroll, John N. on 70-Apr-21 [70-Apr-23: 2B].
Thomas, Mary Rogers m. Summers, Charles S. on 69-Oct-5 [69-Oct-9: 2C].
Thomas, Mary S. m. Smith, John S. on 69-Sep-2 [69-Nov-9: 2C].
Thomas, Morris A. m. Turner, Frank V. on 66-Nov-20 [66-Nov-26: 2C].
Thomas, Nancy (41 yrs.) d. on 70-Jul-26 [70-Jul-27: 4E].
Thomas, Nelson C. m. Stolpp, Carrie L. on 70-Feb-24 [70-Mar-3: 2C; 70-Mar-4: 2C].
Thomas, Oliver H. m. Archer, Nannie H. on 68-Dec-1 [68-Dec-3: 2C].
Thomas, Rachel (41 yrs.) d. on 67-Jun-26 [67-Jun-27: 2B].
Thomas, Raleigh C. m. McDonald, Mary on 68-Nov-25 [68-Nov-30: 2C].
Thomas, Richard C. m. Richards, Mary R. on 69-Jan-12 [69-Jan-29: 2C].
Thomas, Ritty A. (66 yrs.) d. on 68-Mar-15 [68-Mar-19: 2B].
Thomas, Ruth Skinner (1 yr.) d. on 69-Aug-20 [69-Aug-24: 2C].
Thomas, S. Drew (33 yrs.) d. on 68-May-20 [68-May-22: 2C; 68-May-23: 2A].
Thomas, Samuel P. (3 yrs., 4 mos.) d. on 69-Feb-15 [69-Feb-17: 2D].
Thomas, Sarah d. on 70-Nov-2 [70-Nov-4: 2C].

Thomas, Sarah E. d. on 67-Jan-24 [67-Jan-26: 2C].
Thomas, Sarah J. E. m. Skuer, Otto B. on 70-Jan-1 [70-Jan-4: 2C].
Thomas, Sophia (79 yrs.) d. on 68-Nov-30 [68-Dec-2: 2C].
Thomas, Sophie Kerr m. Trippe, Richard on 68-Dec-22 [69-Jan-6: 2C].
Thomas, Susannah d. on 70-Nov-2 [70-Nov-3: 2C].
Thomas, Theodocia m. Waters, James B., Jr. on 70-Feb-17 [70-Feb-22: 2C].
Thomas, Van Beuren m. Bevans, Rachel J. on 66-Feb-23 [66-Mar-2: 2B].
Thomas, Warner (43 yrs.) d. on 70-Aug-30 [70-Sep-1: 2B].
Thomas, Warren Goodloe (1 yr., 4 mos.) d. on 66-Jun-5 [66-Jun-6: 2B].
Thomas, Willey G. (8 yrs., 7 mos.) d. on 69-May-5 [69-May-7: 2C].
Thomas, William (70 yrs.) d. on 67-Sep-16 [67-Sep-17: 2A].
Thomas, William G. (2 yrs., 10 mos.) d. on 67-Jun-12 [67-Jun-13: 2C].
Thomiz, John C. (23 yrs.) d. on 70-Feb-28 Drowned [70-Apr-19: 2B; 70-Apr-21: 2C].
Thompsen, Mary A. m. Franz, John A. on 66-Jan-16 [66-Feb-2: 2C].
Thompson, A. D. m. Marden, Sallie S. on 67-Mar-5 [67-Mar-6: 2C].
Thompson, Ada (7 yrs.) d. [66-Jan-5: 2C].
Thompson, Ada (23 yrs.) d. on 70-Jan-21 [70-Jan-22: 2C].
Thompson, Adaresta A. d. on 69-Oct-7 [69-Oct-14: 2C].
Thompson, Alexander m. Newman, Margaret on 68-Apr-19 [68-Apr-29: 2B].
Thompson, Annie Isabella m. Coyle, Henry H. on 67-Mar-29 [67-May-14: 2B].
Thompson, Arthur D. (48 yrs.) d. on 69-Mar-7 [69-Mar-8: 2C].
Thompson, Avice T. (47 yrs.) d. on 70-Feb-17 [70-Feb-18: 1G; 70-Feb-20: 2C].
Thompson, C. Gratiot m. Underwood, Sophie on 66-Dec-22 [67-Jan-1: 2C].
Thompson, Caroline (38 yrs.) d. on 67-Nov-8 [67-Nov-11: 2C].
Thompson, D. Bowly m. Winn, Achsah Carroll on 68-Nov-19 [68-Nov-24: 2C].
Thompson, Edward (1 yr., 1 mo.) d. [66-Jan-5: 2C].
Thompson, Eliza J. (36 yrs.) d. [66-Jan-5: 2C].
Thompson, Elizabeth Ann (65 yrs.) d. on 70-Nov-10 of Paralysis [70-Nov-12: 4C; 70-Nov-26: 2B, 2C; 70-Nov-12: 2B].
Thompson, Ella H. m. Donaldson, Thomas W. on 67-May-20 [67-May-21: 2B].
Thompson, Ella N. m. Cook, George W. on 66-Jan-9 [66-Jan-13: 2C].
Thompson, Emma (5 yrs.) d. [66-Jan-5: 2C].
Thompson, Emma Belle m. McDonnel, Martin on 67-Apr-3 [67-Apr-15: 2B].
Thompson, Emma G. m. Benny, James W. on 68-Jan-7 [68-Jan-14: 2C].
Thompson, Fanny D. (29 yrs.) d. on 69-Mar-29 [69-Mar-31: 2C].
Thompson, Flora (8 mos.) d. on 67-Jun-27 [67-Jun-28: 2B].
Thompson, Frances Arial m. Gleeson, T. James on 68-May-6 [68-May-25: 2A].
Thompson, George B. m. Gere, Verdie M. on 70-Dec-22 [70-Dec-26: 2C].
Thompson, George W. m. Poole, Debbie on 69-Oct-6 [69-Oct-21: 2B].
Thompson, George W. m. Hurtt, Provie A. on 70-Apr-6 [70-Apr-15: 2B].
Thompson, Gustavus Zane d. on 70-Mar-26 [70-Mar-28: 2B].
Thompson, Hannah J. m. Albaugh, William E. on 70-Jun-8 [70-Jun-13: 2C].
Thompson, Harman Klassen (33 yrs.) d. on 66-Jul-15 [66-Jul-18: 2C].
Thompson, Hattie S. m. Dorsey, B. Harrison on 66-Dec-20 [66-Dec-22: 2A].
Thompson, Helen (3 yrs.) d. [66-Jan-5: 2C].
Thompson, Honnor A. m. Arnold, John J. on 70-Feb-3 [70-Mar-23: 2C].
Thompson, Isabella (81 yrs.) d. on 68-Dec-11 [68-Dec-14: 2C].
Thompson, Isabella m. Saylor, John W on 66-Feb-1 [66-Feb-6: 2D].
Thompson, James (52 yrs.) d. on 70-Jun-24 [70-Jun-25: 2C].
Thompson, James F. m. Swift, Alice A on 66-Nov-22 [66-Nov-24: 2B].
Thompson, James R. (57 yrs.) d. on 68-Nov-3 of Heart disease [68-Nov-7: 1F, 2B].
Thompson, James S. (20 yrs.) d. on 66-Jun-11 of Gunshot wound [66-Jun-13: 2B, 1G].
Thompson, Johannah (28 yrs.) d. on 70-Apr-15 [70-Apr-16: 2B].
Thompson, John D. m. Williams, Kate on 70-Apr-21 [70-Apr-23: 2B].
Thompson, John H. (47 yrs.) d. on 70-Jan-2 [70-Jan-4: 2C].

Thompson, John W. m. Mahaney, Mary on 70-Dec-2 [70-Dec-10: 2B].
Thompson, Joseph, Sr. (60 yrs.) d. on 69-Apr-14 [69-Apr-15: 2B; 69-Apr-16: 2B].
Thompson, Julia (25 yrs.) d. on 68-Jun-15 [68-Jun-16: 2B].
Thompson, Julia (21 yrs.) d. on 69-Jun-3 [69-Jun-4: 2C].
Thompson, Julia Therese m. Keyser, Samuel on 68-Apr-14 [68-Apr-17: 2B].
Thompson, Kate (19 yrs.) d. on 70-Jan-26 [70-Jan-28: 2C].
Thompson, Kate d. on 70-Nov-16 [70-Nov-18: 2C].
Thompson, Lemuel (1 yr., 8 mos.) d. on 68-Feb-24 [68-Mar-2: 2C].
Thompson, Lemuel B. (42 yrs.) d. [66-Jan-5: 2C].
Thompson, Lewis H. (5 yrs.) d. on 70-Aug-14 [70-Aug-15: 2C].
Thompson, Louis Ignatius (4 yrs.) d. on 70-Jan-26 of Typhoid pneumonia [70-Jan-27: 2C].
Thompson, Louisa A. (34 yrs.) d. on 66-Jan-20 [66-Jan-22: 2C; 66-Feb-21: 2D].
Thompson, Martha P. m. Valiant, James on 67-Nov-12 [67-Nov-16: 2B].
Thompson, Mary Ann m. McKeown, John T. on 66-Aug-22 [66-Aug-30: 2B].
Thompson, Mary Carroll m. Inloes, Charles E. on 68-Feb-18 [68-Feb-19: 2C].
Thompson, Mary J. m. Rieger, Francis on 68-Dec-25 [68-Dec-29: 2D].
Thompson, Mary J. m. Wheeler, William S. on 70-Jul-28 [70-Aug-9: 2C].
Thompson, Mary Jackson (73 yrs.) d. on 67-Jul-7 [67-Jul-13: 2B].
Thompson, Mary L. (8 mos.) d. on 70-Jun-28 [70-Jul-2: 2B].
Thompson, Mary M. (60 yrs.) d. on 67-Nov-16 [67-Nov-18: 2B].
Thompson, Mattie J. m. Scarborough, Robert on 66-Feb-1 [66-Feb-21: 2C].
Thompson, Medora H. m. Sitzler, Leonard F. on 70-Jul-14 [70-Jul-27: 2C].
Thompson, Minerva L. (18 yrs.) d. on 70-Sep-19 [70-Oct-3: 2B].
Thompson, Owen m. Diven, Laura V. on 68-Dec-29 [69-Jan-1: 2C].
Thompson, Rebecca m. Rickard, John on 67-Sep-26 [67-Oct-22: 2A].
Thompson, Rebecca A. d. on 70-Feb-6 [70-Feb-7: 2C].
Thompson, Rebecca D. d. on 67-Jun-15 [67-Jun-17: 2C].
Thompson, Regina M. m. Phelps, James G. on 67-Oct-15 [67-Oct-21: 2B].
Thompson, S. M. m. Eareckson, Frederick G. on 67-Feb-28 [67-Mar-21: 2C].
Thompson, Sadie J. (11 mos.) d. on 68-Oct-8 [68-Oct-9: 2C].
Thompson, Sarah E. (56 yrs.) d. on 66-Oct-14 [66-Oct-16: 2B].
Thompson, Sarah M. m. Kugler, Thomas H. on 68-Jul-7 [68-Jul-15: 2B].
Thompson, Susan J. (75 yrs.) d. on 67-Mar-20 [67-Mar-21: 2C].
Thompson, Thomas (49 yrs.) d. on 68-Dec-9 [68-Dec-10: 2D, 4G; 69-Jan-11: 2C].
Thompson, Thomas H. m. Lewin, Sarah L. on 66-Dec-24 [66-Dec-31: 2C].
Thompson, Thomas J. (62 yrs.) d. on 66-Oct-28 [66-Oct-30: 2B].
Thompson, Wallace m. Price, Amelia F. on 68-Jan-7 [68-Jan-29: 2C].
Thompson, William (73 yrs.) d. on 68-Apr-30 [68-May-2: 2C].
Thompson, William (59 yrs.) d. [68-Mar-10: 2C].
Thompson, William d. on 70-Jan-3 in Railroad accident [70-Jan-4: 1H].
Thompson, William m. Woods, Elizabeth on 69-Sep-15 [69-Oct-2: 2B].
Thompson, William m. Hutchinson, Mary T. on 69-Oct-19 [69-Nov-11: 2C].
Thompson, William J. m. Mayes, Mattie J. on 67-Mar-14 [67-Jul-9: 2B].
Thompson, William J. M. m. Cann, Kate on 68-Sep-22 [68-Sep-24: 2B].
Thompson, William Stephen (20 yrs.) d. on 67-Jan-29 [67-Mar-15: 2C].
Thomson, Alexander m. Slack, Minnie on 66-May-10 [66-May-11: 2B].
Thomson, Edwin A. d. on 66-Aug-7 [66-Aug-10: 2C].
Thomson, Meredith D. m. Brockenbaugh, Letice F. on 68-Jun-3 [68-Jun-6: 2A].
Thomson, Robert (91 yrs.) d. on 70-Mar-20 [70-Apr-18: 2B].
Thomson, William J. m. Ross, Jessie on 70-Dec-8 [70-Dec-12: 2C].
Thorburn, Jessie D. m. Lyon, Walter M. on 67-Apr-14 [67-Apr-17: 2B].
Thorburn, Maggie McC. m. Franklin, John, Jr. on 67-Apr-14 [67-Apr-17: 2B].
Thornburg, Elizabeth d. on 69-Dec-19 [69-Dec-31: 2C].
Thorne, Lydia B. m. Wallin, Charles E. on 67-Jul-20 [67-Aug-5: 2B].
Thornley, John m. Payne, Julia H. on 66-Sep-25 [66-Oct-5: 2B].

Thornton, Ariana Charlotte (58 yrs.) d. on 67-Feb-22 [67-Feb-23: 2C].
Thornton, Beniah m. Sturling, Amanda M. on 70-Jun-26 [70-Aug-1: 2C].
Thornton, Elizabeth (31 yrs.) d. on 67-Apr-28 [67-Apr-29: 2B].
Thornton, Elizabeth (39 yrs.) d. on 69-Aug-12 [69-Aug-13: 2C].
Thornton, Harry H. (10 mos.) d. on 68-Dec-18 [68-Dec-19: 2B].
Thornton, Howard F. (76 yrs.) d. on 67-Jul-11 [67-Jul-13: 2B].
Thornton, James A. m. Watkins, Emma V. on 66-Nov-29 [66-Dec-1: 2B].
Thornton, Jane Randolph (28 yrs.) d. on 68-Aug-19 [68-Aug-20: 2B].
Thornton, John C. (57 yrs.) d. on 68-Apr-14 of Typhoid [68-Apr-15: 2B].
Thornton, Marion (1 yr., 4 mos.) d. on 70-Jan-3 [70-Jan-4: 2C].
Thorpe, Gertrude m. Griffith, David I. on 67-Jan-22 [67-Jan-24: 2C].
Thorpe, Mary Louisa m. Dunn, Edward H. on 66-Jul-26 [66-Jul-28: 2C].
Thorpe, Mary M. m. Carver, George W. on 67-May-6 [67-May-11: 2A].
Thorpe, Susanna (56 yrs.) d. on 66-May-22 [66-May-24: 2C].
Thorpe, William W. (28 yrs., 9 mos.) d. on 69-Mar-30 of Paralysis [69-Apr-2: 2C].
Thrasher, Carrie M. (4 yrs.) d. on 67-Dec-5 of Chronic croup [67-Dec-7: 2B].
Thrift, Fleet W. m. Robinson, Rhodie M. on 67-Oct-19 [67-Oct-22: 2A].
Thrift, John Jacob (15 yrs., 3 mos.) d. on 66-Dec-8 [66-Dec-11: 2B].
Thrift, M. R. m. Beale, Joseph L. on 69-Dec-9 [69-Dec-18: 2B].
Throop, Mary C. m. Riggin, William L. P. on 70-Sep-15 [70-Sep-17: 2B].
Thrush, Elizabeth (44 yrs.) d. on 66-Feb-10 [66-Feb-12: 2D; 66-Feb-16: 2B].
Thrush, George R. (44 yrs.) d. on 67-Jan-22 [67-Jan-24: 2C].
Thrush, George R. (44 yrs.) d. on 67-Apr-22 [67-May-8: 2B].
Thrush, Martha V. m. McGowan, Bernard on 66-Sep-20 [66-Oct-3: 2B].
Thrush, William d. on 68-Nov-3 in Railroad accident [68-Nov-11: 1H].
Thuman, Hannah (17 yrs., 8 mos.) d. on 66-Mar-28 [66-Mar-29: 2B].
Thuman, Joanna (49 yrs.) d. on 68-Jan-23 [68-Jan-25: 2B].
Thuman, Margaret d. on 70-Dec-5 [70-Dec-6: 2C].
Thumlert, James E., Jr. (24 yrs., 6 mos.) d. on 66-Dec-27 [66-Dec-29: 2C].
Thumlert, Maggie A. m. Glover, William H. on 69-Jan-21 [69-Jan-23: 2C].
Thumser, Louisa F. m. Gable, Appellius on 68-Dec-31 [69-Jan-9: 2C].
Thurlow, John F. (32 yrs.) d. on 69-Nov-28 [69-Nov-30: 2C].
Thurlow, S. Annie (4 mos.) d. on 70-Sep-14 [70-Sep-15: 2B].
Thurlow, William J. m. Clark, Mollie A. on 68-Feb-6 [68-Feb-10: 2C].
Thurman, Allen W. m. Webb, Hattie A. on 68-Oct-15 [68-Oct-21: 2C].
Thurston, Elizabeth m. Leishear, Adolphus on 70-Mar-30 [70-Apr-16: 2B].
Tibbals, Harry Barrington (1 yr., 3 mos.) d. on 69-Feb-19 [69-Feb-20: 2B].
Tibbs, William (67 yrs.) d. on 68-Jun-24 [68-Jun-25: 2B].
Tice, John K. (28 yrs.) d. on 67-Sep-8 of Consumption [67-Sep-14: 2A].
Tickner, Alonzo (10 yrs.) d. on 68-Sep-7 Struck by stone [68-Sep-8: 1G].
Tickner, Amelia m. Pumphrey, Ebeneezer, Jr. on 67-May-28 [67-Jun-4: 2A].
Tickner, Maria (39 yrs.) d. on 69-Aug-11 [69-Aug-12: 2C].
Tidy, John Stewart (1 yr.) d. on 70-May-1 [70-May-3: 2B].
Tidy, Mary M. m. Macklin, John A. on 68-Oct-29 [68-Nov-7: 2B].
Tidy, Sarah Blanch (7 mos.) d. on 68-Apr-6 [68-Apr-7: 2B].
Tiernan, Gay Bernard (53 yrs.) d. on 68-Dec-13 [68-Dec-18: 2C].
Tierney, James J. d. on 69-Oct-29 in Railroad accident [69-Oct-30: 4B].
Tierney, John (1 yr., 4 mos.) d. on 70-Aug-13 [70-Aug-15: 2C].
Tierney, Patrick E. m. Gildea, Kate on 69-Oct-7 [70-Jan-19: 2C].
Tierney, Thomas (52 yrs.) d. on 69-May-16 [69-May-17: 2B].
Tierney, Thomas m. Gorman, Mary O. on 67-Feb-13 [67-Feb-26: 2C].
Tierney, William (18 yrs.) d. on 68-May-30 of Boiler explosion [68-Jun-1: 1E].
Tiers, Christiana T. (49 yrs.) d. on 66-Mar-24 [66-Mar-28: 2C].
Tietgen, Charles m. Dieckman, Lizzie on 67-Oct-29 [67-Nov-12: 2C].
Tighe, Katey (11 yrs.) d. on 67-Oct-23 [67-Oct-24: 2B].

Tignor, W. J. m. Hazzard, Mary L. on 70-Nov-24 [70-Nov-28: 2C].
Tilden, Thomas E. (62 yrs.) d. on 67-Jan-10 [67-Jan-21: 2C].
Tilghman, Anna M. d. on 70-Dec-13 [70-Dec-23: 2B].
Tilghman, Anna R. m. Slingluff, Trueman C. on 68-Oct-22 [68-Oct-24: 2B].
Tilghman, Eli Ellsworth (8 mos.) d. on 66-Jun-25 [66-Jun-25: 2B].
Tilghman, Fanny A. m. Johnson, Thomas F. on 70-Feb-1 [70-Feb-3: 2B].
Tilghman, Martha A. m. Ritter, John W. on 67-Dec-29 [68-Jan-7: 2B].
Tilghman, Martina d. on 70-Oct-24 of Heart disease [70-Oct-26: 2B].
Tilghman, Mary E. m. Waters, Job W. on 66-Mar-29 [66-Mar-31: 2C].
Tilghman, Richard L. (57 yrs.) d. on 67-Sep-20 of Congestive chills [67-Sep-23: 2A; 67-Sep-25: 2A].
Tilghman, Rosalie m. Shreve, J. Jefferson on 66-Jan-26 [66-Jan-29: 2B].
Tilghman, William Edward (33 yrs.) d. on 69-May-28 [69-May-29: 2B].
Tilley, A. J. m. Bowhan, Ella J. on 66-Aug-16 [66-Sep-4: 2B; 66-Sep-1: 2B].
Tillson, Lizzie M. m. Schoolfield, L. Harrison on 69-Aug-30 [69-Sep-4: 2B].
Tilly, Margaret (55 yrs.) d. on 69-Aug-3 [69-Aug-4: 2C].
Tilmon, Mary E. m. Jones, Nelson on 69-Nov-11 [69-Nov-13: 2B].
Tilton, McLane m. Wells, Annie Maine on 66-Jul-26 [66-Jul-27: 2C].
Tilyard, Angelo (43 yrs.) d. on 69-Aug-7 [69-Aug-9: 2C].
Tilyard, Lizzie M. m. Beacham, Samuel T. on 70-Nov-22 [70-Nov-22: 2C].
Timanus, Cilla J. m. Gross, Harry T. on 70-Oct-27 [70-Oct-29: 2B].
Timanus, Emmie m. Boogher, D. R. on 67-Nov-19 [67-Nov-22: 2C].
Timanus, Fannie m. Ludowieg, A. on 70-Oct-6 [70-Oct-31: 2B].
Timanus, Margaret (66 yrs., 2 mos.) d. on 68-Feb-21 [68-Feb-22: 2B].
Timanus, Mary E. m. Roux, Edwin S. on 68-Jun-18 [68-Jun-24: 2B].
Timbs, John K. (34 yrs.) d. on 66-May-29 [66-May-31: 2B; 66-Jun-1: 2B].
Timbs, Millicent Ann (55 yrs.) d. on 66-Jun-30 [66-Jul-2: 2B].
Timmons, Belle S. d. on 69-Dec-25 [69-Dec-27: 2D].
Timmons, Charles (82 yrs.) d. on 69-Feb-6 [69-Feb-10: 2C].
Timmons, Elizabeth (71 yrs.) d. on 69-Apr-17 [69-Apr-23: 2B].
Timmons, Maggie E. m. Doyle, James M. on 68-Nov-3 [68-Nov-9: 2B].
Timothy, William Henry (2 yrs., 8 mos.) d. on 70-Dec-22 [70-Dec-24: 2B].
Timson, Sarah m. Cooke, Gilbert C. on 67-Jan-3 [67-Jan-4: 2D].
Tindall, Miriam E. m. Riley, Theodore B. on 69-Aug-3 [69-Aug-9: 2B].
Tindle, Robert W. (54 yrs.) d. on 68-Feb-5 [68-Feb-6: 2C].
Tindle, Sarah E. m. Riordan, John B. on 67-Nov-14 [67-Nov-27: 2B].
Tinges, George Herbert (25 yrs.) d. on 70-Mar-8 [70-Mar-9: 2C; 70-Mar-10: 2C].
Tinker, John A. (7 yrs.) d. on 70-Jul-16 [70-Jul-18: 2B].
Tinsley, Lucy (7 mos.) d. on 70-Jun-29 of Cholera infantum [70-Jul-16: 2B].
Tippett, Charles B., Rev. (66 yrs.) d. on 67-Feb-25 of Paralysis [67-Feb-27: 1F, 2C; 67-Feb-28: 2C].
Tipton, Benjamin (71 yrs.) d. on 66-Jun-19 [66-Jun-21: 1G, 2C].
Tipton, Hannah E. m. Taylor, James B. on 67-Jul-18 [67-Jul-20: 2C].
Tipton, J. Emory m. Diffenderfer, Mary on 69-Nov-3 [69-Nov-10: 2C].
Tipton, Jarret (84 yrs.) d. on 66-Apr-5 [66-Apr-19: 2B].
Tipton, Julia A. m. Gill, John W. on 70-Mar-24 [70-Mar-25: 2C].
Tipton, Samuel Hill d. on 66-Oct-20 [66-Oct-30: 2B].
Tipton, W. m. Talbot, Margaret on 67-Jun-24 [67-Jun-26: 2C].
Tipton, William (33 yrs.) d. on 67-Dec-10 [67-Dec-12: 1F, 2B].
Tiralla, Maria (39 yrs.) d. on 67-Feb-2 [67-Feb-4: 2C; 67-Feb-5: 2C].
Tisdale, Elizabeth W. m. Taylor, William H. R. on 68-Oct-13 [68-Oct-20: 2B].
Tise, George m. Wallis, Rachel A. on 68-Sep-3 [68-Sep-8: 2B].
Titchener, Catharine Munder (2 mos.) d. on 68-Oct-2 [68-Oct-3: 2B].
Titchner, A. (37 yrs.) d. on 70-Mar-14 of Consumption [70-Mar-15: 2C].
Titchner, Howard (1 yr., 3 mos.) d. on 67-May-17 [67-May-18: 2A].

Tithin, Mary m. Taylor, William on 68-Sep-18 [68-Sep-22: 2B].
Titlow, Effie J. m. Herron, William on 70-Feb-22 [70-Feb-28: 2C].
Tittle, George T. m. Albaugh, Laura V. on 67-Oct-15 [68-Feb-7: 2C].
Tittle, Virginia E. m. Spencer, Samuel H. on 67-Dec-10 [68-Jul-28: 2B].
Toback, Mary (51 yrs.) d. on 66-Sep-17 in Wagon accident [66-Sep-19: 1F].
Tobin, Daniel d. on 69-Apr-16 [69-Apr-17: 2B].
Tobin, Jeremiah (37 yrs.) d. on 70-Apr-10 of Heart disease [70-Apr-11: 4B; 70-Apr-12: 2B].
Tobin, Mary (45 yrs.) d. on 68-Oct-5 [68-Oct-6: 2B].
Todd, Annie Florence (9 mos.) d. on 66-Jun-14 [66-Jun-15: 2C].
Todd, Elijah, Capt. (31 yrs., 5 mos.) d. on 70-Apr-29 [70-May-3: 2B].
Todd, Gabriel Ludlow (6 mos.) d. on 69-Mar-26 [69-Mar-27: 2B].
Todd, James H. m. Ives, Elizabeth on 67-Sep-3 [67-Sep-7: 2A].
Todd, Jane (55 yrs.) d. on 70-Jul-20 of Heatstroke [70-Jul-21: 1F].
Todd, Jane m. Waterson, William on 70-Dec-8 [70-Dec-13: 2C].
Todd, Mary A. d. on 69-Oct-28 of Consumption [69-Oct-29: 2C].
Todd, Mary Ann (8 yrs., 5 mos.) d. on 67-Jan-28 [67-Jan-29: 2C].
Todd, Mary Elmira (4 yrs., 5 mos.) d. on 70-Nov-10 [70-Nov-11: 2B].
Todd, Mary J. m. Murdock, Albert T. on 68-May-14 [68-May-15: 2B].
Todd, Mary L. (22 yrs., 1 mo.) d. on 70-May-10 [70-May-14: 2B].
Todd, P. A. (32 yrs.) d. on 66-Jun-14 of Lung congestion [66-Jun-15: 2C; 66-Jun-16: 2B; 66-Jul-12: 2C; 66-Jul-13: 2C].
Todd, Ruth m. Grove, Samuel G. on 67-Jun-7 [67-Jun-12: 2B].
Todd, S. Fannie m. Ruskell, William on 70-Jan-12 [70-Jan-18: 2C].
Todd, Sallie E. m. Merritt, Thomas A. on 69-Dec-8 [69-Dec-11: 2B].
Todd, Sallie R. m. Todd, Thomas B. on 66-Feb-1 [66-Feb-21: 2C].
Todd, Sarah E. m. Cooke, William A. on 66-Feb-8 [66-Feb-19: 2B].
Todd, Thomas B. m. Todd, Sallie R. on 66-Feb-1 [66-Feb-21: 2C].
Todd, Thomas R. d. on 66-Dec-27 of Consumption [66-Dec-28: 2C; 66-Dec-29: 2C].
Todd, William T. (40 yrs.) d. on 66-Dec-1 [66-Dec-3: 2C].
Todhunter, Allison Douglas m. Cleveland, James B. on 67-Mar-16 [67-Mar-18: 2B].
Todhunter, Gilbert (3 yrs., 1 mo.) d. on 67-Nov-8 [67-Nov-9: 2B].
Toft, Aggie M. (2 mos.) d. on 69-Nov-16 [69-Nov-17: 2C; 69-Nov-18: 2C].
Toft, John (56 yrs.) d. on 67-Dec-18 [67-Dec-19: 2B].
Toft, L. L. m. Small, Maggie A. on 68-Nov-25 [68-Nov-30: 2C].
Toft, Sarah E. m. Hollinberger, John J. on 67-Oct-1 [67-Oct-4: 2B].
Tolan, Anthony (27 yrs.) d. on 67-Nov-5 Murdered (Stabbing) [67-Nov-6: 1F; 67-Nov-7: 1G, 2C].
Toland, Alviare m. Briscoe, Alexander M. on 68-May-14 [68-Jun-16: 2B].
Tolley, Thomas E. m. Sullivan, Mollie J. on 68-Jul-16 [68-Jul-20: 2B].
Tolloway, Cleary m. Keyton, Thomas on 67-Jan-20 [67-Jan-31: 2C].
Tolson, Ella m. Bellis, William H. on 66-Aug-14 [66-Aug-31: 2B].
Tolson, Georganna m. Kunsman, William H. on 69-Sep-24 [69-Sep-25: 2B].
Tolson, J. Carrow m. Ringgold, Ettie C. on 67-Jul-18 [67-Jul-22: 2C].
Tolson, John R., Rev. (30 yrs.) d. on 70-Jan-29 [70-Feb-4: 2C].
Tolson, Lilian M. m. Richman, Clayton S. on 70-Jun-13 [70-Jun-18: 2B].
Tolson, Margaret E. m. Cushing, Henry M. on 68-Feb-13 [68-Feb-15: 2B].
Tolson, Susannah (27 yrs.) d. on 68-Dec-10 [68-Dec-11: 2C].
Tolson, Thomas H. m. Earhart, Virginia L. on 68-Jun-25 [68-Jun-26: 2B].
Tomer, John (25 yrs.) d. on 66-Jan-13 [66-Jan-15: 2C].
Tomlinson, Alice (21 yrs.) d. on 66-Mar-11 [66-Mar-23: 2C].
Tomlinson, Elenora E. d. on 69-Oct-11 [69-Oct-12: 2C; 69-Oct-13: 2C].
Tomlinson, John W., Capt. (53 yrs.) d. on 69-Aug-27 of Heart disease [69-Aug-28: 1H; 69-Aug-30: 1G, 2B].
Tomlinson, Jonny (6 mos.) d. on 66-Jan-6 [66-Jan-15: 2C].
Tompkins, Amelia C. m. Tompkins, J. G. W. on 69-Aug-19 [69-Aug-21: 2B].

Tompkins, J. G. W. m. Tompkins, Amelia C. on 69-Aug-19 [69-Aug-21: 2B].
Tompkins, John A. m. Shriver, Anne on 67-Feb-26 [67-Feb-27: 2C].
Tompkins, Missouri Brown d. on 68-Nov-21 [68-Nov-23: 2B].
Tompkins, Sallie Ann Elizabeth d. on 70-Oct-26 [70-Oct-27: 2B].
Tompkins, Wesley Kennard (28 yrs.) d. on 68-May-13 [68-May-14: 2B].
Tompson, Mary Rebecca m. Lake, John on 68-Jan-28 [68-Feb-4: 2C].
Toms, Anderson C. (19 yrs., 5 mos.) d. on 67-Aug-15 of Yellow fever [67-Sep-2: 2B].
Toner, Bernard (38 yrs.) d. on 70-May-9 [70-May-10: 2C].
Toner, Harriet (65 yrs.) d. on 68-Jan-29 [68-Jan-31: 2C].
Toner, J. C. m. Shaw, Florence V. on 66-Mar-19 [66-Mar-20: 2C].
Toner, John (1 yr., 2 mos.) d. on 67-Jul-23 [67-Jul-24: 2C].
Toner, John m. Doolittle, Jane on 69-Apr-10 [69-Apr-13: 2B].
Toner, Mary Catherine (17 yrs.) d. on 68-Sep-2 [68-Sep-3: 2B].
Toner, Rebecca m. Eunick, Edward H. on 68-Jan-1 [68-Jan-22: 2C].
Toner, Zachary Taylor (20 yrs.) d. on 66-Oct-14 of Dropsy [66-Oct-15: 2B].
Tonge, Ella R. m. Russell, Charles R. on 69-Sep-16 [69-Sep-18: 2B].
Tonge, Richard H. m. Barling, Annie Linton on 68-Apr-16 [68-Apr-25: 2B].
Tonge, S. Davis d. on 67-Oct-18 [67-Nov-4: 2B].
Tonge, William G. D. m. Taylor, Laura E. on 70-Jun-15 [70-Jun-16: 2B].
Tongue, Johnzie m. Herring, Annie E. on 69-Mar-9 [69-Mar-12: 2C].
Toogood, Elon (44 yrs.) d. on 70-Apr-8 [70-Apr-9: 2B].
Tool, [infant] (2 yrs., 4 mos.) d. on 66-Jul-24 [66-Jul-25: 2C].
Toole, Margaret Ann m. Barnes, George W. on 69-Oct-21 [69-Nov-4: 2B].
Toole, Mary A. (66 yrs.) d. on 68-May-5 [68-May-6: 2B].
Toole, Patrick (48 yrs.) d. on 70-Oct-12 [70-Oct-21: 2C].
Toolen, Patrick (23 yrs.) d. on 67-Apr-1 [67-Apr-2: 2B].
Toomey, Mary C. m. Collins, W. E. on 68-Sep-8 [68-Sep-16: 2B].
Tootell, Leila G. m. King, Patrick J. on 66-Apr-12 [66-Apr-20: 2B].
Topham, John P. m. Hutchins, Lizzie on 67-Sep-3 [67-Oct-1: 2B].
Topham, Joseph L. m. Rodgers, Sarah Frances on 69-Jun-1 [69-Jun-4: 2C].
Topp, Elizabeth D. (52 yrs.) d. on 69-May-8 of Consumption [69-May-10: 2C].
Topping, Josie (5 yrs.) d. on 68-Dec-1 of Scarlet fever [68-Dec-8: 2C].
Topping, Margaret m. on 69-Mar-22 [69-May-11: 2C].
Tormey, Florence C. (11 mos.) d. on 68-Jul-2 [68-Jul-3: 2C].
Tormey, Frank A. m. Demmitt, Florence R. on 66-Sep-14 [66-Sep-24: 2B].
Tormy, John M. m. Curley, Barbara on 66-Apr-26 [66-Apr-27: 2C].
Torphy, Thomas (55 yrs.) d. on 66-Feb-15 [66-Feb-17: 2B].
Torrington, Eleanora m. Hoppell, George W. on 67-Aug-1 [67-Aug-7: 2C].
Torrington, Jane m. Lounsberry, Charles W. on 68-Jan-24 [68-Jan-28: 2D].
Torsch, John W. m. Sutton, Mollie E. on 66-Mar-29 [66-Apr-6: 2B].
Tottle, John m. Colbert, Sophia D. on 66-Apr-10 [66-Apr-14: 2B].
Tottle, William A. m. Holtz, Mollie E. on 69-Jun-15 [69-Jun-16: 2C].
Touchton, William H. m. Pfeltz, Mary on 69-Aug-3 [69-Sep-14: 2B].
Tough, Henrietta E. d. on 69-Feb-18 [69-Feb-19: 2C; 69-Feb-20: 2B].
Toughey, Mary (74 yrs.) d. on 68-Oct-18 [68-Oct-20: 2B].
Toughinbaugh, William m. Cotrell, Rosanna on 68-Dec-24 [68-Dec-25: 2D].
Toulson, J. H. m. Long, Annie on 70-Sep-19 [70-Dec-16: 2C].
Toulson, Laura m. McCormick, William N. on 65-Dec-25 [66-Jan-1: 2C].
Towell, Amelia (85 yrs.) d. on 69-Jun-4 [69-Jun-7: 2B].
Towen, Elizabeth (66 yrs.) d. on 67-Jan-6 [67-Jan-7: 2C].
Tower, Alonzo m. Roberts, Virginia on 70-Nov-10 [70-Nov-19: 2B].
Towler, Martha (82 yrs.) d. on 69-Jul-11 [69-Jul-12: 2D].
Towles, Helen Bertha (8 mos.) d. on 70-Nov-16 [70-Nov-18: 2C].
Towles, John Wickliffe (10 mos.) d. on 66-Feb-5 [66-Feb-6: 2D].
Towles, Octavius Lee (3 yrs., 4 mos.) d. on 66-Jan-25 [66-Jan-27: 2B].

Towner, Ella Chase (13 yrs.) d. on 67-Apr-1 of Typhoid [67-Apr-2: 2B; 67-Apr-3: 2B].
Towner, James L. m. Daicker, Louisa on 68-Feb-20 [68-Feb-22: 2B].
Towner, Laura m. Van Swearingen, Thomas on 66-Dec-26 [66-Dec-27: 2C].
Towner, Lilly Lee (1 yr., 6 mos.) d. on 70-Sep-8 [70-Sep-10: 2B].
Towner, Melissa J. m. Hahn, Daniel H. on 66-Nov-13 [66-Nov-15: 2C].
Townsend, Alpheus A. m. Stuart, Agnes E. on 67-Oct-24 [67-Oct-25: 2B].
Townsend, Calvin D. m. Hacker, Louise on 69-Oct-14 [69-Oct-18: 2C].
Townsend, Eliza (74 yrs.) d. on 68-Feb-26 [68-Feb-29: 2B].
Townsend, Georgie A. m. Geisendaffer, W. J. on 67-Nov-12 [68-Feb-4: 2C].
Townsend, Hannah E. m. Hollis, William B. on 69-May-11 [69-May-13: 2B].
Townsend, Henry (73 yrs.) d. on 67-Dec-9 [67-Dec-11: 2B].
Townsend, J. W. (36 yrs.) d. on 67-Apr-17 in Railroad accident [67-Apr-18: 1E].
Townsend, Jane S. (61 yrs.) d. on 68-Aug-3 [68-Aug-4: 2C; 68-Aug-5: 2B].
Townsend, Jesse M. m. Brookhart, Sarah Jane on 67-Dec-8 [67-Dec-10: 2B].
Townsend, John T. m. Simpson, Sallie on 69-Aug-8 [69-Aug-28: 2B].
Townsend, Joseph C. m. Lee, Belinda on 69-Jun-3 [69-Jun-4: 2C].
Townsend, Josephine m. Rollison, Thomas on 68-Jan-16 [68-Feb-12: 2B].
Townsend, Mary E. m. Henderson, William H. on 69-Dec-21 [70-Jan-11: 2C].
Townsend, Matthias (10 mos.) d. [66-Oct-3: 2B].
Townsend, P. R. (71 yrs.) d. on 69-May-31 [69-Jun-1: 2C].
Townsend, Sarah C. m. Hudson, John M. on 67-Oct-31 [67-Nov-5: 2B].
Townsend, Sarah E. d. on 69-Mar-15 of Consumption [69-Mar-17: 2C].
Townsend, Teackle (73 yrs.) d. on 69-Oct-23 of Heart disease [69-Oct-27: 4B].
Townsend, Thomas (75 yrs.) d. on 66-Aug-6 [66-Aug-13: 2C].
Townsend, Thomas J. (68 yrs.) d. on 67-Oct-4 [67-Oct-5: 2B].
Townshend, James H. m. Smith, Martha J. on 69-Jun-29 [69-Jul-1: 2C].
Townshend, Leander Victor (3 yrs., 10 mos.) d. on 66-Dec-16 [66-Dec-20: 2B].
Towson, Emma K. m. Strong, George W. on 66-Jul-1 [66-Jul-6: 2B; 66-Jul-17: 2C].
Towson, Estelle M. m. Kirkland, Edward M. on 68-Oct-20 [68-Oct-22: 2C].
Towson, James F. d. on 68-Nov-9 [68-Nov-10: 2C; 68-Nov-11: 2C].
Towson, Louisa A. d. on 68-Jul-1 [68-Jul-2: 2C].
Toy, Sallie E. m. Harkins, John H. on 68-Nov-11 [68-Nov-12: 2C].
Toy, Thomas B. m. Haslup, Laura A. on 69-Feb-25 [69-Feb-27: 2C].
Traber, Dorothea (37 yrs.) d. on 68-Aug-23 [68-Aug-24: 2B].
Tracey, Ambrose Patrick (4 yrs., 5 mos.) d. on 66-May-2 [66-May-3: 2C].
Tracey, Ann Eliza (39 yrs.) d. on 69-May-27 [69-May-29: 2B].
Tracey, Catherine Ambrosia (6 yrs., 4 mos.) d. on 66-Apr-17 [66-Apr-18: 2B].
Tracey, Eliza m. Graydon, James on 69-Jan-4 [69-Jan-16: 2C].
Tracey, James d. on 69-Apr-4 [69-Apr-5: 2B].
Tracey, James m. Eggleston, Emily on 67-Sep-15 [67-Sep-17: 2A].
Tracey, John (58 yrs.) d. on 67-May-20 [67-May-27: 2B].
Tracey, Matilda m. Chisholm, James W. H. on 67-Oct-24 [67-Oct-28: 2B].
Tracey, Ruth (68 yrs.) d. on 70-May-23 [70-May-24: 2C].
Tracey, William Charles (2 yrs.) d. on 66-Apr-15 [66-Apr-16: 2B].
Tracy, Edward F. m. Jefferson, Amanda E. on 66-Jun-13 [66-Jun-15: 2C].
Tracy, Emma Elizabeth (1 mo.) d. on 67-Sep-17 [67-Sep-20: 2A].
Tracy, Jane (53 yrs.) d. on 67-Dec-10 of Heart disease [67-Dec-19: 2B].
Tracy, Mary m. Shipley, Charles W. on 66-Nov-8 [66-Nov-9: 2C].
Tracy, Mollie E. m. Castle, Thomas M. on 65-Dec-28 [66-Jan-6: 2B].
Tracy, Samuel W. m. Reynolds, Mary E. on 69-Feb-8 [69-Feb-23: 2C].
Trageaser, C. d. on 68-Nov-15 of Suicide (Jumped from window) [68-Nov-18: 1G].
Trager, John Christian m. Schreiber, Mary on 70-Jul-31 [70-Aug-2: 2C].
Trail, Emilie B. (27 yrs.) d. on 66-Jan-22 [66-Jan-24: 2B].
Trail, Reverdy m. Weed, Maggie J. on 68-Feb-4 [68-Feb-8: 2B].
Trail, William H. m. Hess, Kate [69-Jan-27: 2C].

Traill, Mary V. m. Yellott, John I. [68-Jun-3: 2B].
Trainer, Catherine F. d. on 68-May-19 [68-May-20: 2A; 68-May-21: 2B].
Trainer, John (25 yrs.) d. on 68-Jul-15 [68-Jul-16: 2C].
Trainer, Mary M. m. Gosnell, Walter E. on 69-Jul-20 [69-Aug-16: 2B].
Trainor, Dora Isabella (6 mos.) d. on 69-Mar-15 [69-Mar-17: 2C].
Trammell, Catherine Virginia (28 yrs.) d. on 70-Sep-27 [70-Sep-28: 2B; 70-Sep-29: 2B].
Trammell, Virginia m. Wilson, James H. on 66-Aug-16 [66-Aug-23: 2C].
Trasey, Samuel S. m. Peters, Kate on 70-Jan-5 [70-Jan-8: 2B].
Travers, D. B., Capt. (71 yrs.) d. on 68-Apr-11 [68-Apr-16: 2B].
Travers, Harriet m. Fearing, George R. on 69-Sep-1 [69-Sep-16: 2B].
Travers, Helen M. m. Ruark, Edwin R. on 68-Feb-19 [68-Jun-18: 2B].
Travers, Isabella W. (47 yrs.) d. on 69-Aug-16 [69-Aug-17: 2C].
Travers, John H. (45 yrs.) d. on 70-Apr-6 of Consumption [70-Apr-8: 2C].
Travers, John M. m. Cassidy, Maria G. on 69-Dec-29 [70-Jan-5: 2C].
Travers, Mary Emma m. Holton, John on 68-Nov-17 [68-Nov-19: 2C].
Travers, Medora m. Shorter, P. W. on 66-Jan-4 [66-Jan-6: 2B].
Travers, Samuel H. m. Scheuler, Edna E. on 66-May-15 [66-May-16: 2C].
Travers, Susan (81 yrs.) d. on 70-Apr-27 [70-Apr-29: 2B].
Travers, Thomas M., Capt. (55 yrs.) d. on 70-Apr-7 [70-Aug-8: 2C].
Traverse, Susie M. m. Creighton, William on 66-Dec-13 [66-Dec-15: 2B].
Travis, L. Alonzo m. Matthews, Anna J. on 68-May-20 [68-May-26: 2B].
Travis, Zenophine m. Harman, William H., Jr. on 68-Oct-15 [68-Oct-19: 2B].
Tray, Samuel m. Andrews, Elizabeth on 66-Aug-29 [66-Sep-1: 2B].
Trayser, Elizabeth A. d. on 70-May-1 [70-May-2: 2B; 70-May-3: 2B].
Trayser, Philip (28 yrs.) d. on 68-Jan-1 [68-Apr-27: 2B].
Trazzare, Thomas E. m. Sears, Sarah E. on 66-Sep-11 [66-Sep-18: 2B].
Treadway, Nelson R. m. Franklin, Annie on 70-Apr-7 [70-Apr-9: 2B].
Treadway, Sarah E. m. Fuller, Alvan B. on 66-Dec-13 [66-Dec-17: 2B].
Treadway, Sue m. Wilson, Robert Ewing on 68-Apr-1 [68-Apr-21: 2B].
Treadwell, John m. McCubbin, Sarah Ann on 70-Nov-24 [70-Nov-28: 2C].
Treakle, Etta C. (16 yrs.) d. on 66-Dec-10 [66-Dec-11: 2B].
Tree, Annie F. m. Johnson, C. D. on 65-Oct-2 [66-Mar-24: 2B].
Trego, Albert d. on 70-Oct-6 [70-Oct-7: 2B; 70-Oct-8: 2B].
Trego, Emma Patterson d. on 67-Feb-25 [67-Feb-26: 2C].
Tress, Nelson (23 yrs.) d. on 66-Sep-13 [66-Sep-14: 2B].
Tress, Washington m. Perry, Marion E. on 70-Aug-2 [70-Aug-5: 2C].
Treulieb, J. M. (56 yrs.) d. on 70-Jul-15 Drowned [70-Jul-18: 1F].
Treulieb, John M. (56 yrs.) d. on 70-Jul-15 Drowned [70-Jul-16: 2B].
Trexler, Charles T. m. Smith, Sarah F. on 70-May-26 [70-Jun-7: 2C].
Trey, Lizzie C. M. m. Sherwood, Issac N. on 68-Sep-9 [68-Sep-15: 2B].
Trey, Mary (42 yrs.) d. on 69-Aug-3 [69-Aug-7: 2C].
Trezise, Thomas m. Knight, Rachel on 69-Dec-23 [70-Jan-21: 2C].
Trickle, Louisa (56 yrs.) d. on 68-Mar-1 [68-Mar-3: 2C].
Trimble, Charles T. m. Price, Sarah E. on 70-Aug-30 [70-Sep-3: 2B].
Trimble, Hallie N. m. Rock, Warren T. on 70-Oct-28 [70-Oct-31: 2B].
Trimmer, Alice Gertrude (4 yrs., 1 mo.) d. on 70-Jan-30 [70-Feb-18: 2C].
Trine, Jenny (27 yrs.) d. on 67-Nov-10 of Consumption [67-Nov-11: 2C].
Trine, William H. m. Rea, Annie on 68-Nov-26 [68-Nov-28: 2C].
Triplett, Eliza J. m. McKay, Donald on 70-Feb-1 [70-Feb-2: 2B].
Trippe, Helen m. Lorman, Howell S. on 68-Dec-10 [68-Dec-19: 2B].
Trippe, Mary W. d. on 70-Dec-17 [70-Dec-19: 2C].
Trippe, Richard m. Thomas, Sophie Kerr on 68-Dec-22 [69-Jan-6: 2C].
Trives, Rachel S. m. Handy, James A. on 69-Jun-2 [69-Jun-3: 2B].
Troeger, Louise K. d. on 70-Sep-11 [70-Sep-13: 2B].
Trogler, Mary A. (35 yrs.) d. on 70-Feb-17 [70-Feb-18: 2C].

Troth, Martha A. (38 yrs.) d. on 66-Dec-15 [66-Dec-17: 2B].
Trott, Avarilla Edwards (6 mos.) d. on 69-Dec-30 [69-Dec-31: 2C].
Trott, George Benjamin (4 yrs., 1 mo.) d. on 68-Jun-24 [68-Jun-25: 2B].
Trott, Kate J. (27 yrs.) d. on 68-May-21 [68-May-22: 2C].
Trott, Margaret A. m. Lamley, Charles G. on 69-Dec-14 [69-Dec-23: 2B].
Trott, Mary Louisa m. Marriott, Eugene E. on 70-Jul-7 [70-Jul-8: 2C].
Trott, Samuel (83 yrs.) d. on 66-Oct-31 [66-Nov-2: 2B].
Trotten, Thomas (69 yrs.) d. on 67-Mar-15 [67-Mar-16: 1F, 2B].
Trotter, William m. Jackson, Lucy S. on 68-Oct-21 [68-Nov-2: 2B].
Trotton, Mary d. on 70-Oct-16 [70-Oct-18: 2C].
Troup, Clelia m. Key, Murray on 69-Nov-16 [69-Nov-18: 2C].
Trout, John A. m. Easton, Allie A. on 67-Sep-21 [67-Nov-23: 2B].
Troxell, Martha I. m. Stein, A. T. on 67-Dec-24 [67-Dec-28: 2C].
Trueheart, E. A. (56 yrs.) d. on 68-Dec-7 of Consumption [68-Dec-9: 2C].
Trueman, John (45 yrs.) d. on 70-Feb-7 [70-Feb-8: 4F].
Trueman, Josiah C. m. Sunstrom, Rachel on 69-Jul-28 [69-Jul-31: 2C].
Truett, Oliver (49 yrs.) d. on 69-Apr-7 [69-Apr-8: 2C; 69-Apr-9: 2C; 69-Apr-26: 2C].
Truitt, Elenora H. m. Cullings, James W. on 68-Jan-8 [68-Jan-16: 2C].
Trull, George m. Harvey, Ellen on 66-Nov-6 [66-Nov-9: 2C].
Trumbo, Henry C. (71 yrs.) d. on 70-Mar-22 [70-Mar-23: 2C].
Trumbo, Jane H. m. Dehn, Louis on 68-Feb-9 [68-Feb-13: 2C].
Trumbo, Susan M. m. Keefe, John F. on 66-Apr-17 [66-Apr-20: 2B].
Trumper, Harman d. on 67-Mar-25 Murdered (Stabbing) [67-Mar-26: 1F; 67-Mar-27: 1G].
Trust, Alice M. m. Sickel, Edward on 68-Sep-10 [68-Sep-12: 2B].
Trust, George m. Roese, Mary E. on 68-Jun-30 [68-Jul-7: 2B].
Trust, Jacob Herman (31 yrs.) d. on 69-Nov-7 [69-Nov-17: 2C].
Trust, Josephine d. on 68-Feb-25 of Consumption [68-Feb-27: 2C; 68-Feb-28: 2D].
Trust, Lizzie C. m. Chisholm, Charles H. on 68-Sep-21 [68-Sep-24: 2B].
Trusty, Samuel (70 yrs.) d. on 69-Jan-21 [69-Jan-23: 2C].
Trusty, Samuel (70 yrs.) d. on 70-Jul-19 of Heatstroke [70-Jul-20: 4C].
Truyser, Philip (28 yrs.) d. on 68-Jan-1 [68-Apr-25: 2B].
Tschudi, Elizabeth Clemm (74 yrs.) d. on 68-Apr-25 [68-Apr-27: 2B].
Tschudi, Samuel (82 yrs.) d. on 68-Apr-30 [68-May-5: 1B, 2B].
Tschudy, Theresa m. Becker, Charles on 70-Aug-30 [70-Sep-13: 2B].
Tubble, Mary (80 yrs.) d. on 67-Sep-20 [67-Sep-21: 2A].
Tubman, Carrie G. d. on 70-Aug-30 [70-Aug-31: 2B].
Tubman, F. Eugene m. Coskerry, Carrie G. on 67-Apr-11 [67-Apr-17: 2B].
Tubman, John T. m. Jackson, Mary E. on 66-Aug-8 [66-Aug-10: 2C].
Tubman, Julia L. m. Rennolds, William D. on 66-Nov-15 [66-Nov-19: 2B].
Tubman, Lynn Lackland (10 yrs., 8 mos.) d. on 69-Sep-17 Drowned [69-Sep-20: 2C, 1G].
Tubman, Samuel A. m. Hammond, Nannie on 66-Apr-17 [66-Apr-28: 2A].
Tubman, Sarah A. m. Skinner, Thomas on 69-Feb-18 [69-Feb-20: 2A].
Tubman, Theodore (64 yrs.) d. on 66-May-25 [66-May-30: 2C].
Tubman, William H. (32 yrs.) d. on 70-Aug-24 [70-Aug-26: 2C].
Tubman, Willie A. m. Harding, M. B. on 70-Apr-5 [70-Apr-21: 2B].
Tucker, Ada Kathleen O'Hallora (19 yrs.) d. on 69-Jan-8 [69-Jan-28: 2C].
Tucker, Alfred, Jr. m. Atwell, Susie C. on 66-Nov-20 [66-Dec-3: 2B].
Tucker, Ann Maria m. Staph, Andrew on 66-Oct-29 [66-Nov-1: 2B].
Tucker, Ann Trumbull (90 yrs.) d. on 66-Dec-29 [66-Dec-31: 2C].
Tucker, Anna R. m. Coleman, W. H. on 69-Dec-30 [70-Jan-4: 2C].
Tucker, Cora Belle d. on 67-Mar-20 [67-Mar-25: 2C].
Tucker, David L. m. Stewart, Sallie E. on 70-Nov-15 [70-Nov-26: 2B; 70-Dec-17: 4D; 70-Dec-19: 4C].
Tucker, Enoch (29 yrs.) d. on 69-Mar-13 [69-Mar-16: 2C].
Tucker, Harriet (68 yrs.) d. on 69-May-13 [69-May-15: 2B].

Tucker, Henry Rober d. on 70-Dec-15 [70-Dec-17: 2B; 70-Dec-19: 4C].
Tucker, Ida H. m. Ebaugh, Andrew C. on 70-Apr-21 [70-Jun-2: 2B].
Tucker, Imogene m. Mount, George W. on 67-Nov-26 [67-Nov-28: 2C].
Tucker, Jacob R. m. Peregoy, Sarah Lizzie on 66-Sep-6 [66-Sep-19: 2B].
Tucker, James (83 yrs.) d. on 69-Sep-18 [69-Sep-20: 1G, 2C].
Tucker, James H. m. Bohanon, Mollie R. on 66-Jun-5 [66-Jun-7: 2B].
Tucker, James W. m. Carpenter, Sophronia A. on 69-Sep-2 [69-Sep-6: 2C].
Tucker, Jannett m. Brant, Joseph E. on 68-Apr-12 [68-Apr-28: 2A].
Tucker, John B. (47 yrs.) d. on 66-Jan-4 [66-Jan-6: 2C].
Tucker, Joseph, Jr. (33 yrs.) d. on 69-May-31 [69-Jun-1: 2B].
Tucker, Margaret (55 yrs.) d. on 69-Feb-4 [69-Feb-5: 2C].
Tucker, Maria L. m. Maken, John H. on 67-Dec-15 [67-Dec-23: 2B].
Tucker, Mary A. m. Pennington, E. Burke on 70-Dec-8 [70-Dec-10: 2B].
Tucker, Mary C. (29 yrs.) d. on 68-Sep-28 [68-Sep-29: 2B].
Tucker, Mollie E. m. Holmes, William G., Jr. on 67-Aug-22 [67-Aug-28: 2B].
Tucker, Morton (67 yrs.) d. on 70-Jun-3 [70-Jun-4: 2B].
Tucker, Samuel L. (67 yrs.) d. on 67-Sep-29 [67-Oct-1: 2B].
Tucker, Samuel T. m. Van Meter, Bella M. on 67-Nov-19 [67-Dec-2: 2C].
Tucker, Thomas W. m. O'Halloran, Ada Kathleen on 67-Jul-10 [67-Jul-17: 2C].
Tuckey, Ann Maria (65 yrs.) d. on 66-Nov-4 of Pneumonia [66-Nov-6: 2B].
Tuckley, Lena (11 mos.) d. on 68-Jul-24 [68-Jul-25: 2B].
Tuder, Joseph H. m. Denbow, Annie E. on 70-Aug-29 [70-Aug-31: 2B].
Tudor, Charles H. m. Batch, S. Ollie on 69-Nov-14 [69-Nov-20: 2B].
Tudor, Henry C. m. Farrow, Maria L. on 69-Dec-7 [69-Dec-9: 2C].
Tudor, Issac F. m. Gardner, Rebecca A. on 68-Nov-7 [68-Nov-24: 2C].
Tudor, J. C. m. Johnson, M. A. on 70-Feb-10 [70-Feb-18: 2C].
Tuite, William (55 yrs.) d. on 67-May-28 [67-May-29: 2B].
Tull, Sarah d. on 66-Oct-13 [66-Oct-18: 2B].
Tulley, Martha J. (31 yrs.) d. on 68-Nov-22 [68-Nov-23: 2B].
Tully, Ann m. Lenard, Michael on 67-Mar-4 [67-Mar-23: 2B].
Tully, Harriet Clair (42 yrs., 10 mos.) d. on 70-Jun-26 [70-Jun-28: 2C; 70-Jun-29: 2C].
Tully, Thomas P. (1 yr., 4 mos.) d. on 67-Aug-21 [67-Aug-22: 2B].
Tumbleson, Mary Ellen m. Lowekamp, Charles B. on 68-Oct-8 [68-Oct-19: 2B].
Tumblinson, Lizzie J. m. Roby, Charles J. on 66-Nov-20 [66-Nov-24: 2B].
Tumoney, John (47 yrs.) d. on 70-Mar-9 [70-Mar-10: 2C].
Tunis, Katie G. (17 yrs.) d. on 70-Dec-27 [70-Dec-28: 2D].
Tunis, Samuel W. (62 yrs.) d. on 70-Nov-10 [70-Nov-14: 2B].
Tuomey, Minnie m. Nevius, Reuben S. on 67-Aug-1 [67-Aug-3: 2B].
Turfield, Sarah R. (42 yrs.) d. on 66-Nov-13 [66-Nov-20: 2B].
Turley, Louise B. m. Larrabee, Harrison C. on 68-Sep-30 [68-Oct-2: 2B].
Turnbaugh, Eliza m. Wolf, Henry C. on 69-Oct-13 [69-Oct-21: 2B].
Turnbaugh, Eliza Jane m. Hicks, John W. on 69-Dec-19 [69-Dec-23: 2B].
Turnbull, Alexander d. on 70-Aug-15 [70-Aug-17: 2C].
Turnbull, Anna G. d. on 66-Jan-9 [66-Jan-12: 2C].
Turnbull, Annie E. m. Schutz, Lawrence on 67-Jun-9 [67-Jun-12: 2B].
Turnbull, Hattie m. Childs, N. S. on 67-May-29 [67-May-31: 2B].
Turnbull, John T. m. Cromwell, Ellen on 66-May-30 [66-Jun-8: 2B].
Turnbull, Nesbit m. Criss, Agnes on 69-Oct-12 [69-Oct-21: 2B].
Turner, Adeline (65 yrs.) d. on 68-Aug-9 [68-Aug-11: 2B].
Turner, Ann (44 yrs.) d. on 68-Oct-20 [68-Oct-24: 2B].
Turner, Ann Elizabeth m. Wheeler, Clodius H. on 68-Jun-4 [68-Jun-9: 2B].
Turner, Ann H. (67 yrs.) d. on 69-Feb-25 [69-Feb-26: 2D].
Turner, Annie Lee (1 yr., 1 mo.) d. on 68-Aug-29 [68-Aug-31: 2B].
Turner, Benedick (28 yrs.) d. on 66-Feb-8 [66-Feb-16: 2B].
Turner, Beverly W. m. Boone, Laura V. on 66-Feb-12 [66-Feb-13: 2C].

Turner, Caroline (37 yrs.) d. on 69-Oct-9 [69-Oct-14: 2C].
Turner, Deborah (68 yrs.) d. on 70-May-25 [70-May-31: 2B].
Turner, Eddy (6 mos.) d. on 69-Jun-20 [69-Jun-24: 2C].
Turner, Elizabeth (39 yrs.) d. on 70-Oct-11 [70-Oct-12: 2C].
Turner, Elizabeth Smith d. on 68-Apr-23 [68-Apr-25: 2B].
Turner, Ellen Amanda m. Jones, Evan on 69-Nov-25 [69-Nov-29: 2C].
Turner, Emma A. m. Hood, Steven G. on 66-Oct-25 [66-Oct-27: 2B].
Turner, Emma J. m. Herring, Lewis E. on 69-Jan-13 [69-Jan-27: 2C].
Turner, Frank V. m. Thomas, Morris A. on 66-Nov-20 [66-Nov-26: 2C].
Turner, George (35 yrs.) d. on 70-Jul-29 in Wagon accident [70-Jul-30: 4E].
Turner, George C. m. Agier, Catharine on 67-Jul-29 [67-Oct-15: 2A].
Turner, H. T. m. Harrison, Martha on 68-Jun-11 [68-Jun-23: 2B].
Turner, J. W. m. McKnew, Emma H. on 68-Jun-2 [68-Jun-5: 2B].
Turner, James m. Quigley, Kate on 68-Feb-20 [68-Feb-29: 2B].
Turner, James H. (34 yrs.) d. on 70-Sep-6 [70-Sep-13: 2B].
Turner, John (54 yrs.) d. on 66-May-27 [66-May-29: 2B].
Turner, John, Jr. m. Massey, L. M. on 67-Apr-9 [67-Apr-13: 2B; 67-Apr-15: 2B].
Turner, Joseph (34 yrs.) d. of Smallpox [66-Dec-15: 2B].
Turner, Joseph J. m. Mumford, Virginia A. on 67-Nov-12 [67-Nov-19: 2C].
Turner, Joshua m. Ames, Annie on 66-Feb-12 [66-Feb-17: 2B].
Turner, Lizzie J. m. Bowling, Alexander on 68-Jun-2 [68-Jun-4: 2B].
Turner, Lottie M. m. Ridgely, Richard D. on 68-Mar-25 [68-Mar-30: 2B].
Turner, Lucie H. m. White, George B. on 68-Nov-25 [68-Dec-2: 2C].
Turner, Maggie R. m. Schenck, Alexander D. on 69-May-4 [69-May-6: 2B].
Turner, Margaret (69 yrs.) d. on 69-Sep-16 [69-Sep-17: 2C].
Turner, Maria m. Reynolds, Patrick on 67-May-19 [67-May-23: 2B].
Turner, Mary E. m. Peregoy, Charles F. on 67-Jun-27 [67-Jun-29: 2B].
Turner, Nannie M. (13 yrs.) d. on 66-Jul-21 [66-Jul-24: 2C].
Turner, Prissie m. Gardiner, F. A. on 68-Nov-24 [68-Nov-26: 2B].
Turner, Rodwell m. Reese, Sarah T. on 70-Jun-8 [70-Jun-11: 2B].
Turner, Samuel R. m. Hutchins, Clara V. on 68-Feb-4 [68-Feb-13: 2C].
Turner, Sarah Ann (69 yrs.) d. on 69-Nov-16 [69-Nov-18: 2C].
Turner, Sophie Cook d. on 66-Nov-18 [66-Nov-21: 2C].
Turner, Thomas E. (21 yrs.) d. on 68-Jun-17 [68-Jun-29: 2B].
Turner, William B. m. Nugent, Cecilia M. on 68-Oct-7 [68-Oct-29: 2B].
Turner, William Hamline (19 yrs.) d. on 67-Jun-17 [67-Jun-18: 2B].
Turner, William J. (17 yrs.) d. on 69-Oct-12 [69-Oct-14: 2C].
Turney, Michael (71 yrs.) d. on 68-Sep-13 [68-Sep-14: 2B].
Turpin, Albert S. m. Handley, Mollie A. on 67-Jun-6 [67-Jun-8: 2B].
Turpin, Ann (67 yrs.) d. on 67-Feb-18 [67-Feb-19: 2C].
Turpin, F. T. m. Hackett, Love R. on 70-Dec-15 [70-Dec-31: 2C].
Tuslin, Marian W. m. Terres, Charles E. on 70-Jun-15 [70-Jun-17: 2B].
Tustin, John G. (24 yrs.) d. on 66-Oct-10 of Gunshot wound [66-Oct-11: 2C; 66-Oct-12: 2B; 66-Oct-11: 1G].
Tustin, William H. (40 yrs.) d. on 69-Nov-22 [69-Nov-23: 2C].
Tutt, William Henry (15 yrs.) d. on 69-Feb-3 [69-Feb-5: 2C].
Tuttle, Daniel (72 yrs.) d. on 67-Jan-26 [67-Jan-30: 2C].
Tuttle, Elisha d. on 67-Dec-13 [67-Dec-23: 2B].
Tuttle, Harriet Emily (6 mos.) d. on 66-Jan-19 [66-Jan-22: 2C].
Tuttle, Henry C. (25 yrs.) d. on 68-Sep-19 [68-Sep-21: 2B].
Tuttle, Laura T. m. Weaver, Robert S. on 66-Mar-8 [66-Mar-10: 2B].
Tuttle, Mary (88 yrs.) d. on 68-Apr-25 [68-May-4: 2B].
Tuttle, Mary m. Sinner, David on 70-Jan-7 [70-Jan-11: 2C; 70-Jan-18: 2C].
Tuttle, Oliver C. (25 yrs.) d. on 70-Nov-1 of Typhoid [70-Nov-3: 2C].
Tuxford, Martin (62 yrs.) d. on 68-Dec-17 [68-Dec-18: 2C].

Tuxworth, J. Howard d. on 66-Oct-18 [66-Oct-19: 2B].
Tweedale, Amelia m. Duncan, William Y. on 69-Jun-8 [69-Jun-10: 2C; 69-Jun-12: 2B].
Tweedale, Malisia V. (2 yrs., 11 mos.) d. on 68-Apr-4 [68-Apr-7: 2B].
Tweedale, Sarah Elizabeth (1 yr., 8 mos.) d. on 68-Nov-16 [68-Nov-17: 2C].
Tweedall, Martha A. m. Schultz, William A. on 70-Sep-11 [70-Sep-26: 2B].
Tweeddale, Jacob m. Schaeffer, Caroline on 67-Dec-23 [67-Dec-30: 2C].
Tweedy, Maria Josephine d. on 67-Feb-20 [67-Feb-25: 2C].
Twiford, Harry Sidney (1 yr., 7 mos.) d. on 70-Jun-19 [70-Jun-21: 2C].
Twiford, William (62 yrs.) d. on 66-May-26 of Paralysis [66-May-30: 2C].
Twing, Agnes Carr m. Hoofnagle, William on 68-Mar-1 [68-Mar-5: 2C].
Twist, Henry B. m. Logue, Mary A. on 68-Apr-16 [68-May-5: 2B].
Tydings, John L. m. Robinson, Laura C. on 70-Feb-14 [70-Feb-15: 2C].
Tydings, Thomas J. m. Harvey, Sallie A. on 67-Dec-22 [67-Dec-31: 2C].
Tylee, William C. m. Croghan, Maggie on 69-Dec-21 [70-Jan-14: 2C].
Tyler, Amanda A. d. on 68-Jul-21 [68-Jul-23: 2B].
Tyler, Bettie W. m. Brophy, John P. on 66-Sep-11 [66-Sep-13: 2C].
Tyler, Charles Edwin (8 mos.) d. on 69-Jul-4 [69-Jul-5: 2C].
Tyler, E. Jane d. on 67-Feb-21 [67-Feb-25: 2C].
Tyler, Gordon K. d. on 67-Sep-10 [67-Sep-11: 2B].
Tyler, Hannah m. Carroll, Osborn on 70-Dec-22 [70-Dec-23: 2B].
Tyler, James E. m. Hamer, Ida on 70-Nov-10 [70-Nov-15: 2C].
Tyler, James Milton (8 mos.) d. on 69-Jul-25 [69-Aug-7: 2C].
Tyler, John A. m. Logue, Kate on 66-Feb-15 [66-Feb-17: 2B].
Tyler, Kate E. m. Mace, William on 68-Apr-29 [68-May-5: 2B].
Tyler, Maria m. Belt, T. H., Jr. on 69-Dec-8 [69-Dec-11: 2B].
Tyler, Mary Addison m. Gatchell, Hugh McElderry on 68-Jan-30 [68-Feb-1: 2B].
Tyler, Mattie E. m. Shorey, N. B. on 66-May-17 [66-May-19: 2B].
Tyler, R. Bradley m. Shriver, E. Eme on 69-Mar-11 [69-Mar-13: 2B].
Tyler, Susie m. Pollard, James on 70-Dec-15 [70-Dec-17: 2B].
Tyler, William G. d. on 68-Jun-3 [68-Jun-11: 2B].
Typee, Albert (45 yrs.) d. on 69-Nov-29 [69-Dec-1: 2C; 69-Dec-2: 2C].
Tyson, Charles (15 yrs.) d. on 67-Jun-16 [67-Jun-17: 2C].
Tyson, Cincinnatus Riley (11 yrs., 11 mos.) d. on 70-Feb-27 of Lockjaw [70-Mar-8: 2C].
Tyson, Hannah Ann (69 yrs.) d. on 66-Jan-4 [66-Jan-5: 2C].
Tyson, James d. on 67-Sep-23 in Wagon accident [67-Sep-26: 1F].
Tyson, James E. m. Williams, Fannie E. on 67-Jun-12 [67-Jun-14: 2B].
Tyson, Jane Randolph (1 yr., 6 mos.) d. on 69-May-26 [69-May-27: 2C].
Tyson, Joshua J. H. m. Groff, Mary C. on 69-May-19 [69-May-26: 2C].
Tyson, Margaret (71 yrs.) d. on 66-Jan-18 [66-Jan-20: 2C].
Tyson, Nathan (80 yrs.) d. on 67-Jan-6 [67-Jan-7: 1G, 2C; 67-Jan-8: 2B; 67-Jan-9: 2C].
Tyson, Olive O. B. m. Enos, H. K. on 66-Aug-1 [66-Aug-2: 2C].
Tyson, Patty E. (12 yrs.) d. on 66-Jul-15 [66-Jul-16: 2C].
Tyson, Robert m. Smith, Sallie R. on 69-Nov-25 [69-Nov-29: 2C].
Tyson, William B. (70 yrs.) d. on 70-Sep-10 [70-Sep-12: 2B].
Tyte, Annie E. m. Davis, William H. on 67-Feb-5 [67-Feb-20: 2C].
Uhl, Mary m. McGarvey, William C. on 66-Nov-29 [66-Dec-1: 2B].
Uhler, George W. (60 yrs.) d. on 69-Apr-5 [69-Apr-7: 2C].
Uhler, Hamilton (4 yrs., 8 mos.) d. on 69-Dec-6 [69-Dec-8: 2C].
Uhler, J. H. m. Deeds, Virginia on 69-Aug-3 [69-Aug-4: 2C].
Uhler, Julia m. Berryman, George G. on 68-Nov-19 [68-Nov-23: 2B].
Uhler, Philip R. m. Werdebaugh, Sophia on 67-Dec-5 [67-Dec-9: 2B].
Uhlhorn, Johanna (8 yrs., 2 mos.) d. on 69-Jan-21 [69-Jan-22: 2D; 69-Jan-23: 2C].
Uhrlaub, Edward M., Esq. (55 yrs.) d. on 69-Dec-7 [69-Dec-8: 2C].
Uhthoff, Carrie H. m. Inloes, H. A., Jr. on 67-Apr-25 [67-Apr-27: 2A].
Ulbig, Joseph L. m. Zahn, Fannie N. on 69-Feb-16 [69-Feb-18: 2C].

Ulery, Joseph (4 yrs.) d. on 68-Nov-15 [68-Nov-16: 2C].
Ullbocker, Simon (23 yrs.) d. on 69-Jul-4 Drowned [69-Jul-7: 4C].
Ullman, Mina m. Straus, Solomon on 69-Dec-22 [69-Dec-25: 2C].
Ullrich, Christine (13 yrs.) d. on 70-Aug-17 [70-Aug-18: 2C].
Ullrich, Henry C. m. Peters, Mary C. on 67-Jun-5 [67-Jun-7: 2B].
Ullrich, Mary E. m. Smith, Edward G. on 66-Oct-31 [66-Nov-1: 2B].
Ulman, Bernhard (5 mos.) d. on 68-Jul-16 [68-Jul-18: 2B].
Ulrich, Mary C. m. Mehrs, Harry on 67-Sep-10 [67-Sep-12: 2B].
Umbrage, Josie d. on 69-Jan-15 [69-Jan-16: 2C].
Umstead, Jacob (40 yrs., 3 mos.) d. on 67-May-1 of Typhoid [67-May-4: 2B].
Underwood, Charles (1 yr., 7 mos.) d. on 66-Jul-11 [66-Jul-27: 2C].
Underwood, Eliza Ann (52 yrs.) d. on 70-Dec-16 [70-Dec-17: 2B].
Underwood, Elizabeth (52 yrs.) d. on 66-Sep-1 [66-Sep-3: 2C].
Underwood, George A. m. Kessler, Elizabeth A. on 68-Aug-18 [68-Aug-24: 2B].
Underwood, Joseph Francis (5 yrs.) d. on 70-Jul-18 [70-Aug-9: 2C].
Underwood, Joshua (66 yrs.) d. on 70-May-18 [70-May-19: 2C; 70-May-20: 2C].
Underwood, Loretta Agnes (9 yrs.) d. on 70-Jul-29 [70-Aug-9: 2C].
Underwood, Mary Susanna (5 mos.) d. on 68-Dec-21 [68-Dec-22: 2C].
Underwood, Sarah J. m. Jacobs, Collis F. on 68-Apr-2 [68-Apr-8: 2B].
Underwood, Sophie m. Thompson, C. Gratiot on 66-Dec-22 [67-Jan-1: 2C].
Unduch, H. H. m. Carroll, Minnie on 70-Nov-21 [70-Nov-22: 2B].
Unduch, Mary E. m. Austin, Theodore G. on 66-May-31 [66-Jun-4: 2B].
Unger, Margarethe m. Herpel, John H. on 70-Jul-5 [70-Jul-12: 2B].
Unglaub, Christopher d. on 69-Dec-25 Drowned [70-Jan-28: 1H].
Unglaub, Philip m. Scharp, Mary E. on 69-Sep-12 [69-Sep-14: 2B].
Uniack, Helen M. (1 yr., 4 mos.) d. on 68-Nov-21 of Scarlet fever [68-Nov-26: 2B].
Uniack, Katie H. (6 yrs., 9 mos.) d. on 68-Nov-13 of Scarlet fever [68-Nov-14: 2B; 68-Nov-26: 2B].
Uniack, M. Annie (8 yrs., 3 mos.) d. on 68-Nov-23 of Scarlet fever [68-Nov-26: 2B].
Uniack, Mary m. Sneeringer, William J. on 68-Jun-1 [68-Jun-3: 2B].
Unkle, George m. Swift, Lizzie E. on 70-Mar-29 [70-Mar-30: 2B].
Unruh, Marietta m. Courtney, I. W. on 67-May-13 [67-May-18: 2A].
Unverzagt, George P. m. Cronhardt, Lina on 66-Jun-7 [66-Jun-11: 2B].
Unverzagt, William m. Kalling, Annie Elizabeth on 68-Jul-2 [68-Jul-28: 2B].
Unwin, Edward m. Hughes, Mary on 70-Jun-14 [70-Jun-15: 2B].
Updeheide, Frederica (15 yrs., 2 mos.) d. on 68-Sep-3 [68-Sep-5: 2A].
Uppercu, Thomas S. m. Switzer, Ella F. on 68-Jun-1 [68-Jun-23: 2B].
Uppercue, Maggie m. Adreon, George W. L. on 69-Dec-28 [70-Jan-8: 2B; 70-Jan-11: 2B].
Upperman, Emma m. Covell, Joel E. on 66-May-15 [66-May-23: 2B].
Upperman, Lydia A. m. Poole, John H. on 70-Jun-5 [70-Jun-11: 2B].
Upson, Edward S. m. Williams, Mary on 69-Nov-9 [69-Nov-11: 2C].
Upton, Catherine (8 yrs.) d. on 66-Dec-13 [66-Dec-18: 2B].
Upton, Mary (6 yrs., 1 mo.) d. on 66-Dec-16 [66-Dec-18: 2B].
Upton, Susie R. m. Small, Joseph on 69-Nov-16 [69-Nov-18: 2C].
Urbach, William J. m. Dunn, Amelia S. on 70-Jun-7 [70-Jun-9: 2C].
Urbach, William J. m. Durr, Amelia T. on 70-Jun-7 [70-Jun-14: 2B].
Urban, Brother (74 yrs.) d. on 70-Dec-26 [70-Dec-28: 4E].
Urban, Margaret A. (44 yrs., 9 mos.) d. on 70-Feb-15 [70-Feb-16: 2C; 70-Feb-17: 2C].
Urquhart, John H. (50 yrs.) d. on 67-Mar-10 [67-Mar-14: 2C].
Usher, Elizabeth (68 yrs.) d. on 68-Sep-27 [68-Oct-12: 2B].
Usilton, Esther A. m. Diehl, Theodore on 70-Dec-9 [70-Dec-28: 2C].
Vaden, Anna E. (5 yrs.) d. on 66-Nov-29 of Scarlet fever [66-Dec-4: 2D].
Vaden, Augustus W. (8 yrs.) d. on 66-Nov-29 of Scarlet fever [66-Dec-4: 2D].
Vaden, George (13 yrs.) d. on 66-Dec-1 of Scarlet fever [66-Dec-4: 2D].
Vail, Edward H. (28 yrs.) d. on 67-Oct-14 [67-Oct-15: 2A; 67-Oct-16: 2B].

Vain, Elizabeth J. m. Starkey, William H. on 70-Jul-31 [70-Aug-10: 2B].
Vain, Scott m. Starkey, Charlotte on 70-May-31 [70-Jun-24: 2C].
Vaine, John G. (19 yrs., 6 mos.) d. on 69-Aug-18 [69-Aug-20: 2C].
Vaine, Sarah N. (87 yrs., 2 mos.) d. on 66-Aug-26 [66-Aug-28: 2B].
Valentine, August (17 yrs.) d. on 68-Jan-18 [68-Jan-20: 1F].
Valentine, Mary Ellen m. Wheeler, Zebulon on 70-Jul-7 [70-Jul-16: 2B].
Valentine, Thomas B. m. Dull, Marie A. on 68-Feb-20 [68-Feb-22: 2B].
Valiant, Elizabeth (65 yrs.) d. on 69-Jun-14 [69-Jun-14: 2B].
Valiant, James m. Thompson, Martha P. on 67-Nov-12 [67-Nov-16: 2B].
Valiant, John, Rev. (87 yrs.) d. on 69-Jan-22 [69-Jan-23: 2C; 69-Jan-25: 1G].
Valiant, Mary Sue m. Robertson, William on 70-May-11 [70-May-13: 2C].
Valiant, Sophia Rose (4 mos.) d. on 66-Jul-25 [66-Jul-26: 2C].
Vallee, Mary Ann (38 yrs.) d. on 68-Jan-23 [68-Jan-25: 2B].
Valliant, M. Florence m. Courtenay, Austin M. on 70-Aug-23 [70-Sep-26: 2B; 70-Sep-27: 2B].
Van Bibber, Ann (9 yrs.) d. on 67-Nov-12 [67-Nov-13: 2C].
Van Bibber, Lucretia (80 yrs.) d. on 67-May-16 [67-May-18: 2A].
Van Bokern, Mary Ella m. Sullivan, Henry C. on 66-Jul-17 [66-Jul-21: 2C].
Van Camp, Orsena L. R. m. Zimmerman, Charles A. on 67-Jun-5 [67-Jun-8: 2B].
Van Court, John W. (1 yr., 1 mo.) d. on 70-May-29 [70-May-30: 2B].
Van Daniker, Maria (66 yrs., 3 mos.) d. on 67-Mar-26 [67-Mar-27: 2C].
Van Danniker, Joseph (74 yrs.) d. on 70-Jun-24 [70-Jun-25: 2C].
Van Der Klieft, B. A., Dr. (37 yrs.) d. on 66-Sep-8 [66-Sep-13: 2C; 66-Sep-14: 2B; 66-Sep-17: 4C].
Van Hollen, Ameliaeita (5 yrs., 3 mos.) d. [67-Oct-12: 2A].
Van Hollen, George (33 yrs.) d. on 67-Aug-27 [67-Aug-28: 2B].
Van Horn, Elisha Abert (6 mos.) d. on 70-Jul-14 [70-Jul-15: 2C].
Van Horn, Rebecca m. Hall, George on 70-May-25 [70-May-27: 2B].
Van Kleeck, F. B. m. Hamilton, Estelle Mayer on 69-Jun-10 [69-Jun-11: 2C].
Van Lill, Urith A. (45 yrs.) d. on 69-Dec-18 [69-Dec-23: 2B].
Van Meter, Bella M. m. Tucker, Samuel T. on 67-Nov-19 [67-Dec-2: 2C].
Van Ness, Charles McEvers (20 yrs.) d. on 68-Mar-8 [68-Mar-9: 2C; 68-Mar-11: 2B].
Van Ness, Charles W. (35 yrs.) d. on 70-Jun-26 of Heart disease [70-Jun-27: 1F].
Van Newkirk, Francis M. m. Hudgins, Lucretia on 68-Nov-29 [68-Dec-2: 2C].
Van Newkirk, Joseph m. Price, Sarah Ann on 70-Dec-7 [70-Dec-9: 2C].
Van Newkirk, Mary (50 yrs.) d. on 70-May-27 [70-May-30: 2B].
Van Newkirk, Sarah Lavinia (2 yrs., 8 mos.) d. on 67-Apr-1 Burned [67-Apr-2: 2B; 67-Apr-3: 1G].
Van Norman, Marshall Eugene (26 yrs.) d. on 68-Feb-18 [68-Feb-28: 2D].
Van Norst, Willie H. (10 mos.) d. on 67-Oct-16 [67-Oct-17: 2B].
Van Order, David G. m. Lee, Laura V. on 67-Jul-11 [67-Sep-13: 2B].
Van Order, Mary M. (22 yrs.) d. on 70-Nov-29 [70-Nov-30: 2C].
Van Patten, Hannah M. m. Smith, Amzi on 69-Dec-21 [69-Dec-23: 2B].
Van Reuth, A. P. m. Salom, Mary E. on 67-Feb-21 [67-Feb-23: 2C].
Van Rossum, Ann E. (66 yrs.) d. on 70-Feb-20 [70-Feb-23: 2C].
Van Rossum, John H. m. De Baufre, Mary V. on 67-Feb-28 [67-Mar-2: 2B].
Van Rossum, William E. m. Plummer, Kate on 70-Feb-21 [70-Mar-10: 2C].
Van Ruth, Florus M. m. Hicks, Emily A. on 66-May-16 [66-May-19: 2B].
Van Swearingen, Thomas m. Towner, Laura on 66-Dec-26 [66-Dec-27: 2C].
Van Tromp, John m. Daley, Sallie on 66-Jul-12 [66-Jul-16: 2C].
Van Trump, Volney m. Kirkwood, Mollie J. on 66-Oct-25 [66-Oct-27: 2B].
Van Valzah, Lucy G. m. Elder, C. Maurice on 67-Nov-19 [67-Nov-23: 2B].
Van Vick, Mary E. m. Freeman, James A. on 66-Mar-28 [66-Apr-10: 2C].
Van Wagner, William Henry (21 yrs.) d. on 70-Oct-24 [70-Oct-28: 2C].
Van Wyck, Sarah D. m. Walter, Frelinghuysen on 68-Apr-7 [68-Sep-17: 2B].
Van Zelst, Francis (65 yrs.) d. on 68-Oct-26 [68-Oct-27: 2B].

Vance, Ellen (80 yrs.) d. on 69-Dec-7 [69-Dec-8: 2C].
Vandaniker, John J. (8 mos.) d. on 67-Apr-2 [67-Apr-3: 2B].
Vandaniker, Joseph (22 yrs., 3 mos.) d. on 68-Jul-2 [68-Jul-3: 2B].
Vandaniker, Mary L. (10 mos.) d. on 68-Sep-14 [68-Sep-15: 2B].
Vander Weyde, Jennie m. De Ronceray, Louis on 67-Oct-9 [67-Oct-24: 2B].
Vanderford, William H. m. Neale, Adeline R. on 69-Nov-25 [69-Nov-27: 2B].
Vandergrift, Carrie V. (7 yrs., 2 mos.) d. on 68-Mar-24 [68-Mar-25: 2A].
Vandersloot, F. Edward m. Russell, S. Emma on 69-Sep-27 [69-Sep-29: 2B].
Vandervoort, Eliza D. (64 yrs.) d. on 70-Jun-23 [70-Jun-24: 2C; 70-Jun-25: 2C].
Vanhorn, Eddie (2 yrs.) d. on 69-Oct-27 [69-Oct-28: 2C].
Vanhorn, Lydia V. m. Lancaster, John W. on 66-Sep-25 [66-Oct-3: 2B].
Vanhorn, Samuel A. (5 yrs., 2 mos.) d. on 69-Jul-15 [69-Jul-20: 2C].
Vanni, John (51 yrs.) d. on 69-Sep-22 [69-Sep-23: 2B].
Vanock, William H. m. Lake, Amelia on 66-Sep-26 [66-Dec-15: 2B].
Vanockey, Lewis m. Downey, Henrietta on 68-Nov-26 [68-Dec-22: 2C].
VanReuth, Morris Hicks (1 yr., 8 mos.) d. on 68-Dec-27 [68-Dec-28: 2B].
Vanrossum, John H. (4 mos.) d. on 68-Aug-2 [68-Aug-4: 2C].
Vansant, Augustus L. m. Getz, Mary A. on 66-May-1 [66-May-8: 2B].
Vansant, Dennis B. (11 mos.) d. on 68-Dec-23 [68-Dec-24: 2C].
Vansant, Ellenore K. (1 yr., 5 mos.) d. on 66-Oct-11 [66-Oct-16: 2C].
Vansant, George Elliott (57 yrs.) d. on 69-Jun-4 of Fall from window [69-Jun-5: 1G, 2B].
Vansant, James E. m. Helm, Henrietta on 69-Jan-7 [69-Jan-8: 2C].
Vansant, Joseph (2 yrs.) d. on 70-Mar-24 of Scarlet fever [70-Mar-25: 2C].
Vansant, Kate Beckett (5 yrs., 5 mos.) d. on 70-Mar-22 of Scarlet fever [70-Mar-23: 2C].
Vansant, Mary E. (2 yrs., 2 mos.) d. on 70-May-7 [70-May-9: 2B].
Vansant, Sallie M. d. on 66-Oct-11 [66-Oct-16: 2C].
Vansant, Sarah J. m. Foxwell, Benjamin F. on 66-Apr-22 [66-Apr-26: 2B].
Vanwinkle, Catherine (76 yrs.) d. on 68-Dec-23 [68-Dec-25: 2D].
Vardy, Eliza Jane (42 yrs.) d. on 66-May-31 [66-Jun-2: 2B].
Varina, Edward C. (46 yrs.) d. on 64-May-12 Killed in battle [66-Feb-22: 2B].
Vasmar, Sallie E. (19 yrs., 1 mo.) d. on 66-May-7 [66-May-8: 2B; 66-May-9: 2B].
Vaughan, Henry I. m. Crise, Almira on 68-Feb-25 [68-Mar-2: 2B].
Vaughan, Kate (1 yr., 11 mos.) d. on 67-Nov-8 [67-Nov-9: 2B].
Vaughan, Lottie Amelia m. Melius, Louis on 69-Jun-1 [69-Jun-9: 2C].
Vaughan, Mary E. m. Bowling, Joseph on 67-Mar-12 [67-Apr-11: 2B].
Vaughan, Sarah C. m. Saunders, John Joseph on 66-Feb-13 [66-Feb-20: 2B].
Vaughan, Susan R. (52 yrs.) d. on 67-Jan-6 [67-Jan-14: 2C].
Vaughan, Walter W. m. McNamee, Virginia W. on 70-Dec-15 [70-Dec-21: 2C].
Veasey, Margaret (7 mos.) d. on 70-Sep-13 [70-Sep-14: 2B].
Veasey, Willie M. C. (6 mos.) d. on 70-Apr-16 [70-Apr-18: 2B].
Veazey, Eliza d. on 70-Jan-2 [70-Jan-3: 2C].
Veazey, John Manly (30 yrs.) d. on 68-Oct-21 of Fall from window [68-Oct-22: 1G, 2C].
Veditz, Christina d. on 67-Oct-7 [67-Oct-8: 2B; 67-Oct-9: 2B].
Veeder, Carrie E. m. Phillips, William B. on 69-Feb-22 [69-Feb-25: 2D].
Veeder, Simon d. on 70-Jun-7 [70-Jun-9: 2C].
Veith, Anna Barbara (10 mos.) d. on 68-Sep-1 [68-Sep-2: 2B].
Veith, Catherine Maria (9 yrs., 1 mo.) d. on 68-Jul-14 [68-Jul-16: 2C].
Veith, John m. Schmidt, Rosa on 69-Dec-30 [70-Jan-6: 2C].
Veith, Kate (32 yrs.) d. on 68-Jul-11 [68-Jul-13: 2B].
Verdier, Marie Blanche m. Fuchs, Guido on 67-Jan-21 [67-Feb-5: 2C].
Verena, Juliet M. (20 yrs.) d. on 67-Mar-8 [67-Mar-12: 2C].
Vermillion, George m. Benson, Catherine on 70-Jun-2 [70-Jun-4: 2B].
Vernay, John, Sr. (68 yrs.) d. on 69-Jun-1 [69-Jul-5: 2C].
Vernetson, Harrie E. (1 yr.) d. on 69-Sep-18 [69-Sep-21: 2B].
Vernetson, Harriet (60 yrs.) d. on 68-Jan-15 [68-Jan-16: 2C].

Vernetson, W. E. m. Hellman, Mary E. on 67-May-9 [67-May-11: 2A].
Vernon, Francis Thomas (3 mos.) d. on 70-Feb-11 [70-Feb-12: 2C].
Vernon, Joseph (81 yrs.) d. on 68-Sep-22 [68-Sep-23: 2B].
Vernon, Mary E. (7 yrs., 11 mos.) d. on 66-May-9 [66-May-11: 2B].
Verwayen, Magdalen m. Weber, Arthur on 67-May-18 [67-Jun-25: 2B].
Vey, Louis (18 yrs.) d. on 66-Jul-29 Drowned [66-Jul-30: 4D; 66-Jul-31: 1G].
Vickers, Albert m. Hamner, Jane on 67-Oct-15 [67-Oct-19: 2A].
Vickers, Horace R. m. Lusby, Mary A. on 69-Sep-12 [69-Oct-13: 2C].
Vickers, Mary (63 yrs.) d. on 69-Dec-27 [69-Dec-30: 2C].
Vickers, Mary Rebecca (1 yr., 7 mos.) d. on 68-Aug-14 [68-Aug-25: 2B].
Vickers, Theodore (34 yrs.) d. on 68-Nov-25 [68-Nov-26: 2D].
Vickery, Edward Henderson (2 yrs., 3 mos.) d. on 69-Feb-4 [69-Feb-5: 2C; 69-Feb-6: 2C].
Vickey, Mary (81 yrs.) d. on 66-Sep-13 [66-Sep-14: 2B; 66-Sep-15: 2B].
Victory, Mary Agnes d. on 69-May-3 [69-May-4: 2B; 69-May-5: 2C].
Viese, Maggie (2 yrs.) d. on 69-Apr-27 [69-Apr-28: 2B].
Vieweg, Emma m. Jones, Francis W. on 68-Nov-17 [68-Dec-21: 2B].
Vincell, Mollie m. Stephens, J. J. on 67-Dec-17 [67-Dec-19: 2B].
Vincent, Frances (44 yrs.) d. on 67-Dec-22 [67-Dec-24: 2B].
Vincent, Margaret m. Peregoy, George W. on 68-Mar-3 [68-Mar-24: 2B].
Vincent, Mary (40 yrs.) d. on 67-Mar-12 [67-Mar-14: 1F].
Vincent, Richard m. Merritt, Annie E. on 67-Dec-26 [67-Dec-27: 2D].
Vincent, William H. m. Griffin, Annie L. on 68-Sep-21 [68-Oct-5: 2B].
Vincente, Anna Agatha (6 mos.) d. on 67-Mar-22 [67-Mar-23: 2B].
Vincente, Edward P. m. Stevenson, Maggie on 68-Nov-10 [68-Nov-14: 2B].
Vincente, J. Henry m. Monday, Lottie A. on 70-Jun-2 [70-Jun-9: 2C].
Vincente, Louisa (29 yrs., 2 mos.) d. on 67-Nov-26 [67-Nov-27: 2C; 67-Nov-28: 2C].
Viney, Douglas m. Sapp, Sarah on 69-Oct-17 [69-Oct-20: 2C].
Viney, Jane (73 yrs.) d. on 66-Sep-13 [66-Sep-15: 2B].
Vinson, Annie (73 yrs.) d. on 69-Nov-2 [69-Nov-4: 2C].
Vinton, Robert Spencer, Rev. (74 yrs.) d. on 70-Jul-31 of Dropsy [70-Aug-2: 2C, 4D; 70-Aug-3: 4E].
Virgin, William C. d. [66-Jan-15: 1G].
Virley, Catherine m. Murray, Jesse on 67-Jun-11 [67-Jun-18: 2B].
Virnon, George R. m. Kurtz, Louise DePue on 68-Oct-8 [68-Oct-13: 2C].
Virtue, Emma D. d. on 69-Jan-3 [69-Jan-4: 2C].
Virtue, John m. Hoofnagle, Sarah A. on 68-Sep-29 [68-Oct-1: 2B].
Vivarttas, Aloha m. Redden, Rosa E. on 66-May-1 [66-May-5: 2B].
Vocke, Otto F. (15 yrs.) d. on 69-Jan-12 [69-Jan-13: 2D].
Vogel, Mary m. Mueller, John on 69-Nov-7 [69-Nov-8: 2C].
Vogell, Alvina F. m. Mehlgarten, Charles on 70-Feb-22 [70-Mar-3: 2C].
Vogell, Charles (19 yrs.) d. on 66-Jul-29 Drowned [66-Jul-30: 4D; 66-Jul-31: 1G, 2C].
Vogelman, John L. (79 yrs.) d. on 70-Oct-22 [70-Oct-24: 2B].
Vogelsang, Jacob m. Eberhart, Catharine on 66-Apr-1 [66-Apr-3: 2B].
Vogelsang, John Alexander (5 mos.) d. on 66-Jul-5 [66-Jul-6: 2B].
Vogelsang, William F. (1 yr., 3 mos.) d. on 70-Aug-14 [70-Aug-16: 2C].
Vogelson, Hannah (63 yrs.) d. on 68-Sep-12 [68-Sep-14: 2B].
Vogt, Elizabeth C. M. (37 yrs.) d. on 67-Jan-9 [67-Jan-10: 2C].
Vogt, Gussie M. (1 yr., 7 mos.) d. on 70-Nov-11 [70-Nov-14: 2B].
Vogt, John G. m. Smith, Sarah A on 66-Feb-27 [66-Mar-8: 2B; 66-Mar-9: 2B].
Vogt, Mary E. (38 yrs.) d. on 70-Mar-22 [70-Mar-23: 2C; 70-Mar-24: 2C].
Voice, Oliver H. (1 yr., 6 mos.) d. on 70-May-5 [70-May-7: 2B].
Voight, Elizabeth d. on 66-Dec-17 [66-Dec-19: 2B].
Volans, William C. m. Lambdin, Martha E. on 68-Apr-7 [68-Apr-7: 2B].
Volk, Kayatan m. Kirchmeir, Franziska on 67-Aug-20 [67-Aug-22: 2B].
Volk, Thakla d. on 67-Jul-4 Murdered (Shooting) [67-Jul-6: 4D; 67-Jul-8: 1G].

Volkmar, Elizabeth (87 yrs.) d. on 70-Jun-26 [70-Jun-27: 2C].
Vollandt, Emily (43 yrs.) d. on 68-Jul-4 [68-Jul-6: 2B].
Vollandt, Johanna C. m. Steger, William on 67-Jun-2 [67-Jun-4: 2A].
Vollandt, John M. (75 yrs.) d. on 66-Jan-20 [66-Jan-22: 2C; 66-Jan-23: 2C; 66-Jan-24: 1G].
Vollandt, Maggie m. Stoebe, Herman on 67-Feb-12 [67-Feb-15: 2C].
Vollandt, Mary Dorothy (77 yrs.) d. [68-Jun-3: 2B].
Volz, Mary Lizzie m. Hartmaier, Henry on 67-Jan-8 [67-Jan-10: 2C].
Volz, Peter T. m. Stump, Elizabeth on 67-May-7 [67-May-9: 2A].
Von Brunck, Julius Augustus Fr d. on 70-Jul-26 [70-Aug-8: 2C].
Von Brunck, Otto Frederick (1 yr., 7 mos.) d. on 70-Aug-17 [70-Aug-19: 2C].
Von Culin, Matthew m. Way, M. Elona on 69-May-21 [69-May-29: 2B].
Von Derheyde, Ann (38 yrs.) d. on 68-Sep-10 [68-Oct-11: 2B].
Von Kapff, Harry Rupert d. on 70-Jul-28 [70-Aug-1: 2C].
Von Phul, Philip m. Chatard, Josephine M. on 70-Oct-26 [70-Oct-28: 2C].
Von Santen, Anna (74 yrs.) d. on 67-Oct-20 [67-Oct-22: 2A].
Vonderfer, Matthew W. d. on 68-Oct-26 of Heart disease [68-Oct-28: 1G].
Vondersmith, Daniel (87 yrs.) d. on 70-Aug-29 [70-Aug-30: 2C].
Vondersmith, Willie H. m. Gardner, William F. on 67-Sep-19 [67-Sep-24: 2A].
Voorhees, William Hunter (17 yrs.) d. on 66-Oct-2 [66-Oct-4: 2B].
Voss, Elizabeth (55 yrs.) d. on 66-Aug-23 [66-Aug-24: 2B].
Voyce, Charles m. Weaver, Catherine on 69-Jul-4 [69-Jul-16: 2C].
Voyce, Ellenora m. Sessions, Joseph A. D. on 69-Dec-21 [69-Dec-29: 2D].
Waddell, James (50 yrs.) d. on 69-Aug-28 [69-Aug-30: 2B].
Waddell, Josiah (33 yrs.) d. on 68-Nov-26 [69-Feb-15: 2C].
Waddell, Louisa A. m. Smith, Frederick on 70-May-31 [70-Jun-9: 2C].
Wade, Hugh A. (3 yrs., 5 mos.) d. on 70-Jun-30 [70-Jul-1: 2B].
Wade, Mary Agnes (1 yr., 8 mos.) d. on 68-Dec-30 [69-Jan-1: 2C].
Wade, Matthew (75 yrs.) d. on 70-Apr-14 [70-Apr-15: 2C].
Wade, Walter Clinton (1 yr., 1 mo.) d. on 68-Dec-9 [68-Dec-10: 2D].
Wadhams, A. V. m. Henderson, Carrie E. on 70-Feb-28 [70-Mar-4: 2C].
Waesche, Margaret (90 yrs.) d. on 70-Jan-19 [70-Feb-21: 2B].
Waggaman, Mary d. on 70-Nov-20 [70-Nov-22: 2C].
Waggaman, Samuel J. m. McKee, Mary Theresa on 70-Sep-21 [70-Sep-22: 2C].
Waggner, George E. m. Nicolai, Antoinette Beatrice on 70-Nov-29 [70-Dec-8: 2B].
Waggner, George J., Sr. (64 yrs.) d. on 68-Jun-27 [68-Jun-29: 2B].
Wagner, Mary Olivia m. Crawford, Thomas A. on 66-Aug-9 [66-Aug-20: 2C].
Wagner, Alexander m. Regan, Margaret on 69-Nov-17 [70-Feb-3: 2B].
Wagner, Annie E. m. Hoover, George A. on 65-Jul-20 [66-Jan-6: 2B].
Wagner, Caroline m. Blaney, James J. on 70-Apr-28 [70-Apr-30: 2A].
Wagner, Casper m. Layre, Wilhelmina on 68-Oct-9 [66-Oct-26: 2B].
Wagner, Charles V. m. Yates, Jeannette B. on 70-Nov-1 [70-Nov-3: 2B].
Wagner, Frederick m. Thierrauch, Angeline on 67-Mar-24 [67-Mar-25: 2C].
Wagner, George m. Hart, Victoria A. on 66-Feb-6 [66-Feb-8: 2C].
Wagner, Harry d. on 68-Jul-10 [68-Jul-11: 2B].
Wagner, John (52 yrs.) d. on 66-Feb-19 [66-Feb-20: 2B; 66-Feb-21: 2D].
Wagner, Louisa (27 yrs.) d. on 66-Oct-11 [66-Oct-12: 2B].
Wagner, Maggie m. Jory, John G. on 69-Nov-16 [69-Nov-20: 2B].
Wagner, Mary E. m. Meyer, Jacob on 69-Dec-26 [70-Jan-4: 2C].
Wagner, Rosa C. m. Harman, Edward L. on 69-Nov-18 [69-Nov-20: 2B].
Wagner, Samuel K. (6 mos.) d. on 66-Jan-6 [66-Jan-8: 2B].
Wagner, Thomas C. (43 yrs.) d. on 67-Nov-5 of Heart disease [67-Nov-7: 1G].
Wahl, Georgie m. Shure, Harry W. on 67-Oct-30 [67-Oct-31: 2B].
Wahlmend, George (44 yrs.) d. on 70-Aug-29 of Brain congestion [70-Aug-31: 4E].
Waidner, Amelia M. m. Brandt, Anthony on 70-Sep-1 [70-Oct-4: 2B].
Waidner, Charles Frederick (3 yrs., 3 mos.) d. on 70-Jul-21 [70-Jul-22: 2C].

Waidner, Charles W. m. Frew, Sarah J. on 67-May-23 [67-May-29: 2B].
Waidner, Dollie E. m. Mory, Frederick W. on 67-Oct-13 [67-Dec-17: 2B].
Waidner, Frederick A. m. Thomas, Mary C. on 69-Sep-9 [69-Nov-30: 2C].
Waidner, Jacob B. m. Eggleston, Carrie on 66-Mar-22 [66-Mar-27: 2B].
Waidner, John J. m. Owens, Priscilla on 69-Feb-1 [69-Feb-9: 2C].
Waidner, Louis A., Jr. m. Gruetter, Annie C. on 69-Nov-25 [69-Nov-30: 2C].
Waidner, William F. m. Moore, Margaret K. on 69-Feb-9 [69-Feb-25: 2D].
Wailes, C. A. m. Colton, Hannah Moore on 69-Jan-12 [69-Jan-13: 2D].
Wailes, Stephen C. m. Wise, Rose A. on 69-Sep-22 [69-Sep-23: 2B].
Wain, Daniel m. Kilpatrick, Mary A. on 69-Apr-8 [69-Apr-10: 2B].
Wain, Edward Owen (2 yrs., 6 mos.) d. on 67-Nov-4 [67-Nov-5: 2B].
Wain, Willie M. Monroe (3 yrs., 6 mos.) d. on 70-Dec-7 [70-Dec-8: 2C].
Wait, Elizabeth A. m. Cooper, Samuel on 66-May-21 [66-Jun-2: 2B].
Waite, Annie m. Carr, John B. on 66-Oct-9 [66-Oct-10: 2B].
Waite, Elizabeth B. (16 yrs.) d. on 70-Feb-28 [70-Mar-2: 2C].
Waite, Harrison m. Waters, Anne E. on 67-Jul-30 [67-Aug-13: 2B].
Waite, Matthew Henry (39 yrs.) d. on 70-Apr-13 [70-Apr-14: 2C].
Waits, George J. (2 mos.) d. on 66-Jun-19 [66-Jun-21: 2C].
Waitz, Lauretta A. C. m. Kleinjohn, Charles H. on 69-Jul-17 [69-Jul-27: 2C].
Wakeland, M. C. m. Hanson, F. B. on 67-Jan-10 [67-Jan-18: 2C].
Wakeman, Elizabeth R. B. m. Johnson, James Edward on 68-Sep-8 [68-Sep-19: 2B].
Walbach, Eliza L. m. Marron, Thomas on 66-Apr-26 [66-May-2: 2B].
Walbach, Jno. B. m. Savin, Mary A. on 67-Jun-6 [67-Jun-10: 2B].
Walbach, Mary m. Marron, William L. on 68-Jan-29 [68-Feb-1: 2B].
Walbaum, Martin (26 yrs.) d. on 67-Apr-10 of Suicide (Hanging) [67-Apr-12: 1E].
Walderford, David J. (23 yrs.) d. on 69-Jan-28 [69-Feb-1: 2C].
Walderford, Henry F. Kenney (5 yrs., 4 mos.) d. on 67-Oct-24 [67-Oct-28: 2B].
Waldman, Aggie E. m. Tapman, Harry T. on 67-Jan-1 [67-Jan-5: 2C].
Waldman, George R. m. Burfoot, Mollie W. on 69-Apr-8 [69-Apr-17: 2A].
Waldmann, Emeline M. m. Netre, John G. on 67-Oct-29 [67-Nov-2: 2B].
Waldmann, Mary Clara (5 yrs., 1 mo.) d. [67-Jun-1: 2B].
Waldren, George Edward m. Lum, Isabella on 67-Apr-28 [67-May-7: 2B].
Waldron, Georgia M. m. Junkins, George F. on 69-Jun-8 [69-Jun-12: 2B].
Waldron, Virginia m. Spence, R. T. on 68-Oct-1 [68-Oct-3: 2B].
Waldschmidt, William (23 yrs.) d. on 67-Jan-15 Murdered (Stabbing) [67-Jan-16: 1F].
Waldsmith, Willie Alexander (3 yrs., 10 mos.) d. on 68-Oct-19 [68-Oct-20: 2B].
Wales, Ida (14 yrs., 7 mos.) d. on 70-Sep-10 [70-Sep-14: 2B].
Wales, James C. (34 yrs.) d. on 68-Feb-15 [68-Feb-18: 2C].
Wales, Maggie A. (47 yrs., 3 mos.) d. on 70-Jan-22 [70-Apr-26: 2B; 70-Jan-24: 2C].
Wales, Maggie E. d. on 70-Jan-22 [70-Jan-24: 2C].
Wales, Roseanna (27 yrs.) d. on 68-Dec-27 [68-Dec-28: 2B].
Walker, Adolphiae (19 yrs.) d. on 66-Mar-13 [66-Mar-15: 2C].
Walker, Alexander (1 yr., 8 mos.) d. on 66-Feb-4 of Chronic croup [66-Feb-7: 2C].
Walker, Alverda m. Chesney, Samuel on 70-Aug-18 [70-Aug-20: 2B].
Walker, Bettie m. Stowe, Daniel on 70-Aug-10 [70-Aug-17: 2C].
Walker, Edward M. m. Cameron, Margaret on 66-Jan-4 [66-Jan-20: 2C].
Walker, Edwin (60 yrs.) d. on 70-Jul-12 [70-Jul-16: 2C].
Walker, Eleanor Jane (47 yrs.) d. on 70-Jun-13 [70-Jun-14: 2B].
Walker, Emily J. d. on 67-Jul-4 of Consumption [67-Jul-13: 2B].
Walker, Emma L. m. Robinson, Edmund on 66-May-16 [66-Jul-16: 2C].
Walker, Florence K. m. Patterson, Joseph B. on 66-Jun-5 [67-Feb-9: 2B].
Walker, George m. Russelle, Anna E. on 70-Jun-1 [70-Jun-11: 2B].
Walker, George M. D. m. Young, Laura V. on 70-Mar-10 [70-Mar-24: 2C].
Walker, Issac (28 yrs.) d. on 70-Feb-18 [70-Feb-19: 2B; 70-Feb-21: 1H].
Walker, John (23 yrs.) d. on 69-Jul-27 Drowned [69-Jul-28: 1H].

Walker, John d. on 70-Dec-22 of Pneumonia [70-Dec-29: 2C].
Walker, John H. m. Dunbar, Rachel on 68-Dec-24 [68-Dec-29: 2D].
Walker, John H. m. Braby, Mary J. on 66-Oct-15 [66-Oct-16: 2B].
Walker, John M. m. Cox, Josephine on 70-Oct-20 [70-Oct-22: 2B].
Walker, John Wesley E. (1 yr., 8 mos.) d. on 67-Jan-1 [67-Jan-2: 2C].
Walker, Joseph (35 yrs.) d. on 66-Dec-24 [66-Dec-27: 2C].
Walker, Joseph P. (48 yrs.) d. on 68-Sep-20 [68-Sep-21: 2B].
Walker, Laura V. m. Smith, Owen K. on 67-Oct-16 [67-Oct-17: 2B].
Walker, Margaret S. d. on 70-Dec-17 [70-Dec-19: 2C; 70-Dec-20: 2B].
Walker, Marine Duvall (2 yrs., 1 mo.) d. on 68-Sep-6 [68-Sep-7: 2A].
Walker, Martha J. m. Mackall, Levin C. on 69-Dec-14 [69-Dec-22: 2B].
Walker, Mary Ann M. (56 yrs.) d. on 67-Mar-11 [67-Mar-12: 2C].
Walker, Mary F. m. Jones, Edward C. on 66-Apr-29 [66-May-15: 2C].
Walker, Mary Jane (37 yrs.) d. on 67-Mar-20 of Consumption [67-Mar-21: 2C; 67-Mar-22: 2C].
Walker, Nathaniel C. m. Corletto, Emma F. on 69-May-11 [69-May-9: 2C].
Walker, Patience Sylvinia (10 yrs.) d. on 68-Sep-9 [68-Sep-12: 2B].
Walker, Rachel Beall (71 yrs.) d. on 68-Sep-27 [68-Sep-29: 2B].
Walker, Rebecca F. m. Benkuff, William on 66-Jul-8 [66-Jul-14: 2B].
Walker, Ridgely (31 yrs.) d. on 67-Jul-3 of Erysipelas [67-Jul-10: 2B].
Walker, Susan (73 yrs.) d. on 66-Mar-30 [66-Mar-31: 2C].
Walker, Thaddeus m. Henkel, Louisa on 67-Sep-28 [67-Oct-1: 2B].
Walker, Virginia M. m. Bledsoe, Robert H. on 68-May-11 [68-May-15: 2B].
Walker, Virginia P. m. McCabe, William H. on 70-Feb-18 [70-Feb-25: 2C].
Walker, William J. m. Williams, Kate E. on 69-May-3 [69-May-6: 2B].
Walker, Zedick F. (69 yrs.) d. on 70-Jun-7 in Construction accident [70-Jun-8: 1G, 2C; 70-Jun-9: 2C].
Wall, Amelia m. Fry, Robert J. on 66-Mar-1 [66-Mar-5: 2B].
Wall, Ella Virginia (1 yr., 3 mos.) d. on 69-May-31 [69-Jun-1: 2B].
Wall, Gertrude (9 mos.) d. on 70-Jul-18 [70-Jul-19: 2C].
Wall, H. Clay, Maj. (38 yrs.) d. on 67-Oct-22 of Dropsy [67-Oct-28: 2B].
Wall, Helen A. m. Hess, William U. on 67-Feb-12 [67-Feb-18: 2C].
Wall, J. Edward (35 yrs.) d. on 66-Dec-8 [66-Dec-10: 2C].
Wall, Katie (4 yrs., 8 mos.) d. on 66-Aug-21 [66-Aug-22: 2C].
Wall, Patrick m. Jenkins, M. V. on 69-Dec-27 [70-Jan-1: 2B].
Wall, Prudie E. m. Newberry, Albert S. on 68-Jan-1 [68-Jan-4: 2C].
Wall, William (72 yrs.) d. on 68-Sep-20 [68-Oct-5: 2C].
Wall, William E. m. Dade, Mary C. on 70-Jan-25 [70-Jan-28: 2B].
Wall, William J. (10 mos.) d. on 66-Jun-22 [66-Jun-23: 2B].
Wallace, Celia Jane (1 yr., 4 mos.) d. on 66-Jan-18 of Chronic croup [66-Jan-20: 2C].
Wallace, Charles H. (31 yrs.) d. on 70-Nov-25 [70-Nov-26: 2C].
Wallace, David W. m. Bowers, Mary E. on 68-Dec-9 [68-Dec-11: 2C].
Wallace, Eliza (64 yrs.) d. on 70-Jan-6 [70-Jan-7: 2F].
Wallace, F. Marion (37 yrs.) d. on 70-Dec-11 [70-Dec-31: 2C].
Wallace, George A. m. Harris, Anna Amelia on 70-Nov-29 [70-Dec-2: 2C].
Wallace, George W. m. Marine, Anna T. on 67-Dec-24 [68-Jan-21: 2C].
Wallace, Hugh Grimes (3 yrs., 2 mos.) d. on 69-Dec-9 [69-Dec-11: 2B].
Wallace, Isabella E. m. Eberhart, Henry on 67-Sep-29 [67-Oct-1: 2B].
Wallace, J. m. Barker, Annie Maria on 68-Mar-31 [68-Apr-8: 2B].
Wallace, Maggie A. m. Poe, George, Jr. on 69-Mar-17 [69-Mar-20: 2B].
Wallace, Marian Virginia (3 yrs., 2 mos.) d. on 70-Jul-11 [70-Jul-14: 2B].
Wallace, Mary J. m. Mullen, John on 69-Nov-18 [69-Dec-28: 2C].
Wallace, Mary Jane (51 yrs.) d. on 67-Jun-3 [67-Jun-10: 2B].
Wallace, Matthew (87 yrs.) d. on 66-Jun-8 [66-Jun-25: 2B].
Wallace, Robert B. m. Shannon, Maggie J. on 70-May-10 [70-May-16: 2B].
Wallace, Sallie E. m. Holmes, Byron H. on 68-Oct-27 [68-Nov-9: 2B].

Wallace, Susan Elizabeth (1 yr., 10 mos.) d. on 66-Jul-16 [66-Jul-18: 2C].
Wallace, William, Capt. d. on 69-Dec-26 of Paralysis [69-Dec-27: 2D; 69-Dec-28: 1H].
Wallace, William S. d. on 66-May-13 [66-May-15: 2C].
Wallace, Willie (2 yrs., 6 mos.) d. on 68-Jan-2 [68-Jan-3: 2C].
Waller, Hannah M. m. Heath, William F. on 68-Nov-15 [68-Nov-26: 2B].
Waller, Katie (1 yr., 6 mos.) d. on 69-Feb-1 [69-Feb-3: 2C].
Waller, Sophie m. Miller, Richard A. on 67-Jan-18 [67-Jan-19: 2C].
Wallet, Sarah m. Price, George T. on 66-May-20 [66-Oct-9: 2A].
Wallin, Abijah H. (47 yrs.) d. on 70-Jun-30 [70-Jul-1: 2B].
Wallin, Charles E. m. Thorne, Lydia B. on 67-Jul-20 [67-Aug-5: 2B].
Walling, A. Louisa (37 yrs.) d. on 70-Jan-10 [70-Jan-14: 2C].
Wallis, Elizabeth Custis d. on 67-Jul-12 [67-Jul-13: 2B].
Wallis, J. William m. Scott, Amy E. on 70-Nov-30 [70-Dec-2: 2C].
Wallis, Rachel A. m. Tise, George on 68-Sep-3 [68-Sep-8: 2B].
Wallis, Robert V. m. Ferguson, Mary H. on 69-Sep-23 [69-Sep-24: 2B].
Wallis, Samuel F. d. on 70-Aug-11 [70-Aug-12: 2C].
Wallis, William T. (57 yrs.) d. on 68-Jan-21 of Paralysis [68-Jan-22: 2C, 4E].
Walmsley, Emma E. (4 yrs.) d. on 66-Jul-8 [66-Jul-13: 2C].
Walmsley, Robert H. m. Lloyd, M. Lutie on 67-Jan-15 [67-Jan-31: 2C].
Walsh, Ann Eliza (42 yrs.) d. on 69-May-19 [69-May-20: 2C].
Walsh, Annie m. Barker, C. W. on 69-Aug-23 [69-Sep-24: 2B].
Walsh, Annie C. m. Coll, John on 68-Jun-9 [68-Jun-18: 2B].
Walsh, B. B. m. Carpenter, Rose Ann on 65-Nov-5 [66-Feb-8: 2C].
Walsh, Catherine (26 yrs.) d. on 68-Jan-13 [68-Jan-14: 2C].
Walsh, Catherine (70 yrs.) d. on 66-Mar-15 [66-Mar-17: 2B].
Walsh, Edward (46 yrs.) d. on 67-May-22 [67-May-23: 2C; 67-May-24: 2B].
Walsh, Edward (10 mos.) d. on 70-Jul-24 [70-Jul-25: 2C].
Walsh, Emilie Hughes m. Jones, Eugene W. on 70-Jun-22 [70-Jun-25: 2B].
Walsh, Emma A. m. Moore, H. F. on 69-Feb-2 [69-Feb-5: 2C].
Walsh, Henrietta L. m. Wing, Reginald D. on 68-Jan-23 [68-Feb-19: 2C].
Walsh, Jeff J. m. Gardner, Emma S. on 69-Mar-30 [69-Apr-1: 2C].
Walsh, Jeffrey (56 yrs.) d. on 70-Oct-3 [70-Oct-8: 2B].
Walsh, John J. m. Otten, Sarah Jane on 69-Feb-8 [69-Feb-18: 2C].
Walsh, Julia (34 yrs.) d. on 67-Jun-10 [67-Jun-12: 2B].
Walsh, Kate m. Coady, Thomas [68-Jul-17: 2B].
Walsh, Lawrence (4 yrs., 6 mos.) d. on 68-Dec-6 [68-Dec-7: 2D].
Walsh, Lizzie A. (2 yrs., 6 mos.) d. on 69-Mar-28 [69-Mar-29: 2B].
Walsh, Margaret (83 yrs.) d. on 67-Dec-23 [67-Dec-24: 2B].
Walsh, Margaret (22 yrs.) d. on 66-May-13 [66-May-14: 2B].
Walsh, Martin (90 yrs.) d. on 69-Jul-14 [69-Jul-15: 2C].
Walsh, Martin (8 yrs.) d. on 70-Aug-19 [70-Aug-20: 2B].
Walsh, Mary (38 yrs.) d. on 69-Aug-22 [69-Aug-24: 2C].
Walsh, Mary Donovan (45 yrs.) d. on 70-Feb-22 [70-Feb-24: 2C].
Walsh, Mary Kate (1 yr., 8 mos.) d. on 70-Jun-20 [70-Jun-21: 2C].
Walsh, Thomas d. on 68-Mar-19 of Construction cave-in [68-Mar-20: 1F].
Walsh, Thomas (5 yrs.) d. on 67-Mar-25 [67-Mar-26: 2C].
Walsh, Thomas (87 yrs.) d. on 69-Apr-16 [69-Apr-17: 2B].
Walsh, Thomas m. Gaitley, Mary J. on 70-Apr-26 [70-Apr-27: 2B].
Walsh, William L. m. Anderson, Lizzie on 68-Apr-15 [68-Apr-16: 2B].
Walstrum, Charles E. (11 mos.) d. on 70-Jul-14 [70-Jul-15: 2C].
Walstrum, Clara Ann (1 yr., 6 mos.) d. on 67-Jul-7 of Cholera infantum [67-Jul-23: 2C].
Waltemeyer, Jemimy d. on 68-Sep-3 [68-Sep-4: 2A].
Waltemeyer, William H. m. Cutler, Malinda on 68-Sep-18 [68-Sep-21: 2B].
Walter, Abram m. Jordan, Pauline on 69-Jan-27 [69-Feb-13: 2C].
Walter, Agnes B. m. Cook, J. Glenn on 70-Oct-20 [70-Oct-25: 2B].

Walter, Andrew J. m. Fillinger, Mary J. on 67-Nov-19 [67-Nov-28: 2C].
Walter, Annie V. m. Robinson, William B. on 67-Jan-2 [67-Jan-3: 2B].
Walter, Charles H. m. Blackburn, Lucie on 66-Apr-25 [66-Apr-27: 2C].
Walter, Clara m. Speights, Thomas J. on 69-Nov-8 [70-Jan-7: 2F].
Walter, Edward H. m. McCurley, Fannie on 70-Jan-18 [70-Jan-22: 2B].
Walter, Elizabeth m. Linnenkemper, Herman on 67-Jan-22 [67-Jan-26: 2C].
Walter, Frelinghuysen m. Van Wyck, Sarah D. on 68-Apr-7 [68-Sep-17: 2B].
Walter, George M. m. Walter, Mary E. on 66-Nov-5 [67-Feb-18: 2C].
Walter, George W. (51 yrs.) d. on 70-Nov-27 [70-Nov-29: 2C].
Walter, Hannah m. MacIntosh, William T. on 67-May-22 [67-Sep-11: 2B].
Walter, Henry (11 yrs.) d. on 70-Jul-17 Drowned [70-Jul-18: 4E].
Walter, Henry m. Gross, Lena on 68-May-3 [68-May-12: 2B].
Walter, J. E. m. Schubert, Emily on 69-May-24 [69-May-26: 2C; 69-May-27: 2C].
Walter, James d. on 70-May-9 [70-May-10: 2C].
Walter, John (75 yrs.) d. on 68-Sep-17 [68-Dec-19: 2B].
Walter, Joseph L. m. Lynch, Cinderella on 69-Jul-22 [69-Jul-29: 2C; 69-Jul-30: 2C].
Walter, Laura J. m. Judd, John on 68-Nov-24 [68-Dec-18: 2C].
Walter, Laura J. m. Fugle, James on 70-Feb-15 [70-Feb-19: 2B].
Walter, Maggie m. Parkins, Alfred, Jr. on 67-Jan-2 [67-Jan-3: 2B].
Walter, Margaret (66 yrs.) d. on 69-Mar-12 [69-Mar-13: 2C].
Walter, Mary E. m. Walter, George M. on 66-Nov-5 [67-Feb-18: 2C].
Walter, Rachel (49 yrs., 1 mo.) d. on 67-Nov-12 [67-Nov-13: 2C; 67-Nov-14: 2C].
Walter, Sophia (73 yrs.) d. on 68-Feb-22 [68-Feb-24: 2C].
Walter, William m. Heinekamp, Mary E. on 69-May-25 [69-May-27: 2C].
Walter, William H. m. Durham, Eliza on 70-Apr-20 [70-Apr-29: 2B].
Walter, William H. m. Delphey, Laura V. on 70-May-4 [70-May-10: 2B].
Walters, Benjamin Sherman (2 yrs., 10 mos.) d. on 69-Dec-12 [69-Dec-22: 2B].
Walters, George Frederick (16 yrs.) d. on 69-Mar-11 [69-Mar-12: 2C].
Walters, James C. m. Caldwell, Julia on 69-Apr-13 [69-Apr-28: 2B].
Walters, James E. m. Diffey, Susie V. on 70-Dec-8 [70-Dec-14: 2C].
Walters, John F. m. Brown, Maggie on 66-May-1 [66-Aug-20: 2C].
Walters, John H. m. Wilson, Millie B. on 70-Jan-19 [70-Jan-27: 2C].
Walters, Marietta V. m. Curley, George W. on 70-Jun-16 [70-Jun-21: 2C].
Walters, Mary A. m. Dryden, W. Sidney on 67-Jan-23 [67-Feb-1: 2C].
Walters, Mary E. m. Wright, Owen R. on 67-Mar-28 [67-Apr-2: 2B; 67-Apr-5: 2B].
Walters, Robert B. (59 yrs.) d. on 68-Jul-18 [68-Jul-21: 2C; 68-Jul-20: 1G].
Walters, William P. (38 yrs.) d. on 67-May-14 [67-May-16: 2B].
Walters, Willie Flourance (1 yr., 4 mos.) d. on 66-Apr-9 [66-Apr-13: 2C].
Waltham, C. S. m. Jessop, Georgianna on 66-Jul-5 [66-Jul-16: 2C].
Waltinelar, Joseph d. on 68-Mar-17 [68-Dec-19: 1E].
Waltjen, Annie D. (3 yrs.) d. on 69-Jan-6 [69-Jan-8: 2C].
Waltjen, Catherine J. m. Humphreys, Thomas W. on 67-Nov-20 [68-Jul-17: 2B; 68-Jul-18: 2B].
Waltjen, Fredericka J. m. Wode, Frederick on 70-Feb-20 [70-Mar-29: 2B].
Waltjen, Mary D. m. Shafer, George W. on 66-Aug-29 [66-Sep-5: 2B].
Waltjen, Sophie A. m. Asendorf, George H. on 69-Nov-23 [69-Dec-13: 2C].
Walton, Edward (63 yrs.) d. on 68-Aug-19 [68-Aug-25: 2B].
Walton, Jeanette d. on 69-Aug-5 of Erysipelas [69-Aug-24: 2C].
Walton, Jesse (48 yrs.) d. on 68-Oct-31 [68-Nov-2: 2B].
Walton, Joseph F. m. Faulkner, Cornelia on 66-Feb-11 [66-Feb-15: 2C].
Walton, Mary A. m. Douthat, William H. on 68-May-28 [68-Jun-4: 2B].
Walton, Mollie L. m. McDonough, John A. on 69-Jan-26 [69-Feb-22: 2C].
Waltz, David William (6 mos.) d. on 69-Jan-28 [69-Jan-29: 2C].
Walworth, Harry Irwine (2 mos.) d. on 68-Sep-20 [68-Sep-21: 2B].
Wambach, Emma L. m. Romey, Francis G. on 70-Jul-12 [70-Aug-30: 2B].

Wambach, Emmanuel (52 yrs., 9 mos.) d. on 69-Jul-17 [69-Jul-19: 2D].
Wambach, Margaret Ann (16 yrs.) d. on 67-Feb-28 [67-Mar-2: 2B].
Wambuch, Catharina (54 yrs., 8 mos.) d. on 68-Feb-3 [68-Feb-5: 2D].
Wamsley, J. S. m. Nedwell, M. J. on 69-Feb-23 [69-Mar-16: 2C].
Wands, Alexander H. m. Cleveland, Josephine on 66-Oct-23 [66-Nov-6: 2B].
Wands, Ella W. m. Galt, J. Murray on 68-Jul-28 [68-Nov-30: 2C].
Wann, James H. m. Hammond, Nellie E. on 68-Dec-3 [68-Dec-28: 2B].
Wantland, Mary (68 yrs.) d. on 68-Dec-26 [68-Dec-30: 2D].
Wantz, Lizzie m. Cockey, W. H. on 67-Oct-8 [67-Oct-9: 2B].
Wanzer, George W. (40 yrs.) d. on 68-Feb-28 [68-Feb-29: 2B].
Waples, William A. (35 yrs.) d. on 67-Apr-17 [67-Apr-18: 2B].
Ward, A. Blanche m. Bordley, William J. on 68-Oct-14 [68-Oct-20: 2B].
Ward, Abraham m. Goodwin, Ellen E. on 69-Jun-11 [69-Jun-22: 2C].
Ward, Ade Augusta (4 mos.) d. on 66-Mar-2 [66-Mar-3: 2B].
Ward, Alcinda M. (14 yrs., 4 mos.) d. on 69-Jun-3 of Consumption [69-Jun-4: 2C].
Ward, Alice (35 yrs.) d. on 70-Nov-12 [70-Nov-15: 2C].
Ward, Alice R. m. McCulloh, Chauncey on 70-Aug-6 [70-Aug-25: 2B].
Ward, Alice V. m. Atkins, Thomas on 68-Aug-18 [68-Aug-25: 2B].
Ward, Ann E. d. on 66-Feb-5 [66-Feb-6: 2D].
Ward, Anna Tresia (1 yr., 2 mos.) d. [69-Jun-25: 2C].
Ward, Asa, Jr. m. Ensey, Grace E. on 66-Dec-17 [66-Dec-19: 2B].
Ward, Bridget (37 yrs.) d. on 70-Jul-22 [70-Jul-23: 2B].
Ward, Caroline (68 yrs.) d. on 67-Sep-22 [67-Sep-24: 2A].
Ward, Catherine (45 yrs.) d. on 70-Mar-5 of Consumption [70-Mar-7: 2C].
Ward, Charles W. (34 yrs.) d. on 69-Oct-2 of Consumption [69-Oct-6: 2B].
Ward, Douglass Gordon (2 yrs., 1 mo.) d. on 69-Jan-23 [69-Jan-26: 2C; 69-Jan-27: 2C].
Ward, Edward V. (63 yrs.) d. on 66-Jun-28 [66-Jun-29: 1F, 2C].
Ward, Eliza V. m. Ward, Robert B. on 67-Dec-24 [68-Jan-1: 2C].
Ward, Elizabeth (76 yrs.) d. on 66-Nov-20 [66-Nov-22: 2C].
Ward, Emily E. m. Cullimore, William H. on 68-May-5 [68-May-18: 2B].
Ward, Ernest C. (2 yrs., 9 mos.) d. [66-May-30: 2C].
Ward, George H. (48 yrs.) d. on 68-Mar-6 [68-Mar-18: 2B].
Ward, George H. m. Taylor, Emma H. on 69-Aug-12 [69-Aug-13: 2C].
Ward, George W. (12 yrs.) d. on 66-May-1 Drowned [66-May-2: 1G].
Ward, George W. m. Lowther, Adah Z. on 70-Dec-15 [70-Dec-28: 2C].
Ward, Georgeanna E. (26 yrs.) d. on 69-Jan-21 [69-Jan-23: 2C].
Ward, H. C. m. Wyvill, Mary E. on 68-Jan-23 [68-Jan-25: 2B].
Ward, Harry Gillis (3 yrs., 2 mos.) d. on 69-Jun-8 [69-Jun-14: 2C].
Ward, Helen L. m. Mills, William V. on 66-May-1 [66-May-4: 2C].
Ward, Issac L. m. Forrest, Emma L. on 67-Jul-16 [67-Jul-18: 2C].
Ward, James (1 yr., 3 mos.) d. on 68-Jul-1 [68-Jul-2: 2C].
Ward, James d. on 70-Apr-3 [70-Apr-5: 2B].
Ward, John (68 yrs.) d. on 68-Jul-17 [68-Jul-18: 2B].
Ward, John (99 yrs.) d. on 68-Jul-29 [68-Jul-30: 2B].
Ward, John d. on 70-Apr-11 [70-Apr-12: 2B; 70-Apr-13: 2B].
Ward, John S. (22 yrs., 10 mos.) d. on 68-Sep-12 [68-Sep-18: 2B].
Ward, Joseph W. m. Fosbenner, Ella on 70-Oct-20 [70-Oct-24: 2B].
Ward, Josephine m. Locks, Stephen on 67-Dec-12 [67-Dec-14: 2B].
Ward, K. m. Ziegler, Charles on 70-Mar-7 [70-Apr-19: 2B].
Ward, Laura V. m. Harvey, James E. on 67-Feb-12 [67-Feb-13: 2D].
Ward, Maggie m. Tennis, John M. on 67-Dec-30 [68-Jan-8: 2C].
Ward, Martha E. d. on 68-May-5 [68-May-7: 2B].
Ward, Mary (82 yrs.) d. on 68-May-27 [68-May-29: 2B].
Ward, Mary (49 yrs.) d. on 67-Aug-20 [67-Aug-21: 2B].
Ward, Mary m. Dunn, Edward on 67-Sep-14 [67-Nov-28: 2C].

Ward, Mary Ann (1 yr., 11 mos.) d. on 69-Aug-10 [69-Aug-11: 2C].
Ward, Mary E. m. Mahon, John J. on 70-May-6 [70-May-11: 2B].
Ward, Mary E. E. m. Burbrier, Charles L. on 67-Oct-8 [67-Oct-11: 2B].
Ward, Mary Ellen (11 mos.) d. on 68-Jul-13 [68-Jul-16: 2C].
Ward, Mary J. Wilson d. on 70-Aug-8 [70-Aug-10: 2C].
Ward, Michael (1 yr., 1 mo.) d. on 69-Oct-12 [69-Oct-13: 2C].
Ward, Miranda m. Owings, William G. on 66-Sep-13 [66-Sep-15: 2B].
Ward, Patrick (38 yrs.) d. on 68-Nov-2 [68-Nov-3: 2B].
Ward, Queen m. Poultney, T., Jr. on 67-Jan-3 [67-Jan-14: 2C].
Ward, Richard S. (48 yrs.) d. on 67-Aug-21 of Consumption [67-Aug-23: 2B].
Ward, Robert B. m. Ward, Eliza V. on 67-Dec-24 [68-Jan-1: 2C].
Ward, Sallie m. Glading, Charles F. on 67-Dec-26 [68-Jan-1: 2C].
Ward, Samuel (82 yrs.) d. on 67-Jul-27 [67-Jul-30: 2C; 67-Aug-9: 1G].
Ward, Susie (25 yrs.) d. on 67-Jun-7 [67-Jun-8: 2B].
Ward, Thomas m. Hagerty, Margaret on 67-Apr-22 [68-Feb-11: 2C].
Ward, Thomas m. Killman, Harriet J. on 67-Jun-30 [67-Jul-31: 2C].
Ward, Thomas, Sr. (86 yrs.) d. on 67-Aug-23 [67-Aug-24: 2B; 67-Aug-26: 2D].
Ward, Ulysses, Rev. (76 yrs.) d. on 68-Mar-30 [68-Apr-1: 2C].
Ward, William (50 yrs., 7 mos.) d. on 67-Apr-7 [67-Apr-8: 2B].
Ward, William H. d. on 68-Sep-4 [68-Sep-5: 2A].
Ward, William R. m. Weaver, Mary A. on 69-Jun-8 [69-Jun-10: 2C].
Wardell, Emma m. Emmart, Thomas on 70-Sep-19 [70-Dec-29: 2C].
Wardell, James d. on 67-Aug-24 [67-Aug-26: 2D].
Wardell, Joseph Adrian (6 mos.) d. on 69-Apr-13 [69-Apr-16: 2B].
Wardell, Sarah (46 yrs.) d. on 70-Mar-4 [70-Mar-5: 2B].
Warden, Mary Anne (1 yr., 4 mos.) d. on 69-Jun-7 [69-Jun-8: 2B].
Wardenburg, Helena Marie m. Coster, Robert J. on 66-Apr-3 [66-Apr-5: 2B].
Wardenburg, Mary A. m. Maxwell, George W. on 66-Oct-16 [66-Oct-18: 2B].
Wardenburg, Ra m. Hope, Robert J. on 69-Jan-12 [69-Jan-14: 2D].
Wardenburg, Sallie E. m. Hartley, Howard on 70-Apr-28 [70-May-2: 2B].
Ware, Addie Minerva (2 mos.) d. on 67-Feb-21 [67-Feb-26: 2C].
Ware, Annabel (3 yrs.) d. on 68-Dec-23 [68-Dec-25: 2D].
Ware, Evalina C. (58 yrs.) d. on 66-Mar-14 [66-Apr-13: 2C; 66-Apr-14: 2B].
Ware, Sarah m. Lewis, Alfred E. on 67-Dec-18 [67-Dec-23: 2B].
Ware, Virginia m. Simon, Edmund on 68-Dec-29 [68-Dec-30: 2C].
Ware, William m. Baker, Catherine F. on 66-Jul-24 [66-Jul-30: 2C].
Wareham, Annie m. Fitzpatrick, William on 68-Dec-13 [68-Dec-15: 2C].
Wareham, Issac N. (24 yrs.) d. on 70-Jun-5 [70-Jun-6: 2B].
Wareham, Mary Ann (58 yrs.) d. on 70-Jul-5 [70-Jul-6: 2C].
Warfield, Ann Rebecca (40 yrs.) d. on 66-Aug-27 [66-Aug-28: 2B].
Warfield, Cecilius E. m. Thomas, Laura W. on 70-Jan-18 [70-Jan-27: 2C].
Warfield, Charles A. m. Wilkerson, Jennie F. on 67-Feb-5 [67-Feb-18: 2C].
Warfield, Charles Alexander (82 yrs.) d. on 68-Jul-25 [68-Jul-28: 2B].
Warfield, Clara (3 yrs., 4 mos.) d. on 67-Jan-17 [67-Jan-19: 2C].
Warfield, Daniel (84 yrs.) d. on 67-Jun-21 [67-Jun-22: 2B; 67-Jun-24: 1F].
Warfield, Daniel, Jr. (39 yrs.) d. on 70-Jan-16 [70-Jan-17: 1H, 2C; 70-Jan-19: 1G].
Warfield, Elizabeth Mactier (1 yr., 4 mos.) d. on 66-May-29 [66-May-30: 2C].
Warfield, Emma d. on 70-Aug-28 [70-Sep-3: 2B].
Warfield, Francis M. (26 yrs.) d. on 66-Dec-27 of Consumption [67-Jan-26: 2C].
Warfield, George T. m. Clark, Mary E. on 68-Nov-25 [68-Dec-4: 2D].
Warfield, Gustavus, Dr. (83 yrs.) d. on 66-Aug-8 [66-Aug-10: 2C].
Warfield, Helen m. Fenneman, John T. on 69-May-20 [69-Jun-26: 2B].
Warfield, J. A. m. Jess, Sarah J. on 70-Jun-30 [70-Jul-12: 2B].
Warfield, J. D. m. Dawley, Tonnie on 68-Apr-15 [68-Apr-17: 2B].
Warfield, John Edgar (1 yr., 3 mos.) d. on 66-Dec-31 [67-Jan-3: 2C].

Warfield, Jonathan S. (54 yrs.) d. on 68-Mar-12 [68-Mar-14: 2B].
Warfield, Joshua D. m. Polk, Lizzie C. on 68-Oct-20 [68-Oct-26: 2B].
Warfield, Manelia E. S. m. Jenkins, Henry on 69-Oct-27 [69-Oct-30: 2B].
Warfield, Mary Hutchison d. on 70-Dec-29 [70-Dec-30: 2C; 70-Dec-31: 2C].
Warfield, Milton Eugene (7 yrs.) d. on 68-Nov-1 [68-Nov-2: 2B].
Warfield, Miranda (42 yrs.) d. on 66-Feb-8 [66-Feb-12: 2D].
Warfield, Nancy Mactier (73 yrs.) d. on 68-Mar-16 [68-Mar-18: 2B].
Warfield, Nathan O. m. Day, Laura V. on 69-Dec-7 [69-Dec-8: 2C].
Warfield, Rachel E. (6 yrs., 7 mos.) d. on 69-May-23 [69-May-24: 2B].
Warfield, Sarah Ann (51 yrs.) d. on 70-May-28 [70-Jun-1: 2B].
Warfield, Thomas J. m. Mercer, Ruth E. on 66-Mar-6 [66-Mar-13: 2B].
Warfield, Warner M. (80 yrs.) d. on 67-Jul-28 [67-Aug-3: 2B].
Waring, Benjamin B. (65 yrs.) d. on 67-Feb-6 [67-Feb-20: 2C].
Waring, Carrie F. m. Meade, W. C. on 68-Apr-7 [68-Apr-10: 2B].
Waring, Robert K. m. Saunders, Kate M. on 70-May-3 [70-May-6: 2B].
Warner, Agnes A. m. Jarboe, Walter S. on 68-Jan-9 [68-Jan-11: 2B].
Warner, Andrew E., Capt. (84 yrs.) d. on 70-Jan-15 [70-Jan-17: 1G, 2C; 70-Jan-18: 2C; 70-Jan-19: 1G].
Warner, Anna R. m. Allen, George W. on 69-Sep-23 [69-Sep-25: 2B].
Warner, Annie R. (41 yrs.) d. on 70-Oct-12 [70-Oct-14: 2B].
Warner, Annie S. m. Burbage, John E. on 68-Sep-17 [68-Sep-22: 2B].
Warner, Antoinetta (64 yrs.) d. on 70-Oct-28 [70-Oct-29: 2B].
Warner, Clara Malissa Ross (1 mo.) d. on 66-Nov-10 [66-Nov-14: 2B].
Warner, Elizabeth A. m. McBerryman, Standish on 68-Oct-15 [68-Oct-16: 2B].
Warner, Elizabeth Dorothy (1 yr.) d. on 67-Nov-2 [67-Nov-4: 2B].
Warner, George m. Barnum, Fannie R. on 68-Jan-30 [68-Apr-20: 2B].
Warner, Harriette A. m. Bishop, William M. on 70-Oct-13 [70-Oct-20: 2B].
Warner, J. Philip m. Smith, Mollie A. on 66-Jan-17 [66-Feb-16: 2B].
Warner, John A. (5 yrs.) d. on 68-Nov-19 [68-Nov-21: 2C].
Warner, John S., Capt. d. on 68-Jun-9 [68-Jun-16: 1G, 2B].
Warner, Jonathan m. Smith, Frances A on 68-Aug-18 [68-Aug-27: 2B; 68-Aug-28: 2B].
Warner, Leander A. (70 yrs.) d. on 67-Mar-16 [67-Mar-18: 2B].
Warner, Lucy Hill (4 yrs.) d. on 69-Feb-21 [69-Mar-2: 2C; 69-Feb-23: 2D].
Warner, Maggie d. on 68-Jun-24 [68-Jun-25: 2B].
Warner, Mary Marsleana (11 mos.) d. on 69-Feb-22 [69-Mar-3: 2C].
Warner, Susan Miriam m. Brown, James Andrew on 68-Dec-27 [69-Mar-2: 2C].
Warner, Susie M. m. King, Rufus on 67-Dec-17 [67-Dec-18: 2B].
Warner, Thomas C. (43 yrs.) d. on 67-Nov-4 of Rheumatism and heart disease [67-Nov-22: 2C].
Warner, William m. Godey, Charlotte on 67-Oct-2 [67-Oct-5: 2B].
Warnick, David J. (50 yrs.) d. on 66-Jan-11 [66-Jan-12: 2C].
Warnick, James B. m. Coughlan, Mary E. on 66-Jun-24 [66-Jun-27: 2C].
Warnick, John F. m. Sprowl, Mary A. on 66-Oct-7 [66-Oct-12: 2B].
Warnick, Kate (20 yrs., 4 mos.) d. on 67-May-15 [67-May-16: 2B].
Warnick, Sallie R. m. Finck, Bernard on 68-May-12 [68-May-27: 2B].
Warnick, William B. m. Lynch, Martha M. on 68-Nov-25 [68-Dec-28: 2B].
Warns, Francis G. m. Norris, Georgie O. on 68-Nov-8 [68-Nov-13: 2B].
Warren, James m. Rooney, Mary on 70-May-6 [70-May-11: 2B].
Warren, John A., Rev. (54 yrs.) d. on 70-Jun-15 of Dropsy [70-Jun-20: 1H].
Warren, Lawrence J. m. PARRY, KATE A. on 67-Jun-6 [67-Jun-8: 2B].
Warren, Mary J. m. Harback, Charles on 68-Aug-18 [68-Dec-4: 2D].
Warren, Mary Jane (33 yrs.) d. on 67-Jan-24 [67-Jan-26: 2C].
Warren, Morris Patrick (2 yrs., 7 mos.) d. on 66-Oct-31 [66-Nov-1: 2B].
Warren, P. T. m. Price, Mollie A. on 68-Feb-20 [68-Feb-22: 2B].
Warren, William B. m. Parlett, Lizzie V. on 68-Sep-10 [68-Oct-24: 2B].

Warrick, Accia (76 yrs.) d. on 67-Oct-6 [67-Oct-10: 2B].
Warrick, Ann (78 yrs.) d. on 67-Jul-20 [67-Jul-25: 2C].
Warrington, John T. d. on 68-Jul-5 Drowned [68-Jul-7: 4D].
Warrington, Palmyre m. Brown, James R. on 69-Jan-28 [69-Feb-2: 2C].
Warthen, Ann (66 yrs., 4 mos.) d. on 68-Apr-3 of Consumption [68-Apr-14: 2A].
Wartman, Dorrie m. Jones, J. Preston on 68-Dec-13 [69-Mar-15: 2C].
Wartman, Kate C. (35 yrs.) d. on 69-Jan-6 [69-Jan-8: 2C].
Warwick, Daniel J., Maj. (56 yrs.) d. on 68-Feb-28 of Apoplexy [68-Feb-29: 1G; 68-Mar-2: 1G, 2C].
Warwick, Mary m. Schumacher, H. A. on 66-Dec-25 [66-Dec-28: 2C].
Warwick, Sarah E. m. Clarkston, E. M. on 66-Dec-25 [66-Dec-28: 2C].
Washam, Issac m. Sampson, Amanda V. on 67-May-6 [67-May-8: 2B].
Washbourn, John T. m. Green, Sarah A. on 67-Nov-18 [67-Dec-30: 2C].
Washington, Carrie Virginia d. on 70-May-2 [70-May-4: 2C].
Washington, Ellen (45 yrs.) d. on 67-Feb-12 [67-Feb-13: 2D].
Washington, George d. on 70-Aug-11 of Heatstroke [70-Aug-12: 4D].
Washington, Honnor (65 yrs.) d. on 67-Jan-2 [67-Jan-4: 2D].
Washington, James d. on 68-Aug-15 of Apoplexy [68-Aug-17: 1F].
Washington, James H. (65 yrs.) d. on 68-Aug-15 [68-Aug-17: 2B].
Washington, Joseph m. Barnes, Emily F. on 67-Feb-11 [67-Feb-13: 2D].
Waskey, Mary F. m. Knight, John J. on 68-Dec-23 [68-Dec-24: 2C].
Wasserman, Caroline (57 yrs.) d. on 69-May-30 [69-May-31: 2C].
Watchman, Fanny m. Dickson, William on 66-Dec-24 [67-Mar-28: 2B].
Watchman, John (32 yrs.) d. on 66-Mar-27 [66-Mar-28: 2C].
Watchman, Sarah A. m. May, W. on 69-Mar-24 [69-Mar-27: 2B].
Watchman, William C. m. Yellmann, Amelia C. D. on 70-Apr-20 [70-Apr-22: 2C].
Waterman, Samuel A. (70 yrs.) d. on 70-Oct-17 [70-Oct-18: 2C].
Waterman, Thomas B. m. Crooker, Clara on 67-Jun-20 [67-Jun-22: 2B].
Waters, Anne E. m. Waite, Harrison on 67-Jul-30 [67-Aug-13: 2B].
Waters, Betsey Oudesluys (8 mos.) d. on 68-Aug-13 [68-Aug-14: 2C].
Waters, C. Amanda m. Whitman, C. W. on 69-Apr-4 [69-Apr-8: 2C].
Waters, Cyrus, Rev. (40 yrs.) d. on 67-Sep-24 [67-Sep-26: 2B].
Waters, Elizabeth J. (82 yrs.) d. on 69-May-24 [69-May-28: 2C].
Waters, Fannie E. (22 yrs.) d. on 67-Apr-28 [67-Apr-30: 2A].
Waters, Francis, Rev. (77 yrs.) d. on 68-Apr-23 of Brain softening [68-Apr-24: 1G, 2B; 68-Apr-25: 2B].
Waters, Ignatius, Rev. (56 yrs.) d. on 70-Jan-2 [70-Jan-8: 2B].
Waters, James B., Jr. m. Thomas, Theodocia on 70-Feb-17 [70-Feb-22: 2C].
Waters, Job W. m. Tilghman, Mary E. on 66-Mar-29 [66-Mar-31: 2C].
Waters, John F. m. Rogers, Sarah Jane on 66-May-24 [66-May-26: 2B].
Waters, John H. m. Sherwood, Clara on 70-Apr-28 [70-Apr-30: 2A].
Waters, Julia m. Johnson, William Edward on 70-Aug-8 [70-Aug-13: 2C].
Waters, Maggie M. m. Doughty, Thomas P. on 70-Feb-24 [70-Feb-28: 2C].
Waters, Margaret Jane (9 mos.) d. on 66-Oct-28 [66-Oct-30: 2C].
Waters, Mary m. Edgar, Charles W. on 70-Sep-27 [70-Sep-29: 2B].
Waters, Mary D. d. on 70-Nov-3 [70-Nov-8: 2B].
Waters, Mary Ellen (18 yrs.) d. on 67-Aug-11 Murdered (Stabbing) [67-Aug-12: 1F; 67-Aug-13: 1E].
Waters, Matilda d. on 68-Mar-7 of Chronic croup [68-Mar-9: 2C].
Waters, Matilda (73 yrs.) d. on 68-Dec-23 [68-Dec-24: 2C; 68-Dec-25: 2D].
Waters, Mattie M. m. Talbott, Thomas J., Jr. on 67-Nov-21 [67-Nov-27: 2B].
Waters, Robert Newton, Col. (29 yrs.) d. on 69-Oct-14 [69-Oct-15: 1H, 2C; 69-Oct-16: 2B; 69-Oct-18: 1G].
Waters, Sue M. m. Worley, William N. on 69-Oct-20 [69-Oct-25: 2B].
Waters, T. Sollers m. Grafflin, Amanda P. on 68-Nov-26 [68-Nov-30: 2B].

Waters, Thomas d. on 68-Apr-15 [68-Apr-20: 2B].
Waters, Violetta A. m. Ijams, Joseph A. on 65-Nov-24 [66-Jul-7: 2B].
Waters, Willie Drummond (8 yrs., 1 mo.) d. on 69-Aug-19 [69-Aug-21: 2B].
Waters, Zebulon (85 yrs.) d. on 69-Jan-20 [69-Feb-1: 1H, 2C].
Waterson, William m. Todd, Jane on 70-Dec-8 [70-Dec-13: 2C].
Waterworth, Alexander m. Jones, Annie on 67-May-21 [67-Jun-7: 2B].
Waterworth, Elizabeth E. m. Wilson, Amos C. on 69-Mar-29 [69-May-27: 2C].
Watkins, Amanda F. m. Sharrets, Samuel F. on 69-Jun-2 [69-Jun-10: 2C].
Watkins, Benjamin (64 yrs.) d. on 68-May-20 [68-May-21: 2B].
Watkins, Catherine L. d. on 67-Jun-20 [67-Jun-21: 2B].
Watkins, Clarence Eugene (7 mos.) d. on 70-Jul-19 [70-Jul-21: 2C].
Watkins, Eleanor d. on 66-May-22 of Paralysis [66-May-31: 2B].
Watkins, Elizabeth (86 yrs.) d. on 66-Dec-11 [66-Dec-12: 2B].
Watkins, Elizabeth m. Bell, Andrew J. on 66-Nov-29 [66-Dec-4: 2D].
Watkins, Ellen m. Maccubbin, John T. on 67-Jun-18 [67-Jun-27: 2B].
Watkins, Emily m. Duvall, A. Leslie on 70-Nov-26 [70-Nov-30: 2C].
Watkins, Emma V. m. Reese, Henry O. on 67-Oct-8 [67-Oct-9: 2B].
Watkins, Emma V. m. Thornton, James A. on 66-Nov-29 [66-Dec-1: 2B].
Watkins, Eugenia S. (24 yrs.) d. on 69-Dec-28 [69-Dec-30: 2C].
Watkins, Frank D. m. Lyon, Augusta P. D. on 68-Oct-16 [68-Oct-19: 2B].
Watkins, Gassaway m. Jean, Nellie on 69-Mar-29 [69-Apr-2: 2C].
Watkins, George Lyon (10 mos.) d. on 70-Jun-13 [70-Jun-15: 2B].
Watkins, George N. G. (23 yrs.) d. on 68-Oct-16 [68-Oct-17: 2B].
Watkins, George R. m. Stephens, Anna K. on 67-Oct-3 [67-Oct-4: 2B].
Watkins, George Rust d. on 68-Aug-6 [68-Aug-7: 2B].
Watkins, John B. m. Bagley, Clara A. on 69-Mar-25 [69-Mar-26: 2C; 69-Mar-27: 2B; 69-Mar-29: 2B].
Watkins, John W. m. Esham, F. W. on 68-Sep-29 [68-Oct-2: 2B].
Watkins, Leonard G. m. Dryden, Sarah C. on 66-Nov-12 [66-Nov-15: 2C].
Watkins, Leonard G. m. Hall, Mary V. on 70-Jul-22 [70-Sep-9: 2B].
Watkins, Lydia (67 yrs.) d. of Bilious fever [66-Sep-7: 2B].
Watkins, Margaret A. (48 yrs.) d. on 68-Jan-22 [68-Jan-24: 2D].
Watkins, Mary m. McElhiney, William J. on 67-Jun-4 [67-Jun-5: 2B].
Watkins, Mary Wyan d. on 70-Sep-18 [70-Sep-19: 2B, 4B; 70-Oct-10: 2B].
Watkins, Nicholas W. m. Chamberlain, Mary R. on 68-Oct-29 [68-Nov-3: 2B].
Watkins, Samuel m. Rogers, Ellen on 67-Jan-24 [67-Jan-29: 2C].
Watkins, Sarah C. (23 yrs.) d. on 67-Oct-11 [67-Oct-12: 2A].
Watkins, Sophia H. (15 yrs.) d. on 70-Apr-18 [70-Apr-20: 2B; 70-Apr-30: 2B].
Watkins, Thomas m. Robertson, Mary on 69-Oct-7 [69-Oct-12: 2C].
Watkins, Thomas C. m. Hennick, Annie E. on 68-Dec-6 [69-Jun-2: 2B].
Watkins, William Henry (8 mos.) d. on 68-Aug-5 [68-Aug-6: 2B].
Watkins, Winnifred (23 yrs.) d. on 70-Sep-10 [70-Sep-12: 2C].
Watson, Alice Rebecca McAliste (1 mo.) d. on 70-Jan-31 [70-Feb-2: 2B].
Watson, Anne M. d. on 70-Jul-18 [70-Jul-20: 2C].
Watson, Charles Edwin Randolph (3 mos.) d. on 70-Jun-16 [70-Jun-21: 2C].
Watson, Elizabeth (21 yrs.) d. on 67-May-25 [67-May-29: 2B].
Watson, Ellen N. d. on 68-Jul-10 [68-Jul-24: 2C].
Watson, Frances A. (34 yrs.) d. on 66-May-24 [66-May-25: 2C; 66-May-26: 2B].
Watson, George W. m. Rankin, Susanna on 69-Apr-22 [69-Apr-23: 2B].
Watson, Harry Vincent (1 yr., 1 mo.) d. on 69-Oct-9 [69-Oct-11: 2C].
Watson, Henry F. m. Gorsuch, Amanda on 69-Nov-4 [69-Nov-6: 2B].
Watson, Henry R. (57 yrs.) d. on 68-Mar-15 [68-Mar-16: 2B].
Watson, James (50 yrs.) d. on 69-Feb-25 [69-Feb-26: 2D].
Watson, James m. Coleman, Martha R. on 69-Apr-2 [69-Apr-17: 2A].
Watson, James E. m. Hammontree, Mary on 66-Jul-2 [66-Jul-4: 2B].

Watson, John (29 yrs.) d. on 68-Aug-29 [68-Aug-31: 2B].
Watson, John (79 yrs.) d. on 69-Apr-26 [69-Apr-27: 2C].
Watson, John W. m. Wilmer, Mollie E. on 66-Dec-20 [67-Jan-3: 2B].
Watson, John W. m. Garrett, Margaret on 66-Apr-15 [66-Apr-18: 2B].
Watson, Laura Virginia d. on 69-Oct-20 [69-Oct-22: 2B].
Watson, Maggie S. m. Owings, Perry T. on 70-Apr-28 [70-May-12: 2B].
Watson, Margaret (29 yrs.) d. on 68-May-25 [68-May-26: 2B; 68-May-27: 2B].
Watson, Margaret A. m. Linzey, John H. on 68-Mar-12 [68-Mar-17: 2C].
Watson, Margaret Elizabeth (10 mos.) d. on 67-May-2 [67-May-9: 2A].
Watson, Martha Ann (40 yrs.) d. on 70-Jan-31 [70-Feb-1: 2B; 70-Feb-2: 2B].
Watson, Mary (50 yrs.) d. on 67-May-10 [67-May-11: 2A].
Watson, Mary E. m. Edgerton, Thomas on 66-Aug-21 [66-Aug-23: 2C].
Watson, William, Jr. m. Ballard, Sarah on 70-Sep-5 [70-Mar-14: 2C].
Watson, William H., Dr. (56 yrs.) d. on 68-May-20 of Paralysis [68-May-21: 2B].
Watson, William H. m. Coleson, Lou C. on 70-Dec-26 [70-Dec-31: 2B].
Watters, Emery (87 yrs.) d. on 69-Nov-24 [69-Nov-26: 2D].
Watters, Frank Dela Reintrie (9 yrs., 2 mos.) d. on 68-Aug-29 of Diptheria [68-Sep-1: 2B].
Watters, Harry Granville (2 yrs.) d. on 69-Jan-31 of Pneumonia [69-Feb-1: 2C].
Watters, Sallie D. (26 yrs.) d. on 69-Dec-3 [69-Dec-4: 2C].
Watters, W. J. H. m. Russell, Sallie D. on 67-Nov-19 [67-Nov-27: 2B].
Watts, 'Mother' (103 yrs.) d. on 67-Nov-24 [67-Nov-27: 4E].
Watts, Alice S. d. on 70-Jul-7 [70-Jul-12: 2C].
Watts, Annie S. m. Magruder, F. G. on 67-Jul-2 [67-Jul-24: 2C].
Watts, Charles A. m. Forrest, Mary E. on 69-Feb-18 [69-Apr-19: 2B].
Watts, Clinton Prentice (5 yrs., 3 mos.) d. on 68-Aug-27 [68-Aug-28: 2B].
Watts, Emma m. Lyshear, William H. on 66-Feb-4 [66-Feb-9: 2C].
Watts, Fannie (8 yrs.) d. on 66-Apr-2 [66-Apr-3: 2B].
Watts, Florence Estelle (4 yrs.) d. on 70-Jul-9 [70-Jul-11: 2C].
Watts, Francis G. H. (4 yrs.) d. on 69-Nov-5 [69-Nov-11: 2C].
Watts, George O. m. Dillaway, Genevieve on 69-Oct-28 [69-Nov-4: 2B].
Watts, Howard d. on 66-Apr-6 [66-Apr-7: 2B].
Watts, J. W. m. Fairbanks, Kate on 69-Nov-9 [69-Dec-15: 2B].
Watts, John W. (1 yr., 5 mos.) d. on 69-Jul-21 [69-Jul-26: 2C].
Watts, John W. m. Beziat, Jennie on 69-Aug-24 [69-Sep-7: 2B].
Watts, Josephine m. Gross, Philip T. on 68-Aug-20 [68-Aug-21: 2B].
Watts, Julia A. (68 yrs.) d. on 70-Oct-20 [70-Oct-21: 2C; 70-Oct-22: 2B; 70-Nov-15: 2C].
Watts, Julia A. m. Henderson, William T. on 68-Nov-17 [68-Nov-18: 2C].
Watts, Lula (2 mos.) d. [70-Sep-17: 2B].
Watts, Maggie J. m. Miller, George W. on 69-Dec-8 [69-Dec-9: 2C].
Watts, Marian m. Colton, Lodge on 68-Apr-16 [68-Apr-18: 2A].
Watts, Mary C. m. Mules, Alfred H. on 70-Apr-7 [70-Apr-14: 2B].
Watts, Mary E. H. m. Hardman, Asa S. on 67-Jun-7 [67-Jun-8: 2B].
Watts, Mary Lagora (1 yr., 2 mos.) d. on 70-Oct-6 [70-Oct-7: 2B].
Watts, Nancy m. Bevans, John on 66-Apr-19 [66-Apr-21: 2B].
Watts, Nathaniel m. Logsdon, Imogene on 66-Oct-18 [66-Oct-19: 2B].
Watts, Percy d. on 68-Mar-23 [68-Mar-31: 2B].
Watts, Philip m. Mettam, Kate L. on 68-May-28 [68-May-29: 2B].
Watts, R. Randall Magruder (2 yrs.) d. on 69-Dec-27 [69-Dec-29: 2D].
Watts, Rachel (100 yrs.) d. on 70-Jun-19 [70-Jun-20: 2C].
Watts, Roland (9 mos.) d. on 66-Nov-26 [66-Nov-28: 2C].
Watts, Sarah Elizabeth d. on 67-Mar-2 [67-Mar-7: 2C].
Watts, Talitha (19 yrs.) d. on 68-Sep-22 [68-Sep-29: 2B].
Watts, Thomas m. Correll, Mary R. on 67-May-21 [67-May-25: 2A].
Watts, Thomas B. m. Hogg, Sallie M. on 70-Jan-27 [70-Jan-31: 2C].
Watts, William, Jr. m. Henderson, Hannah Amanda on 66-Feb-13 [66-Feb-17: 2B].

Waugh, Jennie m. Dashields, Thomas on 69-Feb-4 [69-Feb-12: 2C].
Waugh, Jennie m. Matthews, Joshua on 70-Jun-1 [70-Jun-2: 2B].
Waugh, Maggie C. m. Matthews, Wilson on 68-Mar-5 [68-Mar-12: 2B].
Waxter, Estella (11 mos.) d. on 70-Aug-21 [70-Aug-22: 2C].
Way, Catherine (79 yrs.) d. on 69-Jan-7 [69-Jan-9: 2C].
Way, John R. (37 yrs.) d. on 66-Sep-19 [66-Sep-20: 2B].
Way, Lewis E. m. Graves, Sarah Elizabeth on 67-Aug-7 [67-Aug-14: 2B].
Way, M. Elona m. Von Culin, Matthew on 69-May-21 [69-May-29: 2B].
Way, Sarah (63 yrs.) d. on 69-Nov-7 [69-Nov-9: 2C].
Way, Scott m. Heveren, H. A. on 68-Jan-9 [68-Jan-15: 2C].
Way, W. R. m. Childs, Martha E. on 70-Jul-19 [70-Aug-6: 2C].
Way, William (2 yrs., 6 mos.) d. on 69-Aug-15 [69-Aug-16: 2C].
Wayland, Elizabeth d. on 67-Jan-25 [67-Jan-28: 2C].
Wayman, Harriet D. m. Lodge, John H. on 70-May-12 [70-Jun-1: 2B].
Wayman, Sarah Catherine (15 yrs.) d. on 66-Jan-16 [66-Jan-18: 2C].
Ways, Stephen M. (23 yrs.) d. on 69-Mar-16 [69-Mar-17: 2C].
Weatherby, Myrtle Emory (4 mos.) d. on 70-Mar-7 [70-Mar-8: 2C; 70-Mar-9: 2C].
Weathers, Sarah E. m. Bump, Orlando F. on 70-Jul-27 [70-Jul-28: 2C].
Weathers, Virginia A. m. Lewis, Charles H. on 66-Jul-19 [66-Aug-15: 2B].
Weatherstine, Elizabeth (72 yrs.) d. on 66-Dec-13 [66-Dec-15: 2B].
Weatherstine, William Henry (1 yr., 1 mo.) d. on 69-Jul-25 [69-Jul-27: 2C].
Weaver, A. Cornelia m. Frederick, William T. on 68-Oct-12 [68-Oct-16: 2B].
Weaver, Anna Carrie m. Leonard, George W. on 70-Jun-28 [70-Sep-12: 2B].
Weaver, Carey S. (3 yrs., 1 mo.) d. on 69-Mar-2 of Bilious dysentery [69-Mar-3: 2C].
Weaver, Catherine m. Voyce, Charles on 69-Jul-4 [69-Jul-16: 2C].
Weaver, Charles m. Koppelman, Lizzie C. on 66-Jan-16 [66-Jan-19: 2C].
Weaver, Daniel (86 yrs.) d. on 70-Nov-22 [70-Nov-23: 2C, 4D; 70-Nov-24: 2C; 70-Nov-25: 4D].
Weaver, Edmund E. J. m. Lainhart, Juliet F. on 69-Oct-26 [69-Oct-30: 2B].
Weaver, Elizabeth A. m. Lee, George A. on 68-Feb-18 [68-Mar-5: 2C].
Weaver, Elizabeth Thirkel m. Leeke, J. Aldgate on 66-May-29 [66-Jun-6: 2B].
Weaver, Ellen G. m. Hughes, William S. on 66-Nov-19 [66-Nov-27: 2B].
Weaver, George C. m. Winter, Annie on 67-Sep-24 [67-Sep-27: 2B].
Weaver, George H. m. Craeger, Mary Louisa on 67-Feb-18 [68-Feb-20: 2C].
Weaver, Hannah m. Staab, John on 69-Oct-11 [69-Dec-1: 2C].
Weaver, Jacob m. Robinson, Emma on 66-Dec-11 [67-Jan-5: 2C].
Weaver, Jacob B. m. Lloyd, Eliza A. on 69-Nov-29 [69-Dec-1: 2C].
Weaver, James (61 yrs.) d. on 67-Jan-25 [67-Jan-26: 2C].
Weaver, John C. m. Gibson, Laura C. on 70-Mar-19 [70-Mar-26: 2B].
Weaver, John H. (23 yrs.) d. on 66-Oct-7 [66-Oct-9: 2A].
Weaver, Joseph Edward (28 yrs.) d. on 66-Dec-13 [66-Dec-19: 2B].
Weaver, Laura (7 yrs.) d. on 70-Jul-6 [70-Jul-7: 2C].
Weaver, Laura Virginia (1 yr., 10 mos.) d. on 70-Jan-13 [70-Jan-14: 2C].
Weaver, Maggie m. Hill, John T. on 68-Nov-26 [68-Nov-28: 2C].
Weaver, Mary A. m. Ward, William R. on 69-Jun-8 [69-Jun-10: 2C].
Weaver, Mary F. m. Caulk, Joseph on 67-Feb-3 [67-Feb-18: 2C].
Weaver, Mary J. m. Brooks, William W. C. on 67-Apr-11 [67-Apr-24: 2B].
Weaver, Mary Jane (28 yrs.) d. on 67-Aug-20 [67-Aug-21: 2B].
Weaver, Mary L. m. Dunn, Jacob on 70-Jan-12 [70-Feb-5: 2B].
Weaver, Milton Eugene d. on 67-Mar-28 [67-Mar-29: 2B].
Weaver, Robert S. m. Tuttle, Laura T. on 66-Mar-8 [66-Mar-10: 2B].
Weaver, Sue m. Feldhaus, Joseph C. on 69-Nov-18 [69-Nov-24: 2C].
Weaver, Venie J. m. Carter, Charles L. on 68-May-20 [68-Jun-23: 2B].
Weaver, Walter Augustus (1 yr., 11 mos.) d. [70-Feb-19: 2B].
Weaver, Wilhelmina L. (56 yrs.) d. on 66-Jul-28 [66-Jul-30: 2C].
Weaver, William d. on 66-Jun-30 [66-Jul-7: 2C].

Weaver, William E. m. Sullivan, Bessie on 69-Dec-16 [70-Mar-2: 2C].
Webb, Alexander (25 yrs.) d. on 66-May-2 of Suicide (Shooting) [66-May-3: 1F, 2C; 66-Jun-5: 2B].
Webb, Carroll DeFord d. on 67-Aug-19 [67-Aug-21: 2B].
Webb, Cora P. (6 yrs., 8 mos.) d. on 68-Nov-6 of Scarlet fever [68-Nov-7: 2B].
Webb, Emma D. m. Dimmock, Charles W. on 70-Feb-10 [70-Feb-12: 2B].
Webb, Emma Jenavah (2 yrs., 7 mos.) d. on 69-Feb-19 [69-Feb-20: 2B].
Webb, Emma P. m. Hugg, George W. on 70-May-17 [70-Aug-24: 2C].
Webb, Emma W. m. Lambdin, N. B. on 70-May-5 [70-May-25: 2C].
Webb, Fanny Cornelius (32 yrs.) d. on 70-Oct-14 [70-Oct-14: 2B].
Webb, Hattie A. m. Thurman, Allen W. on 68-Oct-15 [68-Oct-21: 2C].
Webb, James Franklin m. Bates, Marcellena on 68-Apr-14 [68-Apr-23: 2B].
Webb, John William (32 yrs.) d. on 66-Jun-4 [66-Jun-5: 2B].
Webb, Joseph Cox (4 yrs., 5 mos.) d. on 66-Sep-18 [66-Sep-19: 2B].
Webb, Katie (3 yrs., 2 mos.) d. on 68-Nov-3 of Scarlet fever [68-Nov-7: 2B].
Webb, Laura V. m. Gambrill, Albert on 70-Oct-27 [70-Nov-1: 2C].
Webb, Levi m. Heyser, Clara on 68-Feb-20 [68-Feb-26: 2C].
Webb, Lizzie (5 mos.) d. on 69-Aug-17 [69-Aug-18: 2C].
Webb, Louis S m. Capron, Julia V. on 68-Aug-23 [68-Aug-25: 2B; 68-Aug-27: 2B].
Webb, Louis S. d. on 68-Aug-25 [68-Aug-27: 2B].
Webb, Louisa C. d. on 67-Jan-22 [67-Jan-24: 1F].
Webb, Mary m. Gough, Charles E. on 70-Nov-21 [70-Nov-22: 2B].
Webb, Mary C. m. Hopper, S. W. T. on 70-May-12 [70-May-14: 2A].
Webb, Mary E. (58 yrs.) d. on 66-May-5 [66-May-7: 2B].
Webb, Mary Elizabeth (17 yrs., 10 mos.) d. on 67-Jun-20 [67-Jun-21: 2B].
Webb, Samuel Evan (6 mos.) d. on 68-May-20 [68-May-21: 2B].
Webb, Thomas W. m. Dukehart, Parthenia B. on 68-Nov-17 [68-Nov-19: 2C; 68-Nov-20: 2C].
Webb, William A., Sr. (57 yrs.) d. on 70-Jun-12 [70-Jun-14: 2B].
Webb, William W. m. Angelmier, Louise on 67-Dec-20 [68-Mar-3: 2C].
Webber, Eliza (42 yrs.) d. on 70-Aug-26 [70-Aug-29: 2C].
Webber, Fanny (87 yrs.) d. on 66-May-7 [66-May-8: 2B].
Webber, George (22 yrs.) d. on 70-Jul-28 of Construction cave-in [70-Jul-25: 4D].
Webber, John Philip m. Marcellett, Mary Josephine on 68-Sep-29 [68-Oct-1: 2B].
Weber, , Mrs. d. on 69-Apr-6 in Railroad accident [69-Apr-7: 1H; 69-Apr-8: 1G].
Weber, Arthur m. Verwayen, Magdalen on 67-May-18 [67-Jun-25: 2B].
Weber, Dorothea (38 yrs.) d. on 69-Mar-14 [69-Mar-16: 2C].
Weber, Henry (35 yrs.) d. on 69-Jan-20 [69-Jan-22: 2D; 69-Jan-23: 2C].
Weber, Henry C. (63 yrs.) d. on 66-Feb-28 [66-Mar-2: 2B].
Weber, Lawrence (9 yrs.) d. on 69-Mar-12 Burned [69-Mar-15: 1G].
Weber, Paul Ferdinand (27 yrs., 5 mos.) d. on 70-May-19 [70-May-20: 2C].
Webersch, Charles William d. on 67-Aug-4 [67-Aug-5: 1E; 67-Aug-6: 1G].
Webert, Mary Lizzie d. on 66-Jan-11 [66-Jan-13: 2C].
Webster, D. A. C. m. Cosby, Sally King on 68-Nov-25 [68-Nov-30: 2B].
Webster, Ella (8 mos.) d. on 69-Mar-14 [69-Mar-25: 2C].
Webster, Ellen (32 yrs.) d. on 68-Sep-18 [68-Sep-24: 2B].
Webster, George m. Guy, Caroline C. on 66-Jun-12 [66-Jul-7: 2B].
Webster, George W., Dr. (45 yrs.) d. on 70-Mar-14 [70-Mar-16: 2C].
Webster, Henry Worthington, Dr (73 yrs.) d. on 69-Oct-23 [69-Oct-25: 2C].
Webster, Jennie S. m. Magraw, Stephen C. on 69-Feb-22 [69-Feb-24: 2C].
Webster, John (31 yrs.) d. on 66-Dec-21 [66-Dec-24: 2B].
Webster, John A. m. Billmyer, Mattie on 69-Aug-8 [69-Sep-20: 2C].
Webster, John T. (46 yrs.) d. on 70-Aug-8 of Apoplexy [70-Aug-9: 2C, 4E].
Webster, Joseph (52 yrs.) d. on 67-Dec-14 [67-Dec-16: 2B; 67-Dec-17: 2B].
Webster, Joseph (63 yrs.) d. on 66-May-30 [66-May-31: 2B].
Webster, Joseph (76 yrs.) d. on 69-May-30 [69-Jun-1: 2B].

Webster, Joseph J. G. m. Jones, Emma on 69-Jul-14 [69-Jul-16: 2C].
Webster, Maggie m. Fisher, George A. on 70-Apr-12 [70-Apr-16: 2B].
Webster, Mattie H. (1 yr., 7 mos.) d. on 68-Mar-13 [68-Mar-18: 2B].
Webster, Richard E. m. Norris, Sophia C. on 67-Jun-6 [67-Jun-8: 2B].
Webster, Sallie m. Bailey, William C. on 67-Jun-4 [67-Jun-10: 2B].
Webster, Sophie Hodges m. Cooke, T. on 67-Mar-20 [67-Apr-5: 2B].
Webster, Thomas T. (45 yrs.) d. on 66-Dec-6 [66-Dec-10: 2C].
Webster, Thomas W. m. Buckingham, M. Florence on 70-Feb-23 [70-Mar-3: 2C].
Weck, John W. m. Steibel, Jeanette on 69-Jul-24 [69-Jul-30: 2C].
Weckesser, Tobias W. (33 yrs.) d. on 68-Sep-1 [68-Sep-2: 2B].
Weddegen, Mary m. Cross, John T. on 70-Jun-20 [70-Nov-18: 2C].
Weddell, George d. on 68-Aug-31 in Railroad accident [68-Sep-2: 1G].
Weed, Maggie J. m. Trail, Reverdy on 68-Feb-4 [68-Feb-8: 2B].
Weeden, Ella Clinton (17 yrs.) d. on 70-Nov-29 [70-Dec-9: 2C].
Weekes, Charles m. Dennis, Mary E. on 67-Nov-19 [67-Nov-20: 2C].
Weeks, Joseph (75 yrs.) d. on 67-Jul-19 [67-Jul-20: 2C].
Weeks, Lizzie Kate (30 yrs., 2 mos.) d. on 69-Apr-15 [69-Apr-28: 2B].
Weeks, Margaretta (2 yrs.) d. on 70-Nov-25 [70-Nov-26: 2C].
Weeks, Mary Ann (56 yrs.) d. on 66-May-19 [66-May-21: 2B].
Weeks, Osborn Meeteer d. on 66-Dec-11 [66-Dec-18: 2B].
Weeks, Robert Stephens (2 yrs., 4 mos.) d. on 67-Jan-12 [67-Jan-24: 2C].
Weems, Betsie Sellman d. on 70-Jul-25 of Consumption [70-Aug-1: 2C].
Weems, Cassandra S. (49 yrs.) d. on 68-Jan-17 [68-Jan-18: 2B].
Weems, Cornelia m. Gibson, John on 69-Sep-2 [69-Sep-2: 2C].
Weems, Eliza (85 yrs.) d. on 67-Oct-13 [67-Oct-17: 2B].
Weems, George W. m. Alderson, Anna on 67-Jun-18 [67-Jul-6: 2B].
Weems, Kate C. m. Sadler, George E. on 69-Dec-23 [69-Dec-25: 2C].
Weems, Mollie S. m. Cann, B. B. on 68-May-14 [68-May-20: 2A].
Weems, Tennyson m. Mann, Josephine on 68-Jun-2 [68-Jun-24: 2B].
Weems, Theodore N. m. Berry, Maggie L. on 69-Sep-16 [69-Sep-17: 2C].
Wegfahrt, Charles (43 yrs.) d. on 69-Dec-6 of Suicide (Stabbing) [69-Dec-8: 1H].
Weglein, Aaron (57 yrs.) d. on 66-Jan-3 [66-Jan-4: 2C; 66-Jan-5: 2C].
Wegner, A., Dr. (74 yrs.) d. on 70-Mar-29 [70-Mar-31: 2C].
Wegner, Charles J. m. Sleepack, Hanna on 68-Jun-9 [68-Jun-13: 2B].
Wehage, Maggie m. Rohleder, Joseph A. on 69-Sep-7 [69-Sep-13: 2B].
Wehn, Annie Louise m. Hayward, Samuel J. on 70-Mar-6 [70-Mar-9: 2C].
Wehn, Emma L. m. Cesterle, Adam on 68-Jun-28 [68-Jun-30: 2C].
Wehr, Catharina (62 yrs.) d. on 68-Sep-26 [68-Sep-28: 2B].
Wehr, Frederick m. Hobleman, Johana on 67-Aug-1 [67-Aug-3: 2B].
Wehr, Herman m. Kabernagle, Mary E. on 67-Apr-16 [67-Apr-20: 2A].
Wehr, Marie (51 yrs.) d. on 66-Oct-14 [66-Oct-16: 2B].
Wehrane, Adele (8 mos.) d. on 68-May-20 [68-May-21: 2B; 68-May-22: 2C].
Wehrhane, Theodore (21 yrs.) d. on 70-Feb-19 [70-Feb-21: 2B].
Weiant, Hannie M. m. Armstrong, William on 69-Oct-27 [69-Nov-1: 2B].
Weiant, Wolsey m. Armstrong, Sallie V. on 69-Apr-15 [69-Apr-19: 2B].
Weidler, Josephine m. Camp, Joseph on 67-Feb-27 [67-Mar-3: 2B].
Weidner, Ellanora M. (5 yrs., 9 mos.) d. on 70-Nov-29 [70-Nov-30: 2C].
Weifforth, Jacob m. Baier, Anna on 66-Sep-3 [66-Sep-5: 2B].
Weigand, Henry C. (36 yrs.) d. on 70-Oct-7 [70-Oct-10: 4B].
Weigel, Christine E. m. Cannoles, John W. on 69-Sep-5 [69-Dec-20: 2C].
Weigel, Mary m. Haigley, Henry on 67-Apr-29 [67-Jun-20: 2B].
Weigel, Rose m. Raborg, Joseph S. on 68-Oct-19 [68-Oct-26: 2B].
Weihrauch, Carrie Louisa (1 yr., 3 mos.) d. on 69-Apr-11 [69-Apr-13: 2B].
Weiker, Augusta M. (42 yrs.) d. on 68-Mar-5 [68-Mar-7: 2C].
Weiker, George Washington (6 mos.) d. on 68-Mar-19 [68-Mar-21: 2A].

Weil, Christina (55 yrs.) d. on 67-Mar-21 [67-Mar-22: 2C].
Weiller, Willie (2 yrs., 3 mos.) d. on 69-Mar-16 [69-Mar-17: 2C].
Weinberg, Israel (47 yrs.) d. on 67-May-30 of Heart disease [67-May-31: 1F].
Weinberger, Nathan (48 yrs., 6 mos.) d. [69-Sep-6: 2C].
Weiner, Annie V. m. Heim, William H. on 68-Oct-20 [68-Oct-24: 2B].
Weiner, Henry M. m. Miller, Fannie A. on 68-May-6 [68-May-8: 2B].
Weir, Benjamin T. m. Chaney, Almira on 67-Jun-24 [67-Jun-26: 2B].
Weir, Isabella m. Simonds, John W. on 66-Apr-8 [66-May-1: 2A].
Weir, James (34 yrs.) d. on 70-May-12 [70-May-13: 2C].
Weirough, George W. (1 yr., 9 mos.) d. on 70-Aug-12 [70-Aug-13: 2C].
Weis, Catherine (71 yrs.) d. on 68-Mar-14 [68-Mar-16: 2B].
Weise, Edward George (15 yrs.) d. on 69-Jul-29 [69-Jul-30: 2C].
Weiser, Bella C. d. on 68-Dec-14 [68-Dec-16: 2C].
Weishampel, Emma C. m. Quail, Charles E. on 67-Jun-4 [67-Jun-6: 2B].
Weisiger, Catherine Suttle (5 mos.) d. on 67-Jun-17 [67-Jun-19: 2B].
Weisiger, Sue S. O'Dell d. on 67-Jan-20 [67-Jan-21: 2C].
Weisman, J. Frank m. Beach, Mary E. on 70-Jun-9 [70-Jun-13: 2C].
Weiss, Caroline m. Lange, William on 69-Oct-26 [69-Nov-23: 2C].
Weiss, William m. Thomas, Mary Margarette on 70-Mar-31 [70-Apr-19: 2B].
Weitlich, John d. on 66-Aug-5 Drowned [66-Aug-6: 1G; 66-Aug-8: 1G].
Weitmyer, Jacob (46 yrs.) d. on 70-May-18 [70-May-27: 2B].
Weitzel, George Peabody d. on 68-Jul-18 [68-Jul-21: 2C].
Weitzel, Jacob (83 yrs.) d. on 68-Sep-14 [68-Sep-15: 2B].
Weitzel, John C. m. Muir, Laura A. on 66-May-7 [66-May-9: 2B].
Weitzel, John C. m. Wilson, Ida A. [69-Mar-22: 2C].
Weitzel, Laura (20 yrs.) d. on 68-Feb-23 [68-Feb-24: 2C; 68-Feb-25: 2C].
Weitzell, Elizabeth (58 yrs.) d. on 66-Feb-9 [66-Feb-10: 2C].
Weitzell, Irene F. (23 yrs.) d. on 67-Aug-16 [67-Aug-17: 2B].
Weitzell, James (17 yrs.) d. on 66-May-20 [66-May-22: 2B].
Weitzell, John (62 yrs., 8 mos.) d. on 69-Feb-10 [69-Feb-15: 2C].
Welby, Anna Maria d. on 68-Aug-13 [68-Aug-17: 2B].
Welby, Charles C. (29 yrs.) d. on 68-Feb-12 of Consumption [68-Feb-13: 2C].
Welch, Annie E. m. Lowell, John B. on 66-Nov-18 [66-Nov-27: 2C].
Welch, Charles (2 mos.) d. on 67-Oct-16 [67-Oct-17: 2B].
Welch, Charles H. (33 yrs.) d. on 68-Jun-22 [68-Jun-27: 2B].
Welch, Edward R. m. Earhart, Laura T. on 67-Oct-21 [67-Oct-23: 2B].
Welch, Elizabeth d. on 67-May-17 of Pneumonia [67-May-23: 2C].
Welch, John (5 yrs., 6 mos.) d. on 68-Jun-28 [68-Jun-30: 2B].
Welch, John m. Buck, Eliza Ann on 68-Jun-2 [68-Jun-4: 2B].
Welch, John W. m. Leiman, Emily J. on 66-Mar-12 [66-Mar-14: 2B].
Welch, Julie J. m. Sank, Corben A. on 66-Apr-4 [66-Apr-7: 2B].
Welch, Mary G. m. German, Benjamin C. on 66-Mar-4 [66-Mar-6: 2B].
Welch, Patrick (48 yrs.) d. on 66-Aug-13 [66-Aug-14: 2C].
Welch, Patrick J. (38 yrs.) d. on 68-Nov-16 [68-Nov-18: 2C].
Welch, Patty (83 yrs.) d. on 69-Mar-5 [69-Mar-8: 2C].
Welch, Robert [of Ben.] (89 yrs.) d. on 66-Nov-19 [66-Nov-23: 2C].
Welch, Ruth E. (39 yrs.) d. on 70-Feb-11 [70-Mar-28: 2B].
Welch, Sallie E. m. Taylor, John W. on 67-Jan-15 [67-Jan-19: 2C].
Welch, Thomas (19 yrs.) d. on 70-May-29 [70-May-30: 2B].
Welch, William C. d. in Railroad accident [67-Aug-15: 1E].
Welden, Charles Warren (1 yr., 3 mos.) d. on 69-Feb-26 [69-Mar-1: 2C].
Welden, Thomas A. (6 mos.) d. on 66-Nov-10 of Pneumonia [66-Nov-13: 2B].
Wellen, Amos F. m. Supple, Sophia C. on 67-May-7 [67-May-14: 2B].
Wellener, Bazil S. m. Donohue, Fannie E. on 69-Dec-28 [70-Jan-6: 2C].
Wellener, Elizabeth (42 yrs.) d. on 68-Aug-30 [68-Aug-31: 2B; 68-Sep-1: 2B].

Wellener, Isabella (75 yrs.) d. on 68-Aug-28 [68-Aug-29: 2B].
Wellener, John T. m. Colbert, Virginia on 69-May-18 [69-May-21: 2C].
Wellener, Mary J. m. Sewell, John T. on 69-Apr-8 [69-Apr-21: 2B].
Weller, Charles m. Bowen, T. Virginia on 70-Mar-17 [70-Apr-5: 2B].
Weller, Charles Edward d. on 70-Jan-16 [70-Jan-18: 2C].
Weller, George P. (45 yrs.) d. on 66-Aug-6 [66-Aug-24: 2B].
Weller, Jacob m. Freeland, Mary J. on 66-Mar-21 [66-Mar-27: 2B].
Weller, Kate m. Hayward, William W. on 66-Oct-4 [66-Oct-5: 2B].
Weller, Mary (75 yrs.) d. on 66-Aug-5 [66-Aug-6: 2C].
Weller, Mary (60 yrs.) d. on 70-Jun-16 [70-Jun-17: 2B].
Wellham, Hezekiah (50 yrs.) d. on 66-Oct-22 of Fits and exposure [66-Oct-23: 2B, 4C].
Welling, Belle C. m. Forsyth, William H. on 68-Jan-21 [68-Jan-23: 2C].
Welling, Elizabeth (15 yrs.) d. on 69-Nov-4 [69-Nov-12: 2C].
Welling, George R., Col. d. on 67-Sep-17 of Yellow fever [67-Oct-19: 2B].
Welling, Mary H. m. Baer, George H. on 67-Nov-5 [67-Nov-12: 2C].
Wellman, Anne Catharine (21 yrs.) d. on 68-Feb-5 [68-Feb-7: 2C].
Wellman, William (74 yrs.) d. on 65-Dec-30 [66-Jan-1: 2C].
Wellmore, Harry Zollicoffer (32 yrs.) d. on 70-Mar-13 of Consumption [70-Mar-24: 2C].
Wells, Alice Mildred d. on 70-Oct-12 [70-Oct-14: 2B].
Wells, Allen m. Caples, Mary on 66-Nov-25 [66-Dec-7: 2B].
Wells, Ann Leonora (37 yrs.) d. on 69-Apr-9 [69-Apr-10: 2B].
Wells, Anna (67 yrs.) d. on 70-Mar-19 [70-Mar-21: 2C].
Wells, Annie Maine m. Tilton, McLane on 66-Jul-26 [66-Jul-27: 2C].
Wells, Caroline B. d. on 70-Mar-25 [70-Apr-16: 2B].
Wells, Catherine (70 yrs.) d. on 69-Aug-23 [69-Aug-26: 2C].
Wells, Catherine A. m. Bone, William W. on 66-May-24 [66-Jul-13: 2C].
Wells, Catherine Eliza (61 yrs.) d. on 70-Apr-2 [70-Apr-5: 2B].
Wells, Charles Hilleary (7 mos.) d. on 68-Jun-25 [68-Jul-3: 2C].
Wells, Charlotte (81 yrs., 2 mos.) d. [66-Mar-30: 2C].
Wells, Clara S. m. Snell, Lorestin on 69-Oct-6 [69-Oct-12: 2C].
Wells, Elizabeth E. m. Conaway, Z. P. on 67-Feb-14 [67-Feb-22: 2D].
Wells, Eugenia m. Berry, George W. on 67-Oct-22 [67-Nov-20: 2C].
Wells, Florence A. m. Pietsch, C. Francis on 66-Jun-14 [66-Jun-26: 2B].
Wells, George m. Hughes, Emily on 67-Sep-5 [67-Sep-7: 2A].
Wells, George Sims d. on 69-Apr-20 [69-Apr-21: 2C].
Wells, Hallie A. m. Smith, Philip H. on 70-Jun-16 [70-Jun-21: 2C].
Wells, Harry J. M. (6 yrs., 2 mos.) d. on 69-Nov-18 [69-Nov-20: 2C].
Wells, Henry S. (60 yrs.) d. on 69-Apr-17 [69-Apr-19: 1F, 2B].
Wells, Howard (4 yrs.) d. on 66-Feb-23 of Diptheria [66-Mar-10: 2B].
Wells, James K. (22 yrs.) d. on 66-May-27 of Typhoid [66-Jun-6: 2B].
Wells, John, Sr. (64 yrs.) d. on 70-Feb-3 of Rheumatism [70-Feb-5: 1G, 2C; 70-Feb-7: 1H].
Wells, L. G. m. Wetmore, Mary E. on 66-Apr-14 [66-Apr-16: 2B].
Wells, Mary (86 yrs.) d. on 69-Jun-20 [69-Jun-21: 2B].
Wells, Mary F. m. Wright, William C. on 68-Dec-3 [69-Apr-20: 2B].
Wells, Mary Wallace m. Giddings, Luther on 69-Jul-15 [69-Jul-17: 2C].
Wells, Nathanies B. (40 yrs.) d. on 67-Jul-29 [67-Jul-30: 2C].
Wells, Oliver McKee m. Leitch, Zorah on 69-Jun-17 [69-Jun-30: 2C].
Wells, Ruth A. m. Reichert, Charles William G. on 69-Jul-13 [69-Jul-27: 2C].
Wells, Sarah (1 yr., 5 mos.) d. on 66-Mar-7 [66-Mar-12: 2B].
Wells, Sarah J. m. Lemcke, Alexander R. on 68-May-6 [68-May-16: 2A].
Wells, Thomas m. Rigger, Mary Clementine on 69-Sep-28 [69-Nov-2: 2B].
Wells, William A. (33 yrs.) d. on 69-May-15 [69-May-17: 2B].
Wells, William A. m. Sherwood, Maggie A. on 66-Oct-25 [66-Oct-27: 2B].
Wells, William H. m. Lamping, F. Emma on 67-Oct-16 [67-Oct-18: 2C].
Wells, William M. m. Simms, Eva A. on 70-Jun-30 [70-Jul-9: 2B].

Wellslager, Anna (28 yrs., 3 mos.) d. on 68-Apr-4 [68-Apr-7: 2B].
Welsh, Allina m. Cole, Moses M. on 68-Oct-14 [68-Oct-27: 2B].
Welsh, Catharine (55 yrs.) d. on 68-Dec-8 [68-Dec-9: 4E].
Welsh, Charles D. m. Garner, Alice F. on 70-May-17 [70-Jun-10: 2B].
Welsh, D. H. m. Law, Annie J. on 70-Feb-7 [70-Mar-1: 2C].
Welsh, David C. m. Frederick, Julia A. Virginia on 70-Nov-29 [70-Dec-7: 2C].
Welsh, Edward m. Billmeyer, Sarah on 70-Dec-27 [70-Dec-31: 2B].
Welsh, Euphemia L. (91 yrs.) d. on 69-Aug-29 [69-Aug-31: 2B].
Welsh, Henrietta d. on 66-May-6 [66-May-8: 2B].
Welsh, Isabella Merriken (1 yr., 9 mos.) d. on 68-Aug-29 [68-Aug-31: 2B].
Welsh, James d. on 66-Nov-20 Drowned [66-Dec-5: 1E].
Welsh, James m. Dunsmore, Mary T. on 70-Nov-22 [70-Dec-15: 2C].
Welsh, John W. m. McSweeny, Sarah on 70-Sep-15 [70-Sep-24: 2B].
Welsh, Lizzie m. Hopkins, William F. on 68-Dec-29 [69-Jan-1: 2C].
Welsh, Lucy Carroll (1 yr., 9 mos.) d. on 67-Nov-14 [67-Nov-16: 2B].
Welsh, Margaret d. [66-May-15: 2C].
Welsh, Margaret (30 yrs.) d. on 70-Aug-23 [70-Aug-24: 2C].
Welsh, Michael (18 yrs.) d. on 66-Oct-14 [66-Oct-16: 2B].
Welsh, Mollie A. m. Holland, Amos T. on 70-Nov-3 [70-Nov-8: 2B].
Welsh, S. Fannie m. Bondarant, H. on 69-Nov-3 [69-Nov-6: 2B].
Welsh, Thomas (11 mos.) d. [68-Aug-19: 2B].
Welsh, Thomas I. d. on 68-Mar-17 [68-Mar-19: 2B].
Welsh, Warner M. m. Smith, Anna J. C. on 70-Dec-22 [70-Dec-23: 2B].
Welsh, William E. m. Fenton, Laura on 70-Mar-31 [70-Apr-2: 2A].
Welshans, Bennett Cole d. on 70-Apr-24 [70-Apr-29: 2B].
Welshons, John F. m. Cole, Susan V. on 68-Dec-17 [68-Dec-22: 2C].
Welslager, Ann Jane (72 yrs.) d. on 66-Sep-15 [66-Sep-17: 2B].
Welton, William J. (48 yrs.) d. on 68-Oct-31 [68-Nov-2: 2B].
Welton, Willie (3 yrs., 7 mos.) d. on 70-Jul-4 [70-Jul-6: 2C].
Welty, F. H. m. Amoss, Alice J. on 68-Jul-18 [68-Oct-3: 2B].
Welty, Hattie R. m. Wheeler, B. L. on 70-Feb-16 [70-Feb-18: 2C].
Wenck, George J. m. Allers, Maggie on 67-Dec-12 [67-Dec-18: 2B].
Wentz, Cecilia m. Smith, Alfred on 68-Feb-18 [68-Mar-7: 2B].
Wentz, Charles Issac (35 yrs.) d. on 67-Nov-9 of Yellow fever [67-Nov-25: 2C].
Wentz, Henry Arthur (1 yr., 4 mos.) d. on 67-Apr-11 [67-Apr-12: 2C; 67-Apr-13: 2B].
Wentz, Kate d. on 68-Aug-16 [68-Aug-17: 2B].
Wentz, Laura Virginia (5 mos.) d. on 67-Dec-27 [67-Dec-28: 2C].
Wentzell, F. A. (27 yrs.) d. on 70-Apr-18 [70-Apr-20: 2B].
Wenzel, Edward Fauth (1 yr., 7 mos.) d. on 69-Aug-26 [69-Aug-28: 2B].
Werb, Mary A. m. Airey, James P. on 70-Jan-29 [70-Jan-3: 2B].
Werdebaugh, Sophia m. Uhler, Philip R on 67-Dec-5 [67-Dec-9: 2B].
Wernal, , Mrs. d. on 68-Jul-10 of Heatstroke [68-Jul-13: 1F].
Werner, Elizabeth (50 yrs.) d. on 66-Jan-3 of Paralysis [66-Jan-6: 2C].
Werner, Gustave m. Newbell, Julia A. on 68-Oct-4 [69-Apr-3: 2B].
Wernex, Mary A. m. Mattfeldt, Charles W. on 66-May-6 [66-Jun-16: 2B].
Wernsing, Mary A. m. Hussman, Charles F. W. on 66-Apr-19 [66-Apr-23: 2B].
Wesley, L. R. m. Shipley, William T. on 69-Nov-25 [69-Nov-26: 2B].
Wessels, Annie E. m. Hartlove, William W. on 69-Nov-18 [69-Nov-20: 2B].
Wessels, Littleton B. m. Armstrong, Belle H. on 70-May-26 [70-Jun-2: 2B].
West, A. C. m. Reed, P. R. on 66-Feb-28 [66-Mar-2: 2B].
West, Alice A. m. Downey, Benjamin F. on 67-Mar-25 [67-Mar-27: 2C].
West, Charles (51 yrs.) d. on 69-Jun-9 [69-Jun-11: 1H, 2C].
West, Charles (24 yrs.) d. on 69-May-26 Drowned [69-Jun-2: 2B].
West, Charles m. Hare, E. on 69-May-13 [69-Jun-2: 2B].
West, Edith (73 yrs.) d. on 69-Oct-26 [69-Oct-28: 2C].

West, Eleanor (69 yrs.) d. on 70-Mar-22 [70-Mar-23: 2C; 70-Mar-24: 2C].
West, Elizabeth (30 yrs.) d. on 67-Nov-5 [67-Nov-6: 2B].
West, George P. m. Sauerwein, Emma on 68-Dec-8 [68-Dec-12: 2C].
West, H. Montgomery m. Skinner, Marianna on 70-Jan-20 [70-Jan-28: 2B].
West, Lidie m. Billmire, W. Oury on 67-Jan-3 [67-Jan-7: 2C].
West, Lizzie Rebecca (1 yr.) d. on 68-Oct-21 [68-Oct-23: 2B].
West, Mary E. (6 yrs.) d. on 67-May-29 [67-May-31: 2B].
West, Mary L. d. on 70-Jun-13 [70-Jun-21: 2C].
West, Otillia R. (53 yrs.) d. on 69-Nov-14 [69-Nov-15: 1H, 2C; 69-Nov-16: 2C].
West, Robert (32 yrs.) d. on 66-Apr-12 [66-Apr-14: 2B].
West, Sophia (95 yrs.) d. on 67-May-30 [67-May-31: 2B].
West, Thomas M. m. Johnson, Annie S. on 70-Nov-22 [70-Nov-24: 2B].
West, Virginia m. Nelson, Martin on 69-Mar-24 [69-Apr-2: 2C].
West, William (83 yrs.) d. on 68-Feb-10 [68-Feb-11: 1G, 2C; 68-Feb-12: 2C].
West, William H. m. Orem, Sophie B. on 70-Oct-27 [70-Nov-1: 2C].
West, William H. H. d. on 64-Jun-3 [66-Apr-25: 2B].
Westcott, James m. Harper, Ann on 66-May-15 [66-May-18: 2C].
Westcott, Nancy (79 yrs.) d. [66-Mar-1: 2B].
Westerman, Allan Robert Henry (2 yrs., 11 mos.) d. on 69-Sep-29 [69-Oct-2: 2B].
Westerman, Francis H. m. Davis, Georgianna on 66-Jan-17 [66-Jan-19: 2C].
Westermyer, Bernard (30 yrs.) d. on 70-Aug-27 Drowned [70-Aug-29: 4D].
Westheimer, David m. Joseph, Babette on 70-Sep-20 [70-Sep-22: 2C].
Westlake, Ada A. (31 yrs.) d. on 70-Apr-7 [70-Apr-9: 2B].
Westlake, Adelaide (1 yr., 1 mo.) d. on 67-Sep-10 [67-Sep-11: 2B].
Westlake, Arthur Willis (1 yr., 4 mos.) d. on 70-Jun-22 of Hydrocephalus [70-Jun-24: 2C].
Westlake, Sarah Lizzie (4 mos.) d. on 68-Jun-24 [68-Jun-25: 2B].
Weston, Cornelius m. Latrobe, Kate on 67-Jul-8 [67-Jul-11: 2C].
Weston, Ellen m. Fredericks, Lewis on 68-Feb-27 [68-Feb-29: 2B].
Weston, John A. m. Kirwan, Georgeanna K. on 70-Apr-20 [70-Apr-22: 2C].
Weston, Nathaniel m. Barney, Annie on 67-Nov-28 [67-Dec-24: 2B].
Westwood, Emily J. d. on 70-Apr-13 [70-Apr-15: 2C].
Wetherald, William d. on 67-Sep-26 [67-Sep-28: 2A].
Wethers, Virginia J. m. Lewis, Charles H. on 66-Jul-19 [66-Jul-27: 2C].
Wethrald, Mary F. m. Balderston, Thomas C. on 70-Nov-23 [70-Nov-28: 2C].
Wetmore, Mary E. m. Wells, L. G. on 66-Apr-14 [66-Apr-26: 2B].
Wetter, Eliza (63 yrs.) d. on 68-Oct-1 [68-Oct-2: 2B].
Wetter, Emma L. m. Sauerhoff, Oscar F. on 69-Sep-14 [69-Sep-28: 2B].
Wetter, John H. (32 yrs.) d. on 66-Dec-17 [66-Dec-19: 2B].
Wettmarshausen, Amelia (16 yrs.) d. on 68-Jan-31 [68-Feb-1: 2C; 68-Feb-12: 2C].
Wetzel, Frederick (48 yrs.) d. on 69-Aug-15 of Suicide (Shooting) [69-Aug-16: 1G; 69-Aug-17: 1G].
Weyforth, George m. Austin, Margaret on 67-Nov-4 [67-Nov-30: 2C].
Weyler, J. Casswell B. (1 yr., 1 mo.) d. on 70-Sep-24 [70-Sep-26: 2B].
Weyler, Mary Matilda (1 yr., 3 mos.) d. on 68-Aug-28 [68-Aug-29: 2B].
Weymouth, Fannie m. Schmick, Philip on 66-Mar-1 [66-Mar-20: 2C].
Weyrauch, Maria Katherine (82 yrs.) d. on 67-Jul-29 of Brain congestion [67-Jul-31: 2C].
Whaland, Frances A. m. Chaires, Samuel on 67-Dec-19 [67-Dec-21: 2B].
Whalay, Ella (6 yrs., 7 mos.) d. on 66-Jul-17 of Heatstroke [66-Jul-18: 2C].
Whalay, James Francis (4 yrs., 6 mos.) d. on 66-Jul-17 of Heatstroke [66-Jul-18: 2C].
Whalen, Anna d. on 70-Jul-11 [70-Jul-12: 2C; 70-Jul-13: 2C].
Whalen, Francis (1 yr., 2 mos.) d. on 67-Jul-22 [67-Jul-23: 2C].
Whalen, Ida Ellsworth (7 yrs., 1 mo.) d. on 69-Apr-11 of Brain congestion [69-Apr-12: 2A].
Whalen, Margaret (80 yrs.) d. on 68-Jul-2 [68-Jul-4: 2C].
Whalen, Mary E. (50 yrs.) d. on 69-Nov-9 of Suicide (Hanging) [69-Nov-10: 1H].
Whalen, Mattie J. m. Boardman, Francis E. on 68-May-5 [68-Oct-9: 2C].

Whalen, Oliver P. (31 yrs.) d. on 70-Sep-28 [70-Sep-30: 2B].
Whalen, Peter (35 yrs.) d. on 69-Sep-7 [69-Sep-8: 2B].
Whaley, Maggie T. m. Blackford, William E. on 69-Jul-3 [69-Nov-18: 2C].
Wharry, Mary J. m. Hush, Samuel C. on 69-Apr-27 [69-May-4: 2B].
Wharton, A. Ophelia d. on 66-Apr-11 [66-Apr-26: 2B].
Wharton, Henry Clifton (28 yrs.) d. on 70-Apr-8 [70-Apr-9: 2B; 70-Apr-11: 2B].
Wharton, Henry W., Maj. d. on 68-Mar-23 [68-Mar-24: 1G, 2B; 68-Mar-25: 2A].
Wharton, Laura Virginia d. on 67-Sep-17 [67-Sep-18: 2B].
Wharton, Theodore C. S. (48 yrs., 11 mos.) d. on 66-Jun-26 [66-Jun-27: 2C].
Whealan, Edward (19 yrs.) d. on 66-May-30 [66-May-31: 2B; 66-Jun-1: 2B].
Whealen, Bridget (56 yrs.) d. on 70-Dec-30 [70-Dec-31: 2C].
Wheat, Julia A. m. Brown, Charles on 67-Nov-12 [67-Nov-14: 2B].
Wheat, Wesley d. on 68-Aug-31 Murdered (Shooting) [68-Sep-2: 1F].
Wheatley, Edith Clifton (7 mos.) d. on 66-Feb-24 [66-Feb-26: 2B].
Wheatley, J. F. (45 yrs.) d. on 68-Mar-10 [68-Mar-11: 2B, 4F].
Wheatley, James R. (48 yrs.) d. on 66-Nov-11 [66-Nov-13: 2B].
Wheatley, Thomas W. m. Colbert, Amelia on 69-Jan-12 [69-Jan-15: 2D].
Wheatley, William F. m. Stoddard, Kate H. on 69-Oct-7 [69-Oct-9: 2C].
Wheeden, Beulah (6 mos.) d. on 66-Oct-7 [66-Oct-8: 2B; 66-Oct-9: 2A].
Wheeden, James M. (56 yrs.) d. on 70-May-25 of Intemperance [70-May-27: 1H].
Wheeden, John Etchberger (1 mo.) d. on 70-Mar-1 of Catarrh [70-Mar-8: 2C].
Wheeden, Leonora (7 mos.) d. on 69-Aug-28 [69-Aug-30: 2B].
Wheeden, Rebecca Jane (1 yr., 8 mos.) d. on 70-Dec-8 [70-Dec-9: 2C].
Wheeden, Thomas Jefferson (3 mos.) d. on 66-Dec-4 of Catarrh [66-Dec-6: 2B].
Wheeler, A. Carroll m. Ramsey, Caroline C. on 68-Nov-5 [68-Nov-7: 2B].
Wheeler, Andrew T. m. Mackinheimer, Laura J. on 69-Aug-12 [69-Aug-14: 2C].
Wheeler, Ann C. (85 yrs.) d. on 69-Apr-4 [69-Apr-6: 2C].
Wheeler, Annie E. (9 mos.) d. on 69-Apr-14 [69-Apr-15: 2B].
Wheeler, B. L. m. Welty, Hattie R. on 70-Feb-16 [70-Feb-18: 2C].
Wheeler, Benjamin F. m. Long, Laura H. on 67-Jun-26 [67-Jun-29: 2B].
Wheeler, Charles (37 yrs.) d. on 66-May-12 [66-May-15: 2C].
Wheeler, Charles Clinton (7 yrs., 6 mos.) d. on 66-Dec-16 [66-Dec-20: 2B].
Wheeler, Charles H. m. Haywood, Victoria on 67-Nov-25 [67-Nov-30: 2C].
Wheeler, Christianetta m. Gray, James on 67-Jun-17 [67-Jun-20: 2B].
Wheeler, Clodius H. m. Turner, Ann Elizabeth on 68-Jun-4 [68-Jun-9: 2B].
Wheeler, Dulton (50 yrs.) d. on 70-Jun-12 [70-Jun-20: 2C].
Wheeler, Elizabeth (69 yrs., 5 mos.) d. on 69-Jul-13 [69-Jul-16: 2C].
Wheeler, Ella m. Robertson, Frank S. on 68-Jan-30 [68-Feb-1: 2B].
Wheeler, Fannie M. m. Lewis, Frank on 69-Nov-4 [69-Nov-6: 2B].
Wheeler, Francis O. (18 yrs.) d. on 70-Mar-29 in Construction accident [70-Mar-31: 1H, 2C].
Wheeler, G. F. m. Jackson, Emma A. on 67-Jun-13 [67-Feb-17: 2B].
Wheeler, George m. Bines, Josephine on 66-Aug-12 [67-Feb-19: 2C].
Wheeler, George C. (26 yrs., 5 mos.) d. on 70-May-24 [70-May-26: 2C].
Wheeler, James H. (49 yrs.) d. on 68-Sep-29 [68-Sep-30: 2B].
Wheeler, Jerome Edgar (2 yrs., 6 mos.) d. on 66-Apr-30 [66-May-1: 2A].
Wheeler, John (52 yrs.) d. on 67-Dec-21 of Heart disease [67-Dec-23: 2B, 4D].
Wheeler, Joseph (45 yrs.) d. on 67-Jun-28 of Brain fever [67-Jun-29: 2A].
Wheeler, Laura J. (35 yrs.) d. on 68-Apr-17 [68-Apr-18: 2C].
Wheeler, Laura J. (5 yrs.) d. on 69-Sep-18 [69-Sep-21: 2B].
Wheeler, Maggie T., Miss m. Tall, S. Columbus, Esq. on 66-Feb-21 [66-Feb-27: 2B].
Wheeler, Maria L. m. Hooper, L. E. on 67-Jan-6 [67-Jan-12: 2C].
Wheeler, Mariah C., Miss m. Brooks, Isaiah C., Esq. on 66-Feb-25 [66-Feb-27: 2B].
Wheeler, Martha F. (3 yrs., 7 mos.) d. on 70-Oct-4 [70-Oct-5: 2B].
Wheeler, Mary Imogen d. on 70-Jan-7 [70-Jan-8: 2B].
Wheeler, Mary T. m. Gordon, F. Skipwith on 66-Jan-9 [66-Jan-11: 2B].

Wheeler, Susannah (40 yrs.) d. on 68-Aug-11 [68-Aug-13: 2B].
Wheeler, Thomas J. m. Brian, Emma V. on 69-Aug-17 [69-Sep-14: 2B].
Wheeler, Tobias K. d. on 69-Mar-29 [69-Mar-31: 2C].
Wheeler, William A. m. Crabson, Anna R. on 67-Aug-28 [67-Sep-21: 2A].
Wheeler, William H. m. Leverton, Annie M. on 66-May-31 [66-Jun-9: 2B].
Wheeler, William S. m. Thompson, Mary J. on 70-Jul-28 [70-Aug-9: 2C].
Wheeler, Zebulon m. Valentine, Mary Ellen on 70-Jul-7 [70-Jul-16: 2B].
Wheelwright, D. Page (18 yrs.) d. [67-Apr-4: 2B].
Whelan, Agnes Olivia m. Kearney, Thomas J. on 67-Dec-25 [68-Jan-6: 2C].
Whelan, Eliza d. on 67-Jan-25 [67-Jan-26: 2C; 67-Jan-28: 2C].
Whelan, Etta m. Cushing, John, Jr. on 70-Apr-26 [70-Apr-28: 2B].
Whelan, Julia (70 yrs.) d. on 66-Jul-31 [66-Aug-2: 2C].
Whelan, Luke (77 yrs.) d. on 68-Nov-20 [68-Nov-21: 2C; 68-Nov-25: 2B].
Wherrett, Albert E. m. Cowen, Louisa on 66-Oct-28 [66-Oct-30: 2B].
Wherrett, Andrew J. m. Sprague, Helen M. on 66-Jun-18 [66-Jun-21: 2B].
Wherrett, Elizabeth Virginia (1 yr., 3 mos.) d. on 67-Aug-28 [67-Aug-29: 2B].
Wherrett, George Z. m. Mankin, Mary J. L. on 67-Dec-3 [67-Dec-6: 2C].
Wherrett, George Zachariah (32 yrs.) d. on 68-Mar-31 [68-Apr-1: 2C].
Wherrett, James M. m. Calwell, Rosanna M. on 69-Oct-14 [69-Oct-19: 2C].
Wherrett, Lizzie (9 mos.) d. on 70-Jun-20 [70-Jun-21: 2C].
Wherrett, Lizzie C. (25 yrs.) d. on 70-Apr-11 of Consumption [70-Apr-12: 2B; 70-Apr-13: 2B].
Wherrett, Lucy A. (36 yrs.) d. on 68-Jul-27 [68-Jul-29: 2B].
Wherrett, Robert M. m. Lacey, Lizzie C. on 66-Sep-23 [66-Sep-27: 2C].
Wherrett, William Zachary (21 yrs., 6 mos.) d. on 68-Feb-7 of Yellow fever [68-Apr-6: 2B].
Wherry, William M. m. Grammer, Alice W. on 68-Jun-10 [68-Jun-12: 2B].
Whippey, C. F. m. Parker, Laura A. on 67-Nov-27 [67-Dec-2: 2C].
Whisman, Willie Howard (1 yr., 4 mos.) d. on 68-Sep-9 [68-Sep-10: 2B].
Whistler, George W. d. on 69-Dec-24 [69-Dec-30: 2C].
Whitaker, Ann Maria (32 yrs.) d. on 67-Mar-11 of Consumption [67-Mar-13: 2C].
Whitaker, Henry M. (38 yrs.) d. on 66-Jul-15 [66-Jul-16: 2C].
Whitaker, Mary (68 yrs.) d. on 67-Feb-17 [67-Mar-23: 2B].
Whitaker, Matilda E. m. Gill, William James on 66-Jun-26 [66-Nov-1: 2B].
Whitaker, Samuel (23 yrs.) d. on 70-Dec-22 [70-Dec-28: 2D].
Whitby, Mary (67 yrs.) d. on 67-Jan-31 [67-Feb-1: 2C].
White, A. V. m. Griffith, A. J. on 68-Nov-10 [68-Nov-11: 2C].
White, Achsah G. m. Bouis, Stephen, Jr. on 68-Dec-24 [69-Jan-14: 2D].
White, Achsah Griffith m. Bouice, Stephen on 68-Dec-24 [68-Dec-31: 2C].
White, Allen Paine (2 yrs., 6 mos.) d. on 66-Jan-20 [66-Jan-22: 2C].
White, Alphonso Disney (1 yr., 1 mo.) d. on 67-Nov-17 of Brain inflammation [67-Nov-18: 2B].
White, Ann (77 yrs.) d. on 70-Aug-24 [70-Aug-31: 2B].
White, Anna H. m. Brook, George E. on 67-May-16 [67-May-18: 2A].
White, Anna Laura (11 mos.) d. on 70-Jul-27 [70-Jul-28: 2C].
White, Artridge (64 yrs., 4 mos.) d. on 66-Dec-26 [66-Dec-27: 2C].
White, Asbury d. on 67-Apr-16 of Blood vessel rupture [67-Apr-18: 1E].
White, C. B. m. Spedden, Virginia on 70-Nov-3 [70-Nov-8: 2B].
White, C. B. m. Hoadley, Frances A. on 69-Dec-21 [70-Jan-3: 2C].
White, Carrie Bell (11 mos.) d. on 69-Mar-1 [69-Mar-3: 2C].
White, Catherine (65 yrs.) d. on 68-Aug-24 [68-Aug-25: 2B].
White, Catherine (82 yrs.) d. on 67-Nov-20 [67-Nov-22: 2C].
White, Catherine E. (21 yrs.) d. on 67-Jan-22 [67-Jan-24: 2C].
White, Charles d. on 69-Jul-3 [69-Sep-21: 2B].
White, Charles m. Young, Josephine on 68-Feb-3 [68-Feb-8: 2B].
White, Charles E. m. Latham, Sarah R. on 68-Oct-13 [68-Oct-17: 2B].
White, D. (35 yrs.) d. on 67-Sep-23 of Heart disease [67-Sep-24: 1E].
White, David H., Capt. (69 yrs.) d. on 66-Jun-10 Murdered (Assault) [66-Jun-13: 2B;

66-Jun-12: 1F, 2B].
White, Denney m. Mills, Thomas H. on 68-May-28 [68-May-30: 2A].
White, E. Blanche m. Selby, Joseph on 68-Feb-19 [68-Feb-21: 2B].
White, Edmond m. Emmons, Antonia on 70-Sep-20 [70-Sep-24: 2B].
White, Edmund m. McKay, Annie J. on 70-Apr-12 [70-Apr-15: 2B].
White, Edward T. m. Bancroft, Lucy D. on 67-May-27 [67-May-29: 2B].
White, Elias A., Dr. (45 yrs.) d. on 66-Feb-18 [66-Feb-19: 2B; 66-Feb-20: 2B].
White, Elizabeth A. (40 yrs.) d. on 67-Jul-28 [67-Jul-30: 2C].
White, Elizabeth A. m. Shipley, Columbus on 68-Jan-2 [68-Jan-17: 2C].
White, Elsie Bankerd (1 yr., 2 mos.) d. on 69-Jul-25 [69-Jul-27: 2C].
White, Emeline m. Lee, Jesse W. on 66-Jan-25 [66-Jan-29: 2B].
White, Emma Wilson (7 yrs.) d. on 68-May-3 [68-May-5: 2B].
White, Frances m. Rountree, William H.H. on 67-Mar-14 [67-May-1: 2B; 67-May-2: 2B].
White, Francis m. Onion, Mary G. on 70-Nov-23 [70-Nov-24: 2B].
White, Francis M. (41 yrs.) d. on 68-Mar-19 [68-Mar-21: 2A].
White, George B. m. Turner, Lucie H. on 68-Nov-25 [68-Dec-2: 2C].
White, George D. m. Cain, Alice on 70-Dec-6 [70-Dec-10: 2B].
White, George R. m. Crowley, Kate E. on 65-Nov-20 [66-Jan-20: 2C].
White, George W. m. Smith, Victorine D. on 69-Jul-25 [70-Mar-14: 2C].
White, Greansbury (32 yrs.) d. on 67-Mar-10 [67-Mar-11: 2C].
White, Hannah R. m. Magers, John M. on 68-Feb-25 [68-Feb-28: 2D].
White, Harvy Elder (1 yr., 3 mos.) d. on 70-May-21 [70-May-24: 2C].
White, Helen V. m. Lillybridge, Octavius C. on 70-Jan-13 [70-Jan-18: 2C].
White, Henrietta Maria m. Chamberlaine, Henry on 68-Nov-10 [68-Nov-11: 2C].
White, Henry F. (37 yrs.) d. on 70-Apr-11 [70-Apr-12: 2B].
White, Hiram F. m. Fifer, Martha on 66-Apr-4 [66-Apr-5: 2B].
White, Irene C. m. Canfield, Charles on 68-Jun-17 [68-Jun-22: 2B].
White, J. Campbell, Rev. d. on 66-Nov-15 [66-Nov-19: 2B].
White, James (61 yrs.) d. on 67-Mar-20 [67-Mar-21: 2C; 67-Mar-22: 2C].
White, James (38 yrs.) d. on 69-Apr-14 of Heart disease [69-Apr-15: 1F].
White, James A. (56 yrs.) d. on 66-Oct-14 [66-Oct-22: 2C].
White, James H. m. Ramsey, Eliza J. on 70-Dec-28 [70-Dec-31: 2B].
White, James McKenny m. Goldsmith, M. M. on 68-Apr-30 [68-May-1: 2B].
White, Jane E. m. Reilly, Peter J. J. on 70-Jan-19 [70-Feb-12: 2C].
White, Jennie A. m. Higgins, J. Richard on 69-Feb-1 [69-Feb-11: 2C].
White, John F. m. Perry, Sarah E. on 67-Jan-6 [67-Jan-18: 2C].
White, John J. m. Carver, Emma V. on 68-Jun-2 [68-Jun-9: 2B].
White, John J. m. Deems, Scotia Anna on 67-Jan-1 [67-Jan-3: 2B].
White, John R. d. on 68-Jul-31 of Scarlet fever [68-Aug-3: 2C].
White, Joseph (77 yrs.) d. on 67-Nov-9 [67-Nov-11: 1F, 2C].
White, Joseph m. Petticord, Sarah Francis on 68-Feb-2 [68-Feb-4: 2C].
White, Joseph K. T. m. Achenbach, Carrie on 69-Nov-19 [69-Nov-20: 2C].
White, Julia A. d. on 67-Nov-28 [67-Nov-30: 2C].
White, Katie (12 yrs., 10 mos.) d. on 70-Mar-27 [70-Mar-29: 2C].
White, L. B. m. Bell, C. H. on 70-Jan-4 [70-Jan-8: 2B].
White, Laura Virginia Wainwrig (7 yrs., 5 mos.) d. on 67-Mar-19 [67-Jul-9: 2B].
White, Letitia V. m. Merecraft, George [69-Sep-15: 2B].
White, Lizzie V. m. Johnson, John D. on 70-Nov-23 [70-Nov-24: 2B].
White, M. E. m. Sessions, W. P. D. on 68-Jan-1 [68-Jan-6: 2C].
White, Maggie M. m. Stump, J. Henry on 67-May-16 [67-May-28: 2B].
White, Martha A. m. Simpson, Charles on 67-Nov-11 [67-Nov-12: 2C].
White, Mary A. (29 yrs.) d. on 67-Jun-13 [67-Jun-20: 2B].
White, Mary Catherine d. on 67-Aug-28 [67-Aug-30: 2B].
White, Mary E. m. Purcell, George K. on 66-Dec-13 [66-Dec-15: 2B].
White, Mary E. m. Forwood, Samuel E. on 69-Dec-16 [69-Dec-18: 2B].

White, Mary F. m. Pearce, Franklin F. on 66-Jul-15 [66-Jul-17: 2C].
White, Mary Grace d. on 70-Aug-18 [70-Aug-23: 2B].
White, Mattee E. m. Bolsom, B. F. on 69-Nov-30 [69-Dec-6: 2C].
White, Nannie Lisle m. Langdon, Thomas P. on 68-Jan-29 [68-Jan-31: 2C].
White, Peter (47 yrs.) d. on 70-Nov-9 [70-Nov-10: 2C].
White, Peter L. m. Smith, Anastasia on 67-Aug-5 [67-Aug-7: 2C].
White, Priscilla Hill (73 yrs.) d. on 68-Apr-10 [68-Apr-16: 2B].
White, Rachel m. Allnutt, Benjamin on 66-Jan-16 [66-Feb-8: 2C].
White, Rachel Maria (29 yrs.) d. on 67-Nov-19 [67-Nov-21: 2C].
White, Rebecca (56 yrs.) d. on 68-Oct-5 [68-Oct-7: 2C].
White, Robert (16 yrs.) d. on 70-Nov-6 [70-Nov-10: 2C].
White, Robert H. m. Murry, Laura V. on 70-Nov-28 [70-Dec-2: 2C].
White, Rose Evelyn (14 yrs., 5 mos.) d. on 67-Apr-9 [67-Apr-10: 2B].
White, Samuel Elanson (9 mos.) d. on 68-Jun-20 [68-Jun-24: 2B].
White, Samuel J., Capt. (24 yrs.) d. on 66-Apr-13 of Lung hemorrhage [66-May-14: 2B].
White, Samuel K. (78 yrs.) d. on 66-Aug-10 [66-Aug-11: 2B].
White, Samuel R. (60 yrs.) d. on 66-Feb-2 [66-Feb-3: 2C].
White, Sarah (57 yrs.) d. on 66-Jan-18 [66-Jan-19: 2C; 66-Jan-20: 2C].
White, Sarah A. m. Hubbard, Andrew J. on 68-Oct-13 [68-Oct-17: 2B].
White, Sarah Elizabeth (23 yrs.) d. on 66-Jan-28 [66-Jan-29: 2C].
White, Sarah L. m. Williams, Charles C. on 68-Oct-13 [68-Oct-26: 2B].
White, Susan P. m. Langley, Hezekiah on 66-Feb-8 [66-Feb-10: 2C].
White, Susannah (82 yrs.) d. on 70-Dec-18 [70-Dec-19: 2C].
White, Thomas G. m. Coyle, Mannie B. on 69-Jul-4 [69-Jul-7: 2C].
White, Valaria V. (18 yrs., 9 mos.) d. on 68-Feb-17 [68-Feb-18: 2C].
White, Virginia Marian (26 yrs.) d. on 68-Aug-30 [68-Aug-31: 2B].
White, Wells M. (33 yrs.) d. on 68-Dec-26 [68-Dec-28: 2C; 68-Dec-29: 2D].
White, William B. (37 yrs.) d. on 67-May-7 Drowned [67-Dec-16: 2B].
White, William Edward (26 yrs.) d. on 69-Jun-17 [69-Aug-11: 2C].
White, William G. m. Smith, Anna M. on 66-Oct-17 [66-Oct-25: 2C; 66-Oct-26: 2B].
White, William H. (32 yrs.) d. on 68-Feb-9 [68-Feb-11: 2C; 68-Feb-12: 2C].
White, William Thomas (29 yrs.) d. on 66-Jun-30 [66-Jul-2: 2B].
White, Willie H. (10 mos.) d. on 69-Jun-25 [69-Jun-26: 2B].
Whiteford, Charles (64 yrs.) d. on 70-Nov-24 [70-Nov-26: 2C].
Whiteford, Dorcas (64 yrs.) d. on 70-Jun-29 [70-Jul-7: 2C].
Whiteford, George Celenna (10 mos.) d. on 67-Jun-18 [67-Jun-20: 2B].
Whiteford, Jennie m. McLaughlin, J. G. on 70-Jun-27 [70-Jun-28: 2C].
Whiteford, M. Crook m. Lucy, Lizzie B. on 69-Jul-27 [69-Aug-4: 2C].
Whiteford, Mary N. (51 yrs.) d. on 68-Mar-6 of Consumption [68-Mar-9: 2C].
Whiteford, Nicholas L. D. (24 yrs.) d. on 70-Jul-5 [70-Jul-7: 2C; 70-Jul-12: 2C].
Whiteford, Solomon Marshall Gu (4 yrs., 8 mos.) d. on 66-Oct-9 [66-Oct-10: 2B].
Whiteford, Virginia A. (34 yrs.) d. on 70-May-15 [70-Jul-15: 2C].
Whiteford, William (61 yrs.) d. on 66-Aug-3 of Paralysis [66-Aug-11: 2B].
Whitehead, Agnes L. m. Lindsay, Granville on 70-Sep-8 [70-Sep-12: 2B].
Whitehead, Edgar L. (4 yrs., 2 mos.) d. on 70-Mar-3 of Scarlet fever [70-Mar-4: 2C].
Whitehead, Emily Susan (7 yrs.) d. on 69-Apr-22 [69-Apr-23: 2B].
Whitehead, Holbrook m. Woods, Lillie J. on 69-Apr-15 [69-Apr-16: 2B].
Whitehead, Willie J. (10 yrs.) d. on 69-Apr-29 [69-Apr-30: 2C].
Whitehill, Julia m. Chappell, Edwin F. on 68-Oct-1 [68-Oct-13: 2C].
Whitehouse, George A. m. Gees, Olivia E. on 67-May-28 [67-Aug-13: 2B].
Whitehouse, James m. Snyder, Louisa C. on 66-Nov-13 [66-Nov-15: 2C].
Whitehouse, Mary Emma m. Kidd, Nelson on 66-Jan-2 [66-Jan-15: 2B].
Whitehouse, William, Mrs. (77 yrs.) d. on 66-Sep-11 [66-Sep-14: 2B].
Whitehurst, Henry W. (35 yrs.) d. on 66-Jun-4 [66-Jun-5: 2B].
Whitehurst, L. H. m. Granberry, Annie M. on 69-Oct-28 [69-Oct-30: 2B].

Whiteley, Arthur J. (66 yrs.) d. on 66-Jun-22 [66-Jun-26: 2B].
Whiteley, David R. (84 yrs.) d. on 70-Jun-23 [70-Jun-24: 2C].
Whiteley, Estelle (2 yrs., 10 mos.) d. on 69-Feb-3 [69-Feb-5: 2C].
Whiteley, Joanna L. (29 yrs.) d. on 66-Aug-20 [66-Aug-21: 2C].
Whiteley, Mary E. m. Baker, Charles E. on 67-Feb-5 [67-Feb-14: 2C].
Whitelock, Eliza Anna (57 yrs., 1 mo.) d. on 67-Mar-14 [67-Mar-16: 2B].
Whitelock, George W. d. on 68-Nov-1 [68-Nov-2: 2B].
Whitemore, J. F. m. Hurley, Fannie H. on 69-Aug-23 [69-Nov-4: 2B].
Whitenack, Carrie V. m. Colburn, W. H. H. on 66-Feb-21 [66-Feb-26: 2B].
Whiteside, A. S. m. Bevier, Katie E. on 66-Aug-22 [66-Sep-1: 2B].
Whiteside, Francis Marion (24 yrs.) d. on 69-Nov-29 [69-Dec-3: 2C].
Whiteside, Issac R. (17 yrs.) d. on 69-Apr-4 [69-Apr-5: 2B].
Whiteside, Mary A. (61 yrs.) d. on 69-Nov-24 [69-Dec-3: 2C].
Whiteside, Samuel m. Crist, Sarah Ella on 67-Dec-17 [67-Dec-27: 2D].
Whitfield, Alexander m. Bailey, Charlotte on 69-Jan-14 [69-Jan-15: 2D].
Whiting, A. Lawrence m. Glanville, Ida M. on 66-May-24 [66-Jun-6: 2B].
Whiting, Ferdinand S. (21 yrs.) d. on 69-Sep-23 [69-Sep-25: 2B].
Whiting, Indiana m. Godwin, Thomas W. on 67-Dec-11 [67-Dec-14: 2B].
Whiting, James A. m. Middleton, Alice S. on 68-Feb-6 [68-Feb-10: 2C].
Whiting, Kate L. m. Gorsuch, John H. on 68-Sep-10 [68-Sep-15: 2B].
Whiting, Mary m. Shaw, Benjamin on 69-Oct-26 [69-Oct-28: 2C].
Whiting, Parmelia Isabella (5 yrs.) d. on 66-Feb-20 [66-Feb-21: 2D].
Whiting, Stephen R. m. Brashears, Laura R. on 68-Jul-2 [68-Jul-7: 2B].
Whiting, William H. m. Schuman, Burwell E. on 68-Nov-5 [68-Nov-9: 2B].
Whitley, Caroline S. (59 yrs.) d. on 69-Mar-18 [69-Mar-20: 2B].
Whitley, Joseph m. Bromwell, Marian on 67-Jul-17 [67-Jul-22: 2C].
Whitley, Julia Ann (70 yrs.) d. on 69-Dec-10 [69-Dec-11: 2B].
Whitley, Marian (18 yrs.) d. [68-Feb-10: 2C].
Whitley, Roseann d. on 69-Aug-12 [69-Aug-14: 2C].
Whitlock, Barbara S. m. Feldhaus, A. J. on 68-Apr-9 [68-Apr-11: 2A].
Whitlock, George m. Riggle, Emily on 68-Aug-16 [68-Aug-19: 2B].
Whitlock, Mary A. m. Dudley, Frederick M. on 67-May-14 [67-May-18: 2A].
Whitman, C. W. m. Waters, C. Amanda on 69-Apr-4 [69-Apr-8: 2C].
Whitman, H. Victorine m. Dorsey, Theodore C on 68-Apr-15 [68-Apr-17: 2B].
Whitman, Louis M. (26 yrs.) d. on 67-Mar-29 [67-Mar-30: 2C; 67-Apr-25: 2B].
Whitman, Malinda F. m. Pretzman, William W. on 68-Nov-11 [68-Nov-25: 2B].
Whitmarsh, Ella m. Rosenbaum, Charles on 69-Jan-17 [69-Jan-22: 2D].
Whitmarsh, Henry C. m. Leggett, Carrie H. on 66-Apr-16 [66-Apr-18: 2B].
Whitney, Alden Weston (17 yrs.) d. on 69-Nov-3 [69-Nov-4: 2C].
Whitney, Annie Bell (8 mos.) d. on 69-Feb-10 [69-Feb-18: 2C].
Whitney, Daniel m. Lowry, Annie on 66-Sep-13 [66-Sep-14: 2B].
Whitney, Emma (2 yrs., 2 mos.) d. on 67-Nov-28 [67-Dec-2: 2C].
Whitney, Georgie A. m. O'Neill, John on 66-Nov-29 [66-Dec-1: 2B].
Whitney, Lydia (68 yrs.) d. on 66-Nov-11 [66-Nov-12: 2C].
Whitney, Maria Louisa m. Stokes, Bradley T. on 69-Oct-21 [69-Oct-25: 2B].
Whitney, Sarah R. m. Roberts, John H. L. on 69-Oct-19 [70-Jan-10: 2C].
Whitney, Thomas B. (6 yrs., 7 mos.) d. on 66-Oct-23 [66-Oct-25: 2C].
Whitney, Walter Shepley (4 mos.) d. on 67-Apr-2 [67-Apr-4: 2B].
Whitridge, Alice D. m. Garrett, T. Harrison on 70-Feb-15 [70-Feb-18: 2C].
Whitridge, Alice Lee m. Thomas, Douglas H. on 70-Jan-25 [70-Jan-27: 2C; 70-Jan-29: 2B].
Whitridge, Henrietta Austin d. on 66-Apr-6 [66-Apr-7: 2B].
Whittaker, Ann Maria d. on 67-Mar-11 [67-Mar-13: 2C].
Whittaker, Avarilla P. m. Temple, William J. on 68-Dec-1 [68-Dec-16: 2C].
Whittaker, Avrilla B. m. Galloway, Absalom on 66-Sep-20 [66-Oct-2: 2B].
Whittaker, George (45 yrs.) d. on 70-Oct-19 of Intemperance and exposure [70-Oct-21: 4D].

Whittaker, Louis d. on 67-Feb-9 Drowned [67-Feb-12: 4C].
Whittelsey, E. J. m. Dunn, Katie P. on 70-Nov-22 [70-Dec-6: 2C].
Whittemore, Fleetwood Francis (1 yr., 2 mos.) d. on 69-Aug-14 [69-Aug-16: 2C].
Whittemore, John S. (46 yrs.) d. on 68-Mar-11 of Suicide (Shooting) [68-Mar-12: 1F; 68-Mar-14: 2B].
Whittemore, Lorman (40 yrs.) d. on 69-Apr-28 [69-Apr-29: 2B].
Whitten, Laura J. m. Higgins, James H. on 66-Apr-19 [66-Apr-29: 2B].
Whitten, Lizzie F. m. France, Henry on 68-Sep-6 [68-Oct-10: 2B].
Whittingham, Eliza d. on 67-May-23 [67-May-28: 2B].
Whittington, A. E. m. Nicholls, E. on 66-Aug-18 [66-Aug-21: 2C].
Whittington, Annie Graham (7 yrs., 7 mos.) d. on 67-Apr-13 [67-Apr-16: 2B].
Whittington, Eveline m. Lee, Henry A. on 68-Oct-6 [68-Oct-28: 2B].
Whittington, Fannie W. (26 yrs.) d. on 67-Apr-9 [67-Apr-12: 2C].
Whittington, Laura Y. m. Bucey, William H. on 66-Mar-21 [66-Mar-22: 2B].
Whittington, Mary Ann d. on 68-Apr-15 [68-Apr-17: 2B].
Whittington, Rosa D. d. on 70-Jan-20 [70-Jan-22: 2C].
Whittington, Samuel H. (64 yrs.) d. on 66-Dec-4 [66-Dec-6: 2B].
Whittington, Virginia M. m. Brown, Henry on 66-Jun-21 [66-Jun-22: 2B].
Whittle, Charles Bernardin (4 yrs., 3 mos.) d. on 69-Nov-30 [69-Dec-2: 2C].
Whittle, Honora (83 yrs.) d. on 70-Jun-21 [70-Jun-22: 2C].
Whittle, Mary Monica (1 mo.) d. on 69-Dec-3 [69-Dec-4: 2C].
Whittlesey, William E. m. Loane, Mary E. on 68-Nov-3 [68-Nov-10: 2C].
Whitworth, Charles, Sr. (65 yrs.) d. on 70-May-21 [70-May-23: 2C].
Whitworth, Isabella m. Young, William H. on 69-Dec-28 [69-Dec-31: 2C].
Wholey, William A. D. (22 yrs.) d. on 66-Oct-26 of Consumption [66-Oct-27: 2B].
Whorton, Amanda M. m. Smith, John F. on 66-Feb-19 [66-Feb-24: 2B].
Whorton, Charles E. (23 yrs.) d. on 70-Oct-27 [70-Oct-29: 2B].
Wiber, Emma Elseworth (7 yrs.) d. on 67-Dec-5 [67-Dec-7: 2B].
Wible, George Henry (32 yrs.) d. on 67-Sep-18 [67-Sep-20: 2A].
Wickens, Mary A. (74 yrs.) d. on 69-Jun-17 [69-Jun-19: 2B].
Wickers, Hampton R. (26 yrs.) d. on 68-Oct-4 [68-Oct-10: 2B].
Wickersham, Susan (75 yrs.) d. on 68-Mar-1 [68-Mar-2: 2B].
Wickert, Margaret J. m. Stansbury, Calvin on 68-Apr-30 [68-May-2: 2C].
Wickes, Sarah V. m. Ringgold, C. F. on 68-Jan-22 [68-Jan-29: 2C].
Wickesser, John (57 yrs.) d. on 67-Aug-3 [67-Aug-7: 2C].
Wickham, John Francis (12 yrs., 7 mos.) d. on 66-Feb-14 [66-Feb-15: 2C].
Wicklein, Charles (57 yrs., 11 mos.) d. on 68-Feb-29 [68-Mar-2: 2C].
Wickliffe, Andrew J. m. Dukehart, Parthenia E. on 69-Oct-21 [69-Oct-23: 2B; 69-Oct-25: 2B].
Wicks, Emma Eugenia (3 yrs., 7 mos.) d. on 69-Jan-22 [69-Jan-29: 2C].
Widerman, Jesse H. (20 yrs., 7 mos.) d. on 67-Jan-1 [67-Jan-2: 2C; 67-Jan-8: 2C].
Wiedfeld, Rebecca E. m. Rosensteel, Ambrose A. on 66-Jun-7 [66-Jun-14: 2B].
Wiegant, John (45 yrs.) d. on 68-Jul-16 of Heatstroke [68-Jul-18: 2B, 1E].
Wiegel, Julia E. m. Swindell, George E. on 70-Jan-13 [70-Jan-17: 2C].
Wieghorst, Elizabeth m. Schwarz, John V. on 66-Jul-10 [66-Jul-13: 2C].
Wieman, Leopold m. Jurgens, Maggie on 70-Apr-26 [70-Apr-28: 2B].
Wiener, Clara (11 yrs., 6 mos.) d. on 69-Oct-1 [69-Oct-2: 2B].
Wier, Florence m. McManus, Frederick A. on 68-Oct-1 [68-Oct-3: 2B].
Wier, Jane E. S. d. on 66-Feb-19 [66-Feb-23: 2C].
Wiesenfeld, Rebecca m. Altmeyer, Abraham on 68-Apr-22 [68-Apr-24: 2B].
Wiesman, William V. m. Holler, Mary on 68-May-12 [68-May-21: 2B].
Wiest, Susanna (83 yrs.) d. on 69-Aug-20 [69-Aug-21: 2B].
Wigart, Henry Bascomb (46 yrs.) d. on 70-Feb-27 of Heart disease [70-Mar-1: 2C].
Wiggin, Reuben Hill (51 yrs.) d. on 66-Dec-8 [66-Dec-10: 2C].
Wiggins, Amanda C. m. Ledley, John C. on 69-Aug-30 [69-Sep-1: 2B].

Wiggins, Lester T. m. De Vere, Sallie M. on 68-Nov-19 [68-Nov-23: 2B].
Wiggins, Mary E. m. Denny, James E. on 70-Dec-14 [70-Dec-23: 2B].
Wiggins, Nannie M. m. Fitch, Edward M. on 66-Oct-15 [66-Oct-18: 2B].
Wigginton, Ellen V.J> (30 yrs., 2 mos.) d. on 67-May-16 of Consumption [67-May-17: 2B].
Wigginton, W. Henry m. Barnes, Carrie E. on 68-Oct-8 [68-Oct-13: 2C].
Wight, John H. (36 yrs.) d. on 69-Aug-10 [69-Aug-11: 2C; 69-Aug-12: 2C].
Wight, William J. (83 yrs.) d. on 67-Feb-27 [67-Mar-1: 2C].
Wightman, Fannie d. on 69-Apr-27 of Consumption [69-Apr-29: 2B].
Wightman, George A. m. Stites, M. Alice on 70-Dec-22 [70-Dec-29: 2C].
Wiker, Annie B.T. m. Carlisle, Nicholas on 67-May-30 [67-May-31: 2B].
Wilber, E. Douglas (30 yrs.) d. on 70-Mar-28 of Typhoid pneumonia [70-Apr-2: 2B].
Wilbur, Asa C. (9 mos.) d. on 68-Dec-16 [68-Dec-18: 2C].
Wilbur, Joseph T. m. Thomas, Ada on 68-Dec-1 [68-Dec-5: 2C].
Wilbur, Mary A.P. m. Arnold, John on 67-Mar-5 [67-Mar-8: 2C].
Wilbur, Mary E. m. Wilderman, Francis M. on 66-Nov-8 [66-Nov-14: 2B].
Wilcox, Andrew J. (36 yrs.) d. on 70-Nov-15 [70-Nov-16: 2C; 70-Nov-17: 2C].
Wilcox, E. B. m. Hopkins, Mary L. on 69-Sep-7 [69-Sep-9: 2B].
Wilcox, Elizabeth Gertrude (9 mos.) d. on 70-Jul-17 [70-Jul-18: 2B].
Wilcox, Thomas S. (27 yrs.) d. on 70-May-21 of Consumption [70-May-23: 2C].
Wild, Frederick W. m. Fehleisen, Bertha M. on 69-Nov-25 [69-Nov-29: 2C; 69-Dec-1: 2C].
Wild, Henry C. m. Herring, Sarah E. on 67-Mar-14 [67-Mar-15: 2C].
Wild, Mary C. Roth (19 yrs., 2 mos.) d. on 66-Mar-3 [66-Mar-5: 2B].
Wilde, Augustin A. m. Bilson, Virginia M. on 68-Dec-22 [69-Jan-11: 2C].
Wilderman, Ellie A. m. Hook, John A. on 65-Dec-14 [66-Jan-24: 2B].
Wilderman, Francis LeRoy (2 mos.) d. on 69-Apr-14 [69-Apr-16: 2B].
Wilderman, Francis M. m. Wilbur, Mary E. on 66-Nov-8 [66-Nov-14: 2B].
Wilderman, George C. (4 mos.) d. on 68-Feb-10 [68-Feb-12: 2C].
Wilderman, John T. m. Bishop, Elvira on 69-Oct-4 [69-Oct-16: 2B].
Wilderman, Mary Blanch (2 mos.) d. on 70-Jun-11 [70-Jun-13: 2C].
Wildey, Augustus (31 yrs.) d. on 66-Mar-13 [66-Mar-14: 2C].
Wildey, Augustus (7 yrs., 5 mos.) d. on 69-Feb-12 [69-Feb-17: 2D].
Wildy, Agnes m. Kinnear, John W. on 68-Apr-22 [68-Apr-25: 2B].
Wile, Charles Lee (10 mos.) d. on 68-Oct-26 [68-Oct-29: 2C].
Wiles, James A. m. Markland, Allie on 66-Dec-11 [67-Jun-3: 2B].
Wiles, James A. m. Wood, Mary E. on 70-Sep-13 [70-Sep-16: 2B].
Wiley, Ann Amelia (86 yrs.) d. on 69-Feb-9 [69-Feb-10: 2C; 69-Feb-11: 2C].
Wiley, Edward P. m. Helsby, Sue on 69-Oct-21 [69-Oct-28: 2C].
Wiley, Eliza Jane m. Talbott, George H. on 69-Oct-6 [69-Nov-1: 2B].
Wiley, M. Josephine d. on 70-Sep-23 [70-Sep-24: 2B].
Wiley, William (46 yrs.) d. on 66-Dec-17 [66-Dec-19: 2B].
Wiley, William J. (22 yrs.) d. on 69-Dec-6 [70-Jan-1: 2B; 70-Jan-3: 1H].
Wilfing, Christopher Henry (68 yrs.) d. on 67-Apr-26 Drowned [67-Aug-29: 2B].
Wilhelm, David Hammond (9 yrs., 4 mos.) d. on 66-Oct-16 [66-Oct-25: 2C].
Wilhelm, George W. R. m. Chandler, Mary E. on 66-Mar-22 [66-Apr-27: 2C].
Wilhelm, H. m. Dorsey, Chloe on 68-Mar-12 [68-Mar-14: 2B].
Wilhelm, James T. m. Dorsey, Julia on 69-Nov-25 [69-Nov-29: 2C].
Wilhelm, Samuel, Jr. d. on 66-Sep-10 [66-Sep-11: 2B].
Wilkens, Auguste F. (5 yrs.) d. on 67-Apr-12 [67-Apr-13: 2B].
Wilkens, Elizabeth O. m. Reed, Benjamin F. on 70-Apr-19 [70-Apr-21: 2B].
Wilkerson, Jennie F. m. Warfield, Charles A. on 67-Feb-5 [67-Feb-18: 2C].
Wilkes, Edward (73 yrs.) d. on 67-Jan-20 [67-Jan-23: 2C].
Wilkes, J. m. Morehead, Martha E. on 67-Aug-1 [67-Aug-31: 2B].
Wilkins, Belmont (10 mos.) d. on 68-Sep-3 [68-Sep-4: 2A].
Wilkins, Charles W. (29 yrs.) d. on 70-Sep-23 [70-Oct-6: 2B].
Wilkins, E. M. m. Merrett, Mary A. on 66-May-8 [66-May-11: 2B].

Wilkins, Frances M. m. Sparklin, William F. on 69-Apr-1 [69-Apr-13: 2B].
Wilkins, James D. m. Paddon, Sarah C. on 66-Oct-25 [66-Oct-29: 2B].
Wilkins, James W. m. Coursey, E. R. on 68-Mar-26 [68-Mar-30: 2B].
Wilkins, John C. (27 yrs.) d. on 69-Nov-2 [69-Nov-3: 2C].
Wilkins, Mary A. m. MacNeal, P. Douglas on 70-Oct-20 [70-Oct-24: 2B].
Wilkins, Mathew Jane m. Robinson, W. T. on 68-Apr-16 [68-Apr-24: 2B].
Wilkins, Richard G. (42 yrs.) d. on 66-Sep-30 [66-Oct-1: 2B].
Wilkins, William A. m. Leavitt, Victoria C. on 66-Mar-21 [66-Mar-28: 2C].
Wilkins, William J. m. Raymond, Lucy E.E. on 67-Dec-24 [67-Dec-27: 2D].
Wilkinson, Anna Catherine d. on 67-Jan-13 [67-Jan-14: 2C].
Wilkinson, Charlotte A. (31 yrs.) d. on 68-Mar-24 [68-Mar-25: 2A; 68-Mar-26: 2B].
Wilkinson, Edmond Gould (2 yrs., 1 mo.) d. on 70-Sep-2 [70-Sep-6: 2B].
Wilkinson, Elenora (5 mos.) d. on 67-Nov-18 [67-Nov-19: 2C].
Wilkinson, Eliza (29 yrs.) d. on 66-Oct-12 [66-Oct-13: 2B].
Wilkinson, George W. (35 yrs.) d. on 70-Jul-20 of Heatstroke [70-Jul-21: 1F, 2C].
Wilkinson, Ida Lavinia (4 mos.) d. on 66-Jun-19 [66-Jun-20: 2C].
Wilkinson, James m. Cummings, Martha A. on 66-Mar-14 [66-Mar-20: 2C].
Wilkinson, John V. (39 yrs.) d. on 69-Apr-4 [69-Apr-5: 2B].
Wilkinson, John Victor (7 mos.) d. on 68-Jul-17 [68-Jul-18: 2B].
Wilkinson, John W.B. m. Clark, Emma on 67-Feb-18 [67-May-30: 2B].
Wilkinson, Julia C. (53 yrs.) d. on 67-Nov-10 [67-Nov-13: 2C].
Wilkinson, Lillian (1 yr., 8 mos.) d. on 70-Jul-8 [70-Jul-12: 2C].
Wilkinson, Maria (63 yrs.) d. on 68-Oct-26 [68-Oct-28: 2B].
Wilkinson, Mary E. (68 yrs.) d. on 68-Feb-12 of Consumption [68-Feb-14: 2C].
Wilkinson, Rebecca Elizabeth (55 yrs.) d. on 66-Nov-16 [66-Nov-16: 2C; 66-Nov-17: 2B].
Wilkinson, Samuel (74 yrs.) d. on 68-Aug-5 [68-Aug-7: 2B].
Wilkinson, Stephen A. m. Frayser, Mary T. on 66-Dec-12 [67-Jan-1: 2C].
Wilkinson, Thomas (78 yrs.) d. on 66-Mar-10 [66-Mar-12: 2B].
Wilkinson, Thomas C. m. Bonn, Emma V. [70-Jun-4: 2B].
Wilkinson, W. H. B. m. Smith, Annie R. on 66-Dec-18 [66-Dec-28: 2C].
Wilkinson, William J. G. m. Dorrett, Susan E. on 68-May-27 [68-May-29: 2B].
Will, Andrew m. Ackland, Mary C. on 66-Sep-13 [66-Sep-15: 2B].
Willard, August (27 yrs., 3 mos.) d. on 70-Mar-23 [70-Mar-25: 2C].
Willard, Emma (83 yrs.) d. on 70-Apr-15 [70-Apr-16: 2B].
Willcox, Edward J. m. Pochon, Sophie on 68-Aug-18 [68-Aug-19: 2B].
Willen, Samuel J. m. Seymour, Nora V. on 66-Nov-5 [66-Nov-6: 2B].
Willett, Drusilla m. Sinclair, Arthur on 67-Sep-3 [67-Sep-5: 2B].
Willey, Marcellus m. North, Mary A. on 70-Dec-27 [70-Dec-29: 2C].
Willey, Mollie E. m. Bancroft, John D. on 68-Jul-14 [68-Jul-16: 2C].
Williams, Alice V. m. Frankland, W. E. on 66-Dec-20 [66-Dec-24: 2B].
Williams, Allison D. d. on 70-Mar-28 [70-Mar-30: 2C; 70-Mar-31: 2C].
Williams, Amelia (73 yrs.) d. on 68-Mar-26 [68-Mar-28: 2B].
Williams, Amelia (101 yrs.) d. on 70-Sep-2 [70-Sep-3: 2B].
Williams, Anna M. m. Yingling, Samuel B. on 69-Nov-16 [69-Nov-17: 2C].
Williams, Annie L. m. Thomas, Luther on 69-Sep-2 [69-Sep-4: 2B].
Williams, Asberry m. Bias, Martha A. on 66-Jun-7 [66-Jun-20: 2C].
Williams, Augustus A. m. Kugler, Octavia A. on 67-Apr-13 [67-Apr-15: 2B].
Williams, Austin Edward (3 yrs., 4 mos.) d. on 66-Feb-5 of Scarlet fever [66-Feb-7: 2C].
Williams, Benjamin (89 yrs.) d. on 67-Apr-4 [67-Apr-5: 1G, 2B].
Williams, Caroline (46 yrs.) d. on 67-Mar-27 [67-Mar-29: 2B].
Williams, Catherine m. Driver, Silas on 69-Sep-30 [69-Oct-2: 2B].
Williams, Cecilia Alberta d. on 70-Jan-1 [70-Jan-3: 2C].
Williams, Charles C. m. White, Sarah L. on 68-Oct-13 [68-Oct-26: 2B].
Williams, Charles Edward (2 yrs., 6 mos.) d. on 69-Jul-4 [69-Jul-5: 2C].
Williams, Charlotte m. Ramsey, Mortimer on 70-Jan-11 [70-May-2: 2B].

Williams, Clara V. m. Woodall, Noble G. W. on 69-Feb-28 [69-Mar-11: 2C].
Williams, Cordelia Carey m. Murray, Herron C. on 68-Oct-26 [68-Nov-24: 2C].
Williams, Dalrymple m. Jacobsen, Emma on 68-Apr-28 [68-Apr-30: 2B].
Williams, Daniel m. Crawford, Martha A. on 67-Jun-6 [67-Jun-10: 2B].
Williams, David (48 yrs.) d. on 67-Feb-8 [67-Feb-9: 2B].
Williams, David E. m. Guy, Alice R. on 67-Jan-29 [67-Feb-11: 2C].
Williams, Denard S. m. Hush, Ida M. on 69-Apr-29 [69-May-3: 2C].
Williams, Edward F. (52 yrs.) d. on 69-Oct-6 [69-Oct-8: 2B].
Williams, Eleanor d. on 70-Sep-27 [70-Sep-28: 2B; 70-Sep-29: 2B].
Williams, Elenora Teresa m. Hanson, Washington R. on 70-May-10 [70-May-25: 2C].
Williams, Eliza m. Boston, Shoff on 70-Jun-28 [70-Jul-9: 2B].
Williams, Elizabeth d. on 68-Feb-28 [68-Apr-3: 2C].
Williams, Elizabeth F. m. Glenn, John H. on 70-Jul-14 [70-Jul-23: 2B].
Williams, Ellanora m. Sheeler, George W. on 67-Oct-15 [67-Oct-17: 2B].
Williams, Ellen Elizabeth m. Dumont, Frank on 66-Feb-15 [66-Feb-24: 2B].
Williams, Ellie m. Stire, Carson on 70-Jan-10 [70-Jan-14: 2C].
Williams, Emma J. d. on 70-Jun-9 [70-Jun-10: 2B].
Williams, Emma R. m. Miles, Abram S. on 69-Apr-22 [69-Apr-26: 2B].
Williams, Fannie E. m. Tyson, James E. on 67-Jun-12 [67-Jun-14: 2B].
Williams, Fannie E. m. Heath, J. B. on 69-May-28 [69-May-29: 2B].
Williams, Francis (47 yrs.) d. on 69-Apr-17 [69-Apr-20: 2B].
Williams, Francis m. Broud, Kate F. on 66-Apr-5 [66-Apr-7: 2B].
Williams, Francis J. (1 yr., 4 mos.) d. on 70-Dec-18 [70-Dec-20: 2B].
Williams, Frank (1 yr., 10 mos.) d. on 70-Apr-23 [70-Apr-26: 2B].
Williams, George d. on 69-Jan-28 of Gunshot wound [69-Jan-29: 1G].
Williams, George W. m. Smithson, Laura A. on 68-Nov-11 [68-Nov-28: 2C].
Williams, Georgeanna m. Green, Samuel on 70-Jan-16 [70-Jan-20: 2C].
Williams, H. B. m. King, Mollie E. on 70-Dec-15 [70-Dec-20: 2B].
Williams, Hannah A. m. Coates, Robert E. on 68-Mar-1 [68-Mar-7: 2B].
Williams, Henry (65 yrs.) d. on 69-Nov-24 [69-Nov-25: 2C].
Williams, Hugh Huntington m. Evans, Mary on 67-Nov-26 [67-Nov-30: 2C].
Williams, J. J. m. Estep, Mary M. on 70-Aug-18 [70-Aug-23: 2B].
Williams, Jacob d. on 70-Dec-4 Murdered (Shooting) [70-Dec-5: 4E].
Williams, James Brooke (7 mos.) d. on 69-Mar-13 [69-Apr-2: 2C].
Williams, James E. A. (43 yrs.) d. on 69-Nov-5 [69-Nov-8: 2C].
Williams, James Henry (1 yr., 2 mos.) d. on 68-Aug-12 [68-Aug-14: 2C].
Williams, James W. (23 yrs.) d. on 69-Dec-3 [69-Dec-4: 2C].
Williams, James Wright (32 yrs.) d. on 70-Mar-30 of Fall from horse [70-Apr-5: 2B].
Williams, John (8 mos.) d. on 66-Nov-26 [66-Nov-29: 2C].
Williams, John m. League, Ella on 70-Jul-5 [70-Jul-7: 2B].
Williams, John H. (46 yrs.) d. on 66-May-31 [66-Jun-1: 2B].
Williams, John H. (25 yrs.) d. on 70-May-21 Drowned [70-May-25: 1H].
Williams, John H. m. Thomas, Lavinia Wm. H. on 70-May-10 [70-May-14: 2A].
Williams, John L. m. Mitchell, Amanda on 68-Jan-21 [68-Jan-25: 2B].
Williams, John Q. m. Rogers, Carrie B. on 66-Sep-20 [66-Sep-22: 2B].
Williams, John R. m. Crawford, Mary F. on 70-Nov-7 [70-Dec-16: 2C].
Williams, John S. m. Winchester, Sarah on 67-Dec-10 [67-Dec-16: 2B].
Williams, John W. m. Williams, S. E. on 66-Feb-6 [66-Feb-22: 2B].
Williams, Julia (1 yr., 9 mos.) d. on 68-Sep-2 [68-Sep-5: 2A].
Williams, Julia (46 yrs.) d. on 70-Oct-16 of Consumption [70-Oct-17: 2B].
Williams, Juliet D. (28 yrs., 9 mos.) d. on 69-Mar-6 [69-Apr-2: 2C].
Williams, Kate m. Thompson, John D. on 70-Apr-21 [70-Apr-23: 2B].
Williams, Kate C. m. Swearer, Benjamin on 68-Jun-2 [68-Jun-3: 2B].
Williams, Kate E. m. Walker, William J. on 69-May-3 [69-May-6: 2B].
Williams, Laura m. Du Barry, Edmund on 68-Nov-12 [68-Nov-14: 2B].

Williams, Lawrence P. (82 yrs.) d. on 68-Jul-17 of Heatstroke [68-Jul-18: 2B, 1E].
Williams, Lena m. Baxley, Claude on 67-Sep-5 [67-Sep-11: 2B].
Williams, Levi m. Hirshback, Mary E. on 68-Aug-24 [68-Sep-7: 2A].
Williams, Levi m. Campbell, Mary E. on 67-Sep-12 [67-Sep-27: 2B].
Williams, Lewis H. (64 yrs.) d. on 66-Jun-17 [66-Jun-19: 2B].
Williams, Littleton (46 yrs.) d. on 66-Sep-27 [66-Sep-28: 2B].
Williams, Lydia C. m. Grumble, John C. on 67-Jun-20 [67-Jul-4: 2B].
Williams, Lydia R. (33 yrs.) d. on 70-Aug-15 [70-Aug-16: 2C].
Williams, Margaret Gordon m. Robinson, George Law on 69-Nov-16 [69-Nov-17: 2C].
Williams, Margaret Jane (1 yr., 9 mos.) d. on 68-Aug-16 [68-Aug-17: 2B].
Williams, Maria m. Snavely, Joseph F. on 68-Nov-12 [68-Nov-14: 2B].
Williams, Maria Dalrymple d. on 68-Sep-19 [68-Sep-21: 2B].
Williams, Marie Cecile (1 yr., 5 mos.) d. on 67-May-11 [67-May-13: 2B].
Williams, Mary d. on 68-Nov-8 [68-Nov-13: 2C].
Williams, Mary (91 yrs.) d. on 67-Jul-29 [67-Jul-30: 2C].
Williams, Mary (50 yrs.) d. [69-Feb-1: 2C].
Williams, Mary m. Hartman, John on 66-Feb-19 [66-Feb-20: 2B].
Williams, Mary m. Upson, Edward S. on 69-Nov-9 [69-Nov-11: 2C].
Williams, Mary A. d. on 67-Mar-11 [67-Mar-12: 2C; 67-Mar-13: 2C].
Williams, Mary A. m. Foster, H. D. on 68-Sep-20 [68-Oct-17: 2B].
Williams, Mary A. m. Woolford, Thomas William on 67-Sep-10 [68-Jun-3: 2B].
Williams, Mary A. m. Klett, R. A. on 66-Jul-3 [66-Jul-18: 2C].
Williams, Mary A. m. Snyder, Azariah H. on 70-Feb-8 [70-Feb-12: 2C].
Williams, Mary C. m. Cameron, John W. on 68-Jun-25 [68-Jun-29: 2B].
Williams, Mary E. m. Cox, Abraham on 70-Mar-22 [70-Mar-26: 2B].
Williams, Mary Eliza J. (25 yrs., 8 mos.) d. on 66-Sep-7 [66-Sep-8: 2B].
Williams, Mary Elizabeth (21 yrs.) d. on 69-Jan-4 [69-Jan-6: 2C].
Williams, Mary Ida Rowe (2 yrs., 10 mos.) d. on 68-Nov-21 [68-Nov-24: 2C].
Williams, Mary S. m. Magee, Samuel C. on 67-Jul-8 [67-Jul-10: 2B].
Williams, Millie V. (33 yrs.) d. on 70-Sep-22 [70-Sep-24: 2B].
Williams, Minerva m. McCleary, Moses Wesley on 69-Feb-25 [69-Mar-3: 2B].
Williams, Mollie m. Pierce, William H. on 68-Jan-15 [68-Jan-16: 2C].
Williams, Nora (20 yrs.) d. on 68-Nov-5 [68-Nov-6: 2C].
Williams, Octavia m. Elder, P. Laurensson on 69-Jan-28 [69-Feb-2: 2C].
Williams, Philip (67 yrs.) d. on 68-Apr-2 [68-Apr-4: 2B].
Williams, Priscilla Caroline (64 yrs.) d. on 70-Jun-13 [70-Jun-14: 2B].
Williams, Robert A. m. Fields, Susan A. on 70-Jul-14 [70-Jul-19: 2B].
Williams, S. E. m. Williams, John W. on 66-Feb-6 [66-Feb-22: 2B].
Williams, Samuel d. on 66-Oct-13 of Cholera [66-Oct-15: 4C].
Williams, Samuel Winchester (1 yr., 3 mos.) d. on 70-Feb-18 [70-Feb-21: 2C].
Williams, Sarah d. on 67-Aug-21 [67-Aug-22: 2C].
Williams, Sarah (82 yrs.) d. on 66-Sep-29 [66-Oct-1: 2B].
Williams, Sarah (53 yrs.) d. on 66-Sep-15 [66-Sep-19: 2B].
Williams, Sarah m. Emmet, Jacob on 67-Jan-28 [67-Feb-8: 2C].
Williams, Sarah A. m. Peppercorn, Francis F. on 67-Nov-1 [67-Nov-4: 2B].
Williams, Sarah B. (58 yrs.) d. on 67-Mar-18 [67-Mar-21: 2C].
Williams, Sarah C. d. on 70-Jun-17 [70-Jun-18: 2B; 70-Jun-20: 1G].
Williams, Sarah Ellen (17 yrs., 8 mos.) d. on 68-Aug-11 [68-Aug-12: 2C].
Williams, Savilla A. m. Fuller, Thomas J. on 66-Dec-13 [66-Dec-17: 2B].
Williams, Stephen, Rev. (84 yrs.) d. on 66-Dec-15 [66-Dec-17: 1G, 2B].
Williams, Thomas (78 yrs.) d. on 68-Apr-4 [68-Apr-6: 2B].
Williams, Thomas B. m. Elliott, Julia A. on 66-Mar-6 [66-Mar-10: 2B].
Williams, Thomas N. (26 yrs.) d. on 68-Dec-31 [69-Jan-1: 2C].
Williams, Thomas W. m. La Porte, Clara E. on 69-Apr-1 [69-Apr-2: 2C; 69-Apr-3: 2B].
Williams, Thomas Whitridge (8 mos.) d. on 68-Sep-19 [68-Sep-22: 2B].

Williams, Washington (25 yrs.) d. on 70-Dec-26 Drowned [70-Dec-28: 4E].
Williams, William (47 yrs.) d. on 68-Sep-9 of Heart disease and dropsy [68-Sep-10: 4B; 68-Sep-12: 2B; 68-Sep-14: 1G].
Williams, William (70 yrs.) d. on 68-Aug-8 [68-Aug-12: 2C].
Williams, William, Rev. (70 yrs.) d. on 69-May-13 [69-May-14: 2C; 69-May-17: 1H].
Williams, William (61 yrs.) d. on 69-Mar-12 [69-Mar-13: 2C].
Williams, William m. Larmour, Margaret A. on 69-Nov-30 [69-Dec-14: 2C].
Williams, William A (28 yrs.) d. on 67-Dec-26 [67-Dec-28: 2C].
Williams, William G. m. Linthicum, Matilda D. on 69-Sep-21 [69-Oct-15: 2C].
Williams, William H. (44 yrs.) d. on 66-Jun-6 [66-Jun-13: 2B].
Williams, William H. m. Lynch, Lizzie on 70-Jul-28 [70-Dec-16: 2C].
Williams, William J., Dr. (58 yrs.) d. on 67-Apr-19 of Apoplexy [67-Apr-20: 1F, 2A].
Williams, Zeddie F. m. Tatham, Sue E. on 66-Apr-11 [66-Apr-17: 2C].
Williamson, Agnes m. Beveridge, Robert on 70-Apr-5 [70-Apr-9: 2B].
Williamson, Bessie M. m. Carr, W. Sanders on 69-Nov-4 [69-Nov-9: 2C].
Williamson, Edward m. Geoghegan, Henrietta on 67-Oct-16 [67-Oct-19: 2A].
Williamson, Emily J. m. Burgess, George R. on 70-Apr-28 [70-May-4: 2C].
Williamson, Emma Louise d. on 66-Sep-24 [66-Sep-25: 2B].
Williamson, Evelyn (5 yrs., 5 mos.) d. on 69-Jan-19 of Scarlet fever [69-Jan-22: 2D].
Williamson, George D. m. Love, Susan on 66-Apr-10 [66-Apr-14: 2B].
Williamson, Henry McIntosh d. on 70-Dec-6 [70-Dec-7: 2C].
Williamson, Henry Seymour (6 yrs., 9 mos.) d. on 66-Sep-26 [66-Sep-27: 2C].
Williamson, J. Pryor m. Woodward, Mary H. on 69-Oct-7 [69-Oct-13: 2C].
Williamson, James A. m. Ross, Eliza on 66-Jun-19 [66-Jun-20: 2C].
Williamson, John B. m. Freshour, Mary C. on 67-May-14 [67-May-27: 2B].
Williamson, L. T. m. Hanitramck, Eliza on 69-Jan-20 [69-Jan-25: 2D].
Williamson, Lavinia, Mrs. m. Pugsley, John H. on 67-Mar-28 [67-Mar-30: 2B].
Williamson, Samuel (45 yrs.) d. on 68-Jul-7 [68-Jul-9: 2B].
Williamson, Walter Alexander B (2 yrs., 4 mos.) d. on 69-Feb-16 [69-Feb-19: 2C].
Williar, Harry D. m. Herring, Carrie E. on 69-Oct-19 [69-Oct-21: 2B].
Williar, Mary E. m. Baldwin, Silas on 68-Apr-28 [68-Apr-30: 2B].
Williar, Mary J. m. Hicks, Joseph on 69-Apr-13 [69-Apr-16: 2B].
Williard, Julius d. on 70-Jan-10 of Lung congestion [70-Jan-12: 1H].
Willick, Mary (75 yrs.) d. on 69-Feb-13 [69-Feb-23: 2D].
Willing, Eddy (9 yrs.) d. on 68-Jul-20 [68-Jul-21: 2C].
Willing, Susan (49 yrs.) d. on 69-Jan-14 of Consumption [69-Jan-16: 2C].
Willingham, Martha A. m. Francis, Charles on 68-Dec-17 [68-Dec-18: 2C].
Willis, Annie S. (44 yrs.) d. on 70-May-23 [70-May-24: 2C; 70-May-25: 2C].
Willis, Columbus C m. Rouse, Virginia F. on 67-Apr-16 [67-Apr-20: 2A].
Willis, Elizabeth m. DeMuth, G. O. on 67-Nov-21 [67-Nov-23: 2B].
Willis, Florence (17 yrs.) d. on 68-Nov-14 [68-Nov-18: 2C].
Willis, Francis H. (42 yrs.) d. on 66-Jun-9 [66-Jun-13: 2B].
Willis, James (35 yrs.) d. on 70-Jun-14 Murdered (Shooting) [70-Jun-15: 1G].
Willis, James m. Goslin, Martha W. on 69-Feb-25 [69-Feb-27: 2C].
Willis, John H. m. Jones, Lillie W. on 70-Apr-5 [70-Oct-11: 2B].
Willis, Lizzie m. Holden, G. W. on 66-Jun-7 [66-Jun-19: 2B].
Willis, Mary L. m. Reynolds, Luther M. on 67-Oct-26 [67-Oct-30: 2B].
Willis, Salisbury (61 yrs.) d. on 69-Dec-27 [69-Dec-28: 2D].
Willis, Virginia (36 yrs.) d. on 67-Dec-26 [67-Dec-27: 2D; 67-Dec-28: 2C].
Willis, W. M. m. Musseter, Harriet J. on 70-Oct-11 [70-Dec-2: 2C].
Willis, Wellie m. Evans, George on 66-Jan-25 [66-Jan-26: 2B].
Willis, Z. L. C. m. Forman, Virginia on 69-Nov-25 [69-Nov-29: 2C].
Willox, Ralph Henri m. Wilson, Sarah L. on 69-Apr-3 [69-Apr-9: 2B].
Wills, Doria Estella (4 mos.) d. on 66-Jun-21 [66-Jun-22: 2B].
Wills, Elizabeth J. m. Finch, George J. on 66-Jun-26 [66-Jun-29: 2C].

Wills, George W. (53 yrs.) d. on 70-Jan-23 [70-Jan-25: 2C].
Wills, Kate (23 yrs.) d. on 69-Apr-4 [69-Apr-5: 2B; 69-Apr-6: 2C].
Wills, Laura m. Wooden, William T. on 68-Sep-6 [68-Sep-22: 2B].
Wills, Mary C. m. Scarborough, James on 69-Oct-18 [69-Dec-28: 2C].
Wills, T. Buchanan (47 yrs.) d. on 68-Apr-9 [68-Apr-11: 2A].
Willson, Arthur (3 mos.) d. on 67-Mar-3 [67-Mar-5: 2C].
Willson, Fayetta H. (47 yrs.) d. on 68-Dec-21 [68-Dec-22: 2C].
Willson, Frank Howard (5 yrs., 9 mos.) d. on 70-Dec-24 [70-Dec-26: 2C].
Willson, James J. m. Money, Margaret J. on 69-May-12 [69-May-15: 2B].
Willson, Josephine (22 yrs.) d. on 70-Apr-25 [70-Apr-28: 2C].
Willson, Margaret m. Hughes, Alexander on 66-May-3 [66-May-30: 2C].
Willson, Mary L. m. Harrison, Phil. L. on 66-Jun-26 [66-Jun-28: 2C].
Wilmer, Ellen d. on 70-May-10 [70-May-11: 2B; 70-May-12: 2B].
Wilmer, Gideon L. m. McMullen, Maggie on 69-Oct-7 [69-Oct-15: 2C].
Wilmer, Mollie E. m. Watson, John W. on 66-Dec-20 [67-Jan-3: 2B].
Wilmer, William B (63 yrs.) d. on 67-Apr-26 [67-May-1: 2B].
Wilmer, William B. m. Kauffman, Helen S. on 70-May-5 [70-May-9: 2B].
Wilmer, William H. d. on 68-Jan-28 [68-Jan-31: 2C].
Wilmore, Fanny E. (19 yrs., 9 mos.) d. on 69-Jun-17 [69-Jun-19: 2B].
Wilmore, Hester m. Jackson, Harold on 68-Oct-1 [68-Oct-3: 2B].
Wilmot, Rebecca E. m. Froelich, John C. on 66-Sep-20 [66-Sep-28: 2B].
Wilson, Agnes (1 mo.) d. on 68-Sep-27 [68-Sep-28: 2B].
Wilson, Agnes B. (38 yrs.) d. on 70-Jun-12 [70-Jun-15: 2B].
Wilson, Alfred A. m. Sharp, Solacie on 69-Feb-7 [69-Feb-10: 2C].
Wilson, Amelia (55 yrs.) d. on 68-Aug-20 [68-Aug-22: 2A].
Wilson, Amos C. m. Waterworth, Elizabeth E. on 69-Mar-29 [69-May-27: 2C].
Wilson, Ann Maria (66 yrs., 2 mos.) d. on 69-Sep-26 [69-Sep-28: 2B].
Wilson, Anna A. m. Martin, John B. on 66-Nov-1 [66-Nov-3: 2B].
Wilson, Anna Belle (1 yr., 2 mos.) d. on 68-Apr-11 [68-Apr-14: 2A].
Wilson, Anna M. (43 yrs.) d. on 68-Feb-28 [68-Mar-3: 2C; 68-Mar-5: 2C].
Wilson, Annie (25 yrs.) d. on 68-Nov-15 [68-Nov-20: 2C].
Wilson, Annie (11 mos.) d. on 70-Aug-25 [70-Aug-27: 2B].
Wilson, Annie m. Clarke, John on 70-Mar-31 [70-May-12: 2B].
Wilson, Annie Estelle (6 mos.) d. on 70-Jul-15 [70-Jul-18: 2C].
Wilson, Annie M. (42 yrs.) d. on 70-May-29 [70-Jun-3: 2B].
Wilson, Annie M. m. Stuart, John B. on 66-Jan-4 [66-Jan-11: 2B].
Wilson, Benjamin, Col. (83 yrs.) d. on 70-Aug-24 [70-Aug-25: 2C].
Wilson, Benjamin m. Gough, Fanny on 67-Oct-17 [67-Oct-21: 2B].
Wilson, Biddy (67 yrs.) d. on 67-Dec-5 [67-Dec-6: 2C].
Wilson, Charles (49 yrs.) d. on 67-May-5 [67-May-7: 2B].
Wilson, Charles E. d. on 66-Oct-22 of Typhoid [66-Nov-10: 2B].
Wilson, Charlie (7 mos.) d. on 67-Jan-21 [67-Jan-22: 2C].
Wilson, Clara Bell (9 yrs., 7 mos.) d. on 68-Aug-15 of Dropsy [68-Aug-17: 2B].
Wilson, Comfort (40 yrs.) d. on 69-Jan-1 [69-Jan-5: 2C].
Wilson, David (57 yrs.) d. on 66-Jul-21 [66-Jul-23: 2C].
Wilson, Douglas J. d. on 69-Apr-20 [69-Apr-22: 2B].
Wilson, Ebeneezer (74 yrs.) d. on 68-Apr-10 [68-Apr-27: 2B].
Wilson, Eberilla (52 yrs.) d. on 68-Apr-8 [68-Apr-10: 2B].
Wilson, Edward H. C. (50 yrs.) d. on 70-Dec-2 [70-Dec-10: 2C].
Wilson, Edwin C. m. Hardesty, Mary E. on 67-Jul-22 [67-Jul-23: 2C].
Wilson, Eliza A. m. Stehl, Justus V. on 69-Oct-27 [69-Nov-1: 2B].
Wilson, Eliza C. (29 yrs.) d. on 68-Apr-6 [68-Apr-7: 2B; 68-Apr-8: 2B].
Wilson, Elizabeth (57 yrs.) d. on 68-Jan-22 [68-Jan-24: 2D; 68-Jan-25: 2B].
Wilson, Elizabeth (85 yrs.) d. on 70-Oct-16 [70-Oct-17: 2B; 70-Oct-18: 2C].
Wilson, Elizabeth Ann m. Foard, Benjamin on 70-Aug-2 [70-Aug-4: 2C; 70-Aug-10: 2C].

Wilson, Elizabeth D. m. Egerton, Samuel E. on 66-Nov-20 [66-Nov-22: 2C].
Wilson, Ellen (29 yrs.) d. on 66-Nov-26 [66-Dec-1: 2B].
Wilson, Francis (5 yrs., 10 mos.) d. on 69-Jul-13 [69-Jul-14: 2D; 69-Jul-15: 2C].
Wilson, Franklin J. (22 yrs.) d. on 69-Apr-23 [69-Apr-26: 2B].
Wilson, Frederick d. on 65-Dec-17 of Consumption [66-Feb-1: 2C].
Wilson, George A. (67 yrs.) d. on 70-Apr-17 [70-Apr-18: 2B; 70-Apr-19: 2B].
Wilson, George H. (28 yrs., 2 mos.) d. on 67-Oct-27 of Dysentery [67-Oct-28: 2C].
Wilson, George H. m. Dixon, Annie E. on 70-Oct-18 [70-Dec-6: 2C].
Wilson, George W., Capt. (33 yrs.) d. on 66-Mar-29 [66-Apr-11: 2B].
Wilson, Greenbury B (75 yrs.) d. on 67-Apr-12 of Heart disease [67-Apr-13: 2B; 67-Apr-15: 1F].
Wilson, Hannah (73 yrs., 5 mos.) d. on 68-Jul-16 [68-Jul-17: 2C].
Wilson, Harry M. (1 yr., 1 mo.) d. on 70-Jul-18 [70-Jul-20: 2C].
Wilson, Henry C. (21 yrs., 4 mos.) d. on 67-May-26 Drowned [67-Nov-28: 2C].
Wilson, Henry P. (42 yrs.) d. on 69-Feb-22 [69-Feb-23: 2D].
Wilson, Ida (4 yrs., 4 mos.) d. on 66-May-3 [66-May-4: 2C].
Wilson, Ida A. m. Weitzel, John C. [69-Mar-22: 2C].
Wilson, Ida Elizabeth (8 mos.) d. on 66-Nov-25 [66-Dec-1: 2B].
Wilson, Ionia May (3 yrs., 6 mos.) d. on 70-Apr-7 of Diptheria and croup [70-Apr-8: 2C].
Wilson, Isabella (63 yrs.) d. on 69-Jun-13 [69-Jun-14: 2B].
Wilson, Isabella G. m. Robinson, William on 66-Sep-13 [66-Sep-18: 2B].
Wilson, Isabella George m. Lee, Richard Henry on 68-Oct-27 [68-Oct-29: 2B].
Wilson, Isabella V. m. Sunstrom, Calvin on 69-May-9 [69-May-11: 2B].
Wilson, J. Oliver (82 yrs.) d. on 70-Apr-27 [70-May-10: 2C].
Wilson, J. Oliver m. Risteau, Annie W. on 68-Aug-4 [68-Aug-5: 2B].
Wilson, James m. Marshall, Lorama on 68-Dec-16 [69-Jan-6: 2C].
Wilson, James H. m. Eagan, Eliza C. on 67-May-26 [67-Jan-4: 2A].
Wilson, James H. m. Trammell, Virginia on 66-Aug-16 [66-Aug-23: 2C].
Wilson, James R. m. Naylor, Susanna on 67-Jun-10 [67-Jul-1: 2B].
Wilson, Jane (67 yrs.) d. on 68-Sep-20 [68-Oct-30: 2C].
Wilson, Jane (79 yrs.) d. on 68-Jul-21 [68-Jul-22: 2C].
Wilson, Jane (58 yrs.) d. on 68-Dec-11 [68-Dec-21: 2C].
Wilson, Jennie m. Lee, Elijah W. on 70-Nov-9 [70-Dec-10: 2B].
Wilson, John (20 yrs.) d. on 69-Oct-30 [69-Nov-1: 2C].
Wilson, John A. (33 yrs.) d. on 70-Jan-10 [70-Jan-12: 2C].
Wilson, John E. (30 yrs., 1 mo.) d. on 67-Nov-20 of Consumption [67-Nov-28: 2C].
Wilson, John Edward (51 yrs.) d. on 68-Jul-13 of Apoplexy [68-Jul-15: 2B].
Wilson, John F. m. Sands, Hattie on 68-Jan-30 [68-Feb-1: 2B].
Wilson, John H. d. on 66-Jul-17 of Heatstroke [66-Jul-19: 1E].
Wilson, John Lee Chapman (2 yrs., 11 mos.) d. on 66-Mar-19 [66-Mar-21: 2C].
Wilson, John W. m. Frazer, Anne G. on 68-Apr-21 [68-Apr-23: 2B].
Wilson, John W. m. Rollins, Harriet E. on 67-Aug-26 [67-Sep-9: 2B].
Wilson, Joseph Addison (13 yrs.) d. on 66-Nov-25 [66-Dec-4: 2D].
Wilson, Joseph H. (59 yrs.) d. on 70-Dec-8 of Paralysis [70-Dec-9: 2C].
Wilson, Joseph Kent m. Nants, Olivia on 69-Jun-15 [69-Jun-17: 2C].
Wilson, Julia A. (80 yrs.) d. on 68-Jun-23 [68-Jun-24: 2B; 68-Jun-25: 2B].
Wilson, Laura Eugenia (17 yrs.) d. on 68-Feb-23 [68-Feb-25: 2C].
Wilson, Lizzie (4 yrs., 5 mos.) d. on 70-Nov-29 [70-Nov-30: 2C].
Wilson, Louise (7 mos.) d. on 67-Jun-30 of Cholera infantum [67-Jul-1: 2B].
Wilson, Lydia (63 yrs.) d. on 69-Jun-12 [69-Jun-14: 2B].
Wilson, M. Cornelia m. Ash, Charles on 69-Oct-27 [69-Nov-2: 2B].
Wilson, Maria B. (63 yrs.) d. on 66-Jul-18 [66-Jul-20: 2D].
Wilson, Marianna m. Crockett, Walter C. on 70-Feb-2 [70-Feb-5: 2B].
Wilson, Marion A m. Woelper, Leonora S on 67-Sep-10 [67-Sep-26: 2B].
Wilson, Martha L. m. Bailey, Charles W. on 69-May-24 [69-Jun-10: 2C].

Wilson, Mary (11 yrs.) d. on 66-Jan-26 [66-Jan-29: 2C].
Wilson, Mary (71 yrs.) d. on 69-Dec-15 [69-Dec-18: 2B].
Wilson, Mary (80 yrs.) d. on 69-Apr-17 [69-Apr-21: 2C].
Wilson, Mary (81 yrs.) d. on 70-Nov-17 [70-Nov-18: 2C; 70-Nov-19: 2B].
Wilson, Mary A. (39 yrs.) d. on 68-Jan-19 [68-Jan-21: 2C].
Wilson, Mary A. m. Ledley, Benjamin P. on 66-Aug-16 [66-Sep-28: 2B].
Wilson, Mary E. m. Howes, E. L. on 66-Mar-7 [66-Mar-10: 2B].
Wilson, Mary J. m. Bennamin, John on 68-Nov-22 [68-Nov-24: 2C].
Wilson, Mary O. (32 yrs.) d. on 67-May-17 [67-May-21: 2B].
Wilson, Matilda (57 yrs.) d. on 70-Dec-4 [70-Dec-8: 2C].
Wilson, Millie B. m. Walters, John H. on 70-Jan-19 [70-Jan-27: 2C].
Wilson, Mollie M. m. Blair, J. A. on 68-Jul-15 [68-Jul-18: 2B].
Wilson, Norval d. on 69-Jan-17 [69-Jan-18: 2D].
Wilson, Paul R. (9 mos.) d. on 70-Jul-6 [70-Jul-7: 2C].
Wilson, Philip Choppell (9 yrs., 1 mo.) d. on 68-Nov-14 [68-Nov-16: 2C].
Wilson, Richard J. (26 yrs.) d. on 66-Mar-6 of Consumption [66-Mar-9: 2B].
Wilson, Robert (31 yrs.) d. on 69-Mar-25 [69-Mar-27: 2B].
Wilson, Robert m. Croshaw, Sue Ann on 70-Jul-11 [70-Jul-16: 2B].
Wilson, Robert E. (43 yrs.) d. on 69-May-9 [69-May-11: 2C].
Wilson, Robert Ewing m. Treadway, Sue on 68-Apr-1 [68-Apr-21: 2B].
Wilson, Ruth N. m. Zell, Thomas J. on 68-Jul-19 [68-Sep-14: 2B].
Wilson, S. Haven m. King, Mary E. on 69-Sep-1 [69-Sep-3: 2B].
Wilson, S. Maria m. Burns, Richard on 66-Jan-4 [66-Jan-6: 2B].
Wilson, Samuel (86 yrs.) d. on 66-Feb-13 [66-Feb-14: 2C].
Wilson, Samuel (67 yrs.) d. on 70-Nov-25 [70-Dec-3: 2B].
Wilson, Samuel G. m. Stevens, Sarah L. on 68-Jun-18 [68-Jun-20: 2B].
Wilson, Samuel James (21 yrs., 3 mos.) d. on 67-Mar-29 [67-Mar-30: 2C].
Wilson, Sarah A. m. Allen, Alexander on 70-Jul-8 [70-Sep-8: 2B].
Wilson, Sarah L. m. Willox, Ralph Henri on 69-Apr-3 [69-Apr-9: 2B].
Wilson, Susan m. Gwinnell, Randolph on 69-Feb-4 [69-Feb-4: 2C].
Wilson, Truston m. Wolf, Laura on 68-Dec-22 [68-Dec-24: 2C].
Wilson, Urith m. Schuchts, James H. on 69-Mar-31 [69-Apr-3: 2B].
Wilson, Vallow m. Chew, Perry on 66-Sep-13 [66-Sep-14: 2B].
Wilson, W. W. m. Phillips, Eliza Jane on 67-May-19 [67-Oct-11: 2B].
Wilson, William (63 yrs.) d. on 66-Sep-26 [66-Sep-27: 2C].
Wilson, William d. on 69-Feb-28 of Heart disease [68-Mar-1: 1G].
Wilson, William G. m. Lee, Frances Anna on 67-Apr-15 [67-Apr-18: 2B].
Wilson, William H. m. Lewis, Frances A. on 68-Dec-31 [69-Jan-9: 2C].
Wilson, William R. m. Philan, Josephine A. on 67-May-21 [67-Feb-9: 2B].
Wilson, William S. (19 yrs.) d. on 70-Jun-18 Drowned [70-Jun-20: 2C].
Wilson, William Samuel (5 mos.) d. on 69-Apr-8 [69-Apr-9: 2C].
Wilson, William T., Rev. (73 yrs.) d. on 69-Sep-1 [69-Sep-4: 2B].
Wilson, William T. m. Pohlan, Augusta on 69-Sep-23 [69-Oct-2: 2B].
Wilson, Willie (8 mos.) d. on 67-Feb-28 [67-Mar-4: 2D].
Wilson, Willie (3 yrs.) d. on 69-Mar-23 [69-Mar-24: 2C].
Wiltberger, Edith M. m. Evans, W. W. on 68-Aug-12 [68-Sep-9: 2B].
Wimmer, Anna M. m. Dettmer, H. on 67-Oct-8 [67-Oct-12: 2A].
Wimpsett, Emma F. M. m. Rumney, Charles W. on 68-Mar-3 [68-Aug-25: 2B].
Wimpsett, Josephine Cicely m. Brodrick, Timothy A. on 69-Dec-30 [70-Jan-1: 1B].
Wimpsett, Mary Paleaner m. Heter, George Lewis on 69-Oct-18 [69-Oct-22: 2B].
Winans, Clinton m. Leveaux, Mathilde Felice on 69-Sep-16 [69-Oct-11: 2C].
Wincent, Agnes (40 yrs.) d. on 70-Mar-10 [70-Mar-12: 2C].
Winchester, A. P. m. Scott, Sue on 67-Nov-6 [67-Nov-9: 2B].
Winchester, Jennie m. Woolf, Harry C. on 69-Jun-9 [69-Jun-11: 2C].
Winchester, John Gordon (6 yrs.) d. on 66-Apr-20 [66-Apr-23: 2B].

Winchester, Sarah m. Williams, John S. on 67-Dec-10 [67-Dec-16: 2B].
Winchester, Sue d. on 68-Dec-25 [68-Dec-28: 2C].
Winchester, William, Jr. (40 yrs.) d. on 70-Mar-10 [70-Apr-30: 2B].
Winchester, William Franklin (6 yrs., 6 mos.) d. on 66-May-21 [66-May-22: 2B].
Winder, Richard B. m. Dorsey, Kate H. on 69-Apr-15 [69-Apr-16: 2B].
Windsor, Clarence (2 yrs., 10 mos.) d. on 69-Apr-30 [69-May-1: 2B].
Windsor, Edith (1 yr., 3 mos.) d. on 69-Apr-25 [69-Apr-26: 2B].
Windsor, Thibedeaux m. Chandler, William E. on 66-May-6 [66-May-8: 2B].
Winer, William I. Kinnersley (1 yr., 9 mos.) d. on 68-Dec-9 [68-Dec-11: 2C].
Wing, Reginald D. m. Walsh, Henrietta L. on 68-Jan-23 [68-Feb-19: 2C].
Wingate, Charles O. (21 yrs.) d. on 70-Feb-1 of Consumption [70-Feb-2: 2B; 70-Feb-3: 2B].
Wingate, Louisa m. Rhea, George W. on 66-Jun-12 [66-Jun-15: 2C].
Wingate, M. Kate m. Skinner, G. B. on 69-Jan-3 [69-Mar-18: 2C].
Wingate, Sarah J. m. Pancoast, Arthur D. on 70-Jun-2 [70-Jun-4: 2B].
Wingate, Susan d. on 69-Jan-26 [69-Jan-28: 2C].
Wingate, Thomas T., Capt. (61 yrs.) d. on 66-May-26 [66-May-28: 1F, 1G, 2B].
Wingate, William E. (12 yrs.) d. on 68-Feb-28 [68-Feb-29: 2B].
Wingrove, Emma m. Bargannini, D. L. on 69-Jun-15 [69-Jun-16: 2C].
Wingrove, Thomas (60 yrs.) d. on 70-May-31 [70-Jun-1: 2B].
Winkel, Henry A. m. Riley, Mary A. on 67-Sep-8 [67-Sep-25: 2B].
Winkelman, Frederick Edwin (1 mo.) d. [67-Aug-27: 2B].
Winkelman, Henrietta m. Feuss, Henry O. on 68-Nov-18 [68-Nov-21: 2C].
Winkelman, John H. m. Ohrenschall, Christina on 69-Mar-23 [69-Mar-29: 2B].
Winkler, Catharine m. Dentz, Simon on 68-Oct-12 [68-Oct-13: 2C].
Winks, Annie E. m. Ross, Alexander on 68-Jun-30 [68-Jul-18: 2B; 68-Jul-21: 2C].
Winks, Cora Rebecca (2 yrs., 7 mos.) d. on 68-Dec-18 of Chronic croup [68-Dec-19: 2C].
Winn, Achsah Carroll m. Thompson, D. Bowly on 68-Nov-19 [68-Nov-24: 2C].
Winn, Agnes (1 yr., 7 mos.) d. on 70-May-7 [70-May-9: 2B].
Winn, Edward d. on 69-Aug-28 of Fall from window [69-Aug-31: 1H].
Winn, Elisha (73 yrs.) d. on 66-Feb-11 [66-Feb-13: 2C].
Winn, Frederick S. m. Miller, Martha J. on 67-Nov-14 [67-Nov-18: 2B].
Winn, Joshua m. Roberts, Margaret Jane on 68-Apr-21 [68-Apr-23: 2B].
Winn, Matilda A. (60 yrs.) d. on 69-Apr-12 [69-Apr-13: 2B; 69-Apr-14: 2B].
Winsett, John G. (63 yrs.) d. on 69-Oct-18 [69-Oct-20: 2C].
Winsett, Mary (59 yrs.) d. on 66-Nov-28 [66-Nov-29: 2C].
Winsett, Mollie L. m. Hopkins, J. Reynolds on 69-Mar-11 [69-Mar-11: 2C].
Winslow, Benjamin F. m. Middleton, Mary P. on 67-Dec-31 [68-Jan-6: 2C].
Winslow, John R., Dr. d. on 66-Feb-13 [66-Feb-15: 2C].
Winter, Annie m. Weaver, George C. on 67-Sep-24 [67-Sep-27: 2B].
Winter, Gabriel (39 yrs.) d. on 66-Jun-20 [66-Jun-23: 2B].
Winter, George m. Roberts, Annie M. on 69-Jan-12 [69-Jan-18: 2C].
Winter, Harry S. m. Adams, Addie on 69-Oct-20 [69-Oct-23: 2B].
Winter, Samuel m. Armstrong, Sarah R. on 69-Sep-30 [69-Oct-7: 2B].
Winter, Samuel G. m. Taylor, Mary V. on 67-May-15 [67-Jun-6: 2B].
Winter, Samuel H. (10 yrs., 1 mo.) d. on 67-May-26 [67-May-27: 2B].
Winter, Scandra R. m. Newcomer, William P. on 70-Aug-30 [70-Sep-6: 2B].
Winter, Tillie m. Schafer, Christian M. S. on 66-Feb-21 [66-Feb-23: 2C].
Winter, Walter Lowry d. on 66-Aug-19 [66-Aug-24: 2B].
Winterbottom, James T. m. Caulk, Hester A. on 66-Dec-27 [66-Dec-29: 2C].
Winterbottom, Margaret (82 yrs.) d. on 70-Sep-8 [70-Sep-10: 2B].
Winternitz, Virginia m. Hechinger, Ferdinand on 70-Jan-20 [70-Jan-25: 2C].
Winters, Benjamin (74 yrs.) d. on 67-Apr-2 [67-Apr-3: 2B].
Winters, James (28 yrs.) d. on 69-Oct-10 [69-Oct-15: 2C].
Winters, James m. England, Carrie A. on 68-Oct-1 [68-Oct-17: 2B].
Winters, Lizzie B. m. Prigg, Julius A. on 70-Apr-19 [70-May-5: 2B].

Winters, Martha H m. Nagle, George O. on 70-Nov-18 [70-Dec-14: 2C].
Winthrop, Harriet R. m. McKim, Haslett on 70-Sep-15 [70-Sep-19: 2B].
Winwood, Milchia d. on 68-Jun-14 [68-Jun-15: 2B].
Wirt, Calvin C. m. Beuhler, Ellen on 70-Dec-13 [70-Dec-16: 2C].
Wirt, Emma R. m. Bradford, John L. on 70-Apr-12 [70-Apr-16: 2B].
Wirt, Jacob (69 yrs.) d. on 69-Nov-8 [69-Nov-12: 2C].
Wirt, William E. (42 yrs.) d. on 70-Jul-28 [70-Aug-6: 2C].
Wirth, Andrew m. Dennis, Mary J. on 69-May-18 [69-May-25: 2C].
Wirth, Frederick (30 yrs.) d. on 67-May-16 of Heart disease [67-May-17: 1G].
Wirth, Jacob (24 yrs.) d. on 68-May-14 [68-May-16: 2B].
Wirts, William T. m. Loney, Ellen L. S. on 69-Aug-31 [69-Sep-20: 2C].
Wirtz, Kate m. Cahill, John on 67-Feb-14 [67-Feb-18: 2C].
Wise, Edward M. d. on 68-Jan-29 [68-Jan-30: 2C].
Wise, Elizabeth (94 yrs.) d. on 67-Mar-25 [67-Mar-28: 2B; 67-Mar-29: 1F].
Wise, Elizabeth m. Gustus, Israel on 68-Feb-18 [68-Feb-19: 2C].
Wise, George (70 yrs.) d. on 70-Nov-27 [70-Nov-28: 2C; 70-Nov-29: 2C].
Wise, Henry A., Rev. d. on 69-Feb-10 [69-Feb-11: 1F; 69-Feb-15: 1G].
Wise, John A. (26 yrs.) d. on 67-Mar-23 in Railroad accident [67-Mar-25: 1F].
Wise, Laura d. on 70-Jul-1 [70-Jul-2: 2B].
Wise, Linnie S. m. Talbot, James A. C. on 66-Mar-27 [66-Apr-12: 2B].
Wise, M. Alice m. Zollinger, George N. on 67-Sep-10 [67-Sep-14: 2A].
Wise, Nicholas J. m. Cummings, Sarah J. on 67-Nov-21 [67-Nov-25: 2C].
Wise, Peyton m. Chilton, Laura Mason on 69-Nov-25 [69-Nov-27: 2B].
Wise, Rosalie m. Gunther, Adolph on 68-Sep-28 [68-Oct-6: 2B].
Wise, Rose A. m. Wailes, Stephen C. on 69-Sep-22 [69-Sep-23: 2B].
Wise, Sarah C. m. Hall, Owen D. on 70-Mar-13 [70-Apr-5: 2B].
Wise, Silas L. m. Erdman, Amanda L. on 69-Aug-5 [69-Aug-7: 2B].
Wise, Wallace Mozart (2 yrs., 1 mo.) d. on 70-Mar-9 [70-Mar-10: 2C].
Wise, William W. m. Bates, Anna Cusic on 68-Dec-22 [68-Dec-24: 2C].
Wiseborough, Benjamin H. (46 yrs.) d. on 68-Jan-25 [68-Jan-27: 2C].
Wiseman, Henry (52 yrs.) d. on 68-Jun-7 [68-Jun-8: 2B].
Wiseman, Margaret (24 yrs.) d. on 69-Apr-30 of Suicide (Poisoning) [69-May-1: 1H; 69-May-3: 1G].
Wisner, H. m. Rickert, Lena on 67-Jun-16 [67-Jun-21: 2B].
Wisnom, Alexander H. m. Clayton, Temperance R. on 69-Jan-11 [69-Mar-3: 2B].
Wissel, Annie M. m. Blair, J. J. on 67-Aug-13 [67-Oct-1: 2B].
Wissman, Marie Adele (71 yrs.) d. [68-Aug-10: 2C].
Witman, Elizabeth Burrows (1 yr., 3 mos.) d. on 70-Feb-20 [70-Feb-22: 2C].
Wittbecker, David Alexander (1 yr.) d. on 67-May-25 [67-May-27: 2B].
Witten, Elea W. m. Smoot, Richard on 66-Oct-4 [66-Oct-16: 2B].
Witters, James, Jr. (47 yrs.) d. on 68-Nov-29 of Consumption [68-Dec-1: 2C].
Witters, James, Sr. (85 yrs.) d. on 70-Nov-22 [70-Nov-24: 2C; 70-Nov-25: 2D].
Wittig, George Edward (1 yr.) d. on 70-Jul-6 [70-Jul-7: 2C].
Wittig, George H. m. Schaaf, Catherine on 68-May-10 [68-May-13: 2B].
Wittington, Charles A. m. Moon, Lucinda on 69-Sep-22 [69-Sep-24: 2B].
Wittler, Mary m. Eagleston, William H. on 69-Dec-12 [69-Dec-24: 2C].
Wittman, August H. (31 yrs., 6 mos.) d. on 68-Oct-27 of Typhoid [68-Oct-31: 2B].
Wittman, George Miltonberger (1 yr., 4 mos.) d. on 66-Aug-8 [66-Aug-9: 2C; 66-Aug-10: 2C].
Witz, William Elliott (4 mos.) d. on 67-Jul-1 of Cholera [67-Jul-6: 2B].
Wivel, Francis P. m. Jones, Mary T. on 66-May-22 [66-May-26: 2B].
Wivle, William (26 yrs.) d. on 70-Oct-24 [70-Oct-25: 2B].
Wix, Harry N. (1 yr., 9 mos.) d. on 66-Nov-9 [66-Nov-14: 2B].
Wode, Frederick m. Waltjen, Fredericka J. on 70-Feb-20 [70-Mar-29: 2B].
Woelper, Emily d. on 67-Aug-7 of Consumption [67-Aug-8: 2B].
Woelper, Leonora S. m. Wilson, Marion A. on 67-Sep-10 [67-Sep-26: 2B].

Wolf, Ann Dorothy (67 yrs.) d. on 68-Oct-27 [68-Oct-28: 2B; 68-Oct-29: 2C].
Wolf, August m. Knickman, Elizabeth on 68-Sep-20 [68-Sep-22: 2B].
Wolf, Augusta (30 yrs.) d. on 70-Dec-20 [70-Dec-22: 2B].
Wolf, Belle m. Mackenhamer, George N. on 67-Sep-11 [67-Sep-17: 2A].
Wolf, Betty (91 yrs.) d. on 70-Jul-19 [70-Jul-20: 2C].
Wolf, Charles P. m. Kenney, Sophia on 66-Dec-6 [66-Dec-21: 2B].
Wolf, Cornelia R. (18 yrs.) d. on 70-Mar-6 [70-Mar-8: 2C].
Wolf, Emma m. Lowenstein, Walter H. on 68-May-4 [68-May-7: 2B].
Wolf, Eugene Bell (7 yrs.) d. on 67-Apr-25 [67-Apr-26: 2B].
Wolf, George Louis m. Leitz, Mary Catherine on 70-Mar-1 [70-Mar-9: 2C].
Wolf, George Penrose (9 mos.) d. on 70-Apr-21 [70-Apr-28: 2C].
Wolf, George W. m. Fredericks, Mary E. on 67-Oct-14 [67-Oct-22: 2A].
Wolf, Harry L. (2 yrs.) d. on 67-Oct-2 of Chronic croup [67-Oct-3: 2B].
Wolf, Heinz d. on 68-Jul-15 of Heatstroke [68-Jul-17: 1D].
Wolf, Henry m. Heck, Adalhaidt on 67-Aug-15 [67-Aug-19: 2C].
Wolf, Henry C. m. Turnbaugh, Eliza on 69-Oct-13 [69-Oct-21: 2B].
Wolf, Isidore m. Lunean, Elise on 67-Jul-9 [67-Jul-10: 2B].
Wolf, John B. m. Mullen, Martha on 69-Jan-11 [69-Jan-13: 2D].
Wolf, Laura m. Wilson, Truston on 68-Dec-22 [68-Dec-24: 2C].
Wolf, Mary m. Eagleston, Charles on 70-Jan-18 [70-Jan-20: 2C].
Wolf, Rebecca m. Adler, Leon on 69-Aug-8 [69-Aug-17: 2C].
Wolf, Samuel Hevener (3 yrs., 8 mos.) d. on 66-Nov-18 [66-Nov-20: 2B].
Wolf, Sarah C. m. Cole, William B. on 70-Mar-1 [70-Sep-1: 2B; 70-Sep-2: 2C].
Wolf, William H. (60 yrs.) d. on 66-Jul-9 [66-Jul-10: 2C].
Wolf, Willie (11 mos.) d. on 69-Jan-24 [69-Jan-26: 2C].
Wolf, Willie R. d. on 68-Dec-30 [68-Dec-31: 2D].
Wolfangel, Frederick William (21 yrs., 11 mos.) d. on 68-Dec-21 of Typhoid [68-Dec-22: 2C; 68-Dec-23: 2C].
Wolfangel, Lenia Christiana (26 yrs.) d. on 69-Jul-20 [69-Jul-21: 2C].
Wolfangel, Mary E. m. Romroser, John G. on 68-Mar-12 [68-Mar-16: 2B].
Wolfe, Francis Eugene (9 mos.) d. on 70-Jul-12 [70-Jul-14: 2B].
Wolfenden, James (85 yrs.) d. on 67-Nov-24 [67-Nov-26: 2B].
Wolff, Alexander m. Meredith, Elizabeth on 68-Oct-1 [68-Oct-2: 2B].
Wolff, Bernard C., Rev. (76 yrs.) d. on 70-Nov-1 [70-Nov-3: 2C].
Wolff, C. C. m. Hume, Maggie J. on 67-Mar-14 [67-Mar-18: 2B].
Wolff, Charlotte (77 yrs.) d. on 69-Dec-3 [69-Dec-11: 2B].
Wolff, Ellen (3 yrs., 10 mos.) d. on 67-May-23 [67-May-25: 2B].
Wolff, Harriet A. d. on 67-Jan-10 [67-Jan-12: 2C].
Wolff, Johanna M. m. Smith, Emil on 69-Sep-2 [69-Sep-4: 2B].
Wolff, Willie R. (1 yr.) d. on 68-Dec-30 [69-Jan-1: 2C].
Wolffe, Bernard L. (82 yrs.) d. on 69-Jun-9 [69-Jun-15: 2C].
Wolfram, Elenora (22 yrs., 3 mos.) d. on 67-May-28 [67-Jun-1: 2B].
Wolfsheimer, Menna (3 yrs., 9 mos.) d. on 68-Dec-31 [69-Jan-2: 2C].
Wolvington, Mary T. m. Aiken, George B. on 70-Jun-9 [70-Jun-14: 2B].
Wonderly, Edward Jacob (10 yrs.) d. on 69-Jun-10 [69-Jun-11: 2C].
Wonderly, Harry m. Abbott, Serena W. on 68-May-26 [68-May-28: 2B].
Wonderly, Isabella (34 yrs.) d. on 69-Oct-18 [69-Oct-19: 2C].
Wonderly, Sophia E. m. Cartlich, George W. A. on 68-Jun-2 [68-Jun-4: 2B].
Wonderoth, Gustave d. on 69-May-9 [69-May-11: 1H].
Wonn, Minnie G. m. Croney, Charles W. G. on 67-Jan-14 [67-Jan-16: 2C].
Wonn, Susannah Turner (31 yrs., 6 mos.) d. on 67-Dec-1 [67-Dec-3: 2C; 67-Dec-4: 2C].
Wonner, Michael m. Bergen, Georgeanna on 67-Sep-15 [67-Oct-14: 2B].
Wood, Adam L. m. Nally, Christa C. on 68-Sep-21 [68-Sep-29: 2B].
Wood, Alexander (56 yrs.) d. on 70-Feb-23 [70-Feb-25: 2C].
Wood, Algernon R. d. on 69-May-9 of Apoplexy [69-May-10: 2C].

Wood, Annie Eliza m. Betts, Albert A. on 65-Oct-25 [66-Apr-17: 2C].
Wood, Annie M. m. Champayre, David W. on 66-Nov-8 [66-Nov-19: 2B].
Wood, Augustus P. (8 mos.) d. on 69-Sep-4 [69-Sep-6: 2C; 69-Sep-7: 2B].
Wood, Catherine J. m. Fennemore, James T. on 69-Dec-2 [69-Dec-4: 2C].
Wood, Charles Whitney (1 yr., 6 mos.) d. on 68-Sep-4 [68-Sep-5: 2A].
Wood, Edward K. m. McCraight, Jane on 70-Jul-26 [70-Jul-28: 2C].
Wood, Ellen Rebecca (22 yrs., 10 mos.) d. on 69-Jan-1 [69-Jan-5: 2C].
Wood, Florence m. Zollinger, William P. on 68-Nov-19 [68-Nov-21: 2C; 68-Nov-23: 2B].
Wood, Franklin m. Burnett, Willienette on 70-Aug-29 [70-Sep-6: 2B].
Wood, George M. D. m. Marston, Mary E. on 66-Sep-11 [66-Sep-17: 2B].
Wood, George W. (49 yrs.) d. on 66-Feb-9 [66-Feb-14: 2C].
Wood, Hattie A. m. Bond, John, Jr. on 68-Oct-15 [68-Oct-19: 2B].
Wood, Henry C. d. on 70-May-26 [70-May-27: 2B].
Wood, Isaiah E. m. Haddaway, Eleanora on 66-Feb-7 [66-Feb-13: 2C].
Wood, J. Alexander m. Adams, Elizabeth on 67-Nov-12 [67-Nov-16: 2B].
Wood, James W. m. Fenemore, Martha A. on 69-Sep-15 [69-Sep-20: 2C].
Wood, John d. on 67-Oct-19 [67-Oct-22: 2A; 67-Oct-24: 2B].
Wood, John F. m. Scales, Carrie on 68-Dec-25 [69-Jan-6: 2C].
Wood, John H. m. Long, Laura on 67-Mar-31 [67-Apr-18: 2B].
Wood, Joseph E. m. Airey, Maggie C. on 67-Nov-19 [67-Nov-26: 2B].
Wood, Lizzie E. m. Sherwood, F. Frank on 68-Oct-29 [68-Nov-3: 2B].
Wood, Mary A. m. Davis, John, Jr. on 67-Dec-30 [68-Mar-3: 2C].
Wood, Mary A. m. Russell, Benjamin F. on 68-Mar-9 [68-Jun-16: 2B].
Wood, Mary E. m. Wiles, James A. on 70-Sep-13 [70-Sep-16: 2B].
Wood, Mary Grace d. on 69-Feb-5 [69-Feb-6: 2C].
Wood, Mary J. m. Heironimus, H. W. on 68-Apr-15 [68-Apr-18: 2A].
Wood, Matilda (72 yrs.) d. on 67-Sep-18 [67-Sep-20: 2A].
Wood, Patrick (55 yrs.) d. on 66-Sep-26 [66-Sep-28: 2B].
Wood, Rebecca R. (72 yrs.) d. on 66-Mar-16 [66-Mar-17: 2B].
Wood, Robert m. Hartze, Charlotte on 66-Sep-13 [66-Sep-18: 2B].
Wood, Susan E. m. Hill, Edward on 66-Sep-24 [66-Sep-29: 2B].
Wood, Thomas A. (24 yrs.) d. on 67-Aug-28 of Typhoid [67-Sep-3: 2B].
Wood, Thomas F. (50 yrs.) d. on 67-Oct-2 [67-Oct-5: 2B; 67-Oct-22: 2A].
Wood, Thomas H. (78 yrs.) d. on 70-Dec-3 [70-Dec-6: 2C, 4G].
Wood, William Davis (28 yrs.) d. on 69-Apr-18 of Consumption [69-Apr-26: 2C].
Woodall, Emma A. m. Woodall, James F. M. on 67-Nov-13 [67-Nov-15: 2B].
Woodall, Frances m. Cromwell, Francis M. on 68-Jan-1 [68-Jan-4: 2C].
Woodall, Frances Ann (22 yrs.) d. on 69-Mar-2 [69-Mar-4: 2C; 69-Mar-5: 2C].
Woodall, Freeman B. (59 yrs.) d. on 68-Jul-27 [68-Jul-31: 2C].
Woodall, James m. Rathie, Lizzie on 66-Jan-30 [66-Feb-7: 2C].
Woodall, James F. M. m. Woodall, Emma A. on 67-Nov-13 [67-Nov-15: 2B].
Woodall, Jennie m. Jeffers, Joseph M. on 69-Jan-28 [69-Feb-5: 2C].
Woodall, John T. (41 yrs.) d. on 68-Nov-25 in Railroad accident [68-Nov-28: 2C, 4D; 68-Nov-30: 1H].
Woodall, Noble G. W. m. Williams, Clara V. on 69-Feb-28 [69-Mar-11: 2C].
Woodall, Priscilla E. m. Brown, Calvert on 69-Jul-6 [69-Jul-7: 2C].
Woodall, Rebecca m. Penington, William Cooper on 67-Dec-4 [67-Dec-5: 2C].
Woodall, Thomas (67 yrs.) d. on 66-Dec-11 [66-Dec-12: 2B; 66-Dec-13: 2B].
Woodall, William T. m. Gray, Sadie E. on 70-Apr-14 [70-Apr-16: 2B].
Woodburn, Charles H., Capt. (40 yrs.) d. on 66-Aug-23 of Fall [66-Sep-8: 2B; 66-Nov-24: 2B; 66-Nov-26: 1G].
Woodcock, Emily W. d. on 70-Feb-15 [70-Feb-24: 2C].
Woodcock, William (75 yrs.) d. on 70-Mar-26 [70-Mar-28: 1H, 2B].
Wooddy, Amanda Elizabeth (25 yrs.) d. on 66-Jun-7 [66-Jun-14: 2B].
Wooddy, Dolly (25 yrs.) d. on 66-Jun-7 [66-Sep-4: 2B].

Wooddy, Maggie C. m. Cosby, DeWitt on 68-Oct-1 [68-Oct-5: 2B].
Wooden, Abbey m. Berry, Nimrod B. on 69-Dec-29 [69-Dec-31: 2C].
Wooden, Elizabeth m. Smith, William on 68-Mar-18 [68-Apr-7: 2B].
Wooden, John T. m. Hopps, Annie E. on 67-Nov-21 [68-Apr-21: 2B].
Wooden, Stephen (56 yrs.) d. on 70-Aug-31 [70-Sep-19: 2B].
Wooden, Susannah M. (34 yrs.) d. on 69-Jun-2 [69-Jun-7: 2B].
Wooden, Wilbur F. m. Stewart, Barbara on 68-Jul-12 [68-Jul-14: 2B].
Wooden, William T. m. Wills, Laura on 68-Sep-6 [68-Sep-22: 2B].
Woodford, Marion m. Joy, G. W. on 68-Dec-31 [69-Jan-1: 2C].
Woodhouse, E. N. m. Moran, Laura E. on 70-Jan-6 [70-Jan-20: 2C].
Woodhull, Alfred A. m. Ellicott, Margaret on 68-Dec-15 [68-Dec-16: 2C].
Woodland, Cassie m. Altvater, Edward Williams on 69-Nov-24 [69-Nov-26: 2B].
Woodland, Lucy C. m. Black, John S. on 70-Aug-10 [70-Aug-29: 2B].
Woodland, Mariah C. m. Smith, William H. on 69-Sep-21 [69-Sep-24: 2B].
Woodrow, J. Frank m. Irwin, Henrietta J. on 68-Aug-25 [68-Aug-28: 2B].
Woodrow, William E. m. Spedden, S. Kate on 66-Jan-22 [66-Jan-25: 2C].
Woods, Alex. P. m. Little, Amelia A. on 67-Jun-12 [67-Jun-18: 2B].
Woods, Bessie Middleton d. on 68-Jul-19 [68-Jul-20: 2B].
Woods, Bridget (75 yrs.) d. on 68-Jul-4 [68-Jul-6: 2B].
Woods, Catherine (60 yrs.) d. on 69-Oct-27 [69-Oct-29: 2C].
Woods, Charles F. m. Coulter, Helen M. on 66-Jun-28 [66-Jul-3: 2C].
Woods, Elizabeth m. Thompson, William on 69-Sep-15 [69-Oct-2: 2B].
Woods, Emma V. m. Malambre, James M. on 67-Dec-31 [68-Jan-17: 2C].
Woods, Frederick Tappan d. on 67-Sep-18 [67-Sep-20: 2A].
Woods, Hudson A. m. Redifer, Emma J. on 66-Dec-27 [67-Jan-3: 2B].
Woods, James C. m. McKeown, Sarah Ann on 66-Dec-5 [66-Dec-11: 2B].
Woods, John m. Glancy, Margaret on 66-May-8 [66-Sep-17: 2B].
Woods, Julia Ann (1 yr., 6 mos.) d. on 69-Aug-30 [69-Sep-1: 2B].
Woods, Lillie J. m. Whitehead, Holbrook on 69-Apr-15 [69-Apr-16: 2B].
Woods, Lotta m. Jones, Israel B. on 69-Jun-1 [69-Jun-8: 2B].
Woods, Mary m. Thomas, Frank on 67-Oct-1 [67-Oct-3: 2B].
Woods, Mary A. m. Eliason, Samuel S. H. on 70-Dec-20 [70-Dec-21: 2B].
Woods, Mary E. m. Francis, Robert on 68-Oct-26 [68-Nov-10: 2C].
Woods, Mary J. m. Dougherty, George W. on 66-Jan-7 [66-Oct-20: 2B].
Woods, Mary Viola (2 mos.) d. on 69-Jul-19 [69-Jul-20: 2C].
Woods, Rebecca (78 yrs.) d. on 68-Mar-8 [68-Mar-10: 2B].
Woods, Samuel Edmonds (1 yr., 4 mos.) d. on 70-Feb-8 [70-Feb-9: 2C].
Woods, Susan m. Foster, Robert on 69-Sep-2 [69-Sep-20: 2C].
Woods, William H. m. Casey, Elenora on 70-Apr-27 [70-Apr-29: 2B].
Woods, William Henry d. [67-Sep-20: 2A].
Woods, William M., Capt. (46 yrs.) d. on 70-May-4 of Pneumonia [70-May-5: 1G, 2B; 70-May-6: 2B].
Woodward, Alice m. Scharf, William on 67-Jun-3 [67-Jun-5: 2B].
Woodward, Ann D. (82 yrs.) d. on 67-Aug-13 [67-Aug-14: 2C].
Woodward, Ann M. (67 yrs.) d. on 67-Jun-26 [67-Jun-27: 2B].
Woodward, D. D. m. Anderson, Virginia on 68-Jan-9 [68-Jan-16: 2C].
Woodward, George S. (2 yrs.) d. on 66-Oct-29 [66-Nov-1: 2B].
Woodward, George W. m. Swan, Alice A. on 68-Jul-21 [68-Aug-19: 2B].
Woodward, Helen m. Sands, Richard on 68-Aug-1 [68-Sep-30: 2B].
Woodward, Irving Hall d. on 70-Dec-15 [70-Dec-21: 2C].
Woodward, J. H. d. on 68-Feb-5 [68-Feb-7: 2C].
Woodward, Joseph P. (1 yr., 11 mos.) d. on 70-Apr-7 of Pneumonia [70-Apr-9: 2B].
Woodward, Louisa Armat (1 yr., 2 mos.) d. on 69-Oct-5 [69-Oct-7: 2B].
Woodward, Maggie A. m. Scharff, Issac Newton on 66-Sep-12 [66-Nov-9: 2C].
Woodward, Martha E. m. Phelps, Charles E. on 68-Dec-29 [68-Dec-31: 2C].

Woodward, Mary B. m. Rogers, Henry C. on 68-Aug-25 [68-Aug-29: 2B].
Woodward, Mary H. m. Williamson, J. Pryor on 69-Oct-7 [69-Oct-13: 2C].
Woodward, Susannah m. Pearsall, John on 66-Jun-3 [67-May-31: 2B].
Woodward, William, Jr. m. Hopkins, Mary Johnson on 68-Dec-10 [68-Dec-31: 2C].
Woodworth, Ella Virginia (24 yrs.) d. on 69-Sep-10 [69-Sep-13: 2B].
Woodworth, Elmer Ferry (8 mos.) d. on 70-May-18 [70-May-19: 2C].
Woodworth, William R. m. Ferry, Ella V. on 67-Jun-13 [67-Jun-18: 2B].
Woolf, Daniel F. m. Layer, Louisa F. on 68-Mar-5 [68-Mar-12: 2B].
Woolf, H. E. m. Frank, Hannah on 69-Apr-11 [69-Apr-20: 2B].
Woolf, Harry C. m. Winchester, Jennie on 69-Jun-9 [69-Jun-11: 2C].
Woolfenden, Ada (1 yr., 4 mos.) d. on 68-Dec-16 of Measles [68-Dec-19: 2B].
Woolfenden, Sadie m. Beutelspacher, George on 66-Aug-5 [67-Mar-27: 2C].
Woolfendon, James m. Maxwell, Margaret A., Mrs. on 67-Mar-28 [67-Mar-30: 2B].
Woolford, A. Augusta m. Jones, Charles W. on 69-May-4 [69-May-15: 2B].
Woolford, Benjamin W. m. Skinner, Emma V. on 70-May-12 [70-May-18: 2B].
Woolford, Harriet J. m. Wright, William R. on 70-May-31 [70-Jun-2: 2B].
Woolford, Lillie G. m. Jordan, Rufus E. on 69-Jun-22 [69-Jun-28: 2C].
Woolford, Napoleon B. m. Merrett, Frances J. on 68-Aug-27 [68-Sep-19: 2B].
Woolford, Thomas E. m. Butler, Amanda H. on 66-Nov-21 [66-Nov-24: 2B].
Woolford, Thomas William m. Williams, Mary A. on 67-Sep-10 [68-Jun-3: 2B].
Woolford, Willie A. d. on 66-Jun-4 [66-Jun-8: 2B].
Woollen, George W. (5 mos.) d. on 69-Aug-4 [69-Aug-5: 2C].
Woollen, James Elmore (2 yrs., 7 mos.) d. on 68-Aug-5 [68-Aug-6: 2B].
Woollen, Maggie (22 yrs.) d. on 68-Dec-3 [68-Dec-7: 2D].
Woollen, Thomas m. Ditzell, Maggie on 67-Mar-11 [67-Apr-15: 2B].
Woolsey, Mary Virginia m. Holmes, Reuben A. on 66-Dec-6 [66-Dec-11: 2B].
Wooton, Elizabeth A. d. on 69-May-23 [69-May-24: 2B].
Wootten, Mary E. m. Lancaster, Louis J. on 68-Feb-20 [68-Mar-17: 2C].
Wootton, Henry E. m. O'Donnell, Ada on 68-Oct-13 [68-Oct-14: 2B].
Worcester, Jessie Hamilton (3 yrs.) d. on 70-Feb-23 [70-Feb-25: 2D].
Worden, Annie m. Lanigan, John on 68-Nov-25 [68-Dec-7: 2C].
Worden, R. m. Maloney, Julia on 68-Sep-1 [68-Sep-4: 2A].
Worden, William H. m. Cook, Mary C. on 70-Sep-20 [70-Sep-30: 2B].
Worick, John H. m. Orem, Mollie L. on 70-Sep-13 [70-Sep-15: 2B].
Work, Eda (3 yrs., 2 mos.) d. on 68-Nov-9 [68-Nov-17: 2C].
Working, George Edward (1 yr., 8 mos.) d. on 66-Nov-23 [66-Nov-24: 2B].
Worley, Clara Emma (6 yrs., 8 mos.) d. on 70-Mar-29 [70-Mar-31: 2C].
Worley, Fannie G. (2 yrs., 5 mos.) d. on 66-Nov-26 [66-Nov-27: 2B].
Worley, William N. m. Waters, Sue M. on 69-Oct-20 [69-Oct-25: 2B].
Wornitz, Emma m. Pflaunlacher, Samuel on 66-Feb-18 [66-Feb-20: 2B].
Worrell, John (82 yrs.) d. on 70-Aug-7 [70-Aug-8: 2C].
Worrell, William H. (42 yrs.) d. on 67-Dec-27 [68-Jan-4: 2C; 68-Jan-6: 2C].
Worth, Melvin H. (7 mos.) d. on 66-Jul-3 [66-Jul-4: 2B].
Worthington, Anna Lee m. Hewes, M. Warren on 67-Jul-23 [67-Jul-25: 2C].
Worthington, Drucie m. Reed, Thomas H. on 66-Dec-20 [67-Jan-4: 2D].
Worthington, James E. S. (18 yrs., 4 mos.) d. on 70-Jun-18 [70-Jun-20: 2C].
Worthington, Joshua F. C. m. Nichols, Blanche on 68-Oct-6 [68-Oct-9: 2C].
Worthington, Laura m. Dorsey, Lloyd E. on 69-Oct-26 [69-Oct-30: 2B].
Worthington, Lavinia m. Price, Beale on 69-Jun-3 [69-Jun-8: 2B].
Worthington, Mary G. m. Hopkins, John H., Jr. on 70-Jun-16 [70-Jun-22: 2C].
Worthington, Nicholas J. m. Simmons, Alice on 67-Oct-17 [67-Oct-19: 2A].
Worthington, Richard J. (63 yrs.) d. on 70-Mar-13 [70-Mar-15: 2C; 70-Mar-21: 1H].
Worthington, Sophia (62 yrs.) d. on 66-Mar-27 [66-Mar-29: 2B].
Worthington, William A. (39 yrs.) d. on 69-Oct-21 [69-Oct-25: 2C].
Worthington, William F. (63 yrs.) d. on 67-Jan-1 [67-Jan-3: 2B; 67-Jan-4: 2D].

Wren, Ann m. Ross, James D. on 65-Dec-28 [66-Jan-3: 2C].
Wright, Albert (4 yrs.) d. on 69-Dec-15 [69-Dec-16: 2C].
Wright, Alice (31 yrs.) d. on 69-Jun-23 [69-Jun-24: 2C].
Wright, Amanda J. m. Hobbs, Yelverton T. on 69-May-20 [69-May-26: 2C].
Wright, Ann (51 yrs.) d. on 69-Jul-21 [69-Jul-22: 2C].
Wright, Annie m. Gaston, Robert on 67-Feb-28 [67-Mar-2: 2B].
Wright, Annie E. m. Seim, Henry, Jr. on 66-Oct-22 [66-Oct-25: 2C].
Wright, Areminta m. Campbell, William H. on 68-Nov-5 [68-Nov-17: 2C].
Wright, Benjamin F. m. Burneston, Mollie F. on 69-Aug-4 [69-Aug-7: 2B].
Wright, Cecilia (22 yrs.) d. on 68-Dec-28 [68-Dec-29: 2D; 68-Dec-30: 2D].
Wright, Charles Albert (24 yrs.) d. on 66-May-15 [66-May-16: 2C; 66-May-21: 2B].
Wright, Clayton (64 yrs.) d. on 67-Nov-4 [67-Nov-15: 2A, 2B].
Wright, David (15 yrs., 4 mos.) d. on 66-Jun-14 [66-Jun-16: 2B].
Wright, David Henderson (9 yrs.) d. on 68-Jun-27 [68-Jun-29: 2B].
Wright, E. Joeline m. Hoffman, John R. on 67-Jul-16 [67-Jul-19: 2C].
Wright, E. Lou m. Legg, Thomas M. on 68-May-25 [68-Jun-9: 2B].
Wright, Edward C. (39 yrs.) d. on 69-Mar-16 [69-Mar-18: 2C].
Wright, Edward Martin (51 yrs.) d. on 69-Dec-12 [69-Dec-13: 2C].
Wright, Elizabeth (32 yrs.) d. on 68-Apr-9 [68-Apr-10: 2B].
Wright, Emily J. d. on 66-Nov-5 [66-Nov-7: 2C].
Wright, Emma N. m. Monroe, David M. on 67-Feb-16 [67-Feb-20: 2C].
Wright, Emory (27 yrs.) d. on 70-Aug-23 Drowned [70-Aug-24: 4D].
Wright, Frances m. Adley, William on 67-Apr-30 [67-May-1: 2B].
Wright, Frances Burnetson d. on 70-Jul-16 [70-Jul-28: 2C; 70-Jul-29: 2C].
Wright, George (38 yrs.) d. on 66-Aug-30 of Stomach inflammation [66-Aug-31: 1F; 66-Sep-6: 2B].
Wright, George E. m. Ripple, Emily W. on 69-Mar-18 [69-Mar-23: 2C].
Wright, George F. m. Oldham, Sallie I. on 65-Aug-17 [66-Jan-30: 2B].
Wright, George S. m. Ross, Laura V. on 67-Sep-17 [67-Sep-24: 2A].
Wright, George W. m. Murdoch, Almira E. on 66-Apr-9 [66-Apr-11: 2B].
Wright, Grace A. m. Stevens, John R. on 67-Jun-6 [67-Jul-9: 2B].
Wright, Henry m. Robbins, Ellen on 66-Jan-17 [66-Jan-22: 2C].
Wright, Isabella M. m. Brown, Waldron P. on 70-Jan-13 [70-Jan-15: 2C].
Wright, Isaiah M. m. Hall, Millie A. on 66-Nov-8 [66-Nov-15: 2C].
Wright, Isarah M. (22 yrs.) d. on 67-Feb-8 [67-Feb-9: 2B].
Wright, J. L. m. Summers, M. Bettie on 70-May-11 [70-May-19: 2C].
Wright, James B. (31 yrs.) d. on 69-Jul-17 [69-Jul-19: 2D].
Wright, James B. (31 yrs.) d. on 70-Apr-21 [70-Apr-22: 2C].
Wright, James B. m. DeFord, Anna on 67-Feb-28 [67-Mar-5: 2C].
Wright, Johanna d. on 70-Jan-6 [70-Jan-7: 2F].
Wright, John, Sr. (74 yrs.) d. on 69-Mar-21 of Dropsy [69-Apr-5: 2B].
Wright, John W. (35 yrs.) d. on 67-Jan-19 of Consumption [67-Jan-21: 2C; 67-Jan-22: 2C; 67-Feb-8: 2C].
Wright, John W. m. Geiglin, Barbara E. on 67-Jan-21 [67-Jan-30: 2C].
Wright, Joseph T. m. Happoldt, Eveleen T. on 70-Dec-8 [70-Dec-20: 2B].
Wright, Joshua J. (48 yrs.) d. on 68-Sep-24 [68-Sep-25: 2B].
Wright, Julia Ann (85 yrs.) d. on 69-Feb-4 [69-Feb-6: 2C].
Wright, Lizzie (29 yrs.) d. on 66-Apr-7 [66-Apr-9: 2B].
Wright, Louisa m. Sapp, Joseph F. on 70-Feb-8 [70-Feb-15: 2C].
Wright, Lucy C. (31 yrs.) d. on 67-Oct-9 [67-Oct-10: 2B].
Wright, Luther (68 yrs.) d. on 67-Jan-28 [67-Jan-29: 1G, 2C; 67-Jan-30: 2C].
Wright, Lydia Gertrude (2 yrs., 2 mos.) d. on 67-Sep-4 [67-Sep-6: 2B].
Wright, Maggie J. m. Tarleton, James R. on 68-Oct-29 [68-Nov-11: 2C].
Wright, Margaret J. (26 yrs.) d. on 66-May-1 of Typhoid [66-May-2: 2B; 66-May-4: 2C].
Wright, Mary A. (75 yrs.) d. on 69-Aug-13 [69-Aug-16: 2C].

Wright, Mary Alenia (28 yrs., 3 mos.) d. on 68-Aug-23 [68-Aug-24: 2B].
Wright, Mary Ann d. on 70-Jan-16 [70-Jan-17: 2C].
Wright, Mary F. m. Leonard, Jonathan on 69-Jan-14 [69-Feb-1: 2C].
Wright, Mary P. m. Grafflin, George W. on 67-Jan-4 [67-Jan-8: 2B].
Wright, Mollie F. d. on 70-Jul-16 [70-Jul-16: 2B].
Wright, Nellie C. m. Cowan, James S on 67-Jun-27 [67-Jul-4: 2B].
Wright, Nelson R. (57 yrs.) d. [66-Oct-17: 2B].
Wright, Olive A. Warren (2 yrs., 6 mos.) d. on 69-May-10 [69-May-11: 2C].
Wright, Owen R. m. Walters, Mary E. on 67-Mar-28 [67-Apr-2: 2B; 67-Apr-15: 2B].
Wright, Perry m. Carmine, Susan on 70-Nov-29 [70-Dec-16: 2C].
Wright, Richard m. Annen, Jennie V. on 70-Feb-11 [70-Mar-23: 2C].
Wright, Sallie E. m. Ford, R. Wesley on 70-Jan-27 [70-Jan-29: 2B; 70-Feb-3: 2B].
Wright, Sarah (61 yrs.) d. on 66-Dec-3 [66-Dec-7: 2B].
Wright, Sarah Ann d. on 69-Oct-3 [69-Oct-5: 2B; 69-Oct-7: 2B].
Wright, Sarah E. m. Maxwell, John W., Jr. on 68-Jan-21 [68-Jan-22: 2C].
Wright, Sarah L. m. Carr, Alexander on 69-Jun-15 [69-Jun-18: 2C].
Wright, Susan E. (35 yrs., 4 mos.) d. on 68-Oct-11 [68-Oct-16: 2B].
Wright, Thomas Clayton m. Taylor, Evelyn Juliett on 68-Nov-18 [68-Nov-21: 2C].
Wright, Thomas J. d. on 67-Jun-11 Drowned [67-Jun-13: 1F].
Wright, Turpin (76 yrs.) d. on 69-Jan-23 [69-Feb-2: 2C].
Wright, William C. m. Wells, Mary F. on 68-Dec-3 [69-Apr-20: 2B].
Wright, William H. m. Gould, Maggie A. on 66-Sep-13 [66-Sep-14: 2B].
Wright, William R. m. Woolford, Harriet J. on 70-May-31 [70-Jun-2: 2B].
Wrightson, Amelia R. m. Holt, Harry C. on 70-Jan-12 [70-Jan-14: 2C; 70-Jan-15: 2C].
Wrightson, Charles Edgar (1 yr., 1 mo.) d. on 70-Aug-8 [70-Aug-9: 2C].
Wrightson, James Edgar (5 yrs., 3 mos.) d. on 67-Nov-14 [67-Nov-16: 2B].
Wroten, Ann (68 yrs.) d. on 67-May-7 [67-May-9: 2A].
Wroten, Augustus m. Rodgers, Elizabeth A. on 68-Mar-9 [68-Mar-28: 2B].
Wroten, Joseph T. (5 yrs., 6 mos.) d. on 66-Feb-19 [66-Feb-21: 2D].
Wroth, Louisa A. d. on 67-Jan-11 [67-Jan-12: 2C; 67-Jan-14: 2C].
Wuehn, Frederick (39 yrs.) d. on 67-Jun-12 [67-Jun-13: 2C].
Wunder, Mollie V. (25 yrs., 8 mos.) d. on 66-May-5 [66-May-11: 2B].
Wunonwer, George (40 yrs.) d. on 68-Jul-16 of Heatstroke [68-Jul-17: 1D].
Wust, Annie (65 yrs.) d. on 70-Mar-13 [70-Mar-14: 2D].
Wyant, Clarinda (48 yrs.) d. on 68-May-18 [68-May-19: 2B].
Wyant, John George (71 yrs.) d. on 66-May-18 [66-May-19: 1F].
Wyant, Joseph m. Blanchard, Mary Ann on 70-Dec-20 [70-Dec-31: 2B].
Wyatt, Edward Winslow d. on 66-Aug-8 [66-Aug-9: 2C].
Wyatt, Emma m. Reigher, James M. on 69-Oct-22 [69-Oct-29: 2B].
Wyatt, Liza Kneeland (29 yrs.) d. on 69-Jul-4 [69-Jul-5: 2C].
Wyatt, Thomas A., Capt. (54 yrs.) d. on 66-Aug-5 [66-Aug-8: 2C].
Wyatt, Thomas J. m. Jones, Mary G. on 67-Dec-3 [67-Dec-5: 2C].
Wyble, Kate m. Rudolf, John A. on 70-May-31 [70-Jun-4: 2B].
Wyle, Rachel (92 yrs.) d. on 67-Oct-29 [67-Oct-30: 2B].
Wylie, Dely Lee (2 yrs., 10 mos.) d. on 70-Mar-5 of Pneumonia [70-Mar-7: 2C].
Wylie, Jane (63 yrs.) d. on 66-Oct-30 [66-Oct-31: 2B].
Wylie, John (71 yrs.) d. on 66-Oct-23 [66-Oct-24: 2C].
Wylie, Mary Frances m. Scott, John C. on 68-May-28 [68-Aug-17: 2B].
Wyman, Edward (68 yrs.) d. on 68-Jan-4 [68-Jan-6: 2C].
Wyman, Frances R. (22 yrs.) d. on 70-Jul-14 [70-Jul-15: 2C].
Wyman, Jesse (57 yrs.) d. on 66-Feb-3 [66-Feb-5: 2C].
Wyman, Walter Dudley (8 mos.) d. on 70-Jun-21 [70-Jul-15: 2C].
Wynkoop, Addie m. Carter, Durus D. on 69-Oct-6 [69-Oct-11: 2C].
Wynn, Thomas Patrick (10 mos.) d. on 69-Oct-15 [69-Oct-16: 2B].
Wysham, John (77 yrs.) d. [69-Dec-1: 2C].

Wysham, Thomas (74 yrs.) d. on 66-Aug-26 [66-Aug-27: 2B].
Wysong, R. m. Bedon, M. C. on 69-Jan-27 [69-Feb-1: 2C].
Wyvill, Mary E. m. Ward, H. C. on 68-Jan-23 [68-Jan-25: 2B].
Wyvill, Samuel W. m. Miller, Henrietta on 67-Feb-13 [67-Feb-18: 2C].
Wyville, Margaret d. on 66-Dec-10 [66-Dec-12: 2B].
Xaupi, Honoraius X., Rev. (83 yrs.) d. on 69-Jul-18 [69-Jul-31: 1H].
Yackel, John (49 yrs.) d. on 68-Feb-3 [68-Feb-5: 2D].
Yager, Kate m. McLanahan, James B. on 69-Nov-9 [69-Nov-30: 2C].
Yakel, Annie Marie (80 yrs.) d. on 70-Aug-6 [70-Aug-9: 2C].
Yakel, Conrad (75 yrs.) d. on 70-Jul-3 [70-Aug-9: 2C].
Yardley, Charles m. McCann, Laura on 67-Jan-24 [67-Jan-25: 2C].
Yater, Henry (86 yrs.) d. on 67-Aug-30 [67-Aug-31: 2B].
Yates, Adelaide (18 yrs., 4 mos.) d. on 70-Apr-14 [70-Apr-15: 2C].
Yates, Charles A. m. Martin, Leila M. on 67-Dec-17 [67-Dec-23: 2B].
Yates, Emily S. m. Dallam, Charles F. on 68-Jan-23 [68-Jan-27: 2C; 68-Jan-29: 2C].
Yates, George (48 yrs.) d. on 66-Aug-5 [66-Aug-6: 2C].
Yates, Jeannette B. m. Wagner, Charles V. on 70-Nov-1 [70-Nov-3: 2B].
Yeagel, Sarah m. Hann, H. Clay on 68-Oct-29 [68-Nov-9: 2B].
Yeager, Alice (20 yrs., 3 mos.) d. on 67-Dec-1 of Consumption [67-Dec-3: 2C].
Yeager, Carrie M. m. Johnson, Jesse on 68-Oct-6 [68-Oct-15: 2C].
Yeager, Daniel (5 yrs.) d. on 68-Apr-21 Murdered (Poisoning) [69-Jan-30: 1G].
Yeager, Elizabeth (70 yrs.) d. on 70-Sep-26 [70-Sep-27: 2B].
Yeager, Ella F. m. Hugg, Emory on 69-Jun-16 [69-Jun-22: 2C].
Yeager, George C. (24 yrs.) d. on 68-Nov-2 [68-Nov-3: 2B].
Yeager, Harry (1 yr., 5 mos.) d. on 69-May-29 [69-Jun-17: 2C].
Yeager, Julie (3 yrs., 3 mos.) d. on 70-Sep-25 [70-Sep-27: 2B].
Yeager, Laura (42 yrs.) d. on 70-Mar-21 [70-Mar-22: 2C].
Yeager, Louis (6 yrs., 8 mos.) d. on 66-Jul-9 [66-Jul-10: 2C].
Yeager, M. B. m. Richey, Maggie S. on 67-May-21 [67-Jun-27: 2B].
Yealdhall, Elizabeth J. m. Pierpont, William T. on 67-Aug-8 [67-Aug-20: 2B].
Yealdhall, Mary (60 yrs.) d. on 68-Apr-30 [68-May-2: 2C].
Yearley, Ann d. on 69-Feb-25 [69-Feb-27: 2C].
Yearley, Catherine E. G. d. on 70-Feb-7 [70-Feb-8: 2C].
Yearley, Elizabeth M. m. Maxwell, William S. on 68-Apr-21 [68-Apr-25: 2B].
Yearley, John F. (48 yrs.) d. on 69-Feb-12 [69-Feb-17: 2D].
Yearley, Sarah J. (24 yrs.) d. on 70-Nov-5 [70-Nov-7: 2B].
Yearley, William H. m. Hall, Emma C. on 67-Jun-27 [67-Jul-6: 2B].
Yearly, Eliza Jane m. Bell, John W. on 66-Apr-24 [66-Apr-26: 2B].
Yeates, John L. P. (35 yrs.) d. on 69-Feb-5 [69-Feb-25: 2D].
Yeatman, Ethielinda (21 yrs.) d. on 67-Dec-3 [67-Dec-4: 2C].
Yeatman, John Weldon (1 yr., 8 mos.) d. on 69-Sep-22 [69-Sep-23: 2C].
Yeatman, Sue A. m. Stansbury, William H. on 69-Jun-24 [69-Jun-30: 2C].
Yeatman, W. Wallace m. Middleton, Mary Julia on 67-Mar-14 [67-Mar-23: 2B].
Yelland, Jonas S. (34 yrs.) d. on 67-Sep-23 [67-Sep-25: 2B].
Yellman, Catherine A. (79 yrs.) d. on 70-Nov-2 [70-Nov-4: 2C].
Yellman, Mary J. m. Boyer, William W. on 68-Nov-17 [68-Nov-19: 2C].
Yellmann, Amelia C. D. m. Watchman, William C. on 70-Apr-20 [70-Apr-22: 2C].
Yellott, Coleman (49 yrs.) d. on 70-Jul-28 [70-Aug-1: 4F, 2C].
Yellott, George Washington, Jr. m. Gittings, Ann Emory [69-Feb-6: 2C].
Yellott, Jane H. m. Pindell, Adolphus T. on 68-Nov-5 [68-Nov-12: 2C].
Yellott, John (55 yrs.) d. on 67-Jul-27 [67-Jul-31: 2C].
Yellott, John I. m. Traill, Mary V. [68-Jun-3: 2B].
Yerkes, William H. m. Booth, Eliza A. on 67-Sep-3 [67-Sep-10: 2B].
Yewell, John (58 yrs.) d. on 70-May-17 [70-May-18: 2B].
Yewell, John W. m. Neviker, Mary C. on 66-Aug-16 [66-Aug-25: 2A].

Yingling, Charles (34 yrs.) d. on 70-Oct-23 [70-Oct-25: 2B].
Yingling, Fannie m. Buckingham, Alfred on 70-Mar-17 [70-Apr-21: 2B].
Yingling, Henrietta (45 yrs.) d. on 66-Dec-2 [66-Dec-7: 2B].
Yingling, Kate V. m. Conrad, T. M. on 67-Oct-17 [67-Nov-6: 2B].
Yingling, Lummie m. Brooks, Joshua on 66-Apr-12 [66-Apr-21: 2B].
Yingling, Mollie M. m. Keller, Josiah G. on 66-Jun-12 [66-Jun-19: 2B].
Yingling, O. H. P. (19 yrs., 5 mos.) d. on 68-Jul-22 [68-Jul-23: 2B].
Yingling, Samuel B. m. Williams, Anna M. on 69-Nov-16 [69-Nov-17: 2C].
Yockel, Charles Frederick (1 yr., 4 mos.) d. on 69-Mar-10 [69-Mar-11: 2C].
Yoe, George A. (30 yrs.) d. on 70-Dec-17 [70-Dec-20: 2B].
Yoe, George P. m. Holland, Annie on 70-May-11 [70-May-12: 2B; 70-May-14: 2A].
Yoe, James F. (49 yrs.) d. on 66-Sep-10 of Typhoid [66-Sep-22: 2B].
Yoe, Mary E. J. (6 mos.) d. on 69-Jul-4 [69-Jul-5: 2C].
Yonge, Mary H. d. on 66-Apr-12 [66-Apr-14: 2B].
York, William m. Morrow, Mary E. on 70-Feb-11 [70-Mar-9: 2C].
Yost, Atwell E. (31 yrs.) d. on 70-Feb-3 [70-Feb-5: 2C].
Yost, Richard D. m. McLean, Margaret Eugenia on 68-Jun-25 [68-Jun-29: 2B].
Yost, Susannah P. d. on 67-Nov-28 [67-Nov-30: 2C].
Yost, Virginia m. Pendleton, Edmund on 69-Jun-23 [69-Jun-28: 2C].
Youce, Clara V. m. Plummer, J. W. on 66-Apr-5 [66-Apr-9: 2B].
Young, Alexena C. m. Smith, William S. on 67-Nov-19 [67-Dec-5: 2C].
Young, Annie E. (29 yrs., 1 mo.) d. on 66-Dec-30 [66-Dec-31: 2B].
Young, Benjamin (37 yrs.) d. on 66-Oct-21 [66-Oct-22: 2C].
Young, Blanche Baker (7 mos.) d. on 70-Oct-5 [70-Oct-26: 2B].
Young, Charles Francis (4 yrs., 1 mo.) d. on 69-Jan-14 [69-Jan-16: 2C].
Young, Charles Randolph Magers (12 yrs., 5 mos.) d. on 70-Jul-30 Drowned [70-Aug-1: 2C, 4F].
Young, Clara Phillips (2 yrs., 9 mos.) d. on 69-Jun-20 [69-Jun-22: 2C].
Young, Cornelius W. (52 yrs.) d. on 66-Apr-10 [66-Apr-11: 2B].
Young, Eliza d. on 67-Mar-18 of Heart disease [67-Mar-19: 1F].
Young, Eliza m. Livingston, Livingus on 68-Apr-28 [68-Apr-30: 2B].
Young, Elizabeth d. on 68-Oct-31 [68-Nov-2: 2B].
Young, Elizabeth (17 yrs.) d. on 68-Feb-29 [68-Mar-2: 2C].
Young, Elizabeth d. on 69-Jul-2 [69-Jul-3: 2B].
Young, Ella R. M. m. Cole, Charles E. on 67-Jun-10 [67-Jun-22: 2B].
Young, F. Garnett m. Crouch, S. Jennie on 70-Jul-14 [70-Jul-19: 2B].
Young, Felicite E. m. Richardson, James O. on 67-Feb-21 [67-Feb-23: 2C].
Young, Floria (7 mos.) d. on 68-Jul-27 [68-Jul-29: 2B].
Young, Francis (30 yrs.) d. on 66-Nov-24 [66-Nov-26: 2C].
Young, George (70 yrs.) d. on 66-Nov-5 [66-Nov-6: 2B].
Young, George H. m. Applegarth, Sarah E., Miss on 68-Feb-6 [68-Feb-8: 2B].
Young, Hannah A. (24 yrs.) d. on 67-Oct-29 [67-Oct-30: 2B; 67-Oct-31: 2B].
Young, Isabella (91 yrs.) d. on 69-Nov-24 [69-Nov-25: 2C].
Young, J. Christopher m. Kraft, Louisa P. on 68-Oct-27 [69-Jan-12: 2C].
Young, James E. m. Burns, Kate on 69-Oct-10 [69-Oct-12: 2C; 69-Oct-30: 2B].
Young, James H. (27 yrs., 6 mos.) d. on 67-Feb-9 Drowned [67-Feb-12: 4C; 67-Feb-18: 2C].
Young, John C. m. Carlton, Hopewell Lynch on 67-Jan-10 [67-Jan-26: 2C].
Young, John Christopher (24 yrs.) d. on 70-Oct-13 [70-Oct-15: 2B].
Young, John W. m. Harrison, Sarah J. on 66-Mar-26 [66-Apr-7: 2B].
Young, Josephine m. White, Charles on 68-Feb-3 [68-Feb-8: 2B].
Young, Kate m. Lantz, Charles on 69-Nov-9 [69-Dec-14: 2C].
Young, Kate H. (34 yrs.) d. on 66-Oct-29 of Consumption [66-Nov-1: 2B].
Young, Laura H. m. Price, James T. on 70-Jan-14 [70-Jan-18: 2C].
Young, Laura V. m. Walker, George M. D. on 70-Mar-10 [70-Mar-24: 2C].
Young, Lydia (87 yrs.) d. on 69-Aug-12 [69-Aug-13: 2C].

Young, Margaret A. m. Bracker, John H. on 68-Jul-6 [68-Jul-7: 2B].
Young, Mary A. m. Rynehart, Samuel, Jr. on 66-Aug-26 [66-Aug-27: 2B; 66-Aug-28: 2B].
Young, Mary Ann (64 yrs.) d. on 67-Sep-4 [67-Sep-5: 2B].
Young, Mary Anne d. on 69-Apr-27 [69-Apr-29: 2B].
Young, Mary E. (21 yrs.) d. on 70-Mar-28 [70-Mar-30: 2C].
Young, R. A. m. Clagett, Fanny on 69-Aug-3 [69-Aug-5: 2B].
Young, Rachel (84 yrs.) d. on 66-Nov-25 [66-Dec-4: 2D].
Young, Rebecca (73 yrs.) d. on 69-Jun-4 [69-Jun-5: 2B].
Young, Samuel (45 yrs.) d. on 66-Jul-30 of Throat cancer [66-Aug-1: 1F].
Young, Sarah Frances (20 yrs.) d. on 68-Dec-24 [68-Dec-29: 2D].
Young, Thomas H. m. Hall, Kate on 69-Nov-30 [69-Dec-2: 2C].
Young, Virginia Ann (31 yrs., 6 mos.) d. on 68-Jan-3 [68-Jan-6: 2C].
Young, William (30 yrs.) d. on 70-May-19 Murdered (Shooting) [70-May-20: 1H; 70-May-21: 1H].
Young, William H. m. Evans, Julia A. on 66-Oct-17 [66-Oct-23: 2B].
Young, William H. m. Whitworth, Isabella on 69-Dec-28 [69-Dec-31: 2C].
Young, William S. m. Forney, Millie on 70-Jun-29 [70-Jul-4: 2C].
Younge, J. (50 yrs.) d. on 70-Jul-28 of Heatstroke [70-Jul-29: 4D].
Younger, Anna m. Arnold, William S. on 69-Jun-16 [69-Jun-26: 2B].
Younger, Jasper (76 yrs.) d. on 68-Oct-23 [68-Oct-24: 2B].
Youngman, M. M. m. Donaldson, J. J. on 65-Nov-16 [66-Jan-4: 2C].
Youngman, Rachel (76 yrs.) d. on 69-Dec-10 [69-Dec-20: 2C].
Youngs, Mary Ellen m. Roe, Thomas B. on 66-Apr-19 [66-Apr-26: 2B].
Youse, William m. Lookingland, Margaret on 68-Dec-28 [68-Dec-30: 2C].
Yundt, Rebecca (60 yrs.) d. on 67-Jan-14 [67-Jan-15: 2C].
Yunger, William (59 yrs.) d. on 66-May-15 [66-May-21: 2B].
Yunker, John George m. Ogden, Josephine on 67-Feb-17 [67-Feb-20: 2C].
Zahn, Fannie N. m. Ulbig, Joseph L. on 69-Feb-16 [69-Feb-18: 2C].
Zahnmesser, Sebastian m. Smith, Elizabeth on 65-Oct-29 [66-Jan-2: 2C].
Zane, Edmund P. m. Loughborough, Maria Louisa on 67-Apr-23 [67-Apr-26: 2B].
Zane, Eliza (80 yrs.) d. on 69-Mar-17 [69-Mar-18: 2C].
Zane, Mary M. S. (60 yrs.) d. on 67-Sep-28 [67-Sep-30: 2B].
Zange, August m. Herold, Amelia F. on 68-Nov-26 [68-Nov-28: 2C].
Zangenberg, George C. J. m. Childs, Martha A. on 66-Feb-22 [66-Feb-24: 2B].
Zantzinger, Mary Augusta (38 yrs.) d. on 70-May-4 [70-May-6: 2B].
Zastrow, Amelia C. m. Carter, Rodney F. on 68-Apr-14 [68-Apr-18: 2C].
Zeigler, Charles (33 yrs.) d. on 70-Jan-7 of Consumption [70-Jan-8: 2B].
Zeigler, David m. Kemp, Mary E. on 69-Jan-26 [69-Jan-30: 2C].
Zeigler, Elizabeth M. m. Greason, Joseph H. on 67-Jun-10 [67-Sep-9: 2B].
Zeigler, George Whitney (3 yrs., 1 mo.) d. on 70-Aug-25 [70-Aug-26: 2C].
Zeigler, Gotlibin H. m. Mudge, William R. on 67-Sep-23 [67-Sep-25: 2B].
Zeigler, Julia A. d. on 69-Oct-28 [69-Nov-27: 2C].
Zeigler, Marion Jane (16 yrs.) d. on 70-Jan-1 [70-Jan-3: 2C].
Zeigler, Mary Elizabeth (7 mos.) d. on 66-Jul-24 [66-Jul-25: 2C].
Zeigler, Mollie F. m. Harris, E. G. on 67-Nov-12 [67-Nov-14: 2B; 67-Nov-15: 2B].
Zeitler, Edward m. Hoffman, Isabella on 66-May-3 [66-May-5: 2B].
Zeitler, Michael (48 yrs.) d. on 69-Sep-28 of Heart disease [69-Sep-29: 1F].
Zell, Amelia (6 yrs.) d. on 67-Mar-8 [67-Mar-9: 2C].
Zell, Barbara A. m. Fefel, George W. on 70-Jul-7 [70-Jul-14: 2B].
Zell, Charles Edward (31 yrs., 1 mo.) d. on 66-May-22 [66-May-23: 2B].
Zell, Christian (40 yrs.) d. on 70-Jul-28 of Consumption [70-Jul-30: 2C].
Zell, Franky (1 yr.) d. on 66-Jul-22 [66-Jul-24: 2C].
Zell, Margaret (29 yrs.) d. on 69-Feb-2 [69-Feb-4: 2C].
Zell, Thomas J. m. Wilson, Ruth N. on 68-Jul-19 [68-Sep-14: 2B].
Zell, Virginia m. Crane, Charles C. on 69-Jun-3 [69-Jun-5: 2B].

Zeller, John W. m. Jordan, Margaret on 68-Nov-19 [68-Nov-21: 2C].
Zellers, John m. Ground, Annie H. on 68-Jul-1 [68-Jul-7: 2B].
Zepp, , Mrs. (21 yrs.) d. on 67-Oct-29 [67-Oct-30: 2B].
Zepp, Charles m. Seymour, Dora on 69-Aug-15 [69-Aug-20: 2C].
Zepp, John H. m. Airey, Mary C. on 67-Apr-11 [67-Apr-20: 2A].
Zepp, Leonard m. Miller, Mary Elizabeth on 68-Jun-9 [68-Jun-10: 2B].
Zerkel, Hettie Estelle (4 yrs., 1 mo.) d. on 70-Feb-25 [70-Feb-26: 2C].
Zerkel, Joseph Winfield (1 yr., 4 mos.) d. on 70-Mar-16 [70-Mar-17: 2C; 70-Mar-18: 2C].
Zerlein, H. d. on 68-Jul-17 of Heatstroke [68-Jul-18: 1E].
Zerweck, Daniel (43 yrs.) d. on 67-Feb-14 of Consumption [67-Feb-16: 2D].
Zerweck, Fannie (8 yrs., 2 mos.) d. on 69-May-20 [69-May-21: 2C].
Zerweck, Mary Ann (77 yrs.) d. on 68-Apr-21 [68-Apr-22: 2B; 68-Apr-23: 2B].
Zerweck, Philip David (31 yrs.) d. on 68-Apr-2 [68-Apr-3: 2C; 68-Apr-4: 2B].
Zerweck, Willie (10 mos.) d. on 67-Mar-9 [67-Mar-14: 2C].
Ziegle, Catharine (62 yrs.) d. on 66-Dec-21 [66-Dec-29: 2C].
Ziegler, Caroline (75 yrs.) d. on 68-Dec-3 [68-Dec-4: 2D].
Ziegler, Charles m. Ward, K. on 70-Mar-7 [70-Apr-19: 2B].
Ziegler, Emma A. m. Downs, John J. on 67-Apr-25 [67-Apr-29: 2B].
Ziegler, Frederick M. m. Hornbrook, Sarah on 70-Nov-17 [70-Nov-28: 2C].
Ziegler, John Frederick d. on 68-Jan-30 of Consumption [68-Jan-31: 2C].
Ziegler, Mary Ann (61 yrs., 8 mos.) d. on 69-Jul-7 [69-Jul-8: 2C].
Ziegler, Susan Annie (3 mos.) d. on 69-Jul-3 of Cholera infantum [69-Jul-8: 2C].
Zielle, Agatha (38 yrs.) d. on 69-Jul-9 of Suicide (Drowning) [69-Jul-12: 1G].
Zigler, Louisa (19 yrs.) d. on 69-Dec-1 [69-Dec-3: 2C].
Zimmer, Henrietta m. Standiford, Issac C. on 69-Jan-4 [69-Mar-8: 2C].
Zimmer, J. Philip (69 yrs.) d. on 69-Mar-21 [69-Mar-22: 2C; 69-Mar-23: 2C].
Zimmer, Maybelle Estelle (1 yr., 4 mos.) d. on 70-Dec-13 of Scarlet fever [70-Dec-15: 2C].
Zimmer, Rosina (81 yrs.) d. on 68-Oct-8 [68-Oct-9: 2C].
Zimmerman, Ann Maria d. on 66-Mar-16 [66-Mar-17: 2B].
Zimmerman, Anna Olivia m. Nicklas, William on 69-Nov-18 [69-Dec-30: 2C].
Zimmerman, Annie m. Pettit, Sylvester on 66-Feb-8 [66-Feb-10: 2C; 66-Feb-13: 2C].
Zimmerman, Charles A. m. Van Camp, Orsena L. R. on 67-Jun-5 [67-Jun-8: 2B].
Zimmerman, Christian (81 yrs.) d. on 66-Sep-22 [66-Sep-24: 2B].
Zimmerman, Dora E. m. Allen, Robert W. on 70-Jun-1 [70-Jun-21: 2C].
Zimmerman, E. Dora m. Harward, William C. on 70-Apr-9 [70-Apr-12: 2B].
Zimmerman, Elizabeth M. m. Bitner, Joseph on 70-Jun-21 [70-Jun-23: 2C].
Zimmerman, Emma Gertrude (4 yrs.) d. on 70-Oct-13 [70-Oct-14: 2B].
Zimmerman, Frances L. (58 yrs.) d. on 70-May-2 [70-May-4: 2C].
Zimmerman, George E. m. Price, Mattie E. on 66-Jan-30 [66-Feb-6: 2D].
Zimmerman, George H. m. Rowe, Nettie A. on 66-Oct-8 [66-Oct-9: 2A].
Zimmerman, George R. m. Disney, Lizzie A. on 69-Nov-25 [69-Nov-27: 2B].
Zimmerman, J. C. m. Hoblitzell, Sue G. on 67-Nov-7 [67-Nov-11: 2C].
Zimmerman, John d. on 68-Nov-10 in Construction accident [68-Nov-11: 1H].
Zimmerman, John C. m. Askey, Susie F. on 67-Mar-3 [67-May-29: 2B].
Zimmerman, Joseph A. H. m. Loftus, Hannah J. on 69-Jan-1 [69-Jan-4: 2C].
Zimmerman, Joseph Frey (21 yrs.) d. on 66-Oct-19 of Yellow fever [66-Nov-3: 2B].
Zimmerman, Julia Agnes (11 mos.) d. on 67-Jan-10 [67-Jan-11: 2C].
Zimmerman, Kate m. Cugle, Edwin on 70-Oct-18 [70-Oct-20: 2B; 70-Oct-21: 2C].
Zimmerman, Lizzie A. m. Brayshaw, John on 68-Apr-28 [68-May-4: 2B].
Zimmerman, Mary A. m. Nalle, Phillip on 69-Feb-24 [69-Feb-26: 2D; 69-Feb-27: 2C].
Zimmerman, Mary Theresie (22 yrs.) d. on 66-Apr-22 [66-Apr-26: 2B].
Zimmerman, Rebecca d. on 69-Mar-20 of Heart disease [69-Mar-22: 4D].
Zimmerman, S. A. m. Fisher, B. F. on 70-Feb-22 [70-Mar-5: 2B].
Zimmerman, S. B. d. on 66-Nov-12 [66-Nov-19: 2B].
Zimmerman, William E. m. Steele, Martha J. on 68-Nov-19 [68-Nov-23: 2B].

Zimmerman, William H. B. (37 yrs.) d. on 68-Apr-24 [68-May-5: 2B].
Zimmisch, William (62 yrs., 9 mos.) d. on 68-Dec-16 [68-Dec-19: 2B].
Zink, Louis m. Labby, Frances A. on 70-Jun-30 [70-Jul-8: 2C].
Zinkand, Margaret (25 yrs.) d. on 70-Jan-23 [70-Jan-31: 2C].
Zinkhahn, John (30 yrs.) d. on 66-Jul-17 of Heatstroke [66-Jul-18: 1F].
Zinkhan, Suzanne (35 yrs.) d. on 66-Jul-30 of Heart disease [66-Aug-1: 1G].
Zirkler, Lizzie m. Rost, Augustus on 67-Mar-27 [67-Apr-12: 2C].
Zirkler, Lydia (1 mo.) d. on 68-Feb-9 [68-Feb-11: 2C].
Zoeller, Mary Katie (10 yrs., 10 mos.) d. on 69-Oct-2 of Scarlet fever [69-Oct-5: 2B].
Zoellers, Kate m. Freedy, Dietrich on 70-Mar-1 [70-Mar-3: 2C].
Zoll, George d. on 70-Dec-17 of Construction cave-in [70-Dec-19: 4C].
Zollickoffer, Spurzheim, Dr. d. on 66-Aug-17 of Cholera [67-Apr-11: 2B].
Zollicoffer, Sallie m. Smith, George M. on 69-Dec-22 [69-Dec-24: 2C].
Zollinger, George N. m. Wise, M. Alice on 67-Sep-10 [67-Sep-14: 2A].
Zollinger, Jacob E. (24 yrs.) d. on 67-Jul-8 [67-Jul-9: 2B; 67-Jul-10: 2B].
Zollinger, Priscilla (83 yrs.) d. on 66-Dec-26 [66-Dec-29: 2C].
Zollinger, William P. m. Wood, Florence on 68-Nov-19 [68-Nov-21: 2C; 68-Nov-23: 2B].
Zorn, Dora d. on 66-Jul-17 of Heatstroke [66-Jul-19: 1F].
Zulauf, Michael, Rev. (50 yrs.) d. on 70-Feb-1 of Typhoid [70-Feb-12: 2C].
Zwanger, John A. (51 yrs.) d. on 68-Mar-14 [68-Mar-16: 1F, 2B].
Zwanzger, Mary B. m. Meeter, John F. on 67-Feb-12 [67-Feb-16: 2D].
Zwanzinger, , Mrs. d. on 66-Oct-1 of Cholera [66-Oct-2: 1G].
Zweisler, Christiana (81 yrs.) d. on 69-Jul-13 [69-Jul-15: 2C].

Addendum to

Index of
Obituaries and Marriages in
The [Baltimore] Sun

1861-1865

Francis P. O'Neill

Published by

FAMILY LINE PUBLICATIONS
Rear 63 East Main Street
Westminster, Maryland 21157

Send or call for a free catalog.

1-800-876-6103

*GENEALOGY * LOCAL HISTORY * EARLY MAPS*

Maryland * Pennsylvania * Delaware
New Jersey * North Carolina
Virginia * West Virginia
Washington, D.C.

Over 1000 titles in stock!

1996

Printed in the United States of America

Abell, Isaiah F. d. on 63-May-2 [63-May-4: 1F].
Abey, Joseph d. on 64-Feb-1 [64-Feb-3: 1G].
Abey, Peter Mowell d. on 61-May-4 [61-May-6: 4E].
Ackwith, Columbus d. on 63-Oct-7 [63-Oct-8: 1F].
Adams, Jane C. d. on 62-Dec-24 [62-Dec-27: 1G].
Adams, John E. d. on 62-Jul-15 [62-Jul-16: 1G].
Adams, John Thomas d. on 64-Mar-22 [64-Mar-23: 1E].
Addison, George C. d. on 63-Oct-6 [63-Oct-8: 1F].
Adler, Clara m. Reinhardt, M. E. on 63-Dec-15 [63-Dec-16: 1D].
Adreon, Annie Reno d. on 63-Jun-26 [63-Jun-30: 2D].
Ady, Francis d. on 65-May-7 [65-May-13: 1G].
Ailley, James d. on 63-Jul-11 [63-Jul-13: 1G].
Akers, Charles d. on 61-Mar-9 [61-Mar-11: 1G; 61-Mar-12: 1G].
Aldon, Adam d. on 63-Feb-2 [63-Feb-3: 2B].
Allen, A. d. on 63-Aug-31 [63-Sep-5: 1G].
Allen, James d. on 64-Sep-3 [64-Sep-5: 1F].
Allen, William G. d. on 65-Dec-23 [65-Dec-29: 1F].
Ambrose, James L. d. on 61-Dec-11 [61-Dec-13: 1F].
Anderson, Charles d. on 64-Feb-22 [64-Feb-24: 1E].
Anderson, John d. on 65-Aug-5 [65-Aug-7: 1G].
Anderson, Mary d. on 62-Apr-23 [62-Apr-28: 4C].
Anderson, Mary d. on 64-Mar-20 [64-Mar-22: 1F].
Annessly, Robert d. on 64-Dec-15 [64-Dec-16: 1G].
Appell, William d. on 64-Sep-26 [64-Sep-27: 1F].
Applegarth, William T. d. on 64-Aug-31 [64-Sep-2: 4B].
Arbin, Catharine, Mrs. d. on 62-Jan-21 [62-Jan-22: 1F].
Archer, James Philip d. on 61-Dec-4 [61-Dec-5: 1F].
Armholt, Gertlip d. on 65-Nov-25 [65-Nov-27: 1F].
Armstrong, Daniel S. d. on 64-Nov-9 [64-Nov-11: 1G].
Armstrong, David d. on 64-Feb-9 [64-Feb-10: 1G].
Armstrong, George d. on 63-Aug-22 [63-Aug-25: 1G].
Armstrong, Robert G. d. on 62-Jan-6 [62-Jan-8: 1G].
Arnold, Henry W. d. on 61-Sep-3 [61-Oct-29: 1G].
Arnold, Peter d. on 63-Aug-9 [63-Sep-8: 1G].
Ashby, Francis d. on 65-Apr-11 [65-Apr-11: 4D; 65-Apr-12: 1F].
Ashley, Millicent Teresa d. on 63-Jun-25 [63-Jun-30: 2D].
Ault, John d. on 63-Jan-12 [63-Jan-13: 1F; 63-Jan-14: 1F].
Austin, Thomas H. B. d. on 65-Jun-26 [65-Jun-27: 1F].
Ayres, James H., Jr. d. on 61-Jan-22 [61-Jan-23: 1F].
Ayres, Martha d. on 61-Dec-6 [61-Dec-7: 1G].
Babylon, Jacob d. on 62-Mar-6 [62-Mar-8: 4F].
Bacon, Mary d. on 61-Feb-1 [61-Feb-2: 1G].
Bailey, Anna d. on 61-Jun-18 [61-Jun-21: 1G].

Baker, Charles d. on 62-Oct-28 [62-Nov-1: 1G].
Baker, John d. on 64-Sep-9 [64-Sep-10: 1G].
Baker, John G. d. on 65-Aug-14 [65-Aug-30: 1G].
Ball, John d. on 63-Apr-4 [63-Apr-6: 1F].
Ballard, Bernhard d. on 65-Nov-16 [65-Nov-17: 1G].
Baltzell, John J. d. on 65-Feb-10 [65-Feb-13: 1G].
Bambaugh, Elizabeth d. on 61-Feb-24 [61-Feb-25: 1G].
Bandel, George S. d. on 64-Feb-13 [64-Feb-16: 1G].
Bangs, John d. on 63-Jun-7 [63-Jun-9: 1H].
Bankard, Jacob d. on 64-Feb-14 [64-Feb-17: 1F].
Bannan, Hugh d. on 61-Oct-18 [61-Oct-19: 1G; 61-Oct-21: 1G; 61-Oct-22: 1F].
Barker, William d. on 61-Oct-12 [61-Nov-16: 1G].
Barling, Joseph d. on 61-Nov-2 [61-Nov-4: 1G].
Barnard, James d. on 64-Apr-26 [64-May-7: 1F].
Barnard, Margaret d. on 64-Apr-27 [64-May-7: 1F].
Barnes, Abraham d. on 63-Apr-10 [63-Apr-13: 1G].
Barnes, Kate L. d. on 63-Jun-26 [63-Jun-30: 2D].
Barr, John Bernard d. on 61-Mar-5 [61-Mar-7: 1F].
Barrill, John d. on 61-Mar-21 [61-Mar-23: 1F].
Barry, George E. d. on 61-May-4 [61-May-7: 1G].
Bartholdt, John d. on 61-Jul-22 [61-Jul-26: 1G].
Bartholomay, John d. on 65-May-20 [65-May-22: 1F].
Bartin, Joshua d. on 64-May-12 [64-May-13: 1H].
Bartlett, William E., Sr. d. on 65-Aug-10 [65-Aug-15: 1G].
Basset, Charles d. on 61-Oct-19 [61-Oct-22: 1F].
Bateman, James O. d. on 63-Sep-6 [63-Sep-7: 1G].
Bathorn, Andrea S. d. on 64-Jul-2 [64-Jul-7: 1G].
Battee, Dennis H. d. on 65-Mar-8 [65-Mar-10: 1G].
Bauer, , Mrs. d. on 65-Jul-27 [65-Jul-29: 1G].
Baughman, John d. on 61-Mar-29 [61-Mar-30: 1F].
Baum, Herman d. on 64-Jun-3 [64-Jun-6: 1F].
Bayer, Lawrence d. on 63-Aug-11 [63-Aug-12: 1F].
Bayer, Lewis d. on 63-Aug-8 [63-Aug-10: 1F].
Bayfield, James H. d. on 62-Mar-10 [62-Mar-14: 1G].
Bayless, William J. d. on 65-Dec-9 [65-Dec-11: 1F].
Beall, Benjamin L. d. on 63-Aug-15 [63-Aug-17: 1F].
Bean, Helena d. on 64-Dec-8 [64-Dec-9: 1F].
Bean, Henry d. on 63-May-28 [63-May-30: 1F].
Beckley, Henry d. on 61-Sep-29 [61-Oct-1: 1F].
Beckwith, E. C. d. on 65-Feb-6 [65-Feb-7: 1F].
Beehler, George d. on 64-Mar-22 [64-Mar-23: 1F].
Behee, Francis d. on 65-May-23 [65-May-26: 1G].

Behering, Henry d. on 63-Feb-2 [63-Feb-4: 1F].
Beho, W. R. d. on 62-Jul-24 [62-Jul-25: 1G].
Bell, Frank d. on 63-Mar-12 [63-Mar-13: 1F].
Bellow, Lawrence d. on 62-Dec-28 [62-Dec-29: 1G].
Bennett, John d. on 61-May-27 [61-Jun-3: 4E].
Bennett, Livingston M. d. on 63-Sep-3 [63-Sep-7: 1F].
Benningham, Mary d. on 61-Dec-31 [62-Jan-3: 1G].
Benteen, Frederick D. d. on 64-Jan-22 [64-Jan-23: 1G].
Bentley, Ambrose d. on 63-Jun-2 [63-Jun-4: 1E].
Bentley, Grafton d. on 63-Sep-4 [63-Sep-5: 1G].
Berger, Joseph W. d. on 62-Jul-1 [62-Jul-15: 1F; 62-Jul-16: 1F].
Berry, Richard S. d. on 61-Apr-10 [61-Apr-15: 4C].
Berryman, John d. on 64-Feb-11 [64-Feb-12: 1F].
Betts, Royston d. on 64-Feb-28 [64-Feb-29: 1G].
Betts, William d. on 61-Dec-22 [61-Dec-24: 1G].
Betz, John d. on 63-Jan-20 [63-Jan-22: 1F; 63-Jan-23: 1G].
Bevan, Stephen d. on 62-Oct-27 [62-Oct-29: 1G].
Biddison, Meshach d. on 61-Dec-14 [61-Dec-16: 1F].
Birkholtz, Charles d. [63-Nov-20: 1G].
Blackman, John H. d. on 61-Jun-18 [61-Jun-21: 1G].
Blakemore, Charles E. d. on 61-Sep-2 [61-Sep-4: 1F].
Blakesly, John d. on 63-May-10 [63-May-12: 1G].
Blakistone, William T. d. on 63-Aug-1 [63-Aug-4: 1G].
Block, Andrew d. on 64-Jul-27 [64-Jul-28: 1G].
Blood, James d. on 65-Mar-24 [65-Mar-27: 1G].
Bloom, Jacob d. on 62-May-15 [62-May-16: 1F].
Bon, Charles d. on 61-Jun-19 [61-Jun-22: 1G].
Bond, Catherine d. on 65-Jan-1 [65-Jan-3: 1F].
Bond, William d. on 63-Jul-20 [63-Jul-22: 1G].
Bortner, Jesse d. on 61-Dec-5 [61-Dec-7: 1G].
Bottomer, Francis T. d. on 62-Aug-16 [62-Aug-18: 1F].
Bowen, Charles H. d. on 65-Mar-29 [65-Mar-30: 1G; 65-Mar-31: 1F].
Bowen, Eliza d. on 63-Nov-11 [63-Nov-12: 1F].
Bowen, John d. on 64-Nov-18 [64-Nov-21: 1F].
Bowen, John d. on 65-Dec-5 [65-Dec-9: 1G].
Bowen, Sarah d. on 62-Sep-25 [62-Sep-26: 1E].
Bower, Augustus d. on 65-Sep-6 [65-Sep-9: 1G].
Bowger, Perry d. on 63-Oct-2 [63-Oct-3: 1F].
Bowie, Maria M. d. on 62-Jun-16 [62-Jun-17: 1G].
Bowman, Edward d. on 61-Jun-27 [61-Jun-29: 1F].
Boyce, Joshua d. on 62-Oct-21 [62-Oct-23: 1G; 62-Oct-22: 1G].
Boyd, Joseph d. on 65-Feb-11 [65-Feb-13: 1G].
Boyd, Joseph C. d. on 61-Aug-6 [61-Aug-7: 1H].

Boyle, John S.   d. on 62-Mar-11 [62-Mar-13: 1G; 62-Mar-14: 1G].
Boyle, Michael   d. [62-Dec-15: 1G].
Boyle, William   d. on 61-Aug-3 [61-Aug-6: 1H].
Bradenbaugh, Charles, Esq.   d. on 62-Apr-16 [62-Apr-16: 1G; 62-Apr-18: 1G].
Bradsman, Conrad   d. on 62-Aug-28 [62-Sep-1: 4B].
Branin, Rachel   d. on 64-Apr-5 [64-Apr-6: 1E; 64-Apr-8: 1G].
Brannan, Randall B.   d. [61-Mar-28: 1E].
Brant, Erastus   d. [63-May-20: 1G].
Braws, Harriet   d. on 62-Apr-29 [62-Apr-30: 4D].
Brazier, Robert B.   d. on 63-Jun-9 [63-Jun-11: 1G].
Breckenridge, Mary C.   d. on 64-Oct-8 [64-Oct-10: 1F].
Breckinridge, John C.   d. on 62-Feb-3 [62-Feb-4: 1F].
Brien, Emily Jane   d. on 62-Dec-24 [62-Dec-25: 1G].
Brigerman, Frederick   d. on 61-Oct-12 [61-Oct-15: 1F].
Briggs, Hosea   d. on 65-Jul-20 [65-Jul-21: 1G].
Broadfoot, William J.   d. on 63-Aug-4 [63-Aug-5: 1G].
Brooks, William   d. on 62-Aug-13 [62-Aug-14: 1G; 62-Feb-15: 1G].
Broughton, Isaac W.   d. on 62-Mar-29 [62-Mar-31: 1G].
Broughton, William   d. on 63-Jun-27 [63-Jun-29: 4B].
Browall, Willie D.   d. on 64-Jul-28 [64-Jul-29: 1G].
Brown, Cassandra   d. on 61-May-27 [61-May-29: 1F].
Brown, Charles E.   d. on 61-Aug-8 [61-Aug-9: 1G].
Brown, Edward   d. on 61-Dec-7 [61-Dec-9: 1G].
Brown, Emmanuel M.   d. on 63-Sep-6 [63-Sep-8: 1G].
Brown, Henry G., Esq.   d. on 62-Jan-8 [62-Jan-10: 1G].
Brown, James   d. on 65-Oct-9 [65-Oct-10: 1F].
Brown, James, Jr.   d. on 63-Jul-3 [63-Jul-16: 4B].
Brown, John   d. on 64-Aug-22 [64-Aug-23: 1G].
Brown, John   d. on 61-Jun-10 [61-Jun-12: 1G].
Brown, John   d. on 63-Aug-11 [63-Aug-12: 1F].
Brown, John N.   d. on 65-Mar-5 [65-Mar-7: 1G].
Brown, Martin   d. [61-Sep-12: 1G].
Brown, Samuel, Sr.   d. on 61-Aug-17 [61-Aug-19: 1G].
Brown, William   d. on 61-May-27 [61-May-28: 1G].
Brown, William   d. on 65-Nov-14 [65-Nov-15: 1F].
Brown, William D.   d. on 63-Jul-10 [63-Jul-14: 1G; 63-Aug-1: 1G].
Bruce, George   d. on 61-Jul-24 [61-Jul-25: 1G].
Brundige, James   d. on 62-Dec-7 [62-Dec-9: 1F].
Brune, Charles   d. [64-Dec-17: 4A].
Bryan, Lewis   d. on 63-Aug-15 [63-Aug-17: 1G].
Bryan, William   d. on 65-Aug-24 [65-Aug-28: 1G].
Buchanan, Mary Ellen   d. on 63-Sep-10 [63-Sep-11: 1F; 63-Sep-12:

1G].
Buck, James d. on 65-Nov-1 [65-Nov-2: 1G].
Buckbaum, John d. on 64-Jul-5 [64-Jul-8: 1G].
Buckholtz, Clementina d. on 63-Aug-5 [63-Aug-8: 1G].
Buckler, Annie d. on 61-Jan-5 [61-Jan-7: 1F].
Buckley, Michael d. on 63-Jul-13 [63-Jul-18: 4C].
Buckley, Paul d. on 62-Feb-2 [62-Feb-7: 1G].
Buker, John d. on 63-Nov-24 [63-Nov-26: 1G].
Bulk, Jarvis W. d. on 64-Mar-2 [64-Mar-3: 1G].
Bull, Ambrose T. d. [61-Nov-5: 1E].
Bull, Randolph d. on 64-May-12 [64-May-18: 1G; 65-Oct-19: 1F].
Bunce, Robert d. on 65-Jul-24 [65-Jul-26: 1G].
Bundy, Wesley S. d. on 61-Jun-2 [61-Aug-19: 1G].
Bunting, Thomas d. on 62-Jul-17 [62-Jul-22: 1G].
Burger, Joseph d. on 63-Jul-9 [63-Jul-10: 1G].
Burgunder, Esther d. on 65-Jun-27 [65-Jun-29: 1F].
Burke, George W. d. on 64-Jun-4 [64-Jun-6: 1G].
Burke, John d. on 61-Nov-27 [61-Nov-30: 1G].
Burke, John d. on 61-May-8 [61-May-9: 1G].
Burke, Patrick d. on 61-Nov-11 [61-Nov-13: 4B].
Burke, William H. d. on 65-May-3 [65-May-4: 1G].
Burnham, William T. d. on 61-Oct-9 [61-Oct-10: 1F].
Burns, Francis d. on 63-Apr-19 [63-Apr-21: 1F].
Burns, John d. on 64-Aug-4 [64-Aug-6: 1G].
Burt, Henry d. on 61-Aug-30 [61-Sep-3: 1G].
Bush, Bernard d. on 61-Oct-17 [61-Oct-19: 1G].
Butler, William d. on 62-Sep-18 [62-Sep-19: 1G].
Byrne, Christopher Joseph d. on 62-Jul-13 [62-Jul-16: 1G].
Byrne, Peter A. d. on 61-Aug-27 [61-Aug-30: 1G].
Byrnes, Edward d. on 62-Sep-15 [62-Sep-17: 1F].
Cademore, John R. d. on 65-Jan-2 [65-Jan-6: 4E].
Camp, Joseph, Sr. d. on 64-Mar-20 [64-Mar-22: 1F].
Campbell, Archibald d. on 63-Jun-13 [63-Jun-15: 1G].
Campbell, Marshall C. d. on 65-Feb-22 [65-Feb-23: 1G].
Cane, Mary d. on 64-Sep-21 [64-Sep-23: 1G].
Caney, John d. on 64-Mar-13 [64-Mar-14: 1G].
Canfield, Edward d. [61-Oct-25: 1G].
Carey, George d. on 65-Feb-11 [65-Feb-13: 1G].
Carmine, George d. on 61-Nov-21 [61-Dec-10: 4F].
Carr, John d. on 64-Feb-11 [64-Feb-12: 1G].
Carroll, Charles d. on 62-Dec-2 [62-Dec-3: 1G].
Carroll, James d. on 64-Mar-4 [64-Mar-9: 1F].
Carroll, Sallie m. Cradock, Thomas on 62-Oct-22 [62-Oct-23: 1F].

Carroll, T. Stapleton d. on 62-Apr-14 [62-Apr-16: 1G; 62-Apr-19: 1G]
Casey, Francis W. d. on 62-Feb-4 [62-Feb-7: 1F].
Casey, Michael d. on 61-Apr-3 [61-Apr-4: 1F].
Cassady, John G. d. on 62-Oct-28 [62-Oct-29: 1G].
Cassard, Emma m. Tyler, G. B. on 65-Nov-21 [65-Nov-22: 1F].
Caton, Edward, Rev. d. on 62-Jun-26 [62-Jul-4: 1G].
Caughey, John H. d. on 62-Aug-24 [62-Aug-26: 1G; 62-Aug-29: 1G].
Caughey, Patrick, Esq. d. on 62-Mar-8 [62-Mar-11: 4D].
Caulk, James d. on 61-Oct-24 [61-Oct-25: 1G].
Chabot, G. H. d. on 63-Oct-2 [63-Oct-3: 1G].
Chambers, Robert F. d. on 64-Sep-9 [64-Sep-12: 1F].
Chambers, Robert M. d. on 64-Aug-14 [64-Aug-16: 1F].
Chambers, William d. on 63-Aug-11 [63-Aug-12: 1F].
Chapman, Joseph d. on 63-Dec-13 [63-Dec-15: 1G].
Chappell, Richard d. [61-Sep-19: 1G].
Chase, David d. on 65-Jul-1 [65-Jul-3: 1G].
Chase, Thorndick d. on 64-Oct-5 [64-Oct-6: 1G].
Cherry, M. Jerome d. on 64-Sep-24 [64-Sep-26: 1G].
Chesney, Benjamin d. on 65-Mar-18 [65-Mar-21: 1F].
Chew, Samuel d. on 63-Dec-25 [63-Dec-26: 1G].
Child, William, Esq. d. on 62-Feb-9 [62-Feb-11: 1G].
Childs, E. J. d. on 65-Dec-24 [65-Dec-27: 1G].
Chisholm, Collins d. on 61-May-6 [61-May-8: 1G].
Choate, Solomon d. on 61-Mar-6 [61-Mar-9: 1G].
Christopher, Harriet d. on 65-Jan-12 [65-Jan-13: 4D; 65-Jan-14: 1G]
Chubb, Anthony d. on 62-May-11 [62-May-12: 1G].
Church, Dolly d. on 61-Feb-1 [61-Feb-4: 1F; 61-Feb-8: 1F].
Church, Edward J. d. on 65-Jan-17 [65-Mar-11: 1G].
Clabby, Patrick d. on 64-Nov-6 [64-Nov-7: 1G].
Clackner, George W. d. on 64-Oct-22 [64-Dec-9: 1G].
Clark, Michael M. d. on 61-May-10 [61-May-11: 1G; 61-May-13: 4B].
Clarke, George d. on 62-Jan-5 [62-Jan-7: 1G; 62-Jan-8: 1G].
Clarke, William d. on 64-Jun-1 [64-Jun-3: 1F].
Clayton, Mary Emma d. on 61-Jun-15 [61-Jun-17: 1G].
Clement, Carter d. on 62-Nov-14 [62-Nov-17: 1G].
Clements, James d. on 61-Apr-2 [61-Apr-4: 1G].
Clemm, John Reese d. on 63-May-19 [63-May-20: 1G].
Clendenin, Alexander d. on 61-Apr-12 [61-Apr-13: 1G].
Cleveland, George W. d. on 65-Jul-14 [65-Jul-17: 1G].
Clipper, Casper d. on 61-Mar-7 [61-Mar-8: 1E].
Coath, Thomas J. d. on 64-Jan-5 [64-Jan-9: 1G].
Cochet, Dominic d. on 63-Jul-24 [63-Jul-25: 1G; 63-Jul-27: 1G].
Cole, Edward V. d. on 61-Dec-13 [61-Dec-20: 1F].

Cole, Frederick d. on 61-Jan-29 [61-Jan-30: 1F].
Cole, John M. d. on 65-Oct-8 [65-Nov-6: 1G].
Coleman, Henry R. d. on 61-May-18 [61-May-20: 1F].
Colgate, Charles d. on 65-Feb-12 [65-Feb-14: 1F].
Colley, John W. d. on 62-Sep-18 [62-Sep-22: 1F; 62-Sep-23: 1G].
Collins, Caroline d. on 61-Aug-22 [61-Aug-24: 1G].
Collins, George d. on 62-Oct-20 [62-Oct-21: 1F].
Collins, James d. on 64-Sep-22 [64-Sep-29: 1G].
Collins, James C. d. on 63-Aug-12 [63-Aug-13: 1F].
Collins, Mary J. d. on 64-Feb-2 [65-Feb-4: 1F].
Coloney, J. B. d. on 64-Oct-9 [64-Oct-12: 1G].
Comegys, Lemuel d. on 65-Mar-4 [65-Mar-8: 1G].
Conain, Louis d. on 65-Feb-18 [65-Feb-20: 1F].
Conlon, Consolata, Sr. d. on 62-Jul-30 [62-Aug-4: 1F].
Connelly, John d. on 64-Aug-4 [64-Aug-6: 1F].
Connelly, Mary d. on 64-Apr-4 [64-Apr-5: 1E].
Connery, John d. on 65-Feb-18 [65-Feb-20: 1G].
Connolly, Michael d. on 64-Sep-28 [64-Oct-1: 1F].
Connolly, Patrick d. on 61-Jul-10 [61-Jul-13: 1F; 61-Jul-15: 1G].
Conradt, C. G. d. on 63-Dec-23 [63-Dec-25: 1G].
Conradt, George M. d. on 63-Aug-4 [63-Aug-5: 1G].
Conradt, George M. d. on 61-Nov-19 [61-Nov-25: 1G].
Conroy, Bridget d. on 62-Mar-6 [62-Mar-10: 4C].
Cook, Charles d. on 65-Jul-1 [65-Jul-3: 1F].
Cook, David W. d. on 65-Aug-19 [65-Aug-21: 1E].
Cook, John W. d. on 62-Oct-30 [62-Oct-31: 1G].
Cooke, Frank d. on 62-Sep-20 [62-Sep-22: 1G].
Cooney, Julia A. d. on 64-Aug-28 [64-Aug-30: 1G].
Cooper, Andrew d. on 62-Aug-7 [62-Aug-8: 1G].
Cooper, Hamilton d. on 61-Jun-6 [61-Jun-13: 1G].
Cooper, J. D. d. on 65-Oct-31 [65-Nov-1: 1F].
Cooper, John d. on 65-Jul-25 [65-Jul-27: 1G].
Cooper, Matthew H., Capt. d. on 62-Jan-18 [62-Jan-20: 1G].
Cooper, T. L., Col. d. on 61-Dec-24 [62-Jan-9: 1D].
Cooper `, James d. [65-Dec-27: 1G].
Copper, Samuel d. on 65-Jan-10 [65-Jan-12: 4C].
Cornelius, John d. on 63-Aug-3 [63-Aug-5: 1G].
Cornthwaite, Edwin Willis d. on 64-Jun-29 [64-Jul-1: 1F].
Corretto, Charles W. d. on 63-Sep-3 [63-Dec-11: 1E].
Cosgrove, John d. on 62-Jul-27 [62-Jul-28: 1F].
Costello, Patrick d. on 65-Jan-6 [65-Jan-7: 1F; 65-Jan-9: 1E].
Costigan, Christopher J. Dorse d. on 62-Nov-10 [63-Jan-2: 1G].
Cottman, James S. d. on 63-Jun-8 [63-Jun-11: 1G].

Coursey, George d. on 65-Feb-14 [65-Feb-15: 1F].
Coursey, Richard d. on 61-Feb-18 [61-Feb-20: 1F].
Courtney, Patrick d. on 63-Mar-6 [63-Mar-7: 1F].
Cousix, John G. d. on 63-May-25 [63-May-27: 1G].
Covey, Richard d. on 64-Dec-23 [64-Dec-24: 1F; 64-Dec-28: 2C].
Cowles, George W. d. on 65-Feb-12 [65-Feb-13: 1G].
Cozine, John T. d. on 61-Dec-10 [61-Dec-13: 1F].
Cozzins, Stephen d. on 63-Aug-11 [63-Aug-12: 1F].
Cradock, Thomas m. Carroll, Sallie on 62-Oct-22 [62-Oct-23: 1F].
Craft, Charles H. d. on 64-Oct-22 [64-Oct-24: 1G].
Craft, Jacob d. on 62-Nov-26 [62-Nov-27: 1G].
Craig, Robert, Mr. d. on 62-Aug-23 [62-Aug-25: 1F].
Crane, Benjamin d. on 64-Oct-27 [64-Oct-28: 1G; 64-Oct-31: 1F].
Crawford, James d. on 63-Mar-5 [63-Mar-6: 1F].
Creamer, Anthony d. on 61-Jan-27 [61-Jan-28: 1F].
Cren, John d. on 63-Jun-2 [63-Jun-5: 1G].
Crocken, James J. d. on 65-Sep-18 [65-Sep-19: 1G].
Crocker, Charles W., Capt. d. on 62-Jun-3 [62-Jun-4: 1G].
Croghan, St George d. [62-Dec-9: 1F].
Cronnelly, Mary d. on 61-Dec-13 [61-Dec-16: 1F].
Crop, Christian d. on 63-Feb-3 [63-Feb-4: 1F].
Cross, George M. d. on 64-Jul-22 [64-Jul-25: 1F].
Crouch, Thomas d. on 64-Jan-18 [64-Jan-20: 1F].
Crouchman, George d. on 63-Jun-24 [63-Jun-25: 1G].
Crowe, Malachi d. on 63-Aug-6 [63-Aug-8: 1F; 63-Aug-10: 1F].
Crummer, Susan d. on 64-Nov-18 [64-Nov-22: 1F].
Crusty, Martin d. on 62-Jul-12 [62-Jul-14: 1F].
Culbertson, George d. on 61-Jun-28 [61-Jul-1: 1G].
Culbertson, James B. d. on 61-Apr-21 [61-Apr-22: 4B].
Cullen, Patrick d. on 63-Aug-10 [63-Aug-11: 1G].
Culley, Robert H. d. on 61-Jan-19 [61-Jan-22: 1E].
Cullison, Joshua d. on 63-Feb-23 [63-Feb-28: 1F].
Cullison, Owen d. on 63-Jan-8 [63-Jan-6: 1F; 63-Jan-9: 4C].
Cullum, John H. W. d. on 65-Aug-19 [65-Aug-21: 1F].
Cunningham, George A. d. on 64-Nov-6 [64-Nov-8: 1G].
Cunningham, George P. d. on 64-Aug-16 [64-Aug-17: 1G].
Cunningham, Thomas A. d. on 64-Jun-26 [64-Jul-19: 1G].
Cunningham, William W. d. on 65-Apr-3 [65-Apr-4: 1F].
Curran, Michael d. on 61-Mar-31 [61-Apr-1: 1F].
Currey, Samuel d. on 61-Oct-20 [61-Oct-21: 1G].
Curry, William d. on 62-Oct-27 [62-Oct-29: 1F].
Curtis, Patrick d. on 61-Apr-1 [61-Apr-2: 1F].
Curtis, Thomas d. on 63-May-31 [63-Jun-6: 1F].

Curtis, William d. on 62-Feb-15 [62-Feb-23: 4D].
Cusick, Francis d. on 61-Nov-22 [61-Nov-26: 1F].
Dail, Daniel d. on 63-Nov-28 [63-Nov-30: 1G].
Daley, Augustus J. d. on 63-Jan-19 [63-Jan-20: 1F; 63-Jan-21: 1F].
Dalrymple, Charles W. d. on 61-Jan-8 [61-Jan-10: 1G].
Danels, Joseph D. d. on 65-Mar-23 [65-Mar-24: 1F].
Daniel, Sophia Delahoy d. on 61-Jun-24 [61-Jun-25: 1F].
Daniels, William E. d. on 63-Jan-21 [63-Jan-24: 1F].
Danvelt, Caroline d. on 65-Jul-29 [65-Jul-31: 1G].
Dappon, Edward d. on 63-Aug-4 [63-Aug-5: 1G].
Darbusky, Henry d. on 64-Feb-20 [64-Feb-22: 1F].
Darling, James d. on 65-Jun-30 [65-Jul-1: 1G].
Davis, John d. on 64-Aug-2 [64-Aug-4: 1G].
Davis, Joseph d. on 63-Jun-28 [63-Jul-3: 1F].
Davis, Lawrence d. on 61-Sep-7 [61-Sep-9: 1F].
Davis, Thomas d. on 65-May-13 [65-May-15: 4B].
Davis, William d. on 65-Dec-26 [65-Dec-27: 1G].
Day, Jacob d. on 61-Aug-6 [61-Aug-7: 1H].
Day, John d. on 63-Aug-11 [63-Aug-12: 1F].
Deaver, John d. on 63-Nov-20 [63-Nov-23: 1G].
Deaver, John B. d. [61-Sep-2: 1G].
Decker, Peter d. on 63-Apr-18 [63-Apr-20: 1F].
Deiner, Elizabeth d. on 62-Dec-21 [62-Dec-22: 1G].
Deirtz, Bernard d. on 64-Jan-18 [64-Feb-14: 1F; 64-Feb-15: 1F].
Deitz, John d. [61-Sep-2: 1G].
DeLaBoiserie, Tanguay d. on 61-Jun-28 [61-Jul-1: 1G].
Delany, William d. on 63-Mar-27 [63-Mar-31: 1F].
Denbey, Rebecca d. on 61-Oct-17 [61-Oct-19: 1F].
Denmead, Adam d. on 64-Aug-10 [64-Aug-11: 1G].
Denny, Jenny d. on 61-Mar-11 [61-Mar-12: 1G; 61-Mar-13: 1F].
Denny, Mary Ann d. on 61-Mar-11 [61-Mar-12: 1G; 61-Mar-13: 1F].
Despeaux, John J. d. on 65-Jan-17 [65-Nov-1: 1G].
Dessler, Charles d. on 65-Dec-11 [65-Dec-12: 1F].
Devalin, Francis d. on 62-Oct-4 [62-Oct-6: 1F].
Dickson, William d. on 62-Jun-2 [62-Jun-4: 1G].
Diffey, Alexander d. on 63-Oct-16 [63-Oct-17: 1G].
Diggs, Beverly d. on 62-Oct-10 [62-Oct-11: 1G].
Disney, John W. d. on 61-Apr-9 [61-Apr-12: 1F].
Disney, Nicholas D. d. on 61-Jun-19 [61-Jun-20: 1G].
Disney, Nicholas D. d. on 61-Jan-13 [61-Jan-14: 1G].
Ditler, David d. on 65-Jul-3 [65-Jul-6: 4C].
Ditman, John J. d. on 63-Jun-29 [63-Jun-30: 2D].
Dittus, Rose Virginia d. on 63-Jun-28 [63-Jun-30: 2D].

Dixon, W. J., Mr.   d. on 62-Aug-13   [62-Aug-14: 1F].
Dobbin, Joseph T.   d. on 64-Dec-7   [64-Dec-8: 4C].
Dobbin, Robert A.   d. on 62-Aug-16   [62-Aug-18: 1C].
Dobbin, William B.   d. on 64-Mar-12   [64-Mar-14: 1F].
Dobson, George   d. on 63-Sep-5   [63-Sep-7: 1G].
Dohm, Charles F.   d. on 61-Dec-9   [61-Dec-20: 1G].
Dollman, George   d. on 65-Jul-29   [65-Jul-31: 1E].
Dolphin, Francis   d. on 63-Oct-15   [63-Oct-16: 1F].
Donahue, Thomas   d. on 61-May-17   [61-May-20: 1G].
Donaldson, Alexander   d. on 64-Jan-22   [64-Jan-26: 1G].
Donaldson, Samuel J.   d. on 65-Nov-26   [65-Nov-27: 1G].
Donnelly, Boy   d. on 61-Jun-16   [61-Jun-28: 1G].
Donohue, Joseph F.   d. on 65-Nov-8   [65-Nov-9: 1F].
Donovan, Joseph S.   d. on 61-Apr-15   [61-Apr-16: 1G].
Donovan, Michael   d. on 63-Nov-28   [63-Dec-2: 1F].
Dorbacker, William   d. on 63-Aug-15   [63-Aug-17: 1G].
Dorsey, Edwin   d. on 63-Nov-20   [63-Nov-21: 1F].
Dorsey, Hammond   d. on 61-Aug-4   [61-Aug-6: 1H].
Dorsey, Maggie A.   m. Sheckells, R. Whatcoat on 63-Jun-21 [63-Jun-30: 2D].
Dorsey, Samuel   d. on 63-Apr-25   [63-May-11: 1G].
Dosh, Adam   d. on 65-Jul-28   [65-Jul-29: 1G].
Doud, James   d. on 63-Jun-18   [63-Jun-20: 1F].
Douglas, Jacob   d. on 64-May-17   [64-May-21: 1F].
Douglas, Peter   d. on 62-Mar-10   [62-Mar-13: 1G].
Dowden, Thomas Heran   d. on 65-Mar-12   [65-Mar-14: 1F].
Dowman, Henry   d. on 62-Nov-22   [62-Nov-24: 1G].
Doyle, Edward   d. on 62-Aug-9   [62-Aug-11: 1F].
Driscoll, Dennis   d. on 62-Sep-24   [62-Sep-25: 1G; 62-Sep-29: 1F].
Driscoll, Georgeanna   d. on 64-Jan-3   [64-Jan-6: 1G].
Ducket, Issac   d. on 65-Mar-27   [65-Mar-29: 1G].
Dugan, Bridget   d. on 63-Aug-10   [63-Aug-11: 1G].
Dukehart, William B.   d. on 61-Feb-18   [61-Feb-19: 1E].
Dulaney, Edward   d. on 61-Dec-22   [61-Dec-25: 4B].
Dulany, Grafton L.   d. on 63-May-19   [63-May-21: 1F].
Duncan, Eliza   d. on 64-Mar-26   [64-Mar-28: 1G].
Dungan, Abel S.   d. on 63-Oct-27   [63-Oct-29: 1F; 63-Oct-30: 1F].
Dungan, Thomas M.   d. on 64-Aug-12   [64-Aug-15: 1F].
Dunn, James   d. on 61-Jan-11   [61-Jan-12: 1F].
Dunnigan, Catherine   d. on 63-Oct-30   [63-Nov-2: 1G].
Dunnigan, Thomas, Capt.   d. on 62-Jul-1   [62-Jul-12: 4C].
Dunning, William S.   d. on 65-Jul-30   [65-Aug-1: 1E].
Durken, Martin   d. on 63-Jun-18   [63-Jun-20: 1F].

Dushane, John d. on 61-Jul-6 [61-Jul-9: 1F].
Dushane, Nathan T. d. on 64-Aug-21 [64-Aug-23: 1F; 64-Aug-24: 4E; 64-Aug-26: 1F].
Duvall, Lemuel d. on 62-Jan-26 [62-Jul-29: 4E].
Dye, Phoebe d. on 64-Jun-27 [64-Jun-29: 1G].
Earle, Patrick d. on 62-Oct-18 [62-Oct-20: 1F].
Early, Mary d. on 62-Apr-15 [62-Apr-26: 1F].
Eaves, James d. on 63-Aug-12 [63-Aug-13: 1F].
Eberstein, Peter F. d. on 63-Dec-10 [63-Dec-11: 1G].
Eck, John d. on 61-Apr-10 [61-Apr-11: 1G].
Eckelberg, Henry d. on 63-Jul-30 [63-Jul-31: 1F].
Edwards, James d. on 63-Jun-2 [63-Jun-4: 1G].
Eggleston, Benjamin d. on 64-Dec-3 [64-Dec-8: 4C].
Eggleston, Josiah d. on 64-Aug-8 [64-Aug-10: 1G].
Ehlen, John H. d. on 64-Jan-8 [64-Jan-9: 1G].
Eichelberger, Itie d. on 63-Jun-14 [63-Jun-15: 1G].
Eickhoff, Theodore d. on 63-Aug-2 [63-Aug-3: 1G].
Ellert, Werner d. on 64-Jan-21 [64-Jan-4: 1F].
Elliott, James M. d. on 63-Nov-24 [63-Nov-25: 1G].
Ely, Hugh d. on 62-Dec-14 [62-Dec-16: 4C].
Ely, John C. d. on 64-Nov-20 [64-Nov-23: 1G].
Emory, A. Walsh d. on 65-Apr-9 [65-Apr-10: 4C].
Ennals, Charles d. on 64-May-27 [64-May-30: 1F].
Ennis, James d. on 63-Jul-16 [63-Jul-18: 4C].
Ensey, Lot d. on 64-Aug-21 [64-Aug-22: 1G].
Ensley, William d. on 65-Nov-10 [65-Nov-11: 1G].
Ensor, Franklin d. on 63-Nov-8 [63-Nov-9: 1G].
Ensor, John T. d. on 63-Jul-14 [63-Jul-15: 4B].
Erp, George d. on 63-Aug-8 [63-Aug-10: 1F].
Ervin, Henry d. on 62-Dec-24 [62-Dec-25: 1F].
Est, Jacob d. on 64-Nov-14 [64-Nov-16: 1F].
Etting, Samuel d. on 62-May-18 [62-May-18: 1G; 62-May-21: 1G].
Evans, Daniel W. d. on 63-Jun-29 [63-Jun-30: 2D].
Evans, Hugh W. d. on 63-Dec-6 [63-Dec-7: 4C].
Everside, Conrad d. on 62-Jan-18 [62-Jan-20: 1F].
Fahey, Bridget d. on 62-Nov-3 [62-Nov-3: 1G].
Fairbank, George d. on 64-May-27 [64-May-30: 1G].
Faithful, Lydia d. on 61-Oct-1 [61-Oct-2: 1F].
Faixall, William d. on 65-Aug-3 [65-Aug-4: 1G].
Falconer, Jonathan d. on 65-Mar-12 [65-Mar-15: 1F].
Farrow, Joseph d. on 61-Apr-30 [61-May-4: 1G].
Fennen, Bernard d. on 63-Feb-9 [63-Feb-11: 1G].
Fenster, John d. on 62-Apr-17 [62-Apr-18: 1G].

Fenton, John   d. on 65-Aug-1   [65-Aug-2: 1G].
Fenton, Michael   d. on 64-Aug-29   [64-Aug-30: 1G].
Ferguson, William   d. on 63-Aug-20   [63-Aug-25: 1G].
Ferranti, Antonio   d. on 61-Mar-10   [61-Mar-21: 1F].
Fieg, Martin   d. on 63-Dec-15   [63-Dec-17: 1F].
Field, Merrick Braufort   d. on 61-Aug-11   [61-Aug-12: 1G; 61-Aug-19: 1G; 61-Nov-21: 1F; 61-Dec-13: 1G].
Fields, William   d. on 64-Jul-15   [64-Jul-16: 1G].
Fiery, Henry   d. on 61-Dec-26   [62-Jan-2: 1G].
Finn, John F.   d. on 61-Feb-1   [61-Feb-4: 1G].
Finn, Margaret   d. on 64-Jan-25   [64-Jan-26: 1F].
Finney, Michael   d. on 63-Aug-6   [63-Aug-8: 1F].
Fisher, Jeremiah   d.   [63-Aug-8: 1F; 63-Aug-26: 1F].
Fisher, William J.   d. on 64-Nov-27   [64-Nov-29: 1F].
Fitzgerald, John B.   d. on 64-Jul-5   [64-Jul-6: 1G].
Fitzpatrick, Michael   d. on 61-May-3   [61-May-6: 4F].
Flaharty, James L.   d. on 64-Dec-16   [64-Dec-17: 4A].
Flannigan, Luke   d. on 62-Aug-7   [62-Aug-11: 1F].
Flarhety, Cornelius   d. on 62-Apr-27   [62-Apr-28: 4B].
Fleisher, Henry   d. on 62-Nov-16   [62-Nov-17: 1G; 62-Nov-18: 1F].
Fletcher, Washington   d. on 62-Dec-8   [62-Dec-9: 1G].
Flint, Thomas, Rev.   d. on 62-Sep-4   [62-Sep-5: 1F].
Flynn, John E.   d. on 61-Apr-6   [61-Apr-8: 1F].
Flynn, William F.   d. on 64-Dec-6   [64-Dec-7: 1G].
Foley, William F.   d. on 64-Jan-1   [64-Jan-4: 1G].
Forbes, William   d. on 65-Jul-29   [65-Jul-31: 1G].
Forbider, Adam   d. on 63-Aug-11   [63-Aug-13: 1F].
Ford, Mary Clare   d. on 65-Jul-1   [65-Jul-3: 1F].
Foreman, Joseph R.   d. on 64-Oct-3   [64-Oct-5: 1F].
Forrester, Barnett   d. on 64-Feb-6   [64-Feb-8: 1F].
Forsyth, Edward S.   d. on 62-Jan-1   [62-Jan-3: 1G].
Foster, James   d.   [62-Sep-15: 1F].
Foulkes, George   d. on 65-Jan-29   [65-Jan-31: 1F].
Foute, George   d. on 61-Dec-15   [61-Dec-16: 1G].
Fowble, Catherine B.   d. on 62-Dec-29   [63-Jan-1: 1G].
Fowler, John   d. on 65-Mar-15   [65-Mar-20: 1F].
Fox, Luther   d. on 62-Mar-20   [62-Mar-25: 4B].
Frailey, Leonard   d. on 64-Jul-25   [64-Jul-26: 1G].
France, Samuel   d. on 61-May-2   [61-May-4: 1G].
Franklin, Harrison T.   d. on 61-Oct-14   [61-Oct-15: 1F].
Franklin, Henry   d. on 65-Sep-5   [65-Sep-7: 1G].
Franklin, Joseph A.   d. on 62-Oct-4   [62-Oct-8: 1F].
Frazier, James   d. on 63-Jun-10   [63-Jun-11: 1G].

Freeland, Thomas d. on 62-Aug-16 [62-Aug-18: 1G].
Freeman, James d. on 64-May-2 [64-May-11: 1F; 64-May-13: 1F].
French, David E. d. on 61-Nov-9 [61-Nov-12: 1F].
Frensch, Adam d. on 61-Nov-25 [61-Nov-27: 1G].
Frew, James d. on 65-Jan-1 [65-Jan-2: 1G].
Friese, Ernest d. on 61-Apr-12 [61-Apr-13: 1G].
Fritz, John d. on 64-Jun-27 [64-Jul-2: 1G].
Fritz, John d. on 65-Apr-22 [65-Apr-23: 4A].
Fritz, William d. on 63-Jul-24 [63-Jul-25: 1G].
Fromherditz, John d. on 61-Apr-5 [61-Apr-8: 1F].
Frothingham, Charles L. d. on 63-May-2 [63-May-4: 1F].
Fryer, Mary d. on 65-Jul-11 [65-Jul-12: 1G].
Fuller, Henry d. on 61-Oct-6 [61-Oct-9: 1G].
Fuller, Josiah R. d. on 65-Sep-3 [65-Sep-6: 1F].
Fulton, George W. d. on 63-Aug-1 [63-Aug-22: 1G].
Fulton, John C. d. on 61-Mar-1 [61-Mar-5: 1G].
Fuss, John d. on 64-Sep-4 [64-Sep-6: 1G].
Gaddess, Alexander, Jr. d. on 65-Mar-31 [65-Apr-8: 1F].
Gadkins, Samuel S. d. on 62-Jan-22 [62-Jan-23: 1G].
Gail, Washington, Capt. d. on 62-Feb-14 [62-May-23: 1F].
Gaines, James d. [62-Aug-2: 1G].
Gaither, Samuel d. on 61-May-18 [61-May-20: 1G].
Gallagher, Francis P. d. on 61-Jan-28 [61-Jan-30: 1F].
Gallar, James d. on 64-Sep-13 [64-Sep-14: 1G].
Gardner, Samuel Oliver d. on 61-Nov-30 [61-Dec-2: 1G; 61-Dec-3: 1F
Gardner, William K. d. on 60-Dec-8 [61-Jan-31: 1G].
Garish, Samuel d. on 63-Dec-6 [63-Dec-8: 1F].
Garrett, John d. on 61-Apr-21 [61-Apr-23: 1G].
Garrett, Mary Sidonia d. on 65-May-12 [65-May-16: 1G].
Garrett, Patrick d. on 62-Apr-17 [62-Apr-21: 1G].
Garrity, Patrick d. on 62-Jul-9 [62-Jul-10: 1G].
Gayle, Joseph R. d. on 63-Jul-22 [63-Oct-7: 1G].
Gehring, , Mrs. d. on 61-Mar-6 [61-Mar-5: 1F; 61-Mar-8: 1F].
Gelling, John d. on 62-Jan-28 [62-Feb-1: 1F].
George, Archibald, Jr. d. on 62-Jan-3 [62-Jan-4: 1F].
George, James d. on 63-Dec-2 [63-Dec-4: 1G].
Gerbrick, Michael d. on 61-Nov-2 [61-Nov-4: 1G].
German, John d. on 65-Aug-11 [65-Aug-3: 1G; 65-Aug-12: 1G].
German, Julia d. on 65-Aug-9 [65-Aug-11: 1F].
German, Margaret d. on 64-Oct-11 [64-Oct-12: 1F].
German, Michael d. on 64-Oct-11 [64-Oct-12: 1F].
Gernhardt, Francis d. on 61-Sep-8 [61-Sep-10: 1F].
Gesner, Charles H. d. on 65-Feb-25 [65-Feb-28: 1F].

Gettier, Jacob d. on 64-Feb-19 [64-Feb-20: 1F].
Gibbons, Nicholas d. on 65-Jul-1 of 651 [65-Jul-3: 1G].
Gibbons, William d. on 64-Sep-24 [64-Sep-26: 1F].
Gibbs, James d. on 63-Feb-24 [63-Feb-25: 1G].
Gibson, David d. on 62-Aug-29 [62-Sep-22: 1G].
Gibson, George d. on 62-Mar-18 [62-Mar-22: 1F].
Gibson, William d. on 62-Oct-31 [62-Nov-1: 1G].
Gibson, William F. d. on 62-Nov-3 [62-Nov-5: 1E].
Gidelman, Maurice d. on 62-Mar-29 [62-Mar-31: 1G].
Gieselman, Charles d. on 61-Dec-5 [61-Dec-7: 1G].
Gilbert, Bennet d. on 62-Dec-16 [62-Dec-19: 1F].
Giles, John R. d. on 61-Mar-5 [61-Mar-6: 1F].
Giles, William Fell d. on 62-Jun-27 [62-Jul-15: 1F; 62-Jul-16: 1F].
Gilfoy, John d. on 62-Aug-12 [62-Aug-16: 1G].
Gill, George d. on 65-Apr-8 [65-Apr-15: 1G].
Gill, Michael d. on 63-Aug-12 [63-Aug-13: 1F; 63-Aug-14: 1F].
Gill, William F. d. on 64-Dec-19 [64-Dec-21: 1G].
Gilman, Charles d. on 61-Sep-9 [61-Sep-11: 1F].
Gilmore, Arthur d. on 65-Mar-26 [65-Mar-29: 1G].
Gittings, Henry N. d. on 62-Oct-31 [63-Feb-20: 1F].
Gittings, Thomas E. d. on 61-Jul-8 [61-Jul-11: 1G].
Gittings, William S. d. [63-Oct-30: 1G].
Given, John C. d. on 62-Jul-27 [62-Sep-12: 1F; 62-Sep-13: 1F].
Glandel, John d. on 63-May-5 [63-May-11: 1G].
Glass, John d. on 63-Jul-17 [63-Jul-20: 4C; 63-Jul-21: 1H].
Gleeson, John P. d. on 63-Oct-2 [63-Oct-7: 1G; 63-Nov-20: 1F].
Glemmon, Charles d. on 61-Nov-4 [61-Nov-5: 1F].
Goldsborough, Charles d. on 63-Dec-18 [63-Dec-19: 1F].
Goldsborough, William J. d. on 63-Aug-3 [63-Aug-4: 1G].
Goodwin, Edward D. d. on 65-Jun-9 [65-Jun-17: 1G].
Goodwin, Richard B. d. on 64-Jun-23 [64-Jun-24: 1F].
Gordon, Alexander B. d. [61-Dec-10: 4F].
Gordon, Francis d. on 65-Oct-13 [65-Oct-14: 1G].
Gordon, Joseph d. on 65-Nov-13 [65-Nov-15: 1F].
Gordon, William d. on 65-Nov-24 [65-Nov-30: 1F].
Gore, George d. on 61-Jan-9 [61-Jan-10: 1G].
Gorsuch, Robert W. d. on 65-May-16 [65-Jun-2: 1G].
Gott, John d. on 62-Aug-6 [62-Aug-8: 1G].
Goud, William d. on 61-Mar-7 [61-Mar-8: 1G].
Goudy, Stephen d. on 63-Sep-5 [63-Sep-14: 1F].
Gough, Alfred d. on 61-Dec-26 [61-Dec-28: 1G].
Gough, Patty Ann d. on 65-Dec-12 [65-Dec-15: 1G].
Gough, William d. on 61-Dec-25 [61-Dec-27: 4C].

Gould, Samuel Francis d. [63-Jan-17: 1F].
Gover, Samuel H., Jr. d. on 64-Mar-8 [64-Mar-10: 1F].
Gover, William L. d. on 64-Mar-1 [64-Mar-10: 1F].
Grabill, Thomas d. on 65-Jan-7 [65-Jan-9: 1E].
Grady, James d. on 63-Jan-12 [63-Jan-14: 1G].
Graff, Benjamin Franklin d. on 62-Jul-9 [62-Jul-10: 1G].
Graham, Jane d. on 64-Mar-10 [64-Mar-14: 1G].
Graham, Jeremiah d. on 61-Jun-15 [61-Jun-17: 1G].
Graham, William d. on 64-Nov-30 [64-Dec-5: 1F; 65-Jan-30: 1G].
Grammar, William H. d. on 62-Jan-11 [62-Jan-17: 2A].
Grant, Edward d. on 62-Feb-8 [62-Feb-15: 1G].
Grant, William d. on 65-Sep-9 [65-Sep-11: 1F].
Grason, John d. [63-Jan-7: 1G].
Gray, Adams d. on 65-Apr-8 [65-Apr-10: 4B].
Gray, James M. d. on 63-Nov-5 [63-Nov-6: 1E].
Grayson, Samuel d. on 62-Jan-22 [62-Jan-24: 1F].
Green, Charles d. on 63-Dec-10 [63-Dec-14: 1G].
Green, Emily d. on 62-Feb-5 [62-Feb-6: 1E].
Green, Mary Joseph d. on 65-Oct-27 [65-Nov-11: 4B].
Green, Richard d. on 61-May-21 [61-May-22: 1F].
Greentree, Asbury d. on 61-Jun-27 [61-Jun-28: 1G].
Greenwell, M. Borromeo d. on 64-Sep-5 [64-Sep-9: 1G].
Gregory, John B. d. on 65-Jun-15 [65-Jun-7: 1G; 65-Jun-10: 1F].
Griest, George d. on 65-Sep-24 [65-Sep-25: 1F].
Griffin, Patrick d. on 61-May-5 [61-May-6: 1F].
Griffith, Israel d. on 62-Aug-9 [62-Aug-11: 1G].
Griffith, John d. on 61-Nov-28 [61-Nov-30: 1F; 61-Dec-2: 1F].
Griffith, John A. d. on 62-Oct-4 [62-Oct-5: 1F].
Grisholm, Elijah d. on 65-Aug-13 [65-Aug-14: 1F].
Groff, Jacob d. on 64-Aug-8 [64-Aug-9: 1G].
Grogan, Patrick d. on 64-Apr-27 [64-Apr-29: 1F].
Grove, Henry B. d. on 65-Oct-29 [65-Oct-30: 1F; 65-Oct-31: 1G].
Grubert, Valentine d. on 62-Jul-13 [62-Jul-14: 1G].
Gunby, Francis A. d. on 64-Dec-19 [64-Dec-21: 1F].
Gundlach, Charles d. on 65-Aug-21 [65-Aug-30: 1G].
Guson, Charles d. on 64-Jul-30 [64-Aug-1: 1G].
Guy, William d. on 62-Feb-22 [62-Feb-24: 1G].
Gwyn, John R. d. [63-Feb-6: 1F].
Haan, Joseph d. on 65-Apr-5 [65-Apr-6: 1G].
Hacker, Henry d. on 63-Nov-14 [63-Nov-16: 1F].
Haff, Abraham d. on 64-Jan-29 [64-Jan-30: 1F].
Hagerty, Edward d. on 65-Sep-26 [65-Sep-27: 1G].
Haig, George H. d. [62-May-26: 1F].

Haight, George A.   d. on 64-Jan-13   [64-Jan-14: 1G].
Haines, Joseph   d. on 61-Nov-22   [61-Nov-23: 1G].
Haker, Paul   d. on 64-Sep-30   [64-Oct-1: 1F].
Hall, Chrity   d. on 61-Sep-24   [61-Sep-25: 1F].
Hall, Edward E.   d. on 61-Aug-6   [61-Aug-7: 1H].
Hall, Edward S.   d. on 61-Aug-6   [61-Aug-8: 1F].
Hall, Jesse, Sr.   d.   [62-Feb-19: 1E].
Hall, John   d. on 61-Aug-17   [61-Aug-20: 1G].
Hall, Nathaniel   d. on 62-Jun-25   [62-Jun-27: 1E].
Hall, Thomas N.   d. on 65-Nov-17   [65-Nov-20: 1F].
Hallack, William   d. on 65-Apr-27   [65-Apr-28: 1G].
Hamilton, Edwin R.   d. on 62-Feb-28   [62-Mar-24: 1G].
Hamilton, George   d. on 63-Sep-19   [63-Sep-21: 1F].
Hamilton, George D.   d. on 64-Apr-5   [64-Apr-7: 1F].
Hammond, John   d.   [62-Jan-4: 1F].
Hamsley, William H.   d. on 61-Nov-11   [61-Nov-13: 4C].
Hanan, John   d. on 65-Nov-11   [65-Nov-13: 1G].
Hance, James   d. on 65-Jul-16   [65-Jul-20: 1G].
Harden, J. M.   d. on 64-May-18   [64-Aug-3: 1G].
Harder, Jerome B.   d. on 65-Feb-25   [65-Feb-28: 1F; 65-Apr-20: 1G].
Hardesty, Mary Oliver   m. Stoneman, George on 61-Nov-21   [61-Nov-22: 1F].
Harding, Richard A.   d. on 65-Apr-12   [65-Apr-14: 1G].
Hare, Catharine   d. on 64-Dec-2   [64-Dec-11: 1G; 64-Dec-13: 1F].
Harlam, William   d. on 63-Jan-31   [63-Feb-2: 1G].
Harman, Francis   d. on 62-Jan-29   [62-Jan-30: 1F; 62-Jan-31: 1F].
Harrigan, John   d. on 61-Dec-24   [61-Feb-28: 1F].
Harrington, , Mrs.   d.   [61-Dec-12: 1F].
Harrington, Eliza   d. on 63-Aug-11   [63-Aug-12: 1F].
Harris, Noah   d. on 61-Dec-29   [61-Dec-31: 1G].
Harris, Richard   d.   [62-Feb-26: 1G].
Harrison, William H.   d. on 62-Nov-15   [62-Nov-19: 1F].
Harryman, Joshua   d. on 64-Sep-14   [64-Sep-15: 1G; 64-Sep-17: 1F].
Hartman, Anis   d. on 65-Aug-26   [65-Aug-28: 1G].
Hartman, Julia   d. on 62-Jan-8   [62-Jan-18: 1G; 62-Jan-20: 1G].
Haubert, Harman V.   d. on 63-Feb-12   [63-Feb-14: 1G].
Hawes, James   d. on 63-Sep-18   [63-Sep-19: 1G].
Hays, John   d. on 62-Sep-30   [62-Oct-1: 1G].
Hays, Stewart   d. on 62-Apr-21   [62-Apr-24: 1F].
Hays, William   d. on 63-Jan-29   [63-Jan-31: 1F].
Heaphy, John   d. on 65-Sep-9   [65-Sep-11: 1G].
Heath, Anna   d. on 65-Jan-14   [65-Jan-16: 4B].
Hedrick, William   d. on 65-Oct-25   [65-Nov-6: 1F].

Heighe, Benjamin M. d. on 61-Nov-20 [61-Nov-21: 1F; 61-Nov-22: 1(
Heilbrun, Michael d. on 61-Mar-10 [61-Mar-12: 1G].
Heiner, Elias d. on 63-Oct-20 [63-Oct-21: 1G].
Heiner, Elizabeth d. on 61-Oct-5 [61-Oct-7: 1F].
Heit, Walburga d. on 61-Feb-20 [61-Feb-21: 1E, 1G; 61-Feb-22: 1G].
Heiter, John, Jr. d. on 63-Nov-20 [63-Nov-21: 1F].
Hellen, Thomas J. d. on 61-May-7 [61-May-9: 1F].
Helmling, George d. on 65-Aug-22 [65-Aug-23: 1G].
Helsby, Hannah A. m. Richards, Joseph T. [63-Jun-30: 2D].
Hemling, James d. on 63-Jan-28 [63-Feb-3: 1F].
Hennick, Frederick A. d. [61-Sep-2: 1G].
Henry, James d. on 64-Jan-30 [64-Feb-2: 1G].
Herbert, Susan A. C. d. on 62-May-2 [62-May-12: 1G].
Hergesheimer, George d. on 61-Aug-5 [61-Aug-7: 1G; 61-Aug-9: 1F].
Herget, John d. on 65-Jun-27 [65-Jun-30: 1F].
Herring, George d. on 64-Aug-22 [64-Aug-23: 1F].
Hersey, John d. on 62-Nov-17 [62-Nov-25: 1G].
Hershberger, William d. on 61-Mar-21 [61-Mar-22: 1E].
Hess, Christina d. on 63-Aug-11 [63-Aug-12: 1F].
Hetz, George d. on 62-Oct-21 [62-Oct-22: 1G].
Hewell, Charles d. on 65-Jul-9 [65-Jul-11: 1F].
Hewing, William d. on 65-Jul-10 [65-Jul-13: 1G].
Hewitt, John T. d. on 63-Oct-17 [63-Oct-19: 1G].
Hewlett, John Q. d. on 64-Nov-5 [64-Nov-7: 1G].
Hickman, John d. on 65-Aug-7 [65-Aug-9: 1G].
Hicks, Thomas Holliday d. on 65-Feb-13 [65-Mar-8: 1F].
Higgins, Patrick d. on 65-Jul-6 [65-Jul-7: 1E; 65-Jul-8: 1F].
Higgins, Rufus M. d. on 61-Jan-9 [61-Feb-5: 1G].
Hilbert, Henry d. on 64-Sep-17 [64-Sep-19: 1G].
Hildebrand, Nicholas d. on 61-Jul-28 [61-Jul-30: 1H].
Hildegrist, Samuel d. on 65-Dec-25 [65-Dec-27: 1G].
Hill, James d. on 63-Mar-4 [63-Mar-5: 1F].
Hill, John d. on 65-Sep-4 [65-Sep-6: 1F].
Hill, Robert d. on 64-Oct-11 [64-Oct-12: 1G].
Hill, Susan d. on 62-Jan-25 [62-Jan-27: 1F].
Hilton, William H. d. on 61-Feb-3 [61-Feb-6: 1F].
Hinks, Charles D. d. on 63-Dec-11 [63-Dec-12: 4B].
Hinternick, Henry d. on 63-Jul-23 [63-Jul-24: 1G].
Hinton, Mary Washington d. on 64-Dec-5 [64-Dec-6: 1F].
Hintze, Frederick E. B. d. on 65-Oct-12 [65-Oct-14: 1F].
Hirst, William, Rev. d. on 62-Aug-10 [62-Aug-11: 1G].
Hiss, Stevenson d. on 65-Jul-12 [65-Jul-12: 1F; 65-Jul-13: 1G].
Hissey, William S. d. on 64-Feb-29 [64-Mar-5: 1G].

Hitzelberger, Agnes d. on 62-Sep-1 [62-Sep-5: 1F].
Hobbs, Thomoson d. on 62-Aug-24 [62-Aug-25: 1F].
Hobbs, William J. d. on 63-Aug-23 [63-Aug-24: 1G].
Hoeflich, Peter d. on 63-Apr-4 [63-Apr-6: 1F].
Hoffman, Henry d. on 64-Jun-7 [64-Jun-9: 1G].
Hoffman, Issac d. on 65-Apr-6 [65-Apr-8: 1F].
Hoffman, John d. on 63-Dec-23 [63-Sep-2: 1F].
Hoffman, John d. on 62-Oct-20 [62-Dec-22: 1G].
Hoffman, John d. on 64-Feb-9 [64-Feb-10: 1G].
Hoffman, John A., Esq. d. on 62-Apr-30 [62-May-2: 1G].
Hoffman, Thomas d. on 65-Nov-13 [65-Nov-14: 1G].
Hoffner, Henry d. on 65-Jun-6 [65-Jun-7: 1G].
Hogan, Edward d. on 65-Aug-29 [65-Oct-17: 1G].
Hogan, John d. on 64-Aug-7 [64-Aug-8: 1F].
Hogg, Edward d. on 62-Jun-3 [62-Jun-4: 1F].
Hogg, James d. on 65-Nov-28 [65-Nov-29: 1G].
Hogg, John d. on 64-Mar-29 [64-Apr-2: 1E].
Holloway, Robert d. on 63-Jul-20 [63-Jul-21: 1G; 63-Jul-23: 1G].
Holman, Daniel d. on 64-Jan-21 [64-Jan-22: 1G].
Holt, Issac d. on 61-Mar-9 [61-Mar-16: 1G].
Holton, Charles A. d. on 63-Dec-3 [63-Dec-9: 1F; 63-Dec-10: 4B].
Holtz, Henry C. m. Walker, Catherine Roseanna on 63-Jun-16 [63-Jun-30: 2D].
Hood, John d. on 62-Sep-25 [62-Sep-26: 1F].
Hook, Marcus R. d. on 61-Nov-12 [61-Nov-13: 4C].
Hooper, William d. on 63-Oct-29 [63-Oct-31: 1F].
Hooper, William H. d. on 62-Aug-2 [62-Aug-6: 1G].
Hoot, Henry d. on 61-Nov-4 [61-Nov-5: 1E].
Hoover, Daniel d. on 64-Apr-13 [64-Apr-15: 1F].
Hopkins, , Mrs. d. on 65-Aug-12 [65-Aug-14: 1E].
Horn, Charles d. on 61-Jun-20 [61-Jun-22: 1G].
Horner, Wilson G. d. on 64-Oct-28 [64-Oct-29: 1F; 64-Oct-31: 1F].
Horveng, Lena d. on 65-Sep-14 [65-Sep-15: 1F].
Hoshall, N. Howard d. on 63-Apr-11 [63-Apr-18: 1E].
Hossefros, George H. d. on 64-Mar-16 [64-Mar-19: 1F].
House, A. G. d. on 64-Aug-3 [64-Aug-6: 1F].
Houston, John d. on 62-Jan-17 [62-Jan-18: 1F].
Howad, Cornelia A. d. on 62-Dec-28 [62-Dec-29: 1G].
Howard, , Mrs. d. on 62-Jan-6 [62-Jan-8: 1G].
Howard, Ann d. on 64-Dec-2 [64-Dec-2: 1G].
Howard, Henry d. on 64-Jul-30 [64-Aug-6: 1G].
Howard, John d. on 62-Jun-18 [62-Jun-20: 1F].
Howard, John E. d. on 61-Dec-11 [61-Dec-13: 1F].

Howard, John Eager   d. on 62-Aug-12   [62-Aug-16: 1G].
Howard, Robert   d. on 65-May-12   [65-May-15: 4B].
Hubbard, George   d. on 63-Aug-12   [63-Aug-13: 1E].
Hubbell, Joseph   d.   [62-Nov-24: 1G].
Hucht, John B.   d. on 63-Aug-2   [63-Aug-3: 1G].
Hudson, Joseph   d. on 63-Sep-26   [63-Sep-28: 1F].
Hudson, Thomas N.   d. on 65-Aug-6   [65-Aug-7: 1F].
Hughes, George W.   d. on 62-Mar-14   [62-May-2: 1F].
Hughes, Michael F.   d. on 61-Nov-12   [61-Nov-13: 4B].
Huk, John   d. on 61-Jul-30   [61-Aug-1: 1H].
Hulme, Joseph   d. on 63-Aug-11   [63-Aug-13: 1F].
Hulse, John   d. on 64-Oct-8   [64-Oct-10: 1F].
Humpft, Catharine   d. on 62-Oct-22   [62-Oct-25: 1F].
Humphreys, Hugh   d. on 63-Oct-16   [63-Oct-17: 1G].
Humphreys, Oliver   d.   [64-May-2: 1F].
Hunnemyer, Christian   d. on 65-Apr-9   [65-Apr-10: 4C].
Hunter, Peter G.   d. on 61-Oct-11   [61-Nov-2: 1E].
Hurley, E. A.   d.   [62-Oct-18: 1F].
Hurley, Michael   d. on 64-Dec-11   [64-Dec-12: 1G].
Hurt, Christopher   d. on 61-Jan-3   [61-Jan-5: 1G].
Hutchins, Joshua   d. on 64-May-1   [64-May-7: 1F].
Hyde, John   d. on 63-Mar-13   [63-Mar-14: 1F].
Hynson, Benjamin Price   d. on 63-Aug-25   [63-Aug-28: 1G].
Hynson, John R.   d. on 64-Nov-28   [64-Nov-30: 1F].
Ing, Caroline   m. Newton, William S. on 63-Apr-16   [63-Jun-30: 2D].
Irons, Lucinda   d. on 63-Dec-28   [63-Dec-30: 1F].
Irwin, Julia   d. on 61-Mar-18   [61-Mar-19: 1G].
Isaacs, Andrew J., Mrs.   d. on 62-Jun-23   [62-Jun-24: 1F].
Jackson, Catharine   d. on 63-Jun-17   [63-Jun-18: 1G].
Jackson, Filmore   d. on 64-Aug-30   [64-Aug-30: 4C].
Jackson, Henry F.   d. on 62-Dec-12   [62-Dec-15: 1F].
Jackson, Jonathan   d. on 62-Dec-6   [62-Dec-8: 1G].
Jackson, Lewis   d. on 65-Jul-19   [65-Jul-20: 1G].
Jackson, Mary S.   d. on 63-Feb-4   [63-Feb-26: 1G].
Jacobsen, Henry G.   d. on 61-Jan-3   [61-Jan-5: 1G].
James, Edward   d. on 64-Oct-17   [64-Oct-24: 1G].
Jameson, Hamilton   d. on 64-Feb-17   [64-Feb-22: 1F].
Jamison, Cecilius C.   d. on 63-Sep-9   [63-Sep-10: 1G].
Jamison, John   d. on 65-Sep-20   [65-Sep-21: 4A].
Jamison, Thomas, Col.   d. on 62-May-5   [62-May-8: 1F].
Jamison, William   d. on 64-Nov-21   [64-Nov-22: 1F].
Jansen, Jacob   d. on 61-Sep-11   [61-Sep-13: 1G].
Jarvis, Nathan S.   d. on 62-May-12   [62-May-16: 1G].

Jay, Edward d. on 64-Jun-23 [64-Jul-2: 1G].
Jenkes, Johannes d. on 65-Aug-30 [65-Sep-1: 1F].
Jenkins, Benjamin d. on 63-Feb-3 [63-Feb-4: 1F].
Jenkins, Hugh d. on 63-Dec-1 [63-Dec-2: 1F; 63-Dec-3: 1F; 63-Dec-4 1G; 63-Dec-21: 1F].
Jenkins, J. Carroll d. [61-Oct-17: 1F].
Jerome, John H. T. d. on 63-Jan-27 [63-Jan-28: 1F; 63-Jan-30: 1F].
Jilmam, Martha d. on 62-Dec-19 [62-Dec-20: 1G].
Johns, L. H. d. on 64-Jun-27 [64-Jun-29: 1G].
Johnson, Finley d. on 64-Apr-27 [64-Apr-29: 1G].
Johnson, Frederica d. on 65-Jan-7 [65-Jan-9: 1F].
Johnson, Hiram d. on 65-Apr-5 [65-Apr-7: 1F].
Johnson, Horace d. on 61-Feb-24 [61-Feb-27: 1F].
Johnson, James d. on 64-Nov-8 [64-Nov-9: 1G].
Johnson, Joseph d. on 62-Jul-24 [62-Jul-25: 1G].
Johnson, Joshua d. on 65-Jun-16 [65-Jun-17: 1F].
Johnson, Julia Ann d. on 65-Mar-3 [65-Mar-4: 1G].
Johnson, Robert d. on 64-Feb-16 [64-Feb-17: 1F].
Johnson, Susan d. on 65-Jun-1 [65-Jun-12: 1F].
Johnson, Thomas d. on 64-Jun-2 [64-Jun-4: 1F].
Johnson, Thomas d. on 65-Nov-7 [65-Nov-7: 1G].
Johnson, Thomas d. on 64-Oct-12 [64-Oct-14: 1G].
Johnson, William Fell, Esq. d. on 62-Apr-15 [62-Apr-17: 1G].
Johnston, John R. d. on 63-Aug-15 [63-Aug-19: 1G; 63-Aug-20: 1G].
Jones, Alfred d. on 65-Mar-8 [65-Mar-11: 1F].
Jones, Ann d. on 63-Sep-6 [63-Sep-7: 1G].
Jones, Edmund d. on 64-Jan-11 [64-Jan-14: 4F].
Jones, Edward R. d. on 61-Feb-17 [61-Feb-19: 1F].
Jones, John d. on 62-Aug-21 [62-Aug-22: 1G].
Jones, Margaret d. on 64-Feb-19 [64-Feb-20: 1G].
Jones, Matthias d. [64-Dec-17: 4A].
Jones, Owen D. d. [61-Sep-14: 1F].
Jones, T. F. d. on 62-Oct-24 [62-Oct-25: 1G; 62-Oct-26: 1F].
Jones, Willie Tell d. on 63-Jun-29 [63-Jun-30: 2D].
Jordan, James Harry d. on 63-Jun-27 [63-Jun-30: 2D].
Jordan, Lewis d. on 65-Jun-7 [65-Jun-8: 1F].
Jordan, Louisa d. on 63-Nov-5 [63-Nov-7: 1G].
Jordon, J. J. d. on 63-May-18 [63-May-19: 1F].
Joslin, Benjamin Franklin, Dr. d. on 61-Dec-31 [62-Jan-9: 1F].
Jubb, Leonora Elizabeth d. on 61-Dec-12 [61-Dec-16: 1G].
Kahler, John d. on 65-Jul-31 [65-Jul-31: 1E].
Kalb, William d. on 63-Jul-20 [63-Jul-22: 1H].
Kauffelt, James B. d. on 64-Jul-17 [64-Jul-18: 1G].

Kaufhalz, George d. on 63-May-28 [63-Jun-1: 1E].
Kavanaugh, Roger d. on 61-Apr-12 [61-Apr-13: 1F].
Kay, Jacob d. on 63-Jul-28 [63-Jul-30: 1G].
Keech, John R. d. on 61-Dec-16 [61-Dec-17: 1G].
Keen, Aquila d. on 61-Mar-31 [61-Apr-2: 1G].
Keen, John d. on 64-May-14 [64-May-16: 4B].
Keene, Benjamin R. d. on 63-Sep-2 [63-Sep-3: 9G].
Keiser, Bennett d. on 64-Aug-18 [64-Aug-20: 1G].
Kelley, Andrew J. d. [64-Apr-22: 1F].
Kelley, James d. on 62-Oct-8 [62-Oct-9: 1F].
Kelley, Lizzie d. on 65-Apr-2 [65-Apr-4: 1F].
Kelley, Simon d. on 62-Feb-10 [62-Mar-11: 4D].
Kelly, Henrietta d. on 63-Sep-15 [63-Sep-16: 1G].
Kelly, James d. on 63-Nov-22 [63-Nov-23: 1G].
Kelly, Michael d. on 65-Jul-28 [65-Jul-31: 1G].
Kelly, Sarah d. on 65-Jul-15 [65-Jul-17: 1G].
Kelly, William F. d. on 65-Jun-9 [65-Jun-28: 1F].
Kelly, William L. d. on 62-Aug-10 [62-Aug-11: 1G].
Kemble, George d. on 63-Aug-10 [63-Aug-11: 1F].
Kemp, Thomas W. d. on 61-Sep-15 [61-Sep-17: 1G].
Kendeline, Margaret d. on 61-Feb-26 [61-Feb-28: 1E; 61-Mar-9: 1F].
Kenly, Edward d. on 61-Apr-29 [61-Apr-30: 1G].
Kennard, Perry d. on 61-Nov-22 [61-Nov-23: 1F].
Kennedy, Philip Clayton d. on 64-Aug-31 [64-Sep-1: 1G].
Kennedy, Samuel d. on 65-Sep-29 [65-Sep-30: 1F].
Kennedy, Sarah d. on 62-Dec-11 [62-Dec-12: 1F].
Kennedy, Thomas d. on 63-Feb-16 [63-Feb-17: 1G].
Kenney, Block d. on 62-May-26 [62-May-27: 1F].
Kenrick, Francis Patrick d. on 63-Jul-7 [63-Jul-9: 1F; 63-Jul-10: 1G; 63-Jul-11: 1G].
Kensett, Amelia Wheeler d. on 64-Nov-17 [64-Nov-18: 1G].
Kent, E. E d. on 64-Aug-9 [64-Aug-16: 1F].
Keplinger, Jonathan d. on 63-Apr-25 [63-Apr-29: 1G].
Kergle, William d. on 64-Feb-13 [64-Feb-15: 1E].
Kernan, , Miss d. on 65-Sep-28 [65-Sep-29: 1G].
Kernan, Edward d. on 63-Jan-28 [63-Feb-3: 1F].
Kernan, Matilda d. on 61-Jul-24 [61-Jul-25: 1G].
Kerns, Thomas d. [62-Sep-16: 1G].
Keuffner, F. A. d. on 65-Aug-15 [65-Aug-16: 1F].
Keyser, , Mr. d. on 64-Aug-6 [64-Aug-9: 1G].
Keyser, Ellen d. on 64-Jul-28 [64-Jul-29: 1G].
Kidd, Joehua H. d. on 64-Oct-6 [64-Oct-7: 1G].
Kidd, William d. on 63-Aug-12 [63-Aug-13: 1E].

Kidmore, John   d. on 64-Sep-27   [64-Sep-29: 1G].
Killman, William   d. on 63-Mar-26   [63-Mar-27: 1F].
King, Joseph, Jr.   d. on 65-Oct-29   [65-Oct-31: 1F].
King, Mary   d. on 63-Aug-2   [63-Aug-3: 1G].
King, Mary   d. on 65-Feb-5   [65-Feb-7: 1F].
King, Thomas   d. on 62-Sep-24   [62-Sep-27: 1G].
Kipp, George, Mrs.   d. on 65-Oct-22   [65-Oct-23: 1G].
Kipp, John, Sr.   d. on 62-Feb-14   [62-Feb-15: 1G].
Kirby, George   d.   [64-Jun-4: 1F].
Kirwan, George W.   d. on 63-Aug-15   [63-Aug-18: 1F].
Kirwan, John   d. on 63-Aug-5   [63-Aug-12: 1G].
Kitsinger, David   d. on 62-Jul-31   [62-Aug-2: 1G].
Klarman, William   d. on 61-Jul-28   [61-Jul-29: 1G].
Klinger, John   d. on 63-Sep-5   [63-Sep-7: 1G].
Knabe, William   d. on 64-May-21   [64-May-23: 1G].
Knapp, Henry   d. on 61-Feb-2   [61-Feb-4: 1F].
Knight, Cornelius D., Dr.   d.   [62-Aug-2: 1G].
Knight, John   d. on 61-Mar-15   [61-Mar-18: 1F].
Knoblock, Frederick   d. on 61-Apr-7   [61-Apr-9: 1F].
Knoll, John   d. on 65-Sep-15   [65-Sep-16: 1G].
Kone, David   d. on 62-Jan-1   [62-Jan-2: 4C].
Kopple, Morris   d. on 62-Jan-30   [62-Feb-3: 1G].
Kraft, Christian   d. on 61-Feb-10   [61-Feb-12: 1G].
Kraft, James   d. on 64-Nov-14   [64-Nov-15: 1G].
Kraft, William   d.   [64-Mar-21: 1F].
Krekel, Henry   d. on 64-Jul-30   [64-Aug-1: 1G].
Krider, Adam   d. on 64-Jan-4   [64-Jan-5: 1F].
Kriesman, William   d. on 61-Sep-21   [61-Sep-24: 1F].
Krug, George   d. on 62-Jan-8   [62-Jan-21: 1E].
Kuhn, Antone   d. on 64-Sep-12   [64-Sep-13: 1G].
Kuhn, George   d. on 64-Apr-30   [64-May-2: 1F].
Kurtz, Benjamin   d. on 65-Dec-29   [65-Dec-30: 1G].
LaFevre, Mary   d. on 62-Jun-12   [62-Jun-13: 1F].
Lankford, David E.   d. on 64-May-30   [64-May-31: 1E].
Lantz, Issac   d. on 65-Jun-1   [65-Jun-3: 1G].
Laroque, Francis Edward   d. on 61-Feb-15   [61-Feb-18: 1F].
Laroque, John M.   d. on 64-Mar-26   [64-Mar-28: 1F].
Latimer, Edward   d. on 64-Feb-14   [64-Feb-16: 1F].
Laypole, Andrew   d. on 64-May-23   [64-May-24: 1G].
Leakin, Sheppard A.   d. on 64-Sep-6   [64-Sep-10: 1G].
Lear, Henry   d. on 65-May-19   [65-May-20: 1F; 65-May-22: 1G].
Lecount, William M   d. on 65-May-27   [65-May-29: 1G; 65-Jun-1: 1F].
Ledlock, Michael   d. on 62-Jan-30   [62-Feb-3: 1G].

Lee, James L. d. on 65-Oct-25 [65-Oct-26: 1G].
Lee, Martha A. d. on 64-Apr-16 [64-Apr-18: 4B].
Lee, Ralph S. d. on 62-Mar-12 [62-Mar-15: 4C].
Leffler, Anne R. d. on 63-Mar-13 [63-Mar-14: 1F; 63-Mar-16: 1G].
Legrand, John C. d. on 61-Dec-29 [61-Dec-30: 4C].
Lehman, Nicholas d. on 63-Mar-29 [63-Apr-1: 1G].
Lemmon, William P. d. on 64-Mar-8 [64-Mar-14: 1F].
Lemon, John d. on 61-Mar-4 [61-Jun-7: 1F; 61-Jun-11: 1F].
Leopold, Isadore d. on 64-May-23 [64-May-24: 1G].
Leutner, Christopher d. on 63-Oct-3 [63-Oct-5: 1F].
Lewis, William T. d. on 65-Oct-26 [65-Nov-2: 1G].
Liemback, August d. on 65-Dec-6 [65-Dec-7: 1G].
Lindsay, James d. [64-Feb-23: 1G].
Lindsay, Richard d. [64-Feb-28: 1G].
Linhard, Philip d. on 62-Apr-19 [62-Apr-21: 1G].
Linn, William d. on 62-Nov-24 [62-Nov-27: 1F].
Lipner, Jane d. on 63-Oct-8 [63-Oct-19: 1G].
Lipp, Stefford d. on 62-Aug-3 [62-Aug-4: 1F].
Littig, Philip d. on 65-Mar-24 [65-Mar-25: 1G].
Little, Thomas d. on 65-Nov-20 [65-Nov-21: 1G].
Lloyd, John d. on 61-Feb-15 [61-Feb-18: 1G].
Lockington, Joshua d. on 61-Oct-15 [61-Oct-17: 1G].
Lockus, Charles d. on 61-Jul-10 [61-Jul-15: 1G].
Lofters, Hannah d. on 63-Apr-10 [63-Apr-13: 1G].
Logue, Bridget d. on 61-Mar-30 [61-Apr-1: 1F].
Loker, Michael J. d. on 61-Aug-14 [61-Aug-16: 1G].
Londheimer, Rebecca d. on 63-Jan-5 [63-Jan-7: 1G].
Long, (son Of Henry) d. on 62-Jan-19 [62-Jan-20: 1G].
Long, Henry d. on 63-Feb-28 [63-Mar-2: 1F].
Long, John H. d. [63-Jun-18: 1G].
Long, Katrina d. on 61-Sep-16 [61-Sep-20: 1G].
Longcope, William d. on 61-Jul-6 [61-Jul-9: 1F].
Loughran, Patrick d. on 63-Nov-7 [63-Nov-9: 1F].
Loura, Barbara, Miss d. on 62-Mar-5 [62-Apr-26: 1F].
Love, George B. d. on 65-Apr-19 [65-Apr-26: 4B].
Lovering, John E. d. on 62-Jan-3 [62-Jan-8: 1G].
Lowe, Thomas W. d. on 62-Nov-9 [62-Nov-11: 1G].
Lowery, John d. on 63-Aug-29 [63-Aug-31: 4B].
Lowndes, James d. on 65-Oct-28 [65-Nov-4: 1F; 65-Nov-6: 1F].
Luscombe, Frank d. on 64-Jan-6 [64-Jan-7: 1F].
Lutz, Melchior d. on 61-Aug-8 [61-Aug-9: 1F].
Lynch, Hannah d. on 63-Jan-1 [63-Jan-2: 1G].
Lynch, Susan d. on 61-Mar-12 [61-Mar-13: 1F].

Lynch, William F.   d. on 65-Oct-17   [65-Oct-18: 1G; 65-Oct-20: 1F].
Lynd, John A.   d. on 64-Jul-23   [64-Jul-25: 1F].
Mackenzie, John P.   d. on 64-Jan-14   [64-Jan-15: 1F; 64-Jan-18: 1F].
Madden, Henry J.   d. on 64-Sep-15   [64-Sep-17: 1F].
Magraw, Charles   d. on 65-Aug-9   [65-Aug-11: 1F].
Magraw, William   d. on 64-Apr-7   [64-Apr-8: 1G; 64-Apr-11: 1F].
Maguire, Julia   d. on 63-Aug-4   [63-Aug-5: 1G].
Mahan, John   d. on 63-May-18   [63-May-20: 1F].
Mahr, [girl]   d. on 61-Sep-3   [61-Sep-6: 1F].
Maitland, Benjamin, Jr.   d. on 60-Dec-30   [61-Jan-3: 1G].
Malcolm, James   d. on 64-May-10   [64-May-11: 1F; 64-May-12: 4B].
Mallon, Annie   d. on 62-Dec-22   [62-Dec-24: 1F].
Mallory, Peter   d. on 62-Dec-13   [62-Dec-15: 1G].
Malone, Daniel   d. on 61-Dec-7   [61-Dec-9: 1G].
Mankin, Isaiah   d. on 64-Apr-14   [64-Apr-20: 1F].
Mann, John, Dr.   d. on 62-Apr-29   [62-Apr-30: 4E].
Manning, James   d. on 65-Aug-10   [65-Aug-11: 1G].
Marquadt, H.   m. Sander, Minna on 63-Jun-25   [63-Jun-30: 2D].
Marriott, Joseph G. W.   d. on 63-Mar-14   [63-Mar-19: 1F].
Marsh, Charles   d. on 62-Jun-9   [62-Jun-10: 1F].
Marsh, Minerva   d. on 61-Apr-25   [61-Apr-27: 4C].
Marshall, Thomas   d. on 64-Sep-6   [64-Sep-7: 1G].
Marshall, Thomas H.   d. on 61-Oct-25   [61-Oct-26: 1G; 61-Oct-27: 1F]
Marson, William F.   d. on 61-Apr-20   [61-May-7: 1G].
Martin, Frederick   d. on 61-Nov-6   [61-Nov-8: 1F].
Martin, James A.   d. on 62-Oct-16   [62-Oct-17: 1F].
Mason, Sarah   d. on 61-Dec-20   [61-Dec-21: 4D].
Matthews, Line   d. on 65-Aug-18   [65-Aug-19: 1G].
Matthews, Thomas   d. on 64-Oct-1   [64-Oct-3: 1F].
Mattingly, John   d. on 65-Aug-15   [65-Aug-16: 1G].
Mattox, Franklin   d. on 62-Aug-2   [62-Aug-4: 1F].
Mattsbacker, James   d. on 61-Jul-1   [61-Jul-2: 1G].
Maund, Frederick, Dr.   d. on 62-Jul-31   [62-Aug-2: 1G].
Maxwell, Ann   d. on 61-Jan-20   [61-Jan-21: 4D].
Maxwell, John   d. on 62-Oct-18   [62-Oct-20: 1F].
Maxwell, Patrick   d. on 62-Dec-12   [62-Dec-13: 1F].
Mayer, Charles F.   d. on 64-Jan-3   [64-Jan-5: 1F].
Mayhew, William E.   d. on 65-Aug-30   [65-Sep-7: 1G].
McAllen, Thomas J.   d. on 61-Aug-10   [61-Aug-13: 1G].
McAllister, Alexander   d. on 62-Oct-26   [62-Dec-13: 1G].
McAllister, William H. W.   d. on 63-Jul-21   [63-Jul-29: 1F].
McAllister, William H. Watson   d.   [65-Jan-6: 4E].
McBlair, Michael   d. on 61-Dec-15   [61-Dec-16: 1G].

McCabe, Henry H. d. on 63-Aug-11 [63-Aug-13: 1F].
McCafferty, Mary d. on 61-Nov-7 [61-Nov-8: 1F].
McCafferty, William d. on 65-Aug-2 [65-Aug-3: 1G].
McCarrier, Mary d. on 65-Apr-22 [65-Apr-23: 4B].
McCauley, George W. d. on 64-Jul-11 [64-Jul-13: 1G].
McClay, John d. on 63-Jan-4 [63-Jan-6: 1G].
McColgan, Julia d. on 63-Dec-20 [63-Dec-22: 4C].
McConkey, James d. on 61-Dec-23 [61-Dec-25: 4B].
McCormack, Archibald d. on 63-Aug-12 [63-Aug-13: 1E].
McCormick, James d. on 62-Jul-9 [62-Jul-10: 1F].
McCormick, Mary d. on 61-Nov-22 [61-Nov-25: 1G].
McDaniels, William d. [64-Aug-8: 1F].
McDermott, Margaret d. on 61-Feb-11 [61-Feb-12: 1F].
McDermott, Michael d. on 65-Jan-12 [65-Jan-13: 4D].
McDonald, George W. d. on 64-Sep-21 [64-Sep-22: 1G].
McDonald, Michael d. on 65-Jul-13 [65-Jul-14: 1G].
McDonald, Thomas d. on 63-Sep-8 [63-Sep-2: 1G; 63-Sep-5: 1G;
  63-Sep-19: 1F].
McDonald, William d. on 64-Sep-6 [64-Sep-8: 1F; 64-Sep-10: 1F].
McDowell, Robert d. on 64-Jul-15 [64-Jul-29: 1G; 64-Aug-10: 1G].
McFadden, Thomas d. on 61-Oct-19 [61-Oct-22: 1F].
McFarland, Malcolm d. on 61-Dec-15 [61-Dec-16: 1G; 61-Dec-17: 1G
  61-Dec-18: 1F].
McFarland, Robert d. on 61-Mar-28 [61-Mar-30: 1G].
McFarrell, Michael d. on 64-Oct-2 [64-Oct-4: 1G].
McFay, Michael d. on 65-Aug-9 [65-Aug-11: 1F].
McGarity, Mary Xavier, Sr. d. on 62-Jun-17 [62-Jun-21: 1F].
McGivney, Michael d. on 64-May-23 [64-May-24: 1F].
McGuire, John d. on 65-Jul-2 [65-Jul-3: 1F].
McJilton, Mary Jane d. on 62-Jul-9 [62-Jul-9: 1F].
McKeldin, William d. on 64-Apr-15 [64-Apr-16: 1G].
McKewen, James d. [61-Oct-25: 1G].
McKiew, Patrick d. on 63-Jul-29 [63-Jul-30: 1G].
McKim, John S. d. on 65-Jan-11 [65-Jan-13: 4D].
McKim, Robert B. d. on 62-May-25 [62-Jun-14: 1F].
McKinley, Hester Ann Mana d. on 63-Feb-10 [63-Feb-11: 1F;
  63-Feb-12: 1F].
McKinsie, Robert d. on 63-May-15 [63-May-16: 1E].
McLaughlin, Andrew d. on 63-Jan-29 [63-Jan-30: 1F; 63-Feb-2: 1F].
McLaughlin, Daniel d. on 63-Nov-1 [63-Nov-3: 1D, 1F].
McLaughlin, John d. on 65-Jun-24 [65-Jun-26: 1G].
McLaughlin, Patrick d. on 64-Apr-18 [64-Apr-20: 1G].
McLean, Cornelius d. on 61-Jun-16 [61-Jun-18: 1F, 1G].

McLoughlin, Hugh d. on 65-Sep-9 [65-Sep-13: 1G].
McMahon, Bridget d. on 63-Jun-29 [63-Jun-30: 2D].
McManus, Mary Angela d. on 65-Nov-8 [65-Nov-24: 1G].
McQuay, Michael d. on 65-Aug-8 [65-Aug-10: 1F].
Meacham, Randall d. [64-Mar-14: 1F].
Means, John d. on 65-Sep-8 [65-Sep-9: 1G].
Medinger, John d. on 62-Aug-2 [62-Aug-4: 1F].
Meekins, Charles E. d. on 65-Jan-18 [65-Jan-19: 1F].
Meekins, Columbus d. on 62-Dec-28 [62-Dec-29: 1G].
Meeks, William d. on 63-Feb-10 [63-Feb-11: 1G].
Meredith, Sarah d. on 62-Feb-5 [62-Feb-6: 1G].
Merksey, Charles d. on 63-Sep-1 [63-Sep-2: 1G].
Merritt, Clara T. d. on 62-Feb-3 [62-Feb-7: 1G].
Metcalf, William M. d. on 62-Feb-11 [62-Feb-12: 1G].
Meyer, August d. on 65-May-7 [65-May-9: 1F].
Meyers, Charles d. on 62-Jun-4 [62-Jun-5: 1F].
Mezick, Baptist d. on 63-Mar-15 [63-Mar-18: 1G].
Michael, Joseph d. on 61-Feb-3 [61-Feb-4: 1G].
Middlekauff, Henry F. d. on 62-Jun-6 [62-Jun-13: 1G].
Miles, Dixon H. d. on 62-Sep-17 [62-Sep-19: 1G; 62-Sep-20: 1F].
Milholland, Edward d. on 63-Jul-10 [63-Jul-11: 1G].
Milholland, Jane F. d. on 65-Jan-14 [65-Jan-16: 4C].
Millard, Mary Eugenia d. on 63-Oct-14 [63-Oct-23: 1F].
Miller, Anton d. on 64-Apr-25 [64-Apr-26: 1F].
Miller, Daniel d. on 62-Nov-25 [62-Nov-27: 1G].
Miller, Elizabeth d. on 64-Dec-5 [64-Dec-6: 1F].
Miller, George d. on 64-May-30 [64-Jun-1: 1G].
Miller, John d. on 63-Sep-3 [63-Sep-4: 1G].
Miller, John d. on 64-Jan-12 [64-Jan-14: 1F].
Miller, Louis d. on 61-Sep-28 [61-Oct-18: 1G].
Miller, Mary d. on 61-Dec-31 [62-Jan-1: 1G].
Miller, Nicholas d. on 63-Oct-3 [63-Oct-6: 1F].
Miller, Thomas F. d. on 61-Dec-15 [61-Dec-17: 1F].
Miller, William B. d. on 65-Sep-5 [65-Sep-6: 1F].
Miller, William C. d. on 61-Apr-16 [61-Apr-17: 1G].
Miller, William F. d. on 64-Aug-16 [64-Aug-26: 1G].
Milliman, John d. on 62-Dec-19 [62-Dec-20: 1G].
Mills, Leah d. on 63-Oct-15 [63-Oct-16: 1G].
Mills, William E. d. on 63-Aug-8 [63-Aug-10: 1F].
Minton, John d. on 65-May-6 [65-May-8: 1F].
Mitchell, Edward d. on 63-Nov-8 [63-Nov-10: 1G].
Mitchell, Eliza Jane d. on 61-Sep-1 [61-Sep-3: 1G].
Mitchell, James, Jr. d. on 61-Jan-29 [61-Feb-1: 1E].

Mitchell, James H. d. on 63-Aug-13 [63-Aug-14: 1F].
Mitchell, William P. d. on 61-Nov-22 [61-Nov-26: 1G].
Modust, Frederick d. on 65-Oct-7 [65-Oct-9: 1G].
Monat, George d. on 61-Dec-30 [61-Dec-31: 1G].
Monroe, Thomas H. W. d. on 64-Jul-28 [64-Jul-30: 1G].
Moore, Elizabeth d. on 61-Aug-3 [61-Aug-5: 1G].
Moore, John F. d. on 63-Aug-16 [63-Aug-17: 1F].
Moore, John R. d. on 64-Apr-3 [64-Apr-4: 1F].
Moore, Margaret Ann d. on 61-Mar-30 [61-Apr-2: 1F; 61-Apr-3: 1G]
Moore, Rachel d. on 64-Feb-19 [64-Feb-20: 1E; 64-Feb-22: 1F].
Moore, Samuel d. on 63-Sep-2 [63-Sep-19: 1G].
Moore, Ulrich d. on 65-Oct-14 [65-Oct-16: 1G].
Moran, John P. d. on 64-Aug-2 [64-Aug-4: 1G].
Moran, Thomas d. on 64-Apr-27 [64-Apr-29: 1F].
Morfit, Henry Mason d. on 65-Dec-1 [65-Dec-16: 1F].
Morgan, John d. on 63-Apr-26 [63-Apr-27: 1F].
Morris, Barney d. on 64-May-11 [64-May-13: 1F; 64-May-14: 4B].
Morris, Charles d. on 65-Dec-27 [65-Dec-29: 1G].
Morris, Gouverneur d. on 65-Dec-25 [65-Dec-27: 1G].
Morris, John W. d. on 64-Jun-2 [64-Jun-3: 1F].
Morris, Thomas A. d. [63-Nov-20: 1G].
Morris, William W. d. on 65-Dec-11 [65-Dec-13: 1G; 65-Dec-14: 4E].
Morrow, William F. d. on 62-Dec-10 [63-Jan-31: 1G].
Morse, Henry d. on 61-Dec-12 [61-Dec-13: 1G].
Morton, Frederick A. d. on 63-Mar-30 [63-Apr-2: 1G; 63-Apr-4: 1G].
Mosenier, William d. on 64-Jun-26 [64-Jun-29: 1F].
Mosher, Max d. on 63-May-25 [63-May-26: 1F].
Moss, John d. on 63-Aug-4 [63-Aug-5: 1G].
Mowell, Christian d. on 63-Aug-11 [63-Aug-13: 1F].
Moxmile, Thomas d. on 62-Oct-19 [62-Oct-21: 1F].
Mullan, James d. on 64-Jul-31 [64-Aug-2: 1G].
Mullin, John d. on 62-Jul-18 [62-Jul-19: 1G].
Mullin, Patrick d. on 64-Aug-10 [64-Aug-12: 1F].
Mumma, David d. on 64-Sep-21 [64-Sep-22: 1G].
Munroe, Nathaniel d. on 61-May-8 [61-May-10: 1G].
Murdoch, Augustus d. on 63-Jan-4 [63-Jan-8: 1G; 63-Apr-13: 1G].
Murphy, Andrew d. on 62-Jun-9 [62-Jun-10: 1F].
Murphy, Dora d. on 64-Sep-17 [64-Sep-19: 1G].
Murphy, Michael d. on 65-May-27 [65-Jun-1: 1F].
Murphy, Thomas d. on 63-Aug-13 [63-Aug-17: 1F; 63-Aug-18: 1F].
Murphy, Thomas L. d. on 61-Mar-16 [61-Mar-18: 1F].
Murray, Albert d. [64-Apr-20: 1G].
Murray, Betsy d. on 64-Mar-18 [64-Mar-19: 1F].

Murray, Catherine d. on 65-Apr-7 [65-Apr-10: 4B].
Murray, James d. on 63-May-29 [63-May-30: 1F].
Murray, John d. on 61-Dec-18 [61-Dec-20: 1F].
Murray, Thomas d. on 65-Aug-15 [65-Aug-19: 1F].
Myers, Charles H. d. on 64-Jan-15 [64-Jan-16: 1G].
Myers, Henry d. on 62-Apr-1 [62-Apr-3: 1G].
Myers, Howard d. on 62-Apr-1 [62-Apr-3: 1G].
Myers, John d. on 65-Aug-14 [65-Aug-16: 1G].
Myrick, Joseph d. on 63-Nov-5 [63-Nov-13: 1F].
Nape, John d. on 65-Apr-5 [65-Apr-8: 1F].
Nash, Thomas d. on 63-Aug-2 [63-Aug-4: 1G].
Nathans, Phebe Ann d. on 62-Jan-24 [62-Jan-27: 1F].
Neal, Charles d. on 65-May-13 [65-May-15: 4B].
Nebur, Wallace d. on 62-Aug-12 [62-Aug-14: 1F].
Neimuller, William d. on 63-Aug-11 [63-Aug-12: 1F].
Nelson, William Franklin d. on 64-Jun-12 [64-Jun-13: 1F].
Newman, John d. on 65-Jul-28 [65-Jul-31: 1E].
Newton, William S. m. Ing, Caroline on 63-Apr-16 [63-Jun-30: 2D].
Nichols, Robert D. d. on 64-Mar-22 [64-Mar-24: 1G].
Nicholson, Charles Henry d. on 65-Sep-9 [65-Sep-11: 1G].
Nicholson, Joseph d. on 63-Sep-17 [63-Sep-18: 1F].
Nicholson, William d. on 62-May-6 [62-May-7: 1F].
Niles, Albert H. d. on 63-Mar-14 [63-Mar-16: 1G].
Niver, Henry d. on 61-Oct-31 [61-Nov-5: 1F].
Nix, Henry d. on 63-Feb-1 [63-Feb-2: 1G].
Nolan, Thomas d. on 61-Oct-4 [61-Oct-5: 1F].
Noonan, Robert, Capt. d. on 62-Mar-23 [62-Mar-27: 1G].
Norman, Francis d. on 63-Mar-28 [63-Mar-30: 1G].
Norris, Charles Sidney d. on 64-Jan-7 [64-Jan-8: 4E; 64-Jan-11: 1G]
Norris, Isaac d. on 62-Aug-23 [62-Aug-26: 1G].
Norris, John d. on 64-Aug-7 [64-Sep-9: 1G].
Norris, William d. on 65-Jun-27 [65-Jun-30: 1F].
Norris, William Pinckney d. on 61-Feb-15 [61-Feb-22: 1F].
North, Edward d. on 62-Feb-24 [62-Feb-26: 1G].
North, Oliver M. d. on 63-Jun-28 [63-Jun-30: 2D].
North, Wesley d. on 63-Feb-2 [63-Feb-3: 2B].
Norton, Edward d. on 65-Jan-10 [65-Jan-12: 4C].
Norton, Thomas d. on 64-Mar-11 [64-Mar-12: 1G].
Norwood, Charles d. on 65-Oct-26 [65-Oct-27: 1F; 65-Oct-28: 1F].
Norwood, John d. on 63-Jan-9 [63-Jan-13: 1G].
Nugent, Bernard d. on 62-Jul-5 [62-Jul-10: 1F].
O'Boyle, Michael d. on 65-Mar-19 [65-Mar-21: 1F].
O'Brien, Edward d. on 61-Jan-5 [61-Jan-7: 1F].

O'Brien, Henry d. on 62-Oct-8 [62-Oct-9: 1G].
O'Callaghan, D. d. on 64-Jan-12 [64-Jan-14: 1F].
O'Connor, James d. on 65-Nov-14 [65-Nov-15: 1F].
O'Hara, John d. on 64-Sep-22 [64-Sep-23: 1F; 64-Sep-24: 1F].
O'Neill, Cornelius d. on 63-Jul-20 [63-Jul-22: 1G; 63-Jul-23: 1G].
O'Neill, Lewis d. on 64-Jul-21 [64-Jul-23: 1F].
Oakley, James d. on 61-Jun-26 [61-Jun-28: 1G].
Oberlinden, Henry d. on 62-Apr-12 [62-Apr-14: 1G].
Obermeyer, Leonard d. on 65-Mar-16 [65-Mar-18: 1G; 65-Mar-22: 1G].
Odell, Anna d. on 63-Dec-23 [63-Dec-24: 1G].
Oehm, Frederick d. on 64-Jul-4 [64-Jul-6: 1G].
Onion, W. F. H. d. on 64-Dec-3 [64-Dec-5: 1F].
Orem, George d. on 61-Mar-3 [61-Mar-6: 1F; 61-Mar-4: 1E].
Orrick, John C. d. on 63-Dec-29 [63-Dec-31: 1F].
Orton, E. T. d. on 64-Feb-29 [64-Mar-2: 1G].
Osborn, Kitty d. on 64-Jun-26 [64-Jun-27: 1F].
Osterin, Phillip d. on 61-Dec-29 [62-Feb-22: 4D].
Ottarson, James d. on 62-Aug-27 [62-Aug-28: 1G].
Owens, Augustus G. W. d. on 65-Jun-25 [65-Jun-29: 1F].
Owens, Robert d. on 65-Jul-22 [65-Jul-24: 1G].
Owings, Jesse d. on 64-Apr-1 [64-Apr-4: 1G].
Paca, John B. d. on 65-Mar-8 [65-Mar-11: 1F].
Palmer, Edward d. on 64-Feb-25 [64-Feb-27: 1F].
Palmer, John d. on 63-Feb-8 [63-Feb-9: 1F].
Parker, James d. on 61-Oct-12 [61-Oct-15: 1F].
Passano, Joseph d. on 65-May-26 [65-May-27: 4A].
Patterson, Benjamin d. on 61-Nov-4 [61-Nov-6: 1G].
Patterson, Edward d. on 65-Sep-24 [65-Sep-26: 1G].
Patterson, Mary d. on 62-Dec-20 [62-Dec-22: 1G].
Patton, William d. on 65-Oct-27 [65-Oct-30: 1G].
Paul, D'Arcy d. on 61-Oct-8 [61-Oct-10: 1F].
Paul, William d. on 64-Jan-20 [64-Jan-21: 1F].
Paxton, George d. on 62-May-12 [62-May-19: 1F].
Paxton, Rosealba d. on 62-May-15 [62-May-16: 1F].
Peacock, Henrietta d. on 61-Apr-26 [61-Apr-27: 4C].
Pearce, Charles R. d. on 61-Aug-11 [61-Aug-13: 1G].
Peck, Henry d. on 65-Feb-13 [65-Feb-15: 1G].
Peck, John D. d. on 65-Jan-21 [65-Jan-23: 1G].
Peduzzi, John d. on 64-Aug-11 [64-Aug-13: 1F].
Pencil, , Mrs. d. on 64-Jun-8 [64-Jun-10: 1G].
Pendleton, Robert W. d. on 61-Apr-17 [61-Apr-19: 4C].
Penn, Elizabeth d. on 62-Aug-16 [62-Aug-18: 1G].

Pennig, Casper   d. on 63-Jul-29   [63-Jul-30: 1G].
Pennington, Charles   d. on 65-Oct-30   [65-Nov-1: 1G].
Pennington, Dorsey   d. on 62-May-3   [62-May-10: 1F].
Pentz, Philip Henry   d. on 64-Feb-15   [64-Feb-16: 1G].
Pepperam, , Mrs.   d. on 61-Jul-21   [61-Jul-22: 1F].
Peregoy, Joseph   d. on 61-Feb-25   [61-Feb-26: 1F].
Perine, Maulden   d. on 65-May-30   [65-May-31: 1F].
Perine, William B.   d. on 63-May-8   [63-May-11: 1E].
Perry, Robert   d. on 63-Aug-8   [63-Aug-11: 1G].
Peters, Edward J.   d. on 64-Dec-7   [64-Dec-9: 1G].
Peters, Louis   d. on 63-Aug-11   [63-Aug-12: 1F].
Peters, William   d. on 63-Nov-27   [63-Nov-28: 4B].
Pettit, Issac   d. on 61-Apr-17   [61-Apr-18: 1G].
Phelan, Patrick   d. on 62-Nov-25   [62-Nov-27: 1G].
Phenix, Dawson   d. on 64-Feb-20   [64-Feb-22: 1F; 64-Feb-24: 1F].
Phillips, Israel B.   d. on 62-Jul-12   [62-Jul-14: 1F].
Phillips, John   d. on 63-May-31   [63-Jun-4: 1G].
Phillips, John Crome   d. on 62-Nov-10   [63-Jan-2: 1G].
Phillips, Llewellyn   d. on 65-Mar-19   [65-Mar-20: 1G].
Phipps, Martha   d. on 64-Feb-20   [64-Feb-20: 1E; 64-Feb-22: 1F].
Pickering, John, Jr.   d. on 63-May-15   [63-May-26: 1F].
Pierce, Harvey L.   d. on 63-Nov-5   [63-Nov-18: 1G].
Piercy, Hannah   d. on 61-Mar-30   [61-Apr-2: 1G].
Piper, Jacob   d. on 61-Apr-16   [61-Apr-18: 1G].
Pitts, Charles H.   d. on 64-Aug-14   [64-Aug-17: 1E].
Plater, Romeli   d. on 64-Jul-30   [64-Aug-1: 1G].
Plowman, James T.   d. on 63-Jan-26   [63-Jan-29: 1G].
Poisal, John R.   d.   [62-Dec-20: 1G].
Pontier, Harry   d. on 64-Apr-26   [64-Apr-28: 1F].
Pontier, Thomas A.   d. on 65-Oct-14   [65-Oct-16: 1G].
Poole, George   d. on 65-Apr-14   [65-Apr-15: 1G].
Pope, Christian   d. on 62-Jun-20   [62-Jun-21: 1G].
Pope, James A.   d. on 63-Aug-1   [63-Aug-3: 1G].
Porter, Robert L.   d. on 61-Apr-9   [61-Apr-10: 1G].
Porter, Thomas   d. on 63-Feb-6   [63-May-9: 1G].
Potter, Cornelius   d. on 64-Sep-24   [64-Sep-26: 1G].
Poumairat, Charles H.   d. on 63-May-2   [63-May-4: 1G; 63-May-5: 1F].
Prentiss, John D.   d. on 61-Aug-31   [61-Sep-1: 1F].
Preston, Timothy   d. on 65-Jan-6   [65-Jan-7: 1F; 65-Jan-9: 1E].
Price, Andrew   d.   [62-Nov-4: 1G].
Price, George W.   d. on 64-Oct-29   [64-Nov-7: 1G].
Price, Henry   d. on 63-Jul-24   [63-Sep-4: 1G].
Pritchett, William   d. on 61-Dec-1   [61-Dec-4: 4B].

Proud, John G. d. on 65-Jul-12 [65-Jul-14: 1G].
Pryor, John d. on 61-Apr-3 [61-Apr-4: 1F; 61-Apr-5: 1E].
Pulley, Washington d. on 64-Dec-6 [64-Dec-13: 1F].
Pumphrey, Alpheus d. on 65-Nov-7 [65-Nov-10: 1G].
Purdy, William d. on 64-Mar-27 [64-Mar-30: 2F].
Purnell, Lemuel H. d. on 61-Jan-10 [61-Jan-14: 1G].
Quail, George K. d. on 64-Mar-27 [64-Mar-28: 1G].
Queen, Mary d. on 61-Nov-13 [61-Nov-15: 4B].
Quigley, Matthew d. on 64-Apr-6 [64-Apr-11: 1F].
Quinlan, John F. d. on 65-Jul-4 [65-Jul-6: 4C].
Quinn, Thomas d. on 63-Apr-30 [63-May-1: 1F].
Raborg, Christopher d. on 62-Jan-21 [62-Jan-22: 1F].
Raborg, George d. [62-Jun-20: 1F].
Raborg, William L. d. on 63-Aug-3 [63-Aug-8: 1F].
Radley, Michael d. on 63-Aug-12 [63-Aug-14: 1F].
Rafton, B. F. d. on 62-Oct-20 [62-Oct-21: 1F].
Raiker, James d. on 63-Feb-1 [63-Feb-2: 1G].
Ramsburg, Israel d. [63-Jan-22: 1G].
Ramsey, Robert d. on 64-Jul-28 [64-Jul-29: 1G; 64-Jul-30: 1G].
Randall, Enoch d. on 61-Aug-20 [61-Aug-21: 4B].
Randall, Samuel d. on 63-May-22 [63-May-22: 1E; 63-May-23: 1G].
Rankaub, Mary, Mrs. d. on 62-Aug-23 [62-Aug-25: 1G].
Rankin, Robert d. on 63-Aug-30 [63-Aug-31: 4C].
Rapp, Thomas J. d. on 63-Dec-19 [63-Dec-21: 1G].
Rash, Agnes d. on 61-Apr-29 [61-Apr-30: 1G].
Rau, John C. d. on 64-May-1 [64-May-2: 1F].
Ray, Frederick d. on 63-Aug-11 [63-Aug-12: 1F].
Rayland, William d. on 62-Dec-30 [62-Dec-31: 1F].
Reach, Edward d. on 64-Jul-14 [64-Jul-18: 1F].
Read, Samuel E. d. on 61-Oct-30 [61-Nov-22: 1F].
Reagg, Henry d. on 63-Jul-10 [63-Jul-13: 1G].
Rederbush, William d. on 65-Aug-2 [65-Aug-3: 1G].
Reed, James d. on 64-Dec-19 [64-Dec-20: 1F; 64-Dec-21: 1F].
Reed, John H. d. on 63-Aug-12 [63-Aug-13: 1R].
Reese, Charles S. d. on 61-Sep-24 [61-Sep-28: 1G].
Reese, Eli Yates d. on 61-Sep-14 [61-Sep-16: 1F; 61-Sep-17: 1F].
Reese, John, Rev. d. on 62-Mar-29 [62-Apr-1: 1F].
Reeves, Francis d. on 61-Aug-13 [61-Aug-19: 1G].
Reeves, Theodore d. on 62-Mar-24 [62-Mar-26: 1G].
Regester, Samuel d. on 65-Mar-18 [65-Mar-20: 1F].
Register, R. Wilson d. on 64-Jul-30 [64-Aug-6: 1G].
Reiley, Charles A. d. on 62-Jan-20 [62-Jan-23: 1G].
Reinhardt, M E. m. Adler, Clara on 63-Dec-15 [63-Dec-16: 1D].

Reisach, Joseph d. on 62-Nov-8 [62-Nov-10: 1G].
Reister, Hester Ann d. on 64-Feb-19 [64-Feb-20: 1F].
Rennous, John A. d. on 61-Oct-19 [61-Oct-25: 1G].
Reynolds, Dennis d. on 65-May-22 [65-May-25: 1F].
Reynolds, William Irving d. on 62-Oct-21 [62-Oct-22: 1F; 62-Oct-24: 1F].
Rhodes, John H. d. on 64-Jan-1 [64-Jan-2: 1G].
Richards, Joseph T. m. Helsby, Hanna A. [63-Jun-30: 2D].
Richardson, Morris d. on 62-Dec-15 [62-Dec-17: 1F].
Richardson, Samuel d. [61-Dec-9: 1G].
Richardson, William d. [62-Apr-14: 1G].
Richmond, Henry d. on 65-Nov-30 [65-Dec-2: 1F].
Rideaway, John E. d. on 61-Aug-23 [61-Aug-26: 1F].
Rider, Moses d. on 64-Jun-26 [64-Jun-27: 1F; 64-Jun-28: 1G].
Rieman, Henry d. on 65-Apr-27 [65-Apr-27: 1G].
Riggin, Israel, Mr. d. on 62-May-27 [62-May-29: 1G].
Riley, Charles d. on 63-Aug-11 [63-Aug-13: 1F].
Riley, James d. on 64-May-30 [64-May-31: 1E].
Riley, John d. on 62-Aug-7 [62-Aug-8: 1G].
Riley, Peter d. on 62-Dec-20 [62-Dec-22: 1G].
Rinehardt, Charles C. d. on 64-Feb-20 [64-Feb-22: 1F].
Roach, John d. on 61-Aug-16 [61-Aug-17: 1F].
Roberts, George d. on 61-Jan-14 [61-Jan-16: 1F].
Roberts, John d. on 61-Aug-10 [61-Aug-12: 1G].
Robertson, John T., Sr. d. on 61-Apr-1 [61-Apr-4: 1G; 61-Apr-5: 1F].
Robinson, Harry d. on 64-Jan-10 [64-Jan-12: 1F].
Robinson, Joseph d. on 63-Mar-17 [63-Mar-18: 1G; 63-Mar-21: 1C].
Robinson, Joseph W. S. d. on 61-Feb-27 [61-Mar-1: 1F].
Robinson, Thomas d. on 62-Jan-15 [62-Jan-17: 1F].
Roche, James d. on 62-Jul-12 [62-Jul-15: 1F].
Rodgers, John d. on 61-Nov-23 [61-Nov-25: 1G; 61-Nov-28: 1F].
Rogers, George d. on 62-Dec-9 [62-Dec-10: 1E].
Rogers, Nathaniel, Jr. d. on 62-Jan-4 [62-Jan-7: 1G].
Rogers, Seth d. on 65-Apr-5 [65-Apr-6: 1G].
Rogers, William, Capt. d. on 62-May-21 [62-May-23: 1F].
Rollins, Emily d. on 63-Mar-13 [63-Mar-14: 1F].
Rollins, William d. on 63-Dec-21 [63-Dec-22: 4C].
Ronsaville, Dayton d. on 65-Jul-27 [65-Jul-29: 1F; 65-Jul-31: 1E].
Rooney, John d. on 63-Jun-5 [63-Jun-6: 1F].
Roppenhier, Christian d. on 65-Feb-21 [65-Feb-24: 1F].
Rose, , Mrs. d. on 61-Nov-29 [61-Nov-30: 1F].
Rose, Robert d. [64-Mar-29: 1F].
Rosefield, Louisa d. on 62-Oct-31 [62-Nov-1: 1G].

Ross, William d. on 65-May-14 [65-May-15: 4B].
Roten, Charles d. on 61-Nov-7 [61-Nov-9: 1G; 61-Nov-13: 4B].
Rothrock, John d. on 65-Jul-14 [65-Jul-17: 1F].
Rough, Michael d. on 64-Nov-29 [64-Nov-30: 1F].
Rouse, Benjamin d. on 63-Aug-22 [63-Aug-26: 1G].
Rowan, Peter d. [62-Mar-25: 1G].
Rrichenberger, Sarah d. on 63-Dec-18 [63-Dec-19: 1G].
Rudolph, Caspar d. on 61-Jul-18 [61-Jul-20: 1G].
Rupp, George d. on 63-Apr-28 [63-Apr-30: 1F].
Ruppel, Conrad d. on 65-Dec-9 [65-Dec-11: 1F].
Russell, Catherine d. on 61-Jul-21 [61-Jul-22: 1G; 61-Jul-25: 1G].
Rust, Charles d. on 60-Nov-21 [61-Jan-18: 1G].
Rust, Samuel d. on 64-Feb-22 [64-Feb-24: 1F].
Rutherford, John W. d. on 64-Jun-10 [64-Jun-14: 1G].
Rutledge, Ida d. on 62-Sep-26 [62-Sep-27: 1G].
Ryan, Robert d. on 63-May-22 [63-May-23: 1G].
Sahm, George d. on 61-Jan-30 [61-Feb-1: 1E].
Sampson, Washington d. on 64-Jul-14 [64-Jul-16: 1G].
Sander, Minna m. Marquadt, H on 63-Jun-25 [63-Jun-30: 2D].
Sandford, Samuel d. on 63-Aug-19 [63-Aug-22: 1F].
Sands, James d. on 62-Sep-5 [62-Sep-6: 1F].
Sanner, George W. d. on 65-Nov-17 [65-Nov-22: 1F].
Sapem, George d. on 62-Aug-11 [62-Aug-12: 1F].
Sarbaugh, Jacob d. on 62-Sep-14 [62-Sep-19: 1G; 62-Oct-13: 1G].
Sargeant, Samuel R. d. on 64-Nov-12 [64-Nov-15: 1F].
Sauerwein, George d. on 64-Oct-3 [64-Oct-4: 1G].
Saulsberry, Andrew d. on 62-Jul-17 [62-Jul-23: 1F].
Scarborough, Henry d. on 65-Jun-17 [65-Jun-19: 1F].
Schaefer, Charles d. on 64-Mar-4 [64-Mar-9: 1F].
Schaefer, William d. on 64-Mar-4 [64-Mar-9: 1F].
Schaffner, Jacob d. on 61-Feb-12 [61-Feb-14: 1G].
Schears, Susanna d. on 64-Apr-1 [64-Apr-4: 1G].
Schilling, Henry d. on 64-Feb-20 [64-Feb-25: 1F].
Schillingham, Antoinette d. on 61-Apr-1 [61-Apr-2: 1F].
Schley, George d. on 64-Jul-6 [64-Jul-7: 1G; 64-Jul-8: 1G].
Schloss, Julius d. on 63-Jun-9 [63-Jun-10: 1F].
Schott, Caspar d. on 63-Oct-14 [63-Oct-15: 1G].
Schribner, John d. on 63-May-13 [63-May-15: 1F].
Schriver, John d. on 65-Aug-19 [65-Aug-21: 1G].
Scott, Elizabeth, Mrs. d. on 62-Apr-4 [62-Apr-5: 1E].
Scott, James H. d. on 63-Oct-2 [63-Oct-5: 1F].
Scott, Otho d. on 64-Mar-9 [64-Mar-11: 1G].
Sechler, Nathan G. d. on 61-Nov-9 [61-Nov-12: 1F].

Seipert, John d. on 64-Dec-11 [64-Dec-13: 1F].
Selden, George L. d. on 64-Feb-14 [64-Feb-17: 1E].
Seth, Robert L. d. on 65-Nov-2 [65-Nov-3: 1G].
Shaffer, Augustus d. on 64-Aug-27 [64-Aug-29: 1G].
Shambar, Theadra d. on 61-Apr-10 [61-Apr-12: 1F].
Sharp, Joseph d. on 65-Nov-6 [65-Nov-7: 1G].
Sharpley, John, Rev. d. on 62-Aug-4 [62-Aug-5: 1F].
Shaubdeis, H. T. d. on 65-Jul-27 [65-Jul-28: 1F].
Shaw, Joseph d. on 65-Apr-24 [65-Apr-26: 4A].
Shay, John d. on 63-Oct-17 [63-Oct-19: 1F].
Sheckells, Charles O. d. on 62-Dec-7 [62-Dec-8: 1G].
Sheckells, R. Whatcoat m. Dorsey, Maggie A. on 63-Jun-21
  [63-Jun-30: 2D].
Sheffield, J. B. d. on 61-Oct-6 [61-Oct-8: 1F; 61-Oct-9: 1F].
Sheriff, James M. d. on 65-Dec-26 [65-Dec-30: 1G].
Shipley, Edwin G. d. on 65-Nov-6 [65-Nov-7: 1G].
Shipley, Peter d. on 64-Dec-6 [64-Dec-7: 1G].
Shipley, Washington d. on 61-Oct-19 [61-Oct-21: 1G].
Shouft, Henry d. on 63-Feb-2 [63-Feb-3: 2B].
Shriner, John d. on 62-Jan-14 [62-Jan-17: 2A].
Shriver, Alexander d. on 64-Feb-8 [64-Feb-9: 1F].
Shriver, Jacob d. on 62-Jul-23 [62-Jul-25: 1F; 62-Jul-26: 1G].
Shutter, John d. on 61-Jul-9 [61-Jul-10: 1G].
Sicke, Henry d. [63-Jan-24: 1F; 63-Jan-26: 1F].
Sidney, Jeremiah d. on 65-Sep-7 [65-Sep-8: 1F].
Sieckken, Charles d. on 63-Nov-7 [63-Nov-9: 1G].
Simpson, Lizabell d. on 65-Oct-25 [65-Oct-26: 1G].
Skinner, Edward d. on 65-Jan-10 [65-Jan-12: 4C].
Skinner, Jeremiah d. on 61-Dec-10 [61-Dec-12: 1F].
Skinner, Thomas Buxton d. [65-Feb-7: 1F].
Slack, William B. d. on 62-Dec-18 [62-Dec-19: 1G].
Slack, William T. d. on 61-Dec-25 [62-Jan-3: 1G].
Slater, Charles Henry d. on 61-Aug-11 [61-Aug-13: 1G].
Slater, William d. on 65-Oct-3 [65-Oct-5: 1G; 65-Oct-7: 1F].
Slaughter, Henry B. d. on 65-Oct-26 [65-Oct-28: 1F].
Slicer, Andrew d. on 65-Jun-20 [65-Jun-21: 1G].
Sloan, Florence d. on 63-Jan-23 [63-Jan-24: 1F].
Sloan, Francis d. on 63-Jan-23 [63-Jan-24: 1F].
Sloane, Ella d. on 64-Mar-5 [64-Mar-7: 1F].
Small, Moses d. on 61-Apr-15 [61-Apr-16: 1F].
Smallwood, John d. on 62-Mar-6 [62-Mar-10: 4C].
Smith, Alexander A. d. on 64-Nov-7 [64-Nov-9: 1F].
Smith, Annie d. on 65-Dec-29 [65-Dec-30: 1G].

Smith, Catharine d. [62-Dec-22: 1G].
Smith, Charles d. on 61-Mar-9 [61-Mar-12: 1F].
Smith, David C. d. on 62-Dec-29 [62-Dec-30: 1G].
Smith, Edward d. on 63-May-28 [63-Apr-29: 1G].
Smith, Elizabeth d. on 61-Aug-30 [61-Aug-31: 1F].
Smith, Emily d. on 64-Nov-19 [64-Nov-21: 1G].
Smith, Francis d. on 62-Dec-8 [62-Dec-9: 1F].
Smith, James d. on 64-Mar-28 [64-Mar-30: 1G].
Smith, James R. d. on 65-Aug-3 [65-Aug-4: 1G].
Smith, John d. on 65-Nov-3 [65-Nov-4: 1F].
Smith, Joseph S. d. on 64-Jan-20 [64-Jan-21: 1F].
Smith, Leonidas L. d. on 65-Nov-1 [65-Nov-3: 1G].
Smith, Levin d. on 62-Jun-14 [62-Jun-16: 1E].
Smith, Matthew d. on 65-Jul-11 [65-Jul-14: 1G].
Smith, Michael d. on 65-Dec-25 [65-Dec-27: 1F].
Smith, Nicholas d. [61-May-27: 1G].
Smith, Nicholas d. on 64-Sep-10 [64-Sep-12: 1G].
Smith, Rachel A. d. on 61-Feb-5 [61-Feb-6: 1E].
Smith, Samuel H. d. on 65-Dec-25 [65-Dec-27: 1G].
Smith, Sarah d. on 63-Apr-7 [63-Apr-9: 1F].
Smith, Thomas J. d. on 63-Aug-22 [63-Aug-25: 1G].
Smith, Walter P. d. on 63-Jul-10 [63-Jul-20: 4B].
Smith, William d. on 63-Feb-2 [63-Feb-3: 2B].
Smith, William H. d. on 61-Oct-20 [61-Nov-2: 1E].
Smith, William M. d. on 64-Jun-25 [64-Jun-27: 1G].
Smithson, Gabriel C. d. on 64-Jan-26 [64-Jan-29: 1G].
Snow, Charles, Capt. d. on 62-Jun-8 [62-Jun-10: 1G].
Snowden, Benjamin d. on 61-Feb-19 [61-Feb-21: 1G].
Snyder, Benjamin d. on 61-Nov-29 [61-Dec-2: 1F].
Snyder, J. d. on 61-May-13 [61-May-14: 1G].
Snyder, John d. on 64-Sep-28 [64-Sep-30: 1F].
Snyder, William d. on 61-Mar-11 [61-Mar-12: 1F; 61-Mar-15: 1F].
Snyder, William d. on 64-Sep-28 [64-Sep-30: 1F].
Sohl, George d. on 62-Aug-20 [62-Aug-22: 1G].
Sollers, James H. d. on 64-Mar-14 [64-Apr-4: 1G].
Spalding, Basil R. d. on 62-Dec-7 [62-Dec-9: 1F].
Spangler, Franklin P. d. on 62-Jun-5 [62-Jun-6: 1F].
Spencer, Oliver J. d. on 61-Feb-8 [61-Apr-16: 1F].
Spicer, Thomas d. on 64-Mar-13 [64-Apr-14: 1F].
Spiegel, Alexander d. on 64-Mar-16 [64-Mar-17: 1G].
Splan, John d. on 63-Jan-15 [63-Jan-16: 1F].
Sprague, Charles d. on 61-Nov-2 [61-Nov-5: 1F].
Sprague, George d. on 65-Mar-14 [65-Mar-15: 1G; 65-Mar-16: 1F].

Spreer, Frederick d. on 65-May-21 [65-May-26: 1G].
Sprigg, Nancy d. on 64-Dec-9 [64-Dec-12: 1G].
Sprigg, William d. on 63-May-4 [63-May-5: 1G].
Spring, Frederick d. on 65-May-20 [65-May-22: 1F].
Sproston, John Glendy, Lt. d. on 62-Jun-8 [62-Jun-20: 1F].
Stalker, John H. d. on 65-Feb-28 [65-Apr-20: 1G].
Stall, Conrad d. on 63-Aug-3 [63-Aug-6: 1G].
Stallings, Joseph d. on 63-May-10 [63-May-11: 1F].
Stansbury, Carville S. d. on 65-Apr-2 [65-Apr-3: 4B].
Stansbury, Jared d. on 61-Nov-20 [61-Nov-23: 1G].
Stanton, Joseph d. on 62-Oct-8 [62-Oct-20: 1G].
Starr, James F. d. on 65-Jul-6 [65-Jul-7: 1E; 65-Jul-8: 1G].
Starr, Lipman d. on 61-Oct-13 [61-Oct-17: 1F].
Staylor, Henry d. on 63-Jan-2 [63-Jan-3: 1G].
Steele, David E. d. on 64-Mar-10 [64-Mar-11: 1F].
Steiger, Adam d. on 62-Jun-22 [62-Jun-24: 1F].
Stephens, Alexander, Sr. d. on 63-May-12 [63-May-4: 1G].
Stephenson, Peter A. d. on 65-May-15 [65-May-17: 1G].
Sterling, John d. on 62-Oct-30 [62-Oct-31: 1G].
Stesch, Adolphus d. on 61-May-12 [61-May-13: 4C].
Steurlein, George d. on 62-Sep-17 [62-Sep-18: 1G].
Steven, James Reverdy d. on 62-Mar-27 [62-Mar-28: 1F].
Stevens, James W. d. on 65-Dec-14 [65-Dec-16: 1F].
Stevens, Joseph d. on 65-Mar-12 [65-Mar-15: 1G].
Stevenson, Louisa d. on 63-May-19 [63-May-20: 1F].
Steward, Edward d. on 62-Oct-28 [62-Oct-29: 1F].
Stewart, James d. on 61-Feb-22 [61-Feb-23: 1G].
Stewart, Mary d. on 62-Jul-24 [62-Jul-25: 1G].
Stieff, Charles M. d. on 62-Jan-1 [62-Jan-3: 1G].
Stigears, George d. on 64-Jul-12 [64-Jul-13: 1G].
Stine, Willie Franklin d. on 63-Jun-6 [63-Jun-9: 1G].
Stinerick, Jacob d. on 65-Mar-16 [65-Mar-20: 1G].
Stinger, Henry d. [61-Dec-17: 1F].
Stinson, William H. d. on 64-Dec-19 [64-Dec-21: 1G].
Stirrat, James d. on 64-Nov-1 [64-Nov-3: 1G; 64-Nov-5: 1G].
Stockbridge, John H. d. on 64-Dec-16 [64-Dec-17: 4A].
Stockett, George Franklin d. on 62-Oct-20 [62-Oct-21: 1F].
Stoeker, John H. d. on 65-Feb-25 [65-Feb-28: 1F].
Stokley, William d. on 63-Dec-7 [64-Jan-4: 1G].
Stone, James H. d. on 63-Aug-21 [63-Sep-9: 4B].
Stone, William J. d. on 61-Jan-18 [61-Jan-21: 4D].
Stoneman, George m. Hardesty, Mary Oliver on 61-Nov-21 [61-Nov-22: 1F].

Stonesifer, Amos d. on 65-Aug-5 [65-Aug-7: 1G].
Stran, , Mr. d. on 64-Nov-18 [64-Nov-19: 1F].
Stratton, Benjamin d. on 64-Sep-11 [64-Sep-12: 1G].
Straughn, L. E. d. on 65-Jun-18 [65-Jun-20: 1G].
Streeter, Sebastian F. d. on 64-Aug-24 [64-Aug-25: 1F; 64-Aug-27: 1F].
Strine, William d. on 61-Oct-14 [61-Oct-22: 1F].
Strobel, Albert d. on 64-Feb-12 [64-Feb-13: 1F].
Strong, Alexander d. on 63-Sep-16 [63-Sep-17: 1F].
Strong, George W. d. on 62-Sep-20 [62-Sep-22: 1F].
Strong, Joseph d. on 61-Mar-15 [61-Mar-18: 1F].
Stubbins, Charles d. on 61-Jun-5 [61-Jun-7: 1G].
Stubbins, Charles d. on 61-Mar-28 [61-Mar-30: 1F].
Stummer, James d. on 61-Mar-18 [61-Mar-19: 1F].
Stump, Henry d. on 65-Oct-29 [65-Oct-30: 1G].
Stunty, Charles H. d. on 63-Jul-3 [63-Jul-15: 4B].
Summer, Elizabeth d. on 61-Mar-24 [61-Mar-26: 1E].
Sunstrom, William d. on 61-Oct-23 [61-Oct-25: 1G].
Sutton, George H. d. on 64-Sep-7 [64-Sep-9: 1F].
Sutton, Mordecai d. on 65-Oct-2 [65-Oct-3: 1G].
Swartz, Caroline d. on 65-Nov-4 [65-Nov-6: 1F].
Sweeny, Dennis d. on 65-Jan-6 [65-Jan-7: 1F; 65-Jan-9: 1E].
Talbott, William d. on 62-Oct-8 [62-Oct-20: 1F].
Taney, Ethelbert d. on 63-Jun-17 [63-Jun-30: 2D].
Taney, John d. on 62-Jan-18 [62-Jan-24: 1A].
Taney, Roger Brooke d. on 64-Oct-12 [64-Oct-17: 1G].
Taskey, Thomas d. on 64-Dec-14 [64-Dec-17: 4A].
Tatem, Joseph d. on 61-May-9 [61-May-10: 1G].
Tayle, Julia d. on 61-Nov-17 [61-Nov-25: 1G].
Taylor, Benjamin d. on 63-Jul-14 [63-Jul-20: 4B].
Taylor, Henry H. d. on 63-Jul-16 [63-Jul-18: 4C].
Taylor, Matthew d. on 64-Jan-25 [64-Jan-26: 1E; 64-Jan-27: 1F].
Taylor, Robert A. d. on 63-Oct-15 [63-Oct-17: 1G].
Taylor, William d. on 65-Dec-25 [65-Dec-27: 1G].
Taylor, William H. d. on 62-Dec-13 [62-Dec-16: 4D].
Teackle, Emma Jane d. on 61-Dec-19 [61-Dec-23: 1G].
Thomas, David d. on 62-Mar-26 [62-Mar-28: 1F].
Thomas, David E. d. on 64-Oct-18 [64-Oct-20: 1G; 64-Oct-22: 1G].
Thomas, Evan d. on 63-Apr-25 [63-Apr-28: 1F].
Thomas, Henry May d. on 63-Oct-18 [63-Oct-21: 1G].
Thomas, John d. on 63-Aug-8 [63-Aug-10: 1F].
Thomas, John d. on 64-Jun-20 [64-Jun-24: 1G].
Thomas, John H. d. on 65-Mar-30 [65-Apr-1: 4A].

Thomas, Joseph d. on 65-Apr-24 [65-Apr-25: 1F; 65-May-1: 1G].
Thomas, Philip E. d. on 61-Sep-1 [61-Sep-2: 1F].
Thomas, Sterling d. on 65-Jan-11 [65-Jan-12: 2C].
Thomas, William B. d. on 62-Nov-16 [62-Nov-19: 1G].
Thompson, Edward N. d. on 65-Jul-20 [65-Jul-21: 1G].
Thompson, John d. on 65-Oct-9 [65-Oct-13: 1G].
Thompson, Lemuel B. d. on 65-Nov-18 [65-Nov-27: 1F].
Thompson, Louis d. on 61-Sep-6 [61-Sep-7: 1F].
Thompson, Samuel d. [63-Jul-14: 1G].
Thompson, William C. d. on 63-Jul-23 [63-Jul-25: 1F].
Thornton, Alfred d. on 63-Oct-13 [64-Oct-14: 1G].
Thornton, Francis A., Capt. d. on 62-Feb-26 [62-Feb-28: 1G].
Thornton, Joseph N. d. on 63-Feb-14 [63-Feb-17: 1F].
Thorpe, John A. J. d. on 62-Jan-8 [62-Jan-10: 1G].
Thrush, Nicholas d. on 65-Apr-4 [65-Apr-6: 1G].
Tice, John d. on 64-Sep-27 [64-Sep-29: 1G].
Tidings, Edwin Randall d. on 64-Dec-6 [64-Dec-7: 1G].
Tiernan, William H. d. on 63-Mar-18 [63-Mar-19: 1F].
Tilly, John d. on 63-Jun-9 [63-Jun-10: 1F].
Tingler, Lucy d. on 65-Aug-25 [65-Aug-26: 1F].
Tobin, Thomas W. d. on 62-Apr-15 [62-Apr-16: 1F].
Todd, Kate d. on 65-Jul-20 [65-Jul-22: 1F; 65-Jul-24: 1G].
Todd, Mary Ann d. on 63-Oct-16 [63-Oct-17: 1G].
Todd, Susan d. on 65-Aug-9 [65-Aug-11: 1F].
Tolson, Will d. on 61-Dec-26 [62-Jan-9: 1F].
Toner, Michael, Mr. d. on 62-Aug-21 [62-Aug-23: 1G].
Toupe, George L. d. on 61-Nov-6 [61-Nov-8: 1F].
Towner, Albert White d. on 63-Jun-6 [63-Jun-8: 1F].
Trainor, John d. on 65-Jun-5 [65-Jun-12: 1G].
Travers, Samuel d. on 64-Dec-9 [64-Dec-10: 1G].
Trilley, Samuel d. on 64-Jul-29 [64-Aug-1: 1G].
Trimble, Edward M. d. on 63-Aug-7 [63-Aug-10: 1F].
Trumbull, S. G. d. [63-May-22: 1F].
Tucker, Frank d. on 61-Dec-23 [61-Dec-24: 1G].
Tufts, George W. d. on 61-Oct-27 [61-Oct-29: 1G].
Tullin, J. d. [61-Nov-5: 1F].
Tumblinson, William, Sr. d. on 63-Apr-26 [63-Apr-27: 1G].
Turnbull, David A. d. on 61-Dec-7 [61-Dec-10: 4E].
Turner, Charles d. on 61-Mar-28 [61-Mar-30: 1G].
Turner, John D. d. on 64-Sep-5 [64-Sep-7: 1F].
Turner, Thomas S. d. on 65-Oct-29 [65-Nov-1: 1G].
Turney, Patrick d. on 65-Jul-24 [65-Jul-25: 1G].
Tuttle, William N. d. on 64-Jun-17 [64-Jun-20: 1G].

Tydings, Richard d. on 61-Dec-25 [62-Jan-1: 1G].
Tyler, G. B. m. Cassard, Emma on 65-Nov-21 [65-Nov-22: 1F].
Tyson, Issac d. on 61-Nov-24 [61-Nov-26: 1F].
Tyson, Issac d. on 63-Nov-13 [64-Jan-30: 1G; 64-Feb-1: 1G].
Tyson, John S. d. on 64-Oct-2 [64-Oct-4: 1G].
Uhl, Lewis d. on 62-May-8 [62-May-10: 1G].
Ulrich, Frederick W. d. on 63-Aug-11 [63-Aug-12: 1F].
Underwood, Albert d. on 64-Aug-25 [64-Aug-27: 1G].
Vacksmoth, August d. on 64-Jan-31 [64-Feb-1: 1G].
Valentine, John d. on 61-Oct-29 [61-Oct-31: 1F].
Van Horn, James d. on 63-Mar-27 [63-Mar-28: 1F; 63-Mar-29: 1F].
Varden, Josiah d. on 63-Jan-15 [63-Jan-17: 1F].
Verrey, Julia Ann d. on 61-Jan-22 [61-Jan-23: 1F].
Vogt, George d. on 61-May-12 [61-May-13: 4C].
Volandt, Christian d. on 63-Aug-31 [63-Sep-10: 1G].
Volmer, Phillip d. on 62-Nov-4 [62-Nov-8: 1F].
Wade, Larkin d. on 65-Jul-4 [65-Jul-6: 4C].
Walker, Catherine Roseanna m. Holtz, Henry C. on 63-Jun-16
  [63-Jun-30: 2D].
Walker, Edward d. on 65-Jul-29 [65-Jul-31: 1E].
Walker, John Wesley d. on 63-Dec-26 [63-Dec-28: 1F].
Walker, Noah Dixon, Jr. d. on 63-May-3 [63-May-15: 1G; 63-May-23
  1G].
Walker, Samuel H. d. on 63-Jun-25 [63-Jun-26: 1G].
Wall, Mary d. on 63-Jul-27 [63-Jul-29: 1G].
Wall, Michael d. on 61-Jan-28 [61-Jan-29: 1E].
Wall, Robert A. d. on 61-Nov-1 [61-Nov-4: 1F].
Wallace, James d. on 63-Mar-25 [63-Mar-26: 1E].
Walsh, T. Yates d. on 65-Jan-20 [65-Jan-22: 1F].
Walter, Charles, Dr. d. on 62-Apr-22 [62-Apr-23: 1F].
Walter, Jacob d. on 65-May-12 [65-May-15: 4B].
Walter, John d. on 62-Jun-26 [62-Jun-27: 1E].
Walters, George d. on 65-Jul-4 [65-Jul-7: 1F].
Walters, S. Ellen d. on 62-Nov-13 [63-Feb-14: 1F].
Wardenberg, William d. on 63-Dec-19 [63-Dec-21: 1F].
Ware, Nathan H. d. on 64-Feb-4 [64-Feb-6: 1G].
Wareham, James d. on 62-Aug-25 [62-Aug-26: 1G].
Warner, Henry d. on 65-Nov-24 [65-Nov-30: 1F].
Warner, Joseph P. d. on 62-Sep-30 [62-Oct-1: 1G; 62-Oct-2: 1G].
Warren, James d. on 65-Mar-18 [65-Mar-20: 1F].
Warrick, George d. on 65-Jul-23 [65-Jul-24: 1F].
Washington, George d. on 63-Nov-30 [63-Dec-1: 1G].
Washington, James H. d. on 65-Aug-22 [65-Sep-28: 1F].

Watchman, John d. on 65-Apr-11 [65-Apr-12: 1F].
Waters, Richard H. d. on 61-Dec-13 [61-Dec-20: 1G].
Waters, William D. d. on 61-Oct-6 [61-Dec-9: 1G].
Watson, David G. d. on 62-Oct-9 [62-Nov-17: 1F].
Watson, John S. d. on 65-Jun-22 [65-Jun-26: 1G].
Watson, Thomas A. d. on 64-Mar-4 [64-Mar-8: 1F].
Waugh, Beverly R. d. on 61-Mar-24 [61-Mar-27: 1E].
Weaver, Lewis d. on 63-Jan-18 [63-Jan-23: 1F].
Weaver, Robert C. d. on 65-Sep-27 [65-Sep-29: 1F].
Webb, Benjamin d. on 61-Aug-31 [61-Aug-5: 1G].
Weber, John d. on 62-Aug-7 [62-Aug-9: 1G].
Weems, George W. d. on 65-Jul-20 [65-Jul-21: 1G].
Weems, J. C. d. on 62-Jan-20 [62-Jan-24: 2A].
Wehr, Peter d. on 64-Nov-14 [64-Nov-15: 1F].
Weiber, William d. on 61-Mar-10 [61-Mar-11: 1G].
Weir, Jon d. on 63-Aug-11 [63-Aug-12: 1F].
Weissinger, Henry d. on 61-Aug-15 [61-Aug-16: 1G].
Welch, John d. on 64-Sep-23 [64-Sep-26: 1G].
Wells, Joshua, Rev. d. on 62-Jan-25 [62-Jan-28: 1F].
Wells, Mary Rebecca d. on 62-Oct-10 [62-Oct-11: 1G].
Wells, Woody W. d. on 64-Aug-4 [64-Aug-6: 1G].
Welsh, Ferdinand d. on 64-Sep-24 [64-Oct-1: 1F].
Welsh, James d. on 64-May-7 [64-May-9: 4B].
Welsh, Michael d. on 63-Mar-7 [63-Mar-9: 1F].
Welsh, Peter d. on 64-Sep-8 [64-Sep-10: 1G].
Welslager, George d. on 62-Feb-11 [62-Feb-13: 4D].
Wenn, Philip d. on 63-Feb-27 [63-Feb-28: 1F].
Wessels, Christian d. on 64-Dec-25 [64-Dec-26: 1F; 64-Dec-28: 4B].
West, George d. on 63-Jul-24 [63-Jul-25: 1G].
West, Joseph d. [63-Jan-31: 1G].
Whalen, Catherine d. on 64-Jul-18 [64-Jul-20: 1G].
Wheeler, George Edward d. on 62-Aug-6 [62-Oct-3: 1F].
Wheeler, Samuel E. d. on 63-Oct-19 [63-Oct-20: 1F].
Whelan, George J., Esq. d. on 62-Jul-1 [62-Jul-23: 1G].
White, Abner d. on 63-Oct-19 [63-Oct-22: 1G; 63-Oct-23: 1F].
White, Daniel d. on 63-Oct-21 [63-Oct-23: 1G].
White, George H. d. on 62-Sep-18 [62-Sep-18: 1G; 62-Sep-19: 1F].
White, James d. on 63-Sep-12 [63-Sep-14: 1F].
White, John H. d. on 63-Aug-11 [63-Aug-15: 1F].
White, Joseph d. on 64-Jul-5 [64-Jul-6: 1G].
White, Leonard d. on 61-Feb-9 [61-Feb-11: 1G].
White, Richard d. on 64-Feb-12 [64-Feb-23: 1G].
White, William d. on 62-Sep-2 [62-Sep-3: 1G].

White, William P. d. on 64-Jan-13 [64-Jan-15: 1F].
Whiteford, David d. on 62-Jun-18 [62-Jun-20: 1F].
Whitehouse, David W. d. on 63-Feb-16 [63-Feb-26: 1G; 63-Feb-27: 1F].
Whitelock, Charles d. on 63-Mar-6 [63-Mar-7: 1F].
Whitely, William H. d. on 61-Mar-20 [61-Mar-22: 1E].
Whiting, George d. on 62-Mar-10 [62-Mar-12: 1F].
Whitney, Charles d. on 63-Oct-20 [63-Oct-29: 1G].
Whitson, David E. d. on 61-Dec-10 [61-Dec-11: 1F; 61-Nov-26: 1F].
Wickes, William, Rev. d. on 62-Apr-7 [62-Apr-11: 1G].
Wiel, Henry d. on 65-Aug-14 [65-Aug-15: 1G].
Wigand, John d. on 63-Sep-6 [63-Sep-7: 1F].
Wigley, William Henry d. on 62-Aug-3 [62-Aug-5: 1G].
Wildey, Thomas d. on 61-Oct-19 [61-Oct-21: 1F; 61-Oct-22: 1E].
Wiley, William d. on 62-Mar-28 [62-Mar-29: 1G].
Wilhelm, John Frank d. on 62-Dec-12 [62-Dec-13: 1G].
Wilkinson, David d. on 63-May-30 [63-Jun-1: 1E].
Willard, Simon d. [64-Jul-28: 1G].
Williams, Amos A. d. on 61-Feb-3 [61-Feb-4: 1G].
Williams, Edward d. on 64-Feb-4 [64-Feb-5: 1F].
Williams, Goodwin G. d. on 64-May-17 [64-May-18: 1G].
Williams, Hester d. on 64-Feb-9 [64-Feb-10: 1G].
Williams, Jacob, Jr. d. on 62-Mar-22 [62-Mar-24: 4B].
Williams, Joseph d. on 64-Oct-31 [64-Nov-2: 1G].
Williams, Julia Ann d. on 62-Jul-10 [62-Jul-12: 1F].
Williams, Mary d. on 61-Jan-29 [61-Jan-30: 1E; 61-Jan-31: 1F].
Williams, Nathaniel d. on 64-Sep-11 [64-Sep-12: 1G].
Williams, Nathaniel F. d. on 64-Dec-25 [64-Dec-26: 1G].
Williams, Thomas d. on 62-Aug-18 [62-Aug-19: 1G].
Williams, Thomas S., Sr. d. on 63-Apr-2 [63-Apr-4: 1F].
Williams, William d. on 65-Jun-4 [65-Jun-13: 1G].
Williamson, Alexander d. on 64-Aug-21 [64-Aug-27: 1G].
Willing, Edward d. on 61-Dec-3 [61-Dec-6: 1F].
Willis, George d. on 61-Nov-6 [61-Nov-8: 1F; 61-Nov-9: 1G].
Wilmot, John G. d. on 64-Aug-31 [64-Sep-1: 1G].
Wilson, Ann d. on 63-Aug-11 [63-Aug-12: 1G].
Wilson, James C. d. on 61-Oct-13 [61-Oct-15: 1F].
Wilson, John W. d. on 64-Sep-28 [64-Sep-30: 1F].
Wilson, John W. d. on 64-Sep-7 [64-Sep-9: 1F].
Wilson, Malcolm d. on 62-Sep-17 [62-Sep-20: 1F].
Wilson, Rebecca d. on 65-Jul-9 [65-Jul-11: 1F].
Wilson, Robert A. d. on 65-Feb-14 [65-Feb-16: 1G].
Wilson, William d. on 65-Jan-10 [65-Jan-12: 4C].

Winans, Celeste Revillon d. on 61-Mar-19 [61-Mar-21: 1E; 61-Mar-2: 1F].
Winans, Ross, Jr. d. on 63-Jun-24 [63-Jun-27: 1G].
Winkelman, Catherine d. on 62-Jan-28 [62-Jan-29: 4D].
Winkleman, John d. on 61-Feb-23 [61-Feb-25: 1F].
Wise, Charles d. on 64-Aug-26 [64-Aug-27: 1G].
Wise, John d. [64-Apr-14: 1G].
Wisner, Angeline d. on 62-Mar-29 [62-Apr-12: 1F].
Wisner, George d. on 62-Apr-5 [62-Apr-12: 1F].
Wisner, John d. on 62-Apr-5 [62-Apr-12: 1F].
Wisner, Lucy d. on 62-Apr-5 [62-Apr-12: 1F].
Wisner, Sarah d. on 62-Apr-12 [62-Apr-12: 1F].
Wood, John d. on 61-Jul-10 [61-Jul-13: 1F].
Wooden, James M. d. on 61-Mar-7 [61-Mar-8: 1F; 61-Mar-11: 1F].
Woodhull, Maxwell d. on 63-Feb-19 [63-Feb-20: 1F].
Woods, Hiram, Sr. d. on 62-Mar-15 [62-Mar-17: 4C].
Woods, Sarah d. on 63-Jan-2 [63-Jan-3: 1G].
Woods, William d. on 64-Jul-12 [64-Jul-13: 1G].
Woodville, William, Sr. d. on 63-Sep-23 [63-Sep-24: 1F; 63-Sep-26: 1G].
Woody, William d. on 63-Aug-24 [63-Aug-26: 1G].
Wooten, Benjamin d. [63-Dec-25: 1G].
Worley, John d. on 62-Dec-23 [62-Dec-25: 1F].
Worth, George d. on 63-Feb-1 [63-Feb-3: 1G].
Wray, Henry d. [61-Oct-29: 1F].
Wright, Charles W., Capt. d. on 62-Jun-12 [62-Jun-13: 1F].
Wright, Samuel d. on 63-Aug-8 [63-Aug-10: 1F].
Wright, Thomas d. on 63-Sep-24 [63-Sep-25: 1G].
Wright, William E. d. on 63-Feb-18 [63-Feb-19: 1G].
Wright, William H. De Courcy d. on 64-Mar-25 [64-Mar-26: 1G].
Wright, William T., Rev. d. [62-May-14: 1G].
Wrisley, Sarah J. d. on 61-Apr-28 [61-Apr-30: 1G].
Wunsch, Xavier d. on 61-Jan-3 [61-Jan-5: 1G].
Wyant, Jeremiah S. d. on 65-Jun-12 [65-Jun-14: 1G].
Wyatt, John d. on 64-Jan-7 [64-Jan-8: 4E].
Wyatt, William E. d. on 64-Jun-24 [64-Jun-25: 1F; 64-Jun-27: 1F].
Wynne, Mary Catherine d. on 61-Sep-29 [61-Oct-5: 1F].
Wyse, William A. d. on 61-Jul-6 [61-Aug-30: 1G].
Yeager, Martin d. on 63-Nov-11 [63-Nov-12: 1F].
Yost, Henry d. on 65-Dec-21 [65-Dec-22: 1F].
Young, Benjamin Walter d. on 63-Jun-27 [63-Jun-30: 2D].
Young, John George d. on 65-Aug-20 [65-Sep-4: 1E].
Young, William Collins d. on 62-Oct-4 [62-Oct-6: 1F].

Young, William H. d. on 64-Jun-22 [64-Jun-23: 1F; 64-Jun-24: 1F; 64-Jun-25: 1F].
Young, William T. d. on 65-Mar-9 [65-Mar-11: 1G; 65-Mar-13: 1G].
Youngman, John d. on 61-Jan-3 [61-Jan-4: 4D].
Zimmerman, Francis d. on 62-Dec-25 [62-Dec-27: 1F].
Zimmerman, John d. on 62-Apr-17 [62-Apr-18: 1G].
Zinkman, A., Mr. d. on 62-Aug-8 [62-Apr-12: 1G].
Zoelner, William d. on 64-Nov-16 [64-Nov-17: 1F].

www.ingramcontent.com/pod-product-compliance
Lightning Source LLC
Chambersburg PA
CBHW071711300426
44115CB00010B/1388